INFORMATION
PLEASE
ALMANAC®
ATLAS & YEARBOOK

45TH EDITION

HOUGHTON MIFFLIN COMPANY BOSTON

1992

Executive Editor
Otto Johnson
Associate Editor
Vera Dailey
Electronic Production Specialist
Christine Frantz
Manuscript Editors
Elizabeth Janice
Kim E. Johnson
Contributing Editors
Arthur Reed, Jr. (Current Events)
Thomas Nemeth, Ph.D. (World Countries)
Dennis M. Lyons (Sports)
Maps
Maps copyright © Hammond Incorporated.
Requests for map use should be sent to Hammond Incorporated, Maplewood, New Jersey 07040.

The Information Please Almanac invites comments and suggestions from readers. Because of the many letters received, however, it is not possible to respond personally to every correspondent. Nevertheless, all suggestions are most welcome, and the editors will consider them carefully. (Information Please Almanac does not rule on bets or wagers.)

ISBN (Hardcover): 0-395-59671-8
ISBN (Paperback): 0-395-59672-6
ISSN: 0073–7860

Previous editions of INFORMATION PLEASE were published in 1990, 1989, 1988, 1987, 1986, 1985, and 1984 by Houghton Mifflin Company, in 1982 by A&W Publishing Company, and in 1981, 1980, and 1979 by Simon & Schuster, in 1978 and 1977 by Information Please Publishing, Inc., and from 1947–1976 by Dan Golenpaul Associates.

Copies of Information Please Almanac may be ordered directly by mail from:
Customer Service Department
Houghton Mifflin Company
Burlington, Ma 01803
Phone toll-free, (800) 225-3362 for price and shipping information. In Massachusetts phone: 272-1500.

INFORMATION PLEASE ALMANAC®
Editorial Office
Houghton Mifflin Company
215 Park Avenue South
New York, N.Y. 10003

Information Please and Information Please Almanac are registered trademarks of Houghton Mifflin Company.

Printed in the United States of America

WP Pa   BP Hbd 10 9 8 7 6 5 4 3 2 1

COMPREHENSIVE INDEX

A

Abacus, 561
Abbreviations:
  Degrees, Academic, 863
  Postal, 992
  Weights and measures, 373–81
Abidjan, Ivory Coast, 173
Abortions, 116, 117, 118, 139, 813
ABSCAM, 117
Absolute zero, 387. 377, 380, 562
Abu Dhabi, United Arab Emirates, 269
Academic costume, 863
Academy Awards, 708–11
Acadia, 99, 164
Acadia National Park, 569
Accidents:
  Aircraft accidents, 357, 383, 388–89
  Deaths from, 382–91, 814–15
  Fires and explosions, 385–387
  Motor vehicle, 814–15
  Railroad accidents, 389–90, 815
  Rates, 814, 815
  Shipwrecks, 387
  See also Disasters
Accra, Ghana, 193
Aconcagua Peak, 150, 468
Acre, 374, 375, 376
Acropolis, 91, 123
ACTION, 650
Actium, Battle of, 92
Actors, actresses:
  Awards for, 708–11, 724, 984
  Famous, 672–700
Adams, John, 652
  See also Headline History; Presidents (U.S.)
Adams, John Quincy, 653
  See also Headline History; Presidents (U.S.)
Adams National Historic Site, 571
Adding machine, 561
Addis Ababa, Ethiopia, 182
Address, forms of, 316–17
Aden, Yemen, 282
Adenauer, Konrad, 192, 672
Administration, Office of, 649
Admirals (U.S.), 303
  First, 122
Adrenaline, isolation of, 561
Adriatic Sea, 148, 209, 246, 283
Advent (season), 587, 588
Advertising, 59
  Expenditures, 59
  Leading agencies, 59
Aegean Islands, 194
Aegean Sea, 194, 267
Aerial combat, first, 357
Aerial photographers, first, 356
Afars and Issas. See Djibouti
Afghanistan, 117, 147, 256
  See also Countries
AFL-CIO, 114, 601
Africa, 465
  Explorations and discoveries, 457
  Map, 488–89
  Population, 136
  Portuguese territory, 243
  Southernmost point, 251
  See also Continents; Countries
Agate (measure), 376
Age:
  Arrests by, 825, 826
  At first marriage, 808
  Death rates by, 816, 818–19
  Life expectancy by, 138, 817, 818–19
  Of unmarried mothers, 811
  Population by, 796–97, 803

School enrollment by, 833
Age limits:
  Driving licenses, 832
  School attendance, 834
Agencies (U.N.), 290–91
Agencies (U.S.), 650–51
Aggtelek Cavern, 475
Agincourt, Battle of, 95
Aging
  See Social Security & Aging
Agnew, Spiro T., 632
  Resignation, 116, 662
Agriculture:
  Animals on farms, 61
  Economic statistics, 46, 60, 61
  Employment, 51, 54, 58
  Farm laborers, 51, 54, 58
  History, 556
  Income, 61
  Production by state, 60
  See also Food
Agriculture, U.S. Dept. of, 649
  Secretaries of, 643–45
AIDS, 80–81, 118
  Cases, 80, 81
  Hot line, 81, 598
  Testing, 81
Air (atmosphere), 334, 351
Air distances, cities, 416–19
Air Force, U.S., 304
  See also Armed Forces
Air Force, U.S. Department of:
  Secretary of, 649
Air Force Academy, U.S., 305
Airlines:
  First scheduled passenger service, 358
  Freight, 65
  Passenger traffic, 360
  Pilots, 360
  See also Travel
Airmail, 989, 991
  Firsts, 122, 357
  International, 991
  Priority mail, 989
  Stamps for, 990
Airplanes:
  Accidents, 388–89
  Exports and imports, 69
  Fastest, 361
  Invention, 356–57, 359
  Passenger traffic, 360
  Pilots, 360
  Records, 362
Air pollution, 6, 563
Airports, world's busiest, 360
Air transport company, first, 356
Akkadian civilization, 89, 91
Alabama, 740
  See also States of U.S.
Alabama–Coosa River, 478
Alamo, Battle of the, 101, 764
Aland Islands, 184
Alaska, 740–41
  Bought, 102, 741, 803
  Discovered, 99, 458, 741
  Gold Rush, 741
  Maps, 481–82
  Mountain peaks, 478
  National parks, 569–70
  Oil, 741
  Volcanoes, 459, 741
  See also States of U.S.
Albania, 147–48, 976
  See also Countries
Alberta, Canada, 163, 164
Albuquerque, New Mexico, 773
  See also Cities (U.S.)
Alcohol. See Liquor
Alcohol abuse, 449, 456
Aldrin, Edwin E., Jr., 115, 326

Aleutian Islands, 100, 459
  Maps, 492, 496
Alexander the Great, 91, 147, 180, 205, 457, 672
Alexandria, Egypt, 180
Alexandria, Pharos of, 123
Alfred the Great, 93, 270
Algeria, 114, 148
  War of Independence, 113, 185
  See also Countries
Alhambra, 124
Ali, Muhammad (Cassius Clay), 898, 916
Aliens, in U.S., 805
Allende, Salvador, 167
Alliance for Progress, 114
All Saints' Day, 586
All-Star Game, Baseball, 950–51
Alpha Centauri, 334
Alps, 152, 185, 209, 261, 283
  Tunnels under, 128
Altamaha–Ocmulgee River, 478
Altamira Cave, 475
Altiplano, 157
Altitude records, aircraft, 362
Altitudes. See Elevations
Aluminum:
  As element, 532
  Manufacture, electrolytic, 554
Alzheimer's Disease, 88
Amazon River, 158, 170, 458, 471
Amendments to Constitution, 620–24
  Civil rights, 620–24
  Right to bear arms, 620
  Search and seizure, 620
American Academy and Institute of Arts and Letters, 602
American Federation of Labor, 114, 601
American folklore, 646
American History. See United States History
American Independent Party, 639
American Indians. See Indians
American League. See Baseball; Football
American Red Cross, 610
American Revolution. See Revolutionary War
American Samoa, 769
American's Creed, The, 628
America's Cup, 945
Amish. See Mennonites
Amman, Jordan, 212
Ampere, 373, 376, 377
Amphetamines, 450, 453
Amphibians, endangered, 565
Amsterdam, Netherlands, 230
Amsterdam-Rhine Canal, 130
Amu Darya River, 472
Amur River, 168, 254, 471
Amusement. See Recreation
Ancient empires, 91
  Map, 90
Ancient history, events, 89–92
Andaman Islands, 201
Andaman Sea, 469
Andes, 150, 167, 170, 239, 468–69
Andorra, 148–49
Andropov, Yuri V., 117, 255, 256
Anesthetic, first use of, 561
Angel Falls, 472
Angkor Wat, 124
Angola, 149, 243
  See also Countries
Angstrom, 374, 376
Anguilla, 274
Animals:
  Classification, 561
  Endangered species, 564–65

7

ELECTIONS

The Hundredth and Second Congress

Composition of 101st and 102nd Congresses

	102nd Congress[2]				101st Congress[1]			
	Dem.	Rep.	Male	Female	Dem.	Rep.	Male	Female
Senate	57	43	98	2	55	45	98	2
House	267	164	403	29	257	176	406	27

1. One seat in House vacant in New Jersey and in Hawaii as of July 1, 1990. 2. Three seats vacant in House, one each from Arizona, Illinois, and Texas as of July 1, 1991. Another will occur in September in Pennsylvania. There is one Independent member of the House.

The Senate

Senior Senator is listed first. The dates in the first column indicate period of service. The date given in parentheses after the Senator's name is year of birth. All terms are for six years and expire in January. Mailing address of Senators: The Senate, Washington, D.C. 20510.

ALABAMA
1979–97 Howell T. Heflin (D) (1921)
1987–93 Richard C. Shelby (D) (1934)
ALASKA
1968–97 Ted Stevens (R) (1923)
1981–93 Frank H. Murkowski (R) (1933)
ARIZONA
1977–95 Dennis DeConcini (D) (1937)
1987–93 John McCain (R) (1936)
ARKANSAS
1975–93 Dale Bumpers (D) (1925)
1979–97 David H. Pryor (D) (1934)
CALIFORNIA
1969–93 Alan Cranston (D) (1914)
1991–92 John Seymour (R) (1937)
COLORADO
1987–93 Timothy E. Wirth (D) (1939)
1991–97 Hank Brown (R) (1940)
CONNECTICUT
1981–93 Christopher J. Dodd (D) (1944)
1989–95 Joseph I. Lieberman (D) (1942)
DELAWARE
1971–95 William V. Roth, Jr. (R) (1921)
1973–97 Joseph R. Biden, Jr. (D) (1942)
FLORIDA
1987–93 Bob Graham (D) (1936)
1989–95 Connie Mack III (R) (1940)
GEORGIA
1972–97 Sam Nunn (D) (1938)
1987–93 Wyche Fowler, Jr. (D) (1940)
HAWAII
1963–93 Daniel K. Inouye (D) (1924)
1990–95 Daniel K. Akaka (D) (1924)
IDAHO
1981–93 Steven D. Symms (R) (1938)
1991–97 Larry E. Craig (R) (1945)
ILLINOIS
1981–93 Alan J. Dixon (D) (1927)
1985–97 Paul Simon (D) (1928)
INDIANA
1977–95 Richard G. Lugar (R) (1932)
1989–97 Dan Coats (R) (1943)
IOWA
1981–93 Charles E. Grassley (R) (1933)
1985–97 Tom Harkin (D) (1939)
KANSAS
1969–93 Robert J. Dole (R) (1923)
1978–97 Nancy Landon Kassebaum (R) (1932)
KENTUCKY
1974–93 Wendell H. Ford (D) (1924)
1985–97 Mitch McConnell (R) (1942)

LOUISIANA
1972–97 J. Bennett Johnson (D) (1932)
1987–93 John B. Breaux (D) (1944)
MAINE
1979–97 William S. Cohen (R) (1940)
1980–95 George J. Mitchell (D) (1933)
MARYLAND
1977–95 Paul Sarbanes (D) (1933)
1987–93 Barbara A. Mikulski (D) (1936)
MASSACHUSETTS
1962–95 Edward M. Kennedy (D) (1932)
1985–97 John F. Kerry (D) (1943)
MICHIGAN
1976–95 Donald W. Riegle, Jr. (D) (1938)
1979–97 Carl Levin (D) (1934)
MINNESOTA
1978–95 David F. Durenberger (R) (1934)
1991–97 Paul Wellstone (D) (1944)
MISSISSIPPI
1978–97 Thad Cochran (R) (1937)
1989–95 Trent Lott (R) (1941)
MISSOURI
1976–95 John C. Danforth (R) (1936)
1987–93 Christopher S. (Kit) Bond (R) (1939)
MONTANA
1978–97 Max Baucus (D) (1941)
1989–95 Conrad Burns (R) (1935)
NEBRASKA
1979–97 J. James Exon (D) (1921)
1989–95 Robert Kerrey (D) (1943)
NEVADA
1987–93 Harry M. Reid (D) (1939)
1989–95 Dick Bryan (D) (1937)
NEW HAMPSHIRE
1980–93 Warren B. Rudman (R) (1930)
1991–97 Robert C. Smith (R) (1941)
NEW JERSEY
1979–97 Bill Bradley (D) (1943)
1982–93 Frank R. Lautenberg (D) (1924)
NEW MEXICO
1973–97 Pete V. Domenici (R) (1932)
1983–95 Jeff Bingaman (D) (1943)
NEW YORK
1977–95 Daniel P. Moynihan (D) (1927)
1981–93 Alfonse M. D'Amato (R) (1937)
NORTH CAROLINA
1973–97 Jesse Helms (R) (1921)
1986–93 Terry Sanford (D) (1917)
NORTH DAKOTA
1960–95 Quentin N. Burdick (D) (1908)
1987–93 Kent Conrad (D) (1948)

OHIO
1974–93 John H. Glenn, Jr. (D) (1921)
1976–95 Howard M. Metzenbaum (D) (1917)
OKLAHOMA
1979–97 David L. Boren (D) (1941)
1981–93 Don Nickles (R) (1948)
OREGON
1967–97 Mark O. Hatfield (R) (1922)
1969–93 Bob Packwood (R) (1932)
PENNSYLVANIA
1981–93 Arlen Specter (R) (1930)
1991–(¹) Harris Wofford (D) (1926)
RHODE ISLAND
1961–97 Claiborne Pell (D) (1918)
1976–95 John H. Chafee (R) (1922)
SOUTH CAROLINA
1956–97 Strom Thurmond (R) (1902)
1966–93 Ernest F. Hollings (D) (1922)
SOUTH DAKOTA
1979–97 Larry Pressler (R) (1942)
1987–93 Thomas A. Daschle (D) (1947)
TENNESSEE
1977–95 James R. Sasser (D) (1936)
1985–97 Albert Gore, Jr. (D) (1948)

TEXAS
1971–95 Lloyd M. Bentsen (D) (1921)
1985–97 Phil Gramm (R) (1942)
UTAH
1974–93 E.J. (Jake) Garn (R) (1932)
1977–95 Orrin G. Hatch (R) (1934)
VERMONT
1975–93 Patrick J. Leahy (D) (1940)
1989–95 James M. Jeffords (R) (1934)
VIRGINIA
1979–97 John W. Warner (R) (1927)
1989–95 Charles Robb (D) (1939)
WASHINGTON
1987–93 Brock Adams (D) (1927)
1989–95 Slade Gorton (R) (1928)
WEST VIRGINIA
1959–95 Robert C. Byrd (D) (1918)
1985–97 John D. (Jay) Rockefeller IV (D) (1937)
WISCONSIN
1981–93 Robert W. Kasten, Jr. (R) (1942)
1989–95 Herbert Kohl (D) (1935)
WYOMING
1977–95 Malcolm Wallop (R) (1933)
1979–97 Alan K. Simpson (R) (1931)

1. Term unknown at press time as date of special election is uncertain.

The House of Representatives

The numerals indicate the Congressional Districts of the states; the designation AL means At Large. All terms end January 1993. Mailing address of Representatives: House of Representatives, Washington, D.C. 20515.

ALABAMA
(7 Representatives)
1. H.L. (Sonny) Callahan (R)
2. William L. Dickinson (R)
3. Glen Browder (D)
4. Thomas Bevill (D)
5. Bud Cramer (D)
6. Ben Erdreich (D)
7. Claude Harris (D)

ALASKA
(1 Representative)
AL Don Young (R)

ARIZONA
(5 Representatives)
1. John J. (Jay) Rhodes III (R)
2. Ed Pastor (D)
3. Bob Stump (R)
4. Jon Kyl (R)
5. Jim Kolbe (R)

ARKANSAS
(4 Representatives)
1. Bill Alexander (D)
2. Ray Thornton (D)
3. John Hammerschmidt (R)
4. Beryl Anthony (D)

CALIFORNIA
(45 Representatives)
1. Frank Riggs (R)
2. Wally Herger (R)
3. Robert T. Matsui (D)
4. Vic Fazio (D)
5. Nancy Pelosi (D)
6. Barbara Boxer (D)
7. George Miller (D)
8. Ronald V. Dellums (D)
9. Fortney H. (Pete) Stark (D)
10. Don Edwards (D)
11. Tom Lantos (D)
12. Thomas J. Campbell (R)
13. Norman Y. Mineta (D)
14. John Doolittle (D)
15. Gary Condit (D)
16. Leon E. Panetta (D)
17. Charles Pashayan, Jr. (R)
18. Richard H. Lehman (D)
19. Robert J. Lagomarsino (R)
20. William M. Thomas (R)
21. Elton Gallegly (R)

22. Carlos J. Moorhead (R)
23. Anthony C. Beilenson (D)
24. Henry A. Waxman (D)
25. Edward R. Roybal (D)
26. Howard L. Berman (D)
27. Mel Levine (D)
28. Julian C. Dixon (D)
29. Maxine Waters (D)
30. Matthew G. Martinez (D)
31. Mervyn M. Dymally (D)
32. Glenn M. Anderson (D)
33. David Dreier (R)
34. Esteban Edward Torres (D)
35. Jerry Lewis (R)
36. George E. Brown, Jr. (D)
37. Al McCandless (R)
38. Robert K. Dornan (R)
39. William E. Dannemeyer (R)
40. Christopher Cox (R)
41. Wiliam Lowery (R)
42. Dana Rohrabacher (R)
43. Ron Packard (R)
44. Randall Cunningham (R)
45. Duncan L. Hunter (R)

COLORADO
(6 Representatives)
1. Patricia Schroeder (D)
2. David E. Skaggs (D)
3. Ben Nighthorse Campbell (D)
4. Wayne Allard (R)
5. Joel Hefley (R)
6. Daniel L. Schaefer (R)

CONNECTICUT
(6 Representatives)
1. Barbara B. Kennelly (D)
2. Sam Gejdenson (D)
3. Rose DeLauro (D)
4. Christopher H. Shays (R)
5. Gary Franks (R)
6. Nancy L. Johnson (R)

DELAWARE
(1 Representative)
AL Thomas R. Carper (D)

FLORIDA
(19 Representatives)
1. Earl D. Hutto (D)
2. Pete Peterson (D)
3. Charles E. Bennett (D)

4. Craig James (R)
5. Bill McCollum (R)
6. Cliff Stearns (R)
7. Sam Gibbons (D)
8. C.W. Bill Young (R)
9. Michael Bilirakis (R)
10. Andy Ireland (R)
11. Jim Bacchus (D)
12. Tom Lewis (R)
13. Porter Goss (R)
14. Harry Johnston (D)
15. E. Clay Shaw, Jr. (R)
16. Larry Smith (D)
17. William Lehman (D)
18. Ileana Ros-Lehtineor (R)
19. Dante B. Fascell (D)

GEORGIA
(10 Representatives)
1. Robert Lindsay Thomas (D)
2. Charles Hatcher (D)
3. Richard Ray (D)
4. Ben Jones (D)
5. John Lewis (D)
6. Newt Gingrich (R)
7. George (Buddy) Darden (D)
8. J. Roy Rowland (D)
9. Edgar L. Jenkins (D)
10. Doug Barnard, Jr. (D)

HAWAII
(2 Representatives)
1. Neil Abercrombie (D)
2. Patsy Mink (D)

IDAHO
(2 Representatives)
1. Larry LaRocco (D)
2. Richard H. Stallings (D)

ILLINOIS
(22 Representatives)
1. Charles A. Hayes (D)
2. Gus Savage (D)
3. Marty Russo (D)
4. George Sangemeister (D)
5. William O. Lipinski (D)
6. Henry J. Hyde (R)
7. Cardiss Collins (D)
8. Dan Rostenkowski (D)
9. Sidney R. Yates (D)

10. John Edward Porter (R)
11. Frank Annunzio (D)
12. Philip M. Crane (R)
13. Harris W. Fawell (R)
14. J. Dennis Hastert (R)
15. Vacancy
16. John Cox Jr. (D)
17. Lane Evans (D)
18. Robert H. Michel (R)
19. Terry L. Bruce (D)
20. Richard Durbin (D)
21. Jerry Costello (D)
22. Glenn Poshard (D)

INDIANA
(10 Representatives)
1. Peter Visclosky (D)
2. Philip R. Sharp (D)
3. Tim Roemer (D)
4. Jill Long (D)
5. Jim Jontz (D)
6. Daniel Burton (R)
7. John T. Meyers (R)
8. Frank McCloskey (D)
9. Lee H. Hamilton (D)
10. Andrew Jacobs, Jr. (D)

IOWA
(6 Representatives)
1. Jim Leach (R)
2. Jim Nussel (R)
3. Dave R. Nagle (D)
4. Neal Smith (D)
5. Jim Ross Lightfoot (R)
6. Fred Grandy (R)

KANSAS
(5 Representatives)
1. Pat Roberts (R)
2. James Slattery (D)
3. Jan Meyers (R)
4. Dan Glickman (D)
5. Richard Nichols (R)

KENTUCKY
(7 Representatives)
1. Carroll Hubbard, Jr. (D)
2. William H. Natcher (D)
3. Romano L. Mazzoli (D)
4. Jim Bunning (R)
5. Harold Rogers (R)
6. Larry J. Hopkins (R)
7. Carl C. Perkins (D)

LOUISIANA
(8 Representatives)
1. Robert L. Livingston, Jr. (R)
2. William J. Jefferson (D)
3. W.J. (Billy) Tauzin (D)
4. Jim McCrery (R)
5. Thomas J. (Jerry) Huckaby (D)
6. Richard Baker (R)
7. Jimmy Hayes (D)
8. Clyde Holloway (R)

MAINE
(2 Representatives)
1. Tom Andrews (D)
2. Olympia J. Snowe (R)

MARYLAND
(8 Representatives)
1. Wayne Gilchrest (R)
2. Helen Delich Bentley (R)
3. Benjamin L. Cardin (D)
4. Thomas McMillen (D)
5. Steny H. Hoyer (D)
6. Beverly B. Byron (D)
7. Kweisi Mfume (D)
8. Constance A. Morella (R)

MASSACHUSETTS
(11 Representatives)
1. John Olver (D)
2. Richard Neal (D)
3. Joseph D. Early (D)
4. Barney Frank (D)

5. Chester G. Atkins (D)
6. Nicholas Mavroules (D)
7. Edward J. Markey (D)
8. Joseph P. Kennedy II (D)
9. Joe Moakley (D)
10. Gerry E. Studds (D)
11. Brian J. Donnelly (D)

MICHIGAN
(18 Representatives)
1. John Conyers, Jr. (D)
2. Carl D. Pursell (R)
3. Howard Wolpe (D)
4. Fred Upton (R)
5. Paul B. Henry (R)
6. Bob Carr (D)
7. Dale E. Kildee (D)
8. Bob Traxler (D)
9. Guy Vander Jagt (R)
10. David Camp (R)
11. Robert W. Davis (R)
12. David E. Bonior (D)
13. Barbara-Rose Collins (D)
14. Dennis M. Hertel (D)
15. William D. Ford (D)
16. John D. Dingell (D)
17. Sander M. Levin (D)
18. William S. Broomfield (R)

MINNESOTA
(8 Representatives)
1. Timothy J. Penny (D)
2. Vin Weber (R)
3. Jim Ramstad (R)
4. Bruce F. Vento (D)
5. Martin Sabo (D)
6. Gerry Sikorski (D)
7. Collin Peterson (D)
8. James L. Oberstar (D)

MISSISSIPPI
(5 Representatives)
1. Jamie L. Whitten (D)
2. Mike Espy (D)
3. G.V. (Sonny) Montgomery (D)
4. Michael Parker (D)
5. Gene Taylor (D)

MISSOURI
(9 Representatives)
1. William L. Clay (D)
2. Joan Horn (D)
3. Richard A. Gephardt (D)
4. Ike Skelton (D)
5. Alan Wheat (D)
6. E. Thomas Coleman (R)
7. Mel Hancock (R)
8. William Emerson (R)
9. Harold L. Volkmer (D)

MONTANA
(2 Representatives)
1. Pat Williams (D)
2. Ron Marlenee (R)

NEBRASKA
(3 Representatives)
1. Douglas K. Bereuther (R)
2. Peter Hoagland (D)
3. Bill Barrett (R)

NEVADA
(2 Representatives)
1. James H. Bilbray (D)
2. Barbara F. Vucanovich (R)

NEW HAMPSHIRE
(2 Representatives)
1. Bill Zeliff (R)
2. Dick Swett (D)

NEW JERSEY
(14 Representatives)
1. Robert Andrews (D)
2. William J. Hughes (D)
3. Frank Pallone (D)
4. Christopher H. Smith (R)

5. Marge Roukema (R)
6. Bernard J. Dwyer (D)
7. Matthew J. Rinaldo (R)
8. Robert A. Roe (D)
9. Robert G. Torricelli (D)
10. Donald Payne (D)
11. Dean A. Gallo (R)
12. Richard Zimmer (R)
13. H. James Saxton (R)
14. Frank Guarini (D)

NEW MEXICO
(3 Representatives)
1. Steve Schiff (R)
2. Joseph R. Skeen (R)
3. William Richardson (D)

NEW YORK
(34 Representatives)
1. George J. Hochbreuckner (D)
2. Thomas J. Downey (D)
3. Robert J. Mrazek (D)
4. Norman F. Lent (R)
5. Raymond J. McGrath (R)
6. Floyd H. Flake (D)
7. Gary L. Ackerman (D)
8. James H. Scheuer (D)
9. Thomas J. Manton (D)
10. Charles E. Schumer (D)
11. Edolphus Towns (D)
12. Major R. Owens (D)
13. Stephen J. Solarz (D)
14. Guy V. Molinari (R)
15. S. William Green (R)
16. Charles B. Rangel (D)
17. Ted Weiss (D)
18. Jose Serrano (D)
19. Elliott Engel (D)
20. Nita Lowey (D)
21. Hamilton Fish, Jr. (R)
22. Benjamin A. Gilman (R)
23. Michael McNulty (D)
24. Gerald B.H. Solomon (R)
25. Sherwood Boehlert (R)
26. David O'B. Martin (R)
27. James Walsh (R)
28. Matther F. McHugh (D)
29. Frank Horton (D)
30. Louise M. Slaughter (D)
31. L. William Paxon (R)
32. John L. LaFalce (D)
33. Henry J. Nowak (D)
34. Amory Houghton, Jr. (R)

NORTH CAROLINA
(11 Representatives)
1. Walter B. Jones (D)
2. Tim Valentine (D)
3. Martin Lancaster (D)
4. David E. Price (D)
5. Stephen L. Neal (D)
6. Howard Coble (R)
7. Charlie Rose (D)
8. W.G. (Bill) Hefner (D)
9. J. Alex McMillan (R)
10. Cass Ballenger (R)
11. Charles Taylor (R)

NORTH DAKOTA
(1 Representative)
AL Byron L. Dorgan (D)

OHIO
(21 Representatives)
1. Charles Luken (D)
2. Willis D. Gradison, Jr. (R)
3. Tony P. Hall (D)
4. Michael G. Oxley (R)
5. Paul Gillmor (R)
6. Bob McEwen (R)
7. David Hobson (R)
8. John Boehner (R)
9. Marcy Kaptur (D)
10. Clarence E. Miller (R)
11. Dennis E. Eckart (D)

12. John R. Kasich (R)
13. Don J. Pease (D)
14. Tom Sawyer (D)
15. Chalmers Wylie (R)
16. Ralph Regula (R)
17. James A. Traficant, Jr. (D)
18. Douglas Applegate (D)
19. Edward F. Feighan (D)
20. Mary Rose Oakar (D)
21. Louis Stokes (D)

OKLAHOMA
(6 Representatives)
1. James M. Inhofe (R)
2. Mike Synar (D)
3. Wesley W. Watkins (D)
4. Dave McCurdy (D)
5. Mickey Edwards (R)
6. Glenn English (D)

OREGON
(5 Representatives)
1. Les AuCoin (D)
2. Robert F. Smith (R)
3. Ronald L. Wyden (D)
4. Peter A. De Fazio (D)
5. Mike Kopetski (D)

PENNSYLVANIA
(23 Representatives)
1. Thomas M. Foglietta (D)
2. William H. Gray III (D)[1]
3. Robert A. Borski (D)
4. Joseph P. Kolter (D)
5. Richard T. Schulze (R)
6. Gus Yatron (D)
7. Curt Weldon (R)
8. Peter H. Kostmayer (D)
9. E.G. Shuster (R)
10. Joseph M. McDade (R)
11. Paul E. Kanjorski (D)
12. John P. Murtha (D)
13. Lawrence Coughlin (R)
14. William J. Coyne (D)
15. Don Ritter (R)
16. Robert S. Walker (R)
17. George W. Gekas (R)
18. Rick Santorum (R)
19. William F. Goodling (R)
20. Joseph M. Gaydos (D)
21. Tom Ridge (R)
22. Austin J. Murphy (D)
23. William F. Clinger (R)

RHODE ISLAND
(2 Representatives)

1. Ronald Machtley (R)
2. Jack Reed (D)

SOUTH CAROLINA
(6 Representatives)
1. Arthur Ravenel, Jr. (R)
2. Floyd Spence (R)
3. Butler Derrick (D)
4. Elizabeth J. Patterson (D)
5. John M. Spratt, Jr. (D)
6. Robin Tallon (D)

SOUTH DAKOTA
(1 Representative)
AL Tim Johnson (D)

TENNESSEE
(9 Representatives)
1. James H. Quillen (R)
2. James Duncan (R)
3. Marilyn Lloyd (D)
4. James Cooper (D)
5. Robert Clement (D)
6. Bart Gordon (D)
7. Don Sundquist (R)
8. John Tanner (D)
9. Harold E. Ford (D)

TEXAS
(27 Representatives)
1. Jim Chapman (D)
2. Charles Wilson (D)
3. Vacancy
4. Ralph M. Hall (D)
5. John Bryant (D)
6. Joe L. Barton (R)
7. William Archer (R)
8. Jack Fields (R)
9. Jack Brooks (D)
10. J.J. Pickle (D)
11. Chet Edwards (D)
12. Pete Green (D)
13. William Sarpalius (D)
14. Greg Laughlin (D)
15. E. (Kika) de la Garza (D)
16. Ronald D. Coleman (D)
17. Charles W. Stenholm (D)
18. Craig Washington (D)
19. Larry Combest (R)
20. Henry B. Gonzalez (D)
21. Lamar Smith (R)
22. Thomas D. Delay (R)
23. Albert G. Bustamante (D)
24. Martin Frost (D)
25. Michael A. Andrews (D)
26. Richard Armey (R)
27. Solomon P. Ortiz (D)

UTAH
(3 Representatives)
1. James V. Hansen (R)
2. Wayne Owens (D)
3. Bill Orton (D)

VERMONT
(1 Representative)
AL Bernie Sanders (Ind)

VIRGINIA
(10 Representatives)
1. Herbert H. Bateman (R)
2. Owen B. Pickett (D)
3. Thomas J. Bliley, Jr. (R)
4. Norman Sisisky (D)
5. L.F. Payne (D)
6. James R. Olin (D)
7. D. French Slaughter (R)
8. Jim Moran (D)
9. Frederick C. Boucher (D)
10. Frank R. Wolf (R)

WASHINGTON
(8 Representatives)
1. John R. Miller (R)
2. Al Swift (D)
3. Jolene Unsoeld (D)
4. Sid W. Morrison (R)
5. Thomas S. Foley (D)
6. Norman D. Dicks (D)
7. James McDermott (D)
8. Rodney Chandler (R)

WEST VIRGINIA
(4 Representatives)
1. Alan B. Mollohan (D)
2. Harley O. Staggers, Jr. (D)
3. Robert Wise (D)
4. Nick J. Rahall (D)

WISCONSIN
(9 Representatives)
1. Les Aspin (D)
2. Scott Klug (R)
3. Steve Gunderson (R)
4. Gerald D. Kleczka (D)
5. James Moody (D)
6. Thomas E. Petri (R)
7. David P. Obey (D)
8. Toby Roth (R)
9. F. James Sensenbrenner, Jr. (R)

WYOMING
(1 Representative)
AL Craig Thomas (R)

1. Vacancy as of September 1, 1991.

Characteristics of Voters in 1988 Presidential Election

(in thousands)

Characteristic	Persons of voting age	Persons reporting they voted		Persons reporting they did not vote	Characteristic	Persons of voting age	Persons reporting they voted		Persons reporting they did not vote
		Total	Percent				Total	Percent	
Male	84,531	47,704	56.4	36,826	North and West	117,373	69,129	58.9	48,243
Female	93,568	54,519	58.3	39,048	South	60,725	33,094	54.5	27,631
White	152,848	90,357	59.1	62,492	Education				
Black	19,692	10,144	51.5	9,548	8 years or less	19,145	7,025	36.7	12,120
Hispanic origin[1]	12,893	3,710	28.8	9,183	9–11 years	21,052	8,698	41.3	12,354
Age: 18–20	10,742	3,570	33.2	7,172	12 years	70,033	38,328	54.7	31,706
21–24	14,827	5,684	38.3	9,142	13–15 years	34,264	22,090	64.5	12,174
25–34	42,677	20,468	48.0	22,210	16 or more	33,604	26,083	77.6	7,521
35–44	35,186	21,550	61.2	13,636	Employed	113,836	66,510	58.4	47,327
45–54	24,277	16,170	66.6	8,107	Unemployed	5,809	2,243	38.6	3,565
55–64	21,585	14,964	69.3	6,621	Not in labor force	58,453	33,471	57.3	24,983
65–74	17,578	12,840	73.0	4,738	**Total**	**178,098**	**102,224**	**57.4**	**75,875**
75 and over	11,226	6,978	62.2	4,248					

1. Persons of Hispanic origin may be of any race. *Source:* Department of Commerce, Bureau of Commerce, Bureau of the Census, *Current Population Survey,* November 1988.

Senate and House Standing Committees, 102nd Congress

Committees of the Senate

Agriculture, Nutrition, and Forestry (18 members)
Chairman: Patrick J. Leahy (Vt.)
Ranking Rep.: Richard G. Luger (Ind.)
Appropriations (29 members)
Chairman: Robert C. Byrd (W.Va.)
Ranking Rep.: Mark O. Hatfield (Ore.)
Armed Services (20 members)
Chairman: Sam Nunn (Ga.)
Ranking Rep.: John Warner (Va.)
Banking, Housing, and Urban Affairs (21 members)
Chairman: Donald W. Riegle (Mich.)
Ranking Rep.: E. J. (Jake) Garn (Utah)
Budget (21 members)
Chairman: James R. Sasser (Tenn.)
Ranking Rep.: Pete V. Domenici (N.M.)
Commerce, Science, and Transportation (20 members)
Chairman: Ernest F. Hollings (S.C.)
Ranking Rep.: John C. Danforth (Mo.)
Energy and Natural Resources (20 members)
Chairman: J. Bennett Johnston (La.)
Ranking Rep.: Malcolm Wallop (Wyom.)
Environment and Public Works (16 members)
Chairman: Quentin N. Burdick (N.D.)
Ranking Rep.: John H. Chafee (R.I.)
Finance (20 members)
Chairman: Lloyd M. Bentsen (Texas)
Ranking Rep.: Bob Packwood (Ore.)
Foreign Relations (18 members)
Chairman: Claiborne Pell (R.I.)
Ranking Rep.: Jesse Helms (N.C.)
Governmental Affairs (14 members)
Chairman: John Glenn (Ohio)
Ranking Rep.: William V. Roth, Jr. (Del.)
Judiciary (14 members)
Chairman: Joseph R. Biden, Jr. (Del)
Ranking Rep.: Strom Thurmond (S.C.)
Labor and Human Resources (17 members)
Chairman: Edward M. Kennedy (Mass.)
Ranking Rep.: Orrin G. Hatch (Utah)
Rules and Administration (16 members)
Chairman: Wendell H. Ford (Ky.)
Ranking Rep.: Ted Stevens (Alas.)
Small Business (18 members)
Chairman: Dale Bumpers (Ark.)
Ranking Rep.: Robert W. Kasten, Jr. (Wisc.)
Veterans' Affairs (12 members)
Chairman: Alan Cranston (Calif.)
Ranking Rep: Arlen Specter (Pa.)

Select and Special Committees

Aging (21 members)
Chairman: David H. Pryor (Ark.)
Ranking Rep.: William S. Cohen (Me.)
Ethics (6 members)
Chairman: Howell T. Heflin (Ala.)
Ranking Rep.: Warren Rudman (N.H.)
Indian Affairs (16 members)
Chairman: Daniel K. Inouye (Hawaii)
Ranking Rep.: John McCain (Ariz.)
Intelligence (15 members)
Chairman: David L. Boren (Okla.)
Ranking Rep.: Frank H. Murkowski (Alas.)

Committees of the House

Agriculture (45 members)
Chairman: E. (Kika) de la Garza (Texas)
Ranking Rep.: E. Thomas Coleman (Mo.)
Appropriations (59 members)
Chairman: Jamie L. Whitten (Miss.)
Ranking Rep.: Joseph M. McDade (Pa.)
Armed Services (54 members)
Chairman: Les Aspin (Wis.)
Ranking Rep.: William L. Dickinson (Ala.)
Banking, Finance, and Urban Affairs (52 members)
Chairman: Henry B. Gonzalez (Texas)
Ranking Rep.: Chalmers P. Wylie (Ohio)
Budget (37 members)
Chairman: Leon E. Panetta (Calif.)
Ranking Rep.: Willis D. Gradison, Jr. (Ohio)
District of Columbia (11 members)
Chairman: Ronald V. Dellums (Calif.)
Ranking Rep.: Thomas J. Bliley, Jr. (Va.)
Education and Labor (37 members)
Chairman: William D. Ford (Mich.)
Ranking Rep.: William F. Goodling (Pa.)
Energy and Commerce (43 members)
Chairman: John D. Dingell (Mich.)
Ranking Rep.: Norman Lent (N.Y.)
Foreign Affairs (45 members)
Chairman: Dante B. Fascell (Fla.)
Ranking Rep.: William S. Broomfield (Mich.)
Government Operations (41 members)
Chairman: John Conyers, Jr. (Mich.)
Ranking Rep.: Frank Horton (N.Y.)
House Administration (24 members)
Chairman: Charlie Rose (N.C.)
Ranking Rep: William M. Thomas (Calif.)
Interior and Insular Affairs (42 members)
Chairman: George Miller (Calif.)
Ranking Rep.: Don Young (Alas.)
Judiciary (34 members)
Chairman: Jack Brooks (Texas)
Ranking Rep.: Hamilton Fish, Jr. (N.Y.)
Merchant Marine and Fisheries (45 members)
Chairman: Walter B. Jones (N.C.)
Ranking Rep.: Robert W. Davis (Mich.)
Post Office and Civil Service (22 members)
Chairman: William (Bill) Clay (Mo.)
Ranking Rep.: Benjamin Gilman (N.Y.)
Public Works and Transportation (55 members)
Chairman: Robert A. Roe (N.J.)
Ranking Rep.: John P. Hammerschmidt (Ark.)
Rules (13 members)
Chairman: John Joseph Moakley (Mass.)
Ranking Rep.: Gerald B.H. Solomon (N.Y.)
Science, Space, and Technology (51 members)
Chairman: George E. Brown, Jr. (Calif.)
Ranking Rep.: Robert S. Walker (Pa.)
Small Business (44 members)
Chairman: John J. LaFalce (N.Y.)
Ranking Rep.: Andy Ireland (Fla.)
Standards of Official Conduct (14 members)
Chairman: Louis Stokes (Ohio)
Ranking Rep.: James V. Hansen (Utah)
Veterans' Affairs (34 members)
Chairman: G. V. (Sonny) Montgomery (Miss.)
Ranking Rep.: Bob Stump (Ariz.)
Ways and Means (36 members)
Chairman: Dan Rostenkowski (Ill.)
Ranking Rep.: William Archer (Texas)

Select Committees

Aging (69 members)
Chairman: Edward Roybal (Calif.)
Ranking Rep.: Matthew J. Rinaldo (N.J.)

Children, Youth, and Families (36 members)
  Chairman: Patricia Schroeder (Colo.)
  Ranking Rep.: Frank R. Wolf (Va.)
Hunger (32 members)
  Chairman: Tony P. Hall (Ohio)
  Ranking Rep.: William Emerson (Mo.)

Intelligence (19 members)
  Chairman: Dave McCurdy (Okla.)
  Ranking Rep.: Bud Shuster (Pa.)
Narcotics Abuse and Control (35 members)
  Chairman: Charles B. Rangel (N.Y.)
  Ranking Rep.: Lawrence Coughlin (Pa.)

Speakers of the House of Representatives

Dates served	Congress	Name and State	Dates served	Congress	Name and State
1789–1791	1	Frederick A. C. Muhlenberg (Pa.)	1869–1869	40	Theodore M. Pomeroy (N.Y.)[5]
1791–1793	2	Jonathan Trumbull (Conn.)	1869–1875	41–43	James G. Blaine (Me.)
1793–1795	3	Frederick A. C. Muhlenberg (Pa.)	1875–1876	44	Michael C. Kerr (Ind.)[6]
1795–1799	4–5	Jonathan Dayton (N.J.)[1]	1876–1881	44–46	Samuel J. Randall (Pa.)
1799–1801	6	Theodore Sedgwick (Mass.)	1881–1883	47	J. Warren Keifer (Ohio)
1801–1807	7–9	Nathaniel Macon (N.C.)	1883–1889	48–50	John G. Carlisle (Ky.)
1807–1811	10–11	Joseph B. Varnum (Mass.)	1889–1891	51	Thomas B. Reed (Me.)
1811–1814	12–13	Henry Clay (Ky.)[2]	1891–1895	52–53	Charles F. Crisp (Ga.)
1814–1815	13	Langdon Cheves (S.C.)	1895–1899	54–55	Thomas B. Reed (Me.)
1815–1820	14–16	Henry Clay (Ky.)[3]	1899–1903	56–57	David B. Henderson (Iowa)
1820–1821	16	John W. Taylor (N.Y.)	1903–1911	58–61	Joseph G. Cannon (Ill.)
1821–1823	17	Philip P. Barbour (Va.)	1911–1919	62–65	Champ Clark (Mo.)
1823–1825	18	Henry Clay (Ky.)	1919–1925	66–68	Frederick H. Gillett (Mass.)
1825–1827	19	John W. Taylor (N.Y.)	1925–1931	69–71	Nicholas Longworth (Ohio)
1827–1834	20–23	Andrew Stevenson (Va.)[4]	1931–1933	72	John N. Garner (Tex.)
1834–1835	23	John Bell (Tenn.)	1933–1934	73	Henry T. Rainey (Ill.)[7]
1835–1839	24–25	James K. Polk (Tenn.)	1935–1936	74	Joseph W. Byrns (Tenn.)[8]
1839–1841	26	Robert M. T. Hunter (Va.)	1936–1940	74–76	William B. Bankhead (Ala.)[9]
1841–1843	27	John White (Ky.)	1940–1947	76–79	Sam Rayburn (Tex.)
1843–1845	28	John W. Jones (Va.)	1947–1949	80	Joseph W. Martin, Jr. (Mass.)
1845–1847	29	John W. Davis (Ind.)	1949–1953	81–82	Sam Rayburn (Tex.)
1847–1849	30	Robert C. Winthrop (Mass.)	1953–1955	83	Joseph W. Martin, Jr. (Mass.)
1849–1851	31	Howell Cobb (Ga.)	1955–1961	84–87	Sam Rayburn (Tex.)[10]
1851–1855	32–33	Linn Boyd (Ky.)	1962–1971	87–91	John W. McCormack (Mass.)[11]
1855–1857	34	Nathaniel P. Banks (Mass.)	1971–1977	92–94	Carl Albert (Okla.)[12]
1857–1859	35	James L. Orr (S.C.)	1977–1987	95–99	Thomas P. O'Neill, Jr. (Mass.)[13]
1859–1861	36	Wm. Pennington (N.J.)	1987–1989	100–101	James C. Wright, Jr. (Tex.)[14]
1861–1863	37	Galusha A. Grow (Pa.)	1989–	101–	Thomas S. Foley (Wash.)
1863–1869	38–40	Schuyler Colfax (Ind.)			

1. George Dent (Md.) was elected Speaker pro tempore for April 20 and May 28, 1798. 2. Resigned during second session of 13th Congress. 3. Resigned between first and second sessions of 16th Congress. 4. Resigned during first session of 23rd Congress. 5. Elected Speaker and served the day of adjournment. 6. Died between first and second sessions of 44th Congress. During first session, there were two Speakers pro tempore: Samuel S. Cox (N.Y.), appointed for Feb. 17, May 12, and June 19, 1876, and Milton Sayler (Ohio), appointed for June 4, 1876. 7. Died in 1934 after adjournment of second session of 73rd Congress. 8. Died during second session of 74th Congress. 9. Died during third session of 76th Congress. 10. Died between first and second sessions of 87th Congress. 11. Not a candidate in 1970 election. 12. Not a candidate in 1976 election. 13. Not a candidate in 1986 election. 14. Resigned during first session of 101st Congress. *Source: Congressional Directory.*

Floor Leaders of the Senate

Democratic	Republican
Gilbert M. Hitchcock, Neb. (Min. 1919–20)	Charles Curtis, Kan. (Maj. 1925–29)
Oscar W. Underwood, Ala. (Min. 1920–23)	James E. Watson, Ind. (Maj. 1929–33)
Joseph T. Robinson, Ark. (Min. 1923–33, Maj. 1933–37)	Charles L. McNary, Ore. (Min. 1933–44)
Alben W. Barkley, Ky. (Maj. 1937–46, Min. 1947–48)	Wallace H. White, Jr., Me. (Min. 1944–47, Maj. 1947–48)
Scott W. Lucas, Ill. (Maj. 1949–50)	Kenneth S. Wherry, Neb. (Min. 1949–51)
Ernest W. McFarland, Ariz. (Maj. 1951–52)	Styles Bridges, N. H. (Min. 1951–52)
Lyndon B. Johnson, Tex. (Min. 1953–54, Maj. 1955–60)	Robert A. Taft, Ohio (Maj. 1953)
Mike Mansfield, Mont. (Maj. 1961–77)	William F. Knowland, Calif. (Maj. 1953–54, Min. 1955–58)
Robert C. Byrd, W. Va. (Maj. 1977–81, Min. 1981–86, Maj. 1987–88)	Everett M. Dirksen, Ill. (Min. 1959–69)
George John Mitchell, Me. (Maj. 1989–)	Hugh Scott, Pa. (Min. 1969–1977)
	Howard H. Baker, Jr., Tenn. (Min. 1977–81, Maj. 1981–84)
	Robert J. Dole, Kan. (Maj. 1985–86, Min. 1987–)

NOTE: Min. = Minority Leader; Maj. = Majority Leader. *Source:* United States Senate, Secretary for the Majority.

Presidential Election of 1988

Principal Candidates for President and Vice President
Republican: George H. Bush; J. Danforth Quayle
Democratic: Michael S. Dukakis; Lloyd Bentsen

State	Total	Bush Rep.	Percent	Dukakis Dem.	Percent	Plurality	Electoral vote R	Electoral vote D
Alabama	1,378,476	815,576	59.17	549,506	39.86	266,070	9	—
Alaska	200,116	119,251	59.59	72,584	36.27	46,667	3	—
Arizona	1,171,873	702,541	59.95	454,029	38.74	248,512	7	—
Arkansas	827,738	466,578	56.37	349,237	42.19	117,341	6	—
California	9,887,065	5,054,917	51.13	4,702,233	47.56	352,684	47	—
Colorado	1,372,394	728,177	53.06	621,453	45.28	106,724	8	—
Connecticut	1,443,394	750,241	51.98	676,584	46.87	73,657	8	—
Delaware	249,891	139,639	55.88	108,647	43.48	30,992	3	—
D.C.	192,877	27,590	14.30	159,407	82.65	131,817	—	3
Florida	4,302,313	2,618,885	60.87	1,656,701	38.51	962,184	21	—
Georgia	1,809,672	1,081,331	59.75	714,792	39.50	366,539	12	—
Hawaii	354,461	158,625	44.75	192,364	54.27	33,739	—	4
Idaho	408,968	253,881	62.08	147,272	36.01	106,609	4	—
Illinois	4,559,120	2,310,939	50.69	2,215,940	48.60	94,999	24	—
Indiana	2,168,621	1,297,763	59.84	860,643	39.69	437,120	12	—
Iowa	1,225,614	545,355	44.50	670,557	54.71	125,202	—	8
Kansas	993,044	554,049	55.79	422,636	42.56	131,413	7	—
Kentucky	1,322,517	734,281	55.52	580,368	43.88	153,913	9	—
Louisiana	1,628,202	883,702	54.27	717,460	44.06	166,242	10	—
Maine	555,035	307,131	55.34	243,569	43.88	63,562	4	—
Maryland	1,714,358	876,167	51.11	826,304	48.20	49,863	10	—
Massachusetts	2,632,805	1,194,635	45.38	1,401,415	53.23	206,780	—	13
Michigan	3,669,163	1,965,486	53.57	1,675,783	45.67	289,703	20	—
Minnesota	2,096,790	962,337	45.90	1,109,471	52.91	147,134	—	10
Mississippi	931,527	557,890	59.89	363,921	39.07	193,969	7	—
Missouri	2,093,713	1,084,953	51.82	1,001,619	47.84	83,334	11	—
Montana	365,674	190,412	52.07	168,936	46.20	21,476	4	—
Nebraska	661,465	397,956	60.16	259,235	39.19	138,721	5	—
Nevada	350,067	206,040	58.86	132,738	37.92	73,302	4	—
New Hampshire	451,074	281,537	62.41	163,696	36.29	117,841	4	—
New Jersey	3,099,553	1,743,192	56.24	1,320,352	42.60	422,840	16	—
New Mexico	521,287	270,341	51.86	244,497	46.90	25,844	5	—
New York[1]	6,485,683	3,081,871	47.52	3,347,882	51.62	266,011	—	36
North Carolina	2,134,370	1,237,258	57.97	890,167	41.71	347,091	13	—
North Dakota	297,261	166,559	56.03	127,739	42.97	38,820	3	—
Ohio	4,393,699	2,416,549	55.00	1,939,629	44.15	476,920	23	—
Oklahoma	1,171,036	678,367	57.93	483,423	41.28	194,944	8	—
Oregon	1,201,694	560,126	46.61	616,206	51.28	56,080	—	7
Pennsylvania	4,536,251	2,300,087	50.70	2,194,944	48.39	105,143	25	—
Rhode Island	404,620	177,761	43.93	225,123	55.64	47,362	—	4
South Carolina	986,009	606,443	61.50	370,554	37.58	235,889	8	—
South Dakota	312,991	165,415	52.85	145,560	46.51	19,855	3	—
Tennessee	1,636,250	947,233	57.89	679,794	41.55	267,439	11	—
Texas	5,427,410	3,036,829	55.95	2,352,748	43.35	684,081	29	—
Utah	647,008	428,442	66.22	207,343	32.05	221,099	5	—
Vermont	243,328	124,331	51.10	115,775	47.58	8,556	3	—
Virginia	2,191,609	1,309,162	59.74	859,799	39.23	449,363	12	—
Washington	1,865,253	903,835	48.46	933,516	50.05	29,681	—	10
West Virginia	653,311	310,065	47.46	341,016	52.20	30,951	—	6
Wisconsin	2,191,608	1,047,499	47.80	1,126,794	51.41	79,295	—	11
Wyoming	176,551	106,867	60.53	67,113	38.01	39,754	3	—
Total	**91,594,809**	**48,886,097**	**53.37**	**41,809,074**	**45.65**	**7,077,023**	**426**	**112**

1. Bush figure is combined Republican and Conservative Party votes; Dukakis figure is combined Democratic and Liberal Party votes. NATIONAL TOTALS OF OTHER CANDIDATES FOR PRESIDENT: Ronald E. Paul, Libertarian, 432,179; Lenora B. Fulani, New Alliance, 217,219; David Duke, Populist, 47,047; Eugene J. McCarthy, Consumer, 30,905; James C. Griffin, American Independent; 27,818; Lyndon H. LaRouche, National Economic, 25,562; William A. Marra, Right to Life, 20,504; Ed Winn, Workers League, 18,693; James Mac Warren, Socialist Workers; 15,604; Herbert Lewin, Peace & Freedom, 10,370; Earl Dodge, Prohibition, 8,002; Larry Holmes, Workers World, 7,846; Willa Kenoyer, Socialist, 3,882; Delmar Dennis, American, 3,475; Jack Herer, GrassRoots, 1,949; Louie G. Youngkeit, Independent, 372; John G. Martin, Third World Assembly, 236; write-ins and None of the Above, 27,975. *Source: Federal Elections 88,* Federal Election Commission.

The Governors of the Fifty States

State	Governor	Current term[1]	State	Governor	Current term[1]
Ala.	Guy Hunt (R)	1991–95	Mont.	Stanley Stephens (R)	1989–93
Alaska	Walter Hickel (Ind.)	1990–94[2]	Neb.	Ben Nelson (D)	1991–95
Ariz.	Fife Symington (R)	1991–95	Nev.	Bob Miller (D)	1991–95
Ark.	Bill Clinton (D)	1991–95	N.H.	Judd Gregg (R)	1991–93
Calif.	Pete Wilson (R)	1991–95	N.J.	James Florio (D)	1990–94
Colo.	Roy Romer (D)	1991–95	N.M.	Bruce King (D)	1991–95
Conn.	Lowell P. Weicker Jr. (Ind.)	1991–95	N.Y.	Mario M. Cuomo (D)	1991–95
Del.	Michael Castle (R)	1989–93	N.C.	James G. Martin (R)	1989–93
Fla.	Lawton Chiles (D)	1991–95	N.D.	George A. Sinner (D)	1989–93
Ga.	Zell Miller (D)	1991–95	Ohio	George Voinovich (R)	1991–95
Hawaii	John Waihee (D)	1990–94[2]	Okla.	David Walters (D)	1991–95
Idaho	Cecil D. Andrus (D)	1991–95	Ore.	Barbara Roberts (D)	1991–95
Ill.	Jim Edgar (R)	1991–95	Pa.	Robert P. Casey (D)	1991–95
Ind.	B. Evan Bayh III (R)	1989–93	R.I.	Bruce Sundlun (D)	1991–93
Iowa	Terry E. Branstad (R)	1991–95	S.C.	Carroll A. Campbell, Jr. (R)	1991–95
Kan.	Joan Finney (D)	1991–95	S.D.	George Mickelson (R)	1991–95
Ky.	Wallace Wilkinson (D)	1987–91[2]	Tenn.	Ned McWherter (D)	1991–95
La.	Charles (Buddy) Roemer (D)	1988–92[3]	Tex.	Ann Richards (D)	1991–95
Me.	John R. McKernan, Jr. (R)	1991–95	Utah	Norman H. Bangerter (R)	1989–93
Md.	William Donald Schaefer (D)	1991–95	Vt.	Howard Dean (D)	1991–95
Mass.	William F. Weld (R)	1991–95	Va.	L. Douglas Wilder (D)	1990–94
Mich.	John Engler (R)	1991–95	Wash.	Booth Gardner (D)	1989–93
Minn.	Arne Carlson (R)	1991–95	W. Va.	Gaston Caperton (D)	1989–93
Miss.	Ray Mabus (D)	1988–92	Wis.	Tommy G. Thompson (R)	1991–95
Mo.	John D. Ashcroft (R)	1989–93	Wyo.	Mike J. Sullivan (D)	1991–95

1. Except where indicated, all terms begin in January. 2. December. 3. March.

Black Elected Officials

Year	U.S. and State Legislatures[1]	City and County Offices[2]	Law Enforcement[3]	Education[4]	Total
1970 (Feb.)	182	715	213	362	1,472
1975 (Apr.)	299	1,878	387	939	3,503
1977 (July)	316	2,497	447	1,051	4,311
1978 (July)	316	2,595	454	1,138	4,503
1979 (July)	315	2,647	486	1,136	4,584
1980 (July)	326	2,832	526	1,206	4,890
1981 (July)	343	2,863	549	1,259	5,014
1982 (July)	342	2,951	563	1,259	5,115
1983 (July)	366	3,197	607	1,369	5,559
1984 (Jan.)	396	3,259	636	1,363	5,654
1985 (Jan.)	407	3,517	661	1,431	6,016[5]
1986 (Jan.)	420	3,824	676	1,504	6,424[5]
1987 (Jan.)	440	3,966	728	1,547	6,681
1988 (July)	436	4,105	738	1,550	6,829
1989 (Jan.)	448	4,406	759	1,612	7,225
1990 (Jan.)	447	4,499	769	1,655	7,370

1. Includes elected State administrators and governors. 2. County commissioners and councilmen, mayors, vice mayors, aldermen, regional officials, and other. 3. Judges, magistrates, constables, marshals, sheriffs, justices of the peace, and other. 4. Members of State education agencies, college boards, school boards, and other. 5. Includes Black elected officials in the Virgin Islands. *Source:* Joint Center for Political and Economic Studies, Washington, D.C., *Black Elected Officials: A National Roster,* Copyright.

Annual Salaries of Federal Officials

President of the U.S.	$200,000[1]	Senators and Representatives	$125,100
Vice President of the U.S.	160,600[2]	President Pro Tempore of Senate	138,900
Cabinet members	138,900	Majority and Minority Leader of the Senate	138,900
Deputy Secretaries of State, Defense, Treasury	125,100	Majority and Minority Leader of the House	138,900
Deputy Attorney General	125,100	Speaker of the House	160,600
Secretaries of the Army, Navy, Air Force	125,100	Chief Justice of the United States	160,600
Under secretaries of executive departments	115,300	Associate Justices of the Supreme Court	153,600

1. Plus taxable $50,000 for expenses and a nontaxable sum (not to exceed $100,000 a year) for travel expenses. 2. Plus taxable $10,000 for expenses. NOTE: All salaries shown above are taxable. Data are as of September 1991. *Source:* Office of Personnel Management.

BUSINESS & ECONOMY

Illiteracy—Cancer of American Society

By Lawrence P. Grayson

The United States is facing the 1990s with the challenge of severe economic competition from productive foreign firms in Europe and Asia. Yet, even as U.S. industry is making major efforts to increase its competitive edge, the nation's young people, those upon whom industry must rely to achieve its goals, lack the basic educational skills for tomorrow's jobs.

Despite the enormous investment of time, effort, and money devoted to education over the past two decades, former Education Secretary Lauro F. Cavazos reported recently that "the reading and writing skills of American students remain dreadfully inadequate. . . . As a nation we should be appalled that we have placed our children in such jeopardy."

Even among our most "educationally advantaged" students, those whose parents have gone to college, the proportion of 17-year-olds who can read advanced materials has declined significantly. Less than 5 percent can understand literary essays, historical documents, scientific materials, and other reading matter of the type encountered in college textbooks.

How can America compete economically against nations in which literacy is almost universal, when 21 million adults in the U.S. cannot read even at the fourth-grade level and many entry-level workers lack the basic skills to study training manuals in business and industry? At Motorola a seventh-grade-level English comprehension test stumps 80 percent of its job applicants. Chrysler Corporation has written its training manuals at an eighth-grade level. But that is beyond the reading ability of more than 25 percent of the people the company already employs.

Over the next decade, 80 percent of the new jobs will require more than a high school education. Yet among those 20 to 24 years old, 40 percent of the Hispanics, 23 percent of the African Americans, and 17 percent of the whites have not completed high school. Even among those who have graduated from high school, 40 percent cannot read at the ninth-grade level.

American industry soon may be forced to hire a million workers a year who cannot read or write at the required levels. The cost to industry to provide remedial education and in lost productivity is estimated to be $25 million per year. This is a tremendous handicap to firms competing in international markets.

The improvement of education is a fundamental, national challenge facing America. Illiteracy undermines our economy, our national defense, our desire to eliminate poverty in the nation, and equal opportunity for all. It is only a few short steps from an ineffective classroom to a future of lost opportunities, unfulfilled dreams, and economic decline. The ability to read and write well enough to function in society is necessary to open doors of hope and expanded opportunity. We must not let illiteracy limit young Americans to lives of pessimism and despair, or the country to a declining standard of living.

We must mount an effort throughout the nation to teach everyone to understand print—to recognize letters, form syllables, link them into words, and know how words form sentences and paragraphs to present ideas—and to be provided with rich, satisfying experiences gained through the reading of articles, stories, and books. This must begin at home, and be continued in every first grade in the United States.

Parents must read to their children, and provide environments in their homes to encourage study. Schools must improve English-language programs based on methods that research and practice have proven effective, and increase the number of well-trained minority teachers, principals, and counselors. The more than 50 programs already funded by the Federal Government to deal with illiteracy should be assessed to determine their effectiveness and revised accordingly. Closer-links must be established between colleges and schools to promote pre-service and in-service training in the most effective approaches for teaching reading. Community groups and businesses must establish new programs of volunteer activities, expand their work/study programs to show the necessity of literacy in the workplace, and reward those who complete their schooling by increasing resources for scholarships. We will not have a competitive America until we improve education for all. We will not have full employment and jobs for everyone who wants to work in this country until each person can read and write. We will not have a true foundation of economic justice in America until everyone has the skills and opportunity to succeed. The American dream is for everyone to have the chance to reach as high as his or her God-given potential allows—and literacy is the key to unlocking that opportunity. □

Dr. Grayson is a former chairman of the board of governors of the American Association of Engineering Societies (an organization representing over 500,000 U.S. engineers in industry, government, and education).

Hispanic-Owned Businesses Are Growing

Hispanic firms grew in number by 81 percent between 1982 and 1987, according to the 1987 Survey of Minority-Owned Businesses, released on May 16, 1991. In 1982 there were 233,975 Hispanic firms; in 1987, there were 422,373. The survey covered only unincorporated businesses and small corporations. Receipts for Hispanic-owned firms increased 110 percent, from $11.8 billion to $24.7 billion.

Individual proprietorships accounted for 94 percent of Hispanic-owned firms in 1987 and accounted for 61 percent of gross receipts. Partnerships made up 3 percent of the firms as did small corporations, accounting for 9 percent and 29 percent of gross receipts, respectively. Service industries, at 44 percent, led the field in numbers but accounted for only 24 percent of gross receipts.

Consumer Price Indexes

(1982–84 = 100)

Year	All items	En-ergy	Food	Shel-ter	Apparel[1]	Trans-porta-tion	Medical care	Fuel oil	Electric-ity	Utility (gas)	Tele-phone	Com-modi-ties
1960	29.6	22.4	30.0	25.2	45.7	29.8	22.3	13.5	29.9	17.6	58.3	33.6
1970	38.8	25.5	39.2	35.5	59.2	37.5	34.0	16.5	31.8	19.6	58.7	41.7
1975	53.8	42.1	59.8	48.8	72.5	50.1	47.5	34.9	50.0	31.1	71.7	58.2
1980	82.4	86.0	86.8	81.0	90.9	83.1	74.9	87.7	75.8	65.7	77.7	86.0
1988	118.3	89.3	118.2	127.1	115.4	108.7	138.6	75.8	111.5	94.5	116.0	111.5
1989	124.0	100.9	125.1	132.8	118.6	114.1	149.3	n.a.	n.a.	n.a.	n.a.	n.a.
1990	130.7	104.5	132.4	140.0	124.1	120.5	162.8	n.a.	n.a.	n.a.	n.a.	n.a.

1. Includes upkeep. *Source: Monthly Labor Review, July 1991.*

Consumer Price Index for All Urban Consumers

(1982–84 = 100)

Group	March 1991	March 1990	Group	March 1991	March 1990
All items	135.0	128.7	Fuel oil, coal, bottled gas	99.3	91.5
Food	135.8	131.5	House operation[1]	115.7	112.8
Alcoholic beverages	142.2	127.8	House furnishings	107.5	106.9
Apparel and upkeep	128.8	125.4	Transportation	122.3	116.8
Men's and boys' apparel	123.0	119.3	Medical care	173.7	158.7
Women's and girls' apparel	129.5	126.8	Personal care	133.6	129.0
Footwear	120.8	116.9	Tobacco products	197.6	175.1
Housing, total	132.6	126.8	Entertainment	136.7	130.9
Rent	142.0	136.5	Personal and educational		
Gas and electricity	110.8	107.9	expenses	179.3	166.3

1. Combines house furnishings and operation. *Source:* Department of Labor, Bureau of Labor Statistics.

Per Capita Personal Income

Year	Amount	Year	Amount	Year	Amount	Year	Amount	Year	Amount
1935	$474	1965	$2,773	1976	6,402	1981	10,949	1986	14,597
1945	1,223	1970	3,893	1977	7,043	1982	11,480	1987	15,471
1950	1,501	1973	4,980	1978	7,729	1983	12,098	1988	16,491
1955	1,881	1974	5,428	1979	8,638	1984	13,114	1989	17,594
1960	2,219	1975	$5,851	1980	$9,910	1985	$13,896	1990[1]	18,685

1. Preliminary. *Source:* Department of Commerce, Bureau of Economic Analysis.

Per Capita Income and Personal Consumption Expenditures

(In current dollars)

Year	Gross national product	Personal income	Disposable personal income	Personal Consumption Expenditures			
				Durable goods	Nondurable goods	Services	Total
1950	$1,900	$1,504	$1,368	$203	$648	$416	$1,267
1955	2,456	1,901	1,687	235	755	570	1,560
1960	2,851	2,265	1,986	240	847	741	1,829
1965	3,268	2,840	2,505	327	987	954	2,268
1970	4,951	4,056	3,489	418	1,318	1,385	3,121
1975	7,401	6,081	5,291	627	1,927	2,135	4,689
1980	11,985	9,916	8,421	963	2,992	3,653	7,607
1985	16,776	13,895	11,861	1,555	3,807	5,622	10,985
1986	17,511	14,592	12,469	1,680	3,898	5,998	11,576
1987	18,508	15,437	13,094	1,735	4,104	6,495	12,334
1988	19,783	16,524	14,123	1,857	4,303	6,984	13,144
1989	20,903	17,621	14,973	1,908	4,541	7,417	13,866
1990	21,737	18,477	15,695	1,910	4,748	7,888	14,547

Source: U.S. Department of Commerce, *Survey of Current Business, July 1991.*

Total Family Income
(figures in percent)

Income range	White 1989	White 1985	White 1975	Black 1989	Black 1985	Black 1975	Hispanic[1] 1989	Hispanic[1] 1985	Hispanic[1] 1975
Families (thousands)[2]	56,590	54,991	49,873	7,470	6,921	5,586	4,840	4,206	2,499
Under $5,000	2.6	3.3	2.2	11.2	11.6	6.9	6.7	7.0	5.6
$5,000 to $9,999	5.1	6.5	6.3	14.7	16.8	18.3	11.9	15.6	13.8
$10,000 to $14,999	7.5	8.5	8.8	12.6	12.8	14.7	12.1	14.0	14.9
$15,000 to $24,999	16.4	18.8	19.7	19.5	21.8	23.2	21.9	22.6	25.3
$25,000 to $34,999	16.8	18.2	20.5	14.4	14.4	16.4	16.5	16.5	19.4
$35,000 to $49,999	20.7	20.6	22.7	13.7	13.1	13.7	16.2	13.5	14.1
$50,000 to $74,999	18.7	16.0	14.3	10.2	7.6	5.8	10.2	8.6	5.4
$75,000 to $99,999	6.9	4.7	3.3	2.8	1.3	0.8	2.9	1.5	0.9
$100,000 and over	5.3	3.3	2.1	0.8	0.6	0.3	1.6	0.8	0.6
Median income	$35,975	$32,051	$31,374	$20,209	$18,455	$19,304	$23,446	$20,919	$21,002

1. Persons of Hispanic origin may be of any race. 2. As of March 1990. *Source:* Department of Commerce, Bureau of the Census.

Median Weekly Earnings of Full-Time Workers by Occupation and Sex

Occupation	Men Number of workers (in thousands)	Men Median weekly earnings	Women Number of workers (in thousands)	Women Median weekly earnings	Total Number of workers (in thousands)	Total Median weekly earnings
Managerial and prof. specialty	12,145	$754	10,632	$520	22,778	$622
Executive, admin, and managerial	6,274	766	4,742	500	11,016	620
Professional specialty	5,871	743	5,891	548	11,762	623
Technical, sales, and admin. support	9,481	497	15,870	337	25,351	383
Technicians and related support	1,704	578	1,371	417	3,075	496
Sales occupations	4,600	502	3,496	299	8,095	404
Administrative support, incl. clerical	3,178	450	11,003	336	14,181	355
Service occupations	4,415	327	4,444	234	8,859	273
Private household	23	([1])	298	169	321	171
Protective service	1,429	496	187	443	1,616	488
Service, except private household and protective	2,963	284	3,959	235	6,922	255
Precision production, craft, and repair	9,992	492	851	315	10,843	481
Mechanics and repairers	3,637	478	145	413	3,781	477
Construction trades	3,402	482	39	([1])	3,441	480
Other precision production, craft, and repair	2,953	514	668	305	3,621	487
Operators, fabricators, and laborers	11,235	383	3,701	265	14,936	345
Machine operators, assemblers, and inspectors	4,458	392	2,793	262	7,251	332
Transportation and material moving occupations	3,873	419	231	325	4,104	415
Handlers, equipment cleaners, helpers, and laborers	2,904	313	677	260	3,581	304
Farming, forestry, and fishing	1,199	268	125	208	1,324	263

1. Data not shown where base is less than 100,000. NOTE: Figures are for the fourth quarter of 1990. *Source:* U.S. Department of Labor, Bureau of Labor Statistics, "Employment and Earnings," January 1991.

Consumer Credit
(installment credit outstanding; in billions of dollars, not seasonally adjusted)

Holder	1990	1989	1988	1987	1986	1985	1980	1975
Commercial banks	347.5	342.8	324.8	287.2	266.8	245.1	147.0	82.9
Finance companies	137.5	140.8	146.2	141.1	134.7	111.9	62.2	32.7
Credit unions	92.9	93.1	88.3	81.0	77.1	72.7	44.0	25.7
Retailers[1]	43.6	44.2	48.4	46.0	43.3	42.9	28.7	18.2
Other[2]	50.4	61.2	67.1	64.4	60.0	53.8	20.1	9.2
Total[3]	748.3	730.9	674.8	619.7	581.9	526.4	302.1	168.7

1. Excludes 30-day charge credit held by retailers, oil and gas companies, and travel and entertainment companies. 2. Includes mutual savings banks, savings and loan associations, and gasoline companies. 3. Beginning 1989, outstanding balances of pools upon which securities have been issued; these balances are no longer on the balance sheets for the loan originators. Data are *not* available historically. *Source:* Federal Reserve Bulletin.

The Public Debt

Year	Gross debt Amount (in millions)	Per capita	Year	Gross debt Amount (in millions)	Per capita
1800 (Jan. 1)	$ 83	$ 15.87	1950	$256,087[1]	$1,688.30
1860 (June 30)	65	2.06	1955	272,807[1]	1,650.63
1865	2,678	75.01	1960	284,093[1]	1,572.31
1900	1,263	16.60	1965	313,819[1]	1,612.70
1920	24,299	228.23	1970	370,094[1]	1,807.09
1925	20,516	177.12	1975	533,189	2,496.90
1930	16,185	131.51	1980	907,701	3,969.55
1935	28,701	225.55	1985	1,823,103	7,598.51
1940	42,968	325.23	1989	2,857,431	11,452.12
1945	258,682	1,848.60	1990	3,233,313	12,823,28

1. Adjusted to exclude issues to the International Monetary Fund and other international lending institutions to conform to the budget presentation. *Source:* Department of the Treasury, Financial Management Service.

Gross National Product or Expenditure[1]

(in billions)

Holder	1990	1989	1988	1987	1985	1980	1970	1960	1950
Gross national product	5,465.1	$5,200.8	$4,880.6	$4,524.3	$4,014.9	$2,732.0	$1,015.5	515.3	288.3
GNP in constant (1982) dollars	4,157.3	4,117.7	4,024.4	3,853.7	3,618.7	3,187.1	2,416.2	1,665.3	1,203.7
Personal consumption expenditures	3,657.3	3,450.1	3,235.1	3,010.8	2,629.0	1,732.6	640.0	330.7	192.1
Durable goods	480.3	474.6	455.2	421.0	372.2	219.3	85.7	43.5	30.8
Nondurable goods	1,193.7	1,130.0	1,052.3	998.1	911.2	681.4	270.3	153.2	98.2
Services	1,983.3	1,845.0	1,727.6	1,591.7	1,345.6	831.9	284.0	134.0	63.2
Gross private domestic investment	741.0	771.2	750.3	699.9	643.1	437.0	148.8	78.2	55.1
Residential	222.0	231.0	232.4	226.4	188.8	122.5	40.5	26.3	20.5
Nonresidential	524.1	511.9	487.2	444.3	442.9	322.8	105.2	48.8	27.8
Change in business inventories	-5.0	28.3	30.6	29.3	11.3	-8.3	3.1	3.1	6.8
Net export of goods and services	-31.2	-46.1	-73.7	-112.6	-78.0	32.1	8.5	5.9	2.2
Government purchases	1,098.1	1,025.6	968.9	926.1	820.8	530.3	218.2	100.6	38.8
Federal	424.0	400.0	381.3	381.6	355.2	208.1	98.8	54.4	19.1
National defense	313.6	301.1	298.0	294.8	259.1	142.7	76.8	45.3	14.3
Other	110.4	98.9	83.3	86.8	96.1	65.4	22.0	9.1	4.8
State and local	674.1	625.6	587.6	544.5	465.6	322.2	119.4	46.1	19.8

1. Current dollars except as noted. *Source:* Department of Commerce, Bureau of Economic Analysis.

Producer Price Indexes by Major Commodity Groups

(1982 = 100)

Commodity	1990	1989	1985	1980	1975	1970
All commodities	116.3	112.2	103.2	89.8	58.4	38.1
Farm products	112.2	110.7	95.1	102.9	77.0	45.8
Processed foods and feeds	121.9	117.8	103.5	95.9	72.6	44.6
Textile products and apparel	114.9	112.3	102.9	89.7	67.4	52.4
Hides, skins, and leather products	141.7	136.3	108.9	94.7	56.5	42.0
Fuels and related products and power	82.2	72.9	91.4	82.8	35.4	15.3
Chemicals and allied products	123.6	123.1	103.7	89.0	62.0	35.0
Rubber and plastic products	113.6	112.6	101.9	90.1	62.2	44.9
Lumber and wood products	129.7	126.7	106.6	101.5	62.1	39.9
Pulp, paper, and allied products	141.3	137.8	113.3	86.3	59.0	37.5
Metals and metal products	123.0	124.1	104.4	95.0	61.5	38.7
Machinery and equipment	120.7	117.4	107.2	86.0	57.9	40.0
Furniture and household durables	119.1	116.9	107.1	90.7	67.5	51.9
Nonmetallic mineral products	114.7	112.6	108.6	88.4	54.4	35.3
Transportation equipment	121.5	117.7	107.9	82.9	56.7	41.9
Miscellaneous products	n.a.	n.a.	109.4	93.6	53.4	39.8

NOTE: n.a. = not available. *Source:* Department of Commerce, Bureau of Economic Analysis, *Survey of Current Businesses, July 1991.*

Weekly Earnings of Full-Time Women Workers

Major occupation group	1990 weekly earnings	% Men's weekly earnings
Managerial and professional specialty	$511	69.9
Executive, administrative, and managerial	485	65.4
Professional specialty	534	74.2
Technical, sales, and administrative support	332	66.9
Technicians and related support	417	73.2
Sales occupations	292	57.8
Administrative support, including clerical	332	75.5
Service occupations	230	71.9
Precision production, craft, and repair	316	64.8
Operators, fabricators, and laborers	262	69.3
Machine operators, assemblers, and inspectors	260	66.5
Transportation and material moving	314	75.1
Handlers, equipment cleaners, helpers, and laborers	250	81.2
Farming, forestry, and fishing	216	82.1
Total; all occupations	**348**	**71.8**

1. Median usual weekly earnings. Half the workers earn more and half the workers usually earn less each week. *Source:* U.S. Department of Labor, Bureau of Labor Statistics.

New Housing Starts[1] and Mobile Homes Shipped

(in thousands)

Year	No. of units started	Year	No. of units started	Year	Mobile homes shipped
1900	189	1970	1,469	1965	216
1910	387	1975	1,171	1970	401
1920	247	1980	1,313	1975	213
1925	937	1982	1,072	1980	222
1930	330	1983	1,712	1983	296
1935	221	1984	1,756	1984	295
1940	603	1985	1,745	1985	284
1945	326	1986	1,807	1986	244
1950	1,952	1987	1,623	1987	233
1955	1,646	1988[2]	1,488	1988	218
1960[1]	1,296	1989	1,376	1989	198
1965	1,510	1990	1,193	1990	188

1. Prior to 1960, starts limited to nonfarm housing; from 1960 on, figures include farm housing. 2. As of 1988 data for housing starts no longer includes public housing starts and only includes private housing starts. *Sources:* Department of Commerce, Housing Construction Statistics, 1900–1965, and Construction Reports, Housing Starts, 1970–83, Manufactured Housing Institute, 1965–76; National Conference of States on Building Codes and Standards.

Median Family Income

(in current dollars)

Year	Income	Percent change	Year	Income	Percent change
1970	$9,867	—	1985	27,144	5.0
1980	21,023	6.9	1986	28,236	4.0
1981	22,388	6.5	1987	29,744	5.3
1982	23,433	4.7	1988	30,992	4.0
1983	24,580	4.9	1989	32,448	4.5
1984	25,948	5.1	1990	33,956	4.4

Source: U.S. Department of Labor, Bureau of Labor Statistics, *Employment and Earnings.*

Expenditures for New Plant and Equipment[1]

(in billions of dollars)

Year	Manufacturing	Transportation[2]	Total nonmanufacturing	Total
1950	$7.73	$2.87	$18.08	$25.81
1955	12.50	3.10	24.58	37.08
1960	16.36	3.54	32.63	48.99
1965	25.41	5.66	45.39	70.79
1970	36.99	7.17	69.16	106.15
1975	53.66	9.95	108.95	162.60
1980	112.60	13.56	205.48	318.08
1984	139.61	13.44	278.77	418.38
1985	152.88	14.57	302.05	454.93
1986	137.95	15.05	309.16	447.11
1987	141.06	15.07	320.45	461.51
1988	163.45	16.63	344.77	508.22
1989	183.80	18.84	380.13	563.93
1990	192.78	21.59	399.52	592.31

1. Data exclude agriculture. 2. Transportation is included in total nonmanufacturing. NOTE: This series was revised in April 1991. *Source:* Department of Commerce, Bureau of the Census.

Life Insurance in Force

(in millions of dollars)

As of Dec. 31	Ordinary	Group	Industrial	Credit	Total
1915	$16,650	$100	$4,279	—	$21,029
1930	78,756	9,801	17,693	$73	106,413
1945	101,550	22,172	27,675	365	151,762
1950	149,071	47,793	33,415	3,844	234,168
1955	216,812	101,345	39,682	14,493	373,332
1960	341,881	175,903	39,563	29,101	586,448
1965	499,638	308,078	39,818	53,020	900,554
1970	734,730	551,357	38,644	77,392	1,402,123
1980	1,760,474	1,579,355	35,994	165,215	3,541,038
1985	3,247,289	2,561,595	28,250	215,973	6,053,107
1989	4,939,964	3,469,498	24,446	260,107	8,694,015
1990	5,366,982	3,753,506	24,071	248,038	9,392,597

Source: American Council of Life Insurance.

Farm Indexes

(1977 = 100)

Year	Prices paid by farmers[1]	Prices rec'd by farmers[2]	Ratio
1950	37	56	151
1955	40	51	128
1960	44	52	118
1965	49	54	115
1970	56	60	109
1975	90	101	113
1980	138	134	97
1985	162	128	79
1989	178	147	83
1990	184	150	82

1. Commodities, interest, and taxes and wage rates. 2. All crops and livestock. *Source:* Department of Agriculture, National Agricultural Statistics Service.

Estimated Annual Retail and Wholesale Sales by Kind of Business
(in millions of dollars)

Kind of business	1990	1989	Kind of business	1990	1989
Retail trade, total	1,807,219	1,741,748	Electrical goods	116,901	112,919
Building materials, hardware, garden			Hardware, plumbing, heating, and		
supplies, and mobile home dealers	92,524	92,700	supplies	44,922	44,047
Automotive dealers	381,961	383,596	Machinery, equipment, supplies	264,382	251,122
Furniture, home furnishings,			Sporting, recreational, photographic		
and equipment stores	92,983	91,493	and hobby goods, toys, supplies	25,234	24,553
General merchandise group stores	211,933	204,387	Metals and minerals except petroleum	90,871	86,937
Food stores	362,410	345,069	Miscellaneous durable goods	72,546	71,588
Gasoline service stations	131,725	117,791	Nondurable goods, total	914,139	885,994
Apparel and accessory stores	94,731	91,426	Paper and paper products	51,454	50,015
Eating and drinking places	182,044	173,894	Drugs, drug proprietaries, and		
Drug and proprietary stores	68,557	62,495	druggists' sundries	47,247	43,040
Liquor stores	20,813	20,033	Apparel, piece goods, & notions	64,186	59,035
Merchant wholesale trade, total	1,790,321	1,728,059	Groceries and related products	238,513	242,684
Durable goods, total	876,182	842,065	Beer, wine, distilled alcoholic		
Motor vehicles and automotive			beverages	44,651	42,925
parts and supplies	174,981	163,614	Farm-product raw materials	122,406	129,499
Furniture and home furnishings	30,251	29,720	Chemical and allied products	41,936	37,584
Lumber and other construction			Petroleum and petroleum products	154,211	140,677
materials	56,094	57,565	Miscellaneous nondurable goods	149,535	140,535

Source: Department of Commerce, Bureau of the Census.

Shareholders in Public Corporations

Characteristic	1990	1985	1983	1981	1980	1975	1970
Individual shareholders (thousands)	51,440	47,040	42,360	32,260	30,200	25,270	30,850
Adult shareowner incidence in population	1 in 4	1 in 4	1 in 4	1 in 5	1 in 5	1 in 6	1 in 4
Median household income	$43,800	$36,800	$33,200	$29,200	$27,750	$19,000	$13,500
Adult shareowners with household							
income: under $10,000 (thousands)	n.a.	2,151	1,460	2,164	1,742	3,420	8,170
$10,000 and over (thousands)	n.a.	40,999	36,261	26,913	25,715	19,970	20,130
$15,000 and over (thousands)	42,920	39,806	33,665	24,376	22,535	15,420	12,709
$25,000 and over (thousands)	38,230	32,690	25,086	17,547	15,605	6,642	4,114
$50,000 and over (thousands)	17,910	11,321	7,918	5,457	3,982	1,216	n.a.
Adult female shareowners (thousands)	17,750	17,547 [1]	20,385	14,154	13,696	11,750	14,290
Adult male shareowners (thousands)	30,220	27,446 [1]	19,226	15,785	14,196	11,630	14,340
Median age	43	44	45	46	46	53	48

NOTE: 1990 results are not strictly comparable with previous studies because of differences in methodologies. 1. Revised to correspond to 1990 methodology. n.a. = not available. *Source:* New York Stock Exchange.

50 Most Active Stocks in 1990

Stock	Share volume	Stock	Share volume	Stock	Share volume
Morris (Philip) (7)	448,780,400	BankAmerica		Unisys Corporation (24)	152,646,600
American Tel. & Tel. (1)	358,179,700	Corporation (21)	179,387,800	Eli Lilly	148,810,800
Int'l Business Machines (2)	341,426,800	Baxter International (27)	178,760,100	Amoco Corporation (47)	147,651,300
General Electric (4)	325,881,200	McDonald's Corporation (20)	177,803,900	Mobil Corporation (36)	146,740,600
Citicorp (14)	323,847,700	Texas Utilities (15)	177,751,400	Motorola Inc.	146,448,100
Federal National		du Pont de Nemours	177,135,800	Archer-Daniels-Midland	146,026,100
Mortgage (30)	282,286,900	Ford Motor (10)	172,246,000	Computer Associates	
American Express (13)	274,643,100	Toys "R" Us	171,965,300	International (32)	144,765,000
Exxon Corporation (5)	246,706,800	Texaco Inc. (3)	167,135,200	Glaxo Holdings	144,220,200
General Motors (12)	243,767,300	Merck & Co. (25)	166,707,800	Digital Equipment (29)	140,010,100
Boeing Company (35)	234,405,000	Coca-Cola Company (50)	165,831,900	Global Marine	139,482,400
Wal-Mart Stores	227,087,600	Dow Chemical (31)	162,559,900	Variety Corporation	138,794,900
Waste Management	221,898,000	COMPAQ Computer (48)	161,092,650	Pfizer Inc.	136,131,300
Bristol-Myers Squibb (16)	218,107,600	GTE Corp.	160,635,200	Schlumberger Limited	135,547,300
Eastman Kodak (8)	208,754,000	USX Corporation (9)	158,890,600	Tandem Computers	132,079,500
Chase Manhattan Corp. (41)	204,899,600	Limited, Inc.	155,931,700	Procter & Gamble	131,496,500
United Telecommunications	192,424,000	Upjohn Company (22)	153,357,000	Unocal Corporation	131,439,300
PepsiCo, Inc. (46)	186,391,100	Johnson & Johnson	153,245,600		

NOTE: 1989 ranking in parentheses, if among top 50. *Source:* New York Stock Exchange.

Geographic Distribution of Shareowners of Public Corporations

Metropolitan Area	Individuals	Households	Metropolitan area	Individuals	Households
New York	2,470,000	1,630,000	Pittsburgh	450,000	300,000
Los Angeles	1,850,000	1,230,000	Denver	440,000	290,000
Chicago	1,610,000	1,070,000	San Jose	420,000	280,000
Detroit	1,240,000	820,000	Cincinnati	410,000	270,000
Philadelphia	1,100,000	720,000	Riverside-San Bernardino	410,000	270,000
Washington D.C.	1,000,000	670,000	Bergan-Passaic, N.J.	400,000	270,000
Boston	940,000	620,000	Milwaukee	400,000	270,000
Houston	880,000	580,000	Kansas City	390,000	260,000
Nassau-Suffolk, N.Y.	750,000	500,000	Seattle	380,000	260,000
Dallas	670,000	440,000	Fort Worth	370,000	240,000
Phoenix	650,000	430,000	Fort Lauderdale	360,000	240,000
St. Louis	640,000	420,000	Columbus	330,000	220,000
Anaheim	630,000	420,000	Portland	310,000	210,000
Atlanta	630,000	410,000	Sacramento	310,000	210,000
Minneapolis	620,000	410,000	Hartford	310,000	210,000
Newark	600,000	400,000	Indianapolis	280,000	190,000
Cleveland	540,000	360,000	Norfolk	280,000	180,000
Baltimore	520,000	350,000	New Orleans	270,000	180,000
San Francisco	490,000	330,000	Orlando	270,000	180,000
Oakland	490,000	320,000	Charlotte	240,000	160,000
Tampa	480,000	320,000	Middlesex, N.J.	230,000	150,000
Miami	470,000	310,000	San Antonio	230,000	150,000
San Diego	450,000	300,000			

New York Stock Exchange Seat Sales for Cash, 1990

Month	Price High	Price Low	Number	Month	Price High	Price Low	Number
January	$400,000	$365,000	3	July	$385,000	$370,000	2
February	360,000	351,000	3	August	330,000	301,000	7
March	360,000	—	1	September	301,000	—	1
April	410,000	390,000	4	October	295,000	—	1
May	410,000	—	1	November	265,000	250,000	2
June	430,000	400,000	2	December	295,000	—	1

NOTE: In addition, there were 12 private seat sales, ranging from a high of $400,000 and a low of $260,000; and 2 EX—OTR private sales. *Source:* New York Stock Exchange.

Largest Businesses, 1990

(in millions of dollars)

Source: FORTUNE © 1991 The Time Inc. Magazine Company. All rights reserved.

50 LARGEST INDUSTRIAL CORPORATIONS

	Sales	Assets
General Motors	126,017.0	180,236.5
Exxon	105,885.0	87,707.0
Fort Motor	98,274.7	173,662.7
Int'l Business Machines	69,018.0	87,568.0
Mobil	58,770.0	41,665.0
General Electric	58,414.0	153,884.0
Philip Morris	44,323.0	46,569.0
Texaco	41,235.0	25,975.0
E.I. Du Pont De Nemours	39,839.0	38,128.0
Chevron	39,262.0	35,089.0
Chrysler	30,868.0	46,374.0
Amoco	28,277.0	32,209.0
Boeing	27,595.0	14,591.0
Shell Oil	24,423.0	28,496.0
Procter & Gamble	24,376.0	18,487.0
Occidental Petroleum	21,947.0	19,743.0
United Technologies	21,783.2	15,918.3
Dow Chemical	20,005.0	23,953.0
USX	19,462.0	17,268.0
Eastman Kodak	19,075.0	24,125.0
Atlantic Richfield	18,819.0	23,864.0
Xerox	18,382.0	31,495.0
Pepsico	17,802.7	17,143.4
McDonnell Douglas	16,351.0	14,965.0
Conagra	15,517.7	4,802.2
Tenneco	14,893.0	19,034.0
Phillips Petroleum	14,032.0	12,130.0
RJR Nabisco Holdings	13,879.0	32,915.0
Hewlett-Packard	13,233.0	11,395.0
Digital Equipment	13,084.5	11,654.8
Minnesota Minning & Mfg.	13,021.0	11,079.0
International Paper	12,960.0	13,669.0
Westinghouse Electric	12,915.0	22,033.0
Georgia-Pacific	12,665.0	12,060.0

Rockwell International	12,442.5	9,738.1
Allied-Signal	12,396.0	10,456.0
Sun	11,909.0	9,000.0
Sara Lee	11,652.0	7,636.4
Caterpillar	11,540.0	11,951.0
Goodyear Tire & Rubber	11,453.1	8,963.6
Johnson & Johnson	11,232.0	9,506.0
Motorola	10,885.0	8,742.0
Aluminum Co. of America	10,865.1	11,413.2
Anheuser-Busch	10,750.6	9,634.3
Unocal	10,740.0	9,762.0
Bristol-Myers Squibb	10,509.0	9,215.0
Coca-Cola	10,406.3	9,278.2
General Dynamics	10,182.0	6,573.0
Unisys	10,111.3	10,288.6
Lockheed	9,977.0	6,860.0

25 LARGEST RETAILING COMPANIES

	Sales	Assets
Sears Roebuck	55,971.7	96,252.8
Wal-Mart Stores	32,601.6	11,388.9
Kmart	32,080.0	13,899.0
American Stores	22,155.5	7,244.7
Kroger	20,261.0	4,118.5
J.C. Penney	17,410.0	12,325.0
Safeway	14,873.6	4,739.1
Dayton Hudson	14,739.0	8,524.0
Great Atlantic & Pacific Tea	11,164.2	2,831.6
May Department Stores	11,027.0	8,295.0
Woolworth	9,789.0	4,305.0
Winn-Dixie	9,744.5	1,732.7
Melville	8,686.8	3,662.2
Albertson's	8,218.6	2,013.5
Southland	8,037.1	2,799.0
R.H. Macy	7,266.8	6,483.3
McDonald's	6,639.6	10,667.5
Supermarkets General Holdings	6,126.0	2,438.8
Walgreen	6,063.0	1,913.6
Publix Super Markets	5,820.7	1,475.7
Food Lion	5,584.5	1,559.5
Toys "R" Us	5,521.2	3,582.4
Price	5,428.8	1,210.1
Vons	5,333.9	1,712.8
The Limited	5,253.5	2,871.9

10 LARGEST TRANSPORTATION COMPANIES

	Operating revenues	Assets
United Parcel Service	13,628.6	8,176.1
AMR	11,803.6	13,353.6
UAL	11,160.1	7,993.8
Delta Air Lines	8,582.2	7,227.0
CSX	8,306.0	12,804.0
NWA	7,257.1	7,273.3
Union Pacific	7,059.2	13,078.4
Federal Express	7,026.2	5,675.1
USAir Group	6,562.8	6,574.2
Continental Airlines Holdings	6,283.6	3,415.4

10 LARGEST DIVERSIFIED FINANCIAL COMPANIES

	Assets	Revenues
American Express	137,682.0	24,332.0
Federal Nat'l Mortgage Ass'n	133,113.0	12,612.0
Salomon	109,877.0	8,946.0
Aetna Life & Casualty	89,300.7	19,428.3
Merrill Lynch	68,129.5	11,213.4
CIGNA	63,691.0	18,344.0
American International Group	58,143.1	15,702.1
Travelers Corp.	55,356.0	12,150.0
Morgan Stanley Group	53,526.5	5,869.6
ITT	49,043.0	20,604.0

10 LARGEST LIFE INSURANCE COMPANIES

	Assets	Premium and annuity income
Prudential of America	133,456.0	24,108.2
Metropolitan Life	103,228.4	19,527.4
Aetna Life	52,342.6	9,591.4
Equitable Life Assurance	50,301.6	4,029.8
Teachers Insurance & Annuity	49,894.1	2,978.9
New York Life	39,876.3	7,709.6
Connecticut General Life	37,407.3	4,418.7
John Hancock Mutual Life	33,749.5	6,822.8
Travelers	33,027.6	4,866.1
Northwestern Mutual Life	31,377.1	4,166.2

10 LARGEST COMMERCIAL BANKS

	Assets	Deposits
Citicorp	216,986.0	142,452.0
BankAmerica Corp.	110,728.0	92,321.0
Chase Manhattan Corp.	98,064.0	70,713.0
J.P. Morgan & Co.	93,103.0	37,557.0
Security Pacific Corp.	84,731.0	58,191.0
Chemical Banking Corp.	73,019.0	48,951.0
NCNB Corp.	65,284.5	50,222.0
Bankers Trust New York Corp.	63,596.0	28,588.0
Manufacturers Hanover Corp.	61,530.0	40,196.0
Wells Fargo & Co.	56,198.5	42,685.0

10 LARGEST UTILITIES

	Assets	Operating revenues
GTE	33,769.0	18,374.0
Bellsouth	30,206.8	14,436.0
Bell Atlantic	27,998.5	12,298.0
US West	27,050.2	9,957.3
NYNEX	26,650.7	13,585.3
Southwestern Bell	22,195.5	9,112.9
Pacific Gas & Electric	21,958.4	9,597.5
American Information Tech.	21,715.1	10,662.5
Pacific Telesis Group	21,581.0	9,716.0
Southern	19,955.0	8,003.0

New Business Concerns and Business Failures

Formations and failures	1988[1]	1987	1986	1985	1984	1983	1982	1980
Business formations								
Index, net formations (1967 = 100)	124.1	121.2	120.4	120.9	121.3	117.5	116.4	129.9
New incorporations (1,000)	68.2	68.5	702	663	635	602	566	534
Failures, number (1,000)	57.1	61.2	61.6	57.1	52.0	31.3	24.9	11.7
Rate per 10,000 concerns	98	102	120	115	107	110	88	42

1. Preliminary. *Sources:* U.S. Bureau of Economic Analysis and Dun & Bradstreet Corporation. NOTE: Data are most recent available.

50 Leading Stocks in Market Value

Stock	Market value (millions)	Listed shares (millions)	Stock	Market value (millions)	Listed shares (millions)
Exxon Corp.	$93,808	1,812.7	Pacific Telesis	$19,585	432.8
International Business Machines	64,591	571.6	American Home Products	18,695	355.2
General Electric	53,272	926.5	Schlumberger Ltd.	17,610	304.3
Morris (Philip)	48,403	935.3	American International Group	17,284	224.8
Merck & Co.	40,940	455.5	Waste Management	16,990	482.0
Coca-Cola Co.	38,947	839.8	Southwestern Bell	16,850	300.9
Bristol-Myers Squibb	35,769	531.9	Texaco Inc.	16,595	274.3
Wal-Mart Stores	34,578	1,143.1	Boeing Co.	15,935	349.3
American Telephone & Telegraph	32,815	1,089.3	US WEST	15,649	402.6
Procter & Gamble	31,444	363.0	Eastman Kodak	15,552	373.6
Johnson & Johnson	27,529	383.7	Dow Chemical	15,538	327.1
BellSouth Corporation	26,703	486.6	Royal Dutch Petroleum	15,283	194.1
Amoco Corp.	26,468	505.3	NYNEX Corp.	14,678	206.4
Mobil Corporation	25,401	438.0	Anheuser-Busch	14,460	335.3
Chevron Corp.	24,846	342.1	Disney (Walt)	13,894	136.7
du Pont de Nemours	24,750	673.5	Pfizer Inc.	13,401	165.4
PepsiCo., Inc.	22,643	862.6	McDonald's Corp.	12,164	417.7
General Motors	21,740	630.2	Ford Motor	11,893	444.6
Bell Atlantic	21,423	399.5	Ralston Purina	11,749	114.6
Eli Lilly	20,721	282.9	Kellogg Co.	11,719	154.5
Atlantic Richfield	20,705	167.7	Schering-Plough Corporation	11,598	261.4
GTE Corp.	20,600	704.3	Warner-Lambert Company	10,822	160.3
Minnesota Mining & Manufacturing	20,238	236.0	Westinghouse Electric	10,544	370.0
Abbott Laboratories	19,692	437.6	Pacific Gas & Electric	10,537	419.4
American Information Technologies (Ameritech)	19,612	293.8	BCE Inc.	10,386	304.4
			Total	**$1,177,048**	**23,023.9**

NOTE: As of Dec. 31, 1990. *Source:* New York Stock Exchange.

Top 50 Banks in the World

Bank	Country	Assets (U.S. dollars)	Bank	Country	Assets (U.S. dollars)
Dai-Ichi Kangyo Bank Ltd., Tokyo	Japan	$428,167,138,042[1]	Hongkong and Shanghai Banking Corp., Hong Kong	Hong Kong	$148,488,419,200[1]
Sumitomo Bank Ltd., Osaka	Japan	409,160,813,636[1]	Commerzbank, Frankfurt	Germany	144,165,990,896[1]
Mitsu Taiyo Kobe Bank Ltd., Tokyo	Japan	408,754,426,386[1]	Toyo Trust & Banking Co., Ltd., Tokyo	Japan	141,744,450,966[2]
Sanwa Bank Ltd., Osaka	Japan	402,698,761,938[1]	Bayerische Vereinsbank, Munich	Germany	137,747,100,000[1]
Fuji Bank, Ltd., Tokyo	Japan	399,545,460,096[1]	Banca Nazionale del Lavoro, Rome	Italy	137,713,846,000[1]
Mitsubishi Bank Ltd., Tokyo	Japan	391,528,117,262[1]	Deutsche Genossenschaftsbank, Frankfurt	Germany	136,453,080,611[1]
Credit Agricole Mutuel, Paris	France	305,205,855,320[1]	Westdeutsche Landesbank Girozentrale, Dusseldorf	Germany	135,824,394,000[1]
Banque Nationale de Paris	France	291,872,593,200[1]	Istituto Bancario San Paola di Torino, Turin	Italy	133,486,857,257[1]
Industrial Bank of Japan, Ltd., Tokyo	Japan	290,067,480,950[1]	Nippon Credit Bank, Ltd., Tokyo	Japan	128,321,129,734[1]
Credit Lyonnais, Paris	France	287,330,254,000[1]	Algemene Bank Nederland, Amsterdam[3]	Netherlands	122,042,365,000[1]
Deutsche Bank, AG, Frankfurt	Germany	266,286,358,959[1]	Rabobank Nederland, Utrecht	Netherlands	119,728,479,000[1]
Barclays Bank Plc., London	United Kingdom	258,983,040,000[1]	Credit Suisse, Zurich	Switzerland	117,345,984,000[1]
Tokai Bank Ltd., Nagoya	Japan	249,751,219,342[1]	Bayerische Hypotheken-und Wechsel-Bank, Munich	Germany	116,410,504,469[1]
Norinchukin Bank, Tokyo	Japan	249,666,548,514	Midland Bank Plc, London	United Kingdom	114,501,120,000[1]
Mitsubishi Trust & Banking Corp., Tokyo	Japan	237,695,564,610[2]	Amsterdam-Rotterdam Bank, Amsterdam[3]	Netherlands	112,460,671,000[1]
National Westminster Bank Plc., London	United Kingdom	232,512,000,000[1]	Banque Paribas, Paris[4]	France	111,555,200,000[1]
Bank of Tokyo, Ltd.	Japan	223,184,576,804[1]	Kyowa Bank, Ltd., Tokyo[5]	Japan	111,546,886,854[1]
Societe Generale, Paris	France	219,983,122,800[1]	Lloyds Bank Plc, London	United Kingdom	105,987,840,000[1]
Sumitomo Trust & Banking Co., Ltd., Osaka	Japan	218,916,041,638[2]	Saitama Bank Ltd., Urawa[5]	Japan	105,634,996,346
Mitsui Trust & Banking Co., Ltd. Tokyo	Japan	210,934,667,188[2]	Bayerische Landesbank Girozentrale, Munich	Germany	103,722,030,945[1]
Long-Term Credit Bank of Japan, Ltd., Tokyo	Japan	200,678,534,326[2]	NMB Postbank Group, N.V., Amsterdam	Netherlands	102,894,395,000[1]
Dresdner Bank, Frankfurt	Germany	186,935,643,693[1]	Shoko Chukin Bank, Tokyo	Japan	102,672,847,684
Union Bank of Switzerland, Zurich	Switzerland	83,442,672,000[1]	Cassa di Risparmio delle Provincie Lombarda, Milan	Italy	99,946,273,000[1]
Yasuda Trust & Banking Co., Ltd., Tokyo	Japan	175,552,377,192[2]			
Daiwa Bank, Ltd., Osaka	Japan	171,238,796,178[2]			
Citibank NA, New York	United States	155,394,000,000			
Swiss Bank Corp., Basel	Switzerland	151,260,090,576[1]			

NOTE: As of Dec. 31, 1990. 1. Consolidated data. 2. Data are not consolidated for affiliates more than 50% owned. 3. A subsidiary of the $231.4 billion-asset ABN Amro Holding N.V., Amsterdam, Netherlands, the 17th largest banking company in the world. 4. A subsidiary of the $185.6-billion-asset Compagnie Financiere de Paribas, Paris, the 25th largest banking company in the world. 5. On April 1, 1991, Kyowa Bank and Saitama Bank merged to form Kyowa Saitama Bank Ltd. *Source: American Banker, July 26, 1991.* Reprinted by permission of American Banker/Bond Buyer.

National Labor Organizations With Membership Over 100,000

Members[1]	Union
921,926	Automobile, Aerospace and Agricultural Implement Workers of America, International Union, United
145,000	Bakery, Confectionery, and Tobacco Workers International Union
106,174	Bricklayers and Allied Craftsmen, International Union of
140,000	Bridge, Structural and Ornamental Iron Workers, International Association of
609,000	Carpenters and Joiners of America, United Brotherhood of
250,000	Clothing and Textile Workers Union, Amalgamated
650,000	Communications Workers of America
2,000,000	Education Association, National (Ind.)
845,000	Electrical Workers, International Brotherhood of
180,000	Electronic, Electrical, Salaried, Machine and Furniture Workers, International Union of
180,000	Fire Fighters, International Association of
1,235,000	Food and Commercial Workers International Union, United
210,000	Government Employees, American Federation of
185,585	Graphic Communications International Union
301,300	Hotel Employees and Restaurant Employees International Union
570,000	Laborers' International Union of North America
150,000	Ladies' Garment Workers' Union, International
315,000	Letter Carriers, National Association of
767,000	Machinists and Aerospace Workers, International Association of
171,000	Mine Workers of America, United (Ind.)
198,000	Nurses Association, American (Ind.)
125,000	Office and Professional Employees International Union
100,000	Oil, Chemical and Atomic Workers International Union
365,000	Operating Engineers, International Union of
155,000	Painters and Allied Trades of the United States and Canada, International Brotherhood of
250,000	Paper Workers International Union, United
325,000	Plumbing and Pipe Fitting Industry of the United States and Canada, United Association of Journeymen and Apprentices of the
330,000	Postal Workers Union, American
130,000	Retail, Wholesale, and Department Store Union
100,000	Rubber, Cork, Linoleum, and Plastic Workers of America, United
950,000	Service Employees International Union
147,000	Sheet Metal Workers' International Association
1,250,000	State, County and Municipal Employees, American Federation of
650,000	Steelworkers of America, United
750,000	Teachers, American Federation of
1,700,000	Teamsters, Chauffeurs, Warehousemen and Helpers of America, International Brotherhood of
165,000	Transit Union, Amalgamated
150,000	Transportation • Communications International Union
100,000	Transportation Union, United

1. Data are for 1991.

Persons in the Labor Force

Year	Labor force[1] Number (thousands)	Labor force[1] % Working-age population	Percent in labor force in[2] Farm occupation	Percent in labor force in[2] Nonfarm occupation	Year	Labor force[1] Number (thousands)	Labor force[1] % Working-age population	Percent in labor force in[2] Farm occupation	Percent in labor force in[2] Nonfarm occupation
1830	3,932	45.5	70.5	29.5	1910	37,371	52.2	31.0	69.0
1840	5,420	46.6	68.6	31.4	1920	42,434	51.3	27.0	73.0
1850	7,697	46.8	63.7	36.3	1930	48,830	49.5	21.4	78.6
1860	10,533	47.0	58.9	41.1	1940	52,789	52.2	17.4	82.6
1870	12,925	45.8	53.0	47.0	1950	60,054	53.5	11.6	88.4
1880	17,392	47.3	49.4	50.6	1960	69,877	55.3	6.0	94.0
1890	23,318	49.2	42.6	57.4	1970	82,049	58.2	3.1	96.9
1900	29,073	50.2	37.5	62.5	1980	106,085	62.0	2.2	97.8

1. For 1830 to 1930, the data relate to the population and gainful workers at ages 10 and over. For 1940 to 1960, the data relate to the population and labor force at ages 14 and over; for 1970 and 1980, the data relate to the population and labor force at age 16 and over. For 1940 to 1980, the data include the Armed Forces. 2. The farm and nonfarm percentages relate only to the experienced civilian labor force. *Source:* Department of Commerce, Bureau of the Census. NOTE: Data are most recent available.

Corporate Profits[1]

(in billions of dollars)

Item	1991[2]	1990	1989	1988	1985	1980	1975	1970
Domestic industries	221.4	236.4	253.5	285.0	190.8	161.9	107.6	62.4
Financial	22.5	18.7	27.3	35.7	21.0	26.9	11.8	12.1
Nonfinancial	198.9	217.7	226.2	249.3	169.7	134.9	95.8	50.2
Manufacturing	67.1	88.8	86.9	98.4	73.0	72.9	52.6	26.6
Wholesale and retail trade	46.2	41.5	39.1	40.1	49.7	23.6	21.3	9.5
Other	43.7	45.9	36.0	36.0	14.0	38.4	21.9	14.1
Rest of world	68.2	56.9	47.8	43.7	31.8	29.9	13.0	6.5
Total	**289.7**	**293.3**	**301.3**	**328.6**	**222.6**	**191.7**	**120.6**	**68.9**

1. Corporate profits with inventory valuation adjustment. 2. Preliminary. *Source:* U.S. Bureau of Economic Analysis, *Survey of Current Business.*

National Income by Type

(in billions of dollars)

Type of share	1990	1989	1985	1980	1975	1970	1965	1960	1950
National income	$4,418.4	$4,223.3	$3,222.3	$2,121.4	$1,215.0	$800.5	$564.3	$414.5	$241.1
Compensation of employees	3,244.2	3,079.0	2,368.2	1,596.5	931.1	603.9	393.8	294.2	154.6
Wages and salaries	2,705.3	2,573.2	1,965.8	1,343.6	805.9	542.0	358.9	270.8	146.8
Supplements to wages and salaries	538.9	505.8	402.4	252.9	125.2	61.9	35.0	23.4	7.8
Proprietors' income[1][2]	402.5	379.3	254.4	130.6	87.0	66.9	57.3	46.2	37.5
Business and professional	352.6	330.7	225.2	107.2	63.5	50.0	42.4	34.2	24.0
Farm	49.9	48.6	29.2	23.4	23.5	16.9	14.8	12.0	13.5
Rental income of persons	6.9[1]	8.2[1]	7.6[1]	31.8	22.4	23.9	19.0	15.8	9.4
Corporate profits[1][2]	298.3	311.6	280.7	182.7	95.9	69.4	76.1	49.9	37.7
Net interest	466.7	445.1	311.4	179.8	78.6	36.4	18.2	8.4	2.0

1. Includes capital consumption adjustment. 2. Includes inventory valuation adjustment. *Source:* Department of Commerce, Bureau of Economic Analysis.

Per Capita Personal Income by States

State	1990[1]	1989	1988	1980	State	1990[1]	1989	1988	1980
Alabama	$14,826	$13,668	$12,845	$7,465	Montana	$15,110	$14,142	$12,896	$8,342
Alaska	21,761	21,365	19,042	13,007	Nebraska	17,221	15,685	14,783	8,895
Arizona	16,297	15,846	15,000	8,854	Nevada	19,416	18,985	17,521	10,848
Arkansas	14,218	12,995	12,212	7,113	New Hampshire	20,789	20,308	19,230	9,150
California	20,795	19,834	18,757	11,021	New Jersey	24,968	23,736	22,146	10,966
Colorado	18,794	17,510	16,465	10,143	New Mexico	14,228	13,196	12,469	7,940
Connecticut	25,358	24,085	23,039	11,532	New York	21,975	20,818	19,261	10,179
Delaware	20,039	18,742	17,693	10,059	North Carolina	16,203	15,283	14,293	7,780
D.C.	24,181	23,131	21,471	12,251	North Dakota	15,255	13,690	12,764	8,642
Florida	18,586	17,710	16,603	9,246	Ohio	17,473	16,446	15,530	9,399
Georgia	16,944	16,057	15,273	8,021	Oklahoma	15,444	14,147	13,355	9,018
Hawaii	20,254	18,413	16,775	10,129	Oregon	17,156	16,003	14,876	9,309
Idaho	15,160	13,761	12,596	8,105	Pennsylvania	18,672	17,392	16,224	9,353
Illinois	20,303	18,873	17,588	10,454	Rhode Island	18,841	18,101	16,846	9,227
Indiana	16,864	15,824	14,856	8,914	South Carolina	15,099	13,641	12,934	7,392
Iowa	17,249	15,864	14,680	9,226	South Dakota	15,872	13,838	12,741	7,800
Kansas	17,986	16,521	15,736	9,880	Tennessee	15,798	14,728	13,859	7,711
Kentucky	14,929	13,823	12,830	7,679	Texas	16,759	15,515	14,592	9,439
Louisiana	14,391	12,926	12,298	8,412	Utah	14,083	14,142	12,180	7,671
Maine	17,200	16,417	15,088	7,760	Vermont	17,436	16,496	15,303	7,957
Maryland	21,864	20,912	19,565	10,394	Virginia	19,746	18,985	17,671	9,413
Massachusetts	22,642	22,234	20,834	10,103	Washington	18,858	17,679	16,452	10,256
Michigan	18,346	17,535	16,544	9,801	West Virginia	13,747	12,439	11,696	7,764
Minnesota	18,731	17,643	16,649	9,673	Wisconsin	17,503	16,532	15,625	9,364
Mississippi	12,735	11,804	11,123	6,573	Wyoming	16,398	14,547	13,634	11,018
Missouri	17,497	16,449	15,458	8,812	**United States**	**18,685**	**17,594**	**16,491**	**9,494**

1. Preliminary. *Source:* U.S. Department of Commerce, Bureau of Economic Analysis, *Survey of Current Business.*

The Federal Budget—Receipts and Outlays

(in billions of dollars)

Description	1992[1]	1991	1990	Description	1992[1]	1991	1990
RECEIPTS BY SOURCE				Commerce & housing credit	92.8	119.5	67.1
Individual income taxes	529.5	492.6	466.9	Transportation	32.7	31.5	29.5
Corporate income taxes	93.5	95.9	93.5	Community development	6.5	7.7	8.5
Social insurance taxes				Education	45.5	42.8	38.5
and contributions	429.4	402.0	380.0	Health	81.3	71.2	57.7
Excise taxes	47.8	44.8	35.3	Medicare	113.7	104.4	98.1
Estate and gift taxes	13.3	12.2	11.5	Income security	184.8	173.2	147.3
Customs duties	19.3	17.7	16.7	Social security	288.6	269.0	248.6
Miscellaneous receipts	23.9	26.2	27.3	Veterans benefits	33.0	31.5	29.1
Total budget receipts	**1,165.0**	**1,091.4**	**1,031.3**	Administration of justice	14.5	12.6	10.0
OUTLAYS BY FUNCTION				General government	13.2	11.2	10.7
National Defense	295.2	298.9	299.3	Net interest	206.3	197.0	184.2
International affairs	17.8	17.0	13.8	Allowances	4.7	8.2	—
Gen. science	17.5	15.8	14.4	Undistributed receipts	−40.8	−39.1	−36.6
Energy	3.7	2.6	2.4	**Total outlays**	**1,445.9**	**1,409.6**	**1,251.7**
Natural resources	19.5	18.8	17.1	**Total deficit**	**−280.9**	**−318.2**	**−220.4**
Agriculture	15.3	15.9	12.0				

1. Estimated. NOTE: The fiscal year is from Oct. 1 to Sept. 30. *Source:* Executive Office of the President, Office of Management and Budget.

Foreign Assistance

(in millions of dollars)

Calendar years	Non-military programs			Military proframs		
	Net new grants	Net new credits	Net other assistance	Net grants	Net credits	Total net assistance[1]
1945–1950[2]	$18,413	$8,086	—	$ 1,525	—	$28,023
1951–60	18,750	2,012	2,767	26,555	49	50,123
1961–70	18,192	14,776	12	21,591	176	54,747
1971–80	27,216	16,399	−1,011	22,602	9,003	74,209
1981–85	29,025	7,071	−2	9,295	10,836	56,226
1986	7,898	298	5	4,125	1,212	13,538
1987	7,419	−2,666	−27	3,131	334	8,191
1988	7,231	202	−36	3,576	−4,205	6,768
1989	7,662	−431	−2	3,728	−1,924	9,033
1990	10,144	372	−34	6,085	−4,644	11,924
Total postwar period	**151,950**	**46,119**	**1,672**	**102,213**	**10,838**	**312,793**

1. Excludes investment in international nonmonetary financial institutions of $20,922 million. 2. Includes transactions after V-J Day (Sept. 2, 1945). NOTE: Detail may not add to total due to rounding. *Source:* Department of Commerce, Bureau of Economic Analysis.

Women in the Civilian Labor Force

(16 years of age and over; in thousands)

Labor force status	1990	1989	1988	1987	1986	1985
In the labor force:	56,554	56,030	54,742	53,658	52,413	51,050
16 to 19 years of age	3,544	3,818	3,872	3,875	3,824	3,767
20 years and over	53,010	52,212	50,870	49,783	48,589	47,283
Employed	53,479	53,027	51,696	50,334	48,706	47,259
16 to 19 years of age	3,024	3,282	3,313	3,260	3,149	3,105
20 years and over	50,455	49,745	48,383	47,075	45,557	44,154
Unemployed	3,075	3,003	3,046	3,324	3,707	3,791
16 to 19 years of age	519	536	558	616	675	661
20 years and over	2,555	2,467	2,487	2,709	3,032	3,129
Not in the labor force:	41,845	41,601	42,014	42,195	42,376	42,686
Women as percent of labor force	45.3	45.2	45.0	44.8	44.5	44.2
Total civilian noninstitutional population	98,399	97,630	96,756	95,853	94,789	93,736

Source: Department of Labor, Bureau of Labor Statistics, annual averages.

Employed Persons 16 Years and Over, by Race and Major Occupational Groups

(number in thousands)

Race and occupational group	1990 Number	1990 Percent distri- bution	1989 Number	1989 Percent distri- bution
WHITE				
Managerial and professional specialty	27,638	27.1	27,459	27.0
Executive, administrative, & managerial	13,539	13.3	13,555	13.3
Professional specialty	14,099	13.8	13,903	13.7
Technical, sales, & administrative support	32,135	31.5	31,619	31.1
Technicians & related support	3,308	3.2	3,125	3.1
Sales occupations	12,857	12.6	12,741	12.5
Administrative support, including clerical	15,970	15.6	15,752	15.5
Service occupations	12,413	12.2	12,237	12.0
Precision production, craft, and repair	12,221	12.0	12,369	12.2
Operators, fabricators, and laborers	14,553	14.3	14,752	14.5
Farming, forestry, fishing	3,127	3.1	3,149	3.1
Total	**102,087**	**100.0**	**101,584**	**100.0**
BLACK				
Managerial and professional specialty	1,913	16.0	1,862	15.6
Executive, administrative, & managerial	853	7.1	840	7.0
Professional specialty	1,060	8.9	1,022	8.5
Technical, sales, & administrative support	3,377	28.2	3,346	28.0
Technicians & related support	349	2.9	347	2.9
Sales occupations	912	7.6	906	7.6
Administrative support, including clerical	2,117	17.7	2,094	17.5
Service occupations	2,728	22.8	2,731	22.9
Precision production, craft, and repair	1,065	8.9	1,089	9.1
Operators, fabricators, and laborers	2,675	22.4	2,714	22.7
Farming, forestry, and fishing	208	1.7	210	1.8
Total	**11,966**	**100.0**	**11,953**	**100.0**

Source: Department of Labor, Bureau of Labor Statistics.

Mothers Participating in Labor Force

(figures in percentage)

Year	Mother with children Under 18 years	Mother with children 6 to 17 years	Mother with children Under 6 years[1]
1955	27.0	38.4	18.2
1965	35.0	45.7	25.3
1975	47.4	54.8	38.9
1980	56.6	64.4	46.6
1981	58.1	65.5	48.9
1982	58.5	65.8	49.9
1983	58.9	66.3	50.5
1984	60.5	68.2	52.1
1985	62.1	69.9	53.5
1986	62.8	70.4	54.4
1987	64.7	72.0	56.7
1988	65.0	73.3	56.1
1989	n.a.	n.a.	n.a.
1990	66.7	74.7	58.2

1. May also have older children. NOTE: For 1955 data are for April; for 1965 and 1975–90, data are for March. *Source:* Department of Labor, Bureau of Labor Statistics. NOTE: Data are most recent available.

Women in the Labor Force

Year	Number[1] (thousands)	% Female population aged 16 and over[1]	% of Labor force population aged 16 and over[1]
1900	5,319	18.8	18.3
1910	7,445	21.5	19.9
1920	8,637	21.4	20.4
1930	10,752	22.0	22.0
1940	12,845	25.4	24.3
1950	18,408	33.9	29.0
1960[2]	23,268	37.8	32.5
1970	31,580	43.4	37.2
1980	45,611	51.6	42.0
1988	54,904	56.6	44.5
1989	56,198	57.5	44.8
1990	56,554	57.5	45.3

1. For 1900–1930, data relate to population and labor force aged 10 and over; for 1940, to population and labor force aged 14 and over; beginning 1950, to population and labor force aged 16 and over. 2. Beginning in 1960, figures include Alaska and Hawaii. *Sources:* Department of Commerce, Bureau of the Census, and Department of Labor, Bureau of Labor Statistics.

Persons Below the Poverty Level, 1970–1989

(in thousands)

Year	All persons	White	Black	Hispanic origin[1]	Year	All persons	White	Black	Hispanic origin[1]
1970	25,420	17,484	7,548	—	1980	29,272	19,699	8,579	3,491
1971	25,559	17,780	7,396	—	1981	31,822	21,553	9,173	3,713
1972	24,460	16,203	7,710	—	1982	34,398	23,517	9,697	4,301
1973	22,973	15,142	7,388	2,366	1983	35,303	23,984	9,882	4,633
1974	23,370	15,736	7,182	2,575	1984	33,700	22,955	9,490	4,806
1975	25,877	17,770	7,545	2,991	1985	33,064	22,860	8,926	5,236
1976	24,975	16,713	7,595	2,783	1986	32,370	22,183	8,983	5,117
1977	24,720	16,416	7,726	2,700	1987[2]	32,221	21,195	9,520	5,422
1978	24,497	16,259	7,625	2,607	1988[2]	31,745	20,715	9,356	5,357
1979	26,072	17,214	8,050	2,921	1989	31,534	20,788	9,305	5,430

1. Persons of Hispanic origin may be of any race. 2. Revised. *Source:* U.S. Department of Commerce, Bureau of the Census.

Manufacturing Industries—Gross Average Weekly Earnings and Hours Worked

Industry	1990 Earnings	1990 Hours worked	1989 Earnings	1989 Hours worked	1985 Earnings	1985 Hours worked	1980 Earnings	1980 Hours worked	1975 Earnings	1975 Hours worked	1970 Earnings	1970 Hours worked
All manufacturing	$442.27	40.8	$429.27	41.0	$385.56	40.5	$288.62	39.7	$189.51	39.4	$133.73	39.8
Durable goods	468.76	41.3	457.60	41.6	415.71	41.2	310.78	40.1	205.09	39.9	143.07	40.3
Primary metal industries	550.83	42.7	531.48	43.0	484.72	41.5	391.78	40.1	246.80	40.0	159.17	40.5
Iron and steel foundries	484.99	42.1	474.99	42.6	429.62	40.8	328.00	40.0	220.99	40.4	151.03	40.6
Nonferrous foundries	413.48	40.3	406.70	41.5	388.74	41.8	291.27	39.9	190.03	39.1	138.16	39.7
Fabricated metal products	447.28	41.3	438.05	41.6	398.96	41.3	300.98	40.4	201.60	40.0	143.67	40.7
Hardware, cutlery, hand tools	440.08	40.9	429.08	41.1	396.42	40.7	275.89	39.3	187.07	39.3	132.33	40.1
Other hardware	448.63	40.6	440.37	40.7	385.40	41.3	195.42	39.4	133.46	40.2		
Structural metal products	416.56	41.0	408.70	41.2	369.00	41.0	291.85	40.2	202.61	40.2	142.61	40.4
Electric and electronic equipment	420.65	40.8	423.50	40.8	384.48	40.6	276.21	39.8	180.91	39.5	130.54	39.8
Machinery, except electrical	494.34	42.0	480.82	42.4	427.04	41.5	328.00	41.0	219.63	40.9	154.95	41.1
Transportation equipment	592.20	42.0	580.88	42.4	542.72	42.7	379.61	40.6	242.61	40.3	163.22	40.3
Motor vehicles and equipment	619.46	42.4	615.47	43.1	584.64	43.5	394.00	40.0	262.68	40.6	170.07	40.3
Lumber and wood products	365.82	40.2	355.29	40.1	326.36	39.8	252.18	38.5	167.35	39.1	117.51	39.7
Furniture and fixtures	333.52	39.1	325.88	39.5	283.29	39.4	209.17	38.1	142.13	37.9	108.58	39.2
Nondurable goods	405.60	40.0	391.55	40.2	342.86	39.5	255.45	39.0	168.78	38.8	120.43	39.1
Textile mill products	320.40	40.0	314.88	41.0	266.39	39.7	203.31	40.1	133.28	39.2	97.76	39.9
Apparel and other textile products	239.88	36.4	234.95	37.0	208.00	36.3	161.42	35.4	111.97	35.1	84.37	35.3
Leather and leather products	258.43	37.4	249.38	37.9	217.09	37.3	169.09	36.7	120.80	37.4	92.63	37.2
Food and kindred products	392.90	40.8	379.73	40.7	341.60	40.0	271.95	39.7	184.17	40.3	127.98	40.5
Tobacco manufactures	645.23	39.2	593.28	38.6	448.26	37.2	294.89	38.1	171.38	38.0	110.00	37.8
Paper and allied products	532.59	43.3	516.57	43.3	466.34	43.1	330.85	42.2	207.58	41.6	144.14	41.9
Printing and publishing	426.38	37.9	410.89	37.8	365.31	37.7	279.36	37.1	198.32	37.0	147.78	37.7
Chemicals and allied products	576.80	42.6	553.74	42.4	484.78	41.9	344.45	41.5	219.63	40.9	153.50	41.6
Petroleum and allied products	723.86	44.6	683.99	44.3	603.72	43.0	422.18	41.8	267.07	41.6	182.76	42.7

Source: Department of Labor, Bureau of Labor Statistics.

Nonmanufacturing Industries—Gross Average Weekly Earnings and Hours Worked

Industry	1990 Earnings	1990 Hours worked	1989 Earnings	1989 Hours worked	1985 Earnings	1985 Hours worked	1975 Earnings	1975 Hours worked	1970 Earnings	1970 Hours worked
Bituminous coal and lignite mining	$740.52	44.0	$696.78	43.0	$630.77	41.4	$284.53	39.2	$186.41	40.8
Metal mining	602.07	42.7	585.08	42.8	547.24	40.9	250.72	42.3	165.68	42.7
Nonmetallic minerals	524.12	45.3	513.91	45.6	451.68	44.5	213.09	43.4	155.11	44.7
Telephone communications	578.74	40.9	561.15	40.9	512.52	41.1	221.18	38.4	131.60	39.4
Radio and TV broadcasting	438.61	34.7	424.86	35.2	381.39	37.1	214.50	39.0	147.45	38.2
Electric, gas, and sanitary services	636.76	41.7	619.28	41.9	534.59	41.7	246.79	41.2	172.64	41.5
Local and suburban transportation	376.65	38.2	369.02	38.4	309.85	38.3	196.89	40.1	142.30	42.1
Wholesale trade	411.48	38.1	395.48	38.1	358.36	38.7	188.75	38.6	137.60	40.0
Retail trade	195.26	28.8	189.01	28.9	177.31	29.7	108.22	32.4	82.47	33.8
Hotels, tourist courts, motels	214.68	30.8	206.82	31.1	176.90	30.5	89.64	31.9	68.16	34.6
Laundries and dry cleaning plants	232.22	34.0	225.04	34.2	198.70	34.2	106.05	35.0	77.47	35.7
General building contracting	487.08	37.7	471.24	37.4	414.78	37.1	254.88	36.0	184.40	36.3

Source: Department of Labor, Bureau of Labor Statistics.

Median Income Comparisons of Year-Round Workers by Educational Attainment 1989
(persons 25 years and over)

Years of school completed	Median income Women	Median income Men	Income gap in dollars	Women's income as a percent of men's	Percent men's income exceeded women's
Elementary school: 8 years or less	$11,712	$17,204	$5,492	68	47
High School: 1 to 3 years	13,222	20,623	7,401	64	56
4 years	16,865	25,859	8,994	65	53
College: 1 to 3 years	20,764	30,406	9,642	68	46
4 years	25,908	36,845	10,937	70	42

Source: Department of Commerce, Bureau of the Census. NOTE: Data are latest available. n.a. = not available.

Money Income of Households with Female Householder, 1989
(No husband present)

Income bracket	Number of Households All	White	Black	Hispanic[1]
Less than $5,000	1,540,000	796,000	708,000	223,000
$5,000 to $9,999	1,921,000	1,113,000	734,000	271,000
$10,000 to $14,999	1,587,000	1,033,000	504,000	161,000
$15,000 to $19,999	1,289,000	883,000	376,000	122,000
$20,000 to $24,999	1,035,000	800,000	226,000	87,000
$25,000 to $29,999	863,000	637,000	197,000	74,000
$30,000 to $34,999	678,000	497,000	167,000	40,000
$35,000 to $39,999	528,000	411,000	99,000	26,000
$40,000 to $44,999	391,000	312,000	78,000	38,000
$45,000 to $49,999	233,000	181,000	43,000	17,000
$50,000 to $54,999	207,000	167,000	33,000	17,000
$55,000 to $59,999	139,000	97,000	36,000	11,000
$60,000 to $64,999	129,000	106,000	18,000	6,000
$65,000 to $69,999	66,000	43,000	17,000	1,000
$70,000 to $74,999	58,000	44,000	12,000	5,000
$75,000 to $79,999	49,000	41,000	6,000	—
$80,000 to $84,999	36,000	29,000	5,000	6,000
$85,000 to $89,999	22,000	21,000	—	4,000
$90,000 to $94,999	18,000	15,000	2,000	—
$95,000 to $99,999	19,000	11,000	6,000	4,000
$100,000 and over	82,000	69,000	10,000	2,000
Median income	$16,442	$18,946	$11,630	$11,745
Mean income	$21,730	$23,866	$16,844	$17,235

1. Persons of Hispanic origin may be of any race. *Source:* Department of Commerce, Bureau of the Census, *Current Population Reports, Consumer Income, Series P-60, No. 172.*

Unemployment by Marital Status, Sex, and Race[1]

	Men		Women	
Marital status and race	Number	Unemployment rate	Number	Unemployment rate
White, 16 years and over	2,866,000	4.8	2,225,000	4.6
Married, spouse present	1,172,000	3.1	984,000	3.6
Widowed, divorced, or separated	382,000	6.2	471,000	5.2
Single (never married)	1,312,000	8.5	770,000	6.8
Black, 16 years and over	793,000	11.8	734,000	10.8
Married, spouse present	197,000	6.2	135,000	5.6
Widowed, divorced, or separated	104,000	10.5	178,000	9.1
Single (never married)	492,000	19.5	421,000	17.3
Total, 16 years and over	3,799,000	5.6	3,075,000	5.4
Married, spouse present	1,429,000	3.4	1,176,000	3.8
Widowed, divorced, or separated	503,000	6.8	671,000	5.9
Single (never married)	1,866,000	10.0	1,228,000	8.6

1. 1990 Annual Averages. *Source: Employment and Earnings*, January 1991, U.S. Department of Labor, Bureau of Labor Statistics.

Earnings Distribution of Year-Round, Full-Time Workers, by Sex, 1989

(persons 15 years old and over as of March 1990)

	Number		Distribution (percent)		Likelihood of a woman in each earnings group (percent)
Earnings group	Women	Men	Women	Men	
$2,499 or less	427,000	548,000	1.4	1.1	1.3
$2,500 to $4,999	440,000	358,000	1.4	0.7	2.0
$5,000 to $7,499	1,274,000	889,000	4.1	1.8	2.3
$7,500 to $9,999	1,982,000	1,454,000	6.3	2.9	2.2
$10,000 to $14,999	6,291,000	5,081,000	20.1	10.2	2.0
$15,000 to $19,999	6,555,000	6,386,000	20.9	12.9	1.6
$20,000 to $24,999	5,169,000	6,648,000	16.5	13.4	1.2
$25,000 to $49,999	8,255,000	20,984,000	26.3	42.1	0.6
$50,000 and over	947,000	7,377,000	3.0	14.9	0.2
Total	**31,340,000**	**49,678,000**	**100.0**	**100.0**	—

Figures obtained by dividing percentages for women by percentages for men. Figures may not add to totals because of rounding. *Source:* Department of Commerce, Bureau of the Census.

Comparison of Median Earnings of Year-Round, Full-Time Workers 15 Years and Over, by Sex, 1960 to 1989

Year	Median earnings		Earnings gap in current dollars	Women's earnings as a percent of men's	Percent men's earnings exceeded women's	Earnings gap in constant 1989 dollars
	Women	Men				
1960	$3,257	$5,368	$2,111	60.7	64.8	8,843
1970	5,323	8,966	3,643	59.4	68.4	11,643
1975	7,504	12,758	5,254	58.8	70.0	12,110
1980	11,197	18,612	7,415	60.2	66.2	11,158
1981	12,001	20,260	8,259	59.2	68.8	11,266
1982	13,014	21,077	8,063	61.7	62.0	10,361
1983	13,915	21,881	7,966	63.6	57.2	9,918
1984	14,780	23,218	8,438	63.7	57.1	10,070
1985	15,624	24,195	8,571	64.7	54.9	9,877
1986	16,232	25,256	9,024	64.3	55.6	10,210
1987	16,911	25,946	9,035	65.2	53.4	9,862
1988	17,606	26,656	9,050	66.0	51.4	9,486
1989	18,778	27,430	8,652	68.0	46.1	8,652

Source: Department of Commerce, Bureau of the Census.

Occupations of Employed Women

(16 years of age and over. Figures are percentage)

Occupations	1990	1989[1]	1988[1]	1987[1]	1986[1]	1985[1]	1984[1]
Managerial and professional	26.2	25.9	25.2	24.4	23.7	23.4	22.5
Technical, sales, administrative support	44.4	44.2	44.6	45.1	45.6	45.5	45.6
Service occupations	17.7	17.7	17.9	18.1	18.3	18.5	18.7
Precision production, craft and repair	2.2	2.2	2.3	2.3	2.4	2.4	2.4
Operators, fabricators, laborers	8,5	8.9	8.9	9.0	8.9	9.1	9.6
Farming, forestry, fishing	1.0	1.1	1.1	1.1	1.1	1.2	1.23

1. Annual averages. NOTE: Details may not add up to totals because of rounding. *Source:* Department of Labor.

Employed and Unemployed Workers by Full- and Part-Time Status, Sex, and Age: 1970 to 1990

(In thousands)

	1990	1989	1988	1987	1985	1980	1975	1970
Total 16 yr and over								
Employed	117,914	117,342	114,968	112,440	107,150	99,303	85,846	78,678
Full time	97,994	97,369	95,214	92,957	88,535	82,564	71,585	66,752
Part time	19,920	19,973	19,754	19,483	18,615	16,742	14,260	11,924
Unemployed	6,874	6,528	6,701	7,425	8,312	7,637	7,929	4,093
Full time	5,541	5,211	5,357	5,979	6,793	6,269	6,523	3,206
Part time	1,332	1,317	1,343	1,446	1,519	1,369	1,408	889
Men, 20 yr and over								
Employed	61,198	60,837	59,781	58,726	56,562	53,101	48,018	45,581
Full time	56,640	56,386	55,353	54,381	52,425	49,699	45,051	43,138
Part time	4,558	4,451	4,427	4,345	4,137	3,403	2,966	2,444
Unemployed	3,170	2,867	2,987	3,369	3,715	3,353	3,476	1,638
Full time	2,936	2,651	2,778	3,147	3,479	3,167	3,255	1,502
Part time	234	215	209	222	236	186	223	137
Women, 20 yr. and over								
Employed	50,455	49,745	48,383	47,074	44,154	38,492	30,726	26,952
Full time	39,036	38,408	37,299	36,121	33,604	29,391	23,242	20,654
Part time	11,419	11,337	11,084	10,953	10,550	9,102	7,484	6,297
Unemployed	2,555	2,467	2,487	2,709	3,129	2,615	2,684	1,349
Full time	2,044	1,963	1,987	2,178	2,536	2,135	2,210	1,077
Part time	511	504	500	530	593	480	474	271
Both sexes 16–19 yr.								
Employed	6,261	6,759	6,805	6,640	6,434	7,710	7,104	6,144
Full time	2,318	2,574	2,562	2,454	2,507	3,474	3,292	2,960
Part time	3,943	4,185	4,243	4,185	3,927	4,237	3,810	3,183
Unemployed	1,149	1,194	1,226	1,347	1,468	1,669	1,767	1,106
Full time	561	596	592	653	777	966	1,057	626
Part time	587	598	634	694	690	701	709	480

Source: U.S. Dept. of Labor, Bureau of Labor Statistics.

Work Stoppages Involving 1,000 Workers or More[1]

Year	Work stoppages	Workers involved (thousands)	Man-days idle (thousands)	Year	Work stoppages	Workers involved (thousands)	Man-days idle (thousands)
1950	424	1,698	30,390	1982	96	656	9,061
1955	363	2,055	21,180	1983	81	909	17,461
1960	222	896	13,260	1984	68	391	8,499
1965	268	999	15,140	1985	61	584	7,079
1970	381	2,468	52,761	1986	72	900	11,861
1975	235	965	17,563	1987	46	174	4,456
1979	235	1,021	20,409	1988	40	118	4,381
1980	187	795	20,844	1989	51	452	16,996
1981	145	729	16,908	1990	44	185	5,926

1. The number of stoppages and workers relate to stoppages that began in the year. Days of idleness include all stoppages in effect. Workers are counted more than once if they were involved in more than one stoppage during the year. *Source:* U.S. Department of Labor. Bureau of Labor Statistics, *Monthly Labor Review. July 1991.*

Leading Advertising Agencies in World Billings

(in thousands of dollars)

Agency	1990	1989
Saatchi & Saatchi Advertising	$5,186,660 [1]	$5,021,859 [2]
Young & Rubicam	5,184,807 [1]	4,472,000 [2]
McCann-Erickson	5,182,872 [1]	4,707,241 [2]
J. Walter Thompson	4,778,255 [1]	4,407,500 [2]
Ogilvy & Mather Worldwide	4,749,888 [1]	4,168,804 [1]
FCB-Publicis	4,713,000 [1]	4,276,500 [1]
Backer Spielvogel Bates Worldwide	4,367,468	4,166,504
BBDO Worldwide	4,043,340 [1]	3,277,114 [2]
Lintas:Worldwide	4,027,238 [1]	3,595,662 [1]
D'Arcy Masius Benton & Bowles	3,810,483 [1]	3,465,656 [2]

1. Estimated. 2. Restated 1989 billings. *Source: Ad Week Magazine,* Top 30 Worldwide Agencies, March 25, 1991 edition. Copyright © Ad Week Magazine Network 1991. All rights reserved.

Unemployment Rate, 1990

Race and age	Women [1]	Men [1]
All races:	5.4	5.6
16 to 19 years	14.7	16.3
20 years and over	4.8	4.9
White	4.6	4.8
16 to 19 years	12.6	14.2
20 years and over	4.1	4.3
Minority races:	9.9	10.0
16 to 19 years	27.3	29.1
20 years and over	8.7	9.3

1. Annual averages. *Source:* Bureau of Labor Statistics, Department of Labor.

Unemployment Rate in the Civilian Labor Force

Year	Unemployment rate	Year	Unemployment rate
1920	5.2	1978	6.0
1924	5.0	1980	7.1
1926	1.8	1981	7.6
1928	4.2	1982	9.7
1930	8.7	1983	9.6
1932	23.6	1984	7.5
1934	21.7	1985	7.2
1936	16.9	1986	7.0
1938	19.0	1987	6.2
1940	14.6	1988	5.4
1942	4.7	1989	5.3
1944	1.2	1990	5.5
1946	3.9	Jan.	5.2
1948	3.8	Feb.	5.2
1950	5.3	March	5.1
1952	3.0	April	5.4
1954	5.5	May	5.3
1956	4.1	June	5.3
1958	6.8	July	5.5
1960	5.5	Aug.	5.6
1962	5.5	Sept.	5.7
1964	5.2	Oct.	5.7
1966	3.8	Nov.	5.9
1968	3.6	Dec.	6.1
1970	4.9	1991	
1972	5.6	Jan.	6.2
1974	5.6	Feb.	6.5
1976	7.7	March	6.8
		April	6.6

NOTE: Estimates prior to 1940 are based on sources other than direct enumeration. *Source:* Department of Labor, Bureau of Labor Statistics.

Employment and Unemployment

(in millions of persons)

Category	1991 [2]	1990	1989	1985	1980	1975	1970	1950	1945	1932	1929
EMPLOYMENT STATUS [1]											
Civilian noninstitutional population	189.4	188.0	186.4	178.2	167.7	153.2	137.1	105.0	94.1	—	—
Civilian labor force	125.7	124.8	123.9	115.5	106.9	93.8	82.8	62.2	53.9	—	—
Civilian labor force participation rate	66.4	66.4	66.5	64.8	63.8	61.2	60.4	59.2	57.2	—	—
Employed	117.4	117.9	117.3	107.2	99.3	85.8	78.7	58.9	52.8	38.9	47.6
Employment-population ratio	62.0	62.7	63.0	60.1	59.2	56.1	57.4	56.1	56.1	—	—
Agriculture	3.2	3.2	3.2	3.2	3.4	3.4	3.5	7.2	8.6	10.2	10.5
Nonagricultural industries	114.2	114.7	14.1	104.0	95.9	82.4	75.2	51.8	44.2	28.8	37.2
Unemployed	8.3	6.9	6.5	8.3	7.6	7.9	4.1	3.3	1.0	12.1	1.6
Unemployment rate	6.6	5.5	5.3	7.2	7.1	8.5	4.9	5.3	1.9	23.6	3.2
Not in labor force	63.7	63.3	62.5	62.7	60.8	59.4	54.3	42.8	40.2	—	—
INDUSTRY											
Total nonagricultural employment	108.7	110.0	108.3	97.5	90.4	76.9	70.9	45.2	40.4	23.6	31.3
Goods-producing industries	23.8	25.0	25.3	24.9	25.7	22.6	23.6	18.5	17.5	8.6	13.3
Mining	0.7	0.7	0.7	0.9	1.0	0.8	0.6	0.9	0.8	0.7	1.1
Construction	4.7	5.1	5.2	4.7	4.3	3.5	3.6	2.4	1.1	1.0	1.5
Manufacturing: Durable goods	10.6	11.1	11.4	11.5	12.2	10.7	11.2	8.1	9.1	—	—
Nondurable goods	7.8	8.0	8.0	7.8	8.1	7.7	8.2	7.2	6.4	—	—
Services-producing industries	84.9	85.0	83.0	72.7	64.7	54.3	47.3	26.7	22.9	15.0	18.0
Transportation and public utilities	5.8	5.8	5.6	5.2	5.1	4.5	4.5	4.0	3.9	2.8	3.9
Trade, Wholesale	6.1	6.2	6.2	5.7	5.3	4.4	4.0	2.6	1.9	—	—
Retail	19.3	19.7	19.5	17.3	15.0	12.6	11.0	6.7	5.4	—	—
Finance, insurance, and real estate	6.7	6.7	6.7	6.0	5.2	4.2	3.6	1.9	1.5	1.3	1.5
Services	28.6	28.2	27.1	22.0	17.9	13.9	11.5	5.4	4.2	2.9	3.4
Federal government	3.0	3.1	3.0	2.9	2.9	2.7	2.7	1.9	2.8	0.6	0.5
State and local government	15.5	15.2	14.8	13.5	13.4	11.9	9.8	4.1	3.1	2.7	2.5

1. For 1929–45, figures on employment status relate to persons 14 years and over; beginning in 1950, 16 years and over. 2. As of April; seasonally adjusted. *Source:* Bureau of Labor Statistics.

Livestock on Farms (in thousands)

Type	1991	1990	1989	1985	1980	1975	1970	1965	1960	1950
Cattle[1]	99,436	98,162	98,065	109,582	111,242	132,028	112,369	109,000	96,236	77,963
Dairy cows[1]	10,159	10,153	10,212	10,311	10,758	11,220	13,303	16,981	19,527	23,853
Sheep[1]	11,200	11,363	10,858	10,716	12,699	14,515	20,423	25,127	33,170	29,826
Swine[2]	52,360	51,150	52,965	54,073	67,318	54,693	57,046	56,106	59,026	58,937
Chickens[3]	1,088,152	3,236,993	3,229,801	4,689,973	4,201,706	3,173,820	3,220,085	2,535,141	1,976,737	535,266
Turkeys[4]	105,800	304,863	242,421	185,427	165,243	124,165	116,139	105,914	84,458	44,134

1. As of Jan. 1. 2. As of Jan. 1 of the previous year for 1950–60; Dec. 1 of the previous year for 1965–85; As of March 1 for 1989–91. 3. As of Jan. 1 of the previous year for 1950–60; Dec. of the previous year for 1965–85; 1989, 1990 totals for calendar year, and 1991 as of April. 4. 1975–89 as of Dec. of previous year, 1990 total for calendar year, 1991 as of April. *Source:* Department of Agriculture, Statistical Reporting Service, Economic Research Service.

Agricultural Output by States, 1990 Crops

State	Corn (1,000 bu)	Wheat (1,000 bu)	Cotton (1,000 ba[1])	Potatoes (1,000 cwt)	Tobacco (1,000 lb)	Cattle[2] (1,000 head)	Swine[3] (1,000 head)
Alabama	13,920	6,650	400.0	1,943	—	1,750	—
Alaska	—	—	—	—	—	8.2	—
Arizona	1,120	9,266	1,015.0	1,794	—	830	—
Arkansas	6,935	49,000	1,100.0	—	—	1,700	—
California	25,600	47,906	2,805.8	17,783	—	4,800	—
Colorado	128,650	86,950	—	24,032	—	2,900	—
Connecticut	—	—	—	—	3,000	76	—
Delaware	19,780	3,060	—	2,009	—	31	—
Florida	5,325	1,815	45.0	9,792	19,040	1,925	—
Georgia	37,400	20,650	410.0	—	103,200	1,400	1,100
Hawaii	—	—	—	—	—	205	—
Idaho	3,900	99,600	—	112,340	—	1,660	—
Illinois	1,320,800	91,200	—	837	—	1,950	5,700
Indiana	703,050	50,440	—	858	13,440	1,250	4,300
Iowa	1,562,400	3,375	—	160	—	4,500	13,800
Kansas	188,500	472,000	1.1	—	—	5,700	1,500
Kentucky	120,000	20,000	—	—	437,153	2,420	920
Louisiana	21,576	12,870	1,180.0	—	—	1,050	—
Maine	—	—	—	20,520	—	116	—
Maryland	53,100	9,880	—	324	9,443	315	—
Massachusetts	—	—	—	650	—	71	—
Michigan	238,050	41,250	—	12,115	—	1,225	1,250
Minnesota	762,600	138,620	—	16,110	—	2,600	4,500
Mississippi	11,200	15,600	1,851.1	—	—	1,370	—
Missouri	205,800	76,000	305.0	957	5,625	4,400	2,800
Montana	855	145,865	—	2,492	—	2,300	4,300
Nebraska	934,400	85,500	—	3,539	—	5,800	—
Nevada	—	980	—	2,345	—	570	—
New Hampshire	—	—	—	—	—	46	—
New Jersey	8,850	1,247	—	1,012	—	70	—
New Mexico	7,975	8,125	126.0	3,400	—	1,360	—
New York	60,760	7,105	—	7,890	—	1,540	—
North Carolina	72,760	22,550	271.0	3,380	639,620	900	2,800
North Dakota	36,800	385,220	—	16,675	—	1,700	—
Ohio	417,450	79,650	—	1,911	20,500	1,650	2,000
Oklahoma	10,032	201,600	380.0	—	—	5,250	—
Oregon	2,700	57,616	—	23,014	—	1,400	—
Pennsylvania	109,610	10,500	—	5,400	19,780	1,860	920
Rhode Island	—	—	—	294	—	7.0	—
South Carolina	14,400	14,440	145.0	—	109,905	590	—
South Dakota	234,000	128,004	—	1,980	—	3,380	1,770
Tennessee	43,860	17,640	490.0	—	99,416	2,300	620
Texas	130,500	130,200	5,085.0	3,072	—	13,200	—
Utah	2,660	7,170	—	1,643	—	780	—
Vermont	—	—	—	—	—	297	—
Virginia	36,500	12,220	6.6	1,980	109,498	1,700	—
Washington	14,000	150,080	—	67,980	—	1,330	—
West Virginia	5,250	552	—	—	2,880	490	—
Wisconsin	354,000	10,085	—	23,075	13,575	4,170	1,200
Wyoming	6,000	6,113	—	561	—	1,220	—
U.S. Total	7,933,068	2,738,594	15,616.6	393,867	1,606,851	98,162	54,362[4]

1. 480-lb net-weight bales. 2. Number on farms as of Jan. 1, 1991. 3. Number on farms as of Dec. 1, 1990. 4. Includes states not listed as individual states as data are not available. The 16 listed states account for approximately 91% of the total. *Source:* Department of Agriculture, Statistical Reporting Service.

Farm Income

(in millions of dollars)

Year	Crops	Livestock, livestock products	Government payments	Total cash income[1]
	Cash receipts from marketings			
1925	5,545	5,476	—	11,021
1930	3,868	5,187	—	9,055
1935	2,977	4,143	$573	7,693
1940	3,469	4,913	723	9,105
1945	9,655	12,008	742	22,405
1950	12,356	16,105	283	28,764
1955	13,523	15,967	229	29,842
1960	15,023	18,989	703	34,958
1965	17,479	21,886	2,463	42,215
1970	20,977	29,532	3,717	54,768
1975	45,813	43,089	807	90,707
1980	71,746	67,991	1,285	143,295
1984	69,471	72,968	8,431	155,253
1985	74,290	69,845	7,705	156,882
1986	64,005	71,534	11,814	152,473
1987	63,751	75,717	16,747	162,023
1988	72,569	78,862	14,480	171,579
1989	75,449	83,724	10,886	170,060

1. Includes items not listed. *Source:* Department of Agriculture, Economic Research Service. NOTE: Figures are latest available.

Per Capita Consumption of Principal Foods[1]

Food	1990	1989	1988
Red meat[2]	112.3	115.9	119.5
Poultry[2]	63.8	60.8	57.4
Fish and shellfish[2]	15.4	15.6	15.2
Eggs	29.6	29.9	31.2
Fluid milk and cream[3]	233.2	236.4	234.6
Ice cream	15.7	16.1	17.3
Cheese (excluding cottage)	24.7	23.9	23.7
Butter (actual weight)	4.4	4.4	4.5
Margarine (actual weight)	10.9	10.2	10.3
Total fats and oils	62.7	61.1	63.0
Selected fresh fruits (farm weight)	92.2	99.7	99.1
Peanuts (shelled)	6.2	7.0	6.9
Selected fresh vegetable	95.2	101.0	98.7
White potatoes[4]	126.8	126.2	123.2
Sugar (refined)	64.2	62.5	62.1
Corn sweeteners (dry weight)	71.9	70.3	69.7
Flour and cereal products	184.8	175.0	172.9
Soft drinks (gal)	n.a.	32.0	31.9
Coffee bean equivalent	10.2	10.3	9.8
Cocoa (chocolate liquor equivalent)	4.2	3.9	3.8

1. As of August 1991. Except where noted, consumption is from commercial sources and is in pounds retail weight. 2. Boneless, trimmed equivalent. 3. Includes milk and cream produced and consumed on farms. 4. Farm-weight equivalent of fresh and processed use. n.a. = not available.

Government Employment and Payrolls

Year and function	Employees (in thousands)				October payrolls (in millions)			
	Total	Federal[1]	State	Local	Total	Federal[1]	State	Local
1940	4,474	1,128		3,346	$566	177		$389
1945	6,556	3,375		3,181	1,110	642		468
1950	6,402	2,117	1,057	3,228	1,528	613	218	696
1955	7,432	2,378	1,199	3,855	2,265	846	326	1,093
1960	8,808	2,421	1,527	4,860	3,333	1,118	524	1,691
1965	10,589	2,588	2,028	5,973	4,884	1,484	849	2,551
1970	13,028	2,881	2,755	7,392	8,334	2,428	1,612	4,294
1975	14,973	2,890	3,271	8,813	13,224	3,584	2,653	6,987
1980	16,213	2,898	3,753	9,562	19,935	5,205	4,285	10,445
1981	15,968	2,865	3,726	9,377	21,193	5,239	4,668	11,287
1982	15,841	2,848	3,744	9,249	23,173	5,959	5,022	12,192
1983	16,034	2,875	3,816	9,344	24,525	6,302	5,346	12,878
1984	16,436	2,942	3,898	9,595	26,904	7,137	5,815	13,952
1985	16,690	3,021	3,984	9,685	28,945	7,580	6,329	15,036
1986	16,933	3,019	4,068	9,846	30,670	7,561	6,810	16,298
1987	17,212	3,091	4,116	10,005	32,669	7,924	7,263	17,482
1988	17,588	3,112	4,236	10,240	34,203	7,976	7,842	18,385
1990, total	18,369	3,105	4,503	10,760	39,228	8,999	9,083	21,146
National defense and international relations	1,038	1,038	[2]	[2]	2,998	2,998	[2]	[2]
Postal service	816	816	[2]	[2]	2,321	2,321	[2]	[2]
Education	7,971	13	1,984	5,974	15,116	37	3,426	11,652
Instructional employees	4,545	n.a.	614	3,931	10,637	n.a.	1,576	9,061
Highways	573	4	261	308	1,199	14	596	588
Health and Hospitals	1,793	291	730	772	3,820	826	1,522	1,472
Police protection	832	79	89	664	2,134	275	257	1,603
Fire protection	327	[2]	[2]	327	739	[2]	[2]	739
Sewerage & solid waste management	238	[2]	2	236	489	[2]	4	484
Parks & recreation	336	24	45	266	464	58	70	336
Natural resources	427	225	164	38	1,074	673	335	66
Financial administration	488	140	147	202	1,045	357	326	362
All other	3,530	475	1,081	1,973	7,829	1,440	2,547	3,844

1. Civilians only. 2. Not applicable. NOTE: n.a. = not available. Detail may not add to totals because of rounding. *Source:* Department of Commerce, Bureau of the Census.

Receipts and Outlays of the Federal Government

(in millions of dollars)

From 1789 to 1842, the federal fiscal year ended Dec. 31; from 1844 to 1976, on June 30; and beginning 1977, on Sept. 30.

Year	Customs (including tonnage tax)[1]	Internal revenue Income and profits tax	Internal revenue Other	Miscellaneous taxes and receipts	Total receipts	Net receipts[2]
		Receipts				
1789–1791	$ 4	—	—	—	$ 4	$ 4
1800	9	—	$ −1	$ 1	11	11
1810	9	—	—	1	9	9
1820	15	—	—	3	18	18
1830	22	—	—	3	25	25
1840	14	—	—	6	20	20
1850	40	—	—	4	44	44
1860	53	—	—	3	56	56
1870	195	—	185	32	411	411
1880	187	—	124	23	334	334
1890	230	—	143	31	403	403
1900	233	—	295	39	567	567
1910	334	—	290	52	675	675
1915	210	$ 80	335	72	698	683
1929	602	2,331	607	493	4,033	3,862
1933	251	746	858	225	2,080	1,997
1939	319	2,189	2,972	188	5,668	4,979
1943	324	16,094	6,050	934	23,402	21,947
1944	431	34,655	7,030	3,325	45,441	43,563
1945	355	35,173	8,729	3,494	47,750	44,362
1950	423	28,263	11,186	1,439	41,311	36,422
1956[4]	705	56,639	20,564	389	78,297	74,547
1960	1,123	67,151	28,266	1,190	97,730	92,492
1965	1,478	79,792	39,996	1,598	122,863	116,833
1970	2,494	138,689	65,276	3,424	209,883	193,743
1975	3,782	202,146	108,371	6,711	321,010	280,997
1980	7,482	359,927	192,436	12,797	572,641	520,050
1985	12,079	474,074	311,092	18,576	815,821	733,996
1986	13,323	412,102	323,779	19,887	(5)	769,091
1987	15,085	476,483	343,268	19,307	(5)	854,143
1988	16,198	495,376	377,469	19,909	(5)	908,953
1989	16,334	549,273	402,200	22,800	(5)	990,691
1990	16,707	560,391	426,893	27,470	(5)	1,031,462

Year	Department of Defense (Army, 1789–1950)	Department of the Navy	Interest on public debt	All other	Net outlays[3]	Surplus (+) or deficit (−)
		Outlays				
1789–1791	$ 1	—	$ 2	$ 1	$ 4	—
1800	3	$ 3	3	1	11	—
1810	2	2	3	1	8	$ +1
1820	3	4	5	6	18	—
1830	5	3	2	5	15	+10
1840	7	6	—	11	24	−4
1850	9	8	4	18	40	+4
1860	16	12	3	32	63	−7
1870	58	22	129	101	310	+101
1880	38	14	96	120	268	+66
1890	45	22	36	215	318	+85
1900	135	56	40	290	521	+46
1910	190	123	21	359	694	−19
1915	202	142	23	379	746	−63
1929	426	365	678	1,658	3,127	+734
1933	435	349	689	3,125	4,598	−2,602
1939	695	673	941	6,533	8,841	−3,862

Year	Outlays Department of Defense (Army, 1789–1950)	Department of the Navy	Interest on public debt	All other	Net outlays[3]	Surplus (+) or deficit (−)
1943	42,526	20,888	1,808	14,146	79,368	−57,420
1944	49,438	26,538	2,609	16,401	94,986	−51,423
1945	50,490	30,047	3,617	14,149	98,303	−53,941
1950	5,789	4,130	5,750	23,875	39,544	−3,122
1956[4]	35,693	—	6,787	27,981	70,460	+4,087
1960	43,969	—	9,180	39,075	92,223	+269
1965	47,179	—	11,346	59,904	118,430	−1,596
1970	78,360	—	19,304	98,924	196,588	−2,845
1975	87,471	—	32,665	205,969	326,105	−45,108
1980	136,138	—	74,860	368,013	579,011	−58,961
1985	244,054	—	178,945	513,810	936,809	−202,813
1986	273,369	—	135,284	581,136	989,789	−220,698
1987	282,016	—	138,519	581,612	1,002,147	−148,004
1988	290,349	—	151,711	621,995	1,064,055	−155,102
1989	303,600	—	169,100	649,943	1,142,643	−123,785
1990	299,355	—	183,790	768,725	1,251,850	−220,388

1. Beginning 1933, tonnage tax is included in "Other receipts." 2. Net receipts equal total receipts less (a) appropriations to federal old-age and survivors' insurance trust fund beginning fiscal year 1939 and (b) refunds of receipts beginning fiscal year 1933. 3. Includes Air Force 1950–65 (in millions): 1950—$3,521; 1956—$16,750; 1960—$19,065; 1965—$18,471. 4. Beginning 1956, computed on unified budget concepts; not strictly comparable with preceding figures. 5. Net receipts are now the total receipts. Public Law 99–177 moved two social security trust funds off-budget. *Source:* Department of the Treasury, Financial Management Service, and *Budget of the United States Government Fiscal Year 1991.* NOTE: Totals figures may not add to totals because of rounding of some items.

Contributions to International Organizations

(for fiscal year 1990 in millions of dollars)

Organization	Amount[1]
United Nations and Specialized Agencies	
United Nations	$206.92
Food and Agriculture Organization	21.80
International Atomic Energy Agency	37.79
International Civil Aviation Organization	7.91
Joint Financing Program	2.46
International Labor Organization	53.16
International Telecommunication Union	5.32
United Nations Industrial Development Organization	19.11
World Health Organization	71.07
World Meteorological Organization	6.68
Others (5 Programs, less than $1 million)	2.38
Peacekeeping Forces	
United Nations Disengagement Observer Force (UNDOF) and UNIFIL	40.75
United Nations Force in Cyprus	8.84
United Nations Iran-Iraq Military Observer Group (UNIMOG)	12.49
United Nations Observer Group in Central America (ONUCA)	17.73
Multinational Force and Observers	23.73
Inter-American Organizations	
Organization of American States	46.33
Inter-American Institute for Cooperation on Agriculture	14.24
Inter-American Tropical Tuna Commission	2.84
Pan American Health Organization	39.20
Others (4 Programs, less than $1 million)	.58
Regional Organizations	
North Atlantic Assembly	1.03
NATO Civilian Headquarters	23.30
Organization for Economic Cooperation and Development	36.08
Others (2 Programs, less than $1 million)	.89
Other International Organizations	

Organization	Amount[1]
Customs Cooperation Council	2.39
General Agreement on Tariffs and Trade	6.65
International Agency for Research on Cancer	1.25
International Criminal Police Organization	1.11
Others (34 Programs, less than $1 million)	6.17
Special Voluntary Programs	
Consultative Group on International Agricultural Research	40.00
International Atomic Energy Agency Technical Assistance Fund	21.55[2]
International Fund for Agricultural Development	34.40
International Organization for Migration	16.21
OAS Special Development Assistance Fund	3.93
OAS Special Multilateral Fund (Education and Science)	4.68
OAS Special Projects fund (Mar del Plata)	1.00
OAS Special Program	2.25
PAHO Special Health Promotion Funds	11.00
United Nations Children's Fund	63.95
United Nations Development Program	105.00
United Nations Environment Program	11.80
U.N. Afghanistan Emergency Trust Fund (UNOCA)	13.28
U.N. Capital Development Fund	1.48
U.N./FAO World Food Program	163.00[3]
U.N. Fund for Drug Abuse Control	4.00
U.N. High Commissioner for Refugees Program:	
Regular Programs (5)	74.32
Special Programs (7)	52.67
United Nations Relief and Works Agency:	
Regular Program	57.00
WHO Special Programs	40.00
WMO Voluntary Cooperation Program	1.97
Others (10 Programs, less than $1 million)	4.32
Total U.S. Contributions	**$1,448.01**

1. Estimated. 2. Includes cash, commodities and services, and $7.32 million for the Safeguards Program and other non-proliferation activities. 3. Includes cash, commodities and services, and $22.1 million for the International Emergency Food Reserve, and $55.9 million for WFP protracted refugee operations.

Social Welfare Expenditures Under Public Programs

(in millions of dollars)

Year and source of funds	Social insurance	Public aid	Health and medical programs[1]	Veterans' programs	Education	Housing	Other social welfare	All health and medical care[2]	Total social welfare	Total social welfare as: Percent of gross national product	Total social welfare as: Percent of total gov't outlays
FEDERAL											
1960	14,307	2,117	1,737	5,367	868	144	417	2,918	24,957	5.0	28.1
1970	45,246	9,649	4,775	8,952	5,876	582	2,259	16,600	77,337	8.1	40.1
1980	191,162	48,666	12,886	21,254	13,452	6,608	8,786	68,989	303,276	11.5	53.2
1981	224,574	55,946	13,596	23,229	13,372	6,045	7,304	80,505	344,066	11.6	54.0
1982	250,551	52,485	14,598	24,463	11,917	7,176	6,500	90,776	367,691	12.0	52.5
1983	274,212	55,895	15,594	25,561	12,397	8,087	7,046	100,274	398,792	12.0	51.9
1984	288,743	58,480	16,622	25,970	13,010	10,226	7,349	103,927	420,399	11.3	50.2
1985	313,108	61,985	18,630	26,704	13,796	11,088	7,548	118,955	452,860	11.5	47.8
1986	326,588	65,615	19,926	27,072	15,022	10,164	7,977	125,730	472,364	11.3	47.6
1987	345,082	69,233	22,219	27,641	16,054	11,110	8,504	143,020	499,844	11.0	50.4
1988	358,412	74,137	22,681	28,845	16,952	14,006	8,112	149,102	523,144	10.9	49.1
STATE AND LOCAL											
1960	4,999	1,984	2,727	112	16,758	33	723	3,478	27,337	5.5	60.1
1970	9,446	6,839	5,132	127	44,970	120	1,886	8,791	68,519	7.1	64.0
1980	38,592	23,133	14,771	212	107,597	601	4,813	31,309	189,720	7.2	66.5
1981	42,821	26,477	17,124	212	114,773	688	4,679	36,327	206,774	7.0	63.1
1982	52,481	28,367	19,195	245	121,957	778	5,154	40,738	228,178	7.4	62.6
1983	56,846	29,935	20,382	265	129,416	1,003	5,438	42,854	243,285	7.3	60.1
1984	52,378	32,206	20,383	301	139,046	1,306	5,946	44,540	251,569	6.8	58.9
1985	59,420	34,792	22,430	338	152,622	1,540	6,398	48,587	277,540	7.0	59.0
1986	63,816	37,464	24,408	373	163,495	1,872	6,728	53,884	298,158	7.1	58.2
1987	69,941	41,462	25,400	410	188,486	2,129	6,773	60,566	344,601	7.4	59.6
1988	73,783	46,237	29,859	409	202,416	2,550	7,368	70,511	362,622	7.6	60.1
TOTAL											
1960	19,307	4,101	4,464	5,479	17,626	177	1,139	6,395	52,293	10.5	38.4
1970	54,691	16,488	9,907	9,078	50,846	701	4,145	25,391	145,856	15.2	48.2
1980	229,754	71,799	27,657	21,466	121,050	7,210	13,599	100,298	492,534	18.7	57.4
1981	267,395	82,424	30,720	23,441	128,145	6,734	11,983	116,832	550,841	18.6	56.9
1982	303,033	80,852	33,793	24,708	133,874	7,954	11,654	131,514	595,869	19.4	55.7
1983	331,058	85,830	35,976	25,826	141,813	9,090	12,484	143,128	642,077	19.3	54.5
1984	341,120	90,685	37,006	26,275	152,056	11,532	13,295	148,467	671,969	18.2	52.8
1985	372,529	96,777	41,060	27,042	166,418	12,627	13,946	167,542	730,399	18.5	51.2
1986	390,404	103,079	44,334	27,445	178,518	12,036	14,705	179,614	770,522	18.4	47.9
1987	415,023	110,695	47,619	28,051	204,540	13,240	15,278	203,586	834,446	18.4	53.5
1988	432,195	120,375	52,540	29,254	219,368	16,556	15,480	219,613	885,766	18.5	52.8
PERCENT OF TOTAL, BY TYPE											
1960	36.9	7.8	8.5	10.5	33.7	0.3	2.2	12.2	100.0	(3)	(3)
1970	37.5	11.3	6.7	6.2	34.9	0.5	3.0	17.2	100.0	(3)	(3)
1980	46.6	14.6	5.6	4.4	24.6	1.5	2.8	20.4	100.0	(3)	(3)
1984	50.9	13.4	5.6	3.9	22.6	1.5	2.0	23.1	100.0	(3)	(3)
1985	51.0	13.2	5.6	3.7	22.8	1.7	1.9	22.9	100.0	(3)	(3)
1986	50.7	13.4	5.8	3.6	23.2	1.6	1.9	23.3	100.0	(3)	(3)
1987	49.7	13.3	5.7	3.4	24.5	1.6	1.8	24.4	100.0	(3)	(3)
1988	48.8	13.6	5.9	3.3	24.8	1.9	1.7	24.8	100.0	(3)	(3)
FEDERAL PERCENT OF TOTAL											
1960	74.1	51.6	38.9	98.0	4.9	81.2	36.6	45.6	47.7	(3)	(3)
1970	82.7	58.5	48.2	98.6	11.6	82.9	54.5	65.4	53.0	(3)	(3)
1980	83.2	67.8	46.6	99.0	11.1	91.7	64.6	68.8	61.6	(3)	(3)
1984	84.7	64.2	43.6	99.0	8.5	87.4	54.7	70.0	62.4	(3)	(3)
1985	84.0	64.0	45.4	98.8	8.3	87.8	54.1	71.0	62.0	(3)	(3)
1986	83.6	63.7	44.9	98.6	8.4	84.4	54.2	70.0	61.3	(3)	(3)
1987	83.1	62.5	46.7	98.5	7.8	83.9	55.7	70.3	59.9	(3)	(3)
1988	82.9	61.6	43.2	98.6	7.7	84.6	52.4	67.9	59.1	(3)	(3)

1. Excludes program parts of social insurance, public aid, veterans, and other social welfare. 2. Combines health and medical programs with medical services provided in connection with social insurance, public aid, veterans, and other social welfare programs. 3. Not applicable. NOTE: Figures are latest available. *Source:* Department of Health and Human Services. *Social Security Bulletin,* May 1991.

Domestic Freight Traffic by Major Carriers

(in millions of ton-miles)[1]

Year	Railrods Ton-miles	Railrods % of total	Inland waterways[2] Ton-miles	Inland waterways[2] % of total	Motor trucks Ton-miles	Motor trucks % of total	Oil pipelines Ton-miles	Oil pipelines % of total	Air carriers Ton-miles	Air carriers % of total
1940	379,201	61.3	118,057	19.1	62,043	10.0	59,277	9.6	14	—
1945	690,809	67.3	142,737	13.9	66,948	6.5	126,530	12.3	91	—
1950	596,940	56.2	163,344	15.4	172,860	16.3	129,175	12.1	318	—
1955	631,385	49.5	216,508	17.0	223,254	17.5	203,244	16.0	481	—
1960	579,130	44.1	220,253	16.8	285,483	21.7	228,626	17.4	778	—
1965	708,700	43.3	262,421	16.0	359,218	21.9	306,393	18.7	1,910	0.1
1970	771,168	39.8	318,560	16.4	412,000	21.3	431,000	22.3	3,274	0.2
1975	759,000	36.7	342,210	16.5	454,000	22.0	507,300	24.6	3,732	0.2
1980	932,000	37.2	420,000	16.9	567,000	22.6	588,000	23.1	4,528	0.2
1983	841,000	36.0	359,000	15.4	575,000	24.6	556,000	23.8	5,870	0.3
1985	895,000	36.4	382,000	15.6	610,000	24.9	564,000	22.9	6,080	0.2
1986	889,000	35.5	393,000	15.7	634,000	25.4	578,000	23.1	7,100	0.3
1987	972,000	36.8	411,000	15.6	661,000	25.1	587,000	22.2	8,670	0.3
1988	1,028,000	37.0	438,000	15.8	699,000	25.1	605,000	21.8	9,300	0.3
1989	1,048,000	37.3	448,000	15.9	716,000	25.4	591,000	21.0	10,210	0.36
1990[3]	1,080,000	37.6	461,000	16.0	735,000	25.6	585,000	20.4	10,480	0.37

1. Mail and express included, except railroads for 1970. 2. Rivers, canals, and domestic traffic on Great Lakes. 3. Preliminary. *Source:* For 1987 on, *Transportation in America, 9th Edition,* Eno Foundation for Transportation.

Tonnage Handled by Principal U.S. Ports

(Over 10 million tons annually; in thousands of tons)

Port	1989	1988	Port	1989	1988
New Orleans	177,523	175,501	Chicago	23,446	22,894
New York	148,590	155,062	Tacoma Harbor, Wash.	22,451	20,668
Houston	125,583	124,887	Newport News, Va.	21,852	21,391
Valdez Harbor, Alaska	95,436	107,145	Seattle	21,763	18,646
Baton Rouge, La.	82,400	78,857	Paulsboro, N.J.	21,446	22,004
Corpus Christi, Texas	60,479	57,932	Detroit	20,701	15,331
Long Beach, Calif.	54,808	46,560	Boston, Port of	18,989	20,641
Norfolk Harbor, Va.	52,055	46,872	Huntington, W.V.	15,707	17,701
Tampa Harbor, Fla.	49,281	50,252	Freeport, Texas	15,176	15,138
Los Angeles	47,272	45,214	Indiana Harbor, Ind.	15,055	16,643
Baltimore Harbor, Md.	44,884	41,926	Jacksonville, Fla.	15,002	15,806
Texas City, Texas	41,272	42,747	Toledo Harbor, Ohio	14,806	14,742
Lake Charles, La.	40,813	37,312	Cleveland	14,688	14,551
Duluth-Superior, Minn.	40,803	40,002	Port Everglades, Fla.	14,685	14,207
Mobile, Ala.	39,980	36,476	Lorain Harbor, Ohio	14,568	17,476
Philadelphia	36,060	37,827	San Juan, P.R.	13,874	13,503
Pittsburgh	33,416	34,373	Anacortes, Wash.	13,169	13,638
Beaumont, Texas	31,668	31,947	Savannah, Ga.	12,830	13,981
Pascagoula, Miss.	31,546	28,528	Presque Isle, Mich.	12,156	11,433
Port Arthur, Texas	31,128	23,801	Memphis, Tenn.	11,844	10,200
Portland, Ore.	30,030	31,971	Galveston, Texas	11,838	12,355
Marcus Hook, Pa.	29,904	29,815	Cincinnati, Ohio	11,557	11,243
St. Louis (Metropolitan)	26,037	29,011	Honolulu, Hawaii	10,360	10,655
Ricmond, Calif.	25,103	18,913	Ashtabula, Ohio	10,322	10,335

Source: Department of the Army, Corps of Engineers.

Annual Railroad Carloadings

Year	Total	Year	Total	Year	Total	Year	Total
1930	30,173,000	1960	27,886,950[1]	1981	21,342,987[1]	1986	19,588,666[1]
1940	36,358,000	1965	28,344,381[1]	1982	18,584,760[1]	1987	20,602,204[1]
1945	41,918,000	1970	27,015,020[1]	1983	19,013,250[1]	1988	22,599,993[1]
1950	38,903,000	1975	22,929,843[1]	1984	20,945,536[1]	1989	21,226,015[1]
1955	32,761,707[1]	1980	22,223,000[1]	1985	19,501,242[1]	1990	21,884,649[1]

1. Only Class 1 railroads. *Source:* Association of American Railroads.

Estimated Motor Vehicle Registration, 1990

(in thousands; including publicly owned vehicles)

State	Autos[1]	Trucks and buses	Motor-cycles	Total	State	Autos[1]	Trucks and buses	Motor-cycles	Total
Alabama	2,720	963	44	3,683	Montana	452	306	27	758
Alaska	233	135	8	368	Nebraska	913	474	22	1,387
Arizona	2,014	837	80	2,851	Nevada	591	256	17	847
Arkansas	929	519	14	1,448	New Hampshire	754	201	36	955
California	17,103	5,073	627	22,176	New Jersey	5,130	463	84	5,593
Colorado	2,355	889	113	3,244	New Mexico	820	499	34	1,319
Connecticut	2,514	158	50	2,672	New York	8,807	1,350	196	10,157
Delaware	408	123	8	531	North Carolina	3,712	1,514	54	5,226
Dist. of Col.	238	16	3	254	North Dakota	370	259	20	629
Florida	9,239	2,293	206	11,532	Ohio	7,567	1,824	248	9,391
Georgia	3,767	1,611	67	5,378	Oklahoma	1,679	913	57	2,592
Hawaii	661	99	19	760	Oregon	1,831	609	64	2,440
Idaho	631	403	42	1,034	Pennsylvania	6,418	1,609	168	8,027
Illinois	6,487	1,636	223	8,123	Rhode Island	554	115	29	669
Indiana	3,222	1,192	93	4,414	South Carolina	1,895	660	30	2,555
Iowa	1,866	733	174	2,599	South Dakota	425	297	29	722
Kansas	1,401	601	70	2,002	Tennessee	3,533	876	83	4,409
Kentucky	1,902	988	32	2,890	Texas	8,649	4,059	175	12,708
Louisiana	2,002	1,011	30	3,013	Utah	806	385	26	1,191
Maine	732	214	39	946	Vermont	348	122	18	470
Maryland	2,942	638	55	3,580	Virginia	3,807	1,175	57	4,982
Massachusetts	3,286	501	53	3,787	Washington	3,002	1,289	126	4,291
Michigan	5,628	1,582	175	7,210	West Virginia	823	399	17	1,222
Minnesota	2,617	724	112	3,341	Wisconsin	2,774	823	216	3,567
Mississippi	1,452	450	27	1,902	Wyoming	290	203	18	493
Missouri	2,741	1,149	59	3,890	**Total**	**145,010**	**45,218**	**4,274**	**190,228**

1. Includes taxicabs. NOTE: Figures are latest available. *Source:* Department of Transportation, Federal Highway Administration.

Passenger Car Production by Make

Companies and models	1990	1989	1985	1980	1975	1970
American Motors Corporation	—	—	109,919	164,725	323,704	276,127
Chrysler Corporation						
Plymouth	212,354	258,847	369,487	293,342	443,550	699,031
Dodge	361,769	453,428	482,388	263,169	354,482	405,699
Chrysler	136,339	203,624	414,193	82,463	102,940	158,614
Imperial	16,280				1,930	10,111
Total	726,742	915,899	1,266,068	638,974	902,902	1,273,455
Ford Motor Company						
Ford	933,466	1,165,886	1,098,627	929,627	1,301,414	1,647,918
Mercury	221,436	297,678	374,446	324,528	405,104	310,463
Lincoln	222,449	213,517	163,077	52,793	101,520	58,771
Total	1,377,351	1,677,081	1,636,150	1,306,948	1,808,038	2,017,152
General Motors Corporation						
Chevrolet	1,025,379	1,196,953	1,691,254	1,737,336	1,687,091	1,504,614
Pontiac	649,255	732,177	702,617	556,429	523,469	422,212
Oldsmobile	418,742	520,981	1,168,982	783,225	654,342	439,632
Buick	405,123	470,052	1,001,461	783,575	535,820	459,931
Cadillac	252,540	293,589	322,765	203,991	278,404	152,859
Saturn	4,245					
Total	2,755,284	3,213,752	4,887,079	4,064,556	3,679,126	2,979,248
Checker Motors Corporation	—	—	—	3,197	3,181	4,146
Volkswagen of America	—	—	96,458	197,106	—	—
Honda	435,437	362,274	238,159	145,337	—	—
Mazda	184,428	216,501	—	—	—	—
Nissan	95,844	115,584	43,810	—	—	—
Toyota	321,523	231,279	—	—	—	—
Diamond Star	148,379		—	—	—	—
Subaru Legacy	32,461					
Industry total	**6,077,449**	**6,823,097**	**8,184,821**	**6,375,506**	**6,716,951**	**6,550,128**

Source: Motor Vehicle Manufacturers Association of the United States.

Motor Vehicle Data

	1989	1988	1980	1970	1960
U.S. passenger cars and taxis registered (thousands)	143,081	141,252	121,724	89,280	61,671
Total mileage of U.S. passenger cars (millions)	1,485,474	1,429,579	1,111,596	916,700	588,083
Total fuel consumption of U.S. passenger cars (millions of gallons)	72,333	71,949	71,883	67,820	41,169
World registration of cars, trucks, and buses (thousands)	556,931	539,790	411,113	246,368	126,955
U.S. registration of cars, trucks, and buses (thousands)	187,261	184,397	155,796	108,418	73,858
U.S. share of world registration of cars, trucks, and buses	33.6%	34.2%	37.9%	44.0%	58.2%

Source: Motor Vehicle Manufacturers Association of the U.S.

Domestic Motor Vehicles Sales

(in thousands)

Type of Vehicle	1988	1987	1986	1985	1984	1983	1980	1975
Passenger Cars								
Passenger car factory sales	7,105	7,085	7,516	8,002	7,621	6,739	6,400	6,713
Passenger car (new) retail sales[1]	10,626	10,278	11,460	11,042	10,390	9,182	8,979	8,640
Domestic[2]	7,526	7,081	8,215	8,205	7,952	6,795	6,581	7,050
Subcompact[3]	1,019	1,101	1,325	1,297	2,322	1,776	1,604	700
Compact[3]	2,781	2,388	2,461	2,563	1,336	1,110	1,659	2,336
Standard[3]	1,722	1,565	1,888	1,882	1,817	1,825	1,358	1,956
Intermediate[3]	2,017	2,026	2,540	2,464	2,484	2,071	1,957	2,058
Imports[4]	3,100	3,197	3,245	2,838	2,439	2,387	2,398	1,587
Trucks								
Truck and bus factory sales	4,121	3,821	3,393	3,357	3,075	2,414	1,667	2,272
Truck and bus retail sales[5]	4,608	4,174	4,031	3,984	3,538	2,709	2,232	2,351
Light duty (up to 14,000 GVW)[6]	4,273	3,885	3,766	3,700	3,261	2,521	1,964	2,076
Med. duty (14,000–26,000 GVW)[6]	83	55	51	53	61	48	92	169
Heavy duty (over 26,000 GVW)[6]	251	234	214	231	216	141	176	106
Motorcycles								
Motorcycles (new) retail sales[7]	710	935	1,045	1,260	1,305	1,185	1,070	940
All-terrain vehicles	290	395	465	550	550	425	n.a.	n.a.
All-terrain vehicle imports	209	320	498	683	635	430	n.a.	n.a.
Motorcycle imports total[8]	287	318	550	733	441	540	1,120	948

1. Based on data from U.S. Dept. of Commerce. 2. Includes domestic models produced in Canada and Mexico. 3. Beginning 1980, cars produced in U.S. by foreign manufacturers are included. 4. Excludes domestic models produced in Canada. 5. Excludes motorcoaches and light-duty imports from foreign manufacturers. Includes imports sold by franchised dealers of U.S. manufacturers. Starting in 1986 includes sales of trucks over 10,000 lbs. GVW by foreign manufacturers. 6. Gross vehicle weight (fully loaded vehicles). 7. Estimates by Motorcycle Industry Council Inc., Costa Mesa, Calif. Includes all-terrain vehicles and scooters. Excludes mopeds/motorized bicycles. 8. *Source:* Motorcycle Industry Council Inc. Data from U.S. Dept. of Commerce. Excludes mopeds/motorized bicycles and all-terrain vehicles. NOTE: n.a. = not available. *Source: Statistical Abstract of the United States 1990.* NOTE: Data are most recent available.

Domestic and Export Factory Sales of Motor Vehicles

(in thousands)

	From plants in United States								
	Passenger cars			Motor trucks and buses			Total motor vehicles		
Year	Total	Domestic	Exports	Total	Domestic	Exports	Total	Domestic	Exports
1970	6,547	6,187	360	1,692	1,566	126	8,239	7,753	486
1975	6,713	6,073	640	2,272	2,003	269	8,985	8,076	909
1980	6,400	5,840	560	1,667	1,464	203	8,067	7,304	763
1985	8,002	7,337	665	3,357	3,126	231	11,359	10,463	896
1986	7,516	6,869	647	3,393	3,130	263	10,909	9,999	910
1987	7,085	6,487	598	3,821	3,509	312	10,906	9,996	910
1988	7,105	6,437	668	4,120	3,795	325	11,225	10,232	993
1989	6,807	6,181	626	4,062	3,752	310	10,869	9,933	936
1990	6,050	5,502	548	3,719	3,448	271	9,769	8,950	819

Source: Motor Vehicle Manufacturers Association of the U.S.

U.S. Direct Investment in EEC Countries, 1990

(in millions of dollars)

Countries	All industries	Petroleum	Manufacturing	Wholesale	Banking	Finance & insurance	Services	Other industries
Belgium	$9,462	$327	$4,331	$2,177	(1)	$2,059	$352	(1)
Denmark	1,633	(1)	286	566	(1)	295	98	-2
France	17,134	(1)	11,051	3,025	174	960	375	(1)
Germany, Federal Republic of	27,715	3,136	17,489	1,505	1,694	2,863	-41	1,069
Greece	300	37	84	71	81	(1)	(1)	(1)
Ireland	6,776	-41	4,885	(1)	4	1,549	352	(1)
Italy	12,971	605	8,535	1,677	361	1,005	298	490
Luxembourg	1,119	22	539	(1)	301	238	0	(1)
Netherlands	22,778	1,636	8,144	2,490	169	8,642	1,439	258
Portugal	590	(1)	285	110	(1)	(1)	(1)	(1)
Spain	7,480	116	4,998	1,011	879	3	312	160
United Kingdom	64,983	11,331	20,636	2,746	3,575	23,071	2,249	1,375
Total	**$172,940**	**$18,761**	**$81,264**	**$15,420**	**$7,504**	**$40,718**	**$5,501**	**$3,772**

1. Suppressed to avoid disclosure of data of individual companies. *Source: Survey of Current Business,* June 1991.

Balance of International Payments

(in billions of dollars)

Item	1990	1989	1988	1985	1980	1975	1970	1965	1960
Exports of goods, services, and income	$652.9	$603.2	$533.4	$366.0	$343.2	$157.9	$68.4	$42.7	$30.5
Merchandise, adjusted, excluding military	389.5	360.5	319.2	214.4	224.0	107.1	42.5	26.5	19.7
Transfers under U.S. military agency sales contracts	9.8	8.3	10.0	9.0	8.2	3.9	1.5	0.8	0.3
Receipts of income on U.S. investments abroad	130.0	127.5	107.8	90.0	75.9	25.4	11.8	7.4	4.6
Other services	123.3	106.9	92.7	45.0	36.5	19.3	9.9	6.4	4.3
Imports of goods and services	-722.7	-689.5	-641.7	-461.2	-333.9	-132.6	-60.0	-32.8	-23.7
Merchandise, adjusted, excluding military	-497.6	-475.3	-446.5	-339.0	-249.3	-98.0	-39.9	-21.5	-14.8
Direct defense expenditures	-17.1	-14.6	-14.6	-12.0	-10.7	-4.8	4.9	-3.0	-3.1
Payments of income on foreign assets in U.S.	-118.1	-128.4	-105.5	-65.0	-43.2	-12.6	-5.5	-2.1	-1.2
Other services	-89.8	-80.0	-75.0	-46.0	-30.7	-17.2	-9.8	-6.2	-4.6
Unilateral transfers, excluding military grants, net	-22.3	-14.7	-14.6	-15.0	-7.0	-4.6	-3.3	-2.9	-2.3
U.S. Government assets abroad, net	2.9	1.2	-3.0	-2.8	-5.2	-3.5	-1.6	-1.6	-1.1
U.S. private assets abroad, net	-58.5	-102.9	-81.5	-26.0	-71.5	-35.4	-10.2	-5.3	-5.1
U.S. assets abroad, net	-57.7	-127.0	-84.2	-27.7	-86.1	-39.7	-9.3	-5.7	-4.1
Foreign assets in U.S., net	86.3	214.6	219.3	127.1	50.3	15.6	6.4	0.7	2.3
Statistical discrepancy	63.5	22.4	-10.6	23.0	29.6	5.5	-0.2	-0.5	-1.0
Balance on goods, services, and income	-69.7	-95.3	-113.8	-106.8	9.5	25.2	8.5	10.0	6.9
Balance on current account	-92.1	-110.0	-126.5	-118.0	3.7	18.4	2.4	5.4	2.8

NOTE: — denotes debits. *Source:* Department of Commerce, Bureau of Economic Analysis.

Foreign Investors in U.S. Business Enterprises

	Number				Investment outlays (millions of dollars)			
	1990[1]	1989	1988	1987	1990[1]	1989	1988	1987
Investments, total	1,565	1,580	1,424	978	$64,423	$71,163	$72,692	$40,310
Acquisitions	796	837	869	543	56,773	59,708	64,855	33,933
Establishments	769	743	555	435	7,651	11,455	7,837	6,377
Investors, total	1,682	1,742	1,542	1,051	64,423	71,163	72,692	40,310
Foreign direct investors	628	727	566	480	12,498	22,538	18,569	11,773
U.S. affilates	1,054	1,015	976	571	51,925	48,625	54,123	28,536

1. Figures are preliminary. *Source:* U.S. Department of Commerce, *Survey of Current Business,* May 1991.

Imports of Leading Commodities
(value in millions of dollars)

Commodity	1990	1989
Food and agricultural commodities	**$17,209.9**	**$16,539.6**
Animal feeds	282.7	279.0
Cocoa	784.3	732.0
Coffee	1,768.8	2,273.5
Corn	23.2	55.1
Cotton, raw	0.5	3.3
Dairy products, eggs	502.2	440.9
Fish	2,011.7	2,132.2
Furskins, undressed	78.2	115.8
Hides and skins, undressed	94.8	97.9
Live animals	1,183.2	869.6
Meat and preparations	2,956.2	2,560.0
Oils and fats, animal	0.5	(z)
Oils and fat, vegetable	717.5	655.5
Rice	71.6	61.9
Soybeans	15.4	23.9
Sugar	852.7	605.3
Tobacco, unmanufactured	696.6	667.6
Vegetables and fruits	5,800.8	4,908.6
Wheat	80.0	57.5
Machinery and transport equipment	**134,849.5**	**132,492.2**
Airplanes	2,836.0	2,947.8
Airplane parts	3,337.8	2,929.1
Cars and trucks	53,556.6	52.960.6
Parts	15,235.1	15,248.3
Spacecraft and parts	204.1	80.0
General industrial machinery	14,483.6	14,486.9
Metalworking machinery	3,687.9	3,867.9
Office machinery	26,917.3	25,714.5
Power generating machinery	14,591.1	14,257.1
Manufactured goods	**118,163.3**	**113,695.4**
Artwork and antiques	2,341.0	2,172.2
Chemicals—fertilizers	955.2	1,003.2
Chemicals—medicinal, pharmaceutical	2,500.2	2,087.6
Chemicals—organic and inorganic	10,625.4	10,248.3
Clothing and footwear	35,108.5	32,931.2
Gem diamonds	3,977.8	4,347.3
Glass	759.5	788.8
Iron and steel mill products	8,810.6	9,392.7
Metal manufactures	6,445.7	6,371.6
Paper, paperboard and articles	8,510.5	8,491.8
Photographic apparatus and supplies	3,359.2	3,435.6
Plastic articles	3,142.3	2,998.6
Pottery	1,222.1	1,243.9
Printed matter	1,670.2	1,617.8
Rubber articles	1,020.8	912.5
Scientific instruments and parts	6,207.6	5,848.9
Textile yarns, fabrics, and articles	6,397.6	6,087.1
Tires and tubes, automotive	2,220.1	2,383.8
Toys, games, sporting goods	9,086.6	8,396.1
Watches, clocks and parts	1,762.2	907.7
Wood manufactures	2,040.2	2,028.7
Mineral fuels and related products	**63,592.2**	**51,638.2**
Coal	86.3	84.1
Natural gas	2,149.4	1,849.7
Petroleum and petroleum products	61,356.5	49,704.4
Crude materials excluding agricultural products	**9,965.3**	**10,416.2**
Cork, wood and lumber	3,126.3	3,499.4
Pulp and waste paper	2,867.0	3,050.4
Metal ores, scrap	3,972.3	3,866.4
Tobacco excluding agricultural, beverages	**1,781.4**	**1,637.0**
Cigarettes	53.6	49.3
Distilled alcoholic beverages	1,727.8	1,587.7
All others	**148,769.4**	**146,792.2**
Total	**495,042.0**	**473,210.8**

Exports of Leading Commodities
(value in millions of dollars)

Commodity	1990	1989
Food and agricultural commodities	**$34,922.3**	**$36,773.9**
Animal feeds	2,855.0	3,081.1
Cocoa	38.2	22.0
Coffee	11.9	12.7
Corn	6,205.2	6,734.2
Cotton, raw	2,782.7	2,244.1
Dairy products, eggs	373.2	446.5
Fish	1,757.4	1,436.8
Furskins, undressed	144.3	173.3
Hides and skins, undressed	1,613.1	1,576.6
Live animals	513.8	531.7
Meat and preparations	3,187.9	2,963.8
Oils and fats, animal	30.6	37.9
Oils and fats, vegetable	664.5	739.6
Rice	801.4	981.4
Soybeans	3,595.2	4,011.5
Sugar	8.2	3.3
Tobacco, unmanufactured	1,441.1	1,339.9
Vegetables and fruits	5,011.6	4,530.4
Wheat	3,887.0	5,907.1
Machinery and transport equipment	**115,244.3**	**106,384.5**
Airplanes	19,615.5	14,432.6
Airplane parts	9,554.1	8,791.6
Cars and trucks	11,901.9	12,267.6
Parts	14,547.7	13,224.8
Spacecraft and parts	894.0	554.0
General industrial machinery	15,688.5	15,034.5
Metalworking machinery	2,747.5	2,738.5
Office machinery	24,725.5	23,992.2
Power generating machinery	15,569.6	15,348.7
Manufactured goods	**70,320.0**	**67,469.7**
Artwork and antiques	2,266.7	1,653.0
Chemicals—fertilizers	2,574.6	2,707.8
Chemicals—medicinal, pharmaceutical	4,103.2	3,692.5
Chemicals—organic and inorganic	14,215.5	14,710.4
Clothing and footwear	2,957.5	2,530.5
Gem diamonds	320.1	1,097.6
Glass	1,058.9	979.0
Iron and steel mill products	3,423.1	3,559.1
Metal manufactures	4,722.7	4,494.4
Paper paperboard and articles	4,991.8	4,585.5
Photographic apparatus and supplies	2,773.4	2,535.0
Plastic articles	1,939.4	1,700.0
Pottery	71.3	69.6
Printed matter	3,158.5	3,002.2
Rubber articles	728.4	670.5
Scientific instruments and parts	12,108.0	11,488.6
Textile yarns, fabrics, and articles	4,922.0	4,301.7
Tires and tubes, automotive	913.6	819.1
Toys, games and sporting goods	1,820.2	1,630.9
Watches, clocks and parts	209.3	177.3
Wood manufactures	1,221.8	1,064.9
Mineral fuels and related products	**11,375.5**	**9,323.7**
Coal	4,464.5	4,087.1
Natural gas	198.7	215.5
Petroleum and petroleum products	6,712.3	5,021.1
Crude material excluding agricultural products	**14,207.4**	**15,118.9**
Cork, wood, lumber	5,224.5	5,203.5
Pulp and waste paper	4,040.2	4,394.5
Metal ores, scrap	4,942.7	5,520.9
Tobacco excluding agricultural, beverages	**5,015.0**	**3,584.8**
Cigarettes	4,761.0	3,362.4
Distilled alcoholic beverages	254.0	222.4
All other	**142,960.4**	**125,156.0**
Total	**394,044.9**	**363,811.5**

Source: Department of Commerce, Bureau of the Census, Foreign Trade Division. NOTE: (z) less than one half unit of measurement shown.

TAXES

History of the Income Tax in the United States

Source: Deloitte & Touche

The nation had few taxes in its early history. From 1791 to 1802, the United States Government was supported by internal taxes on distilled spirits, carriages, refined sugar, tobacco and snuff, property sold at auction, corporate bonds, and slaves. The high cost of the War of 1812 brought about the nation's first sales taxes on gold, silverware, jewelry, and watches. In 1817, however, Congress did away with all internal taxes, relying on tariffs on imported goods to provide sufficient funds for running the Government.

In 1862, in order to support the Civil War effort, Congress enacted the nation's first income tax law. It was a forerunner of our modern income tax in that it was based on the principles of graduated, or progressive, taxation and of withholding income at the source. During the Civil War, a person earning from $600 to $10,000 per year paid tax at the rate of 3%. Those with incomes of more than $10,000 paid taxes at a higher rate. Additional sales and excise taxes were added, and an "inheritance" tax also made its debut. In 1866, internal revenue collections reached their highest point in the nation's 90-year history—more than $310 million, an amount not reached again until 1911.

The Act of 1862 established the office of Commissioner of Internal Revenue. The Commissioner was given the power to assess, levy, and collect taxes, and the right to enforce the tax laws through seizure of property and income and through prosecution. His powers and authority remain very much the same today.

In 1868, Congress again focused its taxation efforts on tobacco and distilled spirits and eliminated the income tax in 1872. It had a short-lived revival in 1894 and 1895. In the latter year, the U.S. Supreme Court decided that the income tax was unconstitutional because it was not apportioned among the states in conformity with the Constitution.

By 1913, with the 16th Amendment to the Constitution, the income tax had become a permanent fixture of the U.S. tax system. The amendment gave Congress legal authority to tax income and resulted in a revenue law that taxed incomes of both individuals and corporations. In fiscal year 1918, annual internal revenue collections for the first time passed the billion-dollar mark, rising to $5.4 billion by 1920. With the advent of World War II, employment increased, as did tax collections—to $7.3 billion. The withholding tax on wages was introduced in 1943 and was instrumental in increasing the number of taxpayers to 60 million and tax collections to $43 billion by 1945.

In 1981, Congress enacted the largest tax cut in U.S. history, approximately $750 billion over six years. The tax reduction, however, was offset by two tax acts, in 1982 and 1984, which attempted to raise approximately $265 billion.

On Oct. 22, 1986, President Reagan signed into law one of the most far-reaching reforms of the United States tax system since the adoption of the income tax. The Tax Reform Act of 1986, as it was called, attempted to be revenue neutral by increasing business taxes and correspondingly decreasing individual taxes by approximately $120 billion over a five-year period.

Following the yearly tradition of new tax acts which began in 1986, the President signed into law the Revenue Reconciliation Act of 1989 on December 19, 1989. As with the '87 and '88 acts, the 1989 act, while providing a number of substantive provisions, was small in comparison with the 1986 act.

Internal Revenue Service

The Internal Revenue Service (IRS), a bureau of the U.S. Treasury Department, is the federal agency charged with the administration of the tax laws passed by Congress. The IRS functions through a national office in Washington, 7 regional offices, 63 district offices, and 10 service centers.

Operations involving most taxpayers are carried out in the district offices and service centers. District offices are organized into Resources Management, Examination, Collection, Taxpayer Service, Employee Plans and Exempt Organizations, and Criminal Investigation. All tax returns are filed with the service centers, where the IRS computer operations are located.

IRS service centers are processing an ever increasing number of returns and documents. In 1990 the number of returns and supplemental documents processed totaled 201.7 million. This represented a 1% increase over 1989.

Prior to 1987, all tax return processing was performed by hand. This process was time consuming and costly. In an attempt to improve the speed and efficiency of the manual processing procedure, the IRS began testing an electronic return filing system beginning with the filing of 1985 returns.

The two most significant results of the test were that refunds for the electronically filed returns were issued more quickly and the tax processing error rate was significantly lower when compared to paper returns.

Electronic filing of individual income tax returns with refunds became an operational program in selected areas for the 1987 processing year. This program is continually expanding. In 1989 1,160,516 individual returns were electronically filed. In 1990 4,193,242 individual returns were filed electronically.

In addition to expanding the program for the electronic filing of individual returns, the IRS has also implemented programs for the electronic filing of partnership, fiduciary, and employee benefit plan returns.

Internal Revenue Service

	1990	1989	1988	1987	1986	1970
U.S. population (in thousands)	251,329	249,412	246,329	244,344	241,995	204,878
Number of IRS employees	111,858	114,758	114,873	102,188	95,880	68,683
Cost to govt. of collecting						
$100 in taxes	$0.52	$0.51	$0.54	$0.49	$0.49	$0.45
Tax per capita	$4,203.12	$4,062.84	$3,792.15	$3,627.22	$3,232.51	$955.31
Collections by principal sources (in thousands of dollars)						
Total IRS collections	$1,056,365,652	$1,013,322,133	$935,106,594	$886,290,590	$782,251,812	$195,722,096
Income and profits taxes						
Individual	540,228,408	515,731,504	473,666,566	465,452,486	416,568,384	103,651,585
Corporation	110,016,539	117,014,564	109,682,554	102,858,985	80,441,620	35,036,983
Employment taxes	367,219,321	345,625,586	318,038,990	277,000,469	244,374,767	37,449,188
Estate and gift taxes	11,761,939	8,973,146	7,784,445	7,667,670	7,194,956	3,680,076
Alcohol taxes	NOTE 4	NOTE 4	NOTE 4	NOTE 4	5,647,485	4,746,382
Tobacco taxes	NOTE 4	NOTE 4	NOTE 4	NOTE 2	4,607,845	2,094,212
Manufacturers' excise taxes	NOTE 3	NOTE 3	NOTE 3	10,221,574	9,927,742	6,683,061
All other taxes	27,139,445	25,977,333	25,934,040	11,991,729	13,489,014	2,380,609

NOTE: For fiscal year ending September 30th. NOTE 2: Alcohol and tobacco tax collections are included in the "All other taxes" amount. NOTE 3: Manufacturers' excise taxes are included in the "All other taxes" amount. NOTE 4: Alcohol and tobacco tax collections are now collected and reported by the Bureau of Alcohol, Tobacco, and Firearms.

Auditing Tax Returns

Most taxpayers' contacts with the IRS arise through the auditing of their tax returns. The Service has been empowered by Congress to inquire about all persons who may be liable for any tax and to obtain for review the books and/or records pertinent to those taxpayers' returns. A wide-ranging audit operation is carried out in the 63 district offices by 15,350 field agents and 2,953 office auditors.

Selecting Returns for Audit

The primary method used by the IRS in selecting returns for audits is a computer program that measures the probability of tax error in each return. The data base (established by an in-depth audit of randomly selected returns in various income categories) consists of approximately 200–250 individual items of information taken from each return. These 200–250 variables individually or in combination are weighted as relative indicators of potential tax change. Returns are then scored according to the weights given the combinations of variables as they appear on each return. The higher the score, the greater the tax change potential. Other returns are selected for examination on the basis of claims for refund, multi-year audits, related return audits, and other audits initiated by the IRS as a result of informants' information, special compliance programs, and the information document matching program.

In 1990, the IRS recommended additional tax and penalties on 883,319 returns, totaling $22 billion.

The Appeals Process

The IRS attempts to resolve tax disputes through an administrative appeals system. Taxpayers who, after audit of their tax returns, disagree with a proposed change in their tax liabilities are entitled to an independent review of their cases. Taxpayers are able to seek an immediate, informal appeal with the Appeals Office. If, however, the dispute arises from a field audit and the amount in question exceeds $10,000, a taxpayer must submit a written protest. Alternatively, the taxpayer can wait for the examiner's report and then request consideration by the Appeals Office and file a protest if necessary. Taxpayers may represent themselves or be represented by an attorney, accountant, or any other advisor authorized to practice before the IRS. Taxpayers can forego their right to the above process and await receipt of a deficiency notice. At this juncture, taxpayers can either (1) not pay the deficiency and petition the Tax Court by a required deadline or (2) pay the deficiency and file a claim for refund with the District Director's office. If the claim is not allowed, a suit for refund may be brought either in the District Court or the Claims Court within a specified period.

Federal Individual Income Tax

Tax Brackets—1991
Taxable Income

Joint return	Single Taxpayer	Rate
$0–$34,000	$0–$20,350	15%
34,001–82,150	20,351–49,300	28%
82,151 and up [1]	49,301 and up [1]	31% [2]

1. The deduction for personal exemptions is phased out as the taxpayer's gross income exceeds $150,000 (for a joint return) and $100,000 for single taxpayers. 2. The 31% rate is effectively increased because total otherwise allowable itemized deductions are reduced by 3% of the taxpayer's adjusted gross income in excess of $100,000.

The Federal individual income tax is levied on the world-wide income of U.S. citizens and resident aliens and on certain types of U.S. source income of non-residents. For a non-itemizer, "tax table income" is adjusted gross income (see below) less $2,150 for each personal exemption and the standard deduction (see below). If a taxpayer itemizes, tax table income is adjusted gross income minus total itemized deductions and personal exemptions. In addition, individuals may also be subject to the alternative minimum tax.

Who Must File a Return[1]

You must file a return if you are:	and your gross income is at least:
Single (legally separated, divorced, or married living apart from spouse with dependent child) and are under 65	$5,500
Single (legally separated, divorced, or married living apart from spouse with dependent child) and are 65 or older	$6,350
A person who can be claimed as a dependent on your parent's return, and who has taxable dividends, interest, or other unearned income	$550
Head of household under age 65	$7,150
Head of household over age 65	$8,000
Married, filing jointly, living together at end of year (or at date of death of spouse), and both are under 65	$10,000
Married, filing jointly, living together at end of year (or at date of death of spouse), and one is 65 or older	$10,650
Married, filing jointly, living together at end of year (or at date of death of spouse), and both are 65 or older	$11,300
Married, filing separate return, or married but not living together at end of year	$2,150
Married, filing separate return, or married but not living together at end of year outer age 65	$2,150

1. In 1991.

Adjusted Gross Income

Gross income consists of wages and salaries, unemployment compensation, tips and gratuities, interest, dividends, annuities, rents and royalties, up to 1/2 of Social Security Benefits if the recipient's income exceeds a base amount, and certain other types of income. Among the items excluded from gross income, and thus not subject to tax, are public assistance benefits and interest on exempt securities (mostly state and local bonds).

Adjusted gross income is determined by subtracting from gross income: alimony paid, penalties on early withdrawal of savings, payments to an I.R.A. (reduced proportionately based upon adjusted gross income levels if taxpayer is an active participant in an employer maintained retirement plan), payments to a Keogh retirement plan and self-employed health insurance payments (25% limit). Employee business expenses and job related moving expenses are now treated as itemized deductions.

Itemized Deductions

Taxpayers may itemize deductions or take the standard deduction. The standard deduction amounts for 1991 are as follows: Married filing jointly and surviving spouses $5,700; Heads of household $5,000; Single $3,400; and Married filing separate returns $2,850. Taxpayers who are age 65 or over or are blind are entitled to an additional standard deduction of $850 for single taxpayers and $650 for a married taxpayer.

In itemizing deductions, the following are major items that may be deducted in 1991: state and local income and property taxes, charitable contributions, employee moving expenses, medical expenses (exceeding 7.5% of adjusted gross income), casualty losses (only the amount over the $100 floor which exceeds 10% of adjusted gross income), mortgage interest, and miscellaneous deductions (deductible only to the extent by which cumulatively they exceed 2% of adjusted gross income).

Personal Exemptions

Personal exemptions are available to the taxpayer for himself, his spouse, and his dependents. The 1991 amount is $2,150 for each individual. Under the 1986 act, no exemption is allowed a taxpayer who can be claimed as a dependent on another taxpayer's return. Additional personal exemptions for taxpayers age 65 or over or blind have been eliminated.

Credits

Taxpayers can reduce their income tax liability by claiming the benefit of certain tax credits. Each dollar of tax credit offsets a dollar of tax liability. The following are a few of the available tax credits:

Certain low-income households with dependent children may claim an Earned Income Credit. The maximum Basic Earned Income Credit is $1,192 for taxpayers with one qualifying child and $1,235 for taxpayers with two or more qualifying children. In addition to the Basic Earned Income Credit, a taxpayer may also be eligible for a Health Insurance Credit which can be taken as a part of the total earned income credit. This maximum credit will be reduced if earned income or adjusted gross income exceeds $11,250, and the credit will be zero for families with incomes over $21,250. The earned income credit is a refundable credit.

A credit for Child and Dependent Care Expenses is available for amounts paid to care for a child or other dependent so that the taxpayer can work. The credit is between 20% and 30% (depending on adjusted gross income) of up to $2,400 of employment-related expenses for one qualifying child or dependent and up to $4,800 of expenses for two or more qualifying individuals.

The elderly and those under 65 who are retired under total disability may be entitled to a credit of up to $750 (if single) or $1,125 (if married and filing jointly). No credit is available if the taxpayer is single and has an adjusted gross income of $17,500 or more, or $5,000 or more in nontaxable Social Security benefits. Similarly, the credit is unavailable to a married couple if their adjusted gross income exceeds $25,000 or if their nontaxable Social Security benefits equal or exceed $7,500.

Free Taxpayer Publications

The IRS publishes over 100 free taxpayer information publications on various subjects. One of these, Publication 910, *Guide to Free Tax Services*, is a catalog of the free services the IRS offers. You can order these publications and any tax forms or instructions you need by calling the IRS toll-free at 1-800-829-3676.

Federal Income Tax Comparisons

Taxes at Selected Rate Brackets After Standard Deductions and Personal Exemptions[1]

Adjusted gross income	Single return listing no dependents				Joint return listing two dependents			
	1991	1990	1989	1975	1991	1990	1989	1975
$ 10,000	$ 668	$ 705	$735	$ 1,506	$−1,235	$ −953[2]	$ −910[2]	$ 829
20,000	2,168	2,205	2,235	4,153	702	926	1,020	2,860
30,000	4,201	4,388	4,561	8,018	2,355	2,453	2,520	5,804
40,000	7,001	7,188	7,361	12,765	3,855	3,953	4,020	9,668
50,000	9,801	9,988	10,161	18,360	5,576	5,960	6,272	14,260

1. For comparison purposes, tax rate schedules were used. 2. Refund based on a basic earned income credit for families with dependent children.

Federal Corporation Taxes

Corporations are taxed under a graduated tax rate structure as shown in the chart. For tax years beginning on or after July 1, 1987, the benefits of the lower rates are phased out for corporations with taxable income between $100,000 and $335,000 and totally eliminated for corporations with income equal to or in excess of $335,000.

If the corporation qualifies, it may elect to be an S corporation. If it makes this election, the corporation will not (with certain exceptions) pay corporate tax on its income. Its income is instead passed through and taxed to its shareholders. There are several requirements a corporation must meet to qualify as an S corporation including having 35 or fewer shareholders, and having only one class of stock.

Tax Years Beginning on or After July 1, 1987

Taxable income	Tax rate
$0–$50,000	15%
$50,001–75,000	25
75,001–100,000	34
100,001–335,000	39
335,001 and up	34

State Corporation Income and Franchise Taxes

All states but Nevada, South Dakota, Washington, and Wyoming impose a tax on corporation net income. The majority of states impose the tax at flat rates ranging from 2.35% to 15%. Several states have adopted a graduated basis of rates for corporations.

Nearly all states follow the federal law in defining net income. However, many states provide for varying exclusions and adjustments.

A state is empowered to tax all of the net income of its domestic corporations. With regard to non-resi-dent corporations, however, it may only tax the net income on business carried on within its boundaries. Corporations are, therefore, required to apportion their incomes among the states where they do business and pay a tax to each of these states. Nearly all states provide an apportionment to their domestic corporations, too, in order that they not be unduly burdened.

Several states tax unincorporated businesses separately.

Federal Estate and Gift Taxes

A Federal Estate Tax Return must be filed for the estate of every U.S. citizen or resident whose gross estate, if the decedent died in 1991, exceeds $600,000. An estate tax return must also be filed for the estate of a non-resident, if the value of his gross estate in the U.S. is more than $60,000 at the date of death. The estate tax return is due nine months after the date of death of the decedent, but a reasonable extension of time to file may be obtained for good reason.

Under the unified federal estate and gift tax structure, individuals who made taxable gifts during the calendar year are required to file a gift tax return by April 15 of the following year.

A unified credit of $192,800 (during 1991) is available to offset both estate and gift taxes. Any part of the credit used to offset gift taxes is not available to offset estate taxes. As a result, although they are still taxable as gifts, lifetime transfers no longer cushion the impact of progressive estate tax rates. Lifetime transfers and transfers made at death are combined for estate tax rate purposes.

Gift taxes are computed by applying the uniform rate schedule to lifetime taxable transfers (after deducting the unified credit) and subtracting the taxes payable for prior taxable periods. In general, estate taxes are computed by applying the uniform rate schedule to cumulative transfers and subtracting the gift taxes paid. An appropriate adjustment is made for taxes on lifetime transfers—such as certain gifts within three years of death—in a decedent's estate.

Among the deductions allowed in computing the amount of the estate subject to tax are funeral expenditures, administrative costs, claims and bequests to religious, charitable, and fraternal organizations or government welfare agencies, and state inheritance taxes. For transfers made after 1981 during life or death, there is an unlimited marital deduction.

An annual gift tax exclusion is provided that permits tax-free gifts to each donee of $10,000 for each year. A husband and wife who agree to treat gifts to third persons as joint gifts can exclude up to $20,000 a year to each donee. An unlimited exclusion for medical expenses and school tuition paid for the benefit of any donee is also available.

Federal Estate and Gift Taxes

Unified Rate Schedule, 1991[1]

If the net amount is:		Tentative tax is:		
From	To	Tax +	%	On excess over
$ 0	$ 10,000	$ 0	18	$ 0
10,001	20,000	1,800	20	10,000
20,001	40,000	3,800	22	20,000
40,001	60,000	8,200	24	40,000
60,001	80,000	13,000	26	60,000
80,001	100,000	18,200	28	80,000
100,001	150,000	23,800	30	100,000
150,001	250,000	38,800	32	150,000
250,001	500,000	70,800	34	250,000
500,001	750,000	155,800	37	500,000
750,001	1,000,000	248,300	39	750,000
1,000,001	1,250,000	345,800	41	1,000,000
1,250,001	1,500,000	448,300	43	1,250,000
1,500,001	2,000,000	555,800	45	1,500,000
2,000,001	2,500,000	780,800	49	2,000,000
2,500,001	3,000,000	1,025,800	53	2,500,000
3,000,001 and up	—	1,290,800	55	3,000,000

1. The estate and gift tax rates are combined in the single rate schedule effective for the estates of decedents dying, and for gifts made, after Dec. 31, 1976.

Recent Legislation

On November 5, 1990, the President signed into law the Revenue Reconciliation Act of 1990 ("the Act"). The emphasis of the Act was increased taxes on the wealthy. Changes imposed by the Act include:

Luxury Tax

A new 10% tax on the purchase of furs and jewelry (over $10,000), automobiles (over $30,000), boats and yachts (over $100,000), and airplanes (over $250,000) was imposed effective January 1, 1991.

Limitation on Itemized Deductions

Total otherwise allowable itemized deductions (other than medical expenses, casualty and theft losses, and investment interest) are reduced by 3% of a taxpayer's adjusted gross income in excess of $100,000. Total itemized deductions may not be reduced by more than 80%.

What if Your Tax Return is Examined?

Source: Internal Revenue Service.

If your return is selected for examination, it does not suggest that you are dishonest. The examination may or may not result in more tax. Your case may be closed without change. Or, you may receive a refund.

Many examinations are handled entirely by mail. For information on this, get Publication 1383, The Correspondence Process (Income Tax Accounts), available free by calling 1-800-829-3676. If the IRS notifies you that your examination is to be conducted through a face-to-face interview, or you request such an interview, you have the right to ask that the examination take place at a reasonable time and place that is convenient for both you and the IRS. If the time or place suggested by the IRS is not convenient, the examiner will try to work out something more suitable. However, in any case, the IRS makes the final determination of how, when, and where the examination will take place.

Throughout the examination, you may represent yourself, have someone else accompany you, or with proper written authorization, have someone represent you in your absence.

You may make a sound recording of the examination if you wish, provided you let the examiner know in advance so that he or she can do the same.

Repeat Examinations

The IRS tries to avoid repeat examinations of the same items, but this sometimes happens. If the IRS examined your tax return for the same items in either of the two previous years and proposed no change to your tax liability, you should contact the IRS as soon as possible so that the agency can see if it should discontinue the repeat examination.

Explanation of Changes

If the IRS proposes any changes to your return, they will explain the reasons for the changes. You should not hesitate to ask about anything that is unclear to you.

Interest

You must pay interest on additional tax that you owe. The interest is figured from the due date of the return. But if an IRS error caused a delay in your case, and this was grossly unfair, you may be entitled to a reduction in the interest. Only delays caused by procedural or mechanical acts that do not involve the exercise of judgment or discretion qualify. If you think the IRS caused such a delay, you should discuss it with the examiner and file a claim. □

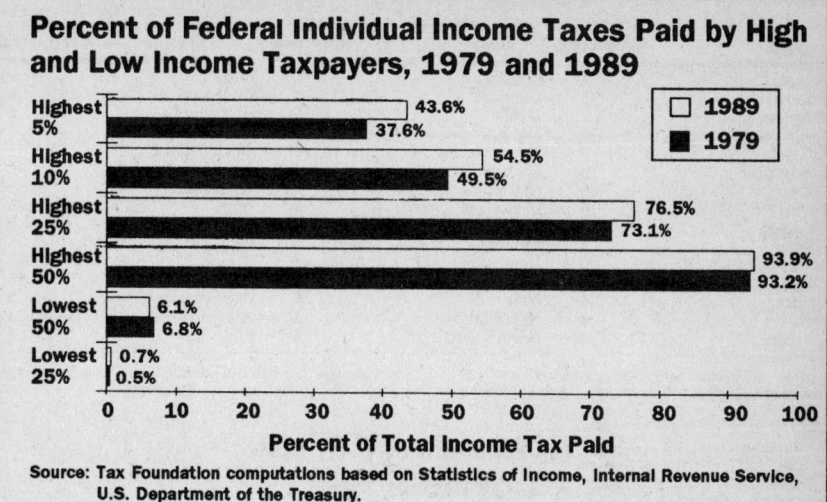

Percent of Federal Individual Income Taxes Paid by High and Low Income Taxpayers, 1979 and 1989

	1989	1979
Highest 5%	43.6%	37.6%
Highest 10%	54.5%	49.5%
Highest 25%	76.5%	73.1%
Highest 50%	93.9%	93.2%
Lowest 50%	6.1%	6.8%
Lowest 25%	0.7%	0.5%

Percent of Total Income Tax Paid

Source: Tax Foundation computations based on Statistics of Income, Internal Revenue Service, U.S. Department of the Treasury.

Top Earners Still Pay Largest Share of Income Tax Bill

The top-earning ten percent of U.S. taxpayers paid nearly 55 percent of the Federal individual income tax bill in 1989, according to a Tax foundation analysis of the recently released 1989 IRS tax return data. Despite all the major tax legislation witnessed over the decade of the 1980s, the fraction of income taxes collected for this top ten percent varied only slightly from year to year between 1979 and 1989 but inched steadily up during the decade.

After paying 49.5 percent of all Federal individual income taxes collected in 1979, these taxpayers, who now number 11.2 million, put a little more into the till most years until in 1989 they paid 54.5 percent. While their adjusted gross income (AGI) rose 89 percent from 1979 to 1989, their average tax payment rose even more—94 percent—and averaged $22,225 in 1989. Their AGI ranged down to $61,780, not exactly "fat cat" status. It still takes millions of middle- and upper-middle income taxpayers to pay the bulk of the total tax bill.

All segments of the top-earning half paid a larger share of the income tax bill over the course of the decade. The top five percent paid 43.6 percent in 1989, up from 37.6 in 1979; the top 25 percent paid 76.5 percent of the taxes paid in 1989, compared to 73.1 percent in 1979; and the top half increased its lion's share from 93.2 to 93.9 percent.

The lower half's share of income taxes paid dropped 11 percent over the decade. These taxpayers, whose AGI ranged from $18,851 down to zero in 1989, paid 6.1 percent of total taxes, down from 6.8 percent in 1979. The lowest 25 percent paid a slightly higher percentage of collections, up from .5 percent in 1979 to .7 percent in 1989.

Trends in Progressivity

The Federal income tax system has remained progressive. Top earners continue to pay a larger share of tax collections despite the alleged upper-income bias of the tax cuts and rate reductions under the Economic Recovery Tax Act of 1981 and the Tax Reform Act of 1986.

Growth in the income base itself has been increasing faster at the upper end of the income scale, resulting in increased income tax receipts from top earners. Naturally, this also results in a higher proportion of the entire population's income being taxed at the highest rate.

The 112 million returns filed for tax year 1989 reported an increase in AGI of $194 billion over 1988. The largest percentage gain in income was from Individual Retirement Account distributions, up 24.3 percent from 1988. Social Security benefits rose 22.4 percent, and taxable interest increased 15.5 percent. Salaries and wages, which constituted 71.6 percent of total positive income for 1989, rose 5.5 percent over 1988. All told, 1989 total individual income taxes rose $23.3 billion over 1988 for a record $439 billion take. □

Taxpayer Rights
Source: Internal Revenue Service.

You have the right to have your personal and financial information kept confidential. You also have the right to know why the IRS is asking you for information, exactly how any information that you give will be used, and what might happen if you do not get the information.

Under the law, the IRS may share your tax information with State tax agencies with which the IRS has information exchange agreements, the Department of Justice and other federal agencies under strict legal guidelines, and certain foreign governments under tax treaty provisions. □

State General Sales and Use Taxes[1]

State	Percent rate	State	Percent rate	State	Percent rate
Alabama	4	Kentucky	6	Ohio	5
Arizona	5	Louisiana	4	Oklahoma	4.5
Arkansas	4.5	Maine	5	Pennsylvania	5
California	4.75	Maryland	5	Rhode Island	7
Colorado	3	Massachusets	5	South Carolina	5
Connecticut	8	Michigan	4	South Dakota	4
D.C.	6	Minnesota	6	Tennessee	5.5
Florida	6	Mississippi	6	Texas	6.25
Georgia	4	Missouri	4.225	Utah	5
Hawaii	4	Nebraska	5	Vermont	5
Idaho	5	New Jersey	7	Virginia	3.5
Illinois	6.25	New Mexico	5	Washington	6.5
Indiana	5	New York	4	West Virginia	6
Iowa	4	North Carolina	3	Wisconsin	5
Kansas	4.25	North Dakota	5	Wyoming	3

1. Local and county taxes, if any, are additional. NOTE: Alaska, Delaware, Montana, New Hampshire, and Oregon have no state-wide sales and use taxes. *Source: Information Please Almanac* questionnaires to the states.

Tax Freedom Day[1] by State

Calendar Years, 1990–91

State	Tax Freedom Day 1990	Tax Freedom Day 1991	Change from 1990 to 1991	State	Tax Freedom Day 1990	Tax Freedom Day 1991	Change from 1990 to 1991
Alabama	April 21	April 25	4	Montana	May 6	May 4	−2
Alaska	May 11	May 11	0	Nebraska	May 1	May 7	6
Arizona	May 2	May 7	5	Nevada	May 9	May 8	−1
Arkansas	April 22	April 26	4	New Hampshire	April 23	April 29	6
California	May 3	May 7	4	New Jersey	May 9	May 14	5
Colorado	April 28	May 2	4	New Mexico	May 4	May 7	3
Connecticut	May 11	May 17	6	New York	May 23	May 26	3
Delaware	May 18	May 21	3	North Carolina	May 1	May 3	2
Dist. of Columbia	May 21	May 26	5	North Dakota	May 5	May 6	1
Florida	May 2	May 4	2	Ohio	May 1	May 6	5
Georgia	April 27	May 3	6	Oklahoma	April 28	May 2	4
Hawaii	May 16	May 16	0	Oregon	May 5	May 10	5
Idaho	April 25	April 28	3	Pennsylvania	May 3	May 7	4
Illinois	May 6	May 9	3	Rhode Island	May 9	May 12	3
Indiana	April 28	May 2	4	South Carolina	April 26	May 1	5
Iowa	May 5	May 7	2	South Dakota	April 28	April 28	0
Kansas	May 1	May 5	4	Tennessee	April 25	April 29	4
Kentucky	April 25	April 29	4	Texas	May 2	May 5	3
Louisiana	April 28	May 4	6	Utah	May 2	May 1	−1
Maine	May 6	May 8	2	Vermont	May 11	May 10	−1
Maryland	May 8	May 11	3	Virginia	April 28	May 2	4
Massachusetts	May 3	May 8	5	Washington	May 9	May 10	1
Michigan	May 8	May 12	4	West Virginia	April 25	May 1	6
Minnesota	May 13	May 14	1	Wisconsin	May 8	May 11	3
Mississippi	April 19	April 24	5	Wyoming	May 2	May 6	4
Missouri	April 25	April 28	3	**U.S. Total**	**May 5**	**May 8**	**3**

1. Tax Freedom Day is the day on which the American taxpayer will have earned enough money to pay his 1991 total taxes. *Source:* Tax Foundation.

Taxes Dominate Average American's Budget

Based on the Government's budget for 1991, the Tax Foundation calculated that the federal tax bill for the average American family with two workers, earning $46,000 and two dependent children, to be $12,984. This 28.2% tax bite from the family's income will cover its direct and indirect federal taxes, but not state or local taxes.

Of the $12,984 that the typical family surrenders to Uncle Sam, nearly 80% will go to just four federal spending categories: Social Security, 32 cents from every dollar; National Defense, 20 cents out of each tax dollar; Interest on the National Debt, 14 cents per dollar; and Health Outlays (mainly Medicare and Medicaid), 13 cents of the family's tax dollar. These four alone will cost the typical family $10,251, or 79 cents of each tax dollar.

Property Tax Collections by State

Per Capita and Per $1,000 of Personal Income
Fiscal Years 1979 and 1989

State	Per capita property tax				Property tax per $1,000 of pers. income			
	Amount		Percent change	Rank 1989	Amount		Percent change	Rank 1989
	1979	1989			1979	1989		
Total	$295	$674	94.6 %	—	$38	$35	−7.5 %	—
Alabama	73	148	104.1	51	12	12	−0.4	51
Alaska	826	1,257	52.2	1	76	66	−12.8	1
Arizona	353	600	70.0	23	50	41	−18.1	19
Arkansas	125	211	68.0	49	21	17	−17.3	48
California	266	543	104.0	27	30	30	−2.1	33
Colorado	326	635	94.6	19	42	39	−7.3	22
Connecticut	456	1,003	119.8	5	51	44	−15.4	15
Delaware	165	276	67.1	44	19	16	−17.6	49
Florida	247	549	122.3	24	34	34	1.0	27
Georgia	209	444	111.8	33	31	30	−6.2	34
Hawaii	191	335	75.9	39	23	20	−13.3	43
Idaho	245	386	57.5	37	36	31	−14.4	31
Illinois	350	657	88.1	18	39	38	−4.3	23
Indiana	247	480	94.6	30	32	32	0.6	29
Iowa	339	624	84.1	20	42	43	0.5	17
Kansas	357	617	72.6	21	46	39	−13.8	21
Kentucky	131	228	74.8	48	20	18	−10.6	47
Louisiana	102	241	137.8	46	15	20	27.6	46
Maine	303	666	120.2	16	48	45	−7.4	13
Maryland	276	546	97.8	25	33	28	−13.9	36
Massachusetts	546	743	36.1	10	69	36	−47.9	24
Michigan	376	764	103.3	9	44	46	4.3	11
Minnesota	311	659	111.8	17	40	40	0.3	20
Mississippi	138	291	111.7	43	25	26	4.3	38
Missouri	205	318	54.9	41	28	21	−26.5	42
Montana	408	679	66.4	15	61	53	−12.7	6
Nebraska	389	698	79.4	14	52	47	−7.9	10
Nevada	355	386	8.8	36	40	23	−41.9	39
New Hampshire	426	1,058	148.5	3	59	56	−5.8	3
New Jersey	506	1,056	108.7	4	58	48	−16.7	9
New Mexico	131	180	37.0	50	20	15	−28.5	50
New York	482	929	92.9	6	58	48	−17.2	8
North Carolina	163	322	97.7	40	25	23	−8.4	40
North Dakota	257	441	71.4	34	36	34	−5.9	26
Ohio	260	476	83.0	31	33	31	−6.9	32
Oklahoma	149	267	78.9	45	21	20	−5.1	45
Oregon	366	795	117.4	8	47	54	16.5	4
Pennsylvania	230	467	103.4	32	30	29	−2.5	35
Rhode Island	399	737	84.7	11	53	44	−17.3	14
South Carolina	181	353	134.3	38	24	28	14.8	37
South Dakota	343	544	58.7	26	50	43	−14.3	16
Tennessee	155	296	90.9	42	24	22	=9.6	41
Texas	274	613	123.8	22	36	42	16.4	18
Utah	230	420	82.1	35	37	35	−5.3	25
Vermont	360	729	102.4	12	56	48	−12.8	7
Virginia	223	541	142.7	29	29	31	5.8	30
Washington	308	542	76.0	28	38	34	−10.6	28
West Virginia	131	237	81.7	47	20	20	0.5	44
Wisconsin	346	710	105.2	13	46	46	−1.1	12
Wyoming	513	870	69.6	7	63	63	0.4	2
Dist. of Columbia	323	1,117	263.8	2	32	54	69.7	5

Source: Department of Commerce, and Tax Foundation computations. Reprinted from *Tax Features*, May–June 1991.

FIRST AID

Information Please Almanac is not responsible and assumes no responsibility for any action undertaken by anyone utilizing the first aid procedures which follow.

The Heimlich Maneuver[1]

Food-Choking

What to look for: Victim cannot speak or breathe; turns blue; collapses.

To perform the Heimlich Maneuver when the victim is standing or sitting:
1. Stand behind the victim and wrap your arms around his waist.
2. Place the thumb side of your fist against the victim's abdomen, slightly above the navel and below the rib cage.
3. Grasp your fist with the other hand and press your fist into the victim's abdomen with a quick upward thrust. Repeat as often as necessary.
4. If the victim is sitting, stand behind the victim's chair and perform the maneuver in the same manner.
5. After the food is dislodged, have the victim seen by a doctor.

When the victim has collapsed and cannot be lifted:
1. Lay the victim on his back.
2. Face the victim and kneel astride his hips.
3. With one hand on top of the other, place the heel of your bottom hand on the abdomen slightly above the navel and below the rib cage.
4. Press into the victim's abdomen with a quick upward thrust. Repeat as often as necessary
5. Should the victim vomit, quickly place him on his side and wipe out his mouth to prevent aspiration (drawing of vomit into the throat).

6. After the food is dislodged, have the victim seen by a doctor.
NOTE: If you start to choke when alone and help is not available, an attempt should be made to self-administer this maneuver.

Burns[2]

First Degree: Signs/Symptoms—reddened skin. **Treatment**—Immerse quickly in cold water or apply ice until pain stops.

Second Degree: Signs/Symptoms—reddened skin, blisters. **Treatment**—(1) Cut away loose clothing, (2) Cover with several layers of cold moist dressings or, if limb is involved, immerse in cold water for relief of pain. (3) Treat for shock.

Third Degree: Signs/Symtoms—skin destroyed, tissues damaged, charring. **Treatment**—(1) Cut away loose clothing (do not remove clothing adhered to skin). (2) Cover with several layers of sterile, cold, moist dressings for relief of pain and to stop burning action. (3) Treat for shock.

Poisons[2]

Treatment—(1) Dilute by drinking large quantities of water. (2) Induce vomiting except when poison is corrosive or a petroleum product. (3) Call the poison control center or a doctor.

Shock[2]

Shock may accompany any serious injury: blood loss, breathing impairment, heart failure, burns. Shock can kill—treat as soon as possible and continue until medical aid is available.

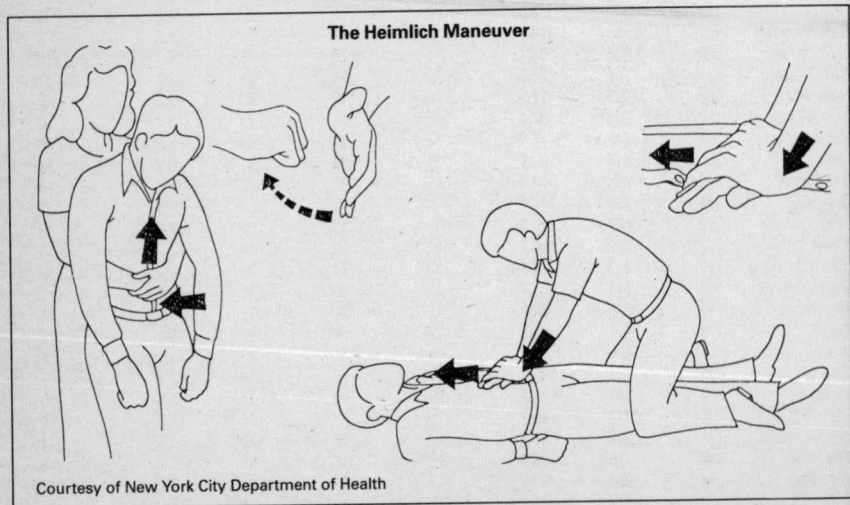

The Heimlich Maneuver

Courtesy of New York City Department of Health

Signs/Symptoms—(1) Shallow breathing. (2) Rapid and weak pulse. (3) Nausea, collapse, vomiting. (4) Shivering. (5) Pale, moist skin. (6) Mental confusion. (7) Drooping eyelids, dilated pupils.

Treatment—(1) Establish and maintain an open airway. (2) Control bleeding. (3) Keep victim lying down. Exception: Head and chest injuries, heart attack, stroke, sun stroke. If no spine injury, victim may be more comfortable and breathe better in a semi-reclining position. If in doubt, keep the victim flat. Elevate the feet unless injury would be aggravated. Maintain normal body temperature. Place blankets under and over victim.

Frostbite[2]

Most frequently frostbitten: toes, fingers, nose, and ears. It is caused by exposure to cold.

Signs/Symptoms—(1) Skin becomes pale or a grayish-yellow color. (2) Parts feel cold and numb. (3) Frozen parts feel doughy.

Treatment—(1) Until victim can be brought inside, he should be wrapped in woolen cloth and kept dry. (2) Do not rub, chafe, or manipulate frostbitten parts. (3) Bring victim indoors. (4) Place in warm water (102° to 105°) and make sure it remains warm. Test water by pouring on inner surface of your forearm. Never thaw if the victim has to go back out into the cold which may cause the affected area to be refrozen. (5) Do not use hot water bottles or a heat lamp, and do not place victim near a hot stove. (6) Do not allow victim to walk if feet are affected. (7) Once thawed, have victim gently exercise parts. (8) For serious frostbite, seek medical aid for thawing because pain will be intense and tissue damage extensive.

Heat Cramps[2]

Affects people who work or do strenous exercises in a hot environment. To prevent it, such people should drink large amounts of cool water and add a pinch of salt to each glass of water

Signs/Symptoms—(1) Painful muscle cramps in legs and abdomen. (2) Faintness. (3) Profuse perspiration.

Treatment—(1) Move victim to a cool place. (2) Give him sips of salted drinking water (one teaspoon of salt to one quart of water). (3) Apply manual pressure to the cramped muscle.

Heat Exhaustion[2]

Signs/Symptoms—(1) Pale and clammy skin. (2) Profuse perspiration. (3) Rapid and shallow breathing. (4) Weakness, dizziness, and headache.

Treatment—(1) Care for victim as if he were in shock. (2) Remove victim to a cool area, do not allow chilling. (3) If body gets too cold, cover victim.

Heat Stroke[2]

Signs/Symptoms—(1) Face is red and flushed. (2) Victim becomes rapidly unconscious. (3) Skin is hot and dry with no perspiration.

Treatment—(1) Lay victim down with head and shoulders raised. (2) Reduce the high body temperature as quickly as possible. (3) Apply cold applications to the body and head. (4) Use ice and fan if available. (5) Watch for signs of shock and treat accordingly. (6) Get medical aid as soon as possible.

Artificial Respiration[3]

(Mouth-to-Mouth Breathing—In Cases Like Drowning, Electric Shock or Smoke Inhalation.)

There is need for help in breathing when breathing movements stop or lips, tongue, and fingernails become blue. When in doubt, apply artificial respiration until you get medical help. No harm can result from its use and delay may cost the patient his life. Start immediately. Seconds count. Clear mouth and throat of any obstructions with your fingers.

For Adults: Place patient on back with face up.

Lift the chin and tilt the head back. If air passage is still closed, pull chin up by placing fingers behind the angles of the lower jaw and pushing forward.

Take deep breath, place you mouth over patient's mouth, making leak-proof seal.

Pinch patient's nostrils closed.

Blow into patient's mouth until you see his chest rise.

—OR—

Take deep breath, place your mouth over patient's nose, making leak-proof seal.

Seal patient's mouth with your hand.

Blow into patient's nose until you see his chest rise.

Remove your mouth and let patient exhale.

Repeat about 12 times a minute. (If the patient's stomach rises markedly, exert moderate hand pressure on the stomach just below the rib cage to keep it from inflating.)

For Infants and Small Children: Place your mouth over patient's mouth and nose. Blow into mouth and nose until you see patient's chest rise normally.

Repeat 20 to 30 times per minute. (Don't exaggerate the tilted position of an infant's head.)

NOTE: For emergency treatment of heart attack, cardiopulmonary resuscitation (CPR) is recommended. Instruction in CPR can be obtained through local health organizations or schools.

Sources: 1. New York City Department of Health. NOTE: Heimlich Maneuver, T.M. Pending. 2. *Firstr Aid,* Mining Enforcement and Safety Administration, U.S. Department of the Interior. 3. *Health Emergency Chart,* Council on Family Health.

NUTRITION & HEALTH

AIDS Among Women to Double by 2000

By the end of the 1990s, the number of women infected with the HIV virus may well double as heterosexual transmission becomes the predominant mode of spread of the virus in most parts of the world, the World Health Organization (WHO) says.

In an analysis of the impact of AIDS and HIV infection on women, WHO estimates that worldwide, some 3 million women are already infected with HIV. Since the start of the pandemic, about one–third of the estimated total of 1.3 million cases of AIDS have been in women. Moreover, WHO says these are probably conservative estimates.

The WHO analysis indicates that, by 1992, a cumulative total of 600,000 women will probably have developed AIDS around the world. In addition, WHO estimates that AIDS will kill at least 2 million women during the 1990s, most of them in sub–Saharan Africa.

The WHO report presented the following picture of the global epidemic of AIDS among women:

• As of 1990, 60 percent off HIV infections worldwide have resulted from heterosexual intercourse. In developing countries, heterosexual sex is the predominant means of HIV transmission. In industrialized countries, the heterosexual spread of HIV is increasing slowly but steadily, especially in groups with high rates of sexually transmitted diseases and drug injecting. By the year 2000, it is projected that 75–80 percent of all HIV infections will result from sexual intercourse between men and women, which will mean dramatic increases in HIV infection among women.

• An estimated 1 in 40 women in sub–Saharan Africa is already infected with HIV. Elsewhere, for example, 1 in 500 women in Latin America and 1 in 700 women in North America is infected. In Asia, and particularly in South and Southeast Asia, recent data indicate that within the past 3 years alone close to 200,000 women may have been infected.

• In some cities in sub–Saharan Africa, up to 40 percent of adults of both sexes may be infected with HIV. These infection levels will cause a doubling or tripling of the total adult mortality rate during the 1990s and will also cause up to a 50–percent increase in the mortality rate of children.

• WHO estimates that approximately 30 percent of infants born to infected mothers will become infected with HIV before, during, or shortly after birth. A cumulative total of as many as 10 million infants will be born infected with HIV worldwide by the year 2000.

• Up to 70 percent of infants born to infected mothers will not be infected. They will not escape the pandemic's impact, however, as their mothers or fathers, or both, die of AIDS. At least 10 million uninfected children under the age of 10 will be orphaned in the 1990s.

□

Understanding AIDS

The Acquired Immune Deficiency Syndrome, or AIDS, was first reported in the United States in mid-1981. The total AIDS cases in the United States (including U.S. territories) as of May 31, 1991, were 179,136, and of these cases, 113,426 deaths were reported, says the Center for Disease Control in Atlanta. According to World Health Organization projections in June 1991, there will be 5-6 million new cases of AIDS by the mid-to-late 1990s and 15-20 million HIV infected adults. It is estimated that 1.5 million people worldwide have AIDS, and that at least 8-10 million are infected with the HIV virus.

AIDS is characterized by a defect in natural immunity against disease. People who have AIDS are vulnerable to serious illnesses which would not be a threat to anyone whose immune system was functioning normally. These illnesses are referred to as "opportunistic" infections or diseases: in AIDS patients the most common of these are Pneumocystis carinii pneumonia (PCP), a parasitic infection of the lungs; and a type of cancer known as Kaposi's sarcoma (KS). Other opportunistic infections include unusually severe infections with yeast, cytomegalovirus, herpes virus, and parasites such as Toxoplasma or Cryptosporidia. Milder infections with these organisms do not suggest immune deficiency.

AIDS is caused by a virus usually known as human immunodeficiency virus, or HIV. Symptoms of full-blown AIDS include a persistent cough, fever, and difficulty in breathing. Multiple purplish blotches and bumps on the skin may indicate Kaposi's sarcoma. The virus can also cause brain damage.

People infected with the virus can have a wide range of symptoms—from none to mild to severe. At least a fourth to a half of those infected will develop AIDS within four to ten years. Many experts think the percentage will be much higher.

AIDS is spread by sexual contact, needle sharing, or less commonly through transfused blood or its components. The risk of infection with the virus is increased by having multiple sexual partners, either homosexual or heterosexual, and sharing of needles among those using illicit drugs. The occurrence of the syndrome in hemophilia patients and persons receiving transfusions provides evidence for transmission through blood. It may be transmitted from infected mother to infant before, during, or shortly after birth (probably through breast milk).

Scientists have discovered how AIDS infects brain cells and have identified genes that affect the AIDS virus. But efforts to devise a treatment or vaccine are complicated by the fact that AIDS is caused by two, perhaps three, similar viruses, and that the virus mutates frequently.

With no cure in sight, prudence could save thousands of people in the U.S. who have yet to be exposed to the virus. Their fate will depend less on science than on the ability of large numbers of human beings to change their behavior in the face of growing danger. Experts believe that couples who have had a totally monogamous relationship for the past decade are safe. A negative blood test would be near-certain evidence of safety.

People who should be tested for AIDS include gay men and intravenous drug users, their sex partners, and anyone who has had several sex partners, if their sexual history is unknown, during any one of the last five years. Anyone who tests positive should see a physician immediately for a medical evaluation. Persons testing positive should inform their sex partners and should use a condom during sex. They should not donate blood, body organs, other tissue or sperm, nor should they share toothbrushes, razors, or other implements that could become contaminated with blood.

Information about where to go for confidential testing for the presence of the AIDS virus is provided by local and state health departments. There is a National AIDS Hot Line: (800) 342-2437 for recorded information about AIDS, or (800) 433-0366 for specific questions. □

Helping a Person With AIDS

No one will require more support and more love than your friend with AIDS. Feel free to offer what you can, without fear of becoming infected. You need to take precautions such as wearing rubber gloves only when blood is present.

If you don't know anyone with AIDS, but you'd still like to offer a helping hand, become a volunteer. You can be sure your help will be appreciated by a person with AIDS.

This might mean dropping by a supermarket to pick up groceries or just being there to talk. Above all, keep an upbeat attitude. It will help you and everyone face the disease more comfortably.

The AIDS Situation Worldwide

Source: The World Health Organization (WHO).

As of May 1, 1991, 359,271 cases of AIDS were reported to the World Health Organization (WHO) from 162 countries and territories. (Another 18 countries and territories reported zero cases.) Taking into account under-diagnosis, under-reporting, and delays in reporting, WHO estimates that more than one million adult AIDS cases may have occurred worldwide since the beginning of the pandemic just over 10 years ago.

In addition, WHO estimated that by early 1991 more than 500,000 pediatric AIDS cases resulting from perinatal transmission may have occurred, with over 90% of this total in sub-Saharan Africa. Perinatal transmission of the human immunodeficiency virus (HIV)—that is, the spread of HIV from an infected mother to her fetus or newborn baby—occurs in approximately one-third of all pregnancies. Thus, WHO estimates that the cumulative global total of AIDS cases by early 1991 is more than 1.5 million.

By April 1991, at least eight to ten million HIV infections may have occurred in adults worldwide and about one million children may have been born infected with HIV.

While the HIV infection rate appears to be slowing in some industrialized countries, the incidence of new infections is increasing markedly in developing countries, especially in sub-Saharan Africa, but also in Asia, Latin America, and the Caribbean.

AIDS takes an average of ten years to develop. Because of this long lag time, AIDS cases will continue to develop from the existing pool of HIV-infected persons for some time to come, no matter how successful the current efforts are to curb the further spread of HIV infections.

Global Projections for 2000

The latest information indicates that there have been about 3 million new HIV infections over the past three years, most of them in sub-Saharan Africa, and in South and South-East Asia. These data suggest that 15 to 20 million adult HIV infections may be reached as soon as the mid-to-late 1990s.

On the basis of these trends, 10 to 20 million new infections may be expected in adults during the 1990s, mostly in the developing world. Thus, for the year 2000, WHO projects a cumulative total of close to 30 million adult HIV infections, of which more than 90% will be in developing countries. During the same decade, WHO projects that close to 10 million or more children will have been born with HIV, the majority of them in sub-Saharan Africa.

The pandemic will have a particularly dramatic effect on the developing countries. Already overburdened health facilities risk being completely overwhelmed. Because of the deaths of millions of young and middle-age adults, over 10 million children will be orphaned and the elderly left without support. The deaths of these adults, who include members of social, economic, and political elites, could lead to economic and even political destabilization. □

Leading Causes of Death by Sex
United States: 1987

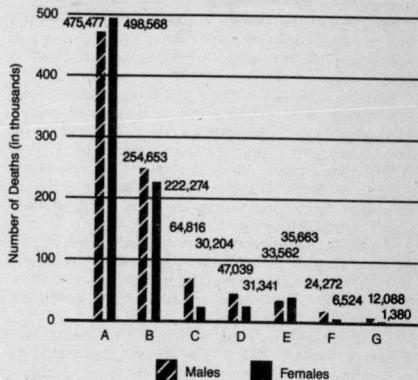

A Cardiovascular Disease
B Cancer
C Accidents
D Chronic Obstructive Pulmonary Disease
E Pneumonia and Influenza
F Suicide
G AIDS

Source: National Center for Health Statistics, U.S. Public Health Service, DHHS and the American Heart Association.

Heart Disease Leading Killer of Americans

Source: American Heart Association, © 1990.

Estimated Annual Number of Americans, by Age and Sex, Experiencing Heart Attack

United States

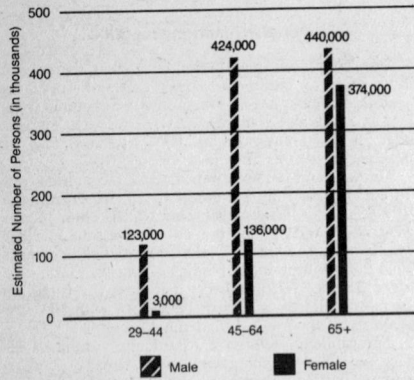

Source: Based on the Framingham Heart Study, 26-year follow-up.

What's the number one killer in America? Millions of people believe it's cancer. They're wrong. Cardiovascular disease holds that deadly distinction.

FACT: In 1988 heart and blood pressure diseases killed nearly one million Americans, almost as many as cancer, accidents, pneumonia, influenza, and all other causes of death combined.

FACT: Almost one in two Americans dies of cardiovascular disease.

FACT: Of the current U.S. population of about 246 million, nearly 68 million people—more than one in four Americans—suffer some form of cardiovascular disease.

Make no mistake. Cancer and other diseases are a real threat. But let's put things in perspective. In 1988 about 488,000 Americans died of cancer. In the same year, more than 16,000 Americans died of AIDS. That's tragic, but the tragedy is compounded if Americans focus on these diseases and neglect a disease that claims more than twice as many victims. Cardiovascular diseases are killers.

Cardiovascular diseases may be discounted, in part, because they're perceived as diseases of the elderly. But that's an over-simplification, because about 175,000 Americans under age 65 die from cardiovascular diseases every year.

Cardiovascular diseases demand attention. Too many people are dying. And many deaths may be preventable—by lowering blood pressure, stopping smoking, reducing the amount of cholesterol in the blood, knowing the warning signs of heart disease. Education is vital.

Death rates from heart attack, stroke and other cardiovascular diseases *are* declining. Advances in medical treatment and healthier lifestyles in recent years have undoubtedly contributed. But there's still a long way to go and no time for complacency. Because someone dies—from cardiovascular disease—every 32 seconds.

Heart Attack—Signals and Action

Know the warning signals of a heart attack:
• Uncomfortable pressure, fullness, squeezing or pain in the center of the chest lasting two minutes or longer.
• Pain spreading to the shoulders, neck or arms.
• Severe pain, lightheadedness, fainting, sweating, nausea or shortness of breath.

Not all these warning signs occur in every heart attack. If some start to occur, however, don't wait. Get help immediately!

Know what to do in an emergency:
• Find out which area hospitals have 24-hour emergency cardiac care.
• Determine (in advance) the hospital or medical facility nearest your home and office, and tell your family and friends to call this facility in an emergency.
• Keep a list of emergency rescue service numbers next to the telephone and in your pocket, wallet or purse.
• If you have chest discomfort that lasts two minutes or longer, call the emergency rescue service.
• If you can get to a hospital faster by going yourself and not waiting for an ambulance, have someone drive you there.

Be a Heart Saver:
• If you're with someone experiencing the signs of a heart attack—and the warning signs last two minutes or longer—act immediately.
• Expect a "denial." It's normal for someone with chest discomfort to deny the possibility of something as serious as a heart attack. But don't take "no" for an answer. Insist on taking prompt action.
• Call the emergency service, or
• Take the person to the nearest hospital emergency room that offers 24-hour emergency cardiac care.
• Give CPR (mouth-to-mouth breathing and chest compression) if it's necessary and you're properly trained. ☐

Estimated Percent of Population with Hypertension by Race and Sex, U.S. Adults Age 18–74

Hypertensives are defined as persons with a systolic level ≥ 140 and/or a diastolic level ≥ 90 or who report using antihypertensive medication.

Source: National Health and Nutrition Examination Survey II, 1976–80.

Cancer Risks You Can Avoid

Source: National Cancer Institute, National Institutes of Health.

What is Cancer?

Cancer is really a group of diseases. There are more than 100 different types of cancer, but they all are a disease of some of the body's cells.

Healthy cells that make up the body's tissues grow, divide, and replace themselves in an orderly way. This process keeps the body in good repair. Sometimes, however, normal cells lose their ability to limit and direct their growth. They divide too rapidly and grow without any order. Too much tissue is produced and *tumors* begin to form. Tumors can be either *benign* or *malignant*.

Benign tumors are not cancer. They do not spread to other parts of the body and they are seldom a threat to life. Often, benign tumors can be removed by surgery, and they are not likely to return.

Malignant tumors are cancer. They can invade and destroy nearby tissue and organs. Cancer cells also can spread, or *metastasize*, to other parts of the body, and form new tumors.

Because cancer can spread, it is important for the doctor to find out as early as possible if a tumor is present and if it is cancer. As soon as a diagnosis is made, treatment can begin.

Signs and Symptoms of Cancer

Cancer and other illnesses often cause a number of problems you can watch for. The most common warning signs of cancer are:

Change in bowel or bladder habits;

A sore that does not heal;

Unusual bleeding or discharge;

Thickening or lump in the breast or elsewhere;

Indigestion or difficulty swallowing;

Obvious change in a wart or mole;

Nagging cough or hoarseness.

These signs and symptoms can be caused by cancer or by a number of other problems. They are *not* a sure sign of cancer. However, it is important to see a doctor if any problem lasts as long as 2 weeks. Don't wait for symptoms to become painful; pain is not an early sign of cancer.

Preventing Cancer

By choosing a lifestyle that avoids certain risks, you can help protect yourself from developing cancer. Many cancers are linked to factors that you can control.

Tobacco—Smoking and using tobacco in any form has been directly linked to cancer. Overall, smoking causes 30 percent of all cancer deaths. The risk of developing lung cancer is 10 times greater for smokers than for nonsmokers. The amount of risk from smoking depends on the number and type of cigarettes you smoke, how long you have been smoking, and how deeply you inhale. Smokers are also more likely to develop cancers of the mouth, throat, esophagus, pancreas, and bladder. And now there is emerging evidence that smoking can also cause cancer of the stomach and cervix.

The use of "smokeless" tobacco (chewing tobacco and oral snuff) increases the risk of cancer of the mouth and pharynx. Once you quit smoking or using smokeless tobacco, your risk of developing cancer begins to decrease right away.

Diet—What you eat may affect your chances of developing cancer. Scientists think there is a link between a high-fat diet and some cancers, particularly those of the breast, colon, endometrium, and prostate. Obesity is thought to be linked with increased death rates for cancers of the prostate, pancreas, breast, and ovary. Still other studies point to an increased risk of getting stomach cancer for those who frequently eat pickled, cured, and smoked foods. The National Cancer Institute believes that eating a well-balanced diet can reduce the risk of getting cancer. Americans should eat more high-fiber foods (such as whole-grain cereals and fruits and vegetables) and less fatty foods.

Sunlight—Repeated exposure to sunlight increases the risk of skin cancer, especially if you have fair skin or freckle easily. In fact, ultraviolet radiation from the sun is the main cause of skin cancer, which is the most common cancer in the United States. Ultraviolet rays are strongest from 11 a.m. to 2 p.m. during the summer, so that is when risk is greatest. Protective clothing, such as a hat and long sleeves, can help block out the sun's harmful rays. You can also use sunscreens to help protect yourself. Sunscreens with a number 15 on the label means most of the sun's harmful rays will be blocked out.

Alcohol—Drinking large amounts of alcohol (one or two drinks a day is considered moderate) is associated with cancers of the mouth, throat, esophagus, and liver. People who smoke cigarettes and drink alcohol have an especially high risk of getting cancers of the mouth and esophagus.

X-rays—Large doses of radiation increase cancer risk. Although individual x-rays expose you to very little radiation, repeated exposure can be harmful. Therefore, it is a good idea to avoid unnecessary x-rays. It's best to talk about the need for each x-ray with your doctor or dentist. If you do need an x-ray, ask if shields can be used to protect other parts of your body.

Industrial Agents and Chemicals—Being exposed to some industrial agents or chemicals increases cancer risk. Industrial agents cause damage by acting alone or together with another cancer-causing agent found in the workplace or with cigarette smoke. For example, inhaling asbestos fibers increases the risk of lung disease and cancer. This risk is especially high for workers who smoke. You should follow work and safety rules to avoid coming in contact with such dangerous materials.

Being exposed to large amounts of household solvent cleaners, cleaning fluids, and paint thinners should be avoided. Some chemicals are especially dangerous if inhaled in high concentrations, particularly in areas that are not well ventilated. In addition, inhaling or swallowing lawn and garden chemicals increases cancer risk. Follow label instructions carefully when using pesticides, fungicides, and other chemicals. Such chemicals should not come in contact with toys or other household items.

Hormones—Taking estrogen to relieve menopausal symptoms (such as hot flashes) has been associated with higher-than-average rates of cancer of the uterus. Numerous studies also have examined the relationship between oral contraceptives (the pill) and a variety of female cancers. Recent studies report that taking the pill does not increase a woman's chance of getting breast cancer. Also, pill users appear to have a lower-than-average risk of cancers of the endometrium and ovary. However, some researchers believe that there may be a higher risk of cancer of the cervix among pill users. Women taking hormones (either estrogens or oral contraceptives) should discuss the benefits and risks with their doctor.

Unavoidable Risks

Certain risk factors for cancer cannot be controlled, but people at high risk can help protect themselves by getting regular checkups. Some groups that have a higher-than-average risk of developing cancer are described below.

(1) Individuals who have close relatives with melanoma or cancer of the breast or colon. A small number of these cancers tend to occur more often in some families. If a close relative has been affected by one of these cancers, you should tell your doctor and be sure to have regular checkups to detect early problems.

(2) Persons who have had x-ray treatment to the head or neck when they were children or young adults. Exposure to these x-ray treatments may result in thyroid tumors, which have been associated with radiation given for an enlarged thymus gland, enlarged tonsils and adenoids, whooping cough, ringworm of the scalp, acne, and other head and neck conditions. Most thyroid tumors are not cancer. If thyroid cancer does develop, it usually can be cured. If you have had such x-rays, you should have a doctor examine your throat and neck every 1 or 2 years.

(3) Daughters and sons whose mothers took a drug called diethylstilbestrol (DES) to prevent miscarriages while they were pregnant with them. DES and some similar drugs given to mothers during pregnancy have been linked to certain unusual tissue formations in the vagina and cervix of their daughters. DES also has caused a rare type of vaginal and cervical cancer in a small number of exposed daughters. Women who took DES and DES-type drugs during pregnancy may themselves have a moderately increased risk of developing breast cancer. DES-exposed daughters and mothers should have examinations at least once a year that include pelvic and breast exams and Pap tests.

No link with cancer due to DES exposure before birth has been found in boys and men. However, there may be an increase in certain reproductive and urinary system problems in DES-exposed sons, who should also be examined regularly by a doctor. □

Dietary Guidelines for Americans

Source: U.S. Dept. of Agriculture, U.S. Dept. of Health and Human Services

What should Americans eat to stay healthy?

These guidelines help answer this question. They are advice for healthy Americans ages 2 years and over—not for younger children and infants, whose dietary needs differ. The guidelines reflect recommendations of nutrition authorities who agree that enough is known about diet's effect on health to encourage certain dietary practices by Americans.

Eat a Variety of Foods

You need more than 40 different nutrients for good health. Essential nutrients include vitamins, minerals, amino acids from protein, certain fatty acids from fat, and sources of calories (protein, carbohydrates, and fat).

These nutrients should come from a variety of foods, not from a few highly fortified foods or supplements. Any food that supplies calories and nutrients can be part of a nutritious diet. The content of the total diet over a day or more is what counts.

No single food can supply all nutrients in the amounts you need. For example, milk supplies calcium but little iron; meat supplies iron but little calcium. To have a nutritious diet, you must eat a variety of foods.

One way to assure variety—and with it, an enjoyable and nutritious diet—is to choose foods each day from the five major food groups.

A Daily Food Guide

Eat a variety of foods daily, choosing different foods from each group. Most people should have at least the lower number of servings suggested from each food group. Some people may need more because of their body size and activity level. Young children should have a variety of foods but may need small servings.

Food Group	Suggested Servings
Vegetables	3–5 servings
Fruits	2–4 servings
Breads, cereals, rice, and pasta	6–11 servings
Milk, yogurt, and cheese	2–3 servings
Meats, poultry, fish, dry beans and peas, eggs, and nuts	2–3 servings

Source: USDA's Food Guide.

People who are inactive or are trying to lose weight may eat little food. They need to take special care to choose lower calorie, nutrient-rich foods from the five major food groups. They also need to eat less of foods high in calories and low in essential nutrients, such as fats and oils, sugars, and alcoholic beverages.

Diets of some groups of people are notably low in some nutrients. Many women and adolescent girls need to eat more calcium-rich foods, such as milk and milk products, to get the calcium they need for healthy bones throughout life. Young children, teen-age girls and women of childbearing age must take care to eat enough iron-rich foods such as lean meats; dry beans; and whole-grain and iron-enriched breads, cereals, and other grain products.

Supplements of some nutrients taken regularly in large amounts can be harmful. Vitamin and mineral supplements at or below the Recommended Dietary Allowances (RDA) are safe, but are rarely needed if you eat a variety of foods. Here are exceptions in which your doctor may recommend a supplement:

• Pregnant women often need an iron supplement. Some older women in their childbearing years may also need an iron supplement to help replace iron lost in menstrual bleeding.

• Certain women who are pregnant or breastfeeding may need a supplement to meet their increased requirements for some nutrients.

• People who are unable to be active and eat little food may need supplements.

Maintain Healthy Weight

If you are too fat or too thin, your chances of developing health problems are increased.

Being too fat is common in the United States. It is linked with high blood pressure, heart disease, stroke, the most common type of diabetes, certain cancers, and other types of illness.

Being too thin is a less common problem. It occurs with anorexia nervosa and is linked with osteoporosis in women and greater risk of illness.

Whether your weight is "healthy" depends on how much of your weight is fat, where in your body the fat is located, and whether you have weight-related medical problems, such as high blood pressure, or a family history of such problems.

What is healthy weight for you? There is no exact answer right now. Researchers are trying to develop more precise ways to describe the guidelines suggested below to help judge if your weight is healthy.

See if your weight is within the range suggested in the table for persons of your age and height. The table shows higher weights for people 35 years and above than for younger adults. This is because recent research suggests that people can be a little heavier as they grow older without added risk to health. Just how much heavier is not yet clear. The weight ranges given in the table are likely to change based on research under way.

Ranges of weights are given in the table because people of the same height may have equal amounts of body fat but differ in muscle and bone. The higher weights in the ranges are suggested for people with more muscle and bone.

Weights above the range are believed to be unhealthy for most people. Weights slightly below the range may be healthy for some small-boned people but are sometimes linked to health problems, especially if sudden weight loss has occurred.

Research also suggests that, for adults, body shape as well as weight is important to health. Excess fat in the abdomen is believed to be of greater health risk than that in the hips and thighs. There are several ways to check body shape. Some require the help of a doctor; others you can do yourself.

A look at your profile in the mirror may be enough to make it clear that you have too much fat in the abdomen. Or you can check your body shape this way:

• Measure around your waist near your navel while you stand relaxed, not pulling in your stomach.

• Measure around your hips, over the buttocks, where they are largest.

• Divide the waist measure by the hips measure to get your waist-to-hip ratio. Research in adults suggests that ratios close to or above one are linked with greater risk for several diseases. However, ratios have not been defined for all populations or age groups.

If your weight is within the range in the table, if your waist-to-hip ratio does to place you at risk, and if you have no medical problem for which your doctor advises you to gain or lose weight, there appears to be no health advantage to changing your weight. If you do not meet all of these conditions, or if you are not sure, you may want to talk to your doctor about how your weight might affect your health and what you should do about it.

Heredity plays a role in body size and shape as do exercise and what you eat. Some people seem to be able to eat more than others and still maintain a good body size and shape.

No one plan for losing weight is best for everyone. If you are not physically active, regular exercise may help you lose weight and keep it off. If you eat too

Suggested Weights for Adults

Height[1]	Weight in pounds[2]	
	19 to 34 years	35 years and over
5'0"	[3]97—128	108—138
5'1"	101—132	111—143
5'2"	104—137	115—148
5'3"	107—141	119—152
5'4"	111—146	122—157
5'5"	114—150	126—162
5'6"	118—155	130—167
5'7"	121—160	134—172
5'8"	125—164	138—178
5'9"	129—169	142—183
5'10"	132—174	146—188
5'11	136—179	151—194
6'0"	140—184	155—199
6'1"	144—189	159—205
6'2"	148—195	164—210
6'3"	152—200	168—216
6'4"	156—205	173—222
6'5"	160—211	177—228
6'6"	164—216	182—234

1. Without shoes. 2. Without clothes. 3. The higher weights in the ranges generally apply to men, who tend to have more muscle and bone; the lower weights more often apply to women, who have less muscle and bone. Source: Derived from National Research Council, 1989.

much, decreasing your calorie intake as advised in the table may help. However, getting enough of some nutrients is difficult in diets of 1,200 calories or less. Long-term success usually depends upon new and better lifelong habits of both exercise and eating.

Do not try to lose weight too fast. A steady loss of 1/2 to 1 pound a week until you reach your goal is generally safe. Avoid crash weight-loss diets that severely restrict the variety of foods or the calories you can have.

Avoid other extreme approaches to losing weight. These include inducing vomiting and using medications such as laxatives, amphetamines, and diuretics. Such approaches are not appropriate for losing weight and can be dangerous.

You probably do not need to try to lose weight if your weight is already below the suggested range in the table and if you are otherwise healthy. If you lose weight suddenly or for unknown reasons, see a doctor. Unexplained weight loss may be an early clue to a health problem.

Children need calories to grow and develop normally; weight-reducing diets are usually not recommended for them. Overweight children may need special help in choosing physical activities they enjoy and nutritious diets with adequate but not excessive calories.

To Decrease Calorie Intake

Eat a variety of foods that is low in calories and high in nutrients:

• Eat less fat and fatty foods.
• Eat more fruits, vegetables, and bread and cereals—without fats and sugars added in preparation and at the table.
• Eat less sugar and sweets.
• Drink little or no alcoholic beverages.
• Eat smaller portions; limit second helpings.

To Increase Calorie Expenditure

Activity	Calories expended per hour[1]	
	Man[2]	Woman[3]
Sitting quietly	100	80
Standing quietly	120	95
Light activity:	300	240
Cleaning house		
Office work		
Playing baseball		
Playing golf		
Moderate activity:	460	370
Walking briskly (3.5 mph)		
Gardening		
Cycling (5.5 mph)		
Dancing		
Playing basketball		
Strenuous activity:	730	580
Jogging (9 min./mile)		
Playing football		
Swimming		
Very strenuous activity:	920	740
Running (7 min./mile)		
Racquetball		
Skiing		

1. May vary depending on environmental conditions. 2. Healthy man, 175 lbs. 3. Healthy woman, 140 lbs. *Source:* Derived from McArdle, et al., Exercise Physiology, 1986.

Choose a Diet Low in Fat, Saturated Fat, and Cholesterol

Most health authorities recommend an American diet with less fat, saturated fat, and cholesterol. The higher levels of saturated fat and cholesterol in our diets are linked to our increased risk for heart disease.

A diet low in fat makes it easier for you to include the variety of foods you need for nutrients without exceeding your calorie needs because fat contains over twice the calories of an equal amount of carbohydrates or protein.

A diet low in saturated fat and cholesterol can help maintain a desirable level of blood cholesterol. For adults this level is below 200 mg/dl. As blood cholesterol increases above this level, greater risk for heart disease occurs. Risk can also be increased by high blood pressure, cigarette smoking, diabetes, a family history of premature heart disease, obesity, and being a male.

The way diet affects blood cholesterol varies among individuals. However, blood cholesterol does increase in most people when they eat a diet high in saturated fat and cholesterol and excessive in calories. Of these, dietary saturated fat has the greatest effect; dietary cholesterol has less.

Suggested goals for fats in American diets are as follows:

Total fat. An amount that provides 30% or less of calories is suggested. Thus, the upper limit on the grams of fat in your diet depends on the calories you need. For example, at 2,000 calories per day, your suggested upper limit is 600 calories from fat (2,000 × .30). This is equal to 67 grams of fat (600 ÷ 9, the number of calories each gram of fat provides).

Saturated fat. An amount that provides less than 10% of calories (less than 22 grams at 2,000 calories per day) is suggested. All fats contain both saturated and unsaturated fat (fatty acids). The fats in animal products are the main sources of saturated fat in most diets, with tropical oils (coconut, palm kernel, and

palm oils) and hydrogenated fats providing smaller amounts.

Cholesterol. Animal products are the source of all dietary cholesterol. Eating less fat from animal sources will help lower cholesterol as well as total fat and saturated fat in your diet.

These goals for fats are not for children under 2 years, who have special dietary needs. As children begin to eat with the family, usually at about 2 years of age or older, they should be encouraged to choose diets that are lower in fat and saturated fat and that provide the calories and nutrients they need for normal growth. Older children and adults with established food habits may need to change their diets gradually toward the goals.

These goals for fats apply to the diet over several days, not to a single meal or food. Some foods that contain fat, saturated fat, and cholesterol, such as meats, milk, cheese, and eggs, also contain high-quality protein and are our best sources of certain vitamins and minerals. Lowfat choices of these foods are lean meat and lowfat milk, and cheeses.

For a Diet Low in Fat, Saturated Fat, and Cholesterol

Fats and Oils

- Use fats and oils sparingly in cooking.
- Use small amounts of salad dressings and spreads, such as butter, margarine, and mayonnaise. One tablespoon of most of these spreads provides 10 to 11 grams of fat.
- Choose liquid vegetable oils most often because they are lower in saturated fat.
- Check labels on foods to see how much fat and saturated fat are in a serving.

Meat, Poultry, Fish, Dry Beans, And Eggs

- Have two or three servings, with a daily total of about 6 ounces. Three ounces of cooked lean beef or chicken without skin—the size of a deck of cards—provides about 6 grams of fat.
- Trim fat from meat; take skin off poultry.
- Have cooked dry beans and peas instead of meat occasionally.
- Moderate the use of egg yolks and organ meats.

Milk And Milk Products

- Have two or three servings daily. (Count as a serving: 1 cup of milk or yogurt or about 1 1/2 ounces of cheese.)
- Choose skim or lowfat milk and fat-free or lowfat yogurt and cheese most of the time. One cup of skim milk has only a trace of fat, 1 cup of 2-percent-fat milk has 5 grams of fat, and 1 cup of whole milk has 8 grams of fat.

Choose a Diet with Plenty of Vegetables, Fruits, and Grain Products

This guideline recommends that adults eat at least three servings of vegetables and two servings of fruit daily. It recommends at least six servings of grain products, such as breads, cereals, pasta, and rice, with an emphasis on whole grains. Children should also be encouraged to eat plenty of these foods.

Vegetables, fruits, and grain products are emphasized in this guideline especially for their complex carbohydrates, dietary fiber, and other food components linked to good health.

These foods are generally low in fats. By choosing the suggested amounts of them, you are likely to in crease carbohydrates and decrease fats in your diet, as health authorities suggest. You will also get more dietary fiber.

Complex carbohydrates, such as starches, are in breads, cereals, pasta, rice, dry beans and peas, and other vegetables, such as potatoes and corn. Dietary fiber—a part of plant foods—is in whole-grain breads and cereals, dry beans and peas, vegetables, and fruits. It is best to eat a variety of these fiber-rich foods because they differ in the kinds of fiber they contain.

Eating foods with fiber is important for proper bowel function and can reduce symptoms of chronic constipation, diverticular disease, and hemorrhoids. Populations like ours with diets low in dietary fiber and complex carbohydrates and high in fat, especially saturated fat, tend to have more heart disease, obesity, and some cancers. Just how dietary fiber is involved is not yet clear.

Some of the benefit from a higher fiber diet may be from the food that provides the fiber, not from fiber alone. For this reason, it's best to get fiber from foods rather than from supplements. In addition, excessive use of fiber supplements is associated with greater risk for intestinal problems and lower absorption of some minerals.

Use Sugars Only in Moderation

Americans eat sugars in many forms. Sugars provide calories and most people like their taste. Some serve as natural preservatives, thickeners, and baking aids in foods. This guideline cautions about eating sugars in large amounts and about frequent snacks of foods containing sugars and starches.

Sugars and many foods that contain them in large amounts supply calories but are limited in nutrients. Thus, they should be used in moderation by most healthy people and sparingly by people with low calorie needs. For very active people with high calorie needs, sugars can be an additional source of calories.

Both sugars and starches—which break down into sugars—can contribute to tooth decay. Sugars and starches are in many foods that also supply nutrients—milk; fruits; some vegetables; and breads, cereals and other foods with sugars and starches as ingredients. The more often these foods—even small amounts—are eaten and the longer they are in the mouth before teeth are brushed, the greater the risk for tooth decay. Thus, eating such foods as frequent between-meal snacks may be more harmful to teeth than having them at meals.

Regular daily brushing with a fluoride toothpaste helps reduce tooth decay by getting fluoride to the teeth. Fluoridated water or other sources of fluoride that a doctor or dentist suggest are especially important for children whose unerupted teeth are forming and growing.

Diets high in sugars have not been shown to cause diabetes. The most common type of diabetes occurs in overweight adults, and avoiding sugars alone will not correct overweight.

Note: Read food labels. A food is likely to be high in sugars if its ingredient list shows one of the above first or second or if it shows several of them.

Use Salt and Sodium Only in Moderation

Table salt contains sodium and chloride—both are essential in the diet. However, most Americans eat more salt and sodium than they need. Food and beverages containing salt provide most of the sodium in our diets, much of it added during processing and manufacturing.

In populations with diets low in salt, high blood pressure is less common than in populations with diets high in salt. Other factors that affect blood pressure are heredity, obesity, and excessive drinking of alcoholic beverages.

In the United States, about one in three adults has high blood pressure. If these people restrict their salt and sodium, usually their blood pressure will fall.

Some people who do not have high blood pressure may reduce their risk of getting it by eating a diet with less salt and other sources of sodium. At present there is no way to predict who might develop high blood pressure and who will benefit from reducing dietary salt and sodium. However, it is wise for most people to eat less salt and sodium because they need much less than they eat and reduction will benefit those people whose blood pressure rises with salt intake.

To Moderate Use of Salt and Sodium

- Use salt sparingly, if at all, in cooking and at the table.
- When planning meals, consider that—
  - fresh and plain frozen vegetables prepared without salt are lower in sodium than canned ones.
  - cereals, pasta, and rice cooked without salt are lower in sodium than ready-to-eat cereals.
  - milk and yogurt are lower in sodium than most cheeses.
  - fresh meat, poultry, and fish are lower in sodium than most canned and processed ones.
  - most frozen dinners and combination dishes, packaged mixes, canned soups, and salad dressings contain a considerable amount of sodium. So do condiments, such as soy and other sauces, pickles, olives, catsup, and mustard.
- Use salted snacks, such as chips, crackers, pretzels, and nuts, sparingly.
- Check labels for the amount of sodium in foods. Choose those lower in sodium most of the time.

Drink Alcohol in Moderation

Alcoholic beverages supply calories but little or no nutrients. Drinking them has no net health benefit, is linked with many health problems, is the cause of many accidents, and can lead to addiction. Their consumption is not recommended. If adults elect to drink alcoholic beverages, they should consume them in moderate amounts.

Some people who should *not* drink alcoholic beverages:

- Women who are pregnant or trying to conceive. Major birth defects have been attributed to heavy drinking by the mother while pregnant. Women who are pregnant or trying to conceive should not drink alcoholic beverages. However, there is no conclusive evidence that an occasional drink is harmful.
- Individuals who plan to drive or engage in other activities that require attention or skill. Most people retain some alcohol in the blood 3 to 5 hours after even moderate drinking.
- Individuals using medicines, even over-the-counter kinds. Alcohol may affect the benefits or toxicity of medicines. Also, some medicines may increase blood alcohol levels or increase alcohol's adverse effect on the brain.
- Individuals who cannot keep their drinking moderate. This is a special concern for recovering alcoholics and people whose family members have alcohol problems.
- Children and adolescents. Use of alcoholic beverages by children and adolescents involves risks to health and other serious problems.

Alzheimer's Disease

Source: American Council on Science and Health.

Alzheimer's disease (AD) is named after Alois Alzheimer, a German physician, who first described the disease in one of his patients in 1906. This patient, a 51-year-old woman, suffered from memory loss, disorientation, depression, and hallucinations. She eventually suffered complete dementia and died five years later. Upon autopsy, her brain revealed extensive lesions of a type now considered characteristic of Alzheimer's disease.

Alzheimer's disease is tragic, not only because it causes untimely death, but because it involves mental deterioration and increases dependency on others. Victims are dependent on other people between 5 and 20 years before death occurs. Caring for an AD victim causes considerable emotional and economic hardship for the care givers, who are usually relatives. Many AD victims become so difficult to care for that they are eventually sent to nursing homes.

Familial Alzheimer's disease is less common than sporadic Alzheimer's disease. It can occur at an early age, as well as at later ages. *Sporadic* Alzheimer's disease, or dementia of the Alzheimer type, is much more common and occurs primarily over age 60, with the majority being age 85 and over. In one recent epidemiological community study, almost 50% of all persons over 75 had been diagnosed with probable Alzheimer's disease. This observation needs to be confirmed by other studies, because former estimates were significantly lower. Nevertheless AD increases exponentially with age. It is not clear whether familial or sporadic AD are one and the same disease or whether they represent two different diseases.

The causes of AD are not known, although many pathogenic mechanisms have been suggested. Inheritance seems to play a role in familial Alzheimer's disease. Defective genes or defective gene products may also play a role in sporadic AD. Environmental factors and aging processes, however, seem to determine whether such a genetic predisposition is expressed. Possible environmental and internal causes and/or contributions to AD are hypothetical. However, scientific knowledge about the events that occur during the course of AD is increasing dramatically.

Treatment of AD focuses mainly on alleviation of the symptoms, such as memory loss and disorientation. Treatment is only moderately successful, and not consistent. No currently known drug can stop the progression of Alzheimer's disease. □

Lyme Disease

Source: American Council on Science and Health.

Lyme disease, an infection caused by the bit of an infected deer tick, is on the rise in the United States and worldwide. Lyme disease is a bacterial infection commonly acquired in wooded and coastal areas of the northeastern, midwestern, southern, and western United States. Scientists distinguished Lyme disease as an entity in 1975, following the discovery of a geographic cluster of children and adults with arthritis in the Lyme, Connecticut area. Later, scientists linked the arthritis to a characteristic skin rash that frequently occurred at the site of the victim's tick bite.

An early indication of Lyme disease is a characteristic rash that appears within 30 days of the tick bite. It typically appears as a bright red ring encircling the bite, often with a clear area at the center in a "bull's eye" pattern. It may also appear as a bright red blotch or patch. The rash can expand gradually up to several inches in diameter and is generally not itchy. Later, in some patients secondary skin lesions may occur away from the original bite. The rash will typically disappear within three weeks even without treatment. From 60 to 80% of people with the rash also experience flu-like symptoms including fatigue, headache, stiff neck, muscle aches and pains, and general malaise. About 20 to 40% of Lyme disease patients never exhibit the typical rash, making accurate diagnosis more difficult and preventive measures more important.

The disease may follow a protracted course and include such complications as facial paralysis, cardiac rhythm disorders and, especially, arthritis. Early treatment with antibiotics usually shortens the course of the disease and reduces the frequency of complications.

Although avoiding endemic areas is the surest way to avoid Lyme disease, following certain precautions will increase individual protection. Preventive measures include frequent skin inspection and immediate removal of any ticks, either by brushing off those unattached or using tweezers to remove those already affixed. Pets should also be checked for ticks. In addition, people entering tick-infested areas should wear clothing that is tight around the ankles and wrists, and use insect repellents.

DO NOT use flame, Vaseline, or nailpolish remover to try to kill the tick before removing it. These methods will either make it more difficult to remove the tick or cause unnecessary delays in removal. □

Tuberculosis Cases Rising

Nearly 24,000 cases of tuberculosis were reported to the U.S. Centers for Disease Control in Atlanta, Georgia, in 1989. What concerns public health authorities is that after decades of declining figures—22,201 cases in 1985, the lowest total in 60 years—the number of cases is beginning to creep up again.

Society's problems—AIDS, homelessness, alcohol and drug abuse, and other factors are reversing the downward trend.

It is estimated that 10 to 15 million Americans are among the 1.7 billion people worldwide who are TB carriers but are not infectious to others. About 90% of TB cases in this country occur when a dormant infection awakens and develops into active TB; only 10% result from a newly acquired infection. Of all infected people, 5% will develop the disease within a year, while another 5% will develop TB later on. Experts are not sure why it happens this way.

TB is usually caused by repeated exposure—usually at home or work—to droplets contaminated with tubercle bacilli that are expelled into the air when a person with active pulmonary TB coughs, sneezes, or even sings, speaks, or laughs. □

HEADLINE HISTORY

In any broad overview of history, arbitrary compartmentalization of facts is self-defeating (and makes locating interrelated people, places, and things that much harder). Therefore, Headline History is designed as a "timeline"—a chronology that highlights both the march of time and interesting, sometimes surprising, juxtapositions.

Also see related sections of *Information Please,* particularly Inventions and Discoveries, Countries of the World, etc.

B.C.

Before Christ or Before Common Era (B.C.E.)

5 billion B.C.   Planet Earth formed.
3 billion B.C.   First signs of primeval life (bacteria and blue-green algae) appear in oceans.
600 million B.C.   Earliest date to which fossils can be traced.
1.7 million B.C.   First discernible hominids (*Australopithecus* and *Homo habilis*). Early hunters and food-gatherers.
500,000 B.C.   *Homo erectus* (crude chopping tools).
70,000 B.C.   Neanderthal man (use of fire and advanced tools).
35,000 B.C.   Neanderthal man being replaced by later groups of *Homo sapiens* (i.e. Cro-Magnon man, etc.).
18,000 B.C.   Cro-Magnons being replaced by later cultures.
15,000 B.C.   Migrations across Bering Straits into the Americas.
10,000 B.C.   Semi-permanent agricultural settlements in Old World.
10,000–4,000 B.C.   Development of settlements into cities and development of skills such as the wheel, pottery and improved methods of cultivation in Mesopatamia and elsewhere.

NOTE: For further information on the geographic development in Earth's prehistory, see the Science section.

4500–3000 B.C.   Sumerians in the Tigris and Euphrates valleys develop a city-state civilization; first phonetic writing (c.3500 B.C.). Egyptian agriculture develops. Western Europe is neolithic, without metals or written records. Earliest recorded date in Egyptian calendar (4241 B.C.). First year of Jewish calendar (3760 B.C.). Copper used by Egyptians and Sumerians.
3000–2000 B.C.   Pharaonic rule begins in Egypt. Cheops, 4th dynasty (2700–2675 B.C.). The Great Sphinx of Giza. Earliest Egyptian mummies. Papyrus. Phoenician settlements on coast of what is now Syria and Lebanon. Semitic tribes settle in Assyria. Sargon, first Akkadian king, builds Mesopotamian empire. The Gilgamesh epic (c.3000 B.C.). Abraham leaves Ur (c.2000 B.C.). Systematic astronomy in Egypt, Babylon, India, China.
2000–1500 B.C.   Hyksos invaders drive Egyptians from Lower Egypt (17th century B.C.). Amosis I frees Egypt from Hyksos (c.1600 B.C.). Assyrians rise to power—cities of Ashur and Nineveh. Twenty-four-character alphabet in Egypt. Israelites enslaved in Egypt. Cuneiform inscriptions used by Hittites. Peak of Minoan culture on Isle of Crete—earliest form of written Greek. Hammurabi, king of Babylon, develops oldest existing code of laws (18th century B.C.). In Britain, Stonehenge erected on some unknown astronomical rationale.
1500–1000 B.C.   Ikhnaton develops monotheistic religion in Egypt (c.1375 B.C.). His successor, Tutankhamen, returns to earlier gods. Moses leads Israelites out of Egypt into Canaan—Ten Commandments. Greeks destroy Troy (c.1193 B.C.). End of Greek civilization in Mycenae with invasion of Dorians. Chinese civilization develops under Shang dynasty. Olmec civilization in Mexico—stone monuments; picture writing.
1000–900 B.C.   Solomon succeeds King David, builds Jerusalem temple. After Solomon's death, kingdom divided into Israel and Judah. Hebrew elders begin to write Old Testament books of Bible. Phoenicians colonize Spain with settlement at Cadiz.
900–800 B.C.   Phoenicians establish Carthage (c.810 B.C.). The *Iliad* and the *Odyssey,* perhaps composed by Greek poet Homer.
800–700 B.C.   Prophets Amos, Hosea, Isaiah. First recorded Olympic games (776 B.C.). Legendary founding of Rome by Romulus (753 B.C.). Assyrian king

Brontosaur

Moses

Egyptian chariots (1500 B.C.)

ANCIENT EMPIRES

	The Egyptian Empire (1400 BC)
	Alexander's Empire (323 BC)
	The Roman Empire (120 AD)
— · · —	Path of the Crusaders (1000-1200 AD)

Some Ancient Civilizations

Name	Approximate dates	Location	Major cities
Akkadian	2350–2230 B.C.	Mesopotamia, parts of Syria, Asia Minor, Iran	Akkad, Ur, Erich
Assyrian	1800–889 B.C.	Mesopotamia, Syria	Assur, Nineveh, Calah
Babylonian	1728–1686 B.C. (old) 625–539 B.C. (new)	Mesopotamia, Syria, Palestine	Babylon
Cimmerian	750–500 B.C.	Caucasus, northern Asia Minor	—
Egyptian	2850–715 B.C.	Nile valley	Thebes, Memphis, Tanis
Etruscan	900–396 B.C.	Northern Italy	—
Greek	900–200 B.C.	Greece	Athens, Sparta, Thebes, Mycenae, Corinth
Hittite	1640–1200 B.C.	Asia Minor, Syria	Hattusas, Nesa
Lydian	700–547 B.C.	Western Asia Minor	Sardis, Miletus
Mede	835–550 B.C.	Iran	Media
Minoan	3000–1100 B.C.	Crete	Knossos
Persian	559–330 B.C.	Iran, Asia Minor, Syria	Persepolis, Pasargadae
Phoenician	1100–332 B.C.	Palestine (colonies: Gibraltar, Carthage Sardinia)	Tyre, Sidon, Byblos
Phrygian	1000–547 B.C.	Central Asia Minor	Gordion
Roman	500 B.C.–A.D. 300	Italy, Mediterranean region, Asia Minor, western Europe	Rome, Byzantium
Scythian	800–300 B.C.	Caucasus	—
Sumerian	3200–2360 B.C.	Mesopotamia	Ur, Nippur

Sargon II conquers Hittites, Chaldeans, Samaria (end of Kingdom of Israel). Earliest written music. Chariots introduced into Italy by Etruscans.

700–600 B.C. End of Assyrian Empire (**616** B.C.)—Nineveh destroyed by Chaldeans (Neo-Babylonians) and Medes (**612** B.C.). Founding of Byzantium by Greeks (**c.660** B.C.). Building of the Acropolis in Athens. Solon, Greek lawgiver (**640–560** B.C.). Sappho of Lesbos, Greek poetess, Lao-Tse, Chinese philosopher and founder of Taoism (born **c.604** B.C.).

600–500 B.C. Babylonian king Nebuchadnezzar builds empire, destroys Jerusalem (**586** B.C.). Babylonian Captivity of the Jews (starting **587** B.C.). Hanging Gardens of Babylon. Cyrus the Great of Persia creates great empire, conquers Babylon (**539** B.C.), frees the Jews. Athenian democracy develops. Aeschylus, Greek dramatist (**525–465** B.C.). Confucius (**551–479** B.C.) develops philosophy-religion in China. Buddha (**563–483** B.C.) founds Buddhism in India.

500–400 B.C. Greeks defeat Persians: battles of Marathon (**490** B.C.), Thermopylae (**480** B.C.), Salamis (**480** B.C.). Peloponnesian Wars between Athens and Sparta (**431–404** B.C.)—Sparta victorious. Pericles comes to power in Athens (**462** B.C.). Flowering of Greek culture during the Age of Pericles (**450–400** B.C.). Sophocles, Greek dramatist (**496–c.406** B.C.). Hippocrates, Greek "Father of Medicine" (born **460** B.C.). Xerxes I, king of Persia (rules **485–465** B.C.).

400–300 B.C. Pentateuch—first five books of the Old Testament evolve in final form. Philip of Macedon assassinated (**336** B.C.) after conquering Greece; succeeded by son, Alexander the Great (**356–323** B.C.), who destroys Thebes (**335** B.C.), conquers Tyre and Jerusalem (**332** B.C.), occupies Babylon (**330** B.C.), invades India, and dies in Babylon. His empire is divided among his generals; one of them, Seleucis I, establishes Middle East empire with capitals at Antioch (Syria) and Seleucia (in Iraq). Trial and execution of Greek philosopher Socrates (**399** B.C.). Dialogues recorded by his student, Plato. Euclid's work on geometry (**323** B.C.). Aristotle, Greek philosopher (**384–322** B.C.). Demosthenes, Greek orator (**384–322** B.C.). Praxiteles, Greek sculptor (**400–330** B.C.).

300–251 B.C. First Punic War (**264–241** B.C.): Rome defeats the Carthaginians and begins its domination of the Mediterranean. Temple of the Sun at Teotihuacan, Mexico (**c.300** B.C.). Invention of Mayan calendar in Yucatán—more

Confucius (551-479 B.C.)

Plato (4277-347 B.C.)

**Archimedes
(287-212 B.C.)**

exact than older calendars. First Roman gladiatorial games (264 B.C.). Archimedes, Greek mathematician (287–212 B.C.).

250–201 B.C. Second Punic War (219–201 B.C.): Hannibal, Carthaginian general (246–142 B.C.), crosses the Alps (218 B.C.), reaches gates of Rome (211 B.C.), retreats, and is defeated by Scipio Africanus at Zama (202 B.C.). Great Wall of China built (c.215 B.C.).

200–151 B.C. Romans defeat Seleucid King Antiochus III at Thermopylae (191 B.C.)—beginning of Roman world domination. Maccabean revolt against Seleucids (167 B.C.).

150–101 B.C. Third Punic War (149–146 B.C.): Rome destroys Carthage, killing 450,000 and enslaving the remaining 50,000 inhabitants. Roman armies conquer Macedonia, Greece, Anatolia, Balearic Islands, and southern France. Venus de Milo (c.140 B.C.). Cicero, Roman orator (106–43 B.C.).

100–51 B.C. Julius Caesar (100–44 B.C.) invades Britain (55 B.C.) and conquers Gaul (France) (c.50 B.C.). Spartacus leads slave revolt against Rome (71 B.C.). Romans conquer Seleucid empire. Roman general Pompey conquers Jerusalem (63 B.C.). Cleopatra on Egyptian throne (51–31 B.C.). Chinese develop use of paper (c.100 B.C.). Virgil, Roman poet (70–19 B.C.). Horace, Roman poet (65–8 B.C.).

50–1 B.C. Caesar crosses Rubicon to fight Pompey (50 B.C.). Herod made Roman governor of Judea (47 B.C.). Caesar murdered (44 B.C.). Caesar's nephew, Octavian, defeats Mark Antony and Cleopatra at Battle of Actium (31 B.C.), and establishes Roman empire as Emperor Augustus—rules 27 B.C.—A.D. 14. Birth of Jesus Christ (variously given from 4 B.C. to A.D. 7). Ovid, Roman poet (43 B.C.—A.D. 18).

A.D.

The Christian or Common Era (C.E.)

**Jesus Christ
(4? B.C.-29? A.D.)**

1–49 After Augustus, Tiberius becomes emperor (dies, 37), succeeded by Caligula (assassinated, 41), who is followed by Claudius. Crucifixion of Jesus (probably 30). Han dynasty in China founded by Emperor Kuang Wu Ti. Buddhism introduced to China.

50–99 Claudius poisoned (54), succeeded by Nero (commits suicide, 68). Missionary journeys of Paul the Apostle (34–60). Jews revolt against Rome; Jerusalem destroyed (70). Roman persecutions of Christians begin (64). Colosseum built in Rome (71–80). Trajan (rules 98–116); Roman empire extends to Mesopotamia, Arabia, Balkans. First Gospels of St. Mark, St. John, St. Matthew.

100–149 Hadrian rules Rome (117–138); codifies Roman law, establishes postal system, builds wall between England and Scotland. Jews revolt under Bar Kokhba (122–135); final *Diaspora* (dispersion) of Jews begins.

150–199 Marcus Aurelius (rules Rome 161–180). Oldest Mayan temples in Central America (c.200)., Mayan civilization develops writing, astronomy, mathematics.

200–249 Goths invade Asia Minor (c.220). Roman persecutions of Christians increase. Persian (Sassanid) empire re-established. End of Chinese Han dynasty.

250–299 Increasing invasions of the Roman empire by Franks and Goths. Buddhism spreads in China.

300–349 Constantine the Great (rules 312–337) reunites eastern and western Roman empires, with new capital (Constantinople) on site of Byzantium (330); issues Edict of Milan legalizing Christianity (313); becomes a Christian on his deathbed (337). Council of Nicaea (325) defines orthodox Christian doctrine. First Gupta dynasty in India (c.320).

350–399 Huns (Mongols) invade Europe (c.360). Theodosius the Great (rules 392–395)—last emperor of a united Roman empire. Roman empire permanently divided in 395: western empire ruled from Rome; eastern empire ruled from Constantinople.

400–449 Western Roman empire disintegrates under weak emperors. Alaric, king of the Visigoths, sacks Rome (410). Attila, Hun chieftain, attacks Roman provinces (433). St. Patrick returns to Ireland (432). St. Augustine's *City of God* (411).

450–499 Vandals destroy Rome (455). Western Roman empire ends as Odoacer, German chieftain, overthrows last Roman emperor, Romulus Augustulus, and becomes king of Italy (476). Ostrogothic kingdom of Italy established by Theodoric the Great (493). Clovis, ruler of the Franks, is converted to Christianity (496). First schism between western and eastern churches (484). Peak of Mayan culture in Mexico (c.460).

500–549 Eastern and western churches reconciled (519). Justinian I, the Great

(483–565), becomes Byzantine emperor (527), issues his first code of civil laws (529), conquers North Africa, Italy, and part of Spain. Plague spreads through Europe (from 542). Arthur, semi-legendary king of the Britons (killed, c.537). Boëthius, Roman scholar (executed, 524).

550–599 Beginnings of European silk industry after Justinian's missionaries smuggle silkworms out of China (553). Mohammed, founder of Islam (570–632). Buddhism in Japan (c.560). St. Augustine of Canterbury brings Christianity to Britain (597). After killing about half the population, plague in Europe subsides (594).

600–649 Mohammed flees from Mecca to Medina (the *Hegira*); first year of the Muslim calendar (622). Muslim empire grows (634). Arabs conquer Jerusalem (637), destroy Alexandrian library (641), conquer Persians (641). Fatima, Mohammed's daughter (606–632).

650–699 Arabs attack North Africa (670), destroy Carthage (697). Venerable Bede, English monk (672–735).

700–749 Arab empire extends from Lisbon to China (by 716). Charles Martel, Frankish leader, defeats Arabs at Tours/Poitiers, halting Arab advance in Europe (732). Charlemagne (742–814).

750–799 Caliph Harun al-Rashid rules Arab empire (786–809): the "golden age" of Arab culture. Vikings begin attacks on Britain (790), land in Ireland (795). Charlemagne becomes king of the Franks (771). City of Machu Picchu flourishes in Peru.

800–849 Charlemagne (Charles the Great) crowned first Holy Roman Emperor in Rome (800). Arabs conquer Crete, Sicily, and Sardinia (826–827). Charlemagne dies (814), succeeded by his son, Louis the Pious, who divides France among his sons (817).

850–899 Norsemen attack as far south as the Mediterranean but are repulsed (859), discover Iceland (861). Alfred the Great becomes king of Britain (871), defeats Danish invaders (878). Russian nation founded by Vikings under Prince Rurik, establishing capital at Novgorod (855–879).

900–949 Vikings discover Greenland (c.900). Arab Spain under Abd ar-Rahman III becomes center of learning (912–961).

950–999 Eric the Red establishes first Viking colony in Greenland (982). Mieczyslaw I becomes first ruler of Poland (960). Hugh Capet elected King of France in 987; Capetian dynasty to rule until 1328. Musical notation systematized (c.990). Vikings and Danes attack Britain (988–999). Holy Roman Empire founded by Otto I, King of Germany since 936, crowned by Pope John XII in 962.

11th century A.D.

c.1000 Hungary and Scandinavia converted to Christianity. Viking raider Leif Ericson discovers North America, calls it *Vinland*. Chinese invent gunpowder. *Beowulf*, Old English epic.

1009 Moslems destroy Holy Sepulchre in Jerusalem.

1013 Danes control England. Canute takes throne (1016), conquers Norway (1028), dies (1035); kingdom divided among his sons: Harold Harefoot (England), Sweyn (Norway), Hardecanute (Denmark).

1040 Macbeth murders Duncan, king of Scotland.

1053 Robert Guiscard, Norman invader, establishes kingdom in Italy, conquers Sicily (1072).

1054 Final separation between Eastern (Orthodox) and Western (Roman) churches.

1055 Seljuk Turks, Asian nomads, move west, capture Baghdad, Armenia (1064), Syria, and Palestine (1075).

1066 William of Normandy invades England, defeats last Saxon king, Harold II, at Battle of Hastings, crowned William I of England ("the Conqueror").

1073 Emergence of strong papacy when Gregory VII is elected. Conflict with English and French kings and German emperors will continue throughout medieval period.

1095 (*See* special material on "The Crusades.")

**Viking Discovery
of Greenland (c.900)**

12th century A.D.

1150–67 Universities of Paris and Oxford founded in France and England.

1162 Thomas à Becket named Archbishop of Canterbury, murdered by Henry II's men (1170). Troubadours (wandering minstrels) glorify romantic concepts of feudalism.

1189 Richard I ("the Lionhearted") succeeds Henry II in England, killed in France (1199), succeeded by King John.

13th century A.D.

1211 Genghis Khan invades China, captures Peking (1214), conquers Persia (1218), invades Russia (1223), dies (1227).

The
MOSLEM WORLD
about 732

Territory overrun by Moslems

The Byzantine Empire

Scale of Miles

0   300   600   900

Indian Ocean

Atlantic Ocean

Aral Sea

Samarkand

Bokhara

PERSIA
644

Indus R.

Volga R.

KHAZARS

SLAVS

AVARS

MAGYARS

FRANKS

Caspian Sea

Black Sea

Dnieper R.

Baltic Sea

ARMENIA

Erzerum

Tabriz

MESOPOTAMIA
641

Bagdad

BABYLONIA
657

Persian Gulf

ARABIA
632

Medina

Mecca

Red Sea

Aden

ABYSSINIA

Nile R.

EGYPT
639-643

Cairo

Alexandria

Jerusalem

Damascus

SYRIA
638

Antioch

CYPRUS

CRETE

Constantinople

BULGARIANS

Danube R.

Adriatic Sea

LOMBARDS

Rome

Naples

SICILY

SARDINIA

Carthage
697-8

BARCA
643

TRIPOLI

MAURETANIA
700-705

Mediterranean Sea

Ceuta

Seville

Cordova

SPAIN
711-713

Toledo

Tagus R.

Almeria

Valencia

Barcelona

SEPTIMANIA

Tours

Oviedo

Ebro R.

1215 King John forced by barons to sign Magna Carta at Runneymede, limiting royal power.

1233 The Inquisition begins as Pope Gregory IX assigns Dominicans responsibility for combatting heresy. Torture used (**1252**). Ferdinand and Isabella establish Spanish Inquisition (**1478**). Tourquemada, Grand Inquisitor, forces conversion or expulsion of Spanish Jews (**1492**). Forced conversion of Moors (**1499**). Inquisition in Portugal (**1531**). First Protestants burned at the stake in Spain (**1543**). Spanish Inquisition abolished (**1834**).

1241 Mongols defeat Germans in Silesia, invade Poland and Hungary, withdraw from Europe after Ughetai, Mongol leader, dies.

1251 Kublai Khan governs China, becomes ruler of Mongols (1259), establishes Yuan dynasty in China (1280), invades Burma (1287), dies (1294).

1271 Marco Polo of Venice travels to China, in court of Kublai Khan (1275–1292), returns to Genoa (1295) and writes *Travels*.

1295 English King Edward I summons the Model Parliament.

14th century A.D.

1312–37 Mali Empire reaches its height in Africa under King Mansa Musa.

1337–1453 Hundred Years' War—English and French kings fight for control of France.

c.1325 The beginning of the Renaissance in Italy: writers Dante, Petrarch, Boccaccio; painter Giotto. Development of *No* drama in Japan. Aztecs establish capital on site of modern Mexico City. Peak of Moslem culture in Spain. Small cannon in use.

1347–1351 At least 25 million people die in Europe's "Black Death" (bubonic plague).

1368 Ming dynasty begins in China.

1376–82 John Wycliffe, pre-Reformation religious reformer and followers translate Latin Bible into English.

1378 The Great Schism (to 1417)—rival popes in Rome and Avignon, France, fight for control of Roman Catholic Church.

c.1387 Chaucer's *Canterbury Tales.*

15th century A.D.

1415 Henry V defeats French at Agincourt. Jan Hus, Bohemian preacher and follower of Wycliffe, burned at stake in Constance as heretic.

1418–60 Portugal's Prince Henry the Navigator sponsors exploration of Africa's coast.

1428 Joan of Arc leads French against English, captured by Burgundians (1430) and turned over to the English, burned at the stake as a witch after ecclesiastical trial (1431).

1438 Inca rule in Peru.

1450 Florence becomes center of Renaissance arts and learning under the Medicis.

1453 Turks conquer Constantinople, end of the Byzantine empire. Hundred Years' War between France and England ends.

1455 The Wars of the Roses, civil wars between rival noble factions, begin in England (to 1485). Having invented printing with movable type at Mainz, Germany, Johann Gutenberg completes first Bible.

1462 Ivan the Great rules Russia until 1505 as first czar; ends payment of tribute to Mongols.

1492 Moors conquered in Spain by troops of Ferdinand and Isabella. Columbus discovers Caribbean islands, returns to Spain (1493). Second voyage to Dominica, Jamaica, Puerto Rico (1493–1496). Third voyage to Orinoco (1498). Fourth voyage to Honduras and Panama (1502–1504).

1497 Vasco da Gama sails around Africa and discovers sea route to India (1498). Establishes Portuguese colony in India (1502). John Cabot, employed by England, reaches and explores Canadian coast. Michelangelo's *Bacchus* sculpture.

John Wycliffe
(1320-1384)

Joan of Arc
(1412-1431)

Christopher Columbus
(1451-1506)

THE CRUSADES (1096–1291)

In 1095 at Council of Clermont, Pope Urban II calls for war to rescue Holy Land from Moslem infidels. *First Crusade* (1096)—about 500,000 peasants led by Peter the Hermit prove so troublesome that Byzantine Emperor Alexius ships them to Asia Minor; only 25,000 survive return after massacre by Seljuk Turks. Followed by organized army, led by nobility, which reaches Constantinople (1097), conquers Jerusalem (1099), Acre (1104), establishes Latin Kingdom protected by Knights of St. John the Hospitaller (1100), and Knights Templar (1123). Seljuk Turks start series of counterattacks (1144). *Second Crusade* (1146) led by King Louis VIII of France and Emperor Conrad III. Crusaders perish in Asia Minor (1147).

Saladin controls Egypt (1171), unites Islam in Holy War *(Jihad)* against Christians, recaptures Jerusalem (1187). *Third Crusade* (1189) under kings of France, England, and Germany fails to reduce Saladin's power. *Fourth Crusade* (1200–1204)—French knights sack Greek Christian Constantinople, establish Latin empire in Byzantium. Greeks re-establish Orthodox faith (1262).

Children's Crusade (1212)—Only 1 of 30,000 French children and about 200 of 20,000 German children survive to return home. Other Crusades—against Egypt (1217), *Sixth* (1228), *Seventh* (1248), *Eighth* (1270). Mamelukes conquer Acre; end of the Crusades (1291).

16th century A.D.

Michelangelo Buonarreti
(1475-1564)

Martin Luther
(1483-1546)

1501 First black slaves in America brought to Spanish colony of Santo Domingo.

c.1503 Leonardo da Vinci paints the *Mona Lisa.*

1506 St. Peter's Church started in Rome; designed and decorated by such artists and architects as Bramante, Michelangelo, da Vinci, Raphael, and Bernini before its completion in **1626.**

1509 Henry VIII ascends English throne. Michelangelo paints the ceiling of the Sistine Chapel.

1517 Turks conquer Egypt, control Arabia. Martin Luther posts his 95 theses denouncing church abuses on church door in Wittenberg—start of the Reformation in Germany.

1519 Ulrich Zwingli begins Reformation in Switzerland. Hernando Cortes conquers Mexico for Spain. Charles I of Spain is chosen Holy Roman Emperor Charles V. Portuguese explorer Fernando Magellan sets out to circumnavigate the globe.

1520 Luther excommunicated by Pope Leo X. Suleiman I ("the Magnificent") becomes Sultan of Turkey, invades Hungary **(1521)**, Rhodes **(1522)**, attacks Austria **(1529)**, annexes Hungary **(1541)**, Tripoli **(1551)**, makes peace with Persia **(1553)**, destroys Spanish fleet **(1560)**, dies **(1566).** Magellan reaches the Pacific, is killed by Philippine natives **(1521).** One of his ships under Juan Sebastián del Cano continues around the world, reaches Spain **(1522).**

1524 Verrazano, sailing under the French flag, explores the New England coast and New York Bay.

1527 Troops of the Holy Roman Empire attack Rome, imprison Pope Clement VII—the end of the Italian Renaissance. Castiglione writes *The Courtier.* The Medici expelled from Florence.

1532 Pizarro marches from Panama to Peru, kills the Inca chieftain, Atahualpa, of Peru **(1533).** Machiavelli's *Prince* published posthumously.

1535 Reformation begins as Henry VIII makes himself head of English Church after being excommunicated by Pope. Sir Thomas More executed as traitor for refusal to acknowledge king's religious authority. Jacques Cartier sails up the St. Lawrence River, basis of French claims to Canada.

1536 Henry VIII executes second wife, Anne Boleyn. John Calvin establishes Presbyterian form of Protestantism in Switzerland, writes *Institutes of the Christian Religion.* Danish and Norwegian Reformations. Michelangelo's *Last Judgment.*

1541 John Knox leads Reformation in Scotland, establishes Presbyterian church **(1560).**

1543 Publication of *On the Revolution of Heavenly Bodies* by Polish scholar Nicolaus Copernicus—giving his theory that the earth revolves around the sun.

1545 Council of Trent to meet intermittently until **1563** to define Catholic dogma and doctrine, reiterate papal authority.

1547 Ivan IV ("the Terrible") crowned as Czar of Russia, begins conquest of Astrakhan and Kazan **(1552)**, battles nobles (boyars) for power **(1564)**, kills his son **(1580)**, dies, and is succeeded by a son who gives power to Boris Godunov **(1584).**

1553 Roman Catholicism restored in England by Queen Mary I, who rules until **1558.** Religious radical Michael Servetus burned as heretic in Geneva by order of John Calvin.

1554 Benvenuto Cellini completes the bronze *Perseus.*

1556 Akbar the Great becomes Mogul emperor of India, conquers Afghanistan **(1581)**, continues wars of conquest (until **1605).**

1558 Queen Elizabeth I ascends the throne (rules to **1603).** Restores Protestantism, establishes state Church of England (Anglicanism). Renaissance will reach height in England—Shakespeare, Marlowe, Spenser.

1561 Persecution of Huguenots in France stopped by Edict of Orleans. French religious wars begin again with massacre of Huguenots at Vassy. St. Bartholomew's Day Massacre—thousands of Huguenots murdered **(1572).** Amnesty granted **(1573).** Persecution continues periodically until Edict of Nantes **(1598)** gives Huguenots religious freedom (until **1685).**

1568 Protestant Netherlands revolts against Catholic Spain; independence will be acknowledged by Spain in **1648.** High point of Dutch Renaissance—painters Rubens, Van Dyck, Hals, and Rembrandt.

1570 Japan permits visits of foreign ships. Queen Elizabeth I excommunicated by Pope. Turks attack Cyprus and war on Venice. Turkish fleet defeated at Battle of Lepanto by Spanish and Italian fleets **(1571).** Peace of Constantinople **(1572)** ends Turkish attacks on Europe.

Anthony Van Dyck
(1559-1641)

1580	Francis Drake returns to England after circumnavigating the globe. Knighted by Queen Elizabeth I **(1581)**. Montaigne's *Essays* published.
1583	William of Orange rules The Netherlands; assassinated on orders of Philip II of Spain **(1584)**.
1587	Mary, Queen of Scots, executed for treason by order of Queen Elizabeth I. Monteverdi's *First Book of Madrigals*.
1588	Defeat of the Spanish Armada by English. Henry, King of Navarre and Protestant leader, recognized as Henry IV, first Bourbon king of France. Converts to Roman Catholicism in **1593** in attempt to end religious wars.
1590	Henry IV enters Paris, wars on Spain **(1595)**, marries Marie de Medici **(1600)**, assassinated **(1610)**. Spenser's *The Faerie Queen*, El Greco's *St. Jerome*. Galileo's experiments with falling objects.
1598	Boris Godunov becomes Russian Czar. Tycho Brahe describes his astronomical experiments.

**Francis Bacon
(1561-1626)**

17th century A.D.

1600	Giordano Bruno burned as a heretic. Ieyasu rules Japan, moves capital to Edo (Tokyo). Shakespeare's *Hamlet* begins his most productive decade. English East India Company established to develop overseas trade.
1607	Jamestown, Virginia, established—first permanent English colony on American mainland.
1609	Samuel de Champlain establishes French colony of Quebec.
1611	Gustavus Adolphus elected King of Sweden. King James Version of the Bible published in England. Rubens paints his *Descent from the Cross*.
1614	John Napier discovers logarithms.
1618	Start of the Thirty Years' War (to **1648**)—Protestant revolt against Catholic oppression; Denmark, Sweden, and France will invade Germany in later phases of war. Kepler proposes his Third Law of planetary motion.
1620	Pilgrims, after three-month voyage in *Mayflower*, land at Plymouth Rock. Francis Bacon's *Novum Organum*.
1633	Inquisition forces Galileo to recant his belief in Copernican theory.
1642	English Civil War. Cavaliers, supporters of Charles I, against Roundheads, parliamentary forces. Oliver Cromwell defeats Royalists **(1646)**. Parliament demands reforms. Charles I offers concessions, brought to trial **(1648)**, beheaded **(1649)**. Cromwell becomes Lord Protector **(1653)**. Rembrandt paints his *Night Watch*.
1644	End of Ming Dynasty in China—Manchus come to power. Descartes' *Principles of Philosophy*. John Milton's *Areopagitica* on the freedom of the press.
1648	End of the Thirty Years' War. German population about half of what it was in **1618** because of war and pestilence.
1658	Cromwell dies; his son, Richard, resigns and Puritan government collapses.
1660	English Parliament calls for the restoration of the monarchy; invites Charles II to return from France.
1661	Charles II is crowned King of England. Louis XIV begins personal rule as absolute monarch; starts to build Versailles.

**Giordano Bruno
(1548-1600)**

**George Washington
(1732-1799)**

THE FOUNDING OF THE AMERICAN NATION

Colonization of America begins: Jamestown, Va. **(1607)**; Pilgrims in Plymouth **(1620)**; Massachusetts Bay Colony **(1630)** New Netherland founded by Dutch West India Company **(1623)**, captured by English **(1664)**. Delaware established by Swedish trading company **(1638)**, absorbed later by Penn family. Proprietorships by royal grants to Lord Baltimore (Maryland, **1632**); Captain John Mason (New Hampshire, **1635**); Sir William Berkeley and Sir George Carteret (New Jersey, **1663**); friends of Charles II (the Carolinas, **1663**); William Penn (Pennsylvania, **1682**); James Oglethorpe and others (Georgia, **1732**).

Increasing conflict between colonists and Britain on western frontier because of royal edict limiting western expansion **(1763)**, and regulation of colonial trade and increased taxation of colonies (Writs of Assistance allow search for illegal shipments, **1761**; Sugar Act, **1764**; Currency Act, **1764**; Stamp Act, **1765**; Quartering Act, **1765**; Duty Act, **1767**.) Boston Massacre **(1770)**. Lord North attempts conciliation **(1770)**. Boston Tea Party **(1773)**, followed by punitive measures passed by Parliament—the "Intolerable Acts."

First Continental Congress **(1774)** sends "Declaration of Rights and Grievances" to king, urges colonies to form Continental Association. Paul Revere's Ride and Lexing-

ton and Concord battle between Massachusetts minutemen and British **(1775)**.

Second Continental Congress **(1775)**, while sending "olive branch" to the king, begins to raise army, appoints Washington commander-in-chief, and seeks alliance with France. Some colonial legislatures urge their delegates to vote for independence. Declaration of Independence **(July 4, 1776)**.

Major Battles of the Revolutionary War: *Long Island*: Howe defeats Putnam's division of Washington's Army in Brooklyn Heights, but Americans escape across East River **(1776)**. *Trenton and Princeton*: Washington defeats Hessians at Trenton. British at Princeton, winters at Morristown **(1776–77)**. Howe winters in Philadelphia; Washington at Valley Forge **(1777–78)**. Burgoyne surrenders British army to General Gates at *Saratoga* **(1777)**.

France recognizes American independence **(1778)**. The War moves south: Savannah captured by British **(1778)**; Charleston occupied **(1780)**; Americans fight successful guerrilla actions under Marion, Pickens, and Sumter. In the West, George Rogers Clark attacks Forts Kaskaskia and Vincennes **(1778–1779)**, defeating British in the region. Cornwallis surrenders at *Yorktown*, Virginia **(Oct. 19, 1781)**. By 1782, Britain is eager for peace because of conflicts with European nations. *Peace of Paris* **(1783)**: Britain recognizes American independence.

HUDSON'S BAY COMPANY

Lake Superior

Lake Michigan

Ottawa R.

Quebec

St. John R.

Proclamation Line of 1763

Montreal

Lake Huron

(1774-1783)

Lake Ontario

Ft. Niagara

Ft. Oswego

Detroit

Lake Erie

Q U E B E C

St. Lawrence

Crown Point

Ft. Ticonderoga

L. George

Oswego

Mohawk R.

(MAINE)

Champlain

Saratoga

Falmouth (Portland)

Portsmouth

N.H.

Albany

Concord

Lexington

Cambridge

Boston

Charlestown

Cherry Valley

MASSACHUSETTS

CONN.

R.I.

Newport

New London

LONG IS.

West Point

Stony Pt.

NEW YORK

Wyoming Valley

Susquehanna R.

Morristown

New York

Brooklyn

N.J.

Princeton

Monmouth

Trenton

Germantown

Philadelphia

Wilmington

Valley Forge

Brandywine

I N D I A N   C O U N T R Y

Ft. Pitt (Pittsburg)

Ohio R.

PENNSYLVANIA

Baltimore

Potomac R.

MARYLAND

DEL.

Mt. Vernon

Kanawha R.

VIRGINIA

James R.

Richmond

Roanoke R.

Williamsburg

Yorktown

Norfolk

Atlantic Ocean

Boonesborough

Harrodsburg

Holston R.

Watauga R.

Proclamation Line of 1763

A P P A L A C H I A N

Guilford Court House

Cape Fear R.

NORTH CAROLINA

New Bern

King's Mt.

Cowpens

Moore's Creek Bridge

Camden

Santee R.

Wilmington

SOUTH CAROLINA

Savannah R.

Chattahoochee R.

GEORGIA

Charleston

Altamaha R.

Savannah

EAST FLORIDA

The
UNITED STATES
during the
REVOLUTION

1664 British take New Amsterdam from the Dutch. English limit "Nonconformity" with re-established Anglican Church. Isaac Newton's experiments with gravity.
1665 Great Plague in London kills 75,000.
1666 Great Fire of London. Molière's *Misanthrope*.
1683 War of European powers against the Turks (to **1699**). Vienna withstands three-month Turkish siege; high point of Turkish advance in Europe.
1685 James II succeeds Charles II in England, calls for freedom of conscience (**1687**). Protestants fear restoration of Catholicism and demand "Glorious Revolution." William of Orange invited to England and James II escapes to France (**1688**). William III and his wife, Mary, crowned. In France, Edict of Nantes of **1598**, granting freedom of worship to Huguenots (French Protestants), is revoked by Louis XIV; thousands of Protestants flee.
1689 Peter the Great becomes Czar of Russia—attempts to westernize nation and build Russia as a military power. Defeats Charles XII of Sweden at Poltava (**1709**). Beginning of the French and Indian Wars (to **1763**), campaigns in America linked to a series of wars between France and England for domination of Europe.
1690 William III of England defeats former King James II and Irish rebels at Battle of the Boyne in Ireland. John Locke's *Human Understanding*.

**John Locke
(1632-1704)**

18th century A.D.

1701 War of the Spanish Succession begins—the last of Louis XIV's wars for domination of the continent. The Peace of Utrecht (**1714**) will end the conflict and mark the rise of the British Empire. Called Queen Anne's War in America, it ends with the British taking New Foundland, Acadia, and Hudson's Bay Territory from France, and Gibraltar and Minorca from Spain.
1704 Deerfield (Conn.) Massacre of English colonists by French and Indians. Bach's first cantata. Jonathan Swift's *Tale of a Tub*. *Boston News Letter*—first newspaper in America.
1707 United Kingdom of Great Britain formed—England, Wales, and Scotland joined by parliamentary Act of Union.
1729 J. S. Bach's *St. Matthew Passion*. Isaac Newton's *Principia* translated from Latin into English.
1735 John Peter Zenger, New York editor, acquitted of libel in New York, establishing press freedom.
1740 Capt. Vitus Bering, Dane employed by Russia, discovers Alaska.
1746 British defeat Scots under Stuart Pretender Prince Charles at Culloden Moor. Last battle fought on British soil.
1751 Publication of the *Encyclopédie* begins in France, the "bible" of the Enlightenment.
1755 Samuel Johnson's *Dictionary* first published. Great earthquake in Lisbon, Portugal—over 60,000 die.
1756 Seven Years' War (French and Indian War in America) (to **1763**), in which Britain and Prussia defeat France, Spain, Austria, and Russia. France loses North American colonies; Spain cedes Florida to Britain in exchange for Cuba. In India, over 100 British prisoners die in "Black Hole of Calcutta."
1757 Beginning of British Empire in India as Robert Clive, British commander, defeats Nawab of Bengal at Plassey.
1759 British capture Quebec from French. Voltaire's *Candide*. Haydn's *Symphony No. 1*.
1762 Catherine II ("the Great") becomes Czarina of Russia. J. J. Rousseau's *Social Contract*. Mozart tours Europe as six-year-old prodigy.
1765 James Watt invents the steam engine.
1769 Sir William Arkwright patents a spinning machine—an early step in the Industrial Revolution.
1772 Joseph Priestley and Daniel Rutherford independently discover nitrogen. Partition of Poland—in **1772**, **1793**, and **1795**, Austria, Prussia, and Russia divide land and people of Poland, end its independence.
1775 The American Revolution (*see* "The Founding of the American Nation"). Priestley discovers hydrochloric and sulfuric acids.
1776 Adam Smith's *Wealth of Nations*. Edward Gibbon's *Decline and Fall of the Roman Empire*. Thomas Paine's *Common Sense*. Fragonard's *Washerwoman*. Mozart's *Haffner Serenade*.
1778 Capt. James Cook discovers Hawaii. Franz Mesmer uses hypnotism.
1781 Immanuel Kant's *Critique of Pure Reason*. Herschel discovers Uranus.
1783 End of Revolutionary War (*see* special material on "The Founding of the

**Catherine II
(1729-1796)**

**Napoleon Bonaparte
(1769-1821)**

American Nation"). William Blake's poems. Beethoven's first printed works.

1784 Crimea annexed by Russia. John Wesley's *Deed of Declaration*, the basic work of Methodism.

1785 Russians settle Aleutian Islands.

1787 The Constitution of the United States signed. Lavoisier's work on chemical nomenclature. Mozart's *Don Giovanni*.

1788 French *Parlement* presents grievances to Louis XVI who agrees to convening of Estates-General in **1789**—not called since **1613**. Goethe's *Egmont*. Laplace's *Laws of the Planetary System*.

1789 French Revolution (*see* special material on the "French Revolution"). In U.S., George Washington elected President with all 69 votes of the Electoral College, takes oath of office in New York City. Vice President: John Adams. Secretary of State: Thomas Jefferson. Secretary of Treasury: Alexander Hamilton.

1790 H.M.S. *Bounty* mutineers settle on Pitcairn Island. Aloisio Galvani experiments on electrical stimulation of the muscles. Philadelphia temporary capital of U.S. as Congress votes to establish new capital on Potomac. U.S. population about 3,929,000, including 698,000 slaves. Lavoisier formulates *Table of 31 chemical elements*.

1791 U.S. Bill of Rights ratified. Boswell's *Life of Johnson*.

1794 Kosciusko's uprising in Poland quelled by the Russians. In U.S., Whiskey Rebellion in Pennsylvania as farmers object to liquor taxes. U.S. Navy and Post Office Department established.

1796 Napoleon Bonaparte, French general, defeats Austrians. In the U.S., Washington's Farewell Address (**Sept. 17**); John Adams elected President; Thomas Jefferson, Vice President. Edward Jenner introduces smallpox vaccination.

1798 Napoleon extends French conquests to Rome and Egypt.

1799 Napoleon leads coup that overthrows Directory, becomes First Consul—one of three who rule France.

19th century A.D.

1800 Napoleon conquers Italy, firmly establishes himself as First Consul in France. In the U.S., Federal Government moves to Washington. Robert Owen's social reforms in England. William Herschel discovers infrared rays. Alessandro Volta produces electricity.

1801 Austria makes temporary peace with France. United Kingdom of Great Britain and Ireland established with one monarch and one parliament; Catholics excluded from voting.

1803 U.S. negotiates Louisiana Purchase from France: For $15 million, U.S. doubles its domain, increasing its territory by 827,000 sq. mi. (2,144,500 sq km), from Mississippi River to Rockies and from Gulf of Mexico to British North America.

**Thomas Jefferson
(1743-1826)**

1804 Haiti declares independence from France; first black nation to gain freedom from European colonial rule. Napoleon proclaims himself emperor of France, systematizes French law under *Code Napoleon*. In the U.S., Alexander Hamilton is mortally wounded in duel with Aaron Burr. Lewis and Clark expedition begins exploration of what is now northwestern U.S.

1805 Lord Nelson defeats the French-Spanish fleets in the Battle of Trafalgar. Napoleon victorious over Austrian and Russian forces at the Battle of Austerlitz.

1807 Robert Fulton makes first successful steamboat trip on *Clermont* between New York City and Albany.

1808 French armies occupy Rome and Spain, extending Napoleon's empire. Britain begins aiding Spanish guerrillas against Napoleon in Peninsular War. In the U.S., Congress bars importation of slaves. Beethoven's *Fifth* and *Sixth Symphonies* performed.

**Alexander Hamilton
(1755-1804)**

1812 Napoleon's Grand Army invades Russia in June. Forced to retreat in winter, most of Napoleon's 600,000 men are lost. In the U.S., war with Britain

---

FRENCH REVOLUTION (1789–1799)

Revolution begins when Third Estate (Commons) delegates swear not to disband until France has a constitution. Paris mob storms Bastille, symbol of royal power (**July 14, 1789**). National Assembly votes for Constitution, Declaration of the Rights of Man, a limited monarchy, and other reforms (**1789–90**). Legislative Assembly elected, Revolutionary Commune formed, and French Republic proclaimed (**1792**). War of the First Coalition—Austria, Prus-

sia, Britain, Netherlands, and Spain fight to restore French nobility (**1792–97**). Start of series of wars between France and European powers that will last, almost without interruption, for 23 years. Louis XVI and Marie Antoinette executed. Committee of Public Safety begins Reign of Terror as political control measure. Interfactional rivalry leads to mass killings. Danton and Robespierre executed. Third French Constitution sets up Directory government (**1795**).

declared over freedom of the seas for U.S. vessels. U.S.S. *Constitution* sinks British frigate. (*See* special material on the "War of 1812.")

1814 French defeated by allies (Britain, Austria, Russia, Prussia, Sweden, and Portugal) in War of Liberation. Napoleon exiled to Elba, off Italian coast. Bourbon King Louis XVIII takes French throne. George Stephenson builds first practical steam locomotive.

1815 Napoleon returns: "Hundred Days" begin. Napoleon defeated by Wellington at Waterloo, banished again to St. Helena in South Atlantic. Congress of Vienna: victorious allies change the map of Europe.

1817 Simón Bolívar establishes independent Venezuela, as Spain loses hold on South American countries. Bolívar named President of Colombia (**1819**). Peru, Guatemala, Panama, and Santo Domingo proclaim independence from Spain (**1821**).

1820 Missouri Compromise—Missouri admitted as slave state but slavery barred in rest of Louisiana Purchase north of 36°30′ N.

1822 Greeks proclaim a republic and independence from Turkey. Turks invade Greece. Russia declares war on Turkey (**1828**). Greece also aided by France and Britain. War ends and Turks recognize Greek independence (**1829**). Brazil becomes independent of Portugal. Schubert's *Eighth Symphony* ("The Unfinished").

1823 U.S. Monroe Doctrine warns European nations not to interfere in Western Hemisphere.

1824 Mexico becomes a republic, three years after declaring independence from Spain. Beethoven's *Ninth Symphony*.

1825 First passenger-carrying railroad in England.

1830 French invade Algeria. Louis Philippe becomes "Citizen King" as revolution forces Charles X to abdicate. Mormon church formed in U.S. by Joseph Smith.

1831 Polish revolt against Russia fails. Belgium separates from the Netherlands. In U.S., Nat Turner leads unsuccessful slave rebellion.

1833 Slavery abolished in British Empire.

1834 Charles Babbage invents "analytical engine," precursor of computer. McCormick patents reaper.

1836 Boer farmers start "Great Trek"—Natal, Transvaal, and Orange Free State founded in South Africa. Mexican army besieges Texans in Alamo. Entire garrison, including Davy Crockett and Jim Bowie, wiped out. Texans gain independence from Mexico after winning Battle of San Jacinto. Dicken's *Pickwick Papers.*

1837 Victoria becomes Queen of Great Britain. Mob kills Elijah P. Lovejoy, Illinois abolitionist publisher.

1839 First Opium War (to **1842**) between Britain and China, over importation of drug into China.

1840 Lower and Upper Canada united.

1841 U.S. President Harrison dies (**April 4**) one month after inauguration; John Tyler becomes first Vice President to succeed to Presidency.

1844 Democratic convention calls for annexation of Texas and acquisition of Oregon ("Fifty-four-forty-or-fight"). Five Chinese ports opened to U.S. ships. Samuel F. B. Morse patents telegraph.

1845 Congress adopts joint resolution for annexation of Texas.

1846 Failure of potato crop causes famine in Ireland. U.S. declares war on Mexico. California and New Mexico annexed by U.S. Brigham Young leads Mormons to Great Salt Lake. W.T. Morton uses ether as anesthetic. Sewing machine patented by Elias Howe.

1848 Revolt in Paris: Louis Philippe abdicates; Louis Napoleon elected President of French Republic. Revolutions in Vienna, Venice, Berlin, Milan, Rome, and Warsaw. Put down by royal troops in **1848–49**. U.S.-Mexico War ends; Mexico cedes claims to Texas, California, Arizona, New Mexico, Utah, Nevada. U.S. treaty with Britain sets Oregon Territory boundary at 49th parallel. Karl Marx and Friedrich Engels' *Communist Manifesto.*

1849 California gold rush begins.

1850 Henry Clay opens great debate on slavery, warns South against secession.

1851 Herman Melville's *Moby Dick*. Harriet Beecher Stowe's *Uncle Tom's Cabin.*

1852 South African Republic established. Louis Napoleon proclaims himself Napoleon III ("Second Empire").

Charles Dickens
(1812-1870)

Henry Clay
(1777-1852)

WAR OF 1812

British interference with American trade, impressment of American seamen, and "War Hawks" drive for western expansion lead to war. American attacks on Canada foiled; U.S. Commodore Perry wins battle of Lake Erie (**1813**). British capture and burn Washington (**1814**) but fail to take Fort McHenry at Baltimore. Andrew Jackson repulses assault on New Orleans after treaty of Ghent ends war (**1815**). War settles little but strengthens U.S. as independent nation.

**Dred Scott
(1795?-1858)**

**Abraham Lincoln
(1809-1865)**

**Ulysses S. Grant
(1822-1885)**

1853 Crimean War begins as Turkey declares war on Russia. Commodore Perry reaches Tokyo.

1854 Britain and France join Turkey in war on Russia. In U.S., Kansas-Nebraska Act permits local option on slavery; rioting and bloodshed. Japanese allow American trade. Antislavery men in Michigan form Republican Party. Tennyson's *Charge of the Light Brigade*. Thoreau's *Walden*.

1855 Armed clashes in Kansas between pro- and anti-slavery forces. Florence Nightingale nurses wounded in Crimea. Walt Whitman's *Leaves of Grass*.

1856 Flaubert's *Madame Bovary*.

1857 Supreme Court, in Dred Scott decision, rules that a slave is not a citizen. Financial crisis in Europe and U.S. Great Mutiny (Sepoy Rebellion) begins in India. India placed under crown rule as a result.

1858 Pro-slavery constitution rejected in Kansas. Abraham Lincoln makes strong antislavery speech in Springfield, Ill.: ". . . this Government cannot endure permanently half slave and half free." Lincoln-Douglas debates. First trans-Atlantic telegraph cable completed by Cyrus W. Field.

1859 John Brown raids Harpers Ferry; is captured and hanged. Work begins on Suez Canal. Unification of Italy starts under leadership of Count Cavour, Sardinian premier. Joined by France in war against Austria. Edward Fitzgerald's *Rubaiyat of Omar Khayyam*. Charles Darwin's *Origin of Species*. J. S. Mill's *On Liberty*

1861 U.S. Civil War begins as attempts at compromise fail (*see* special material on "The Civil War"). Congress creates Colorado, Dakota, and Nevada territories; adopts income tax; Lincoln inaugurated. Serfs emancipated in Russia. Pasteur's theory of germs. Independent Kingdom of Italy proclaimed under Sardinian King Victor Emmanuel II.

1863 French capture Mexico City; proclaim Archduke Maximilian of Austria emperor.

1865 Lincoln fatally shot at Ford's Theater by John Wilkes Booth. Vice President Johnson sworn as successor. Booth caught and dies of gunshot wounds; four conspirators are hanged. Joseph Lister begins antiseptic surgery. Gregor Mendel's Law of Heredity. Lewis Carroll's *Alice's Adventures in Wonderland*.

1866 Alfred Nobel invents dynamite (patented in Britain 1867). Seven Weeks' War: Austria defeated by Prussia and Italy.

1867 Austria-Hungary Dual Monarchy established. French leave Mexico; Maximilian executed. Dominion of Canada established. U.S. buys Alaska from Russia for $7,200,000. South African diamond field discovered. Volume I of Marx's *Das Kapital*. Strauss's *Blue Danube*.

1868 Revolution in Spain; Queen Isabella deposed, flees to France. In U.S., Fourteenth Amendment giving civil rights to blacks is ratified. Georgia under military government after legislature expels blacks.

1869 First U.S. transcontinental rail route completed. James Fisk and Jay Gould attempt to control gold market causes Black Friday panic. Suez Canal opened. Mendeleev's periodic table of elements.

1870 Franco-Prussian War (to **1871**): Napoleon III capitulates at Sedan. Revolt in Paris; Third Republic proclaimed.

THE CIVIL WAR
(The War Between the States or the War of the Rebellion)

Apart from the matter of slavery, the Civil War arose out of both the economic and political rivalry between an agrarian South and an industrial North and the issue of the right of states to secede from the Union.

1861 After South Carolina secedes (**Dec. 20, 1860**), Mississippi, Florida, Alabama, Georgia, Louisiana, and Texas follow, forming the Confederate States of America, with Jefferson Davis as president (**Jan.–March**). War begins as Confederates fire on Fort Sumter (**April 12**). Lincoln calls for 75,000 volunteers. Southern ports blockaded by superior Union naval forces. Virginia, Arkansas, Tennessee, and North Carolina secede to complete 11-state Confederacy. Union army advancing on Richmond repulsed at first Battle of Bull Run (**July**).

1862 Edwin M. Stanton named Secretary of War (**Jan.**). Grant wins first important Union victory in West, at Fort Donelson; Nashville falls (**Feb.**). Ironclads, Union's *Monitor* and Confederate's *Virginia (Merrimac)* duel at Hampton Roads (**March**). New Orleans falls to Union fleet under Farragut; city occupied (**April**). Grant's army escapes defeat at Shiloh. Memphis falls as Union gunboats control upper Mississippi (**June**). Confederate general Robert E. Lee victorious at second Battle of Bull Run (**Aug.**). Union

army under McClellan halts Lee's attack on Washington in the Battle of Antietam (**Sept.**). Lincoln removes McClellan for lack of aggressiveness. Burnside's drive on Richmond fails at Fredericksburg (**Dec.**). Union forces under Rosecrans chase Bragg through Tennessee; battle of Murfreesboro (**Oct.–Jan. 1863**).

1863 Lee defeats Hooker at Chancellorsville; "Stonewall" Jackson, Confederate general, dies (**May**). Confederate invasion of Pennsylvania stopped at Gettysburg by George Meade—Lee loses 20,000 men—the greatest battle of the War (**July**). It and the Union victory at Vicksburg mark the war's turning point. Union general George H. Thomas, the "Rock of Chickamauga," holds Bragg's forces on Georgia-Tennessee border (**Sept.**). Sherman, Hooker, and Thomas drive Bragg back to Georgia. Tennessee restored to the Union (**Nov.**).

1864 Ulysses S. Grant named commander-in-chief of Union forces (**March**). In the Wilderness campaign, Grant forces Lee's Army of Northern Virginia back toward Richmond (**May–June**). Sherman's Atlanta campaign and "march to the sea" (**May–Sept.**). Farragut's victory at Mobile Bay (**Aug.**). Hood's Confederate army defeated at Nashville. Sherman takes Savannah (**Dec.**).

1865 Sheridan defeats Confederates at Five Forks; Confederates evacuate Richmond (**April**). On **April 9**, Lee surrenders to Grant at Appomattox.

1871 France surrenders Alsace-Lorraine to Germany; war ends. German Empire proclaimed with Prussian King as Kaiser Wilhelm I. Fighting with Apaches begins in American West. Boss Tweed corruption exposed in New York. The Chicago Fire, with 250 deaths and $196-million damage. Stanley meets Livingston in Africa.

1872 Congress gives amnesty to most Confederates. Jules Verne's *Around the World in 80 Days*.

1873 Economic crisis in Europe. U.S. establishes gold standard.

1875 First Kentucky Derby.

1876 Sioux kill Gen. George A. Custer and 264 troopers at Little Big Horn River. Alexander Graham Bell patents the telephone.

1877 After Presidential election of **1876,** Electoral Commission gives disputed Electoral College votes to Rutherford B. Hayes despite Tilden's popular majority. Russo-Turkish war (ends in **1878** with power of Turkey in Europe broken). Reconstruction ends in the American South. Thomas Edison patents phonograph.

1878 Congress of Berlin revises Treaty of San Stefano ending Russo-Turkish War; makes extensive redivision of southeastern Europe. First commercial telephone exchange opened in New Haven, Conn.

1880 U.S.-China treaty allows U.S. to restrict immigration of Chinese labor.

1881 President Garfield fatally shot by assassin; Vice President Arthur succeeds him. Charles J. Guiteau convicted and executed (in **1882**).

**Geronimo
(1829-1909)**

1882 Terrorism in Ireland after land evictions. Britain invades and conquers Egypt. Germany, Austria, and Italy form Triple Alliance. In U.S., Congress adopts Chinese Exclusion Act. Rockefeller's Standard Oil Trust is first industrial monopoly. In Berlin, Robert Koch announces discovery of tuberculosis germ.

1883 Congress creates Civil Service Commission. Brooklyn Bridge and Metropolitan Opera House completed.

1885 British Gen. Charles G. "Chinese" Gordon killed at Khartoum in Egyptian Sudan.

1886 Bombing at Haymarket Square, Chicago, kills seven policemen and injures many others. Eight alleged anarchists accused—three imprisoned, one commits suicide, four hanged. (In **1893,** Illinois Governor Altgeld, critical of trial, pardons three survivors.) Statue of Liberty dedicated. Geronimo, Apache Indian chief, surrenders.

1887 Queen Victoria's Golden Jubilee. Sir Arthur Conan Doyle's first Sherlock Holmes story, "A Study in Scarlet."

1888 Historic March blizzard in Northeast U.S.—many perish, property damage exceeds $25 million. George Eastman's box camera (the Kodak). J.B. Dunlop invents pneumatic tire. Jack the Ripper murders in London.

**Samuel Clemens
(Mark Twain)
(1835-1910)**

1889 Second (Socialist) International founded in Paris. Indian Territory in Oklahoma opened to settlement. Thousands die in Johnstown, Pa., flood. Mark Twain's *A Connecticut Yankee in King Arthur's Court*.

1890 Congress votes Sherman Antitrust Act. Sitting Bull killed in Sioux uprising.

1892 Battle between steel strikers and Pinkerton guards at Homestead, Pa.; union defeated after militia intervenes. Silver mine strikers in Idaho fight non-union workers; U.S. troops dispatched. Diesel engine patented.

1894 Sino-Japanese War begins (ends in **1895** with China's defeat). In France, Capt. Alfred Dreyfus convicted on false treason charge (pardoned in **1906**). In U.S., Jacob S. Coxey of Ohio leads "Coxey's Army" of unemployed on Washington. Eugene V. Debs calls general strike of rail workers to support Pullman Company strikers; strike broken, Debs jailed for six months. Thomas A. Edison's kinetoscope given first public showing in New York City.

1895 X-rays discovered by German physicist, Wilhelm Roentgen.

1896 Supreme Court's *Plessy v. Ferguson* decision—"separate but equal" doctrine. Alfred Nobel's will establishes prizes for peace, science, and literature. Marconi receives first wireless patent in Britain. William Jennings Bryan delivers "Cross of Gold" speech at Democratic Convention in

**Thomas A. Edison
(1847-1931)**

SPANISH-AMERICAN WAR (1898–1899)

War fires stoked by "jingo journalism" as American people support Cuban rebels against Spain. American business sees economic gain in Cuban trade and resources and American power zones in Latin America. Outstanding events: Submarine mine explodes U.S. battleship *Maine* in Havana Harbor (**Feb. 15**); 260 killed; responsibility never fixed. Congress declares independence of Cuba (**April 19**). Spain declares war on U.S. (**Apr. 24**); Congress (**Apr. 25**) formally declares nation has been at war with Spain since Apr. 21. Commodore George Dewey wins seven-hour battle of Manila Bay (**May 1**). Spanish fleet destroyed off Santiago, Cuba (**July 3**); city surrenders (**July 17**). Treaty of Paris (ratified by Senate **1899**) ends war. U.S. given Guam and Puerto Rico and agrees to pay Spain $20 million for Philippines. Cuba independent of Spain; under U.S. military control for three years until **May 20, 1902**. Yellow fever is eradicated and political reforms achieved.

Marie Curie
(1867-1934)

Chicago. First modern Olympic games held in Athens, Greece.

1898 Chinese "Boxers," anti-foreign organization, established. They stage uprisings against Europeans in **1900;** U.S. and other Western troops relieve Peking legations. Spanish-American War (*see* special material on the "Spanish-American War"). Pierre and Marie Curie discover radium and polonium.

1899 Boer War (or South African War). Conflict between British and Boers (descendants of Dutch settlers of South Africa). Causes rooted in longstanding territorial disputes and in friction over political rights for English and other "uitlanders" following 1886 discovery of vast gold deposits in Transvaal. (British victorious as war ends in **1902.**) Casualties: 5,774 British dead, about 4,000 Boers. Union of South Africa established in **1908** as confederation of colonies; becomes British dominion in **1910.**

20th century A.D.

1900 Hurricane ravages Galveston, Tex.; 6,000 drown. Sigmund Freud's *The Interpretation of Dreams.*

1901 Queen Victoria dies; succeeded by son, Edward VII. As President McKinley begins second term, he is shot fatally by anarchist Leon Czolgosz. Theodore Roosevelt sworn in as successor.

1902 Enrico Caruso's first gramophone recording.

1903 Wright brothers, Orville and Wilbur, fly first powered, controlled, heavier-than-air plane at Kitty Hawk, N.C. Henry Ford organizes Ford Motor Company.

1904 Russo-Japanese War—competition for Korea and Manchuria: In **1905,** Port Arthur surrenders to Japanese and Russia suffers other defeats; President Roosevelt mediates Treaty of Portsmouth, N.H., ending war with concessions for Japan. *Entente Cordiale:* Britain and France settle their international differences. General theory of radioactivity by Rutherford and Soddy. New York City subway opened.

Theodore Roosevelt
(1858-1919)

1905 General strike in Russia; first workers' soviet set up in St. Petersburg. Sailors on battleship *Potemkin* mutiny; reforms including first Duma (parliament) established by Czar's "October Manifesto." Albert Einstein's special theory of relativity and other key theories in physics. Franz Lehar's *Merry Widow.*

1906 San Francisco earthquake and three-day fire; 500 dead. Roald Amundsen, Norwegian explorer, fixes magnetic North Pole.

1907 Second Hague Peace Conference, of 46 nations, adopts 10 conventions on rules of war. Financial panic of **1907** in U.S.

1908 Earthquake kills 150,000 in southern Italy and Sicily. U.S. Supreme Court, in Danbury Hatters' case, outlaws secondary union boycotts.

1909 North Pole reached by American explorers Robert E. Peary and Matthew Henson.

1910 Boy Scouts of America incorporated.

1911 First use of aircraft as offensive weapon in Turkish-Italian War. Italy defeats Turks and annexes Tripoli and Libya. Chinese Republic proclaimed after revolution overthrows Manchu dynasty. Sun Yat-sen named president. Mexican Revolution: Porfirio Diaz, president since 1877, replaced by Francisco Madero. Triangle Shirtwaist Company fire in New York; 145 killed. Richard Strauss's *Der Rosenkavalier.* Irving Berlin's *Alexander's Ragtime Band.* Amundsen reaches South Pole.

1912 Balkan Wars (**1912–13**) resulting from territorial disputes: Turkey defeated by alliance of Bulgaria, Serbia, Greece, and Montenegro; London peace treaty (**1913**) partitions most of European Turkey among the victors. In second war (**1913**), Bulgaria attacks Serbia and Greece and is defeated after Romania intervenes and Turks recapture Adrianople. *Titanic* sinks on maiden voyage; over 1,500 drown.

Albert Einstein
(1879-1955)

1913 Suffragettes demonstrate in London. Garment workers strike in New York and Boston; win pay raise and shorter hours. Sixteenth Amendment (income tax) and 17th (popular election of U.S. senators) adopted. Bill creating U.S. Federal Reserve System becomes law. Stravinsky's *The Rite of Spring.*

1914 World War I begins (*see* special material on "World War I"). Panama Canal officially opened. Congress sets up Federal Trade Commission, passes Clayton Antitrust Act. U.S. Marines occupy Veracruz, Mexico, intervening in civil war to protect American interests.

1915 U.S. protests German submarine actions and British blockade of Germany. U.S. banks lend $500 million to France and Britain. D. W. Griffith's film *Birth of a Nation.* Albert Einstein's *General Theory of Relativity.*

1916 Congress expands armed forces. Tom Mooney arrested for San Francisco bombing (pardoned in **1939**). Pershing fails in raid into Mexico in quest of

The Partition of Africa ~ 1914

EUROPE

TANGIER (Sp.)
Casablanca
MADEIRA IS. (Port.)
Algiers
TUNISIA
Tripoli
MOROCCO
ALGERIA
LIBYA
Suez Canal
Cairo
CANARY IS. (Spain)
RIO DE ORO
SAHARA
EGYPT (Br. Protect.)
ARABIA
FRENCH WEST AFRICA
ANGLO EGYPTIAN SUDAN
Senegal
Niger
Lake Chad
Khartum
Massawa
ERITREA
Blue Nile
Red Sea
GAMBIA (Br.)
PORT. GUINEA
NIGERIA (Br.)
Adua
FR. SOMALILAND
SIERRA LEONE (Br.)
IVORY COAST
CAMEROUNS (Ger.)
FRENCH EQUATORIAL AFRICA
BR. SOMALILAND
LIBERIA
GOLD COAST (Br.)
TOGOLAND (Ger.)
RIO MUNI (Sp.)
ETHIOPIA
ITAL. SOMALILAND
NILE

EQUATOR

BELGIAN CONGO
Congo R.
UGANDA
L. Victoria Nyanza
BRITISH EAST AFRICA
KENYA
Mombasa
GERMAN EAST AFRICA
Lake Tanganyika
ZANZIBAR (Br.)
ANGOLA (Port.)
NYASALAND
PORT. EAST AFRICA
RHODESIA
MADAGASCAR (Fr.)
GERMAN SOUTHWEST AFRICA
BECHUANALAND
UNION OF SOUTH AFRICA
TRANSVAAL
ORANGE FREE STATE
NATAL
Capetown
CAPE COLONY

European Colonies in Africa ~ 1878

ALGERIA
SENEGAL
GAMBIA
ANGOLA
MOZAMBIQUE
CAPE COLONY

KEY

British	Italian
French	Portuguese
German	Belgian
Spanish	

**Vladimir Lenin
(1870-1924)**

**Woodrow Wilson
(1856-1924)**

rebel Pancho Villa. U.S. buys Virgin Islands from Denmark for $25 million. President Wilson re-elected with "he kept us out of war" slogan. "Black Tom" explosion at munitions dock in Jersey City, N.J., $40,000,000 damages; traced to German saboteurs. Margaret Sanger opens first birth control clinic. Easter Rebellion in Ireland put down by British troops.

1917 First U.S. combat troops in France as U.S. declares war (**April 6**). Russian Revolution—climax of long unrest under czars. February Revolution—Czar forced to abdicate, liberal government created. Kerensky becomes prime minister and forms provisional government (**July**). In October Revolution, Bolsheviks seize power in armed coup d'état led by Lenin and Trotsky. Kerensky flees. Revolutionaries execute the czar and his family (**1918**). Reds set up Third International in Moscow (**1919**). Balfour Declaration promises Jewish homeland in Palestine. Sigmund Freud's *Introduction to Psychoanalysis.*

1918 Russian Civil War between Reds (Bolsheviks) and Whites (anti-Bolsheviks); Reds win in **1920**. Allied troops (U.S., British, French) intervene (**March**); leave in **1919**. Japanese hold Vladivostok until **1922**. World-wide influenza epidemic strikes; by **1920**, nearly 20 million are dead. In U.S. alone, 500,000 perish.

1919 Third International (Comintern) establishes Soviet control over international Communist movements. Paris peace conference. Versailles Treaty, incorporating Wilson's draft Covenant of League of Nations, signed by Allies and Germany; rejected by U.S. Senate. Congress formally ends war in **1921**. Eighteenth (Prohibition) Amendment adopted. Alcock and Brown make first trans-Atlantic non-stop flight.

1920 League of Nations holds first meeting at Geneva, Switzerland. U.S. Dept. of Justice "red hunt" nets thousands of radicals; aliens deported. Women's suffrage (19th) amendment ratified. First Agatha Christie mystery. Sinclair Lewis's *Main Street.*

1921 Reparations Commission fixes German liability at 132 billion gold marks. German inflation begins. Major treaties signed at Washington Disarmament Conference limit naval tonnage and pledge to respect territorial integrity of China. Irish Free State formed in southern Ireland as self-governing dominion of British Empire. In U.S., Nicola Sacco and Bartolomeo Vanzetti, Italian-born anarchists, convicted of armed robbery murder; case stirs world-wide protests; they are executed in **1927**.

1922 Mussolini marches on Rome; forms Fascist government. Irish Free State officially proclaimed.

1923 Adolf Hitler's "Beer Hall Putsch" in Munich fails; in **1924** he is sentenced to five years in prison where he writes *Mein Kampf;* released after eight months. Occupation of Ruhr by French and Belgian troops to enforce reparations payments. Widespread Ku Klux Klan violence in U.S. George Gershwin's *Rhapsody in Blue.*

WORLD WAR I (1914–1918)

Imperial, territorial, and economic rivalries lead to the "Great War" between the Central Powers (Austria-Hungary, Germany, Bulgaria, and Turkey) and the Allies (U.S., Britain, France, Russia, Belgium, Serbia, Greece, Romania, Montenegro, Portugal, Italy, Japan). About 10 million combatants killed, 20 million wounded.

1914 Austrian Archduke Francis Ferdinand and wife assassinated in Sarajevo by Serbian nationalist, Gavrilo Princip (**June 28**). Austria declares war on Serbia (**July 28**). Germany declares war on Russia (**Aug. 1**), on France (**Aug. 3**), invades Belgium (**Aug. 4**). Britain declares war on Germany (**Aug. 4**). Germans defeat Russians in Battle of Tannenberg on Eastern Front (**Aug.**). First Battle of the Marne (**Sept.**). German drive stopped 25 miles from Paris. By end of year, war on the Western Front is "positional" in the trenches.

1915 German submarine blockade of Great Britain begins (**Feb.**). Dardanelles Campaign—British land in Turkey (**April**), withdraw from Gallipoli (**Dec. to Jan. 1916**). Germans use gas at second Battle of Ypres (**April–May**). *Lusitania* sunk by German submarine—1,198 lost, including 128 Americans (**May 7**). On Eastern Front, German and Austrian "great offensive" conquers all of Poland and Lithuania; Russians lose 1 million men (by **Sept. 6**). "Great Fall Offensive" by Allies results in little change from 1914 (**Sept.–Oct.**). Britain and France declare war on Bulgaria (**Oct. 14**).

1916 Battle of Verdun—Germans and French each lose about 350,000 men (**Feb.**). Extended submarine warfare begins (**March**). British-German sea battle of Jutland (**May**); British lose more ships, but German fleet never ventures forth again. On Eastern front, the Brusilov offensive demoralizes Russians, costs them 1 million men (**June–Sept.**). Battle of the Somme—British lose over 400,000; French, 200,000; Germans, about 450,000; all with no strategic results (**July–Nov.**). Romania declares war on Austria-Hungary (**Aug. 27**). Bucharest captured (**Dec.**).

1917 U.S. declares war on Germany (**April 6**). Submarine warfare at peak (**April**). On Italian Front, Battle of Caporetto—Italians retreat, losing 600,000 prisoners and deserters (**Oct.–Dec.**). On Western Front, Battles of Arras, Champagne, Ypres (third battle), etc. First large British tank attack (**Nov.**). U.S. declares war on Austria-Hungary (**Dec. 7**). Armistice between new Russian Bolshevik government and Germans (**Dec. 15**).

1918 Great offensive by Germans (**March–June**). Americans' first important battle role at Château-Thierry—as they and French stop German advance (**June**). Second Battle of the Marne (**July–Aug.**)—start of Allied offensive at Amiens, St. Mihiel, etc. Battles of the Argonne and Ypres panic German leadership (**Sept.–Oct.**). British offensive in Palestine (**Sept.**). Germans ask for armistice (**Oct. 4**). British armistice with Turkey (**Oct.**). German Kaiser abdicates (**Nov.**). Hostilities cease on Western Front (**Nov. 11**).

TERRITORIAL CHANGES
following WORLD WAR I

Territory lost
by Germany   by Russia
by Bulgaria   by Austria-Hungary

1924 Death of Lenin; Stalin wins power struggle, rules as Soviet dictator until death in **1953.** Italian Fascists murder Socialist leader Giacomo Matteotti. Interior Secretary Albert B. Fall and oilmen Harry Sinclair and Edward L. Doheny are charged with conspiracy and bribery in the Teapot Dome scandal, involving fraudulent leases of naval oil reserves. In **1931,** Fall is sentenced to year in prison; Doheny and Sinclair acquitted of bribery. Nathan

Charles A. Lindbergh
(1902-1974)

Herbert Hoover
(1874-1964)

Leopold and Richard Loeb convicted in "thrill killing" of Bobby Franks in Chicago; defended by Clarence Darrow; sentenced to life imprisonment. (Loeb killed by fellow convict in **1936**; Leopold paroled in **1958**, dies in **1971**.)

1925 Nellie Tayloe Ross elected governor of Wyoming; first woman governor elected in U.S. Locarno conferences seek to secure European peace by mutual guarantees. John T. Scopes convicted and fined for teaching evolution in a public school in Tennessee "Monkey Trial"; sentence set aside. John Logie Baird, Scottish inventor, transmits human features by television. Adolf Hitler publishes Volume I of *Mein Kampf.*

1926 General strike in Britain brings nation's activities to standstill. U.S. marines dispatched to Nicaragua during revolt; they remain until **1933**. Gertrude Ederle of U.S. is first woman to swim English Channel.

1927 German economy collapses. Socialists riot in Vienna; general strike follows acquittal of Nazis for political murder. Trotsky expelled from Russian Communist Party. Charles A. Lindbergh flies first successful solo non-stop flight from New York to Paris. Ruth Snyder and Judd Gray convicted of murder of Albert Snyder; they are executed at Sing Sing prison in **1928**. *The Jazz Singer,* with Al Jolson, first part-talking motion picture.

1928 Kellogg-Briand Pact, outlawing war, signed in Paris by 65 nations. Alexander Fleming discovers penicillin. Richard E. Byrd starts expedition to Antarctic; returns in **1930**.

1929 Trotsky expelled from U.S.S.R. Lateran Treaty establishes independent Vatican City. In U.S., stock market prices collapse, with U.S. securities losing $26 billion—first phase of Depression and world economic crisis. St. Valentine's Day gangland massacre in Chicago.

1930 Britain, U.S., Japan, France, and Italy sign naval disarmament treaty. Nazis gain in German elections. Cyclotron developed by Ernest O. Lawrence, U.S. physicist.

1931 Spain becomes a republic with overthrow of King Alfonso XIII. German industrialists finance 800,000-strong Nazi party. British parliament enacts statute of Westminster, legalizing dominion equality with Britain. Mukden Incident begins Japanese occupation of Manchuria. In U.S., Hoover proposes one-year moratorium of war debts. Harold C. Urey discovers heavy hydrogen. Gangster Al Capone sentenced to 11 years in prison for tax evasion (freed in **1939**; dies in **1947**).

1932 Nazis lead in German elections with 230 Reichstag seats. Famine in U.S.S.R. In U.S., Congress sets up Reconstruction Finance Corporation to stimulate economy. Veterans march on Washington—most leave after Senate rejects payment of cash bonuses; others removed by troops under Douglas MacArthur. U.S. protests Japanese aggression in Manchuria. Amelia Earhart is first woman to fly Atlantic solo. Charles A. Lindbergh's baby son kidnapped, killed. (Bruno Richard Hauptmann arrested in **1934**, convicted in **1935**, executed in **1936**.)

1933 Hitler appointed German chancellor, gets dictatorial powers. Reichstag fire in Berlin; Nazi terror begins. (*See* special material on "The Holocaust.") Germany and Japan withdraw from League of Nations. Giuseppe Zangara executed for attempted assassination of President-elect Roosevelt in which

---

THE HOLOCAUST (1933–1945)

"Holocaust" is the term describing the Nazi annihilation of about 6 million Jews (two thirds of the pre-World War II European Jewish population), including 4,500,000 from Russia, Poland, and the Baltic; 750,000 from Hungary and Romania; 290,000 from Germany and Austria; 105,000 from The Netherlands; 90,000 from France; 54,000 from Greece, etc.

The Holocaust was unique in its being *genocide*—the systematic destruction of a people solely because of religion, race, ethnicity, nationality, or homosexuality—on an unmatched scale. Along with the Jews, another 9 to 10 million people—Gypsies, Slavs (Poles, Ukrainians, and Belorussians)—were exterminated.

The only comparable act of genocide in modern times was launched in April 1915, when an estimated 600,000 Armenians were massacred by the Turks.

1933 Hitler named German Chancellor **(Jan.)**. Dachau, first concentration camp, established **(March)**. Boycotts against Jews begin **(April)**.
1935 Anti-Semitic Nuremberg Laws passed by Reichstag **(Sept.)**.

1937 Buchenwald concentration camp opens **(July)**.
1938 Extension of anti-Semitic laws to Austria after annexation **(March)**. *Kristallnacht* (Night of Broken Glass)—anti-Semitic riots in Germany and Austria **(Nov. 9)**. 26,000 Jews sent to concentration camps; Jewish children expelled from schools **(Nov.)**. Expropriation of Jewish property and businesses **(Dec.)**.
1940 As war continues, Nazi acts against Jews extended to German-conquered areas.
1941 Deportation of German Jews begins; massacres of Jews in Odessa and Kiev—68,000 killed **(Nov.)**; in Riga and Vilna—almost 60,000 killed **(Dec.)**.
1942 Unified Jewish resistance in ghettos begins **(Jan.)**. 300,000 Jews from Warsaw Ghetto deported to Treblinka death camp **(July)**.
1943 Warsaw Ghetto uprisings **(Jan. and April)**; Ghetto exterminated **(May)**.
1944 476,000 Hungarian Jews sent to Auschwitz **(May–June)**. D-day **(June 6)**. Soviet Army liberates Maidanek death camp **(July)**. Nazis try to hide evidence of death camps **(Nov.)**.
1945 Americans liberate Buchenwald and British liberate Bergen-Belsen camps **(April)**. Nuremberg War Crimes Trial **(Nov. 1945 to Oct. 1946)**.

The German Attack on Soviet Russia, 1941-1943

Axis occupied areas and Finland, June 22, 41
Russian areas held by Axis-Apr. 15, 43
Retaken by Russia after Nov. 19, '42
(185,300 SQ. miles)

The Pacific Theater of War
1941~1945

Japanese territory 1942
Area retained by Japan after World War II
Allied drives, 1942-45

Chicago Mayor Cermak is fatally shot. Roosevelt inaugurated ("the only thing we have to fear is fear itself"); launches New Deal. Prohibition repealed. U.S.S.R. recognized by U.S.

1934 Chancellor Dollfuss of Austria assassinated by Nazis. Hitler becomes Führer. U.S.S.R. admitted to League of Nations. Dionne sisters, first quintuplets to survive beyond infancy, born in Canada.

1935 Saar incorporated into Germany after plebiscite. Nazis repudiate Versailles Treaty, introduce compulsory military service. Mussolini invades Ethiopia; League of Nations invokes sanctions. Roosevelt opens second phase of New Deal in U.S., calling for social security, better housing, equitable taxation, and farm assistance. Huey Long assassinated in Louisiana

1936 Germans occupy Rhineland. Italy annexes Ethiopia. Rome-Berlin Axis proclaimed (Japan to join in **1940**). Trotsky exiled to Mexico. King George V dies; succeeded by son, Edward VIII, who soon abdicated to marry American-born divorcée, and is succeeded by brother, George VI. Spanish civil war begins. (Franco's fascist forces defeat Loyalist forces by **1939**, when Madrid falls.) War between China and Japan begins, to continue through World War II. Japan and Germany sign anti-Comintern pact; joined by Italy in **1937**.

1937 Hitler repudiates war guilt clause of Versailles Treaty; continues to build German power. Italy withdraws from League of Nations. U.S. gunboat *Panay* sunk by Japanese in Yangtze River. Japan invades China, conquers most of coastal area. Amelia Earhart lost somewhere in Pacific on round-the-world flight.

1938 Hitler marches into Austria; political and geographical union of Germany and Austria proclaimed. Munich Pact—Britain, France, and Italy agree to let Germany partition Czechoslovakia. Douglas "Wrong-Way" Corrigan flies from New York to Dublin.

1939 Germany occupies Bohemia and Moravia; renounces pacts with Poland and England and concludes 10-year non-aggression pact with U.S.S.R. Russo-Finnish War begins; Finns to lose one-tenth of territory in **1940** peace treaty. World War II begins (*see* special material on "World War II"). In U.S., Roosevelt submits $1,319-million defense budget, proclaims U.S. neutrality, and declares limited emergency. Einstein writes FDR about feasibility of atomic bomb. New York World's Fair opens.

1940 Trotsky assassinated in Mexico. Estonia, Latvia, and Lithuania annexed by U.S.S.R. U.S. trades 50 destroyers for leases on British bases in Western Hemisphere. Selective Service Act signed.

**Amelia Earhart
(1898-1937)**

WORLD WAR II (1939–1945)

Axis powers (Germany, Italy, Japan, Hungary, Romania, Bulgaria) *vs.* Allies (U.S., Britain, France, U.S.S.R., Australia, Belgium, Brazil, Canada, China, Denmark, Greece, Netherlands, New Zealand, Norway, Poland, South Africa, Yugoslavia).

1939 Germany invades Poland and annexes Danzig; Britain and France give Hitler ultimatum **(Sept. 1)**, declare war **(Sept. 3)**. Disabled German pocket battleship *Admiral Graf Spee* blown up off Montevideo, Uruguay, on Hitler's orders **(Dec. 17)**. Limited activity ("Sitzkrieg") on Western Front.

1940 Nazis invade Netherlands, Belgium, and Luxembourg **(May 10)**. Chamberlain resigns as Prime Minister; Churchill takes over **(May 10)**. Germans cross French frontier **(May 12)** using air/tank/infantry "Blitzkrieg" tactics. Dunkerque evacuation—about 335,000 out of 400,000 Allied soldiers rescued from Belgium by British civilian and naval craft **(May 26–June 3)**. Italy declares war on France and Britain; invades France **(June 10)**. Germans enter Paris; city undefended **(June 14)**. France and Germany sign armistice at Compiègne **(June 22)**. Nazis bomb Coventry, England **(Nov. 14)**.

1941 Germans launch attacks in Balkans. Yugoslavia surrenders—General Mihajlovic continues guerrilla warfare; Tito leads left-wing guerrillas **(April 17)**. Nazi tanks enter Athens; remnants of British Army quit Greece **(April 27)**. Hitler attacks Russia **(June 22)**. Atlantic Charter—FDR and Churchill agree on war aims **(Aug. 14)**. Japanese attacks on Pearl Harbor, Philippines, Guam force U.S. into war; U.S. Pacific fleet crippled **(Dec. 7)**. U.S. and Britain declare war on Japan. Germany and Italy declare war on U.S.; Congress declares war on those countries **(Dec. 11)**.

1942 British surrender Singapore to Japanese **(Feb. 15)**. U.S. forces on Bataan peninsula in Philippines surrender **(April 9)**. U.S. and Filipino troops on Corregidor island in Manila Bay surrender to Japanese **(May 6)**. Village of Lidice in Czechoslovakia razed by Nazis **(June 10)**. U.S. and

Britain land in French North Africa **(Nov. 8)**.

1943 Casablanca Conference—Churchill and FDR agree on unconditional surrender goal **(Jan. 14–24)**. German 6th Army surrenders at Stalingrad—turning point of war in Russia **(Feb. 1–2)**. Remnants of Nazis trapped on Cape Bon, ending war in Africa **(May 12)**. Mussolini deposed; Badoglio named premier **(July 25)**. Allied troops land on Italian mainland after conquest of Sicily **(Sept. 3)**. Italy surrenders **(Sept. 8)**. Nazis seize Rome **(Sept. 10)**. Cairo Conference: FDR, Churchill, Chiang Kai-shek pledge defeat of Japan, free Korea **(Nov. 22–26)**. Teheran Conference: FDR, Churchill, Stalin agree on invasion plans **(Nov. 28–Dec. 1)**.

1944 U.S. and British troops land at Anzio on west Italian coast and hold beachhead **(Jan. 22)**. U.S. and British troops enter Rome **(June 4)**. D-Day—Allies launch Normandy invasion **(June 6)**. Hitler wounded in bomb plot **(July 20)**. Paris liberated **(Aug. 25)**. Athens freed by Allies **(Oct. 13)**. Americans invade Philippines **(Oct. 20)**. Germans launch counteroffensive in Belgium—Battle of Bulge **(Dec. 16)**.

1945 Yalta Agreement signed by FDR, Churchill, Stalin—establishes basis for occupation of Germany, returns to Soviet Union lands taken by Germany and Japan; U.S.S.R. agrees to friendship pact with China **(Feb. 11)**. Mussolini killed at Lake Como **(April 28)**. Admiral Doenitz takes command in Germany; suicide of Hitler announced **(May 1)**. Berlin falls **(May 2)**. V-E Day—Germany signs unconditional surrender terms at Rheims **(May 7)**. Potsdam Conference—Truman, Churchill, Atlee (after **July 28**), Stalin establish council of foreign ministers to prepare peace treaties; plan German postwar government and reparations **(July 17–Aug. 2)**. A-bomb blasts Hiroshima **(Aug. 6)**. U.S.S.R. declares war on Japan **(Aug. 8)**. Nagasaki hit by A-bomb **(Aug. 9)**. Japan surrenders **(Aug. 14)**. V-J Day—Japanese sign surrender terms aboard battleship *Missouri* **(Sept. 2)**.

D-Day, June 6, 1944

**Winston Churchill,
Franklin D. Roosevelt,
and Joseph V. Stalin
at Yalta**

**Harry S. Truman
(1884–1972)**

1941 Japanese surprise attack on U.S. fleet at Pearl Harbor brings U.S. into World War II. Manhattan Project (atomic bomb research) begins. Roosevelt enunciates "four freedoms," signs lend-lease act, declares national emergency, promises aid to U.S.S.R.

1942 Declaration of United Nations signed in Washington. Women's military services established. Enrico Fermi achieves nuclear chain reaction. Japanese and persons of Japanese ancestry moved inland from Pacific Coast. Coconut Grove nightclub fire in Boston kills 491.

1943 President freezes prices, salaries, and wages to prevent inflation. Income tax withholding introduced.

1944 G.I. Bill of Rights enacted. Bretton Woods Conference creates International Monetary Fund and World Bank. Dumbarton Oaks Conference—U.S., British Commonwealth, and U.S.S.R. propose establishment of United Nations.

1945 Yalta Conference (Roosevelt, Churchill, Stalin) plans final defeat of Germany (**Feb.**). Germany surrenders (**May 7**). San Francisco Conference establishes U.N. (**April–June**). FDR dies (April 12). Potsdam Conference (Truman, Churchill, Stalin) establishes basis of German reconstruction (**July–Aug**). Japan signs surrender (**Sept. 2**).

1946 First meeting of U.N. General Assembly opens in London (**Jan. 10**). League of Nations dissolved (**April**). Italy abolishes monarchy (**June**). Verdict in Nuremberg war trial: 12 Nazi leaders (including 1 tried in absentia) sentenced to hang; 7 imprisoned; 3 acquitted (**Oct. 1**). Goering commits suicide a few hours before 10 other Nazis are executed (**Oct. 15**). Winston Churchill's "Iron Curtain" speech warns of Soviet expansion.

1947 Britain nationalizes coal mines (**Jan. 1**). Peace treaties for Italy, Romania, Bulgaria, Hungary, Finland signed in Paris (**Feb. 10**). Soviet Union rejects U.S. plan for U.N. atomic-energy control (**March 4**). Truman Doctrine proposed—the first significant U.S. attempt to "contain" communist expansion (**March 12**). Marshall Plan for European recovery proposed—a coordinated program to help European nations recover from ravages of war (**June**). (By 1951, this "European Recovery Program" had cost $11 billion.) India and Pakistan gain independence from Britain (**Aug. 15**). Cominform (Communist Information Bureau) founded under Soviet auspices to rebuild contacts among European Communist parties, missing since dissolution of Comintern in 1943 (**Sept.**). (Yugoslav party expelled in 1948 and Cominform disbanded in 1956.)

1948 Gandhi assassinated in New Delhi by Hindu fanatic (**Jan. 30**). Communists seize power in Czechoslovakia (**Feb. 23–25**). Burma and Ceylon granted independence by Britain. Organization of American States (OAS) Charter signed at Bogotá, Colombia (**April 30**). Nation of Israel proclaimed; British mandate ends at midnight; Arab armies attack (**May 14**). Berlin airlift begins (**June 21**); ends May 12, 1949. Stalin and Tito break (**June 28**). Independent Republic of Korea is proclaimed, following election supervised by U.N. (**Aug. 15**). Verdict in Japanese war trial: Tojo and six others sentenced to hang (hanged Dec. 23); 18 imprisoned (**Nov. 12**). United States of Indonesia established as Dutch and Indonesians settled conflict (**Dec. 27**). Alger Hiss, former U.S. State Department official, indicted on perjury charges after denying passing secret documents to communist spy ring. Convicted in second trial (**1950**) and sentenced to five-year prison term.

1949 Cease-fire in Palestine (**Jan. 7**). Truman proposes Point Four Program to help world's backward areas (**Jan. 20**). Israel signs armistice with Egypt (**Feb. 24**). Start of North Atlantic Treaty Organization (NATO)—treaty signed by 12 nations (**April 4**). German Federal Republic (West Germany) established (**Sept. 21**). Truman discloses Soviet Union has set off atomic explosion (**Sept. 23**). Communist People's Republic of China formally proclaimed by Chairman Mao Zedong. (**Oct. 1**).

1950 Truman orders development of hydrogen bomb (**Jan. 31**). Korean War (*see* special material on the "Korean War"). Assassination attempt on President Truman by Puerto Rican nationalists (**Nov. 1**). Brink's robbery in Boston; almost $3 million stolen (**Jan. 17**).

KOREAN WAR (1950–1953)

1950 North Korean Communist forces invade South Korea (June 25). U.N. calls for cease-fire and asks U.N. members to assist South Korea (June 27). Truman orders U.S. forces into Korea (June 27). North Koreans capture Seoul (June 28). Gen. Douglas MacArthur designated commander of unified U.N. forces (July 8). Pusan Beachhead—U.N. forces counterattack and capture Seoul (Aug.–Sept.), capture Pyongyang, North Korean capital (Oct.). Chinese Communists enter war (Oct. 26), force U.N. retreat toward 39th parallel (Dec.).

1951 Gen. Matthew B. Ridgeway replaces MacArthur after he threatens Chinese with massive retaliation (April 11). Armistice negotiations (July) continue with interruptions until June 1953.

1953 Armistice signed (June 26). Chinese troops withdraw from North Korea (Oct. 26, 1958), but over 200 violations of armistice noted in 1959.

1951 Six nations agree to Schuman Plan to pool European coal and steel (**March 19**)—in effect **Feb. 10, 1953.** Julius and Ethel Rosenberg sentenced to death for passing atomic secrets to Russians (**March**). Japanese peace treaty signed in San Francisco by 49 nations (**Sept. 8**). Color television introduced in U.S.

1952 George VI dies; his daughter becomes Elizabeth II (**Feb. 6**). NATO conference approves European army (**Feb.**). AEC announces "satisfactory" experiments in hydrogen-weapons research; eyewitnesses tell of blasts near Enewetak (**Nov.**).

1953 Gen. Dwight D. Eisenhower inaugurated President of United States (**Jan. 20**). Stalin dies (**March 5**). Malenkov becomes Soviet Premier; Beria, Minister of Interior; Molotov, Foreign Minister (**March 6**). Dag Hammarskjold begins term as U.N. Secretary-General (**April 10**). Edmund Hillary, of New Zealand, and Tenzing Norkay, of Nepal, reach top of Mt. Everest (**May 29**). East Berliners rise against Communist rule; quelled by tanks (**June 17**). Egypt becomes republic ruled by military junta (**June 18**). Julius and Ethel Rosenberg executed in Sing Sing prison (**June 19**). Korean armistice signed (**July 27**). Moscow announces explosion of hydrogen bomb (**Aug. 20**).

Dwight D. Eisenhower
(1890-1969)

1954 First atomic submarine *Nautilus*, launched (**Jan. 21**). Five U.S. Congressmen shot on floor of House as Puerto Rican nationalists fire from spectators' gallery; all five recover (**March 1**). Army *vs.* McCarthy inquiry—Senate subcommittee report blames both sides (**Apr. 22–June 17**). Dien Bien Phu, French military outpost in Vietnam, falls to Vietminh army (**May 7**). (*see* special material on the "Vietnam War.") U.S. Supreme Court (in *Brown* v. *Board of Education of Topeka*) unanimously bans racial segregation in public schools (**May 17**). Eisenhower launches world atomic pool without Soviet Union (**Sept. 6**). Eight-nation Southeast Asia defense treaty (SEATO) signed at Manila (**Sept. 8**). West Germany is granted sovereignty, admitted to NATO and Western European Union (**Oct. 23**). Dr. Jonas Salk starts innoculating children against polio. Algerian War of Independence against France begins (**Nov.**); France struggles to maintain colonial rule until 1962 when it agrees to Algeria's independence.

Joseph Stalin
(1879-1953)

1955 Nikolai A. Bulganin becomes Soviet Premier, replacing Malenkov (**Feb. 8**). Churchill resigns; Anthony Eden succeeds him (**April 6**). Federal Republic of West Germany becomes a sovereign state (**May 5**). Warsaw Pact,

---

VIETNAM WAR (1950–1975)

U.S., South Vietnam, and Allies versus North Vietnam and National Liberation Front (Viet Cong). Outstanding events:

1950 President Truman sends 35-man military advisory group to aid French fighting to maintain colonial power in Vietnam.

1954 After defeat of French at Dienbienphu, Geneva Agreements (**July**) provide for withdrawal of French and Vietminh to either side of demarcation zone (DMZ) pending reunification elections, which are never held. Presidents Eisenhower and Kennedy (from **1954** onward) send civilian advisors and, later, military personnel to train South Vietnamese.

1960 Communists from National Liberation Front in South.

1963 Ngo Dinh Diem, South Vietnam's premier, slain in coup (**Nov. 1**).

1961–1963 U.S. military advisors rise from 2,000 to 15,000.

1964 North Vietnamese torpedo boats reportedly attack U.S. destroyers in Gulf of Tonkin (**Aug. 2**). President Johnson orders retaliatory air strikes. Congress approves Gulf of Tonkin resolution (**Aug. 7**) authorizing President to take necessary steps to "maintain peace."

1965 U.S. planes begin combat missions over South Vietnam. In **June**, 23,000 American advisors committed to combat. By end of year over 184,000 U.S. troops in area.

1966 B-52s bomb DMZ, reportedly used by North Vietnam for entry into South (**July 31**).

1967 South Vietnam National Assembly approves election of Nguyen Van Thieu as President (**Oct. 21**).

1968 U.S. has almost 525,000 men in Vietnam. In Tet offensive (**Jan.–Feb.**), Viet Cong guerrillas attack Saigon, Hue, and some provincial capitals. President Johnson orders halt to U.S. bombardment of North Vietnam (**Oct. 31**). Saigon and N.L.F. join U.S. and North Vietnam in Paris peace talks.

1969 President Nixon announces Vietnam peace offer

(**May 14**)—begins troop withdrawals (**June**). Viet Cong forms Provisional Revolutionary Government. U.S. Senate calls for curb on commitments (**June 25**). Ho Chi Minh, 79, North Vietnam president, dies (**Sept. 3**); collective leadership chosen. Some 6,000 U.S. troops pulled back from Thailand and 1,000 marines from Vietnam (announced **Sept. 30**). Massive demonstrations in U.S. protest or support war policies (**Oct. 15**).

1970 Nixon announces sending of troops to Cambodia (**April 30**). Last U.S. troops removed from Cambodia (**June 29**).

1971 Congress bars use of combat troops, but not air power, in Laos and Cambodia (**Jan. 1**). South Vietnamese troops, with U.S. air cover, fail in Laos thrust. Many American ground forces withdrawn from Vietnam combat. *New York Times* publishes Pentagon papers, classified material on expansion of war (**June**).

1972 Nixon responds to North Vietnamese drive across DMZ by ordering mining of North Vietnam ports and heavy bombing of Hanoi-Haiphong area (**April 1**). Nixon orders "Christmas bombing" of north to get North Vietnamese back to conference table (**Dec.**).

1973 President orders halt to offensive operations in North Vietnam (**Jan. 15**). Representatives of North and South Vietnam, U.S., and N.L.F. sign peace pacts in Paris, ending longest war in U.S. history (**Jan. 27**). Last American troops departed in their entirety (**March 29**).

1974 Both sides accuse each other of frequent violations of cease-fire agreement.

1975 Full-scale warfare resumes. Communists victorious (**April 30**). South Vietnam Premier Nguyen Van Thieu resigns (**April 21**). U.S. Marine Embassy guards and U.S. civilians and dependents evacuated (**April 30**). More than 140,000 Vietnamese refugees leave by air and sea, many to settle in U.S. Provisional Revolutionary Government takes control (**June 6**).

1976 Election of National Assembly paves way for reunification of North and South.

Yuri A. Gagarin
(1934-1968)

Fidel Castro
(Aug. 13, 1926)

east European mutual defense agreement, signed **(May 14).** Argentina ousts Perón **(Sept. 19).** President Eisenhower suffers coronary thrombosis in Denver **(Sept. 24).** Martin Luther King, Jr., leads black boycott of Montgomery, Ala., bus system **(Dec. 1);** desegregated service begun **(Dec. 21).** AFL and CIO become one organization—AFL-CIO **(Dec. 5).**

1956 Nikita Khrushchev, First Secretary of U.S.S.R. Communist Party, denounces Stalin's excesses **(Feb. 24).** First aerial H-bomb tested over Namu islet, Bikini Atoll—10 million tons TNT equivalent **(May 21).** Worker's uprising against Communist rule in Poznan, Poland, is crushed **(June 28–30).** Egypt takes control of Suez Canal **(July 26).** Israel launches attack on Egypt's Sinai peninsula and drives toward Suez Canal **(Oct. 29).** British and French invade Egypt at Port Said **(Nov. 5).** Cease-fire forced by U.S. pressure stops British, French, and Israeli advance **(Nov. 6).** Revolt starts in Hungary—Soviet troops and tanks crush anti-Communist rebellion **(Nov.).**

1957 Eisenhower Doctrine calls for aid to Mideast countries which resist armed aggression from Communist-controlled nations **(Jan. 5).** Eisenhower sends troops to Little Rock, Ark., to quell mob and protect school integration **(Sept. 24).** Russians launch *Sputnik I,* first earth-orbiting satellite—the Space Age begins **(Oct. 4).**

1958 Army's Jupiter-C rocket fires first U.S. earth satellite, *Explorer I,* into orbit **(Jan. 31).** Egypt and Syria merge into United Arab Republic **(Feb. 1).** European Economic Community (Common Market) established by Rome Treaty becomes effective **Jan. 1, 1958.** Khrushchev becomes Premier of Soviet Union as Bulganin resigns **(Mar. 27).** Gen. Charles de Gaulle becomes French premier **(June 1),** remaining in power until **1969.** New French constitution adopted **(Sept. 28),** de Gaulle elected president of 5th Republic **(Dec. 21).** Eisenhower orders U.S. Marines into Lebanon at request of President Chamoun, who fears overthrow **(July 15).**

1959 Cuban President Batista resigns and flees—Castro takes over **(Jan. 1).** Tibet's Dalai Lama escapes to India **(Mar. 31).** St. Lawrence Seaway opens, allowing ocean ships to reach Midwest **(April 25).**

1960 American U-2 spy plane, piloted by Francis Gary Powers, shot down over Russia **(May 1).** Khrushchev kills Paris summit conference because of U-2 **(May 16).** Powers sentenced to prison for 10 years **(Aug. 19)**—freed in **February 1962** in exchange for Soviet spy. Top Nazi murderer of Jews, Adolf Eichmann, captured by Israelis in Argentina **(May 23)**—executed in Israel in **1962.** Communist China and Soviet Union split in conflict over Communist ideology. Belgium starts to break up its African colonial empire, gives independence to Belgian Congo (Zaire) on **June 30.** Cuba begins confiscation of $770 million of U.S. property **(Aug. 7).**

1961 U.S. breaks diplomatic relations with Cuba **(Jan. 3).** John F. Kennedy inaugurated President of U.S. **(Jan. 20).** Kennedy proposes Alliance for Progress—10-year plan to raise Latin American living standards **(Mar. 13).** Moscow announces putting first man in orbit around earth, Maj. Yuri A. Gagarin **(April 12).** Cuba invaded at Bay of Pigs by an estimated 1,200 anti-Castro exiles aided by U.S.; invasion crushed **(April 17).** First U.S. spaceman, Navy Cmdr. Alan B. Shepard, Jr., rockets 116.5 miles up in 302-mile trip **(May 5).** Virgil Grissom becomes second American astronaut, making 118-mile-high, 303-mile-long rocket flight over Atlantic **(July 21).** Gherman Stepanovich Titov is launched in Soviet spaceship *Vostok II:* makes 17 1/2 orbits in 25 hours, covering 434,960 miles before landing safely **(Aug. 6).** East Germans erect Berlin Wall between East and West Berlin to halt flood of refugees **(Aug. 13).** U.S.S.R. fires 50-megaton hydrogen bomb, biggest explosion in history **(Oct. 29).**

1962 Lt. Col. John H. Glenn, Jr., is first American to orbit earth—three times in 4 hr 55 min **(Feb. 20).** Adolf Eichmann hanged in Israel for his part in Nazi extermination of six million Jews **(May 31).** France transfers sovereignty to new republic of Algeria **(July 3).** Cuban missile crisis—U.S.S.R. to build missile bases in Cuba; Kennedy orders Cuban blockade, lifts blockade after Russians back down **(Aug.-Nov.).** James H. Meredith, escorted by Federal marshals, registers in University of Mississippi **(Oct. 1).** Pope John XXIII opens Second Vatican Council **(Oct. 11)**—Council holds four sessions, finally closing Dec. 8, 1965. Cuba releases 1,113 prisoners of 1961 invasion attempt **(Dec. 24).**

1963 France and West Germany sign treaty of cooperation ending four centuries of conflict **(Jan. 22).** Pope John XXIII dies **(June 3)**—succeeded June 21 by Cardinal Montini, who becomes Paul VI. U.S. Supreme Court rules no locality may require recitation of Lord's Prayer or Bible verses in public schools **(June 17).** Civil rights rally held by 200,000 blacks and whites in Washington, D.C. **(Aug. 28).** Washington-to-Moscow "hot line" communications link opens, designed to reduce risk of accidental war **(Aug. 30).** President Kennedy shot and killed by sniper in Dallas, Tex. Lyndon B.

Johnson becomes President same day (**Nov. 22**). Lee Harvey Oswald, accused assassin of President Kennedy, is shot and killed by Jack Ruby, Dallas nightclub owner (**Nov. 24**).

1964 U.S. Supreme Court rules that Congressional districts should be roughly equal in population (**Feb. 17**). Jack Ruby convicted of murder in slaying of Lee Harvey Oswald; sentenced to death by Dallas jury (**March 14**)—conviction reversed **Oct. 5, 1966**; Ruby dies **Jan. 3, 1967**, before second trial can be held. Three civil rights workers—Schwerner, Goodman, and Cheney—murdered in Mississippi (**June**). Twenty-one arrests result in trial and conviction of seven by Federal jury. President's Commission on the Assassination of President Kennedy issues Warren Report concluding that Lee Harvey Oswald acted alone.

1965 Rev. Dr. Martin Luther King, Jr., and more than 2,600 other blacks arrested in Selma, Ala., during three-day demonstrations against voter-registration rules (**Feb. 1**). Malcolm X, black-nationalist leader, shot to death at Harlem rally in New York City (**Feb. 21**). U.S. Marines land in Dominican Republic as fighting persists between rebels and Dominican army (**April 28**). Medicare, senior citizens' government medical assistance program, begins (**July 1**). Blacks riot for six days in Watts section of Los Angeles: 34 dead, over 1,000 injured, nearly 4,000 arrested, fire damage put at $175 million (**Aug. 11-16**). Power failure in Ontario plant blacks out parts of eight northeastern states of U.S. and two provinces of southeastern Canada (**Nov. 9**).

John F. Kennedy
(1917-1963)

1966 Black teen-agers riot in Watts, Los Angeles; two men killed and at least 25 injured (**March 15**). Michael E. De Bakey implants artificial heart in human for first time at Houston hospital; plastic device functions and patient lives (**April 21**).

1967 Three Apollo astronauts—Col. Virgil I. Grissom, Col. Edward White II, and Lt. Cmdr. Roger B. Chaffee—killed in spacecraft fire during simulated launch (**Jan. 27**). Israeli and Arab forces battle; six-day war ends with Israel occupying Sinai Peninsula, Golan Heights, Gaza Strip, and east bank of Suez Canal (**June 5**). Red China announces explosion of its first hydrogen bomb (**June 17**). Racial violence in Detroit; 7,000 National Guardsmen aid police after night of rioting. Similar outbreaks occur in New York City's Spanish Harlem, Rochester, N.Y., Birmingham, Ala., and New Britain, Conn. (**July 23**). Thurgood Marshall sworn in as first black U.S. Supreme Court justice (**Oct. 2**). Dr. Christiaan N. Barnard and team of South African surgeons perform world's first successful human heart transplant (**Dec. 3**)—patient dies 18 days later.

1968 North Korea seizes U.S. Navy ship *Pueblo;* holds 83 on board as spies (**Jan. 23**). President Johnson announces he will not seek or accept presidential renomination (**March 31**). Martin Luther King, Jr., civil rights leader, is slain in Memphis (**April 4**)—James Earl Ray, indicted in murder, captured in London on **June 8**. In 1969 Ray pleads guilty and is sentenced to 99 years. Sen. Robert F. Kennedy is shot and critically wounded in Los Angeles hotel after winning California primary (**June 5**)—dies **June 6**. Sirhan B. Sirhan convicted **1969**. Czechoslovakia is invaded by Russians and Warsaw Pact forces to crush liberal regime (**Aug. 20**).

Lyndon B. Johnson
(1908-1973)

1969 Richard M. Nixon is inaugurated 37th President of the U.S. (**Jan. 20**). Apollo 11 astronauts—Neil A. Armstrong, Edwin E. Aldrin, Jr., and Michael Collins—take man's first walk on moon (**July 20**). Sen. Edward M. Kennedy pleads guilty to leaving scene of fatal accident at Chappaquiddick, Mass. (**July 18**) in which Mary Jo Kopechne was drowned—gets two-month suspended sentence (**July 25**).

1970 Biafra surrenders after 32-month fight for independence from Nigeria (**Jan. 12**). Rhodesia severs last tie with British Crown and declares itself a racially segregated republic (**March 1**). Four students at Kent State University in Ohio slain by National Guardsmen at demonstration protesting April 30 incursion into Cambodia (**May 4**). Senate repeals Gulf of Tonkin resolution (**June 24**).

1971 Supreme Court rules unanimously that busing of students may be ordered to achieve racial desegregation (**April 20**). Anti-war militants attempt to disrupt government business in Washington (**May 3**)—police and military units arrest as many as 12,000; most are later released. Twenty-sixth Amendment to U.S. Constitution lowers voting age to 18. U.N. seats Communist China and expels Nationalist China (**Oct. 25**).

Martin Luther King, Jr.
(1929-1968)

1972 President Nixon makes unprecedented eight-day visit to Communist China (**Feb.**). Britain takes over direct rule of Northern Ireland in bid for peace (**March 24**). Gov. George C. Wallace of Alabama is shot by Arthur H. Bremer at Laurel, Md., political rally (**May 15**). Five men are apprehended by police in attempt to bug Democratic National Committee headquarters in Washington D.C.'s Watergate complex—start of the Watergate scandal (**June 17**). Supreme Court rules that death penalty is unconstitutional

**Richard M. Nixon
(Jan. 9, 1913)**

(June 29). Eleven Israeli athletes at Olympic Games in Munich are killed after eight members of an Arab terrorist group invade Olympic Village; five guerrillas and one policeman are also killed **(Sept. 5).**

1973 Great Britain, Ireland, and Denmark enter European Common Market **(Jan. 1).** Nixon, on national TV, accepts responsibility, but not blame, for Watergate; accepts resignations of advisers H. R. Haldeman and John D. Ehrlichman, fires John W. Dean III as counsel. **(April 30).** Greek military junta abolishes monarchy and proclaims republic **(June 1).** U.S. bombing of Cambodia ends, marking official halt to 12 years of combat activity in Southeast Asia **(Aug. 15).** Fourth and biggest Arab-Israeli War begins as Egyptian and Syrian forces attack Israel as Jews mark Yom Kippur, holiest day in their calendar. **(Oct. 6).** Spiro T. Agnew resigns as Vice President and then, in Federal Court in Baltimore, pleads no contest to charges of evasion of income taxes on $29,500 he received in 1967, while Governor of Maryland. He is fined $10,000 and put on three years' probation **(Oct. 10).** In the "Saturday Night Massacre," Nixon fires special Watergate prosecutor Archibald Cox and Deputy Attorney General William D. Ruckelshaus; Attorney General Elliot L. Richardson resigns **(Oct. 20).** Egypt and Israel sign U.S.-sponsored cease-fire accord **(Nov. 11).**

1974 Patricia Hearst, 19-year-old daughter of publisher Randolph Hearst, kidnapped by Symbionese Liberation Army. **(Feb. 5).** House Judiciary Committee adopts three articles of impeachment charging President Nixon with obstruction of justice, failure to uphold laws, and refusal to produce material subpoenaed by the committee **(July 30).** Richard M. Nixon announces he will resign the next day, the first President to do so **(Aug. 8).** Vice President Gerald R. Ford of Michigan is sworn in as 38th President of the U.S. **(Aug. 9).** Ford grants "full, free, and absolute pardon" to ex-President Nixon **(Sept. 8).**

1975 John N. Mitchell, H. R. Haldeman, John D. Ehrlichman, and Robert C. Mardian found guilty of Watergate cover-up. Mitchell, Haldeman, and Ehrlichman are sentenced on Feb. 21 to 30 months-8 years in jail and Mardian to 10 months-3 years **(Jan. 1).** American merchant ship *Mayaguez,* seized by Cambodian forces, is rescued in operation by U.S. Navy and Marines, 38 of whom are killed **(May 15).** *Apollo* and *Soyuz* spacecraft take off for U.S.-Soviet link-up in space **(July 15).** President Ford escapes assassination attempt in Sacramento, Calif., **(Sept. 5).** President Ford escapes second assassination attempt in 17 days. **(Sept. 22).**

1976 Supreme Court rules that blacks and other minorities are entitled to retroactive job seniority **(March 24).** Ford signs Federal Election Campaign Act **(May 11).** Supreme Court rules that death penalty is not inherently cruel or unusual and is a constitutionally acceptable form of punishment **(July 3).** Nation celebrates Bicentennial **(July 4).** Israeli airborne commandos attack Uganda's Entebbe Airport and free 103 hostages held by pro-Palestinian hijackers of Air France plane; one Israeli and several Ugandan soldiers killed in raid **(July 4).** Mysterious disease that eventually claims 29 lives strikes American Legion convention in Philadelphia **(Aug. 4).** Jimmy Carter elected U.S. President **(Nov. 2).**

**Viking I and II
(Launched 1975)**

1977 First woman Episcopal priest ordained **(Jan. 1).** Scientists identify previously unknown bacterium as cause of mysterious "legionnaire's disease" **(Jan. 18).** Carter pardons Vietnam draft evaders **(Jan. 21).** Scientists report using bacteria in lab to make insulin **(May 23).** Supreme Court rules that states are not required to spend Medicaid funds on elective abortions **(June 20).** Deng Xiaoping, purged Chinese leader, restored to power as "Gang of Four" is expelled from Communist Party **(July 22).** Nuclear–proliferation pact, curbing spread of nuclear weapons, signed by 15 countries, including U.S. and U.S.S.R. **(Sept. 21).**

**Voyager I and II
(Launched 1977)**

1978 President chooses Federal Appeals Court Judge William H. Webster as F.B.I. Director **(Jan. 19).** Rhodesia's Prime Minister Ian D. Smith and three black leaders agree on transfer to black majority rule **(Feb. 15).** Former Italian Premier Aldo Moro kidnapped by leftwing terrorists, who kill five bodyguards **(March 16);** he is found slain **(May 9).** U.S. Senate approves Panama Canal neutrality treaty **(March 16);** votes treaty to turn canal over to Panama by year 2000 **(April 18).** Californians in referendum approve Proposition 13 for nearly 60% slash in property tax revenues **(June 6).** Supreme Court, in Bakke case, bars quota systems in college admissions but affirms constitutionality of programs giving advantage to minorities **(June 28).** Pope Paul VI, dead at 80, mourned **(Aug. 6);** new Pope, John Paul I, 65, dies unexpectedly after 34 days in office **(Sept. 28);** succeeded by Karol Cardinal Wojtyla of Poland as John Paul II **(Oct. 16).** "Framework for Peace" in Middle East signed by Egypt's President Anwar el-Sadat and Israel Premier Menachem Begin after 13-day conference at Camp David led by President Carter **(Sept. 17).**

1979 Oil spills pollute ocean waters in Atlantic and Gulf of Mexico **(Jan. 1,**

June 8, July 21). Ohio agrees to pay $675,000 to families of dead and injured in Kent State University shootings **(Jan. 4).** Vietnam and Cambodian insurgents it backs announce fall of Phnom Penh, Cambodian capital, and collapse of Pol Pot regime **(Jan. 7).** Shah leaves Iran after year of turmoil **(Jan. 16);** revolutionary forces under Moslem leader, Ayatollah Ruhollah Khomeini, take over **(Feb. 1** et seq.). Conservatives win British election; Margaret Thatcher new Prime Minister **(March 28).** Nuclear power plant accident at Three Mile Island, Pa., releases radioactivity **(March 28).** Carter and Brezhnev sign SALT II agreement **(June 14).** Nicaraguan President Gen. Anastasio Somoza Debayle resigns and flees to Miami **(July 17);** Sandinistas form government **(July 19).** Earl Mountbatten of Burma, 79, British World War II hero, and three others killed by blast on fishing boat off Irish coast **(Aug. 27);** two I.R.A. members accused **(Aug. 30).** Iranian militants seize U.S. Embassy in Teheran and hold hostages **(Nov. 4).** Soviet invasion of Afghanistan stirs world protests **(Dec. 27).**

Margaret Thatcher
(Oct. 13, 1925)

1980 Six U.S. Embassy aides escape from Iran with Canadian help **(Jan. 29).** F.B.I.'s undercover operation "Abscam" (for Arab scam) implicates public officials **(Feb. 2).** U.S. breaks diplomatic ties with Iran **(April 7).** Eight U.S. servicemen are injured and five are injured as helicopter and cargo plane collide in abortive desert raid to rescue American hostages in Teheran **(April 25).** Supreme Court upholds limits on Federal aid for abortions **(June 30).** Shah of Iran dies at 60 **(July 27).** Anastasio Somoza Debayle, ousted Nicaraguan ruler, and two aides assassinated in Asunción, Paraguay capital **(Sept. 17).** Iraq troops hold 90 square miles of Iran after invasion **(Sept. 19).** Ronald Reagan elected President in Republican sweep **(Nov. 4).** Three U.S. nuns and lay worker found shot in El Salvador **(Dec. 4).** John Lennon of Beatles shot dead in New York City **(Dec. 8).**

1981 U.S.-Iran agreement frees 52 hostages held in Teheran since Nov. 4, 1979 **(Jan. 18);** hostages welcomed back in U.S. **(Jan. 25).** Ronald Reagan takes oath as 40th President **(Jan. 20).** President Reagan wounded by gunman, with press secretary and two law-enforcement officers **(March 30).** Pope John Paul II wounded by gunman **(May 14).** Supreme Court rules, 4-4, that former President Nixon and three top aides may be required to pay monetary damages for unconstitutional wiretap of home telephone of former national security aide **(June 22).** Reagan nominates Judge Sandra Day O'Connor, 51, of Arizona, as first woman on Supreme Court **(July 7).** More than 110 die in collapse of aerial walkways in lobby of Hyatt Regency Hotel in Kansas City; 188 injured **(July 18).** Air controllers strike, disrupting flights **(Aug. 3);** Government dismisses strikers **(Aug. 11).**

Sally K. Ride
(May 26, 1951)

1982 British overcome Argentina in Falklands war **(April 2-June 15).** Israel invades Lebanon in attack on P.L.O. **(June 4).** John W. Hinckley, Jr. found not guilty because of insanity in shooting of President Reagan **(June 21).** Alexander M. Haig, Jr. resigns as Secretary of State **(June 25).** Equal rights amendment fails ratification **(June 30).** Lebanese Christian Phalangists kill hundreds of people in two Palestinian refugee camps in West Beirut **(Sept. 15).** Princess Grace, 52, dies of injuries when car plunges off mountain road; daughter, Stephanie, 17, suffers serious injuries **(Sept. 14).** Leonid I. Brezhnev, Soviet leader, dies at 75 **(Nov. 10).** Yuri V. Andropov, 68, chosen as successor **(Nov. 15).** Artificial heart implanted for first time in Dr. Barney B. Clark, 61, at University of Utah Medical Center in Salt Lake City **(Dec. 2);** Barney Clark dies **(March 23, 1983).**

1983 Pope John Paul II signs new Roman Catholic code incorporating changes brought about by Second Vatican Council **(Jan. 25).** Second space shuttle, *Challenger*, makes successful maiden voyage, which includes the first U.S. space walk in nine years **(April 4).** U.S. Supreme Court declares many local abortion restrictions unconstitutional **(June 15).** Sally K. Ride, 32, first U.S. woman astronaut in space as a crew member aboard space shuttle *Challenger* **(June 18).** U.S. admits shielding former Nazi Gestapo chief, Klaus Barbie, 69, the "butcher of Lyons," wanted in France for war crimes **(Aug. 15).** Benigno S. Aquino, Jr., 50, political rival of Philippines President Marcos, slain in Manila **(Aug. 21).** South Korean Boeing 747 jetliner bound for Seoul apparently strays into Soviet airspace and is shot down by a Soviet SU-15 fighter after it had tracked the airliner for two hours; all 269 aboard are killed, including 61 Americans **(Aug. 30).** Terrorist explosion kills 237 U.S. Marines in Beirut **(Oct. 23).** U.S. and Caribbean allies invade Grenada **(Oct. 25).**

Space Shuttle Columbia
(Launched April 12, 1981)

1984 Bell System broken up **(Jan. 1).** France gets first deliveries of Soviet natural gas **(Jan. 1).** Syria frees captured U.S. Navy pilot, Lieut. Robert C. Goodman, Jr. **(Jan. 3).** U.S. and Vatican exchange diplomats after 116-year hiatus **(Jan. 10).** Reagan orders U.S. Marines withdrawn from Beirut international peacekeeping force **(Feb. 7).** Yuri V. Andropov dies at 69; Konstantin U. Chernenko, 72, named Soviet Union leader **(Feb. 9).** Italy and Vatican agree to end Roman Catholicism as state religion **(Feb. 18).** Reagan ends U.S. role in Beirut by relieving Sixth Fleet from peacekeeping force **(March 30).** Con-

**Indira Gandhi
(1917-1984)**

**Ronald W. Reagan
(Feb. 6, 1911)**

**Mikhail S. Gorbachev
(March 2, 1931)**

gress rebukes President Reagan on use of federal funds for mining Nicaraguan harbors (**April 10**). Soviet Union withdraws from summer Olympic games in U.S., and other bloc nations follow (**May 7 et seq.**). José Napoleón Duarte, moderate, elected president of El Salvador (**May 11**). Three hundred slain as Indian Army occupies Sikh Golden Temple in Amritsar (**June 6**). Thirty-ninth Democratic National Convention, in San Francisco, nominates Walter F. Mondale and Geraldine A. Ferraro (**July 16-19**). Thirty-third Republican National Convention, at Dallas, renominates President Reagan and Vice President Bush (**Aug. 20-25**). Brian Mulroney and Conservative party win Canadian election in landslide (**Sept. 4**). Indian Prime Minister Indira Gandhi assassinated by two Sikh bodyguards; 1,000 killed in anti-Sikh riots; son Rajiv succeeds her (**Oct. 31**). President Reagan re-elected in landslide with 59% of vote (**Nov. 7**). Toxic gas leaks from Union Carbide plant in Bhopal, India, killing 2,000 and injuring 150,000 (**Dec. 3**).

1985   Ronald Reagan, 73, takes oath for second term as 40th President (**Jan. 20**). New Zealand bars U.S. ship when Washington refuses to say whether ship carries nuclear arms (**Feb. 4**). Worldwide Conservative Rabbinical Assembly approves women in clergy (**Feb. 14**). General Westmoreland settles libel action against CBS (**Feb. 18**). Prime Minister Margaret Thatcher addresses Congress, endorsing Reagan's policies (**Feb. 20**). U.S.S.R. leader Chernenko dies at 73 and is replaced by Mikhail Gorbachev, 54 (**March 11**). Secretary of Labor Raymond J. Donovan, facing New York fraud trial, resigns; first sitting Cabinet member to be indicted (**March 15**). Tens of thousands mark 40th anniversary of liberation of Buchenwald death camp (**April 13**). Reagan target of wide attacks by Jewish leaders and others over visit to Bitburg Cemetery, West Germany, where SS troops are buried (**April 18 et seq. May 5**). Two Shiite Moslem gunmen capture TWA airliner with 133 aboard, 104 of them Americans (**June 14**); 39 remaining hostages freed in Beirut (**June 30**). Supreme Court, 5-4, bars public school teachers from parochial schools (**July 1**). Arthur James Walker, 50, retired naval officer, convicted by federal judge of participating in Soviet spy ring (**Aug. 9**). Thousands dead in Mexico earthquake (**Sept. 19**). P.L.O. terrorists hijack *Achille Lauro*, Italian cruise ship, with 80 passengers, plus crew (**Oct. 7**); American, Leon Klinghoffer, killed (**Oct. 8**). Italian government toppled by political crisis over hijacking of *Achille Lauro* (**Oct. 16**). John A. Walker and son, Michael I. Walker, 22, sentenced in Navy espionage case (**Oct. 28**). Volcano eruption leaves 25,000 dead and missing in Colombia (**Nov. 14**). Reagan and Gorbachev meet at summit (**Nov. 19**); agree to step up arms control talks and renew cultural contacts (**Nov. 21**). Terrorists seize Egyptian airliner after takeoff from Athens (**Nov. 23**); 59 dead as Egyptian forces storm plane on Malta (**Nov. 24**). U.S. budget-balancing bill enacted (**Dec. 12**). Newfoundland plane crash kills 248 U.S. soldiers (**Dec. 12**). Terrorists kill 19 at Rome and Vienna airports (**Dec. 30**).

1986   Spain and Portugal join Common Market (**Jan. 1**). President freezes Libyan assets in U.S. (**Jan. 8**). Supreme Court bars racial bias in trial jury selection (**Jan. 14**). Britain and France plan Channel tunnel (**Jan. 20**). *Voyager 2* spacecraft reports secrets of Uranus (**Jan. 26**). Space shuttle *Challenger* explodes after launch at Cape Canaveral, Fla., killing all seven aboard (**Jan. 28**). Haiti President Jean-Claude Duvalier flees to France (**Feb. 7**). President Marcos flees Philippines after ruling 20 years, as newly elected Corazon Aquino succeeds him (**Feb. 26**). Prime Minister Olaf Palme of Sweden shot dead (**Feb. 28**). Kurt Waldheim service as Nazi army officer revealed (**March 3**). Union Carbide agrees to settlement with victims of Bhopal gas leak in India (**March 22**). Two scientific teams report finding AIDS viruses (**March 26**). Halley's Comet yields information on return visit (**April 10**). U.S. planes attack Libyan "terrorist centers" (**April 14**). Desmond Tutu elected Archbishop in South Africa (**April 14**). Major nuclear accident at Soviet Union's Chernobyl power station alarms world (**April 28 et seq.**). Ex-Navy analyst, Jonathan Jay Pollard, 31, guilty as spy for Israel (**June 4**). Supreme Court reaffirms abortion rights (**June 11**). World Court rules U.S. broke international law in mining Nicaraguan waters (**June 27**). Supreme Court voids automatic provisions of budget-balancing law (**July 7**). Jerry A. Whitworth, ex-Navy radioman, convicted as spy (**July 24**). Moslem captors release Rev. Lawrence Martin Jenco (**July 26**). Senate Judiciary Committee approves William H. Rehnquist to be Chief Justice of U.S. (**Aug. 14**). Mexican police torture U.S. narcotics agent (**Aug. 14**). House votes arms appropriations bill rejecting Administration's "star wars" policy (**Aug. 15**). Three Lutheran church groups in U.S. set to merge (**Aug. 29**). Nicholas Daniloff, correspondent for *U.S. News & World Report*, detained in Moscow on espionage charges (**Aug. 30**); released and allowed to leave Soviet Union (**Sept. 29**). Congress overrides Reagan veto of stiff sanctions against South Africa (**Sept. 29 and Oct. 2**). Congress approves immigration bill barring hiring of illegal aliens, with amnesty provision **(Oct. 17)**. Reagan signs $11.7-billion budget reduction measure **(Oct. 21)**. He approves sweeping revision of U.S. tax code **(Oct. 22)**. Democrats triumph in elections, gaining eight seats to win Senate majority **(Nov. 4)**. Secret initiative to send arms to Iran revealed **(Nov. 6 et seq.)**; Reagan denies exchanging arms for hostages and halts arms sales **(Nov. 19)**; diversion of funds from arms sales to Nicaraguan contras revealed **(Nov. 25)**. Walkers, father and son, sentenced in naval spy ring **(Nov. 6)**. Soviet lifts ban on Andrei D. Sakharov, rights activist **(Dec. 19)**. Hotel fire kills 96 in Puerto Rico **(Dec. 31)**.

1987 William Buckley, U.S. hostage in Lebanon, reported slain **(Jan. 20)**. U.S. charges three Wall Street traders with making millions in illegal inside trading **(Feb. 12)**. Reagan admits "mistake" in Iran-Contra affair **(March 4)**. F.D.A. approves drug AZT for treating AIDS victims **(March 20)**. Gene-altered bacteria tested in experiment to aid agriculture **(April 24)**. U.S. puts Austrian President Kurt Waldheim on list of those banned from country **(April 27)**. Quebec accepts Canadian Constitution as "distinct society" **(May 1)**. Supreme Court rules Rotary Clubs must admit women **(May 4)**. Thousands of aliens seek legal status under new amnesty law **(May 5)**. Ulster police slay nine attackers in police station battle **(May 8)**. Three-way heart transplant performed **(May 12)**. Soviet launches world's most powerful rocket **(May 16)**. Iraqi missiles kill 37 in attack on U.S. frigate *Stark* in Persian Gulf **(May 17)**; Iraqi president apologizes **(May 18)**. Prime Minister Thatcher wins rare third term in Britain **(June 11)**. Robert B. Anderson, 77, former Treasury Secretary, sentenced for tax evasion **(June 25)**. Supreme Court Justice Lewis F. Powell, Jr., retires **(June 26)**. Klaus Barbie, 73, Gestapo wartime chief in Lyons, sentenced to life by French court for war crimes **(July 4)**. Marine Lieut. Col. Oliver North, Jr., tells Congressional inquiry higher officials approved his secret Iran-Contra operations **(July 7–10)**. Admiral John M. Poindexter, former National Security Adviser, testifies he authorized use of Iran arms sale profits to aid Contras **(July 15–22)**. George P. Shultz testifies he was deceived repeatedly on Iran-Contra affair **(July 23–24)**. Defense Secretary Caspar W. Weinberger tells inquiry of official deception and intrigue **(July 31, Aug. 3)**. Hundreds killed in clashes at Moslem holy site of Mecca **(Aug. 1)**. Five regional presidents agree on peace accord for Central America **(Aug. 7)**. Reagan says Iran arms-Contra policy went astray and accepts responsibility **(Aug 12)**. Severe earthquake strikes Los Angeles, leaving 100 injured and six dead **(Oct. 1)**. Senate, 58–42, rejects Robert H. Bork as Supreme Court Justice **(Oct. 23)**

1988 U.S. and Canada reach free trade agreement **(Jan. 2)**. Supreme Court, 5–3, backs public school officials' power to censor student activities **(Jan. 13)**. Lyn Nofziger, former Reagan adviser, convicted of violating Federal ethics law **(Feb. 11)**. Marine Lieut. Col. William H. Higgins abducted in Lebanon **(Feb. 17)**. Nine killed in Soviet plane hijacking **(March 10)**. Robert C. McFarlane, former National Security Adviser, pleads guilty in Iran–Contra case **(March 11)**. Congress overrides Reagan veto of civil rights bill **(March 22)**. Arizona Gov. Evan Mecham removed from office after impeachment trial **(April 4)**. Gunmen hijack Kuwaiti airliner **(April 5 et seq.)**. Khalil al-Wazir, P.L.O. official, assassinated in Tunisia **(April 16)**. Israel court dooms John Demjanjuk, 68, "Ivan the Terrible," for Nazi war crimes **(April 25)**. Soviet court clears executed Bolsheviks **(June 13)**. Supreme Court rules against private-club membership restrictions **(June 20)**. U.S. Navy ship shoots down Iranian airliner in Persian Gulf, mistaking it for jet fighter; 290 killed **(July 3)**. Terrorists kill nine tourists on Aegean cruise **(July 11)**. Democratic convention nominates Gov. Michael Dukakis of Massachusetts for President and Texas Senator Lloyd Bentsen for Vice President **(July 17 et seq.)**. Reagan signs law to compensate interned Japanese-Americans **(Aug. 10)**. Republicans nominate George Bush for President and Indiana Senator Dan Quayle for Vice President **(Aug. 15 et seq.)**. Plane blast kills Pakistani President Mohammad Zia ul-Haq **(Aug. 17)**. Michael K. Deaver, Reagan friend, sentenced for lying about lobbying **(Sept. 23)**. Foes defeat Pinochet in Chile's Presidential plebiscite **(Oct. 5)**. Republicans sweep 40 states in election. Vice President Bush beats Gov. Dukakis **(Nov. 8)**. Soviet legislature approves political restructuring and new national legislature **(Dec. 1)**. Benazir Bhutto, first Islamic woman prime minister, chosen to lead Pakistan's government **(Dec. 1)**. Pan-Am 747 explodes from terrorist bomb and crashes in Lockerbie, Scotland, killing all 259 aboard and 11 on ground **(Dec. 21)**.

1989 U.S. planes shoot down two Libyan fighters over international waters in Mediterranean **(Jan. 4)**. Emperor Hirohito of Japan dead at 87 **(Jan. 7)**. George Herbert Walker Bush inaugurated as 41st U.S. President **(Jan. 20)**. Ronald Brown is first black to be elected chairman of Democratic National Committee **(Feb. 10)**. Iran's Ayatollah Khomeini declares author Salman Rushdie's book "The Satanic Verses" offensive and sentences him and his

Corazon C. Aquino
(Jan. 25, 1933)

Kurt Waldheim
(Dec. 21, 1918)

George H. Bush
(June 12, 1924)

**L. Douglas Wilder
(Jan. 17, 1931)**

**Neptune seen from
Voyager 2**

publishers to death (**Feb. 14**). Senate votes, 53–47, to reject Bush nominee, John Tower, as Secretary of Defense (**March 9**). Ruptured tanker *Exxon Valdez* sends 11 million gallons of crude oil into Alaska's Prince William Sound (**March 24**). Blast in a 16-inch gun turret kills 42 on battleship *Iowa* (**April 19**). Tens of thousands of Chinese students take over Beijing's central square in rally for democracy (**April 19** et seq.). More than one million Chinese demonstrators in Beijing put pressure on government for more democracy, crowds demand resignation of Deng Xiaoping, senior leader, and Prime Minister Li Peng. Chaos spreads across nation (**mid-May** et seq.). Mikhail S. Gorbachev named Soviet President (**May 25**). U.S. jury convicts Oliver L. North of crimes stemming from role as covert agent to aid Contras (**May 4**). House Speaker Jim Wright resigns in aftermath of his investigation by House Ethics Committee (**May 31**). Thousands killed as Chinese leaders take hard line toward demonstrators. Arrests and wave of executions begin (**June 4** et seq.). Iranian leader Ayatollah Khomeini, 87, is buried (**June 6**). Lebanese Shiite Moslem terrorists report hanging of Lieut. Col. William R. Higgins, taken hostage in 1988 (**July 31**). Army Gen. Colin R. Powell is first black to become Chairman of Joint Chiefs of Staff (**Aug. 9**). P.W. Botha quits as South Africa's President (**Aug. 14**). *Voyager 2* spacecraft speeds by Neptune after making startling discoveries about planet and its moons (**Aug. 29**). Hurricane Hugo devastates from Caribbean islands to South Carolina (**Sept. 18**). TV evangelist Jim Bakker is convicted of 24 counts of fraud and conspiracy (**Oct. 5**). Space shuttle *Atlantis* launches *Galileo* spacecraft on its trip to Jupiter (**Oct. 18**). L. Douglas Wilder, Democrat, is elected as first black governor of Virginia (**Nov. 7**). Deng Xiaoping resigns from China's leadership after 65-year political career (**Nov. 9**). After 28 years, Berlin Wall is open to West and thousands of jubilant East Germans flood West Berlin and West Germany (**Nov. 11**). Lebanon's President René Moawad is assassinated by car bomb after seventeen days in office (**Nov. 22**). Czech Parliament ends Communists' dominant role in Czechoslovakian society and promises free elections (**Nov. 30**). President Bush and Gorbachev hold shipboard summit off Malta (**Dec. 2–3**). Brent Scowcroft, U.S. National Security Adviser, visits China to mend relations after attacks on pro-democracy protesters (**Dec. 9**). Romanian uprising overthrows Communist government (**Dec. 15** et seq.); President Ceausescu and wife are executed by army (**Dec. 25**). U.S. troops invade Panama, seeking capture of Gen. Manuel Noriega (**Dec. 20**). Noriega takes refuge in Vatican Embassy; resistance to U.S. collapses (**Dec. 24**).

1990 Romania disbands rebellious police force (**Jan. 1**). Gen. Manuel Noriega surrenders in Panama (**Jan. 3**). Soviet Azerbaijan erupts in violence (**Jan. 14** et seq.). Yugoslav Communists end 45-year monopoly of power (**Jan. 22**). Richard V. Secord convicted in Iran–Contra affair (**Jan. 24**). Nicaraguan opposition crushes Sandinistas at polls (**Feb. 5**). Soviet Communists relinquish sole power (**Feb. 7**). Felix S. Bloch, accused in espionage inquiry, dismissed from State Department post (**Feb. 7**). South Africa frees Nelson Mandela, imprisoned 27 1/2 years (**Feb. 11**). U.S. jury indicts Exxon in Alaska oil spill (**Feb. 27**). John M. Poindexter convicted in Iran–Contra affair (**April 7**). Moscow admits Soviet secret police killed thousands in Katyn Forest massacre of 1940 (**April 13**). Michael Milliken convicted in "junk bond" case (**April 20**). Shuttle *Discovery* carries Hubble telescope into space. Space agency acknowledges trouble with defects in telescope (**April 24** et seq.). Violeta Barrios de Chamorro inaugurated as Nicaraguan President (**April 25**). Fire on Navy destroyer *Conynham* kills one and injures 12 (**May 8**). Gorbachev bars independence moves in Latvia and Estonia (**May 14**). U.S.–Soviet summit reaches accord on armaments (**June 1**). South Africa lifts emergency decrees (**June 7**). Supreme Court upsets law

PICTURE CREDITS. The following credits list the names of organizations and individuals who have contributed illustrations to **HEADLINE HISTORY.** The editors wish to thank all of them for their assistance. The credits are arranged alphabetically by picture source, then picture title and page number in **HEADLINE HISTORY.** Credits: AIP Niels Bohr Library, **Marie Curie** and **Albert Einstein,** p. 104; British Information Services, **Margaret Thatcher,** p. 117; Embassy of The Philippines, **Corazon C. Aquino,** p. 119; Harry S. Truman Library, **Harry S. Truman,** p. 112; John Fitzgerald Kennedy Library, Boston, **John F. Kennedy,** p. 115; Matthew Kalmenott, **Brontosaur,** p. 89; NASA Photos, **Charles A. Lindbergh,** p. 108, **Voyager and Viking,** p. 116, **Space Shuttle Columbia,** p. 117; National Portrait Gallery, Smithsonian Institution, **Theodore Roosevelt,** p. 104; Novosti Photos, **Vladimir Lenin,** p. 106, **Yuri A. Gagarin,** p. 114; **Mikhail S. Gorbachev,** p. 118; The Library of Congress Picture Collection, **Christopher Columbus,** p. 95, **Dred Scott,** p. 102, **Geronimo,** p. 103, **Woodrow Wilson,** p. 106, **Herbert C. Hoover,** p. 108, **Amelia Earhart,** p. 111, **Dwight D. Eisenhower,** p. 113, **Lyndon B. Johnson,** p. 115, **Richard M. Nixon,** p. 116; The Permanent Mission of India to the U.N., **Indira Gandhi,** p. 118; Republican National Committee, **Ronald W. Reagan,** p. 118; **George H. Bush,** p. 119; U.S. Army Photos, **D-Day, Yalta Conference,** p. 112, **Joseph Stalin,** p. 113; AP/Wide World Photos, Inc., **Martin Luther King, Jr.,** p. 115 and **Iraqi prisoners,** p. 121; U.N. Photo, **Fidel Castro,** p. 114, U.N. Photo by D. Bur nett, **Kurt Waldheim,** p. 119. **MAP CREDITS.** Maps on pp. 90, 94, 98, 105, 107, 109 and 110 from *An Encyclopedia of World History,* by William L. Langer, The Fifth Edition, Copyright 1940, 1948, 1952, and © 1967, 1972 by Houghton Mifflin Company. Reprinted by permission of Houghton Mifflin Company.

banning flag burning (**June 11**). President Bush breaks with no-tax pledge in budget agreement (**June 26**). Imelda Marcos acquitted in New York of raiding Philippine Treasury (**July 2**). Western Alliance ends cold war and proposes joint action with Soviet Union and Eastern Europe (**July 6**). Gorbachev keeps leadership as Communist General Secretary and President of Soviet Union (**July 14**). U.S. Appeals Court overturns Oliver North's Iran–Contra conviction (**July 20**). U.S. Judge David H. Souter of New Hampshire nominated to Supreme Court (**July 23**); confirmed by Senate (**Oct. 2**). Iraqi troops invade Kuwait and seize petroleum reserves, setting off Persian Gulf crisis (**Aug. 2**)—Highlights: U.N. Security Council orders sweeping trade and financial boycott of Iraq and Kuwait (**Aug. 7**); Washington dispatches troops, planes, and armor to Saudi Arabia against threat of invasion (**Aug. 7**); U.N. Security Council gives U.S. and allies right to enforce embargo by force (**Aug. 25**). Benazir Bhutto government overthrown in Pakistan (**Aug. 6**). U.S. jury convicts Washington Mayor Marion S. Barry on drug possession charge (**Aug. 10**). East and West Germanys reunited as East and West formally end four decades of division (**Aug. 31** et seq.). In Persian Gulf: U.S. deploys combat aircraft in defense of Saudi Arabia (**Sept. 3**); Bush and Gorbachev pledge joint action against Iraq (**Sept. 9**); Security Council votes embargo on air traffic to Iraq (**Sept. 25**). Liberian President Samuel K. Doe, 38, slain by rebels (**Sept. 9**). Charles H. Keating, Jr., savings and loan industry leader, indicted for fraud (**Sept. 18**). Bush and Congressional leaders agree on drastic budget reduction plan (**Sept. 30**). Space shuttle *Discovery* successful after five-month hiatus (**Oct. 6** et seq.). Israel orders inquiry into deaths of 21 Palestinians in Jerusalem Old City (**Oct. 10**). Congress passes deficit-reducing budget measure with new taxes and spending cuts (**Oct. 28**). Forty-three industrial nations vote pact to ban ocean dumping (**Nov. 2**). Militant Rabbi Meir Kahane assassinated in New York (**Nov. 5**). Republicans set back in midterm elections (**Nov. 8**). In Persian Gulf: Bush orders more than 150,000 additional ground, air, and sea forces to area (**Nov. 8**); Iraq sending 250,000 more troops to bolster army in Kuwait and southern Iraq (**Nov. 22**); U.N. Security Council authorizes U.S. and allies to expel Iraq from Kuwait by force unless it leaves by Jan. 1, 1991 (**Nov. 29**). Woman lawyer, Mrs. Mary Robinson, 46, elected president of Ireland (**Nov. 9**). Poland and Germany sign border agreement (**Nov. 14**). Space shuttle *Atlantis* launches spy satellite (**Nov. 15** et seq.). Gorbachev assumes emergency powers (**Nov. 17**). Leaders of 34 nations in Europe and North America proclaim a united Europe (**Nov. 21**). Margaret Thatcher resigns as British Prime Minister (**Nov. 22**); John Major, 47, Chancellor of Exchequer, succeeds her (**Nov. 28**). U.S. unemployment highest in three years (**Dec. 7**). Lech Walesa wins Poland's runoff Presidential election (**Dec. 9**). U.S. and Europe pledge food aid to Soviet Union (**Dec. 10**). F.D.A. approves Norplant, under-skin contraceptive device (**Dec.. 10**). Shuttle *Columbia* lands safely following 10th mission after equipment problems beset flight (**Dec. 11**). Twelve European Community nations move toward unified political ties (**Dec. 15**). Haiti elects leftist priest as President in first democratic election (**Dec. 17**). Eduard A. Shevardnadze, Soviet foreign minister, resigns (**Dec. 20**). Romania expels exiled King Michael on attempted visit (**Dec. 26**). Cold spell destroys California's fruit and vegetable crops (**Dec. 27**).

**Iraqi prisoners
(February 1991)**

THE PERSIAN GULF WAR (Aug. 2, 1990–April 6, 1991)

1990: Iraq invades its tiny neighbor, Kuwait, after talks break down over oil production and debt repayment. Iraqi Pres. Saddam Hussein later annexes Kuwait and declares that Iraq intends to invade Saudi Arabia and take control of the region's oil supplies. He begins organizing a multinational coalition to seek Kuwait's freedom and restoration of its legitimate government. The U.N. Security Council authorizes economic sanctions against Iraq. Pres. Bush orders U.S. troops to protect Saudi Arabia at the Saudis' request and "Operation Desert Shield" begins (**Aug. 6**). 230,000 American troops arrive in Saudi Arabia to take defensive action, but when Iraq continues a huge military buildup in Kuwait, the President orders an additional 200,000 troops deployed to prepare for a possible offensive action by the U.S.-led coalition forces. He subsequently obtains a U.N. Security Council resolution setting a Jan. 15, 1991, deadline for Iraq to withdraw unconditionally from Kuwait (**Nov. 8**).

1991: Pres. Bush wins Congressional approval for his position with the most devastating air assault in history against military targets in Iraq and Kuwait (**Jan. 16**). He rejects a Soviet-Iraq peace plan for a gradual withdrawal that does not comply with all the U.N. resolutions and gives Iraq an ultimatum to withdraw from Kuwait by noon February 23 (**Feb. 22**). The President orders the ground war to begin (**Feb. 24**). In a brilliant and lightning-fast campaign, U.S. and coalition forces smash through Iraq's defenses and defeat Saddam Hussein's troops in only four days of combat. Allies enter Kuwait City (**Feb. 26**). Iraqi army sets fire to over 500 of Kuwait's oil wells as final act of destruction to Kuwait's infrastructure. Pres. Bush orders a unilateral cease-fire 100 hours after the ground offensive started (**Feb. 27**). Allied and Iraq military leaders meet on battlefield to discuss terms for a formal cease-fire to end the Gulf War. Iraq agrees to abide by all of the U.N. resolutions (**Mar. 3**). The first Allied prisoners of war are released (**Mar. 4**). Official cease-fire accepted and signed (**April 6**). 532,000 U.S. forces served in Operation Desert Storm. There were a total of 108 deaths during Operation Desert Shield. There were 266 casualties during Operation Desert Storm: 142 killed in combat, 122 non-hostile deaths, and 2 later died of wounds received in action. No comprehensive casualty figures have been released by Iraq.

Firsts in America

This selection is based on our editorial judgment. Other sources may list different firsts.

Admiral in U.S. Navy: David Glasgow Farragut, 1866.

Air–mail route, first transcontinental: Between New York City and San Francisco, 1920.

Assembly, representative: House of Burgesses, founded in Virginia, 1619.

Bank established: Bank of North America, Philadelphia, 1781.

Birth in America to English parents: Virginia Dare, born Roanoke Island, N.C., 1587.

Black newspaper: *Freedom's Journal,* 1827, edited by John B. Russworm.

Black U.S. diplomat: Ebenezer D. Bassett, 1869, minister-resident to Haiti.

Black elected governor of a state: L. Douglas Wilder, Virginia, 1990.

Black elected to U.S. Senate: Hiram Revels, 1870, Mississippi.

Black elected to U.S. House of Representatives: Jefferson Long, Georgia, 1870.

Black associate justice of U.S. Supreme Court: Thurgood Marshall, Oct. 2, 1967.

Black U.S. cabinet minister: Robert C. Weaver, 1966, Secretary of the Department of Housing and Urban Development.

Botanic garden: Established by John Bartram in Philadelphia, 1728 and is still in existence in its original location.

Cartoon, colored: "The Yellow Kid," by Richard Outcault, in *New York World,* 1895.

College: Harvard, founded 1636.

College to confer degrees on women: Oberlin (Ohio) College, 1841.

College to establish coeducation: Oberlin (Ohio) College, 1833.

Electrocution of a criminal: William Kemmler in Auburn Prison, Auburn, N.Y., Aug. 6, 1890.

Five and Ten Cents Store: Founded by Frank Woolworth, Utica, N.Y., 1879 (moved to Lancaster, Pa., same year).

Fraternity: Phi Beta Kappa; founded Dec. 5, 1776, at College of William and Mary.

Law to be declared unconstitutional by U.S. Supreme Court: Judiciary Act of 1789. Case: *Marbury* v. *Madison,* 1803.

Library, circulating: Philadelphia, 1731.

Newspaper, illustrated daily: *New York Daily Graphic,* 1873.

Newspaper published daily: *Pennsylvania Packet and General Advertiser,* Philadelphia, Sept., 1784.

Newspaper published over a continuous period: *The Boston News–Letter,* April, 1704.

Newsreel: Pathé Frères of Paris, in 1910, circulated a weekly issue of their *Pathé Journal.*

Oil well, commercial: Titusville, Pa., 1859.

Panel quiz show on radio: *Information Please,* May 17, 1938.

Postage stamps issued: 1847.

Public School: Boston Latin School, Boston, 1635.

Railroad, transcontinental: Central Pacific and Union Pacific railroads, joined at Promontory, Utah, May 10, 1869.

Savings bank: The Provident Institute for Savings, Boston, 1816.

Science museum: Founded by Charleston (S.C.) Library Society, 1773.

Skyscraper: Home Insurance Co., Chicago, 1885 (10 floors, 2 added later).

Slaves brought into America: At Jamestown, Va. 1619, from a Dutch ship.

Sorority: Kappa Alpha Theta, at De Pauw University, 1870.

State to abolish capital punishment: Michigan, 1847.

State to enter Union after original 13: Vermont, 1791.

Steam–heated building: Eastern Hotel, Boston, 1845.

Steam railroad (carried passengers and freight): Baltimore & Ohio, 1830.

Strike on record by union: Journeymen Printers, New York City, 1776.

Subway: Opened in Boston, 1897.

"Tabloid" picture newspaper: *The Illustrated Daily News* (now *The Daily News*), New York City, 1919.

Vaudeville theater: Gaiety Museum, Boston, 1883.

Woman astronaut to ride in space: Dr. Sally K. Ride, 1983.

Woman astronaut to walk in space: Dr. Kathryn D. Sullivan, 1984.

Woman cabinet member: Frances Perkins, Secretary of Labor, 1933.

Woman candidate for President: Victoria Claflin Woodhull, nominated by National Woman's Suffrage Assn. on ticket of Nation Radical Reformers, 1872.

Woman candidate for Vice–President: Geraldine A. Ferraro, nominated on a major party ticket, Democratic Party, 1984.

Woman doctor of medicine: Elizabeth Blackwell, M.D. from Geneva Medical College of Western New York, 1849.

Woman elected governor of a state: Nellie Taylor Ross, Wyoming, 1925.

Woman elected to U.S. Senate: Hattie Caraway, Arkansas; elected Nov., 1932.

Woman graduate of law school: Ada H. Kepley, Union College of Law, Chicago, 1870.

Woman member of U.S. House of Representatives: Jeannette Rankin; elected Nov., 1916.

Woman member of U.S. Senate: Rebecca Latimer Felton of Georgia; appointed Oct. 3, 1922.

Woman member of U.S. Supreme Court: Sandra Day O'Connor; appointed July 1981.

Woman suffrage granted: Wyoming Territory, 1869.

Written constitution: *Fundamental Orders of Connecticut,* 1639.

STRUCTURES

The Seven Wonders of the World

(Not all classical writers list the same items as the Seven Wonders, but most of them agree on the following.)

The Pyramids of Egypt. A group of three pyramids, *Khufu, Khafra,* and *Menkaura* at Giza, outside modern Cairo, is often called the first wonder of the world. The largest pyramid, built by Khufu (Cheops), a king of the fourth Dynasty, had an original estimated height of 482 ft (now approximately 450 ft). The base has sides 755 ft long. It contains 2,300,000 blocks; the average weight of each is 2.5 tons. Estimated date of construction is 2800 B.C. Of all the Seven Wonders, the pyramids alone survive.

Hanging Gardens of Babylon. Often listed as the second wonder, these gardens were supposedly built by Nebuchadnezzar about 600 B.C. to please his queen, Amuhia. They are also associated with the mythical Assyrian Queen, Semiramis. Archeologists surmise that the gardens were laid out atop a vaulted building, with provisions for raising water. The terraces were said to rise from 75 to 300 ft.

The Walls of Babylon, also built by Nebuchadnezzar, are sometimes referred to as the second (or the seventh) wonder instead of the Hanging Gardens.

Statue of Zeus (Jupiter) at Olympia. The work of Phidias (5th century B.C.), this colossal figure in gold and ivory was reputedly 40 ft high. All trace of it is lost, except for reproductions on coins.

Temple of Artemis (Diana) at Ephesus. A beautiful structure, begun about 350 B.C. in honor of a non-Hellenic goddess who later became identified with the Greek goddess of the same name. The temple, with Ionic columns 60 ft high, was destroyed by invading Goths in A.D. 262.

Mausoleum at Halicarnassus. This famous monument was erected by Queen Artemisia in memory of her husband, King Mausolus of Caria in Asia Minor, who died in 353 B.C. Some remains of the structure are in the British Museum. This shrine is the source of the modern word "mausoleum."

Colossus at Rhodes. This bronze statue of Helios (Apollo), about 105 ft high, was the work of the sculptor Chares, who reputedly labored for 12 years before completing it in 280 B.C. It was destroyed during an earthquake in 224 B.C.

Pharos of Alexandria. The seventh wonder was the Pharos (lighthouse) of Alexandria, built by Sostratus of Cnidus during the 3rd century B.C. on the island of Pharos off the coast of Egypt. It was destroyed by an earthquake in the 13th century.

Famous Structures

Ancient

The *Great Sphinx of Egypt,* one of the wonders of ancient Egyptian architecture, adjoins the pyramids of Giza and has a length of 240 ft. It was built in the 4th dynasty.

Other Egyptian buildings of note include the *Temples of Karnak* and *Edfu* and the *Tombs at Beni Hassan.*

The *Parthenon of Greece,* built on the Acropolis in Athens, was the chief temple to the goddess Athena. It was believed to have been completed by 438 B.C. The present temple remained intact until the 5th century A.D. Today, though the Parthenon is in ruins, its majestic proportions are still discernible.

Other great structures of ancient Greece were the *Temples at Paestum* (about 540 and 420 B.C.); the *Temple of Poseidon* (about 460 B.C.); the *Temple of Apollo* at Corinth (about 540 B.C.); the *Temple of Apollo* at Bassae (about 450–420 B.C.); the famous *Erechtheum* atop the Acropolis (about 421–405 B.C.); the *Temple of Athena Niké* at Athens (about 426 B.C.); the *Olympieum* at Athens (174 B.C.–A.D. 131); the *Athenian Treasury* at Delphi (about 515 B.C.); the *Propylaea* of the Acropolis at Athens (437–432 B.C.); the *Theater of Dionysus* at Athens (about 350–325 B.C.); the *House of Cleopatra* at Delos (138 B.C.) and the *Theater* at Epidaurus (about 325 B.C.).

The *Colosseum (Flavian Amphitheater) of Rome,* the largest and most famous of the Roman amphitheaters, was opened for use A.D. 80. Elliptical in shape, it consisted of three stories and an upper gallery, rebuilt in stone in its present form in the third century A.D. Its seats rise in tiers, which in turn are buttressed by concrete vaults and stone piers. It could seat between 40,000 and 50,000 spectators. It was principally used for gladiatorial combat.

The *Pantheon* at Rome, begun by Agrippa in 27 B.C. as a temple, was rebuilt in its present circular form by Hadrian (A.D. 110–25). Literally the Pantheon was intended as a temple of "all the gods." It is remarkable for its perfect preservation today, and it has served continuously for 20 centuries as a place of worship.

Famous Roman arches include the *Arch of Constantine* (about A.D. 315) and the *Arch of Titus* (about A.D. 80).

Later European

St. Mark's Cathedral in Venice (1063–67), one of the great examples of Byzantine architecture, was begun in the 9th century. Partly destroyed by fire in 976, it was later rebuilt as a Byzantine edifice.

Other famous Byzantine examples of architecture are *St. Sophia* in Istanbul (A.D. 532–37); *San Vitale* in Ravenna (542); *St. Paul's Outside the Walls,* Rome (5th century); the *Kremlin* baptism and marriage church, Moscow (begun in 1397); and *St. Lorenzo Outside the Walls,* Rome, begun in 588.

The *Cathedral Group* at Pisa (1067–1173), one of the most celebrated groups of structures built in Romanesque-style, consists of the cathedral, the cathedral's baptistery, and the *Leaning Tower*. This trio forms a group by itself in the northwest corner of the city. The cathedral and baptistery are built in varicolored marble. The campanile *(Leaning Tower)* is 179 ft. high and leans more than 16 ft out of the perpendicular. There is little reason to believe that the architects intended to have the tower lean.

Other examples of Romanesque architecture include the *Vézelay Abbey* in France (1130); the *Church of Notre-Dame-du-Port* at Clermont-Ferrand in France (1100); the *Church of San Zeno* (begun in 1138) at Verona, and *Durham Cathedral* in England.

The *Alhambra* (1248–1354), located in Granada, Spain, is universally esteemed as one of the greatest masterpieces of Moslem architecture. Designed as a palace and fortress for the Moorish monarchs of Granada, it is surrounded by a heavily fortified wall more than a mile in perimeter. The location of the Alhambra in the Sierra Nevada provides a magnificent setting for this jewel of Moorish Spain.

The *Tower of London* is a group of buildings and towers covering 13 acres along the north bank of the Thames. The central *White Tower*, begun in 1078 during the reign of William the Conqueror, was originally a fortress and royal residence, but was later used as a prison. The *Bloody Tower* is associated with Anne Boleyn and other notables.

Westminster Abbey, in London, was begun in 1045 and completed in 1065. It was rebuilt and enlarged in 1245–50.

Notre-Dame de Paris (begun in 1163), one of the great examples of Gothic architecture, is a twin-towered church with a steeple over the crossing and immense flying buttresses supporting the masonry at the rear of the church.

Other famous Gothic structures are *Chartres Cathedral* (12th century); *Sainte Chapelle*, Paris (1246–48); *Laon Cathedral*, France (1160–1205); *Reims Cathedral* (about 1210–50; rebuilt after its almost complete destruction in World War I); *Rouen Cathedral* (13th–16th centuries); *Amiens Cathedral* (1218–69); *Beauvais Cathedral* (begun 1247); *Salisbury Cathedral* (1220–60); *York Minster* or the *Cathedral of St. Peter* (begun in the 7th century); *Milan Cathedral* (begun 1386); and *Cologne Cathedral* (13th–19th centuries); badly damaged in World War II.

The Duomo (cathedral) in Florence was founded in 1298, completed by Brunelleschi and consecrated in 1436. The oval-shaped dome dominates the entire structure.

The *Vatican* is a group of buildings in Rome comprising the official residence of the Pope. The *Basilica of St. Peter*, the largest church in the Christian world, was begun in 1450. The *Sistine Chapel*, begun in 1473, is noted for the art masterpieces of Michelangelo, Botticelli, and others. The *Basilica of the Savior* (known as *St. John Lateran*) is the first-ranking Catholic Church in the world, for it is the cathedral of the Pope.

Other examples of Renaissance architecture are the *Palazzo Riccardi*, the *Palazzo Pitti* and the *Palazzo Strozzi* in Florence; the *Farnese Palace* in Rome; *Palazzo Grimani* (completed about 1550) in Venice; the *Escorial* (1563–93) near Madrid; the *Town Hall* of Seville (1527–32); the *Louvre*, Paris; the *Château* at Blois, France; *St. Paul's Cathedral*, London (1675–1710); badly damaged in World War II); the *École Militaire*, Paris (1752); the *Pazzi Chapel*, Flor-

ence, designed by Brunelleschi (1429); the Palace of *Fontainebleau* and the *Château de Chambord* in France.

The *Palace of Versailles*, containing the famous Hall of Mirrors, was built during the reign of Louis XIV and served as the royal palace until 1793.

Outstanding European buildings of the 18th and 19th centuries are the *Superga* at Turin, the *Hôtel-Dieu* in Lyons, the *Belvedere Palace* at Vienna, the *Royal Palace* of Stockholm, the *Opera House* of Paris (1863–75); the *Bank of England*, the *British Museum*, the *University of London*, and the *Houses of Parliament*, all in London; the *Panthéon*, the *Church of the Madeleine*, the *Bourse*, and the *Palais de Justice* in Paris.

The *Eiffel Tower*, in Paris, was built for the Exposition of 1889 by Alexandre Eiffel. It is 984 ft high.[1]

1. 1,056 ft, including the television tower.

Asiatic and African

The *Taj Mahal* (1632–50), at Agra, India, built by Shah Jahan as a tomb for his wife, is considered by some as the most perfect example of the Mogul style and by others as the most beautiful building in the world. Four slim white minarets flank the building, which is topped by a white dome; the entire structure is of marble.

Other examples of Indian architecture are the temples at Benares and Tanjore.

Among famed Moslem edifices are the *Dome of the Rock* or *Mosque of Omar*, Jerusalem (A.D. 691); the *Citadel* (1166), and the *Tombs of the Mamelukes* (15th century), in Cairo; the *Tomb of Humayun* in Delhi; the *Blue Mosque* (1468) at Tabriz, and the *Tamerlane Mausoleum* at Samarkand.

Angkor Wat, outside the city of Angkor Thom, Cambodia, is one of the most beautiful examples of Cambodian or Khmer architecture. The sanctuary was built during the 12th century.

Great Wall of China (228 B.C.?), designed specifically as a defense against nomadic tribes, has large watch towers which could be called buildings. It was erected by Emperor Ch'in Shih Huang Ti and is 1,400 miles long. Built mainly of earth and stone, it varies in height between 18 and 30 ft.

Typical of Chinese architecture are the pagodas or temple towers. Among some of the better-known pagodas are the *Great Pagoda of the Wild Geese* at Sian (founded in 652); *Nan t'a* (11th century) at Fang Shan; the *Pagoda of Sung Yueh Ssu* (A.D. 523) at Sung Shan, Honan.

Other well-known Chinese buildings are the *Drum Tower* (1273), the *Three Great Halls* in the Purple Forbidden City (1627), *Buddha's Perfume Tower* (19th century), the *Porcelain Pagoda*, and the *Summer Palace*, all at Peking.

United States

Rockefeller Center, in New York City, extends from 5th Ave. to the Avenue of the Americas between 48th and 52nd Sts. (and halfway to 7th Ave. between 47th and 51st Sts.). It occupies more than 22 acres and has 19 buildings.

The Cathedral of St. John the Divine, at 112th St and Amsterdam Ave. in New York City, was begun in 1892 and is now in the final stages of completion. When completed, it will be the largest cathedral in the world: 601 ft long, 146 ft wide at the nave, 320 ft wide at the transept. The east end is designed in Romanesque-Byzantine style, and the nave and west ends are Gothic.

St. Patrick's Cathedral, at Fifth Ave. and 50th St. in New York City, has a seating capacity of 2,500. The nave was opened in 1877, and the cathedral was dedicated in 1879.

Louisiana Superdome, in New Orleans, is the largest arena in the history of mankind. The main area can accommodate up to 95,000 people. It is the world's largest steel-constructed room. Unobstructed by posts, it covers 13 acres and reaches 27 stories at its peak.

World Trade Center, in New York City, was dedicated in 1973. Its twin towers are 110 stories high (1,350 ft), and the complex contains over 9 million sq ft of office space. A restaurant is on the 107th floor of the North Tower.

World's Highest Dams

Name	River, Country or State	Structural height (feet)	Structural height (meters)	Gross reservoir capacity (thousands of acre feet)	Gross reservoir capacity (millions of cubic meters)	Year completed
Rogun	Vakhsh, U.S.S.R.	1066	325	9,404	11,600	1985
Nurek	Vakhsh, U.S.S.R.	984	300	8,512	10,500	1980
Grande Dixence	Dixence, Switzerland	935	285	324	400	1962
Inguri	Inguri, U.S.S.R.	892	272	801	1,100	1984
Chicoasén	Grijalva, Mexico	869	265	1,346	1,660	1981
Vaiont	Vaiont, Italy	869	265	137	169	1961
Tehri	Bhagirathi, India	856	261	2,869	3,540	UC
Kinshau	Tons, India	830	253	1,946	2,400	1985
Guavio	Orinoco, Colombia	820	250	811	1,000	1989
Mica	Columbia, Canada	794	242	20,000	24,670	1972
Sayano-Shushensk	Yenisei, U.S.S.R.	794	242	25,353	31,300	1980
Mihoesti	Aries, Romania	794	242	5	6	1983
Chivor	Batá, Colombia	778	237	661	815	1975
Mauvoisin	Drance de Bagnes, Switzerland	777	237	146	180	1957
Oroville	Feather, California	770	235	3,538	4,299	1968
Chirkey	Sulak, U.S.S.R.	764	233	2,252	2,780	1977
Bhakra	Sutlej, India	741	226	8,002	9,870	1963
El Cajón	Humuya, Honduras	741	226	4,580	5,650	1984
Hoover	Colorado, Arizona/Nevada	726	221	28,500	35,154	1936
Contra	Verzasca, Switzerland	722	220	70	86	1965
Mabaklamm	Dorferbach, Austria	722	220	191	235	UC
Mratinje	Piva, Yugoslavia	722	220	713	880	1973
Dworshak	N. Fk. Clearwater, Idaho	717	219	3,453	4,259	1974
Glen Canyon	Colorado, Arizona	710	216	27,000	33,304	1964
Toktogul	Naryn, U.S.S.R.	705	215	15,800	19,500	1978
Daniel Johnson	Manicouagan, Canada	703	214	115,000	141,852	1968
San Roque	Agno, Philippines	689	210	803	990	UC
Luzzone	Brenno di Luzzone, Switzerland	682	208	71	87	1963
Keban	Firat, Turkey	679	207	25,110	31,000	1974
Dez	Dez, Abi, Iran	666	203	2,707	3,340	1963
Almendra	Tormes, Spain	662	202	2,148	2,649	1970
Kölnbrein	Malta, Austria	656	200	166	205	1977
Karun	Karun, Iran	656	200	2,351	2,900	1976
Altinkaya	Kizil Irmak, Turkey	640	195	4,672	5,763	1986
New Bullards Bar	No. Yuba, California	637	194	960	1,184	1968
Lakhwar	Yamuna, India	630	192	470	580	1985
New Melones	Stanislaus, California	625	191	2,400	2,960	1979
Itaipu	Paraná, Brazil/Paraguay	623	190	23,510	29,000	1982
Kurobe 4	Kurobe, Japan	610	186	162	199	1964
Swift	Lewis, Washington	610	186	756	932	1958
Mossyrock	Cowlitz, Washington	607	185	1,300	1,603	1968
Oymopinar	Manavgat, Turkey	607	185	251	310	1983
Atatürk	Firat, Turkey	604	184	39,482	48,700	1990
Shasta	Sacramento, California	602	183	4,550	5,612	1945
Bennett WAC	Peace, Canada	600	183	57,006	70,309	1967
Karakaya	Firat, Turkey	591	180	7,767	9,580	1986
Tignes	Isère, France	591	180	186	230	1952
Amir Kabir (Karad)	Karadj, Iran	591	180	166	205	1962
Tachien	Tachia, Taiwan	591	180	188	232	1974
Dartmouth	Mitta-Mitta, Australia	591	180	3,243	4,000	1978
Özköy	Gediz, Turkey	591	180	762	940	1983
Mosson	Barberine, Switzerland	590	180	184	225	1974
Hillergründl	Ziller, Austria	590	180	73	90	1986
Los Leones	Los Leones, Chile	587	179	86	106	1986
New Don Pedro	Tuolumne, California	585	178	2,030	2,504	1971
Alpa-Gera	Cormor, Italy	584	178	53	65	1965

Name	River, Country or State	Structural height		Gross reservoir capacity		Year completed
		feet	meters	thousands of acre feet	millions of cubic meters	
Kopperston Tailings 3	Jones Branch, West Virginia	580	177	—	—	1963
Takase	Takase, Japan	577	176	62	76	1979
Nader Shah	Marun, Iran	574	175	1,313	1,620	1978
Hasan Ugurlu	Yesil Irmak, Turkey	574	175	874	1,078	1980
Pauti-Mazar	Mazar, Ecuador	540	165	405	500	1984
Hungry Horse	S.Fk., Flathead, Montana	564	172	3,470	4,280	1953
Longyangxia	Huanghe, China	564	172	20,025	24,700	1983
Cabora Bassa	Zambezi, Mozambique	561	171	51,075	63,000	1974
Maqarin	Yarmuk, Jordan	561	171	259	320	1987
Amaluza	Paute, Ecuador	558	170	81	100	1982
Idikki	Periyar, India	554	169	1,618	1,996	1974
Charvak	Chirchik, U.S.S.R.	552	168	1,620	2,000	1970
Gura Apelor Retezat	Riul Mare, Romania	552	168	182	225	1980
Grand Coulee	Columbia, Washington	550	168	9,390	11,582	1942
Boruca	Terraba, Costa Rica	548	167	12,128	14,960	UC
Vidraru	Arges, Romania	545	166	380	465	1965
Kremasta (King Paul)	Achelöus, Greece	541	165	3,850	4,750	1965

NOTE: UC = under construction. *Source:* Department of the Interior, Bureau of Reclamation and *International Water Power and Dam Construction.*

World's Largest Dams

Dam	Location	Volume (thousands)		Year completed
		Cubic meters	Cubic yards	
New Cornelia Tailings	Arizona	209,500	274,015	1973
Poti (Chapetón)	Argentina	200,000	261,590	UC
Tarbela	Pakistan	121,720	159,203	1976
Fort Peck	Montana	96,049	125,628	1940
Atatürk	Turkey	84,500	110,522	1990
Yacyretá-Apipe	Paraguay/Argentina	81,000	105,944	UC
Guri (Raul Leoni)	Venezuela	78,000	102,014	1986
Rogun	U.S.S.R.	75,500	98,750	1985
Oahe	South Dakota	70,339	92,000	1963
Mangla	Pakistan	65,651	85,872	1967
Gardiner	Canada	65,440	85,592	1968
Afsluitdijk	Netherlands	63,400	82,927	1932
Oroville	California	59,639	78,008	1968
San Luis	California	59,405	77,700	1967
Nurek	U.S.S.R.	58,000	75,861	1980
Garrison	North Dakota	50,843	66,500	1956
Cochiti	New Mexico	48,052	62,850	1975
Tabka (Thawra)	Syria	46,000	60,168	1976
Bennett W.A.C.	Canada	43,733	57,201	1967
Tucuruíi	Brazil	43,000	56,242	1984
Boruca	Costa Rica	43,000	56,242	UC
High Aswan (Sadd-el-Aali)	Egypt	43,000	56,242	1970
San Roque	Philippines	43,000	56,242	UC
Kiev	U.S.S.R.	42,841	56,034	1964
Dantiwada Left Embankment	India	41,040	53,680	1965
Saratov	U.S.S.R.	40,400	52,843	1967
Mission Tailings 2	Arizona	40,088	52,435	1973
Fort Randall	South Dakota	38,227	50,000	1953
Kanev	U.S.S.R.	37,860	49,520	1976
Mosul	Iraq	36,000	47,086	1982
Kakhovka	U.S.S.R.	35,640	46,617	1955
Itumbiara	Brazil	35,600	46,563	1980
Lauwerszee	Netherlands	35,575	46,532	1969
Beas	India	35,418	46,325	1974
Oosterschelde	Netherlands	35,000	45,778	1986

NOTE: UC = under construction. *Source:* Department of the Interior, Bureau of Reclamation and *International Water Power and Dam Construction.*

World's Largest Hydroelectric Plants

Name of Dam	Location	Rated capacity (MW) Present	Ultimate	Year of initial operation
Itaipu	Brazil/Paraguay	1,400	12,600	1984
Grand Coulee	Washington	6,480	10,080	1942
Guri (Raul Leoni)	Venezuela	2,800	10,060	1968
Tucuruí	Brazil	—	7,500	1985
Sayano-Shushensk	U.S.S.R.	—	6,400	1980
Krasnoyarsk	U.S.S.R.	6,096	6,096	1968
Corpus-Posadas	Argentina/Paraguay	—	6,000	UC
LaGrande 2	Canada	5,328	5,328	1982
Churchill Falls	Canada	5,225	5,225	1971
Bratsk	U.S.S.R.	4,100	4,600	1964
Ust'—Ilimsk	U.S.S.R.	3,675	4,500	1974
Cabora Bassa	Mozambique	2,075	4,150	1974
Yacyretá-Apipe	Argentina/Paraguay	—	4,050	UC
Rogun	U.S.S.R.	—	3,600	1985
Paulo Afonso	Brazil	3,409	3,409	1954
Salto Santiago	Brazil	1,332	3,333	1980
Pati (Chapetón)	Argentina	—	3,300	UC
Brumley Gap	Virginia	3,200	3,200	1973
Ilha Solteira	Brazil	3,200	3,200	1973
Inga I	Zaire	360	2,820	1974
Gezhouba	China	965	2,715	1981
John Day	Oregon/Washington	2,160	2,700	1969
Nurek	U.S.S.R.	900	2,700	1976
Revelstoke	Canada	900	2,700	1984
Sáo Simao	Brazil	2,680	2,680	1979
LaGrande 4	Canada	2,637	2,637	1984
Mica	Canada	1,736	2,610	1976
Volgograd—22nd Congress	U.S.S.R.	2,560	2,560	1958
Fos do Areia	Brazil	2,511	2,511	1983
Itaparica	Brazil	—	2,500	1985
Bennett W.A.C.	Canada	2,116	2,416	1969
Chicoasén	Mexico	—	2,400	1980
Atatürk	Turkey	—	2,400	1990
LaGrande 3	Canada	2,310	2,310	1982
Volga—V.I. Lenin	U.S.S.R.	2,300	2,300	1955
Iron Gates I	Romania/Yugoslavia	2,300	2,300	1970
Iron Gates II	Romania/Yugoslavia	270	2,160	1983
Bath County	Virginia	—	2,100	1985
High Aswan (Saad-el-Aali)	Egypt	2,100	2,100	1967
Tarbela	Pakistan	1,400	2,100	1977
Piedra del Aquila	Argentina	—	2,100	UC
Itumbiara	Brazil	2,080	2,080	1980
Chief Joseph	Washington	2,069	2,069	1956
McNary	Oregon	980	2,030	1954
Green River	North Carolina	—	2,000	1980
Tehri	India	—	2,000	UC
Cornwall	New York	—	2,000	1978
Ludington	Michigan	1,979	1,979	1973
Robert Moses—Niagara	New York	1,950	1,950	1961
Salto Grande	Argentina/Uruguay	—	1,890	1979

Note: MW = Megawatts, UC = under construction. *Source:* Department of the Interior, Bureau of Reclamation and *International Water Power and Dam Construction.*

Notable U.S. Skyscrapers

City	Building	Stories	Height ft	m	City	Building	Stories	Height ft	m
Chicago	Sears Tower	110	1,454	443	Chicago	John Hancock Center	100	1,127	343
New York	World Trade Center	110	1,377	419	New York	Chrysler	77	1,046	319
New York	Empire State	102	1,250	381	Los Angeles	First Interstate World Center	73	1,017	310
Chicago	AMOCO	80	1,136	346	Houston	Texas	75	1,002	305

City	Building			
Houston	Allied Bank	71	985	300
Chicago	311 South Wacker Drive	65	969	295
New York	American International	66	952	290
Philadelphia	One Liberty Place	62	945	288
Seattle	Columbia Seafirst Center	76	943	287
New York	Citicorp Center	59	915	279
New York	40 Wall Tower	71	900	274
Chicago	Two Prudential Center	64	900	274
Philadelphia	Mellon Bank Center	56	880	268
Chicago	Water Tower Place	74	859	262
Los Angeles	First Interstate Bank	62	858	261
San Francisco	Transamerica Pyramid	61	853	260
Chicago	First National Bank	60	851	259
New York	RCA	70	850	259
Philadelphia	Two Liberty Place	52	845	257
Pittsburgh	USX Tower	64	841	256
Atlanta	One Atlantic Center	50	825	251
New York	Chase Manhattan	60	813	248
New York	Pan Am	59	808	246
New York	Woolworth	55	792	241
Boston	John Hancock Tower	60	790	241
San Francisco	Bank of America	52	779	237
Minneapolis	IDS Tower	57	775	236
New York	One Liberty Plaza	54	775	236
Chicago	Three First National Plaza	57	775	236
New York	One Penn Plaza	57	774	236
Minneapolis	Norwest Center	57	772	235
Miami	Southeast Finan. Ctr.	55	765	233
Atlanta	Westin Peachtree Plaza	73	754	230
New York	Exxon	54	750	229
Boston	Prudential Tower	52	750	229
Dallas	First Interst. Bank Tower	60	744	227
Los Angeles	Security Pacific Plaza	55	743	226
Los Angeles	Wells Fargo Center	54	743	226
Atlanta	Georgia-Pacific Center	52	741	226
Atlanta	191 Peachtree Tower	50	740	225
New York	One Astor Plaza	54	730	222
Chicago	Olympia Centre	63	727	222
Houston	Gulf Tower	52	725	221
New York	Marine Midland	52	724	221
Los Angeles	Mitsui (North Tower) Fudosan Tower	52	716	218
Pittsburgh	One Mellon Bank Center	54	715	218
Houston	One Shell Plaza	50	714	218
Detroit	Detroit Westin Hotel	73	712	220
Indianapolis	Banc One Center Tower	51	711	216
Dallas	Renaissance Tower	56	710	216
Cleveland	Terminal Tower	52	708	216
New York	Union Carbide	52	707	215
New York	General Motors	50	705	215
Seattle	AT&T Gateway Tower	62	702	214
New York	Metropolitan Life	50	700	213
Philadelphia	Blue Cross Tower	50	700	213
Chicago	Leo Burnett Building	46	700	213

NOTE: Height does not include TV towers and antennas. *Source: Information Please* questionnaires.

Notable Tunnels

Name	Location	Length mi.	Length km	Year completed
Railroad, excluding subways				
Seikan	Tsugara Strait, Japan	33.1	53.3	1983
Simplon (I and II)	Alps, Switzerland-Italy	12.3	19.8	1906 & 1922
Apennine	Bologna-Florence, Italy	11.5	18.5	1934
St. Gotthard	Swiss Alps	9.3	14.9	1881
Lötschberg	Swiss Alps	9.1	14.6	1911
Mont Cénis	French Alps	8.5[1]	13.7	1871
New Cascade	Cascade Mountains, Washington	7.8	12.6	1929
Vosges	Vosges, France	7.0	11.3	1940
Arlberg	Austrian Alps	6.3	10.1	1884
Moffat	Rocky Mountains, Colorado	6.2	9.9	1928
Shimuzu	Shimuzu, Japan	6.1	9.8	1931
Rimutaka	Wairarapa, New Zealand	5.5	8.9	1955
Vehicular				
St. Gotthard	Alps, Switzerland	10.2	16.4	1980
Mt. Blanc	Alps, France-Italy	7.5	12.1	1965
Mt. Ena	Japan Alps, Japan	5.3	8.5	1976 [2]
Great St. Bernard	Alps, Switzerland-Italy	3.4	5.5	1964
Mount Royal	Montreal, Canada	3.2	5.1	1918
Lincoln	Hudson River, New York-New Jersey	2.5	4.0	1937
Queensway Road	Mersey River, Liverpool, England	2.2	3.5	1934
Brooklyn-Battery	East River, New York City	2.1	3.4	1950
Holland	Hudson River, New York-New Jersey	1.7	2.7	1927
Fort McHenry	Baltimore, Maryland	1.7	2.7	1985
Hampton Roads	Norfolk, Virginia	1.4	2.3	1957
Queens-Midtown	East River, New York City	1.3	2.1	1940
Liberty Tubes	Pittsburgh, Pennsylvania	1.2	1.9	1923
Baltimore Harbor	Baltimore, Maryland	1.2	1.9	1957
Allegheny Tunnels	Pennsylvania Turnpike	1.2	1.9	1940 [3]

1. Lengthened to its present 8.5 miles in 1881. 2. Parallel tunnel begun in 1976. 3. Parallel tunnel built in 1965, twin tunnel in 1966. NOTE: UC = under construction. *Source:* American Society of Civil Engineers and International Bridge, Tunnel & Turnpike Association.

Notable Modern Bridges

Name	Location	Length of main span		Year completed
		ft	m	
Suspension				
Humber	Hull, Britain	4,626	1,410	1981
Verrazano-Narrows	Lower New York Bay	4,260	1,298	1964
Golden Gate	San Francisco Bay	4,200	1,280	1937
Mackinac Straits	Michigan	3,800	1,158	1957
Bosporus	Istanbul	3,524	1,074	1973
George Washington	Hudson River at New York City	3,500	1,067	1931
Ponte 25 de Abril	Tagus River at Lisbon	3,323	1,013	1966
Second Bosporus Bridge	Turkey	3,322	1,012	1988
Forth Road	Queensferry, Scotland	3,300	1,006	1964
Severn	Severn River at Beachley, England	3,240	988	1966
Tacoma Narrows	Puget Sound at Tacoma, Wash.	2,800	853	1950
Kanmon Strait	Kyushu-Honshu, Japan	2,336	712	1973
Angostura	Orinoco River at Ciudad Bolivar, Venezuela	2,336	712	1967
Transbay (twin spans)	San Francisco Bay	2,310	704	1936
Bronx-Whitestone	East River, New York City	2,300	701	1939
Pierre Laporte	St. Lawrence River at Quebec, Canada	2,190	668	1970
Delaware Memorial (twin bridges)	Delaware River near Wilmington, Del.	2,150	655	1951, 1968
Seaway Skyway	St. Lawrence River at Ogdensburg, N.Y.	2,150	655	1960
Gas Pipe Line	Atchafalaya River, Louisiana	2,000	610	1951
Walt Whitman	Delaware River at Philadelphia	2,000	610	1957
Tancarville	Seine River at Tancarville, France	1,995	608	1959
Lillebaelt	Lillebaelt Strait, Denmark	1,969	600	1970
Ambassador International	Detroit River at Detroit	1,850	564	1929
Throgs Neck	East River, New York City	1,800	549	1961
Benjamin Franklin	Delaware River at Philadelphia	1,750	533	1926
Skjomen	Narvik, Norway	1,722	525	1972
Kvalsund	Hammerfest, Norway	1,722	525	1977
Kleve-Emmerich	Rhine River at Emmerich, West Germany	1,640	500	1965
Bear Mountain	Hudson River at Peekskill, N.Y.	1,632	497	1924
Wm. Preston Lane, Jr., Memorial (twin bridges)	Near Annapolis, Md.	1,600	488	1952, 1973
Williamsburg	East River, New York City	1,600	488	1903
Newport	Narragansett Bay at Newport, R.I.	1,600	488	1969
Brooklyn	East River, New York City	1,595	486	1883
Cantilever				
Quebec Railway	St. Lawrence River at Quebec, Canada	1,800	549	1917
Forth Railway (twin spans)	Queensferry, Scotland	1,710	521	1890
Minato Ohashi	Osaka, Japan	1,673	510	1974
Commodore John Barry	Chester, Pa.	1,644	501	1974
Greater New Orleans (twin spans)	Mississippi River, Louisiana	1,576	480	1958
Howrah	Hooghly River at Calcutta	1,500	457	1943
Transbay Bridge	San Francisco Bay	1,400	427	1936
Baton Rouge	Mississippi River, Louisiana	1,235	376	1968
Tappan Zee	Hudson River at Tarrytown, N.Y.	1,212	369	1955
Longview	Columbia River at Longview, Wash.	1,200	366	1930
Patapsco River	Baltimore Outer Harbor Crossing	1,200	366	1976
Queensboro	East River, New York City	1,182	360	1909
Steel Arch				
New River Gorge	Fayetteville, W. Va.	1,700	518	1977
Bayonne	Kill Van Kull at Bayonne, N.J.	1,675	510	1931
Sydney Harbor	Sydney, Australia	1,670	509	1932
Fremont	Portland, Ore.	1,255	383	1973
Zdákov	Vltava River, Czechoslovakia	1,244	380	1967
Port Mann	Fraser River at Vancouver, British Columbia	1,200	366	1964
Thatcher Ferry	Panama Canal, Panama	1,128	344	1962
Laviolette	St. Lawrence River, Trois Rivieres, Quebec	1,100	335	1967
Runcorn-Widnes	Mersey River, England	1,082	330	1961
Birchenough	Sabi River at Fort Victoria, Rhodesia	1,080	329	1935

Name	Location	Length of main span ft	m	Year completed
Cable-Stayed				
Ikuchi	Honshu-Shikoku, Japan	1,607	490	UC
Alex Fraser	Vancpuver, B.C., Canada	1,525	465	1986
Yokohama-ko-odan	Kanagawa, Japan	1,509	460	UC
Second Hooghly	Calcutta, India	1,500	457	UC
Chao Phya	Thailand	1,476	450	1986
Barrios de Luna	Spain	1,444	440	1983
Hitshuishi-jima and Iwakuro-jima	Honshu-Shikoku, Japan	1,378	420	1988
Meiko Nishi	Aichi, Japan	1,329	405	1985
St. Nazaire	Loire River, St. Nazaire, France	1,325	404	1975
Rande	Rande, Spain	1,312	400	1977
Dame Point	Jacksonville, Florida, U.S.A.	1,300	396	1988
Houston Ship Channel	Baytown, Texas	1,250	381	UC
Hale Boggs Memorial	Luling, Louisiana, U.S.A.	1,222	373	1983
Dusseldorf Flehe	West Germany	1,207	368	1979
Tjörn	Sweden	1,200	366	1981
Sunshine Skyway	Tampa, Florida, U.S.A.	1,200	366	1987
Continuous Truss				
Mark Clark Expressway I-526	Cooper River, at Charleston, S.C.	1,600	487	UC
Astoria	Columbia River at Astoria, Oregon	1,232	376	1966
Oshima	Oshima Island, Japan	1,066	325	1976
Croton Reservoir	Croton, N.Y.	1,052	321	1970
Tenmon	Kumamoto, Japan	984	300	1966
Kuronoseto	Nagashima-Kyushu, Japan	984	300	1974
Ravenswood	Ohio River, Ravenswood, W. Va.	902	275	1981
Dubuque	Mississippi River at Dubuque, Iowa	845	258	1943
Braga Memorial	Taunton River at Somerset, Mass.	840	256	1966
Graf Spee	Germany	839	256	1936
Concrete Arch				
KRK	Zagreb, Yugoslavia	1,280	390	1979
Gladesville	Parramatta River at Sydney, Australia	1,000	305	1964
Amizade	Paraná River at Foz do Iguassu, Brazil	951	290	1964
Arrábida	Porto, Portugal	886	270	1963
Sandö	Angerman River at Kramfors, Sweden	866	264	1943
Shibenik	Krka River, Yugoslavia	808	246	1966
Fiumarella	Catanzaro, Italy	758	231	1961
Zaporozhe	Old Dnepr River, U.S.S.R.	748	228	1952
Novi Sad	Danube River, Yugoslavia	692	211	1961
Segmental Congrete Box Girder				
Jesse H. Jones Memorial	Houston Ship Channel, Texas	750	228	1982

NOTE: UC = under construction. *Source: Encyclopaedia Britannica,* American Society of Civil Engineers, and Bridge Division, Federal Highway Administration.

Famous Ship Canals

Name	Location	Length (miles)[1]	Width (feet)	Depth (feet)	Locks	Year opened
Albert	Belgium	80.0	53.0	16.5	6	1939
Amsterdam-Rhine	Netherlands	45.0	164.0	41.0	3	1952
Beaumont-Port Arthur	United States	40.0	200.0	34.0	—	1916
Chesapeake and Delaware	United States	19.0	250.0	27.0	—	1927
Houston	United States	50.0	[2]	40.0	—	1914
Kiel (Nord-Ostsee Kanal)	Germany	61.3	144.0	36.0	4	1895
Panama	Canal Zone	50.7	110.0	41.0	12	1914
St. Lawrence Seaway	U.S. and Canada	2,400.0[3]	[4]	—	—	1959
Montreal to Prescott	U.S. and Canada	11.5	80.0	30.0	7	1959
Welland	Canada	27.5	80.0	27.0	8	1931
Sault Ste. Marie	Canada	1.2	60.0	16.8	1	1895
Sault Ste. Marie	United States	1.6	80.0	25.0	4	1915
Suez	Egypt	100.6[5]	197.0	36.0	—	1869

1. Statute miles. 2. 300–400 feet. 3. From Montreal to Duluth. 4. 442–550 feet; there are 11.5 miles of locks, 80 feet wide and 30 feet deep. 5. From Port Said lighthouse to entrance channel in Suez roads. *Source:* American Society of Civil Engineers.

WORLD STATISTICS

World Population Continues to Rise

By Nafis Sadik

The 1990s will be a critical decade. The choices of the next 10 years will decide the speed of population growth for much of the next century; they will decide whether world population triples or merely doubles before it finally stops growing; they will decide whether the pace of damage to the environment speeds up or slows down.

The world's population, now 5.3 billion, is increasing by three people every second—about a quarter of a million every day. Between 90 and 100 million people—roughly equivalent to the population of Eastern Europe or Central America—will be added every year during the 1990s; a billion people—a whole extra China—over the decade.

No less than 95% of the global population over the next 35 years will be in the developing countries of Africa, Asia, and Latin America.

It has been more than 20 years since the population growth rate of developing countries reached its peak in 1965–70. But it will be during only the last five years of this century that the additions to total numbers in developing countries will reach their maximum. This 35-year lag is a powerful demonstration of the steamroller momentum of population growth.

Racing to provide services to fast-growing populations is like running up the down escalator: You have to run very fast indeed to maintain upward motion. So far, all the effort put into social programs has not been quite enough to move upward in numerical terms. The absolute total of human deprivation has actually increased, and unless there is a massive increase in family planning and other social spending, the future will be no better.

Population Trends

Southern Asia, with almost a quarter of the current total world population, will account for 31% of the total increase between now and the end of the century; Africa, with 12% of the world's population today, will account for 23% of the increase. By contrast, eastern Asia, which has another 25% of the current world population, will account for only 17% of the total increase. Similarly, the developed countries—Europe (including the Soviet Union), North America, and Japan, which represents 23% of the current world population—will account for only 6% of the increase. The remaining 15% of the world's population, living in developing countries, will produce 23% of the increase.

By and large, the increases will be in the poorest countries—those by definition lease equipped to meet the needs of the new arrivals and invest in the future.

Because of the world's skewed growth patterns, the balance of numbers will shift radically. In 1950, Europe and North America constituted 22% of the world's population. In 2025, they will make up less than 9%. Africa, only 9% of the world population in 1950, will account for just under a fifth of the 2025 total. India will overtake China as the world's most populous country by the year 2030.

Toward the end of the twenty-first century, a number of countries seem set to face severe problems if populations grow as projected. Nigeria could have some 500 million citizens—as many as the whole African continent had around 1982. This would represent more than 10 people for every hectare of arable land. Modern France, with better soils and less erosion, has only three people per hectare. Bangladesh's 116 million inhabitants would grow to 324 million, with density on its arable land more than twice as high as in the Netherlands today. This does not take into account any land that may be lost to sea-level rises caused by global warming.

It should be emphasized that these are not the most pessimistic projections. On the contrary, they assume steadily declining fertility during most of the next 100 years.

Food

Between 1979–81 and 1986–87, cereal production per person actually declined in 51 developing countries and rose in only 43. The total number of malnourished people increased from 460 million to 512 million and is projected to exceed 532 million by the end of the century.

Developing countries as a whole have suffered a serious decline in food self-sufficiency. Their cereal imports in 1969–71 were only 20 million tons. By 1983–85, they had risen to 69 million tons and are projected to total 112 million tons by the end of the century. These deficits have so far been met by corresponding surpluses in the industrialized countries—of which the overwhelming bulk comes from North America.

World food security now depends shakily on the performance of North American farmers. Following the drought-hit U.S. harvest of 1988, world cereal stocks dropped from 451 million tons in 1986–87 to only 290 million tons in 1989, down from a safe 24% of annual consumption to the danger level of 17%.

Poverty

The world produces enough food to feed everyone today—yet malnutrition affects as many as 500 million people. The problem is poverty and the ability to earn a livelihood. The total numbers of the poor have grown over the past two decades to around one billion now.

Absolute poverty has shown a dogged tendency to rise in numerical terms. The poorest fifth of the population still dispose of only 4% of the world's wealth, while the richest dispose of 58%. Economic recession, rising debt burdens, and mistaken priorities have reduced social spending in many countries.

But population growth at over 2% annually has also slowed social progress. So much additional investment has been required to increase the quantity of health, education, and other services to meet the needs of increased populations that the quality of service has suffered.

In many sectors, the proportion of deprived people has declined. But this is a reduced proportion of a higher total population swelled by rapid growth. As a result, the total numbers of deprived people have growth.

The growth of incomes may be affected by population growth. On a regional basis, there is an inverse relationship between population growth and growth of per capita income. There is a lag of 15–20 years between the peak of population growth and the peak growth in the labor force. Already there are severe problems in absorbing new entrants to the labor force in regions such as Africa or South Asia. Yet, in numerical terms, the highest rates of labor-force growth in developing countries lie ahead, in the years 2010–2020.

The labor force in developing countries will grow from around 1.76 billion today to more than 3.1 billion in 2025. Every year, 38 million new jobs will be needed, without counting jobs required to wipe out existing underemployment, estimated at 40% in many developing countries. Complicating the issue will be the spread of new, labor-saving technologies.

The land still provides the livelihood of almost 60% of the population of developing countries. But most of the best and most-accessible land is already in use, and what is left is either less fertile or harder to clear and work. The area available per person actually declined at the rate of 1.9% a year during the 1980s.

Urban and Education Issues

In recent decades, urban growth in developing countries has been even more rapid than overall population growth. Town populations are expanding at 3.6% a year—four and a half times faster than in industrialized countries and 60% faster than rural areas. Rural migrants swell the total, but an increasing share of this growth now comes from natural growth within the cities themselves.

The speed of growth has outpaced the ability of local and national government to provide adequate services. The number of urban households without safe water increased from 138 million in 1970 to 215 million in 1988. Over the same period, households without adequate sanitations ballooned from 98 million to 340 million.

The total number of children out of school grew from 284 million in 1970 to 293 million in 1985 and is projected to rise further to 315 million by the end of the century. Also between 1970 and 1985: The total number of illiterates rose from 742 million to 889 million, and the total number of people without safe sanitation increased from about a billion to 1.75 billion.

Eating Away at the Earth

These increasing numbers are eating away at the earth itself. The combination of fast population growth and poverty in developing countries has begun to make permanent changes to the environment. During the 1990s, these changes will reach critical levels. They include continued urban growth, degradation of land and water resources, massive deforestation, and buildup of greenhouse gases.

Many of these changes are now inevitable because they were not foreseen early enough, or because action was not taken to forestall them. Our options in the present generation are narrower because of the decisions of our predecessors. Our range of choice, as individuals or as nations, is narrower, and the choices are harder.

The 1990s will decide whether the choices for our children narrow yet further—or open up. We know more about population—and interactions among population, resources, and the environment—than any previous generation. We have the basis for action. Failure to use it decisively will ensure only that the problems become much more severe and much more intractable, the choices harder and their price higher.

At the start of the 1990s, the choice must be to act decisively to slow population growth, attack poverty, and protect the environment. The alternative is to hand on to our children a poisoned inheritance. □

Nafis Sadik is executive director of the United Nations Population Fund. This article is adapted from the Fund's "The State of World Population 1990."

Area and Population by Country

Mid-1991 Estimates

Country	Area[1]	Population	Country	Area[1]	Population
Afghanistan	250,000	16,600,000	Cameroon	183,570	11,400,000
Albania	11,100	3,300,000	Canada	3,851,790	26,800,000
Algeria	919,590	26,000,000	Cape Verde	1,560	400,000
Angola	481,350	8,500,000	Central African Republic	240,530	3,000,000
Antigua and Barbuda	170	100,000	Chad	495,750	5,100,000
Argentina	1,068,300	32,700,000	Chile	292,260	13,400,000
Australia	2,967,900	17,500,000	China, People's Republic of	3,705,390	1,151,300,000
Austria	32,370	7,700,000	Colombia	439,730	33,600,000
Bahamas	5,380	300,000	Comoros	690	500,000
Bahrain	240	500,000	Congo	132,050	2,300,000
Bangladesh	55,600	116,600,000	Costa Rica	19,580	3,100,000
Barbados	170	300,000	Côte d'Ivoire	124,500	12,500,000
Belgium	11,750	9,900,000	Cuba	44,420	10,700,000
Belize	8,860	200,000	Cyprus	3,570	700,000
Benin	43,480	4,800,000	Czechoslovakia	49,370	15,700,000
Bhutan	18,150	700,000	Denmark	16,630	5,100,000
Bolivia	424,160	7,500,000	Djibouti	8,490	400,000
Botswana	231,800	1,300,000	Dominica	290	100,000
Brazil	3,268,470	153,300,000	Dominican Republic	18,810	7,300,000
Brunei	2,230	300,000	Ecuador	109,480	10,800,000
Bulgaria	42,820	9,000,000	Egypt	386,660	54,500,000
Burkina Faso	105,870	9,400,000	El Salvador	8,260	5,400,000
Burundi	10,750	5,800,000	Equatorial Guinea	10,830	400,000
Cambodia	69,900	7,100,000	Ethiopia	471,780	53,200,000

Country	Area[1]	Population	Country	Area[1]	Population
Fiji	7,050	700,000	Niger	489,190	8,000,000
Finland	130,130	5,000,000	Nigeria	356,670	122,500,000
France	211,210	56,700,000	Norway	125,180	4,300,000
Gabon	103,350	1,200,000	Oman	82,030	1,600,000
Gambia	4,360	900,000	Pakistan	310,400	117,500,000
Germany	137,800	79,500,000	Panama	29,760	2,500,000
Ghana	92,100	15,500,000	Papua New Guinea	178,260	3,900,000
Greece	50,940	10,100,000	Paraguay	157,050	4,400,000
Grenada	130	100,000	Peru	496,220	22,000,000
Guatemala	42,040	9,500,000	Philippines	115,830	62,300,000
Guinea	94,930	7,500,000	Poland	120,730	38,200,000
Guinea-Bissau	13,950	1,000,000	Portugal	35,550	10,400,000
Guyana	83,000	800,000	Qatar	4,250	500,000
Haiti	10,710	6,300,000	Romania	91,700	23,400,000
Honduras	43,280	5,300,000	Rwanda	10,170	7,500,000
Hungary	35,920	10,400,000	St. Lucia	240	200,000
Iceland	39,770	300,000	St. Vincent and the Grenadines	150	100,000
India	1,269,340	859,200,000	Saudi Arabia	830,000	15,500,000
Indonesia	741,100	181,400,000	Senegal	75,750	7,500,000
Iran	636,290	58,600,000	Sierra Leone	27,700	4,300,000
Iraq	167,920	17,100,000	Singapore	220	2,800,000
Ireland	27,140	3,500,000	Solomon Islands	10,980	300,000
Israel	8,020	4,900,000	Somalia	246,200	7,700,000
Italy	116,310	57,700,000	South Africa	471,440	40,600,000
Jamaica	4,240	2,500,000	Spain	194,900	39,000,000
Japan	143,750	123,800,000	Sri Lanka	26,330	17,400,000
Jordan	35,480	3,400,000	Sudan	967,490	25,900,000
Kenya	224,960	25,200,000	Suriname	63,040	400,000
Korea, North	46,540	21,800,000	Swaziland	6,700	800,000
Korea, South	38,020	43,200,000	Sweden	173,730	8,600,000
Kuwait	6,880	1,400,000	Switzerland	15,940	6,800,000
Laos	91,430	4,100,000	Syria	71,500	12,800,000
Lebanon	4,020	3,400,000	Taiwan	12,460	20,500,000
Lesotho	11,720	1,800,000	Tanzania	364,900	26,900,000
Liberia	43,000	2,700,000	Thailand	196,460	58,800,000
Libya	679,360	4,400,000	Togo	21,930	3,800,000
Luxembourg	990	400,000	Trinidad and Tobago	1,980	1,300,000
Madagascar	226,660	12,400,000	Tunisia	63,170	8,400,000
Malawi	45,750	9,400,000	Turkey	301,380	58,500,000
Malaysia	127,320	18,300,000	Uganda	91,140	18,700,000
Maldives	120	200,000	U.S.S.R.	8,649,500	292,000,000
Mali	478,760	8,300,000	United Arab Emirates	32,280	2,400,000
Malta	120	400,000	United Kingdom	94,530	57,500,000
Mauritania	397,950	2,100,000	United States	3,615,100	252,800,000
Mauritius	790	1,100,000	Uruguay	68,040	3,100,000
Mexico	761,600	85,700,000	Vanuatu	5,700	200,000
Mongolia	604,250	2,200,000	Venezuela	352,140	20,100,000
Morocco	172,410	26,200,000	Vietnam	127,240	67,600,000
Mozambique	309,490	16,100,000	Western Samoa	1,100	200,000
Myanmar	261,220	42,100,000	Yemen[2]	203,850	10,100,000
Namibia	318,260	1,500,000	Yugoslavia	98,760	23,900,000
Nepal	54,360	19,600,000	Zaire	905,560	37,800,000
Netherlands	14,410	15,000,000	Zambia	290,580	8,400,000
New Zealand	103,740	3,500,000	Zimbabwe	150,800	10,000,000
Nicaragua	50,190	3,900,000			

1. Square miles. Source: *1991 World Population Data Sheet*, Population Reference Bureau, Inc., Washington, D.C.

Urban Populations Are Growing Rapidly

Urban populations are growing so fast in many countries that 20 years of growth will result in more people added than there were in the entire country in 1960. For example, expected urban trends will add 56 million to Nigeria's cities during the next two decades, more than Nigeria's entire population of 51 million in 1960. Similar proportional growth is likely in Zaire and Eqypt.

While the largest cities in many developing countries are growing at an unprecedented pace, it is the smaller cities, those with under 2 million inhabitants, that will add the most to the world's population of urban population over the next decade. While the cities of 2 million or more will slightly increase their share of world population from just under 10 percent to just over 10 percent, the smaller cities will increase from 38 percent to 42 percent of the world's people. Rural population will decrease in proportion from 52 percent to 48 percent of the world total.

World's Largest Cities by Rank
(Estimated Mid-Year Population in Thousands)

Rank in 1990	City	1990	1995	2000	Average Annual Growth Rate (%) 1990–95	Area (square miles)
1.	Tokyo-Yokohama, Japan	26,952	28,447	29,971	1.08	1,089
2.	Mexico City, Mexico	20,207	23,913	27,872	3.37	522
3.	Sao Paulo, Brazil	18,052	21,539	25,354	3.53	451
4.	Seoul, South Korea	16,268	19,065	21,976	3.17	342
5.	New York, United States	14,622	14,638	14,648	0.02	1,274
6.	Osaka-Kobe-Kyoto, Japan	13,826	14,060	14,287	0.34	495
7.	Bombay, India	11,777	13,532	15,357	2.78	95
8.	Calcutta, India	11,663	12,885	14,088	1.99	209
9.	Buenos Aires, Argentina	11,518	12,232	12,911	1.20	535
10.	Rio de Janeiro, Brazil	11,428	12,786	14,169	2.25	260
11.	Moscow, Soviet Union	10,367	10,769	11,121	0.76	379
12.	Los Angeles, United States	10,060	10,414	10,714	0.69	1,110
13.	Manila, Philippines	9,880	11,342	12,846	2.76	188
14.	Cairo, Egypt	9,851	11,155	12,512	2.49	104
15.	Jakarta, Indonesia	9,588	11,151	12,804	3.02	76
16.	Tehran, Iran	9,354	11,681	14,251	4.44	112
17.	London, United Kingdom	9,170	8,897	8,574	−0.60	874
18.	Paris, France	8,709	8,764	8,803	0.13	432
19.	Delhi, India	8,475	10,105	11,849	3.52	138
20.	Karachi, Pakistan	7,711	9,350	11,299	3.85	190
21.	Lagos, Nigeria	7,602	9,799	12,528	5.08	56
22.	Essen, Germany	7,474	7,364	7,239	−0.30	704
23.	Shanghai, China	6,873	7,194	7,540	0.91	78
24.	Lima, Peru	6,578	7,853	9,241	3.54	120
25.	Chicago, United States	6,526	6,541	6,568	0.05	762
26.	Taipei, Taiwan	6,513	7,477	8,516	2.76	138
27.	Istanbul, Turkey	6,461	7,624	8,875	3.31	165
28.	Bangkok, Thailand	5,791	6,657	7,587	2.79	102
29.	Madras, India	5,743	6,550	7,384	2.63	115
30.	Beijing, China	5,736	5,865	5,993	0.44	151
31.	Bogota, Colombia	5,710	6,801	7,935	3.50	79
32.	Hong Kong, Hong Kong	5,656	5,841	5,956	0.64	23
33.	Santiago, Chile	5,275	5,812	6,294	1.94	128
34.	Pusan, South Korea	4,838	5,748	6,700	3.45	54
35.	Tianjin, China	4,804	5,041	5,298	0.96	49
36.	Milan, Italy	4,738	4,795	4,839	0.24	344
37.	Nagoya, Japan	4,736	5,017	5,303	1.15	307
38.	St. Petersburg, Soviet Union	4,667	4,694	4,738	0.12	139
39.	Bangalore, India	4,612	5,644	6,764	4.04	50
40.	Madrid, Spain	4,451	4,772	5,104	1.39	66
41.	Shenyang, China	4,248	4,457	4,684	0.96	39
42.	Lahore, Pakistan	4,236	4,986	5,864	3.26	57
43.	Dhaka, Bangladesh	4,224	5,296	6,492	4.52	32
44.	Barcelona, Spain	4,163	4,492	4,834	1.52	87
45.	Manchester, United Kingdom	4,050	3,949	3,827	−0.50	357
46.	Philadelphia, United States	4,007	3,988	3,979	−0.10	471
47.	San Francisco, United States	3,958	4,104	4,214	0.72	428
48.	Baghdad, Iraq	3,941	4,566	5,239	2.94	97
49.	Belo Horizonte, Brazil	3,683	4,373	5,125	3.43	79
50.	Ho Chi Minh City, Vietnam	3,645	4,064	4,481	2.18	31
51.	Ahmadabad, India	3,595	4,200	4,837	3.11	32
52.	Kinshasa, Zaire	3,575	4,520	5,646	4.69	57
53.	Hyderabad, India	3,563	4,149	4,765	3.05	88
54.	Sydney, Australia	3,515	3,619	3,708	0.58	338
55.	Athens, Greece	3,468	3,670	3,866	1.13	116
56.	Miami, United States	3,421	3,679	3,894	1.45	448
57.	Guangzhou, China	3,330	3,485	3,652	0.91	79
58.	Guadalajara, Mexico	3,262	3,839	4,451	3.25	78
59.	Surabaya, Indonesia	3,205	3,428	3,632	1.35	43
60.	Caracas, Venezuela	3,188	3,338	3,435	0.92	54
61.	Wuhan, China	3,169	3,325	3,495	0.96	65
62.	Toronto, Canada	3,108	3,296	3,296	1.17	154
63.	Greater Berlin, Germany	3,022	3,018	3,006	−0.03	274
64.	Rome, Italy	3,021	3,079	3,129	0.38	69
65.	Porto Alegre, Brazil	3,015	3,541	4,109	3.22	231

Rank in 1990	City	1990	1995	2000	Average Annual Growth Rate (%) 1990–95	Area (square miles)
66.	Detroit, United States	2,995	2,865	2,735	−0.89	468
67.	Naples, Italy	2,960	3,051	3,134	0.61	62*
68.	Melbourne, Australia	2,907	2,946	2,968	0.27	327
69.	Alexandria, Egypt	2,899	3,114	3,304	1.43	35
70.	Montreal, Canada	2,896	2,996	3,071	0.68	164
71.	Casablanca, Morocco	2,891	3,327	3,795	2.81	35
72.	Monterrey, Mexico	2,837	3,385	3,974	3.53	77
73.	Rangoon, Burma	2,813	3,075	3,332	1.78	47
74.	Ankara, Turkey	2,782	3,263	3,777	3.19	55
75.	Kiev, Soviet Union	2,751	2,983	3,237	1.62	62
76.	Dallas, United States	2,743	2,972	3,257	1.60	419
77.	Singapore, Singapore	2,695	2,816	2,913	0.88	78
78.	Harbin, China	2,618	2,747	2,887	0.96	30
79.	Washington, United States	2,547	2,637	2,707	0.69	357
80.	Taegu, South Korea	2,529	3,201	4,051	4.71	(n.a.)
81.	Boston, United States	2,475	2,480	2,485	0.04	303
82.	Poona, India	2,447	2,987	3,647	3.99	(n.a.)
83.	Lisbon, Portugal	2,396	2,551	2,717	1.26	(n.a.)
84.	Tashkent, Soviet Union	2,365	2,640	2,947	2.20	(n.a.)
85.	Chengdu, China	2,349	2,465	2,591	0.96	25
86.	Chongqing, China	2,339	2,632	2,961	2.36	(n.a.)
87.	Vienna, Austria	2,313	2,474	2,647	1.35	(n.a.)
88.	Budapest, Hungary	2,301	2,313	2,335	0.10	138
89.	Houston, United States	2,298	2,456	2,651	1.33	310
90.	Salvador, Brazil	2,209	2,694	3,286	3.97	(n.a.)
91.	Birmingham, United Kingdom	2,170	2,130	2,078	−0.37	223
92.	Bucharest, Romania	2,150	2,214	2,271	0.59	52
93.	Havana, Cuba	2,109	2,218	2,333	1.01	(n.a.)
94.	Kanpur, India	2,076	2,356	2,673	2.53	(n.a.)

Source: U.S. Bureau of the Census, 1989, International Data Base. NOTE: For this table cities are defined as population clusters of continuous built-up area with a population density of at least 5,000 persons per square mile. The boundary of the city was determined by examining detailed maps of each city in conjunction with the most recent official population statistics. Exclaves of areas exceeding the minimum population density were added to the city if the intervening gap was less than one mile. To the extent practical, nonresidential areas such as parks, airports, industrial complexes, and water were excluded from the area reported for each city, thus making the population density reflective of the concentrations in the residential portions of the city. By using a consistent definition for the city, it is possible to make comparisons of the cities on the basis of total population, area, and population density.

Political and administrative boundaries were disregarded in determining the population of a city. Berlin includes both East and West Berlin, as well as population from East Germany. Detroit includes Windsor, Canada.

The population of each city was projected based on the proportion each city was of its country total at the time of the last two censuses and projected country populations (U.S. Bureau of the Census 1989).

Population figures for the nine cities with (n.a.) in the area column were derived by a less precise method, not involving the use of detailed maps. In addition, three other cities (Abidjan, Ivory Coast; Khartoum, Sudan; and Medan, Indonesia) were estimated to have at least 2,000,000 inhabitants at midyear 1989. However, projections for these cities could not be prepared because the apparent growth rates indicate that data are not comparable. Thirty-four other cities are projected to have at least 2,000,000 inhabitants by midyear 2000.

Crude Marriage and Divorce Rates for Selected Countries

(per 1,000 population)

Country	Marriage Rate 1989	1988	1987	Divorce Rate 1989	1988	1987	Country	Marriage Rate 1989	1988	1987	Divorce Rate 1989	1988	1987
Australia	7.0	7.1	7.0	n.a.	n.a.	2.44	Italy	5.4	5.5	5.3	n.a.	0.44	0.47
Austria	5.6	4.7	10.1	0.20	1.96	1.93	Japan	5.8	5.8	5.7	1.29	1.25	1.29
Belgium	6.4	6.0	5.8	n.a.	n.a.	n.a.	Luxembourg	5.8	5.5	5.3	n.a.	2.08	1.99
Canada	7.3	7.3	7.1	n.a.	n.a.	3.05	Netherlands	6.1	6.0	6.0	n.a.	1.89	1.90
Czechoslovakia	7.5	7.6	7.8	2.54	2.50	2.54	New Zealand	6.9	7.1	7.5	n.a.	2.63	2.65
Denmark	6.0	6.3	6.1	2.95	2.88	2.80	Norway	4.9	5.2	5.0	n.a.	2.08	2.01
Finland	5.1	5.3	5.4	2.93	2.10	2.10	Poland	6.8	6.5	6.7	1.27	1.27	1.32
France	5.0	4.9	4.8	n.a.	n.a.	1.91	Portugal	n.a.	6.9	6.6	n.a.	0.88	0.87
Germany, East	7.9	8.2	8.5	3.01	2.96	3.04	Spain	n.a.	5.3	5.3	n.a.	n.a.	n.a.
Germany, West	6.6	6.4	6.5	n.a.	2.09	2.13	Sweden	n.a.	5.2	4.9	2.20	2.26	2.19
Greece	6.0	5.2	6.3	n.a.	−n.a.	n.a.	Switzerland	6.8	6.9	6.6	1.95	1.93	1.76
Hungary	6.3	6.2	6.2	n.a.	2.25	2.81	United Kingdom	6.1	6.9	7.0	n.a.	2.89	2.88
Ireland	5.1	5.1	5.1	n.a.	n.a.	n.a.	United States	9.7	9.7	9.9	n.a.	4.80	4.75
Israel	7.0	6.9	6.9	n.a.	1.25	1.19	Yugoslavia	6.7	6.8	7.0	0.89	0.98	0.89

1. Provisional. n.a. = not available. *Sources:* Marriage rates: United Nations, *Monthly Bulletin of Statistics, June 1990;* Divorce rates: United Nations, *Demographic Yearbook 1989.*

Estimates of World Population by Regions

Estimated population in millions

Year	North America[1]	Latin America[2]	Europe[3]	U.S.S.R.	Asia[4]	Africa	Oceania	World total
1650	1	7	103	(5)	257	100	2	470
1750	1	10	144	(5)	437	100	2	694
1850	26	33	274	(5)	656	100	2	1,091
1900	81	63	423	(5)	857	141	6	1,571
1950	166	164	392	180	1,380	219	13	2,513
1960	199	215	425	214	1,683	275	16	3,027
1970	226	283	460	244	2,091	354	19	3,678
1980	252	365	484	266	2,618	472	23	4,478
1985	264	410	492	278	2,831	566	24	4,865
1986	267	419	493	280	2,876	583	25	4,942
1987	270	421	495	284	2,930	601	25	5,026
1988	272	429	497	286	2,995	623	26	5,128
1989	275	438	499	289	3,061	646	26	5,234
1990	278	447	501	291	3,116	661	27	5,321
1991	280	451	502	292	3,155	677	27	5,384

1. U.S. (including Alaska and Hawaii), Bermuda, Canada, Greenland, and St. Pierre and Miquelon. 2. Mexico, Central and South America, and Caribbean Islands. 3. Includes Russia 1650-1900. 4. Excludes Russia (U.S.S.R.). 5. Included in Europe. NOTE: From 1930 on European Turkey included in Asia not Europe. Sources: W.F. Willcox, 1650-1900; United Nations, 1930-70. United States Department of Commerce, Bureau of the Census, 1984; 1986-1991 World Population Data Sheet, Population Reference Bureau, Inc., Washington, D.C.

World's 20 Most Populous Countries: 1991 and 2100

	1991			2100	
Rank	Country	Population	Rank	Country	Population
1.	China	1,151,300,000	1.	India	1,631,800,000
2.	India	859,200,000	2.	China	1,571,400,000
3.	USSR	292,000,000	3.	Nigeria	508,800,000
4.	United States	252,800,000	4.	USSR	375,900,000
5.	Indonesia	181,400,000	5.	Indonesia	356,300,000
6.	Brazil	153,300,000	6.	Pakistan	315,800,000
7.	Japan	123,800,000	7.	United States	308,700,000
8.	Nigeria	122,500,000	8.	Bangladesh	297,100,000
9.	Pakistan	117,500,000	9.	Brazil	293,200,000
10.	Bangladesh	116,600,000	10.	Mexico	195,500,000
11.	Mexico	85,700,000	11.	Ethiopia	173,300,000
12.	Germany	79,500,000	12.	Vietnam	168,100,000
13.	Vietnam	67,600,000	13.	Iran	163,800,000
14.	Philippines	62,300,000	14.	Zaire	138,900,000
15.	Thailand	58,800,000	15.	Japan	127,900,000
16.	Iran	58,600,000	16.	Philippines	125,100,000
17.	Turkey	58,500,000	17.	Tanzania	119,600,000
18.	Italy	57,700,000	18.	Kenya	116,400,000
19.	United Kingdom	57,500,000	19.	Burma	111,700,000
20.	France	56,700,000	20.	Egypt	110,500,000

Sources: 1991 World Population Data Sheet of the Population Reference Bureau, Inc; 2100, World Bank.

The Changing Family Internationally

Far-reaching changes are occurring in family structures and household living arrangements in the developed countries. Families are becoming smaller, and household composition patterns over the past several decades have been away from the traditional nuclear family and toward more single-parent households, more persons living alone, and more couples living together out of wedlock. The one-person household has become the fastest growing type.

Scandinavian countries have been the pacesetters in the development of many of the non-traditional forms of family living, especially births outside of wedlock and cohabitation outside of legal marriage. Women in these societies also have the highest rates of labor force participation.

Japan is the most traditional society of these studied, with very low rates of divorce and births out of wedlock and the highest proportion of married-couple households. But even in Japan, family patterns are changing: sharp drops in fertility have led to much smaller families.

World Population by Country, 1990–2020
(Covers countries with 10 million or more population in 1990)

Country	1990	2000	2010	2020
Afghanistan	15,592,000	24,501,000	31,736,000	39,119,000
Algeria	25,714,000	33,705,000	41,615,000	49,414,000
Argentina	32,291,000	36,036,000	39,885,000	43,462,000
Australia	16,643,000	18,468,000	20,032,000	21,445,000
Bangladesh	117,976,000	153,387,000	191,715,000	230,188,000
Brazil	153,771,000	183,902,000	213,916,000	241,981,000
Burma	41,279,000	49,772,000	58,538,000	67,527,000
Cameroon	11,109,000	14,471,000	18,634,000	23,466,000
Canada	26,527,000	28,233,000	29,423,000	30,232,000
Chile	13,016,000	14,796,000	16,449,000	17,957,000
China				
Mainland	1,130,065,000	1,291,587,000	1,398,189,000	1,523,233,000
Taiwan	20,454,000	22,304,000	23,714,000	24,419,000
Colombia	32,598,000	38,800,000	44,119,000	49,322,000
Cuba	10,582,000	11,488,000	12,086,000	12,501,000
Czechoslovakia	15,695,000	16,204,000	16,619,000	16,820,000
Ecuador	10,506,000	12,993,000	15,522,000	17,966,000
Egypt	54,139,000	68,424,000	84,129,000	100,645,000
Ethiopia	51,375,000	71,132,000	96,385,000	127,589,000
France	56,184,000	57,684,000	58,131,000	57,944,000
Germany[1]	77,555,000	77,227,000	75,358,000	72,567,000
Ghana	15,310,000	20,811,000	27,565,000	36,177,000
Greece	10,066,000	10,271,000	10,317,000	10,142,000
Hungary	10,546,000	10,477,000	10,408,000	10,270,000
India	850,067,000	1,013,280,000	1,166,146,000	1,307,775,000
Indonesia	191,266,000	226,619,000	261,035,000	293,088,000
Iran	55,647,000	75,701,000	100,730,000	130,267,000
Iraq	18,782,000	27,205,000	38,047,000	50,954,000
Italy	57,657,000	58,499,000	58,124,000	56,775,000
Ivory Coast	12,070,000	17,329,000	23,973,000	32,093,000
Japan	123,778,000	129,421,000	132,517,000	130,597,000
Kenya	25,393,000	38,306,000	56,238,000	79,189,000
Madagascar	11,082,000	16,189,000	21,953,000	29,156,000
Malaysia	17,053,000	20,225,000	23,312,000	26,295,000
Mexico	88,335,000	109,448,000	131,092,000	152,241,000
Morocco	26,249,000	33,274,000	40,816,000	48,517,000
Mozambique	14,718,000	20,915,000	27,422,000	35,297,000
Nepal	19,158,000	24,360,000	30,626,000	37,416,000
Netherlands	14,864,000	15,458,000	15,624,000	15,554,000
Nigeria	118,865,000	160,930,000	213,363,000	273,580,000
North Korea	23,059,000	28,388,000	33,538,000	38,536,000
Pakistan	113,163,000	145,266,000	188,961,000	242,169,000
Peru	21,904,000	26,432,000	30,885,000	35,086,000
Philippines	66,647,000	85,527,000	106,933,000	130,665,000
Poland	38,363,000	39,926,000	41,392,000	42,355,000
Portugal	10,528,000	11,031,000	11,286,000	11,392,000
Romania	23,269,000	24,381,000	24,992,000	25,394,000
Saudi Arabia	16,758,000	23,154,000	31,568,000	43,159,000
South Africa	39,550,000	51,528,000	66,369,000	83,456,000
South Korea	43,919,000	49,509,000	54,043,000	57,762,000
Soviet Union	290,939,000	311,637,000	334,004,000	355,093,000
Spain	39,623,000	41,460,000	42,394,000	42,433,000
Sri Lanka	17,135,000	19,384,000	21,778,000	24,003,000
Sudan	25,164,000	34,223,000	44,887,000	56,941,000
Syria	12,471,000	18,157,000	25,797,000	35,435,000
Tanzania	26,070,000	36,646,000	50,948,000	68,788,000
Thailand	54,890,000	61,570,000	67,195,000	71,044,000
Turkey	56,549,000	68,565,000	80,481,000	92,188,000
Uganda	17,593,000	24,662,000	34,144,000	46,406,000
United Kingdom	57,121,000	57,649,000	57,349,000	57,019,000
United States	250,372,000	267,987,000	282,037,000	293,977,000
Venezuela	19,753,000	24,682,00	29,697,000	34,707,000
Vietnam	68,488,000	86,012,000	103,508,000	121,249,000
Yugoslavia	23,864,000	25,040,000	25,707,000	25,930,000
Zaire	35,330,000	47,940,000	64,476,000	84,728,000
Zimbabwe	10,205,000	13,769,000	17,532,000	21,341,000

1. Figure is the total of the populations of East and West Germany. Source: U.S. Department of Commerce, Bureau of the Census.

Expectation of Life by Age and Sex for Selected Countries

Country	Period	Males						Females					
		0	1	10	20	40	60	0	1	10	20	40	60
NORTH AMERICA													
U.S.	1986	71.30	71.10	62.40	52.80	34.50	18.00	78.30	78.00	69.20	59.40	40.20	22.50
Canada	1985–1987	73.02	72.64	63.87	54.26	35.51	18.40	79.79	79.33	70.52	60.71	41.27	23.24
Mexico	1979	62.10	—	—	—	—	—	66.00	—	—	—	—	—
Trinidad & Tobago	1980–1985	66.88	67.34	58.97	49.39	31.13	15.84	71.62	71.64	63.18	53.44	34.55	18.42
CENTRAL AND SOUTH AMERICA													
Brazil	1985–1990 [1]	62.30	—	—	—	—	—	67.50	—	—	—	—	—
Chile	1985–1990	68.05	68.43	59.87	50.27	32.30	16.84	75.05	75.29	66.69	56.93	37.81	20.58
Costa Rica	1985–1990 [1]	72.41	—	—	—	—	—	77.04	—	—	—	—	—
Ecuador	1985 [2]	63.39	67.12	60.43	51.16	33.57	17.76	67.59	70.64	63.09	54.51	36.32	19.43
Guatemala	1979–1980	55.11	59.09	54.38	45.55	30.56	16.57	59.43	62.98	58.74	49.79	33.01	17.50
Panama	1985–1990 [3]	70.15	70.92	63.00	53.58	35.43	18.80	74.10	74.65	66.62	57.03	38.28	20.81
Peru	1980–1985 [4]	56.77	62.32	57.21	48.13	30.97	15.41	66.50	65.67	60.48	51.34	33.82	17.07
Uruguay	1984–1986	68.43	69.67	61.03	51.40	32.68	16.65	74.88	75.89	67.24	57.46	38.27	21.01
Venezuela	1985 [4]	66.68	68.45	60.31	50.92	33.07	17.30	72.80	74.16	65.90	56.23	37.31	20.30
EUROPE													
Austria	1988 [5]	72.03	71.66	62.86	53.26	34.57	17.86	78.63	78.22	69.36	59.51	40.08	21.85
Belgium	1979–1982 [5]	70.04	69.99	61.26	51.64	32.98	16.26	76.79	76.61	67.88	58.08	38.82	20.93
Cyprus	1983–1987	73.90	73.41	65.14	55.47	36.48	19.27	77.82	77.61	68.85	58.99	39.43	21.12
Czechoslovakia	1986 [5]	67.31	67.35	58.61	48.91	30.19	14.58	74.69	74.53	65.72	55.88	36.46	18.71
Denmark[6]	1986–1987 [5]	71.80	71.40	62.60	52.90	34.10	17.40	77.60	77.20	68.40	58.50	39.10	21.70
Finland	1986 [5]	70.49	69.98	61.12	51.42	32.87	16.66	78.72	78.08	69.19	59.33	39.94	21.62
France	1987 [5]	72.03	71.69	62.91	53.24	34.76	18.41	80.27	79.79	70.99	61.16	41.84	23.67
Germany, East[7]	1987–1988 [5]	69.81	69.53	60.77	51.09	32.42	16.09	75.91	75.46	66.67	56.83	37.46	19.55
Germany, West[7]	1985–1987 [5]	71.81	71.52	62.73	53.01	34.07	17.26	78.37	77.97	69.15	59.30	39.87	21.72
Greece	1980 [5]	72.15	72.82	54.13	54.48	35.58	18.17	76.35	76.78	68.24	58.43	38.95	20.63
Hungary	1988	66.16	66.32	57.56	47.86	29.61	15.05	74.03	74.09	65.28	55.44	36.32	19.15
Ireland	1980–1982 [5]	70.14	69.94	61.25	51.58	32.63	15.90	75.62	75.35	66.58	56.75	37.26	19.54
Italy	1985 [5]	72.01	71.92	63.13	53.44	34.36	17.43	78.61	78.38	69.57	59.72	40.18	21.88
Netherlands	1985–1986 [5]	72.95	72.64	63.84	54.08	34.86	17.48	79.55	79.12	70.29	60.43	40.94	22.75
Norway	1987 [5]	72.75	72.42	63.33	53.96	35.08	17.94	79.55	79.16	70.32	60.47	40.93	22.70
Poland	1988	67.15	67.37	58.65	48.96	30.60	15.47	75.67	75.70	66.92	57.07	37.71	20.08
Portugal	1979–1982 [5]	68.35	69.10	60.66	51.31	33.09	16.74	75.20	75.72	67.17	57.46	38.27	20.29
Spain	1980–1982 [5]	72.52	72.54	63.88	54.20	35.35	18.39	78.61	78.44	69.73	59.91	40.46	22.13
Sweden	1987 [5]	74.16	73.66	64.80	55.06	36.12	18.73	80.15	79.60	70.73	60.86	41.39	23.37
Switzerland	1987–1989	73.90	73.50	64.70	55.00	36.40	19.00	80.70	80.20	71.40	61.60	42.20	23.70
U.S.S.R.	1986–1987	65.04	—	—	—	—	—	73.78	—	—	—	—	—
United Kingdom	1985–1987	71.90	71.66	62.86	53.13	33.98	16.80	77.64	77.27	68.45	58.60	39.10	21.16
Yugoslavia	1987–1989 [5]	68.43	69.26	60.66	50.96	32.25	16.28	74.25	75.03	66.39	56.57	37.21	19.39
ASIA													
Bangladesh	1988	56.91	63.66	58.73	49.53	31.58	15.50	55.97	61.50	57.26	48.30	31.44	15.76
India	1976–1980	52.50	58.60	54.80	45.80	28.30	14.10	52.10	58.60	56.60	47.80	31.20	15.90
Iran	1976	55.75	60.78	53.87	45.19	29.19	14.58	55.04	60.14	54.38	44.97	30.47	15.39
Israel[8]	1987	73.60	73.50	64.80	55.10	35.90	18.60	77.00	76.80	68.10	58.20	38.70	20.50
Japan	1988 [9]	75.54	—	66.15	56.40	37.24	19.78	81.30	—	71.84	61.96	42.44	23.88
Korea, South	1989	66.92	66.66	58.18	48.56	30.30	14.87	74.96	74.75	66.23	56.54	37.50	19.87
Pakistan	1976–1978	59.04	66.46	61.34	52.30	34.77	19.25	59.20	65.58	60.68	51.98	35.23	19.27
Sri Lanka	1981	67.78	68.99	60.99	51.64	33.19	17.74	71.66	72.67	64.75	55.36	36.96	19.57
Syria	1976–1979	63.77	66.92	59.88	50.69	32.74	16.16	64.70	67.06	60.14	50.90	32.84	16.23
AFRICA													
Egypt	1985–1990 [1]	59.29	—	—	—	—	—	61.97	—	—	—	—	—
Kenya	1985–1990 [1]	56.50	—	—	—	—	—	60.46	—	—	—	—	—
South Africa	1985–1990 [1]	57.51	—	—	—	—	—	63.48	—	—	—	—	—
OCEANIA													
Australia	1987 [5, 10]	73.03	72.75	63.97	54.35	35.60	18.27	79.46	79.05	70.22	60.40	40.97	22.76
New Zealand	1986–1988	71.03	70.94	62.24	52.75	34.09	17.12	77.27	77.02	68.27	58.50	39.21	21.47

Average future lifetime in years at stated age

1. Estimates prepared in the Population Division of the United Nations. 2. Excluding nomadic Indian tribes. 3. Excluding tribal Indian population numbering 62,187 in 1960. 4. Excluding Indian jungle population. 5. Complete life table. 6. Excluding the Faeroe Islands and Greenland. 7. Including relevant data relating to Berlin. No separate data have been supplied. 8. Including data for East Jerusalem and Israeli residents in certain other territories. 9. For Japanese nationals in Japan only. 10. Excluding full-blooded aborigines, estimated at 49,036 in June 1966. NOTE: Figures are latest available as of August 1991. *Source:* United Nations *Demographic Yearbook, 1988.*

Crude Birth and Death Rates for Selected Countries
(per 1,000 population)

Country	Birth rates					Death rates				
	1989	1988	1985	1980	1975	1989	1988	1985	1980	1975
Australia	14.9	14.9	15.7	15.3	16.9	7.3	7.2	7.5	7.4	7.9
Austria	11.6	11.6	11.6	12.0	12.5	10.9	11.0	11.9	12.2	12.8
Belgium	12.3	n.a.	11.5	12.7	12.2	10.9	n.a.	11.2	11.6	12.2
Canada	n.a.	14.5	14.8	15.4	15.8	n.a.	7.3	7.2	7.2	7.4
Cuba	17.6	18.1	18.0	14.1	n.a.	6.4	6.5	6.4	5.7	n.a.
Czechoslovakia	13.3	13.8	14.5	16.4	19.6	11.6	11.4	11.8	12.1	11.5
Denmark	11.5	11.5	10.6	11.2	14.2	11.6	11.5	11.4	10.9	10.1
Finland	12.8	12.8	12.8	13.1	13.9	9.9	9.9	9.8	9.3	9.3
France	13.6	13.8	13.9	14.8	14.1	9.0	9.4	10.1	10.2	10.6
Germany, East	12.0	12.9	13.7	14.6	10.8	12.4	12.8	13.5	14.2	14.3
Germany, West	11.0	11.0	9.6	10.0	9.7	11.2	11.2	11.5	11.6	12.1
Greece	10.1	10.7	11.7	15.4	15.7	9.3	9.3	9.4	9.1	8.9
Hong Kong	12.1	13.3	14.0	16.9	n.a.	5.0	4.9	4.6	5.1	n.a.
Hungary	11.7	11.7	12.2	13.9	18.4	13.7	13.2	13.9	13.6	12.4
Ireland	14.7	15.3	17.6	21.9	21.5	8.8	8.9	9.4	9.7	10.6
Israel	22.3	22.6	23.5	24.1	28.2	6.3	6.6	6.6	6.7	7.1
Italy	9.7	9.9	10.1	11.2	14.8	9.1	9.3	9.5	9.7	9.9
Japan	10.1	10.7	11.9	13.7	17.2	6.4	6.5	6.2	6.2	6.4
Luxembourg	12.3	12.1	11.2	11.5	11.2	10.5	10.0	11.0	11.5	12.2
Malta	15.8	15.8	16.8	16.0	18.3	7.4	7.8	8.5	8.8	8.8
Mauritius	20.4	19.9	18.8	27.0	25.1	6.7	6.5	6.8	7.2	8.1
Mexico	31.1	n.a.	34.1	35.3	37.5	5.2	n.a.	5.3	6.2	7.2
Netherlands	12.7	12.6	12.3	12.8	13.0	8.7	8.4	8.5	8.1	8.3
New Zealand	17.5	n.a.	15.6	n.a.	18.4	8.2	n.a.	8.4	n.a.	8.1
Norway	14.0	13.7	12.3	12.5	14.1	10.7	10.8	10.7	10.1	9.9
Panama	24.4	24.8	26.6	26.8	32.3	n.a.	n.a.	n.a.	n.a.	n.a.
Poland	14.9	15.5	18.2	19.5	18.9	10.1	9.8	10.3	9.8	8.7
Portugal	n.a.	11.9	12.8	16.4	19.1	n.a.	9.6	9.6	9.9	10.4
Singapore	17.8	20.0	16.6	17.3	17.8	5.2	5.2	5.2	5.2	5.1
Spain	n.a.	n.a.	11.7	16.1	19.1	n.a.	n.a.	8.0	7.7	8.2
Sweden	13.6	13.3	11.8	11.7	12.6	10.8	11.4	11.3	11.0	10.8
Switzerland	12.2	12.2	11.6	11.3	12.3	9.2	9.2	9.2	9.2	8.7
Tunisia	25.2	27.5	31.3	35.2	36.6	n.a.	n.a.	n.a.	n.a.	n.a.
United Kingdom	13.6	13.8	13.3	13.5	12.5	11.5	11.4	11.8	11.8	11.9
United States	16.0	15.9	15.7	16.2	14.0	8.7	8.8	8.7	8.9	8.9
Yugoslavia	14.2	15.0	15.9	17.0	18.2	9.1	9.0	9.1	9.0	8.7

NOTE: n.a. = not available. *Source:* United Nations, *Monthly Bulletin of Statistics,* May 1991.

Legal Abortions in Selected Countries, 1980–1988

Country	1980	1981	1982	1983	1984	1985	1986	1987	1988
Bulgaria	155,876	152,370	147,791	134,165	131,140	132,041	134,686	133,815	—
Canada	65,751	65,053	66,254	61,750	62,291	60,956	62,406	63,585	—
Cuba	103,974	108,559	126,745	116,956	139,588	138,671	160,926	152,704	155,325
Czechoslovakia	100,170	103,517	107,638	108,662	113,802	119,325	124,188	158,451	—
Denmark	23,334	22,779	21,462	20,791	20,742	19,919	20,067	20,830	21,200[1]
Finland	15,037	14,120	13,861	13,360	13,645	13,832	13,310	13,000[1]	—
France	171,218	180,695	181,122	182,862	180,789	173,335	166,797	161,036	163,000
Germany, West	87,702	87,353	91,064	86,529	86,298	83,538	84,274	88,540	83,784
Greece	117	109	—	220	193	180[1]			
Hungary	80,882	78,421	78,682	78,599	82,191	81,970	83,586	84,547	87,106
Iceland	523	597	613	687	745	705	684	691	673
India	346,327	388,405	500,624	492,696	561,033	583,704	—	—	534,870
Israel	14,708	14,514	16,829	15,593	18,948	18,406	17,469	15,290	16,181
Italy	207,644	216,755	231,308	231,061	228,377	210,192	196,969	187,618	—
Netherlands	—	20,897	20,187	19,700	18,700[1]	17,300[1]			
New Zealand	5,945	6,758	6,903	7,198	7,275	7,130	8,056	8,789	10,000[1]
Norway	13,531	13,845	13,496	13,646	14,070	14,599	15,474	15,422	15,852
Poland	133,835	130,070	141,177	130,980	132,844	135,564	129,720	122,536	105,333
Singapore	18,219	18,890	15,548	19,100	22,190	23,512	21,374	21,226	—
Sweden	34,887	33,294	32,604	31,014	30,755	30,838	33,090	34,707	—
United Kingdom	136,782	171,455	171,417	170,620	179,102	180,983	157,168	165,542	178,301
United States	1,297,600	1,300,800	1,304,000	1,269,000	1,333,500	1,328,600	1,328,000[1]	1,354,000[1]	—

1. Provisional. NOTE: Data latest available as of August 1991. *Source:* United Nations, *Demographic Yearbook, 1989.*

Cost of Living of United Nations Personnel in Selected Cities as Reflected by Index of Retail Prices, 1990

(New York City, December 1990 = 100)

City	Index	City	Index	City	Index
Abu Dhabi	92[1]	Dar es Salaam	86[1]	Nassau	112
Addis Ababa	94[1]	Geneva	138	New Delhi	83
Algiers	96[1]	Guatemala City	82	Panama City	80
Amman	89	The Hague	107	Paris	117
Ankara	80	Helsinki	131	Port-au-Prince	89
Athens	92	Islamabad	80	Quito	73
Baghdad	132[1]	Jakarta	82	Rabat	87
Bangkok	79	Kabul	119	Rome	115
Beirut	78	Kathmandu	84	Roseau	95
Belgrade	108	Kingston	71	San Salvador	70
Bogota	83	Kinshasa	87[1]	Santiago	68
Bonn	125	La Paz	62	Seoul	112
Brazzaville	111[1]	Lagos	89[1]	Sofia	60
Brussels	103	Lima	95	Sydney	88
Budapest	54	London	120	Tokyo	137
Buenos Aires	90	Madrid	123	Tripoli	119[1]
Cairo	90	Managua	94	Tunis	81
Caracas	87	Manila	75	Valetta	81
Colombo	78	Mexico City	80	Vienna	117
Copenhagen	116	Montevideo	85	Warsaw	45
Dhaka	81	Montreal	91	Washington, D.C.	92
Dakar	112	Nairobi	85	Yangon	102

1. Calculated on the basis of cost of Government or subsidized housing which is normally lower than prevailing rentals.
Source: United Nations, *Monthly Bulletin of Statistics, March 1991.*

Consumer Price Indexes for All Items for Selected Countries, 1990

(1980 = 100)

Country	Index	Country	Index	Country	Index
Australia	218.0	Germany	129.5	Netherlands	127.2
Austria	141.3	Greece	569.7	Norway	208.5
Burundi	207.4	Hong Kong	217.8	Philippines	359.8
Canada	178.1	Indonesia	112.5	Singapore	124.9
Chile	635.5	Ireland	209.8	South Africa	392.2
Cyprus	160.9	Italy	250.8	Spain	243.5
Czechoslovakia	124.0	Japan	122.5	Sri Lanka	317.0
Denmark	177.4	Jordan	202.1	Sweden	207.6
Egypt	477.3	Korea, South	183.6	United Kingdom	188.6
Finland	191.8	Mexico	15,058.3	United States	158.6
France	184.0	Morocco	201.3	Uruguay	11,422.1

Source: International Labour Office from *Monthly Bulletin of Statistics, July 1991.*

Labor Force Participation Rates by Sex[1]

Country	Females				Males				Females as percent of total labor force			
	1988	1987	1985	1980	1988	1987	1985	1980	1988	1987	1985	1980
Canada	52.6	50.9	48.5	46.2	70.9	70.1	68.7	73.0	43.8	43.2	42.7	39.7
France	n.a.	39.7	39.7	40.0	n.a.	61.1	62.2	68.6	n.a.	42.0	41.6	39.4
Germany, West	n.a.	36.6[2]	39.7	35.5	n.a.	64.1[2]	63.7	68.9	39.6[2]	39.4[2]	38.9	38.0
Italy	28.9[2]	28.6[2]	27.8	27.9	61.9[2]	61.6[2]	62.5	66.0	33.9[2]	33.6	32.7	31.7
Japan	46.6	46.2	46.3	45.7	75.0	74.9	75.9	77.9	39.7	39.6	39.3	38.4
Sweden	62.2[2]	61.6	59.7	58.0	71.5[2]	71.0	70.5	73.6	47.9[2]	47.7	47.1	45.1
United Kingdom	47.3[2]	45.9[2]	44.4[2]	44.8	69.7[2]	68.2[2]	68.0[2]	72.8	42.5[2]	42.4[2]	41.7[2]	40.4
United States	53.4	52.5	50.4	47.7	72.0	71.5	70.9	72.0	45.0	44.8	44.1	42.4

1. Labor force of all ages as percent of population, 15-64 years old. 2. Preliminary. n.a. = not available. *Source: Statistical Abstract of the United States 1990.* NOTE: Data are most recent available.

Unemployment Figures for Selected Countries: 1985–1990

(In thousands except for percentages)

Country	1990 No.	%	1989 No.	%	1988 No.	%	1987 No.	%	1986 No.	%	1985 No.	%
Australia	587.1	6.9	509.1	6.2	576.2	7.2	628.8	8.1	609.9	8.1	601.6	8.3
Austria[1]	165.8	5.4	149.2	5.0	158.6	5.3	164.5	5.6	152.0	5.2	139.5	4.8
Belgium[1,2]	402.8	9.8	419.3	n.a.	459.4	10.9	500.8	11.9	516.8	12.3	557.4	13.5
Canada	1,109.0	8.1	1,018.0	7.5	1,047.0	7.8	1,167.0	8.9	1,236.0	9.6	1,327.9	10.5
Chile[2,7]	281.3	n.a.	249.8	n.a.	285.8	8.1	343.6	7.9	374.3	8.8	273.4	17.0
Cyprus[1]	5.1	n.a.	6.2	n.a.	7.4	n.a.	8.7	3.4	9.2	3.7	8.3	3.3
Denmark[1]	269.1	9.6	264.9	9.4	243.9	8.7	219.4	8.0	217.3	8.0	247.8	9.2
Finland[3]	88.0	3.4	89.0	3.5	116.0	4.5	130.0	5.1	140.0	5.4	163.2	6.3
Germany, West[1]	1,872.0	7.2	2,032.0	7.9	2,236.6	8.7	2,232.5	8.9	2,228.0	9.0	2,304.0	9.3
Hong-Kong[2]	37.0	1.3	30.0	1.1	37.9	1.4	47.5	1.7	76.3	2.8	83.6	3.2
Ireland[4,7]	224.7	17.4	231.6	17.9	241.4	18.6	247.3	19.0	236.4	18.2	230.6	17.7
Israel[5]	n.a.	n.a.	n.a.	n.a.	100.0	6.4	90.0	6.1	104.0	7.1	97.0	6.7
Italy	2,621.0	11.0	2,865.0	12.0	2,885.0	12.0	2,832.0	12.0	2,611.0	11.1	2,471.0	10.6
Japan	1,340.0	2.1	1,420.0	2.3	1,550.0	2.5	1,730.0	2.9	1,670.0	2.8	1,564.3	2.6
Korea[3]	451.0	2.5	459.0	2.6	435.0	2.5	519.0	3.1	611.0	3.8	619.0	4.0
Netherlands[1,6]	346.0	4.9	390.0	n.a.	682.2	n.a.	685.5	11.5	710.7	12.0	761.0	15.6
New Zealand[1]	164.0	7.7	153.6	n.a.	120.9	n.a.	88.1	6.6	67.2	5.0	53.2	4.0
Norway	112.0	4.3	106.0	3.8	69.3	3.2	45.0	2.1	40.0	1.9	51.0	2.5
Portugal	n.a.	n.a.	232.8	5.0	262.2	5.7	319.6	7.1	381.6	8.4	384.7	8.5
Puerto Rico[8]	152.0	14.2	n.a.	n.a.	158.0	15.0	171.0	16.8	188.0	18.9	211.0	21.8
Sweden	69.0	1.6	61.0	1.4	72.0	1.6	84.0	1.9	117.0	2.1	125.0	2.8
Switzerland[1]	18.1	0.6	17.5	0.6	22.2	0.7	24.7	0.8	25.7	0.8	30.3	1.0
United Kingdom[1,9]	1,664.5	5.9	1,800.5	6.4	2,370.4	8.4	2,953.4	10.6	3,289.1	11.9	3,271.2	13.5
United States	6,874.0	5.5	6,528.0	5.3	6,701.0	5.5	7,425.0	6.2	8,237.0	7.0	8,312.0	7.2
Yugoslavia[1]	1,308.5	16.4	1,201.2	14.9	1,131.8	14.1	1,080.6	13.6	1,086.7	13.9	1,040.0	13.8

1. Employment office statistics. All others labor force sample surveys unless otherwise indicated. 2. Scope of series revised as of 1985. 3. Scope of series revised as of 1986. 4. Excluding agriculture, fishing and private domestic services. 5. Including persons who did not work in the country during the previous 12 months. 6. Based on labor force sample surveys beginning 1988 and scope of series revised. 7. Compulsory unemployment insurance statistics. 8. Excluding people temporarily laid off. 9. Excluding persons temporarily laid off. Excluding adult students registered for vacation employment. NOTE: n.a.= not available. *Source:* United Nations, *Monthly Bulletin of Statistics, July 1991.*

Public Expenditure for Education for Selected Countries

Country	Year	Percent of total expenditure	Percent of GNP	Country	Year	Percent of total expenditure	Percent of GNP
Algeria	1987	27.8	9.8	Mexico	1987	n.a.	3.4
Argentina	1987	8.9[2]	1.9[2]	Morocco	1987	25.5	8.3
Australia	1986	12.6	5.8	Nepal	1985	10.8	2.8
Bangladesh	1986	10.5[2]	2.2[2]	Netherlands	1985	16.4	6.8
Brazil	1986	17.7	4.5	Nigeria	1986	12.0[6]	1.4[6]
Canada	1987	15.4	7.2	Philippines	1987	n.a.	2.0
Chile	1987	n.a.	3.6	Poland	1987	12.5	4.4
China	1985	n.a.	2.7	Portugal	1987	n.a.	4.5[2]
Czechoslovakia	1987	8.0	n.a.	Romania	1985	n.a.	2.1
Egypt	1987	n.a.	5.5	Soviet Union	1987	n.a.	7.3[4]
Ethiopia	1986	9.9	4.2	Spain	1987	n.a.	3.2
France	1986	n.a.	5.7[3]	Tanzania	1987	9.7	4.1
Germany, E.	1987	5.4[5]	5.1[4,5]	Thailand	1987	17.9	3.6
Germany, W.	1986	9.2	4.4	Turkey	1987	n.a.	1.7[1]
Hungary	1987	6.3	5.6	UK	1986	n.a.	5.0
India	1986	n.a.	3.4	US	1985	n.a.	6.7[7]
Indonesia	1981	9.3	2.0	Venezuela	1985	21.3	5.4
Italy	1986	8.6[2]	4.0[2]	Yugoslavia	1986	n.a.	3.8
Japan	1986	17.7	5.0	Zaire	1980	32.3[5]	3.4[5]
Korea, S.	1987	26.6	4.2	Zimbabwe	1986	16.2	8.5

1. Expenditure on third-level education is not included. 2. Ministry of Education expenditures only. 3. Metropolitan France only. 4. Percent of net material product. 5. Current expenditures only. 6. Federal government expenditures only. 7. Data refer to total public and private expenditures on education. n.a. = not available. NOTE: Expenditure includes both capital and current expenditures on public education and subsidized private education except as noted above. *Source:* United Nations Educational, Scientific and Cultural Organization, Paris, France, *Statistical Yearbook* (Copyright). From *Statistical Abstract of the United States 1990.* NOTE: Data are most recent available.

Energy, Petroleum, and Coal, by Country

Country	Energy consumed[1] (coal equiv.) Total (mil. metric tons)		Per capita (kilograms)		Electric energy production[2] (bil. kwh)		Crude petroleum production[3] (mil. metric tons)		Coal production[4] (mil. metric tons)	
	1987	1980	1987	1980	1987	1980	1987	1980	1987	1980
Algeria	33.3	24.8	1,441	1,327	13.4	7.1	33.1	47.4	(Z)[5]	(Z)
Argentina	59.5	49.3	1,912	1,746	52.2	39.7	22.0	25.3	.4	.4
Australia[6]	110.6	91.2	6,845	6,195	132.2	96.1	25.1	18.9	147.8	72.5
Austria	30.1	30.5	4,018	4,058	50.2	42.0	1.1	1.5	(Z)	(Z)
Bahrain	6.8	4.4	14,680	12,651	3.0	1.7	2.0	2.4	n.a.	n.a.
Bangladesh	6.9	3.8	64	44	5.9	2.7	(Z)	(Z)	(X)	(X)
Belgium	55.1	59.1	5,560	5,997	62.4	53.6	(X)	(X)	4.4[7]	6.3
Brazil	108.5	92.5	767	763	202.3	139.5	28.5	9.1	6.9	5.2
Bulgaria	53.1	47.3	5,912	5,254	43.5	34.8	.3[5]	.3[5]	.2	.3
Canada	256.5	254.2	9,915	10,547	496.3	377.5	75.2	70.4	32.7	20.2
Chile	11.8	11.4	938	1,025	15.6	11.8	1.3	1.6	1.6	1.0
China	800.8	562.8	749	571	497.3	300.6	134.1	105.9	928.0	595.8
Colombia	24.5	23.8	817	923	35.4	22.9	19.4	6.5	14.6	4.9
Cuba	14.5	13.6	1,442	1,394	13.6	9.9	.9	.3	(X)	(X)
Czechoslovakia	98.2	97.4	6,311	6,364	85.8	72.7	.1	.1	25.7[7]	28.3[7]
Denmark	27.4	26.9	5,346	5,254	29.4	27.1	4.6	.3	(X)	(X)
Ecuador	6.2	5.7	627	708	5.7	3.4	8.9	10.4	n.a.	(NA)
Egypt	33.8	20.1	674	488	32.5	18.9	45.2	29.4	(X)	(X)
Ethiopia	1.2	.9	28	27	.8	.7	(X)	(X)	n.a.	(NA)
Finland	28.1	26.4	5,692	5,514	53.5[8]	38.7[8]	(X)	(X)	(X)	(X)
France[9]	206.9	237.3	3,720	4,409	356.2[8]	246.4[8]	3.2	1.2	16.3[7]	20.2[7]
Germany, East	131.3	121.8	7,891	7,276	114.2	98.8	(Z)	.1	(Z)	(Z)
Germany, West	342.0	359.4	5,624	5,829	415.8	368.8	3.8[10]	4.6	82.4	94.5
Greece	24.5	20.1	2,452	2,088	30.1	22.7	1.1	(Z)	(X)	(X)
Hong Kong	10.6	7.3	1,891	1,448	23.8	12.6	n.a.	(NA)	(X)	(X)
Hungary	40.5	40.6	3,819	3,787	29.7	23.9	1.9	2.0	2.4[7]	3.1[7]
India	220.5	139.4	275	202	217.5	119.3	30.1	9.4	177.0	109.1
Indonesia	47.2	34.7	274	230	34.8	14.2	64.6	77.6	1.7	.3
Iran[11]	65.9	45.7	1,285	1,177	37.9	22.4	113.4	72.7	1.2[5]	.9[5]
Iraq	12.5	10.7	735	807	22.9	11.4	101.8	130.1	n.a.	(NA)
Ireland	12.5	11.1	3,462	3,268	12.6	10.9	(X)	(X)	(Z)	.1
Israel	12.2	8.8	2,794	2,273	17.5	12.5	(Z)	(Z)	(X)	(X)
Italy[12]	204.4	174.9	3,570	3,112	198.3	185.7	3.9	1.8	(Z)	(Z)[5]
Japan	456.1	434.8	3,741	3,726	699.0	577.5	.6[5]	.4	13.0	18.0
Korea, North	57.9	48.5	2,708	2,713	50.2	35.0	(X)	(X)	39.5[5]	36.0[5]
Korea, South	74.2	52.3	1,760	1,373	80.3	40.1	(X)	(X)	24.3	18.6
Kuwait[13]	17.1	6.9	9,191	5,019	18.4	9.4	61.4	84.1	n.a.	n.a.
Libya	11.0	7.3	3,023	2,456	14.3	4.8	46.8	88.3	(X)	(X)
Malaysia	20.8	12.2	1,283	882	17.4	10.2	24.3	13.2	(X)	(X)
Mexico	140.9	118.6	1,697	1,709	104.8[8]	67.0[8]	132.1	99.9	11.1	7.0
Morocco	7.8	6.4	336	319	7.1	4.9	(Z)[5]	(Z)	.8	.7
Myanmar	2.7	2.2	68	62	2.3	1.3	1.0	1.6	(Z)	(Z)
Netherlands	106.0	93.0	7,265	6,543	68.4	64.8	4.3	1.3	(Z)[5 14]	(Z)
New Zealand[18]	12.7	10.0	3,858	3,152	27.0	22.0	1.3	.3	2.1[5]	2.0
Nigeria	16.9	11.0	166	136	9.9	7.2	62.1	104.2	.1[5]	.2
Norway[15]	28.3	26.3	6,782	6,423	103.8	84.1	47.8	24.6	.4	.3
Pakistan	27.8	16.6	250	191	33.5	15.3	2.0	.5	2.4	1.5
Peru	11.7	12.0	564	693	14.2	9.8	8.8	9.6	.2[5]	.1[5]
Philippines	15.4	16.7	265	346	23.9	17.9	.3	.5	1.2	.3
Poland	181.5	176.8	4,810	4,935	145.8	121.9	.1	.3	193.0	193.1
Portugal	13.6	11.2	1,329	1,153	20.1	15.3	(X)	(X)	.3	.2
Romania	106.1	100.0	4,624	4,505	73.1	67.5	10.2[5]	11.5	8.8[5]	8.1
Saudi Arabia[13]	79.4	25.3	6,322	2,745	37.1	18.9	198.1	495.9	n.a.	n.a.
South Africa[16]	107.6	90.2	2,816	2,751	122.5	90.4	(X)	(X)	177.3	116.6
Soviet Union	1,867.2	1,473.1	6,634	5,549	1,664.9	1,293.9	624.0	603.2	519.1	492.9
Spain	81.9	88.4	2,106	2,359	133.2	110.5	1.6	1.6	14.5[7]	13.1[7]
Sudan	1.5	1.5	64	82	1.1	1.0	(X)	(X)	n.a.	n.a.
Sweden	41.8	44.5	5,004	5,376	146.6	96.7	(Z)	(Z)	(Z)	(Z)
Switzerland[17]	24.8	23.3	3,794	3,636	57.0[8]	48.1[8]	(X)	(X)	(X)	(X)
Syria	11.5	7.3	1,025	835	7.2	3.8	12.2	8.3	(X)	(X)
Taiwan[19]	n.a.	37.9	n.a.	2,127	n.a.	42.0	n.a.	.2	(X)	2.6
Tanzania	.9	.8	38	44	.9	.7	(X)	(X)	(Z)	(Z)
Thailand	26.3	17.3	493	372	30.0	15.1	1.0	(Z)	(Z)	(Z)
Trinidad and Tobago	7.1	7.5	5,770	6,992	3.3	2.0	8.1	11.0	n.a.	n.a.

Country	Energy consumed[1] (coal equiv.)				Electric energy production[2] (bil. kwh)		petroleum production[3] (mil. metric tons)		Crude Coal production[4] (mil. metric tons)	
	Total (mil. metric tons)		Per capita (kilograms)							
	1987	1980	1987	1980	1987	1980	1987	1980	1987	1980
Tunisia	5.0	4.1	651	639	4.5	2.8	5.0	5.6	(X)	(X)
Turkey	52.4	31.9	998	718	44.4	23.3	2.6	2.3	3.5	3.6
United Arab Emirates	27.4	16.8	18,832	17,188	13.1	6.3	72.1	82.8	n.a.	n.a.
United Kingdom	290.8	271.0	5,107	4,850	300.2	284.9	117.6	78.9	104.4[7]	130.1[7]
United States	2,322.9	2,364.5	9,542	10,386	2,686[8]	2,354	418.6	424.2	761.1	710.4
Venezuela	55.1	49.0	3,018	3,140	54.7	35.9	95.5	114.8	.1	(Z)
Vietnam	7.4	6.6	118	122	5.3	3.8	n.a.	n.a.	5.6	5.2
Yugoslavia	56.7	48.0	2,423	2,152	80.8	59.4	3.9	4.2	.4	.4
Zaire	2.1	2.0	64	69	5.3	4.2	1.3[5]	1.0	(Z)[5]	.1
Zambia	1.9	2.3	248	403	8.5[8]	9.2	(X)	(X)	.5	.6
World, total	9,653.6	8,544.3	1,921	1,919	10,467	8,247	2,787	2,979	3,334	2,728

n.a. = not available. X = Not applicable. Z = Less than 50,000 metric tons. 1. Based on apparent consumption of coal, lignite, petroleum products, natural gas, and hydro, nuclear, and geothermal electricity. 2. Comprises production by utilities generating primarily for public use, and production by industrial establishments generating primarily for own use. Relates to production at generating centers, including station use and transmission losses. 3. Includes shale oil, but excludes natural gasoline. 4. Excludes lignite and brown coal, except as noted. 5. United Nations Statistical Office estimate. 6. For year ending June 30 of year shown. 7. Includes slurries. 8. Net production, i.e. excluding station use. 9. Includes Monaco. 10. Includes inputs other than crude petroleum and natural gas liquids. 11. For year ending March 20 of year shown. 12. Includes San Marino. 13. Includes share of production and consumption in the Neutral Zone. 14. Includes patent fuel and hard coal briquettes. 15. Includes Svalbard and Jan Mayen Islands. 16. Includes Botswana, Lesotho, Namibia, and Swaziland. 17. Includes Liechtenstein. 18. For year ending March 31 for year shown. 19. *Source:* U.S. Bureau of the Census. Data from Republic of China publications. *Source:* Except as noted, Statistical Office of the United Nations, New York, N.Y., *Energy Statistics Yearbook, 1986* (copyright). From: *Statistical Abstract of the United States, 1990.* NOTE: Data are most recent available.

Wheat, Rice, and Corn—Production for Selected Countries

(in thousands of metric tons)

Country	Wheat			Rice			Corn		
	1986	1985	1984	1986	1985	1984	1986	1985	1984
Argentina	8,900	8,700	13,220	405	410	476	12,400	11,530	9,500
Australia	17,356	16,127	18,666	687	864	632	228	291	238
Belgium[2]	1,265[1]	1,215	1,330	n.a.	n.a.	n.a.	58[1]	90[1]	53
Brazil	5,433	4,323	1,983	10,399	9,019	9,027	20,510	22,020	21,164
Canada	31,850	24,252	21,199	n.a.	n.a.	n.a.	6,694	7,472	7,024
China: Mainland[3]	89,002	85,812	87,817	177,000	171,417	181,193	65,560	64,056	73,600
Egypt	1,929	1,872	1,815	2,450[1]	2,310	2,236	3,801[1]	3,982[1]	3,170
France	26,587	28,890	32,977	60	62	36	10,792	12,409	10,493
Germany, West	10,406	9,866	10,223	n.a.	n.a.	n.a.	1,302	1,204	1,026
Greece	2,200	1,789	2,308	102	103	92	2,070	1,948	2,091
Hungary	5,803	6,578	7,392	44	38	33	7,214	6,818	6,686
India	46,885	44,069	45,476	90,000	96,306	87,553	8,000	6,890	8,442
Indonesia	n.a.	n.a.	n.a.	39,275	39,033	38,136	5,767	4,330	5,288
Iran	7,128	6,661	5,500[3]	1,569	1,523	1,600	50[3]	50[1]	50[1]
Iraq	1,100[1]	1,406	471	145[1]	149	109	36[1]	41	30
Italy	9,070	8,516	10,057	1,082	1,123	1,009	6,560	6,309	6,672
Japan	876	874	741	14,559	14,578	14,848	1	2	2
Korea, South	5[1]	11	17	7,790	7,855	7,970	113	132	133
Mexico	4,772	5,207	4,505	523	809	484	12,154	13,957	12,910
Myanmar	246	206	214	15,000[3]	15,219	14,255	350[3]	323	303
Pakistan	13,923	11,703	10,882	5,241	4,437	4,973	1,067	1,009	1,028
Soviet Union	92,300	78,100	68,600	2,600	2,570	2,720	12,500	14,400	13,600
Sweden	1,714	1,338	1,776	n.a.	n.a.	n.a.	n.a.	n.a.	n.a.
Thailand	n.a.	n.a.	n.a.	19,100	20,264	19,905	4,197	4,934	4,226
United Kingdom	13,874	12,046	14,970	n.a.	n.a.	n.a.	1[3]	1[3]	1[3]
United States	56,792	65,999	70,618	6,097	6,120	6,296	209,632	225,478	194,928
Vietnam	n.a.	n.a.	n.a.	16,197	15,875	15,506	600[1]	600	525
Yugoslavia	4,776	4,859	5,595	48	36	36	12,502	9,896	11,312
World, total	535,842	506,034	516,457	475,533	474,728	470,284	480,609	488,325	452,753

1. Unofficial figure. 2. Includes Luxembourg. 3. FAO estimate. NOTES: Rice data cover rough and paddy. Data for each country pertain to the calendar year in which all or most of the crop was harvested. n.a. = not available. *Source:* Food and Agriculture Organization of the United Nations, Rome, Italy, 1986. *FAO Production Yearbook, vol. 40* (copyright). From: *Statistical Abstract of the United States, 1990.* NOTE: Data are most recent available.

Wheat, Rice and Corn Exports and imports, 1985–1987

(in thousands of metric tons. Countries listed are the 10 leading exporters or importers in 1987)

Exporters	1985	1986	1987	Importers	1985	1986	1987
WHEAT				**WHEAT**			
United States	24,810	24,555	30,638	Soviet Union	20,309	15,745	18,097
Canada	17,007	15,957	22,140	China: Mainland	6,135	6,883	14,050
Australia	15,704	16,109	14,789	Japan	5,510	5,620	5,476
France	16,943	13,367	14,220	Egypt	4,524	4,329	5,162
Argentina	9,583	4,021	4,197	Italy	4,534	5,259	4,617
United Kingdom	1,886	3,987	4,122	South Korea	2,986	3,449	4,121
West Germany	1,045	2,143	2,262	Iran	2,144	1,908	3,600
Soviet Union	1,250	1,181	1,480	Iraq	2,096	2,185	2,900
Hungary	2,002	1,670	1,281	Brazil	4,041	2,255	2,749
Sweden	626	466	691	Poland	1,703	1,662	2,343
RICE				**RICE**			
Thailand	4,062	4,524	4,443	Iran	539	493	800
United States	1,940	2,392	2,472	Soviet Union	321	493	599
Pakistan	719	1,316	1,240	China: Mainland	213	326	559
China: Mainland	1,046	1,123	1,202	Iraq	500	550	524
Italy	727	676	610	Vietnam	422	500	450
Myanmar	452	636	486	Ivory Coast	342	361	401
India	250	200	350	Nigeria	356	320	400
North Korea	200	200	225	Saudi Arabia	428	375	381
Uruguay	242	270	204	Hong Kong	378	368	373
Australia	341	178	186	Senegal	336	378	307
CORN				**CORN**			
United States	44,033	27,099	40,906	Japan	14,225	14,653	16,504
France	4,456	5,799	6,305	Soviet Union	16,600	7,236	9,238
Argentina	7,069	7,411	3,963	China: Mainland	3,108	3,659	5,249
China: Mainland	6,338	5,642	3,917	South Korea	3,406	3,671	4,566
South Africa	400	1,800	2,350	Mexico	1,726	1,704	3,603
Thailand	2,752	3,981	1,628	Egypt	1,907	2,028	2,200
Yugoslavia	900	1,798	1,166	Netherlands	2,374	1,977	1,760
Belgium-Luxembourg	656	364	604	Belgium-Luxembourg	1,930	1,466	1,729
Spain	2	60	459	United Kingdom	1,455	1,482	1,471
Greece	209	580	368	Malaysia	1,182	1,204	1,302

—Represents or rounds to zero. *Source:* U.S. Dept. of Agriculture, Economic Research Service. Data from Food and Agriculture Organization of the United Nations, Rome, Italy, *FOA Trade Yearbook.* From *Statistical Abstract of the United States 1990.* NOTE: Data are most recent available.

Passenger Car Production[1]

(in thousands, monthly averages)

Country	1989	1988	1987	1986	1985	1984	1983
Argentina[2]	—	10.4	13.0	11.7	9.6	11.9	11.0
Australia[2]	27.7	26.2	25.2	26.5	31.8	28.4	30.3
Austria	0.6	0.6	0.6	0.6	0.6	0.6	0.5
Brazil[2]	26.1	32.9	33.1	39.9	38.3	55.5	57.1
Canada	82.0	84.0	67.5	88.4	89.6	86.1	80.9
Czechoslovakia	15.7	13.7	14.5	15.4	15.2	15.0	14.9
France	284.5	261.5	248.5	227.7	232.0	242.5	269.0
Germany, East	18.2	18.2	18.1	18.2	17.5	16.8	15.7
Germany, West	378.6	359.1	361.7	356.1	347.1	315.3	322.9
India	14.8	14.5	12.9	10.8	7.8	7.3	5.7
Italy	164.2	157.0	142.7	136.9	112.8	119.7	116.3
Japan	697.5	683.3	657.6	650.9	637.1	589.4	596.0
Korea, South[2]	70.6	72.3	64.8	38.1	21.8	13.9	10.7
Mexico[2]	37.9	29.0	19.0	16.5	23.8	20.6	17.8
Netherlands	11.2	10.0	10.4	9.9	9.0	9.1	8.9
Poland	23.8	24.5	24.5	24.2	23.6	23.2	22.4
Romania	—	—	10.8	10.3	11.2	10.4	7.5
Spain	141.3	131.3	119.3	108.2	101.4	94.8	92.5
Sweden	—	—	34.7	34.6	33.4	26.2	31.2
U.S.S.R.	—	105.1	108.3	109.9	111.0	110.6	109.6
United Kingdom	108.3	102.2	95.2	84.9	87.3	75.8	87.1
United States[3]	567.3	592.1	590.4	626.3	666.8	635.2	565.1
Yugoslavia	26.0[2]	25.8[2]	25.8[2]	17.5	19.1	15.6	14.0

1. Vehicles built on imported chassis or assembled from imported parts are excluded except for those countries marked. 2. Including assembly. 3. Factory sales. *Source:* United Nations, *Monthly Bulletin of Statistics, January 1991.*

Meat—Production by Country

(in thousands of metric tons)

Country	1980	1985	1987, est.	Country	1980	1985	1987, est.
Argentina	3,220	3,077	2,951	Mexico	2,044	2,289	2,125
Australia[1]	2,332	2,086	2,373	Poland	2,397	2,192	2,502
Brazil	3,115	3,045	3,003	Soviet Union	12,698	14,050	15,210
China	12,664	18,443	20,136	United Kingdom	2,305	2,419	2,440
France	3,823	3,733	3,853	United States	17,680	17,874	17,564
Italy	2,305	2,462	2,413	West Germany	4,759	4,845	5,095
Japan	1,893	2,087	2,155	**World, total**	104,535	115,537	119,724

1. Year ending June 30. NOTE: Covers beef and veal (incl. buffalo meat), pork (incl. bacon and ham), and mutton and lamb (incl. goat meat). Refers to meat from animals slaughtered within the national boundaries irrespective of origin of animals, and relates to commercial and farm slaughter. In terms of carcass weight. Excludes lard, tallow, and edible offals. NOTE: Data are most recent available. *Source:* Statistical Office of the United Nations, New York, NY, *Statistical Yearbook.* (Copyright.) From: *Statistical Abstract of the United States 1990.*

Crude Steel Production and Consumption

Country	Production (mil. metric tons)			Consumption					
				Total (mil. metric tons)			Per capita (kilograms)		
	1987	1986	1985	1987	1986	1985	1987	1986	1985
Argentina	3.6	3.1	2.7	3.0	n.a.	n.a.	95	n.a.	n.a.
Australia	6.1	6.7	6.3[1]	5.8	5.8	5.8	354	363	366
Austria	0.2	0.2	0.3	1.7	2.1	1.8	229	274	235
Bangladesh	0.1	0.1	0.1	0.5	0.3	0.5	5	3	5
Belgium	9.8	9.7	10.7	2.5	0.7	2.8[2]	244	64	275[2]
Brazil	12.0	11.3	11.4	14.0	n.a.	n.a.	99	n.a.	n.a.
Bulgaria	3.0	3.0	2.9	3.4	2.3	3.0	381	258	336
Canada	14.6	14.0	13.4	13.0	11.4	11.9	507	443	471
China: Mainland	56.3	52.2	46.8	69.7	66.2	66.6	64	64	63
Czechoslovakia	15.4	15.1	15.0	11.0	10.3	11.0	703	665	709
France	17.7	17.6	18.8	14.4	14.2	14.2	259	257	258
Germany, East	8.2	8.0	7.9	9.7	4.1	9.5	581	249	574
Germany, West	35.9	36.7	40.1	28.0	28.1	29.3	457	460	481
Greece	0.9	0.9	1.0	1.9	1.7	1.6	189	175	164
India	12.0	11.3	11.0	16.0	n.a.	n.a.	20	n.a.	n.a.
Italy	22.7	22.7	23.7	22.8	20.6	20.7	397	360	362
Japan	97.9	97.6	104.4	71.0	60.3	66.7	582	496	553
Korea, North	6.5	6.5	6.5	6.8	9.2	8.4	316	441	413
Korea, South	2.6	4.1	4.9	13.0	n.a.	n.a.	308	n.a.	n.a.
Mexico	7.0	6.9	7.2	7.6	8.1	8.3	93	102	105
Netherlands	1.8	3.0	3.4	3.9	3.7	4.4	263	254	305
Nigeria	0.2	0.2	0.3	0.8	0.5	0.9	8	5	9
Poland	15.6	15.7	14.8	15.9	15.0	15.2	422	400	409
Romania	13.9	13.5	13.0	n.a.	10.4	10.9	n.a.	451	480
South Africa	8.9	8.0	8.5	6.3	n.a.	n.a.	164	n.a.	n.a.
Soviet Union	161.9	160.6	154.7	164.6	n.a.	n.a.	582	n.a.	n.a.
Spain	11.5	12.0	14.6	8.3	8.0	9.9	214	208	257
Sweden	4.7	4.7	4.8	3.5	3.4	3.2	421	406	384
Turkey	7.0	6.0	4.7	7.7	n.a.	n.a.	149	n.a.	n.a.
United Kingdom	17.2	14.5	15.5	14.7	12.9	14.4	259	227	254
United States	80.9	74.0	80.1[3]	102.9	89.3	107.3	417	370	448
Venezuela	3.7	3.4	3.1	4.1	3.7	3.2	227	208	186
Yugoslavia	1.9	2.0	2.0	4.0	5.1	5.1	170	218	221
World	681.1	665.0	673.5	n.a.	n.a.	n.a.	n.a.	n.a.	n.a.

1. Year ending June 30. 2. Luxembourg included with Belgium. 3. Excludes steel for castings made in foundries operated by companies not producing ingots. n.a. = not available. NOTE: Production data cover both ingots and steel for castings and exclude wrought (puddled) iron. Consumption data represent apparent consumption (i.e. production plus imports minus exports) and do not take into account changes in stock. *Source:* Statistical Office of the United Nations, New York, NY, *Statistical Yearbook.* (Copyright.) From *Statistical Abstract of the United States 1990.* NOTE: Figures are latest available.

China and India Lead in Population

Ninety-two countries have higher birth rates than India, and 134 countries have higher birth rates than China. Nevertheless, more than one-third of the world's births occur in these countries. In 2000 China will rank first in population, as it does now, but in 2100 India will have overtaken it and rank first.

Value of Exports and Imports

(in millions of U.S. dollars)

Country	Exports[1]	Imports[1]
Afghanistan	$238[2]	$798[2]
Algeria	8,164[3]	7,396[3]
Argentina	9,579[2]	4,204[2]
Australia	39,659	38,847
Austria	41,881	50,017
Bahamas	2,786[2]	3,001[2]
Bahrain	2,689[2]	2,866[2]
Bangladesh	1,305[2]	3,524[2]
Barbados	209	705
Belgium-Luxembourg	118,295	120,067
Benin	167[4]	288[4]
Bolivia	900	715
Brazil	34,392[2]	18,281[2]
Bulgaria	13,428	13,089
Burkina Faso	142[3]	489[3]
Burundi	75	236
Cameroon	924[3]	1,271[3]
Canada	126,995	116,461
Cape Verde	7[2]	112[2]
Central African Republic	134[2]	150[2]
Chile	8,580	7,272
Colombia	5,739[2]	5,010[2]
Congo	751[3]	544[3]
Costa Rica	1,362[2]	1,743[2]
Côte d'Ivoire	2,792[3]	2,100[3]
Cuba	5,518[3]	7,579[3]
Cyprus	956	2,558
Czechoslovakia	11,882	13,106
Denmark	35,112	31,766
Dominican Republic	924	1,964
Ecuador	2,722	1,862
Egypt	2,234	9,202
El Salvador	412	902
Ethiopia	446[3]	1,075[3]
Fiji	233	735
Finland	26,743	27,110
France	209,996	233,163
Gabon	1,288[5]	732[5]
Gambia	40[5]	127[5]
Germany, East	17,334[2]	17,778[2]
Germany, West	406,483	349,417
Ghana	1,014[3]	907[3]
Greece	7,543[2]	16,126[2]
Guatemala	1,108[2]	1,654[2]
Guyana	167[6]	248[6]
Haiti	200[3]	344[3]
Honduras	869[3]	933[3]
Hungary	9,707	8,764
Iceland	1,401[2]	1,395[2]
India	17,787	23,396
Indonesia	25,675	21,837
Iran	19,975[7]	9,738[7]
Iraq	21,431[7]	7,257[7]
Ireland	23,778	20,716
Israel	11,576	15,104
Italy	168,680	180,105
Jamaica	1,119	1,848
Japan	286,949	234,800
Jordan	922	2,603
Kenya	1,054	2,227
Korea, South	65,016	69,844
Kuwait	11,476[2]	6,303[2]
Liberia	382[5]	308[5]
Libya	6,683[3]	5,879[3]
Madagascar	312[2]	340[2]
Malawi	418	573
Malaysia	29,418	29,261
Mali	271[2]	500[2]
Malta	858[2]	1,505[2]
Mauritania	437[2]	222[2]
Mauritius	987[2]	1,326[2]
Mexico	22,819[2]	23,633[2]
Morocco	3,308[2]	5,492[2]
Myanmar	325	261
Netherlands	131,839	126,195
New Zealand	9,435	9,489
Nicaragua	300[5]	923[5]
Nigeria	8,138[2]	3,419[2]
Norway	34,072	26,905
Oman	3,933[2]	2,255[2]
Pakistan	5,522	7,356
Panama	321	1,489
Papua-New Guinea	1,281[2]	1,355[2]
Paraguay	1,163[2]	695[2]
Peru	3,274	2,455
Phillippines	8,186	12,206
Poland	13,627	8,160
Portugal	16,348	25,072
Qatar	3,541[6]	1,139[6]
Romania	6,095	9,249
Rwanda	101[3]	369[3]
Saudi Arabia	28,369[2]	21,153[2]
Senegal	606[5]	1,023[5]
Sierra Leone	138[2]	189[2]
Singapore	52,729	60,787
Solomon Islands	75[2]	114[2]
Somalia	104[5]	132[5]
Spain	55,640	87,694
Sri Lanka	1,912	2,634
Sudan	509[3]	1,060[3]
Suriname	301[5]	294[5]
Sweden	57,423	54,580
Switzerland	63,884	69,869
Syria	3,006[2]	2,097[2]
Tanzania	337[3]	1,495[3]
Thailand	22,972	32,746
Togo	242[3]	487[3]
Tonga	9[2]	57[2]
Trinidad	2,049	1,222
Tunisia	3,595	5,550
Turkey	11,626[2]	15,799[2]
Uganda	274[3]	544[3]
U.S.S.R.	104,177	120,651
United Arab Emirates	15,837[8]	6,422[8]
U.K.	185,976	224,938
U.S.	393,893	516,575
Uruguay	1,599[2]	1,203[2]
Vanuatu	20[3]	71[3]
Venezuela	12,983[2]	6,881[2]
Western Samoa	12[2]	67[2]
Yemen	101[5]	1,378[5]
Yugoslavia	14,312	18,890
Zaire	1,249[2]	849[2]
Zambia	1,347[2]	873[2]
Zimbabwe	1,420[5]	1,043[5]

1. 1990 unless otherwise indicated. 2. 1989. 3. 1988. 4. 1984. 5. 1987. 6. 1985. 7. 1979. 8. 1986. *Source:* United Nations, *Monthly Bulletin of Statistics,* July 1991.

COUNTRIES OF THE WORLD

(For late reports, *see* Current Events of 1991)

AFGHANISTAN

Republic of Afghanistan
President: Dr. Najibullah (November 1987)
Area: 250,000 sq mi. (647,500 sq km).
Population (est. mid-1991): 16,600,000 (Average annual rate of natural increase: 2.6%); birth rate: 48/1000; infant mortality rate: 182/1000; density per square mile: 67
Capital: Kabul
Largest cities (est. 1983): Kabul, 750,000; Kandahar, 225,000; Herat, 150,000
Monetary unit: Afghani
Languages: Pushtu, Dari Persian, other Turkic and minor languages
Religion: Islam (Sunni, 74%; Shiite, 25%; other 1%)
National name: Jamhouri Afghanistan
Literacy rate: 12%
Economic summary: Gross domestic product (1989): $3 billion, $200 per capita. Average annual growth rate (1989 est.): .0%. Arable land: 12%; labor force: 4,980,000. Principal products: wheat, cotton, fruits, nuts, wool. Labor force in industry: 10.2%. Major industrial products: carpets and textiles. Natural resources: natural gas, oil, coal, copper, sulfur, lead, zinc, iron, salt, precious and semi-precious stones. Exports: fresh and dried fruits, nuts, natural gas, carpets. Imports: petroleum products and food supplies. Major trading partners: U.S.S.R., Soviet bloc countries, Japan, and China.

Geography. Afghanistan, approximately the size of Texas, lies wedged between the U.S.S.R., China, Pakistan, and Iran. The country is split east to west by the Hindu Kush mountain range, rising in the east to heights of 24,000 feet (7,315 m). With the exception of the southwest, most of the country is covered by high snow-capped mountains and is traversed by deep valleys.

Government. Previously a Marxist "people's republic", a new republic was established following constitutional changes in 1986 and new reforms brought up by Dr. Najibullah after his election as president. Presently a coalition government is functioning under the Premiership of Mr. Fazelhaq Khaliqyar and an effort is being made towards expanding the base of this government through new democratic reforms.

History. Darius I and Alexander the Great were the first conquerors to use Afghanistan as the gateway to India. Islamic conquerors arrived in the 7th century and Genghis Khan and Tamerlane followed in the 13th and 14th centuries.

In the 19th century, Afghanistan became a battleground in the rivalry of imperial Britain and Czarist Russia for the control of Central Asia. The Afghan Wars (1838–42 and 1878–81) fought against the British by Dost Mohammed and his son and grandson ended in defeat.

Afghanistan regained autonomy by the Anglo-Russian agreement of 1907 and full independence by the Treaty of Rawalpindi in 1919. Emir Amanullah founded the kingdom in 1926.

After a coup in 1978, Noor Taraki's attempts to create a Marxist state with Soviet aid brought armed resistance from conservative Muslim opposition.

Taraki was succeeded by Prime Minister Hafizullah Amin. Amin was replaced by Babrak Karmal, who had called for Soviet troops under a mutual defense treaty. Pakistan and other Moslem nations called for a U.N. Security Council session and charged that Amin had been executed on Dec. 27 by Soviet troops already present in Kabul. The Council's call for immediate withdrawal of Soviet troops was vetoed by the U.S.S.R. on Jan. 8, 1980.

The Soviet invasion was met with unanticipated fierce resistance from the Afghan population, resulting in a bloody war. Soviet troops had to fight Afghan tribesmen who called themselves "mujahedeen," or "holy warriors." In the early fighting, many of the guerrillas were armed only with flintlock rifles, but later they acquired more modern weapons, including rockets that they used to attack Soviet installations.

In April 1988, the U.S.S.R., U.S.A., Afghanistan, and Pakistan signed accords calling for an end to outside aid to the warring factions, in return for Soviet withdrawal by 1989. This took place in February of that year but the U.S. and the U.S.S.R. have continued to aid the warring Communist and mujahedeen factions.

At the beginning of April 1991 the rebels scored a psychologically important victory in taking the garrison town of Khost.

ALBANIA

The Republic of Albania
President: Ramiz Alia (1991)
Prime Minister: Ylli Bufi (1991)
Area: 11,100 sq mi. (28,748 sq km)
Population (est. mid-1991): 3,300,000 (average annual rate of natural increase: 1.9%); birth rate: 25/1000; infant mortality rate: 25.2/1000; density per square mile: 299
Capital and largest city (est. 1983): Tirana, 206,100
Monetary unit: Lek
Language: Albanian, Greek
Religions (1980): Sunni Moslem, 99.1%; Roman Catholic, 0.5%; other, 0.4%
Literacy rate 75%
Economic summary: Gross national product (1989 est.): $3.8 billion. Average annual growth rate (1970–78): 4.2%. Per capita income: $1,200. Arable land: 21%; labor force: 1,500,000 (1987). Principal agricultural products: wheat, corn, potatoes, sugar beets, cotton, tobacco. Labor force in industry and commerce: 40%. Major products: textiles, timber, construction materials, fuels, semi-processed minerals. Exports: minerals, metals, fuels, foodstuffs, agricultural materials. Imports: machinery, equipment, and spare parts, minerals, metals, fuels, construction materials, foodstuffs. Major trading partners: Greece, Yugoslavia, Czechoslovakia, Poland, Hungary, Bulgaria, Romania, Germany, France, Italy

147

Geography. Albania is situated on the eastern shore of the Adriatic Sea, with Yugoslavia to the north and east and Greece to the south. Slightly larger than Maryland, it is a mountainous country, mostly over 3,000 feet (914 m) above sea level, with a narrow, marshy coastal plain crossed by several rivers. The centers of population are contained in the interior mountain plateaus and basins.

Government. A multi-party system was installed in March 1991 when free elections were held. Albania's first non-Communist Cabinet was approved June 12, 1991. The Cabinet members are barred from holding office when new elections are held in May or June 1992.

History. Albania proclaimed its independence on Nov. 28, 1912, after a history of Roman, Byzantine, and Turkish domination.

Largely agricultural, Albania is one of the poorest countries in Europe. A battlefield in World War I, after the war it became a republic in which a conservative Moslem landlord, Ahmed Zogu, proclaimed himself President in 1925, and then proclaimed himself King Zog I in a monarchy in 1928. He ruled until Italy annexed Albania in 1939. Communist guerrillas under Enver Hoxha seized power in 1944, near the end of World War II.

His regime closed all of the nation's 2,169 churches and mosques in 1967 in a move to make Albania "the first atheist state in the world."

Hoxha was succeeded by Ramiz Alia, 59, who had been President since 1982.

The elections in March 1991 gave the Communists a decisive majority. But a general strike and street demonstrations soon forced the all-Communist cabinet to resign. A nonpartisan caretaker cabinet was soon appointed.

ALGERIA

Democratic and Popular Republic of Algeria
President: Chadli Bendjedid (1979)
Prime Minister: Sidi Ahmed Ghozali (1991)
Area: 919,595 sq mi. (2,381,751 sq km)
Population (est. mid-1991): 26,000,000 (average annual rate of natural increase: 2.7%); birth rate: 35/1000; infant mortality rate: 74/1000; density per square mile: 28
Capital: Algiers
Largest cities (est. 1987): Algiers, 1,483,000; Oran, 590,000; Constantine, 438,000; Annaba, 310,000
Monetary unit: Dinar
Languages: Arabic (official), French, Berber dialects
Religion: 99% Islam (Sunni)
National name: République Algérienne Democratique et Populaire—El Djemhouria El Djazaïria Demokratia Echaabia
Literacy rate 80%
Economic summary: Gross domestic product (1988): $54.1 billion, $2,235 per capita. Real growth rate: –1.8%. Arable land: 3%; labor force: 3,700,000. Principal products: wheat, barley, oats, wine, citrus fruits, olives, livestock. Labor force in industry: 40%. Major products: petroleum, gas, petrochemicals, fertilizers, iron and steel, textiles, transport equipment. Natural resources: petroleum, natural gas, iron ore, phosphates, lead, zinc, mercury, uranium. Exports: petroleum and gas, iron, wine, phosphates. Imports: food, capital and consumer goods. Major trading partners: U.S., Germany, France, Italy, Belgium, Netherlands, Canada.

Geography. Nearly four times the size of Texas, Algeria is bordered on the west by Morocco and on the east by Tunisia and Libya. To the south are Mauritania, Mali, and Niger. Low plains cover small areas near the Mediterranean coast, with 68% of the country a plateau between 2,625 and 5,250 feet (800 and 1,600 m) above sea level. The highest point is Mount Tahat in the Sahara, which rises 9,850 feet (3,000 m).

Government. Algeria is governed by the President, whose term runs for 5 years. A new Constitution was approved on Feb. 23, 1989. A National Popular Assembly of 295 members exercises legislative power, serving for a five-year term. The National Liberation Front, which led the struggle for independence from France, is the only legal party.

History. As ancient Numidia, Algeria became a Roman colony at the close of the Punic Wars (145 B.C.). Conquered by the Vandals about A.D. 440, it fell from a high state of civilization to virtual barbarism, from which it partly recovered after invasion by the Moslems about 650.

In 1492 the Moors and Jews, who had been expelled from Spain, settled in Algeria. Falling under Turkish control in 1518, Algiers served for three centuries as the headquarters of the Barbary pirates. The French took Algeria in 1830 and made it a part of France in 1848.

On July 5, 1962, Algeria was proclaimed independent. In October 1963, Ahmed Ben Bella was elected President. He began to nationalize foreign holdings and aroused opposition. He was overthrown in a military coup on June 19, 1965, by Col. Houari Boumediène, who suspended the Constitution and sought to restore financial stability.

Boumediène died in December 1978 after a long illness. Chadli Bendjedid, Secretary-General of the National Liberation Front, took the presidency in a smooth transition of power. On July 4, 1979, he released from house arrest former President Ahmed Ben Bella, who had been confined for 14 years since his overthrow.

Nationwide riots in 1988 led the government to introduce democratic reforms. In 1990 numerous political parties appeared. President Bendjedid's originally scheduled parliamentary elections for June 1991 were postponed after violent demonstrations arose in Algiers. Such national voting would be the first multiparty election since independence.

ANDORRA

Principality of Andorra
Episcopal Co-Prince: Msgr. Juan Martí y Alanís, Bishop of Seo de Urgel, Spain (1971)
French Co-Prince: François Mitterrand, President of France (1981)
Head of Government: Josep Pintat Solans (1984)
Area: 175 sq mi. (453 sq km)
Population (est. 1990): 49,974 (average annual growth rate: 2.2%); density per square mile: 282
Capital (est. 1986): Andorra la Vella, 15,639
Monetary units: French franc and Spanish peseta
Languages: Catalán (official); French, Spanish
Religion: Roman Catholic
National names: Les Vallées d'Andorre-Valls d'Andorra

Literacy rate 100%
Economic summary: Arable land: 2%; labor force: NA.
Principal products: oats, barley, cattle, sheep. Major
products: tobacco products and electric power; tour-
ism. Natural resources: water power, mineral water.
Major trading partners: Spain and France.

Geography. Andorra lies high in the Pyrenees
Mountains on the French-Spanish border. The country
is drained by the Valira River.

Government. A General Council of 28 members,
elected for four years, chooses the First Syndic and
Second Syndic. In 1976 the Andorran Democratic
Party, the principality's first political party, was
formed.

History. An autonomous and semi-independent co-
principality, Andorra has been under the joint suzerainty of the French state and the Spanish bishops of
Urgel since 1278.
In 1990 Andorra approved a customs union treaty
with the E.C. permitting free movement of industrial
goods between the two, but Andorra would apply the
E.C.'s external tariffs to third countries.

ANGOLA

People's Republic of Angola
President: José Eduardo dos Santos (1979)
Area: 481,350 sq mi. (1,246,700 sq km)
Population (est. mid-1991): 8,500,000 (average annual
rate of natural increase: 2.8); birth rate: 47/1000; infant
mortality rate: 132/1000; density per square mile: 18
Capital and largest city (est. 1983): Luanda, 525,000
Monetary unit: Kwanza
Languages: Bantu, Portuguese (official)
Religions: 47% Indigenous, 38% Roman Catholic, 15%
Protestant (est.)
Literacy rate: 41%
Economic summary: Gross domestic product (1988 est.):
$5.0 billion, per capita $600; real growth rate 9.2%.
Arable land: 2%. Labor force: 2,783,000; Labor force in
industry: 15%. Principal agricultural products: coffee,
sisal, corn, cotton, sugar, tobacco, bananas, cassava.
Major industrial products: oil, diamonds, processed
fish, tobacco, textiles, cement, processed food and
sugar, brewing. Natural resources: diamonds, gold,
iron, oil. Exports: oil, coffee, diamonds, fish and fish
products, iron ore, timber, corn. Imports: machinery
and electrical equipment, bulk iron, steel and metals,
textiles, clothing, food. Major trading partners: Brazil,
U.S.S.R., Cuba, Portugal, U.S.

Geography. Angola, more than three times the size
of California, extends for more than 1,000 miles
(1,609 km) along the South Atlantic in southwestern
Africa. Zaire is to the north and east, Zambia to the
east, and South-West Africa (Namibia) to the south.
A plateau averaging 6,000 feet (1,829 m) above sea
level rises abruptly from the coastal lowlands. Nearly
all the land is desert or savanna, with hardwood forests in the northeast.

Government. President José Eduardo dos Santos
heads the only official party, the Popular Movement
for the Liberation of Angola–Workers Party, which in
1990 discarded its official Marxism-Leninism in favor of democratic socialism. Large areas in the east

and south are held by the Union for the Total Independence of Angola (Unita), led by Jonas Savimbi.
The Popular Movement won out over Savimbi's
group and a third element in an internal struggle after
Portugal granted its former colony independence on
Nov. 11, 1975. Elections promised at the time of independence have never taken place, and the government relies heavily on Soviet support and Cuban
troops, while Savimbi receives aid from South Africa
and the U.S.

History. Discovered by the Portuguese navigator
Diego Cao in 1482, Angola became a link in trade
with India and the Far East. Later it was a major
source of slaves for Portugal's New World colony of
Brazil. Development of the interior began after the
Treaty of Berlin in 1885 fixed the colony's borders,
and British and Portuguese investment pushed mining, railways, and agriculture.
Following World War II, independence movements
began but were sternly suppressed by military force.
The April revolution of 1974 brought about a reversal
of Portugal's policy, and the next year President
Francisco da Costa Gomes signed an agreement to
grant independence to Angola. The plan called for
election of a constituent assembly and a settlement of
differences by the MPLA and the National Front for
the Liberation of Angola (FNLA) and the National
Union for the Total Independence of Angola (UNI-
TA).
The Organization of African Unity recognized the
MPLA government led by Agostinho Neto on Feb.
11, 1976, and the People's Republic of Angola became the 47th member of the organization.
Although militarily victorious, Neto's regime had
yet to consolidate its power in opposition strongholds
in the east and south.
In March 1977 and May 1978, Zairean refugees in
Angola invaded Zaire's Shaba Province, bringing
charges by Zairean President Mobutu Sese Seko that
the unsuccessful invasions were Soviet-backed with
Angolan help. Angola, the U.S.S.R., and Cuba denied
complicity.
Neto died in Moscow of cancer on Sept. 10, 1979.
The Planning Minister, José Eduardo dos Santos, was
named President.
The South-West Africa People's Organization, or
Swapo, the guerrillas fighting for the independence of
the disputed territory south of Angola also known as
Namibia, fought from bases in Angola and the South
African armed forces also maintained troops there
both to fight the SWAPO guerrillas and to assist the
UNITA guerrillas against Angolan and Cuban troops.
In December 1988, Angola, Cuba, and South Afri-
ca signed agreements calling for Cuban withdrawal
from Angola and South African withdrawal from Namibia by July 1991 and independence for Namibia.
An agreement that would mark a ceasefire and lead
to multiparty elections was signed in early 1991.

ANTIGUA AND BARBUDA

Sovereign: Queen Elizabeth II (1952)
Governor-General: Sir Wilfred E. Jacobs (1981)
Prime Minister: Vere C. Bird, Sr. (1976)
Area: 171 sq mi. (442 sq km)
Population (est. mid-1991): 100,000 (average annual
growth rate: .8%); birth rate: 14/1000; infant mortality
rate: 22/1000; density per square mile: 377
Capital and largest city (est. 1983): St. John's, 30,000
Monetary unit: East Caribbean dollar

Language: English
Religions: Anglican and Roman Catholic
Literacy rate: 90% (est.)
Member of Commonwealth of Nations
Economic summary: Gross domestic product (1989 est.): $353.5 million., per capita $5,500; real growth rate 6.2%. Arable land: 18%; Labor force: 30,000; Labor force in industry: 7% (1983); principal product: cotton, bananas, coconuts, cucumbers, mangoes. Major industry: tourism. Exports: petroleum products, manufactures, machinery and transport equipment. Imports: fuel, food, machinery. Major trading partners: U.K., U.S.

Geography. Antigua, the larger of the two main islands located 295 miles (420 km) south-southeast of San Juan, P.R., is low-lying except for a range of hills in the south that rise to their highest point at Boggy Peak (1,330 ft; 405 m). As a result of its relative flatness, Antigua suffers from cyclical drought, despite a mean annual rainfall of 44 inches. Barbuda is a coral island, well-wooded.

Government. Executive power is held by the Cabinet, presided over by Prime Minister Vere C. Bird, Sr. A 17-member Parliament is elected by universal suffrage. The Antigua Labour Party, led by Prime Minister Bird, holds 15 seats and the remaining two are held by an independent member, H. Frank, and the United National Democratic Party.

History. Antigua was discovered by Christopher Columbus in 1493 and named for the Church of Santa Maria la Antigua in Seville. Colonized by Britain in 1632, it joined the West Indies Federation in 1958. With the breakup of the Federation, it became one of the West Indies Associated States in 1967, self-governing in internal affairs. Full independence was granted Nov. 1, 1981.

Minister of Public Works, Vere Bird, Jr. was removed from office following disclosure that Israeli guns and ammunition had been delivered to Colombia's drug cartel through Antigua.

ARGENTINA

Argentine Republic
President: Carlos S. Menem (1989)
Area: 1,072,067 sq mi. (2,776,654 sq km)
Population (est. mid-1991): 32,700,000 (average annual rate of natural increase: 1.2%); birth rate: 21/1000; infant mortality rate: 31/1000; density per square mile: 31
Capital: Buenos Aires
Largest cities (est. 1983): Buenos Aires, 3,000,000; Córdoba, 1,000,000; Rosario, 950,000; La Plafa, 450,000; San Miguel de Tucumán, 400,000
Monetary unit: Austral
Language: Spanish, English, Italian, German, French
Religion: Predominantly Roman Catholic (nominally)
National name: República Argentina
Literacy rate 94%
Economic summary: Gross national product (1989 est.): $68.8 billion; $2,160 per capita; real growth rate: –5.5%. Arable land: 9%; labor force: 11,500,000. Principal products: grains, oilseeds, livestock products. Labor force in industry: 31%. Major products: processed foods, motor vehicles, consumer durables, textiles, chemicals. Natural resources: minerals, lead, zinc, tin, copper, iron, manganese, oil, uranium. Exports: meats, corn, wheat, wool, hides and industrial products (durables, textiles, airplanes etc.). Imports: machinery,

fuel and lubricating oils, iron and steel, chemical products. Major trading partners: U.S., Brazil, Italy, Germany, Netherlands, Soviet Union, France, Bolivia.

Geography. With an area slightly less than one third of the United States and second in South America only to its eastern neighbor, Brazil, in size and population, Argentina is a plain, rising from the Atlantic to the Chilean border and the towering Andes peaks. Aconcagua (23,034 ft.; 7,021 m) is the highest peak in the world outside Asia. It is bordered also by Bolivia and Paraguay on the north, and by Uruguay on the east.

The northern area is the swampy and partly wooded Gran Chaco, bordering on Bolivia and Paraguay. South of that are the rolling, fertile pampas, rich for agriculture and grazing and supporting most of the population. Next southward is Patagonia, a region of cool, arid steppes with some wooded and fertile sections.

Government. Argentina is a federal union of 22 provinces, one national territory, and the Federal District. Under the Constitution of 1853 (restored by a Constituent National Convention in 1957), the President and Vice President are elected every six years by popular vote through an electoral college. The President appoints his Cabinet. The Vice President presides over the Senate but has no other powers. The Congress consists of two houses: a 46-member Senate and a 254-member Chamber of Deputies.

History. Discovered in 1516 by Juan Díaz de Solis, Argentina developed slowly under Spanish colonial rule. Buenos Aires was settled in 1580; the cattle industry was thriving as early as 1600.

Invading British forces were expelled in 1806–07, and when Napoleon conquered Spain, the Argentinians set up their own government in the name of the Spanish King in 1810. On July 9, 1816, independence was formally declared.

As in World War I, Argentina proclaimed neutrality at the outbreak of World War II, but in the closing phase declared war on the Axis on March 27, 1945, and became a founding member of the United Nations. Juan D. Perón, an army colonel, emerged as the strongman of the postwar era, winning the Presidential elections of 1946 and 1951.

Opposition to Perón's increasing authoritarianism, led to a coup by the armed forces that sent Perón into exile in 1955. Argentina entered a long period of military dictatorships with brief intervals of constitutional government.

The former dictator returned to power in 1973 and his wife was elected Vice-President.

After Peron's death in 1974, his widow became the hemisphere's first woman chief of state, but was deposed in 1976 by a military junta.

In December 1981. Lt. Gen. Leopoldo Galtieri, commander of the army, was named president.

On April 2, 1982, Galtieri landed thousands of troops on the Falkland Islands and reclaimed the Malvinas, their Spanish name, as national territory. By May 21, 5,000 British marines and paratroops landed from the British armada, and regained control of the islands.

Galtieri resigned three days after the surrender of the island garrison on June 14. Maj. Gen. Reynaldo Bignone, took office as President on July 1.

In the presidential election of October 1983, Raúl Alfonsín, leader of the middle-class Radical Civic Union, handed the Peronist Party its first defeat since its founding.

Among the enormous problems facing Alfonsín

after eight years of mismanagement under military rule was a $45-billion foreign debt, the developing world's third largest. After cliff-hanging negotiations with American, European, and Japanese banks representing the country's private creditors, the Alfonsín government agreed on June 29, 1984, to pay $350 million in overdue interest and was moving toward austerity measures.

With the arrears mounting at the rate of $150 million a month, the debt to foreign creditors mounted to $48 billion by mid-1985, and more than $1 billion was past due. On June 11, the Alfonsin government reached agreement with the International Monetary Fund on an austerity program designed to put Argentina into a position to pay its way internationally and keep current with its debt obligations. The agreement opened the door for up to $1.2 billion of new loans to Argentina.

Three days later, on June 14, President Alfonsin announced an "economy of war" to bring the inflation rate down. The program combined the creation of a new currency—the austral, meaning southern— to replace the peso, wage and price controls and a halt to the government's deficit spending. In April 1986, the austral was devalued to spur exports.

Twin economic problems of growing unemployment and quadruple-digit inflation led to a Peronist victory in the elections of May 1989. Inflation of food prices led to riots that induced Alfonsin to step down in June 1989, six months early, in favor of the Peronist, Carlos Menem.

On the eve of a visit by President Bush a group of army leaders and their followers attempted an uprising on December 3, 1990. The rebels attacked important military buildings in the capital in an apparent attempt to take control of the army. Most commanders, however, stood by the legitimate government, and the insurrection was suppressed in less than 24 hours.

AUSTRALIA
Commonwealth of Australia
Sovereign: Queen Elizabeth II (1952)
Governor-General: William Hayden (1989)
Prime Minister: Robert J. L. Hawke (1983)
Area: 2,966,150 sq mi. (7,682,300 sq km)
Population (est. mid-1991): 17,500,000 (average annual rate of natural increase: 0.8%); birth rate: 14/1000; infant mortality rate: 24.3/1000; density per square mile: 6
Capital (est. 1988): Canberra, 297,300
Largest cities (1990): Sydney, 3,656,900; Melbourne, 3,080,000; Brisbane, 1,301,700; Adelaide, 1,049,100; Perth, 1,193,100
Monetary unit: Australian dollar
Language: English
Religions: 26.1% Anglican, 26.0% Roman Catholic, 24.3% other Christian
Literacy rate: 98.5%
Member of Commonwealth of Nations
Economic summary: Gross national product (1989 est.): $240.8 billion, per capita $14,380; real growth rate 4.1%. Arable land: 6%; labor force: 6%. Principal products: wool, meat, cereals, sugar, sheep, cattle, dairy products. Labor force: 7,700,000; Labor force in manufacturing and industry: 16.2% (1987). Major products:

machinery, motor vehicles, iron and steel, chemicals. Natural resources: iron ore, bauxite, zinc, lead, tin, coal, oil, gas, copper, nickel, uranium. Exports: wheat, wool, coal. Imports: meat; iron ore; capital equipment. Major trading partners: Japan, U.S., U.K., New Zealand, Germany, South Korea, Singapore.

Geography. The continent of Australia, with the island state of Tasmania, is approximately equal in area to the United States (excluding Alaska and Hawaii), and is nearly 50% larger than Europe (excluding the U.S.S.R.).

Mountain ranges run from north to south along the east coast, reaching their highest point in Mount Kosciusko (7,308 ft; 2,228 m). The western half of the continent is occupied by a desert plateau that rises into barren, rolling hills near the west coast. It includes the Great Victoria Desert to the south and the Great Sandy Desert to the north. The Great Barrier Reef, extending about 1,245 miles (2,000 km), lies along the northeast coast.

The island of Tasmania (26,178 sq mi.; 67,800 sq km) is off the southeastern coast.

Government. The Federal Parliament consists of a bicameral legislature. The House of Representatives has 148 members elected for three years by popular vote. The Senate has 76 members elected by popular vote for six years. One half of the Senate is elected every three years. Voting is compulsory at 18. Supreme federal judicial power is vested in the High Court of Australia in the Federal Courts, and in the State Courts invested by Parliament with Federal jurisdiction. The High Court consists of seven justices, appointed by the Governor-General in Council. Each of the states has its own judicial system.

History. Dutch, Portuguese, and Spanish ships sighted Australia in the 17th century; the Dutch landed at the Gulf of Carpentaria in 1606. Australia was called New Holland, Botany Bay, and New South Wales until about 1820.

Captain James Cook, in 1770, claimed possession for Great Britain. A British penal colony was set up at what is now Sydney, then Port Jackson, in 1788, and about 161,000 transported English convicts were settled there until the system was suspended in 1839.

Free settlers established six colonies: New South Wales (1786), Tasmania (then Van Diemen's Land) (1825), Western Australia (1829), South Australia (1834), Victoria (1851), and Queensland (1859).

The six colonies became states and in 1901 federated into the Commonwealth of Australia with a Constitution that incorporated British parliamentary tradition and U.S. federal experience. Australia became known for liberal legislation: free compulsory education, protected trade unionism with industrial conciliation and arbitration, the "Australian" ballot facilitating selection, the secret ballot, women's suffrage, maternity allowances, and sickness and old age pensions.

In the election of 1983, Robert Hawke, head of the Labor Party, became Prime Minister. The Labor government was reelected in a Federal election in December 1984.

Prime Minister Hawke survived a challenge to his leadership of the ruling Labor party in early June 1991 from Paul Keating, who thereafter resigned his positions as deputy p.m. and treasurer. A small cabinet reshuffle followed.

Australian External Territories

Norfolk Island (13 sq mi.; 36.3 sq km) was placed under Australian administration in 1914. Population in 1988 was about 1,800.

The Ashmore and Cartier Islands (.8 sq mi.), situated in the Indian Ocean off the northwest coast of Australia, came under Australian administration in 1934. In 1938 the islands were annexed to the Northern Territory. On the attainment of self-government by the Northern Territory in 1978, the islands which are uninhabited were retained as Commonwealth Territory.

The Australian Antarctic Territory (2,360,000 sq mi.; 6,112,400 sq km), comprises all the islands and territories, other than Adélie Land, situated south of lat. 60°S and lying between long. 160° to 45°E. It came under Australian administration in 1936.

Heard Island and the McDonald Islands (158 sq mi.; 409.2 sq km), lying in the sub-Antarctic, were placed under Australian administration in 1947. The islands are uninhabited.

Christmas Island (52 sq mi.; 134.7 sq km) is situated in the Indian Ocean. It came under Australian administration in 1958. Population in 1988 was about 2,000.

Coral Sea Islands (400,000 sq mi.; 1,036,000 sq km, but only a few sq mi. of land) became a territory of Australia in 1969. There is no permanent population on the islands.

AUSTRIA

Republic of Austria
President: Kurt Waldheim (1986)
Chancellor: Franz Vranitzky (1986)
Area: 32,375 sq mi. (83,851 sq km)
Population (est. mid-1991): 7,700,000 (average annual rate of natural increase: 0.1%); birth rate: 12/1000; infant mortality rate: 7.9/1000; density per square mile: 239
Capital: Vienna
Largest cities (est. 1983): Vienna, 1,550,000; Graz, 240,000; Linz, 200,000; Salzburg, 135,000; Innsbruck, 115,000; Klagenfurt, 85,000
Monetary unit: Schilling
Language: German
Religion: Roman Catholic, 85%
Literacy rate: 98%
National name: Republik Österreich
Economic summary: Gross domestic product (1989 est.): $103.2 billion; per capita $13,600; real growth rate 4.2%. Arable land: 17%. Labor force: 3,037,000; 56.4% in services; principal agricultural products: livestock, forest products, grains, sugar beets, potatoes. Principal products: iron and steel, chemicals, machinery, paper and pulp. Natural resources: iron ore, petroleum, timber, magnesite, aluminum, coal, lignite, cement, copper, hydropower. Exports: iron and steel products, timber, paper, textiles, chemical products. Imports: machinery, chemicals, foodstuffs, textiles and clothing, petroleum. Major trading partners: Germany, Italy, Switzerland, U.S., Eastern Europe.

Geography. Slightly smaller than Maine, Austria includes much of the mountainous territory of the eastern Alps (about 75% of the area). The country contains many snowfields, glaciers, and snowcapped peaks, the highest being the Grossglockner (12,530 ft; 3,819 m). The Danube is the principal river. Forests and woodlands cover about 40% of the land area.

Almost at the heart of Europe, Austria has as its neighbors Italy, Switzerland, West Germany, Czechoslovakia, Hungary, Yugoslavia, and Liechtenstein.

Government. Austria is a federal republic composed of nine provinces (Bundesländer), including Vienna. The President is elected by the people for a term of six years. The bicameral legislature consists of the Bundesrat, with 58 members chosen by the provincial assemblies, and the Nationalrat, with 183 members popularly elected for four years. Presidency of the Bundesrat revolves every six months, going to the provinces in alphabetical order.

History. Settled in prehistoric times, the Central European land that is now Austria was overrun in pre-Roman times by various tribes, including the Celts. Charlemagne conquered the area in 788 and encouraged colonization and Christianity. In 1252, Ottokar, King of Bohemia, gained possession, only to lose the territories to Rudolf of Hapsburg in 1278. Thereafter, until World War I, Austria's history was largely that of its ruling house, the Hapsburgs.

Austria emerged from the Congress of Vienna in 1815 as the Continent's dominant power. The *Ausgleich* of 1867 provided for a dual sovereignty, the empire of Austria and the kingdom of Hungary, under Francis Joseph I, who ruled until his death on Nov. 21, 1916. He was succeeded by his grandnephew, Charles I.

During World War I, Austria-Hungary was one of the Central Powers with Germany, Bulgaria, and Turkey, and the conflict left the country in political chaos and economic ruin. Austria, shorn of Hungary, was proclaimed a republic in 1918, and the monarchy was dissolved in 1919.

A parliamentary democracy was set up by the Constitution of Nov. 10, 1920. To check the power of Nazis advocating union with Germany, Chancellor Engelbert Dolfuss in 1933 established a dictatorship, but was assassinated by the Nazis on July 25, 1934. Kurt von Schuschnigg, his successor, struggled to keep Austria independent but on March 12, 1938, German troops occupied the country, and Hitler proclaimed its *Anschluss* (union) with Germany, annexing it to the Third Reich.

After World War II, the U.S. and Britain declared the Austrians a "liberated" people. But the Russians prolonged the occupation. Finally Austria concluded a state treaty with the U.S.S.R. and the other occupying powers and regained its independence on May 15, 1955. The second Austrian republic, established Dec. 19, 1945, on the basis of the 1920 Constitution (amended in 1929), was declared by the federal parliament to be permanently neutral.

On June 8, 1986, former UN Secretary-General Kurt Waldheim was elected to the ceremonial office of President in a campaign marked by controversy over his alleged links to Nazi war-crimes in Yugoslavia.

To the relief of all four political parties President Waldheim announced in June 1991 that he would not seek reelection in 1992. Despite its neutrality Austria permitted the U.S. military to fly aircraft over Austrian airspace during the Persian Gulf war.

BAHAMAS

Commonwealth of the Bahamas
Sovereign: Queen Elizabeth II (1952)
Governor-General: Sir Henry M. Taylor (1988)
Prime Minister: Lynden O. Pindling (1967)
Area: 5,380 sq mi. (13,939 sq km)
Population (1991 census): 254,685 (average annual rate of natural increase: 1.3%); birth rate: 18/1000; infant mortality rate: 22.3/1000; density per square mile: 47
Capital and largest city (1991 census): Nassau, 171,542
Monetary unit: Bahamian dollar
Language: English
Religions: Baptist, 29%; Anglican, 23%; Roman Catholic, 22%, others
Literacy rate: 95%
Member of Commonwealth of Nations
Economic summary: Gross domestic product (1988 est.): $2.4 billion; $9,875 per capita; real growth rate 2.0%. Labor force: 132,600; Principal agricultural products: fruits, vegetables. Major industrial products: fish, refined petroleum, pharmaceutical products; tourism. Natural resources: salt, aragonite, timber. Exports: rum, crawfish, pharmaceuticals, cement, rum. Imports: foodstuffs, manufactured goods, fuels. Major trading partners: U.S., U.K., Nigeria, Canada, Iran.

Geography. The Bahamas are an archipelago of about 700 islands and 2,400 uninhabited islets and cays lying 50 miles off the east coast of Florida. They extend from northwest to southeast for about 760 miles (1,223 km). Only 22 of the islands are inhabited; the most important is New Providence (80 sq mi.; 207 sq km), on which Nassau is situated. Other islands include Grand Bahama, Abaco, Eleuthera, Andros, Cat Island, San Salvador (or Watling's Island), Exuma, Long Island, Crooked Island, Acklins Island, Mayaguana, and Inagua.

The islands are mainly flat, few rising above 200 feet (61 m). There are no fresh water streams. There are several large brackish lakes on several islands including Inagua and New Providence.

Government. The Bahamas moved toward greater autonomy in 1968 after the overwhelming victory in general elections of the Progressive Liberal Party, led by Prime Minister Lynden O. Pindling. The black leader's party won 29 seats in the House of Assembly to only 7 for the predominantly white United Bahamians, who had controlled the islands for decades before Pindling became Premier in 1967.

With its new mandate from the 85%-black population, Pindling's government negotiated a new Constitution with Britain under which the colony became the Commonwealth of the Bahama Islands in 1969. On July 10, 1973, The Bahamas became an independent nation as the Commonwealth of the Bahamas. The islands established diplomatic relations with Cuba in 1974.

In the 1987 election, Pindling's Progressive Liberal Party won 31 of 49 seats in Parliament; the Free National Movement, 16.

The PLP majority rose to 32 seats when Perry Christie reentered the party upon accepting a ministerial portfolio.

History. The islands were reached by Columbus in October 1492, and were a favorite pirate area in the early 18th century. The Bahamas were a crown colony from 1717 until they were granted internal self-government in 1964.

BAHRAIN

State of Bahrain
Emir: Sheik Isa bin-Sulman al-Khalifa (1961)
Prime Minister: Sheik Khalifa bin Sulman al-Khalifa (1970)
Area: 240 sq mi. (620 sq km)
Population (est. mid-1991): 500,000 (average annual rate of natural increase: 2.3%); birth rate: 27/1000; infant mortality rate: 24/1000; density per square mile: 2,243
Capital (est. 1982): Manama, 150,000
Monetary unit: Bahrain dinar
Languages: Arabic (official), English, Farsi, Urdu
Religion: Islam
Literacy rate : 40%
Economic summary: Gross domestic product (1987): $3.5 billion, $7,550 per capita; real growth rate (1988): 0%. Labor force (1982): 140,000; labor force in industry and commerce: 85%. Principal products: eggs, vegetables, fruits. Major products: oil, fish. Natural resources: oil, fish. Exports: oil, aluminum, fish. Imports: machinery, oil-industry equipment, motor vehicles, foodstuffs. Major trading partners: Saudi Arabia, U.S., U.K., Japan.

Geography. Bahrain is an archipelago in the Persian Gulf off the coast of Saudi Arabia. The islands for the most part are level expanses of sand and rock.

Government. A new Constitution was approved in 1973. It created the first elected parliament in the country's history. Called the National Council, it consisted of 30 members elected by male citizens for four-year terms, plus up to 16 Cabinet ministers as ex-officio members. In August 1975, the Amir dissolved the National Council.

History. A sheikdom that passed from the Persians to the al-Khalifa family from Arabia in 1782, Bahrain became, by treaty, a British protectorate in 1820. It has become a major Middle Eastern oil center and, through use of oil revenues, is one of the most developed of the Persian Gulf sheikdoms. The Emir, Sheik Isa bin-Sulman al-Khalifa, who succeeded to the post in 1961, is a member of the original ruling family. Bahrain announced its independence on Aug. 14, 1971.

Expanded use of Bahrain for Allied forces during the Persian Gulf was was granted.

BANGLADESH

People's Republic of Bangladesh
President: Shahabuddin Ahmed
Prime Minister: Khaleda Zia (1991)
Vice President: Moudud Ahmed (1989)
Area: 55,598 sq mi. (143,998 sq km)
Population (est. mid-1991): 116,600,000 (average annual rate of natural increase: 2.4%); birth rate: 37/1000; infant mortality rate: 120/1000; density per square mile: 2,097
Capital and largest city (est 1986): Dhaka, 4,470,000
Monetary unit: Taka
Principal languages: Bangla (official), English
Religions: Islam, (official) 83%; Hindu, 16%
Literacy rate: 29%
Member of Commonwealth of Nations
Economic summary: Gross domestic product (FY89 est.): $20.6 billion, per capita $180; real growth rate 2.1%. Arable land: 67%. Principal products: rice, jute, tea, sugar, potatoes, beef. Labor force: 35,100,000, 11% in industry and commerce. Major industrial products: jute goods, textiles, sugar, fertilizer, paper, processed

foods. Natural resources: natural gas, uranium, timber. Exports: jute, tea, leather, garments. Imports: food grains, fuels, raw cotton, manufactured goods. Major trading partners: U.S., Japan, Middle East, Europe.

Geography. Bangladesh, on the northern coast of the Bay of Bengal, is surrounded by India, with a small common border with Burma in the southeast. It is approximately the size of Wisconsin. The country is low-lying riverine land traversed by the many branches and tributaries of the Ganges and Brahmaputra rivers. Elevations averages less than 600 feet (183 m) above sea level. Tropical monsoons and frequent floods and cyclones inflict heavy damage in the delta region.

Government. Khalida Zia, widow of assassinated President Ziaur Rahman, and her Bangladesh Nationalist Party won the election of late-February 1991. The BNP gained just enough seats in the 330-seat parliament to form a government.

History. The former East Pakistan was part of imperial British India until Britain withdrew in 1947. The two Pakistans were united by religion (Islam), but their peoples were separated by culture, physical features, and 1,000 miles of Indian territory. Bangladesh consists primarily of East Bengal (West Bengal is part of India and its people are primarily Hindu) plus the Sylhet district of the Indian state of Assam. For almost 25 years after independence from Britain, its history was as part of Pakistan (*see* Pakistan).

The East Pakistanis unsuccessfully sought greater autonomy from West Pakistan. The first general elections in Pakistani history, in December 1970, saw virtually all 171 seats of the region (out of 300 for both East and West Pakistan) go to Sheik Mujibur Rahman's Awami League.

Attempts to write an all-Pakistan Constitution to replace the military regime of Gen. Yahya Khan failed. Yahya put down a revolt in March 1971. An estimated one million Bengalis were killed in the fighting or later slaughtered. Ten million more took refuge in India.

In December 1971, India invaded East Pakistan, routed the West Pakistani occupation forces, and created Bangladesh. In February 1974, Pakistan agreed to recognize the independence of Bangladesh.

On March 24, 1982, Gen. Hossain Mohammad Ershad, army chief of staff, took control in a bloodless coup. Ershad assumed the office of President in 1983.

Gen. Ershad resigned on December 6, 1990 amidst protests and numerous allegations of corruption. During his nine-year tenure as president, the country's foreign debt went from $3 billion to $10 billion.

BARBADOS

Sovereign: Queen Elizabeth II
Governor-General: Dame Nita Barrow (June 1990)
Prime Minister: L. Erskine Sandiford (1987)
Area: 166 sq. mi. (431 sq km)
Population (est. mid-1991): 300,000; growth rate: .7%.; birth rate: 16;/1000 infant mortality rate: 9/1000; density per square mile: 1,548
Capital and largest city (est. 1988): Bridgetown, 102,000
Monetary unit: Barbados dollar
Language: English
Religions: Anglican, 70%; Methodist, 9%; Roman Catholic, 4%
Literacy rate: 99%

Member of Commonwealth of Nations
Economic summary: Gross domestic product (1988 est.): $1.3 billion, per capita $5,250; real growth rate (1989 est.) 3.7%). Arable land: 77%. Principal products: sugar cane, subsistence foods. Labor force: 112,300; 37% services and government. Major industrial products: light manufactures, sugar milling, tourism. Exports: sugar and sugar cane byproducts, clothing, electrical parts. Imports: foodstuffs, crude oil, manufactured goods. Major trading partners: U.S., Caribbean nations, U.K., Canada.

Geography. An island in the Atlantic about 300 miles (483 km) north of Venezuela, Barbados is only 21 miles long (34 km) and 14 miles across (23 km) at its widest point. It is circled by fine beaches and narrow coastal plains. The highest point is Mount Hillaby (1,105 ft; 337 m) in the north central area.

Government. The Barbados legislature dates from 1627. It is bicameral, with a Senate of 21 appointed members and an Assembly of 28 elected members. The major political parties are the Democratic Labor Party (18 seats in Assembly), led by Prime Minister L. Erskine Sandiford; Barbados Labor Party (10 seats), led by Henry Deb. Forde and National Democratic Party (0 seats) led by Richie Haynes.

History. Barbados, with a population 90% black, was settled by the British in 1627. It became a crown colony in 1885. It was a member of the Federation of the West Indies from 1958 to 1962. Britain granted the colony independence on Nov. 30, 1966, and it became a parliamentary democracy.

While retaining membership in the Commonwealth of Nations and economic ties with Britain, Barbados seeks broader economic and political relations with Western Hemisphere countries and in particular the developing nations of the Caribbean.

Prime Minister Sandiford handily won a second five-year term as a result of parliamentary elections in January 1991.

BELGIUM

Kingdom of Belgium
Sovereign: King Baudouin I (1951)
Prime Minister: Wilfried Martens (1981)
Area: 11,781 sq mi. (30,513 sq km)
Population (est. mid-1991): 9,900,000 (average annual rate of natural increase: .1%); birth rate: 12/1000; infant mortality rate: 8.6/1000; density per square mile: 842
Capital: Brussels
Largest cities (est. 1987): Brussels, 970,346; Antwerp, 479,748; Ghent, 233,856; Charleroi, 209,395; Liège, 200,891; Bruges, 117,755
Monetary Unit: Belgian franc
Languages: Flemish, 56%; French, 32%; bilingual (Brussels), 11%; German, 1%.
Religion: Roman Catholic, 75%
National name: Royaume de Belgique—Koninkrijk van België
Literacy rate: 98%
Economic summary: Gross domestic product (1989): $166 billion, per capita $17,00; real growth rate 4.5%). Arable land: 24%. Principal products: livestock, poultry, grain, sugar beets, flax, tobacco, potatoes, vegetables, fruits. Labor force: 4,000,000; 37% in industry. Major products: fabricated metal, iron and steel, machinery, textiles, chemicals, food processing. Exports: (Belg.-Luxembourg Econ. Union) iron and steel

products, chemicals, pharmaceuticals, textile products. Imports: (Belg.-Luxembourg Econ. Union) nonelectrical machinery, motor vehicles, textiles, chemicals, fuels. Major trading partners: European Communities, U.S., Eastern Europe.

Geography. A neighbor of France, West Germany, the Netherlands, and Luxembourg, Belgium has about 40 miles of seacoast on the North Sea at the Strait of Dover. In area, it is approximately the size of Maryland. The northern third of the country is a plain extending eastward from the seacoast. North of the Sambre and Meuse Rivers is a low plateau; to the south lies the heavily wooded Ardennes plateau, attaining an elevation of about 2,300 feet (700 m).

The Schelde River, which rises in France and flows through Belgium, emptying into the Schelde estuaries, enables Antwerp to be an ocean port.

Government. Belgium, a parliamentary democracy under a constitutional monarch, consists of nine provinces. Its bicameral legislature has a Senate, with its 181 members elected for four years—106 by general election, 50 by provincial councillors and 25 by the Senate itself. The 212-member Chamber of Representatives is directly elected for four years by proportional representation. There is universal suffrage, and those who do not vote are fined.

Belgium joined the North Atlantic Alliance in 1949 and is a member of the European Community. NATO and the European Community have their headquarters in Brussels.

The sovereign, Baudouin I, was born Sept. 7, 1930; the son of King Leopold III and Queen Astrid. He became King on July 17, 1951, after the abdication of his father. He married Doña Fabiola de Mora y Aragón on Dec. 15, 1960. Since he has no children, his brother, Prince Albert, is heir to the throne.

History. Belgium occupies part of the Roman province of Belgica, named after the Belgae, a people of ancient Gaul. The area was conquered by Julius Caesar in 57–50 B.C., then was overrun by the Franks in the 5th century. It was part of Charlemagne's empire in the 8th century, then in the next century was absorbed into Lotharingia and later into the Duchy of Lower Lorraine. In the 12th century it was partitioned into the Duchies of Brabant and Luxembourg, the Bishopric of Liège, and the domain of the Count of Hainaut, which included Flanders.

In the 16th century, Belgium, with most of the area of the Low Countries, passed to the Duchy of Burgundy and was the marriage portion of Archduke Maximilian of Hapsburg and the inheritance of his grandson, Charles V, who incorporated it into his empire. Then, in 1555, they were united with Spain.

By the treaty of Utrecht in 1713, the country's sovereignty passed to Austria. During the wars that followed the French Revolution, Belgium was occupied and later annexed to France. But with the downfall of Napoleon, the Congress of Vienna in 1815 gave the country to the Netherlands. The Belgians revolted in 1830 and declared their independence.

Germany's invasion of Belgium in 1914 set off World War I. The Treaty of Versailles (1919) gave the areas of Eupen, Malmédy, and Moresnet to Belgium. Leopold III succeeded Albert, King during World War I, in 1934. In World War II, Belgium was overwhelmed by Nazi Germany, and Leopold III was made prisoner. When he attempted to return in 1950, Socialists and Liberals revolted. He abdicated July 16, 1951, and his son, Baudouin, became King the next day.

Despite the increasingly strong divisions between the French- and Flemish-speaking communities, a Christian Democrat-Liberal coalition that took office in December 1981 came close to setting a record for longevity among the 32 governments that had ruled Belgium since World War II. Headed by Prime Minister Wilfried Martens—the fifth government he had led since 1979—it survived several serious political challenges, including the implementation of an unpopular economic austerity program in 1983 and the deployment of NATO cruise missiles in March 1985.

Strife between French and Flemish speakers almost toppled the government in 1986 and 1987. Belgian dithering during the Persian Gulf war saw an outpour of criticism from foreign and domestic sources but proved no danger to the Martens government.

BELIZE

Sovereign: Queen Elizabeth II (1952)
Governor-General: Dame Minita Gordon (1981)
Prime Minister: George Price (1989)
Area: 8,867 sq mi. (22,965 sq km)
Population (est. mid-1991): 200,000 (average annual rate of natural increase: 3.3%); birth rate: 38/1000; infant mortality rate: 35/1000.; density per sq mi.: 27
Capital (1989): Belmopan, 8,000
Largest city (1989): Belize City, 70,000
Monetary unit: Belize dollar
Languages: English (official) and Spanish, Maya, Carib
Religions: 60% Roman Catholic, 40% Protestant
Literacy rate: 93% (est.)
Member of Commonwealth of Nations
Economic summary: Gross domestic product (1989 est.): $225.6 million, per capita $1,285; real growth rate 6%. Arable land: 2%. Principal products: sugar cane, citrus fruits, corn, molasses, rice, bananas, livestock. Labor force: 51,500; 10.3% in manufacturing. Major products: timber, processed foods, furniture, rum, soap. Natural resource: timber, fish. Exports: sugar, molasses, clothing, lumber, citrus fruits, fish. Imports: fuels, transportation equipment, foodstuffs, textiles, machinery. Major trading partners: U.S., U.K., Trinidad and Tobago, Canada, Netherlands Antilles, Mexico.

Geography. Belize (formerly British Honduras) is situated on the Caribbean Sea south of Mexico and east and north of Guatemala. In area, it is about the size of New Hampshire. Most of the country is heavily forested with various hardwoods. Mangrove swamps and cays along the coast give way to hills and mountains in the interior. The highest point is Victoria Peak, 3,681 feet (1,122 m).

Government. Formerly the colony of British Honduras, Belize became a fully independent commonwealth on Sept. 21, 1981, after having been self-governing since 1964. Executive power is nominally wielded by Queen Elizabeth II through an appointed Governor-General but effective power is held by the Prime Minister, who is responsible to a 28-member parliament elected by universal suffrage.

History. Once a part of the Mayan empire, the area was deserted until British timber cutters began exploiting valuable hardwoods in the 17th century. Efforts by Spain to dislodge British settlers, including a major naval attack in 1798, were defeated. The territory was formally named a British colony in 1862 but administered by the Governor of Jamaica until 1884.

Guatemala has long made claims to the territory. A tentative agreement was reached between Britain, Belize, and Guatemala in March 1981 that would offer access to the Caribbean through Belizean territory for Guatemala. The agreement broke down, however.

The prime minister and his People's United Party easily defeated the opposition United Democratic Party in the general elections of Septemebr 1989. Cordial talks held in July 1990 between the Guatemalan president and Prime Minister Price raised hopes of of settling a long-standing border dispute between the two countries.

BENIN

Republic of Benin
President: Nicephore Soglo (1991)
Area: 43,483 sq mi. (112,622 sq km)
Population (est. mid-1991): 4,800,000 (average annual rate of natural increase: 3.0%); birth rate: 49/1000; infant mortality rate: 90/1000; density per square mile: 110
Capital (est. 1984): Porto-Novo, 208,000
Largest city (est. 1982): Cotonou, 490,000
Monetary unit: Franc CFA
Ethnic groups: Fons and Adjas, Baribas, Yorubas, Mahis
Languages: French, African languages
Religions: indigenous, 70%; Christian, 15%; Islam, 15%
National name: Republique Populaire du Benin
Literacy rate (1981): 25.9%
Economic summary: Gross domestic product (1988): $1.7 billion. per capita $335; real growth rate 1.8%. Arable land: 12%. Principal products: oil palms, peanuts, cotton, coffee, tobacco, corn, rice, livestock, fish. Labor force: 1,900,000; less than 2% industry. Major industrial products: processed palm oil, palm kernel oil, textiles, beverages. Natural resources: low-grade iron ore, limestone, some offshore oil. Exports: palm and agricultural products. Imports: beverages, tobacco, consumer goods, fuels, foodstuffs, machinery. Major trading partners: France and other Western European countries, Japan, U.S.

Geography. This West African nation on the Gulf of Guinea, between Togo on the west and Nigeria on the east, is about the size of Tennessee. It is bounded also by Burkina Faso and Niger on the north. The land consists of a narrow coastal strip that rises to a swampy, forested plateau and then to highlands in the north. A hot and humid climate blankets the entire country.

Government. The change in name from Dahomey to Benin was announced by President Mathieu Kerekou on November 30, 1975. Benin commemorates an African kingdom that flourished in the 17th century. At the same time, Kerekou announced the formation of a political organization, the Party of the People's Revolution of Benin, to mark the first anniversary of his declaration of a "new society" guided by Marxist-Leninist principles. Kérékou repudiated Marxism-Leninism in 1989.

History. One of the smallest and most densely populated states in Africa, Benin was annexed by the French in 1893. The area was incorporated into French West Africa in 1904. It became an autonomous republic within the French Community in 1958, and on Aug. 1, 1960, was granted its independence within the Community.

Gen. Christophe Soglo deposed the first president, Hubert Maga, in an army coup in 1963. He dismissed the civilian government in 1965, proclaiming himself chief of state. A group of young army officers seized power in December 1967, deposing Soglo. They promulgated a new Constitution in 1968.

In December 1969, Benin had its fifth coup of the decade, with the army again taking power. In May 1970, a three-man presidential commission was created to take over the government. The commission had a six-year term; each member serves as president for two years. Maga turned over power as scheduled to Justin Ahomadegbe in May 1972, but six months later yet another army coup ousted the triumvirate and installed Lt. Col. Mathieu Kerekou as President.

Student protests and widespread strikes in 1989 and 1990 moved Benin toward multiparty democracy. In March 1991 Prime Minister Soglo won the first free presidential election.

BHUTAN

Kingdom of Bhutan
Ruler: King Jigme Singye Wangchuk (1972)
Area: 18,000 sq mi. (46,620 sq km)
Population (est. mid-1991): 700,000 (average annual rate of natural increase: 2.0%); birth rate: 39/1000; infant mortality rate: 142/1000; density per square mile: 37
Capital (est. 1984): Thimphu, 30,000
Monetary unit: Ngultrum
Language: Dzongkha (official)
Religions: Buddhist, 75%; Hindu, 25%
National name: Druk-yul
Literacy rate: 15%
Economic summary: Gross domestic product (1988 est.): $273 million, per capita $199; real growth rate 8.8%. Arable land: 3%. Labor force in agriculture: 95%. Principal products: rice, barley, wheat, potatoes, fruit. Major industrial product: cement. Natural resources: timber, hydroelectric power. Exports: cardamom, gypsum, timber, handicrafts, cement, fruit. Imports: fuels, machinery, vehicles. Major trading partner: India.

Geography. Mountainous Bhutan, half the size of Indiana, is situated on the southeast slope of the Himalayas, bordered on the north and east by Tibet and on the south and west by India. The landscape consists of a succession of lofty and rugged mountains running generally from north to south and separated by deep valleys. In the north, towering peaks reach a height of 24,000 feet (7,315 m).

Government. Bhutan is a constitutional monarchy. The King rules with a Council of Ministers and a Royal Advisory Council. There is a National Assembly (Parliament), which meets semiannually, but no political parties.

History. British troops invaded the country in 1865 and negotiated an agreement under which Britain undertook to pay an annual allowance to Bhutan on condition of good behavior. A treaty with India in 1949 increased this subsidy and placed Bhutan's foreign affairs under Indian control.

In the 1960s, Bhutan undertook modernization, abolishing slavery and the caste system, emancipating women and enacting land reform. In 1985, Bhutan made its first diplomatic links with non-Asian countries.

Although there were no serious threats to his authority, the King in 1990 took measures to isolate his people further from foreign, Western influences.

BOLIVIA

Republic of Bolivia
President: Jaime Paz Zamora (1989)
Area: 424,162 sq mi. (1,098,581 sq km)
Population (est. mid-1991): 7,500,000 (average annual rate of natural increase: 2.6%; birth rate: 38/1000; infant mortality rate: 93/1000; density per square mile: 18
Judicial capital (est. 1985): Sucre, 86,609
Administrative capital (est. 1985): La Paz, 992,592
Largest cities (est. 1985): Santa Cruz, 441,717; Cochabamba, 317,251; Oruro, 178,393
Monetary unit: Boliviano
Languages: Spanish, Quechua, Aymara
Religion: Roman Catholic, 94%
National name: República de Bolivia
Literacy rate: 63%
Economic summary: Gross national product (1988): $4.6 billion, $660 per capita, real growth rate 2.8%. Arable land: 3%. Labor force in agriculture: 50%. Principal products: potatoes, corn, rice, sugar cane, bananas, coffee. Labor force in manufacturing: 10%. Major products: refined petroleum, processed foods, tin, textiles, clothing. Natural resources: petroleum, natural gas, tin, lead, zinc, copper, tungsten, bismuth, antimony, gold, sulfur, silver, iron ore. Exports: tin, lead, zinc, silver, antimony, coffee, sugar, cotton, soya beans, leather, citrus, natural gas. Imports: foodstuffs, petroleum, consumer goods. Major trading partners: U.S., Argentina.

Geography. Landlocked Bolivia, equal in size to California and Texas combined, lies to the west of Brazil. Its other neighbors are Peru and Chile on the west and Argentina and Paraguay on the south.

The country is a low alluvial plain throughout 60% of its area toward the east, drained by the Amazon and Plata river systems. The western part, enclosed by two chains of the Andes, is a great plateau—the Altiplano, with an average altitude of 12,000 feet (3,658 m). More than 80% of the population lives on the plateau, which also contains La Paz. At an altitude of 11,910 feet (3,630 m), it is the highest capital city in the world.

Lake Titicaca, half the size of Lake Ontario, is one of the highest large lakes in the world, at an altitude of 12,507 feet (3,812 m). Islands in the lake hold ruins of the ancient Incas.

Government. The Bolivian Constitution provides for a democratic, representative, unitary republic, with a government made up of three branches: legislative, executive, and judicial. Executive power is exercised by the president, elected by a direct vote for a four-year term. Legislative power is vested in the National Congress, consisting of the Chamber of Deputies and the Senate. Judicial power is in the hands of the Supreme Court.,

History. Famous since Spanish colonial days for its mineral wealth, modern Bolivia was once a part of the ancient Incan Empire. After the Spaniards defeated the Incas in the 16th century, Bolivia's predominantly Indian population was reduced to slavery. The country won its independence in 1825 and was named after Simón Bolívar, the famed liberator.

Harassed by internal strife, Bolivia lost great slices of territory to three neighbor nations. Several thousand square miles and its outlet to the Pacific were taken by Chile after the War of the Pacific (1879–84). In 1903 a piece of Bolivia's Acre province, rich in rubber, was ceded to Brazil. And in 1938, after a war with Paraguay, Bolivia gave up claim to nearly 100,000 square miles of the Gran Chaco.

In 1965 a guerrilla movement mounted from Cuba and headed by Maj. Ernesto (Ché) Guevara began a revolutionary war. With the aid of U.S. military advisers, the Bolivian army, helped by the peasants, smashed the guerrilla movement, wounding and capturing Guevara on Oct. 8, 1967, and shooting him to death the next day.

Faltering steps toward restoration of civilian government were halted abruptly on July 17, 1980, when Gen. Luis Garcia Meza Tejada seized power. A series of military leaders followed before the military moved, in 1982, to return the government to civilian rule. Hernán Siles Zuazo was inaugurated President on Oct. 10, 1982.

Under Siles' left-of-center government, the country was regularly shut down by work stoppages, the bulk of Bolivia's natural resources—natural gas, gold, lithium, potassium and tungsten—were either sold on the black market or left in the ground, the country had the lowest per-capita income in South America, and inflation approached 3,000 percent. In 1985, the 73-year-old Siles decided he was unable to carry on and quit a year early.

No candidate won a majority in the elections in 1985 and Victor Paz Estensoro, 77, was picked by Congress to become President.

As in 1985 the inconclusive presidential election of 1989 was decided in Congress, where the second place finisher Bánzer threw his support to Paz Zamora, who finished third, in exchange for naming a majority of the new cabinet.

In January 1991 the government started a crop substitution plan aimed at reducing the cultivation of coca plants.

BOPHUTHATSWANA

See South Africa

BOTSWANA

Republic of Botswana
President: Quett K.J. Masire (1980)
Area: 231,800 sq mi. (600,360 sq km)
Population (est. mid-1991): 1,300,000 (average annual rate of natural increase: 2.7%); birth rate: 37/1000; infant mortality rate: 63/1000; density per square mile: 5
Capital and largest city (est. 1984): Gaborone, 79,000
Monetary unit: Pula
Languages: English, Setswana
Religions: Christian, 48%; traditional, 49%
Member of Commonwealth of Nations
Literacy rate: 60%

Economic summary: Gross domestic product (FY88): $1.87 billion, per capita $1,600; real growth rate 8.4%. Arable land: 2%. Principal products: livestock, sorghum, corn, millet, cowpeas, beans. Labor force: 400,000; 163,000 formal sector employees, most others involved in cattle raising and subsistence agriculture. Major industrial products: diamonds, copper, nickel, salt, soda ash, potash, coal, frozen beef; tourism. Natural resources: diamonds, copper, nickel, salt, soda ash, potash, coal, natural gas. Exports: diamonds, cattle, animal products, copper, nickel. Imports: foodstuffs, vehicles, textiles, petroleum products. Major trading partners: South Africa, U.K., U.S., Switzerland.

Geography. Twice the size of Arizona, Botswana is in south central Africa, bounded by Namibia, Zambia, Zimbabwe, and South Africa. Most of the country is near-desert, with the Kalahari occupying the western part of the country. The eastern part is hilly, with salt lakes in the north.

Government. The Botswana Constitution provides, in addition to the unicameral National Assembly, for a House of Chiefs, which has a voice on bills affecting tribal affairs. There is universal suffrage. The major political parties are the Democratic Party (29 of 34 elective seats in 36-man Legislative Assembly), led by President Quett Masire; National Front (4 seats), led by Kenneth Koma; People's Party (1 seat), led by Kenneth Nkhwa.

History. Botswana is the land of the Batawana tribes, which, when threatened by the Boers in Transvaal, asked Britain in 1885 to establish a protectorate over the country, then known as Bechuanaland. In 1961, Britain granted a Constitution to the country. Self-government began in 1965, and on Sept. 30, 1966, the country became independent. Since 1975, it has been an associate member of the European Common Market.

In connection with the release of Nelson Mandela in South Africa Botswana freed 16 detained members of South African liberation movements in February 1990.

BRAZIL

Federative Republic of Brazil
President: Fernando Affonso Collor de Mello (1990)
Area: 3,286,470 sq mi. (8,511,957 sq km)
Population (est. mid-1991): 153,300,000 (average annual rate of natural increase: 1.9%); birth rate: 27/1000; infant mortality rate: 63/1000; density per square mile: 47
Capital (est. 1985): Brasilia, 1,576,657
Largest cities (est. 1985): São Paulo, 10,099,086; Rio de Janeiro, 5,615,149; Salvador, 1,811,367; Belo Horizonte, 2,122,073; Recife, 1,289,627; Porto Alegre, 1,275,483
Monetary unit: Novo cruzado
Language: Portuguese
Religion: Roman Catholic, 90% (nominal)
National name: República Federativa de Brasil
Literacy rate: 76%
Economic summary: Gross national product (1989 est.): $377 billion, per capita $2,500; real growth rate 3%. Arable land: 7%. Principal products: coffee, sugar cane, oranges, cocoa, soybeans, tobacco, cattle. Labor force (1988 est.): 57,000,000; 27% in industry. Major industrial products: steel, chemicals, petrochemicals, machinery, motor vehicles, cement, lumber.

Natural resources: iron ore, manganese, bauxite, nickel, other industrial metals, hydropower, timber. Exports: coffee, iron ore, soybeans, sugar, beef, transport equipment, footwear, orange juice. Imports: crude oil, capital goods, chemical products, foodstuffs, coal. Major trading partners: U.S., Japan, Saudi Arabia, Africa.

Geography. Brazil covers nearly half of South America, extends 2,965 miles (4,772 km) north-south, 2,691 miles (4,331 km), east-west, and borders every nation on the continent except Chile and Ecuador. It is the fifth largest country in the world, ranking after the U.S.S.R., Canada, China, and the U.S.

More than a third of Brazil is drained by the Amazon and its more than 200 tributaries. The Amazon is navigable for ocean steamers to Iquitos, Peru, 2,300 miles (3,700 km) upstream. Southern Brazil is drained by the Plata system—the Paraguay, Uruguay, and Paraná Rivers. The most important stream entirely within Brazil is the São Francisco, navigable for 1,000 miles (1,903 km), but broken near its mouth by the 275-foot (84 m) Paulo Afonso Falls.

Government. The military took control in 1964, ousting the last elected civilian President and installing a series of military men (with the Congress ratifying the junta's choice). Election of a civilian President by the 686-member electoral college took place in January 1985.

A new constitution in 1988 provided for the president to be elected for a five-year term through direct, compulsory and secret suffrage. The National Congress maintains a bicameral structure—a Senate, whose members serve eight-year terms, and a Chamber of Deputies, elected for four-year terms.

History. Brazil is the only Latin American nation deriving its language and culture from Portugal. Adm. Pedro Alvares Cabral claimed the territory for the Portuguese in 1500. He brought to Portugal a cargo of wood, pau-brasil, from which the land received its name. Portugal began colonization in 1532 and made the area a royal colony in 1549.

During the Napoleonic wars, King João VI, then Prince Regent, fled the country in 1807 in advance of the French armies and in 1808 set up his court in Rio de Janeiro. João was drawn home in 1820 by a revolution, leaving his son as Regent. When Portugal sought to reduce Brazil again to colonial status, the prince declared Brazil's independence on Sept. 7, 1822, and became Pedro I, Emperor of Brazil.

Harassed by his parliament, Pedro I abdicated in 1831 in favor of his five-year-old son, who became Emperor in 1840 as Pedro II. The son was a popular monarch, but discontent built up and, in 1889, following a military revolt, he had to abdicate. Although a republic was proclaimed, Brazil was under two military dictatorships during the next four years. A revolt permitted a gradual return to stability under civilian Presidents.

The President during World War I, Wenceslau Braz, cooperated with the Allies and declared war on Germany.

In World War II, Brazil cooperated with the Western Allies, welcoming Allied air bases, patrolling the South Atlantic, and joining the invasion of Italy after declaring war on the Axis.

Gen. João Baptista de Oliveira Figueiredo, became President in 1979 and pledged a return to democracy in 1985.

The electoral college's choice of Tancredo Neves on Jan. 15, 1985, as the first civilian President since 1964 brought a nationwide wave of optimism, but the 75-year-old President-elect was hospitalized and underwent a series of intestinal operations. The civilian government was inaugurated on schedule on March 15, but only Neves' Vice Presidential running mate, José Sarney, was sworn in, and he was widely distrusted because he had previously been a member of the governing military regime's political party. When Neves died on April 21, Sarney became President.

Economically, Brazil's $93-billion foreign debt was the Third World's largest, and inflation reached a staggering 229% annual rate in 1984, almost double the 115% rate in 1983.

Collor de Mello won the election of late 1989 and took office in March 1990 despite his lack of support from a major party. In the campaign he pledged to lower the chronic hyperinflation following the path of free-market economics. Yet an economic recession still saw the inflation rate running at about 400% during the president's first year in office. On the other hand, his program has helped reduce the destruction of the rain forest, and he has successfully faced down the military. Progress has also been slow in renegotiating the payment terms on Brazil's huge foreign debt.

fully sovereign and independent on New Year's Day, 1984, presiding over a Privy Council and Council of Ministers appointed by himself. The Constitution provides for a three-tiered system of indirect elections, but the last elections were held in 1965. The only known opposition leader is in exile. In 1985, the Brunei National Democratic Party (BDNP) was formed but was dissolved by the sultan in 1988.

History. Brunei (pronounced broon-eye) was a powerful state from the 16th to the 19th century, ruling over the northern part of Borneo and adjacent island chains. But it fell into decay and lost Sarawak in 1841, becoming a British protectorate in 1888 and a British dependency in 1905.

The Sultan regained control over internal affairs in 1959, but Britain retained responsibility for the state's defense and foreign affairs until the end of 1983, when the sultanate became fully independent.

Sultain Bolkiah was crowned in 1968 at the age of 22, succeeding his father, Sir Omar Ali Saifuddin, who had abdicated. During his reign, exploitation of the rich Seria oilfield has made the sultanate wealthy.

Warning against opposition to his government, the Islamic religion and himself, the sultan in 1990 said that the laws of the sultanate woudl be restructured into conformity with Islamic law.

BRUNEI DARUSSALAM

State of Brunei Darussalam
Sultan: Hassanal Bolkiah
Area: 2,226 sq mi. (5,765 sq km)
Population (est. mid-1991): 300,000 (annual rate of natural increase: 2.5%); birth rate: 29/1000; infant mortality rate: 7/1000; density per square mile: 119
Capital and largest city (est. 1987): Bandar Seri Begawan, 56,300
Monetary unit: Brunei dollar
Ethnic groups: 64% Malay, 20% Chinese, 16% other
Languages: Malay (official), Chinese, English
Religions: Islam (official religion), 60%; Christian, 8%; Buddhist and local, 32%
Literacy rate: 45%
Member of Commonwealth of Nations, ASEAN, UN, OIC
Economic summary: Gross domestic product (1989 est.): $3.3 billion, per capita $9,600; real growth rate 2.5%. Arable land: 1%; principle agricultural products: fruit, rice, pepper, buffaloes. Labor force: 89,000; 50.4% in production of oil, natural gas and construction. major industrial products: crude petroleum, liquified natural gas. Natural resources: petroleum, natural gas, timber. Exports: crude petroleum, liquified natural gas. Imports: machinery, transport equipment, manufactured goods, foodstuffs. Major trading partners: Japan, U.S., Singapore.

Geography. About the size of Delaware, Brunei is an independent sultanate on the northwest coast of the island of Borneo in the South China Sea, wedged between the Malaysian states of Sabah and Sarawak. Three quarters of the thinly populated country is covered with tropical rain forest; there are rich oil and gas deposits.

Government. Sultan Hassanal Bolkiah is ruler of the state, a former British protectorate which became

BULGARIA

Republic of Bulgaria
Prime Minister: Dimitar Popov (1990)
President: Zhelyu Zhelev (1990)
Area: 42,823 sq mi. (110,912 sq km)
Population (est. mid-1991): 9,000,000 (average annual rate of natural increase: 0.1%); birth rate:13/1000; infant mortality rate: 13.6/1000; density per square mile: 210
Capital: Sofia
Largest cities (est. 1986): Sofia, 1,114,962; Plovdiv, 342,131; Varna, 302,211; Ruse, 183,746; Burgas, 182,570
Monetary unit: Lev
Language: Bulgarian
Religions: Bulgarian Orthodox, 90%; Muslim, Catholic, Protestant, Judaic, Armeno-Gerogorian
National name: Narodna Republika Bulgariya
Literacy rate: 95%
Economic summary: Gross national product (1989 est.): $51.2 billion, per capita $5,710; real growth rate –0.1%. Arable land: 34%. Principal products: grains, tobacco, fruits, vegetables. Labor force: 4,300,000, 33% in industry. Major products: processed agricultural products, machinery, electronics, chemicals. Natural resources: metals, minerals, timber. Exports: machinery and transport equipment, fuels, minerals, raw materials, agricultural products. Imports: machinery and transportation equipment, fuels, raw materials, metals, agricultural raw materials. Major trading partners: U.S.S.R., Eastern European countries, EEC.

Geography. Two mountain ranges and two great valleys mark the topography of Bulgaria, a country the size of Tennessee. Situated on the Black Sea in the eastern part of the Balkan peninsula, it shares borders with Yugoslavia, Romania, Greece, and Turkey. The Balkan belt crosses the center of the country, almost due east-west, rising to a height of 6,888 feet (2,100 m). The Rhodope, Rila and Pirin mountains straightens out along the western and southern border. Between the two ranges, is the valley of the Maritsa, Bulgaria's principal river. Between the Balkan range and the Danube, which forms most of the northern boundary with Romania, is the Danubian tableland.

Southern Dobruja, a fertile region of 2,900 square miles (7,511 sq km), below the Danube delta, is an area of low hills, fens, and sandy steppes.

Government. The 1971 Constitution was radically amended in 1990. The National Assembly, consisting of 400 members elected June 1990 is the legislative body. It elects the President of the Republic and the Council of Ministers.

History. The first Bulgarians, a tribe of wild horsemen akin to the Huns, crossed the Danube from the north in A.D. 679 and subjugated the Slavic population of Moesia. They adopted a Slav dialect and Slavic customs and twice conquered most of the Balkan peninsula between 893 and 1280. After the Serbs subjected their kingdom in 1330, the Bulgars gradually fell prey to the Turks, and from 1396 to 1878 Bulgaria was a Turkish province. In 1878, Russia forced Turkey to give the country its independence; but the European powers, fearing that Bulgaria might become a Russian dependency, intervened. By the Treaty of Berlin in 1878, Bulgaria became autonomous under Turkish sovereignty.

In 1887, Prince Ferdinand of Saxe-Coburg-Gotha was elected ruler of Bulgaria; on Oct. 5, 1908, he declared the country independent and took the title of Tsar.

Bulgaria joined Germany in World War I and lost. On Oct. 3, 1918, Tsar Ferdinand abdicated in favor of his son, Tsar Boris III. Boris assumed dictatorial powers in 1934–35. When Hitler awarded Bulgaria southern Dobruja, taken from Romania in 1940, Boris joined the Nazis in war the next year and occupied parts of Yugoslavia and Greece. Later the Germans tried to force Boris to send his troops against the Russians. Boris resisted and died under mysterious circumstances on Aug. 28, 1943. Simeon II, infant son of Boris, became nominal ruler under a regency. Russia declared war on Bulgaria on Sept. 5, 1944. An armistice was agreed to three days later, after Bulgaria had declared war on Germany. Russian troops streamed in the next day and under an informal armistice a coalition "Fatherland Front" cabinet was set up under Kimon Georgiev.

A Soviet-style people's Republic was established in 1947 and Bulgaria acquired the reputation of being the most slavishly loyal to Moscow of all the East European Communist countries.

Zhikov resigned in 1989 after 35 years in power. His successor, Peter Mladenov, purged the Politburo, ended the Communist monopoly on power and held free elections in May 1990 that led to a surprising victory for the Communists, renamed the Bulgarian Socialist Party. Mladenov was forced to resign in July 1990.

In January 1991 a coalition government of all major political groups was formed embarking on a program of tight monetary policy and committed to political pluralism and reforms aimed at creating a market economy.

BURKINA FASO

Chairman of the Popular Front: Blaise Compaore (1987)
Area: 105,870 sq mi. (274,200 sq km)
Population (est. mid-1991): 9,400,000 (average annual rate of natural increase: 3.3%); birth rate: 50/1000; infant mortality rate: 121/1000; density per square mile: 88
Capital and largest city (est. 1990): Ouagadougou, 500,000
Monetary unit: Franc CFA
Ethnic groups: Mossis, Bobos, Lobis, Fulanis
Languages: French, Tribal languages
Religions: Animist, 65%; Islam, 25%; Roman Catholic, 10%
National name: Burkina Faso
Literacy rate: 13.2%
Economic summary: Gross domestic product (1988): $1.43 billion, per capita $170; real growth rate 7.7%. Arable land: 10%. Labor force in agriculture: 82%. Principal products: millet, sorghum, corn, rice, livestock, peanuts, sugar cane, cotton. Major industrial products: processed agricultural products, light industrial items, brick, brewed products. Natural resources: manganese, limestone, marble, gold, uranium, bauxite, copper. Exports: oilseeds, cotton, live animals, gold. Imports: textiles, food and consumer goods, transport equipment, machinery, fuels. Major trading partners: E.C., Taiwan, Ivory Coast, Africa, U.S.

Geography. Slightly larger than Colorado, Burkina Faso, formerly known as Upper Volta, is a landlocked country in West Africa. Its neighbors are the Ivory Coast, Mali, Niger, Benin, Togo, and Ghana. The country consists of extensive plains, low hills, high savannas, and a desert area in the north.

Government. The former French colony has been governed by a series of military leaders since a coup in November 1980 overthrew the last elected president.

History. The country, called Upper Volta by the French, consists chiefly of the lands of the Mossi Empire, where France established a protectorate over the Kingdom of Ouagadougou in 1897. Upper Volta became a separate colony in 1919, was partitioned among Niger, the Sudan, and the Ivory Coast in 1933 and was reconstituted in 1947. An autonomous republic within the French Community, it became independent on Aug. 5, 1960.

President Maurice Yameògo was deposed on Jan. 3, 1966, by a military coup led by Col. Sangoulé Lamizana, who dissolved the National Assembly and suspended the Constitution. Constitutional rule returned in 1978 with the election of an Assembly and a presidential vote in June in which Gen. Lamizana won by a narrow margin over three other candidates.

On Nov. 25, 1980, there was a bloodless coup which placed Gen. Lamizana under house arrest. Col. Sayé Zerbo took charge as the President of the Military Committee of Reform for National Progress. Maj. Jean-Baptiste Ouedraogo toppled Zerbo in another coup on Nov. 7, 1982. Captain Thomas Sankara, in turn, deposed Ouedraogo a year later. His government changed the country's name on Aug. 3, 1984, to Burkina Faso (the "land of upright men") to sever ties with its colonial past. He was overthrown and killed by Blaise Compaore in 1987.

In June 1991 voters approved a draft constitution providing for three branches of government and presidential elections every seven years. The government has promised a multiparty democracy.

BURMA

See Myanmar

BURUNDI

Republic of Burundi
President: Maj. Pierre Buyoya (1987)
Prime Minister: Adrien Sibomana (1988)
Area: 10,747 sq mi. (27,834 sq km)
Population (est. mid-1991): 5,800,000 (average annual rate of natural increase: 3.2%); birth rate: 47/1000; infant mortality rate: 111/1000; density per square mile: 543
Capital and largest city (1986): Bujumbura, 272,600
Monetary unit: Burundi franc
Languages: Kirundi and French (official), Swahili
Religions: Roman Catholic, 62%; Protestant, 5%; indigenous, 32%
National name: Republika Y'Uburundi
Literacy rate: 33.8%
Economic summary: Gross domestic product (1988): $1.3 billion, per capita $255; real growth rate 2.8%. Arable land: 43%; Principal agricultural products: coffee, tea, cotton, bananas, sorghum. Labor force: 1,900,000 (1983 est.); 93% in agriculture. Major industrial products: light consumer goods. Natural resources: nickel, uranium, rare earth oxide, peat, cobalt, copper, unexploited platinum, vanadium. Exports: coffee, tea, cotton, hides and skins. Imports: food, petroleum products, capital goods, consumer goods. Major trading partners: U.S., Western Europe, Asia.

Geography. Wedged among Tanzania, Zaire, and Rwanda in east central Africa, Burundi occupies a high plateau divided by several deep valleys. It is equal in size to Maryland.

Government. Legislative and executive power is vested in the president.
Burundi's first Constitution, approved July 11, 1974, placed UPRONA (Unity and National Progress), the only political party, in control of national policy.

History. Burundi was once part of German East Africa. An integrated society developed among the Watusi, a tall, warlike people and nomad cattle raisers, and the Bahutu, a Bantu people, who were subject farmers. Belgium won a League of Nations mandate in 1923, and subsequently Burundi, with Rwanda, was transferred to the status of a United Nations trust territory.
In 1962, Burundi gained independence and became a kingdom under Mwami Mwambutsa IV. His son deposed him in 1966 to rule as Ntaré V. He was overthrown by Premier Micombero.
One of Africa's worst tribal wars, which became genocide, occurred in Burundi in April 1972, following the return of Ntare V. He was given a safe-conduct promise in writing by President Micombero but was "judged and immediately executed" by the Burundi leader. His return was apparently attended by an invasion of exiles of Burundi's Hutu tribe. Whether Hutus living in Burundi joined the invasion is unclear, but after it failed, the victorious Tutsis proceeded to massacre some 100,000 persons in six weeks, with possibly 100,000 more slain by summer.
On Nov. 1, 1976, Lt. Col. Jean-Baptiste Bagaye led a coup and assumed the presidency. He suspended the Constitution, and announced that a 30-member Supreme Revolutionary Council would be the governing body.
Bagaza was elected head of the only legal political party in 1979 and was overthrown as party chieftain in 1987.
Intertribal massacres in 1988 led the government to issue a Charter of National Unity, granting the country's three ethnic groups equal rights.

CAMBODIA

President: Prince Norodom Sihanouk (1982)
Prime Minister: Son Sann (1982)
Area: 69,884 sq mi. (181,000 sq km)
Population (est. mid-1991): 7,100,000 (average annual rate of natural increase: 2.2%); birth rate: 38/1000; infant mortality rate: 125/1000; density per square mile: 102
Capital and largest city (est. 1980 for metropolitan area): Phnom Penh, 500,000
Monetary unit: Riel
Ethnic groups: Khmer, 90%; Chinese, 5%; other minorities 5%
Languages: Khmer (official), French
Religion: Theravada Buddhist, 5% others
Literacy rate: 48%
Economic summary: Gross domestic product (1989 est.): $890 million, per capita $130; real growth rate 0%. Arable land: 16%. Principal agricultural products: rice, rubber, corn. Labor force: 2.5–3.0 million; 80% in agriculture; 74% in agriculture. Major industrial products: fish, wood and wood products, milled rice, rubber, cement. Natural resources: timber, gemstones, iron ore, manganese, phosphate. Exports: natural rubber, rice, pepper, wood. Imports: foodstuffs, fuel, consumer goods. Major trading partners: Vietnam, U.S.S.R., Eastern Europe, Japan, India.

Geography. Situated on the Indochinese peninsula, Cambodia is bordered by Thailand and Laos on the north and Vietnam on the east and south. The Gulf of Siam is off the western coast. The country, the size of Missouri, consists chiefly of a large alluvial plain ringed in by mountains and on the east by the Mekong River. The plain is centered on Lake Tonle Sap, which is a natural storage basin of the Mekong.

Government. A bloodless coup toppled Prince Sihanouk in 1970. It was led by Lon Nol and Prince Sisowath Sirik Matak, Sihanouk's cousin. Sihanouk moved to Peking to head a government-in-exile. On Oct. 9, 1970, Lon Nol proclaimed himself President.
The Lon Nol regime was overthrown in April 1975 by Pol Pot, a leader of the Communist Khmer Rouge forces, who instituted a xenophobic reign of terror. Pol Pot was in turn ousted on Jan. 8, 1979, by Vietnamese forces. A new government led by Heng Samrin was installed.

History. Cambodia came under Khmer rule about A.D. 600. Under the Khmers, magnificent temples were built at Angkor. The Khmer kingdom once ruled over most of Southeast Asia, but attacks by the Thai and the Vietnamese almost annihilated the empire until the French joined Cambodia, Laos, and Vietnam into French Indochina.
Under Norodom Sihanouk, enthroned in 1941, and particularly under Japanese occupation during World War II, nationalism revived. After the ouster of the

Japanese, the Cambodians sought independence, but the French returned in 1946, granting the country a Constitution in 1947 and independence within the French Union in 1949. Sihanouk won full military control during the French--Indochinese War in 1953. He abdicated in 1955 in favor of his parents, remaining head of the government, and when his father died in 1960, became chief of state without returning to the throne. In 1963, he sought a guarantee of Cambodia's neutrality from all parties to the Vietnam War.

On March 18, 1970, while Sihanouk was abroad trying to get North Vietnamese and the Vietcong out of border sanctuaries near Vietnam, anti-Vietnamese riots occurred, and Sihanouk was overthrown.

North Vietnamese and Vietcong units in border sanctuaries began moving deeper into Cambodia, threatening rapid overthrow of the new regime headed by Lon Nol. President Nixon sent South Vietnamese and U.S. troops across the border on April 30. U.S. ground forces, limited to 30-kilometer penetration, withdrew by June 30.

The Vietnam peace agreement of 1973 stipulated withdrawal of foreign forces from Cambodia, but fighting continued between Hanoi-backed insurgents and U.S.-supplied government troops. U.S. air support for the government forces was ended by Congress on Aug. 15, 1973.

Fighting reached a quick climax early in 1975, as government troops fell back in bitter fighting, Lon Nol fled by air April 1, leaving the government under the interim control of Premier Long Boret. On April 16, the government's capitulation ended the five-year war, but not the travails of war-ravaged Cambodia.

A new Constitution was proclaimed in December 1975, establishing a 250-member People's Assembly, a State Presidium headed by Pol Pot, and a Supreme Judicial Tribunal. Samphan replaced Sihanouk as head of state in April 1976, and the former monarch was a virtual prisoner until 1979.

In the next two years, from 2 million to 4 million Cambodians are estimated to have died under the brutality of the Pol Pot regime. Border clashes with Vietnam developed into a Vietnamese invasion and by the end of 1978 the Pol Pot government appeared to be collapsing.

Phnom Penh was captured on Jan. 8 and retreating Pol Pot forces and 40,000 refugees were driven into Thailand by May.

At a meeting in Kuala Lumpur, Malaysia, on June 22, 1982, Sihanouk formed an alliance with Son Sann, his former prime minister, and Khieu Samphan, Pol Pot's representative, to oppose the Heng Samrin regime installed by Vietnam.

While Sihanouk remained in exile, about 9,000 noncommunist troops loyal to him and another 15,000 under Son Sann joined about 35,000 communist Pol Pot forces fighting the 170,000 Vietnamese troops supporting the Heng Samrin government. The Cambodian insurgents suffered a major defeat in March 1985 when Vietnamese forces overran their camps in Cambodia and forced them into Thailand.

The Vietnamese plan originally called for them to withdraw by early 1990 and negotiate a political settlement. The main issues were the level of inclusion of the Khmer Rouge, with their record of atrocities, in any new government, the organization and powers of the interim government pending new elections and the role of the United Nations in the transition.

The talks, however, stalled through 1990 on into 1991 with no clear resolution in sight. A continuation of the mid-1991 ceasefire appeared shaky as the warring parties alleged violations by their opponents.

CAMEROON

Republic of Cameroon
President: Paul Biya (1988)
Area: 183,569 sq mi. (475,442 sq km)
Population (est. mid-1991): 11,400,000 (average annual rate of natural increase: 2.6%); birth rate: 42/1000; infant mortality rate: 123/1000; density per square mile: 62
Capital: Yaoundé
Largest cities (est. 1985): Douala, 852,700; Yaoundé, 583,500
Monetary unit: Franc CFA
Languages: French and English (both official); 24 major African language groups
Religions: 51% indigenous beliefs, 33% Christian, 16% Muslim
National name: République du Cameroun
Literacy rate: 56.2%
Economic summary: Gross domestic product (1988): $12.9 billion, per capita $955; real growth rate –8.6%. Arable land: 13%. principal products: coffee, cocoa, timber, corn, peanuts. Labor force in agriculture: 74.4%. Major industrial products: crude oil, small manufacturing, consumer goods, aluminum. Natural resources: timber, some oil, bauxite, hydropower potential. Exports: cocoa, coffee, timber, aluminum, petroleum. Imports: machines and electrical equipment, transport equipment, chemical products, consumer goods. Major trading partners: France, U.S., Western European nations.

Geography. Cameroon is a West African nation on the Gulf of Guinea, bordered by Nigeria, Chad, the Central African Republic, the Congo, Equatorial Guinea, and Gabon. It is nearly twice the size of Oregon.

The interior consists of a high plateau, rising to 4,500 feet (1,372 m), with the land descending to a lower, densely wooded plateau and then to swamps and plains along the coast. Mount Cameroon (13,350 ft.; 4,069 m), near the coast, is the highest elevation in the country. The main rivers are the Benue, Nyong, and Sanaga.

Government. After a 1972 plebiscite, a unitary nation was formed out of East and West Cameroon to replace the former Federal Republic. A Constitution was adopted, providing for election of a president every five years and of a 120-seat National Assembly (later increased to 180), whose nominal five-year term can be extended or shortened by the president. The Cameroon People's Democratic Movement is the only political party.

History. The Republic of Cameroon is inhabited by Hamitic and Semitic peoples in the north, where Islam is the principal religion, and by Bantu peoples in the central and southern regions, where native animism prevails. The tribes were conquered by many invaders.

The land escaped colonial rule until 1884, when treaties with tribal chiefs brought the area under German domination. After World War I, the League of Nations gave the French a mandate over 80% of the area, and the British 20% adjacent to Nigeria. After World War II, when the country came under a U.N. trusteeship in 1946, self-government was granted, and the Cameroun People's Union emerged as the dominant party by campaigning for reunification of French and British Cameroon and for independence. Accused of being under Communist control, it waged a campaign of revolutionary terror from 1955 to 1958, when it was crushed. In British Cameroon, unification was pressed also by the leading party, the Kamerun National Democratic Party, led by John Foncha.

France set up Cameroon as an autonomous state in 1957, and the next year its legislative assembly voted for independence by 1960. In 1959 a fully autonomous government of Cameroon was formed under Ahmadou Ahidjo. Cameroon became an independent republic on Jan. 1, 1960.

Although hesitantly President Biya in the face of repeated calls and demonstrations in 1990 endorsed multiparty democracy. Most political prisoners have been freed, and the country has implemented some basic structural changes in the economy, winning praise from the IMF.

CANADA

Sovereign: Queen Elizabeth II (1952)
Governor General: Raymond John Hnatyshyn (1990)
Prime Minister: Brian Mulroney (1984)
Area: 3,851,809 sq mi. (9,976,186 sq km)
Population (est. mid-1991): 26,832,000 (average annual rate of natural increase: 0.7%); birth rate: 15/1000; infant mortality rate: 7.2/1000; density per square mile: 7
Capital: Ottawa, Ont.
Largest cities (1986 census; metropolitan areas): Toronto, 3,427,168; Montreal, 2,921,357; Vancouver, 1,380,729; Ottawa, 819,263; Edmonton, 785,465; Calgary, 671,326; Winnipeg, 625,304; Quebec, 603,627; Hamilton, 557,029; St. Catherines-Niagara, 343,258
Monetary Unit: Canadian dollar
Languages: English, French
Religions: 46% Roman Catholic, 16% United Church, 10% Anglican
Literacy rate: 99%
Economic Summary: Gross national product (1989 est.): $513.6 billion, per capita $19,600; real growth rate 1%. Arable land: 7.47%. Principal products; wheat, barley, oats, livestock. Labor force (1990): 13,681,000; 75% in manufacturing. Major industrial products; transportation equipment, petroleum, chemicals, wood products. Exports: wheat, petroleum, lumber and wood products, ores, motor vehicles. Imports: electronic equipment, chemicals, processed foods, beverages. Major trading partners: U.S., Japan, U.K., U.S.S.R., Germany, Mexico, South Korea.

Geography. Covering most of the northern part of the North American continent and with an area larger than that of the United States, Canada has an extremely varied topography. In the east the mountainous maritime provinces have an irregular coastline on the Gulf of St. Lawrence and the Atlantic. The St. Lawrence plain, covering most of southern Quebec and Ontario, and the interior continental plain, covering southern Manitoba and Saskatchewan and most of Alberta, are the principal cultivable areas. They are separated by a forested plateau rising from lakes Superior and Huron.

Westward toward the Pacific, most of British Columbia, Yukon, and part of western Alberta are covered by parallel mountain ranges including the Rockies. The Pacific border of the coast range is ragged with fiords and channels. The highest point in Canada is Mount Logan (19,850 ft; 6,050 m), which is in the Yukon.

Canada has an abundance of large and small lakes.

In addition to the Great Lakes on the U.S. border, there are 9 others that are more than 100 miles long (161 km) and 35 that are more than 50 miles long (80 km). The two principal river systems are the Mackenzie and the St. Lawrence. The St. Lawrence, with its tributaries, is navigable for over 1,900 miles (3,058 km).

Government. Canada, a self-governing member of the Commonwealth of Nations, is a federation of 10 provinces (Alberta, British Columbia, Manitoba, New Brunswick, Newfoundland, Nova Scotia, Ontario, Prince Edward Island, Quebec, and Saskatchewan) and two territories (Northwest Territories and Yukon) whose powers were spelled out in the British North America Act of 1867. With the passing of the Constitution Act of 1981, the act and the Constitutional amending power were transferred from the British government to Canada so that the Canadian Constitution is now entirely in the hands of the Canadians.

Actually the Governor General acts only with the advice of the Canadian Prime Minister and the Cabinet, who also sit in the federal Parliament. The Parliament has two houses: a Senate of 104 members appointed for life, and a House of Commons of 295 members apportioned according to provincial population. Elections are held at least every five years or whenever the party in power is voted down in the House of Commons or considers it expedient to appeal to the people. The Prime Minister is the leader of the majority party in the House of Commons—or, if no single party holds a majority, the leader of the party able to command the support of a majority of members of the House. Laws must be passed by both houses of Parliament and signed by the Governor General in the Queen's name.

The 10 provincial governments are nominally headed by Lieutenant Governors appointed by the federal government, but the executive power in each actually is vested in a Cabinet headed by a Premier, who is leader of the majority party. The provincial legislatures are composed of one-house assemblies whose members are elected for four-year terms. They are known as Legislative Assemblies, except in Newfoundland, where it is the House of Assembly, and in Quebec, where it is the National Assembly.

The judicial system consists of a Supreme Court in Ottawa (established in 1875), with appellate jurisdiction, and a Supreme Court in each province, as well as county courts with limited jurisdiction in most of the provinces. The Governor General in Council appoints these judges.

Population by Provinces and Territories

Province	1981 (Census)	1991 (March Estimate)
Alberta	2,237,724	2,501,400
British Columbia	2,744,467	3,185,900
Manitoba	1,026,241	1,092,600
New Brunswick	696,403	725,600
Newfoundland	567,681	571,600
Nova Scotia	847,442	897,500
Ontario	8,625,107	9,840,300
Prince Edward Island	122,506	129,900
Quebec	6,438,403	6,811,800
Saskatchewan	968,313	995,300
Northwest Territories	45,471	54,000
Yukon Territory	23,153	26,500
Total	**24,343,181**	**26,832,400**

Source: Statistics Canada.

Canadian Governors General and Prime Ministers Since 1867

Term of Office	Governor General	Term	Prime Minister	Party
1867–1868	Viscount Monck[1]	1867–1873	Sir John A. MacDonald	Conservative
1869–1872	Baron Lisgar	1873–1878	Alexander Mackenzie	Liberal
1872–1878	Earl of Dufferin	1878–1891	Sir John A. MacDonald	Conservative
1878–1883	Marquess of Lorne	1891–1892	Sir John J. C. Abbott	Conservative
1883–1888	Marquess of Lansdowne	1892–1894	Sir John S. D. Thompson	Conservative
1888–1893	Baron Stanley of Preston	1894–1896	Sir Mackenzie Bowell	Conservative
1893–1898	Earl of Aberdeen	1896	Sir Charles Tupper	Conservative
1898–1904	Earl of Minto	1896–1911	Sir Wilfrid Laurier	Liberal
1904–1911	Earl Grey	1911–1917	Sir Robert L. Borden	Conservative
1911–1916	Duke of Connaught	1917–1920	Sir Robert L. Borden	Unionist
1916–1921	Duke of Devonshire	1920–1921	Arthur Meighen	Unionist
1921–1926	Baron Byng of Vimy	1921–1926	W. L. Mackenzie King	Liberal
1926–1931	Viscount Willingdon	1926	Arthur Meighen	Conservative
1931–1935	Earl of Bessborough	1926–1930	W. L. Mackenzie King	Liberal
1935–1940	Baron Tweedsmuir	1930–1935	Richard B. Bennett	Conservative
1940–1946	Earl of Athlone	1935–1948	W. L. Mackenzie King	Liberal
1946–1952	Viscount Alexander	1948–1957	Louis S. St. Laurent	Liberal
1952–1959	Vincent Massey	1957–1963	John G. Diefenbaker	Conservative
1959–1967	George P. Vanier	1963–1968	Lester B. Pearson	Liberal
1967–1973	Roland Michener	1968–1979	Pierre Elliott Trudeau	Liberal
1974–1979	Jules Léger	1979–1980	Charles Joseph Clark	Conservative
1979–1984	Edward R. Schreyer	1980–1984	Pierre Elliott Trudeau	Liberal
1984–	Jeanne Sauvé	1984–1984	John Turner	Liberal
		1984–	Brian Mulroney	Conservative

1. Became Governor General of British North America in 1861.

History. The Norse explorer Leif Ericson probably reached the shores of Canada (Labrador or Nova Scotia) in A.D. 1000, but the history of the white man in the country actually began in 1497, when John Cabot, an Italian in the service of Henry VII of England, reached Newfoundland or Nova Scotia. Canada was taken for France in 1534 by Jacques Cartier. The actual settlement of New France, as it was then called, began in 1604 at Port Royal in what is now Nova Scotia; in 1608, Quebec was founded. France's colonization efforts were not very successful, but French explorers by the end of the 17th century had penetrated beyond the Great Lakes to the western prairies and south along the Mississippi to the Gulf of Mexico. Meanwhile, the English Hudson's Bay Company had been established in 1670. Because of the valuable fisheries and fur trade, a conflict developed between the French and English; in 1713, Newfoundland, Hudson Bay, and Nova Scotia (Acadia) were lost to England.

During the Seven Years' War (1756–63), England extended its conquest, and the British Maj. Gen. James Wolfe won his famous victory over Gen. Louis Montcalm outside Quebec on Sept. 13, 1759. The Treaty of Paris in 1763 gave England control.

At that time the population of Canada was almost entirely French, but in the next few decades, thousands of British colonists emigrated to Canada from the British Isles and from the American colonies. In 1849, the right of Canada to self-government was recognized. By the British North America Act of 1867, the Dominion of Canada was created through the confederation of Upper and Lower Canada, Nova Scotia, and New Brunswick. Prince Edward Island joined the Dominion in 1873.

In 1869 Canada purchased from the Hudson's Bay Company the vast middle west (Rupert's Land) from which the provinces of Manitoba (1870), Alberta, and Saskatchewan (1905) were later formed. In 1871, British Columbia joined the Dominion. The country was linked from coast to coast in 1885 by the Canadian Pacific Railway.

During the formative years between 1866 and 1896, the Conservative Party, led by Sir John A. MacDonald, governed the country, except during the years 1873–78. In 1896, the Liberal Party took over and, under Sir Wilfrid Laurier, an eminent French Canadian, ruled until 1911.

By the Statute of Westminster in 1931 the British Dominions, including Canada, were formally declared to be partner nations with Britain, "equal in status, in no way subordinate to each other," and bound together only by allegiance to a common Crown.

Newfoundland became Canada's 10th province on March 31, 1949, following a plebiscite. Canada includes two territories—the Yukon Territory, the area north of British Columbia and east of Alaska, and the Northwest Territories, including all of Canada north of 60° north latitude except Yukon and the northernmost sections of Quebec and Newfoundland. This area includes all of the Arctic north of the mainland, Norway having recognized Canadian sovereignty over the Svendrup Islands in the Arctic in 1931.

The Liberal Party, led by William Lyon Mackenzie King, dominated Canadian politics from 1921 until 1957, when it was succeeded by the Progressive Conservatives. The Liberals, under the leadership of Lester B. Pearson, returned to power in 1963. Pearson remained Prime Minister until 1968, when he retired and was replaced by a former law professor, Pierre Elliott Trudeau. Trudeau maintained Canada's defensive alliance with the United States, but began moving toward a more independent policy in world affairs.

Trudeau's election was considered in part a response to the most serious problem confronting the country, the division between French- and English-speaking Canadians, which had led to a separatist movement in the predominantly French province of Quebec. Trudeau, himself a French Canadian, supported programs for bilingualism and an increased measure of provincial autonomy, although he would not tolerate the idea of separatism. In 1974, the provincial government voted to make French the official language of Quebec.

Conflicts over the law establishing French as the dominant language in Quebec, particularly in schooling, kept separatism as a national issue, but by-elections in 1977 produced easy victories for Trudeau's ruling Liberals in four Quebec seats in the national legislature.

Economic problems appeared to take precedence over politics in 1978, as the Sun Life Assurance Company of Canada, the nation's largest insurance firm, announced that it would move its headquarters from Montreal to Toronto. Sun Life was the first business to cite the language law as the reason for its departure.

Despite Trudeau's removal of price and wage controls in 1978, continuing inflation and a high rate of unemployment caused him to delay elections until May 22, 1979. The delay gave Trudeau no advantage—the Progressive Conservatives under Charles Joseph Clark defeated the Liberals everywhere except in Quebec, New Brunswick, and Newfoundland.

Clark took office as the head of Canada's fifth minority government in the last 20 years.

His government collapsed after only six months when a motion to defeat the Tory budget carried by 139–133 on Dec. 13, 1979. On the same day, the Quebec law making French the exclusive official language of the province—an issue which had been expected to provide Clark's first major internal test—was voided by the Canadian Supreme Court.

In national elections Feb. 18, 1980, the resurgent Liberals under Trudeau scored an unexpectedly big victory.

Resolving a dispute that had occupied Trudeau since the beginning of his tenure, Queen Elizabeth II, in Ottawa on April 17, 1982, signed the Constitution Act, cutting the last legal tie between Canada and Britain. Since 1867, the British North America Act required British Parliament approval for any Canadian constitutional change.

The new charter was approved by the federal House of Commons, 246–24, on Dec. 2, 1981, and by a 59–23 vote of the Senate six days later. The Constitution retains Queen Elizabeth as Queen of Canada and keeps Canada's membership in the Commonwealth.

Ending an era, Trudeau retired on June 30, 1984, after 16 years as prime minister, except for the nine-month interruption in 1979–80.

His successor as Liberal Party leader and Prime Minister, John N. Turner, called an early election for a new Parliament after polls showed the Liberals had made a big comeback from the last months of Trudeau's term, despite Canada's continuing recession and 11.2% unemployment, the highest in 40 years.

In the national election on Sept. 4, 1984, the Progressive Conservative Party scored an overwhelming victory, fundamentally changing the country's political landscape. The Conservatives, led by Brian Mulroney, a 45-year-old corporate lawyer, won the highest political majority in Canadian history, Mulroney was sworn in as Canada's 18th Prime Minister on Sept. 17.

The dominant foreign issue was a free trade pact with the U.S., a treaty bitterly opposed by the Liberal and New Democratic parties. The conflict led to elections in Nov. 1988 that solidly re-elected Mulroney and gave him a mandate to proceed with the agreement.

The issue of separatist sentiments in French-speaking Quebec flared up again in 1990 with the failure of the Meech Lake accord. The accord was designed to ease the Quebecers' fear of losing their identity within the English-speaking majority by giving Quebec constitutional status as a "distinct society." The dominant issues during 1991 have been "Whither Canada?" and the continuing effort for a North American free trade zone.

CAPE VERDE

Republic of Cape Verde

President: Antonio Mascarenhas Monteiro (1991)

Premier: Maj. Pedro Pires (1975)

Area: 1,557 sq mi. (4,033 sq km)

Population: (est. mid-1991): 400,000 (average annual rate of natural increase: 3.2%); birth rate: 40/1000; infant mortality rate: 44/1000; density per square mile: 246

Capital (est. 1982): Praia, 37,676

Largest city (est. 1982): Mindelo, 50,000

Monetary unit: Cape Verdean escudo

Language: Portuguese, Criuolo

Religion: Roman Catholic fused with indigenous beliefs

National name: República de Cabo Verde

Literacy rate: 37%

Economic status: Gross domestic product (1987): $158 million, per capita $494; real growth rate 6.1%. Arable land: 9%. Labor force in agriculture: 57%. Principal agricultural products: bananas, corn, sugar cane, beans. Major industry: fishing, salt mining. Natural resources: salt, siliceous rock. Exports: fish, bananas, salt. Imports: petroleum, foodstuffs, consumer goods, industrial products. Major trading partners: Portugal, Angola, Algeria, Belgium/Luxembourg, Italy, Netherlands, Spain, France, U.S., Germany.

Geography: Cape Verde, only slightly larger than Rhode Island, is an archipelago in the Atlantic 385 miles (620 km) west of Dakar, Senegal.

The islands are divided into two groups: Barlavento in the north, comprising Santo Antão (291 sq mi.; 754 sq km), Boa Vista (240 sq mi.; 622 sq km), São Nicolau (132 sq mi.; 342 sq km), São Vicente (88 sq mi.; 246 sq km), Sal (83 sq mi.; 298 sq km), and Santa Luzia (13 sq mi.; 34 sq km); and Sotavento in the south, consisting of São Tiago (383 sq mi.; 992 sq km), Fogo (184 sq mi.; 477 sq km), Maio (103 sq mi.; 267 sq km), and Brava (25 sq mi.; 65 sq km). The islands are mostly mountainous, with the land deeply scarred by erosion. There is an active volcano on Fogo.

Government. The islands became independent on July 5, 1975, under an agreement negotiated with Portugal in 1974. Elections of January 13, 1991 resulted in the ruling African Party for the Independence of Cape Verde losing its majority in the 79-seat parliament. The big winner was the Movement for

Democracy, whose candidate, Antonio Monteiro, won the subsequent presidential election on February 17. These were the first free elections since independence in 1975.

History. Uninhabited upon their discovery in 1456, the Cape Verde islands became part of the Portuguese empire in 1495. A majority of their modern inhabitants are of mixed Portuguese and African ancestry. A coaling station developed during the 19th century on the island of São Vicente has grown in recent years to an oil and gasoline storage depot for ships and aircraft.

CENTRAL AFRICAN REPUBLIC

Head of Government: Gen. André Kolingba (1986)
Area: 241,313 sq mi. (625,000 sq km)
Population (est. mid-1991): 3,000,000 (average annual rate of natural increase: 2.6%); birth rate: 44/1000; infant mortality rate: 141/1000; density per square mile: 12
Capital and largest city (est. 1985): Bangui, 473,000
Monetary unit: Franc CFA
Ethnic groups: Baya, Banda, Sara, Mandjia, Mboum, M'Baka, 6,500 Europeans
Languages: French (official), Sangho, Arabic, Hansa, Swahili
Religions: 24% indigenous beliefs, 50% Protestant and Roman Catholic with animist influence, 15% Muslim, 11% other
National name: République Centrafricaine
Literacy rate: 33%
Economic summary: Gross domestic product (1988 est.): $1.27 billion, per capita $453; real growth rate 2.0%. Arable land: 3%. Principal products: cotton, coffee, peanuts, food crops, livestock. Labor force (1986 est.): 775,413; 85% in agriculture. Major industrial products: timber, textiles, soap, cigarettes, diamonds, processed food, brewed beverages. Natural resources: diamonds, uranium, timber. Exports: diamonds, cotton, timber, coffee. Imports: machinery and electrical equipment, petroleum products, textiles. Major trading partners: France, Japan, U.S., Western Europe, Algeria, Yugoslavia.

Geography. Situated about 500 miles north (805 km) of the equator, the Central African Republic is a landlocked nation bordered by Cameroon, Chad, the Sudan, Zaire, and the Congo. Twice the size of New Mexico, it is covered by tropical forests in the south and semidesert land in the east. The Ubangi and Shari are the largest of many rivers.

Government. On Dec. 4, 1976, the Central African Republic became the Central African Empire. Marshal Jean-Bédel Bokassa, who had ruled the republic since he took power in a military coup Dec. 31, 1965, was declared Emperor Bokassa I. He was overthrown in a coup on Sept. 20, 1979. Former President David Dacko, returned to power and changed the country's name back to the Central African Republic. An army coup on Sept. 1, 1981, deposed Dacko and suspended the Constitution and all political parties. A Military Committee of National Redress was set up to run the country. A new constitution was enacted on Nov. 21, 1986 that extended Kolingba's term another six years and allowed for parliamentary elections in which the Centrafrican Democratic Assembly would be the only party.

History. As the colony of Ubangi-Shari, what is now the Central African Republic was united with Chad in 1905 and joined with Gabon and the Middle Congo in French Equatorial Africa in 1910. After World War II a rebellion in 1946 forced the French to grant self-government. In 1958 the territory voted to become an autonomous republic within the French Community, but on Aug. 13, 1960, President David Dacko proclaimed the republic's independence from France.

Dacko undertook to move the country into Peking's orbit, but was overthrown in a coup on Dec. 31, 1965, by the then Col. Jean-Bédel Bokassa, Army Chief of Staff. In August 1977, the U.S. State Department protested the Emperor's jailing of American and British newsmen.

Politically rather tranquil, relations with Sudan were restored in 1990 after a one-year severance. Falling coffee and timber prices worldwide weakened the economy.

CHAD

Republic of Chad
President: Col Idriss Deby (1991)
Prime Minister: Ousmane Gam
Area: 495,752 sq mi. (1,284,000 sq km)
Population (est. mid-1991): 5,100,000 (average annual rate of natural increase, 2.5%); birth rate: 44/1000; infant mortality rate: 127/1000; density per square mile: 10
Capital and largest city (est. 1991): N'Djamena, 500,000
Monetary unit: Franc CFA
Ethnic groups: Baguirmiens, Kanembous, Saras, Massas, Arabs, Toubous, others
Languages: French and Arabic (official), many tribal languages
Religions: Islam, 44%; Christian, 33%; traditional, 23%
National name: République du Tchad
Literacy rate: 17%
Economic summary: Gross domestic product (1990): $800 million, per capita $150; real growth rate 3%. Arable land: 2%; principal agricultural products: cotton, cattle, sugar, subsistence crops. Labor force in agriculture: 85%. Major products: livestock and livestock products, beer, food processing, textiles, cigarettes. Natural resources: petroleum, unexploited uranium, kaolin. Exports: cotton, livestock and animal products, fish. Imports: food, motor vehicles and parts, petroleum products, machinery, cement, textiles. Major trading partners: France, Nigeria, U.S., Cameroon.

Geography. A landlocked country in north central Africa, Chad is about 85% the size of Alaska. Its neighbors are Niger, Libya, the Sudan, the Central African Republic, Cameroon, and Nigeria. Lake Chad, from which the country gets its name, lies on the western border with Niger and Nigeria. In the north is a desert that runs into the Sahara.

Government. Hissen Habré was overthrown by Gen. Idriss Deby in December 1990.

History. Chad was absorbed into the colony of French Equatorial Africa, as part of Ubangi-Shari, in 1910. France began the country's development after 1920, when it became a separate colony. In 1946,

French Equatorial Africa was admitted to the French Union. By referendum in 1958 the Chad territory became an autonomous republic within the French Union.

A movement led by the first Premier and President, François (later Ngarta) Tombalbaye, achieved complete independence on Aug. 11, 1960.

Tombalbaye was killed in the 1975 coup and was succeeded by Gen. Félix Malloum, who faced a Libyan-financed rebel movement throughout his tenure in office. A ceasefire backed by Libya, Niger, and the Sudan early in 1978 failed to end the fighting.

Nine rival groups meeting in Lagos, Nigeria, in March 1979 agreed to form a provisional government headed by Goukouni Oueddei, a former rebel leader. Fighting broke out again in Chad in March 1980, when Defense Minister Hissen Habré challenged Goukouni and seized the capital. By the year's end, Libyan troops supporting Goukouni recaptured N'djamena, and Libyan President Muammar el-Qaddafi, in January 1981, proposed a merger of Chad with Libya.

The Libyan proposal was rejected and Libyan troops withdrew from Chad but in 1983 poured back into the northern part of the country in support of Goukouni. France, in turn, sent troops into southern Chad in support of Habré.

A Qaddafi-Goukouni break in Nov. 1986 led to the defection of his troops. Government troops then launched an offensive in early 1987 that drove the Libyans out of most of the country.

After the overthrow of Habré's government, Deby, a former defense minister, declared himself president, dissolved the legislature (elected the previous July), and suspended the constitution. He has, however, promised a multiparty democracy despite a widespread belief about Libyan backing.

CHILE

Republic of Chile
President: Patricio Aylwin (1990)
Area: 292,132 sq mi. (756,622 sq km)
Population (est. mid-1991): 13,400,000 (average annual rate of natural increase: 1.8%); birth rate: 23/1000; infant mortality rate: 18.9/1000; density per square mile: 46
Capital: Santiago
Largest cities (est. 1986): Santiago, 4,804,200; Valparaiso, 277,900; Concepción, 292,700; Antofagasta, 203,100; Talcahuano, 229,500; Temuco, 215,400
Monetary unit: Peso
Language: Spanish
Religion: Roman Catholic, 89%; Protestant, 11%; small Jewish and Muslim populations.
National name: República de Chile
Literacy rate: 94%
Economic summary: Gross domestic product (1990): $27.8 billion; $2,111 per capita; 2.1% real growth rate. Arable land: 7%. Principal products: wheat, corn, sugar beets, vegetables, wine, livestock. Labor force: 31.3% in industry. Major industrial products: processed fish, iron and steel, pulp, paper. Natural resources: copper, timber, iron ore, nitrates. Exports: copper, iron ore, paper and wood products, fruits. Imports: wheat, vehicles, petroleum, capital goods, spare parts, raw materials. Major trading partners: U.S., Japan, European Community, Brazil.

Geography. Situated south of Peru and west of Bolivia and Argentina, Chile fills a narrow 1,800-mile (2,897 km) strip between the Andes and the Pacific. Its area is nearly twice that of Montana.

One third of Chile is covered by the towering ranges of the Andes. In the north is the mineral-rich Atacama Desert, between the coastal mountains and the Andes. In the center is a 700-mile-long (1,127 km) valley, thickly populated, between the Andes and the coastal plateau. In the south, the Andes border on the ocean.

At the southern tip of Chile's mainland is Punta Arenas, the southernmost city in the world, and beyond that lies the Strait of Magellan and Tierra del Fuego, an island divided between Chile and Argentina. The southernmost point of South America is Cape Horn, a 1,390-foot (424-m) rock on Horn Island in the Wollaston group, which belongs to Chile. Chile also claims sovereignty over 482,628 sq mi (1,250,000 sq km) of Antarctic territory.

The Juan Fernández Islands, in the South Pacific about 400 miles (644 km) west of the mainland, and Easter Island, about 2,000 miles (3,219 km) west, are Chilean possessions.

Government. Under the 1980 Constitution, the President serves an eight-year term (with the exception of the 1990–1994 term). There is a bicameral legislature which opened its first session in 1990.

History. Chile was originally under the control of the Incas in the north and the fierce Araucanian people in the south. In 1541, a Spaniard, Pedro de Valdivia, founded Santiago. Chile won its independence from Spain in 1818 under Bernardo O'Higgins and an Argentinian, José de San Martin. O'Higgins, dictator until 1823, laid the foundations of the modern state with a two-party system and a centralized government.

The dictator from 1830 to 1837, Diego Portales, fought a war with Peru in 1836–39 that expanded Chilean territory. The Conservatives were in power from 1831 to 1861. Then the Liberals, winning a share of power for the next 30 years, disestablished the church and limited presidential power. Chile fought the War of the Pacific with Peru and Bolivia from 1879 to 1883, winning Antofagasta, Bolivia's only outlet to the sea, and extensive areas from Peru. A revolt in 1890 led by Jorge Montt overthrew, in 1891, José Balmaceda and established a parliamentary dictatorship that existed until a new Constitution was adopted in 1925. Industrialization began before World War I and led to the formation of Marxist groups.

Juan Antonio Ríos, President during World War II, was originally pro-Nazi but in 1944 led his country into the war on the side of the Allies.

A small abortive army uprising in 1969 raised fear of military intervention to prevent a Marxist, Salvador Allende Gossens, from taking office after his election to the presidency on Sept. 4, 1970. Dr. Allende was the first President in a non-Communist country freely elected on a Marxist-Leninist program.

Allende quickly established relations with Cuba and the People's Republic of China and nationalized several American companies.

Allende's overthrow and death in an army assault on the presidential palace in September 1973 ended a 46-year era of constitutional government in Chile.

The takeover was led by a four-man junta headed by Army Chief of Staff Augusto Pinochet Ugarte, who assumed the office of President.

Committed to "exterminate Marxism," the junta embarked on a right-wing dictatorship. It suspended parliament, banned political activity, and broke relations with Cuba.

In 1977, Pinochet, in a speech marking his fourth year in power, promised elections by 1985 if conditions warranted. Earlier, he had abolished DINA, the secret police, and decreed an amnesty for political prisoners.

Pinochet was inaugurated on March 11, 1981, for an eight-year term as President, at the end of which, according to the Constitution adopted six months earlier, the junta would nominate a civilian as successor, although Pinochet announced that he might serve another eight-year term. He stepped down in January 1990 in favor of Patricio Aylwin who was elected Dec. 1989 as the head of a 17-party coalition. President Aylwin in April 1990 charged a commission to examine evidence concerning the disappearance of political prisoners during the early years of Pinochet's rule. In September 1990 the opposition Renovacion Nacional party named a shadow cabinet in a move interpreted as a sign of further democratic consolidation.

CHINA

People's Republic of China
President: Gen. Yang Shangkun (1988)
Premier: Li Peng (1987)
Area: 3,691,521 sq mi. (9,561,000 sq km)[1]
Population (est. mid-1991): 1,151,300,000 (average rate of natural increase: 1.4%); birth rate: 21/1000; infant mortality rate: 33/1000; density per square mile: 311
Capital: Beijing
Largest cities (est. 1983): Shanghai, 11,940,000; Beijing (Peking) 9,330,000; Tianjin (Tientsin) 7,850,000; Canton, 6,840,000; Wuhan, 5,940,000; Shenyang (Mukden), 5,210,000; Nanjing (Nanking), 4,560,000; Chongqing (Chungking), 3,890,000; Harbin; 3,730,000
Monetary unit: Yuan
Languages: Chinese, Mandarin, also local dialects
Religions: Officially atheist but traditional religion contains elements of Confucianism, Taoism, Buddhism
National name: Zhonghua Renmin Gongheguo
Literacy rate: over 75%
Economic summary: Gross national product (1988): $350 billion; $320 per capita; 11% real growth rate. Arable land: 10%. Principal products: rice, wheat, grains, cotton. Labor force: 513,000,000; 61.1% in agriculture. Major industrial products: iron and steel, textiles, armaments, petroleum. Natural resources: coal, natural gas, limestone, marble, metals, hydropower potential. Exports: agricultural products, oil, minerals, metals, manufactured goods. Imports: grains, chemical fertilizer, steel, industrial raw materials, machinery and equipment. Major trading partners: Japan, Hong Kong, U.S., Germany, Singapore, U.S.S.R.

1. Including Manchuria and Tibet.

Geography. China, which occupies the eastern part of Asia, is slightly larger in area than the U.S. Its coastline is roughly a semicircle. The greater part of the country is mountainous, and only in the lower reaches of the Yellow and Yangtze Rivers are there extensive low plains.

The principal mountain ranges are the Tien Shan, to the northwest; the Kunlun chain, running south of the Taklimakan and Gobi Deserts; and the Trans-Himalaya, connecting the Kunlun with the borders of China and Tibet. Manchuria is largely an undulating plain connected with the north China plain by a narrow lowland corridor. Inner Mongolia contains the relatively fertile southern and eastern portions of the Gobi. The large island of Hainan (13,500 sq mi.; 34,380 sq km) lies off the southern coast.

Hydrographically, China proper consists of three great river systems. The northern part of the country is drained by the Yellow River (Huang Ho), 2,109 miles long (5,464 km) and mostly unnavigable. The central part is drained by the Chang Jiang (Yangtze Kiang), the third longest river in the world 2,432 miles (6,300 km). The Zhujiang (Si Kiang) in the south is 848 miles long (2,197 km) and navigable for a considerable distance. In addition, the Amur (1,144 sq mi.; 2,965 km) forms part of the northeastern boundary.

Government. With 2,978 deputies, elected for four-year terms by universal suffrage, the National People's Congress is the chief legislative organ. A State Council has the executive authority. The Congress elects the Premier and Deputy Premiers. All ministries are under the State Council, headed by the Premier.

The Communist Party controls the government.

History. By 2000 B.C. the Chinese were living in the Huang Ho basin, and they had achieved an advanced stage of civilization by 1200 B.C. The great philosophers Lao-tse, Confucius Mo Ti, and Mencius lived during the Chou dynasty (1122–249 B.C.). The warring feudal states were first united under Emperor Ch'in Shih Huang Ti, during whose reign (246–210 B.C.) work was begun on the Great Wall. Under the Han dynasty (206 B.C.–A.D. 220), China prospered and traded with the West.

In the T'ang dynasty (618–907), often called the golden age of Chinese history, painting, sculpture, and poetry flourished, and printing made its earliest known appearance.

The Mings, last of the native rulers (1368–1644), overthrew the Mongol, or Yuan, dynasty (1280–1368) established by Kublai Khan. The Mings in turn were overthrown in 1644 by invaders from the north, the Manchus.

China closely restricted foreign activities, and by the end of the 18th century only Canton and the Portuguese port of Macao were open to European merchants. Following the Anglo-Chinese War of 1839–42, however, several treaty ports were opened, and Hong Kong was ceded to Britain. Treaties signed after further hostilities (1856–60) weakened Chinese sovereignty and removed foreigners from Chinese jurisdiction. The disastrous Chinese-Japanese War of 1894–95 was followed by a scramble for Chinese concessions by European powers, leading to the Boxer Rebellion (1900), suppressed by an international force.

The death of the Empress Dowager Tzu Hsi in 1908 and the accession of the infant Emperor Hsüan T'ung (Pu-Yi) were followed by a nation-wide rebellion led by Dr. Sun Yat-sen, who became first President of the Provisional Chinese Republic in 1911. The Manchus abdicated on Feb. 12, 1912. Dr. Sun resigned in favor of Yuan Shih-k'ai, who suppressed the republicans but was forced by a serious rising in 1915–16 to abandon his intention of declaring himself Emperor. Yuan's death in June 1916 was followed by years of civil war between rival militarists and Dr. Sun's republicans.

Provinces and Regions of China

Name	Area (sq mi.)	Area (sq km)	Capital
Provinces			
Anhui (Anhwei)	54,015	139,900	Hefei (Hofei)
Fujian (Fukien)	47,529	123,100	Fuzhou (Fukien)
Gansu (Kansu)	137,104	355,100	Lanzhou (Lanchow)
Guangdong (Kwangtung)	89,344	231,400	Canton
Guizhou (Kweichow)	67,181	174,000	Guiyang (Kweiyang)
Hebei (Hopei)	81,479	211,030	Shijiazhuang (Shitikiachwang)
Heilongjiang (Heilungkiang)[1]	178,996	463,600	Harbin
Henan (Honan)	64,479	167,000	Zhengzhou (Chengchow)
Hubei (Hupeh)	72,394	187,500	Wuhan
Hunan	81,274	210,500	Changsha
Jiangsu (Kiangsu)	40,927	106,000	Nanjing (Nanking)
Jiangxi (Kiangsi)	63,629	164,800	Nanchang
Jilin (Kirin)[1]	72,201	187,000	Changchun
Liaoning[1]	53,301	138,050	Shenyang
Quinghai (Chinghai)	278,378	721,000	Xining (Sining)
Shaanxi (Shensi)	75,598	195,800	Xian (Sian)
Shandong (Shantung)	59,189	153,300	Jinan (Tsinan)
Shanxi (Shansi)	60,656	157,100	Taiyuan
Sichuan (Szechwan)	219,691	569,000	Chengdu (Chengtu)
Yunnan	168,417	436,200	Kunming
Zhejiang (Chekiang)	39,305	101,800	Hangzhou (Hangchow)
Autonomous Region			
Guangxi Zhuang (Kwangsi Chuang)	85,096	220,400	Nanning
Nei Monggol (Inner Mongolia)[1]	454,633	1,177,500	Hohhot (Huhehot)
Ningxia Hui	30,039	77,800	Yinchuan (Yinchwan)
Xinjiang Uygur (Sinkiang Uighur)[1]	635,829	1,646,800	Urumqi (Urumchi)
Xizang (Tibet)	471,660	1,221,600	Lhasa

1. Together constitute (with Taiwan) what has been traditionally known as Outer China, the remaining territory forming the historical China Proper. NOTE: Names are in Pinyin, with conventional spelling in parentheses.

Nationalist forces, led by Gen. Chiang Kai-shek and with the advice of Communist experts, soon occupied most of China, setting up a Kuomintang regime in 1928. Internal strife continued, however, and Chiang broke with the Communists.

An alleged explosion on the South Manchurian Railway on Sept. 18, 1931, brought invasion of Manchuria by Japanese forces, who installed the last Manchu Emperor, Henry Pu-Yi, as nominal ruler of the puppet state of "Manchukuo." Japanese efforts to take China's northern provinces in July 1937 were resisted by Chiang, who meanwhile had succeeded in uniting most of China behind him. Within two years, however, Japan seized most of the ports and railways. The Kuomintang government retreated first to Hankow and then to Chungking, while the Japanese set up a puppet government at Nanking headed by Wang Jingwei.

Japan's surrender in 1945 touched off civil war between Nationalist forces under Chiang and Communist forces led by Mao Zedong, the party chairman. Despite U.S. aid, the Chiang forces were overcome by the Maoists, backed by the Soviet bloc, and were expelled from the mainland. The Mao regime, established in Peking as the new capital, proclaimed the People's Republic of China on Oct. 1, 1949, with Zhou Enlai as Premier.

After the Korean War began in June 1950, China led the Communist bloc in supporting North Korea, and on Nov. 26, 1950, the Mao regime intervened openly.

In 1958, Mao undertook the "Great Leap Forward"

campaign, which combined the establishment of rural communes with a crash program of village industrialization. These efforts also failed, causing Mao to lose influence to Liu Shaoqi, who became President in 1959, to Premier Zhou, and to Party Secretary Deng Xiaoping.

China exploded its first atomic (fission) bomb in 1964 and produced a fusion bomb in 1967.

Mao moved to Shanghai, and from that base he and his supporters waged what they called a Cultural Revolution. In the spring of 1966 the Mao group formed Red Guard units dominated by youths and students, closing the schools to free the students for agitation.

The Red Guards campaigned against "old ideas, old culture, old habits, and old customs." Often they were no more than uncontrolled mobs, and brutality was frequent. Early in 1967 efforts were made to restore control. The Red Guards were urged to return home. Schools started opening.

Persistent overtures by the Nixon Administration resulted in the dramatic announcement in July that Henry Kissinger, President Richard M. Nixon's national security adviser, had secretly visited Peking and reached agreement on a visit by the President to China.

The movement toward reconciliation, which signaled the end of the U.S. containment policy toward China, provided irresistible momentum for Chinese admission to the U.N. Despite U.S. opposition to expelling Taiwan (Nationalist China), the world body overwhelmingly ousted Chiang in seating Peking.

President Nixon went to Peking for a week early in 1972, meeting Mao as well as Zhou. The summit ended with a historic communiqué on February 28, in which both nations promised to work toward improved relations.

In 1973, the U.S. and China agreed to set up "liaison offices" in each other's capitals, which constituted de facto diplomatic relations. Full diplomatic relations were barred by China as long as the U.S. continued to recognize Nationalist China.

On Jan. 8, 1976, Zhou died. His successor, Vice Premier Deng Xiaoping was supplanted within a month by Hua Guofeng, former Minister of Public Security. Hua became permanent Premier in April. In October he was named successor to Mao as Chairman of the Communist Party.

After Mao died on Sept. 10, a campaign against his widow, Jiang Qing, and three of her "radical" colleagues began. The "Gang of Four" was denounced for having undermined the party, the government, and the economy.

Jiang was brought to trial in 1980 and sentenced on Jan. 25, 1981, to die within two years unless she showed repentance, in which case she would be imprisoned for life.

At the Central Committee meeting of 1977, Deng was reinstated as Deputy Premier, Chief of Staff of the Army, and member of the Central Committee of the Politburo.

At the same time, Jiang Qing, Wang Hongwen, Zhang Chunqiao, and Yao Wenyuan—the notorious "Gang of Four"—were removed from all official posts and banished from the party.

In May 1978, expulsion of ethnic Chinese by Vietnam produced an open rupture. Peking sided with Cambodia in the border fighting that flared between Vietnam and Cambodia, charging Hanoi with aggression.

On Aug. 12, 1978, China and Japan signed a treaty of peace and friendship. Peking and Washington then announced that they would open full diplomatic relations on Jan. 1, 1979 and the Carter Administration abrogated the Taiwan defense treaty. Deputy Premier Deng sealed the agreement with a visit to the United States that coincided with the opening of embassies in both capitals on March 1.

On Deng's return from the U.S. Chinese troops invaded Vietnam to avenge alleged violations of Chinese territory. The action was seen as a reaction to Vietnam's invasion of Cambodia.

The first People's Congress in five years confirmed Zhao Ziyang, an economic planner, as Premier replacing Hua Guofeng, who had held the post since 1976.

After the Central Committee meeting of June 27–29, 1981, Hu Yaobang, a Deng protégé, was elevated to the party chairmanship, replacing Hua Guofeng. Deng became chairman of the military commission of the central committee, giving him control over the army. The committee's 215 members concluded the session with a statement holding Mao Zedong responsible for the "grave blunder" of the Cultural Revolution.

Under Deng Xiaoping's leadership, meanwhile, China's Communist idealogy was almost totally reinterpreted and sweeping economic changes were set in motion in the early 1980s. The Chinese scrapped the personality cult that idolized Mao Zedong, muted Mao's old call for class struggle and exportation of the Communist revolution, and imported Western technology and management techniques to replace the Marxist tenets that retarded modernization.

Also under Deng's leadership, the Chinese Communists worked out an arrangement with Britain for the future of Hong Kong after 1997. The flag of China will be raised but the territory will retain its present social, economic and legal system.

The removal of Hu Yaobang as party chairman in January 1987 was a sign of a hard-line resurgence. He was replaced by former Premier Zhao Ziyang. Conflict between hard-liners and moderates continued and reached a violent climax in 1989. Student demonstrations calling for accelerated liberalization were crushed by military force in June, resulting in several hundred deaths. This was followed by a purge of moderates, including party leader Zhao Ziyang, who was replaced with Jiang Zemin.

In January 1991 a Chinese court convicted and sentenced eight, including the country's leading human rights advocate, to prison for terms of two to seven years for "counterrevolutionary propaganda and incitement." Two additional dissidents were sentenced to 13 years in prison in connection with the Tiananmen protests. Nevertheless, the National People's Congress in April appointed two new deputy prime ministers Zou Jiahua, generally regarded as hard-line, and Zhu Rongji, regarded as reformist.

COLOMBIA

Republic of Colombia
President: César Gaviria Trujillo (1990)
Population (est. mid-1991): 33,600,000 (average annual rate of natural increase, 2.0%); birth rate: 26/1000; infant mortality rate: 37/1000; density per square mile: 76
Capital: Bogotá
Largest cities (est. 1985): Bogotá, 4,208,000; Medellín, 2,069,000; Cali, 1,654,000; Barranquilla, 1,120,000; Bucaramanga, 545,000; Cartagena, 530,000
Monetary unit: Peso
Language: Spanish
Religion: 95% Roman Catholic
National name: República de Colombia
Literacy rate (1985): 88%, Indians about 40%
Economic summary: Gross domestic product (1988): $35.4 billion, per capita $1,110; real growth rate 3.7%. Arable land: 4%. Principal products: coffee, bananas, rice, corn, sugar cane, cotton, tobacco, oilseeds. Labor force: 11,000,000; 21% in industry. Major products: textiles, processed food, beverages, chemicals, cement. Natural resources: petroleum, natural gas, coal, iron ore, nickel, gold, silver. Exports: coffee, fuel oil, cotton, bananas. Imports: machinery, paper products, chemical products, metals and metal products, transportation equipment. Major trading partners: U.S., E.C., Japan, Venezuela, Netherlands, Brazil, Sweden.

Geography. Colombia, in the northwestern part of South America, is the only country on that continent that borders on both the Atlantic and Pacific Oceans. It is nearly equal to the combined areas of California and Texas.

Through the western half of the country, three Andean ranges run north and south, merging into one at the Ecuadorean border. The eastern half is a low, jungle-covered plain, drained by spurs of the Amazon and Orinoco, inhabited mostly by isolated, tropical-forest Indian tribes. The fertile plateau and valley of the eastern range are the most densely populated parts of the country.

Government. Colombia's President, who appoints his own Cabinet, serves for a four-year term. The Senate, the upper house of Congress, has 114 members elected for four years by direct vote. The House of Representatives of 199 members is directly elected for four years.

History. Spaniards in 1510 founded Darien, the first permanent European settlement on the American mainland. In 1538 the Spaniards established the colony of New Granada, the area's name until 1861. After a 14-year struggle, in which Simón Bolívar's Venezuelan troops won the battle of Boyacá in Colombia on Aug. 7, 1819, independence was attained in 1824. Bolívar united Colombia, Venezuela, Panama, and Ecuador in the Republic of Greater Colombia (1819–30), but lost Venezuela and Ecuador to separatists. Bolívar's Vice President, Francisco de Paula Santander, founded the Liberal Party as the Federalists while Bolívar established the Conservatives as the Centralists.

Santander's presidency (1832–36) re-established order, but later periods of Liberal dominance (1849–57 and 1861–80), when the Liberals sought to disestablish the Roman Catholic Church, were marked by insurrection and even civil war. Rafael Nuñez, in a 15-year-presidency, restored the power of the central government and the church, which led in 1899 to a bloody civil war and the loss in 1903 of Panama over ratification of a lease to the U.S. of the Canal Zone. For 21 years, until 1930, the Conservatives held power as revolutionary pressures built up.

The Liberal administrations of Enrique Olaya Herrera and Alfonso López (1930–38) were marked by social reforms that failed to solve the country's problems, and in 1946, insurrection and banditry broke out, claiming hundreds of thousands of lives by 1958. Laureano Gómez (1950–53); the Army Chief of Staff, Gen. Gustavo Rojas Pinilla (1953–56), and a military junta (1956–57) sought to curb disorder by repression.

Government efforts to stamp out the Movement of April 19 (M–19), an urban guerrilla organization, intensified in 1981 with the capture of some of the leaders. A general amnesty offered to the organization failed to bring an end to the movement. The Liberals won a solid majority in 1982, but a split enabled Belisario Betancur Cuartas, the Conservative candidate, to win the presidency on May 31. After his inauguration, he ended the state of siege that had existed almost continuously for 34 years and renewed the general amnesty of 1981.

In an official war against drug trafficking Colombia became a public battleground with bombs, killings and kidnapping. In 1989 a leading presidential candidate, Luis Carlos Galán, was murdered. In an effort to quell the terror President Gaviria proposed lenient punishment in exchange for surrender by the leading drug dealers. In addition in 1991 the constitutional convention voted to ban extradition. In June the most violent trafficker, Pablo Escobar, surrendered.

COMOROS

Federal Islamic Republic of the Comoros
President: Said Mohammed Djohar (1989)
Area: 690 sq mi. (1,787 sq km)

Population (est. 1991): 500,000 (average annual rate of natural increase: 3.5%); birth rate: 47/1000; infant mortality rate: 92/1000; density per square mile: 687
Capital and largest city (est. 1980): Moroni (on Grande Comoro), 20,000
Monetary unit: Franc CFA
Languages: Shaafi Islam, Malagasu, French
Religions: Sunni Muslim, 86%; Roman Catholic, 14%.
National name: République Fédéral Islamique des Comores
Literacy rate (1981): 15%
Economic summary: Gross national product (1988 est.): $207 million, per capita $475; real growth rate 0.1%. Arable land: 35%. Labor force: 140,000 (1982); 80% in agriculture. Principal agricultural products: perfume essences, copra, coconuts, cloves, vanilla, cassava, bananas. Major industrial products: perfume distillations. Exports: perfume essences, vanilla, copra, cloves. Imports: foodstuffs, cement, petroleum products, consumer goods. Major trading partners: France, Germany, U.S., Africa, Pakistan.

Geography. The Comoros Islands—Grande Comoro, Anjouan, Mohéli, and Mayotte (which retains ties to France)—are an archipelago of volcanic origin in the Indian Ocean between Mozambique and Madagascar.

Government. Democratic elections were held in March 1990. The interim president Said Djohar won from among a field of eight candidates. The constitution dates from October 1, 1978, and the country is an Islamic republic with a 42-member unicameral legislature.

History. Under French rule since 1886, the Comoros declared themselves independent July 6, 1975. However, Mayotte, with a Christian majority, voted against joining the other, mainly Islamic, islands, in the move to independence and remains French.

A month after independence, Justice Minister Ali Soilih staged a coup with the help of mercenaries, overthrowing the new nation's first president, Ahmed Abdallah. He was overthrown on May 13, 1978, when a small boatload of French mercenaries, some of whom had aided him three years earlier, seized government headquarters. These mercenaries assassinated Abdallah in a coup attempt in 1989. They were forced to leave by French military pressure.

CONGO

Republic of the Congo
President: Col. Denis Sassou-Neguessou (1979)
Prime Minister: Pierre Moussa (1990)
Area: 132,046 sq mi. (342,000 sq km)
Population (est. mid-1991): 2,300,000 (average annual rate of natural increase: 3.0%); birth rate: 43/1000; infant mortality rate: 112/1000. Density per sq mile: 17
Capital and largest city (est. 1984): Brazzaville, 595,102
Monetary unit: Franc CFA
Ethnic groups: About 15 Bantu groups, Europeans
Languages: French, Lingala, Kikongo, others
Religions: 50% Christian, 48% animist, 2% Muslim
National name: République Populaire du Congo
Literacy rate: 62.9%
Economic summary: Gross domestic product (1988 est.): $2.2 billion, per capita $1,000; real growth rate −3%. Arable land: 2%. Principal agricultural products: cassava, rice, corn, peanuts, coffee, cocoa. Labor force: 79,100; 75% in agriculture. Major industrial products:

crude oil, cigarettes, cement, beverages, milled sugar. Natural resources: wood, potash, petroleum, natural gas. Exports: oil, lumber, tobacco, wood, coffee. Imports: foodstuffs, consumer goods, intermediate manufactures, capital equipment. Major trading partners: France, U.S., Italy, Spain, Brazil, Germany.

Geography. The Congo is situated in west Central Africa astride the Equator. It borders on Gabon, Cameroon, the Central African Republic, Zaire, and the Angola exclave of Cabinda, with a short stretch of coast on the South Atlantic. Its area is nearly three times that of Pennsylvania.

Most of the inland is tropical rain forest, drained by tributaries of the Zaire (Congo) River, which flows south along the eastern border with Zaire to Stanley Pool. The narrow coastal plain rises to highlands separated from the inland plateaus by the 200-mile-wide Niari River Valley, which gives passage to the coast.

Government. Since the coup of September 1968 the country has been governed by a military regime. The Congolese Labor Party is the only party.

History. The inhabitants of the former French Congo, mainly Bantu peoples with Pygmies in the north, were subjects of several kingdoms in earlier times.

The Frenchman Pierre Savorgnan de Brazza signed a treaty with Makoko, ruler of the Bateke people, in 1880, which established French control. The area, with Gabon and Ubangi-Shari, was constituted the colony of French Equatorial Africa in 1910. It joined Chad in supporting the Free French cause in World War II. The Congo proclaimed its independence without leaving the French Community in 1960.

Maj. Marien Ngouabi, head of the National Council of the Revolution, took power as president on Jan. 1, 1969. He was sworn in for a second five-year term in 1975. A visit to Moscow by Ngouabi in March ended with the signing of a Soviet-Congolese economic and technical aid pact.

A four-man commando squad assassinated Ngouabi in Brazzaville on March 18, 1977.

Col. Joachim Yhombi-Opango, Army Chief of Staff, assumed the presidency on April 4. In June, the new government agreed to resume diplomatic relations with the U.S., ending a 12-year rift. Yombhi-Opango resigned on Feb. 4, 1979, and was replaced by Col. Denis Sassou-Neguessou.

In July 1990 the leaders of the ruling party voted to end the one-party system. A national political conference, hailed as a model for sub-Saharan Africa, in 1991 renounced Marxism, rewrote the constitution and scheduled the country's first free elections for 1992.

COSTA RICA

Republic of Costa Rica
President: Rafael Calderón Fournier (1990)
Area: 19,652 sq mi. (50,898 sq km)
Population (est. mid-1991): 3,100,000 (average annual rate of natural increase: 2.4%); birth rate: 28/1000; infant mortality rate: 13.9/1000; density per square mile: 159
Capital and largest city (est. 1984): San José, 278,500
Monetary unit: Colón
Language: Spanish
Religion: 95% Roman Catholic
National name: República de Costa Rica
Literacy rate (1984): 93%

Economic summary: Gross domestic product (1988): $4.7 billion, per capita $1,630; real growth rate 3.8%. Arable land: 6%. Principal products: bananas, coffee, sugar cane, rice, corn, livestock. Labor force: 868,300; 35.1% in industry and commerce. Major products: processed foods, textiles and clothing, construction materials, fertilizer. Natural resource: hydropower potential. Exports: coffee, bananas, beef, sugar, cocoa. Imports: machinery, chemicals, foodstuffs, fuels, fertilizer. Major trading partners: U.S., Central American countries, Germany, Japan, United Kingdom.

Geography. This Central American country lies between Nicaragua to the north and Panama to the south. Its area slightly exceeds that of Vermont and New Hampshire combined.

Most of Costa Rica is tableland, from 3,000 to 6,000 feet (914 to 1,829 m) above sea level. Cocos Island (10 sq mi.; 26 sq km), about 300 miles (483 km) off the Pacific Coast, is under Costa Rican sovereignty.

Government. Under the 1949 Constitution, the president and the one-house Legislative Assembly of 57 members are elected for terms of four years.

The army was abolished in 1949. There is a civil guard and a rural guard.

History. Costa Rica was inhabited by 25,000 Indians when Columbus discovered it and probably named it in 1502. Few of the Indians survived the Spanish conquest, which began in 1563. The region was administered as a Spanish province. Costa Rica achieved independence in 1821 but was absorbed for two years by Agustín de Iturbide in his Mexican Empire. It was established as a republic in 1848.

Except for the military dictatorship of Tomás Guardia from 1870 to 1882, Costa Rica has enjoyed one of the most democratic governments in Latin America.

Rodrigo Carazo Odio, leader of a four-party coalition called the Unity Party, won the presidency in February 1978. His tenure was marked by a disastrous decline in the economy. Luis Alberto Monge Alvarez, a former union organizer and cofounder of the National Liberation Party, swept to victory in the Feb. 7, 1982, national elections.

On Feb. 2, 1986, Oscar Arias Sanchez won the national elections on a neutralist platform. Arias initiated a policy of preventing contra usage of Costa Rican territory. Rafael Calderón won the presidential election of February 4, 1990 with 51% of the vote, his party winning 29 seats in the Assembly. Calderón promised to continue the economic policies of the previous administration.

COTE D'IVOIRE

Republic of Côte d'Ivoire
President: Félix Houphouët-Boigny (1960)
Area: 124,502 sq mi. (322,462 sq km)
Population (est. mid-1991): 12,500,000 (average annual rate of natural increase: 3.5%); birth rate: 50/1000; infant mortality rate: 96/1000; density per square mile: 100
Capital: Yamoussoukro[1]
Monetary unit: Franc CFA
Ethnic groups: 60 different groups: principals are Baoule, Bete, Senoufou, Malinke, Agni
Languages: French and African languages (Diaula esp.)
Religions: 63% indigenous, 25% Christian, 12% Islam

National name: République de la Côte d'Ivoire
Literacy rate: 42.7%
Economic summary: Gross domestic product (1988): $10 billion, per capita $900; real growth rate –6.4%. Arable land: 9%; Labor force: 5,718,000; over 85% in agriculture. Principal products: coffee, cocoa, corn, beans, timber. Major industrial products: food, wood, refined oil, textiles, fertilizer. Natural resources: diamonds, iron ore, crude oil, manganese, cobalt, bauxite, copper. Exports: coffee, cocoa, tropical woods. Imports: raw materials, consumer goods, fuels. Major trading partners: France, U.S., Western European countries, Nigeria.

---

1. Not recognized by U.S. which recognizes Abidjan.

Geography. The Ivory Coast, in western Africa on the Gulf of Guinea, is a little larger than New Mexico. Its neighbors are Liberia, Guinea, Mali, Burkina Faso, and Ghana.

The country consists of a coastal strip in the south, dense forests in the interior, and savannas in the north. Rainfall is heavy, especially along the coast.

Government. The government is headed by a President who is elected every five years by popular vote, together with a National Assembly of 175 members.

History. The Ivory Coast attracted both French and Portuguese merchants in the 15th century. French traders set up establishments early in the 19th century, and in 1842, the French obtained territorial concessions from local tribes, gradually extending their influence along the coast and inland. The area was organized as a territory in 1893, became an autonomous republic in the French Union after World War II, and achieved independence on Aug. 7, 1960.

The Ivory Coast formed a customs union in 1959 with Dahomey (Benin), Niger, and Burkina Faso.

Falling cocoa and coffee prices made this nation the largest per capita debtor in Africa. Massive protests by students, farmers and professionals forced the president to legalize opposition parties and hold the first contested presidential election. In October 1990 Houphouët-Boigny won 81% of the vote. In the first multiparty legislative elections in November the president's Democratic Party won 163 of the 175 seats.

CUBA

Republic of Cuba
President: Fidel Castro Ruz (1976)
Area: 44,218 sq mi. (114,524 sq km)
Population (est. mid-1991): 10,700,000 (average annual rate of natural increase: 1.1%); birth rate: 18/1000; infant mortality rate: 10.7/1000; density per square mile: 243
Capital: Havana
Largest cities (est. 1986): Havana, 2,013,746; Santiago de Cuba, 358,764; Camagüey, 260,782; Holguin, 194,728; Santa Clara, 178,278
Monetary unit: Peso
Language: Spanish
Religion: at least 85% nominally Roman Catholic before Castro assumed power
National name: República de Cuba
Literacy rate: 96%
Economic summary: Gross national product (1989 est.): $20.9 billion, per capita $2,000; real growth rate –1%. Arable land: 23%. Principal products: sugar, tobacco, coffee, rice, fruits. Labor force: 3,300,000; 29% in industry. Major products: processed sugar and tobacco, refined oil products, textiles, chemicals, paper and wood products, metals, consumer products. Natural resources: metals, primarily nickel, timber. Exports: coffee, sugar, nickel, shellfish, tobacco. Imports: capital goods, industrial raw materials, petroleum, foodstuffs. Major trading partners: U.S.S.R., other Communist bloc countries, China.

Geography. The largest island of the West Indies group (equal in area to Pennsylvania), Cuba is also the westernmost—just west of Hispaniola (Haiti and the Dominican Republic), and 90 miles (145 km) south of Key West, Fla., at the entrance to the Gulf of Mexico.

The island is mountainous in the southeast and south central area (Sierra Maestra). Elsewhere it is flat or rolling.

Government. Since 1976, elections have been held every five years to elect the National Assembly, which in turn elects the 31-member Council of States, its President, First Vice-President, five Vice-Presidents, and Secretary. Fidel Castro is President of the Council of State and of the government and First Secretary of the Communist Party of Cuba, the only political party.

History. Arawak Indians inhabiting Cuba when Columbus discovered the island in 1492 died off from diseases brought by sailors and settlers. By 1511, Spaniards under Diego Velásquez were founding settlements that served as bases for Spanish exploration. Cuba soon after served as an assembly point for treasure looted by the conquistadores, attracting French and English pirates.

Black slaves and free laborers were imported to work sugar and tobacco plantations, and waves of chiefly Spanish immigrants maintained a European character in the island's culture. Early slave rebellions and conflicts between colonials and Spanish rulers laid the foundation for an independence movement that turned into open warfare from 1867 to 1878. The poet, José Marti, in 1895 led the struggle that finally ended Spanish rule, thanks largely to U.S. intervention in 1898 after the sinking of the battleship *Maine* in Havana harbor.

A treaty in 1899 made Cuba an independent republic under U.S. protection. The U.S. occupation, which ended in 1902, suppressed yellow fever and brought large American investment. From 1906 to 1909, Washington invoked the Platt Amendment to the treaty, which gave it the right to intervene in order to suppress any revolt. U.S. troops came back in 1912 and again in 1917 to restore order. The Platt Amendment was abrogated in 1934.

Fulgencio Batista, an army sergeant, led a revolt in 1934 that overthrew the regime of President Gerado Machado.

Batista's Cuba was a police state. Corrupt officials took payoffs from American gamblers who operated casinos, demanded bribes from Cubans for various public services and enriched themselves with raids on the public treasury. Dissenters were murdered and their bodies dumped in gutters.

Fidel Castro Ruz, a hulking, bearded attorney in his 30s, landed in Cuba on Christmas Day 1956 with a band of 12 fellow revolutionaries, evaded Batista's soldiers, and set up headquarters in the jungled hills of the Sierra Maestra range. By 1958 his force had grown to about 2,000 guerrillas, for the most part young and middle class. Castro's brother, Raul, and Ernesto (Ché) Guevara, an Argentine physician, were his top lieutenants. Businessmen and landowners who opposed the Batista regime gave financial support to the rebels. The United States, meanwhile, cut off arms shipments to Batista's army.

The beginning of the end for Batista came when the rebels routed 3,000 government troops and captured Santa Clara, capital of Las Villas province 150 miles from Havana, and a trainload of Batista reinforcements refused to get out of their railroad cars. On New Year's Day 1959, Batista flew to exile in the Dominican Republic and Castro took over the government. Crowds cheered the revolutionaries on their seven-day march to the capital.

The United States initially welcomed what looked like the prospect for a democratic Cuba, but a rude awakening came within a few months when Castro established military tribunals for political opponents, jailed hundreds, and began to veer leftward. Castro disavowed Cuba's 1952 military pact with the United States. He confiscated U.S. investments in banks and industries and seized large U.S. landholdings, turning them first into collective farms and then into Soviet-type state farms. The United States broke relations with Cuba on Jan. 3, 1961. Castro thereupon forged an alliance with the Soviet Union.

From the ranks of the Cuban exiles who had fled to the United States, the Central Intelligence Agency recruited and trained an expeditionary force, numbering less than 2,000 men, to invade Cuba, with the expectation that the invasion would spark an uprising of the Cuban populace against Castro. The invasion was planned under the Eisenhower administration and President John F. Kennedy gave the go-ahead for it in the first months of his administration, but rejected a CIA proposal for U.S. planes to provide air support. The landing at the Bay of Pigs on April 17, 1961, was a fiasco. Not only did the invaders fail to receive any support from the populace, but Castro's tanks and artillery made short work of the small force.

A Soviet attempt to change the global power balance by installing in Cuba medium-range missiles—capable of striking targets in the United States with nuclear warheads—provoked a crisis between the superpowers in 1962 that had the potential of touching off World War III. After a visit to Moscow by Cuba's war minister, Raul Castro, work began secretly on the missile launching sites.

Denouncing the Soviets for "deliberate deception," President Kennedy on Oct. 22 announced that the U.S. navy would enforce a "quarantine" of shipping to Cuba and search Soviet bloc ships to prevent the missiles themselves from reaching the island. After six days of tough public statements on both sides and secret diplomacy, Soviet Premier Nikita Khrushchev on Oct. 28 ordered the missile sites dismantled, crated and shipped back to the Soviet Union, in return for a U.S. pledge not to attack Cuba. Limited diplomatic ties were re-established on Sept. 1, 1977.

Emigration increased dramatically after April 1, 1980, when Castro, irritated by the granting of asylum to would-be refugees by the Peruvian embassy in Havana, removed guards and allowed 10,000 Cubans to swarm into the embassy grounds.

As an airlift began taking the refugees to Costa Rica, Castro opened the port of Mariel to a "freedom flotilla" of ships and yachts from the United States, many of them owned or chartered by Cuban-Americans to bring out relatives. More than 125,000 Cubans poured out of Mariel in a mass exodus. It wasn't until after they had reached the United States that it was discovered that the regime had opened prisons and mental hospitals to permit criminals, homosexuals and others unwanted in Cuba to join the refugees.

For most of President Ronald Reagan's first term,

U.S.-Cuban relations were frozen, with Secretary of State Alexander Haig calling Havana the "source" of troubles in Central America. But late in 1984, an agreement was reached between the two countries. Cuba would take back more than 2,700 Cubans who had come to the United States in the Mariel exodus but were not eligible to stay in the country under U.S. immigration law because of criminal or psychiatric disqualification. The United States, in exchange, would reinstitute regular immigration for Cubans to the United States. Castro cancelled it when the U.S. began the Radio Marti broadcasts in May 1985 to bring a non-Communist view to the Cuban people.

In the face of sweeping changes in Eastern Europe and the Soviet Union itself, Cuba has reaffirmed its adherence to Marxism-Leninism. Its economy, furthermore, already under strain, remains heavily indebted to continuing Soviet aid. The last of the Cuban troops left Angola in May 1991, thereby ending a presence begun in 1975 and costing an official count of 2,100 Cuban lives.

CYPRUS

Republic of Cyprus

President: Dr. George Vassiliou (1988)

Area: 3,572 sq mi (9,251 sq km)

Population (est. mid-1991): 700,000 (average annual rate of natural increase: 1.0%); birth rate: 18/1000; infant mortality rate: 11/1000; density per square mile: 200

Capital and largest city: Nicosia, 123,298

Monetary unit: Cyprus pound

Languages: Greek, Turkish, English

Religions: Greek Orthodox, 80%; Islam, 18%; Maronite Latin, 2%

National name: Kypriaki Dimokratia—Kibris Cumhuriyeti

Member of Commonwealth of Nations

Literacy rate (1981): 99%

Economic summary: Gross domestic product (1990 est.): $5.2 billion, per capita $9,000; real growth rate 6.9%. Arable land: 40%. Principal products: vine products, citrus, potatoes, other vegetables. Labor force: 251,406 (in Greek area); 33% in industry. Major products: beverages, footwear, clothing, cement, asbestos mining. Natural resources: copper, asbestos, gypsum, timber, marble, clay, salt. Exports: citrus, potatoes, grapes, wine, cement, clothing. Imports: consumer goods, petroleum and lubricants, food and feed grains, machinery. Major trading partners: U.K., Middle East, North Africa, E.C. (61% exports), U.S., Japan

Geography. The third largest island in the Mediterranean (one and one half times the size of Delaware), Cyprus lies off the southern coast of Turkey and the western shore of Syria. Most of the country consists of a wide plain lying between two mountain ranges that cross the island. The highest peak is Mount Olympus at 6,406 feet (1,953 m).

Government. Under the republic's Constitution, for the protection of the Turkish minority the vice president as well as three of the 10 Cabinet ministers must be from the Turkish community, while the House of Representatives is elected by each community separately, 70% Greek Cypriote and 30% Turkish Cypriote representatives.

The Greek and Turkish communities are self-governing in questions of religion, education, and culture. Other governmental matters are under the jurisdiction of the central government. Each community is entitled to a Communal Chamber.

The Greek Communal Chamber, which had 23 members, was abolished in 1965 and its function was absorbed by the Ministry of Education. The Turkish Communal Chamber, however, has continued to function.

History. Cyprus was the site of early Phoenician and Greek colonies. For centuries its rule passed through many hands. It fell to the Turks in 1571, and a large Turkish colony settled on the island.

In World War I, on the outbreak of hostilities with Turkey, Britain annexed the island. It was declared a crown colony in 1925.

For centuries the Greek population, regarding Greece as its mother country, has sought self-determination and reunion with it *(enosis)*. The resulting quarrel with Turkey threatened NATO. Cyprus became an independent nation on Aug. 16, 1960, with Britain, Greece, and Turkey as guarantor powers.

Archbishop Makarios, president since 1959, was overthrown July 15, 1974, by a military coup led by the Cypriot National Guard. The new regime named Nikos Giorgiades Sampson as president and Bishop Gennadios as head of the Cypriot Church to replace Makarios. The rebels were led by rightist Greek officers who supported *enosis*.

Diplomacy failed to resolve the crisis. Turkey invaded Cyprus by sea and air July 20, 1974, asserting its right to protect the Turkish Cypriote minority.

Geneva talks involving Greece, Turkey, Britain, and the two Cypriote factions failed in mid-August, and the Turks subsequently gained control of 40% of the island. Greece made no armed response to the superior Turkish force, but bitterly suspended military participation in the NATO alliance.

The tension continued after Makarios returned to become President on Dec. 7, 1974. He offered self-government to the Turkish minority, but rejected any solution "involving transfer of populations and amounting to partition of Cyprus."

Turkish Cypriots proclaimed a separate state under Rauf Denktash in the northern part of the island in Nov. 1983, and proposed a "biregional federation."

Makarios died on Aug. 3, 1977, and Spyros Kyprianou was elected to serve the remainder of his term. Kyprianou was subsequently re-elected in 1978, 1983, and 1985. In 1988, George Vassiliou defeated Kyprianou.

On the other hand, talks in New York in 1990 between Vassiliou and Denktash ended in failure. The latter went home espousing a harder than ever line and won a presidential election in his portion of the island.

CZECHOSLOVAKIA

Czech and Slovak Federative Republic
President: Vaclav Havel (1989)
Premier: Marian Calfa (1989)
Area: 49,374 sq mi. (127,896 sq km)
Population (est. mid-1991): 15,700,000 (average annual rate of natural increase: 0.2%); birth rate: 13/1000; infant mortality rate: 11.3/1000; density per square mile: 318
Capital: Prague

Largest cities (est. 1989): Prague, 1,206,098; Bratislava, 429,743; Brno, 388,084; Ostrava, 329,587; Kosice, 229,175
Monetary unit: Koruna
Languages: Czech, Slovak
Religions: Roman Catholic, 50%; Protestant, 20%; Orthodox, 2%; other, 28%
National name: Ceská a Slovenská Federativní Republika
Literacy rate (1981): 99%
Economic summary: Gross national product (1989 est.): $123.2 billion, per capita $7,878; real growth rate 1.0%. Arable land: 40%. Principal products: grains, potatoes, sugar beets, hops, fruit, hogs, cattle, poultry. Labor force: 8,200,000 (1987); 36.9% in industry. Major products: iron and steel, machinery and equipment, cement, sheet glass, motor vehicles, armaments, chemicals, ceramics. Natural resources: coal, timber, lignite, uranium, magnesite. Exports: machinery, chemicals, industrial consumer goods. Imports: machinery, equipment, fuels, raw materials, food, consumer goods. Major trading partners: U.S.S.R. and Eastern Europe, Yugoslavia, Germany, Austria, U.S.

Geography. Czechoslovakia lies in central Europe, a neighbor of East and West Germany, Poland, the U.S.S.R., Hungary, and Austria. It is equal in size to New York State. The principal rivers—the Elbe, Danube, Oder, and Vetava—are vital commercially to this landlocked country, for both waterborne commerce and agriculture, which flourishes in fertile valleys irrigated by these rivers and their tributaries.

Government. Since 1969 the supreme organ of the state has been the Federal Assembly, which has two equal chambers: the Chamber of People, with 150 deputies, and the Chamber of Nations, with 150 deputies. The chief executive is the President, who is elected by the Federal Assembly for a two-year term. The Premier and his Cabinet are appointed by the President but are responsible to the Federal Assembly.

History. Probably about the 5th century A.D., Slavic tribes from the Vistula basin settled in the region of modern Czechoslovakia. Slovakia came under Magyar domination. The Czechs founded the kingdom of Bohemia, the Premyslide dynasty, which ruled Bohemia and Moravia from the 10th to the 16th century. One of the Bohemian kings, Charles IV, Holy Roman Emperor, made Prague an imperial capital and a center of Latin scholarship. The Hussite movement founded by Jan Hus (1369?–1415) linked the Slavs to the Reformation and revived Czech nationalism, previously under German domination. A Hapsburg, Ferdinand I, ascended the throne in 1526. The Czechs rebelled in 1618. Defeated in 1620, they were ruled for the next 300 years as part of the Austrian Empire.

In World War I, Czech and Slovak patriots, notably Thomas G. Masaryk and Milan Stefanik, promoted Czech-Slovak independence from abroad while their followers fought against the Central Powers. On Oct. 28, 1918, Czechoslovakia proclaimed itself a republic. Shortly thereafter Masaryk was unanimously elected first President.

Hitler provoked the country's German minority in the Sudetenland to agitate for autonomy. At the Munich Conference on Sept. 30, 1938, France and the U.K., seeking to avoid World War II, agreed that the Nazis could take the Sudetenland. Dr. Eduard Benes, who had succeeded Masaryk, resigned on Oct. 5, 1938, and fled to London. Czechoslovakia became a state within the German orbit and was known as

Czecho-Slovakia. In March 1939, the Nazis occupied the country.

Soon after Czechoslovakia was liberated in World War II and the government returned in April 1945, it was obliged to cede Ruthenia to the U.S.S.R. In 1946, a Communist, Klement Gottwald, formed a six-party coalition Cabinet. Pressure from Moscow increased until Feb. 23-25, 1948, when the Communists seized complete control in a coup. Following constituent assembly elections in which the Communists and their allies were unopposed, a new Constitution was adopted.

The "people's democracy" was converted into a "socialist" state by a new Constitution adopted June 11, 1960.

After the death of Stalin and the relaxing of Soviet controls, Czechoslovakia witnessed a nationalist awakening. In 1968 conservative Stalinists were driven from power and replaced by more liberal, reform-minded Communists.

Soviet military maneuvers on Czechoslovak soil in May 1968 were followed in July by a meeting of the U.S.S.R. with Poland, Bulgaria, East Germany, and Hungary in Warsaw that demanded an accounting, which Prague refused. Czechoslovak-Soviet talks on Czechoslovak territory, at Cierna, in late July led to an accord. But the Russians charged that the Czechoslovaks had reneged on pledges to modify their policies, and on Aug. 20-21, troops of the five powers, estimated at 600,000, executed a lightning invasion and occupation.

Soviet secret police seized the top Czechoslovak leadership and detained it for several days in Moscow. But Soviet efforts to establish a puppet regime failed. President Ludvik Svoboda negotiated an accord providing for a gradual troop withdrawal in return for "normalization" of political policy.

Czechoslovakia signed a new friendship treaty with the U.S.S.R. that codified the "Brezhnev doctrine," under which Russia can invade any Eastern European socialist nation that threatens to leave the satellite camp.

Anti-government demonstrations reached a head in 1990 when the brutal suppression of a protest on November 17 led to massive popular protests against the Husak regime. Members of the opposition formed the Civic Forum, which pushed for democratization. Marian Colfa became the country's first non-Communist Premier since 1948. Opposition leader Vaclav Havel was elected President on December 29. Opposition groups won a majority in both legislative chambers in the elections of June 1990.

During 1991 strains further developed between the Czech and Slovak regions that threatened to sunder the country in two. In January Czechoslovakia's application to join the Council of Europe was approved unanimously, and the nation moved cautiously toward dismantling the state-run economy. In that month 85% of prices were freed, and the state began the process of auctioning off all state-owned stores. The last Soviet troops left as provided for in negotiations in June 1991.

DENMARK

Kingdom of Denmark
Sovereign: Queen Margrethe II (1972)
Prime Minister: Poul Schlüter (1982)
Area: 16,631 sq mi. (43,075 sq km[1]
Population (est. mid-1991): 5,100,000 (average annual rate of natural increase: 0.0%); birth rate: 12/1000;

infant mortality rate: 8.4/1000; density per square mile: 309
Capital: Copenhagen
Largest cities (est. 1985): Copenhagen, 1,358,540; Aarhus, 252,071; Odense, 171,468; Alborg, 154,750
Monetary unit: Krone
Language: Danish, Faroese, Greenlandic, small German-speaking minority
Religion: 97% Evangelical Lutheran
National name: Kongeriget Danmark
Literacy rate: 99%
Economic summary: Gross domestic product (1990): $125.7 billion; $24,500 per capita; real growth rate, 1.75%. Arable land: 61%. Principal products: meat, dairy products, fish, grains. Labor force: 2,760,000; 34% in industry. Major products: processed foods, machinery and equipment, textiles. Natural resources: crude oil, natural gas, fish, salt, limestone. Exports: meat and dairy products, fish, industrial machinery, chemical products, transportation equipment. Imports: machinery and equipment, transport equipment, petroleum, chemicals, grains and foodstuffs, textiles, paper. Major trading partners: Germany, Sweden, U.K., U.S., Norway, Japan.

---

1. Excluding Faeroe Islands and Greenland.

Geography. Smallest of the Scandinavian countries (half the size of Maine), Denmark occupies the Jutland peninsula, which extends north from Germany between the tips of Norway and Sweden. To the west is the North Sea and to the east the Baltic.

The country also consists of several Baltic islands; the two largest are Sjaelland, the site of Copenhagen, and Fyn. The narrow waters off the north coast are called the Skagerrak and those off the east, the Kattegat.

Government. Denmark has been a constitutional monarchy since 1849. Legislative power is held jointly by the Sovereign and parliament. The Constitution of 1953 provides for a unicameral parliament called the Folketing, consisting of 179 popularly elected members who serve for four years. The Cabinet is presided over by the Sovereign, who appoints the Prime Minister.

The Sovereign, Queen Margrethe II, was born April 16, 1940, and became Queen—the first in Denmark's history—Jan. 15, 1972, the day after her father, King Frederik IX, died at 72 in the 25th year of his reign. Margrethe was the eldest of his three daughters (by Princess Ingrid of Sweden). The nation's Constitution was amended in 1953 to permit her to succeed her father in the absence of a male heir to the throne. (Denmark was ruled six centuries ago by Margrethe I, but she was never crowned Queen since there was no female right of succession.)

History. Denmark emerged with establishment of the Norwegian dynasty of the Ynglinger in Jutland at the end of the 8th century. Danish mariners played a major role in the raids of the Vikings, or Norsemen, on Western Europe and particularly England. The country was Christianized by St. Ansgar and Harald Blaatand (Bluetooth)—the first Christian king—in the 10th century. Harald's son, Sweyn, conquered England in 1013. His son, Canute the Great, who reigned from 1014 to 1035, united Denmark, England, and Norway under his rule; the southern tip of Sweden was part of Denmark until the 17th century. On Canute's death, civil war tore the country until Waldemar I (1157-82) re-established Danish hegemony over the north.

In 1282, the nobles won the Great Charter, and Eric V was forced to share power with parliament and a Council of Nobles. Waldemar IV (1340-75) restored Danish power, checked only by the Hanseatic League of north German cities allied with ports from Holland to Poland. His daughter, Margrethe, in 1397 united under her rule Denmark, Norway, and Sweden. But Sweden later achieved autonomy and in 1523, under Gustavus I, independence.

Denmark supported Napoleon, for which it was punished at the Congress of Vienna in 1815 by the loss of Norway to Sweden. In 1864, Bismarck, together with the Austrians, made war on the little country as an initial step in the unification of Germany. Denmark was neutral in World War I.

In 1940, Denmark was invaded by the Nazis. King Christian X reluctantly cautioned his countrymen to accept the occupation, but there was widespread resistance against the Nazis. In 1944, Iceland declared its independence from Denmark, ending a union that had existed since 1380.

Liberated by British troops in May 1945, the country staged a fast recovery in both agriculture and manufacturing and was a leader in liberalizing trade. It joined the United Nations in 1945 and NATO in 1949.

The Social Democrats largely ran Denmark after the war but were ousted in 1973 in an election dominated by protests against high taxes.

Disputes over economic policy led to elections in 1981 that led to Poul Schlüter coming to power in early 1982. Further disputes over his pro-NATO posture led to elections in May, 1988 that marginally confirmed his position. A dispute over tax reform led the calling of an election in December 1990, after which a Conservative-Liberal coalition government was formed, though it controlled only 61 of the 179 seats in parliament.

Outlying Territories of Denmark

FAEROE ISLANDS

Status: Autonomous part of Denmark
Lagmand (President): Jogran Sundstein (1989)
Area: 540 sq mi. (1,399 sq km)
Population (1989): 47,283 (average annual growth rate: .9%); density per square mile: 87
Capital (est. 1982): Thorshavn, 12,750
Monetary unit: Faeroese krone
Literacy rate: 99%
Economic summary: Gross domestic product (1989 est.): $662 million, per capita $14,000; real growth rate 3%. Arable land: 2%; principal agricultural products: sheep, vegetables. Labor force: 17,585, largely engaged in fishing manufacturing, transportation and commerce. Major industrial products: fish, ships, handicrafts. Exports: fish and fish products. Imports: machinery and transport equipment, foodstuffs, petroleum and petroleum products. Major trading partners: Denmark, U.S., U.K., Germany, Canada, France, Japan.

This group of 18 islands, lying in the North Atlantic about 200 miles (322 km) northwest of the Shetland Islands, joined Denmark in 1386 and has since been part of the Danish kingdom. The islands were occupied by British troops during World War II, after the German occupation of Denmark.

The Faeroes have home rule under a bill enacted in 1948; they also have two representatives in the Danish Folketing.

GREENLAND

Status: Autonomous part of Denmark
Premier: Lars Emil Johansen (1991)
Area: 840,000 sq mi. (incl. 708,069 sq mi. covered by ice-cap) (2,175,600 sq km)
Population (1989): 55,415 (growth rate: 12%)
Capital (est. 1982): Godthaab, 10,000
Monetary unit: Krone
Literacy rate: 99%
Economic summary: Gross national product (1988): $500 million, per capita $9,000; real growth rate 5%. Arable land: 0%; principal agricultural products: hay, sheep, garden produce. Labor force: 22,800, largely engaged in fishing, hunting, sheep breeding. Major industries: fish processing, lead and zinc processing, handicrafts. Natural resources: metals, cryolite, iron ore, coal, uranium, fish. Exports: fish and fish products, metalic ores and concentrates. Imports: petroleum and petroleum products, machinery and transport equipment, foodstuffs. Major trading partners: Denmark, U.S., Germany, Sweden, Japan, Norway.

Greenland, the world's largest island, was colonized in 985–86 by Eric the Red. Danish sovereignty, which covered only the west coast, was extended over the whole island in 1917. In 1941 the U.S. signed an agreement with the Danish minister in Washington, placing it under U.S. protection during World War II but maintaining Danish sovereignty. A definitive agreement for the joint defense of Greenland within the framework of NATO was signed in 1951. A large U.S. air base at Thule in the far north was completed in 1953.

Under 1953 amendments to the Danish Constitution, Greenland became part of Denmark, with two representatives in the Danish Folketing. On May 1, 1979, Greenland gained home rule, with its own local parliament (Landsting), replacing the Greenland Provincial Council.

In February 1982, Greenlanders voted to withdraw from the European Community, which they had joined as part of Denmark in 1973. Danish Premier Anker Jørgensen said he would support the request, but with reluctance.

An election in early March 1991 gave the Siumut Party 11 of the 27 available seats. The early election was called after a scandal allegedly involving overspending by government officials on entertainment.

DJIBOUTI

Republic of Djibouti
President: Hassan Gouled Aptidon (1977)
Prime Minister: Barkat Gourad Hamadou (1978)
Area: 8,490 sq mi. (22,000 sq km)
Population (est. mid-1991): 400,000 (average annual rate of natural increase: 2.9%); birth rate: 46/1000; infant mortality rate: 117/1000; density per square mile: 50
Capital (est. 1980): Djibouti, 200,000
Monetary unit: Djibouti franc
Languages: Arabic, French, Afar, Somali
Religions: Muslim, 94%; Christian, 6%
National name: Jumhouriyya Djibouti
Literacy rate: 20%
Economic summary: Gross domestic product (1986): $333 million, $1,070 per capita; real growth rate –.7%. Arable land: 0%; principal agricultural products: goats, sheep, camels. Labor force: NA. Industries: small-scale enterprises such as dairy products and mineral-

water bottling. Exports: hides, skins, coffee (in transit from Ethiopia). Imports: petroleum, transport equipment, foodstuffs. Major trading partners: Middle East, Africa, Europe, Bahrain, Asia.

Geography. Djibouti lies in northeastern Africa on the Gulf of Aden at the southern entrance to the Red Sea. It borders on Ethiopia and Somalia. The country, the size of Massachusetts, is mainly a stony desert, with scattered plateaus and highlands.

Government. On May 8, 1977, the population of the French Territory of the Afars and Issas voted by more than 98% for independence. Voters also approved a 65-member interim Constituent Assembly. France transferred sovereignty to the new nation of Djibouti on June 27. Later in the year it became a member of the Organization of African Unity and the Arab League. The People's Progress Assembly is the only legal political party.

History. The territory that is now Djibouti was acquired by France between 1843 and 1886 by treaties with the Somali sultans. Small, arid, and sparsely populated, Djibouti is important chiefly because of the capital city's port, the terminal of the Djibouti-Addis Ababa railway that carries 60% of Ethiopia's foreign trade.

Originally known as French Somaliland, the colony voted in 1958 and 1967 to remain under French rule. It was renamed the Territory of the Afars and Issas in 1967 and took the name of its capital city on attaining independence.

The two principal opposition groups in exile banded to form a common front in early 1990. The divisive state of affairs in Somalia caused nervousness in Djibouti lest a large wave of refugees flee into the country.

DOMINICA

Commonwealth of Dominica
President: Sir Clarence Seignoret (1985)
Prime Minister: Mary Eugenia Charles (1980)
Area: 290 sq mi. (751 sq km)
Population (1990): 87,800 (average annual rate of natural increase: 2.9%); birth rate: 26/1000; infant mortality rate: 13/1000; density per square mile: 297
Capital and largest city (est. 1981): Roseau, 20,000
Monetary unit: East Caribbean dollar
Languages: English and French patois
Religions: Roman Catholic, Anglican, Methodist
Member of Commonwealth of Nations
Literacy rate: 80% (est.)
Economic summary: Gross domestic product (1988 est.): $137 million, per capita $1,408; real growth rate 5.6%. Arable land: 9%. Principal products: bananas, citrus fruits, coconuts, cocoa. Labor force: 25,000; 32% in industry and commerce (1984). Major industries: agricultural processing; tourism. Exports: bananas, coconuts, grapefruit, soap, galvanized sheets. Imports: food, oils and fats, chemicals, fuels and lubricants. Major trading partners: U.K., Caribbean countries, U.S.

Geography. Dominica is an island of the Lesser Antilles in the Caribbean south of Guadeloupe and north of Martinique.

Government. Dominica is a republic, with a president elected by the House of Assembly as head of state and a prime minister appointed by the president on the advice of the Assembly. The Freedom Party (11 of 21 seats in the Assembly) is led by Prime Minister Mary Eugenia Charles. The Opposition United Workers Party holds six seats and the United Dominica Labor Party holds four seats.

History. Discovered by Columbus in 1493, Dominica was claimed by Britain and France until 1815, when Britain asserted sovereignty. Dominica, along with other Windward Isles, became a self-governing member of the West Indies Associated States in free association with Britain in 1967.

Dissatisfaction over the slow pace of reconstruction after Hurricane David struck the island in September 1979 brought a landslide victory for the Freedom Party in July 1980. The vote gave the prime ministership to Mary Eugenia Charles, a strong advocate of free enterprise. The Freedom Party won again in 1985 elections, giving Miss Charles a second five-year term as prime minister. She and her party won a third term in elections on May 28, 1990, though with a greatly reduced mandate. The Freedom party retained only 11 seats in the Assembly.

DOMINICAN REPUBLIC

President: Joaquin Balaguer (1986)
Area: 18,704 sq mi. (48,442 sq km)
Population (est. mid-1991): 7,300,000 (average annual rate of natural increase: 2.3%); birth rate: 30/1000; infant mortality rate: 61/1000; density per square mile: 389
Capital: Santo Domingo
Largest cities (est. 1983): Santo Domingo, 1,410,000; Santiago de los Caballeros, 285,000
Monetary unit: Peso
Language: Spanish
Religion: 95% Roman Catholic
National name: República Dominicana
Literacy rate: 74%
Economic summary: Gross domestic product (1988): $5.1 billion, $790 per capita, 0.5% real growth rate. Arable land: 23%. Principal agricultural products: sugar cane, coffee, cocoa, tobacco. Labor force (1986): 2,300,000–2,600,000; 18% in industry. Major industries: tourism, sugar processing, ferronickel and gold mining, textiles, cement, tobacco. Natural resources: nickel, bauxite, gold, silver. Exports: sugar, coffee, cocoa, gold, ferronickel. Imports: foodstuffs, petroleum, cotton and fabrics, chemicals, and pharmaceuticals. Major trading partners: U.S., including Puerto Rico.

Geography. The Dominican Republic in the West Indies, occupies the eastern two thirds of the island of Hispaniola, which it shares with Haiti. Its area equals that of Vermont and New Hampshire combined.

Crossed from northwest to southeast by a mountain range with elevations exceeding 10,000 feet (3,048 m), the country has fertile, well-watered land in the north and east, where nearly two thirds of the population lives. The southwest part is arid and has poor soil, except around Santo Domingo.

Government. The president is elected by direct vote every four years. Legislative powers rest with a Senate and a Chamber of Deputies, both elected by direct vote, also for four years. All citizens must vote when they reach 18 years of age, or even earlier if they are married.

History. The Dominican Republic was discovered by Columbus in 1492. He named it La Española, and his son, Diego, was its first viceroy. The capital, Santo Domingo, founded in 1496, is the oldest European settlement in the Western Hemisphere. Spain ceded the colony to France in 1795, and Haitian blacks under Toussaint L'Ouverture conquered it in 1801.

In 1808 the people revolted and the next year captured Santo Domingo, setting up the first republic. Spain regained title to the colony in 1814. In 1821 the people overthrew Spanish rule, but in 1822 they were reconquered by the Haitians. They revolted again in 1844, threw out the Haitians, and established the Dominican Republic, headed by Pedro Santana. Uprisings and Haitian attacks led Santana to make the country a province of Spain from 1861 to 1865. The U.S. Senate refused to ratify a treaty of annexation. Disorder continued until the dictatorship of Ulíses Heureaux; in 1916, when disorder broke out again, the U.S. sent in a contingent of marines, who remained until 1934.

A sergeant in the Dominican army trained by the marines, Rafaél Leonides Trujillo Molina, overthrew Horacio Vásquez in 1930 and established a dictatorship that lasted until his assassination 31 years later.

A new Constitution was adopted in 1962, and the first free elections since 1924 put Juan Bosch, a leftist leader, in office. However, a right-wing military coup replaced Bosch with a civilian triumvirate.

Leftists rebelled April 24, 1965, and President Lyndon Johnson sent in marines and troops. After an OAS ceasefire request May 6, a compromise installed Hector Garcia-Godoy as provisional president. Joaquin Balaguer won in free elections in 1966 against Bosch, and a peacekeeping force of 9,000 U.S. troops and 2,000 from other countries withdrew. Balaguer restored political and economic stability.

In 1978, the army suspended the counting of ballots when Balaguer trailed in a fourth-term bid. After a warning from President Jimmy Carter, however, Balaguer accepted the victory of Antonio Guzmán of the opposition Dominican Revolutionary Party.

Salvador Jorge Blanco of the Dominican Revolutionary Party was elected President on May 16, 1982, defeating Balaguer and Bosch. Austerity measures imposed by the International Monetary Fund, including sharply higher prices for food and gasoline, provoked rioting in the spring of 1984 that left more than 50 dead.

Saying he feared they would provoke "some kind of revolution," Blanco dragged his feet about putting into effect further IMF demands for higher prices and taxes and devaluation of the peso, and came within weeks of defaulting on several big loans.

Balaguer was elected President in May 1986 and aimed economic policy at diversifying the economy. On May 16, 1990 Balaguer won a sixth presidential term in elections following a non-violent campaign. In its wake Juan Bosch resigned as head of his Dominican Liberation Party.

ECUADOR

Republic of Ecuador
President: Rodrigo Borja Cevallos (1988)
Area: 109,484 sq mi. (270,670 sq km)
Population (est. mid-1991): 10,800,000 (average annual rate of natural increase: 2.4%); birth rate: 31/1000; infant mortality rate: 58/1000; density per square mile: 95
Capital: Quito
Largest cities (est. 1987): Guayaquil, 1,572,615; Quito, 1,137,705; Cuenca, 201,490

Monetary unit: Sucre
Languages: Spanish, Quéchua
Religion: Roman Catholic, 95%
National name: República del Ecuador
Literacy rate: 85%
Economic summary: Gross domestic product (1989). $9.8 billion, $935 per capita; .5% real growth rate. Arable land: 6%; principal agricultural products: bananas, cocoa, coffee, sugar cane, manioc, plantains, potatoes, rice. Labor force (1982): 2,800,000; 21% in manufacturing; major industries: food processing, textiles, chemicals, fishing, timber, petroleum. Exports: petroleum, coffee, bananas, cocoa products, shrimp, fish products. Imports: transport equipment, vehicles, machinery, chemicals, petroleum. Major trading partners: U.S., Latin America, EEC, Caribbean, Japan.

Geography. Ecuador, equal in area to Nevada, is in the northwest part of South America fronting on the Pacific. To the north is Colombia and to the east and south is Peru. Two high and parallel ranges of the Andes, traversing the country from north to south, are topped by tall volcanic peaks. The highest is Chimborazo at 20,577 feet (6,272 m).

The Galápagos Islands (or Colón Archipelago) (3,029 sq mi.; 7,845 sq km) in the Pacific Ocean about 600 miles (966 km) west of the South American mainland, became part of Ecuador in 1832.

Government. A 1978 Constitution returned Ecuador to civilian government after eight years of military rule. The President is elected to a term of four years and a House of Representatives of 71 members is popularly elected for the same period.

History. The tribes in the northern highlands of Ecuador formed the Kingdom of Quito around A.D. 1000. It was absorbed, by conquest and marriage, into the Inca Empire. Pizarro conquered the land in 1532, and through the 17th century a thriving colony was built by exploitation of the Indians. The first revolt against Spain occurred in 1809. Ecuador then joined Venezuela, Colombia, and Panama in a confederacy known as Greater Colombia.

On the collapse of this union in 1830, Ecuador became independent. Subsequent history was one of revolts and dictatorships; it had 48 presidents during the first 131 years of the republic. Conservatives ruled until the Revolution of 1895 ushered in nearly a half century of Radical Liberal rule, during which the church was disestablished and freedom of worship, speech, and press was introduced.

A three-man military junta which had taken power in a 1976 coup, agreed to a free presidential election on July 16, 1978. Jaime Roldós Aguilera won the runoff on April 29, 1979.

The 40-year-old President died in the crash of a small plane May 24, 1981. Vice President Osvaldo Hurtado Larrea became President. León Febres Cordero, was installed President in August 1984. Combined opposition parties won a majority in the 71-member Congress large enough to block significant action, a majority increased in the June 1986 elections.

Problems with the military plagued Febres in 1986–87, and he faced two rebellions.

In 1988, Rodrigo Borja was elected President. He was also able to form a coalition in the House, confirming a leftward shift in the government and promising smoother executive-legislative relations.

Ecuador has been trying to keep out of the drug trafficking trade, which has plagued its neighbors.

EGYPT

Arab Republic of Egypt
President: Hosni Mubarak (1981)
Premier: Dr. Atef Sedky (1986)
Area: 386,900 sq. mi. (1,002,000 sq km)
Population (est. mid-1991): 54,500,000 (average annual rate of natural increase: 2.9%); birth rate: 38/1000; infant mortality rate: 73/1000; density per square mile: 141
Capital: Cairo
Largest cities (est. 1987): Cairo, 12,560,000; (1986 est.): Alexandria, 2,893,000; Giza, 1,670,800; Shubra el Khema, 533,300; El Mahalla el Kubra, 385,300
Monetary unit: Egyptian pound
Language: Arabic
Religions: Islam, 94%; Christian (mostly Coptic), 6%
Literacy rate: 45%
Economic summary: Gross domestic product (1989 est.): $38.3 billion; $700 per capita; 1.0% real growth rate. Arable land: 3%. Principal agricultural products: cotton, wheat, rice, corn, beans. Labor force: 15,000,000; 20% in privately owned services and manufacturing. Major industries: textiles, food processing, tourism, chemicals, petroleum, construction, cement, metals. Natural resources: crude oil, natural gas, iron ore, phosphates, manganese, limestone, gypsum, talc, asbestos, lead, zinc. Exports: cotton, petroleum, yarn, textiles. Imports: foodstuffs, machinery, fertilizers, woods. Major trading partners: U.S., Western Europe, Japan, Eastern Europe.

Geography. Egypt, at the northeast corner of Africa on the Mediterranean Sea, is bordered on the west by Libya, on the south by the Sudan, and on the east by the Red Sea and Israel. It is nearly one and one half times the size of Texas.

The historic Nile flows through the eastern third of the country. On either side of the Nile valley are desert plateaus, spotted with oases. In the north, toward the Mediterranean, plateaus are low, while south of Cairo they rise to a maximum of 1,015 feet (309 m) above sea level. At the head of the Red Sea is the Sinai Peninsula, between the Suez Canal and Israel.

Navigable throughout its course in Egypt, the Nile is used largely as a means of cheap transport for heavy goods. The principal port is Alexandria.

The Nile delta starts 100 miles (161 km) south of the Mediterranean and fans out to a sea front of 155 miles between the cities of Alexandria and Port Said. From Cairo north, the Nile branches into many streams, the principal ones being the Damietta and the Rosetta.

Except for a narrow belt along the Mediterranean, Egypt lies in an almost rainless area, in which high daytime temperatures fall quickly at night.

Government. Executive power is held by the President, who is elected every six years and can appoint one or more Vice Presidents.

The National Democratic Party, led by President Hosni Mubarak, is the dominant political party. Elections on Nov. 29, 1990 confirmed its huge majority. There is also one opposition party and some independents. The major opposition parties boycotted the elections.

History. Egyptian history dates back to about 4000 B.C., when the kingdoms of upper and lower Egypt, already highly civilized, were united. Egypt's "Golden Age" coincided with the 18th and 19th dynasties (16th to 13th centuries B.C.), during which the empire was established. Persia conquered Egypt in 525 B.C.; Alexander the Great subdued it in 332 B.C.; and then the dynasty of the Ptolemies ruled the land until 30 B.C., when Cleopatra, last of the line, committed suicide and Egypt became a Roman province. From 641 to 1517 the Arab caliphs ruled Egypt, and then the Turks took it for their Ottoman Empire.

Napoleon's armies occupied the country from 1798 to 1801. In 1805, Mohammed Ali, leader of a band of Albanian soldiers, became Pasha of Egypt. After completion of the Suez Canal in 1869, the French and British took increasing interest in Egypt.

British troops occupied Egypt in 1882, and British resident agents became its actual administrators, though it remained under nominal Turkish sovereignty. In 1914, this fiction was ended, and Egypt became a protectorate of Britain.

Egyptian nationalism forced Britain to declare Egypt an independent, sovereign state on Feb. 28, 1922, although the British reserved rights for the protection of the Suez Canal and the defense of Egypt. In 1936, by an Anglo-Egyptian treaty of alliance, all British troops and officials were to be withdrawn, except from the Suez Canal Zone. When World War II started, Egypt remained neutral. British imperial troops finally ended the Nazi threat to Suez in 1942 in the battle of El Alamein, west of Alexandria.

In 1951, Egypt abrogated the 1936 treaty and the 1899 Anglo-Egyptian condominium of the Sudan (*See* Sudan). Rioting and attacks on British troops in the Suez Canal Zone followed, reaching a climax in January 1952. The army, led by Gen. Mohammed Naguib, seized power on July 23, 1952. Three days later, King Farouk abdicated in favor of his infant son. The monarchy was abolished and a republic proclaimed on June 18, 1953, with Naguib holding the posts of Provisional President and Premier. He relinquished the latter in 1954 to Gamal Abdel Nasser, leader of the ruling military junta. Naguib was deposed seven months later and Nasser confirmed as President in a referendum on June 23, 1956.

Nasser's policies embroiled his country in continual conflict. In 1956, the U.S. and Britain withdrew their pledges of financial aid for the building of the Aswan High Dam. In reply, Nasser nationalized the Suez Canal and expelled British oil and embassy officials. Israel, barred from the Canal and exasperated by terrorist raids, invaded the Gaza Strip and the Sinai Peninsula. Britain and France, after demanding Egyptian evacuation of the Canal Zone, attacked Egypt on Oct. 31, 1956. Worldwide pressure forced Britain, France, and Israel to halt the hostilities. A U.N. emergency force occupied the Canal Zone, and all troops were evacuated in the spring of 1957.

On Feb. 1, 1958, Egypt and Syria formed the United Arab Republic, which was joined by Yemen in an association known as the United Arab States. However, Syria withdrew from the United Arab Republic in 1961 and Egypt dissolved its ties with Yemen in the United Arab States.

On June 5, 1967, Israel invaded the Sinai Peninsula, the East Bank of the Jordan River, and the zone around the Gulf of Aqaba. A U.N. ceasefire on June 10 saved the Arabs from complete rout.

Nasser declared the 1967 cease-fire void along the Canal in April 1969 and began a war of attrition. The U.S. peace plan of June 19, 1970, resulted in Egypt's agreement to reinstate the cease-fire for at least three months, (from August) and to accept Israel's existence within "recognized and secure" frontiers that might emerge from U.N.-mediated talks. In return, Israel accepted the principle of withdrawing from occupied territories.

Then, on Sept. 28, 1970, Nasser died, at 52, of a heart attack. The new President was Anwar el-Sadat, an associate of Nasser and a former newspaper editor.

The Aswan High Dam, whose financing by the U.S.S.R. was its first step into Egypt, was completed and dedicated in January 1971.

In July 1972, Sadat ordered the expulsion of Soviet "advisors and experts" from Egypt because the Russians had not provided the sophisticated weapons he felt were needed to retake territory lost to Israel in 1967.

The fourth Arab-Israeli war broke out Oct. 6, 1973, while Israelis were commemorating Yom Kippur, the Jewish high holy day. Egypt swept deep into the Sinai, while Syria strove to throw Israel off the Golan Heights.

A U.N.-sponsored truce was accepted on October 22. In January 1974, both sides agreed to a settlement negotiated by U.S. Secretary of State Henry A. Kissinger that gave Egypt a narrow strip along the entire Sinai bank of the Suez Canal. In June, President Nixon made the first visit by a U.S. President to Egypt and full diplomatic relations were established. The Suez Canal was cleared and reopened on June 5, 1975.

Kissinger pursued "shuttle diplomacy" between Cairo and Jerusalem to extend areas of agreement. Israel yielded on three points—the possession of the Mitla and Giddi passes in the Sinai and the Abu Rudeis oil field in the peninsula—and both sides committed themselves to annual renewal of the U.N. peacekeeping force in the Sinai.

In the most audacious act of his career, Sadat flew to Jerusalem at the invitation of Prime Minister Menachem Begin and pleaded before Israel's Knesset on Nov. 20, 1977, for a permanent peace settlement. The Arab world reacted with fury—only Morocco, Tunisia, Sudan, and Oman approved.

Egypt and Israel signed a formal peace treaty on March 26, 1979. The pact ended 30 years of war and established diplomatic and commercial relations.

Egyptian and Israeli officials met in the Sinai desert on April 26, 1979, to implement the peace treaty calling for the phased withdrawal of occupation forces from the peninsula. By mid-1980, two thirds of the Sinai was transferred, but progress here was not matched—the negotiation of Arab autonomy in the Gaza Strip and the West Bank.

Sadat halted further talks in August 1980 because of continued Israeli settlement of the West Bank. On October 6 1981, Sadat was assassinated by extremist Muslim soldiers at a parade in Cairo. Vice President Hosni Mubarak, a former Air Force chief of staff, was confirmed by the parliament as president the next day.

Although feared unrest in Egypt did not occur in the wake of the assassination, and Israel completed the return of the Sinai to Egyptian control on April 25, 1982, Mubarak was unable to revive the autonomy talks. Israel's invasion of Lebanon in June imposed a new strain on him, and brought a marked cooling in Egyptian-Israeli relations, but not a disavowal of the peace treaty.

During 1985, pressures by Moslem fundamentalists to implement Islamic law in Egypt increased. In response, the government began putting all mosques under control of the minister for religious endowments.

While President Mubarak's stand during the Persian Gulf war won wide praise in the West, domestically his position proved far less popular. President Bush proposed writing-off Egypt's large debt to the U.S., but the Congress balked at such a large forgiveness.

Suez Canal. The Suez Canal, in Egyptian territory between the Arabian Desert and the Sinai Peninsula, is an artificial waterway about 100 miles (161 km) long between Port Said on the Mediterranean and Suez on the Red Sea. Construction work, directed by the French engineer Ferdinand de Lesseps, was begun April 25, 1859, and the Canal was opened Nov. 17, 1869. The cost was 432,807,882 francs. The concession was held by an Egyptian joint stock company, *Compagnie Universelle du Canal Maritime de Suez,* in which the British government held 353,504 out of a total of 800,000 shares. The concession was to expire Nov. 17, 1968, but the company was nationalized July 26, 1956, by unilateral action of the Egyptian government.

The Canal was closed in June 1967 after the Arab-Israeli conflict. With the help of the U.S. Navy, work was begun on clearing the Canal in 1974, after the cease-fire ending the Arab-Israeli war. It was reopened to traffic June 5, 1975.

EL SALVADOR

Republic of El Salvador
President: Alfredo Cristiani (1989)
Area: 8,260 sq mi. (21,393 sq km)
Population (est. mid-1991): 5,400,000 (average annual rate of natural increase: 2.7%); birth rate: 35/100; infant mortality rate: 55/1000; density per square mile: 656
Capital: San Salvador
Largest cities (est. 1985): San Salvador, 459,902; Santa Ana, 137,879; Mejicanos, 91,465; San Miguel, 88,520
Monetary unit: Colón
Language: Spanish
Religion: Roman Catholic
National name: República de El Salvador
Literacy rate: 65%
Economic summary: Gross domestic product (1989 est.): $5.5 billion; $1,020 per capita; 0.9% real growth rate. Arable land: 27%. Principal products: coffee, cotton, corn, sugar, rice, sorghum. Labor force: 1,700,000; 15% in manufacturing. Major products: processed foods, clothing and textiles, petroleum products. Natural resources: hydro- and geothermal power, crude oil. Exports: coffee, cotton, sugar, shrimp. Imports: machinery, construction materials, foodstuffs, fertilizer. Major trading partners: U.S., Guatemala, Japan, Germany, Mexico, Venezuela.

Geography. Situated on the Pacific coast of Central America, El Salvador has Guatemala to the west and Honduras to the north and east. It is the smallest of the Central American countries, its area equal to that of Massachusetts, and the only one without an Atlantic coastline.

Most of the country is a fertile volcanic plateau about 2,000 feet (607 m) high. There are some active volcanoes and many scenic crater lakes.

Government. A new Constitution enacted in 1983 vests executive power in a President elected for a nonrenewable, five-year term, and legislative power in a 60-member National Assembly elected by universal suffrage and proportional representation. Judicial power is vested in a Supreme Court, composed of a President and eleven magistrates elected by the Assembly, and subordinate courts.

History. Pedro de Alvarado, a lieutenant of Cortés, conquered El Salvador in 1525. El Salvador, with the other countries of Central America, declared its independence from Spain on Sept. 15, 1821, and was part of a federation of Central American states until that union was dissolved in 1838. Its independent career for decades thereafter was marked by numerous revolutions and wars against other Central American republics.

On Oct. 15, 1979, a junta deposed the President, Gen. Carlos Humberto Romero, seeking to halt increasingly violent clashes between leftist and rightist forces.

On Dec. 4, 1980, three American nuns and an American lay worker were killed in an ambush near San Salvador, causing the Carter Administration to suspend all aid pending an investigation. The naming of José Napoleón Duarte, a moderate civilian, as head of the governing junta brought a resumption of U.S. aid.

Defying guerrilla threats, voters on March 28, 1982, elected a rightist majority to a constituent assembly that dismissed Duarte and replaced him with a centrist physician, Dr. Alvaro Alfredo Magaña. The rightist majority repealed the laws permitting expropriation of land, and critics charged that the land-reform program begun under Duarte was dead.

In an election closely monitored by American and other foreign observers, Duarte was elected President in May 1984.

Duarte's Christian Democratic Party scored an unexpected electoral triumph in national legislative and municipal elections held in March 1985, a winning majority in the new National Assembly. The rightist parties that had been dominant in the previous Constituent Assembly demanded that the vote be nullified, but the army high command rejected their assertion the voting had been fraudulent.

At the same time, U.S. officials said that while the rebels still were far from being defeated, there had been marked improvement in the effectiveness of government troops in the civil war against antigovernment guerrillas that has been waged mainly in the countryside. Talks with the rebels broke down in September 1986. Duarte's inability to find solutions led to the rightwing ARENA party controlling half the seats in the National Assembly, in the elections of March, 1988. The decisive victory of Alfredo Christiani, the ARENA candidate for president, gives the right-wing party effective control of the country, given their political control of most of the municipalities.

U.N.-mediated ceasefire talks in Mexico between the government and rebel forces ended in June 1991 without an agreement, although progress was reportedly made. The 11-year-old civil war has claimed an estimated 75,000 lives.

EQUATORIAL GUINEA

Republic of Equatorial Guinea
President: Col. Teodoro Obiang Nguema Mbasogo (1979)
Prime Minister: Capt. Cristino Seriche Bioko
Area: 10,830 sq mi. (28,051 sq km)
Population (mid-1991): 400,000 (average annual rate of natural increase: 2.6%); birth rate: 43/1000; infant mortality rate: 118/1000; density per square mile: 35
Capital and largest city (est. 1983): Malabo, 37,500
Monetary unit: CFA Franc
Languages: Spanish, pidgin English, Fang, Bubi, Ibo
Religions: Roman Catholic, Protestant, traditional

National name: Républica de Guinea Ecuatorial
Literacy rate: 40%
Economic summary: Gross national product (1987): $103 million, $293 per capita. Arable land: 8%. Principal products: cocoa, wood, coffee; rice, yams. Natural resource: wood, crude oil. Exports: cocoa, wood, coffee. Imports: petroleum, foodstuffs, textiles, machinery. Major trading partners: Spain, Italy, France, the Netherlands.

Geography. Equatorial Guinea, formerly Spanish Guinea, consists of Rio Muni (10,045 sq mi.; 26,117 sq km), on the western coast of Africa, and several islands in the Gulf of Guinea, the largest of which is Bioko (formerly Fernando Po) (785 sq mi.; 2,033 sq km). The other islands are Annobón, Corisco, Elobey Grande, and Elobey Chico. The total area is twice that of Connecticut.

Government. The Constitution of 1973 was suspended after a coup on Aug. 3, 1979. A Supreme Military Council, headed by the president, exercises all power. Political parties were banned until Aug. 1987.

History. Fernando Po and Annobón came under Spanish control in 1778. From 1827 to 1844, with Spanish consent, Britain administered Fernando Po, but in the latter year Spain reclaimed the island. Río Muni was given to Spain in 1885 by the Treaty of Berlin.

Negotiations with Spain led to independence on Oct. 12, 1968.

In 1969, anti-Spanish incidents in Río Muni, including the tearing down of a Spanish flag by national troops, caused 5,000 Spanish residents to flee for their safety, and diplomatic relations between the two nations became strained. A month later, President Masie Nguema Biyogo Negue Ndong charged that a coup had been attempted against him. He seized dictatorial powers and arrested 80 opposition politicians and even several of his Cabinet ministers and the secretary of the National Assembly.

A coup on Aug. 3, 1979, deposed Masie, and a junta led by Lieut. Col. Teodoro Obiang Nguema Mbasogo took over the government. Obiang expelled Soviet technicians and reinstated cooperation with Spain.

In an effort to rehabilitate the country's cocoa production the World Bank devised and was putting into effect a new plan. Spain agreed to provide major economic assistance for the period 1990–93 including help in completing a national television system.

ESTONIA

See page 972

ETHIOPIA

People's Democratic Republic of Ethiopia
President: Meles Zenawi (1991)
Prime Minister: Hailu Yemenu (1989)
Area: 472,432 sq mi. (1,223,600 sq km)
Population (est. mid-1991): 53,200,000 (average annual rate of natural increase: 2.9%); birth rate: 49/1000; infant mortality rate: 130/1000; density per square mile: 113
Capital: Addis Ababa
Largest cities (est. 1984): Addis Ababa, 1,423,111; Asmara, 275,385
Monetary unit: Birr

Languages: Amharic (official), Galligna, Tigrigna
Religions: Ethiopian Orthodox, 35–40%; Islam, 40–45%; animist, 15-20%; other, 5%
Literacy rate: 55.2%
Economic summary: Gross domestic product (FY89 est.): $6.6 billion; $130 per capita; 4.5% real growth rate. Arable land: 12%. Principal products: coffee, barley, wheat, corn, sugar cane, cotton, oilseeds, livestock. Major industrial products: cement, textiles, processed foods, refined oil. Natural resources: potash, gold, platinum, copper. Exports: coffee, hides and skins, oilseeds. Imports: petroleum, foodstuffs. Major trading partners: U.S.S.R., U.S., Germany, Italy, Japan, Djibouti, South Yemen.

Geography. Ethiopia is in east central Africa, bordered on the west by the Sudan, the east by Somalia and Djibouti, the south by Kenya, and the north by the Red Sea. It is nearly three times the size of California.

Over its main plateau land, Ethiopia has several high mountains, the highest of which is Ras Dashan at 15,158 feet (4,620 m). The Blue Nile, or Abbai, rises in the northwest and flows in a great semicircle east, south, and northwest before entering the Sudan. Its chief reservoir, Lake Tana, lies in the northwestern part of the plateau.

Government. On Feb. 22, 1987, a new constitution came into effect. It established a Communist civilian government with a national assembly. A provisional government was formed in Addis Adaba in early July 1991. The leader of the separatist organization in control of Eritrea attended as an observer.

History. Black Africa's oldest state, Ethiopia can trace 2,000 years of recorded history. Its now deposed royal line claimed descent from King Menelik I, traditionally believed to have been the son of the Queen of Sheba and King Solomon. The present nation is a consolidation of smaller kingdoms that owed feudal allegiance to the Ethiopian Emperor.

Hamitic peoples migrated to Ethiopia from Asia Minor in prehistoric times. Semitic traders from Arabia penetrated the region in the 7th century B.C. Its Red Sea ports were important to the Roman and Byzantine Empires. Coptic Christianity came to the country in A.D. 341, and a variant of that communion became Ethiopia's state religion.

Ancient Ethiopia reached its peak in the 5th century, but was isolated by the rise of Islam and weakened by feudal wars. Modern Ethiopia emerged under Emperor Menelik II, who established its independence by routing an Italian invasion in 1896. He expanded Ethiopia by conquest.

Disorders that followed Menelik's death brought his daughter to the throne in 1917, with his cousin, Tafari Makonnen, as Regent, heir presumptive, and strongman. When the Empress died in 1930, Tafari was crowned Emperor Haile Selassie I.

As Regent, Haile Selassie outlawed slavery. As Emperor, he worked for centralization of his diffuse realm, in which 70 languages are spoken, and for moderate reform. In 1931, he granted a Constitution, revised in 1955, that created a parliament with an appointed Senate and an elected Chamber of Deputies, and a system of courts. But basic power remained with the Emperor.

Bent on colonial empire, fascist Italy invaded Ethiopia on Oct. 3, 1935, forcing Haile Selassie into exile in May 1936. Ethiopia was annexed to Eritrea, then an Italian colony, and Italian Somaliland to form Italian East Africa, losing its independence for the first time in recorded history. In 1941, British troops routed the Italians, and Haile Selassie returned to Addis Ababa.

In August 1974, the Armed Forces Committee nationalized Haile Selassie's palace and estates and directed him not to leave Addis Ababa. On Sept. 12, 1974, he was deposed after nearly 58 years as Regent and Emperor. The 82-year-old "Lion of Judah" was placed under guard. Parliament was dissolved and the Constitution suspended.

On Aug. 27, 1975, Haile Selassie died in a small apartment in his former Addis Ababa palace where he had been treated as a state prisoner. He was 83.

Lt. Col. Mengistu Haile Mariam was named head of state Feb. 2, 1977, to replace Brig. Gen. Teferi Benti, who was killed in a factional fight of the Dirgue after having ruled since 1974. The government was losing its fight to hold Eritrea and in the southeastern region of Ogaden, Somali guerrillas backed by Somali regular forces threatened the ancient city of Harar. In October, the U.S.S.R. announced it would end military aid to Somalia and henceforth back its new ally, Ethiopia. This, together with the intervention of Cuban troops in Ogaden, turned the tide for Mengistu. By March 1978, the badly beaten Somalis had retreated to their homeland. This brought an end to large-scale fighting with Somalia, but border skirmishing continued intermittently.

A Communist regime was formally proclaimed on Sept. 10, 1984, with Mengistu as party leader.

Ethiopia became a Marxist state with forced collectivization and relocation of peasants. A cut-off of Soviet aid led to mass animosity, and a rebel offensive began in February 1991. Mengistu resigned and fled the country in May. A group called the Ethiopian People's Revolutionary Democratic Front seized the capital. Also in May a separatist guerrilla organization, the Eritrean People's Liberation Front, took control of the province of Eritrea. The two groups agreed in early July that Eritrea would have an internationally supervised referendum on independence, though probably not for two years to allow for a measure of stability.

FIJI

Republic of Fiji
President: Ratu Sir Penaia Ganilau (1987)
Prime Minister: Ratu Sir Kamisese Mara (1987)
Area: 7,078 sq mi. (18,333 sq km)
Population (est. mid-1991): 700,000 (average annual rate of natural increase: 2.0%); birth rate: 24/1000 infant mortality rate: 21/1000; density per square mile: 104
Capital (1985): Suva (on Viti Levu), 75,000
Monetary unit: Fiji dollar
Languages: Fijian, Hindustani, English
Religions: Christian, 50%; Hindu, 41%; Islam, 8%
Literacy rate: 80%
Economic summary: Gross domestic product (1989 est.): $1.32 billion; $1,750 per capita; real growth rate 12.5%. Arable land: 8%. Principal products: sugar, copra, rice, ginger. Labor force: 176,000; 60% subsistence agriculture; 40% wage earners. Major industrial products: refined sugar, gold, lumber. Natural resources: timber, fish, gold, copper. Exports: sugar, copra, processed fish, lumber. Imports: foodstuffs, machinery, manufactured goods, fuels, chemicals. Major trading partners: U.K., Australia, Japan, New Zealand, U.S.

Geography. Fiji consists of more than 330 islands in the southwestern Pacific Ocean about 1,960 miles (3,152 km) from Sydney, Australia. The two largest islands are Viti Levu (4,109 sq mi.; 10,642 sq km) and Vanua Levu (2,242 sq mi.; 5,807 sq km). The island of Rotuma (18 sq mi.; 47 sq km), about 400 miles (644 km) to the north, is a province of Fiji. Overall, Fiji is nearly as large as New Jersey.

The largest islands in the group are mountainous and volcanic, with the tallest peak being Mount Victoria (4,341 ft; 1,323 m) on Viti Levu. The islands in the south have dense forests on the windward side and grasslands on the leeward.

Government. Military coup leader Major General Sitiveni Rabuka formerly declared Fiji a republic on Oct. 6, 1987. A civilian interium government was established in December 1987. General elections are expected to be held in July 1992.

History. In 1874, an offer of cession by the Fijian chiefs was accepted, and Fiji was proclaimed a possession and dependency of the British Crown.

During World War II, the archipelago was an important air and naval station on the route from the U.S. and Hawaii to Australia and New Zealand.

Fiji became independent on Oct. 10, 1970. The next year it joined the five-island South Pacific Forum, which intends to become a permanent regional group to promote collective diplomacy of the newly independent members.

In Oct., 1987, then Brig. Gen. Sitiveni Rabuka, the coup leader, declared Fiji a republic and removed it from the British Commonwealth.

Rabuka resigned from the cabinet in 1990, and a new constitution came into effect in July that ensured ethnic Fijians a majority of seats in the parliament. Opposition parties condemned this provision and vowed not to participate in elections held under this constitution.

FINLAND

Republic of Finland
President: Mauno H. Koivisto (1982)
Premier: Esko Aho (1991)
Area: 130,119 sq mi. (337,009 sq km)
Population (est. mid-1991): 5,000,000 (average annual rate of natural increase: 0.3%); birth rate: 13/1000; infant mortality rate: 5.8/1000; density per square mile: 38
Capital: Helsinki
Largest cities (est. 1987): Helsinki, 487,749; Tampere, 170,097; Espoo, 162,106; Turku, 160,974
Monetary unit: Markka
Languages: Finnish, Swedish
Religions: Evangelical Lutheran, 97%; Eastern Orthodox, 1.2%
National name: Suomen Tasavalta—Republiken Finland
Literacy rate: almost 100%
Economic summary: Gross domestic product (1989 est.): $74.4 billion; $15,000 per capita; 4.6% real growth rate. Arable land: 8%. Principal products: dairy and meat products, cereals, sugar beets, potatoes. Labor force: 2,556,000; 22.9% mining and manufacturing. Major products: metal manufactures, forestry and wood products, refined copper, ships, electronics. Natural resource: timber. Exports: timber, paper and pulp, ships, machinery, clothing, footwear. Imports: petroleum and petroleum products, chemicals, transportation equipment, machinery, textile yarns, foodstuffs,

fodder grain. Major trading partners: Germany, Sweden, U.S.S.R., U.K., U.S.

Geography. Finland stretches 700 miles (1,127 km) from the Gulf of Finland on the south to Soviet Petsamo, north of the Arctic Circle. The U.S.S.R. extends along the entire eastern frontier while Norway is on her northern border and Sweden lies on her western border. In area, Finland is three times the size of Ohio.

Off the southwest coast are the Aland Islands, controlling the entrance to the Gulf of Bothnia. Finland has more than 200,000 lakes.

The Swedish-populated Aland Islands (581 sq mi.; 1,505 sq km) have an autonomous status under a law passed in 1921.

Government. The president, chosen for six years by the popularly elected Electoral College of 301 members, appoints the Cabinet. The one-chamber Diet, the Eduskunta, consists of 200 members elected for four-year terms by proportional representation.

History. At the end of the 7th century, the Finns came to Finland from their Volga settlements, taking the country from the Lapps, who retreated northward. The Finns' repeated raids on the Scandinavian coast impelled Eric IX, the Swedish King, to conquer the country in 1157 and bring it into contact with Western Christendom. By 1809 the whole of Finland was conquered by Alexander I of Russia, who set up Finland as a Grand Duchy.

The first period of Russification (1809–1905) resulted in a lessening of the powers of the Finnish Diet. The Russian language was made official, and the Finnish military system was superseded by the Russian. The pace of Russification was intensified from 1908 to 1914. When Russian control was weakened as a consequence of the March Revolution of 1917, the Diet on July 20, 1917, proclaimed Finland's independence, which became complete on Dec. 6, 1917.

Finland rejected Soviet territorial demands, and the U.S.S.R. attacked on Nov. 30, 1939. The Finns made an amazing stand of three months and finally capitulated, ceding 16,000 square miles (41,440 sq km) to the U.S.S.R. Under German pressure, the Finns joined the Nazis against Russia in 1941, but were defeated again and ceded the Petsamo area to the U.S.S.R. In 1948, a 20-year treaty of friendship and mutual assistance was signed by the two nations and renewed for another 20 years in 1970.

After 25 years in office, President Urho K. Kekkonen resigned in October 1981 because of ill health. Premier Mauno Koivisto, leader of the Social Democratic Party, was elected President on Jan. 26, 1982, winning decisively over a conservative rival with support from Finnish Communists.

Elections in March 1991 made the Center Party the largest single party in parliament. A center-right coalition government was formed that in June decided to peg the markka to the Ecu and thereby slowly intergate the Finnish economy into that of Western Europe.

FRANCE

French Republic
President: François Mitterrand (1981)
Premier: Edith Cresson (1991)
Area: 211,208 sq mi. (547,026 sq km)
Population (est. mid-1991): 56,700,000 (average annual rate of natural increase: 0.4%); birth rate: 14/1000;

infant mortality rate: 7.2/1000; density per square mile: 268
Capital: Paris
Largest cities (est. 1983): Paris, 2,150,000; (1982 est.): Marseilles, 868,435; Lyons, 410,455; Toulouse, 344,917; Nice, 331,165; Nantes, 237,789; Strasbourg, 247,068; Bordeaux, 201,965
Monetary unit: Franc
Language: French, declining regional dialects
Religion: Roman Catholic, 90%
National name: République Française
Literacy rate: 99%
Economic summary: Gross domestic product (1989 est.): $819.6 billion; $14,600 per capita; 3.4% real growth rate. Arable land: 32%. Principal products: cereals, feed grains, livestock and dairy products, wine, fruits, vegetables, potatoes. Labor force: 24,170,000; 31.3% industry. Major products: chemicals, automobiles, processed foods, iron and steel, aircraft, textiles, clothing. Natural resources: coal, iron ore, bauxite, fish, forests. Exports: textiles and clothing, chemicals, machinery and transport equipment, agricultural products. Imports: machinery, crude petroleum, chemicals, agricultural products. Major trading partners: Germany, Italy, U.S., Belgium-Luxembourg, U.K., Netherlands.

Geography. France (80% the size of Texas) is second in size to the U.S.S.R. among Europe's nations. In the Alps near the Italian and Swiss borders is Europe's highest point—Mont Blanc (15,781 ft; 4,810 m). The forest-covered Vosges Mountains are in the northeast, and the Pyrenees are along the Spanish border.

Except for extreme northern France, which is part of the Flanders plain, the country may be described as four river basins and a plateau. Three of the streams flow west—the Seine into the English Channel, the Loire into the Atlantic, and the Garonne into the Bay of Biscay. The Rhône flows south into the Mediterranean. For about 100 miles (161 km), the Rhine is France's eastern border.

West of the Rhône and northeast of the Garonne lies the central plateau, covering about 15% of France's area and rising to a maximum elevation of 6,188 feet (1,886 m). In the Mediterranean, about 115 miles (185 km) east-southeast of Nice, is Corsica (3,367 sq mi.; 8,721 sq km).

Government. The president is elected for seven years by universal suffrage. He appoints the premier, and the Cabinet is responsible to Parliament. The president has the right to dissolve the National Assembly or to ask Parliament for reconsideration of a law. The Parliament consists of two houses: the National Assembly and the Senate.

History. The history of France, as distinct from ancient Gaul, begins with the Treaty of Verdun (843), dividing the territories corresponding roughly to France, Germany, and Italy among the three grandsons of Charlemagne. Julius Caesar had conquered part of Gaul in 57–52 B.C., and it remained Roman until Franks invaded it in the 5th century.

Charles the Bald, inheritor of *Francia Occidentalis*, founded the Carolingian dynasty, which ruled over a kingdom increasingly feudalized. By 987, the crown passed to Hugh Capet, a princeling who controlled only the Ile-de-France, the region surrounding Paris. For 350 years, an unbroken Capetian line added to its domain and consolidated royal authority until the accession in 1328 of Philip VI, first of the Valois line.

France was then the most powerful nation in Europe, with a population of 15 million.

The missing pieces in Philip's domain were the French provinces still held by the Plantagenet kings of England, who also claimed the French crown. Beginning in 1338, the Hundred Years' War eventually settled the contest. English longbows defeated French armored knights at Crécy (1346) and the English also won the second landmark battle at Agincourt (1415), but the final victory went to the French at Castillon (1453).

Absolute monarchy reached its apogee in the reign of Louis XIV (1643–1715), the Sun King, whose brilliant court was the center of the Western world.

Revolution plunged France into a blood bath beginning in 1789 and ending with a new authoritarianism under Napoleon Bonaparte, who had successfully defended the infant republic from foreign attack and then made himself First Consul in 1799 and Emperor in 1804.

The Congress of Vienna (1815) sought to restore the pre-Napoleonic order in the person of Louis XVIII, but industrialization and the middle class, both fostered under Napoleon, built pressure for change, and a revolution in 1848 drove Louis Phillipe, last of the Bourbons, into exile.

A second republic elected as its president Prince Louis Napoleon, a nephew of Napoleon I, who declared the Second Empire in 1852 and took the throne as Napoleon III. His opposition to the rising power of Prussia ignited the Franco-Prussian War (1870–71), ending in his defeat and abdication.

A new France emerged from World War I as the continent's dominant power. But four years of hostile occupation had reduced northeast France to ruins. The postwar Third Republic was plagued by political instability and economic chaos.

From 1919, French foreign policy aimed at keeping Germany weak through a system of alliances, but it failed to halt the rise of Adolf Hitler and the Nazi war machine. On May 10, 1940, mechanized Nazi troops attacked, and, as they approached Paris, Italy joined with Germany. The Germans marched into an undefended Paris and Marshal Henri Philippe Pétain signed an armistice June 22. France was split into an occupied north and an unoccupied south, the latter becoming a totalitarian state with Pétain as its chief.

Allied armies liberated France in August 1944. The French Committee of National Liberation, formed in Algiers in 1943, established a provisional government in Paris headed by Gen. Charles de Gaulle. The Fourth Republic was born Dec. 24, 1946.

The Empire became the French Union; the National Assembly was strengthened and the presidency weakened; and France joined the North Atlantic Treaty Organization. A war against communist insurgents in Indochina was abandoned after the defeat at Dien Bien Phu. A new rebellion in Algeria threatened a military coup, and on June 1, 1958, the Assembly invited de Gaulle to return as premier with extraordinary powers. He drafted a new Constitution for a Fifth Republic, adopted Sept. 28, which strengthened the presidency and reduced legislative power. He was elected president Dec. 21.

De Gaulle took France out of the NATO military command in 1967 and expelled all foreign-controlled troops from the country. He later went on to attempt to achieve a long-cherished plan of regional reform. This, however, aroused wide opposition. He decided to stake his fate on a referendum. At the voting in April 1969, the electorate defeated the plan.

His successor Georges Pompidou continued the de Gaulle policies of seeking to expand France's influ-

Rulers of France

Name	Born	Ruled[1]
CAROLINGIAN DYNASTY		
Pepin the Short	c. 714	751–768
Charlemagne[2]	742	768–814
Louis I the Debonair[3]	778	814–840
Charles I the Bald[4]	823	840–877
Louis II the Stammerer	846	877–879
Louis III[5]	c. 863	879–882
Carloman[5]	?	879–884
Charles II the Fat[6]	839	884–887 [7]
Eudes (Odo), Count of Paris	?	888–898
Charles III the Simple[8]	879	893–923 [9]
Robert I[10]	c. 865	922–923
Rudolf (Raoul), Duke of Burgundy	?	923–936
Louis IV d'Outremer	c. 921	936–954
Lothair	941	954–986
Louis V the Sluggard	c. 967	986–987
CAPETIAN DYNASTY		
Hugh Capet	c. 940	987–996
Robert II the Pious[11]	c. 970	996–1031
Henry I	1008	1031–1060
Philip I	1052	1060–1108
Louis VI the Fat	1081	1108–1137
Louis VII the Young	c.1121	1137–1180
Philip II (Philip Augustus)	1165	1180–1223
Louis VIII the Lion	1187	1223–1226
Louis IX (St. Louis)	1214	1226–1270
Philip III the Bold	1245	1270–1285
Philip IV the Fair	1268	1285–1314
Louis X the Quarreler	1289	1314–1316
John I[12]	1316	1316
Philip V the Tall	1294	1316–1322
Charles IV the Fair	1294	1322–1328
HOUSE OF VALOIS		
Philip VI	1293	1328–1350
John II the Good	1319	1350–1364
Charles V the Wise	1337	1364–1380
Charles VI the Well–Beloved	1368	1380–1422
Charles VII	1403	1422–1461
Louis XI	1423	1461–1483
Charles VIII	1470	1483–1498
Louis XII the Father of the People	1462	1498–1515
Francis I	1494	1515–1547
Henry II	1519	1547–1559
Francis II	1544	1559–1560
Charles IX	1550	1560–1574
Henry III	1551	1574–1589
HOUSE OF BOURBON		
Henry IV of Navarre	1553	1589–1610
Louis XIII	1601	1610–1643
Louis XIV the Great	1638	1643–1715
Louis XV the Well–Beloved	1710	1715–1774
Louis XVI	1754	1774–1792 [13]
Louis XVII (Louis Charles de France)[14]	1785	1793–1795

Name	Born	Ruled[1]
FIRST REPUBLIC		
National Convention	—	1792–1795
Directory (Directoire)	—	1795–1799
CONSULATE		
Napoleon Bonaparte[15]	1769	1799–1804
FIRST EMPIRE		
Napoleon I	1769	1804–1815 [16]
RESTORATION OF HOUSE OF BOURBON		
Louis XVIII le Désiré	1755	1814–1824
Charles X	1757	1824–1830 [17]
BOURBON-ORLEANS LINE		
Louis Philippe ("Citizen King")	1773	1830–1848 [18]
SECOND REPUBLIC		
Louis Napoleon[19]	1808	1848–1852
SECOND EMPIRE		
Napoleon III (Louis Napoleon)	1808	1852–1870 [20]
THIRD REPUBLIC (PRESIDENTS)		
Louis Adolphe Thiers	1797	1871–1873
Marie E. P. M. de MacMahon	1808	1873–1879
François P. J. Grévy	1807	1879–1887
Sadi Carnot	1837	1887–1894
Jean Casimir–Périer	1847	1894–1895
François Félix Faure	1841	1895–1899
Émile Loubet	1838	1899–1906
Clement Armand Fallières	1841	1906–1913
Raymond Poincaré	1860	1913–1920
Paul E. L. Deschanel	1856	1920–1920
Alexandre Millerand	1859	1920–1924
Gaston Doumergue	1863	1924–1931
Paul Doumer	1857	1931–1932
Albert Lebrun	1871	1932–1940
VICHY GOVERNMENT (CHIEF OF STATE)		
Henri Philippe Pétain	1856	1940–1944
PROVISIONAL GOVERNMENT (PRESIDENTS)		
Charles de Gaulle	1890	1944–1946
Félix Gouin	1884	1946–1946
Georges Bidault	1899	1946–1947
FOURTH REPUBLIC (PRESIDENTS)		
Vincent Auriol	1884	1947–1954
René Coty	1882	1954–1959
FIFTH REPUBLIC (PRESIDENTS)		
Charles de Gaulle	1890	1959–1969
Georges Pompidou	1911	1969–1974
Valéry Giscard d'Estaing	1926	1974–1981
François Mitterrand	1916	1981–

1. For Kings and Emperors through the Second Empire, year of end of rule is also that of death, unless otherwise indicated. 2. Crowned Emperor of the West in 800. His brother, Carloman, ruled as King of the Eastern Franks from 768 until his death in 771. 3. Holy Roman Emperor 814–840. 4. Holy Roman Emperor 875–877 as Charles II. 5. Ruled jointly 879–882. 6. Holy Roman Emperor 881–887 as Charles III. 7. Died 888. 8. King 893–898 in opposition to Eudes. 9. Died 929. 10. Not counted in regular line of Kings of France by some authorities. Elected by nobles but killed in Battle of Soissons. 11. Sometimes called Robert I. 12. Posthumous son of Louis X; lived for only five days. 13. Executed 1793. 14. Titular King only. He died in prison according to official reports, but many pretenders appeared during the Bourbon restoration. 15. As First Consul, Napoleon held the power of government. In 1804, he became Emperor. 16. Abdicated first time June 1814. Re–entered Paris March 1815, after escape from Elba; Louis XVIII fled to Ghent. Abdicated second time June 1815. He named as his successor his son, Napoleon II, who was not acceptable to the Allies. He died 1821. 17. Died 1836. 18. Died 1850. 19. President; became Emperor in 1852. 20. Died 1873.

ence in the Mideast and Africa, selling arms to South Africa (despite the U.N. embargo), to Libya, and to Greece, and in 1971 he endorsed British entry into the Common Market.

Socialist François Mitterrand attained a stunning victory in the May 10, 1981, Presidential election over the Gaullist alliance that had held power since 1958.

The victors immediately moved to carry out campaign pledges to nationalize major industries, halt nuclear testing, suspend nuclear power plant construction, and impose new taxes on the rich. On Feb. 11, 1982, the nationalization bills became law.

The Socialists' policies during Mitterrand's first two years created a 12% inflation rate, a huge trade deficit, and devaluations of the franc. In early 1983, Mitterrand, embarked on an austerity program to control inflation and reduce the trade deficit. He increased taxes and slashed government spending. A halt to economic growth, declining purchasing power for the average Frenchman, and an increase in unemployment to 10% followed. Mitterrand sank lower and lower in the opinion polls.

In March, 1986, a center-right coalition led by Jacques Chirac won a slim majority in legislative elections. Chirac became Premier initiating a period of "co-habitation" between him and the Socialist President, Mitterrand, a cooperation marked by sparring over Chirac's plan to denationalize major industries and effect a harder line on security issues and on New Caledonia.

Mitterrand's decisive reelection in May, 1987, led to Chirac being replaced as Premier by Michel Rocard, a Socialist. Mitterrand called legislative elections for June, 1987 that gave the Socialists a plurality.

Relations, however, cooled with Rocard, and in May 1991 he was replaced with Edith Cresson, France's first female prime minister and like Mitterrand a Socialist. Almost immediately upon taking office she faced a number of economic and social problems that threatened to cut short any honeymoon period. In June France announced it would sign the 1968 Nuclear Nonproliferation Treaty.

Overseas Departments

Overseas Departments elect representatives to the National Assembly, and the same administrative organization as that of mainland France applies to them.

FRENCH GUIANA (including ININI)

Status: Overseas Department
Prefect: Jacques Dewatre (1986)
Area: 35,126 sq mi. (90,976 sq km)
Population (est. mid 1990): 94,702 (average annual growth rate: 3.2%)
Capital (est. 1982): Cayenne, 37,097
Monetary unit: Franc
Language: French
Religion: Roman Catholic
Literacy rate: 73%
Economic summary: Gross domestic product (1982): $210 million; $3,230 per capita. Arable land: NEGL%; principal agricultural products: rice, cassava, bananas, sugar cane. Labor force: 23,265; 21.2% in industry. Major industrial products: timber, rum, rosewood essence, gold mining, processed shrimp. Natural resources: bauxite, timber, cinnabar, kaolin. Exports: shrimp, timber, rum, rosewood essence. Imports:

food, consumer and producer goods, petroleum. Major trading partners: U.S., France, Japan.

French Guiana, lying north of Brazil and east of Suriname on the northeast coast of South America, was first settled in 1604. Penal settlements, embracing the area around the mouth of the Maroni River and the Iles du Salut (including Devil's Island), were founded in 1852; they have since been abolished.

During World War II, French Guiana at first adhered to the Vichy government, but the Free French took over in 1943. French Guiana accepted in 1958 the new Constitution of the French Fifth Republic and remained an Overseas Department of the French Republic.

GUADELOUPE

Status: Overseas Department
Prefect: Yves Bonnet (1986)
Area: 687 sq mi. (1,779 sq km)
Population (est. mid-1991): 300,000 (average annual growth rate 1.4%); birth rate: 21/1000; infant mortality rate: 13/1000
Capital (est. 1983): Basse-Terre, 35,000
Largest city (est. 1982): Pointe-à-Pitre, 50,000
Monetary unit: Franc
Language: French, Creole patois
Religions: Roman Catholic
Literacy rate: over 70%
Economic summary: Gross domestic product (1987): $1.1 billion; $3,300 per capita; n.a. real growth rate. Arable land: 18%; principal agricultural products: sugar cane, bananas, eggplant, flowers. Labor force: 120,000; 25.8% industry. Major industries: construction, public works, sugar, rum, tourism. Exports: sugar, rum, bananas, eggplant, flowerrs. Imports: foodstuffs, clothing, consumer goods, construction materials, petroleum products. Major trading partner: France.

Guadeloupe, in the West Indies about 300 miles (483 km) southeast of Puerto Rico, was discovered by Columbus in 1493. It consists of the twin islands of Basse-Terre and Grande-Terre and five dependencies—Marie-Galante, Les Saintes, La Désirade, St. Barthélemy, and the northern half of St. Martin. The volcano Soufrière (4,813 ft; 1,467 m), also called La Grande Soufrière, is the highest point on Guadeloupe. Violent activity in 1976 and 1977 caused thousands to flee their homes.

French colonization began in 1635. In 1958, Guadeloupe voted in favor of the new Constitution of the French Fifth Republic and remained an Overseas Department of the French Republic.

MARTINIQUE

Status: Overseas Department
Prefect: Edouard LaCroix (1986)
Area: 431 sq mi. (1,116 sq km)
Population (est. mid-1991): 300,000 (average annual growth rate: 1.3%); birth rate: 19/1000; infant mortality rate: 11/1000
Capital (est. 1984): Fort-de-France, 97,814
Monetary unit: Franc
Languages: French, Creole patois
Religion: Roman Catholic
Literacy rate: over 70%
Economic summary: Gross domestic product (1984): $1.3 billion, $3.650 per capita. Average annual growth rate n.a. Arable land: 10%; principal agricultural products:

sugar cane, bananas, rum, pineapples. Labor force: 100,000; 31.7% in service industry. Major industries: sugar, rum, refined oil, cement, tourism. Natural resources: coastal scenery and beaches. Exports: bananas, refined petroleum products, rum, sugar, pineapples. Imports: foodstuffs, clothing and other consumer goods, petroleum products, construction materials. Major trading partners: France, U.S.

Martinique, lying in the Lesser Antilles about 300 miles (483 km) northeast of Venezuela, was probably discovered by Columbus in 1502 and was taken for France in 1635. Following the Franco-German armistice of 1940, it had a semiautonomous status until 1943, when authority was relinquished to the Free French. The area, administered by a Prefect assisted by an elected council, is represented in the French Parliament. In 1958, Martinique voted in favor of the new Constitution of the French Fifth Republic and remained an Overseas Department of the French Republic.

RÉUNION

Status: Overseas Department
Prefect: Jean Anciaux (1986)
Area: 970 sq mi. (2,510 sq km)
Population (est. mid-1991): 600,000 (average annual growth rate, 1.7%); birth rate: 22/1000; infant mortality rate: 13/1000
Capital (est. 1986): Saint-Denis, 109,072
Monetary unit: Franc
Languages: French, Creole
Religion: Roman Catholic
Economic summary: Gross domestic product (1985): $2.4 billion; real growth rate 9% (1987 est.). Arable land: 20%; principal agricultural products: rum, vanilla, bananas, perfume plants. Major industrial products: rum, cigarettes, processed sugar. Exports: sugar, perfume essences, rum, molasses. Imports: manufactured goods, foodstuffs, beverages, machinery and transportation equipment, petroleum products. Major trading partners: France, Mauritius, Bahrain, South Africa, Italy.

Discovered by Portuguese navigators in the 16th century, the island of Réunion, then uninhabited, was taken as a French possession in 1642. It is located about 450 miles (724 km) east of Madagascar, in the Indian Ocean. In 1958, Réunion approved the Constitution of the Fifth French Republic and remained an Overseas Department of the French Republic.

ST. PIERRE AND MIQUELON

Status: Overseas Department
Prefect: Bernard Leurguin (1986)
Area: 93 sq mi. (242 sq km)
Population (est. 1989): 6,303; .4% growth rate.
Capital (est. 1981): Saint Pierre, 5,800
Economic summary: Major industries: fishing, canneries. Exports: fish, pelts. Imports: meat, clothing, fuel, electrical equipment, machinery, building materials. Major trading partners: Canada, France, U.S., U.K., Netherlands.

The sole remnant of the French colonial empire in North America, these islands were first occupied by the French in 1604. Their only importance arises from proximity to the Grand Banks, located 10 miles south of Newfoundland, making them the center of the French Atlantic cod fisheries. On July 19, 1976, the islands became an Overseas Department of the French Republic.

Overseas Territories

Overseas Territories are comparable to Departments, except that their administrative organization includes a locally-elected government.

FRENCH POLYNESIA

Status: Overseas Territory
High Commissioner: Bernard Gerard (1986)
Area: 1,544 sq mi. (4,000 sq km)
Population (mid-1991): 200,000 (average annual growth rate: 2.5%); birth rate: 30/1000; infant mortality rate: 20/1000
Monetary unit: Pacific financial community franc
Language: French
Religions: Protestant, 55%; Roman Catholic, 32%
Capital (est. 1983): Papeete (on Tahiti), 23,496
Economic summary: Gross national product (1986): $2.24 billion. Average annual growth rate n.a. Per capita income (1986): $6,400. Principal agricultural product: copra. Major industries: tourism, maintenance of French nuclear test base. Exports: coconut products, mother of pearl, vanilla. Imports: fuels, foodstuffs, equipment. Major trading partners: France, U.S.

The term French Polynesia is applied to the scattered French possessions in the South Pacific—Mangareva (Gambier), Makatea, the Marquesas Islands, Rapa, Rurutu, Rimatara, the Society Islands, the Tuamotu Archipelago, Tubuai, Raivavae, and the island of Clipperton—which were organized into a single colony in 1903. There are 120 islands, of which 25 are uninhabited.

The High Commissioner is assisted by a Council of Government and a popularly elected Territorial Assembly. The principal and most populous island—Tahiti, in the Society group—was claimed as French in 1768. In 1958, French Polynesia voted in favor of the new Constitution of the French Fifth Republic and remained an Overseas Territory of the French Republic. The natives are mostly Maoris.

The Pacific Nuclear Test Center on the atoll of Mururoa, 744 miles (1,200 km) from Tahiti, was completed in 1966.

MAYOTTE

Status: Territorial collectivity
Prefect: Guy DuPuis (1986)
Area: 146 sq mi. (378 sq km)
Population (est. 1985): 66,282
Capital (est. 1985): Dzaoudzi, 5,675
Principal products: vanilla, ylang-ylang, coffee, copra

The most populous of the Comoro Islands in the Indian Ocean, with a Christian majority, Mayotte voted in 1974 and 1976 against joining the other, predominantly Moslem islands, in declaring themselves independent. It continues to retain its ties to France.

NEW CALEDONIA AND DEPENDENCIES

Status: Overseas Territory
High Commissioner: Ferdinand Wibaux (1986)
Area: 7,374 sq mi. (19,103 sq km)[1]

Population (mid-1991): 200,000 (average annual growth rate: 1.9%); birth rate: 24/1000; infant mortality rate: 21/1000
Capital (est. 1983): Nouméa, 60,112
Monetary unit: Pacific financial community franc
Languages: French, Melanesian and Polynesian dialects
Religion: Roman Catholic, 60%; Protestant, 30%
Literacy rate: Not known
Economic summary: Gross national product (1989 est): $860 million; average annual growth rate 2.4%; per capita income $5,810. Principal agricultural products: coffee, copra, beef, wheat, vegetables. Major industrial product: nickel. Natural resources: nickel, chromite, iron ore. Exports: nickel, chrome. Imports: mineral fuels, machinery, electrical equipment, foodstuffs. Major trading partners: France, Japan, U.S., Australia.

1. Including dependencies.

New Caledonia (6,466 sq mi.; 16,747 sq km), about 1,070 miles (1,722 km) northeast of Sydney, Australia, was discovered by Capt. James Cook in 1774 and annexed by France in 1853. The government also administers the Isle of Pines, the Loyalty Islands (Uvéa, Lifu, and Maré), the Belep Islands, the Huon Island group, and Chesterfield Islands.

The natives are Melanesians; about one third of the population is white and one fifth Indochinese and Javanese. The French National Assembly on July 31, 1984, voted a bill into law that granted internal autonomy to New Caledonia and opened the way to possible eventual independence. This touched off ethnic tensions and violence between the natives and the European settlers, with the natives demanding full independence and sovereignty while the settlers wanted to remain part of France. In June, 1988, France resumed direct administration of the territory and promised a referendum on selfdetermination in 1998. This was agreed to by organizations representing the natives and the French settlers.

SOUTHERN AND ANTARCTIC LANDS

Status: Overseas Territory
Administrator: Claude Corbier
Area: 3,004 sq mi. (7,781 sq km, excluding Adélie Land)
Capital: Port-au-Français

This territory is uninhabited except for the personnel of scientific bases. It consists of Adélie Land (166,752 sq mi.; 431,888 sq km) on the Antarctic mainland and the following islands in the southern Indian Ocean: the Kerguelen and Crozet archipelagos and the islands of Saint-Paul and New Amsterdam.

WALLIS AND FUTUNA ISLANDS

Status: Overseas Territory
Administrator Superior: Roger Dumec (1988)
Area: 106 sq mi. (274 sq km)
Population (July 1990): 14,910
Capital (1980): Wallis (on Uvea), 600

The two islands groups in the South Pacific between Fiji and Samoa were settled by French missionaries at the beginning of the 19th century. A protectorate was established in the 1880s. Following a referendum by the Polynesian inhabitants, the status was changed to that of an Overseas Territory in 1961.

GABON

Gabonese Republic
President: Omar Bongo (1967)
Premier: Oyé Mba Casimir (1990)
Area: 103,346 sq mi. (267,667 sq km)
Population (est. mid-1991): 1,200,000 (average annual rate of natural increase: 2.3%); birth rate: 39/1000; infant mortality rate: 103/1000; density per square mile: 12
Capital and largest city (est. 1983): Libreville, 257,000
Monetary unit: Franc CFA
Ethnic groups: Bateke, Obamba, Bakota, Shake, Pongwés, Adumas, Chiras, Punu, and Lumbu
Languages: French (official) and Bantu dialects
Religions: Roman Catholic, 65%, Protestant, 19%
National name: République Gabonaise
Member of French Community
Literacy rate: 61.6%
Economic summary: Gross domestic product (1989): $3.2 billion; $3,000 per capita; real growth rate 0%. Arable land: 1%. Principal products: cocoa, coffee, wood, palm oil. Labor force: 120,000 salaried; 30% in industry and commerce. Major products: petroleum, natural gas, processed wood, manganese, uranium. Natural resources: wood, petroleum, iron ore, manganese, uranium. Exports: crude petroleum, wood and wood products, minerals. Imports: mining and road-building machinery, electrical equipment, foodstuffs, textiles, transport vehicles. Major trading partners: France, U.S. Germany.

Geography. This West African land with the Atlantic as its western border is also bounded by Equatorial Guinea, Cameroon, and the Congo. Its area is slightly less than Colorado's.

From mangrove swamps on the coast, the land becomes divided plateaus in the north and east and mountains in the north. Most of the country is covered by a dense tropical forest.

Government. The president is elected for a seven-year term. Legislative powers are exercised by a 120-seat National Assembly, which is elected for a seven-year term. After his conversion to Islam in 1973, President Bongo changed his given name, Albert Bernard, to Omar. The Rassemblement Social Démocrate Gabonais is led by President Bongo. He was re-elected without opposition in 1973 and in 1980.

History. Little is known of Gabon's history, even in oral tradition, but Pygmies are believed to be the original inhabitants. Now there are many tribal groups in the country, the largest being the Fang people who constitute a third of the population.

Gabon was first visited by the Portuguese navigator Diego Cam in the 15th century. In 1839, the French founded their first settlement on the left bank of the Gabon Estuary and gradually occupied the hinterland during the second half of the 19th century. It was organized as a French territory in 1888 and became an autonomous republic within the French Union after World War II and an independent republic on Aug. 17, 1960.

Following strikes and riots the president called a national conference in March 1990. In May it adopted a transitional constitution legalizing political parties and calling for free elections. When these took place in September riots arising out of charges of irregularities caused the disqualification of the results. A subsequent round gave the ruling party a victory, but by a narrow margin.

GAMBIA

Republic of the Gambia

President: Sir Dawda K. Jawara (1970)
Area: 4,093 sq mi. (10,600 sq km)
Population (est. mid-1991): 900,000 (average annual rate of natural increase: 2.6%); birth rate: 47/1000; infant mortality rate: 143/1000; density per square mile: 203
Capital (est. 1983): Banjul, 44,188
Monetary unit: Dalasi
Languages: Native tongues, English (official)
Religions: Islam, 90%, Christian, 9%, traditional, 1%
Member of Commonwealth of Nations
Literacy rate: 25.1%
Economic summary: Gross domestic product (FY89 est.): $195 million; $250 per capita; 4.6% real growth rate. Arable land: 16%. Principal products: peanuts, rice, palm kernels. Labor force: 400,000; 18.9% in industry, commerce and services. Major industrial products: processed peanuts, fish, and hides. Natural resources: fish. Exports: peanuts and peanut products, fish. Imports: foodstuffs, fuel, machinery, transport equipment. Major trading partners: U.S., E.C., Asia.

Geography. Situated on the Atlantic coast in westernmost Africa and surrounded on three sides by Senegal, Gambia is twice the size of Delaware. The Gambia River flows for 200 miles (322 km) through Gambia on its way to the Atlantic. The country, the smallest on the continent, averages only 20 miles (32 km) in width.

Government. The president's five-year term is linked to the 35-member unicameral House of Representatives, from which he appoints his Cabinet members and the vice president.

The major political party is the People's Progressive Party (27 seats in House of Representatives), led by President Jawara.

History. During the 17th century, Gambia was settled by various companies of English merchants. Slavery was the chief source of revenue until it was abolished in 1807. Gambia became a crown colony in 1843 and an independent nation within the Commonwealth of Nations on Feb. 18, 1965.

Full independence was approved in a 1970 referendum, and on April 24 of that year Gambia proclaimed itself a republic.

President Dawda K. Jawara won overwhelming re-election to his fifth term on May 5, 1982. Although insisting on his commitment to a multiparty system President Jawara held talks in 1990 with the opposition National Convention Party about the possibility of a party merger.

GERMANY

Federal Republic of Germany

President: Richard von Weizsäcker (1984)
Chancellor: Helmut Kohl (1982)
Area: 137,838 sq mi. (357,000 sq km)
Population (Jan. 1991): 78,700,000 (agerage annual growth rate: –0%; birth rate: 11/1000; infant mortality rate: 7.5/1000; density per square mile: 571
Capital (est. 1990): Berlin, 3,410,000; seat of parliament and government: Bonn[1], 279,000 (1988)
Largest cities (1989 est.): Hamburg, 1,597,500; Munich, 1,206,400; Cologne, 934,400; Frankfurt, 623,700; Essen, 620,000; Dortmund, 584,600; Dusseldorf, 564,400; Stuttgart, 560,100; Bremen, 533,800; Dresden, 501,400; Leipzig, 530,000; Hanover, 497,200

Monetary unit: Deutsche Mark
Language: German
Religions: Protestant, 49%; Roman Catholic, 45%
National name: Bundesrepublik Deutschland
Literacy rate: 99%
Economic summary: Preliminary GNP, West Germany (1990): $1,579 billion; $24,980 est. per capita; GNP 3.6 real growth rate. Arable land: 30%. Principal products: grains, potatoes, sugar beets. Labor force: 27,790,000; 41.6% in industry. Major products: chemicals, machinery, vehicles. Natural resources: iron ore, timber, coal. Exports: machines and machine tools, chemicals, motor vehicles, iron and steel products. Imports: manufactured and agricultural products, raw materials, fuels. Major trading partners: France, Netherlands, Belgium-Luxembourg, Italy, U.S., U.K.
East Germany (1989): $159.5 billion; $9,679 per capita. Arable land: 45%; principal products: grains, potatoes, sugar beets, meat and dairy products. Labor force: 8,960,000; 37.5% in industry; major products: steel, chemicals, machinery, electrical and precision engineering products. Natural resources: brown coal, potash, bauxite. Exports: machinery and equipment, chemical products, textiles, clothing. Imports: raw materials, fuels, agricultural products, machinery and equipment

1. At present, seat of government will eventually move to Berlin.

Geography. The Federal Republic of Germany occupies the western half of the central European area historically regarded as German. This was the part of Germany occupied by the United States, Britain, and France after World War II, when the eastern half of prewar Germany was split roughly between a Soviet-occupied zone, which became the German Democratic Republic, and an area annexed by Poland. After being divided for more than four decades, the two Germanys were reunited on Oct. 3, 1990. The united Federal Republic is about the size of Montana.

Germany's neighbors are France, Belgium, Luxembourg, and the Netherlands on the west, Switzerland and Austria on the south, Czechoslovakia and Poland on the east, and Denmark on the north.

The northern plain, the central hill country, and the southern mountain district constitute the main physical divisions of West Germany, which is slightly smaller than Oregon. The Bavarian plateau in the southwest averages 1,600 feet (488 m) above sea level, but it reaches 9,721 feet (2,962 m) in the Zugspitze Mountains, the highest point in the country.

Important navigable rivers are the Danube, rising in the Black Forest and flowing east across Bavaria into Austria, and the Rhine, which rises in Switzerland and flows across the Netherlands in two channels to the North Sea and is navigable by ocean-going and coastal vessels as far as Cologne. The Elbe, which also empties into the North Sea, is navigable within Germany for smaller vessels. The Weser, flowing into the North Sea, and the Main and Mosel (Moselle), both tributaries of the Rhine, are also important. In addition, the Oder and Neisse Rivers form the border with Poland.

Government. Under the Constitution of May 23, 1949, the Federal Republic was established as a parliamentary democracy. The Parliament consists of the Bundesrat, an upper chamber representing and appointed by the Länder, or states, and the Bundestag, a lower house elected for four years by universal suffrage. A federal assembly composed of Bundestag deputies and deputies from the state parliaments elects the President of the Republic for a five-year term; the Bundestag alone chooses the Chancellor, or Prime Minister. Each of the 16 Länder have a legislature popularly elected for a four-year or five-year term.

The major political parties are the Christian Democratic Union-Christian Social Union (319 of 662 seats in the Bundestag), led by Chancellor Helmut Kohl; Social Democratic Party (239 seats) led by Björn Engholm; and the Free Democratic Party (78 seats), led by Otto Count Larbsdorff, the Alliance 90/Greens (8 seats) and Party of Democratic Socialism (17 seats). Kohl's government is a coalition with the Free Democrats.

History. Immediately before the Christian era, when the Roman Empire had pushed its frontier to the Rhine, what is now Germany was inhabited by several tribes believed to have migrated from Central Asia between the 6th and 4th centuries b.c. One of these tribes, the Franks, attained supremacy in western Europe under Charlemagne, who was crowned Holy Roman Emperor a.d. 800. By the Treaty of Verdun (843), Charlemagne's lands east of the Rhine were ceded to the German Prince Louis. Additional territory acquired by the Treaty of Mersen (870) gave Germany approximately the area it maintained throughout the Middle Ages. For several centuries after Otto the Great was crowned King in 936, the German rulers were also usually heads of the Holy Roman Empire.

Relations between state and church were changed by the Reformation, which began with Martin Luther's 95 theses, and came to a head in 1547, when Charles V scattered the forces of the Protestant League at Mühlberg. Freedom of worship was guaranteed by the Peace of Augsburg (1555), but a Counter Reformation took place later, and a dispute over the succession to the Bohemian throne brought on the Thirty Years' War (1618–48), which devastated Germany and left the empire divided into hundreds of small principalities virtually independent of the Emperor.

Meanwhile, Prussia was developing into a state of considerable strength. Frederick the Great (1740–86) reorganized the Prussian army and defeated Maria Theresa of Austria in a struggle over Silesia. After the defeat of Napoleon at Waterloo (1815), the struggle between Austria and Prussia for supremacy in Germany continued, reaching its climax in the defeat of Austria in the Seven Weeks' War (1866) and the formation of the Prussian-dominated North German Confederation (1867).

The architect of German unity was Otto von Bismarck, a conservative, monarchist, and militaristic Prussian Junker who had no use for "empty phrase-making and constitutions." From 1862 until his retirement in 1890 he dominated not only the German but also the entire European scene. He unified all Germany in a series of three wars against Denmark (1864), Austria (1866), and France (1870–71), which many historians believe were instigated and promoted by Bismarck in his zeal to build a nation through "blood and iron."

On Jan. 18, 1871, King Wilhelm I of Prussia was proclaimed German Emperor in the Hall of Mirrors at Versailles. The North German Confederation, created in 1867, was abolished, and the Second German Reich, consisting of the North and South German states, was born. With a powerful army, an efficient bureaucracy, and a loyal bourgeoisie, Chancellor Bismarck consolidated a powerful centralized state.

Wilhelm II dismissed Bismarck in 1890 and em-

barked upon a "New Course," stressing an intensified colonialism and a powerful navy. His chaotic foreign policy culminated in the diplomatic isolation of Germany and the disastrous defeat in World War I (1914–18).

The Second German Empire collapsed following the defeat of the German armies in 1918, the naval mutiny at Kiel, and the flight of the Kaiser to the Netherlands on November 10. The Social Democrats, led by Friedrich Ebert and Philipp Scheidemann, crushed the Communists and established a moderate republic with Ebert as President.

The Weimar Constitution of 1919 provided for a President to be elected for seven years by universal suffrage and a bicameral legislature, consisting of the Reichsrat, representing the states, and the Reichstag, representing the people. It contained a model Bill of Rights. It was weakened, however, by a provision that enabled the President to rule by decree.

President Ebert died Feb. 28, 1925, and on April 26, Field Marshal Paul von Hindenburg was elected president.

The mass of Germans regarded the Weimar Republic as a child of defeat, imposed upon a Germany whose legitimate aspirations to world leadership had been thwarted by a world conspiracy. Added to this were a crippling currency debacle, a tremendous burden of reparations, and acute economic distress.

Adolf Hitler, an Austrian war veteran and a fanatical nationalist, fanned discontent by promising a Greater Germany, abrogation of the Treaty of Versailles, restoration of Germany's lost colonies, and destruction of the Jews. When the Social Democrats and the Communists refused to combine against the Nazi threat, President Hindenburg made Hitler chancellor on Jan. 30, 1933.

With the death of Hindenburg on Aug. 2, 1934, Hitler repudiated the Treaty of Versailles and began full-scale rearmament. In 1935 he withdrew Germany from the League of Nations, and the next year he reoccupied the Rhineland and signed the anti-Comintern pact with Japan, at the same time strengthening relations with Italy. Austria was annexed in March 1938. By the Munich agreement in September 1938 he gained the Czech Sudetenland, and in violation of this agreement he completed the dismemberment of Czechoslovakia in March 1939. But his invasion of Poland on Sept. 1, 1939, precipitated World War II.

On May 8, 1945, Germany surrendered unconditionally to Allied and Soviet military commanders, and on June 5 the four-nation Allied Control Council became the *de facto* government of Germany.

(For details of World War II, *see* Headline History.)

At the Berlin (or Potsdam) Conference (July 17–Aug. 2, 1945) President Truman, Premier Stalin, and Prime Minister Clement Attlee of Britain set forth the guiding principles of the Allied Control Council. They were Germany's complete disarmament and demilitarization, destruction of its war potential, rigid control of industry, and decentralization of the political and economic structure. Pending final determination of territorial questions at a peace conference, the three victors agreed in principle to the ultimate transfer of the city of Königsberg (now Kaliningrad) and its adjacent area to the U.S.S.R. and to the administration by Poland of former German territories lying generally east of the Oder-Neisse Line.

For purposes of control Germany was divided in 1945 into four national occupation zones, each headed by a Military Governor.

The Western powers were unable to agree with the U.S.S.R. on any fundamental issue. Work of the Allied Control Council was hamstrung by repeated So-

Rulers of Germany and Prussia

Name	Born	Ruled[1]	Name	Born	Ruled[1]
KINGS OF PRUSSIA			**GERMAN FEDERAL REPUBLIC (WEST) (CHANCELLORS)**		
Frederick I[2]	1657	1701–1713	Konrad Adenauer	1876	1949–1963
Frederick William I	1688	1713–1740	Ludwig Erhard	1897	1963–1966
Frederick II the Great	1712	1740–1786	Kurt Georg Kiesinger	1904	1966–1969
Frederick William II	1744	1786–1797	Willy Brandt	1913	1969–1974
Frederick William III	1770	1797–1840	Helmut Schmidt	1918	1974–1984
Frederick William IV	1795	1840–1861	Helmut Kohl	1930	1984–1990
William I	1797	1861–1871 [3]			
			GERMAN DEMOCRATIC REPUBLIC (EAST)		
EMPERORS OF GERMANY			Wilhelm Pieck[5]	1876	1949–1960
William I	1797	1871–1888	Walter Ulbricht[8]	1893	1960–1973
Frederick III	1831	1888–1888	Willi Stoph[9]	1914	1973–1976
William II	1859	1888–1918 [4]	Erich Honecker[9]	1912	1976–1989
			Egon Krenz[9]	1937	1989–1989
HEADS OF THE REICH			Manfred Gerlach[9]		1989–1990
Friedrich Ebert[5]	1871	1919–1925	Sabine Bergman–Pohl[9]		1990–1990
Paul von Hindenburg[5]	1847	1925–1934			
Adolf Hitler[6][7]	1889	1934–1945	**GERMAN FEDERAL REPUBLIC CHANCELLORS**		
Karl Doenitz[6]	1891	1945–1945	Helmut Kohl	1930	1991–

1. Year of end of rule is also that of death, unless otherwise indicated. 2. Was Elector of Brandenburg (1688–1701) as Frederick III. 3. Became Emperor of Germany in 1871. 4. Died 1941. 5. President. 6. Führer. 7. Named Chancellor by President Hindenburg in 1933. 8. Chairman of Council of State. Died 1973. 9. Chairman of Council of State.

viet vetoes; and finally, on March 20, 1948, Russia walked out of the Council. Meanwhile, the U.S. and Britain had taken steps to merge their zones economically (Bizone); and on May 31, 1948, the U.S., Britain, France, and the Benelux countries agreed to set up a German state comprising the three Western Zones.

The U.S.S.R. reacted by clamping a blockade on all ground communications between the Western Zones and Berlin, an enclave in the Soviet Zone. The Western Allies countered by organizing a gigantic airlift to fly supplies into the beleaguered city, assigning 60,000 men to it. The U.S.S.R. was finally forced to lift the blockade on May 12, 1949.

The Federal Republic of Germany was proclaimed on May 23, 1949, with its capital at Bonn. In free elections, West German voters gave a majority in the Constituent Assembly to the Christian Democrats, with the Social Democrats largely making up the opposition. Konrad Adenauer became chancellor, and Theodor Heuss of the Free Democrats was elected first president.

When the Federal Republic of Germany was established in West Germany, the East German states adopted a more centralized constitution for the Democratic Republic of Germany, and it was put into effect on Oct. 7, 1949. The U.S.S.R. thereupon dissolved its occupation zone but Soviet troops remained. The Western Allies declared that the East German Republic was a Soviet creation undertaken without self-determination and refused to recognize it. It was recognized only within the Soviet bloc.

The area that was occupied by East Germany, as well as adjacent areas in Eastern Europe, consists of Mecklenburg, Brandenburg, Lusatia, Saxony, and Thuringia. Soviet armies conquered the five territories by 1945. In the division of 1945 they were allotted to the U.S.S.R. Soviet forces created a State controlled by the secret police with a single party, the Socialist Unity (Communist) Party. The Russians appropriated East German plants to restore their war-ravaged industry.

By 1973, normal relations were established between East and West Germany and the two states entered the United Nations.

The 25-year diplomatic hiatus between East Germany and the U.S. ended Sept. 4, 1974, with the establishment of formal relations.

Agreements in Paris in 1954 giving the Federal Republic full independence and complete sovereignty came into force on May 5, 1955. Under it, West Germany and Italy became members of the Brussels treaty organization created in 1948 and renamed the Western European Union. West Germany also became a member of NATO. In 1955 the U.S.S.R. recognized the Federal Republic. The Saar territory, under an agreement between France and West Germany, held a plebiscite and despite economic links to France voted to rejoin West Germany. It became a state of West Germany on Jan. 1, 1957.

In 1963, Chancellor Adenauer concluded a treaty of mutual cooperation and friendship with France and then retired. He was succeeded by his chief inner-party critic, Ludwig Erhard, who was followed in 1966 by Kurt Georg Kiesinger. He, in turn, was succeeded in 1969 by Willy Brandt, former mayor of West Berlin.

The division between West Germany and East Germany was intensified when the Communists erected the Berlin Wall in 1961. In 1968, the East German Communist leader, Walter Ulbricht, imposed restrictions on West German movements into West Berlin. The Soviet-bloc invasion of Czechoslovakia in August 1968 added to the tension.

A treaty with the U.S.S.R. was signed in Moscow in August 1970 in which force was renounced and respect for the "territorial integrity" of present European states declared.

Three months later, West Germany signed a similar treaty with Poland, renouncing force and setting Poland's western border as the Oder-Neisse Line. It subsequently resumed formal relations with Czechoslovakia in a pact that "voided" the Munich treaty that gave Nazi Germany the Sudetenland.

THE BERLIN WALL (1961–1990)

Major anti-Communist riots broke out in East Berlin in June 1953 and, on Aug. 13, 1961, the Soviet Sector was sealed off by a Communist-built wall, 26 1/2 miles (43 km) long, running through the city. It was built to stem the flood of refugees seeking freedom in the West, 200,000 having fled in 1961 before the wall was erected.

On Nov. 9, 1989, several weeks after the resignation of East Germany's long-time Communist leader, Erich Honecker, the wall's designer and chief defender, the East German government opened its borders to the West and allowed thousands of its citizens to pass freely through the Berlin Wall. They were cheered and greeted by thousands of West Berliners, and many of the jubilant newcomers celebrated their new freedom by climbing on top of the hated wall.

The following day, East German troops began dismantling parts of the wall. It was ironic that this wall was built to keep the citizens from leaving and, 28 years later, it was being dismantled for the same reason.

On Nov. 22, new passages were opened at the north and south of the Brandenburg Gate in an emotional ceremony attended by Chancellor Helmut Kohl of West Germany and Chancellor Hans Modrow of East Germany. The opening of the Brandenburg Gate climaxed the ending of the barriers that had divided the German people since the end of World War II. By the end of 1990, the entire wall had been removed.

Both German states were admitted to the United Nations in 1973.

Brandt, winner of a Nobel Peace Prize for his foreign policies, was forced to resign in 1974 when an East German spy was discovered to be one of his top staff members. Succeeding him was a moderate Social Democrat, Helmut Schmidt.

Helmut Schmidt, Brandt's successor as chancellor, staunchly backed U.S. military strategy in Europe nevertheless, staking his political fate on the strategy of placing U.S. nuclear missiles in Germany unless the Soviet Union reduced its arsenal of intermediate missiles.

The chancellor also strongly opposed nuclear freeze proposals and won 2–1 support for his stand at the convention of Social Democrats in April. The Free Democrats then deserted the Socialists after losing ground in local elections and joined with the Christian Democrats to unseat Schmidt and install Helmut Kohl as chancellor in 1982.

Kohl's tenure has seen a dwindling of the nuclear freeze after the deployment of the U.S. missiles. U.S.-Soviet negotiations in 1987 produced a treaty setting up the removal of medium- and short-range missiles from Europe. An economic upswing in 1986 led to Kohl's re-election.

The fall of the Communist government in East Germany left only Soviet objections to German reunification to be dealt with. This was resolved in July 1990. Soviet objections to a reunified Germany belonging to NATO were dropped in return for German promises to reduce their military and engage in wide-ranging economic cooperation with the Soviet Union.

In ceremonies beginning on the evening of Tuesday, Oct. 2, 1990, and continuing throughout the next day, the German Democratic Republic acceded to the Federal Republic and Germany became a united and sovereign state for the first time since 1945. Some one million people gathered at midnight Oct. 2 at the Reichstag in Berlin. At midnight, a replica of the Liberty Bell, a gift from the United States, rang, and unity was officially proclaimed.

Following unification, the Federal Republic became the second largest country in Europe, after the Soviet Union. A reunited Berlin serves as the official capital, although the government will initially remain in Bonn.

During the national election campaign of late 1990 the central issue remained the cost of unification, including the modernization of the former East German economy. The ruling Christian Democrats promised no tax increases would be needed, while the opposition Social Democrats argued that this was mere wishful thinking.

In the December 2 election the Christian Democrats emerged as the strongest group, taking 43.8% of the vote. Analysts generally considered the vote to be an expression of thanks and support to the Chancellor for his forceful drive for political unity. The Party of Democratic Socialism, formerly the Communist Party, won 17 seats in Parliament.

The new Parliament convened in January 1991 re-electing Helmut Kohl chancellor. Nevertheless it soon became clear that previous official estimates of the cost and time required to absorb eastern Germany were considerably understated. The number of failed enterprises in the east continued to grow, and the exodus of personnel to western Germany ceased to abate.

On June 20, 1991 the German Parliament officially voted in favor of moving the seat of the federal government to Berlin, although given the huge expense of such a move it would be done slowly and require 12 years before Berlin would be a fully functional federal capital.

In foreign affairs Germany signed treaties with Poland establishing and guaranteeing permanent borders. During the Persian Gulf crisis Germany was criticized for what was viewed as its less than full support for the allied cause.

GHANA

Republic of Ghana

Chairman of Provisional National Defense Council:
Flight Lt. Jerry John Rawlings (1981)

Area: 92,100 sq mi. (238,537 sq km)

Population (est. mid-1991): 15,500,000 (average annual rate of natural increase: 3.2%); birth rate: 44/1000; infant mortality rate: 86/1000; density per square mile: 168

Capital: Accra

Largest cities (est. 1984): Accra, 859,600; Kumasi, 348,900; Tamale, 136,800

Monetary unit: Cedi

Languages: English (official), Native tongues (Brong Ahafo, Twi, Fanti, Ga, Ewe, Dagbani)

Religions: indigenous belief, 38%; Islam, 30%; Christian, 24%
Literacy rate: 53.2%
Member of Commonwealth of Nations
Economic summary: Gross national product (1988): $5.2 billion; $400 per capita; 6% real growth rate. Arable land: 5%. Principal products: cocoa, coconuts, coffee, cassava, yams, rice, rubber. Labor force: 3,700,000; 18.7% in industry. Major products: mining products, cocoa products, aluminum. Natural resources: gold, industrial diamonds, bauxite, manganese, timber, fish. Exports: cocoa beans and products, gold, timber, tuna, bauxite, and aluminum. Imports: petroleum, consumer goods, foods, intermediate goods, capital equipment. Major trading partners: U.K., U.S., Germany, France, Japan, South Korea.

Geography. A West African country bordering on the Gulf of Guinea, Ghana has the Ivory Coast to the west, Burkina Faso to the north, and Togo to the east. It compares in size to Oregon.

The coastal belt, extending about 270 miles (435 km), is sandy, marshy, and generally exposed. Behind it is a gradually widening grass strip. The forested plateau region to the north is broken by ridges and hills. The largest river is the Volta.

Government. Ghana returned to military rule after two years of constitutional government when Flight Lt. Jerry Rawlings, who led a coup in 1979 and stepped down voluntarily, seized power on Dec. 31, 1981. Rawlings heads a Provisional National Defense Council, which exercises all power.

History. Created an independent country on March 6, 1957, Ghana is the former British colony of the Gold Coast. The area was first seen by Portuguese traders in 1470. They were followed by the English (1553), the Dutch (1595), and the Swedes (1640). British rule over the Gold Coast began in 1820, but it was not until after quelling the severe resistance of the Ashanti in 1901 that it was firmly established. British Togoland, formerly a colony of Germany, was incorporated into Ghana by referendum in 1956. As the result of a plebiscite, Ghana became a republic on July 1, 1960.

Premier Kwame Nkrumah attempted to take leadership of the Pan-African Movement, holding the All-African People's Congress in his capital, Accra, in 1958 and organizing the Union of African States with Guinea and Mali in 1961. But he oriented his country toward the Soviet Union and China and built an autocratic rule over all aspects of Ghanaian life.

In February 1966, while Nkrumah was visiting Peking and Hanoi, he was deposed by a military coup led by Gen. Emmanuel K. Kotoka.

A series of military coups followed and on June 4, 1979, Flight Lieutenant Jerry Rawlings overthrew Lt. Gen. Frederick Akuffo's military rule on June 4, 1979. Rawlings permitted the election of a civilian president to go ahead as scheduled the following month, and Hilla Limann, candidate of the People's National Party, took office. Charging the civilian government with corruption and repression, Rawlings staged another coup on Dec. 31, 1981. As chairman of the Provisional National Defense Council, Rawlings instituted an austerity program and reduced budget deficits.

On July 11, 1985, a relative of Rawlings, Michael Agbotui Soussoudis, 39, and Sharon M. Scranage, 29, who had been a low-level clerk in the Central Intelligence Agency station in the West African country, were arrested in the United States on espionage charges.

The movement toward multiparty democracy also found expression in Ghana. A new Movement for Freedom and Justice campaigned for democracy. As a member of the Economic Community of West African States Ghana contributed to a peacekeeping force in Liberia.

GREECE

Hellenic Republic
President: Constantine Karamanlis (1990)
Premier: Constantine Mitsotakis (1990)
Area: 50,961 sq mi. (131,990 sq km)
Population (est. mid-1991): 10,100,000 (average annual rate of natural increase: 0.1%); birth rate: 10/1000; infant mortality rate: 9.8/1000; density per square mile: 197
Capital: Athens
Largest cities (1981 census): Athens, 3,027,000; Salonika, 720,000; Patras, 150,000; Larissa, 102,000; Heraklion, 111,000; Volos, 107,000.
Monetary unit: Drachma
Language: Greek
Religion: Greek Orthodox
National name: Elliniki Dimokratia
Literacy rate: 95%
Economic summary: Gross domestic product (1989 est.): $56.3 billion; $5,605 per capita; 2.3% real growth rate. Arable land: 23%. Principal products: grains, fruits, vegetables, olives, olive oil, tobacco, cotton, livestock, dairy products. Labor force: 3,860,000; 20% in manufacturing and mining. Major products: textiles, chemicals, food processing. Natural resources: bauxite, lignite, magnesite, crude oil, marble. Exports: manufactured goods, food and live animals, fuels and lubricants, raw materials. Imports: machinery and automotive equipment, petroleum, consumer goods, chemicals, foodstuffs. Major trading partners: Germany, Italy, France, U.S.A., U.K.

Geography. Greece, on the Mediterranean Sea, is the southernmost country on the Balkan Peninsula in southern Europe. It is bordered on the north by Albania, Yugoslavia, and Bulgaria; on the west by the Ionian Sea; and on the east by the Aegean Sea and Turkey. It is slightly smaller than Alabama.

North central Greece, Epirus, and western Macedonia all are mountainous. The main chain of the Pindus Mountains rises to 10,256 feet (3,126 m) in places, separating Epirus from the plains of Thessaly. Mt. Olympus, rising to 9,570 feet (2,909 m) in the north near the Aegean Sea, is the highest point in the country. Greek Thrace is mostly a lowland region separated from European Turkey by the lower Evros River.

Among the many islands are the Ionian group off the west coast; the Cyclades group to the southeast; other islands in the eastern Aegean, including the Dodecanese Islands, Euboea, Lesbos, Samos, and Chios; and Crete, the fourth largest Mediterranean island.

Government. A referendum in December 1974, five months after the collapse of a military dictatorship, ended the Greek monarchy and established a republic. Ceremonial executive power is held by the president; the Premier heads the government and is responsible to a 300-member unicameral Parliament.

History. Greece, with a recorded history going back to 766 B.C., reached the peak of its glory in the 5th century B.C., and by the middle of the 2nd century B.C., it had declined to the status of a Roman province. It remained within the Eastern Roman Empire until Constantinople fell to the Crusaders in 1204.

In 1453, the Turks took Constantinople, and by 1460 Greece was a Turkish province. The insurrection made famous by the poet Lord Byron broke out in 1821, and in 1827 Greece won independence with sovereignty guaranteed by Britain, France, and Russia.

The protecting powers chose Prince Otto of Bavaria as the first king of modern Greece in 1832 to reign over an area only slightly larger than the Peloponnese Peninsula. Chiefly under the next king, George I, chosen by the protecting powers in 1863, Greece acquired much of its present territory. During his 57-year reign, a period in which he encouraged parliamentary democracy, Thessaly, Epirus, Macedonia, Crete, and most of the Aegean islands were added from the disintegrating Turkish empire. An unsuccessful war against Turkey after World War I brought down the monarchy, to be replaced by a republic in 1923.

Two military dictatorships and a financial crisis brought George II back from exile, but only until 1941, when Italian and German invaders defeated tough Greek resistance. After British and Greek troops liberated the country in October 1944, Communist guerrillas staged a long campaign in which the government received U.S. aid under the Truman Doctrine, the predecessor of the Marshall Plan.

A military junta seized power in April 1967, sending young King Constantine II into exile December 14. Col. George Papadopoulos, as premier, converted the government to republican form in 1973 and as President ended martial law. He was moving to restore democracy when he was ousted in November of that year by his military colleagues. The regime of the "colonels," which had tortured its opponents and scoffed at human rights, resigned July 23, 1974, after having bungled an attempt to seize Cyprus.

Former Premier Karamanlis returned from exile to become premier of Greece's first civilian government since 1967.

On Jan. 1, 1981, Greece became the 10th member of the European Community.

Double-digit inflation and scandals in the Socialist government led to them losing their majority in the elections of June 1989. The opposition New Democracy Party did not gain a majority, however, leading to the creation of a NDP-Communist coalition that initiated an investigation of the scandals. The coalition government was short-lived. Elections in April 1990 finally gave the conservative New Democracy Party a one-seat majority in parliament. Soon afterwards Karamanlis, the founder of that party, was elected president by parliament.

GRENADA

State of Grenada
Sovereign: Queen Elizabeth II
Governor General: Paul Scoon (1978)
Prime Minister: Nicholas Braithwaite (1990)
Area: 133 sq mi. (344 sq km)
Population (est. mid-1991): 100,000 (average annual growth rate, 2.9%); birth rate: 37/1000; infant mortality rate: 30/1000; density per square mile: 634
Capital and largest city (est. 1981): St. George's, 4,800
Monetary unit: East Caribbean dollar
Ethnic groups: Blacks and Indians
Language: English
Religions: Roman Catholic, 64%; Anglican, 21%
Member of Commonwealth of Nations
Literacy rate: 85%
Economic summary: Gross domestic product (1988 est.): $129.7 million; $1,535 per capita; 5% real growth rate.

Arable land: 15%. Principal products: spices, cocoa, bananas. Exports: nutmeg, cocoa beans, bananas, mace. Imports: foodstuffs, machinery, manufactured goods, petroleum. Labor force: 36,000; 31% in services. Major trading partners: U.K., Trinidad and Tobago, U.S., Japan, Canada.

Geography. Grenada (the first "a" is pronounced as in "gray") is the most southerly of the Windward Islands, about 100 miles (161 km) from the South American coast. It is a volcanic island traversed by a mountain range, the highest peak of which is Mount St. Catherine (2,756 ft.; 840 m).

Government. A Governor-General represents the sovereign, Elizabeth II. The Prime Minister is the head of government, chosen by a 15-member House of Representatives elected by universal suffrage every five years.

History. Grenada was discovered by Columbus in 1498. After more than 200 years of British rule, most recently as part of the West Indies Associated States, it became independent Feb. 7, 1974, with Eric M. Gairy as Prime Minister.

Prime Minister Maurice Bishop, a protégé of Cuba's President Castro, was killed in a military coup on Oct. 19, 1983. At the request of five members of the Organization of Eastern Caribbean States, President Reagan ordered an invasion of Grenada on Oct. 25 involving over 1,900 U.S. troops and a small military force from Barbados, Dominica, Jamaica, St. Lucia, and St. Vincent. The troops met strong resistance from Cuban military personnel on the island.

A centrist coalition led by Herbert A. Blaize, a 66-year-old lawyer, won 14 of the 15 seats in Parliament in an election in December 1984, and Blaize became Prime Minister.

None of the four main parties won a clear victory in the election of March 1990. Negotiations led to the National Democratic Congress forming a government with the support of several members from other parties.

GUATEMALA

Republic of Guatemala
President: Jorge Serrano (1991)
Area: 42,042 sq mi. (108,889 sq km)
Population (est. mid-1991): 9,500,000 (average annual rate of natural increase: 3.0%); birth rate: 38/1000; infant mortality rate: 62/1000; density per square mile: 225
Capital and largest city (est. 1982): Guatemala City, 1,250,000
Monetary unit: Quetzal
Languages: Spanish, Indian dialects
Religion: Roman Catholic, Protestant, Mayan.
National name: República de Guatemala
Literacy rate: 50%
Economic summary: Gross domestic product (1990 est.): $12.8 billion; $1,250 per capita; 3.5% real growth rate. Arable land: 12%. Principal products: corn, beans, coffee, cotton, cattle, sugar, bananas, fruits and vegetables. Labor force: 2,500,000; 14% in manufacturing. Principal products: sugar, textiles and clothing, furniture, chemicals, petroleum, metals, rubber. Natural resources: nickel, crude oil, rare woods, fish, chicle. Exports: bananas, cardamom. Imports: manufactured products, machinery, transportation equipment, chem

icals, fuels. Major trading partners: U.S., Central American nations, Caribbean, Mexico.

Geography. The northernmost of the Central American nations, Guatemala is the size of Tennessee. Its neighbors are Mexico on the north, west, and east and Belize, Honduras, and El Salvador on the east. The country consists of two main regions—the cool highlands with the heaviest population and the tropical area along the Pacific and Caribbean coasts. The principal mountain range rises to the highest elevation in Central America and contains many volcanic peaks. Volcanic eruptions are frequent.

The Petén region in the north contains important resources and archaeological sites of the Mayan civilization.

Government. On January 14, 1991 Jorge Serrano was sworn in as president, the first transfer of power from one elected civilian to another. Gustavo Espina, a businessman, was also sworn in as vice president.

Both the President and the Congress are elected for five-year terms and the President may not be re-elected.

History. Once the site of the ancient Mayan civilization, Guatemala, conquered by Spain in 1524, set itself up as a republic in 1839. From 1898 to 1920, the dictator Manuel Estrada Cabrera ran the country, and from 1931 to 1944, Gen. Jorge Ubico Castaneda was the strongman. In 1944 the National Assembly elected Gen. Federico Ponce president, but he was overthrown in October. In December, Dr. Juan José Arévalo was elected as the head of a leftist regime that continued to press its reform program. Jacobo Arbenz Guzmán, administration candidate with leftist leanings, won the 1950 elections.

Arbenz expropriated the large estates, including plantations of the United Fruit Company. With covert U.S. backing, a revolt was led by Col. Carlos Castillo Armas, and Arbenz took refuge in Mexico. Castillo Armas became president but was assassinated in 1957. Constitutional government was restored in 1958, and Gen. Miguel Ydigoras Fuentes was elected president.

A wave of terrorism, by left and right, began in 1967, and in August 1968 U.S. Ambassador John Gordon Mein was killed when he resisted kidnappers. Fear of anarchy led to the election in 1970 of Army Chief of Staff Carlos Araña Osorio, who had put down a rural guerrilla movement at the cost of nearly 3,000 lives. Araña, surprisingly, pledged social reforms when he took office. Another military candidate, Gen. Kjell Laugerud, won the presidency in 1974 amid renewed political violence.

The administration of Gen. Romeo Lucas Garcia, elected president in 1978, ended in a coup by a three-man military junta on March 23, 1982. Lucas Garcia was charged by Amnesty International with responsibility for at least 5,000 political murders in a reign of brutality and corruption that brought a cutoff of U.S. military aid in 1978. Hopes for improvement under the junta faded when Gen. José Efraín Ríos Montt took sole power in June.

President Oscar Mejía Victores, another general, seized power from Rios Montt in an August 1983 coup and pledged to turn over power to an elected civilian President in 1985. A constituent assembly was elected on July 1, 1984, to write a new Constitution.

President Serrano's election was noteworthy for, among other things, he became the first Protestant president in Latin America, and his candidacy at first received hardly any public notice.

GUINEA

Republic of Guinea
President: Brig. Gen. Lansana Conté (1984)
Area: 94,925 sq mi. (245,857 sq km)
Population (est. mid-1991): 7,500,000 (average annual rate of natural increase: 2.6%); birth rate: 47/1000; infant mortality rate: 147/1000; density per square mile: 79
Capital and largest city (est. 1983): Conakry, 656,000
Monetary unit: Guinean franc
Languages: French (official), native tongues (Malinké, Susu, Fulani)
Religions: Islam, 85%; 5% indigenous, 1.5% Christian
National name: République de Guinée
Literacy rate: 20% in Frenchl 48% in local languages
Economic summary: Gross domestic product (1988): $2.5 billion, $350 per capita; real growth rate 5.0%. Arable land: 6%. Principal agricultural products: rice, cassava, millet, corn, coffee, bananas, pineapples. Labor force: 2,400,000 (1983); 11% in industry and commerce. Major industrial products: bauxite, alumina, light manufactured and processed goods, diamonds. Natural resources: bauxite, iron ore, diamonds, gold, water power. Exports: bauxite, alumina, diamonds, pineapples, bananas, coffee. Imports: petroleum, machinery, transport equipment, foodstuffs, textiles. Major trading partners: U.S., U.S.S.R., France, Germany.

Geography. Guinea, in West Africa on the Atlantic, is also bordered by Guinea-Bissau, Senegal, Mali, the Ivory Coast, Liberia, and Sierra Leone. Slightly smaller than Oregon, the country consists of a coastal plain, a mountainous region, a savanna interior, and a forest area in the Guinea Highlands. The highest peak is Mount Nimba at 5,748 ft (1,752 m).

Government. Military government headed by President Lansana Conté, who promoted himself from colonel to brigadier general after a 1984 coup. Although President Conté announced in 1989 that Guinea would move to a multiparty democracy, later details proved the plan disappointing.

History. Previously part of French West Africa, Guinea achieved independence by rejecting the new French Constitution, and on Oct. 2, 1958, became an independent state with Sékou Touré as president. Touré led the country into being the first avowedly Marxist state in Africa. Diplomatic relations with France were suspended in 1965, with the Soviet Union replacing France as the country's chief source of economic and technical assistance.

Prosperity came in 1960 after the start of exploitation of bauxite deposits. Touré was re-elected to a seven-year term in 1974 and again in 1981.

After 26 years as President, Touré died in the United States in March 1984, following surgery. A week later, a military regime headed by Col. Lansana Conté took power with a promise not to shed any more blood after Touré's harsh rule. Conté became President and his co-conspirator in the coup, Col. Diara Traoré, became Prime Minister, but Conté later demoted Traoré to Education Minister. Traoré tried to seize power on July 4, 1985, while Conté was out of the country, but his attempted coup was crushed by troops loyal to Conté.

Along with Sierra Leone and Nigeria, Guinea sent a peacekeeping force to Liberia in August 1990. With Nigeria Guinea deployed troops to Sierra Leone in 1991 to repel invading rebels from Liberia.

GUINEA-BISSAU

Republic of Guinea-Bissau
President of the Council of State: João Bernardo Vieira (1980)
Area: 13,948 sq mi. (36,125 sq km)
Population (est. mid-1991): 1,000,000 (average annual rate of natural increase: 2.0%); birth rate: 43/1000; infant mortality rate: 151/1000; density per square mile: 71
Capital and largest city (est. 1980): Bissau, 110,000
Monetary unit: Guinea-Bissau peso
Language: Portugese Criolo, African languages
Religions: traditional, 65%; Islam, 30%; Christian, 5%
National name: República da Guiné-Bissau
Literacy rate: 34% (1986)
Economic summary: Gross national product (1986): $168 million; $170 per capita; real growth rate –.6%. Arable land: 9%. Principal products: palm kernels, cotton, cashew nuts, peanuts. Labor force: 403,000 (est.). Major industries: food processing, beer, soft drinks. Natural resources: unexploited deposits of bauxite, petroleum, phosphates; fish and timber. Exports: peanuts, cashews, fish, palm kernels. Imports: foodstuffs, manufactured goods, fuels, transportation equipment. Major trading partners: Portugal, Spain, and other European countries.

Geography. A neighbor of Senegal and Guinea in West Africa, on the Atlantic coast, Guinea-Bissau is about half the size of South Carolina.

The country is a low-lying coastal region of swamps, rain forests, and mangrove-covered wetlands, with about 25 islands off the coast. The Bijagos archipelago extends 30 miles (48 km) out to sea. Internal communications depend mainly on deep estuaries and meandering rivers, since there are no railroads. Bissau, the capital, is the main port.

Government. After the overthrow of Louis Cabral in November 1980, the nine-member Council of the Revolution formed an interm government. In 1982, they formed a new government consisting of the President, 2 Vice-Presidents, 18 ministers and 10 state secretaries.

History. Guinea-Bissau was discovered in 1446 by the Portuguese Nuno Tristao, and colonists in the Cape Verde Islands obtained trading rights in the territory. In 1879 the connection with the Cape Verde Islands was broken. Early in the 1900s the Portuguese managed to pacify some tribesmen, although resistance to colonial rule remained.

The African Party for the Independence of Guinea-Bissau and Cape Verde was founded in 1956 and several years later began guerrilla warfare that grew increasingly effective. By 1974 the rebels controlled most of the countryside, where they formed a government that was soon recognized by scores of countries. The military coup in Portugal in April 1974 brightened the prospects for freedom, and in August the Lisbon government signed an agreement granting independence to the province as of Sept. 10. The new republic took the name Guinea-Bissau.

In November 1980, Prémier João Bernardo Vieira headed a coup that deposed Luis Cabral, President since 1974. A Revolutionary Council assumed the powers of government, with Vieira as its head. A dispute with Senegal over territorial waters erupted in April 1990 when Senegal stopped three Guinea-Bissau ships.

GUYANA

Cooperative Republic of Guyana
President: Desmond Hoyte (1985)
Area: 83,000 sq mi. (214,969 sq km)
Population (est. mid-1991): 800,000 (average annual rate of natural increase: 1.8%); birth rate: 25/1000; infant mortality rate: 52/1000; density per square mile: 10
Capital and largest city (est. 1981): Georgetown, 200,000
Monetary unit: Guyana dollar
Languages: English (official), Amerindian dialects
Religions: Hindu, 34%; Protestant, 18%; Islam, 9%; Roman Catholic, 18%; Anglican, 16%
Member of Commonwealth of Nations
Literacy rate: 85%
Economic summary: Gross domestic product (1988 est.): $323 million; $420 per capita; –3.0% real growth rate. Arable land: 3%. Principal products: sugar, rice. Labor force: 268,000; 44.5% industry and commerce. Major products: bauxite, alumina. Natural resources: bauxite, gold, diamonds, hardwood timber, shrimp. Exports: sugar, bauxite, rice, timber, shrimp, gold, molasses, rum. Imports: petroleum, food, machinery. Major trading partners: U.K., U.S., Canada.

Geography. Guyana is situated on the northern coast of South America east of Venezuela, west of Suriname, and north of Brazil. The country consists of a low coastal area and the Guiana Highlands in the south. There is an extensive north-south network of rivers. Guyana is the size of Idaho.

Government. Guyana, formerly British Guiana, proclaimed itself a republic on Feb. 23, 1970, ending its tie with Britain while remaining in the Commonwealth.

Guyana has a unicameral legislature, the National Assembly, with 53 members directly elected for five-year terms and 12 elected by local councils. A 24-member Cabinet is headed by the President.

History. British Guiana won internal self-government in 1952. The next year the People's Progressive Party, headed by Cheddi B. Jagan, an East Indian dentist, won the elections and Jagan became Prime Minister. British authorities deposed him for alleged Communist connections. A coalition ousted Jagan in 1964, installing a moderate Socialist, Forbes Burnham, a black, as Prime Minister. On May 26, 1966, the country became an independent member of the Commonwealth and resumed its traditional name, Guyana.

After ruling Guyana for 21 years, Burnham died on Aug. 6 1985, in a Guyana hospital after a throat operation. Desmond Hoyte, the country's Prime Minister succeeded him under the Guyanese constitution.

On January 8, 1991 Guyana became the 35th member of the Organization of American States.

HAITI

Republic of Haiti
President: Rev. Jean-Bertrand Aristide (1991)
Area: 10,714 sq mi. (27,750 sq km)
Population (est. mid-1991): 6,300,000 (average annual rate of natural increase: 2.3%); birth rate: 45/1000; infant mortality rate: 107/1000; density per square mile: 587
Capital and largest city (est. 1984): Port-au-Prince, city, 461,464; urban area, 738,342
Monetary unit: Gourde
Languages: French, Creole

Religion: Roman Catholic, 80%; Protestant, 10%
National name: République d'Haïti
Literacy rate: 23%
Economic summary: Gross domestic product (1988 est.): $2.4 billion; $380 per capita; 0.3% real growth rate. Arable land: 20%. Principal products: coffee, sugar cane, rice, corn, sorghum. Labor force: 2,300,000; 9% in industry. Major products: refined sugar, textiles, flour, cement, light assembly products. Natural resource: bauxite. Exports: coffee, light industrial products, sugar, cocoa, sisal. Imports: machines and manufactures, food and beverages, petroleum products, fats and oils, chemicals. Major trading partner: U.S.

Geography. Haiti, in the West Indies, occupies the western third of the island of Hispaniola, which it shares with the Dominican Republic. About the size of Maryland, Haiti is two thirds mountainous, with the rest of the country marked by great valleys, extensive plateaus, and small plains. The most densely populated region is the Cul-de-Sac plain near Port-au-Prince.

History. Discovered by Columbus, who landed at Môle Saint Nicolas on Dec. 6, 1492, Haiti in 1697 became a French possession known as Saint Domingue. An insurrection among a slave population of 500,000 in 1791 ended with a declaration of independence by Pierre-Dominique Toussaint l'Ouverture in 1801. Napoleon Bonaparte suppressed the independence movement, but it eventually triumphed in 1804 under Jean-Jacques Dessalines, who gave the new nation the aboriginal name Haiti.

Its prosperity dissipated in internal strife as well as disputes with neighboring Santo Domingo during a succession of 19th-century dictatorships, a bankrupt Haiti accepted a U.S. customs receivership from 1905 to 1941. Direct U.S. rule from 1915 to 1934 brought a measure of stability and a population growth that made Haiti the most densely populated nation in the hemisphere.

In 1949, after four years of democratic rule by President Dumarsais Estimé, dictatorship returned under Gen. Paul Magloire, who was succeeded by François Duvalier in 1957.

Duvalier established a dictatorship based on secret police, known as the "Ton-ton Macoutes," who gunned down opponents of the regime. Duvalier's son, Jean-Claude, or "Baby Doc," succeeded his father in 1971 as ruler of the poorest nation in the Western Hemisphere. Duvalier fled the country in 1986 after strong unrest.

Following the election of December 6, 1990 which he won, Jean-Bertrand Aristide, a Roman Catholic priest, was sworn in as president on February 7, 1991—the country's first freely elected chief executive.

Government. A republic with a bicameral assembly consisting of an upper house or Senate and a lower house, the House of Deputies. The National Assembly consists of 27 senate seats and 83 deputies. The army stopped the first scheduled elections in November and army-sponsored elections led to the election of Leslie Manigat in Jan., 1988. He was overthrown in June 1988 in a military coup led by Namphy, after the former attempted to dismiss him. He was in turn overthrown by Lt. Gen. Prosper Avril.

The ruling council that took power upon the exile of Duvalier was criticized for the inclusion of former Duvalier aides.

Anti-government protests aginst the Avril governments crackdown on opposition leaders forced Avril to resign. Ertha-Trovillot, a former Supreme Court Justice, became President in March 1990.

HONDURAS

Republic of Honduras
President: Rafael L. Callejas (1990)
Area: 43,277 sq mi. (112,088 sq km)
Population (est. mid-1991): 5,300,000 (average annual rate of natural increase: 3.1%); birth rate: 39/1000; infant mortality rate: 48/1000; density per square mile: 122
Capital and largest city (1985): Tegucigalpa, 571,400
Monetary unit: Lempira
Languages: Spanish, some Indian dialects, English in Bay Islands Department
Religion: Roman Catholic
National name: República de Honduras
Literacy rate: 56%
Economic summary: Gross domestic product (1988): $4.4 billion; $890 per capita; 4.0% real growth rate. Arable land: 14%. Principal products: bananas, coffee, timber, beef, shrimp, citrus. Labor force: 1,300,000; 9% in manufacturing. Major industrial products: processed agricultural products, textiles and clothing, wood products. Natural resources: timber, gold, silver, copper, lead, zinc, iron ore, antimony. Exports: bananas, coffee, lumber, shrimp and lobster, minerals. Imports: manufactured goods, machinery, transportation equipment, chemicals, petroleum. Major trading partners: U.S., Caribbean countries, Western Europe, Japan, Latin America.

Geography. Honduras, in the north central part of Central America, has a 400-mile (644-km) Caribbean coastline and a 40-mile (64-km) Pacific frontage. Its neighbors are Guatemala to the west, El Salvador to the south, and Nicaragua to the east. Honduras is slightly larger than Tennessee. Generally mountainous, the country is marked by fertile plateaus, river valleys, and narrow coastal plains.

Government. The President serves a four-year term. There is a 134-member National Congress.

History. Columbus discovered Honduras on his last voyage in 1502. Honduras, with four other countries of Central America, declared its independence from Spain in 1821 and was part of a federation of Central American states until 1838. In that year it seceded from the federation and became a completely independent country.

In July 1969, El Salvador invaded Honduras after Honduran landowners had deported several thousand Salvadorans. The fighting left 1,000 dead and tens of thousands homeless. By threatening economic sanctions and military intervention, the OAS induced El Salvador to withdraw.

Although parliamentary democracy returned with the election of Roberto Suazo Córdova as President in 1982 after a decade of military rule, Honduras faced severe economic problems and tensions along its border with Nicaragua. "Contra" rebels, waging a guerrilla war against the Sandinista regime in Nicaragua, used Honduras as a training and staging area. At the same time, the United States used Honduras as a site for military exercises and built bases to train both Honduran and Salvadoran troops.

In the first democratic transition of power since 1932 Rafael Callejas became president in January 1990. The immediate task was to deal with a deficit caused in part by reduced U.S. aid and the previous government's fiscal policies. The IMF would not grand new loans to the country owing to its arrears on repayment of previous loans.

HUNGARY

Republic of Hungary
President: Arpad Goncz (1990)
Premier: József Antall (1990)
Area: 35,919 sq mi. (93,030 sq km)
Population (1990 census): 10,375,000 (average annual rate of natural increase: –0.2%); birth rate: 12/1000; infant mortality rate: 15.7/1000; density per square mile: 289
Capital: Budapest
Largest cities (1989): Budapest, 2,113,645; Debrecen, 219,151; Miskolc, 207,826; Szeged, 189,484; Pécs, 183,082; Győr, 183,082.
Monetary unit: Forint
Language: Magyar
Religions: Roman Catholic, 67.5%; Protestant, 25%; atheist and others, 7.5%
National name: Magyar Köztársaság
Literacy rate: 99%
Economic summary: Gross national product (1989 est.): $64.6 billion; $6,108 per capita; –1.3% real growth rate. Arable land: 54%. Principal products: corn, wheat, potatoes, sugar beets, sun flowers, livestock, dairy products. Labor force: 4,860,000; 30.9% in industry. Major products: steel, chemicals, pharmaceuticals, textiles, transport equipment. Natural resources: bauxite, coal, natural gas. Exports: machinery and tools, industrial and consumer goods, raw materials. Imports: machinery and transport, fuels, chemical products, manufactured consumer goods. Major trading partners: U.S.S.R., Eastern Europe.

Geography. This central European country the size of Indiana is bordered by Austria to the west, Czechoslovakia to the north, the U.S.S.R. and Romania to the east, and Yugoslavia to the south.

Most of Hungary is a fertile, rolling plain lying east of the Danube River and drained by the Danube and Tisza rivers. In the extreme northwest is the Little Hungarian Plain. South of that area is Lake Balaton (250 sq mi.; 648 sq km).

Government. Hungary is a Republic with legislative power vested in the unicameral National Assembly, whose 386 members are elected directly for four-year terms. The National Assembly elects the President. The supreme body of state power is the 21-member Presidential Council elected by the National Assembly. The supreme administrative body is the Council of Ministers, headed by the Premier.

The major political parties are the Socialist Party, the Hungarian Democratic Forum, the Alliance of Free Democrats, the Independent Socialist Party and the Independent Smallholder's Party.

History. About 2,000 years ago, Hungary was part of the Roman provinces of Pannonia and Dacia. In A.D. 896 it was invaded by the Magyars, who founded a kingdom. Christianity was accepted during the reign of Stephen I (St. Stephen) (997–1038).

The peak of Hungary's great period of medieval power came during the reign of Louis I the Great (1342–82), whose dominions touched the Baltic, Black, and Mediterranean seas.

War with the Turks broke out in 1389, and for more than 100 years the Turks advanced through the Balkans. When the Turks smashed a Hungarian army in 1526, western and northern Hungary accepted Hapsburg rule to escape Turkish occupation. Transylvania became independent under Hungarian princes. Intermittent war with the Turks was waged until a peace treaty was signed in 1699.

After the suppression of the 1848 revolt against

Hapsburg rule, led by Louis Kossuth, the dual monarchy of Austria-Hungary was set up in 1867.

The dual monarchy was defeated with the other Central Powers in World War I. After a short-lived republic in 1918, the chaotic Communist rule of 1919 under Béla Kun ended with the Romanians occupying Budapest on Aug. 4, 1919. When the Romanians left, Adm. Nicholas Horthy entered the capital with a national army. The Treaty of Trianon of June 4, 1920, cost Hungary 68% of its land and 58% of its population. Meanwhile, the National Assembly had restored the legal continuity of the old monarchy; and, on March 1, 1920, Horthy was elected Regent.

Following the German invasion of Russia on June 22, 1941, Hungary joined the attack against the Soviet Union, but the war was not popular and Hungarian troops were almost entirely withdrawn from the eastern front by May 1943. German occupation troops set up a puppet government after Horthy's appeal for an armistice with advancing Soviet troops on Oct. 15, 1944, had resulted in his overthrow. The German regime soon fled the capital, however, and on December 23 a provisional government was formed in Soviet-occupied eastern Hungary. On Jan. 20, 1945, it signed an armistice in Moscow. Early the next year, the National Assembly approved a constitutional law abolishing the thousand-year-old monarchy and establishing a republic.

By the Treaty of Paris (1947), Hungary had to give up all territory it had acquired since 1937 and to pay $300 million reparations to the U.S.S.R., Czechoslovakia, and Yugoslavia. In 1948 the Communist Party, with the support of Soviet troops seized control. Hungary was proclaimed a People's Republic and one-party state in 1949. Industry was nationalized, the land collectivized into state farms, and the opposition terrorized by the secret police.

The terror, modeled after that of the U.S.S.R., reached its height with the trial of Jozsef Cardinal Mindszenty, Roman Catholic primate. He confessed to fantastic charges under duress of drugs or brainwashing and was sentenced to life imprisonment in 1949. Protests were voiced in all parts of the world.

On Oct. 23, 1956, anti-Communist revolution broke out in Budapest. To cope with it, the Communists set up a coalition government and called former Premier Imre Nagy back to head it. But he and most of his ministers were swept by the logic of events into the anti-Communist opposition, and he declared Hungary a neutral power, withdrawing from the Warsaw Treaty and appealing to the United Nations for help.

One of his ministers, János Kádár, established a counter-regime and asked the U.S.S.R. to send in military power. Soviet troops and tanks suppressed the revolution in bloody fighting after 190,000 people had fled the country and Mindszenty, freed from jail, had taken refuge in the U.S. Embassy.

Kádár was succeeded as Premier, but not party secretary, by Gyula Kallai in 1965. Continuing his program of national reconciliation, Kádár emptied prisons, reformed the secret police, and eased travel restrictions.

Hungary developed the reputation of being the freest East European state.

Relations with the U.S. improved in 1972 when World War II debt claims between the two nations were settled. On Jan. 6, 1978, the U.S. returned to Hungary, over anti-Communist protests, the 977-year-old crown of St. Stephen, held at Fort Knox since World War II.

A reform movement in the late-1980s led to the disbanding of the party militia, the withdrawal of po-

litical cells from factories and offices, and free multi-party elections. The new Parliament elected Arpad
Goncz, who had been jailed for his role in the 1956
uprising, as interim President.

Following local and parliamentary elections in October 1990, Jozsef Antall's Hungarian Democratic
Forum and its conservative coalition parties held 60%
of the parliamentary seats. The last Soviet troops left
Hungary in June 1991, thereby ending almost 47
years of military presence.

ICELAND

Republic of Iceland
President: Mrs. Vigdis· Finnbogadottir (1980)
Prime Minister: David Oddsson (1991)
Area: 39,709 sq mi. (102,846 sq km)[1]
Population (Dec. 1990): 255,000 (average annual rate of
natural increase: 1.1%); birth rate: 18/1000; infant mor-
tality rate: 5.3/1000; density per square mile: 7
Capital and largest city (1988): Reykjavik, 95,799
Monetary unit: M.N. króna
Language: Icelandic
Religion: Evangelical Lutheran
National name: Lydveldid Island
Literacy rate: 100%
Economic summary: Gross domestic product (1988): $5.9
billion; $24,031 per capita; −1.8% real growth rate.
Arable land: NEGL%; principal agricultural products:
livestock, potatoes and turnips. Labor force: 134,429;
55.4% in commerce, finance and services. Major prod-
ucts: processed aluminum, fish. Natural resources:
fish, diatomite, hydroelectric and geothermal power.
Exports: fish, animal products, aluminum, diatomite.
Imports: petroleum products, machinery and transportation equipment, food, textiles. Major trading
partners: European Communities (EC) countries, Euro
pean Free Trade Association (EFTA) countries, U.S.,
Japan, and U.S.S.R.

1. Including some offshore islands.

Geography. Iceland, an island about the size of
Kentucky, lies in the north Atlantic Ocean east of
Greenland and just touches the Arctic Circle. It is one
of the most volcanic regions in the world.

Small fresh-water lakes are to be found throughout
the island, and there are many natural phenomena,
including hot springs, geysers, sulfur beds, canyons,
waterfalls, and swift rivers. More than 13% of the
area is covered by snowfields and glaciers, and most
of the people live in the 7% of the island comprising
fertile coastlands.

Government. The president is elected for four years
by popular vote. Executive power resides in the
prime minister and his Cabinet. The Althing (Parliament) is composed of 63 members.

History. Iceland was first settled shortly before 900,
mainly by Norse. A Constitution drawn up about 930
created a form of democracy and provided for an
Althing, or General Assembly.

In 1262–64, Iceland came under Norwegian rule
and passed to ultimate Danish control through the
formation of the Union of Kalmar in 1483. In 1874,
Icelanders obtained their own Constitution. In 1918,
Denmark recognized Iceland as a separate state with
unlimited sovereignty but still nominally under the
Danish king.

On June 17, 1944, after a popular referendum, the

Althing proclaimed Iceland an independent republic.

The British occupied Iceland in 1940, immediately
after the German invasion of Denmark. In 1942, the
U.S. took over the burden of protection. Iceland refused to abandon its neutrality in World War II and
thus forfeited charter membership in the United Nations, but it cooperated with the Allies throughout the
conflict. Iceland joined the North Atlantic Treaty Organization in 1949.

Iceland unilaterally extended its territorial waters
from 12 to 50 nautical miles in 1972, precipitating a
running dispute with Britain known as the "cod war."
An agreement calling for registration of all British
trawlers fishing within 200 miles of Iceland and a
24-hour time limit on incursions was finally reached
in 1976.

Elections to the Althing in April 1991 gave the opposition Independence Party 26 of the 63 seats, up
from 18. Prime Minister Hermannson resigned allowing David Oddsson of the Independence Party to enter into talks with the Social Democrats about a coalition government. None of the parties is interested in
Iceland pursuing membership in the E.C., although it
is a member of the European Free Trade Association.

INDIA

Republic of India
President: Ramaswamy Venkataraman (1987)
Prime Minister: P.V. Narasimha Rao (1991)
Area: 1,229,737 sq mi. (3,185,019 sq km)
Population (est. mid-1991): 859,200,000 (average annual
rate of natural increase: 2.0%); birth rate: 31/1000;
infant mortality rate: 91/1000; density per square mile:
677
Capital (1980 census): New Delhi, 619,417
Largest cities (1981 est.): Calcutta, 9,194,018; Greater
Bombay, 8,243,405; Delhi, 5,729,283; Madras, 4,289,347;
Bangalore, 2,921,751; Ahmedabad, 2,548,057; Kanpur,
1,639,064
Monetary unit: Rupee
Principal languages: Hindi (official), English (official),
Bengali, Gujarati, Kashmiri, Malayalam, Marathi, Ori-
ya, Punjabi, Tamil, Telugu, Urdu, Kannada, Assamese
(all recognized by the Constitution)
Religions: Hindu, 82.6%; Islam, 11.4%; Christian, 2.4%;
Sikh, 2%
National name: Bharat
Literacy rate: 36%
Member of Commonwealth of Nations
Economic summary: Gross national product (1989 est.):
$333 billion; $400 per capita; 5.0% real growth rate.
Arable land: 55%. Principal products: rice, wheat,
oilseeds, cotton, tea, opium poppy (for pharmaceuticals). Labor force: 284,400,000; 67% in agriculture.
Major industrial products: jute, processed food, steel,
machinery, transport machinery, cement. Natural resources: iron ore, coal, manganese, mica, bauxite,
limestone, textiles. Exports: tea, coffee, iron ore, fish
products, manufactures. Imports: petroleum, edible
oils, textiles, clothing, capital goods. Major trading
partners: U.S., U.S.S.R., Japan, E.C., Middle East

Geography. One third the area of the United States,
the Republic of India occupies most of the subcontinent of India in south Asia. It borders on China in
the northeast. Other neighbors are Pakistan on the
west, Nepal and Bhutan on the north, and Burma and
Bangladesh on the east.

The country contains a large part of the great Indo-Gangetic plain, which extends from the Bay of Bengal on the east to the Afghan frontier on the Arabian Sea on the west. This plain is the richest and most densely settled part of the subcontinent. Another distinct natural region is the Deccan, a plateau of 2,000 to 3,000 feet (610 to 914 m) in elevation, occupying the southern portion of the subcontinent.

Forming a part of the republic are several groups of islands—the Laccadives (14 islands) in the Arabian Sea and the Andamans (204 islands) and the Nicobars (19 islands) in the Bay of Bengal.

India's three great river systems, all rising in the Himalayas, have extensive deltas. The Ganges flows south and then east for 1,540 miles (2,478 km) across the northern plain to the Bay of Bengal; part of its delta, which begins 220 miles (354 km) from the sea, is within the republic. The Indus, starting in Tibet, flows northwest for several hundred miles in the Kashmir before turning southwest toward the Arabian Sea; it is important for irrigation in Pakistan. The Brahmaputra, also rising in Tibet, flows eastward, first through India and then south into Bangladesh and the Bay of Bengal.

Government. India is a federal republic. It is also a member of the Commonwealth of Nations, a status defined at the 1949 London Conference of Prime Ministers, by which India recognizes Queen as head of the Commonwealth. Under the Constitution effective Jan. 26, 1950, India has a parliamentary type of government.

The constitutional head of the state is the President, who is elected every five years. He is advised by the Prime Minister and a Cabinet based on a majority of the bicameral Parliament, which consists of a Council of States (Rajya Sabha), representing the constituent units of the republic and a House of the People (Lok Sabha), elected every five years by universal suffrage.

History. The Aryans, or Hindus, who invaded India between 2400 and 1500 b.c. from the northwest found a land already well civilized. Buddhism was founded in the 6th century b.c. and spread through northern India.

In 1526, Moslem invaders founded the great Mogul empire, centered on Delhi, which lasted, at least in name, until 1857. Akbar the Great (1542–1605) strengthened this empire and became the ruler of a greater portion of India than had ever before acknowledged the suzerainty of one man. The long reign of his great-grandson, Aurangzeb (1658–1707), represents both the culmination of Mogul power and the beginning of its decay.

Vasco da Gama, the Portuguese explorer, visited India first in 1498, and for the next 100 years the Portuguese had a virtual monopoly on trade with the subcontinent. Meanwhile, the English founded the East India Company, which set up its first factory at Surat in 1612 and began expanding its influence, fighting the Indian rulers and the French, Dutch, and Portuguese traders simultaneously.

Bombay, taken from the Portuguese, became the seat of English rule in 1687. The defeat of French and Islamic armies by Lord Clive in the decade ending in 1760 laid the foundation of the British Empire in India. From then until 1858, when the administration of India was formally transferred to the British Crown following the Sepoy Mutiny of native troops in 1857, the East India Company suppressed native uprisings and extended British rule.

After World War I, in which the Indian states sent more than 6 million troops to fight beside the Allies, Indian nationalist unrest rose to new heights under the leadership of a little Hindu lawyer, Mohandas K. Gandhi, called Mahatma Gandhi. His tactics called for nonviolent revolts against British authority. He soon became the leading spirit of the All-India Congress Party, which was the spearhead of revolt. In 1919 the British gave added responsibility to Indian officials, and in 1935 India was given a federal form of government and a measure of self-rule.

In 1942, with the Japanese pressing hard on the eastern borders of India, the British War Cabinet tried and failed to reach a political settlement with nationalist leaders. The Congress Party took the position that the British must quit India. In 1942, fearing mass civil disobedience, the government of India carried out widespread arrests of Congress leaders, including Gandhi.

Gandhi was released in 1944 and negotiations for a settlement were resumed. Finally, in February 1947, the Labor government announced its determination to transfer power to "responsible Indian hands" by June 1948 even if a Constitution had not been worked out.

Lord Mountbatten as Viceroy, by June 1947, achieved agreement on the partitioning of India along religious lines and on the splitting of the provinces of Bengal and the Punjab, which the Moslems had claimed.

The Indian Independence Act, passed quickly by the British Parliament, received royal assent on July 18, 1947, and on August 15 the Indian Empire passed into history.

Jawaharlal Nehru, leader of the Congress Party, was made Prime Minister. Before an exchange of populations could be arranged, bloody riots occurred among the communal groups, and armed conflict broke out over rival claims to the princely state of Jammu and Kashmir. Peace was restored only with the greatest difficulty. In 1949 a Constitution, along the lines of the U.S. Constitution, was approved making India a sovereign republic. Under a federal structure the states were organized on linguistic lines.

The dominance of the Congress Party contributed to stability. In 1956 the republic absorbed the former French settlements. Five years later, it forcibly annexed the Portuguese enclaves of Goa, Damao, and Diu.

Nehru died in 1964. His successor, Lal Bahadur Shastri, died on Jan. 10, 1966. Nehru's daughter, Indira Gandhi, became Prime Minister, and she continued his policy of nonalignment.

In 1971 the Pakistani Army moved in to quash the independence movement in East Pakistan that was supported by clandestine aid from India, and some 10 million Bengali refugees poured across the border into India, creating social, economic, and health problems. After numerous border incidents, India invaded East Pakistan and in two weeks forced the surrender of the Pakistani army. East Pakistan was established as an independent state and renamed Bangladesh.

In the summer of 1975, the world's largest democracy veered suddenly toward authoritarianism when a judge in Allahabad, Mrs. Gandhi's home constituency, found her landslide victory in the 1971 elections invalid because civil servants had illegally aided her campaign. Amid demands for her resignation, Mrs. Gandhi decreed a state of emergency on June 26 and ordered mass arrests of her critics, including all opposition party leaders except the Communists.

In 1976, India and Pakistan formally renewed diplomatic relations.

Despite strong opposition to her repressive measures and particularly the resentment against compulsory birth control programs, Mrs. Gandhi in 1977 announced parliamentary elections for March. At the same time, she freed most political prisoners.

The landslide victory of Morarji R. Desai unseated Mrs. Gandhi and also defeated a bid for office by her son, Sanjay.

Mrs. Gandhi staged a spectacular comeback in the elections of January 1980.

In 1984, Mrs. Gandhi ordered the Indian Army to root out a band of Sikh holy men and gunmen who were using the holiest shrine of the Sikh religion, the Golden Temple in Amritsar, as a base for terrorist raids in a violent campaign for greater political autonomy in the strategic Punjab border state. As many as 1,000 people were reported killed in the June 5–6 battle, including Jarnall Singh Bhindranwale, the Khomeini-like militant leader, and 93 soldiers. The perceived sacrilege to the Golden Temple kindled outrage among many of India's 14 million Sikhs and brought a spasm of mutinies and desertions by Sikh officers and soldiers in the army.

On Oct. 31, 1984, Mrs. Gandhi was assassinated by two men identified by police as Sikh members of her bodyguard. The ruling Congress I Party chose her second son, Rajiv Gandhi, to succeed her as Prime Minister.

One week after the resignation of Prime Minister Shekhar, India's president in March 1991 called for national elections, the tenth in its history and the second in less than two years. While at an election rally on May 22 former prime minister Rajiv Gandhi was assassinated. Final phases of the election were postponed a month. When they were resumed the Congress Party and its allies won 236 seats in the lower house, 20 short of a majority. P.V. Narasimha Rao was chosen to form a new government over a strong challenge from within the Congress Party. Ailing with a poor heart, he is widely regarded as a caretaker prime minister.

Native States. Most of the 560-odd native states and subdivisions of pre-1947 India acceded to the new nation, and the central government pursued a vigorous policy of integration. This took three forms: merger into adjacent provinces, conversion into centrally administered areas, and grouping into unions of states. Finally, under a controversial reorganization plan effective Nov. 1, 1956, the unions of states were abolished and merged into adjacent states, and India became a union of 15 states and 8 centrally administered areas. A 16th state was added in 1962, and in 1966, the Punjab was partitioned into two states.

Resolution of the territorial dispute over Kashmir grew out of peace negotiations following the two-week India-Pakistan war of 1971. After sporadic skirmishing, an accord reached July 3, 1972, committed both powers to withdraw troops from a temporary cease-fire line after the border was fixed. Agreement on the border was reached Dec. 7, 1972.

In April 1975, the Indian Parliament voted to make the 300-year-old kingdom of Sikkim a full-fledged Indian state, and the annexation took effect May 16.

Situated in the Himalayas, Sikkim was a virtual dependency of Tibet until the early 19th century. Under an 1890 treaty between China and Great Britain, it became a British protectorate, and was made an Indian protectorate after Britain quit the subcontinent.

INDONESIA

Republic of Indonesia
President: Suharto (1969)[1]
Area: 735,268 sq mi. (1,904,344 sq km)[2]
Population (est. mid-1991): 181,400,000 (average annual rate of natural increase: 1.7%); birth rate: 25/1000; infant mortality rate: 73/1000; density per square mile: 245
Capital: Jakarta
Largest cities (est. 1983): Jakarta, 7,636,000; Surabaja, 2,289,000; Bandung, 1,602,000; Medan, 1,966,000; Semarang, 1,269,000
Monetary unit: Rupiah
Languages: Bahasa Indonesia (official), Dutch, English, and more than 60 regional languages
Religions: Islam, 88%; Christian, 9%; Hindu, 2%; other, 1%
National name: Republik Indonesia
Literacy rate: 62%
Economic summary: Gross national product (1989 est.): $80 billion; $430 per capita; 5.7% real growth rate. Arable land: 8%. Principal products: rice, cassava, peanuts, rubber, coffee. Labor force: 67,000,000; 10% in manufacturing. Major products: petroleum, timber, textiles, cement, fertilizer, rubber. Natural resources: oil, timber, nickel, natural gas, tin, bauxite, copper. Exports: petroleum and liquid natural gas, timber, rubber, coffee, textiles. Imports: chemicals, machinery, manufactured goods. Major trading partners: Japan, U.S., Singapore, E.C.

1. General Suharto served as Acting President of Indonesia from 1967 to 1969. 2. Includes West Irian (former Netherlands New Guinea), renamed Irian Jaya in March 1973 (159,355 sq mi.; 412,731 sq km), and former Portuguese Timor (5,763 sq mi.; 14,925 sq km), annexed in 1976.

Geography. Indonesia is part of the Malay archipelago in Southeast Asia with an area nearly three times that of Texas. It consists of the islands of Sumatra, Java, Madura, Borneo (except Sarawak and Brunei in the north), the Celebes, the Moluccas, Irian Jaya, and about 30 smaller archipelagos, totaling 13,677 islands, of which about 6,000 are inhabited. Its neighbor to the north is Malaysia and to the east Papua New Guinea.

A backbone of mountain ranges extends throughout the main islands of the archipelago. Earthquakes are frequent, and there are many active volcanoes.

Government. The President is elected by the People's Consultative Assembly, whose 1000 members include the functioning legislative arm, the 500-member House of Representatives. Meeting at least once every five years, the Assembly has broad policy functions. The House, 100 of whose members are appointed by the President, meets at least once annually. General Suharto was elected unopposed to a fifth five-year term in 1988.

History. Indonesia is inhabited by Malayan and Papuan peoples ranging from the more advanced Javanese and Balinese to the more primitive Dyaks of Borneo. Invasions from China and India contributed Chinese and Indian admixtures.

During the first few centuries of the Christian era, most of the islands came under the influence of Hindu priests and traders, who spread their culture and religion. Moslem invasions began in the 13th century, and most of the area was Moslem by the 15th. Portuguese traders arrived early in the 16th century but were ousted by the Dutch about 1595. After Napoleon subjugated the Netherlands homeland in 1811, the British seized the islands but returned them to the Dutch in 1816. In 1922 the islands were made an integral part of the Netherlands kingdom.

During World War II, Indonesia was under Japanese military occupation with nominal native self-government. When the Japanese surrendered to the Allies, President Sukarno and Mohammed Hatta, his Vice President, proclaimed Indonesian independence from the Dutch on Aug. 17, 1945. Allied troops—mostly British Indian troops—fought the nationalists until the arrival of Dutch troops. In November 1946, the Dutch and the Indonesians reached a draft agreement contemplating formation of a Netherlands-Indonesian Union, but differences in interpretation resulted in more fighting between Dutch and Indonesian forces.

On Nov. 2, 1949, Dutch and Indonesian leaders agreed upon the terms of union. The transfer of sovereignty took place at Amsterdam on Dec. 27, 1949. In February 1956 Indonesia abrogated the Union with the Netherlands and in August 1956 repudiated its debt to the Netherlands. In 1963, Netherlands New Guinea was transferred to Indonesia and renamed West Irian. In 1973 it became Irian Jaya.

Hatta and Sukarno, the co-fathers of Indonesian independence, split after it was achieved over Sukarno's concept of "guided democracy." Under Sukarno, the country's leading political figure for almost a half century, the Indonesian Communist Party gradually gained increasing influence.

After an attempted coup was put down by General Suharto, the army chief of staff, and officers loyal to him, thousands of Communist suspects were sought out and killed all over the country. Suharto took over the reins of government, gradually eased Sukarno out of office, and took full power in 1967.

Suharto permitted national elections, which moved the nation back to representative government. He also ended hostilities with Malaysia. Under President Suharto, Indonesia has been strongly anticommunist. It also has been politically stable and has made progress in economic development.

Indonesia invaded the former Portuguese half of the island of Timor in 1975, and annexed the territory in 1976. On a visit to Jakarta in July 1984, Secretary of State George P. Shultz expressed concern about reports of human rights abuses being carried out by Indonesian forces in East Timor. More than 100,000 Timorese, a sixth of the mostly Catholic population, were reported to have died from famine, disease, and fighting since the annexation.

Relations with China were normalized in 1990. The army has recently expressed the need for change in the political system. The government has also attempted to liberalize and diversify the economy, relying less on oil export revenue. Indonesia is a member of OPEC.

IRAN

Islamic Republic of Iran
President: Hashemi Rafsanjani (1989)
Area: 636,293 sq mi. (1,648,000 sq km)
Population (est. mid-1991): 58,600,000 (average annual rate of natural increase: 3.3%); birth rate: 41/1000; infant mortality rate: 43/1000; density per square mile: 92
Capital: Teheran
Largest cities (est. 1986): Teheran, 6,037,658; Isfahan, 1,422,308; Mashed, 2,038,388; Tabriz, 1,566,932

Monetary unit: Rial
Languages: Farsi (Persian), Kurdish, Arabic
Religions: Shi'ite Moslem, 95%; Sunni Moslem, 4%
Literacy rate: 48% (est.)
Economic summary: Gross national product (1989): $97.6 billion; $1,800 per capita; real growth rate 0–1%. Arable land: 8%. Principal products: wheat, barley, rice, sugar beets, cotton, dates, raisins, sheep, goats. Labor force: 15,400,000; 21% in manufacturing. Major products: crude and refined oil, textiles, petrochemicals, cement, processed foods, steel and copper fabrication. Natural resources: oil, gas, iron, copper. Exports: petroleum, carpets. Imports: machinery, military supplies, foodstuffs, pharmaceuticals. Major trading partners: Japan, Germany, Netherlands, U.K., Italy, Spain, Turkey.

Geography. Iran, a Middle Eastern country south of the Caspian Sea and north of the Persian Gulf, is three times the size of Arizona. It shares borders with Iraq, Turkey, the U.S.S.R., Afghanistan, and Pakistan.

In general, the country is a plateau averaging 4,000 feet (1,219 m) in elevation. There are also maritime lowlands along the Persian Gulf and the Caspian Sea. The Elburz Mountains in the north rise to 18,603 feet (5,670 m) at Mt. Damavend. From northwest to southeast, the country is crossed by a desert 800 miles (1,287 km) long.

Government. The Pahlavi dynasty was overthrown on Feb. 11, 1979, by followers of the Ayatollah Ruhollah Khomeini. After a referendum endorsed the establishment of a republic, Khomeini drafted a Constitution calling for a President to be popularly elected every four years, an appointed Prime Minister, and a unicameral National Consultative Assembly, popularly elected every four years. A constitutional amendment in 1989 eliminated the post of Prime Minister.

Khomeini also instituted a Revolutionary Council to insure the adherence to Islamic principles in all phases of Iranian life. The Council formally handed over its powers to the Assembly after the organization of the legislature in July 1980, but continued to exercise power behind the scenes.

History. Oil-rich Iran was called Persia before 1935. Its key location blocks the lower land gate to Asia and also stands in the way of traditional Russian ambitions for access to the Indian Ocean. After periods of Assyrian, Median, and Achaemenidian rule, Persia became a powerful empire under Cyrus the Great, reaching from the Indus to the Nile at its zenith in 525 B.C. It fell to Alexander in 331–30 B.C. and to the Seleucids in 312–02 B.C., and a native Persian regime arose about 130 B.C. Another Persian regime arose about A.D. 224, but it fell to the Arabs in 637. In the 12th century, the Mongols took their turn ruling Persia, and in the early part of the 18th century, the Turks occupied the country.

An Anglo-Russian convention of 1907 divided Persia into two spheres of influence. British attempts to impose a protectorate over the entire country were defeated in 1919. Two years later, Gen. Reza Pahlavi seized the government and was elected hereditary Shah in 1925. Subsequently he did much to modernize the country and abolished all foreign extraterritorial rights.

Increased pro-Axis activity led to Anglo-Russian occupation of Iran in 1941 and deposition of the Shah in favor of his son, Mohammed Reza Pahlavi.

Ali Razmara became premier in 1950 and pledged to restore efficient and honest government, but he was assassinated after less than nine months in office and Mohammed Mossadegh took over. Mossadegh was ousted in August 1953, by Fazollah Zahedi, whom the Shah had named premier.

Opposition to the Shah spread, despite the imposition of martial law in September 1978, and massive demonstrations demanded the return of the exiled Ayatollah Ruhollah Khomeini. Riots and strikes continued despite the appointment of an opposition leader, Shahpur Bakhtiar, as premier on Dec. 29. The Shah and his family left Iran on Jan. 16, 1979, for a "vacation," leaving power in the hands of a regency council.

Khomeini returned on Feb. 1 to a nation in turmoil as military units loyal to the Shah continued to support Bakhtiar and clashed with revolutionaries. Khomeini appointed Mehdi Bazargan as premier of the provisional government and in two days of fighting, revolutionaries forced the military to capitulate on Feb. 11.

The new government began a program of nationalization of insurance companies, banks, and industries both locally and foreign-owned. Oil production fell amid the political confusion.

Khomeini, ignoring opposition, proceeded with his plans for revitalizing Islamic traditions. He urged women to return to the veil, or chador; banned alcohol and mixed bathing, and prohibited music from radio and television broadcasting, declaring it to be "no different from opium."

Revolutionary militants invaded the U.S. Embassy in Teheran on Nov. 4, 1979, seized staff members as hostages, and precipitated an international crisis.

Khomeini refused all appeals, even a unanimous vote by the U.N. Security Council demanding immediate release of the hostages.

Iranian hostility toward Washington was reinforced by the Carter administration's economic boycott and deportation order against Iranian students in the U.S., the break in diplomatic relations and ultimately an aborted U.S. raid in April aimed at rescuing the hostages.

As the first anniversary of the embassy seizure neared, Khomeini and his followers insisted on their original conditions: guarantee by the U.S. not to interfere in Iran's affairs, cancellation of U.S. damage claims against Iran, release of $8 billion in frozen Iranian assets, an apology, and the return of the assets held by the former imperial family.

These conditions were largely met and the 52 American hostages were released on Jan. 20, ending 444 days in captivity.

From the release of the hostages onward, President Bani-Sadr and the conservative clerics of the dominant Islamic Republican Party clashed with growing frequency. He was stripped of his command of the armed forces by Khomeini on June 6 and ousted as President on June 22. On July 24, Prime Minister Mohammed Ali Rajai was elected overwhelmingly to the Presidency.

Rajai and Prime Minister Mohammed Javad Bahonar were killed on Aug. 30 by a bomb in Bahonar's office. Hojatolislam Mohammed Ali Khamenei, a clergyman, leader of the Islamic Republican Party and spokesman for Khomeini, was elected President on Oct. 2, 1981.

The sporadic war with Iraq regained momentum in 1982, as Iran launched an offensive in March and regained much of the border area occupied by Iraq in late 1980. Khomeini rejected Iraqi bids for a truce, insisting that Iraq's President Saddam Hussein must leave office first.

Iran continued to be at war with Iraq well into 1988. Although Iraq expressed its willingness to cease fighting, Iran stated that it would not stop the war until Iraq agreed to make payment for war damages to Iran, and punish the Iraqi government leaders involved in the conflict.

On July 20, 1988, Khomeini, after a series of Iranian military reverses, agreed to ceasefire negotiations with Iraq. A cease-fire went into effect Aug. 20, 1988.

Khomeini died in June 1989.

By early 1991 the Islamic Revolution appeared to have lost much of its militancy. Attempting to revive a stagnant economy President Rafsanjani took measures to decentralize the command system and introduce free-market mechanisms. Seeking better relations with the West, and hopefully its money, Iran began making overtures to the European Community.

IRAQ

Republic of Iraq
President: Saddam Hussein (1979)
Area: 167,920 sq mi. (434,913 sq km)
Population (est. mid-1991): 17,100,000 (average annual rate of natural increase: 2.7%); birth rate: 41/1000; infant mortality rate: 69/1000; density per square mile: 102
Capital: Baghdad
Largest cities (est. 1985): Baghdad, 4,648,609; Basra, 616,700; Mosul, 570,926
Monetary unit: Iraqi dinar
Languages: Arabic (official) and Kurdish
Religions: Islam, 97%; Christian or other, 3%
National name: Al Jumhouriya Al Iraqia
Literacy rate: 55–65% (est.)
Economic summary: Gross national product (1989 est.): $35 billion, $1,940 per capita; 5% real growth rate. Arable land: 12%. Principal products: dates, livestock, wheat, barley, cotton, rice. Labor force: 3,400,000 (1984); 28% in industry. Major products: petroleum, chemicals, textiles,, construction materials. Natural resources: oil, natural gas, phosphates, sulfur. Exports: petroleum and refined products, machinery, chemicals, dates. Imports: manufactured goods, food. Major trading partners: France, Italy, Japan, Germany, Brazil, U.K., U.S., Turkey, U.S.S.R.

Geography. Iraq, a triangle of mountains, desert, and fertile river valley, is bounded on the east by Iran, on the north by Turkey, the west by Syria and Jordan, and the south by Saudi Arabia and Kuwait. It is twice the size of Idaho.

The country has arid desertland west of the Euphrates, a broad central valley between the Euphrates and Tigris, and mountains in the northeast. The fertile lower valley is formed by the delta of the two rivers, which join about 120 miles (193 km) from the head of the Persian Gulf. The gulf coastline is 26 miles (42 km) long. The only port for seagoing vessels is Basra, which is on the Shatt-al-Arab River near the head of the Persian Gulf.

Government. Since the coup d'etat of July 1968, Iraq has been governed by the Arab Ba'ath Socialist Party through a Council of Command of the Revolution headed by the President. There is also a Council of Ministers headed by the President.

History. From earliest times Iraq was known as Mesopotamia—the land between the rivers—for it embraces a large part of the alluvial plains of the Tigris and Euphrates.

An advanced civilization existed by 4000 B.C. Sometime after 2000 B.C. the land became the center of the ancient Babylonian and Assyrian empires. It was conquered by Cyrus the Great of Persia in 538 B.C., and by Alexander in 331 B.C. After an Arab conquest in A.D. 637–40, Baghdad became capital of the ruling caliphate. The country was cruelly pillaged by the Mongols in 1258, and during the 16th, 17th, and 18th centuries was the object of repeated Turkish-Persian competition.

Nominal Turkish suzerainty imposed in 1638 was replaced by direct Turkish rule in 1831. In World War I, an Anglo-Indian force occupied most of the country, and Britain was given a mandate over the area in 1920. The British recognized Iraq as a kingdom in 1922 and terminated the mandate in 1932 when Iraq was admitted to the League of Nations. In World War II, Iraq generally adhered to its 1930 treaty of alliance with Britain, but in 1941, British troops were compelled to put down a pro-Axis revolt led by Premier Rashid Ali.

Iraq became a charter member of the Arab League in 1945, and Iraqi troops took part in the Arab invasion of Palestine in 1948.

Faisal II, born on May 2, 1935, succeeded his father, Ghazi I, who was killed in an automobile accident on April 4, 1939. Faisal and his uncle, Crown Prince Abdul-Ilah, were assassinated in August 1958 in a swift revolutionary coup that brought to power a military junta headed by Abdul Karem Kassim. Kassim, in turn, was overthrown and killed in a coup staged March 8, 1963, by the Ba'ath Socialist Party.

Abdel Salam Arif, a leader in the 1958 coup, staged another coup in November 1963, driving the Ba'ath members of the revolutionary council from power. He adopted a new constitution in 1964. In 1966, he, two Cabinet members, and other supporters died in a helicopter crash. His brother, Gen. Abdel Rahman Arif, assumed the presidency, crushed the opposition, and won an indefinite extension of his term in 1967. His regime was ousted in July 1968 by a junta led by Maj. Gen. Ahmed Hassan al-Bakr.

A long-standing dispute over control of the Shatt al-Arab waterway between Iraq and Iran broke into full-scale war on Sept. 20, 1980. Iraqi planes attacked Iranian airfields and the Abadan refinery, and Iraqi ground forces moved into Iran.

Despite the smaller size of its armed forces, Iraq took and held the initiative by seizing Abadan and Khurramshahr together with substantial Iranian territory by December and beating back Iranian counterattacks in January. Peace efforts by the Islamic nations, the nonaligned, and the United Nations failed as 1981 wore on and the war stagnated.

In 1982, the Iraqis fell back to their own country and dug themselves in behind sandbagged defensive fortifications. With massive firepower, they turned back wave after wave of attacking Iranian troops and revolutionary guards, many of them in their teens. From the beginning of the war in September 1980 to September 1984, foreign military analysts estimated that more than 100,000 Iranians and perhaps 50,000 Iraqis had been killed.

The Iraqis clearly wanted to end the war, but the Iranians refused. In March of 1985, Iraq apparently won the largest battle of the long war, crushing a major Iranian offensive in the southern marshes in a week of heavy fighting.

In February 1986, Iranian forces gained on two fronts; but Iraq retook most of the lost ground in 1988 and the war continued a stalemate. In August, Iraq and Iran agreed to hold direct talks after a cease-fire takes effect.

In July 1990, President Hussein claimed that Kuwait was flooding world markets with oil and forcing down prices. A mediation attempt by Arab leaders failed, and on Aug. 2, 1990, over this and territorial claims, Iraqi troops invaded Kuwait and set up a puppet government.

After the Gulf War, Saddam Hussein was still in power. The UN Security Council affirmed an embargo against military supplies to that country and a trade embargo was still in place, pending claims of compensation for damage to Kuwait. (*See* special Current Events article on the Gulf War.)

IRELAND

President: Mary Robinson (1990)
Taoiseach (Prime Minister): Charles J. Haughey (1987)
Area: 27,136 sq mi. (70,282 sq km)
Population (est. mid-1991): 3,600,000 (average annual rate of natural increase: 0.6%); birth rate: 15/1000; infant mortality rate: 7.5/1000; density per square mile: 133
Capital: Dublin
Largest cities (est. 1982): Dublin, 550,000; Cork, 140,000; Limerick, 60,000
Monetary unit: Irish pound (punt)
Languages: Irish, English
Religions: Roman Catholic, 94%; Anglican, 4%; other, 2%
National name: Ireland or Eire in the Irish language
Literacy rate: 99%
Economic summary: Gross national product (1989 est.): $31.4 billion; $8,900 per capita; 4.3% real growth rate. Arable land: 14%. Principal products: cattle and dairy products, pigs, poultry and eggs, sheep and wool, horses, barley, sugar beets. Labor force: 1,310,000; 19.1% in manufacturing and construction. Major products: processed foods, brews, textiles, clothing, chemicals, pharmaceuticals, machinery, transportation equipment, glass and crystal. Natural resources: zinc, lead, natural gas, crude oil, barite, copper, gypsum, limestone, dolomite, peat, silver. Exports: livestock, dairy products, machinery, chemicals, data processing equipment. Imports: food, animtal feed, chemicals, petroleum products, machinery, textile clothing. Major trading partners: U.K., Western European countries, U.S.

Geography. Ireland is situated in the Atlantic Ocean and separated from Britain by the Irish Sea. Half the size of Arkansas, it occupies the entire island except for the six counties which make up Northern Ireland.

Ireland resembles a basin—a central plain rimmed with mountains, except in the Dublin region. The mountains are low, with the highest peak, Carrantuohill in County Kerry, rising to 3,415 feet (1,041 m).

The principal river is the Shannon, which begins in the north central area, flows south and southwest for about 240 miles (386 km), and empties into the Atlantic.

Government. Ireland is a parliamentary democracy. The National Parliament (Oireachtas) consists of the president and two Houses, the House of Representatives (Dáil éireann) and the Senate (Seanad éireann), whose members serve for a maximum term of five years. The House of Representatives has 166 members elected by proportional representation; the Senate has 60 members of whom 11 are nominated by the prime minister, 6 by the universities and the remaining 43 from five vocational panels. The prime minister (Taoiseach), who is the head of government, is appointed by the president on the nomination of the House of Representatives, to which he is responsible.

History. In the Stone and Bronze Ages, Ireland was inhabited by Picts in the north and a people called the Erainn in the south, the same stock, apparently, as in all the isles before the Anglo-Saxon invasion of Britain. About the fourth century B.C., tall, red-haired Celts arrived from Gaul or Galicia. They subdued and assimilated the inhabitants and established a Gaelic civilization.

By the beginning of the Christian Era, Ireland was divided into five kingdoms—Ulster, Connacht, Leinster, Meath, and Munster. St. Patrick introduced Christianity in 432 and the country developed into a center of Gaelic and Latin learning. Irish monasteries, the equivalent of universities, attracted intellectuals as well as the pious and sent out missionaries to many parts of Europe and, some believe, to North America.

Norse depredations along the coasts, starting in 795, ended in 1014 with Norse defeat at the Battle of Clontarf by forces under Brian Boru. In the 12th century, the Pope gave all Ireland to the English Crown as a papal fief. In 1171, Henry II of England was acknowledged "Lord of Ireland," but local sectional rule continued for centuries, and English control over the whole island was not reasonably absolute until the 17th century. By the Act of Union (1801), England and Ireland became the "United Kingdom of Great Britain and Ireland."

A steady decline in the Irish economy followed in the next decades. The population had reached 8.25 million when the great potato famine of 1846–48 took many lives and drove millions to emigrate to America. By 1921 it was down to 4.3 million.

In the meantime, anti-British agitation continued along with demands for Irish home rule. The advent of World War I delayed the institution of home rule and resulted in the Easter Rebellion in Dublin (April 24–29, 1916), in which Irish nationalists unsuccessfully attempted to throw off British rule. Guerrilla warfare against British forces followed proclamation of a republic by the rebels in 1919.

The Irish Free State was established as a dominion on Dec. 6, 1922, with the six northern counties as part of the United Kingdom. Ireland was neutral in World War II.

In 1948, Eamon de Valera, American-born leader of the Sinn Fein, who had won establishment of the Free State in 1921 in negotiations with Britain's David Lloyd George, was defeated by John A. Costello, who demanded final independence from Britain. The Republic of Ireland was proclaimed on April 18, 1949. It withdrew from the Commonwealth but in 1955 entered the United Nations. Since 1949 the prime concern of successive governments has been economic development.

Through the 1960s, two antagonistic currents dominated Irish politics. One sought to bind the wounds of the rebellion and civil war. The other was the effort of the outlawed extremist Irish Republican Army to bring Northern Ireland into the republic. Despite

public sympathy for unification of Ireland, the Dublin government dealt rigorously with IRA guerrillas caught inside the republic's borders.

In the elections of June 11, 1981, Garret M. D. FitzGerald, leader of the Fine Gael, was elected Prime Minister by 81 to 78 with the support of 15 Labor Party members and one independent Socialist added to his own party's 65 members.

FitzGerald resigned Jan. 27, 1982, after his presentation of an austerity budget aroused the opposition of independents who had backed him previously. Former Prime Minister Haughey was sworn in on March 9 and presented a budget with nearly a $1 billion deficit, with additional public spending aimed at stimulating the lagging economy. FitzGerald was re-elected Prime Minister on Dec. 14, 1982 but was unable to solve the problem of unemployment and the elections of 1987 brought Haughey back into power on March 10.

Three candidates vied in the November 1990 presidential election. Although Brian Lenihan of Fianna Fail led in the first round, Mary Robinson, supported by the Labour Party and the Workers Party, won the second round with 52.8% of the vote, becoming the first non-Fianna Fail president since 1945. In local elections of June 1991 the Fianna Fail Party suffered heavy losses.

ISRAEL

State of Israel
President: Chaim Herzog (1988)
Prime Minister: Yitzhak Shamir (1988) (term ends Nov., 1992)
Area: 8,020 sq mi. (20,772 sq km)
Population (est. mid-1991): 4,900,000[1] (average annual rate of natural increase: 1.6%); birth rate: 22/1000; infant mortality rate: 10/1000; density per square mile: 606
Capital: Jerusalem[2]
Largest cities (1989): Jerusalem, 493,500[3]; Tel Aviv, 317,800; Haifa, 222,600
Monetary unit: Shekel
Languages: Hebrew, Arabic, English
Religions: Judaism, 83%; Islam, 13.1%; Christian, 2.3%; Druze, 1.6%
National name: Medinat Yisra'el
Literacy rate: 88% Jews, 70% Arabs
Economic summary: Gross national product (1989): $51.8 billion; $11,296 per capita; 1.5% real growth rate. Arable land: 17%. Principal products: citrus and other fruits, vegetables, beef, dairy and poultry products. Labor force: (1989): 1,348,000; 22.8% in industry, mining and manufacturing. Major products: processed foods, cut diamonds, clothing and textiles, chemicals, metal products, transport and electrical equipment, high-technology electronics. Natural resources: sulfur, copper, phosphates, potash, bromine. Exports: polished diamonds, citrus and other fruits, clothing and textiles, processed foods, high technology products, computerized medical equipment, military hardware, fertilizer and chemical products. Imports: rough diamonds, chemicals, oil, machinery, iron and steel, cereals, textiles, vehicles, ships. Major trading partners: U.S., Germany, U.K., Switzerland, France, Italy, Belgium, Luxembourg.

1. Includes West Bank, Gaza Strip, East Jerusalem. 2. Not recognized by U.S. which recognizes Tel Aviv. 3. Includes East Jerusalem.

Geography. Israel, slightly smaller than Massachusetts, lies at the eastern end of the Mediterranean Sea. It is bordered by Egypt on the west, Syria and Jordan on the east, and Lebanon on the north. Northern Israel is largely a plateau traversed from north to south by mountains and broken by great depressions, also running from north to south.

The maritime plain of Israel is remarkably fertile. The southern Negev region, which comprises almost half the total area, is largely a wide desert steppe area. The National Water Project irrigation scheme is now transforming it into fertile land. The Jordan, the only important river, flows from the north through Lake Hule (Waters of Merom) and Lake Kinneret (Sea of Galilee or Sea of Tiberias), finally entering the Dead Sea, 1,290 feet (393 m) below sea level. This "sea," which is actually a salt lake (394 sq mi.; 1,020 sq km), has no outlet, its water balance being maintained by evaporation.

Government. Israel, which does not have a written constitution, has a republican form of government headed by a president elected for a five-year term by the Knesset. He may serve no more than two terms. The Knesset has 120 members elected by universal suffrage under proportional representation for four years. The government is administered by the Cabinet, which is headed by the prime minister.

The Knesset decided in June 1950 that Israel would acquire a constitution gradually through the years by the enactment of fundamental laws. Israel grants automatic citizenship to every Jew who desires to settle within its borders, subject to control of the Knesset.

History. Palestine, cradle of two great religions and homeland of the modern state of Israel, was known to the ancient Hebrews as the "Land of Canaan." Palestine's name derives from the Philistines, a people who occupied the southern coastal part of the country in the 12th century B.C.

A Hebrew kingdom established in 1000 B.C. was later split into the kingdoms of Judah and Israel; they were subsequently invaded by Assyrians, Babylonians, Egyptians, Persians, Macedonians, Romans, and Byzantines. The Arabs took Palestine from the Byzantine Empire A.D. 634–40. With the exception of a Frankish Crusader kingdom from 1099 to 1187, Palestine remained under Moslem rule until the 20th century (Turkish rule from 1516), when British forces under Gen. Sir Edmund Allenby defeated the Turks and captured Jerusalem Dec. 9, 1917. The League of Nations granted Britain a mandate to govern Palestine, effective in 1923.

Jewish colonies—Jews from Russia established one as early as 1882—multiplied after Theodor Herzl's 1897 call for a Jewish state. The Zionist movement received official approval with the publication of a letter Nov. 2, 1917, from Arthur Balfour, British Foreign Secretary, to Lord Rothschild, a British Jewish leader. Balfour promised support for the establishment of a Jewish homeland in Palestine on the understanding that the civil and religious rights of non-Jewish Palestinians would be safeguarded.

A 1937 British proposal called for an Arab and a Jewish state separated by a mandated area incorporating Jerusalem and Nazareth. Arabs opposed this, demanding a single state with minority rights for Jews, and a 1939 British White Paper retreated, offering instead a single state with further Jewish immigration to be limited to 75,000. Although the White Paper satisfied neither side, further discussion ended on the outbreak of World War II, when the Jewish population stood at nearly 500,000, or 30% of the total. Illegal and legal immigration during the war brought the Jewish population to 678,000 in 1946, compared with 1,269,000 Arabs. Unable to reach a compromise, Britain turned the problem over to the United Nations in 1947, which on November 29 voted for partition—despite strong Arab opposition.

Britain did not help implement the U.N. decision and withdrew on expiration of its mandate May 14, 1948. Zionists had already seized control of areas designated as Jewish, and, on the day of British departure, the Jewish National Council proclaimed the State of Israel.

U.S. recognition came within hours. The next day, Jordanian and Egyptian forces invaded the new nation. At the cease-fire Jan. 7, 1949, Israel increased its original territory by 50%, taking western Galilee, a broad corridor through central Palestine to Jerusalem, and part of modern Jerusalem. (In April 1950, Jordan annexed areas of eastern and central Palestine that had been designated for an Arab state, together with the old city of Jerusalem.)

Chaim Weizmann and David Ben-Gurion became Israel's first president and prime minister. The new government was admitted to the U.N. May 11, 1949.

The next clash with Arab neighbors came when Egypt nationalized the Suez Canal in 1956 and barred Israeli shipping. Coordinating with an Anglo-French force, Israeli troops seized the Gaza Strip and drove through the Sinai to the east bank of the Suez Canal, but withdrew under U.S. and U.N. pressure. In 1967, Israel threatened retaliation against Syrian border raids, and Syria asked Egyptian aid. Egypt demanded the removal of U.N. peace-keeping forces from Suez, staged a national mobilization, closed the Gulf of Aqaba, and moved troops into the Sinai. Starting with simultaneous air attacks against Syrian, Jordanian, and Egyptian air bases on June 5, Israel during a six-day war totally defeated its Arab enemies. Expanding its territory by 200%, Israel at the cease-fire held the Golan Heights, the West Bank of the Jordan River, the Old City, and all of the Sinai and the east bank of the Suez Canal.

Israel insisted that Jerusalem remain a unified city and that peace negotiations be conducted directly, something the Arab states had refused to do because it would constitute a recognition of their Jewish neighbor.

Egypt's President Gamal Abdel Nasser renounced the 1967 cease-fire in 1969 and began a "war of attrition" against Israel, firing Soviet artillery at Israeli forces on the east bank of the canal. Nasser died of a heart attack on Sept. 28, 1970, and was succeeded by Anwar el-Sadat.

In the face of Israeli reluctance even to discuss the return of occupied territories, the fourth Mideast war erupted Oct. 6, 1973, with a surprise Egyptian and Syrian assault on the Jewish high holy day of Yom Kippur. Initial Arab gains were reversed when a cease-fire took effect two weeks later, but Israel suffered heavy losses in manpower.

U.S. Secretary of State Henry A. Kissinger arranged a disengagement of forces on both the Egyptian and Syrian fronts. Geneva talks, aimed at a lasting peace, foundered, however, when Israel balked at inclusion of the Palestine Liberation Organization, a group increasingly active in terrorism directed against Israel.

A second-stage Sinai withdrawal signed by Israel and Egypt in September 1975 required Israel to give up the strategic Mitla and Gidi passes and to return the captured Abu Rudeis oil fields. Egypt guaranteed passage of Israeli cargoes through the reopened Suez Canal, and both sides renounced force in the settlement of disputes. Two hundred U.S. civilian technicians were stationed in a widened U.N. buffer zone to monitor and warn either side of truce violations.

A dramatic breakthrough in the tortuous history of Mideast peace efforts occurred Nov. 9, 1977, when Egypt's President Sadat declared his willingness to go anywhere to talk peace. Prime Minister Menachem Begin on Nov. 15 extended an invitation to the Egyptian leader to address the Knesset. Sadat's arrival in Israel four days later raised worldwide hopes. But optimism ebbed even before Begin was invited to Ismailia by Sadat, December 25–26.

An Israeli peace plan unveiled by Begin on his return, and approved by the Knesset, offered to end military administration in the West Bank and the Gaza Strip, with a degree of Arab self-rule but no relinquishment of sovereignty by Israel. Sadat severed talks on Jan. 18 and, despite U.S. condemnation, Begin approved new West Bank settlements by Israelis.

A PLO raid on Israel's coast on March 11, 1978, killed 30 civilians and provoked a full-scale invasion of southern Lebanon by Israel three days later to attack PLO bases. Israel withdrew three months later, turning over strongpoints to Lebanese Christian militia wherever possible rather than to a U.N. peacekeeping force installed in the area.

On March 14, 1979, after a visit by Carter, the Knesset approved a final peace treaty, and 12 days later Begin and Sadat signed the document, together with Carter, in a White House ceremony. Israel began its withdrawal from the Sinai on May 25 by handing over the coastal town of El Arish and the two countries opened their border on May 29.

One of the most difficult periods in Israel's history began with a confrontation with Syria over the placing by Syria of Soviet surface-to-air missiles in the Bekaa Valley of Lebanon in April 1981. President Reagan dispatched Philip C. Habib to prevent a clash. While Habib was seeking a settlement, Begin ordered a bombing raid against an Iraqi nuclear reactor on June 7, invoking the theory of preemptive self-defense because he said Iraq was planning to make nuclear weapons to attack Israel.

Although Israel withdrew its last settlers from the Sinai in April 1982 and agreed to a Sinai "peace patrol" composed of troops from four West European nations, the fragile peace engineered by Habib in Lebanon was shattered on June 9 by a massive Israeli assault on southern Lebanon. The attack was in retaliation for what Israel charged was a PLO attack that critically wounded the Israeli ambassador to London six days earlier.

Israeli armor swept through UNIFIL lines in southern Lebanon, destroyed PLO strongholds in Tyre and Sidon, and reached the suburbs of Beirut on June 10. As Israeli troops ringed Moslem East Beirut, where 5,000 PLO guerrillas were believed trapped, Habib sought to negotiate a safe exit for them.

A U.S.-mediated accord between Lebanon and Israel, signed on May 17, 1983, provided for Israeli withdrawal from Lebanon. Israeli withdrawal was conditioned on withdrawal of Syrian troops from the Bekaa Valley, however, and the Syrians refused to leave. Israel eventually withdrew its troops from the Beirut area, but kept them in southern Lebanon. Lebanon, under pressure from Syria, canceled the accord in March 1984.

Prime Minister Begin resigned on Sept. 15, 1983.

On Oct. 10, Likud Party stalwart Yitzhak Shamir was elected Prime Minister.

After a close election, the two major parties worked out a carefully balanced power-sharing agreement and the Knesset, on Sept. 14, 1984 approved a national unity government including both the Labor Alignment and the Likud bloc.

In one hopeful development, the coalition government declared an economic emergency on July 1 and imposed sweeping austerity measures intended to break the country's 260% inflation. Key elements were an 18.8% devaluation of the shekel, price increases in such government-subsidized products as gasoline, dismissal of 9,000 government employees, government spending cuts and a wage and price freeze. By the end of Peres' term in October, 1986, the shekel had been revalued and stabilized and inflation was down to less than 20%.

Differences in the approach to take to peace talks started to strain the government in 1987.

In Dec. 1987, riots by Gazan Palestinians led to the current general uprising throughout the occupied territories which consists of low-level violence and civil disobedience. As a consequence, in 1988 the PLO formally declared an independent state. Also, in response to their ostensible recognition of Israel in that year, the U.S. established low-level diplomatic contacts with the PLO.

A deadlock in the elections of Dec. 1988 led to a continuation of the Likud-Labor national unity government. This collapsed in 1990, leading to Shamir forming a right-wing coalition that included the religious parties.

The relaxation of Soviet emigration rules resulted in a massive wave of Jews entering Israel. Citing for one the severe housing shortage, but probably owing as much to political considerations, Israel embarked on constructing new settlements in the West Bank, angering the U.S. Hopes for quick progress on a general Israel-Arab peace after the Persian Gulf War dimmed as many parties to the dispute resumed traditional stances. Opposition leader Shimon Peres expressed disagreement with the official position concerning the settlements. The *intifada* appeared to be losing strength, and the Israelis sensed they were gaining the upperhand.

ITALY

Italian Republic
President: Francesco Cossiga (1985)
Premier: Giulio Andreotti (1989)
Area: 116,500 sq mi. (301,278 sq km)
Population (est. mid-1991): 57,700,000 (average annual rate of natural increase: .1%); birth rate: 10/1000; infant mortality rate: 8.8/1000; density per square mile: 496
Capital: Rome
Largest cities (1984): Rome, 2,826,733; Milan, 1,535,722; Naples, 1,206,955; Turin, 1,049,997; Genoa, 738,099; Palermo, 716,149; Bologna, 442,307; Florence, 435,698; Catania, 377,707; Bari, 368,216.
Monetary unit: Lira
Language: Italian
Religion: Roman Catholic, almost 100%
National name: Repubblica Italiana
Literacy rate: 93%

Economic summary: Gross national product (1990): $1,050 billion; $18,420 per capita; 2.7% real growth rate. Arable land: 32%. Principal products: grapes, olives, citrus fruits, vegetables, wheat, corn. Labor force: 23,670,000; 37.9% in industry. Major products: machinery, iron and steel, autos, textiles, shoes, chemicals. Natural resources: mercury, potash, sulfur, fish, gas, marble. Exports: textiles, wearing apparel, metals, transport equipment, chemicals. Imports: petroleum, industrial machinery, chemicals, food, metals. Major trading partners: United States, E.C., OPEC

Geography. Italy is a long peninsula shaped like a boot bounded on the west by the Tyrrhenian Sea and on the east by the Adriatic. Slightly larger than Arizona, it has for neighbors France, Switzerland, Austria, and Yugoslavia.

Approximately 600 of Italy's 708 miles (1,139 km) of length are in the long peninsula that projects into the Mediterranean from the fertile basin of the Po River. The Apennine Mountains, branching off from the Alps between Nice and Genoa, form the peninsula's backbone, and rise to a maximum height of 9,560 feet (2,912 m) at the Gran Sasso d'Italia (Corno). The Alps form Italy's northern boundary.

Several islands form part of Italy. Sicily (9,926 sq mi.; 25,708 sq km) lies off the toe of the boot, across the Strait of Messina, with a steep and rockbound northern coast and gentler slopes to the sea in the west and south. Mount Etna, an active volcano, rises to 10,741 feet (3,274 m), and most of Sicily is more than 500 feet (3,274 m) in elevation. Sixty-two miles (100 km) southwest of Sicily lies Pantelleria (45 sq mi.; 117 sq km), and south of that are Lampedusa and Linosa. Sardinia (9,301 sq mi.; 24,090 sq km), which is just south of Corsica and about 125 miles (200 km) west of the mainland, is mountainous, stony, and unproductive.

Italy has many northern lakes, lying below the snow-covered peaks of the Alps. The largest are Garda (143 sq mi.; 370 sq km), Maggiore (83 sq mi.; 215 sq km), and Como (55 sq mi.; 142 sq km).

The Po, the principal river, flows from the Alps on Italy's western border and crosses the Lombard plain to the Adriatic.

Government. The president is elected for a term of seven years by Parliament in joint session with regional representatives. The president nominates the premier and, upon the premier's recommendations, the members of the Cabinet. Parliament is composed of two houses: a Senate with 315 elective members and a Chamber of Deputies of 630 members elected by the people for a five-year term.

History. Until A.D. 476, when the German Odoacer became head of the Roman Empire in the west, the history of Italy was largely the history of Rome. From A.D. 800 on, the Holy Roman Emperors, Popes, Normans, and Saracens all vied for control over various segments of the Italian peninsula. Numerous city states, such as Venice and Genoa, and many small principalities flourished in the late Middle Ages.

In 1713, after the War of the Spanish Succession, Milan, Naples, and Sardinia were handed over to Austria, which lost some of its Italian territories in 1735. After 1800, Italy was unified by Napoleon, who crowned himself King of Italy in 1805; but with the Congress of Vienna in 1815, Austria once again became the dominant power in Italy.

Austrian armies crushed Italian uprisings in 1820–1821, and 1831. In the 1830s Giuseppe Mazzini, brilliant liberal nationalist, organized the Risorgimento (Resurrection), which laid the foundation for Italian unity.

Disappointed Italian patriots looked to the House of Savoy for leadership. Count Camille di Cavour (1810–61), Premier of Sardinia in 1852 and the architect of a united Italy, joined England and France in the Crimean War (1853–56), and in 1859, helped France in a war against Austria, thereby obtaining Lombardy. By plebiscite in 1860, Modena, Parma, Tuscany, and the Romagna voted to join Sardinia. In 1860, Giuseppe Garibaldi conquered Sicily and Naples and turned them over to Sardinia. Victor Emmanuel II, King of Sardinia, was proclaimed King of Italy in 1861.

Allied with Germany and Austria-Hungary in the Triple Alliance of 1882, Italy declared its neutrality upon the outbreak of World War I on the ground that Germany had embarked upon an offensive war. In 1915, Italy entered the war on the side of the Allies.

Benito (Il Duce) Mussolini, a former Socialist, organized discontented Italians in 1919 into the Fascist Party to "rescue Italy from Bolshevism." He led his Black Shirts in a march on Rome and, on Oct. 28, 1922, became premier. He transformed Italy into a dictatorship, embarking on an expansionist foreign policy with the invasion and annexation of Ethiopia in 1935 and allying himself with Adolf Hitler in the Rome-Berlin Axis in 1936. He was executed by Partisans on April 28, 1945 at Dongo on Lake Como.

Following the overthrow of Mussolini's dictatorship and the armistice with the Allies (Sept. 3, 1943), Italy joined the war against Germany as a co-belligerent. King Victor Emmanuel III abdicated May 9, 1946, and left the country after having installed his son as King Humbert II. A plebiscite rejected monarchy, however, and on June 13, King Humbert followed his father into exile.

The peace treaty of Sept. 15, 1947, required Italian renunciation of all claims in Ethiopia and Greece and the cession of the Dodecanese to Greece and of five small Alpine areas to France. Much of the Istrian Peninsula, including Fiume and Pola, went to Yugoslavia.

The Trieste area west of the new Yugoslav territory was made a free territory (until 1954, when the city and a 90-square-mile zone were transferred to Italy and the rest to Yugoslavia).

Scandal brought the long reign of the Christian Democrats to an end when Italy's 40th premier since World War II, Arnaldo Forlani, was forced to resign in the wake of disclosure that many high-ranking Christian Democrats and civil servants belonged to a secret Masonic lodge known as "P-2."

When the Socialists deserted the coalition, Forlani was forced to resign on May 26, 1981, leaving to Giovanni Spadolini of the small Republican Party the task of forming a new government. He was succeeded by Amintore Fanfani, a Christian Democrat, the following year. Bettino Craxi, a Socialist, became Premier in 1983.

Craxi was forced to resign on June 27, 1986 following the loss of a key secret-ballot vote in Parliament. After a month of political wrangling, Craxi was able to form a new government on condition that his term end in March, 1987.

In early February 1991 the Italian Communist Party officially changed its name to the Democratic Party of the Left. Though still the second largest party, it has three bitter factions. A political crisis in March led Prime Minister Andreotti to fashion a new coalition in April, Italy's 50th postwar government. The new cabinet represented the same five parties as the previous one. After four days, however, the small Republican Party quit its three relatively low-level appointments.

JAMAICA

Sovereign: Queen Elizabeth II
Governor-General: Hon. Edward Zacca (Acting April 1991)
Prime Minister: Michael Manley (1989)
Area: 4,411 sq mi. (11,424 sq km)
Population (est. mid-1991): 2,500,000 (average annual rate of natural increase: 1.9%); birth rate: 25/1000; infant mortality rate: 18/1000; density per square mile: 587
Capital and largest city (est. 1982): Kingston, 104,000
Monetary unit: Jamaican dollar
Language: English
Religions: Protestant, 71%; Roman Catholic, 10%; Rastafarian, 7%
Member of Commonwealth of Nations
Literacy rate: 74%
Economic summary: Gross domestic product (1990): $1.85 billion; $1,100 per capita; 3.8% real growth rate. Arable land: 19%. Principal products: sugar cane, citrus fruits, bananas, coffee, potatoes, livestock. Labor force: 728,700; 28% in industry and commerce. Major products: bauxite, textiles, processed foods, light manufactures. Natural resources: bauxite, gypsum. Exports: alumina, bauxite, sugar, bananas. Imports: fuels, machinery, consumer goods, construction goods, food. Major trading partners: U.S., U.K., Canada, Venezuela.

Geography. Jamaica is an island in the West Indies, 90 miles (145 km) south of Cuba and 100 miles (161 km) west of Haiti. It is a little smaller than Connecticut.

The island is made up of a plateau and the Blue Mountains, a group of volcanic hills, in the east. Blue Mountain (7,402 ft.; 2,256 m) is the tallest peak.

Government. The legislature is a 60-member House of Representatives elected by universal suffrage and an appointed Senate of 21 members. The Prime Minister is appointed by the Governor-General and must, in the Governor-General's opinion, be the person best able to command the confidence of a majority of the members of the House of Representatives.

History. Jamaica was inhabited by Arawak Indians when Columbus discovered it in 1494 and named it St. Iago. It remained under Spanish rule until 1655, then became a British possession. The island prospered from wealth brought by buccaneers to their base, Port Royal, the capital, until the city disappeared in the sea in 1692 after an earthquake. The Arawaks died off from disease and exploitation, and slaves, mostly black, were imported to work sugar plantations. Abolition of the slave trade (1807), emancipation of the slaves (1833), and a gradual drop in sugar prices led to depressed economic conditions that resulted in an uprising in 1865.

The following year Jamaica's status was changed to that of a colony, and conditions improved considerably. Introduction of banana cultivation made the island less dependent on the sugar crop for its well-being.

On May 5, 1953, Jamaica attained internal autonomy, and in 1958 it led in organizing the West Indies Federation. This effort at Caribbean unification failed. A nationalist labor leader, Sir Alexander Bus-

tamente, led a campaign for withdrawal from the Federation. As the result of a popular referendum in 1961, Jamaica became independent on Aug. 6, 1962.

Michael Manley became Prime Minister in 1972 and initiated a socialist program and in 1977, the government bought 51% of the Kaiser and Reynolds bauxite operations.

The Labor Party defeated Manley's People's National Party in 1980 and its capitalist-oriented leader, Edward P.G. Seaga, became Prime Minister. He instituted measures to encourage private investment.

Like other Caribbean countries, Jamaica was hard-hit by the 1981–82 recession. By 1984, austerity measures that Seaga instituted in the hope of bringing the economy back into balance included elimination of government subsidies. Devaluation of the Jamaican dollar made Jamaican products more competitive on the world market and Jamaica achieved record growth in tourism and agriculture. Manufacturing also grew. But at the same time, the cost of many foods went up 50% to 75% and thousands of Jamaicans fell deeper into poverty.

The PNP decisively won local elections in mid-July, 1987, signaling a weakening in Seaga's position. In 1989, Manley swept back into power with a clear-cut victory. He indicated that he would pursue more centrist policies than he did in his previous administration.

The PNP again decisively won local elections in March 1990. Nevertheless Seaga retained his leadership position in the Labor Party at its annual conference in June.

JAPAN

Emperor: Akihito (1989)
Prime Minister: Toshiki Kaifu (1989)
Area: 145,874 sq mi. (377,815 sq km)
Population (est. mid-1991): 123,800,000 (average annual rate of natural increase: .3%); birth rate: 10/1000; infant mortality rate: 4.5/1000; density per square mile: 849
Capital: Tokyo
Largest cities (1990): Tokyo, 8,163,000; Yokohama, 3,220,000; Osaka, 2,624,000; Nagoya, 2,155,000; Sapporo, 1,672,000; Kobe, 1,477,000; Kyoto, 1,461,000; Fukuoka, 1,237,000; Kawasaki, 1,174,000; Hiroshima, 1,086,000; Kitakyushi, 1,026,000
Monetary unit: Yen
Language: Japanese
Religions: Shintoist, Buddhist
National name: Nippon
Literacy rate: 99%
Economic summary: Gross national product (1989): $2,920 billion; $23,730 per capita; 4.8% real growth rate. Arable land: 13%. Principal products: rice, vegetables, fruits, sugar beets. Labor force: 63,330,000; 33% in manufacturing. Major products: machinery and equipment, metals and metal products, textiles, autos, consumer electronics, chemicals, electrical and electronic equipment. Natural resource: fish. Exports: machinery and equipment, automobiles, metals and metal products, consumer electronics. Imports: fossil fuels, metal ore, raw materials, foodstuffs. Major trading partners: U.S., Middle East, Western Europe, Southeast Asia

Geography. An archipelago extending more than 1,744 miles (2,790 km) from northeast to southwest in the Pacific, Japan is separated from the east coast of Asia by the Sea of Japan. It is approximately the size of Montana.

Japan's four main islands are Honshu, Hokkaido, Kyushu, and Shikoku. The Ryukyu chain to the southwest was U.S.-occupied and the Kuriles to the northeast are Russian-occupied. The surface of the main islands consists largely of mountains separated by narrow valleys. There are about 60 more or less active volcanoes, of which the best-known is Mount Aso. Mount Fuji, seen on postcards, is not active.

Government. Japan's Constitution, promulgated on Nov. 3, 1946, replaced the Meiji Constitution of 1889. The 1946 Constitution, sponsored by the U.S. during its occupation of Japan, brought fundamental changes to the Japanese political system, including the abandonment of the Emperor's divine rights. The Diet (Parliament) consists of a House of Representatives of 511 members, elected for four years, and a House of Councilors of 252 members, half of whom are elected every three years for six-year terms. Executive power is vested in the Cabinet, which is headed by a Prime Minister, nominated by the Diet from its members.

On Jan. 7, 1989, Emperor Hirohito, Japan's longest-reigning monarch died and was succeeded by his son, Akihito (born 1933). He was married in 1959 to Michiko Shoda (the first time a crown prince married a commoner). They have two sons, Hiro and Aya, and a daughter, Nori.

History. A series of legends attributes creation of Japan to the sun goddess, from whom the later emperors were allegedly descended. The first of them was Jimmu Tenno, supposed to have ascended the throne in 660 B.C.

Recorded Japanese history begins with the first contact with China in the 5th century A.D. Japan was then divided into strong feudal states, all nominally under the Emperor, but with real power often held by a court minister or clan. In 1185, Yoritomo, chief of the Minamoto clan, was designated Shogun (Generalissimo) with the administration of the islands under his control. A dual government system—Shogun and Emperor—continued until 1867.

First contact with the West came about 1542, when a Portuguese ship off course arrived in Japanese waters. Portuguese traders, Jesuit missionaries, and Spanish, Dutch, and English traders followed. Suspicious of Christianity and of Portuguese support of a local Japanese revolt, the shoguns prohibited all trade with foreign countries; only a Dutch trading post at Nagasaki was permitted. Western attempts to renew trading relations failed until 1853, when Commodore Matthew Perry sailed an American fleet into Tokyo Bay.

Japan now quickly made the transition from a medieval to a modern power. Feudalism was abolished and industrialization was speeded. An imperial army was established with conscription. The shogun system was abolished in 1868 by Emperor Meiji, and parliamentary government was established in 1889. After a brief war with China in 1894–95, Japan acquired Formosa (Taiwan), the Pescadores Islands, and part of southern Manchuria. China also recognized the independence of Korea (Chosen), which Japan later annexed (1910).

In 1904–05, Japan defeated Russia in the Russo-Japanese War, gaining the territory of southern Sakhalin (Karafuto) and Russia's port and rail rights in Manchuria. In World War I Japan seized Germany's Pacific islands and leased areas in China. The Treaty of Versailles then awarded it a mandate over the islands.

At the Washington Conference of 1921–22, Japan agreed to respect Chinese national integrity. The series of Japanese aggressions that was to lead to the nation's downfall began in 1931 with the invasion of Manchuria. The following year, Japan set up this area as a puppet state, "Manchukuo," under Emperor Henry Pu-Yi, last of China's Manchu dynasty. On Nov. 25, 1936, Japan joined the Axis by signing the anti-Comintern pact. The invasion of China came the next year and the Pearl Harbor attack on the U.S. on Dec. 7, 1941.

(For details of World War II (1939–45), *see* Headline History.)

Japan surrendered formally on Sept. 2, 1945, aboard the battleship *Missouri* in Tokyo Bay after atomic bombs had hit Hiroshima and Nagasaki. Southern Sakhalin and the Kurile Islands reverted to the U.S.S.R., and Formosa (Taiwan) and Manchuria to China. The Pacific islands remained under U.S. occupation. General of the Army Douglas MacArthur was appointed Supreme Commander for the Allied Powers on Aug. 14, 1945.

A new Japanese Constitution went into effect in 1947. In 1949, many of the responsibilities of government were returned to the Japanese. Full sovereignty was granted to Japan by the Japanese Peace Treaty in 1951.

The treaty took effect on April 28, 1952, when Japan returned to full status as a nation. It was admitted into the United Nations in 1958.

Following the visit of Prime Minister Eisaku Sato to Washington in 1969, the U.S. agreed to return Okinawa and other Ryukyu Islands to Japan in 1972, and both nations renewed the security treaty in 1970.

When President Nixon opened a dialogue with Peking in 1972, Prime Minister Kakuei Tanaka, who succeeded Sato in 1972, quickly established diplomatic relations with the mainland Chinese and severed ties with Formosa.

Suzuki was defeated in 1982 by Yasuhiro Nakasone who is considered pro-Western and better relations with the United States have ensued. Despite some opposition to his pro-Western policies in general, his Liberal Democratic party won decisively in the elections of July 7, 1986 and he was granted another year beyond his four-year limit which would have expired in October, 1986. Noboru Takeshita succeeded him in November 1987.

In 1989, an influence-peddling scandal shook the LDP and led to Takeshita's resignation. He was succeeded by Sousuke Uno, who also resigned in scandal.

The general election of July 1989 for the upper house of parliament scored a loss for the ruling Liberal Democratic Party, the first in 35 years. The following month, however, the party's president, Toshiki Kaifu, was elected prime minister. He stressed the need for the government to rid itself of scandal.

Kaifu pledged to provide $9 billion to the U.S. to help defray the expense of the latter's operations in the Persian Gulf. Kaifu's general stance in support of the U.S. drew considerable domestic criticism. The government attempted to push legislation that would have permitted Japan to send a military contingent to the Gulf in noncombat roles. This was defeated amid public outcry against it.

During Soviet President Gorbachev's visit to Tokyo in April 1991 he and Prime Minister Kaifu attempted to resolve a territorial dispute arising out of the last days of World War II. No breakthrough resulted, and the issue still remained at an impasse. President Gorbachev was also unable to convince Japan to grant sizable aid or to engage in large-scale economic cooperation.

JORDAN

The Hashemite Kingdom of Jordan
Ruler: King Hussein I (1952)
Prime Minister: Taher Masri (1991)
Area: 34,573 sq mi (89,544 sq km) excludes West Bank
Population (est. mid-1991): 3,400,000 (average annual
  rate of natural increase: 4.1%); birth rate: 46/1000;
  infant mortality rate: 38/1000; density per square mile:
  105
Capital: Amman
Largest cities (est. 1986): Amman, 972,000; Zarka,
  392,220; Irbid, 271,000; Salt, 134,100
Monetary unit: Jordanian dinar
Languages: Arabic, English
Religions: Islam (Sunni), 92%; Christian, 8%
National name: Al Mamlaka al Urduniya al Hashemiyah
Literacy rate: 79% (est.)
Economic summary: Gross national product (1989): $6.2
  billion; $1,760 per capita; 0% real growth rate (1986).
  Arable land: 4%. Principal products: wheat, fruits, vegetables, olive oil. Labor force: 572,000 (1988); 20% in
  manufacturing and mining. Major products: phosphate, refined petroleum products, cement. Natural
  resources: phosphate, potash. Exports: phosphates,
  fruits, and vegetables, shale oil, fertilizer. Imports:
  petroleum products, textiles, capital goods, motor
  vehicles, foodstuffs. Major trading partners: U.S., Japan, Saudi Arabia, Iraq, E.C.

Geography. The Middle East kingdom of Jordan is
bordered on the west by Israel and the Dead Sea, on
the north by Syria, on the east by Iraq, and on the
south Saudi Arabia. It is comparable in size to Indiana.
  Arid hills and mountains make up most of the
country. The southern section of the Jordan River
flows through the country.

Government. Jordan is a constitutional monarchy
with a bicameral parliament.
  The upper house consists of 40 members appointed
by the king and the lower house is composed of 80
members elected by popular vote. The Constitution
guarantees freedom of religion, speech, press, association, and private property.
  Political parties were legalized in 1991.

History. In biblical times, the country that is now
Jordan contained the lands of Edom, Moab, Ammon,
and Bashan. In A.D. 106 it became part of the Roman
province of Arabia and in 633–36 was conquered by
the Arabs.
  Taken from the Turks by the British in World War
I, Jordan (formerly known as Transjordan) was separated from the Palestine mandate in 1920, and in
1921, placed under the rule of Abdullah ibn Hussein.
  In 1923, Britain recognized Jordan's independence,
subject to the mandate. In 1946, grateful for Jordan's
loyalty in World War II, Britain abolished the mandate. That part of Palestine occupied by Jordanian
troops was formally incorporated by action of the
Jordanian Parliament in 1950.
  King Abdullah was assassinated in 1951. His son
Talal was deposed as mentally ill the next year. Talal's son Hussein, born Nov. 14, 1935, succeeded
him.
  From the beginning of his reign, Hussein had to
steer a careful course between his powerful neighbor
to the west, Israel, and rising Arab nationalism, frequently a direct threat to this throne. Riots erupted
when he joined the Central Treaty Organization (the
Baghdad Pact) in 1955, and he incurred further unpopularity when Britain, France, and Israel attacked

the Suez Canal in 1956, forcing him to place his
army under nominal command of the United Arab
Republic of Egypt and Syria.
  The 1961 breakup of the UAR eased Arab national
pressure on Hussein, who was the first to recognize
Syria after it reclaimed its independence. Jordan was
swept into the 1967 Arab-Israeli war, however, and
lost the old city of Jerusalem and all of its territory
west of the Jordan river, the West Bank. Embittered
Palestinian guerrilla forces virtually took over sections of Jordan in the aftermath of defeat, and open
warfare broke out between the Palestinians and government forces in 1970.
  Despite intervention of Syrian tanks, Hussein's
Bedouin army defeated the Palestinians, suffering
heavy casualties. A U.S. military alert and Israeli armor massed on the Golan Heights contributed psychological weight, but the Jordanians alone drove out
the Syrians and invited the departure of 12,000 Iraqui
troops who had been in the country since the 1967
war. Ignoring protests from other Arab states, Hussein by mid-1971 crushed Palestinian strength in Jordan and shifted the problem to Lebanon, where many
of the guerrillas had fled.
  In October 1974, Hussein concurred in an Arab
summit resolution calling for an independent Palestinian state and endorsing the Palestine Liberation Organization as the "sole legitimate representative of
the Palestinian people." This apparent reversal of
policy changed with the growing disillusion of Arab
states with the P.L.O., however, and by 1977 Hussein
referred again to the unity of people on both banks of
the Jordan.
  As Egypt and Israel neared final agreement on a
peace treaty early in 1979, Hussein met with Yassir
Arafat, the PLO leader, on March 17 and issued a
joint statement of opposition. Although the U.S.
pressed Jordan to break Arab ranks on the issue, Hussein elected to side with the great majority, cutting
ties with Cairo and joining the boycott against Egypt.
  In September 1980, Jordan declared itself with Iraq
in its conflict with Iran and, despite threats from Syria, opened ports to war shipments for Iraq.
  In 1988, Hussein formally renounced all claims to
the West Bank, thus implicitly acknowledging Palestinian claims to statehood and torpedoing USA-spon-
sored efforts at a Palestinian confederation with Jordan.
  Jordan's stance during the Persian Gulf war
strained relations with the U.S. and led to the termination of aid to the former. The signing of a national
charter by King Hussein and leaders of the main political groups in June 1991 meant political parties
were permitted in exchange for acceptance of the
constitution and the monarchy. Also that month Palestinian Taher Masri was named prime minister. Am-
erican-educated Masri was interpreted as an effort to
regain U.S. favor.

KENYA

Republic of Kenya
President: Daniel arap Moi (1978)
Area: 224,960 sq mi. (582,646 sq km)
Population (est. mid-1991): 25,200,000 (average annual
  rate of natural increase: 3.5%); birth rate: 46/1000;
  infant mortality rate: 62/1000; density per square mile:
  112
Capital: Nairobi
Largest cities (est. 1990): Nairobi, 1,200,000; Mombasa,
  800,000

Monetary unit: Kenyan shilling
Languages: English (official), Swahili (national), and several other languages spoken by 40 ethnic groups
Religions: Protestant, 38%; Roman Catholic, 28%; traditional, 26%; Islam, 6%
Literacy rate: 59.2%
Member of Commonwealth of Nations
National name: Jamhuri ya Kenya
Economic summary: Gross domestic product (1989 est.): $8.5 billion; $360 per capita; 4.9% real growth rate. Arable land: 3%. Principal products: coffee, sisal, tea, pineapples, livestock. Labor force: 9,003,000; 22% (1987 est.) in industry and commerce. Major products: textiles, processed foods, consumer goods, refined oil. Natural resources: gold, limestone, minerals, wildlife. Exports: coffee, tea, refined petroleum. Imports: machinery, transport equipment, crude oil, iron and steel products. Major trading partners: Western European countries, Far East, U.S., Africa, Middle East

Geography. Kenya lies on the equator in east central Africa on the coast of the Indian Ocean. It is twice the size of Nevada. Kenya's neighbors are Tanzania, Uganda, the Sudan, Ethiopia, and Somalia.

In the north, the land is arid; the southwestern corner is in the fertile Lake Victoria Basin; and a length of the eastern depression of Great Rift Valley separates western highlands from those that rise from the lowland coastal strip. Large game reserves have been developed.

Government. Under its Constitution Kenya has a one-house National Assembly of 188 members, elected for five years by universal suffrage and 12 nominated and 2 ex-officio, for a total of 202. Since 1969, the president has been chosen by a general election.

The Kenya African National Union (KANU), led by the president, is the only political party allowed.

President Jomo Kenyatta died in his sleep on Aug. 22, 1978. Vice President Daniel arap Moi was elected to succeed him on Oct. 10.

History. Kenya, formerly a British colony and protectorate, was made a crown colony in 1920. The whites' domination of the rich plateau area, the White Highlands, long regarded by the Kikiyu people as their territory, was a factor leading to native terrorism, called the Mau Mau movement, in 1952. In 1954 the British began preparing the territory for African rule and independence. In 1961 Jomo Kenyatta was freed from banishment to become leader of the Kenya African National Union.

Internal self-government was granted in 1963; Kenya became independent on Dec. 12, 1963, with Kenyatta the first president.

Moi's tenure has been marked by a consolidation of power which has included the harassment of political opponents, the banning of secret ballots, and his declaration that KANU was more powerful than the Assembly or the courts.

Calls for electoral reform leading particularly to multiparty democracy resounded repeatedly from different quarters during 1990.

KIRIBATI

Republic of Kiribati
President: Ieremia Tabai (1979)
Area: 277 sq mi. (717 sq km)
Population (est. 1989): 68,828 (average annual growth rate: 1.5%); density per square mile: 245
Capital (1985): Tarawa, 21,393
Monetary unit: Australian dollar

Language: English
Religions: Roman Catholic, 48%; Protestant, 45%
Member of Commonwealth of Nations
Literacy rate: 90%
Economic summary: Gross domestic product (1989): $34 million; $500 per capita; 0% real growth rate. Arable land: NEGL%: Principal agricultural products: copra, vegetables. Exports: fish, copra. Imports: foodstuffs, fuel, transportation equipment. Major trading partners: New Zealand, Australia, Japan, American Samoa, U.K., U.S.

Geography. Kiribati, formerly the Gilbert Islands, consists of three widely separated main groups of Southwest Pacific islands, the Gilberts on the equator, the Phoenix Islands to the east, and the Line Islands further east. Ocean Island, producer of phosphates until it was mined out in 1981, is also included in the two million square miles of ocean, which give Kiribati an important fishery resource.

Government. The president holds executive power. The legislature consists of a House Assembly with 39 members.

History. A British protectorate since 1892, the Gilbert and Ellice Islands became a colony in 1915–16. The two island groups were separated in 1975 and given internal self-government.

Tarawa and others of the Gilbert group were occupied by Japan during World War II. Tarawa was the site of one of the bloodiest battles in U.S. Marine Corps history when Marines landed in November 1943 to dislodge the Japanese defenders.

Princess Anne, representing Queen Elizabeth II, presented the independence documents to the new government on July 12, 1979.

Suffering a huge trade deficit, the nation recently has drawn on its monetary reserves. Similar to other South Pacific island-nations Kiribati is fearful of the effect of global warming on sea levels.

KOREA, NORTH

Democratic People's Republic of Korea
President: Marshal Kim Il Sung (1972)
Premier: Yong Hyong Muk (1989)
Area: 46,768 sq mi. (121,129 sq km)
Population (est. mid-1991): 21,800,000 (average annual rate of natural increase: 1.8%); birth rate: 24/1000; infant mortality rate: 30/1000; density per square mile: 469
Capital and largest city (est. 1982): Pyongyang, 1,500,000
Monetary unit: Won
Language: Korean
Religions: atheist, 68%; traditional, 16%
National name: Choson Minjujuui Inmin Konghwaguk
Literacy rate: 95% (est.)
Economic summary: Gross national product (1989): $28 billion; $1,240 per capita; 3% real growth rate. Arable land: 18%. Principal products: corn, rice, vegetables. Labor force: 9,615,000; 64% nonagricultural. Major industrial products: machines, electric power, chemicals, textiles, processed food, metallurgical products. Natural resources: coal, iron ore, hydroelectric power. Exports: minerals, metallurgical products, agricultural products. Imports: machinery and equipment, petroleum, grain, coking coal. Major trading partners: U.S.S.R., China, Japan.

Geography. Korea is a 600-mile (966 km) peninsula jutting from Manchuria and China (and a small portion of the U.S.S.R.) into the Sea of Japan and the Yellow Sea off eastern Asia. North Korea occupies an area slightly smaller than Pennsylvania north of the 38th parallel.

The country is almost completely covered by a series of north-south mountain ranges separated by narrow valleys. The Yalu River forms part of the northern border with Manchuria.

Government. The elected Supreme People's Assembly, as the chief organ of government, chooses a Presidium and a Cabinet. The Cabinet, which exercises executive authority, is subject to approval by the Assembly and the Presidium.

The Korean Workers (Communist) Party, led by President Kim Il Sung, is the only political party.

History. According to myth, Korea was founded in 2333 B.C. by Tangun. In the 17th century, it became a vassal of China and was isolated from all but Chinese influence and contact until 1876, when Japan forced Korea to negotiate a commercial treaty, opening the land to the U. S. and Europe. Japan achieved control as the result of its war with China (1894–95) and with Russia (1904–05) and annexed Korea in 1910. Japan developed the country but never won over the Korean nationalists.

After the Japanese surrender in 1945, the country was divided into two occupation zones, the U.S.S.R. north of and the U.S. south of the 38th parallel. When the cold war developed between the U.S. and U.S.S.R., trade between the zones was cut off. In 1948, the division between the zones was made permanent with the establishment of separate regimes in the north and south. By mid-1949, the U.S. and U.S.S.R. withdrew all troops. The Democratic People's Republic of Korea (North Korea) was established on May 1, 1948. The Communist Party, headed by Kim Il Sung, was established in power.

On June 25, 1950, the North Korean army launched a surprise attack on South Korea. On June 26, the U.N. Security Council condemned the invasion as aggression and ordered withdrawal of the invading forces. On June 27, President Harry S. Truman ordered air and naval units into action to enforce the U.N. order. The British government did the same, and soon a multinational U.N. command was set up to aid the South Koreans. The North Korean invaders took Seoul and pushed the South Koreans into the southeast corner of their country.

Gen. Douglas MacArthur, U.N. commander, made an amphibious landing at Inchon on September 15 behind the North Korean lines, which resulted in the complete rout of the North Korean army. The U.N. forces drove north across the 38th parallel, approaching the Yalu River. Then Communist China entered the war, forcing the U.N. forces into headlong retreat. Seoul was lost again, then regained; ultimately the war stabilized near the 38th parallel but dragged on for two years while the belligerents negotiated. An armistice was agreed to on July 27, 1953.

In July 1990, North and South Korea signed a historic agreement to meet in September and discuss the easing of political and military confrontations.

Since that time talks have continued repeatedly on and off.

Formerly strenuously opposed to separate membership for the two Koreas in the U.N., the North in May 1991 announced it would, albeit reluctantly, apply for such membership.

KOREA, SOUTH

Republic of Korea
President: Roh Tae Woo (1987)
Premier: Chung Won Shik (1991)
Area: 38,031 sq mi. (98,500 sq km)
Population (est. mid-1991): 43,200,000 (average annual rate of natural increase: 0.9%); birth rate: 15/1000; infant mortality rate: 23/1000; density per square mile: 1,136
Capital: Seoul
Largest cities (est. 1989): Seoul, 10,500,000; Pusan, 3,650,700; Taegu, 2,000,200; Inchon, 1,600,000
Monetary unit: Won
Language: Korean
Religions: strong Confucian tradition, Christian, 28%; Buddhist,
National name: Taehan Min'guk
Literacy rate: over 90%
Economic summary: Gross national product (1989): $200 billion; $4,600 per capita; 6.5% real growth rate. Arable land: 21%. Principal products: rice, barley. Labor force: 16,900,000; 27% in mining and manufacturing. Major products: clothing and textiles, processed foods, automobiles, steel, electronics equipment. Natural resources: molybdenum, lead, tungsten, graphite, coal, hydropower. Exports: Textiles, automobiles, electric and electronics, ships, and steel. Imports: oil, grains, chemicals, machinery, electronics. Major trading partners: U.S., Japan.

Geography. Slightly larger than Indiana, South Korea lies below the 38th parallel on the Korean peninsula. It is mountainous in the east; in the west and south are many harbors on the mainland and offshore islands.

Government. Constitutional amendments enacted in Sept. 1987 called for direct election of a President, who would be limited to a single five-year term, and increased the powers of the National Assembly *vis a vis* the President.

The National Assembly was expanded from 276 to 299 seats, filled by proportional representation.

History. South Korea came into being in the aftermath of World War II as the result of a 1945 agreement making the 38th parallel the boundary between a northern zone occupied by the U.S.S.R. and a southern zone occupied by U.S. forces. (For details, *see* North Korea.)

Elections were held in the U.S. zone in 1948 for a national assembly, which adopted a republican Constitution and elected Syngman Rhee president. The new republic was proclaimed on August 15 and was recognized as the legal government of Korea by the U.N. on Dec. 12, 1948.

On June 25, 1950, South Korea was attacked by North Korean Communist forces. U.S. armed intervention was ordered on June 27 by President Harry S. Truman, and on the same day the U.N. invoked military sanctions against North Korea. Gen. Douglas MacArthur was named commander of the U.N. forces. U.S. and South Korean troops fought a heroic holding action but, by the first week of August, they had been forced back to a 4,000-square-mile beachhead in southeast Korea.

There they stood off superior North Korean forces until September 15, when a major U.N. amphibious attack was launched far behind the Communist lines at Inchon, port of Seoul. By September 30, U.N. forces were in complete control of South Korea. They then invaded North Korea and were nearing the Manchurian and Siberian borders when several hundred thousand Chinese Communist troops entered the conflict in late October. U.N. forces were then forced to retreat below the 38th parallel.

On May 24, 1951, U.N. forces recrossed the parallel and had made important new inroads into North Korea when truce negotiations began on July 10. An armistice was finally signed at Panmunjom on July 27, 1953, leaving a devastated Korea in need of large-scale rehabilitation.

The U.S. and South Korea signed a mutual-defense treaty on Oct. 1, 1953.

Rhee, president since 1948, resigned in 1960 in the face of rising disorders. PoSun Yun was elected to succeed him, but political instability continued. In 1961, Gen. Park Chung Hee took power and subsequently built up the country. The U.S. stepped up military aid, building up South Korea's armed forces to 600,000 men. The South Koreans sent 50,000 troops to Vietnam, at U.S. expense.

Park's assassination on Oct. 26, 1979, by Kim Jae Kyu, head of the Korean Central Intelligence Agency, brought a liberalizing trend as Choi Kyu Hah, the new President, freed imprisoned dissidents. The release of opposition leader Kim Dae jung in February 1980 generated anti-government demonstrations that turned into riots by May. Choi resigned on Aug. 16. Chun Doo Wha, head of a military Special Committee for National Security Measures, was the sole candidate as the electoral college confirmed him as President on Aug. 27.

Elected to a full seven-year term on Feb. 11, Chun had visited Washington on Feb. 2 to receive President Reagan's assurance that U.S. troops would remain in South Korea.

Debate over the Presidential succession in 1988 was the main dispute in 1986–87 with Chun wanting election by the electoral college and the opposition demanding a direct popular vote, charging that Chun could manipulate the college. On April 13, 1987, Chun declared a close on the debate but when, in June, he appointed Roh Toe Woo, the DJP chairman as his successor, violent protests broke out. Roh, and later, Chun, agreed that direct elections should be held. A split in the opposition led to Roh's election on Dec. 16, 1987, with 36.6% of the vote.

Weeks of anti-government protests in May 1991 led to the resignation of then-Prime Minister Ro Ja Bong.

In April President Gorbachev of the Soviet Union became the first Soviet leader to visit South Korea in a bid to win help for his country's own economic problems. At roughly the same time the Soviet Union announced it would not oppose South Korea's application for U.N. membership.

KUWAIT

State of Kuwait

Emir: Sheik Jaber al-Ahmad al-Sabah (1977)
Prime Minister: Sheik Sa'ad Abdullah al-Salim (1978)
Area: 6,880 sq mi. (17,820 sq km)
Population (est. mid-1991): 1,400,000 (average annual rate of natural increase: 3.0%); birth rate: 32/1000; infant mortality rate: 16/1000; density per square mile: 204
Capital (est. 1990): Kuwait, 151,060
Largest city (est. 1980): Hawalli, 152,402

Monetary unit: Kuwaiti dinar
Languages: Arabic and English
Religions: Islam
National name: Dawlat al Kuwayt
Literacy rate: about 71%
Economic summary: Gross domestic product (1988): $20.5 billion; $10,500 per capita; 5% real growth rate. Labor force: 566,000 (1986); 45% in services. Major products: crude and refined oil, petrochemicals, building materials, salt. Natural resources: petroleum, fish, shrimp. Exports: crude and refined petroleum, shrimp. Imports: foodstuffs, automobiles, building materials, machinery, textiles. Major trading partners: U.S., Japan, Italy, Germany, U.K..

Geography. Kuwait is situated northeast of Saudi Arabia at the northern end of the Persian Gulf, south of Iraq. It is slightly larger than Hawaii. The low-lying land is mainly sandy and barren.

Government. Sheik Jaber al-Ahmad al-Sabah rules as Emir of Kuwait and appoints the Prime Minister, who appoints his Cabinet (Council of Ministers). The National Assembly was suspended on July 3, 1986. There are no political parties in Kuwait.

History. Kuwait obtained British protection in 1897 when the Sheik feared that the Turks would take over the area. In 1961, Britain ended the protectorate, giving Kuwait independence, but agreed to give military aid on request. Iraq immediately threatened to occupy the area and Sheik Sabah al-Salem al-Sabah called in British troops in 1961. Soon afterward the Arab League sent in troops, replacing the British. The prize was oil.

Oil was discovered in the 1930s. Kuwait proved to have 20% of the world's known oil resources. It has been a major producer since 1946, the world's second largest oil exporter. The Sheik, who gets half the profits, devotes most of them to the education, welfare, and modernization of his kingdom. In 1966, Sheik Sabah designated a relative, Jaber al-Ahmad al-Sabah, as his successor.

By 1968, the sheikdom had established a model welfare state, and it sought to establish dominance among the sheikdoms and emirates of the Persian Gulf.

A worldwide decline in the price of oil reduced Kuwait's oil income from $18.4 billion in 1980 to only $9 billion in 1984. During the same period Kuwait's support for Iraq in its war with Iran sparked terrorist attacks in Kuwait by radical Shiite Moslem supporters of Iran's Ayatollah Khomeini. The risk of Iranian attack prompted Kuwait to obtain U.S. protection for its tankers in 1987.

In May 1985, a suicide bomber drove into the motorcade of Sheik Jaber al-Ahmed al-Sabah, the ruler. The Sheik escaped with minor cuts and bruises.

In July 1990, Iraq President Hussein blamed Kuwait for falling oil prices. After a failed Arab mediation attempt to solve the dispute peacefully, Iraq invaded Kuwait on Aug. 2, 1990, and set up a pro-Iraqi provisional government.

A coalition of Arab and Western military forces drove Iraqi troops from Kuwait in February 1991. The Emir returned to his country from Saudi Arabia in mid-March. In his first address after that he promised parliamentary elections but gave no precise date. Martial law, in effect since the end of the Gulf war, ended in late June. (*See* special Current Events article on Gulf War.)

LAOS

Lao People's Democratic Republic
President (acting): Phuomi Vongvichit (1986)
Chairman of the Council of Ministers: Kaysone Phomvihane (1975)
Area: 91,429 sq mi. (236,800 sq km)
Population (est. mid-1991): 4,100,000 (average annual rate of natural increase: 2.2%); birth rate: 37/1000; infant mortality rate: 124/1000; density per square mile: 45
Capital and largest city (est. 1984): Vientiane, 200,000
Monetary unit: Kip
Languages: Lao (official), French, English
Religions: Buddhist, 85%; animist and other, 15%
Literacy rate: 85%
Economic summary: Gross domestic product: (1989 est.): $585 million; $150 per capita; 3% real growth rate. Arable land: 4%. Principal products: rice, corn, vegetables. Labor force: 1–1.5 million; 85–90% in agriculture. Major industrial products: tin, timber, electric power. Natural resources: tin, timber, hydroelectric power. Exports: electric power, forest products, tin concentrates, coffee. Imports: rice, foodstuffs, petroleum products, machinery, transport equipment. Major trading partners: Thailand, Malaysia, Vietnam, U.S.S.R., Japan, France, U.S.

Geography. A landlocked nation in Southeast Asia occupying the northwestern portion of the Indochinese peninsula, Laos is surrounded by China, Vietnam, Cambodia, Thailand, and Burma. It is twice the size of Pennsylvania.

Laos is a mountainous country, especially in the north, where peaks rise above 8,000 feet (2,438 m). Dense forests cover the northern and eastern areas. The Mekong River, which forms the boundary with Burma and Thailand, flows entirely through the country for 300 miles (483 km) of its course.

Government. Laos is a people's democratic republic with executive power in the hands of the premier. The monarchy was abolished Dec. 2, 1975, when the Pathet Lao ousted a coalition government and King Sisavang Vatthana abdicated. The King was appointed "Supreme Adviser" to the President, the former Prince Souphanouvong. Former Prince Souvanna Phouma, Premier since 1962, was made an "adviser" to the government. The Lao People's Revolutionary Party (Pathet Lao), led by Chairman Kaysone Phomvihane, is the only political party.

History. Laos became a French protectorate in 1893, and the territory was incorporated into the union of Indochina. A strong nationalist movement developed during World War II, but France reestablished control in 1946 and made the King of Luang Prabang constitutional monarch of all Laos. France granted semiautonomy in 1949 and then, spurred by the Viet Minh rebellion in Vietnam, full independence within the French Union in 1950. In 1951, Prince Souphanouvong organized the Pathet Lao, a Communist independence movement, in North Vietnam. The Viet Minh in 1953 established the Pathet Lao in power at Samneua. Viet Minh and Pathet Lao forces invaded central Laos, and civil war resulted.

By the Geneva agreements of 1954 and an armistice of 1955, two northern provinces were given the Pathet Lao, the royal regime the rest. Full sovereignty was given the kingdom by the Paris agreements of Dec. 29, 1954. In 1957, Prince Souvanna Phouma, the royal Premier, and the Pathet Lao leader, Prince Souphanouvong, the Premier's half-brother, agreed to reestablishment of a unified government, with Pathet Lao participation and integration of Pathet Lao forces into the royal army. The agreement broke down in 1959, and armed conflict broke out again.

In 1960, the struggle became three-way as Gen. Phoumi Nosavan, controlling the bulk of the royal army, set up in the south a pro-Western revolutionary government headed by Prince Boun Oum. General Phoumi took Vientiane in December, driving Souvanna Phouma into exile in Cambodia. The Soviet bloc supported Souvanna Phouma. In 1961, a cease-fire was arranged and the three princes agreed to a coalition government headed by Souvanna Phouma.

But North Vietnam, the U.S. (in the form of Central Intelligence Agency personnel), and China remained active in Laos after the settlement. North Vietnam used a supply line (Ho Chi Minh trail) running down the mountain valleys of eastern Laos into Cambodia and South Vietnam, particularly after the U.S.-South Vietnamese incursion into Cambodia in 1970 stopped supplies via Cambodian seaports.

An agreement, reached in 1973 revived coalition government. The Communist Pathet Lao seized complete power in 1975, installing Souphanouvong as president and Kaysone Phomvihane as premier. Since then other parties and political groups have been moribund and most of their leaders have fled the country.

In July 1985, Laos agreed to help the United States search for U.S. servicemen missing since the Indochina war.

In 1985, border clashes between Laos and Thailand intensified, with over 120 skirmishes reported in 1984 and 1985.

Basically in step with Vietnam's policy of economic but not political reform, Laos has recently dropped all reference to itself as a socialist state. In addition to implementing market-oriented policies, the country has passed laws governing property, inheritance and contracts.

LATVIA

See page 972

LEBANON

Republic of Lebanon
President: Elias Hrawi (1989)
Premier: Omar Karami
Area: 4,015 sq mi. (10,400 sq km)
Population (est. mid-1991): 3,400,000 (average annual rate of natural increase: 2.1%); birth rate: 28/1000; infant mortality rate: 48/1000; density per square mile: 843
Capital: Beirut
Largest cities (est. 1990): Beirut, 1,100,000; Tripoli, 240,000; Sidon, 110,000; Tyre, 60,000; Zahleh, 55,000
Monetary unit: Lebanese pound
Languages: Arabic (official), French, English
Religions: Islam, 75% (5 sects); Christian, 25% (11 sects); Judaism Negl. % (1 sect)
National name: Al-Joumhouriya al-Lubnaniya
Literacy rate: 75%
Economic summary: Gross domestic product (1989 est.): $2.3 billion. Per capita income: $700; Arable land: 21%; principal products: citrus fruits, vegetables, potatoes, tobacco, olives, shrimp. Labor force: 650,000; 79% in industry, commerce and services. Major products: processed foods, textiles, cement, chemicals, refined oil. Exports: fruits, vegetables, textiles. Imports: metals, machinery, foodstuffs. Major trading partners: U.S., Western European and Arab countries.

Geography. Lebanon lies at the eastern end of the Mediterranean Sea north of Israel and west of Syria. It is four fifths the size of Connecticut.

The Lebanon Mountains, which parallel the coast on the west, cover most of the country, while on the eastern border is the Anti-Lebanon range. Between the two lies the Bekaa Valley, the principal agricultural area.

Government. Lebanon is governed by a President, elected by Parliament for a six-year term, and a Cabinet of Ministers appointed by the President but responsible to Parliament.

The unicameral Parliament has 108 members elected for a four-year term by universal suffrage and chosen by proportional division of religious groups.

History. After World War I, France was given a League of Nations mandate over Lebanon and its neighbor Syria, which together had previously been a single political unit in the Ottoman Empire. France divided them in 1920 into separate colonial administrations, drawing a border that separated predominantly Moslem Syria from the kaleidoscope of religious communities in Lebanon in which Maronite Christians were then dominant. After 20 years of the French mandate regime, Lebanon's independence was proclaimed on Nov. 26, 1941, but full independence came in stages. Under an agreement between representatives of Lebanon and the French National Committee of Liberation, most of the powers exercised by France were transferred to the Lebanese government on Jan. 1, 1944. The evacuation of French troops was completed in 1946.

Civil war broke out in 1958, with Moslem factions led by Kamal Jumblat and Saeb Salam rising in insurrection against the Lebanese government headed by President Camille Chamoun, a Maronite Christian. At Chamoun's request, President Eisenhower on July 15 sent U.S. troops to reestablish the government's authority.

Clan warfare between various factions in Lebanon goes back centuries. The hodgepodge includes Maronite Christians, who since independence have dominated the government; Sunni Moslems, who have prospered in business and shared political power; the Druse, a secretive Islamic splinter group; and at the bottom of the heap until recently, Shiite Moslems.

A new—and bloodier—Lebanese civil war that broke out in 1975 resulted in the addition of still another ingredient in the brew—the Syrians. In the fighting between Lebanese factions, 40,000 Lebanese were estimated to have been killed and 100,000 wounded between March 1975 and November 1976. At that point, a Syrian-dominated Arab Deterrent Force intervened and brought large-scale fighting to a halt.

Palestinian guerrillas staging raids on Israel from Lebanese territory drew punitive Israeli raids on Lebanon, and two large-scale Israeli invasions. The Israelis withdrew in June after the U.N. Security Council created a 6,000-man peacekeeping force for the area, called UNIFIL. As they departed, the Israelis turned their strongpoints over to a Christian militia that they had organized, instead of to the U.N. force.

The second Israeli invasion came on June 6, 1982, and this time it was a total one. It was in response to an assassination attempt by Palestinian terrorists on the Israeli ambassador in London.

A U.S. special envoy, Philip C. Habib, negotiated the dispersal of most of the PLO to other Arab nations and Israel pulled back some of its forces. The violence seemed to have come to an end when, on Sept. 14, Bashir Gemayel, the 34-year-old President-elect, was killed by a bomb that destroyed the headquarters of his Christian Phalangist Party.

The day after Gemayel's assassination, Israeli troops moved into west Beirut in force. On Sept. 17 it was revealed that Christian militiamen had massacred hundreds of Palestinians in two refugee camps but Israel denied responsibility.

On Sept. 20, Amin Gemayel, older brother of Bashir Gemayel, was elected President by the parliament.

The massacre in the refugee camps prompted the return of a multinational peacekeeping force composed of U.S. Marines and British, French, and Italian soldiers. Their mandate was to support the central Lebanese government, but they soon found themselves drawn into the struggle for power between different Lebanese factions. During their stay in Lebanon, 260 U.S. Marines and about 60 French soldiers were killed, most of them in suicide bombings of the Marine and French Army compounds on Oct. 23, 1983. The multinational force left in the spring of 1984.

During 1984, Israeli troops remained in southern Lebanon and Syrian troops remained in the Bekaa Valley. By the third anniversary of the invasion, June 6, 1985, all Israeli troops had withdrawn except for several hundred "advisers" to a Christian militia trained and armed by the Israelis.

Events since the Israeli withdrawal included Shiite-PLO fighting resulting from PLO attempts to reestablish its old power base in areas now held by Shiite militia.

In July 1986, Syrian observers took position in Beirut to monitor a peacekeeping agreement. The agreement broke down and fighting between Shiite and Druze militia in West Beirut became so intense that Syrian troops moved in force in February 1987, suppressing militia resistance.

Amin Gemayel's Presidency expired on Sept. 23, 1988. The impossibility of setting up elections led Gemayel to designate a government under army chief Gen. Michael Aoun. Aoun's government was rejected by Prime Minister Selim al-Hoss who established a rival government in Muslim West Beirut.

In October 1989, Lebanese Christian and Moslem deputies approved a tentative peace accord and the new National Assembly selected a President. Christian leader Aoun, charging that the accord didn't place enough pressure on the Syrians to withdraw, refused to recognize the new government.

In early 1991 the Lebanese government, backed by Syria, attempted to regain control over the south and disband all private militias, thereby ending the 16-year civil war. This led in July to clashes with PLO guerrillas, who on July 4 agreed to hand over their weapons. Israel, however, announced it would not withdraw from its self-proclaimed security zone in the south, as Beirut had hoped.

LESOTHO

Kingdom of Lesotho
Sovereign: King Letsie III (1990)
Chairman, Military Council and Council of Ministers:
Col. E.P. Ramaemba (Head of Government)
Area: 11,720 sq mi. (30,355 sq km)
Population (est. mid-1991): 1,800,000 (average annual rate of natural increase: 2.9%); birth rate: 41/1000; infant mortality rate: 95/1000; density per square mile: 156

Capital and largest city (est. 1990): Maseru, 109,382
Monetary unit: Loti
Languages: English and Sesotho (official); also Zulu and Xhosa
Religions: Roman Catholic, 44%; Lesotho Evangelical Church, 30%; Anglican, 12%
Member of Commonwealth of Nations
Literacy rate: 59% (1989)
Economic summary: Gross domestic product (1989FY est.): $412 million; $245 per capita; 8.2% real growth rate. Arable land: 10%. Principal products: corn, wheat, sorghum, barley. Labor force: 689,000; 86.2% in subsistence agriculture. Natural resources: diamonds. Exports: wool, mohair, wheat, cattle, hides and skins. Imports: foodstuffs, building materials, clothing, vehicles, machinery. Major trading partner: South Africa.

Geography. Mountainous Lesotho, the size of Maryland, is surrounded by the Republic of South Africa in the east central part of that country except for short borders on the east and south with two discontinuous units of the Republic of Transkei. The Drakensberg Mountains in the east are Lesotho's principal chain. Elsewhere the region consists of rocky tableland.

Government. A military regime and constitutional monarchy. The king has no legislative or executive powers. The executive branch consists of the monarch, chairman of the Military Council, and the Council of Ministers (cabinet).

History. Lesotho (formerly Basutoland) was constituted a native state under British protection by a treaty signed with the native chief Moshesh in 1843. It was annexed to Cape Colony in 1871, but in 1884 it was restored to direct control by the Crown.

The colony of Basutoland became the independent nation of Lesotho on Oct. 4, 1966.

In the 1970 elections, Ntsu Mokhehle, head of the Basutoland Congress Party, claimed a victory, but Jonathan declared a state of emergency, suspended the Constitution, and arrested Mokhehle. The major issue in the election was relations with South Africa, with Jonathan for close ties to the surrounding white nation, while Mokhehle was for a more independent policy. Jonathan jailed 45 opposition politicians, declared the King had "technically abdicated" by siding with the opposition party, exiled him to the Netherlands, and named his Queen and her seven-year-old son as Regent.

The King returned after a compromise with Jonathan in which the new Constitution would name him head of state but forbid his participation in politics.

After the King refused to approve the replacements in February 1990 of individuals dismissed by Lekhanya, the latter stripped the King of his executive power. Then in early March Lekhanya sent the King into exile. In November the King was dethroned, and his son was sworn in as King Letsie III.

LIBERIA

Republic of Liberia
President: Amos Sawyer (interim) (1990)
Area: 43,000 sq mi. (111,370 sq km)
Population (est. mid-1991): 2,700,000 (average annual rate of natural increase: 3.2%); birth rate: 47/1000; infant mortality rate: 134; density per square mile: 63
Capital and largest city (est. 1984): Monrovia, 425,000

Monetary unit: Liberian dollar
Languages: English (official) and tribal dialects
Religions: traditional, 70%; Christian, 10%; Islam, 20%
Literacy rate: 35%
Economic summary: Gross domestic product (1988): $988 million; $395 per capita; 1.5% real growth rate. Arable land: 1%. Principal products: rubber, rice, palm oil, cassava, coffee, cocoa. Labor force: 510,000; 4.5% in industry and commerce. Major products: iron ore, diamonds, processed rubber, processed food, construction materials. Natural resources: iron ore, gold, timber, diamonds. Exports: iron ore, rubber, timber, coffee. Imports: machinery, petroleum products, transport equipment, foodstuffs. Major trading partners: U.S., E.C., Netherlands, Japan, China.

Geography. Lying on the Atlantic in the southern part of West Africa, Liberia is bordered by Sierra Leone, Guinea, and the Ivory Coast. It is comparable in size to Tennessee.

Most of the country is a plateau covered by dense tropical forests, which thrive under an annual rainfall of about 160 inches a year.

Government. A five-nation West African peacekeeping force installed an interim government in October 1990 and in November made Amos Sawyer interim president. The National Patriotic Front led by Charles Taylor controls most of the country.

History. Liberia was founded in 1822 as a result of the efforts of the American Colonization Society to settle freed American slaves in West Africa. In 1847, it became the Free and Independent Republic of Liberia.

The government of Africa's first republic was modeled after that of the United States, and Joseph J. Roberts of Virginia was elected the first president. He laid the foundations of a modern state and initiated efforts, never too successful but pursued for more than a century, to bring the aboriginal inhabitants of the territory to the level of the emigrants. The English-speaking descendants of U.S. blacks, known as Americo-Liberians, were the intellectual and ruling class. The indigenous inhabitants, divided, constitute 99% of the population.

After 1920, considerable progress was made toward opening up the interior, a process that was spurred in 1951 by the establishment of a 43-mile (69-km) railroad to the Bomi Hills from Monrovia.

In July 1971, while serving his sixth term as president, William V. S. Tubman died following surgery and was succeeded by his long-time associate, Vice President William R. Tolbert, Jr.

Tolbert was ousted in a military coup carried out April 12, 1980, by army enlisted men led by Master Sgt. Samuel K. Doe. Tolbert and 27 other high officials were executed. Doe and his colleagues based their action on the grievances of "native" Liberians against corruption and misrule by the Americo-Liberians who had ruled the country since its founding.

A rebellion led by Charles Taylor, a former Doe aide, started in December 1989 and, by mid-July 1990, had taken most of Liberia's key population and economic centers and surrounded the capital.

A West African peacekeeping force intervened in Liberia and effectively partitioned the country into two zones: One, containing the capital of Monrovia, led by President Sawyer, is backed by virtually all West African nations. The other, led by Mr. Taylor, constitutes about 95% of the territory. The two leaders reached an accord to set aside their differences in June 1990.

LIBYA

Socialist People's Libyan Arab Jamahiriya
Head of State: Col. Muammar el-Qaddafi (1969)
Secretary of the General People's Committee: Abuzeid Omar Dorda (1990)
Area: 679,536 sq mi. (1,759,998 sq km)
Population (est. mid-1991): 4,400,000 (average annual rate of natural increase: 3.1%); birth rate: 37/1000; infant mortality rate: 64/1000; density per square mile: 6
Capital: Tripoli
Largest cities (est. 1980): Tripoli, 587,400; Benghazi, 267,700
Monetary unit: Libyan dinar
Language: Arabic
Religion: Islam
National name: Al-Jumhuria al-Arabia al-Libya
Literacy rate: 50–60%
Economic summary: Gross national product (1988 est.): $20 billion, $5,410 per capita; real growth rate: 0%. Arable land: 1%. Principal products: wheat, barley, olives, dates, citrus fruits, peanuts. Labor force: 1,000,000; 31% in industry. Major products: petroleum, processed foods, textiles, handicrafts. Natural resources: petroleum, natural gas. Exports: petroleum, peanuts, hides. Imports: machinery, foodstuffs, manufactured goods. Major trading partners: Italy, Germany, U.K., France, Spain, Japan.

Geography. Libya stretches along the northeastern coast of Africa between Tunisia and Algeria on the west and Egypt on the east; to the south are the Sudan, Chad, and Niger. It is one sixth larger than Alaska.

A greater part of the country lies within the Sahara. Along the Mediterranean coast and farther inland is arable plateau land.

Government. In a bloodless coup d'etat on Sept. 1, 1969, the military seized power in Libya. King Idris I, who had ruled since 1951, was deposed and the Libyan Arab Republic proclaimed. The official name was changed in 1977 to the Socialist People's Libyan Arab Jamahiriya. The Revolutionary Council that had governed since the coup was renamed the General Secretariat of the General People's Congress. The Arab Socialist Union Organization is the only political party.

History. Libya was a part of the Turkish dominions from the 16th century until 1911. Following the outbreak of hostilities between Italy and Turkey in that year, Italian troops occupied Tripoli; Italian sovereignty was recognized in 1912.

Libya was the scene of much desert fighting during World War II. After the fall of Tripoli on Jan. 23, 1943, it came under Allied administration. In 1949, the U.N. voted that Libya should become independent by 1952.

Discovery of oil in the Libyan Desert promised financial stability and funds for economic development.

The Reagan Administration, accusing Libya of supporting international terrorism, closed the Libyan embassy in Washington on May 6, 1981.

On Aug. 19, 1981, two U.S. Navy F-14's shot down two Soviet-made SU-22's of the Libyan air force that had attacked them in air space above the Gulf of Sidra, claimed by Libya but held to be international by the U.S. In December, Washington asserted that Libyan "hit squads" had been dispatched to the U.S. and security was drastically tightened around President Reagan and other officials. Reagan requested remaining American citizens to leave Libya and nearly all did by Dec. 15. When the Mobil Oil Company abandoned its operations in April 1982, only four U.S. firms were still in Libya, using Libyan or third-country personnel.

Qaddafi's troops also supported rebels in Chad but suffered major military reverses in 1987.

On March 24, 1986, U.S. and Libyan forces skirmished in the Gulf of Sidra, with two Libyan patrol boats being sunk.

On April 14, after a Libyan-backed attack on a West Berlin disco in which two people, including an American serviceman, were killed, Reagan ordered an air raid on Libyan military installations.

A two-year-old U.S. covert policy to destabilize the Libyan government with U.S.-trained Libyan ex-P.O.W.s ended in failure in December 1990 when a Libyan-supplied guerrilla force assumed power in Chad, where the commandos were based, and asked the band to leave. Exiled Prince Idris in March 1991 said he would take control of the paramilitary group, although finding a place of exile for them proved difficult.

LIECHTENSTEIN

Principality of Liechtenstein
Ruler: Prince Hans Adam (1989)
Prime Minister: Hans Brunhart (1978)
Area: 61 sq mi. (157 sq km)
Population (mid-1991): 30,000 (average annual growth rate: 0.7%); birth rate: 13/1000; infant mortality rate: 2.7/1000; density per square mile: 468
Capital and largest city (est. 1986): Vaduz, 4,920
Monetary unit: Swiss franc
Language: German
Religions: Roman Catholic, 82.7%; Protestant, 7.1%; other 10.2%
Literacy rate: 100%
Economic summary: Gross national product: $405 million; $15,000 per capita (1984). Arable land: 25%; Labor force in agriculture: 4%. Principal products: livestock, vegetables, corn, wheat, potatoes, grapes. Labor force: 12,258; 54.4% in industry, trade and building. Major products: electronics, metal products, textiles, ceramics, pharmaceuticals, food products, precision instruments. Natural resource: hydroelectric power. Exports: small specialty machinery, dental products, stamps, hardware, pottery. Imports: machinery, processed foods, metal goods, textiles, motor vehicles. Major trading partners: Switzerland and other Western European countries.

Geography. Tiny Liechtenstein, not quite as large as Washington, D.C., lies on the east bank of the Rhine River south of Lake Constance between Austria and Switzerland. It consists of low valley land and Alpine peaks. Falknis (8,401 ft; 2,561 m) and Naatkopf (8,432 ft; 2,570 m) are the tallest.

Government. The Constitution of 1921, amended in 1972, provides for a legislature, the Landtag, of 25 members elected by direct male suffrage.

History. Founded in 1719, Liechtenstein was a member of the German Confederation from 1815 to 1866, when it became an independent principality. It abolished its army in 1868 and has managed to stay neutral and undamaged in all European wars since then. In a referendum on July 1, 1984, male voters granted women the right to vote, a victory for Prince Hans Adam.

In 1990 the government announced plans to revise the country's banking laws.

LUXEMBOURG

Grand Duchy of Luxembourg
Ruler: Grand Duke Jean (1964)
Premier: Jacques Santer (1984)
Area: 999 sq mi. (2,586 sq km)
Population (est. mid-1991): 400,000 (average annual rate of natural increase: 0.2%); birth rate: 12/1000; infant mortality rate: 9.9/1000; density per square mile: 391
Capital and largest city (est. 1982): Luxembourg, 80,000
Monetary unit: Luxembourg franc
Languages: Luxermbourgish, French, German
Religion: Mainly Roman Catholic
National name: Grand-Duché de Luxembourg
Literacy rate: 100%
Economic summary: Gross national product (1989 est.): $6.3 billion; $17,200 per capita; 4% real growth rate. Arable land: 24%. Principal products: livestock, dairy products, wine. Labor force: 161,000; 24.7% in industry. Major products: banking, steel, processed food, chemicals, metal products, tires, glass. Natural resource: Iron ore. Exports: steel, chemicals, rubber products, glass, aluminum. Imports: minerals, metals, foodstuffs, consumer goods. Major trading partners: European Common Market countries.

Geography. Luxembourg is a neighbor of Belgium on the west, West Germany on the east, and France on the south. The Ardennes Mountains extend from Belgium into the northern section of Luxembourg.

Government. Luxembourg's unicameral legislature, the Chamber of Deputies, consists of 59 members elected for five years.

History. Sigefroi, Count of Ardennes, an offspring of Charlemagne, was Luxembourg's first sovereign ruler. In 1060, the country came under the rule of the House of Luxembourg. From the 15th to the 18th century, Spain, France, and Austria held it in turn. The Congress of Vienna in 1815 made it a Grand Duchy and gave it to William I, King of the Netherlands. In 1839 the Treaty of London ceded the western part of Luxembourg to Belgium.

The eastern part, continuing in personal union with the Netherlands and a member of the German Confederation, became autonomous in 1848 and a neutral territory by decision of the London Conference of 1867, governed by its Grand Duke. Germany occupied the duchy in World Wars I and II. Allied troops liberated the enclave in 1944.

In 1961, Prince Jean, son and heir of Grand Duchess Charlotte, was made head of state, acting for his mother. She abdicated in 1964, and Prince Jean became Grand Duke. Grand Duchess Charlotte died in 1985.

By a customs union between Belgium and Luxembourg, which came into force on May 1, 1922, to last for 50 years, customs frontiers between the two countries were abolished. On Jan. 1, 1948, a customs union with Belgium and the Netherlands (Benelux) came into existence. On Feb. 3, 1958, it became an economic union.

The Luxembourg-based Bank of Credit and Commerce International in 1990 pleaded guilty to charges of money laundering from drug trafficking.

LITHUANIA

See page 973

MADAGASCAR

Democratic Republic of Madagascar
President and Head of State: Didier Ratsiraka (1975)
Prime Minister: Lt. Col. Victor Ramahatra (1988)

Area: 226,660 sq mi. (587,050 sq km)
Population (est. mid-1991): 12,400,000 (average annual rate of natural increase: 3.2%); birth rate: 45/1000; infant mortality rate: 115/1000; density per square mile: 55
Capital and largest city (est. 1983): Antananarivo, 700,000
Monetary unit: Malagasy franc
Languages: Malagasy, French
Ethnic groups: Merina (or Hova), Betsimisaraka, Betsileo, Tsimihety, Antaisaka, Sakalava, Antandroy
Religions: traditional, 52%; Christian, 41%; Islam, 7%
National name: Repoblika Demokratika Malagasy
Literacy rate: 67.5%
Economic summary: Gross domestic product (1988): $1.7 billion; $155 per capita; 2.2% real growth rate. Arable land: 4%. Principal products: rice, livestock, coffee, vanilla, sugar, cloves, cardamom, beans, bananas. Labor force: 4,900,000; 90% in subsistence agriculture. Major industrial products: processed food, textiles, assembled automobiles, soap, cement. Natural resources: graphite, chromium, bauxite, semiprecious stones. Exports: coffee, cloves, vanilla, sugar, petroleum products. Imports: consumer goods, foodstuffs, crude petroleum. Major trading partners: France, U.S., Japan, E.C.

Geography. Madagascar lies in the Indian Ocean off the southeast coast of Africa opposite Mozambique. The world's fourth-largest island, it is twice the size of Arizona. The country's low-lying coastal area gives way to a central plateau. The once densely wooded interior has largely been cut down.

Government. The Constitution of Dec. 30, 1975, approved by referendum following a military coup, provides for direct election by universal suffrage of a president for a seven-year term, a Supreme Council of the Revolution as a policy-making body, a unicameral People's National Assembly of 137 members (elected for five-year terms), and a military Committee for Development. The new constitution followed a period of martial rule that began with the suspension of the republic's original bicameral legislature in 1972.

A decree of March 1990 permitted the formation of political parties. Three new groupings immediately appeared.

History. The present population is of black and Malay stock, with perhaps some Polynesian, called Malagasy. The French took over a protectorate in 1885, and then in 1894–95 ended the monarchy, exiling Queen Rànavàlona III to Algiers. A colonial administration was set up, to which the Comoro Islands were attached in 1908, and other territories later. In World War II, the British occupied Madagascar, which retained ties to Vichy France.

An autonomous republic within the French Community since 1958, Madagascar became an independent member of the Community in 1960. In May 1973, an army coup led by Maj. Gen. Gabriel Ramanantsoa ousted Philibert Tsiranana, president since 1959.

With unemployment and inflation both high, Ramanantsoa resigned Feb. 5, 1975. His leftist-leaning successor, Interior Minister Richard Ratsimandrava, an Army lieutenant colonel, was killed six days later by a machine-gun ambush in Antananarivo, the capital.

On June 15, 1975, Comdr. Didier Ratsiraka was named President. He announced that he would follow a socialist course and, after nationalizing banks and insurance companies, declared all mineral resources nationalized.

An attempted coup in May 1990 was soon put down with a loss of five lives, according to official sources.

MALAWI

Republic of Malawi
President: Hastings Kamuzu Banda (1966)
Area: 45,747 sq mi. (118,484 sq km)
Population (est. mid-1991): 9,400,000 (average annual rate of natural increase: 3.4%); birth rate: 52/1000; infant mortality rate: 136/1000; density per square mile: 206
Capital (est. 1986): Lilongwe, 202,900
Largest city (est. 1986): Blantyre, 378,100
Monetary unit: Kwacha
Languages: English and Chichewa (National); also Tombuka
Religions: Christian, 75%; Islam, 20%
Member of Commonwealth of Nations
Literacy rate: 41.2%
Economic summary: Gross domestic product (1988): $1.4 billion, $180 per capita; growth rate: 3.6%. Arable land: 25%. Principal products: tobacco, tea, sugar, corn, cotton. Labor force: 428,000 wage earners; 16% in manufacturing. Major products: food, tobacco, cement, processed wood, consumer goods. Natural resources: limestone, uranium, coal, bauxite. Exports: tobacco, sugar, tea. Imports: transport equipment, food, petroleum, consumer goods. Major trading partners: U.K., U.S., Japan, Germany, South Africa.

Geography. Malawi is a landlocked country the size of Pennsylvania in southeastern Africa, surrounded by Mozambique, Zambia, and Tanzania. Lake Malawi, formerly Lake Nyasa, occupies most of the country's eastern border. The north-south Rift Valley is flanked by mountain ranges and high plateau areas.

Government. Under a Constitution that came into effect on July 6, 1966, the president is the sole head of state; there is neither a prime minister nor a vice president. The National Assembly has 107 members.

There is only one national party—the Malawi Congress Party led by President Hastings K. Banda, who was designated President for life in 1970.

History. The first European to make extensive explorations in the area was David Livingstone in the 1850s and 1860s. In 1884, Cecil Rhodes's British South African Company received a charter to develop the country. The company came into conflict with the Arab slavers in 1887–89. After Britain annexed the Nyasaland territory in 1891, making it a protectorate in 1892, Sir Harry Johnstone, the first high commissioner, using Royal Navy gunboats, wiped out the slavers.

Nyasaland became the independent nation of Malawi on July 6, 1964. Two years later, it became a republic within the Commonwealth of Nations.

Dr. Hastings K. Banda, Malawi's first Prime Minister, became its first President. He pledged to follow a policy of "discretionary nonalignment." Banda alienated much of black Africa by maintaining good relations with South Africa. He argued that his landlocked country had to rely on South Africa for access to the sea and trade.

In recent years this country's problems have been more economic than political. Malawi's main export crop, tobacco, has sharply dropped in price on world markets producing dramatically lowered foreign earnings.

MALAYSIA

Paramount Ruler: Azlan Muhibuddin Shah, Sultan of Perak (1989)
Prime Minister: D.S. Mahathir bin Mohamed (1981)
Area: 128,328 sq mi. (332,370 sq km)
Population (est. mid-1991): 18,300,000 (average annual rate of natural increase: 2.5%); birth rate: 29/1000; infant mortality rate: 29/1000; density per square mile: 143
Capital: Kuala Lumpur
Largest cities (est. 1980 by U.N.): Kuala Lumpur, 1,000,000; George Town (Pinang), 300,000; Ipoh, 275,000
Monetary unit: Ringgit
Languages: Malay (official), Chinese, Tamil, English
Ethnic divisions: 59% Malay and other indigenous; 32% Chinese; 9% Indian
Religions: Malays nearly all Muslim, Chinese predominantly Buddhists, Indians predominantly Hindu
Member of Commonwealth of Nations
Literacy rate: 65%
Economic summary: Gross domestic product (1989 est.): $37.9 billion; $2,270 per capita; 7.7% real growth rate. Arable land: 3%. Principal products: rice, rubber, palm products. Labor force: 800,000; 17% in manufacturing. Major industrial products: processed rubber, timber, and palm oil, tin, petroleum, light manufactures, electronics equipment. Natural resources: tin, oil, copper, timber. Exports: natural rubber, palm oil, tin, timber, petroleum. Imports: food, crude oil, capital equipment, chemicals. Major trading partners: Japan, Singapore, U.S., Western European countries.

Geography. Malaysia is at the southern end of the Malay Peninsula in southeast Asia. The nation also includes Sabah and Sarawak on the island of Borneo to the southeast. Its area slightly exceeds that of New Mexico.

Most of Malaysia is covered by dense jungle and swamps, with a mountain range running the length of the peninsula. Extensive forests provide ebony, sandalwood, teak, and other woods.

Government. Malaysia is a sovereign constitutional monarchy within the Commonwealth of Nations. The Paramount Ruler is elected for a five-year term by the hereditary rulers of the states from among themselves. He is advised by the prime minister and his cabinet. There is a bicameral legislature. The Senate, whose role is comparable more to that of the British House of Lords than to the U.S. Senate, has 68 members, partly appointed by the Paramount Ruler to represent minority and special interests, and partly elected by the legislative assemblies of the various states.

The House of Representatives, is made up of 180 members, who are elected for five-year terms.

History. Malaysia came into existence on Sept. 16, 1963, as a federation of Malaya, Singapore, Sabah (North Borneo), and Sarawak. In 1965, Singapore withdrew from the federation. Since 1966, the 11 states of former Malaya have been known as West Malaysia, and Sabah and Sarawak have been known as East Malaysia.

The Union of Malaya was established April 1, 1946, being formed from the Federated Malay States of Negri Sembilan, Pahang, Perak, and Selangor; the Unfederated Malay States of Johore, Kedah, Kelantan, Perlis, and Trengganu; and two of the Straits Settlements—Malacca and Penang. The Malay states had been brought under British administration during the late 19th and early 20th centuries.

It became the Federation of Malaya on Feb. 1, 1948, and the Federation attained full independence within the Commonwealth of Nations in 1957.

Sabah, constituting the extreme northern portion of the island of Borneo, was a British protectorate administered under charter by the British North Borneo Company from 1881 to 1946, when it assumed the status of a colony. It was occupied by Japanese troops from 1942 to 1945.

Sarawak extends along the northwestern coast of Borneo for about 500 miles (805 km). In 1841, part of the present territory was granted by the Sultan of Brunei to Sir James Brooke. Sarawak continued to be ruled by members of the Brooke family until the Japanese occupation.

From 1963, when Malaysia became independent, it was the target of guerrilla infiltration from Indonesia, but beat off invasion attempts. In 1966, when Sukarno fell and the Communist Party was liquidated in Indonesia, hostilities ended.

In the late 1960s, the country was torn by communal rioting directed against Chinese and Indians, who controlled a disproportionate share of the country's wealth. Beginning in 1968, the government moved to achieve greater economic balance through a rural development program.

Malaysia felt the impact of the "boat people" fleeing Vietnam early in 1978. Because the refugees were mostly ethnic Chinese, the government was apprehensive about any increase of a minority that previously had been the source of internal conflict in the country. In April 1988, it announced that starting in April 1989 it would accept no more refugees.

General elections were held in October 1990 producing another victory for Prime Minister Mahathir and his Barisan National coalition, which won 127 of the 180 parliamentary seats. Although still more than the two-thirds majority needed to pass constitutional amendments, this total is down from the previous 133 seats.

MALDIVES

Republic of Maldives
President: Maumoon Abdul Gayoom (1978)
Area: 115 sq mi. (298 sq km)
Population (1990 census): 213,215 (average annual rate of natural increase: 3.7%); birth rate: 46/1000; infant mortality rate: 72/1000; density per square mile: 1,951
Capital and largest city (1990): Malé, 55,130
Monetary unit: Maldivian rufiyaa
Language: Dhivehi
Religion: Islam
Literacy rate: 95.04%
Economic summary: Gross domestic product (1988): $136 million; $670 per capita; 9.2% real growth rate. Arable land: 10%. Principal agricultural products: coconuts, corn, sweet potatoes. Labor force: 66,000; 80% in fishing. Major products: fish, processed coconuts, handicraft. Natural resource: fish. Export: fish, clothing. Imports: intermediate and capital goods, consumer goods, petroleum products. Major trading partners: Sri Lanka, Thailand, Western Europe, Japan.

Geography. The Republic of Maldives is a group of atolls in the Indian Ocean about 417 miles (671 km) southwest of Sri Lanka. Its 1,190 coral islets stretch over an area of 35,200 square miles (90,000 sq km). With concerns over global warming and the shrinking of the polar ice caps, Maldives felt directly threatened as none of its islands rises more than six feet above sea level.

Government. The 11-member Cabinet is headed by the president. The Majlis (Parliament) is a unicameral legislature consisting of 48 members. Eight of these are appointed by the president. The others are elected for five-year terms, 2 from the capital island of Malé and 2 from each of the 19 administrative atolls.

There are no political parties in the Maldives.

History. The Maldives (formerly called the Maldive Islands) are inhabited by an Islamic seafaring people. Originally the islands were under the suzerainty of Ceylon. They came under British protection in 1887 and were a dependency of the then colony of Ceylon until 1948. The independence agreement with Britain was signed July 26, 1965.

For centuries a sultanate, the islands adopted a republican form of government in 1952, but the sultanate was restored in 1954. In 1968, however, as the result of a referendum, a republic was again established in the islands.

Ibrahim Nasir, president since 1968, was removed from office by the Majlis in November 1978 and replaced by Maumoon Abdul Cayoom. A national referendum confirmed the new leader.

MALI

Republic of Mali
President of the Republic: Lt. Col. Amadou (1991)
Area: 478,819 sq mi. (1,240,142 sq km)
Population (est. mid-1991): 8,300,000 (average annual rate of natural increase: 3%); birth rate: 51/1000; infant mortality rate: 116/1000; density per square mile: 17
Capital and largest city (est. 1981): Bamako, 750,000
Monetary unit: Franc CFA
Ethnic groups: Bambara, Peul, Soninke, Malinke, Songhai, Dogon, Senoufo, Minianka, Berbers, and Moors
Languages: French (official), African languages
Religions: Islam, 90%; traditional, 9%; Christian, 1%
National name: République de Mali
Literacy rate: 18%
Economic summary: Gross domestic product (1988 est.): $1.94 billion; $220 per capita; –0.9% real growth rate. Arable land: 2%; Principal agricultural products: millet, corn, rice, cotton, peanuts, livestock. Labor force: 2,666,000; 80% in agriculture. Major industrial products: consumer goods, phosphates, gold, fish. Natural resources: bauxite, iron ore, manganese, phosphate, salt, limestone, gold. Exports: livestock, peanuts, dried fish, cotton, skins. Imports: textiles, vehicles, petroleum products, machinery, sugar, cereals. Major trading partners: Western Europe.

Geography. Most of Mali, in West Africa, lies in the Sahara. A landlocked country four fifths the size of Alaska, it is bordered by Guinea, Senegal, Mauritania, Algeria, Niger, Burkina Faso, and the Ivory Coast.

The only fertile area is in the south, where the Niger and Senegal Rivers provide irrigation.

Government. The army overthrew the government on Nov. 19, 1968, and formed a provisional government. The Military Committee of National Liberation consists of 14 members and forms the decision-making body.

In late 1969 an attempted coup was foiled, and Lt. Moussa Traoré, president of the Military Committee took over as chief of state and later as head of government, ousting Capt. Yoro Diakité as Premier.

Soldiers promising a multiparty democracy overthrew the dictatorship of General Traoré in March 1991.

History. Subjugated by France by the end of the 19th century, this area became a colony in 1904 (named French Sudan in 1920) and in 1946 became part of the French Union. On June 20, 1960, it became independent and, under the name of Sudanese Republic, was federated with the Republic of Senegal in the Mali Federation. However, Senegal seceded from the Federation on Aug. 20, 1960, and the Sudanese Republic then changed its name to the Republic of Mali on September 22.

In the 1960s, Mali concentrated on economic development, continuing to accept aid from both Soviet bloc and Western nations, as well as international agencies. In the late 1960s, it began retreating from close ties with China. But a purge of conservative opponents brought greater power to President Modibo Keita, and in 1968 the influence of the Chinese and their Malian sympathizers increased. By a treaty signed in Peking in 1968, China agreed to help build a railroad from Mali to Guinea, providing Mali with vital access to the sea.

Mali, with Mauritania, the Ivory Coast, Senegal, Dahomey (Benin), Niger, and Burkina Faso signed a treaty establishing the Economic Community for West Africa.

Mali and Burkina Faso fought a brief border war from December 25 to 29, 1985.

The leader of the March 1991 coup, Lieut. Col. Amadou Toumani Touré, promised the army would return to the barracks. There were at least 59 casualties after the overnight coup, which France welcomed. A failed coup attempt by Major Lamine Diabira, a member of the ruling council, resulted in his arrest in July.

MALTA

Republic of Malta
President: Dr. Vincent Tabone (1989)
Prime Minister: Dr. Edward Fenech Adami (1987)
Area: 122 sq mi. (316 sq km)
Population (est. mid-1991): 400,000 (average annual rate of natural increase: 0.8%); birth rate: 16/1000; infant mortality rate: 10.4/1000; density per square mile: 2,873
Capital (est. 1987): Valetta, 9,300
Largest city (est. 1987): Birkirkara, 20,300
Monetary unit: Maltese lira
Languages: Maltese and English
Religion: Roman Catholic
National name: Malta
Member of Commonwealth of Nations
Literacy rate: 83%
Economic summary: Gross domestic product (1989): $1.99 billion; $5,645 per capita; 4.9% real growth rate. Arable land: 38%. Principal products: potatoes, wheat, barley, citrus, vegetables, hogs, poultry. Labor force: 125,674; 24% in manufacturing. Major products: textiles, beverages, processed foods, clothing, footwear, tobacco. Natural resources: limestone, salt. Exports: textiles, clothing, footwear. Imports: foods, petroleum, raw material. Major trading partners: Germany, U.K., Italy, U.S.

Geography. The five Maltese islands—with a combined land area smaller than Philadelphia—are in the Mediterranean about 60 miles (97 km) south of the southeastern tip of Sicily.

Government. The government is headed by a Prime Minister, responsible to a 69-member House of Representatives elected by universal suffrage.

The major political parties are the Nationalists (35

of 69 seats in the House,) led by Prime Minister Dr. Dr. Edward Fenech-Adami; Malta Labor Party (34 seats), led by Carmelo Mifsud Bonnici.

History. The strategic importance of Malta was recognized by the Phoenicians, who occupied it, as did in their turn the Greeks, Carthaginians, and Romans. The apostle Paul was shipwrecked there in A.D. 58.

The Knights of St. John (Malta), who obtained the three habitable Maltese islands of Malta, Gozo, and Comino from Charles V in 1530, reached their highest fame when they withstood an attack by superior Turkish forces in 1565.

Napoleon seized Malta in 1798, but the French forces were ousted by British troops the next year, and British rule was confirmed by the Treaty of Paris in 1814.

Malta was heavily attacked by German and Italian aircraft during World War II, but was never invaded by the Axis.

Malta became an independent nation on Sept. 21, 1964, and a republic Dec. 13, 1974, but remained in the British Commonwealth. The Governor-General, Sir Anthony Mamo, was sworn in as first president and Dom Mintoff became prime minister.

After 13 years in office, Mintoff resigned as Prime Minister on Dec. 22, 1984, giving way to chosen successor, Carmelo Mifsud Bonnici, who had been Senior Deputy Prime Minister. Fenech Adami's election in 1987 ended 16 years of Labor rule.

Malta applied for membership in the E.C. in July 1990 and expects to be admitted in the next enlargement.

MARSHALL ISLANDS

See page 771

MAURITANIA

Islamic Republic of Mauritania
Chief of State and Head of Government: Col. Maaouye Ould Sidi Ahmed Taya (1984)
Area: 397,953 sq mi. (1,030,700 sq km)
Population (est. mid-1991): 2,100,000 (average annual rate of natural increase: 2.8%); birth rate: 46/1000; infant mortality rate: 122/1000; density per square mile: 5
Capital and largest city (est. 1981): Nouakchott, 175,000
Monetary unit: Ouguiya
Ethnic groups: Moors, Black/moor mix, 70%; Blacks, 30%.
Languages: Arabic (official) and French
Religion: Islam
National name: République Islamique de Mauritanie
Literacy rate: 17%
Economic summary: Gross domestic product (1988): $1.0 billion; $520 per capita; 3.6% real growth rate. Arable land: 1%; Principal agricultural products: livestock, millet, maize, wheat, dates, rice. Labor force: 465,000 (1981 est.); 45,000 wage earners; 14% in industry and commerce. Major industrial products: iron ore, processed fish. Natural resources: copper, iron ore, gypsum, fish. Exports: iron ore, fish, gum arabic, gypsum. Imports: foodstuffs, petroleum, capital goods. Major trading partners: E.C., Japan, Ivory Coast.

Geography. Mauritania, three times the size of Arizona, is situated in northwest Africa with about 350 miles (592 km) of coastline on the Atlantic Ocean. It is bordered by Morocco on the north, Algeria and Mali on the east, and Senegal on the south.

The country is mostly desert, with the exception of

the fertile Senegal River valley in the south and grazing land in the north.

Government. An Army coup on July 10, 1978, deposed Moktar Ould Daddah, who had been President since Mauritania's independence in 1960. President Mohammed Khouna Ould Haidala, who seized power in the 1978 coup, was in turn deposed in a Dec. 12, 1984, coup by army chief of staff Maaouye Ould Sidi Ahmed Taya, who assumed the title of President.

History. Mauritania was first explored by the Portuguese. The French organized the area as a territory in 1904.

Mauritania became an independent nation on Nov. 28, 1960, and was admitted to the United Nations in 1961 over the strenuous opposition of Morocco, which claimed the territory. With Moors, Arabs, Berbers, and blacks frequently in conflict, the government in the late 1960s sought to make Arab culture dominant to unify the land.

Mauritania acquired administrative control of the southern part of the former Spanish Sahara when the colonial administration withdrew in 1975, under an agreement with Morocco and Spain. Mauritanian troops moved into the territory but encountered resistance from the Polisario Front, a Saharan independence movement backed by Algeria. The task of trying to pacify the area proved a heavy burden. Mauritania signed a peace agreement with the Polisario insurgents in August 1979, withdrew from the territory and renounced territorial claims.

Increased military spending and rising casualties in Western Sahara contributed to the discontent that brought down the civilian government of Ould Daddah in 1978. A succession of military rulers has followed.

In 1989 Mauritania fought a border war with Senegal. In January 1990 Arabic was made the official language of government. Although the country voted in the U.N. to support the embargo against Iraq, the government actually leaned the other way.

MAURITIUS

Sovereign: Queen Elizabeth II
Governor-General: Sir Veerasamy Ringadoo (1986)
Prime Minister: Aneerood Jugnauth (1982)
Area: 787 sq mi. (2,040 sq km)
Population (est. mid-1991): 1,100,000 (average annual rate of natural increase: 1.4%); birth rate: 20/1000; infant mortality rate: 22.7/1000; density per square mile: 1,368
Capital and largest city (est. 1980): Port Louis, 155,000
Monetary unit: Mauritian rupee
Languages: English (official), French, Creole, Hindi, Urdu, Chinese
Religions: Hindu, 51%, Christian, 30%; Islam, 17%; other, 2%
Member of Commonwealth of Nations
Literacy rate: 82.8%
Economic summary: Gross domestic product (1988): $1.9 billion; $1,910 per capita; 6.3% real growth rate. Arable land: 54%. Principal products: sugar cane, tea. Labor force: 335,000; 22% in manufacturing. Major products: processed sugar, wearing apparel, chemical products, textiles. Natural resources: fish. Exports: sugar, light manufactures, textiles. Imports: foodstuffs, manufactured goods. Major trading partners: E.C., S. Africa, U.S.

Geography. Mauritius is a mountainous island in the Indian Ocean east of Madagascar.

Government. Mauritius is a member of the British Commonwealth, with Queen Elizabeth II as head of state. She is represented by a governor-general, who chooses the prime minister from the unicameral Legislative Assembly. The Legislative Assembly has 70 members, 62 of whom are elected by direct suffrage. The remaining 8 are chosen from among the unsuccessful candidates.

History. After a brief Dutch settlement, French immigrants who came in 1715 gave the name of Isle de France to the island and established the first road and harbor infrastructure, as well as the sugar industry, under the leadership of Gov. Mahe de Labourdonnais. Negroes from Africa and Madagascar came as slaves to work in the cane fields. In 1810, the British captured the island and in 1814, by the Treaty of Paris, it was ceded to Great Britain along with its dependencies.

Indian immigration which followed the abolition of slavery in 1835 changed rapidly the fabric of Mauritian society, and the country flourished with the increased cultivation of sugar cane.

Mauritius became independent on March 12, 1968.

The Labor Party government of Sir Seewoosagur Ramgoolam, who had ruled Mauritius since independence, was toppled in a 1982 election by the Movement Militant Mauricien, which had campaigned for recovery of Diego Garcia island, separated from Mauritius during the colonial period and leased by Britain to the United States for a naval base. But an Alliance Party coalition, including the Labor Party, regained power at the end of 1983 and brought back Ramgoolam as Prime Minister. He was succeeded by Aneerood Jugnauth of his party in 1982.

A transformation of the nation from a constitutional monarchy into a republic was attempted in mid-1990 on the understanding that opposition party leader Paul Bérenger would be named president. Public dissent for the move, however, arose, and the required parliamentary vote was never taken.

MEXICO

United Mexican States
President: Carlos Salinas de Gortari (1988)
Area: 761,600 sq mi. (1,972,547 sq km)
Population (est. mid-1991): 85,700,000 (average annual rate of natural increase: 2.3%); birth rate: 29/1000; infant mortality rate: 43/1000; density per square mile: 113
Capital: Federal District (Mexico City)
Largest cities (1989): Federal District, 19,479,000; Guadalajara, 3,186,500; Monterey, 2,858,800; Puebla, 1,707,000; Leon, 1,006,700
Monetary unit: Peso
Languages: Spanish, Indian languages
Religion: nominally Roman Catholic, 97%; Protestant, 3%
Official name: Estados Unidos Mexicanos
Literacy rate: 88%
Economic summary: Gross domestic product (1989): $187.0 billion; $2,165 per capita; 2.5% real growth rate. Arable land: 12%;principal products: corn, cotton, fruits, wheat, beans, coffee, tomatoes, rice. Labor force: 26,100,000 (1988); 12.8% in manufacturing. Ma-

jor products: processed foods, chemicals, basic metals and metal products, petroleum. Natural resources: petroleum, silver, copper, gold, lead, zinc, natural gas, timber. Exports: cotton, shrimp, coffee, petroleum, petroleum products, engines. Imports: grain, metal manufactures, agricultural machinery, electrical equipment. Major trading partners: U.S., Japan, Western European countries.

Geography. The United States' neighbor to the south, Mexico is about one fifth its size. Baja California in the west, an 800-mile (1,287-km) peninsula, forms the Gulf of California. In the east are the Gulf of Mexico and the Bay of Campeche, which is formed by Mexico's other peninsula, the Yucatán.

The center of Mexico is a great, high plateau, open to the north, with mountain chains on east and west and with ocean-front lowlands lying outside of them.

Government. The President, who is popularly elected for six years and is ineligible to succeed himself, governs with a Cabinet of secretaries. Congress has two houses—a 400-member Chamber of Deputies, elected for three years, and a 64-member Senate, elected for six years.

Each of the 31 states has considerable autonomy, with a popularly elected governor, a legislature, and a local judiciary. The President of Mexico appoints the mayor of the Federal District.

History. At least two civilized races—the Mayas and later the Toltecs—preceded the wealthy Aztec empire, conquered in 1519–21 by the Spanish under Hernando Cortés. Spain ruled for the next 300 years until 1810 (the date was Sept. 16 and is now celebrated as Independence Day), when the Mexicans first revolted. They continued the struggle and finally won independence in 1821.

From 1821 to 1877, there were two emperors, several dictators, and enough presidents and provisional executives to make a new government on the average of every nine months. Mexico lost Texas (1836), and after defeat in the war with the U.S. (1846–48) it lost the area comprising the present states of California, Nevada, and Utah, most of Arizona and New Mexico, and parts of Wyoming and Colorado.

In 1855, the Indian patriot Benito Juárez began a series of liberal reforms, including the disestablishment of the Catholic Church, which had acquired vast property. A subsequent civil war was interrupted by the French invasion of Mexico (1861), the crowning of Maximilian of Austria as Emperor (1864), and then his overthrow and execution by forces under Juárez, who again became President in 1867.

The years after the fall of the dictator Porfirio Diaz (1877–80 and 1884–1911) were marked by bloody political-military strife and trouble with the U.S., culminating in the punitive expedition into northern Mexico (1916–17) in unsuccessful pursuit of the revolutionary Pancho Villa. Since a brief period of civil war in 1920, Mexico has enjoyed a period of gradual agricultural, political, and social reforms. Relations with the U.S. were again disturbed in 1938 when all foreign oil wells were expropriated. Agreement on compensation was finally reached in 1941.

The last year of José López Portillo's presidency was shadowed by economic problems caused by falling oil prices.

Miguel de la Madrid Hurtado, candidate of the ruling Partido Revolucionario Institucional, won the July 4 election for a six-year term.

During 1983 and 1984, Mexico suffered its worst financial crisis in 50 years, leading to critically high unemployment and an inability to pay its foreign debt. The collapse of oil prices in 1986 cut into Mexico's export earnings and worsened the situation.

Although the ruling Institutional Revolutionary Party's candidate, Carlos Salinas de Gortari, won the presidential election of 1988, the opposition parties on the left and the right showed unprecedented strength. This continued in mid-1989 when the ruling PRI acknowledged an unprecedented defeat in a gubernatorial election.

In the economic sphere Mexico decided to apply for membership in the Organization for Economic Cooperation & Development and talks began on a comprehensive North American free-trade agreement. The national telephone company was privatized, and the government in 1990 announced it would reprivatize the banks nationalized in 1982.

MICRONESIA

See page 770

MONACO

Principality of Monaco
Ruler: Prince Rainier III (1949)
Minister of State: Jacques Dupont (1991)
Area: 0.73 sq mi. (465 acres)
Population (1989): 28,188 (average annual growth rate: .9%)
Density per square mile: 38,356.2
Capital: Monaco-Ville
Monetary unit: French franc
Languages: French, Monégasque, Italian
Religion: Roman Catholic, 95%
National name: Principauté de Monaco
Literacy rate: 99%

Geography. Monaco is a tiny, hilly wedge driven into the French Mediterranean coast nine miles east of Nice.

Government. Prince Albert of Monaco gave the principality a Constitution in 1911, creating a National Council of 18 members popularly elected for five years. The head of government is the Minister of State.

Prince Rainier III, born May 31, 1923, succeeded his grandfather, Louis II, on the latter's death, May 9, 1949. Rainier was married April 18, 1956, to Grace Kelly, U.S. actress. A daughter, Princess Caroline Louise Marguerite, was born on Jan. 23, 1957 (married to Philippe Junot June 28, 1978 and divorced in 1980; married to Stefano Casiraghi Dec. 29, 1983, and gave birth to a son, Andrea Albert, June 9, 1984); a son, Prince Albert Louis Pierre, on March 14, 1958; and Princess Stéphanie Marie Elisabeth, on Feb. 1, 1965. Princess Grace died Sept. 14, 1982, of injuries received the day before when the car she was driving went off the road near Monte Carlo. She was 52.

The special significance attached to the birth of descendants to Prince Rainier stems from a clause in the Treaty of July 17, 1919, between France and

Monaco stipulating that in the event of vacancy of the Crown, the Monégasque territory would become an autonomous state under a French protectorate.

The National and Democratic Union (all 18 seats in National Council), led by Auguste Medecin, is the only political party.

History. The Phoenicians, and after them the Greeks, had a temple on the Monacan headland honoring Hercules. From *Monoikos,* the Greek surname for this mythological strong man, the principality took its name. After being independent for 800 years, Monaco was annexed to France in 1793 and was placed under Sardinia's protection in 1815. In 1861, it went under French guardianship but continued to be independent.

By a treaty in 1918, France stipulated that the French government be given a veto over the succession to the throne.

Monaco is a little land of pleasure with a tourist business that runs as high as 1.5 million visitors a year. It had popular gaming tables as early as 1856. Five years later, a 50-year concession to operate the games was granted to François Blanc, of Bad Homburg. This concession passed into the hands of a private company in 1898.

Monaco's practice of providing a tax shelter for French businessmen resulted in a dispute between the countries. When Rainier refused to end the practice, France retaliated with a customs tax. In 1967, Rainier took control of the Société des Bains de Mer, operator of the famous Monte Carlo gambling casino, in a program to increase hotel and convention space.

A series of robberies in 1989 led Prince Rainier to appoint a new police commissioner. With the recent tragedies in the royal family speculation has centered on Rainier's grooming of his son Prince Albert to assume the duties of chief of state.

MONGOLIA

Mongolian People's Republic
Chairman of Presidium of the Great People's Khural (President): Punsalmaagiin Ochirbat (1990)
Prime Minister: Dashün Byambasuren (1990)
Area: 604,250 sq mi. (1,565,000 sq km)
Population (est. mid-1991): 2,200,000 (average annual rate of natural increase: 2.7%); birth rate: 36/1000; infant mortality rate: 64/1000; density per square mile: 4
Capital and largest city (est. 1990): Ulan Bator, 550,000
Monetary unit: Tugrik
Language: Mongolian
Religion: predominantly Tibetan Buddhist; Islam about 4%
National name: Bugd Nairamdakh Mongol Ard Uls
Literacy rate: 90% (est.)
Economic summary: Gross domestic product (1989 est.): $1.06 billion; $532 per capita; 3.6% real growth rate. Arable land: 1%. Principal agricultural products: livestock, wheat, potatoes, forage, barley. Major industrial products: coal, copper and molybdenum concentrate. Natural resources: coal, copper, molybdenum, iron, oil, lead, gold, and tungsten. Exports: livestock, animal products, wool, nonferrous metals. Imports: machinery and equipment, clothing, petroleum. Major trading partners: U.S.S.R., China, Japan.

Geography. Mongolia lies in eastern Asia between Soviet Siberia on the north and China on the south. It

is slightly larger than Alaska.

The productive regions of Mongolia—a tableland ranging from 3,000 to 5,000 feet (914 to 1,524 m) in elevation—are in the north, which is well drained by numerous rivers, including the Hovd, Onon, Selenga, and Tula.

Much of the Gobi Desert falls within Mongolia.

Government. The Mongolian People's Republic is a socialist state. The highest organ of state power is the Great People's Hural (Parliament), which is elected for a term of four years and is convened once a year. The powers of the Great People's Hural include the adoption of or making amendments to the constitution, the election of the Baga Hural (standing legislature), the president and vice-president, appointment of the prime minister, the general public prosecutor, and the chief justice of the Supreme Court. In 1990, the Mongolian People's Revolutionary Party, led by Budragchaagiin Dashyondon, gave up its constitutional monopoly on power. Other political parties are the Mongolian Democratic Party, Social Democratic Party, National Progress Party, Party of the Greens, and the Free Labor Party.

History. The Mongolian People's Republic, formerly known as Outer Mongolia, is a Soviet satellite. It contains the original homeland of the historic Mongols, whose power reached its zenith during the 13th century under Kublai Khan. The area accepted Manchu rule in 1689, but after the Chinese Revolution of 1911 and the fall of the Manchus in 1912, the northern Mongol princes expelled the Chinese officials and declared independence under the Khutukhtu, or "Living Buddha."

In 1921, Soviet troops entered the country and facilitated the establishment of a republic by Mongolian revolutionaries in 1924 after the death of the last Living Buddha. China, meanwhile, continued to claim Outer Mongolia but was unable to back the claim with any strength. Under the 1945 Chinese-Russian Treaty, China agreed to give up Outer Mongolia, which, after a plebiscite, became a nominally independent country.

Allied with the U.S.S.R. in its dispute with China, Mongolia has mobilized troops along its borders since 1968 when the two powers became involved in border clashes on the Kazakh-Sinkiang frontier to the west and on the Amur and Ussuri Rivers. A 20-year treaty of friendship and cooperation, signed in 1966, entitled Mongolia to call upon the U.S.S.R. for military aid in the event of invasion.

Free elections were held in August 1990 that produced a multiparty government, though still largely Communist. As a result Mongolia has decided to move toward a market economy with the first step being the auctioning off of many shops and service firms in late June 1991.

MOROCCO

Kingdom of Morocco
Ruler: King Hassan II (1961)
Prime Minister: Azzedine Laraki (1986)
Area: 172,413 sq mi. (446,550 sq km)
Population (est. mid-1991): 26,200,000 (average annual rate of natural increase: 2.5%); birth rate: 34/1000; infant mortality rate: 75/1000; density per square mile: 152
Capital: Rabat
Largest cities: Casablanca, 3,500,000; Rabat-Sale,

1,000,000; Fez, 600,000; Marrakesh, 500,000; Laayoune, 100,000
Monetary unit: Dirham
Languages: Arabic, French, Berber dialects, Spanish
Religions: Islam, 98.7%, Christian, 1.1%; Jewish, 0.2%
National name: al-Mamlaka al-Maghrebia
Literacy rate: 28%
Economic summary: Gross domestic product (1989): $22.5 billion; $800 per capita; 3.4% real growth rate. Arable land: 20%. Products: barley, wheat, citrus fruits, vegetables. Labor force: approx. 7,000,000; 15% in industry. Major products: textiles, processed food, phosphates, leather goods. Natural resources: phosphates, lead, manganese, fisheries. Exports: phosphates, citrus fruits, vegetables, canned fruits and vegetables, canned fish, carpets. Imports: capital goods, fuels, foodstuffs, raw materials, consumer goods. Major trading partners: E.C., U.S.S.R., Japan, U.S.

Geography. Morocco, about one tenth larger than California, is just south of Spain across the Strait of Gibraltar and looks out on the Atlantic from the northwest shoulder of Africa. Algeria is to the east and Mauritania to the south.

On the Atlantic coast there is a fertile plain. The Mediterranean coast is mountainous. The Atlas Mountains, running northeastward from the south to the Algerian frontier, average 11,000 feet (3,353 m) in elevation.

Government. The King, after suspending the 1962 Constitution and dissolving Parliament in 1965, promulgated a new Constitution in 1972. He continued to rule by decree until June 3, 1977, when the first free elections since 1962 took place. The 306-member Chamber of Deputies has 204 elected seats, with the balance chosen by local councils and groups.

History. Morocco was once the home of the Berbers, who helped the Arabs invade Spain in A.D. 711 and then revolted against them and gradually won control of large areas of Spain for a time after 739.

The country was ruled successively by various native dynasties and maintained regular commercial relations with Europe, even during the 17th and 18th centuries when it was the headquarters of the famous Salé pirates. In the 19th century, there were frequent clashes with the French and Spanish. Finally, in 1904, France and Spain divided Morocco into zones of French and Spanish influence, and these were established as protectorates in 1912.

Meanwhile, Morocco had become the object of big-power rivalry, which almost led to a European war in 1905 when Germany attempted to gain a foothold in the rich mineral country. By terms of the Algeciras Conference (1906), Morocco was internationalized economically, and France's privileges were limited.

The Tangier Statute, concluded by Britain, France, and Spain in 1923, created an international zone at the port of Tangier, permanently neutralized and demilitarized. In World War II, Spain occupied the zone, ostensibly to ensure order, but was forced to withdraw in 1945.

Sultan Mohammed V was deposed by the French in 1953 and replaced by his uncle, but nationalist agitation forced his return in 1955. On his death on Feb. 26, 1961, his son, Hassan, became King.

France and Spain recognized the independence and sovereignty of Morocco in 1956. Later the same year,

the Tangier international zone was abolished.

In 1975, tens of thousands of Moroccans crossed the border into Spanish Sahara to back their government's contention that the northern part of the territory was historically part of Morocco. At the same time, Mauritania occupied the southern half of the territory in defiance of Spanish threats to resist such a takeover. Abandoning its commitment to self-determination for the territory, Spain withdrew, and only Algeria protested.

When Mauritania signed a peace treaty with the Algerian-backed Polisario Front in August 1979, Morocco occupied and assumed administrative control of the southern part of the Western Sahara, in addition to the northern part it already occupied. Under pressure from other African leaders, Hassan agreed in mid-1981 to a cease-fire with a referendum under international supervision to decide the fate of the Sahara territory, but the referendum was never carried out.

King Hassan, startled the Reagan Administration in mid-August 1984 by signing a treaty of union with Col. Muammar el-Qaddafi, the Libyan leader.

King Hassan became the second Arab leader to meet with an Israeli leader when, on July 21, 1986, Israeli Prime Minister Shimon Peres came to Morocco. Libyan criticism of the meeting led to King Hassan's abrogation of the treaty with Libya.

Morocco became the first Arab state to condemn the 1990 Iraqi invasion of Kuwait and promised to send an 1,100-men contingent to Saudi Arabia. Public opinion, however, as evidenced by sanctioned marches in Rabat, mounted against Moroccan involvement and demanded withdrawal from the U.S.-led alliance. The official policy remained that the presence of Moroccan troops were exclusively meant to help defend Saudi Arabia.

MOZAMBIQUE

Republic of Mozambique
President: Joaquim Chissano (1986)
Prime Minister: Dr. Mario Machungo (1986)
Area: 303,073 sq mi. (799,380 sq km)
Population (est. mid-1991): 16,100,000 (average annual rate of natural increase: 2.7%); birth rate: 45/1000; infant mortality rate: 136/1000; density per square mile: 52
Capital and largest city (est. mid-1986): Maputo, 882,800
Monetary unit: Metical
Languages: Portuguese (official), Bantu languages
Religions: traditional, 60%; Christian, 30%; Islam, 10%
National name: República Popular de Moçambique
Literacy rate: 38%
Economic summary: Gross national product (1988): $1.6 billion; per capita less than $110; 5% real growth rate. Arable land: 4%. Principal agricultural products: cotton, cashew nuts, sugar, tea, shrimp. Labor force: 90% in agriculture. Major products: processed foods, petroleum products, beverages, textiles, tobacco. Natural resources: coal, titanium. Exports: cashew nuts, sugar, shrimp, copra, citrus. Imports: refined petroleum, food, clothing, farm equipment. Major trading partners: U.S., Western Europe, Japan, U.S.S.R.

Geography. Mozambique stretches for 1,535 miles (2,470 km) along Africa's southeast coast. It is nearly twice the size of California. Tanzania is to the north; Malawi, Zambia, and Zimbabwe to the west; and South Africa and Swaziland to the south.

The country is generally a low-lying plateau broken up by 25 sizable rivers that flow into the Indian Ocean. The largest is the Zambezi, which provides access to central Africa. The principal ports are Maputo and Beira, which is the port for Zimbabwe.

Government. After having been under Portuguese colonial rule for 470 years, Mozambique became independent on June 25, 1975. The first President, Samora Moises Machel, headed the National Front for the Liberation of Mozambique (FRELIMO) in its 10-year guerrilla war for independence. He died in a plane crash on Oct. 19, 1986, and was succeeded by his Foreign Minister, Joaquim Chissano.

History. Mozambique was discovered by Vasco da Gama in 1498, although the Arabs had penetrated into the area as early as the 10th century. It was first colonized in 1505, and by 1510, the Portuguese had control of all the former Arab sultanates on the east African coast.

FRELIMO was organized in 1963. Guerrilla activity had become so extensive by 1973 that Portugal was forced to dispatch 40,000 troops to fight the rebels. A cease-fire was signed in September 1974, when Portugal agreed to grant Mozambique independence.

On Jan. 25, 1985, Mozambique's celebration of a decade of independence from Portugal was not a happy one. The government was locked in a five-year-old, stalemated, paralyzing war with anti-government guerrillas, known as the MNR, backed by the white minority government in South Africa.

President Chissano decided to abandon Marxism-Leninism in 1989. A new constitution was drafted calling for three branches of government and granting civil liberties. The civil war, however, continued through 1990, though hopes for a peaceful settlement emerged in 1991.

MYANMAR

Union of Myanmar
Head of State (Chairman): Gen. Saw Maung (1988)
Area: 261,220 sq mi. (676,560 sq km)
Population (est. mid-1991): 42,100,000 (average annual rate of natural increase: 1.9%); birth rate: 32/1000; infant mortality rate: 95/1000; density per square mile: 161
Capital: Yangon
Largest cities (est. 1983): Yangon, 2,458,712; Mandalay, 532,895; Moulmein, 219,991; Bassein, 144,092
Monetary unit: Kyat
Language: Burmese, minority languages
Religions: Buddhist, 85%; animist, Islam, Christian, or other, 15%
National name: Pyidaungsu Myanmar Naingngandau
Literacy rate: 78%
Economic summary: Gross domestic product (FY 1988): $11.0 billion; $280 per capita; 0.2% (FY1988 est.) real growth rate. Arable land: 15%. Principal products: oilseed, pulses, sugar cane, corn, rice. Labor force: 16,036,000; 14.3% in industry. Major products: textiles, footwear, processed agricultural products, wood and wood products, refined petroleum. Natural resources: timber, tin, antimony, zinc, copper, precious stones, crude oil and natural gas. Exports: rice, teak, oilseeds, metals, rubber, gems. Imports: machinery, transportation equipment, chemicals, food products. Major trading partners: Japan, E.C., China, Southeast Asia.

Geography. Myanmar occupies the northwest portion of the Indochinese peninsula. India lies to the northwest and China to the northeast. Bangladesh,

Laos, and Thailand are also neighbors. The Bay of Bengal touches the southwestern coast.

Slightly smaller than Texas, the country is divided into three natural regions: the Arakan Yoma, a long, narrow mountain range forming the barrier between Myanmar and India; the Shan Plateau in the east, extending southward into Tenasserim; and the Central Basin, running down to the flat fertile delta of the Irrawaddy in the south. This delta contains a network of intercommunicating canals and nine principal river mouths.

Government. On March 2, 1962, the government of U Nu was overthrown and replaced by a Revolutionary Council, which assumed all power in the state. Gen. U Ne Win, as chairman of the Revolutionary Council, became the chief executive. In 1972, Ne Win and his colleagues resigned their military titles. In 1974, Ne Win dissolved the Revolutionary Council and became President under the new Constitution. He voluntarily relinquished the presidency on Nov. 9, 1981.

History. In 1612, the British East India Company sent agents to Burma, but the Burmese long resisted efforts of British traders, and Dutch and Portuguese as well, to establish posts on the Bay of Bengal. By the Anglo-Burmese War in 1824–26 and two following wars, the British East India Company expanded to the whole of Burma by 1886. Burma was annexed to India. It became a separate colony in 1937.

During World War II, Burma was a key battleground; the 800-mile Burma Road was the Allies' vital supply line to China. The Japanese invaded the country in December 1941, and by May 1942 had occupied most of it, cutting off the Burma Road. After one of the most difficult campaigns of the war, Allied forces liberated most of Burma prior to the Japanese surrender in August 1945.

Burma became independent on Jan. 4, 1948. In 1951 and 1952 the Socialists achieved power, and Burma became the first Asian country to introduce social legislation.

In 1968, after the government had made headway against the Communist and separatist rebels, the military regime adopted a policy of strict nonalignment and followed "the Burmese Way" to socialism. But the insurgents continued active.

In July 1988, Ne Win announced his resignation from the Burmese Socialist Program Party (BSPP), the only legal political party.

The civilian government was overthrown in Sept. 1988 by a military junta led by General Saw Maung, an associate of U Ne Win. He changed the name of the party to the National Unity Party.

The new government held elections in May 1990 and the opposition National League for Democracy won in a landslide despite its leaders being in jail or under house arrest.

Since then these leaders have been kept incommunicado, and the military government has consolidated its power. A coalition government-in-exile was formed in December 1990, but no foreign government has recognized it.

NAMIBIA

President: Sam Nujoma (1990)
Status: Independent Country
Area: 318,261 sq mi. (824,296 sq km)
Population (mid-1991): 1,500,000 (average annual growth rate: 3.1%); birth rate: 43/1000; infant mortality rate: 102/1000; density per square mile: 5

Capital (est. 1980): Windhoek, 85,000
Summer capital (est. 1980): Swakopmund, 17,500
Monetary unit: South African rand[1]
Languages: Afrikaans, German, English (all official), several indigenous
Religion: Predominantly Christian
National name: Republic of Namibia
Literacy rate: 58%
Economic summary: Gross national product (1987): $1.54 billion; $1,245 per capita; 2.9% real growth rate. Arable land: 1%. Principal products: corn, millet, sorghum, livestock. Labor force: 500,000; 19% in industry and commerce. Major products: canned meat, dairy products, tanned leather, textiles, clothing. Natural resources: diamonds, copper, lead, zinc, uranium, fish. Exports: diamonds, copper, lead, zinc, beef cattle, karakul pelts. Imports: construction materials, fertilizer, grain, foodstuffs. Major trading partner: South Africa.

1. Namibian dollar to replace Rand in 1992–93.

Geography. Namibia, bounded on the north by Angola and Zambia and on the east by Botswana and South Africa, was discovered for Europeans by the Portuguese explorer Diaz in the late 15th century. It is for the most part a portion of the high plateau of southern Africa with a general elevation of from 3,000 to 4,000 feet.

Government. Namibia became independent in 1990 after its new constitution was ratified. A multi-party democracy with an independent judiciary was established.

History. The territory became a German colony in 1884 but was taken by South African forces in 1915, becoming a South African mandate by the terms of the Treaty of Versailles in 1920.

South Africa's application for incorporation of the territory was rejected by the U.N. General Assembly in 1946 and South Africa was invited to prepare a trusteeship agreement instead. By a law passed in 1949, however, the territory was brought into much closer association with South Africa—including representation in its Parliament.

In 1969, South Africa extended its laws to the mandate over the objection of the U.N., particularly its black African members. When South Africa refused to withdraw them, the Security Council condemned it.

Under a 1974 Security Council resolution, South Africa was required to begin the transfer of power to the Namibians by May 30, 1975, or face U.N. action, but 10 days before the deadline Prime Minister Balthazar J. Vorster rejected U.N. supervision. He said, however, that his government was prepared to negotiate Namibian independence, but not with the South-West African People's Organization, the principal black separatist group. Meanwhile, the all-white legislature of South-West Africa eased several laws on apartheid in public places.

Despite international opposition, the Turnhalle Conference in Windhoek drafted a constitution to organize an interim government based on racial divisions, a proposal overwhelmingly endorsed by white voters in the territory in 1977. At the urging of ambassadors of the five Western members of the Security Council—the U.S., Britain, France, West Germany, and Canada—South Africa on June 11 announced rejection of the Turnhalle constitution and acceptance of the Western proposal to include the South-West Africa People's Organization (SWAPO) in negotiations.

Although negotiations continued between South Africa, the western powers, neighboring black African states, and internal political groups, there was still no agreement on a final independence plan. A new round of talks aimed at resolving the 18-year-old conflict ended in a stalemate on July 25, 1984.

As policemen wielding riot sticks charged demonstrators in a black, South-West Africa township, South Africa handed over limited powers to a new, multiracial administration in the former German colony on June 17, 1985. Installation of the new government ended South Africa's direct rule, but South Africa retained an effective veto over the new government's decisions along with responsibility for the territory's defense and foreign policy, and South Africa's efforts to quell the insurgents seeking independence continued.

An agreement between South Africa, Angola, and Cuba arranged for elections for a Constituent Assembly in Nov. 1989 to establish a new government. SWAPO won 57% of the vote, a majority but not enough to dictate a constitution unilaterally. In February 1990, SWAPO leader Sam Nujoma was elected President and took office when Namibia became independent on March 21, 1990.

On March 14, 1991 delegations from Namibia and South Africa met to discuss the future ownership of Walvis Bay, the chief port along Namibia's coast but which South Africa retained after Namibia's independence. The talks broke off, however, after only a few hours.

NAURU

Republic of Nauru
President: Bernard Dowiyogo (1989)
Area: 8.2 sq mi. (21 sq km)
Population (mid-1989): 9,053 (average annual growth rate: 1.7%)
Density per square mile: 1,086
Capital: Yaren
Monetary unit: Australian dollar
Languages: Nauruan and English
Religions: Protestant, 58%; Roman Catholic, 24%; Confucian and Taoist, 8%
Special relationship within the Commonwealth of Nations
Literacy rate: 99%
Economic summary: Gross national product (1989): more than $90 million; $10,000 per capita. Major industrial products: phosphates. Natural resources: phosphates. Exports: phosphates. Imports: foodstuffs, fuel, machinery. Major trading partners: Australia, New Zealand, U.K., Japan.

Geography. Nauru (pronounced NAH oo roo) is an island in the Pacific just south of the equator, about 2,500 miles (4,023 km) southwest of Honolulu.

Government. Legislative power is invested in a popularly elected 18-member Parliament, which elects the President from among its members. Executive power rests with the President, who is assisted by a five-member Cabinet.

History. Nauru was annexed by Germany in 1888. It was placed under joint Australian, New Zealand, and British mandate after World War I, and in 1947 it became a U.N. trusteeship administered by the same three powers. On Jan. 31, 1968, Nauru became an independent republic.

In elections on December 9, 1989, Bernard Dowiyogo was elected and took office three days later.

NEPAL

Kingdom of Nepal
Ruler: King Birendra Bir Bikram Shah Deva (1972)
Prime Minister: Girija Prasad Koirala (1991)
Area: 54,463 sq mi. (141,059 sq km)
Population (mid-1991): 19,600,000 (average annual rate of natural growth: 2.5%); birth rate: 42/1000; infant mortality rate: 112/1000; density per square mile: 361
Capital and largest city (est. 1980): Katmandu, 400,000
Monetary unit: Nepalese rupee
Languages: Nepali (official), Newari, Bhutia, Maithali
Religions: Hindu, 90%; Buddhist, 5%; Islam, 3%
Literacy rate: 20%
Economic summary: Gross domestic product (FY89): $2.9 billion; $158 per capita; 1.5% real growth rate. Arable land: 17%. Labor force: 4,100,000; 93% in agriculture. Principal products: rice, maize, wheat, millet, jute, sugar cane, oilseed, potatoes. Labor force in industry: 2%. Major products: sugar, textiles, jute, cigarettes, cement. Natural resources: water, timber, hydroelectric potential. Exports: clothing, carpets, leather goods, grain. Imports: petroleum products, fertilizer, machinery. Major trading partners: India, Japan, U.S., Europe.

Geography. A landlocked country the size of Arkansas, lying between India and the Tibetan Autonomous Region of China, Nepal contains Mount Everest (29,108 ft; 8,872 m), the tallest mountain in the world. Along its southern border, Nepal has a strip of level land that is partly forested, partly cultivated. North of that is the slope of the main section of the Himalayan range, including Everest and many other peaks higher than 20,000 feet (6,096 m).

Government. In November, 1990, King Birendra promulgated a new constitution and introduced a multiparty democracy in Nepal. In the May elections of 1991, the Nepali Congress Party won an absolute majority and Mr. Girija Prasad Koirala became the Prime Minister.

History. The Kingdom of Nepal was unified in 1768 by King Prithwi Narayan Shah. A commercial treaty was signed with Britain in 1792, and in 1816, after more than a year's hostilities, the Nepalese agreed to allow British residents to live in Katmandu, the capital. In 1923, Britain recognized the absolute independence of Nepal. Between 1846 and 1951, the country was ruled by the Rana family, which always held the office of prime minister. In 1951, however, the King took over all power and proclaimed a constitutional monarchy.

Mahendra Bir Bikram Shah became King in 1955. After Mahendra, who had ruled since 1955, died of a heart attack in 1972, Prince Birendra, at 26, succeeded to the throne.

In the first election in 22 years, on May 2, 1980, voters approved the continued autocratic rule by the King with the advice of a partyless Parliament. The King, however, permitted the election of a new legislature, in May 1986, to which the Prime Minister and Cabinet are responsible.

A dispute with India over the renewal of a trade and transit treaty led to India closing most of the border crossings, causing severe economic disruption.

In 1990, pro-democracy movement forced King Birendra to lift the ban on political parties and appoint an opposition leader to head an interim government as Prime Minister.

The first free election in three decades provided a victory for the liberal Nepali Congress Party in 1991, although the Communists made a strong showing.

THE NETHERLANDS

Kingdom of the Netherlands
Sovereign: Queen Beatrix (1980)
Premier: Ruud Lubbers (1982)
Area: 16,041 sq mi. (41,548 sq km)
Population (est. mid-1991): 15,000,000 (average annual rate of natural increase: 0.8%); birth rate: 13/1000; infant mortality rate: 6.8/1000; density per square mile: 1,044
Capital: Amsterdam; seat of government: The Hague
Largest cities: Amsterdam, 694,656; Rotterdam, 576,218; 's-Gravenhage, 444,000; Utrecht, 230,738; Eidhoven, 191,500
Monetary unit: Guilder
Language: Dutch
Religions: Roman Catholic, 36%; Protestant, 27%; other, 4%; unaffiliated, 33%
National name: Koninkrijk der Nederlanden
Literacy rate: 99%
Economic summary: Gross national product (1990): $221.8 billion; $28,000 per capita income; 4.2% real growth rate. Arable land; 25%. Principal products: wheat, barley, sugar beets, potatoes, meat and dairy products. Labor force: 6,955,000; 28.2% in manufacturing and construction. Major products: metal fabrication, electrical machinery and equipment, chemicals, electronic equipment, petroleum, fishing. Exports: foodstuffs, natural gas, chemicals, metal products, textiles. Imports: raw materials, consumer goods, transportation equipment, food products, crude petroleum. Major trading partners: Germany, Belgium, France, U.K., U.S.

Geography. The Netherlands, on the coast of the North Sea, has West Germany to the east and Belgium to the south. It is twice the size of New Jersey.

Part of the great plain of north and west Europe, the Netherlands has maximum dimensions of 190 by 160 miles (360 by 257 km) and is low and flat except in Limburg in the southeast, where some hills rise to 300 feet (92 m). About half the country's area is below sea level, making the famous Dutch dikes a requisite to the use of much land. Reclamation of land from the sea through dikes has continued through recent times.

All drainage reaches the North Sea, and the principal rivers—Rhine, Maas (Meuse), and Schelde—have their sources outside the country. The Rhine is the most heavily used waterway in Europe.

Government. The Netherlands and its former colony of the Netherlands Antilles form the Kingdom of the Netherlands.

The Netherlands is a constitutional monarchy with a bicameral Parliament. The Upper Chamber has 75 members elected for six years by representative bodies of the provinces, half of the members retiring every three years. The Lower Chamber has 150 members elected by universal suffrage for four years. The two Chambers have the right of investigation and interpellation; the Lower Chamber can initiate legislation and amend bills.

The Sovereign, Queen Beatrix Wilhelmina Armgard, born Jan. 31, 1938, was married on March 10, 1966, to Claus von Amsberg, a former West German diplomat. The marriage drew public criticism because of the bridegroom's service in the German army during World War II. In 1967, Beatrix gave birth to a son, Willem-Alexander Claus George Ferdinand, the first male heir to the throne since 1884. She also has two other sons, Johan Friso Bernhard Christian David, born in 1968, and Constantijn Christof Frederik Aschwin, born the next year.

History. Julius Caesar found the low-lying Netherlands inhabited by Germanic tribes—the Nervii, Frisii, and Batavi. The Batavi on the Roman frontier did not submit to Rome's rule until 13 B.C., and then only as allies.

A part of Charlemagne's empire in the 8th and 9th centuries A.D., the area later passed into the hands of Burgundy and the Austrian Hapsburgs, and finally in the 16th century came under Spanish rule.

When Philip II of Spain suppressed political liberties and the growing Protestant movement in the Netherlands, a revolt led by William of Orange broke out in 1568. Under the Union if Utrecht (1579), the seven northern provinces became the Republic of United Netherlands.

The Dutch East India Company was established in 1602, and by the end of the 17th century Holland was one of the great sea and colonial powers of Europe.

The nation's independence was not completely established until after the Thirty Years' War (1618–48), after which the country's rise as a commercial and maritime power began. In 1814, all the provinces of Holland and Belgium were merged into one kingdom, but in 1830 the southern provinces broke away to form the Kingdom of Belgium. A liberal Constitution was adopted by the Netherlands in 1848.

In spite of its neutrality in World War II, the Netherlands was invaded by the Nazis in May 1940, and the East Indies were later taken by the Japanese. The nation was liberated in May 1945. In 1948, after a reign of 50 years, Queen Wilhelmina resigned and was succeeded by her daughter Juliana.

In 1949, after a four-year war, the Netherlands granted independence to the East Indies, which became the Republic of Indonesia. In 1963, it turned over the western half of New Guinea to the new nation, ending 300 years of Dutch presence in Asia. Attainment of independence by Suriname on Nov. 25, 1975, left the Dutch Antilles as the Netherlands' only overseas territory.

Prime Minister Van Agt lost his narrow majority in elections on May 26, 1981, in which the major issue was the deployment of U.S. cruise missiles on Dutch soil. Public opposition to the missiles forced the Netherlands, along with Belgium, to reverse its position in 1982 despite the Prime Minister's personal support for the NATO decision to deploy the new weapons in Western Europe. Van Agt lost his centrist coalition in May 1982 in a dispute over economic policy, and was succeeded by Ruud Lubbers as Premier.

Lubbers formed his third government, a center-left coalition, in November 1989. The Netherlands participated in the Persian Gulf war by sending two marine frigates to the Gulf.

Netherlands Autonomous Countries

NETHERLANDS ANTILLES

Status: Part of the Kingdom of the Netherlands
Governor: Mr. J. M. Saleh (1990)
Premier: Maria Liberia Peters
Area: 313 sq mi. (800 sq km)

Population (mid-1991): 200,000 (average annual growth rate: 1.2%); birth rate: 18/1000; infant mortality rate: 13.9/1000
Capital (est. 1978): Willemstad, 152,000
Literacy rate: 95%
Economic summary: Gross national product (1988 est.): $1.0 billion; $5,500 per capita; 3% real growth rate. Arable land: 8%. Principal agricultural products: aloes, sorghum, peanuts. Labor force: 89,000; 28% industry and commerce (1983). Major industries: oil refining, tourism. Natural resource: phosphate. Export: petroleum products. Imports: crude petroleum, food. Major trading partners: U.S., Venezuela.

Geography. The Netherlands Antilles comprise two groups of Caribbean islands 500 miles (805 km) apart: one, about 40 miles (64 km) off the Venezuelan coast, consists of Curaçao (173 sq mi.; 448 sq km), Bonaire (95 sq mi.; 246 sq km), the other, lying to the northeast, consists of three small islands with a total area of 34 square miles (88 sq km).

Government. There is a constitutional government formed by the Governor and Cabinet and an elected Legislative Council. The area has complete autonomy in domestic affairs.

ARUBA

Status: Part of the Kingdom of the Netherlands
Governor: F. B. Tromp
Prime Minister: Nelson Oduber
Area: 75 sq mi. (193 sq km)
Population: (est. mid-1988): 62,322 (average annual growth rate: 0.29%)
Capital (1986): Oranjestad, 19,800
Literacy rate: 95%
Economic summary: Gross national product (1988 est.): $620 million. Real growth rate: 16.7%. Per capita income, $10,000. Little agriculture. Major industries: tourism, light manufacturing (tobacco, beverages, consumer goods.

Geography. Aruba, an island slightly larger than Washington D.C., lies 18 miles (28.9 km) off the coast of Venezuela in the southern Caribbean.

Government. The governmental structure comprises the Governor, appointed by the Queen for a term of six years; the Legislature consisting of 21 members elected by universal suffrage for terms not exceeding four years; and the Council of Ministers, presided over by the Prime Minister, which holds executive power.

NEW ZEALAND

Sovereign: Queen Elizabeth II
Governor-General: Dame Catherine Tizard (1990)
Prime Minister: Hon. Jon Bolger (1990)
Area: 103,884 sq mi. (269,062 sq km) (excluding dependencies)
Population (est. mid-1991): 3,500,000 (average annual growth rate: 0.9%); birth rate: 17/1000; infant mortality rate: 10.6/1000; density per square mile: 33
Capital: Wellington
Largest cities (1989): Auckland, 850,900; Wellington, 324,600; Christchurch, 301,500
Monetary unit: New Zealand dollar
Languages: English, Maori
Religions: Christian, 81%; none or unspecified, 18%; Hindu, Confucian, and other, 1%

Member of Commonwealth of Nations
Literacy rate: 99%
Economic summary: Gross domestic product (1989): $41 billion; $12,555 per capita; real growth rate 2.4%. Arable land: 2%. Principal products: wool, meat, dairy products, livestock. Labor force: 1,591,900: 19.8% in manufacturing. Major products: processed foods, textiles, machinery, transport equipment, wood and paper products, financial services. Natural resources: forests, natural gas, iron ore, coal, gold. Exports: meat, dairy products, wool. Imports: consumer goods, petroleum, motor vehicles, industrial equipment. Major trading partners: Japan, Australia, E.C., U.S.

Geography. New Zealand, about 1,250 miles (2,012 km) southeast of Australia, consists of two main islands and a number of smaller, outlying islands so scattered that they range from the tropical to the antarctic. The country is the size of Colorado.

New Zealand's two main components are North Island and South Island, separated by Cook Strait, which varies from 16 to 190 miles (26 to 396 km) in width. North Island (44,281 sq mi.; 114,688 sq km) is 515 miles (829 km) long and volcanic in its south-central part. This area contains many hot springs and beautiful geysers. South Island (58,093 sq mi.; 150,461 sq km) has the Southern Alps along its west coast, with Mount Cook (12,349 ft; 3,764 m) the highest point.

The largest of the outlying islands are the Auckland Islands (234 sq mi.; 606 sq km), Campbell Island (44 sq mi.; 114 sq km), the Antipodes Islands (24 sq mi.; 62 sq km), and the Kermadec Islands (13 sq mi.; 34 sq km).

Government. New Zealand was granted self-government in 1852, a full parliamentary system and ministries in 1856, and dominion status in 1907. The Queen is represented by a Governor-General, and the Cabinet is responsible to a unicameral Parliament of 97 members, who are elected by popular vote for three years.

History. New Zealand was discovered and named in 1642 by Abel Tasman, a Dutch navigator. Captain James Cook explored the islands in 1769. In 1840, Britain formally annexed them.

From the first, the country has been in the forefront in instituting social welfare legislation. It adopted old age pensions (1898); a national child welfare program (1907); social security for the aged, widows, and orphans, along with family benefit payments; minimum wages; a 40-hour week and unemployment and health insurance (1938); and socialized medicine (1941).

In September 1990 Prime Minister Geoffrey Palmer resigned in the face of a threatened no-confidence vote. He was succeeded by Mike Moore. In the general elections of late October the opposition National Party captured 49% of the vote, winning a 39-seat majority in Parliament. Shortly after becoming the new prime minister, Jim Bolger, abandoning campaign promises, in an effort to revive the economy began severe cutbacks in government social benefits, reductions in health-care coverage and introduced legislation to weaken the country's strong labor unions.

Cook Islands and Overseas Territories

The Cook Islands (93 sq mi.; 241 sq km) were placed under New Zealand administration in 1901. They achieved self-governing status in association with New Zealand in 1965. Population in 1978 was about 19,600. The seat of government is on Rarotonga Island.

The island's chief exports are citrus juice, clothing, canned fruit, and pineapple juice. Nearly all of the trade is with New Zealand.

Niue (100 sq mi.; 259 sq km) was formerly administered as part of the Cook Islands. It was placed under separate New Zealand administration in 1901 and achieved self-governing status in association with New Zealand in 1974. The capital is Alofi. Population in 1980 was about 3,300.

Niue exports passion fruit, copra, plaited ware, honey, and limes. Its principal trading partner is New Zealand.

The Ross Dependency (160,000 sq mi.; 414,400 sq km), an Antarctic region, was placed under New Zealand administration in 1923.

Tokelau (4 sq mi.; 10 sq km) was formerly administered as part of the Gilbert and Ellice Islands colony. It was placed under New Zealand administration in 1925. Its population is about 1,600.

NICARAGUA

Republic of Nicaragua
President: Violeta Barrios de Chamorro (1990)
Area: 50,180 sq mi. (130,000 sq km)
Population (mid-1991): 3,900,000 (average annual rate of natural increase: 3.4%); birth rate: 42/1000; infant mortality rate: 62/1000; density per square mile: 77
Capital and largest city (est. 1985): Managua, 682,111
Monetary unit: Cordoba
Language: Spanish
Religion: Roman Catholic, 95%; Protestant, 5%
National name: República de Nicaragua
Literacy rate: 88%
Economic summary: Gross domestic product (1989 est.): $1.7 billion; $470 per capita; real growth rate –5.0% (1988). Arable land: 9%. Principal products: cotton, coffee, sugar cane, rice, corn, beans, cattle. Labor force: 1,086,000; 13% in industry (1986). Major products: processed foods, chemicals, metal products, clothing and textiles, beverages, footwear. Natural resources: timber, fisheries, gold, silver, copper, tungsten, lead, zinc. Exports: coffee, cotton, seafood, bananas, sugar, meat, chemicals. Imports: machinery, chemicals, food, clothing, petroleum. Major trading partners: Mexico, Germany, Japan, France, U.S., Central America, Caribbean.

Geography. Largest but most sparsely populated of the Central American nations, Nicaragua borders on Honduras to the north and Costa Rica to the south. It is slightly larger than New York State.

Nicaragua is mountainous in the west, with fertile valleys. A plateau slopes eastward toward the Caribbean.

Two big lakes—Nicaragua, about 100 miles long (161 km), and Managua, about 38 miles long (61 km)—are connected by the Tipitapa River. The Pacific coast is volcanic and very fertile. The Caribbean coast, swampy and indented, is aptly called the "Mosquito Coast."

Government. After an election on Nov. 4, 1984, Daniel Ortega began a six-year term as President on

Jan. 10, 1985. He was defeated in general elections held in Feb. 1990 by Violeta Chamorro.

History. Nicaragua, which established independence in 1838, was first visited by the Spaniards in 1522. The chief of the country's leading Indian tribe at that time was called Nicaragua, from whom the nation derived its name. A U.S. naval force intervened in 1909 after two American citizens had been executed, and a few U.S. Marines were kept in the country from 1912 to 1925. The Bryan-Chamorro Treaty of 1916 (terminated in 1970) gave the U.S. an option on a canal route through Nicaragua, and naval bases. Disorder after the 1924 elections brought in the marines again.

A guerrilla leader, Gen. César Augusto Sandino, began fighting the occupation force in 1927. He fought the U.S. troops until their withdrawal in 1933. They trained Gen. Anastasio (Tacho) Somoza García to head a National Guard. In 1934, Somoza assassinated Sandino and overthrew the Liberal President Juan Batista Sacassa, establishing a military dictatorship with himself as president. He spurred the economic development of the country, meanwhile enriching his family through estates in the countryside and investments in air and shipping lines. On his assassination in 1956, he was succeeded by his son Luis, who alternated with trusted family friends in the presidency until his death in 1967. Another son, Maj. Gen. Anastasio Somoza Debayle, became President in 1967.

Sandinista guerrillas, leftists who took their name from Gen. Sandino, launched an offensive in May 1979.

After seven weeks of fighting, Somoza fled the country on July 17, 1979. The Sandinistas assumed power on July 19, promising to maintain a mixed economy, a non-aligned foreign policy, and a pluralist political system. However, the prominence of Cuban President Fidel Castro at the celebration of the first anniversary of the revolution and a five-year delay in holding elections increased debate over the true political color of the Sandinistas.

On Jan. 23, 1981, the Reagan Administration suspended U.S. aid, charging that Nicaragua, with the aid of Cuba and the Soviet Union, was supplying arms to rebels in El Salvador. The Sandinistas denied the charges. Later that year, Nicaraguan guerrillas known as "contras," began a war to overthrow the Sandinistas.

The elections were finally held on Nov. 4, 1984, with Daniel Ortega Saavedra, the Sandinista junta coordinator, winning 63% of the votes cast for President. He began a six-year term on Jan. 10, 1985.

In October 1985, Nicaragua suspended civil liberties and in June 1986, the U.S. Congress voted $100 million in aid, military and non-military, to the contras.

The war intensified in 1986–87, with the re-supplied contras establishing themselves inside the country. Negotiations sponsored by the Contadora (neutral Latin American) nations, but a peace plan sponsored by Arias, the Costa Rican president, led to a treaty signed by the Central American leaders in August 1987, that called for an end to outside aid to guerrillas and negotiations between hostile parties. Congress later cut off military aid to the contras. Although the two sides agreed to a cease-fire in March 1988, further negotiations were inconclusive.

In 1989, an accord established a one-year advance in general elections to Feb. 1990. It also called for easing press restrictions and the release of political prisoners and the disbanding of the contras.

Violetta Chamorro, owner of the opposition paper *La Prensa*, led a broad anti-Sandinista coalition to victory in the presidential and legislative elections, ending 11 years of Sandinista rule.

After a year in office Pres. Chamorro found herself besieged. Business groups were dissatisfied with the pace of reforms; Sandinistas with what they regarded as the dismantling of their earlier achievements and threatened to take up arms again. In Feb. 1991 the president brought the military under her direct command.

NIGER

Republic of Niger
Chief of State: Gen. Ali Saibou (1987)
Area: 489,206 sq mi. (1,267,044 sq km)
Population (est. mid-1991): 8,000,000 (average annual rate of natural increase: 3.3%); birth rate: 51/1000; infant mortality rate: 124/1000; density per square mile: 16
Capital and largest city (est. 1983): Niamey, 399,100
Monetary unit: Franc CFA
Ethnic groups: Hausa, 54%; Djerma and Songhai, 24%; Peul, 11%
Languages: French (official); Hausa, Songhai; Arabic
Religions: Islam, 80%; Animist and Christian, 20%
National name: République du Niger
Literacy rate: 13.9%
Economic summary: Gross domestic product (1988 est.): $2.4 billion; $330 per capita; 7.1% real growth rate. Arable land: 3%. Principal products: peanuts, cotton, livestock, millet, sorghum, cassava, rice. Labor force: 2,500,000 (1982); 90% in agriculture. Major industrial products: uranium, cement, bricks, light industrial products. Natural resources: uranium, coal, iron ore, tin, phosphates. Exports: uranium, cowpeas, livestock, hides, skins. Imports: fuels, machinery, transport equipment, foodstuffs, consumer goods. Major trading partners: France, Nigeria, Japan, Algeria, U.S.

Geography. Niger, in West Africa's Sahara region, is four-fifths the size of Alaska. It is surrounded by Mali, Algeria, Libya, Chad, Nigeria, Benin, and Burkina Faso.

The Niger River in the southwest flows through the country's only fertile area. Elsewhere the land is semiarid.

Government. After a military coup on April 15, 1974, Gen. Seyni Kountché suspended the Constitution and instituted rule by decree. Previously, the President was elected by direct universal suffrage for a five-year term and a National House of Assembly of 50 members was elected for the same term. He died on Nov. 10, 1987, and Col. Saibou, his Chief of Staff, succeeded him.

Demonstrations and strikes in 1990 eventually led to amending the constitution so as to permit a multi-party system. Three underground parties quickly emerged.

History. Niger was incorporated into French West Africa in 1896. There were frequent rebellions, but when order was restored in 1922, the French made the area a colony. In 1958, the voters approved the French Constitution and voted to make the territory an autonomous republic within the French Community. The republic adopted a Constitution in 1959 and the next year withdrew from the Community, proclaiming its independence.

The 1974 army coup ousted President Hamani Diori, who had held office since 1960. He was charged with having mishandled relief for the terrible drought that had devastated Niger and five neighboring sub-Saharan nations for several years. An estimated 2 million people were starving in Niger, but 200,000 tons of imported food, half U.S.-supplied, substantially ended famine conditions by the year's end. The new President, Lt. Col. Seyni Kountché, Chief of Staff of the army, installed a 12-man military government. A predominantly civilian government was formed by Kountché in 1976.

NIGERIA

Federal Republic of Nigeria
President: Gen. Ibrahim Badamasi Babangida (1985)
Area: 356,700 sq mi. (923,853 sq km)
Population (est. mid-1991): 122,500,000 (average annual rate of natural increase: 2.8%); birth rate: 44/1000; infant mortality rate: 119/1000; density per square mile: 343
Capital: Lagos
Largest cities (est. 1983): Lagos, 1,097,000; Ibadan, 1,060,000; Ogbomosho, 527,400; Kano, 487,100
Monetary unit: Naira
Languages: English (official) Hausa, Yoruba, Ibo
Religions: Islam, 50%; Christian, 40%; indigenous, 10%
Member of Commonwealth of Nations
Literacy rate: 42.4%
Economic summary: Gross national product (1989): $30.0 billion; $270 per capita; real growth rate 4%. Arable land: 31%. Principal products: peanuts, rubber, cocoa, grains, fish, yams, cassava, livestock. Labor force: 42,844,000; 19% in industry;. Major products: crude oil, natural gas, coal, tin, processed rubber, cotton, petroleum, hides, textiles, cement, chemicals. Natural resources: petroleum, tin, columbite, iron ore, coal, limestone, lead. Exports: oil, cocoa, palm products, rubber. Imports: consumer goods, capital equipment, raw materials, chemicals. Major trading partners: Western European countries, U.S.

Geography. Nigeria, one-third larger than Texas and black Africa's most populous nation, is situated on the Gulf of Guinea in West Africa. Its neighbors are Benin, Niger, Cameroon, and Chad.

The lower course of the Niger River flows south through the western part of the country into the Gulf of Guinea. Swamps and mangrove forests border the southern coast; inland are hardwood forests.

Government. After 12 years of military rule, a new Constitution re-established democratic government in 1979, but it lasted four years. The military again took over from the democratically elected civilian government on Dec. 31, 1983.

Adopting a U.S.-style constitution the military has pledged to return to the barracks. Two political parties are permitted—the National Republican Convention and the Social Democratic Party. Presidential elections are scheduled for October 1992.

History. Between 1879 and 1914, private colonial developments by the British, with reorganizations of the Crown's interest in the region, resulted in the formation of Nigeria as it exists today. During World War I, native troops of the West African frontier force joined with French forces to defeat the German garrison in the Cameroons.

Nigeria became independent on Oct. 1, 1960.

Organized as a loose federation of self-governing states, the independent nation faced an overwhelming task of unifying a country with 250 ethnic and linguistic groups.

Rioting broke out again in 1966, the military commander was seized, and Col. Yakubu Gowon took power. Also in that year, the Moslem Hausas in the north massacred the predominantly Christian Ibos in the east, many of whom had been driven from the north. Thousands of Ibos took refuge in the Eastern Region. The military government there asked Ibos to return to the region and, in May 1967, the assembly voted to secede from the federation and set up the Republic of Biafra. Civil war broke out.

In January 1970, after 31 months of civil war, Biafra surrendered to the federal government.

Gowon's nine-year rule was ended in 1975 by a bloodless coup that made Army Brigadier Muritala Rufai Mohammed the new chief of state. Mohammed was assassinated the next year 1976 by a group of seven young officers, who failed to seize control of the government.

The return of civilian leadership was established with the election of Alhaji Shehu Shagari, as president in 1979.

A coup on December 31, 1983, restored military rule. The military regime headed by Maj. Gen. Mohammed Buhari was overthrown in a bloodless coup on Aug. 27, 1985, led by Maj. Gen. Ibrahim Babangida, who proclaimed himself president.

He has promised to return to civilian rule in 1992.

NORWAY

Kingdom of Norway
Sovereign: King Harald V (1991)
Prime Minister: Gro Harlem Brundtland (1991)
Area: 125,049 sq mi. (323,877 sq km)
Population (est. 1991): 4,300,000 (average annual growth rate: 0.3%); birth rate: 14/1000; infant mortality rate: 8/1000; density per square mile: 34
Capital: Oslo
Largest cities (1990): Oslo, 457,818; Bergen, 211,866; Trondheim, 137,408; Stavanger, 97,716
Monetary unit: Krone
Language: Norwegian
Religion: Evangelical Lutheran (state), 94%; other Protestant and Roman Catholic, 4%
National name: Kongeriket Norge
Literacy rate: 100%
Economic summary: Gross domestic product (1989 est.): $75.8 billion; $17,900 per capita; 5.7% real growth rate. Arable land: 3%. Principal products: dairy products, livestock, grain, potatoes, furs, wool. Labor force: 2,164,000; 16.6% in mining and manufacturing. Major products: oil and gas, fish, pulp and paper, ships, aluminum, iron, steel, nickel, fertilizers, transportation equipment, hydroelectric power, petrochemicals. Natural resources: fish, timber, hydroelectric power, ores, oil, gas. Exports: oil, natural gas, fish products, ships, pulp and paper, aluminum. Imports: machinery, fuels and lubricants, transportation equipment, chemicals foodstuffs, and clothing. Major trading partners: U.K., Sweden, Germany, U.S., Denmark, Netherlands, Japan.

Geography. Norway is situated in the western part of the Scandinavian peninsula. It extends about 1,100 miles (1,770 km) from the North Sea along the Norwegian Sea to more than 300 miles (483 km) above the Arctic Circle, the farthest north of any European country. It is slightly larger than New Mexico. Sweden borders on most of the eastern frontier, with Finland and the U.S.S.R. in the northeast.

Nearly 70% of Norway is uninhabitable and covered by mountains, glaciers, moors, and rivers. The hundreds of deep fiords that cut into the coastline give Norway an overall oceanfront of more than 12,000 miles (19,312 km). Nearly 50,000 islands off the coast form a breakwater and make a safe coastal shipping channel.

Government. Norway is a constitutional hereditary monarchy. Executive power is vested in the King together with a Cabinet, or Council of State, consisting of a Prime Minister and at least seven other members. The Storting, or Parliament, is composed of 165 members elected by the people under proportional representation. The Storting discusses and votes on political and financial questions, but divides itself into two sections (Lagting and Odelsting) to discuss and pass on legislative matters. The King cannot dissolve the Storting before the expiration of its term.

The sovereign is Harald V, born in 1937, son of Olav V and Princess Martha of Sweden. He succeeded to the throne upon the death of his father in January 1991. He married Sonja Haraldsen, a daughter of a merchant, in 1968.

History. Norwegians, like the Danes and Swedes, are of Teutonic origin. The Norsemen, also known as Vikings, ravaged the coasts of northwestern Europe from the 8th to the 11th century.

In 1815, Norway fell under the control of Sweden. The union of Norway, inhabited by fishermen, sailors, merchants, and peasants, and Sweden, an aristocratic country of large estates and tenant farmers, was not a happy one, but it lasted for nearly a century. In 1905, the Norwegian Parliament arranged a peaceful separation and invited a Danish prince to the Norwegian throne—King Haakon VII. A treaty with Sweden provided that all disputes be settled by arbitration and that no fortifications be erected on the common frontier.

When World War I broke out, Norway joined with Sweden and Denmark in a decision to remain neutral and to cooperate in the joint interest of the three countries. In World War II, Norway was invaded by the Germans on April 9, 1940. It resisted for two months before the Nazis took over complete control. King Haakon and his government fled to London, where they established a government-in-exile. Maj. Vidkun Quisling, whose name is now synonymous with traitor or fifth columnist, was the most notorious Norwegian collaborator with the Nazis. He was executed by the Norwegians on Oct. 24, 1945.

Despite severe losses in the war, Norway recovered quickly. The country led the world in social experimentation. A neighbor of the U.S.S.R., Norway sought to retain good relations with the Soviet Union without losing its identity with the West. It entered the North Atlantic Treaty Organization in 1949.

The Conservative government of Jan Syse resigned in October 1990 over the issue of Norway's future relationship to the E.C. A minority Labor government headed by Gro Brundtland was installed a few days later. The new government promised to be "flexible" in negotiating with the E.C., including allowing changes in the so-called concession laws, which pro-

tect Norwegian sovereignty over domestic resources and industry. Norway is a member of the European Free Trade Association.

Dependencies of Norway

Svalbard (24,208 sq mi.; 62,700 sq km), in the Arctic Ocean about 360 miles north of Norway, consists of the Spitsbergen group and several smaller islands, including Bear Island, Hope Island, King Charles Land, and White Island (or Gillis Land). It came under Norwegian administration in 1925. The population in 1986 was 3,942 of which 1,387 were Norwegians.

Bouvet Island (23 sq mi.; 60 sq km), in the South Atlantic about 1,600 miles south-southwest of the Cape of Good Hope, came under Norwegian administration in 1928.

Jan Mayen Island (147 sq mi.; 380 sq km), in the Arctic Ocean between Norway and Greenland, came under Norwegian administration in 1929.

Peter I Island (96 sq mi.; 249 sq km), lying off Antarctica in the Bellinghausen Sea, came under Norwegian administration in 1931.

Queen Maud Land, a section of Antarctica, came under Norwegian administration in 1939.

OMAN
Sultanate of Oman
Sultan: Qabus Bin Said (1970)
Area: 82,030 sq mi. (212,458 sq km)[1]
Population (est. mid-1991): 1,600,000 (average annual rate of natural increase: 3.8%); birth rate: 46/1000; infant mortality rate: 40/1000; density per square mile: 19
Capital and largest city (est. 1981): Muscat, 70,000
Monetary unit: Omani rial
Language: Arabic (official); also English and Indian languages
Religion: Islam, 86%
National name: Saltonat Uman
Literacy rate: 20%
Economic summary: Gross domestic product (1987 est.): $7.8 billion; $6,006 per capita; –3.0% real growth rate. Principal agricultural products: dates, fruit, cereal, livestock. Labor force: 430,000; 60% in agriculture. Major industries: petroleum drilling, fishing, construction. Natural resources: oil, marble, copper, limestone. Exports: oil. Imports: machinery and transport equipment, food, manufactured goods, livestock, lubricants. Major trading partners: U.K., U.S., Germany, Japan, Korea, Thailand.

1. Excluding the Kuria Muria Islands.

Geography. Oman is a 1,000-mile-long (1,700-km) coastal plain at the southeastern tip of the Arabian peninsula lying on the Arabian Sea and the Gulf of Oman. The interior is a plateau. The country is the size of Kansas.

Government. The Sultan of Oman (formerly called Muscat and Oman), an absolute monarch, is assisted by a council of ministers, six specialized councils, a consultative council and personal advisers.

There are no political parties.

History. Although Oman is an independent state under the rule of the Sultan, it has been under British protection since the early 19th century.

Muscat, the capital of the geographical area known as Oman, was occupied by the Portuguese from 1508 to 1648. Then it fell to Persian princes and later was regained by the Sultan.

In a palace coup on July 23, 1970, the Sultan, Sa'id bin Taimur, who had ruled since 1932, was overthrown by his son, who promised to establish a modern government and use new-found wealth to aid the people of this very isolated state.

The formation of a new consultative council, excluding government officials, was announced in November 1990.

PAKISTAN

Islamic Republic of Pakistan

President: Gulam Ishaq Khan (1988)
Prime Minister: Mian Mohammad Nawaz Sharif (1990)
Area: 310,400 sq mi. (803,936 sq km)[1]
Population (est. mid-1991): 117,500,000 (average annual growth rate: 3%); birth rate: 43/1000; infant mortality rate: 112/1000; density per square mile: 379
Capital (1981 census): Islamabad, 201,000
Largest cities (1981 census for metropolitan area): Karachi, 5,208,100; Lahore, 2,952,700; Faisalabad, (Lyallpur) 1,920,000; Rawalpindi, 920,000; Hyderabad, 795,000
Monetary unit: Pakistan rupee
Principal languages: Urdu (national), English (official), Punjabi, Sindhi, Pashtu, and Baluchi
Religions: Islam, 97%; Hindu, Christian, Buddhist, Parsi
Literacy rate: 26%
Economic summary: Gross national product (FY89): $43.2 billion; $409 per capita; 5.1% real growth rate. Arable land: 26%. Principal products: wheat, rice, cotton, sugarcane. Labor force: 28,900,000; 13% in mining and manufacturing. Major products: cotton textiles, processed foods, petroleum products, construction materials. Natural resources: natural gas, limited petroleum, iron ore. Exports: cotton, rice, textiles, clothing. Imports: edible oil, crude oil, machinery, chemicals, transport equipment. Major trading partners: U.S., E.C., Japan.

1. Excluding Kashmir and Jammu.

Geography. Pakistan is situated in the western part of the Indian subcontinent, with Afghanistan and Iran on the west, India on the east, and the Arabian Sea on the south.

Nearly twice the size of California, Pakistan consists of towering mountains, including the Hindu Kush in the west, a desert area in the east, the Punjab plains in the north, and an expanse of alluvial plains. The 1,000-mile-long (1,609 km) Indus River flows through the country from the Kashmir to the Arabian Sea.

Government. Pakistan is a federal republic with a bicameral legislature—a 217-member National Assembly and an 87-member Senate.

History. Pakistan was one of the two original successor states to British India. For almost 25 years following independence in 1947, it consisted of two separate regions East and West Pakistan, but now comprises only the western sector. It consists of Sind, Baluchistan, the former North-West Frontier Province, western Punjab, the princely state of Bahawalpur, and several other smaller native states.

The British became the dominant power in the region in 1797 following Lord Clive's military victory, but rebellious tribes kept the northwest in turmoil. In the northeast, the formation of the Moslem League in 1906 estranged the Moslems from the Hindus. In 1930, the league, led by Mohammed Ali Jinnah, demanded creation of a Moslem state wherever Moslems were in the majority. He supported Britain during the war. Afterward, the league received almost a unanimous Moslem vote in 1946 and Britain agreed to the formation of Pakistan as a separate dominion.

Pakistan was proclaimed a republic March 23, 1956. Iskander Mirza, then Governor General, was elected Provisional President and H. S. Suhrawardy became the first non-Moslem League Prime Minister.

The election of 1970 set the stage for civil war when Sheik Muuibur told East Pakistanis to stop paying taxes to the central government. West Pakistan troops moved in and fighting began. The independent state of Bangladesh, or Bengali nation, was proclaimed March 26, 1971.

The intervention of Indian troops protected the new state and brought President Yahya Kahn down. Bhutto took over and accepted Bangladesh as an independent entity.

Diplomatically, 1976 saw the resumption of formal relations between India and Pakistan.

Pakistan's first elections under civilian rule took place in March 1977 and provoked bitter opposition protest when Bhutto's party was declared to have won 155 of the 200 elected seats in the 216-member National Assembly. A rising tide of violent protest and political deadlock led to a military takeover on July 5. Gen. Mohammed Zia ul-Haq became Chief Martial Law Administrator.

Bhutto was tried and convicted for the 1974 murder of a political opponent, and despite worldwide protests was executed on April 4, 1979, touching off riots by his supporters. Zia declared himself President on Sept. 16, 1978, a month after Fazel Elahi Chaudhry left office upon the completion of his 5-year term.

A measure of representative government was restored with the election of a new National Assembly in February 1985, although leaders of opposition parties were banned from the election and it was unclear what powers Zia would yield to the legislature.

On December 30, 1985, Zia ended martial law. In May 1988, Zia deposed Prime Minister Mohammed Junejo and dissolved the National Assembly on the grounds that they had not moved quickly enough to establish Islamic law or deal with ethnic strife.

On August 19, 1988, President Zia was killed in a midair explosion of a Pakistani Air Force plane.

Elections at the end of 1988 brought longtime Zia opponent Benazir Bhutto, daughter of Zulfikar Bhutto, to office as Prime Minister.

In August 1990, Pakistan's President dismissed Prime Minister Bhutto on charges of corruption and incompetence and dissolved parliament. Sharif's coalition, the Islamic Democratic Alliance, won the elections of October 1990. Fulfilling a campaign promise, parliament decreed in May 1991 that Islamic law would take precedence over civil legislation. The opposition charged that the bill is undemocratic and would promote sectarianism.

PANAMA

Republic of Panama
President: Guillermo Endara Galimany (1990)
Area: 29,761 sq mi. (77,082 sq km)
Population (est. mid-1991): 2,500,000 (average annual rate of natural increase: 2.1%); birth rate: 26/1000; infant mortality rate: 22/1000; density per square mile: 83
Capital and largest city (est. 1987): Panama City, 440,000
Monetary unit: Balboa
Language: Spanish (official); many bilingual in English
Religions: Roman Catholic, over 93%; Protestant, 6%
National name: República de Panamá
Literacy rate: 90%
Economic summary: Gross domestic product (1989 est.): $3.9 billion; $1,648 per capita; real growth rate −7.5%. Arable land: 6%. Principal products: bananas, corn, sugar, rice, coffee. Labor force: 770,472 (1987); 10.5% in manufacturing and mining. Major industrial products: refined petroleum, sugar, cement, paper products. Natural resources: copper, mahogany, shrimp. Exports: bananas, refined petroleum, sugar, shrimp, coffee. Imports: petroleum, manufactured goods, machinery and transportation equipment, food. Major trading partners: U.S., Central America and the Caribbean, Western Europe, Mexico.

Geography. The southernmost of the Central American nations, Panama is south of Costa Rica and north of Colombia. The Panama Canal bisects the isthmus at its narrowest and lowest point, allowing passage from the Caribbean Sea to the Pacific Ocean.

Panama is slightly smaller than South Carolina. It is marked by a chain of volcanic mountains in the west, moderate hills in the interior, and a low range on the east coast. There are extensive forests in the fertile Caribbean area.

Government. Panama is a centralized republic. The executive power is vested in the president and two vice presidents who exercise power jointly with a cabinet of 12 ministers of state appointed by the president. Presidents and vice presidents are elected for five-year terms and may not succeed themselves. The legislative function is exercised through the National Assembly. The legislators are elected for five-year terms by direct vote and can be reelected.

History. Visited by Columbus in 1502 on his fourth voyage and explored by Balboa in 1513, Panama was the principal transshipment point for Spanish treasure and supplies to and from South and Central America in colonial days. In 1821, when Central America revolted against Spain, Panama joined Colombia, which already had declared its independence. For the next 82 years, Panama attempted unsuccessfully to break away from Colombia. After U.S. proposals for canal rights over the narrow isthmus had been rejected by Colombia, Panama proclaimed its independence with U.S. backing in 1903.

For canal rights in perpetuity, the U.S. paid Panama $10 million and agreed to pay $250,000 each year, increased to $430,000 after devaluation of the U.S. dollar in 1933 and was further increased under a revised treaty signed in 1955. In exchange, the U.S. got the Canal Zone—a 10-mile-wide strip across the isthmus—and a considerable degree of influence in Panama's affairs.

In 1968, Dr. Arnulfo Arias was elected President for the third time in three decades. And for the third time, he was thrown out of office by the military. A two-man junta, Col. José M. Pinilla and Col. Bolivar Urrutia, took control. They were ousted by Gen. Omar Torrijos Herrera, who named a new junta, with Demetrio Lakas Bahas as President.

Panama and the U.S. agreed in 1974 to negotiate the eventual reversion of the canal to Panama, despite strongly expressed opposition in the U.S. Congress. The texts of two treaties—one governing the transfer of the canal and the other guaranteeing its neutrality after transfer—were negotiated by August 1977 and were signed by Pres. Omar Torrijos Herara and President Carter in Washington on September 7. A Panamanian referendum approved the treaties by more than two thirds on October 23, but further changes were insisted upon by the U.S. Senate.

The principal change was a reservation specifying that despite the neutrality treaty's specification that only Panama shall maintain forces in its territory after transfer of the canal Dec. 31, 1999, the U.S. should have the right to use military force to keep the canal operating if it should become obstructed. The Senate approved the treaties in March-April 1978. On June 16, Carter and Torrijos exchanged instruments of ratification in Panama City.

The death of Torrijos in a plane crash on July 31, 1981, left a power vacuum. President Aristides Royo, named by Torrijos in 1978 to a six-year term, clashed with the leadership of the National Guard and was unable to harmonize factions within the ruling Democratic Revolutionary Party. On July 30, 1982, Royo resigned in favor of Vice President Ricardo de la Espriella.

Nicolas Ardito Barletta, Panama's first directly elected President in 16 years, was inaugurated on Oct. 11, 1984, for a five-year term. He lacked the necessary support to solve the country's economic crisis and resigned September 28, 1985. He was replaced by Vice President Eric Arturo Delvalle.

In June 1986, reports surfaced that the behind-the-scenes strongman, Gen. Manuel Noriega, was involved in drug trafficking and the murder of an opposition leader. In 1987, Noriega was accused by his ex-Chief of Staff of assassinating Torrijos in 1981. He was indicted in the U.S. for drug trafficking but when Delvalle attempted to fire him, he forced the National Assembly to replace Delvalle with Manuel Solis Palma. Despite protests and U.S. economic sanctions, Noriega remained in power.

The crisis continued when Noriega called presidential elections for when the current term expired. Despite massive fraud by Noriega, the opposition seemed headed to a landslide. Noriega annulled the elections and suppressed protests by the opposition.

In December 1989, the Assembly named Noriega the "maximum leader" and declared the U.S. and Panama to be in a state of war. A further series of incidents led to a U.S. invasion overthrowing Noriega, who was brought to the U.S. to stand trial for drug trafficking. Guillermo Endara, who probably would have won the election suppressed by Noriega, was instated as President.

A military revolt in December 1990 was easily suppressed, although the leaders eluded capture. The U.S. has pledged to use its troops in Panama if necessary to foil any coup attempt. In May 1991, the Christian Democratic Party, until then largest in the National Assembly, quit the government and went into opposition.

Panama Canal. First conceived by the Spaniards in 1524, when King Charles V of Spain ordered a survey of a waterway across the Isthmus, a construction concession was granted by the Colombian government in 1878 to St. Lucien N. B. Wyse, representing a French company. Two years later, the French Canal Company, inspired by Ferdinand de Lesseps, began construction of what was to have been a sea-level canal. The effort ended in bankruptcy nine years later and the United States ultimately paid the French $40 million for their rights and assets.

The U.S. project, built on territory controlled by the United States, and calling for the creation of an interior lake connected to both oceans by locks, got under way in 1904. Completed in 1914, the Canal is 50.7 miles long and lifts ships 85 feet above sea level through a series of three locks on the Pacific and Atlantic sides. Enlarged in later years, each lock now measures 1,000 feet in length, 110 feet in width, and 40 feet in depth of water.

PAPUA NEW GUINEA

Sovereign: Queen Elizabeth II
Governor General: Sir Serei Eri
Prime Minister: Rabbie Namaliu (1988)
Area: 178,704 sq mi. (462,840 sq km)
Population (est. mid-1991): 3,900,000 (average annual rate of natural increase: 2.3%); birth rate: 34/1000; infant mortality rate: 59/1000; density per square mile: 22
Capital and largest city (est. 1986): Port Moresby, 145,000
Monetary unit: Kina
Languages: English, Melanesian pidgin, Hiri Motu, and 717 distinct native languages
Religions: over half Christian, remainder indigenous
Member of Commonwealth of Nations
Literacy rate: 32%
Economic summary: Gross domestic product (1988 est.): $3.26 billion; $890 per capita; 1.2% real growth rate. Principal products: coffee, copra, palm oil, cocoa, tea, coconuts. Labor force (1980): 1,660,000; 9% industry and commerce. Major industrial products: coconut oil, plywood, wood chips, gold, silver. Natural resources: copper, gold, silver, timber, natural gas. Exports: gold, copper, coffee, palm oil, copra, timber. Imports: food, machinery, transport equipment, fuels. Major trading partners: Australia, U.K., Japan, Germany, Singapore, New Zealand, U.S.

Geography. Papua New Guinea occupies the eastern half of the island of New Guinea, just north of Australia, and many outlying islands. The Indonesian province of Irian Jaya is to the west. To the north and east are the islands of Manus, New Britain, New Ireland, and Bougainville, all part of Papua New Guinea.

Papua New Guinea is about one-tenth larger than California. Its mountainous interior has only recently been explored. The high-plateau climate is temperate, in contrast to the tropical climate of the coastal plains. Two major rivers, the Sepik and the Fly, are navigable for shallow-draft vessels.

Government. Papua New Guinea attained independence Sept. 16, 1975, ending a United Nations trusteeship under the administration of Australia. Parliamentary democracy was established by a Constitution that invests power in a 109-member national legislature.

History. The eastern half of New Guinea was first visited by Spanish and Portuguese explorers in the

16th century, but a permanent European presence was not established until 1884, when Germany declared a protectorate over the northern coast and Britain took similar action in the south. Both nations formally annexed their protectorates and, in 1901, Britain transferred its rights to a newly independent Australia. Australian troops invaded German New Guinea in World War I and retained control under a League of Nations mandate that eventually became a United Nations trusteeship, incorporating a territorial government in the southern region, known as Papua.

Australia granted limited home rule in 1951 and, in 1964, organized elections for the first House of Assembly. Autonomy in internal affairs came nine years later.

In February 1990 guerrillas of the Bougainville Revolutionary Army (BRA) attacked plantations, forcing the evacuation of numerous workers. In May the BRA declared Bougainville's independence, whereupon the government blockaded the island until January 1991.

PARAGUAY

Republic of Paraguay
President: Gen. Andres Rodriguez (1989)
Area: 157,047 sq mi. (406,752 sq km)
Population (est. mid-1991): 4,400,000 (average annual rate of natural increase: 2.8%); birth rate: 34/1000; infant mortality rate: 41/1000; density per square mile: 28
Capital and largest city (est. 1985): Asunción, 477,000
Monetary unit: Guaraní
Languages: Spanish (official), Guaraní
Religion: Roman Catholic, 90%
National name: República del Paraguay
Literacy rate: 81%
Economic summary: Gross domestic product (1989 est.): $8.9 billion; $1,970 per capita; 5.2% real growth rate. Arable land: 20%. Principal products: soybeans, cotton, timber, cassava, tobacco, corn, rice, sugar cane. Labor force: 1,300,000; 34% in industry and commerce. Major products: packed meats, crushed oilseeds, beverages, textiles, light consumer goods, cement. Natural resources: iron ore, timber, manganese, limestone, hydropower. Exports: cotton, soybeans, meat products, timber, coffee, tung oil. Imports: fuels and lubricants, machinery and motors, motor vehicles, beverages, tobacco, foodstuffs. Major trading partners: Argentina, Brazil, U.S., E.C., Japan.

Geography. California-size Paraguay is surrounded by Brazil, Bolivia, and Argentina in south central South America. Eastern Paraguay, between the Paraná and Paraguay Rivers, is upland country with the thickest population settled on the grassy slope that inclines toward the Paraguay River. The greater part of the Chaco region to the west is covered with marshes, lagoons, dense forests, and jungles.

Government. The President is elected by popular vote for five years. The legislature is bicameral, consisting of a Senate of 30 members and a Chamber of Representatives of 60 members. There is also a Council of State, whose members are nominated by the government.

History. In 1526 and again in 1529, Sebastian Cabot explored Paraguay when he sailed up the Paraná and

Paraguay Rivers. From 1608 until their expulsion from the Spanish dominions in 1767, the Jesuits maintained an extensive establishment in the south and east of Paraguay. In 1811, Paraguay revolted against Spanish rule and became a nominal republic under two Consuls.

Actually, Paraguay was governed by three dictators during the first 60 years of independence. The third, Francisco López, waged war against Brazil and Argentina in 1865–70, a conflict in which the male population was almost wiped out. A new Constitution in 1870, designed to prevent dictatorships and internal strife, failed to do so, and not until 1912 did a period of comparative economic and political stability begin.

After World War II, politics became particularly unstable.

Stroessner ruled under a state of siege until 1965, when the dictatorship was relaxed and exiles returned. The Constitution was revised in 1967 to permit Stroessner to be re-elected.

Although oil exploration begun by U.S. companies in the Chaco boreal in 1974 was fruitless, Paraguay found prosperity in another form of energy when construction started in 1978 on the Itaipu Dam on the Parana River as a joint Paraguayan-Brazilian project.

The Stroessner regime was criticized by the U.S. State Department during the Carter administration as a violator of human rights, but unlike Argentina and Uruguay, Paraguay did not suffer cuts in U.S. military aid.

The government was forced to devalue the guarani as a condition for IMF help for the ailing economy.

Stroessner was overthrown by an army leader, Gen. Andres Rodriguez, in 1989. Rodriguez won in Paraguay's first multi-candidate elections in decades. He has promised to hand over power to an elected civilian successor in 1993.

Foreign Minister Luis Argaña was dismissed following condemnation of a speech in July 1990 in which he said that the ruling party would hold on to political power by a new revolution if necessary.

PERU

Republic of Peru
President: Alberto Fujimori (1990)
Premier: Dr. Carlos Torres y Torres Lara (1991)
Area: 496,222 sq mi. (1,285,216 sq km)
Population (est. mid-1991): 22,000,000 (average annual rate of natural increase: 2.3%); birth rate: 31/1000; infant mortality rate: 76/1000; density per square mile: 44
Capital: Lima
Largest cities (est. 1987): Lima, 5,330,800; Arequipa, 572,000; Callao, 545,000; Trujillo, 476,000; Chiclayo, 379,000
Monetary unit: Nuevo Sol (1991)
Languages: Spanish, Quéchua, Aymara, and other native languages
Religion: Roman Catholic
National name: República del Perú
Literacy rate: est. 80%
Economic summary: Gross domestic product (1989 est.): $18.9 billion; $880 per capita; real growth rate –12.2%. Arable land: 3%. Principal products: wheat, potatoes, beans, rice, sugar, cotton, coffee. Labor force: 6,800,000 (1986); 19% in industry (1988 est.). Major products: processed minerals, fish meal, refined petroleum, textiles. Natural resources: silver, gold, iron, copper, fish, petroleum, timber. Exports: copper, fish products, cotton, sugar, coffee, lead, silver, zinc, oil, iron ore. Imports: machinery, foodstuffs, chemicals, pharmaceuticals. Major trading partners: U.S., Japan, Western European, and Latin Americ n countries.

Geography. Peru, in western South America, extends for nearly 1,500 miles (2,414 km) along the Pacific Ocean. Colombia and Ecuador are to the north, Brazil and Bolivia to the east, and Chile to the south.

Five-sixths the size of Alaska, Peru is divided by the Andes Mountains into three sharply differentiated zones. To the west is the coastline, much of it arid, extending 50 to 100 miles (80 to 160 km) inland. The mountain area, with peaks over 20,000 feet (6,096 m), lofty plateaus, and deep valleys, lies centrally. Beyond the mountains to the east is the heavily forested slope leading to the Amazonian plains.

Government. The President, elected by universal suffrage for a five-year term, holds executive power. A Senate of 60 members and a Chamber of Deputies of 180 members, both elected for five-year terms, share legislative power.

History. Peru was once part of the great Incan empire and later the major vice-royalty of Spanish South America. It was conquered in 1531–33 by Francisco Pizarro. On July 28, 1821, Peru proclaimed its independence, but the Spanish were not finally defeated until 1824. For a hundred years thereafter, revolutions were frequent, and a new war was fought with Spain in 1864–66.

Peru emerged from 20 years of dictatorship in 1945 with the inauguration of President José Luis Bustamante y Rivero after the first free election in many decades. But he served for only three years and was succeeded in turn by Gen. Manual A. Odria, Manuel Prado y Ugarteche, and Fernando Belaúnde Terry. On Oct. 3, 1968, Belaúnde was overthrown by Gen. Juan Velasco Alvarado.

Velasco nationalized the nation's second biggest bank and turned two large newspapers over to Marxists in 1970, but he also allowed a new agreement with a copper-mining consortium of four American firms.

In 1975, Velasco was replaced in a bloodless coup by his Premier, Gen. Francisco Morales Bermudez, who promised to restore civilian government. In elections held on May 18, 1980, Belaunde Terry, the last previous civilian President and the candidate of the conservative parties that have traditionally ruled Peru, was elected President again. By the end of his five-year term in 1985, the country was in the midst of acute economic and social crisis.

But Peru's fragile democracy survived this period of stress and when he left office in 1985 Belaunde Terry was the first elected President to turn over power to a constitutionally elected successor since 1945.

In the June run-off to the April 1990 elections Alberto Fujimori won 56.5% of the vote. A newcomer to national politics, Fujimori is the son of Japanese immigrants. The new Cabinet included representatives from the entire political spectrum as well as the military. Nevertheless, two guerrilla groups working separately declared war on the government. Adding to its problems Peru faced a cholera epidemic in 1991, which struck more than 200,000 people, devastating the tourist industry and straining the economy further.

THE PHILIPPINES

Republic of the Philippines
President: Corazon C. Aquino (1986)
Vice President: Salvador H. Laurel (1986)
Area: 115,830 sq mi. (300,000 sq km)
Population (est. mid-1991): 62,300,000 (average annual rate of natural increase: 2.6%); birth rate: 33/1000; infant mortality rate: 54/1000; density per square mile: 538
Capital: Manila
Largest cities (est. 1984): Manila, 1,728,400[1]; Quezon City, 1,326,000; Cebu, 552,200
Monetary unit: Peso
Languages: Filipino (based on Tagalog), English; regional languages: Tagalog, Ilocano, Cebuano, others
Religions: Roman Catholic, 83%; Islam, 3%; Protestant, 9%; Buddhist and other, 3%
National name: Republika ng Pilipinas
Literacy rate: 88% (est.)
Economic summary: Gross domestic product (1989): $40.5 billion; $625 per capita; 5.2% real growth rate. Arable land: 26%. Principal products: rice, corn, coconuts, sugar cane, bananas, pineapple. Labor force: 22,889,000; 20% in industry and commerce. Major products: textiles, pharmaceuticals, chemicals, food processing, electronics assembly. Natural resources: forests, crude oil, metallic and non-metallic minerals. Exports: electrical equipment, coconut products, chemicals, logs and lumber, copper concentrates, nickel. Imports: petroleum, industrial equipment, raw materials. Major trading partners: U.S., Japan, E.C.

---

1. Metropolitan area population is 7,500,000.

Geography. The Philippine Islands are an archipelago of over 7,000 islands lying about 500 miles (805 km) off the southeast coast of Asia. The overall land area is comparable to that of Arizona. The northernmost island, Y'Ami, is 65 miles (105 km) from Taiwan, while the southernmost, Saluag, is 40 miles (64 km) east of Borneo.

Only about 7% of the islands are larger than one square mile, and only one third have names. The largest are Luzon in the north (40,420 sq mi.; 104,687 sq km), Mindanao in the south (36,537 sq mi.; 94,631 sq km), Samar (5,124 sq mi.; 13,271 sq km).

The islands are of volcanic origin, with the larger ones crossed by mountain ranges. The highest peak is Mount Apo (9,690 ft; 2,954 m) on Mindanao.

Government. On February 2, 1987, the Filipino people voted for a new Constitution that established a 24-seat Senate and a 250-seat House of Representatives and gave President Aquino a six-year term. It limits the powers of the President, who can't be re-elected.

History. Fernando Magellan, the Portuguese navigator in the service of Spain, discovered the Philippines in 1521. Twenty-one years later, a Spanish exploration party named the group of islands in honor of Prince Philip, later Philip II of Spain. Spain retained possession of the islands for the next 350 years.

The Philippines were ceded to the U.S. in 1899 by the Treaty of Paris after the Spanish-American War. Meanwhile, the Filipinos, led by Emilio Aguinaldo, had declared their independence. They continued guerrilla warfare against U.S. troops until the capture of Aguinaldo in 1901. By 1902, peace was established except among the Moros.

The first U.S. civilian Governor-General was William Howard Taft (1901–04). The Jones Law (1916) provided for the establishment of a Philippine Legislature composed of an elective Senate and House of Representatives. The Tydings-McDuffie Act (1934) provided for a transitional period until 1946, at which time the Philippines would become completely independent.

Under a Constitution approved by the people of the Philippines in 1935, the Commonwealth of the Philippines came into being, with Manuel Quezon y Molina as President.

On Dec. 8, 1941, the Philippines were invaded by Japanese troops. Following the fall of Bataan and Corregidor, Quezon established a government-in-exile, which he headed until his death in 1944. He was succeeded by Vice President Sergio Osmeña.

U.S. forces led by Gen. Douglas MacArthur reinvaded the Philippines in October 1944 and, after the liberation of Manila in February 1945, Osmeña re-established the government.

The Philippines achieved full independence on July 4, 1946. Manual A. Roxas y Acuña was elected first president. Subsequent presidents have been Elpidio Quirino (1948–53), Ramón Magsaysay (1953–57), Carlos P. García (1957–61), Diosdado Macapagal (1961–65), Ferdinand E. Marcos (1965–86).

The Philippines was one of six nations criticized by the U.S. State Department for human-rights violations in a report made public in 1977, although the department recommended continuing aid because of the importance of U.S. bases in the Philippines.

Marcos, who had freed the last of the national leaders still in detention, former Senator Benigno S. Aquino, Jr., in 1980 and permitted him to go to the United States, ended eight years of martial law on January 17, 1981.

Despite having been warned by First Lady Imelda Marcos that he risked being killed if he came back, opposition leader Aquino returned to the Philippines from self-exile on Aug. 21, 1983. He was shot to death as he was being escorted from his plane by military police at Manila International Airport. The government contended the assassin was a small-time hoodlum allegedly hired by communists, who was in turn shot dead by Filipino troops, but there was widespread suspicion that the Marcos government was involved in the murder.

The assassination sparked huge anti-government rallies and violent clashes between demonstrators and police, which continued intermittently through most of 1984, and helped the fragmented opposition parties score substantial gains in the May 14, 1984, elections for a National Assembly with greater power than a previous interim parliament.

On Jan. 23, 1985, one of Marcos' closest associates, Gen. Fabian C. Ver, the armed forces chief of staff, and 25 others were charged with the 1983 assassination of Aquino. Their trial dragged on through most of the year, with defense attorneys charging the evidence against Ver and the other defendants was fabricated.

In an attempt to re-secure American support, Marcos set Presidential elections for Feb. 7, 1986. After Ver's acquittal, and with the support of the Catholic church, Corazon Aquino, widow of Benigno Aquino, declared her candidacy. Marcos was declared the winner but the vote was widely considered to be rigged and anti-Marcos protests continued. The defection of Defense Minister Juan Enrile and Lt. Gen. Fidel Ramos signaled an end of military support for Marcos, who fled into exile in the U.S. on Feb. 25, 1986.

The Aquino government survived coup attempts by Marcos supporters and other right-wing elements including one, in November, by Enrile. Legislative elections on May 11, 1987, gave pro-Aquino candidates a large majority.

Negotiations on renewal of leases for U.S. military bases threatened to sour relations between the two countries. The volcanic eruptions from Mount Pinatubo, however, severely damaged Clark Air Base. In July 1991 the U.S. decided simply to abandon the base.

President Aquino faced a difficult year passing from one crisis or problem to another compounded by international events and natural disasters.

POLAND

Republic of Poland
President: Lech Walesa (1990)
Prime Minister: Jan Krzysztof Bielecki (1991)
Area: 120,727 sq mi. (312,683 sq km)
Population (est. mid-1991): 38,200,000 (average annual rate of natural increase: .5%); birth rate: 15/1000; infant mortality rate: 15.9/1000; density per square mile: 316
Capital: Warsaw
Largest cities (est. 1986): Warsaw, 1,659,400; Lodz, 847,900; Krakow, 740,100; Wroclaw, 637,200; Poznan, 575,100; Gdansk, 464,600; Szczecin, 392,300
Monetary unit: Zloty
Language: Polish
Religions: Roman Catholic, 95%; Russian Orthodox, Protestant, and other, 5%
National name: Rzeczpospolita Polska
Literacy rate: 98%
Economic summary: Gross national product (1989 est.): $172.4 billion; $4,565 per capita; −1.6% real growth rate. Arable land: 46%. Principal products: rye, rapeseed, potatoes, hogs and other livestock. Labor force: 17,128,000 (1988); 36.5% in industry and construction. Major products: iron and steel, chemicals, textiles, processed foods, machine building. Natural resources: coal, sulfur, copper, natural gas. Exports: coal, machinery and equipment, industrial products. Imports: machinery and equipment, fuels, raw materials, agricultural and food products. Major trading partners: U.S.S.R., Germany, Czechoslovakia.

Geography. Poland, a country the size of New Mexico in north central Europe, borders on East Germany to the west, Czechoslovakia to the south, and the U.S.S.R. to the east. In the north is the Baltic Sea.

Most of the country is a plain with no natural boundaries except the Carpathian Mountains in the south and the Oder and Neisse Rivers in the east. Other major rivers, which are important to commerce, are the Vistula, Warta, and Bug.

Government. The 1952 Constitution describes Poland as the Republic of Poland. The supreme organ of state authority is the Sejm (Parliament), which is composed of 460 members elected for four years.

A 100-seat Senate was established in 1989. A new constitution is scheduled to be passed in 1992, the 200th anniversary of Poland's pre-partition constitution.

History. Little is known about Polish history before the 11th century, when King Boleslaus I (the Brave) ruled over Bohemia, Saxony, and Moravia. Meanwhile, the Teutonic knights of Prussia conquered part of Poland and barred the latter's access to the Baltic. The knights were defeated by Wladislaus II at Tan-

nenberg in 1410 and became Polish vassals, and Poland regained a Baltic shoreline. Poland reached the peak of power between the 14th and 16th centuries, scoring military successes against the Russians and Turks. In 1683, John III (John Sobieski) turned back the Turkish tide at Vienna.

An elective monarchy failed to produce strong central authority, and Prussia and Austria were able to carry out a first partition of the country in 1772, a second in 1792, and a third in 1795. For more than a century thereafter, there was no Polish state, but the Poles never ceased their efforts to regain their independence.

Poland was formally reconstituted in November 1918, with Marshal Josef Pilsudski as Chief of State. In 1919, Ignace Paderewski, the famous pianist and patriot, became the first premier. In 1926, Pilsudski seized complete power in a coup and ruled dictatorially until his death on May 12, 1935, when he was succeeded by Marshal Edward Smigly-Rydz.

Despite a 10-year nonaggression pact signed in 1934, Hitler attacked Poland on Sept. 1, 1939. Russian troops invaded from the east on September 17, and on September 28 a German-Russian agreement divided Poland between Russia and Germany. Wladyslaw Raczkiewicz formed a government-in-exile in France, which moved to London after France's defeat in 1940.

All of Poland was occupied by Germany after the Nazi attack on the U.S.S.R. in June 1941.

The legal Polish government soon fell out with the Russians, and, in 1944, a Communist-dominated Polish Committee of National Liberation received Soviet recognition. Moving to Lublin after that city's liberation, it proclaimed itself the Provisional Government of Poland. Some former members of the Polish government in London joined with the Lublin government to form the Polish Government of National Unity, which Britain and the U.S. recognized.

On Aug. 2, 1945, in Berlin, President Harry S. Truman, Joseph Stalin, and Prime Minister Clement Attlee of Britain established a new *de facto* western frontier for Poland along the Oder and Neisse Rivers. (The border was finally agreed to by West Germany in a nonagression pact signed Dec. 7, 1970.) On Aug. 16, 1945, the U.S.S.R. and Poland signed a treaty delimiting the Soviet-Polish frontier. Under these agreements, Poland was shifted westward. In the east it lost 69,860 square miles (180,934 sq km) with 10,772,000 inhabitants; in the west it gained (subject to final peace-conference approval) 38,986 square miles (100,973 sq km) with a prewar population of 8,621,000.

A New Constitution in 1952 made Poland a "people's democracy" of the Soviet type. In 1955, Poland became a member of the Warsaw Treaty Organization, and its foreign policy became identical with that of the U.S.S.R. The government undertook persecution of the Roman Catholic Church as a remaining source of opposition.

Wladyslaw Gomulka was elected leader of the United Workers (Communist) Party in 1956. He denounced the Stalinist terror, ousted many Stalinists, and improved relations with the church. Most collective farms were dissolved, and the press became freer.

A strike that began in shipyards and spread to other industries in August 1980 produced a stunning victory for workers when the economically hard-pressed government accepted for the first time in a Marxist state the right of workers to organize in independent unions.

Led by Solidarity, a free union founded by Lech

Walesa, workers launched a drive for liberty and improved conditions. A national strike for a five-day week in January 1981 led to the dismissal of Premier Pinkowski and the naming of the fourth Premier in less than a year, Gen. Wojciech Jaruzelski.

Antistrike legislation was approved on Dec. 2 and martial law declared on Dec. 13, when Walesa and other Solidarity leaders were arrested. Ten days later, President Reagan ordered sanctions against the Polish government, stopping food shipments and cutting commercial air traffic. The sanctions were lifted in early 1987.

Martial law was formally ended in 1984 but the government retained emergency powers. On July 21, 1984, the Parliament marked the 40th anniversary of Communist rule in Poland by enacting an amnesty bill authorizing the release of 652 political prisoners—virtually all except for those charged with high treason, espionage, and sabotage—and 35,000 common criminals. On September 10, 1986, the government freed all 225 remaining political prisoners.

Increasing opposition to the government because of the failing economy led to a new wave of strikes in 1988. Unable to totally quell the dissent, it relegalized Solidarity and allowed them to compete in elections.

Solidarity won a stunning victory, taking almost all the seats in the Senate and all of the 169 seats they were allowed to contest in the Sejm. This has given them substantial influence in the new government. Taduesz Mazowiecki was appointed prime minister.

The presidential election of 1990 was essentially a three-way race between Mazowiecki, Solidarity-leader Lech Walesa and an almost unknown businessman Stanislaw Tyminski. In the second round Walesa received 74% of the vote.

Well into 1991 the parliament was still controlled by former Communists. A new election bill was held up until July 1 when President Walesa reluctantly signed it, charging the bill would lead to a weak legislature.

PORTUGAL

Republic of Portugal
President: Mario Soares (1986)
Prime Minister: Anibal Cavaco Silva (1987)
Area: 35,550 sq mi. (92,075 sq km)
Population (est. mid-1991): 10,400,000 (average annual rate of natural increase: 0.2%); birth rate: 12/1000; infant mortality rate: 12.1/1000; density per square mile: 292
Capital: Lisbon
Largest cities (est. 1985): Lisbon, 827,800; Opporto, 344,500
Monetary unit: Escudo
Language: Portuguese
Religion: Roman Catholic 97%, 1% Protestant, 2% other
National name: República Portuguesa
Literacy rate: 83%
Economic summary: Gross domestic product (1989 est.): $72.1 billion; $6,900 per capita; 3.5% real growth rate. Arable land: 32%. Principal products: grains, potatoes, olives, wine grapes. Labor force: 4,605,700; 35% in industry. Major products: textiles, footwear, wood pulp, paper, cork, metal products, refined oil, chemicals, canned fish, wine. Natural resources: fish, cork, tungsten, iron ore. Exports: cotton, textiles, cork and cork products, canned fish, wine, timber and timber products, resin. Imports: petroleum, cotton, foodgrains, industrial machinery, iron and steel, chemicals. Major trading partners: Western European countries, U.S.

Geography. Portugal occupies the western part of the Iberian Peninsula, bordering on the Atlantic Ocean to the west and Spain to the north and east. It is slightly smaller than Indiana.

The country is crossed by many small rivers, and also by three large ones that rise in Spain, flow into the Atlantic, and divide the country into three geographic areas. The Minho River, part of the northern boundary, cuts through a mountainous area that extends south to the vicinity of the Douro River. South of the Douro, the mountains slope to the plains about the Tejo River. The remaining division is the southern one of Alentejo.

The Azores, stretching over 340 miles (547 km) in the Atlantic, consist of nine islands divided into three groups, with a total area of 902 square miles (2,335 sq km). The nearest continental land is Cape da Roca, Portugal, about 900 miles (1,448 km) to the east. The Azores are an important station on Atlantic air routes, and Britain and the U.S. established air bases there during World War II. Madeira, consisting of two inhabited islands, Madeira and Porto Santo, and two groups of uninhabited islands, lie in the Atlantic about 535 miles (861 km) southwest of Lisbon. The Madeiras are 307 square miles (796 sq km) in area.

Government. The Constitution of 1976, revised in 1982, provides for popular election of a President for a five-year term and for a legislature, the Assembly of the Republic, for four years.

History. Portugal was a part of Spain until it won its independence in the middle of the 12th century. King John I (1385–1433) unified his country at the expense of the Castilians and the Moors of Morocco. The expansion of Portugal was brilliantly coordinated by John's son, Prince Henry the Navigator. In 1488, Bartolomew Diaz reached the Cape of Good Hope, proving that the Far East was accessible by sea. In 1498, Vasco da Gama reached the west coast of India. By the middle of the 16th century, the Portuguese Empire was in West and East Africa, Brazil, Persia, Indochina, and Malaya.

In 1581, Philip II of Spain invaded Portugal and held it for 60 years, precipitating a catastrophic decline of Portuguese commerce. Courageous and shrewd explorers, the Portuguese proved to be inefficient and corrupt colonizers. By the time the Portuguese dynasty was restored in 1640, Dutch, English, and French competitors began to seize the lion's share of the world's colonies and commerce. Portugal retained Angola and Mozambique in Africa, and Brazil (until 1822).

The corrupt King Carlos, who ascended the throne in 1889, made Joao Franco the Premier with dictatorial power in 1906. In 1908, Carlos and his heir were shot dead on the streets of Lisbon. The new King, Manoel II, was driven from the throne in the Revolution of 1910 and Portugal became a French-style republic.

Traditionally friendly to Britain, Portugal fought in World War I on the Allied side in Africa as well as on the Western Front. Weak postwar governments and a revolution in 1926 brought Antonio Oliveira Salazar to power. He kept Portugal neutral in World War II but gave the Allies naval and air bases after 1943.

Portugal lost the tiny remnants of its Indian empire—Goa, Daman, and Diu—to Indian military occupation in 1961, the year an insurrection broke out in Angola. For the next 13 years, Salazar, who died in 1970, and his successor, Marcello Caetano, fought independence movements amid growing world criticism. Leftists in the armed forces, weary of a losing battle, launched a successful revolution on April 25, 1974.

In late 1985, a PSP-PSD split ended the Soares coalition government. Cavaco Silva, an advocate of free-market economics, was the Social Democratic candidate. His party emerged with a plurality, unseating the Socialists.

In July 1987, the governing Social Democratic Party was swept back into office with 50.22% of the popular vote, giving Portugal its first majority Government since democracy was restored in 1974.

Mario Soares easily won a second five-year term as president in January 1991 elections.

Portuguese Overseas Territory

After the April 1974 revolution, the military junta moved to grant independence to the territories, beginning with Portuguese Guinea in September 1974, which became the Republic of Guinea-Bissau.

Mozambique and Angola followed, leaving only Portuguese Timor and Macao of the former empire. Despite Lisbon's objections, Indonesia annexed Timor.

MACAO

Status: Territory
Governor: Francisco Nabo (1990)
Area: 6 sq mi. (15.5 sq km)
Population (est. mid-1991): 400,000 (average annual growth rate: 1.4%); birth rate: 17/1000; infant mortality rate: 10/1000
Capital (1970 census): Macao, 241,413
Monetary unit: Pataca
Literacy rate (1981): almost 100% among Portuguese and Macanese, no data on Chinese
Economic summary: Gross domestic product (1989 est.): $2.7 billion, $6,300 per capita; real growth rate 5%. Principal agricultural products: rice and vegetables. Major industrial products: clothing, textiles, plastics, furniture. Exports: textiles, clothing, toys. Imports: raw materials, foodstuffs, capital goods. Major trading partners: Hong Kong, China, U.S., Germany, France.

Macao comprises the peninsula of Macao and the two small islands of Taipa and Colôane on the South China coast, about 35 miles (53 km) from Hong Kong. Established by the Portuguese in 1557, it is the oldest European outpost in the China trade, but Portugal's sovereign rights to the port were not recognized by China until 1887. The port has been eclipsed in importance by Hong Kong, but it is still a busy distribution center and also has an important fishing industry. Portugal will return Macao to China in 1999.

Carlos Melancia resigned as governor in September 1990 after being accused of accepting a bribe from a German firm doing consulting work for a planned airport.

QATAR

State of Qatar
Emir: Sheikh Khalifa bin Hamad al-Thani (1972)
Area: 4,000 sq mi. (11,437 sq km)
Population (est. mid-1991): 500,000 (average annual rate of natural increase: 2.5%); birth rate: 27/1000; infant mortality rate: 24/1000; density per square mile: 122
Capital (est. 1990): Doha, 300,000
Monetary unit: Qatari riyal
Language: Arabic; English is also widely spoken
Religion: Islam, 95%
Literacy rate: 40%
Economic summary: Gross national product (1987): $5.4 billion; $17,070 per capita; 9% real growth rate. Labor force: 104,000. Major industrial product: oil. Natural resources: oil, gas. Export: oil. Imports: foodstuffs, animal and vegetable oils, chemicals, machinery and equipment. Major trading partners: Japan, Western Europe, U.S., Australia, Arab countries.

Geography. Qatar occupies a small peninsula that extends into the Persian Gulf from the east side of the Arabian Peninsula. Saudi Arabia is to the west and the United Arab Emirates to the south. The country is mainly barren.

Government. Qatar, one of the Arabian Gulf states, lies between Bahrain and United Arab Emirates. For a long time, it was under Turkish protection, but in 1916, the Emir accepted British protection. After the discovery of oil in the 1940s and its exploitation in the 1950s and 1960s, political unrest spread to the sheikhdoms. Qatar declared its independence in 1971. The next year the current Sheikh, Khalifa bin Hamad al-Thani, ousted his cousin in a bloodless coup.

History. The emir agreed to the deployment of Arab and Western forces in Qatar following the Iraqi invasion of Kuwait. Also at this time a number of Palestinians were expelled for fear of their support of the PLO's pro-Iraqi position.

ROMANIA

Socialist Republic of Romania
President: Ion Iliescu (1990)
Premier: Petre Roman
Area: 91,700 sq mi. (237,500 sq km)
Population (est. mid-1991): 23,400,000 (average annual rate of natural increase: 0.5%); birth rate: 16/1000; infant mortality rate: 26.9/1000; density per square mile: 255
Capital: Bucharest
Largest cities (est. July 1, 1986): Bucharest, 2,014,359 (1987); Brasov, 351,493; Constanta, 327,676; Timisoara, 325,272; Iasi, 313,060; Cluj-Napoca, 310,017; Galati, 295,372
Monetary unit: Leu
Languages: Romanian, Magyar
Religions: Romanian Orthodox, 80%; Roman Catholic, 6%; 4% others
National name: Republica Socialista România
Literacy rate: 98%
Economic summary: Gross national product (1989 est.): $79.8 billion; $3,445 per capita; –1.5% real growth rate. Arable land: 43%. Principal products: corn, wheat, livestock. Labor force: 10,690,000; 34% in industry. Major products: timber, metal production and processing, chemicals, food processing, petroleum. Natural resources: oil, timber, natural gas, coal, iron ore. Exports: machinery, minerals and metals, foodstuffs, lumber, fuel, manufactures. Imports: machinery, minerals, fuels, agricultural products, consumer goods. Major trading partners: U.S.S.R., Germany, E.C., U.S., China.

Geography. A country in southeastern Europe slightly smaller than Oregon, Romania is bordered on the west by Hungary and Yugoslavia, on the north and east by the U.S.S.R., on the east by the Black Sea, and on the south by Bulgaria.

The Carpathian Mountains divide Romania's upper half from north to south and connect near the center of the country with the Transylvanian Alps, running east and west.

North and west of these ranges lies the Transylvanian plateau, and to the south and east are the plains of Moldavia and Walachia. In its last 190 miles (306 km), the Danube River flows through Romania only. It enters the Black Sea in northern Dobruja, just south of the border with the Soviet Union.

Government. After the overthrow of Nicolae Ceausescu's Communist government at the end of 1989, an interim-government was headed by the National Salvation Front. The sweeping victory of the NSF in May 1990 elections gave the NSF a popular mandate for retaining power yet its legitimacy remains questionable in the eyes of many Romanians.

History. Most of Romania was the Roman province of Dacia from about A.D. 100 to 271. From the 6th to the 12th century, wave after wave of barbarian conquerors overran the native Daco-Roman population. By the 16th century, the main Romanian principalities of Moldavia and Walachia had become satellites within the Ottoman Empire, although they retained much independence. After the Russo-Turkish War of 1828–29, they became Russian protectorates. The nation became a kingdom in 1881 after the Congress of Berlin.

King Ferdinand ascended the throne in 1914. At the start of World War I, Romania proclaimed its neutrality, but later joined the Allied side and in 1916 declared war on the Central Powers. The armistice of Nov. 11, 1918, gave Romania vast territories from Russia and the Austro-Hungarian Empire.

The gains of World War I, making Romania the largest Balkan state, included Bessarabia, Transylvania, and Bukovina. The Banat, a Hungarian area, was divided with Yugoslavia.

In 1925, Crown Prince Carol renounced his rights to the throne, and when King Ferdinand died in 1927, Carol's son, Michael (Mihai) became King under a regency. However, Carol returned from exile in 1930, was crowned King Carol II, and gradually became a powerful political force in the country. In 1938, he abolished the democratic Constitution of 1923.

In 1940, the country was reorganized along Fascist lines, and the Fascist Iron Guard became the nucleus of the new totalitarian party. On June 27, the Soviet Union occupied Bessarabia and northern Bukovina. By the Axis-dictated Vienna Award of 1940, two-fifths of Transylvania went to Hungary, after which Carol dissolved Parliament and granted the new premier, Ion Antonescu, full power. He abdicated and again went into exile.

Romania subsequently signed the Axis Pact on Nov. 23, 1940, and the following June joined in Germany's attack on the Soviet Union, reoccupying Bessarabia. Following the invasion of Romania by the Red Army in August 1944, King Michael led a coup that ousted the Antonescu government. An armistice with the Soviet Union was signed in Moscow on Sept. 12, 1944.

A Communist-dominated government bloc won elections in 1946, Michael abdicated on Dec. 30, 1947, and Romania became a "people's republic." In 1955, Romania joined the Warsaw Treaty Organization and the United Nations. A decade later, with the adoption of a new Constitution emphasizing national autonomy, and especially after Nicolae Ceausescu

came to power in 1967, Bucharest became an increasingly dissident voice in the Soviet bloc. Despite his liberal international record, at home Ceausescu harshly suppressed dissidents calling for freedom of expression in the wake of the Helsinki agreements.

An army-assisted rebellion in Dec. 1989 led to Ceausescu's overthrow. He was tried and executed. Elections in May 1990 led to the head of the interim government, Ion Iliescu, being elected President.

The government remains torn between introducing free-market reforms and its pledges to hold down unemployment and reduce shortages. While some, though few, measures have been implemented, price reforms in November 1990 led to strikes and demonstrations. The opposition remains weak and fragmented.

RWANDA

Republic of Rwanda
President: Maj. Gen. Juvénal Habyarimana (1973)
Area: 10,169 sq mi. (26,338 sq km)
Population (est. mid-1991): 7,500,000 (average annual rate of natural increase: 3.4%); birth rate: 51/1000; infant mortality rate: 117/1000; density per square mile: 739
Capital and largest city (1990): Kigali, 300,000
Monetary unit: Rwanda franc
Languages: Kinyarwanda and French
Religions: Roman Catholic, 56%; Protestant, 18%; Islam, 1%; Animist, 25%
National name: Republika y'u Rwanda
Literacy rate: 46.6%
Economic summary: Gross domestic product (1988 est.): $2.3 billion; $325 per capita; real growth rate –2.5%. Arable land: 29%. Principal products: coffee, tea, bananas, yams, beans. Labor force 3,600,000; in industry: 2%. Major products: processed foods, light consumer goods, minerals. Natural resources: gold, cassiterite, wolfram. Exports: coffee, tea, tungsten, tin, pyrethrum. Imports: textiles, foodstuffs, machinery, and equipment. Major trading partners: Belgium, Germany, Kenya, Japan, France, U.S.

Geography. Rwanda, in east central Africa, is surrounded by Zaire, Uganda, Tanzania, and Burundi. It is slightly smaller than Maryland.

Steep mountains and deep valleys cover most of the country. Lake Kivu in the northwest, at an altitude of 4,829 feet (1,472 m) is the highest lake in Africa. Extending north of it are the Virunga Mountains, which include Volcan Karisimbi (14,187 ft; 4,324 m), Rwanda's highest point.

Government. Grégoire Kayibanda was President from 1962 until he was overthrown in a bloodless coup on July 5, 1973, by the military led by Gen. Juvénal Habyarimana.

In a plebiscite in December 1978, Habyarimana was elected to a five-year term as president and a new constitution adopted that provides for an elected Assembly and a single official party, the National Revolutionary Development Movement.

In 1988, Habyarimana was elected to a third five-year term.

The constitution was revised in 1991 to implement a multiparty system and schedule new elections.

History. Rwanda, which was part of German East Africa, was first visited by European explorers in 1854. During World War I, it was occupied in 1916 by Belgian troops. After the war, it became a Belgian

League of Nations mandate, along with Burundi, under the name of Ruanda-Urundi. The mandate was made a U.N. trust territory in 1946. Until the Belgian Congo achieved independence in 1960, Ruanda-Urundi was administered as part of that colony.

Ruanda became the independent nation of Rwanda on July 1, 1962.

Rebel forces battled with government troops for control of parts of the country during late 1990 and early 1991.

ST. KITTS AND NEVIS

Federation of St. Kitts and Nevis
Sovereign: Queen Elizabeth II
Governor General: Sir Clement Athelston Arrindell (1985)
Prime Minister: Kennedy Alphonse Simmonds (1980)
Area: St. Kitts 65 sq mi. (169 sq km); Nevis 35 sq mi. (93 sq km)
Total population (est. mid-1991): 40,000 (average annual rate of natural increase: 1.1%); birth rate: 21/1000; infant mortality rate: 23/1000
Capital: Basseterre (on St. Kitts), 19,000
Largest town on Nevis: Charlestown, 1,771
Monetary unit: East Caribbean dollar
Economic summary: Gross domestic product (1988 est.): $119 million; $3,240 per capita; 6% real growth rate. Arable land: 22%. Principal agricultural products: sugar, rice, yams. Labor force: 20,000 (1981). Major industries: tourism, sugar processing, salt extraction. Exports: sugar, manufactures, postage stamps. Imports: foodstuffs, manufactured goods, machinery, fuels. Major trading partners: U.S., U.K., Japan, Trinidad and Tobago, Canada.

St. Christopher-Nevis, preferably St. Kitts and Nevis, was formerly part of the West Indies Associated States which were established in 1967 and consisted of Antigua and St. Kitts-Nevis-Anguilla of the Leeward Islands, and Dominica, Grenada, St. Lucia, and St. Vincent of the Windward Islands. Statehood for St. Vincent was held up until 1969 because of local political uncertainties. Anguilla's association with St. Christopher-Nevis ended in 1980.

Two members of the Leeward group—the British Virgin Islands and Montserrat—did not become Associated States.

St. Christopher-Nevis, now St. Kitts and Nevis, became independent on September 19, 1983.

Hurricane Hugo in 1989 inflicted such damage that the sugar crop was sharply reduced in 1990. Tourism and construction, however, have successfully rebounded.

ST. LUCIA

Sovereign: Queen Elizabeth II
Governor-General: (acting) Stanislaus A. James (1989)
Prime Minister: John Compton (1982)
Area: 238 sq mi. (616 sq km)
Population (est. mid-1991): 150,000 (average annual rate of natural increase: 1.6%); birth rate: 21/1000; infant mortality rate: 17.7/1000; density per square mile: 630
Capital (est. 1972): Castries, 45,000
Monetary unit: East Caribbean dollar
Languages: English and patois
Religions: Roman Catholic, 90%; Protestant, 7%; Anglican, 3%

Member of Commonwealth of Nations
Literacy rate: 90%
Economic summary: Gross domestic product (1988 est.): $172 million; $1,258 per capita; 6.8% real growth rate. Arable land: 8%. Principal products: bananas, coconuts, cocoa, citrus fruit. Major industrial products: clothing, assembled electronics, beverages. Exports: bananas, cocoa. Imports: foodstuffs, machinery and equipment, fertilizers, petroleum products. Major trading partners: U.K., U.S., Caribbean countries, Japan.

Geography. One of the Windward Isles of the Eastern Caribbean, St. Lucia lies just south of Martinique. It is of volcanic origin. A chain of wooded mountains runs from north to south, and from them flow many streams into fertile valleys.

Government. A Governor-General represents the sovereign, Queen Elizabeth II. A Prime Minister is head of government, chosen by a 17-member House of Assembly elected by universal suffrage for a maximum term of five years.

History. Discovered by Spain in 1503 and ruled by Spain and then France, St. Lucia became a British territory in 1803. With other Windward Isles, St. Lucia was granted home rule in 1967 as one of the West Indies Associated States. On Feb. 22, 1979, St. Lucia achieved full independence in ceremonies boycotted by the opposition St. Lucia Labor Party, which had advocated a referendum before cutting ties with Britain.

Unrest and a strike by civil servants forced Prime Minister John Compton to hold elections in July, in which his United Workers Party lost its majority for the first time in 15 years.

A Labor Party government was ousted in turn by Compton and his followers, in elections in May 1982.

Formerly dependent on a single crop, bananas, St. Lucia has sought to lower its chronic unemployment and payments deficit. The government provided tax incentives to a U.S. corporation, Amerada Hess, to facilitate location of a $150-million oil refinery and transshipment terminal on the island.

Desmond Fostin, the minister of communications and works, resigned in February 1990 amid charges of corruption in his ministry.

ST. VINCENT AND THE GRENADINES

Sovereign: Queen Elizabeth II
Governor-General: David Jack (1989)
Prime Minister: James Mitchell (1984)
Area: 150 sq mi. (389 sq km)
Population (est. mid-1991): 100,000 (average annual rate of natural increase: 1.6%); birth rate: 23/1000; infant mortality rate: 21.7/1000; density per square mile: 760
Capital and largest city (est. 1984): Kingstown, 18,378
Monetary unit: East Caribbean dollar
Language: English, some French patois
Religions: Anglican, 47%; Methodist, 28%; Roman Catholic, 13%
Member of Commonwealth of Nations
Literacy rate: 82%
Economic summary: Gross domestic product (1988): $160.5 million; $1,413 per capita; 8.4% real growth rate. Arable land: 38%. Principal products: bananas, arrowroot, coconuts. Labor Force: 67,000 (1984 est.).

Major industry: food processing. Exports: bananas, arrowroot, copra. Imports: foodstuffs, machinery and equipment, chemicals, fuels, minerals. Major trading partners: U.K., U.S., Canada, Caribbean nations.

Geography. St. Vincent, chief island of the chain, is 18 miles (29 km) long and 11 miles (18 km) wide. One of the Windward Islands in the Lesser Antilles, it is 100 miles (161 km) west of Barbados. The island is mountainous and well forested. The Grenadines, a chain of nearly 600 islets with a total area of only 17 square miles (27 sq km), extend for 60 miles (96 km) from northeast to southwest between St. Vincent and Grenada, southernmost of the Windwards.

St. Vincent is dominated by the volcano La Soufrière, part of a volcanic range running north and south, which rises to 4,048 feet (1,234 m). The volcano erupted over a 10-day period in April 1979, causing the evacuation of the northern two-thirds of the island. (There is also a volcano of the same name on Basse-Terre, Guadeloupe, which became violently active in 1976 and 1977.)

Government. A Governor-General represents the sovereign, Queen Elizabeth II. A Prime Minister, elected by a 15-member unicameral legislature, holds executive power.

History. Discovered by Columbus in 1498, and alternately claimed by Britain and France, St. Vincent became a British colony by the Treaty of Paris in 1783. The islands won home rule in 1969 as part of the West Indies Associated States and achieved full independence Oct. 26, 1979. Prime Minister Milton Cato's government quelled a brief rebellion Dec. 8, 1979, attributed to economic problems following the eruption of La Soufrière in April 1979. Unlike a 1902 eruption which killed 2,000, there was no loss of life but widespread losses to agriculture.

Recently unemployment has become a major problem as well as the burgeoning debt and trade deficit.

SAN MARINO

Most Serene Republic of San Marino
Co-Regents: Two selected every six months by Grand and General Council
Area: 23.6 sq mi. (62 sq km)
Population (mid-1989): 22,980 (average annual growth rate: 0.6%)
Density per square mile: 974.6
Capital and largest city (est. 1982 for metropolitan area): San Marino, 4,500
Monetary unit: Italian lira
Language: Italian
Religion: Roman Catholic
National name: Repubblica di San Marino
Literacy rate: 97%
Economic summary: Gross national product: NA. Arable land: 17%. Principal products: wheat and other grains, grapes, olives, cheese. Labor force: approx. 4,300. Major industrial products: textiles, leather, cement, wine, olive oil. Exports: building stone, lime, chestnuts, wheat, hides, baked goods. Imports: manufactured consumer goods. Major trading partner: Italy.

Geography. One-tenth the size of New York City, San Marino is surrounded by Italy. It is situated in the Apennines, a little inland from the Adriatic Sea near Rimini.

Government. The country is governed by two co-regents. Executive power is exercised by ten ministers. In 1959, the Grand Council granted women the vote. San Marino is a member of the Conference on Security and Cooperation in Europe.

History. According to tradition, San Marino was founded about A.D. 350 and had good luck for centuries in staying out of the many wars and feuds on the Italian peninsula. It is the oldest republic in the world.

A person born in San Marino remains a citizen and can vote no matter where he lives.

The Communist Party underwent a metamorphosis becoming the Democratic Progressive Party, symbolized by a dove of peace.

SÃO TOMÉ AND PRÍNCIPE

Democratic Republic of São Tomé and Príncipe
President: Miguel Trovoada (1991)
Prime Minister: Celestino Rocha da Costa (1988)
Area: 370 sq mi. (958 sq km)
Population (est. mid-1991): 100,000 (average annual growth rate: 2.5%); birth rate: 35/1000; infant mortality rate: 71.9/1000; density per square mile: 345
Capital and largest city (est. 1984): São Tomé, 34,997
Monetary unit: Dobra
Language: Portuguese
Religions: Roman Catholic, Evangelical Protestant, Seventh-Day Adventist
Literacy rate: 50% (est.)
Economic summary: Gross domestic product (1986): $37.9 million; $340 per capita; 1.8% annual growth rate. Arable land: 1%. Principal agricultural products: cocoa, copra, coconuts, palm oil, coffee, bananas. Labor force: 21,096 (1981): mostly in subsistence agriculture. Major industrial products: shirts, soap, beer, processed fish and shrimp. Exports: cocoa, coffee, copra, palm oil. Imports: textiles, machinery, electrical equipment, fuels, food products. Major trading partners: Netherlands, Portugal, Germany, China.

Geography. The tiny volcanic islands of São Tomé and Príncipe lie in the Gulf of Guinea about 150 miles (240 km) off West Africa. São Tomé (about 330 sq mi.; 859 sq km) is covered by a dense mountainous jungle, out of which have been carved large plantations. Príncipe (about 40 sq mi.; 142 sq km) consists of jagged mountains. Other islands in the republic are Pedras Tinhosas and Rolas.

Government. The Constitution grants supreme power to a People's Assembly composed of members elected for four years. In 1990 a referendum approved a new constitution paving the way for a multi-party democracy.

History. São Tomé and Príncipe were discovered by Portuguese navigators in 1471 and settled by the end of the century. Intensive cultivation by slave labor made the islands a major producer of sugar during the 17th century but output declined until the introduction of coffee and cacao in the 19th century brought new prosperity. The island of São Tomé was the world's largest producer of cacao in 1908 and the crop is still the most important. An exile liberation movement was formed in 1953 after Portuguese landowners quelled labor riots by killing several hundred African workers.

The Portuguese revolution of 1974 brought the end of the overseas empire and the new Lisbon government transferred power to the liberation movement on July 12, 1975.

President Pinto da Costa's ruling party was defeated in multi-party elections in January 1991. A former prime minister and dissident Miguel Trovoada was elected president in March after the withdrawal of the two other candidates.

SAUDI ARABIA

Kingdom of Saudi Arabia
Ruler and Prime Minister: King Fahd bin 'Abdulaziz (1982)
Area: 865,000 sq mi. (2,250,070 sq km)
Population (est. mid-1991): 15,500,000 (average annual rate of natural increase: 3.4%); birth rate: 42/1000; infant mortality rate: 71/1000; density per square mile: 19
Capital: Riyadh
Largest cities (est. 1980): Jeddah, 1,500,000; Riyadh, 1,250,000; Mecca, 750,000
Monetary unit: Riyal
Language: Arabic
Religion: Islam, 100%
National name: Al-Mamlaka al-'Arabiya as-Sa'udiya
Literacy rate: 52%
Economic summary: Gross domestic product (1988): $73 billion; $4,720 per capita; 3.2% real growth rate. Arable land: 1%. Principal products: dates, grains, livestock. Labor force: 4,200,000; about 60% are foreign workers; 28% in industry and oil. Major products: petroleum, cement, plastic products, steel. Natural resources: oil, natural gas, iron ore. Exports: petroleum and petroleum products. Imports: manufactured goods, transport equipment, construction materials, processed food. Major trading partners: U.S., Germany, Great Britain and other Western European countries, South Korea, Taiwan, Japan.

Geography. Saudi Arabia occupies most of the Arabian Peninsula, with the Red Sea and the Gulf of Aqaba to the west, the Arabian Gulf to the east. Neighboring countries are Jordan, Iraq, Kuwait, Qatar, the United Arab Emirates, the Sultanate of Oman, and Yemen.

A narrow coastal plain on the Red Sea rims a mountain range that spans the length of the western coastline. These mountains gradually rise in elevation from north to south. East of these mountains is a massive plateau which slopes gently downward toward the Arabian Gulf. Part of this plateau is covered by the world's largest continuous sand desert, the Rub Al-Khali, or Empty Quarter. Saudi Arabia's oil region lies primarily along the Arabian Gulf.

Government. Saudi Arabia is a monarchy based on the Sharia (Islamic law), as revealed in the Koran (the holy book) and the Hadith (teachings and sayings of the prophet Mohammed). A Council of Ministers was formed in 1953, which acts as a Cabinet under the leadership of the King. There are 20 Ministries.

Royal and ministerial decrees account for most of the promulgated legislation, treaties, and conventions.

There are no political parties.

History. Mohammed united the Arabs in the 7th century, and his followers, led by the caliphs, founded a great empire, with its capital at Medina. Later, the caliphate capital was transferred to Damascus and then Baghdad, but Arabia retained its importance because of the holy cities of Mecca and Medina. In the 16th and 17th centuries, the Turks established at least nominal rule over much of Arabia, and in the middle of the 18th century, it was divided into separate principalities.

The Kingdom of Saudi Arabia is almost entirely the creation of King Ibn Saud (1882–1953). A descendant of earlier Wahabi rulers, he seized Riyadh, the capital of Nejd, in 1901 and set himself up as leader of the Arab nationalist movement. By 1906 he had established Wahabi dominance in Nejd. He conquered Hejaz in 1924–25, consolidating it and Nejd into a dual kingdom in 1926. In 1932, Hejaz and Nejd became a single kingdom, which was officially named Saudi Arabia. A year later the region of Asir was incorporated into the kingdom.

Oil was discovered in 1936, and commercial production began during World War II. Saudi Arabia was neutral until nearly the end of the war, but it was permitted to be a charter member of the United Nations. The country joined the Arab League in 1945 and took part in the 1948–49 war against Israel.

On Ibn Saud's death in 1953, his eldest son, Saud, began an 11-year reign marked by an increasing hostility toward the radical Arabism of Egypt's Gamal Abdel Nasser. In 1964, the ailing Saud was deposed and replaced by the Premier, Crown Prince Faisal, who gave vocal support but no military help to Egypt in the 1967 Mideast war.

Faisal's assassination by a deranged kinsman in 1975 shook the Middle East, but failed to alter his kingdom's course. His successor was his brother, Prince Khalid. Khalid gave influential support to Egypt during negotiations on Israeli withdrawal from the Sinai desert.

King Khalid died of a heart attack June 13, 1982, and was succeeded by his half-brother, Prince Fahd bin 'Abdulaziz, 60, who had exercised the real power throughout Khalid's reign. King Fahd, a pro-Western modernist, chose his 58-year-old half-brother, Abdullah, as Crown Prince.

Saudi Arabia and the smaller, oil-rich Arab states on the Persian Gulf, fearful that they might become Ayatollah Ruhollah Khomeini's next targets if Iran conquered Iraq, made large financial contributions to the Iraqi war effort. They began being dragged into the conflict themselves in the spring of 1984, when Iraq and Iran extended their ground war to attacks on Gulf shipping. First, Iraq attacked tankers loading at Iran's Kharg Island terminal with air-to-ground missiles, then Iran struck back at tankers calling at Saudi Arabia and other Arab countries.

At the same time, cheating by other members of the Organization of Petroleum Exporting Countries, competition from nonmember oil producers, and conservation efforts by consuming nations combined to drive down the world price of oil. Saudi Arabia has one-third of all known oil reserves, but falling demand and rising production outside OPEC combined to reduce its oil revenues from $120 billion in 1980 to $43 billion in 1984 to less the $25 billion in 1985, threatening the country with domestic unrest and undermining its influence in the Gulf area.

Saudi Arabia broke relations with Iran in April 1988 over the issues of riots by Iranian pilgrims in Mecca in July, 1987 and Iranian naval attacks on Saudi vessels in the Persian Gulf.

Following the invasion of Kuwait in August 1990, Saudi Arabia allowed the U.S. to station military forces there ("Operation Desert Shield") to defend its territory against possible Iraqi invasion.

Diplomatic relations with the U.S.S.R. and China were established in 1990, and in November of that year promises were made to revive long-dormant plans for a consultative council. Oil production rose, and government spending substantially increased. (*See* Special Current Events article in the Gulf War.)

SENEGAL

Republic of Senegal
President: Abdou Diouf (1981)
Area: 75,954 sq mi. (196,722 sq km)
Population (est. mid-1991): 7,500,000 (average annual rate of natural increase: 2.8%); birth rate: 46/1000; infant mortality rate: 87/1000; density per square mile: 99
Capital and largest city (est. 1982): Dakar, 975,000
Monetary unit: Franc CFA
Ethnic groups: Wolofs, Sereres, Peuls, Tukulers, and others
Languages: French (official); Wolof, Serer, other ethnic dialects
Religions: Islam, 92%; indigenous, 6%; Christian, 2%
National name: République du Sénégal
Literacy rate: 28.1%
Economic summary: Gross domestic product (1988 est.): $5 billion; $680 per capita; 5.1% real growth rate. Arable land: 27%. Principal products: peanuts, millet, corn, rice, sorghum. Labor force: 2,509,000; 77% subsistence agriculture workers. Major industrial products: processed food, phosphates, refined petroleum, cement, and fish. Natural resources: fish, phosphate, iron ore. Exports: peanuts, phosphate rock, canned fish, petroleum products. Imports: foodstuffs, consumer goods, machinery, transport equipment, petroleum. Major trading partners: U.S., France, Western European countries, African neighbors.

Geography. The capital of Senegal, Dakar, is the westernmost point in Africa. The country, slightly smaller than South Dakota, surrounds Gambia on three sides and is bordered on the north by Mauritania, on the east by Mali, and on the south by Guinea and Guinea-Bissau.

Senegal is mainly a low-lying country, with a semidesert area in the north and northeast and forests in the southwest. The largest rivers include the Senegal in the north and the Casamance in the south tropical climate region.

Government. There is a National Assembly of 120 members, elected every five years. There is universal suffrage and a constitutional guarantee of equality before the law.

History. The Portuguese had some stations on the banks of the Senegal River in the 15th century, and the first French settlement was made at Saint-Louis about 1650. The British took parts of Senegal at various times, but the French gained possession in 1840 and organized the Sudan as a territory in 1904. In 1946, together with other parts of French West Africa, Senegal became part of the French Union. On June 20, 1960, it became an independent republic federated with the Sudanese Republic in the Mali Federation, from which it withdrew two months later.

In 1973, Senegal joined with six other states to create the West African Economic Community.

Pres. Diouf continues his commitment to the austerity measures imposed by the IMF. Senegal's border war with Mauritania still smolders as does the territorial waters dispute with Guinea-Bissau.

SEYCHELLES

Republic of Seychelles
President: France-Albert René (1977)
Area: 175 sq mi. (453 sq km)
Population (est. mid-1991): 100,000 (average annual rate of natural increase: 1.6%); birth rate: 24/1000; infant mortality rate: 18.1/1000; density per square mile: 638
Capital: Victoria, 24,000
Monetary unit: Seychelles rupee
Languages: English and French (official); Creole
Religions: Roman Catholic, 90%; Anglican, 8%
Member of Commonwealth of Nations
Literacy rate: 60%
Economic summary: Gross domestic product (1988 est.): $255 million; $3,720 per capita; 6.2% real growth rate. Arable land: 4%. Principal products: vanilla, coconuts, cinnamon. Labor force: 27,700; 31% in industry and commerce. Major products: processed coconut and vanilla, coir rope. Exports: cinnamon, fish, copra. Imports: food, tobacco, manufactured goods, machinery, petroleum products, transport equipment. Major trading partners: U.K., France, Japan, Pakistan, Reunion, South Africa.

Geography. Seychelles consists of an archipelago of about 100 islands in the Indian Ocean northeast of Madagascar. The principal islands are Mahé (55 sq mi.; 142 sq km), Praslin (15 sq mi.; 38 sq km), and La Digue (4 sq mi.; 10 sq km). The Aldabra, Farquhar, and Desroches groups are included in the territory of the republic.

Government. Seized from France by Britain in 1810, the Seychelles Islands remained a colony until June 29, 1976. The state is an independent republic within the Commonwealth.

On June 5, 1977, Prime Minister Albert René ousted the islands' first President, James Mancham, suspending the Constitution and the 25-member National Assembly. Mancham, whose "lavish spending" and flamboyance were cited by René in seizing power, charged that Soviet influence was at work. The new president denied this and, while more left than his predecessor, pledged to keep the Seychelles in the nonaligned group of countries.

An unsuccessful attempted coup against René attracted international attention when a group of 50 South African mercenaries posing as rugby players attacked the Victoria airport on Nov. 25, 1981. They caused extensive damage before they hijacked an Air India plane and returned to South Africa, where all but five were freed. Only after widespread international protest did the Pretoria government, which denied any responsibility for the attack, reverse the decision and order all the mercenaries tried as hijackers.

Recently experiencing a large trade deficit, partly to supply the tourist industry, the country for this and other reasons has decided to put a ceiling on the number of tourists permitted.

SIERRA LEONE

Republic of Sierra Leone
President: Maj. Gen. Joseph Saidu Momoh (1985)
Area: 27,700 sq mi. (71,740 sq km)

Population (est. mid-1991): 4,300,000 (average annual rate of natural increase: 2.7%); birth rate: 48/1000; infant mortality rate: 147/1000; density per square mile: 154
Capital and largest city (est. 1985): Freetown, 500,000
Monetary unit: Leone
Languages: English (official), Mende, Temne, Krio
Religions: Islam, 30%; indigenous, 30%; Christian, 10%; other, 30%
Member of Commonwealth of Nations
Literacy rate: 31%
Economic summary: Gross domestic product (FY87): $965 million; $250 per capita; real growth rate 1.8%. Arable land: 25%; principal products: coffee, cocoa, palm kernels, rice. Labor force: 1,369,000 (est.); 19% in industry. Major products: diamonds, bauxite, rutile, beverages, cigarettes, textiles, footwear. Natural resources: diamonds, bauxite, iron ore. Exports: diamonds, rutile, bauxite, cocoa, coffee. Imports: food, petroleum, products, capital goods. Major trading partners: U.K., U.S., Western European countries, Japan.

Geography. Sierra Leone, on the Atlantic Ocean in West Africa, is half the size of Illinois. Guinea, in the north and east, and Liberia, in the south, are its neighbors.

Mangrove swamps lie along the coast, with wooded hills and a plateau in the interior. The eastern region is mountainous.

Government. Sierra Leone became an independent nation on April 27, 1961, and declared itself a republic on April 19, 1971.

Sierra Leone became a one party state under the aegis of the All People's Congress Party in April 1978.

History. The coastal area of Sierra Leone was ceded to English settlers in 1788 as a home for blacks discharged from the British armed forces and also for runaway slaves who had found asylum in London. The British protectorate over the hinterland was proclaimed in 1896.

After elections in 1967, the British Governor-General replaced Sir Albert Margai, head of SLPP, which had held power since independence, with Dr. Stevens, head of APC, as prime minister. The Army took over the government; then another coup in April 1968 restored civilian rule and put the military leaders in jail.

A coup attempt early in 1971 by the army commander was apparently foiled by loyal army officers, but the then Prime Minister Stevens called in troops of neighboring Guinea's army, under a 1970 mutual defense pact, to guard his residence. After perfunctorily blaming the U.S. for the coup attempt, Stevens switched Governors-General, changed the Constitution, and ended up with a republic, of which he was first president. He was accused of taking "sweeping dictatorial powers," but was re-elected in 1978. Dr. Stevens' picked successor, Major-General Joseph Saidu Momoh was elected unopposed on Oct. 1, 1985.

A number of organizations in the last year have voiced support for the introduction of multiparty democracy, but President Momoh has opposed the idea.

SINGAPORE

Republic of Singapore
Prime Minister: Goh Chok Tong (1990)
Area: 220 sq mi. (570 sq km)
Population (est. mid-1991): 2,800,000 (average annual rate of natural increase: 1.3%); birth rate: 18/1000;

infant mortality rate: 6.6/1000; density per square mile: 12,307
Capital (est. mid-1988): Singapore, 2,600,000
Monetary unit: Singapore dollar
Languages: Malay, Chinese (Mandarin), Tamil, English
Religions: Islam, Christian, Buddhist, Hindu, Taoist
Member of Commonwealth of Nations
Literacy rate: 90%
Economic summary: Gross domestic product (1989 est.): $27.5 billion; $10,300 per capita; 9.2% real growth rate. Arable land: 4%. Principal products: poultry, rubber, copra, vegetables, fruits. Labor force: 1,324,700; 34.4% in industry. Major industries: petroleum refining, ship repair, electronics, financial services, biotechnology. Exports: petroleum products, rubber, manufactured goods, electronics, computers and computer peripherals. Imports: capital equipment, manufactured goods, petroleum. Major trading partners: U.S., Malaysia, E.C., Japan.

Geography. The Republic of Singapore consists of the main island of Singapore, off the southern tip of the Malay Peninsula between the South China Sea and the Indian Ocean, and 58 nearby islands.

There are extensive mangrove swamps extending inland from the coast, which is broken by many inlets.

Government. There is a Cabinet, headed by the Prime Minister, and a Parliament of 81 members elected by universal suffrage.

The People's Action Party, led by Prime Minister Goh Chok Tong, is the ruling political party in Parliament, holding all but one seat.

History. Singapore, founded in 1819 by Sir Stamford Raffles, became a separate crown colony of Britain in 1946, when the former colony of the Straits Settlements was dissolved. The other two settlements—Penang and Malacca—were transferred to the Union of Malaya, and the small island of Labuan was transferred to North Borneo. The Cocos (or Keeling) Islands were transferred to Australia in 1955 and Christmas Island in 1958.

Singapore attained full internal self-government in 1959. On Sept. 16, 1963, it joined Malaya, Sabah (North Borneo), and Sarawak in the Federation of Malaysia. It withdrew from the Federation on Aug. 9, 1965, and proclaimed itself a republic the next month.

Long-time Prime Minister Lee Kuan Yew stepped down in late November 1990 in order, he said, to make way for a younger team. He remained, however, in the government as a cabinet minister.

SOLOMON ISLANDS

Sovereign: Queen Elizabeth II
Governor-General: Sir George Lepping (1988)
Prime Minister: Solomon Mamaloni (1989)
Area: 11,500 sq mi. (29,785 sq km)
Population (est. mid-1991): 300,000 (average annual rate of natural increase: 3.5%); birth rate: 40/1000; infant mortality rate: 39/1000; density per square mile: 32
Capital and largest city (est. 1986): Honiara (on Guadalcanal), 30,499
Monetary unit: Solomon Islands dollar
Languages: English, Pidgin, 70 other languages and dialects
Religions: Anglican; Roman Catholic; South Seas Evangelical; Seventh-Day Adventist, United (Methodist) Church, other Protestant
Member of British Commonwealth
Literacy rate: 60%

Economic summary: Gross domestic product (1988): $156 million; $500 per capita; 4.3% real growth rate. Arable land: 1%. Principal agricultural products: coconuts, palm oil, rice, cocoa, yams, pigs. Labor force: 23,448; 7% in construction, manufacturing and mining. Major industrial products: processed fish, copra. Natural resources: fish, timber, gold, bauxite. Exports: fish, timber, copra, palm oil. Imports: machinery and transport equipment, foodstuffs, fuel. Major trading partners: Japan, Australia, U.K., Thailand, Singapore.

Geography. Lying east of New Guinea, this island nation consists of the southern islands of the Solomon group: Guadalcanal, Malaita, Santa Isabel, San Cristóbal, Choiseul, New Georgia, and numerous smaller islands.

Government. After 85 years of British rule, the Solomons achieved independence July 7, 1978. The Crown is represented by a Governor-General and legislative power is vested in a unicameral legislature of 38 members, led by the Prime Minister.

History. Discovered in 1567 by Alvaro de Mendana, the Solomons were not visited again for about 200 years. In 1886, Great Britain and Germany divided the islands between them. In 1914, Australian forces took over the German islands and the Solomons became an Australian mandate in 1920. In World War II, most of the islands were occupied by the Japanese. American forces landed on Guadalcanal on Aug. 7, 1942. The islands were the scene of several important U.S. naval and military victories. Although surviving a vote of no-confidence the prime minister resigned from his party and was forced to take five opposition members into his cabinet.

SOMALIA

Somali Democratic Republic
President: Ali Mahdi Mohammed (interim 1991)
Prime Minister: Omar Artan Qalib (1991)
Area: 246,199 sq mi. (637,655 sq km)
Population (est. mid-1991): 7,700,000 (average annual rate of natural increase: 2.9%); birth rate: 49/1000; infant mortality rate: 127/1000; density per square mile: 31
Capital and largest city (est. 1982): Mogadishu, 700,000
Monetary unit: Somali shilling
Language: Somali (official), Arabic, English, Italian
Religion: Islam (Sunni)
National name: Al Jumhouriya As-Somalya al-Dimocradia
Literacy rate: 11.6% (government est.)
Economic summary: Gross domestic product (1988): $1.7 billion; $210 per capita; −1.4% real growth rate. Arable land: 2%. Principal products: livestock, bananas, sorghum, cereals, sugar cane, maize. Labor force: 2,200,000; very few are skilled laborers. A few small industries: sugar refining, textiles, petroleum refining. Natural resources: uranium. Exports: livestock, skins and hides, bananas. Imports: textiles, cereals, construction materials and equipment, petroleum products. Major trading partners: Saudi Arabia, Italy, U.S., U.K.

Geography. Somalia, situated in the Horn of Africa, lies along the Gulf of Aden and the Indian Ocean. It is bounded by Djibouti in the northwest, Ethiopia in the west, and Kenya in the southwest. In area it is slightly smaller than Texas.

Generally arid and barren, Somalia has two chief rivers, the Shebelle and the Juba.

Government. Maj. Gen. Mohamed Siad Barre took power on Oct. 21, 1969, in a coup that established a Supreme Revolutionary Council as the governing body, replacing a parliamentary government. On July 1, 1976, Barre dissolved the Council, naming its members to the Somali Socialist Party, organized that day as the nation's only legal political party. In December 1979, a 171-member People's Assembly was elected under a new Constitution adopted in August. The Assembly confirmed Barre as President for a six-year term. He was re-elected in 1986.

History. From the 7th to the 10th century, Arab and Persian trading posts were established along the coast of present-day Somalia. Nomadic tribes occupied the interior, occasionally pushing into Ethiopian territory. In the 16th century, Turkish rule extended to the northern coast and the Sultans of Zanzibar gained control in the south.

After British occupation of Aden in 1839, the Somali coast became its source of food. The French established a coaling station in 1862 at the site of Djibouti and the Italians planted a settlement in Eritrea. Egypt, which for a time claimed Turkish rights in the area, was succeeded by Britain. By 1920, a British protectorate and an Italian protectorate occupied what is now Somalia. The British ruled the entire area after 1941, with Italy returning in 1950 to serve as United Nations trustee for its former territory.

In mid-1960, Britain and Italy granted independence to their respective sectors, enabling the two to join as the Republic of Somalia on July 1. Somalia broke diplomatic relations with Britain in 1963 when the British granted the Somali-populated Northern Frontier District of Kenya to the Republic of Kenya.

On Oct. 15, 1969, President Abdi Rashid Ali Shermarke was assassinated and the army seized power, dissolving the legislature and arresting all government leaders. Maj. Gen. Mohamed Siad Barre, as President of a renamed Somali Democratic Republic, leaned heavily toward the U.S.S.R.

In 1977, Somalia openly backed rebels in the easternmost area of Ethiopia, the Ogaden desert, which had been seized by Ethiopia at the turn of the century.

Somalia acknowledged defeat in an eight-month war against the Ethiopians, having lost much of its 32,000-man army and most of its tanks and planes.

A U.S. announcement on Jan. 9, 1980, that bases for U.S. ships and planes in the Indian Ocean would be sought in Somalia, Oman, and Kenya, brought a request from Somalia for $1 billion worth of modern arms and an equal amount of economic aid. In August, an agreement was signed giving the U.S. use of military bases in Somalia in return for $25 million in military aid in 1981 and more in subsequent years. In 1988, guerrillas in the north went on the offensive and threatened the northern regional capital.

President Siad Barre fled the country in late January 1991. His departure left Somalia in the hands of a number of clan-based guerrilla groups, none of which trust each other. The installation of Ali Mahdi Mohammed in the capital by the United Somali Congress, based on the Hawye clan, as interim president won the disapproval of other groups. Most of the south is controlled by the Somali Patriotic Movement

SOUTH AFRICA

Republic of South Africa
President: F.W. de Klerk (1989)
Area: 471,440 sq mi. (1,221,030 sq km)
Population (est. mid-1991): 40,600,000 (average annual rate of natural increase: 2.7%); birth rate: 35/1000; infant mortality rate: 52/1000; density per square mile: 86
Administrative capital: Pretoria
Legislative capital: Cape Town
Judicial capital: Bloemfontein
Largest metropolitan areas: Cape Peninsula (Cape Town and surroundings), 1,911,500; Johannesburg/Randburg, 1,609,500; East Rand (Springs, Germiston and surroundings), 1,038,000; Durban/Pinetown/Inanda, 982,075; Pretoria/Wonderboom/Shoshanguve, 822,075
Monetary unit: Rand
Languages: English, Afrikaans (official); Xhosa, Zulu, other African tongues
Religions: Christian; Hindu; Islam
National name: Republic of South Africa
Literacy rate: 99% (whites), 50% blacks (govt. est.)
Economic summary: Gross domestic product (1988): $83.5 billion; $2,380 per capita; 3.2% real growth rate. Arable land: 11.59%. Principal products: corn, wool, wheat, sugar cane, fruits, vegetables. Labor force: 11,000,000; 29% in industry and commerce. Major products: gold, chromium, diamonds, assembled automobiles, machinery, textiles, iron and steel, chemicals, fertilizer. Natural resources: gold, diamonds, platinum, uranium, coal, iron ore, phosphates, manganese. Exports: gold, diamonds, minerals and metals, food, chemicals. Imports: motor vehicle parts, machinery, metals, chemicals, textiles, scientific instruments. Major trading partners: U.S., Germany, other E.C., Japan, U.K., Hong Kong.

Geography. South Africa, on the continent's southern tip, is washed by the Atlantic Ocean on the west and by the Indian Ocean on the south and east. Its neighbors are Namibia in the northwest, Zimbabwe and Botswana in the north, and Mozambique and Swaziland in the northeast. The kingdom of Lesotho forms an enclave within the southeastern part of South Africa. Bophuthatswana, Transkei, Ciskei, and Venda are independent states within South Africa, which occupies an area nearly three times that of California.

The country has a high interior plateau, or veld, nearly half of which averages 4,000 feet (1,219 m) in elevation.

There are no important mountain ranges, although the Great Escarpment, separating the veld from the coastal plain, rises to over 11,000 feet (3,350 m) in the Drakensberg Mountains in the east. The principal river is the Orange, rising in Lesotho and flowing westward for 1,300 miles (2,092 km) to the Atlantic.

The southernmost point of Africa is Cape Agulhas, located in Cape Province about 100 miles (161 km) southeast of the Cape of Good Hope.

Government. A new Constitution in 1984 created a new office of Executive State President, with potentially authoritarian powers. Pieter W. Botha, Prime Minister since 1978, was sworn in as President on Sept. 14, 1984. The President has the power to act at his own discretion (e.g. appoint cabinet members) as well as power that has to be exercised in consultation with the cabinet (e.g. declare war, ratify treaties).

Negotiations are to be initiated between parliamentary and non–parliamentary organizations with the ultimate purpose of establishing a constitution for a non-racial and democratic South Africa based on universal franchise. With regard to the participation in the negotiation process by the six independent homelands and the four independent states within the borders of South Africa, their individual governments will independently decide whether to take part in the negotiations or not and/or whether their states will form part of a unified South Africa once a new constitution has been effected.

The new Constitution brought whites, Indians, and coloreds (mixed-race) into a racially divided Parliament made up of three separate chambers for different racial groups. It provides for selection of the President by an Electoral College made up of representatives from the three chambers. Ten "Bantustans," or black homelands, have unicameral legislatures elected by black voters.

History. The Dutch East India Company landed the first settlers on the Cape of Good Hope in 1652, launching a colony that by the end of the 18th century numbered only about 15,000. Known as Boers or Afrikaners, speaking a Dutch dialect known as Afrikaans, the settlers as early as 1795 tried to establish an independent republic.

After occupying the Cape Colony in that year, Britain took permanent possession in 1814 at the end of the Napoleonic wars, bringing in 5,000 settlers. Anglicization of government and the freeing of slaves in 1833 drove about 12,000 Afrikaners to make the "great trek" north and east into African tribal territory, where they established the republics of the Transvaal and the Orange Free State.

The discovery of diamonds in 1867 and gold nine years later brought an influx of "outlanders" into the republics and spurred Cecil Rhodes to plot annexation. Rhodes's scheme of sparking an "outlander" rebellion to which an armed party under Leander Starr Jameson would ride to the rescue misfired in 1895, forcing Rhodes to resign as prime minister of the Cape colony. What British expansionists called the "inevitable" war with the Boers eventually broke out on Oct. 11, 1899.

The defeat of the Boers in 1902 led in 1910 to the Union of South Africa, composed of four provinces, the two former republics and the old Cape and Natal colonies. Louis Botha, a Boer, became the first Prime Minister.

Jan Christiaan Smuts brought the nation into World War II on the Allied side against Nationalist opposition, and South Africa became a charter member of the United Nations in 1945, but refused to sign the Universal Declaration of Human Rights. Apartheid—racial separation—dominated domestic politics as the Nationalists gained power and imposed greater restrictions on Bantus, Coloreds, and Asians.

Afrikaner hostility to Britain triumphed in 1961 with the declaration on May 31 of the Republic of South Africa and the severing of ties with the Commonwealth. Nationalist Prime Minister H. F. Verwoerd's government in 1963 asserted the power to restrict freedom of those who opposed rigid racial laws. Three years later, amid increasing racial tension and criticism from the outside world, Verwoerd was assassinated. His Nationalist successor, Balthazar J. Vorster, launched a campaign of conciliation toward conservative black African states, offering development loans and trade concessions.

A scandal led to Vorster's resignation on June 4, 1978. Pieter W. Botha succeeded him as Prime Minister, and became President on Sept. 14, 1984.

Protests against apartheid by militant blacks, beginning in the latter half of 1984, led to a state of emergency being declared twice. The first, on July 20, 1985, covered 36 cities and towns and gave the police powers to make arrests without warrants and to detain people indefinitely. The second, declared on June 12, 1986, covered the whole nation. It gave the police a similar extension of powers and banned "subversive" press reports. It was extended for another year in June 1988.

Elections on May 7, 1987, increased the power of Botha's Nationalist party while enabling the far-right Conservative Party to replace the liberal Progressives as the official opposition. The results of the whites-only vote indicated a strong conservative reaction against Botha's policy of limited reform.

A stroke led Botha to step down as leader of his party in 1989 in favor of Frederick de Klerk. De Klerk has accelerated the pace of reform. He unbanned the African National Congress, the principal anti-apartheid organization, and released Nelson Mandela, the ANC deputy chief, after 27 1/2 years imprisonment. Negotiations between the government and the ANC have commenced.

On June 5, 1991 the parliament scrapped the country's apartheid laws concerning property ownership. On June 17 the parliament did the same for the Population Registration Act of 1950, which classified all South Africans at birth by race.

President Bush in early July announced the U.S. was lifting its economic sanctions.

BOPHUTHATSWANA

Republic of Bophuthatswana
President: Kgosi Lucas Mangope (1977)
Area: 15,573 sq mi. (40,333 sq km)
Population (est. 1988): 1,300,000 (average annual growth rate: 2.8%)
Density per square mile: 83.5
Capital: Mmabatho
Largest city (est. 1987): Mabopane, 100,000
Monetary unit: South African rand
Languages: Setswana, English, Afrikaans
Religions: Methodist, Lutheran, Anglican, Presbyterian, Dutch Reformed, Roman Catholic, A.M.E.

Geography. Bophuthatswana consists of six discontinuous areas within the boundaries of South Africa. Most of them share a common border with Botswana.

Government. The republic has a 108-member Legislative Assembly, three quarters of whom are elected and the other 24 nominated by regional authorities. President Mangope's Democratic Party is the majority party.

History. Bophuthatswana was given independence by South Africa on Dec. 6, 1977, following Transkei as the second "homeland" to opt for independence. The new state and Transkei are recognized only by South Africa and each other.

Mangope, as chief minister in the pre-independence period, sought linkage of the seven units into a consolidated area, and has succeeded because Marico Corridor and adjoining farmers have been added and many more farms will be released. A second issue, the citizenship of Batswana in South Africa who wished to remain South African nationals, was settled by enabling them to have citizenship in South African homelands not yet independent.

About two-thirds of the population of Bophuthats-wana live permanently in Bophuthatswana and thousands commute daily to South Africa.

Economy. Bophuthatswana is richer than many other South African homelands, as it has more than half of the republic's platinum deposits. All foreign trade is included with South Africa's, and it is economically interdependent at present with that country.

CISKEI

Republic of Ciskei
Head of State: Brig. Gen. Oupa Gqozo (1990)
Area: 3,282 sq mi. (8,500 sq km)
Population (est. 1982): 675,000
Density per square mile: 205.7
Capital (est. 1980): Zwelitsha, 30,750
Largest city (est. 1981): Mdantsane, 159,000
Monetary unit: South African rand
Languages: Xhosa (official) and English
Religions: Methodist, Lutheran, Anglican, and Bantu Christian

Geography. Ciskei is surrounded by South Africa on three sides, with the Indian Ocean on the south. From a subtropical coastal strip, the land rises through grasslands to the mountainous escarpment that edges the South African interior plateau.

Government. Ruled by a military council installed after Gen Oupa Gqozo seized power in a March 1990 coup. South Africa's State President retains the power to legislate by proclamation and has veto power over the budget.

History. Oral tradition ascribes the origin of the Cape Nguni peoples to the central lakes area of Africa. They arrived in what is now Ciskei in the mid-17th century. White settlers from the Cape Colony first entered the territory a century later, but the Dutch East India Colony sought unsuccessfully to discourage white penetration. Nine wars between whites and the inhabitants, by now known as Xhosas, occurred between 1779 and 1878.

A Ciskeian territorial authority was established in 1961, with 84 chiefs and an executive council exercising limited self-government. In 1972, 20 elected members were added to the legislative assembly and a chief minister and six cabinet members elected by the assembly to function as an executive.

A proposed Constitution was approved by referendum on Oct. 30, 1980, and independence ceremonies held on Dec. 4. No government outside South Africa recognized the new state.

Economy. A subsistence agricultural economy has been superseded by commuter and migratory labor, which accounted for 64% of national income in 1977. There is some light industry and a potential for exploitation of limestone and other minerals.

TRANSKEI

Republic of Transkei
President: Chief Tutor N. Ndamase (1986)
Head of Military Council: Maj. Gen. Bantu Holomisa (1987)
Area: 15,831 sq mi. (41,002 sq km)
Population (est. 1986): 3,609,962 (growth rate: 2.2%)
Density per square mile: 151.6
Capital (est. 1989): Umtala, 57,796

Monetary unit: South African rand
Languages: English, Xhosa, Southern Sotho
Religions: Christian, 66%; tribal, 24%
Economic summary: Gross domestic product: $150 million. Per capita income: $86. Principal agricultural products: tea, corn, sorghum, dry beans. Major industrial products: timber, textiles. Natural resource: timber. Exports: timber, tea, sacks. Imports: foodstuffs, machines, equipment. Major trading partner: South Africa.

Geography. Transkei occupies three discontinuous enclaves within southeast South Africa that add up to twice the size of Massachusetts. It has a 270-mile (435 km) coastline on the Indian Ocean. The capital, Umtala, is connected by rail to the South African port of East London, 100 miles (161 km) to the southwest.

Government. Transkei was granted independence by South Africa as of Oct. 26, 1976. A constitution called for organization of a parliament composed of 77 chiefs and 75 elected members, with a ceremonial president and executive power in the hands of a prime minister.

The Organization of African States and the chairman of the United Nations Special Committee Against Apartheid denounced the new state as a sham and urged governments not to recognize it.

History. British rule was established over the Transkei region between 1866 and 1894, and the Transkeian Territories were formed in 1903. Under the Native Land Act of 1913, the Territories were reserved for black occupation. In 1963, Transkei was given internal self-government and a legislature that elected Paramount Chief Kaiser Matanzima as Chief Minister, a post he retained in elections in 1968 and 1973. Instability led to a coup in Dec. 1987.

Economy. Some 60% of Transkei is cultivated, producing corn, wheat, beans, and sorghum. Grazing is important. Some light industry has been established.

VENDA

Republic of Venda
Chairman of the Council of National Unity: Col. Gabriel Mutheiwana Ramushwana (1990)
Area: 2,510 sq mi. (6,500 sq km)
Population (est. 1982): 400,000 (average annual growth rate: 2.4%)
Density per square mile: 214.5
Capital: Thohoyandou
Largest town (est. 1980): Makearela, 2,500
Monetary unit: South African rand
Languages: Venda, English, Afrikaans
Religions: Christian, tribal
Economic summary: Gross domestic product: $156 million. Per capita income: $312. Principal agricultural products: meat, fruit, sisal, corn. Major industrial products: timber, graphite, magnetite.

Geography. Venda is composed of two noncontiguous territories in northeast South Africa with a total area of about half that of Connecticut. It is mountainous but fertile, well-watered land, with a climate ranging from tropical to subtropical.

Government. The third of South Africa's homelands to be granted independence, Venda became a separate republic on Sept. 13, 1979, unrecognized by any government other than South Africa and its sister homelands, Transkei and Bophuthatswana. The President is popularly elected. An 84-seat legislature is half elected, half appointed.

History. The first European reached Venda in 1816, but the isolation of the area prevented its involvement in the wars of the 19th century between blacks and whites and with other tribes. Venda came under South African administration after the Boer War in 1902. Limited home rule was granted in 1962. Chief Patrick R. Mphephu, leader of one of the 27 tribes that historically made up the Venda nation, became Chief Minister of the interim government in 1973 and President upon independence in 1979. There has been a military regime in power since April 5, 1990.

SOVIET UNION

Union of Soviet Socialist Republics
President: Mikhail S. Gorbachev (1990)
Vice President: Gennady Yanayev (1990)
Prime Minister: Ivan Silayev (1991)
Area[1]: 8,580,545 sq mi. (22,223,509 sq km)
Population (est. 1991[1]): 284,110,000 (average annual rate of natural increase: .8%); birth rate: 18/1000; infant mortality rate: 23/1000; density per square mile[1]: 33.1
Capital: Moscow
Largest cities (1989): Moscow, 8,769,000; St. Petersburg, 4,456,000; Kiev, 2,587,000; Tashkent, 2,073,000; Baku, 1,757,000; Kharkov, 1,611,000; Minsk, 1,589,000; Novosibirsk, 1,436,000; Nizhny Novgorod, 1,438,000; Sverdlovsk, 1,367,000; Tbilisi, 1,260,000; Kuybyshev, 1,257,000; Dnepropetrovsk, 1,179,000
Monetary unit: Ruble
Languages: Russian, Ukranian, Uzbek, Byelorussian, Kazak, Tatar
Religions: Russian Orthodox (predominant), 20%; Islam, 10%; Roman Catholic, Protestant, Georgian Orthodox, Armenian Orthodox, 7%; Jewish, less than 1%; atheist 60% (est.)
National name: Soyuz Sovyetskikh Sotsialisticheskikh Respublik
Literacy rate: 99%
Economic summary[2]: Gross national product (1989 est.): $2,659 billion; $9,211 per capita; 1.4% real growth rate. Arable land: 10%. Principal products: wheat, rye, corn, oats, potatoes, sugar beets, cotton and flax, cattle, pigs, sheep. Labor force: 152,300,000 civilians; 80% in industry. Major products: ferrous and nonferrous metals, fuels and power, building materials, chemicals, machinery. Natural resources: fossil fuels, water power, timber, manganese, lead, zinc, nickel, mercury, potash, phosphate. Exports: petroleum and petroleum products, natural gas, machinery and equipment, manufactured goods. Imports: grain, machinery and equipment, foodstuffs, steel products, consumer manufactures. Major trading partners: E. European countries; E.C., U.S., Cuba, China.

1. Does not include the total areas and population of the former Baltic republics. 2. Includes former Baltic republics.

Geography. The U.S.S.R. is the largest unbroken political unit in the world, occupying more than one-seventh of the land surface of the globe. The greater part of its territory is a vast plain stretching from eastern Europe to the Pacific Ocean. This plain, relieved only occasionally by low mountain ranges (no tably the Urals), consists of three zones running east and west: the frozen marshy tundra of the Arctic; the more temperate forest belt; and the steppes or prairies to the south, which in southern Soviet Asia become sandy deserts.

The topography is more varied in the south, particularly in the Caucasus between the Caspian and

Republics of the U.S.S.R.

Republic and Capital	Area sq mi.	Population 1989 census (thousands)
Russian S.F.S.R. (Moscow)	6,592,800	147,400
Ukraine (Kiev)	233,100	51,707
Kazakhstan (Alma-Ata)	1,049,200	16,536
Byelorussia (Minsk)	80,200	10,200
Uzbekistan (Tashkent)	172,700	19,905
Georgia (Tbilisi)	26,900	5,443
Azerbaijan (Baku)	33,400	7,038
Moldavia (Kishinyov)	13,000	4,338
Kirghizia (Pishpek)	76,600	4,290
Tadzhikistan (Dushanbe)	55,300	5,109
Armenia (Yerevan)	11,500	3,288
Turkmenistan (Ashkhabad)	188,500	3,534

Black Seas, and in the Tien-Pamir mountain system bordering Afghanistan, Sinkiang, and Mongolia. Mountains (Stanovoi and Kolyma) and great rivers (Amur, Yenisei, Lena) also break up the sweep of the plain in Siberia.

In the west, the major rivers are the Volga, Dnieper, Don, Kama, and Southern Bug.

Government. The creation of a new supreme legislature—the 2,250-member Congress of People's Deputies—was approved at the 19th Communist Party Conference, which opened on June 28, 1988. It elected Gorbachev as President in 1990.

Following the abortive coup, the Congress in September 1991 established a transitional government consisting of an executive State Council and two subordinate bodies: a reconstituted parliament and an Inter-Republic Economic Committee. The State Council, led by President Gorbachev, consists of himself and leaders of the ten participating republics. The still vague plan for a new parliament calls for a Council of Republics, wherein each republic is allotted one vote, and a lower-house Council of Union, in which each republic's number of delegates and voting power is in proportion to its population. The Economic Committee, according to the tentative plan, is to oversee the running of the economy on a daily basis. Its leadership and membership are yet to be determined.

At present the State Council is charged with governing the country until the adoption of a new constitution and a new union treaty, which may in turn alter the above arrangement. By accepting the transitional plans the Congress of People's Deputies effectively voted to disband their organization.

History. Tradition says the Viking Rurik came to Russia in A.D. 862 and founded the first Russian dynasty in Novgorod. The various tribes were united by the spread of Christianity in the 10th and 11th centuries; Vladimir "the Saint" was converted in 988. During the 11th century, the grand dukes of Kiev held such centralizing power as existed. In 1240, Kiev was destroyed by the Mongols, and the Russian territory was split into numerous smaller dukedoms, early dukes of Moscow extended their dominions through their office of tribute collector for the Mongols.

In the late 15th century, Duke Ivan III acquired Novgorod and Tver and threw off the Mongol yoke. Ivan IV, the Terrible (1533–84), first Muscovite Tsar, is considered to have founded the Russian state. He crushed the power of rival princes and boyars (great landowners), but Russia remained largely medieval until the reign of Peter the Great (1689–1725), grand-

son of the first Romanov Tsar, Michael (1613–45). Peter made extensive reforms aimed at westernization and, through his defeat of Charles XII of Sweden at the Battle of Poltava in 1709, he extended Russia's boundaries to the west.

Catherine the Great (1762–96) continued Peter's westernization program and also expanded Russian territory, acquiring the Crimea and part of Poland. During the reign of Alexander I (1801–25), Napoleon's attempt to subdue Russia was defeated (1812–13), and new territory was gained, including Finland (1809) and Bessarabia (1812). Alexander originated the Holy Alliance, which for a time crushed Europe's rising liberal movement.

Alexander II (1855–81) pushed Russia's borders to the Pacific and into central Asia. Serfdom was abolished in 1861, but heavy restrictions were imposed on the emancipated class. Revolutionary strikes following Russia's defeat in the war with Japan forced Nicholas II (1894–1917) to grant a representative national body (Duma), elected by narrowly limited suffrage. It met for the first time in 1906, little influencing Nicholas in his reactionary course.

World War I demonstrated tsarist corruption and inefficiency and only patriotism held the poorly equipped army together for a time. Disorders broke out in Petrograd (renamed Leningrad now St. Petersburg) in March 1917, and defection of the Petrograd garrison launched the revolution. Nicholas II was forced to abdicate on March 15, 1917, and he and his family were killed by revolutionists on July 16, 1918.

A provisional government under the successive premierships of Prince Lvov and a moderate, Alexander Kerensky, lost ground to the radical, or Bolshevik, wing of the Socialist Democratic Labor Party. On Nov. 7, 1917, the Bolshevik revolution, engineered by N. Lenin[1] and Leon Trotsky, overthrew the Kerensky government and authority was vested in a Council of People's Commissars, with Lenin as Premier.

The humiliating Treaty of Brest-Litovsk (March 3, 1918) concluded the war with Germany, but civil war and foreign intervention delayed Communist control of all Russia until 1920. A brief war with Poland in 1920 resulted in Russian defeat.

The Union of Soviet Socialist Republics was established as a federation on Dec. 30, 1922.

The death of Lenin on Jan. 21, 1924, precipitated an intraparty struggle between Joseph Stalin, General Secretary of the party, and Trotsky, who favored swifter socialization at home and fomentation of revolution abroad. Trotsky was dismissed as Commissar of War in 1925 and banished from the Soviet Union in 1929. He was murdered in Mexico City on Aug. 21, 1940, by a political agent.

Stalin further consolidated his power by a series of purges in the late 1930s, liquidating prominent party leaders and military officers. Stalin assumed the premiership May 6, 1941.

Soviet foreign policy, at first friendly toward Germany and antagonistic toward Britain and France and then, after Hitler's rise to power in 1933, becoming anti-Fascist and pro-League of Nations, took an abrupt turn on Aug. 24, 1939, with the signing of a nonaggression pact with Nazi Germany. The next month, Moscow joined in the German attack on Poland, seizing territory later incorporated into the Ukrainian and Byelorussian S.S.R.'s. The war with Finland, 1939–40, added territory to the Karelian

---

1. N. Lenin was the pseudonym taken by Vladimir Ilich Ulyanov. It is sometimes given as Nikolai Lenin or V. Lenin.

Rulers of Russia Since 1533

Name	Born	Ruled[1]	Name	Born	Ruled[1]
Ivan IV the Terrible	1530	1533–1584	Alexander II	1818	1855–1881
Theodore I	1557	1584–1598	Alexander III	1845	1881–1894
Boris Godunov	c.1551	1598–1605	Nicholas II	1868	1894–1917 [7]
Theodore II	1589	1605–1605			
Demetrius I[2]	?	1605–1606	**PROVISIONAL GOVERNMENT**		
Basil IV Shuiski	?	1606–1610 [3]	**(PREMIERS)**		
"Time of Troubles"	—	1610–1613	Prince Georgi Lvov	1861	1917–1917
Michael Romanov	1596	1613–1645	Alexander Kerensky	1881	1917–1917
Alexis I	1629	1645–1676			
Theodore III	1656	1676–1682	**POLITICAL LEADERS**		
Ivan V[4]	1666	1682–1689 [5]	N. Lenin	1870	1917–1924
Peter I the Great[4]	1672	1682–1725	Aleksei Rykov	1881	1924–1930
Catherine I	c.1684	1725–1727	Vyacheslav Molotov	1890	1930–1941
Peter II	1715	1727–1730	Joseph Stalin[8]	1879	1941–1953
Anna	1693	1730–1740	Georgi M. Malenkov	1902	1953–1955
Ivan VI	1740	1740–1741 [6]	Nikolai A. Bulganin	1895	1955–1958
Elizabeth	1709	1741–1762	Nikita S. Khrushchev	1894	1958–1964
Peter III	1728	1762–1762	Leonid I. Brezhnev	1906	1964–1982
Catherine II the Great	1729	1762–1796	Yuri V. Andropov	1914	1982–1984
Paul I	1754	1796–1801	Konstantin U. Chernenko	1912	1984–1985
Alexander I	1777	1801–1825	Mikhail S. Gorbachev	1931	1985–
Nicholas I	1796	1825–1855			

1. For Tsars through Nicholas II, year of end of rule is also that of death, unless otherwise indicated. 2. Also known as Pseudo–Demetrius. 3. Died 1612. 4. Ruled jointly until 1689, when Ivan was deposed. 5. Died 1696. 6. Died 1764. 7. Killed 1918. 8. General Secretary of Communist Party, 1924–53.

S.S.R. set up March 31, 1940; the annexation of Bessarabia and Bukovina from Romania became part of the new Moldavian S.S.R. on Aug. 2, 1940; and the annexation of the Baltic republics of Estonia, Latvia, and Lithuania in June 1940 created the 14th, 15th, and 16th Soviet Republics. The illegal annexation of the Baltic republics was never recognized by the U.S. for the 51 years leading up to Soviet recognition of Estonia, Latvia and Lithuania's independence on September 6, 1991. (*See* special Current Events, pages 792–793.) (The number of so-called "Union" republics was reduced to 15 in 1956 when the Karelian S.S.R. became one of the 20 Autonomous Soviet Socialist Republics based on ethnic groups.)

The Soviet-German collaboration ended abruptly with a lightning attack by Hitler on June 22, 1941, which seized 500,000 square miles of Russian territory before Soviet defenses, aided by U.S. and British arms, could halt it. The Soviet resurgence at Stalingrad from November 1942 to February 1943 marked the turning point in a long battle, ending in the final offensive of January 1945.

Then, after denouncing a 1941 nonaggression pact with Japan in April 1945, when Allied forces were nearing victory in the Pacific, the Soviet Union declared war on Japan on Aug. 8, 1945, and quickly occupied Manchuria, Karafuto, and the Kurile islands.

The U.S.S.R. built a cordon of Communist states running from Poland in the north to Albania and Bulgaria in the south, including East Germany, Czechoslovakia, Hungary, and Romania, composed of the territories Soviet troops occupied at the war's end. With its Eastern front solidified, the Soviet Union launched a political offensive against the non-Communist West, moving first to block the Western access to Berlin. The Western powers countered with an airlift, completed unification of West Germany, and organized the defense of Western Europe in the North Atlantic Treaty Organization.

Stalin died on March 6, 1953, and was succeeded the next day by G. M. Malenkov as Premier. His chief rivals for power—Lavrenti P. Beria (chief of the secret police), Nikolai A. Bulganin, and Lazar M. Kaganovich—were named first deputies. Beria was purged in July and executed on Dec. 23, 1953.

The new power in the Kremlin was Nikita S. Khrushchev, First Secretary of the party.

Khrushchev formalized the Eastern European system into a Council for Mutual Economic Assistance (Comecon) and a Warsaw Pact Treaty Organization as a counterweight to NATO.

In its technological race with the U.S., the Soviet Union exploded a hydrogen bomb in 1953, developed an intercontinental ballistic missile by 1957, sent the first satellite into space (Sputnik I) in 1957, and put Yuri Gagarin in the first orbital flight around the earth in 1961.

Khrushchev's downfall stemmed from his decision to place Soviet nuclear missiles in Cuba and then, when challenged by the U.S., backing down and removing the weapons. He was also blamed for the ideological break with China after 1963.

Khrushchev was forced into retirement on Oct. 15, 1964, and was replaced by Leonid I. Brezhnev as First Secretary of the Party and Aleksei N. Kosygin as Premier.

President Nixon visited the U.S.S.R. for summit talks in May 1972, concluding agreements on strategic-arms limitation and a declaration of principles on future U.S.-Soviet relations.

President Carter, actively pursuing both human rights and disarmament, joined with the Soviet Union in September 1977 to declare that the SALT I accord, which would have expired Oct. 1 without further action, be maintained in effect while the two sides sought a new agreement (SALT II).

Brezhnev's 1977 election to the presidency followed publication of a new Constitution supplanting the one adopted in 1936. It specified the dominance of the Communist Party, previously unstated.

Carter and the ailing Brezhnev signed the SALT II treaty in Vienna on June 18, 1979, setting ceilings on each nation's arsenal of intercontinental ballistic missiles. Doubts about Senate ratification grew, and became a certainty on Dec. 27, when Soviet troops invaded Afghanistan. Despite protests from the Moslem and Western worlds, Moscow insisted that Afghan President Hafizullah Amin had asked for aid in quelling a rebellion.

In the face of evidence that Amin had been liquidated by Soviet advisers before the troops arrived, the Soviet Union vetoed a Security Council resolution on Jan. 7, 1980, that called for a withdrawal. Carter ordered a freeze on grain exports and high-technology equipment.

On Jan. 20, Carter called for a world boycott of the Summer Olympic Games scheduled for Moscow. The boycott, less than complete, nevertheless marred the first Olympics to be held in Moscow as the United States, Canada, Japan, and to a partial extent all the western allies except France and Italy shunned the event.

The Soviet Union maintained a stony defense in the face of criticism from Western Europe and the U.S., and a summit meeting of 37 Islamic nations that unanimously condemned the "imperialist invasion" of Afghanistan.

Despite the tension between Moscow and Washington, Strategic Arms Reduction Talks (START) began in Geneva between U.S. and Soviet delegations in mid-1982. Negotiations on intermediate missile reduction also continued in Geneva.

On November 10, 1982, Soviet radio and television announced the death of Leonid Brezhnev. Yuri V. Andropov, who formerly headed the K.G.B., was chosen to succeed Brezhnev as General Secretary. By mid-June 1983, Andropov had assumed all of Brezhnev's three titles.

The Soviet Union broke off both the START talks and the parallel negotiations on European-based missiles in November 1983 in protest against the deployment of medium-range U.S. missiles in Western Europe.

After months of illness, Andropov died in February 1984. Konstantin U. Chernenko, a 72-year-old party stalwart who had been close to Brezhnev, succeeded him as General Secretary and, by mid-April, had also assumed the title of President. In the months following Chernenko's assumption of power, the Kremlin took on a hostile mood toward the West of a kind rarely seen since the height of the cold war 30 years before. Led by Moscow, all the Soviet bloc countries except Romania boycotted the 1984 Summer Olympic Games in Los Angeles—tit-for-tat for the U.S.-led boycott of the 1980 Moscow Games, in the view of most observers.

After 13 months in office, Chernenko died on March 10, 1985. He had been ill much of the time and left only a minor imprint on Soviet history.

Chosen to succeed him as Soviet leader was Mikhail S. Gorbachev, at 54 the youngest man to take charge of the Soviet Union since Stalin. Under Gorbachev, the Soviet Union began its long-awaited shift to a new generation of leadership. Unlike his immediate predecessors, Gorbachev did not also assume the title of President but wielded power from the post of party General Secretary. In a surprise move, Gorbachev elevated Andrei Gromyko, 75, for 28 years the Soviet Union's stony-faced Foreign Minister, to the largely ceremonial post of President. He installed a younger man with no experience in foreign affairs, Eduard Shevardnadze, 57, as Foreign Minister.

A new round of U.S. Soviet arms reduction negotiations began in Geneva in March 1985, this time involving three types of weapons systems.

The Soviet Union took much criticism in early 1986 over the April 24 meltdown at the Chernobyl nuclear plant and its reluctance to give out any information on the accident.

In June 1987, Gorbachev obtained the support of the Central Committee for proposals that would loosen some government controls over the economy and in June 1988, an unusually open party conference approved several resolutions for changes in the structure of the Soviet system. These included a shift of some power from the Party to local soviets, a ten-year limit on the terms of elected government and party officials, and an alteration in the office of the President to give it real power in domestic and 'foreign policy. Gorbachev was elected President in 1989. The elections to the Congress were the first competitive elections in the Soviet Union since 1917. Dissident candidates won a surprisingly large minority although pro-Government deputies maintained a strong lock on the Supreme Soviet.

Glasnost took a new turn when Lithuania declared its independence. The central government responded with an economic blockade. After a stalemate, Lithuania suspended, but didn't revoke, its declaration in return for a lifting of the blockade.

The possible beginning of the fragmentation of the Communist party took place when Boris Yeltsin, leader of the Russian S.S.R. who urges faster reform, left the Communist party along with other radicals.

In March 1991 the Soviet people were asked to vote on a referendum on national unity engineered by President Gorbachev. The resultant victory for the federal government was tempered by the separate approval in Russia for the creation of a popularly-elected republic presidency. In addition, six republics boycotted the vote.

The bitter election contest for the Russian presidency principally between Yeltsin and a Communist loyalist resulted in a major victory for Yeltsin. He took the oath of office for the new position on July 10.

Reversing his relative hard-line position adopted in the autumn of 1990, Gorbachev together with leaders of nine Soviet republics signed an accord, called the Union Treaty, which was meant to preserve the unity of the nation. In exchange the federal government would have turned over control of industrial and natural resources to the individual republics.

An attempted coup d'état took place on August 19 orchestrated by a group of eight senior officials calling itself the State Committee on the State of Emergency. Boris Yeltsin, held up in the Russian Parliament building, defiantly called for a general strike. The next day huge crowds demonstrated in Leningrad, and Yeltsin supporters fortified barricades surrounding the Parliament building. On August 21 the coup committee disbanded, and at least some of its members attempted to flee Moscow. The Soviet Parliament formally reinstated Gorbachev as President. Two days later he resigned from his position as General Secretary of the Communist Party and recommended that its Central Committee be disbanded. On August 29 the Parliament approved the suspension of all Communist Party activities pending an investigation of its role in the failed coup.

SPAIN

Kingdom of Spain
Ruler: King Juan Carlos I (1975)
Prime Minister: Felipe González Márquez (1982)
Area: 194,884 sq mi. (504,750 km)[1]
Population (est. mid-1991): 39,000,000 (average annual growth rate: 0.2%); birth rate: 11/1000; infant mortality rate: 8.3/1000; density per square mile: 200

Capital: Madrid
Largest cities (est. 1987): Madrid, 3,158,800; Barcelona, 1,752,627; Valencia, 774,748; Seville, 645,817
Monetary unit: Peseta
Languages: Spanish, Basque, Catalan, Galician
Religion: Roman Catholic, 99%
National name: Reino de España
Literacy rate: 97%
Economic summary: Gross national product (1989 est.): $398.7 billion; $10,100 per capita; 4.8% real growth rate. Arable land: 31%. Principal products: cereals, vegetables, citrus fruits, wine, olives and olive oil, livestock. Labor force: 14,621,000; 24% in industry. Major products: processed foods, textiles, footwear, petro-chemicals, steel, automobiles, ships. Natural resources: coal, lignite, water power, uranium, mercury, pyrites, fluorspar, gypsum, iron ore, zinc, lead, tungsten, copper. Exports: foodstuffs, live animals, wood, footwear, machinery, chemicals. Imports: machinery and transportation equipment, chemicals, petroleum, timber, iron, steel. Major trading partners: Western European nations, U.S., Middle Eastern countries.

1. Including the Balearic and Canary Islands.

Geography. Spain occupies 85% of the Iberian Peninsula in southwestern Europe, which it shares with Portugal; France is to the northeast, separated by the Pyrenees. The Bay of Biscay lies to the north, the Atlantic Ocean to the west, and the Mediterranean Sea to the south and east: Africa is less than 10 miles (16 km) south at the Strait of Gibraltar.

A broad central plateau slopes to the south and east, crossed by a series of mountain ranges and river valleys.

Principal rivers are the Ebro in the northeast, the Tajo in the central region, and the Guadalquivir in the south.

Off Spain's east coast in the Mediterranean are the Balearic Islands (1,936 sq mi.; 5,014 sq km), the largest of which is Majorca. Sixty miles (97 km) west of Africa are the Canary Islands (2,808 sq mi.; 7,273 sq km).

Government. King Juan Carlos I (born Jan. 5, 1938) succeeded Generalissimo Francisco Franco Bahamonde as Chief of State Nov. 27, 1975.

The Cortes, or Parliament, consists of a Chamber of Deputies of 350 members and a Senate of 208, all elected by universal suffrage. The new Cortes, replacing one that was largely appointed or elected by special constituencies, was organized under a constitution adopted by referendum Dec. 6, 1978.

History. Spain, originally inhabited by Celts, Iberians, and Basques, became a part of the Roman Empire in 206 B.C., when it was conquered by Scipio Africanus. In A.D. 412, the barbarian Visigothic leader Ataulf crossed the Pyrenees and ruled Spain, first in the name of the Roman emperor and then independently. In 711, the Moslems under Tariq entered Spain from Africa and within a few years completed the subjugation of the country. In 732, the Franks, led by Charles Martel, defeated the Moslems near Poitiers, thus preventing the further expansion of Islam in southern Europe. Internal dissension of Spanish Islam invited a steady Christian conquest from the north.

Aragon and Castile were the most important Spanish states from the 12th to the 15th century, consolidated by the marriage of Ferdinand II and Isabella I in 1469. The last Moslem stronghold, Granada, was captured in 1492. Roman Catholicism was established as the official state religion and the Jews (1492) and the Moslems (1502) expelled.

In the era of exploration, discovery, and colonization, Spain amassed tremendous wealth and a vast colonial empire through the conquest of Peru by Pizarro (1532–33) and of Mexico by Cortés (1519–21). The Spanish Hapsburg monarchy became for a time the most powerful in the world.

In 1588, Philip II sent his Invincible Armada to invade England, but its destruction cost Spain its supremacy on the seas and paved the way for England's colonization of America. Spain then sank rapidly to the status of a second-rate power and never again played a major role in European politics. Its colonial empire in the Americas and the Philippines vanished in wars and revolutions during the 18th and 19th centuries.

In World War I, Spain maintained a position of neutrality. In 1923, Gen. Miguel Primo de Rivera became dictator. In 1930, King Alfonso XIII revoked the dictatorship, but a strong antimonarchist and republican movement led to his leaving Spain in 1931. The new Constitution declared Spain a workers' republic, broke up the large estates, separated church and state, and secularized the schools. The elections held in 1936 returned a strong Popular Front majority, with Manuel Azaña as President.

On July 18, 1936, a conservative army officer in Morocco, Francisco Franco Bahamonde, led a mutiny against the government. The civil war that followed lasted three years and cost the lives of nearly a million people. Franco was aided by Fascist Italy and Nazi Germany, while Soviet Russia helped the Loyalist side. Several hundred leftist Americans served in the Abraham Lincoln Brigade on the side of the republic. The war ended when Franco took Madrid on March 28, 1939.

Franco became head of the state, national chief of the Falange Party (the governing party), and Premier and Caudillo (leader). In a referendum in 1947, the Spanish people approved a Franco-drafted succession law declaring Spain a monarchy again. Franco, however, continued as Chief of State.

In 1969, Franco and the Cortes designated Prince Juan Carlos Alfonso Victor María de Borbón (who married Princess Sophia of Greece on May 14, 1962) to become King of Spain when the provisional government headed by Franco came to an end. He is the grandson of Alfonso XIII and the son of Don Juan, pretender to the throne.

Franco died of a heart attack on Nov. 20, 1975, after more than a year of ill health, and Juan Carlos was proclaimed King seven days later.

Over strong rightist opposition, the government legalized the Communist Party in advance of the 1977 elections. Premier Adolfo Suaraz Gonzalez's Union of the Democratic Center, a coalition of a dozen centrist and rightist parties, claimed 34.3% of the popular vote in the election.

Under pressure from Catalonian and Basque nationalists, Suárez granted home rule to these regions in 1979, but centrists aided by him did poorly in the 1980 elections for local assemblies in the two areas. Economic problems persisted, along with new incidents of terrorism, and Suárez resigned on Jan. 29, 1981 and was succeeded by Leopoldo Calvo Sotelo.

With the overwhelming election of Prime Minister Felipe González Márquez and his Spanish Socialist Workers Party in the Oct. 20, 1982, parliamentary elections, the Franco past was finally buried. The thrust of González, a pragmatic moderate, was to modernize rather than radicalize Spain.

A treaty admitting Spain, along with Portugal, to the European Economic Community took effect on Jan. 1, 1986. Later that year, in June, Spain voted to remain in NATO, but outside of its military command.

A cabinet reshuffle in March 1991 effectively meant a shift to the right with a left-wing deputy being replaced by a moderate. Nationwide regional and municipal elections in May produced a setback for the ruling Socialist Party.

SRI LANKA

Democratic Socialist Republic of Sri Lanka
President: Ranasinghe Premadasa (1988)
Prime Minister: Hondoval D. B. Wijetunga (1989)
Area: 25,332 sq mi. (65,610 sq km)
Population (est. mid-1991): 17,400,000 (average annual rate of natural increase: 1.5%); birth rate: 21/1000; infant mortality rate: 19.4/1000; density per square mile: 688
Capital: Sri Jayewardenepura Kotte (Colombo)
Largest cities (est. 1990): Colombo, 1,262,000; Kandy, 200,000; Jafna, 250,000; Galle, 170,000
Monetary unit: Sri Lanka rupee
Languages: Sinhala, Tamil, English
Religions: Buddhist, 69%; Hindu, 15%; Islam, 8%; Christian, 8%
Member of Commonwealth of Nations
Literacy rate: 87%
Economic summary: Gross domestic product (1989): $7 billion; $416 per capita; 6.25% real growth rate (1990). Arable land: 16%. Principal products: tea, coconuts, rubber, rice, spices. Labor force: 6,600,000; 13.3% in mining and manufacturing. Major products: processed rubber, tea, coconuts, textiles, cement, refined petroleum. Natural resources: limestone, graphite, gems. Exports: textiles, tea, rubber, petroleum products, gems and jewelry. Imports: petroleum, machinery, transport equipment, sugar. Major trading partners: Egypt, Iraq, Saudi Arabia, U.S., U.K., Germany, Japan, Singapore, India.

Geography. An island in the Indian Ocean off the southeast tip of India, Sri Lanka is about half the size of Alabama. Most of the land is flat and rolling; mountains in the south central region rise to over 8,000 feet (2,438 m).

Government. Ceylon became an independent country in 1948 after British rule and reverted to the traditional name (resplendent island) on May 22, 1972. A new Constitution was adopted in 1978, replacing that of 1972.

The new Constitution set up the National State Assembly, a 168-member unicameral legislature that serves for six years unless dissolved earlier.

History. Following Portuguese and Dutch rule, Ceylon became an English crown colony in 1798. The British developed coffee, tea, and rubber plantations and granted six Constitutions between 1798 and 1924. The Constitution of 1931 gave a large measure of self-government.

Ceylon became a self-governing dominion of the Commonwealth of Nations in 1948.

Presidential elections were held in December 1982, and won by J.R. Jayewardene.

Tension between the Tamil minority and the Sinhalese majority continued to build and erupted in bloody violence in 1983 that has grown worse since. There are about 2.6 million Tamils in Sri Lanka, while the Sinhalese make up about three-quarters of the 17-million population. Tamil extremists are fighting for a separate nation.

Negotiations broke down in late 1986. A string of Tamil atrocities in early 1987 brought on a government offensive in May-June against guerilla base areas.

The civil war continued during 1990 after a 13-month cease-fire collapsed. The president ruled month to month. The Tamil guerrillas announced a unilateral cease-fire to take effect on January 1, 1991, and the government, too, suspended operations. The cease-fire broke down ten days later. In the early months of 1991 the rebel forces suffered severe casualties.

India had sent soldiers in July 1987 to help enforce an accord granting the Tamil minority limited autonomy. The agreement failed, and Indian troops withdrew at the end of 1989.

SUDAN

Republic of the Sudan
Prime Minister: Brig. Omar Hassam Ahmed Bashir (1989)
Area: 967,491 sq mi. (2,505,802 sq km)
Population (est. mid-1991): 25,900,000 (average annual rate of natural increase: 2.9%); birth rate: 44/1000; infant mortality rate: 104/1000; density per square mile: 27
Capital: Khartoum
Largest cities (est. 1988): Khartoum, 817,000; Omdurman, 527,000; Port Sudan, 207,000
Monetary unit: Sudanese pound
Languages: Arabic, English, tribal dialects
Religions: Islam, 70% (Sunni); indigenous, 20%; Christian, 5%
National name: Jamhuryat es-Sudan
Literacy rate: 31% (1986)
Economic summary: Gross domestic product (FY89 est.): $8.5 billion; $340 per capita (FY87); 7% real growth rate. Arable land: 5%. Principal products: cotton, oil seeds, gum arabic, sorghum, wheat, millet, sheep. Labor force: 6,500,000; 10% in industry and commerce. Major products: cement, textiles, pharmaceuticals, shoes, soap, refined petroleum. Natural resources: crude oil, some iron ore, copper, chrome, industrial metals. Exports: cotton, peanuts, gum arabic, sesame. Imports: petroleum products, machinery and equipment, medicines and chemicals. Major trading partners: Western Europe, Saudi Arabia, Eastern Europe, Japan, U.S.

Geography. The Sudan, in northeast Africa, is the largest country on the continent, measuring about one fourth the size of the United States. Its neighbors are Chad and the Central African Republic on the west, Egypt and Libya on the north, Ethiopia on the east, and Kenya, Uganda, and Zaire on the south. The Red Sea washes about 500 miles of the eastern coast.

The country extends from north to south about 1,200 miles (1,931 km) and west to east about 1,000 miles (1,609 km). The northern region is a continuation of the Libyan Desert. The southern region is fertile, abundantly watered, and, in places, heavily forested. It is traversed from north to south by the Nile, all of whose great tributaries are partly or entirely within its borders.

Government. On January 31, 1991, a criminal code became law that applied Islamic law in the predominantly Moslem north, but not in the more Christian south. The ruling military council passed a decree on

February 4 dividing the country into nine states each administered by a governor and a cabinet of ministers.

History. The early history of the Sudan (known as the Anglo-Egyptian Sudan between 1898 and 1955) is linked with that of Nubia, where a powerful local kingdom was formed in Roman times with its capital at Dongola. After conversion to Christianity in the 6th century, it joined with Ethiopia and resisted Mohammedanization until the 14th century. Thereafter the area was broken up into many small states until 1820–22, when it was conquered by Mohammed Ali, Pasha of Egypt. Egyptian forces were evacuated during the Mahdist revolt (1881–98), but the Sudan was reconquered by the Anglo-Egyptian expeditions of 1896–98, and in 1899 became an Anglo-Egyptian condominium, which was reaffirmed by the Anglo-Egyptian treaty of 1936.

Egypt and Britain agreed in 1953 to grant self-government to the Sudan under an appointed Governor-General. An all-Sudanese Parliament was elected in November-December 1953, and an all-Sudanese government was formed. In December 1955, the Parliament declared the independence of the Sudan, which, with the approval of Britain and Egypt, was proclaimed on Jan. 1, 1956.

In October 1969, Maj. Gen. Gaafar Mohamed Nimeiri, the president of the Council for the Revolution, took over as prime minister. He was elected the nation's first president in 1971.

In 1976, a third coup was attempted against Nimeiri. Nimeiri accused President Muammar el Qaddafi of Libya of having instigated the attempt and broke relations with Libya.

On April 6, 1985, while out of the country on visits to the United States and Egypt, Nimeiri lost power in the same way he gained it 16 years previously—by a military coup headed by his Defense Minister, Gen. Abdel Rahman Siwar el-Dahab.

Among the problems that the new government faced were a debilitating civil war with rebels in the south of the country, other sectarian and tribal conflicts, and a famine.

The government's inability to cope with the war led to disaffections within the army and a military coup in June 1989.

The U.N. estimates that over seven million people in Sudan are threatened with famine as a result of the second successive year of extreme drought and the seven-year civil war. The change to a federal system inaugurated at the beginning of 1991 was part of an attempt to end the war.

SURINAME

Republic of Suriname
President: Johan Kraag (1990)
Vice President and Prime Minister: Henck Aaron (1988)
Area: 63,251 sq mi. (163,820 sq km)
Population (est. mid-1991): 400,000 (average annual rate of natural increase: 2%); birth rate: 26/1000; infant mortality rate: 31/1000; density per square mile: 7
Capital and largest city (est. 1982): Paramaribo, 100,000
Monetary unit: Suriname guilder
Languages: Dutch, Surinamese (lingua franca), English also widely spoken
Religions: Protestant, 25.2%; Roman Catholic, 22.8%; Hindu, 27.4%; Islam, 19.6%; indigenous, about 5%
Literacy rate: 65%
Economic summary: Gross domestic product (1988 est.): $1.27 billion; $3,215 per capita; real growth rate 3.6%.

Arable land: NEGL %. Principal products: rice. Labor force: 104,000 (1984). Major products: aluminum, alumina, processed foods, lumber. Natural resources: bauxite, iron ore, timber, fish, shrimp. Exports: bauxite, alumina, aluminum, rice, shrimp, lumber and wood products. Imports: capital equipment, petroleum, cotton, foodstuffs, consumer goods.Major trading partners: U.S., Trinidad, Netherlands, Norway.

Geography. Suriname lies on the northeast coast of South America, with Guyana to the west, French Guiana to the east, and Brazil to the south. It is about one-tenth larger than Michigan. The principal rivers are the Corantijn on the Guyana border, the Marowijne in the east, and the Suriname, on which the capital city of Paramaribo is situated. The Tumuc-Humac Mountains are on the border with Brazil.

Government. Suriname, formerly known as Dutch Guiana, became an independent republic on Nov. 25, 1975. Elections in November 1987 gave the Front for Democracy and Development coalition an overwhelming majority in the 51-seat National Assembly. The coalition elected Shankar and Aaron as President and Vice-President in January 1988.

A draft constitution approved in September 1987 gave the military a continuing behind-the-scenes role in the government.

History. England established the first European settlement on the Suriname River in 1650 but transferred sovereignty to the Dutch in 1667 in the Treaty of Breda, by which the British acquired New York. Colonization was confined to a narrow coastal strip, and until the abolition of slavery in 1863, African slaves furnished the labor for the plantation economy. After 1870, laborers were imported from British India and the Dutch East Indies.

In 1948, the colony was integrated into the Kingdom of the Netherlands and two years later was granted full home rule in other than foreign affairs and defense. After race rioting over unemployment and inflation, the Netherlands offered complete independence in 1973. Henck A. E. Aaron, leader of a coalition of Creole (Surinamese of African descent) parties, advocated independence, while Jaggernath Lachmon, leader of the Surinamese of East Indian descent, urged delay.

During much of the 1980s Suriname has been under the control of Lieut. Col. Dési Bouterse, who in late December 1990 resigned as commander of the armed forces. The following night Pres. Shenkar was ousted in a bloodless coup. A few days later interim president Johan Krug acted to reinstate Bouterse.

In March 1991 insurgent leader Ronny Brunswijk pledged to end his four-year rebellion. In May national elections gave two parties favoring stronger ties to the Netherlands more than a two-thirds majority.

SWAZILAND

Kingdom of Swaziland
Ruler: King Mswati III (1986)
Prime Minister: Obed Dlamini (1989)
Area: 6,704 sq mi. (17,363 sq km)
Population (est. mid-1991): 800,000 (average annual rate of natural increase: 3.1%); birth rate: 46/1000; infant mortality rate: 101/1000; density per square mile: 122
Capital (est. 1986): Mbabane, 40,000

Monetary unit: Lilangeni
Languages: English and Swazi (official)
Religions: Christian, 60%; indigenous, 40%
Member of Commonwealth of Nations
Literacy rate: 67.9%
Economic summary: Gross national product (1989 est.): $539 million; $750 per capita; 5.7% real growth rate. Arable land: 8%. Principal products: corn, livestock, sugar cane, citrus fruits, cotton, sorghum, peanuts. Labor force: 195,000; about 92,000 wage earners with 14% in manufacturing. Major products: milled sugar, ginned cotton, processed meat and wood. Natural resources: asbestos, diamonds. Exports: sugar, wood pulp, asbestos, citrus fruits. Imports: motor vehicles, transport equipment, petroleum products, foodstuffs, chemicals. Major trading partners: South Africa, U.K., U.S.

Geography. Swaziland, 85% the size of New Jersey, is surrounded by South Africa and Mozambique. The country consists of a high veld in the west and a series of plateaus descending from 6,000 feet (1,829 m) to a low veld of 1,500 feet (457 m).

Government. In 1967, a new Constitution established King Sobhuza II as head of state and provided for an Assembly of 24 members elected by universal suffrage, together with a Senate of 12 members—half appointed by the Assembly and half by the King. In 1973, the King renounced the Constitution, suspended political parties, and took total power for himself. In 1977, he replaced the Parliament with an assembly of tribal leaders. The Parliament reconvened in 1979.

History. Bantu peoples migrated southwest to the area of Mozambique in the 16th century. A number of clans broke away from the main body in the 18th century and settled in Swaziland. In the 19th century they organized as a tribe, partly because they were in constant conflict with the Zulu. Their ruler, Mswazi, applied to the British in the 1840s for help against the Zulu. The British and the Transvaal governments guaranteed the independence of Swaziland in 1881.

South Africa held Swaziland as a protectorate from 1894 to 1899, but after the Boer War, in 1902, Swaziland was transferred to British administration. The Paramount Chief was recognized as the native authority in 1941.

In 1963, the territory was constituted a protectorate, and on Sept. 6, 1968, it became the independent nation of Swaziland.

King Sobhuza died in August 1982.

A substantial drug trade has developed with South Africa.

SWEDEN

Kingdom of Sweden

Sovereign: King Carl XVI Gustaf (1973)
Prime Minister: Ingvar Carlsson (1986)
Area: 173,800 sq mi. (449,964 sq km)
Population (est. mid-1991): 8,600,000 (average annual rate of natural increase: 0.3%); birth rate: 14/1000; infant-mortality rate: 5.8/1000; density per square mile: 50
Capital: Stockholm
Largest cities (est. 1986): Stockholm, 1,435,000; Göteborg, 704,000; Malmö, 458,000
Monetary unit: Krona
Language: Swedish
Religions: Evangelical Lutheran, 93.5%; Roman Catholic, 1%; other, 5.5%
National name: Konungariket Sverige

Literacy rate: 99%
Economic summary: Gross domestic product (1989 est.): $132.7 billion; $15,700 per capita; 2.1% real growth rate. Arable land: 7%. Principal agricultural products: dairy products, grains, sugar beets, potatoes. Labor force: 4,526,000 (1989); 22% in mining and manufacturing. Major products: iron and steel, precision equipment, wood pulp and paper products, automobiles. Natural resources: forests, iron ore, hydroelectric power, zinc, uranium. Exports: machinery, motor vehicles, wood pulp, paper products, iron and steel products. Imports: machinery, petroleum, yarns, foodstuffs, iron and steel, chemicals. Major trading partners: Norway, Germany, U.K., Denmark, U.S.

Geography. Sweden occupies the eastern part of the Scandinavian peninsula, with Norway to the west, Finland and the Gulf of Bothnia to the east, and Denmark and the Baltic Sea in the south. Sweden is the fourth largest country in Europe and is one-tenth larger than California.

The country slopes eastward and southward from the Kjólen Mountains along the Norwegian border, where the peak elevation is Kebnekaise at 6,965 feet (2,123 m) in Lapland. In the north are mountains and many lakes. To the south and east are central lowlands and south of them are fertile areas of forest, valley, and plain.

Along Sweden's rocky coast, chopped up by bays and inlets, are many islands, the largest of which are Gotland and Öland.

Government. Sweden is a constitutional monarchy. Under the 1975 Constitution, the Riksdag is the sole governing body. The prime minister is the political chief executive.

In 1967, agreement was reached on part of a new Constitution after 13 years of work. It provided for a single-house Riksdag of 350 members (later amended to 349 seats) to replace the 104-year old bicameral Riksdag. The members are popularly elected for three years. Ninety-two present members of the Riksdag are women.

The King, Carl XVI Gustaf, was born April 30, 1946, and succeeded to the throne Sept. 19, 1973, on the death at 90 of his grandfather, Gustaf VI Adolf. Carl Gustaf was married on June 19, 1976, to Silvia Sommerlath, a West German commoner. They have three children: Princess Victoria, born July 14, 1977; Prince Carl Philip, born May 13, 1979; and Princess Madeleine, born June 10, 1982. Under the new Act of Succession, effective Jan. 1, 1980, the first child of the reigning monarch, regardless of sex, is heir to the throne.

History. The earliest historical mention of Sweden is found in Tacitus' *Germania*, where reference is made to the powerful king and strong fleet of the Suiones. Toward the end of the 10th century, Olaf Sköttkonung established a Christian stronghold in Sweden. Around 1400, an attempt was made to unite the northern nations into one kingdom, but this led to bitter strife between the Danes and the Swedes.

In 1520, the Danish King, Christian II, conquered Sweden and in the "Stockholm Bloodbath" put leading Swedish personalities to death. Gustavus Vasa (1523–60) broke away from Denmark and fashioned the modern Swedish state.

Sweden played a leading role in the second phase (1630–35) of the Thirty Years' War (1618–48). By the Treaty of Westphalia (1648), Sweden obtained western Pomerania and some neighboring territory on the Baltic. In 1700, a coalition of Russia, Poland, and Denmark united against Sweden and by the Peace of Nystad (1721) forced it to relinquish Livonia, Ingria, Estonia, and parts of Finland.

Sweden emerged from the Napoleonic Wars with the acquisition of Norway from Denmark and with a new royal dynasty stemming from Marshal Jean Bernadotte of France, who became King Charles XIV (1818–44). The artificial union between Sweden and Norway led to an uneasy relationship, and the union was finally dissolved in 1905.

Sweden maintained a position of neutrality in both World Wars.

An elaborate structure of welfare legislation, imitated by many larger nations, began with the establishment of old-age pensions in 1911. Economic prosperity based on its neutralist policy enabled Sweden, together with Norway, to pioneer in public health, housing, and job security programs.

Forty-four years of Socialist government were ended in 1976 with the election of a conservative coalition headed by Thorbjörn Fälldin, a 50-year-old sheep farmer.

Fälldin resigned on Oct. 5, 1978, when his conservative parties partners demanded less restrictions on nuclear power, and his successor, Ola Ullsten, resigned a year later after failing to achieve a consensus on the issue. Returned to office by his coalition partners, Fälldin said he would follow the course directed by a national referendum. On March 23, 1980, voters backed the development of 12 nuclear plants and use of them for at least 25 years to supply 40% of national energy needs while the search for alternative sources continued.

Olof Palme and the Socialists were returned to power in the election of 1982.

In February 1986, Palme was killed by an unknown assailant.

Spiraling inflation coupled with its already high cost of living moved the government in 1990 to act on an austerity package that seriously shook the electorate's confidence in the long-ruling Social Democrats. In July 1991 Sweden formally filed an application for membership in the European Community.

SWITZERLAND

Swiss Confederation
President: Flavio Cotti (1991)
Vice President: René Felber (1991)
Area: 15,941 sq mi. (41,288 sq km)
Population (est. mid-1991): 6,800,000 (average annual rate of natural increase: 0.3%); birth rate: 12/1000; infant mortality rate: 7.3/1000; density per square mile: 424
Capital: Bern
Largest cities (1989): Zurich, 342,900; Basel, 169,600; Geneva, 165,400; Bern, 134,400; Lausanne, 122,600
Monetary unit: Swiss franc
Languages: German, 65%; French, 18%; Italian, 10%; Romansch, 1%
Religions: Roman Catholic, 49%; Protestant, 48%
National name: Schweiz/Suisse/Svizzera/Svizra
Literacy rate: 99%
Economic summary: Gross national product (1989 est.): $119.5 billion; $17,800 per capita; 3.0% real growth rate. Arable land: 10%. Principal products: cheese and other dairy products, livestock. Labor force: 3,220,000; 39% in industry and crafts;. Major products: watches and clocks, precision instruments, machinery, chemicals, pharmaceuticals, textiles. Natural resources: water power, timber, salt. Exports: machinery and equipment, precision instruments, textiles, foodstuffs,

metal products. Imports: transport equipment, foodstuffs, chemicals, textiles, construction material. Major trading partners: U.S., E.C., Japan

Geography. Switzerland, in central Europe, is the land of the Alps. Its tallest peak is the Dufourspitze at 15,203 feet (4,634 m) on the Swiss side of the Italian border, one of 10 summits of the Monte Rose massif in the Apennines. The tallest peak in all of the Alps, Mont Blanc (15,771 ft; 4,807 m), is actually in France.

Most of Switzerland comprises a mountainous plateau bordered by the great bulk of the Alps on the south and by the Jura Mountains on the northwest. About one-fourth of the total area is covered by mountains and glaciers.

The country's largest lakes—Geneva, Constance (Bodensee), and Maggiore—straddle the French, German-Austrian, and Italian borders, respectively.

The Rhine, navigable from Basel to the North Sea, is the principal inland waterway. Other rivers are the Aare and the Rhône.

Switzerland, twice the size of New Jersey, is surrounded by France, West Germany, Austria, Liechtenstein, and Italy.

Government. The Swiss Confederation consists of 23 sovereign cantons, of which three are divided into six half-cantons. Federal authority is vested in a bicameral legislature. The Ständerat, or State Council, consists of 46 members, two from each canton. The lower house, the Nationalrat, or National Council, has 200 deputies, elected for four-year terms.

Executive authority rests with the Bundesrat, or Federal Council, consisting of seven members chosen by parliament. The parliament elects the President, who serves for one year and is succeeded by the Vice President. The federal government regulates foreign policy, railroads, postal service, and the national mint. Each canton reserves for itself important local powers.

A constitutional amendment adopted in 1971 by referendum gave women the vote in federal elections and the right to hold federal office. An equal rights amendment was passed in a national referendum June 14, 1981, barring discrimination against women under canton as well as federal law.

A referendum in March 1990 gave 18-year olds the right to vote in federal elections. A similar referendum failed to pass in 1979.

History. Called Helvetia in ancient times, Switzerland in the Middle Ages was a league of cantons of the Holy Roman Empire. Fashioned around the nucleus of three German forest districts of Schwyz, Uri, and Unterwalden, the Swiss Confederation slowly added new cantons. In 1648 the Treaty of Westphalia gave Switzerland its independence from the Holy Roman Empire.

French revolutionary troops occupied the country in 1798 and named it the Helvetic Republic, but Napoleon in 1803 restored its federal government. By 1815, the French- and Italian-speaking peoples of Switzerland had been granted political equality.

In 1815, the Congress of Vienna guaranteed the neutrality and recognized the independence of Switzerland. In the revolutionary period of 1847, the Catholic cantons seceded and organized a separate union called the *Sonderbund*. In 1848 the new Swiss Constitution established a union modeled upon that of the U.S. The Federal Constitution of 1874 established a strong central government while maintaining large powers of control in each canton.

National unity and political conservatism grew as the country prospered from its neutrality. Its banking system became the world's leading repository for international accounts. Strict neutrality was its policy in World Wars I and II. Geneva was the seat of the League of Nations (later the European headquarters of the United Nations) and of a number of international organizations.

In 1971, the Swiss Supreme Court ruled that Swiss banks must show U.S. tax officials records of U.S. citizens suspected of tax fraud, thus significantly modifying a 1934 law that had seemed to forbid any bank disclosures.

SYRIA

Syrian Arab Republic
President: Hafez al-Assad (1971)
Premier: Mahmoud al-Zubi (1987)
Area: 71,498 sq mi. (185,180 sq km)
Population (est. mid-1991): 12,800,000 (average annual rate of natural increase: 3.8%); birth rate: 43/1000; infant mortality rate: 37/1000; density per square mile: 179
Capital: Damascus
Largest cities (est. 1987): Damascus, 1,292,000; Aleppo, 1,216,000; Homs, 431,000; Hama, 214,000; Latakia, 241,000
Monetary unit: Syrian pound
Language: Arabic
Religions: Islam, 90%; Christian, 10%
National name: Al-Jamhouriya al Arabiya As-Souriya
Literacy rate: 49%
Economic summary: Gross domestic product (1989 est.): $18.5 billion, $1,540 per capita; –2% real growth rate. Arable land: 28%. Principal products: Cotton, wheat, barley, lentils, sheep, goats. Labor force: 2,400,000; 32% in industry. Major products: textiles, phosphate, petroleum, processed food. Natural resources: chrome, manganese, asphalt, iron ore, rock salt, phosphate, oil, gypsum. Exports: petroleum, textiles, phosphates. Imports: machinery and metal products, fuels, foodstuffs. Major trading partners: Italy, Romania, U.S.S.R., U.S., Iran, Libya, France, Germany.

Geography. Slightly larger than North Dakota, Syria lies at the eastern end of the Mediterranean Sea. It is bordered by Lebanon and Israel on the west, Turkey on the north, Iraq on the east, and Jordan on the south.

Coastal Syria is a narrow plain, in back of which is a range of coastal mountains, and still farther inland a steppe area. In the east is the Syrian Desert, and in the south is the Jebel Druze Range. The highest point in Syria is Mount Hermon (9,232 ft; 2,814 m) on the Lebanese border.

Government. Syria's first permanent Constitution was approved in 1973, replacing a provisional charter that had been in force for 10 years. It provided for an elected People's Council as the legislature.

In the first election in 10 years, in 1973, the Ba'ath Arab Socialist Party of President Hafez al-Assad, running on a unified National Progressive ticket with the Communist and Socialist parties, won over 70% of the vote and a commensurate proportion of the seats in the People's Assembly. In 1977 and 1981 elections,

the ruling Ba'athists won by similar margins.

History. Ancient Syria was conquered by Egypt about 1500 b.c., and after that by Hebrews, Assyrians, Chaldeans, Persians, and Greeks. From 64 b.c. until the Arab conquest in a.d. 636, it was part of the Roman Empire except during brief periods. The Arabs made it a trade center for their extensive empire, but it suffered severely from the Mongol invasion in 1260 and fell to the Ottoman Turks in 1516. Syria remained a Turkish province until World War I.

A secret Anglo-French pact of 1916 put Syria in the French zone of influence. The League of Nations gave France a mandate over Syria after World War I, but the French were forced to put down several nationalist uprisings. In 1930, France recognized Syria as an independent republic, but still subject to the mandate. After nationalist demonstrations in 1939, the French High Commissioner suspended the Syrian Constitution. In 1941, British and Free French forces invaded Syria to eliminate Vichy control. During the rest of World War II, Syria was an Allied base.

Again in 1945, nationalist demonstrations broke into actual fighting, and British troops had to restore order. Syrian forces met a series of reverses while participating in the Arab invasion of Palestine in 1948. In 1958, Egypt and Syria formed the United Arab Republic, with Gamal Abdel Nasser of Egypt as President. However, Syria became independent again on Sept. 29, 1961, following a revolution.

In the war of 1967, Israel quickly vanquished the Syrian army. Before acceding to the U.N. cease-fire, the Israeli forces took over control of the fortified Golan Heights commanding the Sea of Galilee.

Syria joined Egypt in attacking Israel in October 1973 in the fourth Arab-Israeli war, but was pushed back from initial successes on the Golan Heights to end up losing more land. However, in the settlement worked out by U.S. Secretary of State Henry A. Kissinger in 1974, the Syrians recovered all the territory lost in 1973 and a token amount of territory, including the deserted town of Quneitra, lost in 1967.

Syrian troops, in Lebanon since 1976 as part of an Arab peacekeeping force whose other members subsequently departed, intervened increasingly during 1980 and 1981 on the side of Moslem Lebanese in their clashes with Christian militants supported by Israel. When Israeli jets shot down Syrian helicopters operating in Lebanon in April 1981, Syria moved Soviet-built surface-to-air (SAM 6) missiles into Lebanon's Bekaa Valley. Israel demanded that the missiles be removed because they violated a 1976 understanding between the governments. The demand, backed up by bombing raids, prompted the Reagan Administration to send veteran diplomat Philip C. Habib as a special envoy to avert a new conflict between the nations.

Habib's carefully engineered cease-fire was shattered by a new Israeli invasion in June 1982, when Israeli aircraft bombed Bekaa Valley missile sites, claiming to destroy all of them along with 25 Syrian planes that had sought to defend the sites. On the ground, Syrian army units were driven back by Israeli armor along the Lebanese coast. The Syrians, who were equipped with Soviet weapons, were outfought everywhere by U.S.-equipped Israelis.

Nevertheless, while the Israelis overran most of the rest of Lebanon, the Syrians retained their positions in the Bekaa Valley. Over the next three years, as the Israelis gradually withdrew their forces, the Syrians remained. As the various Lebanese factions fought each other, the Syrians became the dominant force in the country, both militarily and politically.

The first Arab country to Condemn Iraq's invasion of Kuwait, Syria sent troops to help defend Saudi Arabia from possible Iraq attack. After the Gulf war hope for peace negotiations between Israel and Arab states, particularly Syria, rose then floundered.

In 1990 President Assad ruled out any possibility of legalizing opposition political parties.

TAIWAN

Republic of China

President: Li Teng-hui (1988)
Premier: Hao Po-ts'un (1991)
Area: 13,895 sq mi. (35,988 sq km)
Population (est. mid-1991): 20,500,000 (average annual rate of natural increase: 1.1%); birth rate: 16/1000; infant mortality rate: 6.2/1000; density per square mile: 1,644
Capital: Taipei
Largest cities (1991): Taipei, 2,724,829; Kaohsiung, 1,398,667; Tai Chung, 764,651; Tainan, 685,390; Chilung (Keelung), 353,594
Monetary unit: New Taiwan dollar
Languages: Chinese (Mandarin) and various dialects
Religions: mixture of Buddhist, Confucian, and Taoist, 93%; Christian, 4.5%; other, 2.5%
Literacy rate: 94%
Economic summary: Gross national product (1990): $161.7 billion. Real growth rate (1990): 5.29%. Per capita income (1990): $7,332. Arable land: 24%; principal products: rice, yams, sugar cane, bananas, pineapples, citrus fruits. Labor force: 7,880,000; 41% in industry; major products: textiles, clothing, chemicals, processed foods, electronic equipment, cement, ships, plywood. Natural resources: coal, natural gas, limestone, marble. Exports: textiles, electrical machinery, plywood. Imports: machinery, basic metals, crude oil, chemicals. Major trading partners: U.S., Japan, Hong Kong, Germany.

Geography. The Republic of China today consists of the island of Taiwan, an island 100 miles (161 km) off the Asian mainland in the Pacific; two off-shore islands, Quemoy and Matsu; and the nearby islets of the Pescadores chain. It is slightly larger than the combined areas of Massachusetts and Connecticut.

Taiwan is divided by a central mountain range that runs from north to south, rising sharply on the east coast and descending gradually to a broad western plain, where cultivation is concentrated.

Government. The President and the Vice President are elected by the National Assembly for a term of six years. There are five major governing bodies called Yuans: Executive, Legislative, Judicial, Control, and Examination. Taiwan's internal affairs are administered by the Taiwan Provincial Government under the supervision of the Provincial Assembly, which is popularly elected.

The majority and ruling party is the Kuomintang (KMT) (Nationalist Party) led by President Li Tenghui. The main opposition party is the Democratic Progressive Party (DPP).

History. Taiwan was inhabited by aborigines of Malayan descent when Chinese from the areas now designated as Fukien and Kwangtung began settling it beginning in the 7th century, becoming the majority.

The Portuguese explored the area in 1590, naming it The Beautiful (Formosa). In 1624 the Dutch set up forts in the south, the Spanish in the North. The

Dutch threw out the Spanish in 1641 and controlled the island until 1661, when the Chinese General Koxinga took it over, established an independent kingdom, and expelled the Dutch. The Manchus seized the island in 1683 and held it until 1895, when it passed to Japan after the first Sino-Japanese War. Japan developed and exploited it, and it was heavily bombed by American planes during World War II, after which it was restored to China.

After the defeat of its armies on the mainland, the Nationalist Government of Generalissimo Chiang Kai-shek retreated to Taiwan in December 1949. With only 15% of the population consisting of the 1949 immigrants, Chiang dominated the island, maintaining a 600,000-man army in the hope of eventually recovering the mainland. Japan renounced its claim to the island by the San Francisco Peace Treaty of 1951.

By stationing a fleet in the Strait of Formosa the U.S. prevented a mainland invasion in 1953.

The "China seat" in the U.N., which the Nationalists held with U.S. help for over two decades was lost in October 1971, when the People's Republic of China was admitted and Taiwan ousted by the world body.

Chiang died at 87 of a heart attack on April 5, 1975. His son, Chiang Ching-kuo, continued as Premier and dominant power in the Taipei regime. He assumed the presidency in 1978, and Sun Yun-hsuan became Premier.

President Carter's announcement that the U.S. would recognize only the People's Republic of China after Jan. 1, 1979, and that the U.S. defense treaty with the Nationalists would end aroused protests in Taiwan and in the U.S. Congress. Against Carter's wishes, Congress, in a bill governing future relations with Taiwan, guaranteed U.S. action in the event of an attack on the island. The legislation also provided for the continuation of trade and other relations through an American Institute in Taipei, housed in the former American Embassy.

Although the U.S. had assured Taiwan of continuing arms aid, a communiqué on Aug. 17, 1982, signed by Washington and Peking and promising a gradual reduction of such aid, cast a shadow over Taiwan.

Martial law was lifted in 1987. In April 1991 President Li Teng-hui formally declared an end to emergency rule yet without abandoning his government's claim to be the sole legitimate government of China. All deputies in the National Assembly must retire by the end of 1991.

TANZANIA

United Republic of Tanzania

President: Ali Hassan Mwinyi (1985)
Prime Minister: John Malecela (1990)
Area: 364,879 sq mi. (945,037 sq km)[1]
Population (est. mid-1991): 26,900,000 (average annual rate of natural increase: 3.7%); birth rate: 50/1000; infant mortality rate: 102/1000; density per square mile: 74
Capital and largest city (est. 1984): Dar es Salaam, 1,400,000
Monetary unit: Tanzanian shilling
Languages: Swahili, English, local languages
Religions: Christian, 33%; Islam, 33%; indigenous beliefs, 33%
Member of Commonwealth of Nations
Literacy rate: 79%
Economic summary: Gross domestic product (1989 est.): $5.92 billion; $235 per capita; 4.5% real growth rate.

Arable land: 5%. Principal products: tobacco, corn, cassava, wheat, cotton, coffee, sisal, cashew nuts, pyrethrum, cloves. Labor force: 732,200; 10% in industry and commerce. Major industrial products: textiles, wood products, refined oil, processed agricultural products, diamonds, cement, fertilizer. Natural resources: hydroelectric potential, phosphates, iron and coal. Exports: coffee, cotton, sisal, diamonds, cloves, cashew nuts. Imports: manufactured goods, machinery and transport equipment, crude oil, foodstuffs. Major trading partners: Germany, U.K., U.S., Iran, Japan

1. Including Zanzibar.

Geography. Tanzania is in East Africa on the Indian Ocean. To the north are Uganda and Kenya; to the west, Burundi, Rwanda, and Zaire; and to the south, Mozambique, Zambia, and Malawi. Its area is three times that of New Mexico.

Tanzania contains three of Africa's best-known lakes—Victoria in the north, Tanganyika in the west, and Nyasa in the south. Mount Kilimanjaro in the north, 19,340 feet (5,895 m), is the highest point on the continent.

Government. Under the republican form of government, Tanzania has a President elected by universal suffrage who appoints the Cabinet ministers. The 244-member National Assembly is composed of 119 elected members from the mainland, 50 elected from Zanzibar, 10 members appointed by the President (from both Tanganyika and Zanzibar), 5 national members (elected by the National Assembly after nomination by various national institutions), 20 members elected by Zanzibar's House of Representatives, 25 Regional Commissioners sitting as *ex officio* members, and 15 seats reserved for women (elected by the National Assembly).

The Tanganyika African National Union, the only authorized party on the mainland, and the Afro-Shirazi Party, the only party in Zanzibar and Pemba, merged in 1977 as the Revolutionary Party (Chama Cha Mapinduzi) and elected Julius K. Nyerere as its head.

History. Arab traders first began to colonize the area in A.D. 700. Portuguese explorers reached the coastal regions in 1500 and held some control until the 17th century, when the Sultan of Oman took power. With what are now Burundi and Rwanda, Tanganyika became the colony of German East Africa in 1885. After World War I, it was administered by Britain under a League of Nations mandate and later as a U.N. trust territory.

Although not mentioned in old histories until the 12th century, Zanzibar was believed always to have had connections with southern Arabia. The Portuguese made it one of their tributaries in 1503 and later established a trading post, but they were driven out by Arabs from Oman in 1698. Zanzibar was declared independent of Oman in 1861 and, in 1890, it became a British protectorate.

Tanganyika became independent on Dec. 9, 1961; Zanzibar, on Dec. 10, 1963. On April 26, 1964, the two nations merged into the United Republic of Tanganyika and Zanzibar. The name was changed to Tanzania six months later.

An invasion by Ugandan troops in November 1978 was followed by a counterattack in January 1979, in which 5,000 Tanzanian troops were joined by 3,000 Ugandan exiles opposed to President Idi Amin. Within a month, full-scale war developed.

Nyerere kept troops in Uganda in open support of former Ugandan President Milton Obote, despite protests from opposition groups, until the national elections in December 1980. Although Obote asked that the Tanzanians remain after his victory in order to control guerrilla resistance, Nyerere ordered their withdrawal in May 1981, citing the $1-million-a-month drain on his precarious finances.

In November 1985, Nyerere stepped down as President. Ali Hassan Myinyi, his Vice-President, succeeded him. Nyerere remained chairman of the party. Nyerere resigned as head of the party in August 1990, being replaced by President Mwinyi. Running unopposed Mwinyi was elected president in October. Shortly thereafter plans were announced to study the benefits of instituting a multiparty democracy.

THAILAND

Kingdom of Thailand
Ruler: King Bhumibol Adulyadej (1946)
Prime Minister: Anand Panyarachun (1991)
Area: 198,455 sq mi. (514,000 sq km)
Population (est. mid-1991): 58,800,000 (average annual rate of natural increase: 1.3%); birth rate: 20/1000; infant mortality rate: 39/1000; density per square mile: 296
Capital and largest city (est. 1984): Bangkok, 5,174,682
Monetary unit: Baht
Languages: Thai (Siamese), Chinese, English
Religions: Buddhist, 95.5%; Islam, 4%
National name: Thailand
Literacy rate: 82%
Economic summary: Gross national product (1989 est.): $64.5 billion; $1,160 per capita; 10.8% real growth rate. Arable land: 34%. Principal products: rice, rubber, corn, tapioca, sugar, coconuts. Labor force: 26,000,000; 11% in industry and commerce. Major products: processed food, textiles, furniture, cement, tin, tungsten, jewelry. Natural resources: fish, natural gas, forests, fluorite, tin, tungsten. Exports: rice, tapioca, fishing products, tin, textiles, jewelry. Imports: machinery and parts, petroleum products, iron and steel, electrical appliances, chemicals. Major trading partners: Japan, U.S., Singapore, Malaysia, Netherlands, U.K., Hong Kong, Germany.

Geography. Thailand occupies the western half of the Indochinese peninsula and the northern two-thirds of the Malay peninsula in southeast Asia. Its neighbors are Myanmar on the north and west, Laos on the north and northeast, Cambodia on the east, and Malaysia on the south. Thailand is about the size of France.

Most of the population is supported in the fertile central alluvial plain, which is drained by the Chao Phraya River and its tributaries.

Government. King Bhumibol Adulyadej, who was born Dec. 5, 1927, second son of Prince Mahidol of Songkhla, succeeded to the throne on June 9, 1946, when his brother, King Ananda Mahidol, died of a gunshot wound. He was married on April 28, 1950, to Queen Sirikit; their son, Vajiralongkorn, born July 28, 1952, is the Crown Prince.

History. The Thais first began moving down into their present homeland from the Asian continent in the 6th century A.D. and by the end of the 13th century ruled most of the western portion. During the next 400 years, the Thais fought sporadically with the

Cambodians and the Burmese. The British obtained recognition of paramount interest in Thailand in 1824, and in 1896 an Anglo-French accord guaranteed the independence of Thailand.

A coup in 1932 changed the absolute monarchy into a representative government with universal suffrage. After five hours of token resistance on Dec. 8, 1941, Thailand yielded to Japanese occupation and became one of the springboards in World War II for the Japanese campaign against Malaya.

After the fall of its pro-Japanese puppet government in July 1944, Thailand pursued a policy of passive resistance against the Japanese, and after the Japanese surrender, Thailand repudiated the declaration of war it had been forced to make against Britain and the U.S. in 1942.

Thailand's major problem in the late 1960s was suppressing guerrilla action by Communist invaders in the north.

Although Thailand had received $2 billion in U.S. economic and military aid since 1950 and had sent troops (paid by the U.S.) to Vietnam while permitting U.S. bomber bases on its territory, the collapse of South Vietnam and Cambodia in the spring of 1975 brought rapid changes in the country's diplomatic posture.

At the Thai government's insistence, the U.S. agreed to withdraw all 23,000 U.S. military personnel remaining in Thailand by March 1976. Diplomatic relations with China were established in 1975. Meanwhile, overtures toward an accommodation with the new regime in South Vietnam were initiated.

After three years of civilian government ended with a military coup on Oct. 6, 1976, Thailand reverted to military rule. Political parties, banned after the coup, gained limited freedom in 1980. The same year, the National Assembly elected Gen. Prem Tinsulanonda as prime minister. General elections on April 18, 1983, and July 27, 1986, resulted in Prem continuing as prime minister over a coalition government.

Refugees from Laos, Cambodia, and Vietnam flooded into Thailand in 1978 and 1979, and despite efforts by the United States and other Western countries to resettle them, a total of 130,000 Laotian and Vietnamese refugees were living in camps along the Cambodian border in mid-1980. A drive by Vietnamese occupation forces on western Cambodian areas loyal to the Pol Pot government, culminating in invasions of Thai territory in late June, drove an estimated 100,000 Cambodians across the line as refugees, adding to the 200,000 of their countrymen already in Thailand. The total of 430,000 were being fed by United Nations and church relief organizations but the Thai government complained of the burden of their presence.

On April 3, 1981, a military coup against the Prem government failed. Another coup attempt on Sept. 9, 1985, was crushed by loyal troops after 10 hours of fighting in Bangkok. Four persons were killed and about 60 wounded.

General elections in 1988 led to Prem stepping down in favor of Chatichai Choonharan.

In February 1991 a nonviolent military coup led by Gen. Suchinda Kraprayoon overthrew the democratic government charging corruption. The junta leaders declaring a state of emergency and martial law dismissed the houses of Parliament and abolished the Constitution. The following week the military appointed a well-known businessman and former ambassador, Anand Panyarachun to serve as interim prime minister. Under terms of an interim constitution the junta serves as an equal partner in an administration otherwise dominated by experienced technocrats and diplomats.

TOGO

Republic of Togo
President: Gen. Gnassingbé Eyadema (1967)
Area: 21,925 sq mi. (56,785 sq km)
Population (est. mid-1991): 3,800,000 (average annual rate of natural increase: 3.7%); birth rate: 50/1000; infant mortality rate: 112/1000; density per square mile: 174
Capital and largest city (est. 1982): Lomé, 285,000
Monetary unit: Franc CFA
Languages: Ewé, Mina (south), Kabyé, Cotocoli (north), French (official), and many dialects
Religions: Indigenous beliefs, 70%; Christian, 20%; Islam, 10%
National name: République Togolaise
Literacy rate: 40.7%
Economic summary: Gross domestic product (1988 est.): $1.35 billion; $405 per capita; 4.1% real growth rate. Arable land: 25%. Principal products: yams, cotton, millet, sorghum, cocoa, coffee, rice. Labor force: 78% in agriculture. Major products: phosphate, textiles, processed food. Natural resources: marble, phosphate, limestone. Exports: phosphate, cocoa, coffee. Imports: consumer goods, fuels, machinery, foodstuffs. Major trading partners: E.C., Japan, U.S., Africa

Geography. Togo, twice the size of Maryland, is on the south coast of West Africa bordering on Ghana to the west, Burkina Faso to the north and Benin to the east.

The Gulf of Guinea coastline, only 32 miles long (51 km), is low and sandy. The only port is at Lomé. The Togo hills traverse the central section.

Government. The government of Nicolas Grunitzky was overthrown in a bloodless coup on Jan. 13, 1967, led by Lt. Col. Etienne Eyadema (now Gen. Gnassingbé Eyadema). A National Reconciliation Committee was set up to rule the country. In April, however, Eyadema dissolved the Committee and took over as President. In December 1979, a 67-member National Assembly was voted in by national referendum. The Assembly of the Togolese People is the only political party.

History. Freed slaves from Brazil were the first traders to settle in Togo. Established as a German colony (Togoland) in 1884, the area was split between the British and the French as League of Nations mandates after World War I and subsequently administered as U.N. trusteeships. The British portion voted for incorporation with Ghana.

Togo became independent on April 27, 1960.

Although several independent candidates were elected to the Assembly in March 1990, two opposition leaders were arrested in October. Violent student protests led to further arrests. Sympathy strikes broke out, and the government announced plans to draft a new constitution.

TONGA

Kingdom of Tonga
Sovereign: King Taufa'ahau Tupou IV (1965)
Prime Minister: Prince Fatafehi Tu'ipelehake (1965)
Area: 290 sq mi. (751 sq km)
Population (mid 1989): 100,465 (average annual growth rate: 0.8%)

Density per square mile: 344
Capital (est. 1986): Nuku'alofa, 28,899
Monetary unit: Pa'anga
Languages: Tongan, English
Religions: Christian; Free Wesleyan Church claims over 30,000 adherents
Member of Commonwealth of Nations
Literacy rate: 90–95%
Economic summary: Gross domestic product (FY89 est.): $86 million; $850 per capita; 3.6% real growth rate. Arable land: 25%. Principal products: vanilla, coffee, ginger, black pepper, coconuts, bananas, copra. Labor force: 70% in agriculture. Major industrial products: copra, desiccated coconut. Natural resources: fish. Exports: copra, coconut products, bananas. Imports: foodstuffs, machinery and transport equipment, fuels, chemicals, building materials. Major trading partners: New Zealand, Australia, Fiji, U.S., Japan, E.C.

Geography. Situated east of the Fiji Islands in the South Pacific, Tonga (also called the Friendly Islands) consists of some 150 islands, of which 36 are inhabited.

Most of the islands contain active volcanic craters; others are coral atolls.

Government. Tonga is a constitutional monarchy. Executive authority is vested in the Sovereign, a Privy Council, and a Cabinet headed by the Prime Minister. Legislative authority is vested in the Legislative Assembly. Nine seats are reserved for commoners; the others filled by appointees of the king.

History. The present dynasty of Tonga was founded in 1831 by Taufa'ahau Tupou, who took the name George I. He consolidated the kingdom by conquest and in 1875 granted a Constitution.

In 1900, his great-grandson, George II, signed a treaty of friendship with Britain, and the country became a British protected state. The treaty was revised in 1959.

Tonga became independent on June 4, 1970.

General elections in 1990 were won by reformists charging the government with corruption.

TRANSKEI

See South Africa

TRINIDAD AND TOBAGO

Republic of Trinidad and Tobago
President: Noor Hassanali (1987)
Prime Minister: A.N.R. Robinson (1986)
Area: 1,980 sq mi. (5,128 sq km)
Population (est. mid-1991): 1,300,000 (average annual rate of natural increase: 1.6%); birth rate: 23/1000; infant mortality rate: 11.4/1000; density per square mile: 649
Capital and largest city (est. 1981): Port-of-Spain, 125,000
Monetary unit: Trinidad and Tobago dollar
Languages: English (official); Hindi, French, Spanish
Religions: Christian, 49.3%; Hindu, 23%; Islam, 6%; unknown, 21.7%
Member of Commonwealth of Nations
Literacy rate: 98%
Economic summary: Gross domestic product (1988 est.): $3.75 billion; $3,070 per capita; –2.0% real growth rate. Arable land: 14%. Principal products: sugar cane, cocoa, coffee, citrus. Labor force: 463,900; 14.8% in manufacturing, mining, and quarrying. Major industrial products: petroleum, processed food, cement;

tourism. Natural resources: petroleum, natural gas, asphalt. Exports: petroleum, chemicals, fertilizer. Imports: raw materials, capital goods, consumer goods. Major trading partners: U.S., Caribbean, Latin America, Western Europe.

Geography. Trinidad and Tobago lies in the Caribbean Sea off the northeast coast of Venezuela. The area of the two islands is slightly less than that of Delaware.

Trinidad, the larger, is mainly flat and rolling, with mountains in the north that reach a height of 3,085 feet (940 m) at Mount Aripo. Tobago is heavily forested with hardwood trees.

Government. The legislature consists of a 24-member Senate and a 36-member House of Representatives.

The political parties are the National Alliance for Reconstruction, led by Prime Minister A.N.R. Robinson (33 seats in the House of Representatives); People's National Movement (3 seats).

History. Trinidad was discovered by Columbus in 1498 and remained in Spanish possession, despite raids by other European nations, until it capitulated to the British in 1797 during a war between Britain and Spain.

Trinidad was ceded to Britain in 1802, and in 1899 it was united with Tobago as a colony. From 1958 to 1962, Trinidad and Tobago was a part of the West Indies Federation, and on Aug. 31, 1962, it became independent.

On Aug. 1, 1976, Trinidad and Tobago cut its ties with Britain and became a republic, remaining within the Commonwealth and recognizing Queen Elizabeth II only as head of that organization.

In an attempted coup on July 27, 1990 the prime minister and 54 others were taken hostage. The rebels surrendered, and the hostages freed on August 1. Although the coup had no popular support, 30 people lost their lives.

TUNISIA

Republic of Tunisia
President: Gen. Zine al-Abidine Ben Ali (1987)
Prime Minister: Hamed Karoui (1989)
Area: 63,379 sq mi. (164,152 sq km)
Population (est. mid-1991): 8,400,000 (average annual rate of natural increase: 2.2%); birth rate: 29/1000; infant mortality rate: 48/1000; density per square mile: 132
Capital and largest city (est. 1981): Tunis, 600,000
Monetary unit: Tunisian dinar
Languages: Arabic, French
Religion: Islam (Sunni), 98%; Christian, 1%; Jewish, less than 1%
National name: Al-Joumhouria Attunisia
Literacy rate: 62% (est.)
Economic summary: Gross domestic product (1989 est.): $8.7 billion, $1,105 per capita; 3.1% real growth rate. Arable land: 20%. Principal products: wheat, olives, oranges, grapes, dates. Labor force: 2,250,000; 32% in agriculture. Major industrial products: textiles, leather, chemical fertilizers, petroleum, phosphate, iron ore. Natural resources: oil, phosphates, iron ore, lead, zinc. Exports: petroleum, phosphates and chemicals. Imports: machinery and equipment, consumer goods, foodstuffs. Major trading partners: E.C., U.S.S.R., Middle East, U.S.

Geography. Tunisia, at the northernmost bulge of Africa, thrusts out toward Sicily to mark the division between the eastern and western Mediterranean Sea.

Twice the size of South Carolina, it is bordered on the west by Algeria and by Libya on the south.

Coastal plains on the east rise to a north-south escarpment which slopes gently to the west. Saharan in the south, Tunisia is more mountainous in the north, where the Atlas range continues from Algeria.

Government. Executive power is vested by the Constitution in the president, elected for five years and eligible for re-election to two additional terms. Legislative power is vested in a House of Deputies elected by universal suffrage.

In 1975, the National Assembly amended the Constitution to make Habib Bourguiba president for life. At 71, Bourguiba was re-elected to a fourth five-year term when he ran unopposed in 1974. He was deposed by Gen. Zine Ben Ali in 1987. Ben Ali was elected to a five-year term in April 1989.

History. Tunisia was settled by the Phoenicians and Carthaginians in ancient times. Except for an interval of Vandal conquest in A.D. 439–533, it was part of the Roman Empire until the Arab conquest of 648–69. It was ruled by various Arab and Berber dynasties until the Turks took it in 1570–74. French troops occupied the country in 1881, and the Bey signed a treaty acknowledging a French protectorate.

Nationalist agitation forced France to grant internal autonomy to Tunisia in 1955 and to recognize Tunisian independence and sovereignty in 1956. The Constituent Assembly deposed the Bey on July 25, 1957, declared Tunisia a republic, and elected Habib Bourguiba as president.

Bourguiba maintained a pro-Western foreign policy that earned him enemies. Tunisia refused to break relations with the U.S. during the Israeli-Arab war in June 1967.

Tunisia ended its traditionally neutral role in the Arab world when it joined with the majority of Arab League members to condemn Egypt for concluding a peace treaty with Israel.

Developments in 1986–87 were characterized by a consolidation of power by the 84-year-old Bourguiba and his failure to arrange for a successor. This issue was settled when the then-Prime Minister, Gen. Ben Ali, deposed Bourguiba.

In a surprise move to Western observers President Ben Ali in 1990 expressed his disapproval of U.S.-led actions leading up to the Gulf war. The foreign minister was dismissed, presumably over this issue. Relations between Tunisia and Libya improved, and an attempt was made to do the same with the European Community.

TURKEY

Republic of Turkey
President: Turgut Ozal (1989)
Prime Minister: Mesut Yilmaz (1991)
Area: 300,947 sq mi. (incl. 9,121 in Europe) (779,452 sq km)
Population (est. mid-1991): 58,500,000 (average annual rate of natural increase: 2.2%); birth rate: 30/1000; infant mortality rate: 62/1000; density per square mile: 194
Capital: Ankara
Largest cities (1985 census): Istanbul, 5,858,558; Ankara, 3,462,880; Izmir, 2,316,843; Adana, 1,757,102; Bursa, 1,327,762; Gaziantep, 953,859
Monetary unit: Turkish Lira
Language: Turkish

Religion: Islam (mostly Sunni), 98%
National name: Türkiye Cumhuriyeti
Literacy rate: 70%
Economic summary: Gross domestic product (est. 1989): $75 billion; $1,350 per capita; 1.8% real growth rate. Arable land: 20%. Principal products: cotton, tobacco, cereals, sugar beets, fruits, olives. Labor force: 18,800,000; 14% in industry. Major products: textiles, coal, minerals, processed foods, steel, petroleum. Natural resources: coal, chromite, copper, borate, sulfur. Exports: cotton, tobacco, fruits, nuts, livestock products, textiles. Imports: crude oil, machinery, transport equipment, metals, mineral fuels, fertilizer, chemicals. Major trading partners: Germany, Iraq, France, Italy, U.S., U.K., Iran, Japan.

Geography. Turkey is at the northeastern end of the Mediterranean Sea in southeast Europe and southwest Asia. To the north is the Black Sea and to the west the Aegean Sea. Its neighbors are Greece and Bulgaria to the west, the U.S.S.R. to the north, Iran to the east, and Syria and Iraq to the south. Overall, it is a little larger than Texas.

The Dardanelles, the Sea of Marmara, and the Bosporus divide the country.

Turkey in Europe comprises an area about equal to the state of Massachusetts. It is hilly country drained by the Maritsa River and its tributaries.

Turkey in Asia, or Anatolia, about the size of Texas, is roughly a rectangle in shape with its short sides on the east and west. Its center is a treeless plateau rimmed by mountains.

Government. The President is elected by the Grand National Assembly for a seven-year term and is not eligible for re-election.

In a military coup on Sept. 12, 1980, led by Gen. Kenan Evren, the Chief of General Staff, Premier Süleyman Demirel was ousted, the Grand National Assembly dissolved, and the Constitution suspended. Demirel, former Premier Bülent Ecevit, and some 100 legislators and political figures were detained, but later released. Martial law was declared and all political parties were dissolved. New elections were held in 1983 and a new Assembly was established.

The Prime Minister and his Council of Ministers hold the executive power although the President has the right to veto legislation.

History. The Ottoman Turks first appeared in the early 13th century in Anatolia, subjugating Turkish and Mongol bands pressing against the eastern borders of Byzantium. They gradually spread through the Near East and Balkans, capturing Constantinople in 1453 and storming the gates of Vienna two centuries later. At its height, the Ottoman Empire stretched from the Persian Gulf to western Algeria.

Defeat of the Turkish navy at Lepanto by the Holy League in 1571 and failure of the siege of Vienna heralded the decline of Turkish power. By the 18th century, Russia was seeking to establish itself as the protector of Christians in Turkey's Balkan territories. Russian ambitions were checked by Britain and France in the Crimean War (1854–56), but the Russo-Turkish War (1877–78) gave Bulgaria virtual independence and Romania and Serbia liberation from their nominal allegiance to the Sultan.

Turkish weakness stimulated a revolt of young liberals known as the Young Turks in 1909. They forced Sultan Abdul Hamid to grant a constitution and install a liberal government. Reforms were no barrier to further defeats, however, in a war with Italy

(1911–12) and the Balkan Wars (1912–13). Under the influence of German military advisors, Turkey signed a secret alliance with Germany on Aug. 2, 1914, that led to a declaration of war by the Allied powers and the ultimate humiliation of the occupation of Turkish territory by Greek and other Allied troops.

In 1919, the new Nationalist movement, headed by Mustafa Kemal, was organized to resist the Allied occupation and, in 1920, a National Assembly elected him President of both the Assembly and the government. Under his leadership, the Greeks were driven out of Smyrna, and other Allied forces were withdrawn.

The present Turkish boundaries (with the exception of Alexandretta, ceded to Turkey by France in 1939) were fixed by the Treaty of Lausanne (1923) and later negotiations. The caliphate and sultanate were separated, and the sultanate was abolished in 1922. On Oct. 29, 1923, Turkey formally became a republic, with Mustafa Kemal, who took the name Kemal Atatürk, as its first President. The caliphate was abolished in 1924, and Atatürk proceeded to carry out an extensive program of reform, modernization, and industrialization.

Gen. Ismet Inönü was elected to succeed Atatürk in 1938 and was re-elected in 1939, 1943, and 1946. Defeated in 1950, he was succeeded by Celâl Bayar. In 1939, a mutual assistance pact was concluded with Britain and France. Neutral during most of World War II Turkey, on Feb. 23, 1945, declared war on Germany and Japan, but took no active part in the conflict.

Turkey became a full member of NATO in 1952.

Turkey invaded Cyprus by sea and air July 20, 1974, following the failure of diplomatic efforts to resolve the crisis caused by the ouster of Archbishop Makarios.

Talks in Geneva involving Greece, Turkey, Britain, and Greek Cypriot and Turkish Cypriot leaders broke down in mid-August. Turkey unilaterally announced a cease-fire August 16, after having gained control of 40% of the island. Turkish Cypriots established their own state in the north on Feb. 13, 1975.

In July 1975, after a 30-day warning, Turkey took over control of all the U.S. installations except the big joint defense base at Incirlik, which it reserved for "NATO tasks alone."

The establishment of military government in September 1980 stopped the slide toward anarchy and brought some improvement in the economy.

A Constituent Assembly, consisting of the six-member National Security Council and members appointed by them, drafted a new Constitution that was approved by an overwhelming (91.5%) majority of the voters in a Nov. 6, 1982, referendum. Prime Minister Turgut Özal's Motherland Party came to power in parliamentary elections held in late 1983. Özal was re-elected in November 1987.

During the Persian Gulf war Turkey allowed use of its military bases by the U.S.-led forces principally for air attacks on Iraq. This caused much concern over possible retaliation by Iraq. Despite NATO assurances of protection Turkey openly expressed doubts of the sincerity of such pledges from certain NATO members, particularly Germany.

In the aftermath of the war Turkey kept its borders closed to the flood of Kurds seeking to escape northern Iraq.

The ruling Anap Party chose a new leader in June 1991, Mesut Yilmaz, who reorganized the government, replacing 20 members of the former cabinet.

TUVALU

Sovereign: Queen Elizabeth II
Governor-General: Tupua Leupena (1986)
Prime Minister: Bikenibeu Paeniu (1989)
Area: 10 sq mi. (26 sq km)
Population (mid-1989): 8,624 (average annual growth rate: 1.7%)
Density per square mile: 848
Capital and largest city (est. 1981): Funafuti, 2,500
Monetary unit: Australian dollar
Languages: Tuvaluan, English
Member of the Commonwealth of Nations
Literacy rate: less than 50%
Economic summary: Gross national product (1989 est.): $4.6 million. Per capita income: $530. Principal agricultural products: copra and coconuts. Export: copra. Imports: food, fuels, machinery. Major trading partners: Australia, Fiji, New Zealand

Geography. Formerly the Ellice Islands, Tuvalu consists of nine small islands scattered over 500,000 square miles of the western Pacific, just south of the equator.

Government. Official executive power is vested in a Governor-General, representing the Queen, who is appointed by her on the recommendation of the Tuvalu government. Actual executive power lies with a Prime Minister, who is responsible to a House of Assembly composed of eight elected members.

History. The Ellice Islands became a British protectorate in 1892 and were annexed by Britain in 1915–16 as part of the Gilbert and Ellice Islands Colony. The Ellice Islands were separated in 1975, given home rule, and renamed Tuvalu. Full independence was granted on Sept. 30, 1978.

Prime Minister Paeniu's emphasis since his election in September 1989 has been on opening the economy and making the country more self-sufficient.

UGANDA

Republic of Uganda
President: Yoweri Museveni (1986)
Prime Minister: George Kosmas Adyebo (1991)
Area: 91,459 sq mi. (236,880 sq km)
Population (est. mid-1991): 18,700,000 (average annual rate of natural increase: 3.5%); birth rate: 52/1000; infant mortality rate: 107/1000; density per square mile: 205
Capital and largest city (est. 1980): Kampala, 458,000
Monetary unit: Ugandan shilling
Languages: English (official), Swahili, Luganda, Ateso, Luo
Religions: Christian, 66%; Islam, 16%
Member of Commonwealth of Nations
Literacy rate: 57.3%
Economic summary: Gross domestic product (1988): $4.9 billion; $300 per capita; 6.1% real growth rate. Arable land: 23%. Principal products: coffee, tea, cotton, sugar. Labor force: 4,500,000 (est.); 94% in subsistence activities. Major industrial products: sugar, beer, tobacco, cotton textiles, cement. Natural resources: copper, cobalt, limestone, salt. Exports: coffee, cotton, tea. Imports: petroleum products, machinery, transport equipment, metals, food. Major trading partners: U.S., U.K., Kenya, Italy, France, Spain.

Geography. Uganda, twice the size of Pennsylvania, is in east Africa. It is bordered on the west by Zaire, on the north by the Sudan, on the east by Kenya, and on the south by Tanzania and Rwanda.

The country, which lies across the Equator, is divided into three main areas—swampy lowlands, a fertile plateau with wooded hills, and a desert region. Lake Victoria forms part of the southern border.

Government. The country has been run by the National Resistance Movement (NRM) since January, 1986.

History. Uganda was first visited by European explorers as well as Arab traders in 1844. An Anglo-German agreement of 1890 declared it to be in the British sphere of influence in Africa, and the Imperial British East Africa Company was chartered to develop the area. The company did not prosper financially, and in 1894 a British protectorate was proclaimed.

Uganda became independent on Oct. 9, 1962.

Sir Edward Mutesa was elected the first President and Milton Obote the first Prime Minister of the newly independent country. With the help of a young army officer, Col. Idi Amin, Prime Minister Obote seized control of the government from President Mutesa four years later.

On Jan. 25, 1971, Col. Amin deposed President Obote. Obote went into exile in Tanzania. Amin expelled Asian residents and launched a reign of terror against Ugandan opponents, torturing and killing tens of thousands. In 1976, he had himself proclaimed President for Life. In 1977, Amnesty International estimated that 300,000 may have died under his rule, including church leaders and recalcitrant cabinet ministers.

After Amin held military exercises on the Tanzanian border, angering Tanzania's President Julius Nyerere, a combined force of Tanzanian troops and Ugandan exiles loyal to former President Obote invaded Uganda and chased Amin into exile.

After a series of interim administrations, President Obote led his People's Congress Party to victory in 1980 elections that opponents charged were rigged.

On July, 27, 1985, army troops staged a coup taking over the government. Obote fled into exile. The military regime installed Gen. Tito Okello as chief of state.

The National Resistance Army (NRA), an anti-Obote group led by Yoweri Musevni, kept fighting after being excluded from the new regime. They seized Kampala on January 29, 1986, and Musevni was declared President but strife still continues in the northern part of the country.

President Musevni was chosen chairman of the Organization of African Unity in July 1990 only to be charged with complicity three months later in the Rwandan civil war.

UNION OF SOVIET SOCIALIST REPUBLICS

See Soviet Union

UNITED ARAB EMIRATES

President: Sheik Zayed Bin Sultan Al-Nahayan (1971)
Prime Minister: Sheik Maktum ibn Rashid al-Maktum (1990)
Area: 32,000 sq mi. (82,880 sq km)
Population (est. mid-1991): 2,400,000 (average annual rate of natural increase: 2.7%); birth rate: 30/1000; infant mortality rate: 23/1000; density per square mile: 74
Capital and largest city (est. 1981): Abu Dhabi, 225,000
Monetary unit: Dirham
Language: Arabic; Farsi and English widely spoken
Religion: Islam (Sunni, 80%; Shiite, 16%); other, 4%

Literacy rate: 68%
Economic summary: Gross national product (1989): $23.3 billion, $11,680 per capita; real growth rate –2.1%. Arable land: NEGL%. Principal products: vegetables, dates, poultry, fish. Labor force: 580,000 (1986 est.) 80% is foreign; 85% in industry and commerce. Major products: fish, light manufactures, petroleum, construction materials. Natural resource: oil. Exports: petroleum, dates, fish. Imports: consumer goods, food. Major trading partners: Japan, Western Europe, U.S.

Geography. The United Arab Emirates, in the eastern part of the Arabian Peninsula, extends along part of the Gulf of Oman and the southern coast of the Persian Gulf. The nation is the size of Maine. Its neighbors are Saudi Arabia in the west and south, Qatar in the north, and Oman in the east. Most of the land is barren and sandy.

Government. The United Arab Emirates was formed in 1971 by seven emirates known as the Trucial States—Abu Dhabi (the largest), Dubai, Sharjah, Ajman, Fujairah, Ras al Khaimah and Umm al-Qaiwain.

The loose federation allows joint policies in foreign relations, defense, and development, with each member state keeping its internal local system of government headed by its own ruler. A 40-member legislature consists of eight seats each for Abu Dhabi and Dubai, six seats each for Ras al Khaimah and Sharjah, and four each for the others. It is a member of the Arab League.

History. Originally the area was inhabited by a seafaring people who were converted to Islam in the seventh century. Later, a dissident sect, the Carmathians, established a powerful sheikdom, and its army conquered Mecca. After the sheikdom disintegrated, its people became pirates.

Threatening the sultanate of Muscat and Oman early in the 19th century, the pirates provoked the intervention of the British, who in 1820 enforced a partial truce and in 1853 a permanent truce. Thus what had been called the Pirate Coast was renamed the Trucial Coast.

After a long illness the vice president and ruler of Dubai died. He was succeeded by his son Sheik Maktum, who in November 1990 was appointed prime minister.

UNITED KINGDOM

United Kingdom of Great Britain and Northern Ireland
Sovereign: Queen Elizabeth II (1952)
Prime Minister: John Major (1990)
Area: 94,247 sq mi. (244,100 sq km)
Population (mid-1990): 57,500,000 (average annual rate of natural increase: 0.2%); birth rate: 14/1000; infant mortality rate: 8.4/1000; density per square mile: 609
Capital: London, England
Largest cities (est. 1990): London, 9,170,000; Manchester, 4,050,000; Birmingham, 2,170,000; (est. mid. 1987) Glasgow, 715,621; Leeds, 709,000; Sheffield, 532,300; Liverpool, 476,000; Bradford, 462,500; Edinburgh, 438,232; Bristol, 384,400
Monetary unit: Pound sterling (£)
Languages: English, Welsh, Scots Gaelic
Religions: Church of England (established church); Church of Wales (disestablished); Church of Scotland (established church—Presbyterian); Church of Ireland (disestablished); Roman Catholic; Methodist; Congregational; Baptist; Jewish

Rulers of England and Great Britain

Name	Born	Ruled[1]	Name	Born	Ruled[1]
SAXONS[2]			**HOUSE OF YORK**		
Egbert[3]	c.775	828–839	Edward IV	1442	1461–1483 [5]
Ethelwulf	?	839–858	Edward V	1470	1483–1483
Ethelbald	?	858–860	Richard III	1452	1483–1485
Ethelbert	?	860–866			
Ethelred I	?	866–871	**HOUSE OF TUDOR**		
Alfred the Great	849	871–899	Henry VII	1457	1485–1509
Edward the Elder	c.870	899–924	Henry VIII	1491	1509–1547
Athelstan	895	924–939	Edward VI	1537	1547–1553
Edmund I the Deed-doer	921	939–946	Jane (Lady Jane Grey)[6]	1537	1553–1553
Edred	c.925	946–955	Mary I ("Bloody Mary")	1516	1553–1558
Edwy the Fair	c.943	955–959	Elizabeth I	1533	1558–1603
Edgar the Peaceful	943	959–975			
Edward the Martyr	c.962	975–979	**HOUSE OF STUART**		
Ethelred II the Unready	968	979–1016	James I[7]	1566	1603–1625
Edmund II Ironside	c.993	1016–1016	Charles I	1600	1625–1649
DANES			**COMMONWEALTH**		
Canute	995	1016–1035	Council of State	—	1649–1653
Harold I Harefoot	c.1016	1035–1040	Oliver Cromwell[8]	1599	1653–1658
Hardecanute	c.1018	1040–1042	Richard Cromwell[8]	1626	1658–1659 [9]
SAXONS			**RESTORATION OF HOUSE OF**		
Edward the Confessor	c.1004	1042–1066	**STUART**		
Harold II	c.1020	1066–1066	Charles II	1630	1660–1685
			James II	1633	1685–1688 [10]
HOUSE OF NORMANDY			William III[11]	1650	1689–1702
William I the Conqueror	1027	1066–1087	Mary II[11]	1662	1689–1694
William II Rufus	c.1056	1087–1100	Anne	1665	1702–1714
Henry I Beauclerc	1068	1100–1135			
Stephen of Boulogne	c.1100	1135–1154	**HOUSE OF HANOVER**		
			George I	1660	1714–1727
HOUSE OF PLANTAGENET			George II	1683	1727–1760
Henry II	1133	1154–1189	George III	1738	1760–1820
Richard I Coeur de Lion	1157	1189–1199	George IV	1762	1820–1830
John Lackland	1167	1199–1216	William IV	1765	1830–1837
Henry III	1207	1216–1272	Victoria	1819	1837–1901
Edward I Longshanks	1239	1272–1307			
Edward II	1284	1307–1327	**HOUSE OF SAXE-COBURG**[12]		
Edward III	1312	1327–1377	Edward VII	1841	1901–1910
Richard II	1367	1377–1399 [4]			
			HOUSE OF WINDSOR[12]		
HOUSE OF LANCASTER			George V	1865	1910–1936
Henry IV Bolingbroke	1367	1399–1413	Edward VIII	1894	1936–1936 [13]
Henry V	1387	1413–1422	George VI	1895	1936–1952
Henry VI	1421	1422–1461 [5]	Elizabeth II	1926	1952–

1. Year of end of rule is also that of death, unless otherwise indicated. 2. Dates for Saxon kings are still subject to controversy. 3. Became King of West Saxons in 802; considered (from 828) first King of all England. 4. Died 1400. 5. Henry VI reigned again briefly 1470–71. 6. Nominal Queen for 9 days; not counted as Queen by some authorities. She was beheaded in 1554. 7. Ruled in Scotland as James VI (1567–1625). 8. Lord Protector. 9. Died 1712. 10. Died 1701. 11. Joint rulers (1689–1694). 12. Name changed from Saxe–Coburg to Windsor in 1917. 13. Was known after his abdication as the Duke of Windsor, died 1972.

Literacy rate: 99%

Economic summary: Gross domestic product (1989 est.): $818.0 billion; $14,300 per capita; 2.3% real growth rate. Arable land: 29%. Principal products: wheat, barley, potatoes, sugar beets, livestock, dairy products. Labor force: 28,120,000; 23.6% in manufacturing and construction. Major industrial products: machinery and transport equipment, metals, processed food, paper, textiles, chemicals, clothing. Natural resources: coal, oil, gas. Exports: machinery, transport equipment, chemicals, petroleum. Imports: foodstuffs, machinery, manufactured goods, semifinished goods. Major trading partners: Western European nations, U.S.

Geography. The United Kingdom, consisting of England, Wales, Scotland, and Northern Ireland, is twice the size of New York State. England, in the southeast part of the British Isles, is separated from Scotland on the north by the granite Cheviot Hills; from them the Pennine chain of uplands extends south through the center of England, reaching its highest point in the Lake District in the northwest. To the west along the border of Wales—a land of steep hills and valleys—are the Cambrian Mountains, while the Cotswolds, a range of hills in Gloucestershire, extend into the surrounding shires.

The remainder of England is plain land, though not

necessarily flat, with the rocky sand-topped moors in the southwest, the rolling downs in the south and southeast, and the reclaimed marshes of the low-lying fens in the east central districts.

Scotland is divided into three physical regions—the Highlands, the Central Lowlands, containing two-thirds of the population, and the Southern Uplands. The western Highland coast is intersected throughout by long, narrow sea-lochs, or fiords. Scotland also includes the Outer and Inner Hebrides and other islands off the west coast and the Orkney and Shetland Islands off the north coast.

Wales is generally hilly; the Snowdon range in the northern part culminates in Mount Snowdon (3,560 ft, 1,085 m), highest in both England and Wales.

Important rivers flowing into the North Sea are the Thames, Humber, Tees, and Tyne. In the west are the Severn and Wye, which empty into the Bristol Channel and are navigable, as are the Mersey and Ribble.

Government. The United Kingdom is a constitutional monarchy, with a Queen and a Parliament that has two houses: the House of Lords with about 830 hereditary peers, 26 spiritual peers, about 270 life peers and peeresses, and 9 law-lords, who are hereditary, or life, peers, and the House of Commons, which has 650 popularly elected members. Supreme legislative power is vested in Parliament, which sits for five years unless sooner dissolved.

The executive power of the Crown is exercised by the Cabinet, headed by the Prime Minister. The latter, normally the head of the party commanding a majority in the House of Commons, is appointed by the Sovereign, with whose consent he or she in turn appoints the rest of the Cabinet. All ministers must be members of one or the other house of Parliament; they are individually and collectively responsible to the Crown and Parliament. The Cabinet proposes bills and arranges the business of Parliament, but it depends entirely on the votes in the House of Commons. The Lords cannot hold up "money" bills, but they can delay other bills for a maximum of one year.

By the Act of Union (1707), the Scottish Parliament was assimilated with that of England, and Scotland is now represented in Commons by 71 members. The Secretary of State for Scotland, a member of the Cabinet, is responsible for the administration of Scottish affairs.

Ruler. Queen Elizabeth II, born April 21, 1926, elder daughter of King George VI and Queen Elizabeth, succeeded to the throne on the death of her father on Feb. 6, 1952; married Nov. 20, 1947, to Prince Philip, Duke of Edinburgh, born June 10, 1921; their children are Prince Charles[1] (heir presumptive), born Nov. 14, 1948; Princess Anne, born Aug. 15, 1950; Prince Andrew, born Feb. 19, 1960; and Prince Edward, born March 10, 1964. The Queen's sister is Princess Margaret, born Aug. 21, 1930. Prince William Arthur Philip Louis, son of the Prince and Princess of Wales and second in line to the throne, was born June 21, 1982. A second son, Prince Henry Charles Albert David, was born Sept. 15, 1984, and is third in line.

History. Roman invasions of the 1st century B.C. brought Britain into contact with the Continent. When the Roman legions withdrew in the 5th century

1. The title Prince of Wales, which is not inherited, was conferred on Prince Charles by his mother on July 26, 1958. The investiture ceremony took place on July 1, 1969. The previous Prince of Wales was Prince Edward Albert, who held the title from 1911 to 1936 before he became Edward VIII.

Area and Population of United Kingdom

Subdivision	Area sq mi.	Area sq km	Population (Est. 1988)
England and Wales	58,381	151,207	50,393,000
Scotland	30,414	78,772	5,074,000
Northern Ireland	5,452	14,121	1,598,100
Total	**94,247**	**244,100**	**57,065,400**

A.D., Britain fell easy prey to the invading hordes of Angles, Saxons, and Jutes from Scandinavia and the Low Countries. Seven large kingdoms were established, and the original Britons were forced into Wales and Scotland. It was not until the 10th century that the country finally became united under the kings of Wessex. Following the death of Edward the Confessor (1066), a dispute about the succession arose, and William, Duke of Normandy, invaded England, defeating the Saxon King, Harold II, at the Battle of Hastings (1066). The Norman conquest introduced Norman law and feudalism.

The reign of Henry II (1154–89), first of the Plantagenets, saw an increasing centralization of royal power at the expense of the nobles, but in 1215 John (1199–1216) was forced to sign the Magna Carta, which awarded the people, especially the nobles, certain basic rights. Edward I (1272–1307) continued the conquest of Ireland, reduced Wales to subjection, and made some gains in Scotland. In 1314, however, English forces led by Edward II were ousted from Scotland after the Battle of Bannockburn. The late 13th and early 14th centuries saw the development of a separate House of Commons with tax-raising powers.

Edward III's claim to the throne of France led to the Hundred Years' War (1338–1453) and the loss of almost all the large English territory in France. In England, the great poverty and discontent caused by the war were intensified by the Black Death, a plague that reduced the population by about one-third. The Wars of the Roses (1455–85), a struggle for the throne between the House of York and the House of Lancaster, ended in the victory of Henry Tudor (Henry VII) at Bosworth Field (1485).

During the reign of Henry VIII (1509–47), the Church in England asserted its independence from the Roman Catholic Church. Under Edward VI and Mary, the two extremes of religious fanaticism were reached, and it remained for Henry's daughter, Elizabeth I (1558–1603), to set up the Church of England on a moderate basis. In 1588, the Spanish Armada, a fleet sent out by Catholic King Philip II of Spain, was defeated by the English and destroyed during a storm. During Elizabeth's reign, England became a world power.

Elizabeth's heir was a Stuart—James VI of Scotland—who joined the two crowns as James I (1603–25). The Stuart kings incurred large debts and were forced either to depend on Parliament for taxes or to raise money by illegal means. In 1642, war broke out between Charles I and a large segment of the Parliament; Charles was defeated and executed in 1649, and the monarchy was then abolished. After the death in 1658 of Oliver Cromwell, the Lord Protector, the Puritan Commonwealth fell to pieces and Charles II was placed on the throne in 1660. The struggle between the King and Parliament continued, but Charles II knew when to compromise. His brother, James II (1685–88), possessed none of his ability

British Prime Ministers Since 1770

Name	Term	Name	Term
Lord North (Tory)	1770–1782	William E. Gladstone (Liberal)	1886–1886
Marquis of Rockingham (Whig)	1782–1782	Marquis of Salisbury (Conservative)	1886–1892
Earl of Shelburne (Whig)	1782–1783	William E. Gladstone (Liberal)	1892–1894
Duke of Portland (Coalition)	1783–1783	Earl of Rosebery (Liberal)	1894–1895
William Pitt, the Younger (Tory)	1783–1801	Marquis of Salisbury (Conservative)	1895–1902
Henry Addington (Tory)	1801–1804	Earl Balfour (Conservative)	1902–1905
William Pitt, the Younger (Tory)	1804–1806	Sir H. Campbell–Bannerman (Liberal)	1905–1908
Baron Grenville (Whig)	1806–1807	Herbert H. Asquith (Liberal)	1908–1915
Duke of Portland (Tory)	1807–1809	Herbert H. Asquith (Coalition)	1915–1916
Spencer Perceval (Tory)	1809–1812	David Lloyd George (Coalition)	1916–1922
Earl of Liverpool (Tory)	1812–1827	Andrew Bonar Law (Conservative)	1922–1923
George Canning (Tory)	1827–1827	Stanley Baldwin (Conservative)	1923–1924
Viscount Goderich (Tory)	1827–1828	James Ramsay MacDonald (Labor)	1924–1924
Duke of Wellington (Tory)	1828–1830	Stanley Baldwin (Conservative)	1924–1929
Earl Grey (Whig)	1830–1834	James Ramsay MacDonald (Labor)	1929–1931
Viscount Melbourne (Whig)	1834–1834	James Ramsay MacDonald (Coalition)	1931–1935
Sir Robert Peel (Tory)	1834–1835	Stanley Baldwin (Coalition)	1935–1937
Viscount Melbourne (Whig)	1835–1841	Neville Chamberlain (Coalition)	1937–1940
Sir Robert Peel (Tory)	1841–1846	Winston Churchill (Coalition)	1940–1945
Earl Russell (Whig)	1846–1852	Clement R. Attlee (Labor)	1945–1951
Earl of Derby (Tory)	1852–1852	Sir Winston Churchill (Conservative)	1951–1955
Earl of Aberdeen (Coalition)	1852–1855	Sir Anthony Eden (Conservative)	1955–1957
Viscount Palmerston (Liberal)	1855–1858	Harold Macmillan (Conservative)	1957–1963
Earl of Derby (Conservative)	1858–1859	Sir Alec Frederick Douglas–Home	
Viscount Palmerston (Liberal)	1859–1865	(Conservative)	1963–1964
Earl Russell (Liberal)	1865–1866	Harold Wilson (Labor)	1964–1970
Earl of Derby (Conservative)	1866–1868	Edward Heath (Conservative)	1970–1974
Benjamin Disraeli (Conservative)	1868–1868	Harold Wilson (Labor)	1974–1976
William E. Gladstone (Liberal)	1868–1874	James Callaghan (Labor)	1976–1979
Benjamin Disraeli (Conservative)	1874–1880	Margaret Thatcher (Conservative)	1979–1990
William E. Gladstone (Liberal)	1880–1885	John Major (Conservative)	1990–
Marquis of Salisbury (Conservative)	1885–1886		

and was ousted by the Revolution of 1688, which confirmed the primacy of Parliament. James's daughter, Mary, and her husband, William of Orange, were now the rulers.

Queen Anne's reign (1702–14) was marked by the Duke of Marlborough's victories over France at Blenheim, Oudenarde, and Malplaquet in the War of the Spanish Succession. England and Scotland meanwhile were joined by the Act of Union (1707). Upon the death of Anne, the distant claims of the elector of Hanover were recognized, and he became King of Great Britain and Ireland as George I.

The unwillingness of the Hanoverian kings to rule resulted in the formation by the royal ministers of a Cabinet, headed by a Prime Minister, which directed all public business. Abroad, the constant wars with France expanded the British Empire all over the globe, particularly in North America and India. This imperial growth was checked by the revolt of the American colonies (1775–81).

Struggles with France broke out again in 1793 and during the Napoleonic Wars, which ended at Waterloo in (1815).

The Victorian era, named after Queen Victoria (1837–1901), saw the growth of a democratic system of government that had begun with the Reform Bill of 1832. The two important wars in Victoria's reign were the Crimean War against Russia (1853–56) and the Boer War (1899–1902), the latter enormously extending Britain's influence in Africa.

Increasing uneasiness at home and abroad marked the reign of Edward VII (1901–10). Within four years after the accession of George V in 1910, Britain entered World War I when Germany invaded Belgium. The nation was led by coalition Cabinets, headed first by Herbert Asquith and then, starting in 1916, by the Welsh statesman David Lloyd George. Postwar labor unrest culminated in the general strike of 1926.

King Edward VIII succeeded to the throne on Jan. 20, 1936, at his father's death, but abdicated on Dec. 11, 1936 (in order to marry an American divorcee, Wallis Warfield Simpson) in favor of his brother, who became George VI.

The efforts of Prime Minister Neville Chamberlain to stem the rising threat of Nazism in Germany failed with the German invasion of Poland on Sept. 1, 1939, which was followed by Britain's entry into World War II on September 3. Allied reverses in the spring of 1940 led to Chamberlain's resignation and the formation of another coalition war Cabinet by the Conservative leader, Winston Churchill, who led Britain through most of World War II. Churchill resigned shortly after V-E Day, May 7, 1945, but then formed a "caretaker" government that remained in office until after the parliamentary elections in July, which the Labor Party won overwhelmingly. The government formed by Clement R. Attlee began a moderate socialist program.

For details of World War II (1939–45), *see* Headline History.

In 1951, Churchill again became Prime Minister at the head of a Conservative government. George VI died Feb. 6, 1952, and was succeeded by his daughter Elizabeth II.

Churchill stepped down in 1955 in favor of Sir Anthony Eden, who resigned on grounds of ill health in 1957, and was succeeded by Harold Macmillan and Sir Alec Douglas-Home. In 1964, Harold Wilson led the Labor Party to victory.

A lagging economy brought the Conservatives back to power in 1970. Prime Minister Edward Heath won Britain's admission to the European Community.

Margaret Thatcher became Britain's first woman Prime Minister as the Conservatives won 339 seats on May 3, 1979.

An Argentine invasion of the Falkland Islands on April 2, 1982, involved Britain in a war 8,000 miles from the home islands. Although Argentina had long claimed the Falklands, known as the Malvinas in Spanish, negotiations were in progress until a month before the invasion. The Thatcher government responded to the invasion with a 40-ship task force, which sailed from Portsmouth on April 5. U.S. efforts to settle the dispute failed and United Nations efforts collapsed as the Argentine military government ignored Security Council resolutions calling for a withdrawal of its forces.

When more than 11,000 Argentine troops on the Falklands surrendered on June 14, 1982, Mrs. Thatcher declared her intention to garrison the islands indefinitely, together with a naval presence.

In the general election of June 9, 1983, Prime Minister Thatcher and her Conservative party won a landslide victory over the Laborites and other opponents.

Although there were continuing economic problems and foreign policy disputes, an upswing in the economy in 1986–87 led Thatcher to call elections for June 11 in which she won a near-unprecedented third consecutive term.

Through much, if not all, of 1990 the Conservatives were losing the confidence of the electorate. The unpopularity of her poll tax together with an uncompromising position toward further European integration eroded support within her own party. When John Major won the Conservative Party leadership in November, Mrs. Thatcher resigned, paving the way for the Queen to ask Mr. Major to form a government. In the ensuing months the prime minister has revamped the nation's tax system.

NORTHERN IRELAND

Status: Part of United Kingdom
Secretary of State: Thomas Jeremy King
Area: 5,452 sq mi. (14,121 sq km)
Population (est. 1988): 1,598,100
Density per square mile: 279.7
Capital and largest city (est. mid-1987): Belfast, 303,800
Monetary unit: British pound sterling
Languages: English, Gaelic
Religions: Roman Catholic, 28%; Presbyterian, 22.9%; Church of Ireland, 19%; Methodist, 4%

Geography. Northern Ireland comprises the counties of Antrim, Armagh, Down, Fermanagh, Londonderry, and Tyrone, which make up predominantly Protestant Ulster and form the northern part of the island of Ireland, westernmost of the British Isles. It is slightly larger than Connecticut.

Government. Northern Ireland is an integral part of the United Kingdom (it has 12 representatives in the British House of Commons), but under the terms of

the government of Ireland Act in 1920, it had a semi-autonomous government. But in 1972, after three years of internal strife which resulted in over 400 dead and thousands injured, Britain suspended the Ulster parliament. The Ulster counties became governed directly from London after an attempt to return certain powers to an elected Assembly in Belfast.

The Northern Ireland Assembly was dissolved in 1975 and a Constitutional Convention was elected to write a Constitution acceptable to Protestants and Catholics. The convention failed to reach agreement and closed down the next year.

History. Ulster was part of Catholic Ireland until the reign of Elizabeth I (1558–1603) when, after crushing three Irish rebellions, the crown confiscated lands in Ireland and settled in Ulster the Scot Presbyterians who became rooted there. Another rebellion in 1641–51, crushed as brutally by Oliver Cromwell, resulted in the settlement of Anglican Englishmen in Ulster. Subsequent political policy favoring Protestants and disadvantaging Catholics encouraged further settlement in Northern Ireland.

But the North did not separate from the South until William Gladstone presented in 1886 his proposal for home rule in Ireland as a means of settling the Irish Question. The Protestants in the North, although they had grievances like the Catholics in the South, feared domination by the Catholic majority. Industry, moreover, was concentrated in the north and dependent on the British market.

When World War I began, civil war threatened between the regions. Northern Ireland, however, did not become a political entity until the six counties accepted the Home Rule Bill of 1920. This set up a semiautonomous Parliament in Belfast and a Crown-appointed Governor advised by a Cabinet of the Prime Minister and eight ministers, as well as a 12-member representation in the House of Commons in London.

As the Republic of Ireland gained its sovereignty, relations improved between North and South, although the Irish Republican Army, outlawed in recent years, continued the struggle to end the partition of Ireland. In 1966–69, communal rioting and street fighting between Protestants and Catholics occurred in Londonderry, fomented by extremist nationalist Protestants, who feared the Catholics might attain a local majority, and by Catholics demonstrating for civil rights.

Rioting, terrorism, and sniping killed more than 2,200 people from 1969 through 1984 and the religious communities, Catholic and Protestant, became hostile armed camps. British troops were brought in to separate them but themselves became a target of Catholics.

In 1973, a new British charter created a 78-member Assembly elected by proportional representation that gave more weight to Catholic strength. It created a Province Executive with committee chairmen of the Assembly heading all government departments except law enforcement, which remained under London's control. Assembly elections in 1973 produced a majority for the new Constitution that included Catholic assemblymen.

Ulster's leaders agreed in 1973 to create an 11-member Executive Body with six seats assigned to Unionists (Protestants) and four to members of Catholic parties. Unionist leader Brian Faulkner headed the Executive. Also agreed to was a Council of Ireland, with 14 seats evenly divided between Dublin and Belfast, which could act only by unanimous vote.

Although the Council lacked real authority, its creation sparked a general strike by Protestant extremists in 1974. The two-week strike caused Faulkner's resignation from the Executive and resumption of direct rule from London.

In April 1974, London instituted a new program that responded to some Catholic grievances, but assigned more British troops to cut off movement of arms and munitions to Ulster's violence-racked cities.

Violence continued unabated, with new heights reached early in 1976 when the British government announced the end of special privileges for political prisoners in Northern Ireland. British Prime Minister James Callaghan visited Belfast in July and pledged that Ulster would remain part of the United Kingdom unless a clear majority wished to separate.

In October 1977, the 1976 Nobel Prize for Peace was awarded to Mairead Corrigan and Betty Williams for their campaign for peace in Northern Ireland. Intermittent violence continued, however, and on Aug. 27, 1979, an I.R.A. bomb killed Earl Mountbatten as he was sailing off southern Ireland.

New talks aimed at a restoration of home rule in Northern Ireland began and quickly ended in January 1980. In May, Mrs. Thatcher met with the new Prime Minister of the Irish Republic, Charles Haughey, but she insisted that the future of Ulster must be decided only by its people and the British Parliament. Haughey declared that an internal solution "cannot and will not succeed."

On November 15, 1985, Mrs. Thatcher signed an agreement with Irish Prime Minister Garrett Fitzgerald giving Ireland a consultative role in the affairs of Northern Ireland. It was met with intense disapproval by the Ulster Unionists.

Talks began in June 1991 between leaders of four major Ulster political parties. The hope was that these talks would lead to some degree of home rule in Northern Ireland. On July 3, however, they collapsed.

Dependencies of the United Kingdom

ANGUILLA

Status: Dependency
Governor: B. G. Canty (1989)
Area: 35 sq mi. (91 sq km)
Population (U.N. est. 1988): 8,000
Monetary unit: East Caribbean dollar
Literacy: 80%

Anguilla was originally part of the West Indies Associated States as a component of St. Kitts-Nevis-Anguilla.

In 1967, Anguilla declared its independence from the St. Kitts-Nevis-Anguilla federation. Britain however, did not recognize this action. In February 1969, Anguilla voted to cut all ties with Britain and become an independent republic. In March, Britain landed troops on the island and, on March 30, a truce was signed. In July 1971, Anguilla became a dependency of Britain and two months later Britain ordered the withdrawal of all its troops.

A new Constitution for Anguilla, effective in February 1976, provides for separate administration and a government of elected representatives. The Associated State of St. Kitts-Nevis-Anguilla ended Dec. 19, 1980.

BERMUDA

Status: Self-governing dependency
Governor: Sir Desmond Langley (1988)
Premier: John Swan (1982)
Area: 20 sq mi. (52 sq km)
Population (mid-1989): 58,238 (average annual growth rate: 0.2%)
Capital (1989): Hamilton, 2,000
Monetary unit: Bermuda dollar
Literacy rate: 98%
Economic summary: Gross domestic product (1989 est.): $1.3 billion; $23,000 per capita; 2.0% real growth rate. Arable land: 0%. Principal agricultural products: bananas, vegetables, citrus fruits, dairy products. Labor force: 32,000; 47% clerical and in services. Major industrial products: structural concrete, paints, pharmaceuticals. Natural resource: limestone. Exports: semi-tropical produce, light manufactures. Imports: foodstuffs, fuel, machinery. Major trading partners: U.S., U.K., Canada.

Bermuda is an archipelago of about 360 small islands, 580 miles (934 km) east of North Carolina. The largest is (Great) Bermuda, or Long Island. Discovered by Juan de Bermúdez, a shipwrecked Spaniard, early in the 16th century, the islands were settled in 1612 by an offshoot of the Virginia Company and became a crown colony in 1684.

In 1940, sites on the islands were leased for 99 years to the U.S. for air and navy bases. Bermuda is also the headquarters of the West Indies and Atlantic squadron of the Royal Navy.

In 1968, Bermuda was granted a new Constitution, its first Prime Minister, and autonomy, except for foreign relations, defense, and internal security. The predominantly white United Bermuda Party has retained power in four elections against the opposition—the black-led Progressive Laborites—although Bermuda's population is 60% black. Serious rioting occurred in December 1977 after two blacks were hanged for a series of murders, including the 1973 assassination of the Governor, Sir Richard Sharples, and British troops were summoned to restore order.

BRITISH ANTARCTIC TERRITORY

Status: Dependency
High Commissioner: William Hugh Fullerton (1988)
Area: 500,000 sq mi. (1,395,000 sq km)
Population (1986): no permanent residents

The British Antarctic Territory consists of the South Shetland Islands, South Orkney Islands, and nearby Graham Land on the Antarctic continent, largely uninhabited. They are dependencies of the British crown colony of the Falkland Islands but received a separate administration in 1962, being governed by a British-appointed High Commissioner who is Governor of the Falklands.

BRITISH INDIAN OCEAN TERRITORY

Status: Dependency
Commissioner and Administrator: R. Edis
Administrative headquarters: Victoria, Seychelles
Area: 85 sq mi. (220 sq km)

This dependency, consisting of the Chagos Archipelago and other small island groups, was formed in 1965 by agreement with Mauritius and the Seychelles. There is no permanent civilian population in the territory.

BRITISH VIRGIN ISLANDS

Status: Dependency
Governor: Mark Herdman (1986)
Area: 59 sq mi. (153 sq km)
Population (mid-1989): 12,124 (growth rate: 1.1%)
Capital (est. 1986): Road Town (on Tortola): 2,479
Monetary unit: U.S. dollar

Some 36 islands in the Caribbean Sea northeast of Puerto Rico and west of the Leeward Islands, the British Virgin Islands are economically interdependent with the U.S. Virgin Islands to the south. They were formerly part of the administration of the Leeward Islands. They received a separate administration in 1956 as a crown colony. In 1967 a new Constitution was promulgated that provided for a ministerial system of government headed by the Governor. The principal islands are Tortola, Virgin Gorda, Anegada, and Jost Van Dyke.

CAYMAN ISLANDS

Status: Dependency
Governor: Alan James Scott (1987)
Area: 100 sq mi. (259 sq km)
Population (census 1989): 25,535
Capital (1989): George Town (on Grand Cayman), 12,972
Monetary unit: Cayman Islands dollar

This dependency consists of three islands—Grand Cayman (76 sq mi.; 197 sq km), Cayman Brac (22 sq mi.; 57 sq km), and Little Cayman (20 sq mi.; 52 sq km)—situated about 180 miles (290 km) northwest of Jamaica. They were dependencies of Jamaica until 1959, when they became a unit territory within the Federation of the West Indies. In 1962, upon the dissolution of the Federation, the Cayman Islands became a British dependency.

The islands' chief export is turtle products.

CHANNEL ISLANDS

Status: Crown dependencies
Lieutenant Governor of Jersey: Air Marshall Sir John Sutton (1990)
Lieutenant Governor of Guernsey: Lt. Gen. Sir Michael Wilkins (1990)
Area: 120 sq mi. (311 sq km)
Population (1988): 133,960
Capital of Jersey: St. Helier
Capital of Guernsey: St. Peter Port
Monetary units: Guernsey pound; Jersey pound

This group of islands, lying in the English Channel off the northwest coast of France, is the only portion of the Duchy of Normandy belonging to the English Crown, to which it has been attached since the conquest of 1066. It was the only British possession occupied by Germany during World War II.

For purposes of government, the islands are divided into the Bailiwick of Jersey (45 sq mi.; 117 sq km) and the Bailiwick of Guernsey (30 sq mi.; 78 sq km), including Alderney (3 sq mi.; 7.8 sq km); Sark (2 sq mi.; 5.2 sq km), Herm, Jethou, etc. The islands are administered according to their own laws and customs by local governments. Acts of Parliament in London are not binding on the islands unless they are specifically mentioned. The Queen is represented in each Bailiwick by a Lieutenant Governor.

FALKLAND ISLANDS AND DEPENDENCIES

Status: Dependency
Governor: William Hugh Fullerton (1988)
Chief Executive: R. Sampson
Area: 4,700 sq mi. (12,173 sq km)
Population est. (mid-1989): 1,943 (growth rate: .5%)
Capital (est. 1986): Stanley (on East Falkland), 1,231
Monetary unit: Falkland Island pound

This sparsely inhabited dependency consists of a group of islands in the South Atlantic, about 250 miles (402 km) east of the South American mainland. The largest islands are East Falkland and West Falkland. Dependencies are South Georgia Island (1,450 sq mi.; 3,756 sq km), the South Sandwich Islands, and other islets. Three former dependencies—Graham Land, the South Shetland Islands, and the South Orkney Islands—were established as a new British dependency, the British Antarctic Territory, in 1962.

The chief industry is sheep raising and, apart from the production of wool, hides and skins, and tallow, there are no known resources. The whaling industry is carried on from South Georgia Island.

The chief export is wool.

GIBRALTAR

Status: Self-governing dependency
Governor: Admiral Sir Derek Reffell
Chief Minister: J. Bossano
Area: 2.25 sq mi. (5.8 sq km)
Population (1989): 30,689 (growth rate: .2%)
Monetary unit: Gibraltar pound
Literacy rate: 99% (est.)
Economic summary: Gross national product (FY85 est.): $129 million; $4,450 per capita. Exports: re-exports of tobacco, petroleum, wine. Imports: manufactured goods, fuels, foodstuffs. Major trading partners: U.K., Morocco, Portugal, Netherlands, Spain, U.S.

Gibraltar, at the south end of the Iberian Peninsula, is a rocky promontory commanding the western entrance to the Mediterranean. Aside from its strategic importance, it is also a free port, naval base, and coaling station. It was captured by the Arabs crossing from Africa into Spain in A.D. 711. In the 15th century, it passed to the Moorish ruler of Granada and later became Spanish. It was captured by an Anglo-Dutch force in 1704 during the War of the Spanish Succession and passed to Great Britain by the Treaty of Utrecht in 1713. Most of the inhabitants of Gibraltar are of Spanish, Italian, and Maltese descent.

Spanish efforts to recover Gibraltar culminated in a referendum in 1967 in which the residents voted overwhelmingly to retain their link with Britain. Spain sealed Gibraltar's land border in 1969 and did not open communications until April 1980, after the two governments had agreed to solve their dispute in keeping with a United Nations resolution calling for restoration of the "Rock" to Spain.

HONG KONG

Status: Dependency
Governor: Sir David Wilson (1987)
Area: 398 sq mi. (1,031 sq km)
Population (est. mid-1991): 5,900,000 (average annual rate of natural increase: 0.7%); birth rate: 12/1000; infant mortality rate: 7.4/1000; density per square mile: 14,584
Capital (1976 census): Victoria (Hong Kong Island), 501,700
Monetary unit: Hong Kong dollar
Literacy rate: 75%
Economic summary: Gross domestic product (1989): $57 billion; $10,000 per capita; 3% real growth rate. Arable land: 7%. Principal products: vegetables, rice, dairy products. Labor force: 2,640,000; 35.8% in manufacturing. Major industrial products: textiles, clothing, toys, transistor radios, watches, electronic components. Exports: clothing, textiles, toys, watches, electrical appliances, footwear. Imports: raw materials, transport equipment, food. Major trading partners: U.S., U.K., Japan, Germany, China, Taiwan.

The crown colony of Hong Kong comprises the island of Hong Kong (32 sq mi.; 83 sq km), Stonecutters' Island, Kowloon Peninsula, and the New Territories on the adjoining mainland. The island of Hong Kong, located at the mouth of the Pearl River about 90 miles (145 km) southeast of Canton, was ceded to Britain in 1841.

Stonecutters' Island and Kowloon were annexed in 1860, and the New Territories, which are mainly agricultural lands, were leased from China in 1898 for 99 years. Hong Kong was attacked by Japanese troops Dec. 7, 1941, and surrendered the following Christmas. It remained under Japanese occupation until August 1945.

After two years of painstaking negotiation, authorities of Britain and the People's Republic of China agreed in 1984 that Hong Kong would return to Chinese sovereignty on June 30, 1997, when Britain's lease on the New Territories expires. They also agreed that the vibrant capitalist enclave on China's coast would retain its status as a free port and its social, economic, and legal system as a special administrative region of China. Current laws will remain basically unchanged.

Under a unique "One Country, Two Systems" arrangement, the Chinese government promised that Hong Kong's lifestyle would remain unchanged for 50 years, and that freedoms of speech, press, assembly, association, travel, right to strike, and religious belief would be guaranteed by law. However, the chief executive and some of the legislature will be appointed by Beijing.

Hong Kong will continue to have its own finances and issue its own travel documents, and Peking will not levy taxes.

The crackdown by hard-liners in China has led to apprehension that Hong Kong's autonomy won't be respected.

ISLE OF MAN

Status: Self-Governing Crown Dependency
Lieutenant Governor: Air Marshall Sir Laurence Jones
Area: 227 sq mi. (588 sq km)
Population (mid-1989): 64,728 (growth rate: .2%)
Capital (1986): Douglas, 20,368
Monetary unit: Isle of Man pound

Situated in the Irish Sea, equidistaht from Scotland, Ireland, and England, the Isle of Man is administered according to its own laws by a government composed of the Lieutenant Governor, a Legislative Council, and a House of Keys, one of the most ancient legislative assemblies in the world.

The chief exports are beef and lamb, fish, and livestock.

LEEWARD ISLANDS

See British Virgin Islands; Montserrat

MONTSERRAT

Status: Dependency
Governor: David Taylor (1990)
Area: 38 sq mi. (98 sq km)
Population (mid-1989): 12,428 (growth rate: .3%)
Capital (est. 1988): Plymouth, 3,000
Monetary unit: East Caribbean dollar

The island of Montserrat is in the Lesser Antilles of the West Indies. Until 1956, it was a division of the Leeward Islands. It did not join the West Indies Associated States established in 1967.

The chief exports are cattle, potatoes, cotton, lint, recapped tires, mangoes, and tomatoes.

PITCAIRN ISLAND

Status: Dependency
Governor: David Joseph Moss
Island Magistrate: B. Young
Area: 1.75 sq mi. (4.5 sq km)
Population (April 1990): 65 (growth rate: 0%)
Capital: Adamstown

Pitcairn Island, in the South Pacific about midway between Australia and South America, consists of the island of Pitcairn and the three uninhabited islands of Henderson, Duicie, and Oeno. The island of Pitcairn was settled in 1790 by British mutineers from the ship *Bounty*, commanded by Capt. William Bligh. It was annexed as a British colony in 1838. Overpopulation forced removal of the settlement to Norfolk Island in 1856, but about 40 persons soon returned.

The colony is governed by a 10-member Council presided over by the Island Magistrate, who is elected for a three-year term.

ST. HELENA

Status: Dependency
Governor: Robert F. Stimson (1988)
Area: 120 sq mi. (310 sq km)
Population (mid-1989): 7,200 (growth rate: .6%)
Capital (1987): Jamestown, 1,330
Monetary unit: Pound sterling

St. Helena is a volcanic island in the South Atlantic about 1,100 miles (1,770 km) from the west coast of Africa. It is famous as the place of exile of Napoleon (1815–21).

It was taken for England in 1659 by the East India Company and was brought under the direct government of the Crown in 1834.

St. Helena has two dependencies: Ascension (34 sq mi.; 88 sq km), an island about 700 miles (1,127 km) northwest of St. Helena; and Tristan da Cunha (40 sq mi.; 104 sq km), a group of six islands about 1,500 miles (2,414 km) south-southwest of St. Helena.

TURKS AND CAICOS ISLANDS

Status: Dependency
Governor: Michael Bradley (1987)
Area: 193 sq mi. (500 sq km)
Population (mid-1989): 9,531 (growth rate: 2.4%)
Capital (est. 1988): Grand Turk, 4,500
Monetary unit: U.S. dollar

These two groups of islands are situated at the southeast end of the Bahamas. The principal islands in the Turks group are Grand Turk and Salt Cay; the principal ones in the Caicos group are South Caicos, East Caicos, Middle (or Grand) Caicos, North Caicos, Providenciales, and West Caicos.

The Turks and Caicos Islands were dependencies of Jamaica until 1959, when they became a unit territory within the Federation of the West Indies. In 1962, when Jamaica became independent, the Turks and Caicos became a British crown colony. The present Constitution has been in force since 1969.

Chief exports in 1974 were crayfish (73%) and conch (25%).

VIRGIN ISLANDS

See British Virgin Islands

UNITED STATES

The United States of America
President: George Bush (1989)
Area: 3,540,939 sq mi. (9,171,032 sq km)
Population (1990 census): 248,709,873 (% change 1980–1990: +9.80). White: 199,686,070 (80.3%); Black: 29,986,060 (12.1%); American Indian, Eskimo, or Aleut: 1,959,234 (0.8%); Asian or Pacific Islander: 7,273,662 (2.9%); Other Race: 9,804,847 (3.9%); Hispanic Origin[1]: 22,354,059 (9.0%)
Density per square mile: 70.2
Capital (1990 census): Washington, D.C., 606,900
Largest cities (1990 census): New York, 7,322,564; Los Angeles, 3,485,398; Chicago, 2,783,726; Houston, 1,630,553; Philadelphia, 1,585,577; San Diego, 1,110,549; Detroit, 1,027,974; Dallas, 1,006,877; Phoenix, 983,403; San Antonio, 935,933
Monetary unit: Dollar
Languages: predominantly English, sizable Spanish-speaking minority
Religions: Protestant, 61%; Roman Catholic, 25%; Jewish, 2%; other, 5%; none, 7%
Literacy rate: 99%
Economic summary: Gross national product (1990): $5,465.1 billion; per capita (1990): $21,974; real growth rate: 2.9%. Arable land: 20%. Principal products: corn, wheat, barley, oats, sugar, potatoes, soybeans, fruits, beef, veal, pork. Labor force: 125,557,000. Major industrial products: petroleum products, fertilizers, cement, pig iron and steel, plastics and resins, newsprint, motor vehicles, machinery, natural gas, electricity. Natural resources: coal, oil, copper, gold, silver, minerals, timber. Exports: machinery, chemicals, aircrafts, military equipment, cereals, motor vehicles, grains. Imports: crude and partly refined petroleum, machinery, automobiles. Major trading partners: Canada, Japan.

1. Persons of Hispanic origin can be of any race.

Government. The president is elected for a four-year term and may be re-elected only once. In 1991, the bicameral Congress consisted of the 100-member Senate (57 Democrats, 43 Republicans), elected to a six-year term with one-third of the seats becoming vacant every two years, and the 435-member House of Representatives (267 Democrats, 165 Republicans, 1 Independent),[2] elected every two years. The minimum voting age is 18.

2. As of June 1991 there were 2 vacant House seats.

URUGUAY

Oriental Republic of Uruguay
President: Luis Alberto Lacalle (1990)
Area: 68,040 sq mi. (176,224 sq km)
Population (est. mid-1991): 3,100,000 (average annual rate of natural increase: 0.8%); birth rate: 18/1000; infant mortality rate: 21.9/1000; density per square mile: 46
Capital and largest city (est. 1982): Montevideo, 1,325,000
Monetary unit: Peso
Language: Spanish
Religion: Roman Catholic, 66%; Protestant, 2%; Jewish, 2%
National name: Republica Oriental del Uruguay
Literacy rate: 94%
Economic summary: Gross domestic product (1989 est.): $8.8 billion, $2,950 per capita; 1% real growth rate. Arable land: 8%. Principal products: livestock, grains, Labor force: 1,300,000; 19% in manufacturing;. Major products: processed meats, wool and hides, textiles, shoes, handbags and leather wearing apparel, cement, refined petroleum. Natural resources: hydroelectric power potential. Exports: meat, hides, wool, fish. Imports: crude petroleum, transportation equipment, chemicals, machinery, metals. Major trading partners: U.S., Brazil, Argentina, Germany.

Geography. Uruguay, on the east coast of South America south of Brazil and east of Argentina, is comparable in size to the State of Washington.

The country consists of a low, rolling plain in the south and a low plateau in the north. It has a 120-mile (193 km) Atlantic shore line, a 235-mile (378 km) frontage on the Rio de la Plata, and 270 miles (435 km) on the Uruguay River, its western boundary.

Government. After elections in November 1984, Julio Maria Sanguinetti was inaugurated as President on March 1, 1985, ending 12 years of military rule. Under the Constitution, Presidents serve a single five-year term. The bicameral Congress, dissolved by the military in 1973, also was restored in 1985.

History. Juan Díaz de Solis, a Spaniard, discovered Uruguay in 1516, but the Portuguese were first to settle it when they founded Colonia in 1680. After a long struggle, Spain wrested the country from Portugal in 1778. Uruguay revolted against Spain in 1811, only to be conquered in 1817 by the Portuguese from Brazil. Independence was reasserted with Argentine help in 1825, and the republic was set up in 1828.

Independence, however, did not restore order, and a revolt in 1836 touched off nearly 50 years of factional strife, with occasional armed intervention from Argentina and Brazil.

Uruguay, made prosperous by meat and wool exports, founded a welfare state early in the 20th century. A decline began in the 1950s as successive governments struggled to maintain a large bureaucracy and costly social benefits. Economic stagnation and political frustration followed.

A military coup ousted the civilian government in 1973. The military dictatorship that followed used fear and terror to demoralize the population, taking thousands of political prisoners, probably the highest proportion of citizens jailed for political reasons anywhere in the world.

After ruling for 12 years, the military regime permitted election of a civilian government in November 1984 and relinquished rule in March 1985.

Luis Lacalle became president in March 1990, becoming the first Blanco Party member to assume that office in 23 years. His position, however, became contingent upon accepting four members of the opposition Colorados party into his cabinet.

VANUATU

Republic of Vanuatu
President: Fred Timakata (1989)
Prime Minister: Fr. Walter Lini (1980)
Area: 5,700 sq mi. (14,763 sq km)
Population (est. mid-1991): 200,000 (average annual rate of natural increase: 3.1%); birth rate: 36/1000; infant mortality rate: 36/1000; density per square mile: 30
Capital (est. 1987): Port Vila, 15,100
Monetary unit: Vatu
Religions: Presbyterian, 47%; Roman Catholic, 15%; Anglican, 15%; other Christian, 10%; Animist, 9%
Literacy rate: 10–20% (est.)
Economic Summary: Gross domestic product (1987 est.): $120 million, $820 per capita; real growth rate: 0.7%. Arable land: 1%. Principal agricultural products: copra, cocoa, coffee. Exports: copra, cocoa, coffee, frozen fish. Imports: food, machinery. Major trading partners: France, New Zealand, Japan, Australia, Netherlands.

Geography. Formerly known as the New Hebrides, Vanuatu is an archipelago of some 80 islands lying between New Caledonia and Fiji in the South Pacific. Largest of the islands is Espiritu Santo (875 sq mi.; 2,266 sq km); others are Efate, Malekula, Malo, Pentecost, and Tanna. The population is largely Melanesian of mixed blood.

Government. The constitution by which Vanuatu achieved independence on July 30, 1980, vests executive authority in a President, elected by an electoral college for a five-year term. A unicameral legislature of 39 members exercises legislative power.

History. The islands were discovered by Pedro Fernandes de Queiros of Portugal in 1606 and were charted and named by the British navigator James Cook in 1774. Conflicting British and French interests were resolved by a joint naval commission that administered the islands from 1887. A condominium government was established in 1906.

The islands' plantation economy, based on imported Vietnamese labor, was prosperous until the 1920s, when markets for its products declined. The New Hebrides escaped Japanese occupation in World War II and the French population was among the first to support the Gaullist Free French movement.

A brief rebellion by French settlers and plantation workers on Espiritu Santo led by Jimmy Stevens in May 1980 threatened the scheduled independence of the islands. Britain sent a company of Royal Marines and France a contingent of 50 policemen to quell the revolt, which the new government said was financed by the Phoenix Foundation, a right-wing U.S. group. With the British and French forces replaced by soldiers from Papua New Guinea, independence ceremonies took place on July 30. The next month it was reported that Stevens had been arrested and the revolt quelled.

On the tenth anniversary of independence in 1990 prime minister Lini called for a reexamination of the constitution and existing institutions, claiming that they were forged under colonialism.

VATICAN CITY STATE

Ruler: Pope John Paul II (1978)
Area: 0.17 sq mi. (0.44 sq km)
Population (mid-1989): 755
Density per square mile: 4,424
Monetary unit: Lira
Languages: Latin and Italian
Religion: Roman Catholic
National name: Stato della Città del Vaticano

Geography. The Vatican City State is situated on the Vatican hill, on the right bank of the Tiber River, within the commune of Rome.

Government. The Pope has full legal, executive, and judicial powers. Executive power over the area is in the hands of a Commission of Cardinals appointed by the Pope. The College of Cardinals is the Pope's chief advisory body, and upon his death the cardinals elect his successor for life. The cardinals themselves are created for life by the Pope.

In the Vatican the central administration of the Roman Catholic Church throughout the world (Holy See) is carried on by the Secretariat of State, nine Congregations, three tribunals, twelve councils, and five offices. In its diplomatic relations, the Holy See is represented by the Papal Secretary of State.

History. The Vatican City State, sovereign and independent, is the survivor of the papal states that in 1859 comprised an area of some 17,000 square miles (44,030 sq km). During the struggle for Italian unification, from 1860 to 1870, most of this area became part of Italy.

By an Italian law of May 13, 1871, the temporal power of the Pope was abrogated, and the territory of the Papacy was confined to the Vatican and Lateran palaces and the villa of Castel Gandolfo. The Popes consistently refused to recognize this arrangement and, by the Lateran Treaty of Feb. 11, 1929, between the Vatican and the Kingdom of Italy, the exclusive dominion and sovereign jurisdiction of the Holy See over the city of the Vatican was again recognized, thus restoring the Pope's temporal authority over the area.

The first session of Ecumenical Council Vatican II was opened by John XXIII on Oct. 11, 1962, to plan and set policies for the modernization of the Roman Catholic Church. Pope Paul VI continued the Council, opening the second session on Sept. 29, 1963.

On Aug. 26, 1978, Cardinal Albino Luciani was chosen by the College of Cardinals to succeed Paul VI, who had died of a heart attack on Aug. 6. The new Pope, who took the name John Paul I, was born on Oct. 17, 1912, at Forno di Canale in Italy.

(For a listing of all the Popes, *see* the Index.)

Only 34 days after his election, John Paul I died of a heart attack, ending the shortest reign in 373 years. On Oct. 16, Cardinal Karol Wojtyla, 58, was chosen Pope and took the name John Paul II.

A visit to the Irish Republic and to the United States in September and October 1979, followed by a 12-nation African tour in May 1980 and a visit in July to Brazil, the most populous Catholic nation, further established John Paul's image as a "people's" Pope. On May 13, 1981, a Turkish terrorist shot the Pope in St. Peter's Square, the first assassination attempt against the Pontiff in modern times. Mehmet Ali Agca was sentenced on July 22 to life imprisonment by an Italian Court.

The Pontiff traveled to Britain and Argentina in 1982. He also made a visit to Poland.

On June 3, 1985, the Vatican and Italy ratified a new church-state treaty, known as a concordat, replacing the Lateran Pact of 1929. The new accord affirmed the independence of Vatican City but ended a number of privileges the Catholic Church had in Italy, including its status as the state religion. The treaty ended Rome's status as a "sacred city."

Relations, diplomatic and ecclesiastical, with Eastern Europe have improved dramatically with the fall of communism. Relations with the Soviet Union, while improving, have not yet reached the ambassadorial level.

VENEZUELA

Republic of Venezuela
President: Carlos Andrés Pérez (1989)
Area: 352,143 sq mi. (912,050 sq km)
Population (est. mid-1991): 20,100,000 (average annual rate of natural increase: 2.3%); birth rate: 28/1000; infant mortality rate: 23.3/1000; density per square mile: 57
Capital: Caracas
Largest cities (est. 1981 for metropolitan area): Caracas, 3,000,000; Maracaibo, 890,000; Valencia, 616,000; Barquisimeto, 498,000
Monetary unit: Bolivar
Language: Spanish, Indian dialects in interior
Religion: Roman Catholic
National name: Republica de Venezuela
Literacy rate: 85.6%
Economic summary: Gross domestic product (1989 est.): $52 billion; $2,700 per capita; –8.1% real growth rate. Arable land: 3. Principal products: rice, coffee, corn, sugar, bananas, dairy and meat products. Labor force: 5,800,000; 28% in industry; principal products: refined petroleum products, iron and steel, cement, textiles, transport equipment. Natural resources: petroleum, natural gas, iron ore, hydroelectric power. Exports: petroleum, iron ore. Imports: industrial machinery and equipment, manufactures, chemicals, foodstuffs. Major trading partners: U.S., Japan, Germany, Brazil, Italy.

Geography. Venezuela, a third larger than Texas, occupies most of the northern coast of South America on the Caribbean Sea. It is bordered by Colombia to the west, Guyana to the east, and Brazil to the south.

Mountain systems break Venezuela into four distinct areas: (1) the Maracaibo lowlands; (2) the mountainous region in the north and northwest; (3) the Orinoco basin, with the llanos (vast grass-covered plains) on its northern border and great forest areas in the south and southeast; (4) the Guiana Highlands, south of the Orinoco, accounting for nearly half the national territory. About 80% of Venezuela is drained by the Orinoco and its tributaries.

Government. Venezuela is a federal republic consisting of 20 states, the Federal District, two territories and 72 islands in the Caribbean. There is a bicameral Congress, the 50 members of the Senate and the 201 members of the Chamber of Deputies being elected by popular vote to five-year terms. The President is also elected for five years. He must be a Venezuelan by birth and over 30 years old. He is not eligible for re-election until 10 years after the end of his term.

History. Columbus discovered Venezuela on his third voyage in 1498. A subsequent Spanish explorer gave the country its name, meaning "Little Venice." There were no important settlements until Caracas was founded in 1567. Simón Bolívar, who led the liberation of much of the continent from Spain, was born in Caracas in 1783. With Bolívar taking part, Venezuela was one of the first South American colonies to revolt against Spain, in 1810, but it was not until 1821 that independence was won. Federated at first with Colombia and Ecuador, the country set up a republic in 1830 and then sank for many decades into a condition of revolt, dictatorship, and corruption.

From 1908 to 1935, Gen. Juan Vicente Gómez ruled tyrannically, picking satellites to alternate with him in the presidential palace. Thereafter, there was a struggle between democratic forces and those backing a return to strong-man rule. Dr. Rómulo Betancourt and the liberal Acción Democrática Party won a majority of seats in a constituent assembly to draft a new Constitution in 1946. A well-known writer, Rómulo Gallegos, candidate of Betancourt's party, easily won the presidential election of 1947. But, the army ousted Gallegos the next year and instituted a military junta.

The country overthrew the dictatorship in 1958 and thereafter enjoyed democratic government. Rafael Caldera Rodríguez, President from 1969 to 1974, legalized the Communist Party and established diplomatic relations with Moscow.

Venezuela and neighboring Guyana in 1970 called a 12-year moratorium on their border dispute (Venezuela claimed 50,000 square miles of Guyana's 83,000). In 1974, President Carlos Andrés Perez took office.

In 1976, Venezuela nationalized 21 oil companies, mostly subsidiaries of U.S. firms, offering compensation of $1.28 billion. Oil income in that year was $9.9 billion, and although production decreased 2.2%, revenue remained at the same level in 1977 because of higher prices, largely financing an ambitious social welfare program.

Despite difficulties at home, Pérez continued to play an active foreign role in extending economic aid to Latin neighbors, in backing the human-rights policy of President Carter, and in supporting Carter's return of the Panama Canal to Panama.

Opposition Christian Democrats capitalized on

Pérez's domestic problems to elect Luis Herrera Campíns President in Venezuela's fifth consecutive free election, on Dec. 3, 1978.

Herrera Campins at first supported U.S. policy in Central America, lining up behind the government of El Salvador but he later shifted toward a "political solution" that would include the insurgents. In March 1982, he assailed Reagan's policy as "interventionist."

When the Falklands war broke out, Venezuela became one of the most vigorous advocates of the Argentine cause and one of the sharpest critics of the U.S. decision to back Britain.

Jaime Lusinchi of the Democratic Action party won the country's sixth consecutive free election, on Dec. 4, 1983, and was inaugurated President in March 1984.

In the presidential election of December 1988 former president Carlos Andres Perez of the Democratic Action party easily won. Upon assuming office President Perez introduced an economic austerity program.

VIETNAM

Socialist Republic of Vietnam
President: Vo Chi Cong (1987)
Premier: Vo Van Kiet (1991)
Area: 127,246 sq mi. (329,566 sq km)
Population (est. mid-1991): 67,600,000 (average annual rate of natural increase: 2.3%); birth rate: 32/1000; infant mortality rate: 44/1000; Density per square mile: 531
Capital: Hanoi
Largest cities (est. 1979): Ho Chi Minh City (Saigon),[1] 3,450,000; Hanoi, 2,600,000; Haiphong, 1,280,000; (est. 1973): Da Nang, 492,200; Nha Trang, 216,200; Qui Nho'n, 213,750; Hué 209,000
Monetary unit: Dong
Languages: Vietnamese (official), French, English, Khmer, Chinese
Religions: Buddhist, Roman Catholic, Islam, Taoist, Confucian, Animist
National name: Công Hòa Xa Hôi Chú Nghia Viêt Nam
Literacy rate: 78%
Economic summary: Gross national product (1989 est.): $14.2 billion; $215 per capita; 8% real growth rate. Arable land: 22%. Principal products: rice, rubber, fruits and vegetables, corn, sugar cane, fish. Labor force: 35,000,000 (1989 est.). Major industrial products: processed foods, textiles, cement, chemical fertilizers, glass, tires. Natural resources: phosphates, forests, coal. Exports: agricultural products, coal, minerals. Imports: petroleum, steel products, railroad equipment, chemicals, medicines, raw cotton, fertilizer, grain. Major trading partners: U.S.S.R., Singapore, Japan, Eastern Europe.

1. Includes suburb of Cholon.

Geography. Vietnam occupies the eastern and southern part of the Indochinese peninsula in Southeast Asia, with the South China Sea along its entire coast. China is to the north and Laos and Cambodia to the west. Long and narrow on a north-south axis, Vietnam is about twice the size of Arizona.

The Mekong River delta lies in the south and the Red River delta in the north. Heavily forested mountain and plateau regions make up most of the country.

Government. Less than a year after the capitulation of the former Republic of Vietnam (South Vietnam) on April 30, 1975, a joint National Assembly convened with 249 deputies representing the North and 243 representing the South. The Assembly set July 2, 1976, as the official reunification date. Hanoi became the capital, with North Vietnamese President Ton Duc Thang becoming President of the new Socialist Republic of Vietnam and North Vietnamese Premier Pham Van Dong becoming its head of government. By 1981, the National Assembly had increased to 496 members. Truong Chinh succeeded Thang in 1981.

Dang Cong san Vietnam (Communist Party), led by General Secretary Nguyen Van Linh, is the ruling political party. There are also the Socialist Party and the Democratic Party.

History. The Vietnamese are descendants of Mongoloid nomads from China and migrants from Indonesia. They recognized Chinese suzerainty until the 15th century, an era of nationalistic expansion, when Cambodians were pushed out of the southern area of what is now Vietnam.

A century later, the Portuguese were the first Europeans to enter the area. France established its influence early in the 19th century and within 80 years conquered the three regions into which the country was then divided—Cochin-China in the south, Annam in the center, and Tonkin in the north.

France first unified Vietnam in 1887, when a single governor-generalship was created, followed by the first physical links between north and south—a rail and road system. Even at the beginning of World War II, however, there were internal differences among the three regions.

Japan took over military bases in Vietnam in 1940 and a pro-Vichy French administration remained until 1945. A veteran Communist leader, Ho Chi Minh, organized an independence movement known as the Vietminh to exploit a confused situation. At the end of the war, Ho's followers seized Hanoi and declared a short-lived republic, which ended with the arrival of French forces in 1946.

Paris proposed a unified government within the French Union under the former Annamite emperor, Bao Dai. Cochin-China and Annam accepted the proposal, and Bao Dai was proclaimed emperor of all Vietnam in 1949. Ho and the Vietminh withheld support, and the revolution in China gave them the outside help needed for a war of resistance against French and Vietnamese troops armed largely by the U.S.

A bitter defeat at Dien Bien Phu in northwest Vietnam on May 5, 1954, broke the French military campaign and brought the division of Vietnam at the conference of Geneva that year.

In the new South, Ngo Dinh Diem, Premier under Bao Dai, deposed the monarch in 1955 and established a republic with himself as President. Diem used strong U.S. backing to create an authoritarian regime that suppressed all opposition but could not eradicate the Northern-supplied Communist Viet Cong.

Skirmishing grew into a full-scale war, with escalating U.S. involvement. A military coup, U.S.-inspired in the view of many, ousted Diem Nov. 1, 1963, and a kaleidoscope of military governments followed. The most savage fighting of the war occurred in early 1968, during the Tet holidays.

Although the Viet Cong failed to overthrow the Saigon government, U.S. public reaction to the apparently endless war forced a limitation of U.S. troops to

550,000 and a new emphasis on shifting the burden of further combat to the South Vietnamese. Ho Chi Minh's death on Sept. 3, 1969, brought a quadrumvirate to replace him but no flagging in Northern will to fight.

U.S. bombing and invasion of Cambodia in the summer of 1970—an effort to destroy Viet Cong bases in the neighboring state—marked the end of major U.S. participation in the fighting. Most American ground troops were withdrawn from combat by mid-1971 as heavy bombing of the Ho Chi Minh trail from North Vietnam appeared to cut the supply of men and matériel to the South.

Secret negotiations for peace by Secretary of State Henry A. Kissinger with North Vietnamese officials during 1972 after heavy bombing of Hanoi and Haiphong brought the two sides near agreement in October. When the Northerners demanded the removal of the South's President Nguyen Van Thieu as their price, President Nixon ordered the "Christmas bombing" of the North. The conference resumed and a peace settlement was signed in Paris on Jan. 27, 1973. It called for release of all U.S. prisoners, withdrawal of U.S. forces, limitation of both sides' forces inside South Vietnam, and a commitment to peaceful reunification.

Despite Chinese and Soviet endorsement, the agreement foundered. U.S. bombing of Communist-held areas in Cambodia was halted by Congress in August 1973, and in the following year Communist action in South Vietnam increased.

An armored attack across the 17th parallel in January 1975 panicked the South Vietnamese army and brought the invasion within 40 miles of Saigon by April 9. Thieu resigned on April 21 and fled, to be replaced by Vice President Tran Van Huong, who quit a week later, turning over the office to Gen. Duong Van Minh. "Big Minh" surrendered Saigon on April 30, ending a war that took 1.3 million Vietnamese and 56,000 American lives, at the cost of $141 billion in U.S. aid.

On May 3, 1977, the U.S. and Vietnam opened negotiations in Paris to normalize relations. One of the first results was the withdrawal of U.S. opposition to Vietnamese membership in the United Nations, formalized in the Security Council on July 20. Two major issues remained to be settled, however: the return of the bodies of some 2,500 U.S. servicemen missing in the war and the claim by Hanoi that former President Nixon had promised reconstruction aid under the 1973 agreement. Negotiations failed to resolve these issues.

The new year also brought an intensification of border clashes between Vietnam and Cambodia and accusations by China that Chinese residents of Vietnam were being subjected to persecution. Peking cut off all aid and withdrew 800 technicians.

By June, 133,000 ethnic Chinese were reported to have fled Vietnam, and a year later as many as 500,000 of the 1.8 million Vietnamese of Chinese ancestry were believed to have escaped.

Half of them had gone by land or sea to China. Tens of thousands more had survived boat passage to Thailand, Malaysia, Indonesia, or Hong Kong. U.S. officials said 100,000 may have died. Survivors said they had paid up to $5,000 in bribes to leave Vietnam, and U.S. and British officials charged Hanoi with a deliberate extortion policy.

Hanoi was undoubtedly preoccupied with a continuing war in Cambodia, where 60,000 Vietnamese troops were aiding the Heng Samrin regime in suppressing the last forces of the pro-Chinese Pol Pot regime. In early 1979, Vietnam was conducting a two-front war, defending its northern border against a Chinese invasion and at the same time supporting its army in Cambodia.

Despite Hanoi's claims of total victory, resistance in Cambodia continued through 1984. Vietnam's second conflict, on its border with China, also flared sporadically.

The Hanoi government agreed in July 1984 to resume technical talks with U.S. officials on the possible whereabouts of the 2,490 Americans still listed as missing, most of them believed dead. In August 1985, the North Vietnamese turned over to an American team 26 numbered crates described as containing the remains of 26 U.S. servicemen.

Economic troubles continued, with the government seeking to reschedule its $1.4-billion foreign hard-currency debt, owed mainly to Japan and the International Monetary Fund. In late 1987, a shuffle of the Vietnamese Politburo brought in new leaders who are expected to slightly relax the government grip on the economy and crack down on corruption within the party.

In 1988, Vietnam also began limited troop withdrawals from Laos and Cambodia. Aid from Eastern Europe dropped considerably although in January 1991 the Soviet Union signed a $1 billion trade agreement with Vietnam, which has resisted the pressure for political reform.

(For a Vietnam War chronology, see Headline History.)

WESTERN SAMOA

Independent State of Western Samoa
Head of State: Malietoa Tanumafili II (1962)
Prime Minister: Tofilau Eti Alesana (1988)
Area: 1,093 sq mi. (2,831 sq km)
Population (est. mid-1991): 200,000 (average annual growth rate: 2.8%); birth rate: 34/1000; infant mortality rate: 47/1000; density per square mile: 172
Capital and largest city (1980): Apia, 50,000
Monetary unit: Tala
Languages: Samoan and English
Religions: Christian, 99.7%
National name: Samoa i Sisifo
Member of Commonwealth of Nations
Literacy rate: 90%
Economic summary: Gross domestic product (1989 est.): $112 million; $615 per capita; 0.2% real growth rate. Arable land: 19%. Principal products: copra, coconuts, cocoa, bananas, taro, yams. Labor force: 37,000; 22,000 employed in agriculture (1983 est.). Major industrial products: timber, processed food, fish. Natural resource: timber. Exports: copra, cocoa, coconut oil and cream, timber. Imports: food, manufactured goods, machinery. Major trading partners: New Zealand, Australia, U.S., Fiji, Japan

Geography. Western Samoa, the size of Rhode Island, is in the South Pacific Ocean about 2,200 miles (3,540 km) south of Hawaii midway to Sydney, Australia, and about 800 miles (1,287 km) northeast of Fiji. The larger islands in the Samoan chain are mountainous and of volcanic origin. There is little level land except in the coastal areas, where most cultivation takes place.

Government. Western Samoa has a 47-member Legislature, consisting mainly of the titleholders (chiefs) of family groups, with two non-title members. All members are elected by universal suffrage. When the present Head of State dies, successors will be elected by the Legislature for five-year terms.

History. The Samoan islands were discovered in the 18th century and visited by Dutch and French traders. Toward the end of the 19th century, conflicting interests of the U.S., Britain, and Germany resulted in a treaty signed in 1899. It recognized the paramount interests of the U.S. in those islands east of 171° west longitude (American Samoa) and Germany's interests in the other islands (Western Samoa); the British withdrew in return for recognition of their rights in Tonga and the Solomons.

New Zealand occupied Western Samoa in 1914, and was granted a League of Nations mandate. In 1947, the islands became a U.N. trust territory administered by New Zealand.

Western Samoa became independent on Jan. 1, 1962.

The damage caused by a cyclone in early 1990 worsened the island's already ailing economy.

REPUBLIC OF YEMEN

President: Ali Abdullah Salen
Prime Minister: Haidar Abu Bakr al-Attas
Area: 203,850 sq mi. (527,970 sq km)
Population (est. mid-1991): 10,100,000 (average annual rate of natural increase: 3.5%); birth rate: 51/1000; infant mortality rate: 121/1000; density per square mile: 49
Capital: San'a', 427,185
Monetary unit: Both Dinar and Rial
Largest cities: San'a', 427,185; Aden, 365,000
Language: Arabic
Religion: Islam (Sunni and Shiite)
Literacy rate: 20%
Economic summary: Gross national product (North Yemen) (1988 est.): $5.5 billion, $820 per capita; real growth rate 19.7%; Gross national product (South Yemen) (1988 est.): $1.2 billion. $495 per capita, real growth rate 5.2%; Principal agricultural products: wheat, sorghum, cattle, sheep, cotton, fruits, coffee, dates. Principal industrial products: crude and refined oil, textiles, leather goods, handicrafts, fish. Exports: cotton, coffee, hides, vegetables, dried fish; Imports: textiles, manufactured consumer goods, foodstuffs, sugar, grain, flour. Major trading partners: U.K., U.S.S.R., Japan, Saudi Arabia, Australia, U.S.

Geography. Formerly known as the states of Yemen and the Yemen Arab Republic, the Republic of Yemen occupies the southwestern tip of the Arabian Peninsula on the Red Sea opposite Ethiopia, and extends along the southern part of the Arabian Peninsula on the Gulf of Aden and the Indian Ocean. Saudi Arabia is to the north and Oman is to the east. The country is about the size of France.

It has a 700-mile (1,130-km) narrow coastal plain in the south that gives way to a mountainous region and then a plateau area. Some of the interior highlands in the west attain a height of 12,000 feet (3,660 m).

Government. Parliamentary. There is a five-man ruling Presidential Council consisting of the President, Vice-President, and three other members. They are Salem Saleh Mohammed, the former deputy to the new vice-president, Abdel-Karim al-Arshi, former speaker of Yemen's parliament, and Abdel-Aziz Abdulghani, former Prime Minister of the Yemen Arab Republic. Elections are planned for the end of 1992.

History. The history of Yemen dates back to the Minaean kingdom (1200–650 B.C.). It accepted Islam in A.D. 628, and in the 10th century came under the control of the Rassite dynasty of the Zaidi sect. The Turks occupied the area from 1538 to 1630 and from 1849 to 1918. The sovereign status of Yemen was confirmed by treaties signed with Saudi Arabia and Britain in 1934.

Yemen joined the Arab League in 1945 and established diplomatic relations with the U.S. in 1946.

In 1962, a military revolt of elements favoring President Gamal Abdel Nasser of Egypt broke out. A ruling junta proclaimed a republic, and Yemen became an international battleground, with Egypt and the U.S.S.R. supporting the revolutionaries, and King Saud of Saudi Arabia and King Hussein of Jordan the royalists. The civil war continued until the war between the Arab states and Israel broke out in June 1967. Nasser had to pull out many of his troops and agree to a cease-fire and withdrawal of foreign forces. The war finally ended with the defeat of the royalists in mid-1969.

The People's Republic of Southern Yemen was established Nov. 30, 1967, when Britain granted independence to the Federation of South Arabia. This Federation consisted of the state (once the colony) of Aden and 16 of the 20 states of the Protectorate of South Arabia (once the Aden Protectorate). The four states of the Protectorate that did not join the Federation later became part of Southern Yemen.

The Republic of Yemen was established on May 23, 1990, when pro-western Yemen and Marxist Yemen Arab Republic merged after 300 years of separation to form the new nation. The union had been approved by both governments in November 1989.

The new president, Ali Abdullah Salen of Yemen, was elected by the parliaments of both countries. The parliaments also chose South Yemen's Ali Salem al-Baidh, secretary general of the ruling socialist party, to be the new vice-president.

Since unification a coalition of the People's Congress Party, which ruled in the north, and the Yemen Socialist Party, which ruled in the south, has governed the country. Because of its tight organization the Socialist Party, despite its Marxism, has flourished and become entrenched in the running of the government.

YUGOSLAVIA

Socialist Federal Republic of Yugoslavia
President: Stipe Mesic (1991)
President of Federal Executive Council (Premier): Ante Marković (1989)
Area: 98,766 sq mi. (255,804 sq km)
Population (est. mid-1991): 23,900,000 (average annual rate of natural increase: 0.5%); birth rate: 14/1000; infant mortality rate: 24.3/1000; density per square mile: 242
Capital: Belgrade
Largest cities (est. 1982): Belgrade, 1,250,000; Zagreb, 765,000; Skopje, 505,000; Sarajevo, 450,000; Ljubljana, 255,000; Split, 200,000
Monetary unit: Dinar
Languages: Serbo-Croatian, Slovene, Macedonian (all official)

Religions: Eastern Orthodox, 50%; Roman Catholic, 30%; Islam, 9%; Protestant, 1%; other, 10%
National name: Socijalisticka Federativna Republika Jugoslavija
Literacy rate: 90.5%
Economic summary: Gross national product (1989 est.): $129.5 billion, $5,464 per capita; –1% real growth rate. Arable land: 28%. Principal products: corn, wheat, tobacco, sugar beets. Labor force: 9,600,000; 27% in mining and manufacturing. Major products: wood, processed food, nonferrous metals, machinery, textiles. Natural resources: coal, timber, copper, iron, lead, zinc, bauxite. Exports: leather goods, textiles, machinery. Imports: machinery, chemicals, iron, and steel. Major trading partners: U.S.S.R., E.C., U.S., Czechoslovakia.

Geography. Yugoslavia fronts on the eastern coast of the Adriatic Sea opposite Italy. Its neighbors are Austria, Italy, and Hungary to the north, Romania and Bulgaria to the east, and Greece and Albania to the south. It is slightly larger than Wyoming.

About half of Yugoslavia is mountainous. In the north, the Dinaric Alps rise abruptly from the sea and progress eastward as a barren limestone plateau called the Karst. Montenegro is a jumbled mass of mountains, containing also some grassy slopes and fertile river valleys. Southern Serbia, too, is mountainous. A rich plain in the north and northeast, drained by the Danube, is the most fertile area of the country.

Government. Yugoslavia is a federal republic composed of six socialist republics—Serbia (which includes the provinces of Vojvodina and Kosovo), Croatia, Slovenia, Bosnia-Herzegovina, Macedonia, and Montenegro. Actual administration is carried on by the Federal Executive Council and its secretaries.

The League of Communists and the Socialist Alliance of the Working People are the major political parties.

History. Yugoslavia was formed Dec. 4, 1918, from the patchwork of Balkan states and territories where World War I began with the assassination of Archduke Ferdinand of Austria at Sarajevo on June 28, 1914. The new Kingdom of Serbs, Croats, and Slovenes included the former kingdoms of Serbia and Montenegro; Bosnia-Herzegovina, previously administered jointly by Austria and Hungary; Croatia-Slavonia, a semi-autonomous region of Hungary, and Dalmatia, formerly administered by Austria. King Peter I of Serbia became the first monarch, his son acting as Regent until his accession as Alexander I on Aug. 16, 1921.

Croatian demands for a federal state forced Alexander to assume dictatorial powers in 1929 and to change the country's name to Yugoslavia. Serbian dominance continued despite his efforts, amid the resentment of other regions. A Macedonian associated with Croatian dissidents assassinated Alexander in Marseilles, France, on Oct. 9, 1934, and his cousin, Prince Paul, became Regent for the King's son, Prince Peter.

Paul's pro-Axis policy brought Yugoslavia to sign the Axis Pact on March 25, 1941, and opponents overthrew the government two days later. On April 6 the Nazis occupied the country, and the young King and his government fled. Two guerrilla armies —the Chetniks under Draza Mihajlovic supporting the monarchy and the Partisans under Tito (Josip Broz) leaning toward the U.S.S.R.—fought the Nazis for the duration of the war. In 1943, Tito established an Executive National Committee of Liberation to function as a provisional government.

Tito won the election held in the fall of 1945, as monarchists boycotted the vote. A new Assembly abolished the monarchy and proclaimed the Federal People's Republic of Yugoslavia, with Tito as Prime Minister.

Ruthlessly eliminating opposition, the Tito government executed Mihajlovic in 1946. With Soviet aid, Tito annexed the greater part of Italian Istria under the 1947 peace treaty with Italy but failed in his claim to the key port of Trieste. Zone B of the former free territory of Trieste went to Yugoslavia in 1954.

Tito broke with the Soviet bloc in 1948 and Yugoslavia has since followed a middle road, combining orthodox Communist control of politics and general overall economic policy with a varying degree of freedom in the arts, travel, and individual enterprise. Tito, who became President in 1953 and President for life under a revised Constitution adopted in 1963, played a major part in the creation of a "non-aligned" group of states, the so-called "third world."

The Marshal supported his one-time Soviet mentors in their quarrel with Communist China, but even though he imprisoned the writer Mihajlo Mihajlov and other dissenters at home, he criticized Soviet repression of Czechoslovakia in 1968.

Tito's death on May 4, 1980, three days before his 88th birthday, removed from the scene the last World War II leader. A rotating presidency designed to avoid internal dissension was put into effect immediately, and the feared clash of Yugoslavia's multiple nationalities and regions appeared to have been averted. A collective presidency, rotated annually among the six republics and two autonomous provinces of the federal republic, continued to govern according to a constitutional change made in 1974.

Demonstrations by ethnic Albanians in Kosovo for freedom from Serb rule were met with a forcible response from Serb authorities under the direction of Serb leader Slobodan Miloslovic. Miloslovic has mobilized Serb sentiment not only against the Albanians but also against the central government, raising the spectre of further divisiveness within Yugoslavia. In 1990, elections in the states of Croatia and Slovenia were won by parties advocating greater autonomy.

In May 1991 Croatian voters supported a referendum calling for their republic to become an independent nation. A similar referendum passed in December in Slovenia. In June the respective parliaments in both republics passed declarations of independence. Tensions mounted almost immediately in Yugoslavia, and civil war loomed imminent. Although some fighting did break out, a compromise was accepted in July deferring Slovenia's independence for three months in exchange for talks on a new federal structure.

ZAIRE

Republic of Zaire
President: Mobutu Sese Seko (1965)
Prime Minister: Lunda Bulul (1990)
Area: 905,365 sq mi. (2,344,885 sq km)
Population (est. mid-1991): 37,800,000 (average annual rate of natural increase: 3.1%); birth rate: 46/1000; infant mortality rate: 83/1000; density per square mile: 42

Capital: Kinshasa
Largest cities (est. 1984): Kinshasa, 2,653,558; Lubumbashi, 543,268; Mbuji-Mayi, 423,363; Kananga, 290,898
Monetary unit: Zaire
Languages: French (official), English, Bantu dialects, mainly Swahili, Lingala, Ishiluba, and Kikongo
Religions: Roman Catholic 50%, Protestant 20%, Kimbanguist 10%, Islam 10%; syncretic and traditional, 10%
Ethnic groups: Bantu, Sudanese, Nilotics, Pygmies, Hamites
National name: République du Zaïre
Literacy rate: 55% male, 37% female
Economic summary: Gross domestic product (1988): $6.5 billion; $195 per capita; 2.8% real growth rate. Arable land: 3%. Principal products: coffee, palm oil, rubber, quinine, cassava, bananas, plantains, vegetables, fruits. Labor force: 15,000,000; 13% in industry. Major industrial products: processed and unprocessed minerals, consumer goods. Natural resources: copper, cobalt, zinc, industrial diamonds, manganese, tin, gold, silver, bauxite, iron, coal, crude oil, hydroelectric potential. Exports: copper, cobalt, diamonds, petroleum, coffee. Imports: consumer goods, foodstuffs, mining and other machinery, transport equipment. Major trading partners: Belgium, France, U.S., Germany.

Geography. Zaire is situated in west central Africa and is bordered by the Congo, the Central African Republic, the Sudan, Uganda, Rwanda, Burundi, Tanzania, Zambia, Angola, and the Atlantic Ocean. It is one quarter the size of the U.S.

The principal rivers are the Ubangi and Bomu in the north and the Zaire (Congo) in the west, which flows into the Atlantic. The entire length of Lake Tanganyika lies along the eastern border with Tanzania and Burundi.

Government. Under the Constitution approved by referendum in 1967 and amended in 1974, the third Constitution since 1960, the president and a unicameral Legislature are elected by universal suffrage for five-year terms.

In 1971, the government proclaimed that the Democratic Republic of the Congo would be known as the Republic of Zaire, since the Congo River's name had been changed to the Zaire. In addition, President Joseph D. Mobutu took the name Mobutu Sese Seko and Katanga Province became Shaba.

There is only one political party: the Popular Movement of the Revolution, led by President Mobutu. However, in April 1990, Mobutu lifted the ban on opposition parties.

History. Formerly the Belgian Congo, this territory was inhabited by ancient Negrito peoples (Pygmies), who were pushed into the mountains by Bantu and Nilotic invaders. The American correspondent Henry M. Stanley navigated the Congo River in 1877 and opened the interior to exploration. Commissioned by King Leopold II of the Belgians, Stanley made treaties with native chiefs that enabled the King to obtain personal title to the territory at the Berlin Conference of 1885.

Criticism of forced labor under royal exploitation prompted Belgium to take over administration of the Congo, which remained a colony until agitation for independence forced Brussels to grant freedom on June 30, 1960. Moise Tshombe, Premier of the then

Katanga Province seceded from the new republic on July 11, and another mining province, South Kasai, followed. Belgium sent paratroopers to quell the civil war, and with President Joseph Kasavubu and Premier Patrice Lumumba of the national government in conflict, the United Nations flew in a peacekeeping force.

Kasavubu staged an army coup in 1960 and handed Lumumba over to the Katangan forces. A U.N. investigating commission found that Lumumba had been killed by a Belgian mercenary in the presence of Tshombe. Dag Hammarskjold, U.N. Secretary-General, died in a plane crash en route to a peace conference with Tshombe on Sept. 17, 1961.

U.N. Secretary-General U Thant submitted a national reconciliation plan in 1962 that Tshombe rejected. Tshombe's troops fired on the U.N. force in December, and in the ensuing conflict Tshombe capitulated on Jan. 14, 1963. The peacekeeping force withdrew, and, in a complete about-face, Kasavubu named Tshombe Premier to fight a spreading rebellion. Tshombe used foreign mercenaries and, with the help of Belgian paratroops airlifted by U.S. planes, defeated the most serious opposition, a Communist-backed regime in the northeast.

Kasavubu abruptly dismissed Tshombe in 1965 and was himself ousted by Gen. Joseph-Desiré Mobutu, Army Chief of Staff. The new President nationalized the Union Minière, the Belgian copper mining enterprise that had been a dominant force in the Congo since colonial days. The plane carrying the exiled Tshombe was hijacked in 1967 and he was held prisoner in Algeria until his death from a heart attack was announced June 29, 1969.

Mobutu eliminated opposition to win election in 1970 to a term of seven years, which was renewed in a 1977 election. He invited U.S., South African, and Japanese investment to replace Belgian interests. In 1975, he nationalized much of the economy, barred religious instruction in schools, and decreed the adoption of African names.

On March 8, 1977, invaders from Angola calling themselves the Congolese National Liberation Front pushed into Shaba and threatened the important mining center of Kolwezi. France and Belgium responded to Mobutu's pleas for help with weapons, but the U.S. gave only nonmilitary supplies.

In April, France flew 1,500 Moroccan troops to Shaba to defeat the invaders, who were, Mobutu charged, Soviet-inspired, and Cuban-led. U.S. intelligence sources, however, confirmed Soviet and Cuban denials of any participation and identified the rebels as former Katanga gendarmes who had fled to Angola after their 1963 defeat.

On May 15, 1978, a new assault from Angola resulted in the capture of Kolwezi and the death of 100 whites and 300 blacks. In this second invasion, France and Belgium intervened directly as 1,000 Foreign Legion paratroopers repelled the Katangese and 1,750 Belgian soldiers helped evacuate 2,000 Europeans. The U.S. supplied 18 air transports for both the troop movement and the evacuation.

In April 1990 Mobutu announced he intended to introduce multiparty democracy, but that elections in January 1991 would reduce the number of political parties to two besides his own. Opposition leaders denounced the scheme as giving Mobutu's party an unfair advantage.

A national conference was scheduled for July 1991, but in June three opposition groups announced a boycott and that they would form a parallel government of national union. The conference was postponed.

ZAMBIA

Republic of Zambia
President: Kenneth D. Kaunda (1964)
Prime Minister: Gen. Malimba Masheke (1989)
Area: 290,586 sq mi. (752,618 sq km)
Population (est. mid-1991): 8,400,000 (average annual rate of natural increase: 3.8%); birth rate: 51/1000; infant mortality rate: 76/1000; density per square mile: 29
Capital: Lusaka
Largest cities (est. 1982): Lusaka, 650,000; Kitwe, 345,000; Ndola, 325,000; Chingola, 195,000
Monetary unit: Kwacha
Languages: English and local dialects
Religions: Christian, 50–75%; Islam and Hindu, 1%; remainder indigenous beliefs
Member of Commonwealth of Nations
Literacy rate: 75.7%
Economic summary: Gross domestic product (1988): $4 billion; $530 per capita; real growth rate 6.7%. Arable land: 7%. Principal products: corn, tobacco, rice, sugar cane. Labor force: 2,455,000; 6% in mining, manufacturing and construction. Major products: copper, textiles, chemicals, zinc, fertilizers. Natural resources: copper, zinc, lead, cobalt, coal. Exports: copper, zinc, lead, cobalt, tobacco. Imports: manufactured goods, machinery and transport equipment, foodstuffs. Major trading partners: Western Europe, Japan, South Africa, U.S.

Geography. Zambia, a landlocked country in south central Africa, is about one-tenth larger than Texas. It is surrounded by Angola, Zaire, Tanzania, Malawi, Mozambique, Zimbabwe, Botswana, and Namibia (formerly South-West Africa). The country is mostly a plateau that rises to 8,000 feet (2,434 m) in the east.

Government. Zambia (formerly Northern Rhodesia) is governed by a president, elected by universal suffrage, and a Legislative Assembly, consisting of 125 members elected by universal suffrage and up to 10 additional members nominated by the president.

In December 1990 President Kenneth Kaunda signed constitutional amendments legalizing opposition political parties.

History. Empire builder Cecil Rhodes obtained mining concessions in 1889 from King Lewanika of the Barotse and sent settlers to the area soon thereafter. It was ruled by the British South Africa Company, which he established, until 1924, when the British government took over the administration.

From 1953 to 1964, Northern Rhodesia was federated with Southern Rhodesia and Nyasaland in the Federation of Rhodesia and Nyasaland. On Oct. 24, 1964, Northern Rhodesia became the independent nation of Zambia.

Kenneth Kaunda, the first president, kept Zambia within the Commonwealth of Nations. The country's economy, dependent on copper exports, was threatened when Rhodesia declared its independence from British rule in 1965 and defied U.N. sanctions, which Zambia supported, an action that deprived Zambia of its trade route through Rhodesia. The U.S., Britain, and Canada organized an airlift in 1966 to ship gasoline into Zambia. In 1967, Britain agreed to finance new trade routes for Zambia.

Kaunda visited China in 1967, and China later agreed to finance a 1,000-mile railroad from the copper fields to Dar es Salaam in Tanzania. A pipeline was opened in 1968 from Ndola in Zambia's copper belt to the Indian Ocean at Dar es Salaam, ending the three-year oil drought.

In 1969, Kaunda announced the nationalization of the foreign copper-mining industry, with Zambia to take 51% (over $1 billion, estimated), and an agreement was reached with the companies on payment. He then announced a similar takeover of foreign oil producers.

Zambia suffered heavy damage from bombing raids by the former Rhodesian air force on Zimbabwean guerrilla bases and on its transportation links. These actions, combined with falling prices for copper and cobalt, forced Kaunda to declare a state of economic austerity in January 1981.

With a soaring debt and inflation rate the government in 1990 turned to the International Monetary Fund and the World Bank, with whom an agreement was reached in exchange for economic reforms. Soaring prices in June 1990 led to riots in Lusaka, resulting in a number of killings. Mounting domestic pressure forced Kaunda to move Zambia toward multi-party democracy.

ZIMBABWE

Republic of Zimbabwe
Executive President: Robert Mugabe (1987)
Area: 150,698 sq mi. (390,308 sq km)
Population (est. mid-1991): 10,000,000 (average annual rate of natural increase: 3.1%); birth rate: 41/1000; infant mortality rate: 61/1000; density per square mile: 66
Capital: Harare
Largest cities (est. 1983 for metropolitan area): Harare, 681,000; Bulawayo, 429,000
Monetary unit: Zimbabwean dollar
Languages: English (official), Ndebele, Shona
Religions: Christian, 25%; Animist, 24%; Syncretic, 50%
Literacy rate: 74%
Economic summary: Gross domestic product (1988 est.): $4.6 billion; $470 per capita; 5.3% real growth rate. Arable land: 7%. Principal agricultural products: tobacco, corn, sugar, cotton, livestock. Labor force: 3,100,000; 10% in mining, manufacturing, and construction. Major products: steel, textiles, chemicals, vehicles, gold, copper. Natural resources: gold, copper, chrome, nickel, tin, asbestos. Exports: gold, tobacco, asbestos, copper, meat, chrome, nickel, corn, sugar. Imports: machinery, petroleum products, transport equipment. Major trading partners: South Africa, E.C., U.S.

Geography. Zimbabwe, a landlocked country in south central Africa, is slightly smaller than California. It is bordered by Botswana on the west, Zambia on the north, Mozambique on the east, and South Africa on the south.

A high veld up to 6,000 feet (1,829 m) crosses the country from northeast to southwest. This is flanked by a somewhat lower veld that contains ranching country. Tropical forests that yield hardwoods lie in the southeast.

In the north, on the border with Zambia, is the 175-mile-long (128-m) Kariba Lake, formed by the Kariba Dam across the Zambezi River. It is the site of one of the world's largest hydroelectric projects.

Government. An amendment to the Constitution in October 1987 created the position of Executive President that would combine Presidential and Prime Ministerial functions. Prime Minister Mugabe was the sole candidate and was elected to this post December 30. On December 22, the long negotiated

ZANU-ZAPU merger was promulgated with ZAPU head Joshua Nkomo becoming a Vice President of the renamed ZANU(PF). In August 1987, the Parliament voted to abolish the 20 whites-only seats that had existed since 1980. The remaining 80 members selected replacements who were obliged to support Mugabe's ZANU party.

In March 1990, a constitutional amendment adopted a 150-seat unilateral legislature (House of Assembly) in place of the old bicameral one.

History. Zimbabwe was colonized by Cecil Rhodes's British South Africa Company at the end of the 19th century. In 1923, European settlers voted to become the self-governing British colony of Southern Rhodesia rather than merge with the Union of South Africa. After a brief federation with Northern Rhodesia and Nyasaland in the post-World War II period, Southern Rhodesia chose to remain a colony when its two partners voted for independence in 1963.

On Nov. 11, 1965, the white-minority government of Rhodesia unilaterally declared its independence from Britain.

In 1967, the U.N. imposed mandatory sanctions against Rhodesia. The country moved slowly toward meeting the demands of black Africans. The white-minority regime of Prime Minister Ian Smith withstood British pressure, economic sanctions, guerrilla attacks, and a right-wing assault.

On March 1, 1970, Rhodesia formally proclaimed itself a republic, and within the month nine nations, including the U.S., closed their consulates there.

Heightened guerrilla war and a withdrawal of South African military aid—particularly helicopters—marked the beginning of the collapse of Smith's 11 years of resistance in the spring of 1976. Under pressure from South Africa, Smith agreed with the U.S. that majority rule should come within two years.

In the fall, Smith met with black nationalist leaders in Geneva. The meeting broke up six weeks later when the Rhodesian Premier insisted that whites must retain control of the police and armed forces during the transition to majority rule. A British proposal called for Britons to take over these powers.

Divisions between Rhodesian blacks—Bishop Abel Muzorewa of the African National Congress and Ndabaningi Sithole as moderates versus Robert Mugabe and Joshua Nkomo of the Patriotic Front as advocates of guerrilla force—sharpened in 1977 and no agreement was reached. In July, with white residents leaving in increasing numbers and the economy showing the strain of war, Smith rejected outside mediation and called for general elections in order to work out an "internal solution" of the transfer of power.

On March 3, 1978, Smith, Muzorewa, Sithole, and Chief Jeremiah Chirau signed an agreement to transfer power to the black majority by Dec. 31, 1978.

They constituted themselves an Executive Council, with chairmanship rotating but Smith retaining the title of Prime Minister. Blacks were named to each cabinet ministry, serving as co-ministers with the whites already holding these posts. African nations and the Patriotic Front leaders immediately denounced the action, but Western governments were more reserved, although none granted recognition to the new regime.

White voters ratified a new constitution on Jan. 30, 1979, enfranchising all blacks, establishing a black majority Senate and Assembly, and changing the country's name to Zimbabwe Rhodesia.

Muzorewa agreed to negotiate with Mugabe and Nkomo in British-sponsored talks beginning Sept. 9. By December, all parties accepted a new draft constitution, a cease-fire, and a period of British administration pending a general election.

In voting completed on Feb. 29, 1980, Mugabe's ZANU-Patriotic Front party won 57 of the 80 Assembly seats reserved for blacks. In an earlier vote on Feb. 14, the Rhodesian Front won all 20 seats reserved for whites in the Assembly.

At a ceremony on April 18, Prince Charles of Britain handed to President-elect Rev. Canaan Banana the symbols of independence.

On April 18, 1980, Britain formally recognized the independence of Zimbabwe.

In January 1981, Mugabe dismissed Nkomo as Home Minister and his onetime rival left the government in protest. At the same time, the Prime Minister discharged Edgar Z. Tekere, Manpower and Planning Minister, who had been tried and acquitted of the murder of a white farmer.

Mugabe survived both tests and scored an unprecedented triumph when, in response to his appeal for economic aid, Western nations pledged $1.8 billion for the next three years.

The 1985 harvest was good in Zimbabwe and the country could feed itself. But political turmoil and civil strife continued. In what Western analysts viewed as a free and fair election, President Mugabe's African National Union increased its sizeable majority in the House of Assembly but Mugabe was frustrated because it did not win the 70 seats he sought to cement one-party rule. After the election, Mugabe cracked down on Nkomo's ZAPU-Patriotic Front party.

In April 1990, Mugabe was re-elected and his ZANU(PF) party given virtual unanimity in the Assembly.

In December 1990 the parliament voted by 113 to 3 to amend the original 1980 constitution to allow the compulsory acquisition of white-owned farmland at government-set prices. Indeed, white farmers would have no judiciary recourse.

(For late reports, see Current Events of 1991)

Human Population Growth Threatens The Environment

Source: National Wildlife EnviroAction.

Over the next two decades, 90% of population growth will occur in developing countries in Asia, Africa, and Latin America. While attempting to industrialize and improve the quality of life of their citizens, these nations' explosive population growth will dim prospects for development without destruction of the natural resource base.

Although the United States' population is growing at a much lower rate than most Third World countries, Americans consume resources at a much higher rate. The point is that each person in the industrialized countries represents a large burden on natural resources. At the same time, other countries' populations are growing so fast that they are due to double in less than 25 years. Clearly, environmentally responsible policies must address both consumption and population growth. □

UNITED NATIONS

The 166 Members of the United Nations

Country	Joined U.N.[1]	Country	Joined U.N.[1]	Country	Joined U.N.[1]
Afghanistan	1946	Germany	1973	Niger	1960
Albania	1955	Ghana	1957	Nigeria	1960
Algeria	1962	Greece	1945	Norway	1945
Angola	1976	Grenada	1974	Oman	1971
Antigua and Barbuda	1981	Guatemala	1945	Pakistan	1947
Argentina	1945	Guinea	1958	Panama	1945
Australia	1945	Guinea-Bissau	1974	Papua New Guinea	1975
Austria	1955	Guyana	1966	Paraguay	1945
Bahamas	1973	Haiti	1945	Peru	1945
Bahrain	1971	Honduras	1945	Philippines	1945
Bangladesh	1974	Hungary	1955	Poland	1945
Barbados	1966	Iceland	1946	Portugal	1955
Belgium	1945	India	1945	Qatar	1971
Belize	1981	Indonesia	1950	Romania	1955
Benin	1960	Iran	1945	Rwanda	1962
Bhutan	1971	Iraq	1945	St. Kitts and Nevis	1983
Bolivia	1945	Ireland	1955	St. Lucia	1979
Botswana	1966	Israel	1949	St. Vincent and the Grenadines	1980
Brazil	1945	Italy	1955	São Tomé and Príncipe	1975
Brunei	1984	Jamaica	1962	Saudi Arabia	1945
Bulgaria	1955	Japan	1956	Senegal	1960
Burkina Faso	1960	Jordan	1955	Seychelles	1976
Burundi	1962	Kenya	1963	Sierra Leone	1961
Byelorussian S.S.R.	1945	Korea, North	1991	Singapore	1965
Cambodia	1955	Korea, South	1991	Solomon Islands	1978
Cameroon	1960	Kuwait	1963	Somalia	1960
Canada	1945	Laos	1955	South Africa	1945
Cape Verde	1975	Latvia	1991	Spain	1955
Central African Republic	1960	Lebanon	1945	Sri Lanka	1955
Chad	1960	Lesotho	1966	Sudan	1956
Chile	1945	Liberia	1945	Suriname	1975
China[2]	1945	Libya	1955	Swaziland	1968
Colombia	1945	Liechtenstein	1990	Sweden	1946
Comoros	1975	Lithuania	1991	Syria	1945
Congo	1960	Luxembourg	1945	Tanzania	1961
Costa Rica	1945	Madagascar	1960	Thailand	1946
Côte d'Ivoire	1960	Malawi	1964	Togo	1960
Cuba	1945	Malaysia	1957	Trinidad and Tobago	1962
Cyprus	1960	Maldives	1965	Tunisia	1956
Czechoslovakia	1945	Mali	1960	Turkey	1945
Denmark	1945	Malta	1964	Uganda	1962
Djibouti	1977	Marshall Islands	1991	Ukrainian S.S.R.	1945
Dominica	1978	Mauritania	1961	U.S.S.R.	1945
Dominican Republic	1945	Mauritius	1968	United Arab Emirates	1971
Ecuador	1945	Mexico	1945	United Kingdom	1945
Egypt	1945	Micronesia	1991	United States	1945
El Salvador	1945	Mongolia	1961	Uruguay	1945
Equatorial Guinea	1968	Morocco	1956	Vanuatu	1981
Estonia	1991	Mozambique	1975	Venezuela	1945
Ethiopia	1945	Myanmar	1948	Vietnam	1977
Fiji	1970	Namibia	1990	Western Samoa	1976
Finland	1955	Nepal	1955	Yemen, Republic of	1947
France	1945	Netherlands	1945	Yugoslavia	1945
Gabon	1960	New Zealand	1945	Zaire	1960
Gambia	1965	Nicaragua	1945	Zambia	1964
				Zimbabwe	1980

1. The U.N. officially came into existence on Oct. 24, 1945. 2. On Oct. 25, 1971, the U.N. voted membership to the People's Republic of China, which replaced the Republic of China (Taiwan) in the world body.

Six Official Languages Used by U.N.

There are six official working languages recognized by the United Nations. They are Chinese, English, French, Russian, and Spanish, which have been in use since the world body was organized, and Arabic, which was added by the General Assembly in 1973 and by the Security Council in 1982.

Member Countries' Assessments to U.N. Budget, 1991

Country	Total	Country	Total	Country	Total
Afghanistan	$92,131	Gambia	92,131	Oman	184,262
Albania	92,131	Germany	86,234,389	Pakistan	552,784
Algeria	1,381,962	Ghana	92,131	Panama	184,262
Angola	92,131	Greece	3,685,230	Papua New Guinea	92,131
Antigua and Barbuda	92,131	Grenada	92,131	Paraguay	276,392
Argentina	6,080,629	Guatemala	184,262	Peru	552,784
Australia	14,464,529	Guinea	92,131	Philippines	829,176
Austria	6,817,676	Guinea-Bissau	92,131	Poland	5,159,323
Bahamas	184,262	Guyana	92,131	Portugal	1,658,353
Bahrain	184,262	Haiti	92,131	Qatar	460,653
Bangladesh	92,131	Honduras	92,131	Romania	1,750,484
Barbados	92,131	Hungary	1,934,744	Rwanda	92,131
Belgium	10,779,298	Iceland	276,392	St. Kitts and Nevis	92,131
Belize	92,131	India	3,408,838	St. Lucia	92,131
Benin	92,131	Indonesia	1,381,962	St. Vincent & the Grenadines	92,131
Bhutan	92,131	Iran	6,357,022	São Tomé and Príncipe	92,131
Bolivia	92,131	Iraq	1,105,569	Saudi Arabia	9,397,337
Botswana	92,131	Ireland	1,658,353	Senegal	92,131
Brazil	13,358,959	Israel	1,934,744	Seychelles	92,131
Brunei Darussalam	368,523	Italy	36,760,172	Sierra Leone	92,131
Bulgaria	1,381,962	Jamaica	92,131	Singapore	1,013,439
Burkina Faso	92,131	Japan	104,844,802	Solomon Islands	92,131
Burundi	92,131	Jordan	92,131	Somalia	92,131
Byelorussian S.S.R.	3,040,314	Kenya	92,131	South Africa	4,145,884
Cambodia	92,131	Kuwait	2,671,791	Spain	17,965,497
Cameroon	92,131	Laos	92,131	Sri Lanka	92,131
Canada	28,514,721	Lebanon	92,131	Sudan	92,131
Cape Verde	92,131	Lesotho	92,131	Suriname	92,131
Central African Republic	92,131	Liberia	92,131	Swaziland	92,131
Chad	92,131	Libya	2,579,661	Sweden	11,147,821
Chile	737,046	Liechtenstein	92,131	Syria	368,523
China	7,278,329	Luxembourg	552,784	Tanzania	92,131
Colombia	1,289,830	Madagascar	92,131	Thailand	921,307
Comoros	92,131	Malawi	92,131	Togo	92,131
Congo	92,131	Malaysia	1,013,403	Trinidad and Tobago	460,653
Costa Rica	184,262	Maldives	92,131	Tunisia	276,392
Côte d'Ivoire	184,262	Mali	92,131	Turkey	2,948,720
Cuba	829,176	Malta	92,131	Uganda	92,131
Cyprus	184,262	Mauritania	92,131	Ukrainian S.S.R.	11,516,344
Czechoslovakia	6,080,629	Mauritius	92,131	U.S.S.R.	92,038,626
Denmark	6,357,022	Mexico	8,660,292	United Arab Emirates	1,750,484
Djibouti	92,131	Mongolia	92,131	United Kingdom	44,775,548
Dominica	92,131	Morocco	368,523	United States	271,564,460
Dominican Republic	276,392	Mozambique	92,131	Uruguay	368,523
Ecuador	276,392	Myanmar	92,131	Vanuatu	92,131
Egypt	644,915	Namibia	92,131	Venezuela	5,251,453
El Salvador	92,131	Nepal	92,131	Vietnam	92,131
Equatorial Guinea	92,131	Netherlands	15,201,575	Western Samoa	92,131
Ethiopia	92,131	New Zealand	2,211,138	Yemen Arab Republic	92,131
Fiji	92,131	Nicaragua	92,131	Yugoslavia	4,238,014
Finland	4,698,668	Niger	92,131	Zaire	92,131
France	57,581,723	Nigeria	1,842,615	Zambia	92,131
Gabon	276,392	Norway	5,067,191	Zimbabwe	184,262
				TOTAL	**$962,684,125**

United Nations Headquarters

The first regular session of the General Assembly held at Central Hall, Westminster, London, voted that interim headquarters of the Organization should be located in New York. From London the U.N. moved to Hunter College in the Bronx. In August 1946, an interim headquarters was set up at Lake Success on Long Island. The New York City building at Flushing Meadows, site of the 1939 World's Fair, was converted for the use of the General Assembly. The search for a permanent home ended in December 1946, when the General Assembly accepted an offer from John D. Rockefeller, Jr., of $8,500,000[1] for the purchase of the present Head-

quarters site—an 18-acre tract in Manhattan, alongside the East River. The U.S. Government lent the U.N. $65,000,000 interest free, which is being repaid in annual installments.

Architectural plans drawn up by an international Board of Design were approved by the Assembly, and construction began in September 1948. By mid-1950, the 39-story Secretariat Building was ready for occupancy, and in the spring of 1951 "United Nations, New York" became the Organization's permanent address.

1. This amount paid for two-thirds of the land; New York City gave one-third.

Preamble of the United Nations Charter

The Charter of the United Nations was adopted at the San Francisco Conference of 1945. The complete text may be obtained by writing to the United Nations Sales Section, United Nations, New York, N.Y. 10017, and enclosing $1.

We the peoples of the United Nations determined to save succeeding generations from the scourge of war, which twice in our lifetime has brought untold sorrow to mankind, and

To reaffirm faith in fundamental human rights, in the dignity and worth of the human person, in the equal rights of men and women and of nations large and small, and

To establish conditions under which justice and respect for the obligations arising from treaties and other sources of international law can be maintained, and

To promote social progress and better standards of life in larger freedom, and for these ends

To practice tolerance and live together in peace with one another as good neighbors, and

To unite our strength to maintain international peace and security, and

To insure, by the acceptance of principles and the institution of methods, that armed force shall not be used, save in the common interest, and

To employ international machinery for the promotion of the economic and social advancement of all peoples, have resolved to combine our efforts to accomplish these aims.

Accordingly, our respective Governments, through representatives assembled in the city of San Francisco, who have exhibited their full powers found to be in good and due form, have agreed to the present Charter of the United Nations and do hereby establish an international organization to be known as the United Nations.

Principal Organs of the United Nations

Secretariat

This is the directorate on U.N. operations, apart from political decisions. All members contribute to its upkeep. Its staff of over 6,000 specialists is recruited from member nations on the basis of as wide a geographical distribution as possible. The staff works under the Secretary-General, whom it assists and advises.

Secretaries-General

Javier Pérez de Cuéllar, Peru, Jan. 1, 1982.
Kurt Waldheim, Austria, Jan. 1, 1972, to Dec. 31, 1981.
U Thant, Burma, Nov. 3, 1961, to Dec. 31, 1971.
Dag Hammarskjöld, Sweden, April 11, 1953, to Sept. 17, 1961.
Trygve Lie, Norway, Feb. 1, 1946, to April 10, 1953.

General Assembly

The General Assembly is the world's forum for discussing matters affecting world peace and security, and for making recommendations concerning them. It has no power of its own to enforce decisions.

The Assembly is composed of the 51 original member nations and those admitted since, a total of 159. Each nation has one vote. On important questions including international peace and security, a two-thirds majority of those present and voting is required. Decisions on other questions are made by a simple majority.

The Assembly's agenda can be as broad as the Charter. It can make recommendations to member nations, the Security Council, or both. Emphasis is given on questions relating to international peace and security brought before it by any member, the Security Council, or nonmembers.

The Assembly also maintains a broad program of international cooperation in economic, social, cultural, educational, and health fields, and for assisting in human rights and freedoms.

Among other duties, the Assembly has functions relating to the trusteeship system, and considers and approves the U.N. Budget. Every member contributes to operating expenses according to its means.

Security Council

The Security Council is the primary instrument for establishing and maintaining international peace. Its main purpose is to prevent war by settling disputes between nations.

Under the Charter, the Council is permitted to dispatch a U.N. force to stop aggression. All member nations undertake to make available armed forces, assistance, and facilities to maintain international peace and security.

Any member may bring a dispute before the Security Council or the General Assembly. Any nonmember may do so if it accepts the charter obligations of pacific settlement.

The Security Council has 15 members. There are five permanent members: the United States, the Soviet Union, Britain, France, and China; and 10 tempora ry members elected by the General Assembly for two-year terms, from five different regions of the world.

Voting on procedural matters requires a nine-vote majority to carry. However, on questions of substance, the vote of each of the five permanent members is required.

Current temporary members are (term expires Dec. 31, 1991): Cuba, Yemen, Côte d'Ivoire, Romania, and Zaire; (term expires Dec. 31, 1992): Austria, Belgium, Ecuador, India, and Zimbabwe.

Economic and Social Council

This council is composed of 54 members elected by the General Assembly to 3-year terms. It works closely with the General Assembly as a link with groups formed within the U.N. to help peoples in such fields as education, health, and human rights. It insures that there is no overlapping and sets up commissions to deal with economic conditions and collect facts and figures on conditions over the world. It issues studies and reports and may make recommendations to the Assembly and specialized agencies.

Functional Commissions

Statistical Commission; Population Commission; Commission for Social Development; Commission on Human Rights; Commission on the Status of Women; Commission on Narcotic Drugs.

Regional Commissions

Economic Commission for Europe (ECE); Economic and Social Commission for Asia and the Pacific (ESCAP); Economic Commission for Latin America and the Caribbean (ECLAC); Economic Commission for Africa (ECA); Economic and Social Commission for Western Asia (ESCWA).

Trusteeship Council

This council supervises territories administered by various nations and placed under an international trusteeship system by the United Nations. Each nation is charged with developing the self-government of the territory and preserving and advancing the cultural, political, economic, and other forms of welfare of the people.

The Trusteeship Council is currently composed of 5 members: 1 member—the United States—that administers a trust territory, and 4 members—China, France, the Soviet Union, and the United Kingdom—that are permanent members of the Security Council but do not administer trust territories.

The following countries ceased to be administering members because of the independence of territories they had administered: Italy and France in 1960, Belgium in 1962, New Zealand and the Uni ted Kingdom in 1968 and Australia in 1975. France and the U.K. became nonadministering members.

As of December 1985, there was only one trust territory: the Trust Territory of the Pacific Islands (administered by the United States).

International Court of Justice

The International Court of Justice sits at The Hague, the Netherlands. Its 15-judge bench was established to hear disputes among states, which must agree to accept its verdicts. Its judges, charged with administering justice under international law, deal with cases ranging from disputes over territory to those concerning rights of passage.

Following are the members of the Court and the years in which their terms expire on Feb. 5:

President: Sir Robert Yewdall Jennings, United Kingdom (1994 as president; 2000 term)
Vice President: Shigeru Oda, Japan (1994)
Taslim Olawale Elias, Nigeria (1994)
Jens Evensen, Norway (1994)
Ni Zhengyu, China (1994)
Manfred Lachs, Poland (1994)
Roberto Ago, Italy (1997)
Mohamed Shahabuddeen, Guyana (1997)
Stephen Schwebel, United States (1997)
Mohammed Bedjaoui, Algeria (1997)
Nikolai Tarassov, U.S.S.R. (1997)
Gilbert Guillaume, France (2000)
Andres Aguilar, Venezuela (2000)
Raymond Ranjeva, Madagascar (2000)
Christopher Gregory Weeramantry, Sri Lanka (2000)

Agencies of the United Nations

INTL. ATOMIC ENERGY AGENCY (IAEA)

Established: Statute for IAEA, approved on Oct. 26, 1956, at a conference held at U.N. Headquarters, New York, came into force on July 29, 1957. The Agency is under the aegis of the U.N., but unlike the following, it is not a specialized agency.

Purpose: To promote the peaceful uses of atomic energy; to ensure that assistance provided by it or at its request or under its supervision or control is not used in such a way as to further any military purpose.

Headquarters: Vienna International Center, P.O. Box 100, A-1400 Vienna, Austria

FOOD AND AGRICULTURE ORGANIZATION OF THE UNITED NATIONS (FAO)

Established: October 16, 1945, when constitution became effective.

Purpose: To raise nutrition levels and living standards; to secure improvements in production and distribution of food and agricultural products.

Headquarters: Via delle Terme di Caracalla, 00100, Rome, Italy.

GENERAL AGREEMENT ON TARIFFS AND TRADE (GATT)

Established: Jan. 1, 1948.

Purpose: An International Trade Organization (ITO) was originally planned. Although this agency has not materialized, some of its objectives have been embodied in an international commercial treaty, the General Agreement on Tariffs and Trade. Its purpose is to sponsor trade negotiations.

Headquarters: Centre William Rappard, 154 Rue de Lausanne, CH-1211, Geneva 21, Switzerland.

INTERNATIONAL BANK FOR RECONSTRUCTION AND DEVELOPMENT (IBRD) (WORLD BANK)

Established: December 27, 1945, when Articles of Agreement drawn up at Bretton Woods Conference in July 1944 came into force. Began operations on June 25, 1946.

Purpose: To assist in reconstruction and development of economies of members by facilitating capital investment and by making loans to governments and furnishing technical advice.

Headquarters: 1818 H St., N.W., Washington, D.C. 20433.

INTL. CIVIL AVIATION ORGANIZATION (ICAO)

Established: April 4, 1947, after working as a provisional organization since June 1945.

Purpose: To study problems of international civil aviation; to establish international standards and regulations; to promote safety measures, uniform regulations for operation, simpler procedures at international borders, and the use of new technical methods and equipment. It has evolved standards for meteorological services, traffic control, communications, radio beacons and ranges, search and rescue organization, and other facilities. It has brought about much simplification of customs, immigration, and public health regulations as they apply to international air transport. It drafts international air law conventions, and is concerned with economic aspects of air travel.

Headquarters: 1000 Sherbrooke St. West, Montreal, Quebec, H3A 2R2, Canada.

INTL. DEVELOPMENT ASSOCIATION (IDA)

Established: Sept. 24, 1960. An affiliate of the World Bank, IDA has the same officers and staff as the Bank.

Purpose: To further economic development of its members by providing finance on terms which bear less heavily on balance of payments of members than those of conventional loans.

Headquarters: 1818 H St., N.W., Washington, D.C. 20433.

INTERNATIONAL FINANCE CORPORATION (IFC)

Established: Charter of IFC came into force on July 20, 1956. Although IFC is affiliated with the World Bank, it is a separate legal entity, and its funds are entirely separate from those of the Bank. However, membership in the Corporation is open only to Bank members.

Purpose: To further economic development by encouraging the growth of productive private enterprise in its member countries, particularly in the less developed areas; to invest in productive private enterprises in association with private investors, without government guarantee of repayment where sufficient private capital is not available on reasonable terms; to serve as a clearing house to bring together investment opportunities, private capital (both foreign and domestic), and experienced management.

Headquarters: 1818 H St., N.W., Washington, D.C. 20433.

INTERNATIONAL FUND FOR AGRICULTURAL DEVELOPMENT (IFAD)

Established: June 18, 1976. Began operations in December 1977.

Purpose: To mobilize additional funds for agricultural and rural development in developing countries through projects and programs directly benefiting the poorest rural populations.

Headquarters: 107 Via del Serafico, 00142, Rome, Italy.

INTERNATIONAL LABOR ORGANIZATION (ILO)

Established: April 11, 1919, when constitution was adopted as Part XIII of Treaty of Versailles. Became specialized agency of U.N. in 1946.

Purpose: To contribute to establishment of lasting peace by promoting social justice; to improve labor conditions and living standards through international action; to promote economic and social stability. The U.S. withdrew from the ILO in 1977 and resumed membership in 1980.

Headquarters: 4, route des Morillons, CH-1211 Geneva 22, Switzerland.

INTERNATIONAL MARITIME ORGANIZATION (IMO)

Established: March 17, 1958.

Purpose: To give advisory and consultative help to promote international cooperation in maritime navigation and to encourage the highest standards of safety and navigation. Its aim is to bring about a uniform system of measuring ship tonnage; systems now vary widely in different parts of the world. Other activities include cooperation with other U.N. agencies on matters affecting the maritime field.

Headquarters: 4 Albert Embankment, London SE 1 7SR England.

INTERNATIONAL MONETARY FUND (IMF)

Established: Dec. 27, 1945, when Articles of Agreement drawn up at Bretton Woods Conference in July 1944 came into force. Fund began operations on March 1, 1947.

Purpose: To promote international monetary cooperation and expansion of international trade; to promote exchange stability; to assist in establishment of multilateral system of payments in respect of currency transactions between members.

Headquarters: 700 19th St., N.W., Washington, D.C. 20431.

INTERNATIONAL TELECOMMUNICATION UNION (ITU)

Established: 1865. Became specialized agency of U.N. in 1947.

Purpose: To extend technical assistance to help members keep up with present day telecommunication needs; to standardize communications equipment and procedures; to lower costs. It also works for orderly sharing of radio frequencies and makes studies and recommendations to benefit its members.

Headquarters: Place des Nations, CH-1211 Geneva 20, Switzerland.

UNITED NATIONS EDUCATIONAL, SCIENTIFIC, AND CULTURAL ORGANIZATION (UNESCO)

Established: Nov. 4, 1946, when twentieth signatory to constitution deposited instrument of acceptance with government of U.K.

Purpose: To promote collaboration among nations through education, science, and culture in order to further justice, rule of law, and human rights and freedoms without distinction of race, sex, language, or religion.

Headquarters: UNESCO House. 7, Place de Fontenoy, 75700 Paris, France.

UNITED NATIONS INDUSTRIAL DEVELOPMENT ORGANIZATION (UNIDO)

Established: Nov. 17, 1966. Became specialized agency of the U.N. in 1985.

Purpose: To promote and accelerate the industrialization of the developing countries.

Headquarters: UNIDO, Vienna International Centre, P.O. Box 300, A-1400 Vienna, Austria.

UNIVERSAL POSTAL UNION (UPU)

Established: Oct. 9, 1874. Became specialized agency of U.N. in 1947.

Purpose: To facilitate reciprocal exchange of correspondence by uniform procedures by all UPU members; to help governments modernize and speed up mailing procedures.

Headquarters: Weltpoststrasse 4, CH-3000 Berne 15, Switzerland.

WORLD HEALTH ORGANIZATION (WHO)

Established: April 7, 1948, when 26 members of the U.N. had accepted its constitution, adopted July 22, 1946, by the International Health Conference in New York City.

Purpose: To aid attainment by all people of highest possible level of health.

Headquarters: 20 Avenue Appia, CH-1211 Geneva 27, Switzerland.

WORLD INTELLECTUAL PROPERTY ORGANIZATION (WIPO)

Established: April 26, 1970, when its Convention came into force. Originated as International Bureau of Paris Union (1883) and Berne Union (1886), later succeeded by United International Bureau for the Protection of Intellectual Property (BIRPI). Became a specialized agency of the U.N. in December 1974.

Purpose: To promote legal protection of intellectual property, including artistic and scientific works, artistic performances, sound recordings, broadcasts, inventions, trademarks, industrial designs, and commercial names.

Headquarters: 34 Chemin des Colombettes, 1211 Geneva 20, Switzerland.

WORLD METEOROLOGICAL ORGANIZATION (WMO)

Established: March 23, 1950, succeeding the International Meteorological Organization, a non-governmental organization founded in 1878.

Purpose: To promote international exchange of weather reports and maximum standardization of observations; to help developing countries establish weather services for their own economic needs; to fill gaps in observation stations; to promote meteorological investigations affecting jet aircraft, satellites, energy resources, etc.

Headquarters: 41, Avenue Giuseppe Motta, CH-1211 Geneva 2, Switzerland.

MEDIA

Leading Magazines: United States and Canada

Magazine	Circulation[1]	Magazine	Circulation[1]
American Health—Fitness of Body and Mind	806,172	1,001 Home Ideas	1,662,102
Better Homes and Gardens	8,007,222	Organic Gardening	1,034,842
Bon Appetit	1,397,559	Outdoor Life	1,512,464
Business Week (North America)	894,043	Parents Magazine	1,743,424
Car and Driver	959,395	Penthouse	1,612,574
Changing Times, The Kiplinger Magazine	1,139,738	People Weekly	3,208,668
Chatelaine	921,269	Playboy	3,488,006
Consumers Digest	873,704	Popular Mechanics	1,651,064
Cooking Light	924,499	Popular Photography	911,117
Cosmopolitan	2,600,971	Popular Science	1,807,540
Country Home	1,029,342	Practical Homeowner	750,068
Country Living	1,803,867	Prevention	3,022,108
Discover	1,121,855	Reader's Digest	16,264,547
Ebony	1,810,668	Reader's Digest (Canadian English Edition)	1,290,181
Elle	836,556	Redbook	3,907,221
Essence	850,607	Rolling Stone	1,229,280
Family Circle	5,431,779	Self	1,100,897
The Family Handyman	1,331,696	Seventeen	1,772,362
Field & Stream	2,016,298	Smithsonian	2,234,706
Food & Wine	818,165	Soap Opera Digest	1,447,041
Glamour	2,156,157	Southern Living	2,341,074
Globe	1,200,484	Sport	925,984
Golf Digest	1,357,433	Sports Illustrated	3,220,016
Golf Magazine	1,088,999	Star	3,431,453
Good Housekeeping	5,152,521	Sunset, The Magazine of Western Living	1,409,587
Gourmet	899,549	'Teen	1,175,037
Health	878,994	Tennis	772,190
Home	942,159	Time	4,094,935
Home Mechanix	1,215,178	Travel & Leisure	1,117,412
Homeowner	795,012	True Story	770,103
Hot Rod	876,938	TV Guide	15,604,267
House Beautiful	985,129	TV Guide (Canada)	815,613
Jet	968,545	U.S. News & World Report	2,311,534
Ladies Home Journal	5,001,739	US	1,326,410
Life	1,844,482	Vanity Fair	789,820
Mademoiselle	1,178,116	Victoria	805,983
McCall's	5,020,127	Vogue	1,215,767
Money	1,915,053	Weekly World News	816,676
Motor Trend	892,930	Weight Watchers Magazine	1,020,248
Nation's Business	860,120	Woman's Day	4,802,842
National Enquirer	3,803,607	The Workbasket	1,215,175
National Examiner	805,307	Workbench	862,985
National Geographic Magazine	10,189,703	Working Woman	n.a.
New Woman	1,340,540	Yankee	1,000,784
Newsweek	3,211,958	YM	1,008,522
Omni	838,420		

1. Average total paid circulation for the six-month period ending December 31, 1990. The table lists magazines with combined newsstand and subscription circulation of over 750,000. *Source:* Audit Bureau of Circulations. Publishers' Statements for six-month period ending December 31, 1990.

Major U.S. Daily Newspapers[1]

City and Newspaper	Net paid circulation			
	Morning[1]	All-Day[2]	Evening[2]	Sunday
Akron, Ohio: *Beacon Journal*	158,725		—	225,871
Albany, N.Y.: *Times-Union* (M & S)	108,954		—	163,944
Albuquerque, N.M.: *Journal* (M & S); *Tribune* (E)	123,481[4]		40,812[4]	162,394[4]
Allentown, Pa.: *Call* (M & S)	137,688		—	185,060
Amarillo, Tex.: *News* (M); *Globe-Times* (E); *News-Globe* (S)	44,165		22,144[3]	78,284
Anchorage, Alaska: *News*	44,524		—	45,628
Times	60,445		—	80,323

City and Newspaper	Morning[1]	All-Day[2]	Evening[2]	Sunday
Asbury Park, N.J.: *Press*	—		162,928	224,710
Atlanta: *Constitution* (M); *Journal* (E); *Journal and Constitution* (S)	329,582[3]		189,332[3]	700,739
Atlantic City, N.J.: *Press*	78,442		—	97,572
Augusta, Ga.: *Chronicle* (M); *Herald* (E); *Chronicle—Herald* (S)	71,442[3]		11,961[3]	98,654
Austin, Tex.: *American-Statesman*	177,040[3]		—	227,918
Bakersfield, Calif.: *Californian*	82,879[4]		—	94,696[4]
Baltimore: *Sun*	237,519[3]		159,522[3]	491,924
Bangor, Me.: *News*	76,290[3]		—	92,640[5]
Baton Rouge, La.: *Advocate* (M & S); *State-Times* (E)	84,480[3]		26,633[3]	140,220
Bergen County (Hackensack), N.J.: *Record*	—		172,667[4]	246,317[4]
Beaumont, Tex.: *Enterprise*	70,382		—	86,359
Binghamton, N.Y.: *Press & Sun-Bulletin* (M & S)	70,725		—	92,677
Birmingham, Ala.: *Post-Herald* (M); *News* (E & S)	64,163[3]		168,725[3]	212,529
Boston: *Globe*	516,981[3]		—	798,298
Herald	351,947[3]		—	230,654
Christian Science Monitor	114,873[3]		—	—
Bridgeport, Conn: *Post*	69,077		—	87,387
Buffalo, N.Y.: *News*		314,194[3]	—	383,380
Camden, N.J.: *Courier-Post*	—	102,189[4]		104,658[4]
Canton, Ohio: *Repository*			60,491[4]	78,716[4]
Cedar Rapids, Iowa: *Gazette*	70,208		—	83,196
Charleston, S.C.: *News & Courier* (M); *Evening Post; News & Courier Post* (S)	84,281[3]		35,237[3]	126,698
Charleston, W. Va.: *Gazette* (M); *Mail* (E); *Gazette-Mail* (S)	54,291		49,865	104,130
Charlotte, N.C.: *Observer*	238,555		—	299,451
Chattanooga, Tenn.: *Times* (M); *News-Free Press* (E & S)	44,314		53,002	111,536
Chicago: *Tribune*	741,345[3]		—	1,131,226
Sun-Times	537,780[3]		—	559,093
Daily Herald (M); *Sunday Herald*	103,242		—	101,090
Cincinnati: *Enquirer* (M & S); *Post* (E)	203,033		105,469	351,163
Cleveland: *Plain Dealer*	432,449[3]		—	561,421
Colorado Springs, Colo.: *Gazette Telegraph*	101,575		—	117,004
Columbia, S.C.: *State*	145,365		—	173,636
Columbus, Ohio: *Dispatch*	264,058		—	399,108
Corpus Christi, Tex.: *Caller* (M); *Caller-Times* (S)	69,671[4]		—	92,864[4]
Dallas: *News*	400,553[6]		—	611,716
Times-Herald		210,652[3]	—	308,448
Wall Street Journal (Southwest edition)	190,676[3]		—	—
Davenport, Iowa: *Quad City Times*				
Dayton, Ohio: *News*	184,464		—	233,039
Daytona Beach, Fla.: *News-Journal*	100,668		—	116,514
Denver: *Post*	248,493		—	413,343
Rocky Mountain News	374,009		—	432.502
Des Moines, Iowa: *Register*	206,204		—	344,522
Detroit: *Free Press* (M); *News* (E); *News & Free Press* (S)	622,349[3]		481,766[3]	1,215,149
Duluth, Minn.: *News-Tribune*	60,431		—	84,073
Erie, Pa.: *News* (M); *Times* (E); *Times-News* (S)	30,881[3]		40,321[3]	102,424
El Paso, Tex.: *Times* (M & S); *Herald-Post* (E)				
Eugene, Ore.: *Register-Guard*	74,786		—	79,288
Evansville, Ind.: *Courier* (M); *Press* (E); *Courier & Press* (S)	63,926		34,495	118,400
Fayetteville, N.C.: *Observer-Times* (S)	70,941[4]		—	77,579[4]
Flint, Mich.: *Journal*	—		106,284[3]	124,162
Fort Lauderdale, Fla.: *Sun-Sentinel* (M); *News* (E); *News & Sun-Sentinel* (S)	254,184[3]		7,827[3]	349,737
Fort Myers, Fla.: *News-Press*	100,973		—	127,548
Fort Wayne, Ind.: *Journal-Gazette* (M & S); *News-Sentinel* (E)	63,243		55,405	137,691
Fort Worth: *Star-Telegram*	160,229[3]		90,033[3]	337,446
Fresno, Calif.: *Bee*	154,589[4]		—	187,541[4]
Gary, Ind.: *Post-Tribune*	70,411		—	83,840
Grand Rapids, Mich.: *Press*	—		146,749	191,085
Green Bay, Wis.: *Press-Gazette*	—		59,424	85,336
Greensboro, N.C.: *News & Record*	120,055		—	134,593
Greensburg, Pa.: *Tribune-Review*				
Greenville, S.C.: *News* (M); *Piedmont* (E); *News & Piedmont* (S)	91,219[3]		25,846[3]	137,151
Harrisburg, Pa.: *Patriot* (M); *Evening News; Sunday Patriot-News*	59,880[3]		48,726[3]	175,321

City and newspaper	Morning[1]	All-Day[2]	Evening[2]	Sunday
Hartford, Conn.: *Courant*	231,167		—	320,108
Honolulu: *Advertiser* (M); *Star-Bulletin* (E);				
Star-Bulletin & Advertiser (S)	104,633		88,755	202,678
Houston: *Chronicle*	—	439,574		622,608
Post	310,758		—	358,121
Huntsville, Ala.: *News* (M); *Times* (E & S)	16,875[3]		57,680[3]	80,189
Indianapolis: *Star* (M & S); *News* (E)	231,892[4]		103,455[4]	416,752[4]
Jackson, Miss.: *Clarion-Ledger*	107,787		—	127,440
Jacksonville, Fla.: *Times-Union*	184,394[3]		—	250,112
Kalamazoo, Mich.: *Gazette*			64,201[3]	81,260
Kansas City, Mo.: *Times* (M); *Star* (E & S)	288,571[3]		—	423,305
Knoxville, Tenn.: *Journal* (E); *News-Sentinel* (M & S)	104,545		40,946	172,759
Lakeland, Fla.: *Ledger*	87,547[4]		—	104,919[4]
Lancaster, Pa.: *Intelligencer-Journal* (M); *New Era* (E);				
News (S)	44,980[4]		54,844[4]	104,631[4]
Lansing, Mich.: *State-Journal*	70,652		—	93,689
Las Vegas, Nev.: *Review-Journal*				
Sun	139,735[3]		36,559[3]	212,283
Lexington, Ky.: *Herald-Leader*	124,050		—	161,115
Lincoln, Neb.: *Star* (M); *Journal* (E); *Journal & Star* (S)	38,574[3,7]		41,215[3,7]	83,400
Little Rock, Ark.: *Gazette*	125,207[8]		—	222,072
Democrat	117,403[9]		—	236,093
Long Beach, Calif.: *Press-Telegram*	131,945[10]		—	151,886
Long Island (Melville), N.Y.: *Newsday*		825,512[3]	—	960,308
Los Angeles: *Times*	1,242,864[3]		—	1,576,425
News	202,748[3]		—	223,647
Louisville, Ky.: *Courier-Journal*	238,080		—	328,901
Lubbock, Tex.: *Avalanche-Journal*	68,444		—	76,727
Macon, Ga.: *Telegraph and News*	75,307		—	100,406
Madison, Wis.: *State Journal* (M & S); *Capital Times* (E)	82,450[3]		24,668[3]	157,066
Melbourne, Fla.: *Today*	85,187		—	113,810
Memphis, Tenn.: *Commercial Appeal*	208,313		—	289,444
Miami, Fla.: *Herald*	444,581		—	553,479
Middletown, N.Y.: *Times Herald-Record* (M); *Record* (S)	83,762[4]		—	99,351[4]
Milwaukee: *Sentinel* (M); *Journal* (E & S)	168,995[3]		255,497[3]	490,199
Minneapolis: *Star & Tribune*	413,237		—	673,773
Mobile, Ala.: *Register* (M); *Press* (E); *Press-Register* (S)	62,269[3,4]		44,018[3,4]	114,267[4]
Modesto, Calif.: *Bee*	85,020[4]		—	94,363[4]
Montgomery, Ala. *Advertiser* (M); *Journal* (E);				
Journal & Advertiser (S)	53,859		15,127[3]	79,609
Naperville, Ill.: *Wall Street Journal* (Midwest edition)	526,167[3]		—	—
Nashville, Tenn.: *Tennessean* (M & S); *Banner* (E)	134,607		62,675	268,554
New Haven, Conn.: *Register*	101,563		—	133,547
New Orleans: *Times-Picayune*	—	272,280[3,4]	—	324,241[4]
New York: *News*[11]	n.a.			n.a.
Times	1,209,225[3]			1,762,015
Post	644,738[3]		—	536,694[12]
Wall Street Journal (Eastern edition)	798,515[3]		—	—
National edition	1,919,355[3]		—	—
Women's Wear Daily	57,271[3]		—	—
Newark, N.J.: *Star-Ledger*	485,362[3,4]		—	707,391[4]
Newport News–Hampton, Va.: *Press* (M & S); *Times Herald* (E)	80,863[3,4]		22,792[3,4]	122,643[4]
Norfolk-Portsmouth-Virginia Beach-Chesapeake, Va.:				
Virginian-Pilot (M); *Ledger-Star* (E);				
Virginian-Pilot/Ledger-Star (S)	155,071[3,4]		70,728[3,4]	237,784[4]
Oakland, Calif.: *Tribune* (M & S)	115,296		—	115,116
Oklahoma City: *Oklahoman* (M & S)	231,653			335,319
Omaha, Neb.: *World-Herald*	127,192[3]		97,345[3]	288,666
Orange County (Santa Ana), Calif.: *Register*	—	372,750[3]	—	429,146
Orlando, Fla.: *Sentinel*	—	287,270		388,873
Palo Alto, Calif.: *Wall Street Journal* (Western edition)	403,997[3]		—	—
Peninsula Times Tribune	—		41,332	43,552
Pensacola, Fla.: *News-Journal*	60,680[3,4]		—	80,552[4]
Peoria, Ill.: *Journal Star*	—	90,005[3]	—	114,101
Philadelphia: *Inquirer* (M & S); *Daily News* (E)	515,523[3]		221,855[3]	987,218
Phoenix, Ariz.: *Republic* (M & S); *Gazette* (E)	393,722[4]		96,642[4]	595,413[4]
Pittsburgh: *Post-Gazette, Sun-Telegraph* (M); *Press* (E & S)	161,514[3]		220,465[3]	557,000
Pontiac, Mich.: *Oakland Press*	74,671		—	82,532
Portland, Me.: *Press-Herald* (M); *Express* (E)	60,045[3,13]		19,545[3,13]	—
Telegram (M&S)	71,203[4]		—	139,160

City and newspaper	Morning[1]	All-Day[2]	Evening[2]	Sunday
Portland, Or.: *Oregonian*	—	337,672[3]		440,923
Providence, R.I.: *Journal Bulletin;* Journal (S)	—	200,076[3]	—	264,723
Quincy, Mass.: *Patriot-Ledger*	—		87,966[3, 4]	101,603[4,12]
Raleigh, N.C.: *News & Observer* (M & S)	148,931[4]		—	181,703[4]
Reading, Pa.: *Times* (M); *Eagle* (E & S)	46,036[3]		30,245[3]	113,100
Reno, Nev.: *Gazette Journal*	66,781		—	82,508
Richmond, Va.: *Times-Dispatch* (M & S); *News-Leader* (E)	143,040		103,518	254,331
Riverside, Calif.: *Press-Enterprise* (M & S)	161,126		—	170,092
Roanoke, Va.: *Times & World-News*	86,692[3]		34,363[3]	128,410
Rochester, N.Y.: *Democrat & Chronicle* (M & S); *Times-Union* (E)	133,672[3]		83,342[3]	259,990
Rockford, Ill.: *Register Star*	73,732		—	87,890
Sacramento, Calif.: *Bee*	273,844[4]		—	338,355[4]
Union	n.a.			n.a.
St. Louis: *Post-Dispatch*	391,915[3]		—	585,681
St. Paul: *Pioneer Press*	201,860[3]		—	267,781
St. Petersburg, Fla.: *Times*	389,924[4]		—	500,418[4]
Salt Lake City, Utah: *Tribune* (M & S);	111,994		—	145,371
Deseret News (E & S)	—		63,128	68,464
San Antonio: *Express News*	—	188,377	—	280,048
Light	—	166,722		233,268
San Bernardino, Calif.: *Sun*	93,534		—	104,876
San Bernardino (county): *Inland Valley Bulletin*	—	86,774		89,342
San Diego, Calif.: *Union* (M & S); *Tribune* (E)	279,136[4]		117,084[4]	456,167[4]
San Francisco: *Chronicle* (M); *Examiner* (E);				
Examiner & Chronicle (S)	570,364[3]		137,635[3]	704,322
San Gabriel Valley, Calif.: *Tribune* (M); *Tribune-News* (S)	63,811		—	82,914
San Jose, Calif.: *Mercury-News*	—	290,918[3]	—	338,490
Santa Rosa, Calif.: *Press Democrat*	93,838		—	101,581
Sarasota, Fla.: *Herald-Tribune* (M & S)	142,598[4]		—	171,850[4]
Scranton, Pa.: *Tribune* (M); *Times* (E & S)	31,917[3, 4]		46,345[3, 4]	80,372[4]
Seattle: *Post-Intelligencer* (M); *Times* (E); combined (S)	209,438[3]		237,735[3]	515,347
Shreveport, La.: *Times* (M & S); *Journal* (E)	75,904[4]		16,229[4]	103,822[4]
Savannah, Ga.: *News* (M & S); *Press* (E)	56,443[3]		18,019[3]	81,262
South Bend-Mishawaka, Ind.: *Tribune*	—		89,580[3]	129,214
Spokane, Wash.: *Spokesman-Review* (M & S); *Chronicle* (E)	99,145[3]		22,462[3]	146,928
Springfield, Ill.: *State Journal-Register*	68,930		—	77,735
Springfield, Mass.: *Union News; Republican* (S)	—	113,719	—	156,384
Springfield, Mo.: *News-Leader*	59,179[4]		—	98,644[4]
Staten Island, N.Y.: *Advance* (E&S)			77,777	93,947
Syracuse, N.Y.: *Post-Standard* (M); *Herald-Journal* (E);	88,874		91,802	222,005
Herald-American (S)				
Tacoma, Wash.: *News-Tribune*	121,049[4]		—	139,903[4]
Tallahassee, Fla.: *Democrat*	63,604		—	77,363
Tampa, Fla.: *Tribune* (M); *Tribune & Times* (S)	321,626		—	408,343
Toledo, Ohio: *Blade*	153,062		—	215,490
Trenton, N.J.: *Times* (M&S)	81,243		—	94,157
Trentonian (M & S)	73,050[3]		—	63,019
Tucson, Ariz.: *Star* (M & S); *Citizen* (E)	98,793[4]		52,855[4]	174,987[4]
Tulsa, Okla.: *World* (M & S); *Tribune* (E)	133,902[4]		69,044[4]	241,478[4]
Walnut Creek, Calif.: *Contra Costa Times*	90,360		—	99,567
Washington, D.C.: *Post*	838,902[3]		—	1,165,567
Times[14]	n.a.			
USA Today	1,429,024[8]		—	—
West Palm Beach, Fla.: *Post*	195,523[3]		—	245,809
Wichita, Kan.: *Eagle-Beacon*	122,324		—	198,771
Wilmington, Del.: *News Journal*	—	119,043[3, 4]	—	139,727[4]
Winston-Salem, N.C.: *Journal*	96,250		—	105,021
Worcester, Mass.: *Telegram Gazette; Telegraph* (S)	—	117,047[4]	—	137,347[4]
York, Pa.: *Record* (M); *Dispatch* (E); *News* (S)	42,502[3]		40,398[3]	86,763
Youngstown, Ohio: *Vindicator*	—		88,325[4]	131,954[4]

1. Listing is of cities in which any one edition of a newspaper exceeds an average net paid circulation of 75,000; newspapers of smaller circulation in those cities are also included. 2. Unless otherwise indicated, figures are average Monday-through-Saturday circulation for six-month period ending March 31, 1991. 3. Average Monday-through-Friday circulation. 4. Three-month average for period ending March 31, 1991. 5. Week-end edition. 6. Monday-Thursday, Saturday. 7. (12-22-90 to 3-31-91) 8. Monday-Thursday. 9. Monday, Tuesday, and Thursday. 10. (11-1-90 to 3-31-91). 11. Publishers statement was not filed for the period (six months ending March 31, 1991) because of strike. 12. Saturday edition. 13. (10-1-90 to 12-31-90). 14. Under voluntary temporary suspension of service. n.a. = not avaiable.

English Language Daily and Sunday U.S. Newspapers
(number of newspapers as of Feb. 1, 1991; circulation as reported for Sept. 30, 1990)

State	Morning papers and circulation		Evening papers and circulation		Total M and E and circulation		Sunday papers and circulation	
Alabama	15	308,837	12	457,681	27	766,518	21	766,914
Alaska	4	89,512	4	46,745	7	136,257	4	151,040
Arizona	7	494,737	13	242,645	20	737,382	12	820,907
Arkansas	9	370,658	24	195,356	32	566,014	17	675,215
California	56	5,016,573	63	1,574,716	116	6,591,289	71	6,753,867
Colorado	12	851,424	17	156,461	29	1,007,885	11	1,159,750
Connecticut[1]	11	636,219	12	211,589	21	847,808	11	830,606
Delaware	2	84,371	1	60,326	2	144,697	2	171,880
D.C.	2	877,770	0	0	2	877,770	1	1,137,034
Florida[1]	30	2,910,761	14	264,197	43	3,174,958	36	3,919,849
Georgia	15	745,163	21	466,285	36	1,211,448	18	1,311,556
Hawaii	2	109,424	4	134,842	6	244,266	5	262,028
Idaho	6	118,359	6	90,451	12	208,810	8	226,764
Illinois[1]	15	1,802,638	55	793,981	69	2,596,619	27	2,748,012
Indiana	15	690,062	59	821,892	74	1,511,954	22	1,370,500
Iowa[1]	11	426,385	27	298,481	37	724,866	10	738,089
Kansas	7	279,736	39	251,322	46	531,058	17	492,630
Kentucky	7	454,877	16	207,751	23	662,448	12	673,743
Louisiana[1]	13	479,798	16	300,645	28	780,443	21	892,078
Maine	5	230,081	3	52,182	8	282,263	2	189,747
Maryland	10	485,018	5	253,474	15	738,492	7	679,020
Massachusetts[1]	8	1,188,765	34	827,122	40	2,015,887	14	1,770,072
Michigan	11	789,343	42	1,583,912	52	2,373,255	23	2,431,414
Minnesota[1]	11	660,292	15	289,602	25	949,894	13	1,147,086
Mississippi	6	214,329	16	188,841	22	403,170	14	379,454
Missouri	10	846,142	34	246,449	44	1,092,591	20	1,336,196
Montana	6	151,984	5	36,730	11	188,714	7	193,977
Nebraska	4	192,842	16	278,426	20	471,268	7	436,833
Nevada[1]	3	204,813	5	57,091	8	261,904	4	301,753
New Hampshire	2	80,690	7	134,824	9	215,514	4	158,303
New Jersey[1]	12	1,019,133	13	666,756	23	1,685,889	17	1,925,109
New Mexico	3	157,029	15	157,051	18	314,080	13	289,041
New York[1]	27	6,057,542	47	1,360,517	71	7,418,059	40	5,902,443
North Carolina	12	893,145	41	560,250	53	1,453,395	35	1,452,685
North Dakota	5	136,892	5	50,373	10	187,265	7	185,583
Ohio[1]	13	1,386,214	74	1,359,392	87	2,745,606	34	2,893,165
Oklahoma	11	441,436	38	302,748	49	744,184	43	907,313
Oregon[1]	5	311,336	16	361,796	20	673,132	10	701,058
Pennsylvania[1]	38	1,820,501	54	1,457,348	91	3,277,849	29	3,165,259
Rhode Island	1	102,169	6	192,457	6	294,626	3	306,761
South Carolina	11	552,267	6	123,192	17	675,459	13	727,453
South Dakota	4	104,017	8	64,008	12	168,025	4	136,648
Tennessee[1]	10	593,616	19	375,837	28	969,453	16	1,082,642
Texas[1]	37	2,446,983	65	1,139,270	98	3,586,253	89	4,599,512
Utah	1	109,523	5	175,772	6	285,295	6	327,514
Vermont	4	98,045	5	51,754	9	149,799	3	103,439
Virginia[12]	18	2,056,356	18	469,056	34	2,525,412	15	990,296
Washington[1]	9	577,132	18	604,774	26	1,181,906	15	1,207,659
West Virginia	10	264,193	13	171,810	23	436,003	11	412,013
Wisconsin	7	326,682	29	818,503	36	1,145,185	15	1,118,438
Wyoming	6	65,353	4	30,392	10	95,645	4	74,164
Totals	559	41,311,167	1,084	21,016,795	1,611	62,327,962	863	62,634,512
Total U.S., Sept. 30, 1989	530	40,759,016	1,125	21,890,202	1,626	62,649,218	847	62,008,154
Total U.S., Sept. 30, 1988	520	40,452,815	1,141	22,242,001	1,642	62,694,816	840	61,474,189
Total U.S., Sept. 30, 1987	511	39,123,807	1,166	23,702,466	1,645	62,826,273	820	60,111,863
Total U.S., Sept. 30, 1986	499	37,441,125	1,188	25,060,911	1,657	62,502,036	802	58,924,518
Total U.S., Sept. 30, 1985	482	36,361,561	1,220	26,404,671	1,676	62,766,232	798	58,825,978
Total U.S., Sept. 30, 1984	458	35,424,418	1,257	27,657,322	1,688	63,081,740	783	57,573,979
Total U.S., Sept. 30, 1983	446	33,842,142	1,284	28,802,461	1,701	62,644,603	722	56,747,436
Total U.S., Sept. 30, 1982	434	33,174,087	1,310	29,313,090	1,711	62,487,177	768	56,260,764
Total U.S., Sept. 30, 1981	408	30,552,316	1,352	30,878,429	1,730	61,430,745	755	55,180,004

1. "All-day" newspapers are listed in morning and evening columns but only once in the total, and their circulations are divided between morning and evening figures. Adjustments have been made in state and U.S. total figures. 2. Includes nationally circulated daily. Circulation counted only in the state indicated. *Source: Editor and Publisher International Yearbook, 1991.*

See the Entertainment and Culture section for additional Media information.

WHERE TO FIND OUT MORE

Reference Books and Other Sources

This cannot be a record of all the thousands of available sources of information. Nevertheless, these selected references will enable the reader to locate additional facts about many subjects covered in the *Information Please Almanac*. The editors have chosen sources that they believe will be helpful to the general reader.

General References

Encyclopedias are a unique category, since they attempt to cover most subjects quite thoroughly. The most valuable multivolume encyclopedias are the **Encyclopaedia Britannica** and the **Encyclopedia Americana**. Useful one-volume encyclopedias are the **New Columbia Encyclopedia** and the **Random House Encyclopedia**.

Dictionaries and similar "word books" are also unique: **The American Heritage Dictionary, Second College Edition,** containing 200,000 definitions and specialized usage guidance; **The American Heritage Illustrated Encyclopedic Dictionary,** containing 180,000 entries, 275 boxed encyclopedic features, and 175 colored maps of the world; **Webster's Third New International Dictionary, Unabridged; Webster's II New Riverside University Dictionary,** containing 200,000 definitions plus hundreds of word history paragraphs; and the multivolume **Oxford English Dictionary,** providing definitions in historical order. **Roget's II The New Thesaurus,** containing thousands of synonyms grouped according to meaning, assists writers in choosing just the right word. The quick reference set—**The Word Book III** (over 40,000 words spelled and divided), **The Right Word III** (a concise thesaurus), and **The Written Word III** (a concise guide to writing, style, and usage)—are based on **The American Heritage Dictionary** and are intended for the busy reader needing information fast. Two excellent books of quotations are **Bartlett's Familiar Quotations** and **The Oxford Dictionary of Quotations.**

There are a number of useful atlases: the **New York Times Atlas of the World,** a number of historical atlases (Penguin Books), **Oxford Economic Atlas of the World, Rand McNally Cosmopolitan World Atlas: New Census Edition,** and **Atlas of the Historical Geography of the United States** (Greenwood). Many contemporary road atlases of the United States and foreign countries are also available.

A source of information on virtually all subjects is the United States Government Printing Office (GPO). For information, write: Superintendent of Documents, Washington, D.C. 20402.

For help on any subject, consult: **Subject Guide to Books in Print, The New York Times Index,** and the **Reader's Guide to Periodical Literature** in your library.

Specific References

AIDS Answer Book (Network Publishers)
America Votes (Congressional Quarterly, Inc.)
American Indian, Reference Encyclopedia of the (Todd Publications)
American Recipe Collection (Fell)

American Revolution, The (Houghton Mifflin)
Anatomy, Gray's (Churchill)
Antiques and Collectibles Price List, the Kovels' (Crown)
Architectural & Building Technology, Dictionary of (Elsevier)
Architecture, Encyclopedia of World (Orient Book Distributors)
Art, History of (Prentice-Hall)
Art, Oxford Companion to (Oxford University Press)
Art, Who's Who in American (R.R. Bowker)
Art Directory, American (R.R. Bowker)
Associations, Encyclopedia of (Gale Research Co.)
Astronomy, Peterson First Guide (Houghton Mifflin)
Authors, 1000–1900, European (H.W. Wilson)
Authors, Twentieth Century (H.W. Wilson)
Automobile Facts and Figures (Kallman)
Automotive Yearbook (Wards Communication)
Ballet & Modern Dance: A Concise History (Princeton Book Co.)
Banking and Finance, Encyclopedia of (Bankers Publishing Co.)
Baseball Encyclopedia (Macmillan)
Biographical Dictionary, Cambridge (Cambridge University Press)
Biography Yearbook, Current (H.W. Wilson)
Birds, Field Guide to the, Peterson Field Guide Series (Houghton Mifflin)
Black Americans, Who's Who Among (Gale)
Book Review Digest, 1905– (H.W. Wilson)
Catholic Encyclopedia, New (Publishers Guild)
Chemistry, Encyclopedia of (VanNostrand Rinehold)
Chemistry, Lange's Handbook of, 13th Edition (McGraw Hill)
Christian Church, Oxford Dictionary of the (Oxford University Press)
Citizens Band Radio Rules and Regulations (AMECO)
College Cost Book, 1986–87, The (The College Board)
Composers, Great 1300–1900 (H.W. Wilson)
Composers Since 1900 (H .W. Wilson)
Computer Science and Technology, Encyclopedia of (Dekker)
Computer Software (W.H. Freeman)
Computer Terms, Dictionary of (Barron)
Condo and Co-op Information Book, Complete (Houghton Mifflin)
Congressional Quarterly Almanac (Congressional Quarterly, Inc.)
Consumer Reports (Consumers Union)
Costume, The Dictionary of (Macmillan)
Drama As You Like It (DOK Publications)
Cultural Literacy, The Dictionary of (Houghton Mifflin)
Drama, 20th Century, England, Ireland, the United States (McGraw Hill)
Ecology (Wiley)
Energy: Facts and Future (CRC Printing)
Environmental Politics and Policy, 2nd Edition (Congressional Quarterly)
Environmental Science (Prentice-Hall)

297

Europa World Year Book (Taylor & Francis)
Fact Books, The Rand McNally (Macmillan)
Facts, Famous First (H.W. Wilson)
Facts on File (Facts on File, Inc.)
Film: A Reference Guide (Greenwood)
(Film) **Guide to Movies on Video-cassette** (Consumers Reports)
(Finance) **Touche Ross Guide to Personal Financial Management** (Prentice-Hall)
Football Made Easy (Jonathan David)
Games, Book of (Jazz Press)
Gardening, Encyclopedia of (Revisionist Press)
Gardening, Taylor's Pocket Guides (Houghton Mifflin)
Geography, Dictionary of (Penguin Books)
Government Manual, U.S. (U.S. Office of the Federal Register, Government Printing Office)
History, Album of American (Macmillan)
History, Dictionary of American (Littlefield)
History, Documents of American (Prentice-Hall)
History, Encyclopedia of Latin-American (Greenwood)
History, Encyclopedia of World (Houghton Mifflin)
Hockey, the Illustrated History: An Official Publication of the National Hockey League (Doubleday)
How the World Works, A Guide to Science's Greatest Discoveries (Quill/William Morrow)
Infomania, The Guide to Essential Electronic Services (Houghton Mifflin Company)
Islam, Dictionary of (Orient Book Distributors)
Jazz in the Seventies, Encyclopedia of (Da Capo)
Jewish Concepts, Encyclopedia of (Hebrew Publishers)
Legal Word Book, The (Houghton Mifflin)
Libraries, World Guide to (K. G. Saur)
Library Directory, American (R.R. Bowker)
Literary Market Place (R. R. Bowker)
Literature, Oxford Companion to American (Oxford University Press)
Literature, Oxford Companion to Classical (Oxford University Press)
Literature, Oxford Companion to English (Oxford University Press)
(Literature) **Reader's Adviser: A Layman's Guide to Literature** (R.R. Bowker)
Medical Encyclopedia, Home (Been Porter)
Medical & Health Sciences Word Book (Houghton Mifflin)
Museums of the World (K.G. Saur)
Music and Musicians, Handbook of American (Da Capo)
Music, Concise Oxford Dictionary of (Oxford University Press)
Music, Harvard Dictionary of (Harvard University Press)
Musical Terms, Dictionary of (Gordon Press)
Mystery Writers, Twentieth Century Crime and (St. Martin's Press)
Mythology (Little, Brown and Co.)
National Park Guide (Prentice-Hall)
New Nations: A Student Handbook (Shoe String)
Numismatist's Fireside Companion, Vol. 2 (Bowers & Merena)
Occupational Outlook Handbook (U.S. Bureau of Labor Statistics, Government Printing Office)
Operas, New Milton Cross Complete Stories of the Great (Doubleday)
Performing Arts Information (Kansas State University)
Physics (Wiley)
Pocket Data Book, U.S.A. (U.S. Department of Commerce, Bureau of the Census, Government Printing Office)

Poetry, Granger's Index to (Columbia University Press)
Politics, Almanac of American (Barone & Co.)
Politics, Who's Who in American (R.R. Bowker)
Popular Music, America, Vol. 2 The Age of Rock (Bowling Green University)
Prescription & Non-Prescription Drugs, Complete Guide to (Price Stern)
Private Schools of the United States (Council for American Private Education (CAPE) Schools)
Radon, A Citizen's Guide to (Government Printing Office)
Religions, The Facts on File Dictionary of (Facts on File)
Robert's Rules of Order Revised (Morrow & Co.)
Science, American Men and Women of (R.R. Bowker)
Science and Technology, Asimov's Biographical Encyclopedia of (Doubleday)
Scientific Encyclopedia, VanNostrand's (VanNostrand Reinhold)
Secretary's Handbook, The Professional (Houghton Mifflin)
Senior Citizens Information Resources, Encyclopedia of (Gale Research Co.)
Shakespeare, The Riverside (Houghton Mifflin)
Ships, Boats, & Vessels, Illustrated Encyclopedia of (Overlook Press)
Social Security Handbook (USGPO)
Stamp Collecting for Beginners (Wilshire)
Stars and Planets, Field Guide to the (Houghton Mifflin)
States, Book of the (Council of State Governments)
Statesman's Year-Book (St. Martin's)
Theater, Oxford Companion to the (Oxford University Press)
United Nations, Demographic Yearbook (Unipub)
United Nations, Statistical Yearbook of the (Unipub)
United States, Historical Statistics of the Colonial Times to 1970 (Revisionist Press)
United States, Statistical Abstract of the (U.S. Department of Commerce, Bureau of the Census, Government Printing Office)
Vitamin Book: A No-Nonsense Consumer Guide (Bantam)
Washington Information Directory (Congressional Quarterly, Inc.)
The Way Things Work (Houghton Mifflin)
Who's Who in America (Marquis)
Wines, Dictionary of American (Morrow)
Women, Notable American (Harvard University Press)
World War I (Houghton Mifflin)
World War II (Houghton Mifflin)
Writer's Market (Writers Digest)
Zip Code and Post Office Directory, National (U.S. Postal Service, Government Printing Office)

See the full range of publications of Dun & Bradstreet and Standard & Poor's for corporate financial and stockholder information.

For detailed information on American colleges and universities, see the many publications of the **American Council on Education.**

Also see many other specialized **Who's Who** volumes not listed here for biographies of famous people in many fields.

MILITARY

In March 1941 an inconspicuous, well-dressed young man stepped ashore from a Japanese liner at Honolulu. Posing as a junior consular officer, he was actually a naval officer on the espionage mission of the century—targeting Pearl Harbor for destruction.

Intrigue in the Islands

By Edward Oxford

On a golden, late November afternoon in 1941, time seemed to pause.

Well out from the beach at Waikiki, a solitary swimmer moved with strong, sure strokes in the calm, turquoise waters. A tropic sun played brilliant light on the tranquil sea.

A lean, hard-muscled Japanese in his late twenties, the bather adroitly body-surfed the final yards to shore and then walked to the beach mat he had left on the white sand. Picking up a towel, he dried himself. For a while, he watched the loungers and sunbathers on the storied beach. They had come from around the globe—tourists, honeymooners, businessmen, fanciers of fine places. At casual glance, the observer himself might seem no different. But he was.

He was, in fact, Japan's master-spy in the Hawaiian Islands.

For the past eight months the secret agent had served as Japan's eyes in the strategic island chain. Virtually single-handedly—undetected by U.S. Army and Navy counterintelligence operatives, undiscovered by the Federal Bureau of Investigation (FBI) agents, unnoticed by members of the Honolulu Police espionage squad, and unreported by any of the scores of American informants who ranged the islands—he had maintained a deathwatch on the U.S. Navy's Pacific Fleet. With care, diligence, and cunning—the remarkable extent of which would be revealed only after the passage of decades—the lone spy had pieced together a masterwork of espionage.

Takeo Yoshikawa walked thoughtfully from the beach.

* * *

A graduate of the Imperial Japanese Naval Academy, Yoshikawa had served during the past four years in the Third Bureau, the Naval General Staff's intelligence group. Assigned to the American Desk, the intent ensign amassed an encyclopedic knowledge of that might threaten "the Eastern Sea"—down to the caliber of its every gun and the wingspan of its every airplane. He learned of the land from whence those warships and warplanes came. And he intensified his study of English.

In the summer of 1940, glory of a sort beckoned. Yoshikawa was summoned by his chief in the Third Bureau. The ensign was to be sent to Honolulu on a top-secret mission—to report on the day-to-day readiness of the American forces in and around the Hawaiian Islands.

"Short-wave transmitters are too easily spotted by American radio direction finders," the officer told him. "So you will go as a diplomat. You will transmit

back to us through our diplomatic code. It is the one secure channel of communication. Another thing. From now on your name is no longer Takeo Yoshikawa."

Japan's Foreign Ministry was arranging for a new consul general in Honolulu—Nagao Kita, a forty-six-year-old diplomat then at Canton, China. "Kita can be trusted to cooperate with you," the officer explained. "Kita is the one man in the consulate who knows who you are. He goes to Honolulu first. You follow. Prepare yourself." Yoshikawa bowed and left the room. "In my heart," he would later recall, "I rejoiced."

* * *

Yoshikawa knew that a plan for an attack against Pearl Harbor had been developed by the Imperial Japanese Navy in the early 1930s. He did not know, however, that during his months of espionage work in the Hawaiian Islands the plan would be finalized in detail and in keeping with a precise timetable. As he later put it: "To entrust knowledge of such a vital decision to an expendable espionage agent would have been foolish."

But the perceptive intelligence officer's experience in the Third Bureau led him to believe that the long-envisioned attack would indeed take place—probably during the winter of 1941–42.

On March 27, 1941, the liner *Nitta Maru* docked near Honolulu's Aloha Tower. Its passenger list included one Tadashi Morimura. He carried a diplomat's passport. It identified him as a lower-level consul assigned to the Japanese consulate in Honolulu.

The solemn-faced newcomer wore a plain business suit. Deputy Consul Otojiru Okuda greeted Morimura, placed a lei about his neck, and guided him through customs. A "Royal Taxi Company" cab waited for the two men at pierside. The driver knew where they were going. He drove them the two miles to the two-story white consulate building at 1742 Nuuanu Avenue.

"Morimura" was actually Takeo Yoshikawa, espionage agent. The Hawaiian Islands were soon to become his netherworld.

* * *

To the Japanese, the specks of land on the blue Pacific seemed a rightful, if far removed, part of their homeland. Just as for the Americans, to whom the islands seemed inexorably linked with the U.S. mainland. Possession was in the eye of the beholder.

At the time America annexed the Hawaiian Islands in 1898, more than half of Hawaii's people were natives of Japan. The Japanese were welcomed by plantation owners as a way of stopping the Chinese "threat"—just as Chinese workers had been welcomed to augment the "unruly" Hawaiians. But by 1907 Senator Henry Cabot Lodge, Sr., was expressing fears that the Japanese, arriving in ever-increasing numbers, might "haul their flag up in Hawaii overnight."

The early Japanese immigrants, once their plantation contracts were fulfilled, generally became shop owners and tradesmen. The next generation, with the advantage of education, entered the professional and white-collar ranks. One in five retained dual citizenship. But like other nationalities in Hawaii, the majority of the Japanese there became loyal citizens of America.

As of 1941, about 470,000 people lived in America's Hawaiian Territory. By racial antecedents, the 160,000 Japanese were the most numerous. Along with other Hawaiian residents, most lived on the island of Oahu.

* * *

The mighty naval base at Pearl Harbor, secure behind a narrow channel, was capable of holding, provisioning, repairing, and refitting the entire U.S. Pacific Fleet. Pearl Harbor had undergone a vast transformation during the previous two years. In 1939, the tempo at the once-quiet submarine base and shipyard abruptly picked up with the arrival of a force of heavy cruisers and support ships from the mainland. Engineers deepened and widened the channel into Pearl Harbor, vastly expanded the navy yard with its repaid and drydock facilities, and began construction of underground reservoirs for the base's vital but vulnerable reserves of naval fuel oil.

Then, in the spring of 1940, most major units of the U.S. Fleet—normally based at San Diego and San Pedro, California—began operating continuously in Hawaiian waters, sent there by President Franklin D. Roosevelt for "the deterrent effect" their presence in mid-Pacific might have against Japanese expansion into Southeast Asia. Each week as many as twelve battleships, two or three aircraft carriers, and dozens of cruisers and destroyers cycled in and out of Pearl Harbor, usually on a fixed schedule of several days of battle training at sea, followed by an in-port period of rest and maintenance.* Pearl Harbor was now home port for tens of thousands of naval personnel.

* * *

As thousands of Japanese immigrated to the Hawaiian Islands through the years, their government managed to mingle a few secret agents among them. In response, American counterespionage agencies began to keep lists of Japanese residents they suspected to be undercover agents.

The U.S. military, constantly concerned about the security of its bases on Oahu, made no pretense of a liberal attitude toward the Japanese. The Japanese sampan fleet was ordered to stay clear of the entrance to Pearl Harbor, and Japanese found it almost impossible to secure work within the various military installations on the island. Yet Chinese and Polynesians held jobs on the airfields, inside the navy yard, and even at the secret munitions and fuel dumps. Few Japanese had any doubt of the U.S. government's intense suspicion of them.

But for all the military's vigilance on the bases themselves, almost amusing laxity abounded on the household front. Many military wives had Japanese maids, househelpers, and laundresses. At the dinner table, naval officers talked freely about events at "Pearl," making for useful listening on the part of their Japanese domestics.

Akin to fanciful spy movies, Japanese informers learned a great deal about the island's defenses simply by lounging and listening—in the garish clubs, bars, cafés, red-light houses, and restaurants that brightened Honolulu's jasmined nights. Amidst the soft Hawaiian music and gentle banter, service personnel did not always limit their conversations to nonmilitary matters.

* * *

With Consul General Kita's approval, Yoshikawa cultivated his image as sybarite-about-Honolulu. Wherever he drifted in the island city, the young consul seemed to enjoy the give-and-take of friendly talk, the downing of drinks, and making-tropic-merry under the Hawaiian moon. The shadow-man called his alter-ego "Bobby Make-Believe." But indiscreet as he appeared, Yoshikawa remained extremely circumspect in his "private life within his private life"—his professional pursuits as Japan's Pearl Harbor spy.

Yoshikawa went about his work with exactitude. He had first assured himself that Kita would not interfere with his use of the code room. Kita, though nervous about having Yoshikawa at the consulate in the first place, proved to be cooperative.

"Within a fortnight after arriving in Honolulu, Yoshikawa ranged across Oahu from Ewa to Kohuku Point and from Koena Point to Hanauma Bay. He found vantage points from which he observed the places of interest to his government.

His superiors back in Japan sought details on the number and types of warships in Hawaiian waters and at Pearl Harbor; naval sortie patterns at the base; information on other naval anchorages in the islands; the number and kinds of warplanes present at the various air bases; antiaircraft-gun concentrations; the direction and extent of long-range air patrols; and the deployment of Army forces.

* * *

On October 22, the Honolulu-bound *Taiyo Maru,* with several hundred American families on board, sailed from Yokohama. At Honolulu the ship was to pick up hundreds of Japanese returning to their home country.

The *Taiyo Maru* took an unusual course, first sailing straight north, then turning eastward at the Kurile Islands, where it headed into the North Pacific. Near the International Date Line, the ship veered southward. The *Taiyo Maru,* at the direction of Japanese naval intelligence, was charting the route for the task force set to attack Pearl Harbor.

Commander Toshihide Maejima of the Japanese Imperial Navy, a specialist in submarine warfare, traveled as the ship's doctor. Lieutenant Commander Surguru Suzuki, an aviation expert, posed as the purser. During the voyage the "doctor" and the "purser" moved politely about the liner, raising no suspicion in the minds of the American passengers.

The two naval officers studied the surrounding seas with intense interest. They noted the winds and the atmospheric pressure. They recorded the pitch and roll of the ship. They tried to find calm areas where tankers would be able to refuel warships of the Japanese fleet en route to Pearl Harbor. And they sought to pinpoint the likeliest location for launching planes from aircraft carriers.

Amazingly, they saw not a single ship. Winter's rough seas had persuaded steamers and tankers to

---

*The battleship force consisted of four divisions of three ships each. One of these divisions was shifted to the Atlantic fleet in May 1941 to bolster America's eastern flank against the growing European threat.

more southerly routes. That endlessly clear horizon galvanized the attack-planners back in Tokyo. By following the track of the *Taiyo Maru*, an attacking fleet would have more than a fair chance of sailing undetected all the way from Japan to within a few hundred miles of the Hawaiian Islands.

At nine o'clock in the morning of November 1, the *Taiyo Maru* docked at Pier 8 in Honolulu harbor. This arrival was unlike previous, more festive, landings: no hula girls danced at pierside, and U.S. intelligence agents and FBI men mingled among the customs officials.

The next day, Suzuki met with Consul General Kita and cautioned him that "the day is rapidly approaching." Then he slipped a tiny ball of rice paper into the diplomat's hands. On it were written ninety-seven detailed questions.

Behind locked doors, Yoshikawa worked furiously to write out the answers. In those exhausting hours, the spy brought to bear much of his daringly-won knowledge of Pearl Harbor. His answers provided much of the intelligence upon which the Tokyo strategists based their final attack plan. . . .

* * *

And, though Yoshikawa had no way of knowing whether he had drawn the suspicion of U.S. counterespionage agents, he had in fact played his part well. The Americans kept detailed lists of suspects, which they rated "A," "B," and "C" in order of descending importance. Yoshikawa appeared on none of their lists.

The U.S. counterspies also kept close watch on the Japanese consulate itself. The Honolulu Police espionage unit had two informers among consulate staff members. U.S. Navy Intelligence maintained taps on six of the consulate's desk phones, a tap on Okuda's private line, and even one on the phone in Consul

General Kita's house. Some sixty conversations were recorded each day.

But none of them pointed to Yoshikawa, who was probably the only person at the consulate *not* suspected of being some sort of Japanese spy. American intelligence officers took the innocuous man known to them as "Morimura" as what he appeared to be—a fun-loving young Japanese diplomat who had wangled himself a dream assignment in a tropic paradise.

The master-spy knew not what his enemy spies knew of him. He continued to observe and study and report—come what may.

What distinguished his efforts was the same characteristic that marks the courageous fighting man on the field of battle—utter dedication to duty. As intelligence expert Ladislas Farago later wrote of Yoshikawa in *The Broken Seal*: "Technically competent both as a naval officer and a secret agent, he was indefatigable, conscientious, and an excellent judge of men. He suffered from none of the usual delusions of espionage operations and eschewed the hoary melodrama of their craft. He regarded his mission fatalistically, with the stoic submission of an officer doing his duty."

* * *

For the swimmer who had come ashore at Waikiki Beach on a golden November afternoon, the timeless setting—surf and sand beneath the Hawaiian sun— seemed now a scene to treasure. Somewhere, a fateful hour had been fixed. Somehow, Takeo Yoshikawa sensed the storm of war would soon strike the place of paradise. And what would become of this place, and of America, and of Japan, and of himself—he could not know.

Reprinted through the courtesy of Cowles Magazines, publisher of *American History Illustrated.*

50 Years Later: Pearl Harbor Remembered

About the time that this edition of Information Please Almanac *is published,[1] it will be 50 years since Japan made a devastating air strike against our unprepared military forces in Hawaii. This historic event forced the entry of the United States into World War II and ended in 1945 with the nuclear destruction of Hiroshima and Nagasaki.*

Prelude to War

In July 1940, Japan proclaimed a new order for the East called the Greater East Asia Co-Prosperity Sphere. In the fall, Japan signed "The Tripartite Pact"[2] with Germany and Italy, which gave it a free hand for expansion in the Pacific.

On July 24, 1941, The French Vichy government reluctantly gave in to Japanese demands to take over military air bases in French Indochina. This action threatened the security of the British possessions of

Burma and Malaysia, the Dutch in Indonesia, and the U.S. in the Philippines.

President Roosevelt warned Japan to remove its troops from Indochina and froze Japanese assets in the United States on July 26. This measure was followed by the governments of Britain, Canada, and Holland.

The trade embargo put a stop to Japan's oil supply because almost 90% of its oil was imported from the U.S. and the Dutch East Indies (now Indonesia). Japan did not have enough oil in its strategic reserves to continue its long war with China and for future expansionist plans in the Pacific. The embargo also restricted other vital materials for waging war.

During November, the Japanese government submitted two unsatisfactory proposals to the U.S. to settle the dispute and have the trade embargo lifted but they were not accepted. There was no successful give and take between the two nations and future diplomatic negotiations had become meaningless. Finally, on November 26, the U.S. demanded that Japan withdraw its troops from China making a negotiated settlement with Japan virtually impossible.

Rather than give up its military ambitions, Japan chose the alternative—its long-planned war with the United States of America. A decisive air strike against the American naval base at Pearl Harbor was put into operation. If the surprise attack to knock out the U.S. fleet succeeded, Japan would gain control of

---

1. *Information Please Almanac* is published annually in November.

2. The Tripartite Pact. Japan agreed to recognize and respect Germany and Italy's "new order" in Europe and, in return, they similarly agreed to Japan's right to establish a "new order" in "the sphere of Greater Asia." The three nations also agreed to support each other if any one of them was attacked by a power which was not at the time a participant in the European War or the Sino-Japanese War. This clearly referred to the United States and the Soviet Union.

the Pacific and could seize the American, British, and Dutch possessions there before the United States could recover from the blow and strike back.

The Day of Infamy

Prior to officially declaring war on the United States,[3] Japanese naval warplanes took off at 6:00 a.m. (Hawaiian time), Sunday, Dec. 7, 1941, from six carriers on a mission to destroy the U.S. Pacific Fleet based at Pearl Harbor, Hawaii, some 275 miles away.

The attack consisted of 384 planes in two waves—bombers, dive bombers, torpedo planes, and fighters. The first wave arrived virtually undetected at Pearl Harbor about 7:55 a.m. and met little or no opposition in the initial attack due to the absolute surprise of the assault. The second wave came about 45 minutes later. By 10:00 a.m., the well-planned first strike was completed and the attackers departed, leaving Pearl Harbor devastated and virtually defenseless.

The results of this worst naval catastrophe in U.S. history shocked the American people. In a little less than two hours, the entire battleship force of the U.S. Pacific Fleet (eight battleships) had been damaged or destroyed by a single blow from the air. The battleships *Arizona* and *Oklahoma* were lost along with three destroyers and one target ship.

The *Arizona* sank to the bottom in a vertical position, trapping more than one thousand hapless sailors below the decks without any chance of escape. Today, the protruding and rusted hulk of the *Arizona*

3. The Japanese Government wanted to keep their surprise attack on Pearl Harbor within the bounds of international law. They planned to give the White House a note breaking off peace negotiations at a time which would coincide with 7:30 a.m. (Hawaiian time), Sunday, December 7. This would have given the United States Government practically no time in which to warn their military commanders in Hawaii of the coming war. However, before the Japanese Embassy staff in Washington could finish decoding and translating the lengthy 5,000-word note (received by the Embassy late Saturday night, December 6) and deliver it to the White House, the attack on Pearl Harbor had already begun.

is a shrine to the memory of Pearl Harbor's dead.

On the ground, almost every one of the U.S. aircraft was damaged or destroyed. Most of the Army planes had been lined up in rows on the airfields to prevent possible sabotage, making them perfect targets. Many were wiped out before their pilots could take off and engage the enemy.

The American casualties were high, 2,403 killed (2,008 navy) and 1,178 wounded. The Japanese losses were slight by comparison—only 29 planes and five midget submarines that proved ineffective.

At the time, three U.S. aircraft carriers were away at sea—the *Enterprise*, the *Lexington*, and the *Saratoga*. For the moment, they were the only significant U.S. naval power in the Pacific. Fortunately, most of the damaged ships were later repaired and returned to active duty.

The next day when President Franklin Delano Roosevelt called on Congress to declare war on Japan, he said that Dec. 7, 1941, was "a date which will live in infamy."—*Ed.*

Postscript

For the next six months, there was a Japanese blitzkrieg in the Pacific, and Malaysia, the Dutch East Indies, and the Philippines were overrun. The turning point would come on June 4–6, 1942, during the Battle of Midway.

U.S. carrier aircraft from the greatly outnumbered Pacific Fleet struck a superior task force of the Japanese Navy headed for Midway Island. The ensuing battle became a Pearl Harbor in reverse.

When the fight was over, Japan had lost four of its six aircraft carriers, 322 warplanes, one heavy cruiser, and 3,500 lives. The U.S. suffered the loss of one of its three carriers, a destroyer, 150 aircraft, and 307 lives.

Although few at the time realized it, the United States had put a halt to Japanese expansion in the east and, from then on, Japan would remain on the defensive and its navy would never fully recover from the catastrophic defeat at Midway.—*Ed.*

Remembering America's Korean Veterans

During a three-year duration, June 21, 1950, to July 27, 1953, the United States fought one of its toughest wars under the UN flag in Korea. During this period, 5,720,000 Americans served in the Armed Forces. Of those servicemen and women, 34,000 were killed in action, 8,000 of whom were missing in action, and later declared dead, and 20,000 others died of nonbattle causes, for a total of 54,000 deaths in service. In addition, 103,000 were wounded, and 7,000 were captured or interned. Only 4,000 of the latter were returned by the enemy. The rest are MIAs.

That the total deaths for three years fighting come close to the ten-year total for Vietnam demonstrates the savageness of the fighting.

Just like our Vietnam veterans, they had experienced all the horrors of war and suffered from the same post-traumatic stress when the fighting was over. When the Korean veterans returned home, no special recognition was given them. There were no parades or praise. Unlike those returning from Vietnam, no one harassed them and there were no anti-war activists during the conflict. Theirs was considered a just cause and, as a result of their valor,

South Korea has remained free for over the past forty years.

Unjustly, their great contribution to stopping Communist aggression in that part of the world was simply ignored by our nation. The Korean veterans had fought in what was later called the "Forgotten War."

Legislation was enacted in 1986 to authorize erection of a memorial in the Washington, D.C., area by the American Battle Monuments Commission primarily through private contributions.

So far, $12 million in funds have been received: $1 million from appropriations, $5 million from private contributions (Hyundai Motors America is the largest contributor with over $1 million), $5 million from sales of the Korean War Commemorative Coin, and $1 million in interest.

Isn't it about time that we give the sacrifices of our Korean veterans the long-overdue recognition that they deserve? If you would like to help correct this injustice, write to the American Battle Monuments Commission, Massachusetts Ave., N.W., Washington, D.C. 20314. Attn: Korean War Veteran's Memorial.

The total cost for the monument will be $15 million.

Highest Ranking Officers in the Armed Forces

ARMY[1]
Generals; Colin L. Powell, Chairman of the Joint Chiefs of Staff; Gordon R. Sullivan, Chief of Staff; Robert Riscassi, Vice Chief of Staff; John R. Galvin, Supreme Allied Commander, Europe and Commander-in-Chief, U.S. European Command; Edwin H. Burba, Jr.; John W. Foss; George A. Joulwan; Crosbie E. Saint; Carl W. Stiner; William G.T. Tuttle, Jr.

AIR FORCE
Generals: Merril A. McPeak, Chief of Staff; Jimmie V. Adams; George L. Butler; Michael P.C. Carns; Hansford T. Johnson; Donald J. Kutyna; John M. Loh; James P. McCarthy; Charles C. McDonald; Robert C. Oaks; John A. Shaud; Ronald W. Yates.

NAVY
Admirals: Frank B. Kelso II, Chief of Naval Operations; Leon A. Edney; Bruce DeMars; Jonathan T. Howe; Charles R. Larson; Jerome L. Johnson; Paul D. Miller; William D. Smith; Robert J. Kelly.

MARINE CORPS
Generals: Carl E. Mundy, Jr., Commandant of the Marine Corps; John R. Dailey, Assistant Commandant of the Marine Corps and Chief of Staff; Joseph P. Hoar.
Lieutenant Generals: William Keys, Walter Boomer, Robert Winglass, Royal Moore, Jr., Robert B. Johnston, Henry C. Stackpole, III, Martin Brandtner.

1. On March 15, 1978, George Washington, the commander of the Continental Army in the American Revolution and our first President, was promoted posthumously to the newly-created rank of General of the Armies of the United States. Congress authorized this title to make it clear that Washington is the Army's senior general. *Source:* Department of Defense.

Gen. Colin Luther Powell

Four-star Army general Colin Powell became the 12th chairman of the Joint Chiefs of Staff on Oct. 3, 1989, and is the first black American to hold the nation's highest military honor. U.S. Army Photo.

COAST GUARD
Admiral: Adm. J. William Kime, Commandant.
Vice Admirals: Vice Adm. Martin H. Daniell, Jr., Vice Commandant; Vice Adm. Howard B. Thorsen, Commander Atlantic Area; Vice Adm. A. Bruce Beren, Commander Pacific Area.

History of the Armed Services

Source: Department of Defense.

U.S. Army

On June 14, 1775, the Continental Congress "adopted" the New England Armies—a mixed force of volunteers besieging the British in Boston—appointing a committee to draft "Rules and regulations for the government of the Army" and voting to raise 10 rifle companies as a reinforcement. The next day, it appointed Washington commander-in-chief of the "Continental forces to be raised for the defense of liberty," and he took command at Boston on July 3, 1775. The Continental Army that fought the Revolution was our first national military organization, and hence the Army is the senior service. After the war, the army was radically reduced but enough survived to form a small Regular Army of about 700 men under the Constitution, a nucleus for expansion in the 1790s to successfully meet threats from the Indians and from France. From these humble beginnings, the U.S. Army has developed, normally expanding rapidly by absorbing citizen soldiers in wartime and contracting just as rapidly after each war.

U.S. Navy

The antecedents of the U.S. Navy go back to September 1775, when Gen. Washington commissioned 7 schooners and brigantines to prey on British supply vessels bound for the Colonies or Canada. On Oct. 13, 1775, a resolve of the Continental Congress called for the purchase of 2 vessels for the purpose of intercepting enemy transports. With its passage a Naval Committee of 7 men was formed, and they rapidly obtained passage of legislation calling for procurement of additional vessels. The Continental Navy was supplemented by privateers and ships operated as state navies, but soon after the British surrender it was disestablished.

In 1794, because of dissatisfaction with the payment of tribute to the Barbary pirates, Congress authorized construction of 6 frigates. The first, *United States,* was launched May 10, 1797, but the Navy still remained under the control of the Secretary of War until April 1798, when the Navy Department was created under the Secretary of the Navy with Cabinet rank.

U.S. Air Force

Until creation of the National Military Establishment in September 1947, which united the services under one department, military aviation was a part of the U.S. Army. In the Army, aeronautical operations came under the Signal Corps from 1907 to 1918, when the Army Air Service was established. In 1926, the Army Air Corps came into being and remained until 1941, when the Army Air Forces succeeded it as the Army's air arm. On Sept. 18, 1947, the U.S. Air Force was established as an independent military service under the National Military Establishment. At that time, the name "Army Air Forces" was abolished.

U.S. Coast Guard

Our country's oldest continuous seagoing service, the U.S. Coast Guard, traces its history back to 1790, when the first Congress authorized the construction of ten vessels for the collection of revenue. Known first as the Revenue Marine, and later as the Revenue Cutter Service, the Coast Guard received its present name in 1915 under an act of Congress combining the Revenue Cutter Service with the Life-Saving Service. In 1939, the Lighthouse Service was also consolidated with this unit. The Bureau of Marine Inspection and Navigation was transferred temporarily to the Coast Guard in 1942, permanently in 1946. Through its antecedents, the Coast Guard is one of the oldest organizations under the federal government and, until the Navy Department was established in 1798, served as the only U.S. armed force afloat. In times of peace, it operates under the Department of Transportation, serving as the nation's primary agency for promoting marine safety and enforcing federal maritime laws. In times of war, or on direction of the President, it is attached to the Navy Department.

U.S. Marine Corps

Founded in 1775 and observing its official birthday on Nov. 10, the U.S. Marine Corps was developed to serve on land, on sea, and in the air.

Marines have fought in every U.S. war. From an initial two battalions in the Revolution, the Corps reached a peak strength of six divisions and five aircraft wings in World War II. Its present strength is three active divisions and aircraft wings and a Reserve division/aircraft wing team. In 1947, the National Security Act set Marine Corps strength at not less than three divisions and three aircraft wings.

Service Academies

U.S. Military Academy

Source: U.S. Military Academy.

Established in 1802 by an act of Congress, the U.S. Military Academy is located on the west bank of the Hudson River some 50 miles north of New York City. To gain admission a candidate must first secure a nomination from an authorized source. These sources are:

Congressional Sources

Representatives
Senators
Other: Vice Presidential
District of Columbia
Puerto Rico
Am. Samoa, Guam, Virgin Is.

Military-Service-Connected Sources

Presidential—Sons or daughers of active duty or retired service members
Enlisted members of Army
Enlisted members of Army Reserve/
National Guard
Sons and daughters of deceased and disabled
veterans
Honor military, naval schools
and ROTC
Sons and daughters of persons awarded the
Medal of Honor

Any number of applicants can meet the requirements for a *nomination* in these categories. *Appointments* (offers of admission), however, can only be made to a much smaller number, about 1,200 each year.

Candidates may be nominated for vacancies during the year preceding the day of admission, which occurs in early July. The best time to apply is during the junior year in high school.

Candidates must be citizens of the U.S., be unmarried, be at least 17 but not yet 22 years old on July 1 of the year admitted, have a secondary-school education or its equivalent, and be able to meet the academic, medical, and physical aptitude requirements. Academic qualification is determined by an analysis of entire scholastic record, and performance on either the American College Testing (ACT) Assessment Program Test or the College Entrance Examination Board Scholastic Aptitude Test (SAT). Entrance requirements and procedures for appointment are described in the Admissions Bulletin, available without charge from Admissions, U.S. Military Academy, West Point, N.Y. 10996-1797.

Cadets are members of the Regular Army. As such they receive full scholarships and annual salaries from which they pay for their uniforms, textbooks, and incidental expenses. Upon successful completion of the four-year course, the graduate receives the degree of Bachelor of Science and is commissioned a second lieutenant in the Regular Army with a requirement to serve as an officer for a minimum of six years.

U.S. Naval Academy

Source: U.S. Naval Academy.

The Naval School, established in 1845 at Fort Severn, Annapolis, Md., was renamed the U.S. Naval Academy in 1850. A four-year course was adopted a year later.

The Superintendent is a rear admiral. A civilian academic dean heads the academic program. A captain heads the 4,300-man Brigade of Midshipmen and military, professional, and physical training. The faculty is half military and half civilian.

Graduates are awarded the Bachelor of Science or Bachelor of Science in Engineering and are commissioned as officers in the U.S. Navy or Marine Corps.

Midshipmen are nominated for an appointment from several official sources, which are summarized below. The numbers represent the actual each nominator may have at the academy at any one time. Five each from the Vice President, U.S. Senators, U.S. Representatives, the delegate from Washington, D.C., and the Resident Commissioner of Puerto Rico. Delegates from Guam and the Virgin Islands nominate two each, with one each from the Governor of Puerto Rico, the delegate from American Samoa, and the Office of the Administrator of the Panama Canal Commission.

Annual nominations are from several other sources: Presidential nominations for 100 sons and daughters of career military personnel; 85 each from the regular Navy and Marine corps, and the Navy and Marine Corps reserve; 20 from NROTC/NJROTC/MCJROTC and Honor Military and Naval schools; 65 sons and daughters of disabled veterans or POWs, 600 qualified alternates; and an unlimited number of sons and daughters of Medal of Honor recipients.

To have basic eligibility for admission, candidates must be citizens of the U.S., of good moral character, at least 17 and not more than 22 years of age on July 1 of their entering year, and unmarried.

In order to be considered for admission, a candidate must obtain a nomination from one of the sources of appointments listed above. The Admissions Board at the Naval Academy examines the candidate's school record, College Board or ACT scores, recommendations from school officials, extracurricular activities, and evidence from other sources concerning his or her character, leadership potential, academic preparation, and physical fitness. Qualification for admission is based on all of the above factors.

Tuition, board, lodging, and medical and dental care are provided. Midshipmen receive over $500 a month for books, uniforms, and personal needs.

For general information or answers to specific questions, write: Director of Candidate Guidance, U.S. Naval Academy, Annapolis, Md. 21402-5018.

U.S. Air Force Academy

Source: U.S. Air Force Academy.

The bill establishing the Air Force Academy was signed by President Eisenhower on April 1, 1954. The first class of 306 cadets was sworn in on July 11, 1955, at Lowry Air Force Base, Denver, the Academy's temporary location. The Cadet Wing moved into the Academy's permanent home north of Colorado Springs, Colorado, in 1958.

Cadets receive four years of academic, military, and physical education to prepare them for leadership as officers in the Air Force. The Academy is authorized a total of 4,400 cadets. Each new class averages 1,400. The candidates for the Academy must be at least 17 but less than 22 on July 1 of the year for which they enter the Academy, must be a United States citizen, never married, and be able to meet the mental and physical requirements. A candidate is required to take the following examinations and tests: (1) the Service Academies' Qualifying Medical Examination; (2) either the American College Testing (ACT) Assessment Program test or the College Entrance Examination Board Scholastic Aptitude Test (SAT); and (3) a Physical Aptitude Examination.

Cadets receive their entire education at government expense and, in addition, are paid more than $500 per month base pay. From this sum, they pay for their uniforms, textbooks, tailoring, laundry, entertainment tickets, etc. Upon completion of the four-year program, leading to a Bachelor of Science degree, a cadet who meets the qualifications is commissioned a second lieutenant in the U.S. Air Force. Nearly 65 percent enter pilot or navigator training. For details on admissions, write: Director of Cadet Admissions (RRS), HQ USAF Academy, Colorado Springs, CO 80840-5651.

U.S. Coast Guard Academy

Source: U.S. Coast Guard Academy.

The U.S. Coast Guard Academy, New London, Conn., was founded on July 31, 1876, to serve as the "School of Instruction" for the Revenue Cutter Service, predecessor to the Coast Guard.

The J.C. Dobbin, a converted schooner, housed the first Coast Guard Academy, and was succeeded in 1878 by the barque Chase, a ship built for cadet training. First winter quarters were in a sail loft at New Bedford, Mass. The school was moved in 1900 to Arundel Cove, Md., to provide a more technical education, and in 1910 was moved back to New England to Fort Trumbull, New London, Conn. In 1932 the Academy moved to its present location in New London.

The Academy today offers a four-year curriculum for the professional and academic training of cadets, which leads to a Bachelor of Science degree and a commission as ensign in the Coast Guard.

The U.S. Coast Guard Academy is the only one of the five federal service academies that offers appointments solely on the basis of an annual nationwide competition; there are no congressional nominations or geographical quotas involved. Competition is open to any young American who meets the basic eligibility requirements, which consist of satisfactory Scholastic Aptitude Test (SAT) or American College Testing Program examination (ACT) results, high school standing, and leadership potential. Either the SAT or the ACT must be completed prior to or during the December test administration of the year of application. All cadets must have reached their 17th but not their 22nd birthday by July 1 of the year of entrance to the Academy. All cadets must pass a rigid medical examination before being accepted.

Women were first admitted to the Coast Guard Academy in 1976 and first graduated in 1980. Cadets must be unmarried upon entry and must remain unmarried until after graduation. As ensigns, they must serve a six-year obligation following graduation. Cadets receive a stipend to cover incidentals and uniform expenses. Meals and quarters are provided.

A catalog can be obtained by writing to: Director of Admissions, U.S. Coast Guard Academy, 15 Mohegan Ave., New London, Conn. 06320-4195, or call (203) 444-8501 or (800) 424-8883.

U.S. Merchant Marine Academy

Source: U.S. Merchant Marine Academy.

The U.S. Merchant Marine Academy, situated at Kings Point, N.Y., on the north shore of Long Island, was dedicated Sept. 30, 1943. It is maintained by the Department of Transportation under direction of the Maritime Administration.

The Academy has a complement of approximately 840 men and women representing every state, D.C., the Canal Zone, Puerto Rico, Guam, American Samoa, and the Virgin Islands. It is also authorized to admit up to 12 candidates from the Western Hemisphere and 30 other foreign students at any one time.

Candidates are nominated by Senators and members of the House of Representatives. Nominations to the Academy are governed by a state and territory quota system based on population and the results of the College Entrance Examination Board tests.

A candidate must be a citizen not less than 17 and not yet 22 years of age by July 1 of the year in which admission is sought. Fifteen high school credits, including 3 units in mathematics (from algebra, geometry and/or trigonometry), 1 unit in science (physics or chemistry) and 3 in English are required.

The course is four years and includes one year of practical training aboard a merchant ship. Study includes marine engineering, navigation, satellite navigation and communications, electricity, ship construction, naval science and tactics, economics, business, languages, history, etc.

Upon completion of the course of study, a graduate receives a Bachelor of Science degree, a license as a merchant marine deck or engineering officer, and a commission as an Ensign in the Naval Reserve.

U.S. Casualties in Major Wars

War	Branch of service	Numbers engaged	Battle deaths	Other deaths	Total deaths	Wounds not mortal	Total casualties[1]
Revolutionary War	Army	n.a.	4,044	n.a.	n.a.	6,004	n.a.
1775 to 1783	Navy	n.a.	342	n.a.	n.a.	114	n.a.
	Marines	n.a.	49	n.a.	n.a.	70	n.a.
	Total	**n.a.**	**4,435**	**n.a.**	**n.a.**	**6,188**	**n.a.**
War of 1812	Army	n.a.	1,950	n.a.	n.a.	4,000	n.a.
1812 to 1815	Navy	n.a.	265	n.a.	n.a.	439	n.a.
	Marines	n.a.	45	n.a.	n.a.	66	n.a.
	Total	**286,730**	**2,260**	**n.a.**	**n.a.**	**4,505**	**n.a.**
Mexican War	Army	n.a.	1,721	11,550	13,271	4,102	17,373
1846 to 1848	Navy	n.a.	1	n.a.	n.a.	3	n.a.
	Marines	n.a.	11	n.a.	n.a.	47	n.a.
	Total	**78,718**	**1,733**	**n.a.**	**n.a.**	**4,152**	**n.a.**
Civil War[2]	Army	2,128,948	138,154	221,374	359,528	280,040	639,568
1861 to 1865	Navy	84,415	2,112	2,411	4,523	1,710	6,233
	Marines	148	148	312	460	131	591
	Total	**2,213,363**	**140,414**	**224,097**	**364,511**	**281,881**	**646,392**
Spanish-American War	Army	280,564	369	2,061	2,430	1,594	4,024
1898	Navy	22,875	10	0	10	47	57
	Marines	3,321	6	0	6	21	27
	Total	**306,760**	**385**	**2,061**	**2,446**	**1,662**	**4,108**
World War I	Army	4,057,101	50,510	55,868	106,378	193,663	300,041
1917 to 1918	Navy	599,051	431	6,856	7,287	819	8,106
	Marines	78,839	2,461	390	2,851	9,520	12,371
	Total	**4,734,991**	**53,402**	**63,114**	**116,516**	**204,002**	**320,518**
World War II	Army[3]	11,260,000	234,874	83,400	318,274	565,861	884,135
1941 to 1946	Navy	4,183,466	36,950	25,664	62,614	37,778	100,392
	Marines	669,100	19,733	4,778	24,511	67,207	91,718
	Total	**16,112,566**	**291,557**	**113,842**	**405,399**	**670,846**	**1,076,245**
Korean War	Army	2,834,000	27,704	9,429	37,133	77,596	114,729
1950 to 1953	Navy	1,177,000	458	4,043	4,501	1,576	6,077
	Marine	424,000	4,267	1,261	5,528	23,744	29,272
	Air Force	1,285,000	1,200	5,884	7,084	368	7,452
	Total	**5,720,000**	**33,629**	**20,617**	**54,246**	**103,284**	**157,530**
War in Southeast Asia[4]	Army	4,386,000	30,904	7,270	38,174	96,802	134,976
	Navy[5]	1,842,000	1,634	916	2,552	4,178	6,730
	Marines	794,000	13,079	1,750	14,829	51,392	66,221
	Air Force	1,740,000	1,765	815	2,580	931	3,511
	Total	**8,744,000**	**47,382**	**10,753**	**58,135**	**153,303**	**211,438**

1. Excludes captured or interned and missing in action who were subsequently returned to military control. 2. Union forces only. Totals should probably be somewhat larger as data or disposition of prisoners are far from complete. Final Confederate deaths, based on incomplete returns, were 133,821, to which should be added 26,000–31,000 personnel who died in Union prisons. 3. Army data include Air Force. 4. As of Nov. 11, 1986. 5. Includes a small number of Coast Guard of which 5 were battle deaths. NOTE: All data are subject to revision. For wars before World War I, information represents best data from available records. However, due to incomplete records and possible difference in usage of terminology, reporting systems, etc., figures should be considered estimates. n.a. = not available. *Source:* Department of Defense.

The National Guard

Source: Departments of the Army and the Air Force, National Guard Bureau.

The National Guard of the United States traces its origins to the early colonial militia of 1636 when regiments of the North, South and East Massachusetts Bay Colony first mustered in defense of their newly found territory. Because of its lineage to these early military units, the modern Guard is recognized as the nation's oldest military and is among the oldest in existence anywhere in the world. Guardmembers have served the United States in every major conflict, from the American Revolution to our nation's most recent involvement in the Persian Gulf.

On August 22, 1990, President Bush authorized the call of thousands of National Guard members to federal active duty in response to the escalating crisis in the Middle East. Those first critical months prior to the outbreak of war in January, 1991 saw tens of thousands of National Guardmembers alerted or called to federal active duty. This historic call of the Guard and reserve was the largest since the Korean War, mobilizing close to 70,000 Army and Air Guardmembers to support operational requirements for Operation(s) Desert Shield and Desert Storm. In addition to those formally called, thousands of National Guard volunteers performed missions critical to getting personnel and equipment quickly into the Central Command theater. National Guard units participated in all phases of the operation, to include tactical and strategic airlift, aerial refueling, logistics, communications, as well as by providing combat air and ground units, medical and linguist specialists. Other types of support provided by Army and Air Guard units included mobile aerial port squadrons, transportation, water purification specialists and military police.

At the close of Fiscal Year '90, the Army National Guard had 447,151 people, ranking it the tenth largest army in the world. In that same period, the Air National Guard had close to 117,000 people, ranking the air "arm" of the National Guard as the world's fourth largest Air Force.

In peacetime, the National Guard is commanded by the governors of the respective states/territories and may be called to state active duty by the governor to assist in state emergencies, disasters, and civil disturbances. During a war or national emergency, the National Guard may be called to active duty by the President or Congress. The National Guard serves as the primary source of augmentation for the Army and the Air Force.

Total dollars appropriated to the Guard for fiscal year 91 was in excess of $9 billion. Of that, the Army National Guard operated in fiscal year 1991 with 5.7 billion, the Air Guard budget was $3.6 billion. Although a substantial portion of National Guard funding comes from the federal government, the respective states and territories provide fiscal support in such areas as state missions, recruiting and training administration, armory construction, and funding for state-salaried employees.

The Army National Guard is made up of 3,000 units located in 2,600 communities throughout the 50 states, Puerto Rico, Guam, the Virgin Islands and the District of Columbia.

The Army National Guard provides roughly 43% of the total Army's combat capability and approximately 20 percent of its support units. The Army Guard consists of 10 combat divisions, 14 separate combat brigades, 4 divisional roundout brigades, 4 armored cavalry regiments, 3 medical brigades, 2 special forces groups, 1 infantry scout group (arctic reconnaissance) and 17 major command headquarters units.

The Army National Guard is crucial to the nation's first-line of defense. Over half of the Army's divisional capability is in the Army National Guard. Of the Army's 28 divisions, ten are solely Guard divisions with an additional nine requiring Guard units of battalion or brigade size to bring them to their full combat potential.

The Army National Guard's force structure is broken down into: 10 divisions, 14 separate brigades, five divisional roundout brigades, three armored cavalry regiments, and two special forces groups. In addition, the Army Guard has the Army's only infantry scout group (arctic reconnaissance).

The Air National Guard has 91 flying units and 1,140 mission support units which, upon mobilization, would be gained by one of six major commands of the USAF. The gaining major commands are Tactical Air Command (TAC), Strategic Air Command (SAC), Military Airlift Command (MAC), Air Force Communications Command (AFCC), Pacific Air Forces (PACAF), and Alaskan Air Command (AAC).

The Air National Guard is a vital contributor to the Total Air Force mission. By the close of fiscal year '93, the Air Guard will be performing:

• 100 percent of the Total Air Force air defense mission,
• 100 percent of all Air Force tactical reconnaissance,
• 40 percent of tactical airlift,
• and will represent 30 percent of all U.S. Air Force fighters.

In the mission support areas, the Air National Guard comprises:

• 70 percent of the total Air Forces' combat communications units;
• 70 percent of its engineering and installation forces;
• and 30 percent of the U.S. Air Force civil engineering units.

The National Guard Bureau (NGB), a joint, federal agency headquartered at the Pentagon, serves as both a staff and an operating agency. As a staff agency, NGB participates with the U.S. Army and Air Force staffs in the development and coordination of the programs pertaining to or affecting the National Guard. As an operating agency, NGB formulates and administers the programs for the training, development and maintenance of the Army and Air National Guard of the United States. NGB is the channel of communications between the Departments of Army and Air Force, and the states for non-federalized units and personnel as provided in Title 10 U.S.C. 3015. The Chief, National Guard Bureau is nominated by the President and confirmed by the Senate. The current Chief, National Guard Bureau is Lt. General John B. Conaway, (USAF), an Air Guardsman from Kentucky.

The National Guard offers its members a broad range of educational opportunities. These not only include skill training associated with their military occupational specialty, but in many instances cross over with skills utilized in their civilian occupations. The list of skills is not limited to those that are equipment oriented but includes management, medical, and other career fields. Some of these educational opportunities may even be pursued in civilian institutions, specifically that of the Clinical Specialist, which is compatible with a Licensed Practical Nurse or Licensed Vocational Nurse.

If openings exist, men and women between the ages of 17 and 35 may enlist for an eight-year commitment which can be served both on active and inactive duty. For example, an individual may enlist for a period of three years followed by a five year inactive reserve period. Any of the combinations below are acceptable as long as it meets a total time requirement of eight years:

• initial enlistment of three years, followed by five years inactive reserve duty status;

• or four years, followed by four years inactive reserve duty status;

• or six years, followed by two years inactive reserve duty status;

• or eight years with no inactive duty time.

While on inactive status, the service member is subject to recall should the need arise.

Guard members receive a full day's pay of their military rank for each unit training assembly attended. Additionally, they receive a day's pay of their military rank for each of their 15 days of annual training, plus any other days on active duty for training at military schools or special assignments. All such training counts toward retirement eligibility at age 60 with 20 or more years of qualifying service.

Veterans' Benefits

Although benefits of various kinds date back to Colonial days, veterans of World War I were the first to receive disability compensation, allotments for dependents, life insurance, and vocational rehabilitation. In the 1940's, these benefits were slowly broadened. On March 15, 1989, the Veterans Administration became the Department of Veterans Affairs.

The following benefits available to veterans require certain minimum periods of active duty during qualifying periods of service and generally are applicable only to those whose discharges are not dishonorable. Certain types of discharges are subject to special adjudication to determine eligibility.

For information or assistance in applying for veterans benefits, write, call, or visit a VA Regional Office. Consult your local telephone directory under United States Government, Department of Veterans Affairs (VA) for the address and telephone number. Toll-free telephone service is available in all 50 States.

Unemployment allowances. Every effort is being made to secure employment for Vietnam veterans. Unemployment benefits are administered by the U.S. Department of Labor.

Loan Guaranty. VA will guarantee loans for a variety of purposes, such as: to buy or build a home; to purchase a manufactured home with or without a lot; and to refinance a home presently owned and occupied by the veteran. When the purpose of a refinancing loan is to lower the interest rate on an existing guaranteed loan then prior occupancy by the veteran or spouse will suffice. VA will guarantee the lender against loss up to 50% on loans of $45,000 or less, the lesser of $36,000 or 40% (never less than $22,500) on loans of more than $45,000, and the lesser of $46,000 or 25% on loans of more than $144,000. On manufactured home loans, the amount of the guarantee is 40% of the loan to a maximum of $20,000. The interest rate may not exceed the maximum rate set by VA and in effect when the loan is made.

Compensation and rehabilitation benefits. These are available to those having some service-connected illness or disability.

Disability compensation. VA pays from $80 to $1,620 per month, and for specific conditions up to $4,628 per month, plus allowances for dependents, where the disability is rated 30% or more.

Vocational Rehabilitation. VA provides professional counseling, training and other assistance to help compensably service-disabled veterans, rated 20 percent or more, who have an employment handicap to achieve maximum independence in daily living and, to the extent possible, to obtain and maintain suitable employment. Generally, a veteran may receive up to 48 months of this assistance during the 12 years from the date he or she is notified of entitlement to VA compensation. All the expenses of a veteran's rehabilitation program are paid by VA. In addition, the veteran receives a subsistence allowance which varies based on the rate of training and number of dependents. For example, a single veteran training full time would receive $333 monthly.

Vocational Training for VA Pension Recipients. Veterans who are awarded pension during the period from February 1, 1985, through January 31, 1992, may participate in a program of vocational training essentially identical to that provided in VA's vocational rehabilitation program. Certain veterans awarded pension before February 1, 1985 may also participate in this program. Participants do not receive any direct payments, such as subsistence allowance, while in training.

Medical and dental care. This includes care in VA and, in certain instances, in non-VA, or other federal hospitals. It also covers outpatient treatment at a VA field facility or, in some cases, by an approved private physician or dentist. Full domiciliary care is also provided to veterans with low incomes. Nursing home care may be provided at certain VA medical facilities or in approved community nursing homes. Hospital and other medical care may also be provided for the spouse and child dependents of a veteran who is permanently and totally disabled due to a service-connected disability; or for survivors of a veteran who dies from a service-connected disability; or for survivors of a veteran who at the time of death had a total disability, permanent in nature, resulting from a service-connected disability. These latter benefits are usually provided in nonfederal facilities. Eligibility criteria for veterans' medical benefits vary. Veterans must agree to make a copayment for the care they receive from VA if their incomes exceed levels that vary with number of dependents and they do not have a service-connected disability or service in certain early war periods. Veterans and/or their dependents or survivors should always apply in advance. Contact the nearest VA medical facility.

Readjustment Counseling. VA provides readjustment counseling to veterans of the Vietnam Era in need of assistance in resolving post-war readjustment problems in the areas of employment, family, education, and personal readjustment including post-traumatic stress disorder. Services are provided at community-based Vet Centers and at VA Medical Centers in certain locations. Services include individual family and group counseling, employment and educational counseling, and assistance in obtaining referrals to various governmental and nongovernmental agencies with an interest in assisting Vietnam Era veterans. Contact the nearest Vet Center or VA facility to determine location of Vet Center.

Dependents' educational assistance. VA pays $404 a month for up to 45 months of schooling to spouses and children of veterans who died of service-connected causes or who were permanently and totally disabled from service-connected causes or died while permanently and totally disabled or who are currently missing in action, captured in the line of duty, or forcibly detained or interned in line of duty by a foreign power for more than 90 days. Students must usually be between 18 and 26.

Veterans readjustment education. Veterans and servicepersons who initially entered the military on or after Jan. 1, 1977, and before July 1, 1985, may receive educational assistance under a contributory plan. Individuals contribute $25 to $100 from military pay, up to a maximum of $2,700. This amount is matched by the Federal Government on a 2 for 1 basis. Participants, while on active duty, may make a lump sum contribution. Participants receive monthly payments for the number of months they contributed, or for 36 months, whichever is less. No initial enrollments are permitted after March 31, 1987.

Montgomery GI Bill. This Act provides education benefits for individuals entering the military after June 30, 1985. Servicepersons entering active duty after that date will have their basic pay reduced by $100 a month for the first 12 months of their service, unless they specifically elect not to participate in the program. Servicepersons eligible for post-Korean GI Bill benefits as of December 31, 1989, and who serve 3 years in active duty service after July 1, 1985, are also eligible for the new program, but will not have their basic pay reduced. Servicepersons who, after December 31, 1976, received commissions as officers from service academies or scholarship senior ROTC programs are not eligible for this program.

Active duty for three years (two years, if the initial obligated period of active duty is less than three years), or two years active duty plus four years in the Selected Reserve or National Guard will entitle an individual to $300 a month basic benefits. There is also a targeted, discretionary kicker of up to an additional $700 available. A supplemental benefit of up to an additional $300 with a targeted, discretionary kicker of up to $300 more is also available for certain additional active duty service.

An educational entitlement program is also available for members of the Selected Reserve. Eligibility applies to individuals who, after June 30, 1985 enlist, re-enlist, or extend an enlistment for a six-year pe-

riod. Benefits may be paid to eligible members of the Selected Reserve who complete their initial period of active duty train ing. Full-time payments are $140 a month for 36 months.

Veterans' Benefits Improvement Act of 1989. Veterans awarded 100 percent disability compensation based upon unemployability during the period February 1, 1989, through January 31, 1992, for whom a vocational goal is feasible may participate in a rehabilitation program. Necessary training expenses, special equipment, etc., toward a definite job objective are paid for, plus a monthly allowance up to $333, with increased amounts for dependents, in addition to compensation. In addition, all veterans granted an unemployability rating before February 1, 1985, the start of the special program period, may receive special assistance in securing employment under the Vocational Rehabilitation Program. Any veteran with an unemployability rating who secures gainful employment during the special program period will be protected from reduction until such veteran has worked continuously for 12 months.

Pensions. Pension benefits are payable for wartime veterans permanently and totally disabled from non-service-connected causes. These benefits are based on need. Surviving spouses and children of wartime veterans have the same eligibility status, based on the veteran's honorable wartime service and their need.

Insurance. The VA life insurance programs have approximately 7.2 million policyholders with total coverage of about $216 billion. Detailed information on NSLI (National Service Life Insurance), USGLI (United States Government Life Insurance), and VMLI (Veterans Mortgage Life Insurance) may be obtained at any VA Office. Information regarding SGLI (Servicemen's Group Life Insurance) and VGLI (Veterans Group Life Insurance) may be obtained from the Office of Servicemen's Group Life Insurance, 213 Washington St., Newark, N.J. 07102

Burial benefits. Burial is provided in any VA national cemetery with available grave space to any deceased veteran of wartime or peacetime service, other than for training, who was discharged under conditions other than dishonorable. Also eligible for burial in a national cemetery are the veteran's spouse, widow, widower, minor children, and under certain conditions, unmarried adult children.

Headstone or marker. A government headstone or marker is furnished for any deceased veteran of wartime or peacetime service, other than for training, who was discharged under conditions other than dishonorable and is interred in a national, state veterans', or private cemetery. VA also will furnish markers to veterans' eligible dependents interred in a national or state veterans' cemetery.

Civilian Casualties in Wartime

Unlike Iraq's indiscriminate bombing of civilians with Scud missiles, great effort was made to reduce the level of civilian casualties during the Persian Gulf War by the U.S.-led coalition forces. Although coalition warplanes flew as many as 70,000 sorties in one month, the civilian casualties were astonishingly low by historical comparison even if they actually reached an unconfirmed several thousand. During World War II, over 380,000 civilians were killed every month of the entire war.

During the first large incendiary bombing raid on

Tokyo during the night of March 9–10, 1945, over 300 U.S. B-29 bombers devastated 16 square miles or one-quarter of the heavily defended city, destroying 267,000 structures, and causing about 185,000 civilian casualties. The U.S. lost only 14 aircraft during the action.

Allied bombing raids on the city of Hamburg during one week in 1943 killed between 31,000 to 50,000 residents and caused a million people to flee the burning city. □

Casualties in World War I

Country	Total mobilized forces	Killed or died[1]	Wounded	Prisoners or missing	Total Casualties
Austria-Hungary	7,800,000	1,200,000	3,620,000	2,200,000	7,020,000
Belgium	267,000	13,716	44,686	34,659	93,061
British Empire[2]	8,904,467	908,371	2,090,212	191,652	3,190,235
Bulgaria	1,200,000	87,500	152,390	27,029	266,919
France[2]	8,410,000	1,357,800	4,266,000	537,000	6,160,800
Germany	11,000,000	1,773,700	4,216,058	1,152,800	7,142,558
Greece	230,000	5,000	21,000	1,000	27,000
Italy	5,615,000	650,000	947,000	600,000	2,197,000
Japan	800,000	300	907	3	1,210
Montenegro	50,000	3,000	10,000	7,000	20,000
Portugal	100,000	7,222	13,751	12,318	33,291
Romania	750,000	335,706	120,000	80,000	535,706
Russia	12,000,000	1,700,000	4,950,000	2,500,000	9,150,000
Serbia	707,343	45,000	133,148	152,958	331,106
Turkey	2,850,000	325,000	400,000	250,000	975,000
United States	4,734,991	116,516	204,002	—	320,518

1. Includes deaths from all causes. 2. Official figures. NOTE: For additional U.S. figures, *see* the table on U.S. Casualties in Major Wars in this section.

Casualties in World War II

Country	Men in war	Battle deaths	Wounded
Australia	1,000,000	26,976	180,864
Austria	800,000	280,000	350,117
Belgium	625,000	8,460	55,513[1]
Brazil[2]	40,334	943	4,222
Bulgaria	339,760	6,671	21,878
Canada	1,086,343[7]	42,042[7]	53,145
China[3]	17,250,521	1,324,516	1,762,006
Czechoslovakia	—	6,683[4]	8,017
Denmark	—	4,339	—
Finland	500,000	79,047	50,000
France	—	201,568	400,000
Germany	20,000,000	3,250,000[4]	7,250,000
Greece	—	17,024	47,290
Hungary	—	147,435	89,313
India	2,393,891	32,121	64,354
Italy	3,100,000	149,496[4]	66,716
Japan	9,700,000	1,270,000	140,000
Netherlands	280,000	6,500	2,860
New Zealand	194,000	11,625[4]	17,000
Norway	75,000	2,000	—
Poland	—	664,000	530,000
Romania	650,000[5]	350,000[6]	—
South Africa	410,056	2,473	—
U.S.S.R.	—	6,115,000[4]	14,012,000
United Kingdom	5,896,000	357,116[4]	369,267
United States	16,112,566	291,557	670,846
Yugoslavia	3,741,000	305,000	425,000

1. Civilians only. 2. Army and Navy figures. 3. Figures cover period July 7, 1937–Sept. 2, 1945, and concern only Chinese regular troops. They do not include casualties suffered by guerrillas and local military corps. 4. Deaths from all causes. 5. Against Soviet Russia; 385,847 against Nazi Germany. 6. Against Soviet Russia; 169,822 against Nazi Germany. 7. National Defense Ctr., Canadian Forces Hq., Director of History. NOTE: The figures in this table are unofficial estimates obtained from various sources.

Merchant Marine Casualties in World War II

In 1988, the U.S. Government conferred official veterans status on those who served aboard oceangoing merchant ships in World War II. The officers and crews played a key role in transporting the troops and war material that enabled the United States and its allies to defeat the Axis powers.

During the war, merchant seamen died as a result of enemy attacks at a rate that proportionately ex-

ceeded all branches of the armed services, with the exception of the U.S. Marine Corps.

Enemy action sank more than 700 U.S.-flag merchant ships and claimed the lives of over 6,000 civilian seafarers. Untold thousands of additional seamen were wounded or injured during these attacks, and nearly 600 were made prisoners of war.

U.S. Military Actions Other Than Declared Wars

Hawaii (1893): U.S. Marines, ordered to land by U.S. Minister John L. Stevens, aided the revolutionary Committee of Safety in overthrowing the native government. Stevens then proclaimed Hawaii a U.S. protectorate. Annexation, resisted by the Democratic administration in Washington, was not formally accomplished until 1898.

China (1900): Boxers (a group of Chinese revolutionists) occupied Peking and laid siege to foreign legations. U.S. troops joined an international expedition which relieved the city.

Panama (1903): After Colombia had rejected a proposed agreement for relinquishing sovereignty over the Panama Canal Zone, revolution broke out, aided by promoters of the Panama Canal Co. Two U.S. warships were standing by to protect American privileges. The U.S. recognized the Republic of Panama on November 6.

Dominican Republic (1904): When the Dominican Republic failed to meet debts owed to the U.S. and foreign creditors, President Theodore Roosevelt declared the U.S. intention of exercising "international police power" in the Western Hemisphere whenever necessary. The U.S. accordingly administered customs and managed debt payments of the Dominican Republic from 1905 to 1907.

Nicaragua (1911): The possibility of foreign control over Nicaragua's canal route led to U.S. intervention and agreement. The U.S. landed Marines in Nicaragua (Aug. 14, 1912) to protect American interests there. A small detachment remained until 1933.

Mexico (1914): Mexican dictator Victoriano Huerta, opposed by President Woodrow Wilson, had the support of European governments. An incident involving unarmed U.S. sailors in Tampico led to the landing of U.S. forces on Mexican soil. Veracruz was bombarded by the Navy to prevent the landing of munitions from a German vessel. At the point of war, both powers agreed to mediation by Argentina, Brazil, and Chile. Huerta abdicated, and Venustiano Carranza succeeded to the presidency.

Haiti (1915): U.S. Marines imposed a military occupation. Haiti signed a treaty making it a virtual protectorate of the U.S. until troops were withdrawn in 1934.

Mexico (1916): Raids by Pancho Villa cost American lives on both sides of the border. President Carranza consented to a punitive expedition led by Gen. John J. Pershing, but antagonism grew in Mexico. Wilson withdrew the U.S. force when war with Germany became imminent.

Dominican Republic (1916): Renewed intervention in the Dominican Republic with internal administration by U.S. naval officers lasted until 1924.

Korea (1950): In this undeclared war, which terminated with the July 27, 1953, truce at Panmunjom and the establishment of a neutral nations' supervisory commission, the U.S. and 15 member-nations of the U.N. came to the aid of the Republic of South Korea, whose 38th-parallel border was crossed by the invading Russian Communist-controlled North Koreans, who were later joined by the Chinese Communists.

Lebanon (1958 and 1983): Fearful of the newly formed U.A.R. abetting the rebels of his politically and economically torn country, President Camille Chamoun appealed to the U.S. for military assistance. U.S. troops landed in Beirut in mid-July and left before the end of the year, after internal and external quiet were restored. In September 1983, President Reagan ordered Marines to join an international peacekeeping force in Beirut. On October 23, 241 were killed in the terrorist bombing of the Marine compound. On February 7, 1984, Reagan ordered the Marine contingent withdrawn. He ended the U.S. role in Beirut on March 30 by releasing the Sixth Fleet from the international force.

Dominican Republic (1965): On April 28, when a political coup-turned-civil war endangered the lives of American nationals, President Lyndon B. Johnson rushed 400 marines into Santo Domingo, the beginning of an eventual U.S. peak-commitment of 30,000 troops, constituting the preponderant military strength of the OAS-created Inter-American Peace Force, and 6,500 troops, including 5,000 Americans, remained until after the peaceful inauguration of President Joaquín Balaguer on July 1, 1966, and the entire force left the country on September 20.

Vietnam: This longest war in U.S. history began with economic and technical assistance after 1954 Geneva accords ending the Indochinese War. By 1964 it had escalated into a major conflict.

This involvement spanning the administrations of five Presidents led to domestic discontent in the late 1960s. By April 1969, U.S. troop strength reached a peak of 543,400. Peace negotiations began in Paris in 1968 but proved fruitless. Finally, on Jan. 27, 1973, a peace accord was signed in Paris by the U.S., North and South Vietnam, and the Vietcong. Within 60 days, U.S. POWs were returned, and the U.S. withdrew all military forces from South Vietnam.

Grenada (1983): A left-wing military coup resulted in the intervention of a 1,900-man United States contingent, supported by token forces from Caribbean allies, which engaged an 800-man Cuban Force and secured the island within a few days. The American combat force was brought home two months later although a small non-combat unit was left behind to assist in peacekeeping functions.

Panama (1989): On Dec. 15, the Panamanian legislature proclaimed dictator Gen. Manuel Noriega the nation's "maximum leader," and declared a "state of war" with the United States. On Dec. 20th, following several attacks on Americans, Pres. George Bush ordered over 20,000 U.S. military forces into action in Panama to protect the lives of 35,000 American citizens he considered in "grave danger," to apprehend Gen. Noriega for trial in the U.S. on federal drug trafficking charges, to secure the safety of the Canal, and to defend democracy in Panama. Noriega surrendered to U.S. troops the first week in January 1990.

Persian Gulf War (1990): *See* Headline History p. 121, Current Events p. 974.

The Medal of Honor

Often called the Congressional Medal of Honor, it is the Nation's highest military award for "uncommon valor" by men and women in the armed forces. It is given for actions that are above and beyond the call of duty in combat against an armed enemy. The medal was first awarded by the Army on March 25, 1863, and then by the Navy on April 3, 1863. In April 1991, President Bush awarded posthumously the Medal of Honor to World War I veteran, Army Cpl. Freddie Stowers. He was the first black soldier to receive the nation's highest honor for valor in either World War.

Recipients of the medal receive $200 per month for life, a right to burial at Arlington National Cemetary, admission for them or their children to a service academy if they qualify and quotas permit, and free travel on government aircraft to almost anywhere in the world, on a space-available basis.

In 1989, medals were restored to William F. Cody (Buffalo Bill) and four other scouts who had them revoked in 1917 due to a new ruling.

Medal of Honor Recipients[1]

	Total	Army	Navy	Marines	Air Force	Coast Guard
Civil War	1,520	1,196	307	17	—	—
Indian Wars (1861-98)	428	428	—	—	—	—
Korean Expedition (1871)	15	—	9	6	—	—
Spanish-American War	109	30	64	15	—	—
Philippines/Samoa (1899-1913)	91	70	12	9	—	—
Boxer Rebellion (1900)	59	4	22	33	—	—
Dominican Republic (1904)	3	—	—	3	—	—
Nicaragua (1911)	2	—	—	2	—	—
Mexico (Veracruz) (1914)	55	—	46	9	—	—
Haiti (1915)	6	—	—	6	—	—
Misc. (1865-1920)	166	1	161	4	—	—
World War I	124	96	21	7	—	—
Haitian Action (1919-20)	2	—	—	2	—	—
Misc. (1920-1940)	18	2	15	1	—	—
World War II	433	294	57	81	—	1
Korean War	131	78	7	42	4	—
Vietnam War	238	155	14	57	12	—
Total	**3,400 ***	**3,354**	**735**	**294**	**16**	**1**

1. Total number of actual medals awarded is 3,418. This includes nine awarded to Unknown Soldiers, and some soldiers received more than one medal. *Source:* The Congressional Medal of Honor Society, New York, N.Y.

Average Military Strength[1]

Year	Army	Air Force[2]	Navy	Marine Corps	Total
1942	1,992		416	89	2,498
1943	5,224		1,206	232	6,662
1944	7,507		2,386	398	10,290
1945	8,131		3,205	473	11,809
1950	632	415	412	80	1,539
1953	1,536	971	809	237	3,554
1954	1,477	939	767	242	3,425
1955	1,311	958	692	217	3,178
1960	871	828	617	173	2,489
1965	966	844	669	190	2,668
1970	1,432	834	732	295	3,293
1975	779	628	545	193	2,145
1980	762	561	525	185	2,033
1985	782	601	566	198	2,148
1989	766	575	584	196	2,121
1990	750	550	583	196	2,078

1. In thousands. Data represent averages of month-end strengths. 2. Air Force data prior to June 30, 1948 included with Army data. NOTE: Detail may not add to totals due to rounding. *Source:* Department of Defense.

The Birth of the Ballistic Missile

The forerunner of the modern ballistic missile was the World War II German liquid-fuel rocket bomb called the V-2 (V for "vengeance") first used in 1944. It carried a one-ton warhead of high explosives and could be fired from a mobile launcher. Its range was about 220 miles (354.04 km).

During the war, over 4,000 V-2s were launched against cities in Britain, France, and Belgium. At that time, there was no known defense against them. The United States and the Soviet Union used captured V-2s in post-war research and development of defense programs and space exploration.

WRITER'S GUIDE

A Concise Guide to Style

From *Webster's II New Riverside University Dictionary.* © 1984 by Houghton Mifflin Company.

This section discusses and illustrates the basic conventions of American capitalization, punctuation, and italicization.

Capitalization

Capitalize the following: **1.** the first word of a sentence: Some spiders are poisonous; others are not. Are you my new neighbor?
2. the first word of a direct quotation, except when the quotation is split: Joyce asked, "Do you think that the lecture was interesting?" "No," I responded, "it was very boring." Tom Paine said, "The sublime and the ridiculous are often so nearly related that it is difficult to class them separately."
3. the first word of each line in a poem in traditional verse: Half a league, half a league,/Half a league onward,/All in the valley of Death/Rode the six hundred.—Alfred, Lord Tennyson
4. the names of people, of organizations and their members, of councils and congresses, and of historical periods and events: Marie Curie, Benevolent and Protective Order of Elks, an Elk, Protestant Episcopal Church, an Episcopalian, the Democratic Party, a Democrat, the Nuclear Regulatory Commission, the U.S. Senate, the Middle Ages, World War I, the Battle of Britain.
5. the names of places and geographic divisions, districts, regions, and locales: Richmond, Vermont, Argentina, Seventh Avenue, London Bridge, Arctic Circle, Eastern Hemisphere, Continental Divide, Middle East, Far North, Gulf States, East Coast, the North, the South Shore.
Do not capitalize words indicating compass points unless a specific region is referred to: Turn north onto Interstate 91.
6. the names of rivers, lakes, mountains, and oceans: Ohio River, Lake Como, Rocky Mountains, Atlantic Ocean.
7. the names of ships, aircraft, satellites, and space vehicles: U.S.S. *Arizona, Spirit of St. Louis,* the spy satellite Ferret-D, Voyager II, the space shuttle Challenger.
8. the names of nationalities, races, tribes, and languages: Spanish, Maori, Bantu, Russian.
9. words derived from proper names, except in their extended senses: the Byzantine Empire. *But:* byzantine office politics.
10. words indicating family relationships when used with a person's name as a title: Aunt Toni and Uncle Jack. *But:* my aunt and uncle, Toni and Jack Walker.
11. a title (i.e., civil, judicial, military, royal and noble, religious, and honorary) when preceding a name: Justice Marshall, General Jackson, Mayor Daley, Queen Victoria, Lord Mountbatten, Pope John Paul II, Professor Jacobson, Senator Byrd.
12. all references to the President and Vice President of the United States: The President has entered the hall. The Vice President presides over the Senate.

13. all key words in titles of literary, dramatic, artistic, and musical works: the novel *The Old Man and the Sea,* the short story "Notes from Underground," an article entitled "On Passive Verbs," James Dickey's poem "In the Tree House at Night," the play *Cat on a Hot Tin Roof,* Van Gogh's *Wheat Field and Cypress Trees,* Beethoven's *Emperor Concerto.*
14. *the* in the title of a newspaper if it is a part of the title: *The Wall Street Journal. But:* the New York *Daily News.*
15. the first word in the salutation and in the complimentary close of a letter: My dear Carol, Yours sincerely.
16. epithets and substitutes for the names of people and places: Old Hickory, Old Blood and Guts, The Oval Office, the Windy City.
17. words used in personifications: When is not Death at watch/Within those secret waters?/What wants he but to catch/Earth's heedless sons and daughters?—Edmund Blunden
18. the pronoun *I:* I told them that I had heard the news.
19. names for the Deity and sacred works: God, the Almighty, Jesus, Allah, the Supreme Being, the Bible, the Koran, the Talmud.
20. days of the week, months of the year, holidays, and holy days: Tuesday, May, Independence Day, Passover, Ramadan, Christmas.
21. the names of specific courts: The Supreme Court of the United States, the Massachusetts Appeals Court, the United States Court of Appeals for the First Circuit.
22. the names of treaties, accords, pacts, laws, and specific amendments: Panama Canal Treaty, Treaty of Paris, Geneva Accords, Warsaw Pact countries, Sherman Antitrust Law, Labor Management Relations Act, took the Fifth Amendment.
23. registered trademarks and service marks: Day-Glo, Comsat.
24. the names of geologic eras, periods, epochs, and strata and the names of prehistoric divisions: Paleozoic Era, Precambrian, Pleistocene, Age of Reptiles, Bronze Age, Stone Age.
25. the names of constellations, planets, and stars: Milky Way, Southern Crown, Saturn, Jupiter, Uranus, Polaris.
26. genus but not species names in binomial nomenclature: *Rana pipiens.*
27. New Latin names of classes, families, and all groups higher than genera in botanical and zoological nomenclature: Nematoda.
But do not capitalize derivatives from such names: nematodes.
28. many abbreviations and acronyms: Dec., Tues., Lt. Gen., M.F.A., UNESCO, MIRV.

Italicization

Use italics to:
1. indicate titles of books, plays, and epic poems:

War and Peace, The Importance of Being Earnest, Paradise Lost.

2. indicate titles of magazines and newspapers: *New York* magazine, *The Wall Street Journal,* the New York *Daily News.*

3. set off the titles of motion pictures and radio and television programs: *Star Wars, All Things Considered, Masterpiece Theater.*

4. indicate titles of major musical compositions: Handel's *Messiah,* Adam's *Giselle.*

5. set off the names of paintings and sculpture: *Mona Lisa, Pietà.*

6. indicate words, letters, or numbers that are referred to: The word *hiss* is onomatopoeic. *Can't* means *won't* in your lexicon. You form your *n*'s like *u*'s. A *6* looks like an inverted *9*.

7. indicate foreign words and phrases not yet assimilated into English: *C'est la vie* was the response to my complaint.

8. indicate the names of plaintiff and defendant in legal citations: *Roe* v. *Doe.*

9. emphasize a word or phrase: When you appear on the national news, you are *somebody.*

Use this device sparingly.

10. distinguish New Latin names of genera, species, subspecies, and varieties in botanical and zoological nomenclature: *Homo sapiens.*

11. set off the names of ships and aircraft but not space vehicles: U.S.S. *Arizona, Spirit of St. Louis,* Voyager II, the space shuttle Challenger, the spy satellite Ferret-D.

Punctuation

Apostrophe. 1. indicates the possessive case of singular and plural nouns, indefinite pronouns, and surnames combined with designations such as *Jr., Sr.,* and *II:* my sister's husband, my three sisters' husbands, anyone's guess, They answer each other's phones, John Smith, Jr.'s car.

2. indicates joint possession when used with the last of two or more nouns in a series: Doe and Roe's report.

3. indicates individual possession or authorship when used with each of two or more nouns in a series: Smith's, Roe's, and Doe's reports.

4. indicates the plurals of words, letters, and figures used as such: 60's and 70's; *x*'s, *y*'s, and *z*'s.

5. indicates omission of letters in contractions: aren't, that's, o'clock.

6. indicates omission of figures in dates: the class of '63.

Brackets.

1. enclose words or passages in quoted matter to indicate insertion of material written by someone other than the author: A tough but nervous, tenacious but restless race [the Yankees]; materially ambitious, yet prone to introspection. . . .—Samuel Eliot Morison

2. enclose material inserted within matter already in parentheses: (Vancouver [B.C.] January 1, 19—).

Colon.

1. introduces words, phrases, or clauses that explain, amplify, or summarize what has gone before: Suddenly I realized where we were: Rome.

"There are two cardinal sins from which all the others spring: impatience and laziness."—Franz Kafka

2. introduces a long quotation: In his original draft of the *Declaration of Independence,* Jefferson wrote: "We hold these truths to be sacred and undeniable; that all men are created equal and independent, that

from that equal creation they derive rights inherent and inalienable. . . ."

3. introduces a list: We need the following items: pens, paper, pencils, blotters, and erasers.

4. separates chapter and verse numbers in Biblical references: James 1:4.

5. separates city from publisher in footnotes and bibliographies: Chicago: Riverside Press, 1983.

6. separates hour and minute(s) in time designations: 9:30 a.m., a 9:30 meeting.

7. follows the salutation in a business letter: Gentlemen:

Comma.1. separates the clauses of a compound sentence connected by a coordinating conjunction: A difference exists between the musical works of Handel and Haydn, and it is a difference worth noting.

The comma may be omitted in short compound sentences: I heard what you said and I am furious. I got out of the car and I walked and walked.

2. separates *and* or *or* from the final item in a series of three or more: Red, yellow, and blue may be mixed to produce all colors.

3. separates two or more adjectives modifying the same noun if *and* could be used between them without altering the meaning: a solid, heavy gait. *But:* a polished mahogany dresser.

4. sets off nonrestrictive clauses or phrases (i.e., those that if eliminated would not affect the meaning of the sentences): The burglar, who had entered through the patio, went straight to the silver chest.

The comma should not be used when a clause is restrictive (i.e., essential to the meaning of the sentence): The burglar who had entered through the patio went straight to the silver chest; the other burglar searched for the wall safe.

5. sets off words or phrases in apposition to a noun or noun phrase: Plato, the famous Greek philosopher, was a student of Socrates.

The comma should not be used if such words or phrases precede the noun: The Greek philosopher Plato was a student of Socrates.

6. sets off transitional words and short expressions that require a pause in reading or speaking: Unfortunately, my friend was not well traveled. Did you, after all, find what you were looking for? I live with my family, of course.

7. sets off words used to introduce a sentence: No, I haven't been to Paris. Well, what do you think we should do now?

8. sets off a subordinate clause or a long phrase that precedes a principal clause: By the time we found the restaurant, we were starved. Of all the illustrations in the book, the most striking are those of the tapestries.

9. sets off short quotations and sayings: The candidate said, "Actions speak louder than words." "Talking of axes," said the Duchess, "chop off her head"—Lewis Carroll

10. indicates omission of a word or words: To err is human; to forgive, divine.

11. sets off the year from the month in full dates: Nicholas II of Russia was shot on July 16, 1918.

But note that when only the month and the year are used, no comma appears: Nicholas II of Russia was shot in July 1918.

12. sets off city and state in geographic names: Atlanta, Georgia, is the transportation center of the South. 34 Beach Drive, Bedford, VA 24523.

13. separates series of four or more figures into thousands, millions, etc.: 67,000; 200,000.

14. sets off words used in direct address: "I tell you, folks, all politics is applesauce."—Will Rogers Thank you for your expert assistance, Dolores.

15. Separates a tag question from the rest of a sentence: You forgot your keys again, didn't you?

16. sets off sentence elements that could be misunderstood if the comma were not used: Some time after, the actual date for the project was set.

17. follows the salutation in a personal letter and the complimentary close in a business or personal letter: Dear Jessica, Sincerely yours.

18. sets off titles and degrees from surnames and from the rest of a sentence: Walter T. Prescott, Jr.; Gregory A. Rossi, S.J.; Susan P. Green, M.D., presented the case.

Dash.

1. indicates a sudden break or abrupt change in continuity: "If—if you'll just let me explain—" the student stammered. And the problem—if there really is one—can then be solved.

2. sets apart an explanatory, a defining, or an emphatic phrase: Foods rich in protein—meat, fish, and eggs—should be eaten on a daily basis.

More important than winning the election, is governing the nation. That is the test of a political party—the acid, final test.—Adlai E. Stevenson

3. sets apart parenthetical matter: Wolsey, for all his faults—and he had many—was a great statesman, a man of natural dignity with a generous temperament. . . .—Jasper Ridley

4. marks an unfinished sentence: "But if my bus is late—" he began.

5. sets off a summarizing phrase or clause: The vital measure of a newspaper is not its size but its spirit—that is its responsibility to report the news fully, accurately, and fairly.—Arthur H. Sulzberger

6. sets off the name of an author or source, as at the end of a quotation: A poet can survive everything but a misprint.—Oscar Wilde

Ellipses.

1. indicate, by three spaced points, omission of words or sentences within quoted matter: Equipped by education to rule in the nineteenth century, . . . he lived and reigned in Russia in the twentieth century.—Robert K. Massie

2. indicate, by four spaced points, omission of words at the end of a sentence: The timidity of bureaucrats when it comes to dealing with . . . abuses is easy to explain. . . .—*New York*

3. indicate, when extended the length of a line, omission of one or more lines of poetry:

Roll on, thou deep and dark blue
    ocean—roll!
. . . .
Man marks the earth with ruin—his
    control
Stops with the shore.—Lord Byron

4. are sometimes used as a device, as for example, in advertising copy:

To help you Move and Grow
    with the Rigors of
Business in the 1980's . . .
    and Beyond.—*Journal of Business Strategy*

Exclamation Point.

1. terminates an emphatic or exclamatory sentence: Go home at once! You've got to be kidding!

2. terminates an emphatic interjection: Encore!

Hyphen. 1. indicates that part of a word of more than one syllable has been carried over from one line to the next:

During the revolution, the nation was
beset with problems—looting, fighting, and famine.

2. joins the elements of some compounds: great-grandparent, attorney-at-law, ne'er-do-well.

3. joins the elements of compound modifiers preceding nouns: high-school students, a fire-and-brim-

stone lecture, a two-hour meeting.

4. indicates that two or more compounds share a single base: four- and six-volume sets, eight- and nine-year olds.

5. separates the prefix and root in some combinations; check the Dictionary when in doubt about the spelling: anti-Nazi, re-elect, co-author, re-form/reform, re-cover/recover, re-creation/-recreation.

6. substitutes for the word *to* between typewritten inclusive words or figures: pp. 145–155, the Boston-New York air shuttle.

7. punctuates written-out compound numbers from 21 through 99: forty-six years of age, a person who is forty-six, two hundred fifty-nine dollars.

Parentheses. 1. enclose material that is not essential to a sentence and that if not included would not alter its meaning: After a few minutes (some say less) the blaze was extinguished.

2. often enclose letters or figures to indicate subdivisions of a series: A movement in sonata form consists of the following elements: (1) the exposition, (2) the development, and (3) the recapitulation.

3. enclose figures following and confirming written-out numbers, especially in legal and business documents: The fee for my services will be two thousand dollars ($2,000.00).

4. enclose an abbreviation for a term following the written-out term, when used for the first time in a text: The patient is suffering from acquired immune deficiency syndrome (AIDS).

Period. 1. terminates a complete declarative or mild imperative sentence: There could be no turning back as war's dark shadow settled irrevocably across the continent of Europe.—W. Bruce Lincoln. Return all the books when you can. Would you kindly affix your signature here.

2. terminates sentence fragments: Gray clouds—and what looks like a veil of rain falling behind the East German headland. A pair of ducks. A tired or dying swan, head buried in its back feathers, sits on the sand a few feet from the water's edge.—Anthony Bailey

3. follows some abbreviations: Dec., Rev., St., Blvd., pp., Co.

Question Mark. 1. punctuates a direct question: Have you seen the new play yet? Who goes there? *But:* I wonder who said "Nothing is easy in war." I asked if they planned to leave.

2. indicates uncertainty: Ferdinand Magellan (1480?–1521), Plato (427?–347 B.C.).

Quotation Marks. 1. Double quotation marks enclose direct quotations: "What was Paris like in the Twenties?" our daughter asked. "Ladies and Gentlemen," the Chief Usher said, "the President of the United States." Robert Louis Stevenson said that "it is better to be a fool than to be dead." When advised not to become a lawyer because the profession was already overcrowded, Daniel Webster replied, "There is always room at the top."

2. Double quotation marks enclose words or phrases to clarify their meaning or use or to indicate that they are being used in a special way: This was the border of what we often call "the West" or "the Free World." "The Windy City" is a name for Chicago.

3. Double quotation marks set off the translation of a foreign word or phrase: *die Grenze,* "the border."

4. Double quotation marks set off the titles of series of books, of articles or chapters in publications, of essays, of short stories and poems, of individual radio and television programs, and of songs and short musical pieces: "The Horizon Concise History" series; an article entitled "On Reflexive Verbs in

English"; Chapter Nine, "The Prince and the Peasant"; Pushkin's "The Queen of Spades"; Tennyson's "Ode on the Death of the Duke of Wellington"; "The Bob Hope Special"; Schubert's "Death and the Maiden."

5. Single quotation marks enclose quotations within quotations: The blurb for the piece proclaimed, "Two years ago at Geneva, South Vietnam was virtually sold down the river to the Communists. Today the spunky little . . . country is back on its own feet, thanks to "a mandarin in a sharkskin suit who's upsetting the Red timetable.' "—Frances FitzGerald

Put commas and periods inside quotation marks; put semicolons and colons outside. Other punctuation, such as exclamation points and question marks, should be put inside the closing quotation marks only if part of the matter quoted.

Semicolon. 1. separates the clauses of a compound sentence having no coordinating conjunction: Do not let us speak of darker days; let us rather speak of sterner days.—Winston Churchill

2. separates the clauses of a compound sentence in which the clauses contain internal punctuation, even when the clauses are joined by conjunctions: Skis in hand, we trudged to the lodge, stowed our lunches, and donned our boots; and the rest of our party waited for us at the lifts.

3. separates elements of a series in which items already contain commas: Among those at the diplomatic reception were the Secretary of State; the daughter of the Ambassador to the Court of St. James's, formerly of London; and two United Nations delegates.

4. separates clauses of a compound sentence joined by a conjunctive adverb, such as *however, nonetheless,* or *hence:* We insisted upon a hearing; however, the Grievance Committee refused.

5. may be used instead of a comma to signal longer pauses for dramatic effect: But I want you to know that when I cross the river my last conscious thought will be of the Corps; and the Corps; and the Corps.—General Douglas MacArthur

Virgule. 1. separates successive divisions in an extended date: fiscal year 1983/84.

2. represents *per:* 35 km/hr, 1,800 ft/sec.

3. means *or* between the words *and* and *or:* Take water skis and/or fishing equipment when you visit the beach this summer.

4. separates two or more lines of poetry that are quoted and run in on successive lines of a text: The student actress had a memory lapse when she came to the lines "Double, double, toil and trouble/Fire burn and cauldron bubble/Eye of newt and toe of frog/Wool of bat and tongue of dog" and had to leave the stage in embarrassment.

Forms of Address[1]

Source: Webster's II New Riverside University Dictionary. Copyright © 1984 by Houghton Mifflin Company.

Academics

Dean, college or university. *Address:* Dean _____. *Salutation:* Dear Dean _____
President. *Address:* President _____ _____. *Salutation:* Dear President _____.
Professor, college or university. *Address:* Professor _____. *Salutation:* Dear Professor _____.

Clerical and Religious Orders

Abbot. *Address:* The Right Reverend _____ _____ O.S.B. Abbot of _____. *Salutation:* Right Reverend Abbot or Dear Father Abbot.
Archbishop, Eastern Orthodox. *Address:* The Most Reverend Joseph, Archbishop of _____. *Salutation:* Your Eminence.
Archbishop, Roman Catholic. The Most Reverend _____, Archbishop of _____. *Salutation:* Your Excellency.
Archdeacon, Episcopal. *Address:* The Venerable _____, Archdeacon of _____. *Salutation:* Venerable Sir or Dear Archdeacon _____.
Bishop, Episcopal. *Address:* The Right Reverend _____, Bishop of _____. *Salutation:* Right Reverend Sir or Dear Bishop _____.
Bishop, other Protestant. *Address:* The Reverend _____. *Salutation:* Dear Bishop _____.
Bishop, Roman Catholic. *Address:* The Most Reverend _____, Bishop of _____. *Salutation:* Your Excellency or Dear Bishop _____.
Brotherhood, Roman Catholic. *Address:* Brother _____, C.F.C. *Salutation:* Dear Brother or Dear Brother Joseph.
Brotherhood, superior of. *Address:* Brother Joseph C.F.C. Superior. *Salutation:* Dear Brother Joseph.
Cardinal. *Address:* His Eminence Joseph Cardinal Stone. *Salutation:* Your Eminence.

Clergyman/woman, Protestant. *Address:* The Reverend _____ _____ or The Reverend _____ _____, D.D. *Salutation:* Dear Mr./Ms. _____ or Dear Dr. _____.
Dean of a cathedral, Episcopal. *Address:* The Very Reverend _____ _____, Dean of _____. *Salutation:* Dear Dean _____.
Monsignor. *Address:* The Right Reverend Monsignor _____ _____. *Salutation:* Dear Monsignor.
Patriarch, Greek Orthodox. *Address:* His All Holiness Patriarch Joseph. *Salutation:* Your All Holiness.
Patriarch, Russian Orthodox. *Address:* His Holiness the Patriarch of _____. *Salutation:* Your Holiness.
Pope. *Address:* His Holiness The Pope. *Salutation:* Your Holiness or Most Holy Father.
Priest, Roman Catholic. *Address:* The Reverend _____ _____, S.J. *Salutation:* Dear Reverend Father or Dear Father.
Rabbi, man or woman. *Address:* Rabbi _____ _____ or _____ _____ D.D.. *Salutation:* Dear Rabbi _____ or Dear Dr. _____.
Sisterhood, Roman Catholic. *Address:* Sister _____ _____, C.S.J. *Salutation:* Dear Sister or Dear Sister _____.
Sisterhood, superior of. *Address:* The Reverend Mother Superior, S.C. *Salutation:* Reverend Mother.

Diplomats

Ambassador, U.S. *Address:* The Honorable _____ _____ The Ambassador of the United States. *Salutation:* Sir/Madam or Dear Mr./Madam Ambassador.
Ambassador to the U.S. *Address:* His/Her Excellency _____ _____, The Ambassador of _____. *Salutation:* Excellency or Dear Mr./Madam Ambassador.

Chargé d'Affaires, U.S. *Address:* The Honorable
_____ _____ , United States Chargé d'Affaires.
Salutation: Dear Mr./Ms. _____ .
Consul, U.S. *Address:* _____ , Esq., United
States Consul. *Salutation:* Dear Mr./Ms. _____ .
Minister, U.S. or to U.S. *Address:* The Honorable
_____ _____ , The Minister of _____ . *Saluta-
tion:* Sir/Madam or Dear Mr./Madame Minister.
Secretary General, United Nations. *Address:* His/
Her Excellency _____ , Secretary Gener-
al of the United Nations. *Salutation:* Dear
Mr./Madam/Madame Secretary General.
United Nations Representative (Foreign). *Ad-
dress:* His/Her Excellency _____ _____ Repre-
sentative of _____ to the United Nations. *Salu-
tation:* Excellency or My dear Mr./Madame
_____

United Nations Representative (U.S.) *Address:*
The Honorable _____ _____ , United States
Representative to the United Nations. *Saluta-
tion:* Sir/Madam or Dear Mr./Ms. _____ .

Government Officials

Assemblyman. *Address:* The Honorable
_____ . *Salutation:* Dear Mr./Ms. _____ .
Associate Justice, U.S. Supreme Court. *Address:*
Mr./Madam Justice _____ . *Salutation:* Dear
Mr./Madam Justice or Sir/Madam.
Attorney General, U.S. *Address:* The Honorable
_____ _____ , Attorney General of the United
States. *Salutation:* Dear Mr./Madam or Attorney
General.
Cabinet member: *Address:* The Honorable _____
_____ , Secretary of _____ . *Salutation:* Sir/Ma-
dam or Dear Mr./Madam Secretary.
Chief Justice, U.S. Supreme Court. *Address:* The
Chief Justice of the United States. *Salutation:*
Dear Mr. Chief Justice.
Commissioner (federal, state, local). *Address:*
The Honorable _____ _____ . *Salutation:* Dear
Mr./Ms. _____ .
Governor. *Address:* The Honorable _____ _____ ,
Governor of _____ . *Salutation:* Dear Governor
_____
Judge, Federal: *Address:* The Honorable _____
_____ , Judge of the United States District
Court for the _____ , District of _____ .

Salutation: Sir/Madam or Dear Judge _____ .
Judge, state or local. *Address:* The Honorable _____
_____ , Judge of the Court of _____ . *Salutation:*
Dear Judge
Lieutenant Governor. *Address:* The Honorable
_____ , Lieutenant Governor of _____ .
Salutation: Dear Mr./Ms. _____ .
Mayor. *Address:* The Honorable _____ _____ ,
Mayor of _____ . *Salutation:* Dear Mayor _____
President, U.S. *Address:* The President. *Saluta-
tion:* Dear Mr. President.
President, U.S., former. *Address:* The Honorable
_____ _____ . *Salutation:* Dear Mr. _____ .
Representative, state. *Address:* The Honorable
_____ _____ . *Salutation:* Dear Mr./Ms. _____ .
Representative, U.S. *Address:* The Honorable
_____ _____ , United States House of Repre-
sentatives. *Salutation:* Dear Mr./Ms. _____ .
Senator, state. *Address:* The Honorable _____ _____ ,
The State Senate, State Capitol. *Salutation:*
Dear Senator _____ .
Senator, U.S. *Address:* The Honorable _____
_____ , United States Senate. *Salutation:* Dear
Senator _____ .
Speaker, U.S. House of Representatives. *Ad-
dress:* The Honorable _____ _____ , Speaker of
the House of Representatives. *Salutation:* Dear
Mr./Madam Speaker.
Vice President, U.S. *Address:* The Vice President
of the United States. *Salutation:* Sir or Dear Mr.
Vice President.

Military and Naval Officers

Rank. *Address:* Full rank, USN (or USCG, USAF,
USA, USMC). *Salutation:* Dear (full rank)
_____ .

Professions

Attorney. *Address:* Mr./Ms. _____ _____ , Attorney at law or _____ _____ , Esq. *Salutation:*
Dear Mr./Ms. _____ .
Dentist. *Address:* _____ _____ , D.D.S. *Salutation:* Dear Dr. _____ .
Physician. *Address:* _____ _____ , M.D. *Salutation:* Dear Dr. _____ .
Veterinarian. *Address:* _____ _____ , D.V.M. *Salutation:* Dear Dr. _____ .

1. Forms of address do not always follow set guidelines; the type of salutation is often determined by the relationship between correspondents or by the purpose and content of the letter. However, a general style applies to most occasions. In highly formal salutations, when the addressee is a woman, "Madam" should be substituted for "Sir." When the salutation is informal, "Ms.," "Miss," or "Mrs." should be substituted for "Mr." If a woman addressee has previously indicated a preference for a particular form of address, that form should be used.

Selecting Child Care

Choosing child care is an important issue for parents. Here are some questions parents may want to ask when looking for child care:
1. What are the licensing laws for day care providers in your city, county, or state? Your local consumer protection office is a good place to check for this information.
2. Do caregivers have references? What about special training in child development and education? How many children does each adult look after?
3. Is the home or center clean? Is there enough space inside and outside for the children to play? Is the playground fenced?
4. If the center is large, do visitors and children sign in and out? What are the safety precautions in case of fire or other emergencies?
5. What about sick children? Do they stay home?

What if a child needs medical help?
6. How does the staff discipline children? How much of each day is filled with planned activities? Are activities geared to children's ages and development?
7. What are the fees for half-days, overtime, or sick children?
8. Are kids' pictures or projects hung up and changed often?
9. Do caregivers tell you what your child did that day? How he or she is doing overall?

After your child is in a program, you may wish to ask:
1. Does your child talk happily about the program?
2. Do you know new employees? Do they talk to your child?

SPACE

Above: Artist's concept of Space Station Freedom's U.S. and international laboratories and U.S. habitation module. The U.S. laboratory and living modules are in bottom left of the illustration. The Japanese Experiment Module is top right, and the European Space Agency (ESA) laboratory module is top left. Shown mated to the node between the U.S. lab and the ESA module is the Assured Crew Return Vehicle used for emergency returns to Earth of space station crew members. NASA photo.

NASA Plans a Streamlined Space Station

NASA's new design for Space Station Freedom will be cheaper, smaller, easier to assemble in orbit, and will require fewer Shuttle flights to build. Ambitious plans call for the station to be completed by the turn of the century, and the first elements of the space station to be launched into orbit in early 1996. The program calls for man-tended capability to be achieved in 1997. Space station Freedom should be ready for permanent occupancy by a four-man live-in crew in the year 2000.

In the man-tended phase, astronauts brought up to Freedom by the Space Shuttle will be able to work inside the U.S. laboratory for two-week periods and will then return to Earth with the Shuttle. Six Shuttle flights will be required to achieve the man-tended configuration.

The permanently manned configuration will consist of a U.S. laboratory and habitat, as well as European and Japanese laboratories, a Canadian Mobile Servicing System, and accommodations for the live-in crew of four. A new feature of the space station will be the provision of an Assured Crew Return Vehicle to provide the space station astronauts with the means to return to Earth in an emergency. Seventeen shuttle flights will be needed to build the permanently manned configuration.

The pressurized laboratory and living modules being built by the U.S. are 27 feet long and 14.5 feet in diameter. The over-all width of Space Station Freedom will be 353 feet. Two other pressurized laboratory modules are being built, one by the European Space Agency and the other by Japan. □

Mars Observer Mission

A long-awaited NASA mission to study the surface, atmosphere, interior, and magnetic field of Mars for a full Martian Year is scheduled for a 1992 launch at the Jet Propulsion Laboratory, Pasadena, California. Called the *Mars Observer,* it will be the first in a planned series of Planetary Observer missions that will use a new class of spacecraft derived from Earth-orbiter designs. These missions will be of modest cost and are intended to explore objects of the inner solar system such as Venus, the Moon, Mars, and near-Earth asteroids and comets.

The *Mars Observer* will continue NASA's exploration of the red planet, which began with the *Mariner 4* mission in 1964–65, and continued with *Mariners 6* and *7* in 1969 and *Mariner 9* in 1971–72. This program reached its peak with the *Viking* orbiters and landers of 1975–82.

The new global studies of the planet's geology and atmosphere are expected to give scientists more information about the planet's evolution. One subject of particular interest is the role that water once played on Mars. While there is no liquid water on the surface of Mars now, the *Mariner* and *Viking* missions found ample evidence that liquid flowed there long ago.

If all goes well in September 1992, an expendable commercial *Titan III* launch vehicle will carry *Mars Observer* and its booster into Earth orbit. From there, the Transfer Orbit Stage will boost the spacecraft into an interplanetary orbit leading to Mars.

After an 11-month cruise, *Mars Observer* will arrive at the red planet and be placed in a special orbit that will circle above Mars about every two hours. This mapping orbit will be sun-synchronized, so that sunlight will be at the same angle (early afternoon directly below the spacecraft) on the day side throughout the long observation period.

The mission will last for one Martian year (almost 687 Earth days) to allow the spacecraft to examine the planet through its four seasons.

The scientific objectives of the Mars mission are to: determine the global elemental and mineralogical character of the surface material; define the global topography and gravitational field; establish the nature of the magnetic field; determine the time and space distribution, abundance, sources and sinks of volatile material and dust over a seasonal cycle; and to explore the structure and aspects of the circulation of the atmosphere.

In addition, *Mars Observer* will participate in an ambitious international Mars investigation through an agreement with France and the Soviet Union. The participation is the Mars Balloon Relay Experiment. The Soviet Mars '94 mission will deploy balloon-borne instrument packages in the atmosphere of Mars. (*See* The Mars Balloon, p. 322.) ☐

ULYSSES

Ulysses is an international project to study the poles of the Sun and interstellar space above and below the poles. *Ulysses*, will launch a single 814-lb (370-kg) spacecraft into an orbit at right angles to the solar system's ecliptic plane. (The ecliptic is the plane in which the Earth and most of the planets orbit the Sun.) This special orbit will allow the spacecraft to examine for the first time the regions of the Sun's north and south poles. Besides examining the Sun's energy fields, instruments on *Ulysses* will study other phenomena from the Milky Way and beyond.

While scientists have studied the Sun for centuries, they know very little about matter reaching the solar system from other nearby stars. This is because particles reaching the Sun's magnetic field from beyond the solar system are greatly changed by the Sun's magnetic field and by collision with particles flowing outward from the Sun. No spacecraft has ever left the solar system to make actual measurements of the interstellar medium.

The *Ulysses* spacecraft was launched from the space shuttle *Discovery* on Oct. 6, 1990, and will make its first solar encounter between June to October 1994. A second encounter will take place from June to September 1995.

Major Eileen Marie Collins

Major Collins, USAF, is the only female candidate in training as an astronaut pilot. When her training is completed, she will be qualified to become the first woman to pilot a space shuttle.

A native of Elmira, New York, Maj. Collins has an associate in science degree in Mathematics/Science from Corning Community College, a bachelor of arts degree in Mathematics and Economics from Syracuse University, a master of science degree in Operations Research from Stanford University, and a master of arts degree in Space Systems Management from Webster University.

She has been a T-38 instructor pilot at Vance AFB, Oklahoma, and a C-141 aircraft commander and instructor pilot at Travis AFB, California. She was an assistant professor in mathematics and a T-41 instructor pilot at the U.S. Air Force Academy, and was selected for the astronaut program while attending Air Force Test Pilot School at Edwards AFB, California, from which she graduated. ☐

THE CRAF/CASSINI MISSION

These projects combine two missions that will use both NASA's new *Mariner Mark II* spacecraft and greatly reduce the total cost. NASA plans to launch *Cassini* in December 1995 and follow it with the CRAF mission in February 1996.

Comet Rendezvous Asteroid Flyby (CRAF)

This mission will send a spacecraft to encounter the comet *Tempel 2* and fly alongside the comet for more than two years. This mission will mark the first time that a spacecraft has flown in formation with a comet. Most of the phenomena associated with comets will be the target of CRAF's instruments.

The Cassini Mission

The ringed planet Saturn, its major moon Titan, and complex system of at least 18 other satellites[1] will be the destination for NASA's and the European

Space Agency's Cassini Mission. Cassini is named for the Italian-French astronomer, Gian Domenico Cassini (1625–1712), who discovered four of Saturn's major moons and a dark, narrow gap ("Cassini's Division") splitting the planet's rings.

Early during the spacecraft's four-year tour orbiting Saturn, it will launch a parachuted probe decending through Titan's dense atmosphere to the surface of the satellite which has unique organic-like chemistry that could provide clues to the origin of life on Earth.

Current plans call for Cassini to be launched in December 1995. NASA will provide the expendable Titan-Centaur launch vehicle and the Cassini orbiter spacecraft and the European Space Agency (ESA) will contribute the Titan probe. NASA and ESA member countries will provide science instruments for both the orbiter and probe.

In November 1990, Congress approved $145 million for the mission.

In order to reach Saturn, Cassini will first execute flybys of the Earth and Jupiter to gain "gravity assist" boosts in velocity to send it on its way. The first flyby of Earth will take place 26 months after launch, followed by the Jupiter flyby some 19 months later. During the first leg of its trip, before its first Earth flyby, Cassini will navigate through part of the asteroid belt and could perform an encounter with the asteroid Maja in March 1997. Maja is a carbonaceous, or "C" type asteroid about 50 miles (78 kilometers) in diameter. Two small a steroids are being considered as possible additional argets, but only one of them could be visited.

The spacecraft's final encounter before proceeding to Saturn will be with Jupiter, which it will pass at a distance of about 2.2 million miles (3.6 million kilo-

meters). Its flight path will take it for 130 days down through a region that no spacecraft has explored more than briefly—the giant planet's magnetotail. Cassini will fly down the magnetotail[2] of Jupiter, performing studies complementing NASA's CRAF mission and the Galileo mission to Jupiter.

Upon reaching Saturn, the spacecraft will begin the first of some three dozen highly elliptical orbits during the remainder of its mission. Eighty-five days later, it will release its probe to Titan. Eleven days later, the probe will enter Titan's dense atmosphere and descend to the surface by parachute.

The $260-million probe is called *Huygens* after the famous Dutch astronomer Christiaan Huygens (1629–1695) who was the first to correctly interpret the rings of Saturn. He was also the discoverer of Saturn's largest satellite, *Titan*.

Because of the dense atmosphere shrouding the moon Titan, little is known of its surface. At Titan, scientists hope to gain a better understanding of abundances of elements and compounds in its atmosphere, winds, and temperatures, and its surface state and composition.

After relaying to Earth data from the Titan probe's experiments, Cassini will continue with orbits of Saturn and flybys of most of the planet's 16 or more moons. In addition to 36 close encounters with Titan, the spacecraft's orbits will allow it to study Saturn's polar regions after examining the planet's equatorial zone. ☐

1. The International Astronomical Union has officially recognized 18 Saturnian moons. Photographs from *Voyager* flybys suggest that others may exist. 2. A tube of Jupiter's energy field, which trails away from the sun for several million miles.

GALILEO

Galileo is a project to orbit Jupiter and send an instrumented probe into the giant planet's atmosphere. The Galileo mission will allow scientists to study—at close range and for almost two years—the largest planet in the solar system, its satellites and massive energy field. The project is named after the Italian astronomer Galileo Galilei, who on Jan. 7, 1610, discovered three of Jupiter's moons and later on January 13th discovered a fourth satellite. These four "Galilean" satellites—Io, Europa, Ganymede, and Callisto, are major targets for the mission. The spacecraft will study the chemical composition and physical state of Jupiter's atmosphere and the four moons, as well as the structure and dynamics of the Jovian magnetosphere.

During the 22–month life of the mission, the orbiter will complete 10 orbits of Jupiter while making a close flyby of at least one Galilean satellite on each orbit.

The spacecraft was carried aloft by the space shuttle *Atlantis* and launched toward Jupiter on Oct. 18, 1989. After a six-year journey, it will reach the planet in 1995.

Galileo will make the first spacecraft encounter with an asteroid in later October 1991 when it passes within 901 miles (1,450 kilometers) of asteroid *Gaspora*. In August 1993 Galileo will fly by asteroid *Ida* within 584 miles (940 kilometers).

Using special maneuvers to gain speed with gravity assists, Galileo passed Venus in Feb. 1990, Earth in Dec. 1990, and will make one last fly-by of Earth in Dec. 1992, passing about 186 miles (300 kilometers) above Earth at a speed of 8.7 miles per second (14.1 kilometers per second).

A problem with opening Galileo's main antenna developed in April 1991. If it is not solved, the spacecraft will only be able to send back a fraction of the data planned.

The Canadian Astronauts

Shown in the above photo are six members of the Canadian Astronaut Corps. Standing, left to right, are Ken Money, Roberta Bondar, and Bjarni Tryggvason. Seated astronauts are Bob Thirsk, Steve MacLean, and Marc Garneau. Marc Garneau was a payload specialist on a shuttle flight in October 1984. Roberta Bondar will be a payload specialist on the space shuttle *Discovery* in January 1992. She will be the first Canadian woman in space. Astronaut MacLean is scheduled for a shuttle mission in April 1992. The others are awaiting flight assignments.

THE GALILEO PROBE. In this artist's rendering, the Galileo probe with its heat shield below and a parachute above enters the turbulent upper atmosphere of Jupiter. About 150 days before Galileo's arrival at Jupiter, the probe will separate from the orbiter and travel unattended toward entry. The orbiter's trajectory will be corrected to send it past the moon Io and then into Jupiter orbit. The probe will strike the uper atmosphere at about 30 miles per second. Data from its six instruments will be relayed to Earth via the orbiter during the probe's expected 75 minutes of operation before Jupiter's temperature and pressure destroy it. NASA illustration.

MAGELLAN
Venus Radar Mapper

On May 4, 1989, NASA'S unmanned spacecraft *Magellan* was launched from the shuttle *Discovery*. It was the first time a space probe was launched from a shuttle. *Magellan* is a spacecraft equipped with an imaging radar system designed to "see" through Venus' thick cloud-like cover and obtain detailed photographlike images of 90% or more of the planet's surface. *Magellan* reached Venus on Aug. 10, 1990, and although there were problems with its radio transmissions, it began taking the sharpest images of the planet ever seen. The spacecraft was placed in an elliptical orbit, circling Venus once every 3.1 hours and the radar was planned to operate once each orbit for approximately 40 minutes, from an altitude of 190 to 1060 miles (300 to 1,700 kilometers). The mapping was scheduled for 243 days.

The spacecraft's first objective in radar probing Venus was completed on May 15, 1991, after 1,789 orbits during which 84% of the planet's susrface was mapped in fantastic detail. The planet's entire terrain should be mapped by the end of 1991.

Magellan's mapping revealed a surface covered with enormous lava flows, thousands of craters, and unusual features not found on Earth. Over 600 large craters were found on Venus. The largest crater yet found was a double-ring basin, 170.8 miles (275 kilometers) across. It has been proposed that it be named after Margaret Mead, the American anthropologist.

Is There Ice on the Moon?

Unlike the rest of the Moon's surface, the temperature of its polar regions remains pe rmanently about –390° to –315° F and some of its craters remain perpetually in the dark. Some scientists have speculated that ice may have accumulated in the dark craters over long eons of time.

NASA would like to launch a polar lunar orbiter known as the *Lunar Observer* in the mid-1990s to study the unknown regions of the Moon's poles and search for water, ice, and other useful volatiles that may exist on the Moon.

In December 1992, the U.S. *Galileo* spacecraft, during its first Earth flyby, will travel over the Moon's North Pole, presenting an opportunity to find signs of ice in the dark craters.

The Mars Balloon

The ambitious Mars 94 program calls for two launches in October 1994 for arrival in September 1995. During the mission, the spacecraft will drop one or two balloons which will carry several scientific packages for analyzing Martian meteorological and surface conditions over a wide range of the planet.

The balloon segment of the mission is a joint U.S.S.R., France, and United States undertaking, which has greatly benefitted from the successful balloon deployed at Venus in 1985 under the Soviet VEGA program.

The American effort is being led by the Planetary Society and Titan Systems, Inc.

The balloon will carry both a suspended payload (gondola) and a distributed payload (SNAKE) which will come into contact with the planet's surface as the balloon descends during the Martian night. The SNAKE will carry its own instruments to investigate the Martian surface. The sun's light will heat the gases within the lightweight balloon during the daytime, causing the balloon to rise and drift with the winds above the planet's surface. At right, the gases will cool, causing the balloon to descend and rest on the Martian soil.

The French Space Agency, The Centre National d'Etudes Spatials (CENES) is building the balloon that will carry the SNAKE.

The total mass of the balloon system is targeted for 60 to 65 kilograms (130 to 134 pounds). The gondola will weigh about 15 kilograms (33 pounds).

U.S. Unmanned Planetary and Lunar Programs

Lunar Orbiter. Series of spacecraft designed to orbit the Moon, taking pictures and obtaining data in support of the subsequent manned Apollo landings. The U.S. launched five *Lunar Orbiters* between Aug. 10, 1966 and Aug. 2, 1967.

Mariner. Designation for a series of spacecraft designed to fly past or orbit the planets, particularly Mercury, Venus, and Mars. *Mariners* provided the early information on Venus and Mars. *Mariner 9,* orbiting Mars in 1971, returned the most startling photographs of that planet and helped pave the way for a *Viking* landing in 1976. *Mariner 10* explored Venus and Mercury in 1973 and was the first probe to use a planet's gravity to whip it toward another.

Pioneer. Designation for the United States' first series of sophisticated interplanetary spacecraft. *Pioneers 10* and *11* reached Jupiter in 1973 and 1974 and continued on to explore Saturn and the other outer planets. *Pioneer 11,* renamed *Pioneer Saturn,* examined the Saturn system in September 1979. Significant discoveries were the finding of a small new moon and a narrow new ring. In 1986, *Pioneer 10* was the first man-made object to escape the solar system. *Pioneer Venus 1* and *2* reached Venus in 1978 and provided detailed information about that planet's surface and atmosphere.

Ranger. NASA's earliest moon exploration program. Spacecraft were designed for a crash landing on the Moon, taking pictures and returning scientific data up to the moment of impact. Provided the first closeup views of the lunar surface. The *Rangers* provided more than 17,000 closeup pictures, giving us more information about the Moon in a few years than in all the time that had gone before.

Surveyor. Series of unmanned spacecraft designed to land gently on the Moon and provide information on the surface in preparation for the manned lunar landings. Their legs were instrumented to return data on the surface hardness of the Moon. *Surveyor* dispelled the fear that Apollo spacecraft might sink several feet or more into the lunar dust.

Viking. Designation for two spacecraft designed to conduct detailed scientific examination of the planet Mars, including a search for life. *Viking 1* landed on July 20, 1976; *Viking 2,* Sept. 3, 1976. More was learned about the Red Planet in a few short months than in all the time that had gone before. But the question of life on Mars remains unresolved.

Voyager. Designation for two spacecraft designed to explore Jupiter and the other outer planets. *Voyager 1* and *Voyager 2* passed Jupiter in 1979 and sent back startling color TV images of that planet and its moons. They took a total of about 33,000 pictures. *Voyager 1* passed Saturn November 1980. *Voyager 2* passed Saturn August 1981 and Uranus in January 1986.

It encountered Neptune on August 29, 1989 and made many startling discoveries. Found four rings around the planet, six new moons, a Great Giant Spot, and evidence of volcanic-like activity on its largest moon, Triton. The spacecraft sent back over 9,000 pictures of the planet and its system.

On February 13, 1990, at a distance of 3.7 billion miles, *Voyager 1* took its final pictures—the sun and six of its planets as seen from deep space. NASA released the extraordinary images to the public on June 6, 1990. Only Mercury, Mars, and Pluto were not seen.

Notable Unmanned Lunar and Interplanetary Probes

Spacecraft	Launch date	Destination	Remarks
Pioneer 3 (U.S.)	Dec. 6, 1958	Moon	Max. alt.: 66,654 mi. Discovered outer Van Allen layer.
Luna 2 (U.S.S.R.)	Sept. 12, 1959	Moon	Impacted on Sept. 14. First space vehicle to reach moon.
Luna 3 (U.S.S.R.)	Oct. 4, 1959	Moon	Flew around Moon and transmitted first pictures of lunar far side, Oct. 7.
Mariner 2 (U.S.)	Aug. 27, 1962	Venus	Venus probe. Successful mid-course correction. Passed 21,648 mi. from Venus Dec. 14, 1962. Reported 800°F. surface temp. Contact lost Jan. 3, 1963 at 54 million mi.
Mariner 4 (U.S.)	Nov. 28, 1964	Mars	Transmitted first close-up pictures on June 14, 1965, from altitude of 6,000 mi.
Ranger 7 (U.S.)	July 28, 1964	Moon	Impacted near Crater Guericke 68.5 h after launch. Sent 4,316 pictures during last 15 min of flight as close as 1,000 ft above lunar surface.
Luna 9 (U.S.S.R.)	Jan. 31, 1966	Moon	3,428 lb. Instrument capsule of 220 lb soft-landed Feb. 3, 1966. Sent back about 30 pictures.

Spacecraft	Launch date	Destination	Remarks
Surveyor 1 (U.S.)	May 30, 1966	Moon	Landed June 2, 1966. Sent almost 10,400 pictures, a number after surviving the 14-day lunar night.
Lunar Orbiter 1 (U.S.)	Aug. 10, 1966	Moon	Orbited Mo on Aug. 14. 21 pictures sent.
Surveyor 3 (U.S.)	April 17, 1967	Moon	Soft-landed 65 h after launch on Oceanus Procellarum. Scooped and tested lunar soil.
Venera 4 (U.S.S.R.)	June 12, 1967	Venus	Arrived Oct. 17. Instrument capsule sent temperature and chemical data.
Surveyor 5 (U.S.)	Sept. 8, 1967	Moon	Landed near lunar equator Sept. 10. Radiological analysis of lunar soil. Mechanical claw for digging soil.
Surveyor 7 (U.S.)	Jan. 6, 1968	Moon	Landed near Crater Tycho Jan. 10. Soil analysis. Sent 3,343 pictures.
Pioneer 9 (U.S.)	Nov. 8, 1968	Sun Orbit	Achieved orbit. Six experiments returned solar radiation data.
Venera 5 (U.S.S.R.)	Jan. 5, 1969	Venus	Landed May 16, 1969. Returned atmospheric data.
Mariner 6 (U.S.)	Feb. 24, 1969	Mars	Came within 2000 mi. of Mars July 31, 1969. Sent back data & TV pictures.
Luna 16 (U.S.S.R.)	Sept. 12, 1970	Moon	Soft-landed Sept. 20, scooped up rock, returned to Earth Sept. 24.
Luna 17 (U.S.S.R.)	Nov. 10, 1970	Moon	Soft-landed on Sea of Rains Nov. 17. Lunokhod 1, self-propelled vehicle, used for first time. Sent TV photos, made soil analysis, etc.
Mariner 9 (U.S.)	May 30, 1971	Mars	First craft to orbit Mars, Nov. 13. 7,300 pictures, 1st close-ups of Mars' moon. Transmission ended Oct. 27, 1972.
Luna 20 (U.S.S.R.)	Feb. 14, 1972	Moon	Soft-landed Feb. 21 in Sea of Fertility. Returned Feb. 25 with rock samples.
Pioneer 10 (U.S.)	March 3, 1972	Jupiter	620-million-mile flight path through asteroid belt passed Jupiter Dec. 3, 1973, to give man first closeup of planet. In 1986, it became first man-made object to escape solar system.
Luna 21 (U.S.S.R.)	Jan. 8, 1973	Moon	Soft-landed Jan. 16. Lunokhod 2 (moon-car) scooped up soil samples, returned them to Earth Jan. 27.
Mariner 10 (U.S.)	Nov. 3, 1973	Venus, Mercury	Passed Venus Feb. 5, 1974. Arrived Mercury March 29, 1974, for man's first closeup look at planet. First time gravity of one planet (Venus) used to whip spacecraft toward another (Mercury).
Viking 1 (U.S.)	Aug. 20, 1975	Mars	Carrying life-detection labs. Landed July 20, 1976, for de-tailed scientific research, including pictures. Designed to work for only 90 days, it operated for almost 6 1/2 years before it went silent in November 1982.
Viking 2 (U.S .)	Sept. 9, 1975	Mars	Like Viking 1. Landed Sept. 3, 1976. Functioned 3 1/2 years.
Luna 24 (U.S.S.R.)	Aug. 9, 1976	Moon	Soft-landed Aug. 18, 1976. Returned soil samples Aug. 22, 1976
Voyager 1 (U.S.)	Sept. 5, 1977	Jupiter, Saturn	Fly-by mission. Reached Jupiter in March 1979; passed Saturn Nov. 1980; passed Uranus 1986.
Voyager 2 (U.S.)	Aug. 20, 1977	Jupiter, Saturn, Uranus	Launched before *Voyager 1*. Encountered Jupiter in July 1979; flew by Saturn Aug. 1981; passed Uranus January 1986; scheduled to pass Neptune Aug. 24, 1989.
Pioneer Venus 1 (U.S.)	May 20, 1978	Venus	Arrived Dec. 4 and orbited Venus, photographing surface and atmosphere.
Pioneer Venus 2 (U.S.)	Aug. 8, 1978	Venus	Four-part multi-probe, landed Dec. 9.
Venera 13 (U.S.S.R.)	Oct. 30, 1981	Venus	Landed March 1, 1982. Took first X-ray fluorescence analysis of the planet's surface. Transmitted data 2 hours 7 minutes.
VEGA 1 (U.S.S.R.)	Deployed on Venus, June 10, 1985	Encounter with Halley's comet	In flyby over Venus while enroute to encounter with Halley's Comet, VEGA 1 and 2 dropped scientific capsules onto Venus to study atmosphere and surface material. Encoun-tered Halley's Comet on March 6 and March 9, 1986. Took TV pictures, and studied comet's dust particles.
VEGA 2 (U.S.S.R.)	Deployed on Venus, June 14, 1985		
Suisei (Japan)	Encountered Halley's Comet March 8, 1986	Halley's Comet	Spacecraft made fly-by of comet and studied atmosphere with ultraviolet camera. Observed rotation nucleus.
Sakigake (Japan)	Encountered Halley's Comet March 10, 1986	Halley's Comet	Spacecraft made fly-by to study solar wind and magnetic fields. Detected plasma waves.
Giotto (ESA)	Encountered Halley's Comet March 13, 1986	Halley's Comet	European Space Agency spacecraft made closest approach to comet. Studied atmosphere and magnetic fields. Sent back best pictures of nucleus.
Phobos Mission (U.S.S.R.)	July 7 and July 12, 1988	Mars and Phobos	Two spacecraft to probe Martian moon Phobos starting April 1989. Were to study orbit, soil chemistry, send TV pictures and data of planet. Contact was lost with Phobos 1 in August 1988 and later with Phobos 2 in March 1989 after it reached the Martian moon.

Spacecraft	Launch date	Destination	Remarks
Magellan (U.S.)	May 4, 1989	Venus	Arrived at Venus on Aug. 10, 1990 and made a geologic map of planet with a powerful radar.
Galileo (U.S.)	Oct. 18, 1989	Jupiter	To study Jupiter's atmosphere and its moons during 22-month mission. It will reach the planet in 1995.
Hiten (Japan)	Jan. 24, 1990	Moon	First Japanese unmanned spacecraft carried two small satellites without scientific instruments. One satellite placed in lunar orbit called *Hagoromo;* its transmitter later failed. The other in Earth orbit for future missions but contact was lost. Project was a practice test for later scientific missions in the 1990s.
Hubble Space Telescope (U.S., E.S.A.)[2]	April 25, 1990	Earth Orbit	Studies distant stars and galaxies and search for evidence of planets in other solar systems.
Ulysses *U.S., ESA	Oct. 6, 1990	The Sun	To study the poles of the Sun and interstellar space above and below the poles. First solar encounter to be in 1994. Second encounter to be in 1995.
Gamma-Ray Observatory (U.S.)	April 7, 1991	Eart Orbit	To make first survey of gamma ray sources across the whole sky, sturying explosive energic sources such as supernovae, quasars, neutron stars, pulsars, and black holes.
Mars Observer (U.S.)	Sept. 1992[1]	Mars	Spacecraft to arrive at Mars Aug. 1993 and orbit the planet for one full Martian year to study atmosphere and surface change during the planet's seasons.
Mars '94 (U.S.S.R.)	Oct. 1994[1]	Mars	Two spacecraft to study Mars over an 18-month period. Will investigate Martian surface and deploy a balloon-borne package to study the planet's atmosphere.

1. Tentative launch date. To be deployed by Space Shuttle. 2. European Space Agency (E.S.A.) responsible for furnishing the solar arrays, the Faint Object Camera, and participation in flight operations aspects of the mission.

U.S. Manned Space Flight Projects

Mercury. *Project Mercury,* initiated in 1958 and completed in 1963, was the United States' first man-in-space program. It was designed to further knowledge about man's capabilities in space.

In April 1959, seven military jet test pilots were introduced to the public as America's first astronauts. They were: Lt. M. Scott Carpenter, USN; Capt. L. Gordon Cooper, Jr., USAF; Lt. Col. John H. Glenn, Jr., USMC; Cap. Virgil I. Grissom, USAF; Lt. Comdr. Walter M. Shirra, Jr., USN; Lt. Comdr. Alan B. Shepard, Jr., USN; and Capt. Donald K. Slayton, USAF. Six of the original seven would make a Mercury flight. Slayton was grounded for medical reasons, but remained a director of the astronaut office. He returned to flight status in 1975 as Docking Module Pilot on the Apollo-Soyuz flight.

Flight Summary

Each astronaut named his capsule and added the numeral 7 to denote the teamwork of the original astronauts.

May 5, 1961. Alan B. Shepard, Jr., makes a suborbital flight in *Freedom 7* and becomes the first American in space. Time: 15 minutes, 22 seconds.

July 21, 1961. Virgil I. Grissom makes the second successful suborbital flight on *Liberty Bell 7*, but spacecraft sank shortly after splashdown. Time: 15 minutes, 37 seconds. Grissom was later killed in *Apollo 1* fire, Jan. 27, 1967.

February 20, 1962. John H. Glenn, Jr., makes a three-orbit flight and becomes the first American in orbit. Time: 4 hours, 55 minutes.

May 24, 1962. M. Scott Carpenter duplicates Glenn's flight in *Aurora 7*. Time: 4 hours, 56 minutes.

October 3, 1962. Walter M. Schirra, Jr., makes a six-orbit engineering test flight in *Sigma 7*. Time: 9 hours, 13 minutes.

May 15–16, 1963. L. Gordon Cooper, Jr., performs the last *Mercury* mission and completes 22 orbits in *Faith 7* to evaluate effects of one day in space. Time: 34 hours, 19 minutes.

Gemini. *Gemini* was an extension of *Project Mercury,* to determine the effects of prolonged space flight on man—two weeks or longer—the time it takes to reach the Moon and return. "Walks in space" provided invalua ble information for astronauts' later walks on the Moon. The *Gemini* spacecraft, twice as large as the *Mercury* capsule, accommodated two astronauts. Its crew named the project *Gemini* for the third constellation of the Zodiac and its twin stars, Castor and Pollus. The capsule differed from the *Mercury* spacecrafts in that it had hatches above the capsules so that the astronauts could leave the spacecraft and perform spacewalks or extra vehicular activities (EVAs).

There were ten manned flights in the *Gemini* program, starting with *Gemini 3* on March 23, 1965, and ending with the *Gemini 12* mission on Nov. 15, 1966. *Gemini 1* and *2* were unmanned test flights of the equipment.

When the *Gemini* program ended, U.S. astronauts had perfected rendezvous and docking maneuvers with other orbiting vehicles.

Apollo. *Apollo* was the designation for the United States' effort to land a man on the Moon and return him safely to Earth. The goal was successfully accomplished with *Apollo 11* on July 20, 1969, culminating eight years of rehearsal and centuries of dreaming. Astronauts Neil A. Armstrong and Col. Edwin E. Aldrin, Jr., scooped up and brought back the first lunar rocks ever seen on Earth—about 47 pounds.

Tragedy struck Jan. 27, 1967, on the launch pad during a preflight test of what would have become *Apollo 1*, the first manned mission. Astronauts Lt. Col. Virgil "Gus" Grissom, Lt. Col. Edward H. White, and Lt. Cdr. Roger Chafee lost their lives when a fire swept through the command module.

Six *Apollo* flights followed, ending with *Apollo 17* in December, 1972. The last three *Apollos* carried mechanized vehicles called lunar rovers for wide-ranging surface exploration of the Moon by astronauts. The rendezvous and docking of an *Apollo* spacecraft with a Russian *Soyuz* craft in Earth orbit on July 18, 1975, closed out the *Apollo* program.

During the Apollo project, the following 12 astronauts explored the lunar terrain:

Col. Edwin E. "Buzz" Aldrin, Jr., and Neil A. Armstrong, *Apollo 11;* Cdr. Alan L. Bean and Cdr. Charles Conrad, Jr., *Apollo 12;* Edgar D. Mitchell and Alan B. Shepard, *Apollo 14;* Lt. Col. James B. Irwin and Col. David R. Scott, *Apollo 15;* Col. Charles M. Duke, Jr., and Capt. John W. Young, *Apollo 16;* and Capt. Eugene A. Cernan and Dr. Harrison H. Schmitt, *Apollo 17.*

Apollo was a three-part spacecraft: the command module (CM), the crew's quarters and flight control section; the service modules (SM) for the propulsion and spacecraft support systems (when together, the two modules were called CSM); and the lunar module (LM) to take two of the crew to the lunar surface, support them on the Moon, and return them to the CSM in orbit. The crews that made the lunar flights where both command modules and lunar modules were involved selected call names for the vehicles. The call names for the spacecraft in the six lunar landing missions with the command module and lunar module designations respectively were:

Apollo 11, Columbia and *Eagle; Apollo 12, Yankee Clipper* and *Intrepid;* (NOTE: The third lunar attempt, *Apollo 13,* April 11–17, 1970, 5 days, 22.9 hours, was aborted after the service module oxygen tank ruptured. The *Apollo 13* crew members were James A. Lovell, Jr., John L. Swigert, Jr., and Fred W. Haise, Jr. The mission was classified as a "Successful failure," because the crew was rescued. The call names for their spacecraft were *Odyssey* (CM) and *Aquarius* (LM).) *Apollo 14, Kitty Hawk* and *Antares; Apollo 15, Endeavor* and *Falcon; Apollo 16, Casper* and *Orion;* and *Apollo 17, America* and *Challenger.*

Skylab. America's first Earth-orbiting space station. *Project Skylab* was designed to demonstrate that men can work and live in space for prolonged periods without ill effects. Originally the spent third stage of a Saturn 5 moon rocket, *Skylab* measured 118 feet from stem to stern, and carried the most varied assortment of experimental equipment ever assembled in a single spacecraft. Three three-man crews visited the space stations, spending more than 740 hours observing the Sun and bringing home more than 175,000 solar pictures. These were the first recordings of solar activity above Earth's obscuring atmosphere. *Skylab* also evaluated systems designed to gather information on Earth's resources and environmental conditions. *Skylab* biomedical findings indicated that man adapts well to space for at least a period of three months, provided he has a proper diet and adequately programmed exercise, sleep, work, and recreation periods. *Skylab* orbited Earth at a distance of about 300 miles. Five years after the last *Skylab* mission, the 77-ton space station's orbit began to deteriorate faster than expected, owing to unexpectedly high sunspot activity. On July 11, 1979, the parts of *Skylab* that did not burn up in the atmosphere came crashing down on parts of Australia and the Indian Ocean. No one was hurt.

Space Shuttle. The *Space Shuttle* (also known as the National Space Transportation System or STS) is a manned spacecraft design developed by NASA to reduce the cost of using space for commercial, scientific, and defense needs. The *Shuttle* is a manned rocket which, after depositing its payload in space, can be flown back to Earth like a conventional airplane and be available for re-use. Although its cargoes are unmanned, the *Shuttle* can serve as an inhabited Earth-orbiting laboratory for up to 30 days. The NASA orbiter is 122.2 feet long and has a wingspan of 78.6 feet.

The *Space Shuttle Columbia* was successfully launched on April 12, 1981. It made five flights (the first four were test runs), the last completed on November 16, 1982. The second shuttle, *Challenger,* made its maiden flight on April 4, 1983. In April 1984, crew members of the *Challenger* captured, repaired, and returned the Solar Max satellite to orbit, making it the first time a disabled satellite had been repaired in space. The third shuttle, *Discovery,* made its first flight on August 30, 1984. The fourth space shuttle, *Atlantis,* made its maiden flight on Oct. 3, 1985.

A tragedy occurred on Jan. 28, 1986, when the shuttle *Challenger* exploded, killing the crew of seven 73 seconds after takeoff. It was the world's worst space flight disaster.

The first U.S. space mission since the *Challenger* disaster was launched 32 months later on Sept. 29, 1988, with the flight of *Discovery.* It had a crew of five and deployed a TDRS (Tracking Data Relay Satellite) communications satellite.

A new orbiter, the *Endeavour,* named after British explorer James Cook's first ship, is being built by Rockwell International, Inc. to replace the *Challenger.* The maiden voyage of *Endeavor* is scheduled for September 1992.

Soviet Manned Space Flight Programs

Vostok. The Soviets' first manned capsule, roughly spherical, used to place the first six cosmonauts in Earth orbit (1961–65).

Voskhod. Adaptation of the *Vostok* capsule to accommodate two and three cosmonauts. *Voskhod 1* orbited three persons, and *Voskhod 2* orbited two persons performing the world's first manned extra-vehicular activity.

Soyuz. Late-model manned spacecraft with provisions for three cosmonauts and a "working compartment" accessible through a hatch. Soyuz is the Russian word for "union." Since 1973, all *Soyuz* spacecraft have carried two cosmonauts. *Soyuz 19,* launched July 15, 1975, docked with the American *Apollo* spacecraft.

Salyut. Earth-orbiting space station intended for prolonged occupancy and re-visitation by cosmonauts. They are usually launched by Soviet Proton rockets. *Salyut 1* was launched April 19, 1971. *Salyut 2,* launched April 3, 1973, malfunctioned in orbit and was never occupied. *Salyut 3* was launched June 25, 1974. *Salyut 4* was launched Dec. 26, 1974. *Salyut 5* was launched June 22, 1976. *Salyut 6* was launched on Sept. 29, 1977. *Salyut 7* was launched on April 19, 1982 and is still in orbit. It is slowly descending, and will re-enter the Earth's atmosphere in 1991. A record breaking Russian endurance flight was set (Feb. 8, 1984–Oct. 2, 1985) when Soviet astronauts spent 237 days in orbit aboard *Salyut-7.*

Mir. The latest Soviet space station was launched into orbit on Feb. 20, 1986. Since that time, two space endurance records have been set in the *Mir.* On Dec. 29, 1987, Col. Yuri Romanenko set a single-mission record of 326.5 days in space. On Dec. 21, 1989, Col. Vladimir Titov and Musa Manarov returned to Earth after spending 366 days aboard the orbiting space station.

Notable Manned Space Flights

Designation and country	Date	Astronauts	Flight time (h/min)	Remarks
Vostok 1(U.S.S.R.)	April 12, 1961	Yuri A. Gagarin	1/48	First manned orbital flight
MR III (U.S.)	May 5, 1961	Alan B. Shepard, Jr.	0/15	Range 486 km (302 mi.), peak 187 km (116.5 mi); capsule recovered. First American in space.
Vostok 2 (U.S.S.R.)	Aug. 6–7, 1961	Gherman S. Titov	25/18	First long-duration flight
MA VI (U.S.)	Feb. 20, 1962	John H. Glenn, Jr.	4/55	First American in orbit
MA IX (U.S.)	May 15–16, 1963	L. Gordon Cooper, Jr.	34/20	Longest Mercury flight
Vostok 6 (U.S.S.R.)	June 16–19, 1963	Valentina V. Tereshkova	70/50	First orbital flight by female cosmonaut
Voskhod 1 (U.S.S.R.)	Oct. 12, 1964	Vladimir M. Komarov; Konstantin P. Feoktistov; Boris G. Yegorov	24/17	First 3-man orbital flight; also first flight without space suits
Voskhod 2 (U.S.S.R.)	March 18, 1965	Alexei A. Leonov; Pavel I. Belyayev	26/2	First "space walk" (by Leonov), 10 min
GT III (U.S.)	March 23, 1965	Virgil I. Grissom; John W. Young	4/53	First manned test of Gemini spacecraft
GT IV (U.S.)	June 3–7, 1965	James A. McDivitt; Edward H. White, 2d	97/48	First American "space walk" (by White), lasting slightly over 20 min
GT VIII (U.S.)	March 16–17, 1966	Neil A. Armstrong; David R. Scott	10/42	First docking between manned spacecraft and an unmanned space vehicle (an orbiting Agena rocket).
Apollo 7 (U.S.)	Oct. 11–22, 1968	Walter M. Schirra, Jr.; Donn F. Eisele; R. Walter Cunningham	260/9	First manned test of Apollo command module; first live TV transmissions from orbit
Soyuz 3 (U.S.S.R.)	Oct. 26–30, 1968	Georgi T. Bergeovoi	94/51	First manned rendezvous and possible docking by Soviet cosmonaut
Apollo 8 (U.S.)	Dec. 21–27, 1968	Frank Borman; James A. Lovell, Jr.; William A. Anders	147/00	First spacecraft in circumlunar orbit; TV transmissions from this orbit. The three astronauts were also the first men to view the Earth whole.
Apollo 9 (U.S.)	Mar. 3–13, 1969	James A. McDivitt; David R. Scott; Russell A. Schweikart	241/1	First manned flight of Lunar Module
Apollo 10 (U.S.)	May 18–26, 1969	Thomas P. Stafford; Eugene A. Cernan; John W. Young	192/3	First descent to within 9 miles of moon's surface by manned craft
Apollo 11 (U.S.)	July 16–24, 1969	Neil A. Armstrong; Edwin E. Aldrin, Jr.; Michael Collins	195/18	First manned landing and EVA on Moon; soil and rock samples collected; experiments left on lunar surface
Soyuz 6 (U.S.S.R.)	Oct. 11–16, 1969	Gorgiy Shonin; Valriy Kabasov	118/42	Three spacecraft and seven men put into earth orbit simultaneously for first time
Apollo 12 (U.S.)	Nov. 14–24, 1969	Charles Conrad, Jr.; Richard F. Gordon, Jr.; Alan Bean	244/36	Manned lunar landing mission; investigated Surveyor 3 spacecraft; collected lunar samples. EVA time: 15 h 30 min
Apollo 13 (U.S.)	April 11–17, 1970	James A. Lovell, Jr.; Fred W. Haise, Jr.; John L. Swigert, Jr.	142/54	Third manned lunar landing attempt; aborted due to pressure loss in liquid oxygen in service module and failure of fuel cells
Apollo 14 (U.S.)	Jan. 31–Feb. 9, 1971	Alan B. Shepard; Stuart A. Roosa; Edgar D. Mitchell	216/42	Third manned lunar landing: returned largest amount of lunar material
Soyuz 11 (U.S.S.R.)	June 6–30, 1971	Georgiy Tomofeyevich Dobrovolskiy; Vladislav Nikolayevich Volkov; Viktor Ivanovich Patsyev	569/40	Linked up with first space station, Salyut 1. Astronauts died just before re-entry due to loss of pressurization in spacecraft
Apollo 15 (U.S.)	July 26–Aug. 7, 1971	David R. Scott; James B. Irwin; Alfred M. Worden	295/12	Fourth manned lunar landing; first use of Lunar Rover propelled by Scott and Irving; first live pictures of LM lift-off from Moon; exploration time: 18 hours
Apollo 16 (U.S.)	April 16–27, 1972	John W. Young; Thomas K. Mattingly; Charles M. Duke, Jr.	265/51	Fifth manned lunar landing; second use of Lunar Rover Vehicle, propelled by Young and Duke Total exploration time on the Moon was 20 h 14 min, setting new record. Mattingly's in-flight "walk in space" was 1 h 23 min. Approximately 213 lb of lunar rock returned
Apollo 17 (U.S.)	Dec. 7–19, 1972	Eugene A. Cernan; Ronald E. Evans; Harrison H. Schmitt	301/51	Sixth and last manned lunar landing; third to carry lunar rover. Cernan and Schmitt, during three EVA's, completed total of 22 h 05 min 3 sec. USS Ticonderoga recovered crew and about 250 lbs of lunar samples
Skylab SL-2 (U.S.)	May 25–June 22, 1973	Charles Conrad, Jr.; Josep P. Kerwin; Paul J. Weitz	672/50	First manned Skylab launch. Established Skylab Orbital Assembly and conducted scientific and medical experiments
Skylab SL-3 (U.S.)	July 28–Sept. 25, 1973	Alan L. Bean, Jr.; Jack R. Lousma; Owen K. Garriott	1427/9	Second manned Skylab launch. New crew remained in space for 59 days, continuing scientific and medical experiments and earth observations from orbit

Designation and country	Date	Astronauts	Flight time (h/min)	Remarks
Skylab SL-4 (U.S.)	Nov. 16, 1973– Feb. 8, 1974	Gerald Carr; Edward Gibson; William Pogue	2017/16	Third manned Skylab launch; obtained medical data on crew for use in extending the duration of manned space flight; crews "walked in space" 4 times, totaling 44 h 40 min. Longest space mission yet—84 d 1 h 16 min. Splashdown in Pacific, Feb. 9, 1974
Apollo/Soyuz Test Project (U.S. and U.S.S.R.)	July 15–24, 1975 (U.S.)	U.S.: Brig. Gen. Thomas P. Stafford, Vance D. Brand, Donald K. Slayton	216/05	World's first international manned rendezvous and docking in space; aimed at developing a space rescue capability
	July 15–21, 1975 (U.S.S.R.)	U.S.S.R.: Col. A. A. Leonov, V. N. Kubasov	223/35	Apollo and Soyuz docked and crewmen exchanged visits on July 17, 1975. Mission duration for Soyuz: 142 h 31 min. For Apollo: 217 h, 28 min.
Columbia (U.S.)	April 12–14, 1981	Capt. Robert L. Crippen; John W. Young	54/20	Maiden voyage of *Space Shuttle,* the first spacecraft designed specifically for re-use up to 100 times
Salyut 7 (U .S.S.R.)	Feb. 8, 1984– Oct. 2, 1985	Leonid Kizim; Vladimir Solovyov; Oleg Atkov	237 days	Record Soviet team endurance flight in orbiting space station
Mir (U.S.S.R.)	Feb. 8, 1987– Dec. 29, 1987	Yuri V. Romanenko[2]	326.5 days	Record Soviet single endurance flight in orbiting space station.
Mir (U.S.S.R.)	Dec. 21, 1988– Dec. 21, , 1988	Col. Vladimir Titov and Musa Manarov[3]	366 days	Record Soviet team endurance flight in orbiting space station.

1. Approximate time. NOTE: The letters MR stand for Mercury (capsule) and Redstone (rocket); MA, for Mercury and Atlas (rocket); GT, for Gemini (capsule) and Titan-II (rocket). The first astronaut listed in the Gemini and Apollo flights is the command pilot. The Mercury capsules had names: MR-III was *Freedom 7,* MR-IV was *Liberty Bell 7,* MA-VI was *Friendship 7,* MA-VII was *Aurora 7,* MA-VIII was *Sigma 7,* and MA-IX was *Faith 7.* The figure 7 referred to the fact that the first group of U.S. astronauts numbered seven men. Only one Gemini capsule had a name: GT-III was called *Molly Brown* (after the Broadway musical *The Unsinkable Molly Brown*); thereafter the practice of naming the capsules was discontinued. 2. Returned to earth with two fellow cosmonauts, Aleksandr P. Aleksandrov and Anatoly Levchenko, who had spent a shorter stay aboard the *Mir.* 3. Also returned to earth with French astronaut Jean-Loup Chrétien who spent 3-1/2 weeks aboard the *Mir.*

The Soviet Space Shuttle *Buran*

The successful test flight of the Soviet Union's first reusable space shuttle *Buran* (Russian for "snowstorm") (Shown at right on launch pad. Novosti photo) was made on Nov. 15, 1988. The unmanned flight circled the Earth for two orbits and lasted 3 hr 25 min.

The Soviet and American space shuttles closely resemble each other in size and appearance and have similar delta wings and vertical tail structures. Some major differences between the two shuttles are that the Soviet craft has no large rocket engines of its own. It uses the giant disposable *Energiya* rocket for most of its propulsion, and has only small rockets for maneuvering. The United States space shuttles have three reusable main engines to help lift it into orbit. The *Buran* also has larger payload capabilities than NASA's orbiters.

Unlike the American version, the *Buran* is designed for fully automatic flight, from takeoff to landing, a difficult engineering feat. By comparison, U.S. astronauts take control of their shuttles when making the final landing approach.

The crew cabin of *Buran* can accommodate two to four astronauts and has seats for six passengers or other crew members. The U.S. space shuttle can accommodate up to eight crew members. The Soviet shuttle is being adapted for docking with the *Mir* space station.

The Soviet craft is 19 ft (5.6 m) in diameter compared with NASA's shuttle, 17 ft (5.2 m). The wingspan is 79.2 ft (24 m). NASA's orbiter is 78.6 ft (23.79 m). *Buran's* length is 119 ft (36 m), the U.S. shuttle is 122.2 ft long (37.24 m).

The Soviets had planned to make ten to twelve shuttle flights a year, but the *Buran* program was delayed due to economic considerations. Manned *Buran* missions will start in 1992.

A second *Buran* flight is unlikely to take place before the end of 1991. A third *Buran* mission with a two-cosmonaut crew is planned for 1992. The Soviets are assembling two additional *Buran* space shuttles. Cosmonaut Igor Vold will be the pilot of the first manned *Buran* flight. He has flown test flight missions of the Soviet space shuttle.

ASTRONOMY

The Gamma Ray Observatory after launching by the space shuttle *Atlantis*. NASA illustration.

The Gamma Ray Observatory

The Gamma Ray Observatory (GRO) launched from the space shuttle *Atlantis* April 7, 1991, is the second of the four "Great Observatories" NASA planned for studying the Universe. The first of the "Great Observatories" was the Hubble Space Telescope, launched April 24, 1990. The others are the Advanced X-ray Astrophysics Facility (AXAF) expected to launch in 1997, and the Space Infrared Telescope Facility (SIRTF) planned to launch in 1999 or 2000.

Before the Gamma Ray Observatory could be launched into orbit, mission specialists Air Force Lieut. Col. Jerry L. Ross and Dr. Jerome Apt made an emergency trip to the cargo bay of the *Atlantis* to free one of the GRO's antennas that had jammed. It was the first American space walk in five years.

The GRO was the heaviest NASA science payload (about 35,000 pounds or 15.3 metric tons) ever deployed by the Shuttle in low earth orbit. Its four large telescopes—some nearly the size of a compact car—each recognize gamma rays within a specific energy range. Because these ranges overlap, astronomers can observe most of the gamma-ray spectrum and can compare data from different instruments.

Unlike visible radiation and radio waves, gamma rays cannot be focused with telescopes. Instead, gamma rays are detected when they interact with matter. Their passage through the detectors on the GRO convert the rays to flashes of visible light which are counted and measured. From those flashes, scientists can determine their energy level and source. Gamma rays cannot be detected on Earth because they do not penetrate the atmosphere.

The $617-million spacecraft was built by TRW and measures 70 feet (21 meters) between the tips of its solar arrays. The solar arrays provide 1800 watts of electrical power required for the operation of the observatory. The spacecraft is designed to have a minimum life of two years, but it is expected to operate for at least six years.

What Are Gamma Rays?

Gamma rays are the highest energy radiations in the electromagnetic spectrum, ranging from tens of thousands to tens of billions of electron volts (eV). An eV is a measure of the amount of energy impacted to an electron when subjected to an electrical potential of 1 volt. In contrast, visible light corresponds to only a few electron volts. These gamma rays provide a means of studying some of the primary forces of change in the astrophysical processes.

Gamma rays are thought to originate with the "Big Bang" and subsequent expansion of the universe we witness today. Through these gamma-ray observations, we may witness the birth of elements and deaths of stars, gain clues into the mysteries of quasars, pulsars, neutron stars, and get a glimpse into the spacetime precipice of a black hole. In all these cases, large amounts of energy are released and gamma rays produced.

Some Sources of Gamma Rays

Gamma rays are generated by **supernovas** and by their very dense remains, **neutron stars.** These stars spin very rapidly, some—perhaps all—emit radiation in pulses and are known as pulsars. Pulsars are thought to be remnants of supernova explosions. One of the fastest known **pulsars** makes 643 complete rotations in one second. How these stars convert their rotational energy to gamma rays is not known. Since the first pulsar was discovered in 1968, we now have located more than 500 of them.

Quasi-stellar objects (**quasars** for short) are the most energetic objects in the universe. No other entity emits more energy. They also flicker, and their radiation can change from day to day. Astronomers are uncertain about the nature of quasars. One quasar has been observed emitting vast numbers of gamma rays, and many others may do so as well.

The **Milky Way Galaxy** emits a glow of gamma rays, although the sources of this glow is not fully understood.

Active galaxies, unlike the Milky Way, shine brightest in radio waves, X-rays, or even gamma rays, and the intensity of their radiation may change from week to week. Scientists want to know why these galaxies vary so much.

Bursters and other **transient sources** also produce gamma rays. These intense bursts are particularly hard to study because they cannot be predicted and last a very short time. In 1979 one gamma-ray burst observed near the Large Magellanic Cloud, our nearest galactic neighbor, unleashed in just one-tenth of a second more gamma-ray energy than our sun can pump out in every form over the next 1,000 years. It is not known why these bursts occur.

Black holes are theoretical points of space where gravity is so strong that even light cannot escape. Scientists think that, if black holes do exist, matter drawn into them will give off gamma rays just as it disappears. □

Advanced X-Ray Astrophysics Facility

In 1997 or 1998, the last of NASA's "great observatories," the Advanced X-Ray Astrophysics Facility (SIRTF) will be deployed, providing astronomers with a 100-fold increase in resolution over previous orbiting satellites in the X-ray region of the electromagnetic spectrum.

SIRTF will open a new window on the universe. From its vantage point of 62,000 miles (100,000 kilometers) above the Earth's surface, the telescope will conduct a wide range of investigations in the realm of infrared light.

SIRTF will be a challenging mission. The telescope's unique position in space, its five-year operational lifetime and its ability to provide 1,000 to 10,000 times the sensitivity of previous orbiting satellites will allow SIRTF to gaze back in time to ancient galaxies at nearly the beginning of the universe.

The super-cooled SIRTF space telescope will be free from the infrared emissions of Earth's atmosphere and emissions that would be produced by the warm optics of an ambient-temperature telescope. Infrared light is not visible to the human eye because the radiation has longer wavelengths and lower frequencies (fewer vibrations per second) than does red visible light. To detect this radiation, specialized infrared detectors, most often composed of crystals of germanium or silicon laced with other elements, will be constructed for use in the telescope.

The telescope measures 18.15 feet (5.5 meters) in length by 9.24 feet (2.8 meters) in diameter and weighs approximately 7,590 pounds (3,450 kilograms) without the cryogenic fluid.

The SIRTF telescope and its instruments will be housed within a cylindrical cryogen tank. The hollow walls of the tank contain 570 kilograms (1,040 gallons or 4,000 liters) of superfluid helium that will be used to cool detectors, optics and other key parts of the telescope to a few degrees above absolute zero. The colder the detectors, the colder and fainter the objects they will be able to detect.

The Space Infrared Telescope Facility will be launched by a Titan 4-Centaur launch vehicle into a high-altitude, circular orbit well above Earth's trapped radiation zone. □

Astronomical Terms

Planet is the term used for a body in orbit around the Sun. Its origin is Greek; even in antiquity it was known that a number of "stars" did not stay in the same relative positions to the others. There were five such restless "stars" known—Mercury, Venus, Mars, Jupiter, and Saturn—and the Greeks referred to them as *planetes*, a word which means "wanderers." That the earth is one of the planets was realized later. The additional planets were discovered after the invention of the telescope.

Satellite (or *moon*) is the term for a body in orbit around a planet. As long as our own Moon was the only moon known, there was no need for a general term for the moons of planets. But when Galileo Galilei discovered the four main moons of the planet Jupiter, Johannes Kepler (in a letter to Galileo) suggested "satellite" (from the Latin *satelles,* which means attendant) as a general term for such bodies. The word is used interchangeably with "moons": astronomers speak and write about the moons of Neptune, Saturn, etc. A satellite may be any size.

Orbit is the term for the path traveled by a body in space. It comes from the Latin *orbis,* which means circle, circuit, etc., and *orbita,* which means a rut or a wheel track. Theoretically, four mathematical figures are possible orbits: two are open (hyperbola and parabola) and two are closed (ellipse and circle), but in reality all closed orbits are ellipses. These ellipses can be nearly circular, as are the orbits of most planets, or very elongated, as are the orbits of most comets. In these orbits, the Sun is in one focal point of the ellipse, and the other focal point is empty. In the orbits of satellites, the planet stands in one focal point of the orbit. The *primary* of an orbit is the body in the focal point. For planets, the point of the orbit closest to the Sun is the *perihelion,* and the point farthest from the Sun is the *aphelion.* For orbits around the Earth, the corresponding terms are *perigee* and *apogee;* for orbits around other planets, corresponding terms are coined when necessary.

Two heavenly bodies are in *inferior* or *superior conjunction* when they have the same Right Ascension, or are in the same meridian; that is, when one is due north or south of the other. If the bodies appear near each other as seen from the Earth, they will rise and set at the same time. They are in *opposition* when they are opposite each other in the he avens: when one rises as the other is setting. *Greatest elongation* is the greatest apparent angular distance from the Sun, when a planet is most favorably suited for observation. Mercury can be seen with the naked eye only at about this time. An *occultation* of a planet or star is an eclipse of it by some other body, usually the Moon.

Stars are the basic units of population in the universe. Our Sun is the nearest star. Stars are very large (our Sun has a diameter of 865,400 miles—a comparatively small star). Stars are composed of intensely hot gasses, deriving their energy from nuclear reactions going on in their interiors.

Galaxies are immense systems containing billions of stars. All that you can see in the sky (with a very few exceptions) belongs to our galaxy—a system of roughly 200 billion stars. The few exceptions are other galaxies. Our own galaxy, the rim of which we see as the "Milky Way," is about 100,000 light-years in diameter and about 10,000 light-years in thickness. Its shape is roughly that of a thick lens; more precisely it is a "spiral nebula," a term first used for other galaxies when they were discovered and before it was realized that these were separate and distant galaxies. The spiral galaxy nearest to ours is in the constellation Andromeda. It is somewhat larger than our own galaxy and is visible to the naked eye.

Recent developments in radio astronomy have revealed additional celestial objects that are still incompletely understood.

Quasars ("quasi-stellar" objects), originally thought to be peculiar stars in our own galaxy, are now believed to be the most remote objects in the Universe. Spectral studies of quasars indicate that some are 9 billion light years away and moving away from us at the incredible rate of 150,000 miles per second. Quasars emit tremendous amounts of light and microwave radiation. Although they appear to be far smaller than ordinary galaxies, some quasars emit as much as 100 times more energy. Some astronomers believe that quasars are the cores of violently exploding galaxies.

Pulsars are believed to be rapidly spinning neutron stars, so crushed by their own gravity that a million tons of their matter would hardly fill a thimble. Pulsars are so named because they emit bursts of radio energy at regular intervals. Some have pulse rates as rapid as 10 per second.

A *black hole* is the theoretical end-product of the total gravitational collapse of a massive star or group of stars. Crushed even smaller than an incredibly dense neutron star, such a body may become so dense that not even light can escape its gravitational field. It has been suggested that black holes may be detectable in proximity to normal stars when they draw matter away from their visible neighbors. Strong sources of X-rays in our galaxy and beyond may also indicate the presence of black holes. One possible black hole now being studied is the invisible companion to a supergiant star in the constellation Cygnus.

Origin of the Universe

Evidence uncovered in recent years tends to confirm that the universe began its existence about 15 billion years ago as a dense, hot globule of gas expanding rapidly outward. At that time, the universe contained nothing but hydrogen and a small amount of helium. There were no stars and no planets. The first stars probably began to condense out of the primordial hydrogen when the universe was about 100 million years old and continued to form as the universe aged. The Sun arose in this way 4.6 billion years ago. Many stars came into being before the Sun was formed; many others formed after the Sun appeared. This process continues, and through telescopes we can now see stars forming out of compressed pockets of hydrogen in outer space.

Birth and Death of a Star

When a star begins to form as a dense cloud of gas, the individual hydrogen atoms fall toward the center of the cloud under the force of the star's gravity. As they fall, they pick up speed, and their energy increases. The increase in energy heats the gas. When this process has continued for some millions of years, the temperature reaches about 20 million degrees Fahrenheit. At this temperature, the hydrogen within the star ignites and burns in a continuing series of nuclear reactions in which all the elements in the universe are manufactured from hydrogen and helium. The onset of these reactions marks the birth of a star. When a star begins to exhaust its hydrogen supply, its life nears an end. The first sign of old age is a swelling and reddening of its outer regions. Such an aging, swollen star is called a red giant. The Sun, a middle-aged star, will probably swell to a red giant in 5 billion years, vaporizing the earth and any creatures that may be left on its surface. When all its fuel has been exhausted, a star cannot generate sufficient pressure at its center to balance the crushing force of gravity. The star collapses under the force of its own weight; if it is a small star, it collapses gently and remains collapsed. Such a collapsed star, at its life's end, is called a white dwarf. The Sun will probably end its life in this way. A different fate awaits a large star. Its final collapse generates a violent explosion, blowing the innards of the star out into space. There, the materials of the exploded star mix with the primeval hydrogen of the universe. Later in the history of the galaxy, other stars are formed out of this mixture. The Sun is one of these stars. It contains the debris of countless other stars that exploded before the Sun was born.

Supernova 1987A

On Feb. 24, 1987, Canadian astronomer Ian Shelter at the Las Campas Observatory in Chile discovered a supernova—an exploding star—from a photograph taken on Feb. 23 of the Large Megallanic Cloud, a galaxy some 160,000 light years away from Earth. Astronomers believe that the dying star was Sanduleak –69°202, a 10-million-year-old blue supergiant.

Supernova 1987A was the closest and best studied supernova in almost 400 years. The last known one was observed by Johannes Kepler in 1604, four years before the telescope was invented.

Formation of the Solar System

The sun's age was calculated in 1989 to be 4.49 billion years old, less than the 4.7 billion years pre-

Astronomical Constants

Light–year (distance traveled by light in one year)	5,880,000,000,000 mi.
Parsec (parallax of one second, for stellar distances)	3.259 light-yrs.
Velocity of light	186,281.7 mi./sec.
Astronomical unit (A.U.), or mean distance earth-to-sun	ca. 93,000,000 mi.[1]
Mean distance, earth to moon	238,860 mi.
General precession	50".26
Obliquity of the ecliptic	23° 27'8".26–0".4684(t–1900)[2]
Equatorial radius of the earth	3963.34 statute mi.
Polar radius of the earth	3949.99 statute mi.
Earth's mean radius	3958.89 statute mi.
Oblateness of the earth	1/297
Equatorial horizontal parallax of the moon	57' 2".70
Earth's mean velocity in orbit	18.5 mi./sec.
Sidereal year	365d.2564
Tropical year	365d.2422
Sidereal month	27d.3217
Synodic month	29d.5306
Mean sidereal day	23h56m4s.091 of mean solar time
Mean solar day	24h3m56s.555 of sidereal time

1. Actual mean distance derived from radar bounces: 92,935,700 mi. The value of 92,897,400 mi. (based on parallax of 8,.80) is used in calculations. 2. *t* refers to the year in question, for example, 1991.

viously believed. It was formed from a cloud of hydrogen mixed with small amounts of other substances that had been manufactured in the bodies of other stars before the Sun was born. This was the parent cloud of the solar system. The dense hot gas at the center of the cloud gave rise to the Sun; the outer regions of the cloud—cooler and less dense—gave birth to the planets.

Our solar system consists of one star (the Sun), nine planets and all their moons, several thousand minor planets called asteroids or planetoids, and an equally large number of comets.

The Sun

All the stars, including our Sun, are gigantic balls of superheated gas, kept hot by atomic reactions in their centers. In our Sun, this atomic reaction is hydrogen fusion: four hydrogen atoms are combined to form one helium atom. The temperature at the core of our Sun must be 20 million degrees centigrade, the surface temperature is around 6,000 degrees centigrade, or about 11,000 degrees Fahrenheit. The diameter of the sun is 865,400 miles, and its surface area is approximately 12,000 times that of the Earth. Compared with other stars, our Sun is just a bit below average in size and temperature. Its fuel supply (hydrogen) is estimated to last for another 5 billion years.

Our Sun is not motionless in space; in fact it has two proper motions. One is a seemingly straight-line motion in the direction of the constellation Hercules at the rate of about 12 miles per second. But since the Sun is a part of the Milky Way system and since the whole system rotates slowly around its own center, the Sun also moves at the rate of 175 miles per second as part of the rotating Milky Way system.

In addition to this motion, the Sun rotates on its axis. Observing the motion of sun spots (darkish areas which look like enormous whirling storms) and solar flares, which are usually associated with sun spots, has shown that the rotational period of our Sun is just short of 25 days. But this figure is valid for the Sun's equator only; the sections near the Sun's poles seem to have a rotational period of 34 days. Naturally, since the Sun generates its own heat and light, there is no temperature difference between poles and equator.

What we call the Sun's "surface" is technically known as the photosphere. Since the whole Sun is a ball of very hot gas, there is really no such thing as a surfac e; it is a question of visual impression. The next layer outside the photosphere is known as the chromosphere, which extends several thousand miles beyond the photosphere. It is in steady motion, and often enormous prominences can be seen to burst from it, extending as much as 100,000 miles into space. Outside the chromosphere is the corona. The corona consists of very tenuous gases (essentially hydrogen) and makes a magnificent sight when the Sun is eclipsed.

The Moon

Mercury and Venus do not have any moons. Therefore, the Earth is the planet nearest the Sun to be orbited by a moon.

The next planet farther out, Mars, has two very small moons. Jupiter has four major moons and twelve minor ones. Saturn, the ringed planet, has eighteen known moons (and possibly more), of which one (Titan) is larger than the planet Mercury. Uranus has fifteen moons, (four of them large) as well as rings, while Neptune has one large and seven small moons. Pluto has one moon, discovered in 1978. Some astronomers still consider Pluto to be a "runaway moon" of Neptune.

Our own Moon, with a diameter of 2,160 miles, is one of the larger moons in our solar system and is especially large when compared with the planet that it orbits. In fact, the common center of gravity of the Earth-Moon system is only about 1,000 miles below the Earth's surface. The closest our Moon can come to us (its perigee) is 221,463 miles; the farthest it can go away (its apogee) is 252,710 miles. The period of rotation of our Moon is equal to its period of revolution around the Earth. Hence from Earth we can see only one hemisphere of the Moon. Both periods are 27 days, 7 hours, 43 minutes and 11.47 seconds. But while the rotation of the Moon is constant, its velocity in its orbit is not, since it moves more slowly in apogee than in perigee. Consequently, some portions

(Continued on page 333)

Quasars and Cosmology

Source: A Field Guide to the Stars and Planets, Donald H. Menzel and Jay M. Pasachoff.

The Milky Way in Sagittarius. Astonomers believe that there may be a large black hole at the center of our own galaxy, the Milk Way, 30,000 light years away.

Quasars

It came as a surprise in 1960 when some of the sources of celestial radio waves appeared to be point-like—"quasi-stellar"—instead of looking like galaxies. These "quasi-stellar radio sources"—*quasars,* for short—were discovered three years later to be extremely far away, when Maarten Schmidt discovered that the spectrum of one of them showed an extreme redshift. A class of radio-quiet quasars—quasi-stellar objects with huge redshifts—has since been discovered. We now know of over a thousand quasars.

The redshift can be expressed as the fraction or percentage by which the wavelengths of light are shifted. For speeds much slower than the speed of light, this fraction is the same as the fraction that the recession speed of the quasar is of the speed of light. For example, a redshift (called z) of 0.2 means that the wavelengths are shifted toward the red by 0.2 times (20% of) the original wavelength. It is also true that the galaxy or quasar emitting such light is receding from us at 0.2 times the speed of light, or 60,000 km/sec. A quasar with redshift of 1.0 has its wavelengths shifted by 1.0 times (100% of) the original wavelength; each wavelength is doubled. But Einstein's formulas from the special theory of relativity must be used to calculate how fast the quasars are receding; their velocities are always less than the speed of light.

The most distant quasar is redshifted by $z = 3.78$.[1] Few quasars with redshifts greater than 3 (300%) have been found, even though instruments exist that would be sensitive enough to do so. The farther out the quasar is, the farther back in time the light reach

ing us was emitted. That few quasars of the largest redshifts are found indicates that we are seeing back to the instant at which the first quasars were formed—somewhat over 10 billion years ago.

Since quasars are so far away yet still send us some visible light and relatively strong radio radiation, the quasars must be astonishingly bright. Astronomers now agree that giant black holes are probably present in the centers of quasars. These black holes would contain millions of times the mass of the sun. As gas is sucked into the black holes, it heats up and gives off energy. Quasars may be a stage in the evolution of galaxies, for there is evidence that some quasars have structure around them not unlike that of galaxies. Since we see most quasars quite far away, we are seeing them far back in time, and we can conclude that the epoch at which quasars were brightest took place long ago.

Cosmology

Hubble's observations that the most distant galaxies are receding from us faster than closer galaxies can be explained if the universe were expanding in a way similar to the way a giant loaf of raisin bread rises. If you picture yourself as sitting on a raisin, all the other raisins will recede from you as the bread rises. Since there is more dough between you and the more distant raisins, the dough will expand more and the distant raisins will recede more rapidly than closer ones. Similarly, the universe is expanding. We have the same view no matter which raisin or galaxy we are on, so the fact that all raisins and galaxies seem to be receding doesn't say that we are at the center of the universe. Indeed, the universe has no center. (We would have to picture a loaf of raisin bread extending infinitely in all directions to get a more accurate analogy.)

Since the universe is uniformly expanding now, we can ask what happened in the past. As we go back in time, the universe must have been more compressed, until it was at quite a high density 15 billion or so years ago. Most models of the origin of the universe say that there then was a *big bang* that started the expansion. A new model—the *inflationary universe*—holds that the early universe grew larger rapidly for a short time before it settled down to its current rate of expansion. The big bang itself may not have occurred; the first matter could have formed as a chance fluctuation in the nothingness of space.

Astronomers ask what will happen to the universe in the future. The evidence is not all in. One possibility is that the universe is *open*—it will continue to expand forever. Another possibility is that the universe will eventually stop its expansion and begin to contract. We know that this cannot happen for at least 50 billion years more—at least three times longer than the current age of the universe—because we can observe the rate at which the universe is now expanding. Still, if the universe does contract in the long run, then we have a *closed universe* that will wind up in a *big crunch*. The inflationary model indicates that the universe will expand forever, but at a decreasing rate. □

---

1. Astronomers recently discovered a quasar with a redshift of about 4.9 making it the most distant object known. Another newly detected quasar called BR 1202-07 is the most brilliant known object in the universe. Light from this quasar takes 12 million years to reach the Earth.—*Ed.*

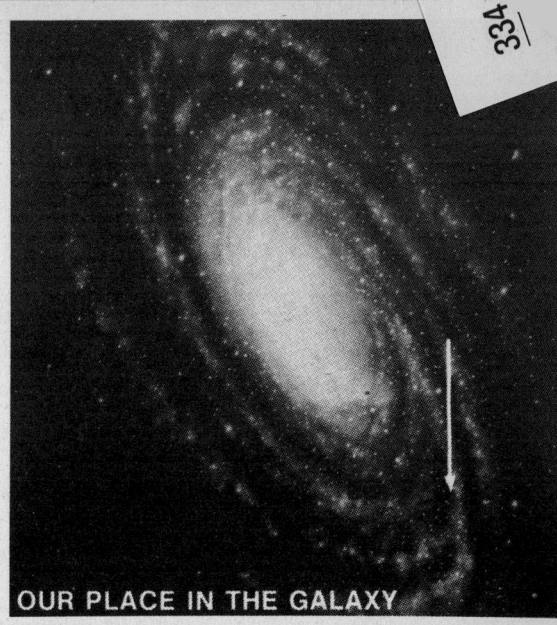

THE MILKY WAY GALAXY. Our sun is one of 200-billion stars banded together by gravity in an enormous spiral disk called the Milky Way Galaxy. The arrow indicates our position three-fifths of the way out from the center. It takes light 100,000 years to traverse our Galaxy, one of billions of galaxies in the universe. Copyright © 1984, Hansen Planetarium, Salt Lake City, Utah. Reproduced with Permission.

OUR PLACE IN THE GALAXY

(Continued from page 331)

near the rim which are not normally visible will appear briefly. This phenomenon is called "libration," and by taking advantage of the librations, astronomers have succeeded in mapping approximately 59% of the lunar surface. The other 41% can never be seen from the earth but has been mapped by American and Russian Moon-orbiting spacecraft.

Though the Moon goes around the Earth in the time mentioned, the interval from new Moon to new Moon is 29 days, 12 hours, 44 minutes and 2.78 seconds. This delay of nearly two days is due to the fact that the Earth is moving around the Sun, so that the Moon needs two extra days to reach a spot in its orbit where no part is illuminated by the Sun, as seen from Earth.

If the plane of the Earth's orbit around the Sun (the ecliptic) and the plane of the Moon's orbit around the Earth were the same, the Moon would be eclipsed by the Earth every time it is full, and the Sun would be eclipsed by the Moon every time the Moon is "new" (it would be better to call it the "black Moon" when it is in this position). But because the two orbits do not coincide, the Moon's shadow normally misses the Earth and the Earth's shadow misses the Moon. The inclination of the two orbital planes to each other is 5 degrees. The tides are, of course, caused by the Moon with the help of the Sun, but in the open ocean they are surprisingly low, amounting to about one yard. The very high tides which can be observed near the shore in some places are due to funnelling effects of the shorelines. At new Moon and at full Moon the tides raised by the Moon are reinforced by the Sun; these are the "spring tides." If the Sun's tidal power acts at right angles to that of the Moon (quarter moons) we get the low "neap tides."

Our Planet Earth

The Earth, circling the Sun at an average distance of 93 million miles, is the fifth largest planet and the

third from the Sun. It orbits the Sun at a speed of 67,000 miles per hour, making one revolution in 365 days, 5 hours, 48 minutes, and 45.51 seconds. The Earth completes one rotation on its axis every 23 hours, 56 minutes, and 4.09 seconds. Actually a bit pear-shaped rather than a true sphere, the Earth has a diameter of 7,927 miles at the Equator and a few miles less at the poles. It has an estimated mass of about 6.6 sextillion tons, with an average density of 5.52 grams per cubic centimeter. The Earth's surface area encompasses 196,949,970 square miles of which about three-fourths is water.

Origin of the Earth. The Earth, along with the other planets, is believed to have been born 4.5 billion years ago as a solidified cloud of dust and gases left over from the creation of the Sun. For perhaps 500 million years, the interior of the Earth stayed solid and relatively cool, perhaps 2000° F. The main ingredients, according to the best available evidence, were iron and silicates, with small amounts of other elements, some of them radioactive. As millions of years passed, energy released by radioactive decay—mostly of uranium, thorium, and potassium—gradually heated the Earth, melting some of its consituents. The iron melted before the silicates, and, being heavier, sank toward the center. This forced upward the silicates that it found there. After many years, the iron reached the center, almost 4,000 miles deep, and began to accumulate. No eyes were around at that time to view the turmoil which must have taken place on the face of the Earth—gigantic heaves and bubbling of the surface, exploding volcanoes, and flowing lava covering everything in sight. Finally, the iron in the center accumulated as the core. Around it, a thin but fairly stable crust of solid rock formed as the Earth cooled. Depressions in the crust were natural basins in which water, rising from the interior of the planet through volcanoes and fissures, collected

The Brightest Stars

Star	Constellation	Mag.	Dist. (l.-y.)	Star	Constellation	Mag.	Dist. (l.-y.)
Sirius	Canis Major	−1.6	8	Antares	Scorpius	1.2	170
Canopus	Carina	−0.9	650	Fomalhaut	Piscis Austrinus	1.3	27
Alpha Centauri	Centaurus	+0.1	4	Deneb	Cygnus	1.3	465
Vega[1]	Lyra	0.1	23	Regulus	Leo	1.3	70
Capella	Auriga	0.2	42	Beta Crucis	Crux	1.5	465
Arcturus	Boötes	0.2	32	Eta Carinae	Carina	1–7	—
Rigel	Orion	0.3	545	Alpha-one Crucis	Crux	1.6	150
Procyon	Canis Minor	0.5	10	Castor	Gemini	1.6	44
Achernar	Eridanus	0.6	70	Gamma Crucis	Crux	1.6	—
Beta Centari	Centaurus	0.9	130	Epsilon Canis Majoris	Canis Major	1.6	325
Altair	Aquila	0.9	18	Epsilon Ursae Majoris	Ursa Major	1.7	50
Betelgeuse	Orion	0.9	600	Bellatrix	Orion	1.7	215
Aldebaran	Taurus	1.1	54	Lambda Scorpii	Scorpius	1.7	205
Spica	Virgo	1.2	190	Epsilon Carinae	Carina	1.7	325
Pollux	Gemini	1.2	31	Mira	Cetus	2–10	250

1. In 1984, the discovery of a possible planetary system around Vega was reported.

to form the oceans. Slowly the Earth acquired its present appearance.

The Earth Today. As a result of radioactive heating over millions of years, the Earth's molten *core* is probably fairly hot today, around 11,000° F. By comparison, lead melts at around 800° F. Most of the Earth's 2,100-mile-thick core is liquid, but there is evidence that the center of the core is solid. The liquid outer portion, about 95% of the core, is constantly in motion, causing the Earth to have a magnetic field that makes compass needles point north and south. The details are not known, but the latest evidence suggests that planets which have a magnetic field probably have a solid core or a partially liquid one.

Outside the core is the Earth's *mantle,* 1,800 miles thick, and extending nearly to the surface. The mantle is composed of heavy silicate rock, similar to that brought up by volcanic eruptions. It is somewhere between liquid and solid, slightly yielding, and therefore contributing to an active, moving Earth. Most of the Earth's radioactive material is in the thin *crust* which covers the mantle, but some is in the mantle and continues to give off heat. The crust's thickness ranges from 5 to 25 miles.

Scientists recently discovered that the Earth's core is not a perfect sphere. X-ray like images of inside the Earth show that there are vast mountains six to seven miles high and deep valleys on the core. These features are in an upside down relationship to the Earth's surface.

Continental Drift. A great deal of recent evidence confirms the theory that the continents of the Earth, made mostly of relatively light granite, float in the slightly yielding mantle, like logs in a pond. For many years it had been noticed that if North and South America could be pushed toward western and southern Europe and western Africa, they would fit like pieces in a jigsaw puzzle. Today, there is little question—the continents have drifted widely and continue to do so.

In 10 million years, the world as we know it may be unrecognizable, with California drifting out to sea, Florida joining South America, and Africa moving farther away from Europe and Asia.

The Earth's Atmosphere. The thin blanket of atmosphere that envelops the Earth extends several hundred miles into space. From sea level—the very bottom of the ocean of air—to a height of about 60 miles, the air in the atmosphere is made up of the same gases in the same ratio: about 78% nitrogen, 21% oxygen, and the remaining 1% being a mixture of argon, carbon dioxide, and tiny amounts of neon, helium, krypton, xenon, and other gases. The atmosphere becomes less dense with increasing altitude: more than three-fourths of the Earth's huge envelope is concentrated in the first 5 to 10 miles above the surface. At sea level, a cubic foot of the atmosphere weighs about an ounce and a quarter. The entire atmosphere weighs 5,700,000,000,000,000 tons, and the force with which gravity holds it in place causes it to exert a pressure of nearly 15 pounds per square inch. Going out from the Earth's surface, the atmosphere is divided into five regions. The regions, and the heights to which they extend, are: *Troposphere,* 0 to 7 miles (at middle latitudes); *stratosphere,* 7 to 30 miles; *mesosphere,* 30 to 50 miles; *thermosphere,* 50 to 400 miles; and *exosphere,* above 400 miles. The boundaries between each of the regions are known respectively as the *tropopause, stratopause, mesopause,* and *thermopause.* Alternate terms often used for the layers above the troposphere are *ozonosphere* (for stratosphere) and *ionosphere* for the remaining upper layers.

The Seasons. Seasons are caused by the 23.4 degree tilt of the Earth's axis, which alternately turns the North and South Poles toward the Sun. Times when the Sun's apparent path crosses the Equator are known as *equinoxes.* Times when the Sun's apparent path is at the greatest distance from the Equator are known as *solstices.* The lengths of the days are most extreme at each solstice. If the Earth's axis were perpendicular to the plane of the Earth's orbit around the Sun, there would be no seasons, and the days always would be equal in length. Since the Earth's axis is at an angle, the Sun strikes the Earth directly at the Equator only twice a year: in March (vernal equinox) and September (autumnal equinox). In the Northern Hemisphere, spring begins at the vernal equinox, summer at the summer solstice, fall at the autumnal equinox, and winter at the winter solstice. The situation is reversed in the Southern Hemisphere.

PLANET SIZES

PLANET SIZES. Shown from left to right: Mercury, Venus, Earth, Mars, Ju piter, Saturn, Uranus, Neptune, and Pluto.

Copyright © 1984 Hansen Planetarium, Salt Lake City, Utah. Reproduced with Permission.

Basic Planetary Data

	Mercury	Venus	Earth	Mars	Jupiter
Mean distance from Sun (Millions of kilometers)	57.9	108.2	149.6	227.9	778.3
(Millions of miles)	36.0	67.24	92.9	141.71	483.88
Period of revolution	88 days	224.7 days	365.2 days	687 days	11.86 yrs
Rotation period	59 days	243 days retrograde	23 hr 56 min 4 sec	24 hr 37 min	9 hr 55 min 30 sec
Inclination of axis	Near 0°	3°	23°27′	25°12′	3°5′
Inclination of orbit to ecliptic	7°	3.4°	0°	1.9°	1.3°
Eccentricity of orbit	.206	.007	.017	.093	.048
Equatorial diameter (Kilometers)	4,880	12,100	12,756	6,794	142,800
(Miles)	3,032.4	7,519	7,926.2	4,194	88,736
Atmosphere (Main components)	Virtually none	Carbon dioxide	Nitrogen oxygen	Carbon dioxide	Hydrogen helium
Satellites	0	0	1	2	16
Rings	0	0	0	0	1

	Saturn	Uranus	Neptune	Pluto
Mean distance from Sun (Millions of kilometers)	1,427	2,870	4,497	5,900
(Millions of miles)	887.14	1,783.98	2,796.46	3,666
Period of revolution	29.46 yrs	84 yrs	165 yrs	248 yrs
Rotation period	10 hr 40 min 24 sec	16.8 hr(?) retrograde	16 hr 11 min(?)	6 days 9 hr 18 mins retrograde
Inclination of axis	26°44′	97°55′	28°48′	60° (?)
Inclination of orbit to ecliptic	2.5°	0.8°	1.8°	17.2°
Eccentricity of orbit	.056	.047	.009	.254
Equatorial diameter (Kilometers)	120,660	51,810	49,528	2,290 (?)
(Miles)	74,978	32,193	30,775	1,423 (?)
Atmosphere (Main components)	Hydrogen helium	He lium hydrogen methane	Hydrogen helium methane	None detected
Satellites	18+[1]	15	8	1
Rings	1,000 (?)	11	4	?

1. 1981 S13 discovered from *Voyager* photos in 1990. *Source:* Basic NASA data and other sources.

THE SOLAR SYSTEM

THE SOLAR SYSTEM. Orbiting around the Sun are Mercury, Venus, Earth, Mars, Jupiter, Saturn, Uranus, Neptune, and Pluto. Our Solar System was born nearly five billion years ago out of a cloud of interstellar gas and dust. Gravity caused this nebula to contract and flatten into a spinning disk. Near the center, where the density was greatest, a body formed which was so massive that its internal pressures ignited and sustained a nuclear reaction, creating a star we call the Sun. Elsewhere in the cloud, smaller bodies coalesced and cooled—nine planets, perhaps fifty moons, millions of asteroids, and billions of comets. Within our Milky Way Galaxy, there may be billions of other solar systems. Copyright © 1984 Hansen Planetarium, Salt Lake City, Utah. Reproduced with Permission.

Mercury

Mercury is the planet nearest the Sun. Appropriately named for the wing-footed Roman messenger of the gods, Mercury whizzes around the Sun at a speed of 30 miles per second completing one circuit in 88 days. The days and nights are long on Mercury. It takes 59 Earth days for Mercury to make a single rotation. It spins at a rate of about 10 kilometers (about 6 miles) per hour, measured at the equator, as compared to the Earth's spin of about 1,600 kilometers (about 1,000 miles) per hour at the equator.

The photographs *Mariner 10* (1974–75) radioed back to Earth revealed an ancient, heavily cratered surface on Mercury, closely resembling our own Moon. The pictures showed huge cliffs, or scarps, crisscrossing the planet. These apparently were created when Mercury's interior cooled and shrank, compressing the planet's crust. The cliffs are as high as two kilometers (1.2 miles) and as long as 1,500 kilometers (932 miles). Another unique feature is the Caloris Basin, a large impact crater about 1,300 kilometers (808 miles) in diameter.

Mercury, like the Earth, appears to have a crust of light silicate rock. Scientists believe it has a heavy iron-rich core that makes up about half of its volume. Instruments onboard *Mariner 10* discovered that the planet has a weak magnetic field and a trace of atmosphere—a trillionth the density of the Earth's and comp osed chiefly of argon, neon, and helium. The spacecraft reported temperatures ranging from 510° C (950° F) on Mercury's sunlit side to –210° C (–346° F) on the dark side. Mercury literally bakes in daylight and freezes at night.

Until the *Mariner 10* probe, little was known about the planet. Even the best telescopic views from Earth showed Mercury as an indistinct object lacking any surface detail. The planet is so close to the Sun that it is usually lost in the Sun's glare.

• Mercury is a naked eye object at morning or evening twilight when it is at greatest elongation.

Venus

Although Venus is Earth's closest neighbor, very little is known about the planet because it is permanently covered with thick clouds. In 1962, Soviet and American space probes, coupled with Earth-based radar and infrared spectroscopy, began slowly unraveling some of the mystery surrounding Venus. Twenty-eight years later, the *Magellan* spacecraft sent by the United States arrived at Venus in August 1990 and began radar-mapping the planet's surface in greater detail.

According to the latest results, Venus' atmosphere exerts a pressure at the surface 94.5 times greater than Earth's. Walking on Venus would be as difficult as walking a half-mile beneath the ocean. Because of a thick blanket of carbon dioxide, a "greenhouse effect" exists on Venus. Venus intercepts twice as much of the Sun's light as does the Earth. The light enters freely through the carbon dioxide gas and is changed to heat radiation in molecular collisions. But carbon dioxide prevents the heat from escaping. Consequently, the temperature of the surface of Venus is over 800° F, hot enough to melt lead.

The atmospheric composition of Venus is about 96% carbon dioxide, 4% nitrogen, and minor amounts of water, oxygen, and sulfur compounds. There are at least four distinct cloud and haze layers that exist at different altitudes above the planet's surface. The haze layers contain small aerosol particles, possibly droplets of sulfuric acid. A concentration of sulfur dioxide above the cloud tops has been observerd to be decreasing since 1978. The source of sulfur dioxide at this altitude is unknown; it may be injected by volcanic explosions or atmospheric overturning.

Measurements of the Venusian atmosphere and its cloud patterns reveal nearly constant high-speed zonal winds, about 100 meters per second (220 miles per hour) at the equator. The winds decrease toward the poles so that the atmosphere at cloud-top level rot ates almost like a solid body. The wind speeds at the equator correspond to Venus' rotation period of four to five days at most latitudes. The circulation is always in the same direction—east to west—as Venus' slow retrograde motion. Earth's winds blow from west to east, the same direction as its rotation.

Venus is quite round, very different from the other planets and from the Moon. Venus has neither polar flattening nor an equatorial bulge. The diameter of Venus is 12,100 kilometers (7,519 miles). Venus has a retrograde axial rotation period of 243.1 Earth days. The surface atmospheric pressure is 1,396 pounds per square inch (95 Earth atmospheres). The planet's mean distance from the Sun is 108.2 million kilometers (67.2 million miles). The period of its revolution around the Sun is 224.7 days.

The highest point on Venus is the summit of Maxwell Montes, 10.8 kilometers (6.71 miles) above the mean level, more than a mile taller than Mount Everest. There is some evidence that this huge mountain is an active volcano. The lowest point is in the rift valley, Diana Chasma, 2.9 kilometers (1.8 miles) below the mean level. This point is about one-fifth the greatest depth on Earth in the Marianas Trench.

Venus has an extreme lowland basin, Atalanta Planitia, which is about the size of Earth's North Atlantic Ocean basin. The smooth surface of the Atalanta Planitia resembles the mare basins of the Moon.

There are only two highland or continental masses on Venus: Ishtar Terra and Aphrodite Terra. Ishtar Terra is 11 kilometers (6.8 miles) at its highest points (the highest peaks on Venus) and those of Aphrodite Terra rise to about 5 kilometers (3.10 miles) above the planet. Ishtar Terra is about the size of the continental United States and Aphrodite Terra is about the size of Africa.

Scientists are yet uncertain if Venus is geologically active. Lightning which was interpreted to result from active volcanism has been inferred from *Pioneer Venus Orbiter* electric measurements but the signals attributed to lightning may be the result of other causes.

The unmanned NASA spacecraft *Magellan* was launched on May 4, 1989, from the shuttle *Atlantis* and arrived at Venus Aug. 10, 1990, to map most of the planet. Despite some problems with its radio transmissions, the results of the radar mapping delighted scientists and provided them with the sharpest images ever taken of the planet's surface. Images taken from *Magellan* show ten times more detail than ever seen before.

By May 15, 1991, *Magellan* completed its first radar probings around Venus and had successfully mapped 84% of the planet's surface. By the end of 1991, all of the planet will have been mapped. (Also see *Magellan* in the Space Section.)

• Venus is the brightest of all the planets and is often visible in the morning or evening, when it is frequently referred to as the Morning Star or Evening Star. At its brightest, it can sometimes be seen with the naked eye in full daylight, if one knows where to look.

Magellan radar image of Western Ishtar Terra, an Australia-sized highland in the planet's northern hemisphere. The highland is centered on a 1.5 to 2.5 miles (2.5 to 4 kilometer) high plateau, Lakshmi Planum which can be seen in the distance and to the right. Black stripes reflect area where information was not collected. NASA.

Magellan radar image of Golubkina Crater on Venus. The impact crater is 20.4 miles (34 kilometers) in diameter. NASA.

Giant Olympus Mons, the tallest volcano on Mars, is also the highest mountain in the solar system. It is 540 kilometers (336 miles) across and rises 10 miles higher than Mount Everest. NASA photo.

Phobos, Mars' tiny inner moon, is covered with a large number of craters.

Mars

Mars, on the other side of the Earth from Venus, is Venus' direct opposite in terms of physical properties. Its atmosphere is cold, thin, and transparent, and readily permits observation of the planet's features. We know more about Mars than any other planet except Earth. Mars is a forbidding, rugged planet with huge volcanoes and deep chasms. The largest volcano, Olympus Mons (Olympic Mountain) rises 78,000 feet above the surface, higher than Mount Everest. The plains of Mars are pockmarked by the hits of thousands of meteors over the years.

Most of our information about Mars comes from the Mariner 9 spacecraft, which orbited the planet in 1971. Mariner 9, photographing 100% of the planet, uncovered spectacular geological formations, including a Martian Grand Canyon that dwarfs the one on Earth. Called Valles Marineris (Mariner Valley) it stretches more than 3,000 miles along the equatorial region of Mars and is over 4 kilometers (2.5 miles) deep in places and 80 to 100 kilometers (50 to 62 miles) wide. The spacecraft's cameras also recorded what appeared to be dried riverbeds, suggesting the onetime presence of water on the planet. The latter idea gives encouragement to scientists looking for life on Mars, for where there is water, there may be life. However, to date, no evidence of life has been found. Temperatures near the equator range from –17 degrees F. in the daytime to –130 degrees F. at night.

None of these probes have clearly shown whether Mars has its own magnetic field. Scientists hope that the *Mars Observer*, scheduled for a 1992 launch, will provide a conclusive answerr. (See *Mars Observer* in Space Section.)

Mars rotates upon its axis in nearly the same period as Earth—24 hours, 37 minutes—so that a Mars day is almost identical to an Earth day. Mars takes 687 days to make one trip around the Sun. Because of its eccentric orbit Mars' distance from the Sun can vary by about 36 million miles. Its distance from Earth can vary by as much as 200 million miles. The atmosphere of Mars is much thinner than Earth's; atmospheric pressure is about 1% that of our planet. Its gravity is one-third of Earth's. Major constituents are carbon dioxide and nitrogen. Water vapor and oxygen are minor constituents. Mars' polar caps, composed mostly of frozen carbon dioxide (dry ice), recede and advance according to the Martian seasons.

Scientists have not yet determined if the Martian snow (as water ice or carbon dioxide particles) actually crystallizes on the polar caps or whether it falls from the clouds over them.

Mars has four seasons like Earth, but they are much longer. For example, in the northern hemisphere, the Martian spring is 198 days, and the winter season lasts 158 days.

Mars was named for the Roman god of war, because when seen from Earth its distinct red color reminded the ancient people of blood. We know now that the reddish hue reflects the oxidized (rusted) iron in the surface material. The landing of two robot Viking spacecraft on the surface of Mars in 1976 provided more information about Mars in a few months than in all the time that has gone before.

The Martian Moons

Mars has two very small elliptical-shaped moons, Deimos and Phobos—the Greek names for the companions of the God Mars: Deimos (Terror) and Phobos (Fear). They were discovered in August 1877 by the American astronomer Asaph Hall (1829–1907) of the U.S. Naval Observatory in Washington, D.C.

The inner satellite Phobos is 27 kilometers (16.78 miles) long and it revolves around the planet in 7.6 hours. The outer moon, Deimos, is 15 kilometers (9.32 miles) long and it circles the planet in 30.35 hours. The short orbital period of Phobos means that the satellite travels around Mars twice in a Martian day. If an observer were suitably situated on the planet, he would see Phobos rise and set twice in a day.

Recent studies of Phobos indicate that its orbit is slowly decreasing downward and that in approximately 40 million years, it will crash into the planet's surface.

In 1988, the Soviet Union launched two spacecraft to study the geology, climate, and atmosphere of Mars, and explore its moon, Phobos. The attempt was unsuccessful as contact was lost with both spacecraft.

The Soviet Union plans to make unmanned studies of the Martian atmosphere and surface during 1994 to 1996. (*Also see* Space Section.)

Meteorites From Mars

Our knowledge of the origin and history of Mars has been greatly enhanced by recent research showing that a group of eight meteorites, labeled SNC[1] (named for towns where they were found: Shergotty, India, in 1865; Nakhla, Egypt, in 1911; and Chassigny, France, in 1815), are probably samples of Mars. This hypothesis is based largely on the composition of noble gases (particularly argon and xenon) trapped in the meteorites, and the Shergottites in particular, which resemble measurements of the Martian atmosphere made by the *Viking* spacecraft. Major element compositions of the SNCs are also similar to Martian soil analyses made by *Viking*.

These meteorites suggest that the Martian mantle is two to four times richer than Earth in moderately volatile elements such as potassium, rubidium, chlorine, bromine, sodium, zinc, and lead. In contrast, nitrogen, carbon dioxide, and the noble gases are more depleted than expected in the Martian atmosphere, suggesting an episode of severe atmospheric loss at some time in its history.

The relatively young isotopic ages of the SNC meteorites (1.3 billion years or less) suggest that Mars has been volcanically active during its recent past.

Scientists do not know how the meteorites were thrown off the Martian surface.

1. Pronounced "snick."

Jupiter

Jupiter is the largest planet in the solar system—a gaseous world as large as 1,300 Earths. Its equatorial diameter is 142,800 kilometers (88,736 miles), while from pole to pole, Jupiter measures only 133,500 kilometers (84,201 miles). For comparison, the diameter of the Earth is 12,756 kilometers (7,926.2 miles). The massive planet rotates at a dizzying speed—once every 9 hours and 55 minutes. It takes Jupiter almost 12 Earth years to complete a journey around the Sun.

The giant planet appears as a banded disk of turbulent clouds with all of its stripes running parallel to its bulging equator. Large dusky gray regions surround each pole. Darker Gray or brown stripes called belts intermingle with lighter, yellow-white stripes called zones. The belts are regions of descending air

Jupiter's ring. A line has been drawn around a photograph of Jupiter to show the position of the extremely thin faint ring. NASA photo.

masses and the zones are rising cloudy air masses. The strongest winds—up to 400 kilometers (250 miles) per hour—are found at boundaries between the belts and zones.

This uniquely colorful atmosphere is mainly hydrogen and helium. It contains small amounts of methane, ammonia, ethane, acetylene, phosphene, germanium tetrahydride, and possibly hydrogen cyanide.

Cloud-type lightning bolts similar to those on Earth have been found in the Jovian atmosphere. At the polar regions, auroras have been observed. A very thin ring of material less than one kilometer (0.6 mile) in thickness and about 6,000 kilometers (4,000 miles) in radial extent has been observed circling the planet about 55,000 kilometers (35,000 miles) above the cloud tops.

The most prominent feature on Jupiter is its Great Red Spot, an oval larger than the planet Earth. It is a tremendous atmospheric storm that rotates counter-clockwise with one revolution every six days at the outer edge, while at the center almost no motion can be seen. The Spot is about 25,000 kilometers (16,000 miles) on its long axis, and would cover three Earths. The outer rim shows streamline shapes of 360-kilometer (225-mile) winds. Wind currents on the top flow east to west and currents on the top flow east to west and currents on the bottom flow west to east. The color of the Great Red Spot may indicate that it extends deep into the Jovian atmosphere.

The Spot was first seen more than three centuries ago. During the years, it has changed its color and size, and it escaped detection for nearly 50 years in the 1700s. *Voyager 1* and *2* found the Great Red Spot to be cooler at the top than the surrounding clouds, indicating that the Spot may tower above them.

Jupiter emits 67% more heat than it absorbs from the Sun. This heat is thought to be accumulated during the planet's formation several billion years ago.

Jovian Moons

The four great moons of Jupiter were discovered by Galileo Galilei (1564–1642) in January 1610, and are called the Galilean satellites after their discoverer. Their names are Io, Europa, Ganymede, and Callisto. Like our Moon, the satellites always keep the same face turned toward the Earth. Jupiter has 16 known satellites.

Ganymede

Ganymede, 5,270 kilometers (3,275 miles) in diameter, is Jupiter's largest moon, and also it is the largest satellite in the solar system. Ganymede is about one and one-half times the size of our Moon. It is heavily cratered and probably has the greatest variety of geologic process recorded on its surface. Ganymede is half water and half rock, resulting in a density about two-thirds that of Europa, an ice-coated satellite. No atmosphere has been detected on it.

Europa

Europa, 3,130 kilometers (1,945 miles) in diameter, the brightest of Jupiter's Galilean satellites, may have a surface of thin ice crust overlying water or softer ice, with large-scale fracture and ridge systems appearing in the crust. Europa has a density about three times that of water, suggesting that it is a mixture of silicate rock and some water. Very few impact craters are visible on the surface, implying a continual resurfacing process, perhaps by the production of fresh ice or snow along cracks and cold glacier-like flows.

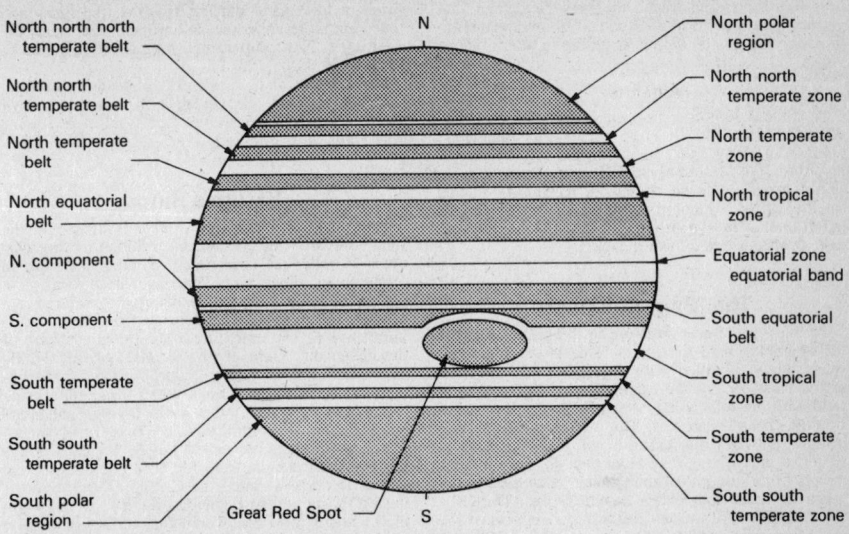

North north north temperate belt

North north temperate belt

North temperate belt

North equatorial belt

N. component

S. component

South temperate belt

South south temperate belt

South polar region

Great Red Spot

N

S

North polar region

North north temperate zone

North temperate zone

North tropical zone

Equatorial zone equatorial band

South equatorial belt

South tropical zone

South temperate zone

South south temperate zone

Schematic diagram of Jupiter's major features. NASA illustration.

Ganymede, Jupiter's largest satellite and also the largest known moon in the solar system. Its diverse surface indicates several periods of geologic activity.

A computer-generated image of Io, the most volcanically active planetary body known in the solar system. Io's volcanoes and lava lakes cover the landscape and continually reface it, so that many impact craters have disappeared. NASA photo.

Callisto

Callisto, 4,840 kilometers (3,008 miles) in diameter, is the least active geologically of the Galilean satellites. Its icy, dirt-laden surface appears to be very ancient and heavily cratered. Callisto's density (less than twice that of water) is very close to that of Ganymede, yet there is little or no evidence of the crustal motion and internal activity that is visible on Ganymede.

Io

Io, 3,640 kilometers (2,262 miles) in diameter, is the most spectacular of the Galilean moons. Its bril-

liant colors of red, orange, and yellow set it apart from any other planet. Eight active volcanoes have been detected on Io, with some plumes extending up to 320 kilometers (200 miles) above the surface. The relative smoothness of Io's surface and its volcanic activity suggest that it has the youngest surface of Jupiter's moons. Its surface is composed of large amounts of sulfur and sulfur-dioxide frost, which account for the primarily yellow-orange surface color.

The volcanoes seem to eject a sufficient amount of sulfur dioxide to form a doughnut-shaped ring (torus) of ionized sulfur and oxygen atoms around Jupiter near Io's orbit. The Jovian magnetic field lines that go through the torus allow particles to precipitate into the polar regions of Jupiter, resulting in intense ultraviolet and visible auroras.

Amalthea

Amalthea, Jupiter's most innermost satellite, was discovered in 1892. It is so small—265 kilometers (165 miles) long and 150 kilometers (90 miles) wide—that it is extremely difficult to observe from Earth. Amalthea is an elongated, irregularly shaped satellite of reddish color. It orbits the planet every 12 hours and is in synchronous rotation, with its long axis always oriented toward Jupiter.

The Magnetosphere

Perhaps the largest structure in the solar system is the magnetosphere of Jupiter. This is the region of space which is filled with Jupiter's magnetic field and is bounded by the interaction of that magnetic field with the solar wind, which is the Sun's outward flow of charged particles. The plasma of electrically charged particles that exists in the magnetosphere is flattened into a large disk more than 4.8 million kilometers (3 million miles) in diameter, is coupled to the magnetic field, and rotates around Jupiter. The Galilean satellites are located in the inner regions of the magnetosphere and are subjected to intense radiation bombardment.

The intense radiation field that surrounds Jupiter is fatal to humans. If astronauts were one day able to approach the planet as close as the *Voyager 1* spacecraft did, they would receive a dose of 400,000 rads or roughly 1,000 times the lethal dose for humans.

In 1989, evidence from ground-based infrared spectra of Io indicated that the Jovian moon has hydrogen sulfide (H_2S) on its surface and in its atmosphere. It is the first time that the presence of H_2S has been detected outside the Earth.

• Even when nearest the Earth, Jupiter is still almost 400 million miles away. But because of its size, it may rival Venus in brilliance when near. Jupiter's four large moons may be seen through field glasses, moving rapidly around Jupiter and changing their position from night to night.

The United States launched its *Galileo* spacecraft toward Jupiter on Oct. 18, 1989. The unmanned spacecraft will reach Jupiter in 1995 and make a 22-month study of the planet.

Saturn

Saturn, the second largest planet in the solar system, is the least dense. Its mass is 95 times the mass of the Earth and its density is 0.70 gram per cubic centimeter, so that it would float in an ocean if there were one big enough to hold it.

Saturn radiates more energy than it receives from the Sun, about 80% more. However, the excess thermal energy cannot be primarily attributed to Saturn's primordial heat loss, as is speculated for Jupiter.

Saturn's diameter is 120,660 kilometers (74,978 miles) but 10% less at the poles, a consequence of its rapid rotation. Its axis of rotation is tilted by 27 degrees and the length of its day is 10 hours, 39 minutes, and 24 seconds.

Saturn is composed primarily of liquid metallic hydrogen (about 80%) and the second most common element is believed to be helium.

Saturn's atmospheric appearance is very similar to Jupiter's with dark and light cloud markings and

swirls, eddies, and curling ribbons; the belts and zones are more numerous and a thick haze mutes the markings. The temperature ranges from 80° K to 90° K (176° F to −203° F).

Winds blow at extremely high speeds on Saturn. Near the equator, the *Voyagers* measured winds of about 500 meters per second (1,100 miles per hour). The winds blow primarily in an eastward direction.

Saturn's Rings

Saturn's spectacular ring system is unique in the solar system, with uncountable billions of tiny particles of water ice (with traces of other material) in orbit around the planet. The ring particles range in size from smaller than grains of sugar to as large as a house. The main rings stretch out from about 7,000 kilometers (4,350 miles) to above the atmosphere of the planet out to the F ring, a total span of 74,000 kilometers (45,984 miles). Saturn's rings can be likened to a phonograph, rings within rings numbering in the hundreds, and spokes in the B rings, and shepherding satellites controlling the F ring.

The main rings are called the A, B, and C rings moving from outside to inside. The gap between the A and B rings is called the Cassini Division and is named for the Italian-French astronomer, Gian Domenico Cassini, who discovered four of Saturn's major moons and the dark, narrow gap, "Cassini's Division," splitting the planet's rings.

Saturn's magnetic field has well-defined north and south magnetic poles, and is aligned with Saturn's axis of rotation to within one degree.

Saturn's Moons

Saturn has 18 recognized moons and there is evidence for several more. The five largest moons, Tethys, Dione, Rhea, Titan, and Iapetus, range from 1060 to 5150 kilometers (650 to 3,200 miles) in diameter. The planet's outstanding satellite is Titan, first discovered by the Dutch astronomer Christiaan Huygens in 1656.

Titan

Titan is remarkable because it is the only known moon in the solar system that has a substantial atmosphere—largely nitrogen with a minor amount of methane and a rich variety of other hydrocarbons. Its surface is completely hidden from view (except at infrared and radio wavelengths) by a dense, hazy atmosphere.

The diameter of Titan is 5,150 kilometers (3,200 miles) and it is the second largest satellite in the solar system after Jupiter's Ganymede. Titan is larger than the planet Mercury.

Titan's surface temperature is about −175° C (−280° F) and its surface pressure is about 50% greater than the surface pressure of the Earth. After the Voyager I flyby in 1980, scientists hypothesized that Titan may have an ocean of liquid hydrogen covering its surface. However, in 1990 it was shown that Titan's surface reflects and scatters radio waves, suggesting that the satellite has a solid surface with the possibility of small hydrocarbon lakes.

The new data was obtained by using NASA's 70-meter antenna in California to transmit powerful radio waves to Titan, and the Very Large Array in New Mexico as the receiver of the reflected waves.

NASA plans to send a scientific probe to the surface of Titan in August 2002 as part of its Cassini Mission. The probe will be provided by the European

Photo of icy Mimias shows the largest meteorite crater which is about one-quarter the diameter of the entire moon. A huge mountain can be seen rising up almost 20,000 feet from the center of the crater. The crater's walls average 16,000 feet in height. NASA photo.

NASA illustration of the divisions in Saturn's ring system.

Space Agency (ESA). For further details, see the "Cassini Mission" in the special *Space* section of *Information Please Almanac.*

Other Notable Saturnian Moons

The other four largest moons of Saturn are: Tethys, Dione, Rhea, and Iapetus.

Tethys is 1,060 kilometers (650 miles) in diameter. Its surface is heavily cratered and it has a huge, globe-girdling canyon, Ithaca Chasma. Part of the canyon stretches over three-quarters of the satellite's surface. Ithaca Chasma is about 2,500 kilometers (1,550 miles) long. It has an average width of about 100 kilometers (62 miles) and a depth of 3 to 5 kilometers (1.8 to 3.1 miles).

Tethys also has a huge impact crater named Odysseus, 400 kilometers (244 miles) in diameter, or more than one-third its diameter.

Dione is slightly larger than Tethys, 1,120 kilometers (696 miles) and is more than half composed of water ice. It has bright, wispy markings resembling thin veils covering its features.

Rhea, the largest of the inner satellites, is 1,530 kilometers (951 miles) in diameter. It is composed mainly of water ice, causing its reflective surface to present an almost uniform white appearance.

Iapetus is the outermost of Saturn's icy satellites. Its appearance is unique because it has one dark and one bright hemisphere. The origin of the black coating of its dark face is unknown. Iapetus has a diameter of 1,460 kilometers (907 miles).

Other notable moons of Saturn are Mimas, Enceladus, Hyperion, and Phoebe.

Mimas is small, only 329 kilometers (244 miles) in diameter. It has a huge impact crater, Herschel, nearly one-third its diameter. The crater is about 130 kilometers (81 miles) wide and its icy peak rises almost 10 kilometers (6.2 miles) above the floor.

Mimas is believed to be composed mainly of water ice and to co ntain between 20 to 50% rock.

Enceladus is remarkable in that its surface shows signs of extensive and recent geological activity. There may be active water volcanism. The surface is extremely bright, reflecting more than 90% of incident sunlight. This suggests that its surface is composed of extremely pure ice without dust or rocks to contaminate it.

Enceladus has a diameter of 500 kilometers (310 miles).

Hyperion orbits between Iapetus and Titan. It is irregular in shape, measuring about 400 by 250 by 200 kilometers (248 by 155 by 124 miles). It may be a remnant of a much larger object which was shattered by impact with another space body. It appears that Hyperion is composed primarily of water ice.

Hyperion orbits Saturn in a randon-like motion ("chaotic tumbling").

Phoebe is Saturn's outermost satellite. It travels in a retrograde orbit at a distance of over 10 million kilometers (6.2 million miles) away from the planet. It is the darkest moon of Saturn and is the planet's only known satellite that does not keep the same face always turned to Saturn. It has been speculated that it is an asteroid that was captured by the planet.

The Uranian moon Miranda is one of the strangest objects in the solar system. Photo shows some of its complex surface terrain. NASA photo.

Phoebe rotates in about nine hours and orbits Saturn in 406 days. It has a diameter of 200 kilometers (124 miles).

1981 S13 discovered in 1990 from *Voyager 2* photos taken in 1981. An official name, Pan, is to be approved by the International Astronomical Union. The satellite is estimated to be about 20 kilometers (12.43 miles) in diameter, which makes it the planet's smallest known moon. It orbits within the Encke Gap, a 325-kilometer (202 mile) division in Saturn's A ring. It was identified by Johann Franz Encke (1791–1865) in 1837.

The remaining eight moons range from 25 to 190 kilometers (15 to 120 miles) in diameter. They are all non-spherical in shape.

NASA's planned Cassini Mission to Saturn in the later 1990s will shed more light on the planet's mysteries. (*See* Cassini Mission in the Space Section.)

• Saturn is the last of the planets visible to the naked eye. Saturn is never an object of overwhelming brilliance, but it looks like a bright star. The rings can be seen with a small telescope.

Uranus

Uranus, the first planet discovered in modern times by Sir William Herschel in 1781, is the seventh planet from the Sun, twice as far out as Saturn. Its mean distance from the Sun is 2,869 million kilometers (1,783 million miles). Uranus's equatorial diameter is 51,810 kilometers (32,200 miles). The axis of Uranus is tilted at 97 degrees, so it goes around the Sun nearly lying on its side.

Due to Uranus' unusual inclination, the polar regions receive more sunlight during a Uranus year of 84 Earth years. Scientists had thought that the temperature of its poles would be warmer than that at its equator, but *Voyager 2* discovered that the equatorial temperatures were similar to the temperatures at the poles, –209° C (–344° F), implying that some redistribution of heat toward the equatorial region must oc-

cur within the atmosphere. The wind patterns are much like Saturn's, flowing parallel to the equator in the direction of the planet's rotation.

Ninety-eight percent of the upper atmosphere is composed of hydrogen and helium; the remaining two percent is methane. Scientists speculate that the bulk of the lower atmosphere is composed of water (perhaps as much as 50%), methane, and ammonia. Methane is responsible for Uranus' blue-green color because it selectively absorbs red sunlight and condenses to form clouds of ice crystals in the cooler, higher regions of Uranus' atmosphere.

It was also discovered that the planet's magnetic field was 60 degrees tilted from the planet's axis of rotation and offset from the planet's center by one-third of Uranus' radius. It may be generated at a depth where water is under sufficient pressure to be electrically conductive.

The Uranian Rings

Voyager 2 also expanded the body of information pertaining to the rings and moons of Uranus. *Voyager*'s cameras obtained the first images of nine previously known narrow rings and discovered at least two new rings, one narrow and one broadly diffused, bringing the total known rings to eleven. It was found that a highly structured distribution of fine dust exists throughout the ring system.

The outermost (epsilon) ring contains nothing smaller than fist-sized particles. It is flanked by two small moons discovered interior to the orbit of the Uranian moon Miranda. The moons exert a shepherding influence on the epsilon ring and on the outer edges of the gamma and delta rings.

All of the rings lie within one planetary radius[1] of Uranus' cloud tops. Most of Uranus' rings are narrow, ranging in width from 1 to 93 kilometers (0.6 to 58 miles) and are only a few kilometers thick. The Uranian rings are colorless and extremely dark. The dark material may be either irradiated methane ice or organic-rich minerals mixed with water-impregnated, silicon-based compounds. There is evidence that incomplete rings, or "ring arcs," exist at Uranus.

The Uranian Moons

There are 15 known moons of Uranus. In order of decreasing distance from the planet, the moons are Oberon, Titania, Umbriel, Ariel, Miranda, Puck, Belinda, Cressida, Portia, Rosalind, Desdemona, Juliet, Bianca, Ophelia, and Cordelia. Nine of the new moons range in size from 26 to 108 kilometers (16 to 67 miles) in diameter and, being closer to the planet, have faster periods of revolution (8 to 15 hours) than their more distant relatives.

Oberon and Titania

The two largest moons, Oberon, 1,516 kilometers (942 miles) in diameter, and Titania (1,580 kilometers (982 miles) in diameter, are less than half the diameter of Earth's moon. Titania, the reddest of Uranus' moons, may have endured global tectonics as evidenced by complex valleys and fault lines etched into its surface. Smooth sections indicate that volcanic resurfacing has taken place.

---

1. The equatorial radius of Uranus is 25,560 kilometers (15,880 miles) at a pressure of 1 bar.

ABOVE LEFT: The rugged terrain of Triton, Neptune's largest moon. *Voyager 2* photographed geyser-like eruptions of nitrogen gas on Triton. **ABOVE RIGHT: High-altitude clouds in Neptune's atmosphere. BELOW RIGHT: The Great Dark Spot is the most prominent feature in the planet's atmosphere. It is a counter-clockwise storm about the size of the Earth.**

Umbriel and Ariel

Umbriel and Ariel are roughly three-fourths the size of Oberon and Titania. Umbriel is the darkest of the large moons with huge craters peppering its surface. Umbriel has a paucity of what are known as bright ray craters, which are formed on an older darker surface when bright submerged ice is excavated and sprayed by meteroid impacts.

In contrast, the surface of Ariel, the brightest of the Uranian moons, is relatively free of pockmarks due to volcanism which periodically erases the damage done by foreign projectiles. However, there are several extremely deep cuts on Ariel's surface.

Miranda

The smallest of Uranus' large moons, Miranda, 472 kilometers (293 miles) in diameter, has been described as "the most bizarre body in the solar system," with the most geologically complex surface. Miranda's remarkable terrain consists of rolling, heavily cratered plains (the oldest known in the Uranian system) adjoined by three huge, 200 to 300 kilometer (120 to 180 mile) oval-to-trapezoidal regions known as coronae, which are characterized by networks of concentric canyons.

Puck

Puck was the first new moon discovered by *Voyager*, and is 154 kilometers (96 miles) in diameter and makes a trip around Uranus every 18 hours. Puck is shaped somewhat like a potato with a huge impact crater marring roughly one-fourth of its surface.

- Uranus can—on rare occasions—become bright enough to be seen with the naked eye, if one knows exactly where to look; normally, a good set of field glasses or a small portable telescope is required.

Neptune

Little was known about Neptune until August 1989, when NASA's *Voyager 2* became the first spacecraft to observe the planet. Passing about 4,950 kilometers (3,000 miles) above Neptune's north pole, *Voyager 2* made its closest approach to any planet since leaving Earth twelve years prior. The spacecraft passed about 40,000 kilometers (25,000 miles) from Neptune's largest moon, Triton, the last solid body that *Voyager 2* will have studied.

Nearly 4.5 billion kilometers (3 billion miles) from the Sun, Neptune orbits the Sun once in 165 years, and therefore has made not quite a full circle around the Sun since it was discovered.[1]

With an equatorial diameter of 49,528 kilometers (30,775 miles), Neptune is the smallest of our solar system's four gas giants.[2] Even so, its volume could hold nearly 60 Earths. Neptune is also denser than the other gas giants—Jupiter, Saturn, and Uranus, about 64% heavier than if it were composed entirely of water.

Neptune has a blue color as a result of methane in its atmosphere. Methane preferentially absorbs the longer wavelengths of sunlight (those near the red end of the spectrum). What are left to be reflected are colors at the blue end of the spectrum.

The atmosphere of Neptune is mainly composed of hydrogen, with helium and traces of methane and ammonia.

Neptune is a dynamic planet even though it receives only three percent as much sunlight as Jupiter does. Several large, dark spots are prominent features on the planet. The largest spot is about the size of the Earth and was designated the "Great Dark Spot" by its discoverers. It appears to be an anticyclone similar to Jupiter's Great Red Spot. While Neptune's Great Dark Spot is comparable in size, relative to the planet, and at the same latitude (22° south latitude) as Jupiter's Great Red Spot, it is far more variable in size and shape than its Jovian counterpart. Bright, wispy "cirrus-type" clouds overlay the Great Dark Spot at its southern and northeastern boundaries.

At about 42° south, a bright, irregularly shaped, eastward-moving cloud circles much faster than does the Great Dark Spot, "scooting" around Neptune in about 16 hours. This "scooter" may be a cloud plume rising between cloud decks.

Another spot, designated "D2," is located far to the south of the Great Dark Spot at 55° S latitude. It is almond-shaped, with a bright central core, and moves eastward around the planet in about 16 hours.

The atmosphere above Neptune's clouds is hotter near the equator, cooler in the mid-latitudes, and warm again at the south pole. Temperatures in the stratosphere were measured to be 750 kelvins (900° F), while at the 100 millibar pressure level, they were measured to be 55° K (–360° F).

Long, bright clouds, reminiscent of cirrus clouds on Earth, were seen high in Neptune's atmosphere. They appear to form above most of the methane, and consequently are not blue.

At northern low latitudes (27° N), *Voyager* captured images of cloud streaks casting their shadows on cloud decks estimated to be about 50 to 100 kilometers (30 to 60 miles) below. The widths of these cloud streaks range from 50 to 200 kilometers (30 to 125 miles). Cloud streaks were also seen in the southern polar regions (71° S) where the cloud heights were about 50 kilometers (30 miles).

Most of the winds on Neptune blow in a westward direction, which is retrograde, or opposite to the rotation of the planet. Near the Great Dark Spot, there are retrograde winds blowing up to 1,500 miles an hour—the strongest measured on any planet.

The Magnetic Field

Neptune's magnetic field is tilted 47 degrees from the planet's rotation axis, and is offset at least 0.55 radii (about 13,500 kilometers or 8,500 miles) from the physical center. The dynamo electric currents produced within the planet, therefore, must be relatively closer to the surface than for Earth, Jupiter, or Saturn. Because of its unusual orientation, and the tilt of the planet's rotation axis, Neptune's magnetic field goes through dramatic changes as the planet rotates in the solar wind.

Voyager's planetary radio astronomy instrument measured the periodic radio waves generated by the magnetic field and determined that the rotation rate of the interior of Neptune is 16 hours 7 minutes.

Voyager also detected auroras, similar to the northern and southern lights on Earth, in Neptune's atmosphere. Unlike those on Earth, due to Neptune's complex magnetic field, the auroras are extremely complicated processes that occur over wide regions of the planet, not just near the planet's magnetic poles.

Neptune's Moons

Triton

The largest of Neptune's eight known satellites, Triton is different from all other icy moons that *Voyager* has studied. Triton circles Neptune in a tilted, circular, retrograde orbit, completing an orbit in 5.875 days at an average distance of 330,000 kilometers (205,000 miles) above the planet's cloud tops.

Triton shows evidence of a remarkable geologic history, and *Voyager 2* images show active geyser-like eruptions spewing invisible nitrogen gas and dark dust particles 2 to eight kilometers (1 to 5 miles) into space.

Triton is about three-quarters the size of Earth's moon and has a diameter of about 2,705 kilometers (1,680 miles), and a mean density of about 2.066 grams per cubic centimeter. (The density of water is 1.0 gram per cubic centimeter.) This means that Triton contains more rock in its interior than the icy satellites of Saturn and Uranus do.

The relatively high density and the retrograde orbit offer strong evidence that Triton did not originate near Neptune, but is a captured object.

An extremely thin atmosphere extends as much as 800 kilometers (500 miles) above the satellite's surface. Tiny nitrogen ice particles may form thin clouds a few kilometers above the surface. Triton is very bright, reflecting 60 to 95% of the sunlight that strikes it. (By comparison, Earth's moon reflects only 11 percent.)

The atmospheric pressure at Triton's surface is about 14 microbars, a mere 1/70,000th the surface pressure on Earth. Temperature at the surface is about 38 kelvins (–391° F), making it the coldest surface of any body yet visited in the solar system.

The Smaller Satellites

In addition to the previously known moons Triton and Nereid, *Voyager 2* found six more satellites, making the total eight.

Nereid

Nereid was discovered in 1948 through Earth-based telescopes. Little is known about Nereid, which is slightly smaller than 1989N1[3], having a diameter of 340 kilometers (211 miles). The satellite's surface reflects about 14% of the sunlight that strikes it. Nereid's orbit is the most eccentric in the solar system, ranging from about 1,353,600 km (841,100 miles) to 9,623,700 (5,980,200 mi.).

---

1. Astronomers have studied Neptune since Sept. 23, 1846, when Johann Gottfried Galle, of the Berlin Observatory, and Louis d'Arrest, an astronomy student, discovered the eighth planet on the basis of mathematical predictions by Urbain Jean Joseph Le Verrier. Similar predictions were made independently by John Couch Adams. Galileo Galilei had seen Neptune during several nights of observing Jupiter, in January 1613, but didn't realize he was seeing a new planet.

2. These four planets are about 4 to 12 times greater in diameter than Earth. They have no solid surfaces, but possess massive atmospheres that contain substantial amounts of hydrogen and helium with traces of other gases.

3. All of the new satellites have no t yet been named. The temporary designations give the year of discovery, the planet that they are associated with, and the order of discovery. For example, 1989N1 was the first satellite of Neptune found that year.

1989N1 to 1989N6

1989N1 (Proteus[4]). Like all six of Neptune's newly discovered small satellites, it is one of the darkest objects in the solar system—"as dark as soot" is a good description. It reflects only 6% of the sunlight that strikes it. 1989N1 is an ellipsoid about 258 kilometers (415 miles) in diameter, larger than Nereid. It circles Neptune at a distance of about 92,800 kilometers (57,700 miles) above the cloud tops, and completes one orbit in 26 hours 54 minutes. Scientists say that it is about as large as a satellite can be without being pulled into a spherical shape by its own gravity.

1989N2. This object is only about 48,800 kilometers (30,300 miles) from Neptune and circles the planet in 13 hours 18 minutes. Its diameter is 190 kilometers (120 miles).

1989N3 (Despina[4]). The satellite is 27,700 kilometers (17,200 miles) from Neptune's clouds and makes one orbit every 8 hours. Its diameter is about 150 kilometers (90 miles).

1989N4. It lies 37,200 kilometers (23,100 miles) from Neptune. Its diameter is 180 kilometers (110 miles) and it completes an orbit in 10 hours 18 minutes.

1989N5 (Thalassa[4]). The satellite appears to be about 80 kilometers (50 miles) in diameter. It orbits Neptune in 7 hours 30 minutes some 25,200 kilometers (15,700 miles) above the cloud tops.

1989N6 (Naiad[4]). The last satellite discovered, it is about 60 kilometers (37 miles) in diameter and orbits Neptune about 23,200 kilometers (14,400 miles) above the clouds in 7 hours 6 minutes.

1989N1 and its tiny companions are cratered and irregularly shaped—they are not round—and show no signs of any geologic modifications. All circle the planet in the same direction as Neptune rotates, and remain close to Neptune's equatorial plane.

Neptune's Rings

Voyager found four rings and evidence of ring *arcs* or incomplete rings. The "Main Ring" orbits Neptune at about 38,100 kilometers (23,700 miles) above the

4. Satellite's temporary new name, subject to confirmation by The International Astronomical Union.

cloud tops. The "Inner Ring " is about 28,400 kilometers (17,700 miles) from Neptune's cloud tops. An "Inside Diffuse Ring"—a complete ring—is located about 17,100 kilometers (10,600 miles) from the planet's cloud tops. Some scientists suspect that this ring may extend all the way down to Neptune's cloud tops. An area called "the Plateau" is a broad, diffuse sheet of fine material just outside the so-called "Inner Ring." The fine material is approximately the size of smoke particles. All other rings contain a greater proportion of larger material.

Pluto

Pluto, the outermost and smallest planet in the solar system, is the only planet not visited by an exploring spacecraft. So little is known about it that it is difficult to classify. Its distance is so great that the Hubble Space Telescope cannot reveal its surface features. Appropriately named for the Roman god of the underworld, it must be frozen, dark, and dead. Pluto's mean distance from the Sun is 5,900 million kilometers (3,666 million miles).

In 1978, light curve studies gave evidence of a moon revolving around Pluto with the same period as Pluto's rotation. Therefore, it stays over the same point on Pluto's surface. In addition, it keeps the same face toward the planet. The satellite was later named Charon and is estimated to be about 1,284 kilometers (798 miles) in diameter. Recent estimates indicate Pluto's diameter is about 2,290 kilometers (1,423 miles), making the pair more like a double planet than any other in the solar system. Previously, the Earth-Moon system held this distinction. The density of Pluto is slightly greater than that of water.

There is evidence that Pluto has an atmosphere containing methane and polar ice caps that increase and decrease in size with the planet's seasons. It is not known to have water.

Pluto was predicted by calculation when Percival Lowell (1855–1916) noticed irregularities in the orbits of Uranus and Neptune. Clyde Tombaugh (1906–   ) discovered the planet in 1930, precisely where Lowell predicted it would be. The name Pluto was chosen because the first two letters represent the initials of Percival Lowell.

• Pluto has the most eccentric orbit in the solar system, bringing it at times closer to the Sun than Neptune. Pluto approached the perihelion of its orbit on Sept. 5, 1989, and for the rest of this century will be closer to the Sun than Neptune. Even then, it can be seen only with a large telescope.

Are We Alone?

Source: U.S. Naval Observatory.

Seventeen years ago, on November 16, 1974, the people of the planet Earth sent a purposeful message to interstellar space. Using a giant radio telescope in Puerto Rico, we beamed up a 3-minute message about ourselves to anyone listening in a cluster of stars in the constellation **Hercules.** We told them all about the solar system we live in, about the population of the world at the time, and about the atomic elements we're made of. We haven't heard back from anyone.

Moving outward, our message has traveled 17 light

years so far, nearly four times the distance to the nearest star, *Alpha Centauri,* but needs at least another 24,983 years to get to the 300,000 closely packed stars in the Hercules cluster. Then it will be another 25,000 before we should expect to hear anything back.

Finding a signal from the great beyond would be momentous, a turning point. Definitively finding that there existed intelligent life elsewhere in our Universe would perhaps be the greatest event in all of human history.   □

The First Ten Minor Planets (Asteroids)

Name	Year of discovery	Mean Distance from sun (millions of miles)	Orbital period (years)	Diameter (miles)	Magnitude
1. Ceres	1801	257.0	4.60	485	7.4
2. Pallas	1802	257.4	4.61	304	8.0
3. Juno	1804	247.8	4.36	118	8.7
4. Vesta	1807	219.3	3.63	243	6.5
5. Astraea	1845	239.3	4.14	50	9.9
6. Hebe	1847	225.2	3.78	121	8.5
7. Iris	1847	221.4	3.68	121	8.4
8. Flora	1847	204.4	3.27	56	8.9
9. Metis	1848	221.7	3.69	78	8.9
10. Hygeia	1849	222.6	5.59	40 (?)	9.5

The Asteroids

Between the orbits of Mars and Jupiter are an estimated 30,000 pieces of rocky debris, known collectively as the asteroids, or planetoids. The first and, incidentally, the largest (Ceres) was discovered during the New Year's night of 1801 by the Italian astronomer Father Piazzi (1746–1826), and its orbit was calculated by the German mathematician Karl Friedrich Gauss (1777–1855). Gauss invented a new method of calculating orbits on that occasion. A German amateur astronomer, the physician Olbers (1748–1840), discovered the second asteroid, Pallas. The number now known, catalogued, and named is over 2,000; the estimated total is about 20 times that figure. A few asteroids do not move in orbits beyond the orbit of Mars, but in orbits which cross the orbit of Mars. The first of them was named Eros because of this peculiar orbit. It had become the rule to bestow female names on the asteroids, but when it was found that Eros crossed the orbit of a major planet, it received a male name. Since then around two dozen orbit-crossers have been discovered, and they are often referred to as the "male asteroids." A few of them—Albert, Adonis, Apollo, Amor, and Icarus—cross the orbit of the Earth, and two of them may come closer than our Moon; but the crossing is like a bridge crossing a highway, not like two highways intersecting. Hence there is very little danger of collision from these bodies. They are all small, three to five miles in diameter, and therefore very difficult objects to identify, even when quite close. Some scientists believe the asteroids represent the remains of an exploded planet.

Comets

Comets, according to the noted astronomer, Fred L. Whipple (1906–), are enormous "snowballs" of frozen gases (mostly carbon dioxide, methane, and water vapor) and contain very little solid material. The whole behavior of comets can then be explained as the behavior of frozen gas being heated by the Sun. When the comet Kohoutek made its first appearance to man in 1973, its behavior seemed to confirm this theory and later, the international study by five spacecraft that encountered Comet Halley in March 1986 confirmed Whipple's idea of the make-up of comets.

Since comets appear in the sky without any warning, people in classical times and especially during the Middle Ages believed that they had a special meaning, which, of course, was bad. Since a natural catastrophe of some sort of a military conflict occurs every year, it was quite simple to blame the comet that happened to be visible. But even in the past, there were some people who used logical reasoning. When, in Roman times, a comet was blamed for the loss of a battle and hence was called a "bad omen," a Roman writer observed that the victors in the battle probably did not think so.

Up until the middle of the sixteenth century, comets were believed to be phenomena of the upper atmosphere; they were usually "explained" as "burning vapors" which had risen from "distant swamps." That nobody had ever actually seen burning vapors rise from a swamp did not matter.

But a large comet which appeared in 1577 was carefully observed by Tycho Brahe (1546–1601), a Danish astronomer who is often, and with the best of reasons, called "eccentric" but who insisted on precise measurements for everything. It was Tycho Brahe's accumulation of literally thousands of precise measurements which later enable his younger collaborator, Johannes Kepler (1571–1630), to discover the laws of planetary motion. Measuring the motion of the comet of 1577, Tycho Brahe could show that it had been far beyond the atmosphere, even though he could not give figures for the distance. Tycho Brahe's work proved that comets were astronomical and not meteorological phenomena.

In 1682, the second Astronomer Royal of Great Britain, Dr. Edmond Halley (1656–1742), checked the orbit of a bright comet that was in the sky then and compared it with earlier comet orbits which were known in part. Halley found that the comet of 1682 was the third to move through what appeared to be the same orbit. And the three appearances were roughly 76 years apart. Halley concluded that this was the same comet, moving around the Sun in a closed orbit, like the planets. He predicted that it would reappear in 1758 or 1759. Halley himself died in 1742, but a large comet appeared sixteen years after his death as predicted and was immediately referred to as "Halley's comet."

In the Spring of 1973, the discovery of comet Kohoutek, apparently headed for a close-Christmastime rendezvous with the Sun, created worldwide excitement. The comet was a visual disappointment, but turned out to be a treasure trove of information on these little-understood celestial objects. Given an unprecedented advance notice of nine months on the advent of the fiery object, scientists were able to study the comet in visible, ultraviolet and infrared light; with optical telescopes, radio telescopes, and radar. They observed it from the ground, from high-flying aircraft, with instruments aboard unmanned satellites, with sounding rockets, and telescopes and cameras on the Earth-orbiting Skylab space station.

Halley's Comet appeared again in 1986, sparking a worldwide effort to study it up close. Five satellites in all took readings from the comet at various distances. Two Soviet craft, *Vega 1* and *Vega 2*, went in close to provide detailed pictures of the comet, including the first of the comet's core. The European Space Agency's craft, *Giotto*, entered the comet itself, coming to within 450 miles of the comet's center and successfully passing through its tail. In addition, two Japanese craft, the *Suisei* and the *Sakigake*, passed at a longer distance in order to analyze the cloud and tail of the comet and the effect of solar radiation upon it. The United States declined to launch a similar mission, citing budgetary constraints imposed by the shuttle program. A space telescope was to study Halley's Comet but was destroyed in the *Challenger* disaster.

The information gained included measurements of the size of the nucleus, an idea of its configuration and the rate of its rotation. The gas and dust of the comet were analyzed as was the material of the tail. This information is considered important because comets are believed to be debris from the formation of the solar system and to have changed little since then.

Astronomers refer to comets as "periodic" or as "non-periodic" comets, but the latter term does not mean that these comets have no period; it merely means that their period is not known. The actual periods of comets run from 3.3 years (the shortest known) to many thousands of years. Their orbits are elliptical, like those of the planets, but they are very eccentric, long and narrow ellipses. Only comet Schwassmann-Wachmann has an orbit which has such a low eccentricity (for a cometary orbit) that it could be the orbit of a minor planet.

When a comet, coming from deep space, approaches the Sun, it is at first indistinguishable from a minor planet. Somewhere between the orbits of Mars and Jupiter its outline becomes fuzzy; it is said to develop a "coma" (the word used here is the Latin word *coma*, which means "hair," not the phonetically identical Greek word which means "deep sleep"). Then, near the orbit of Mars, the comet develops its tail, which at first trails behind. This grows steadily as the comet comes closer and closer to the Sun. As it rounds the Sun (as first noticed by Girolamo Fracastoro, 1483–1553) the tail always points away from the Sun so that the comet, when moving away from the Sun, points its tail ahead like the landing lights of an airplane.

The reason for this behavior is that the tail is pushed in these directions by the radiation pressure of the Sun. It sometimes happens that a comet loses its tail at perihelion; it then grows another one. Although the tail is clearly visible against the black of the sky, it is very tenuous. It has been said that if the tail of Halley's comet could be compressed to the density of iron, it would fit into a small suitcase.

Although very low in mass, comets are among the largest members of the solar system. The nucleus of a comet may be up to 10,000 miles in diameter; its coma between 10,000 and 50,000 miles in diameter; and its tail as long as 28 million miles.

Meteors and Meteorites

The term "meteor" for what is usually called a "shooting star" bears an unfortunate resemblance to the term "meteorology," the science of weather and weather forecasting. This resemblance is due to an ancient misunderstanding which wrongly considered meteors an atmospheric phenomenon. Actually, the streak of light in the sky that scientists call a meteor is essentially an astronomical phenomenon: the entry of a small piece of cosmic matter into our atmosphere.

The distinction between "meteors" and "fireballs" (formerly also called "bolides") is merely one of convenience; a fireball is an unusually bright meteor. Incidentally, it also means that a fireball is larger than a faint meteor.

Bodies which enter our atmosphere become visible when they are about 60 miles above the ground. The fact that they grow hot enough to emit light is not due to the "friction" of the atmosphere, as one can often read. The phenomenon responsible for the heating is one of compression. Unconfined air cannot move faster than the speed of sound. Since the entering meteorite moves with 30 to 60 times the speed of sound, the air simply cannot get out of the way. Therefore, it is compressed like the air in the cylinder of a Diesel engine and is heated by compression. This heat—or part of it—is transferred to the moving body. The details of this process are now fairly well understood as a result of re-entry tests with ballistic-missile nose cones.

The average weight of a body producing a faint "shooting star" is only a small fraction of an ounce. Even a bright fireball may not weigh more than 2 or 3 pounds. Naturally, the smaller bodies are worn to dust by the passage through the atmosphere; only rather large ones reach the ground. Those that are found are called meteorites. (The "meteor," to repeat, is the term for the light streak in the sky.)

The largest meteorite known is still imbedded in the ground near Grootfontein in SW Africa and is estimated to weight 70 tons. The second largest known is the 34-ton Anighito (on exhibit in the Hayden Planetarium, New York), which was found by Admiral Peary at Cape York in Greenland. The largest meteorite found in the United States is the Willamette meteorite (found in Oregon, weight ca. 15 tons), but large portions of this meteorite weathered away before it was found. Its weight as it struck the ground may have been 20 tons.

All these are iron meteorites (an iron meteorite normally contains about 7% nickel), which form one class of meteorites. The other class consists of the stony meteorites, and between them there are the so-called "stony irons." The so-called "tektites" consist of glass similar to our volcanic glass obsidian, and because of the similarity, there is doubt in a number of cases whether the glass is of terrestrial or of extra-terrestrial origin.

Though no meteorite larger than the Grootfontein is actually known, we do know that the Earth has, on occasion, been struck by much larger bodies. Evidence for such hits are the meteorite craters, of which an especially good example is located near the Cañon Diablo in Arizona. Another meteor crater in the United States is a rather old crater near Odessa, Texas. A large number of others are known, especially in eastern Canada; and for many "probables," meteoric origin has now been proved.

The 88 Recognized Constellations

In astronomical works, the Latin names of the constellations are used. The letter N or S following the Latin name indicates whether the constellation is located to the north or south of the Zodiac. The letter Z indicates that the constellation is within the Zodiac.

Latin name	Letter	English version	Latin name	Letter	English version	Latin name	Letter	English version
Andromeda	N	Andromeda	Delphinus	N	Dolphin	Pavo	S	Peacock
Antlia	S	Airpump	Dorado	S	Swordfish	Pegasus	N	Pegasus
Apus	S	Bird of Paradise			(Goldfish)	Perseus	N	Perseus
Aquarius	Z	Water Bearer	Draco	N	Dragon	Phoenix	S	Phoenix
Aquila	N	Eagle	Equuleus	N	Filly	Pictor	S	Painter (or his
Ara	S	Altar	Eridanus	S	Eridanus (river)			Easel)
Aries	Z	Ram	Fornax	S	Furnace	Pisces	Z	Fishes
Auriga	N	Charioteer	Gemini	Z	Twins	Piscis		
Boötes	N	Herdsmen	Grus	S	Crane	Austrinus	S	Southern Fish
Caelum	S	Sculptor's Tool	Hercules	N	Hercules	Puppis	S	Poop (of Argo)[1]
Camelopardalis	N	Giraffe	Horologium	S	Clock	Pyxis	S	Mariner's
Cancer	Z	Crab	Hydra	N	Sea Serpent			Compass
Canes Venatici	N	Hunting Dogs	Hydrus	S	Water Snake	Reticulum	S	Net
Canis Major	S	Great Dog	Indus	S	Indian	Sagitta	N	Arrow
Canis Minor	S	Little Dog	Lacerta	N	Lizard	Sagittarius	Z	Archer
Capricornus	Z	Goat (or Sea-Goat)	Leo	Z	Lion	Scorpius	Z	Scorpion
			Leo Minor	N	Little Lion	Sculptor	S	Sculptor
Carina	S	Keel (of Argo)[1]	Lepus	S	Hare	Scutum	N	Shield
Cassiopeia	N	Cassiopeia	Libra	Z	Scales	Serpens	S	Serpent
Centaurus	S	Centaur	Lupus	S	Wolf	Sextans	S	Sextant
Cepheus	N	Cepheus	Lynx	N	Lynx	Taurus	Z	Bull
Cetus	S	Whale	Lyra	N	Lyre (Harp)	Telescopium	S	Telescope
Chameleon	S	Chameleon	Mensa	S	Table	Triangulum	N	Triangle
Circinus	S	Compasses			(mountain)	Triangulum	S	Southern
Columba	S	Dove	Microscopium	S	Microscope	Australe		Triangle
Coma Berenices	N	Berenice's Hair	Monoceros	S	Unicorn	Tucana	S	Toucan
Corona Australis	S	Southern Crown	Musca	S	Southern Fly	Ursa Major	N	Big Dipper
Corona Borealis	N	Northern Crown	Norma	S	Rule	Ursa Minor	N	Little Dipper
Corvus	S	Crow (Raven)			(straightedge)	Vela	S	Sail (of Argo)[1]
Crater	S	Cup	Octans	S	Octant	Virgo	Z	Virgin
Crux	S	Southern Cross	Ophiuchus	N	Serpent-Bearer	Volans	S	Flying Fish
Cygnus	N	Swan	Orion	S	Orion	Vulpecula	N	Fox

1. The original constellation Argo Navis (the Ship Argo) has been divided into Carina, Puppis, and Vela. Normally the brightest star in each constellation is designated by alpha, the first letter of the Greek alphabet, the second brightest by beta, the second letter of the Greek alphabet, and so forth. But the Greek letters run through Carina, Puppis, and Vela as if it were still one constellation.

The meteor showers are caused by multitudes of very small bodies travelling in swarms. The Earth travels in its orbit through these swarms like a car driving through falling snow. The point from which the meteors seem to emanate is called the *radiant* and is named for the constellation in that area. The Perseid meteor shower in August is the most spectacular of the year, boasting at peak roughly 60 meteors per hour under good atmospheric conditions. The presence of a bright moon diminishes the number of visible meteors.

The Constellations

Constellations are groupings of stars which form patterns that can be easily recognized and remembered, for example, Orion and the Big Dipper. Actually, the stars of the majority of all constellations do not "belong together." Usually they are at greatly varying distances from the Earth and just happen to lie more or less in the same line of sight as seen from our solar system. But in a few cases the stars of a constellation are actually associated; most of the bright stars of the Big Dipper travel together and form what astronomers call an open cluster.

If you observe a planet, say Mars, for one complete revolution, you will see that it passes succes-

sively through twelve constellations. All planets (except Pluto at certain times) can be observed only in these twelve constellations, which form the so-called Zodiac, and the Sun also moves through the Zodiacal signs, though the Sun's apparent movement is actually caused by the movement of the Earth.

Although the constellations are due mainly to the optical accident of line of sight and have no real significance, astronomers have retained them as reference areas. It is much easier to speak of a star in Orion than to give its geometrical position in the sky. During the Astronomical Congress of 1928, it was decided to recognize 88 constellations. A description of their agreed-upon boundaries was published at Cambridge, England, in 1930, under the title *Atlas Céleste.*

The Auroras

The "northern lights" (*Aurora borealis*) as well as the "southern lights" (*Aurora australis*) are upper-atmosphere phenomena of astronomical origin. The auroras center around the magnetic (not the geographical) poles of the Earth, which explains why, in the Western Hemisphere, they have been seen as far to the south as New Orleans and Florida while the

equivalent latitude in the Eastern Hemisphere never sees an aurora. The northern magnetic pole happens to be in the Western Hemisphere.

The lower limit of an aurora is at about 50 miles. Upper limits have been estimated to be as high as 400 miles. Since about 1880, a connection between the auroras on Earth and the sun spots has been suspected and has gradually come to be accepted. It was said that the sun spots probably eject "particles" (later the word *electrons* was substituted) which on striking the Earth's atmosphere, cause the auroras. But this explanation suffered from certain difficulties. Sometimes a very large sun spot group on the Sun, with individual spots bigger than the Earth itself, would not cause an aurora. Moreover, even if a sun spot caused an aurora, the time that passed between the appearance of the one and the occurrence of the other was highly unpredictable.

This problem of the time lag is, in all probability, solved by the discovery of the Van Allen layer by artificial satellite *Explorer I*. The Van Allen layer[1] is a double layer of charged sub-atomic particles around the Earth. The inner layer, with its center some 1,500 miles from the ground, reaches from about 40° N. to about 40° S. and does not touch the atmosphere. The outer layer, much larger and with its center several thousand miles from the ground, does touch the atmosphere in the vicinity of the magnetic poles.

It seems probable that the "leakage" of electrons from the outer Van Allen layer causes the auroras. A new burst of electrons from the Sun seems to be caught in the outer layer first. Under the assumption that all electrons are first caught in the outer layer, the time lag can be understood. There has to be an "overflow" from the outer layer to produce an aurora.

The Atmosphere

Astronomically speaking, the presence of our atmosphere is deplorable. Though reasonably transparent to visible light, the atmosphere may absorb as much as 60% of the visible and near-visible light. It is opaque to most other wave-lengths, except certain fairly short radio waves. In addition to absorbing much light, our atmosphere bends light rays entering at a slant (for a given observer) so that the true position of a star close to the horizon is not what it seems to be. One effect is that we see the Sun above the horizon before it actually is. And the unsteady movement of the atmosphere causes the "twinkling" of the stars, which may be romantic but is a nuisance when it comes to observing.

The composition of our atmosphere near the ground is 78% nitrogen and 21% oxygen, the remaining 1% consisting of other gases, most of it argon. The composition stays the same to an altitude of at least 70 miles (except that higher up two impurities, carbon dioxide and water vapor, are missing), but the pressure drops very fast. At 18,000 feet, half of the total mass of the atmosphere is below, and at 100,000 feet, 99% of the mass of the atmosphere is below. The upper limit of the atmosphere is usually given as 120 miles; no definitive figure is possible, since there is no boundary line between the incredibly attenuated gases 120 miles up and space.

Astronomical Telescopes

Optical telescopes used in astronomy are of two basic kinds: refracting and reflecting. In the *refractor*

---

1. Named after the American physicist, James Alfred Van Allen (1914–   ) who discovered the broad bands of intense radiation surrounding the Earth in 1958.

telescope, a lens is used to collect light from a distant object and bring it to a focus. A second lens, the eyepiece, then magnifies the image which may be examined visually or photographed directly. The *reflector telescope* uses a concave mirror instead of a lens, which reflects the light rays back toward the upper end of the telescope where they are magnified and observed or photographed. Most large optical telescopes now being built are reflectors.

Radio telescopes are used to study radio waves coming from outside the Earth's atmosphere. The waves are gathered by an antenna or "dish," which is a parabolic reflecting surface made of metal or finely meshed wire. Radio signals have been received from the Sun, Moon, and planets, and from the center of our galaxy and other galaxies. Radio signals are the means by which the distant and mysterious quasars and pulsars were discovered.

Very Large Telescope

In December 1987, the European Southern Observatory (ESO) agreed to build a super telescope called the Very Large Telescope in the mountains of northern Chile. It will be the world's largest ground-based optical telescope and will consist of four 8-meter (26.24 ft) telescopes whose mirrors will combine their images to simulate a single mirror of 16-meter (52 .49 ft) diameter.

It will take at least ten years to complete construction of the super telescope and will cost about $235 million.

The Hubble Space Telescope

The Edwin P. Hubble Space Telescope was released by the space shuttle *Discovery* on April 25, 1990. It is able to peer far out in space and back in time, producing imagery of unprecedented clarity, of galaxies, star systems, and some of the universe's more intriguing objects: quasars, pulsars, and exploding galaxies. It can distinguish fine details—in planetary atmospheres or nearby star fields—with ten times the clarity of the best ground observatories. When pointed at Jupiter, for example, the telescope will provide images comparable to those from Voyager flybys.

The $1.6-billion Space Telescope has a primary mirror 2.4 m (94 inches) in diameter. The mirror is almost half the diameter of the 5-m (200 inch) telescope at Mt. Palomar, the most powerful ground-based telescope in the western world.

After it was placed in orbit at 380 miles (611.5 km) altitude, the Hubble Telescope became the principal tool for exploring the universe through this decade and the next.

The Space telescope can view galaxies and quasars over distances up to 14 billion light years. Seeing that far will show us the universe as it was early in its lifetime and will reveal how matter has evolved over the eons. It will also teach us more about the large structure of the universe, providing clues as to whether the universe will continue to expand.

The first two test images taken by the orbiting telescope of an open star cluster, NGC 3535, in the southern-sky constellation Carina (the Ship's Keel) revealed a double star previously suspected but not seen before.

It was discovered in June 1990 that there was a spherical aberration in one of the telescope's mirrors and this defect may not be repaired until a late 1993 shuttle mission. In 1991, two of the craft's six gyroscopes failed, causing additional problems. In the meantime, observations are continuing with the equipment that is working correctly.

Conversion of Universal Time (U. T.) to Civil Time

U.T.	E.D.T.[1]	E.S.T.[2]	C.S.T.[3]	M.S.T.[4]	P.S.T.[5]	U.T.	E.D.T.[1]	E.S.T.[2]	C.S.T.[3]	M.S.T.[4]	P.S.T.[5]
00	*8P	*7P	*6P	*5P	*4P	12	8A	7A	6A	5A	4A
01	*9P	*8P	*7P	*6P	*5P	13	9A	8A	7A	6A	5A
02	*10P	*9P	*8P	*7P	*6P	14	10A	9A	8A	7A	6A
03	*11P	*10P	*9P	*8P	*7P	15	11A	10A	9A	8A	7A
04	M	*11P	*10P	*9P	*8P	16	N	11A	10A	9A	8A
05	1A	M	*11P	*10P	*9P	17	1P	N	11A	10A	9A
06	2A	1A	M	*11P	*10P	18	2P	1P	N	11A	10A
07	3A	2A	1A	M	*11P	19	3P	2P	1P	N	11A
08	4A	3A	2A	1A	M	20	4P	3P	2P	1P	N
09	5A	4A	3A	2A	1A	21	5P	4P	3P	2P	1P
10	6A	5A	4A	3A	2A	22	6P	5P	4P	3P	2P
11	7A	6A	5A	4A	3A	23	7P	6P	5P	4P	3P

1. Eastern Daylight Time. 2. Eastern Standard Time, same as Central Daylight Time. 3. Central Standard Time, same as Mountain Daylight Time. 4. Mountain Standard Time, same as Pacific Daylight Time. 5. Pacific Standard Time. NOTES: *denotes previous day. N = noon. M = midnight.

Phenomena, 1992

Configurations of Sun, Moon, and Planets

NOTE: The hour listings are in Universal Time. For conversion to United States time zones, see conversion table above.

JANUARY

d	h	
1	12	Venus 5° N of Moon
3	01	Mercury 3° N of Moon
3	10	Mars 0°.8 N of Moon (Occn.)
3	15	Earth at perihelion
4	23	NEW MOON (Eclipse)
5	01	Uranus in conjunction with Sun
6	12	Moon at apogee
6	23	Saturn 3° S of Moon
7	13	Neptune in conjunction with Sun
7	19	Venus 7° N of Antares
7	23	Juno 0°.2 S of Moon (Occn.)
10	20	Mercury 0°.6 N of Mars
13	03	FIRST QUARTER
19	21	FULL MOON
19	22	Moon at perigee
20	03	Mercury 0°.6 S of Uranus
21	11	Mercury 1°.9 S of Neptune
23	01	Jupiter 7° N of Moon
26	15	LAST QUARTER
29	20	Vesta stationary
29	21	Mars 0°.4 S of Uranus
29	22	Saturn in conjunction with Sun
31	17	Venus 1°.0 N of Moon (Occn.)

FEBRUARY

1	08	Mars 1°.5 S of Neptune
1	09	Uranus 0°.9 S of Moon (Occn.)
1	12	Neptune 0°.03 N of Moon (Occn.)
1	13	Mars 1°.5 S of Moon
2	12	Moon at apogee
3	19	NEW MOON
7	07	Venus 0°.9 N of Uranus
8	15	Venus 0°.3 S of Neptune
11	16	FIRST QUARTER
12	09	Mercury in superior conjunction
17	11	Moon at perigee
18	08	FULL MOON
19	07	Jupiter 6° N of Moon
19	22	Venus 0°.9 N oof Mars

25	08	LAST QUARTER
28	02	Pluto stationary
28	18	Uranus 1°.2 S of Moon
28	21	Neptune 0°.2 S of Moon (Occn.)
29	01	Jupiter at opposition
29	02	Venus 0°.1 N of Saturn
29	21	Moon at apogee

MARCH

1	18	Mars 4° S of Moon
2	01	Saturn 4° S of Moon
2	06	Venus 4° S of Moon
4	13	NEW MOON
6	06	Mercury 4° S of Moon
8	12	Juno in conjunction with Sun
9	04	Vesta at opposition
9	21	Mercury greatest elong. E (18°)
12	03	FIRST QUARTER
16	15	Mercury stationary
16	18	Moon at perigee
17	12	Jupiter 6° N of Moon
18	18	FULL MOON
20	09	Equinox
26	02	LAST QUARTER
26	15	Mercury in inferior conjunction
27	03	Uranus 1°.5 S of Moon
27	05	Neptune 0°.5 S of Moon (Occn.)
28	14	Moon at apogee
29	14	Saturn 4° S of Moon
31	01	Mars 6° S of Moon

APRIL

1	19	Venus 7° S of Moon
2	08	Mercury 4° S of Moon
3	05	NEW MOON
5	23	Mercury 2° N of Venus
8	01	Mercury stationary
10	10	FIRST QUARTER
13	07	Moon at perigee
13	16	Jupiter 6° N of Moon
17	05	FULL MOON
20	11	Neptune stationary
22	01	Uranus stationary

23	12	Uranus 1°.8 S of Moon
23	14	Neptune 0°.7 S of Moon (Occn.)
23	15	Mercury greatest elong. W (27°)
24	04	Pallas stationary
24	22	LAST QUARTER
25	10	Moon at apogee
26	02	Saturn 5° S of Moon
27	07	Vesta stationary
29	07	Mars 7° S of Moon
30	21	Mercury 8° S of Moon

MAY

1	05	Jupiter stationary
2	18	NEW MOON
8	12	Moon at perigee
9	16	FIRST QUARTER
10	22	Jupiter 6° N of Moon
12	01	Pluto at opposition
16	16	FULL MOON
20	20	Uranus 2° S of Moon
20	21	Neptune 0°.9 S of Moon (Occn.)
23	05	Moon at apogee
23	12	Saturn 5° S of Moon
24	16	LAST QUARTER
28	09	Mars 7° S of Moon
29	03	Saturn stationary
31	16	Mercury in superior conjunction

JUNE

1	04	NEW MOON
4	02	Moon at perigee
7	07	Jupiter 7° N of Moon
7	12	Ceres stationary
7	21	FIRST QUARTER
13	16	Venus in superior conjunction
15	05	FULL MOON (Eclipse)
17	01	Uranus 1°.9 S of Moon
17	04	Neptune 0°.9 S of Moon (Occn.)
18	23	Pallas at opposition
19	19	Saturn 5° S of Moon

19	22	Moon at apogee
21	03	Solstice
23	02	Mercury 5° S of Pollux
23	08	LAST QUARTER
26	08	Mars 6° S of Moon
30	12	NEW MOON (Eclipse)

JULY

2	01	Moon at perigee
2	10	Mercury 4° N of Moon
3	12	Earth at aphelion
4	20	Jupiter 7° N of Moon
6	01	Mercury greatest elong. E (26°)
7	03	FIRST QUARTER
7	23	Uranus at opposition
9	13	Neptune at opposition
14	06	Uranus 1°.8 S of Moon
14	09	Neptune 0°.8 S of Moon (Occn.)
14	19	FULL MOON
16	23	Saturn 5° S of Moon
17	11	Moon at apogee
19	03	Mercury stationary
22	22	LAST QUARTER
25	04	Mars 4° S of Moon
25	15	Mercury 6°S of Venus
25	22	Ceres at opposition
29	20	NEW MOON
30	08	Moon at perigee

AUGUST

1	12	Jupiter 7°N of Moon
2	21	Mercury in inferior conjunction
4	09	Pluto stationary
5	11	FIRST QUARTER
6	18	Venus 1°.1 N of Regulus
7	10	Saturn at opposition
10	10	Uranus 1°.8 S of Moon
10	14	Neptune 0°.8 S of Moon (Occn.)
11	09	Mars 5° N of Aldebaran
12	13	Mercury stationary
13	01	Saturn 5° S of Moon
13	10	FULL MOON
13	16	Moon at apogee
14	01	Pallas stationary
21	02	Mercury greatest elong. W (18°)
21	10	LAST QUARTER

22	21	Mars 1°.4 S of Moon
23	03	Venus 0°.3 N of Jupiter
27	01	Mercury 5° N of Moon
27	18	Moon at perigee
28	03	NEW MOON
29	19	Venus 7° N of Moon

SEPTEMBER

2	23	Mercury 1°.2 N of Regulus
3	23	FIRST QUARTER
6	15	Uranus 1°.9 S of Moon
6	19	Neptune 0°.9 S of Moon (Occn.)
9	03	Saturn 5° S of Moon
9	19	Moon at apogee
12	02	FULL MOON
15	04	Mercury in superior conjunction
16	12	Ceres stationary
17	19	Jupiter in conjunction with Sun
19	05	Venus 3° N of Spica
19	20	LAST QUARTER
20	09	Mars 0°.9 N of Moon (Occn.)
22	19	Equinox
23	00	Uranus stationary
25	03	Moon at perigee
26	11	NEW MOON
27	16	Neptune stationary
28	15	Venus 4° N of Moon

OCTOBER

2	22	Mercury 2° N of Spica
3	14	FIRST QUARTER
3	22	Uranus 2° S of Moon
4	02	Neptune 1°.2 S of Moon (Occn.)
6	08	Saturn 5° S of Moon
7	06	Moon at apogee
11	18	FULL MOON
16	04	Saturn stationary
18	15	Mars 3° N of Moon
19	04	LAST QUARTER
23	05	Moon at perigee
24	00	Jupiter 7° N of Moon
25	21	NEW MOON
27	07	Venus 3° N of Antares
27	15	Mercury 0°.5 S of Moon (Occn.)

28	15	Venus 0°.4 S of Moon (Occn.)
31	07	Uranus 2° S of Moon
31	10	Neptune 1°.4 S of Moon
31	16	Mercury greatest elong. E (24°)

NOVEMBER

2	09	FIRST QUARTER
2	16	Saturn 5° S of Moon
3	23	Moon at apogee
4	21	Mars 5° S of Pollux
10	09	FULL MOON
11	14	Mercury stationary
15	00	Pluto in conjunction with Sun
15	12	Mars 5° N of Moon
17	04	Juno stationary
17	12	LAST QUARTER
19	00	Moon at perigee
20	16	Jupiter 7° N of Moon
21	22	Mercury in injerior conjunction
24	09	NEW MOON
26	12	Venus 1°.9 S of Uranus
27	13	Venus 3° S of Neptune
27	18	Uranus 3° S of Moon
29	16	Mars stationary
30	03	Saturn ° S of Moon

DECEMBER

1	06	Mercury stationary
1	20	Moon at apogee
2	06	FIRST QUARTER
4	10	Vesta in conjunction with Sun
9	14	Mercury greatest elong. W (21°)
10	00	FULL MOON
12	19	Mars 6° N of Moon
13	21	Moon at perigee
16	19	LAST QUARTER
18	05	Jupiter 7° N of Moon
19	03	Mercury 6°N of Antares
21	15	Solstice
21	16	Venus 1°.5 N of Pollux
22	11	Mercury 1°.5 N of Moon
22	21	Mars 3° S of Pollux
24	01	NEW MOON (Eclipse)
27	17	Saturn 6° S of Moon
28	02	Juno at opposition
28	07	Venus 7° S of Moon
29	17	Moon at apogee

Eclipses of the Sun and the Moon, 1992

Jan. 4–5. Annular eclipse of the Sun. Visible in Oceania, Philippines, Japan, the extreme coast of northeast Asia, northern Australia, and the west coast of North America.

June 15. Partial eclipse of the Moon. The beginning of the umbral phase visible in South America, Central America, the United States except in the northwest, southeastern Canada, Antarctica, the eastern South Pacific Ocean, extreme western Europe, Africa except the northeast, and the Atlantic Ocean; the end visible in New Zealand, Hawaii, South America, Central America, North America except Alaska and northern Canada, Antarctica, extreme western Africa, the South Pacific Ocean, the southeastern North Pacific Ocean, and most of the Atlantic Ocean except the northeast.

June 30. Total eclipse of the Sun. Visible in Central South America, and in Southwest Africa.

Dec. 10–11. Total eclipse of the Moon. The beginning of the umbral phase visible in northeastern South America, eastern and northern North America, Greenland, the Arctic regions, Africa, Europe, most of Asia, most of the Atlantic Ocean, and the Indian Ocean; the end visible in South America, Central America, most of North America, Greenland, the Arctic regions, Africa, Europe, northern and western Asia, the eastern Pacific Ocean, the Atlantic Ocean, and the Western Indian Ocean.

Dec. 23–24. Partial eclipse of the Sun. Visible in eastern China, Korea, Japan, the extreme eastern part of the U.S.S.R., and southwestern Alaska.

DECLINATIONS OF SUN AND PLANETS, 1992

Visibility of Planets, 1992

Mercury can only be seen low in the east before sunrise, or low in the west after sunset (about the time of the beginning or end off civil twilight). It is visible in the mornings between the following approximate dates: January 1 to January 30, April 3 to May 24, August 11 to September 6, and November 28 to December 31. The planet is brighter at the end of each period, (the best conditions in low northern latitudes occur for a few days in early January and during the third week in August and in most northern latitudes for the first three weeks in December, and in southern latitudes from the second week in April until mid-May). It is visible in the evenings between the following approximate dates: February 23 to March 19, June 8 to July 26, and September 27 to November 16. The planet is brighter at the beginning of each period, (the best conditions in northern latitudes occur during the first half of March and in southern latitudes from the third week in June until the third week in July and second week in October until just before mid-November).

Venus is a brilliant object in the morning sky from the beginning of the year until the second week in May when it becomes too close to the Sun for observation. During the second half of July it reappears in the evening sky where it stays until the end of the year. Venus is in conjunction with Mars on February 19, with Saturn on February 29 and December 21, with Mercury on April 5 and July 25 and with Jupiter on August 23.

Mars can be seen at the very beginning of January in the morning sky in Ophiuchus then it passes through Sagittarius, Capricornus, Aquarius, Pisces, briefly into Cetus and back into Pisces, on to Aries and Taurus (passing 5° N of *Aldebaran* on August 11), Gemini (passing 5° S of *Pollux* on November 4 by which time it can be seen for more than half the night), Cancer and back into Gemini in mid December where it remains for the rest of the year

(passing 3° S of *Pollux* on December 22). Mars is in conjunction with Mercury on January 10, with Venus on February 19 and with Saturn on March 6.

Jupiter can be seen in January for more than half of the night in Leo, its westward elongation gradually increases until it is at opposition on February 29 when it can be seen throughout the night. Its eastward elongation then gradually decreases until by early June it can be seen only in the evening sky. In early September it becomes too close to the Sun for observation until the beginning of October when it reappears in the morning sky in Virgo in which constellation it remains for the rest of the year. Jupiter is in conjunction with Venus on August 23.

Saturn can be seen in the evening sky in Capricornus until mid-January then it becomes too close to the Sun for observation. It reappears in the morning sky in mid-February still in Capricornus, in which constellation it remains throughout the year. Its westward elongation gradually increases until it is at opposition on August 7 when it is visible throughout the night. Its eastward elongation then gradually decreases until from early November it can only be seen in the evening sky. Saturn is in conjunction with Venus on February 29 and December 21 and with Mars on March 6.

Uranus is too close to the Sun for observation until towards the end of January when it appears in the morning sky in Sagittarius, in which constellation it remains throughout the year. It is at opposition on July 7 when it can be seen throughout the night, after which its eastward elongation gradually decreases. From early October it can only be seen in the evening sky until the second half of December when it again becomes too close to the Sun for observation.

Neptune is too close to the Sun for observation until late January when it can be seen in the morning sky shortly before sunrise in Sagittarius, in which constellation it remains throughout the year. It is at opposition on July 9 when it can be seen throughout the night. From mid-October it can only be seen in the evening sky until mid-December when it again becomes too close to the Sun for observation.

Do not confuse (1) Mercury with Mars during the first half of January, the reddish tint of Mars should assist in its identification. (2) Venus with Mars from mid-February to early March, with Saturn from late February to early March and mid-December to late December, with Mercury in early April and in the third week of May and with Jupiter late August, in all occasions Venus is the brighter object. (3) Mars with Saturn for the first half of March when Mars is the brighter object. ☐

Visibility of Planets in Morning and Evening Twilight

Morning			Evening		
Venus	January 1	— May 7	Venus	July 20	— December 31
Mars	January 1	— December 31	Jupiter	February 29	— September 4
Jupiter	January 1	— February 29	Saturn	January 1	— January 13
	October 1	— December 31		August 7	— December 31
Saturn	February 16	— August 7			

A Lesson in Astronomy

Reprinted by courtesy of the U.S. Naval Observatory

To understand where things are in the sky, and how the locations of the planets relate to each other, you have to understand one of the most basic things about astronomy—the *celestial sphere*.

Imagine, if you will, all the things in the sky—the Sun, Moon, planets, stars, etc.—no matter how far away they actually are, being on a gigantic transparent sphere, with the Earth at its center. The early Greeks believed this celestial sphere to be made out of some crystalline material, at a very great distance from the Earth.

From here things get easy. As the Earth rotates on its axis, we perceive the celestial sphere to be moving, and not the Earth. The sphere has two points around which it rotates, and we call them the celestial poles. The celestial poles are where the Earth's axis penetrates the celestial sphere. The north celestial pole is marked by Polaris, the North Star, which is relatively close to the pole. The south celestial pole has no bright star nearby to mark its place in the sky. Now, if we extend the Earth's equator on to the celestial sphere, we get the celestial equator. The celestial equator is 90° from the celestial poles. Straight up from where you happen to be is called the zenith, and straight down is called the nadir. The zenith forms the apex of the hemisphere of the celestial sphere that is above your horizon at any given time.

Now for something not so easy. As we watch the Sun rise and set on any given day it marks a path in the sky called a diurnal circle. In fact, any object on the celestial sphere will make a diurnal circle—the apparent path of an object made through the course of a day. If you marked the position of the Sun (in Right Ascension and Declination) against the background of stars through the course of a year you would see another path on the celestial sphere—we call it the ecliptic. The ecliptic is the apparent path the Sun makes on the celestial sphere due to the Earth's revolution around the Sun. The ecliptic also represents the plane of the solar system. The inclination of the orbits of all other objects in the solar system are measured against it.

How do astronomers measure things on the celestial sphere? There are two ways. The first way is probably most familiar, called the altitude-azimuth, or horizon system. Altitude is the object's position in degrees above the horizon, and azimuth is the object's direction, measured in degrees from north (0°), moving east (just like a compass, east is 90°, south is 180°, etc.). Altitude-azimuth is always measured from the observer's position, and does not give you a universal position for an object. The best way to mark an object's position in the heavens is to use a fixed set of coordinates, much like the Earth's latitude and longitude. The celestial coordinate system most used is the Right Ascension and Declination system.

Right Ascension is measured in hours, not degrees, starting at the vernal equinox, a zero point equivalent to 0° longitude on the Earth, and is marked in one hour increments, measured east. Each one hour increment equals 15°, and there are 24 hours of Right Ascension. Declination is a measurement of degrees north or south of the celestial equator. Positive is above the celestial equator, and negative is below. For example, the bright star Sirius in the winter sky has a position of 6 hours, 44 minutes Right Ascension, and –16 degrees, 42 minutes Declination (abbreviated 6h 44m and –16° 42′).

The orientation of the observer to the celestial sphere is an important factor you cannot overlook. The first thing you should do is find the North Star. Once you have that in your sights, everything else will fall into place. If you know your latitude, you're in good shape, because your latitude marks your position north of the equator (if you are in the northern hemisphere). Your latitude is equal to the altitude of the North Star above the northern horizon. Subtract your latitude from 90° and you will have the altitude of the celestial equator above your southern horizon. It is best to have a star chart handy during an evening observing session, as most will have the ecliptic charted among the evening constellations. ☐

Radio Signals May Detect New Planet

In July 1991, British astronomers studying radio emissions from Pulsar PSR 1829-10 reported evidence of a planet-size object orbiting the Pulsar which is some 33,000 light years from Earth. They speculate that the planet is about twelve times the Earth's mass and is possibly two to three times the Earth's diameter.

If their findings can be confirmed, it would be the first time that a planet was discovered beyond our solar system.

AVIATION

Famous Firsts in Aviation

Cayley's Helicopter

Sir George Cayley's Helicopter design

Sir George Cayley of England (1773-1857) designed the first practical helicopter in 1842-43. His remarkable machine had twin contra-rotating rotors which served as wings and two pusher-type propellers at the back to give the aircraft forward motion.

Cayley designed and built the first successful man-carrying glider in 1853 and sent his coachman aloft in it on its first flight. He also formulated the basic principles of modern aerodynamics and is the father of British aeronautics.

1782 **First balloon flight.** Jacques and Joseph Montgolfier of Annonay, France, sent up a small smoke-filled balloon about mid-November.

1783 **First hydrogen-filled balloon flight.** Jacques A. C. Charles, Paris physicist, supervised construction by A. J. and M. N. Robert of a 13-ft diameter balloon that was filled with hydrogen. It got up to about 3,000 ft and traveled about 16 mi. in a 45-min flight (Aug. 27).

First human balloon flights. A Frenchman, Jean Pilâtre de Rozier made the first captive-balloon ascension (Oct. 15). With the Marquis d'Arlandes, Pilâtre de Rozier made the first free flight, reaching a peak altitude of about 500 ft, and traveling about 5 1/2 mi. in 20 min (Nov. 21).

1784 **First powered balloon.** Gen. Jean Baptiste Marie Meusnier developed the first propeller-driven and elliptically-shaped balloon—the crew cranking three propellers on a common shaft to give the craft a speed of about 3 mph.

First woman to fly. Mme. Thible, a French opera singer (June 4).

1793 **First balloon flight in America.** Jean Pierre Blanchard, a French pilot, made it from Philadelphia to near Woodbury, Gloucester County, N.J., in a little over 45 min (Jan. 9).

1794 **First military use of the balloon.** Jean Marie Coutelle, using a balloon built for the French Army, made two 4-hr observation ascents. The military purpose of the ascents seems to have been to damage the enemy's morale.

1797 **First parachute jump.** André-Jacques Garnerin dropped from about 6,500 ft over Monceau Park in Paris in a 23-ft diameter parachute made of white canvas with a basket attached (Oct. 22).

1843 **First air transport company.** In London, William S. Henson and John Stringfellow filed articles of incorporation for the Aerial Transit Company (March 24). It failed.

1852 **First dirigible.** Henri Giffard, a French engineer, flew in a controllable (more or less) steam-engine powered balloon, 144 ft long and 39 ft in diameter, inflated with 88,000 cu ft of coal gas. It reached 6.7 mph on a flight from Paris to Trappe (Sept. 24).

1860 **First aerial photographers.** Samuel Archer King and William Black made two photos of Boston, still in existence.

1872 **First gas-engine powered dirigible.** Paul Haenlein, a German engineer, flew in a semi-rigid-frame dirigible, powered by a 4-cylinder internal-combustion engine running on coal gas drawn from the supporting bag.

1873 **First transatlantic attempt.** *The New York Daily Graphic* sponsored the attempt with a 400,000 cu ft balloon carrying a lifeboat. A rip in the bag during inflation brought collapse of the balloon and the project.

1897 **First successful metal dirigible.** An all-metal dirigible, designed by David Schwarz, a Hungarian, took off from Berlin's Tempelhof Field and, powered by a 16-hp Daimler engine, got several miles before leaking gas caused it to crash (Nov. 13).

1900 **First Zeppelin flight.** Germany's Count Ferdinand von Zeppelin flew the first of his long series of rigid-frame airships. It attained a speed of 18 mi. per h and got 3 1/2 mi. before its steering gear failed (July 2).

1903 **First successful heavier-than-air machine flight.** Aviation was really born on the sand dunes at Kitty Hawk, N.C., when Orville Wright crawled to his prone position between the wings of the biplane he and his brother Wilbur had built, opened the throttle of their homemade 12-hp engine and took to the air. He covered 120 ft in 12 sec. Later that day, in one of four flights, Wilbur stayed up 59 sec and covered 852 ft (Dec. 17).

Did the Wrights Fly First?

Supporters of Gustave A. Whitehead are seeking to prove that the German-born inventor flew a powered-batwing aircraft on Aug. 14, 1901, in Bridgeport, Conn., two years before the Wright Brothers made their first powered flight.

While photographs of Whitehead's plane exist, none of them show it flying, nor is there much useful evidence to prove or disprove this claim.

Although Whitehead supporters have built what they claim is a replica of his plane and have flown it on several short hops in 1986, it should be noted that blueprints of Whitehead's actual craft do not exist.

The current opinion of the Smithsonian is that none of Gustave Whitehead's planes actually flew and the controversy remains.

Dec. 17, 1903. Orville Wright at the controls, Wilbur runs alongside him. (National Air and Space Museum, Smithsonian Institution)

1904 First airplane maneuvers. Orville Wright made the first turn with an airplane (Sept. 15); 5 days later his brother Wilbur made the first complete circle.

1905 First airplane flight over half an hour. Orville Wright kept his craft up 33 min 17 sec (Oct. 4).

1906 First European airplane flight. Alberto Santos-Dumont, a Brazilian, flew a heavier-than-air machine at Bagatelle Field, Paris (Sept. 13).

1908 First airplane fatality. Lt. Thomas E. Selfridge, U.S. Army Signal Corps, was in a group of officers evaluating the Wright plane at Fort Myer, Va. He was up about 75 ft with Orville Wright when the propeller hit a bracing wire and was broken, throwing the plane out of control, killing Selfridge and seriously injuring Wright (Sept. 17).

1909 First cross-Channel flight. Louis Blériot flew in a 25-hp Blériot VI monoplane from Les Baraques near Calais, France, and landed near Dover Castle, England, in a 26.61-mi. (38-km) 37-min flight across the English Channel (July 25).

First International Aviation Competition Meeting. American Glenn Curtis narrowly beats France's Louis Blériot in main event and wins the Gordon Bennett Cup. Meet held at Rheims, France (Aug. 22–28).

1910 First licensed woman pilot. Baroness Raymonde de la Roche of France, who learned to fly in 1909, received ticket No. 36 on March 8.

First flight from shipboard. Lt. Eugene Ely, USN, took a Curtiss plane off from the deck of cruiser *Birmingham* at Hampton Roads, Va., and flew to Norfolk (Nov. 14). The following January, he reversed the process, flying from Camp Selfridge to the deck of the armored cruiser *Pennsylvania* in San Francisco Bay (Jan. 18).

1911 First U.S. woman pilot. Harriet Quimby, a magazine writer, got ticket No. 37, making her the second licensed female pilot in the world.

1912 First woman's cross-Channel flight. Harriet Quimby flew from Dover, England, across the English Channel, and landed at Hardelot, France (25 mi. south of Calais) in a Blériot

Harriet Quimby was the leading woman aviator of her day. (Leslie's Weekly Illustrated Newspaper)

monoplane loaned to her by Louis Blériot (April 16). She was later killed in a flying accident over Dorchester Bay during a Harvard-Boston aviation meet on July 1, 1912.

1913 First multi-engined aircraft. Built and flown by Igor Ivan Sikorsky while still in his native Russia.

1914 First aerial combat. In August, Allied and German pilots and observers started shooting at each other with pistols and rifles—with negligible results.

1915 First air raids on England. German Zeppelins started dropping bombs on four English communities (Jan. 19).

1918 First U.S. air squadron. The U.S. Army Air Corps made its first independent raids over enemy lines, in DH-4 planes (British-designed) powered with 400-hp American-designed Liberty engines (April 8).

First regular airmail service. Operated for the Post Office Department by the Army, the first regular service was inaugurated with one round trip a day (except Sunday) between Washington, D.C., and New York City (May 15).

1919 First transatlantic flight. The NC-4, one of four Curtiss flying boats commanded by Lt. Comdr. Albert C. Read, reached Lisbon, Portugal, (May 27) after hops from Trepassy Bay, Newfoundland, to Horta, Azores (May 16–17), to Ponta Delgada (May 20). The Liberty-powered craft was piloted by Walter Hinton.

First nonstop transatlantic flight. Capt. John Alcock and Lt. Arthur Whitten Brown, British World War I flyers, made the 1,900 mi. from St. John's, Newfoundland, to Clifden, Ireland, in 16 h 12 min in a Vickers-Vimy bomber with two 350-hp Rolls-Royce engines (June 15–16).

First lighter-than-air transatlantic flight. The British dirigible R-34, commanded by Maj. George H. Scott, left Firth of Forth, Scotland, (July 2) and touched down at Mineola, L.I., 108 h later. The eastbound trip was made in 75 h (completed July 13).

First scheduled London-Paris passenger service (using airplanes). Aircraft Travel and Transport inaugurated London-Paris service (Aug. 25). Later the company started the first trans-channel mail service on the same route (Nov. 10).

1921 First naval vessel sunk by aircraft. Two battleships being scrapped by treaty were sunk by bombs dropped from Army planes in demonstration put on by Brig. Gen. William S. Mitchell (July 21).

First helium balloon. The C-7, non-rigid Navy dirigible was first to use non-inflammable helium as lifting gas, making a flight from Hampton Roads, Va., to Washington, D.C. (Dec. 1).

1922 First member of Caterpillar Club. Lt. (later Maj. Gen.) Harold Harris bailed out of a crippled plane he was testing at McCook Field, Dayton, Ohio (Oct. 20), and became the first man to join the Caterpillar Club—those whose lives have been saved by parachute.

1923 First nonstop transcontinental flight. Lts. John A. Macready and Oakley Kelly flew a single-engine Fokker T-2 nonstop from New York to San Diego, a distance of just over 2,500 mi. in 26 h 50 min (May 2–3).

First autogyro flight. Juan de la Cierva, a brilliant Spanish mathematician, made the first successful flight in a rotary wing aircraft in Madrid (June 9).

1924 First round-the-world flight. Four Douglas Cruiser biplanes of the U.S. Army Air Corps took off from Seattle under command of Maj. Frederick Martin (April 6). 175 days later, two of the planes (Lt. Lowell Smith's and Lt. Erik Nelson's) landed in Seattle after a circuitous route—one source saying 26,345 mi., another saying 27,553 mi.

1926 First polar flight. Then-Lt. Cmdr. Richard E. Byrd, acting as navigator, and Floyd Bennett as pilot, flew a trimotor Fokker from Kings Bay, Spitsbergen, over the North Pole and back in 15 1/2 h (May 8–9).

1927 First solo, nonstop transatlantic flight. Charles Augustus Lindbergh lifted his Wright-powered Ryan monoplane, *Spirit of St. Louis,* from Roosevelt Field, L.I., to stay aloft 33 h 39 min and travel 3,600 mi. to Le Bourget Field outside Paris (May 20–21).

First transatlantic passenger. Charles A. Levine was piloted by Clarence D. Chamberlin from Roosevelt Field, L.I., to Eisleben, Germany, in a Wright-powered Bellanca (June 4–5).

1928 First east-west transatlantic crossing. Baron Guenther von Huenefeld, piloted by German Capt. Hermann Koehl and Irish Capt. James Fitzmaurice, left Dublin for New York City (April 12) in a single-engine all-metal Junkers-monoplane. Some 37 h later, they crashed on Greely Island, Labrador. Rescued.

Charles A. Lindbergh and *The Spirit of St. Louis.* (National Air and Space Museum, Smithsonian Institution)

First U.S.-Australia flight. Sir Charles Kingsford-Smith and Capt. Charles T. P. Ulm, Australians, and two American navigators, Harry W. Lyon and James Warner, crossed the Pacific from Oakland to Brisbane. They went via Hawaii and the Fiji Islands in a trimotor Fokker (May 31–June 8).

First transarctic flight. Sir Hubert Wilkins, an Australian explorer and Carl Ben Eielson, who served as pilot, flew from Point Barrow, Alaska, to Spitsbergen (mid-April).

1929 First of the endurance records. With Air Corps Maj. Carl Spaatz in command and Capt. Ira Eaker as chief pilot, an Army Fokker, aided by refueling in the air, remained aloft 150 h 40 min at Los Angeles (Jan. 1–7).

First round-the-world airship flight. The LZ-127, known as the *Graf Zeppelin,* flew 21,300 miles in 20 days and 4 hours. Also set distance record (August).

First blind flight. James H. Doolittle proved the feasibility of instrument-guided flying when he took off and landed entirely on instruments (Sept. 24).

First rocket-engine flight. Fritz von Opel, a German auto maker, stayed aloft in his small rocket-powered craft for 75 sec, covering nearly 2 mi. (Sept. 30).

First South Pole flight. Comdr. Richard E. Byrd, with Bernt Balchen as pilot, Harold I. June, radio operator, and Capt. A. C. McKinley, photographer, flew a trimotor Fokker from the Bay of Whales, Little America, over the South Pole and back (Nov. 28–29).

1930 First Paris-New York nonstop flight. Dieudonné Coste and Maurice Bellonte, French pilots, flew a Hispano-powered Breguet biplane from Le Bourget Field to Valley Stream, L.I., in 37 h 18 min. (Sept. 2–3).

1931 First flight into the stratosphere. Auguste Piccard, a Swiss physicist, and Charles Knipfer ascended in a balloon from Augsburg, Germany, and reached a height of 51,793 ft in a 17-h flight that terminated on a glacier near Innsbruck, Austria (May 27).

First nonstop transpacific flight. Hugh Herndon and Clyde Pangborn took off from Sabishiro Beach, Japan, dropped their landing gear, and flew 4,860 mi. to near Wenatchee, Wash., in 41 h 13 min. (Oct. 4–5).

1932 **First woman's transatlantic solo.** Amelia Earhart, flying a Pratt & Whitney Wasp-powered Lockheed Vega, flew alone from Harbor Grace, Newfoundland, to Ireland in approximately 15 h (May 20–21).

First westbound transatlantic solo. James A. Mollison, a British pilot, took a de Havilland Puss Moth from Portmarnock, Ireland, to Pennfield, N.B. (Aug. 18).

First woman airline pilot. Ruth Rowland Nichols, first woman to hold three international records at the same time—speed, distance, altitude—was employed by N.Y.-New England Airways.

1933 **First round-the-world solo.** Wiley Post took a Lockheed Vega, *Winnie Mae*, 15,596 mi. around the world in 7 d 18 h 49 1/2 min (July 15–22).

1937 **First successful helicopter.** Hanna Reitsch, a German pilot, flew Dr. Heinrich Focke's FW-61 in free, fully controlled flight at Bremen (July 4).

1939 **First turbojet flight.** Just before their invasion of Poland, the Germans flew a Heinkel He-178 plane powered by a Heinkel S3B turbojet (Aug. 27).

1942 **First American jet plane flight.** Robert Stanley, chief pilot for Bell Aircraft Corp., flew the Bell XP-59 *Airacomet* at Muroc Army Base, Calif. (Oct. 1).

1944 **The first production stage rocket-engine fighter plane,** the German Messerschmitt Me 163B *Komet* (test flown 1941) becomes operational in June 1944. Some 350 of these delta-wing fighters were built before WW II in Europe ended.

1947 **First piloted supersonic flight in an airplane.** Capt. Charles E. Yeager, U.S. Air Force, flew the X-1 rocket-powered research plane built by Bell Aircraft Corp., faster than the speed of sound at Muroc Air Force Base, California (Oct. 14).

1949 **First round-the-world nonstop flight.** Capt. James Gallagher and USAF crew of 13 flew a Boeing B-50A Superfortress around the world nonstop from Ft. Worth, returning to same point: 23,452 mi. in 94 h 1 min, with 4 aerial refuelings enroute (Feb. 27–March 2).

1950 **First nonstop transatlantic jet flight.** Col. David C. Schilling (USAF) flew 3,300 mi. from England to Limestone, Maine, in 10 h 1 min (Sept. 22).

1951 **First solo across North Pole.** Charles F. Blair, Jr., flew a converted P-51 (May 29).

1952 **First jetliner service.** De Havilland Comet flight inaugurated by BOAC between London and Johannesburg, South Africa (May 2). Flight, including stops, took 23 h 38 min.

First transatlantic helicopter flight. Capt. Vincent H. McGovern and 1st Lt. Harold W. Moore piloted 2 Sikorsky H-19s from Westover, Mass., to Prestwick, Scotland (3,410 mi.). Trip was made in 5 steps, with flying time of 42 h 25 min (July 15–31).

First transatlantic round trip in same day. British Canberra twin-jet bomber flew from Aldergrove, Northern Ireland, to Gander, Newfoundland, and back in 7 h 59 min flying time (Aug. 26).

1955 **First transcontinental round trip in same day.** Lt. John M. Conroy piloted F-86 Sabrejet across U.S. (Los Angeles-New York) and back—5,085 mi.—in 11 h 33 min 27 sec (May 21).

1957 **First round-the-world, nonstop jet plane flight.** Maj. Gen. Archie J. Old, Jr., USAF, led a flight

Chuck Yeager alongside the Bell X-1 named *Glamorous Glennis* after his wife. (National Air and Space Museum, Smithsonian Institution)

of 3 Boeing B-52 bombers, powered with 8 10,000-lb. thrust Pratt & Whitney Aircraft J57 engines around the world in 45 h 19 min; distance 24,325 mi.; average speed 525 mph. (Completed Jan. 18.)

1958 **First transatlantic jet passenger service.** BOAC, New York to London (Oct. 4). Pan American started daily service, N.Y. to Paris (Oct. 26).

First domestic jet passenger service. National Airlines inaugurated service between New York and Miami (Dec. 10).

1968 **Prototype of world's first supersonic** airliner, the Soviet-designed Tupolev Tu-144 made first flight, Dec. 31. It first achieved supersonic speed on June 5, 1969.

1973 **First female pilot of a U.S. major scheduled airline.** Emily H. Warner became employed by Frontier Airlines on January 29 as second officer on a Boeing 737.

1976 **First regularly-scheduled commercial supersonic transport (SST) flights begin.** Air France and British Airways inaugurate service (January 21). Air France flies the Paris-Rio de Janeiro route; B.A., the London-Bahrain. Both airlines begin SST service to Washington, D.C. (May 24).

1977 **First successful man-powered aircraft.** Paul MacCready, an aeronautical engineer from Pasadena, Calif., was awarded the Kremer Prize for creating the world 's first successful man-powered aircraft. The *Gossamer Condor* was flown by Bryan Allen over the required 3-mile course on Aug. 23.

1978 **First successful transatlantic balloon flight.** Three Albuquerque, N.M., men, Ben Abruzzo, Larry Newman, and Maxie Anderson, completed the crossing (Aug. 16. Landed, Aug. 17) in their helium-filled balloon, *Double Eagle II*.

1979 **First man-powered aircraft to fly across the English Channel.** The Kremer Prize for the Channel crossing was won by Bryan Allen who flew the *Gossamer Albatross* from Folkestone, England to Cap Gris-Nez, France, in 2 h 55 min (June 12).

1980 **First successful balloon flight over the North Pole.** Sidney Conn and his wife Eleanor, in hot-air balloon *Joy of Sound* (April 11).

First nonstop transcontinental balloon flight, and also record for longest overland voyage in a balloon. Maxie Anderson and his son, Kris, completed four-day flight from Fort Baker, Calif., to successful landing outside Matane, Quebec, on May 12 in their helium-filled balloon, *Kitty Hawk*.

First long-distance solar-powered flight. Janice Brown, 98-lb. former teacher, flew tiny exper-

World 25 Busiest Airports in 1990

	Airport	Passengers[1]	Cargo		Operations	
1.	Chicago, Ill. (O'Hare)	59,936,137	986,673	(5)	810,865	(1)
2.	Dallas/Ft. Worth, Texas	48,515,464	556,749	(16)	731,036	(3)
3.	Atlanta, Georgia	48,024,566	610,450	(14)	790,502	(2)
4.	Los Angeles (International)	45,810,221	1,164,926	(4)	679,861	(4)
5.	London (Heathrow)	42,964,200	779,400	(8)	390,485	(18)
6.	Tokyo, Japan (Haneda)	40,233,031	614,610	(13)	183,950	(77)
7.	San Francisco (International)	31,059,820	566,068	(15)	430,253	(11)
8.	New York (Kennedy)	29,786,657	1,322,353	(2)	302,038	(36)
9.	Frankfurt, Germany	28,912,145	1,259,398	(3)	324,387	(27)
10.	Denver, Colorado	27,432,989	280,136	(32)	484,040	(8)
11.	Miami, Fla. (International)	25,837,445	966,443	(6)	480,987	(9)
12.	Paris (Orly)	24,329,700	287,895	(30)	193,451	(74)
13.	Osaka, Japan	23,511,611	493,947	(19)	130,550	(128)
14.	Honolulu, Oahu, Hawaii	23,367,770	374,901	(23)	407,048	(15)
15.	Boston, Massachusetts	22,935,844	364,275	(24)	424,568	(12)
16.	New York (LaGuardia)	22,753,812	116,844	(62)	354,229	(24)
17.	Detroit (Metro Wayne Co.)	22,585,156	191,421	(44)	387,848	(19)
18.	Paris (Charles De Gaulle)	22,506,107	647,369	(10)	235,350	(52)
19.	Newark, N.J. (International)	22,255,002	504,980	(18)	379,432	(22)
20.	Phoenix, Arizona	21,718,068	114,238	(65)	498,752	(6)
21.	London (Gatwick)	21,185,400	228,000	(35)	203,200	(69)
22.	Minneapolis/St. Paul, Minn.	20,381,314	266,355	(34)	379,785	(21)
23.	Toronto, Ont. (Pearson)	20,304,271	322,929	(26)	353,682	(25)
24.	St. Louis, Missouri	20,065,737	108,047	(67)	439,002	(10)
25.	Tokyo, Japan (Narita)	19,264,650	1,387,552	(1)	125,187	(136)

1. Enplaned, deplaned, and transfer, in millions. NOTE: Figures in ( ) next to cargo and operations totals represent rank for those categories. *Source:* Airport Operators Council International.

imental solar-powered aircraft, *Solar Challenger* six miles in 22-min near Marana, Ariz. (Dec. 3). The craft was powered by a 2.75-hp engine.

First solar-powered aircraft to fly across the English Channel. Stephen R. Ptacek flew the 210-lb *Solar Challenger* at the average speed of 30 mph from Cormeilles-en-Vexin near Paris to the Royal Manston Air Force Base on England's southeastern coast in 5 h 30 min (July 7).

1984 First solo transatlantic balloon flight. Joe W. Kittinger landed Sept. 18 near Savona, Italy, in his helium-filled balloon *Rosie O'Grady's Balloon of Peace* after a flight of 3,535 miles from Caribou, Me.

1986 First nonstop flight around the world without refueling. From Edwards AFB, Calif., Dick Rutan and Jeana Yeager flew in *Voyager* around the world (24,986.727 mi.), returning to Edwards in 216 h 3 min 44 s (Dec. 14–23).

1987 First Transatlantic Hot-Air Balloon Flight. Richard Branson and Per Lindstrand flew 2,789.6 miles from Sugarloaf Mt., Maine, to Ireland in the hot-air balloon *Virgin Atlantic Flyer* (July 2–4).

1991 First Transpacific hot-air balloon flight. Richard Branson and Per Lindstrand flew about 6,700 miles from Miyakonyo, Japan, to 150 miles west of Yellowknift, Northwest Territories, Canada (Jan. 15–17). Record pending verification.

World Class Helicopter Records

Selected records. *Source:* National Aeronautic Association.

Great Circle Distance Without Landing
International: 2,213.04 mi.; 3,561.55 km.
Robert G. Ferry (U.S.) in Hughes YOH-6A helicopter powered by Allison T-63-A-5 engine; from Culver City, Calif., to Ormond Beach, Fla., April 6–7, 1966.

Distance, Closed Circuit
International: 1,739.96 mi.; 2,800.20 km.
Jack Schweibold (U.S.) in Hughes YOH-6A helicopter powered by Allison T-62-A-5 engine; Edwards Air Force Base, Calif., March 26, 1966.

Altitude
International: 40,820 ft; 12,442 m.
Jean Boulet (France) in Alouette SA 315-001 "Lama" powered by Artouste IIIB 735 KW engine; Istres, France, June 21, 1972.

Altitude in Horizontal Flight
International: 36,122 ft; 11,010 m.
CWO James K. Church, (U.S.) in Sikorsky CH-54B helicopter powered by 2 P&W JFTD-12 engines; Stratford, CT., Nov. 4, 1971.

Speed Around the World
35.40 mph; 56.97 kph.
H. Ross Perot, Jr., pilot; J.W. Coburn, co-pilot (U.S.) in Bell 206 L-II Long Ranger, powered by one Allison 250-C28B of 435 hp. Elapsed time: 29 days 3 h 8 min 13 sec, Sept. 10–30, 1982.

Active Pilot Certificates Held[1]

(as of January 1)

Year	Total	Airline transport	Commercial	Private
1970	720,028	31,442	176,585	299,491
1975	733,728	41,002	192,425	305,848
1980	814,667	63,652	182,097	343,276
1985	722,376	79,192	155,929	320,086
1987	699,653	91,287	143,635	300,949
1988	694,016	96,968	143,030	299,786
1989	700,010	102,087	144,540	293,179
1990	702,659	107,732	149,666	299,111

1. Includes other pilot categories—helicopter, glider and recreational (17,487), and students (128,663). *Source:* Department of Transportation, Federal Aviation Administration.

THE WORLD'S FASTEST AIRCRAFT. The Lockheed SR-71 A/B "Blackbird" first produced in January 1966 was moth-balled in 1989. It is the world's fastest and highest flying production aircraft built. The Blackbird was unarmed and had a crew of two seated in tandem. The dimensions are: span 55 ft 7 in.; length 107 ft 5 in.; and height 18 ft 6 in. Its estimated maximum speed at 78,750 feet is over Mach 3, and its operational ceiling is above 80,000 feet. In a reconnaissance mission, the SR-71 could cover up to a 100,000 sq.-mi. area in one hour.

Before it was donated to the Smithsonian Institution, one of the SR-71's set a transcontinental speed record on March 6, 1990, distance: 2,404 miles, time: 1 hr 7 min 53.69 seconds, speed: 2,124.51 miles per hour. □

THE F-117A STEALTH FIGHTER is the world's first operational military aircraft designed to attack targets undetected by enemy radar defenses. During the Persian Gulf War, the bat-shaped F-117A easily slipped past Iraq's Soviet-made radar unseen, resulting in the destruction of numerous military targets with HARM surface-to-air missiles and laser-guided bombs. During the conflict, none of the stealth fighters was ever shot down by the enemy. The F-117A is flown by the 37th Tactical Fighter Wing at Tonopah Test Range Airfield, Nevada. USAF photo. □

Absolute World Records

(Maximum Performance in Any Class)
Source: National Aeronautic Association

These official Absolute World Records are the supreme achievements of all the hundreds of records open to flying machines. They are the most outstanding of all the major types, and thus warrant the highest respect.

All types of airplanes are eligible for these few very special records. Airplanes may be powered by piston, turboprop, turbojet, rocket engines or a combination. They may be landplanes, seaplanes or amphibians; they may be lightplanes, business planes, military or commercial airplanes.

Over the years, many different categories of aircraft have held these records. In the past, the cost of developing high-performance aircraft has been so great that only airplanes created for military purposes have held these records. There have been two exceptions to this situation.

Most recently and most dramatically, the Rutan designed "Voyager" shattered the theory that only a complicated military behemoth could hold an Absolute World Record. The Voyager team and its nonstop, non-refueled flight around the world proved that the dreams of dedicated individuals, combined with creative engineering, new technology, and hard work, could conquer the world.

The other exception was the X-15 rocket-powered research airplane. Holder of one record, it was used for both civilian and military research during its highly productive lifetime.

Within the seven basic categories of Absolute Records for airplanes, again the Voyager stands out as a special achievement. This amateur, hand-built, experimental aircraft deserves special recognition because the others were are all military/civilian aircraft designed and built by major government facilities. They are: the little-known Soviet E-266M a rocket-boosted version of the MiG-25 "Foxbat" interceptor, which holds the absolute altitude record, the aforementioned North American X-15 which holds the record for carrier-launched altitude, and the Lockheed SR-71 "Blackbird" photoreconnaisance airplane which holds three records for speed and altitude.

As evidence of the exceptional status of these records, note that several are more than 10 years old. Since the performance of many new government-backed a irplanes which might be superior to these is wrapped in a blanket of national security, the breaking of some of these records will depend as much on political considerations as on technical ones.

Speed Around the World, Nonstop, Nonrefueled

Speed (mph)	Date	Type Plane	Pilots	Place
115.65	Dec. 14-23, 1986	*Voyager*	Dick Rutan & Jeana Yeager (U.S.)	Edwards AFB, Calif.—Edwards AFB, Calif.

Distance, Great Circle Without Landing, also Distance, Closed Circuit Without Landing

Distance (mi.)	Date	Pilots	Place
24,986.727	Dec. 14-23, 1986	Dick Rutan & Jeana Yeager (U.S.)	Edwards AFB, Calif.—Edwards AFB, Calif.

Speed Over a Straight Course

Speed (mph)	Date	Type Plane	Pilot	Place
2,193.16	July 28, 1976	Lockheed SR-71A	Capt. Eldon W. Joersz (USAF)	Beale AFB, Calif.

Speed Over A Closed Circuit

Speed (mph)	Date	Type Plane	Pilot	Place
2,092.294	July 27,1976	Lockheed SR-71A	Maj. Adolphus H. Bledsoe, Jr. (USAF)	Beale, AFB, Calif.

Altitude

Height (ft)	Date	Type Plane	Pilot	Place
123,523.58	Aug. 31, 1977	MIG-25, E-266M	Alexander Fedotov (U.S.S.R.)	U.S.S.R.

Altitude in Horizontal Flight

Height (ft)	Date	Pilot	Place
85,068.997	July 28, 1976	Capt. Robert C. Helt (USAF)	Beale AFB, Calif.

Altitude, Aircraft Launched From A Carrier Airplane

Height (ft)	Date	Type Plane	Pilot	Place
314,750.00	July 17, 1962	N. American X-15-1	Maj. Robert White (USAF)	Edwards AFB, Calif.

WEATHER & CLIMATE

Climate of 100 Selected U.S. Cities

| City | Average Monthly Temperature (°F)[1] | | | | Precipitation | | Snowfall | |
	Jan.	April	July	Oct	Average (in.)[1]	annual (days)[2]	Average annual (in.)[2]	Years[2]
Albany, N.Y.	21.1	46.6	71.4	50.5	35.74	134	65.5	38
Albuquerque, N.M.	34.8	55.1	78.8	57.4	8.12	59	10.6	45
Anchorage, Alaska	13.0	35.4	58.1	34.6	15.20	115	69.2	41[3]
Asheville, N.C.	36.8	55.7	73.2	56.0	47.71	124	17.5	20
Atlanta, Ga.	41.9	61.8	78.6	62.2	48.61	115	1.9	50
Atlantic City, N.J.	31.8	51.0	74.4	55.5	41.93	112	16.4	40[3]
Austin, Texas	49.1	68.7	84.7	69.8	31.50	83	0.9	43
Baltimore, Md.	32.7	54.0	76.8	56.9	41.84	113	21.8	34
Baton Rouge, La.	50.8	68.4	82.1	68.2	55.77	108	0.1	34[3]
Billings, Mont.	20.9	44.6	72.3	49.3	15.09	96	57.2	50
Birmingham, Ala.	42.9	62.8	80.1	62.6	54.52	117	1.3	41
Bismark, N.D.	6.7	42.5	70.4	46.1	15.36	96	40.3	45
Boise, Idaho	29.9	48.6	74.6	51.9	11.71	92	21.4	45
Boston, Mass.	29.6	48.7	73.5	54.8	43.81	127	41.8	49[3]
Bridgeport, Conn.	29.5	48.6	74.0	56.0	41.56	117	26.0	36
Buffalo, N.Y.	23.5	45.4	70.7	51.5	37.52	169	92.2	41
Burlington, Vt.	16.6	42.7	69.6	47.9	33.69	153	78.2	41
Caribou, Maine	10.7	37.3	65.1	43.1	36.59	160	113.3	45
Casper, Wyom.	22.2	42.1	70.9	47.1	11.43	95	80.5	34
Charleston, S.C.	47.9	64.3	80.5	65.8	51.59	113	0.6	42
Charleston, W.Va.	32.9	55.3	74.5	55.9	42.43	151	31.5	37
Charlotte, N.C.	40.5	60.3	78.5	60.7	43.16	111	6.1	45
Cheyenne, Wyom.	26.1	41.8	68.9	47.5	13.31	98	54.1	49
Chicago, Ill.	21.4	48.8	73.0	53.5	33.34	127	40.3	26
Cleveland, Ohio	25.5	48.1	71.6	53.2	35.40	156	53.6	43
Columbia, S.C.	44.7	63.8	81.0	63.4	49.12	109	1.9	37
Columbus, Ohio	27.1	51.4	73.8	53.9	36.97	137	28.3	37[3]
Concord, N.H.	19.9	44.1	69.5	48.3	36.53	125	64.5	43
Dallas–Ft. Worth, Texas	44.0	65.9	86.3	67.9	29.46	78	3.1	31
Denver, Colo.	29.5	47.4	73.4	51.9	15.31	88	59.8	50
Des Moines, Iowa	18.6	50.5	76.3	54.2	30.83	107	34.7	45
Detroit, Mich.	23.4	47.3	71.9	51.9	30.97	133	40.4	26
Dodge City, Kan.	29.5	54.3	80.0	57.7	20.66	78	19.5	42
Duluth, Minn.	6.3	38.3	65.4	44.2	29.68	135	77.4	41[3]
El Paso, Texas	44.2	63.6	82.5	63.6	7.82	47	5.2	45
Fairbanks, Alaska	−12.7	30.2	61.5	25.1	10.37	106	67.5	33
Fargo, N.D.	4.3	42.1	70.6	46.3	19.59	100	35.9	42
Grand Junction, Colo.	25.5	51.7	78.9	54.9	8.00	72	26.1	38
Grand Rapids, Mich.	22.0	46.3	71.4	50.9	34.35	143	72.4	21
Hartford, Conn.	25.2	48.8	73.4	52.4	44.39	127	50.0	30
Helena, Mont.	18.1	42.3	67.9	45.1	11.37	96	47.9	44
Honolulu, Hawaii	72.6	75.7	80.1	79.5	23.47	100	0.0	38[3]
Houston, Texas	51.4	68.7	83.1	69.7	44.76	105	0.4	50
Indianapolis, Ind.	26.0	52.4	75.1	54.8	39.12	125	23.1	53[3]
Jackson, Miss.	45.7	65.1	81.9	65.0	52.82	109	1.2	21
Jacksonville, Fla.	53.2	67.7	81.3	69.5	52.76	116	T	43
Juneau, Alaska	21.8	39.1	55.7	41.8	53.15	220	102.8	41
Kansas City, Mo.	28.4	56.9	80.9	59.6	29.27	98	20.0	43
Knoxville, Tenn .	38.2	59.6	77.6	59.5	47.29	127	12.3	42
Las Vegas, Nev.	44.5	63.5	90.2	67.5	4.19	26	1.4	36
Lexington, Ky.	31.5	55.1	75.9	56.8	45.68	131	16.3	40
Little Rock, Ark.	39.9	62.4	82.1	63.1	49.20	104	5.4	42
Long Beach, Calif.	55.2	60.9	72.8	67.5	11.54	32	T	41[3]
Los Angeles, Calif.	56.0	59.5	69.0	66.3	12.08	36	T	49
Louisville, Ky.	32.5	56.6	77.6	-57.7	43.56	125	17.5	37
Madison, Wisc.	15.6	45.8	70.6	49.5	30.84	118	40.8	36
Memphis, Tenn.	39.6	62.6	82.1	62.9	51.57	107	5.5	34
Miami, Fla.	67.1	75.3	82.5	77.9	57.55	129	0.0	42
Milwaukee, Wisc.	18.7	44.6	70.5	50.9	30.94	125	47.0	44

363

City	Average Monthly Temperature (°F)[1]				Precipitation		Snowfall	
	Jan.	April	July	Oct	Average (in.)[1]	annual (days)[2]	Average annual (in.)[2]	Years[2]
Minneapolis–St. Paul, Minn.	11.2	46.0	73.1	49.6	26.36	115	48.9	46
Mobile, Ala.	50.8	68.0	82.2	68.5	64.64	123	0.3	43
Montgomery, Ala.	46.7	65.2	81.7	65.3	49.16	108	0.3	40
Mt. Washington, N.H.	5.1	22.4	48.7	30.5	89.92	209	246.8	52
Nashville, Tenn.	37.1	59.7	79.4	60.2	48.49	119	11.1	43
Newark, N.J.	31.2	52.1	76.8	57.2	42.34	122	28.2	43
New Orleans, La.	52.4	68.7	82.1	69.2	59.74	114	0.2	38[3]
New York, N.Y.	31.8	51.9	76.4	57.5	42.82	119	26.1	40[3]
Norfolk, Va.	39.9	58.2	78.4	61.3	45.22	115	7.9	36
Oklahoma City, Okla.	35.9	60.2	82.1	62.3	30.89	82	9.0	45
Olympia, Wash.	37.2	47.3	63.0	50.1	50.96	164	18.0	43
Omaha, Neb.	20.2	52.2	77.7	54.5	30.34	98	31.1	49[3]
Philadelphia, Pa.	31.2	52.9	76.5	56.5	41.42	117	21.9	42[3]
Phoenix, Ariz.	52.3	68.1	92.3	73.4	7.11	36	T	47[3]
Pittsburgh, Pa.	26.7	50.1	72.0	52.5	36.30	154	44.6	32
Portland, Maine	21.5	42.8	68.1	48.5	43.52	128	72.4	44
Portland, Ore.	38.9	50.4	67.7	54.3	37.39	154	6.8	44
Providence, R.I.	28.2	47.9	72.5	53.2	45.32	124	37.1	31
Raleigh, N.C.	39.6	59.4	77.7	59.7	41.76	112	7.7	40
Reno, Nev.	32.2	46.4	69.5	50.3	7.49	51	25.3	42
Richmond, Va.	36.6	57.9	77.8	58.6	44.07	113	14.6	47
Roswell, N.M.	41.4	61.9	81.4	61.7	9.70	52	11.4	37[3]
Sacramento, Calif.	45.3	58.2	75.6	63.9	17.10	58	0.1	36[3]
Salt Lake City, Utah	28.6	49.2	77.5	53.0	15.31	90	59.1	56
San Antonio, Texas	50.4	69.6	84.6	70.2	29.13	81	0.4	42
San Diego, Calif.	56.8	61.2	70.3	67.5	9.32	43	T	44
San Francisco, Calif.	48.5	54.8	62.2	60.6	19.71	63	T	57
Savannah, Ga.	49.1	66.0	81.2	66.9	49.70	111	0.3	34
Seattle–Tacoma, Wash.	39.1	48.7	64.8	52.4	38.60	158	12.8	40
Sioux Falls, S.D.	12.4	46.4	74.0	49.4	24.12	96	39.9	39
Spokane, Wash.	25.7	45.8	69.7	47.5	16.71	114	51.5	37
Springfield, Ill.	24.6	53.3	76.5	56.0	33.78	114	24.5	37
St. Louis, Mo.	28.8	56.1	78.9	57.9	33.91	111	19.8	48[3]
Tampa, Fla.	59.8	71.5	82.1	74.4	46.73	107	T	38
Toledo, Ohio	23.1	47.8	71.8	51.7	31.78	137	38.3	29
Tucson, Ariz.	51.1	64.9	86.2	70.4	11.14	52	1.2	44
Tulsa, Okla.	35.2	61.0	83.2	62.6	38.77	89	9.0	46
Vero Beach, Fla.	61.9	71.7	81.1	75.2	51.41	n.a.	n.a.	0
Washington, D.C.	35.2	56.7	78.9	59.3	39.00	112	17.0	41[3]
Wilmington, Del.	31.2	52.4	76.0	56.3	41.38	117	20.9	37
Wichita, Kan.	29.6	56.3	81.4	59.1	28.61	85	16.4	31

1. Based on 30 year period 1951–80. Data latest available. 2. Data through 1984 based on number of years as indicated in Years column. 3. For snowfall data where number of years differ from that for precipitation data. T = trace. n.a. = not available. *Source:* National Oceanic and Atmospheric Administration.

Wind Chill Factors

Wind speed (mph)	Thermometer reading (degrees Fahrenheit)																
	35	30	25	20	15	10	5	0	–5	–10	–15	–20	–25	–30	–35	–40	–45
5	33	27	21	19	12	7	0	–5	–10	–15	–21	–26	–31	–36	–42	–47	–52
10	22	16	10	3	–3	–9	–15	–22	–27	–34	–40	–46	–52	–58	–64	–71	–77
15	16	9	2	–5	–11	–18	–25	–31	–38	–45	–51	–58	–65	–72	–78	–85	–92
20	12	4	–3	–10	–17	–24	–31	–39	–46	–53	–60	–67	–74	–81	–88	–95	–103
25	8	1	–7	–15	–22	–29	–36	–44	–51	–59	–66	–74	–81	–88	–96	–103	–110
30	6	–2	–10	–18	–25	–33	–41	–49	–56	–64	–71	–79	–86	–93	–101	–109	–116
35	4	–4	–12	–20	–27	–35	–43	–52	–58	–67	–74	–82	–89	–97	–105	–113	–120
40	3	–5	–13	–21	–29	–37	–45	–53	–60	–69	–76	–84	–92	–100	–107	–115	–123
45	2	–6	–14	–22	–30	–38	–46	–54	–62	–70	–78	–85	–93	–102	–109	–117	–125

NOTES: This chart gives equivalent temperatures for combinations of wind speed and temperatures. For example, the combination of a temperature of 10° Fahrenheit and a wind blowing at 10 mph has a cooling power equal to –9° F. Wind speeds of higher than 45 mph have little additional cooling effect.

World and U.S. Extremes of Climate

Highest recorded temperature

	Place	Date	Degree Fahrenheit	Degree Centigrade
World (Africa)	El Azizia, Libya	Sept. 13, 1922	136	58
North America (U.S.)	Death Valley, Calif.	July 10, 1913	134	57
Asia	Tirat Tsvi, Israel	June 21, 1942	129	54
Australia	Cloncurry, Queensland	Jan. 16, 1889	128	53
Europe	Seville, Spain	Aug. 4, 1881	122	50
South America	Rivadavia, Argentina	Dec. 11, 1905	120	49
Canada	Midale and Yellow Grass, Saskatchewan	July 5, 1937	113	45
Persian Gulf (sea–surface)		August 5, 1924	96	36
South Pole		Dec. 27, 1978	7.5	−14
Antarctica	Vanda Station	Jan. 5, 1974	59	15

Lowest recorded temperature

	Place	Date	Degree Fahrenheit	Degree Centigrade
World (Antarctica)	Vostok	July 21, 1983	−129	−89
Asia	Verkhoyansk/Oimekon	Feb. 6, 1933	−90	−68
Greenland	Northice	Jan. 9, 1954	−87	−66
North America (excl. Greenland)	Snag, Yukon, Canada	Feb. 3, 1947	−81	−63
Alaska	Prospect Creek, Endicott Mts.	Jan. 23, 1971	−80	−62
U.S., excluding Alaska	Rogers Pass, Mont.	Jan. 20, 1954	−70	−56.5
Europe	Ust 'Shchugor, U.S.S.R.	n.a.	−67	−55
South America	Sarmiento, Argentina	Jan. 1, 1907	−27	−33
Africa	Ifrane, Morocco	Feb. 11, 1935	−11	−24
Australia	Charlotte Pass, N.S.W.	July 22, 1947	−8	−22
United States	Prospect Creek, Alaska	Jan. 23, 1971	−80	−62

Greatest rainfalls

	Place	Date	Inches	Centimeters
1 minute (World)	Unionville, Md.	July 4, 1956	1.23	3.1
20 minutes (World)	Curtea–de–Arges, Romania	July 7, 1889	8.1	20.5
42 minutes (World)	Holt, Mo.	June 22, 1947	12	30.5
12 hours (World)	Foc–Foc, La Réunion	Jan. 7–8, 1966	45	114
24 hours (World)	Foc–Foc, La Réunion	Jan. 7–8, 1966	72	182.5
24 hours (N. Hemisphere)	Paishih, Taiwan	Sept. 10–11, 1963	49	125
24 hours (Australia)	Bellenden Ker, Queensland	Jan. 4, 1979	44	114
24 hours (U.S.)	Alvin, Texas	July 25–26, 1979	43	109
24 hours (Canada)	Ucluelet Brynnor Mines, British Columbia	Oct. 6, 1967	19	49
5 days (World)	Commerson, La Réunion	Jan. 23–28, 1980	156	395
1 month (World)	Cherrapunji, India	July 1861	366	930
12 months (World)	Cherrapunji, India	Aug. 1860–Aug. 1861	1,042	2,647
12 months (U.S.)	Kukui, Maui, Hawaii	Dec. 1981–Dec. 1982	739	1878

Greatest snowfalls

	Place	Date	Inches	Centimeters
1 month (U.S.)	Tamarack, Calif.	Jan. 1911	390	991
24 hours (N. America)	Silver Lake, Colo.	April 14–15, 1921	76	192.5
24 hours (Alaska)	Thompson Pass	Dec. 29, 1955	62	157.5
19 hours (France)	Bessans	April 5–6, 1969	68	173
1 storm (N. America)	Mt. Shasta Ski Bowl, Calif.	Feb. 13–19, 1959	189	480
1 storm (Alaska)	Thompson Pass	Dec. 26–31, 1955	175	445.5
1 season (N. America)	Paradise Ranger Sta., Wash.	1971–1972	1,122	2,850
1 season (Alaska)	Thompson Pass	1952–1953	974.5	2,475
1 season (Canada)	Revelstoke Mt. Copeland, British Columbia	1971–1972	964	2,446.5

Source: U.S. Army Corps of Engineers, Engineer Topographic Laboratories.

Tropical Storms and Hurricanes, 1886–1990

	Jan.–April	May	June	July	Aug.	Sept.	Oct.	Nov.	Dec.	Total
Number of tropical storms (incl. hurricanes)	3	14	56	68	215	299	186	42	6	889
Number of tropical storms that reached hurricane intensity	1	3	23	36	149	188	95	21	3	519

Other Recorded Extremes

Highest average annual mean temperature (World): Dallol, Ethiopia (Oct. 1960–Dec. 1966), 94° F (35° C). **(U.S.):** Key West, Fla. (30–year normal), 78.2° F (25.7° C).

Lowest average annual mean temperature (Antarctica): Plateau Station −70° F (−57° C). **(U.S.):** Barrow, Alaska (30–year normal), 9.3° F (−13° C).

Greatest average yearly rainfall (U.S.): Mt. Waialeale, Kauai, Hawaii (32–year avg), 460 in. (1,168 cm). **(India):** Cherrapunji (74–year avg), 450 in. (1,143 cm).

Minimum average yearly rainfall (Chile): Arica (59–year avg), 0.03 in. (0.08 cm) (no rainfall for 14 consecutive years). **(U.S.):** Death Valley, Calif. (42–year avg), 1.63 in. (4.14 cm). Bagdad, Calif., holds the U.S. record for the longest period with no measurable rain, 767 days, from Oct. 3, 1912 to Nov. 8, 1914).

Hottest summer avg in Western Hemisphere (U.S.): Death Valley, Calif., 98° F (36.7° C).

Longest hot spell (W. Australia): Marble Bar, 100° F (38° C) (or above) for 162 consecutive days, Oct. 30, 1923–Apr. 7, 1924.

Largest hailstone (U.S.): Coffeyville, KS, 17.5 in. (44.5 cm), Sept. 3, 1979.

Weather Glossary

blizzard: storm characterized by strong winds, low temperatures, and large amounts of snow.

blowing snow: snow lifted from ground surface by wind; restricts visibility.

cold wave warning: indicates that a change to abnormally cold weather is expected; greater than normal protective measures will be required.

cyclone: circulation of winds rotating counterclockwise in the northern hemisphere and clockwise in the southern hemisphere. Hurricanes and tornadoes are both examples of cyclones.

drifting snow: strong winds will blow loose or falling snow into significant drifts.

drizzle: uniform close precipitation of tiny drops with diameter of less than .02 inch.

flash flood: dangerous rapid rise of water levels in streams, rivers, or over land area.

freezing rain or drizzle: rain or drizzle that freezes on contact with the ground or other objects forming a coating of ice on exposed surfaces.

gale warning: winds in the 33–48 knot (38–55 mph) range forecast.

hail: small balls of ice falling separately or in lumps; usually associated with thunderstorms and temperatures that may be well above freezing.

hazardous driving warnings: indicates that drizzle, freezing rain, snow, sleet, or strong winds make driving conditions difficult.

heavy snow warnings: issued when 4 inches or more of snow are expected to fall in a 12–hour period or when 6 inches or more are anticipated in a 24–hour period.

hurricane: devastating cyclonic storm; winds over 74 mph near storm center; usually tropical in origin; called cyclone in Indian Ocean, typhoon in the Pacific.

hurricane warning: winds in excess of 64 knots (74 mph) in connection with hurricane.

rain: precipitation of liquid particles with diameters larger than .02 inch.

sleet: translucent or transparent ice pellets; frozen rain; generally a winter phenomenon.

small craft warning: indicates winds as high as 33 knots (38 mph) and sea conditions dangerous to small boats.

snow flurries: snow falling for a short time at intermittent periods; accumulations are usually small.

snow squall: brief, intense falls of snow, usually accompanied by gusty winds.

storm warnings: winds greater than 48 knots (55 mph) are forecast.

temperature–humidity index (THI): measure of personal discomfort based on the combined effects of temperature and humidity. Most people are uncomfortable when the THI is 75. A THI of 80 produces acute discomfort for almost everyone.

tidal waves: series of ocean waves caused by earthquakes; can reach speeds of 600 mph; they grow in height as they reach shore and can crest as high as 100 feet.

thunder: the sound produced by the rapid expansion of air heated by lightning.

tornado: dangerous whirlwind associated with the cumulonimbus clouds of severe thunderstorms; winds up to 300 mph.

tornado warning: tornado has actually been detected by radar or sighted in designated area.

tornado watch: potential exists in the watch area for storms that could contain tornadoes.

travelers' warning: *see* hazardous driving warning.

tsunami: *see* tidal waves.

wind–chill factor: combined effect of temperature and wind speed as compared to equivalent temperature in calm air .

During a Hurricane

Source: Federal Emergency Management Agency and NOAA.

Remain indoors during a hurricane. Blowing debris can injure and kill. Travel is extremely dangerous. Be especially wary of the "eye" of the hurricane. If the storm center passes directly overhead, there will be a lull in the wind lasting from a few minutes to half-an-hour or more. At the other side of the "eye" the winds will increase rapidly to hurricane force, and will come from the opposite direction.

Record Highest Temperatures by State

State	Temp. °F	Temp °C	Date	Station	Elevation, feet
Alabama	112	44	Sept. 5, 1925	Centerville	345
Alaska	100	38	June 27, 1915	Fort Yukon	est. 420
Arizona	127	53	July 7, 1905*	Parker	345
Arkansas	120	49	Aug. 10, 1936	Ozark	396
California	134	57	July 10, 1913	Greenland Ranch	−178
Colorado	118	48	July 11, 1888	Bennett	5,484
Connecticut	105	41	July 22, 1926	Waterbury	400
Delaware	110	43	July 21, 1930	Millsboro	20
D.C.	106	41	July 20, 1930	Washington	410
Florida	109	43	June 29, 1931	Monticello	207
Georgia	113	45	May 27, 1978	Greenville	860
Hawaii	100	38	Apr. 27, 1931	Pahala	850
Idaho	118	48	July 28, 1934	Orofino	1,027
Illinois	117	47	July 14, 1954	E. St. Louis	410
Indiana	116	47	July 14, 1936	Collegeville	672
Iowa	118	48	July 20, 1934	Keokuk	614
Kansas	121	49	July 24, 1936*	Alton (near)	1,651
Kentucky	114	46	July 28, 1930	Greensburg	581
Louisiana	114	46	Aug. 10, 1936	Plain Dealing	268
Maine	105	41	July 10, 1911*	North Bridgton	450
Maryland	109	43	uly 10, 1936*	Cumberland & Frederick	623;325
Massachusetts	107	42	Aug. 2, 1975	New Bedford & Chester	120;640
Michigan	112	44	July 13, 1936	Mio	963
Minnesota	114	46	July 6, 1936*	Moorhead	904
Mississippi	115	46	July 29, 1930	Holly Springs	600
Missouri	118	48	July 14, 1954*	Warsaw & Union	687;560
Montana	117	47	July 5, 1937	Medicine Lake	1,950
Nebraska	118	48	July 24, 1936*	Minden	2,169
Nevada	122	50	June 23, 1954*	Overton	1,240
New Hampshire	106	41	July 4, 1911	Nashua	125
New Jersey	110	43	July 10, 1936	Runyon	18
New Mexico	116	47	July 14, 1934*	Orogrande	4,171
New York	108	42	July 22, 1926	Troy	35
North Carolina	110	43	Aug. 21, 1983	Fayetteville	81
North Dakota	121	49	July 6, 1936	Steele	1,857
Ohio	113	45	July 21, 1934*	Gallipolis (near)	673
Oklahoma	120	49	July 26, 1943*	Tishomingo	670
Oregon	119	48	Aug. 10, 1898	Pendleton	1,074
Pennsylvania	111	44	July 10, 1936*	Phoenixville	100
Rhode Island	104	40	Aug. 2, 1975	Providence	51
South Carolina	111	44	June 28, 1954*	Camden	170
South Dakota	120	49	July 5, 1936	Gannvalley	1,750
Tennessee	113	45	Aug. 9, 1930*	Perryville	377
Texas	120	49	Aug. 12, 1936	Seymour	1,291
Utah	117	47	July 5, 1895	Saint George	2,880
Vermont	105	41	July 4, 1911	Vernon	310
Virginia	110	43	July 15, 1954	Balcony Falls	725
Washington	118	48	Aug. 5, 1961*	Ice Harbor Dam	475
West Virginia	112	44	July 10, 1936*	Martinsburg	435
Wisconsin	114	46	July 13, 1936	Wisconsin Dells	900
Wyoming	114	46	July 12, 1900	Basin	3,500

*Also on earlier dates at the same or other places. *Source:* National Climatic Data Center, Atlanta, and Storm Phillips, STORMFAX, INC.

Record Lowest Temperatures by State

State	Temp. °F	Temp °C	Date	Station	Elevation, feet
Alabama	−27	−33	Jan. 30, 1966	New Market	760
Alaska	−80	−62	Jan. 23, 1971	Prospect Creek	1,100
Arizona	−40	−40	Jan. 7, 1971	Hawley Lake	8,180
Arkansas	−29	−34	Feb. 13, 1905	Pond	1,250
California	−45	−43	Jan. 20, 1937	Boca	5,532
Colorado	−60	−51	Jan. 1, 1979*	Maybell	5,920
Connecticut	−32	−36	Feb. 16, 1943	Falls Village	585
Delaware	−17	−27	Jan. 17, 1893	Millsboro	20
D.C.	−15	−26	Feb. 11, 1899	Washington	410
Florida	−2	−19	Feb. 13, 1899	Tallahassee	193
Georgia	−17	−27	Jan. 27, 1940	CCC Camp F−16	est. 1,000
Hawaii	14	−11	Jan. 2, 1961	Haleakala, Maui Is	9,750
Idaho	−60	−51	Jan. 18, 1943	Island Park Dam	6,285
Illinois	−35	−37	Jan. 22, 1930	Mount Carroll	817
Indiana	−35	−37	Feb. 2, 1951	Greensburg	954
Iowa	−47	−44	Jan. 12, 1912	Washta	1,157
Kansas	−40	−40	Feb. 13, 1905	Lebanon	1,812
Kentucky	−34	−37	Jan. 28, 1963	Cynthiana	684
Louisiana	−16	−27	Feb. 13, 1899	Minden	194
Maine	−48	−44	Jan. 19, 1925	Van Buren	510
Maryland	−40	−40	Jan. 13, 1912	Oakland	2,461
Massachusetts	−34	−37	Jan. 18, 1957	Birch Hill Dam	840
Michigan	−51	−46	Feb. 9, 1934	Vanderbilt	785
Minnesota	−59	−51	Feb. 16, 1903*	Pokegama Dam	1,280
Mississippi	−19	−28	Jan. 30, 1966	Corinth	420
Missouri	−40	−40	Feb. 13, 1905	Warsaw	700
Montana	−70	−57	Jan. 20, 1954	Rogers Pass	5,470
Nebraska	−47	−44	Feb. 12, 1899	Camp Clarke	3,700
Nevada	−50	−46	Jan. 8, 1937	San Jacinto	5,200
New Hampshire	−46	−43	Jan. 28, 1925	Pittsburg	1,575
New Jersey	−34	−37	Jan. 5, 1904	River Vale	70
New Mexico	−50	−46	Feb. 1, 1951	Gavilan	7,350
New York	−52	−47	Feb. 18, 1979*	Old Forge	1,720
North Carolina	−29	−37	Jan. 30, 1966	Mt. Mitchell	6,525
North Dakota	−60	−51	Feb. 15, 1936	Parshall	1,929
Ohio	−39	−39	Feb. 10, 1899	Milligan	800
Oklahoma	−27	−33	Jan. 18, 1930	Watts	958
Oregon	−54	−48	Feb. 10, 1933*	Seneca	4,700
Pennsylvania	−42	−41	Jan. 5, 1904	Smethport	est. 1,500
Rhode Island	−23	−31	Jan. 11, 1942	Kingston	100
South Carolina	−20	−28	Jan. 18, 1977	Caesars Head	3,100
South Dakota	−58	−50	Feb. 17, 1936	McIntosh	2,277
Tennessee	−32	−36	Dec. 30, 1917	Mountain City	2,471
Texas	−23	−31	Feb. 8, 1933*	Seminole	3,275
Utah	−50	−51	Jan. 5, 1913*	Strawberry Tunnel	7,650
Vermont	−50	−46	Dec. 30, 1933	Bloomfield	915
Virginia	−29	−34	Feb. 10, 1899	Monterey	—
Washington	−48	−44	Dec. 30, 1968	Mazama & Winthrop	2,120;1,765
West Virginia	−37	−38	Dec. 30, 1917	Lewisburg	2,200
Wisconsin	−54	−48	Jan. 24, 1922	Danbury	908
Wyoming	−63	−53	Feb. 9, 1933	Moran	6,770

*Also on earlier dates at the same or other places. *Source:* National Climatic Data Center, Atlanta, and Storm Phillips, STORMFAX, INC.

Record High and Low Temperature in U.S. for Each Month

Source: National Climatic Data Center, Atlanta, and Storm Phillips, STORMFAX, Inc.

January

The highest temperature ever recorded for the month of January occurred on January 17, 1936, again in 1954, in Laredo, Tex. (elevation 421 ft) where the temperature reached 98° F.

The lowest temperature ever recorded for the month of January occurred on January 20, 1954, in Rogers Pass, Mont. (elevation 5,470 ft) where the temperature fell to –70° F.

February

The highest temperature ever recorded for the month of February occurred on February 3, 1963, in Montezuma, Ariz. (elevation 735 ft) where the temperature reached 105° F.

The lowest temperature ever recorded for the month of February occurred on February 9, 1933, at the Riverside Ranger Station in Montana (elevation 6,700 ft) where the temperature fell to –66° F.

March

The highest temperature ever recorded for the month of March occurred on March 31, 1954, in Rio Grande City, Tex. (elevation 168 ft) where the temperature reached 108° F.

The lowest temperature ever recorded for the month of March occurred on March 17, 1906, in Snake River, Wyo. (elevation 6,862 ft) where the temperature dropped to –50° F.

April

The highest temperature ever recorded for the month of April occurred on April 25, 1898, at Volcano Springs, Calif. (elevation –220 ft) where the temperature reached 118° F.

The lowest temperature ever recorded for the month of April occurred on April 5, 1945, in Eagle Nest, N. Mex. (elevation 8,250 ft) where the temperature dropped to –36° F.

May

The highest temperature ever recorded for the month of May occurred on May 27, 1896, in Salton, Calif. (elevation –263 ft) where the temperature reached 124° F.

The lowest temperature ever recorded for the month of May occurred on May 7, 1964, in White Mountain 2, Calif. (elevation 12,470 ft) where the temperature dropped to –15° F.

June

The highest temperature ever recorded for the month of June occurred on June 15, 1896, at Fort Mohave, Ariz. (elevation 555 ft) where the temperature reached 127° F.

The lowest temperature ever recorded for the month of June occurred on June 13, 1907, in Tamarack, Calif. (elevation 8,000 ft) where the temperature dropped to 2° F.

July

The highest temperature ever recorded for the month of July occurred on July 10, 1913, at Greenland Ranch, Calif. (elevation –178 ft) where the temperature reached 134° F.

The lowest temperature ever recorded for the month of July occurred on July 21, 1911, at Painter, Wyo. (elevation 6,800 ft) where the temperature fell to 10° F.

August

The highest temperature ever recorded for the month of August occurred on August 17, 1885, at Amos, Calif. (elevation –172 ft) where the temperature reached 130° F.

The lowest temperature ever recorded for the month of August occurred on August 25, 1910, in Bowen, Mont. (elevation 6,080 ft) where the temperature fell to 10° F.

September

The highest temperature ever recorded for the month of September occurred on September 2, 1950, in Mecca, Calif. (elevation –175 ft) where the temperature reached 126° F.

The lowest temperature ever recorded for the month of September occurred on September 24, 1926, at Riverside Ranger Station, Mont. (elevation 6,700 ft) where the temperature fell to –9 F.

October

The highest temperature ever recorded for the month of October occurred on October 5, 1917, in Sentinel, Ariz. (elevation 685 ft) where the temperature reached 116° F.

The lowest temperature ever recorded for the month of October occurred on October 29, 1917, in Soda Butte, Wyo. (elevation 6,600 ft) where the temperature fell to –33° F.

November

The highest temperature ever recorded for the month of November occurred on November 12, 1906, in Craftonville, Calif. (elevation 1,759 ft) where the temperature reached 105° F.

The lowest temperature ever recorded for the month of November occurred on November 16, 1959, at Lincoln, Mont. (elevation 5,130 ft) where the temperature fell to –53° F.

December

The highest temperature ever recorded for the month of December occurred on December 8, 1938, in La Mesa, Calif. (elevation 539 ft) where the temperature reached 100° F.

The lowest temperature ever recorded for the month of December occurred on December 19, 1924, at Riverside Ranger Station, Mont. (elevation 6,700 ft) where the temperature fell to –59° F.

Temperature Extremes in The United States

Source: National Oceanic and Atmospheric Administration, Environmental Data and Information Service, and National Center Climatic Center

The Highest Temperature Extremes

Greenland Ranch, California, with 134° F (56.67° C) on July 10, 1913, holds the record for the highest temperature ever officially observed in the United States. This station was located in barren Death Valley, 178 feet below sea level. Death Valley is about 140 miles long, four to six miles wide, and oriented north to south in southwestern California. Much of the valley is below sea level and is flanked by towering mountain ranges with Mt. Whitney, the highest landmark in the 48 conterminous states, rising to 14,495 feet above sea level, less than 100 miles to the west. Death Valley has the hottest summers in the Western Hemisphere, and is the only known place in the United States where nightime temperatures sometimes remain above 100° F (37.78° C).

The highest annual normal (1941–70 mean) temperature in the United States, 78.2° F (25.67° C), and the highest summer (June–August) normal temperature, 92.8° F (33.78° C), are for Death Valley, California. The highest winter (December–February) normal temperature is 72.8° F (22.67° C) for Honolulu, Hawaii.

Amazing temperature rises of 40° to 50° (4.44 to 10° C) in a few minutes occasionally may be brought about by chinook winds.

Some Outstanding Temperature Rises

In 12 hours: 83° F (46.11° C), Granville, N.D., Feb. 21, 1918, from −33° F to 50° F (−36.11 to 10° C) from early morning to late afternoon.

In 15 minutes: 42° F (23.34° C), Fort Assiniboine, Mont., Jan. 19, 1892, from −5° F to 37° F (−20.56 to 2.78° C).

In seven minutes: 34° F (1.11° C), Kipp, Mont., Dec. 1, 1896. The observer also reported that a total rise of 80° F (26.67° C) occurred in a few hours and that 30 inches of snow disappeared in one–half day.

In two minutes: 49° F (27.22° C), Spearfish, S.D., Jan. 22, 1943 from −4° F (20° C) at 7:30 a.m. to 45° F (7.22° C) at 7:32 a.m.

The Lowest Temperature Extremes

The lowest temperature on record in the United States, −79.8° F (−62.1° C), was observed at Prospect Creek Camp in the Endicott Mountains of northern Alaska (latitude 66° 48′N, longitude 150° 40′W) on Jan. 23, 1971. The lowest ever recorded in the conterminous 48 states, −69.7° F (−56.5° C), occurred at Rogers Pass, in Lewis and Clark County, Mont., on Jan. 20, 1954. Rogers Pass is in mountainous and heavily forested terrain about one–half mile east of and 140 feet below the summit of the Continental Divide.

The lowest annual normal (1941–70 mean) temperature in the United States is 9.3° F (−12.68° C) for Barrow, Alaska, which lies on the Arctic coast. Barrow also has the coolest summers (June–August) with a normal temperature of 36.4° F (2.44° C). The lowest winter (December–February) normal temperature, is −15.7° F (−26.5° C) for Barter Island on the arctic coast of northeast Alaska.

In the 48 conterminous states, Mt. Washington, N.H. (elevation 6,262 feet) has the lowest annual normal temperature 26.9° F (−2.72° C) and the lowest normal summer temperature, 46.8° F (8.22° C). A few stations in the northeastern United States and in the upper Rocky Mountains have normal annual temperatures in the 30s; summer normal temperatures at these stations are in the low 50s. Winter normal temperatures are lowest in northeastern North Dakota, 5.6° F (−14.23° C) for Langdon Experiment Farm, and in northwestern Minnesota, 5.3° F (−14.83° C) for Hallock.

Some Outstanding Temperature Falls

In 24 hours: 100° F (55.57° C), Browing, Mont., Jan. 23–24, 1916, from 44° to −56° F (6.67° to −48.9° C).

In 12 hours: 84° F (46.67° C), Fairfield, Mont., Dec. 24, 1924, from 63° (17.22° C) at noon to −21° F (−29.45° C) at midnight.

In 2 hours: 62° F (34.45° C), Rapid City, S.D., Jan. 12, 1911, from 49° F (9.45° C) at 6:00 a.m. to −13° F (−25° C) at 8:00 a.m.

In 27 minutes: 58° F (32.22° C), Spearfish, S.D., Jan. 22, 1943, from 54° F (12.22 ° C) at 9:00 a.m. to −4° F (−20° C) at 9:27 a.m.

In 15 minutes: 47° F (26.11° C), Rapid City, S.D., Jan. 10, 1911, from 55° F (12.78° C) at 7:00 a.m. to 8° F (−13.33° C). at 7:15 a.m.

1. A warm, dry wind that descends from the eastern slopes of the Rocky Mountains, causing a rapid rise in temperature.

Winter Indoor Comfort and Relative Humidity

Compared to summer when the moisture content of the air (relative humidity) is an important factor of body discomfort, air moisture has a lesser effect on the human body during outdoor winter activities. But it is a big factor for winter indoor comfort because it has a direct bearing on health and energy consumption.

The colder the outdoor temperature, the more heat must be added indoors for body comfort. However, the heat that is added will cause a drying effect and lower the indoor relative humidity, unless an indoor moisture source is present.

While a room temperature between 71° and 77° F may be comfortable for short periods of time under very dry conditions, prolonged exposure to dry air has varying effects on the human body and usually causes discomfort. The moisture content of the air is important, and by increasing the relative humidity to

Average Indoor Relative Humidity, %, for January

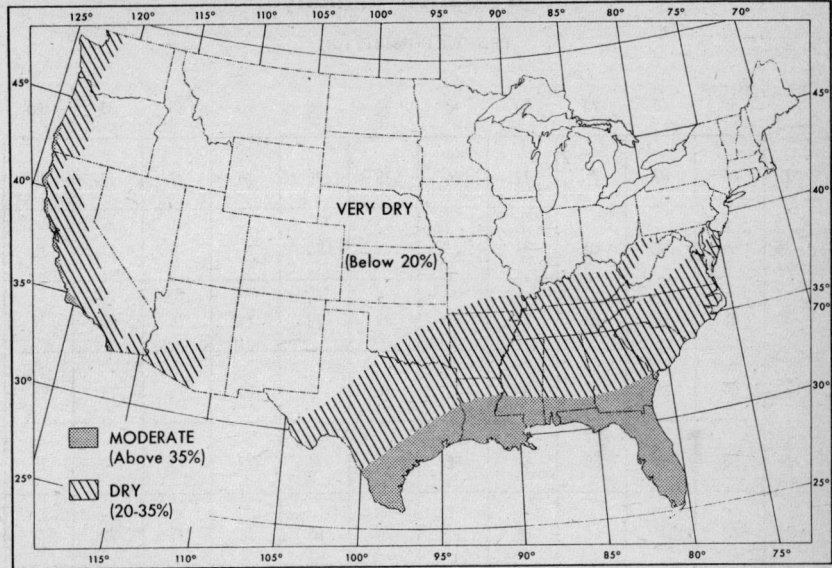

Source: National Oceanic and Atmospheric Administration, Environmental Data and Information Service, National Climatic Center.

above 50% within the above temperature range, 80% or more of all average dressed persons would feel comfortable.050

Effects of Dry Air on the Body

Studies have shown that dry air has four main effects on the human body:

1. Breathing dry air is a potential health hazard which can cause such respiratory ailments as asthma, bronchitis, sinusitis, and nosebleeds, or general dehydration since body fluids are depleted during respiration.

2. Skin moisture evaporation can cause skin irritations and eye itching.

3. Irritative effects, such as static electricity which causes mild shocks when metal is touched, are common when the air moisture is low.

4. The "apparent temperature" of the air is lower than what the thermometer indicates, and the body "feels" colder.

These problems can be reduced by simply increasing the indoor relative humidity. This can be done through use of humidifiers, vaporizers, steam generators, sources such as large pans, or water containers made of porous ceramics. Even wet towels or water in a bathtub will be of some help. The lower the room temperature the easier the relative humidity can be brought to its desired level. A relative humidity indicator (hygrometer) may be of assistance in determining the humidity in the house.

Referring to item 4, a more detailed discussion is necessary. While the indoor temperature as read from a thermometer may be 75° F, the apparent temperature (what it feels like) may be warmer or colder depending on the moisture content of the air. Apparent temperature can vary as much as 8° F within a relative humidity range of 10 to 80 percent (these limits are generally possible in a closed room). Because of evaporation the human body cools when exposed to dry air, and the sense of coldness increases as the humidity decreases. With a room temperature of 70° F, for example, a person will feel colder in a dry room than in a moist room; this is especially noticeable when entering a dry room after bathing.

The table on the following page gives apparent temperatures for various combinations of room temperature and relative humidity. As an example of how to read the table, a room temperature of 70° F combined with a relative humidity of 10% feels like 64° F, but at 80% it feels like 71° F.

Although degrees of comfort vary with age, health, activity, clothing, and body characteristics, the table can be used as a general guideline when raising the apparent temperature and the level of comfort through an increase in room moisture, rather than by an addition of heat to the room. This method of changing the apparent temperature can give the direct benefit of reducing heating costs because comfort can be maintained with a lower thermostat setting if moisture is added. For example, an apparent comfortable temperature can be maintained with a thermostat setting of 75° F with 20% relative humidity or with a 70° F setting with 80 percent humidity. A relative humidity of 20 percent is common for homes without a humidifier during winter in the northern United States.

Apparent Temperature for Values of Room Temperature and Relative Humidity

RELATIVE HUMIDITY (%)

ROOM TEMPERATURE (F)	0	10	20	30	40	50	60	70	80	90	100
75	68	69	71	72	74	75	76	76	77	78	79
74	66	68	69	71	72	73	74	75	76	77	78
73	65	67	68	70	71	72	73	74	75	76	77
72	64	65	67	68	70	71	72	73	74	75	76
71	63	64	66	67	68	70	71	72	73	74	75
70	63	64	65	66	67	68	69	70	71	72	73
69	62	63	64	65	66	67	68	69	70	71	72
68	61	62	63	64	65	66	67	68	69	70	71
67	60	61	62	63	64	65	66	67	68	68	69
66	59	60	61	62	63	64	65	66	67	67	68
65	59	60	61	61	62	63	64	65	65	66	67
64	58	59	60	60	61	62	63	64	64	65	66
63	57	58	59	59	60	61	62	62	63	64	64
62	56	57	58	58	59	60	61	61	62	63	63
61	56	57	57	58	59	59	60	60	61	61	62
60	55	56	56	57	58	58	59	59	60	60	61

Source: National Oceanic and Atmospheric Administration, Environmental Data and Information Service and National Climatic Center.

WEIGHTS & MEASURES

Measures and Weights

Source: Department of Commerce, National Bureau of Standards.

The International System (Metric)

The International System of Units is a modernized version of the metric system, established by international agreement, that i.e. provides a logical and interconnected framework for all measurements in science, industry, and commerce. The system is built on a foundation of seven basic units, and all other units are derived from them. (Use of metric weights and measures was legalized in the United States in 1866, and our customary units of weights and measures are defined in terms of the meter and kilogram.)

Length. Meter. Up until 1893, the meter was defined as 1,650,764.73 wavelengths in vacuum of the orange-red line of the spectrum of krypton-86. Since then, it is equal to the distance traveled by light in a vacuum in 1/299,792,458 of a second.

Time. Second. The second is defined as the duration of 9,192,631,770 cycles of the radiation associated with a specified transition of the cesium 133 atom.

Mass. Kilogram. The standard for the kilogram is a cylinder of platinum-iridium alloy kept by the International Bureau of Weights and Measures at Paris. A duplicate at the National Bureau of Standards serves as the mass standard for the United States. The kilogram is the only base unit still defined by a physical object.

Temperature. Kelvin. The kelvin is defined as the fraction 1/273.16 of the thermodynamic temperature of the triple point of water; that is, the point at which water forms an interface of solid, liquid and vapor. This is defined as 0.01°C on the Centigrade or Celsius scale and 32.02°F on the Fahrenheit scale. The temperature 0°K is called "absolute zero."

Electric Current. Electric current. The ampere is defined as that current that, if maintained in each of two long parallel wires separted by one meter in free space, would produce a force between the two wires (due to their magnetic fields) of 2×10^{-7} newton for each meter of length. (A newton is the unit of force which when applied to one kilogram mass would experience an acceleration of one meter per second per second.)

Luminous Intensity. Candela. The candela is defined as the luminous intensity of 1/600,000 of a square meter of a cavity at the temperature of freezing platinum (2,042K).

Amount of Substance. Mole. The mole is the amount of substance of a system that contains as many elementary entities as there are atoms in 0.012 kilogram of carbon-12.

Tables of Metric Weights and Measures

LINEAR MEASURE

10 millimeters (mm) =	1 centimeter (cm)
10 centimeters =	1 decimeter (dm) = 100 millimeters
10 decimeters =	1 meter (m) = 1,000 millimeters
10 meters =	1 dekameter (dam)
10 dekameters =	1 hectometer (hm) = 100 meters
10 hectometers =	1 kilometer (km) = 1,000 meters

AREA MEASURE

100 square millimeters (mm²) =	1 sq centimeter (cm²)
10,000 square centimeters =	1 sq meter (m²) = 1,000,000 sq millimeters
100 square meters =	1 are (a)
100 ares =	1 hectare (ha) = 10,000 sq meters
100 hectares =	1 sq kilometer (km²) = 1,000,000 sq meters

VOLUME MEASURE

10 milliliters (ml) =	1 centiliter (cl)
10 centiliters =	1 deciliter (dl) = 100 milliliters

10 deciliters =	1 liter (l) = 1,000 milliliters
10 liters =	1 dekaliter (dal)
10 dekaliters =	1 hectoliter (hl) = 100 liters
10 hectoliters =	1 kiloliter (kl) = 1,000 liters

CUBIC MEASURE

1,000 cubic millimeters (mm³) =	1 cu centimeter (cm³)
1,000 cubic centimeters =	1 cu decimeter (dm³) = 1,000,000 cu millimeters
1,000 cubic decimeters =	1 cu meter (m³) = 1 stere = 1,000,000 cu centimeters = 1,000,000,000 cu millimeters

WEIGHT

10 milligrams (mg) =	1 centigram (cg)
10 centigrams =	1 decigram (dg) = 100 milligrams
10 decigrams =	1 gram (g) = 1,000 milligrams
10 grams =	1 dekagram (dag)
10 dekagrams =	1 hectogram (hg) = 100 grams
10 hectograms =	1 kilogram (kg) = 1,000 grams
1,000 kilograms =	1 metric ton (t)

Tables of Customary U.S. Weights and Measures

LINEAR MEASURE

12 inches (in.) =	1 foot (ft)
3 feet =	1 yard (yd)
5 1/2 yards =	1 rod (rd), pole, or perch (16 1/2 ft)
40 rods =	1 furlong (fur) = 220 yds = 660 ft
8 furlongs =	1 statute mile (mi.) = 1,760 yds = 5,280 ft
3 land miles =	1 league
5,280 feet =	1 statute or land mile
6,076.11549 feet =	1 international nautical mile

AREA MEASURE

144 square inches =	1 sq ft
9 square feet =	1 sq yd = 1,296 sq in.
30 1/4 square yards =	1 sq rd = 272 1/4 sq ft
160 square rods =	1 acre = 4,840 sq yds = 43,560 sq ft
640 acres =	1 sq mi.
1 mile square =	1 section (of land)
6 miles square =	1 township = 36 sections = 36 sq mi.

CUBIC MEASURE

1,728 cubic inches =	1 cu ft
27 cubic feet =	1 cu yd

LIQUID MEASURE

When necessary to distinguish the liquid pint or quart from the dry pint or quart, the word "liquid" or the abbreviation "liq" should be used in combination with the name or abbreviation of the liquid unit.

4 gills (gi) =	1 pint (pt) (= 28.875 cu in.)
2 pints =	1 quart (qt) (= 57.75 cu in.)
4 quarts =	1 gallon (gal) (= 231 cu in.) = 8 pts = 32 gills

APOTHECARIES' FLUID MEASURE

60 minims (min.) =	1 fluid dram (fl dr) (= 0.2256 cu in.)
8 fluid drams =	1 fluid ounce (fl oz) (= 1.8047 cu in.)
16 fluid ounces =	1 pt (= 28.875 cu in.) = 128 fl drs
2 pints =	1 qt (= 57.75 cu in.) = 32 fl oz = 256 fl drs
4 quarts =	1 gal (= 231 cu in.) = 128 fl oz = 1,024 fl drs

DRY MEASURE

When necessary to distinguish the dry pint or quart from the liquid pint or quart, the word "dry" should be used in combination with the name or abbreviation of the dry unit.

2 pints =	1 qt (=67.2006 cu in.)
8 quarts =	1 peck (pk) (=537.605 cu in.) = 16 pts
4 pecks =	1 bushel (bu) (= 2,150.42 cu in.) = 32 qts

AVOIRDUPOIS WEIGHT

When necessary to distinguish the avoirdupois dram from the apothecaries dram, or to distinguish the avoirdupois dram or ounce from the fluid dram or ounce, or to distinguish the avoirdupois ounce or pound from the troy or apothecaries, ounce or pound, the word "avoirdupois" or the abbreviation "avdp" should be used in combination with the name or abbreviation of the avoirdupois unit. (The "grain" is the same in avoirdupois, troy, and apothecaries weights.)

27 11/32 grains =	1 dram (dr)
16 drams =	1 oz = 437 1/2 grains
16 ounces =	1 lb = 256 drams = 7,000 grains
100 pounds =	1 hundredweight (cwt)[1]
20 hundredweights =	1 ton (tn) = 2,000 lbs[1]

In "gross" or "long" measure, the following values are recognized:

112 pounds =	1 gross or long cwt[1]
20 gross or long hundredweights =	1 gross or long ton = 2,240 lbs[1]

1. When the terms "hundredweight" and "ton" are used unmodified, they are commonly understood to mean the 100–pound hundredweight and the 2,000–pound ton, respectively; these units may be designated "net" or "short" when necessary to distinguish them from the corresponding units in gross or long measure.

UNITS OF CIRCULAR MEASURE

Second (″) =	—
Minute (′) =	60 seconds
Degree (°) =	60 minutes
Right angle =	90 degrees
Straight angle =	180 degrees
Circle =	360 degrees

TROY WEIGHT

24 grains =	1 pennyweight (dwt)
20 pennyweights =	1 ounce troy (oz t) = 480 grains
12 ounces troy =	1 pound troy (lb t) = 240 pennyweights = 5,760 grains

APOTHECARIES' WEIGHT

20 grains =	1 scruple (s ap)
3 scruples =	1 dram apothecaries' (dr ap) = 60 grains
8 drams apothecaries =	1 ounce apothecaries' (oz ap) = 24 scruples = 480 grains
12 ounces apothecaries =	1 pound apothecaries' (lb ap) = 96 drams apothecaries' = 288 scruples = 5,760 grains

GUNTER'S OR SURVEYOR'S CHAIN MEASURE

7.92 inches =	1 link (li)
100 links =	1 chain (ch) = 4 rods = 66 ft
80 chains =	1 statute mile = 320 rods = 5,280 ft

Metric and U.S. Equivalents

1 angstrom[1] (light wave measurement)	0.1 millimicron 0.000 1 micron 0.000 000 1 millimeter 0.000 000 004 inch	1 decimeter	3.937 inches
		1 dekameter	32.808 feet
1 cable's length	120 fathoms 720 feet 219.456 meters	1 fathom	6 feet 1.8288 meters
		1 foot	0.3048 meter
1 centimeter	0.3937 inch	1 furlong	10 chains (surveyor's) 660 feet 220 yards 1/8 statute mile 201.168 meters
1 chain (Gunter's or surveyor's)	66 feet 20.1168 meters		

1 inch	2.54 centimeters	**CAPACITIES OR VOLUMES**	
1 kilometer	0.621 mile	1 barrel, liquid	31 to 42 gallons[2]
1 league (land)	3 statute miles 4.828 kilometers	1 barrel, standard for fruits, vegetables,	7,056 cubic inches 105 dry quarts
1 link (Gunter's or surveyor's)	7.92 inches 0.201 168 meter	and other dry commodities except cranberries	3.281 bushels, struck measure
1 meter	39.37 inches 1.094 yards	1 barrel, standard, cranberry	5.286 cubic inches 86 45/64 dry quarts
1 micron	0.001 millimeter 0.000 039 37 inch		2.709 bushels, struck measure
1 mil	0.001 inch 0.025 4 millimeter	1 bushel (U.S.) struck measure	2,150.42 cubic inches 35.238 liters
1 mile (statute or land)	5,280 feet 1.609 kilometers	1 bushel, heaped (U.S.)	2,747.715 cubic inches 1.278 bushels, struck measure[3]
1 mile (nautical international)	1.852 kilometers 1.151 statute miles 0.999 U.S. nautical miles	1 cord (firewood)	128 cubic feet
1 millimeter	0.03937 inch	1 cubic centimeter	0.061 cubic inch
1 millimicron (m+GRKm)	0.001 micron 0.000 000 039 37 inch	1 cubic decimeter	61.024 cubic inches
1 nanometer	0.001 micrometer or 0.000 000 039 37 inch	1 cubic foot	7.481 gallons 28.316 cubic decimeters
1 point (typography)	0.013 837 inch 1/72 inch (approximately) 0.351 millimeter	1 cubic inch	0.554 fluid ounce 4.433 fluid drams 16.387 cubic centimeters
1 rod, pole, or perch	16 1/2 feet 5.0292 meters	1 cubic meter	1.308 cubic yards
1 yard	0.9144 meter	1 cubic yard	0.765 cubic meter
AREAS OR SURFACES		1 cup, measuring	8 fluid ounces 1/2 liquid pint
1 acre	43,560 square feet 4,840 square yards 0.405 hectare	1 dram, fluid or liquid (U.S.)	1/8 fluid ounces 0.226 cubic inch 3.697 milliliters 1.041 British fluid drachms
1 are	119.599 square yards 0.025 acre	1 dekaliter	2.642 gallons 1.135 pecks
1 hectare	2.471 acres	1 gallon (U.S.)	231 cubic inches 3.785 liters 0.833 British gallon 128 U.S. fluid ounces
1 square centimeter	0.155 square inch		
1 square decimeter	15.5 square inches		
1 square foot	929.030 square centimeters	1 gallon (British Imperial)	277.42 cubic inches 1.201 U.S. gallons 4.546 liters 160 British fluid ounces
1 square inch	6.4516 square centimeters		
1 square kilometer	0.386 square mile 247.105 acres	1 gill	7.219 cubic inches 4 fluid ounces 0.118 liter
1 square meter	1.196 square yards 10.764 square feet	1 hectoliter	26.418 gallons 2.838 bushels
1 square mile	258.999 hectares	1 liter	1.057 liquid quarts 0.908 dry quart 61.024 cubic inches
1 square millimeter	0.002 square inch		
1 square rod, square pole or square perch	25.293 square meters	1 milliliter	0.271 fluid dram 16.231 minims 0.061 cubic inch
1 square yard	0.836 square meters	1 ounce, fluid or liquid (U.S.)	1.805 cubic inch 29.574 milliliters 1.041 British fluid ounces

1 peck	8.810 liters	1 hundredweight, net or short	100 pounds 45.359 kilograms
1 pint, dry	33.600 cubic inches 0.551 liter	1 kilogram	2.205 pounds
1 pint, liquid	28.875 cubic inches 0.473 liter	1 microgram [µg (the Greek letter mu in combination with the letter g)]	0.000 001 gram
1 quart, dry (U.S.)	67.201 cubic inches 1.101 liters 0.969 British quart	1 milligram	0.015 grain
1 quart, liquid (U.S.)	57.75 cubic inches 0.946 liter 0.833 British quart	1 ounce, avoirdupois	437.5 grains 0.911 troy or apothecaries, ounce 28.350 grams
1 quart (British)	69.354 cubic inches 1.032 U.S. dry quarts 1.201 U.S. liquid quarts	1 ounce, troy or apothecaries	480 grains 1.097 avoirdupois ounces 31.103 grams
1 tablespoon, measuring	3 teaspoons 4 fluid drams 1/2 fluid ounce	1 pennyweight	1.555 grams
1 teaspoon, measuring	1/3 tablespoon 1 1/3 fluid drams	1 point	0.01 carat 2 milligrams
1 assay ton[4]	29.167 grams	1 pound, avoirdupois	7,000 grains 1.215 troy or apothecaries pounds 453.592 37 grams
1 carat	200 milligrams 3.086 grains	1 pound, troy or apothecaries	5,760 grains 0.823 avoirdupois pound 373.242 grams
1 dram, apothecaries'	60 grains 3.888 grams	1 ton, gross or long[5]	2,240 pounds 1.12 net tons 1.016 metric tons
1 dram, avoirdupois	27 11/32 (=27.344) grains 1.772 grams	1 ton, metric	2,204.623 pounds 0.984 gross ton 1.102 net tons
1 grain	64.798 91 milligrams		
1 gram	15.432 grains 0.035 ounce, avoirdupois	1 ton, net or short	2,000 pounds 0.893 gross ton 0.907 metric ton
1 hundredweight, gross or long[5]	112 pounds 50.802 kilograms		

1. The angstrom is basically defined as 10^{-10} meter. 2. There is a variety of "barrels" established by law or usage. For example, federal taxes on fermented liquors are based on a barrel of 31 gallons; many state laws fix the "barrel for liquids" at 31 1/2 gallons; one state fixes a 36–gallon barrel for cistern measurement; federal law recognizes a 40–gallon barrel for "proof spirits"; by custom, 42 gallons comprise a barrel of crude oil or petroleum products for statistical purposes, and this equivalent is recognized "for liquids" by four states. 3. Frequently recognized as 1 1/4 bushels, struck measure. 4. Used in assaying. The assay ton bears the same relation to the milligram that a ton of 2,000 pounds avoirdupois bears to the ounce troy; hence the weight in milligrams of precious metal obtained from one assay ton of ore gives directly the number of troy ounces to the net ton. 5. The gross or long ton and hundredweight are used commercially in the United States to only a limited extent, usually in restricted industrial fields. These units are the same as the British "ton" and "hundredweight."

Miscellaneous Units of Measure

Acre: An area of 43,560 square feet. Originally, the area a yoke of oxen could plow in one day.

Agate: Originally a measurement of type size (5 1/2 points). Now equal to 1/14 inch. Used in printing for measuring column length.

Ampere: Unit of electric current. A potential difference of one volt across a resistance of one ohm produces a current of one ampere.

Astronomical Unit (A.U.): 93,000,000 miles, the average distance of the earth from the sun. Used for astronomy.

Bale: A large bundle of goods. In the U.S., the ap-

proximate weight of a bale of cotton is 500 pounds. The weight varies in other countries.

Board Foot (fbm): 144 cubic inches (12 in. × 12 in. × 1 in.). Used for lumber.

Bolt: 40 yards. Used for measuring cloth.

Btu: British thermal unit. Amount of heat needed to increase the temperature of one pound of water by one degree Fahrenheit (252 calories).

Carat (c): 200 milligrams or 3.086 grains troy. Originally the weight of a seed of the carob tree in the Mediterranean region. Used for weighing precious stones. See also Karat.

Chain (ch): A chain 66 feet or one–tenth of a furlong in length, divided into 100 parts called links. One mile is equal to 80 chains. Used in surveying and sometimes called Gunter's or surveyor's chain.

Cubit: 18 inches or 45.72 cm. Derived from distance between elbow and tip of middle finger.

Decibel: Unit of relative loudness. One decibel is the smallest amount of change detectable by the human ear.

Ell, English: 1 1/4 yards or 1/32 bolt. Used for measuring cloth.

Freight, Ton (also called Measurement Ton): 40 cubic feet of merchandise. Used for cargo freight.

Great Gross: 12 gross or 1728.

Gross: 12 dozen or 144.

Hand: 4 inches or 10.16 cm. Derived from the width of the hand. Used for measuring the height of horses at withers.

Hertz: Modern unit for measurement of electromagnetic wave frequencies (equivalent to "cycles per second").

Hogshead (hhd): 2 liquid barrels or 14,653 cubic inches.

Horsepower: The power needed to lift 33,000 pounds a distance of one foot in one minute (about 1 1/2 times the power an average horse can exert). Used for measuring power of steam engines, etc.

Karat (kt): A measure of the purity of gold, indicating how many parts out of 24 are pure. For example: 18 karat gold is 3/4 pure. Sometimes spelled *carat*.

Knot: Not a distance, but the rate of speed of one nautical mile per hour. Used for measuring speed of ships.

League: Rather indefinite and varying measure, but usually estimated at 3 miles in English-speaking countries.

Light-Year: 5,880,000,000,000 miles, the distance light travels in a vacuum in a year at the rate of 186,281.7 miles (299,792 kilometers) per second. (If an astronomical unit were represented by one inch, a light-year would be represented by about one mile.) Used for measurements in interstellar space.

Magnum: Two-quart bottle. Used for measuring wine, etc.

Ohm: Unit of electrical resistance. A circuit in which a potential difference of one volt produces a current of one ampere has a resistance of one ohm.

Parsec: Approximately 3.26 light-years of 19.2 million miles. Term is combination of first syllables of *par*allax and *sec*ond, and distance is that of imaginary star when lines drawn from it to both earth and sun form a maximum angle or parallax of one second (1/3600 degree). Used for measuring interstellar distances.

Pi (π): 3.14159265+. The ratio of the circumference of a circle to its diameter. For practical purposes, the value is used to four decimal places: 3.1416.

Pica: 1/6 inch or 12 points. Used in printing for measuring column width, etc.

Pipe: 2 hogsheads. Used for measuring wine and other liquids.

Point: .013837 (approximately 1/72) inch or 1/12 pica. Used in printing for measuring type size.

Quintal: 100,000 grams or 220.46 pounds avoirdupois.

Quire: Used for measuring paper. Sometimes 24 sheets but more often 25. There are 20 quires to a ream.

Ream: Used for measuring paper. Sometimes 480 sheets, but more often 500 sheets.

Roentgen: International Unit of radiation exposure produced by X-rays.

Score: 20 units.

Sound, Speed of: Usually placed at 1,088 ft per second at 32°F at sea level. It varies at other temperatures and in different media.

Span: 9 inches or 22.86 cm. Derived from the distance between the end of the thumb and the end of the little finger when both are outstretched.

Square: 100 square feet. Used in building.

Stone: Legally 14 pounds avoirdupois in Great Britain.

Therm: 100,000 Btu's.

Township: U.S. land measurement of almost 36 square miles. The south border is 6 miles long. The east and west borders, also 6 miles long, follow the meridians, making the north border slightly less than 6 miles long. Used in surveying.

Tun: 252 gallons, but often larger. Used for measuring wine and other liquids.

Watt: Unit of power. The power used by a current of one ampere across a potential difference of one volt equals one watt.

Kelvin Scale

Absolute zero, –273.16° on the Celsius (Centigrade) scale, is 0° Kelvin. Thus, degrees Kelvin are equivalent to degrees Celsuis plus 273.16. The freezing point of water, 0°C. and 32°F., is 273.16°K. The conversion formula is $K° = C° + 273.16$.

Conversion of Miles to Kilometers and Kilometers to Miles

Miles	Kilometers	Miles	Kilometers	Miles	Kilometers	Kilometers	Miles	Kilometers	Miles	Kilometers	Miles
1	1.6	8	12.8	60	96.5	1	0.6	8	4.9	60	37.2
2	3.2	9	14.4	70	112.6	2	1.2	9	5.5	70	43.4
3	4.8	10	16.0	80	128.7	3	1.8	10	6.2	80	49.7
4	6.4	20	32.1	90	144.8	4	2.4	20	12.4	90	55.9
5	8.0	30	48.2	100	160.9	5	3.1	30	18.6	100	62.1
6	9.6	40	64.3	1,000	1609	6	3.7	40	24.8	1,000	621
7	11.2	50	80.4			7	4.3	50	31.0		

Bolts and Screws: Conversion from Fractions of an Inch to Millimeters

Inch	mm	Inch	mm	Inch	mm	Inch	mm
1/64	0.40	17/64	6.75	33/64	13.10	49/64	19.45
1/32	0.79	9/32	7.14	17/32	13.50	25/32	19.84
3/64	1.19	19/64	7.54	35/64	13.90	51/64	20.24
1/16	1.59	5/16	7.94	9/16	14.29	13/16	20.64
5/64	1.98	21/64	8.33	37/64	14.69	53/64	21.03
3/32	2.38	11/32	8.73	19/32	15.08	27/32	21.43
7/64	2.78	23/64	9.13	39/64	15.48	55/64	21.83
1/8	3.18	3/8	9.53	5/8	15.88	7/8	22.23
9/64	3.57	25/64	9.92	41/64	16.27	57/64	22.62
5/32	3.97	13/32	10.32	21/32	16.67	29/32	23.02
11/64	4.37	27/64	10.72	43/64	17.06	59/64	23.42
3/16	4.76	7/16	11.11	11/64	17.46	15/16	23.81
13/64	5.16	29/64	11.51	45/64	17.86	61/64	24.21
7/32	5.56	15/32	11.91	23/32	18.26	31/32	24.61
15/64	5.95	31/64	12.30	47/64	18.65	63/64	25.00
1/4	6.35	1/2	12.70	3/4	19.05	1	25.40

U.S.—Metric Cooking Conversions

U.S. customary system				Metric			
Capacity		Weight		Capacity		Weight	
1/5 teaspoon	1 milliliter	1 fluid oz	30 milliliters	1 milliliter	1/5 teaspoon	1 gram	.035 ounce
1 teaspoon	5 ml		28 grams	5 ml	1 teaspoon	100 grams	3.5 ounces
1 tablespoon	15 ml	1 pound	454 grams	15 ml	1 tablespoon	500 grams	1.10 pounds
1/5 cup	50 ml			34 ml	1 fluid oz	1 kilogram	2.205
1 cup	240 ml						pounds
2 cups (1 pint)	470 ml			100 ml	3.4 fluid oz		35 oz
4 cups (1 quart)	.95 liter			240 ml	1 cup		
4 quarts (1 gal.)	3.8 liters			1 liter	34 fluid oz		
					4.2 cups		
					2.1 pints		
					1.06 quarts		
					0.26 gallon		

Cooking Measurement Equivalents

16 tablespoons =	1 cup	2 tablespoons =	1/8 cup
12 tablespoons =	3/4 cup	2 tablespoons + 2 teaspoons =	1/6 cup
10 tablespoons + 2 teaspoons =	2/3 cup	1 tablespoon =	1/16 cup
8 tablespoons =	1/2 cup	2 cups =	1 pint
6 tablespoons =	3/8 cup	2 pints =	1 quart
5 tablespoons + 1 teaspoon =	1/3 cup	3 teaspoons =	1 tablespoon
4 tablespoons =	1/4 cup	48 teaspoons =	1 cup

Prefixes and Multiples

Prefix	Suffix	Equivalent	Multiple/submultiple	Prefix	Suffix	Equivalent	Multiple/submultiple
atto	a	quintillionth part	10^{-18}	deci	d	tenth part	10^{-1}
femto	f	quadrillionth part	10^{-15}	deka	da	tenfold	10
pico	p	trillionth part	10^{-12}	hecto	h	hundredfold	10^2
nano	n	billionth part	10^{-9}	kilo	k	thousandfold	10^3
micro	μ	millionth part	10^{-6}	mega	M	millionfold	10^6
milli	m	thousandth part	10^{-3}	giga	G	billionfold	10^9
centi	c	hundredth part	10^{-2}	tera	T	trillionfold	10^{12}

Common Formulas

Circumference

Circle: $C = \pi d$, in which π is 3.1416 and d the diameter.

Area

Triangle: $A = \dfrac{ab}{2}$, in which a is the base and b the height.

Square: $A = a^2$, in which a is one of the sides.

Rectangle: $A = ab$, in which a is the base and b the height.

Trapezoid: $A = \dfrac{h(a+b)}{2}$, in which h is the height, a the longer parallel side, and b the shorter.

Regular pentagon: $A = 1.720a^2$, in which a is one of the sides.

Regular hexagon: $A = 2.598a^2$, in which a is one of the sides.

Regular octagon: $A = 4.828a^2$, in which a is one of the sides.

Circle: $A = \pi r^2$, in which π is 3.1416 and r the radius.

Volume

Cube: $V = a^3$, in which a is one of the edges.

Rectangular prism: $V = abc$, in which a is the length, b is the width, and c the depth.

Pyramid: $V = \dfrac{Ah}{3}$, in which A is the area of the base and h the height.

Cylinder: $V = \pi r^2 h$, in which π is 3.1416, r the radius of the base, and h the height.

Cone: $V = \dfrac{\pi r^2 h}{3}$, in which π is 3.1416, r the radius of the base, and h the height.

Sphere: $V = \dfrac{4\pi r^3}{3}$, in which π is 3.1416 and r the radius.

Miscellaneous

Distance in feet traveled by falling body: $d = 16t^2$, in which t is the time in seconds.

Speed in sound in feet per second through any given temperature of air:
$V = \dfrac{1087\sqrt{273+t}}{16.52}$ in which t is the temperature Centigrade.

Cost in cents of opperration of electrical device: $C = \dfrac{Wtc}{1000}$, in which W is the number of watts, t the time in hours, and c the cost in cents per hilowatt-hour.

Conversion of matter into energy (Einstein's Theorem): $E = mc^2$, in which E is the energy in ergs, m the mass of the matter in grams, and c the speed of light in centimeters per second. ($C^2 = 9.10^{20}$).

Decimal Equivalents of Common Fractions

1/2	.5000	1/10	.1000	2/7	.2857	3/11	.2727	5/9	.5556	7/11	.6364
1/3	.3333	1/11	.0909	2/9	.2222	4/5	.8000	5/11	.4545	7/12	.5833
1/4	.2500	1/12	.0833	2/11	.1818	4/7	.5714	5/12	.4167	8/9	.8889
1/5	.2000	1/16	.0625	3/4	.7500	4/9	.4444	6/7	.8571	8/11	.7273
1/6	.1667	1/32	.0313	3/5	.6000	4/11	.3636	6/11	.5455	9/10	.9000
1/7	.1429	1/64	.0156	3/7	.4286	5/6	.8333	7/8	.8750	9/11	.8182
1/8	.1250	2/3	.6667	3/8	.3750	5/7	.7143	7/9	.7778	10/11	.9091
1/9	.1111	2/5	.4000	3/10	.3000	5/8	.6250	7/10	.7000	11/12	.9167

Conversion Factors

To change	To	Multi–ply by	To change	To	Multi–ply by
acres	hectares	.4047	liters	pints (dry)	1.8162
acres	square feet	43,560	liters	pints (liquid)	2.1134
acres	square miles	.001562	liters	quarts (dry)	.9081
atmospheres	cms. of mercury	76	liters	quarts (liquid)	1.0567
BTU	horsepower-hour	.0003931	meters	feet	3.2808
BTU	kilowatt-hour	.0002928	meters	miles	.0006214
BTU/hour	watts	.2931	meters	yards	1.0936
bushels	cubic inches	2150.4	metric tons	tons (long)	.9842
bushels (U.S.)	hectoliters	.3524	metric tons	tons (short)	1.1023
centimeters	inches	.3937	miles	kilometers	1.6093
centimeters	feet	.03281	miles	feet	5280
circumference	radians	6.283	miles (nautical)	miles (statute)	1.1516
cubic feet	cubic meters	.0283	miles (statute)	miles (nautical)	.8684
cubic meters	cubic feet	35.3145	miles/hour	feet/minute	88
cubic meters	cubic yards	1.3079	millimeters	inches	.0394
cubic yards	cubic meters	.7646	ounces avdp.	grams	28.3495
degrees	radians	.01745	ounces	pounds	.0625
dynes	grams	.00102	ounces (troy)	ounces (avdp)	1.09714
fathoms	feet	6.0	pecks	liters	8.8096
feet	meters	.3048	pints (dry)	liters	.5506
feet	miles (nautical)	.0001645	pints (liquid)	liters	.4732
feet	miles (statute)	.0001894	pounds ap or t	kilograms	.3782
feet/second	miles/hour	.6818	pounds avdp	kilograms	.4536
furlongs	feet	660.0	pounds	ounces	16
furlongs	miles	.125	quarts (dry)	liters	1.1012
gallons (U.S.)	liters	3.7853	quarts (liquid)	liters	.9463
grains	grams	.0648	radians	degrees	57.30
grams	grains	15.4324	rods	meters	5.029
grams	ounces avdp	.0353	rods	feet	16.5
grams	pounds	.002205	square feet	square meters	.0929
hectares	acres	2.4710	square kilometers	square miles	.3861
hectoliters	bushels (U.S.)	2.8378	square meters	square feet	10.7639
horsepower	watts	745.7	square meters	square yards	1.1960
hours	days	.04167	square miles	square kilometers	2.5900
inches	millimeters	25.4000	square yards	square meters	.8361
inches	centimeters	2.5400	tons (long)	metric tons	1.016
kilograms	pounds avdp or t	2.2046	tons (short)	metric tons	.9072
kilometers	miles	.6214	tons (long)	pounds	2240
kilowatts	horsepower	1.341	tons (short)	pounds	2000
knots	nautical miles/hour	1.0	watts	Btu/hour	3.4129
knots	statute miles/hour	1.151	watts	horsepower	.001341
liters	gallons (U.S.)	.2642	yards	meters	.9144
liters	pecks	.1135	yards	miles	.0005682

Fahrenheit and Celsius (Centigrade) Scales

Zero on the Fahrenheit scale represents the temperature produced by the mixing of equal weights of snow and common salt.

	F	C
Boiling point of water	212°	100°
Freezing point of water	32°	0°
Absolute zero	−459.6°	−273.1°

Absolute zero is theoretically the lowest possible temperature, the point at which all molecular motion would cease.

To convert Fahrenheit to Celsius (Centigrade), subtract 32 and multiply by 5/9.

To convert Celsius (Centigrade) to Fahrenheit, multiiply by 9/5 and add 32.

°Centi–grade	°Fahren–heit	°Centi–grade	°Fahren–heit
−273.1	−459.6	30	86
−250	−418	35	95
−200	−328	40	104
−150	−238	45	113
−100	−148	50	122
−50	−58	55	131
−40	−40	60	140
−30	−22	65	149
−20	−4	70	158
−10	14	75	167
0	32	80	176
5	41	85	185
10	50	90	194
15	59	95	203
20	68	100	212
25	77		

Roman Numerals

Roman numerals are expressed by letters of the alphabet and are rarely used today except for formality or variety.

There are three basic principles for reading Roman numerals:

1. A letter repeated once or twice repeats its value that many times (XXX = 30, CC = 200, etc.).

2. One or more letters placed after another letter of greater value increases the greater value by the amount of the smaller. (VI = 6, LXX = 70, MCC = 1200, etc.).

3. A letter placed before another letter of greater value decreases the greater value by the amount of the smaller. (IV = 4, XC = 90, CM = 900, etc.).

Letter	Value	Letter	Value	Letter	Value	Letter	Value	Letter	Value
I	1	VII	7	XXX	30	LXXX	80	$\overline{\text{V}}$	5,000
II	2	VIII	8	XL	40	XC	90	$\overline{\text{X}}$	10,000
III	3	IX	9	L	50	C	100	$\overline{\text{L}}$	50,000
IV	4	X	10	LX	60	D	500	$\overline{\text{C}}$	100,000
V	5	XX	20	LXX	70	M	1,000	$\overline{\text{D}}$	500,000
VI	6							$\overline{\text{M}}$	1,000,000

Mean and Median

The mean, also called the average, of a series of quantities is obtained by finding the sum of the quantities and dividing it by the number of quantities. In the series 1, 3, 5, 18, 19, 20, 25, the mean or average is 13—i.e., 91 divided by 7.

The median of a series is that point which so divided it that half the quantities are on one side, half on the other. In the above series, the median is 18.

The median often better expresses the common-run, since it is not, as is the mean, affected by an excessively high or low figure. In the series 1, 3, 4, 7, 55, the median of 4 is a truer expression of the common-run than is the mean of 14.

Prime Numbers Between 1 and 1,000

2	3	5	7	11	13	17	19	23
29	31	37	41	43	47	53	59	61	67
71	73	79	83	89	97	101	103	107	109
113	127	131	137	139	149	151	157	163	167
173	179	181	191	193	197	199	211	223	227
229	233	239	241	251	257	263	269	271	277
281	283	293	307	311	313	317	331	337	347
349	353	359	367	373	379	383	389	397	401
409	419	421	431	433	439	443	449	457	461
463	467	479	487	491	499	503	509	521	523
541	547	557	563	569	571	577	587	593	599
601	607	613	617	619	631	641	643	647	653
659	661	673	677	683	691	701	709	719	727
733	739	743	751	757	761	769	773	787	797
809	811	821	823	827	829	839	853	857	859
863	877	881	883	887	907	911	919	929	937
941	947	953	967	971	977	983	991	997	(1009)

Definitions of Gold Terminology

The term "fineness" defines a gold content in parts per thousand. For example, a gold nugget containing 885 parts of pure gold, 100 parts of silver, and 15 parts of copper would be considered 885-fine.

The word "karat" indicates the proportion of solid gold in an alloy based on a total of 24 parts. Thus, 14-karat (14K) gold indicates a composition of 14 parts of gold and 10 parts of other metals.

The term "gold-filled" is used to describe articles of jewelry made of base metal which are covered on one or more surfaces with a layer of gold alloy. No article having a gold alloy portion of less than one twentieth by weight may be marked "gold-filled." Articles may be marked "rolled gold plate" provided the proportional fraction and fineness designations are also shown.

Electroplated jewelry items carrying at least 7 millionths of an inch of gold on significant surfaces may be labeled "electroplate." Plate thicknesses less than this may be marked "gold-flashed" or "gold-washed."

Portraits and Designs of U.S. Paper Currency[1]

Currency	Portrait	Design on back	Currency	Portrait	Design on back
$1	Washington	ONE between obverse and reverse of Great Seal of U.S.	$50	Grant	U.S. Capitol
			$100	Franklin	Independence Hall
$2[2]	Jefferson	Monticello	$500	McKinley	Ornate FIVE HUNDRED
$2[3]	Jefferson	"The Signing of the Declaration of Independence"	$1,000	Cleveland	Ornate ONE THOUSAND
			$5,000	Madison	Ornate FIVE THOUSAND
$5	Lincoln	Lincoln Memorial	$10,000	Chase	Ornate TEN THOUSAND
$10	Hamilton	U.S. Treasury Building	$100,000[4]	Wilson	Ornate ONE HUNDRED THOUSAND
$20	Jackson	White House			

1. Denominations of $500 and higher were discontinued in 1969. 2. Discontinued in 1966. 3. New issue, April 13, 1976. 4. For use only in transactions between Federal Reserve System and Treasury Department.

GREAT DISASTERS

The following lists are not all-inclusive due to space limitations. Only disasters involving great loss of life and/or property, historical interest, or unusual circumstances are listed. Data as of Aug. 1, 1991. For later disasters see *Current Events*.

Earthquakes and Volcanic Eruptions

A.D. 79 Aug. 24, Italy: eruption of Mt. Vesuvius buried cities of Pompeii and Herculaneum, killing thousands.

1556 Jan. 24, Shaanxi (Shensi) Province, China: most deadly earthquake in history; 830,000 killed.

1755 Nov. 1, Portugal: one of the most severe of recorded earthquakes leveled Lisbon and was felt as far away as southern France and North Africa; 10,000–20,000 killed in Lisbon.

1883 Aug. 26–28, Netherlands Indies: eruption of Krakatau; violent explosions destroyed two thirds of island. Sea waves occurred as far away as Cape Horn, and possibly England. Estimated 36,000 dead.

1902 May 8, Martinique, West Indies: Mt. Pelée erupted and wiped out city of St. Pierre; 40,000 dead.

1908 Dec. 28, Messina, Sicily: about 85,000 killed and city totally destroyed.

1915 Jan. 13, Avezzano, Italy: earthquake left 29,980 dead.

1920 Dec. 16, Gansu (Kansu) Province, China: earthquake killed 200,000.

1923 Sept. 1, Japan: earthquake destroyed third of Tokyo and most of Yokohama; more than 140,000 killed.

1933 March 10, Long Beach, Calif.: 117 left dead by earthquake.

1935 May 31, India: earthquake at Quetta killed an estimated 50,000.

1939 Jan. 24, Chile: earthquake razed 50,000 sq mi.; about 30,000 killed.
Dec. 27, Northern Turkey: severe quakes destroyed city of Erzingan; about 100,000 casualties.

1950 Aug. 15, India: earthquake affected 30,000 sq mi. in Assam; 20,000–30,000 believed killed.

1963 July 26, Skoplje, Yugoslavia: four fifths of city destroyed; 1,011 dead, 3,350 injured.

1964 March 27, Alaska: strongest earthquake ever to strike North America hit 80 miles east of Anchorage; followed by seismic wave 50 feet high that traveled 8,445 miles at 450 miles per hour; 117 killed.

1970 May 31, Peru: earthquake left 50,000 dead, 17,000 missing.

1972 April 10, Iran: 5,000 killed in earthquake 60 0 miles south of Teheran.
Dec. 22, Managua, Nicaragua: earthquake devastated city, leaving up to 6,000 dead.

1976 Feb. 4, Guatemala: earthquake left over 23,000 dead.
July 28, Tangshan, China: earthquake devastated 20-sq-mi. area of city leaving estimated 242,000 dead.
Aug. 17, Mindanao, Philippines: earthquake and tidal wave left up to 8,000 dead or missing.

1977 March 4, Bucharest: earthquake razed most of downtown Bucharest; 1,541 reported dead, over 11,000 injured.

1978 Sept. 16, Tabas, Iran: earthquake destroyed city in eastern Iran, leaving 25,000 dead.

1980 Nov. 23, Naples, Italy: 2,735 killed when earthquake struck southern Italy.

1982 Dec. 13, Yemen: 2,800 reported dead in earthquake.

1985 Sept. 19–20, Mexico: earthquake registering 8.1 on Richter scale struck central and southwestern regions, devastating part of Mexico City and three coastal states. An estimated 25,000 killed.
Nov. 14–16, Colombia: eruption of Nevada del Ruiz, 85 miles northwest of Bogotá, caused mud slides which buried most of the town of Armero and devastated Chinchiná. An estimated 25,000 were killed.

1988 Dec. 7, Armenia: an earthquake measuring 6.9 on the Richter scale killed nearly 25,000, injured 15,000, and left at least 400,000 homeless.

1989 Oct. 17, San Francisco Bay Area: an earthquake measuring 7.1 on the Richter Scale killed 67 and injured over 3,000. The quake damaged or destroyed over 100,000 buildings and caused billions of dollars of damage.

1990 June 21, Northwestern Iran: an earthquake measuring 7.7 on the Richter Scale destroyed cities, towns, and villages in Caspian Sea area. At least 50,000 dead, over 60,000 injured, and 400,000 homeless.
July 16, Luzon Island, The Philippines: an earthquake measuring 7.7 on the Richter scale claimed the lives of over 1,600 people and injured nearly 3,000 others.

Major U.S. Epidemics

1793 Philadelphia. More than 4,000 residents died from yellow fever.

1832 July–August, New York City. Over 3,000 people killed in a cholera epidemic. **October, New Orleans.** Cholera took the lives of 4,340 persons.

1848 New York City. More than 5,000 deaths caused by cholera.

1853 New Orleans. Yellow fever killed 7,790 residents.

1867 New Orleans. 3,093 persons perished from yellow fever.

1878 Southern States. Over 13,000 people died from yellow fever in lower Mississippi Valley.

1916 Nationwide. Over 7,000 deaths occurred and 27,363 cases were reported of polio (infantile paralysis) in America's worst polio epidemic.

1918 March–November, Nationwide. Outbreak of influenza killed over 500,000 people in the worst single U.S. epidemic.

1949 Nationwide. 2,720 deaths occurred from polio and 42,173 cases were reported.

1952 Nationwide. Polio killed 3,300; 57,628 cases reported; worst epidemic since 1916.

1981 To present. Total AIDS cases reported in the U.S. and its territories as of May 31, 1991, were 179,136, and of these cases, 113,426 died. The Center for Disease Control estimates that AIDS cases will rise to between 390,000 and 480,000 by the end of 1993.

WORST UNITED STATES DISASTERS

Aircraft
1979 May 25, Chicago: American Airlines DC-10 lost left engine upon take-off and crashed seconds later, killing all 272 persons aboard and three on the ground in worst U.S. air disaster.

Dam
1928 March 12, Santa Paula, Calif.: collapse of St. Francis Dam left 450 dead.

Drought
1930s Many states: longest drought of the 20th century. Peak periods were 1930, 1934, 1936, 1939, and 1940. During 1934, dry regions stretched solidly from New York and Pennsylvania across the Great Plains to the California coast. A great "dust bowl" covered some 50 million acres in the south central plains during the winter of 1935–1936.

Earthquake
1906 April 18, San Francisco: earthquake accompanied by fire razed more than 4 sq mi.; more than 500 dead or missing.

Epidemic
1918 Nationwide: Spanish influenza killed over 500,000 Americans.

Explosion
1947 April 16–18, Texas City, Texas: Most of the city destroyed by a fire and subsequent explosion on the French freighter *Grandcamp* carrying a cargo of ammonium nitrate. At least 516 were killed and over 3,000 injured.

Fire
1871 Oct. 8, Peshtigo, Wis.: over 1,200 lives lost and 2 billion trees burned in forest fire.

Flood
1889 May 31, Johnstown, Pa.: more than 2,200 died in flood.

Hurricane
1900 Aug. 27–Sept. 15, Galveston, Tex.: over 6,000 died from devastation due to both winds and tidal wave.

Marine
1865 April 27, *Sultana*: boiler explosion on Mississippi River steamboat near Memphis, 1,547 killed.

Mine
1907 Dec. 6, Monongha, W. Va.: coal mine explosion killed 361.

Oil Spill
1989 Mar. 24, Prince William Sound, Alaska: Tanker, *Exxon Valdez*, hit an undersea reef and released 10 million plus gallons of oil into the waters, causing the worst oil spill in U.S. history.

Railroad
1918 July 9, Nashville, Tenn.: 101 killed in a two-train collision near Nashville.

Submarine
1963 April 10, *Thresher*: atomic-powered submarine sank in North Atlantic: 129 dead.

Tornado
1925 March 18, Great Tri-State Tornado: Missouri, Illinois, and Indiana; 695 deaths. Eight additional tornadoes in Kentucky, Tennessee, and Alabama raised day's toll to 792 dead.

Floods, Avalanches, and Tidal Waves

1228 Holland: 100,000 persons reputedly drowned by sea flood in Friesland.

1642 China: rebels destroyed Kaifeng seawall; 300,000 drowned.

1896 June 15, Sanriku, Japan: earthquake and tidal wave killed 27,000.

1953 Northwest Europe: storm followed by floods devastated North Sea coastal areas. Netherlands was hardest hit with 1,794 dead.

1959 Dec. 2, Frejus, France: flood caused by collapse of Malpasset Dam left 412 dead.

1960 Agadir, Morocco: 10,000–12,000 dead as earthquake set off tidal wave and fire, destroying most of city.

1962 Jan. 10, Peru: avalanche down Huascaran, extinct Andean volcano, killed more than 3,000 persons.

1963 Oct. 9, Italy: landslide into the Vaiont Dam; flood killed about 2,000.

1966 Oct. 21, Aberfan, Wales: avalanche of coal, waste, mud, and rocks killed 144 persons, including 116 children in school.

1969 Jan. 18–26, Southern California: floods and mudslides from heavy rains caused widespread property damage; at least 100 dead. Another downpour (Feb. 23–26) caused further floods and mudslides; at least 18 dead.

1970 Nov. 13, East Pakistan: 200,000 killed by cyclone-driven tidal wave from Bay of Bengal. Over 100,000 missing.

1971 Sept. 29, Orissa State, India: cyclone and tidal wave off Bay of Bengal killed as many as 10,000.

1972 Feb. 26, Man, W. Va.: more than 118 died when slag-pile dam collapsed under pressure of torrential rains and flooded 17-mile valley.
June 9–10, Rapid City, S.D.: flash flood caused 237 deaths and $160 million in damage.
June 20, Eastern Seaboard: tropical storm Agnes, in 10-day rampage, caused widespread flash floods. Death toll was 129, 115,000 were left homeless, and damage estimated at $3.5 billion.

1976 Aug. 1, Loveland, Colo.: Flash flood along Route 34 in Big Thompson Canyon left 139 dead.

1977 Nov. 19, Andhra Pradesh State, India: cyclone and flood from Bay of Bengal left 7,000–10,000 dead.

1988 August-September, Bangladesh: Heaviest monsoon in 70 years innundates three-fourths of country, killing more than 1,300 people and leaving 30 million homeless. Damage is estimated at over $1 billion.

Tropical Storms

Cyclones, typhoons, and hurricanes are the same kind of tropical storms but are called by different names in different areas of the world. For example: a typhoon is a severe tropical hurricane that occurs in the western Pacific and China Sea.

Cyclones

1864 Oct. 5, India: most of Calcutta denuded by cyclone; 70,000 killed.

1942 Oct. 16, India: cyclone devastated Bengal; about 40,000 lives lost.

1960 Oct. 10, East Pakistan: cyclone and tidal wave killed about 6,000.
October 31, East Pakistan: another cyclone hit Chittagong and surrounding area. 6,000 believed killed.

1963 May 28–29, East Pakistan: cyclone killed about 22,000 along coast.

1964 Dec. 22–23, India and Ceylon: cyclone and tidal wave killed 1,800.

1965 May 11–12 and June 1–2, East Pakistan: cyclones killed about 47,000.
Dec. 15, Karachi: cyclone killed about 10,000.

1970 Nov. 12–13, East Pakistan: cyclone and tidal waves killed 200,000 and another 100,000 were reported missing.

1971 Sept. 29, Orissa State, India: cyclone and tidal wave off Bay of Bengal killed as many as 10,000.

1974 Dec. 25, Darwin, Australia: cyclone destroyed nearly the entire city, causing mass evacuation; 50 reported dead.

1977 Nov. 19, Andhra Pradesh, India: cyclone and tidal wave claimed lives of 20,000.

1978 Nov. 23, Sri Lanka and southern India: cyclone claimed at least 1,500 deaths.

1985 May 25, Bay of Bengal, Bangladesh: cyclone and tidal waves may have killed as many as 11,000 although official death toll was 2,540.

1988 Nov. 29, Bangladesh and India: cyclone took as many as 3,000 lives.

1991 April 30, southeastern Bangladesh: cyclone killed more than 125,000 and left as many as 9 million homeless. Thousands of survivors died from hunger and water borne disease.

U.S. Hurricanes

(U.S. deaths only except where noted)

1775 Sept. 2–Sept. 9, North Carolina to Nova Scotia: called the "Hurricane of Independence," it is believed that 4,170 in the U.S. and Canada died in the storm.

1856 Aug. 11, Last Island, La.: 400 died.

1893 Aug. 28, Savannah, Ga., Charleston, S.C., Sea Islands, S.C.: at least 1,000 died.

1900 Aug. 27–Sept. 15, Galveston, Tex. and Texas Gulf Coast: more than 6,000 died in hurricane and tidal wave.

1909 Sept. 10–21, Louisiana and Mississippi: 350 deaths.

1915 Aug. 5–23, East Texas and Louisiana: 275 killed.

1919 Sept. 2–15, Florida, Louisiana and Texas: 287 deaths, and 488 deaths at sea.

1926 Sept. 11–22, Florida and Alabama: 243 deaths.

1928 Sept. 6–20, Southern Florida: 1,836 died and 1,870 injured.

1935 Aug. 29–Sept. 10, Southern Florida: 408 killed.

1938 Sept. 10–22, Long Island and Southern New England: 600 deaths; 1,764 injured.

1944 Sept. 9–16, North Carolina to New England: 46 deaths, and 344 deaths at sea.

1947 Sept. 4–21, Florida and Mid-Gulf Coast: 51 killed.

1954 Aug. 25–31, North Carolina to New England: "Carol" killed 60 and injured 1,000 in Long Island–New England area.
Oct. 5–18, South Carolina to New York: "Hazel" killed 95 in U.S.; about 400-1000 in Haiti; 78 in Canada.

1955 Aug. 7–21, North Carolina to New England: "Diane" took 184 lives.

1957 June 25–28, Texas to Alabama: "Audrey" wiped out Cameron, La., causing 390 deaths.

1960 Aug. 29–Sept. 13, Florida to New England: "Donna" killed 50 in the United States. 115 deaths in Antilles—mostly from flash floods in Puerto Rico.

1961 Sept. 3–15, Texas coast: "Carla" devastated Texas gulf cities, taking 46 lives.

1965 Aug. 27–Sept. 12, Southern Florida and Louisiana: "Betsy" killed 75 people.

1969 Aug. 14–22, Mississippi, Louisiana, Alabama, Virginia, W. Virginia: 256 killed and 68 persons missing as a result of "Camille."

1972 June 14–23, Florida to New York: "Agnes" caused 117 deaths (50 in Pennsylvania).

1979 Aug. 25–Sept. 7, Caribbean Islands to New England: "David" caused 5 U.S. deaths; 1,200 in the Dominican Republic.

1980 Aug. 3–10, Caribbean Islands to Texas Gulf: "Allen" killed 28 in the U.S.; over 200 killed in Caribbean.

1989 Sept. 10–22, Caribbean Sea and South and North Carolina: "Hugo" claimed 49 U.S. lives (71 killed overall) and set record for high dollar damages.

Other Hurricanes

1926 Oct. 20, Cuba: worst hurricane in 80 years, 650 reported dead.

1930 Sept. 3 Santo Domingo: hurricane killed about 2,000 and injured 6,000.

1934 Sept. 21, Japan: hurricane killed more than 4,000 on Honshu.

1955 Sept. 19, Mexico: Hurricane "Hilda" took 200 lives.
Sept. 22–28, Caribbean: Hurricane "Janet" killed 200 in Honduras and 300 in Mexico.

1961 Oct. 31, British Honduras: Hurricane "Hattie" devastated capital Belize, killed at least 400.

1963 Oct. 2–7, Caribbean: Hurricane "Flora" killed up to 7,000 in Haiti and Cuba.

1966 Sept. 24–30, Caribbean area: Hurricane "Inez" killed 293.

1974 Sept. 20, Honduras: Hurricane "Fifi" struck northern section of country, leaving 8,000 dead, 100,000 homeless.

1988 Sept. 12–17, Caribbean Sea and Gulf of Mexico: Hurricane "Gilbert," worst Atlantic storm ever recorded, took at least 260 lives and caused some 39 tornadoes in Texas.

Tornadoes

1884 Feb. 19: tornadoes in Mississippi, Alabama, North and South Carolina, Tennessee, Kentucky and Indiana caused estimated 800 deaths.

Nuclear Power Plant Accidents

1952 Dec. 12, Chalk River, near Ottawa, Canada: A partial meltdown of the reactor's uranium fuel core resulted after the accidental removal of four control rods. Although millions of gallons of radioactive water accumulated inside the reactor, there were no injuries.

1957 Oct. 7, Windscale Pile No. 1, north of Liverpool, England: Fire in a graphite-cooled reactor spewed radiation over the countryside, contaminating a 200 sq mi area.

South Ural Mountains: Explosion of radioactive wastes at Soviet nuclear weapons factory 12 miles from city of Kyshtym forces the evacuation of over 10,000 people from a contaminated area. No casualties were reported by Soviet officials.

1976 near Greifswald, East Germany. Radioactive core of reactor in the Lubmin nuclear power plant nearly melted down due to the failure of safety systems during a fire.

1979 March 28, Three Mile Island, near Harrisburg, Pa.: One of two reactors lost its coolant, which caused the radioactive fuel to overheat and caused a partial meltdown. Some radioactive material was released.

1986 April 16, Chernobyl, near Kiev, U.S.S.R.: Explosion and fire in the graphite core of one of four reactors released radioacti ve material which spread over part. of the Soviet Union, Eastern Europe, Scandinavia, and later Western Europe, in the worst such accident to date.

1925 Mar. 18: tornadoes in Missouri, Illinois, Indiana, Kentucky, Tennessee, and Alabama killed 792.

1932 March 21: outbreak of tornadoes in Alabama, Mississippi, Georgia, and Tennessee killed 268.

1936 April 5–6: series of tornadoes in Arkansas, Alabama, Tennessee, Georgia, and South Carolina killed 498.

1952 March 21–22: tornadoes in Arkansas, Tennessee, Missouri, Mississippi, Alabama, and Kentucky caused 343 deaths.

1953 May 11: a single tornado struck Wako, Texas, killing 114.

June 8: another tornado killed 116 in Flint, Michigan.

1965 April 11: Tornadoes in Iowa, Illinois, Indiana, Ohio, Michigan, and Wisconsin caused 256 deaths.

1974 April 3–4: a series of tornadoes in East, South, and Midwest killed approximately 315.

Typhoons

1906 Sept. 18, Hong Kong: typhoon with tsunami killed an estimated 10,000 persons.

1949 Dec. 5, Off Korea: typhoon struck fishing fleet; several thousand men reported dead.

1953 Sept. 25, Vietnam: typhoon killed an estimated 1,000.

1959 Aug. 20, Fukien Province, China: Typhoon "Iris" killed 2,334.

Sept. 27, Honshu, Japan: Typhoon "Vera" killed an estimated 4,464.

1960 June 9, Fukien Province, China: Typhoon "Mary" caused at least 1,600 deaths.

1984 Sept. 2–3, Philippines: Typhoon "Ike" hit seven major islands leaving 1,300 dead.

Fires and Explosions

1666 Sept. 2, England: "Great Fire of London" destroyed St. Paul's Church, etc. Damage £10 million.

1835 Dec. 16, New York City: 530 buildings destroyed by fire.

1871 Oct. 8, Chicago: the "Chicago Fire" burned 17,450 buildings, killed 250 persons; $196 million damage.

1872 Nov. 9, Boston: fire destroyed 800 buildings; $75-million damage.

1876 Dec. 5, New York City: fire in Brooklyn Theater killed more than 300.

1881 Dec. 8, Vienna: at least 620 died in fire at Ring Theatre.

1894 Sept. 1, Minnesota: forest fire over 480-square-mile area destroyed six towns and killed 480 people.

1900 May 1, Scofield, Utah: explosion of blasting powder in coal mine killed 200.

June 30, Hoboken, N.J.: piers of North German Lloyd Steamship line burned; 326 dead.

1903 Dec. 30, Chicago: Iroquois Theatre fire killed 602.

1906 March 10, France: explosion in coal mine in Courrières killed 1,060.

1907 Dec. 19, Jacobs Creek, Pa.: explosion in coal mine left 239 dead.

1909 Nov. 13, Cherry, Ill.: explosion in coal mine killed 259.

1911 March 25, New York City: fire in Triangle Shirtwaist Factory fatal to 145.

1913 Oct. 22, Dawson, N.M.: coal mine explosion left 263 dead.

1917 April 10, Eddystone, Pa.: explosion in munitions plant killed 133.

Dec. 6, Canada: 1,600 people died when French ammunition ship *Mont Blanc* collided with Belgium steamer in Halifax Harbor.

1930 April 21, Columbus, Ohio: fire in Ohio State Penitentiary killed 320 convicts.

1937 March 18, New London, Tex.: explosion destroyed schoolhouse; 294 killed.

1942 April 26, Manchuria: explosion in Honkeiko Colliery killed 1,549.

Nov. 28, Boston: Cocoanut Grove nightclub fire killed 491.

1944 July 6, Hartford, Conn.: fire and ensuing stampede in main tent of Ringling Brothers Circus killed 168, injured 487.

July 17, Port Chicago, Calif.: 322 killed as ammunition ships explode.

Oct. 20, Cleveland: liquid-gas tanks exploded, killing 130.

1946 Dec. 7, Atlanta: fire in Winecoff Hotel killed 119.

1948 Dec. 3, Shanghai: Chinese passenger ship *Kiangya*, carrying refugees fleeing Communist troops during civil war, struck an old mine, exploded, and sank off Shanghai. Over 3,000 people are believed killed.

THE WORST MARINE DISASTER IN U.S. HISTORY.

The Mississippi sidewheeler *Sultana* had a total capacity of 376 passengers and crew. On this occasion, the ship was jammed with some 2,400 Union soldiers who had recently been released from Confederate prison camps. The Civil War had ended several weeks before and the troops were cheerfully looking forward to returning home. There were about 100 civilian passengers aboard, men, women, and children, who occupied first-class cabins. The boat also had a cargo of horses, mules, hogs, and, surprisingly, a live ten-foot alligator that was kept in a wooden crate. On April 27, 1865, eight miles out of Memphis, Tennes-see, the boiler exploded and the ship burst into flames. During the night, the *Sultana* burned down to the water line, while its survivors clung to floating debris. Some passengers were trapped aboard the flaming ship and died in the inferno. During the shipboard fire, one desperate individual managed to kill the alligator with a knife and used the crate to float to safety. Exactly how many people died in the disaster is not known. At least 1,547 lives were lost, exceeding the total of 1,513 for the 1912 sinking of the *Titanic*. Illustration: Courtesy of Mariners Museum.

1949 Sept. 2, China: fire on Chongqing (Chungking) waterfront killed 1,700.

1954 May 26, off Quonset Point, R.I.: explosion and fire aboard aircraft carrier *Bennington* killed 103 crewmen.

1956 Aug. 7, Colombia: about 1,100 reported killed when seven army ammunition trucks exploded at Cali.

Aug. 8, Belgium: 262 died in coal mine fire at Marcinelle.

1960 Jan. 21, Coalbrook, South Africa: coal mine explosion killed 437.

Nov. 13, Syria: 152 children killed in moviehouse fire.

1961 Dec. 17, Niteroi, Brazil: circus fire fatal to 323.

1962 Feb. 7, Saarland, West Germany: coal mine gas explosion killed 298.

1963 Nov. 9, Japan: explosion in coal mine at Omuta killed 447.

1965 May 28, India: coal mine fire in state of Bihar killed 375.

June 1, near Fukuoka, Japan: coal mine explosion killed 236.

1967 May 22, Brussels: fire in L'Innovation, major department store, left 322 dead.

July 29, off North Vietnam: fire on U.S. carrier *Forrestal* killed 134.

1969 Jan. 14, Pearl Harbor, Hawaii: nuclear aircraft carrier *Enterprise* ripped by explosions; 27 dead, 82 injured.

1970 Nov. 1, Saint-Laurent-du-Pont, France: fire in dance hall killed 146 young people.

1972 May 13, Osaka, Japan: 118 people died in fire in nightclub on top floor of Sennichi department store.

June 6, Wankie, Rhodesia: explosion in coal mine killed 427.

1973 Nov. 29, Kumamoto, Japan: fire in Taiyo department store killed 101.

1974 Feb. 1, Sao Paulo, Brazil: fire in upper stories of bank building killed 189 persons, many of whom leaped to death.

1975 Dec. 27, Dhanbad, India: explosion in coal mine followed by flooding from nearby reservoir left 372 dead.

1977 May 28, Southgate, Ky.: fire in Beverly Hills Supper Club; 167 dead.

1978 July 11, Tarragona, Spain: 140 killed at coastal campsite when tank truck carrying liquid gas overturned and exploded.

Aug. 20, Abadan, Iran: nearly 400 killed when arsonists set fire to crowded theater.

1982 Dec. 18–21, Caracas, Venezuela: power-plant fire leaves 128 dead.

Space Accidents

1967 Jan. 27, Apollo 1: A fire aboard the space capsule on the ground at Cape Kennedy, Fla. killed astronauts Virgil I. Grissom, Edward H. White, and Roger Chaffee.
April 23–24, Soyuz 1: Vladimir M. Komarov was killed when his craft crashed after its parachute lines, released at 23,000 feet for re-entry, became snarled.
1971 June 6–30, Soyuz 11: Three cosmonauts, Georgi T. Dolrovolsky, Vladislav N. Volkov, and Viktor I. Patsayev, found dead in the craft after its automatic landing. Apparently the cause of death was loss of pressurization in the space craft during re-entry

into the earth's atmosphere.
1980 March 18, U.S.S.R. A Vostok rocket exploded on its launch pad while being refueled, killing 50 at the Plesetsk Space Center.
1986 Jan 28, Challenger Space Shuttle: Exploded 73 seconds after lift off, killing all seven crew members. They were: Christa McAuliffe, Francis R. Scobee, Michael J. Smith, Judith A. Resnick, Ronald E. McNair, Ellison S. Onizuka, and Gregory B. Jarvis. A booster leak ignited the fuel, causing the explosion.

1986 Dec. 31, San Juan, P. R.: arson fire in Dupont Plaza Hotel set by three hotel employees kills 96.
1989 April 19, off Puerto Rico: A gun turret on the battleship *Iowa* exploded during a test-firing while participating in training excercises in the Atlantic about 330 miles northeast of Puerto Rico; 47 crew members were killed. *Also see* Wartime Disasters, *U.S.S. Mississippi.*
June 3, Ural Mountains: Liquified petroleum gas leaking from a pipeline running alongside the Trans-Siberian railway near Uta, 720 miles east of Moscow, exploded and destroyed two passing passenger trains. About 500 travelers were killed and 723 injured of an estimated 1,200 passengers on both trains.
Oct. 23, Pasadena, Texas. A huge explosion followed by a series of others and a raging fire at a plastics manufacturing plant owned by Phillips Petroleum Co. killed 22 and injured more than 80 persons. A large leak of ethylene was presumed to be the cause.
1990 Jan. 14, Zaragoza, Spain. A fire at a discotheque killed 43 with poisonous smoke fumes.
March 25, New York City. Arson fire in illegal *Happy Land Social Club*, Bronx, killed 87.

Shipwrecks

1833 May 11, *Lady of the Lake:* bound from England to Quebec, struck iceberg; 215 perished.
1853 Sept. 29 *Annie Jane:* emigrant vessel off coast of Scotland; 348 died.
1898 Nov. 26, *City of Portland:* Loss of 157 off Cape Cod.
1904 June 15, *General Slocum:* excursion steamer burned in East River, New York; 1,021 perished.
1912 March 5, *Principe de Asturias:* Spanish steamer struck rock off Sebastien Point; 500 drowned.
April 15, *Titanic:* sank after colliding with iceberg; 1,513 died.
1914 May 29, *Empress of Ireland:* sank after collision in St. Lawrence River; 1,024 perished.
1915 July 24, *Eastland:* Great Lakes excursion steamer overturned in Chicago River; 812 died.
1928 Nov. 12, *Vestris:* British steamer sank in gale off Virginia; 110 died.
1931 June 14: French excursion steamer overturned in gale off St. Nazaire; approximately 450 died.
1934 Sept. 8, *Morro Castle:* 134 killed in fire off

Asbury Park, N.J.
1939 May 23, *Squalus:* submarine with 59 men sank off Hampton Beach, N.H.; 33 saved.
June 1, Submarine *Thetis:* sank in Liverpool Bay, England; 99 perished.
1942 Oct. 2, *Queen Mary:* ramm ed and sank a British cruiser; 338 aboard the cruiser died.
1945 April 9: U.S. ship, loaded with aerial bombs, exploded at Bari, Italy; at least 360 killed.
1947 November, Yingkow: Unidentified Chinese troopship evacuating Nationalist troops from Manchuria sank, killing an estimated 6,000 persons.
1949 Sept. 17, *Noronic:* Canadian Great Lakes cruise ship burned at Toronto dock; about 130 died.
1952 April 26, *Hobson:* minesweeper collided with aircraft carrier *Wasp* and sank during night maneuvers in mid-Atlantic; 176 persons lost.
1953 Jan. 9, *Chang Tyong-Ho:* South Korean ferry foundered off Pusan; 249 reported dead.
Jan. 31, *Princess Victoria:* British ferry sank in Irish Sea; 133 lost.
1956 July 25, *Andrea Doria:* Italian liner collided with Swedish liner *Stockholm* off Nantucket Island, Mass., sinking next day; 52, mostly passengers on Italian ship, dead or unaccounted for; over 1,600 rescued.
1962 April 8, *Dara,* British liner, exploded and sank in Persian Gulf; 236 persons dead. Caused by time bomb.
1963 May 4: U.A.R. ferry capsized and sank in upper Nile; over 200 died.
1968 Late May, *Scorpion:* nuclear submarine sank in Atlantic 400 miles S.W. of Azores; 99 dead. (Located Oct. 31.)
1970 Dec. 15: ferry in Korean Strait capsized; 261 lost.
1976 Oct. 20, Luling, La.: *George Prince,* Mississippi River ferry, rammed by Norwegian tanker *Frosta;* 77 dead.
1983 May 25, *10th of Ramadan,* Nile steamer, caught fire and sank in Lake Nasser, near Aswan, Egypt; 272 dead and 75 missing.
1987 March 9, Belgium: British ferry capsizes after leaving Belgian port of Zeebrugge with 500 abroad; 134 drowned. Water rushing through open bow is believed to be probable cause.
1987 Dec. 20. Manila: Over 1,500 people killed when passenger ferry *Dona Paz* collided with oil tanker *Victor* off Mindoro Is., 110 miles south of Manila.

1989 **April 7, Norwegian Sea:** Fourty-two seamen died when Soviet Mike-class nuclear-powered submarine sank more than 300 miles off coast of Norway after an undersea accident and fire. Twenty-seven crew members were rescued.

1990 **April 7, Skagerrak Strait off Norway.** Suspected arson fire aboard Danish-owned North Sea ferry, *Scandinavian Star*, kills at least 110 passengers.

April 7, Myanmar (Burma). Double-decker ferry sinks in Gyaing River during a storm and 215 persons are believed drowned.

Aircraft Accidents

1921 **Aug. 24, England:** *AR-2* British dirigible, broke in two on trial trip near Hull; 62 died.

1925 **Sept. 3, Caldwell, Ohio:** U.S. dirigible *Shenandoah* broke apart; 14 dead.

1930 **Oct. 5, Beauvais, France:** British dirigible R 101 crashed, killing 47.

1933 **April 4, New Jersey Coast:** U.S. dirigible *Akron* crashed; 73 died.

1937 **May 6, Lakehurst, N.J.:** German zeppelin *Hindenburg* destroyed by fire at tower mooring; 36 killed.

1945 **July 28, New York City:** U.S. Army bomber crashed into Empire State Building; 13 dead.

1952 **Jan. 22, Elizabeth, N.J.:** 29 killed, including former Secretary of War Robert P. Patterson, when airliner hit apartments; seven of dead were on ground.

1953 **June 18, near Tokyo:** crash of U.S. Air Force "Globemaster" killed 129 servicemen.

1960 **Dec. 16, New York City:** United and Trans World planes collided in fog, crashed in two boroughs, killing 134 in air and on ground.

1961 **Feb. 15, near Brussels:** 72 on board and farmer on ground killed in crash of Sabena plane; U.S. figure skating team wiped out.

1966 **March 5, Japan:** British airliner caught fire and crashed into Mt. Fuji; 124 dead.

Dec. 24, Binh Thai, South Vietnam: crash of military-chartered plane into village killed 129.

1970 **Nov. 14, Huntington, W. Va.:** chartered plane carrying 43 players and coaches of Marshall University football team crashed; 75 dead.

1971 **July 30, Morioka, Japan:** Japanese Boeing 727 and F-86 fighter collided in mid-air; toll was 162.

Sept. 4, near Juneau, Alaska: Alaska Airlines Boeing 727 crashed into Chilkoot Mountains; 111 killed.

1972 **Aug. 14, East Berlin, East Germany:** Soviet-built East German Ilyushin plane crashed, killing 156.

Dec. 3, Santa Cruz de Tenerife, Canary Islands: Spanish charter jet carrying West German tourists crashed on take-off; all 155 aboard killed.

Dec. 30, Miami, Fla.: Eastern Airlines Lockheed 1011 TriStar Jumbo jet crashed into Everglades; 101 killed, 75 survived.

1973 **Jan. 22, Kano, Nigeria:** 171 Nigerian Moslems returning from Mecca and five crewmen died in crash.

1973 **Feb. 21:** Civilian Libyan Arab Airlines Boeing 727 shot down by Israeli fighters over Sinai after it had strayed off course; 108 died, five survived. Officials claimed that the pilot had ignored fighters' warnings to land.

April 10, Hochwald, Switzerland: British airliner carrying tourists to Swiss fair crashed in blizzard; 106 dead.

July 11, Paris: Boeing 707 of Varig Airlines, en route to Rio de Janeiro, crashed near airport, killing 122 of 134 passengers.

1974 **March 3, Paris:** Turkish DC-10 jumbo jet crashed in forest shortly after take-off; all 346 passengers and crew killed.

Dec. 4, Colombo, Sri Lanka: Dutch DC-8 carrying Moslems to Mecca crashed on landing approach, killing all 191 persons aboard.

1975 **April 4, near Saigon, Vietnam:** Air Force Galaxy C-5A crashed after take-off, killing 172, mostly Vietnamese children.

Aug. 3, Agadir, Morocco: Chartered Boeing 707, returning Moroccan workers home after vacation in France, plunged into mountainside; all 188 aboard killed.

1976 **Sept. 10, Zagreb, Yugoslavia:** midair collision between British Airways Trident and Yugoslav charter DC-9 fatal to all 176 persons aboard; worst mid-air collision on record.

1977 **March 27, Santa Cruz de Tenerife, Canary Islands:** Pan American and KLM Boeing 747s collided on runway. All 249 on KLM plane and 333 of 394 aboard Pan Am jet killed. Total of 582 is highest for any type of aviation disaster.

1978 **Jan. 1, Bombay:** Air India 747 with 213 aboard exploded and plunged into sea minutes after takeoff.

Sept. 25, San Diego, Calif.: Pacific Southwest plane collided in midair with Cessna. All 135 on airliner, 2 in Cessna, and 7 on ground killed for total of 144.

Nov. 15, Colombo, Sri Lanka: Chartered Icelandic Airlines DC-8, carrying 249 Moslem pilgrims from Mecca, crashed in thunderstorm during landing approach; 183 killed.

1979 **Nov. 26, Jidda, Saudi Arabia:** Pakistan International Airlines 707 carrying pilgrims returning from Mecca crashed on take-off; all 156 aboard killed.

Nov. 28, Mt. Erebus, Antarctica: Air New Zealand DC-10 crashed on sightseeing flight; 257 killed.

1980 **March 14, Warsaw:** LOT Polish Airlines Ilyushin 62 crashed while attempting landing; 22 boxers and officials of a U.S. amateur boxing team killed along with 65 others.

April 25, Santa Cruz de Tenerife, Canary Islands: Chartered Boeing 727 carrying 138 British vacationers and crew of 8 crashed into mountain while approaching for landing; all killed.

Aug. 19, Riyadh, Saudi Arabia: all 301 aboard Saudi Arabian jet killed when burning plane made safe landing but passengers were unable to escape.

1981 **Dec. 1, Ajaccio, Corsica:** Yugoslav DC-9 Super 80 carrying tourists crashed into mountain on landing approach, killing all 178 aboard.

1983 **June 28, near Cuenca, Ecuador:** Ecuadorean jetliner crashed in mountains, killing 119.

**Aug. 30, near island of Sakhalin off Siberia, South Korean civilian jetliner shot down by Soviet fighter after it strayed off course into Soviet airspace. All 269 people aboard killed.

Nov. 26, Madrid: A Columbian Avianca Boeing 747 crashed near Mejorada del Campó Airport killing 183 persons aboard. Eleven people survived the accident.

1985 **June 23:** Air-India Boeing 747 exploded over the Atlantic off the coast of Ireland, all 329 aboard killed.

Aug. 12, Japan Air Lines Boeing 747 crashed

into a mountain, killing 520 of the 524 aboard.

Dec. 12, A chartered Arrow Air DC-8, bringing American soldiers home for Christmas, crashed on takeoff from Gander, Newfoundland. All 256 aboard died.

1987 May 9, Poland: Polish airliner, Ilyushin 62M on charter flight to New York, crashes after takeoff from Warsaw killing 183.

Aug. 16, Detroit: Northwest Airlines McDonnell Douglas MD-30 plunges to heavily traveled boulevard, killing 156. Girl 4, only survivor.

Nov. 26: South African Airways Boeing 747 goes down south of Mauritius in rough seas; 160 die.

Nov. 29: Korean Air Boeing 747 jetliner explodes from bomb planted by North Korean agents and crashes into sea off Burma, killing all 115 aboard.

1988 July 3, Persian Gulf: U.S. Navy cruiser *Vincennes* shot down Iran Air A300 Airbus, killing 290 persons, after mistaking it for an attacking jet fighter.

Aug. 28, Ramstein Air Force Base, West Germany: Three jets from Italian Air Force acr obatic team collided in mid-air during air show and crashed, killing 70 persons, including the pilots and spectators on the ground. It is worst air-show disaster in history.

Dec. 21, Lockerbie, Scotland: A New-York-bound Pan-Am Boeing 747 exploded in flight from a terrorist bomb and crashed into Scottish village, killing all 259 aboard and 11 persons on the ground. Passengers included 38 Syracuse University students and many U.S. military personnel.

1989 Feb. 24, UAL 811: About 100 miles southwest of Hawaii, a 10- × 40-ft hole blew open in the fuselage of a United Airlines Boeing 747. Nine passengers were sucked out of the jet liner to their deaths 20,000 ft over the Pacific; 27 other passengers were injured.

June 7, Paramaribo, Suriname: A Surinam Airways DC-8 carrying 174 passengers and nine crew members crashed into the jungle while making a third attempt to land in a thick fog, killing 168 aboard.

1991 July 11, Jedda, Saudi Arabia: Canadian-chartered DC-8 carrying pilgrims returning to Nigeria crashes after takeoff, killing 261 persons.

Railroad Accidents

NOTE: Very few passengers were killed in a single U.S. train wreck up until 1853. These early trains ran slowly, made short trips, night travel was rare, and there were not many of them in operation.

1831 June 17: The boiler exploded on America's first passenger locomotive, *The Best Friend of Charleston*, killing the fireman. He was the first person in America to be killed in a railroad accident.

1833 Nov. 8, near Heightstown, N.J.: the world's first train wreck and the first passenger fatalities recorded. A 24-passenger Camden & Amboy train was derailed due to a broken axle, killing two passengers and injuring all others. Former president, John Quincy Adams and Cornelius Vanderbilt, who later made a fortune in railroads, were aboard the train.

1853 May 6, Norwalk, Conn: a New Haven Railroad train ran through an open drawbridge and plunged into the Norwalk River. Forty-six passengers were crushed to death or drowned. This was the first major drawbridge accident.

1856 July 17, Camp Hill, Pa.: two Northern Penn trains crashed head-on. Sixty-six church school children bound for a picnic died in the flaming wreckage.

1876 Dec. 29, Ashtabula, Ohio: a Lake Shore train fell into the Ashtabula River when a bridge it was crossing collapsed during a snowstorm. Ninety-two were killed.

1887 Aug. 10, near Chatsworth, Ill.: a burning railroad trestle collapsed while a Toledo, Peoria & Western train was crossing, killing 81 and injuring 372.

1904 Aug. 7, Eden, Colo.: Train derailed on bridge during flash flood; 96 killed.

1910 March 1, Wellington, Wash.: two trains swept into canyon by avalanche; 96 dead.

1915 May 22, Gretna, Scotland: two passenger trains and troop train collided; 227 killed.

1917 Dec. 12, Modane, France: nearly 550 killed in derailment of troop train near mouth of Mt. Cenis tunnel.

1918 Nov. 1, New York City: derailment of subway train in Malbone St. tunnel in Brooklyn left 92 dead.

1939 Dec. 22, near Magdeburg, Germany: more than 125 killed in collision; 99 killed in another wreck near Friedrichshafen.

1943 Dec. 16, near Rennert, N.C.: 72 killed in derailment and collision of two Atlantic Coast Line trains.

1944 March 2, near Salerno, Italy: 521 suffocated when Italian train stalled in tunnel.

1949 Oct. 22, near Nowy Dwor, Poland: more than 200 reported killed in derailment of Danzig-Warsaw express.

1950 Nov. 22, Richmond Hill, N.Y.: 79 died when one Long Island Rail Road commuter train crashed into rear of another.

1951 Feb. 6, Woodbridge, N.J.: 85 died when Pennsylvania Railroad commuter train plunged through temporary overpass.

1952 Oct. 8, Harrow-Wealdstone, England: two express trains crashed into commuter train; 112 dead.

1953 Dec. 24, near Sakvice, Czechoslovakia: two trains crashed; over 100 dead.

1957 Sept. 1, near Kendal, Jamaica: about 175 killed when train plunged into ravine.

Sept. 29, near Montgomery, West Pakistan: express train crashed into standing oil train; nearly 300 killed.

Dec. 4, St. John's, England: 92 killed, 187 injured as one commuter train crashed into another in fog.

1960 Nov. 14, Pardubice, Czechoslovakia: two trains collided; 110 dead, 106 injured.

1962 May 3, near Tokyo: 163 killed and 400 injured when train crashed into wreckage of collision between inbound freight train and outbound commuter train.

1963 Nov. 9, near Yokohama, Japan: two passenger trains crashed into derailed freight, killing 163.

1964 July 26, Custoias, Portugal: passenger train derailed; 94 dead.

1970 Feb. 4, near Buenos Aires: 236 killed when express train crashed into standing commuter train.

1972 July 21, Seville, Spain: head-on crash of two passenger trains killed 76.

Oct. 6, near Saltillo, Mexico: train carrying religious pilgrims derailed and caught fire, killing 204 and injuring over 1,000.

Oct. 30, Chicago: two Illinois Central commuter trains collided during morning rush hour; 45 dead and over 200 injured.

1974 Aug. 30, Zagreb, Yugoslavia: train entering station derailed, killing 153 and injuring over 60.

1977 Feb. 4, Chicago: 11 killed and over 180 injured when elevated train hit rear of another, sending two cars to street.

1981 June 6, Near Mansi, India: Driver of train carrying over 500 passengers, braked to avoid hitting cow, causing train to plunge off a bridge into Baghmati River; 268 passengers were reported killed, but at least 300 more were missing.

1982 Jan. 26, Algeria: Derailment on Algiers—Oran line leaves up to 120 dead.

July 11, Tepic, Mexico: Nogales-Guadalajara train plunges down mountain gorge killing 120.

1988 Dec. 12, South London: A commuter train crashed into the rear of a stopped train killing 33 and injuring more than 110 passengers.

1989 Jan. 15, Maizdi Khan, Bangladesh: A train carrying Muslim pilgrims crashed head-on with a mail train killing at least 110 persons and injuring as many as 1,000. Many people were riding on the roof of the trains and between the cars.

1989 Aug. 10, near Los Mochis, Mexico: A second-class passenger train traveling from Mazatlán to Mexicali, plunged off a bridge at Puente del Rio Bamoa into the river and killed an estimated 85 people and injured 107.

1990 Jan. 4, Sangi village, Sindh province, Pakistan: An overcrowded sixteen-car passenger train was switched to the wrong track and rammed into a standing freight train. At least 210 persons were killed and 700 were believed injured in what is said to be Pakistan's worst train disaster.

March 7, Philadelphia. Three passengers were killed and 162 injured when a six-car subway train derailed and crashed into a tunnel support beam.

April 15, near Kumrahar, Bihar State, India. An explosion aboard a moving commuter train caused a fire when a match was lit near a leaking gas cylinder, killing at least 80 people and injuring 65 others.

Oil Spills

1978 March 16, off Portsall, France: Wrecked supertanker *Amoco Cadiz* spilled 68 million gallons causing widespread environmental damage over 100 miles of coast of Brittany. Is world's largest tanker disaster.

1979 June 8, Gulf of Mexico: Exploratory oil well, Ixtoc 1, blew out, spilling an estimated 140 million gallons of crude into the open sea. Although it is the largest known oil spill, it had a low environmental impact.

1989 Dec. 19. Off Las Palmas, the Canary Islands. An explosion in Iranian supertanker, the *Kharg-5*, tore through its hull and caused 19 million gallons of crude oil to spill out into the Atlantic Ocean about 400 miles north of Las Palmas, forming a 100-square-mile oil slick.

Wartime Spills

1991 Jan. 25, Southern Kuwait: during the Persian Gulf War, Iraq deliberately released an estimated 460 million gallons of crude oil into the Persian Gulf from tankers at Mina al-Ahmadi and Sea Island Terminal 10 miles off Kuwait. Spill had little military significance. On Jan. 27, U.S. warplanes bombed pipe systems to stop the flow of oil.

Sports

1955 June 11, Le Mans, France: Racing car in Grand Prix hurtled into grandstand, killing 82 spectators.

1964 May 24, Lima, Peru: More than 300 soccer fans killed and over 500 injured during riot and panic following unpopular ruling by referee in Peru vs. Argentina soccer game. It is worst soccer disaster on record.

1971 Jan. 2, Glasgow, Scotland: Sixty-six persons killed in a crush at the Glasgow Rangers home stadium when fans trying to leave encountered fans trying to return to the stadium after hearing that a late goal had been scored.

1982 Oct. 20, Moscow: According to *Sovietsky Sport*, as many as 340 persons were killed at Lenin Stadium when exiting soccer fans collided with returning fans after final goal was scored. All the fans had been crowded into one section of stadium by police.

1985 May 11, Bradford, England: 56 persons burned to death and over 200 injured when fire engulfed the main grandstand at Bradford's soccer stadium.

May 29, Brussels, Belgium: Drunken group of British soccer fans supporting Liverpool club stormed stand filled with Italian supporters of Juventus team before European Champion's Cup final. While British fans attacked rival spectators at the Heysel Stadium, concrete retaining wall collapsed and 39 persons were crushed or trampled to death, 32 of them Italians. More than 400 persons were injured.

1988 March 12, Katmandu, Nepal: Some 80 soccer fans seeking cover during a violent hail storm at the national stadium were trampled to death in a stampede because the stadium doors were locked.

1989 April 15, Sheffield, England: Ninety-four people were killed and 170 injured at Hillsborough stadium when throngs of Liverpool soccer fans, many without tickets, collapsed a stadium barrier in a mad rush to see the game between Liverpool and Nottingham Forest. It was Britain's worst soccer disaster.

Miscellaneous

1958 January–October, Austria, France, Germany, Italy, and Switzerland: 283 people were killed in mountain climbing accidents in Alps Mountains.

1980 Jan. 20, Sincelejo, Colombia: Bleachers at a bullring collapsed, leaving 222 dead.

March 30, Stavanger, Norway: Floating hotel in North Sea collapsed, killing 123 oil workers.

1981 July 18, Kansas City, Mo.: suspended walkway in Hyatt Regency Hotel collapses; 113 dead, 186 injured.

1984 Dec. 3, Bhopal, India: Toxic gas, methyl isocyanate, seeped from Union Carbide insecticide plant, killing more than 2,000; injuring about 150,000.

1987 Sept. 18. Goiânia, Brazil: 244 people contaminated with cesium-137 removed from steel cylinder taken from cancer-therapy machine in abandoned clinic and sold as scrap. Four people died in worst radiation disaster in Western Hemisphere.

1988 July 6, North Sea off Scotland: 166 workers killed in explosion and fire on Occidental Petroleum's Piper Alpha rig in North Sea off Scottish coast; 64 survivors rescued. It is the world's worst offshore oil disaster.

1990 July 2, Mecca, Saudi Arabia: a stampede in a 1,800 foot-long pedestrian tunnel leading from Mecca to a tent city for pilgrims, killed 1,426 pilgrims who were trampled to death.

Wartime Disasters

1915 May 6: Despite German warnings in newspapers, the Cunard Liner *Lusitania* sailed from New York for Liverpool, England, on May 1st and was sunk off the coast of Ireland by a German submarine. 1,198 passengers and crew, 128 of them Americans, died. Unknown to the passengers, the ship was carrying a cargo of small arms. The disaster contributed to the entry of the United States into World War I.

1916 Feb. 26: 3,100 people died when the French cruiser *Provence* was sunk by a German submarine in the Mediterranean.

1940 Sept. 13. The luxury liner *S.S. City of Benares* sailed from Liverpool with over 90 British children who were being evacuated to Canada to escape harm during World War II. About 600 miles out to sea, the ship was torpedoed by a German submarine during the night and only 13 of the children survived the disaster.[1]

1943 November, Gilbert Islands: While battleship *U.S.S. Mississippi* was bombarding Makin Atoll in Pacific during WW II, an accidental gun turret explosion killed 43 of her crew.

1944 Sept. 12, South China Sea: U.S. submarines torpedoed and sank two Japanese troop ships[2], the *Kachidoki Maru* and the *Rakuyo Maru*. Unknown to the submarines, the Japanese, in disregard for the rules of treatment of prisoners of war, had forced 2,000 British, Australian, and American POWs into the holds of the ships

which were designed to hold only 300 troops. Later, when the subs discovered the tragedy, they sought to rescue as many survivors as possible. Japanese vessels picked up most of *Kachidoki Maru*'s prisoners but abandoned those from the *Rakuyo Maru*, taking only the Japanese survivors. Of the 1,300 POWs aboard the *Rakuyo Maru*, 159 were rescued, but only seven lived.

Oct. 24, South China Sea: The *Arisan Maru*[2] carrying 1,800 American prisoners was torpedoed by a U.S. submarine and sunk. The Japanese destroyer escort rescued Japanese military and civilian personnel and left the POWs to their fate. It is estimated that only ten prisoners survived the disaster.

Dec. 17–18, Philippine Sea: A typhoon struck U.S. Third Fleet's Task Force 38, sank three destroyers, damaged seven other ships, destroyed 186 aircraft, and killed 800 officers and men.

1945 Jan. 30: 7,700 persons died in world's largest marine disaster when the Nazi passenger ship *Wilhelm Gustoff* carrying Germans fleeing Poland was torpedoed in the Baltic by a Soviet submarine.

May 3, *Cap Arcona*: Several days before World War II ended in Europe, the German passenger ship carrying about 6,000, of which an estimated 5,000 were concentration camp prisoners, was sunk by British aircraft. An estimated 5,000 persons were killed, most of them prisoners who were about to gain their freedom.

July 29, near Leyte Gulf: The heavy cruiser *Indianapolis* was torpedoed and sunk by a Japanese submarine. Of the crew of 1,199 men, only 316 survived. Several days earlier, the *Indianapolis* had delivered a lead cylinder containing uranium (U-235) and the firing mechanism for the first atomic bomb to Tinian Island. Had the ship been sunk earlier while delivering its special cargo, WW II would have ended differently.

1991 February, Kuwait: during the Persian Gulf War, Iraqi troops dynamited and set fire to over 500 of Kuwait's 950 oil wells, causing the world's worst man-made environmental disaster.

---

1. During the war (1939-1945), some 10,000 children were evacuated to say with foster parents in the United States and Canada. The sinking of the *City of Benares* ended the British government's evacuation program.
2. The ships had no identification that they were transporting prisioners of war.

How Columbus Avoided a Great Disaster

Source: American Weather Stories.

Christopher Columbus was intimately acquainted with hurricanes. Arriving off Hispaniola on his fourth and final voyage in the summer of 1502, the aging Admiral, now fallen from favor, read the signs of an approaching storm. He requested the shelter of Santo Domingo harbor, but was refused. Instead, ignoring Columbus' warning, some 30 vessels, many loaded with gold and slaves, sailed proudly out of the harbor for Spain. Francisco de Bobadilla, Columbus' mortal enemy, sailed on the flagship.

Twenty ships and over 500 men, including de Bobadilla, were never seen again. Only one vessel reached Spain—a small, leaky ship grudgingly assigned to carry back to Spain the proceeds from the sale of Columbus' few remaining island properties, his guarantee of an independent old age.

Columbus himself, a weatherwise seaman, rode out the hurricane safely at anchor in an island cove. Meanwhile, Santo Domingo was smashed flat—for the first of many times. □

RELIGION

The National Survey of Religious Identification, 1989–1990

Conducted by CUNY Graduate Center Researchers

This major study, the first of its kind, gives us a detailed religious profile of 20th Century America. The survey, which includes a representative sample of 113,000 adults across the continental United States, was directed by Prof. Barry A. Kosmin, a senior researcher at the City University Graduate Center, in cooperation with Prof. Seymour P. Lachman, CUNY Dean for Community Development. Highlights of the report are summarized herein for *Information Please Almanac* readers.

Nationwide, 26.2% of Americans identify themselves as Roman Catholic, while 60.3% are Protestant (with the overwhelming majority identifying themselves with a particular Protestant denomination). Among non-Christians, religious Jews make up approximately 2% of the population and those identifying themselves as Muslim make up about 0.5% of the population.

Other major findings include: The percentage of respondents in western states who said they had no religious identification was double the national average at 13% in California, 14% in Washington and 17% in Oregon. The population most identified with religion is found in the South.

According to the study, the major churches in the country are Roman Catholic (26.2%), Baptist (19.4%), Methodist (8%) and Lutheran (5.2%). In the national picture the much publicized cults and new religions practically vanish into statistical insignificance.

Some religious denominations are particularly strong on regional and state levels. For example, Catholics are a majority in Connecticut, Massachusetts and Rhode Island; outside the Northeast they are strongest in Louisiana (47%). Baptists form a majority in Alabama, Georgia and Mississippi.

Half of all Black Americans profess to be Baptists. More than 9% of Blacks are Catholic, and they are nearly 6% of all American Catholics.

Mormons, though only 1.4% of all Americans, comprise 69% of Utah's population and are a plurality (31%) in neighboring Idaho. The other major denominations evidencing state pluralities are the Lutherans in North Dakota (36%) and Minnesota (34%) and Methodists in Delaware (27%).

Most who say they are of Irish ancestry are actually Protestants, not Catholics. Presumably many, though not all, are of Scots-Irish or Northern Irish descent. On the other hand, ethnic intermarriage produces a good proportion of Italian and Polish Protestants and Scandinavian Catholics. Hispanics, one of America's rapidly growing groups, comprise 14% of all Catholics, but one-third of Hispanics adhere to other religions. Americans who claim to be of Jewish ethnic origin number 6.8 million, but only two-thirds of them say they actually follow the Jewish religion.

Of the 1.5 million Arab-Americans more than half are Christians, including most people of Lebanese and Iraqi descent. Of the country's 1.4 million Muslims, 40% are Black, though less than 2% of the total Black population is Muslim. Moreover, Muslims are only slightly more numerous than Buddhists, and

Self-Described Religious Adherence of U.S. Adult Population 1990

Christians	Number
Christian (no denomination supplied)	8,073,000
Roman Catholic	46,004,000
Protestant (no denomination supplied)	17,214,000
Baptist	33,964,000
Methodist	14,116,000
Lutheran	9,110,000
Presbyterian	4,985,000
Pentecostal	3,116,000
Episcopalian/Anglican	3,042,000
Mormon/LDS	2,487,000
Church of Christ	1,769,000
Jehovah Witness	1,381,000
Seventh Day Adventist	668,000
Assembly of God	660,000
Holiness/Holy	610,000
Nazarene	549,000
Unitarian	463,000
Evangelical/Born Again	446,000
Church of God	442,000
Congregational	438,000
Greek Orthodox	384,000
Quaker/Mennonite	302,000
Christian Science	214,000
Brethren	206,000
Disciples of Christ	144,000
New Apostolic	117,000
Worldwide Church of God	116,000
Russian Orthodox	85,000
Charismatic	75,000
Wesleyan	58,000
Christian Reform	40,000
Eastern Orthodox	33,000
Church of God in Christ	32,000
Fundamentalist	27,000
Independent Church	25,000
Four Square Gospel	24,000
Dutch Reform	19,000
Covenant	16,000
Church of America	11,000
Four Square	4,000
Open Bible	4,000
Non-Denominational	195,000
Total Christian	**151,668,000**

Non-Christians	Number
Jewish	3,137,000
Muslim/Islamic	527,000 *
Buddhist	401,000 *
Hindu	227,000 *
Bahai	28,000
Taoist	23,000
Rastafarian	14,000
Wiccan	8,000

Deity	6,000
Agnostic	1,186,000
Scientology	45,000
Humanist	29,000
New Age	20,000
Eckankar	18,000
Other unclassified	889,000
No religion	13,116,000
Refused	4,031,000
U.S. Total	**175,440,000**

*Adjustments for undercounts due to language problems.

Hindus are growing rapidly. Buddhist strength is centered in the West, and Hindus are concentrated in the Northeast.

Most Asian-Americans are not Buddhists, Hindus or Muslims but Christians, particularly Catholics and Baptists, similar to other Americans.

People without a religious affiliation are the least likely to marry. Mormons have the highest proportion of married adults and the largest number of children. They are also the most Republican in their political affiliation.

While Baptists and Jews are the most Democratic in their political affiliation, Jews are the most urbanized of the religious groups, and Baptists are the most rural.

The most highly educated groups, in terms of the proportion of college graduates, are Jews, Hindus, Episcopalians, Presbyterians and Buddhists.

Pentecostals and Baptists have the youngest populations and Methodists and Presbyterians the oldest.

Rates of marriage break-up are surprisingly uniform across all religious groups. The Greek Orthodox have the lowest rate of divorce and the Unitarians the highest. Roman Catholics have rates similar to Lutherans and other mainstream Protestant denominations. □

Major Religions of the World

Judaism

The determining factors of Judaism are: descendance from Israel, the *Torah,* and Tradition.

The name Israel (Jacob, a patriarch) also signifies his descendants as a people. During the 15th–13th centuries B.C., Israelite tribes, coming from South and East, gradually settled in Palestine, then inhabited by Canaanites. They were held together by Moses, who gave them religious unity in the worship of *Jahweh,* the God who had chosen Israel to be his people.

Under Judges, the 12 tribes at first formed an am-

phictyonic covenant. Saul established kingship (circa 1050 B.C.), and under David, his successor (1000–960 B.C.), the State of Israel comprised all of Palestine with Jerusalem as religio-political center. A golden era followed under Solomon (965–926 B.C.), who built *Jahweh* a temple.

After Solomon's death, the kingdom separated into Israel in the North and Judah in the South. A period of conflicts ensued, which ended with the conquest of Israel by Assyria in 722 B.C. The Babylonians defeated Judah in 586 B.C., destroying Jerusalem and its temple, and deporting many to Babylon.

Estimated Membership of the Principal Religions of the World

Statistics of the world's religions are only very rough approximations. Aside from Christianity, few religions, if any, attempt to keep statistical records; and even Protestants and Catholics employ different methods of counting members. All persons of whatever age who have received baptism in the Catholic Church are counted as members, while in most Protestant Churches only those who "join" the church are numbered. The compiling of statistics is further complicated by the fact that in China one may be at the same time a Confucian, a Taoist, and a Buddhist. In Japan, one may be both a Buddhist and a Shintoist.

Religion	Africa	Asia	Europe[1]	South America	North America	Oceania	World
Christians	310,600,000	252,800,000	518,800,000	419,078,000	235,500,000	22,000,000	1,758,778,000
Roman Catholics	116,670,000	118,900,000	266,580,000	390,050,000	95,600,000	7,980,000	995,780,000
Protestants	82,900,000	78,380,000	83,200,000	16,600,000	94,900,000	7,310,000	363,290,000
Orthodox	27,100,000	3,516,000	128,150,000	1,696,000	5,920,000	560,000	166,942,000
Anglicans	25,500,000	680,000	32,760,300	1,250,000	7,230,000	5,560,000	72,980,300
Other Christians	58,430,000	51,324,000	8,109,700	9,482,000	31,850,000	590,000	159,785,700
Muslims	264,132,000	612,768,000	51,100,000	1,300,000	5,600,000	100,000	935,000,000
Nonreligious	1,800,000	686,600,000	135,800,000	16,500,000	22,100,000	3,200,000	866,000,000
Hindus	1,400,000	700,448,000	702,000	850,000	1,250,000	350,000	705,000,000
Buddhists	20,000	301,215,000	670,000	520,000	550,000	25,000	303,000,000
Atheists	300,000	155,280,000	72,500,000	3,100,000	1,300,000	520,000	233,000,000
Chinese folk religionists	12,000	179,717,000	61,000	70,000	120,000	20,000	180,000,000
New-Religionists	20,000	136,009,000	51,000	510,000	1,400,000	10,000	138,000,000
Tribal religionists	67,006,000	24,000,000	1,000	900,000	40,000	65,000	92,012,000
Sikhs	25,000	17,577,500	230,500	8,000	250,000	9,000	18,100,000
Jews	320,000	5,375,000	3,660,000	1,050,000	6,900,000	95,000	17,400,000
Shamanists	1,000	9,844,500	252,000	1,000	1,000	500	10,100,000
Confucians	1,000	5,766,000	4,000	2,000	26,000	1,000	5,800,000
Baha'is	1,420,000	2,578,000	97,000	770,000	360,000	75,000	5,300,000
Jains	50,000	3,576,000	15,000	4,000	4,000	1,000	3,650,000
Shintoists	200	3,097,200	600	900	1,000	500	3,100,000
Other religionists	410,800	11,824,800	1,787,900	3,432,500	478,000	4,000	17,938,000
Total Population	**647,518,000**	**3,108,476,000**	**785,732,000**	**448,096,000**	**275,880,000**	**26,476,000**	**5,292,178,000**

1. Includes the U.S.S.R. *Source: Britiannica Book of the Year, 1991.*

The era of the kings is significant also in that the great prophets worked in that time, emphasizing faith in *Jahweh* as both God of Israel and God of the universe, and stressing social justice.

When the Persians permitted the Jews to return from exile (539 B.C.), temple and cult were restored in Jerusalem. The Persian rulers were succeeded by the Seleucides. The Maccabaean revolt against these Hellenistic kings gave independence to the Jews in 128 B.C., which lasted till the Romans occupied the country.

Important groups that exerted influence during these times were the Sadducees, priests in the temple in Jerusalem; the Pharisees, teachers of the Law in the synagogues; Essenes, a religious order (from whom Dead Sea Scrolls, discovered in 1947, came); Apocalyptists, who were expecting the heavenly Messiah; and Zealots, who were prepared to fight for national independence.

When the latter turned against Rome in A.D. 66, Roman armies under Titus suppressed the revolt, destroying Jerusalem and its temple in A.D. 70. The Jews were scattered in the *diaspora* (Dispersion), subject to oppressions until the Age of the Enlightenment (18th century) brought their emancipation, although persecutions did not end entirely.

The fall of the Jerusalem temple was an important event in the religious life of the Jews, which now developed around *Torah* (Law) and synagogue. Around A.D. 100 the Sacred Scriptures were codified. Synagogue worship became central, with readings from *Torah* and prophets. Most important prayers are the *Shema* (Hear) and the Prayer of the 18 Benedictions.

Religious life is guided by the commandments contained in the *Torah:* circumcision and *Sabbath,* as well as other ethical and ceremonial commandments.

The *Talmud,* based on the *Mishnah* and its interpretations, took shape over many centuries in the Babylonian and Palestinian Schools. It was a strong binding force of Judaism in the Dispersion.

In the 12th century, Maimonides formulated his "13 Articles of Faith," which carried great authority. Fundamental in this creed are: belief in God and his oneness *(Sherma),* belief in the changeless *Torah,* in the words of Moses and the prophets, belief in reward and punishment, the coming of the Messiah, and the resurrection of the dead.

Judaism is divided into theological schools, the main divisions of which are Orthodox, Conservative, and Reform.

Christianity

Christianity is founded upon Jesus Christ, to whose life the New Testament writings testify. Jesus, a Jew, was born in about 7 B.C. and assumed his public life, after his 30th year, in Galilee. The Gospels tell of many extraordinary deeds that accompanied his ministry. He proclaimed the Kingdom of God, a future reality that is at the same time already present. Nationalistic-Jewish expectations of the Messiah he rejected. Rather, he referred to himself as the "Son of Man," the Christ, who has power to forgive sins now and who shall also come as Judge at the end of time. Jesus set forth the religio-ethical demands for participation in the Kingdom of God as change of heart and love of God and neighbor.

At the Last Supper he signified his death as a sacrifice, which would inaugurate the New Covenant, by which many would be saved. Circa A.D. 30 he died on a cross in Jerusalem. The early Church carried on Jesus' proclamation, the apostle Paul emphasizing his death and resurrection.

The person of Jesus is fundamental to the Christian faith since it is believed that in his life, death, and resurrection, God's revelation became historically tangible. He is seen as the turning point in history, and man's relationship to God as determined by his attitude to Jesus.

Historically Christianity thus arose out of Judaism, claiming fulfillment of the promises of the Old Testament in Jesus. The early Church designated itself as "the true Israel," which expected the speedy return of Jesus. The mother church was at Jerusalem, but churches were soon founded in many other places. The apostle Paul was instrumental in founding and extending a Gentile Christianity that was free from Jewish legalism.

The new religion spread rapidly throughout the eastern and western parts of the Roman Empire. In coming to terms with other religious movements within the Empire, Christianity began to take definite shape as an organization in its doctrine, liturgy, and ministry circa A.D. 200. In the 4th century the Catholic Church had taken root in countries stretching from Spain in the West to Persia and India in the East. Christians had been repeatedly subject to persecution by the Roman state, but finally gained tolerance under Constantine the Great (A.D. 313). Since that time, the Church became favored under his successors and in 380 the Emperor Theodosius proclaimed Christianity the State religion. Paganism was suppressed and public life was gradually molded in accordance with Christian ethical demands.

It was in these years also that the Church was able to achieve a certain unity of doctrine. Due to differences of interpretation of basic doctrines concerning Christ, which threatened to divide the Catholic Church, a standard Christian Creed was formulated by bishops at successive Ecumenical Councils, the first of which was held in A.D. 325 (Nicaea). The chief doctrines formulated concerned the doctrine of the Trinity, i.e., that there is one God in three persons: Father, Son, and Holy Spirit (Constantinople, A.D. 381); and the nature of Christ as both divine and human (Chalcedon, A.D. 541).

Through differences and rivalry between East and West the unity of the Church was broken by schism in 1054. In 1517 a separation occurred in the Western Church with the Reformation. From the major Protestant denominations [Lutheran, Presbyterian, Anglican (Episcopalian)], many Free Churches separated themselves in an age of individualism.

In the 20th century, however, the direction is toward unity. The Ecumenical Movement led to the formation of the World Council of Churches in 1948 (Amsterdam), which has since been joined by many Protestant and Orthodox Churches.

Through its missionary activity Christianity has spread to most parts of the globe.

Eastern Orthodoxy

Eastern Orthodoxy comprises the faith and practice of Churches stemming from ancient Churches in the Eastern part of the Roman Empire. The term covers Orthodox Churches in communion with the See of Constantinople and Nestorian and Monophysite Churches.

The Orthodox, Catholic, Apostolic Church is the direct descendant of the Byzantine State Church and consists of a series of independent national churches that are united by Doctrine, Liturgy, and Hierarchical organization (deacons and priests, who may either be married or be monks before ordination, and bishops, who must be celibates). The heads of these Churches

U.S. Church Membership

Religious group	Members
Protestant bodies and others	79,386,506
Roman Catholics	57,019,948
Jewish congregations[1]	5,944,000
Eastern churches	4,077,011
Old Catholic, Polish National Catholic, Armenian churches	979,831
Buddhists	19,441
Miscellaneous	200,329
Total[2]	**147,607,394**

1. Includes Orthodox, Conservative, and Reform. 2. As reported in the *1991 Yearbook of American & Canadian Churches* from statistics furnished by 219 religious bodies in the United States.

are patriarchs or metropolitans; the Patriarch of Constantinople is only "first among equals." Rivalry between the Pope of Rome and the Patriarch of Constantinople, aided by differences and misunderstandings that existed for centuries between the Eastern and Western parts of the Empire, led to a schism in 1054. Repeated attempts at reunion have failed in past centuries. The mutual excommunication pronounced in that year was lifted in 1965, however, and because of greater interaction in theology between Orthodox Churches and those in the West, a climate of better understanding has been created in the 20th century. First contacts were with Anglicans and Old Catholics. Orthodox Churches belong to the World Council of Churches.

The Eastern Orthodox Churches recognize only the canons of the seven Ecumenical Councils (325–787) as binding for faith and they reject doctrines that have been added in the West.

The central worship service is called the Liturgy, which is understood as representation of God's acts of salvation. Its center is the celebration of the Eucharist, or Lord's Supper.

In their worship icons (sacred pictures) are used that have a sacramental meaning as representation. The Mother of Christ, angels, and saints are highly venerated.

The number of sacraments in the Orthodox Church is the same as in the Western Catholic Church.

Orthodox Churches are found in the Balkans and the Soviet Union also, since the 20th century, in Western Europe and other parts of the world, particularly in America.

Eastern Rite Churches

These include the Uniate Churches that recognize the authority of the Pope but keep their own traditional liturgies and those Churches dating back to the 5th century that emancipated themselves from the Byzantine State Church: the Nestorian Church in the Near East and India and the Monophysite Churches (Coptic, Ethiopian, Syrian, Armenian, and the Mar Thoma Church in India).

Roman Catholicism

Roman Catholicism comprises the belief and practice of the Roman Catholic Church. The Church stands under the authority of the Bishop of Rome, the Pope, and is ruled by him and bishops who are held to be, through ordination, successors of Peter and the Apostles, respectively. Fundamental to the structure of the Church is the juridical aspect: doctrine and sacraments are bound to the power of jurisdiction and

consecration of the hierarchy. The Pope, as the head of the hierarchy of archbishops, bishops, priests, and deacons, has full ecclesiastical power, granted him by Christ, through Peter. As successor to Peter, he is the Vicar of Christ. The powers that others in the hierarchy possess are delegated.

Roman Catholics believe their Church to be the one, holy, catholic, and apostolic Church, possessing all the properties of the one, true Church of Christ.

The faith of the Church is understood to be identical with that taught by Christ and his Apostles and contained in Bible and Tradition, i.e. the original deposit of faith, to which nothing new may be added. New definitions of doctrines, such as the Immaculate Conception of Mary (1854) and the bodily Assumption of Mary (1950), have been declared by Popes, however, in accordance with the principle of development (implicit-explicit doctrine).

At Vatican Council I (1870) the Pope was proclaimed "endowed with infallibility, *ex cathedra,* i.e., when exercising the office of Pastor and Teacher of all Christians."

The center of Roman Catholic worship is the celebration of the Mass, the Eucharist, which is the commemoration of Christ's sacrificial death and of his resurrection. Other sacraments are Baptism, Confirmation, Confession, Matrimony, Ordination, and Extreme Unction, seven in all. The Virgin Mary and saints, and their relics, are highly venerated and prayers are made to them to intercede with God, in whose presence they are believed to dwell.

The Roman Catholic Church is the largest Christian organization in the world, found in most countries.

Since Vatican Council II (1962–65), and the effort to "update" the Church, many interesting changes and developments have been taking place.

Protestantism

Protestantism comprises the Christian churches that separated from Rome during the Reformation in the 16th century, initiated by an Augustinian monk, Martin Luther. "Protestant" was originally applied to followers of Luther, who protested at the Diet of Spires (1529) against the decree which prohibited all further ecclesiastical reforms. Subsequently, Protestantism came to mean rejection of attempts to tie God's revelation to earthly institutions, and a return to the Gospel and the Word of God as sole authority in matters of faith and practice. Central in the biblical message is the justification of the sinner by faith alone. The Church is understood as a fellowship and the priesthood of all believers stressed.

The Augsburg Confession (1530) was the principal statement of Lutheran faith and practice. It became a model for other Confessions of Faith, which in their turn had decisive influence on Church polity. Major Protestant denominations are Lutheran, Reformed (Calvinist), Presbyterian, and Anglican (Episcopal). Smaller ones are the Mennonite, Schwenkfeldians, and Unitarians. In Great Britain and America there are the Congregationalists, Baptists, Quakers, Methodists, and other free church types of communities. (In regarding themselves as being faithful to original biblical Christianity, these Churches differ from such religious bodies as Unitarians, Mormons, Jehovah's Witnesses, and Christian Scientists, who either teach new doctrines or reject old ones.)

Since the latter part of the 19th century, national councils of churches have been established in many countries, e.g. the Federal Council of Churches of Christ in America in 1908. Denominations across countries joined in federations and world alliances, beginning with the Anglican Lambeth Conference in 1867.

Protestant missionary activity, particularly strong in the last century, resulted in the founding of many younger churches in Asia and Africa. The Ecumenical Movement, which originated with Protestant missions, aims at unity among Christians and churches.

Islam

Islam is the religion founded in Arabia by Mohammed between 610 and 632. Its more than 600 million adherents are found in countries stretching from Morocco in the West to Indonesia in the East.

Mohammed was born in A.D. 570 at Mecca and belonged to the Quraysh tribe, which was active in caravan trade. At the age of 25 he joined the caravan trade from Mecca to Syria in the employment of a rich widow, Khadiji, whom he married. Critical of the idolatry of the inhabitants of Mecca, he began to lead a contemplative life in the deserts. There he received a series of revelations. Encouraged by Khadiji, he gradually became convinced that he was given a God-appointed task to devote himself to the reform of religion and society. Idolatry was to be abandoned.

The *Hegira (Hijra)* (migration) of Mohammed from Mecca, where he was not honored, to Medina, where he was well received, occurred in 622 and marks the beginning of the Muslim era. In 630 he marched on Mecca and conquered it. He died at Medina in 632. His grave there has since been a place of pilgrimage.

Mohammed's followers, called Moslems, revered him as the prophet of *Allah* (God), beside whom there is no other God. Although he had no close knowledge of Judaism and Christianity, he considered himself succeeding and completing them as the seal of the Prophets. Sources of the Islamic faith are the *Qur'an,* regarded as the uncreated, eternal Word of God, and Tradition *(hadith)* regarding sayings and deeds of the prophet.

Islam means surrender to the will of *Allah.* He is the all-powerful, whose will is supreme and determines man's fate. Good deeds will be rewarded at the Last Judgment in paradise and evil deeds will be punished in hell.

The Five Pillars, primary duties, of Islam are: witness; confessing the oneness of God and of Mohammed, his prophet; prayer, to be performed five times a day; almsgiving to the poor and the mosque (house of worship); fasting during daylight hours in the month of Ramadan; and pilgrimage to Mecca at least once in the Moslem's lifetime.

Islam, upholding the law of brotherhood, succeeded in uniting an Arab world that had disintegrated into tribes and castes. Disagreements concerning the succession of the prophet caused a great division in Islam between *Sunnis* and *Shias.* Among these, other sects arose *(Wahhabi).* Doctrinal issues also led to the rise of different schools of thought in theology. Nevertheless, since Arab armies turned against Syria and Palestine in 635, Islam has expanded successfully under Mohammed's successors. Its rapid conquests in Asia and Africa are unsurpassed in history. Turning against Europe, Moslems conquered Spain in 713. In 1453 Constantinople fell into their hands and in 1529 Moslem armies besieged Vienna. Since then, Islam has lost its foothold in Europe.

In modern times it has made great gains in Africa.

Hinduism

In India alone there are more than 625 million adherents of Hinduism. In contrast to other religions, it has no founder. Considered the oldest religion in the world, it dates back, perhaps, to prehistoric times.

Hinduism is hard to define, there being no common creed, no one doctrine to bind Hindus together. Intellectually there is complete freedom of belief, and one can be monotheist, polytheist, or atheist. What matters is the social system: a Hindu is one born into a caste.

As a religion, Hinduism is founded on the sacred scriptures, written in Sanskrit and called the *Vedas (Veda-*knowledge). There are four Vedic books, among which the *Rig Veda* is the most important. It speaks of many gods and also deals with questions concerning the universe and creation. The dates of these works are unknown (1000 B.C.?).

The *Upanishads* (dated 1000–800 B.C.), commentaries on the Vedic texts, have philosophical speculations on the origin of the universe, the nature of deity, of *atman* (the human soul), and its relationship to *Brahman* (the universal soul).

Brahman is the principle and source of the universe who can be indicated only by negatives. As the divine intelligence, he is the ground of the visible world, a presence that pervades all beings. Thus the many Hindu deities came to be understood as manifestations of the one *Brahman* from whom everything proceeds and to whom everything ultimately returns. The religio-social system of Hinduism is based on the concept of reincarnation and transmigration in which all living beings, from plants below to gods above, are caught in a cosmic system that is an everlasting cycle of becoming and perishing.

Life is determined by the law of *karma,* according to which rebirth is dependent on moral behavior in a previous phase of existence. The doctrine of transmigration thus provides a rationale for the caste system. In this view, life on earth is regarded as transient *(maya)* and a burden. The goal of existence is liberation from the cycle of rebirth and redeath and entrance into the indescribable state of what in Buddhism is called *nirvana* (extinction of passion).

Further important sacred writings are the Epics *(puranas),* which contain legendary stories about gods and men. They are the *Mahabharata* (composed between 200 B.C. and A.D. 200) and the *Ramayana.* The former includes the *Bhagavad-Gita* (Song of the Lord), its most famous part, that tells of devotion to *Krishna* (Lord), who appears as an *avatar* (incarnation) of the god *Vishnu,* and of the duty of obeying caste rules. The work begins with a praise of the *yoga* (discipline) system.

The practice of Hinduism consists of rites and ceremonies, performed within the framework of the caste system and centering on the main socio-religious occasions of birth, marriage, and death. There are many Hindu temples, which are dwelling places of the deities and to which people bring offerings. There are also places of pilgrimages, the chief one being Benares on the Ganges, most sacred among the rivers in India.

In modern times work has been done to reform and revive Hinduism. One of the outstanding reformers was Ramakrishna (1836–86), who inspired many followers, one of whom founded the Ramakrishna mission, which seeks to convert others to its religion. The mission is active both in India and in other countries.

Buddhism

Founded in the 6th century B.C. in northern India by Gautama Buddha, who was born in southern Nepal as son to a king. His birth is surrounded by many legends, but Western scholars agree that he lived from 563 to 483 B.C. Warned by a sage that his son would become an ascetic or a universal monarch, the king confined him to his home. He was able to escape and began the life of a homeless wanderer in search of peace, passing through many disappointments until he finally came to the Tree of Enlightenment, under which he lived in meditation till enlightenment came to him and he became a Buddha (enlightened one).

Now he understood the origin of suffering, summarized in the *Four Noble Truths*, which constitutes the foundation of Buddhism. The Four are the truth of suffering, which all living beings must endure; of the origin of suffering, which is craving and which leads to rebirth; that it can be destroyed; and of the way that leads to cessation of pain, i.e., the *Noble Eightfold Way*, which is the rule of practical Buddhism: right views, right intention, right speech, right action, right livelihood, right effort, right concentration, and right ecstasy.

Nirvana is the goal of all existence, the state of complete redemption, into which the redeemed enters. Buddha's insight can free every man from the law of reincarnation through complete emptying of the self.

The nucleus of Buddha's church or association was originally formed by monks and lay-brothers, whose houses gradually became monasteries used as places for religious instruction. The worship service consisted of a sermon, expounding of Scripture, meditation, and confession. At a later stage pilgrimages to the holy places associated with the Buddha came into being, as well as veneration of relics.

In the 3rd century B.C., King Ashoka made Buddhism the State religion of India but, as centuries passed, it gradually fell into decay through splits, persecutions, and the hostile Brahmans. Buddhism spread to countries outside India, however.

At the beginning of the Christian era, there occurred a split that gave rise to two main types: *Hinayana* (Little Vehicle), or southern Buddhism, and *Mahayana* (Great Vehicle), or northern Buddhism. The former type, more individualistic, survived in Ceylon and southern Asia. *Hinayana* retained more closely the original teachings of the Buddha, which did not know of a personal god or soul. *Mahayana*, more social, polytheistic, and developing a pluralistic pompous cult, was strong in the Himalayas, Tibet, Mongolia, China, Korea, and Japan.

In the present century, Buddhism has found believers also in the West and Buddhist associations have been established in Europe and the U.S.

Confucianism

Confucius (K'ung Fu-tzu), born in the state of Lu (northern China), lived from 551 to 479 B.C. Tradition, exaggerating the importance of Confucius in life, has depicted him as a great statesman but, in fact, he seems to have been a private teacher. Anthologies of ancient Chinese classics, along with his own Analects *(Lun Yu),* became the basis of Confucianism. These Analects were transmitted as a collection of his sayings as recorded by his students, with whom he discussed ethical and social problems. They developed into men of high moral standing, who served the State as administrators.

In his teachings, Confucius emphasized the importance of an old Chinese concept *(li),* which has the connotation of proper conduct. There is some disagreement as to the religious ideas of Confucius, but he held high the concepts handed down from centuries before him. Thus he believed in Heaven *(T'ien)* and sacrificed to his ancestors. Ancestor worship he

indeed encouraged as an expression of filial piety, which he considered the loftiest of virtues.

Piety to Confucius was the foundation of the family as well as the State. The family is the nucleus of the State, and the "five relations," between king and subject, father and son, man and wife, older and younger brother, and friend and friend, are determined by the virtues of love of fellow men, righteousness, and respect.

An extension of ancestor worship may be seen in the worship of Confucius, which became official in the 2nd century B.C. when the emperor, in recognition of Confucius' teachings as supporting the imperial rule, offered sacrifices at his tomb.

Mencius (Meng Tse), who lived around 400 B.C., did much to propagate and elaborate Confucianism in its concern with ordering society. Thus, for two millennia, Confucius' doctrine of State, with its emphasis on ethics and social morality, rooted in ancient Chinese tradition and developed and continued by his disciples, has been standard in China and the Far East.

With the revolution of 1911 in China, however, students, burning Confucius in effigy, called for the removal of "the old curiosity shop."

Shintoism

Shinto, the Chinese term for the Japanese *Kami no Michi,* i.e., the Way of the Gods, comprises the religious ideas and cult indigenous to Japan. *Kami,* or gods, considered divine forces of nature that are worshipped, may reside in rivers, trees, rocks, mountains, certain animals, or, particularly, in the sun and moon. The worship of ancestors, heroes, and deceased emperors was incorporated later.

After Buddhism had come from Korea, Japan's native religion at first resisted it. Then there followed a period of compromise and amalgamation with Buddhist beliefs and ceremonies, resulting, since the 9th century A.D., in a syncretistic religion, a Twofold Shinto. Buddhist deities came to be regarded as manifestations of Japanese deities and Buddhist priests took over most of the Shinto shrines.

In modern times Shinto regained independence from Buddhism. Under the reign of the Emperor Meiji (1868–1912) it became the official State religion, in which loyalty to the emperor was emphasized. The line of succession of emperors is traced back to the first Emperor Jimmu (660 B.C.) and beyond him to the Sun-goddess *Amaterasuomikami.*

The centers of worship are the shrines and temples in which the deities are believed to dwell and believers approach them through *torii* (gateways). Most important among the shrines is the imperial shrine of the Sun-goddess at Ise, where state ceremonies were once held in June and December. The *Yasukuni* shrine of the war dead in Tokyo is also well known.

Acts of worship consist of prayers, clapping of hands, acts of purification, and offerings. On feast days processions and performances of music and dancing take place and priests read prayers before the gods in the shrines, asking for good harvest, the well-being of people and emperor, etc. In Japanese homes there is a god-shelf, a small wooden shrine that contains the tablets bearing the names of ancestors. Offerings are made and candles lit before it.

After World War II the Allied Command ordered the disestablishment of State Shinto. To be distinguished from State Shinto is Sect Shinto, consisting of 13 recognized sects. These have arisen in modern times. Most important among them is *Tenrikyo* in Tenri City (Nara), in which healing by faith plays a central role.

Taoism

Taoism, a religion of China, was, according to tradition, founded by Lao Tse, a Chinese philosopher, long considered one of the prominent religious leaders from the 6th century B.C.

Data about him are for the most part legendary, however, and the *Tao Te Ching* (the classic of the Way and of its Power), traditionally ascribed to him, is now believed by many scholars to have originated in the 3rd century B.C. The book is composed in short chapters, written in aphoristic rhymes. Central are the word *Tao*, which means way or path and, in a deeper sense, signifies the principle that underlies the reality of this world and manifests itself in nature and in the lives of men, and the word *Te* (power).

The virtuous man draws power from being absorbed in *Tao*, the ultimate reality within an ever-changing world. By non-action and keeping away from human striving it is possible for man to live in harmony with the principles that underlie and govern the universe. *Tao* cannot be comprehended by reason and knowledge, but only by inward quiet.

Besides the *Tao Te Ching*, dating from approximately the same period, there are two Taoist works, written by Chuang Tse and Lieh Tse.

Theoretical Taoism of this classical philosophical movement of the 4th and 3rd centuries B.C. in China differed from popular Taoism, into which it gradually degenerated. The standard of theoretical Taoism was maintained in the classics, of course, and among the upper classes it continued to be alive until modern times.

Religious Taoism is a form of religion dealing with deities and spirits, magic and soothsaying. In the 2nd century A.D. it was organized with temples, cult, priests, and monasteries and was able to hold its own in the competition with Buddhism that came up at the same time.

After the 7th century A.D., however, Taoist religion further declined. Split into numerous sects, which often operate like secret societies, it has become a syncretistic folk religion in which some of the old deities and saints live on.

Roman Catholic Pontiffs

St. Peter, of Bethsaida in Galilee, Prince of the Apostles, was the first Pope. He lived first in Antioch and then in Rome for 25 years. In AD 64 or 67, he was martyred. St. Linus became the second Pope.

Name	Birthplace	Reigned From	Reigned To	Name	Birthplace	Reigned From	Reigned To
St. Linus	Tuscia	67	76	St. Boniface I	Rome	418	422
St. Anacletus (Cletus)	Rome	76	88	St. Celestine I	Campania	422	432
St. Clement	Rome	88	97	St. Sixtus III	Rome	432	440
St. Evaristus	Greece	97	105	St. Leo I (the Great)	Tuscany	440	461
St. Alexander I	Rome	105	115	St. Hilary	Sardinia	461	468
St. Sixtus I	Rome	115	125	St. Simplicius	Tivoli	468	483
St. Telesphorus	Greece	125	136	St. Felix III (II)[2]	Rome	483	492
St. Hyginus	Greece	136	140	St. Gelasius I	Africa	492	496
St. Pius I	Aquileia	140	155	Anastasius II	Rome	496	498
St. Anicetus	Syria	155	166	St. Symmachus	Sardinia	498	514
St. Soter	Campania	166	175	St. Hormisdas	Frosinone	514	523
St. Eleutherius	Epirus	175	189	St. John I	Tuscany	523	526
St. Victor I	Africa	189	199	St. Felix IV (III)	Samnium	526	530
St. Zephyrinus	Rome	199	217	Boniface II	Rome	530	532
St. Callistus I	Rome	217	222	John II	Rome	533	535
St. Urban I	Rome	222	230	St. Agapitus I	Rome	535	536
St. Pontian	Rome	230	235	St. Silverius	Campania	536	537
St. Anterus	Greece	235	236	Vigilius	Rome	537	555
St. Fabian	Rome	236	250	Pelagius I	Rome	556	561
St. Cornelius	Rome	251	253	John III	Rome	561	574
St. Lucius I	Rome	253	254	Benedict I	Rome	575	579
St. Stephen I	Rome	254	257	Pelagius II	Rome	579	590
St. Sixtus II	Greece	257	258	St. Gregory I (the Great)	Rome	590	604
St. Dionysius	Unknown	259	268	Sabinianus	Tuscany	604	606
St. Felix I	Rome	269	274	Boniface III	Rome	607	607
St. Eutychian	Luni	275	283	St. Boniface IV	Marsi	608	615
St. Caius	Dalmatia	283	296	St. Deusdedit (Adeodatus I)	Rome	615	618
St. Marcellinus	Rome	296	304	Boniface V	Naples	619	625
St. Marcellus I	Rome	308	309	Honorius I	Campania	625	638
St. Eusebius	Greece	309[1]	309[1]	Severinus	Rome	640	640
St. Meltiades	Africa	311	314	John IV	Dalmatia	640	642
St. Sylvester I	Rome	314	335	Theodore I	Greece	642	649
St. Marcus	Rome	336	336	St. Martin I	Todi	649	655
St. Julius I	Rome	337	352	St. Eugene I[3]	Rome	654	657
Liberius	Rome	352	366	St. Vitalian	Segni	657	672
St. Damasus I	Spain	366	384	Adeodatus II	Rome	672	676
St. Siricius	Rome	384	399	Donus	Rome	676	678
St. Anastasius I	Rome	399	401	St. Agatho	Sicily	678	681
St. Innocent I	Albano	401	417				
St. Zozimus	Greece	417	418				

Name	Birthplace	Reigned From	To	Name	Birthplace	Reigned From	To
St. Leo II	Sicily	682	683	Gregory VI	Rome	1045	1046
St. Benedict II	Rome	684	685	Clement II	Saxony	1046	1047
John V	Syria	685	686	Benedict IX	—	1047	1048
Conon	Unknown	686	687	(3rd time)			
St. Sergius I	Syria	687	701	Damasus II	Bavaria	1048	1048
John VI	Greece	701	705	St. Leo IX	Alsace	1049	1054
John VII	Greece	705	707	Victor II	Germany	1055	1057
Sisinnius	Syria	708	708	Stephen IX (X)	Lorraine	1057	1058
Constantine	Syria	708	715	Nicholas II	Burgundy	1059	1061
St. Gregory II	Rome	715	731	Alexander II	Milan	1061	1073
St. Gregory III	Syria	731	741	St. Gregory VII	Tuscany	1073	1085
St. Zachary	Greece	741	752	Bl. Victor III	Benevento	1086	1087
Stephen II (III)[4]	Rome	752	757	Bl. Urban II	France	1088	1099
St. Paul I	Rome	757	767	Paschal II	Ravenna	1099	1118
Stephen III (IV)	Sicily	768	772	Gelasius II	Gaeta	1118	1119
Adrian I	Rome	772	795	Callistus II	Burgundy	1119	1124
St. Leo III	Rome	795	816	Honorius II	Flagnano	1124	1130
Stephen IV (V)	Rome	816	817	Innocent II	Rome	1130	1143
St. Paschal I	Rome	817	824	Celestine II	Città di	1143	1144
Eugene II	Rome	824	827		Castello		
Valentine	Rome	827	827	Lucius II	Bologna	1144	1145
Gregory IV	Rome	827	844	Bl. Eugene III	Pisa	1145	1153
Sergius II	Rome	844	847	Anastasius IV	Rome	1153	1154
St. Leo IV	Rome	847	855	Adrian IV	England	1154	1159
Benedict III	Rome	855	858	Alexander III	Siena	1159	1181
St. Nicholas I	Rome	858	867	Lucius III	Lucca	1181	1185
(the Great)				Urban III	Milan	1185	1187
Adrian II	Rome	867	872	Gregory VIII	Benevento	1187	1187
John VIII	Rome	872	882	Clement III	Rome	1187	1191
Marinus I	Gallese	882	884	Celestine III	Rome	1191	1198
St. Adrian III	Rome	884	885	Innocent III	Anagni	1198	1216
Stephen V (VI)	Rome	885	891	Honorius III	Rome	1216	1227
Formosus	Portus	891	896	Gregory IX	Anagni	1227	1241
Boniface VI	Rome	896	896	Celestine IV	Milan	1241	1241
Stephen VI (VII)	Rome	896	897	Innocent IV	Genoa	1243	1254
Romanus	Gallese	897	897	Alexander IV	Anagni	1254	1261
Theodore II	Rome	897	897	Urban IV	Troyes	1261	1264
John IX	Tivoli	898	900	Clement IV	France	1265	1268
Benedict IV	Rome	900	903	Bl. Gregory X	Piacenza	1271	1276
Leo V	Ardea	903	903	Bl. Innocent V	Savoy	1276	1276
Sergius III	Rome	904	911	Adrian V	Genoa	1276	1276
Anastasius III	Rome	911	913	John XXI[7]	Portugal	1276	1277
Landus	Sabina	913	914	Nicholas III	Rome	1277	1280
John X	Tossignano	914	928	Martin IV[8]	France	1281	1285
Leo VI	Rome	928	928	Honorius IV	Rome	1285	1287
Stephen VII (VIII)	Rome	928	931	Nicholas IV	Ascoli	1288	1292
John XI	Rome	931	935	St. Celestine V	Isernia	1294	1294
Leo VII	Rome	936	939	Boniface VIII	Anagni	1294	1303
Stephen VIII (IX)	Rome	939	942	Bl. Benedict XI	Treviso	1303	1304
Marinus II	Rome	942	946	Clement V	France	1305	1314
Agapitus II	Rome	946	955	John XXII	Cahors	1316	1334
John XII	Tusculum	955	964	Benedict XII	France	1334	1342
Leo VIII[5]	Rome	963	965	Clement VI	France	1342	1352
Benedict V[5]	Rome	964	966	Innocent VI	France	1352	1362
John XIII	Rome	965	972	Bl. Urban V	France	1362	1370
Benedict VI	Rome	973	974	Gregory XI	France	1370	1378
Benedict VII	Rome	974	983	Urban VI	Naples	1378	1389
John XIV	Pavia	983	984	Boniface IX	Naples	1389	1404
John XV	Rome	985	996	Innocent VII	Sul mona	1404	1406
Gregory V	Saxony	996	999	Gregory XII	Venice	1406	1415
Sylvester II	Auvergne	999	1003	Martin V	Rome	1417	1431
John XVII	Rome	1003	1003	Eugene IV	Venice	1431	1447
John XVIII	Rome	1004	1009	Nicholas V	Sarzana	1447	1455
Sergius IV	Rome	1009	1012	Callistus III	Jativa	1455	1458
Benedict VIII	Tusculum	1012	1024	Pius II	Siena	1458	1464
John XIX	Tusculum	1024	1032	Paul II	Venice	1464	1471
Benedict IX[6]	Tusculum	1032	1044	Sixtus IV	Savona	1471	1484
Sylvester III	Rome	1045	1045	Innocent VIII	Genoa	1484	1492
Benedict IX	—	1045	1045	Alexander VI	Jativa	1492	1503
(2nd time)				Pius III	Siena	1503	1503

Name	Birthplace	Reigned From	To	Name	Birthplace	Reigned From	To
Julius II	Savona	1503	1513	Alexander VIII	Venice	1689	1691
Leo X	Florence	1513	1521	Innocent XII	Spinazzola	1691	1700
Adrian VI	Utrecht	1522	1523	Clement XI	Urbino	1700	1721
Clement VII	Florence	1523	1534	Innocent XIII	Rome	1721	1724
Paul III	Rome	1534	1549	Benedict XIII	Gravina	1724	1730
Julius III	Rome	1550	1555	Clement XII	Florence	1730	1740
Marcellus II	Montepulciano	1555	1555	Benedict XIV	Bologna	1740	1758
Paul IV	Naples	1555	1559	Clement XIII	Venice	1758	1769
Pius IV	Milan	1559	1565	Clement XIV	Rimini	1769	1774
St. Pius V	Bosco	1566	1572	Pius VI	Cesena	1775	1799
Gregory XIII	Bologna	1572	1585	Pius VII	Cesena	1800	1823
Sixtus V	Grottammare	1585	1590	Leo XII	Genga	1823	1829
Urban VII	Rome	1590	1590	Pius VIII	Cingoli	1829	1830
Gregory XIV	Cremona	1590	1591	Gregory XVI	Belluno	1831	1846
Innocent IX	Bologna	1591	1591	Pius IX	Senegallia	1846	1878
Clement VIII	Florence	1592	1605	Leo XIII	Carpineto	1878	1903
Leo XI	Florence	1605	1605	St. Pius X	Riese	1903	1914
Paul V	Rome	1605	1621	Benedict XV	Genoa	1914	1922
Gregory XV	Bologna	1621	1623	Pius XI	Desio	1922	1939
Urban VIII	Florence	1623	1644	Pius XII	Rome	1939	1958
Innocent X	Rome	1644	1655	John XXIII	Sotto il Monte	1958	1963
Alexander VII	Siena	1655	1667	Paul VI	Concesio	1963	1978
Clement IX	Pistoia	1667	1669	John Paul I	Forno di Canale	1978	1978
Clement X	Rome	1670	1676	John Paul II	Wadowice, Poland	1978	
Bl. Innocent XI	Como	1676	1689				

1. Or 310. 2. He should be called Felix II, and his successors of the same name should be numbered accordingly. The discrepancy was caused by the erroneous insertion in some lists of the name of St. Felix of Rome, Martyr. 3. He was elected during the exile of St. Martin I, who endorsed him as Pope. 4. After St. Zachary died, a Roman priest named Stephen was elected but died before his consecration as Bishop of Rome. His name is not included in all lists for this reason. In view of this historical confusion, the *National Catholic Almanac* lists the true Stephen II as Stephen II (III), the true Stephen III as Stephen III (IV), etc. 5. Confusion exists concerning the legitimacy of claims. If the deposition of John was invalid, Leo was an antipope until after the end of Benedict's reign. If the deposition of John was valid, Leo was the legitimate Pope and Benedict an antipope. 6. If the triple removal of Benedict IX was not valid, Sylvester III, Gregory VI, and Clement II were antipopes. 7. Elimination was made of the name of John XX in an effort to rectify the numerical designation of Popes named John. The error dates back to the time of John XV. 8. The names of Marinus I and Marinus II were construed as Martin. In view of these two pontificates and the earlier reign of St. Martin I, this pontiff was called Martin IV. *Source: National Catholic Almanac, from Annuarto Pontificio.*

Books of the Bible

NEW TESTAMENT

Matthew
Mark
Luke
John
Acts
Romans
1 Corinthians
2 Corinthians
Galatians
Ephesians
Phillipians
Colossians
1 Thessalonians
2 Thessalonians
1 Timothy
2 Timothy
Titus
Philemon
Hebrews
James
1 Peter
2 Peter
1 John
2 John
3 John
Jude
Revelation

OLD TESTAMENT

Genesis
Exodus
Leviticus
Numbers
Deuteronomy
Joshua
Judges
Ruth
I Samuel
2 Samuel
I Kings
2 Kings
I Chronicles
2 Chronicles
Ezra
Nehemiah
[1]Tobit
[1]Judith
Esther
[1]1 Maccabees
[1]2 Maccabees
Job
Psalms
Proverbs
Ecclesiastes
Song of Songs/Solomon
[1]Wisdom
[1]Sirach/Ecclesiasticus
Isaiah
Jeremiah
Lamentations
[1]Baruch
Ezekiel
Daniel
Hosea
Joel
Amos
Obadiah
Jonah
Micah
Nahum
Habakkuk
Zephaniah
Haggai
Zechariah
Malachi

1. These books are generally not accepted in the Protestant canon of Scripture, and Protestants refer to them as "Apocrypha." Catholic bibles include these books and refer to them as "Deuterocanonical." These disputed books were included in pre–Reformation Bibles.

Air Safety
What You Can Do, What You Can't

About one in every million commercial airline flights in the U.S. each year results in fatalities. The risk is small, but can you tilt the odds more in your favor by choosing one airline over another? Frankly, nobody knows. Crashes occur so infrequently that there isn't enough data to call any domestic airline safer than any other.

Maintenance records aren't of much help either. Though consumers might reasonably suspect that an airline going through a financial crisis would be tempted to skimp on maintenance, the Federal Aviation Administration says it conducts more frequent inspections of financially troubled carriers, possibly mitigating any potential danger. It also says it steps up inspections of carriers involved in labor disputes.

How about aging aircraft? Older planes can be harder to maintain. But many experts say an old plane that's well taken care of can fly indefinitely. Further, a plane is the sum of many parts, quite a few of which may be brand new.

Are Commuters Riskier?

One sector of the industry—commuter airlines—has historically had a worse accident record than that of major airlines. Commuter airlines fly short routes between hubs and small airports, often using planes with 30 or fewer seats. Between 1980 and 1990, fatal commuter-airline crashes were about four times more frequent than those of large carriers (2.2 crashes per million flights versus 0.58 crashes per million flights).

Most accidents occur during take-off or landing: commuter planes are more vulnerable to accidents because the airports they use sometimes lack up-to-date air-traffic control systems. Commuter airlines also hire young, inexperienced pilots, and traditionally their turnover rate has been high.

But the safety record of commuter carriers is improving. Last year, the rate of accidents among scheduled commuter flights was slightly lower than that of the larger carriers. And the FAA has proposed stricter pilot standards, which should mean a greater margin of safety.

Still, if you're concerned, ask the travel agent if you'll be flying a commuter during any leg of your trip. Though your ticket may say Continental, for example, you could be on a commuter airline that shares Continental's booking code.

Improving Your Odds

Regardless of which airline you fly, you can reduce your risk through common sense. If you have a choice—and a refundable ticket—put off the flight when bad weather is predicted at either end.

Despite folk wisdom that passengers seated in the back of a plane are most likely to survive a plane crash, statisticians have found that no particular part of the plane is safest. It all depends on how the plane hits. The best advice is to choose a seat that offers the easiest escape route, such as an aisle seat in the emergency exit row., Plan an escape strategy. Note how many seats separate you from the emergency exits, fore and aft; in a dark or smoke-filled cabin, you may have to feel your way to the emergency exit.

Wear the safety belt snug, but not painfully tight. Don't unbuckle it except to go to the lavatory. Unexpected turbulence has caused injuries and some deaths.

How you dress can also affect your likelihood of surviving an accident. Flat, non-slip shoes are best; high heels can slow an escape and puncture evacuation slides. Clothing that covers most of your body can protect against burns. Tightly woven, natural fibers burn more slowly than synthetics. Consider wearing a chain on your glasses so you won't lose them. A handkerchief—or better, a wet washcloth in a plastic bag—can serve as a primitive filter against poisonous fumes.

A few safety groups have recommended the use of smoke hoods that fit like a ski mask and are said to filter out suffocating particles and noxious fumes. Three or four brands are available, most through mail-order, but at prices as high as $89. Their makers claim they can provide the wearer with up to 20 minutes of additional breathing time. However, the jury is out on their usefulness. If you were to survive the initial impact of an airplane crash, the seconds you would then spend trying to put a mask on might be better spent trying to get out of the plane.

Flying With Kids

Traveling with children requires special consideration. Though children under the age of two may fly free if they sit on a parent's lap, we don't recommend that. The force of a crash can wrench a child from your arms. If you can afford to, buy your child a ticket and bring aboard a child safety seat that carries the FAA's seal of approval for air travel. All the airlines in our survey say they allow such seats. If you can't afford a ticket for your infant, most airlines (Southwest is an exception) will allow you to b ring the safety seat aboard free if there is an unsold seat next to you. □

Warning on Taking Pets Abroad

Pets taken out of the U.S. and returned are subject to the same requirements as those entering for the first time. Pets excluded from entry into the United States will be exported or destroyed.

The U.S. Public Health Service requires that pets—particularly dogs, cats, and turtles—brought into this country be examined at the first port of entry for possible evidence of disease that can be transmitted to humans.

For information on requirements of the country into which you will take your pet, contact the specific embassy or nearest consular office. □

U.S. Passport and Customs Information

Source: Department of State, Bureau of Consular Affairs and Department of the Treasury, Customs Service.

Passports

With a few exceptions, a passport is required for all U.S. citizens to depart and enter the United States and to enter most foreign countries. A valid U.S. passport is the best documentation of U.S. citizenship available. Persons who travel to a country where a U.S. passport is not required should be in possession of documentary evidence of their U.S. citizenship and identity to facilitate reentry into the United States. Travelers should check passport and visa requirements with consular officials of the countries to be visited well in advance of their departure date.

Application for a passport may be made at a passport agency; to a clerk of any Federal court or State court of record; or a judge or clerk of any probate court accepting applications; or at a post office selected to accept passport applications. Passport agencies are located in Boston, Chicago, Honolulu, Houston, Los Angeles, Miami, New Orleans, New York, Philadelphia, San Francisco, Seattle, Stamford, Conn., and Washington, D.C.

All persons are required to obtain individual passports in their own names. Neither spouses nor children may be included in each others' passports. Applicants between the ages of 13 and 18 must appear in person before the clerk or agent executing the application. For children under the age of 13, a parent or legal guardian may execute an application for them.

First time passport applicants must apply in person. Applicants must present evidence of citizenship (e.g., a certified copy of birth certificate), personal identification (e.g., a valid driver's license), two identical black and white or color photographs taken within six months (2 × 2 inches, with the image size measured from the bottom of the chin to the top of the head [including hair] not less than 1 inch nor more than 1 3/8 inches on a plain white or off–white background, vending machine photographs not acceptable), plus a completed passport application (DSP–11). If you were born abroad, you may also use as proof of citizenship: a Certificate of Naturalization, a Certificate of Citizenship, a Report of Birth abroad of a Citizen of the United States of America or a Certification of Birth. A fee of $35 plus a $7 execution fee is charged for adults 18 years and older for a passport valid for ten years from the date of issue. The fee for minor children under 18 years of age is $20 for a five–year passport plus $7 for the execution of the application.

You may apply for a passport by mail if you have been the bearer of a passport issued within 12 years prior to the date of a new application, are able to submit your most recent U.S. passport with your new application, and your previous passport was not issued before your 16th birthday. If you are eligible to apply by mail, include your previous passport, a completed, signed, and dated DSP–82 "Application for Passport by Mail," new photographs, and the passport fee of $35. The $7 execution fee is not required when applying by mail. Mail the application and attachments to one of the 13 passport agencies.

Passports may be presented for amendment to show a married name or legal change of name or to correct descriptive data. Any alterations to the passport by the bearer *other than* in the spaces provided for change of address and next of kin data are forbidden.

Loss, theft or destruction of a passport should be reported to Passport Services, 1425 K Street, N.W., Washington, D.C. 20524 immediately, or to the nearest passport agency. If you are overseas, report to the nearest U.S. Embassy or consulate and to local police authorities. Your passport is a valuable citizenship and identity document. It should be carefully safeguarded. Its loss could cause you unnecessary travel complications as well as significant expense. It is advisable to photocopy the data page of your passport and keep it in a place separate from your passport to facilitate the issuance of a replacement passport should one be necessary.

Customs

United States residents must declare all articles acquired abroad and in their possession at the time of their return. In addition, articles acquired in the U.S. Virgin Islands, American Samoa, or Guam and not accompanying you must be declared at the time of your return. The wearing or use of an article acquired abroad does *not* exempt it from duty. Customs declaration forms are distributed on vessels and planes, and should be prepared in advance of arrival for presentation to the customs inspectors.

If you have not exceeded the duty–free exemption allowed, you may make an oral declaration to the customs inspector. A written declaration is necessary when (1) total fair retail value of articles exceeds $1,400 ($400 duty–free exemption plus $1,000 dutiable at a flat 10% rate) (keep your sales slips); (2) over 1 liter of liquor, 200 cigarettes, or 100 cigars are included; (3) items are not intended for your personal or household use, or articles brought home for another person; and (4) when a customs duty or internal revenue tax is collectible on any article in your possession.

An exception to the above are regulations applicable to articles purchased in the U.S. Virgin Islands, American Samoa, or Guam where you may receive a customs exemption of $1,200. Not more than $400 of this exemption may be applied to merchandise obtained elsewhere than in these islands or $600 if acquired in a beneficiary country. Five liters of alcoholic beverages and 1000 cigarettes may be included provided not more than one liter and 200 cigarettes were acquired elsewhere than in these islands. Articles acquired in and sent from these islands to the United States may be claimed under your duty–free personal exemption if properly declared at the time of your return. For information on rules applying to beneficiary countries and a list of them check with your customer officer or write for the pamphlet "GSP and the Traveler" from the Department of the Treasury, U.S. Customs Services, Washington, D.C. 20229. Since rules change it is always wise to check with customs before leaving, to get information pertinent to the areas you will be visiting.

Articles accompanying you, in excess of your personal exemption, up to $1000 will be assessed at a flat rate of duty of 10% based on fair retail value in country of acquisition. (If articles were acquired in the insular possessions, the flat rate of duty is 5% and these goods may accompany you or be shipped home.) These articles must be for your personal use or for use as gifts and not for sale. This provision may be used every 30 days, excluding the day of your last arrival. Any items which have a "free" duty rate will be excluded before duty is calculated.

Other exemptions include in part: automobiles, boats, planes, or other vehicles taken abroad for non-commercial use. Foreign–made personal articles (e.g., watches, cameras, etc.) taken abroad should be registered with Customs before departure. Customs will register anything with a serial number identifying marks or documented by sales receipt or insurance document. Gifts of not more than $50 can be shipped back to the United States tax and duty free ($100 if mailed from the Virgin Islands, American Samoa, or Guam). Household effects and tools of trade which you take out of the United States are duty free at time of return.

Prohibited and restricted articles include in part: absinthe, narcotics and dangerous drugs, obscene articles and publications, seditious and treasonable materials, hazardous articles (e.g., fireworks, dangerous toys, toxic and poisonous substances, and switchblade knives), biological materials of public health or veterinary importance, fruit, vegetables and plants, meats, poultry and products thereof, birds, monkeys, and turtles.

If you understate the value of an article you declare, or if you otherwise misrepresent an article in your declaration, you may have to pay a penalty in addition to payment of duty. Under certain circumstances, the article could be seized and forfeited if the penalty is not paid.

If you fail to declare an article acquired abroad, not only is the article subject to seizure and forfeiture, but you will be liable for a personal penalty in an amount equal to the value of the article in the United States. In addition, you may also be liable to criminal prosecution.

If you carry more than $10,000 into or out of the United States in currency (either United States or foreign money), negotiable instruments in bearer form, or travelers checks, a report must be filed with United States Customs at the time you arrive or depart with such amounts.

Foreign Embassies in the United States

Source: U.S. Department of State

Embassy of the Republic of Afghanistan, 2341 Wyoming Ave., N.W., Washington, D.C. 20008. Phone: (202) 234–3770, 3771.

Embassy of the Democratic & Popular Republic of Algeria, 2118 Kalorama Rd., N.W., Washington, D.C. 20008. Phone: (202) 265–2800.

Embassy of Antigua & Barbuda, 3400 International Dr., N.W., Suite 4M, Washington, D.C. 20008. Phone: (202) 362–5211, 5166, 5122.

Embassy of the Argentine Republic, 1600 New Hampshire Ave., N.W., Washington, D.C. 20009. Phone: (202) 939–6400 to 6403, inclusive.

Embassy of Australia, 1601 Massachusetts Ave., N.W., Washington, D.C. 20036. Phone: (202) 797–3000.

Embassy of Austria, 2343 Massachusetts Ave., N.W., Washington, D.C. 20008. Phone: (202) 483–4474.

Embassy of the Commonwealth of the Bahamas, 2220 Massachusetts Ave., N.W., Washington, D.C. 20008. Phone: (202) 319-2660.

Embassy of the State of Bahrain, 3502 International Dr., N.W., Washington, D.C. 20008. Phone: (202) 342–0741, 0742.

Embassy of the People's Republic of Bangladesh, 2201 Wisconsin Ave., N.W., Washington, D.C. 20007. Phone: (202) 342–8372 to 8376.

Embassy of Barbados, 2144 Wyoming Ave., N.W., Washington, D.C. 20008. Phone: (202) 939–9218, 9219.

Embassy of Belgium, 3330 Garfield St., N.W., Washington, D.C. 20008. Phone: (202) 333–6900.

Embassy of Belize, 3400 International Dr., N.W., Suite 2J, Washington, D.C. 20008. Phone: (202) 363–4505.

Embassy of the People's Republic of Benin, 2737 Cathedral Ave., N.W., Washington, D.C. 20008. Phone: (202) 232–6656.

Embassy of Bolivia, 3014 Massachusetts Ave., N.W., Washington, D.C. 20008. Phone: (202) 483–4410, 4411, 4412.

Embassy of the Republic of Botswana, 3400 International Dr., N.W., Suite 7M, Washington, D.C. 20008. Phone: (202) 244–4990, 4991.

Brazilian Embassy, 3006 Massachusetts Ave., N.W., Washington, D.C. 20008. Phone: (202) 745–2700.

Embassy of the State of Brunei Darussalam, 2600 Virginia Ave., N.W., Suite 300, Washington, D.C. 20037. Phone: (202) 342–0159.

Embassy of the Republic of Bulgaria, 1621 22nd St., N.W., Washington, D.C. 20008. Phone: (202) 387–7969.

Embassy of Burkina Faso, 2340 Massachusetts Ave., N.W., Washington, D.C. 20008. Phone: (202) 332–5577, 6895.

Embassy of the Republic of Burundi, 2233 Wisconsin Ave., N.W., Suite 212, Washington, D.C. 20007. Phone: (202) 342–257 4.

Embassy of the Republic of Cameroon, 2349 Massachusetts Ave., N.W., Washington, D.C. 20008. Phone: (202) 265–8790 to 8794.

Embassy of Canada, 501 Pennsylvania Ave., N.W., Washington, D.C. 20001. Phone: (202) 682–1740.

Embassy of the Republic of Cape Verde, 3415 Massachusetts Ave., N.W., Washington, D.C. 20007. Phone: (202) 965–6820.

Embassy of Central African Republic, 1618 22nd St. N.W., Washington, D.C. 20008. Phone: (202) 483–7800, 7801.

Embassy of the Republic of Chad, 2002 R St., N.W., Washington, D.C. 20009. Phone: (202) 462–4009.

Embassy of Chile, 1732 Massachusetts Ave., N.W., Washington, D.C. 20036. Phone: (202) 785–1746.

Embassy of the People's Republic of China, 2300 Connecticut Ave., N.W., Washington, D.C. 20008. Phone: (202) 328–2500, 2501, 2502.

Embassy of Colombia, 2118 Leroy Pl., N.W., Washington, D.C. 20008. Phone: (202) 387–8338.

Embassy of the Federal and Islamic Republic of Comoros, c/o Permanent Mission of the Federal and Islamic Republic of Comoros to the United Nations, 336 E. 45th St., 2nd floor, New York, N.Y. 10017. Phone: (212) 972–8010.

Embassy of the People's Republic of the Congo, 4891 Colorado Ave., N.W., Washington, D.C.

20011. Phone: (202) 726–5500, 5501.

Embassy of Costa Rica, 1825 Connecticut Ave., 70 N.W., Suite 211, Washington, D.C. 20009. Phone: (202) 234–2945 to 2947.

Embassy of the Republic of Cote d'Ivoire, 2424 Massachusetts Ave., N.W., Washington, D.C. 20008. Phone: (202) 797–0300.

Embassy of the Republic of Cyprus, 2211 R St. N.W., Washington, D.C. 20008. Phone: (202) 462–5772.

Embassy of the Czech and Slovak Federal Republic, 3900 Linnean Ave., N.W., Washington, D.C. 20008. Phone: (202) 363–6315, 6316.

Cuban Interests Section, 2630 and 2639 16th St., N.W., Washington, D.C. 20009. Phone: (202) 797–8518 to 8520, 8609, 8610.

Royal Danish Embassy, 3200 Whitehaven St., N.W., Washington, D.C. 20008. Phone: (202) 234–4300.

Embassy of the Republic of Djibouti, 1156 15th St., N.W., Suite 515, Washington, D.C. 20005. Phone: (202) 331-0270.

Embassy of the Dominican Republic, 1715 22nd St., N.W., Washington, D.C. 20008. Phone: (202) 332–6280.

Embassy of Ecuador, 2535 15th St., N.W., Washington, D.C. 20009. Phone: (202) 234–7200.

Embassy of the Arab Republic o f Egypt, 2310 Decatur Pl., N.W., Washington, D.C. 20008. Phone: (202) 232–5400.

Embassy of El Salvador, 2308 California St., N.W., Washington, D.C. 20008. Phone: (202) 265–9671, 9672.

Embassy of Equatorial Guinea, 801 Second Ave., Suite 1403, New York, N.Y. 10017.

Legation of Estonia, 9 Rockefeller Plaza, New York, N.Y. 10020. Phone: (212) 247–1450.

Embassy of Ethiopia, 2134 Kalorama Rd., N.W., Washington, D.C. 20008. Phone: (202) 234–2281, 2282.

Embassy of the Republic of Fiji, 2233 Wisconsin Ave., N.W., Suite 240, Washington, D.C. 20007. Phone: (202) 337–8320.

Embassy of Finland, 3216 New Mexico Ave., N.W., Washington, D.C. 20016. Phone: (202) 363–2430.

Embassy of France, 4101 Reservoir Rd., N.W., Washington, D.C. 20007. Phone: (202) 944–6000.

Embassy of the Gabonese Republic, 2034 20th St., N.W., Washington, D.C. 20009. Phone: (202) 797–1000.

Embassy of The Gambia, 1030 15th St., N.W., Suite 720, Washington, D.C. 20005. Phone: (202) 842–1356, 1359.

Embassy of the Federal Republic of Germany, 4645 Reservoir Rd., N.W., Washington, D.C. 20007. Phone: (202) 298–4000.

Embassy of Ghana, 3512 International Dr., N.W., Washington, D.C. 20008 (202) 686–4520.

Embassy of Greece, 2221 Massachusetts Ave., N.W., Washington, D.C. 20008. Phone (202) 939–5800.

Embassy of Grenada, 1701 New Hampshire Ave., N.W., Washington, D.C. 20009. Phone: (202) 265–2561.

Embassy of Guatemala, 2220 R St., N.W., Washington, D.C. 20008. Phone: (202) 745–4952 to 4954.

Embassy of the Republic of Guinea, 2112 Leroy Pl., N.W., Washington, D.C. 20008. Phone: (202) 483–9420.

Embassy of the Republic of Guinea–Bissau, 918 16th St., N.W., Mezzanine Suite, Washington, D.C. 20006. Phone: (202) 872-4222.

Embassy of Guyana, 2490 Tracy Pl., N.W. Washington, D.C. 20008. Phone: (202) 265–6900, 6903.

Embassy of Haiti, 2311 Massachusetts Ave., N.W., Washington, D.C. 20008. Phone: (202) 332–4090 to 4092.

Apostolic Nunciature of the Holy See, 3339 Massachusetts Ave., N.W., Washington, D.C. 20008. Phone: (202) 333–7121.

Embassy of Honduras, 3007 Tilden St., N.W., Washington, D .C. 20008. Phone: (202) 966–7702, 2604, 5008, 4596.

Embassy of the Republic of Hungary, 3910 Shoemaker St., N.W., Washington, D.C. 20008. Phone: (202) 362–6730.

Embassy of Iceland, 2022 Connecticut Ave., N.W., Washington, D.C. 20008. Phone: (202) 265–6653 to 6655.

Embassy of India, 2107 Massachusetts Ave., N.W., Washington, D.C. 20008. Phone: (202) 939–7000.

Embassy of the Republic of Indonesia, 2020 Massachusetts Ave., N.W., Washington, D.C. 20036. Phone: (202) 775–5200.

Embassy of the Republic of Iraq, 1801 P St., N.W., Washington, D.C. 20036. Phone: (202) 483–7500.

Embassy of Ireland, 2234 Massachusetts Ave., N.W., Washington, D.C. 20008. Phone: (202) 462–3939.

Embassy of Israel, 3514 International Dr., N.W., Washington, D.C. 20008. Phone: (202) 364–5500.

Embassy of Italy, 1601 Fuller St., N.W., Washington, D.C. 20009. Phone: (202) 328–5500.

Embassy of Jamaica, 1850 K St., N.W., Suite 355, Washington, D.C. 20006. Phone: (202) 452–0660.

Embassy of Japan, 2520 Massachusetts Ave., N.W., Washington, D.C. 20008. Phone: (202) 939–6700.

Embassy of the Hashemite Kingdom of Jordan, 3504 International Dr., N.W., Washington, D.C. 20008. Phone: (202) 966–2664.

Embassy of Kenya, 2249 R St., N.W., Washington, D.C. 20008. Phone: (202) 387–6101.

Embassy of Korea, 2370 Massachusetts Ave., N.W., Washington, D.C. 20008. Phone: (202) 939–5600.

Embassy of the State of Kuwait, 2940 Tilden St., N.W., Washington, D.C. 20008. Phone: (202) 966–0702.

Embassy of the Lao People's Democratic Republic, 2222 S St., N.W., Washington, D.C. 20008. Phone: (202) 332–6416, 6417.

Legation of Latvia, 4325 17th St., N.W., Washington, D.C. 20011. Phone: (202) 726–8213, 8214.

Embassy of Lebanon, 2560 28th St., N.W., Washington, D.C. 20008. Phone: (202) 939–6300.

Embassy of the Kingdom of Lesotho, 2511 Massachusetts Ave., N.W., Washington, D.C. 20008. Phone: (202) 797–5534 to 5536.

Embassy of the Republic of Liberia, 5201 16th St., N.W., Washington, D.C. 20011. Phone: (202) 291–0761.

Legation of Lithuania, 2622 16th St., N.W., Washington, D.C. 20009. Phone: (202) 234–5860, 2639.

Embassy of Luxembourg, 2200 Massachusetts Ave., N.W., Washington, D.C. 20008. Phone: (202) 265–4171.

Embassy of the Democratic Republic of Madagascar, 2374 Massachusetts Ave., N. W., Washington, D.C. 20008. Phone: (202) 265–5525, 5526.

Malawi Embassy, 2408 Massachusetts Ave., N.W., Washington, D.C. 20008. Phone: (202) 797–1007.

Embassy of Malaysia, 2401 Massachusetts Ave., N.W., Washington, D.C. 20008. Phone: (202) 328–2700.

Embassy of the Republic of Mali, 2130 R St., N.W., Washington, D.C. 20008. Phone: (202) 332–2249; (202) 939–8950.

Embassy of Malta, 2017 Connecticut Ave., N.W., Washington, D.C. 20008. Phone: (202) 462–3611, 3612.

Embassy of the Republic of the Marshall Islands, 2433 Massachusetts Ave., N.W., Washington, D.C. 20008. Phone: (202) 234-5414.

Embassy of the Islamic Republic of Mauritania, 2129 Leroy Pl., N.W., Washington, D.C. 20008. Phone: (202) 232–5700.

Embassy of Mauritius, 4301 Connecticut Ave., N.W., Suite 134, Washington, D.C. 20008. Phone: (202) 244–1491, 1492.

Embassy of Mexico, 1911 Pennsylvania Ave., N.W., 20006, Washington, D.C. Phone: (202) 728–1600.

Embassy of the Federated States of Micronesia, 1725 N St., N.W., Washington, D.C. 20036. Phone: (202) 223-4383.

Embassy of the Mongolian People's Republic, Washington, D.C. Phone: (202) 983-1962.

Embassy of Morocco, 1601 21st St., N.W., Washington, D.C. 20009. Phone: (202) 462–7979 to 7982, inclusive.

Embassy of the People's Republic of Mozambique, 1990 M St., N.W., Suite 570, Washington, D.C. 20036. Phone: (202) 293–7146.

Embassy of the Union of Myanmar, 2300 S St., N.W., Washington, D.C. 20008. Phone: (202) 332–9044, 9045.

Embassy of the Republic of Namibia, 1413 K St., N.W., 7th floor, Washington, D.C. 20005. Phone: (202) 289-3871.

Royal Nepalese Embassy, 2131 Leroy Pl., N.W., Washington, D.C. 20008. Phone: (202) 667–4550.

Embassy of the Netherlands, 4200 Linnean Ave., N.W., Washington, D.C. 20008. Phone: (202) 244–5300; after 6 p.m. (202) 244–5304.

Embassy of New Zealand, 37 Observatory Circle, N.W., Washington, D.C. 20008. Phone: (202) 328–4800.

Embassy of Nicaragua, 1627 New Hampshire Ave., N.W., Washington, D.C. 20009. Phone: (202) 939–6570.

Embassy of the Republic of Niger, 2204 R St., N.W., Washington, D.C. 20008. Phone: (202) 483–4224 to 4227, inclusive.

Embassy of the Federal Republic of Nigeria, 2201 M St., N.W., Washington, D.C. 20037. Phone: (202) 822–1500.

Royal Norwegian Embassy, 2720 34th St., N.W., Washington, D.C. 20008. Phone: (202) 333–6000.

Embassy of the Sultanate of Oman, 2342 Massachusetts Ave., N.W., Washington, D.C. 20008. Phone: (202) 387–1980 to 1982.

Embassy of Pakistan, 2315 Massachusetts Ave., N.W., Washington, D.C. 20008. Phone: (202) 939–6200.

Embassy of Panama, 2862 McGill Terrace, N.W., Washington, D.C. 20008. Phone: (202) 483–1407.

Embassy of Papua New Guinea, 1615 New Hampshire Ave., N.W., 3rd floor, Washington, D.C. 20009. Phone: (202) 745-3680.

Embassy of Paraguay, 2400 Massachusetts Ave., N.W., Washington, D.C. 20008. Phone: (202) 483–6960 to 6962.

Embassy of Peru, 1700 Massachusetts Ave., N.W., Washington, D.C. 20036. Phone: (202) 833–9860 to 9869.

Embassy of the Philippines, 1617 Massachusetts Ave., N.W., Washington, D.C. 20036. Phone: (202) 483–1414.

Embassy of the Republic of Poland, 2640 16th St., N.W., Washington, D.C. 20009. Phone: (202) 234–3800 to 3802.

Embassy of Portugal, 2125 Kalorama Rd., N.W., Washington, D.C. 20008. Phone: (202) 328–8610.

Embassy of the State of Qatar, 600 New Hampshire Ave., N.W., Suite 1180, Washington, D.C. 20037. Phone: (202) 338–0111.

Embassy of Romania, 1607 23rd St., N.W., Washington, D.C. 20008. Phone: (202) 232–4747, 6593, 6634.

Embassy of the Republic of Rwanda, 1714 New Hampshire Ave., N.W., Washington, D.C. 20009. Phone: (202) 232–2882.

Embassy of Saint Kitts and Nevis, 2100 M St., N.W., Suite 608, Washington, D.C. 20037. Phone: (202) 833-3550.

Embassy of Saint Lucia, 2100 M St., N.W., Suite 309, Washington, D.C. 20037. Phone: (202) 463–7378, 7379.

Embassy of Saint Vincent and the Grenadines, 1717 Massachusetts Ave., N.W., Suite 102, Washington, D.C. 20036. Phone: (202) 462-7806, 7846.

Embassy of São Tomé and Príncipe, 801 Second Ave., Suite 603, New York, N.Y. 10017 (temporary address). Phone: (212) 697–4211.

Embassy of Saudi Arabia, 601 New Hampshire Ave., N.W., Washington, D.C. 20037. Phone: (202) 342–3800.

Embassy of the Republic of Senegal, 2112 Wyoming Ave., N.W., Washington, D.C. 20008. Phone: (202) 234–0540, 0541.

Embassy of the Republic of Seychelles, c/o Permanent Mission of Seychelles to the United Nations, 820 Second Ave., Suite 900F, New York, N.Y. 10017. Phone: (212) 687–9766/9767.

Embassy of Sierra Leone, 1701 19th St., N.W., Washington, D.C. 20009. Phone: (202) 939–9261.

Embassy of the Republic of Singapore, 1824 R St., N.W., Washington, D.C. 20009. Phone: (202) 667–7555.

Embassy of the Solomon Islands, c/o Permanent Mission of the Solomon Islands to the United Nations, 820 Second Ave., Suite 800, New York, N.Y. 10017. Phone: (212) 599-6193.

Embassy of the Somali Democratic Republic, 600 New Hampshire Ave., N.W., Suite 710, Washington, D.C. 20037. Phone: (202) 342–1575.

Embassy of South Africa, 3051 Massachusetts Ave., N.W., Washington, D.C. 20008. Phone: (202) 232–4400.

Embassy of Spain, 2700 15th St., N.W., Washington, D.C. 20009. Phone: (202) 265–0190, 0191.

Embassy of the Democratic Socialist Republic of Sri Lanka, 2148 Wyoming Ave., N.W., Washington, D.C. 20008. Phone: (202) 483–4025 to 4028.

Embassy of the Republic of the Sudan, 2210 Massachusetts Ave., N.W., Washington, D.C. 20008. Phone: (202) 338–8565 to 8570.

Embassy of the Republic of Suriname, 4301 Connecticut Ave., N.W., Suite 108, Washington, D.C. 20008. Phone: (202) 244–7488, 7490 to 7492.

Embassy of the Kingdom of Swaziland, 3400 International Drive, N.W., Washington, D.C. 20008. Phone: (202) 362–6683, 6685.

Embassy of Sweden, 600 New Hampshire Ave., N.W., Suites 1200 and 715, Washington, D.C. 20037. Phone: (202) 944–5600.

Embassy of Switzerland, 2900 Cathedral Ave., N.W., Washington, D.C. 20008. Phone: (202) 745–7900.

Embassy of the Syrian Arab Republic, 2215 Wyoming Ave., N.W., Washington, D.C. 20008. Phone: (202) 232–6313.

Embassy of the United Republic of Tanzania, 2139 R St., N.W., Washington, D.C. 20008. Phone: (202) 939–6125.

Embassy of Thailand, 2300 Kalorama Rd., N.W., Washington, D.C. 20008. Phone: (202) 483–7200.

Embassy of the Republic of Togo, 2208 Massachusetts Ave., N.W., Washington, D.C. 20008. Phone: (202) 234–4212, 4213.

Embassy of Trinidad and Tobago, 1708 Massachusetts Ave., N.W., Washington, D.C. 20036. Phone: (202) 467–6490.

Embassy of Tunisia, 1515 Massachusetts Ave., N.W., Washington, D.C. 20005. Phone: (202) 862–1850.

Embassy of the Republic of Turkey, 1714 Massachusetts Ave. N.W., Washington, D.C. 20036. Phone: (202) 659–8200.

Embassy of the Republic of Uganda, 5909 16th St., N.W., Washington, D.C. 20011. Phone: (202) 726–7100 to 7102.

Embassy of the Union of Soviet Socialist Republics, 1125 16th St., N.W., Washington, D.C. 20036. Phone: (202) 628–7551, 8548.

Embassy of the United Arab Emirates, 600 New Hampshire Ave., N.W., Suite 740, Washington, D.C. 20037. Phone: (202) 338–6500.

United Kingdom of Great Britain & Northern Ireland—British Embassy, 3100 Massachusetts Ave., N.W., Washington, D.C. 20008. Phone: (202) 462–1340.

Embassy of Uruguay, 1 918 F St., N.W., Washington D.C. 20006. Phone: (202) 331–1313 to 1316, inclusive.

Embassy of Venezuela, 1099 30th St., N.W., Washington D.C. 20007. Phone: (202) 342-2214.

Embassy of Western Samoa, 1155 15th St. N.W., # 510, Washington, D.C. 20005. Phone: (202) 833–1743.

Embassy of the Republic of Yemen, 600 New Hampshire Ave., N.W., Suite 840, Washington, D.C. 20037. Phone: (202) 965–4760, 4761.

Embassy of the Socialist Federal Republic of Yugoslavia, 2410 California St., N.W., Washington, D.C. 20008. Phone: (202) 462–6566.

Embassy of the Republic of Zaire, 1800 New Hampshire Ave., N.W., Washington, D.C. 20009. Phone: (202) 234–7690, 7691.

Embassy of the Republic of Zambia, 2419 Massachusetts Ave., N.W., Washington, D.C. 20008. Phone: (202) 265–9717 to 9721.

Embassy of Zimbabwe, 1608 New Hampshire Ave., N.W., Washington, D.C. 20009. Phone: (202) 332–7100.

Diplomatic Personnel To and From the U.S.

Country	U.S. Representative to[1]	Rank	Representative from[2]	Rank
Afghanistan	—	—	Abdul Ghafoor Jawshan	Min.-Consl.
Algeria	Christopher W. S. Ross	Amb.	Abderrahmane Bensid	Amb.
Antigua and Barbuda	(Vacancy)	Amb.	Paul O. Spencer	Min.-Consl.
Argentina	Terance A. Todman	Amb.	Carlos Ortiz de Rosas	Amb.
Australia	Melvin F. Sembler	Amb.	Michael John Cook	Amb.
Austria	Roy Michael Huffington	Amb.	Friedrich Hoess	Amb.
Bahamas	Chic Hecht	Amb.	Margaret E. McDonald	Amb.
Bahrain	Charles W. Hostler	Amb.	Ghazi Mohamed Algosaibi	Amb.
Bangladesh	William B. Milam	Amb.	A.H.S. Ataul Karim	Amb.
Barbados	G. Philip Hughes	Amb.	Sir William Douglas	Amb.
Belgium	Maynard W. Gitman	Amb.	Jean Cassiers	Amb.
Belize	Eugene L. Scassa	Amb.	James V. Hyde	Amb.
Benin	Harriet W. Isom	Amb.	Candide Pierre Ahouansou	Amb.
Bolivia	Robert S. Gelbard	Amb.	Jorge Crespo–Velasco	Amb.
Botswana	David Passage	Amb.	Botsweletse Kingsley Sebele	Amb.
Brazil	Richard H. Melton	Amb.	Marcilio Marques Moreira	Amb.
Brunei	Christopher H. Phillips	Amb.	Dato Haji Mohammad Kassim	Amb.
Bulgaria	H. Kenneth Hill	Amb.	Ognian Raytchev Pishev	Amb.
Burkina Faso	Edward P. Byrnn	Amb.	Paul–Désiré Kabore	Amb.
Burundi	Cynthia S. Perry	Amb.	Julien Kavakure	Amb.
Cameroon	Frances D. Cook	Amb.	Paul Pondi	Amb.
Canada	Edward N. Ney	Amb.	Derek H. Burney	Amb.
Cape Verde	Francis T. McNamara	Amb.	Jorge M. Custodio Dos Santos	Amb.
Central African Republic	Daniel H. Simpson	Amb.	Jean–Pierre Sohahong–Kombet	Amb.
Chad	Richard W. Bogosian	Amb.	Mahamat Ali Adoum	Amb.
Chile	Charles A. Gillespie Jr.	Amb.	Patricio Silva	Amb.
China	James R. Lilley	Amb.	Qizhen Zhu	Amb.
Colombia	Thomas E. McNamara	Amb.	Jaime Garcia-Parra	Amb.
Comoros	Kenneth N. Peltier	Amb.	Amini Ali Moumin	Amb.
Congo, People's Republic of	James D. Phillips	Amb.	Roger Issombo	Amb.
Costa Rica	(Vacancy)	Amb.	Gonzalo J. Facio	Amb.
Côte d'Ivoire	Kenneth L. Brown	Amb.	Charles Gomis	Amb.
Cyprus	Robert E. Lamb	Amb.	Michael E. Sherifis	Amb.
Czechoslovakia	Shirley Temple Black	Amb.	Rita Klimova	Amb.
Denmark	Keith L. Brown	Amb.	Peter P. Dyvig	Amb.

Country	U.S. Representative to[1]	Rank	Representative from[2]	Rank
Djibouti	Robert S. Barrett IV	Amb.	Roble Olhaye	Amb.
Dominica	—	—	Edward I. Watty	Amb.
Dominican Republic	Paul D. Taylor	Amb.	Dr. Dario Suro	Min.
Ecuador	Paul C. Lambert	Amb.	Jaime Moncayo	Amb.
Egypt	Frank G. Wisner	Amb.	El Sayed Abdel Raouf El Reedy	Amb.
El Salvador	William G. Walker	Amb.	Miguel Angel Salaverria	Amb.
Equatorial Guinea	(Vacancy)	Amb.	Damaso Obiang Ndong	Amb.
Ethiopia	Robert G. Houdek	Cd'A.	Girma Amare	Consul.
Fiji	Evelyn I. H. Teegen	Amb.	Ratu Finau Mara	Consul.
Finland	John G. Weinmann	Amb.	Jukka Valtasaari	Amb.
France	Alan P. Larson	Amb.	Jacques Andreani	Amb.
Gabon	Keith L. Wauchope	Amb.	Alexandre Sambat	Amb.
Gambia	Arlene Render	Amb.	Ousman A. Sallah	Amb.
Germany	Vernon A. Walters	Amb.	Juergen Ruhfus	Amb.
Ghana	Raymond C. Ewing	Amb.	Dr. Joseph L.S. Abbey	Amb.
Greece	Michael G. Sotirhos	Amb.	Christo Zacharakis	Amb.
Grenada	(Vacancy)	Cd'A.	Denneth Modeste	Amb.
Guatemala	Thomas F. Stroock	Amb.	Norma J. Vazques	Min.-Consl.
Guinea	Dane F. Smith, Jr.	Amb.	Camara Ansoumane	Consl.
Guinea–Bissau	William H. Jacobsen, Jr.	Amb.	Alfredo Lopes Cabral	Amb.
Guyana	(Vacancy)	Amb.	Dr. Cedric Hilburn Grant	Amb.
Haiti	Alvin P. Adams, Jr.	Amb.	Louis Harold Joseph	Min.–Consl.
Holy See	Thomas P. Melady	Amb.	Most Rev. Agostino Cacciavillan	Pro–Nuncio
Honduras	Cresencio S. Arcos	Amb.	Jorge Ramon Hernandez–Alcerro	Min.-Consl.
Hungary	Charles H. Thomas	Amb.	Eniko Bollobas	Min.-Consl.
Iceland	Charles E. Cobb, Jr.	Amb.	Tomas A. Tomasson	Amb.
India	William Clark, Jr.	Amb.	Abid Hussain	Amb.
Indonesia	John C. Monjo	Amb.	Abdul Rachman Ramly	Amb.
Iraq	—	—	—	—
Ireland	Richard A. Moore	Amb.	Padraic N. MacKernan	Amb.
Israel	William A. Brown	Amb.	Zalman Shoval	Amb.
Italy	Peter F. Secchia	Amb.	Rinaldo Petrignani	Amb.
Jamaica	Glen A. Holden	Amb.	Richard Leighton Bernal	Amb.
Japan	Michael H. Armacost	Amb.	Ryohei Murata	Amb.
Jordan	Roger G. Harrison	Amb.	Hussein A. Hammami	Amb.
Kenya	Smith Hempstone, Jr.	Amb.	Denis D. Afande	Amb.
Korea, South	Donald P. Gregg	Amb.	Hong-Choo Hyun	Amb.
Kuwait	Edward Gnehm	Amb.	Shaikh Saud Nasir Al–Sabah	Amb.
Laos	Charles B. Salmon, Jr.	Cd'A.	Linthong Phetsavan	1st Secy.
Lebanon	Ryan C. Crocker	Amb.	Nassib S. Lahoud	Amb.
Lesotho	Leonard H.O. Spearman, Sr.	Amb.	W. T. Van Tonder	Amb.
Liberia	Peter J. de Vos	Amb.	Eugenia A. Wordsworth–Stevenson	Amb.
Luxembourg	Edward M. Rowell	Amb.	Andre Philippe	Amb.
Madagascar	Howard K. Walker	Amb.	Pierrot J. Rajaonarivelo	Amb.
Malawi	George A. Trail, III	Amb.	Robert B. Mbaya	Amb.
Malaysia	Paul M. Cleveland	Amb.	A.R. Ahmad Fuzi	Min.
Mali	Herbert Donald Gelber	Amb.	Mohamed Alhousseyni Toure	Amb.
Malta	Sally J. Novetzke	Amb.	Salv. J. Stellini	Amb.
Marshall Islands	William Bodde, Jr.	Cd'A.	Wilfred I. Kendall	Amb.
Mauritania	William H. Twaddell	Amb.	Abdellah Ould Daddah	Amb.
Mauritius	Penne Percy Korth	Amb.	Chitmansing Jesseramsing	Amb.
Mexico	John D. Negroponte	Amb.	Gustavo Petricioli	Amb.
Micronesia	Aurelia Brazeal	Amb.	Jesse B. Marehalau	Amb
Mongolia	Joseph E. Lake	Amb.	Gendengiin Nyamdoo	Amb.
Morocco	E. Michael Ussery	Amb.	Mohamed Belkhayat	Amb.
Mozambique	Townsend B. Friedman, Jr.	Amb.	Hipolito Pereira Zozimo Patricio	Amb.
Myanmar (Burma)	Burton Levin	Amb.	U Hla Myint OO	Consl.
Namibia	Genta Hawkins Holmes	Amb.	Hinyangerwa Pius Asheeke	Min.
Nepal	Julia Chang Bloch	Amb.	Mohan Man Sainju	Amb.
Netherlands	C. Howard Wilkins, Jr.	Amb.	Johan H. Meesman	Amb.
New Zealand	Della M. Newman	Amb.	Denis Bazeley Gordon McLean	Amb.
Nicaragua	Harry W. Shlaudeman	Amb.	Ernesto Palazio	Amb.
Niger	Carl C. Cundiff	Amb.	Moumouni Adamou Djermakoye	Amb.
Nigeria	Lannon Walker	Amb.	Kevin Efiong Efretei	Min.
Norway	Loret Miller Ruppe	Amb.	Kjeld Vibe	Amb.
Oman	Richard W. Boehm	Amb.	Awadh Bader Al–Shanfari	Amb.
Pakistan	Robert B. Oakley	Amb.	Najmuddin A. Shaikh	Amb.
Panama	Deane R. Hinton	Amb.	Miguel A. Corro	Min.-Consl.
Papua New Guinea	Robert W. Farrand	Amb.	Margaret Taylor	Amb.
Paraguay	Timothy L. Towell	Amb.	Marcos Martinez Mendieta	Amb.
Peru	Anthony C.E. Quainton	Amb.	Roberto MacLean	Amb.

Country	U.S. Representative to[1]	Rank	Representative from[2]	Rank
Philippines	Nicholas Platt	Amb.	Emmanuel Pelaez	Amb.
Poland	Thomas W. Simons, Jr.	Amb.	Kazimierz Dziewanowski	Amb.
Portugal	Everett Ellis Briggs	Amb.	Joao Eduardo M. Pereira Bastos	Amb.
Qatar	Mark G. Hambley	Amb.	Dr. Hamad Abdelaziz Al–Kawari	Amb.
Romania	Alan Green, Jr.	Amb.	Virgil Constantinescu	Amb.
Rwanda	Robert A. Flaten	Amb.	Aloys Uwimana	Amb.
Saint Kitts and Nevis	—		Erstein M. Edwards	Amb.
Saint Lucia	—		Dr. Joseph Edsel Edmunds	Amb.
Saint Vincent and the Grenadines	—	—	Kingsley C.A. Layne	Amb.
São Tomé and Príncipe	—		Joaquim Rafael Branco	Amb.
Saudi Arabia	Charles W. Freeman, Jr.	Amb.	Prince Bandar Bin Sultan	Amb.
Senegal	George E. Moose	Amb.	Ibra Deguene Ka	Amb.
Seychelles	James B. Moran	Amb.	Marc R. Marengo	2nd Secy.
Sierra Leone	Johnny Young	Amb.	Dr. George Carew	Amb.
Singapore	Robert D. Orr	Amb.	S.R. Nathan	Amb.
Solomon Islands	Robert W. Farrand	Amb.	Francis Bugotu	Amb.
Somalia	—	—	Embassy ceased operations	
South Africa	William L. Swing	Amb.	Harry Heinz Schwarz	Amb.
Spain	Joseph Zappala	Amb.	Jaime de Ojeda y Eiseley	Amb.
Sri Lanka	Marion V. Creekmore, Jr.	Amb.	W. Susanta DeAlwis	Amb.
Sudan	James R. Cheek	Amb.	Abdalla Ahmed Abdalla	Amb.
Suriname	John P. Leonard	Amb.	Willem A. Udenhout	Amb.
Swaziland	Stephen H. Rogers	Amb.	Absalom Vusani Mamba	Amb.
Sweden	Charles E. Rednam	Amb.	Anders Ingmar Thunborg	Amb.
Switzerland	Joseph B. Gildenhorn	Amb.	Edouard Brunner	Amb.
Syria	Edward P. Djerejian	Amb.	Walid Al-Moualem	Amb.
Tanzania	Edward DeJarnette,	Amb.	Charles Musama Nyirabu	Amb.
Thailand	Daniel A. O'Donohue	Amb.	Krit Garnjana-Goonchorn	Min.
Togo	Harmon E. Kirby	Amb.	Ellom–Kodjo Schuppius	Amb.
Trinidad and Tobago	Charles A. Gargano	Amb.	Angus Albert Khan	Amb.
Tunisia	Robert H. Pelletreau, Jr.	Amb.	Ismail Khelil	Amb.
Turkey	Morton I. Abramowitz	Amb.	Nuzhet Kandemir	Amb.
Uganda	John A. Burroughs, Jr.	Amb.	Stephen Kapimpina Katenta–Apuli	Amb.
U.S.S.R.	Robert S. Strauss	Amb.	Viktor Georgievich Komplektov	Amb.
United Arab Emirates	Edward S. Walker, Jr.	Amb.	Abdulla bin Zayed Al–Nahayyan	Amb.
United Kingdom	Raymond G.H. Seitz	Amb.	Sir Robin Renwick	Amb.
Uruguay	Richard C. Brown	Amb.	Dr. Eduardo MacGillycuddy	Amb.
Venezuela	Michael M. Skol	Amb.	Simon Alberto Consalvi	Amb.
Western Samoa	Della Newman	Amb.	Tuaopepe Fili Wendt	Amb.
Yemen	Charles F. Dunbar	Amb.	Mohsin A. Alaini	Amb.
Yugoslavia	Warren Zimmerman	Amb.	Dzevad Mujezinovic	Amb.
Zaire	William C. Harrop	Amb.	Tatanene Manata	Amb.
Zambia	Gordon L. Street	Amb.	Dr. Paul J.F. Lusaka	Amb.
Zimbabwe	(Vacancy)	Amb.	Stanislaus Garikai Chigwedere	Amb.

1. As of May, 1991. 2. As of May 1991. NOTE: Amb.=Ambassador; Cd'A.=Charge d'Affaires; Secy.=Secretary; Consl.=Counselor; Min.=Minister; P.O.=Principal Officer. *Source:* U.S. Department of State.

Health Hints for the International Traveler

Source: U.S. Department of Health and Human Services, Public Health Service, Centers for Disease Control

Introduction

This article includes practical information on how to avoid potential health problems. Some of these recommendations are common–sense precautions; others have been scientifically documented.

Personal and specific preventive measures against certain diseases may require advance planning and advice from a physician concerning immunization and prophylaxis. If more specific information is needed, travelers should contact their local health department or physician.

Travelers who take prescription medications should carry an adequate supply accompanied by a signed and dated statement from a physician; the statement should indicate the major health problems and dosage of such medications, to provide information for medical authorities in case of emergency. The traveler should take an extra pair of glasses or lens prescription, and a card, tag, or bracelet that identifies any physical condition that may require emergency care.

Medical Care

If medical care is needed abroad, travel agents or the American Embassy or Consulate can usually provide names of hospitals, physicians, or emergency medical service agencies. Prior to departure, travelers should contact their own insurance companies concerning their coverage.

WHO Blood Transfusion Guidelines

There is a growing public awareness of the AIDS epidemic, and a resulting concern about acquiring the AIDS virus through blood transfusion. Systematic screening of blood donations is not yet feasible in all developing countries. Requests have been made by persons planning international travels, to have their own blood, or blood from their home country, available to them in case of urgent need. These requests raise logistic, technical and ethical issues which are not easy to resolve. Ultimately, the safety of blood for such persons will depend upon the quality of blood transfusion services in the host country. The strengthening of these services is of the highest priority. While efforts are being made to achieve this end, other approaches are also needed.

Basic Principles:

1. Unexpected, emergency, blood transfusion is rarely required. It is needed only in situations of massive hemorrhage like severe trauma, gynecological and obstetric emergency, or gastrointestinal bleeding.

2. In many cases, resuscitation can be achieved by use of colloid or crystalloid plasma expanders[1] instead of blood.

3. Blood transfusion is not free of risk, even in the best of conditions. In most developing countries, the risk is increased by limited technical resources for screening blood donors for HIV infection and other diseases transmissible by blood.

4. The international shipment of blood for transfusion is practical only when handled by agreement between two responsible organizations, such as national blood transfusion services. This mechanism is not useful for emergency needs of individual patients and should not be attempted by private individuals or organizations not operating recognized blood programs.

Therefore:

1. There are no medical indications for travelers to take blood with them from their home country.

2. The limited storage period of blood and the need for special equipment negate the feasibility of independent blood banking for individual travelers or small groups.

3. Blood should be transfused only when absolutely indicated. This applies even more forcefully in those countries where screening of blood for transmissible diseases is not yet widely performed.

Proposed Options:

1. When urgent resuscitation is necessary, the use of plasma expanders rather than blood should always be considered.

2. In case of emergency need of blood, use of plasma expanders and urgent evacuation home may be the actions of choice.

3. When blood transfusion cannot be avoided, the attending physician should make every effort to ensure that the blood has been screened for transmissible diseases, including HIV.

4. International travelers should: (a) take active steps to minimize the risk of injury; (b) establish a plan for dealing with medical emergencies; (c) support the development within countries of safe and adequate blood supplies.

This information is taken from the WHO publication "World Health Organization

Global Programme on AIDS: Blood transfusion guidelines for international travelers."

Motion Sickness

Travelers with a history of motion sickness or sea sickness can attempt to avoid symptoms by taking anti–motion–sickness pills or antihistaminics before departure.

Pregnant Women

The problems that a pregnant woman might encounter during international travel are basically the same problems that other international travelers have. These have to do with exposure to infectious diseases and availability of good medical care. There is the additional potential problem that air travel late in pregnancy might precipitate labor.

Potential health problems vary from country to country; therefore, if the traveler has specific questions, she should be advised to check with the embassy or local consulate general office of the country in question before traveling.

Disabled Travelers

The Airport Operators Council International, Incorporated, publishes "Access Travel: A Guide to Accessibility of Terminals." The 40–page guide lists design features, facilities, and services for handicapped persons in 472 airport terminals in over 50 countries. Single copies are available at no cost from the Architectural and Transportation Barriers Compliance Board. For a copy, you may write or call, ATBCB, 1111 18th Street, N.W., Suite 50, Washington, D.C. 20036–3894, (202) 653–7834.

Risks From Food and Drink

Contaminated food and drink are common sources for the introduction of infection into the body. Among the more common infections that travelers may acquire from contaminated food and drink are *Escherichia coli* infections, shigellosis or bacillary dysentery, giardiasis, cryptosporidiosis, and hepatitis A. Other less common infectious disease risks for travelers include typhoid fever and other salmonelloses, cholera, infections caused by rotaviruses and Norwalk–like viruses, and a variety of protozoan and helminth parasites (other than those that cause giardiasis and cryptosporidiosis). Many of the infectious diseases transmitted in food and water can also be acquired directly through the fecal–oral route.

Water

Water that has been adequately chlorinated, using minimum recommended water–works standards as practiced in the United States, will afford significant protection against viral and bacterial waterborne diseases. However, chlorine treatment alone, as used in the routine disinfection of water, may not kill some enteric viruses and the parasitic organisms that cause giardiasis and amebiasis. In areas where chlorinated tap water is not available, or where hygiene and sanitation are poor, travelers should be advised that only the following may be safe to drink:

1. Beverages, such as tea and coffee, made with boiled water.

2. Canned or bottled *carbonated* beverages, including *carbonated* bottled water and soft drinks.

3. Beer and wine.

Where water may be contaminated, ice (or containers for drinking) also should be considered contaminated. Thus, in these areas ice should not be used in beverages. If ice has been in contact with containers used for drinking, the containers should be thoroughly cleaned, preferably with soap and hot water, after the ice has been discarded.

Treatment of Water With Tincture of Iodine

Tincture of iodine (from medicine chest or first aid kit)	Drops* to be added per quart or litre	
	Clear water	Cold or cloudy water+
2%	5	10

*1 drop = 0.05 ml
Let stand for 30 minutes.
Water is safe to use.
+Very turbid or cloudy water may require prolonged contact time; let stand up to several hours prior to use, if possible.

It is safer to drink directly from a can or bottle of a beverage than from a questionable container. However, water on the outside of cans or bottles of beverages might be contaminated. Therefore, wet cans or bottles should be dried before being opened, and surfaces which are contacted directly by the mouth in drinking should first be wiped clean. Where water may be contaminated, travelers should avoid brushing their teeth with tap water.

Treatment of Water

Boiling is by far the most reliable method to make water of uncertain purity safe for drinking. Water should be brought to a vigorous boil and allowed to cool to room temperature—do not add ice. At very high altitudes, for an extra margin of saf ety, boil for several minutes or use chemical disinfection. Adding a pinch of salt to each quart, or pouring the water several times from one container to another will improve the taste.

Chemical disinfection with iodine is an alternative method of water treatment when it is not feasible to boil water. Two well-tested methods for disinfection with iodine are the use of tincture of iodine (*See* table), and the use of tetraglycine hydroperiodide tablets (Globaline, Potable–Agua, Coghlan's,[2] etc.). The tablets are available from pharmacies and sporting goods stores. The manufacturer's instructions should be followed. If water is cloudy, the number of tablets should be doubled; if water is extremely cold, an attempt should be made to warm the water, and the recommended contact time should be increased to achieve reliable disinfection. Cloudy water should be strained through a clean cloth into a container to remove any sediment or floating matter, and then the water should be treated with heat or iodine. Chlorine, in various forms, has also been used for chemical disinfection. However, its germicidal activity varies greatly with pH, temperature, and organic content of the water to be purified, and is less reliable than iodine.

There are a variety of portable filters currently on the market which according to the manufacturers' data will provide safe drinking water. Although the iodide–impregnated resins and the microstrainer type filters will kill and/or remove many micoorganisms, there are very few published reports in the scientific literature dealing both with the methods used and the results of the tests employed to evaluate the efficacy of these filters against water–borne pathogens. Until there is sufficient independent verification of the efficacy of these filters, The Centers for Disease Control

makes no recommendation regarding their use.

As a last resort, if no source of safe drinking water is available or can be obtained, tap water that is uncomfortably hot to touch is usually safe. After allowing such hot water to cool to room temperature in a thoroughly cleaned container, it may be used for brushing teeth, as well as for drinking.

Food

To avoid illness, food should be selected with care. All raw food is subject to contamination. Particularly in areas where hygiene and sanitation are inadequate, the traveler should be advised to avoid salads, uncooked vegetables, unpasteurized milk and milk products such as cheese, and to eat only food that has been cooked and is still hot, or fruit that has been peeled by the traveler. Undercooked and raw meat, fish, and shellfish may carry various intestinal pathogens.

The easiest way to guarantee a safe food source for an infant less than 6 months of age is to have the child breast-feed. If the infant has already been weaned from the breast, formula prepared from commercial powder and boiled water is the safest and most practical food.

Some species of fish and shellfish can contain poisonous biotoxins, even when well cooked. The most common type of fish poisoning in travelers is ciguatera fish poisoning. Red snapper, grouper, barracuda, amberjack, sea bass, and a wide range of tropical reef fish contain the toxin at unpredictable times. The potential for ciguatera poisoning exists in all subtropical and tropical insular areas of the West Indies, Pacific and Indian Oceans where the implicated fish species are consumed. □

1. See World Health Organization documents LAB/81,5: "Use of plasma volume substitutes and plasma in developing countries," for further details, and WHO/GPA/INF/88.5 "Guidelines for Treatment of Acute Blood Loss."

2. Use of trade names is for identification only and does not imply endorsement by the Public Health Service or the U.S. Department of Health and Human Services.

Travel Tips

The booklet, *Your Trip Abroad,* contains some valuable information on loss and theft of a passport as well as other travel tips. To obtain a copy, write to the Superintendent of Documents, U.S. Government Printing Office, Washington, D.C. 20402 and ask for publication #8969. The single copy price is $1.

State and City Tourism Offices

The following is a selected list of state, tourism o ffices. Where a toll–free 800 number is available, it is given. However, the numbers are subject to change.

ALABAMA
Bureau of Tourism & Travel
401 Adams Ave.
Montgomery, AL
36104-4331
205–242–4169 or
1–800–ALABAMA

ALASKA
Alaska Division of Tourism
P.O. Box E
Juneau, AK 99811
907–465–2010

ARIZONA
Arizona Office of Tourism
1100 West Washington
Phoenix, AZ 85007
602 542–TOUR

ARKANSAS
Arkansas Department of
Parks and Tourism
1 Capitol Mall
Little Rock, AR 72201
501–682–7777 or
1–800–NATURAL
(both in and out of state)

CALIFORNIA
California Office of Tourism
Department of Com-
merce
801 K Street
Suite 1600
Sacramento, CA 95814
Write or phone for free
200–page Guide Infor-
mation Packet: (Outside
Calif.) 800–862–2543

COLORADO
Colorado Tourism Board
1625 Broadway, Suite 1700
Denver, CO 80202
303–592–5410
For a vacation planning kit,
call Toll–free
1–800–433–2656

CONNECTICUT
Tourism Promotion Service
CT Dept. of Economic
Development
865 Brook Street
Rocky Hill, CT 06067–3405
203–258–4355 or 800–CT
BOUND (nationwide)

DELAWARE
Delaware Tourism Office
Delaware Development
Office
99 Kings Highway
P.O. Box 1401 Dept. RB
Dover, DE 19903
302–736–4271 or
1–800–441–8846
(out of state)

DISTRICT OF COLUMBIA
Washington Convention
and Visitors Association
1212 New York Ave., NW
Washington, D.C. 20005
202–789–7000

FLORIDA
Department of Commerce
Visitors Inquiry
126 Van Buren St.
Tallahassee, FL 32399–2000
904–487–1462

GEORGIA
Tourist Division
P.O. Box 1776
Atlanta, GA 30301-1776
404–656–3590
1-800-VISIT GA
(1-800-847-4842)

HAWAII
Hawaii Visitors Bureau
2270 Kalakaua Ave., Suite
801
Honolulu, HI 96815
808–923–1811

IDAHO
Department of Commerce
700 W. State St.
Second Floor
Boise, ID 83720
208–334–2470 or
1–800–635–7820

ILLINOIS
Illinois Dep artment of
Commerce and
Community
Affairs, Bureau of
Tourism
620 East Adams Street
Springfield, IL 62701
217–782–7139

INDIANA
Indiana Dept. of Commerce
Tourism & Film Develop-
ment Division
One North Capitol
Suite 700
Indianapolis, IN
46204–2288
317–232–8860 or
1–800–289–ONIN

IOWA
Iowa Department of
Economic Development
Division of Tourism
200 East Grand Avenue
Des Moines, IA 50309
515–242-4705
1-800-345-IOWA

KANSAS
Travel & Tourism Develop-
ment Division
Department of Commerce
400 W. 8th St., 5th Floor
Topeka, KS 66603
913–296–2009
1-800-2 KANSAS

KENTUCKY
Department of Travel
Development
550 Mero Street
2200 Capital Plaza Tower
Frankfort, KY 40601-1968
502–564–4930 or
1–800–225–TRIP
(Continental United States
and provinces of Ontario
and Quebec, Canada)

LOUISIANA
Office of Tourism
P.O. Box 94291
Baton Rouge, LA
70804–9291
504–342–8119 or
1–800–33GUMBO

MAINE
Maine Publicity Bureau
97 Winthrop St., P.O. Box
2300
Hallowell, ME 04347–2300
207–289–6070

MARYLAND
Office of Tourism
Development
217 E. Redwood St.
Baltimore, MD 21202
1–800–543–1036

MASSACHUSETTS
Office of Travel and
Tourism
100 Cambridge St., 13th
Floor
Boston, MA 02202
617–727–3201

MICHIGAN
Travel Bureau
Department of Commerce
P.O. Box 30226
Lansing, MI 48909
1–800–5432–YES

MINNESOTA
Minnesota Office of
Tourism
375 Jackson St.
250 Skyway Level
Farm Credit Services Bldg.
St. Paul, MN 55101-1848
612–296–5029 or
1–800–657–3700

MISSISSIPPI
Department of Economic
and Community
Development
Tourism Development
P.O. Box 22825
Jackson, MS 39205-2825
601–359–3297 or
1–800–647–2290

Average Daily Temperatures (°F) in Tourist Cities

Location	January High	January Low	April High	April Low	July High	July Low	October High	October Low
U.S. CITIES (See Weather and Climate Section)								
CANADA								
Ottawa	21	3	51	31	81	58	54	37
Quebec	18	2	45	29	76	57	51	37
Toronto	30	16	50	34	79	59	56	40
Vancouver	41	32	58	40	74	54	57	44
MEXICO								
Acapulco	85	70	87	71	89	75	88	74
Mexico City	66	42	78	52	74	54	70	50
OVERSEAS								
Australia (Sydney)	78	65	71	58	60	46	71	56
Austria (Vienna)	34	26	57	41	75	59	55	44
Bahamas (Nassau)	77	65	81	69	88	75	85	73
Bermuda (Hamilton)	68	58	71	59	85	73	79	69
Brazil (Rio de Janeiro)	84	73	80	69	75	63	77	66
Denmark (Copenhagen)	36	29	50	37	72	55	53	42
Egypt (Cairo)	65	47	83	57	96	70	86	65
France (Paris)	42	32	60	41	76	55	59	44
Germany (Berlin)	35	26	55	38	74	55	55	41
Greece (Athens)	54	42	67	52	90	72	74	60
Hong Kong	64	56	75	67	87	78	81	73
India (Calcutta)	80	55	97	76	90	79	89	74
Italy (Rome)	54	39	68	46	88	64	73	53
Israel (Jerusalem)	55	41	73	50	87	63	81	59
Japan (Tokyo)	47	29	63	46	83	70	69	55
Nigeria (Lagos)	88	74	89	77	83	74	85	74
Netherlands (Amsterdam)	40	34	52	43	69	59	56	48
Puerto Rico (San Juan)	81	67	84	69	87	74	87	73
South Africa (Cape Town)	78	60	72	53	63	45	70	52
Spain (Madrid)	47	33	64	44	87	62	66	48
United Kingdom (London)	44	35	56	40	73	55	58	44
United Kingdom (Edinburgh)	43	35	50	39	65	52	53	44
U.S.S.R. (Moscow)	21	9	47	31	76	55	46	34
Venezuela (Caracas)	75	56	81	60	78	61	79	61
Yugoslavia (Belgrade)	37	27	64	45	84	61	65	47

MISSOURI
Missouri Division of Tourism
Truman State Office Bldg.
301 W. High St.
P.O. Box 1055
Jefferson City, MO 65102
314–751–4133

MONTANA
Department of Commerce
Travel Montana
1424 9th Avenue
Helena, MT 59620
406–444–2654 or
1–800–541–1447

NEBRASKA
Dept. of Economic Development
Division of Travel and Tourism
301 Centennial Mall South
P.O. Box 94666
Lincoln, NE 68509
402–471–3796 or
1–800–742–7595 (in state) or 1–800–228–4307 (out of state)

NEVADA
Commission on Tourism
Capitol Complex

Carson City, NV 89710
1–800–Nevada–8

NEW HAMPSHIRE
Office of Vacation Travel
P.O. Box 856
Concord, NH 03302
603–271–2666
or for recorded weekly events, ski conditions, foliage reports
1–800–258–3608
Toll free number is for northeast only

NEW JERSEY
Division of Travel and Tourism
CN–826
Trenton, NJ 08625
1–800–JERSEY–7

NEW MEXICO
New Mexico Department of Tourism
Joseph M. Montoya Bldg.
Room 1057
1100 St. Francis Dr.
Santa Fe, NM 87503
505–827–0291 or
1–800–545–2040

NEW YORK
Division of Tourism
1 Commerce Plaza
Albany, NY 12245
Toll free from anywhere in the U.S. and its territorial possessions
1–800–225–5697. From Canada, call (518) 474–4116

NORTH CAROLINA
Travel and Tourism Division
Department of Economic and Community Development
430 North Salisbury St.
Raleigh, NC 27611
919–733–4171 or
1–800–VISIT NC

NORTH DAKOTA
North Dakota Tourism Promotion
Liberty Memorial Building
Capitol Grounds
604 E. Boulevard
Bismarck, ND 58505
701–224–2525 or
1–800–437–2077 (out of state)
1–800–537–8879 (Canada)

OHIO
Ohio Division of Travel and
Tourism
P.O. Box 1001
Columbus, OH 43266–0001
614–466–8844 (Business
Office)
1–800–BUCKEYE
(National
Toll–Free Travel Hotline)

OKLAHOMA
Oklahoma Tourism and
Recreation Dept.
Literature Distribution
Center
P.O. Box 60000
Oklahoma City, OK 73146
405–521–2409 (In
Oklahoma
City area) or nationwide
at 1–800–652–6552

OREGON
Tourism Division
Oregon Economic
Development Dept.
775 Summer St. NE
Salem, OR 97310
503–373–1270 or
1–800–547–7842 (Out of
state); 1–800–543–8838
(in–state)

PENNSYLVANIA
Bureau of Travel Marketing
453 Forum Building
Harrisburg, PA 17120
717–787–5453 (Business
Office)
1–800–VISIT PA, ext. 257
(To order single free copy
of PA Travel Guide)

RHODE ISLAND
Rhode Island Tourism
Division

7 Jackson Walkway
Providence, RI 02903
401–277–2601 or
1–800–556–2484

SOUTH CAROLINA
South Carolina Division of
Tourism
Box 71
Columbia, SC 29202
803–734–0235

SOUTH DAKOTA
Department of Tourism
Capitol Lake Plaza
Pierre, South Dakota 57501
605–773–3301 or
1–800–843–1930

TENNESSEE
Department of Tourist
Development
P.O. Box 23170
Nashville, TN 37202
615–741–2158

TEXAS
Travel Information Services
State Highway Department
P.O. Box 5064
Austin, TX 78763–5064
512–483–3705

UTAH
Utah Travel Council
Council Hall, Capitol Hill
Salt Lake City, UT 84114
801–538–1030

VERMONT
Agency of Development
and Community Affairs
Travel Division
134 State St.
Montpelier, VT 05602
802–828–3236

VIRGINIA
Virginia Division of Tourism
1021 East Cary St.
Richmond, VA 23219
804–786–4484
1–800–VISIT-VA

WASHINGTON
Washington State Dept. of
Trade and Economic
Development
101 General Administration
Bldg.
AX–13
Olympia, WA 98504–0613
206–753–5630

WASHINGTON, D.C.
See District of Columbia

WEST VIRGINIA
Division of Tourism
and Parks
2101 Washington St. E.
Charleston, WV 25305
304–348–2286 or
1–800–CALL–WVA

WISCONSIN
Department of
Development
Division of Tourism
Development
Box 7606
Madison, WI 53707
Toll free in WI and neigh-
bor states 1–800–372–2737
others: 608–266–2161
Nationally 1–800–432–TRIP

WYOMING
Wyoming Division of
Tourism
I–25 at College Drive
Cheyenne, WY 82002–0660
307–777–7777 or
1–800–225–5996

Travel Advisories

Source: U.S. Department of State.

The Department of State tries to alert American travelers to adverse conditions abroad—including violence—through the travel advisory program. In consultation with our embassies and consulates overseas, and various bureaus of the Department of State, the Office of Overseas Citizens Services in the Bureau of Consular Affairs is sues travel advisories about conditions in specific countries. Advisories generally do not pertain to isolated international terrorist incidents since these can occur anywhere and at any time. Some mention conditions of political or civil unrest which could pose a threat to personal safety.

There are only a few advisories in effect which advise avoiding all travel to a particular country because of a high incidence of terrorism within the region or because a long–term problem exists. Most of the security–related advisories do not recommend against travel to an entire country but suggest avoiding specific areas within a country where unrest is endemic.

Ask about current travel advisories for specific countries at any of the 13 regional U.S. passport agencies and at U.S. Embassies and consulates abroad. Travel advisories are also widely disseminated to interested organizations, travel associations, and airlines.

Travel advisories may be heard by calling (24 hours a day) the State Department's Citizens Emergency Center at 202–647–5225. ☐

Passport Travel Tips

The American Society of Travel Agents (ASTA) advises those traveling abroad to photocopy important pages in their passports, especially the pages featuring their photos and passport numbers, and dates and places of issue. Also copy those pages containing visas of countries you plan to visit.

In the case of a lost passport, U.S. embassies will usually accept photocopies as proof that you actually possess a passport. Losing a passport abroad can be a time–consuming and expensive process to replace.

Keep a list of your credit cards and other important numbers (driver's license, traveler's cheques) in a separate location from your cards in case they are lost. ☐

Road Mileages Between U.S. Cities[1]

Cities	Birmingham	Boston	Buffalo	Chicago	Cleveland	Dallas	Denver
Birmingham, Ala.	—	1,194	947	657	734	653	1,318
Boston, Mass.	1,194	—	457	983	639	1,815	1,991
Buffalo, N.Y.	947	457	—	536	192	1,387	1,561
Chicago, Ill.	657	983	536	—	344	931	1,050
Cleveland, Ohio	734	639	192	344	—	1,205	1,369
Dallas, Tex.	653	1,815	1,387	931	1,205	—	801
Denver, Colo	1,318	1,991	1,561	1,050	1,369	801	—
Detroit, Mich.	754	702	252	279	175	1,167	1,301
El Paso, Tex.	1,278	2,358	1,928	1,439	1,746	625	652
Houston, Tex.	692	1,886	1,532	1,092	1,358	242	1,032
Indianapolis, Ind.	492	940	510	189	318	877	1,051
Kansas City, Mo.	703	1,427	997	503	815	508	616
Los Angeles, Calif.	2,078	3,036	2,606	2,112	2,424	1,425	1,174
Louisville, Ky.	378	996	571	305	379	865	1,135
Memphis, Tenn.	249	1,345	965	546	773	470	1,069
Miami, Fla.	777	1,539	1,445	1,390	1,325	1,332	2,094
Minneapolis, Minn.	1,067	1,402	955	411	763	969	867
New Orleans, La.	347	1,541	1,294	947	1,102	504	1,305
New York, N.Y.	983	213	436	840	514	1,604	1,780
Omaha, Neb.	907	1,458	1,011	493	819	661	559
Philadelphia, Pa.	894	304	383	758	432	1,515	1,698
Phoenix, Ariz.	1,680	2,664	2,234	1,729	2,052	1,027	836
Pittsburgh, Pa.	792	597	219	457	131	1,237	1,411
St. Louis, Mo.	508	1,179	749	293	567	638	871
Salt Lake City, Utah	1,805	2,425	1,978	1,458	1,786	1,239	512
San Francisco, Calif.	2,385	3,179	2,732	2,212	2,540	1,765	1,266
Seattle, Wash.	2,612	3,043	2,596	2,052	2,404	2,122	1,373
Washington, D.C.	751	440	386	695	369	1,372	1,635

Cities	Detroit	El Paso	Houston	Indianapolis	Kansas City	Los Angeles	Louisville
Birmingham, Ala.	754	1,278	692	492	703	2,078	378
Boston, Mass.	702	2,358	1,886	940	1,427	3,036	996
Buffalo, N.Y.	252	1,928	1,532	510	997	2,606	571
Chicago, Ill.	279	1,439	1,092	189	503	2,112	305
Cleveland, Ohio	175	1,746	1,358	318	815	2,424	379
Dallas, Tex.	1,167	625	242	877	508	1,425	865
Denver, Colo.	1,310	652	1,032	1,051	616	1,174	1,135
Detroit, Mich.	—	1,696	1,312	290	760	2,369	378
El Paso, Tex.	1,696	—	756	1,418	936	800	1,443
Houston, Tex.	1,312	756	—	1,022	750	1,556	981
Indianapolis, Ind.	290	1,418	1,022	—	487	2,096	114
Kansas City, Mo.	760	936	750	487	—	1,609	519
Los Angeles, Calif.	2,369	800	1,556	2,096	1,609	—	2,128
Louisville, Ky.	378	1,443	981	114	519	2,128	—
Memphis, Tenn.	756	1,095	586	466	454	1,847	396
Miami, Fla.	1,409	1,957	1,237	1,225	1,479	2,757	1,111
Minneapolis, Minn.	698	1,353	1,211	600	466	2,041	716
New Orleans, La.	1,101	1,121	365	839	839	1,921	725
New York, N.Y.	671	2,147	1,675	729	1,216	2,825	785
Omaha, Neb.	754	1,015	903	590	204	1,733	704
Philadelphia, Pa.	589	2,065	1,586	647	1,134	2,743	703
Phoenix, Ariz.	1,986	402	1,158	1,713	1,226	398	1,749
Pittsburgh, Pa.	288	1,778	1,395	360	847	2,456	416
St. Louis, Mo.	529	1,179	799	239	255	1,864	264
Salt Lake City, Utah	1,721	877	1,465	1,545	1,128	728	1,647
San Francisco, Calif.	2,475	1,202	1,958	2,299	1,882	403	2,401
Seattle, Wash.	2,339	1,760	2,348	2,241	1,909	1,150	2,355
Washington, D.C.	526	1,997	1,443	565	1,071	2,680	601

1. These figures represent estimates and are subject to change.

Road Mileages Between U.S. Cities

Cities	Memphis	Miami	Minne-apolis	New Orleans	New York	Omaha	Phila-delphia
Birmingham, Ala.	249	777	1,067	347	983	907	894
Boston, Mass.	1,345	1,539	1,402	1,541	213	1,458	304
Buffalo, N.Y.	965	1,445	955	1,294	436	1,011	383
Chicago, Ill.	546	1,390	411	947	840	493	758
Cleveland, Ohio	773	1,325	763	1,102	514	819	432
Dallas, Tex.	470	1,332	969	504	1,604	661	1,515
Denver, Colo.	1,069	2,094	867	1,305	1,780	559	1,698
Detroit, Mich.	756	1,409	698	1,101	671	754	589
El Paso, Tex.	1,095	1,957	1,353	1,121	2,147	1,015	2,065
Houston, Tex.	586	1,237	1,211	365	1,675	903	1,586
Indianapolis, Ind.	466	1,225	600	839	729	590	647
Kansas City, Mo.	454	1,479	466	839	1,216	204	1,134
Los Angeles, Calif.	1,847	2,757	2,041	1,921	2,825	1,733	2,743
Louisville, Ky.	396	1,111	716	725	785	704	703
Memphis, Tenn.	—	1,025	854	401	1,134	658	1,045
Miami, Fla.	1,025	—	1,801	892	1,328	1,683	1,239
Minneapolis, Minn.	854	1,801	—	1,255	1,259	373	1,177
New Orleans, La.	401	892	1,255	—	1,330	1,043	1,241
New York, N.Y.	1,134	1,328	1,259	1,330	—	1,315	93
Omaha, Neb.	658	1,683	373	1,043	1,315	—	1,233
Philadelphia, Pa.	1,045	1,239	1,177	1,241	93	1,233	—
Phoenix, Ariz.	1,464	2,359	1,644	1,523	2,442	1,305	2,360
Pittsburgh, Pa.	810	1,250	876	1,118	386	932	304
St. Louis, Mo.	295	1,241	559	696	968	459	886
Salt Lake City, Utah	1,556	2,571	1,243	1,743	2,282	967	2,200
San Francisco, Calif.	2,151	3,097	1,997	2,269	3,036	1,721	2,954
Seattle, Wash.	2,363	3,389	1,641	2,606	2,900	1,705	2,818
Washington, D.C.	902	1,101	1,114	1,098	229	1,170	140

Cities	Phoenix	Pitts-burgh	St. Louis	Salt Lake City	San Francisco	Seattle	Wash-ington
Birmingham, Ala.	1,680	792	508	1,805	2,385	2,612	751
Boston, Mass.	2,664	597	1,179	2,425	3,179	3,043	440
Buffalo, N.Y.	2,234	219	749	1,978	2,732	2,596	386
Chicago, Ill.	1,729	457	293	1,458	2,212	2,052	695
Cleveland, Ohio	2,052	131	567	1,786	2,540	2,404	369
Dallas, Tex.	1,027	1,237	638	1,239	1,765	2,122	1,372
Denver, Colo.	836	1,411	871	512	1,266	1,373	1,635
Detroit, Mich.	1,986	288	529	1,721	2,475	2,339	526
El Paso, Tex.	402	1,778	1,179	877	1,202	1,760	1,997
Houston, Tex.	1,158	1,395	799	1,465	1,958	2,348	1,443
Indianapolis, Ind.	1,713	360	239	1,545	2,299	2,241	565
Kansas City, Mo.	1,226	847	255	1,128	1,882	1,909	1,071
Los Angeles, Calif.	398	2,456	1,864	728	403	1,150	2,680
Louisville, Ky.	1,749	416	264	1,647	2,401	2,355	601
Memphis, Tenn.	1,464	810	295	1,556	2,151	2,363	902
Miami, Fla.	2,359	1,250	1,241	2,571	3,097	3,389	1,101
Minneapolis, Minn.	1,644	876	559	1,243	1,997	1,641	1,114
New Orleans, La.	1,523	1,118	696	1,743	2,269	2,626	1,098
New York, N.Y.	2,442	386	968	2,282	3,036	2,900	229
Omaha, Neb.	1,305	932	459	967	1,721	1,705	1,178
Philadelphia, Pa.	2,360	304	886	2,200	2,954	2,818	140
Phoenix, Ariz.	—	2,073	1,485	651	800	1,482	2,278
Pittsburgh, Pa.	2,073	—	599	1,899	2,653	2,517	241
St. Louis, Mo.	1,485	599	—	1,383	2,137	2,164	836
Salt Lake City, Utah	651	1,899	1,383	—	754	883	2,110
San Francisco, Calif.	800	2,653	2,137	754	—	817	2,864
Seattle, Wash.	1,482	2,517	2,164	883	817	—	2,755
Washington, D.C.	2,278	241	836	2,110	2,864	2,755	—

Air Distances Between U.S. Cities in Statute Miles

Cities	Birming–ham	Boston	Buffalo	Chicago	Cleveland	Dallas	Denver
Birmingham, Ala.	—	1,052	776	578	618	581	1,095
Boston, Mass.	1,052	—	400	851	551	1,551	1,769
Buffalo, N. Y.	776	400	—	454	173	1,198	1,370
Chicago, Ill.	578	851	454	—	308	803	920
Cleveland, Ohio	618	551	173	308	—	1,025	1,227
Dallas, Tex.	581	1,551	1,198	803	1,025	—	663
Denver, Colo.	1,095	1,769	1,370	920	1,227	663	—
Detroit, Mich.	641	613	216	238	90	999	1,156
El Paso, Tex.	1,15 2	2,072	1,692	1,252	1,525	572	557
Houston, Tex.	567	1,605	1,286	940	1,114	225	879
Indianapolis, Ind.	433	807	435	165	263	763	1,000
Kansas City, Mo.	579	1,251	861	414	700	451	558
Los Angeles, Calif.	1,802	2,596	2,198	1,745	2,049	1,240	831
Louisville, Ky.	331	826	483	269	311	726	1,038
Memphis, Tenn.	217	1,137	803	482	630	420	879
Miami, Fla.	665	1,255	1,181	1,188	1,087	1,111	1,726
Minneapolis, Minn.	862	1,123	731	355	630	862	700
New Orleans, La.	312	1,359	1,086	833	924	443	1,082
New York, N. Y.	864	188	292	713	405	1,374	1,631
Omaha, Neb.	732	1,282	883	432	739	586	488
Philadelphia, Pa.	783	271	279	666	360	1,299	1,579
Phoenix, Ariz.	1,456	2,300	1,906	1,453	1,749	887	586
Pittsburgh, Pa.	608	483	178	410	115	1,070	1,320
St. Louis, Mo.	400	1,038	662	262	492	547	796
Salt Lake City, Utah	1,466	2,099	1,699	1,260	1,568	999	371
San Francisco, Calif.	2,013	2,699	2,300	1,858	2,166	1,483	949
Seattle, Wash.	2,082	2,493	2,117	1,737	2,026	1,681	1,021
Washington, D.C.	661	393	292	597	306	1,185	1,494

Cities	Detroit	El Paso	Houston	Indian–apolis	Kansas City	Los Angeles	Louisville
Birmingham, Ala.	641	1,152	567	433	579	1,802	331
Boston, Mass.	613	2,072	1,605	807	1,251	2,596	826
Buffalo, N. Y.	216	1,692	1,286	435	861	2,198	483
Chicago, Ill.	238	1,252	940	165	414	1,745	269
Cleveland, Ohio	90	1,525	1,114	263	700	2,049	311
Dallas, Tex.	999	572	225	763	451	1,240	726
Denver, Colo.	1,156	557	879	1,000	558	831	1,038
Detroit, Mich.	—	1,479	1,105	240	645	1,983	316
El Paso, Tex.	1,479	—	676	1,264	839	701	1,254
Houston, Tex.	1,105	676	—	865	644	1,374	803
Indianapolis, Ind.	240	1,264	865	—	453	1,809	107
Kansas City, Mo.	645	839	644	453	—	1,356	480
Los Angeles, Calif.	1,983	701	1,374	1,809	1,356	—	1,829
Louisville, Ky.	316	1,254	803	107	480	1,829	—
Memphis, Tenn.	623	976	484	384	369	1,603	320
Miami, Fla.	1,152	1,643	968	1,024	1,241	2,339	919
Minneapolis, Minn.	543	1,157	1,056	511	413	1,524	605
New Orleans, La.	939	983	318	712	680	1,673	623
New York, N. Y.	482	1,905	1,420	646	1,097	2,451	652
Omaha, Neb.	669	878	794	525	166	1,315	580
Philadelphia, Pa.	443	1,836	1,341	585	1,038	2,394	582
Phoenix, Ariz.	1,690	346	1,017	1,499	1,049	357	1,508
Pittsburgh, Pa.	205	1,590	1,137	330	781	2,136	344
St. Louis, Mo.	455	1,034	679	231	238	1,589	242
Salt Lake City, Utah	1,492	689	1,200	1,356	925	579	1,402
San Francisco, Calif.	2,091	995	1,645	1,949	1,506	347	1,986
Seattle, Wash.	1,938	1,376	1,891	1,872	1,506	959	1,943
Washington, D.C.	396	1,728	1,220	494	945	2,300	476

Source: National Geodetic Survey.

Air Distances Between U.S. Cities in Statute Miles

Cities	Memphis	Miami	Minne– apolis	New Orleans	New York	Omaha	Phila– delphiae
Birmingham, Ala.	217	665	862	312	864	732	783
Boston, Mass.	1,137	1,255	1,123	1,359	188	1,282	271
Buffalo, N.Y.	803	1,181	731	1,086	292	883	279
Chicago, Ill.	482	1,188	355	833	713	432	666
Cleveland, Ohio	630	1,087	630	924	405	739	360
Dallas, Tex.	420	1,111	862	443	1,374	586	1,299
Denver, Colo.	879	1,726	700	1,082	1,631	488	1,579
Detroit, Mich.	623	1,152	543	939	482	669	443
El Paso, Tex.	976	1,643	1,157	983	1,905	878	1,836
Houston, Tex.	484	968	1,056	318	1,420	794	1,341
Indianapolis, Ind.	384	1,024	511	712	646	525	585
Kansas City, Mo.	369	1,241	413	680	1,097	166	1,038
Los Angeles, Calif.	1,603	2,339	1,524	1,673	2,451	1,315	2,394
Louisville, Ky.	320	919	605	623	652	580	582
Memphis, Tenn.	—	872	699	358	957	529	881
Miami, Fla.	872	—	1,511	669	1,092	1,397	1,019
Minneapolis, Minn.	699	1,511	—	1,051	1,018	290	985
New Orleans, La.	358	669	1,051	—	1,171	847	1,089
New York, N.Y.	957	1,092	1,018	1,171	—	1,144	83
Omaha, Neb.	529	1,397	290	847	1,144	—	1,094
Philadelphia, Pa.	881	1,019	985	1,089	83	1,094	—
Phoenix, Ariz.	1,263	1,982	1,280	1,316	2,145	1,036	2,083
Pittsburgh, Pa.	660	1,010	743	919	317	836	259
St. Louis, Mo.	240	1,061	466	598	875	354	811
Salt Lake City, Utah	1,250	2,089	987	1,434	1,972	833	1,925
San Francisco, Calif.	1,802	2,594	1,584	1,926	2,571	1,429	2,523
Seattle, Wash.	1,867	2,734	1,395	2,101	2,408	1,369	2,380
Washington, D.C.	765	923	934	966	205	1,014	123

Cities	Phoenix	Pitts– burgh	St. Louis	Salt Lake City	San Francisco	Seattle	Wash– ington
Birmingham, Ala.	1,456	608	400	1,466	2,013	2,082	661
Boston, Mass.	2,300	483	1,038	2,099	2,699	2,493	393
Buffalo, N.Y.	1,906	178	662	1,699	2,300	2,117	292
Chicago, Ill.	1,453	410	262	1,260	1,858	1,737	597
Cleveland, Ohio	1,749	115	492	1,568	2,166	2,026	306
Dallas, Tex.	887	1,070	547	999	1,483	1,681	1,185
Denver, Colo.	586	1,320	796	371	949	1,021	1,494
Detroit, Mich.	1,690	205	455	1,492	2,091	1,938	396
El Paso, Tex.	346	1,590	1,034	689	995	1,376	1,728
Houston, Tex.	1,017	1,137	679	1,200	1,645	1,891	1,220
Indianapolis, Ind.	1,499	330	231	1,356	1,949	1,872	494
Kansas City, Mo.	1,049	781	238	925	1,506	1,506	945
Los Angeles, Calif.	357	2,136	1,589	579	347	959	2,300
Louisville, Ky.	1,508	344	242	1,402	1,986	1,943	476
Memphis, Tenn.	1,263	660	240	1,250	1,802	1,867	765
Miami, Fla.	1,982	1,010	1,061	2,089	2,594	2,734	923
Minneapolis, Minn.	1,280	743	466	987	1,584	1,395	934
New Orleans, La.	1,316	919	598	1,434	1,926	2,101	966
New York, N.Y.	2,145	317	875	1,972	2,571	2,408	205
Omaha, Neb.	1,036	836	354	833	1,429	1,369	1,014
Philadelphia, Pa.	2,083	259	811	1,925	2,523	2,380	123
Phoenix, Ariz.	—	1,828	1,272	504	653	1,114	1,983
Pittsburgh, Pa.	1,828	—	559	1,668	2,264	2,138	192
St. Louis, Mo.	1,272	559	—	1,162	1,744	1,724	712
Salt Lake City, Utah	504	1,668	1,162	—	600	701	1,848
San Francisco, Calif.	653	2,264	1,744	600	—	678	2,442
Seattle, Wash.	1,114	2,138	1,724	701	678	—	2,329
Washington, D.C.	1,983	192	712	1,848	2,442	2,329	—

Source: National Geodetic Survey.

Air Distances Between World Cities in Statute Miles

Cities	Berlin	Buenos Aires	Cairo	Calcutta	Cape Town	Caracas	Chicago
Berlin	—	7,402	1,795	4,368	5,981	5,247	4,405
Buenos Aires	7,402	—	7,345	10,265	4,269	3,168	5,598
Cairo	1,795	7,345	—	3,539	4,500	6,338	6,129
Calcutta	4,368	10,265	3,539	—	6,024	9,605	7,980
Cape Town, South Africa	5,981	4,269	4,500	6,024	—	6,365	8,494
Caracas, Venezuela	5,247	3,168	6,338	9,605	6,365	—	2,501
Chicago	4,405	5,598	6,129	7,980	8,494	2,501	—
Hong Kong	5,440	11,472	5,061	1,648	7,375	10,167	7,793
Honolulu, Hawaii	7,309	7,561	8,838	7,047	11,534	6,013	4,250
Istanbul	1,078	7,611	768	3,638	5,154	6,048	5,477
Lisbon	1,436	5,956	2,363	5,638	5,325	4,041	3,990
London	579	6,916	2,181	4,947	6,012	4,660	3,950
Los Angeles	5,724	6,170	7,520	8,090	9,992	3,632	1,745
Manila	6,132	11,051	5,704	2,203	7,486	10,620	8,143
Mexico City	6,047	4,592	7,688	9,492	8,517	2,232	1,691
Montreal	3,729	5,615	5,414	7,607	7,931	2,449	744
Moscow	1,004	8,376	1,803	3,321	6,300	6,173	4,974
New York	3,965	5,297	5,602	7,918	7,764	2,132	713
Paris	545	6,870	1,995	4,883	5,807	4,736	4,134
Rio de Janeiro	6,220	1,200	6,146	9,377	3,773	2,810	5,296
Rome	734	6,929	1,320	4,482	5,249	5,196	4,808
San Francisco	5,661	6,467	7,364	7,814	10,247	3,904	1,858
Shanghai, China	5,218	12,201	5,183	2,117	8,061	9,501	7,061
Stockholm	504	7,808	2,111	4,195	6,444	5,420	4,278
Sydney, Australia	10,006	7,330	8,952	5,685	6,843	9,513	9,272
Tokyo	5,540	11,408	5,935	3,194	9,156	8,799	6,299
Warsaw	320	7,662	1,630	4,048	5,958	5,517	4,667
Washington, D.C.	4,169	5,218	5,800	8,084	7,901	2,059	597

Cities	Hong Kong	Honolulu	Istanbul	Lisbon	London	Los Angeles	Manila
Berlin	5,440	7,309	1,078	1,436	579	5,724	6,132
Buenos Aires	11,472	7,561	7,611	5,956	6,916	6,170	11,051
Cairo	5,061	8,838	768	2,363	2,181	7,520	5,704
Calcutta	1,648	7,047	3,638	5,638	4,947	8,090	2,203
Cape Town, South Africa	7,375	11,534	5,154	5,325	6,012	9,992	7,486
Caracas, Venezuela	10,167	6,013	6,048	4,041	4,660	3,632	10,620
Chicago	7,793	4,250	5,477	3,990	3,950	1,745	8,143
Hong Kong	—	5,549	4,984	6,853	5,982	7,195	693
Honolulu, Hawaii	5,549	—	8,109	7,820	7,228	2,574	5,299
Istanbul	4,984	8,109	—	2,012	1,552	6,783	5,664
Lisbon	6,853	7,820	2,012	—	985	5,621	7,546
London	5,982	7,228	1,552	985	—	5,382	6,672
Los Angeles, Calif.	7,195	2,574	6,783	5,621	5,382	—	7,261
Manila	693	5,299	5,664	7,546	6,672	7,261	—
Mexico City	8,782	3,779	7,110	5,390	5,550	1,589	8,835
Montreal	7,729	4,910	4,789	3,246	3,282	2,427	8,186
Moscow	4,439	7,037	1,091	2,427	1,555	6,003	5,131
New York	8,054	4,964	4,975	3,364	3,458	2,451	8,498
Paris	5,985	7,438	1,400	904	213	5,588	6,677
Rio de Janeiro	11,021	8,285	6,389	4,796	5,766	6,331	11,259
Rome	5,768	8,022	843	1,161	887	6,732	6,457
San Francisco	6,897	2,393	6,703	5,666	5,357	347	6,967
Shanghai, China	764	4,941	4,962	6,654	5,715	6,438	1,150
Stockholm	5,113	6,862	1,348	1,856	890	5,454	5,797
Sydney, Australia	4,584	4,943	9,294	11,302	10,564	7,530	3,944
Tokyo	1,794	3,853	5,560	6,915	5,940	5,433	1,866
Warsaw	5,144	7,355	863	1,715	899	5,922	5,837
Washington, D.C.	8,147	4,519	5,215	3,562	3,663	2,300	8,562

Source: Encyclopaedia Britannica.

Air Distances Between World Cities in Statute Miles

Cities	Mexico City	Montreal	Moscow	New York	Paris	Rio de Janeiro	Rome
Berlin	6,047	3,729	1,004	3,965	545	6,220	734
Buenos Aires	4,592	5,615	8,376	5,297	6,870	1,200	6,929
Cairo	7,688	5,414	1,803	5,602	1,995	6,146	1,320
Calcutta	9,492	7,607	3,321	7,918	4,883	9,377	4,482
Cape Town, South Africa	8,517	7,931	6,300	7,764	5,807	3,773	5,249
Caracas, Venezuela	2,232	2,449	6,173	2,132	4,736	2,810	5,196
Chicago	1,691	744	4,974	713	4,134	5,296	4,808
Hong Kong	8,782	7,729	4,439	8,054	5,985	11,021	5,768
Honolulu	3,779	4,910	7,037	4,964	7,438	8,285	8,022
Istanbul	7,110	4,789	1,091	4,975	1,400	6,389	843
Lisbon	5,390	3,246	2,427	3,364	904	4,796	1,161
London	5,550	3,282	1,555	3,458	213	5,766	887
Los Angeles	1,589	2,427	6,003	2,451	5,588	6,331	6,732
Manila	8,835	8,186	5,131	8,498	6,677	11,259	6,457
Mexico City	—	2,318	6,663	2,094	5,716	4,771	6,366
Montreal	2,318	—	4,386	320	3,422	5,097	4,080
Moscow	6,663	4,386	—	4,665	1,544	7,175	1,474
New York	2,094	320	4,665	—	3,624	4,817	4,281
Paris	5,716	3,422	1,544	3,624	—	5,699	697
Rio de Janeiro	4,771	5,097	7,175	4,817	5,699	—	5,684
Rome	6,366	4,080	1,474	4,281	697	5,684	—
San Francisco	1,887	2,539	5,871	2,571	5,558	6,621	6,240
Shanghai, China	8,022	7,053	4,235	7,371	5,754	11,336	5,677
Stockholm	5,959	3,667	762	3,924	958	6,651	1,234
Sydney, Australia	8,052	9,954	9,012	9,933	10,544	8,306	10,136
Tokyo	7,021	6,383	4,647	6,740	6,034	11,533	6,135
Warsaw	6,365	4,009	715	4,344	849	6,467	817
Washington, D.C.	1,887	488	4,858	205	3,829	4,796	4,434

Cities	San Francisco	Shanghai	Stockholm	Sydney	Tokyo	Moscow	Washington
Berlin	5,661	5,218	504	10,006	5,540	320	4,169
Buenos Aires	6,467	12,201	7,808	7,330	11,408	7,662	5,218
Cairo	7,364	5,183	2,111	8,952	5,935	1,630	5,800
Calcutta	7,814	2,117	4,195	5,685	3,194	4,048	8,084
Cape Town, South Africa	10,247	8,061	6,444	6,843	9,156	5,958	7,901
Caracas, Venezuela	3,904	9,501	5,420	9,513	8,799	5,517	2,059
Chicago	1,858	7,061	4,278	9,272	6,299	4,667	597
Hong Kong	6,897	764	5,113	4,584	1,794	5,144	8,147
Honolulu	2,393	4,941	6,862	4,943	3,853	7,355	4,519
Istanbul	6,703	4,962	1,348	9,294	5,560	863	5,215
Lisbon	5,666	6,654	1,856	11,302	6,915	1,715	3,562
London	5,357	5,715	890	10,564	5,940	899	3,663
Los Angeles	347	6,438	5,454	7,530	5,433	5,922	2,300
Manila	6,967	1,150	5,797	3,944	1,866	5,837	8,562
Mexico City	1,887	8,022	5,959	8,052	7,021	6,365	1,887
Montreal	2,539	7,053	3,667	9,954	6,383	4,009	488
Moscow	5,871	4,235	762	9,012	4,647	715	4,858
New York	2,571	7,371	3,924	9,933	6,740	4,344	205
Paris	5,558	5,754	958	10,544	6,034	849	3,829
Rio de Janeiro	6,621	11,336	6,651	8,306	11,533	6,467	4,796
Rome	6,240	5,677	1,234	10,136	6,135	817	4,434
San Francisco	—	6,140	5,361	7,416	5,135	5,841	2,442
Shanghai, China	6,140	—	4,825	4,899	1,097	4,951	7,448
Stockholm	5,361	4,825	—	9,696	5,051	501	4,123
Sydney, Australia	7,416	4,899	9,696	—	4,866	9,696	9,758
Tokyo	5,135	1,097	5,051	4,866	—	5,249	6,772
Warsaw	5,841	4,951	501	9,696	5,249	—	4,457
Washington, D.C.	2,442	7,448	4,123	9,758	6,772	4,457	—

Source: Encyclopaedia Britannica.

PERSONAL FINANCE

The articles and opinions in this section are for general information only and are not intended to provide specific advice or recommendations for any individual.

When an Insured Bank Fails

Facts on Protecting Depositors and Collecting Loans in a Failed Bank

Source: Federal Deposit Insurance Corporation (FDIC).

Bank Failure and Deposit Payoff

How is a depositor notified?

When an insured bank has been closed for liquidation and a payoff is to be made, the FDIC is required to notify each depositor in writing at the customer's last address on record with the bank. This notification is mailed within a few days after the bank closes. Every effort also is made to inform the public through the news media. In a situation where the failed bank is merged with another institution, depositors are notified by the assuming bank. This notification usually is mailed with the first bank statement after the assumption

What does the FDIC do?

It balances the bank's books and credits interest earned on all accounts through the date of closing. FDIC claim agents determine how much each depositor is owed and then prepare a list of all deposits. This list is flagged to indicate those depositors who require special handling because they have past due loans, overdrafts or deposits pledged as collateral and depositors who have funds in excess of the insured limit. Checks then are prepared for each depositor up to the insured maximum.

When can a depositor expect to receive payment?

In the case of a payoff, the FDIC begins paying depositors generally within a few days after a bank has closed. In the case of a merger, the funds usually are available on the next business day.

Where does the depositor obtain payment?

The information is posted on the doors of the closed bank, publicized in the press and, in the case of a payoff, in the notice sent to insured depositors. In the case of a deposit assumption the funds are immediately available at the assuming bank.

How are claims established?

In a payoff the depositor provides evidence of deposit ownership, such as a passbook, certificate of deposit, or the last statement (with cancelled checks if applicable), and then fills out a claim form at the bank. FDIC claim agents are on hand to assist in filing the claim. Passbooks, certificates of deposits and other documents used to establish claims against a closed bank must be surrendered upon receipt of the deposit insurance payment. Those depositors whose accounts have not been flagged for special attention are directed to a teller's window where their claims are quickly processed. In the case of a merger, customers continue to carry on business as usual, using the deposit slips and checks from the failed bank until new ones are provided by the assuming bank.

What happens when your account is flagged?

In the case of a payoff, persons with deposits in excess of the insured limit are directed to claim agents who will explain deposit insurance coverage to them, pay the insured portions of their deposits and assist them in filing claims against the estate of the closed bank for the uninsured balances. Depositors whose accounts have been flagged are referred to another area where the Receiver will explain how their accounts are handled. In the case of a deposit assumption, the FDIC freezes the flagged accounts and they are not transferred until cleared by the claim agent.

Must a claim be filed in person?

No. those who are unable to appear in person may file claims by mail. This correspondence should be addressed to the claim agent in charge of the closed bank. All claim forms for amounts in excess of $50 not signed in the presence of an FDIC claim agent must be notarized. No claims are required in a deposit assumption since the customers of the old bank automatically become customers of the assuming bank.

When do you file a claim?

Claims are required to be filed in all payoffs. A depositor is allowed 18 months from the date a Receiver is appointed to file a claim for deposit insurance. However, claims should be filed as soon as possible after the bank's closing.

How is the insurance payment made?

The FDIC makes payment to the depositor by check or it may use other means such as establishing an account for the depositor in an operating bank in the local area. These funds are available for immediate withdrawal.

If a depositor has more than the insured limit, what happens to the amount in excess of $100,000?

If, for example, a depositor has a total claim of $105,000, he or she would be paid $100,000 and would retain a claim against the estate of the closed bank for the remaining $5,000. For this $5,000, the depositor would be given a Receiver's Certificate as proof of his or her claim and would receive **pro rata** payments as the assets of the bank are collected or sold. In a deposit assumption all accounts, insured and uninsured, are transferred to the assuming bank.

How can the correct balance in a checking account be determined?

Final statements with cancelled checks are available to depositors prior to the filing of their claims. These are made available at the closed bank when the payoff begins or are mailed promptly. This allows a review of the final charges against the account from the date of the last regular statement for reconciliation with the depositor's checkbook.

What happens to checks that do not clear an account before the bank is closed?

In a payoff those checks are not paid or charged against the account because the FDIC freezes all accounts at the time the bank is closed. Such checks are returned and usually will be marked "drawee bank closed." This does not reflect on the credit standing of any bank depositor. However, it is the depositor's responsibility to make funds available to creditors who received checks that were returned and did not clear through the depositor's account because of the closing. When the closed bank's deposits are assumed by another bank and the offices reopen the next business day there usually is no interruption in the processing of checks drawn on the failed bank. If the reopening is delayed a few days the checks may be handled as in a payoff.

When can the holders of safe deposit boxes gain access to their property?

Access to safe deposit boxes usually is granted to all box holders when the payoff of depositors begins, and immediately in the case of a deposit assumption. In deposit payoff cases access to safe deposit boxes is discouraged until the payoff begins. However, if the customer has a genuine emergency, access to the safe deposit box can be gained on a case-by-case basis.

Can a bank customer with, for example, $150,000 on deposit and a $50,000 loan balance offset the portion of the deposit that exceeds the $100,000 insurance limit against the balance due on the loan?

In most states a depositor can offset his or her deposit account including any uninsured portion, against a loan if the loan and deposit are held by the same person or persons. If the loan is past due at the time of a deposit payoff, the FDIC is required to make the offset in calculating the insured deposit. FDIC offset specialists will be available at the bank to determine whether an offset can or must be made. In the case of a deposit assumption, the account in question would be flagged and an FDIC specialist would make a determination on how the loan balance would be treated.

Loan Customers

What happens to a borrower who owes money to a bank when its deposits are assumed by another bank?

When deposits of a failed bank are assumed by a healthy institution, the assuming bank normally is required to purchase the consumer installment loans, real estate loans, and certain other loans. The assuming bank then has thirty days to select the loans it wants from the rest of the portfolio. The borrower maintains the same payment schedule and makes the payments to the assuming bank on the loans it has taken over. The other loans are retained by the FDIC and payments are made to it on the contracted schedule. In the case of a payoff, all loans are retained by the FDIC and payments made to it as Receiver for the failed bank.

What happens if the borrower is delinquent at the time of the bank failure?

The loan probably would be rejected by the assuming bank and would be taken over by the FDIC for collection. An FDIC representative would meet with the borrower and try to work out a payment schedule to bring the payments current. The borrower might be asked to provide additional collateral or cosigners. At some point the FDIC may attempt to sell the note and payments then would be made to the new holder of the note.

What happens in the case of a deposit transfer or direct payoff?

In a deposit transfer, if the loans are purchased by the bank receiving the insured deposits, selected loans may be moved with the insured deposits to the new institution. Payments then continue to the new institution under the existing schedule. Those loans not moved are retained by the FDIC and payments are made to it. In the case of a direct payoff to depositors, all loans are retained by the FDIC as Receiver of the failed bank. Those that are current are maintained on the same schedule, with payments made to the FDIC.

What if the loan is delinquent at the time of deposit transfer or payoff?

In either a deposit transfer or payoff, the FDIC retains all delinquent loans plus selected other loans. The FDIC representative meets with the borrower and attempts to work out a payment schedule to make the note current. If such an arrangement cannot be agreed to, payments are made to the FDIC until the note is paid off. If it is not possible to work out an acceptable payment program with the borrower, the FDIC has the same options for collecting as any lending institution. It is important to note here that there are many reasons other than delinquency for the FDIC to retain a note after a bank is closed. The assuming bank has thirty days to select the loans it wants to assume and the FDIC retains the loans during that period and keeps the ones that are not selected for a longer period. Loans might be rejected because they do not fit the loan portfolio maintained by the acquiring bank. Commercial loans normally are not transferred in bulk to an assuming bank, even though they may be current in their payments.

Deposit Insurance Coverage

What is the basic insurance protection?

The basic insured amount for a depositor under current law is $100,000. Deposits maintained in different rights or capacities, or forms of ownership, each are separately insured up to $100,000. Thus, a person may hold or have an interest in more than one separately insured account in the same insured bank.

What types of deposits are insured?

All types of deposits received by a bank in its usual course of business are insured, including savings deposits, checking accounts, deposits in NOW accounts, Christmas savings and other open-account time deposits, time certificates of deposit, uninvested trust funds, certified checks, cashier's checks, officer's checks, money orders and drafts and travelers' checks for which an insured bank is primarily liable.

If a depositor has an account in the main office of a bank and also at a branch office, are these accounts separately insured?

No. The main office and all of its branches are considered to be one bank. Therefore, the accounts would be added together and insured only to the $100,000 maximum.

Is the insurance protection increased by placing funds in two or more types of deposit accounts in the same bank?

No. Deposit insurance is not increased merely by dividing funds owned in the same right and capacity among the types of deposits available. For example, checking and savings accounts owned by the same depositor are added together and insured up to $100,000.

If a depositor has accounts in several different insured banks, will the deposits be added together in determining insurance coverage?

No. The maximum insurance of $100,000 is applicable to each insured depositor in each insured bank, without regard to deposits held in any other insured bank.

What insurance coverage is provided for IRA and Keogh account deposits?

IRA and Keogh funds, when held by a bank in a trust or custodial capacity, are insured separately from other deposits. IRA and Keogh funds held in time or savings deposits are insured up to the maximum $100,000 and funds held in demand deposits are, in most cases, separately insured to the maximum of $100,000. Alternatively, IRA and Keogh funds held by a nonbank trustee or custodian and deposited in a time or savings deposit in an insured bank are separately insured to the maximum of $100,000. □

Managing Family Debt

By BankCard Holders of America

If you are up to your ears in debt, you have plenty of company—hundreds of thousands of Americans are in serious financial difficulty. These people are as diverse as the country itself, and cannot be dismissed as lazy, irresponsible types who are irregularly employed, or have otherwise unsteady lives. Many of these debt-ridden Americans are hard-working people with stable families.

In these times of fast and easy credit, many people with good credit histories find their mailboxes flooded with offers for "pre-approved" credit. It is easy to get into financial trouble by responding to even a few of these offers, charging those special items that you've been wanting, and suddenly finding yourself overwhelmed by debt.

People in financial crises typically are employed, hold about eight credit cards (the national average), a mortgage, and car loans. According to credit counselors, about 75% of debt-ridden individuals got into trouble through situations beyond their control, including: large medical bills, an uninsured accident or theft, a large tax bill, a period of disability or unemployment, or income loss from separation or divorce. Just one of these incidents, combined with a lack of savings and insurance, can turn a normally tight budget into a credit crisis.

Signs of Trouble

When should you be concerned about excessive debt? Consider the following questions concerning your family's debt, to decide if you have a debt problem.

• **Could you pay all of your debt (excluding mortgage) in 18 to 24 months?** If not, you may be over-extended.

• **Are you an impulse buyer?** Do you buy things on credit that you wouldn't buy with cash? Your family's spending habits can be the central reason behind a debt problem. Spendaholics are people who shop and spend for emotional reasons rather than actual need. If you find yourself shopping to relax, shopping to ease the stress in your life, or buying something you really can't afford because "you deserve it", you may need to reevaluate your spending. Debtors Anonymous, and groups like it, help spendaholics stop impulse buying, and change their attitude about spending.

• **Do you routinely pay only the minimum payments to all creditors?** If you cannot manage to pay all of your monthly minimums, you have a definite problem. Even if you are easily able to pay your minimums, you may not be paying enough to reduce your debt significantly. Many people charge purchases until their credit has reached its limit, only to find that they can pay no more than the monthly minimum. It is important to remember, though, that paying only the minimums on revolving credit accounts does not really do much to reduce your total debt. For example, it would take *eight years* to pay off a $1,000 credit card purchase (on a card with an interest rate of 19.8%), if you only paid the minimum payment each month.

• **Have you responded to an offer for additional credit cards because all of your current credit cards are charged up to their limit?** Acquiring additional credit when you are already having trouble reducing your total debt is a good way to get deeper into trouble. If you're having difficulty paying off your credit cards, do not apply for more credit until your total debt is paid.

• **Do you sometimes have to choose which bills to pay?** This is a sure sign that something is wrong and you should be seeking assistance. Unfortunately, many people who aren't able to pay a bill do nothing to inform the creditor. Hiding from the problem will not make it disappear. If you cannot pay a bill, contact the creditor and explain the problem. Assure them of your intent to pay the bill, and negotiate a reasonable payment period. It is much better to establish relations with a creditor before the account goes into collection, and bill collectors are knocking on your door.

• **Do you take cash advances on your credit card to pay other bills, or to purchase staples such as food, gas, or utilities?** Again, this is a sure sign that something is wrong. Cash advances are an expensive way to borrow money because of the high interest rates, and per-transaction fees charged by many banks. In addition, cash advances can send your balance up to its credit limit very quickly and only worsen your debt burden. Remember that cash advances accrue interest charges immediately. There is no interest-free "grace period" on cash advances as there is on purchases.

Face the Problem

The first step in managing family debt is to face the problem, and stop purchasing with credit. The family should sit down together, determine their total monthly income, and compare that to their total indebtedness, as well as their total monthly payments, If you are easily tempted to "break out the plastic," you should consider cutting up your cards. Or, lock them in a safety deposit box, out of reach, but accessible in an emergency. Adopt a pay-as-you-go philosophy, and agree not to purchase anything on credit until the full debt is repaid. Some families may want to consider additional sources of income such as a part-time job. It is also a good idea for consumers to pay off their highest interest rate credit cards first. Because of the high interest rate, these are the most expensive loans to be carrying and they increase total debt faster.

When your debt problem is too serious to be solved by a tight budget and frugality, other options are available: debt consolidation, a second mortgage or home equity loan, and the best choice: credit counseling. Bankruptcy is a drastic step to take, and should be considered a last resort, taken only after all other avenues have been exhausted.

Debt Consolidation

"Worried about all those unpaid bills? We can get you out of debt."

Advertising by debt consolidation services is enticing. It sounds wonderfully simple. All your bills are pooled into a single, lower payment, and the consolidation service pays your creditors. Using a debt consolidation loan to pay debt works like this: the money borrowed is used to payoff all outstanding debt, and the borrower then makes only one monthly payment to the lender. That payment should be less than the total of the individual monthly payment to creditors. Unfortunately, this is not as inexpensive and easy as it appears. Debt consolidation services are often expensive, and some may do nothing more than lead the family father into debt. The following example describes one couple's experience with a debt consolidation service:

Bob and Joan had a large debt and found themselves unable to meet their monthly payments. They were several months behind on some bills, and receiving letters daily from creditors. They responded to an advertisement from "Friendly Financial Services" which offered them a debt consolidation loan under which they agreed to pay the company a certain amount each month. The company, in turn, agreed to pay their creditors. Although the interest was very high, and they had to pay $300 up-front as an installment fee, they thought it was the only way out.

"Friendly Financial" did write the creditors, saying that its attorneys now represented Bob and Joan. The company also proposed that the creditors accept lower monthly payments and agree to forgo all interest payments. Some creditors refused to deal with "Friendly Financial" and continued to send delinquent notices to Bob and Joan. Since they had already signed for the loan, they were stuck with the same payments as before, plus a payment to "Friendly Financial"

All debt consolidation services are not as bad as "Friendly Financial," but it is a good idea to check out the company with your state's attorney general's office or your area Better Business Bureau before you do business with them. Most states prohibit debt consolidation companies from operating on a for-profit basis. If you choose a debt consolidation loan, try to verify that all of your creditors will agree to the loan company's deal before you sign the contract. Ask the service what proportion of your monthly payment actually goes to your creditors, and how much is taken by the company as a fee for its services. Be sure to check the interest rate and compare it to rates available through your bank or credit union.

Finally, in order to make a debt consolidation loan work, you must change your spending habits. The pay-as-you-go, cash only, lifestyle is the only way that the debt consolidation loan can work to make you debt-free. You cannot continue to purchase with credit because, very quickly, you will be faced with the same overwhelming bills.

Home Equity and Second Mortgage Loans

Home equity and second mortgage loans are similar types of loans of which homeowners can take advantage. A second mortgage is a set amount of money borrowed, paid back over a set length of time, with a fixed interest rate. Home equity loans generally carry variable interest rates (the interest fluctuates as interest rates in the economy change). With these types of loans, there can be high up-front costs such as application fees, appraisal fees, and annual fees for home equity lines of credit.

More people are considering these loans because, under the current tax laws, the interest on them is generally tax-deductible, while the credit card interest is no longer deductible. As a means of paying off debt, however, these loans are not the best choice. If you need money right away, a second mortgage or home equity loan is a good way to get it. But, because these are long-term loans you will be paying them off for many years to come. (A better use for home equity or second mortgage money is home improvement, or other appreciating investments.)

Regardless of the type and cost of the loan chosen to pay off debt, the biggest danger to borrowers is that once the loan is in place, they may feel free to return to their old spending habits. They may once again use their plastic cards to purchase items that they cannot buy with cash. Quickly, the family can be faced again with monthly payments that exceed their disposable income.

Bankruptcy

Filing bankruptcy protects you from creditor's legal claims, and allows you to start over, debt free. While bankruptcy does not carry quite the stigma that it used to, it is not an inconsequential magic way to get out of debt. Bankruptcy holds serious consequences for a family, including the possible loss of your home and property. A bankruptcy completely ruins your credit record for at least 10 years (after that time, it drops off your credit record, but potential creditors can research farther back into your file if you are applying for a large loan). Bankruptcy is the most negative information that can appear on a credit report. It makes it nearly impossible to obtain credit of any type and can even affect you when applying for a new job, or getting utility services in a new home.

Credit Counseling

Credit counseling is the best, lease expensive, and for many, most satisfying method for managing family debt that has gotten out of control. Non-profit credit counselors function in several capacities. First, they take a detailed account of the family's living expenses and debt, and create a repayment plan and budget. Second, if necessary, the counselor contacts each of the family's creditors on behalf of the family, and reschedules the debt by establishing smaller payments over a longer period of time. The family agrees to make one monthly payment to the counseling service, out of which the service pays the creditors. The entire amount of the payment goes to repaying the debt. Non-profit credit counseling centers are funded by voluntary contributions from the business community (who benefit greatly from individuals repaying their debt through counseling rather than defaulting), and fees charged to their clients (usually small, and based on their ability to pay).

Families in credit counseling morally commit to repay their debt, and live on a cash-only basis. Credit counselors teach the family how to budget and record expenses. The counselors also teach the family to have a new attitude about money, and how to stop impulsive spending habits.

Where To Go for Help

You must develop the discipline to spend and live within your means, in order to prevent your family from falling into debt. In these times of easy credit, it is not easy to maintain spending discipline. Individuals and families having difficulty should seek help by asking their local government consumer affairs office for information about credit counseling in their community.

BHA offers a continuing education program, including newsletters, pamphlets, and personalized credit advice to consumers seeking to manage credit debt, and personal finances in general. The National Foundation for Consumer Credit can also give you the name and address of a non-profit credit counseling service near you. They may be contacted at: National Foundation for Consumer Credit, 8701 Georgia Avenue, Silver Spring, Md. 20910 (1-800-388-CCCS). Another organization to help people attempting to change their excessive spending habits is: Debtors Anonymous, General Service Board, P.O. Box 20322, New York, N.Y. 10025. ☐

Making Bank Deposits

When Will Your Money Be Available?
Source: Board of Governors of the Federal Reserve System.

In 1987, Congress passed a law that limits how long financial institutions may delay a customer's ability to use deposited funds. The law, called the Expedited Funds Availability Act, balances the risk to financial institutions with the needs of customers. As of September 1, 1988, all banks, savings and loan associations, savings banks, and credit unions must let you use funds deposited in checking, share draft, or NOW accounts within a fixed number of days. They also must tell you, in writing, how soon you may use the money after making a deposit.

The law does not require an institution to delay your ability to use deposited funds; it only limits how long the delay may last. Many institutions have always let their long–term customers use deposited funds right away, and they may continue to do so under the new law. Even those institutions that do delay their customers' use of funds may make funds available sooner than the limits set in the new law. Some institutions, of course, may now take as much time as the established schedule allows. So, if availability of funds is a consideration for you, you may want to compare the policies of different institutions before deciding where you will deposit your funds.

How Soon Are Your Deposited Funds Available?

How quickly the funds must be available depends on the type of check you deposit and on the likelihood that it will be paid. For example, you may be able to use the money sooner when you deposit a U.S. Treasury check than when you deposit a check from an individual or a business. The time you have to wait may also depend on where the individual or business that gave you the check has their checking account. Your institution can expect to find out more quickly from a hometown institution than from a distant, out–of–state institution whether a check is backed by sufficient funds.

The following are usually the longest times that institutions can delay your use of deposited funds under the new law.

These times, based on business days, include all days except Saturdays, Sundays, and federal holidays.

Now let's look at how these rules affect the availability of your funds. Let's say that your institution

Type of deposit	When the funds must be available to you
• cash • the first $100 of any deposit of checks • government, cashier's, certified, or teller's checks • checks written on another account at the same institution • direct deposit and other electronic credits	the next business day after the day of deposit (certain conditions may apply—check with your institution
• checks written on local institutions	the second business day after the day of deposit
• checks written on non-local institutions • deposits made at an automated teller machine not belonging to your institution	the fifth business day after the day of deposit

decides to hold deposited funds for the longest time allowed by law. If you deposit a local check* on a Monday, you can use the deposited funds on Thursday—the third business day after the day of deposit. If you deposit the check on a Wednesday, however, you will have to wait until Monday to use your funds, because Saturday and Sunday are not business days and are not counted in figuring the time. If you deposit the check on a day when your institution is closed, on a Saturday, or on any business day after the cut–off time (usually 2 p.m.), the institution may treat the deposit as though you actually made it on the following business day.

At the end of the waiting period, your institution will pay checks that you have written, but it may not allow you to withdraw all the money in cash right

---

*Under the law, a check is a local check if it is deposited in an institution located in the same Federal Reserve check processing region as the paying bank. There are 48 Federal Reserve check processing regions in the nation.

away. Contact your institution to see whether it has special rules for cash withdrawals.

Deposits at an automated teller machine not belonging to your institution must be available on the same schedule as other deposits.

Are There Special Rules for New Accounts?

When you open an account, be sure to ask whether the institution has special rules regarding availability of funds for new customers. An institution may delay a new customer's use of deposited funds longer because it is not familiar with that person's history in using a checking account. These longer delays are allowed only during the first 30 days the account is open.

May an Institution Delay Your Use of Deposited Funds Beyond the Usual Limits?

In certain instances, the law allows an institution to delay a customer's use of deposited funds longer than the usual limits, generally for four more business days. This longer limit gives an institution extra time to make sure a deposit is backed by sufficient funds. An institution may use this longer limit in the following circumstances:

- you redeposit a check that was returned unpaid.
- you have overdrawn your account repeatedly in the previous six months. (That is, you have not had

enough money in the account to cover checks you wrote.)

- you deposit checks totalling more than $5,000 on any one day.
- your institution has reason to believe that the check you are depositing will not be paid.

If your institution uses the longer limit, it must tell you why it has done so and when you will be able to use the deposited funds.

Additional Information

All institutions must send a notice explaining to their customers when they must use deposited funds. When you receive the notice, take the time to review it carefully. If you do not understand it, ask someone at your institution for help. If you write checks against funds not yet available for your use, you could end up owing charges on returned checks to your institution, as well as to the merchants or others who receive these checks from you.

Keep in mind that you are responsible should a check you deposit be returned unpaid. If you have already used some or all of the funds, you will have to reimburse your institution promptly.

The way you endorse a check for deposit could help hasten its clearing. When you endorse a check, make sure that your signature is near the edge of the left side on the back of the check. This will leave room for all the financial institutions handling the check to make their endorsements and move the check more quickly. □

A Guide to Life Insurance

By Virginia Applegarth

Individual Policies

In addition to Social Security[1] and group coverage, the third main type of insurance is individual coverage. This coverage is purchased by you as an individual, either through an agent or directly from an insurance company. Individual life insurance policies generally have many more options and many more variations than group insurance.

Term Insurance

There are two basic types of life insurance policies—term and permanent. They both provide protection against death.

Term insurance offers pure insurance protection; all of the premium goes toward purchasing the risk coverage. The premium typically increases periodically (either every year, every five years, 10 years, etc.) and becomes very expensive by age 65 or so as the risk of death increases. There ar e several different types of term insurance to choose from.

Nonrenewable versus renewable. With nonrenewable term insurance, the policy is good for only a limited period of time (typically 5 to 20 years). This is usually the cheapest form of term insurance you can buy, but you cannot renew it. Even if you need insurance after the policy expires, you must apply for a new policy, take a new medical exam, and hope that you are healthy enough to qualify.

Renewable insurance is just that: it is renewable at the option of the policyholder regardless of his or her health, usually at least until age 70. Even if you are

on your deathbed, the company must renew your policy. Renewable term contracts are generally more expensive than nonrenewable. However, because it is hard to predict your future health or insurance needs, you should select a renewable policy.

Convertible versus nonconvertible. With a convertible policy, you can trade in your term insurance policy for a permanent insurance policy (offering protection plus an investment element) without having to prove you are healthy. This feature is especially useful if you know that you need permanent protection but you cannot afford the premiums right now. Nonconvertible policies offer no such option.

Death benefits. In a level term policy, the death benefit stays the same as long as the policy stays in force. With decreasing term, on the other hand, the amount payable upon death will decrease to zero at the end of the term period. One of the most common decreasing term policies is a mortgage insurance policy.

Revertible versus nonrevertible. With a revertible policy, you can get a break on premiums if you can continue to prove your good health (which means additional paperwork every few years). If you cannot, premiums generally will be higher than if you had chosen a policy without this feature (a nonrevertible policy. With a revertible policy, you are gambling that you will stay healthy; with a nonrevertible policy, you are not.

With all of these options to choose from, a good general recommendation is level death benefit, annual renewable and convertible term, nonrevertible and renewable to at least age 70.

Permanent Insurance

In contrast to term insurance, permanent insurance offers protection for your whole life. One major benefit of permanent insurance is that no matter how long you live, premiums will never increase. The insurance company accomplishes this by charging higher premiums than for term insurance in the early years and building up a reserve to help pay premiums in future years, when term premiums start to go up dramatically.

A permanent insurance policy offers protection against death coupled with a savings or investment account. In other words, you get something back whether you live or die. Permanent insurance is also attractive because under current tax laws the investment portion within the policy grows at a tax-deferred rate, so income taxes on the gains do not have to be paid unless and until the policy is cashed in.

Different types of permanent policies have different savings vehicles. However, they are all based on the concept that extra premiums paid in the early years go toward a savings or cash value account. This is why, if both policies were issued at the same age, the premium for a $100,000 permanent policy is more than for a $100,000 term policy in the early years and usually much less in later years.

Whole life. The best known type of permanent insurance (because it has been around for more than 100 years) is whole life, ordinary life, or straight life—all different names for the same product. It is called whole life because the death benefits continue for your entire life, although there are ways to stop payments earlier. W hole life offers a guaranteed premium and death benefit as well as a guaranteed minimum cash value, which you can borrow against if necessary.

Having cash value is like having a savings account within the policy that grows each year. If you die, the policy pays the death benefit amount. However, you can cancel the policy at any time during your life and get back the current cash value. This option can be helpful to supplement retirement income. In addition, many policies pay dividends that can increase your cash values and/or death benefits substantially.

Insurance companies are either stock companies (the stockholders own the company) or mutual companies (the policyholders technically own the company). If your whole life policy is with a mutual company, you will probably qualify for dividends. Dividends are technically a partial return of premium, so they are not taxable.070

Interest-sensitive policies. A decade ago, thanks to competition and a changing investment environment, interest-sensitive permanent life insurance products were introduced. With interest-sensitive policies, the cash value part can fluctuate more widely than in whole life policies because it is more directly tied to interest rates. The distinguishing feature of interest-sensitive insurance contracts is that they separate out the insurance portion (the protection part) and the investment portion (the savings part). The policyholder receives periodic statements that list all charges taken out of his or her premiums, such as expenses, the cost of insurance, etc. The remaining premium goes into the investment portion.

Interest-sensitive products are more directly linked to the investment environment, which can sometimes make their value vary a great deal over short periods

of time. With interest-sensitive products as a whole, you are assuming more risk than with a standard whole life policy. In return, however, you may enjoy greater investment returns than with a traditional product.

Universal life. The most popular type of interest-sensitive product today is universal life. You can have flexible premium payments, and there is a minimum guaranteed death benefit and interest rate. When a premium is paid, expense, insurance, and maintenance charges are deducted; the balance is put into your investment account. The insurance company decides wh ich types of investments to make, and investment earnings are credited to the savings part after a variety of charges are taken out. Because you can sometimes skip payments on a universal life policy, you could easily find yourself suddenly faced with a large premium due to save the policy. It is crucial to have the self-discipline to pay the premium as originally planned.

Variable life. Another type of interest-sensitive insurance policy that allows the individual more investment flexibility is variable life. This product allows you to pick the type of investment you want. For the investment account, you typically can choose among money market, stock, bond, and real estate funds. You can also periodically change your investments in the account. However, although there is a guaranteed death benefit, there is very little premium flexibility and no minimum guaranteed cash value. Variable life is best suited to you if you are willing to take a fair amount of investment risk.

Variable universal life. A new contender in the interest-sensitive market is variable universal life, which combines features of both variable and universal products. Variable universal life contracts offer flexible premiums (like universal policies), as well as the ability to direct how your investment account is invested (like variables).

Special "Mostly Investment" Policies

Single Premium Life

With a single premium life policy, which can be single premium whole life or variable life, you pay one premium and immediately get a paid-up contract. In other words, you never have to pay another premium for the insurance coverage. The advantages are that the investment grows on a tax-deferred basis and, like traditional insurance products, the death benefit is income tax-free. The disadvantage is that new tax regulations (on policies issued after June 21, 1988) penalize many types of withdrawals from single premium policies, so you do not have ready access to your investment until age 59 1/2. Consult your tax adviser before purchasing such a policy.

Annuities

The other type of special policy is an annuity. With an annuity, you pay premiums and, in return, receive regular income for your life and sometimes even beyond, to your beneficiary. In buying an annuity, usually for retirement income, there are three basic decisions to make.

Single premium versus annual premium. Like a single premium life insurance contract, a single premium annuity requires only one premium and the policy is paid up. With an annual premium contract, however, annual premiums are paid for a defined period of time before the policy becomes paid up.

When benefits begin. With an immediate annuity, almost as soon as the insurance company receives the premium it begins to pay benefits. A deferred annuity means that benefit payments will be deferred for a specified period of time.

Fixed versus variable payments. With a fixed annuity, the insurance company agrees to pay a fixed monthly amount regardless of changes in inflation and investments. Variable annuity payments will fluctuate up and down, depending on the company's investment results and other factors. Each monthly payment may be different, or payments may vary on a yearly basis. With variable annuities, however, you still receive a minimum guaranteed monthly payment. Like single premium life contracts, annuities have the same disadvantages on many kinds of withdrawals before age 59 1/2. However, they also provide an in-

come throughout your retirement, no matter how long you live, and sometimes even to your beneficiary. ☐

Excerpts from HOW TO MAKE BASIC INVESTMENT DECISIONS by Neal Oschsner part of the REAL LIFE, REAL ANSWERS series. Copyright © 1990 by Lee Simmons Associates. Reprinted by permission of Houghton Mifflin Co. REAL LIFE, REAL ANSWERS is a Registered Trademark of the John Hancock Mutual Life Insusrance Company.

Although this article is designed to provide accurate and authoritative information in regard to the subject matter covered, neither the author and general editors nor the publisher are engaged in renderinglegal, accounting, or other professional service. If legal advice or other expert assistance is required, the services of a competent professional should be sought.

1. Social Security information is provided in-depth in the special section on "Social Security & Aging," prepared by the editors of *Information Please Almanac*.

Additional Considerations

Source: A Consumer's Guide to Life Insurance, published by the American Council of Life Insurance.

Before the Purchase

When buying life insurance, you should read the contract carefully and, if necessary, ask your agent for a point–by–point explanation of the language. To help the consumer, many insurance companies have rewritten their contracts to make them more understandable. Keep in mind that these are legal documents and you should be familiar with what they promise, even though some technical terms are used.

In addition, the National Association of Insurance Commissioners and many state insurance departments have prepared buyer's guides to help you further understand life insurance terms, benefits and relative costs. Buyer's guides are distributed through your agent and insurance company, so be sure to ask for one. If you have more questions about companies or policies, you can check with your state insurance commissioner's office.

No matter how they are put together, however, li fe insurance policies can be divided into three parts. There's The First Page, which outlines the basic features of the contract; The Details, which spell out the basic agreement; and The Application, which is the information you give the company about yourself and which becomes part of the policy.

After the Purchase

After purchasing new life insurance, keep in mind that you have a 10–day "free look," which entitles you to change your mind. If you do so, the company will return your premium, without penalty.

It's a good idea to provide your beneficiaries with a photocopy of your policy, and your agent's name. If you

have a lawyer, he or she should likewise have this information and know who your beneficiaries are.

Your beneficiaries should know where your policy is kept, because it may have to be sent to the company upon your death, along with a copy of the death certificate, in order to obtain the life insurance proceeds. You should keep your policy in a safe place at home and the name of the company and policy number in a safe deposit box in case your policy is misplaced or lost.

Your beneficiaries need not take your insurance proceeds in one lump sum. Many people select other options, such as a monthly income and a specific sum set aside for other purposes, perhaps retirement or college costs. Ask your agent about the settlement options available to you.

Switching Policies

If you already own life insurance, think twice if someone suggests that you replace it. Before you give up this protection make sure you are still insurable (check medical and any other qualification requirements). Also remember that you are now older than when you first purchased your policy, and a new one will cost more because of your age. Moreover, an older policy may have provisions that are not duplicated in some new ones. This does not mean that you should reject the idea of replacing a policy you already have, but rather that you should proceed with caution. It is recommended that you ask your agent or company for an opinion about the new proposal, so you hear both sides of the matter. ☐

Facts You Should Know
About Currency Transaction Reports Required by Federal Law

Source: American Bankers Association

Federal Law

In 1970 the U.S. Congress enacted into law the Bank Secrecy Act. As a result of the regulations promulgated pursuant to this law, all financial institutions are required to report transactions involving over $10,000 in cash to the Internal Revenue Service (IRS) by preparing Government Form 4789—Currency Transaction Report (CTR).

Examples of reportable transactions include deposits; withdrawals; exchanges of currency; check cash-

ing; cash purchases of cashiers' checks, money orders and travelers checks; and other financial services involving the physical transfer of over $10,000 in cash from one person to another.

The Form 4789 (CTR) which a financial institution is obligated to prepare and file with the IRS must include identifying information about the individual or individuals conducting the transaction, such as name, street address, Social Security Number, and specific occupation. In addition, the financial institution must examine and record the information from at least one identification document of the individual (e.g., a driver's license).

If an individual conducts the cash transaction on behalf of another person or business, the CTR Form must include information which identifies both the individual presenting the transaction and the person or entity for whom the transaction is conducted. Furthermore, this Form is to include some specific details regarding the nature of the transaction.

Exemptions

The Bank Secrecy Act regulations permit commercial banks, savings banks, savings and loans, and credit unions to exempt from the cash reporting requirements the deposits to or withdrawals from accounts of established depositors who routinely have cash transactions over $10,000. However, the regulations place certain qualifying restrictions upon the types of established depositors whose transactions to or from an account may be exempted. The most common type of deposits or withdrawals which may qualify for exemption are those made by or on behalf of a United States resident who operates a retail business which is primarily engaged in providing goods to ultimate consumers, and for which the business is paid in substantial portion by cash.

When a financial institution exempts the deposits or withdrawals of an established depositor from the reporting requirements, it must set a specific limit on the amount for which the transactions are exempted. This amount must be commensurate with the customary conduct of the lawful, domestic business of that depositor. Should a transaction occur which exceeds the set amount exempted, a CTR Form must be prepared for the transaction. Furthermore, a financial institution may not exempt a depositor's transactions without first preparing a written statement, to be signed by the depositor, describing the customary conduct of the lawful, domestic business of that depositor.

1986 Legislation

In October 1986, Congress enacted Public Law 99-750, known as the Anti-Drug Abuse Act. The new law contains provisions under which it is a criminal violation of Federal law if, for the purpose of evading a currency transaction reporting requirement, a person:

"(1) cause(s) or attempt(s) to cause a domestic financial institution to fail to file a (currency transaction) report;

"(2) cause(s) or attempt(s) to cause a domestic financial institution to file a (currency transaction) report . . . that contains a material omission or misstatement of fact; or

"(3) structure(s) or assist(s) in structuring, or attempt(s) to structure or assist in structuring, any transaction with one or more domestic financial institutions." □

The Biweekly Mortgage
An Easy, Affordable Way To Own Your Own Home
Source: Fannie Mae.

How would you like a mortgage that pays off in about 20 years, can save you thousands of dollars, and offers convenient, affordable payments? If you're looking for excellent value in a mortgage, you'll want to consider the biweekly mortgage.

How It Works

The biweekly mortgage gets its name from the frequency of its payments, which occur every two weeks. Each payment, however, is equivalent to *half* the amount of a comparable monthly payment.

A traditional 30-year fixed-rate mortgage has 12 monthly mortgage payments a year. A biweekly mortgage, on the other hand, with payments due every 2 weeks, requires an average of 26 payments over the course of a year. The 26 biweekly payments are equivalent to 13 monthly payments a year—or, in effect, one "extra monthly payment" as compared with a traditional 30-year fixed-rate mortgage.

The biweekly's "extra monthly payment," along with its more frequent application of payments to the loan balance (or amortizaton), greatly increases the speed with which the loan pays off and results in several significant advantages for you.

The Biweekly's Advantages

Fast Equity Build-up. The extra payments under the biweekly mortgage, along with the more frequent payment schedule, pay the loan off much faster than a traditional 30-year fixed-rate monthly payment. Loans that ordinarily take 30 years to amortize will pay off in as few as 19 to 21 years when paid on a biweekly basis. This means that you can own your home a lot sooner.

Interest Savings. Because of its faster amortization,the biweekly mortgage offers you significant interest savings. With the loan being paid off faster, you pay interest on a smaller balance. And because the loan amortizes so fast, you also pay interest for a shorter period of time—closer to 20 rather than 30 years. Over the life of the loan, this adds up to significant savings for you.

The actual term and interest savings for a biweekly mortgage depend on the interest rate of the loan. The higher the rate of the loan, the shorter the term of the biweekly. Check the chart at the end of this article to see the actual term and interest savings for various mortgage amounts.

Affordable Payments. The biweekly mortgage, for all its benefits, costs about one monthly payment more per year than a fixed-rate mortgage. And because the two to three extra biweekly payments are distributed throughout the year, the extra cost is easier to manage.

This combination of advantages is attracting a great deal of interest to the biweekly mortgage.

Commonly Asked Questions

Why does the biweekly pay off so much faster than a 30-year fixed-rate mortgage?

The biweekly pays faster than a 30-year fixed-rate mortgage because of:

• the two or three extra biweekly payments each year, and,

• the biweekly, as opposed to monthly, amortization of the loan.

These two factors, over the life of the loan, account for a dramatic reduction in the biweekly's loan term and interest expense.

Is qualifying for a biweekly mortgage any different than for a 30-year fixed-rate mortgage?

Because of the two or three additional biweekly payments each year, the income requirements for the biweekly mortgage are higher than for a comparable 30-year fixed-rate mortgage.

The following table illustrates just how well the biweekly mortgage compares with a 30-year fixed-rate mortgage.

Biweekly Mortgage Comparison
($70,000 Mortgage)

	30-year FRM	Biweekly
Interest rate	10.5%	10.5%
Payment amount	$640	$320[1]
Qualifying income[2]	$27,429	$29,714

1. Biweekly payment equivalent to one-half of fixed-rate monthly payment. 2. Based on 28 percent payment-to-income underwriting ratio (or 1/12 of total annual biweekly payments) cannot exceed 28 percent of your gross monthly income.

Will I need to send an additional mortgage check every month?

The ease of making biweekly payments is another one of its important advantages. With a biweekly mortgage, your lending institution automatically drafts the payment directly from your bank account. If you are paid every two weeks, each biweekly payment will correspond to the deposit of your paycheck. Because automatic drafting eliminates the effort of writing checks and mailing in payments, most people find biweekly payments very convenient.

Why does a biweekly mortgage with a higher interest rate have a shorter loan term than a biweekly with a lower interest rate?

As the interest rate increases, so does the biweekly payment amount, and a greater portion of the biweekly payment is applied to the principal balance. This results in faster payoff of the mortgage. The chart at the end of this article illustrates the various loan terms (in months) for different interest rates.

How does the biweekly compare with the 15-year fixed-rate mortgage?

The biweekly mortgage and the 15-year mortgage are two alternatives to the traditional 30-year fixed-rate mortgage. Both offer faster equity build-up and reduced interest costs. The biweekly has a longer term than the 15-year fixed-rate mortgage, but the payments are more affordable.

For more information on the 15-year fixed-rate mortgage, refer to Fannie Mae's brochure, "A Mortgage You Can Bank On: How a 15-year mortgage can help you save for the future." To receive your copy, ask your lender or write: Fannie Mae 15-Year Mortgage Consumer Brochure, P.O. Box 2335, Baltimore, Md. 21203.

The table below illustrates the amount of time it takes to pay off a biweekly mortgage and the total amount of interest saved when compared with a 30-year fixed-rate mortgage based on varying mortgage amounts and interest rates.

Are all biweekly mortgage programs alike?

No. You should be aware that some programs call themselves "biweekly" because they draft your account every two weeks, but they apply only one payment per month to your loan's unpaid principal balance. With "true" biweekly mortgages, including those purchased by Fannie Mae, funds are applied directly to your loan's unpaid principal balance as they are drafted from your account.

For more information on how a biweekly mortgage can meet your home financing needs, see your Fannie Mae-approved mortgage lender. □

Fannie Mae

Fannie Mae's position as the nation's largest single investor in conventional home mortgages enables it to offer a broad range of mortgage products to local lenders.

Fannie Mae does not lend money to consumers, but buys mortgages from a national network of 4,000 approved lenders who do originate mortgage loans, including mortgage bankers, savings and loan institutions, and commercial banks.

Biweekly Payment Amount and Total Interest Saved*

Interest Rate, Term in Months	$60,000 Biweekly Payment Amount	$60,000 Total Interest Savings[1]	$80,000 Biweekly Payment Amount	$80,000 Total Interest Savings[1]	$100,000 Biweekly Payment Amount	$100,000 Total Interest Savings[1]	$120,000 Biweekly Payment Amount	$120,000 Total Interest Savings[1]
9.00%[2] 264 mos.[3]	241	36,244	322	48,332	402	60,417	483	72,500
9.50%[2] 258 mos.[3]	252	40,994	336	54,668	420	68,329	505	82,003
10.00%[2] 252 mos.[3]	263	46,088	351	61,450	439	76,806	527	92,180
10.50%[2] 246 mos.[3]	274	51,503	366	68,663	457	85,843	549	103,014
11.00%[2] 240 mos.[3]	286	57,229	381	76,318	476	95,396	571	114,480
11.50%[2] 234 mos.[3]	297	63,264	396	84,353	495	105,442	594	126,550
12.00%[3] 229 mos.[3]	309	69,596	411	92,770	514	115,975	617	139,190
12.50%[2] 223 mos.[3]	320	76,166	427	101,572	534	126,962	640	152,364
13.00%[2] 217 mos.[3]	332	83,016	442	110,688	553	138,360	664	166,033

1. As compared with a 30-year fixed-rate mortgage. 2. Interest rate. 3. Length of loan term (in months). *All figures are approximate,.

Mortgage Highlights

Type	Description	Considerations
Fixed rate mortgage	Fixed interest rate, usually long–term; equal mnthly payments of principl and interest until debt is paid in full.	Offers stability and long–term tax advantages. Interest rates may be higher than other types of financing. New fixed rates are rarely assumable.
Fifteen–year mortgage	Fixed interest rate. Requires down payment or monthly payments higher than 30–year loan. Loan is fully repaid over 15–year term.	Frequently offered at slightly reduced interest rate. Offers faster accumulation of equity than traditional fixed rate mortgage but has higher monthly payments. Involves paying less interest but this may result in fewer tax deductions.
Adjustable rate mortgage	Interest rate changes over the life of the loan, resulting in possible changes in your monthly payments, loan term, and/or principal. Some plans have rate or interest caps.	Starting interest rate is slightly below market, but payments can increase sharply and frequently if index increases. Payment caps prevent wide fluctuations in payments but may cause negative amortization. Rate caps limit total amount debt can expand
Renegotiable rate mortgage (roll–over)	Interest rate and monthly payments are constant for several years; changes possible thereafter. Long–term mortgage.	Less frequent changes in interest rate offer some stability.
Balloon mortgage	Monthly payments based on fixed interest rate; usually short–term; payments may cover interest only with principal due in full at term end.	Offers low monthly payments but possibly no equity until loan is fully paid. When due, loan must be paid off or refinanced. Refinancing poses high risk if rates climb.
Graduated payment mortgage	Lower monthly payments rise gradually (usually over 5–10 years), then level off for duration of term. With adjustable interest rate, additional payment changes possible if index changes.	Easier to qualify for. Buyer's income must be able to keep pace with scheduled payment increases. With an adjustable rate, payment increases beyond the graduated payments can result in additional negative amortization..
Shared appreciation mortgage	Below–market interest rate and lower monthly payments, in exchange for a share of profits when property is sold or on a specified date. Many variations.	If home appreciates greatly, total cost of loan jumps. If home fails to appreciate, projected increase in value may still be due, requiring refinancing at possibly higher rates.
Assumable mortgage	Buyer takes over seller's original, below–market rate mortgage.	Lowers monthly payments. May be prohibited if "due on sale" clause is in original mortgage. Not permitted on most new fixed rate mortgages.
Seller take–back	Seller provides all or part of financing with a first or second mortgage.	May offer a below–market interest rate; may have a balloon payment requiring full payment in a few years or refinancing at market rates, which could sharply increase debt.
Wraparound	Seller keeps original low rate mortgage. Buyer makes payments to seller who forwards a portion to the lender holding original mortgage. Offers lower effective interest rate on total transaction.	Lender may call in old mortgage and require higher rate. If buyer defaults, seller must take legal action to collect debt.
Growing equity mortgage (rapid payoff mortgage)	Fixed interest rate but monthly payments may vary according to agreed–upon scchedule or index.	Permits rapid payoff of debt because payment increases reduce principal. Buyer's income must be able to keep up with payment increases.
Land contract	Seller retains original mortgage. No transfer of title until loan is fully paid. Equal monthly payments based on below–market interest rate with unpaid principal due at loan end.	May offer no equity until loan is fully paid. Buyer has few protections if conflict arises during loan.
Buy–down	Developer (or other party) provides an interest subsidy which lowers monthly payments during the first few years of the loan. Can have fixed or adjustable interest rate.	Offers a break from higher payments during early years. Enables buyer with lower income to qualify. With adjustable rate mortgage, payments may jump substantially at end of subsidy. Developer may increase selling price.
Rent with option	Renter pays "option fee" for right to purchase property at specified time and agreed–upon price. Rent may or may not be applied to sales price.	Enables renter to buy time to obtain down payment and decide whether to purchase. Locks in price during inflationary times. Failure to take option means loss of option fee and rental payments.
Reverse annuity mortgage (equity conversion)	Borrower owns mortgage–free property and needs income. Lender makes monthly payments to borrower, using property as collateral.	Can provide homeowners with needed cash. At end of term, borrower must have money available to avoid selling property or refinancing.

Source: The Mortgage Money Guide, Federal Trade Commission.

Mortgage Payment Tables

Source: *The Mortgage Money Guide,* Federal Trade Commission.

8% Annual Percentage Rate

Amount Financed	Monthly payments (principal and interest)*					
	5 Years	10 Years	15 Years	20 Years	25 Years	30 Years
$ 25,000	506.91	303.32	238.91	209.11	192.95	183.44
30,000	608.29	363.98	286.70	250.93	231.54	220.13
35,000	709.67	424.65	334.48	292.75	270.14	256.82
40,000	811.06	485.31	382.26	334.58	308.73	293.51
45,000	912.44	545.97	430.04	376.40	347.32	330.19
50,000	1013.82	606.64	477.83	418.22	385.91	366.88
60,000	1216.58	727.97	573.39	501.86	463.09	440.26
70,000	1419.35	849.29	668.96	585.51	540.27	513.64
80,000	1622.11	970.62	764.52	669.15	617.45	587.01
90,000	1824.88	1091.95	860.09	752.80	694.63	660.39
100,000	2027.64	1213.28	955.65	836.44	771.82	733.76

9% Annual Percentage Rate

Amount Financed	Monthly payments (principal and interest)*					
	5 Years	10 Years	15 Years	20 Years	25 Years	30 Years
$ 25,000	518.96	316.69	253.57	224.93	209.80	201.16
30,000	622.75	380.03	304.28	269.92	251.76	241.39
35,000	726.54	443.36	354.99	314.90	293.72	281.62
40,000	830.33	506.70	405.71	359.89	335.68	321.85
45,000	934.13	570.04	456.42	404.88	377.64	362.08
50,000	1037.92	633.38	507.13	449.86	419.60	402.31
60,000	1245.50	760.05	608.56	539.84	503.52	482.77
70,000	1453.08	886.73	709.99	629.81	587.44	563.24
80,000	1660.67	1013.41	811.41	719.78	671.36	643.70
90,000	1868.25	1140.08	912.84	809.75	755.28	724.16
100,000	2075.84	1266.76	1014.27	899.73	839.20	804.62

10% Annual Percentage Rate

Amount Financed	Monthly payments (principal and interest)*					
	5 Years	10 Years	15 Years	20 Years	25 Years	30 Years
$ 25,000	531.18	330.38	268.65	241.26	227.18	219.39
30,000	637.41	396.45	322.38	289.51	272.61	263.27
35,000	743.65	462.53	376.11	337.76	318.05	307.15
40,000	849.88	528.60	429.84	386.01	363.48	351.03
45,000	956.12	594.68	483.57	434.26	408.92	394.91
50,000	1062.35	660.75	537.30	482.51	454.35	438.79
60,000	1274.82	792.90	644.76	579.01	545.22	526.54
70,000	1487.29	925.06	752.22	675.52	636.09	614.30
80,000	1699.76	1057.20	859.68	772.02	726.96	702.06
90,000	1912.23	1189.36	967.14	868.52	817.83	789.81
100,000	2124.70	1321.51	1074.61	965.02	908.70	877.57

Losing Ground

Source: *The Mortgage Money Guide,* Federal Trade Commission.

Repaying debt gradually through payments of principal and interest is called amortization. Today's economic climate has given rise to a reverse process called negative amortization.

Negative amortization means that you are losing—not gaining—value, or equity. This is because your monthly payments may be too low to cover the interest rate agreed upon in the mortgage contract. Instead of paying the full interest costs now, you'll pay them later—either in larger payments or in more payments. You will also be paying interest on that interest.

In other words, the lender postpones collection of the money you owe by increasin g the size of your debt. In extreme cases, you may even lose the equity

11% Annual Percentage Rate

Monthly payments (principal and interest)*

Amount Financed	5 Years	10 Years	15 Years	20 Years	25 Years	30 Years
$ 25,000	543.56	344.38	284.15	258.05	245.03	238.08
30,000	652.27	413.25	340.98	309.66	294.03	285.70
35,000	760.98	482.13	397.81	361.27	343.04	333.31
40,000	869.70	551.00	454.64	412.88	392.05	380.93
45,000	978.41	619.88	511.47	464.48	441.05	428.55
50,000	1087.12	688.75	568.30	516.09	490.06	476.16
60,000	1304.54	826.50	681.96	619.31	588.07	571.39
70,000	1521.97	964.25	795.62	722.53	686.08	666.63
80,000	1739.39	1102.00	909.28	825.75	784.09	761.86
90,000	1956.81	1239.75	1022.94	928.97	882.10	857.09
100,000	2174.24	1377.50	1136.60	1032.19	980.11	952.32

12% Annual Percentage Rate

Monthly payments (principal and interest)*

Amount Financed	5 Years	10 Years	15 Years	20 Years	25 Years	30 Years
$ 25,000	556.11	358.68	300.05	275.28	263.31	257.16
30,000	667.33	430.42	360.06	330.33	315.97	308.59
35,000	778.56	502.15	420.06	385.39	368.63	360.02
40,000	889.78	573.89	480.07	440.44	421.29	411.45
45,000	1001.00	645.62	540.08	495.49	473.96	462.88
50,000	1112.22	717.36	600.09	550.55	526.62	514.31
60,000	1334.67	860.83	720.11	660.66	631.93	617.17
70,000	1557.11	1004.30	840.12	770.77	737.26	720.03
80,000	1779.56	1147.77	960.14	880.87	842.58	822.90
90,000	2002.00	1291.24	1080.15	990.98	947.90	925.75
100,000	2224.44	1434.71	1200.17	1101.09	1053.23	1028.62

13% Annual Percentage Rate

Monthly payments (principal and interest)*

Amount Financed	5 Years	10 Years	15 Years	20 Years	25 Years	30 Years
$ 25,000	568.83	373.28	316.32	292.90	281.96	276.55
30,000	682.60	447.94	379.58	351.48	338.36	331.86
35,000	796.36	522.59	442.84	410.06	394.75	387.17
40,000	910.13	597.25	506.10	468.64	451.14	442.48
45,000	1023.89	671.90	569.36	527.21	507.53	497.79
50,000	1137.66	746.56	632.63	585.79	563.92	553.10
60,000	1365.19	895.87	759.15	702.95	676.71	663.72
70,000	1592.72	1045.18	885.67	820.11	789.49	774.34
80,000	1820.25	1194.49	1012.20	937.27	902.27	884.96
90,000	2047.78	1343.80	1138.72	1054.42	1015.05	995.58
100,000	2275.31	1493.11	1265.25	1171.58	1127.84	1106.20

you purchased with your down payment, leaving you in worse financial shape a few years after you purchase your home than when you bought it.

Suppose you signed an adjustable rate mortgage for $50,000 in 1978. The index established your initial rate at 9.15%. It nearly doubled to 17.39% by 1981. If your monthly payments had kept pace with the index, they would have risen from $408 to $722. But because of a payment cap they stayed at $408. By 1981 your mortgage had swelled from $50,000 to $58,350, even though you had dutifully paid $408 every month for 48 months. In other words, you paid out $20,000 but you were $8,000 more in debt than you were three years earlier. During the next few years, despite the fact that the index fell gradually, you were still paying off the increases made to your principal from earlier years.

Certain loans, such as graduated payment mortgages, are structured so that you regain the lost ground with payments that eventually rise high enough to fully pay off your debt. And you may also be able to pay off the extra costs if your home is gaining rapidly in value or if your income is rising fast enough to meet the increased obligation. But if it isn't, you may realize a loss if, for example, you sign a below–market adjustable rate mortgage in January and try to sell the home in August when interest rates are higher. You could end up owing more than you'd make on the sale. □

14% Annual Percentage Rate

Amount Financed	Monthly payments (principal and interest)*					
	5 Years	10 Years	15 Years	20 Years	25 Years	30 Years
$ 25,000	581.71	388.17	332.94	310.89	300.95	296.22
30,000	698.05	465.80	399.53	373.06	361.13	355.47
35,000	814.39	543.44	466.11	435.24	421.32	414.71
40,000	930.74	621.07	532.70	497.41	481.51	473.95
45,000	1047.08	698.70	599.29	559.59	541.70	533.20
50,000	1163.42	776.34	665.88	621.77	601.89	592.44
60,000	1396.10	931.60	799.05	746.12	722.26	710.93
70,000	1628.78	1086.87	932.22	870.47	842.64	829.42
80,000	1861.47	1242.14	1065.40	994.82	963.01	947.90
90,000	2094.14	1397.40	1198.57	1119.17	1083.38	1066.38
100,000	2326.83	1552.67	1331.75	1243.53	1203.77	1184.88

15% Annual Percentage Rate

Amount Financed	Monthly payments (principal and interest)*					
	5 Years	10 Years	15 Years	20 Years	25 Years	30 Years
$ 25,000	594.75	403.34	349.90	329.20	320.21	316.12
30,000	713.70	484.01	419.88	395.04	384.25	379.34
35,000	832.65	564.68	489.86	460.88	448.30	442.56
40,000	951.60	645.34	559.84	526.72	512.34	505.78
45,000	1070.55	726.01	629.82	592.56	576.38	569.00
50,000	1189.50	806.68	699.80	658.40	640.42	632.23
60,000	1427.40	968.01	839.76	790.08	768.50	758.67
70,000	1665.30	1129.35	979.72	921.76	896.59	885.12
80,000	1903.20	1290.68	1119.67	1053.44	1024.67	1011.56
90,000	2141.09	1452.01	1259.63	1185.11	1152.75	1138.00
100,000	2379.00	1613.35	1399.59	1 316.79	1280.84	1264.45

*For loans that fully pay off the debt over the loan term.

Know Homebuying Lingo

Source: National Association of Realtors

Amortization. The gradual repayment of a mortgage by periodic installments.

Annual percentage rate (APR). The total finance charge (interest, loan fees, points) expressed as a percentage of the loan amount.

Assessed value. The valuation placed on property by a public tax assessor as the basis of property taxes.

Binder. An agreement, accompanied by a deposit, whereby the buyer evidences good faith.

Cap. The maximum amount an interest or monthly payment can change, either at adjustment time or over the life of the mortgage.

Closing. The final step in transferring ownership of a property from the seller to the buyer.

Closing costs. Fees and expenses, not including the price of the home, payable by the sell er and the buyer at the closing (e.g. brokerage commissions, title insurance premiums, and inspection, appraisal, recording, and attorney's fees).

Deed. A legal document conveying title to a property.

Escrow. The placement of money or documents with a third party for safekeeping pending the fulfilment or performance of a specified act or condition.

Lien. A legal claim against a property that must be paid when the property is sold.

Loan–to–value–ratio. The relationship between the amount of a home loan and the total value of the property. Lenders may limit their maximum loan to 80–95 percent of value.

Lock–in rate. A commitment made by lenders on a mortgage loan to "lock in" a certain rate pending loan approval. Lock–in periods vary.

Points. A dollar amount paid to the lender as a consideration for making the loan. A point is one percent of the loan amount; also called discount points.

Principal, interest, taxes, and insurance (PITI) payment. A periodic (typically monthly) payment that includes the principal and interest payment plus a contribution to the escrow account established by the lender to pay insurance premiums and property taxes on the mortgaged property.

Private mortgage insurance (PMI). Insurance issued to a lender by a private company to protect the lender against loss on a defaulted mortgage loan. Its use is usually limited to loans with high loan–to–value ratios. The borrower pays the premiums.

Shared equity mortgage. A home loan in which an investor is granted a share of the equity, thereby allowing the investor to participate in the proceeds from resale.

Title. A document that's evidence of ownership.

Title insurance. Protection for lenders and homeowners against financial loss resulting from legal debts in the title.

SOCIAL SECURITY & AGING

Is There a Lifeline in Your Future?

By Barry Robinson

Wouldn't it be wonderful if there were some way to make it possible for old people to continue living in their own homes with the comforting assurance of knowing that, if anything terrible should happen to them—such as falling down and being hurt or suddenly becoming ill—all they would have to do to summon help in such an emergency is simply press a button?

That, in brief, is the dream behind—if not always the ultimate reality of—what have come to be known as lifelines or personal alarms (frequently referred to generically as Personal Emergency Response Systems or PERS). Out of these devices has developed an evolving industry that is still seeking to define itself in terms of technical, professional, and ethical standards. In the process, it has spawned an array of products and services that, while conceived principally with the elderly in mind could also be potentially beneficial for younger adults and children.

At its simplest, a PERS consists of an electronic device that automatically sends a prearranged phone call for help if a person at home cannot use normal means to communicate in an emergency. Although some of the basic technology essential for implementing the lifeline concept has existed for years, it wasn't until the mid-1970s that parallel development of the first PERS systems began both in Sweden and the United States.

Since then, the field has grown to where it is now estimated that there are as many as 100 manufacturers of PERS products in the 12 industrialized nations where the concept has caught on most strongly, thousands of community-based programs utilizing them, and hundresds of thousands of older persons using them. In the United States alone, there are 40 PERS manufacturers, but many of them are relatively small companies.

Commonalities and Contradictions

Another indication of the field's growth is that, in June 1990, some 50 of the world's leading PERS practitioners came together in Washington at the American Lifeline Institute's *First International Symposium on Emergency Response Services for Frail Persons Living Alone* to assess where they are and where they're going. Among the conferees were health care planners, government officials, business executives, and social service administrators from England, Germany, Canada, Holland, Sweden, Denmark, Scotland, Wales, Japan, New Zealand, Israel, and the United States.

The most striking similarity among all of the countries represented at the symposium was that primary PERS users tend to be women in their 70s and 80s, who live alone and suffer from cardiac and/or muscoloskeletal problems, and who may be subject to falls. While this preponderance of female clients may be simply a reflection of the demographic reality of there being far more women (often living alone) in this age bracket than men, it may also indicate a greater willingness among older women than among older men to accept—and take steps to deal with—their own vulnerability.

Usage: While some maintain that as much as 40% of all people over age 75 may need PERS, the highest estimated actual use is 12% in the United Kingdom countries, with Canada, Holland, and Sweden averaging 3%. U.S. usage is currently pegged at 350,000 people or 2% of the nation's 75+ population.

Costs: Average prices for home PERS units range from $600 through $1,200 (although some American systems reportedly sell for as much as $4,000), plus $10–$40 monthly monitoring fees. At least one U.S. company also makes its units available on a rental basis for $35 a month, including monitoring. Payment for PERS by government or social service agencies is more common in Europe, but some support is beginning to be available in the U.S.

Benefit: Although people's lives have literally been saved through PERS-related intervention, perhaps the greatest saving has been of individual lifestyles, with psychological benefits for both users and their families. Occasionally, this can have unanticipated consequences. In Sweden, notes Bo Stenberg of Tele Larm Inc., it "has also contributed to family members feeling more secure—sometimes family members feel so secure and reassured that they tend to visit the person concerned less often."

A Link to Life for Some

Although other PERS applications will probably be developed in the near future for individuals of all ages in a variety of situations, today's lifeline systems are mostly associated with the elderly for whom they serve as a link to help and assistance in times of need. While systems and programs vary immensely from place to place and provider to provider, there are generally three parts to the process.

First, there is the electronic hardware which normally consists of a telephone plus a remote device which a person can carry or wear like a pendant or clipped to clothing. This is not an ordinary telephone, but a so-called "smart" phone which has been programmed to transmit a message to either a specified

Barry Robinson is associate editor of *Ageing International*, the journal of the International Federation on Ageing, from which this article is excerpted, and international liaison for the American Association of Retired Persons (AARP). He is the author of *Options for Older Americans, On The Beat: Policemen at Work,* and "The Vision of Aging: Sight and Insight" in *Aging and Human Visual Function,* plus numerous articles in American and Japanese periodicals.

or central receiver identifying itself and its location (and, in some cases, depending upon the technological sophistication of the system, forwarding additional information about the PERS user). In many cases, the unit can also be used as a normal telephone so it has a dual utilitarian value. The remote device is essentially an extension of the phone.

When someone needs help, all he or she has to do is press a button on the phone unit itself or on the remote device. Either way, the pressed button triggers the transmitter to send a signal to a prearranged destination which may be as near as the front desk in an apartment building's lobby or as far as a regional monitoring center.

It is in the second stage that the greatest variations exist. Depending upon the system provider and the local program, the receiving station might relay the message to a local response agency (such as a rescue or first aid squad) for follow-up or, in an apartment house, building managers might investigate directly themselves. Some units are equipped with speakerphones which enable the party receiving the signal to attempt to make voice contact with the individual seeking help. Obviously, if a person lapses into unconsciousness after pressing the button, conversation is not possible, but that in itself tells the monitor something about the seriousness of the situation. Once the nature of the problem has been determined, the third stage of the process involves dispatching appropriate assistance.

Some systems go beyond this in the kind of linkage they provide or at least make possible. In Japan, for instance, there are ongoing experiments with *Hana-Chan*, a "human contact service." (Hana is a name common among older women, and chan is an endearing form of address usually used with children.)

"Beyond allowing emergency signals to be sent by only a single touch of the stick," explains Masayuki Abe of Nippon Telegraph and Telephone Corp. (NTT), "the Hana-Chan telephone center makes phone calls twice a day to ask after users and relay messages. . . . A further enrichment is planned to provide users with living information and health information from the center." Eventually, this could extend beyond telephone contact to a more ambitious system which "offers consultations to help members meet the needs of daily life and provides information on living, health, and other needs, such as an escort service to the hospital in cases of non-emergencies."

Of course, all of this costs money and, at a time when governments around the world are looking for ways to restrain burgeoning health care and social welfare expenditures, there is some question about how much farther they will be willing to go in paying for such helpful, but not necessarily essential, programs.

All of this sounds good, but no one really knows for sure how well the lifeline concept will work over the long run—or, for that matter, right now. Because PERS is still in a relatively early stage of development, much of what is known about it usually tends to be anecdotal with few meaningful statistics available. There have been some attempts to measure its effectiveness in terms of use, client satisfaction, and whether the presence off a PERS unit in a household prevents or postpones individual institutionalization. By these criteria, PERS generally does well, but there are shortcomings stemming from the nature of the devices and the nature of human beings.

Most of the PERS at present in use around the world utilize "active" devices which send for help only when the user activates them. If a person sud-

denly loses consciousness and is unable to push the remote button—or if the remote unit isn't available on his or her person—no signal is transmitted. "Passive" systems are one way of avoiding this gap. However, this more effective means of determining if and when a person needs help is also the most intrusive—and therefore the least acceptable.

In "passive" systems, electronic sensors monitor such things as the opening of refrigerator and bathroom doors, any sudden motion at or near floor level, the flushing of toilets, etc., and then relay the information to the PERS center for analysis on a regular basis. The absence of activity acts as an indication that something may be wrong. Practitioners and planners tend to think such innovations are wonderful; the elderly themselves, however, are not so sure. In Japan, for instance, older people responded quite positively to survey questions about their perceptions of the usefulness of passive PERS devices, but very few Japanese elders have agreed to allow them in their homes, preferring the active models instead.

Doing Well By Doing Good?

When it succeeds in its mission, the PERS industry serves as a catalyst in which commerce and conscience come conveniently together for the benefit of all. This, however, is not always the case, and reports of consumer abuse and outright fraud are beginning to surface in the U.S. For instance, grisly details about a crime that never actually occurred were allegedly used to sell systems to people in San Francisco. And, in Baltimore, some 200 PERS units were sold to older women for $1,295 each, a price which was supposed to include prepaid monitoring service for three years. The firm, however, failed to pay the company that would be doing the actual monitoring, thereby making the products useless for all intents and purposes.

"This is not a problem industry in that the units usually work well," commented John Nethercut, an Assistant Attorney General of Maryland, to *The New York Times*, "but it is a dangerous industry because the consumers tend to be old and scared and vulnerable."

Exploiting old peoples' self-perception of fear and vulnerability is not confined to unscrupulous salesmen seeking to sell individuals a more or less basically sound product which, although they may or may not actually need it, will not necessarily do them harm other than financial distress. This same exploitation of human emotions is at the root of a controversial television commercial that has become fodder for comedians, disc jockeys, and late night talk show hosts. In the commercial, an older woman with a PERS button hanging around her neck, is shown lying on the floor as she cries out: "I've fallen and I can't get up."

In all fairness, it should be pointed out that the commercial's star, Edith Fore, of Camden, N.J., is not a professional actress, and the situation she portrays is real. In fact, something similar actually happened to her, so there is a very definite element of truth in at least this advertising. Mrs. Fore plays "Mrs. Fletcher" who has an accident in her home and sends for help via PERS. Not long after being widowed, Mrs. Fore fell down in *her* home and sent for help by pressing the button on the device she was wearing.

While the commercial is not specifically based on her own experience, this coincidence may have weighed in her favor when she was auditioning for the commercial.

Before Lifecall Systems discovered Mrs. Fore, its TV commercials featured one of America's most famous entertainers, the 95-year-old comedian George Burns, who puffed on his cigar and told a few jokes, but did not lie on the floor. With Mrs. Fore on the floor, Lifecall's sales accelerated, and Mrs. Fore herself blossomed into a sort of *camp* comedy cult figure who now appears at nightclubs, judging talent contests featuring people trying to mimic her. T-shirts bearing her now-famous line have become hot items in novelty shops. For her role in the commercial, she was only paid a flat fee of $1,000 but, because of it, Edith Fore has become a celebrity. In the approximate words of Andy Warhol who coined the idea of everyone being famous for at least a quarter of an hour—Mrs. Fore, *this* is *your* 15 minutes.

A Lifeline to the Future?

It is doubtful if anyone actually intended to make a commercial people would laugh at, and that worries some of us in the aging field. If an old person in distress in a television portrayal is now perceived as an object of ridicule by a sizable segment of the public, how will they react to the real thing? Will old people with real problems evoke the same scorn as the woman on TV?

While sales pitches utilizing scare tactics seem to attract the most public attention due to their sensational aspects, most advertising and promotion for PERS systems actually tends to be generally benign, stressing serenity rather than fear in slogans like "peace of mind for the whole family." There is also some emphasis on the secondary convenience features of PERS in which one's telephone can be programmed to do a variety of chores.

"There is a need [for PERS] by many groups, including unsupervised children, younger disabled persons, and anyone in a threatening environment, such as employees alone at night or those subject to marital violence or racial harassment," observes Andrew Dibner, president of the American Lifeline Institute and former president of Lifeline Systems Inc., who is widely credited in the United States with being the inventor—or, at least, the innovator of—PERS. "Equipment must be developed to meet the special needs of these groups, and marketing and distribution needs to sensitively present it to assure its acceptance as a new aid."

Adding automatic dialing and remote radio control to the old familiar telephone led to the creation of PERS. And what will PERS lead to?

With lifeline technology expanding and extending into new and unanticipated area, there will, of course, be still more questions about the trade-off of sacrificing personal privacy for security and lifestyle enhancements, and speculation about where all this is going to lead in terms of personal autonomy vs. societal control.

Not to many years ago, there were jokes about how Social Security would eventually develop to the point where, as soon as a person was born, he or she would be assigned his or her own number and card. With Americans now being registered for Social Security at earlier and earlier ages, no one jokes about that possibility anymore.

So it is not inconceivable that the time may come when everyone has his or her own portable PERS unit that they wear at all times so that, at any given moment, a central monitoring station can know where they are and what they're doing, and can send help right away, whether they need it or not. Relax. It's only a joke . . . now.

For More Information:

The Consumer Affairs section of the American Association of Retired Persons (AARP) has been monitoring the development of the lifeline services industry since the first products came on the market, and is developing a new publication about PERS which is expected to be available in early 1992. For information, write to AARP Consumer Affairs, 601 E Street N.W., Washington, D.C. 20049.

Condensed excerpts of presentations from the *First International Symposium on Emergency Response Services for Frail Persons Living Alone* mentioned earlier in this article are featured in the *International Journal of Technology & Aging*'s special Spring/Summer 1991 issue on "Personal Response Systems." Check your local public or college library, or contact Human Sciences Press, 233 Spring Street, New York, N.Y. 10013-1578. □

Barriers to Employment of Older Workers

Source: U.S. Department of Agriculture

Early retirement (labor force withdrawal prior to age 65) has become the norm. By age 62, almost half of all people are out of the labor force, that is, neither working nor looking for a job. Anticipating a dramatic decline in the ratio of workers to retirees as the baby-boom generation becomes eligible for retirement early in the next century, Federal policy has been directed toward encouraging workers to extend their work lives. However, older workers who might want to work still face various institutional barriers through (1) the impact of Social Security regulations and pension policies on work activity, (2) the market for part-time jobs, and (3) age discrimination.

The Social Security amendments of 1983 contained several long-term provisions, designed to remove work disincentives. These include:

• Beginning in the year 2000, the retirement age at which beneficiaries are eligible to receive full benefits will increase gradually from 65 to 67.

• Reduced benefits will continue to be available at age 62, but reduction factors will be revised to a maximum of 30 percent (for workers entitled at 62 when the normal retirement age is 67) compared to the prior 20 percent reduction.

• The delayed retirement credit will increase by half a percentage point for every other year, from 3 percent for workers age 62 prior to 1987 to 8 percent per year for workers age 62 after 2004.

• Beginning in 1990, the withholding rate decreased from $1 of every $2 above the exempt amount for persons who attain full retirement age to $1 of every three dollars. □

Social Security

The original Social Security Act was passed in 1935 and amended in 1939, 1946, 1950, 1952, 1954, 1956, 1958, 1960, 1961, 1965, 1967, 1969, 1972, 1974, 1977, 1980-1984, 1986, and 1988-1989.

The act is administered by the Social Security Administration and the Health Care Financing Administration, and other agencies within the Department of Health and Human Services.

For purposes of clarity, the explanations given below will describe the provisions of the act as amended.

Old Age, Disability, and Survivors Insurance

Practically everyone who works fairly regularly is covered by social security. Most state and local government employees are covered under voluntary agreements between states and the Secretary of Health and Human Services. Workers not covered include most federal civilian employees hired prior to January 1984, career railroad workers, and a few other exceptions.

Cash tips count for Social Security if they amount to $20 or more in a month from employment with a single employer.

To qualify for benefits or make payments possible for your survivors, you must be in work covered by the law for a certain number of "quarters of coverage." Before 1978, a quarter of coverage was earned if a worker was paid $50 or more wages in a 3-month calendar quarter. A self-employed person got 4 "quarters of coverage" for a year in which his net earnings were $400 or more.

In 1978, a worker, whether employed or self-employed, received one quarter of coverage for each $250 of covered annual earnings up to a maximum of four for a year. The quarter of coverage measure was increased to $260 in 1979 and $290 in 1980, $310 in 1981, $340 in 1982, $370 in 1983, $390 in 1984, $410 in 1985, $440 in 1986, $460 in 1987, $470 in 1988, $500 in 1989, $520 in 1990, $540 in 1991, and will increase automatically in future years to keep pace with increases in average wages. The number of quarters needed differs for different persons and depends on the date of your birth; in general, it is related to the number of years after 1950, or after the year you reach 21, if later, and up to the year you reach 62, become disabled, or die. One "quarter of coverage" is required for each such year in order for you or your family to get benefits. No one will need more than 40 quarters. Your local Social Security office can tell you how long you need to work.

Who Pays for the Insurance?

Both workers and their employers pay for the workers' insurance. Self-employed persons pay their own social security contributions annually along with their income tax. The rates include the cost of Medicare hospital insurance. The contribution and benefit base is $53,400 for 1991 for retirement, survivor and disability coverage, and $125,000 for Medicare coverage, and will increase automatically in future years as earnings levels rise. The contribution rate schedules under present law are shown in a table in this section.

Social Security Contribution and Rate Schedule
(percent of covered earnings)

Year	Retirement survivors, and disability insurance	Hospital insurance	Year
EMPLOYERS AND EMPLOYEES			
1978	4.95 %	1.10 %	6.05 %
1979-80	5.08	1.05	6.13
1981	5.35	1.30	6.65
1982-83	5.40	1.30	6.70
1984	5.70	1.30	7.00
1985	5.70	1.35	7.05
1986-87	5.70	1.45	7.15
1988-89	6.06	1.45	7.51
1990 & later	6.20	1.45	7.65
SELF-EMPLOYED			
1978	7.00 %	1.10 %	8.10 %
1979-80	7.05	1.05	8.10
1981	8.00	1.30	9.30
1982	8.05	1.30	9.35
1983	8.05	1.30	9.35
1984	11.40	2.60	*14.00
1985	11.40	2.70	*14.10
1986-87	11.40	2.90	*14.30
1988-89	12.12	2.90	*15.02
1990 & later	12.40	2.90	*15.30

*The law provides credit against self-employment tax liability in the following manner: 2.7% in 1984; 2.3% in 1985; 2.09% 1986-1989 and, beginning with the 1990 taxable year, the credit is replaced.

The separate payroll contribution to finance hospital insurance is placed in a separate trust fund in the U.S. Treasury. In addition, the medical insurance premiums, currently $29.90 a month in 1991, and the government's shares go into another separate trust fund.

How to Apply for Benefits

You apply for benefits by filing a claim either in person, by mail, or by telephone at any social security office. You can get the address either from the post office or from the phone book under the listing, United States Government—Department of Health and Human Services—Social Security Administration. You will need certain kinds of proof, depending upon the type of benefit you are claiming. If it is a retirement benefit, you should provide a birth certificate, or religious record. If you are unable to get these documents, other old documents showing your age or date of birth—such as census records, school records, early naturalization certificate, etc.—may be acceptable. A widow, or widower, 60 or older who is claiming widow's benefits based on his or her spouse's earnings should have both proof of age and a copy of the marriage certificate. A child claiming child's benefits should provide a birth certificate. If formal proof is not available, the Social Security office will tell you what kinds of information will be acceptable.

Delayed Retirement Credit Rates

Age 62	Monthly percentage	Yearly percentage
Prior to 1979	1/12 of 1%	1%
1979-1986	1/4 of 1%	3%
1987-1988	7/24 of 1%	3.5%
1989-1990	1/3 of 1%	4%
1991-1992	3/8 of 1%	4.5%
1993-1994	5/12 of 1%	5%
1995-1996	11/24 of 1%	5.5%
1997-1998	1/2 of 1%	6%
1999-2000	13/24 of 1%	6.5%
2001-2002	7/12 of 1%	7%
2003-2004	5/8 of 1%	7.5%
2005 or later	2/3 of 1%	8%

What Does Social Security Offer?

The Social Security contribution you pay gives you four different kinds of protection: (1) retirement benefits, (2) survivors' benefits, (3) disability benefits, and (4) Medicare hospital insurance benefits.

Retirement benefits. Currently, a worker becomes eligible for the full amount of his retirement benefits at age 65, if he has retired under the definition in the law. A worker may retire at 62 and get 80% of his full benefit. The closer he is to age 65 when he starts collecting his benefit, the larger is the fraction of his full benefit that he will get.

The amount of the retirement benefit you are entitled to at 65 is the key to all other benefits under the program. The retirement benefit is based on covered earnings, generally those after 1950. Your covered earnings will be updated (indexed) to the second year before you reach age 62, become disabled, or die, and will reflect the increases in average wages that have occurred since the earnings were paid.

A worker who delays his retirement past age 65, or who does not receive a benefit for some months after age 65 because of high earnings will get a special credit that can mean a larger benefit. The credit adds to a worker's benefits 1% (3% for workers age 62 after 1978) for each year (1/12 of 1% for each month) from age 65 to age 70 for which he did not get benefits. (*See* table.)

The law provides a special minimum benefit at retirement for people who worked under Social Security for many years. The provision will help people who had low incomes, but above a specific level, in their working years. The amount of the special minimum depends on the number of years of coverage. For a worker retiring at 65 in Jan. 1991 with 30 or more years of coverage, the special minimum benefit would be $461.20 (effective December 1984). These benefits are reduced if a worker is under 65 and are increased automatically for increases in the cost of living.

If you retired at age 65 in Jan. 1991 with average earnings, you would get a benefit of $750.50.

If your spouse is also 65, then he or she will get a spouse's benefit that is equal to half your benefit. So if your benefit is $750.50, your spouse gets $375.20.

If your spouse is between ages 62 and 65, he or she can draw a reduced benefit; the amount depends on the number of months before 65 that he or she starts getting checks. If he or she draws his or her benefit when he or she is 62, he or she will get about 3/8 of your basic benefit, or $281.40. (He or she will get this amount for the rest of his or her life, unless you should die first; then he or she can start getting widow's or widower's benefits, described below.)

If the spouse is entitled to a worker's retirement benefit on his or her own earnings, he or she can draw whichever amount is larger. If the spouse is entitled to a retirement benefit which is less than the spouse's benefit, he or she will receive his or her own retirement benefit plus the difference between the retirement benefit and the spouse's benefit.

If you have children under 18 or a child under age 19 in full-time attendance at an elementary or secondary school or a son or daughter who became totally disabled prior to reaching age 22, when you retire they will get a benefit equal to half your full retirement benefits (subject to maximum payments that can be made to a family). If your spouse is caring for a child who is under 16 or who became disabled before 22 (and getting benefits too), he or she is eligible for benefits, even if he or she is under 62.

In general, the highest retirement check that can be paid to a worker who retired at 65 in Jan. 1991 is about $1022.90 a month. Maximum payment to the family of this retired worker is about $1,790.60 in Jan. 1991. When your children reach age 18, their benefits will stop except for children under age 19 attending an elementary or secondary school and except for a benefit that is going to a son or daughter who became totally disabled before attaining age 22. Such a person can continue to get his benefits as long as his disability meets the definition in the law.

If you are divorced, you can get Social Security benefits (the same as a spouse or widow, or widower), based on your ex-spouse's earnings record if you were married at least 10 years and your ex-spouse has retired, become disabled, or died. If a divorced spouse has been divorced for at least 2 years, the spouse may be eligible for benefits even if the worker is not receiving benefits. However, both the worker and spouse must be age 62 or over and the worker must be fully insured.

Survivor benefits. This feature of the social security program gives your family valuable life insurance protection—in some cases benefits to a family could amount to $100,000 or more over a period of years. The amount of protection is again geared to what the worker would be entitled to if he had been age 65 when he died. Your survivors could get:

1. A one-time cash payment. [NOTE: There is no restriction on the use of the lump-sum death payment.] This "lump-sum death payment" is $255.

2. A benefit for each child until he reaches 18, or 19 if the child is in full-time attendance at an elementary or secondary school or at any age if disabled before 22. Each eligible child receives 75% of the basic benefit (subject to reduction for the family maximum). A disabled child can continue to collect benefits after age 22.) If certain conditions are met, dependent grandchildren of insured workers can receive survivor or dependent benefits.

3. A benefit for your widow(er) at any age, if she/he has children under 16 or disabled in care. Her/his benefit is also 75% of the basic benefit. She/he can collect this as long as she/he has a child under 16 or disabled now "in care." Payments stop then (they will start again upon application when she/he is 60 at a slightly lower amount).

Total family survivor benefits are estimated to be as high as $2,183.20 a month if the worker dies in 1991.

4. If there are no children either under 16 or disabled, your spouse can get a widow's, or widower's benefit starting at age 60. This would come to 71 1/2% of the basic amount at age 60. A widow, or widower, who first becomes entitled at 65 or later may get 100% of his or her deceased spouse's basic amount (provided neither he nor she ever drew reduced benefits).

5. Dependent parents can sometimes collect survivors' benefits. They are usually eligible if: (a) they were getting at least half their support from the deceased worker at (1) the time of the worker's death if the worker did not qualify for disability benefits before death, or (2) if the worker had been entitled to disability benefits which had not been terminated before death either at the beginning of the period of disability or at the time of death; (b) they have reached 62; and (c) they are not eligible for a greater retirement benefit based on their own earnings. A single surviving parent can then get 82 1/2% of the basic benefit. If two parents are eligible, each would get 75%.

Here is an example of survivors' benefits in one family situation: John Jones died at age 29 in June 1990 leaving a wife and two children aged one and three. He had average covered earnings under Social Security. Family survivors' benefits would include: (1) a cash lump-sum death payment of $255, and (2) a total monthly benefit of $1,317 for the family. When the children reach 18, their benefits stop unless they are attending an elementary or secondary school full time, in which case payments continue up to age 19. When the older child no longer collects benefits, the widow and younger child continue to get benefits until that child is 16. He will still get a benefit until age 18 (or age 19, if he continues in elementary or secondary school), but Mrs. Jones' checks will stop. When Mrs. Jones becomes 60 (assuming she has not remarried), she will be able to get a reduced widow's benefit if she so chooses, or she can wait until age 65 to get a full benefit.

If in addition to your Social Security benefit as a wife, husband, widow, or widower you receive a pension based on your work in employment not covered by Social Security, your benefit as a spouse or survivor will be reduced by 2/3rds of the amount of that pension. Under an exception in the law, your government pension will not affect your spouse's or survivor's benefit if you became eligible for that pension before December 1982 and if, at the time you apply or become entitled to your social security benefit as a spouse or survivor, you could have qualified for that benefit if the law in effect in January 1977 had remained in effect (i.e., at that time, men had to prove they were dependent upon their wives for support to be eligible for benefits as a spouse or survivor.) There are also several other exceptions in the law. Your government pension, however, currently will not affect any Social Security benefit based on your own work covered by social security.

Disability Benefits. Disability benefits can be paid to several groups of people:

Disabled workers under 65 and their families.

Persons disabled before 22 who continue to be disabled. These benefits are payable as early as 18 when a parent (or grandparent under certain circumstances) receives social security retirement or disability benefits or when an insured parent dies.

Work Credit for Disabilty Benefits

Born after 1929, become disabled at age	Born before 1930, become disabled before 62 in	Years of work credit you need
42 or younger	1971	5
44	1973	5 1/2
46	1975	6
48	1977	6 1/2
50	1979	7
51	1980	7 1/4
52	1981	7 1/2
54	1983	8
56	1985	8 1/2
58	1987	9
60	1989	9 1/2
62 or older	1991 or later	10

NOTE: Five years of this credit must have been earned in the 10 years ending when you became disabled; years need not be continuous or in units of full years.

Disabled widows and widowers and (under certain conditions) disabled surviving divorced spouses of workers who were insured at death. These benefits are payable as early as 50.

A disabled person is eligible for Medicare after being entitled to disability payments for 24 months.

If you are a worker and become severely disabled, you will be eligible for monthly benefits if you have worked under Social Security long enough and recently enough. The amount of work you will need depends on your age when you become disabled:

Before 24: You need credit for 1 1/2 years of work in the 3-year period ending when your disability begins.

24 through 30: You need credit for having worked half the time between 21 and the time you become disabled.

31 or older: All workers disabled at 31 or older—except the blind—need the amount of credit shown in the chart.

To be considered disabled under the social security law you must be: (1) unable to engage in any substantial activity because of any medically determinable physical or mental impairment which can be expected to result in death or has lasted for 12 continuous months, or (2) blind. A person whose vision is no better than 20/200 even with glasses, or who has a limited visual field of 20 degrees or less, is considered "blind" under the social security law.

If you meet these conditions, you may be able to get payments even if your recovery from the disability is expected.

The medical evidence from your physician or other sources will show the severity of your condition and the extent to which it prevents you from doing substantial gainful work. Your age, education, training, and work experience also may be considered in deciding whether you are able to work. If you can't do your regular work but can do other substantial gainful work, you will not be considered disabled.

While you are receiving benefits as a disabled worker, payments can also be made to certain members of your family. These family members include:

Your unmarried children under 18.

Your children under 19 if they are unmarried and

attending an elementary or secondary school full time.

Your unmarried children 18 or older who were disabled before reaching 22 and continue to be disabled.

Your spouse at any age if she/he has in-care a child who is under 16 or disabled and who is getting benefits based on your social security record.

Your spouse 62 or older even if there are no children entitled to benefits.

A child may be eligible on a grandparent's social security record only if the child's parents are disabled or deceased and the child was living with and receiving 1/2 support from the grandparent at the time the grandparent qualified for benefits.

Benefits begin after a waiting period of 5 full calendar months. No benefits can be paid for these first 5 months of disability; therefore, the first payment is for the 6th full month. If you are disabled more than 6 full months before you apply, back benefits may be payable, but not before the 6th full month of disability. It is important to apply soon after the disability starts because back payments are limited to the 12 months preceding the month you apply.

Certain disabled people under 65 are eligible for Medicare. They include disabled workers at any age, persons who became disabled before age 22, and disabled widows and widowers age 50 or over who have been entitled to disability checks for 2 years or more.

Medicare protection generally ends when monthly disability benefits end, and can continue an additional 3 years after benefits stop because an individual returns to gainful work. (Under certain circumstances, former disability beneficiaries may purchase continued Medicare coverage. *See* "Do You Qualify for Hospital Insurance?" in this section.)

If a person becomes entitled to disability benefits again, Medicare coverage starts at the same time if a worker becomes disabled again within 5 years after benefits end (or within 7 years for a disabled widow, widower, or person disabled before age 22).

Benefits to workers disabled after 1978 and their dependents are based, in part, on earnings that have been adjusted to take account of increases in average wages since they were earned. The adjusted earnings are averaged together and a formula is applied to the adjusted average to figure the benefit rate.

Monthly benefits in Jan. 1991 or later can be as high as $1,214.20 for a worker and as high as $1,821.30 for a worker with a family. Once a person starts receiving benefits, the amount will increase automatically in future years to keep pace with the rising cost of living.

If you receive benefits as a disabled worker, an adult disabled since childhood, or a disabled widow or widower, you are not subject to the general rule under which some benefits are withheld if you have substantial earnings. There are special rules, which include medical considerations, for determining how any work you do might affect your disability payments.

If one of your dependents who is under 65 and who is not disabled works and earns more than $7,080 in 1991, some of the dependent's benefits may be withheld. In general, $1 in benefits is withheld for each $2 over $7,080. Different rules apply to your dependents who are 65 or over. A person 65 or over can earn $9,720 in 1991 without having benefits withheld. For persons 65 or over, $1 in benefits is withheld for $3 in earnings over $9,720.

The amount a person can earn without having any benefits withheld will increase in future years as the level of average wages rises.

If you are receiving disability benefits, you are required by law to let the Social Security Administration know if your condition improves or if you return to work no matter how little you earn.

If at any time medical evidence shows that you no longer meet the requirements for entitlement to disability benefits, you will still receive benefits for a 3-month period of adjustment. Benefits will then be stopped.

Whether or not you report a return to work or that your condition has improved, Social Security will review your claim periodically to see if you continue to meet the requirements for benefits.

If you are a disabled worker or a person disabled in childhood and you return to work in spite of a severe condition, your benefits may continue to be paid during a trial work period of up to 9 months—not necessarily consecutive months. This will give you a chance to test your ability to work. If after 9 service months it is decided that you are able to do substantial gainful work, your benefits will be paid for an adjustment period of 3 additional months.

Thus, if you go to work in spite of your disability, you may continue to receive disability benefits for up to 12 months, even though the work is substantial gainful work. If it is decided that the work you are able to do is not substantial and gainful, you may continue to receive benefits. Of course, should you no longer meet the requirements for entitlement to disability, your benefits would be stopped after a 3-month adjustment period even though your trial work period might not be over.

Disabled widows and widowers also can have a trial work period. If your benefits are stopped because you return to work and you become unable to continue working within the next 33 months, your benefits can be restarted automatically. You do not have to file a new disability application.

You Can Earn Income Without Losing Benefits

If you are 70 or over you can earn any amount and still get all your benefits. If you are under 70, you can receive all benefits if your earnings do not exceed the annual exempt amount. The annual amount for 1991 is $9,720 for people 65 or over and $7,080 for people under 65.

If your earnings go over the annual amount, $1 in benefits is withheld for each $2 ($3 if age 65-69) of earnings above the limit.

The monthly measure used for 1977 and earlier years to determine whether benefits could be paid for any month during which they earned 1/12 or less of the annual exempt amount and did not substantial work in their business has been eliminated. A person can now use the monthly test only in the first year that he or she has a month in which earnings do not exceed 1/12 of the annual exempt amount or does not perform substantial services in self-employment. If such a month occurs in 1991, a benefit can be paid for any month in which you earn $810 or less (if 65 or older) or $590 (if under 65) and don't perform substantial services in self-employment even though your total yearly earnings exceed the annual amount.

The annual exempt amount will increase automatically as the level of average wages rises.

If a worker's earnings exceed the exempt amount, social security benefits to his dependents may be reduced. However, a dependent's benefits will not be reduced if another dependent has excess earnings.

Anyone earning over the annual exempt amount a year while receiving benefits (and under age 70) must report these earnings to the Social Security Administration. If you continue to work after you have applied for social security, your additional earnings may increase the amount of your monthly payment. This will be done automatically by the Social Security Administration. You need not ask for it.

Medicare

The Medicare program is administered by the Health Care Financing Administration.

Most people 65 and over and many under 65 who have been entitled to disability checks for at least 2 years have Medicare protection. So do insured people and their dependents who need a kidney transplant or dialysis treatment because of permanent kidney failure.

The hospital insurance part of Medicare helps pay the cost of inpatient hospital care and certain kinds of follow-up care. The medical insurance part helps pay for the cost of doctors' services, outpatient hospital services, and for certain other medical items and services.

A person who is eligible for monthly benefits at 65 gets hospital insurance automatically and does not have to pay a premium. He does pay a monthly premium for medical insurance.

Supplemental Security Income

The supplemental security income (SSI) program is a federally funded program administered by the Social Security Administration. Its basic purpose is to assure a minimum level of income to people who are elderly (65 or over), blind or disabled, and who have limited income and resources.

In 1991, the maximum Federal SSI payment was $407 a month for an individual and $610 a month for a couple. But in many States, SSI payments are much higher because the State adds to the Federal payment.

Countable resources must be valued at $2,000 or less for an individual or $3,000 or less for a couple. But not all the things people own count for SSI. For instance, the house a person lives in and the land around it, and usually, one car does not count.

Generally, depending on the State, people who get SSI can also get Medicaid to pay for their health care costs as well as food stamps and other social services. And in many States an application for SSI is an application for Medicaid, so people do not have to make separate applications. Certain people can also apply for food stamps at the same Social Security office where they apply for SSI.

Social Security representatives will need information about the income and resources and the citizenship or alien status of people applying for benefits. If the person is living with a spouse, or the application is for a disabled child living with parents, the same information is needed about the spouse/parents.

People who are age 65 or over will need proof of their age such as a birth certificate, or religious record. And if a person who is filing is disabled or blind, Social Security will need information about the impairment and its treatment history.

It helps if people have this information and evidence with them when they talk to their Social Security representative. But they do not need to have **any** of these things to **start** their application. All they need to do is to call Social Security to find out if they are eligible for SSI payments and the other benefits that come with it. Benefits are not retroactive, so delay can cost money.

The Social Security representative will explain just what information/evidence is needed for the SSI claim, and will provide help in getting it if help is needed. Most Social Security offices will make an appointment for an office visit or for a telephone interview if that is more convenient. Or people can just walk in, and wait until someone is free to help them.

Over 4.8 million people receive SSI benefits now. Many receive both SSI and Social Security. Do not wait. Call 1-800-234-5SSA, and find out more about SSI. Even the call is free!

How to Protect Your Social Security Record

Always show your Social Security card when you start a new job. In that way you will be sure that your earnings will be credited to *your* Social Security record and not someone else's. If you lose your Social Security card, contact Social Security to find out how to apply for a new one. When a woman marries, she should apply for a new card showing her married name (and the same number).

Public Assistance

The Federal government makes grants to the states to help them provide financial assistance, medical care, and social services to certain persons in need, including children dependent because of the death, absence from home, incapacity, or (in some states) unemployment of a parent. In addition, some help is provided from only state and/or local funds to some other needy persons.

Federal sharing in state cash assistance expenditures made in accordance with the Social Security Act is based on formulas which are set forth in the Act. The Social Security Act gives the states the option of using one of two formulas, whichever is to its benefit. One formula limits the amount of assistance payment in which there is federal sharing. The other formula permits federal sharing without a limit on the amount of assistance payment. Administrative costs in all the programs are shared equally by the federal and state governments.

Within these and other general patterns set by the requirements of the Social Security Act and their administrative interpretations, each state initiates and administers its own public assistance programs, including the determination of who is eligible to receive assistance, and how much can be granted and under what conditions. Assistance is in the form of cash payments made to recipients, except that direct payments are used for medical care, and restricted payments may be used in cases of mismanagement. Other social services are provided, in some instances, to help assistance recipients increase their capacity for self-care and self-support or to strengthen family life.

In the medical assistance Medicaid program, federal funds pay 50% to 83% of the costs for medical care. If it is to a state's benefit, it may use the Medicaid formula for federal sharing for its money payment programs, ignoring the maximum on dollar amounts per recipient.

Medicare Program

The Medicare program is a federal health-insurance program for persons 65 and over, disabled people under 65 who have been entitled to social security disability benefits at least 24 months, or have worked long enough in Federal employment to be insured for Medicare, and insured workers and their dependents at any age who need dialysis treatment or a kidney transplant because of permanent kidney failure.

Enacted under the Social Security Amendments of 1965, Medicare's official name is Title XVIII of the Social Security Act. These amendments also carried Title XIX, providing federal assistance to state medical-aid programs, which has come to be known as Medicaid.

Medicare

It will be helpful to your understanding of the Medicare program if you keep the following points in mind:

- The federal health-insurance program does not of itself offer medical services. It helps pay hospital, doctor, and other medical bills. You choose your own doctor, who prescribes your treatment and place of treatment. But, you should always make sure that health care facilities or persons who provide you with treatment or services are participating in Medicare. Usually, Medicare cannot pay for care from non-participating health care organizations.
- There are two parts of the program: (1) The hospital insurance part for the payment of most of the cost of covered care provided by participating hospitals, skilled nursing facilities, and home health agencies. (2) The medical insurance part which helps pay doctors' bills and certain other expenses.
- Another important point to remember: While Medicare pays the major share of the costs of many illnesses requiring hospitalization, it does not offer adequate protection for long-term illness or mental illness.
- Therefore, it may be advisable not to cancel any private health insurance you now carry. You may wish to cancel a policy whose benefits are duplicated by the federal program, and consider a new policy that will provide for the payment of costs not covered by the federal program. Private insurance companies offer policies supplementing the protection offered by the federal program.
- If you want help in deciding whether to buy private supplemental insurance, ask at any social security office for the pamphlet, *Guide to Health Insurance for People with Medicare*. This free pamphlet describes the various types of supplemental insurance available.

Do You Qualify for Hospital Insurance?

If you're entitled to monthly social security or railroad retirement checks (as a worker, dependent, or survivor), you have hospital insurance protection automatically when you're 65. Disabled people under 65 will have hospital insurance automatically after they have been entitled to social security disability benefits for 24 months. Effective July 1, 1990, for-mer disability beneficiaries will be able to purchase hospital insurance after their premium-free coverage stops due to work activity. Federal employees who are disabled before 65 may be eligible on the basis of Federal employment. (Disabled people who get railroad annuities must meet special requirements.) People 65 or older who are not entitled to monthly benefits must have worked long enough under Social Security or the railroad retirement system or in covered Federal employment to get hospital insurance without paying a monthly premium. If they do not have enough work, they can buy hospital insurance. The premium is $177 a month in 1991. People are eligible at any age if they need maintenance dialysis or a kidney transplant for permanent kidney failure and are getting monthly Social Security or railroad retirement benefits or have worked long enough.

To be sure your protection will start the month you reach 65, apply for Medicare insurance 3 months before reaching 65, even if you don't plan to retire.

Do You Qualify for Voluntary Medical Insurance?

The voluntary medical insurance plan is a vital supplement to the hospital plan. It helps pay for doctors' and other medical services. Many people have not been able to obtain such insurance from private companies because they could not afford it or because of their medical histories.

One difference between the hospital insurance plan and the medical insurance plan is that you do not have to be under the social security or railroad retirement systems to enroll in the medical plan. Almost anyone who is 65 or older or who is eligible for hospital insurance can enroll in medical insurance.

People who get social security benefits or retirement benefits under the railroad retirement system will be enrolled automatically for medical insurance—unless they say they don't want it—when they become entitled to hospital insurance. Automatic enrollment does not apply to people who plan to continue working past 65, who are disabled widows or widowers between 50 and 65 who aren't getting disability checks, who are 65 but have not worked long enough to be eligible for hospital insurance, who have permanent kidney failure, who are eligible for Medicare on the basis of Federal employment, or who live in Puerto Rico or foreign countries. These people have to apply for medical insurance if they want it. People who have medical insurance pay a monthly premium covering part of the cost of this protection. The other part is paid from general federal revenues. The basic premium for enrollees is $29.90 a month in 1991.

Is Other Insurance Necessary?

As already indicated, Medicare provides only partial reimbursement. Therefore, you should know how much medical cost you can bear and perhaps arrange for other insurance.

In 1991, for the first 60 days of inpatient hospital care in each benefit period, hospital insurance pays for all covered services except for the first $628. For the 61st through 90th day of a covered inpatient hospital stay, hospital insurance pays for all covered services except for $157 a day. People who need to be in a hospital for more than 90 days in a benefit period can use some or all of their 60 lifetime reserve days. Hospital insurance pays for all covered services except for $314 a day for each reserve day used. Hospital insurance also does not pay the full cost of an inpatient stay in a skilled nursing facility.

Under medical insurance, the patient must meet an annual deductible. In 1991, the annual deductible is $100. After the patient has met the deductible, each year, medical insurance generally pays 80% of the approved amounts for any additional covered services the patient receives during the rest of the year.

How You Obtain Coverage

If you are receiving Social Security or railroad retirement monthly benefits, you will receive from the government information concerning Medicare about 3 months before you become entitled to hospital insurance.

All other eligible people have to file an application for Medicare. They should contact a social security office to apply for Medicare.

New in 1991

Breast Cancer Screening (Mammography): Medicare medical insurance now helps pay for X-ray screenings to detect breast cancer. Women 65 or older can use the benefit ever other year. Younger disabled women covered by Medicare can use it more frequently. Medicare will pay 80 percent of up to $55 for each screening.

Physician Payment Reforms: In 1991, physicians who do not accept assignment may not charge you for office and hospital visits more than 140 percent of the Medicare prevailing charge for non-participating physicians. For most other services (surgery, for example) the limit is 125 percent. Physicians who knowingly charge more than these amounts are subject to sanctions.

You no longer have to file claims to Medicare for covered medical insurance services received after September 1, 1990. Doctors, suppliers, and other providers of services must submit the claims to Medicare within one year of providing the service to you or be subject to certain penalties. □

Social Security Facts

By Gwendolyn S. King

I have a unique responsibility as Commissioner to ensure that the current discussion on Social Security edifies, and does not confuse or mislead, the public on America's most important and successful social program. Based on much inaccurate information that has been disseminated to the public recently on this issue, I believe it is necessary to set the record straight on what is fact, and what is fiction.

Fiction: Social Security reserves are being used to finance general government operating expenses and, thus, are nothing more than worthless IOUs. They are not being invested for the public's benefit.

Fact: Section 201 of the Social Security Act stipulates that Social Security reserves are to be invested exclusively in interest-bearing U.S. government obligations. The law's creators intended that the public's money should be placed in the safest possible investment, backed by the full faith and credit of the U.S. government.

Because Social Security trust funds are invested in Treasury obligations, the money, after investment, has always been available to the government for its general operating needs.

Social Security dollars do draw interest. The Treasury pays the Social Security Trust Fund substantial interest payments—9.7 percent in the year ending June 30, 1989.

Fiction: Social Security reserves are sufficiently high, allowing a payroll tax cut and a return to the pay-as-you-go system.

Fact: The 1983 Social Security Rescue Amendments were adopted because of a realization that the pay-as-you-go philosophy left the system vulnerable to the effects of economic downturns. Back-to-back recessions in the late '70s and early '80s moved Social Security dangerously close to fiscal catastrophe. At one point, the contingency reserve contained only

14 percent of the next year's benefit expenditures, necessitating interfund borrowing from the Hospital Insurance Trust Fund.

At the begining of 1990, the Social Security Trust Fund had accumulated $188 billion. That money represents only nine months' worth of benefit payments. There is general agreement that a contingency of 100-150 percent of the funds needed to pay one year's worth of benefits should accumulate before changes in system financing are even discussed.

Fiction: The Social Security pay-roll tax is a regressive tax.

Fact: Social Security provides significant protection to surviving spouses and children, as well as to insured workers and their families in the event of disability. In fact, about 40 percent of Social Security benefit payments are in these non-retirement categories.

The Social Security benefit structure is highly progressive. It provides considerably higher benefits for low earners, in relation to their pre-retirement earnings, than for high-income workers. For workers retiring at age 65, Social Security benefits replace approximately 58 percent of earnings, 42 percent for mid-income Americans, and 24 percent for high-income earners.

Today, a low-income worker retiring at age 65 will gain back his or her lifetime Social Security tax contributions, plus interest, in about four years. High-income workers will gain their contribution back with interest in about seven years. □

Gwendolyn S. King is Commissioner of the Social Security Administration.

Source: Tax Federation. These opinions are not necessarily those of the Tax Federation or the *Information Please Almanac.*

DRUGS & DRUG ABUSE

Prenatal Substance Abuse

By Josephine Gittler and Dr. Merle McPherson

Incidence and Prevalence

The most frequently cited national estimate of the number of drug-exposed newborns stems from a 1988 nationwide survey of 36 hospitals conducted by the National Association of Perinatal Addiction, Research and Education. Based on this survey, it was estimated that 11 percent of all newborns, or 375,000 newborns, had been exposed perinatally to illegal drugs. There was a variation in the rates, ranging from less than 1 percent to 27 percent, reported by the hospitals surveyed.

A similar 1988 survey of 18 hospitals (14 public and 4 private) in 15 large urban areas was conducted by the U.S. House of Representatives Select Committee on Children, Youth and Families. This survey found that at 15 of the 18 hospitals surveyed, births of drug-exposed infants had substantially increased since 1985. The survey further found that at the hospitals surveyed, the reported proportions of newborns who had been exposed to drugs in utero ranged from 4 percent to 18 percent.

It should be noted that the aforementioned statistics concerning drug-exposed newborns include newborns who have been exposed perinatally not only to crack, but also to illegal drugs such as heroin, methadone, cocaine, amphetamines, PCP and marijuana. It should also be noted that many of the hospitals surveyed are located in major metropolitan areas and were not necessarily representative of hospitals in the nation as a whole.

There are several national estimates of babies specifically exposed to crack in utero. The President's National Drug Control Strategy Report has estimated that 100,000 crack-exposed babies are born annually. One national expert has arrived at the somewhat lower estimate of 1 to 2 percent of all babies born each year, or 30,000 to 50,000 babies, perinatally exposed to crack.

Data concerning the incidence and prevalence of newborns exposed to illegal drugs, including but not limited to crack, are fragmentary and incomplete. Moreover, the accuracy of the statistics that do exist are open to question. Nevertheless, these available statistics, derived primarily from reports of selected hospitals, indicate that the incidence and prevalence of perinatal drug exposure is substantial and rising.

Demographic Characteristics

Existing reports indicate that mothers of drug-exposed infants, particularly crack-exposed babies, most often are in their twenties and thirties rather than being teenagers and that they most often are not first-time mothers. The extensive abuse of crack among low-income and minority women living in the nation's large inner city neighborhoods has received a great deal of attention, but there is some evidence that drug abuse during pregnancy cuts across socioeconomic lines and occurs among a significant number of middle-income and upper-income women.

Relationship Between Drug Abuse and AIDS

There are also definite linkages between drug abuse and the birth of infants infected with the human immunodeficiency virus (HIV) that leads to AIDS. Intravenous (IV) drug users are at risk of contracting AIDS because the HIV infection is spread through contaminated needles shared by IV drug users. Pregnant women and adolescents who are or have been IV drug users or whose sexual partners are IV drug users may become HIV infected and these women and adolescents may then transmit the infection to their babies during pregnancy or at birth.

In addition, a growing number of female crack abusers are becoming infected with syphilis and AIDS because they are engaging in unsafe sex, including prostitution, to support their crack habits. Accordingly, there is a risk that newborns who are drug-exposed may also be HIV infected.

Effects of Drug Exposure

The effects of the perinatal exposure of a newborn to drugs may be divided into two categories: prenatal effects and postnatal effects, and the latter may be divided into effects on infants, toddlers, pre-school children and school children.

Reliable research data about the effects of in utero exposure to crack are limited. Since extensive crack abuse among pregnant women is a fairly recent phenomenon, it is not surprising that more is known about its short-term effects than its long-term effects. Furthermore, the perinatal effects of crack exposure are difficult to separate from the effects of other factors, such as poor maternal health, inadequate nutrition and lack of prenatal care. Similarly, the postnatal effects of crack exposure are difficult to separate from the effects of other factors such as family dysfunction, poverty and environmental deprivation. There is need for more rigorous studies to be conducted before a definite conclusion can be reached about the long-term as well as short-term effects of exposure, and the relationship between the effects of exposure and the effects of other associated factors. Yet, available research data and clinical observations indicate that crack-exposed babies run an increased risk of mortality, morbidity, and problems in development and behavior.

Babies exposed to crack during their mother's pregnancy are more likely to be premature and abnormally smaller for gestational age, and have an increased risk of genital-urinary abnormalities. They are often hypersensitive and irritable, demonstrate altered sleep and wake cycles and have movement disorders and fine motor deficits. Toddlers exposed to crack during their mother's pregnancy frequently "are irritable and display poor impulse control and less goal-directed behavior . . . are distractible and easily frustrated," "have expressive language difficulties," "demonstrate less free play," and "are less securely attached to caretaker." There is also some preliminary research which suggests that children exposed to drugs in utero are more "vulnerable to developmental problems that may affect learning."

Risk of Abandonment, Neglect and Abuse

Crack-exposed babies whose mothers continue to abuse crack after their birth run an increased risk of abandonment, neglect and abuse. These babies often require more than normal care because of the effects of in utero exposure to drugs. However, addiction to crack may substantially impair a mother's ability and willingness to provide even minimal care to her baby. Moreover, the mothers addicted to crack may well have a variety of other difficulties, such as poverty, lack of family and social support systems and psychosocial problems that interfere with effective parenting. Therefore, it is not surprising that many crack-exposed babies are abandoned or are found to be neglected or abused.

Impact on Existing Services Systems

The care of large numbers of drug-exposed newborns, primarily crack babies, is severely straining the resources of hospitals in large urban areas serving the poor and minorities. Since drug-exposed newborns frequently are premature or low-birth weight and may suffer from drug withdrawal symptoms, many receive care in intensive care nurseries and have long hospital stays.

* * *

Many drug-exposed newborns and children whose families are involved with drug abuse are being referred to child welfare authorities. In some large cities, there has been a great growth in the child welfare caseloads of social service agencies—an increase attributable to parental drug abuse from 2,627 cases in 1986 to 8,251 cases in 1988 in New York City. And estimates of the proportion of new child welfare cases involving parental drug abuse in Boston and San

Francisco are 64 percent and 76 percent, respectively.

* * *

In some areas the already over-burdened foster care system is being overwhelmed by the large number of drug-exposed newborns pouring into foster care. It appears that 30 to 50 percent of identified crack-exposed babies go into foster care. Some cities have witnessed a tremendous rise in total foster placements of children from families involved in drug abuse.

Although there has been an expansion in foster care placements, this expansion has not kept pace with the rise in the population of children needing such placements. Moreover, drug-exposed infants may need specialized foster care due to the effects of drug exposure, and such specialized foster care is in short supply.

Early intervention programs and the public schools are also having to deal with children who were exposed to drugs, particularly crack, during their mother's pregnancies. Many of these children will need early intervention services. Since widespread crack abuse first occurred about 5 years ago, public schools are just beginning to see the first large group of these children. It can be anticipated that some of these children will be classified as special education students because of physical, learning and behavior problems. Others will be classified as regular education students but will need special handling and attention in the classroom. □

Josephine Gittler is a Professor of Law at the University of Iowa and Co-Director of the National Maternal and Child Health Resource Center. Merle McPherson, M.D., is Director of the Division of Services for Children with Special Health Needs, Maternal and Child Health Bureau, Public Health Services, U.S. Department of Health and Human Services.

This article was excerpted from an article of the same title, published in *Children Today,* a publication of the Office of Human Development Services, Department of Health and Human Services.

A Primer on Drugs of Abuse

Main Sources: U.S. Department of Justice, Drug Enforcement Administration, U.S. Department of Education, National Institute on Drug Abuse.

NARCOTICS

The term narcotic in its medical meaning refers to opium and opium derivatives or synthetic substitutes.[1]

Narcotics are essential in the practice of medicine: they are the most effective agents known for the relief of intense pain. They are also used as cough suppressants as well as a centuries-old remedy for diarrhea.

Under medical supervision, narcotics are administered orally or by intramuscular injection. As drugs of abuse, however, they also are sniffed, smoked, or self-administered by the more direct routes of subcutaneous ("skin-popping") and intravenous ("mainlining") injection.

The relief of suffering, whether of physical or psychological origin, may result in a short-lived state of

euphoria. The initial effects, however, are often unpleasant, leading many to conclude that those who persist in their illicit use may have latent personality disturbances. Narcotics tend to induce pinpoint pupils and reduced vision, together with drowsiness, apathy, decreased physical activity, and constipation. A larger dose may induce sleep, but there is an increasing possibility of nausea, vomiting, and respiratory depression—the major toxic effect of the opiates. Except in cases of acute intoxication, there is no loss of motor coordination or slurred speech as in the case of the depressants.

To the extent that the response may be felt to be pleasurable, its intensity may be expected to increase with the amount of the dose administered. Repeated use, however, will result in increasing tolerance: the user must administer progressively larger doses to attain the desired effect, thereby reinforcing the compulsive behavior known as drug dependence.

---

1. Cocaine, ecgonine, and coca leaves, classified as narcotics under the Controlled Substances Act (CSA), are discussed in the text on stimulants.

Physical dependence refers to an alteration of the normal functions of the body that necessitates the continued presence of a drug in order to prevent the withdrawal or abstinence syndrome, which is characteristic of each class of addictive drugs. The intensity of physical symptoms experienced during the withdrawal period is related directly to the amount of narcotic used each day.

Deprivation of an addictive drug causes increased excitability of those same bodily functions that have been depressed by its habitual use.

With the deprivation of narcotics, the first withdrawal signs are usually experienced shortly before the time of the next scheduled dose. Complaints, pleas, and demands by the addict are prominent, increasing in intensity and peaking from 36 to 72 hours after the last dose, then gradually subsiding. Symptoms, such as watery eyes, runny nose, yawning, and perspiration, appear about 8 to 12 hours after the last dose. Thereafter, the addict may fall into a restless sleep. As the abstinence syndrome progresses, restlessness, irritability, loss of appetite, insomnia, goose flesh, tremors, and finally yawning and severe sneezing occur. These symptoms reach their peak at 48 to 72 hours. The patient is weak and depressed, with nausea and vomiting. Stomach cramps and diarrhea are common. Heart rate and blood pressure are elevated. Chills alternating with flushing and excessive sweating are also characteristic symptoms. Pains in the bones and muscles of the back and extremities occur as do muscle spasms and kicking movements, which may be the source of the expression "kicking the habit." At this time an individual may become suicidal. Without treatment the syndrome eventually runs its course and most of the symptoms will disappear in 7 to 10 days. How long it takes to restore physiological and psychological equilibrium, however, is unpredictable. For a few weeks following withdrawal the addict will continue to think and talk about his use of drugs and be particularly susceptible to an urge to use them again.

The withdrawal syndrome may be avoided by reducing the dose of narcotic over a one-to-three-week period. Detoxification of an addict can be accomplished by substituting oral methadone for the illicit narcotic and gradually reducing the dose. However, since the addict's entire pattern of life usually is built around drug taking, narcotic dependence is never entirely resolved by withdrawal alone.

Since addicts tend to become preoccupied with the daily ritual of obtaining and taking drugs, they often neglect themselves and may suffer from malnutrition, infections, and unattended diseases or injuries. Among the hazards of narcotic addiction are toxic reactions to contaminants, such as quindine, sugars, and talcum power, as well as unsterile needles and injection techniques, resulting in abscesses, blood poisoning, hepatitis, and AIDS.

Since there is no simple way to determine the purity of a drug that is sold on the street, the potency is unpredictable, posing the ever present danger of an unintentional overdose. A person with a mild overdose may be stuporous or asleep. Larger doses may induce a coma with slow, shallow respiration. The skin becomes clammy cold, the body limp, and the jaw relaxed; there is a danger that the tongue may fall back, blocking the air passageway. If the condition is sufficiently severe, convulsions may occur, followed by respiratory arrest and death. Specific antidotes for narcotic poisoning are available at hospitals.

NARCOTICS OF NATURAL ORIGIN

The poppy *Papaver somniferum* is the main source of the nonsynthetic narcotics. It was grown in the Mediterranean region as early as 300 B.C. and has since been cultivated in countries around the world, such as Hungary, Turkey, India, Burma, China, Lebanon, Pakistan, Afghanistan, Laos, and Mexico.

The milky fluid that oozes from incisions in the unripe seedpod has, since ancient times, been scraped by hand and air dried to produce opium gum. A more modern method of harvesting is by the industrial poppy straw process of extracting alkaloids from the mature dried plant. The extract may be in either liquid, solid, or powder form. Most poppy straw concentrate made available commercially is a fine brownish powder with a distinct odor. More than 400 tons of opium or its equivalent in poppy straw concentrate are legally imported annually into the United States

Opium

There were no legal restrictions on the importation or use of opium until the early 1900s. In those days, patent medicines often contained opium without any warning label. Today, there are state, federal, and international laws governing the production and distribution of narcotics substances, and there is little abuse of opium in the United States.

At least 25 alkaloids can be extracted from opium. These fall into two general categories, each producing markedly different effects. The first, known as the phenanthrene alkaloids, represented by morphine and codeine, are used as analgesics and cough suppressants; the second, the isoquinoline alkaloids, represented by papaverine (an intestinal relaxant) and noscapine (a cough suppressant), have no significant influence on the central nervous system and are not regulated under the Controlled Substances Act (CSA).

Although a small amount of opium is used to make antidiarrheal preparations, such as paregoric, virtually all the opium imported into this country is broken down into its alkaloid constituents, principally morphine and codeine.

Morphine

The principal constituent of opium, ranging in concentration from 4 to 21 percent, morphine is one of the most effective drugs known for the relief of pain. It is marketed in the form of white crystals, hypodermic tablets, and injectable preparations. Its licit use is restricted primarily to hospitals. Morphine is odorless, tastes bitter, and darkens with age. It may be administered subcutaneously, intramuscularly, or intravenously, the latter method being the one most frequently resorted to by addicts. Tolerance and dependence develop rapidly in the user. Only a small part of the morphine obtained from opium is used medically. Most of it is converted to codeine and, secondarily, to hydromorphone.

Codeine

This alkaloid is found in raw opium in concentrations ranging from 0.7 to 2.5 percent. It was first isolated in 1832 as an impurity in a batch of morphine. Although it occurs naturally, most codeine is produced from morphine. As compared with morphine, codeine produces less analgesia, sedation, and respiratory depression. It is widely distributed in products of two general types. Codeine for the relief of moderate pain may consist of codeine tablets or be combined with other products, such as aspirin or acetaminophen (Tylenol). Some examples of liquid codeine preparations for the relief of coughs (antitussives) are Robitussin AC, Cheracol, and elixir of terpin hydrate with codeine. Codeine is also manufactured to a lessèr extent in injectable form for the relief of pain. It is by far the most widely used naturally occurring narcotic in medical treatment.

Thebaine

A minor constituent of opium, thebaine is the principal alkaloid present in another species of poppy, *Papaver bracteatum*, which has been grown experimentally in the United States as well as in other parts of the world. Although chemically similar to both codeine and morphine, it produces stimulant rather than depressant effects. Thebaine is not used in this country for medical purposes, but it is converted into a variety of medically important compounds, including codeine, hydrocodone, oxycodone, oxymorphone, nalbuphine, naloxone, and the Bentley compounds. It is controlled in Schedule II of the CSA as well as under international law.

SEMI-SYNTHETIC NARCOTICS

The following narcotics are among the more significant synthetic substances that have been derived by modification of the chemicals contained in opium.

Heroin

First synthesized from morphine in 1874, heroin was not extensively used in medicine until the beginning of this century. The Bayer Company in Germany first started commercial production of the new pain remedy in 1898. While it received widespread accep-tance, the medical profession for years remained unaware of its potential for addiction. The first comprehensive control of heroin in the United States was established with the Harrison Narcotic Act of 1914.

Pure heroin is a white powder with a bitter taste. Illicit heroin may vary in both form and color. Most illicit heroin is a powder which may vary in color from white to dark brown because of impurities left from the manufacturing process or the presence of additives, such as food coloring, cocoa, or brown sugar.

Pure heroin is rarely sold on the street. A "bag"—slang for a single dosage unit of heroin—may weigh about 100 mg, usually containing about five percent heroin. To increase the bulk of the material sold to the addict, diluents are mixed with the heroin in ratios ranging from 9 to 1 to as much as 99 to 1. Sugars, starch, powdered milk, and quinine are among the diluents used.

Another form of heroin known as "black tar" heroin has also become increasingly available in recent years, especially in the western United States. Black tar heroin is a crudely processed form of heroin illicitly manufactured in Mexico. It may be sticky like roofing tar or hard like coal, and it is dark brown to black in color. Black tar heroin is often sold on the street in its tar-like state, sometimes at purities ranging as high as 40 to 80 percent. Black tar heroin is sometimes diluted, however, by adding materials of similar consistency (such as burnt cornstarch), or by converting the tar heroin into a powder and adding conventional diluents, such as mannitol or quinine. It is most commonly used through injection.

The Controlled Substances Act

The Controlled Substances Act (CSA), Title II of the Comprehensive Drug Abuse Prevention and Control Act of 1970, is the legal foundation of the Government's fight against abuse of drugs and other substances. This law is a consolidation of numerous laws regulating the manufacture and distribution of narcotics, stimulants, depressants, and hallucinogens.

The CSA places all substances which were in some manner regulated under existing federal law into one of five schedules. This placement is based upon the substance's medical use, potential for abuse, and safety or dependence liability. The Act also provides a mechanism for substances to be controlled, or added to a schedule; decontrolled, or removed from control; and rescheduled or transferred from one schedule to another.

The five schedules are as follows:

Schedule I

√ The drug or other substance has a high potential for abuse.
√ The drug or other substance has no currently accepted medical use in treatment in the United States.
√ There is a lack of accepted safety for use of the drug or other substance under medical supervision.

Schedule II

√ The drug or other substance has a high potential for abuse.
√ The drug or other substance has a currently accepted medical use in treatment in the United States or a currently accepted medical use with severe restrictions.

√ Abuse of the drug or other substance may lead to severe psychological or physical dependence.

Schedule III

√ The drug or other substance has a potential for abuse less than the drugs or other substances in Schedules I and II.
√ The drug or other substance has a currently accepted medical use in treatment in the United States.
√ Abuse of the drug or other substance may lead to moderate or low physical dependence or high psychological dependence.

Schedule IV

√ The drug or other substance has a low potential for abuse relative to the drugs or other substances in Schedule III.
√ The drug or other substance has a currently accepted medical use in treatment in the United States.
√ Abuse of the drug or other substance may lead to limited physical dependence or psychological dependence relative to the drugs or other substances in Schedule III.

Schedule V

√ The drug or other substance has a low potential for abuse relative to the drugs or other substances in Schedule IV.
√ The drug or other substance has a currently accepted medical use in treatment in the United States.
√ Abuse of the drug or other substances may lead to limited physical dependence or psychological dependence relative to the drugs or other substances in Schedule IV.

What Americans Spend on Illegal Drugs

(in billions of dollars)

Drug	1988	1989	1990
Cocaine	$22.9	$22.5	$17.5
Heroin	$15.8	$15.5	$12.3
Marijuana	$11.1	$10.0	$8.8
Other	$1.8	$1.8	$1.8
Total	**$51.6**	**$49.8**	**$40.4**

Source: "What America's Users Spend on Illegal Drugs," an Office of National Drug Control Policy Technical Paper, June 1991.

Although these estimates are imprecise, they are reliable enough to imply that the trade in illicit substances is immense—roughly $40 billion to $50 billion. To put this amount into perspective, consider that Americans spend $44 billion on alcohol products and another $37 billion on tobacco products. Federal, State, and local governments spend $46 billion on the criminal justice system and $183 billion on public elementary and secondary education.

The social costs from drug consumption greatly exceed the $40 billion to $50 billion spent on illicit drugs. Drug use fosters crime, both property crime to support consumption and violent crime to support drug distribution networks. Drug use intensifies catastrophic health problems, ranging from hepatitis and endocarditis to crack babies and AIDS. And drug use promotes general social disorganization as it disrupts or severs personal, familial, and legitimate economic relationships. The public bears much of the burden of these indirect costs by financing the criminal justice response to drug-related crime, maintaining a public treatment system, and educating the impressionable about the dangers of drug use. □

Estimates of Production and Supply of Cocaine

(in metric tons and billions of dollars)

Item	1988	1989	1990
Coca leaf crop[1]	293,700 MT	298,090 Mt	310,150 MT
Cocaine HCL produced	829 MT	836 MT	873 MT
Transshipment, foreign seizures	38 MT	64 MT	92 MT
Cocaine shipped to the U.S.	418–593 MT	388–557 MT	376–544 MT
Cocaine seized by Federal authorities	57 MT	95 MT	101–113 MT
Cocaine available for consumption in the U.S.	361–536 MT	293–462 MT	263–443 MT
Retail value, U.S.	$36–$54 billion	$29–$46 billion	$26–$44 billion

1. From South America. *Source:* "What America's Users Spend on Illegal Drugs," an Office of National Drug Control Policy Technical Paper, June 1991.

Hydromorphone

Most commonly sold as Dilaudid, hydromorphone is the second oldest semi-synthetic narcotic analgesic. Marketed both in tablet and injectable form, it is shorter acting and more sedating than morphine, but its potency is from two to eight times as great. It is, therefore, a highly abusable drug, much sought after by narcotic addicts, who usually obtain it through fraudulent prescription or theft. The tablets, stronger than available liquid forms, may be dissolved and injected.

Oxycodone

Oxycodone is synthesized from thebaine. It is similar to codeine, but more potent and with a higher dependence potential. It is effective orally and is marketed in combination with aspirin as Percodan for the relief of pain. Addicts take Percodan orally or dissolve tablets in water, filter out the insoluble material, and "mainline" the active drug.

What High School Students Spend on Illegal Drugs

(in millions of dollars)

Drug	1988	1989	1990
Cocaine	$303	$299	$276
Heroin		Insignificant	
Marijuana	$360	$358	$343
Other	$36	$37	$32

Source: "What America's Users Spend on Illegal Drugs," an Office of National Drug Control Policy Technical Paper, June 1991.

During 1990, students in grades 6 though 12 consumed an estimated 2,800 kg (6,172.8 lb) of cocaine. They consumed 34,000 (74,956.4 lb) kg of marijuana, and an insignificant amount of heroin. Roughly 15% of high school students drop out. This figure implies that about 420 kg (925.9 lb) of cocaine was consumed by schoolage dropouts during 1990. It is also assumed that the estimate of 15% is accurate for heroin, marijuana, and other drugs as well.

The retail value of drugs consumed by high school dropouts in 1990 was: cocaine, $41 million; marijuana, $51 million; and other, $5 million. □

What College Students Spend on Illegal Drugs

(in millions of dollars)

Drug	1988	1989	1990
Cocaine	$651	$644	$594
Heroin		Insignificant	
Marijuana	$453	$451	$431
Other	$22	$23	$20

Source: "What America's Users Spend on Illegal Drugs," an Office of National Drug Control Policy Technical Paper, June 1991.

It has been estimated that during 1988 college students consumed about 8,000 kg (17,636.8 lb) of pure cocaine, and 46,000 kg (101,411.6 lb) of marijuana. Heroin use is rare among college students and was excluded from these estimates. □

Trends in Annual Prevalence of Fourteen Types of Drugs

Among College Students 1–4 Years Beyond High School

	Percent who used in last twelve months							
	1980	1985	1986	1987	1988	1989	1990	'89–'90 change
Any illicit drug[e]	56.2	46.3	45.0	40.1	37.4	36.7	33.3	–3.4
Any illicit drug[e] other than marijuana	32.3	26.7	25.0	21.3	19.2	16.4	15.2	–1.2
Marijuana	51.2	41.7	40.9	37.0	34.6	33.6	29.4	–4.2
Inhalants[b]	3.0	3.1	3.9	3.7	4.1	3.7	3.9	+0.2
Hallucinogens	8.5	5.0	6.0	5.9	5.3	5.1	5.4	+0.3
LSD	6.0	2.2	3.9	4.0	3.6	3.4	4.3	+0.9
Cocaine	16.8	17.3	17.1	13.7	10.0	8.2	5.6	–2.6
Crack[c]	n.a.	n.a.	1.3	2.0	1.4	1.5	0.6	–0.9
MDMA ("Ecstasy")[f]	n.a.	n.a.	n.a.	n.a.	n.a.	2.3	2.3	0.0
Heroin	0.4	0.2	0.1	0.2	0.2	0.1	0.1	0.0
Other opiates[a]	5.1	2.4	4.0	3.1	3.1	3.2	2.9	–0.3
Stimulants[a]	22.4	n.a.	n.a.	n.a.	n.a.	n.a.	n.a.	n.a.
Stimulants, adjusted[a,d]	n.a.	11.9	10.3	7.2	6.2	4.6	4.5	–0.1
Crystal methamphetamine[g]	n.a.	n.a.	n.a.	n.a.	n.a.	n.a.	0.1	n.a.
Sedatives[a]	8.3	2.5	2.6	1.7	1.5	1.0	n.a.	n.a.
Barbiturates[a]	2.9	1.3	2.0	1.2	1.1	1.0	1.4	+0.4
Methaqualone[a]	7.2	1.4	1.2	0.8	0.5	0.2	n.a.	n.a.
Tranquilizers[a]	6.9	3.6	4.4	3.8	3.1	2.6	3.0	+0.4
Alcohol	90.5	92.0	91.5	90.9	89.6	89.6	89.0	–0.6
Cigarettes	36.2	35.0	35.3	38.0	36.6	34.2	35.5	+1.3

a. Only drug use which was not under a doctor's orders is included here. b. This drug was asked about in four of the five questionnaire forms in 1980–89, and in five of the six questionnaire forms in 1990. c. This drug was asked about in one of the five questionnaire forms in 1986, and in two of the five questionnaire forms in 1987–89, and in all six forms in 1990. d. Based on the data from the revised question, which attempts to exclude the inappropriate reporting of non-prescription stimulants.'e. Use of "any illicit drug" includes any use of marijuana, hallucinogens, cocaine, and heroin, or any use of other opiates, stimulants, barbiturates, methaqualone (until 1990); or tranquilizers not under a doctor's orders. f. This drug was asked about in two of the five questionnaire forms in 1989, and in two of the six questionnaire forms in 1990. g. This drug was asked about in two of the six questionnaire forms. NOTE: n.a. = data not available.

Source: The University of Michigan 1990 annual study titled "Monitoring the Future," conducted under a series of research grants from the National Institute on Drug Abuse to the U–M Institute for Social Research.

Etorphine and Diprenorphine

Two of the Bentley compounds, these substances are both made from thebaine. Etorphine is more than one thousand times as potent as morphine in its analgesic, sedative, and respiratory depressant effects. For human use, its potency is a distinct disadvantage because of the danger of overdose. Etorphine hydrochloride (M99) is used by veterinarians to immobilize large wild animals. Diprenorphine hydrochloride (M50-50), acting as an antagonist, counteracts the effects of etorphine. The manufacture and distribution of both substances are strictly regulated under the CSA.

SYNTHETIC NARCOTICS

In contrast to pharmaceutical products derived directly or indirectly from narcotics of natural origin, synthetic narcotics are produced entirely within the laboratory. A continuing search for a product that will retain the analgesic properties of morphine without the consequent dangers of tolerance and dependence has yet to yield a drug that is not susceptible to abuse. The two that are most widely available are meperidine and methadone.

Meperidine (Pethidine)

The first synthetic narcotic, meperidine, is chemically dissimilar to morphine but resembles it in its analgesic effect. It is probably the most widely used drug for the relief of moderate to severe pain. Available in pure form as well as in products containing other medicinal ingredients, it is administered either orally or by injection, the latter method being the most widely abused. Tolerance and dependence develop with chronic use, and large doses can result in convulsions or death.

Methadone and Related Drugs

German scientists synthesized methadone during World War II because of a shortage of morphine. Although chemically unlike morphine or heroin, it produces many of the same effects. Introduced into the United States in 1947 as an analgesic and distributed under such names as Amidone, Dolophine, and Methadone, it became widely used in the 1960s in the treatment of narcotic addicts. The effects of methadone differ from morphine-based drugs in that they have a longer duration of action, lasting up to 24 hours, thereby permitting administration only once a day in heroin detoxification and maintenance programs. Moreover, methadone is almost as effective when administered orally as it is by injection. But tolerance and dependence may develop, and withdrawal symptoms, though they develop more slowly and are less severe, are more prolonged. Ironically, methadone, designed to control narcotic addiction, has emerged in some metropolitan areas as a major cause of overdose deaths.

Closely related chemically to methadone is the synthetic compound levo-alpha-acetylmethadol (LAAM), which has an even longer duration of action (from 48 to 72 hours), permitting a further reduction in clinic visits and the elimination of take-home medication. Its potential in the treatment of narcotic addicts is under investigation.

Another close relative of methadone is propoxyphene, first marketed in 1957 under the trade name Darvon for the relief of mild to moderate pain. Less dependence-producing than the other opiates, it is less effective as an analgesic. Propoxyphene is in Schedule II and preparations containing it are in Schedule IV

How Long Drugs Stay in Urine

Nicotine	24 to 48 hours
Marijuana	10 to 35 days
Cocaine	24 to 36 hours
Amphetamines	38 to 72 hours
PCP	48 to 78 hours
Valium, et al.	48 to 76 hours
Heroin	48 to 72 hours
Phenylpropanolamine*	24 to 48 hours

*The most commonly abused over the counter drug. Source: The National Parents' Resource Institute for Drug Education, Inc. (PRIDE).

Narcotic Antagonists

The deliberate effort to find an effective analgesic that is not dependence-producing led to the development of compounds known as narcotic antagonists. These drugs, as the name implies, block or reverse the effects of narcotics. Naloxone (Narcan), having no morphine-like effects, was removed from the CSA when introduced as a specific antidote for narcotic poisoning in 1971. Nalorphine (Nalline), introduced into clinical medicine in 1951 and now in Schedule III, is called a narcotic agonist-antagonist. In a drug-free individual, it produces morphine-like effects; it counteracts these effects in an individual under the influence of narcotics.

Another agonist-antagonist is pentazocine (Talwin). Introduced as an analgesic in 1967, it was determined to be an abusable drug and placed under Schedule IV in 1979. On the street, pentazocine is frequently used in combination with another drug: tripelennamine. This combination is commonly referred to as "T's and B's" or "T's and Blues" with "T" referring to Talwin and "B" indicating the blue PBZ (tripelennamine) tablet.

A further attempt at reducing the abuse of this drug was made in 1983 with the addition of naloxone to the pentazocine tablets. The new product, Talwin Nx, contains a quantity of antagonist sufficient to counteract the morphine-like effects of pentazocine if the tablets are dissolved and injected.

DEPRESSANTS

Substances regulated under the CSA as depressants have a potential for abuse associated with both physical and psychological dependence. Taken as prescribed by a physician, depressants may be beneficial for the relief of anxiety, irritability, and tension, and for the symptomatic treatment of insomnia. In excessive amounts, however, they produce a state of intoxication that is remarkably similar to that of alcohol.

As in the case of alcohol, these effects may vary not only from person to person but from time to time in the same individual. Low doses produce mild sedation. Higher doses, insofar as they relieve anxiety or stress, may produce a temporary sense of well-being; they may also produce mood depression and apathy. In marked contrast to the effects of narcotics, however, intoxicating doses invariably result in impaired judgment, slurred speech, and loss of motor coordination. In addition to the dangers of disorientation, resulting in a high incidence of highway accidents, recurrent users incur risks of long-term involvement with depressants.

Tolerance to the intoxicating effects develops rapidly, leading to a progressive narrowing of the margin of safety between an intoxicating and lethal dose. The person who is unaware of the dangers of increasing dependence will often increase the daily dose up to 10 or 20 times the recommended therapeutic level. The source of supply may be no farther than the family medicine cabinet. Depressants are also frequently obtained by theft, illegal prescription, or purchase on the illicit market.

In the world of illicit drug use, depressants often are used as self-medication to soothe jangled nerves brought on by the use of stimulants, to quell the anxiety of "flashbacks" resulting from prior use of hallucinogens, or to ease withdrawal from heroin. The dangers, it should be stressed, are compounded when depressants are used in combination with alcohol or other drugs. Chronic intoxication, though it affects every age group, is not common in middle age. The problem often remains unrecognized until the user exhibits recurrent confusion or an obvious inability to function. Depressants also serve as a means of suicide, a pattern particularly common among women.

The depressants vary with respect to their potential for overdose. Moderate depressant poisoning closely resembles alcoholic inebriation. The symptoms of severe depressant poisoning are coma, a cold clammy skin, a weak and rapid pulse, and a slow to rapid but shallow respiration. Death will follow if the reduced respiration and low blood pressure are not counteracted by proper medical treatment.

The abrupt cessation or reduction of high-dose depressant intake may result in a characteristic withdrawal syndrome, which should be recognized as a medical emergency more serious than that of any other drugs of abuse. An apparent improvement in the patient's condition may be the initial result of detoxification. Within 24 hours, however, minor withdrawal symptoms manifest themselves, among them anxiety and agitation, loss of appetite, nausea and vomiting, increased heart rate and excessive sweating, tremulousness and abdominal cramps. The symptoms usually peak during the second or third day of abstinence from the short-acting barbiturates or meprobamate; they may not be reached until the seventh or eighth day of abstinence from the long-acting barbiturates or benzodiazepines. It is during the peak period that the major withdrawal symptoms usually occur. The patient may experience convulsions indistinguishable from those occurring in grand mal epilepsy. More than half of those who experience convulsions will go on to develop delirium, often resulting in a psychotic state identical to the delirium tremens associated with the alcohol withdrawal syndrome. Detoxification and treatment must therefore be carried out under close medical supervision. While treatment techniques vary to some extent, they share common objectives: stabilization of the drug-dependent state to allay withdrawal symptoms followed by gradual withdrawal to prevent their recurrence.

Among the depressants that give rise to the general conditions described are chloral hydrate, a broad array of barbiturates, glutethimide, methaqualone, meprobamate, and the benzodiazepines.

Chloral Hydrate

The oldest of the hypnotic (sleep-inducing) drugs, chloral hydrate was first synthesized in 1862 and soon supplanted alcohol, opium, and cannabis preparations for inducing sedation and sleep. Its popularity declined after the introduction of the barbiturates. It has a penetrating, slightly acrid odor, and a bitter caustic taste. Its depressant effects, as well as resulting tolerance and dependence, are comparable to those of alcohol, and withdrawal symptoms resemble delirium tremens. Chloral hydrate is a liquid, marketed in the form of syrups and soft gelatin capsules. Cases of poisoning have occurred from mixing chloral hydrate with alcoholic drinks. Chloral hydrate is not a street drug of choice. Its main misuse is by older adults.

Barbiturates

Among the drugs most frequently prescribed to induce sedation and sleep by both physicians and veterinarians are the barbiturates. About 2,500 derivatives of barbituric acid have been synthesized, but of these only about 15 remain in medical use. Small therapeutic doses tend to calm nervous conditions, and larger dozes cause sleep 20 to 60 minutes after oral administration. As in the case of alcohol, some individuals may experience a sense of excitement before sedation takes effect. If dosage is increased, however, the effects of the barbiturates may progress through successive stages of sedation, sleep, and coma to death from respiratory arrest and cardiovascular complications.

Barbiturates are classified as ultrashort, short, intermediate, and long-acting. The ultrashort-acting barbiturates produce anesthesia within one minute after intravenous administration. The rapid onset and brief duration of action make them undesirable for purposes of abuse. Those in current medical use are hexobarbital (Sombulex), methohexital (Brevital), thiamylal (Surital), and thiopental (Pentothal).

Among the short-acting and intermediate-acting barbiturates are pentobarbital (Nembutal), secobarbital (Seconal), and amobarbital (Amytal)—three of the drugs in the depressant category most sought after by abusers. The group also includes butabarbital (Butisol), talbutal (Lotusate), and aprobarbital (Alurate). After oral administration, the onset time of action is from 15 to 40 minutes and duration of action is up to 6 hours. Physicians prescribe short-acting barbiturates to induce sedation or sleep. Veterinarians use pentobarbital for anesthesia and euthanasia.

Long-acting barbiturates, which include phenobarbital (Luminal), mephobarbital or methylphenobarbital (Mebaral), and metharbital (Gemonil), have onset times of up to one hour and durations of action up to 16 hours. They are used medicinally as sedatives, hypnotics, and anticonvulsants. Their slow onset of action discourages their use for episodic intoxication, and they are not ordinarily distributed on the illicit market except when sold as something else. It should be emphasized, however, that all barbiturates result in a buildup of tolerance, and dependence on them is widespread.

Glutethimide

When glutethimide (Doriden) was introduced in 1954, it was said to be a safe barbiturate substitute without an addiction potential. Experience has shown, however, that glutethimide is yet another depressant having no particular advantage over the barbiturates and several important disadvantages. The sedative effects of glutethimide begin about 30 minutes after oral administration and last for 4 to 8 hours. Glutethimide is marketed as Doriden in 250 and 500 mg tablets. Because the effects of this drug are of long duration, it is exceptionally difficult to reverse overdoses, which often result in death.

Methaqualone

Methaqualone is a synthetic sedative chemically unrelated to the barbiturates, glutethimide, or chloral hydrate. It has been widely abused and has caused many cases of serious poisoning. It was placed in Schedule II in 1973 and rescheduled to Schedule I in 1984. It is administered orally and is rapidly absorbed from the digestive tract. Large doses can cause coma, which may be accompanied by thrashing movements or convulsions. Continued heavy use of large doses leads to tolerance and dependence.

Methaqualone was marketed in the United States under various brand names, such as Quaalude, Parest, Mequin, Optimil, Somnafac, and Sopor. Mandrax is a European name for methaqualone in combination with an antihistamine.

Mecloqualone, a chemical similar to methaqualone in all significant respects, is not legally sold in the United States and is in Schedule I.

Meprobamate

Meprobamate, first synthesized in 1950, introduced the era of mild or "minor" tranquilizers. In the United States today more than 70 tons of meprobamate are distributed annually under its generic name, as well as under brand names such as Miltown, Equanil, and SK-Bamate. Meprobamate is prescribed primarily for the relief of anxiety, tension, and associated muscle spasms. Its onset and duration of action are like those of the intermediate-acting barbiturates; it differs from them in that it is a muscle relaxant, does not produce sleep at therapeutic doses, and is relatively less toxic. Excessive use, however, can result in psychological and physical dependence.

Benzodiazepines

The benzodiazepine family of depressants relieve anxiety, tension, and muscle spasms, produce sedation, and prevent convulsions. These substances are marketed as anxiolytics (mild or minor tranquilizers), sedatives, hypnotics or anticonvulsants based to some extent on differences in their duration of action. Twelve members of this group currently are marketed in the United States. They are alprazolam (Xanax), chlordiazepoxide (Librium), clonazepam (Clonopin), clorazepate (Tranxene), diazepam (Valium), flurazepam (Dalmane), halazepam (Paxipam), lorazepam (Ativan), midazolam (Versed), oxazepam (Serax), prazepam (Centrax), quazepam (Dormalin), temazepam (Restoril), and triazolam (Halcion). While the margin of safety associated with these drugs is considerable, overdose can occur, and continuous use for several months can result in psychic or physical dependence.

Librium and Valium are among the most widely prescribed drugs in this country. These drugs have a relatively slow onset but long duration of action. Prolonged use of excessive doses may result in physical and psychological dependence. Withdrawal symptoms develop approximately one week to 10 days after continual high doses are abruptly discontinued. The delay in appearance of the abstinence syndrome is due to the slow elimination of the drug from the body. When these drugs are used to obtain a "high," they are usually taken in conjunction with another drug, such as alcohol.

STIMULANTS

The two most prevalent stimulants are nicotine in tobacco products and caffeine, the active ingredient of coffee, tea, and some bottled beverages that are sold in every supermarket. When used in moderation, these stimulants tend to relieve fatigue and increase alertness. They are an accepted part of our culture.

There are, however, more potent stimulants that because of their dependence-producing potential are under the regulatory control of the CSA. These controlled stimulants are available by prescription for medical purposes; they are also clandestinely manufactured for distribution on the illicit market.

Users tend to rely on stimulants to feel stronger, more decisive, and self-possessed. Because of the cumulative effects of the drugs, chronic users often follow a pattern of taking "uppers" in the morning and "downers," such as alcohol or sleeping pills, at night. Such chemical manipulation interferes with normal body processes and can lead to mental and physical illness.

Individuals who resort to stimulants for their euphoric effects consume large doses sporadically, over weekends or at night, often going on to experiment with other drugs of abuse. The consumption of stimulants may result in a temporary sense of exhilaration, superabundant energy, hyperactivity, extended wakefulness, and a loss of appetite. It may also induce irritability, anxiety, and apprehension. These effects are greatly intensified with administration by intravenous injection, which may produce a sudden sensation known as a "flash" or "rush." The protracted use of stimulants is followed, however, by a period of depression known as "crashing" that is invariably described as unpleasant. Since the depression can be easily counteracted by a further injection of stimulant, this abuse pattern becomes increasingly difficult to break. Heavy users may inject themselves every few hours, a process sometimes continued to the point of delirium, psychosis, or physical exhaustion.

Tolerance to both the euphoric and appetite suppressant effects develops rapidly. Doses large enough to overcome the insensitivity that develops may cause various mental aberrations, the early signs of which include repetitive grinding of the teeth, touching and picking the face and extremities, performing the same task over and over, a preoccupation with one's own processes, suspiciousness, and a sense of being watched. Paranoia with auditory and visual hallucinations characterizes the toxic syndrome resulting from continued high doses. Dizziness, tremor, agitation, hostility, panic, headache, flushed skin, chest pain with palpitations, excessive sweating, vomiting, and abdominal cramps are among the symptoms of a sublethal overdose. In the absence of medical intervention, high fever, convulsions, and cardiovascular collapse may precede the onset of death. It should be added that physical exertion increases the hazards of stimulant use since accidental death is due in part to their effects on the cardiovascular and temperature regulating systems. Fatalities under conditions of extreme exertion have been reported among athletes who have taken stimulants in moderate amounts.

If withdrawn from stimulants, chronic high-dose users exhibit profound depression, apathy, fatigue, and disturbed sleep for up to 20 hours a day. The immediate withdrawal syndrome may last for several days. There may also be a lingering impairment of perception and thought processes. Anxiety, an incapacitating tenseness, and suicidal tendencies may persist for weeks or months. Many experts now interpret these symptoms as indicating that stimulant drugs are capable of producing physical dependence. Whether the withdrawal syndrome is physical or psychological in origin is, in this instance, academic since the stimulants are recognized as among the most potent agents of reward and reinforcement that underlie the problem of dependence.

Cocaine

The most potent stimulant of natural origin, cocaine is extracted from the leaves of the coca plant (Erythroxylon coca), which has been grown in the Andean highlands of South America since prehistoric times. The leaves of the plant are chewed in the region for refreshment and relief from fatigue.

Pure cocaine, the principal psychoactive ingredient, was first isolated in the 1880s. It was used as an anesthetic in eye surgery for which no previously known drug had been suitable. It became particularly useful in surgery of the nose and throat because of its ability to anesthetize tissue while simultaneously constricting blood vessels and limiting bleeding. Many of its therapeutic applications are now obsolete because of the development of safer drugs as local anesthetics.

Illicit cocaine is usually distributed as a white crystalline powder, often diluted by a variety of other ingredients, the most common of which are sugars such as lactose, inositol, mannitol, and local anesthetics such as lidocaine. The frequent adulteration is to increase volume and thus to multiply profits.

The drug is most commonly administered by being "snorted" through the nasal passages. Symptoms of repeated use in this manner may resemble the congested nose of a common cold.

The intensity of the psychological effects of cocaine, as with many psychoactive drugs, depends on the rate of entry into the blood. Intravenous injection or smoking produces an almost immediate intense experience. Cocaine hydrochloride, the usual form in which cocaine is sold, while soluble in water and sometimes injected, is fairly insensitive to heat. Conversion of cocaine hydrochloride to cocaine base yields a substance that will become more volatile when heated. "Crack," or cocaine base in the form of chips, chunks or "rocks," is usually vaporized in a pipe or smoked with plant material in a cigarette or a "joint." Inhalation of the cocaine fumes produces effects that are very fast in onset, very intense, and are quickly over. These intense effects are often followed within minutes by a dysphoric "crash," leading to frequently repeated doses and rapid addiction.

Because of the intensity of its pleasurable effects, cocaine has the potential for extraordinary psychic dependency. Recurrent users may resort to larger doses at shorter intervals until their lives are entirely committed to their drug addiction. Anxiety, restlessness, and extreme irritability may indicate the onset of a toxic psychosis similar to paranoid schizophrenia. Tactile hallucinations so afflict some chronic users that they injure themselves in attempting to remove imaginary insects from under the skin. Others feel persecuted and fear that they are being watched and followed.

Excessive doses of cocaine may cause seizures and death from, for example, respiratory failure, stroke, cerebral hemorrhage, or heart failure. There is no specific treatment for cocaine overdose. Nor does tolerance develop to the toxic effects of cocaine. In fact, there are studies which indicate that repeated use lowers the dose at which toxicity occurs. There is no "safe" dose of cocaine.

Amphetamines

Amphetamine, dextroamphetamine, and methamphetamine are so similar in the effects they induce that they can be differentiated from one another only by laboratory analysis. Amphetamine was first used clinically in the mid-1930s to treat narcolepsy, a rare disorder resulting in an uncontrollable tendency to sleep. After the introduction of the amphetamines into medical practice, the number of conditions for which they were prescribed multiplied, as did the quantities made available.

For a time, they were sold without prescription in inhalers and other over-the-counter preparations. Abuse became popular. Many segments of the population, especially those concerned with extensive or irregular hours, were among those who used amphetamines orally in excessive amounts. "Speed freaks," who injected amphetamines, became known for their bizarre and often violent behavior. Over-the-counter availability (except inhalers) was terminated and amphetamines now are available only by prescription. Inhalers still are available over-the-counter.

Whereas a prescribed dose is between 2.5 and 15 mg per day, those on a "speed" binge have been known to inject as much as 1,000 mg every 2 or 3 hours. Recognition of the deleterious effects of these drugs and their limited therapeutic value led to a marked reduction in their use by the medical profession. The medical use of amphetamines is now limited to narcolepsy, attention deficit disorders in children, and certain cases of obesity—as a short-term adjunct to a restricted diet for patients resistant to other forms of therapy.

Their illicit use closely parallels that of cocaine in the range of its short-term and long-term effects. Despite broad recognition of the risks, clandestine laboratories produce vast quantities of amphetamines, particularly methamphetamine, for distribution on the illicit market.

Methamphetamine Abusers

According to a recent study by the National Institute on Drug Abuse, abusing populations are predominantly white, lower middle income, high school educated, young adults ranging in age from 20 to 35 years. Although clients in drug treatment programs for methamphetamine abuse report that the drug is commonly used by adolescent males, that group is not observed in morbidity and mortality data. Abuse patterns suggest an estimated two- to four-year latency period from first use to full addiction. Most treatment clients interviewed initiated use by intranasal snorting, but then turned to intravenous (IV) administration. Compulsive usage accelerates with IV use because of the drug's rapid onset of action in a pattern similar to crack cocaine abuse. Although crack is not injected, inhalation of its vapors provides a rapid pulmonary delivery of the drug in concentrated dose to the brain promoting an intensified onset of action. This method, like IV methamphetamine use, triggers an initial, short-term jolt which compels the user to repeat drug use again and again in a futile attempt to re-experience the drug's exhilarating effects. Additionally, needle sharing with methamphetamine appears common despite users' knowledge of HIV transmission risk. Thus, methamphetamine has been characterized as "white man's version of crack" and a "gateway to needle use and sharing."

Dosage levels reported by those interviewed varied according to how long methamphetamine had been used, the purity of the drug, and its route of administration. Doses tended to increase significantly with continued use, particularly with IV administration. The smallest unit of purchase was usually 1/4 gram, which would provide approximately 4 doses to the first time, intranasal user. Quantities used by study participants ranged from less than 1/4 gram to 4 grams per day. A common unit of sale is called an *eightball*, reported to be 1/8 of an ounce or 3.5 grams which usually sold for $150. Prices for an eightball were mentioned as low as $90 and as high as $200.

Phenmetrazine (Preludin) and Methylphenidate (Ritalin)

The medical indications, patterns of abuse, and adverse effects of phenmetrazine (Preludin) and methylphenidate (Ritalin) compare closely with those of the other stimulants. Phenmetrazine is medically used only as an appetite suppressant and methylphenidate mainly for treatment of attention deficit disorders in children. They have been subject to abuse in countries where freely available, as they are here in localities where medical practitioners write prescriptions on demand. While the abuse of these drugs involves both oral and intravenous use, most of the abuse involves the injection of tablets dissolved in water. Complications arising from such use are common since the tablets contain insoluble materials which, when injected, block small blood vessels and cause serious damage, especially in the lungs and retina of the eye.

Anorectic Drugs

In recent years, a number of drugs have been manufactured and marketed to replace amphetamines as appetite suppressants. These so-called anorectic drugs include benzphetamine (Didrex), chlorphentermine (Pre-Sate, etc.), clortermine (Voranil), diethylpropion (Tenuate, Tepanil, etc.), fenfluramine (Pondimin), mazindol (Sanorex, Mazanor), phendimetrazine (Plegine, Bacarate, Melfiat, Statobex, Tanorex, etc.), phentermine (Ionamin, Adipex-P, etc.). They produce many of the effects of the amphetamines, but are generally less potent. All are controlled because of the similarity of their effects to those of the amphetamines. Fenfluramine differs somewhat from the others in that at low doses it produces sedation.

CANNABIS

Cannabis sativa L., the hemp plant, grows wild throughout most of the tropic and temperate regions of the world. It is a single species. This plant has long been cultivated for the tough fiber of the stem, the seed used in feed mixtures, and the oil as an ingredient of paint, as well as for its biologically active substances, most highly concentrated in the leaves and resinous flowering tops.

The plant material has been used as a drug for centuries. In 1839, it entered the annals of western medicine with the publication of an article surveying its therapeutic potential, including possible uses as an analgesic and anticonvulsant agent. It was alleged to be effective in treating a wide range of physical and mental ailments during the remainder of the 19th century. With the introduction of many new synthetic drugs in the 20th century, interest in it as a medication waned.

The controls imposed with the passage of the Marihuana Tax Act of 1937 further curtailed its use in treatment, and by 1941 it had been deleted from the *U.S. Pharmacopoeia* and the *National Formulary*, the official compendia of drugs. But advances continued to be made in the chemistry of cannabis. Among the many cannabinoids synthesized by the plant are cannabinol, cannabidiol, cannabinolidic acids, cannabigerol, cannabichromene, and several isomers of tetrahydrocannabinol, one of which is believed responsible for most of its characteristic psychoactive effects. This is delta-9-tetrahydrocannabinol (THC), one of 61 cannabinoids which are unique chemicals found only in cannabis.

Cannabis products are usually smoked in the form of loosely rolled cigarettes ("joints"). They may be used alone or in combination with other substances. They may also be administered orally, but are reported to be about three times more potent when smoked. The effects are felt within minutes, reach their peak in 10 to 30 minutes, and may linger for 2 or 3 hours.

A condensed description of these effects is apt to be inadequate or even misleading. So much depends upon the experience and expectations of the individual as well as the activity of the drug itself. Low doses tend to induce restlessness and an increasing sense of well-being, followed by a dreamy state of relaxation, and frequently hunger, especially a craving for sweets. Changes of sensory perception—a more vivid sense of sight, smell, touch, taste, and hearing—may be accompanied by subtle alterations in thought formation and expression. Stronger doses intensify reactions. The individual may experience shifting sensory imagery, rapidly fluctuating emotions, a flight of fragmentary thoughts with disturbed associations, an altered sense of self-identity, impaired memory, and a dulling of attention despite an illusion of heightened insight. This state of intoxication may not be noticeable to an observer. High doses may result in image distortion, a loss of personal identity, and fantasies and hallucination. Very high doses may result in a toxic psychosis.

During the past 20 to 25 years, there has been a resurgence in the scientific study of cannabis, one goal of which has been to develop therapeutic agents which, if used as directed in medical treatment, will not produce harmful side effects. THC can be synthesized in the laboratory. Because it is a liquid insoluble in water and it decomposes on exposure to air and light, it is administered in soft gelatin capsules. Research has resulted in development and marketing of a product containing THC for the control of nausea and vomiting caused by chemotherapeutic agents used in the treatment of cancer. None of the synthetic cannabinoids have so far been detected in the drug traffic.

Three drugs that come from cannabis are currently distributed on the U.S. illicit market. Having no currently accepted medical use in treatment in the United States, they remain under Schedule I of the CSA.

Marijuana

The term marijuana is used in this country to refer to the cannabis plant and to any part or extract of it that produces somatic or psychic changes in humans. A tobacco-like substance produced by drying the leaves and flowering tops of the plant, marijuana varies significantly in its potency, depending on the source and selectivity of plant materials used. Most wild U.S. cannabis is considered inferior because of a low concentration of THC, usually less than 0.5 per-

cent. Jamaican, Colombian, and Mexican varieties range between 0.5 and 7 percent. The most selective produce is reputed to be sinsemilla (Spanish, *sin semilla:* without seed), prepared from the unpollinated female cannabis plant, samples of which have been found to contain up to 20 percent THC. Southeast Asian "Thai sticks," consisting of marijuana buds bound on short sections of bamboo, are encountered infrequently on the U.S. illicit market.

Hashish

The Middle East is the main source of hashish. It consists of the drug-rich resinous secretions of the cannabis plant, which are collected, dried, and then compressed into a variety of forms, such as balls, cakes, or cookie-like sheets. The THC content of hashish in the United States averages 3 percent.

Hashish Oil

The name is used by illicit drug users and dealers but is a misnomer in suggesting any resemblance to hashish other than its objective of further concentration. Hashish oil is produced by a process of repeated extraction of cannabis plant materials to yield a dark viscious liquid, current samples of which average about 20 percent THC. In terms of its psychoactive effect, a drop or two of this liquid on a cigarette is equal to a single "joint" of marijuana.

HALLUCINOGENS

Hallucinogenic drugs, both natural and synthetic, are substances that distort the perception of objective reality. They induce a state of excitation of the central nervous system, manifested by alterations of mood, usually euphoric, but sometimes severely depressive. Under the influence of hallucinogens, the senses of direction, distance, and time becomes disoriented. A user may speak of "seeing" sounds and "hearing" colors. If taken in a large enough dose, the drug produces delusions and visual hallucinations. Occasionally, depersonalization and depression are so severe that suicide is possible, but the most common danger is impaired judgment, leading to rash decisions and accidents. Persons in hallucinogenic states should, therefore, be closely supervised and upset as little as possible to keep them from harming themselves and others. Acute anxiety, restlessness, and sleeplessness are common until the drug wears off.

Long after hallucinogens are eliminated from the body, users may experience flashbacks—fragmentary recurrences of psychedelic effects—such as the intensification of a perceived color, the apparent motion of a fixed object, or the mistaking of one object for another. Recurrent use produces tolerance, which tends to encourage resorting to greater amounts. Although no evidence of physical dependence is detectable when the drugs are withdrawn, recurrent use tends to produce psychic dependence, varying according to the drug, the dose, and the individual user. It should be stressed that the hallucinogens are unpredictable in their effects each time they are used.

The abuse of hallucinogens in the United States reached a peak of popularity in the late 1960s, and a subsequent decline was attributed to broader awareness of their hazardous effects. Their abuse, however, reemerged in the late 1970s and has continued in this decade.

Peyote and Mescaline

The primary active ingredient of the peyote cactus is the hallucinogen *mescaline*. It is derived from the fleshy parts or buttons of this plant, which has been employed by Indians in northern Mexico from the earliest recorded time as a part of traditional religious rites. The Native American Church, which uses peyote in religious ceremonies, has been exempted from certain provisions of the CSA. Peyote, or mescal buttons, and mescaline should not be confused with mescal, the colorless Mexican liquor distilled from the leaves of maguey plants. Usually ground into a powder, peyote is taken orally. Mescaline can also be produced synthetically. A dose of 350 to 500 mg of mescaline produces illusions and hallucinations lasting from 5 to 12 hours.

DOM, DOB, MDA, and MDMA

Many chemical variations of mescaline and amphetamine have been synthesized in the laboratory, certain of which at various times have won acceptance among illicit drug users and traffickers. DOM (4-methyl-2,5-dimethoxyamphetamine), synthesized in 1963, was introduced in 1967 into the Haight-Asbury drug scene in San Francisco. At first named STP after a motor oil additive, the acronym was quickly reinterpreted to stand for "Serenity, Tranquility, and Peace." A host of related chemicals are illicitly manufactured, including DOB (4-bromo-2,5-dimethoxyamphetamine), MDA (3, 4-methylenedioxyamphetamine), and MDMA (3, 4-methylenedioxymethamphetamine) (XTC). These drugs differ from one another in their speed of onset, duration of action, potency, and capacity to modify mood with or without producing hallucinations. They are usually taken orally, sometimes "snorted," and rarely injected intravenously. Because they are produced in clandestine laboratories, they are seldom pure, and the dose in a tablet, in a capsule, or on a square of impregnated paper may be expected to vary considerably. The names of these drugs are sometimes used to misrepresent other chemicals.

Psilocybin and Psilocyn

Like the peyote cactus, Psilocybe mushrooms have been used for centuries in traditional Indian rites. When they are eaten, these "sacred" or "magic" mushrooms affect mood and perception in a manner similar to mescaline and LSD. Their active ingredients, psilocybin and psilocyn, are chemically related to LSD. They can now be made synthetically, but much of what is sold under these names on the illicit market consists of other chemical compounds.

LSD (LSD-25, lysergide)

LSD is an abbreviation of the German expression for lysergic acid diethylamide. It is produced from lysergic acid, a substance derived from the ergot fungus which grows on rye or from lysergic acid amide, a chemical found in morning glory seeds. Both of these precursor chemicals are in Schedule III of the CSA.

LSD was first synthesized in 1938. Its psychotomimetic effects were discovered in 1943 when a chemist accidentally took some LSD. As he began to experience the effects now known as a "trip," he was aware of vertigo and an intensification of light. Closing his eyes, he saw a stream of fantastic images of extraordinary vividness accompanied by a kaleidoscopic play of colors. This condition lasted for about two hours.

Because of the extremely high potency of LSD, its structural relationship to a chemical which is present in the brain, and its similarity in effects to certain aspects of psychosis, LSD was used as a tool of research to study the mechanism of mental illness. Although there was a marked decline from its initial popularity in illicit channels during the 1960s, there are indications that its illicit use once again may be increasing to some extent.

LSD is usually sold in the form of tablets, thin squares of gelatin ("window panes"), or impregnated paper ("blotter acid"). The average effective oral dose is from 30 to 50 micrograms, but the amount per dosage unit varies greatly. The effects of higher doses persist for 10 or 12 hours. Tolerance develops rapidly.

Phencyclidine (PCP) and Related Drugs

Phencyclidine was investigated in the 1950s as a human anesthetic, but, because of side effects of confusion and delirium, its development for human use was discontinued. It became commercially available for use in veterinary medicine in the 1960s under the trade name Sernylan. In 1978, however, the manufacturer stopped production. That same year phencyclidine was transferred from Schedule III to Schedule II of the CSA, together with two previously unscheduled precursor chemicals. Most, if not all, phencyclidine on the U.S. illicit market is produced in clandestine laboratories.

More commonly known as PCP, it is sold under at least 50 other names, including Angel Dust, Crystal, Supergrass, Killer Weed, Embalming Fluid, and Rocket Fuel, that reflect the range of its bizarre and volatile effects. It is also frequently misrepresented as mescaline, LSD, or THC. In its pure form, it is a white crystalline powder that readily dissolves in water. Most PCP now contains contaminants resulting from its makeshift manufacture, causing the color to range from tan to brown and the consistency from a powder to a gummy mass. Although sold in tablets and capsules, as well as in powder and liquid form, it is commonly applied to a leafy material, such as parsley, mint, oregano, or marijuana, and smoked.

The drug is as variable in its effects as it is in its appearance. A moderate amount often produces in the user a sense of detachment, distance, and estrangement from the surroundings. Numbness, slurred or blocked speech, and a loss of coordination may be accompanied by a sense of strength and invulnerability. A blank stare, rapid and involuntary eye movements, and an exaggerated gait are among the more common observable effects. Auditory hallucinations, image distortion as in a fun-house mirror, and severe mood disorders may also occur, producing in some acute anxiety and a feeling of impending doom, in others paranoia and violent hostility. PCP is unique among popular drugs of abuse in its power to produce psychoses indistinguishable from schizophrenia. Although such extreme psychic reactions are usually associated with repeated use of the drug, they have been known to occur in some cases after only one dose and to last, or recur intermittently, long after the drug has left the body. Phencyclidine now poses greater risks to the user than any other drug of abuse, with the possible exception of crack—the smokable form of cocaine—whose street distribution and use by inhalation parallels that of PCP.

Modification of the manufacturing process may further yield chemically related analogues capable of producing, so far as is known, similar psychic effects. Three of these analogues have so far been encountered on the U.S. illicit market, where they have been sold as PCP. In view of the severe behavioral toxicity of phencyclidine and its analogues, in November 1978 the Congress passed legislation increasing the penalties for manufacture, distribution, and possession with intent to distribute these chemicals. The penalties for manufacture, distribution, and possession with intent to distribute PCP were further increased by the Controlled Substances Penalties Amendments Act of 1984 and the Narcotics Penalties and Enforcement Act of 1986. There are enhanced penalties for violations involving specified quantities of PCP or substances containing PCP.

1. The chemicals are 1-phenylcyclohexylamine and 1-piperidinocyclohexanecarbonitrile (PCC).
2. The analogues are N-ethyl-1-phenylcyclohexaylamine (PCE), 1-(2-phenylcyclohexyl)-pyrrolidine (PCP; PHP), and 1-[1-(2-thienyl-cyclohexyl)-piperdine)] (TPCP; PCP).

ALCOHOL

Source: U.S. Department of Education.

Effects.—Alcohol consumption causes a number of marked changes in behavior. Even low doses significantly impair the judgment and coordination required to drive a car safely, increasing the likelihood that the driver will be involved in an accident. Low to moderate doses of alcohol also increase the incidence of a variety of aggressive acts, including spouse and child abuse. Moderate to high doses of alcohol cause marked impairments in higher mental functions, severely altering a person's ability to learn and remember information. Very high doses cause respiratory depression and death. If combined with other depressants of the central nervous system, much lower doses of alcohol will produce the effects just described.

Repeated use of alcohol can lead to dependence. Sudden cessation of alcohol intake is likely to produce withdrawal symptoms, including severe anxiety, tremors, hallucinations, and convulsions. Alcohol withdrawal can be life-threatening. Long-term consumption of large quantities of alcohol, particularly when combined with poor nutrition, can also lead to permanent damage to vital organs such as the brain and the liver.

Mothers who drink alcohol during pregnancy may give birth to infants with fetal alcohol syndrome. These infants have irreversible physical abnormalities and mental retardation. In addition, research indicates that children of alcoholic parents are at greater risk than other youngsters of becoming alcoholics.

Youth and Alcohol

Alcohol is the number one drug problem among youth. The easy availability, widespread acceptability, and extensive promotion of alcoholic beverages within our society make alcohol the most widely used and abused drug.

• Alcohol use is widespread. By their senior year of high school almost all students will have tried alcoholic beverages; 2 out of 3 will be current users; 1 in 20 will be daily users; and almost 4 out of 10 will consume 5 or more drinks in a row at least once every 2 weeks.

• Early alcohol use is associated with subsequent alcohol dependence and related health problems. Youth who use alcohol at a younger age are more likely to use alcohol heavily and to experience alcohol-related problems affecting their relationships with family and friends by late adolescence. Their school performance is likely to suffer, and they are more

likely to be truant. They are also more likely to abuse other drugs and to get in trouble with the law, or, if they are girls, to become pregnant.

TOBACCO

Source: U.S. Department of Education.

Effects.—The smoking of tobacco products is the chief avoidable cause of death in our society. Smokers are more likely than nonsmokers to contract heart disease—some 170,000 die each year from smoking-related coronary heart disease. Lung, larynx, esophageal, bladder, pancreatic, and kidney cancers also strike smokers at increased rates. Some 30 percent of cancer deaths (130,000 per year) are linked to smoking. Chronic obstructive lung diseases such as emphysema and chronic bronchitis are 10 times more likely to occur among smokers than among nonsmokers.

Smoking during pregnancy also poses serious risks. Spontaneous abortion, preterm birth, low birth weights, and fetal and infant deaths are all more likely to occur when the pregnant woman/mother is a smoker.

Cigarette smoke contains some 4,000 chemicals, several of which are known carcinogens. Other toxins and irritants found in smoke can produce eye, nose, and throat irritations. Carbon monoxide, another component of cigarette smoke, combines with hemoglobin in the blood stream to form carboxyhemoglobin, a substance that interferes with the body's ability to obtain and use oxygen.

Perhaps the most dangerous substance in tobacco smoke is nicotine. Although it is implicated in the onset of heart attacks and cancer, its most dangerous role is reinforcing and strengthening the desire to smoke. Because nicotine is highly addictive, addicts find it very difficult to stop smoking. Of 1,000 typical smokers, fewer than 20 percent succeed in stopping on the first try.

Although the harmful effects of smoking cannot be questioned, people who quit can make significant strides in repairing damage done by smoking. For pack-a-day smokers, the increased risk of heart attack dissipates after 10 years. The likelihood of contracting lung cancer as a result of smoking can also be greatly reduced by quitting.

Sources of Information

American Council for Drug Education.—This organization provides information on drug use, develops media campaigns, reviews scientific findings, publishes books and a newsletter, and offers films and curriculum materials for preteens. 204 Monroe St., Rockville, Md. 20850. Telephone (301) 294-0600.

Parents' Resource Institute for Drug Education, Inc. (PRIDE)—This national resource and information center offers consultant services to parent groups, school personnel, and youth groups, and provides a drug-use survey service. Membership is $25, $45 international. The Hurt Building, 50 Hurt Plaza, Suite 210, Atlanta, Ga. 30303. Telephone (404) 577-4500.

U.S. Clearinghouse.—(A publication list is available on request, along with placement on a mailing list for new publications. Single copies are free.) National Clearinghouse for Alcohol and Drug Information (NCADI), P.O. Box 2345, Rockville, Md. 20852. Telephone (301) 468-2600

GEOGRAPHY

World Geography
Explorations and Discoveries
(All years are A.D. unless B.C. is specified.)

Country or place	Event	Explorer or discoverer	Date
AFRICA			
Sierra Leone	Visited	Hanno, Carthaginian seaman	c. 520 B.C.
Zaire River (Congo)	Mouth discovered	Diogo Cão, Portuguese	c. 1484
Cape of Good Hope	Rounded	Bartolomeu Diaz, Portuguese	1488
Gambia River	Explored	Mungo Park, Scottish explorer	1795
Sahara	Crossed	Dixon Denham and Hugh Clapperton, English explorers	1822–23
Zambezi River	Discovered	David Livingstone, Scottish explorer	1851
Sudan	Explored	Heinrich Barth, German explorer	1852–55
Victoria Falls	Discovered	Livingstone	1855
Lake Tanganyika	Discovered	Richard Burton and John Speke, British explorers	1858
Zaire River (Congo)	Traced	Sir Henry M. Stanley, British explorer	1877
ASIA			
Punjab (India)	Visited	Alexander the Great	327 B.C.
China	Visited	Marco Polo, Italian traveler	c. 1272
Tibet	Visited	Odoric of Pordenone, Italian monk	c. 1325
Southern China	Explored	Niccolò dei Conti, Venetian traveler	c. 1440
India	Visited (Cape route)	Vasco da Gama, Portuguese navigator	1498
Japan	Visited	St. Francis Xavier of Spain	1549
Arabia	Explored	Carsten Niebuhr, German explorer	1762
China	Explored	Ferdinand Richthofen, German scientiest	1868
Mongolia	Explored	Nikolai M. Przhevalsky, Russian explorer	1870–73
Central Asia	Explored	Sven Hedin, Swedish scientist	1890–1908
EUROPE			
Shetland Islands	Visited	Pytheas of Massilia (Marseille)	c. 325 B.C.
North Cape	Rounded	Ottar, Norwegian explorer	c. 870
Iceland	Colonized	Norwegian noblemen	c. 890–900
NORTH AMERICA			
Greenland	Colonized	Eric the Red, Norwegian	c. 985
Labrador; Nova Scotia(?)	Discovered	Leif Ericson, Norse explorer	1000
West Indies	Discovered	Christopher Columbus, Italian	1492
North America	Coast discovered	Giovanni Caboto (John Cabot), for British	1497
Pacific Ocean	Discovered	Vasco Núñez de Balboa, Spanish explorer	1513
Florida	Explored	Ponce de León, Spanish explorer	1513
Mexico	Conquered	Hernando Cortés, Spanish adventurer	1519–21
St. Lawrence River	Discovered	Jacques Cartier, French navigator	1534
Southwest U. S.	Explored	Francisco Coronado, Spanish explorer	1540–42
Colorado River	Discovered	Hernando de Alarcón, Spanish explorer	1540
Mississippi River	Discovered	Hernando de Soto, Spanish explorer	1541
Frobisher Bay	Discovered	Martin Frobisher, English seaman	1576
Maine Coast	Explored	Samuel de Champlain, French explorer	1604

Country or place	Event	Explorer or discoverer	Date
Jamestown, Va.	Settled	John Smith, English colonist	1607
Hudson River	Explored	Henry Hudson, English navigator	1609
Hudson Bay (Canada)	Discovered	Henry Hudson	1610
Baffin Bay	Discovered	William Baffin, English navigator	1616
Lake Michigan	Navigated	Jean Nicolet, French explorer	1634
Arkansas River	Discovered	Jacques Marquette and Louis Jolliet, French explorers	1673
Mississippi River	Explored	Sieur de La Salle, French explorer	1682
Bering Strait	Discovered	Vitus Bering, Danish explorer	1728
Alaska	Discovered	Vitus Bering	1741
Mackenzie River (Canada)	Discovered	Sir Alexander Mackenzie, Scottish–Canadian explorer	1789
Northwest U. S.	Explored	Meriwether Lewis and William Clark	1804–06
Northeast Passage (Arctic Ocean)	Navigated	Nils Nordenskjöld, Swedish explorer	1879
Greenland	Explored	Robert Peary, American explorer	1892
Northwest Passage	Navigated	Roald Amundsen, Norwegian explorer	1906
SOUTH AMERICA			
Continent	Visited	Columbus, Italian	1498
Brazil	Discovered	Pedro Alvarez Cabral, Portuguese	1500
Peru	Conquered	Francisco Pizarro, Spanish explorer	1532–33
Amazon River	Explored	Francisco Orellana, Spanish explorer	1541
Cape Horn	Discovered	Willem C. Schouten, Dutch navigator	1615
OCEANIA			
Papua New Guinea	Visited	Jorge de Menezes, Portuguese explorer	1526
Australia	Visited	Abel Janszoon Tasman, Dutch navigator	1642
Tasmania	Discovered		
Australia	Explored	John McDouall Stuart, English explorer	1828
Australia	Explored	Robert Burke and William Wills, Australian explorers	1861
New Zealand	Sighted (and named)	Abel Janszoon Tasman	1642
New Zealand	Visited	James Cook, English navigator	1769
ARCTIC, ANTARCTIC, AND MISCELLANEOUS			
Ocean exploration	Expedition	Magellan's ships circled globe	1519–22
Galápagos Islands	Visited	Diego de Rivadeneira, Spanish captain	1535
Spitsbergen	Visited	Willem Barents, Dutch navigator	1596
Antarctic Circle	Crossed	James Cook, English navigator	1773
Antarctica	Discovered	Nathaniel Palmer, U. S. whaler (archipelago) and Fabian Gottlieb von Bellingshausen, Russian admiral (mainland)	1820–21
Antarctica	Explored	Charles Wilkes, American explorer	1840
North Pole	Reached	Robert E. Peary, American explorer	1909
South Pole	Reached	Roald Amundsen, Norwegian explorer	1911

The Continents

A continent is defined as a large unbroken land mass completely surrounded by water, although in some cases continents are (or were in part) connected by land bridges.

The hypothesis first suggested late in the 19th century was that the continents consist of lighter rocks that rest on heavier crustal material in about the same manner that icebergs float on water. That the rocks forming the continents are lighter than the material below them and under the ocean bottoms is now established. As a consequence of this fact, Alfred Wegener (for the first time in 1912) suggested that the continents are slowly moving, at a rate of about one yard per century, so that their relative positions are not rigidly fixed. Many geologists that were originally skeptical have come to accept this theory of Continental Drift.

When describing a continent, it is important to remember that there is a fundamental difference between a deep ocean, like the Atlantic, and shallow seas, like the Baltic and most of the North Sea, which are merely flooded portions of a continent. Another and entirely different point to remember is that political considerations have often overridden geographical facts when it came to naming continents.

Geographically speaking, Europe, including the British Isles, is a large western peninsula of the continent of Asia; and many geographers, when referring to Europe and Asia, speak of the Eurasian Continent. But traditionally, Europe is counted as a separate continent, with the Ural and the Caucasus mountains forming the line of demarcation between Europe and Asia.

To the south of Europe, Asia has an odd-shaped peninsula jutting westward, which has a large number of political subdivisions. The northern section is taken up by Turkey; to the south of Turkey there are Syria, Iraq, Israel, Jordan, Saudi Arabia, and a number of smaller Arab countries. All this is part of Asia. Traditionally, the island of Cyprus in the Mediterranean is also considered to be part of Asia, while the island of Crete is counted as European.

The large islands of Java, Borneo, and Sumatra and the smaller islands near them are counted as part of "tropical Asia," while New Guinea is counted as related to Australia. In the case of the Americas, the problem arises as to whether they should be considered one or two continents. There are good arguments on both sides, but since there is now a land bridge between North and South America (in the past it was often flooded) and since no part of the sea east of the land bridge is deep ocean, it is more logical to consider the Americas as one continent.

Politically, based mainly on history, the Americas are divided into North America (from the Arctic to the Mexican border), Central America (from Mexico to Panama, with the Caribbean islands), and South America. Greenland is considered a section of North America, while Iceland is traditionally counted as a European island because of its political ties with the Scandinavian countries.

The island groups in the Pacific are often called "Oceania," but this name does *not* imply that scientists consider them the remains of a continent.

The seven continents are North America, South America, Europe, Asia, Africa, Australia, and Antarctica.

Volcanoes of the World

About 500 volcanoes have had recorded eruptions within historical times. Almost two thirds of these are in the Northern Hemisphere. Most volcanoes occur at the boundaries of the earth's crustal plates, such as the famous "Ring of Fire" that surrounds the Pacific Ocean plate. Of the world's active volcanoes, about 60% are along the perimeter of the Pacific, about 17% on mid-oceanic islands, about 14% in an arc along the south of the Indonesian islands, and about 9% in the Mediterranean area, Africa, and Asia Minor. Many of the world's volcanoes are submarine and have unrecorded eruptions.

Pacific "Ring of Fire"

NORTHWEST
Japan: At least 33 active vents.
Aso (5,223 ft; 1,592 m), on Kyushu, has one of the largest craters in the world.
Asama (over 8,300 ft; 2,530 m), on Honshu, is continuously active; violent eruption in 1783.
Azuma (nearly 7,700 ft; 2,347 m), on Honshu, erupted in 1900.
Chokai (7,300 ft; 2,225 m), on Honshu, erupted in 1974 after having been quiescent since 1861.
Fujiyama (Fujisan) (12,385 ft; 3,775 m), on Honshu, southwest of Tokyo. Symmetrical in outline, snow-covered. Regarded as a sacred mountain.
On-take (3,668 ft; 1,118 m), on peninsula of Kyushu. Strong smoke emissions and explosions began November 1973 and continued through 1974.
Mt. Unzen (4,500 ft; 1,371 m), on Kyushu erupted on June 3, 1991. Last eruption was in 1792.
U.S.S.R.: Kamchatka peninsula, 14–18 active volcanoes. Klyuchevskaya (Kluchev) (15,500 ft; 4,724 m) reported active in 1974.
Kurile Islands: At least 13 active volcanoes and several submarine outbreaks.

SOUTHWEST
New Zealand: Mount Tarawera (3,645 ft; 1,112 m), on North Island, had a severe eruption in 1886 that destroyed the famous Pink and White sinter terraces of Rotomahana, a hot lake.
Ngauruhoe (7,515 ft; 2,291 m), on North Island, emits steam and vapor constantly. Erupted 1974.
Papua New Guinea: Karkar Island (4,920 ft; 1,500 m). Mild eruptions 1974.

Philippine Islands: About 100 eruptive centers; Hibok Hibok, on Camiguin, erupted September 1950 and again in December 1951, when about 750 were reported killed or missing; eruptions continued during 1952–53.
Taal (4,752 ft; 1,448 m), on Luzon. Major eruption in 1965 killed 190; erupted again, 1968.
Mt. Pinatubo (4,795 ft; 1,462 m), on Luzon erupted on June 10, 1991. Last major eruption in 1380.
Volcano Islands: Mount Suribachi (546 ft; 166 m), on Iwo Jima. A sulfurous steaming volcano. Raising of U.S. flag over Mount Suribachi was one of the dramatic episodes of World War II.

NORTHEAST
Alaska: Mount Wrangell (14,163 ft; 4,317 m) and Mount Katmai (about 6,700 ft; 2,042 m). On June 6, 1912, a violent eruption (Nova Rupta) of Mount Katmai occurred, during which the "Valley of Ten Thousand Smokes" was formed.
Aleutian Islands: There are 32 active vents known and numerous inactive cones. Akutan Island (over 4,000 ft; 1,220 m) erupted in 1974, with ash and debris rising over 300 ft.
Great Sitkin (5,741 ft; 1,750 m). Explosive activity February-September 1974, accompanied by earthquake originating at volcano that registered 2.3 on Richter scale.
Augustine Island: Augustine volcano (4,000 ft; 1,220 m) erupted March 27, 1986. It last erupted in 1976.
California, Oregon, Washington: Lassen Peak (10,453 ft; 3,186 m) in California is one of two observed active volcanoes in the U.S. outside Alaska and Hawaii. The last period of activity was 1914–17. Mt. St. Helens (9,677 ft; 2,950 m) in the Cascade Range of southwest Washington became active on March 27, 1980, and erupted on May 18 after being inactive since 1857. From April 15 through May 1, 1986, weak activity began for the first time in two years. Other mountains of volcanic origin include Mount Shasta (California), Mount Hood (Oregon), Mount Mazama (Oregon)—the mountain containing Crater Lake, Mount Rainier (Washington), and Mount Baker (Washington), which has been steaming since

Continued on page 462

The Pacific Ocean "Ring of Fire"

Bezmianny

Vesuvius

Vulcano

Mt. Etna Stromboli

Barren Island

Mt. Fiji

Myōjin-shō

Mayon

Taal

Ulawun

Mt. Sinabung

Krakatau

Bouvet

Heard

0°   60°   120°

Earthquake Fatalities Rose in 1990

Source: U.S. Department of the Interior, U.S. Geological Survey.

According to the U.S. Geological Survey, over 52,000 people were killed in earthquakes during 1990, almost reaching the ten-year total of over 57,000 deaths for the 1980s. None of the fatalities were in the United States. An estimated 50,000 of those deaths resulted from an Iranian earthquake on June 21.

During the past three decades, the worldwide death toll from earthquakes has averaged about 30,000 people a year.

Sixty-eight significant earthquakes occurred throughout the world in 1990, six more than the annual average during the 1980s. The USGS defines significant earthquakes as those that register 6.5 or

Source: U.S. Department of the Interior, U.S. Geological Survey.

larger in magnitude, or smaller earthquakes that cause casualties or significant damage. Forty of the significant earthquakes in 1990 occurred in the world's most prolific earthquake zone—the Ring of Fire rimming the Pacific Ocean.

The strongest earthquake in the world in 1990 occurred July 16 on Luzon Island in the Philippines, registering a magnitude of 7.8 and leaving more than 1,600 people dead.

According to the USGS, there are probably several million earthquakes occurring each year, but most are so small or occur in such remote areas that they are undetected even by the most sensitive instruments in the world.

October 1975, but gives no sign of an impending eruption.

SOUTHEAST

Chile and Argentina: About 25 active or potentially active.

Colombia: Huila (nearly 18,900 ft; 5,760 m), a vapor-emitting volcano, and Tolima (nearly 18,500 ft; 5,640 m). Eruption of Puracé (15,600 ft; 4,755 m) in 1949 killed 17 people. Nevado del Ruiz (16,200 ft; 4,938 m.), erupted Nov. 13, 1985, sending torrential floods of mud and water engulfing the town of Armero and killing more than 22,000 people.

Ecuador: Cayambe (nearly 19,000 ft; 5,791 m). Almost on the equator.

Cotopaxi (19,344 ft; 5,896 m). Perhaps highest active volcano in the world. Possesses a beautifully formed cone.

Reventador (11,434 ft; 3,485 m). Observed in active state in late 1973.

El Salvador: Izalco ("beacon of Central America") (7,830 ft; 2,387 m) first appeared in 1770 and is still growing (erupted in 1950, 1956; last erupted in October-November 1966). San Salvador (6,187 ft; 1,886 m) had a violent eruption in 1923. Conchagua (about 4100 ft; 1,250 m) erupted with considerable damage early in 1947.

Guatemala: Santa Maria Quezaltenango (12,361 ft; 3,768 m). Frequent activity between 1902–08 and 1922–28 after centuries of quiescence. Most dangerously active vent of Central America. Other volcanoes include Tajumulco (13,814 ft; 4,211 m) and Atitlán (11,633 ft; 3,546 m).

Mexico: Boquerón ("Big Mouth"), on San Benedicto, about 250 mi. south of Lower California. Newest volcano in Western Hemisphere, discovered September 1952.

Colima (about 14,000 ft; 4,270 m), in group that has had frequent eruptions.

Orizaba (Citlaltépetl) (18,701 ft; 5,700 m).

Parícutin (7,450 ft; 2,270 m). First appeared in February 1943. In less than a week, a cone over 140 ft high developed with a crater one quarter mile in circumference. Cone grew more than 1,500 ft (457 m) in 1943. Erupted 1952.

Popocatépetl (17,887 ft; 5,452 m). Large, deep, bell-shaped crater. Not entirely extinct; steam still escapes.

El Chinchonal (7,300 ft; 1,005.6 m) about 15 miles from Pichucalco. Long inactive, it erupted in March 1982.

Nicaragua: Volcanoes include Telica, Coseguina, and Momotombo. Between Momotombo on the west shore of Lake Managua and Coseguina overlooking the Gulf of Fonseca, there is a string of more than 20 cones, many still active. One of these, Cerro Negro, erupted in July 1947, with considerable damage and loss of life, and again in 1971.

Concepción (5,100 ft; 1,555 m). Ash eruptions 1973–74.

Mid-oceanic Islands

Canary Islands: Pico de Teide (12,192 ft; 3,716 m), on Tenerife.

Cape Verde Islands: Fogo (nearly 9,300 ft; 2,835 m). Severe eruption in 1857; quiescent until 1951.

Caribbean: La Soufrière (4,813 ft; 1,467 m), on Basse-Terre, Guadeloupe. Also called La Grande Soufrière. Violent activity in July-August 1976 caused evacuation of 73,000 people; renewed activity in April 1977 again caused thousands to flee their homes.

La Soufrière (4,048 ft; 1,234 m), on St. Vincent. Major eruption in 1902 killed over 1,000 people. Eruptions over 10-day period in April 1979 caused evacuation of northern two thirds of island.

Comoros: One volcano, Karthala (nearly 8,000 ft; 2,440 m), is visible for over 100 miles. Last erupted in 1904.

Hawaii: Mauna Loa ("Long Mountain") (13,680 ft; 4,170 m), on Hawaii, discharges from its high side vents more lava than any other volcano. Largest volcanic mountain in the world in cubic content. Area of crater is 3.7 sq mi. Violent eruption in June 1950, with lava pouring 25 miles into the ocean. Last major eruption in March 1984.

Mauna Kea (13,796 ft; 4,205 m), on Hawaii. Highest mountain in state.

Kilauea (4,090 ft; 1,247 m) is a vent in the side of Mauna Loa, but its eruptions are apparently independent. One of the most spectacular and active craters. Crater has an area of 4.14 sq mi. Earthquake in July 1975 caused major eruption. Eruptions began in September 1977 and reached a height of 980 ft (300 m). Activity ended Oct. 1. Became active again in January 1983, exploding in earnest in March 1983 forming the volcanic cone Pu'u O which has erupted periodically ever since. By May 1990, the lava flow had traveled 20 miles, obliterating the community of Kalapana on the southeast coast. By summer it had reached the Pacific Ocean. Over 36,000 people.

Iceland: At least 25 volcanoes active in historical times. Very similar to Hawaiian volcanoes. Askja (over 4,700 ft; 1,433 m) is the largest. Hekla, one of the most active volcanoes in Iceland, erupted on Jan. 17, 1990 after 10 years of repose.

Lesser Antilles (West Indian Islands): Mount Pelée (over 4,500 ft; 1,370 m), northwestern Martinique. Eruption in 1902 destroyed town of St. Pierre and killed approximately 40,000 people.

Réunion Island (east of Madagascar): Piton de la Fournaise (Le Volcan) (8,610 ft; 2,624 m). Large lava flows. Last erupted in 1972.

Samoan archipelago: Savai'i Island had an eruption in 1905 that caused considerable damage. Niuafoo (Tin Can), in the Tonga Islands, has a crater that extends 6,000 feet below and 600 feet above water.

Indonesia

Sumatra: Ninety volcanoes have been discovered; 12 are now active. The most famous, Krakatau, is a small volcanic island in the Sunda Strait. Numerous volcanic discharges occurred in 1883. One extremely violent explosion caused the disappearance of the highest peak and the northern part of the island. Fine dust was carried around the world in the upper atmosphere. Over 36,000 persons lost their lives in resultant tidal waves that were felt as far away as Cape Horn. Active in 1972.

Mediterranean Area

Italy: Mount Etna (10,902 ft; 3,323 m), eastern Sicily. Two new craters formed in eruptions of February-March 1947. Worst eruption in 50 years occurred November 1950–January 1951. Erupted again in 1974, 1975, 1977, 1978, 1979, and 1983.

Stromboli (about 3,000 ft; 914 m), Lipari Islands (north of Sicily). Called "Lighthouse of the Mediterranean." Reported active in 1971.

Mount Vesuvius (4,200 ft; 1,280 m), southeast of Naples. Only active volcano on European mainland. Pompeii buried by an eruption, A.D. 79.

Antarctica

The discovery of two small active volcanoes in 1982 brings to five the total number known on Antarctica. The new ones, 30 miles apart, are on the Weddell Sea side of the Antarctic Peninsula. The largest, Mount Erebus (13,000 ft; 3,962 m), rises from McMurdo Sound. Mount Melbourne (9,000 ft; 2,743 m) is in Victoria Land. The fifth, off the northern tip of the Antarctic Peninsula, is a crater known as Deception Island.

Principal Types of Volcanoes

(*Source:* U.S. Dept. of Interior, Geological Survey.)

The word "volcano" comes from the little island of Vulcano in the Mediterranean Sea off Sicily. Centuries ago, the people living in this area believed that Vulcano was the chimney of the forge of Vulcan—the blacksmith of the Roman gods. They thought that the hot lava fragments and clouds of dust erupting from Vulcano came from Vulcan's forge. Today, we know that volcanic eruptions are not supernatural but can be studied and interpreted by scientists.

Geologists generally group volcanoes into four main kinds—cinder cones, composite volcanoes, shield volcanoes, and lava domes.

Cinder Cones

Cinder cones are the simplest type of volcano. They are built from particles and blobs of congealed lava ejected from a single vent. As the gas-charged lava is blown violently into the air, it breaks into small fragments that solidify and fall as cinders around the vent to form a circular or oval cone. Most cinder cones have a bowl-shaped crater at the summit and rarely rise more than a thousand feet or so above their surroundings. Cinder cones are numerous in western North America as well as throughout other volcanic terrains of the world.

Composite Volcanoes

Some of the Earth's grandest mountains are composite volcanoes—sometimes called *stratovolcanoes*. They are typically steep-sided, symmetrical cones of large dimension built of alternating layers of lava flows, volcanic ash, cinders, blocks, and bombs and may rise as much as 8,000 feet above their bases. Some of the most conspicuous and beautiful mountains in the world are composite volcanoes, including Mount Fuji in Japan, Mount Cotopaxi in Ecuador, Mount Shasta in California, Mount Hood in Oregon, and Mount St. Helens and Mount Rainier in Washington.

Most composite volcanoes have a crater at the summit which contains a central vent or a clustered group of vents. Lavas either flow through breaks in the crater wall or issue from fissures on the flanks of the cone. Lava, solidified within the fissures, forms *dikes* that act as ribs which greatly strengthen the cone.

The essential feature of a composite volcano is a conduit system through which magma from a reservoir deep in the Earth's crust rises to the surface. The volcano is built up by the accumulation of material erupted through the conduit and increases in size as lava, cinders, ash, etc., are added to its slopes.

Shield Volcanoes

Shield volcanoes, the third type of volcano, are built almost entirely of fluid lava flows. Flow after flow pours out in all directions from a central summit vent, or group of vents, building a broad, gently sloping cone of flat, domical shape, with a profile much like that of a warrior's shield. They are built up slowly by the accretion of thousands of flows of highly fluid basaltic (from *basalt*, a hard, dense dark volcanic rock) lava that spread widely over great distances, and then cool as thin, gently dipping sheets. Lavas also commonly erupt from vents along fractures (rift zones) that develop on the flanks of the cone. Some of the largest volcanoes in the world are shield volcanoes. In northern California and Oregon, many shield volcanoes have diameters of 3 or 4 miles and heights of 1,500 to 2,000 feet. The Hawaiian Islands are composed of linear chains of these volcanoes, including Kilauea and Mauna Loa on the island of Hawaii.

In some shield-volcano eruptions, basaltic lava pours out quietly from long fissures instead of central vents and floods the surrounding countryside with lava flow upon lava flow, forming broad plateaus. Lava plateaus of this type can be seen in Iceland, southeastern Washington, eastern Oregon, and southern Idaho.

Lava Domes

Volcanic or lava domes are formed by relatively small, bulbous masses of lava too viscous to flow any great distance; consequently, on extrusion, the lava piles over and around its vent. A dome grows largely by expansion from within. As it grows its outer surface cools and hardens, then shatters, spilling loose fragments down its sides. Some domes form craggy knobs or spines over the volcanic vent, whereas others form short, steep-sided lava flows known as "coulees." Volcanic domes commonly occur within the craters or on the flanks of large composite volcanoes. The nearly circular Novarupta Dome that formed during the 1912 eruption of Katmai Volcano, Alaska, measures 800 feet across and 200 feet high. The internal structure of this dome—defined by layering of lava fanning upward and outward from the center—indicates that it grew largely by expansion from within. Mount Pelée in Martinique, West Indies, and Lassen Peak and Mono domes in California, are examples of lava domes.

Submarine Volcanoes

Submarine volcanoes and volcanic vents are common features on certain zones of the ocean floor. Some are active at the present time and, in shallow water, disclose their presence by blasting steam and rock-debris high above the surface of the sea. Many others lie at such great depths that the tremendous weight of the water above them results in high, confining pressure and prevents the formation and release of steam and gases. Even very large, deepwater eruptions may not disturb the ocean floor.

The famous black sand beaches of Hawaii were created virtually instantaneously by the violent interaction between hot lava and sea water.

Plate-Tectonics Theory—The Lithosphere Plates of the Earth

Source: U.S. Department of the Interior, U.S. Geological Survey.

World Population, Land Areas, and Elevations

Area	Estimated population, mid-1991	Approximate Land area sq mi.	Percent of total land area	Population density per sq mi.	Elevation, feet	
					Highest	Lowest
WORLD	5,384,000,000	58,433,000	100.0	92.1 [1]	Mt. Everest, Asia, 29,108	Dead Sea, Asia, 1,290 below sea level
ASIA, incl. Philippines, Indonesia, and European and Asiatic Turkey; excl. Asiatic U.S.S.R	3,155,000,000	10,644,000	18.2	296.4	Mt. Everest, Tibet-Nepal, 29,108	Dead Sea, Israel-Jordan, 1,290 below sea level
AFRICA	677,000,000	11,707,000	20.0	57.8	Mt. Kilimanjaro, Tanzania, 19,340	Lake Assal, Djibouti, 571 below sea level
NORTH AMERICA, including Hawaii, Central America, and Caribbean region	430,000,000	9,360,000	16.0	45.9	Mt. McKinley; Alaska, 20,320	Death Valley, Calif., 282 below sea level
SOUTH AMERICA	302,000,000	6,883,000	11.8	43.9	Mt. Aconcagua, Arg.-Chile, 23,034	Valdes Peninsula, 131 below sea level
ANTARCTICA	—	6,000,000	10.3	—	Vinson Massif, Sentinel Range, 16,863	Sea level
EUROPE, incl. Iceland; excl. European U.S.S.R. and European Turkey	502,000,000	1,905,000	3.3	263.5	Mont Blanc, France, 15,781	Sea level
OCEANIA, incl. Australia, New Zealand, Melanesia, Micronesia, and Polynesia[2]	27,000,000	3,284,000	5.6	8.2	Wilhelm, Papua New Guinea, 14,793	Lake Eyre, Australia, 38 below sea level
U.S.S.R., both European and Asiatic	292,000,000	8,647,000	14.8	33.8	Communism Peak, Pamir, 24,590	Caspian Sea, 96 below sea level

1. In computing density per square mile, the area of Antarctica is omitted. 2. Although Hawaii is geographically part of Oceania, its population is included in the population figure for North America. *Source:* Population Reference Bureau, Inc.

Plate-Tectonics Theory

(*Source:* U.S. Dept. of the Interior, Geological Survey.)

According to the generally accepted "plate-tectonics" theory, scientists believe that the Earth's surface is broken into a number of shifting slabs or plates, which average about 50 miles in thickness. These plates move relative to one another above a hotter, deeper, more mobile zone at average rates as great as a few inches per year. Most of the world's active volcanoes are located along or near the boundaries between shifting plates and are called "plate-boundary" volcanoes. However, some active volcanoes are not associated with plate boundaries, and many of these so-called "intra-plate" volcanoes form roughly linear chains in the interior of some oceanic plates. The Hawaiian Islands provide perhaps the best example of an "intra-plate" volcanic chain, developed by the northwest-moving Pacific plate passing over an inferred "hot spot" that initiates the magma-generation and volcano-formation process. The peripheral areas

of the Pacific Ocean Basin, containing the boundaries of several plates, are dotted by many active volcanoes that form the so-called "Ring of Fire." The "Ring" provides excellent examples of "plate-boundary" volcanoes, including Mount St. Helens.

The accompanying figure on page 464 shows the boundaries of lithosphere plates that are active at present. The double lines indicate zones of spreading from which plates are moving apart. The lines with barbs show zones of underthrusting (subduction), where one plate is sliding beneath another. The barbs on the lines indicate the overriding plate. The single line defines a strike-slip fault along which plates are sliding horizontally past one another. The stippled areas indicate a part of a continent, exclusive of that along a plate boundary, which is undergoing active extensional, compressional, or strike-slip faulting.

The Severity of an Earthquake

(*Source:* U.S. Dept. of the Interior, Geological Survey.)

The Richter Magnitude Scale

The Richter magnitude scale was developed in 1935 by Charles F. Richter of the California Institute of Technology as a mathematical device to compare the size of earthquakes. The magnitude of an earthquake is determined from the logarithm of the amplitude of waves recorded by seismographs. Adjustments are included in the magnitude formula to compensate for the variation in the distance between the various seismographs and the epicenter of the earthquakes. On the Richter Scale, magnitude is expressed in whole numbers and decimal fractions. For example, a magnitude of 5.3 might be computed for a moderate earthquake, and a strong earthquake might be rated as magnitude 6.3.

Because of the logarithmic basis of the scale, each whole-number increase in magnitude represents a tenfold increase in measured amplitude; as an estimate of energy, each whole number step in the magnitude scale corresponds to the release of about 31 times more energy than the amount associated with the preceding whole number value.

Earthquakes with magnitudes of about 2.0 or less are usually called microearthquakes; they are not commonly felt by people and are generally recorded only on local seismographs. Events with magnitudes of about 4.5 or greater—there are several thousand such shocks annually—are strong enough to be recorded by sensitive seismographs all over the world.

Great earthquakes, such as the 1906 Good Friday earthquake in San Francisco, have magnitudes of 8.0 or higher. On the average, one earthquake of such size occurs somewhere in the world each year. Although the Richter Scale has no upper limit, the largest known shocks have had magnitudes in the 8.8 to 8.9 range.

The Richter Scale is not used to express damage. An earthquake in a densely populated area which results in many deaths and considerable damage may have the same magnitude as a shock in a remote area that does nothing more than frighten the wildlife. Large-magnitude earthquakes that occur beneath the oceans may not even be felt by humans.

The Modified Mercalli Intensity Scale

The effect of an earthquake on the Earth's surface is called the intensity. The intensity scale consists of a series of certain key responses such as people awakening, movement of furniture, damage to chimneys, and finally—total destruction. Although numerous *intensity scales* have been developed over the last several hundred years to evaluate the effects of earthquakes, the one currently used in the United States is the Modified Mercalli (MM) Intensity Scale. It was developed in 1931 by the American seismologists Harry Wood and Frank Neumann. This scale, composed of 12 increasing levels of intensity that range from imperceptible shaking to catastrophic destruction, is designated by Roman numerals. It does not have a mathematical basis; instead it is an arbitrary ranking based on observed effects.

The Modified Mercalli Intensity value assigned to a specific site after an earthquake has a more meaningful measure of severity to the nonscientist than the magnitude because intensity refers to the effects actually experienced at that place. After the occurrence of widely-felt earthquakes, the Geological Survey mails questionnaires to postmasters in the disturbed area requesting the information so that intensity values can be assigned. The results of this postal canvass and information furnished by other sources are used to assign an intensity value, and to compile isoseismal maps that show the extent of various levels of intensity within the felt area. The maximum observed intensity generally occurs near the epicenter.

The *lower* numbers of the intensity scale generally deal with the manner in which the earthquake is felt by people. The *higher* numbers of the scale are based on observed structural damage. Structural engineers usually contribute information for assigning intensity values of VIII or above.

The Mexico City earthquake on September 19, 1985, was assigned an intensity of IX on the Mercalli Scale.

The following is an abbreviated description of the 12 levels of Modified Mercalli intensity.

I. Not felt except by a very few under especially favorable conditions.

II. Felt only by a few persons at rest, especially on upper floors of buildings. Delicately suspended objects may swing.

III. Felt quite noticeably by persons indoors, especially on upper floors of buildings. Many people do not recognize it as an earthquake. Standing motor cars may rock slightly. Vibration similar to the passing of a truck. Duration estimated.

IV. Felt indoors by many, outdoors by few during the day. At night, some awakened. Dishes, windows, doors disturbed; walls make cracking sound. Sensation like heavy truck striking building. Standing motor cars rocked noticeably.

V. Felt by nearly everyone; many awakened. Some dishes, windows broken. Unstable objects overturned. Pendulum clocks may stop.

VI. Felt by all, many frightened. Some heavy furniture moved; a few instances of fallen plaster. Damage slight.

VII. Damage negligible in buildings of good design and construction; slight to moderate in well-built ordinary structures; considerable damage in poorly built or badly designed structures; some chimneys broken.

VIII. Damage slight in specially designed structures; considerable damage in ordinary substantial buildings with partial collapse. Damage great in poorly built structures. Fall of chimneys, factory stacks, columns, monuments, walls. Heavy furniture overturned.

IX. Damage considerable in specially designed structures; well-designed frame structures thrown out of plumb. Damage great in substantial buildings, with partial collapse. Buildings shifted off foundations.

X. Some well-built wooden structures destroyed; most masonry and frame structures destroyed with foundations. Rails bent.

XI. Few, if any (masonry) structures remain standing. Bridges destroyed. Rails bent greatly.

XII. Damage total. Lines of sight and level are distorted. Objects thrown into the air.

Latitude and Longitude of World Cities

(and time corresponding to 12:00 noon, eastern standard time)

City	Lat. °	Lat. ′	Long. °	Long. ′	Time	City	Lat. °	Lat. ′	Long. °	Long. ′	Time
Aberdeen, Scotland	57	9 n	2	9 w	5:00 p.m.	Leeds, England	53	45 n	1	30 w	5:00 p.m.
Adelaide, Australia	34	55 s	138	36 e	2:30 a.m.[1]	Leningrad	59	56 n	30	18 e	8:00 p.m.
Algiers	36	50 n	3	0 e	6:00 p.m.	Lima, Peru	12	0 s	77	2 w	2:00 noon
Amsterdam	52	22 n	4	53 e	6:00 p.m.	Lisbon	38	44 n	9	9 w	5:00 p.m.
Ankara, Turkey	39	55 n	32	55 e	7:00 p.m.	Liverpool, England	53	25 n	3	0 w	5:00 p.m.
Asunción, Paraguay	25	15 s	57	40 w	1:00 p.m.	London	51	32 n	0	5 w	5:00 p.m.
Athens	37	58 n	23	43 e	7:00 p.m.	Lyons, France	45	45 n	4	50 e	6:00 p.m.
Auckland, New Zealand	36	52 s	174	45 e	5:00 a.m.[1]	Madrid	40	26 n	3	42 w	6:00 p.m.
Bangkok, Thailand	13	45 n	100	30 e	midnight[1]	Manchester, England	53	30 n	2	15 w	5:00 p.m.
Barcelona	41	23 n	2	9 e	6:00 p.m.	Manila	14	35 n	120	57 e	1:00 a.m.[1]
Belém, Brazil	1	28 s	48	29 w	2:00 p.m.	Marseilles, France	43	20 n	5	20 e	6:00 p.m.
Belfast, Northern Ireland	54	37 n	5	56 w	5:00 p.m.	Mazatlán, Mexico	23	12 n	106	25 w	10:00 a.m.
Belgrade, Yugoslavia	44	52 n	20	32 e	6:00 p.m.	Mecca, Saudi Arabia	21	29 n	39	45 e	8:00 p.m.
Berlin	52	30 n	13	25 e	6:00 p.m.	Melbourne	37	47 s	144	58 e	3:00 a.m.[1]
Birmingham, England	52	25 n	1	55 w	5:00 p.m.	Mexico City	19	26 n	99	7 w	11:00 a.m.
Bogotá, Colombia	4	32 n	74	15 w	12:00 noon	Milan, Italy	45	27 n	9	10 e	6:00 p.m.
Bombay	19	0 n	72	48 e	10:30 p.m.	Montevideo, Uruguay	34	53 s	56	10 w	2:00 p.m.
Bordeaux, France	44	50 n	0	31 w	6:00 p.m.	Moscow	55	45 n	37	36 e	8:00 p.m.
Bremen, W. Germany	53	5 n	8	49 e	6:00 p.m.	Munich, Germany	48	8 n	11	35 e	6:00 p.m.
Brisbane, Australia	27	29 s	153	8 e	3:00 a.m.[1]	Nagasaki, Japan	32	48 n	129	57 e	2:00 a.m.[1]
Bristol, England	51	28 n	2	35 w	5:00 p.m.	Nagoya, Japan	35	7 n	136	56 e	2:00 a.m.[1]
Brussels	50	52 n	4	22 e	6:00 p.m.	Nairobi, Kenya	1	25 s	36	55 e	8:00 p.m.
Bucharest	44	25 n	26	7 e	7:00 p.m.	Nanjing (Nanking), China	32	3 n	118	53 e	1:00 a.m.[1]
Budapest	47	30 n	19	5 e	6:00 p.m.	Naples, Italy	40	50 n	14	15 e	6:00 p.m.
Buenos Aires	34	35 s	58	22 w	2:00 p.m.	Newcastle-on-Tyne, Eng.	54	58 n	1	37 w	5:00 p.m.
Cairo	30	2 n	31	21 e	7:00 p.m.	Odessa, U.S.S.R.	46	27 n	30	48 e	8:00 p.m.
Calcutta	22	34 n	88	24 e	10:30 p.m.	Osaka, Japan	34	32 n	135	30 e	2:00 a.m.[1]
Canton, China	23	7 n	113	15 e	1:00 a.m.[1]	Oslo	59	57 n	10	42 e	6:00 p.m.
Cape Town, South Africa	33	55 s	18	22 e	7:00 p.m.	Panama City, Panama	8	58 n	79	32 w	12:00 noon
Caracas, Venezuela	10	28 n	67	2 w	1:00 p.m.	Paramaribo, Surinam	5	45 n	55	15 w	1:30 p.m.
Cayenne, French Guiana	4	49 n	52	18 w	1:00 p.m.	Paris	48	48 n	2	20 e	6:00 p.m.
Chihuahua, Mexico	28	37 n	106	5 w	11:00 a.m.	Peking	39	55 n	116	25 e	1:00 a.m.[1]
Chongqing, China	29	46 n	106	34 e	1:00 a.m.[1]	Perth, Australia	31	57 s	115	52 e	1:00 a.m.[1]
Copenhagen	55	40 n	12	34 e	6:00 p.m.	Plymouth, England	50	25 n	4	5 w	5:00 p.m.
Córdoba, Argentina	31	28 s	64	10 w	2:00 p.m.	Port Moresby, Papua New Guinea	9	25 s	147	8 e	3:00 a.m.[1]
Dakar, Senegal	14	40 n	17	28 w	5:00 p.m.	Prague	50	5 n	14	26 e	6:00 p.m.
Darwin, Australia	12	28 s	130	51 e	2:30 a.m.[1]	Reykjavik, Iceland	64	4 n	21	58 w	4:00 p.m.
Djibouti	11	30 n	43	3 e	8:00 p.m.	Rio de Janeiro	22	57 s	43	12 w	2:00 p.m.
Dublin	53	20 n	6	15 w	5:00 p.m.	Rome	41	54 n	12	27 e	6:00 p.m.
Durban, South Africa	29	53 s	30	53 e	7:00 p.m.	Salvador, Brazil	12	56 s	38	27 w	2:00 p.m.
Edinburgh, Scotland	55	55 n	3	10 w	5:00 p.m.	Santiago, Chile	33	28 s	70	45 w	1:00 p.m.
Frankfurt	50	7 n	8	41 e	6:00 p.m.	Sao Paulo, Brazil	23	31 s	46	31 w	2:00 p.m.
Georgetown, Guyana	6	45 n	58	15 w	1:15 p.m.	Shanghai, China	31	10 n	121	28 e	1:00 a.m.[1]
Glasgow, Scotland	55	50 n	4	15 w	5:00 p.m.	Singapore	1	14 n	103	55 e	0:30 a.m.[1]
Guatemala City, Guatemala	14	37 n	90	31 w	11:00 a.m.	Sofia, Bulgaria	42	40 n	23	20 e	7:00 p.m.
Guayaquil, Ecuador	2	10 s	79	56 w	12:00 noon	Stockholm	59	17 n	18	3 e	6:00 p.m.
Hamburg	53	33 n	10	2 e	6:00 p.m.	Sydney, Australia	34	0 s	151	0 e	3:00 a.m.[1]
Hammerfest, Norway	70	38 n	23	38 e	6:00 p.m.	Tananarive, Madagascar	18	50 s	47	33 e	8:00 p.m.
Havana	23	8 n	82	23 w	12:00 noon	Teheran, Iran	35	45 n	51	45 e	8:30 p.m.
Helsinki, Finland	60	10 n	25	0 e	7:00 p.m.	Tokyo	35	40 n	139	45 e	2:00 a.m.[1]
Hobart, Tasmania	42	52 s	147	19 e	3:00 a.m.[1]	Tripoli, Libya	32	57 n	13	12 e	7:00 p.m.
Iquique, Chile	20	10 s	70	7 w	1:00 p.m.	Venice	45	26 n	12	20 e	6:00 p.m.
Irkutsk, U.S.S.R.	52	30 n	104	20 e	1:00 a.m.	Veracruz, Mexico	19	10 n	96	10 w	11:00 a.m.
Jakarta, Indonesia	6	16 s	106	48 e	0:30 a.m.[1]	Vienna	48	14 n	16	20 e	6:00 p.m.
Johannesburg, South Africa	26	12 s	28	4 e	7:00 p.m.	Vladivostok, U.S.S.R.	43	10 n	132	0 e	3:00 a.m.[1]
Kingston, Jamaica	17	59 n	76	49 w	12:00 noon	Warsaw	52	14 n	21	0 e	6:00 p.m.
Kinshasa, Zaire	4	18 s	15	17 e	6:00 p.m.	Wellington, New Zealand	41	17 s	174	47 e	5:00 a.m.[1]
La Paz, Bolivia	16	27 s	68	22 w	1:00 p.m.	Yangon, Myanmar	16	50 n	96	0 e	11:30 p.m.
						Zürich	47	21 n	8	31 e	6:00 p.m.

1. On the following day.

Highest Mountain Peaks of the World

(For U.S. peaks, see Index)

Mountain peak	Range	Location	Height feet	meters
Everest	Himalayas	Nepal-Tibet	29,108[1]	8,872
Godwin Austen (K-2)	Karakoram	Kashmir	29,064	8,858
Kanchenjunga	Himalayas	Nepal-Sikkim	28,208	8,598
Lhotse	Himalayas	Nepal-Tibet	27,890	8,501
Makalu	Himalayas	Tibet-Nepal	27,790	8,470
Dhaulagiri I	Himalayas	Nepal	26,810	8,172
Manaslu	Himalayas	Nepal	26,760	8,156
Cho Oyu	Himalayas	Nepal	26,750	8,153
Nanga Parbat	Himalayas	Kashmir	26,660	8,126
Annapurna I	Himalayas	Nepal	26,504	8,078
Gasherbrum I	Karakoram	Kashmir	26,470	8,068
Broad Peak	Karakoram	Kashmir	26,400	8,047
Gasherbrum II	Karakoram	Kashmir	26,360	8,033
Gosainthan	Himalayas	Tibet	26,291	8,013
Gasherbrum III	Karakoram	Kashmir	26,090	7,952
Annapurna II	Himalayas	Nepal	26,041	7,937
Gasherbrum IV	Karakoram	India	26,000	7,925
Kangbachen	Himalayas	Nepal	25,925	7,902
Gyachung Kang	Himalayas	Nepal	25,910	7,897
Himal Chuli	Himalayas	Nepal	25,895	7,893
Disteghil Sar	Karakoram	Kashmir	25,868	7,885
Nuptse	Himalayas	Nepal	25,850	7,829
Kunyang Kish	Karakoram	Kashmir	25,760	7,852
Dakum (Peak 29)	Himalayas	Nepal	25,760	7,852
Masherbrum	Karakoram	Kashmir	25,660	7,821
Nanda Devi	Himalayas	India	25,645	7,817
Chomolonzo	Himalayas	Nepal-Tibet	25,640	7,815
Rakaposhi	Karakoram	Kashmir	25,550	7,788
Batura	Karakoram	Kashmir	25,540	7,785
Kanjut Sar	Karakoram	Kashmir	25,460	7,760
Kamet	Himalayas	India-Tibet	25,447	7,756
Namche Barwa	Himalayas	Tibet	25,445	7,756
Dhaulagiri II	Himalayas	Nepal	25,427	7,750
Saltoro Kangri	Karakoram	India	25,400	7,742
Gurla Mandhata	Himalayas	Tibet	25,355	7,728
Ulugh Muztagh	Kunlun	Tibet	25,341	7,724
Trivor	Karakoram	Kashmir	25,330	7,721
Jannu	Himalayas	Nepal	25,294	7,710
Tirich Mir	Hindu Kush	Pakistan	25,230	7,690
Saser Kangri	Karakoram	India	25,170	7,672
Makalu II	Himalayas	Nepal	25,130	7,660
Chogolisa	Karakoram	India	25,110	7,654
Dhaulagiri IV	Himalayas	Nepal	25,064	7,639
Fang	Himalayas	Nepal	25,013	7,624
Kula Kangri	Himalayas	Bhutan	24,783	7,554
Changtse	Himalayas	Tibet	24,780	7,553
Muztagh Ata	Muztagh Ata	China	24,757	7,546
Skyang Kangri	Himalayas	Kashmir	24,750	7,544
Communism Peak	Pamir	U.S.S.R.	24,590	7,495
Victory Peak	Pamir	U.S.S.R.	24,406	7,439
Sia Kangri	Himalayas	Kashmir	24,340	7,419
Chamlang	Himalayas	Nepal	24,012	7,319
Alung Gangri	Himalayas	Tibet	23,999	7,315
Chomo Lhari	Himalayas	Tibet-Bhutan	23,996	7,314
Muztagh (K-5)	Kunlun	China	23,891	7,282
Amne Machin	Kunlun	China	23,490	7,160
Gaurisankar	Himalayas	Nepal-Tibet	23,440	7,145
Lenin Peak	Pamir	U.S.S.R.	23,405	7,134
Korzhenevski Peak	Pamir	U.S.S.R.	23,310	7,105
Kangto	Himalayas	Tibet	23,260	7,090
Dunagiri	Himalayas	India	23,184	7,066
Pauhunri	Himalayas	India-Tibet	23,180	7,065
Aconcagua	Andes	Argentina-Chile	23,034	7,021
Revolution Peak	Pamir	U.S.S.R.	22,880	6,974
Kangchenjhan	Himalayas	India	22,700	6,919
Siniolchu	Himalayas	India	22,620	6,895

Mountain peak	Range	Location	Height feet	Height meters
Ojos des Salado	Andes	Argentina-Chile	22,588	6,885
Bonete	Andes	Argentina-Chile	22,546	6,872
Simvuo	Himalayas	India	22,346	6,811
Tup	Andes	Argentina	22,309	6,800
Kungpu	Himalayas	Bhutan	22,300	6,797
Falso-Azufre	Andes	Argentina-Chile	22,277	6,790
Moscow Peak	Pamir	U.S.S.R.	22,260	6,785
Veladero	Andes	Argentina	22,244	6,780
Pissis	Andes	Argentina	22,241	6,779
Mercedario	Andes	Argentina-Chile	22,211	6,770
Huascarán	Andes	Peru	22,198	6,766
Tocorpuri	Andes	Bolivia-Chile	22,162	6,755
Karl Marx Peak	Pamir	U.S.S.R.	22,067	6,726
Llullaillaco	Andes	Argentina-Chile	22,057	6,723
Libertador	Andes	Argentina	22,047	6,720
Kailas	Himalayas	Tibet	22,027	6,714
Lingtren	Himalayas	Nepal-Tibet	21,972	6,697
Incahuasi	Andes	Argentina-Chile	21,719	6,620
Carnicero	Andes	Peru	21,689	6,611
Kurumda	Pamir	U.S.S.R.	21,686	6,610
Garmo Peak	Pamir	U.S.S.R.	21,637	6,595
Sajama	Andes	Bolivia	21,555	6,570
Ancohuma	Andes	Bolivia	21,490	6,550
El Muerto	Andes	Argentina-Chile	21,456	6,540
Nacimiento	Andes	Argentina	21,302	6,493
Illimani	Andes	Bolivia	21,184	6,457
Antofalla	Andes	Argentina-Chile	21,129	6,440
Coropuña	Andes	Peru	21,079	6,425
Cuzco (Ausangate)	Andes	Peru	20,995	6,399
Toro	Andes	Argentina-Chile	20,932	6,380
Parinacota	Andes	Bolivia-Chile	20,768	6,330
Chimboraso	Andes	Ecuador	20,702	6,31
Salcantay	Andes	Peru	20,575	6,271
General Manuel Belgrano	Andes	Argentina	20,505	6,250
Chañi	Andes	Argentina	20,341	6,200
Caca Aca	Andes	Bolivia	20,328	6,196
McKinley	Alaska	Alaska	20,320	6,194
Vudor Peak	Pamir	U.S.S.R.	20,118	6,132
Condoriri	Andes	Bolivia	20,095	6,125
Solimana	Andes	Peru	20,069	6,117
Nevada	Andes	Argentina	20,023	6,103

1. Mt. Everest grows about 1 centimeter (.394 inch) higher each year.

Oceans and Seas

Name	Area sq mi.	Area sq km	Average depth feet	Average depth meters	Greatest known depth feet	Greatest known depth meters	Place greatest known depth
Pacific Ocean	64,000,000	165,760,000	13,215	4,028	36,198	11,033	Mariana Trench
Atlantic Ocean	31,815,000	82,400,000	12,880	3,926	30,246	9,219	Puerto Rico Trough
Indian Ocean	25,300,000	65,526,700	13,002	3,963	24,460	7,455	Sunda Trench
Arctic Ocean	5,440,200	14,090,000	3,953	1,205	18,456	5,625	77° 45′ N; 175° W
Mediterranean Sea[1]	1,145,100	2,965,800	4,688	1,429	15,197	4,632	Off Cape Matapan, Greece
Caribbean Sea	1,049,500	2,718,200	8,685	2,647	22,788	6,946	Off Cayman Islands
South China Sea	895,400	2,319,000	5,419	1,652	16,456	5,016	West of Luzon
Bering Sea	884,900	2,291,900	5,075	1,547	15,659	4,773	Off Buldir Island
Gulf of Mexico	615,000	1,592,800	4,874	1,486	12,425	3,787	Sigsbee Deep
Okhotsk Sea	613,800	1,589,700	2,749	838	12,001	3,658	146° 10′ E; 46° 50′ N
East China Sea	482,300	1,249,200	617	188	9,126	2,782	25° 16′ N; 125° E
Hudson Bay	475,800	1,232,300	420	128	600	183	Near entrance
Japan Sea	389,100	1,007,800	4,429	1,350	12,276	3,742	Central Basin
Andaman Sea	308,100	797,700	2,854	870	12,392	3,777	Off Car Nicobar Island
North Sea	222,100	575,200	308	94	2,165	660	Skagerrak
Red Sea	169,100	438,000	1,611	491	7,254	2,211	Off Port Sudan
Baltic Sea	163,000	422,200	180	55	1,380	421	Off Gotland

1. Includes Black Sea and Sea of Azov. NOTE: For Caspian Sea, *see* Large Lakes of World elsewhere in this section.

World's Greatest Man-Made Lakes[1]

Name of dam	Loaction	Millions of cubic meters	Thousands of acre-feet	Year completed
Owen Falls	Uganda	204,800	166,000	1954
Kariba	Zimbabwe	181,592	147,218	1959
Bratsk	U.S.S.R.	169,270	137,220	1964
High Aswan (Sadd-el-Aali)	Egypt	168,000	136,200	1970
Akosombo	Ghana	148,000	120,000	1965
Daniel Johnson	Canada	141,852	115,000	1968
Guri (Raul Leoni)	Venezuela	136,000	110,256	1986
Krasnoyarsk	U.S.S.R.	73,300	59,425	1967
Bennett W.A.C.	Canada	70,309	57,006	1967
Zeya	U.S.S.R.	68,400	55,452	1978
Cabora Bassa	Mozambique	63,000	51,075	1974
LaGrande 2	Canada	61,720	50,037	1982
LaGrande 3	Canada	60,020	48,659	1982
Ust'—Ilimsk	U.S.S.R.	59,300	48,075	1980
Volga—V.I. Lenin	U.S.S.R.	58,000	47,020	1955
Caniapiscau	Canada	53,790	43,608	1981
Poti (Chapetón)	Argentina	53,700	43,535	UC
Upper Wainganga	India	50,700	41,103	1987
Sáo Felix	Brazil	50,600	41,022	1986
Bukhtarma	U.S.S.R.	49,740	40,325	1960
Atatürk (Karababa)	Turkey	48,700	39,482	1990
Cerros Colorados	Argentina	48,000	38,914	1973
Irkutsk	U.S.S.R.	46,000	37,290	1956
Tucuruí	Brazil	36,375	29,489	1984
Vilyuy	U.S.S.R.	35,900	29,104	1967
Sanmenxia	China	35,400	28,700	1960
Hoover	Nevada/Arizona	35,154	28,500	1936
Sobridinho	Brazil	34,200	27,726	1981
Glen Canyon	Arizona	33,304	27,000	1964
Jenpeg	Canada	31,790	25,772	1975

1. Formed by construction of dams. NOTE: UC = under construction, *Source:* Department of the Interior, Bureau of Reclamation and *International Water Power and Dam Construction.*

Large Lakes of the World

Name and location	Area		Length		Maximum depth	
	sq mi.	km	mi.	km	feet	meters
Caspian Sea, U.S.S.R.-Iran[1]	152,239	394,299	745	1,199	3,104	946
Superior, U.S.-Canada	31,820	82,414	383	616	1,333	406
Victoria, Tanzania—Uganda	26,828	69,485	200	322	270	82
Aral, U.S.S.R.	25,659	66,457	266	428	223	68
Huron, U.S.-Canada	23,010	59,596	247	397	750	229
Michigan, U.S.	22,400	58,016	321	517	923	281
Tanganyika, Tanzania-Zaire	12,700	32,893	420	676	4,708	1,435
Baikal, U.S.S.R.	12,162	31,500	395	636	5,712	1,741
Great Bear, Canada	12,000	31,080	232	373	270	82
Nyasa, Malawi-Mozambique-Tanzania	11,600	30,044	360	579	2,316	706
Great Slave, Canada	11,170	28,930	298	480	2,015	614
Chad,[2] Chad-Niger-Nigeria	9,946	25,760	—	—	23	7
Erie, U.S.-Canada	9,930	25,719	241	388	210	64
Winnipeg, Canada	9,094	23,553	264	425	204	62
Ontario, U.S.-Canada	7,520	19,477	193	311	778	237
Balkash, U.S.S.R.	7,115	18,428	376	605	87	27
Ladoga, U.S.S.R.	7,000	18,130	124	200	738	225
Onega, U.S.S.R.	3,819	9,891	154	248	361	110
Titicaca, Bolivia-Peru	3,141	8,135	110	177	1,214	370
Nicaragua, Nicaragua	3,089	8,001	110	177	230	70
Athabaska, Canada	3,058	7,920	208	335	407	124
Rudolf, Kenya	2,473	6,405	154	248	—	—
Reindeer, Canada	2,444	6,330	152	245	—	—
Eyre, South Australia	2,400[3]	6,216	130	209	varies	varies
Issyk-Kul, U.S.S.R.	2,394	6,200	113	182	2,297	700
Urmia,[2] Iran	2,317	6,001	81	130	49	15
Torrens, South Australia	2,200	5,698	130	209	—	—
Vänern, Sweden	2,141	5,545	87	140	322	98

Name and location	Area		Length		Maximum depth	
	sq mi.	km	mi.	km	feet	meters
Winnipegosis, Canada	2,086	5,403	152	245	59	18
Mobutu Sese Seko, Uganda	2,046	5,299	100	161	180	55
Nettilling, Baffin Island, Canada	1,950	5,051	70	113	—	—
Nipigon, Canada	1,870	4,843	72	116	—	—
Manitoba, Canada	1,817	4,706	140	225	22	7
Great Salt, U.S.	1,800	4,662	75	121	15/25	5/8
Kioga, Uganda	1,700	4,403	50	80	about 30	9
Koko-Nor, China	1,630	4,222	66	106	—	—

1. The Caspian Sea is called "sea" because the Romans, finding it salty, named it *Mare Caspium*. Many geographers, however, consider it a lake because it is land-locked. 2. Figures represent high-water data. 3. Varies with the rainfall of the wet season. It has been reported to dry up almost completely on occasion.

Principal Rivers of the World

(For other U.S. rivers, see Index)

River	Source	Outflow	Approx. length	
			miles	km
Nile	Tributaries of Lake Victoria, Africa	Mediterranean Sea	4,180	6,690
Amazon	Glacier-fed lakes, Peru	Atlantic Ocean	3,912	6,296
Mississippi-Missouri-Red Rock	Source of Red Rock, Montana	Gulf of Mexico	3,880	6,240
Yangtze Kiang	Tibetan plateau, China	China Sea	3,602	5,797
Ob	Altai Mts., U.S.S.R.	Gulf of Ob	3,459	5,567
Huang Ho (Yellow)	Eastern part of Kunlan Mts., west China	Gulf of Chihli	2,900	4,667
Yenisei	Tannu-Ola Mts., western Tuva, U.S.S.R.	Arctic Ocean	2,800	4,506
Paraná	Confluence of Paranaiba and Grande rivers	Río de la Plata	2,795	4,498
Irtish	Altai Mts., U.S.S.R.	Ob River	2,758	4,438
Zaire (Congo)	Confluence of Lualab and Luapula rivers, Zaire	Atlantic Ocean	2,716	4,371
Heilong (Amur)	Confluence of Shilka (U.S.S.R.) and Argun (Manchuria) rivers	Tatar Strait	2,704	4,352
Lena	Baikal Mts., U.S.S.R.	Arctic Ocean	2,652	4,268
Mackenzie	Head of Finlay River, British Columbia, Canada	Beaufort Sea (Arctic Ocean)	2,635	4,241
Niger	Guinea	Gulf of Guinea	2,600	4,184
Mekong	Tibetan highlands	South China Sea	2,500	4,023
Mississippi	Lake Itasca, Minnesota	Gulf of Mexico	2,348	3,779
Missouri	Confluence of Jefferson, Gallatin, and Madison rivers, Montana	Mississippi River	2,315	3,726
Volga	Valdai plateau, U.S.S.R.	Caspian Sea	2,291	3,687
Madeira	Confluence of Beni and Maumoré rivers, Bolivia-Brazil boundary	Amazon River	2,012	3,238
Purus	Peruvian Andes	Amazon River	1,993	3,207
São Francisco	Southwest Minas Gerais, Brazil	Atlantic Ocean	1,987	3,198
Yukon	Junction of Lewes and Pelly rivers, Yukon Territory, Canada	Bering Sea	1,979	3,185
St. Lawrence	Lake Ontario	Gulf of St. Lawrence	1,900	3,058
Rio Grande	San Juan Mts., Colorado	Gulf of Mexico	1,885	3,034
Brahmaputra	Himalayas	Ganges River	1,800	2,897
Indus	Himalayas	Arabian Sea	1,800	2,897
Danube	Black Forest, W. Germany	Black Sea	1,766	2,842

River	Source	Outflow	Approx. length	
			miles	km
Euphrates	Confluence of Murat Nehri and Kara Su rivers, Turkey	Shatt-al-Arab	1,739	2,799
Darling	Central part of Eastern Highlands, Australia	Murray River	1,702	2,739
Zambezi	11°21′S, 24°22′E, Zambia	Mozambique Channel	1,700	2,736
Tocantins	Goiás, Brazil	Pará River	1,677	2,699
Murray	Australian Alps, New South Wales	Indian Ocean	1,609	2,589
Nelson	Head of Bow River, western Alberta, Canada	Hudson Bay	1,600	2,575
Paraguay	Mato Grosso, Brazil	Paraná River	1,584	2,549
Ural	Southern Ural Mts., U.S.S.R.	Caspian Sea	1,574	2,533
Ganges	Himalayas	Bay of Bengal	1,557	2,506
Amu Darya (Oxus)	Nicholas Range, Pamir Mts., U.S.S.R.	Aral Sea	1,500	2,414
Japurá	Andes, Colombia	Amazon River	1,500	2,414
Salween	Tibet, south of Kunlun Mts.	Gulf of Martaban	1,500	2,414
Arkansas	Central Colorado	Mississippi River	1,459	2,348
Colorado	Grand County, Colorado	Gulf of California	1,450	2,333
Dnieper	Valdai Hills, U.S.S.R.	Black Sea	1,419	2,284
Ohio-Allegheny	Potter County, Pennsylvania	Mississippi River	1,306	2,102
Irrawaddy	Confluence of Nmai and Mali rivers, northeast Burma	Bay of Bengal	1,300	2,092
Orange	Lesotho	Atlantic Ocean	1,300	2,092
Orinoco	Serra Parima Mts., Venezuela	Atlantic Ocean	1,281	2,062
Pilcomayo	Andes Mts., Bolivia	Paraguay River	1,242	1,999
Xi Jiang (Si Kiang)	Eastern Yunnan Province, China	China Sea	1,236	1,989
Columbia	Columbia Lake, British Columbia, Canada	Pacific Ocean	1,232	1,983
Don	Tula, R.S.F.S.R., U.S.S.R.	Sea of Azov	1,223	1,968
Sungari	China-North Korea boundary	Amur River	1,215	1,955
Saskatchewan	Canadian Rocky Mts.	Lake Winnipeg	1,205	1,939
Peace	Stikine Mts., British Columbia, Canada	Great Slave River	1,195	1,923
Tigris	Taurus Mts., Turkey	Shatt-al-Arab	1,180	1,899

Highest Waterfalls of the World

Waterfall	Location	River	Height	
			miles	km
Angel	Venezuela	Tributary of Caroni	3,281	1,000
Tugela	Natal, South Africa	Tugela	3,000	914
Cuquenán	Venezuela	Cuquenán	2,000	610
Sutherland	South Island, N.Z.	Arthur	1,904	580
Takkakaw	British Columbia	Tributary of Yoho	1,650	503
Ribbon (Yosemite)	California	Creek flowing into Yosemite	1,612	491
Upper Yosemite	California	Yosemite Creek, tributary of Merced	1,430	436
Gavarnie	Southwest France	Gave de Pau	1,384	422
Vettisfoss	Norway	Mörkedola	1,200	366
Widows' Tears (Yosemite)	California	Tributary of Merced	1,170	357
Staubbach	Switzerland	Staubbach (Lauterbrunnen Valley)	984	300

Waterfall	Location	River	Height miles	km
Middle Cascade (Yosemite)	California	Yosemite Creek, tributary of Merced	909	277
King Edward VIII	Guyana	Courantyne	850	259
Gersoppa	India	Sharavati	829	253
Kaieteur	Guyana	Potaro	822	251
Skykje	Norway	In Skykjedal (valley of Inner Hardinger Fjord)	820	250
Kalambo	Tanzania-Zambia	—	720	219
Fairy (Mount Rainier Park)	Washington	Stevens Creek	700	213
Trummelbach	Switzerland	Trummelbach (Lauterbrunnen Valley)	700	213
Aniene (Teverone)	Italy	Tiber	680	207
Cascata delle Marmore	Italy	Velino, tributary of Nera	650	198
Maradalsfos	Norway	Stream flowing into Ejkisdalsvand (lake)	643	196
Feather	California	Fall River	640	195
Maletsunyane	Lesotho	Maletsunyane	630	192
Bridalveil (Yosemite)	California	Yosemite Creek	620	189
Multnomah	Oregon	Multnomah Creek, tributary of Columbia	620	189
Vøringsfos	Norway	Bjoreia	597	182
Nevada (Yosemite)	California	Merced	594	181
Skjeggedal	Norway	Tysso	525	160
Marina	Guyana	Tributary of Kuribrong, tributary of Potaro	500	152
Tequendama	Colombia	Funza, tributary of Magdalena	425	130
King George's	Cape of Good Hope, South Africa	Orange	400	122
Illilouette (Yosemite)	California	Illilouette Creek, tributary of Merced	370	113
Victoria	Rhodesia-Zambia boundary	Zambezi	355	108
Handöl	Sweden	Handöl Creek	345	105
Lower Yosemite	California	Yosemite	320	98
Comet (Mount Rainier Park)	Washington	Van Trump Creek	320	98
Vernal (Yosemite)	California	Merced	317	97
Virginia	Northwest Territories, Canada	South Nahanni, tributary of Mackenzie	315	96
Lower Yellowstone	Wyoming	Yellowstone	310	94

NOTE: Niagara Falls (New York-Ontario), though of great volume, has parallel drops of only 158 and 167 feet.

Large Islands of the World

Island	Location and status	Area sq mi.	sq km
Greenland	North Atlantic (Danish)	839,999	2,175,597
New Guinea	Southwest Pacific (Irian Jaya, Indonesian, west part; Papua New Guinea, east part)	316,615	820,033
Borneo	West mid-Pacific (Indonesian, south part, Brunei and Malaysian, north part)	286,914	743,107
Madagascar	Indian Ocean (Malagasy Republic)	226,657	587,042
Baffin	North Atlantic (Canadian)	183,810	476,068
Sumatra	Northeast Indian Ocean (Indonesian)	182,859	473,605
Honshu	Sea of Japan-Pacific (Japanese)	88,925	230,316
Great Britain	Off coast of NW Europe (England, Scotland, and Wales)	88,758	229,883
Ellesmere	Arctic Ocean (Canadian)	82,119	212,688
Victoria	Arctic Ocean (Canadian)	81,930	212,199
Celebes	West mid-Pacific (Indonesian)	72,986	189,034
South Island	South Pacific (New Zealand)	58,093	150,461
Java	Indian Ocean (Indonesian)	48,990	126,884
North Island	South Pacific (New Zealand)	44,281	114,688

Island	Location and status	Area sq mi.	Area sq km
Cuba	Caribbean Sea (republic)	44,218	114,525
Newfoundland	North Atlantic (Canadian)	42,734	110,681
Luzon	West mid-Pacific (Philippines)	40,420	104,688
Iceland	North Atlantic (republic)	39,768	102,999
Mindanao	West mid-Pacific (Philippines)	36,537	94,631
Ireland	West of Great Britain (republic, south part; United Kingdom, north part)	32,597	84,426
Hokkaido	Sea of Japan—Pacific (Japanese)	30,372	78,663
Hispaniola	Caribbean Sea (Dominican Republic, east part; Haiti, west part)	29,355	76,029
Tasmania	South of Australia (Australian)	26,215	67,897
Sri Lanka (Ceylon)	Indian Ocean (republic)	25,332	65,610
Sakhalin (Karafuto)	North of Japan (U.S.S.R.)	24,560	63,610
Banks	Arctic Ocean (Canadian)	23,230	60,166
Devon	Arctic Ocean (Canadian)	20,861	54,030
Tierra del Fuego	Southern tip of South America (Argentinian, east part; Chilean, west part)	18,605	48,187
Kyushu	Sea of Japan—Pacific (Japanese)	16,223	42,018
Melville	Arctic Ocean (Canadian)	16,141	41,805
Axel Heiberg	Arctic Ocean (Canadian)	15,779	40,868
Southampton	Hudson Bay (Canadian)	15,700	40,663

Principal Deserts of the World

Desert	Location	Approximate size	Approx. elevation, ft
Atacama	North Chile	400 mi. long	7,000–13,500
Black Rock	Northwest Nevada	About 1,000 sq mi.	2,000–8,500
Colorado	Southeast California from San Gorgonio Pass to Gulf of California	200 mi. long and a maximum width of 50 mi.	Few feet above to 250 below sea level
Dasht-e-Kavir	Southeast of Caspian Sea, Iran	—	2,000
Dasht-e-Lūt	Northeast of Kerman, Iran	—	1,000
Gobi (Shamo)	Covers most of Mongolia	500,000 sq mi.	3,000–5,000
Great Arabian	Most of Arabia	1,500 mi. long	—
An Nafud (Red Desert)	South of Jauf	400 mi. by avg of 140 mi.	3,000
Dahna	Northeast of Nejd	400 mi. by 30 mi.	—
Rub' al-Khali	South portion of Nejd	Over 200,000 sq. mi.	—
Syrian (Al-Hamad)	North of lat. 30°N	—	1,850
Great Australian	Western portion of Australia	About one half the continent	600–1,000
Great Salt Lake	West of Great Salt Lake to Nevada—Utah boundary	About 110 mi. by 50 mi.	4,500
Kalahari	South Africa—South-West Africa	About 120,000 sq mi.	Over 3,000
Kara Kum (Desert of Kiva)	Southwest Turkmen, U.S.S.R.	115,000 sq mi.	—
Kyzyl Kum	Uzbek and Kazakh, U.S.S.R.	Over 100,000 sq. mi.	160 near Lake Aral to 2,000 in southeast
Libyan	Libya, Egypt, Sudan	Over 500,000 sq mi.	—
Mojave	North of Colorado Desert and south of Death Valley, southeast California	15,000 sq mi.	2,000
Nubian	From Red Sea to great west bend of the Nile, Sudan	—	2,500
Painted Desert	Northeast Arizona	Over 7,000 sq mi.	High plateau, 5,000
Sahara	North Africa to about lat. 15°N and from Red Sea to Atlantic Ocean	3,200 mi. greatest length along lat. 20°N; area over 3,500,000 sq mi.	440 below sea level to 11,000 above; avg elevation, 1,400–1,600
Takla Makan	South central Sinkiang, China	Over 100,000 sq mi.	—
Thar (Indian)	Pakistan-India	Nearly 100,000 sq mi.	Over 1,000

Interesting Caves and Caverns of the World

Aggtelek. In village of same name, northern Hungary. Large stalactitic cavern about 5 miles long.

Altamira Cave. Near Santander, Spain. Contains animal paintings (Old Stone Age art) on roof and walls.

Antiparos. On island of same name in the Grecian Archipelago. Some stalactites are 20 ft long. Brilliant colors and fantastic shapes.

Blue Grotto. On island of Capri, Italy. Cavern hollowed out in limestone by constant wave action. Now half filled with water because of sinking coast. Name derived from unusual blue light permeating the cave. Source of light is a submerged opening, light passing through the water.

Carlsbad Caverns. Southeast New Mexico. Largest underground labyrinth yet discovered. Three levels: 754, 900, and 1,320 ft below the surface.

Fingal's Cave. On island of Staffa off coast of western Scotland. Penetrates about 200 ft inland. Contains basaltic columns almost 40 ft high.

Ice Cave. Near Dobsina, Czechoslovakia. Noted for its beautiful crystal effects.

Jenolan Caves. In Blue Mountain plateau, New South Wales, Australia. Beautiful stalactitic formations.

Kent's Cavern. Near Torquay, England. Source of much information on Paleolithic man.

Luray Cavern. Near Luray, Va. Has large stalactitic and stalagmitic columns of many colors.

Mammoth Cave. Limestone cavern in central Kentucky. Cave area is about 10 miles in diameter but has over 300 miles of irregular subterranean passageways at various levels. Temperature remains fairly constant at 54°F.

Peak Cavern or Devil's Hole. Derbyshire, England. About 2,250 ft into a mountain. Lowest part is about 600 ft below the surface.

Postojna (Postumia) Grotto. Near Postumia in Julian Alps, about 25 miles northeast of Trieste. Stalactitic cavern, largest in Europe. Piuca (Pivka) River flows through part of it. Caves have numerous beautiful stalactites.

Singing Cave. Iceland. A lava cave; name derived from echoes of people singing in it.

Wind Cave. In Black Hills of South Dakota. Limestone caverns with stalactites and stalagmites almost entirely missing. Variety of crystal formations called "boxwork."

Wyandotte Cave. In Crawford County, southern Indiana. A limestone cavern with five levels of passages; one of the largest in North America. "Monumental Mountain," approximately 135 ft high, is believed to be one of the world's largest underground "mountains."

U.S. Geography

Miscellaneous Data for the United States

Source: Department of the Interior, U.S. Geological Survey.

Highest point: Mount McKinley, Alaska	20,320 ft (6,198 m)
Lowest point: Death Valley, Calif.	282 ft (86 m) below sea level
Approximate mean altitude	2,500 ft (763 m)
Points farthest apart (50 states):	5,859 mi. (9,429 km)
Log Point, Elliot Key, Fla., and Kure Island, Hawaii	
Geographic center (50 states):	44° 58′ N. lat.103° 46′ W. long.
In Butte County, S.D. (west of Castle Rock)	
Geographic center (48 conterminous states):	39° 50′ N. lat.98° 35′ W. long.
In Smith County, Kan. (near Lebanon)	
Boundaries:	
Between Alaska and Canada	1,538 mi. (2,475 km)
Between the 48 conterminous states and Canada (incl. Great Lakes)	3,987 mi. (6,416 km)
Between the United States and Mexico	1,933 mi. (3,111 km)

Extreme Points of the United States (50 States)

Extreme point	Latitude	Longitude	Distance[1] mi.	km
Northernmost point: Point Barrow, Alaska	71°23′ N	156°29′ W	2,507	4,034
Easternmost point: West Quoddy Head, Me.	44°49′ N	66°57′ W	1,788	2,997
Southernmost point: Ka Lae (South Cape), Hawaii	18°55′ N	155°41′ W	3,463	5,573
Westernmost point: Pochnoi Point, Alaska (Semisopochnoi Island)	51°17′ N	172°09′ E	3,372	5,426

1. From geographic center of United States (incl. Alaska and Hawaii), west of Castle Rock, S.D., 44°58′ N. lat., 103°46′ W long.

Highest, Lowest, and Mean Altitudes in the United States

State	Altitude ft[1]	Highest point	Altitude ft[1]	Lowest point	Altitude ft[1]
Alabama	500	Cheaha Mountain	2,405	Gulf of Mexico	Sea level
Alaska	1,900	Mount McKinley	20,320	Pacific Ocean	Sea level
Arizona	4,100	Humphreys Peak	12,633	Colorado River	70
Arkansas	650	Magazine Mountain	2,753	Ouachita River	55
California	2,900	Mount Whitney	14,491[2]	Death Valley	282[3]
Colorado	6,800	Mount Elbert	14,433	Arkansas River	3,350
Connecticut	500	Mount Frissell, on south slope	2,380	Long Island Sound.	Sea level
Delaware	60	On Ebright Road	442	Atlantic Ocean	Sea level
D.C.	150	Tenleytown, at Reno Reservoir	410	Potomac River	1
Florida	100	Sec. 30, T6N, R20W[4]	345	Atlantic Ocean	Sea level
Georgia	600	Brasstown Bald	4,784	Atlantic Ocean	Sea level
Hawaii	3,030	Puu Wekiu, Mauna Kea	13,796	Pacific Ocean	Sea level
Idaho	5,000	Borah Peak	12,662	Snake River	710
Illinois	600	Charles Mound	1,235	Mississippi River	279[5]
Indiana	700	Franklin Township, Wayne County	1,257	Ohio River	320[5]
Iowa	1,100	Sec. 29, T100N, R41W[6]	1,670	Mississippi River	480
Kansas	2,000	Mount Sunflower	4,039[7]	Verdigris River	679
Kentucky	750	Black Mountain	4,139	Mississippi River	257[5]
Louisiana	100	Driskill Mountain	535	New Orleans	8[3]
Maine	600	Mount Katahdin	5,267	Atlantic Ocean	Sea level
Maryland	350	Backbone Mountain	3,360	Atlantic Ocean	Sea level
Massachusetts	500	Mount Greylock	3,487	Atlantic Ocean	Sea level
Michigan	900	Mount Arvon	1,979	Lake Erie	572[5]
Minnesota	1,200	Eagle Mountain	2,301	Lake Superior	600
Mississippi	300	Woodall Mountain	806	Gulf of Mexico	Sea level
Missouri	800	Taum Sauk Mountain	1,772	St. Francis River	230[5]
Montana	3,400	Granite Peak	12,799	Kootenai River	1,800
Nebraska	2,600	Johnson Township, Kimball County	5,424	Missouri River	840
Nevada	5,500	Boundary Peak	13,140	Colorado River	479
New Hampshire	1,000	Mount Washington	6,288	Atlantic Ocean	Sea level
New Jersey	250	High Point	1,803[7]	Atlantic Ocean	Sea level
New Mexico	5,700	Wheeler Peak	13,161	Red Bluff Reservoir	2,842
New York	1,000	Mount Marcy	5,344	Atlantic Ocean	Sea level
North Carolina	700	Mount Mitchell	6,684	Atlantic Ocean	Sea level
North Dakota	1,900	White Butte	3,506	Red River	750
Ohio	850	Campbell Hill	1,549	Ohio River	455[5]
Oklahoma	1,300	Black Mesa	4,973	Little River	289
Oregon	3,300	Mount Hood	11,239	Pacific Ocean	Sea level
Pennsylvania	1,100	Mount Davis	3,213	Delaware River	Sea level
Rhode Island	200	Jerimoth Hill	812	Atlantic Ocean	Sea level
South Carolina	350	Sassafras Mountain	3,560	Atlantic Ocean	Sea level
South Dakota	2,200	Harney Peak	7,242	Big Stone Lake	966
Tennessee	900	Clingmans Dome	6,643	Mississippi River	178[5]
Texas	1,700	Guadalupe Peak	8,749	Gulf of Mexico	Sea level
Utah	6,100	Kings Peak	13,528	Beaverdam Wash	2,000
Vermont	1,000	Mount Mansfield	4,393	Lake Champlain	95
Virginia	950	Mount Rogers	5,729	Atlantic Ocean	Sea level
Washington	1,700	Mount Rainier	14,411	Pacific Ocean	Sea level
West Virginia	1,500	Spruce Knob	4,861	Potomac River	240
Wisconsin	1,050	Timms Hill	1,951	Lake Michigan	579[5]
Wyoming	6,700	Gannett Peak	13,804	Belle Fourche River	3,099
United States	2,500	Mount McKinley (Alaska)	20,320	Death Valley (California)	282[3]

1. Approximate mean altitude. 2. National Geodetic Survey. 3. Below sea level. 4. Walton County. 5. Corps of Engineers 6. Osceola County. 7. State Surveys *Source:* Department of the Interior, U.S. Geological Survey.

The Continental Divide

The Continental Divide is a ridge of high ground which runs irregularly north and south through the Rocky Mountains and separates eastward-flowing from westward-flowing streams. The waters which flow eastward empty into the Atlantic Ocean, chiefly by way of the Gulf of Mexico; those which flow westward empty into the Pacific.

Mason and Dixon's Line

Mason and Dixon's Line (often called the Mason-Dixon Line) is the boundary between Pennsylvania and Maryland, running at a north latitude of 39°43'19.11". The greater part of it was surveyed from 1763–67 by Charles Mason and Jeremiah Dixon, English astronomers who had been appointed to settle a dispute between the colonies. As the line was partly the boundary between the free and the slave states, it has come to signify the division between the North and the South.

Latitude and Longitude of U.S. and Canadian Cities

(and time corresponding to 12:00 noon, eastern standard time)

City	Lat. °	Lat. ′	Long. °	Long. ′	Time	City	Lat. °	Lat. ′	Long. °	Long. ′	Time
Albany, N.Y.	42	40	73	45	12:00 noon	Memphis, Tenn	35	9	90	3	11:00 a.m.
Albuquerque, N.M.	35	05	106	39	10:00 a.m.	Miami, Fla.	25	46	80	12	12:00 noon
Amarillo, Tex.	35	11	101	50	11:00 a.m.	Milwaukee	43	2	87	55	11:00 a.m.
Anchorage, Alaska	61	13	149	54	7:00 a.m.	Minneapolis	44	59	93	14	11:00 a.m.
Atlanta	33	45	84	23	12:00 noon	Mobile, Ala.	30	42	88	3	11:00 a.m.
Austin, Tex.	30	16	97	44	11:00 a.m.	Montgomery, Ala.	32	21	86	18	11:00 a.m.
Baker, Ore.	44	47	117	50	9:00 a.m.	Montpelier, Vt.	44	15	72	32	12:00 noon
Baltimore	39	18	76	38	12:00 noon	Montreal, Que.	45	30	73	35	12:00 noon
Bangor, Me.	44	48	68	47	12:00 noon	Moose Jaw, Sask.	50	37	105	31	10:00 a.m.
Birmingham, Ala.	33	30	86	50	11:00 a.m.	Nashville, Tenn.	36	10	86	47	11:00 a.m.
Bismarck, N.D.	46	48	100	47	11:00 a.m.	Nelson, B.C.	49	30	117	17	9:00 a.m.
Boise, Idaho	43	36	116	13	10:00 a.m.	Newark, N.J.	40	44	74	10	12:00 noon
Boston	42	21	71	5	12:00 noon	New Haven, Conn.	41	19	72	55	12:00 noon
Buffalo, N.Y.	42	55	78	50	12:00 noon	New Orleans	29	57	90	4	11:00 a.m.
Calgary, Alberta	51	1	114	1	10:00 a.m.	New York	40	47	73	58	12:00 noon
Carlsbad, N.M.	32	26	104	15	10:00 a.m.	Nome, Alaska	64	25	165	30	6:00 a.m.
Charleston, S.C.	32	47	79	56	12:00 noon	Oakland, Calif.	37	48	122	16	9:00 a.m.
Charleston, W. Va.	38	21	81	38	12:00 noon	Oklahoma City	35	26	97	28	11:00 a.m.
Charlotte, N.C.	35	14	80	50	12:00 noon	Omaha, Neb.	41	15	95	56	11:00 a.m.
Cheyenne, Wyo.	41	9	104	52	10:00 a.m.	Ottawa, Ont.	45	24	75	43	12:00 noon
Chicago	41	50	87	37	11:00 a.m.	Philadelphia	39	57	75	10	12:00 noon
Cincinnati	39	8	84	30	12:00 noon	Phoenix, Ariz.	33	29	112	4	10:00 a.m.
Cleveland	41	28	81	37	12:00 noon	Pierre, S.D.	44	22	100	21	11:00 a.m.
Columbia, S.C.	34	0	81	2	12:00 noon	Pittsburgh	40	27	79	57	12:00 noon
Columbus, Ohio	40	0	83	1	12:00 noon	Port Arthur, Ont.	48	30	89	17	12:00 noon
Dallas	32	46	96	46	11:00 a.m.	Portland, Me.	43	40	70	15	12:00 noon
Denver	39	45	105	0	10:00 a.m.	Portland, Ore.	45	31	122	41	9:00 a.m.
Des Moines, Iowa	41	35	93	37	11:00 a.m.	Providence, R.I.	41	50	71	24	12:00 noon
Detroit	42	20	83	3	12:00 noon	Quebec, Que.	46	49	71	11	12:00 noon
Dubuque, Iowa	42	31	90	40	11:00 a.m.	Raleigh, N.C.	35	46	78	39	12:00 noon
Duluth, Minn.	46	49	92	5	11:00 a.m.	Reno, Nev.	39	30	119	49	9:00 a.m.
Eastport, Me.	44	54	67	0	12:00 noon	Richfield, Utah	38	46	112	5	10:00 a.m.
El Centro, Calif.	32	38	115	33	9:00 a.m.	Richmond, Va.	37	33	77	29	12:00 noon
El Paso	31	46	106	29	10:00 a.m.	Roanoke, Va.	37	17	79	57	12:00 noon
Eugene, Ore.	44	3	123	5	9:00 a.m.	Sacramento, Calif.	38	35	121	30	9:00 a.m.
Fargo, N.D.	46	52	96	48	11:00 a.m.	St. John, N.B.	45	18	66	10	1:00 p.m.
Flagstaff, Ariz.	35	13	111	41	10:00 a.m.	St. Louis	38	35	90	12	11:00 a.m.
Fort Worth, Tex.	32	43	97	19	11:00 a.m.	Salt Lake City, Utah	40	46	111	54	10:00 a.m.
Fresno, Calif.	36	44	119	48	9:00 a.m.	San Antonio	29	23	98	33	11:00 a.m.
Grand Junction, Colo.	39	5	108	33	10:00 a.m.	San Diego, Calif.	32	42	117	10	9:00 a.m.
Grand Rapids, Mich.	42	58	85	40	12:00 noon	San Francisco	37	47	122	26	9:00 a.m.
Havre, Mont.	48	33	109	43	10:00 a.m.	San Jose, Calif.	37	20	121	53	9:00 a.m.
Helena, Mont.	46	35	112	2	10:00 a.m.	San Juan, P.R.	18	30	66	10	1:00 p.m.
Honolulu	21	18	157	50	7:00 a.m.	Santa Fe, N.M.	35	41	105	57	10:00 a.m.
Hot Springs, Ark.	34	31	93	3	11:00 a.m.	Savannah, Ga.	32	5	81	5	12:00 noon
Houston, Tex.	29	45	95	21	11:00 a.m.	Seattle	47	37	122	20	9:00 a.m.
Idaho Falls, Idaho	43	30	112	1	10:00 a.m.	Shreveport, La.	32	28	93	42	11:00 a.m.
Indianapolis	39	46	86	10	12:00 noon	Sioux Falls, S.D.	43	33	96	44	11:00 a.m.
Jackson, Miss.	32	20	90	12	11:00 a.m.	Sitka, Alaska	57	10	135	15	9:00 a.m.
Jacksonville, Fla.	30	22	81	40	12:00 noon	Spokane, Wash.	47	40	117	26	9:00 a.m.
Juneau, Alaska	58	18	134	24	9:00 a.m.	Springfield, Ill.	39	48	89	38	11:00 a.m.
Kansas City, Mo.	39	6	94	35	11:00 a.m.	Springfield, Mass.	42	6	72	34	12:00 noon
Key West, Fla.	24	33	81	48	12:00 noon	Springfield, Mo.	37	13	93	17	11:00 a.m.
Kingston, Ont.	44	15	76	30	12:00 noon	Syracuse, N.Y.	43	2	76	8	12:00 noon
Klamath Falls, Ore.	42	10	121	44	9:00 a.m.	Tampa, Fla.	27	57	82	27	12:00 noon
Knoxville, Tenn.	35	57	83	56	12:00 noon	Toledo, Ohio	41	39	83	33	12:00 noon
Las Vegas, Nev.	36	10	115	12	9:00 a.m.	Toronto, Ont.	43	40	79	24	12:00 noon
Lewiston, Idaho	46	24	117	2	9:00 a.m.	Tulsa, Okla.	36	09	95	59	11:00 a.m.
Lincoln, Neb.	40	50	96	40	11:00 a.m.	Victoria, B.C.	48	25	123	21	9:00 a.m.
London, Ont.	43	2	81	34	12:00 noon	Virginia Beach, Va.	36	51	75	58	12:00 noon
Long Beach, Calif.	33	46	118	11	9:00 a.m.	Washington, D.C.	38	53	77	02	12:00 noon
Los Angeles	34	3	118	15	9:00 a.m.	Wichita, Kan.	37	43	97	17	11:00 a.m.
Louisville, Ky.	38	15	85	46	12:00 noon	Wilmington, N.C.	34	14	77	57	12:00 noon
Manchester, N.H.	43	0	71	30	12:00 noon	Winnipeg, Man.	49	54	97	7	11:00 a.m.

Named Summits in the U.S. Over 14,000 Feet Above Sea Level

Name	State	Height	Name	State	Height	Name	State	Height
Mt. McKinley	Alaska	20,320	Castle Peak	Colo.	14,265	Mt. Eolus	Colo.	14,083
Mt. St. Elias	Alaska	18,008	Quandary Peak	Colo.	14,265	Windom Peak	Colo.	14,082
Mt. Foraker	Alaska	17,400	Mt. Evans	Colo.	14,264	Mt. Columbia	Colo.	14,073
Mt. Bona	Alaska	16,500	Longs Peak	Colo.	14,255	Mt. Augusta	Alaska	14,070
Mt. Blackburn	Alaska	16,390	Mt. Wilson	Colo.	14,246	Missouri Mtn.	Colo.	14,067
Mt. Sanford	Alaska	16,237	White Mtn.	Calif.	14,246	Humboldt Peak	Colo.	14,064
Mt. Vancouver	Alaska	15,979	North Palisade	Calif.	14,242	Mt. Bierstadt	Colo.	14,060
South Buttress	Alaska	15,885	Mt. Cameron	Colo.	14,238	Sunlight Peak	Colo.	14,059
Mt. Churchill	Alaska	15,638	Shavano Peak	Colo.	14,229	Split Mtn.	Calif.	14,058
Mt. Fairweather	Alaska	15,300	Crestone Needle	Colo.	14,197	Handies Peak	Colo.	14,048
Mt. Hubbard	Alaska	14,950	Mt. Belford	Colo.	14,197	Culebra Peak	Colo.	14,047
Mt. Bear	Alaska	14,831	Mt. Princeton	Colo.	14,197	Mt. Lindsey	Colo.	14,042
East Buttress	Alaska	14,730	Mt. Yale	Colo.	14,196	Ellingwood Point	Colo.	14,042
Mt. Hunter	Alaska	14,573	Mt. Bross	Colo.	14,172	Little Bear Peak	Colo.	14,037
Browne Tower	Alaska	14,530	Kit Carson Mtn.	Colo.	14,165	Mt. Sherman	Colo.	14,036
Mt. Alverstone	Alaska	14,500	Mt. Wrangell	Alaska	14,163	Redcloud Peak	Colo.	14,034
Mt. Whitney	Calif.	14,494 [1]	Mt. Shasta	Calif.	14,162	Mt. Langley	Calif.	14,026
University Peak	Alaska	14,470	El Diente Peak	Colo.	14,159	Conundrum Peak	Colo.	14,022
Mt. Elbert	Colo.	14,433	Point Success	Wash.	14,158	Mt. Tyndall	Calif.	14,019
Mt. Massive	Colo.	14,421	Maroon Peak	Colo.	14,156	Pyramid Peak	Colo.	14,018
Mt. Harvard	Colo.	14,420	Tabeguache Mtn.	Colo.	14,155	Wilson Peak	Colo.	14,017
Mt. Rainier	Wash.	14,411	Mt. Oxford	Colo.	14,153	Wetterhorn Peak	Colo.	14,015
Mt. Williamson	Calif.	14,370	Mt. Sill	Calif.	14,153	North Maroon Peak	Colo.	14,014
La Plata Peak	Colo.	14,361	Mt. Sneffels	Colo.	14,150	San Luis Peak	Colo.	14,014
Blanca Peak	Colo.	14,345	Mt. Democrat	Colo.	14,148	Middle Palisade	Calif.	14,012
Uncompahgre Peak	Colo.	14,309	Capitol Peak	Colo.	14,130	Mt. Muir	Calif.	14,012
Crestone Peak	Colo.	14,294	Liberty Cap	Wash.	14,112	Mt. of the Holy Cross	Colo.	14,005
Mt. Lincoln	Colo.	14,286	Pikes Peak	Colo.	14,110	Huron Peak	Colo.	14,003
Grays Peak	Colo.	14,270	Snowmass Mtn.	Colo.	14,092	Thunderbolt Peak	Calif.	14,003
Mt. Antero	Colo.	14,269	Mt. Russell	Calif.	14,088	Sunshine Peak	Colo.	14,001
Torreys Peak	Colo.	14,267						

1. National Geodetic Survey. *Source:* Department of the Interior, U.S. Geological Survey.

Rivers of the United States

(350 or more miles long)

Alabama-Coosa (600 mi.; 966 km): From junction of Oostanula and Etowah R. in Georgia to Mobile R.

Altamaha-Ocmulgee (392 mi.; 631 km): From junction of Yellow R. and South R., Newton Co. in Georgia to Atlantic Ocean.

Apalachicola-Chattahoochee (524 mi.; 843 km): From Towns Co. in Georgia to Gulf of Mexico in Florida.

Arkansas (1,459 mi.; 2,348 km): From Lake Co. in Colorado to Mississippi R. in Arkansas.

Brazos (923 mi.; 1,490 km): From junction of Salt Fork and Double Mountain Fork in Texas to Gulf of Mexico.

Canadian (906 mi.; 1,458 km): From Las Animas Co. in Colorado to Arkansas R. in Oklahoma.

Cimarron (600 mi.; 966 km): From Colfax Co. in New Mexico to Arkansas R. in Oklahoma.

Colorado (1,450 mi.; 2,333 km): From Rocky Mountain National Park in Colorado to Gulf of California in Mexico.

Colorado (862 mi.; 1,387 km): From Dawson Co. in Texas to Matagorda Bay.

Columbia (1,243 mi.; 2,000 km): From Columbia Lake in British Columbia to Pacific Ocean (entering between Oregon and Washington).

Colville (350 mi.; 563 km): From Brooks Range in Alaska to Beaufort Sea.

Connecticut (407 mi.; 655 km): From Third Connecticut Lake in New Hampshire to Long Island Sound in Connecticut.

Cumberland (720 mi.; 1,159 km): From junction of Poor and Clover Forks in Harlan Co. in Kentucky to Ohio R.

Delaware (390 mi.; 628 km): From Schoharie Co. in New York to Liston Point, Delaware Bay.

Gila (649 mi.; 1,044 km): From Catron Co. in New Mexico to Colorado R. in Arizona.

Green (360 mi.; 579 km): From Lincoln Co. in Kentucky to Ohio R. in Kentucky.

Green (730 mi.; 1,175 km): From Sublette Co. in Wyoming to Colorado R. in Utah.

Illinois (420 mi.; 676 km): From St. Joseph Co. in Indiana to Mississippi R. at Grafton in Illinois.

James (sometimes called *Dakota*) (710 mi.; 1,143 km): From Wells Co. in North Dakota to Missouri R. in South Dakota.

Kanawha-New (352 mi.; 566 km): From junction of North and South Forks of New R. in North Carolina, through Virginia and West Virginia (New River becoming Kanawha River), to Ohio River.

Koyukuk (470 mi.; 756 km): From Brooks Range in Alaska to Yukon R.

Kuskokwim (724 mi.; 1,165 km): From Alaska Range in Alaska to Kuskokwim Bay.

Licking (350 mi.; 563 km): From Magoffin Co. in Kentucky to Ohio R. at Cincinnati in Ohio.

Little Missouri (560 mi.; 901 km): From Crook Co. in Wyoming to Missouri R. in North Dakota.

Milk (625 mi.; 1,006 km): From junction of forks in Alberta Province to Missouri R.

Coastline of the United States

State	Lengths, statute miles		State	Lengths, statute miles	
	General coastline[1]	Tidal shoreline[2]		General coastline[1]	Tidal shoreline[2]
Atlantic Coast:			Gulf Coast:		
Maine	228	3,478	Florida (Gulf)	770	5,095
New Hampshire	13	131	Alabama	53	607
Massachusetts	192	1,519	Mississippi	44	359
Rhode Island	40	384	Louisiana	397	7,721
Connecticut	—	618	Texas	367	3,359
New York	127	1,850	Total Gulf coast	1,631	17,141
New Jersey	130	1,792	Pacific Coast:		
Pennsylvania	—	89	California	840	3,427
Delaware	28	381	Oregon	296	1,410
Maryland	31	3,190	Washington	157	3,026
Virginia	112	3,315	Hawaii	750	1,052
North Carolina	301	3,375	Alaska (Pacific)	5,580	31,383
South Carolina	187	2,876	Total Pacific coast	7,623	40,298
Georgia	100	2,344	Arctic Coast:		
Florida (Atlantic)	580	3,331	Alaska (Arctic)	1,060	2,521
Total Atlantic coast	2,069	28,673	Total Arctic coast	1,060	2,521
			States Total	**12,383**	**88,633**

1. Figures are lengths of general outline of seacoast. Measurements made with unit measure of 30 minutes of latitude on charts as near scale of 1:1,200,000 as possible. Coastline of bays and sounds is included to point where they narrow to width of unit measure, and distance across at such point is included. 2. Figures obtained in 1939–40 with recording instrument on largest–scale maps and charts then available. Shoreline of outer coast, offshore islands, sounds, bays, rivers, and creeks is included to head of tidewater, or to point where tidal waters narrow to width of 100 feet. *Source:* Department of Commerce, National Oceanic and Atmospheric Administration, National Ocean Service.

Mississippi (2,340 mi.; 3,766 km): From Lake Itasca in Minnesota to mouth of Southwest Pass in La.

Mississippi-Missouri-Red Rock (3,710 mi.; 5,970 km): From source of Red Rock R. in Montana to mouth of Southwest Pass in Louisiana.

Missouri (2,315 mi.; 3,726 km): From junction of Jefferson R., Gallatin R., and Madison R. in Montana to Mississippi R. near St. Louis.

Missouri-Red Rock (2,540 mi.; 4,090 km): From source of Red Rock R. in Montana to Mississippi R. near St. Louis.

Mobile-Alabama-Coosa (645 mi.; 1,040 km): From junction of Etowah R. and Oostanula R. in Georgia to Mobile Bay.

Neosho (460 mi.; 740 km): From Morris Co. in Kansas to Arkansas R. in Oklahoma.

Niobrara (431 mi.; 694 km): From Niobrara Co. in Wyoming to Missouri R. in Nebraska.

Noatak (350 mi.; 563 km): From Brooks Range in Alaska to Kotzebue Sound.

North Canadian (800 mi.; 1,290 km): From Union Co. in New Mexico to Canadian R. in Oklahoma.

North Platte (618 mi.; 995 km): From Jackson Co. in Colorado to junction with So. Platte R. in Nebraska to form Platte R.

Ohio (981 mi.; 1,579 km): From junction of Allegheny R. and Monongahela R. at Pittsburgh to Mississippi R. between Illinois and Kentucky.

Ohio-Allegheny (1,306 mi.; 2,102 km): From Potter Co. in Pennsylvania to Mississippi R. at Cairo in Illinois.

Osage (500 mi.; 805 km): From east-central Kansas to Missouri R. near Jefferson City in Missouri.

Ouachita (605 mi.; 974 km): From Polk Co. in Arkansas to Red R. in Louisiana.

Pearl (411 mi.; 661 km): From Neshoba County in Mississippi to Gulf of Mexico (Mississippi-Louisiana).

Pecos (926 mi.; 1,490 km): From Mora Co. in New Mexico to Rio Grande in Texas.

Pee Dee-Yadkin (435 mi.; 700 km): From Watauga

Co. in North Carolina to Winyah Bay in South Carolina.

Pend Oreille-Clark Fork (531 mi.; 855 km): Near Butte in Montana to Columbia R. on Washington-Canada border.

Porcupine (569 mi.; 916 km): From Yukon Territory, Canada, to Yukon R. in Alaska.

Potomac (383 mi.; 616 km): From Garrett Co. in Md. to Chesapeake Bay at Point Lookout in Md.

Powder (375 mi.; 603 km): From junction of forks in Johnson Co. in Wyoming to Yellowstone R. in Montana.

Red (1,290 mi.; 2,080 km): From source of Tierra Blanca Creek in Curry County, New Mexico to Mississippi R. in Louisiana.

Red (also called *Red River of the North*) (545 mi.; 877 km): From junction of Otter Tail R. and Bois de Sioux R. in Minnesota to Lake Winnipeg in Manitoba.

Republican (445 mi.; 716 km): From junction of North Fork and Arikaree R. in Nebraska to junction with Smoky Hill R. in Kansas to form the Kansas R.

Rio Grande (1,900 mi.; 3,060 km): From San Juan Co. in Colorado to Gulf of Mexico.

Roanoke (380 mi.; 612 km): From junction of forks in Montgomery Co. in Virginia to Albemarle Sound in North Carolina.

Sabine (380 mi.; 612 km): From junction of forks in Hunt Co. in Texas to Sabine Lake between Texas and Louisiana.

Sacramento (377 mi.; 607 km): From Siskiyou Co. in California to Suisun Bay.

Saint Francis (425 mi.; 684 km): From Iron Co. in Missouri to Mississippi R. in Arkansas.

Salmon (420 mi.; 676 km): From Custer Co. in Idaho to Snake R.

San Joaquin (350 mi.; 563 km): From junction of forks in Madera Co. in California to Suisun Bay.

San Juan (360 mi.; 579 km): From Archuleta Co. in Colorado to Colorado R. in Utah.

Santee-Wateree-Catawba (538 mi.; 866 km):

From McDowell Co. in North Carolina to Atlantic Ocean in South Carolina.

Smoky Hill (540 mi.; 869 km): From Cheyenne Co. in Colorado to junction with Republican R. in Kansas to form Kansas R.

Snake (1,038 mi.; 1,670 km): From Ocean Plateau in Wyoming to Columbia R. in Washington.

South Platte (424 mi.; 682 km): From Park Co. in Colorado to junction with North Platte R. in Nebraska to form Platte R.

Susquehanna (444 mi.; 715 km): From Otsego Lake in New York to Chesapeake Bay in Maryland.

Tanana (659 mi.; 1,060 km): From Wrangell Mts. in Yukon Territory, Canada, to Yukon R. in Alaska.

Tennessee (652 mi.; 1,049 km): From junction of Holston R. and French Broad R. in Tennessee to Ohio R. in Kentucky.

Tennessee-French Broad (870 mi.; 1,400 km): From Bland Co. in Virginia to Ohio R. at Paducah in Kentucky.

Tombigbee (525 mil; 845 km): From junction of forks in Itawamba Co. in Mississippi to Mobile R. in Alabama.

Trinity (360 mi.; 579 km): From junction of forks in Dallas Co. in Texas to Galveston Bay.

Wabash (512 mi.; 824 km): From Darke Co. in Ohio to Ohio R. between Illinois and Indiana.

Washita (500 mi.; 805 km): From Hemphill Co. in Texas to Red R. in Oklahoma.

White (722 mi.; 1,160 km): From Madison Co. in Arkansas to Mississippi R.

Wisconsin (430 mi.; 692 km): From Vilas Co. in Wisconsin to Mississippi R.

Yellowstone (692 mi.; 1,110 km): From Park Co. in Wyoming to Missouri R. in North Dakota.

Yukon (1,979 mi.; 3,185 km): From junction of Lewes R. and Pelly R. in Yukon Territory, Canada, to Bering Sea in Alaska.

Geysers in The United States

Geysers are natural hot springs that intermittently eject a column of water and steam into the air. They exist in many parts of the volcanic regions of the world such as Japan and South America but their greatest development is in Iceland, New Zealand, and Yellowstone National Park.

There are 120 named geysers in Yellowstone National Park, Wyoming, and perhaps half that numebr unnamed. Most of the geysers and the 4,000 or more hot springs are located in the western portion of the park. The most important are the following:

Norris Geyser Basin has 24 or more active geysers; the number varies. There are scores of steam vents and hot springs. *Valentine* is highest, erupting 50–75 ft at intervals varying from 18 hr to 3 days or more. *Minuté* erupts 15–20 ft high, several hours aprt. Others include *Steamboat, Fearless, Veteran, Vixen, Corporal, Whirligig, Little Whirligig,* and *Pinwheel.*

Lower Geyser Basin has at least 18 active geysers. *Fountain* throws water 50–75 ft in all directions at unpredictable intervals. *Clepsydra* erupts violently from four vents up to 30 ft. *Great Fountain* plays every 8 to 15 hr in spurts from 30 to 90 ft high.

Midway Geyser Basin has vast steaming terraces of red, orange, pink and other colors; there are pools and springs, including the beautiful *Grand Prismatic Spring. Excelsior* crater discharges boiling water into Firehole River at the rate of 6 cu ft per second.

Giant erupts up to 200 ft at intervals of 2 1/2 days to 3 mo; eruptions last about 1 1/2 hr. *Daisy* sends water up to 75 ft but is irregular and frequently inactive.

Old Faithful sends up a column varying from 116 to 175 ft at intervals of about 65 min, varying from 33 to 90 min. Eruptions last about 4 min, during which time about 12,000 gal are discharged.

Giantess seldom erupts, but during its active period sends up streams 150–200 ft.

Lion Group: *Lion* plays up to 60 ft every 2–4 days when active; *Little Cub* up to 10 ft every 1–2 hr. *Big Cub* and *Lioness* seldom erupt.

Mammoth Hot Springs: There are no geysers in this area. The formation is travertine. Sides of a hill are steps and terraces over which flow the steaming waters of hot springs laden with minerals. Each step is tinted by algae to many shades of orange, pink, yellow, brown, green, and blue. Terraces are white where no water flows.

Loihi: Hawaii's Newest Volcano

Source: Department of the Interior/U.S. Geological Survey

Hawaii's worldwide image as an idyllic tropical paradise is well deserved. What is less well known, however, is that the islands exist only because of nearly continuous volcanic activity.

Since the beginning of a historical record early in the 19th century, eruptions have occurred frequently at Mauna Loa and Kilauea; these two volcanoes on the Big Island are among the most active in the world. Nearby Loihi Seamount, off the Big Island's south coast, is the newest Hawaiian volcano, not yet visible above the ocean surface.

Loihi rises 10,100 feet above the ocean floor to within 3,100 feet of the water surface. recent detailed mapping shows Loihi to be similar in form to Kilauea and Mauna Loa. Photographs taken by deep–sea camera show that Loihi's summit area has fresh-appearing, coherent pillow-lava flows and talus blocks. Examination of samples dredged from Loihi indicates that the pillow-lava fragments have fresh glassy crusts, indicative of their recent formation. The exact ages of the sampled Loihi flows are not yet known, but certainlyl some cannot be more than a few hundred years old. In fact, the occurrence of earthquake swarms at Loihi during 1971–1972, 1975, and 1984–85 suggests major submarine eruptions or magma intrusions into the upper part of Loihi. Thus Loihi appears to be a historically active, but as yet submarine, volcano.

Studies of Loihi provide a unique opportunity to decipher the youthful submarine stage in the formation and evolution of Hawaiian volcanoes. When might the still-growing Loihi emerge above the surface of the Pacific to become Hawaii's newest volcano island? It will almost certainly take several tens of thousands of years, if the growth rate for Loihi is comparable to that of other Hawaiian volcanoes.

NORTH AMERICA

LAMBERT AZIMUTHAL EQUAL-AREA
PROJECTION

SCALE OF MILES

0   200   400   600   800   1000

SCALE OF KILOMETERS

0   200   400   600   800   1000

Capitals .... ⊛
International Boundaries .... —·—·—
Canals ....

© Copyright HAMMOND INCORPORATED, Maplewood, N.J.

483

UNITED STATES

POLYCONIC PROJECTION

SCALE OF MILES

0 50 100 200 300 400

SCALE OF KILOMETERS

0 100 200 300 400

Capitals of Countries .... ☆
State Capitals .... △
International Boundaries .... _____

© Copyright HAMMOND INCORPORATED, Maplewood, N.J.

Longitude 95° West of Greenwich 90°

CANADA

CONIC PROJECTION

SCALE OF MILES
0 100 200 300 400 500

SCALE OF KILOMETERS
0 100 200 300 400 500

Capitals of Countries ⊛
Provincial & Territorial
  Capitals ⊙
Administrative Centers ⊙

© Copyright HAMMOND INCORPORATED, Maplewood, N.J.

MIDDLE AMERICA

BONNE PROJECTION

Copyright by C. S. HAMMOND & Co., N. Y.

SCALE OF MILES

Capitals of Countries
Other Capitals
International Boundaries

487

SOUTH AMERICA

LAMBERT AZIMUTHAL EQUAL-AREA PROJECTION

SCALE OF MILES
0   100   200   400   600

SCALE OF KILOMETERS
0 100 200   400   600

Capitals of Countries ✩
International Boundaries
Canals

Copyright by C. S. HAMMOND & CO., N.Y.

EUROPE

LAMBERT AZIMUTHAL EQUAL AREA PROJECTION

SCALE OF MILES

SCALE OF KILOMETERS

Capitals of Countries .... ☆
International Boundaries ...... —··—··—
Canals ....

Copyright by C. S. HAMMOND & CO., N.Y.

491

ASIA

LAMBERT AZIMUTHAL EQUAL-AREA PROJECTION

SCALE OF MILES

SCALE OF KILOMETERS

Capitals of Countries.................☆
International Boundaries.................
Canals.................

TIME ZONES OF THE WORLD

NOTE: Standard time zones in the U.S.S.R. are always advanced one hour.

STANDARD TIME ZONES

Areas using half hour deviations.

Areas not using zone system.

© Copyright HAMMOND INCORPORATED, Maplewood, N.J.

NEAR and
MIDDLE EAST
CONIC PROJECTION
SCALE OF MILES
100   200   300   400
KILOMETERS
100 200   300   400

Capitals of Countries .... ⊛
International Boundaries .... ____
Other Boundaries ....

496

THE YEAR IN PICTURES

MISSILE DAMAGE—Residents survey damage caused by Iraqi SCUD in the January 18, 1991, attack on Tel Aviv.

BRIEFING—General Norman Schwarzkopf points to troop position 150 miles outside of Baghdad on the evening of February 24, 1991, stating nothing could have stopped them had the mission been to take Baghdad.

ON THE MOVE—U.S. Army's 3rd Armored Division heads toward occupied Iraq against a backdrop of burning oilwells.

TIME OUT FOR PRAYER—A Kuwaiti oilfield worker kneels for midday prayer near a burning oil field near Kuwait City.

POLLUTED—A Saudi government official skims oil off a beach-side pool, one result of the massive release of oil by the Iraqis.

DESTROYED—A shopowner stands amid the ruins of his shop in Kuwait City where rows of shops were looted and destroyed.

PRISONERS OF WAR—A Kuwaiti helicopter herds Iraqi prisoners across a stream in southeastern Kuwait.

NO GENERAL—Saddam Hussein is "not a soldier, not a great general, and not a great tactician" Central Command Chief Gen. Norman Schwarzkopf tells press at briefing.

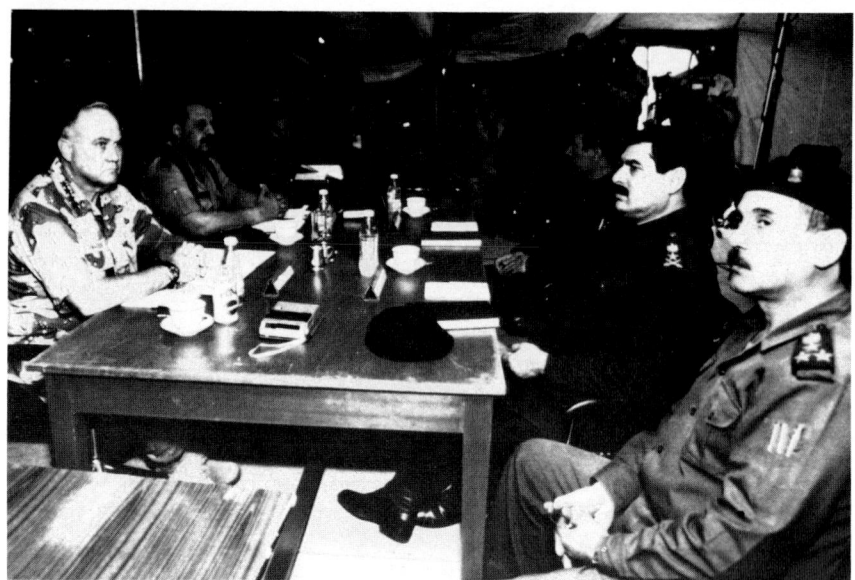

SETTING TERMS—General Schwarzkopf meets with top Iraqi military leaders to set terms for a permanent cease-fire in the Gulf War.

TENT CITY—Kurdish refugees settle in at a camp set up by Turkish authorities on the Iraq border.

HOME AGAIN—Former U.S. prisoners of war arrive at Andrews Air Force Base in Maryland.

WELCOME—Spectators are on hand to greet the returnees at Andrews Air Force Base.

OPERATION WELCOME HOME—Ticker tape showers on Desert Storm leaders as parade makes its way along lower Broadway in New York City.

CROWDS DEFY BAN—Tens of thousands of Soviet citizens rally to support Boris Yeltsin in defiance of Gorbachev's ban on demonstrations.

ANTI-COMMUNIST DEMONSTRATION—Demonstrators wave the three-fingered sign of the opposition Serbian Renewal Movement at a rally in Belgrade, Yugoslavia.

VOTING—Soviet President Gorbachev casts his vote in a national referendum to support strong central control over the republics.

EVACUATION—Eruption of Mount Pinatubo, in the background, forces evacuation of U.S. military forces from Clark Air Force Base in the Philippines.

WHITE HOUSE GUESTS—Polish President Lech Walesa and his wife Danuta listen to President Bush as first lady Barbara Bush looks on.

TREATY SIGNING—President George Bush and Soviet President Mikhail Gorbachev sign the START Treaty at the end of their Moscow summit meeting.

DERAILMENT—Railroad officials survey the wreckage of an Amtrak passenger train that resulted in the death of at least seven people.

RESIGNED—Thurgood Marshall resigns from the Supreme Court after 24 years on the bench.

ECLIPSE—The corona of a total solar eclipse as seen passing over the Baja Peninsula in Mexico.

CONGRATULATIONS—Soviet President Gorbachev congratulates Boris Yeltsin after his inauguration as the president of the Russian Republic.

HOME AT LAST—Former hostage John McCarthy, a television journalist, arrives at the Royal Air Force base at Lyneham, England, following his release in Beirut after five years of captivity.

FREED—Edwin Austin Tracy, an American held hostage for nearly five years, leaves the foreign ministry building in Damascus, Syria, following his release to Syrian officials in Beirut, Lebanon.

ECONOMIC SUMMIT—Soviet President Mikhail Gorbachev joins the G-7 leaders at the end of their 1991 conference. From left front: President Bush, Gorbachev, British Prime Minister Major, French President Mitterrand, and German Chancellor Kohl. From left rear: Economic Community President Delors, Italian Prime Minister Andreotti, Canadian Prime Minister Mulroney, Japanese Prime Minister Kaifu, and Dutch Prime Minister Lubbers.

CELEBRATION—Thousands of Muscovites march to Red Square carrying an old Russian flag in celebration of the failure of the coup which had attempted to remove President Gorbachev.

CROSSWORD PUZZLE GUIDE

First Aid to Crossword Puzzlers

We cannot begin to list all the odd words you will meet with in your daily and Sunday crossword puzzles, for such words run into many thousands. But we have tried to include those that turn up most frequently, as well as many others that should be of help to you when you are unable to go any further.

Also, we do not guarantee that the definitions in your puzzle will be exactly the same as ours, although we have checked every word with a standard dictionary and have followed its definition.

In nearly every case, we have used as the key word the principal noun of the definition, rather than any adjective, adjective phrase, or noun used as an adjective. And, to simplify your searching, we have grouped the words according to the number of spaces you have to fill.

For a list of Foreign Phrases, *see* Index. For Rulers of England and Great Britain, France, Germany and Prussia, and Russia, *see* Countries of the World.

Words of Two Letters

Ambary, DA
And (French, Latin), ET
Article (Arabic), AL
    (French), LA, LE, UN
    (Spanish), EL, LA, UN
At the (French), AU
    (Spanish), AL
Behold, LO
Bird: Hawaiian, OO
Birthplace: Abraham's, UR
Bone, OS
Buddha, FO
Butterfly: Peacock, IO
Champagne, AY
Chaos, NU
Chief: Burmese, BO
Coin: Roman, AS
    Siamese, AT
Concerning, RE
Dialect: Chinese, WU
Double (Egy. relig.), KA
Drama: Japanese, NO
Egg (comb. form), OO
Esker, OS
Eye (Scotch), EE
Factor: Amplification, MU
Fifty (Greek), NU
Fish: Carplike, ID
Force, OD
Forty (Greek), MU
From (French, Latin, Spanish), DE

(Latin prefix), AB
From the (French), DU
God: Babylonian, EA, ZU
    Egyptian sun, RA
    Hindu unknown, KA
    Semitic, EL
Goddess: Babylonian, AI
    Greek earth, GE
Gold (heraldry), OR
Gulf: Arctic, OB
Heart (Egy. relig.), AB
Indian: South American, GE
King: Of Bashan, OG
Language: Artificial, RO
    Assamese, AO
Lava: Hawaiian, AA
Letter: Greek, MU, NU, PI, XI
    Hebrew, HE, PE
Lily: Palm, TI
Measure: Annamese, LY
    Chinese, HO, HU, KO, LI, MU, PU,
    TO, TU
    Japanese, GO, JO, MO, RI, SE, TO
    Metric land, AR
    Netherlands, EL
    Portuguese, PE
    Siamese, WA
    Swedish, AM
    Type, EM, EN
Monk: Buddhist, BO
Month: Jewish, AB

Mouth, OS
Mulberry: Indian, AL
Native: Burmese, WA
Note: Of Scale, DO, FA, MI, LA, RE, TI
Of (French, Latin, Spanish), DE
Of the (French), DU
One (Scotch), AE
Pagoda: Chinese, TA
Plant: East Indian fiber, DA
Ridge: Sandy, AS, OS
River: Russian, OB
Sloth: Three-toed, AI
Soul (Egy. relig.), BA
Sound: Hindu mystic, OM
Suffix: Comparative, ER
The. *See* Article
To the: French, AU
    Spanish, AL
Tree: Buddhist sacred, BO
Tribe: Assamese, AO
Type: Jumbled, PI
Weight: Annamese, TA
    Chinese, LI
    Danish, ES
    Japanese, MO
    Roman, AS
Whirlwind: Faeroe Is., OE
Yes (German), JA
    (Italian, Spanish), SI
    (Russian), DA

Words of Three Letters

Adherent: IST
Again, BIS
Age, ERA
Antelope: African, GNU, KOB
Apricot: Japanese, UME
Article (German), DAS, DEM, DEN,
    DER, DES, DIE, EIN
    (French), LES, UNE
    (Spanish), LAS, LOS, UNA
Banana: Polynesian, FEI
Barge, HOY
Bass: African, IYO
Beak, NEB, NIB
Beard: Grain, AWN
Beetle: June, DOR
Being, ENS
Berry: Hawthorn, HAW
Beverage: Hawaiian, AVA
Bird: Australian, EMU
    Crowlike, JAY
    Extinct, MOA

Fabulous, ROC
Frigate, IWA
Parson, POE, TUE, TUI
Sea, AUK
Blackbird, ANI, ANO
Born, NEE
Bronze: Roman, AES
Bugle: Yellow, IVA
By way of, VIA
Canton: Swiss, URI
Cap: Turkish, FEZ
Catnip, NEP
Character: In "Faerie Queene," UNA
Coin: Afghan, PUL
    Albanian, LEK
    British Guiana, BIT
    Bulgarian, LEV, LEW
    French, ECU, SOU
    Indian, PIE
    Japanese, SEN, YEN
    Korean, WON

Lithuanian, LIT
Macao, Timor, AVO
Palestinian, MIL
Persian, PUL
Peruvian, SOL
Rumanian, BAN, LEU, LEY
Scandinavian, ORE
Siamese, ATT
    See also Money of account
Collection: Facts, ANA
Commune: Belgian, ANS, ATH
    Netherlands, EDE, EPE
Community: Russian, MIR
Constellation: Southern, ARA
Contraction: Poetic, EEN, EER, OER
Covering: Apex of roof, EPI
Crab: Fiddler, UCA
Crag: Rocky, TOR
Cry: Crow, rook, raven, CAW
Cup: Wine, AMA
Cymbal, Oriental, TAL, ZEL

513

Disease: Silkworm, UJI
Division: (Danish territorial, AMT
   Geologic, EON
Doctrine, ISM
Dowry, DOT
Dry (French), SEC
Dynasty: Chinese, CHI, HAN, SUI,
   WEI, YIN
Eagle: Sea, ERN
Earth (comb. form), GEO
Egg: Louse, NIT
Eggs: Fish, ROE
Emmet, ANT
Enzyme, ASE
Equal (comb. form), ISO
Extension: building, ELL
Far (comb. form), TEL
Farewell, AVE
Fiber: Palm, TAL
Finial, EPI
Fish: Carplike, IDE
   Pikelike, GAR
Flatfish, DAB
Fleur-de-lis, LIS, LYS
Food: Hawaiian, POI
Formerly, NEE
Friend (French), AMI
Game: Card, LOO
Garment: Camel-hair, ABA
Gateway, DAR
Gazelle: Tibetan, GOA
Genus: Ducks, AIX
   Grasses, POA
   Grasses (maize), ZEA
   Herbs or shrubs, IVA
   Lizards, UTA
   Rodents (incl. house mice), MUS
   Ruminants (incl. cattle), BOS
   Swine, SUS
Gibbon: Malay, LAR
God: Assyrian, SIN
   Babylonian, ABU, ANU, BEL, HEA,
    SIN, UTU
   Irish sea, LER
   Phrygian, MEN
   Polynesian, ORO
Goddess: Babylonian, AYA
   Etruscan, UNI
   Hindu, SRI, UMA, VAC
   Teutonic, RAN
Governor: Algerian, DEY
   Turkish, BEY
Grampus, ORC
Grape, UVA
Grass: Meadow, POA
Gypsy, ROM
Hail, AVE
Hare: Female, DOE
Hawthorn, HAW
Hay: Spread for drying, TED
Herb: Japanese, UDO
   Perennial, PIA
   Used for blue dye, WAD
Herd: Whales, GAM, POD
Hero: Spanish, CID
High (music), ALT
Honey (pharm.), MEL
Humorist: American, ADE
I (Latin), EGO
I love (Latin), AMO
Indian: Algonquian, FOX, SAC, WEA
   Chimakuan, HOH
   Keresan, SIA
   Mayan, MAM
   Shoshonean, UTE
   Siouan, KAW, OTO
   South American, ITE, ONA, URO,
    URU, YAO
   Tierra del Fuego, ONA
   Wakashan, AHT
Ingot, PIG
Inlet: Narrow, RIA
Island: Cyclades, IOS
   Dodecanese, COS, KOS
   (French), ILE
   River, AIT

Jackdaw, DAW
John (Gaelic), IAN
Keelbill, ANI, ANO
Kiln, OST
King: British legendary LUD
Kobold, NIS
Lace: To make, TAT
Lamprey, EEL
Language: Artificial, IDO
   Bantu, ILA
   Siamese, LAO, TAI
Leaf: Palm, OLA, OLE
Leaving, ORT
Left: Cause to turn, HAW
Letter: Greek, CHI, ETA, PHI, PSI,
   RHO, TAU
   Hebrew, MEM, NUN, SIN, TAV, VAU
Lettuce, COS
Life (comb. form), BIO
Lily: Palm, TOI
Lizard, EFT
Louse: Young, NIT
Love (Anglo-Irish), GRA
Lute: Oriental, TAR
Macaw: Bralizian, ARA
Marble, TAW
Match: Shooting (French), TIR
Meadow, LEA
Measure: Abyssinian, TAT
   Algerian, PIK
   Annamese, GON, MAU, NGU,
    VUO, SAO, TAO, TAT
   Arabian, DEN, SAA
   Belgian, VAT
   Bulgarian, OKA, OKE
   Chinese, FEN, TOU, YIN
   Cloth, ELL
   Cyprus, OKA, OKE, PIK
   Czech, LAN, SAH
   Danish, FOD, MIL, POT
   Dominican Republic, ONA
   Dutch, old, AAM
   East Indian, KIT
   Egyptian, APT, HEN, PIK, ROB
   Electric, MHO, OHM
   Energy, ERG
   English, PIN
   Estonian, TUN
   French, POT
   German, AAM
   Greek, PIK
   Hebrew, CAB, HIN, KOR, LOG
   Hungarian, AKO
   Icelandic, FET
   Indian, GAZ, GUZ, JOW, KOS
   Japanese, BOO, CHO, KEN, RIN,
    SHO, SUN, TAN
   Malabar, ADY
   Metric land, ARE
   Netherlands, KAN, KOP, MUD,
    VAT, ZAK
   Norwegian, FOT, POT
   Persian, GAZ, GUZ, MOU, ZAR, ZER
   Polish, CAL
   Rangoon, DHA, LAN
   Roman, PES, URN
   Russian, FUT, LOF
   Scotch, COP
   Siamese, KEN, NIU, RAI, SAT,
    SEN, SOK, WAH, YOT
   Somaliland, TOP
   Spanish, PIE
   Straits Settlements, PAU, TUN
   Swedish, ALN, FOT, MIL, REF, TUM
   Swiss, POT
   Tunisian, SAA
   Turkish, OKA, OKE, PIK
   Wire, MIL
   Württemberg, IMI
   Yarn, LEA
   Yugoslavian, OKA, RIF
Milk, LAC
Milkfish, AWA
Moccasin, PAC
Money: Yap stone, FEI
Money of Account: Anglo-Saxon, ORA,

ORE
   French, SOU
   Indian, LAC
   Japanese, RIN
   Oman, GAJ
   Virgin Islands, BIT
   See also Coin
Monkey: Capuchin, SAI
Morsel, ORT
Mother: Peer Gynt's, ASE
Mountain: Asia Minor, IDA
Mulberry: Indian, AAL, ACH, AWL
Muttonbird: New Zealand, OII
Nahoor, SNA
Native: Mindanao, ATA
Neckpiece, BOA
Newt, EFT
No (Scotch), NAE
Note: Guido's highest, ELA
   Of scale, SOL
Nursemaid: Oriental, AMA, IYA
Ocher: Yellow, SIL
One (Scotch), YIN
Ornament: Pagoda, TEE
Oven: Polynesian, UMU
Ox: Tibetan, YAK
Pagoda: Chinese, TAA
Parrot: Hawk, HIA
   New Zealand, KEA
Part: Footlike, PES
Particle: Electrified, ION
Pasha, DEY
Pass: Mountain, COL
Paste: Rice, AME
Pea: Indian split, DAL
Peasant: Philippine, TAO
Penpoint, NEB, NIB
Piece out, EKE
Pigeon, NUN
Pine: Textile screw, ARA
Pistol (slang), GAT
Pit: Baking, IMU
Plant: Pepper, AVA
Play: By Capek, RUR
Poem: Old French, DIT
Porgy: Japanese, TAI
Priest: Biblical high, ELI
Prince Ethiopian, RAS
Pseudonym: Dickens', BOZ
Queen: Fairy, MAB
Quince: Bengal, BEL
Record: Ship's, LOG
Refuse: Flax (Scotch), PAB, POB
Resin, LAC
Resort, SPA
Revolver (slang), GAT
Right: Cause to turn, GEE
River: Scotch or English, DEE
   (Spanish), RIO
   Swiss, AAR
Room: Harem, ODA
Rootstock: Fern, ROI
Rose (Persian), GUL
Ruff: Female, REE
Rule: Indian, RAJ
Sailor, GOB, TAR
Saint: Female (abbr.), STE
   Mohammedan, PIR
Salt, SAL
Sash: Japanese, OBI
Scrap, ORT
Seed: Poppy, MAW
   Small, PIP
Self, EGO
Serpent: Vedic sky, AHI
Sesame, TIL
Sheep: Female, EWE
   Indian, SHA
   Male, RAM
Sheepfold (Scotch), REE
Shelter, LEE
Shield, ECU
Shooting match (French), TIR
Shrew: European, ERD
Shrub: Evergreen, YEW
Silkworm, ERI

Snake, ASP, BOA
Soak, RET
Son-in-law: Mohammed's, ALI
Sorrel: Wood, OCA
Spade: Long, narrow, LOY
Spirit: Malignant, KER
Spot: Playing-card, PIP
Spread for drying, TED
Spring: Mineral, SPA
Sprite: Water, NIX
Statesman: Japanese, ITO
Stern: Toward, AFT
Stomach: Bird's, MAW
Street (French), RUE
Summer (French), ETE
Sun, SOL
Swamp, BOG, FEN
Swan: Male, COB
Tea: Chinese, CHA
Temple: Shinto, SHA
The. *See* Article
Thing (law), RES
Title: Etruscan, LAR
  Monk's, FRA
  Portuguese, DOM
  Spanish, DON
  Turkish, AGA, BEY
Tool: Cutting, ADZ, AXE
  Mining, GAD
  Piercing, AWL
Tree: Candlenut, AMA
  Central American, EBO
  East Indian, SAJ, SAL

Evergreen, YEW
Hawaiian, KOA, KOU
Indian, BEL, DAR
Linden, LIN
New Zealand, AKE
Philippine, DAO, TUA, TUI
Rubber, ULE
  South American, APA
Tribe: New Zealand, ATI
Turmeric, REA
Twice, BIS
Twin: Siamese, ENG
Uncle (dialect), EAM, EME
Veil: Chalice, AER, AIR
Vessel: Wine, AMA
Vestment: Ecclesiastical, ALB
Vetch: Bitter, ERS
Victorfish, AKU
Vine: New Zealand, AKA
  Philippine, IYO
Wallaba, APA
Wapiti, ELK
Water (French), EAU
Waterfall, LIN
Watering place: Prussian, EMS
Weave: Designating plain, UNI
Weight: Annamese, CAN
  Bulgarian, OKA, OKE
  Burmese, MOO, VIS
  Chinese, FEN, HAO, KIN, SSU,
    TAN, YIN
  Cyprus, OKA, OKE
  Danish, LOD, ORT, VOG

East Indian, TJI
Egyptian, KAT, OKA, OKE
English, for wool, TOD
German, LOT
Greek, MNA, OKA, OKE
Indian, SER
Japanese, FUN, KIN, RIN, SHI
Korean, KON
Malacca, KIP
Mongolian, LAN
Netherlands, ONS
Norwegian, LOD
Polish, LUT
Rangoon, PAI
Roman, BES
Russian, LOT
Siamese, BAT, HAP, PAI
Swedish, ASS, ORT
Turkish, OKA, OKE
Yugoslavian, OKA, OKE
Whales: Herd, GAM, POD
Wildebeest, GNU
Wing, ALA
Witticism, MOT
Wolframite, CAL
Worm: African, LOA
Wreath: Hawaiian, LEI
Yale, ELI
Yam: Hawaiian, HOI
Yes (French), OUI
Young: Bring forth, EAN
Z (letter), ZED

Words of Four Letters

Aborigine: Borneo, DYAK
Agave, ALOE
Animal: Footless, APOD
Ant: White, ANAI, ANAY
Antelope: African, ASSE, BISA,
  GUIB,KOBA, KUDU, ORYX, POKU,
  PUKU, TOPI, TORA
Apoplexy: Plant, ESCA
Apple, POME
Apricot, ANSU
Ardor, ELAN
Armadillo, APAR, PEBA, PEVA, TATU
Ascetic: Mohammedan, SUFI
Association: Chinese, TONG
Astronomer: Persian, OMAR
Avatar: Of Vishnu, RAMA
Axillary, ALAR
Band: Horizontal (heraldry), FESS
Barracuda, SPET
Bark: Mulberry, TAPA
Base: Column, DADO
Bearing (heraldry), ORLE
Beer: Russian, KVAS
Beige, ECRU
Being, ESSE
Beverage: Japanese rice, SAKE
Bird: Asian, MINA, MYNA
  Egyptian sacred, IBIS
  Extinct, DODO, MAMO
  Flightless, KIWI
  Gull-like, TERN
  Hawaiian, IIWI, MAMO
  Parson, KOKO
  Unfledged, EYAS
Birds: As class, AVES
Black, EBON
  (French), NOIR
Blackbird: European, MERL
Boat: Flat-bottomed, DORY
Bone: Forearm, ULNA
Bones, OSSA
Box, Japanese, INRO
Bravo (rare), EUGE
Buffalo: Indian wild, ARNA
Bull (Spanish), TORO
Burden, ONUS
Cabbage: Sliced, SLAW

Caliph: Mohammedan, OMAR
Canoe: Malay, PRAU, PROA
Cap: Military, KEPI
Cape, NESS
Capital: Ancient Irish, TARA
Case: Article, ETUI
Cat: Wild, BALU, EYRA
Chalcedony, SARD
Chamber: Indian ceremonial, KIVA
Channel: Brain, ITER
Cheese: Dutch, EDAM
Chest: Sepulchral stone, CIST
Chieftain: Arab, EMIR
Church: Part of, APSE, NAVE
  (Scotch), KIRK
Claim (law), LIEN
Cluster: Flower, CYME
Coin: Chinese, TAEL, YUAN
  German, MARK
  Indian, ANNA
  Iranian, RIAL
  Italian, LIRA
  Moroccan, OKIA
  Siamese, BAHT
  South American, PESO
  Spanish, DURO, PESO
  Turkish, PARA
Commune: Belgian, AATH
Composition: Musical, OPUS
Compound: Chemical, DIOL
Constellation: Southern, PAVO
Council: Russian, DUMA
Counsel, REDE
Covering: Seed, ARIL
Cross: Egyptian, ANKH
Cry: Bacchanalian, EVOE
Cup (Scotch), TASS
Cupbearer, SAKI
Dagger, DIRK
  Malay, KRIS
Dam: River, WEIR
Dash, ELAN
Date: Roman, IDES
Dawn: Pertaining to, EOAN
Dean: English, INGE
Decay: In fruit, BLET
Deer: Sambar, MAHA

Disease: Skin, ACNE
Disk: Solar, ATEN
Dog: Hunting, ALAN
Drink: Hindu intoxicating, SOMA
Duck, SMEE, SMEW, TEAL
Dynasty: Chinese, CHEN, CHIN,
  CHOU, CHOW, HSIA, MING, SUNG,
  TANG, TSIN
  Mongol, YUAN
Eagle: Biblical, GIER
  Sea, ERNE
Egyptian: Christian, COPT
Ear: Pertaining to, OTIC
Entrance: Mine, ADIT
Esau, EDOM
Escutcheon: Voided, ORLE
Eskers, OSAR
Evergreen: New Zealand, TAWA
Fairy: Persian, PERI
Family: Italian, ESTE
Far (comb. form), TELE
Farewell, VALE
Father (French), PERE
Fennel: Philippine, ANIS
Fever: Malarial, AGUE
Fiber: East Indian, JUTE
Firn, NEVE
Fish: Carplike, DACE
  Hawaiian, ULUA
  Herringlike, SHAD
  Mackerellike, CERO
  Marine, HAKE
  Sea, LING, MERO, OPAH
  Spiny-finned, GOBY
Food: Tropical, TARO
Foot: Metric, IAMB
Formerly, ERST
Founder: Of Carthage, DIDO
France: Southern, MIDI
Furze, ULEX
Gaelic, ERSE
Gaiter, SPAT
Game: Card, FARO, SKAT
Garlic: European wild, MOLY
Garment: Hindu, SARI
  Roman, TOGA
Gazelle, CORA

Gem, JADE, ONYX, OPAL, RUBY
Genus: Amphibians (incl. frogs), RANA
  Amphibians (incl. tree toads), HYLA
  Antelopes, ORYX
  Auks, ALCA, URIA
  Bees, APIS
  Birds (American ostriches), RHEA
  Birds (cranes), CRUS
  Birds (magpies), PICA
  Birds (peacocks), PAVO
  Cetaceans, INIA
  Ducks (incl. mallards), ANAS
  Fishes (burbots), LOTA
  Fishes (incl. bowfins), AMIA
  Geese (snow geese), CHEN
  Gulls, XEMA
  Herbs, ARUM, GEUM
  Insects (water scorpions), NEPA
  Lilies, ALOE
  Mammals (mankind), HOMO
  Orchids, DISA
  Owls, ASIO, BUBO, OTUS
  Palms, NIPA
  Sea birds, SULA
  Sheep, OVIS
  Shrubs, Eurasian, ULEX
  Shrubs (hollies), ILEX
  Shrubs (incl. Virginia Willow), ITEA
  Shrubs, tropical, EVEA
  Snakes (sand snakes), ERYX
  Swans, OLOR
  Trees, chocolate, COLA
  Trees (ebony family), MABA
  Trees (incl. maples), ACER
  Trees (olives), OLEA
  Trees, tropical, EVEA
  Turtles, EMYS
Goat: Wild, IBEX, KRAS, TAHR, TAIR, THAR
God: Assyrian, ASUR
  Babylonian, ADAD, ADDU, ENKI, ENZU, IRRA, NABU, NEBO, UTUG
  Celtic, LLEU, LLEW
  Hindu, AGNI, CIVA, DEVA, DEWA, KAMA, RAMA, SIVA, VAYU
  Phrygian, ATYS
  Semitic, BAAL
  Teutonic, HLER
Goddess: Babylonian, ERUA, GULA
  Hawaiian, PELE
  Hindu, DEVI, KALI, SHRI, VACH
Gooseberry: Hawaiian, POHA
Gourd, PEPO
Grafted (heraldry), ENTE
Grandfather (obsolete), AIEL
Grandparents: Pertaining to, AVAL
Grass: Hawaiian, HILO
Gray (French), GRIS
Green (heraldry), VERT
Groom: Indian, SYCE
Half (prefix), DEMI, HEMI, SEMI
Hamlet, DORP
Hammer-head: Part of, PEEN
Handle, ANSA
Harp: Japanese, KOTO
Hartebeest, ASSE, TORA
Hautboy, OBOE
Hawk: Taken from nest (falconry), EYAS
Hearing (law), OYER
Heater: For liquids, ETNA
Herb: Aromatic, ANET, DILL
  Fabulous, MOLY
  Perennial, GEUM, SEGO
  Pot, WORT
  Used for blue dye, WADE, WOAD
Hill: Flat-topped, MESA
  Sand, DENE, DUNE
Hoarfrost, RIME
Hog: Immature female, GILT
Holly, ILEX
House: Cow, BYRE
  (Spanish), CASA
Ice: Floating, FLOE
Image, ICON, IKON
Incarnation: Of Vishnu, RAMA

Indian: Algonquian, CREE, SAUK
  Central American, MAYA
  Iroquoian, ERIE
  Mexican, CORA
  Peruvian, CANA, INCA, MORO
  Shoshonean, HOPI
  Siouan, OTOE
  Southwestern, HOPI, PIMA, YUMA, ZUNI
Insect: Immature, PUPA
Instrument: Stringed, LUTE, LYRE
Ireland, EIRE, ERIN
Jacket: English, ETON
Jail (British), GAOL
Jar, OLLA
Judge: Mohammedan, CADI
Juniper: European, CADE
Kiln, OAST, OVEN
King: British legendary, LUDD, NUDD
Kiss, BUSS
Knife: Philippine, BOLO
Koran: Section of, SURA
Laborer: Spanish American, PEON
Lake: Mountain, TARN
  (Scotch), LOCH
Lamp: Miner's, DAVY
Landing place: Indian, GHAT
Language: Buddhist, PALI
  Japanese, AINU
Latvian, LETT
Layer: Of iris, UVEA
Leaf: Palm, OLAY, OLLA
Legislature: Ukrainian, RADA
Lemur, LORI
Leopard, PARD
Let it stand, STET
Letter: Greek, BETA, IOTA, ZETA
  Hebrew, AYIN, BETH, CAPH, KOPH, RESH, SHIN, TETH, YODH
  Papal, BULL
Lily, ALOE
Literature: Hindu sacred, VEDA
Lizard, GILA
  Monitor, URAN
Loquat, BIWA
Magistrate: Genoese or Venetian, DOGE
Man (Latin), HOMO
Mark: Omission, DELE
  armoset: South American, MICO
Meadow: Fertile, VEGA
Measure: Electric, VOLT, WATT
  Force, DYNE
  Hebrew, OMER
  Printing, PICA
  Spanish or Portuguese, VARA
  Swiss land, IMMI
Medley, OLIO
Merganser, SMEW
Milk (French), LAIT
Molding, GULA
  Curved, OGEE
Mongoose: Crab-eating, URVA
Monk: Tibetan, LAMA
Monkey: African, MONA, WAAG
  Ceylonese, MAHA
  Cochin-China, DOUC
  South American, SAKI, TITI
Monkshood, ATIS
Month: Jewish, ADAR, ELUL, IYAR
Mother (French), MERE
Mountain: Thessaly, OSSA
Mouse: Meadow, VOLE
Mythology: Norse, EDDA
Nail (French), CLOU
Native: Philippine, MORO
Nest: Of pheasants, NIDE
Network, RETE
No (German), NEIN
Noble: Mohammedan, AMIR
Notice: Death, OBIT
Novel: By Zola, NANA
Nursemaid: Oriental AMAH, AYAH, EYAH
Nut: Philippine, PILI

Oak: Holm, ILEX
Oil (comb. form), OLEO
Ostrich: American, RHEA
Oven, KILN, OAST
Owl: Barn, LULU
Ox: Celebes wild, ANOE
  Extinct wild, URUS
Palm, ATAP, NIPA, SAGO
Parliament, DIET
Parrot: New Zealand, KAKA
Pass: Indian mountain, GHAT
Passage: Closing (music), CODA
Peach: Clingstone, PAVY
Peasant: Indian, RYOT
  Old English, CARL
Pepper: Australasian, KAVA
Perfume, ATAR
Persia, IRAN
Person: Extraordinary, ONER
Pickerel or pike, ESOX
Pitcher, EWER
Plant: Aromatic, NARD
  Century, ALOE
  Indigo, ANIL
  Pepper, KAVA
Platform: Raised, DAIS
Plum: Wild, SLOE
Pods: Vegetable, OKRA, OKRO
Poem: Epic, EPOS
Poet: Persian, OMAR
  Roman, OVID
Poison, BANE
  Arrow, INEE
Porkfish, SISI
Portico: Greek, STOA
Premium, AGIO
Priest: Mohammedan, IMAM
Prima donna, DIVA
Prong: Fork, TINE
Pseudonym: Lamb's, ELIA
Queen: Carthaginian, DIDO
  Hindu, RANI
Rabbit, CONY
Race: Of Japan, AINU
Rail: Ducklike, COOT
  North American, SORA
Redshank, CLEE
Refuse: After pressing, MARC
Regiment: Turkish, ALAI
Reliquary, ARCA
Resort: Italian, LIDO
Ridges: Sandy, ASAR, OSAR
River: German, ELBE, ODER
  Italian, ADDA
  Siberian, LENA
Road: Roman, ITER
Rockfish: California, RENA
Rodent: Mouselike, VOLE
  South American, PACA
Rootstock, TARO
Salamander, NEWT
Salmon: Silver, COHO
  Young, PARR
Same (Greek), HOMO
  (Latin), IDEM
Sauce: Fish, ALEC
School: English, ETON
Seaweed, AGAR, ALGA, KELP
Secular, LAIC
Sediment, SILT
Seed: Dill, ANET
  Of vetch, TARE
Serf, ILOT
Sesame, TEEL
Settlement: Eskimo, ETAH
Shark: Atlantic, GATA
  European, TOPE
Sheep: Wild, UDAD
Sheltered, ALEE
Shield, EGIS
Ship: Jason's, ARGO
  Left side of, PORT
  Two-masted, BRIG
Shrine: Buddhist, TOPE
Shrub: New Zealand, TUTU

Sign: Magic, RUNE
Silkworm, ERIA
Skin: Beaver, PLEW
Skink: Egyptian, ADDA
Slave, ESNE
Sloth: Two-toed, UNAU
Smooth, LENE
Snow: Glacial, NEVE
Soapstone, TALC
Society: African secret, EGBO, PORO
Son: Of Seth, ENOS
Song (German), LIED
   Unaccompanied, GLEE
Sound: Lung, RALE
Sour, ACID
Sow: Young, GILT
Spike: Brad-shaped, BROB
Spirit: Buddhist evil, MARA
Stake: Poker, ANTE
Star: Temporary, NOVA
Starch: East Indian, SAGO
Stone: Precious, OPAL
Strap: Bridle, REIN
Strewn (heraldry), SEME
Sweetsop, ATES, ATTA
Sword: Fencing, EPEE, FOIL
Tambourine: African, TAAR
Tapir: Brazilian, ANTA
Tax, CESS
Tea: South American, MATE
Therefore (Latin), ERGO
Thing: Extraordinary, ONER
Three (dice, cards, etc.), TREY
Thrush: Hawaiian, OMAO

Tide, NEAP
Tipster: Racing, TOUT
Tissue, TELA
Title: Etruscan, LARS
   Hindu, BABU
   Indian, RAJA
   Mohammedan, EMIR, IMAM
   Persian, BABA
   Spanish, DONA
   Turkish, AGHA, BABA
Toad: Largest-known, AGUA
   Tree, HYLA
Tool: Cutting, ADZE
Track: Deer, SLOT
Tract: Sandy, DENE
Tree: Apple, SORB
   Central American, EBOE
   East Indian, TEAK
   Eucalyptus, YATE
   Guiana and Trinidad, MORA
   Javanese, UPAS
   Linden, LIME, LINN, TEIL, TILL
   Sandarac, ARAR
   Sassafras, AGUE
   Tamarisk salt, ATLE
Tribe: Moro, SULU
Trout, CHAR
Urchin: Street, ARAB
Vessel: Arab, DHOW
Vestment: Ecclesiastical, COPE
Vetch, TARE
Vine: East Indian, SOMA
Violinist: Famous, AUER

Vortex, EDDY
Wampum, PEAG
Wapiti, STAG
Waste: Allowance for, TRET
Watchman: Indian, MINA
Water (Spanish), AGUA
Waterfall, LINN
Wavy (heraldry), ONDE, UNDE
Wax, CERE
   Chinese, PELA
Weed: Biblical, TARE
Weight: Ancient, MINA
   Danish (pl.), ESER
   East Asian, TAEL
   Greek, MINA
   Siamese, BAHT
Well done (rare), EUGE
Whale, CETE
   Killer, ORCA
   White, HUSE, HUSO
Whirlpool, EDDY
Wife: Of Geraint, ENID
Willow: Virginia, ITEA
Wine, PORT
Winged, ALAR
   (Heraldry), AILE
Wings, ALAE
Withered, SERE
Without (French), SANS
Wool: To comb, CARD
Work, OPUS
Wrong: Civil, TORT
Young: Bring forth, YEAN

Words of Five Letters

Abode of dead: Babylonian, ARALU
Aborigine: Borneo DAYAK
Aftersong, EPODE
Aloe, AGAVE
Animal: Footless, APODE
Ant, EMMET
Antelope: African, ADDAX, BEISA, CAAMA, ELAND,
   GUIBA, ORIBI, TIANG
   Goat, GORAL, SEROW
   Indian, SASIN
   Siberian, SAIGA
Arch: Pointed, OGIVE
Armadillo, APARA, POYOU, TATOU
Arrowroot, ARARU
Artery: Trunk, AORTA
Association: Russian, ARTEL
   Secret, CABAL
Author: English, READE
Automaton, GOLEM, ROBOT
Award: Motion-picture, OSCAR
Basket: Fishing, CREEL
Beer: Russian, KVASS
Bible: Mohammedan, KORAN
Bird: Asian, MINAH, MYNAH
   Indian, SHAMA
   Larklike, PIPIT
   Loonlike, GREBE
   Oscine, VIREO
   South American, AGAMI
   Swimming, GREBE
Black: (French), NOIRE
   (Heraldry), SABLE
Blackbird: European, MERLE, OUSEL, OUZEL
Block: Glacial, SERAC
Blue (heraldry), AZURE
Boat: Eskimo, BIDAR, UMIAK
Bobwhite, COLIN, QUAIL
Bone (comb. form), OSTEO
   Leg, TIBIA
   Thigh, FEMUR
Broom: Twig, BESOM
Brother (French), FRERE
   Moses, AARON
Canoe: Eskimo, BIDAR, KAYAK
Cape: Papal, FANON, ORALE
Caravansary, SERAI

Card: Old playing, TAROT
Caterpillar: New Zealand, AWETO
Catkin, AMENT
Cavity: Stone, GEODE
Cephalopod, SQUID
Cetacean, WHALE
Chariot, ESSED
Cheek: Pertaining to, MALAR
Chieftain: Arab, EMEER
Child (Scotch), BAIRN
Cigar, CLARO
Coating: Seed, TESTA
Cockatoo: Palm, ARARA
Coin: Costa Rican, COLON
   Danish, KRONE
   Ecuadorian, SUCRE
   English, GROAT, PENCE
   French, FRANC
   German, KRONE, TALER
   Hungarian, PENGO
   Icelandic, KRONA
   Indian, RUPEE
   Iraqi, DINAR
   Norwegian, KRONE
   Polish, ZLOTY
   Russian, COPEC, KOPEK, RUBLE
   Swedish, KRONA
   Turkish, ASPER
   Yugoslav, DINAR
Collar: Papal, FANON, ORALE
   Roman, RABAT
Commune: Italian, TREIA
Composition: Choral, MOTET
Compound: Chemical, ESTER
Conceal (law), ELOIN
Council: Ecclesiastical, SYNOD
Court: Anglo-Saxon, GEMOT
   Inner, PATIO
Crest: Mountain, ARETE
Crown: Papal, TIARA
Cuttlefish, SEPIA
Date: Roman, NONES
Decree: Mohammedan, IRADE
   Russian, UKASE
Deposit: Loam, LOESS
Desert: Gobi, SHAMO

Devilfish, MANTA
Disease: Cereals, ERGOT
Disk, PATEN
Dog: Wild, DHOLE, DINGO
Dormouse, LEROT
Drum, TABOR
Duck: Sea, EIDER
Dynasty: Chinese, CHING, LIANG, SHANG
Earthquake, SEISM
Eel, ELVER, MORAY
Ermine: European, STOAT
Ether: Crystalline, APIOL
Fabric: Velvetlike, PANNE
Fabulist, AESOP
Family: Italian, CENCI
Fiber: West Indian, SISAL
Fig: Smyrna, ELEME, ELEMI
Figure: Of speech, TROPE
Finch: European, SERIN
Fish: American small, KILLY
Flower: Garden, ASTER
Friend (Spanish), AMIGO
Fruit: Tropical, MANGO
Fungus: Rye, ERGOT
Furze, GORSE
Gateway, TORAN, TORII
Gem, AGATE, BERYL, PEARL, TOPAZ
Genus: Barnacles, LEPAS
  Bears, URSUS
  Birds (loons), GAVIA
  Birds (nuthatches), SITTA
  Cats, FELIS
  Dogs, CANIS
  Fishes (chiros), ELOPS
  Fishes (perch), PERCA
  Geese, ANSER
  Grasses, STIPA
  Grasses (incl. oats), AVENA
  Gulls, LARUS
  Hares, rabbits, LEPUS
  Hawks, BUTEO
  Herbs, old world, INULA
  Herbs, trailing or climbing, APIOS
  Herbs, tropical, TACCA, URENA
  Horses, EQUUS
  Insects (olive flies), DACUS
  Lice, plant, APHIS
  Lichens, USNEA
  Lizards, AGAMA
  Moles, TALPA
  Mollusks, OLIVA
  Monkeys, CEBUS
  Palms, ARECA
  Pigeons, GOURA
  Plants (amaryllis family), AGAVE
  Ruminants (goats), CAPRA
  Shrubs, Asiatic, SABIA
  Shrubs (heath), ERICA
  Shrubs (incl. raspberry), RUBUS
  Shrubs, tropical, IXORA, TREMA, URENA
  Ticks, ARGAS
  Trees (of elm family), TREMA, ULMUS
  Trees, tropical, IXORA, TREMA
Goat: Bezoar, PASAN
God: Assyrian, ASHIR, ASHUR, ASSUR
  Babylonian, DAGAN, SIRIS
  Gaelic, DAGDA
  Hindu, BHAGA, INDRA, SHIVA
  Japanese, EBISU
  Philistine, DAGON
  Phrygian, ATTIS
  Teutonic, AEGIR, GYMIR
  Welsh, DYLAN
Goddess: Babylonian, ISTAR, NANAI
  Hindu, DURGA, GAURI, SHREE
Group: Of six, HEXAD
Grove: Sacred to Diana, NEMUS
Growing out, ENATE
Guitar: Hindu, SITAR
Gull: PEWEE, PEWIT
Hartebeest, CAAMA
Headdress: Jewish or Persian, TIARA
  Liturgical, MITER, MITRE
Heath, ERICA
Herb: Grasslike marsh, SEDGE

Heron, EGRET
Hog: Young, SHOAT, SHOTE
Image, EIKON
Indian: Cariban, ARARA
  Iroquoian, HURON
  Mexican, AZTEC, OPATA, OTOMI
  Muskhogean, CREEK
  Siouan, OSAGE, TETON
  Spanish American, ARARA, CARIB
Inflorescence: Racemose, AMENT
Insect: Immature, LARVA
Intrigue, CABAL
Iris: Yellow, SEDGE
Juniper, GORSE, RETEM
Kidneys: Pertaining to, RENAL
King: British legendary, LLUDD
Kite: European, GLEDE
Kobold, NISSE
Land: Cultivated, ARADA, ARADO
Landholder (Scotch), LAIRD, THANE
Language: Dravidian, TAMIL
Lariat, LASSO, REATA
Laughing, RIANT
Lawgiver: Athenian, DRACO, SOLON
Leaf: Calyx, SEPAL
  Fern, FROND
Lemur, LORIS
Letter: English, AITCH
  Greek, ALPHA, DELTA, GAMMA, KAPPA, OMEGA, SIGMA, THETA
  Hebrew, ALEPH, CHETH, GIMEL, SADHE, ZAYIN
Lichen, USNEA
Lighthouse, PHARE
Lizard: Old World, AGAMA
Loincloth, DHOTI
Louse: Plant, APHID
Macaw: Brazilian, ARARA
Mahogany: Philippine, ALMON
Mammal: Badgerlike, RATEL
  Civetlike, GENET
  Giraffelike, OKAPI
  Raccoonlike, COATI
Man (French), HOMME
Marble, AGATE
Mark: Insertion, CARET
Market place: Greek, AGORA
Marsupial: Australian, KOALA
Measure: Electric, FARAD, HENRY
  Energy, JOULE
  Metric, LITER, STERE
  Printing, AGATE
  Russian, VERST
Mixture: Smelting, MATTE
Mohicans: Last of, UNCAS
Molding: Convex, OVOLO, TORUS
Mole, TALPA
Monkey: African, PATAS
  Capuchin, SAJOU
  Howling, ARABA
Monkshood, ATEES
Month: Jewish, NISAN, SIVAN, TEBET
Museum (French), MUSEE
Musketeer, ATHOS
Native: Aleutian, ALEUT
  New Zealand, MAORI
Neckpiece: Ecclesiastical, AMICE
Nerve (comb. form), NEURO
Nest: Eagle's or hawk's, AERIE
  Insect's, NIDUS
Net: Fishing, SEINE
Newsstand, KIOSK
Nitrogen, AZOTE
Noble: Mohammedan, AMEER
Nodule: Stone, GEODE
Nostrils, NARES
Notched irregularly, EROSE
Nymph: Mohammedan, HOURI
Official: Roman, EDILE
Oleoresin, ELEMI
Opening: Mouthlike, STOMA
Oration: Funeral, ELOGE
Ostiole, STOMA
Page: Left-hand, VERSO
  Right-hand, RECTO
Palm, ARECA, BETEL

Park: Colorado, ESTES
Perfume, ATTAR
Philosopher: Greek, PLATO
Pillar: Stone, STELA, STELE
Pinnacle: Glacial, SERAC
Plain, LLANO
Plant: Century, AGAVE
   Climbing, LIANA
   Dwarf, CUMIN
   East Asian perennial, RAMIE
   Medicinal, SENNA
   Mustard family, CRESS
Plate: Communion, PATEN
Poem: Lyric, EPODE
Point: Lowest, NADIR
Poplar, ABELE, ALAMO, ASPEN
Porridge: Spanish American, ATOLE
Post: Stair, NEWEL
Priest: Mohammedan, IMAUM
Protozoan, AMEBA
Queen: (French), REINE
   Hindu, RANEE
Rabbit, CONEY
Rail, CRAKE
Red (heraldry), GULES
Religion: Moslem, ISLAM
Resin, ELEMI
Revoke (law), ADEEM
Rich man, MIDAS, NABOB
Ridge: Sandy, ESKAR, ESKER
River: French, LOIRE, SEINE
Rockfish: California, REINA
Rootstock: Fragrant, ORRIS
Ruff: Female, REEVE
Sack: Pack, KYACK
Salt: Ethereal, ESTER
Saltpeter, NITER, NITRE
Salutation: Eastern, SALAM
Sandpiper: Old World, TEREK
Scented, OLENT
School: Fish, SHOAL
   French public, LYCEE
Scriptures: Mohammedan, KORAN
Seaweeds, ALGAE
Seed: Aromatic, ANISE
Seraglio, HAREM, SERAI
Serf, HELOT
Sheep: Wild, AUDAD
Sheeplike, OVINE
Shield, AEGIS
Shoe: Wooden, SABOT
Shoots: Pickled bamboo, ACHAR
Shot: Billiard, CAROM, MASSE
Shrine: Buddhist, STUPA
Shrub: Burning bush, WAHOO
   Ornamental evergreen, TOYON
   Used in tanning, SUMAC
Silk: Watered, MOIRE
Sister (French), SOEUR
   (Latin), SOROR
Six: Group of, HEXAD

Skeleton: Marine, CORAL
Slave, HELOT
Snake, ABOMA, ADDER, COBRA, RACER
Soldier: French, POILU
   Indian, SEPOY
Sour, ACERB
Spirit: Air, ARIEL
Staff: Shepherd's, CROOK
Starwort, ASTER
Steel (German), STAHL
Stockade: Russian, ETAPE
Stop (nautical), AVAST
Storehouse, ETAPE
Subway: Parisian, METRO
Tapestry, ARRAS
Tea: Paraguayan, YERBA
Temple: Hawaiian, HEIAU
Terminal: Positive, ANODE
Theater: Greek, ODEON, ODEUM
Then (French), ALORS
Thread: Surgical, SETON
Thrush: Wilson's, VEERY
Title: Hindu, BABOO
   Indian, RAJAH, SAHEB, SAHIB
   Mohammedan, EMEER, IMAUM
Tree: Buddhist sacred, PIPAL
   East Indian cotton, SIMAL
   Hickory, PECAN
   Light-wooded, BALSA
   Malayan, TERAP
   Mediterranean, CAROB
   Mexican, ABETO
   Mexican pine, OCOTE
   New Zealand, MAIRE
   Philippine, ALMON
   Rain, SAMAN
   South American, UMBRA
   Tamarack, LARCH
   Tamarisk salt, ATLEE
   West Indian, ACANA
Trout, CHARR
Troy, ILION, ILIUM
Twin: Siamese, CHANG
Vestment: Ecclesiastical, STOLE
Violin: Famous, AMATI, STRAD
Volcano: Mud, SALSE
Wampum, PEAGE
War cry: Greek, ALALA
Wavy (heraldry), UNDEE
Weight: Jewish, GERAH
Wen, TALPA
Wheat, SPELT
Wheel: Persian water, NORIA
Whitefish, CISCO
Willow, OSIER
Window: Bay, ORIEL
Wine, MEDOC, RHINE, TINTA, TOKAY
Winged, ALATE
Woman (French), FEMME
Year: Excess of solar over lunar, EPACT
Zoroastrian, PARSI

Words of Six or More Letters

Agave, MAGUEY
Alkaloid: Crystalline, ESERIN, ESERINE
Alligator, CAYMAN
Amphibole, EDENITE, URALITE
Ant: White, TERMITE
Antelope: African, DIKDIK, DUIKER, GEMSBOK, IMPA-LA, KOODOO
   European, CHAMOIS
   Indian, NILGAI, NILGAU, NILGHAI, NILGHAU
Ape: Asian or East Indian, GIBBON
Appendage: Leaf, STIPEL, STIPULE
Armadillo, PELUDO, TATOUAY
Arrowroot, ARARAO
Ascetic: Jewish, ESSENE
Ass: Asian wild, ONAGER
Avatar: Of Vishnu, KRISHNA
Babylonian, ELAMITE
Badge: Shoulder, EPAULET
Baldness, ALOPECIA

Barracuda, SENNET
Bark: Aromatic, SINTOC
Bearlike, URSINE
Beetle, ELATER
Bible: Zoroastrian, AVESTA
Bird: Sea, PETREL
   South American, SERIEMA
   Wading, AVOCET, AVOSET
Bone: Leg, FIBULA
Branched, RAMATE
Brother (Latin), FRATER
Bunting: European, ORTOLAN
Call: Trumpet, SENNET
Canoe: Eskimo, BAIDAR, OOMIAK
Caravansary, IMARET
Cat: Asian or African, CHEETAH
   Leopardlike, OCELOT
Cenobite: Jewish, ESSENE
Centerpiece: Table, EPERGNE

Cetacean, DOLPHIN, PORPOISE
Chariot, ESSEDA, ESSEDE
Chief: Seminole, OSCEOLA
Claim: Release as (law), REMISE
Clock: Water, CLEPSYDRA
Cloud, CUMULUS, NIMBUS
Coach: French hackney, FIACRE
Coin: Czech, KORUNA
 Ethiopian, TALARI
 Finnish, MARKKA
 German, THALER
 Greek, DRACHMA
 Haitian, GOURDE
 Honduran, LEMPIRA
 Hungarian, FORINT
 Indo-Chinese, PIASTER
 Netherlands, GUILDER
 Panamanian, BALBOA
 Paraguayan, GUARANI
 Portuguese, ESCUDO
 Russian, COPECK, KOPECK, ROUBLE
 Spanish, PESETA
 Venezuelan, BOLIVAR
Communion: Last holy, VIATICUM
Conceal (law), ELOIGN
Confection, PRALINE
Construction: Sentence, SYNTAX
Convexity: Shaft of column, ENTASIS
Court: Anglo-Saxon, GEMOTE
Cow: Sea, DUGONG, MANATEE
Cylindrical, TERETE
Dagger, STILETTO
 Malay, CREESE, KREESE
Date: Roman, CALENDS, KALENDS
Deer, CARIBOU, WAPITI
Disease: Plant, ERINOSE
Doorkeeper, OSTIARY
Dragonflies: Order of, ODANATA
Drink: Of gods, NECTAR
Drum: TABOUR
 Moorish, ATABAL, ATTABAL
Duck: Fish-eating, MERGANSER
 Sea, SCOTER
Dynasty: Chinese, MANCHU
Eel, CONGER
Edit, REDACT
Envelope: Flower, PERIANTH
Eskimo, AMERIND
Ether: Crystalline, APIOLE
Excuse (law), ESSOIN
Eyespots, OCELLI
Fabric, ESTAMENE, ESTAMIN, ETAMINE
Falcon: European, KESTREL
Figure: Used as column, CARYATID, TELAMON
Fine: For punishment, AMERCE
Fish: Asian fresh-water, GOURAMI
 Pikelike, BARRACUDA
Five: Group of, PENTAD
Fly: African, TSETSE
Foot: Metric, ANAPEST, IAMBUS
Foxlike, VULPINE
Frying pan, SPIDER
Fur, KARAKUL
Galley: Greek or Roman, BIREME, TRIREME
Game: Card, ECARTE
Garment: Greek, CHLAMYS
Gateway, GOPURA, TORANA
Genus: Birds (ravens, crows), CORVUS
 Eels, CONGER
 Fishes, ANABAS
 Foxes, VULPES
 Herbs, ANEMONE
 Insects, CICADA
 Lemurs, GALAGO
 Mints (incl. catnip), NEPETA
 Mollusks, ANOMIA, ASTARTE, TEREDO
 Mollusks (incl. oysters), OSTREA
 Monkeys (spider monkeys), ATELES
 Thrushes (incl. robins), TURDUS
 Trees (of elm family), CELTIS
 Trees (inc. dogwood), CORNUS
 Trees, tropical American, SAPOTA
 Wrens, NANNUS
Gibbon, SIAMANG, WOUWOU
Gland: Salivary, RACEMOSE

Goat: Bezoar, PASANG
Goatlike, CAPRINE
God: Assyrian, ASHSHUR, ASSHUR
 Babylonian, BABBAR, MARDUK, MERODACH,
  NANNAR, NERGAL, SHAMASH
 Hindu, BRAHMA, KRISHNA, VISHNU
 Tahitian, TAAROA
Goddess: Babylonian, ISHTAR
 Hindu, CHANDI, HAIMAVATI, LAKSHMI, PARVATI,
  SARASVATI, SARASWATI
Government, POLITY
Governor: Persian, SATRAP
Grandson (Scotch), NEPOTE
Group: Of five, PENTAD
 Of nine, ENNEAD
 Of seven, HEPTAD
Hare: in first year, LEVERET
Harpsichord, SPINET
Herb: Alpine, EDELWEISS
 Chinese, GINSENG
 South African, FREESIA
Hermit, EREMITE
Hero: Legendary, PALADIN
Heron, BITTERN
Horselike, EQUINE
Hound: Short-legged, BEAGLE
House (French), MAISON
Idiot, CRETIN
Implement: Stone, NEOLITH
Incarnation: Hindu, AVATAR
Indian, APACHE, COMANCHE, PAIUTE, SENECA
Inn: Turkish, IMARET
Insects: Order of, DIPTERA
Instrument: Japanese banjolike, SAMISEN
 Musical, CLAVIER, SPINET
Interstice, AREOLA
Ironwood, COLIMA
Juniper: Old Testament, RAETAM
Kettledrum, ATABAL
King: Fairy, OBERON
Kneecap, PATELLA
Knife, MACHETE
Langur: Sumatran, SIMPAI
Legislature: Spanish, CORTES
Lemur: African, GALAGO
 Madagascar, AYEAYE
Letter: Greek, EPSILON, LAMBDA, OMICRON, UPSILON
 Hebrew, DALETH, LAMEDH, SAMEKH
Lighthouse, PHAROS
Lizard, IGUANA
Llama, ALPACA
Lockjaw, TETANUS
Locust, CICADA, CICALA
Macaw: Brazilian, MARACAN
Maid: Of Astolat, ELAINE
Mammal: Madagascar, TENDRAC, TENREC
Man (Spanish), HOMBRE
Marmoset: South American, TAMARIN
Marsupial, BANDICOOT, WOMBAT
Massacre, POGROM
Mayor: Spanish, ALCALDE
Measure: Electric, AMPERE, COULOMB, KILOWATT
Medicine: Quack, NOSTRUM
Member: Religious order, CENOBITE
Molasses, TREACLE
Monkey: African, GRIVET, NISNAS
 Asian, LANGUR
 Philippine, MACHIN
 South American, PINCHE, SAIMIRI, SAMIRI, SAPAJOU
Monster, CHIMERA, GORGON
 (Comb. form), TERATO
 Cretan, MINOTAUR
Month: Jewish, HESHVAN, KISLEV, SHEBAT, TAMMUZ,
 TISHRI, VEADAR
Mountain: Asia Minor, ARARAT
Mulct, AMERCE
Musketeer, ARAMIS, PORTHOS
Nearsighted, MYOPIC
Net, TRAMMEL
New York City, GOTHAM
Nine: Group of, ENNEAD
Nobleman: Spanish, GRANDEE
Official: Roman, AEDILE
Onyx: Mexican, TECALI
Order: Dragonflies, ODANATA

Insects, DIPTERA
Organ: Plant, PISTIL
Ornament: Shoulder, EPAULET
Overcoat: Military, CAPOTE
Ox: Wild, BANTENG
Oxidation: Bronze or copper, PATINA
Paralysis: Incomplete, PARESIS
Pear: Alligator, AVOCADO
Persimmon: Mexican, CHAPOTE
Pipe: Peace, CALUMET
Plaid (Scotch), TARTAN
Plain, PAMPAS, STEPPE, TUNDRA
Plant: Buttercup family, ANEMONE
   Century, MAGUEY
   On rocks, LICHEN
Plowing: Fit for, ARABLE
Poem: Heroic, EPOPEE
   Six-lined, SESTET
Point: Highest, ZENITH
Potion: Love, PHILTER, PHILTRE
Protozoan, AMOEBA
Punish, AMERCE
Purple (heraldry), PURPURE
Queen: Fairy, TITANIA
Race: Skiing, SLALOM
Rat, BANDICOOT, LEMMING
Retort, RIPOST, RIPOSTE
Ring: Harness, TERRET
   Little, ANNULET
Rodent: Jumping, JERBOA
   Spanish American, AGOUTI, AGOUTY
Sailor: East Indian, LASCAR
Salmon: Young, GRILSE
Salutation: Eastern, SALAAM
Sandpiper, PLOVER
Sandy, ARENOSE
Sapodilla, SAPOTA, SAPOTE
Saw: Surgical, TREPAN
Seven: Group of, HEPTAD
Sexes: Common to both, EPICENE
Shawl: Mexican, SERAPE
Sheathing: Flower, SPATHE
Sheep: Wild, AOUDAD, ARGALI
Shipworm, TEREDO
Shoes: Mercury's winged, TALARIA
Shortening: Syllable, SYSTOLE
Shrub, SPIRAEA

Sickle-shaped, FALCATE
Silver (heraldry), ARGENT
Snake, ANACONDA
Speech: Loss of, APHASIA
Spiral, HELICAL
Staff: Bishop's, CROSIER, CROZIER
Stalk: Plant, PETIOLE
State: Swiss, CANTON
Studio, ATELIER
Swan: Young, CYGNET
Swimming, NATANT
Sword-shaped, ENSATE
Terminal: Negative, CATHODE
Third (music), TIERCE
Thrust: Fencing, RIPOST, RIPOSTE
Tile: Pertaining to, TEGULAR
Tomb: Empty, CENOTAPH
Tooth (comb. form), ODONTO
Tower: Mohammedan, MINARET
Tree: African timber, BAOBAB
   Black gum, TUPELO
   East Indian, MARGOSA
   Locust, ACACIA
   Malayan, SINTOC
   Marmalade, SAPOTE
Urn: Tea, SAMOVAR
Vehicle, LANDAU, TROIKA
Verbose, PROLIX
Viceroy: Egyptian, KHEDIVE
Vulture: American, CONDOR
Warehouse (French), ENTREPOT
Whale: White, BELUGA
Whirlpool, VORTEX
Will: Addition to, CODICIL
   Having left, TESTATE
Wind, CHINOOK, MONSOON, SIMOOM, SIMOON, SI
ROCCO
Window: In roof, DORMER
Wine, BARBERA, BURGUNDY, CABERNET, CHABLIS,
CHIANTI, CLARET, MUSCATEL, RIESLING,
SAUTERNE, SHERRY, ZINFANDEL
Wolfish, LUPINE
Woman: Boisterous, TERMAGANT
Woolly, LANATE
Workshop, ATELIER
Zoroastrian, PARSEE

Old-Testament Names

(We do not pretend that this list is all-inclusive. We include only those names which in our opinion one meets most often in crossword puzzles.)

Aaron: First high priest of Jews; son of Amram; brother of Miriam and Moses; father of Abihu, Eleazer, Ithamar, and Nadab.

Abel: Son of Adam; slain by Cain.

Abigail: Wife of Nabal; later, wife of David.

Abihu: Son of Aaron.

Abimelech: King of Gerar.

Abner: Commander of army of Saul and Ishbosheth; slain by Joab.

Abraham (or Abram): Patriarch; forefather of the Jews; son of Terah; husband of Sarah; father of Isaac and Ishmael.

Absalom: Son of David and Maacah; revolted against David; slain by Joab.

Achish: King of Gath; gave refuge to David.

Achsa (or Achsah): Daughter of Caleb; wife of Othniel.

Adah: Wife of Lamech.

Adam: First man; husband of Eve; father of Cain, Abel, and Seth.

Adonijah: Son of David and Haggith.

Agag: King of Amalek; spared by Saul; slain by Samuel.

Ahasuerus: King of Persia; husband of Vashti and, later, Esther; sometimes identified with Xerxes the Great.

Ahijah: Prophet; foretold accession of Jeroboam.

Ahinoam: Wife of David.

Amasa: Commander of army of David; slain by Joab.

Amnon: Son of David and Ahinoam; ravished Tamar; slain by Absalom.

Amram: Husband of Jochebed; father of Aaron, Mi-

riam and Moses.

Asenath: Wife of Joseph.

Asher: Son of Jacob and Zilpah.

Balaam: Prophet; rebuked by his donkey for cursing God.

Barak: Jewish captain; associated with Deborah.

Baruch: Secretary to Jeremiah.

Bathsheba: Wife of Uriah; later, wife of David.

Belshazzar: Crown prince of Babylon.

Benaiah: Warrior of David; proclaimed Solomon King.

Ben-Hadad: Name of several kings of Damascus.

Benjamin: Son of Jacob and Rachel.

Bezaleel: Chief architect of tabernacle.

Bilhah: Servant of Rachel; mistress of Jacob.

Bildad: Comforter of Job.

Boaz: Husband of Ruth; father of Obed.

Cain: Son of Adam and Eve; slayer of Abel; father of Enoch.

Cainan: Son of Enos.

Caleb: Spy sent out by Moses to visit Canaan; father of Achsa.

Canaan: Son of Ham.

Chilion: Son of Elimelech; husband of Orpah.

Cush: Son of Ham; father of Nimrod.

Dan: Son of Jacob and Bilhah.

Daniel: Prophet; saved from lions by God.

Deborah: Hebrew prophetess; helped Israelites conquer Canaanites.

Delilah: Mistress and betrayer of Samson.

Elam: Son of Shem.

Eleazar: Son of Aaron; succeeded him as high priest.

Eli: High priest and judge; teacher of Samuel; father of Hophni and Phinehas.

Eliakim: Chief minister of Hezekiah.

Eliezer: Servant of Abraham.

Elihu: Comforter of Job.

Elijah (or Elias): Prophet; went to heaven in chariot of fire.

Elimelech: Husband of Naomi; father of Chilion and Mahlon.

Eliphaz: Comforter of Job.

Elisha (or Eliseus): Prophet; successor of Elijah.

Elkanah: Husband of Hannah; father of Samuel.

Enoch: Son of Cain.

Enoch: Father of Methuselah.

Enos: Son of Seth; father of Cainan.

Ephraim: Son of Joseph.

Esau: Son of Isaac and Rebecca; sold his birthright to his brother Jacob.

Esther: Jewish wife of Ahasuerus; saved Jews from Haman's plotting.

Eve: First woman; created from rib of Adam.

Ezra (or Esdras): Hebrew scribe and priest.

Gad: Son of Jacob and Zilpah.

Gehazi: Servant of Elisha.

Gideon: Israelite hero; defeated Midianites.

Goliath: Philistine giant; slain by David.

Hagar: Handmaid of Sarah; concubine of Abraham; mother of Ishmael.

Haggith: Mother of Adonijah.

Ham: Son of Noah; father of Cush, Mizraim, Phut, and Canaan.

Haman: Chief minister of Ahasuerus; hanged on gallows prepared for Mordecai.

Hannah: Wife of Elkanah; mother of Samuel.

Hanun: King of Ammonites.

Haran: Brother of Abraham; father of Lot.

Hazael: King of Damascus.

Hephzi-Bah: Wife of Hezekiah; mother of Mannaseh.

Hiram: King of Tyre.

Holofernes: General of Nebuchadnezzar; slain by Judith.

Hophni: Son of Eli.

Isaac: Hebrew patriarch; son of Abraham and Sarah; half brother of Ishmael; husband of Rebecca; father of Esau and Jacob.

Ishmael: Son of Abraham and Hagar; half brother of Isaac.

Issachar: Son of Jacob and Leah.

Ithamar: Son of Aaron.

Jabal: Son of Lamech and Adah.

Jabin: King of Hazor.

Jacob: Hebrew patriarch, founder of Israel; son of Isaac and Rebecca; husband of Leah and Rachel; father of Asher, Benjamin, Dan, Gad, Issachar, Joseph, Judah, Levi, Naphtali, Reuben, Simeon, and Zebulun.

Jael: Slayer of Sisera.

Japheth: Son of Noah.

Jehoiada: High priest; husband of Jehoshabeath; revolted against Athaliah and made Joash King of Judah.

Jehoshabeath (or Jehosheba): Daughter of Jehoram of Judah; wife of Jehoiada.

Jephthah: Judge in Israel; sacrificed his only daughter because of vow.

Jesse: Son of Obed; father of David.

Jethro: Midianite priest; father of Zipporah.

Jezebel: Phoenician princess; wife of Ahab; mother of Ahaziah, Athaliah, and Jehoram.

Joab: Commander in chief under David; slayer of Abner, Absalom, and Amasa.

Job: Patriarch; underwent many afflictions; comforted by Bildad, Elihu, Eliphaz and Zophar.

Jochebed: Wife of Amram.

Jonah: Prophet; cast into sea and swallowed by great fish.

Jonathan: Son of Saul; friend of David.

Joseph: Son of Jacob and Rachel; sold into slavery by his brothers; husband of Asenath; father of Ephraim and Manassah.

Joshua: Successor of Moses; son of Nun.

Jubal: Son of Lamech and Adah.

Judah: Son of Jacob and Leah.

Judith: Slayer of Holofernes.

Kish: Father of Saul.

Laban: Father of Leah and Rachel.

Lamech: Son of Methuselah; father of Noah.

Lamech: Husband of Adah and Zillah; father of Jabal, Jubal, and Tubal-Cain.

Leah: Daughter of Laban; wife of Jacob.

Levi: Son of Jacob and Leah.

Lot: Son of Haran; escaped destruction of Sodom.

Maacah: Mother of Absalom and Tamar.

Mahlon: Son of Elimelech; first husband of Ruth.

Manasseh: Son of Joseph.

Melchizedek: King of Salem.

Methuselah: Patriarch; son of Enoch; father of Lamech.

Michal: Daughter of Saul; wife of David.

Miriam: Prophetess; daughter of Amram; sister of Aaron and Moses.

Mizraim: Son of Ham.

Mordecai: Uncle of Esther; with her aid, saved Jews from Haman's plotting.

Moses: Prophet and lawgiver; son of Amram; brother of Aaron and Miriam; husband of Zipporah.

Naaman: Syrian captain; cured of leprosy by Elisha.

Nabal: Husband of Abigail.

Naboth: Owner of vineyard; stoned to death because he would not sell it to Ahab.

Nadab: Son of Aaron.

Nahor: Father of Terah.

Naomi: Wife of Elimelech; mother-in-law of Ruth.

Naphtali: Son of Jacob and Bilhah.

Nathan: Prophet; reproved David for causing Uriah's death.

Nebuchadnezzar (or Nebuchadrezzar): King of Babylon; destroyer of Jerusalem.

Nehemiah: Jewish leader; empowered by Artaxerxes to rebuild Jerusalem.

Nimrod: Mighty hunter; son of Cush.

Noah: Patriarch; Son of Lamech; escaped Deluge by building Ark; father of Ham, Japheth and Shem.

Nun (or Non): Father of Joshua.

Obed: Son of Boaz; father of Jesse.

Og: King of Bashan.

Orpah: Wife of Chilion.

Othniel: Kenezite; judge of Israel; husband of Achsa.

Phinehas: Son of Eleazer.

Phinehas: Son of Eli.

Phut (or Put): Son of Ham.

Potiphar: Egyptian official; bought Joseph.

Rachel: Wife of Jacob.

Rebecca (or Rebekah): Wife of Isaac.

Reuben: Son of Jacob and Leah.

Ruth: Wife of Mahlon, later of Boaz; daughter-in-law of Naomi.

Samson: Judge of Israel; famed for strength; betrayed by Delilah.

Samuel: Hebrew judge and prophet; son of Elkanah.

Sarah (or Sara, Sarai): Wife of Abraham.

Sennacherib: King of Assyria.

Seth: Son of Adam; father of Enos.

Shem: Son of Noah; father of Elam.

Simeon: Son of Jacob and Leah.

Sisera: Canaanite captain; slain by Jael.

Tamar: Daughter of David and Maachah; ravished by Amnon.

Terah: Son of Nahor; father of Abraham.

Tubal-Cain: Son of Lamech and Zillah.

Uriah: Husband of Bathsheba; sent to death in battle by David.

Vashti: Wife of Ahasuerus; set aside by him.

Zadok: High priest during David's reign.

Zebulun (or Zabulon): Son of Jacob and Leah.

Zillah: Wife of Lamech.

Zilpah: Servant of Leah; mistress of Jacob.

Zipporah: Daughter of Jethro; wife of Moses.

Zophar: Comforter of Job.

Kings of Judah and Israel

Kings Before Division of Kingdom

Saul: First King of Israel; son of Kish; father of Ish-Bosheth, Jonathan and Michal.

Ish-Bosheth (or Eshbaal): King of Israel; son of Saul.

David: King of Judah; later of Israel; son of Jesse; husband of Abigail, Ahinoam, Bathsheba, Michal, etc.; father of Absalom, Adonijah, Amnon, Solomon, Tamar, etc.

Solomon: King of Israel and Judah; son of David; father of Rehoboam.

Rehoboam:
Son of Solomon; during his reign the kingdom was divided into Judah and Israel.

Kings of Judah (Southern Kingdom)

Rehoboam: First King.

Abijah (or Abijam or Abia): Son of Rehoboam.

Asa: Probably son of Abijah.

Jehoshaphat: Son of Asa.

Jehoram (or Joram): Son of Jehoshaphat; husband of Athaliah.

Ahaziah: Son of Jehoram and Athaliah.

Athaliah: Daughter of King Ahab of Israel and Jezebel; wife of Jehoram.

Joash (or Jehoash): Son of Ahaziah.

Amaziah: Son of Joash.

Uzziah (or Azariah): Son of Amaziah.

Jotham: Regent, later King; son of Uzziah.

Ahaz: Son of Jotham.

Hezekiah: Son of Ahaz; husband of Hephzi-Bah.

Manasseh: Son of Hezekiah and Hephzi-Bah.

Amon: Son of Manasseh.

Josiah (or Josias): Son of Amon.

Jehoahaz (or Joahaz): Son of Josiah.

Jehoiachin: Son of Jehoiakim.

Jehoiakim: Son of Josiah.

Zedekiah: Son of Josiah; kingdom overthrown by Babylonians under Nebuchadnezzar.

Kings of Israel (Northern Kingdom)

Jeroboam I: Led secession of Israel.

Nadab: Son of Jeroboam I.

Baasha: Overthrew Nadab.

Elah: Son of Baasha.

Zimri: Overthrew Elah.

Omri: Overthrew Zimri.

Ahab: Son of Omri; husband of Jezebel.

Ahaziah: Son of Ahab.

Jehoram (or Joram): Son of Ahab.

Jehu: Overthrew Jehoram.

Jehoahaz (or Joahaz): Son of Jehu.

Jehoash (or Joash): Son of Jehoahaz.

Jeroboam II: Son of Jehoash.

Zechariah: Son of Jeroboam II.

Shallum: Overthrew Zechariah.

Menahem: Overthrew Shallum.

Pekahiah: Son of Menahem.

Pekah: Overthrew Pekahiah.

Hoshea: Overthrew Pekah; kingdom overthrown by Assyrians under Sargon II.

Prophets

Major.—Isaiah, Jeremiah, Ezekiel, Daniel.

Minor.—Hosea, Obadiah, Nahum, Haggai, Joel, Jonah, Habakkuk, Zechariah, Amos, Micah, Zephaniah, Malachi.

Greek and Roman Mythology

(Most of the Greek deities were adopted by the Romans, although in many cases there was a change of name. In the list below, information is given under the Greek name; the name in parentheses is the Latin equivalent. However, all Latin names are listed with cross references to the Greek ones. In addition, there are several deities which were exclusively Roman.)

Acheron: *See* Rivers.

Achilles: Greek warrior; slew Hector at Troy; slain by Paris, who wounded him in his vulnerable heel.

Actaeon: Hunter; surprised Artemis bathing; changed by her to stag and killed by his dogs.

Admetus: King of Thessaly; his wife, Alcestis, offered to die in his place.

Adonis: Beautiful youth loved by Aphrodite.

Aeacus: One of three judges of dead in Hades; son of Zeus.

Aeëtes: King of Colchis; father of Medea; keeper of Golden Fleece.

Aegeus: Father of Theseus; believing Theseus killed in Crete, he drowned himself, Aegean Sea named for him.

Aegisthus: Son of Thyestes; slew Atreus; with Clytemnestra, his paramour, slew Agamemnon; slain by Orestes.

Aegyptus: Brother of Danaus; his sons, except Lynceus, slain by Danaides.

Aeneas: Trojan; son of Anchises and Aphrodite; after fall of Troy, led his followers eventually to Italy; loved and deserted Dido.

Aeolus: *See* Winds.

Aesculapius: *See* Asclepius.

Aeson: King of Iolcus; father of Jason; overthrown by his brother Pelias; restored to youth by Medea.

Aether: Personification of sky.

Aethra: Mother of Theseus.

Agamemnon: King of Mycenae; son of Atreus; brother of Menelaus; leader of Greeks against Troy; slain on his return home by Clytemnestra and Aegisthus.

Agiaia: *See* Graces.

Ajax: Greek warrior; killed himself at Troy because Achilles' armor was awarded to Odysseus.

Alcestis: Wife of Admetus; offered to die in his place but saved from death by Hercules.

Alcmene: Wife of Amphitryon; mother by Zeus of Hercules.

Alcyone: *See* Pleiades.

Alecto: *See* Furies.

Alectryon: Youth changed by Ares into cock.

Althaea: Wife of Oeneus; mother of Meleager.

Amazons: Female warriors in Asia Minor; supported Troy against Greeks.

Amor: *See* Eros.

Amphion: Musician; husband of Niobe; charmed stones to build fortifications for Thebes.

Amphitrite: Sea goddess; wife of Poseidon.

Amphitryon: Husband of Alcmene.

Anchises: Father of Aeneas.

Ancile: Sacred shield that fell from heavens; palladium of Rome.

Andraemon: Husband of Dryope.

Andromache: Wife of Hector.

Andromeda: Daughter of Cepheus; chained to cliff for monster to devour; rescued by Perseus.

Anteia: Wife of Proetus; tried to induce Bellerophon to elope with her.

Anteros: God who avenged unrequited love.

Antigone: Daughter of Oedipus; accompanied him to Colonus; performed burial rite for Polynices and hanged herself.

Antinoüs: Leader of suitors of Penelope; slain by Odysseus.

Aphrodite (Venus): Goddess of love and beauty; daughter of Zeus; mother of Eros.

Apollo: God of beauty, poetry, music; later identified with Helios as Phoebus Apollo; son of Zeus and Leto.

Aquilo: *See* Winds.

Arachne: Maiden who challenged Athena to weaving contest; changed to spider.

Ares (Mars): God of war; son of Zeus and Hera.

Argo: Ship in which Jason and followers sailed to Colchis for Golden Fleece.

Argus: Monster with hundred eyes; slain by Hermes; his eyes placed by Hera into peacock's tail.

Ariadne: Daughter of Minos; aided Theseus in slaying Minotaur; deserted by him on island of Naxos and married to Dionysus.

Arion: Musician; thrown overboard by pirates but saved by dolphin.

Artemis (Diana): Goddess of moon; huntress; twin sister of Apollo.

Asclepius (Aesculapius): Mortal son of Apollo; slain by Zeus for raising dead; later deified as god of medicine. Also known as Asklepios.

Astarte: Phoenician goddess of love; variously identified with Aphrodite, Selene, and Artemis.

Astraea: Goddess of Justice; daughter of Zeus and Themis.

Atalanta: Princess who challenged her suitors to a foot race; Hippomenes won race and married her.

Athena (Minerva): Goddess of wisdom; known poetically as Pallas Athene; sprang fully armed from head of Zeus.

Atlas: Titan; held world on his shoulders as punishment for warring against Zeus; son of Iapetus.

Atreus: King of Mycenae; father of Menelaus and Agamemnon; brother of Thyestes, three of whose sons he slew and served to him at banquet; slain by Aegisthus.

Atropos: *See* Fates.

Aurora: *See* Eos.

Auster: *See* Winds.

Avernus: Infernal regions; name derived from small vaporous lake near Vesuvius which was fabled to kill birds and vegetation.

Bacchus: *See* Dionysus.

Bellerophon: Corinthian hero; killed Chimera with aid of Pegasus; tried to reach Olympus on Pegasus and was thrown to his death.

Bellona: Roman goddess of war.

Boreas: *See* Winds.

Briareus: Monster of hundred hands; son of Uranus and Gaea.

Briseis: Captive maiden given to Achilles; taken by Agamemnon in exchange for loss of Chryseis, which caused Achilles to cease fighting, until death of Patroclus.

Cadmus: Brother of Europa; planter of dragon seeds from which first Thebans sprang.

Calliope: *See* Muses.

Calypso: Sea nymph; kept Odysseus on her island Ogygia for seven years.

Cassandra: Daughter of Priam; prophetess who was never believed; slain with Agamemnon.

Castor: *See* Dioscuri.

Celaeno: *See* Pleiades.

Centaurs: Beings half man and half horse; lived in mountains of Thessaly.

Cephalus: Hunter; accidentally killed his wife Procris with his spear.

Cepheus: King of Ethiopia; father of Andromeda.

Cerberus: Three-headed dog guarding entrance to Hades.

Ceres: *See* Demeter.

Chaos: Formless void; personified as first of gods.

Charon: Boatman on Styx who carried souls of dead to Hades; son of Erebus.

Charybdis: Female monster; personification of whirlpool.

Chimera: Female monster with head of lion, body of goat, tail of serpent; killed by Bellerophon.

Chiron: Most famous of centaurs.

Chronos: Personification of time.

Chryseis: Captive maiden given to Agamemnon; his refusal to accept ransom from her father Chryses caused Apollo to send plague on Greeks besieging Troy.

Circe: Sorceress; daughter of Helios; changed Odysseus' men into swine.

Clio: *See* Muses.

Clotho: *See* Fates.

Clytemnestra: Wife of Agamemnon, whom she slew with aid of her paramour, Aegisthus; slain by her son Orestes.

Cocytus: *See* Rivers.

Creon: Father of Jocasta; forbade burial of Polynices; ordered burial alive of Antigone.

Creüsa: Princess of Corinth, for whom Jason deserted Medea; slain by Medea, who sent her poisoned robe; also known as Glauke.

Creusa: Wife of Aeneas; died fleeing Troy.

Cronus (Saturn): Titan; god of harvests; son of Uranus and Gaea; dethroned by his son Zeus.

Cupid: *See* Eros.

Cybele: Anatolian nature goddess; adopted by Greeks and identified with Rhea.

Cyclopes: Race of one-eyed giants (singular: Cyclops).

Daedalus: Athenian artificer; father of Icarus; builder of Labyrinth in Crete; devised wings attached with wax for him and Icarus to escape Crete.

Danae: Princess of Argos; mother of Perseus by Zeus, who appeared to her in form of golden shower.

Danaïdes: Daughters of Danaüs; at his command, all except Hypermnestra slew their husbands, the sons of Aegyptus.

Danaüs: Brother of Aegyptus; father of Danaïdes; slain by Lynceus.

Daphne: Nymph; pursued by Apollo; changed to laurel tree.

Decuma: *See* Fates.

Deino: *See* Graeae.

Demeter (Ceres): Goddess of agriculture; mother of Persephone.

Diana: *See* Artemis.

Dido: Founder and queen of Carthage; stabbed herself when deserted by Aeneas.

Diomedes: Greek hero; with Odysseus, entered Troy and carried off Palladium, sacred statue of Athena.

Diomedes: Owner of man-eating horses, which Hercules, as ninth labor, carried off.

Dione: Titan goddess; mother by Zeus of Aphrodite.

Dionysus (Bacchus): God of wine; son of Zeus and Semele.

Dioscuri: Twins Castor and Pollux; sons of Leda by Zeus.

Dis: *See* Hades.

Dryads: Wood nymphs.

Dryope: Maiden changed to Hamadryad.

Echo: Nymph who fell hopelessly in love with Narcissus; faded away except for her voice.

Electra: Daughter of Agamemnon and Clytemnestra; sister of Orestes; urged Orestes to slay Clytemnestra and Aegisthus.

Electra: *See* Pleiades.

Elysium: Abode of blessed dead.

Endymion: Mortal loved by Selene.

Enyo: *See* Graeae.

Eos (Aurora): Goddess of dawn.

Epimetheus: Brother of Prometheus; husband of Pandora.

Erato: *See* Muses.

Erebus: Spirit of darkness; son of Chaos.

Erinyes: *See* Furies.

Eris: Goddess of discord.

Eros (Amor or Cupid): God of love; son of Aphrodite.

Eteocles: Son of Oedipus, whom he succeeded to rule alternately with Polynices; refused to give up throne at end of year; he and Polynices slew each other.

Eumenides: *See* Furies.

Euphrosyne: *See* Graces.

Europa: Mortal loved by Zeus, who, in form of white bull, carried her off to Crete.

Eurus: *See* Winds.

Euryale: *See* Gorgons.

Eurydice: Nymph; wife of Orpheus.

Eurystheus: King of Argos; imposed twelve labors on Hercules.

Euterpe: *See* Muses.

Fates: Goddesses of destiny; Clotho (Spinner of thread of life), Lachesis (Determiner of length), and Atropos (Cutter of thread); also called Moirae. Identified by Romans with their goddesses of fate; Nona, Decuma, and Morta; called Parcae.

Fauns: Roman deities of woods and groves.

Faunus: *See* Pan.

Favonius: *See* Winds.

Flora: Roman goddess of flowers.

Fortuna: Roman goddess of fortune.

Furies: Avenging spirits; Alecto, Megaera, and Tisiphone; known also as Erinyes or Eumenides.

Gaea: Goddess of earth; daughter of Chaos; mother of Titans; known also as Ge, Gea, Gaia, etc.

Galatea: Statue of maiden carved from ivory by Pygmalion; given life by Aphrodite.

Galatea: Sea nymph; loved by Polyphemus.

Ganymede: Beautiful boy; successor to Hebe as cupbearer of gods.

Glaucus: Mortal who became sea divinity by eating magic grass.

Glauke: *See* Creüsa.

Golden Fleece: Fleece from ram that flew Phrixos to Colchis; Aeëtes placed it under guard of dragon; carried off by Jason.

Gorgons: Female monsters; Euryale, Medusa, and Stheno; had snakes for hair; their glances turned mortals to stone. *See* Medusa.

Graces: Beautiful goddesses: Aglaia (Brilliance), Euphrosyne (Joy), and Thalia (Bloom); daughters of Zeus.

Graeae: Sentinels for Gorgons; Deino, Enyo, and Pephredo; had one eye among them, which passed from one to another.

Hades (Dis): Name sometimes given Pluto; also, abode of dead, ruled by Pluto.

Haemon: Son of Creon; promised husband of Antigone; killed himself in her tomb.

Hamadryads: Tree nymphs.

Harpies: Monsters with heads of women and bodies of birds.

Hebe (Juventas): Goddess of youth; cupbearer of gods before Ganymede; daughter of Zeus and Hera.

Hecate: Goddess of sorcery and witchcraft.

Hector: Son of Priam; slayer of Patroclus; slain by Achilles.

Hecuba: Wife of Priam.

Helen: Fairest woman in world; daughter of Zeus and Leda; wife of Menelaus; carried to Troy by Paris, causing Trojan War.

Heliades: Daughters of Helios; mourned for Phaëthon and were changed to poplar trees.

Helios (Sol): God of sun; later identified with Apollo.

Helle: Sister of Phrixos; fell from ram of Golden Fleece; water where she fell named Hellespont.

Hephaestus (Vulcan): God of fire; celestial blacksmith; son of Zeus and Hera; husband of Aphrodite.

Hera (Juno): Queen of heaven; wife of Zeus.

Hercules: Hero and strong man; son of Zeus and Alcmene; performed twelve labors or deeds to be free from bondage under Eurystheus; after death, his mortal share was destroyed, and he became immortal. Also known as Herakles or Heracles. Labors: (1) killing Nemean lion; (2) killing Lernaean Hydra; (3) capturing Erymanthian boar; (4) capturing Cerynean hind; (5) killing man-eating Stymphalian birds; (6) procuring girdle of Hippolyte; (7) cleaning Augean stables; (8) capturing Cretan bull; (9) capturing man-eating horses of Diomedes; (10) capturing cattle of Geryon; (11) procuring golden apples of Hesperides; (12) bringing Cerberus up from Hades.

Hermes (Mercury): God of physicians and thieves; messenger of gods; son of Zeus and Maia.

Hero: Priestess of Aphrodite; Leander swam Hellespont nightly to see her; drowned herself at his death.

Hesperus: Evening star.

Hestia (Vesta): Goddess of hearth; sister of Zeus.

Hippolyte: Queen of Amazons; wife of Theseus.

Hippolytus: Son of Theseus and Hippolyte; falsely accused by Phaedra of trying to kidnap her; slain by Poseidon at request of Theseus.

Hippomenes: Husband of Atalanta, whom he beat in race by dropping golden apples, which she stopped to pick up.

Hyacinthus: Beautiful youth accidentally killed by Apollo, who caused flower to spring up from his blood.

Hydra: Nine-headed monster in marsh of Lerna; slain by Hercules.

Hygeia: Personification of health.

Hyman: God of marriage.

Hyperion: Titan; early sun god; father of Helios.

Hypermnestra: Daughter of Danaüs; refused to kill her husband Lynceus.

Hypnos (Somnus): God of sleep.

Iapetus: Titan; father of Atlas, Epimetheus, and Prometheus.

Icarus: Son of Daedalus; flew too near sun with wax-attached wings and fell into sea and was drowned.

Io: Mortal maiden loved by Zeus; changed by Hera into heifer.

Iobates: King of Lycia; sent Bellerophon to slay Chimera.

Iphigenia: Daughter of Agamemnon; offered as sacrifice to Artemis at Aulis; carried by Artemis to Tauris where she became priestess; escaped from there with Orestes.

Iris: Goddess of rainbow; messenger of Zeus and Hera.

Ismene: Daughter of Oedipus; sister of Antigone.

Iulus: Son of Aeneas.

Ixion: King of Lapithae; for making love to Hera he was bound to endlessly revolving wheel in Tartarus.

Janus: Roman god of gates and doors; represented with two opposite faces.

Jason: Son of Aeson; to gain throne of Ioclus from Pelias, went to Colchis and brought back Golden Fleece; married Medea; deserted her for Creüsa.

Jocasta: Wife of Laius; mother of Oedipus; unwittingly became wife of Oedipus; hanged herself when relationship was discovered.

Juno: *See* Hera.

Jupiter: *See* Zeus.

Juventas: *See* Hebe.

Lachesis: *See* Fates.

Laius: Father of Oedipus, by whom he was slain.

Laocoön: Priest of Apollo at Troy; warned against bringing wooden horse into Troy; destroyed with his two sons by serpents sent by Athena.

Lares: Roman ancestral spirits protecting descendants and homes.

Lavinia: Wife of Aeneas after defeat of Turnus.

Leander: Swam Hellespont nightly to see Hero; drowned in storm.

Leda: Mortal loved by Zeus in form of Swan; mother of Helen, Clytemnestra, Dioscuri.

Lethe: *See* Rivers.

Leto (Latona): Mother by Zeus of Artemis and Apollo.

Lucina: Roman goddess of childbirth; identified with Juno.

Lynceus: Son of Aegyptus; husband of Hypermnestra; slew Danaüs.

Maia: Daughter of Atlas; mother of Hermes.

Maia: *See* Pleiades.

Manes: Souls of dead Romans, particularly of ancestors.

Mars: *See* Ares.

Marsyas: Shepherd; challenged Apollo to music contest and lost; flayed alive by Apollo.

Medea: Sorceress; daughter of Aeëtes; helped Jason obtain Golden Fleece; when deserted by him for Creüsa, killed her children and Creüsa.

Medusa: Gorgon; slain by Perseus, who cut off her head.

Megaera: *See* Furies.

Meleager: Son of Althaea; his life would last as long as brand burning at his birth; Althaea quenched and saved it but destroyed it when Meleager slew his uncles.

Melpomene: *See* Muses.

Memnon: Ethiopian king; made immortal by Zeus; son of Tithonus and Eos.

Menelaus: King of Sparta; son of Atreus; brother of Agamemnon; husband of Helen.

Mercury: *See* Hermes.

Merope: *See* Pleiades.

Mezentius: Cruel Etruscan king; ally of Turnus against Aeneas; slain by Aeneas.

Midas: King of Phrygia; given gift of turning to gold all he touched.

Minerva: *See* Athena.

Minos: King of Crete; after death, one of three judges of dead in Hades; son of Zeus and Europa.

Minotaur: Monster, half man and half beast, kept in Labyrinth in Crete; slain by Theseus.

Mnemosyne: Goddess of memory; mother by Zeus of Muses.

Moirae: *See* Fates.

Momus: God of ridicule.

Morpheus: God of dreams.

Mors: *See* Thanatos.

Morta: *See* Fates.

Muses: Goddesses presiding over arts and sciences: Calliope (epic poetry), Clio (history), Erato (lyric and love poetry), Euterpe (music), Melpomene (tragedy), Polymnia or Polyhymnia (sacred poetry), Terpsichore (choral dance and song), Thalia (comedy and bucolic poetry), Urania (astronomy); daughters of Zeus and Mnemosyne.

Naiads: Nymphs of waters, streams, and fountains.

Napaeae: Wood nymphs.

Narcissus: Beautiful youth loved by Echo; in punishment for not returning her love, he was made to fall in love with his image reflected in pool; pined away and became flower.

Nemesis: Goddess of retribution.

Neoptolemus: Son of Achilles; slew Priam; also known as Pyrrhus.

Neptune: *See* Poseidon.

Nereids: Sea nymphs; attendants on Poseidon.

Nestor: King of Pylos; noted for wise counsel in expedition against Troy.

Nike: Goddess of victory.

Niobe: Daughter of Tantalus; wife of Amphion; her children slain by Apollo and Artemis; changed to stone but continued to weep her loss.

Nona: *See* Fates.

Notus: *See* Winds.

Nox: *See* Nyx.

Nymphs: Beautiful maidens; inferior deities of nature.

Nyx (Nox): Goddess of night.

Oceanids: Ocean nymphs; daughters of Oceanus.

Oceanus: Eldest of Titans; god of waters.

Odysseus (Ulysses): King of Ithaca; husband of Penelope; wandered ten years after fall of Troy before arriving home.

Oedipus: King of Thebes; son of Laius and Jocasta; unwittingly murdered Laius and married Jocasta; tore his eyes out when relationship was discovered.

Oenone: Nymph of Mount Ida; wife of Paris, who abandoned her; refused to cure him when he was poisoned by arrow of Philoctetes at Troy.

Ops: *See* Rhea.

Oreads: Mountain nymphs.

Orestes: Son of Agamemnon and Clytemnestra; brother of Electra; slew Clytemnestra and Aegisthus; pursued by Furies until his purification by Apollo.

Orion: Hunter; slain by Artemis and made heavenly constellation.

Orpheus: Famed musician; son of Apollo and Muse Calliope; husband of Eurydice.

Pales: Roman goddess of shepherds and herdsmen.

Palinurus: Aeneas' pilot; fell overboard in his sleep and was drowned.

Pan (Faunus): God of woods and fields; part goat; son of Hermes.

Pandora: Opener of box containing human ills; mortal wife of Epimetheus.

Parcae: *See* Fates.

Paris: Son of Priam; gave apple of discord to Aphrodite, for which she enabled him to carry off Helen; slew Achilles at Troy; slain by Philoctetes.

Patroclus: Great friend of Achilles; wore Achilles' armor and was slain by Hector.

Pegasus: Winged horse that sprang from Medusa's body at her death; ridden by Bellerophon when he slew Chimera.

Pelias: King of Ioclus; seized throne from his brother Aeson; sent Jason for Golden Fleece; slain unwittingly by his daughters at instigation of Medea.

Pelops: Son of Tantalus; his father cooked and served him to gods; restored to life; Peloponnesus named for him.

Penates: Roman household gods.

Penelope: Wife of Odysseus; waited faithfully for him for ten years while putting off numerous suitors.

Pephredo: *See* Graeae.

Periphetes: Giant; son of Hephaestus; slain by Theseus.

Persephone (Proserpine): Queen of infernal regions; daughter of Zeus and Demeter; wife of Pluto.

Perseus: Son of Zeus and Danaë; slew Medusa; rescued Andromeda from monster and married her.

Phaedra: Daughter of Minos; wife of Theseus; caused the death of her stepson, Hippolytus.

Phaethon: Son of Helios; drove his father's sun chariot and was struck down by Zeus before he set world on fire.

Philoctetes: Greek warrior who possessed Hercules' bow and arrows; slew Paris at Troy with poisoned arrow.

Phineus: Betrothed of Andromeda; tried to slay Perseus but turned to stone by Medusa's head.

Phlegethon: *See* Rivers.

Phosphor: Morning star.

Phrixos: Brother of Helle; carried by ram of Golden Fleece to Colchis.

Pirithous: Son of Ixion; friend of Theseus; tried to carry off Persephone from Hades; bound to enchanted rock by Pluto.

Pleiades: Alcyone, Celaeno, Electra, Maia, Merope, Sterope or Asterope, Taygeta; seven daughters of Atlas; transformed into heavenly constellation, of which six stars are visible (Merope is said to have hidden in shame for loving a mortal).

Pluto (Dis): God of Hades; brother of Zeus.

Plutus: God of wealth.

Pollux: *See* Dioscuri.

Polymnia: *See* Muses.

Polynices: Son of Oedipus; he and his brother Eteocles killed each other; burial rite, forbidden by Creon, performed by his sister Antigone.

Polyphemus: Cyclops; devoured six of Odysseus' men; blinded by Odysseus.

Polyxena: Daughter of Priam; betrothed to Achilles, whom Paris slew at their betrothal; sacrificed to shade of Achilles.

Pomona: Roman goddess of fruits.

Pontus: Sea god; son of Gaea.

Poseidon (Neptune): God of sea; brother of Zeus.

Priam: King of Troy; husband of Hecuba; ransomed Hector's body from Achilles; slain by Neoptolemus.

Priapus: God of regeneration.

Procris: Wife of Cephalus, who accidentally slew her.

Procrustes: Giant; stretched or cut off legs of victims to make them fit iron bed; slain by Theseus.

Proetus: Husband of Anteia; sent Bellerophon to lobates to be put to death.

Prometheus: Titan; stole fire from heaven for man. Zeus punished him by chaining him to rock in Caucasus where vultures devoured his liver daily.

Proteus: Sea god; assumed various shapes when called on to prophesy.

Psyche: Beloved of Eros; punished by jealous Aphrodite; made immortal and united with Eros.

Pygmalion: King of Cyprus; carved ivory statue of maiden which Aphrodite gave life as Galatea.

Pyramus: Babylonian youth; made love to Thisbe through hole in wall; thinking Thisbe slain by lion, killed himself.

Pyrrhus: *See* Neoptolemus.

Python: Serpent born from slime left by Deluge; slain by Apollo.

Quirinus: Roman war god.

Remus: Brother of Romulus; slain by him.

Rhadamanthus: One of three judges of dead in Hades; son of Zeus and Europa.

Rhea (Ops): Daughter of Uranus and Gaea; wife of Cronus; mother of Zeus; identified with Cybele.

Rivers of Underworld: Acheron (woe), Cocytus (wailing), Lethe (forgetfulness), Phlegethon (fire), Styx (across which souls of dead were ferried by Charon).

Romulus: Founder of Rome; he and Remus suckled in infancy by she-wolf; slew Remus; deified by Romans.

Sarpedon: King of Lycia; son of Zeus and Europa; slain by Patroclus at Troy.

Saturn: *See* Cronus.

Satyrs: Hoofed demigods of woods and fields; companions of Dionysus.

Sciron: Robber; forced strangers to wash his feet, then hurled them into sea where tortoise devoured them; slain by Theseus.

Scylla: Female monster inhabiting rock opposite Charybdis; menaced passing sailors.

Selene: Goddess of moon.

Semele: Daughter of Cadmus; mother by Zeus of Dionysus; demanded Zeus appear before her in all his splendor and was destroyed by his lightnings.

Sibyls: Various prophetesses; most famous, Cumaean sibyl, accompanied Aeneas into Hades.

Sileni: Minor woodland deities similar to satyrs (singular: silenus). Sometimes Silenus refers to eldest of satyrs, son of Hermes or of Pan.

Silvanus: Roman god of woods and fields.

Sinis: Giant; bent pines, by which he hurled victims against side of mountain; slain by Theseus.

Sirens: Minor deities who lured sailors to destruction with their singing.

Sisyphus: King of Corinth; condemned in Tartarus to roll huge stone to top of hill; it always rolled back down again.

Sol: *See* Helios.

Somnus: *See* Hypnos.

Sphinx: Monster of Thebes; killed those who could not answer her riddle; slain by Oedipus. Name also refers to other monsters having body of lion, wings, and head and bust of woman.

Sterope: *See* Pleiades.

Stheno: *See* Gorgons.

Styx: *See* Rivers.

Symplegades: Clashing rocks at entrance to Black Sea; Argo passed through, causing them to become forever fixed.

Syrinx: Nymph pursued by Pan; changed to reeds, from which he made his pipes.

Tantalus: Cruel king; father of Pelops and Niobe; condemned in Tartarus to stand chin-deep in lake surrounded by fruit branches; as he tried to eat or drink, water or fruit always receded.

Tartarus: Underworld below Hades; often refers to Hades.

Taygeta: *See* Pleiades.

Telemachus: Son of Odysseus; made unsuccessful journey to find his father.

Tellus: Roman goddess of earth.

Terminus: Roman god of boundaries and landmarks.

Terpsichore: *See* Muses.

Terra: Roman earth goddess.

Thalia: *See* Graces; Muses.

Thanatos (Mors): God of death.

Themis: Titan goddess of laws of physical phenomena; daughter of Uranus; mother of Prometheus.

Theseus: Son of Aegeus; slew Minotaur; married and deserted Ariadne; later married Phaedra.

Thisbe: Beloved of Pyramus; killed herself at his death.

Thyestes: Brother of Atreus; Atreus killed three of his sons and served them to him at banquet.

Tiresias: Blind soothsayer of Thebes.

Tisiphone: *See* Furies.

Titans: Early gods from which Olympian gods were derived; children of Uranus and Gaea.

Tithonus: Mortal loved by Eos; changed into grasshopper.

Triton: Demigod of sea; son of Poseidon.

Turnus: King of Rutuli in Italy; betrothed to Lavinia; slain by Aeneas.

Ulysses: *See* Odysseus.

Urania: *See* Muses.

Uranus: Personification of Heaven; husband of Gaea; father of Titans; dethroned by his son Cronus.

Venus: *See* Aphrodite.

Vertumnus: Roman god of fruits and vegetables; husband of Pomona.

Vesta: *See* Hestia.

Vulcan: *See* Hephaestus.

Winds: Aeolus (keeper of winds), Boreas (Aquilo) (north wind), Eurus (east wind), Notus (Auster) (south wind), Zephyrus (Favonius) (west wind).

Zephyrus: *See* Winds.

Zeus (Jupiter): Chief of Olympian gods; son of Cronus and Rhea; husband of Hera.

Norse Mythology

Aesir: Chief gods of Asgard.

Andvari: Dwarf; robbed of gold and magic ring by Loki.

Angerbotha (Angrbotha): Giantess; mother by Loki of Fenrir, Hel, and Midgard serpent.

Asgard (Asgarth): Abode of gods.

Ask (Aske, Askr): First man; created by Odin, Hoenir, and Lothur.

Asynjur: Goddesses of Asgard.

Atli: Second husband of Gudrun; invited Gunnar and Hogni to his court, where they were slain; slain by Gudrun.

Audhumia (Audhumbla): Cow that nourished Ymir, created Buri by licking ice cliff.

Balder (Baldr, Baldur): God of light, spring, peace, joy; son of Odin; slain by Hoth at instigation of Loki.

Bifrost: Rainbow bridge connecting Midgard and Asgard.

Bragi (Brage): God of poetry; husband of Ithunn.

Branstock: Great oak in hall of Volsungs; into it, Odin thrust Gram, which only Sigmund could draw forth.

Brynhild: Valkyrie; wakened from magic sleep by Sigurd; married Gunnar; instigated death of Sigurd; killed herself and was burned on pyre beside Sigurd.

Bur (Bor): Son of Buri; father of Odin, Hoenir, and Lothur.

Buri (Bori): Progenitor of gods; father of Bur; created by Audhumla.

Embla: First woman; created by Odin, Hoenir, and Lothur.

Fafnir: Son of Rodmar, whom he slew for gold in Otter's skin; in form of dragon, guarded gold; slain by Sigurd.

Fenrir: Wolf; offspring of Loki; swallows Odin at Ragnarok and is slain by Vitharr.

Forseti: Son of Balder.

Frey (Freyr): God of fertility and crops; son of Njorth; originally one of Vanir.

Freya (Freyja): Goddess of love and beauty; sister of Frey; originally one of Vanir.

Frigg (Frigga): Goddess of sky; wife of Odin.

Garm: Watchdog of Hel; slays, and is slain by, Tyr at Ragnarok.

Gimle: Home of blessed after Ragnarok.

Giuki: King of Nibelungs; father of Gunnar, Hogni, Guttorm, and Gudrun.

Glathsehim (Gladsheim): Hall of gods in Asgard.

Gram (meaning "Angry"): Sigmund's sword; rewelded by Regin; used by Sigurd to slay Fafnir.

Greyfell: Sigmund's horse; descended from Sleipnir.

Grimhild: Mother of Gudrun; administered magic potion to Sigurd which made him forget Brynhild.

Gudrun: Daughter of Giuki; wife of Sigurd; later wife of Atli and Jonakr.

Gunnar: Son of Giuki; in his semblance Sigurd won Brynhild for him; slain at hall of Atli.

Guttorm: Son of Giuki; slew Sigurd at Brynhild's request.

Heimdall (Heimdallr): Guardian of Asgard.

Hel: Goddess of dead and queen of underworld; daughter of Loki.

Hiordis: Wife of Sigmund; mother of Sigurd.

Hoenir: One of creators of Ask and Embla; son of Bur.

Hogni: Son of Giuki; slain at hall of Atli.

Hoth (Hoder, Hodur): Blind god of night and darkness; slayer of Balder at instigation of Loki.

Ithunn (Ithun, Iduna): Keeper of golden apples of youth; wife of Bragi.

Jonakr: Third husband of Gudrun.

Jormunrek: Slayer of Swanhild; slain by sons of Gudrun.

Jotunnheim (Jotunheim): Abode of giants.

Lif and Lifthrasir: First man and woman after Ragnarok.

Loki: God of evil and mischief; instigator of Balder's death.

Lothur (Lodur): One of creators of Ask and Embla.

Midgard (Midgarth): Abode of mankind; the earth.

Midgard Serpent: Sea monster; offspring of Loki; slays, and is slain by, Thor at Ragnarok.

Mimir: Giant; guardian of well in Jotunnheim at root of Yggdrasill; knower of past and future.

Mjollnir: Magic hammer of Thor.

Nagifar: Ship to be used by giants in attacking Asgard atRagnarok; built from nails of dead men.

Nanna: Wife of Balder.

Nibelungs: Dwellers in northern kingdom ruled by Giuki.

Niflheim (Nifelheim): Outer region of cold and darkness; abode of Hel.

Njorth: Father of Frey and Freya; originally one of Vanir.

Norns: Demigoddesses of fate: Urth (Urdur) (Past), Verthandi (Verdandi) (Present), Skuld (Future).

Odin (Othin): Head of Aesir; creator of world with Vili and Ve; equivalent to Woden (Wodan, Wotan) in Teutonic mythology.

Otter: Son of Rodmar; slain by Loki; his skin filled with gold hoard of Andvari to appease Rodmar.

Ragnarok: Final destruction of present world in battle between gods and giants; some minor gods will survive, and Lif and Lifthrasir will repeople world.

Regin: Blacksmith; son of Rodmar; foster-father of Sigurd.

Rerir: King of Huns; son of Sigi.

Rodmar: Father of Regin, Otter, and Fafnir; demanded Otter's skin be filled with gold; slain by Fafnir, who stole gold.

Sif: Wife of Thor.

Siggeir: King of Goths; husband of Signy; he and his sons slew Volsung and his sons, except Sigmund; slain by Sigmund and Sinflotli.

Sigi: King of Huns; son of Odin.

Sigmund: Son of Volsung; brother of Signy, who bore him Sinflotli; husband of Hiordis, who bore him Sigurd.

Signy: Daughter of Volsung; sister of Sigmund; wife of Siggeir; mother by Sigmund of Sinflotli.

Sigurd: Son of Sigmund and Hiordis; wakened Brynhild from magic sleep; married Gudrun; slain by Guttorm at instigation of Brynhild.

Sigyn: Wife of Loki.

Sinflotli: Son of Sigmund and Signy.

Skuld: *See* Norns.

Sleipnir (Sleipner): Eight-legged horse of Odin.

Surt (Surtr): Fire demon; slays Frey at Ragnarok.

Svartalfaheim: Abode of dwarfs.

Swanhild: Daughter of Sigurd and Gudrun; slain by Jormunrek.

Thor: God of thunder; oldest son of Odin; equivalent to Germanic deity Donar.

Tyr: God of war; son of Odin; equivalent to Tiu in Teutonic mythology.

Ull (Ullr): Son of Sif; stepson of Thor.

Urth: *See* Norns.

Valhalla (Valhall): Great hall in Asgard where Odin received souls of heroes killed in battle.

Vali: Odin's son: Ragnarok survivor.

Valkyries: Virgins, messengers of Odin, who selected heroes to die in battle and took them to Valhalla; generally considered as nine in number.

Vanir: Early race of gods; three survivors, Njorth, Frey, and Freya, are associated with Aesir.

Ve: Brother of Odin; one of creators of world.

Verthandi: *See* Norns.

Vili: Brother of Odin; one of creators of world.

Vingolf: Abode of goddesses in Asgard.

Vitharr (Vithar): Son of Odin; survivor of Ragnarok.

Volsung: Descendant of Odin, and father of Signy, Sigmund; his descendants were called Volsungs.

Yggdrasill: Giant ash tree springing from body of Ymir and supporting universe; its roots extended to Asgard, Jotunnheim, and Niffheim.

Ymir (Ymer): Primeval frost giant killed by Odin, Vili, and Ve; world created from his body; also, from his body sprang Yggdrasill.

Egyptian Mythology

Aaru: Abode of the blessed dead.

Amen (Amon, Ammdn): One of chief Theban deities; united with sun god under form of Amen-Ra.

Amenti: Region of dead where souls were judged by Osiris.

Anubis: Guide of souls to Amenti; son of Osiris; jackal-headed.

Apis: Sacred bull, an embodiment of Ptah; identified with Osiris as Osiris-Apis or Serapis.

Geb (Keb, Seb): Earth god; father of Osiris; represented with goose on head.

Hathor (Athor): Goddess of love and mirth; cowheaded.

Horus: God of day; son of Osiris and Isis; hawk-headed.

Isis: Goddess of motherhood and fertility; sister and wife of Osiris.

Khepera: God of morning sun.

Khnemu (Khnum, Chnuphis, Chnemu, Chnum): Ramheaded god.

Khonsu (Khensu, Khuns): Son of Amen and Mut.

Mentu (Ment): Solar deity, sometimes considered god of war; falcon-headed.

Min (Khem, Chem): Principle of physical life.

Mut (Maut): Wife of Amen.

Nephthys: Goddess of the dead; sister and wife of Set.

Nu: Chaos from which world was created, personified as a god.

Nut: Goddess of heavens; consort of Geb.

Osiris: God of underworld and judge of dead; son of Geb and Nut.

Ptah (Phtha): Chief deity of Memphis.

Ra: God of the Sun, the supreme god; son of Nut; Pharaohs claimed descent from him; represented as lion, cat, or falcon.

Serapis: God uniting attributes of Osiris and Apis.

Set (Seth): God of darkness or evil; brother and enemy of Osiris.

Shu: Solar deity; son of Ra and Hathor.

Tem (Atmu, Atum, Tum): Solar deity.

Thoth (Dhouti): God of wisdom and magic; scribe of gods; ibis-headed

Modern Wedding Anniversary Gift List

Anniversay	Gift	Anniversay	Gift	Anniversay	Gift
1st	Gold jewelry	10th	Diamond jewelry	19th	Aquamarine
2nd	Garnet	11th	Turquoise	20th	Emerald
3rd	Pearls	12th	Jade	25th	Silve jubilee
4th	Blue topaz	13th	Citrine	30th	Pearl jubilee
5th	Sapphire	14th	Opal	35th	Emerald
6th	Amethyst	15th	Ruby	40th	Ruby
7th	Onyx	16th	Peridot	45th	Sapphire
8th	Tourmaline	17th	Watches	50th	Golden jubilee
9th	Lapis	18th	Cat's-eye	60th	Diamond jubilee

Source: Jewelry Industry Council

Computers at Arm's Length

While computer technology has sped forward, our knowledge about its health effects on humans has not kept pace. One potential hazard in particular worries scientists and the people who work at computers: the risk posed by the electromagnetic radiation emitted from computer screens—also called video display terminals, or VDTs. The debate about this risk heated up last year [1990] when *Macworld,* an independently owned magazine for the users of Apple Macintosh computers, reported that cathode-ray-tube VDTs, the most common type, emit relatively high levels of electromagnetic fields, which some researchers have associated with an increased incidence of certain cancers, miscarriages, and birth defects. Since millions of workers and entire industries depend on computers, any changes in the way they are used could entail enormous economic and social costs.

What Are Electromagnetic Fields?

Wherever there's electricity—be it overhead power lines, home appliances, or computers—there are low-frequency electromagnetic fields (EMFs). These imperceptible energy emissions, located at the low end of the electromagnetic spectrum, are produced by alternating current as it surges in electric wieres. As the term "electromagnetic" suggests, EMFs have two components, an electric charge and a magentic attraction. Low-frequency EMFs are less blatantly damaging to living cells than higher-frequency forms of radiation such as X-rays, microwaves, or ultraviolet rays, which contain more energy.

It is very difficult to determine what subtle effect, if any, low-frequency fields may have on living tissue over long periods. It is known that the body's cells have their own electric fields, and some laboratory studies have shown that these internal fields can be disrupted by exposure to even low-energy EMFs. Some scientists hypothesize that subsequent cell changes—notably in cell membranes, genetic material, immune function, and/or hormonal and enzyme activity—may lead to an increased risk of cancer. However, it's hard to extrapolate from test-tube studies on isolated cells to human beings living in the real world.

Why Single Out Computers?

Most electric appliances emit EMFs, but exposure to them tends to be brief (as with hair dryers or toasters) and/or at a distance (at least several feet away, as with TVs). In contrast, millions of people, year after year, spend most of their working hours within a foot or two of VDTs, which have relatively strong fields.

The mechanism by which a VDT displays images on its screen generates electric and magnetic fields in what are called the very-low-frequency (VLF) and extremely-low-frequency (ELF) range, which pass right through the machine's case. It's the magentic fields that scientists are most concerned about and that are hardest to shield. Various appliances produce similar energy fields, but the distinctive type from

VDTs is emitted in sharp bursts—in what's called a pulsed "sawtooth" pattern—which, some researchers hypothesize, may allow them to have a greater effect on tissue.

A number of studies have looked at the potential health hazard posed by the long-term exposure of both animals and humans to low-frequency electromagnetic radiation. Although some studies have found, for instance, a link between EMFs and increased birth defect in animals, or an increased risk of cancer (especially leukemia, lymphomas, and brain cancer) in electrical workers or even in children living near high-voltage power lines, other studies have found no clear link. Earlier this year [1991] the Environmental Protection Agency concluded that EMFs are "a possible, but not proven, cause of cancer in people." *At this time, it is impossible to say whether EMFs pose any risk, and if they do, at what dose.*

Concern specifically about VDTs began in the late 1970s, when reports appeared about computer operators having high rates of headaches, miscarriages, and other health problems. Yet over the years, studies on VDTs have yielded contradictory or inconsistent results. And those that have found an increased incidence of cancers and birth disorders, for instance, generally suggest that the risk is statistically small. In Sweden, meanwile, the government and labor organizations have set up stringent low-radiation standards for VDTs. There are no such standards on loq-frequency VDT emissions in the U.S., though some researchers are now advocating such guidelines.

The only consensus among scientists is that more research needs to be done. A number of long-term studies are currently underway (including ones at the Universit of California at Berkeley and the Mt. Sinai School of Medicine in New York) and may help clarify matters.

What to Do

Until we know more, it's probably prudent to minimize your exposure if your work involves heavy computer use. Though the evidence about birth defects and miscarriages remains inconclusive, pregnant women in particular should take these steps:

Sit farther from the screen—in most cases this is all you have to do. A few inches can make a significant difference. Electromagnetic radiation falls off rapidly with distance from the source. Try to work at least 28 inches (about arm's length) from the screen. The fields are almost always considerably stronger at the sides and rear of the machines, so sit at least four feet from your colleagues' monitors. (Magnetic-field emissions pass through partitions, walls, and even lead barriers.) In some offices, it may be necessary to rearrange work stations.

An adjustable computer desk with a shelf that pulls out to hold the keyboard will let you sit farther from the screen. If you have trouble reading the screen at that distance, enlarge the type size. If your computer

A long-awaited study released by the National Institute of Occupational Safety and Health (NIOSH) released in March 1991, concluded that there was no increase in the risk of miscarriages with the occupational use of VDTs or their electromagnetic fields. The NIOSH report was criticized by advocates of VDT users as flawed and inconclusive.

Critics of the study urge further investigation into VDT reproductive research. More than 7 million U.S. women of reproductive age use VDTs on the job. Since 1980, several clusters of miscarriages have occurred among VDT users.—Ed.

program can't do this, you can buy a special large-type program, a magnifying screen, or a pair of eyeglasses that will let you focus at a distance of 28 inches or more from the screen (regular reading glasses focus at about 18 inches).

Turn off the VDT when you're not using it but sitting nearby. Dimming the screen won't reduce the emissions.

Don't fall for the ads for anti-glare screens that claim to block "radiation." Though these costly devices can block low-frequency electric fields, a *Macworld* study found that they don't block the magnetic fields, which worry scientists most.

Don't trust a bargain-basement EMF meter to give you an accurate reading on your computer's emissions. In any case, if you sit far enough from your VDT, you needn't worry. If you or your employer nevertheless wants to test your monitors, be prepared to spend at least several hundred dollars.

When Shopping for a New Computer

If you're thinking of buying a new VDT, look for one with lower electromagnetic emissions, such as the following:

• *Models that meet the "Swedish standards."* Several American manufacturers are now marketing "low-radiation" VDTs originally designed for sale in Sweden, where there are strict specifications for VDT emissions. Thanks to consumer demand, more such models will undoubtedly be available soon in the U.S.—apparently at little or no added cost.

• *Liquid crystal display (LCD) monitors.* Nonbacklist LCDs, which contain no cathode ray tube, generate extremely low magnetic fields. They are generally employed in laptop models, but are also becoming available in some larger models.

• *Monochromatic screens.* These generally give off less radiation than color monitors. A small monitor, however, doesn't necessarily emit a weaker field than a large one; an undamaged old VDT isn't necessarily worse than a new one.

For an information packet and other data about VDTs, contact the Labor Occupational Health Program at the University of California at Berkeley (2521 Channing Way, Berkeley, CA 94720; telephone 415–642–5507). ▢

Manufacturers, FDA Study ELF

Makers of electric blankets and the FDA will work together to help the manufacturers voluntarily reduce the appliances' emissions of extremely low frequency (ELF) electric and magnetic fields, under a plan endorsed by the Technical Electronic Product Radiation Safety Standards Committee, an expert advisory panel to FDA.

There has been concern about possible health hazards from ELF fields from electric power lines and household appliances—particularly electric blankets, since they are used close to the body for long periods.

While some human studies suggest a link between ELF emissions and certain types of cancer, other human and animal research does not. Studies have not determined the levels of emissions received, nor established an increased risk to the fetus. The committee decided that the scientific evidence does not warrant regulatory action. ▢

Federal Investment in Biotechnology Increased

The biotechnology revolution began in the 1970s and 1980s when scientists learned new techniques to alter precisely the genetic constitution of living organisms. Biotechnology is an ancient practice that includes such familiar applications as the use of yeast in baking bread and cultures in making cheese. The newer, most innovative biotechnologies are tremendously diverse and include gene transfer, embryo manipulation and transfer, plant regeneration, and perhaps the most widely known, recombinant DNA technology (rDNA) or "genetic engineering."

The 1992 Federal budget proposes $4,107 million for biotechnology research and development, an increase of $319 million or 8% over 1991.

Just a decade and a half after its beginnings, the U.S. biotechnology industry produced pharmaceuticals, diagnostic tests, and agricultural products worth close to $2 billion.

Scientific advances from biotechnology have not been limited to medicines. Biotechnology is expected to play a major role in improving U.S. agriculture and protecting the environment. Cell fusion, the merging of the genetic material of two cells of different species, can accelerate the selective breeding process for producing hardier and more fruitful crops and livestock. Enhancements of certain characteristics in vegetables are expected to provide increased resistance to insects, thus reducing the need for chemical pesticides. Companies are field-testing a variety of crops with enhanced resistance to specific viruses, insect pests, and safer herbicides.

Biotechnology holds great promise for the environment, including products that will clean up the ecosystem, provide alternatives to chemicals, and perform other tasks such as mineral recovery.

Bioremediation is a process that involves the use of microorganisms for cleanup of the environment. Certain microorganisms will feed on and degrade hazardous or toxic chemicals and produce environmentally safe substances as by-products. Recent experiments using bioremediation have demonstrated the value of microbes for cleanup of oil spills. Bioremediation is also used for cleansing soil contaminated with gasoline.

In 1992, the total Federal investment in biotechnology-related research is proposed at approximately $4.1 billion. ▢

Table of Geological Periods

It is now generally assumed that planets are formed by the accretion of gas and dust in a cosmic cloud, but there is no way of estimating the length of this process. Our earth acquired its present size, more or less, between 4,000 and 5,000 million years ago. Life on earth originated about 2,000 million years ago, but there are no good fossil remains from periods earlier than the Cambrian, which began about 550 million years ago. The largely unknown past before the Cambrian Period is referred to as the Pre-Cambrian and is subdivided into the Lower (or older) and Upper (or younger) Pre-Cambrian—also called the Archaeozoic and Proterozoic Eras.

The known geological history of the earth since the beginning of the Cambrian Period is subdivided into three "eras," each of which comprises a number of "periods." They, in turn, are subdivided into "subperiods." In a subperiod, a certain section may be especially well known because of rich fossil finds. Such a section is called a "formation," and it is usually identified by a place name.

Paleozoic Era

This era began 550 million years ago and lasted for 355 million years. The name was compounded from Greek *palaios* (old) and zoön *(animal).*

Period	Duration[1]	Subperiods	Events
Cambrian (from *Cambria,* Latin name for Wales)	70	Lower Cambrian Middle Cambrian Upper Cambrian	Invertebrate sea life of many types, proliferating during this and the following period
Ordovician (from Latin *Ordovices,* people of early Britain)	85	Lower Ordovician Upper Ordovician	
Silurian (from Latin *Silures,* people of eary Wales)	40	Lower Silurian Upper Silurian	First known fishes; gigantic sea scorpions
Devonian (from Devonshire in England)	50	Lower Devonian Upper Devonian	Prliferation of fishes and other forms of sea life, land still largely lifeless
Carboniferous (from Latin *carbo* = coal + *fero* = to bear)	85	Lower or Mississippian Upper or Pennsylvanian	Period of maximum coal formation in swampy forests; early insects and first known amphibians
Permian (from district of Perm in Russia)	25	Lower Permian Upper Permian	Early reptiels and mammals; earliest form of turtles

Mesozoic Era

This era began 195 million years ago and lasted for 135 million years. The name was compounded form Greek *mesos* (middle) and zoön (animal). Popular name: Age of Reptiles.

Period	Duration[1]	Subperiods	Events
Triassic (from *trias* = triad)	35	Lower or Buntsandstein (from German *bunt* = colorful + *Sandstein* = sandstone) Middle of Muschelkalk (from German *Muschel* = clam + *Kalk* = limestone) Upper or Keuper (old miner's term)	Early saurians
Jurrassic (from Jura Mountains)	35	Lower of Black Jurassic, or Lias (from French *liais* = hard stone) Middle or Brown Jurassic, or Dogger (old provincial English for ironstone) Upper or White Jurasic, or Malm (Middle English for sand)	Man sea-going reptiles; early large dinosaurs; somewhat later, flying reptile (pterosaurs), earliest known birds
Cretaceous (from Latin *creta* = chalk)	65	Lower Cretaceous Upper Cretaceous	Maximum development of dinosaurs; birds proliferating; oppossum-like mammals

Cenozoic Era

This era began 60 million years ago and includes the geological present. The name was compounded from Greek *kainos* (new) and *zoön* (animal). Popular name: Age of Mammals.

Period	Duration[1]	Subperiods	Events
Tertiary (originally thought to be the third of only three periods)	c. 60	Palecene (from Greek *palaios* = old + *kainos* = new)	First mammals other than marsupials
		Eocene (from Greek *eos* = dawn + *kainos* = new)	Formation of amber; rich insect fauna; early bats
		Oligocene (from Greek *oligos* = few + *kainos* = new)	Steady increase of large mammals
		Miocene (from Greek *meios* = less + *kainos* = new)	
		Pliocene (from Greek *pleios* = more + *kainos* = new)	Mammals closely resembling present types; protohumans
Pleistocene (from Greek *pleistos* = most + *kainos* = new) (popular name: Ice Age)	1	Four major glaciations, named Günz, Mindel, Riss, and Würm originally the name of rivers Last glaciation ended 10,000 to 15,000 years ago	Various forms of early man
Holocene (from Greek *holos* = entire + *kainos* = new)		The present	The last 3,000 years are called "history"

1. In millions of years.

Chemical Elements

Element	Symbol	Atomic no.	Atomic weight	Specific gravity	Melting point °C	Boiling point °C	Number of isotopes[1]	Discoverer	Year
Actinium	Ac	89	227[2]	10.07[2]	1050	3200±300	11	Debierne	1899
Aluminum	Al	13	26.9815	2.6989	660.37	2467	8	Wöhler	1827
Americum	Am	95	243[6]	13.67	994 ±4	2607	13[3]	Seaborg et al.	1944
Antimony	Sb	51	121.75	6.61	630.74	1750	29	Early historic times	—
Argon	Ar	18	39.948	1.7837[4]	−189.2	−185.7	8	Rayleigh and Ramsay	1894
Arsenic (gray)	As	33	74.9216	5.73	817 (28 atm.)	613[5]	14	Albertus Magnus	1250?
Astatine	At	85	−210		302	337	21	Corson et al.	1940
arium	Ba	56	137.34	3.5	725	1640	25	Davy	1808
Berkelium	Bk	97	247[6]	14.00[7]			8[3]	Seaborg et al.	1949
Berylium	Be	4	9.01218	1.848	1278 ±5	2970 (5 mm.)	6	Vauquelin	1798
Bismuth	Bi	83	208.9806	9.747	271.3	1560±5	19	Geoffroy	1753
Boron	B	5	10.81	2.37[8]	2300	2550[5]	6	Gay-Lussac and Thénard; Davy	1808
Bromine	Br	35	79.904	3.12[4]	−7.2	58.78	19	Balard	1826
Cadmium	Cd	48	112.40	8.65	320.9	765	22	Stromeyer	1817
Calcium	Ca	20	40.08	1.55	839 ±2	1484	14	Davy	1808
Californium	Cf	98	251[6]				12[3]	Seaborg et al.	1950
Carbon	C	6	12.011	1.8–3.5[9]	−3550	4827	7	Prehistoric	—
Cerium	Ce	58	140.12	6.771	798 ±3	3257	19	Berzelius and Hisinger; Klaproth	1803
Cesium	Cs	55	132.9055	1.873	28.40	678.4	22	Bunsen and Kirchoff	1860
Chlorine	Cl	17	35.453	1.56[4]	−100.98	−34.6	11	Scheele	1774
Chromium	Cr	24	51.996	7.18–7.20	1857 ±20	2672	9	Vauquelin	1797
Cobalt	Co	27	58.9332	8.9	1495	2870	14	Brandt	c.1735
Copper	Cu	29	63.546	8.96	1083.4±0.2	2567	11	Prehistoric	—
Curium	Cm	96	247[6]	13.51[2]	1340 ±40		13[3]	Seaborg et al.	1944
Dysprosium	Dy	66	162.50	8.540	1409	2335	21	Boisbaudran	1886
Einsteinium	Es	99	254[6]				12[3]	Ghiorso et al.	1952
Erbium	Er	68	167.26	9.045	1522	2510	16	Mosander	1843
Europium	Eu	63	151.96	5.283	822 ±5	1597	21	Demarcay	1896
Fermium	Fm	100	257[6]				10[3]	Ghiorso et al.	1953
Fluorine	F	9	18.9984	1.108[4]	−219.62	−188.14	6	Moissan	1886
Francium	Fr	87	223[6]		27[2]	677[2]	21	Perey	1938
Gadolinium	Gd	64	157.25	7.898	1311 ±1	3233	17	Marignac	1880
Gallium	Ga	31	69.72	5.904	29.78	2403	14	Boisbaudran	1875
Germanium	Ge	32	72.59	5.323	937.4	2830	17	Winkler	1886
Gold	Au	79	196.9665	19.32	1064.43	2807	21	Prehistoric	—
Hafnium	Hf	72	178.49	13.31	2227 ±20	4602	17	Coster and von Hevesy	1923
Helium	He	2	4.00260	0.1785[4]	−272.2 (26 atm.)	−268.934	5	Janssen	1868
Holmium	Ho	67	164.9303	8.781	1470	2720	29	Delafontaine and Soret	1878
Hydrogen	H	1	1.0080	0.070[4]	−259.14	−252.87	3	Cavendish	1766

Element	Symbol	Atomic no.	Atomic weight	Specific gravity	Melting point °C	Boiling point °C	Number of isotopes[1]	Discoverer	Year
Indium	In	49	114.82	7.31	156.61	2080	34	Reich and Richter	1863
Iodine	I	53	126.9045	4.93	113.5	184.35	24	Cortois	1811
Iridium	Ir	77	192.22	22.42	2410	4130	25	Tennant	1803
Iron	Fe	26	55.847	7.894	1535	2750	10	Prehistoric	—
Krypton	Kr	36	83.80	3.733[4]	-156.6	-152.30+0.10	23	Ramsay and Travers	1898
Lanthanum	La	57	138.9055	6.166	920 +5	3454	19	Mosander	1839
Lawrenceium	Lr	103	257[6]	—	—	—	20[3]	Ghiorso et al.	1961
Lead	Pb	82	207.2	11.35	327.502	1740	29	Prehistoric	—
Lithium	Li	3	6.941	0.534	180.54	1347	5	Arfvedson	1817
Lutetium	Lu	71	174.97	9.835	1656 +5	3315	22	Urbain	1907
Magnesium	Mg	12	24.305	1.738	648.8+0.5	1090	8	Black	1755
Manganese	Mn	25	54.9380	7.21–7.44[10]	1244 +3	1962	11	Gahn, Scheele, and Bergman	1774
Mendelevium	Md	101	256[6]	—	—	—	3[3]	Ghiorso et al.	1955
Mercury	Hg	80	200.59	13.546	-38.87	356.58	26	Prehistoric	—
Molybdenum	Mo	42	95.94	10.22	2617	4612	20	Scheele	1778
Neodymium	Nd	60	144.24	6.80 & 7.004[10]	1010	3127	16	von Welsbach	1885
Neon	Ne	10	20.179	0.89990 (g/1 0°C/1 atm)	-248.67	-246.048	8	Ramsay and Travers	1898
Neptunium	Np	93	237.0482	20.25	640 +1	3902	15[3]	McMillan and Abelson	1940
Nickel	Ni	28	58.71	8.902	1453	2732	11	Cronstedt	1751
Niobium (Columbium)	Nb	41	92.9064	8.57	2468 +10	4742	24	Hatchett	1801
Nitrogen	N	7	14.0067	0.808[4]	-209.86	-195.8	8	Rutherford	1772
Nobelium	No	102	254[6]	—	—	—	7[3]	Ghiorso et al.	1957
Osmium	Os	76	190.2	22.57	3045 +30	5027+100	19	Tennant	1803
Oxygen	O	8	15.9994	1.14[4]	-218.4	-182.962	8	Priestley	1774
Palladium	Pd	46	106.4	12.02	1552	3140	21	Wollaston	1803
Phosphorous	P	15	30.9738	1.82 (white)	44.1	280	7	Brand	1669
Platinum	Pt	78	195.09	21.45	1772	3827+100	32	Ulloa	1735
Plutonium	Pu	94	244[6]	19.84	641	3232	16[3]	Seaborg et al.	1940
Poionium	Po	84	210[6]	9.32	254	962	34	Curie	1898
Potassium	K	19	39.102	0.862	63.65	774	10	Davy	1807
Praseodymium	Pr	59	140.9077	6.772	931 +4	3212	15	von Weisbach	1885
Promethium	Pm	61	145[6]	—	≈1080	2460?	14	Marinsky et al.	1945
Protactinium	Pa	91	231.0359	15.37[2]	<1600	—	14	Hahn and Meitner	1917
Radium	Ra	88	226.0254	5.0?	700	1140	15	P. and M. Curie	1898
Radon	Rn	86	222[6]	4.4[4]	-71	-61.8	20	Dorn	1900
Rhenium	Re	75	186.2	21.02	3180	5627	21	Noddack, Berg, and Tacke	1925
Rhodium	Rh	45	102.9055	12.41	1966 +3	3727+100	20	Wollaston	1803
Rubidium	Rb	37	85.4678	1.532	38.89	688	20	Bunsen and Kirchoff	1861
Ruthenium	Ru	44	101.07	12.44	2310	3900	16	Klaus	1844
Samarium	Sm	62	150.4	7.536	1072 +5	1778	17	Boisbaudran	1879
Scandium	Sc	21	44.9559	2.989	1539	2832	15	Nilson	1879
Selenium	Se	34	78.96	4.79 (gray)	217	684.9+1	20	Berzelius	1817
Silicon	Si	14	28.086	2.33	1410	2355	8	Berzelius	1824
Silver	Ag	47	107.868	10.5	961.93	2212	27	Prehistoric	—
Sodium	Na	11	22.9898	0.971	97.81+0.03	882.9	7	Davy	1807
Strontium	Sr	38	87.62	2.54	769	1384	18	Davy	1808
Sulfur	S	16	32.06	2.07[11]	112.8	444.674	10	Prehistoric	—
Tantalum	Ta	73	180.9479	16.654	2996	5425+100	19	Ekeberg	1801
Technetium	Tc	43	98.062	11.50[2]	2172	4877	23	Perrier and Segré	1937
Tellurium	Te	52	127.60	6.24	449.5+0.3	989.8+3.8	29	von Reichenstein	1782
Terbium	Tb	65	158.9254	8.234	1360 +4	3041	24	Mosander	1843
Thallium	Tl	81	204.37	11.85	303.5	1457+10	28	Crookes	1861
Thorium	Th	90	232.0381	11.72	1750	4790	12	Berzelius	1828
Thulium	Tm	69	168.9342	9.314	1545 +15	1727	18	Cleve	1879
Tin	Sn	50	118.69	7.31 (white)	231.9681	2270	28	Prehistoric	—
Titanium	Ti	22	47.90	4.55	1660 +10	3287	9	Gregor	1791
Tungsten (Wolfram)	W	74	183.85	19.3	3410 +20	5660	22	J. and F. d'Elhuyar	1783
Uranium	U	92	238.029	-18.95	1132.3+0.8	3818	15	Peligot	1841
Vanadium	V	23	50.9414	6.11	1890 +10	3380	9	del Rio	1801
Xenon	Xe	54	131.30	3.52[4]	-111.9	-107.1+3	31	Ramsay and Travers	1898
Ytterbium	Yb	70	173.04	6.972	824 +5	1193	16	Marignac	1878
Yttrium	Y	39	88.9059	4.457	1523 +8	3337	21	Gadolin	1794
Zinc	Zn	30	65.38	7.133	419.58	907	15	Prehistoric	—
Zirconium	Zr	40	91.22	6.506[2]	1852 +2	4377	20	Klaproth	1789

Elements No. 104, 105, and 106—See NOTE at end of footnotes.

1. Isotopes are different forms of the same element having the same atomic number but different atomic weights. 2. Calculated figure. 3. Artificially produced. 4. Liquid 5. Sublimation point. 6. Mass number of the isotope of longest known life. 7. Estimated. 8. Amorphous. 9. Depending on whether amorphous, graphite or diamond. 10. Depending on allotropic form. 11. Rhombic. ≈ Is approximately. < Is less than. NOTE: There is a dispute between groups at the Lawrence Berkeley Laboratory of the University of California and at the Dubna Laboratory in the Soviet Union concerning the discovery of elements 104, 105, and 106. The Lawrence Berkeley Laboratory claims that 104 and 105 were discovered in 1969 and 1970, respectively, by Ghiorso et al. and has suggested the names Rutherfordium and Hahnium. The U.S. laboratory claims also that Ghiorso et al. discovered element 106 in 19734. No name has yet been suggested for this element. Names will not be official until the controversy is resolved and they have been approved by the International Union of pure and Applied Chemistry.

SCIENCE & LEARNING

A Chronology of Major Developments from 1450 to the Present

Text from AN ENCYCLOPEDIA OF WORLD HISTORY by William L. Langer, The Fifth Edition, Copyright 1940, 1948, 1952, and © 1967, 1972 by Houghton Mifflin Company. Reprinted by permission of Houghton Mifflin Company.

Science

1469. Publication of Pliny's *Historia naturalis*, the first scientific book to be printed.

1527-1541. Philippus Paracelsus [Theophrastus von Hohenheim] (1493-1541) crusaded for the use of chemicals in the treatment of disease. He introduced the system of salt, sulfur, and mercury as the three prime "elements," from which all things are made.

1540. Posthumous publication of *De la pirotechnica*, a handbook of metallurgy containing information about smelting and ore reduction compiled by **Vannoccio Biringuccio** (1480-1539).

1543. Nicolaus Copernicus [Niklas Kopernik] (1473-1543) published *De revolutionibus orbium coelestium*, which asserted that the planets, including the earth, circle around a stationary sun. He believed this theory represented the true structure of the world.

1543. Andreas Vesalius (1514-1564) produced *De fabrica corporis humani*, an illustrated, systematic study of the human body. This work is a union of Renaissance artistic endeavor and of a revived interest in the empirical study of **human anatomy**.

1545. Jerome Cardan (1501-1576) published the solution of the **cubic equation** in *Ars Magna*. This solution, the first major advance in mathematics in the European Renaissance, was due to **Niccolò Tartaglia** (?1500-1557), and was used without his permission.

1546. Georgius Agricola [Georg Bauer] (1494-1555) applied observation rather than mere speculation to the study of rocks, publishing *De natura fossilium*, an early handbook of mineralogy, and *De re metallica* (1556), which dealt with mining and metallurgy.

1546. Girolamo Fracastoro (?1483-1553) developed the theory that **contagion** (infectious disease) is caused by a living agent transmitted from person to person.

1551-1587. Conrad Gesner (1516-1565) amassed in the first great Renaissance encyclopedia, *Historia animalium*, ancient and contemporary knowledge of the animal kingdom.

1554. Jean Fernel (1497-1558) codified the practical and theoretical medicine of the Renaissance, rejecting magic and astrology but emphasizing the functions of organs.

1572. Tycho Brahe (1546-1601) observed a bright new star, a *super nova*, and determined that it was beyond the moon, thereby destroying the prevailing Aristotelian notion that no change occurred in celestial regions. Through systematic observation, using instruments designed by himself, Tycho

Johannes Kepler

Johannes Kepler, German astronomer and mathematician, was the founder of modern astronomy. He was born on Dec. 27, 1571, in the village of Weil-der-Stadt in the Duchy of Württenberg, Swabia. He studied mathematics, philosophy, theology, and astronomy at the University of Tüblingen, earning his M.A. in 1591.

Kepler became a teacher of mathematics and astronomy at Gratz, the Austrian province of Styria from 1594 to 1600. His writings on celestial orbits impressed the famous Danish astronomer Tycho Brahe who invited Kepler to join him at Prague. Kepler accepted and assisted Tycho in preparing new planetary tables. When Brahe died in 1601, Kepler succeeded him as Imperial Mathematician. He had access to all of Tycho Brahe's papers and 20 years of precise observations which he used to form the foundation of his three laws of planetary motion *(Kepler's Laws)* published between 1609 and 1618.

They are: (1) the path of a planet is an ellipse with the sun at one focus; (2) a line from the sun to a planet sweeps out equal areas in equal time periods; and (3) the square of the orbital period of a planet is proportional to the cube of its average distance from the sun.

Kepler spent the latter part of his life as a professor of mathematics at Linz, Austria. He died at Regensburg, Bavaria, on Nov. 15, 1630. ☐

accumulated very accurate data on planetary and lunar positions and produced the **first modern star catalog.**

1583. Andrea Cesalpino (1519-1603) compiled the first modern **classification of plants** based on a comparative study of forms.

1585. Simon Stevin (1548-1620) published *La disme,* introducing decimal fractions into arithmetic. A year later he published treatises on **statics and hydrostatics.** The work on statics gave a mathematical proof of the law of the lever, elegantly proved the law of the inclined plane, and showed that two unequal weights fell through the same distance in the same time.

1591. François Viète [Vieta] **(1540-1603)** introduced **literal notation** in algebra, i.e., the systematic use of letters to represent both coefficients and unknown quantities in algebraic equations.

c. 1600. Dutch lens-grinders in Middleburg are thought to have constructed the **first refracting telescope** and the **compound microscope.**

1600. William Gilbert (1540-1603) provided in *De magnete* a methodical experimental study of the **electric and magnetic properties of bodies,** and established that the earth itself is a magnet.

1603. Johann Bayer (1572-1625) produced a **celestial atlas** which introduced the use of Greek letters to indicate the brightest stars in every constellation.

1609. Johannes Kepler (1571-1630) announced in *Astronomia nova* his first two **laws of planetary motion:** planets move in ellipses with the sun in one focus; the radius vector from the sun to a planet sweeps out equal areas in equal times. In *Harmonices mundi* (1619) he added his third law: the squares of the periods of revolution of all planets are proportional to the cubes of their mean distances from the sun.

1610. Galileo Galilei (1564-1642), in *Sidereus nuncius,* revealed the results of the first telescopic observations of celestial phenomena. He used these observations to destroy the Aristotelian-Ptolemaic cosmology and to argue for the plausibility of the Copernican system.

1614. John Napier (1550-1617) introduced **logarithms** as a computational tool.

1627. Kepler, on the basis of Tycho Brahe's observations and his own theories, compiled the *Rudolphine Tables (Tabulae Rudolfinae)* which made possible the calculation of future planetary positions and other astronomical events; they were standard for over a century.

1628. William Harvey (1578-1657) in his classic *Exercitatio anatomica de motu cordis et sanguinis in animalibus* blended reason, comparative observation, and experimentation to demonstrate the **circulation of the blood.**

1632. Galileo fashioned in *Dialogo sopra i due massimi sistemi del mondo Tolemaico e Copernicano* a brilliant polemical masterpiece, which clearly showed the superiority of the Copernican system over the Ptolemaic system of the world. This work led to **Galileo's trial and recantation** before the Roman Inquisition of the Catholic Church.

1637. René Descartes (1596-1650) published *Discours de la méthode,* an introduction to his philosophy, which served as a preface to his works on dioptrics, meteorology, and geometry. In the same year he published *La géometrie,* setting forth an **analytic geometry,** i.e., representation of geometric figures by algebraic equations and algebraic equations by geometric figures. **Pierre de Fermat (?1608-1665)** simultaneously and independently developed an analytic geometry. Both Descartes and Fermat applied analytic geometry to the finding of tangents to curves; Fermat also devised a general method for finding maxima and minima.

1638. Galileo in *Discorsi e demonstrazione matematiche intorno a due nuove scienze* established the basic principles of a mathematical description of falling bodies and projectile motion.

1642-1671. Blaise Pascal (1623-1662) constructed the first **adding machine** that could perform the operation of carrying. Some thirty years later, **Gottfried Wilhelm Leibniz (1646-1716)** invented a more complex calculating machine which would multiply rapidly by repeated additions.

Galileo Galilei

The great Italian scientist, Galileo Galilei, was born in Pisa on Feb. 15, 1564. He taught mathematics at the University of Pisa from 1589 to 1592. He discovered that all falling bodies, large or small, descend with an equal velocity, but the famous story that he demonstrated this by experimenting with weights dropped from the Leaning Tower of Pisa is believed not to be true. From 1592 to 1610, he was a professor of mathematics at the University of Padua. After hearing about a simple magnifying device that was constructed in Holland, he was able to make the first complete astronomical telescope in 1609. Within a year, Galileo made some spectacular discoveries from his celestial observations. They included the four largest moons of Jupiter, the phases of Venus, the mountains and craters of the Moon, and the finding that the Milky Way is made up of myriads of single stars. Galileo's discovery that Venus goes through a complete cycle of phases was a major proof of Copernicus's idea that the sun rather than the Earth is the center of the solar system. His support of Copernicus's views conflicted with church dogma and, in 1616, he was ordered to refrain from teaching Copernicus's heliocentric view of the heavens. Despite the warning, he continued to support Copernican ideas, and in 1633, was summoned to Rome and tried by the Holy Inquisition. Galileo was convicted and made to recant his "false" belief that the Earth moves round the Sun. He was placed in house arrest at his retreat at Arcetri near Florence, where he remained until his death on Jan. 8, 1642. ☐

Sir Isaac Newton

Sir Isaac Newton, the English mathematician and philosopher was born in Woolsthrope, Lincolnshire, on Christmas day 1642. He earned his B.A. degree at Trinity College, Cambridge University in 1665. During this time he made his first discovery on fluxions but did not publish it. However, it has been established that he devised calculus independently of the German philosopher and mathematician Gottfried W. Leibnitz.

In 1666, according to the popular story, he was working in his garden at Woolsthorpe, when he supposedly reflected on the fall of an apple and it suggested to him the law of universal gravitation.

Newton's subsequent investigations include the nature of light. He experimented with sunlight refracted through a prism in a darkened room and discovered that ordinary white light contains the colors of the rainbow. His study of the laws of refraction and reflection led him to construct the first reflecting telescope in 1668.

Newton's other achievements were in the field of mechanics with his discovery of the second and third laws of motion. He became a member of the Royal Society in 1672.

He published his greatest work, "The Mathematical Principle of Natural Philosophy" in 1687 which presented his law of gravitation and laws of motion. He was knighted by Queen Anne in 1705.

Newton was elected president of the Royal Society in 1703 and remained in that office until his death in London on Mar. 20, 1727. He was given a national funeral and was the first scientist to be buried in Westminster Abbey. ☐

1648. Jan Baptista van Helmont (1577-1644), in his posthumously published collected works, *Ortus medicinae,* assigned the name "gas" to the "wild spirits" which were produced in various chemical processes and argued that acid fermentation, not "innate heat," was the operative agent of digestion.

1654. Correspondence between Pascal and Fermat on mathematical treatment of games of chance resulted in the beginning of **probability theory.**

1655. John Wallis (1616-1703) published *Arithmetica infinitorum,* which studied infinite series, infinite products, solved problems of quadratures, and found tangents by use of infinitesimals.

1657. The foundation of the **Accademia del Cimento** of Florence, the first organized scientific academy and a center for the new experimental science which stemmed from the work of Galileo.

1659. Christiaan Huygens (1629-1695) revealed, in *Systema Saturnium,* that Saturn is surrounded by a thin, flat ring.

1660-1674. Robert Boyle (1627-1691) described his first **pneumatic pump,** an improvement on that invented by **Otto von Guericke** (1602-1686), in *New Experiments Physicomechanical, Touching the Spring of the Air.* In the second edition (1662) Boyle noted the relation between pressure and volume now called **Boyle's Law.** With this pump Boyle showed that animals die from a lack of air, not from the accumulation of noxious vapors. So began an era in respiration studies that included the elucidation of lung structure (1661) by **Marcello Malpighi** (1628-1694), the proof that fresh air is necessary for respiration (1667) by **Robert Hooke** (1635-1703), the observation that blood changes color when in contact with air (1667-1669) by **Richard Lower** (1631-1691), and the demonstration that the volume of air is reduced in respiration (1674) by **John Mayow** (1640-1679).

1662. Charles II of England chartered **The Royal Society of London,** an independent organization that became the major center of English scientific activity during the 17th and 18th centuries.

1662. Jeremiah Horrocks (1619-1641) predicted and was the first man to observe (1639) **a transit of Venus** across the disk of the sun. His work was posthumously published in *Venus in sole visa* (1662).

1665. Robert Hooke published *Micrographia,* containing descriptions of his microscopic observations. He first used the word *cells* to describe the lacework of rigid walls seen in cork. The observations of Hooke and other classical microscopists— **Marcello Malpighi, Nehemiah Grew** (1641-1712), **Jan Swammerdam** (1637-1680), **Antony van Leeuwenhoek** (1632-1723)—revealed the complex minute structure of living matter and the existence of micro-organisms.

1666. Louis XIV of France founded the **Académie Royale des Sciences,** a government-controlled and financed organization dedicated to experimental science. The activity of the Académie was regularly recorded in the *Journal des Savants,* one of the earliest scientific periodicals. In 1667 the king founded the **Observatoire de Paris** and named the Italian astronomer **Giovanni Domenico Cassini** (1625-1712) as its first director (1669).

1669. Isaac Newton (1642-1727) announced his calculus, in *De analysi per aequationes numero terminorum infinitas,* which circulated in manuscript but was first published in 1711. He further developed the calculus in *Methodus fluxionum et serierum infinitarum* (1671, published 1736), using as fundamental notions "fluxions" (time derivatives) and "fluents" (inverse of fluxions), fluents being interpreted as areas.

1671-1684. Cassini discovered four new **satellites of Saturn** and observed a dark marking in Saturn's ring.

1672. Newton presented to the Royal Society a **reflecting telescope** which he constructed on principles learned in his optical studies. Newton also published his "New Theory about Light and Colors" showing notably that white light is composed of the various spectral colors, each of which has a different index of refraction.

1673. Christiaan Huygens announced in *Horologium oscillatorium* the invention and theory of the **pendulum clock.** This work included theorems on centrifugal force in circular motion.

1675. Olaus Roemer (1644-1710), by studying the eclipses of Jupiter's moons, determined that light is transmitted with a finite, though very great, speed.

1675. Charles II of England established the **Royal Observatory, Greenwich** and designated **John Flamsteed** (1646-1719) as the first Astronomer Royal.

1678. Robert Hooke provided an account of the law of elastic force, *ut tensio, sic vis* (stress is proportional to strain), which is now known by his name.

1679. Edmé Mariotte (?1620-1684) announced his discovery of the constant **relation between the pressure and volume** of an enclosed quantity of air (discovered independently of Robert Boyle).

1684. Leibniz first published his **differential calculus,** based on work done independently of Newton during the period 1673-1676. Leibniz based his calculus on the finding of differentials, which he understood as infinitesimal differences, and defined the integral as an infinite sum of infinitesimals; the operations of summing and of finding the differences were mutually inverse. His vision of a universal symbolic language led him to devise notation of great heuristic power, such as *d* for differential and ∫ for integral.

1686-1704. John Ray (1627-1705) in the three volumes of *Historia generalis plantarum* provided an able account of the structure, physiology, and distribution of plants and laid the foundations of modern **systematic classification.**

1687. Newton in his *Philosophiae naturalis principia mathematica* founded mechanics, both celestial and terrestrial, on his three axioms or **laws of motion.** He demonstrated that the sun attracts the planets and the earth attracts the moon with a force inversely proportional to the square of the distance between them. In his **principle of universal gravitation** he states that any two bodies attract each other with a force proportional to the product of their masses and inversely proportional to the square of the distance between them.

1688. Francesco Redi (1621-1697) challenged the ancient belief in spontaneous generation and began a two-century-long debate on the subject by his controlled experimentation on the production of maggots.

1696. Guillaume de L'Hôpital (1661-1704) published the first textbook of the **infinitesimal calculus,** *Analyse des infiniment petits,* based on the lectures of his teacher, **Johann Bernoulli** (1667-1748).

1697. Bernoulli showed that the curve of quickest descent was the cycloid, thereby solving the first problem of the **calculus of variations.**

1700. Gottfried Wilhelm Leibniz (1646-1716) was instrumental in the foundation of the **Berlin Academy,** Germany's first stable scientific organization.

1701-1713. Jakob (Jacques) Bernoulli (1654-1705) worked on problems (1701) which later became the calculus of variations. His *Ars conjectandi,* posthumously published in 1713, on probability theory, permutations and combinations, and binomial distribution.

Scientific Thought

1704. Isaac Newton (1642-1727), reporting on the optical researches he had undertaken since the 1660s, published his *Opticks.* He treated experimentally of the reflection, refraction, diffraction, and spectra of light.

He investigated the dispersion and composition of white light, showing that it is not homogeneous, as was traditionally thought, but decomposable into simple colors. The *Opticks* concluded with a group of "Queries," which in later editions developed Newton's speculations and conjectures concerning heat, chemical affinity, pneumatics, physiology, atomism, the nature of gravitation and the aether, the relation of the world of nature to God, and the proper manner of scientific inquiry. These speculations determined much of the experimental science of the 18th century.

1705. Edmund Halley (1656-1742) noted the resemblance in the paths of the comets of 1531, 1607, and 1682, and conjectured that these were different appearances of the same comet, now called *Halley's Comet.* He correctly predicted the return of this comet in 1758.

1708. Hermann Boerhaave (1668-1738) systematized physiology in the mechanistic terms of chemistry. As teacher of theoretical medicine at Leyden he influenced a whole generation of physicians.

1715. Brook Taylor (1685-1731) published *Methodus incrementorum directa et inversa,* the first treatise on finite differences and the source of *Taylor's series.* The series took on great importance in the work of **Leonhard Euler** (1707-1783) and **Joseph-Louis Lagrange** (1736-1813).

1717. Gabriel D. Fahrenheit (1686-1736) proposed the *Fahrenheit System* and a mode of calibrating thermometers.

1718. Etienne F. Geoffroy (1672-1731) published the first table of *chemical affinities,* a chart designed to indicate the reactivity of individual chemicals toward each other.

1725. Peter the Great founded the **Academy of Sciences** at St. Petersburg. The original resident membership of sixteen included thirteen Germans, two Swiss, and one Frenchman.

1725. John Flamsteed's (1646-1719) *Historia coelestis britannica,* a catalog of the positions of nearly 3,000 stars published posthumously. This replaced the catalog of **Tycho Brahe** as the standard reference source.

1727-1733. Stephen Hales (1677-1761) in *Vegetable Staticks* (1727) and *Haemastaticks* (1733) recorded a series of experiments in plant and animal physiology and demonstrated that biological phenomena, such as blood pressure, could be investigated on a quantitative basis. He also invented a pneumatic trough, an indispensible apparatus for collecting gases.

1728. James Bradley (1693-1762) explained an anomalous motion of the fixed stars by his discovery of the aberration of light.

1732. Boerhaave published *Elementa chemiae,* a standard chemistry textbook influential until the end of the 18th century.

1736. Leonhard Euler published *Mechanica sive motus analytice exposita,* generally considered to be the first systematic textbook of mechanics. During his life, Euler made fundamental contributions in many areas of analytical mechanics, e.g., the theory of the motion of rigid bodies, hydrodynamics, the application of variational principles in mechanics, and celestial mechanics.

1738. Pierre de Maupertuis (1698-1759) published *Sur la figure de la terre,* a report of a scientific expedition to Lapland which confirmed Newton's view that the earth is a spheroid flattened near the poles with a bulge near the equator.

1738. Daniel Bernoulli (1700-1782), in *Hydrodynamica,* presented investigations of the forces exerted by fluids, and presented an early version of the **kinetic theory of gases.**

1743. Alexis Clairaut (1713-1765) presented his *Théorie de la figure de la terre,* a mathematical investigation on hydrostatic principles of the shape of the earth.

1743-1744. Benjamin Franklin (1706-1790) was instrumental in the establishment of the **American Philosophical Society** at Philadelphia, America's first scientific society, devoted to "the promotion of useful knowledge."

1748. James Bradley reported his discovery, made earlier, of the **mutation of the earth's axis.**

1748. Euler published *Introductio in analysin infinitorum,* systematizing the calculus and emphasizing the study of functions, classifying differential equations, and treating trigonometric functions and equations of curves without reference to diagrams. He gave an elegant and highly influential exposition of the Leibnizian calculus, together with many new results of his own, in his *Institutiones calculi differentialis* (1755) and *Institutiones calculi integralis* (1768-1770).

1748. John Tuberville Needham (1713-1781), in *Observations upon the Generation, Composition, and Decomposition of Animal and Vegetable Substances,* reported that boiled, sealed flasks of broth teemed with "little animals" when opened. His rival Lazzaro Spallanzani (1729-1799) devised controlled experiments to test such factors as the amount of heating necessary to kill micro-organisms.

1750. Thomas Wright (1711-1786) suggested that the appearance of the Milky Way from the earth is due to the distribution of the visible stars in a disc.

1751. Robert Whytt (1714-1764) explicitly distinguished voluntary from involuntary motions, recognized that only a segment of the spinal cord is necessary for reflex action, and established the **study of reflexes** as a distinct branch of physiology.

1751-1754. Franklin published *Experiments and Observations on Electricity,* in which he explained his theory that electricity is a single fluid and used it to account for the properties of the Leyden jar and other known electrical phenomena. He deduced the principle of the **conservation of electric charge** from his theory, and established that lightning is identical with electricity produced by friction.

1755. Mikhail Lomonosov (1711-1765) played a leading role in the founding of **Moscow University.** Known for his work in chemistry, electricity, mechanics, and history, his major contribution was the establishment of the scientific tradition in Russia.

1756-1762. Joseph Black (1728-1799), in *Experiments upon Magnesia Alba* (1756), announced the isolation of a new gas, "fixed air" (carbon dioxide). In researches conducted between 1759 and 1762, but published posthumously (1803) in his *Lectures on the Elements of Chemistry,* he distinguished between temperature and quantity of heat,

and introduced the terms and concepts *latent heat, heat of fusion, thermal capacity,* and *caloric.*

1756. Johann Lehmann (d. 1767) contributed to knowledge of geological succession by classifying orders of strata. Similar work was carried on by **Giovanni Arduino** (1713-1795), who gave the names *primitive, secondary,* and *tertiary* to lithologically distinct sequences of strata; and earlier by **John Strachey** (1671-1743), whose "Observations on the Strata in the Somersetshire Coal Fields" (1719) established stratigraphical divisions and offered an early attempt at a structure section.

1758. Carl Linnaeus (1707-1778) in the tenth edition of his *Systema naturae* catalogued all known flora and fauna, (including man), and laid the basis for modern taxonomy by his consistent use of a **binomial nomenclature.**

1760-1761. Joseph-Louis Lagrange presented a complete *calculus of variations,* incorporating both old and new results in an elegant and systematic treatment.

1761. Giovanni Morgagni (1682-1771) presented in *De sedibus et causis morborum* a correlation of clinical symptoms and anatomic lesions challenging the notion of disease as an imbalance of humors.

1768-1779. Captain James Cook (1728-1779), an English naval officer, led three expeditions opening the Pacific to scientific explorers and collectors.

1771. Charles Messier (1730-1817) published the first installment of a star catalog which eventually recorded 103 nebulae and clusters.

1771-1794. John Hunter (1728-1793) raised surgery from a technical trade to the ranks of a science by connecting morphology with physiology and emphasizing the natural healing powers of the body.

1773-1784. Pierre Laplace (1749-1827) and **Lagrange** in a long series of papers finally solved the "long-term inequality" of Jupiter and Saturn, thus giving important evidence for the stability of the solar system.

1774-1817. Abraham Werner (1749/50-1817) propagated his view that features of the earth's crust are of aqueous origin (neptunism). Werner's methodical systematization of rocks and their formations helped found mineralogy as a science.

1774. Nicholas Desmarest (1725-1815) established the igneous origin of basalt in a study of the Auvergne volcanoes, thereby challenging neptunism.

1774-1786. Joseph Priestley (1733-1804) in his *Experiments and Observations on Different Kinds of Air* reported his studies on gases and announced the discovery of a number of water soluble gases, including ammonia, sulfur dioxide, and hydrogen chloride. In 1774 Priestley isolated **oxygen,** which he called "dephlogisticated air," in experiments with red calx of mercury.

1777. Carl Scheele (1742-1786) published his *Chemische Abhandlung von der Luft und dem Feuer.* He reported on his production of hydrogen in 1770 ("inflammable air"), his isolation of oxygen in 1773 ("fire air"), and his discoveries of many new and important substances, both organic and inorganic.

1779. Jan Ingenhousz (1730-1799) showed that plants make the atmosphere fit for breathing by producing oxygen during the day, that green leaves and stalks are the functional parts in this process, and that plants carry out respiration concomitantly with photosynthesis.

1780-1781. Claude Berthollet (1748-1822) and **Antoine Lavoisier** (1743-1794), using the new chemical techniques of pneumatic and combustion analysis, isolated carbon, oxygen, and hydrogen as the elements of organic substances. Their work opened a new era in elementary organic analysis and physiological chemistry.

1781. William Herschel (1738-1822) discovered by telescopic observation the planet **Uranus,** the first planet to be discovered in recorded history.

1783. John Goodricke (1764-1786) observed regular variations in the brightness of the star Algol and demonstrated that Algol was an eclipsing binary.

1784. René-Just Haüy (1743-1821/22) gave an exposition of the laws of crystal form in *Essai d'une théorie sur la structure des crystaux.*

1784. Henry Cavendish (1731-1810) published *Experiments on Air,* in which he showed from experimental results obtained in 1781 that the explosion of a mixture of two volumes of "inflammable air" (hydrogen) with one volume of "dephlogisticated air" (oxygen) produced water.

1784. Lavoisier and **Laplace** measured the amount of oxygen consumed and of carbon dioxide and heat produced in respiration and combustion.

1785-1789. Charles Augustin de Coulomb (1736-1806) published *Mémoires sur l'électricité et le magnétisme,* in which, by using a torsion balance, he measured the force of electric and magnetic attraction and repulsion and found it inversely proportional to the square of the distance between point charges or magnetic poles.

1788. Lagrange published *Méchanique analitique,* a strictly analytical treatment of mechanics. Here statics is founded on the principle of virtual velocities and dynamics on d'Alembert's principle.

1789. Lavoisier published his *Traité élémentaire de chimie* rejecting the phlogiston theory. He championed his new **theory of combustion** which maintained that oxygen supports combustion and respiration, and combines with metals to form a calx. He also presented a new and empirically determined list of chemical elements. Two years earlier, in collaboration with **Guyton de Morveau** (1737-1816), **Claude-Louis Berthollet** (1748-1822), and **Antoine Fourcroy** (1757-1809), he published a treatise outlining a new method of chemical nomenclature, essentially the one used today.

1790-1801. The revolutionary government of France decreed the adoption of a decimal system of weights, measures, and coinage (the **metric system**).

1791. Luigi Galvani (1737-1798) in a series of experiments reported in *De viribus electricitatis in motu musculari animalium,* postulated the existence of "animal electricity."

1793. The Académie Royale des Sciences was first suppressed by the revolutionary government and then reopened as a section of the **Institut de France.** Motivated by a new concern for applied science, the government established the **école Polytechnique** (1794), providing training and posts for eminent French scientists.

1795. James Hutton (1726-1797) published his *Theory of the Earth,* setting forth the uniformitarian principle that geological change is produced by continuous natural forces.

1798. Edward Jenner (1749-1823) described his success at using the scrapings from cowpox as a "vaccination" against smallpox.

1799. Carl Friedrich Gauss (1777-1855) gave the first rigorous proof of the fundamental theorem of algebra, that an nth degree algebraic equation with real coefficients has n roots.

1799. Joseph Louis Proust (1754-1826) announced the **law of definite proportions,** according to which the same chemical compound, however it is prepared, always contains the same elements combined in the same proportions by weight.

1800. Alessandro Volta (1745-1827), in his essay "On the Electricity Excited by the mere Contact of Conducting Substances of Different Kinds," disagreeing with **Luigi Galvani** (1791), showed that the electrically produced effects in muscular contraction arise not from an innate animal electricity, but from the moist contact of different metals. This observation led him to construct the voltaic pile, the forerunner of the modern battery and the first source of a continuous electric current.

Mathematics, Physics, and Astronomy

1799-1825. Pierre Laplace (1749-1827) published his *Traité de mécanique céleste,* in which he aimed at presenting analytically all of the developments in gravitational astronomy since the time of Newton.

1800. The Royal Institution of Great Britain, center for the diffusion of technical and scientific knowledge, was founded by the American **Benjamin Thompson (Count Rumford)** (1753-1814).

1801. Giuseppi Piazzi (1746-1826) discovered the first asteroid *Ceres;* its orbit was computed by Gauss.

1801. Carl Friedrich Gauss (1777-1855) published *Disquisitiones arithmeticae,* developing the theory of congruences, quadratic forms, and quadratic residues, using methods and concepts basic to the subsequent progress of number theory and algebra.

1802. Thomas Young (1773-1829) demonstrated in his paper "On the Theory of Light and Colours" that the properties of light, including interference phenomena, are satisfactorily explained by considering it as a periodic wave motion in an aether.

1803-1804. William Herschel (1738-1822) reported observations on six cases of double stars, and concluded that each was a binary or connected pair of stars in which each member influenced the motion of the other. This was the first observation of changes taking place under gravity beyond the solar system.

1815-1821. Augustin Fresnel (1788-1827), through a series of mathematical and experimental researches on interference, diffraction, polarization, and double refraction, was able to establish the **transverse wave theory of light.**

1820. Hans Oersted (1777-1851) showed that a magnetic needle placed near a current-carrying wire deviated from its position, and that the direction of deviation depended on the direction of current flow.

1820. André-Marie Ampère (1775-1836) repeated Oersted's experiments (1820), and reported his discovery that two current-carrying wires exercise a reciprocal action upon one another. He later established a mathematical theory of known electrical phenomena, and experimentally demonstrated the principles of the electrodynamics of adjacent current-carrying conductors.

Michael Faraday

Michael Faraday, the distinguished English physicist and chemist, was born of poor parents in Newington Butts on Sept. 22, 1791. Due to his family's poverty, his formal education was only in reading, writing, and the rudiments of mathematics.

At the age of 13, Faraday was apprenticed to a bookbinder and, because of the opportunities given him while learning the trade, he was able to read extensively about science during his free time.

In 1812, he obtained employment as laboratory assistant to Sir Humphrey Davy, the celebrated chemist and inventor, and was launched on his scientific career that led to many important discoveries.

Faraday discovered electromagnetic induction and developed the first dynamo. It was a simple device consisting of a copper disk that rotated between the poles of a permanent magnet. He also formulated the laws of electrolysis. Faraday gave us the familiar terms: *electrode, cathode, anode, anion, cation, ion, ionization, electrolyte,* and *electrolysis.*

He became a member of the Royal Institution in 1823 and was made a Fellow of the Royal Society in 1824. He was offered knighthood, and the presidency of the Royal Society but declined both honors. Michael Faraday died at Hampton Court, near London, on Aug. 25, 1867. ☐

1821-1859. Michael Faraday (1791-1867) demonstrated electromagnetic rotation (1821) and discovered electromagnetic induction (1831). He independently discovered self-induced currents (1834), found two years earlier by **Joseph Henry** (1797-1878). He found the laws of electrochemical decomposition and conduction, and established a general theory of electrolysis. He also introduced the concept of *field* into physics. These and other investigations were collected in his *Experimental Researches in Electricity* (1839-1855) and in his *Experimental Researches in Chemistry and Physics* (1859).

1821-1823. Augustin-Louis Cauchy (1789-1857), who successfully sought rigor in analysis, gave the first essentially correct definition of limit in *Cours*

d'analyse (1821). This work also contained the first systematic study of convergence of series and general tests for it, and the first theory of functions of a complex variable. He defined the derivative and integral in terms of limit, and obtained the fundamental theorem of calculus (1823).

1822. Joseph Fourier (1768-1830) published *Théorie analytique de la chaleur,* giving a mathematical theory of heat conduction. He introduced trigonometric series, *Fourier series* of arbitrary, piecewise, continuous functions, thus extending the notion of function.

1824. Nicolas Sadi Carnot (1796-1832) published *Réflexions sur la puissance motrice du feu.* Here he showed that the transformation of heat into motive power depends on the quantity of heat ("caloric"), and the temperature difference between the source and sink of heat. He also introduced the reversible cycle of a heat engine—now called the *Carnot cycle.*

1827. Georg S. Ohm (1789-1854) found that the ratio of electromotive force to the current, in an electric circuit, is a constant *(Ohm's Law)* and called this constant the resistance of the circuit.

1829-1832. Nikolai Lobacheyskii (1793-1856) and **János Bólyai** (1802-1860) independently developed the first **non-Euclidean geometries.**

1831. The foundation of the **British Association for the Advancement of Science,** dedicated to the promotion and professionalization of British science. The B.A.A.S. was based on a German model, **Gesellschaft deutscher Naturforscher,** and served as an example for the **American Association for the Advancement of Science** (1848).

1833. Charles Babbage (1792-1871) conceived an "analytical engine" (a large-scale digital calculator). In 1822, he had made a working model of a smaller, "difference engine" to calculate tables of functions by finite difference methods.

1833. Gauss, in his *Intensitas vis magnetica terrestris,* presented a rigorous mathematical analysis of the earth's magnetic field, and proposed a system of absolute units for the measurement of terrestrial magnetism.

1834. Adolphe Quetelet (1796-1874) initiated the **London Statistical Society,** and later helped found several other such groups. He applied the theory of probability to the statistics of society, especially in *Sur l'homme* (1835).

1835. Cauchy published the first existence proof for the solution of a differential equation.

1838-1839. Friedrich Bessel (1784-1846), **Friedrich Struve** (1793-1864), and **Thomas Henderson** (1798-1844) measured *stellar parallax* for the first time.

1842. Julius von Mayer (1814-1878) stated that the total amount of energy in the universe is constant (a form of the **first law of thermodynamics**), and that in natural processes energy is never lost, but only transformed from one kind to another.

1843-1846. John Adams (1819-1892) and **Urbain LeVerrier** (1811-1877) independently predicted the existence of a new planet and constructed its orbit from a consideration of irregularities in the motion of Uranus. This planet, later named *Neptune,* was sighted in 1846 by **Johann Galle** (1812-1910)—a great triumph for gravitational astronomy.

1843. James Joule (1818-1889) sought the connection between electricity, heat, and mechanical energy in "The Calorific Effects of Magneto-Electricity, and the Mechanical Value of Heat," and determined by four different procedures the mechanical equivalent of heat. In 1847 he enunciated the principle of the **conservation of energy.**

1846. The **Smithsonian Institution** for the increase and diffusion of knowledge was established by the United States Congress, utilizing the funds bequeathed by England's **James Smithson** (1765-1829).

1847. Hermann Helmholtz (1821-1894) announced the principle of the conservation of energy in *über die Erhaltung der Kraft*. He discussed the principle in great theoretical detail and elucidated its meaning.

1848. William Thomson (Lord Kelvin) (1824-1907) established the absolute thermodynamic scale of temperature, which is named after him.

1849. Armand Fizeau (1819-1896) for the first time successfully measured the **speed of light** by observations which do not involve astronomical constants.

1849. Jean Bernard Foucault (1819-1868) measured the speed of light accurately in media other than air, and thereby determined that the speed of light in air is greater than in water. Later, in a famous pendulum experiment, he demonstrated that the earth rotates (1851).

1850. William Cranch Bond (1789-1859), using the Harvard College Observatory's 15-inch refractor, took the first photograph of a star.

1850. Rudolph Clausius (1822-1888) announced the **second law of thermodynamics:** heat cannot of itself pass from a colder to a warmer body. In *über die bewegende Kraft der Wärme* (1865) he introduced the term *entropy,* stating that the entropy of the universe tends to increase.

1854. Bernhard Riemann (1826-1866) established the mathematical importance of non-Euclidean geometries, discussing them in his general theory of manifolds. In the same year he gave the most comprehensive and general definition of the classical definite integral, since called the *Riemann integral.*

1854. George Boole (1815-1864) published *The Laws of Thought,* an expansion of his 1847 work, *The Mathematical Analysis of Logic,* which marks the beginning of **symbolic logic,** i.e., the attempt to express the laws of thought in algebraic symbols.

Hermann von Helmholtz

Hermann Ludwig Ferdinand von Helmholtz, one of the 19th century's greatest scientists, was born in Potsdam, Germany, on Aug. 31, 1821. He studied medicine at the Royal Institute for Medicine and Surgery, Berlin, from 1838 to 1842. He later taught physics at the University of Berlin (1871-1894) and became the first director of the Physio-Technical Institute at Charlottenburg (1888-1894).

Helmholtz's studies led him to reject the doctrine of vitalism (*see* Vitalism, p. 454) and he concluded that all forces could be reduced ultimately to matter and motion. His famous paper, "On the Conservation of Force," published in 1847, included his mathematical formulation on the principle of conservation of energy, making him one of the originators of this idea.

Helmholtz also made many important contributions to physiology, optics, electrodynamics, and mathematics. He invented the opthalmoscope and opthalmometer.

He died in Charlottenburg on Sept. 8, 1894. □

James Clerk Maxwell

James Clerk Maxwell, the British physicist and creator of the electromagnetic theory of light, was born in Edinburgh, Scotland, on June 13, 1831. He studied at the University of Edinburgh and Trinity College, Cambridge, graduating in 1854. In 1855, he became a Fellow of Trinity, and was appointed Professor of Natural Philosophy and Astronomy at King's College London in 1860. He left King's College in 1865 to retire to private life and devote himself to research and writing on electricity and magnetism.

In 1871, Maxwell became the first Cavendish professor of experimental physics at Cambridge and directed the organization of the Cavendish laboratory which opened in 1874.

Basing his own study and research on that of Michael Faraday, he developed the mathematical interpretation of Faraday's electromagnetic field concepts. He published his famous *Treatise on Electricity and Magnetism* in 1873 which expounded a set of four equations that were applicable to electricity, magnetism, and light.

Maxwell also made important contributions to theoretical physics in the kinetic theory of gases.

He is also known for his studies of color and color blindness. He invented the "Maxwell" disk and color box. Maxwell showed that you could produce any given color from a combination of three selected colors taken from the spectrum.

James Clerk Maxwell's work on electromagnetic theory ranks next to Newton's work on mechanics. He died on Nov. 5, 1879, at Cambridge. □

Max Planck

Max Carl Ernst Ludwig Planck was born on April 23, 1858, in Kiel, Germany. He studied at the University of Munich from 1874 to 1877. In 1877 he went to the University of Berlin where he received his Ph.D. for his dissertation on the second law of thermodynamics when he was 21 years old. He subsequently taught at the University of Munich and Kiel University.

In 1889, he became a professor at the University of Berlin, where he remained until 1928 when he retired.

While investigating the problem of black body[1] radiation, Planck discovered the algebraic equation that described it. Since his findings did not conform to the classical laws of physics, he continued to study the problem and, in 1900, announced his revolutionary theory that energy was not a continuous entity but came in discontinuous small bundles that he called quanta. His discovery had provided an understanding of the nature of light and of radiation in general.

Later research by scientists such as Albert Einstein and Niels Bohr confirmed his basic hypothesis and established the Quantum Theory of modern physics.

Planck was awarded the Nobel prize in physics in 1918 for his work on black body radiation. He died at the age of 89 on Oct. 3, 1947, in Göttingen.

1. Black body: a theoretically perfect absorber of all radiation falling on it, reflecting or transmitting none.

1860-1877. James Clerk Maxwell (1831-1879) and **Ludwig Boltzmann** (1844-1906) developed statistical mechanics, a theory of the behavior of a gas considered as a collection of large numbers of molecules obeying the laws of classical mechanics.

1863. The United States Congress approved creation of the **National Academy of Sciences** as a scientific adviser to the federal government and promoter of scientific research.

1868. William Huggins (1824-1910), noting a slight shift toward the red in the spectrum of Sirius, calculated the radial velocity of a star for the first time.

1870-1883. Georg Cantor (1845-1918) published his major works, founding the **theory of sets** (1870) and the **theory of transfinite numbers** (1883).

1872-1882. Richard Dedekind (1831-1916) gave arithmetic definitions of irrational numbers (the *Dedekind cut*), constituting the first rigorous theory of irrationals.

1873. Maxwell published his *Treatise on Electricity and Magnetism* where he described the properties of the electromagnetic field in a series of equations *(Maxwell equations)* which entailed the electromagnetic theory of light.

1877. Giovanni Schiaparelli (1835-1910) observed long, narrow, straight, intersecting, dark lines on Mars, which he called *canali*.

1877-1893. Francis Galton (1822-1911) and **Karl Pearson** (1857-1936) developed the major statistical tools of present-day social science, e.g. regression (Galton, 1877), correlation coefficients (Galton, 1888), moments and standard deviation (Pearson, 1893).

1878. William Crookes (1832-1919) showed that cathode rays proceed in straight lines are capable of turning a small wheel, can be deflected by a magnet, excite fluorescence in certain substances, and heat and sometimes even melt some metals.

1887. Heinrich Hertz (1857-1894) demonstrated the existence of electromagnetic waves in the space about a discharging Leyden jar, and found that electromagnetic waves were propagated with the velocity of light as Maxwell had predicted (1873). Hertz's work led to modern radio communications.

1895. Wilhelm K. Röntgen (1845-1923) announced the discovery of x-rays in *Eine neue Art von Strahlen.*

1895. John W. Strutt (Lord Rayleigh) (1842-1919) and **William Ramsay** (1852-1916) discovered the "inert" or "noble" gas *argon.* Ramsay later discovered the other noble gases: helium, krypton, neon, xenon, and radon.

1896. Alfred B. Nobel (1833-1896) endowed prizes for outstanding achievements in physics, chemistry, medicine, and physiology. The first prizes were awarded in 1901.

1896. Antoine H. Becquerel (1852-1908) discovered radioactivity in uranium compounds.

1897. Joseph John Thomson (1856-1940) announced the discovery of the **electron,** the first sub-atomic particle, and determined experimentally the ratio of its mass to its charge.

1900. Max Planck (1858-1947) stated that energy is not emitted continuously from radiating bodies, but in discrete parcels, or **quanta.**

1904. Marie Sklodowska Curie (1867-1934) showed that pitchblende (uranium ore) contained two new radioactive elements: **radium** and **polonium.**

Second from left: Albert Einstein, third from left: Max Planck

Albert Einstein

Albert Einstein, one of the greatest intellects in the history of mankind, was born of Jewish parents in Ulm, Wurttemberg, Germany, on March 14, 1879. Contrary to a popular legend that he failed math in his youth, Einstein was a gifted student in mathematics and physics. He earned his doctorate at the University of Zurich, Switzerland, in 1905. During the same year, he published four papers of major importance in physics, which included his special and general theory of relativity.

He became a Swiss citizen and taught at the University of Zurich in 1909, the German University of Prague in 1911, and returned to Zurich in 1912. In 1913, Einstein accepted the posts of titular professor of physics and director of theoretical physics at the Kaiser Wilhelm Institute in Berlin and renewed his German citizenship.

One of his predictions on the general theory of relativity, which concerned the bending of light rays from stars by the sun as they passed on their way to the earth, was verified in 1919 by British scientists studying a solar eclipse and brought him international fame.

Einstein was awarded the 1921 Nobel Prize in Physics for his work on the photoelectric effect.

After Hitler's rise to power in 1933, he was persecuted by the Nazi government and he gave up his German citizenship. Fortunately, he had accepted the post as head of the school of mathematics at the Institute for Advanced Study at Princeton in 1933 and remained there until his death. He eventually became a U.S. citizen.

Although Einstein was an ardent pacifist, he wrote to President Roosevelt in 1939 to investigate the use of atomic energy in bombs. He did this at the request of other scientists including Niels Bohr who suspected that the Nazis were developing a nuclear-fission device. After the war, Einstein was a leader in seeking international governmental control of nuclear energy.

A Zionist, Einstein was offered the presidency of Israel by David Ben-Gurion in 1952, but declined. He died in Princeton, N.J., on April 18, 1955. ☐

1905. Albert Einstein (1879-1955) announced his **special theory of relativity,** which required a fundamental revision in the traditionally held Newtonian views of space and time, and introduced the celebrated equation $E = mc^2$.

1905. Einstein attributed to radiation itself a particle structure, and by supposing each particle of light **(photon)** to carry a quantum of energy, explained the photoelectric effect.

1910-1913. Bertrand Russell (1872-1970) and **Alfred North Whitehead** (1861-1947) published *Principia Mathematica,* carrying out the reduction of arithmetic to symbolic logic. This work is the foundation of the calculus of propositions and modern symbolic logic.

1911. Robert A. Millikan (1868-1953) established that electric charge always consists of an integral multiple of a unit charge, which he determined with great accuracy, in his oil-drop experiment.

1911. Ernest Rutherford (1871-1937) introduced the nuclear **model of the atom,** i.e., a small positively charged nucleus, containing most of the mass of the atom, surrounded by electrons.

1911-1913. Ejnar Hertzsprung (1873-1967) studied double stars and their colors, especially in the Pléiades, and with **Henry Norris Russell** (1877-1957) devised the Hertzsprung-Russell Diagram, a graphic way of grouping stars by the relation between their absolute magnitudes and spectral types.

1912. Max von Laue (1879-1960) discovered **X-ray diffraction,** a powerful technique for directly observing the atomic structure of crystals.

1913. Niels Bohr (1885-1962) devised a new model of the atom by applying quantum theory to Rutherford's nuclear atom. Although this model violated classical electromagnetic theory it successfully accounted for the spectrum of hydrogen.

Niels Henrik David Bohr

Niels Bohr, the founder of the modern theory of atomic structure was born in Copenhagen on Oct. 7, 1885. He received his Ph.D in physics from the University of Copenhagen in 1911. His thesis on the electron theory of metals remains a classic today.

From 1912 to 1916, Bohr worked at Manchester University with Ernest Rutherford (1871-1937) who in 1911 had introduced the nuclear model of the atom, i.e., a small positively charged nucleus surrounded by negatively charged electrons. Bohr applied Planck's quantum theory to Rutherford's atomic structure, and in 1913, proposed a radical new concept of atomic structure (known as the Bohr atom) in which electrons travel around the nucleus in orbits that are determined by quantum conditions and not by classical laws alone. He left Manchester in 1916 to take a professorship at the University of Copenhagen, and in 1920 he assumed the directorship of the Institute of Theoretical Physics created for him at the University and remained in that position for the rest of his academic career.

His brilliant work on atomic structure won him the Nobel Prize for physics in 1922.

During World War II, Bohr escaped from the Nazi occupation of Denmark to Sweden in 1943, and from there to England. The same year, he visited the United States and made some technical contributions to atomic bomb research. However, he was greatly concerned for the future of the world and the control of these terrible weapons.

After the war, he returned to Denmark. He continued his efforts to further world peace and mutual understanding. He received the first Atoms for Peace award in 1957.

Bohr died in Copenhagen on Nov. 18, 1962. □

1915. Einstein announced his **general theory of relativity**, which explained the advance of Mercury's perihelion, and predicted the subsequently observed bending of light rays near the sun.

1918. Harlow Shapley (1885-1972), from an extensive study of the distribution of globular clusters and cepheid variable stars, increased the estimated size of our galaxy about ten times. He envisioned the galaxy as a flattened lens-shaped system of stars in which the solar system occupied a position far from the center.

1919. Rutherford found that the collision of alpha particles with nitrogen atoms resulted in the disintegration of the nitrogen and the production of hydrogen nuclei (protons) and an isotope of oxygen. He was the first person to achieve artificial transmutation of an element.

1919. Arthur S. Eddington (1882-1944) and others, by studying data obtained during a total solar eclipse, verified Einstein's prediction of the bending of light rays by the gravitational field of large masses.

1919-1929. Edwin P. Hubble (1889-1953) detected cepheid variable stars in the Andromeda Nebula, a discovery that allowed him to determine the distances between galaxies.

1924. Louis-Victor de Broglie (1892-1987) determined from theoretical considerations that the electron, which had been considered a particle, should behave as a wave under certain circumstances. Experimental confirmation was obtained in 1927 by **Clinton Davisson** (1881-1958) and **Lester H. Germer**.

1925. Wolfgang Pauli (1900-1958) announced the **exclusion principle** (in any atom no two electrons have identical sets of quantum numbers). This principle was an important aid in determining the electron structure of the heavier elements.

1925-1926. Werner Karl Heisenberg and **Erwin Schrödinger** (1887-1960) independently, and in different ways, laid the theoretical foundations of the new **quantum mechanics** which, though violating classical notions of causality, successfully predicts the behavior of atomic particles.

1927. George Lemaître in order to explain the red shift in the spectra from distant galaxies, introduced the concept of the **expanding universe. Eddington** pursued research in this subject from 1930.

1928. Paul A. Dirac by combining quantum mechanics and relativity theory, devised a relativistic **theory of the electron.**

1930. Vannevar Bush (1890-1974) and his associates placed into operation a "differential analyzer," the first modern analog computer.

1931. Ernest O. Lawrence (1901-1958) invented the **cyclotron,** a device for accelerating atomic particles, which has become the fundamental research tool in high-energy physics and has made possible the creation of trans-uranium elements.

1932. Karl Jansky reported the reception of radio waves from cosmic sources, making **radio astronomy** possible.

1938-1939. Otto Hahn (1879-1968) and **Otto Strassmann** bombarded uranium with neutrons and found an isotope of barium in the product (1938). **Lise Meitner** (1878-1968) and **Otto Frisch** explained this result by assuming the fission of the uranium nucleus **(nuclear fission).**

1942. Enrico Fermi (1901-1954) and associates built the first controlled self-sustaining **nuclear reactor.** Fermi was one of the chief architects of the theory of the atomic nucleus.

1944. Mark I, the Harvard-IBM Automatic Sequence Controlled Calculator, was put into operation at Harvard University. This was the first large-scale digital calculating machine.

1945. Vannevar Bush issued the report *Science: The Endless Frontier,* recommending the creation of a United States foundation for the support and encouragement of basic research and education in science. In 1950 the United States Congress established the **National Science Foundation** to implement this recommendation.

1946. The foundation of the **United States Atomic Energy Commission** assured civilian control of United States developments in atomic energy.

1946. ENIAC (Electronic Numerical Integrator and Calculator) was put into operation at the University of Pennsylvania, the first electronic high speed digital calculating machine.

1951. Harold I. Ewen and **Edward M. Purcell** detected the 21-centimeter hydrogen spectral line in galactic radiation, which had been predicted in 1944 by **Hendrik van de Hulst.** This discovery has enabled astronomers to map the structure of the Milky Way.

Chemistry, Biology, and Geology

1799-1805. Georges Cuvier (1769-1832) founded **comparative anatomy** on functional grounds maintaining that the parts of the organism are correlated to the functioning whole.

1800-1802. Marie-François Bichat (1771-1802) stimulated the separate and systematic study of each anatomical structure and physiological function by his classification of the body into textures or *tissus* each with its particular vital property.

1801. Claude Berthollet (1748-1822) opposed the prevailing doctrine of elective affinities with his **law of mass action.**

1802. John Playfair (1748-1819), friend and disciple of **James Hutton** (1726-1797), produced *Illustrations of the Huttonian Theory of the Earth*, bringing a clear exposition of uniformitarianism to a wide audience and establishing this philosophy as the basis of modern geology.

1804. Nicholas de Saussure (1767-1845) explained the process of photosynthesis in terms of the new chemistry of **Antoine Lavoisier** (1743-1794).

1807. Humphry Davy (1778-1829), using the new voltaic battery, isolated the metals potassium and sodium.

1807. Establishment of **United States Coast Survey,** the first United States scientific agency.

1807. Foundation of the **Geological Society of London,** which served as a center for research and discussion and as a model for similar societies in other countries.

1808. John Dalton (1766-1844) published his *New System of Chemical Philosophy,* which established the quantitative atomic theory in chemistry.

1808. Joseph Gay-Lussac (1778-1850) announced his discovery of the law of combining volumes for gases, i.e., the ratios of the volumes of reacting gases are small whole numbers.

1809. Jean-Baptiste Lamarck (1744-1829), in *Philosophie zoologique*, gave the most complete explanation of his **theory of evolution.** He argued that through a combination of unconscious striving, the physiological effects of use and disuse, and the influence of the environment, anatomical parts became modified. Furthermore, he believed that by the "inheritance of acquired characteristics" living forms evolved in an ever-ascending scale of perfection.

1811. Amedeo Avogadro (1776-1856) concluded that equal volumes of all gases at the same temperature and pressure contain equal numbers of molecules; in effect his hypothesis distinguished between atoms and molecules, but his ideas were neglected until 1858.

1815. William Smith (1769-1839) published his famous **geological map of England and Wales,** and

Edwin Powell Hubble

Edwin Powell Hubble, the American astronomer who revolutionized our understanding of the universe was born in Marshfield, Mo., on Nov. 20, 1889. He studied physics at the University of Chicago and law at Oxford. After a brief practice at law, he returned to Chicago to work for a doctorate in astronomy.

Hubble did research at Yerkes Observatory, Williams Bay, Wis., from 1914 to 1917, and joined the Army following America's entrance in the war. He accepted a position on the staff of Mt. Wilson Observatory, Pasadena, Calif., in 1919 where at that time and up until 1948 the observatory's 100-inch Hooker reflector telescope was the most powerful in the world.

Hubble spend the rest of his life at Mt. Wilson and eventually became its director. He took time out from his work during World War II when he did research on ballistics (1942-1946).

During 1923-1924, Hubble studied the Andromeda nebula from photographs taken through the 100-inch telescope and discovered that it contained short-period variable stars. This observation led him to conclude that Andromeda was not part of our own Milky Way galaxy, but was an independent star system at a very great distance from our own. He went on to study many remote galaxies along with other astronomers, and in 1929 found the first observational evidence to support the theories that the universe is expanding. Hubble also classified galaxies according to their shapes and investigated many of their properties. He died at San Marino, Calif., on Sept. 28, 1953.

established that specific strata can be identified by their fossil content, the principle upon which historical geology is founded. He also worked out the main divisions of the **Secondary** or **Mesozoic** strata.

Charles Darwin

Charles Robert Darwin, the English naturalist, was born in Shrewsbury, England, on Feb. 12, 1809. When he was sixteen, he attended Edinburgh University to study medicine and, in 1827, attended Christ's College, Cambridge, to prepare for the ministry. Although he received a B.A. degree in 1831, he was disinterested in both professions. However, while at Cambridge, he became keenly interested in natural history.

An important change took place in his life when, in 1831, he was able to obtain a position as official naturalist aboard the H.M.S. *Beagle* bound on an around-the-world scientific expedition. During the five-year voyage (1831-1836), Darwin saw many natural wonders and made many important observations which he recorded in voluminous notes. This great scientific adventure was the beginning of his career as one of England's leading biologists and provided him with the basis for his evolutionary theory of natural selection.

In 1859, he published his controversial book on the "Origin of Species." It soon received wide and stormy attention. His book on the "Descent of Man," published in 1871, proposed the idea that man descended from ape-like ancestors and added to the furor as it contradicted divine scripture.

When Charles Darwin died on April 19, 1882, many scientists had accepted his basic theories. He was buried at Westminster Abbey. ☐

1819. Pierre Dulong (1785-1838) and **Alexis Petit** (1791-1820) formulated the rule that the product of the relative atomic weight and the specific heat of an element is a constant. This made possible the experimental determination of relative atomic weights.

1819. René Laënnec (1781-1826) invented the **stethoscope.**

1822. François Magendie (1783-1855) showed that the sensory and motor functions arise from different spinal roots. He was anticipated in 1811 by the more discursive work of **Charles Bell** (1774-1842).

1828. Karl von Baer (1792-1876) founded modern comparative embryology with the publication of *über Entwickelungsgeschichte der Thiere.* Here he proclaimed that embryonic development is the history of increasing specificity.

1831-1836. Charles Darwin (1809-1882), as naturalist aboard *H. M. S. Beagle,* studied South American flora and fauna, and gathered information he was later to use in his theory of evolution.

c. 1831-1852. Roderick Murchison (1792-1871) and **Adam Sedgwick** (1785-1873) described the succession of Paleozoic strata in Wales, Murchison defining the *Silurian* system (1839) and Sedgwick defining the *Cambrian* system.

1838-1842. The **United States Exploring Expedition,** under the command of Lieut. **Charles Wilkes** (1798-1877), explored the Pacific Ocean, the first example of a United States government-sponsored scientific maritime venture.

1839. Theodor Schwann (1810-1882) extended the 1838 observations on plants cells of **Matthias Schleiden** (1804-1881) into the generalization that cells are the common structural and functional unit of all living organisms.

1840. Louis Agassiz (1807-1873) elucidated the role of glaciers in geological change and enunciated his ice age theory.

1846. William T. G. Morton (1819-1868) gave the first public demonstration of the use of **ether as an anaesthetic** in surgery.

1847. Carl Ludwig (1816-1895) perfected the **kymograph,** which became an invaluable measuring instrument for physiology.

1848. Louis Pasteur (1822-1895), in a series of brilliantly conceived and executed experiments, demonstrated the connection between the optical activity of organic molecules and crystalline structure, thus founding **stereochemistry.**

1848. Claude Bernard (1813-1878) demonstrated the ability of the liver to store sugar in the form of glycogen. His widely read *Introduction à l'étude de la médecine expérimentale* (1865) influenced literary men as well as scientists.

1852. Edward Frankland (1825-1899) announced his **theory of valency,** i.e., each atom has a certain "valency," or capacity for combining with a definite number of other atoms.

1856-1864. Bernard evolved the concept of the *milieu interieur,* envisioning that cells were autonomous physiological units, yet were dependent upon and protected by the internal environment of the whole organism.

1856-1866. Hermann Helmholtz (1821-1894) extended the doctrine of specific nerve energies developed by **Johannes Müller** to vision and hearing, indicating the penetration of physics and physiology into psychology.

1857-1860. Louis Pasteur demonstrated that fermentation was a product of yeast cell activity. This challenged the view of Liebig that the ferment was merely an unstable chemical substance.

1858. Rudolph Virchow (1821-1902) in *Die Cellularpathologie* declared that disease reflects an impairment of cellular organization. Here, too, he stated his famous generalization *"omnis cellula e cellula"* (all cells arise from cells) and described the cell as the basic element of the life process.

1858. Friedrich A. Kekulé (1829-1896) published *über die Konstitution und die Metamorphosen der chemischen Verbindungen und über die chemische Natur des Kohlenstoffs,* in which he recognized that carbon is quadrivalent, and that carbon atoms link together to form long chains that serve as skeletons for organic molecules.

1859. Gustav R. Kirchhoff (1824-1887) and **Robert**

W. Bunsen (1811-1899) began researches that made **spectrum analysis** a powerful method for the investigation of matter. They showed that a chemical element was clearly characterized by its spectrum, and by spectrum analysis they were able to discover previously unknown elements.

1859. Darwin amassed twenty-five years of careful research in *The Origin of Species*. Inspired by the evidence in geology, paleontology, zoogeography, and domestic animal breeding, he declared that species evolved through variation and the natural selection of those individuals best suited to survive in given environmental conditions. A similar theory was developed independently by **Alfred R. Wallace** (1823-1913).

1860. Marcelin Berthelot (1827-1907) published *Chimie organique fondée sur la synthèse*, which showed that total synthesis of all classes of organic compounds from the elements carbon, hydrogen, oxygen, and nitrogen was possible.

1861. Alexander M. Butlerov (1828-1886) introduced the term "chemical structure" at a chemical meeting in Germany. Butlerov shares credit with **Kekulé** for the development of the theory of the structure of organic compounds.

1861. Pasteur, in a classic paper "Mémoire sur les corpuscles organisés qui existent dans l'atmosphère," described a series of experiments which confuted the doctrine of the spontaneous generation of micro-organisms.

1862-1877. Pasteur investigated several types of micro-organisms to advance the **germ theory of disease.** His evidence encouraged **Joseph Lister** (1827-1912) to initiate the practice of **antiseptic surgery** (1865).

1865. Gregor Mendel (1822-1884), an Augustinian monk, described cross-breeding experiments with peas which demonstrated the particulate nature of inheritance. He concluded that many traits segregated into dominant and recessive alternatives and that combined traits assorted independently. Little attention was paid to his results until 1900 when cytological work suggested such unit characters existed.

1869. Dmitri I. Mendeleev (1834-1907), in *Principles of Chemistry*, devised his periodic table of the chemical elements, which arranged the elements in the order of increasing atomic weight, noted the periodic recurrence of similar properties in groups of elements, and successfully predicted the properties of elements yet to be discovered.

1872-1876. *H. M. S. Challenger* made an extended voyage of scientific investigation, led by **Wyville Thomson** (1830-1882). The information gathered and reported largely by **John Murray** (1841-1914) gave much impetus to the science of **oceanography.**

1879. Ivan P. Pavlov (1849-1936) showed the production of gastric juices could be achieved without the introduction of food into the stomach. His work in the physiology of digestion led him to develop the concept of the acquired or *conditioned reflex.*

1879. The **United States Geological Survey** was founded, consolidating under one office the several surveys which had been gaining valuable information in western North America for over a decade. Under the directorship of **John W. Powell** (1834-1902) after 1881, the survey grew into a powerful agency for the progress of science in the United States.

1880. John Milne (1850-1913) developed the first accurate **seismograph,** permitting the careful study

Louis Pasteur

Louis Pasteur, the French chemist and microbiologist for whom the pasteurization process was named, was born in Dole, France on December 27, 1822. He received his doctorate of sciences at the école Normale Supérieure in 1847 and at the age of 26 launched his career as a scientific innovator—showing the Paris Academy that certain chemical compounds split into mirror-image components. This finding formed the basis for his theory of molecular asymmetry showing that atomical arrangement affects the biological properties of chemicals.

By 1857 Pasteur was director of scientific studies at his alma mater; in 1863 he became dean of the science faculty at the University of Lille, where he began to study fermentation. Once proving that germs in air putrefy food, he devised a way to destroy germs with heat—a process now known as pasteurization.

In the following years Pasteur found ways to protect France's valued silkworms against disease, beer against decomposition, farm animals against various illnesses. On April 27, 1882 he was elected to the Académie Française, where he began his most significant study—into the prevention of rabies—and three years later saved the life of a nine-year-old boy. In 1888 the Pasteur Institute for the research, treatment and prevention of rabies was inaugurated in Paris. Pasteur headed the institute until his death on September 28, 1895.

of earthquakes and opening the way to new knowledge of the earth's interior.

1882. **Robert Koch** (1843-1910) described the etiology of the **tubercle bacillus.** This discovery led him (1884) ɪo state *Koch's postulates,* a method for isolating micro-organisms and proving that they are specific causes, not merely concomitants, of disease.

1883. **Ilia I. Mechnikov** (1845-1916) described the action of phagocytic cells in transparent starfish larvae. His discovery led to a general explanation of local inflammation.

1883. **Edouard van Beneden** (1845-1901) described how the chromosomes are derived in equal number

The Double Helix—DNA

The Double Helix—DNA

bers from the conjugating germ cells. This led to the discovery of reduction division in the formation of the gametes.

1887. Svante A. Arrhenius (1859-1927) announced his theory of electrolytic dissociation, according to which most of the molecules of an electrolyte are immediately dissociated into two ions when dissolved.

1890. Emil von Behring (1854-1917) and **Shíbasaburo Kitasato** (1856-1931) demonstrated that the serum of immunized rabbits neutralized the toxin of tetanus. This discovery opened the possibility that disease could be prevented through the stimulation of specific antibody production.

1892. August Weismann (1834-1914) described in *Das Keimplasma* his theory of the continuity of the germ plasm and a scheme for the unfolding of a particulate hereditary pattern in embryogenesis.

1893. Theobald Smith (1859-1934), in "Investigations into the Nature, Causation and Prevention of Southern Cattle Fever," demonstrated that parasites could act as vectors of disease.

1895. Wilhelm K. Röntgen (1845-1923) discovered x-rays and immediately realized that his discovery had a practical application in medicine.

1897. Eduard Buchner (1860-1917) discovered that *zymase*, a cell-free yeast extract, caused fermentation, thus resolving a long-standing controversy over "vital" and "inorganic" ferments.

1909. Paul Ehrlich (1854-1915) showed that the synthetic compound, *Salvarsan*, was an effective treatment for syphilis. This discovery was a tremendous stimulus to the field of chemotherapy. In 1935 **Gerhard Domagk** (1895-1964) made the fundamental discovery which led to the introduction and widespread use of **sulfa drugs.**

1911. Thomas H. Morgan (1866-1945) claimed that certain traits were genetically linked on the chromosome, thus visualizing a linear arrangement of genes and stimulating the construction of genetic maps.

1915. Alfred Wegener (1880-1930) gave the classic expression of the controversial theory of continental drift in *Die Entstehung der Kontinente und Ozeane.*

1927. Hermann J. Muller (1890-1967) announced that he had successfully induced mutations in fruit flies with x-rays. This provided a useful experimental tool, yet in retrospect gave warning to the generations of the 1940s and 1950s of a danger in the release of atomic energy.

1929. Alexander Fleming (1881-1955) announced that the common mold *Penicillium* had an inhibitory effect on certain pathogenic bacteria. It was not until 1943 under the pressures of World War II, however, that the first antibiotic, penicillin, was successfully developed.

1930. Ronald A. Fisher (1890-1962) established in *The Genetical Theory of Natural Selection* that superior genes have a significant selective advantage, thus testifying that Darwinian evolution was compatible with genetics.

1944. Ostwald T. Avery (1877-1955) and collaborators announced they had transmuted one type of pneumococcus bacteria into a second type by the transfer of DNA molecules.

1946. Willard F. Libby (1908-1980), and associates, developed *radiocarbon dating,* a method for ascertaining the absolute age of materials containing carbon.

1953. Francis H. C. Crick (1916-) and **James D. Watson** (1928-) offered a model for the structure of DNA which accounted for gene replication and conceived a biochemical code that could transmit a great variety of genetic information.

INVENTIONS & TECHNOLOGY

A Chronology of Major Developments from 1450 to the Present

Text from AN ENCYCLOPEDIA OF WORLD HISTORY by William L. Langer, The Fifth Edition, Copyright 1940, 1948, 1952, and 1967, 1972 by Houghton Mifflin Company. Reprinted by permission of Houghton Mifflin Company.

c. 1450. Printing with moveable type introduced into Europe by **Johannes Gutenberg** (?1400–1468). **Laurens Coster** (1440), cheapened and widened the diffusion of knowledge. This development accompanied an increased use of wood-block illustrations.

1485. Publication of **Leon Battista Alberti's** (1404–1472) De reaedificora exemplifies the extended interests of Renaissance architects and artists in the realm of applied science. A more famous example is **Leonardo da Vinci** (1452–1519), who was a military engineer and speculated on various types of machines. Structural theory did not advance until the work of **Galileo Galilei** (*Dialogues concerning Two New Sciences*, 1638), **Christopher Wren,** and **Robert Hooke.** The revival of interest in classical architecture, sparked by the rediscovery of the works of Vitruvius, led architects to develop new techniques, flat ceiling, and the dome. Some architects of the period were **Filippo Brunelleschi** (?1377–1446), **Franois Mansard** (1598–1666), **Claude Perrault** (1613–1688), **François Blondel** (1617–1686), **Inigo Jones** (1573–1652), and **Christopher Wren** (1632–1723).

1500. The expansion of trade brought a **development in ship construction.** Galleys were in use until the 17th century but the fully rigged ship with stern-post rudder developed during the 15th century, and by 1700 the four-masted galleon had evolved.

c. 1510. First of the handbooks on metallurgy appeared, *Probierbergbüchlein* on assaying, *Bergbüchlein* on mining. In 1540 **Vannocio Biringuccio's** (1480–1539) *Pyrotechnica* published, the first practical, comprehensive metallurgy text by a professional metallurgist. Included were descriptions of alloying and cannon-molding processes. In 1556 *De re metallica* of Agricola (Georg Bauer), a physician in the mining area of Saxony, appeared. It covered all aspects of mining from the survey of the site through the equipment and methods of mining to assaying, blast and glass furnace descriptions as well as the treatment of iron, copper, and glass. Agricola was concerned with miners' health, and described the diseases to which they are prone.

1520. Wheel lock invented, probably in Italy, one of the steps to a single-handed pistol. **Rifling** of the gun barrel was a known technique, 1525, and by 1697 iron cannon were cast directly from the blast furnace.

1533. The principle of **triangulation** in surveying discovered by **Gemma Frisius,** a German. More technical maps began to appear to replace the earlier Portalan maps (first **road map of Europe** appeared in Germany, 1511). **Maritime charts** were improved; in 1536 **Pedro Nuñez** (1492–1577) wrote on the errors in the plain charts used at sea. In 1569 **Gerhard Mercator** [Kremer] (1512–1594) devised the mercator chart; in 1600 the first seaman's calendar appeared. The **telescope,** invented c. 1590, and the back-staff (1595) of **John Davis** (?1550–1605), superseded the older navigational instruments, the astrolabe and cross-staff.

The true Effigies of Iohn Guttemberg Delineated from the Original Painting at Mentz in Germanie.

Johannes Gutenberg.

c. 1589. William Lee (d. 1610) invented the first frame **knitting machine,** slowly accepted during the 17th century.

1560–1660. Increased **use of coal,** especially in England, as a power source. The output of coal in Newcastle rose from 32,951 tons in 1563–1564 to 529,032 tons in 1658–1659. The use of coal was dictated by serious deforestation both in England and on the Continent. By 1615 wood-fired glass furnaces were illegal in England; thus technology was stimulated by the necessity of using coal.

1575–1680. The evolution of the **glass-maker's "chair."** Many new techniques were introduced into glass-making, including those of producing ruby glass (before 1620), lead and white glass (1679).

1603. Cannon were bored in Spain. By 1650 lead shot was molded by means of a split mold.

1698. Thomas Savery's (?1650–1715) steam engine. The steam mill of **Giovanni Branca,** 1629, was ill conceived, and the engine of **Denis Papin,** 1688, was not developed and had no effect on the Industrial Revolution.

1700. By this date many **foods and crops** were exchanged between Europe, Asia, and the Americas.

From the New World came the **potato** (in Spain c. 1570), maize, tea, chocolate, **tobacco. Coffee** grew wild in Ethiopia (known c. 1450) and was introduced into Europe (in England by 1650). By this date **sugar** was a common, cheap commodity in England; cane was shipped to America to form the basis of the industry in the Caribbean in the 18th century. **Cotton** was exported to America where it became an important crop.

Technical achievements of this century in agriculture, mining, metallurgy, and machinery (prime movers, textiles, and machine tools) laid the groundwork for the Industrial Revolution, commencing about the mid-century, which was markedly to change the nature of society and civilization. Industrialization, commencing first in England and first in the textile industry, was to urbanize society, transform the international power structure, and put its mark upon every aspect of modern life.

c. 1700. Christopher Polhem (1661–1751), the "Father of Swedish Technology," developed an improved **rolling mill** and utilized water power for primitive mass production.

1709–1717. Abraham Darby (1677–1717) produced iron from a **coke-fired blast furnace** at Coalbrookdale; despite shortage of charcoal, it took 50 years and improvements made in the method by his son Abraham Darby II before coke was regularly used for this purpose.

1712. Low pressure **steam pump** ("atmospheric engine") of **Thomas Newcomen** (1663–1729) used to pump water from mines. Newcomen utilized some features of **Denis Papin's** (1647–1714) atmospheric engine of 1695, but his invention was quite independent of **Thomas Savery's** (?1650–1715) first useful "fire-engine" of 1698. **John Smeaton** (1724–1792) made many empirical improvements of the Newcomen engine; he also designed bridges, harbors, canals, and the Eddystone Lighthouse (1759), and lowered the price of iron by his water-powered bellows (1761).

1716. Corps des Ponts et Chaussées established in France for civil engineering works; clear distinction made between civil engineer and architect. First improvements in **road-making** since Roman times with work of **P.M.J. Trésaguet** (1716–1794) in France, and **John L. McAdam** (1756–1836) ("metalled" or "macadamized" roads) and **Thomas Telford** (1757–1834) in England. Trésaguet and Telford emphasized a road foundation of large stones, with smaller stones for top layer; McAdam stressed a roadtop impervious to water.

1722. First technical treatise on iron, *L'Art de conver-*

tir le fer forgé en acier et l'art d'adoucir le fer fondu, by **René A. F. de Réaumur** (1683–1757). **Metallurgical techniques** developed during this century included **Benjamin Huntsman's** (1704–1776) crucible process for casting steel (1751), utilized for cutlery and instruments but not commercially successful until 1770; **Henry Cort's** (1740–1800) puddling process to produce wrought (bar) iron from cast iron in a reverberatory furnace (1784); and Cort's perfected rolling mill with grooved rollers (1784).

1732. Publication of **Jethro Tull's** (1674–1741) *New Horse Hoeing Husbandry* in which he described his innovations in **scientific cultivation:** seed drill (1701) to plant seed in rows rather than the older, casual method of tossing seeds; the horse-hoe (introduced by Tull from France in 1714); and the technique of soil pulverization. **Robert Bakewell** (1725–1795) introduced selective breeding of livestock, and **Charles Townshend** (1674–1738) introduced useful new crops, turnips and clover, for winter fodder. The work of these pioneers in scientific cultivation, publicized by **Arthur Young** (1741–1820), helped to produce the **Agricultural Revolution,** which effected radical transformations in agricultural crops and techniques and a large increase in the production of foodstuffs and animal materials (wool, hides).

1733. John Kay (d. 1764?) patented the **flying shuttle,** the first of a series of inventions which were to transform the manufacture of textiles, substitute the factory system for the older method of domestic production, introduce power-driven machinery into manufacturing processes, and mark the first steps in the Industrial Revolution. Other landmarks in the industrialization of textile production were the **spinning jenny** invented (1764) by **James Hargreaves** (d. 1778); the spinning machine (**waterframe**) developed (1769) by **Richard Arkwright** (1732–1792), perhaps based on earlier machines for roller spinning (especially that devised by Lewis Paul in 1733 with some assistance from John Wyatt), and which made Arkwright Lancashire's largest cotton-manufacturer and one of England's richest men; the **spinning "mule"** (1784) of **Samuel Crompton** (1753–1827); the power-loom (1785) of **Edmund Cartwright** (1743–1823), and the cotton gin (1793) of **Eli Whitney** (1765–1825).

1753. Publication by **Johann Heinrich Pott** of the *Lithogeoginoise pyrotechnique* on the **ceramic arts,** which developed during this period as Euro-

Major Developments 1450–1789

Development	See year	Development	See year	Development	See year
Architecture	1485	Flush toilet	1707	Roadmaps	1533
Agricultural developments	1732	Glassmaking	1575–1680	Rolling mill	1700
		Knitting machines	1589	Ship construction	1500
Blast furnace	1709–17	Lithography	1798	Semaphore	1793
Bleaching	1785	Mapmaking	1533	Steam engines	1698,1776
Boring mill	1774	Marine chronometer	1797	Soda	1789
Cannon	1520,1603	Metallurgy	c.1510,1722	Telescope	1533
Canal building	1770	Optical glass	1798	Textile production	1733
Crops, New World	1700	Pumps	1712	Toolmaking	1797
Ceramics	1753	Road construction	1716	Wheel lock	1520

Watt's Steam Engine, 1784. His improved engines helped usher in the Industrial Revolution

peans sought to reproduce the much admired Chinese porcelain introduced to Europe in the later 17th century. First to produce quality china were the **Meissen** works in Saxony (Dresden China), followed by the French state manufactory at **Sèvres** (1768). The English developed bone-china (utilizing bone-ash as an ingredient): **Josiah Wedgwood** (1730–1795) was appointed royal potter (1762) and established his **Etruria** works in 1769. By the 1750's The Potteries, a series of towns in Staffordshire, had become the center of world production of inexpensive earthenware.

1754. Society for the Encouragement of Arts, Manufactures and Commerce (later, **The Royal Society of Arts**) established, inspiring the organization of similar societies in France, Netherlands, and Russia. The first exhibition of the industrial arts was held in Paris (1763). The French *Encyclopédie* (1751–1772) provided a comprehensive treatise, with illustrations, of contemporary technology.

1770. Completion of the English **Grand Trunk Canal** linking the Trent and the Mersey Rivers, giving the industrial towns of the Midlands a direct water route for exports and initiating a **canal-building** fever in England, which reached America and France in the early 19th century. Principal English canal engineers were **James Brindley** (1716–1772), **John Rennie** (1761–1821), and **Thomas Telford** (1757–1834).

1774. **John Wilkinson** (1728–1808) invented the **boring-mill.** Originally designed to bore cannon, this machine was to find its most important use in the boring of cylinders for

1776. The **steam engine** of **James Watt** (1736–1819). Based upon the older Newcomen engine, the first working model (1768, patented 1769) contained the separate steam condenser. Put into practical use in 1776, Watt's engine was not a commercial success until 1785, when Watt went into partnership with the entrepreneur **Matthew Boulton** (1728–1809) and only after further improvements had been made: the epicyclic (sun-and-planet) gear (1781) producing rotary motion by the reciprocal piston action, and the

double-acting expansive engine (1782). (The "steam engine," actually a two-cylinder atmospheric pressure engine, of the Russian **Polzunov** [1729–1766] operated only for a short time [1767] and had no influence on subsequent engine development.)

1785. Introduction of **chemical bleaching** with chlorine *(eau de Javel)* by the French chemist **C. L. Berthollet** (1748–1822).

1789. The **Leblanc process** for obtaining soda from common salt invented by **Nicolas Leblanc** (1742–1806) in France, but first exploited in England.

1793. **Claude Chappe** (1763–1805) developed the **semaphore** (visual telegraph); rapid spread after success of first line from Paris-Lille.

1794. Establishment of **École Polytechnique,** premier institution of higher technological education in France; emphasis upon mathematics and applied science.

1797. **Henry Maudslay** (1771–1831) designed a **screw-cutting lathe,** made entirely of metal and utilizing a slide-rest. This tool was the culmination of much previous precision tool development, including the drill and lathe (1768–1780) of **Jacques de Vaucanson** (1709–1782), the screw-cutting lathe (1770) of **Jesse Ramsden** (1735–1800); the marine chronometer (1759) of **John Harrison** (1693–1776); the spring-winding machine of **Joseph Bramah** (1748–1814), who also invented the modern water closet (1778) and a hydraulic press (1796).

1798. **P. L. Guinand** (1748–1824), a Swiss, patented a stirring process for making optical glass which became the foundation of the great German **optical industry** of the 19th century.

1798. **Aloys Senefelder** (1771–1834) of Prague invented **lithography.**

The Industrial Revolution

The Industrial Revolution, begun in the latter half of the 18th century, expanded into new geographical areas, revolutionized older technologies, created new ones, and continued to transform society and human life during the 19th and 20th centuries. Although historians might debate as to whether several industrial revolutions occurred during this two-century span, whether there were different phases of the same revolution, or whether industrialization had reached the point of a "continuing revolution," there was no doubt that technological advances from the mid-18th century to the present had given man greatly increased mastery over his environment, while at the same time posing problems and even threats to man's continued existence.

The culmination of Britain's leadership in the Industrial Revolution was reached at the **Great Exhibition of 1851** in London; after that Britain's position declined relatively while new industrial giants, America and Germany near the close of the 19th century, and Russia in the 20th century, gained in technological strength.

Energy and Power

1800. The **galvanic cell,** or Voltaic pile, of **Alessandro Volta** (1745–1827) was the first electric battery (converting chemical energy into electrical energy).

1802. **Richard Trevithick** (1771–1833) built the first **high-pressure steam engine,** although the American **Oliver Evans** (1755–1819) had patented one

Drake's oil well. He struck oil on August 27, 1859, at a depth of 69 feet.

in the United States in 1797. Other advances in steam-engine technology included the compound engine (adding a high pressure cylinder to the original Watt engine) by **William McNaught** (1813–1881) in 1845.

1806. First gas-lighting of cotton mills. Improvements made in production and distribution of gas as heat source (**Bunsen burner,** 1855) and for illumination (**Welsbach gas-mantle,** 1885).

1827. **Benoit Fourneyron** (1802–1867) developed the **water-turbine.**

1832. The first mechanical generation of electricity by **Hippolyte Pixii.** Major improvements in **electric generators** followed: the improved armature (1856) designed by **Werner von Siemens** (1816–1892); and the ring-armature (1870) of **Zénobe T. Gramme** (1826–1901), which represented the first practical dynamo.

1854. **Abraham Gesner** (1797–1864) manufactured kerosene.

1859. **William M. J. Rankine** (1820–1872) published the first comprehensive manual of the steam engine. The steam engine stimulated theoretical studies in thermodynamics by Clapeyron, Clausius, Joule, Lord Kelvin, and Gibbs.

1859. **Edwin L. Drake** (1819–1880) drilled the first oil well in Titusville, Pennsylvania, opening up the Pennsylvania oil field and starting the large-scale

commercial exploitation of petroleum. **First oil pipeline** (two-inch diameter, six miles long) constructed 1865 in Pennsylvania.

1876. **Nicholas August Otto** (1832–1891) built the first practical gas engine, working upon the so-called **Otto cycle,** which is now almost universally employed for all internal combustion engines. Otto's work was based upon previous engines of **Étienne Lenoir** (1822–1900) and **Alphonse Beau de Rochas** (1815–1891). The Otto cycle was employed in the gasoline engine patented (1885) by **Gottlieb Daimler** (1834–1900).

1882. The Pearl Street (New York City) electric generating station, a pioneer central power station designed by **Thomas A. Edison** (1847–1931), commenced operations a few months after Edison dynamos had been installed at Holborn Viaduct Station in England.

1884. **Charles A. Parsons** (1854–1931) patented the **steam turbine.** The steam turbine (1887) of the Swede **Gustav de Laval** (1845–1913) proved successful for engines of smaller power.

1886. Beginning of the first great **hydroelectric installation** at Niagara Falls.

1888. **Nikola Tesla** (1856–1943) invented the **alternating current electric motor;** he also made possible the polyphase transmission of power over long distances and pioneered the invention of radio.

1892. **Rudolf Diesel** (1858–1913) patented his heavy oil engine, first manufactured successfully in 1897.

1921. **Tetraethyl lead,** gasoline anti-knock additive, produced by **Thomas Midgley** (1889–1944).

1930–1937. Development of gas turbine unit for jet propulsion in aircraft by **Frank Whittle.**

1930–1935. Development of first commercially practicable **catalytic cracking system** for petroleum by **Eugene J. Houdry** (1892–1962).

1942. Dawn of the Nuclear Age. The first self-sustaining **nuclear chain reaction** achieved at Stagg Field, Chicago, by **Enrico Fermi** (1901–1954). The first full-scale use of nuclear fuel to produce electricity occurred at Calder Hall (England) in 1956.

1954. The **solar battery** developed by Bell Telephone Laboratories, making it possible to convert sunlight directly to electric power.

Materials and Construction

1800. Pioneer **suspension bridge,** hung by iron chains, built by **James Finley** (c. 1762–1828) in Pennsylvania; wire suspension employed by **Marc Seguin** (1786–1875) in bridge near Lyons (1825). The American, **Ithiel Town** (1784–1844), patented

Major Developments in Energy and Power Sources

Development	See year	Development	See year	Development	See year
Catalytic Cracking	1930–35	Hydroelectric installation	1886	Tetraethyl lead	1921
Electric battery	1800	Kerosine	1854	Turbine, steam	1884
A.C. motor	1888	Diesel engine	1892	Turbine, jet-propulsion	1930–37
Electric generators	1832	Nuclear chain reaction	1942	Turbine, water	1827
Electric generating station	1882	Oil well	1859	Solar battery	1954
Gasoline engines	1876	Oil pipeline	1865		
Gas lightning	1806	Steam engine	1802, 1859		

Low-cost Bessemer steelmaking established the foundation of the modern steel industry.

his truss bridge (1820).

1817–1825. Building of the **Erie Canal,** the first great American civil engineering work.

1818. The **Institute of Civil Engineers** (London), the first professional engineering society, founded.

Marc Isambard Brunel (1769–1849) patented the cast-iron **tunnel shield; Thomas Cochrane** (1830) used this shield to construct foundations on marshy ground.

1824. Joseph Aspdin (1779–1855) patented **Portland cement,** a hydraulic cement (impervious to water) as durable as that employed by the Romans.

1827. *Gay-Lussac tower* introduced in manufacture of sulfuric-acid, largely replacing John Roebuck's lead-chamber process (1746). **Herman Frasch** (1851–1914) developed process (1891) for mining sulfur (by superheated water and pumping to the surface).

1836. Galvanized iron introduced by Sorel in France. Galvanized fencing and barbed wire (c. 1880) helped to fence off large tracts of cattle land in American west during latter part of 19th century.

1839. Charles Goodyear (1800–1860) **vulcanized rubber.** Although introduced into Europe in 1615, rubber had not been commercially successful until a solvent for the latex was found (1765); bonding of rubber to cloth to produce raincoats (macintoshes) had been developed (1824) by **Charles Macintosh** (1766–1843).

1855. John A. Roebling (1806–1869) completed **wire cable bridge** at Niagara; Roebling utilized this same method for the **Brooklyn Bridge** (completed by his son, W.A. Roebling, in 1883), and it became standard construction technique for all great suspension bridges.

1856. Henry Bessemer (1813–1898) perfected the technique *(Bessemer process)* for converting pig iron into steel by directing an air blast upon the molten metal.

1856. *Mauve,* first of the **aniline** (coal-tar) **dyes,** discovered by **William H. Perkin** (1838–1907). Beginning of the synthetic dye industry, which was to develop greatly in Germany.

1861. Ernest Solvay (1838–1922) patented the Solvay ammonia process for the manufacture of soda.

1863. The **open-hearth process** for the manufacture of steel developed by the Martin brothers in France using the regenerative furnace devised (1856) by **Frederick Siemens** (1826–1904) (also known as the Siemens-Martin process).

1867. Alfred Nobel (1833–1896) manufactured **dynamite.** Guncotton and nitroglycerine both discovered in 1846, had previously been used for blasting purposes. In 1875 Nobel discovered blasting gelatine, from which arose the gelignite industry. Cordite, another explosive, patented 1889 by Frederick Abel and James Dewar.

1863. Henry Clifton Sorby (1826–1908) of Sheffield discovered the microstructure of steel, marking the beginning of **modern metallurgical science.**

1868. Robert F. Mushet (1811–1891) began the manufacture of **tungsten steel.** Other steel alloys also developed: chromium steel (France, 1877); manganese steel (Robert Hadfield, England, 1882); nickel steel (France, 1888); stainless steel (many inventors, 1911–1920).

1872. John W. Hyatt (1837–1920) began commer-

Major Developments in Materials and Construction

Development	See year	Development	See year	Development	See year
Aluminum	1886	Dynamite	1867	Solvay ammonia process	1861
Aniline dyes	1856	Eiffel Tower	1889	Steelmaking, basic oxygen	1950
Bridge, wire cable	1855	Erie Canal	1817–25	Steelmaking, Bessemer	1856
Bridge, suspension	1800	Galvanized iron	1836	Steel-frame building	1928
Bridge, truss	1800	Institue of Civil Engineers	1818	Sulfuric acid	1827
Celluloid	1872	Modern metallurgy	1863	Tungsten steel	1868
Casting, shell molding	1941	Polymer	1909	Vulcanized rubber	1839
Cantilever technique, buildings	1947	Reinforced concrete	1947		
		Silicones	1945		

cial production of celluloid, discovered by Alexander Parkes (1855).

1877. Joseph Monier (1823–1906) patented a **reinforced concrete** beam. In the 1890s two other Frenchmen, Edmond Coignet and Francois Hennibique, utilized reinforced concrete for pipes, aqueducts, bridges, tunnels; E. L. Ransome employed it extensively in building construction.

1879. Percy Gilchrist (1851–1935) and **Sidney G. Thomas** (1850–1885) developed a method for making steel from phosphoric iron ores, thereby doubling in effect the world's potential steel production.

1886. Charles M. Hall (1863–1914) developed the electrolytic method of obtaining aluminum from its oxide (bauxite).

1889. Completion of the **Eiffel Tower;** wrought-iron superstructure on reinforced concrete base. Cast iron used for building construction earlier in the century by James Bogardus (1800–1874) for office buildings in New York and by Joseph Paxton (1801–1865) for Crystal Palace at Great Exhibition of 1851 (also employing wrought iron and glass, and prefabricated units). The first complete steel-frame structure was built in Chicago in 1890; steel made possible skyscrapers, as did the earlier invention (1854) of the elevator by **Elisha G. Otis** (1811–1861).

1902. Arthur D. Little (1863–1935) patented rayon, the **first cellulose fiber,** and also artificial silk. Earlier (1884) Louis, Count of Chardonet (1839–1924), had produced an artificial thread which was woven into a silk-like material. Cellophane developed by J. E. Brandenberger (1912); further developed by W.H. Church and K. E. Prindle (1926).

1909. The first polymer, **Bakelite,** discovered by Leo **H. Baekeland** (1863–1944). Subsequent development of polymers include neoprene, arising from work of Father Julius A. Nieuwland beginning in 1906; nylon, developed by Wallace H. Carothers and first manufactured in 1938; acrilan; orlon; dynel; and dacron (called terylene by its British inventors, J. R. Whinfield and J. T. Dickson, 1941). Synthetic polymers include elastomers, fibers, plastics. Silicon polymers developed c. 1945.

1928. The first steel-frame, glass-curtain-wall building completed. By 1960 this technique was practically universal for high buildings; developed particularly by **L. Mies van der Rohe** (1886–1969).

1941. Shell molding, a revolutionary process produc-

ing more accurate castings cheaply, invented by **Johannes Croning.** Powder metallurgy, although known since Wollaston's work at the beginning of the 19th century, achieved extensive application in mid-20th century.

1945. Industrial development of silicones proceeded apace for a wide variety of applications, including lubricants for exceedingly high and low temperatures; binding of fiberglass; water-repellent agents; etc.

1947. Frank Lloyd Wright (1869–1959) extended pure cantilever technique (earlier employed with iron and steel construction in bridges) by using concrete slab cantilevers for S. C. Johnson Research Building (Racine, Wisconsin).

1950. Basic-oxygen process for manufacture of steel developed in Austria.

Machines and Industrial Techniques

1800. Eli Whitney (1765–1825) credited with introduction of **interchangeable parts** for manufacturing muskets. Although it had European precedents, the system of interchangeable parts became known as "the American system" because it was most fully exploited in the United States and became the foundation of the mass production characteristic of American industry at a later date.

1801. Joseph M. Jacquard (1752–1834) invented a loom for figured silk fabrics, later introduced into the making of worsteds. **William Horrocks** (1776–1849) developed the power loom (1813), improved (1822) by **Richard Roberts** (1789–1864). Machine combing of wool developed (1845); ring spinning frame (1830); the Brussels power loom invented by Erastus B. Bigelow (1814–1879) of Massachusetts for the weaving of carpets (1845); and the loom of J. H. Northrop of Massachusetts (1892), which was almost completely automatic.

1810. Friedrich Koenig's (1774–1833) **power-driven press** in use, followed by the flat bed press (1811). Other developments leading to mass production of printed matter, especially newspapers, were the rotary press of Robert Hoe (1846) and the web printing press, allowing for printing on a continuous roll (web) of paper by a rotary press, invented (1865) by William A. Bullock. In 1885 the linotype of **Ottmar Mergenthaler** (1854–1899) replaced monotype.

1823–1843. Charles Babbage (1792–1871) attempted to build calculating machines (following the lead of Thomas de Colmar, who built the first

Major Developments in Machines and Industrial Techniques

Development	See year	Development	See year	Development	See year
Adding machines	1884	Electric driven machinery	1873	Printing presses and automatic typesetting	1810
Armament	1837	Interchangable manufacturing parts	1849–54	Refrigeration	1895
Automation	1947	Interchangeable firearm parts	1800	Resistance welder	1877
Ballpoint pen	1938	Laser	1920	Razors	1895
Bottlemaking	1898	Liquid air plant	1895	Screw gauge	1830
Calculators	1823–43	Looms	1801	Sewing machines	1846
Computers	1944, 1953	Managerial techniques	1920	Steam hammer	1839
Continuous rolling, steel sheet	1923	Milling machine	1855	Tanks	1915
Electric appliances	1882	Mass production	1914	Turret lathe	1855
Electric precipitation	1905–10			Zipper	1913

practical calculating machine in 1820); Babbage's machines were never completed, being too advanced for the technology of the time, but his theories formed a basis for later work in this field.

1830. Joseph Whitworth (1803–1887) developed the **standard screw gauge** and a machine to measure one-millionth of an inch, for standards. Made possible more precise machine tools for planing, gear-cutting, and milling.

1837. Rapid **development of armament**, keeping pace with improvements in metallurgy, machines, and explosives: **Henri J. Paixhans'** (1783–1854) shell-gun, adopted by France, 1837; rifled, breech-loading artillery used by Piedmont, 1845; the French '75, the first quick-firing artillery piece, firing both shrapnel and high explosive, 1898; the cast steel breech-loading Prussian artillery manufactured by the Krupps from 1849 on. In small arms, there was the Colt revolver (1835), the Dreyse needle-gun (1841), the Minié bullet (1849), Winchester repeating rifle (1860), Gatling machine gun (1861), French Chassepot (1866), and the Maxim gun (1884). The self-propelled torpedo was invented by Robert Whitehead (1823–1905) in 1864; smokeless powder appeared in 1884.

1839. Steam hammer invented by **James Nasmyth** (1808–1890). Also developments in drop-forging and die-stamping at this time.

1846. Elias Howe (1819–1867) invented the lock-stitch sewing machine; in 1851 **Isaac M. Singer** (1811–1875) invented the first practical domestic **sewing machine**. This became the first major consumer appliance, soon followed by the **carpet sweeper** of M. R. Bissell (1876), and the **vacuum cleaner** (I. W. McGaffey, 1869; J. Thurman, 1899).

1849–1854. Exploiting the increasing accuracy of machine tools, **Samuel Colt** (1814–1862) and **Elisha Root** (1808–1865) developed a practical system for manufacturing interchangeable parts, especially in connection with Colt's revolver.

1855. Development of **turret lathe** by American machine-tool makers. First true **universal milling machine** designed (1862) by **Joseph R. Brown** (1810–1876). Other machine-tool improvements included Mushet's tool steel, increasing the cutting speed (high speed tool steel, 1898, by Taylor and White), gear-box mechanisms for better control, multiple-spindle lathes (1890), and tungsten carbide tools (1926).

1873. First **use of electricity to drive machinery**, Vienna. Quickly adopted, usually with the motor incorporated into the machine rather than separate.

1877. Elihu Thomson invented a **resistance welder.** N. W. Bernardos of Russia patented carbon-arc welding, although arc welding (most popularly employed process today) did not come into its own until invention of the coated electrode in the 1920s. Oxyacetylene torch (invented in 1900 by Edmund Fouche) and gas welding was the dominant process until recently. Development of inert-gas-shielded arc welding after 1942.

1882. Invention and use of electric appliances for consumer market: electric fan (S.S. Wheeler); flatiron (H. W. Seely, 1882); stove (W. S. Hadaway, 1896); separate attachable plug (H. Hubbell, 1904); sewing machine (Singer Co., 1889); washing machine (Hurling Co., 1907).

1884. Dorr E. Felt (1862–1930) made first accurate **comptometer. William S. Burroughs** (1857–1898) developed first successful recording **adding machine** (1888); Brunsviga calculating machine (1892).

1895. Carl Linde established liquid air plant. He had previously (1876) introduced the ammonia compressor machine (the first vapor compression machine invented by Jacob Perkins, 1834). Other refrigerating machines were: ammonia absorption machine (Carré, 1860), air refrigerator (Gorrie, 1845; improved by Kirk, 1862), open-cycle air machine (Giffard, 1873), and later by Bell and Coleman).

1895. King C. Gillette (1855–1932) invented **safety razor** with throwaway blades. **J. Schick** invented **electric razor** (1928). Stainless steel throwaway blades invented in Sweden (1962).

1898. M. J. Owens (1859–1923) invented automatic **bottle-making machine.**

1905–1910. Electric precipitation equipment for prevention of atmospheric pollution by industry, developed by Frederick G. Cottrell (1877–1948).

1913. G. Sundback invented a slide fastener (**zipper**); earlier version patented by W. L. Judson (1891).

1914. Conveyer-belt mass production employed in the United States most dramatically in Henry Ford's assembly line for Model T Ford automobile, which became the symbol for American industrial technique.

1915. Development of **tank in warfare** by British (Sir Ernest Swinton).

1920. Managerial **techniques** improved through development of "Scientific Management," whose principles were first enunciated by **Frederick W. Taylor** (1856–1915) in the first decade of the century. Taylor concentrated on time-motion studies. Other proponents of "rationalized" production were Frank Gilbreth and Charles Bedaux. Quality control developed 1926.

1920. J. C. Shaw developed a **sensing device**, controlled by a servomechanism, for a milling machine. Hydraulic trace of J. W. Anderson (1927) allowed the reproduction of complex shapes. Machine tools further supplemented by electrolytic and ultrasonic machines, and cutting machines guided by an electron beam. **Development of laser** (light amplification by simulated emission of radiation) by Theodore N. Maiman (1960), also used for precision cutting.

1923. First mill for hot continuous wide strip rolling of steel, based on work of John B. Tytus.

1938. Ladislao J. and George Biro patented the **ball-point pen.**

1944. Harvard IBM Automatic Sequence Controlled Calculator, the first automatic general-purpose **digital computer**, completed. ENIAC (electronic numerical integrator and calculator), the first electronic digital computer, built in 1946. Development of special purpose computers and data processor (1950), including programmed **teaching machines.**

1947. Word **Automation** coined by John Diebold and D. S. Harder, to define "self-powered, self-guiding and correcting mechanism," and later extended to include all elements of "automated factory" and extension to office and clerical procedures.

1953. Electronic computers with feedback mechanism (servomechanisms), made possible new field of **Cybernetics**, defined by **Norbert Wiener** (1953) as "the study of control and communication in the animal and the machine."

Agricultural Production and Food Technology

1801. Franz K. Achard (1753–1821) built the first **sugar-beet factory** (Silesia). Sugar-beet cultivation and beet-sugar industry developed primarily in France and Germany.

Major Developments in Agriculture and Food Technology

Development	See year	Development	See year	Development	See year
Artificial insemination	1940	DDT	1939	Plows	1837
Cream separator	1877	Evaporated milk	1860	Poultry farming	1950
Canning	1810	Farm implements	1850–80	Reapers	1834
Chemical fertilizers	1880	Frozen foods	1917	Refrigeration	1865
Cotton picker	1889	Hydrogenation	1902	Sugarbeet industry	1801
		Pasteurization	1861	Tractors	1892

1810. Nicolas Appert (c. 1750–1840) described system for food preservation by canning, using glass jars. Tin cans introduced 1811.

1834. Cyrus H. McCormick (1809–1884) patented his **reaper**, and began commercial manufacture c. 1840. Obed Hussey (1792–1860) invented a similar reaper simultaneously and independently.

1837. John Deere (1804–1886) introduced the **steel plow.** In 1819 Jethro Wood (1774–1834) had developed a cast-iron plow; and John Lane had introduced a steel-blade plowshare in 1833. James Oliver's (1823–1908) chilled plow of 1855 was improved by the Marsh brothers (1857). Mechanical power applied to plowing with the introduction of **cable plowing** (1859); by 1858 John Fowler had introduced the **steam plow.**

1850–1880. Improvements in **farm implements** included the revolving disc harrow (1847), binder (1850), corn planter (1853), two-horsestraddle-row cultivator (1856), combine harvester (1860), combine seed drill (1867), and sheaf-biding harvester (1878).

1860. Gail Borden (1801–1874) opened the first factory for the production of **evaporated milk.**

1861. After Louis Pasteur's work on microorganisms, **pasteurization** was introduced as a preservative for beer, wine, and milk.

1865. Development of **mechanical refrigeration** for preservation of food products, especially Thaddeus Lowe's (1832–1913) compression ice machine (1865) and Linde's ammonia compression refrigerator (1873).

1869. Transcontinental railway aided development of **meat-packing industry** in Chicago.

1877. Gustav de Laval (1845–1913) invented the centrifugal **cream separator.**

1880. Application of **chemical fertilizers** increased food production. J. B. Lawes manufactured superphosphates (1842); Chilean sodium nitrate beds exploited from c. 1870 until methods of fixing atmospheric nitrogen were developed after 1900 by Fritz Haber (1868–1934); use of potash as an inorganic fertilizer from Strassfurt deposits.

1889. Angus Campbell tested the first spindle type **cotton picker;** this type of machine was not fully developed and marketed successfully until the 1940s, competing with the machine devised by John and Mack Rust in 1924 and also commercially produced in the 1940s.

1892. Gasoline **tractor** came into use for farming. **Caterpillar tractor** developed 1931.

1902. W. Normann patented a process for hardening liquid fats by hydrogenation, making available an ample supply of solid fats for soap and food.

1917. Clarence Birdseye (1886–1956) began development of method for quick **freezing of foods** in small containers; placed on market in 1929.

1939. Paul Muller synthesized DDT for use as an insecticide. Othmar Zeidler had prepared DDT in 1874, but its insecticidal qualities had not been suspected.

1940. Development of **artificial insemination** to improve livestock breeding.

1945. Unit **packaging of foodstuffs** improved by development of plastic packaging films. Trend toward prepared "convenience" foods for household use.

1950. Mass-production, battery-raising of poultry increased production, lowered prices, and converted chicken and turkey from a holiday and Sunday luxury to an everyday food item.

Transportation and Communication

1802. Richard Trevithick (1771–1833) patented a steam carriage; earlier attempts to use steam power for transport purposes had been made by Nicolas Cugnot in France (1769); William Murdock in England (1785), and Oliver Evans in the United States. In 1804 Trevithick designed and built a locomotive to run on rails.

1807. Robert Fulton (1765–1815) sailed the *Clermont* from New York to Albany. This was by no means the first steamboat: the Marquis Claude de Jouffroy d'Abbans (1751–1832) had built a paddle-wheel steamer in France (1783); John Fitch (1743–1798) had launched a steamboat on the Delaware (1787); James Rumsey (1743–1792) on the Potomac (1787); and John Stevens (1749–1838) had designed a successful screw-propeller steamboat (1802). However, Fulton's boat was the first steamboat to represent a commercial success. By 1819 steam augmented sail on the first transatlantic steamship crossing of the *Savannah*.

1814. George Stephenson (1781–1848) built his **first locomotive**, and in 1829 his *Rocket*, designed with the aid of his son Robert (1803–1859), won out in

Cugnot's steam carriage, 1770.

Stephenson's Rocket averaged 16 m.p.h. with a maximum speed of 29 m.p.h.

a competition with locomotives of other design and thereby set the pattern for future locomotive developments.

1825. Opening of the **Stockton-Darlington Railway,** the first successful railroad system, using a steam engine built by Stephenson. In 1829 the first railroads were opened in the United States (Pennsylvania) and France (Lyon-St. étienne), both employing English-built locomotives. The first American locomotive was built (1830) by Peter Cooper (1791–1883).

1837. Charles Wheatstone (1802–1875) and **William F. Cooke** (1806–1879) patented the telegraph, which was also independently invented by the American **Samuel F. B. Morse** (1791–1872), whose **telegraphic code** was universally adopted. By 1866, **Cyrus W. Field** (1819–1892) succeeded in laying a **transatlantic cable,** after two previous failures and after overcoming tremendous financial and technical difficulties.

1839. Louis J. M. Daguerre (1787–1851) evolved the **daguerreotype photographic process,** based on the work of Joseph Nicéphore Niepce (1765–1833). Although **William H. F. Talbot** (1800–1877) produced paper positives (1841), the first fully practical medium for photography was the wet collodion plate process (1851) of Frederick S. Archer (1813–1857).

1860. Construction began on the **London underground railway** system, which was electrified in 1905. Construction began on the Paris *metro* in 1898, on New York City subway in 1900.

1864. George M. Pullman (1831–1897) built the first **sleeping car** specially constructed for that purpose.

1867. Ernest Michaux invented the **velocipede,** the first bicycle to put cranks and pedals directly on the front wheel; the "safety" bicycle with the geared chain-drive to rear wheel was introduced in 1885.

1869. Union Pacific and Central Pacific Railroads met to complete the **first transcontinental line** in America. The **Trans-Siberian Railway** was begun in 1891.

1869. Opening of the Suez Canal, the work of the French engineer **Ferdinand de Lesseps** (1805–1894).

1873. The Remington Company began manufacture of the **typewriter** patented by **Christopher L. Sholes** (1819–1890); shift-key system, with capital and small letters on same type bar, introduced in 1878.

1874. Stephen D. Field's (1846–1913) electrically powered **streetcar** began operation in New York City, replacing the horsecars introduced in 1832. The cable streetcar, invented by Andrew S. Hallidie (1836–1900), was put into use in San Francisco (1873). The first streetcars with overhead trolley lines were in use in Germany by 1884 and first installed in the United States at Richmond, Virginia, in 1888.

1876. Alexander Graham Bell (1847–1922) patented the **telephone.** The first telephone exchange installed in New Haven (1877) and an automatic switching system introduced in 1879. Much previous experimentation had been done on telephones, including that of Philip Reis of Germany (1861), Antonio Meucci of Italy (1857), and Elisha Gray (simultaneously with Bell). The periodic in-

Bell demonstrating the long-distance capability of his invention at Salem, Mass., on March 15, 1877. A hook-up was made with Boston, 18 miles away, and an extended conversation took place between the two cities.

sertion of loading coils (inductors), originated by M. I. Pupin (1899), made possible long distance transmission of telephone calls.

1878–1879. Joseph W. Swan (1828–1914) of England made the first successful carbon filament **electric lamp** in 1878; working independently Thomas A. Edison patented his **incandescent bulb** in 1879. Improved vacuum in the lamp bulb made possible by the high vacuum mercury pump developed by Hermann Springel (1865). At the same time successful experiments in public lighting were carried on with the use of arc lamps, the most successful systems being those of P. Jablochkoff (Paris, 1876) and Charles F. Brush (Cleveland, 1879). Tungsten filament lamp introduced in 1913.

1885. Karl Benz (1844–1929) produced the prototype of the **automobile** using an internal combustion motor operating on the Otto four-stroke cycle principle; the same year Gottlieb Daimler (1834–1900) also patented his **gasoline engine,** trying it first on a motorcycle, then on a four-wheeled vehicle. These may be said to have been the first automobiles, although there had been experiments with battery-powered electric automobiles from 1851 on and some previous internal combustion vehicles had been attempted by the Frenchman étienne Lenoir (1859) and the Austrian Siegfried Marcus (1864). Other automobile pioneers included the Frenchmen Peugeot and Panhard. The first automobile patent in the United States was taken out by George B. Selden (1879), but the Duryea (1895) was the first auto made for sale in the United States. Henry Ford (1863–1947)

made his first car in 1896 and founded the Ford Motor Co. in 1903. Important in the development of the automobile was the invention (1888) of the **pneumatic tire** by John B. Dunlop (1840–1921).

1889–1890. Thomas Edison improved on his first **phonograph** (patented 1878) by substituting wax for the tinfoil-coated cylinders and by adding a loudspeaker to amplify the sounds produced by the diaphragm. Emile Berliner (1851–1929) improved the quality of sound reproduction (1890) by utilizing disk-records and better cutting technique.

1888. George Eastman (1854–1932) perfected the **hand camera** *(Kodak);* he had previously invented the first successful roll film (1880). Leo Backeland perfected (1893) a photographic paper *(Velox)* sufficiently sensitive to be printed by artificial light. Work of Rudolph Fischer and Siegrist in dye-coupler color processes (1910–1914) provided the basis for the development of a commercially practicable color film *(Kodachrome)* by Leopold Godowsky, Jr., and Leopold Mannes (1935).

1895. The first public **motion picture** showing in Paris, by Louis (1864–1948) and Auguste (1862–1954) Lumière, inventors of the **cinématographe.** This followed by a year the opeineing of Edison's Kinetoscope Parlor (New York City) where the motion picture (peepshow) could be viewed by but one person at a time. Both these successful attempts at motion pictures had been preceded by earlier devices: the "thaumatrope" of J. A. Paris (1826); the magic lantern, devised by A. Kircher (1645) and improved by Pieter van Musschenbroek (1736); the multi-camera apparatus of

Edward Muybridge (1872); the "photographic gun" of E. J. Marey (1882); the celluloid motion-picture film of William Friese-Green (1889). Prototype of the modern **film projector** was the Vitascope (1896), devised by **Charles Francis Jenkins** (1867–1934) and Thomas Armat on the basis of Edison's kinetoscope.

1895. Guglielmo Marconi (1874–1937) invented the **wireless telegraph,** based on the discovery (1887) of radio waves by Heinrich Hertz (1857–1894) (existence of these waves had been deduced by James Clerk Maxwell in 1873). Other contributors to wireless development were E. Branly, Thomas Edison, Alexander Popov (who contributed the aerial), Reginald E. Fessenden (improved transmitter, 1901). In 1901 Marconi succeeded in sending a wireless signal across the Atlantic.

1898. Valdemar Poulsen of Denmark invented the **magnetic recording of sound** (1898). F. Pfleumer of Germany replaced steel wire by plastic tape coated with magnetic material (1930's), and Marvin Camras of the United States made further developments in magnetic recording (1940s).

1904. John Ambrose Fleming (1849–1945) devised the diode thermionic valve **(radio tube); Lee de Forest** (1873–1961) invented the Audion (1906), a three-electrode vacuum tube (triode amplifier), thereby providing the basis for the development of **electronics.**

1911. Charles F. Kettering (1876–1958), who had previously invented lighting and ignition systems for the automobile, perfected the **electric self-starter.** The first fully **automatic transmission,** perfected by Earl A. Thompson, was introduced commercially in 1939. Harry Vickers and Francis W. Davis began work on hydraulic **power-assisted steering** systems in 1925 and 1926 respectively, and in 1951 power steering was introduced for passenger cars.

1913. Diesel-electric railway engines first used in Sweden. Coming into use in the United States during the later 1930's, they have largely replaced steam-locomotives.

1920. Frank Conrad (1874–1941) of the Westinghouse Co. began broadcasting radio programs in Pittsburgh, marking the **beginning of radio** as a mass communication medium.

1922. Herbert T. Kalmus developed **Technicolor,** first commercially successful color process for motion pictures.

1926. Sound Motion Pictures. Although Edison had attempted to put together his phonograph and motion picture inventions for sound movies as early as 1904, it was 1923 before de Forest successfully demonstrated his phono-film system for recording sound on the motion picture film. The first motion picture with sound accompaniment was publicly shown in 1926, the first talking picture in 1927.

1926. John L. Baird (1888–1946) successfully demonstrated **television** in England. His mechanical system of television, similar to that of C. F. Jenkins in the United States, was based on Paul von Nipkov's rotating disk (1886), but had technical limitations; modern electronic television developed from the cathode-ray tube (1897) of Ferdinand Braun and A. A. Campbell-Swinton's proposals (1911) for use of a cathode ray to scan an image. The crucial invention was the Iconoscope of the Russian-American **Vladimir Zworykin** (1889–1982), the device which transmits television images quickly and effectively. Philo Farnsworth of the United States contributed the image disector tube (1927). General broadcasting of television began in England in 1936, in the United States in 1941, but languished until after World War II. Peter C. Goldmark of Columbia Broadcasting System demonstrated (1940) sequential method of color television which gave way to compatible electronic system developed by R. C. A. in the 1950s.

1932. Edwin H. Land (1909–1991) invented the first practical synthetic light-polarizing material (**polaroid glass**), found useful in sunglasses, cameras, and scientific optical instruments. In 1947 he invented the **Polaroid Land camera,** which developed the film inside the camera and produced a photograph print within one minute; in 1962 he introduced color film for his camera.

1933. Fluorescent lamps introduced for floodlighting and advertising. Developments leading up to this included experiments by George Stokes (1852) and Alexandre Becquerel (1859) to excite fluorescent materials by ultraviolet rays or in a discharge tube; Peter Cooper-Hewitt's invention of the mercury vapor lamp (1901); the introduction of the **Neon lamp** by Georges Claude and the work on cathodes

Major Developments in Transportation and Communication

Development	See year	Development	See year	Development	See year
Aviation (see Aviation section)		Hand-held camera	1888	Sound recording	1898
Automobiles	1885	Polariod glass, camera	1932	Steam power	1802
Self-starter	1911	Radar	1940–45	Steamboat	1807
Bicycles	1867	Radio tube	1904	Streetcar	1874
Electric lamp	1878–79	Radio broadcasts	1920	Submarine, nuclear	1950
Fluorescent lamp	1933	FM (frequency modulation)	1933	Suez Canal	1869
Maser	1954	Railroad system, first	1825	Telegraph	1837
Motion pictures	1895	Diesel-electric engines	1913	Wireless	1895
Technicolor	1922	Sleeping car	1864	Telephone	1876
3-D films	1953	Locomotive	1814	Television	1926
Cinerama	1953	London railway system	1860	Transistor	1948
Phonograph	1888–90	Transcontinental, first	1869	Typewriter	1873
Long-playing records	1948	Space (see Space section)		Xerography	1937
Photography, Daguerrotype	1839	Satellite	1957		

**The world's first liquid-fuel rocket, 1926
(Smithsonian Institution photo)**

by D. M. Moore and Wehnelt in the 1900's; and J. Risler's application of powder to the outside of tubular discharge lamps (1923). Subsequent developments have included increased cathode life and improved fluorescent powders.

1933. Edwin H. Armstrong (1890–1954), pioneer radio inventor (regenerative, i.e., feedback, circuit, 1912, and superheterodyne circuit, 1918), perfected **frequency modulation (FM)** providing static-free radio reception.

1937. Chester Carlson patented a new dry photographic process *(Xerography)* based upon principles of photoconductivity and electrostatics.

1939. Igor Sikorsky (1889–1972) flew the first **helicopter** of his design. The first helicopter capable of flight was the work of Ellehammer of Denmark (1912), based on C. Rendard's articulated rotor blade (1904) and G. A. Croco's cyclic pitch control (1906). Juan de la Cierva invented the autogiro (1922), differing from the helicopter in that its rotor auto-rotated and the engine drove a normal propeller. Further development work was done (1934–1936) by Louis Breguet and Heinrich Focke.

1939. First test flight of a **turbo-jet airplane** (Heinkel) with an engine designed by Hans von Ohain. Simultaneous and parallel work on jet airplanes in Britain, based on turbo-jet engine designed by Frank Whittle (1930). (Also see special section on Aviation for additional information.)

1940–1945. Development of radar ("radio-detec-

tion-and-ranging") stimulated by World War II, for detection of aircraft, blind-bombing techniques, and naval search equipment. Based on Heinrich Hertz's demonstration (1887) that radio waves are reflected similarly to light rays, the technique was first applied by Edward Appleton in Britain (1924) and G. Breit and M. A. Tuve in the United States (1925) for investigating ionization in the upper atmosphere. Robert A. Watson-Watt showed the possibilities of employing radio waves to detect aircraft (1935); J. T. Randall and H. A. H. Boot developed the cavity magnetron for high-power microwave transmission. Simultaneously, radar development had been going on in Germany and the United States, including the development of equipment by Robert H. Page of the Naval Laboratory. After 1940 Britain and the United States co-operated in radar development, much of the work being done at the Radiation Laboratory in Cambridge, Mass.

1941–1945. Construction of 2,500 miles of large diameter (20-inch–24-inch) **pipelines** to deliver petroleum from oil-producing regions in Southwest United States to East Coast depots. Development of welding of steelpipe sections (1913–1914) cut leakage and made possible large-scale pipeline construction.

1948. Long-playing phonograph record introduced, based on Peter Goldmark's development of the narrow-groove vinyl plastic record, a light-weight pickup, and a slow-speed (33-1/3 r.p.m.), silent turntable.

1948. Basic research in semi-conductors at the Bell Telephone Laboratories resulted in the invention of the **transistor** by a group which included William Shockley, John Bardeen, and Walter H. Brattain. This tiny, rugged, amplifying device was increasingly used to replace vacuum tubes in electronic instruments. In 1954 the silicon transistor was developed.

1950. Development of **nuclear propulsion** for submarines and surface ships. The United States submarine *Nautilus* (1955), built under the stimulus exerted by Admiral Hyman Rickover, was the first submarine to pass under the North Polar ice cap. The Soviet icebreaker *Lenin* was the first nuclear-powered surface vessel.

1953. "Cinerama" system (invented and developed by Fred Waller) to produce three-dimensional films, released for commercial exhibition. At about the same time Cinemascope, employing a single large concave screen, and stereophonic sound were introduced for motion picture exhibition.

1954. Charles H. Townes (1915–   ) invented the **maser** (microwave amplification by the simulated emission of radiation), making it possible to transmit signals over great distances.

1957. Launching of first **man-made satellite**, *Sputnik I*, by Russia (Oct. 4) marked the beginning of the **Space Age.** This was the product of millennia of human dreams but, more materially, of the rocket researches of **Robert H. Goddard** (1882–1945) of the United States (first liquid-fuel rocket launched, 1926), the theoretical studies of the Russian **Konstantin Tsiolkovsky** (1903), and the German **Herman Oberth** (1923). (Also see special section on Space for additional information.)

Selected Scientific Inventions, Discoveries, and Theories

Abacus: *See* Calculating machine

Adding machine: *See* Calculating machine; Computer

Adrenaline: (isolation of) John Jacob Abel, U.S., 1897

Anesthetic: (first use of anesthetic—ether—on man) Crawford W. Long, U.S., 1842

Antibiotics: (first demonstration of antibiotic effect) Louis Pasteur, Jules-François Joubert, France, 1887; (penicillin, first modern antibiotic) Alexander Fleming, England, 1928

Antiseptic: (surgery) Joseph Lister, England, 1867

Antitoxin, diphtheria: Emil von Behring, Germany, 1890

Atomic theory: (ancient) Leucippus, Democritus, Greece, c.500 B.C.; Lucretius, Rome, c.100 B.C.; (modern) John Dalton, England, 1808

Bacteria: Anton van Leeuwenhoek, The Netherlands, 1683

Barometer: Evangelista Torricelli, Italy, 1643

Bicycle: Karl D. von Sauerbronn, Germany, 1816; (first modern model) James Starley, England, 1884

Bifocal lens: *See* Lens, bifocal

Blood, circulation of: William Harvey, England, 1628

Braille: Louis Braille, France, 1829

Bullet: (conical) Claude Minié, France, 1849

Calculating machine: (Abacus) China, c.190; (logarithms: made multiplying easier and thus calculators practical) John Napier, Scotland, 1614; (slide rule) William Oughtred, England, 1632; (digital calculator) Blaise Pascal, 1642; (multiplication machine) Gottfried Leibnitz, Germany, 1671; (important 19th-century contributors to modern machine) Frank S. Baldwin, Jay R. Monroe, Dorr E. Felt, W. T. Ohdner, William Burroughs, all U.S.; ("analytical engine" design, included concepts of programming, taping) Charles Babbage, England, 1835. *See also* Computer

Classification of plants and animals: (by genera and species) Carolus Linnaeus, Sweden, 1737–53

Clock, pendulum: Christian Huygens, The Netherlands, 1656

Combustion: (nature of) Antoine Lavoisier, France, 1777

Computer: (differential analyzer, mechanically operated) Vannevar Bush, U.S., 1928; (Mark I, first information-processing digital computer) Howard Aiken, U.S., 1944; (ENIAC, Electronic Numerical Integrator and Calculator, first all-electronic) J. Presper Eckert, John W. Mauchly, U.S., 1946; (stored-program concept) John von Neumann, U.S., 1947

Conditioned reflex: Ivan Pavlov, Russia, c.1910

Cosmetics: Egypt, c.4000 B.C.

Crossbow: China, c.300 B.C.

Cyclotron: Ernest O. Lawrence, U.S., 1931

Deuterium: (heavy hydrogen) Harold Urey, U.S., 1931

DNA: (deoxyribonucleic acid) Friedrich Meischer, Germany, 1869; (determination of double-helical structure) F. H. Crick, England, James D. Watson, U.S., 1953

Electromagnet: William Sturgeon, England, 1823

Electron: Sir Joseph J. Thompson, England, 1897

$E = mc^2$: (equivalence of mass and energy) Albert Einstein, Switzerland, 1907

Section of Charles Babbage's Difference Engine, an ingenious calculating machine.

Falling bodies, law of: Galileo Galilei, Italy, 1590

Fermentation: (micro-organisms as cause of) Louis Pasteur, France, c.1860

Geometry, elements of: Euclid, Alexandria, Egypt, c.300 B.C.

Gravitation, law of: Sir Isaac Newton, England, c.1665 (published 1687)

Gunpowder: China, c.700

Gyrocompass: Elmer A. Sperry, U.S., 1905

Gyroscope: Léon Foucault, France, 1852

Helium first observed on sun: Sir Joseph Lockyer, England, 1868

Heredity, laws of: Gregor Mendel, Austria, 1865

Induction, electric: Joseph Henry, U.S., 1828

Insulin: Sir Frederick G. Banting, J. J. R. MacLeod, Canada, 1922

Intelligence testing: Alfred Binet, Theodore Simon, France, 1905

Isotopes: (concept of) Frederick Soddy, England, 1912; (stable isotopes) J. J. Thompson, England, 1913; (existence demonstrated by mass spectrography) Francis W. Ashton, 1919

Laser: (theoretical work on) Charles H. Townes, Arthur L. Schawlow, U.S., N. Basov, A. Prokhorov, U.S.S.R., 1958; (first working model) T. H. Maiman, U.S., 1960

Lens, bifocal: Benjamin Franklin, U.S., c.1760

Light, nature of: (wave theory) Christian Huygens, The Netherlands, 1678; (electromagnetic theory) James Clerk Maxwell, England, 1873

Lightning rod: Benjamin Franklin, U.S., 1752

Logarithms: *See* Calculating machine

Loom: (horizontal, two-beamed) Egypt, c.4400 B.C.; (Jacquard drawloom, pattern controlled by punch cards) Jacques de Vaucanson, France, 1745, Joseph-Marie Jacquard, 1801; (flying shuttle) John Kay, England, 1733; (power-driven loom) Edmund Cartwright, England, 1785

Machine gun: James Puckle, England, 1718; Richard J. Gatling, U.S., 1861

Match: (phosphorus) François Derosne, France, 1816; (friction) Charles Sauria, France, 1831; (safety) J. E. Lundstrom, Sweden, 1855

Mendelian law: *See* Heredity

Microscope: (compound) Zacharias Janssen, The Netherlands, 1590; (electron) Vladimir Zworykin et al., U.S., Canada, Germany, 1932–1939

Neptunium: (first transuranic element, synthesis of) Edward M. McMillan, Philip H. Abelson, U.S., 1940

Neutron: James Chadwick, England, 1932

Neutron-induced radiation: Enrico Fermi et al., Italy, 1934

Nuclear fission: Otto Hahn, Fritz Strassmann, Germany, 1938

Ohm's law: (relationship between strength of electric current, electromotive force, and circuit resistance) Georg S. Ohm, Germany, 1827

Ozone: Christian Schönbein, Germany, 1839

Paper: China, c.100 B.C.

Parachute: Louis S. Lenormand, France, 1783

Pen: (fountain) Lewis E. Waterman, U.S., 1884; (ball-point, for marking on rough surfaces) John H. Loud, U.S., 1888; (ball-point, for handwriting) Lazlo Biro, Argentina, 1944

Penicillin: *See* Antibiotics

Periodic law: (that properties of elements are functions of their atomic weights) Dmitri Mendeleev, Russia, 1869

Periodic table: (arrangement of chemical elements based on periodic law) Dmitri Mendeleev, Russia, 1869

Plow, forked: Mesopotamia, before 3000 B.C.

Plutonium, synthesis of: Glenn T. Seaborg, Edwin M. McMillan, Arthur C. Wahl, Joseph W. Kennedy, U.S., 1941

Polio, vaccine against: (vaccine made from dead virus strains) Jonas E. Salk, U.S., 1954; (vaccine made from live virus strains) Albert Sabin, U.S., 1960

Positron: Carl D. Anderson, U.S., 1932

Pressure cooker: (early version) Denis Papin, France, 1679

Printing: (block) Japan, c.700; (movable type) Korea, c.1400; Johann Gutenberg, Germany, c.1450 (lithography, offset) Aloys Senefelder, Germany, 1796; (rotary press) Richard Hoe, U.S., 1844; (linotype) Ottmar Mergenthaler, U.S., 1884

Programming, information: *See* Calculating machine

Propeller, screw: Sir Francis P. Smith, England, 1836; John Ericsson, England, worked independently of and simultaneously with Smith, 1837

Proton: Ernest Rutherford, England, 1919

Psychoanalysis: Sigmund Freud, Austria, c.1904

Quantum theory: Max Planck, Germany, 1901

Rabies immunization: Louis Pasteur, France, 1885

Radioactivity: (X-rays) Wilhelm K. Roentgen, Germany, 1895; (radioactivity of uranium) Henri Becquerel, France, 1896; (radioactive elements, radium and polonium in uranium ore) Marie Sklodowska-Curie, Pierre Curie, France, 1898; (classification of alpha and beta particle radiation) Pierre Curie, France, 1900; (gamma radiation) Paul-Ulrich Villard, France, 1900; (carbon dating) Willard F. Libby et al., U.S., 1955

Relativity: (special and general theories of) Albert Einstein, Switzerland, Germany, U.S., 1905–53

Roller bearing: (wooden for cartwheel) Germany or France, c.100 B.C.

Safety match: *See* Match

Solar system, universe: (sun-centered universe) Nicolaus Copernicus, Warsaw, 1543; (establishment of planetary orbits as elliptical) Johannes Kepler, Germany, 1609; (infinity of universe) Giordano Bruno, Italian monk, 1584

Spectrum: (heterogeneity of light) Sir Isaac Newton, England, 1665–66

Spermatozoa: Anton van Leeuwenhoek, The Netherlands, 1683

Spinning: (spinning wheel) India, introduced to Europe in Middle Ages; (Saxony wheel, continuous spinning of wool or cotton yarn) England, c.1500–1600; (spinning jenny) James Hargreaves, England, 1764; (spinning frame) Sir Richard Arkwright, England, 1769; (spinning mule, completed mechanization of spinning, permitting production of yarn to keep up with demands of modern looms) Samuel Crompton, England, 1779

Sulfa drugs: (parent compound, para-aminobenzenesulfanomide) Paul Gelmo, Austria, 1908; (antibacterial activity) Gerhard Domagk, Germany, 1935

Syphilis, test for: *See* Wassermann test

Thermometer: (open-column) Galileo Galilei, c.1593; (clinical) Santorio Santorio, Padua, c.1615; (mercury, also Fahrenheit scale) Gabriel D. Fahrenheit, Germany, 1714; (centigrade scale) Anders Celsius, Sweden, 1742; (absolute-temperature, or Kelvin, scale) William Thompson, Lord Kelvin, England, 1848

Toilet, flush: Product of Minoan civilization, Crete, c.2000 B.C. Alleged invention by "Thomas Crapper" is untrue.

Tractor: Benjamin Holt, U.S., 1900

Transformer, electric: William Stanley, U.S., 1885

Uncertainty principle: (that position and velocity of an object cannot both be measured exactly, at the same time) Werner Heisenberg, Germany, 1927

Vaccination: Edward Jenner, England, 1796

Van Allen (radiation) Belt: (around the earth) James Van Allen, U.S., 1958

Vitamins: (hypothesis of disease deficiency) Sir F. G. Hopkins, Casimir Funk, England, 1912; (vitamin A) Elmer V. McCollum, M. Davis, U.S., 1912–14; (vitamin B) Elmer V. McCollum, U.S., 1915–16; (thiamin, B_1) Casimir Funk, England, 1912; (riboflavin, B_2) D. T. Smith, E. G. Hendrick, U.S., 1926; (niacin) Conrad Elvehjem, U.S., 1937; (B_6) Paul Gyorgy, U.S., 1934; (vitamin C) C. A. Hoist, T. Froelich, Norway, 1912; (vitamin D) Elmer V. McCollum, U.S., 1922; (folic acid) Lucy Wills, England, 1933

Wassermann test: (for syphilis) August von Wassermann, Germany, 1906

Weaving, cloth: *See* Loom

Wheel: (cart, solid wood) Mesopotamia, c.3800–3600 B.C.

Windmill: Persia, c.600

X-ray: *See* Radioactivity

Zero: India, c.600; (absolute zero, cessation of all molecular energy) William

ENVIRONMENT

1991 Environmental Quality Index

Source: Copyright 1991 by the National Wildlife Federation.

Reprinted from the February-March issue of *National Wildlife Magazine.*

National Wildlife's annual Environmental Quality Index is a subjective analysis of the state of the nation's natural resources. The information included in each section is based on personal interviews, news reports, and the most current scientific studies. The judgments on resource trends represent the collective thinking of the editors and the National Wildlife Federation staff, based on consultation with government experts, private specialists, and academic researchers.

Wildlife: Worse. Despite administration promises, wetlands and endangered species protection efforts came under repeated attack. Last June [1990] the U.S. Fish and Wildlife Service officially listed the northern spotted owl as a threatened species. On June 26 the White House rejected plans developed by an interagency committee for protecting the owl's habitat and rewrote the plan purportedly to better balance economic and biological considerations. Then came a recommendation that the law [Endangered Species Act] be changed to make economic disruption grounds for withholding protection for declining species. Meanwhile biologists were discussing a new report by the World Resources Institute predicting that if trends continue, one-fourth of all plant and animal species existing in the mid-1980s would be extinct in 25 years.

Air: Worse. While urban pollution problems mounts, U.S. lawmakers finally pass a new version of the Clean Air Act. The news from New York City was ominous: After nearly two decades of struggling toward compliance with clean-air standards, new figures showed the city was losing ground on all fronts. New York's failure was no surprise to Connecticut. Officials there insisted that, because of the pollution from New York City, they could not meet clean-air standards even if they stopped all manufacturing and traffic in their state. The implacable enemy is the automobile. Although the nation's fleet is cleaner and more efficient that it was in 1970, it is so much larger that it is still degrading air quality. The Bush Administration got a Clean Air Bill through Congress that contained the nation's first regulations of emissions linked to acid rain and the first tightening in 20 years of standards for tailpipe emissions.

Water: Worse. As U.S. officials turn their attentions to Great Lakes pollution, drinking water threats surface elsewhere. EPA Administrator William Reilly announced his agency's next top priority: cleaning up the Great Lakes. According to a Conservation Fund study, the entire Great Lakes basin "is deteriorating from the impacts of toxic chemicals and other stresses." Among the stresses, an average of 425 oil spills and 75 chemical spills every month. Conservationists are particularly concerned about the long-term effects of such potent toxics as PCBs, DDT, and dioxin. Meanwhile the EPA was under fire for lack of effort in another realm: drinking water. The National Wildlife Federation sued the EPA for relaxing rules that require states to comply with the Safe Drinking Water Act. Throughout much of the western half of the country, authorities were more concerned about the health and quantity of their diminishing underground water supplies. Aquifers in many areas are not only being polluted but also are being pumped faster than they can recharge naturally.

Forests: Worse. Controversy centers on ancient forests, but federal timber harvest reductions signal overall policy shifts. The heated controversy over the northern spotted owl and the Endangered Species Act tended to obscure what the fight was really over: the rapidly dwindling, irreplaceable ancient forest ecosystem of the Northwest. Since there are no laws protecting endangered forests, conservationists have had to rely on those protecting the habitat of endangered species, such as the spotted owl. A National Research Council study took the Forest Service to task for concentrating its research on tree production when "The number one job today is creating a livable environment." The Forest Service response: it unveiled a new master plan calling for a substantial reduction of logging in national forests from the current average annual cut of 12.2 billion board feet to 10.8 billion board feet by 1995. The plan would halve clear-cutting in national forests, and would put greater emphasis on wildlife protection and recreation. Though the focus of much controversy about forestry issues, national forests are the source of only about 20 percent of the annual timber harvest; private woods provide about half the harvest and company-owned land the rest. In the private sector, timber companies face a squeeze far more formidable than that of wildlife habitat: land developers.

Energy: Worse. A new Middle East crisis creates a predictable response but not changes in U.S. energy policy. When the crisis came [Iraq's invasion of Kuwait] the most significant proposal in energy policy to deal with the changed world was made by Interior Secretary Lujan. "There is no reason why we should not explore in the Arctic National Wildlife Refuge." The loss of oil from Iraq and Kuwait made worse a situation that was already becoming gloomy. During a year that saw demands for petroleum rising implacably—by 800,000 barrels per day among Pacific Rim countries alone—production in this country and the Soviet Union was declining just as irreversibly. Environmentalists pointed out that the solution to the oil dilemma is not to increase drilling but rather to use supplies more efficiently. Better energy conservation, they said, is the county's greatest untapped resource. One area where vast amounts of oil could be saved is in car fuel efficiency. But the administration actively opposed a bill that would require automobiles to increase gas mileage of all cars sold in this country by 40 percent by the year 2001. Two months before the Iraqi surprise, President Bush declared a moratorium until the turn of the century on offshore oil and gas drilling near the West Coast, Florida and the Georges Bank area of the North Atlantic.

Soil: Same. Topsoil erosion is down thanks to recent programs and many farmers are rethinking use of chemicals. After years of reports about consistent high losses to erosion, there was good news in 1990. According to the Worldwatch Institute in Washington, D.C., America's farmers have reduced soil erosion by more than one-third since 1985, largely because of new programs instituted by the federal Farm Bill passed that year. By last year [1990] the rate of soil loss had been reduced to about one billion tons annually. That remains a staggering loss and there are worries about the future of the program. American farmers are not only trying harder to keep their soil, but they are increasingly reluctant to douse it with chemicals. One half of the farmers in a recent poll expressed concern about the dangers of using too many agricultural chemicals on their land. The revised Farm Bill that eventually won approval did break new ground in environmental protection, particularly in regard to pesticide control and forest and wetland protection programs.

Quality of Life: Worse. The quality of life that Americans experienced in 1990 depended to a great extent on where they lived, and what they knew. Residents of Chattanooga, Tenn., for example, had reason to feel pretty good. A citizens' movement there that spans two decades has helped turn one of the nation's worst environments into one of the best. In northeast Detroit, on the other hand, the picture was not so rosy. Residents there suffered under a constant drizzle of oily soot coming from a steel plant operating in what Wayne County officials described as "gross violation" of pollution standards. Living in New England, according to one study of relative environmental health, was in general more wholesome than living in the South.

Endangered Species

The number of threatened animal taxa identified by International Union for Conservation of Nature and Natural Resources (IUCN) is just over 5,000, comprised of 698 mammals, 1,047 birds, 191 reptiles, 63 amphibians, 762 fishes, and 2,250 invertebrates. However, except for birds, for which International Council for Bird Preservation (ICBP)/IUCN have now attempted a global review, these numbers represent only those taxa whose threatened status is known to IUCN; many, many more taxa, particularly invertebrates, are threatened, and becoming extinct every year undescribed and unknown to the scientific and conservation communities. Thus the number of threatened taxa identified by IUCN represents only the visible fraction of a much greater problem.

The following list comprises some of the more familiar species that are endangered. Due to space limitations, it does not include all mammals, birds, reptiles, amphibians, and fish on the 1990 IUCN Red List nor does it include any clams, crustaceans, snails, insects, or plants.

Some Endangered and Threatened Species of the World[1]

Common Name	Scientific Name	Listed range
MAMMALS		
Bear, Baluchistan	Selenarctos thibetanus gedrosianus	Iran, Pakistan
Bear, Polar[2]	Ursus maritimus	Arctic
Cat, Pardel lynx	Felis pardina	Portugal, Spain
Cat, little spotted[2]	Felis tigrina	Central & South America
Cheetah[2]	Acinonyx jubatus	Africa, Middle East Iran, [India]
Chimpanzee, West African	Pan troglodytes verus	West Africa
Cougar, Florida	Felis concolor coryi	U.S.
Deer, Key[4]	Odocoileus virginiaus clavium	U.S.
Deer, marsh[2]	Blastocerus dichotomus	Central America
Elephant, Indian	Elephas maximus	Asia
Gazelle, Clark's (Dibatag)[2]	Ammodorcas clarkei	Ethiopia, Somalia
Gazelle, slender-horned	Gazella leptoceros	Sahara/Sahel
Gorilla, mountain	Gorilla gorilla beringei	Rwanda, Uganda, Zaire
Ibex, Walia	Capra walie	Ethiopia
Jaguar[2]	Panthera onca	U.S., Central & South America
Leopard[3]	Panthera pardus	Africa, Middle East, Asia
Leopard, snow	Panthera uncia	Asia
Lion, Asiatic	Panthera leo persica	Gujarat (India)
Mandrill[2]	Mandrillus sphinx	Cameroon, Congo, Eq. Guinea, Gabon
Monkey, long-haired spider[2]	Ateles belzebuth	South America
Ocelot[2]	Felis pardalis	U.S., Central & South America
Prairie dog, Utah[2]	Cynomys parvidens	U.S.
Pronghorn, Sonoran	Antilocapra americana sonoriensis	Mexico, U.S.

Common Name	Scientific Name	Listed range
Rat, Morro Bay kangaroo	Dipodomys heermanni morroensis	California
Rhinoceros, great Indian	Rhinoceros unicornis	India, Nepal
Sloth, maned	Bradypus torquatus	Brazil
Tiger	Panthera tigris	Asia
Wallaby, bridled nailtail	Onychogalea fraenata	Australia
Whale, humpback[2]	Megaptera novaeangliae	All oceans
Wolf, gray[2]	Canis lupus	North America, Middle East, Eurasia
Wolf, red	Canis rufus	U.S.
Zebra, Cape Mountain	Equus zebra zebra	South Africa
BIRDS		
Albatross, short-tailed[4]	Diomedea albatrus	Japan
Condor, California	Gymnogyps californianus	U.S.
Crane, whooping	Grus americana	Canada, U.S.
Crow, Hawaiian	Corvus tropicus	Hawaiian Islands
Kestrel, Mauritius	Falco punctatus	Mauritius
Parrot, paradise	Psephotus pulcherrimus	Australia
Stork, oriental white[4]	Ciconia boyciana	China, Japan, South Korea, U.S.S.R.
Woodpecker, ivory-billed	Campephilus principalis	Cuba, U.S.
REPTILES		
Crocodile, American	Crocodylus acutus	Caribbean, Central America, U.S.
Iguana, Anegada ground	Cyclura pinguis	British Virgin Is.
Python, Indian[2]	Python molurus	South & Southeast Asia
Snake, Atlantic saltmarsh[4]	Nerodia fasciata taeniata	U.S.
AMPHIBIANS		
Frog, Israel painted[5]	Discoglossus nigriventer	Israel
Toad, Mount Nimba viviparous[2]	Nectophrynoides occidentalis	Guinea, Cote d'Ivoire
FISH		
Catfish, giant[2]	Pangasianodon gigas	Mekong Basin
Trout, cutthroat[2]	Salmo clarki (subspecies)	U.S.

1. Unless otherwise indicated the species is rated endangered. 2. Vulnerable. 3. Threatened. 4. Rare. 5. Extinct? *[Former distribution]* Source: *1990 IUCN Red List of Threatened Animals,* published by the International Union for Conservation of Nature and Natural Resources/United Nations Environment Programme, Avenue du Mont-Blanc, CH-1196 Gland, Switzerland.

Zoological Gardens

North America abounds in zoos from Canada to Mexico. The Metro Toronto Zoo, opened in 1974, is one of the largest in the world. Its six pavilions simulate the animals' natural habitats. So does the Calgary Zoo which also has a children's zoo. Mexico City's Chapultepec Park includes a large zoo featuring one of the few pairs of pandas outside of Red China, and a children's zoo.

The first zoological garden in the United States was established in Philadelphia in 1874. Since that time nearly every large city in the country has acquired a zoo. Among the largest are San Diego's on the West Coast; Chicago's Brookfield Zoo and those of St. Louis and Kansas City in the Middle West; New Orleans' Audubon Park and Zoological Garden in the South; and in the East the New York Zoological Society's park in the Bronx. The National Zoological Park in Washington, D.C., in a beautiful setting of hills, woods, and streams, was established in 1890 by an act of Congress. The major U.S. zoos now have created large naturalhabitat areas for their collections.

In Europe, zoological gardens have long been popular public institutions. The modern concept of zoo keeping may be dated from 1752 with the founding of the Imperial Menagerie at the Schönbrunn Palace in Vienna. It was opened to the public in 1765 and is still in operation. In 1793 the zoological collection of the Jardin des Plantes was established in Paris in the Bois de Boulogne. At Antwerp the Royal Zoological Society founded a large menagerie in 1843. Now its aviary is noted for the principle of lighted and darkened spaces for confining the birds. Germany's famous Tiergarten zoo, in West Berlin, was founded in 1841 and officially opened in 1844. East Berlin has founded its own zoo.

In the British Isles, the Zoological Society of London established its collection in Regent's Park in 1828. It was also responsible for the establishment of the prototype of the openrange zoo, Whipsnade Park, in 1932. Edinburgh's zoo is famous for its collection of penguins, the largest colony in captivity.

U.S. Zoos and Aquariums

Source: The facilities listed are members of, and accredited by, the American Association of Zoological Parks and Aquariums to ensure that they are maintaining professional standards. It also accredits facilities outside of the United States.

Abilene Zoological Gardens, Texas
Akron Zoological Park, Ohio
Alexandria Zoological Park, La.
Arizona-Sonora Desert Museum, Tucson
Audubon Park and Zoological Garden, New Orleans
John Ball Zoological Gardens, Grand Rapids, Mich.
Baltimore Zoo, Md.
Beardsley Zoological Gardens, Bridgeport, Conn.
Belle Isle Zoo and Aquarium, Detroit
Bergen County Zoological Park, Paramus, N.J.
Binder Park Zoo, Battle Creek, Mich.
Birmingham Zoo, Ala.
Blank Park Zoo of Des Moines, Iowa
Brandywine Zoo, Wilmington, Del.
Brookgreen Gardens, Murrells Inlet, S.C.
Buffalo Zoological Gardens, N.Y.
Burnet Park Zoo, Syracuse, N.Y.
Busch Gardens, Tampa, Fla.
Caldwell Zoo, Tyler, Texas
Cape May County Park Zoo, Cape May Court House, N.J.
Central Florida Zoological Park, Lake Monroe, Fla.
Central Park Zoo, New York, N.Y.
Central Texas Zoo, Waco, Texas
Chaffee Zoological Gardens of Fresno, Calif.
Cheyenne Mountain Zoological Park, Colorado Springs
Chicago Zoological Park, Brookfield, Ill.
Cincinnati Zoo and Botanical Garden, Ohio
Cleveland Metroparks Zoological Park, Ohio
Columbus Zoological Gardens, Ohio
Dallas Aquarium, Texas
Dallas Zoo, Texas
Denver Zoological Gardens, Colo.
Detroit Zoological Park, Mich.
Dickerson Park Zoo, Springfield, Mo.
Discovery Island Zoological Park, Lake Buena Vista, Fla.
Dreher Park Zoo, West Palm Beach, Fla.
El Paso Zoo, Texas
Emporia Zoo, Kan.
Erie Zoological Gardens, Pa.
Folsom Children's Zoo & Botanical Gardens, Lincoln, Neb.
Fort Wayne Children's Zoo, Ind.
Fort Worth Zoological Park, Texas
Fossil Rim Wildlife Center, Glen Rose, Texas
Franklin Park Zoo, Boston
Glen Oak Zoo, Peoria, Ill.
Great Plains Zoo & Musem, Sioux Falls, S.D.
Greater Baton Rouge Zoo, La.
Greenville Zoo, S.C.
Hogle Zoological Gardens, Salt Lake City, Utah
Honolulu Zoo, Hawaii
Houston Zoological Gardens, Texas
Indianapolis Zoo, Ind.
International Crane Foundation, Baraboo, Wis.
Jackson Zoological Park, Miss.
Jacksonville Zoological Park, Fla.
Kansas City Zoological Gardens, Mo.
Knoxville Zoological Gardens, Tenn.
Lake Superior Zoological Gardens, Duluth, Minn.
Lincoln Park Zoological Gardens, Chicago
Little Rock Zoological Gardens, Ark.
Living Desert, The, Palm Desert, Calif.
Los Angeles Zoo, Calif.

Louisville Zoological Garden, Ky.
Lowry Park Zoological Garden, Tampa, Fla.
Marine World Africa USA, Vallejo, Calif.
Memphis Zoological Garden and Aquarium, Tenn.
Mesker Park Zoo, Evansville, Ind.
Metro Washington Park Zoo, Portland, Ore.
Miami Metrozoo, Fla.
Micke Grove Zoo, Lodi, Calif.
Miller Park Zoo, Bloomington, Ill.
Milwaukee County Zoological Gardens, Wis.
Minnesota Zoological Garden, Apple Valley, Minn.
Monkey Jungle, Miami, Fla.
Monterey Bay Aquarium, Calif.
Montgomery Zoo, Ala.
Mystic Marinelife Aquarium, Mystic, Conn.
National Aquarium in Baltimore, Md.
National Zoological Park, Washington, D.C.
New England Aquarium, Boston
New York Aquarium, Brooklyn
New York Zoological Park, Bronx
North Carolina Aquarium at Fort Fisher, Kure Beach
North Carolina Aquarium at Pine Knoll Shores, Atlantic Beach
North Carolina Aquarium on Roanoke Island, Manteo
North Carolina Zoological Park, Asheboro, N.C.
Northwest Trek Wildlife Park, Eatonville, Wash.
Oakland Zoo, Calif.
Oglebay's Good Children's Zoo, Wheeling, W.Va.
Oklahoma City Zoological Park, Okla.
Omaha's Henry Doorly Zoo, Neb.
Charles Paddock Zoo, Atascadero, Calif.
Parrot Jungle and Gardens, Miami, Fla.
Clyde Peeling's Reptiland Ltd., Allenwood, Pa.
Philadelphia Zoological Garden, Pa.
Phoenix Zoo, The Ariz.
Pittsburgh Aviary, Pa.
Pittsburgh Zoo, Pa.
Point Defiance Zoo and Aquarium, Tacoma, Wash.
Gladys Porter Zoo, Brownsville, Texas
Potawatomi Zoo, South Bend, Ind.
Potter Park Zoological Gardens, Lansing, Mich.
Racine Zoological Gardens, Wis.
Reid Park Zoo, Tucson, Ariz.
Lee Richardson Zoo, Garden City, Kan.
Rio Grande Zoological Park, Albuquerque, N.M.
Riverbanks Zoological Park, Columbia, S.C.
Riverside Zoo, Scottsbluff, Neb.
Henson Robinson Zoo, Springfield, Ill.
Roosevelt Zoo, Minot, N.D.
Ross Park Zoo, Binghamton, N.Y.
Sacramento Zoo, Calif.
St. Augustine Alligator Farm, Fla.
St. Louis Zoological Park, Mo.
St. Paul's Como Zoo, Minn.
Salisbury Zoological Park, Md.
San Antonio Zoological Gardens and Aquarium, Texas
San Diego Wild Animal Park, Calif.
San Diego Zoo, Calif.
San Francisco Zoological Gardens, Calif.
Santa Ana Zoo, Calif.
Santa Barbara Zoological Gardens, Calif.
Sante Fe Teaching Zoo, Gainesville, Fla.
Sea Life Park, Waimanalo, Hawaii

Sea World of California, San Diego
Sea World of Florida, Orlando
Sea World of Ohio, Aurora
Sea World of Texas, San Antonio
The Seattle Aquarium, Wash.
Sedgwick County Zoo and Botanical Garden, Wichita, Kan.
Seneca Park Zoo, Rochester, N.Y.
John G. Shedd Aquarium, Chicago
Staten Island Zoo, N.Y.
Sunset Zoological Park, Manhattan, Kan.
The Texas Zoo, Victoria, Texas
Toledo Zoological Gardens, Ohio
Topeka Zoological Park, Kan.
Tracy Aviary, Salt Lake City, Utah
Trevor Zoo, Millbrook, N.Y.

Ellen Trout Zoo, Lufkin, Texas
Tulsa Zoological Park, Okla.
Utica Zoo, N.Y.
Henry Vilas Zoo, Madison, Wis.
Virginia Zoological Park, Norfolk, Va.
Waikiki Aquarium, Hawaii
Wild Animal Habitat, Kings Island, Ohio
Wildlife Safari, Winston, Ore.
Wildlife World Zoo, Litchfield Park, Ariz.
Roger Williams Park Zoo, Providence, R.I.
Woodland Park Zoological Gardens, Seattle
The ZOO, Gulf Breeze, Fla.
Zoo Atlanta, Ga.
ZOOAMERICA North American Wildlife Park, Hershey, Pa.

Gestation, Incubation, and Longevity of Certain Animals

Animal	Gestation or incubation, in days & (average)	Longevity, in years & record exceptions)	Animal	Gestation or incubation, in days & (average)	Longeveity, in years & record exceptions)
Ass	365	18–20 (63)	Horse	329–345 (336)	20–25 (50+)
Bear	180–240[1]	15–30 (47)	Kangaroo	32–39[1]	4–6 (23)
Cat	52–69 (63)	10–12 (26+)	Lion	105–113 (108)	10 (29)
Chicken	22	7–8 (14)	Man	253–303	(2)
Cow	c. 280	9–12 (39)	Monkey	139–270[1]	12–15[1](29)
Deer	197–300[1]	10–15 (26)	Mouse	19–31[1]	1–3 (4)
Dog	53–71 (63)	10–12 (24)	Parakeet (Budgerigar)	17–20 (18)	8 (12+)
Duck	21–35[1](28)	10 (15)	Pig	101–130 (115)	10 (22)
Elephant	510–730 (624)[1]	30–40 (71)	Pigeon	11–19	10–12 (39)
Fox	51–63[1]	8–10 (14)	Rabbit	30–35 (31)	6–8 (15)
Goat	136–160 (151)	12 (17)	Rat	21	3 (5)
Groundhog	31–32	4–9	Sheep	144–152 (151)[1]	12 (16)
Guinea pig	58–75 (68)	3 (6)	Squirrel	44	8–9 (15)
Hamster, golden	15–17	2 (8)	Whale	365–547[1]	
Hippopotamus	220–255 (240)	30 (49+)	Wolf	60–63	10–12 (16)

1. Depending on kind. 2. For life expectancy charts, *see* Index. *Source:* James Doherty, Curator of Mammals, N.Y. Zoological Society.

Speed of Animals

Most of the following measurements are for maximum speeds over approximate quarter–mile distances. Exceptions—which are included to give a wide range of animals—are the lion and elephant, whose speeds were clocked in the act of charging; the whippet, which was timed over a 200–yard course; the cheetah over a 100–yard distance; man for a 15–yard segment of a 100–yard run; and the black mamba, six–lined race runner, spider, giant tortoise, three–toed sloth, and garden snail, which were measured over various small distances.

Animal	Speed mph	Animal	Speed mph	Animal	Speed mph
Cheetah	70	Mongolian wild ass	40	Man	27.89
Pronghorn antelope	61	Greyhound	39.35	Elephant	25
Wildebeest	50	Whippet	35.5	Black mamba snake	20
Lion	50	Rabbit (domestic)	35	Six–lined race runner	18
Thomson's gazelle	50	Mule deer	35	Squirrel	12
Quarter horse	47.5	Jackal	35	Pig (domestic)	11
Elk	45	Reindeer	32	Chicken	9
Cape hunting dog	45	Giraffe	32	Spider (Tegenearia atrica)	1.17
Coyote	43	White–tailed deer	30	Giant Tortoise	0.17
Gray fox	42	Wart hog	30	Three–toed sloth	0.15
Hyena	40	Grizzly bear	30	Garden snail	0.03
Zebra	40	Cat (domestic)	30		

Source: Natural History Magazine, March 1974, copyright 1974. The American Museum of Natural History; and James Doherty, Curator of Mammals, N.Y. Zoological Society.

Animal Group Terminology

Source: James Doherty, Curator of Mammals, N.Y. Zoological Society, and Information Please data.

ants: colony
bears: sleuth, sloth
bees: grist, hive, swarm
birds: flight, volery
cattle: drove
cats: clutter, clowder
chicks: brood, clutch
clams: bed
cranes: sedge, seige
crows: murder
doves: dule
ducks: brace, team
elephants: herd
elks: gang
finches: charm
fish: school, shoal, draught
foxes: leash, skulk
geese: flock, gaggle, skein
gnats: cloud, horde
goats: trip

gorillas: band
hares: down, husk
hawks: cast
hens: brood
hogs: drift
horses: pair, team
hounds: cry, mute, pack
kangaroos: troop
kittens: kindle, litter
larks: exaltation
lions: pride
locusts: plague
magpies: tidings
mules: span
nightingales: watch
oxen: yoke
oysters: bed
parrots: company
partridges: covey

peacocks: muster, ostentation
pheasants: nest, bouquet
pigs: litter
ponies: string
quail: bevy, covey
rabbits: nest
seals: pod
sheep: drove, flock
sparrows: host
storks: mustering
swans: bevy, wedge
swine: sounder
toads: knot
turkeys: rafter
turtles: bale
vipers: nest
whales: gam, pod
wolves: pack, route
woodcocks: fall

Animal Names: Male, Female, and Young

Animal	Male	Female	Young	Animal	Male	Female	Young	Animal	Male	Female	Young
Ass	Jack	Jenny	Foal	Duck	Drake	Duck	Duckling	Sheep	Ram	Ewe	Lamb
Bear	Boar	Sow	Cub	Elephant	Bull	Cow	Calf	Swan	Cob	Pen	Cygnet
Cat	Tom	Queen	Kitten	Fox	Dog	Vixen	Cub	Swine	Boar	Sow	Piglet
Cattle	Bull	Cow	Calf	Goose	Gander	Goose	Gosling	Tiger	Tiger	Tigress	Cub
Chicken	Rooster	Hen	Chick	Horse	Stallion	Mare	Foal	Whale	Bull	Cow	Calf
Deer	Buck	Doe	Fawn	Lion	Lion	Lioness	Cub	Wolf	Dog	Bitch	Pup
Dog	Dog	Bitch	Pup	Rabbit	Buck	Doe	Bunny				

Source: James Doherty, Curator of Mammals, N.Y. Zoological Society.

Cleaner Motor Vehicle Fuels

By Richard D. Wilson, Director of EPA's Office of Mobile Sources

Compared to cleaning up the emissions from cars, less has been done on cleaning up the fuels they use. It is not difficult to understand how the quality of fuel burned in an engine affects its emissions. The most environmentally successful fuel–related program, to date, has been the virtual elimination of lead in gasoline. Another Environmental Protection Agency (EPA) program, which took effect all across the country in the summer of 1989, reduced the volatility of gasoline. Reducing volatility means that less fumes evaporate into the atmosphere on hot–weather days which, in turn, means significantly reduced smog levels. The 1990 Clean Air Act amendments require that additional steps be taken by fuel producers to improve fuel quality.

During summer months, beginning in 1992, all gasoline in the country will evaporate less rapidly, as required by a second step in the volatility–reduction program.

Beginning in the winter of 1992–1993, the amendments mandate the addition of oxygen to all gasoline sold during the winter months in any city with carbon monoxide problems. Adding oxygen, in the form of alcohols or ethers, greatly reduces carbon monoxide emissions from all cars, new and old.

Oil refiners will be required to reduce the amount of sulfur in diesel fuel as of October 1, 1993.

Beginning in 1995, all gasoline sold year–round in the nine cities with the worst air pollution must be reformulated to reduce smog–forming and toxic pollutants. For example, the amount of benzene, a component of gasoline known to cause cancer, will be lowered. Other cities may choose to have this "clean" gasoline sold within their boundaries as well.

The law establishes a California Pilot Program to encourage and demonstrate the production of even cleaner fuels and vehicles. Beginning in 1996, auto companies must sell 150,000 cars in California that have emission levels one–half that allowed for other new cars. The number of cars increases to 300,000 a year in 1999; in 2001 emission levels are reduced by half again.

As early as 1988, a percentage of new vehicles purchased in centrally fueled fleets in 22 polluted cities must meet tailpipe standards that are about one-third of those in place for general passenger cars. This program is intended to stimulate development of new, low-polluting fuel/vehicle combinations. □

This article is excerpted from *EPA Journal*, January-February 1991, "Motor Vehicles and Fuels: The Strategy" by Richard D. Wilson.

The National Park System

Source: Department of the Interior, National Park Service.

The National Park System of the United States is administered by the National Park Service, a bureau of the Department of the Interior. Started with the establishment of Yellowstone National Park in 1872, the system includes not only the most extraordinary and spectacular scenic exhibits in the United States but also a large number of sites distinguished either for their historic or prehistoric importance or scientific interest, or for their superior recreational assets. The number and extent of the various types of areas that make up the system follow.

Type of area	Number	Total acreage[1]	Type of area	Number	Total acreage[1]
International Historic Site	1	35.39	National Parkways	4	168,619.50
National Battlefields	11	12,843.31	National Preserves	13	22,152,181.34
National Battlefield Parks	3	5,725.30	National Recreation Areas	18	3,697,315.38
National Battlefield Site	1	1.00	National Reserve	1	14,407.19
National Historic Sites	69	18,551.19	National Rivers	5	360,113.07
National Historical Parks	31	150,616.70	National Scenic Trails	3	172,376.55
National Lakeshores	4	227,306.73	National Seashores	10	592,508.65
National Memorials	26	7,976.54	National Wild and Scenic Rivers	9	212,612.45
National Military Parks	9	35,873.21	Parks (other)	11	38,721.26
National Monuments	78	4,848,652.27	**Total**	**357**	**80,115,984.18**
National Parks	50	47,436,577.18			

1. Acreages as of December 30, 1990.

National Parks

Name, location, and year authorized	Acreage	Outstanding characteristics
Acadia (Maine), 1919	41,488.00	Rugged seashore on Mt. Desert Island and adjacent mainland
Arches (Utah), 1971	73,378.98	Unusual stone arches, windows, pedestals caused by erosion
Badlands (S.D.), 1978	242,756.00	Arid land of fossils, prairie, bison, deer, bighorn, antelope
Big Bend (Tex.), 1935	801,163.00	Mountains and desert bordering the Rio Grande
Biscayne (Fla.), 1980	173,467.00	Aquatic, coral reef park south of Miami was a national monument, 1968–80
Bryce Canyon (Utah), 1924	35,835.08	Area of grotesque eroded rocks brilliantly colored
Canyonlands (Utah), 1964	337,570.43	Colorful wilderness with impressive red-rock canyons, spires, arches
Capitol Reef (Utah), 1971	241,904.26	Highly colored sedimentary rock formations in high, narrow gorges
Carlsbad Caverns (N.M.), 1930	46,775.00	The world's largest known caves
Channel Islands (Calif.) 1980	249,353.77	Area is rich in marine mammals, sea birds, endangered species and archeology
Crater Lake (Ore.), 1902	183,224.05	Deep blue lake in heart of inactive volcano
Denali (Alaska), 1917	4,716,726.00	Mt. McKinley National Park was renamed and enlarged by Act of Dec. 2, 1980. Contains Mt. McKinley, N. America's highest mountain (20,320 ft)
Everglades (Fla.), 1934	1,506,499.00	Subtropical area with abundant bird and animal life
Gates of the Arctic (Alaska), 1980	7,523,888.00	Diverse north central wilderness contains part of Brooks Range
Glacier (Mont.), 1910	1,013,572.42	Rocky Mountain scenery with many glaciers and lakes
Glacier Bay (Alaska), 1980	3,225,284.00	Park was a national monument (1925–1980) popular for wildlife, whale-watching, glacier-calving, and scenery
Grand Canyon (Ariz.), 1919	1,218,375.24	Mile-deep gorge, 4 to 18 miles wide, 217 miles long
Grand Teton (Wyo.), 1929	309,993.93	Picturesque range of high mountain peaks
Great Basin (Nev.), 1986	77,100.00	Exceptional scenic, biologic, and geologic attractions
Great Smoky Mts. (N.C.-Tenn) 1926	520,269.44	Highest mountain range east of Black Hills; luxuriant plant life
Guadalupe Mountains (Tex.), 1966	86,416.01	Contains highest point in Texas: Guadalupe Peak (8,751 ft)
Haleakala (Hawaii), 1960	28,655.25	World-famous 10,023-ft. Haleakala volcano (dormant)
Hawaii Volcanoes (Hawaii), 1916	229,177.03	Spectacular volcanic area; luxuriant vegetation at lower levels
Hot Springs (Ark.), 1921	5,839.24	47 mineral hot springs said to have therapeutic value
Isle Royale (Mich.), 1931	571.790.11	Largest wilderness island in Lake Superior; moose, wolves, lakes
Katmai (Alaska), 1980	3,716,000.00	Expansion may assure brown bear's preservation. Park was national monument 1918–80; is known for fishing, 1912 eruption, bears

Name, location, and year authorized	Acreage	Outstanding characteristics
Kenai Fjords (Alaska), 1980	669,541.00	Mountain goats, marine mammals, birdlife are features at this seacoast park near Seward
Kings Canyon (Calif.), 1940	461,901.20	Huge canyons; high mountains; giant sequoias
Kobuk Valley (Alaska), 1980	1,750,421.00	Native culture and anthropology center around the broad Kobuk River in northwest Alaska
Lake Clark (Alaska), 1980	2,636,839.00	Park provides scenic and wilderness recreation across Cook Inlet from Anchorage
Lassen Volcanic (Calif.), 1916	106,372.36	Exhibits of impressive volcanic phenomena
Mammoth Cave (Ky.), 1926	52,419.00	Vast limestone labyrinth with underground river
Mesa Verde (Colo.), 1906	52,122.00	Best-preserved prehistoric cliff dwellings in United States
Mount Rainier (Wash.), 1899	235,612.00	Single-peak glacial system; dense forests, flowered meadows
North Cascades (Wash.), 1968	504,780.94	Roadless Alpine landscape; jagged peaks; mountain lakes; glaciers
Olympic (Wash.), 1938	922,654.00	Finest Pacific Northwest rain forest; scenic mountain park
Petrified Forest (Ariz.), 1962	93,532.57	Extensive natural exhibit of petrified wood
Redwood (Calif.), 1968	110,132.40	Coastal redwood forests; contains world's tallest known tree (369.2 ft)
Rocky Mountain (Colo.), 1915	265,198.00	Section of the Rocky Mountains; 107 named peaks over 10,000 ft
Samoa (American Samoa)	9,000.00	Samoa National Park, American Samoa: two rain forest preserves and a coral reef on the island of Ofu are home to unique tropical animals. The park also includes several thousand acres on the islands of Tutuila and Ta'u.
Sequoia (Calif.), 1890	402,482.38	Giant sequoias; magnificent High Sierra scenery, including Mt. Whitney
Shenandoah (Va.), 1926	195,039.00	Tree-covered mountains; scenic Skyline Drive
Theodore Roosevelt (N.D.), 1978	70,447.00	Scenic valley of Little Missouri River; T.R. Ranch; Wildlife
Virgin Islands (U.S. V.I.), 1956	14,688.87	Beaches; lush hills; prehistoric Carib Indian relics
Voyageurs (Minn.), 1971	218,035.93	Wildlife, canoeing, fishing, and hiking
Wind Cave (S.D.), 1903	28,295.00	Limestone caverns in Black Hills; buffalo herd
Wrangell-St. Elias (Alaska), 1980	8,331,604.00	Largest Park System area has abundant wildlife, second highest peak in U.S. (Mt. St. Elias); adjoins Canadian park
Yellowstone (Wyo.-Mont.-Idaho), 1872	2,219,790.71	World's greatest geyser area; abundant falls, wildlife, and canyons
Yosemite (Calif.), 1890	761,170.20	Mountains; inspiring gorges and waterfalls; giant sequoias
Zion (Utah), 1919	146,597.64	Multicolored gorge in heart of southern Utah desert

NATIONAL HISTORICAL PARKS

Name and location	Total acreage
Appomattox Court House (Va.)	1,325.08
Boston (Mass.)	41.03
Chaco Culture (N.M.)	33,974.29
Chesapeake and Ohio Canal (Md.-W.Va.-D.C.)	20,781.00
Colonial (Va.)	9,327.37
Cumberland Gap (Ky.-Tenn.-Va.)	20,274.42
George Rogers Clark (Ind.)	26.17
Harpers Ferry (W.Va.-Md.)	2,238.60
Independence (Pa.)	44.85
Jean Lafitte (La.)	20,020.00
Kalaupapa (Hawaii)	10,778.88
Klondike Goldrush (Alaska, Wash.)	13,191.35
Kaloko-Honokohau (Hawaii)	1,160.91
Lowell (Mass.)	136.04
Lyndon B. Johnson (Tex.)	1,570.61
Minute Man (Mass.)	750.00
Morristown (N.J.)	1,670.61
Natchez (Miss.)	80.00
Nez Perce (Idaho)	2,108.89
Pecos (N.M.)	6,547.00
Púuchonua o Honaunau (Hawaii)	181.80
San Antonio Missions (Tex.)	492.66
San Fransico Maritime (Calif.)	50.00
San Juan Island (Wash.)	1,751.99
Saratoga (N.Y.)	3,392.82
Sitka (Alaska)	106.83
Tumacacori (Ariz.)	16.52
Valley Forge (Pa.)	3,468.06
War in the Pacific (Guam)	1,960.15

Name and location	Total acreage
Women's Rights (N.Y.)	5.54
Zuni-Cibola (N.M.)	800.00

NATIONAL MONUMENTS

Agate Fossil Beds (Neb.)	3,055.22
Alibates Flint Quarries (Tex.)	1,370.97
Aniakchak (Alaska)	137,176.00
Aztec Ruins (N.M.)	319.03
Bandelier (N.M.)	32,737.20
Black Canyon (Colo.)	20,766.14
Booker T. Washington (Va.)	223.92
Buck Island Reef (U.S. V.I.)	880.00
Cabrillo (Calif.)	137.06
Canyon de Chelly (Ariz.)	83,840.00
Cape Krusenstern (Alaska)	659,807.00
Capulin Volcano (N.M.)	792.84
Casa Grande (Ariz.)	472.50
Castillo de San Marcos (Fla.)	20.48
Castle Clinton (N.Y.)	1.00
Cedar Breaks (Utah)	6,154.60
Chiricahua (Ariz.)	11,984.80
Colorado (Colo.)	20,453.93
Congaree Swamp (S.C.)	22,200.00
Craters of the Moon (Idaho)	53,545.05
Custer Battlefield (Mont.)	765.34
Death Valley (Calif.-Nev.)	2,067,627.68
Devils Postpile (Calif.)	798.46

Name and location	Total acreage
Devils Tower (Wyo.)	1,346.91
Dinosaur (Utah-Colo.)	210,844.02
Effigy Mounds (Iowa)	1,481.39
El Malpais (N.M.)	114,335.00
El Morro (N.M.)	1,278.72
Florissant Fossil Beds (Colo.)	5,998.09
Fort Frederica (Ga.)	216.35
Fort Jefferson (Fla.)	64,700.00
Fort Matanzas (Fla.)	227.76
Fort McHenry (Md.)	43.26
Fort Pulaski (Ga.)	5,623.10
Fort Stanwix (N.Y.)	15.52
Fort Sumter (S.C.)	194.00
Fort Union (N.M.)	720.60
Fossil Butte (Wyo.)	8,198.00
George Washington Birthplace (Va.)	553.00
George Washington Carver (Mo.)	210.00
Gila Cliff Dwellings (N.M.)	533.13
Grand Portage (Minn.)	709.97
Great Sand Dunes (Colo.)	38,662.18
Hagerman Fossil Beds (Idaho)	4,280.00
Hohokam Pima (Ariz.)	1,690.00
Homestead (Neb.)	194.57
Hovenweep (Utah-Colo.)	784.93
Jewel Cave (S.D.)	1,273.51
John Day Fossil Beds (Ore.)	14,014.10
Joshua Tree (Calif.)	559,954.50
Lava Beds (Calif.)	46,559.87
Montezuma Castle (Ariz.)	857.69
Mound City Group (Ohio)	270.20
Muir Woods (Calif.)	553.55
Natural Bridges (Utah)	7,636.49
Navajo (Ariz.)	360.00
Ocmulgee (Ga.)	683.48
Oregon Caves (Ore.)	487.98
Organ Pipe Cactus (Ariz.)	330,688.86
Petroglyph (N.M.)	5,207.00
Pinnacles (Calif.)	16,265.44
Pipe Spring (Ariz.)	40.00
Pipestone (Minn.)	281.78
Poverty Point	910.85
Rainbow Bridge (Utah)	160.00
Russell Cave (Ala.)	310.45
Saguaro (Ariz.)	83,573.88
Salinas (N.M.)	1,076.94
Scotts Bluff (Neb.)	2,997.08
Statue of Liberty (N.Y.-N.J.)	58.38
Sunset Crater (Ariz.)	3,040.00
Timpanogos Cave (Utah)	250.00
Tonto (Ariz.)	1,120.00
Tuzigoot (Ariz.)	800.62
Walnut Canyon (Ariz.)	2,249.46
White Sands (N.M.)	143,732.92
Wupatki (Ariz.)	35,253.24
Yucca House (Colo.)	10.00

NATIONAL PRESERVES

Aniakchak (Alaska)	465,603.00
Bering Land Bridge (Alaska)	2,784,960.00
Big Cypress (Fla.)	716,000.00
Big Thicket (Tex.)	85,736.00
Denali (Alaska)	1,311,365.00
Gates of the Arctic (Alaska)	948,629.00
Glacier Bay (Alaska)	57,884.00
Katmai (Alaska)	374,000.00
Lake Clark (Alaska)	1,407,293.00
Noatak (Alaska)	6,574,481.00
Timucuan Ecological and Historic Preserve (Fla.)	46,000.00
Wrangell-St Elias (Alaska)	4,856,720.99
Yukon-Charley (Alaska)	2,523,509.00

Name and location	Total acreage

NATIONAL RESERVE

City of Rocks (Idaho)	14.407.19

NATIONAL MILITARY PARKS

Chickamauga and Chattanooga (Ga.-Tenn.)	8,106.04
Fredericksburg and Spotsylvania (Va.)	5,907.45
Gettysburg (Pa.)	3,895.70
Guilford Courthouse (N.C.)	220.25
Horseshoe Bend (Ala.)	2,040.00
Kings Mountain (S.C.)	3,945.29
Pea Ridge (Ark.)	4,300.35
Shiloh (Tenn.)	3,837.50
Vicksburg (Miss.)	1,619.89

NATIONAL BATTLEFIELDS

Antietam (Md.)	3,244.42
Big Hole (Mont.)	655.61
Cowpens (S.C.)	841.56
Fort Donelson (Tenn.)	536.66
Fort Necessity (Pa.)	902.80
Monocacy (Md.)	1,647.01
Moores Creek (N.C.)	86.52
Petersburg (Va.)	2,735.38
Stones River (Tenn.)	402.91
Tupelo (Miss.)	1.00
Wilson's Creek (Mo.)	1,749.91

NATIONAL BATTLEFIELD PARKS

Kennesaw Mountain (Ga.)	2,884.52
Manassas (Va.)	5,071.61
Richmond (Va.)	769.16

NATIONAL BATTLEFIELD SITE

Brices Cross Roads (Miss.)	1.00

NATIONAL HISTORIC SITES

Abraham Lincoln Birthplace (Ky.)	116.50
Adams (Mass.)	9.82
Allegheny Portage Railroad (Pa.)	1,246.97
Andersonville (Ga.)	475.72
Andrew Johnson (Tenn.)	16.68
Bent's Old Fort (Colo.)	799.80
Boston African American (Mass.)	0.00
Carl Sandburg Home (N.C.)	263.52
Charles Pinckney (S.C.)	25.00
Christiansted (V.I.)	27.15
Clara Barton (Md.)	8.59
Edgar Allan Poe (Pa.)	0.52
Edison (N.J.)	21.25
Eisenhower (Pa.)	690.46
Eleanor Roosevelt (N.Y.)	180.50
Eugene O'Neill (Calif.)	13.19
Ford's Theatre (Lincoln Museum) (D.C.)	0.29
Fort Bowie (Ariz.)	1,000.00
Fort Davis (Tex.)	460.00
Fort Laramie (Wyo.)	832.85
Fort Larned (Kan.)	718.39
Fort Point (Calif.)	29.00
Fort Raleigh (N.C.)	157.27
Fort Scott (Kan.)	16.69
Fort Smith (Ark.-Okla.)	75.00
Fort Union Trading Post (N.D.-Mont.)	442.45
Fort Vancouver (Wash.)	208.89
Frederick Douglass Home (D.C.)	8.53
Frederick Law Olmsted (Mass.)	1.75
Friendship Hill (Pa.)	674.56
Golden Spike (Utah)	2,735.28
Grant-Kohrs Ranch (Mont.)	1,498.65
Hampton (Md.)	62.04

Name and location	Total acreage
Harry S Truman (Mo.)	0.78
Herbert Hoover (Iowa)	186.80
Home of F. D. Roosevelt (N.Y.)	290.34
Hopewell Furnace (Pa.)	848.06
Hubbell Trading Post (Ariz.)	160.09
James A. Garfield (Ohio)	7.82
Jimmy Carter (Ga.)	69.55
John F. Kennedy (Mass.)	0.09
John Muir (Calif.)	338.90
Knife River Indian Villages (N.D.)	1,293.35
Lincoln Home (Ill.)	12.24
Longfellow (Mass.)	1.98
Maggie L. Walker (Va.)	1.29
Martin Luther King, Jr. (Ga.)	23.18
Martin Van Buren (N.Y.)	39.58
Ninety Six (S.C.)	989.14
Palo Alto Battlefield (Tex.)	50.00
Pennsylvania Avenue (D.C.)	0.00
Puukohola Heiau (Hawaii)	80.47
Sagamore Hill (N.Y.)	83.02
Saint-Gaudens (N.H.)	148.23
Saint Paul's Church (N.Y.)	6.13
Salem Maritime (Mass.)	8.95
San Juan (P.R.)	75.13
Saugus Iron Works (Mass.)	8.51
Springfield Armory (Mass.)	54.93
Steamtown (Pa.)	42.30
Theodore Roosevelt Birthplace (N.Y.)	0.11
Theodore Roosevelt Inaugural (N.Y.)	1.03
Thomas Stone (Md.)	328.25
Tuskegee Institute (Ala.)	74.39
Ulysses S. Grant (Mo.)	9.65
Vanderbilt Mansion (N.Y.)	211.65
Weir Farm (Conn.)	62.00
Whitman Mission (Wash.)	98.15
William Howard Taft (Ohio)	3.07

NATIONAL MEMORIALS

Arkansas Post (Ark.)	389.18
Arlington House, the Robert E. Lee Memorial (Va.)	27.91
Chamizal (Tex.)	54.90
Coronado (Ariz.)	4,750.22
De Sota (Fla.)	26.84
Federal Hall (N.Y.)	0.45
Fort Caroline (Fla.)	138.39
Fort Clatsop (Ore.)	125.20
General Grant (N.Y.)	0.76
Hamilton Grange (N.Y.)	0.11
Jefferson National Expansion Memorial (Mo.)	190.58
John F. Kennedy Center for Performing Arts (D.C.)	17.50
Johnstown Flood (Pa.)	164.12
Lincoln Boyhood (Ind.)	199.65
Lincoln Memorial (D.C.)	109.63
Lyndon Baines Johnson Memorial Grove on the Potomac (D.C.)	17.00
Mount Rushmore (S.D.)	1,278.45
Perry's Victory and International Peace Memorial (Ohio)	25.38
Roger Williams (R.I.)	4.56
Thaddeus Kosciuszko (Pa.)	0.02
Theodore Roosevelt Island (D.C.)	88.50
Thomas Jefferson Memorial (D.C.)	18.36
USS Arizona Memorial (Hawaii)	0.00
Vietnam Veterans Memorial (D.C.)	2.00
Washington Monument (D.C.)	106.01
Wright Brothers (N.C.)	431.40

NATIONAL CEMETERIES[1]

Antietam (Md.)	11.36
Battleground (D.C.)	1.03

Fort Donelson (Tenn.)	15.34
Fredericksburg (Va.)	12.00
Gettysburg (Pa.)	20.58
Poplar Grove (Va.)	8.72
Shiloh (Tenn.)	10.05
Stones River (Tenn.)	20.09
Vicksburg (Miss.)	116.28
Yorktown (Va.)	2.91

1. The National Cemeteries are not independent areas of the National Park System; each is part of a military park, battlefield, etc., except Battleground. Their acreage is kept separately. Arlington National Cemetery is under the Department of the Army. *See* Index.

NATIONAL SEASHORES

Assateague Island (Md.-Va.)	39,630.93
Canaveral (Fla.)	57,661.69
Cape Cod (Mass.)	43,557.24
Cape Hatteras (N.C.)	30,319.43
Cape Lookout (N.C.)	28,243.36
Cumberland Island (Ga.)	36,415.09
Fire Island (N.Y.)	19,578.55
Gulf Islands (Fla.-Miss.)	136,618.00
Padre Island (Tex.)	130,434.27
Point Reyes (Calif.)	71,050.00

NATIONAL PARKWAYS

Blue Ridge (Va.-N.C.)	86,941.00
George Washington Memorial (Va.-Md.)	7,159.00
John D. Rockefeller, Jr., Memorial (Wyo.)	23,777.22
Natchez Trace (Miss.-Tenn.-Ala.)	51,742.00

NATIONAL LAKESHORES

Apostle Islands (Wis.)	69,371.89
Indiana Dunes (Ind.)	13,845.00
Pictured Rocks (Mich)	72,903.00
Sleeping Bear Dunes (Mich.)	71,188.00

NATIONAL WILD AND SCENIC RIVERS

Alagnak Wild River (Alaska)	24,038.00
Bluestone National Scenic River (W. Va.)	0.00
Delaware (N.Y.-N.J.-Pa.)	1,973.33
Lower St. Croix (Minn.-Wis.)	9,474.93
Missouri National Recreational River (Neb., S.D.)	0.00
Obed Wild & Scenic River (Tenn.)	5,074.85
Rio Grande Wild & Scenic (Tex.)	9,600.00
St. Croix (Minn.-Wis.)	67,379.00
Upper Delaware (N.Y., N.J.-Pa.)	75,000.00

NATIONAL RIVERS

Big South Fork National River & Recreation Area (Ky.-Tenn.)	122,960.00
Buffalo (Ark.)	94,218.57
Mississippi National River & Recreation Area (Minn.)	50,000.00
New River Gorge (W.Va.)	62,144.00
Ozark (Mo.)	80,791.00

OTHER PARKS

Catoctin Mountain (Md.)	5,770.22
Constitution Gardens, (D.C.)	52.00
Fort Washington Park (Md.)	341.00
Greenbelt Park (Md.)	1,175.99
Piscataway (Md.)	4,262.52
Prince William Forest (Va.)	18,571.55
Rock Creek Park (D.C.)	1,754.37
Wolf Trap Farm Park for the Performing Arts (Va.)	130.28

NATIONAL RECREATION AREAS

Amistad (Tex.)	57,292.44
Bighorn Canyon (Wyo.-Mont.)	120,296.22

Name and location	Total acreage
Chattahoochee River (Ga.)	9,263.64
Chickasaw (Okla.)	9,521.91
Coulee Dam (Wash.)	100,390.31
Curecanti (Colo.)	42,114.47
Cuyahoga Valley (Ohio)	32,525.00
Delaware Water Gap (Pa.-N.J.)	66,651.86
Gateway (N.Y.-N.J.)	26,310.93
Gauley River (W. Va.)	10,300.00
Glen Canyon (Ariz.-Utah)	1,236,880.00
Golden Gate (Calif.)	73,122.00
Lake Chelan (Wash.)	61,882.76
Lake Mead (Ariz.-Nev.)	1,495,665.52
Lake Meredith (Tex.)	44,977.63
Ross Lake (Wash.)	117,574.09
Santa Monica Mountains (Calif.)	150,050.00
Whiskeytown-Shasta-Trinity (Calif.)	42,503.46

NATIONAL SCENIC TRAIL

Appalachian (Maine, N.H., Vt., Mass., Conn., N.Y., N.J., Pa., Md., W.Va., Va., N.C., Tenn., Ga.)	161,382.00
Natchez Trace (Ga.-Ala.-Tenn.)	10,995.00
Potomac Heritage (D.C.-Md.-Va.-Pa.)	0.00

NATIONAL MALL

National Mall (D.C.)	146.35

INTERNATIONAL HISTORIC SITE

Saint Croix Island (Maine)	35.39

AFFILIATED AREAS

(National Historic Sites unless otherwise noted.)

American Memorial Park (N. Mariana Is.)	0.00
Benjamin Franklin (Pa.)[1]	0.00
Blackstone River Valley National Heritage Corridor (Mass., R.I.)	0.00
Chicago Portage (Ill.)	91.20

Name and location	Total acreage
Chimney Rock (Neb.)	83.36
David Berger (Ohio)[1]	0.00
Delaware and Lehigh Navigation Canal National Heritage Corridor (Pa.)	0.00
Ebey's Landing (Wash.)	8,000.00
Father Marquette (Mich.)[1]	52.00
Gloria Dei Church (Pa.)	3.71
Green Springs Historic District (Va.)	5,490.59
Historic Camden (S.C.)	0.00
Ice Age Scenic Trail (Wis.)	0.00
Ice Age (Wis.)[2]	32,500.00
Iditarod National Historic Trail (Alaska)	0.00
Illinois and Michigan Canal National Heritage Corridor	0.00
International Peace Garden (N.D.)	2,330.30
Jamestown (Va.)	20.63
Lewis & Clark Natl. Historic Trail (Ill., Mo., Kan., Neb., Iowa, Idaho, S.D., N.D., Mont., Ore., Wash.)	39.11
M. McLeod Bethune Council House (D.C.)	0.00
McLoughlin House (Ore.)	0.63
Mormon Pioneer Natl. Historic Trail (Ill., Iowa, Neb., Wyo., Utah)	0.00
North Country Nat'l Scenic Trail (N.Y., Pa., Ohio, Mich., Wis., Minn., N.D.)	0.00
Oregon Natl. Historic Trail (Mo., Kan., Neb., Wyo., Idaho, Ore., Wash.)	0.00
Overmountain Victory Trail (Mo. to Ore.)	0.00
Pinelands Natl. Reserve (N.J.)	0.00
Red Hill Patrick Henry (Va.)[1]	0.00
Roosevelt-Campobello International Park (Canada)	2,721.50
Santa Fe National Historic Trail (Mo. to N.M.)	0.00
Sewell-Belmont House National Historic Site (D.C.)	0.35
Touro Synagogue (R.I.)	0.23
Trail of Tears National Historic Trail (N.C. to Okla.)	0.00

1. National Memorial. 2. National Scientific Reserve.

Don't Eat the Flowers

There are more than 700 species of plants that grow in the United States that have been identified as dangerous if eaten. Among them are some that are commonly favored by gardeners—buttercups, daffodils, lily of the valley, sweet peas, oleander, azalea, bleeding heart, delphinium, and rhododendron. According to a survey of the nation's poison control centers, next to medicines, plants are the leading cause of poisoning in children under five years of age. A threefold increase in plant poisoning, from 1971 levels, is attributed to the house plant explosion and back-to-nature dining.

Water Supply of the World[1]

The Antarctic Icecap is the largest supply of fresh water, nearly 2 percent of the world's total of fresh and salt water. As can be seen from the table below, the amount of water in our atmosphere is over ten times as large as the water in all the rivers taken together. The fresh water actually available for human use in lakes and rivers and the accessible ground water amounts to only about one third of one percent of the world's total water supply.

	Surface area (square miles)	Volume (cubic miles)	Percentage of total
Salt Water			
The oceans	139,500,000	317,000,000	97.2
Inland seas and saline lakes	270,000	25,000	0.008
Fresh Water			
Freshwater lakes	330,000	30,000	0.009
All rivers (average level)	—	300	0.0001
Antarctic Icecap	6,000,000	6,300,000	1.9
Arctic Icecap and glaciers	900,000	680,000	0.21
Water in the atmosphere	197,000,000	3,100	0.001
Ground water within half a mile from surface	—	1,000,000	0.31
Deep-lying ground water	—	1,000,000	0.31
Total (rounded)	—	**326,000,000**	**100.00**

1. All figures are estimated. *Source:* Department of the Interior, Geological Survey.

RECYCLING

Here Today . . . Here Tomorrow:
The Degradable Plastics Scam
By William C. Burns

In the past few years, the American people's concern about protecting the environment has increased dramatically. In recent surveys, more than 75% of those polled have indicated that they believe that a "major effort" must be made to improve the quality of the environment, and that programs to accomplish this should be implemented "regardless of cost." As consumers, we have also indicated that we are willing to pay a premium for "environmentally friendly" products, leading to the production of many more "green" products by industry.

Unfortunately, some corporations, eager to cash in on America's new environmental ethic, appear to be far more concerned about a different kind of "green." This has led to deceptive and misleading product claims that could lead to a backlash against the environmental movement in this country. The recent marketing of so-called "degradable bags" provides an excellent case study to demonstrate the point that all that glitters is not necessarily "green."

Degradable Plastics: In The Bag?

In response to surveys that indicated that 70–90% of Americans were willing to pay more for degradable products, companies such as First Brand, the producer of "Glad" trash bags, and Mobil Corporation, maker of "Hefty" bags, rushed to market lines of "degradable" trash bags. In just two years, these products captured 10–20% of the market for trash, grocery, and merchandise bags, although they cost up to 14% more than "non degradable" products. Producers of degradable bags confidently claimed that their products would begin to disintegrate within six months and "continue to break down into harmless particles even after they are buried in a landfill." Unfortunately, it has become clear in the last two years that degradable bags are simply a "green marketing" illusion that can do nothing to solve the municipal solid waste crisis, and may actually worsen the situation.

Degradable plastics fall into two categories: biodegradable and photodegradable. Biodegradable plastics are produced by embedding cornstarch within the polymer chains that make up plastic materials. In theory, when a product made of such materials is discarded, hungry microorganisms will attack the starch and consume it, breaking down the links of the polymer chains, leaving behind a "plastic swiss cheese." An oxidizing agent added to the plastic is then supposed to come into play, breaking down the plastic molecules into even smaller pieces. Ultimately, these smaller pieces should eventually become small enough to degrade naturally into carbon dioxide and water.

Photodegradable plastics rely on the sun's ultraviolet light to break down a plastic's polymer chains, rendering the plastic brittle and hastening its disintegration. Chemicals, such as carbon monoxide, are added to the plastics to trigger this process in the presence of sunlight.

Unfortunately, while degradable plastics may break down under ideal laboratory conditions, this is not what generally happens in landfills. Landfills are designed to minimize the presence of oxygen and water. The microorganisms essential for the biodegradation process are not likely to thrive in such an environment. Landfills are also very dark places; thus, the sunlight necessary for photodegradation will also be absent. Several recent studies have demonstrated that degradable plastics do not break down under landfill or composting conditions, or in marine environments. Even if some degradable plastics technologies prove effective, they may harm the environment. Plastic bags often are made with fillers and additives which contain toxic heavy metals such as cadmium, lead, chromium, copper, and beryllium. As plastics disintegrate, these metals may leach into the soil or groundwater. For example, cadmium found in a municipal compost operation in Nebraska was ultimately traced to yellow dye in degradable bags used to hold leaves and grass clippings. Several researchers have expressed concern that the plastic dust that remains after plastics degrade could harm wildlife if ingested. There has been virtually no research on this subject.

Finally, the starch added to biodegradable plastics makes it difficult to recycle such products because the added starch clumps up and weakens recycled plastic. Also, as Jeanne Wirka of Environmental Action suggests, degradable plastics "work at cross-purposes to recycling" because they may convince people that they can simply discard items and they will disappear, crippling the perceived need for recycling.

* * *

Finally, in the face of the threat of lawsuits by attorney generals in several states, as well as efforts by environmental groups to organize a boycott of degradable plastics, three of the largest manufacturers of such products, Dow Chemical Company, Mobil Chemical Company, and First Brands announced that they would remove the word "degradable" from the packages of their products.

* * *

Is there anything that a consumer can do in the face of this determination to press ahead with an unproven and potentially hazardous technology? The answer is yes. First, you should not purchase plastic products, or products in plastic packaging, that claim to be "degradable," until such time as these claims are supported by solid scientific research that demonstrates the effectiveness and the environmental soundness of such products. Second, you should write your state and federal representatives and urge them to oppose governmental purchases of degradable plastic products at this time. Third, you should work to establish plastics recycling facilities in your community to reduce the need for degradable products. Finally, we must carefully scrutinize the "green claims" that any manufacturer makes for its products. If we fail to do so the "degradable bags scam" will only be the first in a long series of green hoaxes in the 1990s. □

William C. Burns is Director, Environmental Affairs, Earth Care Paper, Inc., P.O. Box 14140, Madison, WI 53714-0140. Reprinted from "Recycles!," with permission, Earth Care Paper Inc.

Incineration: The Rush to Burn
By William C. Burns

The United States faces a solid waste crisis of unprecedented proportions in the 1990s. The Environmental Protection Agency estimates that more than a third of the nation's municipalities will run out of landfill space in the next two or three years and more than half will exhaust available space within the next ten years. According to the Association of State and Territorial Solid Waste Management Officials, virtually every state in the union suffers from a shortage of landfill space.

In the face of such limited landfill capacity, many cities are rushing to build incineration plants to dispose of solid waste. More than a hundred incineration plants are currently being built or planned, at a cost of more than $30 billion. By the middle of this decade almost half of our municipal solid waste may be incinerated.

Unfortunately, incinerators have their own environmental costs. Researchers who surveyed 45 municipal solid waste incinerators in Denmark concluded that these facilities were the major source of carcinogenic dioxin and furans in the atmosphere. A recent study by the government of the Netherlands similarly concluded that the general public was exposed to hazardous levels of dioxin through the consumption of products which originated near dioxin emission sources, such as incinerators. The Center For Biology of Natural Systems at Queens College, New York, has also concluded that incinerators are a major contributor to environmental exposure to dioxin and furans in this country.

Incinerators only burn 70% of solid waste, and the residual ash must be buried in landfills. This residual is often more dangerous than the original garbage because it contains hazardous levels of heavy metals such as lead and cadmium, which may leak into groundwater supplies or the atmosphere. It has been estimated that by 1992, more than 200 incinerators in the United States will generate about 55,000 tons of ash a day. In spite of this, the EPA has failed to issue guidelines to regulate the disposal of incinerator ash.

Finally, the smokestacks of incinerators emit potentially hazardous levels of other toxins, including arsenic, mercury and carbon monoxide. Proponents of incineration plants argue that the technology exists to design facilities that will not produce such adverse environmental effects. However, the experience of many nations renders such claims questionable. In Sweden, the inability to develop environmentally benign incinerators led to a moratorium on their construction in 1984. More recently, the state of Michigan placed a hold on funding for incineration facilities citing environmental concerns—including higher than expected levels of toxic emissions from the plant smokestacks and high levels of lead in the ash residues.

Of course, if we adopt a "go slow" approach on incinerators, we must find a way to dispose of an ever-increasing mountain of trash. Three long-term solutions are recycling, composting, and reductions in packaging of products. Recycling success stories, such as Seattle, which has a current recycling rate of 34% and aims to recycle 60% of its waste by 1998, can serve as an inspiration for other municipalities who seek an alternative to incineration. Recent studies have also demonstrated incineration can be as much as six times more expensive than recycling when factors including energy saved by recycling and the costs of building incineration facilities are taken into account. Many communities throughout the country have dramatically reduced the volume of yard waste sent to landfills through composing operations. Such programs often provide an additional source of revenue to participating cities and towns.

Packaging comprises some 50% of the volume, and 30% of the weight of the household waste stream; the average American discards about 600 pounds of product packaging each year. Many of the products on the market today are overpackaged, use environmentally damaging materials such as polyvinyl chlorides, or consist of multilayer resins which makes the materials impossible to recycle. Consumers should avoid such products and express their displeasure to the manufacturer. We should also seek to buy products packaged in recycled materials. Environmentally conscious lifestyle choices can help us avoid the adoption of questionable technologies, such as incineration. □

Organizations to contact for additional information:

Center For the Biology of
  Natural Systems
Queens College
Flushing, NY 11367
(718) 670-4180

Environmental Defense Fund
256 Park Ave. South
New York, NY 10010
(212)M 505-2100

William C. Burns is Director, Environmental Affairs, Earth Care Paper, Inc., P.O. Box 14140, Madison, WI 53714-0140. Reprinted from "Recycles!," with permission, Earth Care Paper Inc.

Waste Reducing Recipes

Source: "New York's Waste Reduction Handbook."

Here are substitutes for many household products that contain toxic chemicals. These common solutions, plus some elbow grease, are reliable and effective ways to get the hob done while reducing excess packaging and toxic waste.

Clogs: Unclog drains by pouring boiling water with a few tablespoons of baking soda and a large splash of vinegar down drains. This treatment once-a-week prevents clogs too.

Ceramic tile cleaner: Mix one-quarter cup while vinegar with one gallon of water.

Furniture polish: Mix three parts olive oil with one part lemon juice or vinegar and apply with a clean, soft cloth.

Oven cleaner: Sprinkle water, then a layer of baking soda on oven surfaces. Rub gently with very fine steel wool for tough spots.

Toilet cleaner: Sprinkle some baking soda into the bowl, then drizzle with vinegar and scour with a toilet brush. □

Paper Chase

Source: "Conservation 90," The Environmental Digest for the Resource Conservation Alliance,
National Wildlife Federation

From forests to waterways to landfills, the production and use of paper is an environmental nightmare. Growing demand for paper has led to poor forest management, polluted water from pulp and paper mills, and overflowing landfills—where paper makes up more than 40 percent of the waste. As people have become aware of these problems, recycled paper has emerged as a solution. Most recycled paper, however, does little to reduce paper's harmful effects. The paper we put in recycling bins rarely ends up in the "recycled" paper we buy for printing and writing. Instead, the paper we recycle is used to make low-grade paper products like wall insulation, while recycled printing and writing paper is made from scraps from the mill—industrial left-overs that have always been recycled. And most paper—recycled or not—is bleached with harmful chemicals that poison lakes and rivers and threaten public health. There are signs these problems will change, but it depends on consumer demand: people need to ask for environmentally sound paper and recycle the paper they use.

Paper Perfection

What is environmentally sound paper? Ideally, it is recycled, made with a high percentage of "post-consumer waste"—paper that has reached the consumer and then been retrieved for recycling before it reaches a landfill or incinerator. Environmentally sound paper also has not been bleached with chlorine during the recycling process or in the original pulping process.

Using post-consumer waste in recycled paper is important because it encourages people to recycle. By placing a premium on people's waste paper, the use of post-consumer waste in recycled paper provides an incentive to separate paper from other garbage for recycling. Buying paper with a high post-consumer waste content completes the circle: it perpetuates the incentive to recycle, saves trees, and lessens the burden on our overflowing landfills.

In the United States, most paper is made from wood fibers bleached with chlorine. In the bleaching process, chlorine combines with organic molecules from the wood to form organochlorines, a group of toxic chlorine compounds that includes cancer-causing and chromosome-damaging chemicals. Organochlorines, such as dioxins and furans, are released into the environment in the effluent and sludge produced by pulp and paper mills and are also found in bleached paper products.

Despite its obvious environmental benefits, recycled paper made with a high percentage of post-consumer waste that is not bleached with chlorine during the recycling process is about as common as a spotted owl in a clear cut. Environmentally sound paper is hard to find because the federal government has loosely defined recycled paper, the paper industry has been slow to respond to consumer demand, and the recycling infrastructure is not yet capable of handling the amount of post-consumer waste required to make available large quantities of environmentally sound paper.

Paper Hype

Most recycled paper is made with "pre-consumer waste"—industrial waste paper recovered from paper and printing plants. The paper industry has always recycled pre-consumer waste to make high-grade paper, so pre-consumer waste has not contributed to landfill problems. In response to increasing demand for recycled paper, the paper industry started labelling paper made from per-consumer waste as "recycled." In the past, this paper was not labeled as such because the industry believed people would not buy it.

Recycled paper made from pre-consumer waste is a market ploy designed to placate the demands of an increasingly environmentally aware society. Such paper satisfies the increasing demand, but not the environmental need. The paper industry was prompted to put the "recycled" label on many of its products when the Environmental Protection Agency (EPA) finally released guidelines in 1988 for the purchase of recycled paper by government agencies. The guidelines, which were required by the Resource Conservation and Recovery Act of 1976, recommend a minimum recycled fiber content of 50 percent for high-grade bleached printing and writing paper.

The paper industry interpreted this guidelines loosely. Because paper is only about 70 percent wood fibers (the rest is filler), industry determined that recycled paper could comply with EPA guidelines if half of the fibers, or 35 percent of the paper content, were recycled pre-consumer waste.

Environmentalists believe that the EPA is undermining the market for recycled printing and writing paper instead of acting as a leader. Mills are being rewarded for doing what they have done all along—that is, recycle material that has not left the mill. Until the federal government redefines its guidelines to encourage the production of environmentally friendly paper, it is unlikely that Americans will see recycled printing and writing paper with high post-consumer content. ☐

The Ink Dilemma

A key step in making high-quality recycled paper from post-consumer waste is the removal of ink from the waste paper. The "de-inking" process, however, presents environmental problems of its own: forty tons of potentially toxic sludge are created to produce 100 tons of de-inked fiber.

Because some ink contains heavy metals like lead and cadmium to give it color, the de-inking sludge is often contaminated. In the last decade, however, the amount of toxic heavy metals in ink has been substantially reduced. Paper companies claim that sludge from de-inking that tests as non-toxic can be used to fertilize soil. Some environmental groups, however, feel that the potential toxicity of the sludge is enough of a hazard that post consumer waste recycling should be done without de-inking at all.

In addition to containing heavy metals, printing inks can emit volatile organic compounds which harm air quality and human health. Traditional petroleum-based ink emits much higher levels of these compounds than ink made from vegetable oils. Vegetable-based ink, although it is made with some proportion of petroleum, is easier to de-ink. Made from soybeans, cottonseed or other vegetables, vegetable-based ink comes from farm-grown plants instead of spill-prone imported oil. And, according to industry consultant Michael Mangan, vegetable-based ink performs better on the printing press and reduces printing costs.

Source Directory

For information about recycled paper and bleaching:

Earth Care Paper, Inc.
P.O. Box 3335
Madison, WI 53704
(608) 256-5522
(catalog of recycled paper products)

E.H. Pechan and Assoc., Inc.
5528 Hempstead Way
Springfield, VA 22151
(800) 941-5542
(lists of mills where you can get recycled paper, and guidelines from states that have implemented recycling programs)

Environmental Defense Fund
257 Park Ave. South
New York, NY 10010
(800) 225-5333
(free recycling brochure)

Environmental Protection Agency
Office of Solid Waste
401 M St., SW
Washington, D.C. 20460
(800) 424-9346 (from Washington, D.C. 382-3000)
(information about your state's recycling coordinator)

Greenpeace
Northwest Office

Good Shepard Center
4649 Sunnyside Avenue N
Seattle, WA 98103
(*The Greenpeace Guide to Paper*, one of the best sources of information about the papermaking process and issues surrounding recycled paper and pulp and paper bleaching; cost $3.00)

National Wildlife Federation
COOL IT!
1400 16th St., NW
Washington, D.C. 20036-2266
(NWF's COOL IT! program has a packet of information for college students who want to start a campus recycling program)

San Francisco Recycling Program
271 City Hall
San Francisco, CA 94102
(415) 554-6193
(*Your Office Paper Recycling Guide*, a guide to help you start an office recycling program, $5.00, but free to residences and government offices in San Francisco)

For information about soy inks:

American Soybean Association
540 Maryville Center Drive
St. Louis, MO 63141
(314) 576-1770

Information Resources For Starting A Community Recycling Program
By William C. Burns, Director, Environmental Affairs, Earth Care Paper Inc.

Information and support to help you start a community recycling program is readily available. The groups listed below will be happy to share their expertise and success stories with you. Also, where relevant, we have listed some helpful publications available from these organizations. While this list does not include all such resources, it will provide a starting point for your local recycling efforts.

Organizations that assist in the establishment of recycling programs

1. Governmental Refuse Collection and Disposal Association (GRCDA): Established by GRCDA and the National Recycling Coalition and funded by the U.S. Environmental Protection Agency, GRCDA administers a "peer match program" that provides a network of advisors for every aspect of community projects—from solid waste analysis to choosing recycling machinery. GRCDA, Attention EPA Peer Match Program, P.O. Box 7219, Silver Spring, MD 20910, (800) 456-GRCD.

2. National Recycling Coalition: The NRC brings together individuals, state and local governments, industry and environment groups to promote recycling programs. Ask for their information packet for communities interested in recycling. Include a self-addressed, stamped envelope. 1101 30th St., N.W., Suite 305, Washington, DC 20009, (202) 625-6406. NRC also shares the cost of sending qualified experts to appear before audiences seeking information on recycling programs.

3. Conservation and Renewable Energy Inquiry and Referral Service (CAREIRS): Ask for their free community recycling packet. P.O. Box 8900, Silver Spring, MD 20907 (800) 523-2929.

4. Institute For Local Reliance: Ask for *Community-Based Recycling: How To Get Started in Your Community* ($3.50), 2425 18th St., N.W., Washington, DC 20009, (202) 232-4108.

5. Citizens For A Better Environment: 647 W. Virginia St., #303, Milwaukee, WI 53204, (414) 271-7280. C.B.E. is actively involved in a wide array of projects related to source reduction and recycling. Write the organization for a list of current publications.

Publications

Publications About Recycling Available From Earth Care:

1. Concern, Inc., *Waste: Choices For Communities* ($3.00).

2. Environmental Defense Fund, *Coming Full Circle: Successful Recycling Today* ($20.00).

Publications Available From Other Sources:

1. Staff of *Biocycle* Magazine, *The Biocycle Guide To Collecting, Processing And Marketing Recyclables* (paperback $49.95/hardcover $59.95), Biocycle, P.O. Box 351, Emmaus, PA 18029.

2. American Paper Institute, *Starting A Recycling Program* (free), American Paper Institute, 260 Madison Ave., New York, NY 10016-2499, (212) 340-0600.

CALENDAR & HOLIDAYS

1992

JANUARY

S	M	T	W	T	F	S
			1	2	3	4
5	6	7	8	9	10	11
12	13	14	15	16	17	18
19	20	21	22	23	24	25
26	27	28	29	30	31	

1 — New Year's Day
6 — Epiphany
20 — Martin Luther King Jr. Day

FEBRUARY

S	M	T	W	T	F	S
						1
2	3	4	5	6	7	8
9	10	11	12	13	14	15
16	17	18	19	20	21	22
23	24	25	26	27	28	29

2 — Groundhog Day
12 — Lincoln's Birthday
14 — Valentine's Day
17 — Washington's Birthday Observed

MARCH

S	M	T	W	T	F	S
1	2	3	4	5	6	7
8	9	10	11	12	13	14
15	16	17	18	19	20	21
22	23	24	25	26	27	28
29	30	31				

4 — Ash Wednesday
6 — 1st Day of Ramadan
17 — St. Patrick's Day
19 — Purim

APRIL

S	M	T	W	T	F	S
			1	2	3	4
5	6	7	8	9	10	11
12	13	14	15	16	17	18
19	20	21	22	23	24	25
26	27	28	29	30		

5 — Daylight Savings Time begins
12 — Palm Sunday
17 — Good Friday
18 — 1st Day of Passover
19 — Easter

MAY

S	M	T	W	T	F	S
					1	2
3	4	5	6	7	8	9
10	11	12	13	14	15	16
17	18	19	20	21	22	23
24	25	26	27	28	29	30
31						

10 — Mother's Day
28 — Ascension Day
30 — Memorial Day

JUNE

S	M	T	W	T	F	S
	1	2	3	4	5	6
7	8	9	10	11	12	13
14	15	16	17	18	19	20
21	22	23	24	25	26	27
28	29	30				

7 — 1st Day of Shavuot and Pentecost
14 — Flag Day
21 — Father's Day

JULY

S	M	T	W	T	F	S
			1	2	3	4
5	6	7	8	9	10	11
12	13	14	15	16	17	18
19	20	21	22	23	24	25
26	27	28	29	30	31	

1 — Canada Day
4 — Independence Day

AUGUST

S	M	T	W	T	F	S
						1
2	3	4	5	6	7	8
9	10	11	12	13	14	15
16	17	18	19	20	21	22
23	24	25	26	27	28	29
30	31					

SEPTEMBER

S	M	T	W	T	F	S
		1	2	3	4	5
6	7	8	9	10	11	12
13	14	15	16	17	18	19
20	21	22	23	24	25	26
27	28	29	30			

7 — Labor day
28 — 1st Day of Rosh Hashana

OCTOBER

S	M	T	W	T	F	S
				1	2	3
4	5	6	7	8	9	10
11	12	13	14	15	16	17
18	19	20	21	22	23	24
25	26	27	28	29	30	31

7 — Yom Kippur
12 — Columbus Day and Thanksgiving Day (Canada)
25 — Daylight Savings Time ends
31 — Halloween

NOVEMBER

S	M	T	W	T	F	S
1	2	3	4	5	6	7
8	9	10	11	12	13	14
15	16	17	18	19	20	21
22	23	24	25	26	27	28
29	30					

1 — All Saints Day
3 — Election Day
11 — Veterans Day
26 — Thanksgiving
29 — 1st Sunday of Advent

DECEMBER

S	M	T	W	T	F	S
		1	2	3	4	5
6	7	8	9	10	11	12
13	14	15	16	17	18	19
20	21	22	23	24	25	26
27	28	29	30	31		

20 — 1st Day of Hanukkah
25 — Christmas

Seasons for the Northern Hemisphere, 1992

Eastern Standard Time

March 19, 7:48 p.m., sun enters sign of Aries; spring begins

June 20, 10:14 p.m., sun enters sign of Cancer; summer begins

Sept. 22, 1:43 p.m., sun enters sign of Libra; fall begins

Dec. 21, 9:43 a.m., sun enters sign of Capricorn; winter begins

1991

JANUARY
S	M	T	W	T	F	S
		1	2	3	4	5
6	7	8	9	10	11	12
13	14	15	16	17	18	19
20	21	22	23	24	25	26
27	28	29	30	31		

FEBRUARY
S	M	T	W	T	F	S
					1	2
3	4	5	6	7	8	9
10	11	12	13	14	15	16
17	18	19	20	21	22	23
24	25	26	27	28		

MARCH
S	M	T	W	T	F	S
					1	2
3	4	5	6	7	8	9
10	11	12	13	14	15	16
17	18	19	20	21	22	23
24	25	26	27	28	29	30
31						

APRIL
S	M	T	W	T	F	S
	1	2	3	4	5	6
7	8	9	10	11	12	13
14	15	16	17	18	19	20
21	22	23	24	25	26	27
28	29	30				

MAY
S	M	T	W	T	F	S
			1	2	3	4
5	6	7	8	9	10	11
12	13	14	15	16	17	18
19	20	21	22	23	24	25
26	27	28	29	30	31	

JUNE
S	M	T	W	T	F	S
						1
2	3	4	5	6	7	8
9	10	11	12	13	14	15
16	17	18	19	20	21	22
23	24	25	26	27	28	29
30						

JULY
S	M	T	W	T	F	S
	1	2	3	4	5	6
7	8	9	10	11	12	13
14	15	16	17	18	19	20
21	22	23	24	25	26	27
28	29	30	31			

AUGUST
S	M	T	W	T	F	S
				1	2	3
4	5	6	7	8	9	10
11	12	13	14	15	16	17
18	19	20	21	22	23	24
25	26	27	28	29	30	31

SEPTEMBER
S	M	T	W	T	F	S
1	2	3	4	5	6	7
8	9	10	11	12	13	14
15	16	17	18	19	20	21
22	23	24	25	26	27	28
29	30					

OCTOBER
S	M	T	W	T	F	S
		1	2	3	4	5
6	7	8	9	10	11	12
13	14	15	16	17	18	19
20	21	22	23	24	25	26
27	28	29	30	31		

NOVEMBER
S	M	T	W	T	F	S
					1	2
3	4	5	6	7	8	9
10	11	12	13	14	15	16
17	18	19	20	21	22	23
24	25	26	27	28	29	30

DECEMBER
S	M	T	W	T	F	S
1	2	3	4	5	6	7
8	9	10	11	12	13	14
15	16	17	18	19	20	21
22	23	24	25	26	27	28
29	30	31				

1993

JANUARY
S	M	T	W	T	F	S
					1	2
3	4	5	6	7	8	9
10	11	12	13	14	15	16
17	18	19	20	21	22	23
24	25	26	27	28	29	30
31						

FEBRUARY
S	M	T	W	T	F	S
	1	2	3	4	5	6
7	8	9	10	11	12	13
14	15	16	17	18	19	20
21	22	23	24	25	26	27
28						

MARCH
S	M	T	W	T	F	S
	1	2	3	4	5	6
7	8	9	10	11	12	13
14	15	16	17	18	19	20
21	22	23	24	25	26	27
28	29	30	31			

APRIL
S	M	T	W	T	F	S
				1	2	3
4	5	6	7	8	9	10
11	12	13	14	15	16	17
18	19	20	21	22	23	24
25	26	27	28	29	30	

MAY
S	M	T	W	T	F	S
						1
2	3	4	5	6	7	8
9	10	11	12	13	14	15
16	17	18	19	20	21	22
23	24	25	26	27	28	29
30	31					

JUNE
S	M	T	W	T	F	S
		1	2	3	4	5
6	7	8	9	10	11	12
13	14	15	16	17	18	19
20	21	22	23	24	25	26
27	28	29	30			

JULY
S	M	T	W	T	F	S
				1	2	3
4	5	6	7	8	9	10
11	12	13	14	15	16	17
18	19	20	21	22	23	24
25	26	27	28	29	30	31

AUGUST
S	M	T	W	T	F	S
1	2	3	4	5	6	7
8	9	10	11	12	13	14
15	16	17	18	19	20	21
22	23	24	25	26	27	28
29	30	31				

SEPTEMBER
S	M	T	W	T	F	S
		1	2	3	4	
5	6	7	8	9	10	11
12	13	14	15	16	17	18
19	20	21	22	23	24	25
26	27	28	29	30		

OCTOBER
S	M	T	W	T	F	S
					1	2
3	4	5	6	7	8	9
10	11	12	13	14	15	16
17	18	19	20	21	22	23
24	25	26	27	28	29	30
31						

NOVEMBER
S	M	T	W	T	F	S
	1	2	3	4	5	6
7	8	9	10	11	12	13
14	15	16	17	18	19	20
21	22	23	24	25	26	27
28	29	30				

DECEMBER
S	M	T	W	T	F	S
			1	2	3	4
5	6	7	8	9	10	11
12	13	14	15	16	17	18
19	20	21	22	23	24	25
26	27	28	29	30	31	

Pre-Columbian Calendar Systems

The Mayans and the Aztecs both used two calendars—a sacred or ceremonial calendar of 260 days and a 365-day secular calendar that was divided into 18 months of 20 days each. An additional five days were added to complete the 365-day year. The Mayans were able to approximate the true length of the tropical year with a greater accuracy than does the Gregorian calendar year we now use. The tropical year is 365.2422 days. The Mayans determined it to be 365.2420 days, whereas the Gregorian calendar year is 365.2425.

Very little is known about the Inca calendar. Because the Incas did not have a written language, early reports about their calendar cannot be verified.

PERPETUAL CALENDAR

1800 .. 4	1844 .. 9	1888 .. 8	1932 .. 13	1976 .. 12	2020 .. 11
1801 .. 5	1845 .. 4	1889 .. 3	1933 .. 1	1977 .. 7	2021 .. 6
1802 .. 6	1846 .. 5	1890 .. 4	1934 .. 2	1978 .. 1	2022 .. 7
1803 .. 7	1847 .. 6	1891 .. 5	1935 .. 3	1979 .. 2	2023 .. 1
1804 .. 8	1848 .. 14	1892 .. 13	1936 .. 11	1980 .. 10	2024 .. 9
1805 .. 3	1849 .. 2	1893 .. 1	1937 .. 6	1981 .. 5	2025 .. 4
1806 .. 4	1850 .. 3	1894 .. 2	1938 .. 7	1982 .. 6	2026 .. 5
1807 .. 5	1851 .. 4	1895 .. 3	1939 .. 1	1983 .. 7	2027 .. 6
1808 .. 13	1852 .. 12	1896 .. 11	1940 .. 9	1984 .. 8	2028 .. 14
1809 .. 1	1853 .. 7	1897 .. 6	1941 .. 4	1985 .. 3	2029 .. 2
1810 .. 2	1854 .. 1	1898 .. 7	1942 .. 5	1986 .. 4	2030 .. 3
1811 .. 3	1855 .. 2	1899 .. 1	1943 .. 6	1987 .. 5	2031 .. 4
1812 .. 11	1856 .. 10	1900 .. 2	1944 .. 14	1988 .. 13	2032 .. 12
1813 .. 6	1857 .. 5	1901 .. 3	1945 .. 2	1989 .. 1	2033 .. 7
1814 .. 7	1858 .. 6	1902 .. 4	1946 .. 3	1990 .. 2	2034 .. 1
1815 .. 1	1859 .. 7	1903 .. 5	1947 .. 4	1991 .. 3	2035 .. 2
1816 .. 9	1860 .. 8	1904 .. 13	1948 .. 12	1992 .. 11	2036 .. 10
1817 .. 4	1861 .. 3	1905 .. 1	1949 .. 7	1993 .. 6	2037 .. 5
1818 .. 5	1862 .. 4	1906 .. 2	1950 .. 1	1994 .. 7	2038 .. 6
1819 .. 6	1863 .. 5	1907 .. 3	1951 .. 2	1995 .. 1	2039 .. 7
1820 .. 14	1864 .. 13	1908 .. 11	1952 .. 10	1996 .. 9	2040 .. 8
1821 .. 2	1865 .. 1	1909 .. 6	1953 .. 5	1997 .. 4	2041 .. 3
1822 .. 3	1866 .. 2	1910 .. 7	1954 .. 6	1998 .. 5	2042 .. 4
1823 .. 4	1867 .. 3	1911 .. 1	1955 .. 7	1999 .. 6	2043 .. 5
1824 .. 12	1868 .. 11	1912 .. 9	1956 .. 8	2000 .. 14	2044 .. 13
1825 .. 7	1869 .. 6	1913 .. 4	1957 .. 3	2001 .. 2	2045 .. 1
1826 .. 1	1870 .. 7	1914 .. 5	1958 .. 4	2002 .. 3	2046 .. 2
1827 .. 2	1871 .. 1	1915 .. 6	1959 .. 5	2003 .. 4	2047 .. 3
1828 .. 10	1872 .. 9	1916 .. 14	1960 .. 13	2004 .. 12	2048 .. 11
1829 .. 5	1873 .. 4	1917 .. 2	1961 .. 1	2005 .. 7	2049 .. 6
1830 .. 6	1874 .. 5	1918 .. 3	1962 .. 2	2006 .. 1	2050 .. 7
1831 .. 7	1875 .. 6	1919 .. 4	1963 .. 3	2007 .. 2	2051 .. 1
1832 .. 8	1876 .. 14	1920 .. 12	1964 .. 11	2008 .. 10	2052 .. 9
1833 .. 3	1877 .. 2	1921 .. 7	1965 .. 6	2009 .. 5	2053 .. 4
1834 .. 4	1878 .. 3	1922 .. 1	1966 .. 7	2010 .. 6	2054 .. 5
1835 .. 5	1879 .. 4	1923 .. 2	1967 .. 1	2011 .. 7	2055 .. 6
1836 .. 13	1880 .. 12	1924 .. 10	1968 .. 9	2012 .. 8	2056 .. 14
1837 .. 1	1881 .. 7	1925 .. 5	1969 .. 4	2013 .. 3	2057 .. 2
1838 .. 2	1882 .. 1	1926 .. 6	1970 .. 5	2014 .. 4	2058 .. 3
1839 .. 3	1883 .. 2	1927 .. 7	1971 .. 6	2015 .. 5	2059 .. 4
1840 .. 11	1884 .. 10	1928 .. 8	1972 .. 14	2016 .. 13	2060 .. 12
1841 .. 6	1885 .. 5	1929 .. 3	1973 .. 2	2017 .. 1	2061 .. 7
1842 .. 7	1886 .. 6	1930 .. 4	1974 .. 3	2018 .. 2	2062 .. 1
1843 .. 1	1887 .. 7	1931 .. 5	1975 .. 4	2019 .. 3	2063 .. 2

DIRECTIONS: The number given with each year in the key above is number of calendar to use for that year

1

```
       JANUARY                FEBRUARY                 MARCH                   APRIL
S  M  T  W  T  F  S     S  M  T  W  T  F  S     S  M  T  W  T  F  S     S  M  T  W  T  F  S
 1  2  3  4  5  6  7              1  2  3  4              1  2  3  4                          1
 8  9 10 11 12 13 14     5  6  7  8  9 10 11     5  6  7  8  9 10 11     2  3  4  5  6  7  8
15 16 17 18 19 20 21    12 13 14 15 16 17 18    12 13 14 15 16 17 18     9 10 11 12 13 14 15
22 23 24 25 26 27 28    19 20 21 22 23 24 25    19 20 21 22 23 24 25    16 17 18 19 20 21 22
29 30 31                26 27 28                26 27 28 29 30 31       23 24 25 26 27 28 29
                                                                        30
         MAY                     JUNE                    JULY                   AUGUST
S  M  T  W  T  F  S     S  M  T  W  T  F  S     S  M  T  W  T  F  S     S  M  T  W  T  F  S
    1  2  3  4  5  6              1  2  3                          1           1  2  3  4  5
 7  8  9 10 11 12 13     4  5  6  7  8  9 10     2  3  4  5  6  7  8     6  7  8  9 10 11 12
14 15 16 17 18 19 20    11 12 13 14 15 16 17     9 10 11 12 13 14 15    13 14 15 16 17 18 19
21 22 23 24 25 26 27    18 19 20 21 22 23 24    16 17 18 19 20 21 22    20 21 22 23 24 25 26
28 29 30 31             25 26 27 28 29 30       23 24 25 26 27 28 29    27 28 29 30 31
                                                30 31
      SEPTEMBER                 OCTOBER                NOVEMBER                DECEMBER
S  M  T  W  T  F  S     S  M  T  W  T  F  S     S  M  T  W  T  F  S     S  M  T  W  T  F  S
             1  2        1  2  3  4  5  6  7              1  2  3  4                    1  2
 3  4  5  6  7  8  9     8  9 10 11 12 13 14     5  6  7  8  9 10 11     3  4  5  6  7  8  9
10 11 12 13 14 15 16    15 16 17 18 19 20 21    12 13 14 15 16 17 18    10 11 12 13 14 15 16
17 18 19 20 21 22 23    22 23 24 25 26 27 28    19 20 21 22 23 24 25    17 18 19 20 21 22 23
24 25 26 27 28 29 30    29 30 31                26 27 28 29 30          24 25 26 27 28 29 30
                                                                        31
```

2

```
       JANUARY                FEBRUARY                 MARCH                   APRIL
S  M  T  W  T  F  S     S  M  T  W  T  F  S     S  M  T  W  T  F  S     S  M  T  W  T  F  S
 1  2  3  4  5  6                 1  2  3                 1  2  3        1  2  3  4  5  6  7
 7  8  9 10 11 12 13     4  5  6  7  8  9 10     4  5  6  7  8  9 10     8  9 10 11 12 13 14
14 15 16 17 18 19 20    11 12 13 14 15 16 17    11 12 13 14 15 16 17    15 16 17 18 19 20 21
21 22 23 24 25 26 27    18 19 20 21 22 23 24    18 19 20 21 22 23 24    22 23 24 25 26 27 28
28 29 30 31             25 26 27 28             25 26 27 28 29 30 31    29 30
         MAY                     JUNE                    JULY                   AUGUST
S  M  T  W  T  F  S     S  M  T  W  T  F  S     S  M  T  W  T  F  S     S  M  T  W  T  F  S
       1  2  3  4  5              1  2        1  2  3  4  5  6  7                 1  2  3  4
 6  7  8  9 10 11 12     3  4  5  6  7  8  9     8  9 10 11 12 13 14     5  6  7  8  9 10 11
13 14 15 16 17 18 19    10 11 12 13 14 15 16    15 16 17 18 19 20 21    12 13 14 15 16 17 18
20 21 22 23 24 25 26    17 18 19 20 21 22 23    22 23 24 25 26 27 28    19 20 21 22 23 24 25
27 28 29 30 31          24 25 26 27 28 29 30    29 30 31                26 27 28 29 30 31
      SEPTEMBER                 OCTOBER                NOVEMBER                DECEMBER
S  M  T  W  T  F  S     S  M  T  W  T  F  S     S  M  T  W  T  F  S     S  M  T  W  T  F  S
                1        1  2  3  4  5  6              1  2  3                          1
 2  3  4  5  6  7  8     7  8  9 10 11 12 13     4  5  6  7  8  9 10     2  3  4  5  6  7  8
 9 10 11 12 13 14 15    14 15 16 17 18 19 20    11 12 13 14 15 16 17     9 10 11 12 13 14 15
16 17 18 19 20 21 22    21 22 23 24 25 26 27    18 19 20 21 22 23 24    16 17 18 19 20 21 22
23 24 25 26 27 28 29    28 29 30 31             25 26 27 28 29 30       23 24 25 26 27 28 29
30                                                                      30 31
```

3

```
       JANUARY                FEBRUARY                 MARCH                   APRIL
S  M  T  W  T  F  S     S  M  T  W  T  F  S     S  M  T  W  T  F  S     S  M  T  W  T  F  S
       1  2  3  4  5                    1  2                    1  2              1  2  3  4  5  6
 6  7  8  9 10 11 12     3  4  5  6  7  8  9     3  4  5  6  7  8  9     7  8  9 10 11 12 13
13 14 15 16 17 18 19    10 11 12 13 14 15 16    10 11 12 13 14 15 16    14 15 16 17 18 19 20
20 21 22 23 24 25 26    17 18 19 20 21 22 23    17 18 19 20 21 22 23    21 22 23 24 25 26 27
27 28 29 30 31          24 25 26 27 28          24 25 26 27 28 29 30    28 29 30
                                                31
         MAY                     JUNE                    JULY                   AUGUST
S  M  T  W  T  F  S     S  M  T  W  T  F  S     S  M  T  W  T  F  S     S  M  T  W  T  F  S
          1  2  3  4                    1        1  2  3  4  5  6                    1  2  3
 5  6  7  8  9 10 11     2  3  4  5  6  7  8     7  8  9 10 11 12 13     4  5  6  7  8  9 10
12 13 14 15 16 17 18     9 10 11 12 13 14 15    14 15 16 17 18 19 20    11 12 13 14 15 16 17
19 20 21 22 23 24 25    16 17 18 19 20 21 22    21 22 23 24 25 26 27    18 19 20 21 22 23 24
26 27 28 29 30 31       23 24 25 26 27 28 29    28 29 30 31             25 26 27 28 29 30 31
                        30
      SEPTEMBER                 OCTOBER                NOVEMBER                DECEMBER
S  M  T  W  T  F  S     S  M  T  W  T  F  S     S  M  T  W  T  F  S     S  M  T  W  T  F  S
 1  2  3  4  5  6  7        1  2  3  4  5                    1  2        1  2  3  4  5  6  7
 8  9 10 11 12 13 14     6  7  8  9 10 11 12     3  4  5  6  7  8  9     8  9 10 11 12 13 14
15 16 17 18 19 20 21    13 14 15 16 17 18 19    10 11 12 13 14 15 16    15 16 17 18 19 20 21
22 23 24 25 26 27 28    20 21 22 23 24 25 26    17 18 19 20 21 22 23    22 23 24 25 26 27 28
29 30                   27 28 29 30 31          24 25 26 27 28 29 30    29 30 31
```

4

```
       JANUARY                FEBRUARY                 MARCH                   APRIL
S  M  T  W  T  F  S     S  M  T  W  T  F  S     S  M  T  W  T  F  S     S  M  T  W  T  F  S
          1  2  3  4                       1                       1              1  2  3  4  5
 5  6  7  8  9 10 11     2  3  4  5  6  7  8     2  3  4  5  6  7  8     6  7  8  9 10 11 12
12 13 14 15 16 17 18     9 10 11 12 13 14 15     9 10 11 12 13 14 15    13 14 15 16 17 18 19
19 20 21 22 23 24 25    16 17 18 19 20 21 22    16 17 18 19 20 21 22    20 21 22 23 24 25 26
26 27 28 29 30 31       23 24 25 26 27 28       23 24 25 26 27 28 29    27 28 29 30
                                                30 31
         MAY                     JUNE                    JULY                   AUGUST
S  M  T  W  T  F  S     S  M  T  W  T  F  S     S  M  T  W  T  F  S     S  M  T  W  T  F  S
             1  2  3     1  2  3  4  5  6  7              1  2  3  4  5              1  2
 4  5  6  7  8  9 10     8  9 10 11 12 13 14     6  7  8  9 10 11 12     3  4  5  6  7  8  9
11 12 13 14 15 16 17    15 16 17 18 19 20 21    13 14 15 16 17 18 19    10 11 12 13 14 15 16
18 19 20 21 22 23 24    22 23 24 25 26 27 28    20 21 22 23 24 25 26    17 18 19 20 21 22 23
25 26 27 28 29 30 31    29 30                   27 28 29 30 31          24 25 26 27 28 29 30
                                                                        31
      SEPTEMBER                 OCTOBER                NOVEMBER                DECEMBER
S  M  T  W  T  F  S     S  M  T  W  T  F  S     S  M  T  W  T  F  S     S  M  T  W  T  F  S
    1  2  3  4  5  6              1  2  3  4                       1        1  2  3  4  5  6
 7  8  9 10 11 12 13     5  6  7  8  9 10 11     2  3  4  5  6  7  8     7  8  9 10 11 12 13
14 15 16 17 18 19 20    12 13 14 15 16 17 18     9 10 11 12 13 14 15    14 15 16 17 18 19 20
21 22 23 24 25 26 27    19 20 21 22 23 24 25    16 17 18 19 20 21 22    21 22 23 24 25 26 27
28 29 30                26 27 28 29 30 31       23 24 25 26 27 28 29    28 29 30 31
                                                30
```

5

```
       JANUARY                FEBRUARY                 MARCH                   APRIL
S  M  T  W  T  F  S     S  M  T  W  T  F  S     S  M  T  W  T  F  S     S  M  T  W  T  F  S
             1  2  3     1  2  3  4  5  6  7     1  2  3  4  5  6  7              1  2  3  4
 4  5  6  7  8  9 10     8  9 10 11 12 13 14     8  9 10 11 12 13 14     5  6  7  8  9 10 11
11 12 13 14 15 16 17    15 16 17 18 19 20 21    15 16 17 18 19 20 21    12 13 14 15 16 17 18
18 19 20 21 22 23 24    22 23 24 25 26 27 28    22 23 24 25 26 27 28    19 20 21 22 23 24 25
25 26 27 28 29 30 31                            29 30 31                26 27 28 29 30
         MAY                     JUNE                    JULY                   AUGUST
S  M  T  W  T  F  S     S  M  T  W  T  F  S     S  M  T  W  T  F  S     S  M  T  W  T  F  S
                1  2challenge 1  2  3  4  5  6              1  2  3  4                          1
 3  4  5  6  7  8  9     7  8  9 10 11 12 13     5  6  7  8  9 10 11     2  3  4  5  6  7  8
10 11 12 13 14 15 16    14 15 16 17 18 19 20    12 13 14 15 16 17 18     9 10 11 12 13 14 15
17 18 19 20 21 22 23    21 22 23 24 25 26 27    19 20 21 22 23 24 25    16 17 18 19 20 21 22
24 25 26 27 28 29 30    28 29 30                26 27 28 29 30 31       23 24 25 26 27 28 29
31                                                                      30 31
      SEPTEMBER                 OCTOBER                NOVEMBER                DECEMBER
S  M  T  W  T  F  S     S  M  T  W  T  F  S     S  M  T  W  T  F  S     S  M  T  W  T  F  S
       1  2  3  4  5              1  2  3        1  2  3  4  5  6  7              1  2  3  4  5
 6  7  8  9 10 11 12     4  5  6  7  8  9 10     8  9 10 11 12 13 14     6  7  8  9 10 11 12
13 14 15 16 17 18 19    11 12 13 14 15 16 17    15 16 17 18 19 20 21    13 14 15 16 17 18 19
20 21 22 23 24 25 26    18 19 20 21 22 23 24    22 23 24 25 26 27 28    20 21 22 23 24 25 26
27 28 29 30             25 26 27 28 29 30 31    29 30                   27 28 29 30 31
```

6

```
       JANUARY                FEBRUARY                 MARCH                   APRIL
S  M  T  W  T  F  S     S  M  T  W  T  F  S     S  M  T  W  T  F  S     S  M  T  W  T  F  S
                1  2     1  2  3  4  5  6        1  2  3  4  5  6              1  2  3
 3  4  5  6  7  8  9     7  8  9 10 11 12 13     7  8  9 10 11 12 13     4  5  6  7  8  9 10
10 11 12 13 14 15 16    14 15 16 17 18 19 20    14 15 16 17 18 19 20    11 12 13 14 15 16 17
17 18 19 20 21 22 23    21 22 23 24 25 26 27    21 22 23 24 25 26 27    18 19 20 21 22 23 24
24 25 26 27 28 29 30    28                      28 29 30 31             25 26 27 28 29 30
31
         MAY                     JUNE                    JULY                   AUGUST
S  M  T  W  T  F  S     S  M  T  W  T  F  S     S  M  T  W  T  F  S     S  M  T  W  T  F  S
                   1              1  2  3  4  5              1  2  3     1  2  3  4  5  6  7
 2  3  4  5  6  7  8     6  7  8  9 10 11 12     4  5  6  7  8  9 10     8  9 10 11 12 13 14
 9 10 11 12 13 14 15    13 14 15 16 17 18 19    11 12 13 14 15 16 17    15 16 17 18 19 20 21
16 17 18 19 20 21 22    20 21 22 23 24 25 26    18 19 20 21 22 23 24    22 23 24 25 26 27 28
23 24 25 26 27 28 29    27 28 29 30             25 26 27 28 29 30 31    29 30 31
30 31
      SEPTEMBER                 OCTOBER                NOVEMBER                DECEMBER
S  M  T  W  T  F  S     S  M  T  W  T  F  S     S  M  T  W  T  F  S     S  M  T  W  T  F  S
          1  2  3  4              1  2        1  2  3  4  5  6              1  2  3  4
 5  6  7  8  9 10 11     3  4  5  6  7  8  9     7  8  9 10 11 12 13     5  6  7  8  9 10 11
12 13 14 15 16 17 18    10 11 12 13 14 15 16    14 15 16 17 18 19 20    12 13 14 15 16 17 18
19 20 21 22 23 24 25    17 18 19 20 21 22 23    21 22 23 24 25 26 27    19 20 21 22 23 24 25
26 27 28 29 30          24 25 26 27 28 29 30    28 29 30                26 27 28 29 30 31
                        31
```

7

JANUARY
```
S  M  T  W  T  F  S
               1
 2  3  4  5  6  7  8
 9 10 11 12 13 14 15
16 17 18 19 20 21 22
23 24 25 26 27 28 29
30 31
```

FEBRUARY
```
S  M  T  W  T  F  S
    1  2  3  4  5
 6  7  8  9 10 11 12
13 14 15 16 17 18 19
20 21 22 23 24 25 26
27 28
```

MARCH
```
S  M  T  W  T  F  S
    1  2  3  4  5
 6  7  8  9 10 11 12
13 14 15 16 17 18 19
20 21 22 23 24 25 26
27 28 29 30 31
```

APRIL
```
S  M  T  W  T  F  S
             1  2
 3  4  5  6  7  8  9
10 11 12 13 14 15 16
17 18 19 20 21 22 23
24 25 26 27 28 29 30
```

MAY
```
S  M  T  W  T  F  S
 1  2  3  4  5  6  7
 8  9 10 11 12 13 14
15 16 17 18 19 20 21
22 23 24 25 26 27 28
29 30 31
```

JUNE
```
S  M  T  W  T  F  S
          1  2  3  4
 5  6  7  8  9 10 11
12 13 14 15 16 17 18
19 20 21 22 23 24 25
26 27 28 29 30
```

JULY
```
S  M  T  W  T  F  S
             1  2
 3  4  5  6  7  8  9
10 11 12 13 14 15 16
17 18 19 20 21 22 23
24 25 26 27 28 29 30
31
```

AUGUST
```
S  M  T  W  T  F  S
    1  2  3  4  5  6
 7  8  9 10 11 12 13
14 15 16 17 18 19 20
21 22 23 24 25 26 27
28 29 30 31
```

SEPTEMBER
```
S  M  T  W  T  F  S
          1  2  3
 4  5  6  7  8  9 10
11 12 13 14 15 16 17
18 19 20 21 22 23 24
25 26 27 28 29 30
```

OCTOBER
```
S  M  T  W  T  F  S
                1
 2  3  4  5  6  7  8
 9 10 11 12 13 14 15
16 17 18 19 20 21 22
23 24 25 26 27 28 29
30 31
```

NOVEMBER
```
S  M  T  W  T  F  S
    1  2  3  4  5
 6  7  8  9 10 11 12
13 14 15 16 17 18 19
20 21 22 23 24 25 26
27 28 29 30
```

DECEMBER
```
S  M  T  W  T  F  S
          1  2  3
 4  5  6  7  8  9 10
11 12 13 14 15 16 17
18 19 20 21 22 23 24
25 26 27 28 29 30 31
```

8

JANUARY
```
S  M  T  W  T  F  S
 1  2  3  4  5  6  7
 8  9 10 11 12 13 14
15 16 17 18 19 20 21
22 23 24 25 26 27 28
29 30 31
```

FEBRUARY
```
S  M  T  W  T  F  S
       1  2  3  4
 5  6  7  8  9 10 11
12 13 14 15 16 17 18
19 20 21 22 23 24 25
26 27 28 29
```

MARCH
```
S  M  T  W  T  F  S
          1  2  3
 4  5  6  7  8  9 10
11 12 13 14 15 16 17
18 19 20 21 22 23 24
25 26 27 28 29 30 31
```

APRIL
```
S  M  T  W  T  F  S
 1  2  3  4  5  6  7
 8  9 10 11 12 13 14
15 16 17 18 19 20 21
22 23 24 25 26 27 28
29 30
```

MAY
```
S  M  T  W  T  F  S
       1  2  3  4  5
 6  7  8  9 10 11 12
13 14 15 16 17 18 19
20 21 22 23 24 25 26
27 28 29 30 31
```

JUNE
```
S  M  T  W  T  F  S
             1  2
 3  4  5  6  7  8  9
10 11 12 13 14 15 16
17 18 19 20 21 22 23
24 25 26 27 28 29 30
```

JULY
```
S  M  T  W  T  F  S
 1  2  3  4  5  6  7
 8  9 10 11 12 13 14
15 16 17 18 19 20 21
22 23 24 25 26 27 28
29 30 31
```

AUGUST
```
S  M  T  W  T  F  S
          1  2  3  4
 5  6  7  8  9 10 11
12 13 14 15 16 17 18
19 20 21 22 23 24 25
26 27 28 29 30 31
```

SEPTEMBER
```
S  M  T  W  T  F  S
                1
 2  3  4  5  6  7  8
 9 10 11 12 13 14 15
16 17 18 19 20 21 22
23 24 25 26 27 28 29
30
```

OCTOBER
```
S  M  T  W  T  F  S
    1  2  3  4  5  6
 7  8  9 10 11 12 13
14 15 16 17 18 19 20
21 22 23 24 25 26 27
28 29 30 31
```

NOVEMBER
```
S  M  T  W  T  F  S
          1  2  3
 4  5  6  7  8  9 10
11 12 13 14 15 16 17
18 19 20 21 22 23 24
25 26 27 28 29 30
```

DECEMBER
```
S  M  T  W  T  F  S
                1
 2  3  4  5  6  7  8
 9 10 11 12 13 14 15
16 17 18 19 20 21 22
23 24 25 26 27 28 29
30 31
```

9

JANUARY
```
S  M  T  W  T  F  S
    1  2  3  4  5  6
 7  8  9 10 11 12 13
14 15 16 17 18 19 20
21 22 23 24 25 26 27
28 29 30 31
```

FEBRUARY
```
S  M  T  W  T  F  S
          1  2  3
 4  5  6  7  8  9 10
11 12 13 14 15 16 17
18 19 20 21 22 23 24
25 26 27 28
```

MARCH
```
S  M  T  W  T  F  S
          1  2  3
 4  5  6  7  8  9 10
11 12 13 14 15 16 17
18 19 20 21 22 23 24
25 26 27 28 29 30 31
```

APRIL
```
S  M  T  W  T  F  S
 1  2  3  4  5  6  7
 8  9 10 11 12 13 14
15 16 17 18 19 20 21
22 23 24 25 26 27 28
29 30
```

MAY
```
S  M  T  W  T  F  S
       1  2  3  4  5
 6  7  8  9 10 11 12
13 14 15 16 17 18 19
20 21 22 23 24 25 26
27 28 29 30 31
```

JUNE
```
S  M  T  W  T  F  S
             1  2
 3  4  5  6  7  8  9
10 11 12 13 14 15 16
17 18 19 20 21 22 23
24 25 26 27 28 29 30
```

JULY
```
S  M  T  W  T  F  S
 1  2  3  4  5  6  7
 8  9 10 11 12 13 14
15 16 17 18 19 20 21
22 23 24 25 26 27 28
29 30 31
```

AUGUST
```
S  M  T  W  T  F  S
          1  2  3  4
 5  6  7  8  9 10 11
12 13 14 15 16 17 18
19 20 21 22 23 24 25
26 27 28 29 30 31
```

SEPTEMBER
```
S  M  T  W  T  F  S
                1
 2  3  4  5  6  7  8
 9 10 11 12 13 14 15
16 17 18 19 20 21 22
23 24 25 26 27 28 29
30
```

OCTOBER
```
S  M  T  W  T  F  S
    1  2  3  4  5  6
 7  8  9 10 11 12 13
14 15 16 17 18 19 20
21 22 23 24 25 26 27
28 29 30 31
```

NOVEMBER
```
S  M  T  W  T  F  S
          1  2  3
 4  5  6  7  8  9 10
11 12 13 14 15 16 17
18 19 20 21 22 23 24
25 26 27 28 29 30
```

DECEMBER
```
S  M  T  W  T  F  S
                1
 2  3  4  5  6  7  8
 9 10 11 12 13 14 15
16 17 18 19 20 21 22
23 24 25 26 27 28 29
30 31
```

10

JANUARY
```
S  M  T  W  T  F  S
       1  2  3  4  5
 6  7  8  9 10 11 12
13 14 15 16 17 18 19
20 21 22 23 24 25 26
27 28 29 30 31
```

FEBRUARY
```
S  M  T  W  T  F  S
             1  2
 3  4  5  6  7  8  9
10 11 12 13 14 15 16
17 18 19 20 21 22 23
24 25 26 27 28
```

MARCH
```
S  M  T  W  T  F  S
             1  2
 3  4  5  6  7  8  9
10 11 12 13 14 15 16
17 18 19 20 21 22 23
24 25 26 27 28 29 30
31
```

APRIL
```
S  M  T  W  T  F  S
    1  2  3  4  5  6
 7  8  9 10 11 12 13
14 15 16 17 18 19 20
21 22 23 24 25 26 27
28 29 30
```

MAY
```
S  M  T  W  T  F  S
          1  2  3  4
 5  6  7  8  9 10 11
12 13 14 15 16 17 18
19 20 21 22 23 24 25
26 27 28 29 30 31
```

JUNE
```
S  M  T  W  T  F  S
                1
 2  3  4  5  6  7  8
 9 10 11 12 13 14 15
16 17 18 19 20 21 22
23 24 25 26 27 28 29
30
```

JULY
```
S  M  T  W  T  F  S
    1  2  3  4  5  6
 7  8  9 10 11 12 13
14 15 16 17 18 19 20
21 22 23 24 25 26 27
28 29 30 31
```

AUGUST
```
S  M  T  W  T  F  S
          1  2  3
 4  5  6  7  8  9 10
11 12 13 14 15 16 17
18 19 20 21 22 23 24
25 26 27 28 29 30 31
```

SEPTEMBER
```
S  M  T  W  T  F  S
 1  2  3  4  5  6  7
 8  9 10 11 12 13 14
15 16 17 18 19 20 21
22 23 24 25 26 27 28
29 30
```

OCTOBER
```
S  M  T  W  T  F  S
       1  2  3  4  5
 6  7  8  9 10 11 12
13 14 15 16 17 18 19
20 21 22 23 24 25 26
27 28 29 30 31
```

NOVEMBER
```
S  M  T  W  T  F  S
             1  2
 3  4  5  6  7  8  9
10 11 12 13 14 15 16
17 18 19 20 21 22 23
24 25 26 27 28 29 30
```

DECEMBER
```
S  M  T  W  T  F  S
 1  2  3  4  5  6  7
 8  9 10 11 12 13 14
15 16 17 18 19 20 21
22 23 24 25 26 27 28
29 30 31
```

11

JANUARY
```
S  M  T  W  T  F  S
          1  2  3  4
 5  6  7  8  9 10 11
12 13 14 15 16 17 18
19 20 21 22 23 24 25
26 27 28 29 30 31
```

FEBRUARY
```
S  M  T  W  T  F  S
                1
 2  3  4  5  6  7  8
 9 10 11 12 13 14 15
16 17 18 19 20 21 22
23 24 25 26 27 28
```

MARCH
```
S  M  T  W  T  F  S
                1
 2  3  4  5  6  7  8
 9 10 11 12 13 14 15
16 17 18 19 20 21 22
23 24 25 26 27 28 29
30 31
```

APRIL
```
S  M  T  W  T  F  S
       1  2  3  4  5
 6  7  8  9 10 11 12
13 14 15 16 17 18 19
20 21 22 23 24 25 26
27 28 29 30
```

MAY
```
S  M  T  W  T  F  S
          1  2  3
 4  5  6  7  8  9 10
11 12 13 14 15 16 17
18 19 20 21 22 23 24
25 26 27 28 29 30 31
```

JUNE
```
S  M  T  W  T  F  S
 1  2  3  4  5  6  7
 8  9 10 11 12 13 14
15 16 17 18 19 20 21
22 23 24 25 26 27 28
29 30
```

JULY
```
S  M  T  W  T  F  S
       1  2  3  4  5
 6  7  8  9 10 11 12
13 14 15 16 17 18 19
20 21 22 23 24 25 26
27 28 29 30 31
```

AUGUST
```
S  M  T  W  T  F  S
             1  2
 3  4  5  6  7  8  9
10 11 12 13 14 15 16
17 18 19 20 21 22 23
24 25 26 27 28 29 30
31
```

SEPTEMBER
```
S  M  T  W  T  F  S
    1  2  3  4  5  6
 7  8  9 10 11 12 13
14 15 16 17 18 19 20
21 22 23 24 25 26 27
28 29 30
```

OCTOBER
```
S  M  T  W  T  F  S
          1  2  3  4
 5  6  7  8  9 10 11
12 13 14 15 16 17 18
19 20 21 22 23 24 25
26 27 28 29 30 31
```

NOVEMBER
```
S  M  T  W  T  F  S
                1
 2  3  4  5  6  7  8
 9 10 11 12 13 14 15
16 17 18 19 20 21 22
23 24 25 26 27 28 29
30
```

DECEMBER
```
S  M  T  W  T  F  S
    1  2  3  4  5  6
 7  8  9 10 11 12 13
14 15 16 17 18 19 20
21 22 23 24 25 26 27
28 29 30 31
```

12

JANUARY
```
S  M  T  W  T  F  S
          1  2  3
 4  5  6  7  8  9 10
11 12 13 14 15 16 17
18 19 20 21 22 23 24
25 26 27 28 29 30 31
```

FEBRUARY
```
S  M  T  W  T  F  S
 1  2  3  4  5  6  7
 8  9 10 11 12 13 14
15 16 17 18 19 20 21
22 23 24 25 26 27 28
29
```

MARCH
```
S  M  T  W  T  F  S
    1  2  3  4  5  6
 7  8  9 10 11 12 13
14 15 16 17 18 19 20
21 22 23 24 25 26 27
28 29 30 31
```

APRIL
```
S  M  T  W  T  F  S
          1  2  3
 4  5  6  7  8  9 10
11 12 13 14 15 16 17
18 19 20 21 22 23 24
25 26 27 28 29 30
```

MAY
```
S  M  T  W  T  F  S
                1
 2  3  4  5  6  7  8
 9 10 11 12 13 14 15
16 17 18 19 20 21 22
23 24 25 26 27 28 29
30 31
```

JUNE
```
S  M  T  W  T  F  S
       1  2  3  4  5
 6  7  8  9 10 11 12
13 14 15 16 17 18 19
20 21 22 23 24 25 26
27 28 29 30
```

JULY
```
S  M  T  W  T  F  S
          1  2  3
 4  5  6  7  8  9 10
11 12 13 14 15 16 17
18 19 20 21 22 23 24
25 26 27 28 29 30 31
```

AUGUST
```
S  M  T  W  T  F  S
 1  2  3  4  5  6  7
 8  9 10 11 12 13 14
15 16 17 18 19 20 21
22 23 24 25 26 27 28
29 30 31
```

SEPTEMBER
```
S  M  T  W  T  F  S
          1  2  3  4
 5  6  7  8  9 10 11
12 13 14 15 16 17 18
19 20 21 22 23 24 25
26 27 28 29 30
```

OCTOBER
```
S  M  T  W  T  F  S
             1  2
 3  4  5  6  7  8  9
10 11 12 13 14 15 16
17 18 19 20 21 22 23
24 25 26 27 28 29 30
31
```

NOVEMBER
```
S  M  T  W  T  F  S
    1  2  3  4  5  6
 7  8  9 10 11 12 13
14 15 16 17 18 19 20
21 22 23 24 25 26 27
28 29 30
```

DECEMBER
```
S  M  T  W  T  F  S
          1  2  3  4
 5  6  7  8  9 10 11
12 13 14 15 16 17 18
19 20 21 22 23 24 25
26 27 28 29 30 31
```

13

JANUARY
```
S  M  T  W  T  F  S
                1  2
 3  4  5  6  7  8  9
10 11 12 13 14 15 16
17 18 19 20 21 22 23
24 25 26 27 28 29 30
31
```

FEBRUARY
```
S  M  T  W  T  F  S
    1  2  3  4  5  6
 7  8  9 10 11 12 13
14 15 16 17 18 19 20
21 22 23 24 25 26 27
28 29
```

MARCH
```
S  M  T  W  T  F  S
       1  2  3  4  5
 6  7  8  9 10 11 12
13 14 15 16 17 18 19
20 21 22 23 24 25 26
27 28 29 30 31
```

APRIL
```
S  M  T  W  T  F  S
                1  2
 3  4  5  6  7  8  9
10 11 12 13 14 15 16
17 18 19 20 21 22 23
24 25 26 27 28 29 30
```

MAY
```
S  M  T  W  T  F  S
 1  2  3  4  5  6  7
 8  9 10 11 12 13 14
15 16 17 18 19 20 21
22 23 24 25 26 27 28
29 30 31
```

JUNE
```
S  M  T  W  T  F  S
          1  2  3  4
 5  6  7  8  9 10 11
12 13 14 15 16 17 18
19 20 21 22 23 24 25
26 27 28 29 30
```

JULY
```
S  M  T  W  T  F  S
                1  2
 3  4  5  6  7  8  9
10 11 12 13 14 15 16
17 18 19 20 21 22 23
24 25 26 27 28 29 30
31
```

AUGUST
```
S  M  T  W  T  F  S
    1  2  3  4  5  6
 7  8  9 10 11 12 13
14 15 16 17 18 19 20
21 22 23 24 25 26 27
28 29 30 31
```

SEPTEMBER
```
S  M  T  W  T  F  S
          1  2  3
 4  5  6  7  8  9 10
11 12 13 14 15 16 17
18 19 20 21 22 23 24
25 26 27 28 29 30
```

OCTOBER
```
S  M  T  W  T  F  S
                1
 2  3  4  5  6  7  8
 9 10 11 12 13 14 15
16 17 18 19 20 21 22
23 24 25 26 27 28 29
30 31
```

NOVEMBER
```
S  M  T  W  T  F  S
    1  2  3  4  5
 6  7  8  9 10 11 12
13 14 15 16 17 18 19
20 21 22 23 24 25 26
27 28 29 30
```

DECEMBER
```
S  M  T  W  T  F  S
          1  2  3
 4  5  6  7  8  9 10
11 12 13 14 15 16 17
18 19 20 21 22 23 24
25 26 27 28 29 30 31
```

14

JANUARY
```
S  M  T  W  T  F  S
                1
 2  3  4  5  6  7  8
 9 10 11 12 13 14 15
16 17 18 19 20 21 22
23 24 25 26 27 28 29
30 31
```

FEBRUARY
```
S  M  T  W  T  F  S
    1  2  3  4  5
 6  7  8  9 10 11 12
13 14 15 16 17 18 19
20 21 22 23 24 25 26
27 28
```

MARCH
```
S  M  T  W  T  F  S
    1  2  3  4  5
 6  7  8  9 10 11 12
13 14 15 16 17 18 19
20 21 22 23 24 25 26
27 28 29 30 31
```

APRIL
```
S  M  T  W  T  F  S
             1  2
 3  4  5  6  7  8  9
10 11 12 13 14 15 16
17 18 19 20 21 22 23
24 25 26 27 28 29 30
```

MAY
```
S  M  T  W  T  F  S
 1  2  3  4  5  6  7
 8  9 10 11 12 13 14
15 16 17 18 19 20 21
22 23 24 25 26 27 28
29 30 31
```

JUNE
```
S  M  T  W  T  F  S
          1  2  3  4
 5  6  7  8  9 10 11
12 13 14 15 16 17 18
19 20 21 22 23 24 25
26 27 28 29 30
```

JULY
```
S  M  T  W  T  F  S
             1  2
 3  4  5  6  7  8  9
10 11 12 13 14 15 16
17 18 19 20 21 22 23
24 25 26 27 28 29 30
31
```

AUGUST
```
S  M  T  W  T  F  S
    1  2  3  4  5  6
 7  8  9 10 11 12 13
14 15 16 17 18 19 20
21 22 23 24 25 26 27
28 29 30 31
```

SEPTEMBER
```
S  M  T  W  T  F  S
          1  2  3
 4  5  6  7  8  9 10
11 12 13 14 15 16 17
18 19 20 21 22 23 24
25 26 27 28 29 30
```

OCTOBER
```
S  M  T  W  T  F  S
                1
 2  3  4  5  6  7  8
 9 10 11 12 13 14 15
16 17 18 19 20 21 22
23 24 25 26 27 28 29
30 31
```

NOVEMBER
```
S  M  T  W  T  F  S
    1  2  3  4  5
 6  7  8  9 10 11 12
13 14 15 16 17 18 19
20 21 22 23 24 25 26
27 28 29 30
```

DECEMBER
```
S  M  T  W  T  F  S
          1  2  3
 4  5  6  7  8  9 10
11 12 13 14 15 16 17
18 19 20 21 22 23 24
25 26 27 28 29 30 31
```

The Calendar

History of the Calendar

The purpose of a calendar is to reckon time in advance, to show how many days have to elapse until a certain event takes place—the harvest, a religious festival, or whatever. The earliest calendars, naturally, were crude, and they must have been strongly influenced by the geographical location of the people who made them. In the Scandinavian countries, for example, where the seasons are pronounced, the concept of the year was determined by the seasons, specifically by the end of winter. The Norsemen, before becoming Christians, are said to have had a calendar consisting of ten months of 30 days each.

But in warmer countries, where the seasons are less pronounced, the Moon became the basic unit for time reckoning; an old Jewish book actually makes the statement that "the Moon was created for the counting of the days." All the oldest calendars of which we have reliable information were lunar calendars, based on the time interval from one new moon to the next—a so-called "lunation." But even in a warm climate there are annual events that pay no attention to the phases of the Moon. In some areas it was a rainy season; in Egypt it was the annual flooding of the Nile. It was, therefore, necessary to regulate daily life and religious festivals by lunations, but to take care of the annual event in some other manner.

The calendar of the Assyrians was based on the phases of the Moon. The month began with the first appearance of the lunar crescent, and since this can best be observed in the evening, the day began with sunset. They knew that a lunation was 29 1/2 days long, so their lunar year had a duration of 354 days, falling eleven days short of the solar year.[1] After three years such a lunar calendar would be off by 33 days, or more than one lunation. We know that the Assyrians added an extra month from time to time, but we do not know whether they had developed a special rule for doing so or whether the priests proclaimed the necessity for an extra month from observation. If they made every third year a year of 13 lunations, their three-year period would cover 1,091 1/2 days (using their value of 29 1/2 days for one lunation), or just about four days too short. In one century this mistake would add up to 133 days by their reckoning (in reality closer to 134 days), requiring four extra lunations per century.

We now know that an eight-year period, consisting of five years with 12 months and three years with 13 months would lead to a difference of only 20 days per century, but we do not know whether such a calendar was actually used.

The best approximation that was possible in antiquity was a 19-year period, with seven of these 19 years having 13 months. This means that the period contained 235 months. This, still using the old value for a lunation, made a total of 6,932 1/2 days, while 19 solar years added up to 6,939.7 days, a difference of just one week per period and about five weeks per century. Even the 19-year period required constant adjustment, but it was the period that became the basis of the religious calendar of the Jews. The Arabs used the same calendar at first, but Mohammed forbade shifting from 12 months to 13 months, so that the Islamic religious calendar, even today, has a lunar year of 354 days. As a result the Islamic religious festivals run through all the seasons of the year three times per century.

The Egyptians had a traditional calendar with 12 months of 30 days each. At one time they added five extra days at the end of every year. These turned into a five-day festival because it was thought to be unlucky to work during that time.

When Rome emerged as a world power, the difficulties of making a calendar were well known, but the Romans complicated their lives because of their superstition that even numbers were unlucky. Hence their months were 29 or 31 days long, with the exception of February, which had 28 days. However, four months of 31 days, seven months of 29 days, and one month of 28 days added up to only 355 days. Therefore, the Romans invented an extra month called Mercedonius of 22 or 23 days. It was added every second year.

Even with Mercedonius, the Roman calendar was so far off that Caesar, advised by the astronomer Sosigenes, ordered a sweeping reform in 45 B.C. One year, made 445 days long by imperial decree, brought the calendar back in step with the seasons. Then the solar year (with the value of 365 days and 6 hours) was made the basis of the calendar. The months were 30 or 31 days in length, and to take care of the six hours, every fourth year was made a 366-day year. Moreover, Caesar decreed, the year began with the first of January, not with the vernal equinox in late March.

This was the Julian calendar, named after Julius Caesar. It is still the calendar of the Eastern Orthodox churches.

However, the year is 11 1/2 minutes shorter than the figure written into Caesar's calendar by Sosigenes, and after a number of centuries, even 11 1/2 minutes add up. *See* table.

While Caesar could decree that the vernal equinox should not be used as the first day of the new year, the vernal equinox is still a fact of Nature that could not be disregarded. One of the first (as far as we know) to become alarmed about this was Roger Bacon. He sent a memorandum to Pope Clement IV, who apparently was not impressed. But Pope Sixtus IV (reigned 1471 to 1484) decided that another reform was needed and called the German astronomer Regiomontanus to Rome to advise him. Regiomontanus arrived in 1475, but one year later he died in an epidemic, one of the recurrent outbreaks of the plague. The Pope himself survived, but his reform plans died with Regiomontanus.

Less than a hundred years later, in 1545, the Council of Trent authorized the then Pope, Paul III, to reform the calendar once more. Most of the mathematical and astronomical work was done by Father Christopher Clavius, S.J. The immediate correction, advised by Father Clavius and ordered by Pope Gregory XIII, was that Thursday, Oct. 4, 1582, was to be the last day of the Julian calendar. The next day was Friday, with the date of October 15. For long-range accuracy, a formula suggested by the Vatican librarian Aloysius Giglio (latinized into Lilius) was adopted: every fourth year is a leap year *unless* it is a century year like 1700 or 1800. Century years can be

---

1. The correct figures are: lunation: 29 d, 12 h, 44 min, 2.8 sec (29.530585 d); solar year: 365 d, 5 h, 48 min, 46 sec (365.242216 d); 12 lunations: 354 d, 8 h, 48 min, 34 sec (354.3671 d).

Drift of the Vernal Equinox in the Julian Calendar

Date	Julian year	Date	Julian year	Date	Julian Year
March 21	325 A.D.	March 17	837 A.D.	March 13	1349 A.D.
March 20	453 A.D.	March 16	965 A.D.	March 12	1477 A.D.
March 19	581 A.D.	March 15	1093 A.D.	March 11	1605 A.D.
March 18	709 A.D.	March 14	1221 A.D.		

leap years *only* when they are divisible by 400 (e.g., 1600). This rule eliminates three leap years in four centuries, making the calendar sufficiently correct for all ordinary purposes.

Unfortunately, all the Protestant princes in 1582 chose to ignore the papal bull; they continued with the Julian calendar. It was not until 1698 that the German professor Erhard Weigel persuaded the Protestant rulers of Germany and of the Netherlands to change to the new calendar. In England the shift took place in 1752, and in Russia it needed the revolution to introduce the Gregorian calendar in 1918.

The average year of the Gregorian calendar, in spite of the leap year rule, is about 26 seconds longer than the earth's orbital period. But this discrepancy will need 3,323 years to build up to a single day.

Modern proposals for calendar reform do not aim at a "better" calendar, but at one that is more convenient to use, especially for commercial purposes. A 365-day year cannot be divided into equal halves or quarters; the number of days per month is haphazard; the months begin or end in the middle of a week; a holiday fixed by date (e.g., the Fourth of July) will wander through a week; a holiday fixed in another manner (e.g., Easter) can fall on thirty-five possible dates. The Gregorian calendar, admittedly, keeps the calendar dates in reasonable unison with astronomical events, but it still is full of minor annoyances. Moreover, you need a calendar every year to look up dates; an ideal calendar would be one that you can memorize for one year and that is valid for all other years, too.

In 1834 an Italian priest, Marco Mastrofini, suggested taking one day out of every year. It would be made a holiday and *not* be given the name of a weekday. That would make every year begin with January 1 as a Sunday. The leap-year day would be treated the same way, so that in leap years there would be two unnamed holidays at the end of the year.

About a decade later the philosopher Auguste Comte also suggested a 364-day calendar with an extra day, which he called Year Day.

Since then there have been other unsuccessful attempts at calendar reform.

Time and Calendar

The two natural cycles on which time measurements are based are the year and the day. The year is defined as the time required for the Earth to complete one revolution around the Sun, while the day is the time for the Earth to complete one turn upon its axis. Unfortunately the Earth needs 365 days plus about six hours to go around the Sun once, so that the year does not consist of so and so many days; the fractional day has to be taken care of by an extra day every fourth year.

But because the Earth, while turning upon its axis, also moves around the Sun there are two kinds of days. A day may be defined as the interval between the highest point of the Sun in the sky on two succes-

sive days. This, averaged out over the year, produces the customary 24-hour day. But one might also define a day as the time interval between the moments when a certain point in the sky, say a conveniently located star, is directly overhead. This is called:

Sidereal time. Astronomers use a point which they call the "vernal equinox" for the actual determination. Such a sidereal day is somewhat shorter than the "solar day," namely by about 3 minutes and 56 seconds of so-called "mean solar time."

Apparent solar time is the time based directly on the Sun's position in the sky. In ordinary life the day runs from midnight to midnight. It begins when the Sun is invisible by being 12 hours from its zenith. Astronomers use the so-called "Julian Day," which runs from noon to noon; the concept was invented by the astronomer Joseph Scaliger, who named it after his father Julius. To avoid the problems caused by leap-year days and so forth, Scaliger picked a conveniently remote date in the past and suggested just counting days without regard to weeks, months, and years. The Julian Day for 0^h Jan. 31, 1992 is 244 8621.5. The reason for having the Julian Day run from noon to noon is the practical one that astronomical observations usually extend across the midnight hour, which would require a change in date (or in the Julian Day number) if the astronomical day, like the civil day, ran from midnight to midnight.

Mean solar time, rather than apparent solar time, is what is actually used most of the time. The mean solar time is based on the position of a fictitious "mean sun." The reason why this fictitious sun has to be introduced is the following: the Earth turns on its axis regularly; it needs the same number of seconds regardless of the season. But the movement of the Earth around the Sun is not regular because the Earth's orbit is an ellipse. This has the result (as explained in the section The Seasons) that the Earth moves faster in January and slower in July. Though it is the Earth that changes velocity, it looks to us as if the Sun did. In January, when the Earth moves faster, the *apparent* movement of the Sun looks faster. The "mean sun" of time measurements, then, is a sun that moves regularly all year round; the real Sun will be either ahead of or behind the "mean sun." The difference between the real Sun and the fictitious mean sun is called the *equation of time.*

When the real Sun is west of the mean sun we have the "sun fast" condition, with the real Sun crossing the meridian ahead of the mean sun. The opposite is the "sun slow" situation when the real Sun crosses the meridian after the mean sun. Of course, what is observed is the real Sun. The equation of time is needed to establish mean solar time, kept by the reference clocks.

But if all clocks were actually set by mean solar time we would be plagued by a welter of time differences that would be "correct" but a major nuisance. A clock on Long Island, correctly showing mean solar time for its location (this would be *local civil time*), would be slightly ahead of a clock in Newark, N.J. The Newark clock would be slightly ahead of a

The Names of Days

Latin	Saxon	English	French	Itralian	Spanish	German
Dies Solis	Sun's Day	Sunday	dimanche	domenica	domingo	Sonntag
Dies Lunae	Moon's Day	Monday	lundi	lunedi	lunes	Montag
Dies Martis	Tiw's Day	Tuesday	mardi	martedi	martes	Dienstag
Dies Mercurii	Woden's Day	Wednesday	mercredi	mercoledi	miércoles	Mittwoch
Dies Jovis	Thor's Day	Thursday	jeudi	giovedi	jueves	Donnerstag
Dies Veneris	Frigg's Day	Friday	vendredi	venedri	viernes	Freitag
Dies Saturni	Seterne's Day	Saturday	samedi	sabato	sáabado	Sonnabend

NOTE: The Romans gave one day of the week to each planet known, the Sun and Moon being considered planets in this connection. The Saxon names are a kind of translation of the Roman names: Tiw was substituted for Mars, Woden (Wotan) for Mercury, Thor for Jupiter (Jove), Frigg for Venus, and Seterne for Saturn. The English names are adapted Saxon. The Spanish and Italian names, which are normally not capitalized, and the French are derived from the Latin. The German names follow the Saxon pattern with two exceptions: Wednesday is Mittwoch (Middle of the Week), and Saturday is Sonnabend (Sunday's Eve).

clock in Trenton, N.J., which, in turn, would be ahead of a clock in Philadelphia. This condition actually prevailed in the past until 1883, when *standard time* was introduced. Standard time is the correct mean solar time for a designated meridian, and this time is used for a certain area to the east and west of this meridian. In the U.S. four meridians have been designated to supply standard times; they are 75°, 90°, 105°, and 120° west of Greenwich. The 75° meridian determines Eastern Standard Time. It happens to run through Camden, N.J., where standard time, therefore, is also mean solar time and local civil time. The 90° meridian (which happens to pass through the western part of Memphis, Tenn.) determines Central Standard Time, the 105° meridian (passing through Denver) determines Mountain Standard Time, and the 120° meridian (which runs through Lake Tahoe) determines Pacific Standard Time.

Canada, extending over more territory from west to east, adds one time zone on either side: Atlantic Standard Time (based on 60° west of Greenwich) for New Brunswick, Nova Scotia, and Quebec, and Yukon Standard Time (determined by the 135° meridian) for its extreme West. Alaska, extending still farther to the west, adds two more time zones, Alaska Standard Time (determined by the 150° meridian that passes through Anchorage) and Nome Standard Time, based on the 165° meridian just east of Nome.

In general the Earth is divided into 24 such time zones, which run one hour apart. For practical purposes the time zones sometimes show indentations, and there are a few "subzones" that differ from the neighboring zone by only half an hour, e.g., Newfoundland.

The date line. While the time zones are based on the natural event of the Sun crossing the meridian,

the date must be an arbitrary decision. The meridians are traditionally counted from the meridian of the observatory of Greenwich in England, which is called the zero meridian. The logical place for changing the date is 12 hours, or 180° from Greenwich. Fortunately, the 180th meridian runs mostly through the open Pacific. The date line makes a zigzag in the north to incorporate the eastern tip of Siberia into the Siberian time system and then another one to incorporate a number of islands into the Alaska time system. In the south there is a similar zigzag for the purpose of tying a number of British-owned islands to the New Zealand time system. Otherwise the date line is the same as 180° from Greenwich. At points to the east of the date line the calendar is one day earlier than at points to the west of it. A traveller going eastward across the date line from one island to another would not have to re-set his watch because he would stay inside the time zone (provided he does so where the date line does *not* coincide with the 180° meridian), but it would be the same time of the previous day.

The Seasons

The seasons are caused by the tilt of the Earth's axis (23.4°) and not by the fact that the Earth's orbit around the Sun is an ellipse. The average distance of the Earth from the Sun is 93 million miles; the difference between aphelion (farthest away) and perihelion (closest to the Sun) is 3 million miles, so that perihelion is about 91.4 million miles from the Sun. The Earth goes through the perihelion point a few days after New Year, just when the northern hemisphere has winter. Aphelion is passed during the first days in July. This by itself shows that the distance from the

The Names of the Months

January: named after Janus, protector of the gateway to heaven
February: named after Februalia, a time period when sacrifices were made to atone for sins
March: named after Mars, the god of war, presumably signifying that the campaigns interrupted by the winter could be resumed
April: from *aperire,* Latin for "to open" (buds)
May: named after Maia, the goddess of growth of

plants
June: from *juvenis,* Latin for "youth"
July: named after Julius Caesar
August: named after Augustus, the first Roman Emperor
September: from *septem,* Latin for "seven"
October: from *octo,* Latin for "eight"
November: from *novem,* Latin for "nine"
December: from *decem,* Latin for "ten"

NOTE: The earliest Latin calendar was a 10-month one; thus September was the seventh month, October, the eighth, etc. July was originally called Quintilis, as the fifth month; August was originally called Sextilis, as the sixth month.

Sun is not important within these limits. What is important is that when the Earth passes through perihelion, the northern end of the Earth's axis happens to tilt away from the Sun, so that the areas beyond the Tropic of Cancer receive only slanting rays from a Sun low in the sky.

The tilt of the Earth's axis is responsible for four lines you find on every globe. When, say, the North Pole is tilted away from the Sun as much as possible, the farthest points in the North which can still be reached by the Sun's rays are 23 1/2° from the pole. This is the Arctic Circle. The Antarctic Circle is the corresponding limit 23.4° from the South Pole; the Sun's rays cannot reach beyond this point when we have mid-summer in the North.

When the Sun is vertically above the equator, the day is of equal length all over the Earth. This happens twice a year, and these are the "equinoxes" in March and in September. After having been over the equator in March, the Sun will seem to move northward. The northernmost point where the Sun can be straight overhead is 23.4° north of the equator. This is the Tropic of Cancer; the Sun can never be vertically overhead to the north of this line. Similarly the Sun cannot be vertically overhead to the south of a line 23.4° south of the equator—the Tropic of Capricorn.

This explains the climatic zones. In the belt (the Greek word *zone* means "belt") between the Tropic of Cancer and the Tropic of Capricorn, the Sun can be straight overhead; this is the tropical zone. The two zones where the Sun cannot be overhead but will be above the horizon every day of the year are the two temperate zones; the two areas where the Sun will not rise at all for varying lengths of time are the two polar areas, Arctic and Antarctic.

Holidays

Religious and Secular, 1992

Since 1971, by federal law, Washington's Birthday, Memorial Day, Columbus Day, and Veterans' Day have been celebrated on Mondays to create three-day weekends for federal employees. Many states now observe these holidays on the same Mondays. The dates given for the holidays listed below are the traditional ones.

New Year's Day, Wednesday, Jan. 1. A legal holiday in all states and the District of Columbia, New Year's Day has its origin in Roman Times, when sacrifices were offered to Janus, the two-faced Roman deity who looked back on the past and forward to the future.

Epiphany, Monday, Jan. 6. Falls the twelfth day after Christmas and commemorates the manifestation of Jesus as the Son of God, as represented by the adoration of the Magi, the baptism of Jesus, and the miracle of the wine at the marriage feast at Cana. Epiphany originally marked the beginning of the carnival season preceding Lent, and the evening (sometimes the eve) is known as Twelfth Night.

Martin Luther King, Jr.'s Birthday, Wednesday, Jan. 15. Honors the late civil rights leader. Became a legal public holiday in 1986.

Ground-hog Day, Sunday, Feb. 2. Legend has it that if the ground-hog sees his shadow, he'll return to his hole, and winter will last another six weeks.

Lincoln's Birthday, Wednesday, Feb. 12. A legal holiday in many states, this day was first formally observed in Washington, D.C., in 1866, when both houses of Congress gathered for a memorial address in tribute to the assassinated President.

St. Valentine's Day, Friday, Feb. 14. This day is the festival of two third-century martyrs, both named St. Valentine. It is not known why this day is associated with lovers. It may derive from an old pagan festival about this time of year, or it may have been inspired by the belief that birds mate on this day.

Washington's Birthday, Saturday, Feb. 22. The birthday of George Washington is celebrated as a legal holiday in every state of the Union, the District of Columbia, and all territories. The observance began in 1796.

Shrove Tuesday, March 3. Falls the day before Ash Wednesday and marks the end of the carnival season, which once began on Epiphany but is now usually celebrated the last three days before Lent. In France, the day is known as Mardi Gras (Fat Tuesday), and Mardi Gras celebrations are also held in several American cities, particularly in New Orleans. The day is sometimes called Pancake Tuesday by the English because fats, which were prohibited during Lent, had to be used up.

Ash Wednesday, March 4. The first day of the Lenten season, which lasts 40 days. Having its origin sometime before A.D. 1000, it is a day of public penance and is marked in the Roman Catholic Church by the burning of the palms blessed on the previous year's Palm Sunday. With his thumb, the priest then marks a cross upon the forehead of each worshipper. The Anglican Church and a few Protestant groups in the United States also observe the day, but generally without the use of ashes.

St. Patrick's Day, Tuesday, March 17. St. Patrick, patron saint of Ireland, has been honored in America since the first days of the nation. There are many dinners and meetings but perhaps the most notable part of the observance is the annual St. Patrick's Day parade on Fifth Avenue in New York City.

Purim (Feast of Lots), Thursday, March 19. A day of joy and feasting celebrating deliverance of the Jews from a massacre planned by the Persian minister Haman. The Jewish Queen Esther interceded with her husband, King Ahasuerus, to spare the life of her uncle, Mordecai, and Haman was hanged on the same gallows he had built for Mordecai. The holiday is marked by the reading of the Book of Esther (megillah), and by the exchange of gifts, donations to the poor, and the presentation of Purim plays.

Palm Sunday, April 12. Is observed the Sunday

before Easter to commemorate the entry of Jesus into Jerusalem. The procession and the ceremonies introducing the benediction of palms probably had their origin in Jerusalem.

Good Friday, April 17. This day commemorates the Crucifixion, which is retold during services from the Gospel according to St. John. A feature in Roman Catholic churches is the Liturgy of the Passion; there is no Consecration, the Host having been consecrated the previous day. The eating of hot cross buns on this day is said to have started in England.

First Day of Passover (Pesach), Saturday, April 18. The Feast of the Passover, also called the Feast of Unleavened Bread, commemorates the escape of the Jews from Egypt. As the Jews fled they ate unleavened bread, and from that time the Jews have allowed no leavening in the houses during Passover, bread being replaced by matzoh.

Easter Sunday, April 19. Observed in all Christian churches, Easter commemorates the Resurrection of Jesus. It is celebrated on the first Sunday after the full moon which occurs on or next after March 21 and is therefore celebrated between March 22 and April 25 inclusive. This date was fixed by the Council of Nicaea in A.D. 325. The Orthodox Church celebrates Easter on April 26, 1992.

Mother's Day, Sunday, May 10. Observed the second Sunday in May, as proposed by Anna Jarvis of Philadelphia in 1907.

Ascension Day, Thursday, May 28. Took place in the presence of His apostles 40 days after the Resurrection of Jesus. It is traditionally held to have occurred on Mount Olivet in Bethany.

Memorial Day, Saturday, May 30. Also known as Decoration Day, Memorial Day is a legal holiday in most of the states and in the territories, and is also observed by the armed forces. In 1868, Gen. John A. Logan, Commander in Chief of the Grand Army of the Republic, issued an order designating the day as one in which the graves of soldiers would be decorated. The holiday was originally devoted to honoring the memory of those who fell in the Civil War, but is now also dedicated to the memory of all war dead.

First Day of Shavuot (Hebrew Pentecost), Sunday, June 7. This festival, sometimes called the Feast of Weeks, or of Harvest, or of the First Fruits, falls 50 days after Passover and originally celebrated the end of the seven-week grain harvesting season. In later tradition, it also celebrated the giving of the Law to Moses on Mount Sinai.

Pentecost (Whitsunday), Sunday, June 7. This day commemorates the descent of the Holy Ghost upon the apostles 50 days after the Resurrection. The sermon by the Apostle Peter, which led to the baptism of 3,000 who professed belief, originated the ceremonies that have since been followed. "Whitsunday" is believed to have come from "white Sunday" when, among the English, white robes were worn by those baptized on the day.

Flag Day, Sunday, June 14. This day commemorates the adoption by the Continental Congress on June 14, 1777, of the Stars and Stripes as the U.S. flag. Although it is a legal holiday only in Pennsylvania, President Truman, on Aug. 3, 1949, signed a bill re-

questing the President to call for its observance each year by proclamation.

Father's Day, Sunday, June 21. Observed the third Sunday in June. First celebrated June 19, 1910.

Independence Day, Saturday, July 4. The day of the adoption of the Declaration of Independence in 1776, celebrated in all states and territories. The observance began the next year in Philadelphia.

Labor Day, Monday, Sept. 7. Observed the first Monday in September in all states and territories, Labor Day was first celebrated in New York in 1882 under the sponsorship of the Central Labor Union, following the suggestion of Peter J. McGuire, of the Knights of Labor, that the day be set aside in honor of labor.

First Day of Rosh Hashana (Jewish New Year), Monday, Sept. 28. This day marks the beginning of the Jewish year 5753 and opens the Ten Days of Penitence closing with Yom Kippur.

Yom Kippur (Day of Atonement), Wednesday, Oct. 7. This day marks the end of the Ten Days of Penitence that began with Rosh Hashana. It is described in *Leviticus* as a "Sabbath of rest," and synagogue services begin the preceding sundown, resume the following morning, and continue to sundown.

First Day of Sukkot (Feast of Tabernacles) Monday, Oct. 12. This festival, also known as the Feast of the Ingathering, originally celebrated the fruit harvest, and the name comes from the booths or tabernacles in which the Jews lived during the harvest, although one tradition traces it to the shelters used by the Jews in their wandering through the wilderness. During the festival many Jews build small huts in their back yards or on the roofs of their houses.

Columbus Day, Monday, Oct. 12. A legal holiday in many states, commemorating the discovery of America by Columbus in 1492. Quite likely the first celebration of Columbus Day was that organized in 1792 by the Society of St. Tammany, or Columbian Order, widely known as Tammany Hall.

Simhat Torah (Rejoicing of the Law), Tuesday, Oct. 20. This joyous holiday falls on the eighth day of Sukkot. It marks the end of the year's reading of the Torah (Five Books of Moses) in the synagogue every Saturday and the beginning of the new cycle of reading.

United Nations Day, Saturday, Oct. 24. Marking the founding of the United Nations.

Halloween, Saturday, Oct. 31. Eve of All Saints' Day, formerly called All Hallows and Hallowmass. Halloween is traditionally associated in some countries with old customs such as bonfires, masquerading, and the telling of ghost stories. These are old Celtic practices marking the beginning of winter.

All Saints' Day, Sunday, Nov. 1. A Roman Catholic and Anglican holiday celebrating all saints, known and unknown.

Election Day, (legal holiday in certain states), Tuesday, Nov. 3. Since 1845, by Act of Congress, the first

Tuesday after the first Monday in November is the date for choosing Presidential electors. State elections are also generally held on this day.

Veterans Day, Wednesday, Nov. 11. Armistice Day was established in 1926 to commemorate the signing in 1918 of the Armistice ending World War I. On June 1, 1954, the name was changed to Veterans Day to honor all men and women who have served America in its armed forces.

Thanksgiving, Thursday, Nov. 26. Observed nationally on the fourth Thursday in November by Act of Congress (1941), the first such national proclamation having been issued by President Lincoln in 1863, on the urging of Mrs. Sarah J. Hale, editor of *Godey's Lady's Book.* Most Americans believe that the holiday dates back to the day of thanks ordered by Governor Bradford of Plymouth Colony in New England in 1621, but scholars point out that days of thanks stem from ancient times.

First Sunday of Advent, Nov. 29. Advent is the season in which the faithful must prepare themselves for the advent of the Saviour on Christmas. The four Sundays before Christmas are marked by special church services.

First Day of Hanukkah (Festival of Lights), Sunday, Dec. 20. This festival was instituted by Judas Maccabaeus in 165 B.C. to celebrate the purification of the Temple of Jerusalem, which had been desecrated three years earlier by Antiochus Epiphanes, who set up a pagan altar and offered sacrifices to Zeus Olympius. In Jewish homes, a light is lighted on each night of the eight-day festival.

Christmas (Feast of the Nativity), Friday, Dec. 25. The most widely celebrated holiday of the Christian year, Christmas is observed as the anniversary of the birth of Jesus. Christmas customs are centuries old. The mistletoe, for example, comes from the Druids, who, in hanging the mistletoe, hoped for peace and good fortune. Use of such plants as holly comes from the ancient belief that such plants blossomed at Christmas. Comparatively recent is the Christmas tree, first set up inGermany in the 17th century, and the use of candles on trees developed from the belief that candles appeared by miracle on the trees at Christmas. Colonial Manhattan Islanders introduced the name Santa Claus, a corruption of the Dutch name for the 4th-century Asia Minor St. Nicholas.

State Observances

January 6, Three Kings' Day: Puerto Rico.
January 8, Battle of New Orleans Day: Louisiana.
January 11, De Hostos' Birthday: Puerto Rico.
January 19, Robert E. Lee's Birthday: Arkansas, Florida, Kentucky, Louisiana, South Carolina, **(third Monday)** Alabama, Mississippi.
January 19, Confederate Heroes Day: Texas.
January (third Monday): Lee-Jackson-King Day: Virginia.
January 30, F.D. Roosevelt's Birthday: Kentucky.
February 15, Susan B. Anthony's Birthday: Florida, Minnesota.
March (first Tuesday), Town Meeting Day: Vermont.
March 2, Texas Independence Day: Texas.
March (first Monday), Casimir Pulaski's Birthday: Illinois.
March 17, Evacuation Day: Massachusetts (in Suffolk County).
March 20 (First Day of Spring), Youth Day: Oklahoma.
March 22, Abolition Day: Puerto Rico.
March 25, Maryland Day: Maryland.
March 26, Prince Jonah Kuhio Kalanianaole Day: Hawaii.
March (last Monday), Seward's Day: Alaska.
April 2, Pascua Florida Day: Florida
April 13, Thomas Jefferson's Birthday: Alabama, Oklahoma.
April 16, De Diego's Birthday: Puerto Rico.
April (third Monday), Patriots' Day: Maine, Massachusetts.
April 21, San Jacinto Day: Texas.
April 22, Arbor Day: Nebraska.
April 22, Oklahoma Day: Oklahoma.
April 26, Confederate Memorial Day: Florida, Georgia.
April (fourth Monday), Fast Day: New Hampshire.
April (last Monday), Confederate Memorial Day: Alabama, Mississippi.
May 1, Bird Day: Oklahoma.
May 8, Truman Day: Missouri.
May 11, Minnesota Day: Minnesota.

May 20, Mecklenburg Independence Day: North Carolina.
June (first Monday), Jefferson Davis's Birthday: Alabama, Mississippi.
June 3, Jefferson Davis's Birthday: Florida, South Carolina.
June 3, Confederate Memorial Day: Kentucky, Louisiana.
June 9, Senior Citizens Day: Oklahoma.
June 11, King Kamehameha I Day: Hawaii.
June 15, Separation Day: Delaware.
June 17, Bunker Hill Day: Massachusetts (in Suffolk County).
June 19, Emancipation Day: Texas.
June 20, West Virginia Day: West Virginia.
July 17, Muñoz Rivera's Birthday: Puerto Rico.
July 24, Pioneer Day: Utah.
July 25, Constitution Day: Puerto Rico.
July 27, Barbosa's Birthday: Puerto Rico.
August (first Sunday), American Family Day: Arizona.
August (first Monday), Colorado Day: Colorado.
August (second Monday), Victory Day: Rhode Island.
August 16, Bennington Battle Day: Vermont.
August (third Friday), Admission Day: Hawaii.
August 27, Lyndon B. Johnson's Birthday: Texas.
August 30, Huey P. Long Day: Louisiana.
September 9, Admission Day: California.
September 12, Defenders' Day: Maryland.
September 16, Cherokee Strip Day: Oklahoma.
September (first Saturday after full moon), Indian Day: Oklahoma.
October 10, Leif Erickson Day: Minnesota.
October 10, Oklahoma Historical Day: Oklahoma.
October 18, Alaska Day: Alaska.
October 31, Nevada Day: Nevada.
November 4, Will Rogers Day: Oklahoma.
November (week of the 16th), Oklahoma Heritage Week: Oklahoma.
November 19, Discovery Day: Puerto Rico.
December 7, Delaware Day: Delaware.

Movable Holidays, 1992–1995

CHRISTIAN AND SECULAR

Year	Ash Wednesday	Easter	Pentecost	Labor Day	Election Day	Thanksgiving	1st Sun. Advent
1992	March 4	April 19	June 7	Sept. 7	Nov. 3	Nov. 26	Nov. 29
1993	Feb. 24	April 11	May 30	Sept. 6	Nov. 2	Nov. 25	Nov. 28
1994	Feb. 16	April 3	May 22	Sept. 5	Nov. 8	Nov. 24	Nov. 27
1995	March 1	April 16	June 4	Sept. 4	Nov. 7	Nov. 23	Dec. 3

Shrove Tuesday: 1 day before Ash Wednesday
Palm Sunday: 7 days before Easter
Maundy Thursday: 3 days before Easter
Good Friday: 2 days before Easter

Holy Saturday: 1 day before Easter
Ascension Day: 10 days before Pentecost
Trinity Sunday: 7 days after Pentecost
Corpus Christi: 11 days after Pentecost

NOTE: Easter is celebrated on April 26, 1992, by the Orthodox Church.

JEWISH

Year	Purim[1]	1st day Passover[2]	1st day Shavuot[3]	1st day Rosh Hashana[4]	Yom Kippur[5]	1st day Sukkot[6]	Simhat Torah[7]	1st day Hanukkah[8]
1992	March 19	April 18	June 7	Sept. 28	Oct. 7	Oct. 12	Oct. 20	Dec. 20
1993	March 7	April 6	May 26	Sept. 16	Sept. 25	Sept. 30	Oct. 8	Dec. 9
1994	Feb. 25	March 27	May 16	Sept. 6	Sept. 15	Sept. 20	Sept. 28	Nov. 28
1995	March 16	April 15	June 4	Sept. 25	Oct. 4	Oct. 9	Oct. 17	Dec. 18

1. Feast of Lots. 2. Feast of Unleavened Bread. 3. Hebrew Pentecost; or Feast of Weeks, or of Harvest, or of First Fruits. 4. Jewish New Year. 5. Day of Atonement. 6. Feast of Tabernacles, or of the Ingathering. 7. Rejoicing of the Law. 8. Festival of Lights.

Length of Jewish holidays (O=Orthodox, C=Conservative, R=Reform):

Passover: O & C, 8 days (holy days: first 2 and last 2); R, 7 days (holy days: first and last)
Shavuot: O & C, 2 days; R, 1 day
Rosh Hashana: O & C, 2 days; R, 1 day.
Yom Kippur: All groups, 1 day

Sukkot: All groups, 7 days (holy days: O & C, first 2; R, first only) O & C observe two additional days: Shemini Atseret (Eighth Day of the Feast) and Simhat Torah. R observes Shemini Atseret but not Simhat Torah
Hanukkah: All groups, 8 days

NOTE: All holidays begin at sundown on the evening before the date given.

Islamic 1992

March 6 First day of the month of Ramadan
April 5 'Id al Fitr (Festival of end of Ramadan)
June 12 'Id al-Adha (Festival of Sacrifice at time of annual pilgrimage to Mecca)

July 2 First day of month of Muharram (beginning of liturgical year)
Sept. 11 Mawlid al-Nabi (Anniversary of Prophet Mohammed's birthday)

NOTE: All holidays begin at sundown on the evening before the date given.

Chinese Calendar

The Chinese lunar year is divided into 12 months of 29 or 30 days. The calendar is adjusted to the length of the solar year by the addition of extra months at regular intervals.

The years are arranged in major cycles of 60 years.

Each successive year is named after one of 12 animals. These 12-year cycles are continuously repeated. The Chinese New Year is celebrated at the first new moon after the sun enters Aquarius—sometime between Jan. 21 and Feb. 19.

Rat	Ox	Tiger	Cat (Rabbit)	Dragon	Snake	Horse	Sheep (Goat)	Monkey	Rooster	Dog	Pig
1864	1865	1866	1867	1868	1869	1870	1871	1872	1873	1874	1875
1876	1877	1878	1879	1880	1881	1882	1883	1884	1885	1886	1887
1888	1889	1890	1891	1892	1893	1894	1895	1896	1897	1898	1899
1900	1901	1902	1903	1904	1905	1906	1907	1908	1909	1910	1911
1912	1913	1914	1915	1916	1917	1918	1919	1920	1921	1922	1923
1924	1925	1926	1927	1928	1929	1930	1931	1932	1933	1934	1935
1936	1937	1938	1939	1940	1941	1942	1943	1944	1945	1946	1947
1948	1949	1950	1951	1952	1953	1954	1955	1956	1957	1958	1959
1960	1961	1962	1963	1964	1965	1966	1967	1968	1969	1970	1971
1972	1973	1974	1975	1976	1977	1978	1979	1980	1981	1982	1983
1984	1985	1986	1987	1988	1989	1990	1991	1992	1993	1994	1995

National Holidays Around the World, 1992

Country	Date	Country	Date	Country	Date
Afghanistan	April 27	Gabon	Aug. 17	Pakistan	March 23
Albania	Nov. 29	Gambia	Feb. 18	Panama	Nov. 3
Algeria	Nov. 1	Ghana	March 6	Papua New Guinea	Sept. 16
Angola	Nov. 11	Greece	March 25	Paraguay	May 14
Antigua and Barbuda	Nov. 1	Grenada	Feb. 7	Peru	July 28
Argentina	May 25	Guatemala	Sept. 15	Philippines	June 12
Australia	Jan. 26	Guinea	Oct. 2	Poland	July 22
Austria	Oct. 26	Guinea-Bissau	Sept. 24	Portugal	June 10
Bahamas	July 10	Guyana	Feb. 23	Qatar	Sept. 3
Bahrain	Dec. 16	Haiti	Jan. 1	Romania	Dec. 1
Bangladesh	March 26	Honduras	Sept. 15	Rwanda	July 1
Barbados	Nov. 30	Hungary	March 15	St. Kitts and Nevis	Sept. 19
Belgium	July 21	Iceland	June 17	St. Lucia	Feb. 22
Belize	Sept. 21	India	Jan. 26	St. Vincent and	
Benin	Nov. 30	Indonesia	Aug. 17	the Grenadines	Oct. 27
Bhutan	Dec. 17	Iran	Feb. 11	São Tomé and Príncipe	July 12
Bolivia	Aug. 6	Iraq	July 17	Saudi Arabia	Sept. 23
Botswana	Sept. 30	Ireland	March 17	Senegal	April 4
Brazil	Sept. 7	Israel	May 7[1]	Seychelles	June 5
Brunei	Feb. 23	Italy	June 2	Sierra Leone	April 27
Bulgaria	March 3	Jamaica	Aug. 3[2]	Singapore	Aug. 9
Burkina Faso	Aug. 4	Japan	April 29	Solomon Islands	July 7
Burundi	July 1	Jordan	May 25	Somalia	Oct. 21
Cambodia	April 17	Kenya	Dec. 12	South Africa	May 31
Cameroon	May 20	Kuwait	Feb. 25	Spain	Oct. 12
Canada	July 1	Laos	Dec. 2	Sri Lanka	Feb. 4
Cape Verde	Sept. 12	Lebanon	Nov. 22	Sudan	Jan. 1
Central African Republic	Dec. 1	Lesotho	Oct. 4	Suriname	Nov. 25
Chad	June 7	Liberia	July 26	Swaziland	Sept. 6
Chile	Sept. 18	Libya	Sept. 1	Sweden	June 6
China	Oct. 1	Luxembourg	June 23	Switzerland	Aug. 1
Colombia	July 20	Madagascar	June 26	Syria	April 17
Comoros	July 6	Malawi	July 6	Tanzania	April 26
Congo	Aug. 15	Malaysia	Aug. 31	Thailand	Dec. 5
Costa Rica	Sept. 15	Maldives	July 26	Togo	April 27
Côte d'Ivoire	Dec. 7	Mali	Sept. 22	Trinidad and Tobago	Aug. 31
Cuba	Jan. 1	Malta	March 31	Tunisia	June 1
Cyprus	Oct. 1	Mauritania	Nov. 28	Turkey	Oct. 29
Czechoslovakia	May 9,	Mauritius	March 12	Uganda	Oct. 9
	Oct. 28	Mexico	Sept. 16	U.S.S.R.	Nov. 7
Denmark	April 16	Mongolia	July 11	United Arab Emirates	Dec. 2
Djibouti	June 27	Morocco	March 3	United Kingdom	June 13[3]
Dominica	Nov. 3	Mozambique	June 25	United States	July 4
Dominican Republic	Feb. 27	Myanmar	Jan. 4	Uruguay	Aug. 25
Ecuador	Aug. 10	Nepal	Dec. 28	Vanuatu	July 30
Egypt	July 23	Netherlands	April 30	Venezuela	July 5
El Salvador	Sept. 15	New Zealand	Feb. 6	Viet Nam	Sept. 2
Equatorial Guinea	Oct. 12	Nicaragua	Sept. 15	Western Samoa	June 1
Ethiopia	Sept. 12	Niger	Dec. 18	Yemen, Republic of	Sept. 26
Fiji	Oct. 10	Nigeria	Oct. 1	Yugoslavia	Nov. 29
Finland	Dec. 6	Norway	May 17	Zaire	June 30
France	July 14	Oman	Nov. 18	Zambia	Oct. 24
				Zimbabwe	April 18

1. Changes yearly according to Hebrew calendar. 2. Celebrated on first Monday in August. 3. Celebrated the second Saturday in June.

The Basic Unit of the World Calendar

Days	First month					Second Month					Third month				
Sunday	1	8	15	22	29	—	5	12	19	26	—	3	10	17	24
Monday	2	9	16	23	30	—	6	13	20	27	—	4	11	18	25
Tuesday	3	10	17	24	31	—	7	14	21	28	—	5	12	19	26
Wednesday	4	11	18	25	—	1	8	15	22	29	—	6	13	20	27
Thursday	5	12	19	26	—	2	9	16	23	30	—	7	14	21	28
Friday	6	13	20	27	—	3	10	17	24	—	1	8	15	22	29
Saturday	7	14	21	28	—	4	11	18	25	—	2	9	16	23	30

CONSUMER'S RESOURCE GUIDE

Building a Better Credit Record

Source: Federal Trade Commission in cooperation with Associated Credit Bureaus, Inc., National Foundation for Consumer Credit, U.S. Office of Consumer Affairs.

Understanding Your Credit History

If you have ever used a major credit card or financed an expensive purchase, such as a car, you probably have a record at a local credit bureau. This record of your credit history allows creditors to check your payment habits before they give you credit.

If you have been denied credit because of information that was supplied by a credit bureau, the Fair Credit Reporting Act requires the creditor to give you the name and address of the credit bureau that supplied the information. If you contact that bureau to learn what is in your file within 30 days of receiving a denial notice, the information is free. If not, the credit bureau may charge you a small fee.

You always are entitled to learn what is in your credit file, but credit bureaus vary in how they disclose this information. Most will send you a printed copy of your credit report. Some, however, will ask you to visit the bureau to review your record or will give you information over the telephone once you have provided proper identification.

This article tells you how to reach the credit bureau that has your file to review your credit history. It also explains how credit bureaus work and how you can conduct your own credit check-up from information your local credit bureau has collected.

How Credit Bureaus Work

Credit reporting agencies, often called credit bureaus, are companies that gather information on credit users and sell that information in the form of credit reports to credit grantors, such as banks, finance companies, and retailers. Credit bureaus keep records of consumers' debts and how regularly these debts are repaid. They gather information from creditors who send computer tapes or other payment data to credit bureaus, usually on a monthly basis, showing what each account-holder owes or has paid. The data show if payments are up-to-date or overdue, and if any action has been taken to collect overdue bills. The credit bureau adds this data to existing information in consumer files, creating a month-by-month history of activity on consumer accounts.

Credit bureaus cooperate with each other, passing information on to other bureaus when people move, for example. But, as businesses, they also compete for subscribers (credit grantors), who judge credit bureaus on the completeness of their records and the quality of their service.

Checking Your Credit File

Even if you have not been denied credit, you may wish to find out what information is in your credit file. Some financial advisors suggest that consumer review their credit reports every three or four years to check for inaccuracies or omissions. This could be especially important if you are considering making a major purchase, such as buying a home. Checking in advance on the accuracy of information in your credit file could speed the credit-granting process.

To find which credit bureaus have your file, check the Yellow Pages under Credit Bureaus or Credit Reporting Agencies for the phone numbers and addresses of the bureaus near you.

When you contact them, give all identifying information, such as your full name, Social Security number, current address, former address, and spouse's name (if applicable). Ordinarily, a credit bureau will charge $5 to $15 to give you your credit file information. To get a complete credit picture, ask all local credit bureaus if they maintain a file on you.

If you are married, you and your spouse probably have individual credit files. These files may contain identical or different information, depending on whether you and your spouse have shared or separate accounts. You and your spouse may find it helpful to review and compare your credit histories together.

Credit information on accounts opened before June 1, 1977, that are shared by a husband and wife often are reported only in the husband's name. However, creditors must report the credit history individually, in the name of each spouse, if you ask them to do so. Newer accounts should be reported on an individual basis automatically. If you find this is not the case, write to the creditor and request that the account be reported in both names. This will help both of you build a credit history.

Understanding Your Credit Report

1. **Identification and employment data.** Your name, birthdate, address, Social Security number, employer, and spouse's name are routinely noted. The bureau also may provide other information, such as your employment history, home ownership, income, and previous address, if a creditor requests it.

2. **Payment history.** Your account record with different creditors is listed, showing how much credit has been extended and how you have repaid it. Related events, such as referral of an overdue account to a collection agency, may be noted as well.

3. **Inquiries.** Credit bureaus are required to maintain a record of all creditors who have requested your credit history within the past six months. They normally include such credit inquiries in your credit file for at least this long.

4. **Public record information.** Events that are a matter of public record and are related to your creditworthiness, such as bankruptcies, foreclosures, or tax liens, may also appear in your report.

How to Correct Errors

Your credit file may contain errors that can affect your chances of obtaining credit in the future. Under the Fair Credit Reporting Act, you are entitled to have incomplete or inaccurate information corrected without charge.

If you dispute information in your report, the credit bureau must reinvestigate it within a "reasonable period of time," unless it believes the dispute is "frivolous or irrelevant." To check on the accuracy of a disputed item, the credit bureau will ask the creditor in question what its records show. If the disputed item is on the public record, the credit bureau will check there instead. If a disputed item cannot be verified, the credit bureau must delete it. If an item contains erroneous information, the credit bureau must correct the error. If the item is incomplete, the bureau must complete it. For example, if your file showed accounts that belong to another person, the credit bureau would have to delete them. If it showed that you were late in making payments but failed to show that you are no longer delinquent, the credit bureau would have to add information to show that your payments are now current. Also, at your request, the credit bureau must send a notice of the correction to any creditor who had checked your file in the past six months.

If the reinvestigation does not resolve your dispute, the Fair Credit Reporting Act permits you to file a statement of up to 100 words with the credit bureau explaining your side of the story. Employees of the credit bureau often are available to help you word your statement. The credit bureau must include this explanation in your report each time it sends it out.

Adding Omissions

Your credit file may not contain information on all of the accounts you have with creditors. Although most national department store and all-purpose bank credit card accounts will be included in your file, not all creditors supply information to credit bureaus. For example, some travel-and-entertainment and gasoline card companies, local retailers, and credit unions do not report to credit bureaus.

If you have been told that you were denied credit because of an "insufficient credit file" and you have accounts with creditors that do not appear in your credit file, you can ask the credit bureau to add this information to future reports. Although they are not required to do so, for a fee many credit bureaus will add other accounts, if verifiable, to your credit file.

Time Affects Your Credit Report

Under the Fair Credit Reporting Act, credit bureaus can report most negative information for no more than seven years. The seven-year period runs from the date of the last regularly scheduled payment that was made before the account became delinquent *unless* the creditor later took action on the account, such as charging it off or obtaining a judgment for the amount due. If a creditor took such an action, the seven years would run from the date of that event. For example, if a retailer turned over your past-due account to a collection agency in 1985, a credit bureau may report this event until 1992. You should be aware that if you made a payment after 1985 on this account, your action would *not* extend the permissible reporting period beyond 1992.

There are exceptions to the seven-year rule. Bankruptcies may be reported for 10 years. Also, any negative credit-history information may be reported indefinitely in three circumstances:

- If you apply for $50,000 or more in credit;
- If you apply for a life insurance policy with a face amount of $50,000 or more;
- If you apply for a job paying $20,000 or more (and the employer requests a credit report in connection with the application).

You can contact the credit bureau if you believe negative information is being reported beyond the permitted period and ask that it be removed.

Dealing With Problems

Before creditors will give you credit, they look at how you have paid your bills in the past. Negative information in your credit file may lead creditors to deny you credit. Information that is considered negative includes late payments, repossessions, accounts turned over to a collection agency, charge-offs (accounts viewed as a "loss" by a creditor), judgments, liens, and bankruptcy.

A poor credit history that is accurate cannot be changed. There is nothing that you (or anyone else) can do to require a credit bureau to remove accurate information from your credit report until the reporting period has expired. However, this does not necessarily mean that you will be unable to obtain credit during the period. Because creditors set their own credit-granting standards, not all of them look at your credit history in the same way. Some creditors may look only at more recent years to evaluate you for credit, and they may grant you credit if your bill-paying history has improved. Before applying for credit, it may be useful to contact creditors informally to discuss their credit standards.

If you cannot obtain credit based on your own credit history, you may be able to do so if someone who has a good credit history co-signs a loan for you—this means the co-signer agrees to pay if you do not. Or you may be able to obtain a small loan or a credit card with a low dollar limit by using your savings account as collateral. If you pay promptly and your creditor reports to a credit bureau, this new information will improve your credit history picture.

Dealing With Mounting Bills

A sudden illness or the loss of your job may make it impossible for you to pay your bills on time. Whatever your situation, if you find that you cannot make your payments, contact your creditors at once. Try to work out a modified payment plan with your creditors that reduces your payments to a more manageable level. If you have paid promptly in the past, they may be willing to work with you. Do not wait until your account is turned over to a debt collector. At that point, the creditor has given up on you.

If you do work out a debt-repayment plan, ask your creditors to report your new, smaller payments to the credit bureau as timely. Otherwise, the credit bureau may report these payments as delinquent because you are paying less than the amount agreed to in your original credit agreement..

Automobile loans may present special problems. Most automobile financing agreements permit your creditor to repossess your car at any time that you are in default on your payments. No advance notice is required. If your car is repossessed, you may have to pay the full balance due on the loan, as well as towing and storage costs, to get it back. If you cannot do this, the creditor may sell the car. Do not wait until you are in default. Try to solve the problem with your creditor when you realize you will not be able to meet your payments. It may be better to sell the car yourself and pay off your debt. This would avoid the added costs of repossession and a negative entry on your credit report.

Finding Low-Cost Help

If you cannot resolve your credit problems yourself or need additional assistance, you may want to contact a Consumer Credit Counseling Service (CCCS). This is a non-profit organization with more than 280 offices located in 44 states that counsels indebted consumers. CCCS counselors will try to arrange a repayment plan that is acceptable to you and your creditors. They also will help you set up a realistic budget and plan expenditures. These counseling offices, which are funded by contributions from credit-granting institutions, are offered at little or no cost to consumers. You can find the CCCS office nearest you by checking the White Pages of your telephone directory or by sending a self-addressed stamped envelope to: National Foundation for Consumer Credit, 8701 Georgia Ave., Suite 507, Silver Spring, Md. 20910 (301) 589-5600.

In addition, non-profit counseling programs are sometimes operated by universities, military bases, credit union, and housing authorities. They are likely to charge little or nothing for their assistance. Or, you can check with your local bank or consumer protection office to see if it has a listing of reputable, low-cost financial counseling services.

Copyrights

Source: Library of Congress, Copyright Office.

U.S. is a Member of the Berne Union

On March 1, 1989, the United States joined the Berne Union by entering into an international treaty called the Berne Convention, whose full title is the Berne Convention for the Protection of Literary and Artistic Works. Also on that date, amendments to the U.S. copyright law that satisfy U.S. treaty obligations under the Convention took effect and some of them are listed herein. Contact the U.S. Copyright Office for details of Berne Convention obligations.

The U.S. Law continues to govern the protection and registration of works in the United States.

Beginning March 1, 1989, copyright in the works of U.S. authors is protected automatically in all member nations of the Berne Union and the works of foreign authors who are nationals of a Berne Union country, and works first published in a Berne Union country are automatically protected in the United States.

In order to fulfill its Berne Convention obligations, the United States made certain changes in its copyright law by passing the Berne Convention Implementation Act of 1988. These changes are not retroactive and are effective only on and after March 1, 1989.

The copyright law (Title 17 of the United States Code) was amended by the enactment of a statute for its general revision, Public Law 94–553 (90 Stat. 2541), which was signed by the President on October 19, 1976. The new law superseded the copyright act of 1909, as amended, which remained effective until the new enactment took effect on January 1, 1978.

Under the new law, all copyrightable works, whether published or unpublished, are subject to a single system of statutory protection which gives a copyright owner the exclusive right to reproduce the copyrighted work in copies or phonorecords and distribute them to the public by sale, rental, lease, or lending. Among the other rights given to the owner of a copyright are the exclusive rights to prepare de-

rivative works based upon the copyrighted work, to perform the work publicly if it be literary, musical, dramatic, choreographic, a pantomime, motion picture, or other audiovisual work, and in the case of literary, musical, dramatic, and choreographic works, pantomimes, and pictorial, graphic, or sculptural works, including the individual images of a motion picture or other audiovisual work, to display the copyrighted work publicly. All of these rights are subject to certain exceptions, including the principle of "fair use" which the new statute specifically recognizes.

Special provisions are included which permit compulsory licensing for the recording of musical compositions, noncommercial transmissions by public broadcasters of published musical and graphic works, performances of copyrighted music by jukeboxes, and the secondary transmission of copyrighted works on cable television systems.

Copyright protection under the new law extends to original works of authorship fixed in a tangible medium of expression, from which they can be perceived, reproduced, or otherwise communicated, either directly or with the aid of a machine or device. Works of authorship include books, periodicals and other literary works, musical compositions with accompanying lyrics, dramas and dramatico-musical compositions, pantomimes and choreographic works, motion pictures and other audiovisual works, sound recordings, and works of the visual arts.

As a mandatory condition of copyright protection under the law in effect before 1978, all published copies of a work were required to bear a copyright notice. The 1976 Act provides for a notice on published copies, but omission or errors will not immediately result in forfeiture of the copyright, and can be corrected within certain time limits. Innocent infringers misled by the omission or error may be shielded from liability.

In accordance with the Berne agreement, mandatory notice of copyright has been abolished for works published for the first time on or after March 1, 1989.

Failure to place a notice of copyright on copies or phonorecords of such works can no longer result in the loss of copyright.

Voluntary use of notice is encouraged. Placing a notice of copyright on published works is still strongly recommended. One of the benefits is that an infringer will not be able to claim that he or she "innocently infringed" a work. (A successful innocent infringement claim may result in a reduction in damages for infringement that the copyright owner would otherwise receive.)

A sample notice of copyright is: © 1991 John Brown.

The notice requirement for works incorporating a predominant portion of U.S. government work has been eliminated as of March 1, 1989. For these works to receive the evidentiary benefit of voluntary notice, in addition to the notice, a statement is required on the copies identifying what is copyrighted.

A sample is: © 1991 Jane Brown. Copyright claimed in Chapters 7–10, exclusive of U.S. government maps.

Notice Unchanged for Works Published Before March 1, 1989

The Berne Convention Implementation Act is not retroactive. Thus, the notice requirements that were in place before March 1, 1989, govern all works first published during that period (regardless of national origin).

• Works first published between January 1, 1978, and February 28, 1989: If a work was first published without notice during this period, it is still necessary to register the work before or within five years after publication and add the notice to copies distributed in the United States after discovery of the omission.

• Works first published before January 1, 1978: If a work was first published without the required notice before 1978, copyright was lost immediately (with the possible exception of works seeking "ad interim" protection). Once copyright is lost, it can never be restored in the United States, except by special legislation.

Registration in the Copyright Office is not a condition of copyright protection but will be a prerequisite to bringing an action in a court of law for infringement. With certain exceptions, the remedies of statutory damages and attorney's fees will not be available for infringements occurring before registration. Most copies or phonorecords published in the United States with notice of copyright are required to be deposited for the collections of the Library of Congress, not as a condition of copyright protection, but under provisions of the law subjecting the copyright owner to certain penalties for failure to deposit after a demand by the Register of Copyrights. Registration is permissive, but may be made either at the time the depository requirements are satisfied or at any other time during the subsistence of the copyright.

For works already under statutory protection, the new law retains the present term of copyright of 28 years from first publication (or from registration in some cases), renewable by certain persons for a second period of protection, but it increases the length of the second period to 47 years. Copyrights in their first term on January 1, 1978, must still be renewed during the last (28th) year of the original copyright term to receive the maximum statutory term of 75 years (a first term of 28 years plus a renewal term of 47 years).

Copyrights in their second term on January 1, 1978, are automatically extended up to a maximum of 75 years. Unpublished works that are already in existence on January 1, 1978, but are not protected by statutory copyright and have not yet gone into the public domain, will generally obtain automatic Federal copyright protection for the author's life, plus an additional 50 years after the author's death, but in any event, for a minimal term of 25 years (that is, until December 31, 2002), and if the work is published before that date, then for an additional term of 25 years, through the end of 2027.

For works created on or after January 1, 1978, the new law provides a term lasting for the author's life, plus an additional 50 years after the author's death. For works made for hire, and for anonymous and pseudonymous works (unless the author's identity is revealed in Copyright Office records), the new term will be 75 years from publication or 100 years from creation, whichever is shorter. The new law provides that all terms of copyright will run through the end of the calendar year in which they would otherwise expire. This will not only affect the duration of copyrights, but also the time-limits for renewal registrations.

Works already in the public domain cannot be protected under the new law. The 1976 Act provides no procedure for restoring protection to works in which copyright has been lost for any reason. In general, works published before January 1, 1916, are not under copyright protection in the United States, at least insofar as any version published before that date is concerned.

The new law requires that all visually perceptible copies published in the United States or elsewhere bear a notice of copyright affixed in such manner and location as to give reasonable notice of the claim of copyright. (Abolished in or after March 1, 1989, according to the Berne agreement) The notice consists of the symbol © (the letter C in a circle), the word "Copyright," or the abbreviation "Copr.," and the year of first publication of the work, and the name of the owner of copyright in the work. EXAMPLE: © *1991 John Doe.*

The notice of copyright prescribed for sound recordings consists of the symbol ℗ (the letter P in a circle), the year of first publication of the sound recording, and the name of the owner of copyright in the sound recording, placed on the surface of the phonorecord, or on the phonorecord label or container, in such manner and location as to give reasonable notice of the claim of copyright. EXAMPLE: ℗ *1991 Doe Records, Inc.*

According to the Berne Agreement, copyright owners must deposit in the Copyright Office two complete copies or phonorecords of the best edition of all works subject to copyright that are publicly distributed in the United States, whether or not the work contains a notice of copyright. In general, this deposit requirement may be satisfied by registration. For more information about mandatory deposit, request Circular 7d.

Renewal Is Still Required

Works first federally copyrighted before 1978 must still be renewed in the 28th year in order to receive the second term of 47 years. If such a work is not timely renewed, it will fall into the public domain in the United States at the end of the 28th year.

Recordation

Recordation as a Prerequisite to an Infringement Suit. The copyright owner no longer has to record a transfer before bringing a copyright lawsuit in that owner's name.

Benefits of recordation. The benefits of recordation in the Copyright Office are unchanged:

• Under certain conditions, recordation establishes priorities between conflicting transfers and nonexclusive licenses;

• Under certain conditions, recordation establishes priority between conflicting transfers; and,

• Recordation establishes a public record of the contents of the transfer or document.

Jukebox Licenses

Section 116 of the 1976 Copyright Act provides for a compulsory license to publicly perform nondramatic musical works by means of coin-operated phonorecord players (jukeboxes). The Berne Convention Implementation Act amends the law to provide for negotiated licenses between the user (the jukebox operator) and the copyright owner. If necessary, the parties are encouraged to submit to arbitration to facilitate negotiated licenses. Such licenses take precedence over the compulsory license.

For detailed information about the admendments to U.S. copyright law under the Berne Convention agreement, request circulars 93, "Highlights of U.S. Adherence to the Berne Convention," and 93a, "The United States Joins The Berne Union" from the Copyright Office.

For publications, call the Forms and Publications Hotline, 202-707-9100, or write:

Copyright Office
Publications Section, LM-455
Library of Congress
Washington, D.C. 20559

To speak with an information specialist or to request further information, call 202-479-0700, or write:

Copyright Office
Information Section, LM-401
Library of Congress
Washington, D.C. 20559

Counterfeit Products

Source: U.S. Office of Consumer Affairs.

Counterfeit products include any product bearing an unauthorized representation of a manufacturer's trademark or trade name. Examples of products which have been counterfeited include prescription and over-the-counter drugs, clothing, credit cards, watches, pacemakers, and machine and automobile replacement parts. Because counterfeit products are often of sub-standard quality, there are potential safety risks which may cause personal injury as well as economic loss.

Avoiding counterfeit products takes practice. The following are usually associated with counterfeit products:

• incorrect, smeared or blurred product packaging
• incorrect spelling of brand name
• no warranty or guarantee available
• "unbelievably" low prices

Unemployment Insurance

Unemployment insurance is managed jointly by the states and the federal government. Most states began paying benefits in 1938 and 1939.

Under What Conditions Can the Worker Collect?

The laws vary from state to state. In general, a waiting period of one week is required after a claim is filed before collecting unemployment insurance; the worker must be able to work, must not have quit without good cause or have been discharged for misconduct; he must not be involved in a labor dispute; above all, he must be ready and willing to work. He may be disqualified if he refuses, without good cause, to accept a job which is suitable for him in terms of his qualifications and experience, unless the wages, hours and working conditions offered are substantially less favorable than those prevailing for similar jobs in the community.

The unemployed worker must go to the local state employment security office and register for work. If that office has a suitable opening available, he must accept it or lose his unemployment payments, unless he has good cause for the refusal. If a worker moves out of his own state, he can still collect at his new residence; the state in which he is now located will act as agent for the other state, which will pay his benefits.

Benefits are paid only to unemployed workers who

have had at least a certain amount of recent past employment or earnings in a job covered by the state law. The amount of employment or earnings, and the period used to measure them, vary from state to state, but the intent of the various laws is to limit benefits to workers whose recent records indicate that they are members of the labor force. The amount of benefits an unemployed worker may receive for any week is also determined by application to his past wages of a formula specified in the law. The general objective is to provide a weekly benefit which is about half the worker's customary weekly wages, up to a maximum set by the law (see table). In a majority of states, the total benefits a worker may receive in a 12-month period is limited to a fraction of his total wages in a prior 12-month period, as well as to a stated number of weeks. Thus, not all workers in a state are entitled to benefits for the number of weeks shown in the table.

Who Pays for the Insurance?

The total cost is borne by the employer in all but a few states. Each state has a sliding scale of rates. The standard rate is set at 6.2% of taxable payroll in most states. But employers with records of less unemployment (that is, with fewer unemployment benefits paid to their former workers) are rewarded with rates lower than the standard state rate.

During periods of high unemployment in a state,

federal-state extended benefits are available to workers who have exhausted their regular benefits. An unemployed worker may receive benefits equal to the weekly benefit he received under the state program for one half the weeks of his basic entitlement to benefits up to a maximum (including regular benefits) of 39 weeks.

Federal Programs

Amendments to the Social Security Act provided unemployment insurance for Federal civilian employees (1954) and for ex-servicemen (1958). Benefits under these programs are paid by state employment security agencies as agents of the federal government under agreements with the Secretary of Labor. For federal civilian employees, eligibility for benefits and the amount of benefits paid are determined according to the terms and conditions of the applicable state unemployment insurance law. Ex-servicemen are subject to specific eligibility and benefit payment provisions: benefits are not payable before the fifth week subsequent to the week of release or discharge from service and such benefits are limited to 13 weeks of duration.

State Unemployment Compensation Maximums, 1991

State	Weekly benefit[1]	Maximum duration, weeks	State	Weekly benefit[1]	Maximum duration, weeks
Alabama	150	26	Nebraska	144	26
Alaska	212–284	26	Nevada	202	26
Arizona	165	26	New Hampshire	168	26
Arkansas	220	26	New Jersey	291	26
California	210	26	New Mexico	177	26
Colorado	229	26	New York	260	26
Connecticut	270–320	26	North Carolina	245	26
Delaware	225	26	North Dakota	198	26
D.C.	293	26	Ohio	196–291	26
Florida	225	26	Oklahoma	197	26
Georgia	185	26	Oregon	247	26
Hawaii	275	26	Pennsylvania	291–299	26
Idaho	206	26	Puerto Rico	120	20
Illinois	206–270	26	Rhode Island	269–336	26
Indiana	96–161	26	South Carolina	175	26
Iowa	186–228	26	South Dakota	154	26
Kansas	222	26	Tennessee	165	26
Kentucky	199	26	Texas	224	26
Louisiana	181	26	Utah	221	26
Maine	188–282	26	Vermont	182	26
Maryland	215	26	Virgin Islands	191	26
Massachusetts	282–423	30	Virginia	198	26
Michigan	276	26	Washington	246	30
Minnesota	260	26	West Virginia	251	26
Mississippi	145	26	Wisconsin	225	26
Missouri	170	26	Wyoming	200	26
Montana	193	26			

1. Maximum amounts. When two amounts are shown, higher includes dependents' allowances. *Source:* Department of Labor, Employment and Training Administration.

Trademarks

Source: Department of Commerce, Patent and Trademark Office.

A trademark may be defined as a word, letter, device, or symbol, as well as some combination of these, which is used in connection with merchandise and which points distinctly to the origin of the goods.

Certificates of registration of trademarks are issued under the seal of the Patent and Trademark Office and may be registered by the owner if he is engaged in interstate or foreign commerce which may lawfully be regulated by Congress since any Federal jurisdiction over trademarks arises under the commerce clause of the Constitution. Effective November 16, 1989, applications to register may also be based on a "bona fide intention to use the mark in commerce." Trademarks may be registered by foreign owners who comply with our law, as well as by citizens of foreign countries with which the U.S. has treaties relating to trademarks. American citizens may register trademarks in foreign countries by complying with the laws of those countries. The right to registration and protection of trademarks in many foreign countries is guaranteed by treaties.

General jurisdiction in trademark cases involving Federal Registrations is given to Federal courts. Adverse decisions of examiners on applications for registration are appealable to the Trademark Trial and Appeal Board, whose affirmances, and decisions in *inter partes* proceedings, are subject to court review. Before adopting a trademark, a person should make a search of prior marks to avoid infringing unwittingly upon them.

The duration of a trademark registration is 10 years, but it may be renewed indefinitely for 10-year periods, provided the trademark is still in use at the time of expiration.

The application fee is $175.

Patents

Source: Department of Commerce, Patent and Trademark Office.

A patent, in the most general sense, is a document issued by a government, conferring some special right or privilege. The term is now restricted mainly to patents for inventions; occasionally, land patents.

The grant of a patent for an invention gives the inventor the privilege, for a limited period of time, of excluding others from making, using, or selling a certain article. However, it does not give him the right to make, use, or sell his own invention if it is an improvement on some unexpired patent whose claims are infringed thereby.

In the U.S., the law provides that a patent may be granted, for a term of 17 years, to any person who has invented or discovered any new and useful art, machine, manufacture, or composition of matter, as well as any new and useful improvements thereof. A patent may also be granted to a person who has invented or discovered and asexually reproduced a new and distinct variety of plant (other than a tuber-propagated one) or has invented a new, original and ornamental design for an article of manufacture.

A patent is granted only upon a regularly filed application, complete in all respects; upon payment of the fees; and upon determination that the disclosure is complete and that the invention is new, useful, and, in view of the prior art, unobvious to one skilled in the art. The disclosure must be of such nature as to enable others to reproduce the invention.

A complete application, which must be addressed to the Commissioner of Patents and Trademarks, Washington, D.C. 20231, consists of a specification with one or more claims; oath or declaration; drawing (whenever the nature of the case admits of it); and a basic filing fee of $315.[1] The filing fee is not returned to the applicant if the patent is refused. If the patent is allowed, another fee of $525[1] is required before the patent is issued. The fee for design patent application is $125; the issue fee is $185[1]. Maintenance fees are required on utility patents at stipulated intervals.

Applications are ordinarily considered in the order in which they are received. Patents are not granted for printed matter, for methods of doing business, or for devices for which claims contrary to natural laws are made. Applications for a perpetual-motion machine have been made from time to time, but until a working model is presented that actually fulfills the claim, no patent will be issued.

1. Fees quoted are for small entities. Fees are double for corporations.

Beware of Illegal Patent Services

It is illegal under patent law (35 USC 33) for anyone to hold himself out as qualified to prepare and prosecute patent applications unless he is registered with the Patent Office. Also, Patent Office regulations forbid registered practitioners advertising for patent business. Some inventors, unaware of this, enter into binding contracts with persons and firms which advertise their assistance in making patent searches, preparing drawings, specifications, and patent applications, only to discover much later that their applications require the services of fully qualified agents or attorneys.

Birthstones

Month	Stone	Month	Stone
January	Garnet	July	Ruby or Star Ruby
February	Amethyst	August	Peridot or Sardonyx
March	Aquamarine or Bloodstone	September	Sapphire or Star Sapphire
April	Diamond	October	Opal or Tourmaline
May	Emerald	November	Topaz or Citrine
June	Pearl, Alexandrite or Moonstone	December	Turquoise, Lapis Lazuli, Blue Zircon or Blue Topaz

Source: Jewelry Industry Council.

Additional Consumer Information

Consult the following special sections of *Information Please Almanac* for specific consumer information

837	Accredited Senior Colleges	574	Recycling
42	Business & Economy	529	Science
578	Calendar & Holidays	434	Social Security & Aging
444	Drugs & Drug Abuse	401	Travel
34	Elections	70	Taxes
666	Energy	598	Toll–Free Numbers
78	First Aid	601	U.S. Societies & Associations
80	Nutrition & Health	297	Where to Find out More
420	Personal Finance	311	Writer's Guide
989	Postage	373	Weights & Measures

How to Write a Complaint Letter

Source: United States Office of Consumer Affairs.

• Include your name, address, and home and work phone numbers.

• Type your letter if possible. If it is handwritten, make sure it is neat and easy to read.

• Make your letter brief and to the point. Include all important facts about your purchase, including the date and place where you made the purchase and any information you can give about the product or service such as serial or model numbers or specific type of service.

• State exactly what you want done about the problem and how long you are willing to wait to get it resolved. Be reasonable.

• Include all documents regarding your problem. Be sure to send COPIES, not originals.

• Avoid writing an angry, sarcastic, or threatening letter. The person reading your letter probably was not responsible for your problem, but may be very helpful in resolving it.

• Keep a copy of the letter for your records.

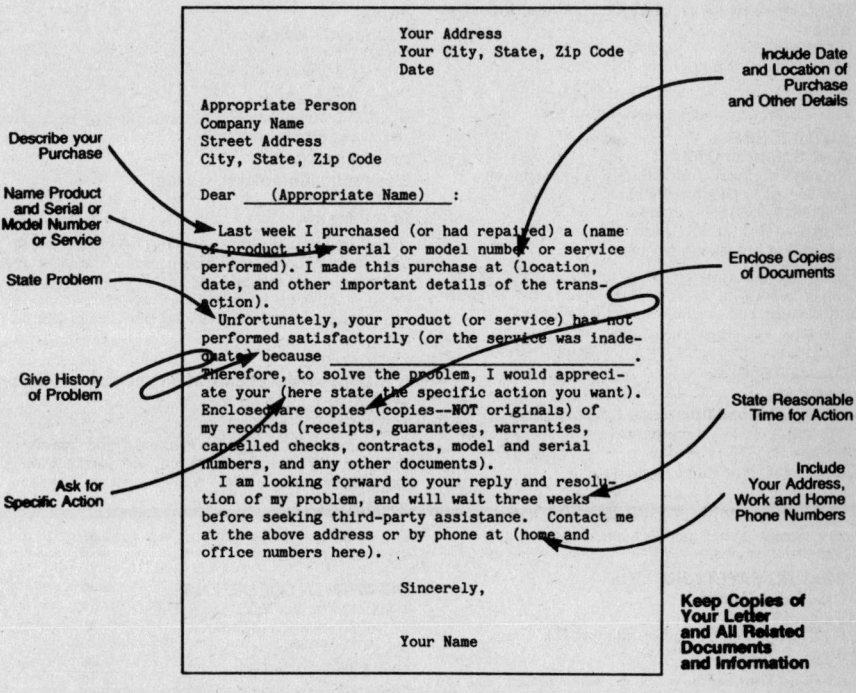

Buying a Used Car

Source: Consumer's Resource Handbook.

Look for and read the "buyer's guide," which must be displayed in the window of all used cars sold by dealers. The buyer's guide explains who must pay for repairs after the purchase. It will tell you if there is a warranty on the car, what the warranty covers, and whether a service contract is available.

Comparison shop for price, condition, warranty, and mileage for the model(s) you are interested in buying. Also compare available interest rates and other terms of financing agreements.

To estimate the total cost of the car, add in any interest rates for financing, the cost of a service con-

tract (if any), and any service or repair expenses you will be likely to pay.

Before buying the car, you might want to consider having a mechanic inspect it.

Check the reliability of the dealer with your state or local consumer protection agency. Also check the local Better Business Bureau to see if there are a large number of complaints against the dealer.

Finally, when purchasing a used car from someone other than a dealer, get a bill of sale, the proper title and registration, and copies of all financial transactions. □

TOLL-FREE NUMBERS

AIDS
National AIDS Hotline
U.S. Public Health Service
1-800-342-2437
Hours: 24 hours, 7 days
SIDA (Spanish line) 1-800-344-7432
8 a.m.–2 a.m. EST
TTY (hearing impaired) 1-800-243-7889
10 a.m.–10 p.m. EST

Provides the latest information to the public about Acquired Immune Deficiency Syndrome (AIDS).

AIDS Drugs Hotline
National Institute of Allergies and Infectious Diseases
1-800-874-2572
Hours: 9 a.m.–7 p.m., Mon.-Fri.

Callers learn the status of research and how to get into a government-sponsored clinical trial.

AUTOMOBILE
Auto Safety Hotline
National Highway Traffic Safety Administration
202-366-0123 (Washington, D.C.)
1-800-424-9393 (Elsewhere)
Hours: 8:00–4:00, EST Mon.–Fri.
Answering service after hours

Handles complaints on safety-related defects, and receives reports of vehicle safety problems. Provides information and in some cases literature on:
• motor vehicle safety recalls • car seats • automobile equipment • tires • motor homes • drunk driving • gas mileage

BANKING
Federal Deposit Insurance Corporation
202-898-3536 (Washington, D.C.)
1-800-424-5488 (Elsewhere)
Hours: 9:00–4:00, EST Mon.–Fri.

Provides general banking information on consumer banking laws. Will refer consumer to proper regulatory agency that supervises institution complaint is being filed against.

BOATING SAFETY HOTLINE
U.S. Coast Guard
1-800-368-5647
1-202-267-0973, 0780 (Washington, D.C.)
Hours: 8:00–4:00 EST Mon.-Fri.

Provides information on boats, safe boating, and associated equipment involved in safety defect (recall) campaigns for past five model years. Takes complaints about possible safety defects. Cannot resolve non-safety problems between consumer and manufacturer and cannot recommend or endorse specific boats or products.

BLIND
National Federation of the Blind
1-800-638-7518, 8-5 EST, Mon.-Fri.
1-301-659-9314 (Maryland)

Provides job information. Concerned about the rights of the blind. Free package of information about blindness.

CHEMICALS
Chemical Referral Center
1-800-262-8200
1-202-887-1315 (Washington, D.C.)
Hours: 9:00-6:00, EST, Mon.-Fri.

Refers callers to health and safety contacts at chemical manufacturers.

CHILD ABUSE
Parents Anonymous
1-800-352-0386 (California)—machine on 24 hours—can leave message
1-800-421-0353 (Elsewhere) provides referrals for all states
Hours: 8:30–5:00 Mon.–Fri., PST

CIVICS
National Civic League
1-800-223-6004
303-571-4343 in Colorado
Hours: 8 A.M.—5 P.M. MST, Mon.-Fri.

Nonprofit organization that seeks to improve state and local governments.

CIVIL RIGHTS
Civil Rights Complaint Hotline
1-800-368-1019
Answering machine

Accepts complaints regarding discrimination on the basis of race, color, national origin, handicap, or age occurring in Health and Human Services programs, i.e. in admission to hospitals, nursing homes, day care centers, or federally funded state health care assistance.

EDUCATION
U.S. Department of Education's Inspector General's Office
1-800-MIS-USED

This number is to report suspected fraud, waste, or abuse involving Federal student aid funds. Callers may remain anonymous.

1-800-433-3243

For complaints on procedure a school is using to distribute financial aid.

DEPARTMENT OF DEFENSE
1-800-424-9098 (Washington, D.C.)
223-5080 (Autovon Line)
693-5080 (FTS)
Hours: 8:00–4:30, EST

Operated for citizens to report suspected cases of fraud and waste involving the Department of Defense. The anonymity of callers will be respected.

DRUG ABUSE
National Institute on Drug Abuse
1-800-662-HELP
Hours: 9:00–3:00 Monday to Friday), 12:00-3:00 (Saturday & Sunday).

Provides information on drug abuse, and treatment referrals.

National Cocaine Hotline
1-800-COCAINE
Hours: 24 hours—7days

Provides information on cocaine and drug-related problems for cocaine abusers.

ALCOHOLISM
National Council on Alcoholism and Drug Dependence Hotline
1-800-622-2255
Hours: 24 hours—7 days

The National Council on Alcoholism, Inc. (NCA), is a national nonprofit organization that combats alcoholism, other drug addictions, and related problems. The council provides an automated referral service for affiliate offices and will mail information. All names and addresses are kept confidential.

Mothers Against Drunk Driving (MADD)
1-800-438-6233
Hours: 24-hours (Business hours: 8 A.M.—5 P.M. Central Time, Mon.-Fri.)
In New York state, call 1-800-245-6233 8:30—5 P.M.

Provides counseling, victim hotline, and nearest chapter referrals. Sends free literature.

"Just Say No Clubs" Hotline (Drug Abuse)
"Just Say No" International
1-800-258-2766
Hours: 8:00 A.M.—5:00 P.M., PCT, Mon.-Fri.

These nationwide clubs provide support and positive peer reinforcement to youngsters through workshops, seminars, newsletters, walk-a-thons, and a variety of other activities. Clubs are organized by schools, communities, and parent groups.

ELECTIONS
Federal Election Commission
Clearinghouse on Election Administration
1-800-424-9530
202-376-3120 (Wash. D.C., Alaska, and Hawaii)
Hours: 8:30—5:30, EST Mon.-Fri.

Provides information on campaign financing.

ENERGY
Conservation and Renewable Energy Inquiry and Referral Service
1-800-523-2929
Hours: 9:00–5:00, EST Mon.–Fri.

Provides non-technical information on solar, wind, and other energy heating and cooling technologies, energy conservation, and alcohol fuels.

ENVIRONMENT
Hazardous Waste
RCRA Superfund Hotline
Environmental Protection Agency
202-382-3000 (Washington, D.C.)
1-800-424-9346 (Elsewhere)
Hours: 8:30–7:30, EST Mon.–Fri.

Provides information and interpretation of federal hazardous waste regulations. Will provide referrals regarding other hazardous waste matters.

Pesticide Hotline
National Pesticide Telecommunications Network
1-800-858-7378
Hours: 24 hours—7 days

Provides information on health hazards, cleanup and disposal of pesticides. Will refer callers to human and animal poison control centers in their states if necessary.

FOOD
The Meat and Poultry Hotline
U.S. Department of Agriculture
1-800-535-4555
202-447-3333 in Washington, D.C.
Hours: 10 A.M.—4 P.M. EST, Mon.-Fri.

Provides information on proper handling, preparation, storing, and cooking of meat, poultry, and eggs. Answers questions about the safe cooking of poultry and meat in microwave ovens.

HEALTH CARE
ALZHEIMER'S DISEASE
Alzheimer's Disease and Related Disorders Association, Inc.
1-800-621-0379
1-800-572-6037 (Illinois)
Hours: 8 a.m.–5:30 p.m., M–F CST

Information and referral service. Provides support for patients and their families, aids research efforts, etc.

Cancer Information Service
National Cancer Institute
National Institutes of Health
Department of Health & Human Services
1-800-638-6694 (National)
1-800-4-Cancer (State)
Hours: 9:00 A.M.–10:00 P.M., EST Mon.–Fri.

Provides information on cancer, prevention, treatment and ongoing research; fills requests for pamphlets and other literature on cancer.

National Health Information Center
Department of Health & Human Services
301-565-4167 (Maryland)
1-800-336-4797 (Elsewhere)
Hours: 9:00–5:00 EST Mon.–Fri.

Provides referrals to sources of information on health-related issues.

Sexually Transmitted Diseases (STDs)
National STD Hotline
Operated by The American Social Health Association
1-800-227-8922
Hours: 8 A.M.—11 P.M. EST Mon.-Fri.

Provides latest information about STDs (sometimes called VD) and where to get confidential, free treatment in your area.

HOUSING
Fair Housing Discrimination Hotline
Fair Housing and Equal Opportunity
Department of Housing and Urban Development
202-708-3500 (Washington, D.C.)
1-800-669-9777 (Elsewhere)
Hours: 8:45—5:15, EST Mon.—Fri.

Receives housing discrimination complaints due to race, color, religion, sex, familial status, handicap, or national origin.

INSURANCE
Federal Crime Insurance
Federal Emergency Management Administration
1-800-638-8780 (National Number)
Hours: 8:30–5:00, EST Mon.–Fri.
Answering service after hours.

Provides information on federal crime insurance for both homes and businesses which have been robbed or burglarized.

National Insurance Consumer Helpline
Sponsored by insurance industry trade associations
1-800-942-4242
Hours: 8:00–8:00 EST Mon.–Fri.

Trained personnel provide answers on a wide range of questions about various insurance matters, are able to refer consumer complaints to appropriate sources, and send consumer brochures upon reqeust.

National Flood Insurance
1-800-492-6605 (Maryland)
1-800-638-6831 (Alaska, Hawaii, Puerto Rico, Virgin Islands, Guam)
1-800-638-6620 (Elsewhere)
Hours: 8:00–8:00, EST Mon.–Fri.

Provides information on community participation in the flood program (emergency or regular). If the community does not have a program, it is not eligible for government-subsidized insurance relief. Complaints are referred to the proper office within the agency.

PREGNANCY
Pro-Choice
Abortion Hotline
National Abortion Federation
1-800-772-9100
Hours: 9:30 A.M.—5:30 P.M. EST, Mon.-Fri.

Provides facts about abortion, counseling, and referrals to member clinics.

RIGHT-TO-LIFE
Birthright, Inc. (U.S.A.)
1-800-848-LOVE
1-800-328-LOVE in Canada
Hours: 8 A.M.—3 A.M., EST 7-days

Birthright, Inc. provides alternative advice to abortion. Operates crisis centers, and provides help such as pregnancy testing, housing, medical care, and adoption referral.

PRODUCT SAFETY
Consumer Product Safety Commission
1-800-638-2772
Hours: 10:30–4:00, EST Mon.–Fri.

Provides recorded information on the safety of consumer products. Receives reports of product-related deaths, illnesses, and injuries. Products are not rated or recommended.

RUNAWAYS
Runaway Hotline
1-800-231-6946 (U.S.A. except Texas)
1-800-392-3352 (Texas)
Hours: 24 hours, 7 days

Helps runaways by referring them to shelters, clinics, local hotlines. Will relay messages from the runaway to the parent.

SOCIAL SECURITY AND MEDICARE FRAUD
Inspector General's Hotline
Department of Health and Human Services
1-800-368-5779
Hours: 10:00–4:00, EST Mon.-Fri.

Takes calls on fraud in Social Security payments or abuse, Medicaid and Medicare fraud and other HHS programs. Recording machine after hours.

1-800-234-5772
Hours: 9:00–4:30, EST Mon–Fri.

Provides Social Security information.

VIETNAM VETERANS
Vietnam Veterans of America
1-800-424-7275 (answering machine)
202-332-2700 (Washington, D.C.)
Hours: 9:00–5:30, EST Mon.-Fri.

Answering machine takes messages for information and help. Provides information on Agent Orange, post-traumatic stress disorder, and other maters. Will answer questions on direct line.

Veterans of the Vietnam War, Inc.
1-800-VIETNAM
1-800-NAM-9090 (Pennsylvania)
Hours: 8 a.m.–6 p.m., Mon.-Fri., service after hours

Provides information on filing claims against the Agent Orange Settlement, filing claims for veterans benefits with the VA, how to take the VA to court, and information on MIAs and POWs. Veterans newsletter is available, also provides Veterans location services.

Tips For Shopping by Mail, Telephone, or Television

Source: Consumer's Resource Handbook, United States Office of Consumer Affairs.

Be suspicious of exaggerated product claims or very low prices, and read product descriptions carefully—sometimes pictures of products are misleading. If you have any doubt about the company, check with the U.S. Postal Service, your state or local consumer protection agency, or Better Business Bureau before ordering.

Ask about the firm's return policy. If it is not stated, ask before you order. For example, does the company pay charges for shipping and return? Is a warranty or guarantee available? Does the company sometimes substitute comparable goods for the product you want to order?

Keep a record of your order, including the company's name, address, and telephone number, the price of the items ordered, any handling or other charges, the date you mailed (or telephoned) in the order, and your method of payment. Keep copies of canceled checks and/or statements.

If you order by mail, your order should be shipped within 30 days after the company receives your complete order, unless another period is agreed upon when placing the order or is stated in an advertisement. If your order is delayed, a notice of delay should be sent to you within the promised shipping period along with an option to cancel the order.

If you buy a product through a television shopping program, check the cost of the same item sold by other sources, including local stores, catalogs, etc.

If you want to buy a product based on a telephone call from the company, ask for the name, address, and phone number where you can reach the caller after considering the offer. Never give your credit card or social security number over the telephone as proof of your identity.

Postal regulations allow you to write a check payable to the sender, rather than the delivery company, for cash on delivery (C.O.D.) orders. If, after examining the merchandise, you feel there has been a misrepresentation or fraud, you can stop payment on the check and file a complaint with the U.S. Postal Inspector's Office.

You can have a charge removed from your bill if you did not receive the goods or services or if your order was obtained through misrepresentation or fraud. You must notify the credit card company in writing, at the billing/inquiries/disputes address, within 60 days after the charge first appeared on your bill. ☐

U.S. SOCIETIES & ASSOCIATIONS

Source: Information Please questionnaires to organizations. Names are listed alphabetically according to key word in title; figure in parentheses is year of founding; other figure is membership. An asterisk (*) before a name indicates that up-to-date information has not been provided.

The following is a partial list selected for general readership interest. A comprehensive listing of approximately 20,000 national and international organizations can be found in the **"Encyclopedia of Associations,"** 20th Ed., 1986, Vol. I, Parts 1-3 (Katherine Gruber, Editor; Iris Cloyd, Research Editor), published by Gale Research Company, Book Tower, Detroit, Mich. 48226, available in most public libraries.

Abortion Federation, National (1977): 1436 U St. N.W., Suite 103, Washington, D.C., 20009. Phone: (202) 667-5881.

Abortion Rights Action League, National (1969): 1101 14th St. N.W., Washington, D.C. 20005. 400,000. Phone: (202) 408-4600.

Accountants, American Institute of Certified Public (1887): 1211 Avenue of the Americas, New York, N.Y. 10036. 304,000. Phone: (212) 575-6200.

Accountants, National Association of (1919): 10 Paragon Dr., Montvale, N.J., 07645-1760. Phone: (201) 573-9000.

Acoustical Society of America (1929): 500 Sunnyside Blvd., Woodbury, N.Y. 11797. 6,700. Phone: (516) 349-7800.

ACSM: American Congress on Surveying and Mapping (1941): 5410 Grosvenor Lane, Bethesda, Md. 20814. 10,000. Phone: (301) 493-0200.

Actors' Equity Association (1913): 165 W. 46th St., New York, N.Y. 10036. Phone: (212) 869-8530.

Actuaries, Society of (1949): 475 N. Martingale Rd., Suite 800, Schaumburg, Ill. 60173-2226. 13,000. Phone: (708) 706-3500.

Adirondack Mountain Club (1922): RD 3, Box 3055, Luzerne Rd., Lake George, N.Y. 12845. 17,000. Phone: (518) 668-4447.

Aeronautic Association, National (1905): 1815 N. Fort Myer Dr., Arlington, Va. 22209. 300,000. Phone: (703) 527-0226.

Aeronautics and Astronautics, American Institute of (1932): The Aerospace Center, 370 L'Enfant Promenade S.W., Washington, D.C. 20024. 40,000+. Phone: (202) 646-7400.

Aerospace Industries Association of America (1919): 1250 Eye St. N.W., Washington, D.C. 20005. 55 companies. Phone: (202) 371-8400.

Aerospace Medical Association (1929): 320 S. Henry St., Alexandria, Va. 22314-3524. 4,350. Phone: (703) 739-2240.

African-American Institute, The (1953): 833 United Nations Plaza, New York, N.Y. 10017. Phone: (212) 949-5666.

AFS Intercultural Programs (American Field Service) (1947): 313 E. 43rd St., New York, N.Y. 10017. 100,000. Phone: (212) 949-4242 or (800) AFS-INFO.

Aging Association, American (1970): 600 S. 42nd St., Omaha, Neb. 68198-4635. 500. Phone: (402) 559-4416.

Agricultural Engineers, American Society of (1907): 2950 Niles Rd., St. Joseph, Mich. 49085. 12,000. Phone: (616) 429-0300.

Agricultural History Society (1919): 1301 New York Ave. N.W., Washington, D.C. 20005-4788. 1,400. Phone: (202) 219–0787.

Agronomy, American Society of (1907): 677 S. Segoe Rd., Madison, Wis. 53711-1086. 13,000. Phone: (608) 273-8080.

Air & Waste Management Association (1907): P.O. Box 2861, Pittsburgh, Pa. 15230. 11,000. Phone: (412) 232-3444.

Aircraft Association, Experimental (1953): 3000 Poberezny Rd., Oshkosh, Wis. 54903-3086. 125,000. Phone: (414) 426-4800.

Aircraft Owners and Pilots Association (1939): 421 Aviation Way, Frederick, Md. 21701-4798. 300,000. Phone: (301) 695-2000.

Air Force Association (1946): 1501 Lee Highway, Arlington, Va., 22209-1198. 194,000. Phone: (703) 247-5800.

Air Line Pilots Association (1931): 1625 Massachusetts Ave. N.W., Washington, D.C. 20036 and 535 Herndon Pkwy., Herndon, Va. 22070. 43,000. Phone: (703) 689-2270.

Air Transport Association of America (1936): 1709 New York Ave. N.W., Washington, D.C. 20006. 21 airlines. Phone: (202) 626-4000.

Al-Anon Family Group Headquarters, Inc. For families and friends of alcoholics. (1951): P.O. Box 862, Midtown Station, New York, N.Y. 10018-0862. 31,000 groups worldwide. Phone: (800) 356-9996.

Alateen. For children of alcoholics: P.O. Box 862, Midtown Station, New York, N.Y. 10018-0862. 3,500 groups worldwide. Phone: 1 (800) 356–9996.

Alcoholics Anonymous (1935): P.O. Box 459, Grand Central Station, New York, N.Y. 10163. 1,800,000. Address communications to General Service Office. Phone: (212) 686-1100.

Alcoholism, and Drug Dependence, National Council on (1944): 12 W. 21st St., New York, N.Y. 10010. 200 affiliates. Phone: (212) 206-6770.

Alcohol Problems, American Council on (1895): 3426 Bridgeland Dr., Bridgeton, Mo. 63044. 3,500. Phone: (314) 739-5944.

Alexander Graham Bell Association for the Deaf (1890): 3417 Volta Place N.W., Washington, D.C. 20007. 6,000. Phone: (202) 337-5220.

Allergy and Immunology, American Academy of (1943): 611 E. Wells St., Milwaukee, Wis. 53202. 4,200. Phone: (414) 272-6071.

Alzheimer's Disease and Related Disorders Association, Inc. (1980): 70 E. Lake St., Suite 600, Chicago, Ill. 60601-5997. More than 200 Chapters and Affiliates, over 1,600 Family Support Groups. Toll-free information: (800) 621-0379; in Illinois: (800) 572-6037.

American Federation of Labor and Congress of Industrial Organizations (AFL-CIO) (1955): 815 16th St. N.W., Washington, D.C. 20006. 14,100,000. Phone: (202) 637-5010.

American Film and Video Association (formerly Educational Film Library Assn.) (1943): 920 Barnsdale Rd., Suite 152, La Grange Park, Ill. 60525. 1,400. Phone: (708) 482-4000.

American Foundrymen's Society, Inc. (1896): 505 State St., Des Plaines, Ill. 60016-8399. 14,000. Phone: (708) 824-0181.

American Friends Service Committee (1917): 1501 Cherry St., Philadelphia, Pa. 19102-1479. Phone: (215) 241-7000.

American Historical Association (1884): 400 A St. S.E., Washington, D.C. 20003. 19,000. Phone: (202) 544-2422.

American Indian Affairs, Association on (1923): 245 Fifth Ave., New York, N.Y. 10016. 35,000. Phone: (212) 689-8720.

American Legion, The (1919): P.O. Box 1055, Indianapolis, Ind. 46206. 2,900,000. Phone: (317) 635-8411.

American Legion Auxiliary (1919): 777 N. Meridian St., Indianapolis, Ind. 46204. 963,483. Phone: (317) 635-6291.

American Mensa, Ltd. (1960): 2626 E. 14th St., Brooklyn, N.Y. 11235-3992. 55,000. Phone: (718) 934-3700.

American Montessori Society (1960): 150 Fifth Ave., New York, N.Y. 10011. 12,000. Phone: (212) 924-3209.

American Philosophical Society (1743): 104 S. 5th St., Philadelphia, Pa. 19106-3387. 682. Phone: (215) 440-3400.

American Planning Association (1909): 1776 Massachusetts Ave. N.W., Washington, D.C. 20036 (headquarters). 26,000. Phone: (202) 872-0611. Membership office: 1313 E. 60th St., Chicago, Ill. 60637. Phone: (312) 955-9100.

Americans for Democratic Action, Inc. (1947): 1511 "K" St. N.W., Suite 941, Washington, D.C. 20005. 40,000. Phone: (202) 638-6447.

American Society for Public Administration (ASPA) (1939): 1120 G St. N.W., Suite 500, Washington, D.C. 20005. 16,000. Phone: (202) 393-7878.

American Society of CLU & ChFC (1928): 270 Bryn Mawr Ave., Bryn Mawr, Pa. 19010-2195. Phone: (215) 526-2500.

American Universities, Association of (1900): One Dupont Circle N.W., Suite 730, Washington, D.C. 20036. Phone: (202) 466-5030.

AMIDEAST (America-Mideast Educational and Training Services) (1951): 1100 17th St. N.W., Washington, D.C. 20036-4601. 217 institutional members. Phone: (202) 785-0022.

Amnesty International/USA (1961): 322 Eighth Ave., New York, N.Y. 10001-4808. 385,000. Phone: (212) 807-8400.

AMVETS (American Veterans of World War II, Korea, and Vietnam) (1944): 4647 Forbes Blvd., Lanham, Md. 20706. 200,000. Phone: (301) 459-9600.

Animal Protection Institute of America (1968): 2831 Fruitridge Rd., P.O. Box 22505, Sacramento, Calif. 95822. Phone: (916) 731-5521.

Animals, Fund For (1967): 200 W. 57th St., New York, N.Y. 10019. 175,000. Phone: (212) 246-2096.

Animals, The American Society for the Prevention of Cruelty to (ASPCA) (1866): 441 E. 92nd St., New York, N.Y. 10128. 400,000+. Phone: (212) 876-7700..

Animal Welfare Institute (1951): P.O. Box 3650, Washington, D.C. 20007. 8,600. Phone: (202) 337-2332.

Anthropological Association, American (1902): 1703 New Hampshire Ave. N.W., Washington, D.C. 20009. 11,500. Phone: (202) 232-8800.

Anti-Defamation League of B'nai B'rith (1913): 823 United Nations Plaza, New York, N.Y. 10017-3560. Phone: (212) 490-2525.

Antiquarian Society, American (1812): 185 Salisbury St., Worcester, Mass. 01609. 543. Phone: (508) 755-5221.

Anti-Vivisection Society, The American (1883): Suite 204, Noble Plaza, 801 Old York Rd., Jenkintown, Pa. 19046-1685. 15,000. Phone: (215) 887-0816.

Appraisers, American Society of (1936): P.O. Box 17265, Washington, D.C. 20041. 6,000. Phone: (703) 478-2228.

Arbitration Association, American (1926): 140 W. 51st St., New York, N.Y. 10020-1203. 5,500. Phone: (212) 484-4000.

Arboriculture, International Society of (1924): 303 W. University, Urbana, Ill. 61801-1746. 6,000. Phone: (217) 328-2032.

Archaeological Institute of America (1879): 675 Commonwealth Ave., Boston, Mass. 02215. 10,000. Phone: (617) 353-9361.

Architects, The American Institute of (1857): 1735 New York Ave. N.W., Washington, D.C. 20006. 56,000. Phone: (202) 626-7300.

Architectural Historians, Society of (1940): 1232 Pine St., Philadelphia, Pa. 19107-5944. 4,000. Phone: (215) 735-0224.

Army, Association of the United States (1950): 2425 Wilson Blvd., Arlington, Va. 22210-0860. 150,000. Phone: (703) 841-4300.

Arthritis Foundation (1948): 1314 Spring St. N.W., Atlanta, Ga. 30309. 70 local chapters. Phone: (404) 872-7100.

Arts, National Endowment for the (1965): 1100 Pennsylvania Ave. N.W., Washington, D.C. 20506. Phone: (202) 682-5400.

Arts, The American Federation of (1909): 41 E. 65th St., New York, N.Y. 10021. 1,400. Phone: (212) 988-7700.

Arts and Letters, American Academy and Institute of (1898): 633 W. 155th St., New York, N.Y. 10032. 250. Phone: (212) 368-5900.

ASM International® (1913): Materials Park, Ohio 44073. 54,000. Phone: (216) 338-5151.

Association for Investment Management and Research (1947): 1633 Broadway, 16th Floor, New York, N.Y. 10019. 17,500. Phone: (212) 957-2860.

Astronomical Society, American (1899): Astronomy Program, University of Maryland, College Park, Md. 20742. 5,700. Phone: (301) 405-1818.

Atheists, American (1963): P.O. Box 140195, Austin, Tex. 78714-0195. 40,000 Families. Phone: (512) 458-1244.

Auctioneers Association, National (1949): 8880 Ballentine, Overland Park, Kan. 66214-1985. 6,000. Phone: (913) 541-8084.

Audubon Society, National (1905): 950 Third Ave., New York, N.Y. 10022. 546,000. Phone: (212) 832-3200.

Authors League of America (1912): 330 W. 42nd St., 29th Floor, New York, N.Y. 10036-6902. 14,000. Phone: (212) 564-8350.

Autism Society of America (1965): 8601 Georgia Ave., Suite 503, Silver Spring, Md. 20910. 10,000. Phone: (301) 565-0433.

Automobile Association, American (1902): 1000 AAA Dr., Heathrow, Fla., 32746-5063. Phone: (407) 444-7000.

Automobile Club, National (1924): Bayside Plaza, 188 The Embarcadero, #300, San Francisco, Calif. 94105. 300,000. Phone: (415) 777-4000.

Automotive Hall of Fame (1939): P.O. Box 1727, Midland, Mich. 48641-1727. Phone: (517) 631-5760.

Bar Association, American (1878): 750 N. Lake Shore Dr., Chicago, Ill. 60611-4497. 371,000. Phone: (312) 988-5000.

Barber Shop Quartet Singing in America, Society for the Preservation and Encouragement of (1938): 6315 Third Ave., Kenosha, Wis., 53143-5199. 38,000. Phone: (414) 656-8440.

***Better Business Bureaus, Council of** (1970): 4200 Wilson Blvd., Suite 800, Arlington, Va. 22203. Phone: (703) 276-0100.

Bible Society, American (1816): 1865 Broadway, New York, N.Y. 10023-9980. 320,000. Phone: (212) 408-1200.

Biblical Literature, Society of (1880): 1549 Clairmont Rd., Suite 204, Decatur, Ga. 30033-4635. 7,000. Phone: (404) 636-4744.

Bibliographical Society of America (1904): P.O. Box 397, Grand Central Station, New York, N.Y. 10163. 1,300. Phone: (212) 995-9151.

Bide-A-Wee Home Association, Inc. (1903): 410 E. 38th St., New York, N.Y. 10016. Phone: Adoptions (pets) (212) 532-4455; Clinic and Hospital (212) 532-5884.

Big Brothers/Big Sisters of America (1977): 230 N. 13th St., Philadelphia, Pa. 19107. Phone: (215) 567-7000.

Biochemistry and Molecular Biology, American Society for (1906): 9650 Rockville Pike, Bethesda, Md. 20814. 8,200. Phone: (301) 530-7145.

Biological Sciences, American Institute of (1947): 730 11th St. N.W., Washington, D.C. 20001-4521. 14,000. Phone: (202) 628-1500.

Blind, American Council of the (1961): 1155 15th St. N.W., Suite 720, Washington, D.C. 20005. 20,000. Phone: (202) 467–5081.

Blind, National Federation of the (1940): 1800 Johnson St., Baltimore, Md. 21230. 50,000. Phone: (301) 659-9314.

Blindness, National Society to Prevent (1908): 500 E. Remington Rd., Schaumburg, Ill. 60173-4557. 26 affiliates. Phone: (708) 843-2020.

Blindness, Research to Prevent (1960): 598 Madison Ave., New York, N.Y. 10022. 3,300. Phone: (212) 752-4333.

Blue Cross and Blue Shield Association (1948 and 1946): 676 N. St. Clair St., Chicago, Ill. 60611. 74 Plans. Phone: (312) 440-6000.

B'nai B'rith International (1843): 1640 Rhode Island Ave. N.W., Washington, D.C. 20036-3278. 500,000. Phone: (202) 857-6500.

Booksellers Association, American (1900): 137 W. 25th St., New York, N.Y. 10001. 8,298. Phone: (212) 463-8450.

Botanical Gardens & Arboreta, American Association of (1940): 786 Church Rd., Wayne, Pa. 19087. 2,000. Phone: (215) 688-1120.

Boys & Girls Clubs of America (1906): 771 First Ave., New York, N.Y. 10017. 1,410,99 5. Phone: (212) 351-5900.

Boy Scouts of America (1910): 1325 W. Walnut Hill Lane, P.O. Box 152079, Irving, Tex. 75015-2079. 5,448,197. Phone: (214) 580-2000.

Bridge, Tunnel, and Turnpike Association, International (1932): 2120 L St. N.W., Suite 305, Washington, D.C. 20037-1527. 215 agencies. Phone: (202) 659-4620.

Broadcasters, National Association of (1922): 1771 N St. N.W., Washington, D.C. 20036. 6,000. Phone: (202) 429-5300.

Brookings Institution, The (1916): 1775 Massachusetts Ave. N.W., Washington, D.C. 20036-2188. Phone: (202) 797-6000.

Brooks Bird Club, Inc., The (1932): 707 Warwood Ave., Wheeling, W. Va. 26003. 1,000. Phone: (304) 547-5253.

Business Clubs, National Association of American (1922): 3315 No. Main St., High Point, N.C. 27265. 7,000. Phone: (919) 869-2166.

Business Education Association, National (1946): 1914 Association Dr., Reston, Va. 22091-1596. 16,000. Phone: (703) 860-8300.

Business Women's Association, American (1949): 9100 Ward Parkway, P.O. Box 8728, Kansas City, Mo. 64114-0728. More than 100,000. Phone: (816) 361-6621.

Campers & Hikers Association, National (1949): 4804 Transit Rd., Bldg. 2, Depew, N.Y. 14043-4906. 24,000 families. Phone: (716) 668-6242.

Camp Fire Boys and Girls (1910): 4601 Madison Ave., Kansas City, Mo. 64112-1278. 600,000. Phone: (816) 756-1950.

Camping Association, The American (1910): 5000 State Rd. 67 N., Martinsville, Ind. 46151-7902. 5,500. Phone: (317) 342-8456.

Cancer Society, American (1913): 1599 Clifton Rd., N.E.. Atlanta Ga. 30329. 2,646,070 volunteers. Phone: (800) ACS-2345 or check local listings.

CARE, Inc. (1945): 660 First Ave., New York, N.Y. 10016. 19 agencies plus 22 public members. Phone: (212) 686-3110.

Carnegie Endowment for International Peace (1910): 2400 N St. N.W., Washington, D.C. 20037. Phone: (202) 862-7900.

Cartoonists Society, National (1946): 157 W. 57th St., Suite 904, New York, N.Y. 10019. Phone: (212) 333-7606.

Catholic Charities USA (1910): 1731 King St., Alexandria, Va. 22314. 4,000 individuals, 735 agencies and institutions. Phone: (703) 549-1390.

Catholic Daughters of the Americas (1903): 10 W. 71st St., New York, N.Y. 10023. 150,000. Phone: (212) 877-3041.

Catholic Historical Society, American (1884): 263 S. Fourth St., Philadelphia, Pa. 19106. 950. Phone: (215) 925-5752.

Catholic War Veterans of the U.S.A. Inc. (1935): 419 N. Lee St., Alexandria, Va. 22314. 30,000. Phone: (703) 549-3622.

Ceramic Society, Inc., The American (1899): 757 Brooksedge Plaza Dr., Westerville, Ohio 43081-6136. Phone: (614) 890-4700.

Cerebral Palsy Associations, Inc., United (1949): 7 Penn Plaza, Suite 804, New York, N.Y. 10001. 163 affiliates. Phone: (800) USA IUCP.

Chamber of Commerce of the U.S. (1912): 1615 H St. N.W., Washington, D.C. 20062. 180,000. Phone: (202) 659-6000.

Chemical Engineers, American Institute of (1908): 345 E. 47th St., New York, N.Y. 10017. 52,000. Phone: (212) 705-7338.

Chemical Manufacturers Association, Inc. (1872): 2501 M St. N.W., Washington, D.C. 20037. 185 companies. Phone: (202) 887-1100.

Chemical Society, American (1876): 1155 16th St. N.W., Washington, D.C. 20036. 140,089. Phone: (202) 872-4600.

Chemists, American Institute of (1923): 7315 Wisconsin Ave., Bethesda, Md. 20814. 5,000. Phone: (301) 652-2447.

Chess Federation, United States (1939): 186 Rt. 9W, New Windsor, N.Y. 12553. 60,000. Phone: (914) 562-8350/(800) 388–KING.

Child Labor Committee, National (1904): 1501 Broadway, Rm. 1111, New York, N.Y. 10036. Phone: (212) 840-1801.

Children, American Association for Protecting (a Div. of the American Humane Association) (1877): 63 Inverness Dr. East, Englewood, Colo. 80112. Phone: (303) 792-9900.

Children's Aid Society, The (1853): 105 E. 22nd St., New York, N.Y. 10010. Child welfare services, community centers, camps and health services. Phone: (212) 949-4800.

Children's Book Council (1945): 568 Broadway, Suite 404, New York, N.Y. 10012. 61 publishing houses. Phone: (212) 966-1990.

Child Welfare League of America (1920): 440 First St. N.W., Suite 310, Washington, D.C. 20001-2085. Phone: (202) 638-2952.

Chiropractic Association, American (1963): 1701 Clarendon Blvd., Arlington, Va. 22209. 21,300. Phone: (703) 276-8800.

Christians and Jews, National Conference of (1927): 71 Fifth Ave., New York, N.Y. 10003. 200,000. Phone: (212) 206-0006.

Churches of Christ in the USA, National Council of the (1950): 475 Riverside Drive, New York, N.Y. 10115. 32 Protestant and Orthodox communions. Phone: (212) 870-2511.

Cities, National League of (1924): 1301 Pennsylvania Ave. N.W., Washington, D.C. 20004. 16,000 cities and towns. Phone: (202) 626-3000.

Civil Air Patrol (1941): Maxwell AFB, Ala. 36112-5572. 61,720. Phone: (205) 953-5463.

Civil Engineers, American Society of (1852): 345 E. 47th St., New York, N.Y. 10017. 110,000. Phone: (212) 705-7496.

Civil Liberties Union, American (1920): 132 W. 43rd St., New York, N.Y. 10036. 290,000. Phone: (212) 944-9800.

Clinical Chemistry, Inc., American Association for (1948): 2029 K St. N.W., 7th Floor, Washington, D.C. 20006. 9,000. Phone (202) 857-0717.

Clinical Pathologists, American Society of (1922): 2100 W. Harrison St., Chicago, Ill. 60612. 50,000. Phone: (312) 738-1336.

Collectors Association, American (1939): Box 39106, Minneapolis, Minn. 55439-0106. Over 3,690 debt collection agencies. Phone: (612) 926-6547.

College Board, The (1900): 45 Columbus Ave., New York, N.Y. 10023-6992. 2,800 institutions. Phone: (212) 713-8000.

College Placement Council (1956): 62 E. Highland Ave., Bethlehem, Pa. 18017. 3,100. Phone: (215) 868-1421.

Common Cause (1970): 2030 M St. N.W., Washington, D.C. 20036. 270,000. Phone: (202) 833-1200.

Community and Junior Colleges, American Association of (1920): One Dupont Circle N.W., Suite 410, Washington, D.C. 20036-1176. 1,124 institutions. Phone: (202) 728-0200.

Community Cultural Center Association, American (1978): 19 Foothills Dr., Pompton Plains, N.J. 07444. Phone: (201) 835-2661.

Composers, Authors, and Publishers, American Society of (ASCAP) (1914): One Lincoln Plaza, New York, N.Y. 10023. 48,000. Phone: (212) 621-6000.

Composers/USA, National Association of (1932): P.O. Box 49652, Barrington Station, Los Angeles, Calif. 90049. 550. Phone: (213) 541-8213.

*Congress of Racial Equality (CORE) (1942): 1457 Flatbush Ave., Brooklyn, N.Y. 11210. Nationwide network of chapters. Phone: (718) 434-3580.

Conscientious Objectors, Central Committee for (1948): 2208 South St., Philadelphia, Pa. 19146. Phone: (215) 545-4626.

Conservation Engineers, Association of (1961): Alabama Dept. of Cons. & Natural Resources, Engineering Section, 64 N. Union St., Montgomery, Ala. 36130. Phone: (205) 242-3476.

Consulting Chemists & Chemical Engineers, Inc., Association of (1928): 295 Madison Ave., 27th Floor, New York, N.Y. 10017. 130. Phone: (212) 983-3160.

Consulting Organizations, Council of (1989): 230 Park Ave., Suite 544, New York, N.Y. 10169. 2,100 individual members in DMC Division, 50 firms in ACME Division. Phone: (212) 697-9693.

Consumer Federation of America (1968): 1424 16th St. N.W., Suit 604, Washington, D.C. 20036. 240 member organizations. Phone: (202) 387-6121.

Consumer Interests, American Council on (1953): 240 Stanley Hall, Univ. of Missouri, Columbia, Mo. 65211. 1,800. Phone: (314) 882-3817.

Consumers League, National (1899): 815 15th St. N.W., Suite 928-N, Washington, D.C. 20005. Phone: (202) 639-8140.

Consumers Union (1936): 101 Truman Ave., Yonkers, N.Y. 10703-1057. 4,900,000 subscribers to *Consumer Reports*. Phone: (914) 378-2000.

Contract Bridge League, American (1927): 2990 Airways Blvd., Memphis, Tenn. 38116-3847. Phone: (901) 332-5586.

Cooperative Business Association, National (formerly Cooperative League of the U.S.A) (1916): 1401 New York Ave. N.W., Suite 1100, Washington, D.C. 20005. Phone: (202) 638-6222.

Counselors and Family Therapists, National Academy of (1972): 55 Morris Ave., Springfield, N.J. 07081-1422. Phone: (201) 379-7496.

Country Music Association (1958): One Music Circle South, Nashville, Tenn. 37203. 6,000. Phone: (615) 244-2840.

Credit Association, International (1912): P.O. Box 27357, St. Louis, Mo. 63141-1757. 11,500 members, 125 local associations. Phone: (314) 991-3030.

Credit Management, National Association of (1896): 8815 Centre Park Dr., Suite 200, Columbia, Md. 21045. Phone: (301) 740-5560.

Credit Union National Association (1934): P.O. Box 431, Madison, Wis. 53701. 52 state leagues representing 14,500 credit unions. Phone: (608) 231-4000.

*Crime and Delinquency, National Council on (1907): 685 Market St., #620, San Francisco, Calif. 94105. Nationwide membership. Phone: (415) 896-6223.

CSA/USA, Celiac Sprue Association/United States of America: P.O. Box 31700, Omaha, Neb. 68131-0700. 6 regions in U.S., 36 chapters, 60 active resource units. Phone: (402) 558-0600.

Dairy Council, National (1915): 6300 N. River Rd., Rosement, Ill. 60018. Phone: (708) 696-1020.

Daughters of the American Revolution, National Society (1890): 1776 D St. N.W., Washington, D.C. 20006. 200,000. Phone: (202) 628-1776.

Daughters of the Confederacy, United (1894): 328

N. Boulevard, Richmond, Va. 23220-4057. 27,000. Phone: (804) 355-1636.

Deaf, National Association of the (1880): 814 Thayer Ave., Silver Spring, Md. 20910. Phone: (301) 587-1788; (301) 587-1789 TDD.

Defenders of Wildlife (1947): 1244 19th St. N.W., Washington, D.C. 20036. 84,000 members and supporters. Phone: (202) 659-9510.

Defense Preparedness Association, American (1919): Two Colonial Place, Suite 400, 2101 Wilson Blvd., Arlington, Va. 22201-3061. 45,000 individual, 1,000 corporate. Phone: (703) 522-1820.

Dental Association, American (1859): 211 E. Chicago Ave., Chicago, Ill. 60611. 150,000. Phone: (312) 440-2500.

Diabetes Association, American (1940): 1660 Duke St., Alexandria, Va. 22314. Phone: (703) 549-1500.

Dignity (1969): 1500 Massachusetts Ave. N.W., Suite 11, Washington, D.C. 20005. 5,000. Phone: (202) 861-0017.

Disabled American Veterans (1920): 807 Maine Ave. S.W., Washington, D.C. 20024. Phone: (202) 554-3501.

Dowsers, Inc., The American Society of (1961): P.O. Box 24, Danville, Vt. 05828-0024. 3,500. Phone: (802) 684-3417.

Drug, Chemical, & Allied Trades Association, Inc., The (1890): 2 Roosevelt Ave., Syosset, N.Y. 11791. 575. Phone (516) 496-3317.

Ducks Unlimited, Inc. (1937): One Waterfowl Way, Long Grove, Ill. 60047. 550,000. Phone: (708) 438-4300.

Earthwatch (1971): 680 Mt. Auburn St., Box 403N, Watertown, Mass. 02272. 75,000. Phone: (617) 926-8200.

Eastern Star, Order of, General Grand Chapter (1876): 1618 New Hampshire Ave. N.W., Washington, D.C. 20009. 2,087,063. Phone: (202) 667-4737.

Easter Seal Society, The National (1921): 70 E. Lake St., Chicago, Ill. 60601. 58 affiliated state societies and Puerto Rico. Phone: (312) 726-6200 and (312) 726-4258 TDD.

Economic Association, American (1885): 2014 Broadway, Suite 305, Nashville, Tenn. 32703. 21,000. 6,000 inst. subscribers. Phone: (615) 322-2595.

Economic Development, Committee for (1942): 477 Madison Ave., New York, N.Y. 10022. 250 trustees. Phone: (212) 688-2063.

Edison Electric Institute (1933): 701 Pennsylvania Ave. N.W., Washington, D.C. 20004-2696.

Education, American Council on (1918): One Dupont Circle N.W., Washington, D.C. 20036. 1,750 institutional members. Phone: (202) 939-9300.

Education, Council for Advancement and Support of (CASE) (1974): 11 Dupont Circle N.W., Suite 400, Washington, D.C. 20036-1207. 14,000. Phone: (202) 328-5900.

Educational Exchange, International, Council on (1947): 205 E. 42nd St., New York, N.Y. 10017. 203. Phone: (212) 661-1414.

Educational Research Association, American (1916): 1230 17th St. N.W., Washington, D.C. 20036. 17,000. Phone: (202) 223-9485.

Education Association, National (1857): 1201 16th St. N.W., Washington, D.C. 20036-3290. 2 million. Phone: (202) 833-4000.

Electrochemical Society, The (1902): 10 S. Main St., Pennington, N.J. 08534-2896. 6,274. Phone: (609) 737-1902.

Electronic Industries Association (1924): 2001 Pennsylvania Ave. N.W., Washington, D.C. 20006-1813. 1,000 member companies. Phone: (202) 457-4900.

Electroplaters and Surface Finishers Society, American (1909): 12644 Research Pkwy., Orlando, Fla. 32826. 10,000. Phone: (407) 281-6441.

Elks of the U.S.A., Benevolent and Protective Order of the (1868): 2750 Lake View Ave., Chicago, Ill. 60614. 1,400,000. Phone: (312) 477-2750.

Energy Engineers, Association of (1977): 4025 Pleasantdale Rd., Suite 420, Atlanta, Ga. 30340. 7,500. Phone: (404) 447-5083.

English-Speaking Union of the United States (1920): 16 E. 69th St., New York, N.Y. 10021. 25,000. Phone: (212) 879-6800.

Entomological Society of America (1889): 9301 Annapolis Rd., Lanham, Md. 20706-3115. 9,000. Phone: (301) 731-4535.

Esperanto League for North America, The (1952): P.O. Box 1129, El Cerrito, Calif. 94530. Over 1,000. Phone: (415) 653-0998.

Exceptional Children, The Council for (1922): 1920 Association Dr., Reston, Va. 22091. 54,000. Phone: (703) 620-3660.

Experimental Test Pilots, The Society of (1956): 44814 Elm St., Lancaster, Calif. 93534. 1,800. Phone: (805) 942-9574.

Exploration Geophysicists, Society of (1930): P.O. Box 702740, Tulsa, Okla. 74170-2740. 15,000. Phone: (918) 493-3516.

Family Physicians, American Academy of (1947): 8880 Ward Pkwy., Kansas City, Mo. 64114-2797. 70,000. Phone: (816) 333-9700.

Family Relations, National Council on (1938): 3989 Central Ave. N.E., #550, Minneapolis, Minn. 55421-3921. 3,800. Phone: (612) 781-9331.

Family Service America (1911): 11700 W. Lake Park Dr., Park Place, Milwaukee, Wis. 53224. Approximately 300 member agencies. Phone: (414) 359-1040.

Farm Bureau Federation, American (1919): 225 Touhy Ave., Park Ridge, Ill. 60068. 3.8 million member families. Phone: (312) 399-5700.

Farmer Cooperatives, National Council of (1929): 50 F St. N.W., Washington, D.C. 20001. 135. Phone: (202) 626-8700.

Federal Bar Association (1920): 1815 H St. N.W., Suite 408, Washington, D.C. 20006-3697. 15,000. Phone: (202) 638-0252.

Federal Employees, National Federation of (1917): 1016 16th St. N.W., Washington, D.C. 20036. Rep. 150,000. Phone: (202) 862-4400.

Feline and Canine Friends, Inc. (1973): 505 N. 70Bush St., Anaheim, Calif. 92805. 1,000. Phone: (714) 635-7975.

Fellowship of Reconciliation (1915): Box 271, Nyack, N.Y. 10960. 36,000. Phone: (914) 358-4601.

Female Executives, National Association for (1972): 127 W. 24th St., New York, N.Y. 10011. 250,000. Phone: (212) 645-0770.

FFA Organization, National (1928): 5632 Mt. Vernon Memorial Hwy., P.O. Box 15160, Alexandria, Va. 22309-0160. 387,042. Phone: (703) 360-3600.

Fire Protection Association, National (1896): One Batterymarch Park, P.O. Box 9101, Quincy, Mass. 02269-9101. 56,000. Phone: (617) 770-3999.

Flag Foundation, National (1968): Flag Plaza, Pittsburgh, Pa. 15219-3630. 3,000+. Phone: (412) 261-1776.

Fleet Reserve Association (1924): 125 N. West St., Alexandria, Va. 22314-2754. 153,000. Phone:

(703) 683-1400.

Flight Test Engineers, Society of (1968): P.O. Box 4047, Lancaster, Calif. 93539. 1,100. Phone: (805) 948-3067.

Foreign Policy Association (1918): 729 Seventh Ave., New York, N.Y. 10019. Phone: (212) 764-4050.

Foreign Relations, Council on (1921): 58 E. 68th St., New York, N.Y. 10021. 2,600. Phone: (212) 734-0400.

Foreign Study, American Institute for (1965): 102 Greenwich Ave., Greenwich, Conn. 06830. Phone: (203) 869-9090/(800) 727-AIFS.

Foreign Trade Council, Inc., National (1914): 100 E. 42nd St., New York, N.Y. 10017. Over 550 companies. Phone: (212) 867-5630. Also, 1625 K St. N.W., Washington, D.C. 20006. Phone: (202) 887-0278.

Forensic Sciences, American Academy of (1948): 218 E. Cache La Poudre/80903, P.O. Box 669, Colorado Springs, Colo. 80901-0669. 3,500. Phone: (719) 636-1100.

Forest Council, American (1932): 1250 Connecticut Ave. N.W., Suite 320, Washington, D.C. 20036. 100. Phone: (202) 463-2455.

Foresters, Society of American (1900): 5400 Grosvenor Lane, Bethesda, Md. 20814-2198. 19,000. Phone: (301) 897-8720.

Forestry Association, American (1875): 1516 P St. N.W., Washington, D.C. 20005. 35,000. Phone: (202) 667-3300.

Fortean Organization, International (1965): P.O. Box 367, Arlington, Va. 22210-0367. 900. Phone: (703) 522-9232.

Foster Parents Plan International (1937). Box 804, East Greenwich, R.I. 02818. Phone: (401) 826-2500.

4-H Program (early 1900s): Room 3860-S, U.S. Department of Agriculture, Washington, D.C. 20250. 5,492,120. Phone: (202) 447-5853.

Freedom of Information Center (1958): 20 Walter Williams Hall, Univ. of Missouri, Columbia, Mo. 65211. Phone: (314) 882-4856.

French-American Chamber of Commerce in the U.S. Inc. (1896): 509 Madison Ave., Suite 1900, New York, N.Y. 10022. 605. Membership Association. Phone: (212) 371-4466.

French Institute/Alliance Française (1911): 22 E. 60th St., New York, N.Y. 10022-1077. 9,000. Phone: (212) 355-6100.

Friendship and Good Will, International Society of (Esperanto) (1978): 211 W. Fourth Ave., P.O. Box 2637, Gastonia, N.C. 28053-2637. 3,922 in 166 countries. Phone: (704) 864-7906.

Friends of Animals Inc. (1957): P.O. Box 1244, Norwalk, Conn. 06856. 104,000. Phone: (203) 866-5223. For low-cost spay/neuter info. call: (800) 321-PETS.

Friends of the Earth (1969): 218 D St. S.E., Washington, D.C. 20003. Phone: (202) 544-2600.

Future Homemakers of America, Inc. (1945): 1910 Association Dr., Reston, Va. 22091. 280,000. Phone: (703) 476-4900.

Gamblers Anonymous: Box 17173, Los Angeles, Calif. 90017. Phone: (213) 386-8789.

Genealogical Society, National (1903): 4527 17th St. N., Arlington, Va. 22207-2399. 10,000. Phone: (703) 525-0050.

Genetic Association, American (1903): P.O. Box 39, Buckeystown, Md. 21717. 1,600. Phone: (301) 695-9292.

Geographers, Association of American (1904): 1710 16th St. N.W., Washington, D.C. 20009-3198. 6,300. Phone: (202) 234-1450.

Geographical Society, The American (1851): 156 Fifth Ave., Suite 600, New York, N.Y. 10010-7002. 1,500. Phone: (212) 242-0214.

Geographic Education, National Council for (1915): Indiana University of Pennsylvania, Indiana, Pa. 15705. 3,700. Phone: (412) 357-6290.

Geographic Society, National (1888): 17th and M Sts. N.W., Washington, D.C. 20036. 10,000,000. Phone: (202) 857-7000.

Geological Institute, American (1948): 4220 King St., Alexandria, Va. 22302-1507. 20 member societies representing 70,000 geoscientists. Phone: (703) 379-2480.

Geological Society of America, Inc. (1888): 3300 Penrose Pl., P.O. Box 9140, Boulder, Colo. 80301. 17,000. Phone: (303) 447-2020.

Geriatrics Society, American (1942): 770 Lexington Ave., Suite 300, New York, N.Y. 10021. 6,200. Phone: (212) 308-1414.

German American National Congress, The (Deutsch-Amerikanischer National Congress—D.A.N.K.) (1958): 4740 N. Western Ave., Chicago, Ill. 60625. 30,000, plus Associates. Phone: (312) 275-1100.

Gideons International, The (1889): 2900 Lebanon Rd., Nashville, Tenn. 37214-0800. 105,000. Phone: (615) 883-8533.

Gifted, The Association for the (1958): The Council for Exceptional Children, 1920 Association Dr., Reston, Va. 22091. 2,200. Phone: (703) 620-3660.

Girls Incorporated (1945): 30 E. 33rd St., New York, N.Y. 10016. 250,000. Phone: (212) 689-3700.

Girl Scouts of the U.S.A. (1912): 830 Third Ave., New York, N.Y. 10022-7522. 3,268,630. Phone: (212) 940-7500.

Graphic Artists, Society of American (1916): 32 Union Square, Rm. 1214, New York, N.Y. 10003. Phone: (212) 260-5706.

Graphoanalysis Society, International (1929): 111 N. Canal St., Chicago, Ill. 60606. 10,000. Phone: (312) 930-9446.

Gray Panthers Project Fund (1970): 1424 16th St. N.W., Suite 602, Washington, D.C. 20036. Over 80 chapters (networks). Phone: (202) 387-3111.

Greenpeace U.S.A. (1979): 1436 U St. N.W., Washington, D.C. 20009. 800,000. Phone: (202) 462-1177.

Group Psychotherapy Association, American (1942): 25 E. 21st St., 6th Floor, New York, N.Y. 10010. 3,500 Phone: (212) 477-2677.

Guide Dog Foundation for the Blind, Inc. (1946): 371 E. Jericho Turnpike, Smithtown, N.Y. 11787-2976. 15,000. Phone: (516) 265-2121; outside N.Y. city call (800) 548-4337.

Hadassah, The Women's Zionist Organization of America (1912): 50 W. 58th St., New York, N.Y. 10019. 385,000. Phone: (212) 355-7900.

Handgun Control, Inc. (1974): 1225 Eye St. N.W., Washington, D.C. 20005. 250,000. Phone: (202) 898-0792.

Health, Physical Education, Recreation, and Dance, American Alliance for (1885): 1900 Association Dr., Reston, Va. 22091. 35,000. Phone: (703) 476-3400.

Heart Association, American (1924): 7320 Greenville Ave., Dallas, Tex. 75231-4599. 3,200,000 volunteers. Phone: (214) 373-6300.

Heating, Refrigerating, and Air-Conditioning Engineers, Inc., American Society of (1894): 1791 Tullie Circle N.E., Atlanta, Ga. 30329. 50,000.

Phone: (404) 636-8400.

Helicopter Association International (1948): 1619 Duke St., Alexandria, Va. 22314-3439. Phone: (703) 683-4646.

Hemispheric Affairs, Council on (1975): 724 9th St. N.W., Rm. 401, Washington, D.C. 20001. Phone: (202) 393-3322.

Historians, The Organization of American (1907): Indiana Univ., 112 N. Bryan St., Bloomington, Ind. 47408. 9,000. Phone: (812) 855-7311.

Historic Preservation, National Trust for (1949): 1785 Massachusetts Ave. N.W., Washington, D.C. 20036. 230,000. Phone: (202) 673-4000.

Home Economics Association, American (1909): 1555 King St., Alexandria, Va. 22314. 23,000. Phone: (800) 424-8080.

Horse Council, Inc., American (1969): 1700 K St. N.W., #300, Washington, D.C. 20006. More than 180 organizations and 2,400 individuals. Phone: (202) 296-4031.

Horse Shows Association, Inc., American (1917): 220 E. 42nd St., New York, N.Y. 10017-5806. 55,000. Phone: (212) 972-2472.

Horticultural Association, National Junior (1935): 441 E. Pine, Freemont, Mich. 49412. 12,500. Phone: (616) 924-5237.

Horticultural Society, American (1922): Box 0105, Mt. Vernon, Va. 22121. 20,000. Phone: (703) 768-5700 or (800) 777-7931.

Hospital Association, American (1898): 840 N. Lake Shore Dr., Chicago, Ill. 60611. 5,500 institutions. Phone: (312) 280-6000.

Housing Science, International Association for (1972): P.O. Box 340254, Coral Gables/Miami, Fla. 33114. 500 professionals. Phone: (305) 448-3532.

Humane Association, American (1877): P.O. Box 1266, Denver, Colo. 80201-1266. Phone: (303) 792-9900.

Humane Society of the United States (1954): 2100 L St. N.W., Washington, D.C. 20037. 1,000,000. Phone: (202) 452-1100.

Humanities, National Endowment for the (1965): 1100 Pennsylvania Ave. N.W., Washington, D.C. 20506. Phone: (202) 786-0443.

Hydrogen Energy, International Association for (1975): P.O. Box 248266, Coral Gables, Fla. 33124. 2,500. Phone: (305) 284-4666.

Illustrators, Society of (1901): 128 E. 63rd St., New York, N.Y. 10021. 975. Phone: (212) 838-2560 .

Industrial Engineers, Institute of (1948): 25 Technology Park/Atlanta, Norcross, Ga. 30092. 40,000. Phone: (404) 449-0460.

Interfraternity Conference, National (1909): 3901 W. 86th St., Suite 390, Indianapolis, Ind. 46268. 59. Phone: (317) 872-1112.

Iron and Steel Institute, American (1908): 1133 15th St. N.W., Suite 300, Washington, D.C. 20005-2701. 1,200. Phone: (202) 452-7100.

Izaak Walton League of America (1922): 1401 Wilson Blvd., Level B, Arlington, Va. 22209. 53,000. Phone: (703) 528-1818.

Jaycees, The United States (The U.S. Junior Chamber of Commerce) (1920): P.O. Box 7, Tulsa, Okla. 74121. 234,000. Phone: (918) 584-2481.

Jewish Community Centers, World Confederation of (1946): 12 Hess St., Jerusalem, Israel 94185. Phone: (02) 231 371/221 265.

Jewish Community Centers Association of North America (1917): 15 E. 26th St., New York, N.Y. 10010-1579. 275 affiliated Jewish Community Centers, YM-YWHAs, and camps. Phone: (212) 532-4949.

Jewish Congress, American (1918): 15 E. 84th St., New York, N.Y. 10028. 50,000. Phone: (212) 879-4500.

Jewish Historical Society, American (1892): 2 Thornton Rd., Waltham, Mass. 02154. 3,500. Phone: (617) 891-8110.

Jewish War Veterans of the U.S.A. (1896): 1811 R St. N.W., Washington, D.C. 20009-1659. Phone: (202) 265-6280.

Jewish Women, National Council of (1893): 53 W. 23rd St., New York, N.Y. 10010. 100,000. Phone: (212) 645-4048.

John Birch Society (1958): P.O. Box 8040, Appleton, Wis. 54913. Under 100,000. Phone: (414) 749-3780.

Journalists, Society of Professional, (1909): 16 S. Jackson, Greencastle, Ind. 46135-0077. 20,000. Phone: (317) 653-3333.

Journalists and Authors, American Society of (1948): 1501 Broadway, Suite 302, New York, N.Y. 10036. 800. Phone: (212) 997-0947.

Judaism, American Council for (1943): P.O. Box 9009, Alexandria, Va. 22304. 10,000. Phone: (703) 836-2546.

Junior Achievement Inc. (1919): 45 East Clubhouse Dr., Colorado Springs, Colo. 80906. 1.5 million. Phone: (719) 540-8000.

Junior Leagues International, Inc., Association of (1921): 660 First Ave., New York, N.Y. 10016-3241. 276 Leagues, 188,000 members. Phone: (212) 683-1515.

Junior Statesmen of America (1934): 650 Bair Island Rd., Suite 201, Redwood City, Calif. 94063. 10,000. Phone: (415) 366-2700.

Kennel Club, American (1884): 51 Madison Ave., New York, N.Y. 10010. 473 member clubs. Phone: (212) 696-8200.

Kiwanis International (1915): 3636 Woodview Trace, Indianapolis, Ind. 46268-3196. 323,000. Phone: (317) 875-8755.

Knights of Columbus (1882): One Columbus Plaza, New Haven, Conn. 06507-0901. 1,509,641. Phone: (203) 772-2130.

Knights of Pythias, Supreme Lodge (1864): 2785 E. Desert Inn Rd. #150, Las Vegas, Nev. 89121. 89,000. Phone: (702) 735-3302.

Knights Templar, Grand Encampment of (1816): 14 E. Jackson Blvd., Suite 1700, Chicago, Ill. 60604. 340,000. Phone: (312) 427-5670.

La Leche League International (1956): 9616 Minneapolis Ave., Franklin Park, Ill. 60131-8209. 40,000. Phone: (708) 455-7730.

Law, American Society of International (1906): 2223 Massachusetts Ave. N.W., Washington, D.C. 20008. 4,500. Phone: (202) 265-4313.

League of Women Voters of the U.S. (1920): 1730 M St. N.W., Washington, D.C. 20036. 114,000. Phone: (202) 429-1965.

Legal Aid and Defender Association, National (1911): 1625 K St. N.W., Suite 800, Washington, D.C. 20006. 5,000. Phone: (202) 452-0620.

Legal Secretaries, National Association of (1950): 2250 E. 73rd St., Suite 550, Tulsa, Okla. 74136-6864. 18,000. Phone: (918) 493-3540.

Leukemia Society of America (1949): 733 Third Ave., New York, N.Y. 10017. Phone: (212) 573-8484.

Library Association, American (1876): 50 E. Huron St., Chicago, Ill. 60611. 51,500. Phone: (312) 944-6780.

Life Insurance, American Council of (1976): 1001

Pennsylvania Ave. N.W., Washington, D.C. 20004-2599. 617. Phone: (202) 624-2000.

Life Underwriters, National Association of (1890): 1922 F St. N.W., Washington, D.C. 20006-4387. Phone: (202) 331-6000.

Lions Clubs International (1917): 300 22nd St., Oak Brook, Ill. 60521-8842. 1,376,470. Phone: (708) 571-5466.

Longwave Club of America (1974): 45 Wildflower Rd., Levittown, Pa. 19057. 530. Phone: (215) 945-0543.

Lung Association, American (1904): 1740 Broadway, New York, N.Y. 10019-4374. 132 constituent and affiliate associations. Phone: (212) 315-8700.

Magazine Editors, American Society of (1963): 575 Lexington Ave., New York, N.Y. 10022. 700. Phone: (212) 752-0055.

Magazine Publishers of America (1919): 575 Lexington Ave., New York, N.Y. 10022. 197 companies, 725 publications. Phone: (212) 752-0055.

Management Association, American (1923): 135 W. 50th St., New York, N.Y. 10020-1201. 75,000. Phone: (212) 586-8100.

Manufacturers, National Association of (1895): 1331 Pennsylvania Ave. N.W., Suite 1500-North Lobby, Washington, D.C. 20004-1703. 13,500. Phone: (202) 637-3065.

Manufacturers' Agents National Association (MANA) (1947): 23016 Mill Creek Rd., P.O. Box 3467, Laguna Hills, Calif. 92654. 9,000. Phone: (714) 859-4040.

March of Dimes Birth Defects Foundation (1938): 1275 Mamaroneck Ave., White Plains, N.Y. 10605. 133 chapters. Phone: (914) 428-7100.

Marine Conservation, Center for (1972): 1725 De Sales St. N.W., Suite 500, Washington, D.C. 20036. 110,000. Phone: (202) 429-5609.

Marine Corps Association (1913): Bldg. #715, Marine Corps Base, Quantico, Va. 22134. 104,419. Phone: (800) 336-0291.

Marine Corps League (1923): 8626 Lee Hwy., Fairfax, Va. Correspondence address: P.O. Box 3070, Merrifield, Va. 22116. 30,000. Phone: (703) 207-9588 or (703) 207-9589.

Marine Technology Society (1963): 1825 K St. N.W., Suite 218, Washington, D.C. 20006. 2,700. Phone: (202) 775-5966.

Masons, Ancient and Accepted Scottish Rite, Northern Masonic Jurisdiction, Supreme Council 33 (1813): 33 Marrett Rd., Lexington, Mass. 02173. 412,612. Phone: (617) 862-4410.

Masons, Ancient and Accepted Scottish Rite, Southern Jurisdiction, Supreme Council (1801): 1733 16th St. N.W., Washington, D.C. 20009. 575,746. Phone: (202) 232-3579.

Masons, Royal Arch, General Grand Chapter International (1797): P.O. Box 489, 111 S. Fourth St., Danville, Ky. 40422. 277,340. Phone: (606) 236-0757.

Massachusetts Audubon Society (1896): South Great Rd., Lincoln, Mass. 01773. 49,000 member households. Phone: (508) 259-9500.

Mathematical Association of America (1915): 1529 18th St. N.W., Washington, D.C. 20036. 33,000. Phone: (202) 387-5200.

Mathematical Society, American (1888): P.O. Box 6248, Providence, R.I. 02940-6248. 28,710. Phone: (401) 455-4000.

Mathematical Statistics, Institute of (1935): 3401 Investment Blvd. #7, Hayward, Calif. 94545. 3,800. Phone: (415) 783-8141.

Mayflower Descendants, General Society of

(1897): 4 Winslow St., P.O. Box 3297, Plymouth, Mass. 02361. 25,000. Phone: (508) 746-3188.

Mayors, U.S. Conference of (1932): 1620 Eye St. N.W., Washington, D.C. 20006. 8 standing committees. Phone: (202) 293-7330.

Mechanical Engineers, American Society of (1880): 345 E. 47th St., New York, N.Y. 10017. 118,000. Phone: (212) 705-7722.

Mechanics, American Academy of (1969): 4205 EBIU, AMES, 0411, University of CA, San Diego, 9500 Gilman Dr., La Jolla, Calif. 92093-0411. 1,600. Phone: (619) 534-2036.

Medical Association, American (1847): 515 N. State St., Chicago, Ill. 60610-4377. Phone: (312) 464-5000.

Medical Library Association (1898): Six N. Michigan Ave., Suite 300, Chicago, Ill. 60602. 5,000. Phone: (312) 419-9094.

Mental Health Association, National (1909): 1021 Prince St., Alexandria, Va., 22314-2971. 1,000,000. Phone: (703) 684-7722.

Meteorological Society, American (1919): 45 Beacon St., Boston, Mass. 02108-3693. 10,000. Phone: (617) 227-2425.

Military Chaplains Association of the U.S.A. (1925): P.O. Box 42660, Washington, D.C. 20015-0660. 1,500. Phone: (202) 574-2423.

Mining, Metallurgy and Exploration, Society for; The Minerals, Metals & Materials Society (1871): 345 E. 47th St., New York, N.Y. 10017. 4 Member Societies: Society of Mining Engineers, The Minerals, Metals and Materials Society, Iron & Steel Society, Society of Petroleum Engineers. Phone: (212) 705-7695.

Mining and Metallurgical Society of America (1910): 9 Escalle Lane, Larkspur, Calif. 94939. 300. Phone: (415) 924-7441.

Model Aeronautics, Academy of (1936): 1810 Samuel Morse Dr., Reston, Va. 22090. 150,000. Phone: (703) 435-0750.

Modern Language Association of America (1883): 10 Astor Place, New York, N.Y. 10003. 33,285. Phone: (212) 475-9500.

Modern Woodmen of America (1883): 1701 1st Ave., Rock Island, Ill. 61201. 649,000. Phone: (309) 786-6481.

Moose, Loyal Order of (1888): Mooseheart, Ill. 60539. 1,804,198. Phone: (708) 859-2000.

Mothers Against Drunk Driving (MADD) (1980): P.O. box 541688, Dallas, Tex. 75354-1688. 2.95 million. Phone: (214) 744-6233.

Motion Picture & Television Engineers, Society of (1916): 595 W. Hartsdale Ave., White Plains, N.Y. 10607. 9,500. Phone: (914) 761-1100.

Motion Picture Arts & Sciences, Academy of (1927): 8949 Wilshire Blvd., Beverly Hills, Calif. 90211-1972. Phone: (213) 247-3000.

Multiple Sclerosis Society, National (1946): 205 E. 42nd St., New York, N.Y. 10017-5706. 400,000. Phone: (212) 986-3240.

Muscular Dystrophy Association (1950): 3561 East Sunrise Dr., Tucson, Ariz. 85718. 2,300,000 volunteers. Phone: (602) 529-2000.

Museum of Natural History, American (1869): Central Park West at 79th St., New York, N.Y. 10024-5192. 520,000. Phone: (212) 769-5100.

Museums, American Association of (1906): 1225 Eye St. N.W., Suite 200, Washington, D.C. 20005. 11,500. Phone: (202) 289-1818.

Music Council, National (1940): P.O. Box 5551, Englewood, N.J. 07631-5551. 50 National Music Organizations. Phone: (201) 871-9088.

Musicians, American Federation of (1896): 1501 Broadway, Suite 600 Paramount Bldg., New York, N.Y. 10036. Phone: (212) 869-1330.

Music Publishers Association, Inc., National (1917): 205 E. 42nd St., New York, N.Y. 10017. Trade Organization/Harry Fox Agency-Licensing Organization. Phone: (212) 370-5330.

Muzzle Loading Rifle Association, National (1933): P.O. Box 67, Friendship, Ind. 47021. 30,000. Phone: (812) 667-5131.

NAFSA: Association of International Educators (1948): 1875 Connecticut Ave. N.W., Suite 1000, Washington, D.C. 20009-5728. 6,500. Phone: (202) 462-4811.

Narcolepsy and Cataplexy Foundation of America (1975): 445 E. 68th St., Suite 12L, New York, N.Y. 10021. 3,991. Phone: (212) 628-6315.

National Association for the Advancement of Colored People (1909): 4805 Mt. Hope Dr., Baltimore, Md. 21215. 500,000+. Phone: (301) 358-8900.

National Grange, The (1867): 1616 H St. N.W., Washington, D.C. 20006. 330,000. Phone: (202) 628-3507.

National PTA (National Congress of Parents and Teachers) (1897): 700 N. Rush St., Chicago, Ill. 60611. 7.0 million. Phone: (312) 787-0977.

National Rifle Association of America (1871): 1600 Rhode Island Ave. N.W., Washington, D.C. 20036. 3,000,000. Phone: (202) 828-6000.

Natural Science for Youth Foundation (1961): 130 Azalea Dr., Roswell, Ga. 30075. 350. Phone: (404) 594-9367.

Nature Conservancy, The (1951): 1815 N. Lynn St., Arlington, Va. 22209. 680,000. Phone: (703) 841-5300.

Naval Architects and Marine Engineers, The Society of (1893): 601 Pavonia Ave., Jersey City, N.J. 07306. 12,200. Phone: (201) 798-4800.

Naval Engineers, American Society of (1888): 1452 Duke St., Alexandria, Va. 22314. 7,500. Phone: (703) 836-6727.

Naval Institute, United States (1873): Annapolis, Md. 21402. 100,000. Phone: (301) 268-6110.

Navigation, The Institute of (1945): 1026 16th St. N.W., Suite 104, Washington, D.C. 20036. 3,200. Phone: (202) 783-4121.

Navy League of the United States (1902): 2300 Wilson Blvd., Arlington, Va. 22311. 70,500; Dudley L. Carlson, Vice Admiral, USN (Ret.), Executive Director.

Neurofibromatosis Foundation, The National (1978): 141 Fifth Ave., Suite 7-S, New York, N.Y. 10010. 27,000. Phone: (212) 460-8980; toll-free (800) 323-7938.

Newspaper Editors, American Society of (1922): P.O. Box 17004, Washington, D.C. 20041. 1,000. Phone: (703) 648-1144.

Newspaper Publishers Association, American (1887): The Newspaper Center, P.O. Box 17407, Dulles International Airport, Washington, D.C. 20041. 1,400. Phone: (703) 648-1000.

Ninety-Second Street Young Men's and Young Women's Hebrew Association (1874): 1395 Lexington Ave., New York, N.Y. 10128. Phone: (212) 427-6000.

Nondestructive Testing, Inc., The American Society for (1941): 1711 Arlingate Lane, P.O. Box 28518, Columbus, Ohio 43228-0518. 10,841. Phone: Natl. (800) 222-ASNT; Ohio (800) NDT-OHIO.

North American Shortwave Assn. (1964): 45 Wildflower Rd., Levittown, Pa. 19057. 1,800.

Phone: (215) 945-0543.

NOT SAFE (National Organization Taunting Safety and Fairness Everywhere) (1980): P.O. Box 5743, Montecito, Calif. 93108. 975. Phone: (805) 969-6217.

Nuclear Society, American (1954): 555 N. Kensington Ave., La Grange Park, Ill. 60525. 16,000. Phone: (708) 352-6611.

Numismatic Association, American (1891): 818 N. Cascade Ave., Colorado Springs, Colo. 80903-3279. 34,000. Phone: (719) 632-2646.

Nurses Association, American (1896): 2420 Pershing Rd., Kansas City, Mo. 64108. 200,000. Phone: (816) 474-5720.

Nutrition, American Institute of (1928): 9650 Rockville Pike, Bethesda, Md. 20814. 2,950. Phone: (301) 530-7050.

Odd Fellows, Sovereign Grand Lodge, Independent Order of (1819): 422 Trade St., Winston-Salem, N.C. 27101-2830. 500,000. Phone: (919) 725-5955.

Olympic Committee, United States (1921): 1750 East Boulder St., Colorado Springs, Colo. 80909-5760. Phone: (719) 632-5551.

Optical Society of America (1916): 2010 Massachusetts Ave. N.W., Washington, D.C. 20036. 11,000. Phone: (202) 223-8130.

Optimist International (1919): 4494 Lindell Blvd., St. Louis, Mo. 63108. 170,000. Phone: (314) 371-6000.

Optometric Association, American (1898): 243 N. Lindbergh Blvd., St. Louis, Mo. 63141. 28,000. Phone: (314) 991-4100.

*Organization of American States, General Secretariat (1890): 1889 F St. N.W., Washington, D.C. 20006. 32 member nations. Phone: (202) 458-3000.

Ornithologists' Union, American (1883): c/o National Museum of Natural History, Smithsonian Institution, Washington, D.C. 20560. 5,000. Phone: (202) 357-1970.

ORT Federation, American (1922): 817 Broadway, 10th Floor, New York, N.Y. 10003. 160,000. Phone: (212) 677-4400.

Overeaters Anonymous (1960): P.O. Box 92870, Los Angeles, Calif. 90009. 150,000. Phone: (213) 542-8363.

Parents Without Partners (1957): 8807 Colesville Rd., Silver Spring, Md. 20910. 115,000. Phone: (301) 588-9354 or (800) 637-7974.

Parks & Conservation Association, National (1919): 1015 31st St. N.W., Washington, D.C. 20007. 289,000. Phone: (202) 944-8530.

Pathologists, American Association of (1976): 9650 Rockville Pike, Bethesda, Md. 20814-3993. 2,300. Phone: (301) 530-7130.

People for the American Way (1980): 2000 M St. N.W., Suite 400, Washington, D.C. 20036. 280,000. Phone: (202) 467-4999.

Petroleum Geologists, American Association of (1917): P.O. Box 979, Tulsa, Okla. 74101-0979. 34,700. Phone: (918) 584-2555.

Pharmaceutical Association, American (1852): 2215 Constitution Ave. N.W., Washington, D.C. 20037. 40,000. Phone: (202) 628-4410.

Philatelic Society, American (1886): P.O. Box 8000, State College, Pa. 16803. 57,000. Phone: (814) 237-3803.

Photogrammetry and Remote Sensing, American Society for (1934): 5410 Grosvenor Lane, Suite 210, Bethesda, Md. 20814-2160. Phone: (301) 493-0290.

Photographic Society of America (1934): 3000 United Founders Blvd., Suite 103, Oklahoma

City, Okla. 73112. Phone: (405) 843-1437.

Photography, International Center of (1974): 1130 Fifth Ave., New York, N.Y. 10128. Midtown branch: 1133 Avenue of the Americas, New York, N.Y. 10036. Phone: (212) 860-1777.

Physical Society, American (1899): 335 E. 45th St., New York, N.Y. 10017-3483. 39,000. Phone: (212) 682-7341.

Physical Therapy Association, American (APTA) (1921): 1111 N. Fairfax St., Alexandria, Va. 22314. 50,000. Phone: (703) 684-2782.

Physics, American Institute of (1931): 335 E. 45th St., New York, N.Y. 10017. 102,500. Phone: (212) 661-9404.

Pilot Club International (1921): Pilot International World Headquarters, 244 College St., P.O. Box 4844, Macon, Ga. 31213-0599. 21,000. Phone: (912) 743-7403.

Planetary Society, The (1979): 65 N. Catalina Ave., Pasadena, Calif. 91106. 120,000. Phone: (818) 793-5100.

Planned Parenthood® Federation of America, Inc., (1916): 810 Seventh Ave., New York, N.Y. 10019. 171 affiliates. Phone: (212) 541-7800.

Plastics Engineers, Society of (1942): 14 Fairfield Dr., Brookfield, Conn. 06804-0403. 35,000. Phone: (203) 775-0471.

Police, American Federation of (1966): Records Center, 3801 Biscayne Blvd., Miami, Fla. 33137. 55,000. Phone: (305) 573-0070.

Police, International Association of Chiefs of (1893): 1110 N. Glebe Rd., Suite 200, Arlington, Va. 22201. 13,000. Phone (703) 243-6500.

Police Hall of Fame, American (1960): 3801 Biscayne Blvd., Miami, Fla. 33137. 55,000. Phone: (305) 573-0070.

Political and Social Science, American Academy of (1889): 3937 Chestnut St., Philadelphia, Pa. 19104. Phone: (215) 386-4594.

Political Science, Academy of (1880): 475 Riverside Dr., Suite 1274, New York, N.Y. 10115-0012. 9,000. Phone: (212) 870-2500.

Powder Metallurgy Institute, American (1958): 105 College Rd. East, Princeton, N.J. 08540. 2,800. Phone: (609) 452-7700.

Practical Nurse Education and Service, National Association for (1941): 1400 Spring St., Suite 310, Silver Spring, Md. 20910. Phone: (301) 588-2491.

Press Club, National (1908): National Press Bldg., 529 14th St. N.W., Washington, D.C. 20045. 4,800. Phone: (202) 662-7500.

Professional Engineers, National Society of (1934): 1420 King St., Alexandria, Va. 22314. 75,000. Phone: (703) 684-2800.

Professional Photographers of America, Inc. (1880): 1090 Executive Way, Des Plaines, Ill. 60018. 17,000. Phone: (708) 299-8161.

Psychiatric Association, American (1844): 1400 K St. N.W., Washington, D.C. 20005. 36,900. Phone: (202) 682-6000.

Psychoanalytic Association, The American (1911): 309 E. 49th St., New York, N.Y. 10017. 3,000 psychoanalysts. Phone: (212) 752-0450.

Psychological Association, American (1892): 1200 17th St. N.W., Washington, D.C. 20036. 108,000. Phone: (202) 955-7600.

Public Health Association, American (1872): 1015 15th St. N.W., Washington, D.C. 20005. 50,000+. Phone: (202) 789-5600.

Puppeteers of America (1937): 5 Cricklewood Path, Pasadena, Calif. 91107-1002. Phone: (818) 797-5748.

Quality Control, The American Society for (1946): 310 W. Wisconsin Ave., Milwaukee, Wis. 53203. 80,184. Phone: (414) 272-8575.

Railroads, Association of American (1934): 50 F St. N.W., Washington, D.C. 20001-1564. Phone: (202) 639-2100.

Recording Arts and Sciences, Inc., National Academy of (1958): 303 N. Glenoaks Blvd., Suite 140, Burbank, Calif. 91502-1178. 8,200. Phone: (213) 849-1313.

Red Cross, American (1881): 17th and D Sts. N.W., Washington, D.C. 20006. Over 2,800 chapters. Phone: (202) 737-8300.

Rehabilitation Association, National (1925): 633 S. Washington St., Alexandria, Va. 22314-4193. 18,000. Phone: (703) 836-0850.

Research and Enlightenment, Association for (1931): 67th St. & Atlantic Ave. (P.O. Box 595), Virginia Beach, Va. 23451. 75,000. Phone: (804) 428-3588.

Reserve Officers Association of the United States (1922): 1 Constitution Ave. N.E., Washington, D.C. 20002. 125,000. Phone: (202) 479-2200.

Retarded Citizens of the United States, Association for (1950): P.O. Box 1047, Arlington, Tex. 76004. 1,200 chapters. Phone: (817) 261-6003.

Retired Federal Employees, National Association of (1921): 1533 New Hampshire Ave. N.W., Washington, D.C. 20036-1279. 500,000. Phone: (202) 234-0832.

*Retired Persons, American Association of (1958): 1909 K St. N.W., Washington, D.C. 20049. 29,000,000. Phone: (202) 872-4700.

Reye's Syndrome Foundation, National (1974): 426 N. Lewis St., Bryan, Ohio 43506. Phone: (800) 233-7393. In Ohio: (800) 231-7393.

RID-USA (Remove Intoxicated Drivers) (1978): Box 520, Schenectady, N.Y. 12301. Over 155/42 state chapters. Phone: (518) 372-0034.

Right to Life, National Committee (1973): 419 7th St. N.W., Washington, D.C. 20004. Phone: (202) 626-8800.

Rotary International (1905): One Rotary Center, 1560 Sherman Ave., Evanston, Ill. 60201. 1,116,000 in 172 countries. Phone: (708) 866-3000.

SAE International (1905): 400 Commonwealth Dr., Warrendale, Pa. 15096-0001. 60,000. Phone: (412) 776-4841.

Safety Council, National (1913): 444 N. Michigan Ave., Chicago, Ill. 60611. Phone: (312) 527-4800.

Salvation Army, The (1865): National Headquarters, 615 Slaters Lane, Alexandria, Va. 22314. 445,566. Phone: (703) 979-3380.

SANE/FREEZE: Campaign for Global Security (a merger of SANE and the Nuclear Weapons Freeze Campaign) (1957): 1819 H St. N.W., Suite 640, Washington, D.C. 20006-3603. 170,000. Phone: (202) 862-9740.

Save-the-Redwoods League (1918): 114 Sansome St., Suite 605, San Francisco, Calif. 94104. 45,000. Phone: (415) 362-2352.

Savings Institutions, National Council of (1920): 1101 15th St. N.W., Suite 400, Washington, D.C. 20005-5070. Phone: (202) 857-3100.

Science, American Association for the Advancement of (1848): 1333 H St. N.W., Washington, D.C. 20005. 133,000. Phone: (202) 326-6400.

Science and Health, American Council on (1978): 1995 Broadway, 16th Floor, New York, N.Y. 10023-5860. Phone: (212) 362-7044.

Science Fiction Society, World (1939): c/o Southern California Institute for Fan Interests, P.O. Box 8442, Van Nuys, Calif. 91409. 6,000. Phone:

(818) 366-3827.

Science Writers, Inc., National Association of (1934): P.O. Box 294, Greenlawn, N.Y. 11740. 1,650. Phone: (516) 757-5664.

Scientists, Federation of American (FAS) (1945): 307 Massachusetts Ave. N.E., Washington, D.C. 20002. 4,000. Phone: (202) 546-3300.

SCRABBLE® Association, National (1972): P.O. Box 700, Front Street Garden, Greenport, N.Y. 11944. 15,000. Phone: (516) 477-0033.

Screen Actors Guild (1933): 7065 Hollywood Blvd., Hollywood, Calif. 90028-6065. 76,000. Phone; (213) 465-4600.

Sculpture Society, National (1893): 15 E. 26th St., New York, N.Y. 10010. 350. Phone: (212) 889-6960.

Seeing Eye Inc., The (1929): P.O. Box 375. Morristown, N.J. 07963-0375. Phone: (201) 539-4425.

Senior Citizens, National Alliance of (1974): 2525 Wilson Blvd., Arlington, Va. 22201. 65,000. Phone: (703) 528-4380.

Separationists, Society of (1963): P.O. Box 140195, Austin, Tex. 78714-0195. 37,216 families. Phone: (512) 458-1244.

Shriners of North America and Shriners Hospitals for Crippled Children, The (1872): Box 31356, Tampa, Fla. 33631-3356. 750,000. Phone: (813) 281-0300.

Sierra Club (1892): 730 Polk St., San Francisco, Calif. 94109. 650,000. Phone: (415) 776-2211.

SIETAR INTERNATIONAL (1974) 733 15th St. N.W., Suite 900, Washington, D.C. 20005. 1,500. Phone: (202) 737-5000.

Simon Wiesenthal Center (1978): 9760 W. Pico Blvd., Los Angeles, Calif. 90035. 375,000. Phone: (213) 553-9036.

Small Business United, National (1937): 1155 15th St. N.W., #710, Washington, D.C. 20005. 50,000. Phone: (202) 293-8830.

Social Work Education, Council on (1919): 1600 Duke St., Alexandria, Va. 22314-3421. Phone: (703) 683-8080.

Social Workers, National Association of (1955): 7981 Eastern Ave., Silver Spring, Md. 20910. Phone: (301) 565-0333.

Sociological Association, American (1905): 1722 N St. N.W., Washington, D.C. 20036-2981. 13,000. Phone: (202) 833-3410.

Soil and Water Conservation Society (1945): 7515 N.E. Ankeny Rd., Ankeny, Iowa 50021. 13,000. Phone: (515) 289-2331.

Songwriters Guild of America, The (1931): 276 Fifth Ave., Suite 306, New York, N.Y. 10001. 4,200. Phone: (212) 686-6820.

Sons of Italy in America, Order (1905): 219 E St. N.E., Washington, D.C. 20002. 175,000. Phone: (202) 547-2900.

Sons of the American Revolution, National Society of the (1889): 1000 S. 4th St., Louisville, Ky. 40203. 26,000. Phone: (502) 589-1776.

Soroptimist International of the Americas (1921): 1616 Walnut St., Philadelphia, Pa. 19103. 50,000. Phone: (215) 732-0512.

Southern Association on Children Under Six (1948): Box 5403, Brady Station, Little Rock, Ark. 72215. 16,000. Phone: (501) 663-0353.

Space Education Association, U.S. (1973): 746 Turnpike Rd., Elizabethtown, Pa. 17022-1161. 1,000. Phone: (717) 367-3265.

Space Society, National (1974): 922 Pennsylvania Ave. S.E., Washington, D.C. 20003. 30,000. Phone: (202) 543-1900.

Special Olympics International (1968): 1350 New York Ave. N.W., Suite 500, Washington, D.C., 20005. 1,000,000. Phone: (202) 628-3630.

Speech-Language-Hearing Association, American (1925): 10801 Rockville Pike, Rockville, Md. 20852. 62,000. Phone: (301) 897-5700.

Sports Car Club of America Inc. (1944): 9033 E. Easter Place, Englewood, Colo. 80112-2105. 54,000. Phone: (303) 694-7222.

State Garden Clubs, Inc., National Council of (1929): 4401 Magnolia Ave., St. Louis, Mo. 63110. 280,992. Phone: (314) 776-7574.

*State Governments, The Council of (1933): P.O. Box 11910, Iron Works Pike, Lexington, Ky. 40578-1910. All state officials, all 50 states. Phone: (606) 231-1939.

Statistical Association, American (1839): 1429 Duke St., Alexandria, Va. 22314. 15,103.

Student Association, United States (1947): 1012 14th St. N.W., #207, Washington, D.C. 20005. Phone: (202) 347-8772.

Surgeons, American College of (1913): 55 E. Erie, St., Chicago, Ill. 60611-2797. 50,000+. Phone: (312) 664-4050.

Symphony Orchestra League, American (1942): 777 Fourteenth St. N.W., Suite 500, Washington, D.C. 20005. 4,713. Phone: (202) 628-0099.

TASH: The Association for Persons with Severe Handicaps (1973): 7010 Roosevelt Way N.E., Seattle, Wash. 98115. 9,000. Phone: (206) 523-8446.

Tax Foundation, Inc. (1937): 470 L'Enfant Plaza S.W., Suite 7112, Washington, D.C. 20024. Phone: (202) 863-5454.

Teachers, American Federation of (1916): 555 New Jersey Ave. N.W., Washington, D.C., 20001. 660,000. Phone: (202) 879-4400.

Television Arts and Sciences, National Academy of (1948): 111 W. 57th St., New York, N.Y., 10019. 15,000. Phone: (212) 586-8424.

Testing & Materials, American Society for (1898): 1916 Race St., Philadelphia, Pa. 19103. 32,000. Phone: (215) 299-5400.

Theatre Guild (1919): 226 W. 47th St., New York, N.Y. 10036. 105,000. Phone: (212) 869-5470.

Theosophical Society in America, The (1875): P.O. Box 270, Wheaton, Ill. 60189-0270. 5,600. Phone: (708) 668-1571.

Tin Can Sailors, Inc. (1976): Battleship Cove, Fall River, Mass. 02721. 14,000. Phone: (617) 678-1905.

Toastmasters International (1924): P.O. Box 9052, Mission Viejo, Calif. 92690-7052, and 23182 Arroyo Vista, Rancho Santa Margarita, Calif. 92688. 160,000. Phone: (714) 542-6793 and (714) 858-8255.

TOUGHLOVE International (1977): P.O. Box 1069, Doylestown, Pa. 18901. 750 registered groups. Phone: (215) 348-7090.

TransAfrica Forum (1982): 545 Eighth St. S.E., Suite 200, Washington, D.C. 20003. Phone: (202) 547-2550.

Travel Agents, American Society of (ASTA) (1931): P.O. Box 23992, Washington, D.C. 20026-3992. 20,000. Phone: (703) 739-2782.

Travelers Aid Services (1905/1982); 2 Lafayette St., New York, N.Y. 10007. Lucy N. Friedman, Executive Director. (Result of merger of Travelers Aid Society of New York and Victim Services Agency in 1982). Phone: (212) 577-7700. **Client Services:** Times Square Office, 158-160 W. 42nd St., Manhattan (212) 944-0013; JFK Airport Office, International Arrivals Bldg., Jamaica, Queens (718) 656-4870; 24-hour Crime Victims

Hotline (212) 577-7777; Immigration Hotline (718) 899-4000.

Tuberous Sclerosis Association, Inc., National (1975): 8000 Corporate Dr., Suite 120, Landover, Md. 20785. 5,000. Phone: (301) 459-9888 or (800) 225-6872.

UFOs, National Investigations Committee on (1967): 14617 Victory Blvd., Suite 4, Van Nuys, Calif. 91411. Phone: (818) 989-5942.

UNICEF, U.S. Committee for (1947): 333 E. 38th St., New York, N.Y. 10016. 20,000 volunteers. Phone: (212) 686-5522.

Union of Concerned Scientists (1969): 26 Church St., Cambridge, Mass. 02238. 90,000. Phone: (617) 547-5552.

United Jewish Appeal (1939): 99 Park Ave., New York, N.Y. 10016. Phone: (212) 818-9100.

United Negro College Fund Inc. (1944): 500 E. 62nd St., New York, N.Y. 10021. Phone: (212) 326-1100.

United Way of America (1918): 701 N. Fairfax St., Alexandria, Va. 22314-2045. 2,300 local United Ways. Phone: (703) 836-7100.

University Foundation, International (1973): 1301 S. Noland Rd., Independence, Mo. 64055. 35,000. Phone: (816) 461-3633.

University Women, American Association of (1881): 1111 16th St. N.W., Washington, D.C. 20036. 140,000. Phone: (202) 785-7700.

Urban League, National (1910): 500 E. 62nd St., New York, N.Y. 10021. 116. Phone: (212) 310-9000.

USO (United Service Organizations) (1941): World Headquarters, 601 Indiana Ave. N.W., Washington, D.C. 20004. Phone: (202) 783-8121.

Variety Clubs International (1927): 1560 Broadway, Suite 1209, New York, N.Y. 10036. 15,000. Phone: (212) 704-9872.

Veterans Committee, American (AVC) (1944): 6309 Bannockburn Dr., Bethesda, Md. 20817. 15,000. Phone: (301) 320-6490.

Veterans of Foreign Wars of the U.S. (1899): V.F.W. Bldg., 34th and Broadway, Kansas City, Mo. 64111. V.F.W. and Auxiliary, 2,850,000. Phone: (816) 756-3390.

Veterinary Medical Association, American (1863): 930 N. Meacham Rd., Schaumburg, Ill. 60196-1074. 50,000. Phone: (708) 605-8070.

Visually Handicapped, Division for the (1948): The Council for Exceptional Children, 1920 Association Dr., Reston, Va. 22091. 1,000. Phone: (703) 620-3660.

Volunteers of America (1896): 3813 N. Causeway Blvd., Metairie, La. 70002. Provides human services in over 200 communities. Phone: (504) 837-2652.

War Resisters League (1923): 339 Lafayette St., New York, N.Y. 10012. 18,000. Phone: (212) 228-0450.

Washington Legal Foundation (1976): 1705 N St. N.W., Washington, D.C. 20036. 200,000. Phone: (202) 857-0240.

Water Quality Association (1974): 4151 Naperville Rd., Lisle, Ill. 60532. Phone: (708) 505-0160.

Water Resources Association, American (1964): 5410 Grosvenor Lane, Suite 220, Bethesda, Md. 20814. 4,000. Phone: (301) 493-8600.

Welding Society, American (1919): 550 N.W. Le-

Jeune Rd., Miami, Fla. 33126. 38,000. Phone: (305) 443-9353; toll free (800) 443-9353.

Wildlife Federation, National (1936): 1400 16th St. N.W., Washington, D.C. 20036-2266. 5,600,000. Phone: (202) 797-6800.

Wildlife Fund, World (1961): 1250 24th St. N.W., Washington, D.C. 20037. 1.1 million. Phone: (202) 293-4800.

Woman's Christian Temperance Union, National (1874): 1730 Chicago Ave., Evanston, Ill. 60201. Under 50,000. Phone: (708) 864-1396.

Women, National Organization for (NOW) (1966): 1000 16th St. N.W., Suite 700, Washington, D.C. 20036-5705. 270,000. Phone: (202) 331-0066.

Women's American ORT (1927): 315 Park Ave. South, New York, N.Y. 10010. Over 1,000 Chapters. Phone: (212) 505-7700.

Women's Clubs, General Federation of (1890): 1734 N St., N.W., Washington, D.C. 20036-2990. 400,000. Phone: (202) 347-3168.

Women's Educational and Industrial Union (1877): 356 Boylston St., Boston, Mass. 02116. 2,200. Phone: (617) 536-5651.

Women's International League for Peace and Freedom (1915): 1213 Race St., Philadelphia, Pa. 19107-1691. 50,000. Phone: (215) 563-7110.

World Future Society (1966): 4916 Saint Elmo Ave., Bethesda, Md. 20814. 30,000. Phone: (301) 656-8274.

World Health, American Association for (1951): 2001 S St. N.W., Suite 530, Washington, D.C. 20009. 800. Phone: (202) 265-0286.

World Peace, International Association of Educators for (1969): P.O. Box 3282, Mastin Lake Station, Huntsville, Ala. 35810. 20,000. Phone: (205) 534-5501.

World Peace Foundation (1910): 22 Batterymarch St., Boston, Mass. 02109. Phone: (617) 482-3875.

Worldwatch Institute (1974): 1776 Massachusetts Ave. N.W., Washington, D.C. 20036. Research organization. Phone: (202) 452-1999.

Writers Union, National (1983): 13 Astor Pl., 7th Fl., New York, NY 10003. 3,000. Phone: (212) 254-0279.

YMCA of the USA (1844): 101 N. Wacker Dr., Chicago, Ill. 60606. 12,800,000. Phone: (312) 977-0031.

*Young Women's Christian Association of the U.S.A. (1858 in U.S.A., 1855 in England): 726 Broadway, New York, N.Y. 10003. 2,030,922. Phone: (212) 614-2846.

Youth Hostels, Inc., American (1934): P.O. Box 37613, Washington, D.C. 20013-7613. 100,000. Phone: (202) 783-6161.

Zero Population Growth (1968): 1400 Sixteenth St. N.W., Suite 320, Washington, D.C. 20036. 33,000. Phone: (202) 332-2200.

Zionist Organization of America (1897): ZOA House, 4 E. 34th St., New York, N.Y. 10016. 135,000. Phone: (212) 481-1500.

Zoological Parks and Aquariums, American Association of (1924): Oglebay Park, Wheeling, W. Va. 26003. 6,000. Phone: (304) 242-2160.

Zoologists, American Society of (1890): 104 Sirius Circle, Thousand Oaks, Calif. 91360. 4,000. Phone: (805) 492-3585.

Conservation Hall of Fame

The new headquarters office of the National Wildlife Federation features a Conservation Hall of Fame which is open to the public Monday through Friday, 8:00 a.m. to 4:30 p.m., except during previously scheduled meetings or conferences. For further information contact the conference coordinator: (202) 797-6800.

U.S. HISTORY & GOVERNMENT

THE DECLARATION OF INDEPENDENCE

In Congress, July 4, 1776

The unanimous Declaration of the thirteen united States of America.

When in the Course of human events it becomes necessary for one people to dissolve the political bands which have connected them with another, and to assume among the powers of the earth, the separate and equal station to which the Laws of Nature and of Nature's God entitle them, a decent respect to the opinions of mankind requires that they should declare the causes which impel them to the separation.

We hold these truths to be self-evident, that all men are created equal, that they are endowed by their Creator with certain unalienable Rights, that among these are Life, Liberty and the pursuit of Happiness.—That to secure these rights, Governments are instituted among Men, deriving their just powers from the consent of the governed,—That whenever any Form of Government becomes destructive of these ends, it is the Right of the People to alter or to abolish it, and to institute new Government, laying its foundation on such principles and organizing its powers in such form, as to them shall seem most likely to effect their Safety and Happiness. Prudence, indeed, will dictate that Governments long established should not be changed for light and transient causes; and accordingly all experience hath shewn that mankind are more disposed to suffer, while evils are sufferable, than to right themselves by abolishing the forms to which they are accustomed. But when a long train of abuses and usurpations, pursuing invariably the same Object evinces a design to reduce them under absolute Despotism, it is their right, it is their duty, to throw off such Government, and to provide new Guards for their future security.—Such has been the patient sufferance of these Colonies; and such is now the necessity which constrains them to alter their former Systems of Government. The history of the present King of Great Britain is a history of repeated injuries and usurpations, all having in direct object the establishment of an absolute Tyranny over these States. To prove this, let Facts be submitted to a candid world.

He has refused his Assent to Laws, the most wholesome and necessary for the public good.

He has forbidden his Governors to pass Laws of immediate and pressing importance, unless suspended in their operation till his Assent should be obtained; and when so suspended, he has utterly neglected to attend to them.

He has refused to pass other Laws for the accommodation of large districts of people, unless those people would relinquish the right of Representation in the Legislature, a right inestimable to them and formidable to tyrants only.

He has called together legislative bodies at places unusual, uncomfortable, and distant from the depository of their Public Records, for the sole purpose of fatiguing them into compliance with his measures.

He has dissolved Representative Houses repeatedly, for opposing with manly firmness his invasions on the rights of the people.

He has refused for a long time, after such dissolutions, to cause others to be elected; whereby the Legislative Powers, incapable of Annihilation, have returned to the People at large for their exercise; the State remaining in the mean time exposed to all the dangers of invasion from without, and convulsions within.

He has endeavoured to prevent the population of these States; for that purpose obstructing the Laws for Naturalization of Foreigners; refusing to pass others to encourage their migrations hither, and raising the conditions of new Appropriations of Lands.

He has obstructed the Administration of Justice, by refusing his Assent to Laws for establishing Judiciary Powers.

He has made Judges dependent on his Will alone, for the tenure of their offices, and the amount and payment of their salaries.

He has erected a multitude of New Offices, and sent hither swarms of Officers to harass our people, and eat out their substance.

He has kept among us, in times of peace, Standing Armies without the Consent of our legislatures.

He has affected to render the Military independent of and superior to the Civil Power.

He has combined with others to subject us to a jurisdiction foreign to our constitution, and unacknowledged by our laws; giving his Assent to their Acts of pretended Legislation:

For quartering large bodies of armed troops among us:

For protecting them, by a mock Trial, from punishment for any Murders which they should commit on the Inhabitants of these States:

For cutting off our Trade with all parts of the

NOTE: On April 12, 1776, the legislature of North Carolina authorized its delegates to the Continental Congress to join with others in a declaration of separation from Great Britain; the first colony to instruct its delegates to take the actual initiative was Virginia on May 15. On June 7, 1776, Richard Henry Lee of Virginia offered a resolution to the Congress to the effect "that these United Colonies are, and of right ought to be, free and independent States. . . ." A committee, consisting of Thomas Jefferson, John Adams, Benjamin Franklin, Robert R. Livingston, and Roger Sherman was organized to "prepare a declaration to the effect of the said first resolution." The Declaration of Independence was adopted on July 4, 1776.

Most delegates signed the Declaration August 2, but George Wythe (Va.) signed August 27; Richard Henry Lee (Va.), Elbridge Gerry (Mass.), and Oliver Wolcott (Conn.) in September; Matthew Thornton (N.H.), not a delegate until September, in November; and Thomas McKean (Del.), although present on July 4, not until 1781 by special permission, having served in the army in the interim.

world:

For imposing Taxes on us without our Consent:

For depriving us in many cases, of the benefits of Trial by Jury:

For transporting us beyond Seas to be tried for pretended offences:

For abolishing the free System of English Laws in a neighbouring Province, establishing therein an Arbitrary government, and enlarging its Boundaries so as to render it at once an example and fit instrument for introducing the same absolute rule into these Colonies:

For taking away our Charters, abolishing our most valuable Laws and altering fundamentally the Forms of our Governments:

For suspending our own Legislatures, and declaring themselves invested with power to legislate for us in all cases whatsoever.

He has abdicated Government here, by declaring us out of his Protection and waging War against us.

He has plundered our seas, ravaged our Coasts, burnt our towns, and destroyed the lives of our people.

He is at this time transporting large Armies of foreign Mercenaries to compleat the works of death, desolation, and tyranny, already begun with circumstances of Cruelty & Perfidy scarcely paralleled in the most barbarous ages, and totally unworthy the Head of a civilized nation.

He has constrained our fellow Citizens taken Captive on the high Seas to bear Arms against their Country, to become the executioners of their friends and Brethren, or to fall themselves by their Hands.

He has excited domestic insurrections amongst us, and has endeavoured to bring on the inhabitants of our frontiers, the merciless Indian Savages, whose known rule of warfare, is an undistinguished destruction of all ages, sexes and conditions.

In every stage of these Oppressions We have Petitioned for Redress in the most humble terms: Our repeated Petitions have been answered only by repeated injury. A Prince, whose character is thus marked by every act which may define a Tyrant, is unfit to be the ruler of a free people.

Nor have We been wanting in attentions to our Brittish brethren. We have warned them from time to time of attempts by their legislature to extend an unwarrantable jurisdiction over us. We have reminded them of the circumstances of our emigration and settlement here. We have appealed to their native justice and magnanimity, and we have conjured them by the ties of our common kindred to disavow these usurpations, which would inevitably interrupt our connections and correspondence. They too have been deaf to the voice of justice and of consanguinity. We must, therefore, acquiesce in the necessity, which denounces our Separation, and hold them, as we hold the rest of mankind, Enemies in War, in Peace Friends.

We, therefore, the Representatives of the United States of America, in General Congress, Assembled, appealing to the Supreme Judge of the world for the rectitude of our intentions, do, in the Name, and by Authority of the good People of these Colonies, solemnly publish and declare, That these United Colonies are, and of Right ought to be Free and Independent States; that they are Absolved from all Allegiance to the British Crown, and that all political connection between them and the State of Great Britain, is and ought to be totally dissolved; and that as Free and Independent States, they have full Power to levy War, conclude Peace, contract Alliances, establish Commerce, and to do all other Acts and Things which Independent States may of right do.—And for the support of this Declaration, with a firm reliance on the protection of Divine Providence, we mutually pledge to each other our Lives, our Fortunes and our sacred Honor.

—John Hancock

New Hampshire
Josiah Bartlett
Wm. Whipple
Matthew Thornton

Rhode Island
Step. Hopkins
William Ellery

Connecticut
Roger Sherman
Sam'el Huntington
Wm. Williams
Oliver Wolcott

New York
Wm. Floyd
Phil. Livingston
Frans. Lewis
Lewis Morris

New Jersey
Richd. Stockton
Jno. Witherspoon
Fras. Hopkinson
John Hart
Abra. Clark

Pennsylvania
Robt. Morris
Benjamin Rush
Benj. Franklin
John Morton
Geo. Clymer
Jas. Smith
Geo. Taylor
James Wilson
Geo. Ross

Massachusetts-Bay
Saml. Adams
John Adams
Robt. Treat Paine
Elbridge Gerry

Delaware
Caesar Rodney
Geo. Read
Tho. M'Kean

Maryland
Samuel Chase
Wm. Paca
Thos. Stone
Charles Carroll of Carrollton

Virginia
George Wythe
Richard Henry Lee
Th. Jefferson
Benj. Harrison
Ths. Nelson, Jr.
Francis Lightfoot Lee
Carter Braxton

North Carolina
Wm. Hooper
Joseph Hewes
John Penn

South Carolina
Edward Rutledge
Thos. Heyward, Junr.
Thomas Lynch, Junr.
Arthur Middleton

Georgia
Button Gwinnett
Lyman Hall
Geo. Walton

Constitution of the United States of America

(Historical text has been edited to conform to contemporary American usage.
The bracketed words are designations for your convenience; they are not part of the Constitution.)

The oldest federal constitution in existence was framed by a convention of delegates from twelve of the thirteen original states in Philadelphia in May, 1787, Rhode Island failing to send a delegate. George Washington presided over the session, which lasted until September 17, 1787. The draft (originally a preamble and seven Articles) was submitted to all thirteen states and was to become effective when ratified by nine states. It went into effect on the first Wednesday in March, 1789, having been ratified by New Hampshire, the ninth state to approve, on June 21, 1788. The states ratified the Constitution in the following order:

Delaware	December 7, 1787	South Carolina	May 23, 1788
Pennsylvania	December 12, 1787	New Hampshire	June 21, 1788
New Jersey	December 18, 1787	Virginia	June 25, 1788
Georgia	January 2, 1788	New York	July 26, 1788
Connecticut	January 9, 1788	North Carolina	November 21, 1789
Massachusetts	February 6, 1788	Rhode Island	May 29, 1790
Maryland	April 28, 1788		

[Preamble]

We the people of the United States, in order to form a more perfect Union, establish justice, insure domestic tranquility, provide for the common defence, promote the general welfare, and secure the blessings of liberty to ourselves and our posterity, do ordain and establish this Constitution for the United States of America.

Article I

Section 1

[Legislative powers vested in Congress.] All legislative powers herein granted shall be vested in a Congress of the United States, which shall consist of a Senate and House of Representatives.

Section 2

[Composition of the House of Representatives.— 1.] The House of Representatives shall be composed of members chosen every second year by the people of the several States, and the electors in each State shall have the qualifications requisite for electors of the most numerous branch of the State Legislature.

[Qualifications of Representatives.—2.] No Person shall be a Representative who shall not have attained to the age of twenty-five years, and been seven years a citizen of the United States, and who shall not, when elected, be an inhabitant of that State in which he shall be chosen.

[Apportionment of Representatives and direct taxes—census.[1]—3.] (Representatives and direct taxes shall be apportioned among the several States which may be included within this Union, according to their respective numbers, which shall be determined by adding to the whole number of free persons, including those bound to service for a term of years, and excluding Indians not taxed, three fifths of all other persons.) The actual enumeration shall be made within three years after the first meeting of the Congress of the United States, and within every subsequent term of ten years, in such manner as they shall by law direct. The number of Representatives shall not exceed one for every thirty thousand, but each State shall have at least one Representative; and until such enumeration shall be made, the State of New Hampshire shall be entitled to choose three,

Massachusetts eight, Rhode-Island and Providence Plantations one, Connecticut five, New York six, New Jersey four, Pennsylvania eight, Delaware one, Maryland six, Virginia ten, North Carolina five, South Carolina five, and Georgia three.

[Filling of vacancies in representation.—4.] When vacancies happen in the representation from any State, the Executive Authority thereof shall issue writs of election to fill such vacancies.

[Selection of officers; power of impeachment.— 5.] The House of Representatives shall choose their Speaker and other officers; and shall have the sole power of impeachment.

Section 3[2]

[The Senate.—1.] The Senate of the United States shall be composed of two Senators from each State, chosen by the Legislature thereof, for six years; and each Senator shall have one vote.

[Classification of Senators; filling of vacancies.—2.] Immediately after they shall be assembled in consequence of the first election, they shall be divided as equally as may be into three classes. The seats of the Senators of the first class shall be vacated at the expiration of the second year, of the second class at the expiration of the fourth year, and of the third class at the expiration of the sixth year, so that one-third may be chosen every second year; and if vacancies happen by resignation, or otherwise, during the recess of the Legislature of any State, the Executive thereof may make temporary appointments (until the next meeting of the Legislature, which shall then fill such vacancies).

[Qualification of Senators.—3.] No person shall be a Senator who shall not have attained to the age of thirty years, and been nine years a citizen of the United States, and who shall not, when elected, be an inhabitant of that State for which he shall be chosen.

[Vice President to be President of Senate.—4.] The Vice President of the United States shall be President of the Senate, but shall have no vote, unless they be equally divided.

[Selection of Senate officers; President pro tempore.—5.] The Senate shall choose their other officers, and also a President pro tempore, in the absence of the Vice President, or when he shall exercise the office of President of the United States.

[Senate to try impeachments.—6.] The Senate

shall have the sole power to try all impeachments. When sitting for that purpose, they shall be on oath or affirmation. When the President of the United States is tried, the Chief Justice shall preside: and no person shall be convicted without the concurrence of two thirds of the members present.

[**Judgment in cases of Impeachment.—7.**] Judgment in cases of impeachment shall not extend further than to removal from office, and disqualification to hold and enjoy any office of honor, trust, or profit under the United States: but the party convicted shall nevertheless be liable and subject to indictment, trial, judgment and punishment, according to Law.

Section 4

[**Control of congressional elections.—1.**] The times, places, and manner of holding elections for Senators and Representatives, shall be prescribed in each State by the Legislature thereof; but the Congress may at any time by law make or alter such regulations, except as to the places of choosing Senators.

[**Time for assembling of Congress.[3]—2.**] The Congress shall assemble at least once in every year, and such meeting shall be on the first Monday in December, unless they shall by law appoint a different day.

Section 5

[**Each house to be the judge of the election and qualifications of its members; regulations as to quorum.—1.**] Each House shall be the judge of the elections, returns, and qualifications of its own members, and a majority of each shall constitute a quorum to do business; but a smaller number may adjourn from day to day, and may be authorized to compel the attendance of absent members, in such manner, and under such penalties as each House may provide.

[**Each house to determine its own rules.—2.**] Each House may determine the rules of its proceedings, punish its members for disorderly behavior, and, with the concurrence of two thirds, expel a member.

[**Journals and yeas and nays.—3.**] Each House shall keep a journal of its proceedings, and from time to time publish the same, excepting such parts as may in their judgment require secrecy; and the yeas and nays of the members of either House on any question shall, at the desire of one fifth of those present, be entered on the journal.

[**Adjournment.—4.**] Neither House, during the session of Congress, shall, without the consent of the other, adjourn for more than three days, nor to any other place than that in which the two Houses shall be sitting.

Section 6

[**Compensation and privileges of members of Congress.—1.**] The Senators and Representatives shall receive a compensation for their services, to be ascertained by law, and paid out of the Treasury of the United States. They shall in all cases, except treason, felony, and breach of the peace, be privileged from arrest during their attendance at the session of their respective Houses, and in going to and returning from the same; and for any speech or debate in either House, they shall not be questioned in any other place.

[**Incompatible offices; exclusions.—2.**] No Senator or Representative shall, during the time for which he was elected, be appointed to any civil office under the authority of the United States, which shall have been created, or the emoluments whereof shall have

been increased during such time; and no person holding any office under the United States shall be a member of either House during his continuance in office.

Section 7

[**Revenue bills to originate in House.—1.**] All bills for raising revenue shall originate in the House of Representatives; but the Senate may propose or concur with amendments as on other bills.

[**Manner of passing bills; veto power of President.—2.**] Every bill which shall have passed the House of Representatives and the Senate, shall, before it becomes a law, be presented to the President of the United States; if he approve he shall sign it, but if not he shall return it, with his objections to that House in which it shall have originated, who shall enter the objections at large on their journal, and proceed to reconsider it. If after such reconsideration two thirds of that House shall agree to pass the bill, it shall be sent, together with the objections, to the other House, by which it shall likewise be reconsidered, and if approved by two thirds of that House, it shall become a law. But in all such cases the votes of both Houses shall be determined by yeas and nays, and the names of the persons voting for and against the bill shall be entered on the journal of each house, respectively. If any bill shall not be returned by the President within ten days (Sundays excepted) after it shall have been presented to him, the same shall be a law, in like manner as if he had signed it, unless the Congress by their adjournment prevent its return, in which case it shall not be a law.

[**Concurrent orders or resolutions, to be passed by President.—3.**] Every order, resolution, or vote to which the concurrence of the Senate and House of Representatives may be necessary (except on a question of adjournment) shall be presented to the President of the United States; and before the same shall take effect, shall be approved by him, or being disapproved by him, shall be repassed by two thirds of the Senate and House of Representatives, according to the rules and limitations prescribed in the case of a bill.

Section 8

[**General powers of Congress.[4]**]
[**Taxes, duties, imposts, and excises.—1.**] The Congress shall have power to lay and collect taxes, duties, imposts and excises, to pay the debts and provide for the common defense and general welfare of the United States; but all duties, imposts and excises shall be uniform throughout the United States;

[**Borrowing of money.—2.**] To borrow money on the credit of the United States;

[**Regulation of commerce.—3.**] To regulate commerce with foreign nations, and among the several States, and with the Indian tribes;

[**Naturalization and bankruptcy.—4.**] To establish a uniform rule of naturalization, and uniform laws on the subject of bankruptcies throughout the United States;

[**Money, weights and measures.—5.**] To coin money, regulate the value thereof, and of foreign coin, and fix the standard of weights and measures;

[**Counterfeiting.—6.**] To provide for the punishment of counterfeiting the securities and current coin of the United States;

[**Post offices.—7.**] To establish post offices and post roads;

[**Patents and copyrights.—8.**] To promote the

progress of science and useful arts, by securing for limited times to authors and inventors the exclusive right to their respective writings and discoveries;

[**Inferior courts.—9.**] To constitute tribunals inferior to the Supreme Court;

[**Piracies and felonies.—10.**] To define and punish piracies and felonies committed on the high seas, and offences against the law of nations;

[**War; marque and reprisal.—11.**] To declare war, grant letters of marque and reprisal, and make rules concerning captures on land and water;

[**Armies.—12.**] To raise and support armies, but no appropriation of money to that use shall be for a longer term than two years;

[**Navy.—13.**] To provide and maintain a navy;

[**Land and naval forces.—14.**] To make rules for the government and regulation of the land and naval forces;

[**Calling out militia.—15.**] To provide for calling forth the militia to execute the laws of the Union, suppress insurrections, and repel invasions;

[**Organizing, arming, and disciplining militia.—16.**] To provide for organizing, arming, and disciplining, the militia, and for governing such part of them as may be employed in the service of the United States, reserving to the States, respectively, the appointment of the officers, and the authority of training the militia according to the discipline prescribed by Congress;

[**Exclusive legislation over District of Columbia.—17.**] To exercise exclusive legislation in all cases whatsoever, over such district (not exceeding ten miles square) as may, by cession of particular States, and the acceptance of Congress, become the seat of the Government of the United States, and to exercise like authority over all places purchased by the consent of the Legislature of the State in which the same shall be, for the erection of forts, magazines, arsenals, dock-yards, and other needful buildings;—And

[**To enact laws necessary to enforce Constitution.—18.**] To make all laws which shall be necessary and proper for carrying into execution the foregoing powers, and all other powers vested by this Constitution in the Government of the United States, or in any department or officer thereof.

Section 9

[**Migration or importation of certain persons not to be prohibited before 1808.—1.**] The migration or importation of such persons as any of the States now existing shall think proper to admit, shall not be prohibited by the Congress prior to the year one thousand eight hundred and eight, but a tax or duty may be imposed on such importation, not exceeding ten dollars for each person.

[**Writ of habeas corpus not to be suspended; exception.—2.**] The privilege of the writ of habeas corpus shall not be suspended, unless when in cases of rebellion or invasion the public safety may require it.

[**Bills of attainder and ex post facto laws prohibited.—3.**] No bill of attainder or ex post facto law shall be passed.

[**Capitation and other direct taxes.—4.**] No capitation, or other direct, tax shall be laid, unless in proportion to the census or enumeration herein before directed to be taken.[5]

[**Exports not to be taxed.—5.**] No tax or duty shall be laid on articles exported from any State.

[**No preference to be given to ports of any States; interstate shipping.—6.**] No preference shall be given by any regulation of commerce or revenue to the ports of one State over those of another: nor shall vessels bound to, or from, one State, be obliged to enter, clear, or pay duties in another.

[**Money, how drawn from treasury; financial statements to be published.—7.**] No money shall be drawn from the Treasury, but in consequence of appropriations made by law; and a regular statement and account of the receipts and expenditures of all public money shall be published from time to time.

[**Titles of nobility not to be granted; acceptance by government officers of favors from foreign powers.—8.**] No title of nobility shall be granted by the United States: and no person holding any office of profit or trust under them, shall, without the consent of the Congress, accept of any present, emolument, office, or title, of any kind whatever, from any king, prince, or foreign state.

Section 10

[**Limitations of the powers of the several States.—1.**] No State shall enter into any treaty, alliance, or confederation; grant letters of marque and reprisal; coin money; emit bills of credit; make any thing but gold and silver coin a tender in payment of debts; pass any bill of attainder, ex post facto law, or law impairing the obligation of contracts, or grant any title of nobility.

[**State imposts and duties.—2.**] No State shall, without the consent of the Congress, lay any imposts or duties on imports or exports, except what may be absolutely necessary for executing its inspection laws; and the net produce of all duties and imposts, laid by any State on imports or exports, shall be for the use of the Treasury of the United States; and all such laws shall be subject to the revision and control of the Congress.

[**Further restrictions on powers of States.—3.**] No State shall, without the consent of Congress, lay any duty of tonnage, keep troops, or ships of war in time of peace, enter into any agreement or compact with another state, or with a foreign power, or engage in war, unless actually invaded, or in such imminent danger as will not admit of delay.

Article II

Section 1

[**The President; the executive power.—1.**] The executive power shall be vested in a President of the United States of America. He shall hold his office during the term of four years, and, together with the Vice President, chosen for the same term, be elected, as follows

[**Appointment and qualifications of presidential electors.—2.**] Each State shall appoint, in such manner as the Legislature thereof may direct, a number of electors, equal to the whole number of Senators and Representatives to which the State may be entitled in the Congress: but no Senator or Representative, or person holding an office of trust or profit under the United States, shall be appointed an elector.

[**Original method of electing the President and Vice President.[6]**] (The electors shall meet in their respective States, and vote by ballot for two persons, of whom one at least shall not be an inhabitant of the same State with themselves. And they shall make a list of all the persons voted for, and of the number of votes for each; which list they shall sign and certify, and transmit sealed to the seat of the Government of the United States, directed to the President of the

Senate. The President of the Senate shall, in the presence of the Senate and House of Representatives, open all the certificates, and the votes shall then be counted. The person having the greatest number of votes shall be the President, if such number be a majority of the whole number of electors appointed; and if there be more than one who have such majority, and have an equal number of votes, then the House of Representatives shall immediately choose by ballot one of them for President; and if no person have a majority, then from the five highest on the list the said House shall in like manner choose the President. But in choosing the President, the votes shall be taken by States, the representation from each State having one vote; A quorum for this purpose shall consist of a member or members from two thirds of the States, and a majority of all the states shall be necessary to a choice. In every case, after the choice of the President, the person having the greatest number of votes of the electors shall be the Vice President. But if there should remain two or more who have equal votes, the Senate should choose from them by ballot the Vice President.)

[Congress may determine time of choosing electors and day for casting their votes.—3.] The Congress may determine the time of choosing the electors, and the day on which they shall give their votes; which day shall be the same throughout the United States.

[Qualifications for the office of President.[7]—4.] No person except a natural born citizen, or a citizen of the United States, at the time of the adoption of this Constitution, shall be eligible to the office of President; neither shall any person be eligible to that office who shall not have attained to the age of thirty-five years, and been fourteen years a resident within the United States.

[Filling vacancy in the office of President.[8]—5.] In case of the removal of the President from office, or of his death, resignation, or inability to discharge the powers and duties of the said office, the same shall devolve on the Vice President, and the Congress may by law provide for the case of removal, death, resignation or inability, both of the President and Vice President, declaring what officer shall then act as President, and such officer shall act accordingly, until the disability be removed, or a President shall be elected.

[Compensation of the President.—6.] The President shall, at stated times, receive for his services, a compensation, which shall neither be increased nor diminished during the period for which he shall have been elected, and he shall not receive within that period any other emolument from the United States, or any of them.

[Oath to be taken by the President.—7.] Before he enter on the execution of his office, he shall take the following oath or affirmation:—"I do solemnly swear (or affirm) that I will faithfully execute the office of President of the United States, and will to the best of my ability, preserve, protect, and defend the Constitution of the United States."

Section 2

[The President to be commander in chief of army and navy and head of executive departments; may grant reprieves and pardons.—1.] The President shall be Commander in Chief of the Army and Navy of the United States, and of the militia of the several States, when called into the actual service of the United States; he may require the opinion, in writing, of the principal officer in each of the executive departments, upon any subject relating to the duties of their respective offices, and he shall have power to grant reprieves and pardons for offences against the United States, except in cases of impeachment.

[President may, with concurrence of Senate, make treaties, appoint ambassadors, etc.; appointment of inferior officers, authority of Congress over.—2.] He shall have power, by and with the advice and consent of the Senate, to make treaties, provided two thirds of the Senators present concur; and he shall nominate, and by and with the advice and consent of the Senate, shall appoint ambassadors, other public ministers and consuls, judges of the Supreme Court, and all other officers of the United States, whose appointments are not herein otherwise provided for, and which shall be established by law: but the Congress may by law vest the appointment of such inferior officers, as they think proper, in the President alone, in the courts of law, or in the heads of departments.

[President may fill vacancies in office during recess of Senate.—3.] The President shall have power to fill up all vacancies that may happen during the recess of the Senate, by granting commissions which shall expire at the end of their session.

Section 3

[President to give advice to Congress; may convene or adjourn it on certain occasions; to receive ambassadors, etc.; have laws executed and commission all officers.] He shall from time to time give to the Congress information of the state of the Union, and recommend to their consideration such measures as he shall judge necessary and expedient; he may, on extraordinary occasions, convene both Houses, or either of them, and in case of disagreement between them, with respect to the time of adjournment, he may adjourn them to such time as he shall think proper; he shall receive ambassadors and other public ministers: he shall take care that the laws be faithfully executed, and shall commission all the officers of the United States.

Section 4

[All civil officers removable by impeachment.] The President, Vice President, and all civil officers of the United States shall be removed from office on impeachment for, and conviction of, treason, bribery, or other high crimes and misdemeanors.

Article III

Section 1

[Judicial powers; how vested; term of office and compensation of judges.] The judicial Power of the United States, shall be vested in one Supreme Court, and in such inferior courts as the Congress may from time to time ordain and establish. The judges, both of the supreme and inferior courts, shall hold their offices during good behavior, and shall, at stated times, receive for their services, a compensation, which shall not be diminished during their continuance in office.

Section 2

[Jurisdiction of Federal courts[9]—1.] The judicial power shall extend to all cases, in law and equity, arising under this Constitution, the laws of the United States, and treaties made, or which shall be made, under their authority; to all cases affecting ambassadors, other public ministers and consuls; to all cases of admiralty and maritime jurisdiction; to controversies to which the United States, shall be a party; to controversies between two or more States; between a State and citizens of another State; between citizens of different States; between citizens of the same State claiming lands under grants of different states, and between a State, or the citizens thereof, and foreign states, citizens, or subjects.

[**Original and appellate jurisdiction of Supreme Court.—2.**] In all cases affecting ambassadors, other public ministers and consuls, and those in which a State shall be party, the Supreme Court shall have original jurisdiction. In all the other cases before mentioned, the Supreme Court shall have appellate jurisdiction, both as to law and fact, with such exceptions, and under such regulations, as the Congress shall make.

[**Trial of all crimes, except impeachment, to be by jury.—3.**] The trial of all crimes, except in cases of impeachment, shall be by jury; and such trial shall be held in the State where the said crimes shall have been committed; but when not committed within any State, the trial shall be at such place or places as the Congress may by law have directed.

Section 3

[**Treason defined; conviction of.—1.**] Treason against the United States, shall consist only in levying war against them, or, in adhering to their enemies, giving them aid and comfort. No person shall be convicted of treason unless on the testimony of two witnesses to the same overt act, or on confession in open court.

[**Congress to declare punishment for treason; proviso.—2.**] The Congress shall have power to declare the punishment of treason, but no attainder of treason shall work corruption of blood, or forfeiture except during the life of the person attained.

Article IV

Section 1

[**Each State to give full faith and credit to the public acts and records of other States.**] Full faith and credit shall be given in each State to the public acts, records, and judicial proceedings of every other State. And the Congress may by general laws prescribe the manner in which such acts, records, and proceedings shall be proved, and the effect thereof.

Section 2

[**Privileges of citizens.—1.**] The citizens of each State shall be entitled to all privileges and immunities of citizens in the several States.

[**Extradition between the several States.—2.**] A person charged in any State with treason, felony, or other crime, who shall flee from justice, and be found in another State, shall on demand of the Executive authority of the State from which he fled, be delivered up, to be removed to the State having jurisdiction of the crime.

[**Persons held to labor or service in one State, fleeing to another, to be returned.—3.**] No person held to service or labor in one State, under the laws thereof, escaping into another, shall, in consequence of any law or regulation therein, be discharged from such service or labor, but shall be delivered up on claim of the party to whom such service or labor may be due.

Section 3

[**New States.—1.**] New States may be admitted by the Congress into this Union; but no new State shall be formed or erected within the jurisdiction of any other State; nor any State be formed by the junction of two or more States, or parts of States, without the consent of the Legislatures of the States concerned as well as of the Congress.

[**Regulations concerning territory.—2.**] The Congress shall have power to dispose of and make all needful rules and regulations respecting the territory or other property belonging to the United States; and nothing in this Constitution shall be so construed as to prejudice any claims of the United States, or of any particular State.

Section 4

[**Republican form of government and protection guaranteed the several States.**] The United States shall guarantee to every State in this Union a Republican form of government, and shall protect each of them against invasion; and on application of the Legislature, or of the Executive (when the Legislature cannot be convened) against domestic violence.

Article V

[**Ways in which the Constitution can be amended.**] The Congress, whenever two thirds of both Houses shall deem it necessary, shall propose amendments to this Constitution, or, on the application of the Legislatures of two thirds of the several States shall call a convention for proposing amendments, which, in either case, shall be valid to all intents and purposes, as part of this Constitution, when ratified by the Legislatures of three fourths of the several States, or by conventions in three fourths thereof, as the one or the other mode of ratification may be proposed by the Congress; provided that no amendment which may be made prior to the year one thousand eight hundred and eight shall in any manner affect the first and fourth clauses in the ninth Section of the first Article; and that no State, without its consent, shall be deprived of its equal suffrage in the Senate.

Article VI

[**Debts contracted under the confederation secured.—1.**] All debts contracted and engagements entered into, before the adoption of this Constitution, shall be as valid against the United States under this Constitution, as under the Confederation.

[**Constitution, laws, and treaties of the United States to be supreme.—2.**] This Constitution, and the laws of the United States which shall be made in pursuance thereof; and all treaties made, or which shall be made, under the authority of the United States, shall be the supreme law of the land; and the judges in every State shall be bound thereby, any thing in the Constitution or laws of any State to the

1. The clause included in parentheses is amended by the 14th Amendment, Section 2. 2. The first paragraph of this section and the part of the second paragraph included in parentheses are amended by the 17th Amendment. 3. Amended by the 20th Amendment, Section 2. 4. By the 16th Amendment, Congress is given the power to lay and collect taxes on income. 5. See the 16th Amendment. 6. This clause has been superseded by the 12th Amendment. 7. For qualifications of the Vice President, see 12th Amendment. 8. Amended by the 20th Amendment, Sections 3 and 4. 9. This section is abridged by the 11th Amendment. 10. See the 13th Amendment.

contrary notwithstanding.

[Who shall take constitutional oath; no religious test as to official qualification.—3.] The Senators and Representatives before mentioned, and the members of the several State Legislatures, and all executive and judicial officers, both of the United States and of the several States, shall be bound by oath or affirmation, to support this Constitution; but no religious test shall ever be required as a qualification to any office or public trust under the United States.

Article VII

[Constitution to be considered adopted when ratified by nine States.] The ratification of the conventions of nine States shall be sufficient for the establishment of this Constitution between the States so ratifying the same.

Done in convention by the unanimous consent of the States present the seventeenth day of September in the year of our Lord one thousand seven hundred and eighty seven and of the independence of the United States of America the Twelfth. In witness whereof we have hereunto subscribed our names.

GEORGE WASHINGTON
President and Deputy from Virginia

NEW HAMPSHIRE
John Langdon   Nicholas Gilman

MASSACHUSETTS
Nathaniel Gorham   Rufus King

CONNECTICUT
Wm. Saml. Johnson   Roger Sherman

NEW YORK
Alexander Hamilton

NEW JERSEY
Wil. Livingston   Wm. Paterson
David Brearley   Jona. Dayton

PENNSYLVANIA
B. Franklin   Thomas Mifflin
Robt. Morris   Geo. Clymer
Thos. FitzSimons   Jared Ingersoll
James Wilson   Gouv. Morris

DELAWARE
Geo. Read   Gunning Bedford Jun.
John Dickinson   Richard Bassett
Jaco. Broom

MARYLAND
James McHenry   Dan. of St. Thos. Jenifer
Danl. Carroll

VIRGINIA
John Blair   James Madison, Jr.

NORTH CAROLINA
Wm. Blount   Richd Dobbs Spaight
Hu. Williamson

SOUTH CAROLINA
J. Rutledge   Charles Cotesworth
Charles Pinckney   Pinckney
                                Pierce Butler

GEORGIA
William Few   Abr. Baldwin
Attest: William Jackson, Secretary

Amendments to the Constitution
of the United States

(Amendments I to X inclusive, popularly known as the Bill of Rights, were proposed and sent to the states by the first session of the First Congress. They were ratified Dec. 15, 1791.)

Article I

[Freedom of religion, speech, of the press, and right of petition.] Congress shall make no law respecting an establishment of religion, or prohibiting the free exercise thereof; or abridging the freedom of speech, or of the press; or the right of the people peaceably to assemble, and to petition the Government for a redress of grievances.

Article II

[Right of people to bear arms not to be infringed.] A well regulated militia, being necessary to the security of a free State, the right of the people to keep and bear arms, shall not be infringed.

Article III

[Quartering of troops.] No soldier shall, in time of peace be quartered in any house, without the consent of the owner, nor in time of war, but in a manner to be prescribed by law.

Article IV

[Persons and houses to be secure from unreasonable searches and seizures.] The right of the people to be secure in their persons, houses, papers, and effects, against unreasonable searches and seizures, shall not be violated, and no warrants shall issue, but upon probable cause, supported by oath or affirmation, and particularly describing the place to be searched, and the persons or things to be seized.

Article V

[Trials for crimes; just compensation for private property taken for public use.] No person shall be held to answer for a capital, or otherwise infamous crime, unless on a presentment or indictment of a Grand Jury, except in cases arising in the land or naval forces, or in the militia, when in actual service in time of war or public danger; nor shall any person be subject for the same offence to be twice put in jeopardy of life or limb; nor shall be compelled in any criminal case to be a witness, against himself, nor be deprived of life, liberty, or property, without due process of law; nor shall private property be taken for public use, without just compensation.

Article VI

[Civil rights in trials for crimes enumerated.] In all criminal prosecutions, the accused shall enjoy the right to a speedy and public trial, by an impartial jury of the State and district wherein the crime shall have been committed, which district shall have been previously ascertained by law, and to be informed of the nature and cause of the accusation; to be confronted with the witnesses against him; to have compulsory process for obtaining witnesses in his favor, and to have the assistance of counsel for his defense.

Article VII

[Civil rights in civil suits.] In suits at common law, where the value in controversy shall exceed twenty dollars, the right of trial by jury shall be preserved, and no fact tried by a jury, shall be otherwise re-examined in any court of the United States, than according to the rules of the common law.

Article VIII

[Excessive bail, fines, and punishments prohibited.] Excessive bail shall not be required, nor excessive fines imposed, nor cruel and unusual punishments inflicted.

Article IX

[Reserved rights of people.] The enumeration in the Constitution, of certain rights, shall not be construed to deny or disparage others retained by the people.

Article X

[Powers not delegated, reserved to states and people respectively.] The powers not delegated to the United States by the Constitution, nor prohibited by it to the States, are reserved to the States, respectively, or to the people.

Article XI

(The proposed amendment was sent to the states Mar. 5, 1794, by the Third Congress. It was ratified Feb. 7, 1795.)

[Judicial power of United States not to extend to suits against a State.] The judicial power of the United States shall not be construed to extend to any suit in law or equity, commenced or prosecuted against one of the United States by citizens of another State, or by citizens or subjects of any foreign state.

Article XII

(The proposed amendment was sent to the states Dec. 12, 1803, by the Eighth Congress. It was ratified July 27, 1804.)

[Present mode of electing President and Vice-President by electors.[1]] The electors shall meet in their respective states, and vote by ballot for President and Vice President, one of whom, at least, shall not be an inhabitant of the same state with themselves; they shall name in their ballots the person voted for as President, and in distinct ballots the person voted for as Vice President, and they shall make distinct lists of all persons voted for as President, and of all persons voted for as Vice President, and of the number of votes for each, which lists they shall sign and certify, and transmit sealed to the seat of the government of the United States, directed to the President of the Senate; the President of the Senate shall, in the presence of the Senate and House of Representatives, open all the certificates and the votes shall then be counted; the person having the greatest number of votes for President, shall be the President, if such number be a majority of the whole number of electors appointed; and if no person have such majority, then from the persons having the highest numbers not exceeding three on the list of those voted for as President, the House of Representatives shall choose immediately, by ballot, the President. But in choosing the President, the votes shall be taken by states, the representation from each State having one vote; a quorum for this purpose shall consist of a member or members from two thirds of the states, and a majority of all the states shall be necessary to a choice. And if the House of Representatives shall not choose a President whenever the right of choice shall devolve upon them, before the fourth day of March next following, then the Vice President shall act as President, as in the case of the death or other constitutional disability of the President. The person having the greatest number of votes as Vice President, shall be the Vice President, if such number be a majority of the whole number of electors appointed, and if no person have a majority, then from the two highest numbers on the list, the Senate shall choose the Vice President; a quorum for the purpose shall consist of two thirds of the whole number of Senators, and a majority of the whole number shall be necessary to a choice. But no person constitutionally ineligible to the office of President shall be eligible to that of Vice President of the United States.

Article XIII

(The proposed amendment was sent to the states Feb. 1, 1865, by the Thirty-eighth Congress. It was ratified Dec. 6, 1865.)

Section 1

[Slavery prohibited.] Neither slavery nor involuntary servitude, except as a punishment for crime whereof the party shall have been duly convicted, shall exist within the United States, or any place subject to their jurisdiction.

Section 2

[Congress given power to enforce this article.] Congress shall have power to enforce this article by appropriate legislation.

Article XIV

(The proposed amendment was sent to the states June 16, 1866, by the Thirty-ninth Congress. It was ratified July 9, 1868.)

Section 1

[Citizenship defined; privileges of citizens.] All persons born or naturalized in the United States, and subject to the jurisdiction thereof, are citizens of the United States and of the State wherein they reside. No State shall make or enforce any law which shall abridge the privileges or immunities of citizens of the United States; nor shall any State deprive any person of life, liberty, or property, without due process of law; nor deny to any person within its jurisdiction the equal protection of the laws.

Section 2

[**Apportionment of Representatives.**] Representatives shall be apportioned among the several States according to their respective numbers, counting the whole number of persons in each State, excluding Indians not taxed. But when the right to vote at any election for the choice of electors for President and Vice President of the United States, Representatives in Congress, the executive and judicial officers of a State, or the members of the Legislature thereof, is denied to any of the male inhabitants of such State, being twenty-one years of age, and citizens of the United States, or in any way abridged, except for participation in rebellion, or other crime, the basis of representation therein shall be reduced in the proportion which the number of such male citizens shall bear to the whole number of male citizens twenty-one years of age in such State.

Section 3

[**Disqualification for office; removal of disability.**] No person shall be a Senator or Representative in Congress, or elector of President and Vice President, or hold any office, civil or military, under the United States, or under any State, who, having previously taken an oath, as a member of Congress, or as an officer of the United States, or as a member of any State Legislature, or as an executive or judicial officer of any State, to support the Constitution of the United States, shall have engaged in insurrection or rebellion against the same, or given aid or comfort to the enemies thereof. But Congress may, by a vote of two thirds of each House, remove such disability.

Section 4

[**Public debt not to be questioned; payment of debts and claims incurred in aid of rebellion forbidden.**] The validity of the public debt of the United States, authorized by law, including debts incurred for payment of pensions and bounties for services in suppressing insurrection or rebellion, shall not be questioned. But neither the United States nor any State shall assume or pay any debt or obligation incurred in aid of insurrection or rebellion against the United States, or any claim for the loss or emancipation of any slave; but all such debts, obligations, and claims shall be held illegal and void.

Section 5

[**Congress given power to enforce this article.**] The Congress shall have power to enforce, by appropriate legislation, the provisions of this article.

Article XV

(The proposed amendment was sent to the states Feb. 27, 1869, by the Fortieth Congress. It was ratified Feb. 3, 1870.)

Section 1

[**Right of certain citizens to vote established.**] The right of citizens of the United States to vote shall not be denied or abridged by the United States or by any State on account of race, color, or previous condition of servitude.

Section 2

[**Congress given power to enforce this article.**] The Congress shall have power to enforce this article by appropriate legislation.

Article XVI

(The proposed amendment was sent to the states July 12, 1909, by the Sixty-first Congress. It was ratified Feb. 3, 1913.)

[**Taxes on income; Congress given power to lay and collect.**] The Congress shall have power to lay and collect taxes on incomes, from whatever source derived, without apportionment among the several States, and without regard to any census or enumeration.

Article XVII

(The proposed amendment was sent to the states May 16, 1912, by the Sixty-second Congress. It was ratified April 8, 1913.)

[**Election of United States Senators; filling of vacancies; qualifications of electors.**] The Senate of the United States shall be composed of two Senators from each State, elected by the people thereof, for six years; and each Senator shall have one vote. The electors in each State shall have the qualifications requisite for electors of the most numerous branch of the State Legislatures.

When vacancies happen in the representation of any State in the Senate, the executive authority of such State shall issue writs of election to fill such vacancies: Provided, that the legislature of any State may empower the executive thereof to make temporary appointment until the people fill the vacancies by election as the legislature may direct.

This amendment shall not be so construed as to affect the election or term of any Senator chosen before it becomes valid as part of the Constitution.

Article XVIII[2]

(The proposed amendment was sent to the states Dec. 18, 1917, by the Sixty-fifth Congress. It was ratified by three quarters of the states by Jan. 16, 1919, and became effective Jan. 16, 1920.)

Section 1

[**Manufacture, sale, or transportation of intoxicating liquors, for beverage purposes, prohibited.**] After one year from the ratification of this article the manufacture, sale, or transportation of intoxicating liquors within, the importation thereof into, or the exportation thereof from the United States and all territory subject to the jurisdiction thereof for beverage purposes is hereby prohibited.

Section 2

[**Congress and the several States given concurrent power to pass appropriate legislation to enforce this article.**] The Congress and the several States shall have concurrent power to enforce this article by appropriate legislation.

Section 3

[**Provisions of article to become operative, when adopted by three fourths of the States.**] This article shall be inoperative unless it shall have been ratified as an amendment to the Constitution by the legislatures of the several States, as provided in the Constitution, within seven years from the date of the submission hereof to the States by Congress.

Article XIX

(The proposed amendment was sent to the states June 4, 1919, by the Sixty-sixth Congress. It was ratified Aug. 18, 1920.)

[The right of citizens to vote shall not be denied because of sex.] The right of citizens of the United States to vote shall not be denied or abridged by the United States or by any State on account of sex.

[Congress given power to enforce this article.] Congress shall have power to enforce this article by appropriate legislation.

Article XX

(The proposed amendment, sometimes called the "Lame Duck Amendment," was sent to the states Mar. 3, 1932, by the Seventy-second Congress. It was ratified Jan. 23, 1933; but, in accordance with Section 5, Sections 1 and 2 did not go into effect until Oct. 15, 1933.)

Section 1

[Terms of President, Vice President, Senators, and Representatives.] The terms of the President and Vice President shall end at noon on the twentieth day of January, and the terms of Senators and Representatives at noon on the third day of January, of the years in which such terms would have ended if this article had not been ratified; and the terms of their successors shall then begin.

Section 2

[Time of assembling Congress.] The Congress shall assemble at least once in every year, and such meeting shall begin at noon on the third day of January, unless they shall by law appoint a different day.

Section 3

[Filling vacancy in office of President.] If, at the time fixed for the beginning of the term of the President, the President-elect shall have died, the Vice President-elect shall become President. If a President shall not have been chosen before the time fixed for the beginning of his term, or if the President-elect shall have failed to qualify, then the Vice President shall have qualified; and the Congress may by law provide for the case wherein neither a President-elect nor a Vice President-elect shall have qualified, declaring who shall then act as President, or the manner in which one who is to act shall be selected, and such person shall act accordingly until a President or Vice President shall have qualified.

Section 4

[Power of Congress in Presidential succession.] The Congress may by law provide for the case of the death of any of the persons from whom the House of Representatives may choose a President whenever the right of choice shall have devolved upon them, and for the case of the death of any of the persons from whom the Senate may choose a Vice President whenever the right of choice shall have devolved upon them.

Section 5

[Time of taking effect.] Sections 1 and 2 shall take effect on the 15th day of October following the ratification of this article.

Section 6

[Ratification.] This article shall be inoperative unless it shall have been ratified as an amendment to the Constitution by the legislatures of three fourths of the several States within seven years from the date of its submission.

Article XXI

(The proposed amendment was sent to the states Feb. 20, 1933, by the Seventy-second Congress. It was ratified Dec. 5, 1933.)

Section 1

[Repeal of Prohibition Amendment.] The eighteenth article of amendment to the Constitution of the United States is hereby repealed.

Section 2

[Transportation of intoxicating liquors.] The transportation or importation into any State, territory, or possession of the United States for delivery or use therein of intoxicating liquors, in violation of the laws thereof, is hereby prohibited.

Section 3

[Ratification.] This article shall be inoperative unless it shall have been ratified as an amendment to the Constitution by convention in the several States, as provided in the Constitution, within seven years from the date of the submission thereof to the States by the Congress.

Article XXII

(The proposed amendment was sent to the states Mar. 21, 1947, by the Eightieth Congress. It was ratified Feb. 27, 1951.)

Section 1

[Limit to number of terms a President may serve.] No person shall be elected to the office of the President more than twice, and no person who has held the office of President, or acted as President, for more than two years of a term to which some other person was elected President shall be elected to the office of the President more than once. But this article shall not apply to any person holding the office of President when this article was proposed by the Congress, and shall not prevent any person who may be holding the office of President, or acting as President, during the term within which this article becomes operative from holding the office of President or acting as President during the remainder of such term.

Section 2

[Ratification.] This article shall be inoperative unless it shall have been ratified as an amendment to the Constitution by the legislatures of three fourths of the several States within seven years from the date of its submission to the States by the Congress.

Article XXIII

(The proposed amendment was sent to the states June 16, 1960, by the Eighty-sixth Congress. It was ratified March 29, 1961.)

Section 1

[Electors for the District of Columbia.] The District constituting the seat of Government of the United States shall appoint in such manner as the Congress may direct: A number of electors of President and Vice President equal to the whole number of Senators and Representatives in Congress to which the District would be entitled if it were a State, but in no event more than the least populous State; they shall be in addition to those appointed by the States, but they shall be considered, for the purposes of the election of President and Vice President, to be electors appointed by a State; and they shall meet in the District and perform such duties as provided by the twelfth article of amendment.

Section 2

[Congress given power to enforce this article.] The Congress shall have the power to enforce this article by appropriate legislation.

Article XXIV

(The proposed amendment was sent to the states Aug. 27, 1962, by the Eighty-seventh Congress. It was ratified Jan. 23, 1964.)

Section 1

[Payment of poll tax or other taxes not to be prerequisite for voting in federal elections.] The right of citizens of the United States to vote in any primary or other election for President or Vice President, for electors for President or Vice President, or for Senator or Representative in Congress, shall not be denied or abridged by the United States or any State by reasons of failure to pay any poll tax or other tax.

Section 2

[Congress given power to enforce this article.] The Congress shall have the power to enforce this article by appropriate legislation.

Article XXV

(The proposed amendment was sent to the states July 6, 1965, by the Eighty-ninth Congress. It was ratified Feb. 10, 1967.)

Section 1

[Succession of Vice President to Presidency.] In case of the removal of the President from office or of his death or resignation, the Vice President shall become President.

Section 2

[Vacancy in office of Vice President.] Whenever there is a vacancy in the office of the Vice President, the President shall nominate a Vice President who shall take office upon confirmation by a majority vote of both Houses of Congress.

Section 3

[Vice President as Acting President.] Whenever the President transmits to the President pro tempore of the Senate and the Speaker of the House of Representatives his written declaration that he is unable to discharge the powers and duties of his office, and un-

til he transmits to them a written declaration to the contrary, such powers and duties shall be discharged by the Vice President as Acting President.

Section 4

[Vice President as Acting President.] Whenever the Vice President and a majority of either the principal officers of the executive departments or of such other body as Congress may by law provide, transmit to the President pro tempore of the Senate and the Speaker of the House of Representatives their written declaration that the President is unable to discharge the powers and duties of his office, the Vice President shall immediately assume the powers and duties of the office as Acting President.

Thereafter, when the President transmits to the President pro tempore of the Senate and the Speaker of the House of Representatives his written declaration that no inability exists, he shall resume the powers and duties of his office unless the Vice President and a majority of either the principal officers of the executive department or of such other body as Congress may by law provide, transmit within four days to the President pro tempore of the Senate and the Speaker of the House of Representatives their written declaration that the President is unable to discharge the powers and duties of his office. Thereupon Congress shall decide the issue, assembling within forty-eight hours for that purpose if not in session. If the Congress, within twenty-one days after receipt of the latter written declaration, or, if Congress is not in session, within twenty-one days after Congress is required to assemble, determines by two thirds vote of both Houses that the President is unable to discharge the powers and duties of his office, the Vice President shall continue to discharge the same as Acting President; otherwise, the President shall resume the powers and duties of his office.

Article XXVI

(The proposed amendment was sent to the states Mar. 23, 1971, by the Ninety-second Congress. It was ratified July 1, 1971.)

Section 1

[Voting for 18-year-olds.] The right of citizens of the United States, who are 18 years of age or older, to vote shall not be denied or abridged by the United States or by any state on account of age.

Section 2

[Congress given power to enforce this article.] The Congress shall have power to enforce this article by appropriate legislation.

1. Amended by the 20th Amendment, Sections 3 and 4. 2. Repealed by the 21st Amendment.

The White House

Source: Department of the Interior, U.S. National Park Service.

The White House, the official residence of the President, is at 1600 Pennsylvania Avenue in Washington, D.C. 20500. The site, covering about 18 acres, was selected by President Washington and Pierre Charles L'Enfant, and the architect was James Hoban. The design appears to have been influenced by Leinster House, Dublin, and James Gibb's *Book of Architecture.* The cornerstone was laid Oct. 13, 1792, and the first residents were President and Mrs. John Adams in November 1800. The building was fired by the British in 1814.

From December 1948 to March 1952, the interior of the White House was rebuilt, and the outer walls were strengthened.

The rooms for public functions are on the first floor; the second and third floors are used as the residence of the President and First Family. The most celebrated public room is the East Room, where formal receptions take place. Other public rooms are the Red Room, the Green Room, and the Blue Room. The State Dining Room is used for formal dinners. There are 132 rooms.

The Mayflower Compact

On Sept. 6, 1620, the *Mayflower,* a sailing vessel of about 180 tons, started her memorable voyage from Plymouth, England, with about 100[1] pilgrims aboard, bound for Virginia to establish a private permanent colony in North America. Arriving at what is now Provincetown, Mass., on Nov. 11 (Nov. 21, new style calendar), 41 of the passengers signed the famous "Mayflower Compact" as the boat lay at anchor in that Cape Cod harbor. A small detail of the pilgrims, led by William Bradford, assigned to select a place for permanent settlement landed at what is now Plymouth, Mass., on Dec. 21 (n.s.).

The text of the compact follows:

In the name of God, Amen. We, whose names are underwritten, the Loyal Subjects of our dread Sovereign Lord, King *James,* by the Grace of God, of *Great Britain, France and Ireland,* King, *Defender of the Faith, &*

Having undertaken for the Glory of God, and Advancement of the Christian Faith, and the Honour of our King and Country, a voyage to plant the first colony in the northern Parts of Virginia; do by these Presents, solemnly and mutually in the Presence of God and one of another, covenant and combine ourselves together into a civil Body Politick, for our better Ordering and Preservation, and Furtherance of the Ends aforesaid; And by Virtue hereof to enact, constitute, and frame, such just and equal Laws, Ordinances, Acts, Constitutions and Offices, from time to time, as shall be thought most meet and convenient for the General good of the Colony; unto which we promise all due Submission and Obedience.

In Witness whereof we have hereunto subscribed our names at *Cape Cod* the eleventh of *November,* in the Reign of our Sovereign Lord, King *James* of *England, France* and *Ireland,* the eighteenth, and of *Scotland* the fifty-fourth. *Anno Domini,* 1620

John Carver	William Mullins	John Billington	Peter Brown
Digery Priest	Thomas English	Thomas Tinker	John Turner
William Brewster	John Howland	Samuel Fuller	Edward Tilly
Edmund Margesson	Stephen Hopkins	Richard Clark	John Craxton
John Alden	Edward Winslow	John Allerton	Thomas Rogers
George Soule	Gilbert Winslow	Richard Warren	John Goodman
James Chilton	Miles Standish	Edward Liester	Edward Fuller
Francis Cooke	Richard Bitteridge	William Bradford	Richard Gardiner
Moses Fletcher	Francis Eaton	Thomas Williams	William White
John Ridgate	John Tilly	Isaac Allerton	Edward Doten
Christopher Martin			

1. Historians differ as to whether 100, 101, or 102 passengers were aboard.

The Monroe Doctrine

The Monroe Doctrine was announced in President James Monroe's message to Congress, during his second term on Dec. 2, 1823, in part as follows:

"In the discussions to which this interest has given rise, and in the arrangements by which they may terminate, the occasion has been deemed proper for asserting as a principle in which rights and interests of the United States are involved, that the American continents, by the free and independent condition which they have assumed and maintain, are henceforth not to be considered as subjects for future colonization by any European power. . . . We owe it, therefore, to candor and to the amicable relations existing between the United States and those powers to declare that we should consider any attempt on their part to extend their system to any portion of this hemisphere as dangerous to our peace and safety. With the existing colonies or dependencies of any European power we have not interfered and shall not interfere. But with the governments who have declared their independence and maintain it, and whose independence we have, on great consideration and on just principles, acknowledged, we could not view any interposition for the purpose of oppressing them or controlling in any other manner their destiny by any European power in any other light than as the manifestation of an unfriendly disposition toward the United States."

Order of Presidential Succession

1. The Vice President
2. Speaker of the House
3. President pro tempore of the Senate
4. Secretary of State
5. Secretary of the Treasury
6. Secretary of Defense
7. Attorney General
8. Secretary of the Interior
9. Secretary of Agriculture
10. Secretary of Commerce
11. Secretary of Labor
12. Secretary of Health and Human Services
13. Secretary of Housing and Urban Development
14. Secretary of Transportation
15. Secretary of Energy
16. Secretary of Education

NOTE: An official cannot succeed to the Presidency unless that person meets the Constitutional requirements.

The Star-Spangled Banner

Francis Scott Key, 1814

O say, can you see, by the dawn's early light,
What so proudly we hail'd at the twilight's last gleaming?
Whose broad stripes and bright stars, thro' the perilous fight,
O'er the ramparts we watch'd, were so gallantly streaming?
And the rockets' red glare, the bombs bursting in air,
Gave proof thro' the night that our flag was still there.
O say, does that star-spangled banner yet wave
O'er the land of the free and the home of the brave?

On the shore dimly seen thro' the mists of the deep,
Where the foe's haughty host in dread silence reposes,
What is that which the breeze, o'er the towering steep,
As it fitfully blows, half conceals, half discloses?
Now it catches the gleam of the morning's first beam,
In full glory reflected, now shines on the stream:
'T is the star-spangled banner: O, long may it wave
O'er the land of the free and the home of the brave!

And where is that band who so vauntingly swore
That the havoc of war and the battle's confusion,
A home and a country should leave us no more?
Their blood has wash'd out their foul footsteps' pollution.
No refuge could save the hireling and slave
From the terror of flight or the gloom of the grave:
And the star-spangled banner in triumph doth wave
O'er the land of the free and the home of the brave.

O thus be it ever when free-men shall stand
Between their lov'd home and the war's desolation;
Blest with vict'ry and peace, may the heav'n-rescued land
Praise the Pow'r that hath made and preserv'd us a nation!
Then conquer we must, when our cause it is just,
And this be our motto: "In God is our trust!"
And the star-spangled banner in triumph shall wave
O'er the land of the free and the home of the brave!

On Sept. 13, 1814, Francis Scott Key visited the British fleet in Chesapeake Bay to secure the release of Dr. William Beanes, who had been captured after the burning of Washington, D.C. The release was secured, but Key was detained on ship overnight during the shelling of Fort McHenry, one of the forts defending Baltimore. In the morning, he was so delighted to see the American flag still flying over the fort that he began a poem to commemorate the occasion. First published under the title "Defense of Fort M'Henry," and later as "The Star-Spangled Banner," the poem soon attained wide popularity as sung to the tune "To Anacreon in Heaven." The origin of this tune is obscure, but it may have been written by John Stafford Smith, a British composer born in 1750. "The Star-Spangled Banner" was officially made the National Anthem by Congress in 1931, although it had been already adopted as such by the Army and the Navy.

The Emancipation Proclamation

January 1, 1863

By the President of the United States of America:

A Proclamation.

Whereas on the 22d day of September, A.D. 1862, a proclamation was issued by the President of the United States, containing, among other things, the following, to wit:

"That on the 1st day of January, A.D. 1863, all persons held as slaves within any State or designated part of a State the people whereof shall then be in rebellion against the United States shall be then, thenceforward, and forever free; and the executive government of the United States, including the military and naval authority thereof, will recognize and maintain the freedom of such persons, and will do not act or acts to repress such persons, or any of them, in any efforts they may make for their actual freedom.

"That the executive will on the 1st day of January aforesaid, by proclamation, designate the States and parts of States, if any, in which the people thereof, respectively, shall then be in rebellion against the United States; and the fact that any State or the people thereof shall on that day be in good faith represented in the Congress of the United States by members chosen thereto at elections wherein a majority of the qualified voters of such States shall have participated shall, in the absence of strong countervailing testimony, be deemed conclusive evidence that such State and the people thereof are not then in rebellion against the United States."

Now, therefore, I, Abraham Lincoln, President of

the United States, by virtue of the power in me vested as Commander-in-Chief of the Army and Navy of the United States in time of actual armed rebellion against the authority and government of the United States, and as a fit and necessary war measure for suppressing said rebellion, do, on this 1st day of January, A.D. 1863, and in accordance with my purpose so to do, publicly proclaimed for the full period of one hundred days from the first day above mentioned, order and designate as the States and parts of States wherein the people thereof, respectively, are this day in rebellion against the United States the following, to wit:

Arkansas, Texas, Louisiana (except the parishes of St. Bernard, Plaquemines, Jefferson, St. John, St. Charles, St. James, Ascension, Assumption, Terrebonne, Lafourche, St. Mary, St. Martin, and Orleans, including the city of New Orleans), Mississippi, Alabama, Florida, Georgia, South Carolina, North Carolina, and Virginia (except the forty-eight counties designated as West Virginia, and also the counties of Berkeley, Accomac, Northhampton, Elizabeth City, York, Princess Anne, and Norfolk, including the cities of Norfolk and Portsmouth), and which excepted parts are for the present le____ lamation were not issued.

And by virtue of the p____ aforesaid, I do order and de____ as slaves within said desig____ States are, and henceforward the Executive Government ____ cluding the military and naval ____ thereof, will recognize and maintain the freedom of said persons.

And I hereby enjoin upon the people so declared to be free to abstain from all violence, unless in necessary self-defense; and I recommend to them that, in all cases when allowed, they labor faithfully for reasonable wages.

And I further declare and make known that such persons of suitable condition will be received into the armed service of the United States to garrison forts, positions, stations, and other places, and to man vessels of all sorts in said service.

And upon this act, sincerely believed to be an act of justice, warranted by the Constitution upon military necessity, I invoke the considerate judgment of mankind and the gracious favor of Almighty God.

The Confederate States of America

State	Seceded from Union	Readmitted to Union[1]	State	Seceded from Union	Readmitted to Union[1]
1. South Carolina	Dec. 20, 1860	July 9, 1868	7. Texas	March 2, 1861	March 30, 1870
2. Mississippi	Jan. 9, 1861	Feb. 23, 1870	8. Virginia	April 17, 1861	Jan. 26, 1870
3. Florida	Jan. 10, 1861	June 25, 1868	9. Arkansas	May 6, 1861	June 22, 1868
4. Alabama	Jan. 11, 1861	July 13, 1868	10. North Carolina	May 20, 1861	July 4, 1868
5. Georgia	Jan. 19, 1861	July 15, 1870[2]	11. Tennessee	June 8, 1861	July 24, 1866
6. Louisiana	Jan. 26, 1861	July 9, 1868			

1. Date of readmission to representation in U.S. House of Representatives. 2. Second readmission date. First date was July 21, 1868, but the representatives were unseated March 5, 1869. NOTE: Four other slave states—Delaware, Kentucky, Maryland, and Missouri—remained in the Union.

Lincoln's Gettysburg Address

The Battle of Gettysburg, one of the most noted battles of the Civil War, was fought on July 1, 2, and 3, 1863. On Nov. 19, 1863, the field was dedicated as a national cemetery by President Lincoln in a two-minute speech that was to become immortal. At the time of its delivery the speech was relegated to the inside pages of the papers, while a two-hour address by Edward Everett, the leading orator of the time, caught the headlines.

The following is the text of the address revised by President Lincoln from his own notes:

Fourscore and seven years ago our fathers brought forth on this continent a new nation conceived in liberty and dedicated to the proposition that all men are created equal. Now we are engaged in a great civil war testing whether that nation, or any nation so conceived and so dedicated, can long endure. We are met on a great battlefield of that war. We have come to dedicate a portion of that field as a final resting-place for those who here gave their lives that that nation might live. It is altogether fitting and proper that we should do this. But, in a larger sense, we cannot dedicate, we cannot consecrate, we cannot hallow this ground. The brave men, living and dead, who struggled here have consecrated it far above our poor power to add or detract. The world will little note nor long remember what we say here, but it can never forget what they did here. It is for us the living rather to be dedicated here to the unfinished work which they who fought here have thus far so nobly advanced. It is rather for us to be here dedicated to the great task remaining before us—that from these honored dead we take increased devotion to that cause for which they gave the last full measure of devotion—that we here highly resolve that these dead shall not have died in vain, that this nation under God shall have a new birth of freedom, and that government of the people, by the people, for the people shall not perish from the earth.

The Early Congresses

..t the urging of Massachusetts and Virginia, the .irst Continental Congress met in Philadelphia on Sept. 5, 1774, and was attended by representatives of all the colonies except Georgia. Patrick Henry of Virginia declared: "The distinctions between Pennsylvanians, New Yorkers and New Englanders are no more. I am not a Virginian but an American." This Congress, which adjourned Oct. 26, 1774, passed intercolonial resolutions calling for extensive boycott by the colonies against British trade.

The following year, most of the delegates from the colonies were chosen by popular election to attend the Second Continental Congress, which assembled in Philadelphia on May 10. As war had already begun between the colonies and England, the chief problems before the Congress were the procuring of military supplies, the establishment of an army and proper defenses, the issuing of continental bills of credit, etc. On June 15, 1775, George Washington was elected to command the Continental army. Congress adjourned Dec. 12, 1776.

Other Continental Congresses were held in Baltimore (1776–77), Philadelphia (1777), Lancaster, Pa. (1777), York, Pa. (1777–78), and Philadelphia (1778–81).

In 1781, the Articles of Confederation, although establishing a league of the thirteen states rather than a strong central government, provided for the continuance of Congress. Known thereafter as the Congress of the Confederation, it held sessions in Philadelphia (1781–83), Princeton, N.J. (1783), Annapolis, Md. (1783–84), and Trenton, N.J. (1784). Five sessions were held in New York City between the years 1785 and 1789.

The Congress of the United States, established by the ratification of the Constitution, held its first meeting on March 4, 1789, in New York City. Several sessions of Congress were held in Philadelphia, and the first meeting in Washington, D.C., was on Nov. 17, 1800.

Presidents of the Continental Congresses

Name	Elected	Brith and Death Dates	Name	Elected	Birth and Death Dates
Peyton Randolph, Va.	9/5/1774	c.1721–1775	John Hanson, Md.	11/5/1781	1715–1783
Henry Middleton, S.C.	10/22/1774	1717–1784	Elias Boudinot, N.J.	11/4/1782	1740–1821
Peyton Randolph, Va.	5/10/1775	c.1721–1775	Thomas Mifflin, Pa.	11/3/1783	1744–1800
John Hancock, Mass.	5/24/1775	1737–1793	Richard Henry Lee, Va.	11/30/1784	1732–1794
Henry Laurens, S.C.	11/1/1777	1724–1792	John Hancock, Mass.[1]	11/23/1785	1737–1793
John Jay, N.Y.	12/10/1778	1745–1829	Nathaniel Gorham, Mass.	6/6/1786	1738–1796
Samuel Huntington, Conn.	9/28/1779	1731–1796	Arthur St. Clair, Pa.	2/2/1787	1734–1818
Thomas McKean, Del.	7/10/1781	1734–1817	Cyrus Griffin, Va.	1/22/1788	1748–1810

1. Resigned May 29, 1786, never having served, because of continued illness.

The Great Seal of the U.S.

On July 4, 1776, the Continental Congress appointed a committee consisting of Benjamin Franklin, John Adams, and Thomas Jefferson "to bring in a device for a seal of the United States of America." After many delays, a verbal description of a design by William Barton was finally approved by Congress on June 20, 1782. The seal shows an American bald eagle with a ribbon in its mouth bearing the device *E pluribus unum* (One out of many). In its talons are the arrows of war and an olive branch of peace. On the reverse side it shows an unfinished pyramid with an eye (the eye of Providence) above it. Although this description was adopted in 1782, the first drawing was not made until four years later, and no die has ever been cut.

The American's Creed

William Tyler Page

"I believe in the United States of America as a government of the people, by the people, for the people; whose just powers are derived from the consent of the governed; a democracy in a republic; a sovereign Nation of many sovereign States; a perfect union, one and inseparable; established upon those principles of freedom, equality, justice, and humanity for which American patriots sacrificed their lives and fortunes.

"I therefore believe it is my duty to my country to love it, to support its Constitution, to obey its laws, to respect its flag, and to defend it against all enemies."

NOTE: William Tyler Page, Clerk of the U.S. House of Representatives, wrote "The American's Creed" in 1917. It was accepted by the House on behalf of the American people on April 3, 1918.

U.S. Capitol

When the French architect and engineer Maj. Pierre L'Enfant first began to lay out the plans for a new Federal city (now Washington, D.C.), he noted that Jenkins' Hill, overlooking the area, seemed to be "a pedestal waiting for a monument." It was here that the U.S. Capitol would be built. The basic structure as we know it today evolved over a period of more than 150 years. In 1792 a competition was held for the design of a capitol building. Dr. William Thornton, a physician and amateur architect, submitted the winning plan, a simple, low-lying structure of classical proportions with a shallow dome. Later, internal modifications were made by Benjamin Henry Latrobe. After the building was burned by the British in 1814, Latrobe and architect Charles Bulfinch were responsible for its reconstruction. Finally, under Thomas Walter, who was Architect of the Capitol from 1851 to 1865, the House and Senate wings and the imposing cast iron dome topped with the Statue of Freedom were added, and the Capitol assumed the form we see today. It was in the old Senate chamber that Daniel Webster cried out, "Liberty and Union, now and forever, one and inseparable!" In Statuary Hall, which used to be the old House chamber, a small disk on the floor marks the spot where John

Quincy Adams was fatally stricken after more than 50 years of service to his country. A whisper from one side of this room can be heard across the vast space of the hall. Visitors can see the original Supreme Court chamber a floor below the Rotunda.

In addition to its historical association, the Capitol Building is also a vast artistic treasure house. The works of such famous artists as Gilbert Stuart, Rembrandt Peale, and John Trumbull are displayed on the walls. The Great Rotunda, with its 180-foot- (54.9-m-) high dome, is decorated with a massive fresco by Constantino Brumidi, which extends some 300 feet (90 m) in circumference. Throughout the building are many paintings of events in U.S. history and sculptures of outstanding Americans. The Capitol itself is situated on a 68-acre (27.5-ha) park designed by the 19th-century landscape architect Frederick Law Olmsted. There are free guided tours of the Capitol, which include admission to the House and Senate galleries. Those who wish to visit the visitors' gallery in either wing without taking the tour may obtain passes from their Senators or Congressmen. Visitors may ride on the monorail subway that joins the House and Senate wings of the Capitol with the Congressional office buildings.

Washington Monument

Construction of this magnificent Washington, D.C., monument, which draws some two million visitors a year, took nearly a century of planning, building, and controversy. Provision for a large equestrian statue of George Washington was made in the original city plan, but the project was soon dropped. After Washington's death it was taken up again, and a number of false starts and changes of design were made. Finally, in 1848, work was begun on the monument that stands today. The design, by architect Robert Mills, then featured an ornate base. In 1854, however, political squabbling and a lack of money brought construction to a halt. Work was resumed in 1880, and the monument was completed in 1884 and opened to the public in 1888. The tapered shaft, faced with white marble and rising from walls 15 feet thick (4.6 m) at the base was modeled after the obelisks of ancient Egypt. The monument, one of the tallest masonry constructions in the world, stands just over 555 feet (169 m). Memorial stones from the 50 States, foreign countries, and organizations line the interior walls. The top, reached only by elevator, commands a panoramic view of the city.

The Liberty Bell

The Liberty Bell was cast in England in 1752 for the Pennsylvania Statehouse (now named Independence Hall) in Philadelphia. It was recast in Philadelphia in 1753. It is inscribed with the words, "Proclaim liberty throughout all the land unto all the inhabitants thereof" (Lev. 25:10). The bell was rung on July 8, 1776, for the first public reading of the Declaration of Independence. Hidden in Allentown during the British occupation of Philadelphia, it was replaced in Independence Hall in 1778. The bell cracked on July 8, 1835, while tolling the death of Chief Justice John Marshall. In 1976 the Liberty Bell was moved to a special exhibition building near Independence Hall.

Arlington National Cemetery

Arlington National Cemetery occupies 612 acres in Virginia on the Potomac River, directly opposite Washington. This land was part of the estate of John Parke Custis, Martha Washington's son. His son, George Washington Parke Custis, built the mansion which later became the home of Robert E. Lee. In 1864, Arlington became a military cemetery. More than 216,000 servicemembers and their dependents are buried there. Expansion of the cemetery began in 1966, using a 180-acre tract of land directly east of the present site.

In 1921, an Unknown American Soldier of World War I was buried in the cemetery; the monument at the Tomb was opened to the public without ceremony in 1932. Two additional Unknowns, one from World War II and one from the Korean War, were buried May 30, 1958. The Unknown Serviceman of Vietnam was buried on May 28, 1984. The inscription carved on the Tomb of the Unknowns reads:

> HERE RESTS IN
> HONORED GLORY
> AN AMERICAN
> SOLDIER
> KNOWN BUT TO GOD

History of the Flag

Source: Encyclopaedia Britannica.

The first official American flag, the Continental or Grand Union flag, was displayed on Prospect Hill, Jan. 1, 1776, in the American lines besieging Boston. It had 13 alternate red and white stripes, with the British Union Jack in the upper left corner.

On June 14, 1777, the Continental Congress adopted the design for a new flag, which actually was the Continental flag with the red cross of St. George and the white cross of St. Andrew replaced on the blue field by 13 stars, one for each state. No rule was made as to the arrangement of the stars, and while they were usually shown in a circle, there were various other designs. It is uncertain when the new flag was first flown, but its first official announcement is believed to have been on Sept. 3, 1777.

The first public assertion that Betsy Ross made the first Stars and Stripes appeared in a paper read before the Historical Society of Pennsylvania on March 14, 1870, by William J. Canby, a grandson. However, Mr. Canby on later investigation found no official documents of any action by Congress on the flag before June 14, 1777. Betsy Ross's own story, according to her daughter, was that Washington, Robert Morris, and George Ross, as representatives of Congress, visited her in Philadelphia in June 1776, showing her a rough draft of the flag and asking her if she could make one. However, the only actual record of the manufacture of flags by Betsy Ross is a voucher in Harrisburg, Pa., for 14 pounds and some shillings for flags for the Pennsylvania navy.

On Jan. 13, 1794, Congress voted to add two stars and two stripes to the flag in recognition of the admission of Vermont and Kentucky to the Union. By 1818, there were 20 states in the Union, and as it was obvious that the flag would soon become unwieldy, Congress voted April 18 to return to the original 13 stripes and to indicate the admission of a new state simply by the addition of a star the following July 4. The 49th star, for Alaska, was added July 4, 1959; and the 50th star, for Hawaii, was added July 4, 1960.

The first Confederate flag, adopted in 1861 by the Confederate convention in Montgomery, Ala., was called the Stars and Bars; but because of its similarity in colors to the American flag, there was much confusion in the Battle of Bull Run. To remedy this situation, Gen. G. T. Beauregard suggested a battle flag, which was used by the Southern armies throughout the war. The flag consisted of a red field on which was placed a blue cross of St. Andrew separated from the field by a white fillet and adorned with 13[1] white stars for the Confederate states. In May 1863, at Richmond, an official flag was adopted by the Confederate Congress. This flag was white and twice as long as wide; the union, two-thirds the width of the flag, contained the battle flag designed for Gen. Beauregard. A broad transverse stripe of red was added Feb. 4, 1865, so that the flag might not be mistaken for a signal of truce.

1. 11 states formally seceded, and unofficial groups in Kentucky and Missouri adopted ordinances of secession. On this basis, these two states were admitted to the Confederacy, although the official state governments remained in the Union.

The Pledge of Allegiance[1] to the Flag

"I pledge allegiance to the Flag of the United States of America, and to the Republic for which it stands, one Nation under God,[2] indivisible, with liberty and justice for all."

1. The original pledge was published in the Sept. 8, 1892, issue of *The Youth's Companion* in Boston. For years, the authorship was in dispute between James B. Upham and Francis Bellamy of the magazine's staff. In 1939, after a study of the controversy, the United States Flag Association decided that authorship be credited to Bellamy. 2. The phrase "under God" was added to the pledge on June 14, 1954.

The Statue of Liberty

The Statue of Liberty ("Liberty Enlightening the World") is a 225-ton, steel-reinforced copper female figure, 152 ft in height, facing the ocean from Liberty[1] Island in New York Harbor. The right hand holds aloft a torch, and the left hand carries a tablet upon which is inscribed: "July IV MDCCLXXVI."

The statue was designed by Frédéric Auguste Bartholdi of Alsace as a gift to the United States from the people of France to memorialize the alliance of the two countries in the American Revolution and their abiding friendship. The French people contributed the $250,000 cost.

The 150-foot pedestal was designed by Richard M. Hunt and built by Gen. Charles P. Stone, both Americans. It contains steel underpinnings designed by Alexander Eiffel of France to support the statue. The $270,000 cost was borne by popular subscription in this country. President Grover Cleveland accepted the statue for the United States on Oct. 28, 1886.

On Sept. 26, 1972, President Richard M. Nixon dedicated the American Museum of Immigration, housed in structural additions to the base of the stat-

1. Called Bedloe's Island prior to 1956.

ue. In 1984 scaffolding went up for a major restoration and the torch was extinguished on July 4. It was relit with much ceremony July 4, 1986 to mark its centennial.

On a tablet inside the pedestal is engraved the following sonnet, written by Emma Lazarus (1849–1887):

The New Colossus

Not like the brazen giant of Greek fame.
With conquering limbs astride from land to land;
Here at our sea-washed, sunset gates shall stand
A mighty woman with a torch, whose flame
Is the imprisoned lightning, and her name
Mother of Exiles. From her beacon-hand
Glows world-wide welcome; her mild eyes command
The air-bridged harbor that twin cities frame.
"Keep, ancient lands, your storied pomp!" cries she
With silent lips. "Give me your tired, your poor,
Your huddled masses yearning to breathe free,
The wretched refuse of your teeming shore.
Send these, the homeless, tempest-tost to me,
I lift my lamp beside the golden door!"

Presidents

Name and (party)[1]	Term	State of birth	Born	Died	Religion	Age at inaug.	Age at death
1. Washington (F)[2]	1789–1797	Va.	2/22/1732	12/14/1799	Episcopalian	57	67
2. J. Adams (F)	1797–1801	Mass.	10/30/1735	7/4/1826	Unitarian	61	90
3. Jefferson (DR)	1801–1809	Va.	4/13/1743	7/4/1826	Deist	57	83
4. Madison (DR)	1809–1817	Va.	3/16/1751	6/28/1836	Episcopalian	57	85
5. Monroe (DR)	1817–1825	Va.	4/28/1758	7/4/1831	Episcopalian	58	73
6. J. Q. Adams (DR)	1825–1829	Mass.	7/11/1767	2/23/1848	Unitarian	57	80
7. Jackson (D)	1829–1837	S.C.	3/15/1767	6/8/1845	Presbyterian	61	78
8. Van Buren (D)	1837–1841	N.Y.	12/5/1782	7/24/1862	Reformed Dutch	54	79
9. W. H. Harrison (W)[3]	1841	Va.	2/9/1773	4/4/1841	Episcopalian	68	68
10. Tyler (W)	1841–1845	Va.	3/29/1790	1/18/1862	Episcopalian	51	71
11. Polk (D)	1845–1849	N.C.	11/2/1795	6/15/1849	Methodist	49	53
12. Taylor (W)[3]	1849–1850	Va.	11/24/1784	7/9/1850	Episcopalian	64	65
13. Fillmore (W)	1850–1853	N.Y.	1/7/1800	3/8/1874	Unitarian	50	74
14. Pierce (D)	1853–1857	N.H.	11/23/1804	10/8/1869	Episcopalian	48	64
15. Buchanan (D)	1857–1861	Pa.	4/23/1791	6/1/1868	Presbyterian	65	77
16. Lincoln (R)[4]	1861–1865	Ky.	2/12/1809	4/15/1865	Liberal	52	56
17. A. Johnson (U)[5]	1865–1869	N.C.	12/29/1808	7/31/1875	(6)	56	66
18. Grant (R)	1869–1877	Ohio	4/27/1822	7/23/1885	Methodist	46	63
19. Hayes (R)	1877–1881	Ohio	10/4/1822	1/17/1893	Methodist	54	70
20. Garfield (R)[4]	1881	Ohio	11/19/1831	9/19/1881	Disciples of Christ	49	49
21. Arthur (R)	1881–1885	Vt.	10/5/1830	11/18/1886	Episcopalian	50	56
22. Cleveland (D)	1885–1889	N.J.	3/18/1837	6/24/1908	Presbyterian	47	71
23. B. Harrison (R)	1889–1893	Ohio	8/20/1833	3/13/1901	Presbyterian	55	67
24. Cleveland (D)[7]	1893–1897	—	—	—	—	55	—
25. McKinley (R)[4]	1897–1901	Ohio	1/29/1843	9/14/1901	Methodist	54	58
26. T. Roosevelt (R)	1901–1909	N.Y.	10/27/1858	1/6/1919	Reformed Dutch	42	60
27. Taft (R)	1909–1913	Ohio	9/15/1857	3/8/1930	Unitarian	51	72
28. Wilson (D)	1913–1921	Va.	12/28/1856	2/3/1924	Presbyterian	56	67
29. Harding (R)[3]	1921–1923	Ohio	11/2/1865	8/2/1923	Baptist	55	57
30. Coolidge (R)	1923–1929	Vt.	7/4/1872	1/5/1933	Congregationalist	51	60
31. Hoover (R)	1929–1933	Iowa	8/10/1874	10/20/1964	Quaker	54	90
32. F. D. Roosevelt (D)[3]	1933–1945	N.Y.	1/30/1882	4/12/1945	Episcopalian	51	63
33. Truman (D)	1945–1953	Mo.	5/8/1884	12/26/1972	Baptist	60	88
34. Eisenhower (R)	1953–1961	Tex.	10/14/1890	3/28/1969	Presbyterian	62	78
35. Kennedy (D)[4]	1961–1963	Mass.	5/29/1917	11/22/1963	Roman Catholic	43	46
36. L. B. Johnson (D)	1963–1969	Tex.	8/27/1908	1/22/1973	Disciples of Christ	55	64
37. Nixon (R)[8]	1969–1974	Calif.	1/9/1913	—	Quaker	56	—
38. Ford (R)	1974–1977	Neb.	7/14/1913	—	Episcopalian	61	—
39. Carter (D)	1977–1981	Ga.	10/1/1924	—	Southern Baptist	52	—
40. Reagan (R)	1981–1989	Ill.	2/6/1911	—	Disciples of Christ	69	—
41. Bush (R)	1989–	Mass.	6/12/24	—	Episcopalian	64	—

1. F—Federalist; DR—Democratic-Republican; D—Democratic; W—Whig; R—Republican; U—Union. 2. No party for first election. The party system in the U.S. made its appearance during Washington's first term. 3. Died in office. 4. Assassinated in office. 5. The Republican National Convention of 1864 adopted the name Union Party. It renominated Lincoln for President; for Vice President it nominated Johnson, a War Democrat. Although frequently listed as a Republican Vice President and President, Johnson undoubtedly considered himself strictly a member of the Union Party. When that party broke apart after 1868, he returned to the Democratic Party. 6. Johnson was not a professed church member; however, he admired the Baptist principles of church government. 7. Second nonconsecutive term. 8. Resigned Aug. 9, 1974.

Vice Presidents

Name and (party)[1]	Term	State of birth	Birth and death dates	President served under
1. John Adams (F)[2]	1789–1797	Massachusetts	1735–1826	Washington
2. Thomas Jefferson (DR)	1797–1801	Virginia	1743–1826	J. Adams
3. Aaron Burr (DR)	1801–1805	New Jersey	1756–1836	Jefferson
4. George Clinton (DR)[3]	1805–1812	New York	1739–1812	Jefferson and Madison
5. Elbridge Gerry (DR)[3]	1813–1814	Massachusetts	1744–1814	Madison
6. Daniel D. Tompkins (DR)	1817–1825	New York	1774–1825	Monroe
7. John C. Calhoun[4]	1825–1832	South Carolina	1782–1850	J. Q. Adams and Jackson
8. Martin Van Buren (D)	1833–1837	New York	1782–1862	Jackson
9. Richard M. Johnson (D)	1837–1841	Kentucky	1780–1850	Van Buren
10. John Tyler (W)[5]	1841	Virginia	1790–1862	W. H. Harrison
11. George M. Dallas (D)	1845–1849	Pennsylvania	1792–1864	Polk
12. Millard Fillmore (W)[5]	1849–1850	New York	1800–1874	Taylor
13. William R. King (D)[3]	1853	North Carolina	1786–1853	Pierce
14. John C. Breckinridge (D)	1857–1861	Kentucky	1821–1875	Buchanan

Name and (party)[1]	Term	State of birth	Birth and death dates	President served under
15. Hannibal Hamlin (R)	1861–1865	Maine	1809–1891	Lincoln
16. Andrew Johnson (U)[5]	1865	North Carolina	1808–1875	Lincoln
17. Schuyler Colfax (R)	1869–1873	New York	1823–1885	Grant
18. Henry Wilson (R)[3]	1873–1875	New Hampshire	1812–1875	Grant
19. William A. Wheeler (R)	1877–1881	New York	1819–1887	Hayes
20. Chester A. Arthur (R)[5]	1881	Vermont	1830–1886	Garfield
21. Thomas A. Hendricks (D)[3]	1885	Ohio	1819–1885	Cleveland
22. Levi P. Morton (R)	1889–1893	Vermont	1824–1920	B. Harrison
23. Adlai E. Stevenson (D)	1893–1897	Kentucky	1835–1914	Cleveland
24. Garrett A. Hobart (R)[3]	1897–1899	New Jersey	1844–1899	McKinley
25. Theodore Roosevelt (R)[5]	1901	New York	1858–1919	McKinley
26. Charles W. Fairbanks (R)	1905–1909	Ohio	1852–1918	T. Roosevelt
27. James S. Sherman (R)[3]	1909–1912	New York	1855–1912	Taft
28. Thomas R. Marshall (D)	1913–1921	Indiana	1854–1925	Wilson
29. Calvin Coolidge (R)[5]	1921–1923	Vermont	1872–1933	Harding
30. Charles G. Dawes (R)	1925–1929	Ohio	1865–1951	Coolidge
31. Charles Curtis (R)	1929–1933	Kansas	1860–1936	Hoover
32. John N. Garner (D)	1933–1941	Texas	1868–1967	F. D. Roosevelt
33. Henry A. Wallace (D)	1941–1945	Iowa	1888–1965	F. D. Roosevelt
34. Harry S. Truman (D)[5]	1945	Missouri	1884–1972	F. D. Roosevelt
35. Alben W. Barkley (D)	1949–1953	Kentucky	1877–1956	Truman
36. Richard M. Nixon (R)	1953–1961	California	1913–	Eisenhower
37. Lyndon B. Johnson (D)[5]	1961–1963	Texas	1908–1973	Kennedy
38. Hubert H. Humphrey (D)	1965–1969	South Dakota	1911–1978	Johnson
39. Spiro T. Agnew (R)[6]	1969–1973	Maryland	1918–	Nixon
40. Gerald R. Ford (R)[7]	1973–1974	Nebraska	1913–	Nixon
41. Nelson A. Rockefeller (R)[8]	1974–1977	Maine	1908–1979	Ford
42. Walter F. Mondale (D)	1977–1981	Minnesota	1928–	Carter
43. George Bush (R)	1981–1989	Massachusetts	1924–	Reagan
44. J. Danforth Quayle (R)	1989–	Indiana	1947–	Bush

1. F—Federalist; DR—Democratic-Republican; D—Democratic; W—Whig; R—Republican; U—Union. 2. No party for first election. The party system in the U.S. made its appearance during Washington's first term as President. 3. Died in office. 4. Democratic-Republican with J. Q. Adams; Democratic with Jackson. Calhoun resigned in 1832 to become a U.S. Senator. 5. Succeeded to presidency on death of President. 6. Resigned Oct. 10, 1973, after pleading no contest to Federal income tax evasion charges. 7. Nominated by Nixon on Oct. 12, 1973, under provisions of 25th Amendment. Confirmed by Congress on Dec. 6, 1973, and was sworn in same day. He became President Aug. 9, 1974, upon Nixon's resignation. 8. Nominated by Ford Aug. 20, 1974; confirmed by Congress on Dec. 19, 1974, and was sworn in same day.

Burial Places of the Presidents

President	Burial place	President	Burial place
Washington	Mt. Vernon, Va.	Grant	New York City
J. Adams	Quincy, Mass.	Hayes	Fremont, Ohio
Jefferson	Charlottesville, Va.	Garfield	Cleveland, Ohio
Madison	Montpelier Station, Va.	Arthur	Albany, N.Y.
Monroe	Richmond, Va.	Cleveland	Princeton, N.J.
J. Q. Adams	Quincy, Mass.	B. Harrison	Indianapolis
Jackson	The Hermitage, nr. Nashville, Tenn.	McKinley	Canton, Ohio
		T. Roosevelt	Oyster Bay, N.Y.
Van Buren	Kinderhook, N.Y.	Taft	Arlington National Cemetery
W. H. Harrison	North Bend, Ohio	Wilson	Washington National Cathedral
Tyler	Richmond, Va.	Harding	Marion, Ohio
Polk	Nashville, Tenn.	Coolidge	Plymouth, Vt.
Taylor	Louisville, Ky.	Hoover	West Branch, Iowa
Fillmore	Buffalo, N.Y.	F. D. Roosevelt	Hyde Park, N.Y.
Pierce	Concord, N.H.	Truman	Independence, Mo.
Buchanan	Lancaster, Pa.	Eisenhower	Abilene, Kan.
Lincoln	Springfield, Ill.	Kennedy	Arlington National Cemetery
A. Johnson	Greeneville, Tenn.	L. B. Johnson	Stonewall, Tex.

"In God We Trust"

"In God We Trust" first appeared on U.S. coins after April 22, 1864, when Congress passed an act authorizing the coinage of a 2-cent piece bearing this motto. Thereafter, Congress extended its use to other coins. On July 30, 1956, it became the national motto.

Wives and Children of the Presidents

President	Wife's name	Year an place of wife's birth	Married	Wife died	Children of President[1] Sons	Children of President[1] Daughters
Washington	Martha Dandridge Custis	1732, Va.	1759	1802	—	—
John Adams	Abigail Smith	1744, Mass.	1764	1818	3	2
Jefferson	Martha Wayles Skelton	1748, Va.	1772	1782	1	5
Madison	Dorothy "Dolley" Payne Todd	1768, N.C.	1794	1849	—	—
Monroe	Elizabeth "Eliza" Kortright	1768, N.Y.	1786	1830	—	2
J. Q. Adams	Louisa Catherine Johnson	1775, England	1797	1852	3	1
Jackson	Mrs. Rachel Donelson Robards	1767, Va.	1791	1828	—	—
Van Buren	Hannah Hoes	1788, N.Y.	1807	1819	4	—
W. H. Harrison	Anna Symmes	1775, N.J.	1795	1864	6	4
Tyler	Letitia Christian	1790, Va.	1813	1842	3	4
	Julia Gardiner	1820, N.Y.	1844	1889	5	2
Polk	Sarah Childress	1803, Tenn.	1824	1891	—	—
Taylor	Margaret Smith	1788, Md.	1810	1852	1	5
Fillmore	Abigail Powers	1798, N.Y.	1826	1853	1	1
	Caroline Carmichael McIntosh	1813, N.J.	1858	1881	—	—
Pierce	Jane Means Appleton	1806, N.H.	1834	1863	3	—
Buchanan	(Unmarried)	—	—	—	—	—
Lincoln	Mary Todd	1818, Ky.	1842	1882	4	—
A. Johnson	Eliza McCardle	1810, Tenn.	1827	1876	3	2
Grant	Julia Dent	1826, Mo.	1848	1902	3	1
Hayes	Lucy Ware Webb	1831, Ohio	1852	1889	7	1
Garfield	Lucretia Rudolph	1832, Ohio	1858	1918	5	2
Arthur	Ellen Lewis Herndon	1837, Va.	1859	1880	2	1
Cleveland	Frances Folsom	1864, N.Y.	1886	1947	2	3
B. Harrison	Caroline Lavinia Scott	1832, Ohio	1853	1892	1	1
	Mary Scott Lord Dimmick	1858, Pa.	1896	1948	—	1
McKinley	Ida Saxton	1847, Ohio	1871	1907	—	2
T. Roosevelt	Alice Hathaway Lee	1861, Mass.	1880	1884	—	1
	Edith Kermit Carow	1861, Conn.	1886	1948	4	1
Taft	Helen Herron	1861, Ohio	1886	1943	2	1
Wilson	Ellen Louise Axson	1860, Ga.	1885	1914	—	3
	Edith Bolling Galt	1872, Va.	1915	1961	—	—
Harding	Florence Kling DeWolfe	1860, Ohio	1891	1924	—	—
Coolidge	Grace Anna Goodhue	1879, Vt.	1905	1957	2	—
Hoover	Lou Henry	1875, Iowa	1899	1944	2	—
F. D. Roosevelt	Anna Eleanor Roosevelt	1884, N.Y.	1905	1962	5	1
Truman	Bess Wallace	1885, Mo.	1919	1982	—	1
Eisenhower	Mamie Geneva Doud	1896, Iowa	1916	1979	2	—
Kennedy	Jacqueline Lee Bouvier	1929, N.Y.	1953		—	2	1
L. B. Johnson	Claudia Alta "Lady Bird" Taylor	1912, Tex.	1934		—	—	2
Nixon	Thelma Catherine "Pat" Ryan	1912, Nev.	1940		—	—	2
Ford	Elizabeth "Betty" Bloomer Warren	1918, Ill.	1948		—	3	1
Carter	Rosalynn Smith	1928, Ga.	1946		—	3	1
Reagan	Jane Wyman	1914, Mo.	1940[2]		—	1[3]	1
	Nancy Davis	1921 (?)[4], N.Y.	1952		—	1	1
Bush	Barbara Pierce	1925, N.Y.	1945		—	4	2

1. Includes children who died in infancy. 2. Divorced in 1948. 3. Adopted. 4. Birthday officially given as 1923 but her high school and college records show 1921 for year of birth.

Elections

How a President Is Nominated and Elected

The National Conventions of both major parties are held during the summer of a presidential-election year. Earlier, each party selects delegates by primaries, conventions, committees, etc.

For their 1992 National Convention, the Republicans allow each state a base of 6 delegates at large; the District of Columbia, 14; Puerto Rico, 14; Guam and the Virgin Islands, 4 each. In addition, each state receives 3 district delegates for each representative it has in the House of Representatives, regardless of po-

litical affiliation. This did not apply to the District of Columbia, Puerto Rico, Guam and the Virgin Islands.

Each state is awarded additional delegates at large on the basis of having supported the Republican candidate for President in 1988 and electing Republican candidates for Senator, Governor, and U.S. Representative between 1988 and 1991 inclusive.

The number of delegates at the 1992 convention, to be held in Houston starting August 17, will be 2,206.[1]

Following is the apportionment of delegates:

Alabama	38	Florida	97	Kentucky	35	Montana	20	Ohio	83	Texas	121
Alaska	19	Georgia	52	Louisiana	38	Nebraska	24	Oklahoma	34	Utah	27
Arizona	37	Guam	4	Maine	22	Nevada	21	Oregon	23	Vermont	19
Arkansas	27	Hawaii	14	Maryland	42	N.H.	23	Pa.	90	V.I.	4
California	201	Idaho	22	Mass.	38	N. Jersey	60	P.R.	14	Virginia	54
Colorado	37	Illinois	85	Michigan	72	New Mexico	25	R.I.	15	Washington	35
Connecticut	35	Indiana	51	Minnesota	32	New York	100	S.C.	36	W. Va.	18
Delaware	19	Iowa	23	Mississippi	32	N.C.	57	S.D.	19	Wisconsin	35
D.C.	14	Kansas	30	Missouri	47	N.D.	17	Tennessee	45	Wyoming	20

1. Includes 4 delegates from American Samoa.

The Democrats base the number of delegates on a state's showing in the 1988 and 1990 elections. At the 1992 convention, to be held in New York starting July 13, there will be 4,313[1,2] delegates casting 4,282 votes. Following is the apportionment by states:

Alabama	62	Florida	160	Kentucky	62	Montana	22	Ohio	167	Texas	214
Alaska	18	Georgia	88	Louisiana	69	Nebraska	31	Oklahoma	52	Utah	28
Arizona	47	Guam	10[1]	Maine	30	Nevada	23	Oregon	53	Vermont	19
Arkansas	43	Hawaii	26	Maryland	80	N. H.	24	Pa.	188	V.I.	10[1]
California	382	Idaho	24	Mass.	107	New Jersey	117	P.R.	57	Virginia	92
Colorado	54	Illinois	183	Michigan	148	New Mexico	33	R.I.	28	Washington	80
Connecticut	61	Indiana	86	Minnesota	87	New York	268	S.C.	50	W. Va.	38
Delaware	19	Iowa	57	Mississippi	45	N.C.	93	S.D.	20	Wisconsin	91
D. C.	29	Kansas	42	Missouri	86	N.D.	20	Tennessee	77	Wyoming	19

1. Fractional votes. 2. Includes 22[1] delegates for Democrats Abroad and 10[1] for American Samoa. As of March 26, 1991.

The Conventions

At each convention, a temporary chairman is chosen. After a credentials committee seats the delegates, a permanent chairman is elected. The convention then votes on a platform, drawn up by the platform committee.

By the third or fourth day, presidential nominations begin. The chairman calls the roll of states alphabetically. A state may place a candidate in nomination or yield to another state.

Voting, again alphabetically by roll call of states, begins after all nominations have been made and seconded. A simple majority is required in each party, although this may require many ballots.

Finally, the vice-presidential candidate is selected. Although there is no law saying that the candidates *must* come from different states, it is, practically, necessary for this to be the case. Otherwise, according to the Constitution (*see* Amendment XII), electors from that state could vote for only one of the candidates and would have to cast their other vote for some person of another state. This could result in a presidential candidate's receiving a majority electoral vote and his running mate's failing to.

The Electoral College

The next step in the process is the nomination of electors in each state, according to its laws. These electors must not be Federal office holders. In the November election, the voters cast their votes for electors, not for President. In some states, the ballots include only the names of the presidential and vice-presidential candidates; in others, they include only names of the electors. Nowadays, it is rare for electors to be split between parties. The last such occurrence was in North Carolina in 1968[1]; the last before that, in Tennessee in 1948. On three occasions (1824, 1876, and 1888), the presidential candidate with the largest popular vote failed to obtain an electoral-vote majority.

Each state has as many electors as it has Senators and Representatives. For the 1988 election, the total electors were 538, based on 100 Senators, 435 Representatives, plus 3 electoral votes from the District of Columbia as a result of the 23rd Amendment to the Constitution.

On the first Monday after the second Wednesday in December, the electors cast their votes in their respective state capitols. Constitutionally they may vote for someone other than the party candidate but usually they do not since they are pledged to one party and its candidate on the ballot. Should the presidential or vice-presidential candidate die between the November election and the December meetings, the electors pledged to vote for him could vote for whomever they pleased. However, it seems certain that the national committee would attempt to get an agreement among the state party leaders for a replacement candidate.

The votes of the electors, certified by the states, are sent to Congress, where the president of the Senate opens the certificates and has them counted in the presence of both Houses on January 6. The new President is inaugurated at noon on January 20.

Should no candidate receive a majority of the electoral vote for President, the House of Representatives chooses a President from among the three highest candidates, voting, not as individuals, but as states, with a majority (now 26) needed to elect. Should no vice-presidential candidate obtain the majority, the Senate, voting as individuals, chooses from the highest two.

1. In 1956, 1 of Alabama's 11 electoral votes was cast for Walter B. Jones. In 1960, 6 of Alabama's 11 electoral votes and 1 of Oklahoma's 8 electoral votes were cast for Harry Flood Byrd. (Byrd also received all 8 of Mississippi's electoral votes.)

National Political Conventions Since 1856

Opening date	Party	Where held	Opening date	Party	Where held
June 17, 1856	Republican	Philadelphia	June 12, 1928	Republican	Kansas City
June 2, 1856	Democratic	Cincinnati	June 26, 1928	Democratic	Houston
May 16, 1860	Republican	Chicago	June 14, 1932	Republican	Chicago
April 23, 1860	Democratic	Charleston and Baltimore	June 27, 1932	Democratic	Chicago
			June 9, 1936	Republican	Cleveland
June 7, 1864	Republican[1]	Baltimore	June 23, 1936	Democratic	Philadelphia
Aug. 29, 1864	Democratic	Chicago	June 24, 1940	Republican	Philadelphia
May 20, 1868	Republican	Chicago	July 15, 1940	Democratic	Chicago
July 4, 1868	Democratic	New York City	June 26, 1944	Republican	Chicago
June 5, 1872	Republican	Philadelphia	July 19, 1944	Democratic	Chicago
June 9, 1872	Democratic	Baltimore	June 21, 1948	Republican	Philadelphia
June 14, 1876	Republican	Cincinnati	July 12, 1948	Democratic	Philadelphia
June 28, 1876	Democratic	St. Louis	July 17, 1948	[3]	Birmingham
June 2, 1880	Republican	Chicago	July 22, 1948	Progressive	Philadelphia
June 23, 1880	Democratic	Cincinnati	July 7, 1952	Republican	Chicago
June 3, 1884	Republican	Chicago	July 21, 1952	Democratic	Chicago
July 11, 1884	Democratic	Chicago	Aug. 20, 1956	Republican	San Francisco
June 19, 1888	Republican	Chicago	Aug. 13, 1956	Democratic	Chicago
June 6, 1888	Democratic	St. Louis	July 25, 1960	Republican	Chicago
June 7, 1892	Republican	Minneapolis	July 11, 1960	Democratic	Los Angeles
June 21, 1892	Democratic	Chicago	July 13, 1964	Republican	San Francisco
June 16, 1896	Republican	St. Louis	Aug. 24, 1964	Democratic	Atlantic City
July 7, 1896	Democratic	Chicago	Aug. 5, 1968	Republican	Miami Beach
June 19, 1900	Republican	Philadelphia	Aug. 26, 1968	Democratic	Chicago
July 4, 1900	Democratic	Kansas City	July 10, 1972	Democratic	Miami Beach
June 21, 1904	Republican	Chicago	Aug. 21, 1972	Republican	Miami Beach
July 6, 1904	Democratic	St. Louis	July 12, 1976	Democratic	New York City
June 16, 1908	Republican	Chicago	Aug. 16, 1976	Republican	Kansas City, Mo.
July 7, 1908	Democratic	Denver	Aug. 11, 1980	Democratic	New York City
June 18, 1912	Republican	Chicago	July 14, 1980	Republican	Detroit
June 25, 1912	Democratic	Baltimore	Aug. 20, 1984	Republican	Dallas
June 7, 1916	Republican	Chicago	July 16, 1984	Democratic	San Francisco
June 14, 1916	Democratic	St. Louis	July 18, 1988	Democratic	Atlanta
June 8, 1920	Republican	Chicago	Aug. 15, 1988	Republican	New Orleans
June 28, 1920	Democratic	San Francisco	July 13, 1992	Democratic	New York City
June 10, 1924	Republican	Cleveland	Aug. 17, 1992	Republican	Houston
June 24, 1924[2]	Democratic	New York City			

1. The Convention adopted name Union party to attract War Democrats and others favoring prosecution of war. 2. In session until July 10, 1924. 3. States' Rights delegates from 13 Southern states.

National Committee Chairmen Since 1944

Chairman and (state)	Term	Chairman and (state)	Term
REPUBLICAN		**DEMOCRATIC**	
Herbert Brownell, Jr. (N.Y.)	1944–46	Robert E. Hannegan (Mo.)	1944–47
Carroll Reece (Tenn.)	1946–48	J. Howard McGrath (R.I.)	1947–49
Hugh D. Scott, Jr. (Pa.)	1948–49	William M. Boyle, Jr. (Mo.)	1949–51
Guy G. Gabrielson (N.J.)	1949–52	Frank E. McKinney (Ind.)	1951–52
Arthur E. Summerfield (Mich.)	1952–53	Stephen A. Mitchell (Ill.)	1952–54
Wesley Roberts (Kan.)	1953–	Paul M. Butler (Ind.)	1955–60
Leonard W. Hall (N.Y.)	1953–57	Henry M. Jackson (Wash.)	1960–61
Meade Alcorn (Conn.)	1957–59	John M. Bailey (Conn.)	1961–68
Thruston B. Morton (Ky.)	1959–61	Lawrence F. O'Brien (Mass.)	1968–69
William E. Miller (N.Y.)	1961–64	Fred R. Harris (Okla.)	1969–70
Dean Burch (Ariz.)	1964–65	Lawrence F. O'Brien (Mass.)	1970–72
Ray C. Bliss (Ohio)	1965–69	Jean Westwood (Utah)	1972
Rogers C. B. Morton (Md.)	1969–71	Robert S. Strauss (Tex.)	1972–77
Robert Dole (Kan.)	1971–73	Kenneth M. Curtis (Me.)	1977
George H. Bush (Tex.)	1973–74	John C. White (Tex.)	1977–81
Mary Louise Smith (Iowa)	1974–77	Charles T. Manatt (Calif.)	1981–85
William E. Brock III (Tenn.)	1977–81	Paul G. Kirk, Jr. (Mass.)	1985–89
Richard Richards (Utah)	1981–83	Ronald H. Brown (D.C.)	1989–
Frank J. Fahrenkopf, Jr. (Nevada)	1983–89		
Lee Atwater (S.C.)	1989–91		
Clayton K. Yeutter (Neb.)	1991		

Republican National Committee: 310 First St., S.E., Washington, D.C. 20003.
Democratic National Committee: 430 South Capitol St., S.E., Washington, D.C. 20003.

Presidential Elections, 1789 to 1988

For the original method of electing the President and the Vice President (elections of 1789, 1792, 1796, and 1800), see Article II, Section 1, of the Constitution. The election of 1804 was the first one in which the electors voted for President and Vice President on separate ballots. (See Amendment XII to the Constitution.)

Year	Presidential candidates	Party	Electoral vote	Year	Vice-presidential candidates	Party	Electoral vote
1789[1]	George Washington	(no party)	69	1796	John Adams	Federalist	71
	John Adams	(no party)	34		Thomas Jefferson	Dem.-Rep.	68
	Scattering	(no party)	35		Thomas Pinckney	Federalist	59
	Votes not cast		8		Aaron Burr	Dem.-Rep.	30
					Scattering		48
1792	George Washington	Federalist	132				
	John Adams	Federalist	77	1800[2]	Thomas Jefferson	Dem.-Rep.	73
	George Clinton	Anti-Federalist	50		Aaron Burr	Dem.-Rep.	73
	Thomas Jefferson	Anti-Federalist	4		John Adams	Federalist	65
	Aaron Burr	Anti-Federalist	1		Charles C. Pinckney	Federalist	64
	Votes not cast		6		John Jay	Federalist	1

Year	Presidential candidates	Party	Electoral vote	Vice-presidential candidates	Party	Electoral vote
1804	Thomas Jefferson	Dem.-Rep.	162	George Clinton	Dem.-Rep.	162
	Charles C. Pinckney	Federalist	14	Rufus King	Federalist	14
1808	James Madison	Dem.-Rep.	122	George Clinton	Dem.-Rep.	113
	Charles C. Pinckney	Federalist	47	Rufus King	Federalist	47
	George Clinton	Dem.-Rep.	6	John Langdon	Ind. (no party)	9
	Votes not cast		1	James Madison	Dem.-Rep.	3
				James Monroe	Dem.-Rep.	3
				Votes not cast		1
1812	James Madison	Dem.-Rep.	128	Elbridge Gerry	Dem.-Rep.	131
	De Witt Clinton	Federalist	89	Jared Ingersoll	Federalist	86
	Votes not cast		1	Votes not cast		1
1816	James Monroe	Dem.-Rep.	183	Daniel D. Tompkins	Dem.-Rep.	183
	Rufus King	Federalist	34	John E. Howard	Federalist	22
	Votes not cast		4	James Ross	Ind. (no party)	5
				John Marshall	Federalist	4
				Robert G. Harper	Ind. (no party)	3
				Votes not cast		4
1820	James Monroe	Dem-Rep	231	Daniel D. Tompkins	Dem.-Rep.	218
	John Quincy Adams	Ind. (no party)	1	Richard Stockton	Ind. (no party)	8
	Votes not cast		3	Daniel Rodney	Ind. (no party)	4
				Richard Rush	Ind. (no party)	1
				Robert G. Harper	Ind. (no party)	1
				Votes not cast		3
1824[3]	John Quincy Adams	(no party)	84	John C. Calhoun	(no party)	182
	Andrew Jackson	(no party)	99	Nathan Sanford	(no party)	30
	William H. Crawford	(no party)	41	Nathaniel Macon	(no party)	24
	Henry Clay	(no party)	37	Andrew Jackson	(no party)	13
				Martin Van Buren	(no party)	9
				Henry Clay	(no party)	2
				Votes not cast		1
1828	Andrew Jackson	Democratic	178	John C. Calhoun	Democratic	171
	John Quincy Adams	Natl. Rep.	83	Richard Rush	Natl. Rep.	83
				William Smith	Democratic	7
1832	Andrew Jackson	Democratic	219	Martin Van Buren	Democratic	189
	Henry Clay	Natl. Rep.	49	John Sergeant	Natl. Rep.	49
	John Floyd	Ind. (no party)	11	Henry Lee	Ind. (no party)	11
	William Wirt	Antimasonic[4]	7	Amos Ellmaker	Antimasonic	7
	Votes not cast		2	William Wilkins	Ind. (no party)	30
				Votes not cast		2

Year	Presidential candidates	Party	Electoral vote	Vice-presidential candidates	Party	Electoral vote
1836	Martin Van Buren	Democratic	170	Richard M. Johnson[5]	Democratic	147
	William H. Harrison	Whig	73	Francis Granger	Whig	77
	Hugh L. White	Whig	26	John Tyler	Whig	47
	Daniel Webster	Whig	14	William Smith	Ind. (no party)	23
	W. P. Mangum	Ind. (no party)	11			
1840	William H. Harrison[6]	Whig	234	John Tyler	Whig	234
	Martin Van Buren	Democratic	60	Richard M. Johnson	Democratic	48
				L. W. Tazewell	Ind. (no party)	11
				James K. Polk	Democratic	1
1844	James K. Polk	Democratic	170	George M. Dallas	Democratic	170
	Henry Clay	Whig	105	Theo. Frelinghuysen	Whig	105
1848	Zachary Taylor[7]	Whig	163	Millard Fillmore	Whig	163
	Lewis Cass	Democratic	127	William O. Butler	Democratic	127
1852	Franklin Pierce	Democratic	254	William R. King	Democratic	254
	Winfield Scott	Whig	42	William A. Graham	Whig	42
1856	James Buchanan	Democratic	174	John C. Breckinridge	Democratic	174
	John C. Fremont	Republican	114	William L. Dayton	Republican	114
	Millard Fillmore	American[8]	8	A. J. Donelson	American[8]	8
1860	Abraham Lincoln	Republican	180	Hannibal Hamlin	Republican	180
	John C. Breckinridge	Democratic	72	Joseph Lane	Democratic	72
	John Bell	Const. Union	39	Edward Everett	Const. Union	39
	Stephen A. Douglas	Democratic	12	H. V. Johnson	Democratic	12
1864	Abraham Lincoln[9]	Union[10]	212	Andrew Johnson	Union[15]	212
	George B. McClellan	Democratic	21	G. H. Pendleton	Democratic	21
1868	Ulysses S. Grant	Republican	214	Schuyler Colfax	Republican	214
	Horatio Seymour	Democratic	80	Francis P. Blair, Jr.	Democratic	80
	Votes not counted[11]		23	Votes not counted[11]		

Year	Presidential candidates	Party	Electoral vote	Popular vote	Vice-presidential candidates and party
1872	Ulysses S. Grant	Republican	286	3,597,132	Henry Wilson—R
	Horace Greeley	Dem., Liberal Rep.	([12])	2,834,125	B. Gratz Brown—D, LR—(47)
	Thomas A. Hendricks	Democratic	42		Scattering—(19)
	B. Gratz Brown	Dem., Liberal Rep.	18		Votes not counted—(14)
	Charles J. Jenkins	Democratic	2		
	David Davis	Democratic	1		
	Votes not counted		17		
1876[13]	Rutherford B. Hayes	Republican	185	4,033,768	William A. Wheeler—R
	Samuel J. Tilden	Democratic	184	4,285,992	Thomas A. Hendricks—D
	Peter Cooper	Greenback	0	81,737	Samuel F. Cary—G
1880	James A. Garfield[14]	Republican	214	4,449,053	Chester A. Arthur—R
	Winfield S. Hancock	Democratic	155	4,442,035	William H. English—D
	James B. Weaver	Greenback	0	308,578	B. J. Chambers—G
1884	Grover Cleveland	Democratic	219	4,911,017	Thomas A. Hendricks—D
	James G. Blaine	Republican	182	4,848,334	John A. Logan—R
	Benjamin F. Butler	Greenback	0	175,370	A. M. West—G
	John P. St. John	Prohibition	0	150,369	William Daniel—P
1888	Benjamin Harrison	Republican	233	5,440,216	Levi P. Morton—R
	Grover Cleveland	Democratic	168	5,538,233	A. G. Thurman—D
	Clinton B. Fisk	Prohibition	0	249,506	John A. Brooks—P
	Alson J. Streeter	Union Labor	0	146,935	Charles E. Cunningham—UL
1892	Grover Cleveland	Democratic	277	5,556,918	Adlai E. Stevenson—D
	Benjamin Harrison	Republican	145	5,176,108	Whitelaw Reid—R
	James B. Weaver	People's[15]	22	1,041,028	James G. Field—Peo
	John Bidwell	Prohibition	0	264,133	James B. Cranfill—P

Year	Presidential candidates	Party	Electoral vote	Popular vote	Vice-presidential candidates and party
1896	William McKinley	Republican	271	7,035,638	Garret A. Hobart—R
	William J. Bryan	Dem., People's[15]	176	6,467,946	Arthur Sewall—D—(149)
					Thomas E. Watson—Peo—(27)
	John M. Palmer	Natl. Dem.	0	133,148	Simon B. Buckner—ND
	Joshua Levering	Prohibition	0	132,007	Hale Johnson—P
1900	William McKinley[16]	Republican	292	7,219,530	Theodore Roosevelt—R
	William J. Bryan	Dem., People's[15]	155	6,358,071	Adlai E. Stevenson—D, Peo
	Eugene V. Debs	Social Democratic	0	94,768	Job Harriman—SD
1904	Theodore Roosevelt	Republican	336	7,628,834	Charles W. Fairbanks—R
	Alton B. Parker	Democratic	140	5,084,491	Henry G. Davis—D
	Eugene V. Debs	Socialist	0	402,400	Benjamin Hanford—S
1908	William H. Taft	Republican	321	7,679,006	James S. Sherman—R
	William J. Bryan	Democratic	162	6,409,106	John W. Kern—D
	Eugene V. Debs	Socialist	0	402,820	Benjamin Hanford—S
1912	Woodrow Wilson	Democratic	435	6,286,214	Thomas R. Marshall—D
	Theodore Roosevelt	Progressive	88	4,126,020	Hiram Johnson—Prog
	William H. Taft	Republican	8	3,483,922	Nicholas M. Butler—R[17]
	Eugene V. Debs	Socialist	0	897,011	Emil Seidel—S
1916	Woodrow Wilson	Democratic	277	9,129,606	Thomas R. Marshall—D
	Charles E. Hughes	Republican	254	8,538,221	Charles W. Fairbanks—R
	A. L. Benson	Socialist	0	585,113	G. R. Kirkpatrick—S
1920	Warren G. Harding[18]	Republican	404	16,152,200	Calvin Coolidge—R
	James M. Cox	Democratic	127	9,147,353	Franklin D. Roosevelt—D
	Eugene V. Debs	Socialist	0	917,799	Seymour Stedman—S
1924	Calvin Coolidge	Republican	382	15,725,016	Charles G. Dawes—R
	John W. Davis	Democratic	136	8,385,586	Charles W. Bryan—D
	Robert M. LaFollette	Progressive, Socialist	13	4,822,856	Burton K. Wheeler—Prog S
1928	Herbert Hoover	Republican	444	21,392,190	Charles Curtis—R
	Alfred E. Smith	Democratic	87	15,016,443	Joseph T. Robinson—D
	Norman Thomas	Socialist	0	267,420	James H. Maurer—S
1932	Franklin D. Roosevelt	Democratic	472	22,821,857	John N. Garner—D
	Herbert Hoover	Republican	59	15,761,841	Charles Curtis—R
	Norman Thomas	Socialist	0	884,781	James H. Maurer—S
1936	Franklin D. Roosevelt	Democratic	523	27,751,597	John N. Garner—D
	Alfred M. Landon	Republican	8	16,679,583	Frank Knox—R
	Norman Thomas	Socialist	0	187,720	George Nelson—S
1940	Franklin D. Roosevelt	Democratic	449	27,244,160	Henry A. Wallace—D
	Wendell L. Willkie	Republican	82	22,305,198	Charles L. McNary—R
	Norman Thomas	Socialist	0	99,557	Maynard C. Krueger—S
1944	Franklin D. Roosevelt[19]	Democratic	432	25,602,504	Harry S. Truman—D
	Thomas E. Dewey	Republican	99	22,006,285	John W. Bricker—R
	Norman Thomas	Socialist	0	80,518	Darlington Hoopes—S
1948	Harry S. Truman	Democratic	303	24,179,345	Alben W. Barkley—D
	Thomas E. Dewey	Republican	189	21,991,291	Earl Warren—R
	J. Strom Thurmond	States' Rights Dem.	39	1,176,125	Fielding L. Wright—SR
	Henry A. Wallace	Progressive	0	1,157,326	Glen Taylor—Prog
	Norman Thomas	Socialist	0	139,572	Tucker P. Smith—S
1952	Dwight D. Eisenhower	Republican	442	33,936,234	Richard M. Nixon—R
	Adlai E. Stevenson	Democratic	89	27,314,992	John J. Sparkman—D
1956	Dwight D. Eisenhower	Republican	457	35,590,472	Richard M. Nixon—R
	Adlai E. Stevenson	Democratic	73[20]	26,022,752	Estes Kefauver—D
1960	John F. Kennedy[22]	Democratic	303	34,226,731	Lyndon B. Johnson—D
	Richard M. Nixon	Republican	219[21]	34,108,157	Henry Cabot Lodge—R

Year	Presidential candidates	Party	Electoral vote	Popular vote	Vice-presidential candidates and party
1964	Lyndon B. Johnson	Democratic	486	43,129,484	Hubert H. Humphrey—D
	Barry M. Goldwater	Republican	52	27,178,188	William E. Miller—R
1968	Richard M. Nixon	Republican	301	31,785,480	Spiro T. Agnew—R
	Hubert H. Humphrey	Democratic	191	31,275,166	Edmund S. Muskie—D
	George C. Wallace	American Independent	46	9,906,473	Curtis F. LeMay—AI
1972	Richard M. Nixon[23]	Republican	520[24]	47,169,911	Spiro T. Agnew—R
	George McGovern	Democratic	17	29,170,383	Sargent Shriver—D
	John G. Schmitz	American	0	1,099,482	Thomas J. Anderson—A
1976	Jimmy Carter	Democratic	297	40,830,763	Walter F. Mondale—D
	Gerald R. Ford	Republican	240[25]	39,147,973	Robert J. Dole—R
	Eugene J. McCarthy	Independent	0	756,631	None
1980	Ronald Reagan	Republican	489	43,899,248	George Bush—R
	Jimmy Carter	Democratic	49	36,481,435	Walter F. Mondale—D
	John B. Anderson	Independent	0	5,719,437	Patrick J. Lucey—I
1984	Ronald Reagan	Republican	525	54,455,075	George Bush—R
	Walter F. Mondale	Democratic	13	37,577,185	Geraldine A. Ferraro—D
1988	George H. Bush	Republican	426	48,886,097	J. Danforth Quayle—R
	Michael S. Dukakis	Democratic	111[26]	41,809,074	Lloyd Bentsen—D

1. Only 10 states participated in the election. The New York legislature chose no electors, and North Carolina and Rhode Island had not yet ratified the Constitution. 2. As Jefferson and Burr were tied, the House of Representatives chose the President. In a vote by states, 10 votes were cast for Jefferson, 4 for Burr; 2 votes were not cast. 3. As no candidate had an electoral-vote majority, the House of Representatives chose the President from the first three. In a vote by states, 13 votes were cast for Adams, 7 for Jackson, and 4 for Crawford. 4. The Antimasonic Party on Sept. 26, 1831, was the first party to hold a nominating convention to choose candidates for President and Vice-President. 5. As Johnson did not have an electoral-vote majority, the Senate chose him 33–14 over Granger, the others being legally out of the race. 6. Harrison died April 4, 1841, and Tyler succeeded him April 6. 7. Taylor died July 9, 1850, and Fillmore succeeded him July 10. 8. Also known as the Know-Nothing Party. 9. Lincoln died April 15, 1865, and Johnson succeeded him the same day. 10. Name adopted by the Republican National Convention of 1864. Johnson was a War Democrat. 11. 23 Southern electoral votes were excluded. 12. See Election of 1872 in *Unusual Voting Results* under Elections, Presidential, in Index. 13. See Election of 1876 in *Unusual Voting Results* under Elections, Presidential, in Index. 14. Garfield died Sept. 19, 1881, and Arthur succeeded him Sept. 20. 15. Members of People's Party were called Populists. 16. McKinley died Sept. 14, 1901, and Roosevelt succeeded him the same day. 17. James S. Sherman, Republican candidate for Vice President, died Oct. 30, 1912, and the Republican electoral votes were cast for Butler. 18. Harding died Aug. 2, 1923, and Coolidge succeeded him Aug. 3. 19. Roosevelt died April 12, 1945, and Truman succeeded him the same day. 20. One electoral vote from Alabama was cast for Walter B. Jones. 21. Sen. Harry F. Byrd received 15 electoral votes. 22. Kennedy died Nov. 22, 1963, and Johnson succeeded him the same day. 23. Nixon resigned Aug. 9, 1974, and Gerald R. Ford succeeded him the same day. 24. One electoral vote from Virginia was cast for John Hospers, Libertarian Party. 25. One electoral vote from Washington was cast for Ronald Reagan. 26. One electoral vote from West Virginia was cast for Lloyd Bentsen.

Qualifications for Voting

The Supreme Court decision of March 21, 1972, declared lengthy requirements for voting in state and local elections unconstitutional and suggested that 30 days was an ample period. Most of the states have changed or eliminated their durational residency requirements to comply with the ruling, as shown.

NO DURATIONAL RESIDENCY REQUIREMENT

Alabama,[6] Arkansas, Connecticut,[13] Delaware,[12] District of Columbia,[16] Florida,[5] Georgia,[2] Hawaii,[2] Iowa,[6] Louisiana,[8] Maine, Maryland,[3] Massachusetts,[3] Missouri,[4] Nebraska,[9] New Hampshire,[17] New Mexico,[7] North Carolina, Oklahoma, South Carolina,[22] South Dakota,[10] Tennessee,[20] Texas, Virginia, West Virginia,[2] Wyoming[2]

30-DAY RESIDENCY REQUIREMENT

Alaska,[18] Arizona,[11] Idaho,[17] Illinois, Indiana, Kentucky,[2] Michigan, Mississippi,[21] Montana, Nevada, New Jersey, New York, North Dakota,[3] Ohio, Pennsylvania, Rhode Island, Utah, Washington

OTHER

California,[19] Colorado,[1] Kansas, Minnesota[15] and Oregon, 20 days; Vermont, 17 days;[14] Wisconsin, 10 days

1. 32 days. 2. 30-day registration requirement. 3. No residency required to register to vote. 4. Must be registered by the fourth Wednesday prior to election. 5. 30-day registration requirement for national elections; 30-day for state elections. 6. 10-day registration requirement. In-person registration by 5 PM, eleven days before election date. 7. Must register 28 days before election. 8. 24 days prior to any election. 9. Registration requirement, 2nd Friday prior to elections. 10. 15-day registration requirement. 11. Residency in the state 29 days next preceding the election. 12. Must reside in Delaware and register by the last day that the books are open for registration. 13. Registration deadline 21st day before election; registration and party enrollment deadline the day before primary; unaffiliated voters may vote in Republican primaries for *some* offices. 14. Administrative cut-off date for processing applications. 15. Permits registration and voting on election day with approved ID. 16. Registration stops 30 days before any election and until 15 days after. Voters must inform Board of Elections of change of address within 30 days of moving. 17. Registration requirement, 10 days prior

to elections. 18. If otherwise qualified but has not been a resident of the election district for at least 30 days preceding the date of a presidential election, is entitled to register and vote for presidential and vice^NDpresidential candidates. 19. 29 days before an election. 20. Must be resident of state for a period of at least 20 days prior to registration. *Source: Information Please* questionnaires to the states. 21. 30 days registration required, 60 days if registration is by mail. 22. Registration certificate not valid for 30 days but if you move within the state you can vote in old precinct during the 30 days.

Unusual Voting Results

Election of 1872

The presidential and vice-presidential candidates of the Liberal Republicans and the northern Democrats in 1872 were Horace Greeley and B. Gratz Brown. Greeley died Nov. 29, 1872, before his 66 electors voted. In the electoral balloting for President, 63 of Greeley's votes were scattered among four other men, including Brown.

Election of 1876

In the election of 1876 Samuel J. Tilden, the Democratic candidate, received a popular majority but lacked one undisputed electoral vote to carry a clear majority of the electoral college. The crux of the problem was in the 22 electoral votes which were in dispute because Florida, Louisiana, South Carolina, and Oregon each sent in two sets of election returns. In the three southern states, Republican election boards threw out enough Democratic votes to certify the Republican candidate, Hayes. In Oregon, the Democratic governor disqualified a Republican elector, replacing him with a Democrat. Since the Senate was Republican and the House of Representatives Democratic, it seemed useless to refer the disputed returns to the two houses for solution. Instead Congress appointed an Electoral Commission with five representatives each from the Senate, the House, and the Supreme Court. All but one Justice was named, giving the Commission seven Republican and seven Democratic members. The naming of the fifth Justice was left to the other four. He was a Republican who first favored Tilden but, under pressure from his party, switched to Hayes, ensuring his election by the Commission voting 8 to 7 on party lines.

Minority Presidents

Fifteen candidates have become President of the

United States with a popular vote less than 50% of the total cast. It should be noted, however, that in elections before 1872, presidential electors were not chosen by popular vote in all states. Adams' election in 1824 was by the House of Representatives, which chose him over Jackson, who had a plurality of both electoral and popular votes, but not a majority in the electoral college.

Besides Jackson in 1824, only two other candidates receiving the largest popular vote have failed to gain a majority in the electoral college—Samuel J. Tilden (D) in 1876 and Grover Cleveland (D) in 1888.

The "minority" Presidents follow:

Vote Received by Minority Presidents

Year	President	Electoral Percent	Popular vote Percent
1824	John Q. Adams	31.8	29.8
1844	James K. Polk (D)	61.8	49.3
1848	Zachary Taylor (W)	56.2	47.3
1856	James Buchanan (D)	58.7	45.3
1860	Abraham Lincoln (R)	59.4	39.9
1876	Rutherford B. Hayes (R)	50.1	47.9
1880	James A. Garfield (R)	57.9	48.3
1884	Grover Cleveland (D)	54.6	48.8
1888	Benjamin Harrison (R)	58.1	47.8
1892	Grover Cleveland (D)	62.4	46.0
1912	Woodrow Wilson (D)	81.9	41.8
1916	Woodrow Wilson (D)	52.1	49.3
1948	Harry S. Truman (D)	57.1	49.5
1960	John F. Kennedy (D)	56.4	49.7
1968	Richard M. Nixon (R)	56.1	43.4

How a Bill Becomes a Law

When a Senator or a Representative introduces a bill, he sends it to the clerk of his house, who gives it a number and title. This is the *first reading*, and the bill is referred to the proper committee.

The committee may decide the bill is unwise or unnecessary and *table* it, thus killing it at once. Or it may decide the bill is worthwhile and hold hearings to listen to facts and opinions presented by experts and other interested persons. After members of the committee have debated the bill and perhaps offered amendments, a vote is taken; and if the vote is favorable, the bill is sent back to the floor of the house.

The clerk reads the bill sentence by sentence to the house, and this is known as the *second reading*. Members may then debate the bill and offer amendments. In the House of Representatives, the time for debate is limited by a *cloture rule*, but there is no such restriction in the Senate for cloture, where 60 votes are required. This makes possible a *filibuster*, in which one or more opponents hold the floor to defeat the bill.

The *third reading* is by title only, and the bill is put to a vote, which may be by voice or roll call, depending on the circumstances and parliamentary rules. Members who must be absent at the time but who wish to record their vote may be paired if each negative vote has a balancing affirmative one.

The bill then goes to the other house of Congress, where it may be defeated, or passed with or without amendments. If the bill is defeated, it dies. If it is passed with amendments, a joint Congressional committee must be appointed by both houses to iron out the differences.

After its final passage by both houses, the bill is sent to the President. If he approves, he signs it, and the bill becomes a law. However, if he disapproves, he *vetoes* the bill by refusing to sign it and sending it back to the house of origin with his reasons for the veto. The objections are read and debated, and a roll-call vote is taken. If the bill receives less than a two-thirds vote, it is defeated and goes no farther. But if it receives a two-thirds vote or greater, it is sent to the other house for a vote. If that house also passes it by a two-thirds vote, the President's veto is *overridden,* and the bill becomes a law.

Should the President desire neither to sign nor to veto the bill, he may retain it for ten days, Sundays excepted, after which time it automatically becomes a law without signature. However, if Congress has adjourned within those ten days, the bill is automatically killed, that process of indirect rejection being known as a *pocket veto.*

Government Officials

Cabinet Members With Dates of Appointment

Although the Constitution made no provision for a President's advisory group, the heads of the three executive departments (State, Treasury, and War) and the Attorney General were organized by Washington into such a group; and by about 1793, the name "Cabinet" was applied to it. With the exception of the Attorney General up to 1870 and the Postmaster General from 1829 to 1872, Cabinet members have been heads of executive departments.

A Cabinet member is appointed by the President, subject to the confirmation of the Senate; and as his term is not fixed, he may be replaced at any time by the President. At a change in Administration, it is customary for him to tender his resignation, but he remains in office until a successor is appointed.

The table of Cabinet members lists only those members who actually served after being duly commissioned.

The dates shown are those of appointment. "Cont." indicates that the term continued from the previous Administration for a substantial amount of time.

With the creation of the Department of Transportation in 1966, the Cabinet consisted of 12 members. This figure was reduced to 11 when the Post Office Department became an independent agency in 1970 but, with the establishment in 1977 of a Department of Energy, became 12 again. Creation of the Department of Education in 1980 raised the number to 13. Creation of the Department of Veterans' Affairs in 1989 raised the number to 14.

WASHINGTON

Secretary of State	Thomas Jefferson 1789
	Edmund Randolph 1794
	Timothy Pickering 1795
Secretary of the Treasury	Alexander Hamilton 1789
	Oliver Wolcott, Jr. 1795
Secretary of War	Henry Knox 1789
	Timothy Pickering 1795
	James McHenry 1796
Attorney General	Edmund Randolph 1789
	William Bradford 1794
	Charles Lee 1795

J. ADAMS

Secretary of State	Timothy Pickering (Cont.)
	John Marshall 1800
Secretary of the Treasury	Oliver Wolcott, Jr. (Cont.)
	Samuel Dexter 1801
Secretary of War	James McHenry (Cont.)
	Samuel Dexter 1800
Attorney General	Charles Lee (Cont.)
Secretary of the Navy	Benjamin Stoddert 1798

JEFFERSON

Secretary of State	James Madison 1801
Secretary of the Treasury	Samuel Dexter (Cont.)
	Albert Gallatin 1801
Secretary of War	Henry Dearborn 1801
Attorney General	Levi Lincoln 1801
	Robert Smith 1805
	John Breckinridge 1805
	Caesar A. Rodney 1807
Secretary of the Navy	Benjamin Stoddert (Cont.)
	Robert Smith 1801

MADISON

Secretary of State	Robert Smith 1809
	James Monroe 1811
Secretary of the Treasury	Albert Gallatin (Cont.)
	George W. Campbell 1814
	Alexander J. Dallas 1814
	William H. Crawford 1816
Secretary of War	William Eustis 1809
	John Armstrong 1813
	James Monroe 1814
	William H. Crawford 1815

Attorney General	Caesar A. Rodney (Cont.)
	William Pinckney 1811
	Richard Rush 1814
Secretary of the Navy	Paul Hamilton 1809
	William Jones 1813
	B. W. Crowninshield 1814

MONROE

Secretary of State	John Quincy Adams 1817
Secretary of the Treasury	William H. Crawford (Cont.)
Secretary of War	John C. Calhoun 1817
Attorney General	Richard Rush (Cont.)
	William Wirt 1817
Secretary of the Navy	B. W. Crowninshield (Cont.)
	Smith Thompson 1818
	Samuel L. Southard 1823

J. Q. ADAMS

Secretary of State	Henry Clay 1825
Secretary of the Treasury	Richard Rush 1825
Secretary of War	James Barbour 1825
	Peter B. Porter 1828
Attorney General	William Wirt (Cont.)
Secretary of the Navy	Samuel L. Southard (Cont.)

JACKSON

Secretary of State	Martin Van Buren 1829
	Edward Livingston 1831
	Louis McLane 1833
	John Forsyth 1834
Secretary of the Treasury	Samuel D. Ingham 1829
	Louis McLane 1831
	William J. Duane 1833
	Roger B. Taney[3] 1833
	Levi Woodbury 1834
Secretary of War	John H. Eaton 1829
	Lewis Cass 1831
Attorney General	John M. Berrien 1829
	Roger B. Taney 1831
	Benjamin F. Butler 1833
Postmaster General[1]	William T. Barry 1829
	Amos Kendall 1835
Secretary of the Navy	John Branch 1829
	Levi Woodbury 1831
	Mahlon Dickerson 1834

VAN BUREN

Secretary of State	John Forsyth (Cont.)
Secretary of the Treasury	Levi Woodbury (Cont.)
Secretary of War	Joel R. Poinsett 1837
Attorney General	Benjamin F. Butler (Cont.)
	Felix Grundy 1838
	Henry D. Gilpin 1840
Postmaster General	Amos Kendall (Cont.)
	John M. Niles 1840
Secretary of the Navy	Mahlon Dickerson (Cont.)
	James K. Paulding 1838

W. H. HARRISON

Secretary of State	Daniel Webster 1841
Secretary of the Treasury	Thomas Ewing 1841
Secretary of War	John Bell 1841
Attorney General	John J. Crittenden 1841
Postmaster General	Francis Granger 1841
Secretary of the Navy	George E. Badger 1841

TYLER

Secretary of State	Daniel Webster (Cont.)
	Abel P. Upshur 1843
	John C. Calhoun 1844
Secretary of the Treasury	Thomas Ewing (Cont.)
	Walter Forward 1841
	John C. Spencer[3] 1843
	George M. Bibb 1844
Secretary of War	John Bell (Cont.)
	John C. Spencer 1841
	James M. Porter[3] 1843
	William Wilkins 1844
Attorney General	John J. Crittenden (Cont.)
	Hugh S. Legaré 1841
	John Nelson 1843
Postmaster General	Francis Granger (Cont.)
	Charles A. Wickliffe 1841
Secretary of the Navy	George E. Badger (Cont.)
	Abel P. Upshur 1841
	David Henshaw[3] 1843
	Thomas W. Gilmer 1844
	John Y. Mason 1844

POLK

Secretary of State	James Buchanan 1845
Secretary of the Treasury	Robert J. Walker 1845
Secretary of War	William L. Marcy 1845
Attorney General	John Y. Mason 1845
	Nathan Clifford 1846
	Isaac Toucey 1848
Postmaster General	Cave Johnson 1845
Secretary of the Navy	George Bancroft 1845
	John Y. Mason 1846

TAYLOR

Secretary of State	John M. Clayton 1849
Secretary of the Treasury	William M. Meredith 1849
Secretary of War	George W. Crawford 1849
Attorney General	Reverdy Johnson 1849
Postmaster General	Jacob Collamer 1849
Secretary of the Navy	William B. Preston 1849
Secretary of the Interior	Thomas Ewing 1849

FILLMORE

Secretary of State	Daniel Webster 1850
	Edward Everett 1852
Secretary of the Treasury	Thomas Corwin 1850
Secretary of War	Charles M. Conrad 1850
Attorney General	John J. Crittenden 1850
Postmaster General	Nathan K. Hall 1850
	Samuel D. Hubbard 1852
Secretary of the Navy	William A. Graham 1850
	John P. Kennedy 1852
Secretary of the Interior	Thos. M. T. McKennan 1850
	Alex. H. H. Stuart 1850

PIERCE

Secretary of State	William L. Marcy 1853
Secretary of the Treasury	James Guthrie 1853
Secretary of War	Jefferson Davis 1853

Attorney General	Caleb Cushing 1853
Postmaster General	James Campbell 1853
Secretary of the Navy	James C. Dobbin 1853
Secretary of the Interior	Robert McClelland 1853

BUCHANAN

Secretary of State	Lewis Cass 1857
	Jeremiah S. Black 1860
Secretary of the Treasury	Howell Cobb 1857
	Philip F. Thomas 1860
	John A. Dix 1861
Secretary of War	John B. Floyd 1857
	Joseph Holt 1861
Attorney General	Jeremiah S. Black 1857
	Edwin M. Stanton 1860
Postmaster General	Aaron V. Brown 1857
	Joseph Holt 1859
	Horatio King 1861
Secretary of the Navy	Isaac Toucey 1857
Secretary of the Interior	Jacob Thompson 1857

LINCOLN

Secretary of State	William H. Seward 1861
Secretary of the Treasury	Salmon P. Chase 1861
	William P. Fessenden 1864
	Hugh McCulloch 1865
Secretary of War	Simon Cameron 1861
	Edwin M. Stanton 1862
Attorney General	Edward Bates 1861
	James Speed 1864
Postmaster General	Montgomery Blair 1861
	William Dennison 1864
Secretary of the Navy	Gideon Welles 1861
Secretary of the Interior	Caleb B. Smith 1861
	John P. Usher 1863

A. JOHNSON

Secretary of State	William H. Seward (Cont.)
Secretary of the Treasury	Hugh McCulloch (Cont.)
Secretary of War	Edwin M. Stanton (Cont.)
	John M. Schofield 1868
Attorney General	James Speed (Cont.)
	Henry Stanbery 1866
	William M. Evarts 1868
Postmaster General	William Dennison (Cont.)
	Alexander W. Randall 1866
Secretary of the Navy	Gideon Welles (Cont.)
Secretary of the Interior	John P. Usher (Cont.)
	James Harlan 1865
	Orville H. Browning 1866

GRANT

Secretary of State	Elihu B. Washburne 1869
	Hamilton Fish 1869
	George S. Boutwell 1869
	William A. Richardson 1873
	Benjamin H. Bristow 1874
	Lot M. Morrill 1876
Secretary of War	John A. Rawlins 1869
	William W. Belknap 1869
	Alphonso Taft 1876
	James D. Cameron 1876
Attorney General	Ebenezer R. Hoar 1869
	Amos T. Akerman 1870
	George H. Williams 1871
	Edwards Pierrepont 1875
	Alphonso Taft 1876
Postmaster General	John A. J. Creswell 1869
	Marshall Jewell 1874
	James N. Tyner 1876
Secretary of the Navy	Adolph E. Borie 1869
	George M. Robeson 1869
Secretary of the Interior	Jacob D. Cox 1869
	Columbus Delano 1870
	Zachariah Chandler 1875

HAYES

Secretary of State	William M. Evarts 1877
Secretary of the Treasury	John Sherman 1877
Secretary of War	George W. McCrary 1877
	Alexander Ramsey 1879

Attorney General	Charles Devens 1877
Postmaster General	David M. Key 1877
	Horace Maynard 1880
	Richard W. Thompson 1877
	Nathan Goff, Jr. 1881
Secretary of the Interior	Carl Schurz 1877

GARFIELD

Secretary of State	James G. Blaine 1881
Secretary of the Treasury	William Windom 1881
Secretary of War	Robert T. Lincoln 1881
Attorney General	Wayne MacVeagh 1881
Postmaster General	Thomas L. James 1881
Secretary of the Navy	William H. Hunt 1881
Secretary of the Interior	Samuel J. Kirkwood 1881

ARTHUR

Secretary of State	James G. Blaine (Cont.)
	F. T. Frelinghuysen 1881
Secretary of the Treasury	William Windom (Cont.)
	Charles J. Folger 1881
	Walter Q. Gresham 1884
	Hugh McCulloch 1884
Secretary of War	Robert T. Lincoln (Cont.)
Attorney General	Wayne MacVeagh (Cont.)
	Benjamin H. Brewster 1881
Postmaster General	Thomas L. James (Cont.)
	Timothy O. Howe 1881
	Walter Q. Gresham 1883
	Frank Hatton 1884
Secretary of the Navy	William H. Hunt (Cont.)
	William E. Chandler 1882
Secretary of the Interior	Samuel J. Kirkwood (Cont.)
	Henry M. Teller 1882

CLEVELAND

Secretary of State	Thomas F. Bayard 1885
Secretary of the Treasury	Daniel Manning 1885
	Charles S. Fairchild 1887
Secretary of War	William C. Endicott 1885
Attorney General	Augustus H. Garland 1885
Postmaster General	William F. Vilas 1885
	Don M. Dickinson 1888
Secretary of the Navy	William C. Whitney 1885
Secretary of the Interior	Lucius Q. C. Lamar 1885
	William F. Vilas 1888
Secretary of Agriculture	Norman J. Colman 1889

B. HARRISON

Secretary of State	James G. Blaine 1889
	John W. Foster 1892
Secretary of the Treasury	William Windom 1889
	Charles Foster 1891
Secretary of War	Redfield Proctor 1889
	Stephen B. Elkins 1891
Attorney General	William H. H. Miller 1889
Postmaster General	John Wanamaker 1889
Secretary of the Navy	Benjamin F. Tracy 1889
Secretary of the Interior	John W. Noble 1889
Secretary of Agriculture	Jeremiah M. Rusk 1889

CLEVELAND

Secretary of State	Walter Q. Gresham 1893
	Richard Olney 1895
Secretary of the Treasury	John G. Carlisle 1893
Secretary of War	Daniel S. Lamont 1893
Attorney General	Richard Olney 1893
	Judson Harmon 1895
Postmaster General	Wilson S. Bissell 1893
	William L. Wilson 1895
Secretary of the Navy	Hilary A. Herbert 1893
Secretary of the Interior	Hoke Smith 1893
	David R. Francis 1896
Secretary of Agriculture	Julius Sterling Morton 1893

MCKINLEY

Secretary of State	John Sherman 1897
	William R. Day 1898
	John Hay 1898
Secretary of the Treasury	Lyman J. Gage 1897
Secretary of War	Russell A. Alger 1897
	Elihu Root 1899

Attorney General	Joseph McKenna 1897
	John W. Griggs 1898
	Philander C. Knox 1901
Postmaster General	James A. Gary 1897
	Charles E. Smith 1898
Secretary of the Navy	John D. Long 1897
Secretary of the Interior	Cornelius N. Bliss 1897
	Ethan A. Hitchcock 1898
Secretary of Agriculture	James Wilson 1897

T. ROOSEVELT

Secretary of State	John Hay (Cont.)
	Elihu Root 1905
	Robert Bacon 1909
Secretary of the Treasury	Lyman J. Gage (Cont.)
	Leslie M. Shaw 1902
	George B. Cortelyou 1907
Secretary of War	Elihu Root (Cont.)
	William H. Taft 1904
	Luke E. Wright 1908
Attorney General	Philander C. Knox (Cont.)
	William H. Moody 1904
	Charles J. Bonaparte 1906
Postmaster General	Charles E. Smith (Cont.)
	Henry C. Payne 1902
	Robert J. Wynne 1904
	George B. Cortelyou 1905
	George von L. Meyer 1907
Secretary of the Navy	John D. Long (Cont.)
	William H. Moody 1902
	Paul Morton 1904
	Charles J. Bonaparte 1905
	Victor H. Metcalf 1906
	Truman H. Newberry 1908
Secretary of the Interior	Ethan A. Hitchcock (Cont.)
	James R. Garfield 1907
Secretary of Agriculture	James Wilson (Cont.)
Secretary of Commerce and Labor	George B. Cortelyou 1903
	Victor H. Metcalf 1904
	Oscar S. Straus 1906

TAFT

Secretary of State	Philander C. Knox 1909
Secretary of the Treasury	Franklin MacVeagh 1909
Secretary of War	Jacob M. Dickinson 1909
	Henry L. Stimson 1911
Attorney General	George W. Wickersham 1909
Postmaster General	Frank H. Hitchcock 1909
Secretary of the Navy	George von L. Meyer 1909
Secretary of the Interior	Richard A. Ballinger 1909
	Walter L. Fisher 1911
Secretary of Agriculture	James Wilson (Cont.)
Secretary of Commerce and Labor	Charles Nagel 1909

WILSON

Secretary of State	William J. Bryan 1913
	Robert Lansing 1915
	Bainbridge Colby 1920
Secretary of the Treasury	William G. McAdoo 1913
	Carter Glass 1918
	David F. Houston 1920
Secretary of War	Lindley M. Garrison 1913
	Newton D. Baker 1916
Attorney General	James C. McReynolds 1913
	Thomas W. Gregory 1914
	A. Mitchell Palmer 1919
Postmaster General	Albert S. Burleson 1913
Secretary of the Navy	Josephus Daniels 1913
Secretary of the Interior	Franklin K. Lane 1913
	John B. Payne 1920
Secretary of Agriculture	David F. Houston 1913
	Edwin T. Meredith 1920
Secretary of Commerce	William C. Redfield 1913
	Joshua W. Alexander 1919
Secretary of Labor	William B. Wilson 1913

HARDING

Secretary of State	Charles E. Hughes 1921
Secretary of the Treasury	Andrew W. Mellon 1921
Secretary of War	John W. Weeks 1921
Attorney General	Harry M. Daugherty 1921
Postmaster General	Will H. Hays 1921

	Hubert Work 1922
	Harry S. New 1923
Secretary of the Navy	Edwin Denby 1921
Secretary of the Interior	Albert B. Fall 1921
	Hubert Work 1923
Secretary of Agriculture	Henry C. Wallace 1921
Secretary of Commerce	Herbert Hoover 1921
Secretary of Labor	James J. Davis 1921

COOLIDGE

Secretary of State	Charles E. Hughes (Cont.)
	Frank B. Kellogg 1925
Secretary of the Treasury	Andrew W. Mellon (Cont.)
Secretary of War	John W. Weeks (Cont.)
	Dwight F. Davis 1925
Attorney General	Harry M. Daughtery (Cont.)
	Harlan F. Stone 1924
	John G. Sargent 1925
Postmaster General	
	Harry S. New (Cont.)
Secretary of the Navy	Edwin Denby (Cont.)
	Curtis D. Wilbur 1924
Secretary of the Interior	Hubert Work (Cont.)
	Roy O. West 1928
Secretary of Agriculture	Henry C. Wallace (Cont.)
	Howard M. Gore 1924
	William M. Jardine 1925
Secretary of Commerce	Herbert Hoover (Cont.)
	William F. Whiting 1928
Secretary of Labor	James J. Davis (Cont.)

HOOVER

Secretary of State	Frank B. Kellogg (Cont.)
	Henry L. Stimson 1929
Secretary of the Treasury	Andrew W. Mellon (Cont.)
	Ogden L. Mills 1932
Secretary of War	James W. Good 1929
	Patrick J. Hurley 1929
Attorney General	William D. Mitchell 1929
Postmaster General	Walter F. Brown 1929
Secretary of the Navy	Charles F. Adams 1929
Secretary of the Interior	Ray Lyman Wilbur 1929
Secretary of Agriculture	Arthur M. Hyde 1929
Secretary of Commerce	Robert P. Lamont 1929
	Roy D. Chapin 1932
Secretary of Labor	James J. Davis (Cont.)
	William N. Doak 1930

F. D. ROOSEVELT

Secretary of State	Cordell Hull 1933
	E. R. Stettinius, Jr. 1944
Secretary of the Treasury	William H. Woodin 1933
	Henry Morgenthau, Jr. 1934
Secretary of War	George H. Dern 1933
	Harry H. Woodring 1936
	Henry L. Stimson 1940
Attorney General	Homer S. Cummings 1933
	Frank Murphy 1939
	Robert H. Jackson 1940
	Francis Biddle 1941
Postmaster General	James A. Farley 1933
	Frank C. Walker 1940
Secretary of the Navy	Claude A. Swanson 1933
	Charles Edison 1940
	Frank Knox 1940
	James Forrestal 1944
Secretary of the Interior	Harold L. Ickes 1933
Secretary of Agriculture	Henry A. Wallace 1933
	Claude R. Wickard 1940
Secretary of Commerce	Daniel C. Roper 1933
	Harry L. Hopkins 1938
	Jesse H. Jones 1940
	Henry A. Wallace 1945
Secretary of Labor	Frances Perkins 1933

TRUMAN

Secretary of State	E. R. Stettinius, Jr. (Cont.)
	James F. Byrnes 1945
	George C. Marshall 1947
	Dean Acheson 1949
Secretary of the Treasury	Henry Morgenthau, Jr. (Cont.)
	Frederick M. Vinson 1945
	John W. Snyder 1946
Secretary of Defense	James Forrestal 1947

	Louis A. Johnson 1949
	George C. Marshall 1950
	Robert A. Lovett 1951
Attorney General	Francis Biddle (Cont.)
	Tom C. Clark 1945
	J. Howard McGrath 1949
	James P. McGranery 1952
Postmaster General	Frank C. Walker (Cont.)
	Robert E. Hannegan 1945
	Jesse M. Donaldson 1947
Secretary of the Interior	Harold L. Ickes (Cont.)
	Julius A. Krug 1946
	Oscar L. Chapman 1949
Secretary of Agriculture	Claude R. Wickard (Cont.)
	Clinton P. Anderson 1945
	Charles F. Brannan 1948
Secretary of Commerce	Henry A. Wallace (Cont.)
	W. Averell Harriman 1946
	Charles Sawyer 1948
Secretary of Labor	Frances Perkins (Cont.)
	Lewis B. Schwellenbach 1945
	Maurice J. Tobin 1948
Secretary of War [2]	Henry L. Stimson (Cont.)
	Robert P. Patterson 1945
	Kenneth C. Royall 1947
Secretary of the Navy [2]	James Forrestal 1945

EISENHOWER

Secretary of State	John Foster Dulles 1953
	Christian A. Herter 1959
Secretary of the Treasury	George M. Humphrey 1953
	Robert B. Anderson 1957
Secretary of Defense	Charles E. Wilson 1953
	Neil H. McElroy 1957
	Thomas S. Gates, Jr. 1959
Attorney General	Herbert Brownell, Jr. 1953
	William P. Rogers 1958
Postmaster General	Arthur E. Summerfield 1953
Secretary of the Interior	Douglas McKay 1953
	Frederick A. Seaton 1956
Secretary of Agriculture	Ezra Taft Benson 1953
Secretary of Commerce	Sinclair Weeks 1953
	Lewis L. Strauss[3] 1958
	Frederick H. Mueller 1959
Secretary of Labor	Martin P. Durkin 1953
	James P. Mitchell 1953
Secretary of Health, Education, and Welfare	Oveta Culp Hobby 1953
	Marion B. Folsom 1955
	Arthur S. Flemming 1958

KENNEDY

Secretary of State	Dean Rusk 1961
Secretary of the Treasury	C. Douglas Dillon 1961
Secretary of Defense	Robert S. McNamara 1961
Attorney General	Robert F. Kennedy 1961
Postmaster General	J. Edward Day 1961
	John A. Gronouski 1963
Secretary of the Interior	Stewart L. Udall 1961
Secretary of Agriculture	Orville L. Freeman 1961
Secretary of Commerce	Luther H. Hodges 1961
Secretary of Labor	Arthur J. Goldberg 1961
	W. Willard Wirtz 1962
Secretary of Health, Education, and Welfare	Abraham A. Ribicoff 1961
	Anthony J. Celebrezze 1962

L. B. JOHNSON

Secretary of State	Dean Rusk (Cont.)
Secretary of the Treasury	C. Douglas Dillon (Cont.)
	Henry H. Fowler 1965
	Joseph W. Barr[4] 1968
Secretary of Defense	Robert S. McNamara (Cont.)
	Clark M. Clifford 1968
Attorney General	Robert F. Kennedy (Cont.)
	N. de B. Katzenbach 1965
	Ramsey Clark 1967
Postmaster General	John A. Gronouski (Cont.)
	Lawrence F. O'Brien 1965
	W. Marvin Watson 1968
Secretary of the Interior	Stewart L. Udall (Cont.)
Secretary of Agriculture	Orville L. Freeman (Cont.)
Secretary of Commerce	Luther H. Hodges (Cont.)
	John T. Connor 1964

	A. B. Trowbridge 1967
	C. R. Smith 1968
Secretary of Labor	W. Willard Wirtz (Cont.)
Secretary of Health, Education, and Welfare	Anthony J. Celebrezze (Cont.)
	John W. Gardner 1965
	Wilbur J. Cohen 1968
Secretary of Housing and Urban Development	Robert C. Weaver 1966
	Robert C. Wood[4] 1969
Secretary of Transportation	Alan S. Boyd 1966

NIXON

Secretary of State	William P. Rogers 1969
	Henry A. Kissinger 1973
Secretary of the Treasury	David M. Kennedy 1969
	John B. Connally 1971
	George P. Shultz 1972
	William E. Simon 1974
Secretary of Defense	Melvin R. Laird 1969
	Elliot L. Richardson 1973
	James R. Schlesinger 1973
Attorney General	John N. Mitchell 1969
	Richard G. Kleindienst 1972
	Elliot L. Richardson 1973
	William B. Saxbe 1974
Postmaster General[5]	William M. Blount 1969
Secretary of the Interior	Walter J. Hickel 1969
	Rogers C. B. Morton 1971
Secretary of Agriculture	Clifford M. Hardin 1969
	Earl L. Butz 1971
Secretary of Commerce	Maurice H. Stans 1969
	Peter G. Peterson 1972
	Frederick B. Dent 1973
Secretary of Labor	George P. Shultz 1969
	James D. Hodgson 1970
	Peter J. Brennan 1973
Secretary of Health, Education, and Welfare	Robert H. Finch 1969
	Elliot L. Richardson 1970
	Caspar W. Weinberger 1973
Secretary of Housing and Urban Development	George Romney 1969
	James T. Lynn 1973
Secretary of Transportation	John A. Volpe 1969
	Claude S. Brinegar 1973

FORD

Secretary of State	Henry A. Kissinger (Cont.)
Secretary of the Treasury	William E. Simon (Cont.)
Secretary of Defense	James R. Schlesinger (Cont.)
	Donald H. Rumsfeld 1975
Attorney General	William B. Saxbe (Cont.)
	Edward H. Levi 1975
Secretary of the Interior	Rogers C. B. Morton (Cont.)
	Stanley K. Hathaway 1975
	Thomas S. Kleppe 1975
Secretary of Agriculture	Earl L. Butz (Cont.)
	John Knebel 1976
Secretary of Commerce	Frederick B. Dent (Cont.)
	Rogers C. B. Morton 1975
	Elliot L. Richardson 1976
Secretary of Labor	Peter J. Brennan (Cont.)
	John T. Dunlop 1975
	William J. Usery, Jr. 1976
Secretary of Health, Education, and Welfare	Caspar W. Weinberger (Cont.)
	F. David Mathews 1975
Secretary of Housing and Urban Development	James T. Lynn (Cont.)
	Carla A. Hills 1975
Secretary of Transportation	Claude S. Brinegar (Cont.)
	William T. Coleman, Jr. 1975

CARTER

Secretary of State	Cyrus R. Vance 1977
	Edmund S. Muskie 1980
Secretary of the Treasury	W. Michael Blumenthal 1977
	G. William Miller 1979
Secretary of Defense	Harold Brown 1977
Attorney General	Griffin B. Bell 1977
	Benjamin R. Civiletti 1979
Secretary of the Interior	Cecil D. Andrus 1977
Secretary of Agriculture	Bob S. Bergland 1977
Secretary of Commerce	Juanita M. Kreps 1977
	Philip M. Klutznick 1979
Secretary of Labor	F. Ray Marshall 1977
Secretary of Health and Human Services[6]	Joseph A. Califano, Jr. 1977
	Patricia Roberts Harris 1979
Secretary of Housing and Urban Development	Patricia Roberts Harris 1977
	Moon Landrieu 1979
Secretary of Transportation	Brock Adams 1977
	Neil E. Goldschmidt 1979
Secretary of Energy	James R. Schlesinger 1977
	Charles W. Duncan, Jr. 1979
Secretary of Education	Shirley Mount Hufstedler 1979

REAGAN

Secretary of State	Alexander M. Haig, Jr. 1981
	George P. Shultz 1982
Secretary of the Treasury	Donald T. Regan 1981
	James A. Baker 3rd 1985
	Nicholas F. Brady 1988
Secretary of Defense	Caspar W. Weinberger 1981
	Frank C. Carlucci 1987
Attorney General	William French Smith 1981
	Edwin Meese 3rd 1985
	Richard L. Thornburgh 1988
Secretary of the Interior	James G. Watt 1981
	William P. Clark 1983
	Donald P. Hodel 1985
Secretary of Agriculture	John R. Block 1981
	Richard E. Lyng 1986
Secretary of Commerce	Malcolm Baldrige 1981
	C. William Verity, Jr. 1987
Secretary of Labor	Raymond J. Donovan 1981
	William E. Brock 1985
	Ann Dore McLaughlin 1987
Secretary of Health and Human Services	Richard S. Schweiker 1981
	Margaret M. Heckler 1983
	Otis R. Bowen 1985
Secretary of Housing and Urban Development	Samuel R. Pierce, Jr. 1981
Secretary of Transportation	Andrew L. Lewis, Jr. 1981
	Elizabeth H. Dole 1983
	James H. Burnley 4th 1987
Secretary of Energy	James B. Edwards 1981
	Donald P. Hodel 1983
	John S. Herrington 1985
Secretary of Education	T. H. Bell 1981
	William J. Bennett 1985
	Lauro F. Cavazos 1988

BUSH

Secretary of State	James A. Baker 3d 1989
Secretary of the Treasury	Nicholas F. Brady (Cont.)
Secretary of Defense	Richard Cheney 1989
Attorney General	Richard L. Thornburgh (Cont.)
	William P. Barr (acting)
Secretary of the Interior	Manuel Lujan Jr. 1989
Secretary of Agriculture	Clayton K. Yeutter 1989
	Edward Madigan 1991
Secretary of Commerce	Robert A. Mosbacher Sr. 1989
Secretary of Labor	Elizabeth H. Dole 1989
	Lynn Martin 1991
Secretary of Health and Human Services	Louis W. Sullivan 1989
Secretary of Housing and Urban Development	Jack F. Kemp 1989
Secretary of Transportation	Samuel K. Skinner 1989
Secretary of Energy	James D. Watkins 1989
Secretary of Education	Lauro F. Cavazos (Cont.)
	Lamar Alexander 1991
Secretary of Veterans Affairs	Edward J. Derwinski 1989

1. The Postmaster General did not become a Cabinet member until 1829. Earlier Postmasters General were: Samuel Osgood (1789), Timothy Pickering (1791), Joseph Habersham (1795), Gideon Granger (1801), Return J. Meigs, Jr. (1814), and John McLean (1823). 2. On July 26, 1947, the Departments of War and of the Navy were incorporated into the Department of Defense. 3. Not confirmed by the Senate. 4. Recess appointment. 5. The Postmaster General is no longer a Cabinet member. 6. Known as Department of Health, Education, and Welfare until May 1980.

Figures and Legends in American Folklore

Appleseed, Johnny (John Chapman, 1774–1847): Massachusetts-born nurseryman; reputed to have spread seeds and seedlings from which rose orchards of the Midwest.

Billy the Kid (William H. Bonney, 1859–1881): New York-born desperado; killed his first man before he reached his teens; after short life of crime in Wild West, was gunned down by Sheriff Pat Garrett; symbol of lawless West.

Boone, Daniel (1734–1820): Frontiersman and Indian fighter, about whom legends of early America have been built; figured in Byron's *Don Juan.*

Brodie, Steve (1863–1901): Reputed to have dived off Brooklyn Bridge on July 23, 1886. (Whether he actually did so has never been proved.)

Buffalo Bill (William F. Cody, 1846–1917): Buffalo hunter and Indian scout; much of legend about him and Wild West stems from his own Wild West show, which he operated in late 19th century.

Bunyan, Paul: Mythical lumberjack; subject of tall tales throughout timber country (that he dug Grand Canyon, for example).

Crockett, David (1786–1836): Frontiersman and member of U.S. Congress, about whom legends have been built of heroic feats; died in defense of Alamo.

Fritchie (or Frietchie), Barbara: Symbol of patriotism; in ballad by John Greenleaf Whittier, 90-year-old Barbara Fritchie defiantly waves Stars and Stripes as "Stonewall" Jackson's Confederate troops march through Frederick, Md.

James, Jesse (1847–1882): Bank and train robber; folklore has given him quality of American Robin Hood.

Jones, Casey (John Luther Jones, 1863–1900): Example of heroic locomotive engineer given to feats of prowess; died in wreck with his hand on brake lever when his Illinois Central "Cannonball" express hit freight train at Vaughan, Miss.

Ross, Betsy (1752–1836): Member of Philadelphia flag-making family; reported to have designed and sewn first American flag. (Report is without confirmation.)

Uncle Sam: Personification of United States and its people; origin uncertain; may be based on inspector of government supplies in Revolutionary War and War of 1812.

Assassinations and Attempts in U. S. Since 1865

Cermak, Anton J. (Mayor of Chicago): Shot Feb. 15, 1933, in Miami by Giuseppe Zangara, who attempted to assassinate Franklin D. Roosevelt; Cermak died March 6.

Ford, Gerald R. (President of U.S.): Escaped assassination attempt Sept. 5, 1975, in Sacramento, Calif., by Lynette Alice (Squeaky) Fromm, who pointed but did not fire .45-caliber pistol. Escaped assassination attempt in San Francisco, Calif., Sept. 22, 1975, by Sara Jane Moore, who fired one shot from a .38-caliber pistol that was deflected.

Garfield, James A. (President of U.S.): Shot July 2, 1881, in Washington, D.C., by Charles J. Guiteau; died Sept. 19.

Jordan, Vernon E., Jr. (civil rights leader): Shot and critically wounded in assassination attempt May 29, 1980, in Fort Wayne, Ind.

Kennedy, John F. (President of U.S.): Shot Nov. 22, 1963, in Dallas, Tex., allegedly by Lee Harvey Oswald; died same day. Injured was Gov. John B. Connally of Texas. Oswald was shot and killed two days later by Jack Ruby.

Kennedy, Robert F. (U.S. Senator from New York): Shot June 5, 1968, in Los Angeles by Sirhan Bishara Sirhan; died June 6.

King, Martin Luther, Jr. (civil rights leader): Shot April 4, 1968, in Memphis by James Earl Ray; died same day.

Lincoln, Abraham (President of U.S.): Shot April 14, 1865, in Washington, D.C., by John Wilkes Booth; died April 15.

Long, Huey P. (U.S. Senator from Louisiana): Shot Sept. 8, 1935, in Baton Rouge by Dr. Carl A. Weiss; died Sept. 10.

McKinley, William (President of U.S.): Shot Sept. 6, 1901, in Buffalo by Leon Czolgosz; died Sept. 14.

Reagan, Ronald (President of U.S.): Shot in left lung in Washington by John W. Hinckley, Jr., on March 30, 1981; three others also wounded.

Roosevelt, Franklin D. (President-elect of U.S.): Escaped assassination unhurt Feb. 15, 1933, in Miami. *See* Cermak.

Roosevelt, Theodore (ex-President of U.S.): Escaped assassination (though shot) Oct. 14, 1912, in Milwaukee while campaigning for President.

Seward, William H. (Secretary of State): Escaped assassination (though injured) April 14, 1865, in Washington, D.C., by Lewis Powell (or Paine), accomplice of John Wilkes Booth.

Truman, Harry S. (President of U.S.): Escaped assassination unhurt Nov. 1, 1950, in Washington, D.C., as 2 Puerto Rican nationalists attempted to shoot their way into Blair House.

Wallace, George C. (Governor of Alabama): Shot and critically wounded in assassination attempt May 15, 1972, at Laurel, Md., by Arthur Herman Bremer. Wallace paralyzed from waist down.

Impeachments of Federal Officials

Source: Congressional Directory

The procedure for the impeachment of Federal officials is detailed in Article I, Section 3, of the Constitution. See Index

The Senate has sat as a court of impeachment in

the following cases:

William Blount, Senator from Tennessee; charges dismissed for want of jurisdiction, January 14, 1799.
John Pickering, Judge of the U.S. District Court for New Hampshire; removed from office March 12, 1804.
Samuel Chase, Associate Justice of the Supreme Court; acquitted March 1, 1805.
James H. Peck, Judge of the U.S. District Court for Missouri; acquitted Jan. 31, 1831.
West H. Humphreys, Judge of the U.S. District Court for the middle, eastern, and western districts of Tennessee; removed from office June 26, 1862.
Andrew Johnson, President of the United States; acquitted May 26, 1868.
William W. Belknap, Secretary of War; acquitted Aug. 1, 1876.
Charles Swayne, Judge of the U.S. District Court for the northern district of Florida; acquitted Feb. 27, 1905.

Robert W. Archbald, Associate Judge, U.S. Commerce Court; removed Jan. 13, 1913.
George W. English, Judge of the U.S. District Court for eastern district of Illinois; resigned Nov. 4, 1926; proceedings dismissed.
Harold Louderback, Judge of the U.S. District Court for the northern district of California; acquitted May 24, 1933.
Halsted L. Ritter, Judge of the U.S. District Court for the southern district of Florida; removed from office April 17, 1936.
Harry E. Claiborne, Judge of the U.S. District Court for the district of Nevada; removed from office October 9, 1986.
Alcee L. Hastings, Judge of the U.S. District Court for the southern district of Florida; removed from office October 20, 1989.
Walter L. Nixon, Jr., Judge of the U.S. District Court for Mississippi; removed from office November 3, 1989.

Members of the Supreme Court of the United States

Name; apptd. from	Service		Birth		Died	Religion
	Term	Yrs	Place	Date		
CHIEF JUSTICES						
John Jay, N.Y.	1789–1795	5	N.Y.	1745	1829	Episcopal
John Rutledge, S.C.	1795	0	S.C.	1739	1800	Church of England
Oliver Ellsworth, Conn.	1796–1800	4	Conn.	1745	1807	Congregational
John Marshall, Va.	1801–1835	34	Va.	1755	1835	Episcopal
Roger B. Taney, Md.	1836–1864	28	Md.	1777	1864	Roman Catholic
Salmon P. Chase, Ohio	1864–1873	8	N.H.	1808	1873	Episcopal
Morrison R. Waite, Ohio	1874–1888	14	Conn.	1816	1888	Episcopal
Melville W. Fuller, Ill.	1888–1910	21	Me.	1833	1910	Episcopal
Edward D. White, La.	1910–1921	10	La.	1845	1921	Roman Catholic
William H. Taft, Conn.	1921–1930	8	Ohio	1857	1930	Unitarian
Charles E. Hughes, N.Y.	1930–1941	11	N.Y.	1862	1948	Baptist
Harlan F. Stone, N.Y.	1941–1946	4	N.H.	1872	1946	Episcopal
Frederick M. Vinson, Ky.	1946–1953	7	Ky.	1890	1953	Methodist
Earl Warren, Calif.	1953–1969	15	Calif.	1891	1974	Protestant
Warren E. Burger, Va.	1969–1986	17	Minn.	1907	—	Presbyterian
William H. Rehnquist, Ariz.	1986–		Wis.	1924	—	Lutheran
ASSOCIATE JUSTICES						
James Wilson, Pa.	1789–1798	8	Scotland	1742	1798	Episcopal
John Rutledge, S.C.	1790–1791	1	S.C.	1739	1800	Church of England
William Cushing, Mass.	1790–1810	20	Mass.	1732	1810	Unitarian
John Blair, Va.	1790–1796	5	Va.	1732	1800	Presbyterian
James Iredell, N.C.	1790–1799	9	England	1751	1799	Episcopal
Thomas Johnson, Md.	1792–1793	0	Md.	1732	1819	Episcopal
William Paterson, N.J.	1793–1806	13	Ireland	1745	1806	Protestant
Samuel Chase, Md.	1796–1811	15	Md.	1741	1811	Episcopal
Bushrod Washington, Va.	1799–1829	30	Va.	1762	1829	Episcopal
Alfred Moore, N.C.	1800–1804	3	N.C.	1755	1810	Episcopal
William Johnson, S.C.	1804–1834	30	S.C.	1771	1834	Presbyterian
Brockholst Livingston, N.Y.	1807–1823	16	N.Y.	1757	1823	Presbyterian
Thomas Todd, Ky.	1807–1826	18	Va.	1765	1826	Presbyterian
Gabriel Duval, Md.	1811–1835	23	Md.	1752	1844	French Protestant
Joseph Story, Mass.	1812–1845	33	Mass.	1779	1845	Unitarian
Smith Thompson, N.Y.	1823–1843	20	N.Y.	1768	1843	Presbyterian
Robert Trimble, Ky.	1826–1828	2	Va.	1777	1828	Protestant
John McLean, Ohio	1830–1861	31	N.J.	1785	1861	Methodist-Epis.
Henry Baldwin, Pa.	1830–1844	14	Conn.	1780	1844	Trinity Church
James M. Wayne, Ga.	1835–1867	32	Ga.	1790	1867	Protestant
Philip P. Barbour, Va.	1836–1841	4	Va.	1783	1841	Episcopal
John Catron, Tenn.	1837–1865	28	Pa.	1786	1865	Presbyterian
John McKinley, Ala.	1837–1852	14	Va.	1780	1852	Protestant
Peter V. Daniel, Va.	1841–1860	18	Va.	1784	1860	Episcopal
Samuel Nelson, N.Y.	1845–1872	27	N.Y.	1792	1873	Protestant
Levi Woodbury, N.H.	1845–1851	5	N.H.	1789	1851	Protestant
Robert C. Grier, Pa.	1846–1870	23	Pa.	1794	1870	Presbyterian

Name; apptd. from	Service Term	Yrs	Brith Place	Date	Died	Religion
Benjamin R. Curtis, Mass.	1851–1857	5	Mass.	1809	1874	([2])
John A. Campbell, Ala.	1853–1861	8	Ga.	1811	1889	Episcopal
Nathan Clifford, Maine	1858–1881	23	N.H.	1803	1881	([1])
Noah H. Swayne, Ohio	1862–1881	18	Va.	1804	1884	Quaker
Samuel F. Miller, Iowa	1862–1890	28	Ky.	1816	1890	Unitarian
David Davis, Ill.	1862–1877	14	Md.	1815	1886	([4])
Stephen J. Field, Calif.	1863–1897	34	Conn.	1816	1899	Episcopal
William Strong, Pa.	1870–1880	10	Conn.	1808	1895	Presbyterian
Joseph P. Bradley, N.J.	1870–1892	21	N.Y.	1813	1892	Presbyterian
Ward Hunt, N.Y.	1872–1882	9	N.Y.	1810	1886	Episcopal
John M. Harlan, Ky.	1877–1911	33	Ky.	1833	1911	Presbyterian
William B. Woods, Ga.	1880–1887	6	Ohio	1824	1887	Protestant
Stanley Matthews, Ohio	1881–1889	7	Ohio	1824	1889	Presbyterian
Horace Gray, Mass.	1882–1902	20	Mass.	1828	1902	([3])
Samuel Blatchford, N.Y.	1882–1893	11	N.Y.	1820	1893	Presbyterian
Lucius Q. C. Lamar, Miss.	1888–1893	5	Ga.	1825	1893	Methodist
David J. Brewer, Kan.	1889–1910	20	Asia Minor	1837	1910	Protestant
Henry B. Brown, Mich.	1890–1906	15	Mass.	1836	1913	Protestant
George Shiras, Jr., Pa.	1892–1903	10	Pa.	1832	1924	Presbyterian
Howell E. Jackson, Tenn.	1893–1895	2	Tenn.	1832	1895	Baptist
Edward D. White, La.	1894–1910	16	La.	1845	1921	Roman Catholic
Rufus W. Peckham, N.Y.	1895–1909	13	N.Y.	1838	1909	Episcopal
Joseph McKenna, Calif.	1898–1925	26	Pa.	1843	1926	Roman Catholic
Oliver W. Holmes, Mass.	1902–1932	29	Mass.	1841	1935	Unitarian
William R. Day, Ohio	1903–1922	19	Ohio	1849	1923	Protestant
William H. Moody, Mass.	1906–1910	3	Mass.	1853	1917	Episcopal
Horace H. Lurton, Tenn.	1909–1914	4	Ky.	1844	1914	EpiscopalCharles
E. Hughes, N.Y.	1910–1916	5	N.Y.	1862	1948	Baptist
Willis Van Devanter, Wyo.	1910–1937	26	Ind.	1859	1941	Episcopal
Joseph R. Lamar, Ga.	1910–1916	4	Ga.	1857	1916	Ch. of Disciples
Mahlon Pitney, N.J.	1912–1922	10	N.J.	1858	1924	Presbyterian
James C. McReynolds, Tenn.	1914–1941	26	Ky.	1862	1946	Disciples of Christ
Louis D. Brandeis, Mass.	1916–1939	22	Ky.	1856	1941	Jewish
John H. Clarke, Ohio	1916–1922	5	Ohio	1857	1945	Protestant
George Sutherland, Utah	1922–1938	15	England	1862	1942	Episcopal
Pierce Butler, Minn.	1923–1939	16	Minn.	1866	1939	Roman Catholic
Edward T. Sanford, Tenn.	1923–1930	7	Tenn.	1865	1930	Episcopal
Harlan F. Stone, N.Y.	1925–1941	16	N.H.	1872	1946	Episcopal
Owen J. Roberts, Pa.	1930–1945	15	Pa.	1875	1955	Episcopal
Benjamin N. Cardozo, N.Y.	1932–1938	6	N.Y.	1870	1938	Jewish
Hugo L. Black, Ala.	1937–1971	34	Ala.	1886	1971	Baptist
Stanley F. Reed, Ky.	1938–1957	19	Ky.	1884	1980	Protestant
Felix Frankfurter, Mass.	1939–1962	23	Austria	1882	1965	Jewish
William O. Douglas, Conn.	1939–1975	36	Minn.	1898	1980	Presbyterian
Frank Murphy, Mich.	1940–1949	9	Mich.	1890	1949	Roman Catholic
James F. Byrnes, S.C.	1941–1942	1	S.C.	1879	1972	Episcopal
Robert H. Jackson, Pa.	1941–1954	13	N.Y.	1892	1954	Episcopal
Wiley B. Rutledge, Iowa	1943–1949	6	Ky.	1894	1949	Unitarian
Harold H. Burton, Ohio	1945–1958	13	Mass.	1888	1964	Unitarian
Tom C. Clark, Tex.	1949–1967	17	Tex.	1899	1977	Presbyterian
Sherman Minton, Ind.	1949–1956	7	Ind.	1890	1965	Roman Catholic
John M. Harlan, N.Y.	1955–1971	16	Ill.	1899	1971	Presbyterian
William J. Brennan, Jr., N.J.	1956–1990	33	N.J.	1906	—	Roman Catholic
Charles E. Whittaker, Mo.	1957–1962	5	Kan.	1901	1973	Methodist
Potter Stewart, Ohio	1958–1981	23	Mich.	1915	1985	Episcopal
Byron R. White, Colo.	1962–	—	Colo.	1917	—	Episcopal
Arthur J. Goldberg, Ill.	1962–1965	2	Ill.	1908	—	Jewish
Abe Fortas, Tenn.	1965–1969	3	Tenn.	1910	1982	Jewish
Thurgood Marshall, N.Y.[5]	1967–1991	24	Md.	1908	—	Episcopalian
Harry A. Blackmun, Minn.	1970–	—	Ill.	1908	—	Methodist
Lewis F. Powell, Jr., Va.	1972–1987	15	Va.	1907	—	Presbyterian
William H. Rehnquist, Ariz.	1972–1986	14	Wis.	1924	—	Lutheran
John Paul Stevens, Ill.	1975–	—	Ill.	1920	—	Protestant
Sandra Day O'Connor, Ariz.	1981–	—	Tex.	1930	—	Episcopal
Antonin Scalia, D.C.	1986–	—	N.J.	1936	—	Roman Catholic
Anthony M. Kennedy, Calif.	1988–	—	Calif.	1936	—	n.a.
David H. Souter, N.H.	1990–	—	Mass.	1939	—	Episcopalian

1. Congregational; later Unitarian. 2. Unitarian; then Episcopal. 3. Unitarian or Congregational. 4. Not a member of any church. 5. Clarence Thomas nominated to fill vacancy. *See* Current Events for confirmation or another nomination.
NOTE: n.a. = not available.

Executive Departments and Agencies

Source: Congressional Directory, 1991–1992
Unless otherwise indicated, addresses shown are in Washington, D.C.

CENTRAL INTELLIGENCE AGENCY (CIA)
Washington, D.C. (20505).
Established: 1947.
Director: Vacancy.[1]

COUNCIL OF ECONOMIC ADVISERS (CEA)
Room 314, Old Executive Office Bldg. (20500).
Members: 3.
Established: Feb. 20, 1946.
Chairman: Michael J. Boskin.

COUNCIL ON ENVIRONMENTAL QUALITY
722 Jackson Pl., N.W. (20503).
Members: 3.
Established: 1969.
Chairman: Michael R. Deland.

NATIONAL SECURITY COUNCIL (NSC)
Old Executive Office Bldg. (20506).
Members: 4.
Established: July 26, 1947.
Chairman: The President.
Other members: Vice President; Secretary of State; Secretary of Defense.

OFFICE OF ADMINISTRATION
Old Executive Office Bldg. (20500).
Established: Dec. 12, 1977.
Director: Paul Bateman.

OFFICE OF MANAGEMENT AND BUDGET
Old Executive Office Bldg. (20503).
Established: July 1, 1970.
Director: Richard Darman.

OFFICE OF SCIENCE AND TECHNOLOGY POLICY
Executive Office Building (20506).
Established: May 11, 1976.
Director: D. Allan Bromley.

OFFICE OF THE UNITED STATES TRADE REPRESENTATIVE
600 17th St., N.W. (20506).
Established: Jan. 15, 1963.
Trade Representative: Carla A. Hills.

OFFICE OF POLICY DEVELOPMENT
1600 Pennsylvania Ave., N.W. (20500).
Established: Jan. 21, 1981.
Director: William L. Roper.

OFFICE OF NATIONAL DRUG CONTROL POLICY
Suite 1011, 1825 Connecticut Ave., N.W. (20009).
Established: March 13, 1989.
Director: Robert Martinez.

Executive Departments

DEPARTMENT OF STATE
2201 C St., N.W. (20520).
Established: 1781 as Department of Foreign Affairs; reconstituted, 1789, following adoption of Constitution; name changed to Department of State Sept. 15, 1789.
Secretary: James A. Baker III.
Deputy Secretary: Lawrence S. Eagleburger.
Chief Delegate to U.N.: Thomas R. Pickering.

DEPARTMENT OF THE TREASURY
15th St. & Pennsylvania Ave., N.W. (20220).
Established: Sept. 2, 1789.
Secretary: Nicholas F. Brady.
Deputy Secretary: John E. Robson.
Treasurer of the U.S.: Catalina Vasquez Villalpando.
Comptroller of the Currency: Robert L. Clarke.

DEPARTMENT OF DEFENSE
The Pentagon (20301).
Established: July 26, 1947, as National Department Establishment; name changed to Department of Defense on Aug. 10, 1949. Subordinate to Secretary of Defense are Secretaries of Army, Navy, Air Force.
Secretary: Richard Cheney.
Deputy Secretary: Donald J. Atwood.
Secretary of Army: Michael P.W. Stone
Secretary of Navy: H. Lawrence Garrett III.
Secretary of Air Force: Donald B. Rice.
Commandant of Marine Corps: Gen. Alfred M. Gray.
Joint Chiefs of Staff: Gen. Colin L. Powell, Chairman; Adm. Frank B. Kelso II, Navy; Gen. Merrill A. McPeak, Air Force; Gen. Gordon Russell Sullivan, Army; Lt. Gen. Carl E. Mundy, Jr., Marine Corps.

DEPARTMENT OF JUSTICE
Constitution Ave. between 9th & 10th Sts., N.W. (20530).
Established: Office of Attorney General was created Sept. 24, 1789. Although he was one of original Cabinet members, he was not executive department head until June 22, 1870, when Department of Justice was established.
Attorney General: William P. Barr (acting).
Deputy Attorney General: Vacancy.
Solicitor General: Kenneth W. Starr.
Director of FBI: William Steele Sessions.

DEPARTMENT OF THE INTERIOR
C St. between 18th & 19th Sts., N.W. (20240).
Established: March 3, 1849.
Secretary: Manuel Lujan, Jr.
Under Secretary: Frank A. Bracken.

DEPARTMENT OF AGRICULTURE
Independence Ave. between 12th & 14th Sts., S.W. (20250).
Established: May 15, 1862. Administered by Commissioner of Agriculture until 1889, when it was made executive department.
Secretary: Edward Madigan.
Deputy Secretary: Ann M. Veneman.

DEPARTMENT OF COMMERCE
14th St. between Constitution Ave. & E St., N.W. (20230).
Established: Department of Commerce and Labor was created Feb. 14, 1903. On March 4, 1913, all labor activities were transferred out of Department of Commerce and Labor and it was renamed Department of Commerce.
Secretary: Robert A. Mosbacher.
Deputy Secretary: Rockwell Schnabel.

DEPARTMENT OF LABOR
200 Constitution Ave., N.W. (20210).
Established: Bureau of Labor was created in 1884 under Department of the Interior; later became independent department without executive rank. Returned to bureau status in Department of Commerce and Labor, but on March 4, 1913, became independent executive department under its present name.
Secretary: Lynn Morley Martin.
Deputy Secretary: Roderick DeArment.

DEPARTMENT OF HEALTH AND HUMAN SERVICES[1]
200 Independence Ave., S.W. (20201).
Established: April 11, 1953, replacing Federal Security Agency created in 1939.

Secretary: Louis W. Sullivan.
Surgeon General: Dr. Antonia Novello.
1. Originally Department of Health, Education and Welfare. Name changed in May 1980 when Department of Education was activated.

DEPARTMENT OF HOUSING AND URBAN DEVELOPMENT
451 7th St., S.W. (20410).
Established: 1965, replacing Housing and Home Finance Agency created in 1947.
Secretary: Jack Kemp.
Under Secretary: Alfred A. Dellibovi.

DEPARTMENT OF TRANSPORTATION
400 7th St., S.W. (20590).
Established: Oct. 15, 1966, as result of Department of Transportation Act, which became effective April 1, 1967.
Secretary: Samuel K. Skinner.
Deputy Secretary: Elaine L. Chao.

DEPARTMENT OF ENERGY
1000 Independence Ave., S.W. (20585).
Established: Aug. 1977.
Secretary: James D. Watkins.
Deputy Secretary: W. Henson Moore.

DEPARTMENT OF EDUCATION
400 Maryland Avenue, S.W. (20202).
Established: Oct. 17, 1979.
Secretary: Lamar Alexander.
Under Secretary: Ted Sanders.

DEPARTMENT OF VETERANS' AFFAIRS
810 Vermont Avenue, N.W. (20420).
Established: March 15, 1989, replacing Veterans Administration created in 1930.
Secretary: Edward J. Derwinski.
Deputy Secretary: Anthony J. Principi.

Major Independent Agencies

ACTION
1100 Vermont Ave., N.W. (20525).
Established: July 1, 1971.
Director: Jane Kenny.

CONSUMER PRODUCT SAFETY COMMISSION
5401 Westbard Ave., Bethesda, Md. (20207).
Members: 5.
Established: Oct. 27, 1972.
Chairman: Jacqueline Jones-Smith.

ENVIRONMENTAL PROTECTION AGENCY (EPA)
401 M St., S.W. (20460).
Established: Dec. 2, 1970.
Administrator: William K. Reilly.

EQUAL EMPLOYMENT OPPORTUNITY COMMISSION (EEOC)
1801 L St., N.W. (20507).
Members: 5.
Established: July 2, 1965.
Chairman: Evan J. Kemp, Jr.

FARM CREDIT ADMINISTRATION (FCA)
1501 Farm Credit Dr., McLean, Va. (22102).
Members: 13.
Established: July 17, 1916.
Chairman of Federal Farm Credit Board: Harold B. Steele.

FEDERAL COMMUNICATIONS COMMISSION (FCC)
1919 M St., N.W. (20554).
Members: 7.
Established: 1934.
Chairman: Alfred C. Silkes.

FEDERAL DEPOSIT INSURANCE CORPORATION (FDIC)
550 17th St., N.W. (20429).
Members: 3.
Established: June 16, 1933.

Chairman: L. William Seidman.

FEDERAL ELECTION COMMISSION (FEC)
999 E St., N.W. (20463).
Members: 6.
Established: 1974.
Chairman: John W. McGarry.

FEDERAL MARITIME COMMISSION
1100 L St., N.W. (20573).
Members: 5.
Established: Aug. 12, 1961.
Chairman: Christopher L. Koch.

FEDERAL MEDIATION AND CONCILIATION SERVICE (FMCS)
2100 K St., N.W. (20427).
Established: 1947.
Director: Bernard E. DeLury.

FEDERAL RESERVE SYSTEM (FRS), BOARD OF GOVERNORS OF
20th St. & Constitution Ave., N.W. (20551).
Members: 7.
Established: Dec. 23, 1913.
Chairman: Alan Greenspan.

FEDERAL TRADE COMMISSION (FTC)
Pennsylvania Ave. at 6th St., N.W. (20580).
Members: 5.
Established: Sept. 26, 1914.
Chairman: Janet D. Steiger.

GENERAL SERVICES ADMINISTRATION (GSA)
18th and F Sts., N.W. (20405).
Established: July 1, 1949.
Administrator: Richard G. Austin.

INTERSTATE COMMERCE COMMISSION (ICC)
12th St. & Constitution Ave., N.W. (20423).
Members: 7.
Established: Feb. 4, 1887.
Chairman: Edward Philbin.

NATIONAL AERONAUTICS AND SPACE ADMINISTRATION (NASA)
600 Independence Ave. (20546).
Established: 1958.
Administrator: Vice Adm. Richard H. Truly (Ret.).

NATIONAL FOUNDATION ON THE ARTS AND THE HUMANITIES
1100 Pennsylvania Ave., N.W., (20506).
Established: 1965.
Chairmen: National Endowment for the Arts, John E. Frohnmayer; National Endowment for the Humanities, Lynne V. Cheney.

NATIONAL LABOR RELATIONS BOARD (NLRB)
1717 Pennsylvania Ave., N.W. (20570).
Members: 5.
Established: July 5, 1935.
Chairman: James M. Stephens.

NATIONAL MEDIATION BOARD
Suite 910, 1425 K St., N.W. (20572).
Members: 3.
Established: June 21, 1934.
Chairman: Joshua M. Javits.

NATIONAL SCIENCE FOUNDATION (NSF)
1800 G St., N.W. (20550).
Established: 1950.
Director: Walter E. Massey.

NATIONAL TRANSPORTATION SAFETY BOARD
800 Independence Ave., S.W. (20594).
Members: 5.
Established: April 1, 1975.
Chairman: James L. Kolstad (acting).

NUCLEAR REGULATORY COMMISSION (NRC)
Rockville, Md. (20852).
Members: 5.
Established: Jan. 19, 1975.
Chairman: Kenneth Carr.

OFFICE OF PERSONNEL MANAGEMENT (OPM)
1900 E St., N.W. (20415).
  Members: 3.
  Established: Jan. 1, 1979.
  Director: Constance B. Newman.
SECURITIES AND EXCHANGE COMMISSION (SEC)
450 5th St., N.W. (20549).
  Members: 5.
  Established: July 2, 1934.
  Chairman: Richard C. Breeden.
SELECTIVE SERVICE SYSTEM (SSS)
National Headquarters 1023 31st., N.W. (20435).
  Established: Sept. 16, 1940.
  Director: Gen. Samuel K. Lessey, Jr.
SMALL BUSINESS ADMINISTRATION (SBA)
409 3rd St., N.W. (20416).
  Established: July 30, 1953.
  Administrator: Patricia Saiki.
TENNESSEE VALLEY AUTHORITY (TVA)
400 West Summit Hill Drive, Knoxville, Tenn. (37902).
Washington office: Capitol Hill Office Bldg., 412 First St., S.E. (20444).
  Members of Board of Directors: 3.
  Established: May 18, 1933.
  Chairman: Marvin Runyon.
U.S. AGENCY FOR INTERNATIONAL DEVELOPMENT
520 21st St., N.W. (20523).
  Established: Oct. 1, 1979.
  Administrator: Ronald Roskens.
U.S. ARMS CONTROL AND DISARMAMENT AGENCY
520 21st St., N.W., (20451).
  Established: Sept. 26, 1961.
  Director: Ronald F. Lehman II.
U.S. COMMISSION ON CIVIL RIGHTS
1121 Vermont Avenue, N.W. (20425).
  Members: 8.
  Established: 1957.
  Chairman: Arthur A. Fletcher.
U.S. INFORMATION AGENCY
301 Fourth St., S.W. (20547).
  Established: Aug. 1, 1953. Reorganized April 1, 1978.
  Director: Henry E. Catto (acting).
U.S. INTERNATIONAL TRADE COMMISSION
500 E St., N.W. (20436).
  Members: 6.
  Established: Sept. 8, 1916.
  Chairman: Anne E. Brunsdale (acting).
U.S. POSTAL SERVICE
475 L'Enfant Plaza West, S.W. (20260).
  Postmaster General: Anthony M. Frank.
  Deputy Postmaster General: Michael S. Coughlin.
  Established: Office of Postmaster General and temporary post office system created in 1789. Act of Feb. 20, 1792, made detailed provisions for Post Office Department. In 1970 became independent agency headed by 11-member board of governors.

Other Independent Agencies

Administrative Conference of the United States—Suite 500, 2120 L St., N.W. (20037).
American Battle Monuments Commission—5127 Pulaski Bldg. 20 Massachusetts Ave., N.W. (20314).
Appalachian Regional Commission—1666 Connecticut Ave., N.W. (20235).

Board for International Broadcasting—Suite 400, 1201 Connecticut Ave., N.W. (20036).
Commission of Fine Arts—Pension Bldg. 441 F St., N.W. (20001).
Commodity Futures Trading Commission—2033 K St., N.W. (20581).
Export-Import Bank of the United States—811 Vermont Ave., N.W. (20571).
Federal Emergency Management Agency—500 C St., S.W. (20472).
Federal Home Loan Bank Board—1700 G St., N.W. (20552).
Federal Labor Relations Authority—500 C St., S.W. (20424).
Inter-American Foundation—1515 Wilson Blvd., Arlington, Va. (22209).
Merit Systems Protection Board—1120 Vermont Ave., N.W. (20419).
National Commission on Libraries and Information Science—Suite 310, 111 18th st., N.W. (20036).
National Credit Union Administration—1776 G St., N.W. (20456).
Occupational Safety and Health Review Commission—1825 K St., N.W. (20006).
Panama Canal Commission—Suite 550, 2000 L St., N.W. (20036).
Peace Corps—1990 K St., N.W. (20526).
Pension Benefit Guaranty Corporation—2020 K St., N.W. (20006).
Postal Rate Commission—Suite 300, 1333 H St., N.W. (20268).
President's Committee on Employment of the Handicapped—1111 20th St., N.W. (20036).
President's Council on Physical Fitness and Sports—450 5th St., N.W. (20001).
Railroad Retirement Board (RRB)—844 Rush St., Chicago, Ill. (60611); Washington Liaison Office: Suite 558, 2000 L St. (20036).
U.S. Parole Commission—Room 420, 5550 Friendship Blvd., Chevy Chase, Md. (20815).

Legislative Department

Architect of the Capitol—U.S. Capitol Building (20515).
General Accounting Office (GAO)—441 G St., N.W. (20548).
Government Printing Office (GPO)—North Capitol & H Sts., N.W. (20401).
Library of Congress—10 First St. S.E. (20540).
Office of Technology Assessment—600 Pennsylvania Ave., S.E. (20510).
United States Botanic Garden—Office of Director, 245 First St., S.W. (20024).

Quasi-Official Agencies

American National Red Cross—430 17th St., N.W. (20006).
Legal Services Corporation—400 Virginia Ave. S.W. (20024).
National Academy of Sciences, National Academy of Engineering, National Research Council, Institute of Medicine—2101 Constitution Ave., N.W. (20418).
National Railroad Passenger Corporation (Amtrak)—60 Massachusetts Ave., N.E. (20002).
Smithsonian Institution—1000 Jefferson Dr., S.W. (20560).

---

1. Robert M. Gates nominated but confirmation hearings delayed until September 1991.

Biographies of the Presidents

GEORGE WASHINGTON was born on Feb. 22, 1732 (Feb. 11, 1731/2, old style) in Westmoreland County, Va. While in his teens, he trained as a surveyor, and at the age of 20 he was appointed adjutant in the Virginia militia. For the next three years, he fought in the wars against the French and Indians, serving as Gen. Edward Braddock's aide in the disastrous campaign against Fort Duquesne. In 1759, he resigned from the militia, married Martha Dandridge Custis, a widow, and settled down as a gentleman farmer at Mount Vernon, Va.

As a militiaman, Washington had been exposed to the arrogance of the British officers, and his experience as a planter with British commercial restrictions increased his anti-British sentiment. He opposed the Stamp Act of 1765 and after 1770 became increasingly prominent in organizing resistance. A delegate to the Continental Congress, Washington was selected as commander in chief of the Continental Army and took command at Cambridge, Mass., on July 3, 1775.

Inadequately supported and sometimes covertly sabotaged by the Congress, in charge of troops who were inexperienced, badly equipped, and impatient of discipline, Washington conducted the war on the policy of avoiding major engagements with the British and wearing them down by harrassing tactics. His able generalship, along with the French alliance and the growing weariness within Britain, brought the war to a conclusion with the surrender of Cornwallis at Yorktown, Va., on Oct. 19, 1781.

The chaotic years under the Articles of Confederation led Washington to return to public life in the hope of promoting the formation of a strong central government. He presided over the Constitutional Convention and yielded to the universal demand that he serve as first President. He was inaugurated on April 30, 1789, in New York, the first national capital. In office, he sought to unite the nation and establish the authority of the new government at home and abroad. Greatly distressed by the emergence of the Hamilton-Jefferson rivalry, Washington worked to maintain neutrality but actually sympathized more with Hamilton. Following his unanimous re-election in 1792, his second term was dominated by the Federalists. His Farewell Address on Sept. 17, 1796 (published but never delivered) rebuked party spirit and warned against "permanent alliances" with foreign powers.

He died at Mount Vernon on Dec. 14, 1799.

JOHN ADAMS was born on Oct. 30 (Oct. 19, old style), 1735, at Braintree (now Quincy), Mass. A Harvard graduate, he considered teaching and the ministry but finally turned to law and was admitted to the bar in 1758. Six years later, he married Abigail Smith. He opposed the Stamp Act, served as lawyer for patriots indicted by the British, and by the time of the Continental Congresses, was in the vanguard of the movement for independence. In 1778, he went to France as commissioner. Subsequently he helped negotiate the peace treaty with Britain, and in 1785 became envoy to London. Resigning in 1788, he was elected Vice President under Washington and was re-elected in 1792.

Though a Federalist, Adams did not get along with Hamilton, who sought to prevent his election to the presidency in 1796 and thereafter intrigued against his administration. In 1798, Adam's independent policy averted a war with France but completed the break with Hamilton and the right-wing Federalists; at the same time, the enactment of the Alien and Sedition Acts, directed against foreigners and against critics of the government, exasperated the Jeffersonian opposition. The split between Adams and Hamilton resulted in Jefferson's becoming the next President. Adams retired to his home in Quincy. He and Jefferson died on the same day, July 4, 1826, the 50th anniversary of the signing of the Declaration of Independence.

His *Defence of the Constitutions of Government of the United States* (1787) contains original and striking, if conservative, political ideas.

THOMAS JEFFERSON was born on April 13 (April 2, old style), 1743, at Shadwell in Goochland (now Albemarle) County, Va. A William and Mary graduate, he studied law, but from the start showed an interest in science and philosophy. His literary skill and political clarity brought him to the forefront of the revolutionary movement in Virginia. As delegate to the Continental Congress, he drafted the Declaration of Independence. In 1776, he entered the Virginia House of Delegates and initiated a comprehensive reform program for the abolition of feudal survivals in land tenure and the separation of church and state.

In 1779, he became governor, but constitutional limitations on his power, combined with his own lack of executive energy, caused an unsatisfactory administration, culminating in Jefferson's virtual abdication when the British invaded Virginia in 1781. He retired to his beautiful home at Monticello, Va., to his family. His wife, Martha Wayles Skelton, whom he married in 1772, died in 1782.

Jefferson's *Notes on Virginia* (1784-85) illustrate his many-faceted interests, his limitless intellectual curiosity, his deep faith in agrarian democracy. Sent to Congress in 1783, he helped lay down the decimal system and drafted basic reports on the organization of the western lands. In 1785 he was appointed minister to France, where the Anglo-Saxon liberalism he had drawn from John Locke, the British philosopher, was stimulated by contact with the thought that would soon ferment in the French Revolution. In 1789, Washington appointed him Secretary of State. While favoring the Constitution and a strengthened central government, Jefferson came to believe that Hamilton contemplated the establishment of a monarchy. Growing differences resulted in Jefferson's resignation on Dec. 31, 1793.

Elected vice president in 1796, Jefferson continued to serve as spiritual leader of the opposition to Federalism, particularly to the repressive Alien and Sedition Acts. He was elected President in 1801 by the House of Representatives as a result of Hamilton's decision to throw the Federalist votes to him rather than to Aaron Burr, who had tied him in electoral votes. He was the first President to be inaugurated in Washington, which he had helped to design.

The purchase of Louisiana from France in 1803, though in violation of Jefferson's earlier constitutional scruples, was the most notable act of his administration. Re-elected in 1804, with the Federalist Charles C. Pinckney opposing him, Jefferson tried desperately to keep the United States out of the Napoleonic Wars in Europe, employing to this end the unpopular embargo policy.

After his retirement to Monticello in 1809, he developed his interest in education, founding the University of Virginia and watching its development with never-flagging interest. He died at Monticello on July 4, 1826. Jefferson had an enormous variety of interests and skills, ranging from education and science to architecture and music.

JAMES MADISON was born in Port Conway, Va., on March 16, 1751 (March 5, 1750/1, old style). A Princeton graduate, he joined the struggle for independence on his return to Virginia in 1771. In the 1770s and 1780s he was active in state politics, where he championed the Jefferson reform program, and in the Continental Congress. Madison was influential in the Constitutional Convention as leader of the group favoring a strong central government and as recorder of the debates; and he subsequently wrote, in collaboration with Alexander Hamilton and John Jay, the *Federalist* papers to aid the campaign for the adoption of the Constitution.

Serving in the new Congress, Madison soon emerged as the leader in the House of the men who opposed Hamilton's financial program and his pro-British leanings in foreign policy. Retiring from Congress in 1797, he continued to be active in Virginia and drafted the Virginia Resolution protesting the Alien and Sedition Acts. His intimacy with Jefferson made him the natural choice for Secretary of State in 1801.

In 1809, Madison succeeded Jefferson as President, defeating Charles C. Pinckney. His attractive wife, Dolley Payne Todd, whom he married in 1794, brought a new social sparkle to the executive mansion. In the meantime, increasing tension with Britain culminated in the War of 1812—a war for which the United States was unprepared and for which Madison lacked the executive talent to clear out incompetence and mobilize the nation's energies. Madison was re-elected in 1812, running against the Federalist De Witt Clinton. In 1814, the British actually captured Washington and forced Madison to flee to Virginia.

Madison's domestic program capitulated to the Hamiltonian policies that he had resisted 20 years before and he now signed bills to establish a United States Bank and a higher tariff.

After his presidency, he remained in retirement in Virginia until his death on June 28, 1836.

JAMES MONROE was born on April 28, 1758, in Westmoreland County, Va. A William and Mary graduate, he served in the army during the first years of the Revolution and was wounded at Trenton. He then entered Virginia politics and later national politics under the sponsorship of Jefferson. In 1786, he married Elizabeth (Eliza) Kortright.

Fearing centralization, Monroe opposed the adoption of the Constitution and, as senator from Virginia, was highly critical of the Hamiltonian program. In 1794, he was appointed minister to France, where his ardent sympathies with the Revolution exceeded the wishes of the State Department. His troubled diplomatic career ended with his recall in 1796. From 1799 to 1802, he was governor of Virginia. In 1803, Jefferson sent him to France to help negotiate the Louisiana Purchase and for the next few years he was active in various negotiations on the Continent.

In 1808, Monroe flirted with the radical wing of the Republican Party, which opposed Madison's candicacy; but the presidential boom came to naught and, after a brief term as governor of Virginia in 1811, Monroe accepted Madison's offer to become Secretary of State. During the War of 1812, he vainly sought a field command and instead served as Secretary of War from September 1814 to March 1815.

Elected President in 1816 over the Federalist Rufus King, and re-elected without opposition in 1820, Monroe, the last of the Virginia dynasty, pursued the course of systematic tranquilization that won for his administrations the name "the era of good feeling." He continued Madison's surrender to the Hamiltonian domestic program, signed the Missouri Compromise, acquired Florida, and with the able assistance of his Secretary of State, John Quincy Adams, promulgated the Monroe Doctrine in 1823, declaring against foreign colonization or intervention in the Americas. He died in New York City on July 4, 1831, the third president to die on the anniversary of Independence.

JOHN QUINCY ADAMS was born on July 11, 1767, at Braintree (now Quincy), Mass., the son of John Adams, the second President. He spent his early years in Europe with his father, graduated from Harvard, and entered law practice. His anti-Jeffersonian newspaper articles won him political attention. In 1794, he became minister to the Netherlands, the first of several diplomatic posts that occupied him until his return to Boston in 1801. In 1797, he married Louisa Catherine Johnson.

In 1803, Adams was elected to the Senate, nominally as a Federalist, but his repeated displays of independence on such issues as the Louisiana Purchase and the embargo caused his party to demand his resignation and ostracize him socially. In 1809, Madison rewarded him for his support of Jefferson by appointing him minister to St. Petersburg. He helped negotiate the Treaty of Ghent in 1814, and in 1815 became minister to London. In 1817 Monroe appointed him Secretary of State where he served with great distinction, gaining Florida from Spain without hostilities and playing an equal part with Monroe in formulating the Monroe Doctrine.

When no presidential candidate received a majority of electoral votes in 1824, Adams, with the support of Henry Clay, was elected by the House in 1825 over Andrew Jackson, who had the original plurality. Adams had ambitious plans of government activity to foster internal improvements and promote the arts and sciences, but congressional obstructionism, combined with his own unwillingness or inability to play the role of a politician, resulted in little being accomplished. After being defeated for re-elected by Jackson in 1828, he successfully ran for the House of Representatives in 1830. There though nominally a Whig, he pursued as ever an independent course. He led the fight to force Congress to receive antislavery petitions and fathered the Smithsonian Institution.

Stricken on the floor of the House, he died on Feb. 23, 1848. His long and detailed *Diary* gives a unique picture of the personalities and politics of the times.

ANDREW JACKSON was born on March 15, 1767, in what is now generally agreed to be Waxhaw, S.C. After a turbulent boyhood as an orphan and a British prisoner, he moved west to Tennessee, where he soon qualified for law practice but found time for such frontier pleasures as horse racing, cockfighting, and dueling. His marriage to Rachel Donelson Robards in 1791 was complicated by subsequent legal uncertainties about the status of her divorce. During the 1790s, Jackson served in the Tennessee Constitutional Convention, the United States House of Representatives and Senate, and on the Tennessee Supreme Court.

After some years as a country gentleman, living at the Hermitage near Nashville, Jackson in 1812 was given command of Tennessee troops sent against the Creeks. He defeated the Indians at Horseshoe Bend in 1814; subsequently he became a major general and won the Battle of New Orleans over veteran British troops, though after the treaty of peace had been signed at Ghent. In 1818, Jackson invaded Florida, captured Pensacola, and hanged two Englishmen named Arbuthnot and Ambrister, creating an international incident. A presidential boom began for him in 1821, and to foster it, he returned to the Senate (1823–25). Though he won a plurality of electoral votes in 1824, he lost in the House when Clay threw his strength to Adams. Four years later, he easily defeated Adams.

As President, Jackson greatly expanded the power and prestige of the presidential office and carried through an unprecedented program of domestic reform, vetoing the bill to extend the United States Bank, moving toward a hard-money currency policy, and checking the program of federal internal improvements. He also vindicated federal authority against South Carolina with its doctrine of nullification and against France on the question of debts. The support given his policies by the workingmen of the East as well as by the farmers of the East, West, and South resulted in his triumphant re-election in 1832 over Clay.

After watching the inauguration of his handpicked successor, Martin Van Buren, Jackson retired to the Hermitage, where he maintained a lively interest in national affairs until his death on June 8, 1845.

MARTIN VAN BUREN was born on Dec. 5, 1782, at Kinderhook, N.Y. After graduating from the village school, he became a law clerk, entered practice in 1803, and soon became active in state politics as state senator and attorney general. In 1820, he was elected to the United States Senate. He threw the support of his efficient political organization, known as the Albany Regency, to William H. Crawford in 1824 and to Jackson in 1828. After leading the opposition to Adams's administration in the Senate, he served briefly as governor of New York (1828–29) and resigned to become Jackson's Secretary of State. He was soon on close personal terms with Jackson and played an important part in the Jacksonian program.

In 1832, Van Buren became vice president; in 1836, President. The Panic of 1837 overshadowed his term. He attributed it to the overexpansion of the credit and favored the establishment of an independent treasury as repository for the federal funds. In 1840, he established a 10-hour day on public works. Defeated by Harrison in 1840, he was the leading contender for the Democratic nomination in 1844 until he publicly opposed immediate annexation of Texas, and was subsequently beaten by the Southern delegations at the Baltimore convention. This incident increased his growing misgivings about the slave power.

After working behind the scenes among the anti-slavery Democrats, Van Buren joined in the movement that led to the Free-Soil Party and became its candidate for President in 1848. He subsequently returned to the Democratic Party while continuing to object to its pro-Southern policy. He died in Kinderhook on July 24, 1862. His *Autobiography* throws valuable sidelights on the political history of the times.

His wife, Hannah Hoes, whom he married in 1807, died in 1819.

WILLIAM HENRY HARRISON was born in Charles City County, Va., on Feb. 9, 1773. Joining the army in 1791, he was active in Indian fighting in the Northwest, became secretary of the Northwest Territory in 1798 and governor of Indiana in 1800. He married Anna Symmes in 1795. Growing discontent over white encroachments on Indian lands led to the formation of an Indian alliance under Tecumseh to resist further aggressions. In 1811, Harrison won a nominal victory over the Indians at Tippecanoe and in 1813 a more decisive one at the Battle of the Thames, where Tecumseh was killed.

After resigning from the army in 1814, Harrison had an obscure career in politics and diplomacy, ending up 20 years later as a county recorder in Ohio. Nominated for President in 1835 as a military hero whom the conservative politicians hoped to be able to control, he ran surprisingly well against Van Buren in 1836. Four years later, he defeated Van Buren but caught pneumonia and died in Washington on April 4, 1841, a month after his inauguration. Harrison was the first president to die in office.

JOHN TYLER was born in Charles City County, Va., on March 29, 1790. A William and Mary graduate, he entered law practice and politics, serving in the House of Representatives (1817–21), as governor of Virginia (1825–27), and as senator (1827–36). A strict constructionist, he supported Crawford in 1824 and Jackson in 1828, but broke with Jackson over his United States Bank policy and became a member of the Southern state-rights group that co-operated with the Whigs. In 1836, he resigned from the Senate rather than follow instructions from the Virginia legislature to vote for a resolution expunging censure of Jackson from the Senate record.

Elected vice president on the Whig ticket in 1840, Tyler succeeded to the presidency on Harrison's death. His strict-constructionist views soon caused a split with the Henry Clay wing of the Whig party and a stalemate on domestic questions. Tyler's more considerable achievements were his support of the Webster-Ashburton Treaty with Britain and his success in bringing about the annexation of Texas.

After his presidency he lived in retirement in Virginia until the outbreak of the Civil War, when he emerged briefly as chairman of a peace convention and then as delegate to the provisional Congress of the Confederacy. He died on Jan. 18, 1862. He married Letitia Christian in 1813 and, two years after her death in 1842, Julia Gardiner.

JAMES KNOX POLK was born in Mecklenburg County, N.C., on Nov. 2, 1795. A graduate of the University of North Carolina, he moved west to Tennessee, was admitted to the bar, and soon became prominent in state politics. In 1825, he was elected to the House of Representatives, where he opposed Adams and, after 1829, became Jackson's floor leader in the fight against the Bank. In 1835, he became Speaker of the House. Four years later, he was elected governor of Tennessee, but was beaten in tries for re-election in 1841 and 1843.

The supporters of Van Buren for the Democratic

nomination in 1844 counted on Polk as his running mate; but, when Van Buren's stand on Texas alienated Southern support, the convention swung to Polk on the ninth ballot. He was elected over Henry Clay, the Whig candidate. Rapidly disillusioning those who thought that he would not run his own administration, Polk proceeded steadily and precisely to achieve four major objectives—the acquisition of California, the settlement of the Oregon question, the reduction of the tariff, and the establishment of the independent treasury. He also enlarged the Monroe Doctrine to exclude all non-American intervention in American affairs, whether forcible or not, and he forced Mexico into a war that he waged to a successful conclusion.

His wife, Sarah Childress, whom he married in 1824, was a woman of charm and ability. Polk died in Nashville, Tenn., on June 15, 1849.

ZACHARY TAYLOR was born at Montebello, Orange County, Va., on Nov. 24, 1784. Embarking on a military career in 1808, Taylor fought in the War of 1812, the Black Hawk War, and the Seminole War, meanwhile holding garrison jobs on the frontier or desk jobs in Washington. A brigadier general as a result of his victory over the Seminoles at Lake Okeechobee (1837), Taylor held a succession of Southwestern commands and in 1846 established a base on the Rio Grande, where his forces engaged in hostilities that precipitated the war with Mexico. He captured Monterrey in September 1846 and, disregarding Polk's orders to stay on the defensive, defeated Santa Anna at Buena Vista in February 1847, ending the war in the northern provinces.

Though Taylor had never cast a vote for president, his party affiliations were Whiggish and his availability was increased by his difficulties with Polk. He was elected president over the Democrat Lewis Cass. During the revival of the slavery controversy, which was to result in the Compromise of 1850, Taylor began to take an increasingly firm stand against appeasing the South; but he died in Washington on July 9, 1850, during the fight over the Compromise. He married Margaret Mackall Smith in 1810. His bluff and simple soldierly qualities won him the name Old Rough and Ready.

MILLARD FILLMORE was born at Locke, Cayuga County, N.Y., on Jan. 7, 1800. A lawyer, he entered politics with the Anti-Masonic Party under the sponsorship of Thurlow Weed, editor and party boss, and subsequently followed Weed into the Whig Party. He served in the House of Representatives (1833–35 and 1837–43) and played a leading role in writing the tariff of 1842. Defeated for governor of New York in 1844, he became State comptroller in 1848, was put on the Whig ticket with Taylor as a concession to the Clay wing of the party, and became president upon Taylor's death in 1850.

As president, Fillmore broke with Weed and William H. Seward and associated himself with the pro-Southern Whigs, supporting the Compromise of 1850. Defeated for the Whig nomination in 1852, he ran for president in 1856 as candidate of the American, or Know-Nothing Party, which sought to unite the country against foreigners in the alleged hope of diverting it from the explosive slavery issue. Fillmore opposed Lincoln during the Civil War. He died in Buffalo on March 8, 1874.

He was married in 1826 to Abigail Powers, who died in 1853, and in 1858 to Caroline Carmichael McIntosh.

FRANKLIN PIERCE was born at Hillsboro, N.H., on Nov. 23, 1804. A Bowdoin graduate, lawyer, and Jacksonian Democrat, he won rapid political advancement in the party, in part because of the prestige of his father, Gov. Benjamin Pierce. By 1831 he was Speaker of the New Hampshire House of Representatives; from 1833 to 1837, he served in the federal House and from 1837 to 1842 in the Senate. His wife, Jane Means Appleton, whom he married in 1834, disliked Washington and the somewhat dissipated life led by Pierce; in 1842 Pierce resigned from the Senate and began a successful law practice in Concord, N.H. During the Mexican War, he was a brigadier general.

Thereafter Pierce continued to oppose antislavery tendencies within the Democratic Party. As a result, he was the Southern choice to break the deadlock at the Democratic convention of 1852 and was nominated on the 49th ballot. In the election, Pierce overwhelmed Gen. Winfield Scott, the Whig candidate.

As president, Pierce followed a course of appeasing the South at home and of playing with schemes of territorial expansion abroad. The failure of his foreign and domestic policies prevented his renomination; and he died in Concord on Oct. 8, 1869, in relative obscurity.

JAMES BUCHANAN was born near Mercersburg, Pa., on April 23, 1791. A Dickinson graduate and a lawyer, he entered Pennsylvania politics as a Federalist. With the disappearance of the Federalist Party, he became a Jacksonian Democrat. He served with ability in the House (1821–31), as minister to St. Petersburg (1832–33), and in the Senate (1834–45), and in 1845 became Polk's Secretary of State. In 1853, Pierce appointed Buchanan minister to Britain, where he participated with other American diplomats in Europe in drafting the expansionist Ostend Manifesto.

He was elected president in 1856, defeating John C. Frémont, the Republican candidate, and former President Millard Fillmore of the American Party. The growing crisis over slavery presented Buchanan with problems he lacked the will to tackle. His appeasement of the South alientated the Stephen Douglas wing of the Democratic Party without reducing Southern militancy on slavery issues. While denying the right of secession, Buchanan also denied that the federal government could do anything about it. He supported the administration during the Civil War and died in Lancaster, Pa., on June 1, 1868.

The only president to remain a bachelor throughout his term, Buchanan used his charming niece, Harriet Lane, as White House hostess.

ABRAHAM LINCOLN was born in Hardin (now Larue) County, Ky., on Feb. 12, 1809. His family moved to Indiana and then to Illinois, and Lincoln gained what education he could along the way. While reading law, he worked in a store, managed a mill, surveyed, and split rails. In 1834, he went to the Illinois legislature as a Whig and became the party's floor leader. For the next 20 years he practiced law in Springfield, except for a single term (1847–49) in Congress, where he denounced the Mexican War. In 1855, he was a candidate for senator annd the next year he joined the new Republican Party.

A leading but unsuccessful candidate for the vice-presidential nomination with Frémont, Lincoln gained national attention in 1858 when, as Republican candidate for senator from Illinois, he engaged in a series of debates with Stephen A. Douglas, the Democratic candidate. He lost the election, but continued to prepare the way for the 1860 Republican convention and was rewarded with the presidential nomination on the third ballot. He won the election over three opponents.

From the start, Lincoln made clear that, unlike Buchanan, he believed the national government had the power to crush the rebellion. Not an abolitionist, he held the slavery issue subordinate to that of preserving the Union, but soon perceived that the war could not be brought to a successful conclusion without freeing the slaves. His administration was hampered by the incompetence of many Union generals, the inexperience of the troops, and the harassing political tactics both of the Republican Radicals, who favored a hard policy toward the South, and the Democratic Copperheads, who desired a negotiated peace. The Gettysburg Address of Nov. 19, 1863, marks the high point in the record of American eloquence. Lincoln's long search for a winning combination finally brought Generals Ulysses S. Grant and William T. Sherman on the top; and their series of victories in 1864 dispelled the mutterings from both Radicals and Peace Democrats that at one time seemed to threaten Lincoln's re-election. He was re-elected in 1864, defeating Gen. George B. McClellan, the Democratic candidate. His inaugural address urged leniency toward the South: "With malice toward none, with charity for all . . . let us strive on to finish the work we are in; to bind up the nation's wounds . . ." This policy aroused growing opposition on the part of the Republican Radicals, but before the matter could be put to the test, Lincoln was shot by the actor John Wilkes Booth at Ford's Theater, Washington, on April 14, 1865. He died the next morning.

Lincoln's marriage to Mary Todd in 1842 was often unhappy and turbulent, in part because of his wife's pronounced instability.

ANDREW JOHNSON was born at Raleigh, N.C., on Dec. 29, 1808. Self-educated, he became a tailor in Greeneville, Tenn., but soon went into politics, where he rose steadily. He served in the House of Representatives (1843–54), as governor of Tennessee (1853–57), and as a senator (1857–62). Politically he was a Jacksonian Democrat and his specialty was the fight for a more equitable land policy. Alone among the Southern Senators, he stood by the Union during the Civil War. In 1862, he became war governor of Tennessee and carried out a thankless and difficult job with great courage. Johnson became Lincoln's running mate in 1864 as a result of an attempt to give the ticket a nonpartisan and nonsectional character. Succeeding to the presidency on Lincoln's death, Johnson sought to carry out Lincoln's policy, but without his political skill. The result was a hopeless conflict with the Radical Republicans who dominated Congress, passed measures over Johnson's vetoes, and attempted to limit the power of the executive concerning appointments and removals. The conflict culminated with Johnson's impeachment for attempting to remove his disloyal Secretary of War in defiance of the Tenure of Office Act which required senatorial concurrence for such dismissals. The opposition failed by one vote to get the two thirds necessary for conviction.

After his presidency, Johnson maintained an interest in politics and in 1875 was again elected to the Senate. He died near Carter Station, Tenn., on July 31, 1875. He married Eliza McCardle in 1827.

ULYSSES SIMPSON GRANT was born (as Hiram Ulysses Grant) at Point Pleasant, Ohio, on April 27, 1822. He graduated from West Point in 1843 and served without particular distinction in the Mexican War. In 1848 he married Julia Dent. He resigned from the army in 1854, after warnings from his commanding officer about his drinking habits, and for the next six years held a wide variety of jobs in the Middle West. With the outbreak of the Civil War, he sought a command and soon, to his surprise, was made a brigadier general. His continuing successes in the western theaters, culminating in the capture of Vicksburg, Miss., in 1863, brought him national fame and soon the command of all the Union armies. Grant's dogged, implacable policy of concentrating on dividing and destroying the Confederate armies brought the war to an end in 1865. The next year, he was made full general.

In 1868, as Republican candidate for president, Grant was elected over the Democrat, Horatio Seymour. From the start, Grant showed his unfitness for the office. His Cabinet was weak, his domestic policy was confused, many of his intimate associates were corrupt. The notable achievement in foreign affairs was the settlement of controversies with Great Britain in the Treaty of London (1871), negotiated by his able Secretary of State, Hamilton Fish.

Running for re-election in 1872, he defeated Horace Greeley, the Democratic and Liberal Republican candidate. The Panic of 1873 graft scandals close to the presidency created difficulties for his second term.

After retiring from office, Grant toured Europe for two years and returned in time to accede to a third-term boom, but was beaten in the convention of 1880. Illness and bad business judgment darkened his last years, but he worked steadily at the *Personal Memoirs,* which were to be so successful when published after his death at Mount McGregor, near Saratoga, N.Y., on July 23, 1885.

RUTHERFORD BIRCHARD HAYES was born in Delaware, Ohio, on Oct. 4, 1822. A graduate of Kenyon College and the Harvard Law School, he practiced law in Lower Sandusky (now Fremont) and then in Cincinnati. In 1852 he married Lucy Webb. A Whig, he joined the Republican party in 1855. During the Civil War he rose to major general. He served in the House of Representatives from 1865 to 1867 and then confirmed a reputation for honesty and efficiency in two terms as Governor of Ohio (1868–72). His election to a third term in 1875 made him the logical candidate for those Republicans who wished to stop James G. Blaine in 1876, and he was nominated.

The result of the election was in doubt for some time and hinged upon disputed returns from South Carolina, Louisiana, Florida, and Oregon. Samuel J. Tilden, the Democrat, had the larger popular vote but was adjudged by the strictly partisan decisions of the Electoral Commission to have one fewer electoral vote, 185 to 184. The national acceptance of this result was due in part to the general understanding that Hayes would pursue a conciliatory policy toward the South. He withdrew the troops from the South, took a conservative position on financial and labor issues, and urged civil service reform.

Hayes served only one term by his own wish and

spent the rest of his life in various humanitarian endeavors. He died in Fremont on Jan. 17, 1893.

JAMES ABRAM GARFIELD, the last president to be born in a log cabin, was born in Cuyahoga County, Ohio, on Nov. 19, 1831. A Williams graduate, he taught school for a time and entered Republican politics in Ohio. In 1858, he married Lucretia Rudolph. During the Civil War, he had a promising career, rising to major general of volunteers; but he resigned in 1863, having been elected to the House of Representatives, where he served until 1880. His oratorical and parliamentary abilities soon made him the leading Republican in the House, though his record was marred by his unorthodox acceptance of a fee in the DeGolyer paving contract case and by suspicions of his complicity in the Crédit Mobilier scandal.

In 1880, Garfield was elected to the Senate, but instead became the presidential candidate on the 36th ballot as a result of a deadlock in the Republican convention. In the election, he defeated Gen. Winfield Scott Hancock, the Democratic candidate. Garfield's administration was barely under way when he was shot by Charles J. Guiteau, a disappointed office seeker, in Washington on July 2, 1881. He died in Elberton, N.J., on Sept. 19.

CHESTER ALAN ARTHUR was born at Fairfield, Vt., on Oct. 5, 1830. A graduate of Union College, he became a successful New York lawyer. In 1859, he married Ellen Herndon. During the Civil War, he held administrative jobs in the Republican state administration and in 1871 was appointed collector of the Port of New York by Grant. This post gave him control over considerable patronage. Though not personally corrupt, Arthur managed his power in the interests of the New York machine so openly that President Hayes in 1877 called for an investigation and the next year Arthur was suspended.

In 1880 Arthur was nominated for vice president in the hope of conciliating the followers of Grant and the powerful New York machine. As president upon Garfield's death, Arthur, stepping out of his familiar role as spoilsman, backed civil service reform, reorganized the Cabinet, and prosecuted political associates accused of post office graft. Losing machine support and failing to gain the reformers, he was not nominated for a full term in 1884. He died in New York City on Nov. 18, 1886.

STEPHEN GROVER CLEVELAND was born at Caldwell, N.J., on March 18, 1837. He was admitted to the bar in Buffalo, N.Y., in 1859 and lived there as a lawyer, with occasional incursions into Democratic politics, for more than 20 years. He did not participate in the Civil War. As mayor of Buffalo in 1881, he carried through a reform program so ably that the Democrats ran him successfully for governor in 1882. In 1884 he won the Democratic nomination for President. The campaign contrasted Cleveland's spotless public career with the uncertain record of James G. Blaine, the Republican candidate, and Cleveland received enough Mugwump (independent Republican) support to win.

As president, Cleveland pushed civil service reform, opposed the pension grab and attacked the high tariff rates. While in the White House, he married Frances Folsom in 1886. Renominated in 1888, Cleveland was defeated by Benjamin Harrison, polling more popular but fewer electoral votes. In 1892, he was elected over Harrison. When the Panic of 1893 burst upon the country, Cleveland's attempts to solve it by sound-money measures alienated the free-silver wing of the party, while his tariff policy alienated the protectionists. In 1894, he sent troops to break the Pullman strike. In foreign affairs, his firmness caused Great Britain to back down in the Venezuela border dispute.

In his last years Cleveland was an active and much-respected public figure. He died in Princeton, N.J., on June 24, 1908.

BENJAMIN HARRISON was born in North Bend, Ohio, on Aug. 20, 1833, the grandson of William Henry Harrison, the ninth president. A graduate of Miami University in Ohio, he took up the law in Indiana and became active in Republican politics. In 1853, he married Caroline Lavinia Scott. During the Civil War, he rose to brigadier general. A sound-money Republican, he was elected senator from Indiana in 1880. In 1888, he received the Republican nomination for President on the eighth ballot. Though behind on the popular vote, he won over Grover Cleveland in the electoral college by 233 to 168.

As President, Harrison failed to please either the bosses or the reform element in the party. In foreign affairs he backed Secretary of State Blaine, whose policy foreshadowed later American imperialism. Harrison was renominated in 1892 but lost to Cleveland. His wife died in the White House in 1892 and Harrison married her niece, Mary Scott (Lord) Dimmick, in 1896. After his presidency, he resumed law practice. He died in Indianapolis on March 13, 1901.

WILLIAM McKINLEY was born in Niles, Ohio, on Jan. 29, 1843. He taught school, then served in the Civil War, rising from the ranks to become a major. Subsequently he opened a law office in Canton, Ohio, and in 1871 married Ida Saxton. Elected to Congress in 1876, he served there until 1891, except for 1883–85. His faithful advocacy of business interests culminated in the passage of the highly protective McKinley Tariff of 1890. With the support of Mark Hanna, a shrewd Cleveland businessman interested in safeguarding tariff protection, McKinley became governor of Ohio in 1892 and Republican presidential candidate in 1896. The business community, alarmed by the progressivism of William Jennings Bryan, the Democratic candidate, spent considerable money to assure McKinley's victory.

The chief event of McKinley's administration was the war with Spain, which resulted in our acquisition of the Philippines and other islands. With imperialism an issue, McKinley defeated Bryan again in 1900. On Sept. 6, 1901, he was shot at Buffalo, N.Y., by Leon F. Czolgosz, an anarchist, and he died there eight days later.

THEODORE ROOSEVELT was born in New York City on Oct. 27, 1858. A Harvard graduate, he was early interested in ranching, in politics, and in writing picturesque historical narratives. He was a Republican member of the New York Assembly in 1882–84, an unsuccessful candidate for mayor of New York in 1886, a U.S. Civil Service Commissioner under Benjamin Harrison, Police Commissioner of New York City in 1895, and Assistant Secretary of the Navy under McKinley in 1897. He resigned in 1898 to help organize a volunteer regiment, the Rough Riders, and take a more direct part in the war with Spain. He was elected governor of New York in 1898 and vice president in 1900, in spite of lack of enthusiasm on the part of the bosses.

Assuming the presidency of the assassinated McKinley in 1901, Roosevelt embarked on a wide-ranging program of government reform and conservation of natural resources. He ordered antitrust suits against several large corporations, threatened to intervene in the anthracite coal strike of 1902, which prompted the operators to accept arbitration, and, in general, championed the rights of the "little man" and fought the "malefactors of great wealth." He was also responsible for such progressive legislation as the Elkins Act of 1901, which outlawed freight rebates by railroads; the bill establishing the Department of Commerce and Labor; the Hepburn Act, which gave the I.C.C. greater control over the railroads; the Meat Inspection Act; and the Pure Food and Drug Act.

In foreign affairs, Roosevelt pursued a strong policy, permitting the instigation of a revolt in Panama to dispose of Colombian objections to the Panama Canal and helping to maintain the balance of power in the East by bringing the Russo-Japanese War to an end, for which he won the Nobel Peace Prize, the first American to achieve a Nobel prize in any category. In 1904, he decisively defeated Alton B. Parker, his conservative Democratic opponent.

Roosevelt's increasing coldness toward his successor, William Howard Taft, led him to overlook his earlier disclaimer of third-term ambitions and to re-enter politics. Defeated by the machine in the Republican convention of 1912, he organized the Progressive Party (Bull Moose) and polled more votes than Taft, though the split brought about the election of Woodrow Wilson. From 1915 on, Roosevelt strongly favored intervention in the European war. He became deeply embittered at Wilson's refusal to allow him to raise a volunteer division. He died in Oyster Bay, N.Y., on Jan. 6, 1919. He was married twice: in 1880 to Alice Hathaway Lee, who died in 1884, and in 1886 to Edith Kermit Carow.

WILLIAM HOWARD TAFT was born in Cincinnati on Sept. 15, 1857. A Yale graduate, he entered Ohio Republican politics in the 1880s. In 1886 he married Helen Herron. From 1887 to 1890, he served on the Ohio Superior Court; 1890–92, as solicitor general of the United States; 1892–1900, on the federal circuit court. In 1900 McKinley appointed him president of the Philippine Commission and in 1901 governor general. Taft had great success in pacifying the Filipinos, solving the problem of the church lands, improving economic conditions, and establishing limited self-government. His period as Secretary of War (1904–08) further demonstrated his capacity as administrator and conciliator, and he was Roosevelt's hand-picked successor in 1908. In the election, he polled 321 electoral votes to 162 for William Jennings Bryan, who was running for the presidency for the third time.

Though he carried on many of Roosevelt's policies, Taft got into increasing trouble with the progressive wing of the party and displayed mounting irritability and indecision. After his defeat in 1912, he became professor of constitutional law at Yale. In 1921 he

was appointed Chief Justice of the United States. He died in Washington on March 8, 1930.

THOMAS WOODROW WILSON was born in Staunton, Va., on Dec. 28, 1856. A Princeton graduate, he turned from law practice to post-graduate work in political science at Johns Hopkins University, receiving his Ph.D. in 1886. He taught at Bryn Mawr, Wesleyan, and Princeton, and in 1902 was made president of Princeton. After an unsuccessful attempt to democratize the social life of the university, he welcomed an invitation in 1910 to be the Democratic gubernatorial candidate in New Jersey, and was elected. His success in fighting the machine and putting through a reform program attracted national attention.

In 1912, at the Democratic convention in Baltimore, Wilson won the nomination on the 46th ballot and went on to defeat Roosevelt and Taft in the election. Wilson proceeded under the standard of the New Freedom to enact a program of domestic reform, including the Federal Reserve Act, the Clayton Antitrust Act, the establishment of the Federal Trade Commission, and other measures designed to restore competition in the face of the great monopolies. In foreign affairs, while privately sympathetic with the Allies, he strove to maintain neutrality in the European war and warned both sides against encroachments on American interests.

Re-elected in 1916 as a peace candidate, he tried to mediate between the warring nations; but when the Germans resumed unrestricted submarine warfare in 1917, Wilson brought the United States into what he now believed was a war to make the world safe for democracy. He supplied the classic formulations of Allied war aims and the armistice of Nov. 11, 1918 was negotiated on the basis of Wilson's Fourteen Points. In 1919 he strove at Versailles to lay the foundations for enduring peace. He accepted the imperfections of the Versailles Treaty in the expectation that they could be remedied by action within the League of Nations. He probably could have secured ratification of the treaty by the Senate if he had adopted a more conciliatory attitude toward the mild reservationists; but his insistence on all or nothing eventually caused the diehard isolationists and diehard Wilsonites to unite in rejecting a compromise.

In September 1919 Wilson suffered a paralytic stroke that limited his activity. After leaving the presidency he lived on in retirement in Washington, dying on Feb. 3, 1924. He was married twice—in 1885 to Ellen Louise Axson, who died in 1914, and in 1915 to Edith Bolling Galt.

WARREN GAMALIEL HARDING was born in Morrow County, Ohio, on Nov. 2, 1865. After attending Ohio Central College, Harding became interested in journalism and in 1884 bought the *Marion* (Ohio) *Star*. In 1891 he married a wealthy widow, Florence Kling De Wolfe. As his paper prospered, he entered Republican politics, serving as state senator (1899–1903) and as lieutenant governor (1904–06). In 1910, he was defeated for governor, but in 1914 was elected to the Senate. His reputation as an orator made him the keynoter at the 1916 Republican convention.

When the 1920 convention was deadlocked between Leonard Wood and Frank O. Lowden, Harding became the dark-horse nominee on his solemn affirmation that there was no reason in his past that he should not be. Straddling the League question, Harding was easily elected over James M. Cox, his Democratic opponent. His Cabinet contained some able men, but also some manifestly unfit for public office. Harding's own intimates were mediocre when they were not corrupt. The impending disclosure of the Teapot Dome scandal in the Interior Department and illegal practices in the Justice Department and Veterans' Bureau, as well as political setbacks, profoundly worried him. On his return from Alaska in 1923, he died unexpectedly in San Francisco on Aug. 2.

JOHN CALVIN COOLIDGE was born in Plymouth, Vt., on July 4, 1872. An Amherst graduate, he went into law practice at Northampton, Mass., in 1897. He married Grace Anna Goodhue in 1905. He entered Republican state politics, becoming successively mayor of Northampton, state senator, lieutenant governor and, in 1919, governor. His use of the state militia to end the Boston police strike in 1919 won him a somewhat undeserved reputation for decisive action and brought him the Republican vice-presidential nomination in 1920. After Harding's death Coolidge handled the Washington scandals with care and finally managed to save the Republican Party from public blame for the widespread corruption.

In 1924, Coolidge was elected without difficulty, defeating the Democrat, John W. Davis, and Robert M. La Follette running on the Progressive ticket. His second term, like his first, was characterized by a general satisfaction with the existing economic order. He stated that he did not choose to run in 1928.

After his presidency, Coolidge lived quietly in Northampton, writing an unilluminating *Autobiography* and conducting a syndicated column. He died there on Jan. 5, 1933.

HERBERT CLARK HOOVER was born at West Branch, Iowa, on Aug. 10, 1874, the first president to be born west of the Mississippi. A Stanford graduate, he worked from 1895 to 1913 as a mining engineer and consultant throughout the world. In 1899, he married Lou Henry. During World War I, he served with distinction as chairman of the American Relief Committee in London, as chairman of the Commission for Relief in Belgium, and as U.S. Food Administrator. His political affiliations were still too indeterminate for him to be mentioned as a possibility for either the Republican or Democratic nomination in 1920, but after the election he served Harding and Coolidge as Secretary of Commerce.

In the election of 1928, Hoover overwhelmed Gov. Alfred E. Smith of New York, the Democratic candidate and the first Roman Catholic to run for the presidency. He soon faced the worst depression in the nation's history, but his attacks upon it were hampered by his devotion to the theory that the forces that brought the crisis would soon bring the revival and then by his belief that there were too many areas in which the federal government had no power to act. In a succession of vetoes, he struck down measures proposing a national employment system or national relief, he reduced income tax rates, and only at the end of his term did he yield to popular pressure and set up agencies such as the Reconstruction Finance Corporation to make emergency loans to assist business.

After his 1932 defeat, Hoover returned to private business. In 1946, President Truman charged him

with various world food missions; and from 1947 to 1949 and 1953 to 1955, he was head of the Commission on Organization of the Executive Branch of the Government. He died in New York City on Oct. 20, 1964.

FRANKLIN DELANO ROOSEVELT was born in Hyde Park, N.Y., on Jan. 30, 1882. A Harvard graduate, he attended Columbia Law School and was admitted to the New York bar. In 1910, he was elected to the New York State Senate as a Democrat. Reelected in 1912, he was appointed Assistant Secretary of the Navy by Woodrow Wilson the next year. In 1920, his radiant personality and his war service resulted in his nomination for vice president as James M. Cox's running mate. After his defeat, he returned to law practice in New York. In August 1921, Roosevelt was stricken with infantile paralysis while on vacation at Campobello, New Brunswick. After a long and gallant fight, he recovered partial use of his legs. In 1924 and 1928, he led the fight at the Democratic national conventions for the nomination of Gov. Alfred E. Smith of New York, and in 1928 Roosevelt was himself induced to run for governor of New York. He was elected, and was re-elected in 1930.

In 1932, Roosevelt received the Democratic nomination for president and immediately launched a campaign that brought new spirit to a weary and discouraged nation. He defeated Hoover by a wide margin. His first term was characterized by an unfolding of the New Deal program, with greater benefits for labor, the farmers, and the unemployed, and the progressive estrangement of most of the business community.

At an early stage, Roosevelt became aware of the menace to world peace posed by totalitarian fascism, and from 1937 on he tried to focus public attention on the trend of events in Europe and Asia. As a result, he was widely denounced as a warmonger. He was re-elected in 1936 over Gov. Alfred M. Landon of Kansas by the overwhelming electoral margin of 523 to 8, and the gathering international crisis prompted him to run for an unprecedented third term in 1940. He defeated Wendell L. Willkie.

Roosevelt's program to bring maximum aid to Britain and, after June 1941, to Russia was opposed, until the Japanese attack on Pearl Harbor restored national unity. During the war, Roosevelt shelved the New Deal in the interests of conciliating the business community, both in order to get full production during the war and to prepare the way for a united acceptance of the peace settlements after the war. A series of conferences with Winston Churchill and Joseph Stalin laid down the bases for the postwar world. In 1944 he was elected to a fourth term, running against Gov. Thomas E. Dewey of New York.

On April 12, 1945, Roosevelt died of a cerebral hemorrhage at Warm Springs, Ga., shortly after his return from the Yalta Conference. His wife, Anna Eleanor Roosevelt, whom he married in 1905, was a woman of great ability who made significant contributions to her husband's policies.

HARRY S. TRUMAN was born on a farm near Lamar, Mo., on May 8, 1884. During World War I, he served in France as a captain with the 129th Field Artillery. He married Bess Wallace in 1919. After engaging briefly and unsuccessfully in the haberdashery business in Kansas City, Mo., Truman entered local politics. Under the sponsorship of Thomas Pendergast, Democratic boss of Missouri, he held a number of local offices, preserving his personal honesty in the midst of a notoriously corrupt political machine. In 1934, he was elected to the Senate and was re-elected in 1940. During his first term he was a loyal but quiet supporter of the New Deal, but in his second term, an appointment as head of a Senate committee to investigate war production brought out his special qualities of honesty, common sense, and hard work, and he won widespread respect.

Elected vice president in 1944, Truman became president upon Roosevelt's sudden death in April 1945 and was immediately faced with the problems of winding down the war against the Axis and preparing the nation for postwar adjustment.

The years 1947–48 were distinguished by civil-rights proposals, the Truman Doctrine to contain the spread of Communism, and the Marshall Plan to aid in the economic reconstruction of war-ravaged nations. Truman's general record, highlighted by a vigorous Fair Deal campaign, brought about his unexpected election in 1948 over the heavily favored Thomas E. Dewey.

Truman's second term was primarily concerned with the Cold War with the Soviet Union, the implementing of the North Atlantic Pact, the United Nations police action in Korea, and the vast rearmament program with its accompanying problems of economic stabilization.

On March 29, 1952, Truman announced that he would not run again for the presidency. After leaving the White House, he returned to his home in Independence, Mo., to write his memoirs. He further busied himself with the Harry S. Truman Library there. He died in Kansas City, Mo., on Dec. 26, 1972.

DWIGHT DAVID EISENHOWER was born in Denison, Tex., on Oct. 14, 1890. His ancestors lived in Germany and emigrated to America, settling in Pennsylvania, early in the 18th century. His father, David, had a general store in Hope, Kan., which failed. After a brief time in Texas, the family moved to Abilene, Kan.

After graduating from Abilene High School in 1909, Eisenhower did odd jobs for almost two years. He won an appointment to the Naval Academy at Annapolis, but was too old for admittance. Then he received an appointment in 1910 to West Point, from which he graduated as a second lieutenant in 1915.

He did not see service in World War I, having been stationed at Fort Sam Houston, Tex. There he met Mamie Geneva Doud, whom he married in Denver on July 1, 1916, and by whom he had two sons: Doud Dwight (died in infancy) and John Sheldon Doud.

Eisenhower served in the Philippines from 1935 to 1939 with Gen. Douglas MacArthur. Afterward, Gen. George C. Marshall, the Army Chief of Staff, brought him into the War Department's General Staff and in 1942 placed him in command of the invasion of North Africa. In 1944, he was made Supreme Allied Commander for the invasion of Europe.

After the war, Eisenhower served as Army Chief of Staff from November 1945 until February 1948, when he was appointed president of Columbia University.

In December 1950, President Truman recalled Eisenhower to active duty to command the North Atlantic Treaty Organization forces in Europe. He held his post until the end of May 1952.

At the Republican convention of 1952 in Chicago, Eisenhower won the presidential nomination on the first ballot in a close race with Senator Robert A. Taft of Ohio. In the election, he defeated Gov. Adlai E. Stevenson of Illinois.

Through two terms, Eisenhower hewed to moderate domestic policies. He sought peace through Free World strength in an era of new nationalisms, nuclear missiles, and space exploration. He fostered alliances pledging the United States to resist Red aggression in Europe, Asia, and Latin America. The Eisenhower Doctrine of 1957 extended commitments to the Middle East.

At home, the popular president lacked Republican Congressional majorities after 1954, but he was re-elected in 1956 by 457 electoral votes to 73 for Stevenson.

While retaining most Fair Deal programs, he stressed "fiscal responsibility" in domestic affairs. A moderate in civil rights, he sent troops to Little Rock, Ark., to enforce court-ordered school integration.

With his wartime rank restored by Congress, Eisenhower returned to private life and the role of elder statesman, with his vigor hardly impaired by a heart attack, an ileitis operation, and a mild stroke suffered while in office. He died in Washington on March 28, 1969.

JOHN FITZGERALD KENNEDY was born in Brookline, Mass., on May 29, 1917. His father, Joseph P. Kennedy, was Ambassador to Great Britain from 1937 to 1940.

Kennedy was graduated from Harvard University in 1940 and joined the Navy the next year. He became skipper of a PT boat that was sunk in the Pacific by a Japanese destroyer. Although given up for lost, he swam to a safe island, towing an injured enlisted man.

After recovering from a war-aggravated spinal injury, Kennedy entered politics in 1946 and was elected to Congress. In 1952, he ran against Senator Henry Cabot Lodge, Jr., of Massachusetts, and won.

Kennedy was married on Sept. 12, 1953, to Jacqueline Lee Bouvier, by whom he had three children: Caroline, John Fitzgerald, Jr., and Patrick Bouvier (died in infancy).

In 1957 Kennedy won the Pulitzer Prize for a book he had written earlier, *Profiles in Courage.*

After strenuous primary battles, Kennedy won the Democratic presidential nomination on the first ballot at the 1960 Los Angeles convention. With a plurality of only 118,574 votes, he carried the election over Vice President Richard M. Nixon and became the first Roman Catholic president.

Kennedy brought to the White House the dynamic idea of a "New Frontier" approach in dealing with problems at home, abroad, and in the dimensions of space. Out of his leadership in his first few months in office came the 10-year Alliance for Progress to aid Latin America, the Peace Corps, and accelerated programs that brought the first Americans into orbit in the race into space.

Failure of the U.S.-supported Cuban invasion in April 1961 led to the entrenchment of the Communist-backed Castro regime, only 90 miles from United States soil. When it became known that Soviet offensive missiles were being installed in Cuba in 1962, Kennedy ordered a naval "quarantine" of the island and moved troops into position to eliminate this threat to U.S. security. The world seemed on the brink of a nuclear war until Soviet Premier Khrushchev ordered the removal of the missiles.

A sudden "thaw," or the appearance of one, in the cold war came with the agreement with the Soviet Union on a limited test-ban treaty signed in Moscow on Aug. 6, 1963.

In his domestic policies, Kennedy's proposals for medical care for the aged, expanded area redevelopment, and aid to education were defeated, but on minimum wage, trade legislation, and other measures he won important victories.

Widespread racial disorders and demonstrations led to Kennedy's proposing sweeping civil rights legislation. As his third year in office drew to a close, he also recommended an $11-billion tax cut to bolster the economy. Both measures were pending in Congress when Kennedy, looking forward to a second term, journeyed to Texas for a series of speeches.

While riding in a procession in Dallas on Nov. 22, 1963, he was shot to death by an assassin firing from an upper floor of a building. The alleged assassin, Lee Harvey Oswald, was killed two days later in the Dallas city jail by Jack Ruby, owner of a strip-tease place.

At 46 years of age, Kennedy became the fourth president to be assassinated and the eighth to die in office.

LYNDON BAINES JOHNSON was born in Stonewall, Tex., on Aug. 27, 1908. On both sides of his family he had a political heritage mingled with a Baptist background of preachers and teachers. Both his father and his paternal grandfather served in the Texas House of Representatives.

After his graduation from Southwest Texas State Teachers College, Johnson taught school for two years. He went to Washington in 1932 as secretary to Rep. Richard M. Kleberg. During this time, he married Claudia Alta Taylor, known as "Lady Bird." They had two children: Lynda Bird and Luci Baines.

In 1935, Johnson became Texas administrator for the National Youth Administration. Two years later, he was elected to Congress as an all-out supporter of Franklin D. Roosevelt, and served until 1949. He was the first member of Congress to enlist in the armed forces after the attack on Pearl Harbor. He served in the Navy in the Pacific and won a Silver Star.

Johnson was elected to the Senate in 1948 after he had captured the Democratic nomination by only 87 votes. He was 40 years old. He became the Senate Democratic leader in 1953. A heart attack in 1955 threatened to end his political career, but he recovered fully and resumed his duties.

At the height of his power as Senate leader, Johnson sought the Democratic nomination for president in 1960. When he lost to John F. Kennedy, he surprised even some of his closest associates by accepting second place on the ticket.

Johnson was riding in another car in the motorcade when Kennedy was assassinated in Dallas on Nov. 22, 1963. He took the oath of office in the presidential jet on the Dallas airfield.

With Johnson's insistent backing, Congress finally adopted a far-reaching civil-rights bill, a voting-rights bill, a Medicare program for the aged, and measures to improve education and conservation. Congress also began what Johnson described as "an all-out war" on poverty.

Amassing a record-breaking majority of nearly 16 million votes, Johnson was elected president in his own right in 1964, defeating Senator Barry Goldwater of Arizona.

The double tragedy of a war in Southeast Asia and urban riots at home marked Johnson's last two years in office. Faced with disunity in the nation and challenges within his own party, Johnson surprised the country on March 31, 1968, with the announcement that he would not be a candidate for re-election. He died of a heart attack suffered at his LBJ Ranch on Jan. 22, 1973.

RICHARD MILHOUS NIXON was born in Yorba Linda, Calif., on Jan. 9, 1913, to Midwestern-bred parents, Francis A. and Hannah Milhous Nixon, who raised their five sons as Quakers.

Nixon was a high school debater and was undergraduate president at Whittier College in California, where he was graduated in 1934. As a scholarship student at Duke University Law School in North Carolina, he graduated third in his class in 1937.

After five years as a lawyer, Nixon joined the Navy in August 1942. He was an air transport officer in the South Pacific and a legal officer stateside before his discharge in 1946 as a lieutenant commander.

Running for Congress in California as a Republican in 1946, Nixon defeated Rep. Jerry Voorhis. As a member of the House Un-American Activities Committee, he made a name as an investigator of Alger Hiss, a former high State Department official, who was later jailed for perjury. In 1950, Nixon defeated Rep. Helen Gahagan Douglas, a Democrat, for the Senate. He was criticized for portraying her as a Communist dupe.

Nixon's anti-Communism, his Western base, and his youth figured in his selection in 1952 to run for vice president on the ticket headed by Dwight D. Eisenhower. Demands for Nixon's withdrawal followed disclosure that California businessmen had paid some of his Senate office expenses. He televised rebuttal, known as "the Checkers speech" (named for a cocker spaniel given to the Nixons), brought him support from the public and from Eisenhower. The ticket won easily in 1952 and again in 1956.

Eisenhower gave Nixon substantive assignments, including missions to 56 countries. In Moscow in 1959, Nixon won acclaim for his defense of U.S. interests in an impromptu "kitchen debate" with Soviet Premier Nikita S. Khrushchev.

Nixon lost the 1960 race for the presidency to John F. Kennedy.

In 1962, Nixon failed in a bid for California's governorship and seemed to be finished as a national candidate. He became a Wall Street lawyer, but kept his old party ties and developed new ones through constant travels to speak for Republicans.

Nixon won the 1968 Republican presidential nomination after a shrewd primary campaign, then made Gov. Spiro T. Agnew of Maryland his surprise choice for vice president. In the election, they edged out the Democratic ticket headed by Vice President Hubert H. Humphrey by 510,314 votes out of 73,212,065 cast.

Committed to wind down the U.S. role in the Vietnamese War, Nixon pursued "Vietnamization"—training and equipping South Vietnamese to do their own fighting. American ground combat forces in Vietnam fell steadily from 540,000 when Nixon took office to none in 1973 when the military draft was ended. But there was heavy continuing use of U.S. air power.

Nixon improved relations with Moscow and re-opened the long-closed door to mainland China with a good-will trip there in February 1972. In May of that year, he visited Moscow and signed agreements on arms limitation and trade expansion and approved plans for a joint U.S.-Soviet space mission in 1975.

Inflation was a campaign issue for Nixon, but he failed to master it as president. On Aug. 15, 1971, with unemployment edging up, Nixon abruptly announced a new economic policy: a 90-day wage-price freeze, stimulative tax cuts, a temporary 10% tariff, and spending cuts. A second phase, imposing guidelines on wage, price and rent boosts, was announced October 7.

The economy responded in time for the 1972 campaign, in which Nixon played up his foreign-policy achievements. Played down was the burglary on June 17, 1972, of Democratic national headquarters in the Watergate apartment complex in Washington. The Nixon-Agnew re-election campaign cost a record $60 million and swamped the Democratic ticket headed by Senator George McGovern of South Dakota with a plurality of 17,999,528 out of 77,718,554 votes. Only Massachusetts, with 14 electoral votes, and the District of Columbia, with 3, went for McGovern.

In January 1973, hints of a cover-up emerged at the trial of six men found guilty of the Watergate burglary. With a Senate investigation under way, Nixon announced on April 30 the resignations of his top aides, H. R. Haldeman and John D. Ehrlichman, and the dismissal of White House counsel John Dean III. Dean was the star witness at televised Senate hearings that exposed both a White House cover-up of Watergate and massive illegalities in Republican fund-raising in 1972.

The hearings also disclosed that Nixon had routinely tape-recorded his office meetings and telephone conversations.

On Oct. 10, 1973, Agnew resigned as vice president, then pleaded no-contest to a negotiated federal charge of evading income taxes on alleged bribes. Two days later, Nixon nominated the House minority leader, Rep. Gerald R. Ford of Michigan, as the new vice president. Congress confirmed Ford on Dec. 6, 1973.

In June 1974, Nixon visited Israel and four Arab nations. Then he met in Moscow with Soviet leader Leonid I. Brezhnev and reached preliminary nuclear arms limitation agreements.

But, in the month after his return, Watergate ended the Nixon regime. On July 24 the Supreme Court ordered Nixon to surrender subpoenaed tapes. On July 30, the Judiciary Committee referred three impeachment articles to the full membership. On August 5, Nixon bowed to the Supreme Court and released tapes showing he halted an FBI probe of the Watergate burglary six days after it occurred. It was in effect an admission of obstruction of justice, and impeachment appeared inevitable.

Nixon resigned on Aug. 9, 1974, the first president ever to do so. A month later, President Ford issued an unconditional pardon for any offenses Nixon might have committed as president, thus forestalling possible prosecution.

In 1940, Nixon married Thelma Catherine (Pat) Ryan. They had two daughters, Patricia (Tricia) Cox and Julie, who married Dwight David Eisenhower II, grandson of the former president.

GERALD RUDOLPH FORD was born in Omaha, Neb., on July 14, 1913, the only child of Leslie and Dorothy Gardner King. His parents were divorced in 1915. His mother moved to Grand Rapids, Mich., and married Gerald R. Ford. The boy was renamed for his stepfather.

Ford captained his high school football team in Grand Rapids, and a football scholarship took him to the University of Michigan, where he starred as varsity center before his graduation in 1935. A job as assistant football coach at Yale gave him an opportunity to attend Yale Law School, from which he graduated in the top third of his class in 1941.

He returned to Grand Rapids to practice law, but entered the Navy in April 1942. He saw wartime service in the Pacific on the light aircraft carrier *Monterey* and was a lieutenant commander when he returned to Grand Rapids early in 1946 to resume law practice and dabble in politics.

Ford was elected to Congress in 1948 for the first of his 13 terms in the House. He was soon assigned to the influential Appropriations Committee and rose to become the ranking Republican on the subcommittee on Defense Department appropriations and an expert in the field.

As a legislator, Ford described himself as "a moderate on domestic issues, a conservative in fiscal affairs, and a dyed-in-the-wool internationalist." He carried the ball for Pentagon appropriations, was a hawk on the war in Vietnam, and kept a low profile on civil-rights issues.

He was also dependable and hard-working and popular with his colleagues. In 1963, he was elected chairman of the House Republican Conference. He served in 1963–64 as a member of the Warren Commission that investigated the assassination of John F. Kennedy. A revolt by dissatisfied younger Republicans in 1965 made him minority leader.

Ford shelved his hopes for the Speakership on Oct. 12, 1973, when Nixon nominated him to fill the vice presidency left vacant by Agnew's resignation under fire. It was the first use of the procedures for filling vacancies in the vice presidency laid down in the 25th Amendment to the Constitution, which Ford had helped enact.

Congress confirmed Ford as vice president on Dec. 6, 1973. Once in office, he said he did not believe Nixon had been involved in the Watergate scandals, but criticized his stubborn court battle against releasing tape recordings of Watergate-related conversations for use as evidence.

The scandals led to Nixon's unprecedented resignation on Aug. 9, 1974, and Ford was sworn in immediately as the 38th president, the first to enter the White House without winning a national election.

Ford assured the nation when he took office that "our long national nightmare is over" and pledged "openness and candor" in all his actions. He won a warm response from the Democratic 93rd Congress when he said he wanted "a good marriage" rather than a honeymoon with his former colleagues. In December 1974 Congressional majorities backed his choice of former New York Gov. Nelson A. Rockefeller as his successor in the again-vacant vice presidency.

The cordiality was chilled by Ford's announcement on Sept. 8, 1974, that he had granted an unconditional pardon to Nixon for any crimes he might have committed as president. Although no formal charges were pending, Ford said he feared "ugly passions" would be aroused if Nixon were brought to trial. The pardon was widely criticized.

To fight inflation, the new president first proposed fiscal restraints and spending curbs and a 5% tax sur-charge that got nowhere in the Senate and House. Congress again rebuffed Ford in the spring of 1975 when he appealed for emergency military aid to help the governments of South Vietnam and Cambodia re-sist massive Communist offensives.

In November 1974, Ford visited Japan, South Ko-rea, and the Soviet Union, where he and Soviet lead-er Leonid I. Brezhnev conferred in Vladivostok and reached a tentative agreement to limit the number of strategic offensive nuclear weapons. It was Ford's first meeting as president with Brezhnev, who planned a return visit to Washington in the fall of 1975.

Politically, Ford's fortunes improved steadily in the first half of 1975. Badly divided Democrats in Con-gress were unable to muster votes to override his ve-toes of spending bills that exceeded his budget. He faced some right-wing opposition in his own party, but moved to pre-empt it with an early announce-ment—on July 8, 1975—of his intention to be a can-didate in 1976.

Early state primaries in 1976 suggested an easy victory for Ford despite Ronald Reagan's bitter at-tacks on administration foreign policy and defense programs. But later Reagan primary successes threat-ened the President's lead. At the Kansas City conven-tion, Ford was nominated by the narrow margin of 1,187 to 1,070. But Reagan had moved the party to the right, and Ford himself was regarded as a caretak-er president lacking in strength and vision. He was defeated in November by Jimmy Carter.

In 1948, Ford married Elizabeth Anne (Betty) Bloomer. They had four children, Michael Gerald, John Gardner, Steven Meigs, and Susan Elizabeth.

JAMES EARL CARTER, JR., was born in the tiny village of Plains, Ga., Oct. 1, 1924, and grew up on the family farm at nearby Archery. Both parents were fifth-generation Georgians. His father, James Earl Carter, was known as a segregationist, but treated his black and white workers equally. Carter's mother, Lillian Gordy, was a matriarchal presence in home and community and opposed the then-prevailing code of racial inequality. The future President was baptized in 1935 in the conservative Southern Baptist Church and spoke often of being a "born again" Christian, although committed to the separation of church and state.

Carter married Rosalynn Smith, a neighbor, in 1946. Their first child, John William, was born a year later in Portsmouth, Va. Their other children are James Earl III, born in Honolulu in 1950; Donnel Jef-frey, born in New London, Conn., in 1952, and Amy Lynn, born in Plains in 1967.

In 1946 Carter was graduated from the U.S. Naval Academy at Annapolis and served in the nuclear-sub-marine program under Adm. Hyman G. Rickover. In 1954, after his father's death, he resigned from the Navy to take over the family's flourishing warehouse and cotton gin, with several thousand acres for grow-ing seed peanuts.

Carter was elected to the Georgia Senate in 1962. In 1966 he lost the race for Governor, but was elected in 1970. His term brought a state government reorganization, sharply reduced agencies, increased economy and efficiency, and new social programs, all with no general tax increase. In 1972 the peanut farmer-politician set his sights on the Presidency and in 1974 built a base for himself as he criss-crossed the country as chairman of the Democratic Campaign Committee, appealing for revival and reform. In 1975 his image as a typical Southern white was erased when he won support of most of the old Southern civil-rights coalition after endorsement by Rep. An-drew Young, black Democrat from Atlanta, who had been the closest aide to the Rev. Martin Luther King, Jr. At Carter's 1971 inauguration as Governor he had called for an end to all forms of racial discrimination.

In the 1976 spring primaries, he won 19 out of 31 with a broad appeal to conservatives and liberals, black and white, poor and well-to-do. Throughout his campaigning Carter set forth his policies in his soft Southern voice, and with his electric-blue stare faced down skeptics who joked about "Jimmy Who?" His toothy smile became his trademark. He was nomi-nated on the first roll-call vote of the 1976 Bicenten-nial Democratic National Convention in New York, and defeated Gerald R. Ford in November. Likewise, in 1980 he was renominated on the first ballot after vanquishing Senator Edward M. Kennedy of Massa-chusetts in the primaries. At the convention he de-feated the Kennedy forces in their attempt to block a party rule that bound a large majority of pledged delegates to vote for Carter. In the election campaign, Carter attacked his rivals, Ronald Reagan and John B. Anderson, independent, with the warning that a Reagan Republican victory would heighten the risk of war and impede civil rights and economic opportuni-ty. In November Carter lost to Reagan, who won 489 Electoral College votes and 51% of the popular tally, to 49 electoral votes and 41% for Carter.

In his one term, Carter fought hard for his pro-grams against resistance from an independent-minded Democratic Congress that frustrated many pet proj-ects although it overrode only two vetoes. Many of his difficulties were traced to his aides' brusqueness in dealing with Capitol Hill and insensitivity to Con-gressional feelings and tradition. Observers generally viewed public dissatisfaction with the "stagflation" economy as a principal factor in his defeat. Others included his jittery performance in the debate Oct. 28 with Reagan and the final uncertainties in the negoti-ations for freeing the Iranians' hostages, along with earlier staff problems, friction with Congress, long gasoline lines, and the months-long Iranian crisis, in-cluding the abortive sally in April 1980 to free the hostages. The President, however, did deflect criti-cism resulting from the activities of his brother, Billy. Yet, assessments of his record noted many positive elements. There was, for one thing, peace throughout his term, with no American combat deaths and with a brake on the advocates of force. Regarded as perhaps his greatest personal achievements were the Camp David accords between Israel and Egypt and the re-sulting treaty—the first between Israel and an Arab neighbor. The treaty with China and the Panama Ca-nal treaties were also major achievements. Carter worked for nuclear-arms control. His concern for in-ternational human rights was credited with saving lives and reducing torture, and he supported the Brit-ish policy that ended internecine warfare in Rhodesia, now Zimbabwe. Domestically, his environmental re-cord was a major accomplishment. His judicial ap-pointments won acclaim; the Southerner who had for-sworn racism made 265 choices for the Federal bench that included minority members and women. On en-ergy, he ended by price decontrols the practice of holding U.S. petroleum prices far below world levels.

—Arthur P. Reed, Jr.

RONALD WILSON REAGAN rode to the Presidency in 1980 on a tide of resurgent right-wing sentiment among an electorate battered by winds of unwanted change, longing for a distant, simpler era.

He left office in January 1989 with two-thirds of the American people approving his performance during his two terms. It was the highest rating for any retiring President since World War II. In his farewell speech, Reagan exhorted the nation to cling to the revival of patriotism that he had fostered. And he spoke proudly of the economic recovery during his Administrations, although regretting the huge budget deficit, for which, in part, many blamed his policies.

Reagan had retained the public's affection as he applied his political magic to policy goals. His place in history will rest, perhaps, on the short- and intermediate-range missile treaty consummated on a cordial visit to the Soviet Union that he had once reviled as an "evil empire." Its provisions, including a ground-breaking agreement on verification inspection, were formulated in four days of summit talks in Moscow in May 1988 with the Soviet leader, Mikhail S. Gorbachev.

And Reagan can point to numerous domestic achievements: sharp cuts in income tax rates, sweeping tax reform; creating economic growth without inflation, reducing the unemployment rate, among others. He failed, however, to win the "Reagan Revolution" on such issues as abortion and school prayer, and he seemed aloof from "sleazy" conduct by some top officials.

In his final months Reagan campaigned aggressively to win election as President for his two-term Vice President, George Bush.

Reagan's popularity with the public dipped sharply in 1986 when the Iran-Contra scandal broke, shortly after the Democrats gained control of the Senate. Observers agreed that Reagan's presidency had been weakened, if temporarily, by the two unrelated events. Then the weeks-long Congressional hearings in the summer of 1987 heard an array of Administration officials, present and former, tell their tales of a White House riven by deceit and undercover maneuvering. Yet no breath of illegality touched the President's personal reputation; on Aug. 12, 1987, he told the nation that he had not known of questionable activities but agreed that he was "ultimately accountable."

Ronald Reagan, actor turned politician, New Dealer turned conservative, came to the films and politics from a thoroughly Middle-American background—middle class, Middle West and small town. He was born in Tampico, Ill., Feb. 6, 1911, the second son of John Edward Reagan and Nelle Wilson Reagan, and the family later moved to Dixon, Ill. The father, of Irish descent, was a shop clerk and merchant with Democratic sympathies. It was an impoverished family; young Ronald sold homemade popcorn at high school games and worked as a lifeguard to earn money for his college tuition. When the father got a New Deal WPA job, the future President became an ardent Roosevelt Democrat.

Reagan won a B.A. degree in 1932 from Eureka (Ill.) College, where a photographic memory aided in his studies and in debating and college theatricals. In a Depression year, he was making $100 a week as a sports announcer for radio station WHO in Des Moines, Iowa, from 1932 to 1937. His career as a film and TV actor stretched from 1937 to 1966, and his salary climbed to $3,500 a week. As a World War II captain in Army film studios, Reagan recoiled from what he saw as the laziness of Civil Service workers, and moved to the Right. As president of the Screen Actors Guild, he resisted what he considered a Communist plot to subvert the film industry. With advancing age, Reagan left leading-man roles and became a television spokesman for the General Electric Company at $150,000.

With oratorical skill his trademark, Reagan became an active Republican. At the behest of a small group of conservative Southern California businessmen, he ran for governor with a pledge to cut spending, and was elected by almost a million votes over the political veteran, Democratic Gov. Edmund G. Brown, father of the later governor.

In the 1980 election battle against Jimmy Carter, Reagan broadened his appeal by espousing moderate policies, gaining much of his support from disaffected Democrats and blue-collar workers. The incoming Administration immediately set out to "turn the government around" with a new economic program. Over strenuous Congressional opposition, Reagan triumphed on his "supply side" theory to stimulate production and control inflation through tax cuts and sharp reductions in government spending.

The President won high acclaim for his nomination of Sandra Day O'Connor as the first woman on the Supreme Court. His later nominations met increasing opposition but did much to tilt the Court's orientation to the Right.

In 1982, the President's popularity had slipped as the economy declined into the worst recession in 40 years, with persistent high unemployment and interest rates. Initial support for "supply side" economics faded but the President won crucial battles in Congress.

Internationally, Reagan confronted numerous critical problems in his first term. The successful invasion of Grenada accomplished much diplomatically. But the intervention in Lebanon and the withdrawal of Marines after a disastrous terrorist attack were regarded as military failures.

The popular President won reelection in the 1984 landslide, with the economy improving and inflation under control. Domestically, a tax reform bill that Reagan backed became law. But the constantly growing budget deficit remained a constant irritant, with the President and Congress persistently at odds over priorities in spending for defense and domestic programs. His foreign policy met stiffening opposition, with Congress increasingly reluctant to increase spending for the Nicarguan "Contras" and the Pentagon and to expand the development of the MX missile. But even severe critics praised Reagan's restrained but decisive handling of the crisis following the hijacking of an American plane in Beirut by Moslem extremists. The attack on Libya in April 1986 galvanized the nation, although it drew scathing disapproval from the NATO alliance.

Barely three months into his first term, Reagan was the target of an assassin's bullet; his courageous comeback won public admiration.

Reagan is devoted to his wife, Nancy, whom he married after his divorce from the screen actress Jane Wyman. The children of the first marriage are Maureen, his daughter by Miss Wyman, and Michael, an adopted son. In the present marriage the children are Patricia and Ron.

—Arthur P. Reed, Jr.

GEORGE H. BUSH became President on January 20, 1989, with his theme harmony and conciliation after the often-turbulent Reagan years. With his calm and unassuming manner, he emerged from his subordinate Vice-Presidential role with an air of quiet authority. His Inaugural address emphasized "A new breeze is blowing, and the old bipartisanship must be made new again."

In his first months, the President, the nation's 41st, established himself as his own man and all but erased memories of what many had regarded as his fiercely abrasive Presidential election campaign of 1988 and questionable tactics against his Democratic opponent. People liked his easy style and readiness to compromise even as he remained a staunch conservative, although that readiness had disconcerted some conservatives.

In 1991, the 67-year-old President emerged as the leader of an international coalition of Western democracies, Japan, and even some Arab states that freed invaded Kuwait and vanquished, at least for a time, Iraq's President Saddam Hussein and his armies.

A nation grateful at feeling the end of the "Vietnam syndrome" gave the President an over-all rating of 89 percent in a Gallup poll in March after the end of the war. The approval rate fell as the year went on, but a solid majority continued to approve the President's performance, although with growing concern about the faltering economy and other domestic problems. And there were nagging doubts about the Persian Gulf war, its motives and conduct, and about the ensuing refugee crisis.

A major Bush accomplishment in 1991 was the Strategic Arms Reduction Treaty (Start), signed in July with Soviet President Mikhail S. Gorbachev at their fourth summit conference, marking the end of the long weapons buildup. Succeeding events in the Soviet Union and the apparent disintegration of the Communist empire could only enhance his status.

The year also saw the President undergoing treatment for Graves' disease, a thyroid disorder, from which he suffered serious side effects.

Bush's early Cabinet choices reflected a pragmatic desire for an efficient nonideological Government.

But in his second year, 1990, the President confronted a mounting array of problems, the most critical being on the domestic side. Chief among them were the staggering and mushrooming budget deficit and the savings and loan crisis. Other vexing issues were the question of cutting defense expenditures with consequent economic dislocation, the war on drugs, and the environment.

With his usual cautious instinct, the President nominated to the Supreme Court the scholarly David Souter, with broadly conservative views. Souter was confirmed without a bruising battle.

At home, the President's popularity slipped sharply from its near record 76 percent public approval following the invasion of Panama in late 1989. This plunge followed Bush's recantation of his "no new taxes" pledge as he sat down with Congressional leaders to tame the budget deficit and deal with a faltering economy.

In his first year Bush, a World War II hero, had won plaudits at home and abroad for his confident, competent conduct at the NATO 40th anniversary summit meeting at Brussels, the Paris economic conference, on his tour of Eastern Europe, and at the Malta conference with Gorbachev. Grave challenges in that year were the Lebanon hostage crisis and the ongoing war on the drug traffic.

Domestically, the President had to cope with such issues as the Exxon Valdez oil spill in Alaska and the dispute over flag-burning restrictions, which was resolved, if only for a time, in mid-1990.

Bush, scion of an aristocratic New England family, came to the White House after a long career in public service, in which he held top positions in national and international organizations. As Vice President, he avoided the appearance of direct involvement in the Iran-Contra affair while not seeming to shy away from the President.

Earlier, in the 1960s, Bush won two contests for a Texas Republican seat in the House of Representatives, but lost two bids for a Senate seat and one for the Presidency. After his second race for the Senate, President Nixon appointed him U.S. delegate to the United Nations with the rank of Ambassador and he later became Republican National Chairman. He headed the United States liaison office in Beijing before becoming Director of Central Intelligence.

In 1980 Bush became Reagan's running mate despite earlier criticism of Reagan "voodoo economics" and by the 1984 election had won acclaim for devotion to Reagan's conservative agenda despite his own reputation as somewhat more liberally inclined. Nevertheless, die-hard right-wingers could find satisfaction in Bush's war record and his Government service, particularly with the C.I.A. Throughout he remained influential in White House decisions, particularly in foreign affairs.

In the 1988 campaign, Bush's choice of Senator Dan Quayle of Indiana for Vice President surprised his friends and provoked criticism and ridicule that continued even after the Administration was established in office. Nonetheless Bush strongly defended his choice.

The future President joined the Navy after war broke out and at 18 became the Navy's youngest commissioned pilot, serving from 1942 to 1945. The man later derided by some as a "wimp" fought the Japanese on 58 missions and was shot down once. He won the Distinguished Flying Cross.

Throughout his whole career, Bush had the backing of an established family, headed by his father, the autocratic and wealthy Prescott Bush, who was elected to the Senate from Connecticut in 1952. And his family helped the young patrician became established in his early business ventures, a rich uncle raising most of the capital required for founding a new oil company in Texas.

George Herbert Walker Bush was born June 12, 1924, in Milton, Mass., to Prescott and Dorothy Bush. The family later moved to Connecticut. The youth studied at the elite Phillips Academy in Andover, Mass., before entering the Navy.

After the war, Bush earned an economics degree and a Phi Beta Kappa key in two and a half years at Yale University. While there he captained the baseball team and was initiated into "Skull and Bones," the prestigious Yale secret society.

In 1945 Bush married Barbara Pierce of Rye, N.Y., daughter of a magazine publisher. With his bride, Bush moved to Texas instead of entering his father's investment banking business. There he founded his oil company and in 1980 reported an estimated wealth of $1.4 million.

The Bushes have lived in 17 cities and more than a score of homes and have traveled in as many countries. In her husband's frequent absences during the early years, Mrs. Bush was often matriarch of a family of four boys and a girl. Bush is close to his immediate family and to 10 grandchildren, a sister, and three brothers.

Bush sold his Houston home several years ago and moved from the Vice President's dwelling to the White House, and lives there and at the family estate at Kennebunkport, Maine.

—Arthur P. Reed, Jr.

ENERGY

Cool Energy
The Renewable Solution to Global Warming
By the Union of Concerned Scientists

There is a strong consensus within the scientific community than an increasing concentration of heat-trapping gases in the atmosphere will cause the earth's climate to get warmer. The buildup of these gases—carbon dioxide (CO_2), chlorofluorocarbons (CFCs), nitrous oxide, methane, and ozone (smog)—will increase the atmosphere's natural "greenhouse effect," bringing on global warming. Resulting changes in surface temperature, precipitation, sea level, and other aspects of our climate could cause severe disruption of natural and economic systems throughout the world.

Our society uses enormous amounts of energy to heat our homes and offices, to power our industrial economy, and to move us rapidly from place to place. The burning of fossil fuels (coal, oil, and natural gas) to supply this energy is responsible for the buildup of the most common greenhouse gas—carbon dioxide. Fossil-fuel burning releases 5.6 billion tons of carbon—at least 70 percent of total carbon emissions from human sources—into the atmosphere each year. It is also a major source of nitrous oxide, methane, and ozone.

Fortunately, we can reduce these greenhouse-gas emissions and slow down the climate change without major changes in our way of life.

Renewable Energy

Renewable energy sources have several advantages over fossil fuels and nuclear power. They are enormous and inexhaustible, produce little or no pollution or hazardous waste, and pose few risks to public safety. Further, they are entirely a domestic resource and thus would be virtually immune to foreign disruptions like the 1973 Arab oil embargo. They also provide a hedge against energy-price inflation caused by the depletion of fossil-fuel reserves. And, unlike coal and nuclear plants, which take 8–15 years to put into operation, large-scale, renewable-energy technologies can be installed quickly, in six months to two years.

The United States already relies on renewable energy sources for about 7.5 percent of its energy needs. The vast majority of this energy comes from two sources that have reached commercial maturity: hydroelectric power and wood. In the future, a much larger portion will be supplied by the emerging technologies of solar, wind, and biomass-derived fuels.

Solar. Solar technologies can provide both electricity and heat and thus are suitable for a variety of energy applications. Passive-solar home-heating systems, solar water heaters, large-scale solar-thermal electric systems (which convert solar heat to electricity), and photovoltaic cells (which generate electricity directly) have all met with some commercial success in the past decade.

Most solar technologies are much less expensive today than just a few years ago, and they are likely to become more competitive in the next few years. For example, the price of photovoltaic electricity has fallen tenfold since 1976, to about 25–35 cents per kilowatt-hour, in 10 years the cost could reach 6–12 cents per kilowatt-hour, low enough to compete with most conventional electricity sources for generating peak daytime power.

Solar-thermal electric systems already produce electricity at a cost of about 12 cents per kilowatt-hour, and the cost is expected to drop to 8 cents per kilowatt-hour when larger plants now under construction are completed. By the end of the 1990s, a variety of solar-thermal electric designs, including parabolic-trough collectors, parabolic-dish collectors, and central receivers, could be generating electricity at economic prices.

Wind. Wind power, one of the oldest and most environmentally benign energy sources, has been one of the most successful in the past 10 years. Between 1981 and 1988, over 15,000 wind turbines with a total peak electric capacity of almost 1,500 megawatts were installed in California—where the vast majority of U.S. and world wind-power development has taken place—and in 1987 these turbines generated about as much electricity as San Francisco consumes in a year.

Wind power offers the potential for meeting a large fraction of U.S. electricity needs. Estimates of the total potential vary, but it appears that at least 20 percent of current U.S. electricity demand could be met by wind turbines installed on the Great Plains, along coasts, and in other windy areas.

Wind turbines are among the most economical of the emerging renewable-energy technologies. At a good site, modern turbines can produce electricity at a cost of 7–9 cents per kilowatt-hour. Within the next few years the cost could fall to 4–6 cents per kilowatt-hour. This would make wind power competitive with a broad range of conventional electricity sources.

Biomass. Biomass use—capturing the solar energy in wood and vegetation—is now 4–5 percent of annual U.S. energy consumption. Ultimately, biomass resources could supply 15–30 percent of U.S. energy consumption. Agricultural, forestry, and municipal wastes, plus plants and trees grown on "energy plantations," would supply the raw materials.

In the future, biomass is likely to be most important as a source of liquid fuels for transportation. Automobiles and trucks could run on these fuels with only minor modifications to their engines and fuel tanks. (Currently about 8 percent of gasoline sold in the United States contains ethanol, derived from corn or other grains, in a mixture known as gasohol.) In addition, biomass-derived gases such as methane (the major constituent of natural gas) and a mixture of carbon monoxide and hydrogen can be readily burned in existing natural-gas-fired steam boilers and furnaces.

Most biomass fuels are still too expensive to succeed commercially, but their costs are falling steadily, and the Department of Energy projects that biomass fuels could become competitive with petroleum-based fuels around the turn of the century.

As long as biomass that is consumed for energy is replaced by new growth, so that the carbon dioxide released in combustion is reabsorbed, biomass's net contribution to global warming will be negligible. More than most renewable energy sources, however, biomass carries some environmental risks, including air pollution, toxic residues and ash, and depletion of soil nutrients. These issues must therefore be studied carefully and appropriate standards and regulations developed.

Stimulating the Renewable-Energy Economy

The transition to a renewable-energy economy will require the implementation of a new national energy policy, changes in government programs, and a restructuring of some aspects of our taxation system. There are a number of options for action at the federal, state, and local levels that will help to stimulate large-scale commercialization of renewable energy sources.

Federal Funding for Research, Development, and Demonstration. Despite massive cuts under the Reagan administration, federally funded R&D has contributed to continuing gains in solar, wind, and biomass technologies. What is needed now is a steady annual increase of perhaps 20–30 percent in the Department of Energy renewable-energy budget. There is also a need for greater emphasis on near-term commercialization, including cost-sharing efforts with the private sector, demonstration projects, and the purchase of renewable energy in large quantities to supply power to government facilities.

Leveling the "Playing Field." Renewable energy sources are forced to compete in a rigged market because our economic system fails to account for the environmental and social damage caused by energy technologies. These "external" costs—such as the acid rain and air pollution caused by coal burning—are not included in the prices we pay for fossil fuels. This means that relatively harmful energy sources, like coal, are given an unfair market advantage over relatively benign sources, like wind power. If the hidden costs of energy technologies were included in their price—rather than in our taxes and health-insurance costs—renewable-energy technologies would be in a far better position to compete with their conventional counterparts.

The playing field can be at least partially leveled through the utility rate-setting procedure (where the "external" costs would be "internalized"); by federal and state support, whether direct or through tax credits, to bring down the costs of renewable energy sources; and by modest taxes on the use of fossil fuels.

Encouraging Private Investment. The short-term focus that has run rampant in American industry and financial circles also places renewable energy sources at a disadvantage. The high initial costs of solar collectors, wind turbines, and other renewable technologies make them more expensive than conventional technologies in the short term, even though their costs in the long run are likely to be lower.

These barriers can be lowered by the use of tax credits for renewable-energy investments and by educational programs on the federal, state, and local levels.

Conclusion

The global development of renewable energy sources, along with improvements in energy efficiency, could greatly slow the pace of global warming, cutting the projected temperature increase over the next 100 years by nearly 50 percent, according to a recent EPA study. In order to accomplish this, however, government leadership, particularly by the U.S., will be crucial. The United States must increase its support for renewable energy sources. The relatively minor initial investments required will be more than offset by the long-term economic and environmental benefits. □

This material is adapted from a 1990 Union of Concerned Scientists report of the same title, available from the UCS Publications Department.

The Union of Concerned Scientists is a nonprofit 501(c)(3) organization supported by donations from some 100,000 individuals, including many thousands of scientists. For more information, contact: Union of Concerned Scientists, 26 Church Street, Cambridge, Mass., 02238, (617) 547-5552.

Renewable Energy Consumption Estimates, 1989–1990
(Quadrillion Btu, Except as Noted)

	1989	1990
Reported consumption	3.10	3.15
Hydroelectric power	2.88	2.94
Electric utilities	2.74	2.89
Industrial	0.03	0.03
Imported electricity	0.27	0.21
Exported electricity	0.17	0.19
Geothermal energy at electric utilities	0.20	0.18
Wood and waste energy at electric utilities	0.02	0.02
Wind energy at electric utilities	([1])	([1])
Additional consumption estimates	3.19	3.55
Biofuels	2.90	3.23
Residential, commercial, and industrial	2.83	3.15
Transportation use	0.07	0.08
Geothermal energy (non-electric utilities)	0.14	0.16
Solar energy (non-electric utilities)	0.09	0.08
Wind energy (non-electric utilities)	0.03	0.04
Hydroelectric power (additional industrial use)	0.03	0.04
Total consumption estimates	6.29	6.70

1. Less than 0.005 quadrillion Btu. *Source: Annual Energy Review, 1990,* Energy Information Administration.

Renewable Energy Consumption

In 1990, electric utilities and other consumers reported 3.2 quadrillion Btu of renewable energy consumption, most of which was hydroelectric power. Additional renewable energy consumption estimates of about 3.6 quadrillion Btu per year consisted primarily of non-electric utility use of biofuels such as wood, waste, and alcohol fuels. When U.S. total energy consumption is adjusted by the addition of the estimates, total renewable energy consumption accounted for an 8-percent share.

Wood and Other Biofuels

Energy derived from wood totaled 2.5 quadrillion Btu in 1989. Almost 1.6 quadrillion Btu of wood was consumed by the industrial sector. Industries with ready access to wood and wood byproducts, such as the paper and lumber industries, relied heavily on wood as an energy source. Energy derived from other biofuels, such as agricultural and solid wastes and alcohol fuels, totaled 0.4 quadrillion Btu in 1989.

Solar Energy

Solar energy is an inexhaustible, universally available source of energy. Converting solar energy to useful forms, however, requires large collection areas, and therefore the amount that can be harnessed is limited. Producer shipments of equipment are used as one measure of solar energy consumption. Shipments of low-temperature collectors, used primarily for heating swimming pools, peaked at 12 million square feet in 1980 but totaled only 4.3 million square feet in 1989. Shipments of medium-temperature, special, and other collectors, used primarily for domestic hot water, peaked at 12 million square feet in 1983 and 1984 but, following the expiration of the Federal energy tax credit in 1985, fell to 0.7 million square feet in 1988. In 1989,

2 million square feet were shipped. Shipments of photovoltaic modules totaled 13 thousand peak kilowatts in 1989.

Geothermal Energy

Most geothermal energy is trapped below the Earth's crust in layers of molten rock, but where the crust is thinner, geothermal energy can be harnessed. Geothermal energy may be used directly, for purposes such as space heating, or converted to electricity. In 1960, The Geysers in California became the first U.S. utility to generate electricity from geothermal steam. Subsequently, electricity generation from geothermal sources trended upward and peaked at 10.8 billion kilowatthours of electricity in 1987. From 1988 to 1990, however, electricity generation from geothermal sources declined, falling to 8.6 billion kilowatthours in 1990.

Solar Thermal Collector Shipments by Type

	Low–Temperature Collectors			Medium–Temperature, Special, and Other Collectors		
Year	No. of manufacturers	Quantity shipped (million square feet)	Average shipments per manufacturer (thousand square feet)	No. of manufacturers	Quantity shipped (million square feet)	Average shipments per manufacturer (thousand square feet)
1974	6	1.14	189.5	39	0.14	3.5
1975	13	3.03	232.8	118	0.72	6.1
1976	19	3.88	204.0	203	1.93	9.5
1977	52	4.74	91.2	297	5.57	18.8
1978	69	5.87	85.1	204	4.99	24.5
1979	84	8.39	100.0	257	5.86	22.8
1980	79	12.23	154.8	250	7.17	28.7
1981	75	8.68	115.7	263	11.46	43.6
1982	61	7.48	122.6	248	11.15	44.9
1983	55	4.85	88.2	179	11.98	66.9
1984	48	4.48	93.3	206	11.94	58.0
1986	22	3.75	170.5	87	1.11	12.8
1987	12	3.16	263.1	50	0.96	19.1
1988	8	3.33	415.8	45	0.73	16.2
1989	10	4.28	428.3	36	1.99	55.3

Note: Manufacturers producing more than one type of collector are accounted for in both groups. No data are avialable for 1985. *Sources:* **Number of Manufacturers:** Energy Information Administration (EIA), "Annual Solar Thermal Collector Manufacturers Survey." **Other Data:** • 1974 through 1976—Federal Energy Administration, *Solar Collector Manufacturing Activity,* semi-annual. • 1977-EIA, *Solar Collector Manufacturing Activity, July through December, 1981,* March 1982 (semi-annual). • 1978 and forward—EIA, *Solar Collector Manufacturing Activity,* annual.

Households That Burn Wood, 1980–1982, 1984, and 1987[1]

	1980	1982	1984	1987
Households that burn wood				
Numbers of households (millions)	21.6	21.4	22.9	22.5
Percent of all U.S. households	26.4	25.6	26.6	24.8
Number of cords burned (millions)	42.7	48.6	49.0	42.6
Average number of cords burned per household				
Mean	2.0	2.3	2.1	1.9
Median	0.7	1.0	1.0	0.7
Wood energy consumed (trillion Btu)	854	971	981	853
Households that burn wood as main heating fuel				
Number of households (millions)	4.7	5.6	6.4	5.0
Percent of all U.S. households	5.8	6.7	7.5	5.6
Number of cords burned (millions)	22.4	28.7	29.4	23.5
Average number of cords burned per household				
Mean	4.7	5.1	4.6	4.7
Median	3.3	4.0	4.0	4.0
Wood energy consumed (trillion Btu)	448	574	589	470
Households that burn wood as secondary heating fuel and for other purposes				
Number of households (millions)	16.9	15.9	16.5	17.4
Percent of all U.S. households	20.6	18.9	19.1	19.3
Number of cords burned (millions)	20.3	19.9	19.6	19.2
Average number of cords burned per household				
Mean	1.2	1.3	1.2	1.1
Median	0.3	0.5	0.5	0.5
Wood energy consumed (trillion Btu)	406	397	392	383

1. Data are for the heating season beginning with the latter part of the previous year shown. NOTE: Consumption estimates are based on respondent reports and may be subject to reporting biases. NOTE: No data are available for 1983, 1985, or 1986. *Source:* Energy Information Administratio, Form EIA-457, "Residential Energy Consumption Survey."

Simplified diagram of a nuclear reactor. Laurel Cook, Boston, MA.

Largest Nuclear Power Plants in the United States
(over a million kilowatts)

Plant	Operating utility	Capacity (kilowatts)	Year operative
South Texas 1, TX	Houston Lighting & Power	1,250,000	1988
South Texas 2	Houston Lighting	1,250,000	1989
Palo Verde 1, AZ	Arizona Public Service	1,221,000	1986
Palo Verde 2, AZ	Arizona Public Service	1,221,000	1986
Palo Verde 3, AZ	Arizona Public Service	1,221,000	1988
Perry 1, OH	Cleveland Electric Illumination	1,205,000	1987
Sequoyah 1, TN	Tennessee Valley Authority	1,148,000	1981
Sequoyah 2, TN	Tennessee Valley Authority	1,148,000	1982
Callaway, MO	Union Electric	1,145,000	1984
Grand Gulf 1, MS	System Energy Resources	1,142,000	1985
Millstone 3, CT	Northeast Nuclear Energy	1,142,000	1986
Catawba 1, SC	Duke Power Co.	1,129,000	1985
Catawba 2, SC	Duke Power Co.	1,129,000	1986
McGuire 1, NC	Duke Power Co.	1,129,000	1981
McGuire 2, NC	Duke Power Co.	1,129,000	1984
Wolf Creek 1, KS	Wolf Creek Nuclear Operating	1,128,000	1985
Braidwood 1, IL	Commonwealth Edison	1,120,000	1988
Braidwood 2, IL	Commonwealth Edison	1,120,000	1988
Salem 1, DE	Public Service Electric & Gas	1,106,000	1977
Salem 2, DE	Public Service Electric & Gas	1,106,000	1981
Byron 1, IL	Commonwealth Edison	1,105,000	1985
Byron 2, IL	Commonwealth Edison	1,105,000	1987
Vogtle 2	Georgia Power	1,083,000	1989
Trojan, OR	Portland General Electric	1,095,000	1976
Fermi 2, OH	Detroit Edison	1,093,000	1988
Diablo Canyon 2	Pacific Gas & Electric	1,087,000	1986
N ine Mile Point 2, NY	Niagara Mohawk Power	1,080,000	1988
San Onofre 3, CA	Southern California Edison	1,080,000	1984
Vogtle 1, GA	Georgia Power	1,079,000	1987
Waterford 3, LA	Louisiana Power & Light	1,075,000	1985
Diablo Canyon 1, CA	Pacific Gas & Electric	1,073,000	1985
San Onofre 2, CA	Southern California Edison	1,070,000	1983
Hope Creek 1, DE	Public Service Electric & Gas	1,067,000	1986
Browns Ferry 1, AL	Tennessee Valley Authority	1,065,000	1974
Browns Ferry 2, AL	Tennessee Valley Authority	1,065,000	1975
Browns Ferry 3, AL	Tennessee Valley Authority	1,065,000	1977
Limerick 2	Philadelphia Elec	1,065,000	1990
Cook 2, MI	Indiana & Michigan Power	1,060,000	1978
Limerick 1, PA	Philadelphia Electric	1,055,000	1986
Peach Bottom 2, PA	Philadelphia Electric	1,051,000	1974
Zion 1, IL	Commonwealth Edison	1,040,000	1973

Plant	Operating utility	Capacity (kilowatts)	Year operative
Zion 2, IL	Commonwealth Edison	1,040,000	1974
La Salle 1, IL	Commonwealth Edison	1,036,000	1984
La Salle 2, IL	Commonwealth Edison	1,036,000	1984
Peach Bottom 3, PA	Philadelphia Gas & Electric	1,035,000	1974
Susquehanna 1, PA	Pennsylvania Power & Light	1,032,000	1983
Susquehanna 2, PA	Pennsylvania Power & Light	1,032,000	1985
Comanche Peak 1, TX	Texas Utilities	1,159,000	1990
Seabrook 1, NH	Public Service of N.H.	1,150,000	1990

Source: Nuclear Regulatory Commission.

Production of Crude Petroleum by Countries

(in thousands of 42–gallon barrels)

Area and country	Est. 1991[1]	1990[1]	Est. percent change	Area and country	Est. 1991[1]	1990[1]	Est. percent change
Western Hemisphere	5,914,460	5,675,750	4.2	Iraq	94,170	1,123,105	−91.6
Argentina	178,485	173,010	3.2	Kuwait	55,845	647,510	−91.4
Bolivia	8,395	6,395	21.1	Neutral Zone	15,330	147,825	−89.6
Brazil	237,980	229,585	3.7	Oman	266,450	233,600	14.1
Canada	548,595	542,755	1.1	Qatar	136,510	136,875	−0.3
Chile	6,935	7,300	−5.0	Saudi Arabia	2,991,175	2,007,500	49.0
Colombia	145,635	149,650	−2.7	Syria	166,075	135,050	23.0
Ecuador	107,310	102,200	5.0	United Arab Emirates	904,835	751,535	20.4
Mexico	985,052	954,840	5.8	Yemen	76,650	69,350	10.5
Peru	42,340	45,625	−7.2	Asia Pacific	2,354,615	2,289,280	2.9
Trinidad	52,925	55,480	−4.6	Australia	187,610	223,015	−15.9
United States	2,709,030	2,664,865	1.7	Brunei	49,275	51,465	−4.3
Venezuela	857,750	734,745	16.7	China	1,022,365	1,004,845	1.7
Western Europe	1,539,570	1,461,095	5.4	India	241,630	254,040	−4.9
Austria	7,665	8,760	−12.5	Indonesia	528,155	456,250	15.8
Denmark	48,910	41,975	16.5	Japan	4,745	4,380	8.3
France	21,170	23,360	−9.4	Malaysia	237,250	226,300	4.8
Germany	27,375	28,470	−3.8	Myanmar	4,380	4,628	−7.7
Greece	5,475	6,205	−11.8	New Zealand	13,140	13,870	−5.3
Italy	34,675	37,230	−6.9	Pakistan	24,820	21,170	17.2
Netherlands	22,995	27,375	−16.0	Thailand	16,790	14,965	12.2
Norway	680,725	570,860	19.2	Vietnam	22,265	10,950	103.3
Spain	4,745	5,840	−18.8	Africa	2,313,370	2,183,065	6.0
Turkey	31,390	21,535	45.8	Algeria	292,000	295,650	−1.2
United Kingdom	654,445	689,485	−5.1	Angola	180,675	166,805	6.0
Eastern Europe	4,055,515	4,466,140	−9.2	Cameroon	57,305	63,145	−9.2
Albania	14,600	14,600	—	Congo	55,480	58,765	−5.6
Hungary	14,235	14,235	—	Egypt	325,215	311,710	4.3
Romania	58,400	58,400	—	Gabon	109,500	94,900	15.4
U.S.S.R.	3,942,000	4,352,625	−9.4	Libya	547,500	483,260	13.3
Yugoslavia	22,995	22,995	—	Nigeria	693,500	657,000	5.6
Middle East	5,790,360	6,340,050	−8.7	Tunisia	39,055	36,135	8.1
Bahrain	15,330	15,695	−2.3	Zaire	10,950	9,855	11.1
Iran	1,067,990	1,072,005	−0.4	**World Total**	**21,967,890**	**22,415,380**	**−2.0**

1. Based on Jan.–Feb. average. 2. Shared by Kuwait and Saudi Arabia. 3. An enclave in West Africa on Atlantic coast between the Congo and Angola. 4. Based on data prior to union into Republic of Yemen. Totals may not add up due to rounding.

Energy Equivalents

(*Source:* Energy Information Administration.)

1 Btu of energy: one match tip, 250 calories (International Steam Table), or 0.25 kilocalories (food calories).

1,000 Btu of energy: two five–ounce glasses of table wine; 250 kilocalories (food calories), or 0.80 peanut butter and jelly sandwiches.

1 million Btu of energy: 90 pounds of coal, 120 pounds of oven dried hardwood, 8 gallons of motor gasoline, 10 therms of natural dry gas, 11 gallons of propane, 1.2 days of U.S. energy consumption per capita (1984), or

two months dietary intake of a laborer.

1 barrel of crude oil: 14 days U.S. petroleum consumption per capita, 5.6 thousand cubic feet of dry natural gas, 0.26 short tons (520 pounds) of coal, or 1,700 kilowatts of electricity.

1 short ton of coal: 102 days of U.S. petroleum consumption per capita, 3.8 barrels of crude oil, 21 thousand cubic feet of dry natural gas, or 6,500 kilowatt-hours of electricity.

Petroleum Imports by Country of Origin, 1980–1990

(Thousand barrels per day)

Year	Nigeria	Saudi Arabia	Vene-zuela	Other OPEC[1]	Total OPEC[2]	Total Arab OPEC[3]	Canada	Mexico	United Kingdom	Virgin Is. and Puerto Rico
1980	857	1,261	481	865	4,300	2,551	455	533	176	476
1981	620	1,129	406	491	3,323	1,848	447	522	375	389
1982	514	552	412	250	2,146	854	482	685	456	366
1983	302	337	422	223	1,862	632	547	826	382	322
1984	216	325	548	294	2,049	819	630	748	402	336
1985	293	168	605	264	1,830	472	770	816	310	275
1986	440	685	793	329	2,837	1,162	807	699	350	265
1987	535	751	804	390	3,060	1,274	848	655	352	294
1988	618	1,064	794	538	3,520	1,839	999	747	315	264
1989[4]	815	1,224	873	776	4,140	2,130	931	767	215	353
1990[4]	797	1,337	1,020	729	4,275	2,232	921	752	184	315

Source: 1. "Other OPEC" consists of Ecuador, Gabon, Iran, Iraq, Kuwait, Libya, Qatar, and United Arab Emirates. Prior to 1988, imports from the Neutral Zone between Kuwait and Saudi Arabia are included in imports from Saudi Arabia. From 1988 forward, those imports are included in imports from "Other OPEC." 2. "Total OPEC" consists of Ecuador, Gabon, Indonesia, Iran, Nigeria, and Venezuela, as well as the Arab members. "Total OPEC" imports exclude petroleum imported into the United States indirectly from OPEC countries, primarily from Caribbean and West European refining areas, as petroleum products that were refined from crude oil produced in OPEC countries. 3. "Total Arab OPEC" consists of Algeria, Iraq, Kuwait, Libya, Qatar, Saudi Arabia, and United Arab Emirates. Imports from the Neutral Zone are included in imports from "Total Arab OPEC." 4. Previous-year data may have been revised. Current-year data are preliminary. Note: Sum of components may not equal total due to independent rounding. Sources: 1980—Energy Information Administration (EIA), Energy Data Reports, *P.A.D. Districts Supply/Demand, Annual.* •1981 through 1989—EIA, *Petroleum Supply Annual.* •1990—EIA, *Petroleum Supply Monthly,* Feb. 1991.

Petroleum Exports by Country of Destination, 1980–1990

(Thousand Barrels per Day)

Year	Canada	Japan	Mexico	Nether-lands	Belgium[1]	Italy	United Kingdom	France	Brazil	Virgin Is./ Puerto Rico
1980	108	32	28	23	20	14	7	11	4	220
1981	89	38	26	42	12	22	5	15	1	221
1982	85	68	53	85	17	32	14	24	8	211
1983	76	104	24	49	22	35	8	23	2	144
1984	83	92	35	37	21	39	14	18	1	152
1985	74	108	61	44	26	30	14	11	3	161
1986	85	110	56	58	30	39	8	11	3	112
1987	83	120	70	39	17	42	6	12	2	126
1988	84	124	70	26	25	29	9	12	3	147
1989	92	122	89	36	23	37	9	11	5	141
1990[2]	98	92	89	54	20	48	11	17	2	101

1. Including Luxembourg. 2. Preliminary. NOTE: Sum of components may not equal total due to independent rounding. *Source:* 1980—Energy Information Administration (EIA), Energy Data Reports, *Petroleum Statement, Annual.* • 1981 through 1989—EIA, *Petroleum Supply Annual.* • 1990—EIA, *Petroleum Supply Monthly,* Feb. 1991.

U.S. Motor Vehicle Fuel Consumption and Related Data

(1989 estimate)

Type of vehicle	Total travel (million vehicle miles)	Number of registered vehicles	Average miles traveled per vehicle	Fuel consumed (thousand gallons)	Average fuel con-sumption per vehicle (gallons)
All passenger vehicles	1,501,584	148,140,398	10,136	73,490,430	496
Total personal passenger vehicles	1,495,899	147,515,358	10,141	72,541,348	492
Cars	1,485,474	143,081,443	10,382	72,332,848	506
Motorcycles	10,425	4,433,915	2,351	208,500	47
All buses	5,685	625,040	9,095	949,082	1,518
All cargo vehicles	605,456	43,554,064	13,901	58,374,395	1,340
Single unit trucks	509,889	41,964,779	12,150	40,482,694	965
Combination	95,567	1,589,285	60,132	17,891,701	11,258
All motor vehicles	2,107,040	191,694,462	10,992	131,864,825	688

Source: Department of Transportation, Federal Highway Administration.

PEOPLE

Many public figures not listed here may be found elsewhere in the *Information Please Almanac*.

A name in parentheses is the original name or form of name. Localities are places of birth. Country name in parenthesis is the present-day name. Dates of birth appear as month/day/year. **Boldface** years in parentheses are dates of (**birth-death**).

Information has been gathered from many sources, including the individuals themselves. However, the *Information Please Almanac* cannot guarantee the accuracy of every individual item.

A

Aalto, Alvar (architect); Kuortane, Finland **(1898-1976)**
Abbado, Claudio (orchestra conductor); Milan, Italy, 1933
Abbott, Bud (William) (comedian); Asbury Park, N.J. **(1898-1974)**
Abbott, George (stage producer); Forestville, N.Y., 6/25/1887
Abel, Walter (actor); St. Paul **(1898-1987)**
Abelard, Peter (theologian); nr. Nantes, France **(1079-1142)**
Abernathy, Ralph (civil rights leader); Linden, Ala., **(1926-1990)**
Acheson, Dean (statesman); Middletown, Conn. **(1893-1971)**
Acuff, Roy Claxton (musician); nr. Maynardsville, Tenn. 9/15/1903
Adams, Charles Francis (diplomat); Boston **(1807-1886)**
Adams, Don (actor); New York City, 4/19/1926
Adams, Edie (Edie Enke) (actress); Kingston, Pa., 4/16/1929
Adams, Franklin Pierce (columnist and author); Chicago **(1881-1960)**
Adams, Henry Brooks (historian); Boston **(1838-1918)**
Adams, Joey (comedian); New York City, 1/6/1911
Adams, Mason (actor); New York City, 2/26/19
Adams, Maude (Maude Kiskadden) (actress); Salt Lake City, **(1872-1953)**
Adams, Samuel (American Revolutionary patriot); Boston **(1722-1803)**
Adamson, Joy (naturalist); Troppau, Silesia **(1910-1980)**
Addams, Charles (cartoonist); Westfield, N.J., **(1912-1988)**
Addams, Jane (social worker); Cedarville, Ill. **(1860-1935)**
Adderley, Julian "Cannonball" (jazz saxophonist); Tampa, Fla. **(1928-1975)**
Ade, George (humorist); Kentland, Ind. **(1866-1944)**
Adenauer, Konrad (statesman); Cologne, Germany **(1876-1967)**
Adler, Alfred (psychoanalyst); Vienna **(1870-1937)**
Adler, Larry (musician); Baltimore, 2/10/1914
Adler, Richard (songwriter); New York City, 8/3/1921
Adoree, Renée (Renée La Fonte) (actress); Lille, France **(1898-1933)**
Aeschylus (dramatist); Eleusis (Greece) **(525-456** B.C.)
Aesop (fabulist); birthplace unknown (**lived c. 600** B.C.)
Aherne, Brian (actor); King's Norton, England **(1902-1986)**
Aiello, Danny (actor); New York City, 6/20/33
Aiken, Conrad (poet); Savannah, Ga. **(1889-1973)**
Ailey, Alvin (c horeographer); Rogers, Tex., **(1931-1989)**
Albanese, Licia (operatic soprano); Bari, Italy, 7/22/1913
Albee, Edward (playwright); Washington, D.C., 3/12/1928
Albers, Josef (painter); Bottrop, Germany (1888-1976)
Albert, Eddie (Edward Albert Heimberger) (actor); Rock Island, Ill., 4/22/1908
Albert, Edward (actor); Los Angeles, 2/20/51
Albertson, Jack (actor); Malden, Mass. **(1910?-1981)**
Albright, Lola (actress); Akron, Ohio, 7/20/1925
Alcott, Louisa May (novelist); Germantown, Pa. **(1832-1888)**
Alda, Alan (actor); New York City, 1/28/1936
Alda, Robert (Alphonso d'Abruzzo) (actor); New York City **(1914-1986)**
Alden, John (American Pilgrim); England **(1599?-1687)**
Alexander, Jane (Quigley) (actress); Boston, 10/28/39
Alexander the Great (monarch and conqueror); Pella, Macedonia (Greece) **(356-323** B.C.)
Alger, Horatio (author); Revere, Mass. **(1834-1899)**
Algren, Nelson (novelist); Detroit **(1909-1981)**
Allen, Debbie (dancer-choreographer, actress); Houston, Tex., 1/16/50
Allen, Ethan (American Revolutionary soldier); Litchfield, Conn. **(1738-1789)**
Allen, Fred (John Florence Sullivan) (comedian); Cambridge, Mass. **(1894-1956)**
Allen, Gracie (Grace Ethel Cecile Rosalie Allen) (comedienne); San Francisco **(1906-1964)**
Allen, Mel (Melvin Israel) (sportscaster); Birmingham, Ala., 2/14/1913
Allen, Peter (actor); Tenterfield, Australia, 2/10/1944
Allen, Steve (TV entertainer); New York City, 12/26/1921
Allen, Woody (Allen Stewart Konigsberg) (actor, writer, and director); Brooklyn, N.Y., 12/1/1935
Alley, Kirstie (actress); Wichita, Kan., 1/12/55
Allison, Fran (actress); LaPorte City, Iowa, **(1908?-1989)**
Allman, Gregg (singer); Nashville, Tenn., 12/8/1947
Allyson, June (Jan Allyson) (actress); New York City, 10/7/1923
Alonso, Alicia (ballerina); Havana, 12/21/1921(?)
Alpert, Herb (band leader); Los Angeles, 3/31/1935(?)
Alsop, Joseph W., Jr. (journalist); Avon, Conn., **(1910-1989)**
Alsop, Stewart (journalist); Avon, Conn. **(1914-1974)**
Altman, Robert (film director); Kansas City, Mo., 2/20/1925
Amati, Nicola (violin maker); Cremona, Italy **(1596-1684)**
Ambler, Eric (suspense writer); London, 6/28/1909
Ameche, Don (Dominic Amici) (actor); Kenosha, Wis., 5/31/1908
Ames, Leon (actor); Portland, Ind., 1/20/03
Amis, Kingsley (novelist); London, 4/16/1922
Amory, Cleveland (writer and conservationist); Nahant, Mass., 9/2/1917
Amos (Freeman F. Gosden) (radio comedian); Richmond, Va., **(1899-1982)**
Amos, John (actor); Newark, N.J., 12/27/41
Amsterdam, Morey (actor); Chicago, 12/14/1914
Andersen, Hans Christian (author of fairy-tales); Odense, Denmark **(1805-1875)**
Anderson, Eddie. *See* Rochester
Anderson, Harry (actor); Newport, R.I., 10/14/52
Anderson, Ib (ballet dancer); Copenhagen, 12/14/1954
Anderson, Jack (journalist); Long Beach, Calif., 10/19/1922
Anderson, Dame Judith (actress); Adelaide, Australia, 2/10/1898
Anderson, Lindsay (Gordon) (director); Bangalore, India, 4/17/1923
Anderson, Loni (actress); St. Paul, Minn. 8/5/45
Anderson, Lynn (singer); Grand Forks, N.D., 9/26/1947
Anderson, Marian (contralto); Philadelphia, 2/17/1902
Anderson, Maxwell (dramatist); Atlantic, Pa. **(1888-1959)**
Anderson, Richard Dean (actor); Minneapolis, Minn., 1/23/50
Anderson, Robert (playwright); New York City, 4/28/1917
Andersson, Bibi (actress); Stockholm, 11/11/1935
Andress, Ursula (actress); Switzerland, 3/19/1938
Andrews, Dana (actor); Collins, Miss., 1/1/1909
Andrews, Julie (Julia Wells) (actress and singer); Walton-on-Thames, England, 10/1/1935
Andrews, La Verne (singer); Minneapolis **(1916-1967)**
Andrews, Maxene (singer); Minneapolis, 1/3/1918
Andrews, Patti (singer); Minneapolis, 2/16/1920
Andy (Charles J. Correll) (radio comedian); Peoria, Ill. **(1890-1972)**
Angeles, Victoria de los (Victoria Gamez Cima) (operatic soprano); Barcelona, 11/1/1924
Anka, Paul (singer and composer); Ottawa, 7/30/1941
Ann-Margret (Ann-Margret Olsson) (actress); Valsjobyn, Sweden, 4/28/1941
Annabella (actress); Paris, 1912
Anouilh, Jean (playwright); Bordeaux, France **(1910-1987)**
Anthony, Susan Brownell (woman suffragist); Adams, Mass. **(1820-1906)**
Antonioni, Michelangelo (director); Ferrara, Italy, 9/2 9/1912
Antony, Mark (Marcus Antonius) (statesman); Rome **(83?-30** B.C.)
Anuszkiewicz, Richard (painter); Erie, Pa., 5/23/1930
Aquinas, St. Thomas (philosopher); nr. Aquino (Italy) **(1225?-1274)**
Arbuckle, Roscoe "Fatty" (actor and director); San Jose, Calif. **(1887-1933)**
Archimedes (physicist and mathematician); Syracuse, Sicily **(287?-212** B.C.)
Archipenko, Alexandre (sculptor); Kiev, Russia **(1887-1964)**
Arden, Elizabeth (Florence Nightingale Graham) (cosmetics executive); Woodbridge, Canada **(1891-1966)**

Arden, Eve (Eunice Quedens) (actress); Mill Valley, Calif. **(1907–1990)**
Arendt, Hannah (historian); Hannover, Germany **(1906-1975)**
Aristophanes (dramatist); Athens (448?-380 B.C.)
Aristotle (philosopher); Stagirus, Macedonia **(384-322** B.C.)
Arkin, Alan (actor and director); New York City, 3/26/1934
Arledge, Roone (TV executive); Forest Hills, N.Y., 7/8/1931
Arlen, Harold (Hyman Arluck) (composer); Buffalo, N.Y. **(1905-1986)**
Arlen, Richard (actor); Charlottesville, Va. **(1900-1976)**
Arliss, George (actor); London **(1868-1946)**
Armstrong, Louis ("Satchmo") (musician); New Orleans **(1900-1971)**
Armstrong-Jones, Anthony. See Snowdon, Earl of
Arnaz, Desi (Desiderio) (actor and producer); Santiago, Cuba **(1917-1986)**
Arness, James (James Aurness) (TV actor); Minneapolis, 5/26/1923
Arno, Peter (cartoonist); New York City **(1904-1968)**
Arnold, Benedict (American Revolutionary War general, charged with treason); Norwich, Conn. **(1741-1801)**
Arnold, Eddy (singer); Henderson, Tenn., 5/15/1918
Arnold, Edward (actor); New York City **(1890-1956)**
Arnold, Matthew (poet and critic); Laleham, England **(1822-1888)**
Arp, Jean (sculptor and painter); Strasbourg (France) **(1887-1966)**
Arpino, Gerald (choreographer); Staten Island, N.Y., 1/14/28
Arquette, Cliff ("Charley Weaver") (actor); Toledo, Ohio **(1905-1974)**
Arquette, Rosanna (actress); New York City, 8/10/59
Arrau, Claudio (pianist); Chillán, Chile **(1903–1991)**
Arroyo, Martina (soprano); New York City, 2/2/1940
Arthur, Bea (Bernice Frankel) (actress); New York City, 5/13/1926(?)
Arthur, Jean (Gladys Greene) (actress); New York City **(1900–1991)**
Asch, Sholem (novelist); Kutno, Poland **(1880-1957)**
Ashcroft, Dame Peggy (actress); Croydon, England **(1907–1991)**
Ashkenazy, Vladimir (concert pianist); Gorki, U.S.S.R., 7/6/1937
Ashley, Elizabeth (actress); Ocala, Fla., 8/30/1939
Ashton, Sir Frederick William Mallandaine (choreographer); Guayaquil, Ecuador **(1904-1988)**
Asimov, Isaac (author); Petrovichi, Russia, 1/2/1920
Asner, Edward (actor); Kansas City, Mo., 11/15/1929
Astaire, Fred (Frederick Austerlitz) (dancer and actor); Omaha, Neb. **(1899-1987)**
Astin, John (actor, director); Baltimore, Md., 3/30/30
Astor, John Jacob (financier); Waldorf (Germany) **(1763-1848)**
Astor, Mary (Lucile Langhanke) (actress); Quincy, Ill. **(1906-1987)**
Atkins, Chet (guitarist); nr. Luttrell, Tenn., 6/20/1924
Atkinson, Brooks (drama critic); Melrose, Mass. **(1894-1984)**
Attenborough, Richard (actor-director) Cambridge, England, 8/29/1923
Attila (King of Huns, called "Scourge of God") **(406?-453)**
Attlee, Clement R ichard (statesman); London **(1883-1967)**
Atwill, Lionel (actor); Croydon, England, **(1885-1946)**
Auberjonois, Rene (actor); New York City, 6/1/40
Auchincloss, Louis (author); Lawrence, N.Y., 9/27/1917
Auden, W(ystan) H(ugh) (poet); York, England **(1907-1973)**
Audubon, John James (naturalist and painter); Haiti **(1785-1851)**
Auer, Leopold (violinist and teacher); Veszprém, Hungary **(1845-1930)**
Auer, Mischa (actor); St. Petersburg, Russia **(1905-1967)**
Augustine, Saint (Aurelius Augustinus) (theologian); Tagaste, Numidia (Algeria) **(354-430)**
Augustus (Gaius Octavius) (Roman emperor); Rome (63 B.C.-A.D. **14)**
Aumont, Jean-Pierre (actor); Paris, 1/5/1913
Austen, Jane (novelist); Steventon, England **(1775-1817)**
Autry, Gene (singer and actor); Tioga, Tex., 9/29/1907
Avalon, Frankie (singer); Philadelphia, 9/18/1940
Avedon, Richard (photographer); New York City, 5/15/1923
Avery, Milton (painter); Alt mar, N.Y. **(1893-1965)**
Ax, Emanuel (pianist); Lvov, U.S.S.R., 6/8/1949
Axelrod, George (playwright); New York City, 6/9/1922
Ayckbourn, Alan (playwright); London, 4/12/1939
Ayckroyd, Dan (actor); Ottawa, Ont., Canada, 7/1/1952
Ayres, Agnes (actress); Carbondale, Ill., **(1896-1940)**
Ayres, Lew (actor); Minneapolis, 12/28/1908
Aznavour, Charles (singer, composer); Paris, France 5/22/24

B

Bacall, Lauren (Betty Joan Perske) (actress); New York City, 9/16/1924
Bach, Johann Sebastian (composer); Eisenach (East Germany) **(1685-1750)**
Bach, Karl Phillipp Emanuel (composer); Weimar (East Germany) **(1714-1788)**
Bacharach, Burt (songwriter); Kansas City, Mo., 5/12/1929
Backus, Jim (actor); Cleveland, **(1913-1989)**
Bacon, Francis (painter); Dublin, 1910
Bacon, Francis (philosopher and essayist); London **(1561-1626)**

Bacon, Roger (philosopher and scientist); Ilchester, England **(1214?-1294)**
Baedeker, Karl (travel-guidebook publisher); Essen (Germany) **(1801-1859)**
Baez, Joan (folk singer); Staten Island, N.Y., 1/9/1941
Bagnold, Enid (novelist); Rochester, England **(1889-1981)**
Bailey, F. Lee (lawyer); Waltham, Mass., 6/10/1933
Bailey, Pearl (singer); Newport News, Va. **(1918-1990)**
Bain, Conrad (actor); Lethbridge, Alberta, Canada, 2/4/23
Bainter, Fay (actress); Los Angeles **(1891-1968)**
Baio, Scott (actor); Brooklyn, N.Y., 9/22/61
Baird, Bil (William B.) (puppeteer); Grand Island, Neb **(1904-1987)**
Baker, Anita (singer); Toledo, Ohio, 1958
Baker, Carroll (actress); Johnstown, Pa., 5/28/1931
Baker, Josephine (singer and dancer); St. Louis **(1906-1975)**
Baker, Russell (columnist); Loudoun County, Va., 8/14/1925
Balanchine, George (choreographer); St. Petersburg, Russia **(1904-1983)**
Balboa, Vasco Nuñez de (explorer); Jerez de los Caballeros (Spain) **(1475-1517)**
Baldwin, Faith (novelist); New Rochelle, N.Y. **(1893-1978)**
Baldwin, James (novelist); New York City **(1924-1987)**
Balenciaga, Cristóbal (fashion designer); Guetaria, Spain **(1895–972)**
Ball, Lucille (Désirée) (actress and producer); Celoron (nr. Jamestown), N.Y. **(1911-1989)**
Ballard, Kaye (Catherine Gloria Balotta) (actress); Cleveland, 11/20/1926
Balmain, Pierre (fashion designer); St.-Jean-de-Maurienne, France **(1914-1982)**
Balsam, Martin (actor); New York City, 11/4/1919
Balzac, Honoré de (novelist); Tours, France **(1799-1850)**
Bancroft, Anne (Annemarie Italiano) (actress); New York City, 9/17/1931
Bancroft, George (actor); Philadelphia **(1882-1956)**
Bankhead, Tallulah (actress); Huntsville, Ala. **(1903-1963)**
Banneker, Benjamin (almanacker and mathematician-astronomer on District of Columbia site survey); Ellicott, Md. **(1731-1806)**
Banting, Fredrick Grant (physiologist); Alliston, Ont., Canada **(1891-1941)**
Bara, Theda (Theodosia Goodman) (actress); Cincinnati **(1890-1955)**
Barber, Red (Walter Lanier) (sportscaster); Columbus, Miss., 2/17/1908
Barber, Samuel (composer); West Chester, Pa. **(1910-1981)**
Bardot, Brigitte (actress); Paris, 1935
Barenboim, Daniel (concert pianist and conductor); Buenos Aires, 11/15/1942
Bari, Lynn (actress); Roanoke, Va., 12/18/13 (?)
Barker, Bob (host); Darrington, Wash., 12/12/23
Barnard, Christiaan N. (heart surgeon); Beauford West, South Africa, 1923
Barnes, Priscilla (actress); Fort Dix, N.J., 12/7/55
Barnum, Phineas Taylor (showman); Bethel, Conn. **(1810-1891)**
Barr, Roseanne (actress); Salt Lake City, 11/3/1952
Barrie, Sir James Matthew (author); Kirriemuir, Scotland **(1860-1937)**
Barrie, Wendy (actress); Hong Kong **(1913-1978)**
Barry, Gene (Eugene Klass) (actor); New York City, 6/4/1922
Barry, John (naval officer); County Wexford, Ireland **(1745-1803)**
Barrymore, Diana (actress); New York City **(1921-1960)**
Barrymore, Ethel (Ethel Blythe) (actress); Philadelphia **(1879-1959)**
Barrymore, Georgiana Drew (actress); Philadelphia **(1856-1893)**
Barrymore, John (John Blythe) (actor); Philadelphia **(1882-1942)**
Barrymore, Lionel (Lionel Blythe) (actor); Philadelphia **(1878-1954)**
Barrymore, Maurice (Herbert Blythe) (actor and playwright); Agra, India **(1847-1905)**
Barthelme, Donald (novelist); Philadelphia **(1931 -1989)**
Barthelmess, Richard (actor); New York City **(1897-1963)**
Bartholomew, Freddie (actor); London, 3/28/1924
Bartók, Béla (composer); Nagyszentmiklos (Romania) **(1881-1945)**
Barton, Clara (founder of American Red Cross); Oxford, Mass. **(1821-1912)**
Baruch, Bernard Mannes (statesman); Camden, S.C. **(1870-1965)**
Baryshnikov, Mikhail Nikolayevich (ballet dancer and artistic director); Riga, Latvia, 1/27/1948
Basehart, Richard (actor); Zanesville, Ohio **(1914-1984)**
Basie, Count (William) (band leader); Red Bank, N.J. **(1904-1984)**
Basinger, Kim (actress); Athens, Ga., 12/8/53
Bassey, Shirley (singer); Cardiff, Wales, 1/8/1937
Batchelor, Clarence Daniel (political cartoonist); Osage City, Kan. **(1888-1977)**
Bateman, Jason (actor); Rye, N.Y. 1/14/69
Bateman, Justine (actress); Rye, N.Y., 2/19/66
Bates, Alan (actor); Allestree, England, 2/17/1934
Battle, Kathleen (soprano); Portsmouth, Ohio, 8/13/48
Baudelaire, Charles Pierre (poet); Paris **(1821-1867)**

Baudouin (King); Palace of Laeken, Belgium, 9/7/1930
Baxter, Anne (actress); Michigan City, Ind. **(1923-1985)**
Baxter, Warner (actor); Columbus, Ohio **(1891-1951)**
Baxter-Birney, Meredith (actress); Los Angeles, 6/21/47
Bean, Orson (Dallas Frederick Burrows) (actor); Burlington, Vt., 7/22/1928
Beardsley, Aubrey Vincent (illustrator); Brighton, England **(1872-1898)**
Beaton, Cecil (photographer and designer); London **(1904-1980)**
Beatty, Clyde (animal trainer); Chillicothe, Ohio **(1903-1965)**
Beatty, Warren (actor and producer); Richmond, Va., 3/30/1937
Beaumont, Francis (dramatist); Grace-Dieu, England **(1584-1616)**
Beavers, Louise (actress); Cincinnati, Ohio **(1902-1962)**
Becket, Thomas à (Archbishop of Canterbury); London **(1118?-1170)**
Beckett, Samuel (playwright); Dublin **(1906-1989)**
Beckmann, Max (painter); Leipzig, Germany **(1884-1950)**
Bede, Saint ("The Venerable Bede") (scholar); Monkwearmouth, England **(673-735)**
Beecham, Sir Thomas (conductor); St. Helens, England **(1879-1961)**
Beecher, Henry Ward (clergyman); Litchfi eld, Conn. **(1813-1887)**
Beerbohm, Sir Max (author); London **(1872-1956)**
Beery, Noah (actor); Kansas City, Mo. **(1884-1946)**
Beery, Noah, Jr. (actor); New York City, 8/10/1916
Beery, Wallace (actor); Kansas City, Mo. **(1886-1949)**
Beethoven, Ludwig von (composer); Bonn (Germany) **(1770-1827)**
Begley, Ed (actor); Hartford, Conn. **(1901-1970)**
Belafonte, Harry (singer and actor); New York City, 3/1/1927
Belafonte-Harper, Shari (actress); New York City, 9/22/54
Belasco, David (dramatist and producer); San Francisco **(1854-1931)**
Bel Geddes, Barbara (actress); New York City, 10/31/22
Bell, Alexander Graham (inventor); Edinburgh, Scotland **(1847-1922)**
Bellamy, Edward (author); Chicopee Falls, Mass. **(1850-1898)**
Bellamy, Ralph (actor); Chicago, 6/17/1904
Bellini, Giovanni (painter); Venice **(c.1430-1516)**
Bellow, Saul (novelist); Lachine, Quebec, Canada, 6/10/1915
Bellows, George Wesley (painter and lithographer); Columbus, Ohio **(1882-1925)**
Belmondo, Jean-Paul (actor); Neuilly-sur-Seine, France, 4/9/1933
Belushi, Jim (actor); Chicago, 6/15/54
Belushi, John (comedian, actor); Chicago **(1949-1982)**
Benchley, Peter Bradford (novelist); New York City, 5/8/1940
Benchley, Robert Charles (humorist); Worcester, Mass. **(1889-1945)**
Bendix, William (actor); New York City **(1906-1964)**
Benedict, Dirk (actor); Helena, Mont., 3/1/44
Benes, Eduard (statesman); Kozlany (Czechoslovakia) **(1884-1948)**
Benét, Stephen Vincent (poet and story writer); Bethlehem, Pa. **(1898-1943)**
Benét, William Rose (poet and novelist); Ft. Hamilton, Brooklyn, N.Y. **(1886-1950)**
Ben-Gurion, David (David Green) (statesman); Plónsk (Poland) **(1886-1973)**
Benjamin, Richard (actor); New York City, 5/22/1938
Bennett, Constance (actress); New York City **(1905-1965)**
Bennett, Enoch Arnold (novelist and dramatist); Hanley, England **(1867-1931)**
Bennett, James Gordon (editor); Keith, Scotland **(1795-1872)**
Bennett, Joan (actress); Palisades, N.J. **(1910-1990)**
Bennett, Robert Russell (composer); Kansas City, Mo., **(1894-1981)**
Bennett, Tony (Anthony Benedetto) (singer); Astoria, Queens, N.Y., 8/3/1926
Benny, Jack (Benjamin Kubelsky) (comedian); Chicago **(1894-1974)**
Benson, Robby (actor); Dallas, Tex., 1/21/56
Bentham, Jeremy Heinrich (economist); London **(1748-1832)**
Benton, Thomas Hart (painter); Neosho, Mo. **(1889-1975)**
Berg, Alban (composer); Vienna **(1885-1935)**
Berg, Gertrude (writer and actress); New York City **(1899-1966)**
Bergen, Candice (actress); Beverly Hills, Calif., 5/9/1946
Bergen, Edgar (ventriloquist); Chicago, **(1903-1978)**
Bergen, Polly (actress and singer); Knoxville, Tenn., 7/14/1930
Bergerac, Cyrano de (poet); Paris **(1619-1655)**
Bergman, Ingmar (film director); Uppsala, Sweden, 7/14/1918
Bergman, Ingrid (actress); Stockholm **(1918-1982)**
Bergson, Henri (philosopher); Paris **(1859-1941)**
Berkeley, Busby (choreographer, director); Los Angeles **(1885-1976)**
Berle, Milton (Milton Berlinger) (comedian); New York City, 7/12/1908
Berlin, Irving (Israel Baline) (songwriter); Temum, Russia **(1888-1989)**
Berlioz, Louis Hector (composer); La Côte-Saint-André, France **(1803-1869)**
Berman, Lazar (concert pianist); Leningrad, 1930.
Berman, Shelley (Sheldon) (comedian); Chicago, 2/3/1926
Bernardi, Herschel (actor); New York City **(1922-1986)**
Bernhardt, Sarah (Rosine Bernard) (actress); Paris **(1844-1923)**
Bernini, Gian Lorenzo (sculptor and painter); Naples (Italy)

(1598-1680)
Bernoulli, Jacques (scientist); Basel, Switzerland **(1654-1705)**
Bernsen, Corbin (actor); North Hollywood, Calif., 7/7/?
Bertinelli, Valerie (actress); Wilmington, Del., 4/23/60
Bernstein, Leonard (conductor); Lawrence, Mass. **(1918-1990)**
Berry, Chuck (Charles Edward Berry) (singer and guitarist); San Jose, Calif., 1/15/1926
Berry, Ken (actor); Moline, Ill., 11/3/30
Betjeman, Sir John (Poet Laureate); London **(1906-1984)**
Bettelheim, Bruno (psychoanalyst); Vienna **(1903-1990)**
Bickford, Charles (actor); Cambridge, Mass. **(1889-1967)**
Bierce, Ambrose Gwinnett (journalist); Meigs County, Ohio **(1842-1914?)**
Bikel, Theodore (actor and folk singer); Vienna, 5/2/1924
Bing, Sir Rudolf (opera manager); Vienna, 1/9/1902
Bingham, George Caleb (painter); Augusta Co., Va. **(1811-1879)**
Bishop, Joey (Joseph Gottlieb) (comedian); New York City, 2/3/1919
Bismarck-Schönhausen, Prince Otto Eduard Leopold von (statesman); Schönhausen (East Germany) **(1815-1898)**
Bisset, Jacqueline (actress); Weybridge, England, 9/13/1944
Bixby, Bill (actor); San Francisco, 1/22/1934
Bizet, Georges (Alexandre César Léopold Bizet) (composer); Paris **(1838-1875)**
Bjoerling, Jussi (tenor); Stora Tuna, Sweden **(1911-1960)**
Black, Cilla (singer and actress); Liverpool, England, 5/27/1943
Black, Karen (actress); Park Ridge, Ill., 7/1/1942
Black, Shirley Temple (former actress); Santa Monica, Calif., 4/23/1928
Blackmer, Sidney (actor); Salisbury, N.C. **(1898-1973)**
Blackstone, Sir William (jurist); London **(1723-1780)**
Blaine, Vivian (actress and singer); Newark, N.J., 11/21/1924
Blair, Janet (actress); Altoona, Pa., 4/23/1921
Blake, Amanda (Beverly Louise Neill) (actress); Buffalo, N.Y. **(1929-1989)**
Blake, Eubie (James Hubert) (pianist); Baltimore, **(1883-1983)**
Blake, Robert (Michael Gubitosi) (actor); Nutley, N.J., 9/18/1933
Blake, William (poet and artist); London **(1757-1827)**
Blanc, Mel(vin Jerome) (actor and voice specialist); San Francisco **(1908-1989)**
Blass, Bill (fashion designer); Fort Wayne, Ind., 6/22/1922
Bloch, Ernest (composer); Geneva **(1880-1959)**
Blondell, Joan (actress); New York City **(1909-1979)**
Bloom, Claire (actress); London, 2/15/1931
Bloomgarden, Kermit (producer); Brooklyn, N.Y. **(1904-1976)**
Blore, Eric (actor); London **(1887-1959)**
Blue, Monte (actor); Indianapolis **(1890-1963)**
Blyth, Ann (actress); New York City, 8/16/1928
Boccaccio, Giovanni (author); Paris **(1313-1375)**
Boccherini, Luigi (Rodolfo) (composer); Lucca, Italy **(1743-1805)**
Boccioni, Umberto (painter and sculptor); Reggio di Calabria, Italy **(1882-1916)**
Bock, Jerry (composer); New Haven, Conn., 11/23/1928
Bogarde, Dirk (Derek Van den Bogaerde) (film actor and director); London, 3/28/1921
Bogart, Humphrey DeForest (actor); New York City **(1899-1957)**
Bogdanovich, Peter (producer and director); Kingston, N.Y., 7/30/1939
Bohlen, Charles E. (diplomat); Clayton, N.Y. **(1904-1974)**
Bohr, Niels (atomic physicist); Copenhagen **(1885-1962)**
Boland, Mary (actress); Philadelphia, Pa. **(1880-1965)**
Boles, John (actor); Greenville, Tex. **(1895-1969)**
Bolger, Ray (dancer and actor); Dorchester, Mass **(1904-1987)**
Bolivar, Simón (South American liberator); Caracas, Venezuela **(1783-1830)**
Bologna, Giovanni da (sculptor); Douai (France) **(1529-1608)**
Bombeck, Erma (author, columnist); Dayton, Ohio 2/21/1927
Bonaparte, Napoleon (Emperor of the French); Ajaccio, Corsica (France) **(1769-1821)**
Bond, Julian (Georgia legislator); Nashville, Tenn., 1/14/1940
Bondi, Beulah (actress); Chicago **(1883-1981)**
Bonet, Lisa (actress); San Francisco, 11/16/67
Bonnard, Pierre (painter); Fontenayaux-Roses, France **(1867-1947)**
Bon Jovi, Jon (musician, singer); Sayreville, N.J., 3/2/62
Bono, Sonny (Salvatore) (singer); Detroit, 2/16/1935
Boone, Daniel (frontiersman); nr. Reading, Pa. **(1734-1820)**
Boone, Pat (Charles) (singer); Jacksonville, Fla., 6/1/1934
Boone, Richard (actor); Los Angeles **(1917-1981)**
Booth, Edwin Thomas (actor); Bel Air, Md. **(1833-1893)**
Booth, Evangeline Cory (religious leader); London **(1865-1950)**
Booth, John Wilkes (actor; assassin of Lincoln); Harford County, Md. **(1838-1865)**
Booth, Shirley (Thelma Booth Ford) (actress); New York City, 8/30/1907
Bordoni, Irene (actress); Ajaccio (France) **(1895-1953)**
Borge, Victor (pianist and comedian); Copenhagen, 1/3/1909

Borgia, Cesare (nobleman and soldier); Rome **(1475?-1507)**
Borgia, Lucrezia (Duchess of Ferrara); Rome **(1480-1519)**
Borgnine, Ernest (actor); Hamden, Conn., 1/24/1917
Borromini, Francesco (architect); Bissone (Italy) **(1599-1667)**
Bosch, Hieronymus (Hieronymus van Aeken) (painter); Hertogen-bosch (Netherlands) **(c.1450-1516)**
Bosley, Tom (actor); Chicago, 10/1/1927
Bostwick, Barry (actor); San Mateo, Calif., 2/24/45
Boswel I, Connee (singer); New Orleans **(1907-1976)**
Boswell, James (diarist and biographer); Edinburgh, Scotland **(1740-1795)**
Botticelli, Sandro (Alessandro di Mariano dei Filipepi) (painter); Florence (Italy) **(1444?-1510)**
Bottoms, Joseph (actor); Santa Barbara, Calif., 4/16/33
Bottoms, Timothy (actor); Santa Barbara, Calif., 8/30/50
Boulez, Pierre (conductor); Montbrison, France, 3/26/1925
Bourke-White, Margaret (photographer); New York City **(1906-1971)**
Bow, Clara (actress); Brooklyn, N.Y. **(1905-1965)**
Bowen, Catherine Drinker (biographer); Haverford, Pa. **(1897-1973)**
Bowes, Edward (radio show director); San Francisco **(1874-1946)**
Bowie, David (David Robert Jones) (actor and musician); London, 1/8/1947(?)
Bowie, James (soldier); Burke County, Ga. **(1799-1836)**
Bowles, Chester (diplomat); Springfield, Mass. **(1901-1986)**
Boxleitner, Bruce (actor); Elgin, Ill., 5/12/50
Boyce, William (composer); London? **(1710-1779)**
Boyd, Bill (William) ("Hopalong Cassidy") (actor); Cambridge, Ohio **(1898-1972)**
Boyd, Stephen (Stephen Millar) (actor); Belfast, Northern Ireland **(1928-1977)**
Boyer, Charles (actor); Figeac, France **(1899-1978)**
Boy George (George Alan O'Dowd) (singer); London, 1961
Boyle, Peter (actor); Philadelphia, 10/18/33
Boyle, Robert (scientist); Lismore Castle, Munster, Ireland **(1627-1691)**
Bracken, Eddie (actor); Astoria, Queens, N.Y., 2/7/1920
Bradbury, Ray Douglas (science-fiction writer); Waukegan, Ill., 8/22/1920
Bradlee, Benjamin C. (editor); Boston, 8/26/1921
Bradley, Ed (broadcast journalist); Philadelphia, Pa., 6/22/1941
Bradley, Omar N. (5-star general); Clark, Mo. **(1893-1981)**
Brady, Alice (actress); New York City **(1892-1939)**
Brady, Scott (actor); Brooklyn, N.Y., **(1924-1985)**
Brahe, Tycho (astronomer); Knudstrup, Denmark **(1546-1601)**
Brahms, Johannes (composer); Hamburg **(1833-1897)**
Braille, Louis (teacher of blind); Coupvray, France **(1809-1862)**
Brailowsky, Alexander (pianist); Kiev, Russia **(1896-1976)**
Bramante, Donato D'Agnolo (architect); Monte Asdrualdo (now Fermignano, Italy) **(1444-1514)**
Brancusi, Constantin (sculptor); Pestisansi, Romania **(1876-1957)**
Brando, Marlon (actor); Omaha, Neb., 4/3/1924
Brandt, Willy (Herbert Frahm) (ex-Chancellor); Lübeck, Germany, 12/18/1913
Braque, Georges (painter); Argenteuil, France **(1882-1963)**
Brazzi, Rossano (actor); Bologna, Italy, 9/18/1916
Brecht, Bertolt (dramatist and poet); Augsburg, Bavaria **(1898-1956)**
Brel, Jacques (singer and composer); Brussels, **(1929-1978)**
Brennan, Walter (actor); Lynn, Mass. **(1894-1974)**
Brent, George (actor); Dublin **(1904-1979)**
Breslin, Jimmy (journalist); Jamaica, Queens, N.Y., 10/17/1930
Breuer, Marcel (architect and designer); Pécs, Hungary **(1902-1981)**
Brewer, Teresa (singer); Toledo, Ohio, 5/7/1931
Brewster, Kingman, Jr. (ex-president of Yale); Longmeadow, Mass. **(1919-1988)**
Brezhnev, Leonid I. (Communist Party Secretary); Dneprodzerzhinsk, Ukraine **(1906-1982)**
Brice, Fanny (Fannie Borach) (comedienne); New York City **(1892-1951)**
Bridges, Beau (actor); Los Angeles, 12/9/1941
Bridges, Jeff (actor); Los Angeles, 12/4/49
Bridges, Lloyd (actor); San Leandro, Calif. 1/15/1913
Brinkley, David (TV newscaster); Wilmington, N.C., 7/10/1920
Britt, May (Maybritt Wilkins) (actress); Sweden, 3/22/1936
Britten, Benjamin (composer); Lowestoft, England **(1913-1976)**
Britton, Barbara (actress); Long Beach, Calif. **(1920-1980)**
Broderick, Helen (actress); Philadelphia, Pa. **(1891-1959)**
Brolin, James (actor); Los Angeles, 7/18/40
Bromfield, Louis (novelist); Mansfield, Ohio **(1896-1956)**
Bronson, Charles (Charles Buchinsky) (actor); Ehrenfield, Pa., 11/3/1922(?)
Brontë, Charlotte (novelist); Thornton, England **(1816-1855)**
Brontë, Emily Jane (novelist); Thornton, England **(1818-1848)**
Bronzino, Agnolo (painter); Monticelli (Italy) **(1503-1572)**
Brook, Peter (director); London, 3/21/1925
Brooke, Rupert (poet); Rugby, England **(1887-1915)**

Brooks, Geraldine (Geraldine Stroock) (actress); New York City **(1925-1977)**
Brooks, Gwendolyn (poet); Topeka, Kan., 6/7/1917
Brooks, Mel (Melvin K aminsky) (writer and film director); Brooklyn, N.Y., 1926(?)
Brosnan, Pierce (actor); County Meath, Ireland, 5/16/52
Brothers, Joyce (Bauer) (psychologist, author, radio-TV personality); New York City, 1927(?)
Broun, Matthew Heywood Campbell (journalist); Brooklyn, N.Y. **(1888-1939)**
Brown, Helen Gurley (author); Green Forest, Ark., 2/18/1922
Brown, James (singer); Augusta, Ga., 5/3/1934
Brown, Joe E. (comedian); Holgate, Ohio **(1892-1973)**
Brown, John (abolitionist); Torrington, Conn. **(1800-1859)**
Brown, John Mason (critic); Louisville, Ky. **(1900-1969)**
Brown, Les (band leader); Reinerton, Pa., 1912
Brown, Pamela (actress); London **(1918-1975)**
Brown, Vanessa (Smylla Brind) (actress); Vienna, 3/24/1928
Browne, Jackson (singer and guitarist); Heidelberg, Germany, 10/9/late 1940s
Browning, Elizabeth Barrett (poet); Durham, England **(1806-1861)**
Browning, Robert (poet); London **(1812-1889)**
Brubeck, Dave (musician); Concord, Calif., 12/6/1920
Bruce, Lenny (comedian); Long Island, N.Y. **(1926-1966)**
Bruce, Nigel (actor); Ensenada, Mexico **(1895-1953)**
Bruce, Virginia (actress); Minneapolis, Minn. **(1910-1982)**
Brueghel, Pieter (painter); nr. Breda, Flanders (Netherlands) **(1520?-1569)**
Bruhn, Erik (Belton Evers) (ballet dancer); Copenhagen **(1928-1986)**
Brunelleschi, Filippo (architect); Florence (Italy) **(1377-1446)**
Bruno, Giordano (philosopher); Nola, Italy **(1548-1600)**
Brutus, Marcus Junius (Roman politician); (85?-42 b.c.)
Bryan, William Jennings (orator and politician); Salem, Ill. **(1860-1925)**
Bryant, Anita (singer); Barnsdall, Okla., 3/25/1940
Bryant, William Cullen (poet and editor); Cummington, Mass. **(1794-1878)**
Brynner, Yul (Taidje Khan) (actor); Sakhalin Island, Russia **(1920-1985)**
Brzezinski, Zbigniew (ex-presidential adviser); Warsaw, 3/28/1928
Buber, Martin (philosopher and theologian); Vienna **(1878-1965)**
Bucchanan, Jack (actor); Glasgow, Scotland **(1891-1957)**
Buchanan, Edgar (actor); Humansville, Mo., **(1903-1979)**
Buchholz, Horst (actor); Berlin, 12/4/1933
Buchwald, Art (Arthur) (columnist); Mount Vernon, N.Y., 10/20/1925
Buck, Pearl S(ydenstricker) (author); Hillsboro, W. Va. **(1892-1973)**
Buckley, William F., Jr. (journalist); New York City, 11/24/1925
Buddha. *See* Gautama Buddha
Buffalo Bill (William Frederick Cody) (scout); Scott County, Iowa **(1846-1917)**
Bujold, Genevieve (actress); Montreal, 7/1/1942
Bujones, Fernando (ballet dancer); Miami, Fla., 3/9/1955
Bullins, Ed (playwright); Philadelphia, 7/2/1935
Bullock, Jm J. (actor); Casper Wyom., 2/9?
Bumbry, Grace (mezzo-soprano); St. Louis, 1/4/1937
Bunche, Ralph J. (statesman); Detroit **(1904-1971)**
Bundy, McGeorge (educator); Boston, 3/30/1919
Bundy, William Putnam (editor); Washington, D.C., 9/24/1917
Buñuel, Luis (film director); Calanda, Spain, **(1900-1983)**
Bunyan, John (preacher and author); Elstow, England **(1628-1688)**
Burbank, Luther (horticulturist); Lancaster, Mass. **(1849-1926)**
Burke, Adm. Arleigh A. (ex-Chief of Naval Operations); Boulder, Colo., 10/19/1901
Burke, Billie (comedienne); Washington, D.C. **(1885-1970)**
Burke, Delta (actress); Orlando, Fla., 7/30/56
Burke, Edmund (statesman); Dublin **(1729-1797)**
Burne-Jones, Edward Coley (painter); Birmingham, England **(1833-1898)**
Burnett, Carol (comedienne); San Antonio, 4/26/1933
Burnette, Smiley (Lester Alvin) (actor); Summum, Ill. **(1911-1967)**
Burney, Fanny (Frances) (writer); King's Lynn, England **(1752-1840)**
Burns, George (Nathan Birnbaum) (comedian); New York City, 1/20/1896
Burns, Robert (poet); Alloway, Scotland **(1759-1796)**
Burr, Aaron (political leader); Newark, N.J. **(1756-1836)**
Burr, Raymond (William Stacey Burr) (actor); New Westminster, British Columbia, Canada, 5/21/1917
Burroughs, Edgar Rice (novelist); Chicago **(1875-1950)**
Burrows, Abe (playwright and director); New York City, **(1910-1985)**
Burstyn, Ellen (Edna Rae Gillooly) (actress); Detroit, 12/7/1932
Burton, LaVar (actor); Landsthul, Germany, 2/16/57
Burton, Richard (Richard Jenkins) (actor); Pontrhydfen, Wales **(1925-1984)**
Bush, Vannevar (scientist); Everett, Mass. **(1890-1974)**
Bushman, Francis X. (actor); Baltimore **(1883-1966)**
Butkus, Dick (actor); Chicago, 12/9/42

Butler, Samuel (author); Langar, England **(1835-1902)**
Butterworth, Charles (actor); South Bend, Ind. **(1896-1946)**
Buttons, Red (Aaron Chwatt) (actor); New York City, 2/5/1919
Buzzi, Ruth (comedienne); Wequetequock, Conn., 7/24/1936
Byington, Spring (actress); Colorado Springs, Colo. **(1893-1971)**
Byrd, Richard Evelyn (polar explorer); Winchester, Va. **(1888-1957)**
Byron, George Gordon (6th Baron Byron) (poet); London **(1788-1824)**

C

Caan, James (actor); The Bronx, N.Y., 3/26/1939
Caballé, Montserrat (soprano); Barcelona, Spain, 4/12/33
Cabot, Bruce (actor); Carlsbad, N.M. **(1904-1972)**
Cabot, John (Giovanni Caboto) (navigator); Genoa (?) **(1450-1498)**
Cabot, Sebastian (navigator); Venice **(1476?-1557)**
Cadmus, Paul (painter and etcher); New York City, 12/17/1904
Caesar, Gaius Julius (statesman); Rome **(100?-44** B.C.)
Caesar, Sid (comedian); Yonkers, N.Y., 9/8/1922
Cagney, James (actor); New York City **(1899-1986)**
Cahn, Sammy (songwriter); New York City, 6/18/1913
Caine, Michael (Maurice J. Micklewhite) (actor); London, 3/14/1933
Calder, Alexander (sculptor); Lawnton, Pa. **(1898-1976)**
Calderón del al Barca, Pedro (dramatist); Madrid **(1600-1681)**
Caldwell, Erskine (novelist); White Oak, Ga. **(1903-1987)**
Caldwell, Sarah (opera director and conductor); Maryville, Mo., 1928
Caldwell, Taylor (novelist); Manchester, England **(1900-1985)**
Caldwell, Zoe (actress); Hawthorn, Australia, 9/14/1933
Calhern, Louis (Carl Henry Vogt) (actor); Brooklyn, N.Y. **(1895-1956)**
Calhoun, John Caldwell (statesman); nr. Calhoun Mills, S.C. **(1782-1850)**
Calisher, Hortense (novelist); New York City, 12/20/1911
Callas, Maria (Maria Calogeropoulos) (dramatic soprano); New York City **(1923-1977)**
Calloway, Cab (Cabell) (band leader); Rochester, N.Y., 12/25/1907
Calvet, Corinne (actress); Paris, 4/30/1926
Calvin, John (Jean Chauvin) (religious reformer); Noyon, Picardy **(1509-1564)**
Cambridge, Godfrey (comedian); New York City **(1933-1976)**
Cameron, Rod (Rod Cox) (actor); Calgary, Alberta, Canada, **(1912-1983)**
Campbell, Glen (singer); nr. Delight, Ark., 4/22/1938
Campbell, Mrs. Patrick (Beatrice Stella Tanner) (actress); London **(1865-1940)**
Camus, Albert (author); Mondovi, Algeria **(1913-1960)**
Canaletto, (Giovanni Antonio Canale); (painter) Venice **(1697-1768)**
Candy, John (actor, comedian); Toronto, Ont., Canada, 10/31/50
Caniff, Milton (cartoonist); Hillsboro, Ohio **(1907-1988)**
Cannon, Dyan (actress); Tacoma, Wash., 1/4/1937
Canova, Judy (comedienne); Jacksonville, Fla., **(1916-1983)**
Cantinflas (Mario Moreno) (comedian); Mexico City, 8/12/1911
Cantor, Eddie (Edward Iskowitz) (actor); New York City **(1892-1964)**
Cantrell, Lana (singer); Sydney, Australia, 1944
Capote, Truman (novelist); New Orleans **(1924-1984)**
Capp, Al (Alfred Gerald Caplin) (cartoonist); New Haven, Conn. **(1909-1979)**
Capra, Frank (film producer, director); Palermo, Italy **(1897–1991)**
Caravaggio, Michelangelo Merisi da (painter); Caravaggio (Italy) **(1573-1610)**
Cardin, Pierre (fashion designer); nr. Venice, 7/7/1922
Cardinale, Claudia (actress); Tunis, Tunisia, 1939
Carey, Harry (actor); New York City **(1878-1947)**
Carey, Macdonald (actor); Sioux City, Iowa, 3/15/1913
Carlin, George (comedian); Bronx, N.Y., 5/12/37
Carlisle, Kitty (singer and actress); New Orleans, 9/3/1915
Carlson, Richard (actor); Albert Lea, Minn., **(1912-1977)**
Carlyle, Thomas (essayist and historian); Ecclefechan, Scotland **(1795-1881)**
Carmichael, Hoagy (Hoagland Howard) (songwriter); Bloomington, Ind. **(1899-1981)**
Carne, Judy (Joyce Botterill) (singer); Northampton, England, 1939
Carnegie, Andrew (industrialist); Dunfermline, Scotland **(1835-1919)**
Carney, Art (actor); Mt. Vernon, N.Y., 11/4/1918
Carnovsky, Morris (actor); St. Louis, 9/5/1897
Caron, Leslie (actress); Paris, 7/1/1931
Carr, Vikki (singer); El Paso, 7/19/1942
Carracci, Annibale (painter); Bologna (Italy) **(1560-1609)**
Carracci, Lodovico (painter); Bologna (Italy) **(1555-1619)**
Carradine, David (actor); Holly wood, Calif., 12/8/1936
Carradine, John (actor); New York City **(1906-1988)**
Carradine, Keith (actor); San Mateo, Calif., 8/8/49
Carreras, José (tenor); Barcelona, Spain, 12/5/1946
Carrillo, Leo (actor); Los Angeles **(1881-1961)**
Carroll, Diahann (Carol Diahann Johnson) (singer and actress); Bronx, N.Y., 7/17/1935

Carroll, Leo G. (actor); Weedon, England **(1892-1972)**
Carroll, Lewis (Charles Lutwidge Dodgson) (author and mathematician); Daresbury, England **(1832-1898)**
Carroll, Madeleine (actress); West Bromwich, England **(1906-1987)**
Carroll, Nancy (actress); New York City **(1904-1965)**
Carroll, Pat (comedienne); Shreveport, La., 5/5/1927
Carson, Jack (actor); Carmen, Man., Canada **(1910-1963)**
Carson, Johnny (TV entertainer); Corning, Iowa, 10/23/1925
Carson, Kit (Christopher) (scout); Madison County, Ky. **(1809-1868)**
Carson, Rachel (biologist and author); Springdale, Pa. **(1907-1964)**
Carter, Dixie (actress); McLemoresville, Tenn., 5/25/39
Carter, Jack (comedian); New York City, 1923
Carter, Lynda (actress); Phoenix, Ariz., 7/24/51
Cartier, Jacques (explorer); Saint-Malo, Brittany (France) **(1491-1557)**
Cartier-Brisson, Henri (photographer); Chanteloup, France, 8/22/1908
Cartland, Barbara (author); England, 7/9/1901
Caruso, Enrico (Errico) (tenor); Naples, Italy **(1873-1921)**
Carver, George Washington (botanist); Missouri **(1864-1943)**
Cary, Arthur Joyce Lunel (novelist); Londonderry, Ireland **(1888-1957)**
Casals, Pablo (cellist); Vendrell, Spain **(1876-1973)**
Casanova de Seingalt, Giovanni Jacopo (adventurer); Venice **(1725-1798)**
Cash, Johnny (singer); nr. Kingsland, Ark., 2/26/1932
Cass, Peggy (comedienne); Boston, 5/21/1924
Cassatt, Mary (painter); Allegheny, Pa. **(1844-1926)**
Cassavetes, John (actor and director); New York City **(1929-1989)**
Cassidy, David (singer); New York City, 4/12/1950
Cassidy, Jack (actor); Richmond Hill, Queens, N.Y. **(1927-1976)**
Cassidy, Shaun (actor); Los Angeles, 9/27/58
Cassini, Oleg (Oleg Lolewski-Cassini) (fashion designer); Paris, 4/11/1913
Castagno, Andrea del (painter); San Martino a Corella (Italy) (c.1421-1457)
Castellano, Richard (actor); New York City **(1934-1988)**
Castle, Irene (Irene Foote) (actress and dancer); New Rochelle, N.Y. **(1893-1969)**
Castle, Vernon Blythe (dancer and aviator); Norwich, England **(1887-1918)**
Castro Ruz, Fidel (Premier); Mayari, Oriente, Cuba, 8/13/1926
Cather, Willa Sibert (novelist); Winchester, Va. **(1876-1947)**
Cato, Marcus Porcius (called Cato the Elder) (statesman); Tusculum (Italy) **(234-149** B.C.)
Catt, Carrie Chapman Lane (woman suffragist); Ripon, Wis. **(1859-1947)**
Catton, Bruce (historian); Petoskey, Mich. **(1899-1978)**
Cauldfield, Joan (actress); East Orange, N.J. **(1927–1991)**
Cavallaro, Carmen (band leader); New York City, 1913
Cavett, Dick (Richard) (TV entertainer); Gibbon, Neb., 11/19/1936
Cellini, Benvenuto (goldsmith and sculptor); Florence (Italy) **(1500-1571)**
Cervantes Saavedra, Miguel de (novelist); Alcalá de Henares, Spain **(1547-1616)**
Cézanne, Paul (painter); Aix-en-Provence, France **(1839-1906)**
Chagall, Marc (painter); Vitebsk, Russia, **(1887-1985)**
Chaliapin, Feodor Ivanovitch (operatic basso); Kazan, Russia **(1873-1938)**
Chamberlain, Arthur Neville (statesman); Edgbaston, England **(1869-1940)**
Chamberlain, Richard (actor); Los Angeles, 3/31/1935(?)
Champion, Gower (choreographer); Geneva, Ill. **(1921-1980)**
Champion, Marge (actress and dancer); Los Angeles, 9/2/1923
Champlain, Samuel de (explorer); nr. Rochefort, France **(1567?-1635)**
Chancellor, John (TV commentator); Chicago, 7/14/1927
Chandler, Jeff (actor); Brooklyn, N.Y. **(1918-1961)**
Chandler, Raymond (writer); Chicago **(1883-1959)**
Chanel, "Coco" (Gabriel Bonheur) (fashion designer); Issoire, France **(1883-1971)**
Chaney, Lon (actor); Colorado Springs, Colo. **(1883-1930)**
Channing, Carol (actress); Seattle, 1/31/1923
Channing, Stockard (actress); New York City, 2/13/44
Chaplin, Geraldine (actress); Santa Monica, Calif., 7/31/1944
Chaplin, Sir Charles (actor); London **(1889-1977)**
Charisse, Cyd (Tula Finklea) (dancer and actress); Amarillo, Tex., 3/8/1923
Charlemagne (Holy Roman Emperor); birthplace unknown **(742-814)**
Charles, Ray (Ray Charles Robinson) (pianist, singer, and songwriter); Albany Ga., 9/23/1930
Charo (Maria Rosario Pilar Martinez) (actress); Murcia, Spain 1/15/51
Chase, Charlie (actor, director); Baltimore, Md. **(1893-1940)**
Chase, Chevy (Cornelius Crane Chase) (comedian); New York City, 10/8/1943

Chase, Ilka (author and actress); New York City **(1905-1978)**
Chase, Lucia (founder Ballet Theatre [now American Ballet Theatre]); Waterbury, Conn. **(1907-1986)**
Chatterton, Ruth (actress); New York City **(1893-1961)**
Chaucer, Geoffrey (poet); London **(1340?-1400)**
Chávez, Carlos (composer); nr. Mexico City **(1899-1978)**
Chavez, Cesar (labor leader); nr. Yuma, Ariz., 3/31/1927
Chayefsky, Paddy (Sidney) (playwright); New York City, **(1923-1981)**
Checker, Chubby (Ernest Evans) (performer); Philadelphia, 10/3/1941
Cheever, John (novelist); Quincy, Mass. **(1912-1982)**
Chekhov, Anton Pavlovich (dramatist and short-story writer); Taganrog, Russia **(1860-1904)**
Cher (Cherilyn LaPiere) (singer); El Centro, Calif., 5/20/1946
Cherubini, Luigi (composer); Florence **(1760-1842)**
Chesterton, Gilbert Keith (author); Kensington, England **(1874-1936)**
Chevalier, Maurice (entertainer); Paris **(1888-1972)**
Chiang Kai-shek (Chief of State); Feng-hwa, China **(1887-1975)**
Child, Julia (food expert); Pasadena, Calif., 8/15/1912
Chippendale, Thomas (cabinet-maker); Otley, England **(1718?-1779)**
Chirico, Giorgio de (painter); Vólos, Greece, **(1888-1978)**
Chopin, Frédéric François (composer); nr. Warsaw **(1810-1849)**
Chou En-lai. *See* Zhou Enlai
Christian, Linda (Blanca Rosa Welter) (actress); Tampico, Mexico, 11/13/1924
Christie, Agatha (mystery writer); Torquay, England, **(1890-1976)**
Christie, Julie (actress); Chukua, India, 4/14/1941
Christopher, Jordon (actor and musician); Youngstown, Ohio, 1941
Christy, June (singer); Springfield, Ill., 1925
Churchill, Sir Winston Leonard Spencer (statesman); Blenheim Palace, Oxfordshire, England **(1874-1965)**
Cicero, Marcus Tullius (orator and statesman); Arpinum (Italy) **(106-43** B.C.)
Cid, El (Rodrigo [or Ruy] DíezdeBivar)(Spanish nationl hero); nr. Burgos, Spain **(1040?-1099)**
Cilento, Diane (actress); Queensland, Australia, 10/5/1933
Cimabue, Giovanni (painter); Florence (Italy) **(c.1240-c.1302)**
Cimino, Michael (film director); New York City, 1943(?)
Clair, René (René Chomette) (film director); Paris **(1898-1981)**
Claire, Ina (Ina Fagan) (actress); Washington, D.C., **(1895-1985)**
Clapton, Eric (singer and guitarist); Ripley, England, 3/30/1945
Clark, Bobby (comedian, actor); Springfield, Ohio **(1888-1960)**
Clark, Dane (Barney Zanville) (actor); New York City, 2/18/1915
Clark, Dick (TV personality); Mt. Vernon, N.Y., 11/30/1929
Clark, Mark W. (general); Madison Barracks, N.Y. **(1896-1984)**
Clark, Petula (singer); Epsom, England, 11/15/1934
Clark, Roy (country music artist); Meherrin, Va., 4/15/1933
Clark, William (explorer); Caroline County, Va. **(1770-1838)**
Clarke, Arthur C. (science fiction writer); Minehead, England, 12/16/1917
Clary, Robert (actor); Paris, France, 3/1/26
Claude Lorrain (Claude Gellée) (painter); Champagne, France **(1600-1682)**
Clausewitz, Karl von (military strategist); Burg (East Germany) **(1780-1831)**
Clay, Henry (statesman); Hanover County, Va. **(1777-1852)**
Clay, Lucius D. (banker, ex-general); Marietta, Ga. **(1897-1978)**
Clayburgh, Jill (actress); New York City, 4/30/1944
Cleese, John (writer, actor); Weston-super-Mare, England, 10/27/39
Clemenceau, Georges (statesman); Mouilleron-en-Pareds, Vondée, France **(1841-1929)**
Clemens, Samuel L. *See* Mark Twain
Cleopatra (Queen of Egypt); Alexandria, Egypt **(69-30** B.C.)
Cliburn, Van (Harvey Lavan Cliburn, Jr.) (concert pianist); Shreveport, La., 7/12/1934
Clifford, Clark M. (ex-Secretary of Defense); Ft. Scott, Kan., 12/25/1906
Clift, Montgomery (actor); Omaha, Neb. **(1920-1966)**
Clooney, Rosemary (singer); Maysville, Ky., 5/23/1928
Close, Glenn (actress); Greenwich, Conn., 3/19/1947
Clurman, Harold (stage producer); New York City **(1901-1980)**
Cobb, Irvin Shrewsbury (humorist); Paducah, Ky. **(1876-1944)**
Cobb, Lee J. (Leo Jacob) (actor); New York City **(1911-1976)**
Coburn, Charles Douville (actor); Savannah, Ga. **(1877-1961)**
Coburn, James (actor); Laurel, Neb., 8/31/1928
Coca, Imogene (comedienne); Philadelphia, 11/18/1908
Cocker, Joe (John Robert Cocker) (singer); Sheffield, England, 5/20/1944
Coco, James (actor); New York City **(1929-1987)**
Cocteau, Jean (author); Maison-Lafitte, France **(1891-1963)**
Cody, W. F. *See* Buffalo Bill
Cohan, George Michael (actor and dramatist); Providence, R.I. **(1878-1942)**
Cohn, Mindy (actress); Los Angeles, 5/20/66
Colbert, Claudette (Lily Chauchoin) (actress); Paris, 9/13/1903
Colby, William E. (ex-Director of CIA); St. Paul, 1/4/1920

Cole, Nat "King" (singer); Montgomery, Ala. **(1919-1965)**
Cole, Natalie (singer); Los Angeles, 2/6/1950
Cole, Thomas (painter); Lancashire, England **(1801-1848)**
Coleman, Dabney (actor); Corpus Christi, Tex., 1/2/32
Coleman, Gary (actor); Zion, Ill., 2/8/68
Coleridge, Samuel Taylor (poet); Ottery St. Mary, England **(1772-1834)**
Colette (Sidonie-Gabrielle Colette) (novelist); St.-Sauveur, France **(c.1873-1954)**
Collier, Constance (actress); Windsor, England **(1878-1955)**
Collingwood, Charles (TV commentator); Three Rivers, Mich. **(1917-1985)**
Collins, Dorothy (Marjorie Chandler) (singer); Windsor, Ontario, Canada, 11/18/1926
Collins, Joan (actress); London 5/23/1933
Collins, Judy (singer); Seattle, 5/1/1939
Colman, Ronald (actor); Richmond, England **(1891-1958)**
Colonna, Jerry (comedian); Boston **(1905-1986)**
Columbo, Russ (singer, bandleader); San Francisco **(1908-1934)**
Columbus, Christopher (Cristoforo Colombo) (discoverer of America); Genoa (Italy) **(1451-1506)**
Comden, Betty (writer); New York City, 5/3/1919
Comenius, Johann Amos (educational reformer) Nivnice, Moravia (Czechoslovakia) **(1592-1670)**
Commager, Henry Steele (historian); Pittsburgh, 10/25/1902
Como, Perry (Pierino) (singer); Canonsburg, Pa., 5/18/1912
Compton, Karl Taylor (phy sicist); Wooster, Ohio **(1887-1954)**
Comte, Auguste (philosopher); Montpellier, France **(1798-1857)**
Conant, James B. (educator and statesman); Dorchester, Mass. **(1893-1978)**
Condon, Eddie (jazz musician); Goodland, Ind. **(1905-1973)**
Confucius (K'ung Fu-tzu) (philosopher); Shantung province, China **(c.551-479** B.C.)
Congreve, William (dramatist); nr. Leeds, England **(1670-1729)**
Connelly, Marc (playwright); McKeesport, Pa. **(1890-1980)**
Connery, Sean (actor); Edinburgh, Scotland, 8/25/1930
Conniff, Ray (band leader); Attleboro, Mass., 11/6/1916
Connolly, Walter (actor); Cincinnati, Ohio **(1887-1940)**
Connors, Chuck (actor); Brooklyn, N.Y., 4/10/1921
Connors, Mike (actor); Fresno, Calif., 8/15/1925
Conrad, Joseph (Teodor Jozef Konrad Korzeniowski) (novelist); Berdichev, Ukraine **(1857-1924)**
Conrad, Robert (Conrad Robert Falk) (actor); Chicago, 3/1/1935
Conrad, William (actor); Louisville, Ky., 9/27/1920
Conried, Hans (Frank Foster) (actor); Baltimore **(1915-1982)**
Constable, John (painter); East Bergholt, Suffolk, England **(1776-1837)**
Constantine II (ex-king); Athens, 6/2/1940
Constantine, Michael (actor); Reading, Pa., 5/22/27
Conte, Richard (actor); New York City **(1916-1975)**
Conti, Tom (actor); Paisley, Scotland, 11/22/1941
Converse, Frank (actor); St. Louis, 1938
Convy, Bert (actor, host); St. Louis, Mo. **(1933–1991)**
Conway, Tim (comedian); Chagrin Falls, Ohio, 12/15/1933
Coogan, Jackie (actor); Los Angeles **(1914-1984)**
Cook, Peter (actor, writer); Torquay, England, 11/17/37
Cooke, Alistair (Alfred Alistair); (TV narrator and journalist); Manchester, England, 11/20/1908
Cooley, Denton A(rthur) (heart surgeon); Houston, Tex., 8/22/1920
Coolidge, Rita (singer); Nashville, Tenn., 1944
Cooper, Alice (Vincent Furnier) (rock musician); Detroit, 2/4/1948
Cooper, Gary (Frank James Cooper) (actor); Helena, Mont. **(1901-1961)**
Cooper, Dame Gladys (actress); Lewisham, England **(1898-1971)**
Cooper, Jackie (actor and director); Los Angeles, 9/15/1922
Cooper, James Fenimore (novelist); Burlington, N.J. **(1789-1 851)**
Cooper, Peter (industrialist and philanthropist); New York City **(1791-1883)**
Copernicus, Nicolaus (Mikolaj Kopernik) (astronomer); Thorn, Poland **(1473-1543)**
Copland, Aaron (composer); Brooklyn, N.Y. **(1900–1990)**
Copley, John Singleton (painter); Boston, Mass. **(1738-1815)**
Copperfield, David (illusionist); Matuchen, N.J., 9/16/1956
Coppola, Francis Ford (film director); Detroit, 4/7/1939
Corelli, Arcangelo (composer); Fusignano, Italy **(1653-1713)**
Corelli, Franco (operatic tenor); Ancona, Italy, 4/8/1923
Corneille, Pierre (dramatist); Rouen, France **(1606-1684)**
Cornell, Katharine (actress); Berlin **(1893-1974)**
Coret, Jean Baptiste Camille (painter); Paris **(1796-1875)**
Correggio, Antonio Allegri da (painter); Correggio (Italy) **(1494-1534)**
Corsaro, Frank (opera director); New York harbor, 12/22/1924
Cortés (or Cortez), Hernando (explorer); Medellin, Spain **(1485-1547)**
Cosby, Bill (actor); Philadelphia, 7/12/1937
Cosell, Howard (Howard Cohen) (sportscaster); Winston-Salem, N.C., 3/25/1920

Costa-Gavras, Henri (Kostantinos Gavras) (film director); Athens, 1933
Costello, Dolores (actress); Pittsburgh, Pa. **(1905-1979)**
Costello, Elvis (Declan Patrick McManus) (singer, musician, songwriter); London, 1954
Costello, Lou (comedian); Paterson, N.J. **(1908-1959)**
Costello, Maurice (actor); Pittsburgh **(1877-1950)**
Cotten, Joseph (actor); Petersburg, Va., 5/15/1905
Couperin, François (composer); Paris **(1668-1733)**
Courbet, Gustave (painter); Ornans, France **(1819-1877)**
Courrssèges, André (fashion designer); Pau, France, 3/9/1923
Courtenay, Tom (actor); Hull, England, 2/25/1937
Cousins, Norman (publisher); Union Hill, N.J. **(1915-1990)**
Cousteau, Jacques-Yves (marine explorer); St. André-de-Cubzac, France, 6/11/1910
Coward, Sir Noel (playwright and actor); Teddington, England **(1899-1973)**
Cowl, Jane (actress); Boston **(1887-1950)**
Cowles, Gardner, Jr. (newspaper publisher); Algona, Iowa, **(1903-1985)**
Cowper, William (poet); Great Berkhamstead, England **(1731-1800)**
Cox, Wally (actor); Detroit, Mich. **(1924-1973)**
Cozzens, James Gould (novelist); Chicago **(1903-1978)**
Crabbe, Buster (Clarence) (actor); Oakland, Calif. **(1908-1983)**
Crain, Jeanne (actress); Barstow, Calif., 5/25/1925
Cranach, Lucas, the elder (painter); Kronach (Germany) **(1472-1553)**
Crane, Hart (poet); Garrettsville, Ohio **(1899-1932)**
Crane, Stephen (novelist and poet); Newark, N.J. **(1871-1900)**
Cranmer, Thomas (churchman); Aslacton, England **(1489-1556)**
Crawford, Broderick (actor); Philadelphia **(1911-1986)**
Crawford, Cheryl (stage producer); Akron, Ohio **(1902-1986)**
Crawford, Joan (Lucille LeSueur) (actress and business executive); San Antonio **(1908-1977)**
Cregar, Laird (actor); Philadelphia, Pa. **(1916-1944)**
Crenna, Richard (actor); Los Angeles, 11/30/1927
Crespin, Régine (operatic soprano); Marseilles, France, 2/23/1929
Crichton, (John) Michael (novelist); Chicago, 10/23/1942
Crisp, Donald (actor); London **(1880-1974)**
Croce, Benedetto (philosopher); Peseasseroli, Aquila, Italy **(1866-1952)**
Croce, Jim (singer); Philadelphia **(1942-1973)**
Crockett, Davy (David) (frontiersman); Greene County, Tenn. **(1786-1836)**
Cromwell, Oliver (statesman); Huntingdon, England **(1599-1658)**
Cronin, A. J. (Archibald J. Cronin) (novelist); Cardross, Scotland **(1896-1981)**
Cronkite, Walter (TV newscaster); St. Joseph, Mo., 11/4/1916
Cronyn, Hume (actor); London, Ontario, Canada, 7/18/1911
Crosby, Bing (Harry Lillis) (singer, actor); Tacoma, Wash. **(1904-1977)**
Crosby, Bob (musician); Spokane, Wash., 8/23/1913
Crosby, Cathy Lee (actress); Los Angeles, 12/2/48
Crosby, Norm (comedian); Boston, 9/15/27
Cross, Ben (Bernard) (actor); Paddington, England, 12/16/1947
Cross, Milton (opera commentator); New York City **(1897-1975)**
Crouse, Russel (playwright); Findlay, Ohio **(1893-1966)**
Cruise, Tom (actor); Syracuse, N.Y., 7/3/1962
Crystal, Billy (comedian, actor); Long Beach, L.I., N.Y., 3/14/47
Cugat, Xavier (band leader); Barcelona, Spain **(1900-1990)**
Cukor, George (film director); New York City **(1899-1983)**
Cullen , Bill (William Lawrence Cullen) (radio and TV entertainer); Pittsburgh **(1920-1990)**
Culp, Robert (actor); Berkeley, Calif., 8/16/1930
Cummings, E. E. (Edward Estlin Cummings) (poet); Cambridge, Mass. **(1894-1962)**
Cummings, Robert (actor); Joplin, Mo. **(1908-1990)**
Curie, Marie (Marja Sklodowska) (physical chemist); Warsaw **(1867-1934)**
Curie, Pierre (physicist); Paris **(1859-1906)**
Curtin, Jane (actress); Cambridge, Mass., 9/6/47
Curtin, Phyllis (soprano); Clarksburg, W.Va., 12/3/1927
Curtis, Jamie Lee (actress); Los Angeles, 11/22/58
Curtis, Tony (Bernard Schwartz) (actor); Bronx, N.Y., 6/3/1925
Curzon, Clifford (concert pianist); London **(1907-1982)**
Custer, George Armstrong (army officer); New Rumley, Ohio **(1839-1876)**

D

da Gama, Vasco (explorer); Sines, Portugal **(1460-1524)**
Daguerre, Louis (photographic pioneer); nr. Paris **(1787-1851)**
Dahl, Arlene (actress); Minneapolis, 8/11/1928
Dailey, Dan (actor and dancer); New York City, **(1917-1978)**
Dale, Jim (actor, singer, songwriter); Rothwell, England, 8/15/35

Daley, Richard J. (Mayor of Chicago); Chicago **(1902-1976)**
Dali, Salvador (painter); Figueras, Spain **(1904-1989)**
Dalton, Abby (actress); Las Vegas, Nev., 8/15/32
Dalton, John (chemist); nr. Cockermouth, England **(1766-1844)**
Daly, James (actor); Wisconsin Rapids, Wis. **(1918-1978)**
Daly, John (radio and TV news analyst); Johannesburg, South Africa **(1914–1991)**
Daly, Tyne (actress); Madison, Wis. 2/21/47
d'Amboise, Jacques (ballet dancer); Dedham, Mass., 7/28/1934
Damone, Vic (Vito Farinola) (singer); Brooklyn, N.Y., 6/12/1928
Damrosch, Walter Johannes (orchestra conductor); Breslau (Poland) **(1862-1950)**
Dana, Charles Anderson (editor); Hinsdale, N.H. **(1819-1897)**
Dandridge, Dorothy (actress); Cleveland **(1923-1965)**
Dangerfield, Rodney (comedian); Babylon, L.I., N.Y., 1921
Daniels, Bebe (Virginia Daniels) (actress); Dallas **(1901-1971)**
Daniels, William (actor); Brooklyn, N.Y., 3/31/27
Danilova, Alexandra (ballerina); Peterhof, Russia, 1/20/1904
Dannay, Frederic (novelist, pseudonym Ellery Queen); Brooklyn, N.Y. **(1905-1982)**
Danner, Blythe (actress); Philadelphia, 1944(?)
D'Annunzio, Gabriele (soldier and author); Francaville at Mare, Pescara, Italy **(1863-1938)**
Danson, Ted (actor); San Diego, Calif., 12/29/47
Dante (or Durante) Alighieri (poet); Florence (Italy) **(1265-1321)**
Danton, Georges Jacques (French Revolutionary leader); Arcis-sur-Aube, France **(1759-1794)**
Danza, Tony (actor); Brooklyn, N.Y., 4/21/51
Darnell, Linda (actress); Dallas **(1921-1965)**
Darren, James (actor); Philadelphia, 6/8/1936
Darrieux, Danielle (actress); Bordeaux, France, 5/1/1917
Darrow, Clarence Seward (lawyer); Kinsman, Ohio **(1857-1938)**
Darwell, Jane (actress); Palmyra, Mo. **(1879-1967)**
Darwin, Charles Robert (naturalist); Shrewsbury, England **(1809-1882)**
daSilva, Howard (actor); Cleveland **(1909-1986)**
Dassin, Jules (film director); Middletown, Conn., 12/18/1911
Daumier, Honoré (caricaturist); Marseilles, France **(1808-1879)**
Dauphin, Claude (actor); Corbeil, France **(1903-1978)**
Davenport, Harry (actor); New York City **(1866-1949)**
David, Jacques-Louis (painter); Paris **(1748-1825)**
David (King of Israel and Judah) **(died c. 973** B.C.**)**
Davidson, John (singer and actor); Pittsburgh, 12/13/1941
Davies, Marion (Marion Douras) (actress); New York City **(1898?-1961)**
da Vinci, Leonardo (painter and scientist); Vinci, Tuscany (Italy) **(1452-1519)**
Davis, Ann B. (actress); Schenectady, N.Y., 5/5/26
Davis, Bette (actress); Lowell, Mass. **(1908-1989)**
Davis, Elmer Holmes (radio commentator); Aurora, Ind. **(1890-1958)**
Davis, Jefferson (President of the Confederacy); Christian (now Todd) County, Ky. **(1808-1889)**
Davis, Joan (actress); St. Paul, Minn., **(1907-1961)**
Davis, Mac (singer); Lubbock, Tex., 1/21/1942
Davis, Miles (jazz trumpeter); Alton, Ill., 5/25/1926
Davis, Ossie (actor and writer); Cogdell, Ga., 12/18/1917
Davis, Sammy, Jr. (actor and singer); New York City **(1925-1990)**
Davis, Skeeter (Mary Francis Penick) (singer); Dry Ridge, Ky., 12/30/1931
Davis, Stuart (painter); Philadelphia **(1894-1964)**
Dawber, Pam (actress); Farmington Hills, Mich., 10/18/51
Dawson, Richard (actor, host); Gosport, Hampshire, England, 11/20/32
Day, Dennis (singer); New York City **(1917-1988)**
Day, Doris (Doris von Kappelhoff) (singer and actress); Cincinnati, 4/3/1924
Day, Laraine (La Raine Johnson) (actress); Roosevelt, Utah, 10/13/1920
Dayan, Moshe (ex-Defense Minister of Israel); Dagania, Palestine **(1915-1981)**
Dean, James (actor); Marion, Ind. **(1931-1955)**
Dean, Jimmy (singer); Seth Ward, nr. Plainview, Tex., 8/10/1928
De Bakey, Michael E. (heart surgeon); Lake Charles, La., 9/7/1908
de Beauvoir, Simone (novelist and philosopher); Paris **(1908-1986)**
Debs, Eugene Victor (Socialist leader); Terre Haute, Ind. **(1855-1926)**
Debussy, Claude Achille (composer); St. Germain-en-Laye, France **(1862-1918)**
DeCamp, Rosemary (actress); Prescott, Ariz., 11/14/14(?)
De Carlo, Yvonne (Peggy Yvonne Middleton) (actress); Vancouver, B.C., Canada, 9/1/1924
de Chirico, Giorgio (painter); Volos, Greece, **(1888-1978)**
Dee, Francis (actress); Los Angeles, 11/26/07
Dee, Ruby (actress); Cleveland, Ohio, 10/27/23(?)
Dee, Sandra (Alexandra Zuck) (actress); Bayonne, N.J., 4/23/1942
Defoe, Daniel (novelist); London **(1659?-1731)**

Defore, Don (actor); Cedar Rapids, Iowa, 8/25/17
Degas, Hilaire Germain Edgar (painter); Paris **(1834-1917)**
de Gaulle, Charles André Joseph Marie (soldier and statesman); Lille, France **(1890-1970)**
DeHaven, Gloria (actress); Los Angeles, 7/23/1925
de Havilland, Olivia (actress); Tokyo, 7/1/1916
Dekker, Albert (actor); Brooklyn, N.Y. **(1904-1968)**
de Kooning, Willem (painter); Rotterdam, 4/24/1904
Delacroix, Eugène (painter); Charenton-St. Maurice, France **(1798-1863)**
de la Renta, Oscar (fashion designer); Santo Domingo, Dominican Republic, 7/22/1932
Delaunay, Robert (painter); Paris **(1885-1941)**
De Laurentiis, Dino (film producer); Torre Annunziata, Bay of Naples, Italy, 8/8/1919
della Robbia, Andrea (sculptor) Florence **(1435-1525)**
della Robbia, Luca (sculptor); Florence **(1400-1482)**
Delon, Alain (actor); Sceaux, France, 11/8/1935
Del Rio, Dolores (Dolores Ansunsolo) (actress); Durango, Mexico **(1905-1983)**
DeLuise, Dom (comedian); Brooklyn, N.Y., 8/1/1933
Demarest, William (actor); St. Paul **(1892-1983)**
de Mille, Agnes (choreographer); New York City 9/18/1905
De Mille, Cecil Blount (film director); Ashfield, Mass. **(1881-1959)**
Demosthenes (orator); Athens **(385?-322** B.C.)
Deneuve, Catherine (actress); Paris, 10/22/1943
De Niro, Robert (actor); New York City, 8/17/1943
Dennehy, Brian (actor); Brigeport, Conn., 7/9/40
Denning, Richard (actor); Poughkeepsie, N.Y., 3/27/14
Dennis, Sandy (actress); Hastings, Neb., 4/27/1937
Denny, Reginald (actor); Richmond, England **(1891-1967)**
Denver, John (Henry John Deutschendorf, Jr.) (singer); Roswell, N.M., 12/31/1943
De Palma, Brian (film director); Newark, N.J., 9/11/1940
Derain, André (painter); Chatou, Seine-et-Oise, France **(1880-1954)**
Derek, John (actor, director); Los Angeles, 8/12/26
Dern, Bruce (actor); Chicago, 6/4/1936
Descartes, René (philosopher and mathematician); La Haye, France **(1596-1650)**
De Seversky, Alexander P. (aviator); Tiflis, Russia **(1894-1974)**
De Sica, Vittorio (film director); Sora, Italy **(1901-1974)**
Desmond, Johnny (composer); Detroit **(1921-1985)**
Desmond, William (actor); Dublin **(1878-1949)**
De Soto, Hernando (explorer); Barcarrota, Spain **(1500?-1542)**
De Valera, Eamon (ex-President of Ireland); New York City **(1882-1975)**
Devane, William (actor); Albany, N.Y., 9/5/39
Devine, Andy (actor); Flagstaff, Ariz. **(1905-1977)**
DeVito, Danny (Daniel Michael); (actor, director); Neptune, N.J., 11/17/1944
De Vries, Peter (novelist); Chicago, 2/27/1910
de Waart, Edo (conductor); Amsterdam, the Netherlands, 6/1/41
Dewey, George (admiral); Montpelier, Vt. **(1837-1917)**
Dewey, John (philosopher and educator); Burlington, Vt. **(1859-1952)**
Dewey, Thomas E. (politician); Owosso, Mich. **(1902-1971)**
Dewhurst, Colleen (actress); Montreal **(1924-1991)**
De Wilde, Brandon (actor); Brookly, N.Y. **(1942-1972)**
DeWitt, Joyce (actress); Wheeling W.Va., 4/23/49
De Wolfe, Billy (actor); Wollaston, Mass. **(1907-1974)**
Dey, Susan (actress); Pekin, Ill., 12/10/52
Diamond, Neil (singer); Brooklyn, N.Y., 1/24/1941
Diana (Diana Frances Spencer) (Princess of Wales); Sandringham, England, 7/1/61
Dichter, Misha (pianist); Shanghai, 9/27/1945
Dickens, Charles John Huffam (novelist); Portsea, England **(1812-1870)**
Dickey, James (poet); Atlanta, 2/2/1923
Dickinson, Angie (Angeline Brown) (actress); Kulm, N.D., 9/30/1932
Dickinson, Emily Elizabeth (poet); Amherst, Mass. **(1830-1886)**
Diddley, Bo (Elias McDaniel) (guitarist); McComb, Miss., 12/30/1928
Diderot, Denis (encyclopedist); Langres, France **(1713-1784)**
Diefenbaker, John G. (ex-Prime Minister); Grey County, Ontario, Canada **(1895-1979)**
Dietrich, Marlene (Maria Magdalena von Losch) (actress); Berlin, 12/27/1901
Diggs, Dudley (actor); Dublin **(1879-1947)**
Diller, Phyllis (Phyllis Driver) (comedienne); Lima, Ohio, 7/17/1917
Dillman, Bradford (actor); San Francisco, 4/14/1930
Dine, Jim (painter); Cincinnati, 6/16/1935
Diogenes (philosopher); Sinope (Turkey) **(412?-323** B.C.)
Dion (Dion DiMucci) (singer); Bronx, N.Y., 7/18/1939
Dior, Christian (fashion designer); Granville, France **(1905-1957)**
Disney, Walt(er) Elias (film animator and producer); Chicago **(1901-1966)**
Disraeli, Benjamin (Earl of Beaconsfield) (statesman); London

(1804-1881)
Dix, Dorothea (civil rights reformer); Hampden, Me. **(1802-1887)**
Dix, Richard (Ernest Carlton Brimmer) (actor); St. Paul **(1894-1949)**
Dixon, Jeane (Jeane Pinckert) (seer); Medford, Wis., **1918**
Dobbs, Mattiwilda (soprano); Atlanta, Ga., 7/11/1925
Doctorow, E(dgar) L(aurence) (novelist); New York City, 1/6/1931
Dodgson, C. L. *See* Carroll, Lewis.
Dolin, Anton (dancer); Slinfold, England **(1904-1983)**
Domingo, Placido (tenor); Madrid, 1/21/1941
Domino, Fats (Antoine) (musician); New Orleans, 2/26/1928
Donahue, Phil (television personality); Cleveland, 12/21/1935
Donahue, Troy (actor); New York City, 1/27/36(?)
Donat, Robert (actor); Withington, England **(1905-1958)**
Donatello (Donato Niccolò di Betto Bardi) (sculptor); Florence **(c.1386-1466)**
Donlevy, Brian (actor); Portadown, Ireland **(1899-1972)**
Donovan (Donovan Leitch) (singer and songwriter); Glasgow, Scotland, 2/10/1946
Donne, John (poet); London **(1573-1631)**
Doolittle, James H. (ex-Air Force general); Alameda, Calif., 12/14/1896
Dorati, Antal (orchestra conductor); Budapest **(1906-1988)**
Dorsey, Jimmy (band leader); Shenandoah, Pa. **(1904-1957)**
Dorsey, Tommy (band leader); Mahonoy Plains, Pa. **(1905-1956)**
Dos Passos, John (author); Chicago **(1896-1970)**
Dostoevski, Fyodor Mikhailovich (novelist); Moscow **(1821-1881)**
Dotrice, Roy (actor); Guernsey, Channel Islands, England, 5/26/23
Douglas, Helen Gahagan (ex-Representative); Boonton, N.J. **(1900-1980)**
Douglas, Kirk (Issur Danielovitch) (actor); Amsterdam, N.Y., 12/9/1916
Douglas, Melvyn (Melvyn Hesselberg) (actor); Macon, Ga., **(1901-1981)**
Douglas, Michael (actor; movie producer); New Brunswick, N.J., 9/25/1944
Douglas, Mike (Michael D. Dowd, Jr.) (TV personality); Chicago, 8/11/1925
Douglas, Paul (actor); Philadelphia **(1907-1959)**
Douglas, Stephen Arnold (politician); Brandon, Vt. **(1813-1861)**
Dowling, Eddie (Edward Goucher) (actor and stage producer); Woonsocket, R.I., **(1894-1976)**
Down, Lesley-Anne (actress); London, England, 3/17/54
Downs, Hugh (TV entertainer); Akron, Ohio, 2/14/1921
Doyle, Sir Arthur Conan (novelist and spiritualist); Edinburgh, Scotland **(1859-1930)**
Doyle, David (actor); Omaha, Neb., 12/1/25
Drake, Alfred (singer and actor); New York City, 10/7/1914
Drake, Sir Francis (navigator); Tavistock, England **(1545-1596)**
Dreiser, Theodore (writer); Terre Haute, Ind. **(1871-1945)**
Dressler, Marie (Leila Koeber) (actress); Cobourg, Ontario, Canada **(1869-1934)**
Dreyfus, Alfred (French army officer); Mulhouse (France) **(1859-1935)**
Dreyfuss, Richard (actor); Brooklyn, N.Y., 10/29/1947
Drury, Allen (novelist); Houston, 9/2/1918
Dryden, John (poet); Northamptonshire, England **(1631-1700)**
Dryer, Fred (actor); Hawthorne, Calif., 7/6/46
Dru, Joan (actress); Logan, W. Va., 1/31/23
Dubček, Alexander (ex-President of Czechoslovakia); Uhroved (Czechoslovakia), 11/27/1921
Dubinsky, David (David Dobnievski) (labor leader); Brest-Litovsk (U.S.S.R.) **(1892-1982)**
Duchamp, Marcel (painter); Blainville, France **(1887-1968)**
Duchin, Eddy (pianist, bandleader); Cambridge, Mass. **(1909-1951)**
Duchin, Peter (pianist and band leader); New York City, 7/28/1937
Dufay, Guillaume (composer); Cambrai, France **(c. 1400-1474)**
Duff, Howard (actor); Bremerton, Wash. **(1917-1990)**
Duffy, Julia (actress); Minneapolis, Minn., 6/27/50
Dufy, Raoul (painter); Le Havre, France **(1877-1953)**
Duke, James B. (industrialist); nr. Durham, N.C. **(1856-1925)**
Duke, Patty (Anna Marie Duke) (actress); New York City, 12/14/1946
Dullea, Keir (actor); Cleveland, 5/30/1936(?)
Dulles, Allen Welsh (ex-Director of CIA); Watertown, N.Y. **(1893-1969)**
Dulles, John Foster (statesman); Washington, D.C. **(1888-1959)**
Dumas, Alexandre (called Dumas fils) (novelist); Paris **(1824-1895)**
Dumas, Alexandre (called Dumas père) (novelist); Villers-Cotterets, France **(1802-1870)**
du Maurier, Daphne (novelist); London **(1907-1989)**
du Maurier, George Louis Palmella Busson (novelist); Paris **(1834-1896)**
Dumont, Margaret (actress); **(1889-1965)**
Dunaway, Faye (actress); Bascom, Fla., 1/14/1941
Duncan, Isadora (dancer); San Francisco **(1878-1927)**
Duncan, Sandy (actress); Henderson, Tex., 2/20/1946
Dunham, Katherine (dancer, choreographer); Chicago, 1914

Dunn, James (actor); Santa Monica, Calif. **(1905-1967)**
Dunne, Irene (actress); Louisville, Ky. **(1901?-1990)**
Dunnock, Mildred (actress); Baltimore **(1901–1991)**
Duns Scotus, John (theologian); Duns, Scotland **(1265-1303)**
Du Pont, Pierre S. (economist); Paris **(1739-1817)**
Durante, Jimmy (comedian); New York City **(1893-1980)**
Durbin, Deanna (Edna Mae) (actress); Winnipeg, Canada, 12/4/1922
Dürer, Albrecht (painter and engraver); Nürnberg (Germany) **(1471-1528)**
Durning, Charles (actor); Highland Falls, N.Y., 2/28/23
Durrell, Lawrence George (novelist); Julundur, India **(1912–1990)**
Duryea, Dan (actor); White Plains, N.Y. **(1907-1968)**
Duse, Eleonora (actress); Chioggia, Italy **(1859-1924)**
Dussault, Nancy (actress); Pensacola, Fla., 6/30/36
Duvalier, Jean-Claude (ex-President; son of "Papa Doc"); Port-au-Prince, Haiti, 7/3/1951
Duvall, Robert (actor); San Diego, Calif., 1931
Duvall, Shelley (actress); Houston, Tex., 1950
Dvořák, Antonin (composer); Nelahozeves (Czechoslovakia) **(1841-1904)**
Dylan, Bob (Robert Zimmerman) (folk singer and composer); Duluth, Minn., 5/24/1941
Dysart, Richard (actor); Brighton, Mass., 3/30/?

E

Eagels, Joanne (actress); Kansas City, Mo. **(1894-1929)**
Eakins, Thomas (painter and sculptor); Philadelphia, **(1844-1916)**
Earhart, Amelia (aviator); Atchison, Kan. **(1898-1937)**
Eastman, George (inventor); Waterville, N.Y. **(1854-1932)**
Eastwood, Clint (actor); San Francisco, 5/31/1930
Ebert, Roger (film critic); Urbana, Ill., 6/18/42
Ebsen, Buddy (Christian Ebsen, Jr.) (actor); Belleville, Ill., 4/2/1908
Eckstine, Billy (singer); Pittsburgh, 7/8/1914
Eddy, Mary Baker (founder of Christian Science Church); Bow, N.H. **(1821-1910)**
Eddy, Nelson (baritone and actor); Providence, R.I. **(1901-1967)**
Eden, Sir Anthony (Earl of Avon) (ex-Prime Minister); Durham, England **(1897-1977)**
Eden, Barbara (actress); Tucson, Ariz., 8/23/34
Edison, Thomas Alva (inventor); Milan, Ohio **(1847-1931)**
Edwards, Anthony (actor); Santa Barbara, Calif., 7/19/?
Edwards, Blake (film writer-producer); Tulsa, Okla. 7/26/1922
Edwards, Jonathan (theologian); East Windsor, Conn. **(1703-1758)**
Edwards, Ralph (TV and radio producer); Merino, Colo., 1913
Edwards, Vincent (actor); Brooklyn, N.Y., 7/7/1928
Egan, Richard (actor); San Francisco, **(1923-1987)**
Eggar, Samantha (actress); London, 5/3/1939
Eglevsky, André (ballet dancer); Moscow **(1917-1977)**
Ehrlich, Paul (bacteriologist); Strzelin (Poland) **(1854-1915)**
Eikenberry, Jill (actress); New Haven, Conn., 1/21/47
Einstein, Albert (physicist); Ulm, Germany **(1879-1955)**
Eisenhower, Milton S. (educator); Abilene, Kan., **(1899-1985)**
Eisenstaedt, Alfred (photographer and photojournalist); Dirschau (Poland), 12/6/1898
Ekberg, Anita (actress); Malmö, Sweden, 9/29/1931
Ekland, Britt (Britt-Marie) (actress); Stockholm, Sweden, 1942
Eldridge, Florence (Florence McKechnie) (actress); Brooklyn, N.Y., **(1901-1988)**
Elgar, Sir Edward (composer); Worcester, England **(1857-1934)**
Elgart, Larry (band leader); New London, Conn., 3/20/1922
El Greco (Domenicos Theotocopoulos) (painter); Candia, Crete (Greece) **(c.1541-1614)**
Eliot, George (Mary Ann Evans) (novelist); Chilvers Coton, England **(1819-1880)**
Eliot, Thomas Stearns (poet); St. Louis **(1888-1965)**
Ellington, Duke (Edward Kennedy) (jazz musician); Washington, D.C. **(1899-1974)**
Elliot, "Mama" Cass (Ellen Naomi Cohen) (singer); Baltimore **(1941-1974)**
Elliott, Denholm (actor); London, 5/31/22
Elliott, Sam (actor); Californa, 8/9/44
Elman, Mischa (violinist); Stalnoye, Ukraine **(1891-1967)**
Emerson, Ralph Waldo (philosopher and poet); Boston **(1803-1882)**
Enesco, Georges (composer); Dorohoi, Romania **(1881-1955)**
Engels, Friedrich (Socialist writer); Barmen (Germany) **(1820-1895)**
Englund, Robert (actor); Glendale, Calif., 6/6/49
Entremont, Philippe (concert pianist); Rheims, France, 6/7/1934
Epicurus (philosopher); Samos (Greece) **(341-270** B.C.)
Epstein, Sir Jacob (sculptor); New York City **(1880-1959)**
Erasmus, Desiderius (Gerhard Gerhards) (scholar); Rotterdam **(1466?-1536)**
Erhard, Ludwig (ex-Chancellor); Furth, Germany **(1897-1977)**
Erickson, Leif (actor); Alameda, Calif. **(1911-1986)**
Ericson, Leif (navigator); **(c. 10th century** A.D.)

Erikson, Erik H. (psychoanalyst); Frankfurt, Germany, 6/15/1902
Ernst, Max (painter); Bruhl, Germany **(1891-1976)**
Erté (Romain de Tirtoff) (artist, designer); St. Petersburg, Russia **(1892-1990)**
Estrada, Erik (actor); New York City, 3/16/49
Euclid (mathematician); Megara (Greece) **(c. 300** B.C.)
Euler, Leonhard (mathematician); Basel, Switzerland **(1707-1783)**
Euripides (dramatist); Salamis (Greece) **(c.484-407** B.C.)
Evans, Dale (Frances Butts) (actress and singer); Uvalde, Tex., 10/31/1912
Evans, Dame Edith (actress); London **(1888-1976)**
Evans, Linda (actress); Hartford, Conn., 11/18/1942
Evans, Maurice (actor); Dorchester, England **(1901-1989)**
Everett, Chad (actor); (Raymon Lee Cramton) South Bend, Ind., 6/11/1936
Evers, Charles (civil rights leader); Decatur, Miss., 9/14/1923(?)
Evers, Medgar (civil rights leader); Decatur, Miss. **(1925-1963)**
Evigan, Greg (actor); South Amboy, N.J., 10/14/53
Ewell, Tom (Yewell Tompkins) (actor); Owensboro, Ky., 4/29/1909

F

Fabares, Shelley (actress); Santa Monica, Calif., 1/19/44
Fabian (Fabian Anthony Forte) (singer); Philadelphia, 2/6/1943
Fabray, Nanette (Nanette Fabarés) (actress); San Diego, Calif., 10/27/1922
Fadiman, Clifton (literary critic); Brooklyn, N.Y., 5/15/1904
Fahrenheit, Gabriel (German physicist); Danzig (Poland) **(1686-1736)**
Fairbanks, Douglas (Douglas Ulman) (actor); Denver **(1883-1939)**
Fairbanks, Douglas, Jr. (actor); New York City, 12/9/1909
Fairchild, Morgan (actress); Dallas, Tex., 2/3/50
Faith, Percy (conductor); Toronto **(1908-1976)**
Falk, Peter (actor); New York City, 9/16/1927
Falla, Manuel de (composer); Cadiz, Spain **(1876-1946)**
Faraday, Michael (physicist); Newington, England **(1791-1867)**
Farber, Barry (radio-TV broadcaster); Baltimore, Md., 1930
Farentino, James (actor); Brooklyn, N.Y., 2/24/1938
Farmer, Frances (actress); Seattle, Wash. **(1913-1970)**
Farmer, James (civil rights leader); Marshall, Tex., 1/12/1920
Farnum, William (actor); Boston **(1876-1953)**
Farr, Jamie (actor); Toledo, Ohio, 7/1/34
Farrar, Geraldine (soprano, actress); Melrose, Mass. **(1882-1967)**
Farrell, Charles (actor); Onset Bay, Mass. **(1901-1990)**
Farrell, Eileen (operatic soprano); Willimantic, Conn., 2/13/1920
Farrell, Glenda (actress); Enid, Okla. **(1904-1971)**
Farrell, James T. (novelist); Chicago **(1904-1979)**
Farrell, Mike (actor); St. Paul, Minn., 2/6/39
Farrell, Suzanne (Roberta Sue Ficker) (ballerina); Cincinnati, 8/16/1945
Farrow, Mia (actress); Los Angeles, 2/9/1946
Fasanella, Ralph (painter); New York City, 9/2/1914
Fassbinder, Rainer Werner (film and stage director); Bad Wörishofen, West Germany **(1946-1982)**
Fast, Howard (novelist); New York City, 11/11/1914
Faulkner, William (novelist); New Albany, Miss. **(1897-1962)**
Fauré, Gabriel Urbain (composer); Pamiers, France **(1845-1924)**
Fawcett, Farrah (actress); Corpus Christi, Tex., 2/2/1947(?)
Faye, Alice (Ann Leppert) (actress); New York City, 5/5/1912
Feiffer, Jules (cartoonist); New York City, 1/26/1929
Feininger, Lyonel (painter); New York City **(1871-1956)**
Feldman, Marty (actor, screenwriter, director); London **(1938-1982)**
Feldon, Barbara (actress); Pittsburgh, 3/12/1941
Feliciano, José (singer); Larez, Puerto Rico, 9/10/1945
Felker, Clay S. (editor and publisher); St. Louis, 10/2/1925(?)
Fell, Norman (actor); Philadelphia, 3/24/23
Fellini, Federico (film director); Rimini, Italy, 1/20/1920
Fender, Freddie (Baldemar Huerta) (singer); San Benito, Tex., 1937
Ferber, Edna (novelist); Kalamazoo, Mich. **(1885-1968)**
Ferguson, Maynard (jazz trumpeter); Verdun, Quebec, Canada, 5/4/1928
Fermi, Enrico (atomic physicist); Rome **(1901-1954)**
Fernandel (Fernand Joseph Desire Contandin) (actor); Marseilles, France **(1903-1971)**
Ferrer, José (actor and director); Santurce, Puerto Rico, 1/8/1912
Ferrer, Mel (actor); Elberon, N.J., 8/25/1917
Ferrigno, Lou (actor); Brooklyn, N.Y., 11/9/52
Fetchit, Stepin (Lincoln Theodore Perry) (comedian); Key West, Fla. **(1902-1985)**
Fiedler, Arthur (conductor); Boston **(1894-1979)**
Field, Betty (actress); Boston **(1918-1973)**
Field, Eugene (poet); St. Louis **(1850-1895)**
Field, Marshall (merchant); nr. Conway, Mass. **(1834-1906)**
Field, Sally (actress); Pasadena, Calif., 11/6/1946

Fielding, Henry (novelist); nr. Glastonbury, England **(1707-1754)**
Fields, Gracie (comedienne); Rochdale, England **(1898-1979)**
Fields, Totie (comedienne); Hartford, Conn. **(1931-1978)**
Fields, W. C. (William Claude Dukenfield) (comedian); Philadelphia **(1880-1946)**
Fierstein, Harvey (Forbes) (playwright and actor); Brooklyn, 6/6/1954
Filene, Edward A. (merchant); **(1860-1937)**
Finch, Peter (actor); Kensington, England **(1916-1977)**
Finney, Albert (actor); Salford, England, 5/9/1936
Firkusny, Rudolf (pianist); Napajedia (Czechoslovakia), 2/11/1912
Fischer-Dieskau, Dietrich (baritone); Berlin, 5/28/1925
Fisher, Carrie (actress); Los Angeles, 10/21/56
Fisher, Eddie (Edwin) (singer); Philadelphia, 8/10/1928
Fitzgerald, Barry (William Joseph Shields) (actor); Dublin **(1888-1961)**
Fitzgerald, Edward (radio broadcaster); Troy, N.Y. **(1898(?)-1982)**
Fitzgerald, Ella (singer); Newport News, Va., 4/25/1918
Fitzgerald, F. Scott (Francis Scott Key) (novelist); St. Paul, Minn. **(1896-1940)**
Fitzgerald, Geraldine (actress); Dublin, 11/24/1914
Fitzgerald, Pegeen (radio broadcaster); Norcatur, Kan. **(1910-1989)**
Flack, Roberta (singer); Black Mountain, N.C., 2/10/1940
Flagstad, Kirsten (Wagnerian soprano); Hamar, Norway **(1895-1962)**
Flatt, Lester Raymond (bluegrass musician); Overton County, Tenn. **(1914-1979)**
Flaubert, Gustave (novelist); Rouen, France **(1821-1880)**
Fleming, Sir Alexander (bacteriologist); Lochfield, Scotland **(1881-1955)**
Fleming, Rhonda (Marilyn Louis) (actress); Los Angeles, 8/10/1923
Fletcher, John (dramatist); Rye? England **(1579-1625)**
Flynn, Errol (actor); Hobart, Tasmania **(1909-1959)**
Foch, Nina (actress); Leyden, Netherlands, 4/20/1924
Fodor, Eugene (violinist); Turkey Creek, Colo., 3/5/1950
Fokine, Michel (dancer, choreographer); St. Petersburg, Russia **(1880-1942)**
Fonda, Henry (actor); Grand Island, Neb. **(1905-1982)**
Fonda, Jane (actress); New York City, 12/21/1937
Fonda, Peter (actor); New York City, 2/23/1939
Fontaine, Frank (singer and comedian); Cambridge, Mass. **(1920-1979)**
Fontaine, Joan (Joan de Havilland) (actress); Tokyo, 10/22/1917
Fontanne, Lynn (actress); London, **(1887-1983)**
Fonteyn, Dame Margot (Margaret Hookham) (ballerina); Reigate, England **(1919–1991)**
Forbes, Malcolm S(tevenson) (publisher and sportsman); Brooklyn, N.Y. **(1919-1990)**
Ford, Glenn (Gwyllyn Ford) (actor); Quebec, 5/1/1916
Ford, Harrison (actor); Chicago, 7/13/1942
Ford, Henry (industrialist); Greenfield, Mich. **(1863-1947)**
Ford, Henry, II (auto maker); Detroit **(1917-1987)**
Ford, John (film director); Cape Elizabeth, Me. **(1895-1973)**
Ford, Paul (actor); Baltimore **(1901-1976)**
Ford, Tennessee Ernie (Ernie Jennings Ford) (singer); Bristol, Tenn., 2/13/1919
Forrester, Maureen (contralto); Montreal, 7/25/1930
Forsythe, John (actor); Penn's Grove, N.J., 1/29/1918
Fosdick, Harry Emerson (clergyman); Buffalo, N.Y. **(1878-1968)**
Fosse, Bob (Robert Louis) (choreographer and director); Chicago **(1927-1987)**
Foster, Jodie (actress); Bronx, N.Y., 1963
Foster, Preston (actor); Ocean City, N.J. **(1900-1970)**
Foster, Stephen Collins (composer); nr. Pittsburgh **(1826-1864)**
Fox, Michael J. (actor); Edmonton, Alta., Canada, 6/9/1961
Foxx, Redd (John Elroy Sanford) (actor and comedian); St. Louis, 12/9/1922
Foy, Eddie, Jr. (dancer and actor); New Rochelle, N.Y. **(1905-1983)**
Fra Angelico (Giovanni da Fiesole) (painter); Vicchio in the Mugello, Tuscany (Italy) **(c.1387-1455)**
Fracci, Carla (ballerina); Milan, Italy, 8/20/1936
Fragonard, Jean Honoré (painter); Grasse, France **(1732-1806)**
Frampton, Peter (rock musician); Beckenham, England, 4/20/1950
France, Anatole (Jacques Anatole François Thibault) (author); Paris **(1844-1924)**
Francescatti, Zino (violinist); Marseilles, France **(1902–1991)**
Franciosa, Anthony (Anthony Papaleo) (actor); New York City, 10/25/1928
Francis, Anne (actress); Ossining, N.Y., 7/16/30
Francis, Arlene (Arlene Francis Kazanjian) (actress); Boston, 10/20/1908
Francis, Connie (Concetta Franconero) (singer); Newark, N.J., 12/12/1938
Francis, Genie (actress); Englewood, N.J., 5/26/62
Francis, Kay (Katherine Edwina Gibbs) (actress); Oklahoma City **1903-1968)**
Francis of Assisi, Saint (Giovanni Francesco Barnardone) (founder of Franciscans); Assisi, Italy **(1182-1226)**

Franck, César Auguste (composer); Liège (Belgium) **(1822-1890)**
Franco Bahamonde, Francisco (Chief of State); El Ferrol, Spain **(1892-1975)**
Franklin, Aretha (singer); Memphis, Tenn., 3/25/1942
Franklin, Benjamin (statesman and scientist); Boston **(1706-1790)**
Franklin, Bonnie (actress); Santa Monica, Calif., 1/6/44
Frann, Mary (actress); St. Louis, Mo., 2/27/43
Frazer, Sir James George (anthropologist); Glasgow, Scotland **(1854-1941)**
Freud, Sigmund (psychoanalyst); Moravia (Czechoslovakia) **(1856-1939)**
Friedan, Betty (Betty Naomi Goldstein) (feminist); Peoria, Ill., 2/4/1921
Fromm, Erich (psychoanalyst); Frankfurt-am-Main, Germany **(1900-1980)**
Frost, David (TV entertainer); Tenterden, England, 4/7/1939
Frost, Robert Lee (poet); San Francisco **(1874-1963)**
Fry, Christopher (playwright); Bristol, England, 12/18/1907
Frye, David (impressionist); Brooklyn, N.Y., 1934
Fugard, Athol (playwright); Middleburg, South Africa, 6/11/1932
Fuller, R(ichard) Buckminster (Jr.) (architect and educator); Milton, Mass. **(1895-1983)**
Fulton, Robert (inventor); Lancaster County, Pa. **(1765-1815)**
Funicello, Annette (actress); Los Angeles, 10/22/42
Funt, Allen (TV producer); Brooklyn, N.Y., 9/16/1914
Furness, Betty (Elizabeth) (ex-actress and consumer advocate); New York City, 1/3/1916

G

Gabel, Martin (actor and producer); Philadelphia **(1912-1986)**
Gabin, Jean (actor); Paris **(1904-1976)**
Gable, (William) Clark (actor); Cadiz, Ohio **(1901-1960)**
Gabo, Naum (sculptor); Briansk, Russia **(1890-1977)**
Gabor, Eva (actress); Budapest, 2/11/1926(?)
Gabor, Zsa Zsa (Sari) (actress); Budapest, 2/6/1919(?)
Gabrieli, Giovanni (composer); Venice **(c.1557-1612)**
Gainsborough, Thomas (painter); Sudbury, Suffolk, England **(1727-1788)**
Galbraith, John Kenneth (economist); Iona Station, Ontario, Canada, 10/15/1908
Galilei, Galileo (astronomer and physicist); Pisa (Italy) **(1564-1642)**
Gallico, Paul (novelist); New York City **(1897-1976)**
Gallup, George H. (poll taker); Jefferson, Iowa **(1901-1984)**
Galsworthy, John (novelist and dramatist); Coombe, England **(1867-1933)**
Galway, James (flutist); Belfast, Northern Ireland, 12/8/1939
Gambling, John A. (radio broadcaster); New York City, 1930
Gandhi, Indira (Indira Nehru) (Prime Minister); Allahabad, India **(1917-1984)**
Gandhi, Mohandas Karamchand (called Mahatma Gandhi) (Hindu leader); Porbandar, India **(1869-1948)**
Gannett, Frank E. (editor and publisher); **(1876-1957)**
Garagiola, Joe (Joseph Henry) (sportscaster); St. Louis, 2/12/1926
Garbo, Greta (Greta Gustafsson) (actress); Stockholm **(1905-1990)**
Garcia Lorca, Frederico (author); Fuente Vaqueros, Spain **(1898-1936)**
Garden, Mary (soprano); Aberdeen, Scotland **(1874-1967)**
Gardenia, Vincent (actor); Naples, Italy, 1/7/22
Gardner, Ava (actress); Smithfield, N.C. **(1922-1990)**
Gardner, Erle Stanley (novelist); Malden, Mass. **(1889-1970)**
Garfield, John (Jules Garfinkle) (actor); New York City **(1913-1952)**
Garfunkel, Art (Arthur) (singer); Newark, N.J., 11/5/1941
Gargan, William (actor); Brooklyn, N.Y., **(1905-1979)**
Garibaldi, Giuseppe (Italian nationalist leader); Nice, France **(1807-1882)**
Garland, Judy (Frances Gumm) (actress and singer); Grand Rapids, Minn. **(1922-1969)**
Garner, Erroll (jazz pianist); Pittsburgh **(1921-1977)**
Garner, James (James Bumgarner) (actor); Norman, Okla., 4/7/1928
Garner, Peggy Ann (actress); Canton, Ohio **(1932-1984)**
Garr, Teri (actress); Lakewood, Ohio, 12/11/49
Garrett, Betty (actress); St. Joseph, Mo., 5/23/1919
Garrick, David (actor); Hereford, England **(1717-1779)**
Garrison, William Lloyd (abolitionist); Newburyport, Mass. **(1805-1879)**
Garroway, Dave (TV host); Schenectady, N.Y. **(1913-1982)**
Garson, Greer (actress); County Down, Northern Ireland, 9/29/1912(?)
Gary, John (singer); Watertown, N.Y., 11/29/1932
Gassman, Vittorio (film actor and director); Genoa, Italy, 9/1/1922
Gaudi, Antonio (architect); Reus, Spain **(1852-1926)**
Gauguin, Eugène Henri Paul (painter); Paris **(1848-1903)**
Gautama Buddha (Prince Siddhartha) (philosopher); Kapilavastu (India) **(563?-?483** B.C.)

Gavin, John (actor, diplomat); Los Angeles, 4/8/1935

Gayle, Crystal (Brenda Gayle Webb) (singer); Paintsville, Ky., 1/9/51

Gaynor, Janet (actress); Philadelphia **(1906-1984)**

Gaynor, Mitzi (Francesca Mitzi Marlene de Czanyi von Gerber) (actress); Chicago, 9/4/1931

Gazzara, Ben (Biago Anthony Gazzara) (actor); New York City, 8/28/1930

Gebel-Williams, Gunther (animal trainer); Schweidnitz (Poland), 1934

Gedda, Nicolai (tenor); Stockholm, Sweden, 7/11/25

Geddes, Barbara Bel (actress); New York City, 10/31/1922

Genet, Jean (playwright); Paris **(1910-1986)**

Genghis Khan (Temujin) (conqueror); nr. Lake Baikal, Russia **(1162-1227)**

Genn, Leo (actor); London **(1905-1978)**

Gentry, Bobbie (Roberta Streeter) (singer); Chickasaw Co., Miss., 7/27/1944

George, David Lloyd (statesman); Manchester, England **(1863-1945)**

Gere, Richard (actor); Philadelphia, 1950

Gericault, Jean Louis (painter); Rouen, France **(1791-1824)**

Geronimo (Goyathlay) (Apache chieftain); Arizona **(1829-1909)**

Gershwin, George (composer); Brooklyn, N.Y. **(1898-1937)**

Gershwin, Ira (lyricist); New York City, **(1896-1983)**

Getty, J. Paul (oil executive); Minneapolis **(1892-1976)**

Getz, Stan (saxophonist); Philadelphia **(1927–1991)**

Ghiberti, Lorenzo (goldsmith and sculptor); Florence **(1378-1455)**

Ghostley, Alice (actress); Eve, Mo., 8/14/26

Giacometti, Alberto (sculptor); Switzerland **(1901-1966)**

Giannini, Giancarlo (actor); La Spezia, Italy, 8/1/1942

Gibbon, Edward (historian); Putney, England **(1737-1794)**

Gibson, Charles Dana (illustrator); Roxbury, Mass. **(1867-1944)**

Gibson, Henry (actor, comedian); Germantown, Pa., 9/21/35

Gibson, Hoot (Edward) (actor); Tememah, Neb. **(1892-1962)**

Gibson, Mel (actor); Peekskill, N.Y., 1/3/56

Gide, André (author); Paris **(1869-1951)**

Gielgud, Sir John (actor); London, 4/14/1904

Gilbert, John (movie actor); Logan, Utah **(1897-1936)**

Gilbert, Melissa (actress); Los Angeles, 5/8/64

Gilbert, Sir William Schwenck (librettist); London **(1836-1911)**

Gilels, Emil (concert pianist); Odessa, Ukraine **(1916-1985)**

Gillespie, Dizzy (John Birks Gillespie) (jazz trumpeter); Cheraw, S.C., 10/21/1917

Gillette, William (actor); Hartford, Conn. **(1855-1932)**

Gimbel, Bernard F. (merchant); Vincennes, Ind. **(1885-1966)**

Gingold, Hermione (actress and comedienne); London **(1897-1987)**

Ginsberg, Allen (poet); Newark, N.J., 6/3/1926

Giordano, Luca (painter); Naples, Italy **(1632-1705)**

Giorgione (painter); Castelfranco, (Italy) **(c.1477-1510)**

Giotto di Bondone (painter); Vespignamo (Italy) **(c.1266-1337)**

Giovanni, Nikki (poet); Knoxville, Tenn., 6/7/1943

Giroud, Françoise (French government official); Geneva, 9/21/1916

Gish, Dorothy (actress); Massillon, Ohio **(1898-1968)**

Gish, Lillian (Lillian de Guiche) (actress); Springfield, Ohio, 10/14/1896(?)

Givenchy, Hubert (fashion designer); Beauvais, France, 2/21/1927

Gladstone, William Ewart (statesman); Liverpool, England **(1809-1898)**

Glaser, Paul Michael (actor, director); Cambridge, Mass., 3/25/43

Glass, Philip (composer); Baltimore, 1/31/1937

Gleason, Jackie (comedian); Brooklyn, N.Y. **(1916-1987)**

Gleason, James (actor); New York City **(1886-1959)**

Gless, Sharon (actress); Los Angeles, 5/31/43

Gluck, Christoph Willibald (composer); Erasbach (Germany) **(1714-1787)**

Gobel, George (comedian); Chicago **(1920–1991)**

Godard, Jean Luc (film director); Paris, 12/3/1930

Goddard, Robert Hutchings (father of modern rocketry); Worcester, Mass. **(1882-1945)**

Goddard, Paulette (Marion Levy) (actress); Great Neck, N.Y. **(1911?-1990)**

Godfrey, Arthur (entertainer); New York City **(1903-1983)**

Godunov, Alexander (ballet dancer); Sakhalin, U.S.S.R. 11/28/1949

Goebbels, Joseph Paul (Nazi leader); Rheydt, Germany **(1897-1945)**

Goering, Hermann (Nazi leader); Rosenheim, Germany **(1893-1946)**

Goethals, George Washington (engineer); Brooklyn, N.Y. **(1858-1928)**

Goethe, Johann Wolfgang von (poet and playwright); Frankfurt-am-Main, Germany **(1749-1832)**

Gogol, Nikolai Vasilievich (novelist); nr. Mirgorod, Ukraine **(1809-1852)**

Goldberg, Rube (cartoonist); San Francisco **(1883-1970)**

Goldberg, Whoopi (actress); New York City, **1949 (?)**

Goldblum, Jeff (actor); Pittsburgh, Pa., 10/22/52

Golden, Harry (Harry Goldhurst) (auth or); New York City **(1902-1981)**

Goldsmith, Oliver (dramatist and poet); County Longford, Ireland **(1728-1774)**

Goldwyn, Samuel (Samuel Goldfish) (film producer); Warsaw **(1882-1974)**

Golenpaul, Dan (creator of Information Please radio show and editor of almanac of same name); New York City **(1900-1974)**

Gompers, Samuel (labor leader); London **(1850-1924)**

Goodall, Jane (Baroness van Lawick-Goodall) (ethologist); London, 4/3/1934

Goodman, Benny (clarinetist); Chicago **(1909-1986)**

Goodyear, Charles (inventor); New Haven, Conn. **(1800-1860)**

Gorbachev, Mikhail Sergeyevich (Soviet leader); Privolnoye, U.S.S.R., 3/2/1931

Gordimer, Nadine (novelist and short-story writer); Springs, South Africa, 12/20/1923

Gordon, Max (stage producer); New York City; **(1892-1978)**

Gordon, Ruth (actress); Wollaston, Mass. **(1896-1985)**

Gordy, Berry, Jr. (record company executive); Detroit, 11/28/1929

Gore, Lesley (singer); Tenafly, N.J., 1946

Goren, Charles H. (bridge expert); Philadelphia **(1901–1991)**

Gorki, Maxim (Alexei Maximovich Peshkov) (author); Nizhni Novgorod, Russia **(1868-1936)**

Gorky, Arshile (painter); Armenia **(1904-1948)**

Gormé, Eydie (singer); Bronx, N.Y., 8/16/1932

Gorshin, Frank (actor); Pittsburgh, 4/5/1934

Gosden, Freeman F. *See* Amos

Gossett, Louis, Jr. (actor); Brooklyn, N.Y., 5/27/36

Gottschalk, Louis Moreau (pianist, composer); New Orleans, La. **(1829-1869)**

Gould, Chester (cartoonist); Pawnee, Okla. **(1900-1985)**

Gould, Elliott (Elliott Goldstein) (actor); Brooklyn, N.Y., 8/29/1938

Gould, Glenn (concert pianist); Toronto, **(1932-1982)**

Gould, Morton (composer); Richmond Hill, Queens, N.Y., 12/10/1913

Goulet, Robert (singer); Lawrence, Mass., 11/26/1933

Gounod, Charles François (composer); Paris **(1818-1893)**

Goya y Lucientes, Francisco José de (painter); Fuendetodos, Spain **(1746-1828)**

Grable, Betty (actress); St. Louis **(1916-1973)**

Grace, Princess of Monaco (Grace Kelly) (ex-actress); Philadelphia **(1929-1982)**

Graham, Bill (Wolfgang Grajonca) (rock impresario); Berlin, 1931

Graham, Billy (William F.) (ev angelist); Charlotte, N.C., 11/7/1918

Graham, Katharine Meyer (newspaper publisher); New York City, 6/16/1917

Graham, Martha (choreographer); Pittsburgh **(1894–1991)**

Graham, Virgina (actress,host); Chicago, 7/4/13

Grahame, Gloria (Gloria Hallwood) (actress); Los Angeles **(1929-1981)**

Grainger, Percy Aldridge (pianist and composer); Melbourne, Australia **(1882-1961)**

Gramm, Donald (Grambach) (bass-baritone); Milwaukee **(1927-1983)**

Granger, Farley (actor); San Jose, Calif., 7/1/1925

Granger, Stewart (James Stewart) (actor); London, 5/6/1913

Grant, Cary (Alexander Archibald Leach) (actor); Bristol, England **(1904-1986)**

Grant, Kathryn (actress); Houston, Tex. 1933

Grant, Lee (Lyova Haskell Rosenthal) (actress); New York City, 10/31/1930

Granville, Bonita (actress); New York City **(1923-1988)**

Grass, Günter (novelist); Danzig (Poland), 10/16/1927

Grauer, Ben (radio and TV announcer); New York City **(1908-1977)**

Graves, Peter (Peter Arness) (actor); Minneapolis, 3/18/1926

Graves, Robert (writer); London **(1895-1985)**

Gray, Barry (Bernard Yaroslaw) (radio interviewer); Atlantic City, N.J., 7/2/1916

Gray, Dolores (singer and actress); Chicago, 6/7/1930

Gray, Linda (actress); Santa Monica, Calif., 9/12/40

Gray, Thomas (poet); London **(1716-1771)**

Grayson, Kathryn (Zelma Hednick) (singer and actress); Winston-Salem, N.C., 2/9/1923

Greco, Buddy (singer); Philadelphia, 8/14/1926

Greco, José (dancer); Montorio nei Frentani, Itály, 12/23/1918

Greeley, Horace (journalist and politician); Amherst, N.H. **(1811-1872)**

Green, Adolph (actor and lyricist); New York City, 12/2/1915

Green, Al (singer); Forrest City, Ark., 4/13/1946

Greene, Graham (novelist); Berkhamsted, England **(1904–1991)**

Greene, Lorne (actor); Ottawa **(1915-1987)**

Greene, Martyn (actor); London **(1899-1975)**

Greene, Michele (actress); Las Vegas, Nev., 2/3/?

Greene, Shecky (comedian, actor); Chicago, 4/8/25

Greenstreet, Sydney (actor); Sandwich, England **(1879-1954)**

Greenwood, Charlotte (actress); Philadelphia, Pa. **(1893-1978)**

Greenwood, Joan (actress and director); London **(19 21-1987)**

Greer, Germaine (feminist); Melbourne, 1/29/1939

Gregory, Cynthia (ballerina); Los Angeles, 7/8/1946

Gregory, Dick (comedian); St. Louis, 1932

Greuze, Jean-Baptiste (painter); Tournus, France **(1725-1805)**
Grey, Joel (Joel Katz) (actor); Cleveland, 4/11/1932
Grey, Zane (author); Zanesville, Ohio **(1875-1939)**
Grieg, Edvard Hagerup (composer); Bergen, Norway **(1843-1907)**
Grier, Roosevelt (entertainer and former athlete); Cuthbert, Ga., 7/14/1932
Griffin, Merv (TV entertainer); San Mateo, Calif., 7/6/1925
Griffith, Andy (actor); Mount Airy, N.C., 6/1/1926
Griffith, David Lewelyn Wark (film producer); La Grange, Ky. **(1875-1948)**
Griffith, Melanie (actress); New York City, 8/9/57
Grigorovich, Yuri (choreographer); Leningrad, 1/1/1927
Grimes, Tammy (actress); Lynn, Mass., 1/30/1934
Grimm, Jacob (author of fairy tales); Hanau (Germany) **(1785-1863)**
Grimm, Wilhelm (author of fairy tales); Hanau (Germany) **(1786-1859)**
Gris, Juan (José Victoriano González) (painter); Madrid **(1887-1927)**
Grizzard, George (actor); Roanoke Rapids, N.C., 4/1/1928
Grodin, Charles (actor); Pittsburgh, Pa., 4/21/35
Groh, David (actor); Brooklyn, N.Y., 5/21/39
Gromyko, Andrei A. (diplomat); Starye Gromyki, Russia **(1909-1989)**
Gropius, Walter (architect); Berlin **(1883-1969)**
Gropper, William (painter, illustrator); New York City **(1897-1977)**
Gross, Michael (actor); Chicago, 6/21/47
Grosz, George (painter); Germany **(1893-1959)**
Guardino, Harry (actor); New York City, 12/23/1925
Guggenheim, Meyer (capitalist); Langnau, Switzerland **(1828-1905)**
Guillaume, Robert (actor); St. Louis, Mo. 11/30/27
Guinness, Sir Alec (actor); London, 4/2/1914
Guitry, Sacha (Alexandre) (actor and film director); St. Petersburg, Russia **(1885-1957)**
Gumbel, Bryant Charles (TV newscaster); New Orleans, 9/29/1948
Gunther, John (author); Chicago **(1901-1970)**
Gutenberg, Johannes (printer); Mainz (Germany) **(1400?-?1468)**
Guthrie, Arlo (singer); New York City, 7/10/1947
Guthrie, Woody (folk singer and composer); Okemah, Okla. **(1912-1967)**
Gwenn, Edmund (actor); London **(1875-1959)**
Gwynne, Fred (actor); New York City, 7/10/26

H

Hackett, Bobby (trumpeter); Providence, R.I. **(1915-1976)**
Hackett, Buddy (Leonard Hacker) (comedian and actor); Brooklyn, N.Y., 8/31/1924
Hackman, Gene (actor); San Bernardino, Calif., 1/30/1931
Hagen, Uta (actress); Göttingen, Germany, 6/12/1919
Haggard, Merle (songwriter); Bakersfield, Calif., 4/6/1937
Hagman, Larry (actor); Weatherford, Tex., 1931
Haig, Alexander Meigs, Jr. (ex-Secretary of State and ex-general); Bala-Cynwyd, Pa., 12/2/1924
Haile Selassie (Ras Tafari Makonnen) (ex-Emperor); Ethiopia **(1892-1975)**
Hailey, Arthur (novelist); Luton, England, 4/5/1920
Halberstam, David (journalist); New York City, 4/10/1934
Hale, Alan (actor, director); Washington, D.C. **(1892-1950)**
Hale, Barbara (actress); DeKalb, Ill., 4/18/21
Hale, Edward Everett (clergyman and author); Boston **(1822-1909)**
Hale, Nathan (American Revolutionary officer); Coventry, Conn. **(1755-1776)**
Halevi, Judah (Jewish poet); Toledo, Spain **(1085-1140)**
Haley, Alex (writer); Ithaca, N.Y., 8/11/1921
Haley, Jack (actor); Boston **(1899-1979)**
Hall, Arsenio (comedian); Cleveland, Ohio, 2/12/?
Hall, Donald (Andrew, Jr.) (poet) New Haven, Conn., 9/20/1928
Hall, Huntz (actor); New York City, 1920
Hall, Monty (TV personality); Winnipeg, Canada, 1923
Halley, Edmund (astronomer); London **(1656-1742)**
Hals, Frans (painter); Antwerp (Netherlands) **(1580?-1666)**
Halsey, William Frederick, Jr. (naval officer); Elizabeth, N.J. **(1882-1959)**
Hamel, Veronica (actress); Philadelphia, Pa., 11/20/43
Hamill, Pete (journalist); Brooklyn, N.Y., 6/24/1935
Hamilton, Alexander (statesman); Nevis, British West Indies **(1757?-1804)**
Hamilton, George (actor); Memphis, Tenn., 8/12/1939
Hamilton, Margaret (actress); Cleveland **(1902-1985)**
Hamlin, Harry (actor); Pasadena, Calif., 10/30/51
Hamlisch, Marvin (composer and pianist); New York City, 6/2/1944
Hammarskjöld, Dag (U.N. Secretary-General); Jönköping, Sweden **(1905-1961)**
Hammerstein, Oscar, II (librettist and stage producer); New York City **(1895-1960)**
Hampden, Walter (Walter Hampden Dougherty) (actor); Brooklyn, N.Y. **(1879-1955)**

Hampshire, Susan (actress); London, 5/12/38
Hampton, Lionel (vibraharpist and band leader); Birmingham, Ala., 4/12/1913
Hamsun, Knut (Knut Pedersen) (novelist); Lom, Norway **(1859-1952)**
Hancock, John (statesman); Braintree, Mass. **(1737-1793)**
Hand, Learned (jurist); Albany, N.Y. **(1872-1961)**
Handel, George Frederick (Georg Friedrich Händel) (composer); Halle (East Germany) **(1685-1759)**
Handy, William Christopher (blues composer); Florence, Ala. **(1873-1958)**
Hanks, Tom (actor); Concord, Calif., 7/9/1956
Hannibal (Carthaginian general); North Africa **(247-182** B.C.)
Hanson, Howard (conductor); Wahoo, Neb., **(1896-1981)**
Harburg, E. Y. "Yip" (songwriter); New York City **(1896-1981)**
Harding, Ann (actress); San Antonio, Tex. **(1902-1981)**
Hardwicke, Sir Cedric (actor); Stourbridge, England **(1893-1964)**
Hardy, Oliver (comedian); Atlanta **(1892-1957)**
Hardy, Thomas (novelist); Dorsetshire, England **(1840-1928)**
Harkness, Edward S. (capitalist); Cleveland **(1874-1940)**
Harlow, Jean (Harlean Carpentier) (actress); Kansas City, Mo. **(1911-1937)**
Harnick, Sheldon (lyricist); Chicago, 4/30/1924
Harper, Valerie (actress); Suffern, N.Y., 8/22/1940(?)
Harrell, Lynn (cellist); New York City, 1/30/1944
Harriman, W. (William) Averell (ex-Governor of New York); New York City **(1891-1986)**
Harrington, Pat., Jr. (actor, comedian); New York City, 8/13/29
Harris, Barbara (actress); Evanston, Ill., 1935
Harris, Emmylou (singer); Birmingham, Ala., 1949
Harris, Julie (actress); Grosse Pointe Park, Mich., 12/2/1925
Harris, Phil (actor and band leader); Linton, Ind., 6/24/1906
Harris, Richard (actor); Limerick, Ireland, 10/1/1933
Harris, Rosemary (actress); Ashby, England, 9/19/1930
Harris, Roy (composer); Lincoln County, Okla. **(1898-1979)**
Harrison, George (singer and songwriter); Liverpool, England, 2/25/1943
Harrison, Gregory (actor); Avalon, Catalina Island, Calif., 5/31/50
Harrison, Sir Rex (Reginald Carey) (actor); Huyton, England, **(1908-1990)**
Hart, Lorenz (lyricist); New York **(1895-1943)**
Hart, Mary (host); Sioux Falls, S.D., c.1950
Hart, Moss (playwright); New York City **(1904-1961)**
Hart, William S. (actor); Newburgh, N.Y. **(1862-1946)**
Harte, Bret (Francis Brett Harte) (author); Albany, N.Y. **(1836-1902)**
Hartford, Huntington (George Huntington Hartford II) (A.&P. heir); New York City, 4/18/1911
Hartford, John (singer and banjoist); New York City, 12/30/1937
Hartley, Mariette (actress); New York City, 6/21/40
Hartman, David Downs (TV newscaster); Pawtucket, R.I., 5/19/1935
Hartman, Elizabeth (actress); Youngstown, Ohio **(1941-1987)**
Hartman, Lisa (actress); Houston, Tex., 6/1/56
Harvey, Laurence (Larushka Skikne) (actor); Joniskis, Lithuania **(1928-1973)**
Harvey, William (physician); Folkestone, England **(1578-1657)**
Hasselhoff, David (actor); Baltimore, Md., 7/17/52
Hasso, Signe (actress); Stockholm, 8/15/1915
Havoc, June (June Hovick) (actress); Seattle, 1916
Haver, June (actress); Rock Island, Ill., 6/10/1926
Hawkins, Jack (actor); London **(1910-1973)**
Hawn, Goldie (actress); Washington, D.C., 11/21/1945
Haworth, Jill (actress); Sussex, England, 1945
Hawthorne, Nathaniel (novelist); Salem, Mass. **(1804-1864)**
Hay, John Milton (statesman); Salem, Ind. **(1838-1905)**
Hayakawa, Sessue (actor); Honshu, Japan **(1890-1973)**
Hayden, Melissa (ballerina); Toronto, 4/25/1923
Hayden, Sterling (Sterling Relyea Walter) (actor and writer); Montclair, N.J. **(1916-1986)**
Haydn, Franz Joseph (composer); Rohrau (Austria) **(1732-1809)**
Hayes, Helen (Helen Hayes Brown) (actress); Washington, D.C., 10/10/1900
Hayes, Isaac (composer); Covington, Tenn., 8/20/1942
Hayes, Peter Lind (comedian, singer); San Francisco, 6/25/15
Haymes, Dick (singer, actor); Buenos Aires **(1916-1980)**
Hayward, Leland (producer); Nebraska City, Neb. **(1902-1971)**
Hayward, Louis (actor); Johannesburg, South Africa **(1909-1985)**
Hayward, Susan (Edythe Marrener) (actress); Brooklyn, N.Y. **(1919?-1975)**
Hayworth, Rita (Margarita Cansino) (actress); New York City **(1918-1987)**
Head, Edith (costume designer); Los Angeles **(1907-1981)**
Hearst, William Randolph (publisher); San Francisco **(1863-1951)**
Hearst, William Randolph, Jr. (publisher); New York City, 1/27/1908
Heath, Edward (ex-Prime Minister); Broadstairs, England, 7/9/1916
Heatherton, Joey (actress); Rockville Centre, N.Y., 9/14/1944

Hecht, Ben (author); New York City **(1894-1964)**
Heckart, Eileen (actress); Columbus, Ohio, 3/29/1919
Heflin, Van (Emmet Evan Heflin) (actor); Walters, Okla. **(1910-1971)**
Hefner, Hugh (publisher); Chicago, 4/9/1926
Hegel, Georg Wilhelm Friedrich (philosopher); Stuttgart (Germany) **(1770-1831)**
Heifetz, Jascha (concert violinist); Vilna, Russia **(1901-1987)**
Heine, Heinrich (Harry) (poet); Düsseldorf (Germany) **(1797-1856)**
Heinemann, Gustav (ex-President of Germany); Schweim, Germany **(1899-1976)**
Heisenberg, Werner Karl (physicist); Würzburg, Germany **(1901-1976)**
Held, Anna (comedienne); Paris, France **(1873(?)-1918)**
Heller, Joseph (novelist); Brooklyn, N.Y., 5/1/1923
Hellman, Lillian (playwright); New Orleans **(1905-1984)**
Helmond, Katherine (actress); Galveston, Tex., 7/5/34(?)
Hemingway, Ernest Miller (novelist); Oak Park, Ill. **(1899-1961)**
Hemingway, Margaux (actress); Portland, Ore., Feb. 1955
Hemmings, David (actor); Guilford, England, 11/2/1941
Henderson, Florence (actress); Dale, Ind., 2/14/1934
Henderson, Skitch (Lyle Russell Cedric) (conductor and pianist); Birmingham, England(?), 1/27/1918
Hendrix, Jimi (James Marshall Hendrix) (guitarist); Seattle **(1942-1970)**
Henley, Beth (playwright-actress); Jackson, Miss., 5/8/1952
Henner, Marilu (actress); Chicago, 4/6/52
Henning, Doug (magician and actor); Winnipeg, Canada, 1947(?)
Henreid, Paul (actor); Trieste, 1/10/1908
Henri, Robert (painter); Cincinnati **(1865-1926)**
Henry, O. (William Sydney Porter) (story writer); Greensboro, N.C. **(1862-1910)**
Henry, Patrick (statesman); Hanover County, Va. **(1736-1799)**
Henson, Jim (puppeteer); Greenville, Miss. **(1936-1990)**
Hepburn, Audrey (actress); Brussels, Belgium, 5/4/1929
Hepburn, Katharine (actress); Hartford, Conn., 11/8/1909
Hepplewhite, George (furniture designer); England **(?-1786)**
Hepworth, Barbara (sculptor); Wakefield, England **(1903-1975)**
Herachel, William (Frederich Wilhelm) (astronomer); Hanover, Germany **(1738-1822)**
Herbert, George (poet); Montgomery Castle, Wales **(1593-1633)**
Herbert, Victor (composer); Dublin **(1859-1924)**
Herblock (Herbert L. Block) (political cartoonist); Chicago, 10/13/1909
Herman, Pee-wee (Paul Reubens) (comedian); Peekskill, N.Y., 1952
Herman, Woody (Woodrow Charles) (band leader); Milwaukee **(1913-1987)**
Herod (Herodes) (called Herod the Great) (King of Judea) (73?-4 **60**B.C.)
Herodotus (historian); Halicarnassus, Asia Minor (Turkey) **(c. 484-425** B.C.)
Herrick, Robert (poet); London? **(1591-1674)**
Hershey, Barbara (actress); Hollywood, Calif., 2/5/48(?)
Hershfield, Harry (humorist and raconteur); Cedar Rapids, Iowa **(1885-1974)**
Hersholt, Jean (actor); Copenhagen **(1886-1956)**
Hesburgh, Theodore M. (educator); Syracuse, N.Y., 5/2/1917
Hesseman, Howard (actor); Salem, Ore., 2/27/40
Heston, Charlton (actor); Evanston, Ill., 10/4/1924
Heyerdahl, Thor (ethnologist and explorer); Larvik, Norway, 10/6/1914
Hildegarde (Hildegarde Loretta Sell) (singer); Adell, Wis., 2/1/1906
Hill, Arthur (actor); Melfort, Canada, 8/1/1922
Hill, Benny (comedian); Southampton, England, 1/21/25
Hillary, Sir Edmund (mountain climber); New Zealand, 7/20/1919
Hiller, Wendy (actress); Bramhall, England, 8/15/1912
Hillerman, John (actor); Denison, Tex., 12/20(?)/32
Hilliard, Harriet. *See* Nelson, Harriet
Hindemith, Paul (composer); Hanau, Germany **(1895-1963)**
Hines, Earl "Fatha" (jazz pianist); Duquesne, Pa. **(1905-1983)**
Hines, Gregory (dancer, actor); New York City, 2/14/46
Hines, Jerome (Jerome Heinz) (basso); Los Angeles, 11/8/1921
Hingle, Pat (actor); Denver, 7/19/1924
Hippocrates (physician); Cos, Greece **(c. 460-c. 377** B.C.)
Hirohito (Emperor); Tokyo, **(1901-1989)**
Hiroshige, Ando (pain ter); Edo? (Tokyo) **(1797-1858)**
Hirsch, Judd (actor); New York City, 3/15/1935
Hirschfeld, Al (Albert) (cartoonist); St. Louis, 6/21/1903
Hirschhorn, Joseph Herman (financier, speculator, and art collector); Mitau, Latvia **(1899-1981)**
Hirt, Al (trumpeter); New Orleans, 11/7/1922
Hitchcock, Alfred J. (film director); London **(1899-1980)**
Hitler, Adolf (German dictator); Braunau, Austria **(1889-1945)**
Hitzig, William Maxwell (physician); Austria, 12/15/1904
Hobbes, Thomas (philosopher); Westport, England **(1588-1679)**
Hobson, Laura Z. (Laura K. Zametkin) (novelist); New York City **(1900-1986)**

Hockney, David (artist); Bradford, England, 7/9/1937
Hodges, Eddie (actor); Hattiesburg, Miss., 3/5/1947
Hoffa, James R(iddle) (labor leader); Brazil, Ind. **(1913-75?)** presumed murdered.
Hoffman, Dustin (film actor and director); Los Angeles, 8/8/1937
Hofmann, Hans (painter); Germany **(1880-1966)**
Hogan, Paul (actor); Lightning Ridge, NSW, Australia, 1941 (?)
Hogarth, William (painter and engraver); London **(1697-1764)**
Hokusai, Katauhika (artist); Yedo, Japan **(1760-1849)**
Holbein, Hans (the Elder) (painter); Augsburg (Germany) **(1465?-1524)**
Holbein, Hans (the Younger) (painter); Augsburg (Germany) **(1497?-1543)**
Holbrook, Hal (actor); Cleveland, 2/17/1925
Holden, William (William Franklin Beedle, Jr.) (actor); O'Fallon, Ill. **(1918-1981)**
Holder, Geoffrey (dancer); Port-of-Spain, Trinidad, 8/1/1930
Holiday, Billie (Eleanora Fagan) (jazz-blues singer); Baltimore **(1915-1959)**
Holliday, Judy (Judith Tuvim) (comedienne); New York City **(1922-1965)**
Holliday, Polly (actress); Jasper, Ala., 7/2/37
Holliman, Earl (actor); Delhi, La., 9/11/28
Holloway, Stanley (actor); London **(1890-1982)**
Holloway, Sterling (actor); Cedartown, Ga., 1905
Holm, Celeste (actress); New York City, 4/29/1919
Holmes, Oliver Wendell (jurist); Boston **(1841-1935)**
Holt, Jack (actor); Winchester, Va. **(1888-1951)**
Holt, Tim (actor); Beverly Hills, Calif. **(1918-1973)**
Holtz, Lou (comedian); San Francisco **(1898-1980)**
Home, Lord (Alexander Frederick Douglas-Home) (diplomat); London, 7/2/1903
Homeier, Skip (George Vincent Homeier) (actor); Chicago, 10/5/1930
Homer, Winslow (painter); Boston, Mass. **(1836-1910)**
Homer (Greek poet) **(c.850** B.C.?)
Homolka, Oscar (actor); Vienna **(1898-1978)**
Honegger, Arthur (composer); Le Havre, France **(1892-1955)**
Hook, Sidney (philosopher); New York City, **(1902-1989)**
Hoover, J. Edgar (FBI director); Washington, D.C. **(1895-1972)**
Hope, Bob (Leslie Townes Hope) (comedian); London, 5/29/1903
Hopkins, Anthony (actor); Port Talbot, Wales, 12/31/1937
Hopkins, Gerald Manley (poet); Stratford, England **(1844-1899)**
Hopkins, Johns (financier); Anne Arundel County, Md. **(1795-1873)**
Hopkins, Miriam (actress); Bainbridge, Ga. **(1902-1972)**
Hopper, Dennis (actor); Dodge City, Kan., 5/17/1936
Hopper, Edward (painter); Nyack, N.Y. **(1882-1967)**
Horace (Quintus Horatius Flaccus) (poet); Venosa (Italy) **(65-8** B.C.)
Horne, Lena (singer); Brooklyn, N.Y., 6/30/1917
Horne, Marilyn (mezzo-soprano); Bradford, Pa., 1/16/1934
Horowitz, Vladimir (pianist); Kiev, Russia **(1903-1989)**
Horsley, Lee (actor); Muleshoe, Tex., 5/15/55
Horton, Edward Everett (comedian); Brooklyn, N.Y. **(1887-1970)**
Hoskins, Bob (actor); Bury St. Edminds, England, 10/26/42
Houdini, Harry (Ehrich Weiss) (magician); Appleton, Wis. **(1874-1926)**
Houseman, John (Jacques Haussmann) (producer, director, and actor); Bucharest **(1902-1988)**
Housman, A(lfred) E(dward) (poet); Fockburg, England **(1859-1936)**
Houston, Samuel (political leader); Rockbridge County, Va. **(1793-1863)**
Houston, Whitney (singer); Newark, N.J., 8/9/63
Howard, Ken (actor); El Centro, Calif., 3/28/44
Howard, Leslie (Leslie Stainer) (actor); London **(1893-1943)**
Howard, Ron (actor, producer, director); Duncan, Okla., 3/1/54
Howard, Trevor (actor); Kent, England **(1916-1988)**
Howe, Elias (inventor); Spencer, Mass. **(1819-1867)**
Howe, Irving (literary critic); New York City, 6/11/1920
Howe, Julia Ward (poet and reformer); New York City **(1819-1910)**
Howes, Sally Ann (actress); London, 7/20/1934
Hudson, Henry (English navigator) **(?-1611)**
Hudson, Rock (born Roy Scherer, Jr.; took Roy Fitzgerald as legal name) (actor); Winnetka, Ill., **(1925-1985)**
Hughes, Barnard (actor); Bedford Hills, N.Y., 7/16/15
Hughes, Charles Evans (jurist); Glens Falls, N.Y. **(1862-1948)**
Hughes, Howard (industrialist and film producer); Houston **(1905-1976)**
Hughes, Langston (poet); Joplin, Mo. **(1902-1967)**
Hugo, Victor Marie (author); Besançon, France **(1802-1885)**
Hulce, Tom (actor); Detroit, Mich., 12/6/53
Hull, Henry (actor); Louisville, Ky. **(1890-1977)**
Hume, David (philosopher); Edinburgh, Scotland **(1711-1776)**
Humperdinck, Engelbert (Arnold Dorsey) (singer); Madras, India, 5/2/1936
Humperdinck, Engelbert (composer); Siegburg (Germany) **(1854-1921)**
Hunt, H. L. (industrialist); nr. Vandalia, Ill. **(1889-1974)**

Hunt, Marsha (actress); Chicago, 10/17/1917
Hunter, Kim (Janet Cole) (actress); Detroit, 11/12/1922
Hunter, Tab (Arthur Andrew Gelien) (actor); New York City, 7/11/1931
Huntley, Chet (TV newscaster); Cardwell, Mont. **(1911-1974)**
Hurok, Sol (Solomon) (impresario); Pogar, Russia **(1884-1974)**
Hurst, Fannie (novelist); Hamilton, Ohio **(1889-1968)**
Hurt, John (actor); Shirebrook, England, 1/22/1940
Hurt, William (actor); Washington, D.C., 3/20/50
Hus, Jan (Bohemian religious reformer); Husinetz, nr. Budweis (Czechoslovakia) **(c.1369-1415)**
Husing, Ted (sportscaster); New York City **(1901-1962)**
Hussein I (King); Jordan, 11/14/1935
Hussey, Ruth (Ruth Carol O'Rourke) (actress); Providence, R.I., 10/30/14
Huston, John (film director and writer); Nevada, Mo. **(1906-1987)**
Huston, Walter (Walter Houghston) (actor); Toronto **(1884-1950)**
Hutchins, Robert M. (educator); Brooklyn, N.Y. **(1899-1977)**
Hutton, Barbara (Woolworth heiress); New York City **(1912-1979)**
Hutton, Betty (Betty Thornburg) (actress); Battle Creek, Mich., 2/26/1921
Hutton, Lauren (actress, model); Charleston, S.C., 11/17/43
Hutton, Timothy (actor); Los Angeles, 8/16/1960
Huxley, Aldous (au thor); Godalming, England **(1894-1963)**
Huxley, Sir Julian S. (biologist and author); London **(1887-1975)**
Huxley, Thomas Henry (biologist); Ealing, England **(1825-1895)**

I

Ian, Janis (singer); New York City, 5/7/1951
Ibsen, Henrik (dramatist); Skien, Norway **(1828-1906)**
Inge, William (playwright); Independence, Kan. **(1913-1973)**
Ingres, Jean Auguste Dominique (painter); Montauban, France **(1780-1867)**
Inness, George (painter); nr. Newburgh, N.Y. **(1825-1894)**
Ionesco, Eugene (playwright); Slatina, Romania, 11/26/1912
Ireland, Jill (actress); London, **(1936-1990)**
Ireland, John (actor); Vancouver, B.C., Canada, 1/30/1915
Irons, Jeremy (actor); Cowes, Isle of Wight, England, 9/19/1948
Irving, Amy (actress); Palo Alto, Calif., 9/10/1953
Irving, John (Winslow) (writer); Exeter, N.H., 3/2/1942
Irving, Washington (author); New York City **(1783-1859)**
Isherwood, Christopher (novelist and playwright); nr. Dilsey and High Lane, England **(1904-1986)**
Iturbi, José (concert pianist); Valencia, Spain **(1895-1980)**
Ives, Burl (Icle Ivanhoe) (singer); Hunt, Ill., 6/14/1909
Ives, Charles E(dward) (composer); Danbury, Conn. **(1874-1954)**

J

Jackson, Anne (actress); Millvale, Pa., 9/3/1926
Jackson, Glenda (actress); Hoylake, England, 1937(?)
Jackson, Gordon (actor); Glasgow, Scotland, **(1923-1990)**
Jackson, Rev. Jesse (civil rights leader); Greenville, S.C., 10/8/1941
Jackson, Kate (actress); Birmingham, Ala., 10/29/1949
Jackson, Mahalia (gospel singer); New Orleans **(1911-1972)**
Jackson, Michael (singer); Gary, Ind., 8/29/1958
Jackson, Thomas Jonathan ("Stonewall") (general); Clarksburg, Va. (now W. Va.) **(1824-1863)**
Jacobi, Derek (actor); Leytonstone, England, 10/22/38
Jacobi, Lou (actor); Toronto, 12/26/1913
Jacobs, Jane (urbanologist); Scranton, Pa., 5/1/1916
Jaffe, Sam (actor); New York City **(1891-1984)**
Jagger, Dean (actor); Lima, Ohio **(1903-1991)**
Jagger, Mick (Michael Phillip) (singer); Dartford, England, 7/26/1944
James, Harry (trumpeter); Albany, Ga. **(1916-1983)**
James, Henry (novelist); New York City **(1843-1916)**
James, Jesse Woodson (outlaw); Clay County, Mo. **(1847-1882)**
James, William (psychologist); New York City **(1842-1910)**
Jameson, (Margaret) Storm (novelist); Whitby, England **(1897-1986)**
Janis, Byron (pianist); McKeesport, Pa., 3/24/1928
Janis, Conrad (actor, musician); New York City, 2/11/28
Jannings, Emil (actor); Brooklyn, N.Y. **(1886-1950)**
Janssen, David (David Meyer) (actor); Naponee, Neb. **(1930-1980)**
Jay, John (statesman and jurist); New York City **(1745-1829)**
Jeanmaire, Renée (dancer); Paris, 4/29/1924
Jenner, Edward (physician); Berkeley, England **(1749-1823)**
Jennings, Waylon (singer); Littlefield, Tex., 1937
Jessel, George (entertainer); New York City **(1898-1981)**
Jessup, Philip C. (diplomat); New York City, 1/5/1897
Jiang Qing (political leader); Chucheng, China, 1913 (?)
Jillian, Ann (actress); Cambridge, Mass., 1/29/51
Joan of Arc (Jeanne d'Arc) (saint and patriot); Domremy-la-Pucelle, France **(1412-1431)**

Joel, Billy (singer); New York City, 5/9/1949
Joffrey, Robert (Abdullah Jaffa Bey Khan) (choreographer); Seattle **(1930-1988)**
John, Elton (Reginald Kenneth Dwight) (singer and pianist); Pinner, England, 3/25/1947
Johns, Glynis (actress); Pretoria, South Africa, 10/5/1923
Johns, Jasper (painter and sculptor); Augusta, Ga., 5/15/1930
Johnson, Don (actor); Flatt Creek, Mo., 12/15/49
Johnson, James Weldon (author and educator); Jacksonville, Fla. **(1871-1938)**
Johnson, Philip Cortalyou (architect); Cleveland, Ohio, 7/8/1906
Johnson, Samuel (lexicographer and author); Lichfield, England **(1709-1784)**
Johnson, Van (actor); Newport, R.I., 8/20/1916
Joliot-Curie, Frédéric (physicist); Paris **(1900-1958)**
Joliot-Curie, Irène (Irène Curie) (physicist); France **(1897-1956)**
Jolliet (or Joliet), Louis (explorer); Beaupré, Canada **(1645-1700)**
Jolson, Al (Asa Yoelson) (actor and singer); St. Petersburg, Russia **(1886-1950)**
Jones, Allan (singer, actor); Old Forge, Pa., 10/14/08
Jones, Buck (Charles Frederick Gebhart) (actor); Vincennes, Ind. **(1889-1942)**
Jones, Carolyn (singer and actress); Amarillo, Tex., **(1933-1983)**
Jones, Dean (actor); Morgan County, Ala., 1/25/1935
Jones, George (singer); Saratoga, Tex., 9/12/1931
Jones, Inigo (architect); London **(1573-1652)**
Jones, James (novelist); Robinson, Ill. **(1921-1977)**
Jones, James Earl (actor); Arkabutla, Miss., 1/17/1931
Jones, Jennifer (Phyllis Isley) (actress); Tulsa, Okla., 3/2/1919
Jones, John Paul (John Paul) (naval officer); Scotland **(1747-1792)**
Jones, Quincy (composer); Chicago, 3/14/1933
Jones, Shirley (singer and actress); Smithtown, Pa., 3/31/1934
Jones, Spike (host, orchestra leader); Long Beach, Calif. **(1911-1965)**
Jones, Tom (Thomas Jones Woodward) (singer); Pontypridd, Wales, 6/7/1940
Jong, Erica (writer); New York City, 3/26/1942
Jonson, Ben (Benjamin) (poet and dramatist); Westminster, England **(1572-1637)**
Joplin, Janis (singer); Port Arthur, Tex. **(1943-1970)**
Jordan, James Edward (radio actor-Fibber McGee); Peoria, Ill. **(1896-1988)**
Jordan, Marian (radio actress-Molly of Fibber McGee and Molly); Peoria, Ill. **(1898-1961)**
Jory, Victor (actor); Dawson City, Yukon, Canada **(1902-1982)**
Josquin des Prés (usually known as Josquin) (composer); Conde-sur-L'Escaut?, Hainaut (France or Belgium) **(c.1445-1521)**
Jourdan, Louis (Louis Gendre) (actor); Marseilles, France, 6/19/1920
Joyce, James (novelist); Dublin **(1882-1941)**
Juárez, Benito Pablo (statesman); Guelatao, Mexico **(1806-1872)**
Julia, Raul (Raúl Rafael Carlos Julia y Arcelay) (actor); San Juan, Puerto Rico, 3/9/1940
Juliana (Queen); The Hague, Netherlands, 4/30/1909
Jung, Carl Gustav (psychoanalyst); Basel, Switzerland **(1875-1961)**
Jurado, Katy (actress); Guadalajara, Mexico, 1927

K

Kabalevsky, Dmitri (composer); St. Petersburg, Russia **(1904-1987)**
Kafka, Franz (author); Prague **(1883-1924)**
Kádár, János (Communist Party leader); Hungary, 1912
Kahn, Gus (songwriter); Coblenz, Germany **(1886-1941)**
Kahn, Louis I. (architect); Oesel Island, Estonia **(1901-1974)**
Kahn, Madeline (actress); Boston, 9/29/1942
Kaminska, Ida (actress); Odessa, Russia **(1899-1980)**
Kandinsky, Wassily (painter); Moscow **(1866-1944)**
Kane, Helen (actress, singer); Bronx, N.Y. **(1903-1966)**
Kanin, Garson (playwright); Rochester, N.Y., 11/24/1912
Kant, Immanuel (philosopher); Königsberg (Kaliningrad, U.S.S.R.) **(1724-1804)**
Kantor, MacKinlay (novelist); Webster City, Iowa **(1904-1977)**
Kaplan, Gabe (Gabriel) (actor); Brooklyn, N.Y., 3/31/1945
Karloff, Boris (William Henry Pratt) (actor); London **(1887-1969)**
Kasem, Casey (disc jockey); Detroit, Mich., 4/27/1932
Katt, William (actor); Los Angeles, 2/16/50
Kaufman, George S. (playwright); Pittsburgh **(1889-1961)**
Kavner, Julie (actress); Los Angeles, 9/7/51
Kaye, Danny (David Daniel Kominski) (comedian); Brooklyn, N.Y. **(1913-1987)**
Kaye, Sammy (band leader); Cleveland **(1910-1987)**
Kazan, Elia (director); Constantinople, Turkey, 9/7/1909
Kazan, Lainie (Levine) (singer); New York City, 5/15/1940
Keach, Stacy (actor); Savannah, Ga., 6/2/1941
Kean, Edmund (actor); London **(1787-1833)**
Keaton, Buster (Joseph Frank Keaton) (comedian); Piqua, Kan.

(1896-1966)
Keaton, Diane (actress); Los Angeles, 1/5/1946
Keats, John (poet); London **(1795-1821)**
Keel, Howard (singer and actor); Gillespie, Ill., 4/13/1919
Keeler, Ruby (Lehy Keeler) (actress and dancer); Halifax, Nova Scotia, Canada, 8/25/1910
Kefauver, Estes (legislator); Madisonville, Tenn. **(1903-1963)**
Keith, Brian (actor); Bayonne, N.J., 11/14/1921
Keller, Helen Adams (author and educator); Tuscumbia, Ala. **(1880-1968)**
Kellerman, Sally (actress); Long Beach, Calif., 6/2/1938
Kelley, DeForest (actor); Atlanta, Ga., 1/20/20
Kelly, Emmett (clown); Sedan, Kan., **(1898-1979)**
Kelly, Gene (dancer and actor); Pittsburgh, 8/23/1912
Kelly, Grace. *See* Grace, Princess of Monaco.
Kelly, Nancy (actress); Lowell, Mass., 3/25/21
Kelly, Patsy (actress and comedienne); Brooklyn, N.Y. **(1910-1981)**
Kelly, Walt (cartoonist); Philadelphia **(1913-1973)**
Kemal Ataturk (Mustafa Kemal) (Turkish soldier and statesman); Salonika (Greece) **(1881-1938)**
Kemble, Fanny (F rances Anne) (actress); London **(1809-1893)**
Kempis, Thomas à (mystic); Kempis, Prussia (Germany) **(1380-1471)**
Kennan, George F. (diplomat); Milwaukee, 2/16/1904
Kennedy, Arthur (actor); Worcester, Mass. **(1914-1990)**
Kennedy, George (actor); New York City, 2/18/1925
Kennedy, Jacqueline. *See* Onassis, Jacqueline
Kennedy, Joseph P. (financier); Boston **(1888-1969)**
Kennedy, Robert Francis (legislator); Brookline, Mass. **(1925-1968)**
Kennedy, Rose Fitzgerald (President's mother); Boston, 7/22/1890
Kent, Allegra (ballerina); Santa Monica, Calif., 8/11/38
Kent, Rockwell (painter); Tarrytown Heights, N.Y. **(1882-1971)**
Kenton, Stan (Stanley Newcomb) (jazz musician); Wichita, Kan. **(1912-1979)**
Kepler, Johannes (astronomer); Weil (Germany) **(1571-1630)**
Kercheval, Ken (actor); Wolcottville, Ind., 7/15/35
Kerensky, Alexander Fedorovich (statesman); Simbirks, Russia **(1881-1970)**
Kern, Jerome David (composer); New York City **(1885-1945)**
Kerns, Joanna (actress); San Francisco, 2/12/53
Kerr, Deborah (actress); Helensburgh, Scotland, 9/30/1921
Kettering, Charles F. (engineer and inventor); nr. Loudonville, Ohio **(1876-1958)**
Key, Francis Scott (lawyer and author of national anthem); Frederick (now Carroll) County, Md. **(1779-1843)**
Keyes, Frances Parkinson (novelist); Charlottesville, Va. **(1885-1970)**
Keynes (1st Baron of Tilton) (John Maynard Keynes) (economist); Cambridge, England **(1883-1946)**
Khachaturian, Aram (composer); Tiflis, Russia **(1903-1978)**
Khrushchev, Nikita S. (Soviet leader); Kalinovka, nr. Kursk, Ukraine **(1894-1971)**
Kibbee, Guy (actor); El Paso **(1886-1956)**
Kidd, Michael (choreographer); Brooklyn, N.Y., 1917
Kidd, William (called Captain Kidd) (pirate); Greenock, Scotland **(1645?-1701)**
Kidder, Margot (actress); Yellowknife, N.W.T., Canada, 10/17/48
Kiepura, Jan (tenor); Sosnowiec, Poland **(1904(?)-1966)**
Kieran, John (writer); New York City **(1892-1981)**
Kierkegaard, Sören Aalys (philosopher); Copenhagen **(1813-1855)**
Kiesinger, Kurt Georg (diplomat); Ebingen, Germany **(1904-1988)**
Kiley, Richard (actor and singer); Chicago, 3/31/1922
Kilmer, Alfred Joyce (poet); New Brunswick, N.J. **(1886-1918)**
King, Alan (Irwin Alan Kniberg) (entertainer); Brooklyn, N.Y., 12/26/1927
King, B.B. (Riley King) (guitarist); Itta Bena, Miss., 9/16/1925
King, Carole (singer and songwriter); Brooklyn, N.Y., 2/9/1941
King, Coretta Scott (civil rights leader); Marion, Ala., 4/27/1927
King, Dennis (actor, singer); Coventry, England **(1897-1971)**
King, Martin Luther, Jr. (civil rights leader); Atlanta **(1929-1968)**
King, Pee Wee (Frank) (singer); Abrams, Wis., 2/18/1914
King, Stephen (writer); Portland, Maine, 9/21/1947
Kingsley, Ben (Krishna Bhanji) (actor); Snainton, England, 12/31/1943
Kingsley, Sidney (Sidney Kirschner) (playwright); New York City, 10/18/1906
Kinski, Nastassja (Nastassja Nakszynski) (actress); West Berlin, 1/24/1961
Kipling, Rudyard (author); Bombay **(1865-1936)**
Kipnis, Alexander (basso); Ukraine, **(1891-1978)**
Kirby, George (comedian); Chicago, 1923(?)
Kirk, Grayson (educator); Jeffersonville, Ohio, 10/12/1903
Kirk, Lisa (actress and singer); Charleroi, Pa. **(1925-1990)**
Kirk, Phyllis (actress); Plainfield, N.J., 9/18/1930
Kirkland, Gelsey (ballerina); Bethlehem, Pa., 12/29/1952
Kirkpatrick, Jeane Jordan (educator-public affairs); Duncan, Okla., 11/19/1926
Kirkpatrick, Ralph (harpsichordist); Leominster, Mass. **(1911-1984)**

Kirkwood, James (actor); Grand Rapids, Mich. **(1883-1963)**
Kirsten, Dorothy (soprano); Montclair, N.J., 7/6/1919
Kissinger, Henry (Heinz Alfred Kissinger) (ex-Secretary of State); Furth, Germany, 5/27/1923
Kitt, Eartha (singer); North, S.C., 1/26/1928
Klee, Paul (painter); Münchenbuchsee, nr. Bern, Switzerland **(1879-1940)**
Klein, Calvin (fashion designer); Bronx, N.Y., 11/19/1942
Klein, Robert (comedian); New York City, 2/8/1942
Kline, Kevin (actor); St. Louis, Mo., 10/24/47
Kleist, Henrich von (poet); Frankfurt an der Oder (East Germany) **(1777-1811)**
Klemperer, Otto (conductor); Breslau (Poland) **(1885-1973)**
Klemperer, Werner (actor); Cologne, Germany, 3/22/1920
Klugman, Jack (actor); Philadelphia, 4/27/1922
Knievel, Evel (Robert Craig) (daredevil motorcyclist); Butte, Mont., 10/17/1938
Knight, Gladys (singer); Atlanta, 5/28/1944
Knight, Ted (Tadeus Wladyslaw Konopka) (actor); Terryville, Conn., **(1923-1986)**
Knight, John S. (publisher); Bluefield, W. Va. **(1894-1981)**
Knopf, Alfred A. (publisher); New York City, **(1892-1984)**
Knotts, Don (actor); Morgantown, W.Va., 7/21/1924
Knox, John (religious reformer); Haddington, East Lothian, Scotland **(1505-1572)**
Koch, Robert (physician); Klausthal (Germany) **(1843-1910)**
Koestler, Arthur (novelist); Budapest **(1905-1983)**
Kokoschka, Oskar (painter); Pöchlarn Austria **(1886-1980)**
Kooper, Al (singer and pianist); Brooklyn, N.Y., 2/5/1944
Kopell, Bernie (actor); New York City, 6/21/33
Koppel, Ted (broadcast journalist); Lancashire, England, 2/8/1940
Korman, Harvey (actor); Chicago, 2/15/1927
Kosciusko, Thaddeus (Tadeusz Andrzej Bonawentura Kosciuszko) (military officer); Grand Duchy of Lithuania **(1746-1817)**
Kossuth, Lajos (patriot); Monok, Hungary **(1802-1894)**
Kostelanetz, André (orchestra conductor); St. Petersburg, Russia **(1901-1980)**
Kosygin, Aleksei N. (Premier); St. Petersburg, Russia **(1904-1980)**
Koussevitzky, Serge (Sergei) Alexandrovitch (orchestra conductor); Vishni Volochek, Tver, Russia **(1874-1951)**
Kovacs, Ernie (comedian); Trenton, N.J. **(1919-1962)**
Kramer, Stanley E. (film producer and director); New York City, 9/29/1913
Kràus, Lili (pianist); Budapest **(1905-1986)**
Kreisler, Fritz (violinist and composer); Vienna **(1875-1962)**
Kresge, S. S. (merchant); Bald Mount, Pa. **(1867-1966)**
Krips, Josef (orchestra conductor); Vienna **(1902-1974)**
Kristofferson, Kris (singer); Brownsville, Tex., 6/22/1936
Kruger, Otto (actor); Toledo, Ohio **(1885-1974)**
Krupa, Gene (drummer); Chicago **(1909-1973)**
Krupp, Alfred (munitions magnate); Essen, Germany **(1812-1887)**
Kubelik, Rafael (conductor); Bychory (Czechoslovakia), 6/29/1914
Kublai Khan (Mongol conqueror) **(1216-1294)**
Kubrick, Stanley (producer and director); New York City, 7/26/1928
Kuralt, Charles (TV journalist); Wilmington, N.C., 9/10/1934
Kurosawa, Akira (film director); Tokyo, 3/23/1910
Kurtz, Efrem (conductor); St. Petersburg, Russia, 11/7/1900
Kurtz, Swoosie (actress); Omaha, Neb., 9/6/44
Ky, Nguyen Cao (ex-Vice President of South Vietnam); Son Tay (Vietnam), 9/8/1930

L

LaBelle, Patti (singer, actress); Philadelphia, Pa., 10/4/44
Ladd, Alan (actor); Hot Springs, Ark. **(1913-1964)**
Ladd, Cheryl (Cheryl Stoppelmoor) (actress); Huron, S.D., 7/12/1951
Ladd, Diane (actress); Meridian, Miss., 11/29/32
Lafayette, Marquis de (Marie Joseph Paul Yves Roch Gilbert du Motier) (military officer); Auvergne, France **(1757-1834)**
Lafitte, Jean (pirate); Bayonne? France **(1780-1826)**
La Follette, Robert Marin (politician); Primrose, Wis. **(1855-1925)**
La Guardia, Fiorello Henry (Mayor of New York); New York City **(1882-1947)**
Lahr, Bert (Irving Lahrheim) (comedian); New York City **(1895-1967)**
Laine, Cleo (Clementina Dinah Campbell) (singer, actress); Southall, England, 10/28/27
Laine, Frankie (Frank Paul LoVecchio) (singer); Chicago, 3/30/1913
Laird, Melvin (ex-Secretary of Defense); Omaha, Neb., 9/1/1922
Lake, Veronica (actress); Brooklyn, N.Y. **(1919-1973)**
Lamarck, Chevalier de (Jean Baptiste Pierre Antoine de Monet) (naturalist); Bazantin, France **(1744-1829)**
Lamarr, Hedy (Hedwig Kiesler) (actress); Vienna, 1915
Lamas, Fernando (actor); Buenos Aires, **(1915-1982)**
Lamas, Lorenzo (actor); Los Angeles, 1/20/58

Lamb, Charles (Elia) (essayist); London **(1775-1834)**
L'Amour, Louis (author); Jamestown, N.D., **(1908-1988)**
Lamour, Dorothy (Dorothy Kaumeyer) (actress); New Orleans, 10/10/1914
Lancaster, Burt (actor); New York City, 11/2/1913
Lanchester, Elsa (Elsa Sullivan) (actress); London **(1902-1986)**
Landau, Martin (actor); Brooklyn, N.Y. 1934
Landers, Ann (columnist); Sioux City, Iowa, 7/4/1918
Landon, Michael (Eugene Maurice Orowitz) (actor); Forest Hills, Queens, N.Y. **(1936—1991)**
Lane, Abbe (singer); New York City, 1933
Lang, Fritz (film director); Vienna **(1890-1976)**
Lang, Paul Henry (music critic); Budapest, 8/28/1901
Lange, Hope (actress); Redding Ridge, Conn., 11/28/1933
Lange, Jessica (actress); Cloquet, Minn., 4/20/49
Langella, Frank (actor); Bayonne, N.J., 1/1/1940
Langford, Frances (singer); Lakeland, Fla., 4/4/1913
Langmuir, Irving (chemist); Brooklyn, N.Y. **(1881-1957)**
Langtry, Lillie (Emily Le Breton) (actress); Island of Jersey **(1852-1929)**
Lansbury, Angela (actress); London, 10/16/1925
Lansing, Robert (Robert Howell Brown) (actor); San Diego, Calif., 6/5/1928
Lanza, Mario (Alfred Arnold Cocozza) (singer and actor); Philadelphia **(1921-1959)**
Lao-Tzu (or Lao-Tse) (Li Erh) (philosopher); Honan Province, China **(c. 604-531** B.C.)
Lardner, Ring (Ringgold Wilmar Lardner) (story writer); Niles, Mich. **(1885-1933)**
La Rochefoucauld, Francois duc de (author); Paris **(1613-1680)**
Larroquette, John (actor); New Orleans, 11/25/47
La Salle, Sieur de (Robert Cavelier) (explorer); Rouen, France **(1643-1687)**
Lasser, Louise (actress); New York City, 1940(?)
Lauder, Sir Harry (Harry MacLennan) (singer); Portobello, Scotland **(1870-1950)**
Laughton, Charles (actor); Scarborough, England **(1899-1962)**
Lauper, Cyndi (singer); New York City, 6/20/53
Laurel, Stan (Arthur Jefferson) (comedian); Ulverston, England **(1890-1965)**
Laurents, Arthur (playwright); New York City, 7/14/1918
Laurie, Piper (Rosetta Jacobs) (actress); Detroit, 1/22/1932
Lavin, Linda (actress); Portland, Me., 10/15/37
Lavoisier, Antoine-Laurent (chemist); Paris **(1743-1794)**
Lawford, Peter (actor); London **(1923-1984)**
Lawrence, David Herbert (novelist); Nottingham, England **(1885-1930)**
Lawrence, Gertrude (Gertrud Klasen) (actress); London **(1900-1952)**
Lawrence, Marjorie (singer); Deans Marsh, Australia **(1908-1979)**
Lawrence, Steve (Sidney Leibowitz) (singer); Brooklyn, N.Y., 7/8/1935
Lawrence of Arabia (Thomas Edward Lawrence, later changed to Shaw) (author and soldier); Tremadoc, Wales **(1888-1935)**
Lawrence, Vicki (actress); Inglewood, Calif., 3/26/49
Leach, Robin (host, producer); London, c.1941
Leachman, Cloris (actress); Des Moines, Iowa, 4/30/1926(?)
Lean, David (film director); Croydon, En gland **(1908—1991)**
Lear, Edward (nonsense poet); London **(1812-1888)**
Lear, Evelyn (Shulman) (soprano); Brooklyn, N.Y., 1/8/29(?)
Lear, Norman (TV producer); New Haven, Conn., 7/27/22
Learned, Michael (actress); Washington, D.C., 4/9/39
le Carré, John (David John Moore Cornwell) (novelist); Poole, England, 10/19/1931
Le Corbusier (Charles Edouard Jeanneret) (architect); La Chaux-de-Fonds, Switzerland **(1887-1965)**
Lederer, Francis (actor); Prague, 11/6/1906
Lee, Christopher (actor); London, 5/27/1922
Lee, Gypsy Rose (Rose Louise Hovick) (entertainer); Seattle **(1914-1970)**
Lee, Manfred B. (novelist, pseudonym Ellery Queen); Brooklyn, N.Y. **(1905-1971)**
Lee, Michele (actress, singer); Los Angeles, 6/24/42
Lee, Peggy (Norma Engstrom) (singer); Jamestown, N.D., 5/26/1920
Lee, Robert Edward (Confederate general); Stratford Estate, Va. **(1807-1870)**
Leeuwenhoek, Anton van (zoologist); Delft (Netherlands) **(1632-1723)**
Le Gallienne, Eva (actress); London **(1899—1991)**
Lehár Franz (composer); Komárom (Czechoslovakia) **(1870-1948)**
Lehman, Herbert H. (Governor and Senator); New York City **(1878-1963)**
Lehmann, Lotte (soprano); Perleberg (Germany) **(1888-1976)**
Leibniz, Gottfried W. von (scientist); Leipzig (East Germany) **(1646-1716)**
Leigh, Janet (Jeanetta Morrison) (actress); Merced, Calif., 7/6/1927
Leigh, Vivien (Vivien Mary Hartley) (actress); Darjeeling, India **(1913-1967)**
Leighton, Margaret (actress); nr. Birmingham, England **(1922-1976)**
Leinsdorf, Erich (conductor); Vienna, 2/4/1912
Lemmon, Jack (actor); Boston, 2/8/1925
Lenin, Vladimir (Vladimir Ilich Ulyanov) (Soviet leader); Simbirsk, Russia **(1870-1924)**
Lennon, Dianne (singer); Los Angeles, 12/1/39
Lennon, Janet (singer); Culver City, Calif., 11/15/46
Lennon, John (singer and songwriter); Liverpool, England **(1940-1980)**
Lennon, Kathy (singer); Santa Monica, Calif., 8/22/42
Lennon, Peggy (singer); Los Angeles, 4/8/41
Leno, Jay (comedian, T.V. host); New Rochelle, N.Y., 4/28/1950
Lenya, Lotte (Karoline Blamauer) (singer and actress); Vienna, Austria **(1898-1981)**
Leonard, Sheldon (act or and director); New York City, 2/22/1907
Lerner, Alan Jay (lyricist); New York City **(1918-1986)**
Lerner, Max (columnist); Minsk, Russia, 12/20/1902
Le Roy, Mervyn (film producer); San Francisco **(1900-1987)**
Leslie, Joan (actress); Detroit, 1/26/1925
Lessing, Doris (novelist); Kermanshah, Iran, 10/22/1919
Lester, Mark (actor); Richmond, England, 1958
Letterman, David (TV personality); Indianapolis, 1947
Levant, Oscar (pianist); Pittsburgh **(1906-1972)**
Levene, Sam (actor); New York City **(1905-1980)**
Levenson, Sam (humorist); New York City **(1911-1980)**
Levi, Carlo (novelist); Turin, Italy **(1902-1975)**
Levine, James (music director, Metropolitan Opera); Cincinnati, 6/23/1943
Levine, Joseph E. (film producer); Boston **(1905-1987)**
Lewis, Jerry (Joseph Levitch) (comedian and film director); Newark, N.J., 3/16/1926
Lewis, Jerry Lee (singer); Ferriday, La., 9/29/1935
Lewis, John Llewellyn (labor leader); Lucas, Iowa **(1880-1969)**
Lewis, Meriwether (explorer); Albemarle Co., Va. **(1774-1809)**
Lewis, Shari (Shari Hurwitz) (puppeteer); New York City, 1/17/1934
Lewis, Sinclair (novelist); Sauk Centre, Minn. **(1885-1951)**
Lewis, Ted (entertainer); Circleville, Ohio **(1891-1971)**
Ley, Willy (science writer); Berlin **(1906-1969)**
Liberace (Wladziu Liberace) (pianist); West Allis, Wis. **(1919-1987)**
Lichtenstein, Roy (painter); New York City, 10/27/1923
Lie, Trygve Halvdan (first U.N. Secretary-General); Oslo **(1896-1968)**
Light, Judith (actress); Trenton, N.J., 2/9/49
Lightfoot, Gordon (singer and songwriter); Orillia, Ontario, Canada, 11/17/1938
Lillie, Beatrice (Lady Peel) (actress and comedienne); Toronto **(1898-1989)**
Lin Yutang (author); Changchow, China **(1895-1976)**
Lind, Jenny (Johanna Maria Lind) (soprano); Stockholm **(1820-1887)**
Lindbergh, Anne Morrow (author); Englewood, N.J., 6/22/1906
Lindbergh, Charles A. (aviator); Detroit **(1902-1974)**
Linden, Hal (Harold Lipshitz) (actor); New York City, 3/20/1931
Lindfors, Viveca (actress); Uppsala, Sweden, 12/29/20
Lindsay, Howard (playwright); Waterford, N.Y. **(1889- 1968)**
Lindsay, John Vliet (ex-Mayor of New York City); New York City, 11/24/1921
Lindstrom, Pia (TV newscaster); Stockholm, 11/?/1938
Linkletter, Art (radio-TV personality); Moose Jaw, Saskatchewan, Canada, 7/17/1912
Linnaeus, Carolus (Carl von Linné (botanist); Råshult, Sweden **(1707-1778)**
Lipchitz, Jacques (sculptor); Druskieniki, Latvia **(1891-1973)**
Lippi, Fra Filippo (painter); Florence **(1406-1469)**
Lippmann, Walter (columnist, author, and political analyst); New York City **(1889-1974)**
Lister, (1st Baron of Lyme Regis) (Joseph Lister) (surgeon); Upton, England **(1827-1912)**
Liszt, Franz (composer and pianist); Raiding (Hungary) **(1811-1886)**
Lithgow, John (actor); Rochester, N.Y., 6/6/45
Little, Cleavon (actor and comedian); Chickasha, Okla., 6/1/1939
Little, Rich (impressionist); Ottawa, 11/26/1938
Livesey, Roger (actor); Barry, Wales **(1906-1976)**
Livingstone, David (missionary and explorer); Lanarkshire, Scotland **(1813-1873)**
Livingstone, Mary (Sadye Marks) (comedienne); Seattle **(1909-1983)**
Llewellyn, Richard (novelist); St. David's, Wales **(1906-1983)**
Lloyd, Harold (comedian); Burchard, Neb. **(1894-1971)**
Lloyd George, David (Earl of Dwyfor) (statesman); Manchester, England **(1863-1945)**
Lloyd Webber, Andrew (composer); London, England, 3/22/1948
Locke, John (philosopher); Somersetshire, England **(1632-1704)**
Lockhart, Gene (actor); London, Ontario, Canada **(1891-1957)**
Lockhart, June (actress); New York City, 6/25/1925
Lockwood, Margaret (actress); Karachi (Pakistan) **(1916-1990)**
Lodge, Henry Cabot (legislator); Boston **(1850-1924)**
Lodge, Henry Cabot, Jr. (diplomat); Nahant, Mass. **(1902-1985)**

Loesser, Frank (composer); New York City (1910-1969)
Loewe, Frederick (composer); Vienna (1901-1988)
Logan, Joshua (director and producer); Texarkana, Tex. (1908-1988)
Lollobrigida, Gina (actress); Subiaco, Italy, 1928
Lombard, Carole (Carol Jane Peters) (actress); Ft. Wayne, Ind. (1908-1942)
Lombardo, Guy (band leader); London, Ontario, Canada (1902-1977)
London, George (baritone); Montreal (1920-1985)
London, Jack (John Griffith London) (novelist); San Francisco (1876-1916)
London, Julie (Julie Peck) (singer and actress); Santa Rosa, Calif., 9/26/1926
Long, Huey Pierce (politician); Winnfield, La. (1893-1935)
Long, Shelly (actress); Fort Wayne, Ind., 8/23/49
Longfellow, Henry Wadsworth (poet); Portland, Me. (1807-1882)
Longworth, Alice Roosevelt (social figure); New York City (1884-1980)
Loos, Anita (novelist); Sissons, Calif., (1888-1981)
Lopez, Trini (singer); Dallas, Tex., 5/15/37
Lopez, Vincent (band leader); Brooklyn, N.Y. (1895-1975)
Lord, Jack (John Joseph Ryan) (actor); New York City, 12/30/1930
Loren, Sophia (Sofia Scicolone) (actress); Rome, 9/20/1934
Lorre, Peter (Laszlo Löewenstein) (actor); Rosenberg (Czechoslovakia) (1904-1964)
Loudon. Dorothy (actress, singer); Boston, 9/17/1933
Louise, Tina (actress); New York City, 2/11/1937
Lovecraft, Howard Phillips (author); Providence, R.I., (1890-1937)
Lowe, Edmund (actor); San Jose, Calif. (1892-1971)
Lowell, Amy (poet); Brookline, Mass. (1874-1925)
Lowell, James Russell (poet); Cambridge, Mass. (1819-1891)
Lowell, Robert (poet); Boston (1917-1977)
Loy, Myrna (Myrna Williams) (actress); nr. Helena, Mont., 8/2/1905
Loyola, St. Ignatius of (Iñigo de Oñez y Loyola) (founder of Jesuits); Gúipuzcoa Province, Spain (1491-1556)
Lubitsch, Ernst (film director); Berlin (1892-1947)
Lucas, George (film director); Modesto, Calif., 5/14/44
Lucci, Susan (actress); Scarsdale, N.Y., 12/23/1948
Luce, Clare Boothe (playwright and former Ambassador); New York City (1903-1987)
Luce, Henry Robinson (editor and publisher); Tengchow, China (1898-1967)
Ludlum, Robert (author); New York City, 5/25/1927
Lugosi, Bela (Bela Lugosi Blasko) (actor); Logos, Hungary (1888-1956)
Lukas, Paul (actor); Budapest (1895-1971)
Lully, Jean Baptiste (French composer); Florence (1639-1687)
Lumet, Sidney (film and TV director); Philadelphia, 6/25/1924
Lunden, Joan (TV host); Fair Oaks, Calif., 9/19/1950
Lunt, Alfred (actor); Milwaukee (1892-1977)
Lupino, Ida (actress and director); London, 2/4/1918
LuPone, Patti (actress; singer); Northport, N.Y., 4/21/1949
Luther, Martin (religious reformer); Eisleben (East Germany) (1483-1546)
Lynde, Paul (comedian); Mt. Vernon, Ohio (1926-1982)
Lynley, Carol (actress); New York City, 2/13/1942
Lynn, Jeffrey (actor); Auburn, Mass., 1909
Lynn, Loretta (singer); Butcher's Hollow, Ky., 4/14/1935

M

Ma, Yo-Yo (cellist); Paris, 10/7/1955
Maazel, Lorin (conductor); Neuilly, France, 3/5/1930
MacArthur, Charles (playwright); Scranton, Pa. (1895-1956)
MacArthur, Douglas (five-star general); Little Rock Barracks, Ark. (1880-1964)
MacArthur, James (actor); Los Angeles, 12/8/1937
Macaulay, Thomas Babington (author); Rothley Temple, England (1800-1859)
MacCorkindale, Simon (actor); Ely, England, 2/12/53
MacDermot, Galt (composer); Montreal, 12/19/1928
MacDonald, James Ramsay (statesman); Lossiemouth, Scotland (1866-1937)
MacDonald, Jeanette (actress and soprano); Philadelphia (1907-1965)
Macdonald, Ross (Kenneth Millar) (mystery writer); Los Gatos, Calif. (1915-1983)
MacDowell, Edward Alexander (composer); New York City (1861-1908)
Macfadden, Bernarr (physical culturist); nr. Mill Spring, Mo. (1868-1955)
MacGraw, Ali (actress); New York City, 4/1/1939
Machaut, Guillaume de (composer); Marchault, France (1300-1377)
Machiavelli, Niccolò (political philosopher); Florence (Italy) (1469-1527)
Mack, Ted (TV personality); Greeley, Colo. (1904-1976)

MacKenzie, Gisele (Marie Marguerite Louise Gisele LaFleche) (singer and actress); Winnipeg, Manitoba, Canada, 1/10/1927
Mackie, Bob (designer); Monterey Park, Calif., 3/24/1940
MacLaine, Shirley (Shirley MacLean Beatty) (actress); Richmond, Va., 4/24/1934
MacLeish, Archibald (poet); Glencoe, Ill. (1892-1982)
Macmillan, Harold (ex-Prime Minister); London (1894-1986)
MacMurray, Fred (actor); Kankakee, Ill., 8/30/1908
MacNeil, Cornell (baritone); Minneapolis, 1925
MacRae, Gordon (singer); East Orange, N.J. (1921-1986)
MacRae, Sheila (comedienne); London, 9/24/1924
Madison, Guy (Robert Moseley) (actor); Bakersfield, Calif., 1/19/1922
Madonna (Madonna Louise Ciccone) (singer); Bay City, Mich., 8/16/58
Maeterlinck, Count Maurice (author); Ghent, Belgium (1862-1949)
Magellan, Ferdinand (Fernando de Magalhaes) (navigator); Sabrosa, Portugal (1480?-1521)
Magnani, Anna (actress); Rome (1908-1973)
Magritte, René (painter); Belgium (1898-1967)
Magsaysay, Ramón (statesman); Iba, Luzon, Philippines (1907-1957)
Mahan, Alfred Thayer (naval historian); West Point, N.Y. (1840-1914)
Mahler, Gustav (composer and conductor); Kalischt (Czechoslovakia) (1860-1911)
Mailer, Norman (novelist); Long Branch, N.J., 1/31/1923
Maillol, Aristide (sculptor); Banyuls-sur-Mer, Rousillion, France (1861-1944)
Maimonides, Moses (Jewish philosopher); Cordoba, Spain (1135-1204)
Main, Marjorie (Mary Tomlinson Krebs) (actress); Acton, Ind. (1890-1975)
Mainbocher (Main Rousseau Bocher) (fashion designer); Chicago (1891-1976)
Majors, Lee (actor); Wyandotte, Mich., 4/23/1940
Makarova, Natalia (ballerina); Leningrad, 11/21/1940
Makeba, Miriam (singer); Johannesburg, South Africa, 3/4/1932
Malamud, Bernard (novelist); Brooklyn, N.Y., (1914-1986)
Malden, Karl (Miaden Sekulovich) (actor); Chicago, 3/22/1913
Malkovich, John (actor); Christopher, Ill., 12/9/53
Malle, Louis (director); Thumeries, France, 10/30/32
Malone, Dorothy (actress); Chicago, 1/30/1925
Malraux, André (author); Paris (1901-1976)
Malthus, Thomas Robert (economist); nr. Dorking, England (1766-1834)
Mamet, David (playwright); Chicago, 11/30/1947
Manchester, Melissa (singer); Bronx, N.Y., 2/15/1951
Manchester, William (writer); Attleboro, Mass., 4/1/1922
Mancini, Henry (composer and conductor); Cleveland, 4/16/1924
Mandela, Nelson (Rolihlahla) (South African political activist) Umtata, Transkei, 1918
Mandela, Winnie (Nomzamo) (South African political activist); Pondoland district of the Transkei, 1936(?)
Mandrell, Barbara (singer); Houston, 12/25/1948
Manet, Edouard (painter); Paris (1832-1883)
Mangano, Silvana (actress); Rome (1930-1989)
Mangione, Chuck (hornist, pianist, and composer); Rochester, N.Y., 11/29/1940
Manilow, Barry (singer); Brooklyn, N.Y., 6/17/1946
Mankiewicz, Frank F. (columnist); New York City, 5/16/1924
Mankiewicz, Joseph L. (film writer and director); Wilkes-Barre, Pa., 2/11/1909
Mann, Horace (educator); Franklin, Mass. (1796-1859)
Mann, Thomas (novelist); Lübeck, Germany (1875-1955)
Mannes, Marya (writer); New York City, 11/14/1904
Mansfield, Jayne (Jayne Palmer) (actress); Bryn Mawr, Pa. (1932-1967)
Mansfield, Katherine (story writer); Wellington, New Zealand (1888-1923)
Mantovani, Annunzio (conductor); Venice (1905-1980)
Mao Zedong (Tse-tung) (Chinese leader); Shao Shan, China (1893-1976)
Mapplethorpe, Robert (photographer); Floral Park, Queens, N.Y. (1946-1989)
Marat, Jean Paul (French revolutionist); Boudry, Neuchâtel, Switzerland (1743-1793)
Marceau, Marcel (mime); Strasbourg, France, 3/22/1923
March, Fredric (Frederick Bickel) (actor); Racine, Wis. (1897-1975)
Marchand, Nancy (actress); Buffalo, N.Y., 6/19/28
Marconi, Guglielmo (inventor); Bologna, Italy (1874-1937)
Marcus Aurelius (Marcus Annius Verus) (Roman emperor); Rome (121-180)
Marcuse, Herbert (philosopher); Berlin, (1898-1979)
Margaret Rose (Princess); Glamis Castle, Angus, Scotland, 8/21/1930
Margrethe II (Queen); Copenhagen, 4/16/1940

Marie Antoinette (Josephe Jeanne Marie Antoinette) (Queen of France); Vienna **(1755-1793)**

Marisol (sculptor); Venezuela, 1930

Markham, Edwin (poet); Oregon City, Ore. **(1852-1940)**

Markova, Dame Alicia (Lilian Alice Marks) (ballerina); London 12/1/1910

Marley, Bob (reggae singer and songwriter); Kingston, Jamaica **(1945-1981)**

Marlowe, Christopher (dramatist); Canterbury, England **(1564-1593)**

Marlowe, Julia (Sarah Frances Frost) (actress); Cumberlandshire, England **(1866-1950)**

Marquand, J(ohn) P(hillips) (novelist); Wilmington, Del. **(1893-1960)**

Marquette, Jacques (missionary and explorer); Laon, France **(1637-1675)**

Marriner, Neville (conductor); Lincoln, England, 4/15/1924

Marsalis, Wynton (musician); New Orleans, La., 10/18/61

Marsh, Jean (actress); Stoke Newington, England, 7/1/1934

Marshall, E.G. (actor); Owatonna, Minn., 6/18/1910

Marshall, George Catlett (general); Uniontown, Pa. **(1880-1959)**

Marshall, Herbert (actor); London **(1890-1968)**

Marshall, John (jurist); nr. Germantown, Va. **(1755-1835)**

Marshall, Penny (actress); New York City, 10/15/1942

Martin, Dean (Dino Crocetti) (singer and actor); Steubenville, Ohio, 6/17/1917

Martin, Mary (singer and actress); Weatherford, Tex. **(1931–1990)**

Martin, Steve (comedian); Waco, Tex., 1945(?)

Martin, Tony (Alvin Morris) (singer); San Francisco, 12/25/1913

Martinelli, Giovanni (tenor); Montagnana, Italy **(1885-1969)**

Martins, Peter (dancer-choreographer); Copenhagen, 10/27/1945

Marvell, Andrew (poet); Winestead, England **(1621-1678)**

Marvin, Lee (actor); New York City **(1924-1987)**

Marx, Chico (Leonard) (comedian); New York City **(1891-1961)**

Marx, Groucho (Julius) (comedian); New York City **(1890-1977)**

Marx, Harpo (Arthur) (comedian); New York City **(1893-1964)**

Marx, Karl (Socialist writer); Treves (Germany) **(1818-1883)**

Marx, Zeppo (Herbert) (comedian); New York City **(1901-1979)**

Mary Stuart (Queen of Scotland); Linlithgow, Scotland **(1542-1587)**

Masaryk, Jan Garrigue (statesman); Prague (Czechoslovakia) **(1886-1948)**

Masaryk, Thomas Garrigue (statesman); Hodonin (Czechoslovakia) **(1850-1937)**

Masefield, John (poet); Ledbury, England **(1878-1967)**

Masekela, Hugh (trumpeter); Wilbank, South Africa, 4/4/1939

Mason, Jackie (comedian); Sheboygan, Wis., 6/9/30(?)

Mason, James (actor); Huddersfield, England **(1909-1984)**

Mason, Marsha (actress); St. Louis, Mo., 4/3/42

Massenet, Jules Emile Frédéric (composer); Montaud, France **(1842-1912)**

Massey, Raymond (actor); Toronto, **(1896-1983)**

Massine, Léonide (choreographer); Moscow, **(1895-1979)**

Masters, Edgar Lee (poet); Garnett, Kan. **(1869-1950)**

Mastroianni, Marcello (actor); Fontana Liri, Italy, 9/28/1924

Mather, Cotton (clergyman); Boston **(1663-1728)**

Mathis, Johnny (singer); San Francisco, 9/30/1935

Matisse, Henri (painter); Le Cateau, France **(1869-1954)**

Matthau, Walter (Walter Matuschanskayasky) (actor); New York City, 10/1/1920

Mature, Victor (actor); Louisville, Ky., 1/19/1916

Maugham, W(illiam) Somerset (author); Paris **(1874-1965)**

Mauldin, Bill (political cartoonist); Mountain Park, N.M., 10/29/1921

Maupassant, Henri René Albert Guy de (story writer); Normandy, France **(1850-1893)**

Maurois, André (Emile Herzog) (author); Elbauf, France **(1885-1967)**

Maximilian (Ferdinand Maximilian Joseph) (Emperor of Mexico); Vienna **(1832-1867)**

Maxwell, James Clerk (physicist); Edinburgh, Scotland **(1831-1879)**

May, Elaine (Elaine Berlin) (entertainer-writer); Philadelphia, 4/21/1932

May, Rollo (psychologist); Ada, Ohio, 4/21/1909

Mayall, John (singer and songwriter); Manchester, England, 11/29/1933

Mayer, Louis B. (motion picture executive); Minsk, Russia **(1885-1957)**

Mayo, Charles H. (surgeon); Rochester, Minn. **(1865-1939)**

Mayo, Charles W. (surgeon); Rochester, Minn. **(1898-1968)**

Mayo, Virginia (Jones) (actress); St. Louis, 1920

Mayo, William J. (surgeon); Le Sueur, Minn. **(1861-1939)**

Mayron, Melanie (actress); Philadelphia, 10/20/1952

Mazzini, Giuseppe (patriot); Genoa **(1805-1872)**

McBride, Mary Margaret (radio personality); Paris, Mo. **(1899-1976)**

McBride, Patricia (ballerina); Teaneck, N.J., 8/23/1942

McCallum, David (actor); Glasgow, Scotland, 9/19/1933

McCambridge, Mercedes (actress); Joliet, Ill., 3/17/1918

McCarthy, Eugene J. (ex-Senator); Watkins, Minn., 3/29/1916

McCarthy, Joseph Raymond (Senator); Grand Chute, Wis. **(1908-1957)**

McCarthy, Kevin (actor); Seattle, 2/15/1914

McCarthy, Mary (novelist); Seattle **(1912-1989)**

McCartney, Paul (singer and songwriter); Liverpool, England, 6/18/1942

McClanahan, Rue (actress); Healdton, Okla., 2/21/1935

McClellan, George Brinton (general); Philadelphia **(1826-1885)**

McClintock, Barbara (geneticist); Hartford, Conn., 6/16/1902

McCloy, John J. (lawyer and banker); Philadelphia, 3/31/1895

McClure, Doug (actor); Glendale, Calif., 5/11/1938

McCormack, John (tenor); Athlone, Ireland **(1884-1945)**

McCormack, John W. (ex-Speaker of House); Boston **(1891-1980)**

McCormack, Patty (actress); New York City, 8/21/1945

McCormick, Cyrus Hall (inventor); Rockbridge County, Va. **(1809-1884)**

McCormick, Myron (actor); Albany, Ind. **(1907-1962)**

McCoy, Col. Tim (actor); Saginaw, Mich. **(1891-1978)**

McCracken, James (dramatic tenor); Gary, Ind. **(1926-1988)**

McCrea, Joel (actor); Los Angeles **(1905–1990)**

McCullers, Carson (novelist); Columbus, Ga. **(1917-1967)**

McDaniel, Hattie (actress); Wichita, Kan. **(1895-1952)**

McDowall, Roddy (actor); London, 9/17/1928

McDowell, Malcolm (actor); Leeds, England, 6/19/1943

McFarland, Spanky (George Emmett) (actor); Fort Worth, Tex., 10/2/28

McGavin, Darren (actor); San Joaquin, Calif., 5/7/1922

McGinley, Phyllis (poet and writer); Ontario, Ore. **(1905-1978)**

McGoohan, Patrick (actor); Astoria, Queens, N.Y., 1928

McGovern, Maureen (singer); Youngstown, Ohio, 7/27/1949

McGuire, Dorothy (actress); Omaha, Neb. 6/14/1919

McKellen, Ian (actor); Burnley, England, 5/25/1939

McKenna, Siobhan (actress); Belfast, Northern Ireland **(1923-1986)**

McKeon, Rod (singer and composer); Oakland, Calif., 4/29/1933

McLaglen, Victor (actor); Tunbridge Wells, Kent, England **(1886-1959)**

McLaughlin, John (guitarist); Yorkshire, England, 1942

McLean, Don (singer and songwriter); New Rochelle, N.Y., 10/2/1945

McLuhan, Marshall (Herbert Marshall) (communications writer); Edmonton, Canada **(1911-1980)**

McMahon, Ed (TV personality); Detroit, 3/6/1923

McNamara, Robert S. (former president of World Bank); San Francisco, 6/9/1916

McQueen, Butterfly (Thelma) (actress); Tampa, Fla., 1/8/11

McQueen, Steve (Terence Stephen McQueen) (actor); Indianapolis **(1930-1980)**

McRaney, Gerald (actor); Collins, Miss., 8/19/47

Mead, Margaret (anthropologist); Philadelphia, **(1901-1978)**

Meadows, Audrey (actress); Wu Chang, China, 1922(?)

Meadows, Jayne (actress); Wu Chang, China 9/27/1926

Meany, George (labor leader); New York City **(1894-1980)**

Meara, Anne (actress); New York City, 1929

Medici, Lorenzo de' (called Lorenzo the Magnificent) (Florentine ruler); Florence (Italy) **(1449-1492)**

Meek, Donald (actor); Glasgow, Scotland **(1880-1946)**

Meeker, Ralph (Ralph Rathgeber) (actor); Minneapolis, **(1920-1988)**

Mehta, Zubin (conductor); Bombay, 4/29/1936

Meir, Golda (Golda Myerson, nee Mabovitz) (ex-Premier of Israel); Kiev, Russia **(1898-1978)**

Melanie (Melanie Safka) (singer and songwriter); New York City, 2/3/1947

Melba, Dame Nellie (Helen Porter Mitchell) (soprano); nr. Melbourne **(1861-1931)**

Melchior, Lauritz (Lebrecht Hommel) (heroic tenor); Copenhagen **(1890-1973)**

Mellon, Andrew William (financier); Pittsburgh **(1855-1937)**

Melville, Herman (novelist); New York City **(1819-1891)**

Mencken, Henry Louis (writer); Baltimore **(1880-1956)**

Mendel, Gregor Johann (geneticist); Heinzendorf, Austrian Silesia **(1822-1884)**

Mendeleyev, Dmitri Ivanovich (chemist); Tobolsk, Russia **(1834-1907)**

Mendelssohn-Bartholdy, Jakob Ludwig Felix (composer); Hamburg **(1809-1847)**

Mendès-France, Pierre (ex-Premier); Paris **(1905-1982)**

Menjou, Adolphe (actor); Pittsburgh **(1890-1963)**

Mennin, Peter (Peter Mennini) (composer); Erie, Pa. **(1923-1983)**

Menninger, William C. (psychiatrist); Topeka, Kan. **(1899-1966)**

Menotti, Gian Carlo (composer); Cadegliano, Italy, 7/7/1911

Menuhin, Yehudi (violinist and conductor); New York City, 4/22/1916

Menzies, Robert Gordon (ex-Prime Minister); Jeparit, Australia **(1894-1978)**

Mercer, Johnny (songwriter); Savannah, Ga. **(1909-1976)**

Mercer, Mabel (singer); Burton-on-Trent, England **(1900-1984)**

Mercer, Marian (actress, singer); Akron, Ohio, 11/26/35

Mercouri, Melina (actress); Athens, 10/18/1925

Meredith, Burgess (actor); Cleveland, 11/16/1908

Merkel, Una (actress); Covington, Ky. **(1903-1986)**

Merman, Ethel (Ethel Zimmerman) (singer and actress); Astoria, Queens, N.Y. **(1909-1984)**

Merrick, David (David Margulois) (stage producer); St. Louis, 11/27/1912

Merrill, Dina (actress); New York City, 12/9/1925

Merrill, Gary (actor); Hartford, Conn. **(1915-1990)**

Merrill, Robert (baritone); Brooklyn, N.Y., 6/4/1919

Merton, Thomas (clergyman and writer); France **(1915-1968)**

Mesmer, Franz Anton (physician); Itzmang, nr. Constance (Germany) **(1733-1815)**

Mesta, Perle (social figure); Sturgis, Mich. **(1889-1975)**

Metternich, Prince Klemens Wenzel Nepomuk Lothar von (statesman); Coblenz (Germany) **(1773-1859)**

Michelangelo Buonarroti (painter, sculptor, and architect); Caprese (Italy) **(1475-1564)**

Michener, James A. (novelist); New York City, 2/3/1907

Mickiewicz, Adam (Polish poet); Zozie, Belorussia (U.S.S.R.) **(1798-1855)**

Midler, Bette (singer); Honolulu, 1945

Mielziner, Jo (stage designer); Paris **(1901-1976)**

Mies van der Rohe, Ludwig (architect and designer); Aachen, Germany **(1886-1969)**

Mikoyan, Anastas I. (diplomat); Sanain, Armenia, **(1895-1978)**

Miles, Sarah (actress); Essex, England, 12/31/1943

Miles, Sylvia (actress); New York City, 9/9/1932

Miles, Vera (Vera Ralston) (actress); nr. Boise City, Okla., 8/23/1930

Milhaud, Darius (composer); Aix-en-Provence, France **(1892-1974)**

Mill, John Stuart (philosopher); London, **(1806-1873)**

Milland, Ray (Reginald Truscott-Jones) (actor); Neath, Wales **(1907-1986)**

Millay, Edna St. Vincent (poet); Rockland, Me. **(1892-1950)**

Miller, Ann (Lucille Ann Collier) (dancer and actress); Cherino, Tex., 4/12/1923

Miller, Arthur (playwright); New York City, 10/17/1915

Miller, Glenn (band leader); Clarinda, Iowa **(1904-1944)**

Miller, Henry (novelist); New York City **(1891-1980)**

Miller, Jason (John Miller) (playwright); New York City, 1939(?)

Miller, Marilyn (dancer-singer, actress); Evansville, Ind. **(1898-1936)**

Miller, Mitch (Mitchell) (musician); Rochester, N.Y., 7/4/1911

Miller, Roger (singer); Fort Worth, 1/2/1936

Millet, Jean François (painter); Gruchy, France **(1814-1875)**

Millett, Kate (feminist); St. Paul, 9/14/1934

Millikan, Robert A. (physicist); Morrison, Ill. **(1869-1953)**

Mills, Donna (actress); Chicago, 12/11/41

Mills, Hayley (actress); London, 4/18/1946

Mills, John (actor); Felixstowe, England, 2/22/1908

Mills, Juliet (actress); London, 11/21/41

Milne, A(lan) A(lexander) (author); London **(1882-1956)**

Milner, Martin (actor); Detroit, Mich., 12/28/1931

Milnes, Sherrill (baritone); Downers Grove, Ill., 1/10/35

Milstein, Nathan (concert violinist); Odessa, Russia, 12/31/1904

Milton, John (poet); London **(1608-1674)**

Mimieux, Yvette (actress); Hollywood, Calif., 1/8/1941

Mineo, Sal (actor); New York City **(1939-1976)**

Minnelli, Liza (singer and actress); Hollywood, Calif., 3/12/1946

Minnelli, Vincente (film director); Chicago **(1913-1986)**

Minuit, Peter (Governor of New Amsterdam); Wesel (Germany) **(1580-1638)**

Miranda, Carmen (Maria do Carmo da Cunha) (singer and dancer); Lisbon **(1913-1955)**

Miró Joan (painter); Barcelona **(1893-1983)**

Mitchell, Cameron (actor); Dallastown, Pa., 4/11/1918

Mitchell, Guy (actor); Detroit, 2/27/1927

Mitchell, John N. (former Attorney General); Detroit **(1913-1988)**

Mitchell, Joni (Roberta Joan Anderson) (singer and songwriter); Ft. Macleod, Canada, 11/7/1943

Mitchell, Margaret (novelist); Atlanta **(1900-1949)**

Mitchell, Thomas (actor); Elizabeth, N.J. **(1892-1962)**

Mitchum, Robert (actor); Bridgeport, Conn., 8/6/1917

Mitropoulos, Dimitri (orchestra conductor); Athens **(1896-1960)**

Mix, Tom (actor); Mix Run, Pa. **(1880-1940)**

Modigliani, Amedeo (painter); Leghorn, Italy **(1884-1920)**

Moffo, Anna (soprano); Wayne, Pa., 6/27/1934

Mohammed (prophet); Mecca (Saudi Arabia) **(570-632)**

Molière (Jean Baptiste Poquelin) (dramatist); Paris **(1622-1673)**

Moll, Richard (actor); Pasadena, Calif. 1/13/(?)

Molnar, Ferenc (dramatist); Budapest **(1878-1952)**

Molotov, Vyacheslav M. (V. M. Skryabin) (diplomat); Kukarka, Russia **(1890-1986)**

Mondrian, Piet (painter); Amersfoort, Netherlands **(1872-1944)**

Monet, Claude (painter); Paris **(1840-1926)**

Monk, Meredith (choreographer-composer-performing artist); Lima, Peru, 11/20/1942

Monk, Thelonious (pianist); Rocky Mount, N.C. **(1918-1982)**

Monroe, Marilyn (Norma Jean Mortenson or Baker) (actress); Los Angeles **(1926-1962)**

Monroe, Vaughn (Wilton) (band leader); Akron, Ohio **(1912-1973)**

Monsarrat, Nicholas (novelist); Liverpool, England, **(1910-1979)**

Montaigne, Michel Eyquem de (essayist); nr. Bordeaux, France **(1533-1592)**

Montalban, Ricardo (actor); Mexico City, 11/25/1920

Montand, Yves (Yvo Montand Livi) (actor and singer); Monsummano, Italy, 10/13/1921

Montesquieu, Charles-Louis de Secondat, baron de La Brède and de, (philosopher) nr. Borleaux, France **(1689-1755)**

Monteux, Pierre (conductor); Paris **(1875-1964)**

Monteverdi, Claudio (composer); Cremona? Italy **(1567-1643)**

Montez, Maria (actress); Dominican Republican **(1918-1951)**

Montezuma II (Aztec emperor); Mexico **(1480?-1520)**

Montgomery, Elizabeth (actress); Hollywood, Calif., 4/15/1933

Montgomery, George (George Montgomery Letz) (actor); Brady, Mont., 8/29/1916

Montgomery, Robert (Henry, Jr.) (actor); Beacon, N.Y. **(1904-1981)**

Montgomery of Alamein, 1st Viscount of Hindhead (Sir Bernard Law Montgomery) (military leader); London **(1887-1976)**

Montoya, Carlos (guitarist); Madrid, 12/13/1903

Moore, Clement Clarke (author); New York City **(1779-1863)**

Moore, Dudley (actor-writer-musician); Dagenham, England, 4/19/1935

Moore, Garry (Thomas Garrison Morfit) (TV personality); Baltimore, 1/31/1915

Moore, Grace (soprano); Jellico, Tenn. **(1901-1947)**

Moore, Henry (sculptor); Castleford, England **(1898-1986)**

Moore, Marianne (poet); Kirkwood, Mo. **(1887-1972)**

Moore, Mary Tyler (actress); Brooklyn, N.Y., 12/29/1937

Moore, Melba (Beatrice) (singer and actress); New York City, 10/27/1945

Moore, Roger (actor); London, 10/14/1927(?)

Moore, Thomas (poet); Dublin **(1779-1852)**

Moore, Victor (actor); Hammonton, N.J. **(1876-1962)**

Moorehead, Agnes (actress); Clinton, Mass. **(1906-1974)**

More, Henry (philosopher); Grantham, England **(1614-1687)**

More, Sir Thomas (statesman and author); London **(1478-1535)**

Moreau, Jeanne (actress); Paris, 1/23/1928

Moreno, Rita (Rosita Dolores Alverio) (actress); Humacao, Puerto Rico, 12/11/1931

Morgan, Dennis (actor); Prentice, Wis., 12/10/1920

Mo rgan, Frank (actor); New York City **(1890-1949)**

Morgan, Harry (actor); Detroit, 4/10/1915

Morgan, Helen (singer); Danville, Ohio **(1900?-1941)**

Morgan, Henry (comedian); New York City, 3/31/1915

Morgan, Jane (Florence Currier) (singer); Boston, 1920

Morgan, John Pierpont (financier); Hartford, Conn. **(1837-1913)**

Morgan, Ralph (actor); New York City **(1882-1956)**

Moriarty, Michael (actor); Detroit, 4/5/1941

Morini, Erica (concert violinist); Vienna, 1/5/1910

Morison, Samuel Eliot (historian); Boston **(1887-1976)**

Morley, Christopher Darlington (novelist); Haverford, Pa. **(1890-1957)**

Morley, Robert (actor); Semley, England, 5/26/1908

Morris, Chester (actor); New York City **(1901-1970)**

Morris, Wayne (actor); Los Angeles, Calif. **(1914-1959)**

Morrison, Jim (James Douglas Morrison) (singer and songwriter); Melbourne, Fla. **(1943-1971)**

Morse, Marston (mathematician); Waterville, Me. **(1892-1977)**

Morse, Robert (actor); Newton, Mass., 5/18/1931

Morse, Samuel Finley Breese (painter and inventor); Charlestown, Mass. **(1791-1872)**

Moses, Grandma (Mrs. Anna Mary Robertson Moses) (painter); Greenwich, N.Y. **(1860-1961)**

Moses, Robert (urban planner); New Haven, Conn., **(1888-1981)**

Mostel, Zero (Samuel Joel Mostel) (actor); Brooklyn, N.Y. **(1915-1977)**

Moussorgsky, Modest Petrovich (composer); Karev, Russia **(1839-1881)**

Mowbray, Alan (actor); London **(1896-1969)**

Moyers, Bill D. (Billy Don) (journalist); Hugo, Okla., 6/5/1934

Moynihan, Daniel Patrick (New York Senator); Tulsa, Okla., 3/16/1927

Mozart, Wolfgang Amadeus (Johannes Chrysostomus Wolfgangus Theophilus Mozart) (composer); Salzburg (Austria) **(1756-1791)**

Mudd, Roger (TV newscaster); Washington, D.C., 2/9/1928

Muggeridge, Malcolm (Thomas) (writer); Croydon, England **(1903-1990)**

Muhammad, Elijah (Elijah Poole) (religious leader); Sandersville, Ga. **(1897-1975)**

Mulgrew, Kate (actress); Dubuque, Iowa, 4/?/1929

Mulhare, Edward (actor); Ireland, 1923

Mumford, Lewis (cultural historian and city planner); Flushing, Queens, N.Y. **(1895-1990)**

Munch, Edvard (painter); Löt en, Norway **(1863-1944)**

Munchhausen, Karl Friedrick Hieronymus, baron von (anecdotist); Hanover, Germany **(1720-1797)**

Muni, Paul (Muni Weisenfreund) (actor); Lemburg (Ukraine) **(1895-1967)**

Munsel, Patrice (soprano); Spokane, Wash., 5/14/1925

Murdoch, Iris (novelist); Dublin, 7/15/1919

Murdoch, Rupert (publisher); Melbourne, 3/11/1931

Murillo, Bartolomé Esteban (painter); Seville, Spain **(1617-1682)**

Murphy, Audie (actor and war hero); Kingston, Tex. **(1924-1971)**

Murphy, Eddie (actor-comedian); Brooklyn, N.Y. 4/3/61

Murphy, George (actor, dancer, and ex-Senator); New Haven, Conn., 7/4/1902

Murray, Arthur (dance teacher); New York City **(1895–1991)**

Murray, Bill (actor-comedian); Wilmette, Ill. 9/21/1950

Murray, Kathryn (dance teacher); Jersey City, N.J., 1906

Murray, Ken (Don Court) (producer); Nyack, N.Y. **(1903-1988)**

Murray, Mae (Marie Adrienne Koenig) (actress); Portsmouth, Va. **(1890-1965)**

Murrow, Edward R. (commentator and government official); Greensboro, N.C. **(1908-1965)**

.**Mussolini,** Benito (Italian dictator); Dovia, Forli, Italy **(1883-1945)**

Muti, Riccardo (orchestra conductor); Naples, Italy, 7/28/41

Mutter, Anne-Sophie (violinist); Rheinfelden, West Germany, 6/29/63

Myerson, Bess (consumer advocate); Bronx, N.Y., 1924

Myrdal, Gunnar (sociologist and economist); Gustaf Parish, Sweden **(1898-1987)**

N

Nabokov, Vladimir (novelist); St. Petersburg, Russia **(1899-1977)**

Nabors, Jim (actor and singer); Sylacauga, Ala., 6/12/1932

Nader, Ralph (consumer advocate); Winsted, Conn., 2/27/1934

Nagel, Conrad (actor); Keokuk, Iowa **(1897-1970)**

Naish, J. Carrol (actor); New York City **(1900-1973)**

Naldi, Nita (Anita Donna Dooley) (actress); New York City **(1899-1961)**

Napoleon Bonaparte. *See* Bonaparte, Napoleon

Nash, Graham (singer); Blackpool, England, 1942

Nash, Ogden (poet); Rye, N.Y. **(1902-1971)**

Nasser, Gamal Abdel (statesman); Beni Mor, Egypt **(1918-1970)**

Nast, Thomas (cartoonist); Landau (Germany) **(1840-1902)**

Nation, Carry Amelia (temperance leader); Garrard County, Ky. **(1846-1911)**

Natwick, Mildred (actress); Baltimore, 6/19/1908

Nazimova, Alla (actress); Yalta, Crimea, Russia **(1879-1945)**

Neagle, Anna (Marjorie Robertson) (actress); London **(1908-1986)**

Neal, Patricia (actress); Packard, Ky., 1/20/1926

Neff, Hildegarde (actress); Ulm, Germany, 12/28/1925

Negri, Pola (Apolina Mathias-Chalupec) (actress); Bromberg (Poland) **(1899-1987)**

Nehru, Jawaharlal (first Prime Minister of India); Allahabad, India **(1889-1964)**

Nelligan, Kate (actress); London, Ont., Canada, 3/16/51

Nelson, Barry (Neilsen) (actor); San Francisco, 1920

Nelson, David (actor); New York City, 10/24/1936

Nelson, Harriet Hilliard (Peggy Lou Snyder) (actress); Des Moines, Iowa, 1914

Nelson, Ozzie (Oswald) (actor); Jersey City, N.J. **(1907-1975)**

Nelson, Ricky (Eric) (singer and actor); Teaneck, N.J. **(1940-1985)**

Nelson, Viscount Horatio (naval officer); Burnham Thorpe, England **(1758-1805)**

Nelson, Willie (singer); Waco, Texas, 4/30/1933

Nenni, Pietro (Socialist leader); Faenza, Italy **(1891-1980)**

Nero (Nero Claudius Caesar Drusus Germanicus) (Roman emperor); Antium (Italy) **(37-68)**

Nero, Peter (pianist); New York City, 5/22/1934

Nesbitt, Cathleen (actress); Cheshire, England **(1889-1982)**

Nevelson, Louise (sculptor); Kiev, Russia **(1899-1988)**

Newhart, Bob (entertainer); Chicago, 9/5/1929

Newhouse, Samuel I. (publisher); New York City **(1895-1979)**

Newley, Anthony (actor and song writer); London, 9/24/1931

Newman, Edwin (news commentator); New York City, 1/25/1919

Newman, John Henry (prelate); London **(1801-1890)**

Newman, Paul (actor and director); Cleveland, 1/26/1925

Newman, Randy (singer); Los Angeles, 11/28/1943

Newton, Huey (black activist); New Orleans, 2/17/1942

Newton, Sir Isaac (mathematician and scientist); nr. Grantham, England **(1642-1727)**

Newton, Wayne (singer); Norfolk, Va., 4/3/1942

Newton-John, Olivia (singer); Cambridge, England, 9/26/1948

Nichols, Mike (Michael Peschkowsky) (stage and film director); Berlin, 11/6/1931

Nicholson, Jack (actor); Neptune, N.J., 4/22/1937

Nietzsche, Friedrich Wilhelm (philosopher); nr. Lützen Saxon y (East Germany) **(1844-1900)**

Nightingale, Florence (nurse); Florence (Italy) **(1820-1910)**

Nijinsky, Vaslav (ballet dancer); Warsaw **(1890-1950)**

Nilsson, Birgit (soprano); West Karup, Sweden, 5/17/1923

Nilsson, Harry (singer and songwriter); Brooklyn, N.Y., 6/15/1941

Nimitz, Chester W. (naval officer); Fredericksburg, Tex. **(1885-1966)**

Nimoy, Leonard (actor); Boston, 3/26/1931

Nin, Anais (author and diarist); Neuilly, France **(1903-1977)**

Niven, David (actor); Kirriemuir, Scotland, **(1910-1983)**

Nizer, Louis (lawyer and author); London, 2/6/1902

Nobel, Alfred Bernhard (industrialist); Stockholm **(1833-1896)**

Noguchi, Isamu (sculptor); Los Angeles **(1904-1988)**

Nolan, Lloyd (actor); San Francisco **(1902-1985)**

Nolte, Nick (actor); Omaha, Neb., 1942

Norell, Norman (Norman Levinson) (fashion designer); Noblesville, Ind. **(1900-1972)**

Norman, Jessye (soprano); Augusta, Ga., 9/15/45

Norman, Marsha (Marsha Williams) (playwright); Louisville, Ky., 9/21/1947

Normand, Mabel (actress); Boston **(1894-1930)**

Norstad, Gen. Lauris (ex-commander of NATO forces); Minneapolis **(1907-1988)**

North, John Ringling (circus director); Baraboo, Wis. **(1903-1985)**

North, Sheree (actress); Los Angeles, 1/17/1933

Norton, Eleanor Holmes (New York City government official, lawyer); Washington, D.C., 6/13/1937

Nostradamus (Michel de Notredame) (astrologer); St. Rémy, France **(1503-1566)**

Novaes, Guiomar (pianist); São João de Boa Vista, Brazil **(1895-1979)**

Novak, Kim (Marilyn Novak) (actress); Chicago, 2/13/1933

Novarro, Ramon (Ramon Samaniegoes) (actor); Durango, Mexico **(1899-1968)**

Novello, Ivor (actor, playwright, composer); Cardiff, Wales **(1893-1951)**

Nugent, Elliott (actor and director); Dover, Ohio, **(1899-1980)**

Nureyev, Rudolf (ballet dancer); U.S.S.R., 3/17/1938

Nuyen, France (actress); Marseilles, France, 7/31/1939

Nyro, Laura (singer and songwriter); Bronx, N.Y., 1947

O

Oakie, Jack (actor); Sedalia, Mo. **(1903-1978)**

Oakley, Annie (Phoebe Anne Oakley Mozee) (markswoman); Darke County, Ohio **(1860-1926)**

Oates, Joyce Carol (novelist); Lockport, N.Y., 6/16/1938

Oberon, Merle (Estelle Merle O'Brien Thompson) (actress); Calcutta, India **(1911-1979)**

Oberth, Hermann (rocketry and space flight pioneer); Hermannstadt, Romania **(1894-1989)**

O'Brian, Hugh (Hugh J. Krampe) (actor); Rochester, N.Y., 4/19/1930

O'Brien, Edmond (actor); New York City **(1915-1985)**

O'Brien, Margaret (Angela Maxine O'Brien) (actress); San Diego, Calif., 1/15/1937

O'Brien, Pat (William Joseph O'Brien, Jr.) (actor); Milwaukee, **(1899-1983)**

O'Casey, Sean (playwright); Dublin **(1881-1964)**

Ochs, Adolph Simon (publisher); Cincinnati **(1858-1935)**

O'Connor, Carroll (actor); New York City, 8/2/1924

O'Connor, Donald (actor); Chicago, 8/28/1925

Odets, Clifford (playwright); Philadelphia **(1906-1963)**

Odetta (Odetta Holmes) (folk singer and actress); Birmingham, Ala., 12/31/1930

Offenbach, Jacques (composer); Cologne, Germany **(1819-1880)**

O'Hara, John (novelist); Pottsville, Pa. **(1905-1970)**

O'Hara, Maureen (Maureen FitzSimons) (actress); Dublin, 8/17/1921

Ohlsson, Garrick (pianist); Bronxville, N.Y., 4/3/1948

Ohrbach, Jerry (actor-singer); Bronx, N.Y., 10/20/1935

Oistrakh, David (concert violinist); Odessa, Russia **(1908-1974)**

O'Keefe, Dennis (actor); Fort Madison, Iowa **(1908-1968)**

O'Keeffe, Georgia (painter); Sun Prairie, Wis. **(1887-1986)**

Oland, Warner (actor); Umea, Sweden **(1880-1938)**

Olav V (King of Norway); Sandringham, England, 7/2/1903

Oldenburg, Claes (painter); Stockholm, Sweden, 1/28/1929

Oliver, Edna May (actress); Malden, Mass. **(1883-1942)**

Olivier, Lord (Laurence) (actor); Dorking, England **(1907-1989)**

Olmsted, Frederick Law (landscape architect); Hartford, Conn. **(1822-1903)**

Olsen, Ole (John Sigvard Olsen) (comedian); Peru, Ind. **(1892-1963)**

Omar Khayyam (poet and astronomer); Nishapur (Iran) **(died c. 1123)**

Onassis, Aristotle (shipping executive); Smyrna, Turkey **(1906-1975)**

Onassis, Christina (shipping executive); New York City **(1950-1988)**

Onassis, Jacqueline Kennedy (Jacqueline Bouvier) (President's widow); Southampton, N.Y., 7/28/1929

O'Neal, Ryan (Patrick) (actor); Los Angeles, 4/20/1941
O'Neal, Tatum (actress); Los Angeles, Calif., 11/5/1963
O'Neill, Eugene Gladstone (playwright); New York City (1888-1953)
O'Neill, Jennifer (actress); Rio de Janeiro, 2/20/1949
Oppenheimer, J. Robert (nuclear physicist); New York City (1904-1967)
Orff, Carl (composer); Munich, Germany (1895-1982)
Orlando, Tony (Michael Anthony Orlando Cassavitis) (singer); New York City, 4/3/1944
Ormandy, Eugene (conductor); Budapest (1899-1985)
Orozco, José Clemente (painter); Zapotlán, Jalisco, Mexico (1883-1949)
Orwell, George (Eric Arthur Blair) (British author); Motihari, India (1903-1950)
Osborn, Paul (playwright); Evansville, Ind. (1901-1988)
Osborne, John (playwright); London, 12/12/1929
Osler, Sir William (physician); Bondhead, Ontario, Canada (1849-1919)
Osmond, Donny (singer); Ogden, Utah, 12/9/1957
Osmond, Marie (singer); Ogden, Utah, 1959
O'Sullivan, Maureen (actress); County Roscommon, Ireland, 5/17/1911
Otis, Elisha (inventor); Halifax, Vt. (1811-1861)
O'Toole, Peter (actor); Connemara, Ireland, 8/2/1933
Ouspenskaya, Maria (actress); Tula, Russia (1876-1949)
Ovid (Publius Ovidius Naso) (poet); Sulmona (Italy) (43 B.C.-?A.D. 17)
Owen, Reginald (actor); Wheathampstead, England (1887-1972)
Owens, Buck (Alvis Edgar Owens) (singer); Sherman, Tex., 8/12/1929
Ozawa, Seiji (orchestra conductor); Hoten, Japan, 9/1/35

P

Paar, Jack (TV personality); Canton, Ohio, 5/1/1918
Pacino, Al (Alfred) (actor); New York City, 4/25/1940
Packard, Vance (author); Granville Summit, Pa., 5/22/1914
Paderewski, Ignace Jan (pianist and statesman); Kurylowka, Russian Podolia (1860-1941)
Paganini, Nicolò (violinist); Genoa (Italy) (1782-1840)
Page, Geraldine (actress); Kirksville, Mo. (1924-1987)
Page, Patti (Clara Ann Fowler) (singer and entertainer); Claremore, Okla., 11/8/1927
Paige, Janis (actress); Tacoma, Wash., 9/16/1922
Paine, Thomas (political philosopher); Thetford, England (1737-1809)
Palance, Jack (Walter Palanuik) (actor); Lattimer, Pa., 2/18/1920
Palestrina, Giovanni Pierluigi da (composer); Palestrina, Italy (1526-1594)
Paley, William S. (broadcasting executive); Chicago (1901–1990)
Palladio, Andrea (architect); Padua or Vicenza (Italy) (1508-1580)
Pallette, Eugene (actor); Winfield, Kan. (1889-1954)
Palmer, Betsy (actress); East Chicago, Ind., 1929
Palmer, Lilli (Lilli Peiser) (actress); Posen (Germany) (1914-1986)
Palmerston, Henry John Templeton (3rd Viscount) (statesman); Broadlands, England (1784-1865)
Pangborn, Franklin (actor); Newark, N.J. (1893-1958)
Papanicolaou, George N. (physician); Coumi, Greece (1883-1962)
Papas, Irene (actress); Chiliomodion, Greece, 1929
Papp, Joseph (Joseph Papirofsky) (stage producer and director); Brooklyn, N.Y., 6/22/1921
Paracelaus, Philippus (Aureolus Theophrastus Bombastus von Hohenheim) (physican); Einsiedeln, Switzerland (1493-1541)
Park, Chung Hee (President of South Korea); Sangmo-ri, Korea (1917-1979)
Parker, Dorothy (Dorothy Rothschild) (author); West End, N.J. (1893-1967)
Parker, Eleanor (actress); Cedarville, Ohio, 6/26/1922
Parker, Fess (actor); Fort Worth, Tex., 1925
Parker, Jean (actress); Butte, Mont., 8/11/12
Parker, Suzy (model and actress); San Antonio, 10/28/1933
Parkinson, C(yril) Northcote (historian); Durham, England, 7/30/1909
Parks, Bert (Bert Jacobson) (entertainer); Atlanta, 12/30/1914
Parks, Gordon (film director); Ft. Scott, Kan., 11/30/1912
Parnell, Charles Stewart (statesman); Avondale, Ireland (1846-1891)
Parnis, Mollie (Mollie Parnis Livingston) (fashion designer); New York City, 3/18/1905
Parsons, Estelle (actress); Marblehead, Mass., 11/20/1927
Parton, Dolly (singer); Locust Ridge, Tenn. 1/19/1946
Pascal, Blaise (philosopher); Clermont, France (1623-1662)
Pasternak, Boris Leonidovich (author); Moscow (1890-1960)
Pasternak, Joseph (film producer); Silagy-Somlyo, Romania (1901–1991)
Pasteur, Louis (chemist); Dôle, France (1822-1895)
Pastor, Tony (Antonio) (actor, theater manager); New York City (1837-1908)

Paton, Alan (author); Pietermaritzburg, South Africa (1903-1988)
Patti, Adelina (soprano); Madrid (1843-1919)
Patton, George Smith, Jr. (general); San Gabriel, Calif., (1885-1945)
Paul, Les (Lester William Polfus) (guitarist); Waukesha, Wis., 6/9/1915
Paul VI (Giovanni Battista Montini) (Pope); Concesio, nr. Brescia, Italy (1897-1978)
Pauley, Jane (TV newscaster); Indianapolis, 10/31/1950
Pauling, Linus Carl (chemist); Portland, Ore., 2/28/1901
Pavarotti, Luciano (tenor); Modena, Italy, 10/12/1935
Pavlov, Ivan Petrovich (physiologist); Ryazan district, Russia (1849-1936)
Pavlova, Anna (ballerina); St. Petersburg, Russia (1885-1931)
Paxinou, Katina (actress); Piraeus, Greece (1900-1973)
Payne, John (actor); Roanoke, Va. (1912-1989)
Peale, Norman Vincent (clergyman); Bowersville, Ohio, 5/31/1898
Pearl, Minnie (Sarah Ophelia Colley Cannon) (comedienne and singer); Centerville, Tenn., 10/25/1912
Pears, Peter (tenor); Farnham, England (1910-1986)
Pearson, Drew (Andrew Russel Pearson) (columnist); Evanston, Ill. (1897-1969)
Pearson, Lester B. (statesman); Toronto (1897-1972)
Peary, Robert Edwin (explorer); Cresson, Pa. (1856-1920)
Peck, Gregory (actor); La Jolla, Calif., 4/5/1916
Peckinpah, Sam (film director); Fresno, Calif. (1925-1984)
Peerce, Jan (tenor); New York City (1904-1984)
Pegler, (James) Westbrook (columnist); Minneapolis, (1894-1969)
Pei, I(eoh) M(ing) (architect); Canton, China, 4/26/1917
Penn, Arthur (stage and film director); Philadelphia, 9/27/1922
Penn, William (American colonist); London (1644-1718)
Penner, Joe (comedian); Hungary (1904-1941)
Penney, James C. (merchant); Hamilton, Mo. (1875-1971)
Peppard, George (actor); Detroit, 10/1/1928
Pepys, Samuel (diarist); Bampton, England (1633-1703)
Perelman, S(idney) J(oseph) (writer); Brooklyn, N.Y. (1904-1979)
Pergolesi, Giovanni Battista (composer); Jesi, Italy (1710-1736)
Pericles (statesman); Athens (died 429 B.C.)
Perkins, Osgood (actor); West Newton, Mass. (1892-1937)
Perkins, Tony (Anthony) (actor); New York City, 4/14/1932
Perlman, Itzhak (violinist); Tel Aviv, Israel, 8/31/1945
Perlman, Rhea (actress); Brooklyn, N.Y., 3/31/48
Perón, Isabel (María Estela Martínez Cartas) (former chief of state); La Rioja, Argentina, 2/4/1931
Perón, Juan D. (statesman); nr. Lobos, Argentina (1895-1974)
Perón, Maria Eva Duarte de (political leader); Los Toldos, Argentina (1919-1952)
Perrine, Valerie (actress and dancer); Galveston, Tex., 9/3/1943
Pershing, John Joseph (general); Linn County, Mo. (1860-1948)
Pestalozzi, Johann (educator); Zurich, Switzerland (1746-1827)
Peters, Bernadette (Bernadette Lazzara) (actress); New York City, 2/28/1944
Peters, Brock (actor-singer); New York City, 7/2/1927
Peters, Jean (actress); Canton, Ohio, 10/15/1926
Peters, Roberta (Roberta Peterman) (soprano); New York City, 5/4/1930
Petit, Roland (choreographer and dancer); Villemombe, France, 1924
Petrarch (Francesco Petrarca) (poet); Arezzo (Italy) (1304-1374)
Pfeiffer, Michelle (actress); Santa Ana, Calif., 4/29/58
Philip (Philip Mountbatten) (Duke of Edinburgh); Corfu, Greece, 6/10/1921
Piaf, Edith (Edith Gassion) (chanteuse); Paris (1916-1963)
Piatigorsky, Gregor (cellist); Ekaterinoslav, Russia (1903-1976)
Piazza, Ben (actor); Little Rock, Ark., 7/30/1934
Piazza, Marguerite (soprano); New Orleans, 5/6/1926
Picasso, Pablo (painter and sculptor); Málaga, Spain (1881-1973)
Pickford, Jack (Jack Smith) (actor); Toronto (1896-1933)
Pickford, Mary (Gladys Mary Smith) (actress); Toronto (1893-1979)
Picon, Molly (actress); New York City, 6/1/1898
Pidgeon, Walter (actor); East St. John, New Brunswick, Canada (1898-1984)
Pinter, Harold (playwright); London, 10/10/1930
Pinza, Ezio (basso); Rome (1892-1957)
Pirandello, Luigi (dramatist and novelist); nr. Girgenti, Italy (1867-1936)
Piranesi, Giambattista (artist); Mestre, Italy (1720-1778)
Pissaro, Camille Jacob (painter); St. Thomas (U.S. Virgin Islands) (1830-1903)
Piston, Walter (composer); Rockland, Me. (1894-1976)
Pitman, Sir (Isaac) James (educator a nd publisher); Bath, England, 8/14/1901
Pitt, William ("Younger Pitt") (statesman); nr. Bromley, England (1759-1806)
Pitts, ZaSu (actress); Parsons, Kan. (1898-1963)
Pius XII (Eugenio Pacelli) (Pope); Rome (1876-1958)
Pizarro, Francisco (explorer); Trujillo, Spain (1470?-1541)

Planck, Max (physicist); Kiel, Germany **(1858-1947)**
Plato (Aristocles) (philosopher); Athens (?) **(427?-347** B.C.**)**
Pleasence, Donald (actor); Worksop, England, 10/5/1919
Pleshette, Suzanne (actress); New York City, 1/31/1937
Plimpton, George (author); New York City, 3/18/1927
Plisetskaya, Maya (ballerina); Moscow, 11/20/1925
Plowright, Joan (actress); Brigg, England, 10/28/1929
Plummer, Christopher (actor); Toronto, 12/13/1929
Plutarch (biographer); Chaeronea (Greece) **(46?-?120)**
Pocahontas (Matoaka) (American Indian princess); Virginia (?) **(1595?-1617)**
Podhoretz, Norman (author); Brooklyn, N.Y., 1/16/1930
Poe, Edgar Allan (poet and story writer); Boston, Mass. **(1809-1849)**
Poitier, Sidney (film actor and director); Miami, Fla., 2/20/1927
Polanski, Roman (film director); Paris, 8/18/1933
Pollard, Michael J. (actor); Passaic, N.J., 5/30/1939
Pollock, Jackson (painter); Cody, Wyo. **(1912-1956)**
Polo, Marco (traveler); Venice **(1254?-?1324)**
Pompadour, Mme. de (Jeanne Antoinette Poisson) (courtesan); Versailles **(1721-1764)**
Pompey (Gnaeus Pompeius Magnus) (general); Rome (?) **(106-48** B.C.**)**
Ponce de León, Juan (explorer); Servas, Spain **(1460?-1521)**
Pons, Lily (coloratura soprano); Cannes, France **(1904-1976)**
Ponselle, Rosa (soprano); Meriden, Conn. **(1897-1981)**
Ponti, Carlo (director); Milan, Italy, 12/11/1913
Pope, Alexander (poet); London **(1688-1744)**
Porter, Cole (songwriter); Peru, Ind. **(1892?-1964)**
Porter, Katherine Anne (novelist); Indian Creek, Tex. **(1891-1980)**
Post, Wiley (aviator); Grand Plain, Tex. **(1900-1935)**
Poston, Tom (actor); Columbus, Ohio, 10/17/1927
Potëmkin, Grigori Aleksandrovich, Prince (statesman); Khizovo (Khizov, Belorussia, U.S.S.R.) **(1 739-1791)**
Potok, Chaim (author); New York City, 2/17/1929
Poulenc, Francis (composer); Paris **(1899-1963)**
Pound, Ezra (poet); Hailey, Idaho **(1885-1972)**
Poussin, Nicolas (painter); Villers, France **(1594-1665)**
Powell, Adam Clayton, Jr. (Congressman); New Haven, Conn. **(1908-1972)**
Powell, Dick (actor); Mt. View, Ark. **(1904-1963)**
Powell, Eleanor (actress and tap dancer); Springfield, Mass. **(1912-1982)**
Powell, Jane (Suzanne Burce) (actress and singer); Portland, Ore., 4/1/1929
Powell, William (actor); Pittsburgh, **(1892-1984)**
Power, Tyrone (actor); Cincinnati, Ohio **(1914-1958)**
Powers, Stephanie (Taffy Paul) (actress); Hollywood, Calif., 11/12/1942
Praxiteles (sculptor); Athens **(c.370-c.330** B.C.**)**
Preminger, Otto (film director and producer); Vienna **(1906-1986)**
Prentiss, Paula (Paula Ragusa) (actress); San Antonio, 1939
Presley, Elvis (singer and actor); Tupelo, Miss. **(1935-1977)**
Presley, Priscilla (actress); Brooklyn, N.Y., 5/24/45
Preston, Robert (Robert Preston Meservey) (actor); Newton Highlands, Mass **(1918-1987)**
Previn, André (conductor); Berlin, 4/6/1929
Previn, Dory (singer); Rahway, N.J., 10/22/1929(?)
Price, Leontyne (Mary) (soprano); Laurel, Miss., 2/10/1927
Price, Ray (country music artist); Perryville, Tex., 1/12/1926
Price, Vincent (actor); St. Louis, 5/27/1911
Pride, Charley (singer); Sledge, Miss., 3/18/1938(?)
Priestley, J. B. (John B.) (author); Bradford, England **(1894-1984)**
Priestley, Joseph (chemist); nr. Leeds, England **(1733-1804)**
Primrose, William (violist); Glasgow, Scotland **(1904-1982)**
Prince (Prince Roger Nelson) (singer); Minneapolis, 6/7/58
Prince, Harold (stage producer); New York City, 1/30/1928
Principal, Victoria (actress); Fukuoka, Japan, 1/3/45(?)
Prinze, Freddie (actor); New York City **(1954-1977)**
Pritchett, V(ictor) S(awdon) (literary critic); Ipswich, England, 12/16/1900
Procter, William (scientist); Cincinnati **(1872-1951)**
Prokofiev, Sergei Sergeevich (composer); St. Petersburg, Russia **(1891-1953)**
Proust, Marcel (novelist); Paris **(1871-1922)**
Provine, Dorothy (actress); Deadwood, S. Dak., 1/20/1937
Prowse, Juliet (actress); Bombay, 9/25/1936
Pryor, Richard (comedian); Peoria, Ill., 12/1/1940
Ptolemy (Claudius Ptolemaeus) (astronomer and geographer); Ptolemais Hermii (Egypt) **(2nd century** A.D.**)**
Pucci, Emilio (Marchese di Barsento) (fashion designer); Naples, Italy, 11/20/1914
Puccini, Giacomo (composer); Lucca, Italy **(1858-1924)**
Puente, Tito (band leader); New York City, 4/20/1923
Pulaski, Casimir (military officer); Podolia, Poland **(1748-1779)**
Pulitzer, Joseph (publisher); Makó (Hungary) **(1847-1911)**
Pullman, George (inventor); Brockton, N.Y. **(1831-1897)**

Purcell, Henry (composer); London **(1658-1695)**
Pusey, Nathan M. (educator); Council Bluffs, Iowa, 4/4/1907
Pushkin, Alexander Sergeevich (poet and dramatist); Moscow **(1799-1837)**
Puzo, Mario (novelist); New York City, 10/15/1921
Pyle, Ernest Taylor (journalist); Dana, Ind. **(1900-1945)**
Pythagoras (mathematician and philosopher); Samos (Greece) **(6th century** B.C.**)**

Q

Quaid, Randy, (actor); Houston, Texas, 10/1/1950
Quayle, Anthony (actor); Ainsdale, England **(1913-1989)**
Queen, Ellery: pen name of the late Frederic Dannay and the late Manfred B. Lee
Queler, Eve (conductor); New York City, 1/1/1936
Quennell, Peter Courtney (biographer); Bromley, England, 3/9/1905
Quinn, Anthony (actor); Chihuahua, Mexico, 4/21/1916

R

Rabe, David (playwright); Dubuque, Iowa, 3/10/1940
Rabelais, François (satirist); nr. Chinon, France **(1494?-1553)**
Rabi, I(sidor) I(saac) (physicist); Rymanow (Poland) **(1898-1988)**
Rachmaninoff, Sergei Wassilievitch (pianist and composer); Oneg Estate, Novgorod, Russia **(1873-1943)**
Racine, Jean Baptiste (dramatist); La Ferté-Milon, France **(1639-1699)**
Radner, Gilda (comedienne); Detroit **(1946-1989)**
Raft, George (actor); New York City **(1895-1980)**
Rainer, Luise (actress); Vienna, 1912
Raines, Ella (actress); Snoqualmie Falls, Wash. **(1921-1988)**
Rainier III (Prince); Monaco, 5/31/1923
Rains, Claude (actor); London **(1 889-1967)**
Raitt, Bonnie (singer); Burbank, Calif., 11/8/1949
Raitt, John (actor,singer); Santa Ana, Calif., 1/29(?)/17
Raleigh, Sir Walter (courtier and navigator); London **(1552?-1618)**
Rambeau, Marjorie (actress); San Francisco **(1889-1970)**
Rameau, Jean-Philippe (composer); Dijon? France **(1683-1764)**
Rampal, Jean-Pierre (Louis) (flutist); Marseilles, France, 7/1/22
Randall, Tony (Leonard Rosenberg) (actor); Tulsa, Okla., 2/26/1920
Randolph, A(sa) Philip (labor leader); Crescent City, Fla. **(1889-1979)**
Raphael (Raffaello Santi) (painter and architect); Urbino (Italy) **(1483-1520)**
Rasputin, Grigori Efimovich (monk); Tobolsk Province, Russia **(1871?-1916)**
Rathbone, Basil (actor); Johannesburg, South Africa **(1892-1967)**
Rather, Dan (TV newscaster); Wharton, Tex., 10/31/1931
Ratoff, Gregory (film director); St. Petersburg, Russia **(1897-1960)**
Rattigan, Terence (playwright); London **(1911-1977)**
Rauschenberg, Robert (painter); Port Arthur, Tex., 10/22/1925
Ravel, Maurice Joseph (composer); Ciboure, France **(1875-1937)**
Rawls, Lou (singer); Chicago, 12/1/1935
Ray, Aldo (DaRe) (actor); Pen Argyl, Pa. **(1926–1991)**
Ray, Gene Anthony (actor, dancer); Harlem, N.Y., 5/24/63
Ray, Man (painter); Philadelphia **(1890-1976)**
Ray, Satyajit (film director); Calcutta, 5/2/1922
Rayburn, Gene (TV personality); Christopher, Ill., 12/22/1917
Raye, Martha (Margie Yvonne Reed) (comedienne and actress); Butte, Mont., 8/27/1916
Raymond, Gene (actor); New York City, 8/13/1908
Reasoner, Harry (TV commentator); Dakota City, Iowa **(1923–1991)**
Redding, Otis (singer); Dawson, Ga. **(1941-1967)**
Reddy, Helen (singer); Melbourne, 10/25/1941
Redford, Robert (Charles Robert Redford, Jr.) (actor); Santa Monica, Calif., 8/18/1937
Redgrave, Lynn (actress); London, 3/8/1943
Redgrave, Sir Michael (actor); Bristol, England **(1908-1985)**
Redgrave, Vanessa (actress); London, 1/30/1937
Reed, Donna (actress); Denison, Iowa **(1921-1986)**
Reed, Rex (critic); Ft. Worth, 10/2/1940
Reed, Walter (army surgeon); Belroi, Va. **(1851-1902)**
Reese, Della (Deloreese Patricia Early) (singer); Detroit, 7/6/1932
Reeve, Christopher (actor); New York City, 9/25/52
Reeves, Jim (singer); Panola County, Tex. **(1923-1964)**
Reich, Steve (composer); New York City, 10/3/1936
Reid, Wallace (actor); St. Louis **(1891-1923)**
Reiner, Carl (actor); New York City, 3/20/1922
Reiner, Fritz (conductor); Budapest **(1888-1963)**
Reiner, Robert (actor); Bronx, N.Y., 1945
Reinhardt, Max (Max Goldmann) (theater producer); nr. Vienna **(1873-1943)**

Remarque, Erich Maria (novelist); Osnabrück, Germany **(1898-1970)**
Rembrandt (Rembrandt Harmensz van Rijn) (painter); Leyden (Netherlands) **(1605-1669)**
Remick, Lee (Ann) (actress); Boston **(1935–1991)**
Rennert, Günther (opera director and producer); Essen, Germany, 4/1/1911
Rennie, Michael (actor); Bradford, England **(1909-1971)**
Renoir, Jean (film director and writer); Paris, **(1894-1979)**
Renoir, Pierre Auguste (painter); Limoges, France **(1841-1919)**
Resnais, Alain (film director); Vannes, France, 6/3/1922
Resnik, Regina (mezzo-soprano); New York City, 8/30/1922
Respighi, Ottorino (composer); Bologna, Italy **(1879-1936)**
Reston, James (journalist); Clydebank, Scotland, 11/3/1909
Reuther, Walter (labor leader); Wheeling, W. Va. **(1907-1970)**
Revere, Paul (silversmith and hero of famous ride); Boston **(1735-1818)**
Revson, Charles (business executive); Boston **(1906-1975)**
Reynolds, Burt (actor); Waycross, Ga., 2/11/1936
Renolds, Debbie (Marie Frances Reynolds) (actress); El Paso, 4/1/1932
Reynolds, Sir Joshua (painter); nr. Plymouth, England **(1723-1792)**
Reynolds, Marjorie (Goodspeed) (actress); Buhl, Idaho, 8/12/21
Rhodes, Cecil John (South African statesman); Bishop Stortford, England **(1853-1902)**
Rice, Elmer (playwright); New York City **(1892-1967)**
Rice, Grantland (sports writer); Murfreesboro, Tenn. **(1880-1954)**
Rich, Buddy (Bernard) (drummer); Brooklyn, N.Y. **(1917-1987)**
Rich, Charlie (singer); Colt, Ark., 12/14/1932
Richardson, Elliot L. (ex-Cabinet member); Boston, 7/20/1920
Richardson, Sir Ralph (actor); Cheltenham, England **(1902-1983)**
Richardson, Tony (director); Shipley, England, 6/5/1928
Richelieu, Duc de (Armand Jean du Plessis) (cardinal); Paris **(1585-1642)**
Richie, Lionel (singer-songwriter); Tuskegee, Ala., 1949 (?)
Richter, Charles Francis (seismologist); Hamilton, Canada **(1900-1985)**
Richter, Sviatoslav (pianist); Zhitomir, Ukraine, 3/20/1914
Rickenbacker, Edward V. (aviator); Columbus, Ohio **(1890-1973)**
Rickles, Don (comedian); New York City, 5/8/1926
Rickover, Vice Admiral Hyman G. (atomic energy expert); Russia **(1900-1986)**
Riddle, Nelson (composer); Hackensack, N.J. **(1921-1985)**
Ride, Sally K(risten) (astronaut, astrophysicist); Encino, Calif., 5/26/1951
Ridgway, General Matthew B. (ex-Army Chief of Staff); Ft. Monroe, Va., 3/3/1895
Rigg, Diana (actress); Doncaster, England, 7/20/1938
Riley, James Whitcomb (poet); Greenfield, Ind. **(1849-1916)**
Rimsky-Korsakov, Nikolai Andreevich (composer); Tikhvin, Russia **(1844-1908)**
Rinehart, Mary (née Roberts) (novelist); Pittsburgh **(1876-1958)**
Ritchard, Cyril (actor and director); Sydney, Australia **(1898-1977)**
Ritter, John (Jonathan) (actor); Burbank, Calif., 9/17/1948
Ritter, Tex (Woodward Maurice Ritter) (singer); Panola County, Tex., **(1905-1973)**
Ritter, Thelma (actress); Brooklyn, N.Y. **(1905-1969)**
Rivera, Chita (Dolores Conchita Figuero del Rivero) (dancer-actress-singer); Washington, D.C. 1/23/1933
Rivera, Diego (painter); Guanajuato, Mexico **(1886-1957)**
Rivera, Geraldo (Miguel) (TV newscaster); New York City, 7/3/1943
Rivers, Joan (comedienne); Brooklyn, N.Y., 6/8/1933
Rivers, Larry (Yitzroch Loiza Grossberg) (painter); New York City, 8/17/1923
Robards, Jason, Jr. (actor); Chicago, 7/26/1922
Robards, Jason, Sr. (actor); Hillsdale, Mich. **(1892-1963)**
Robbins, Harold (Harold Rubin) (novelist); New York City, 5/21/1916
Robbins, Jerome (Jerome Rabinowitz) (choreographer); New York City, 10/11/1918
Robbins, Marty (singer); Glendale, Ariz., **(1925-1982)**
Roberts, Eric (actor); Bilox, Miss., 4/18/1956
Roberts, (Granville) Oral (evangelist and publisher); nr. Ada, Okla., 1/24/1918
Robertson, Cliff (actor); La Jolla, Cal if., 9/9/1925
Robertson, Dale (Dayle) (actor); Oklahoma City, 7/14/1923
Robeson, Paul (singer and actor); Princeton, N.J., **(1898-1976)**
Robespierre, Maximilien François Marie Isidore de (French Revolutionist); Arras, France **(1758-1794)**
Robinson, Bill "Bojangles" (Luther) (dancer); Richmond, Va. **(1878-1949)**
Robinson, Edward G. (Emanuel Goldenberg) (actor); Bucharest **(1893-1973)**
Robinson, Edwin Arlington (poet); Head Tide, Me. **(1869-1935)**
Robson, Dame Flora (actress); South Shields, England **(1902-1984)**
Robson, May (actress); Melbourne, Australia **(1858-1942)**
Rochester (Eddie Anderson) (actor); Oakland, Calif. **(1905-1977)**

Rockefeller, David (banker); New York City, 6/12/1915
Rockefeller, John Davison (capitalist); Richford, N.Y. **(1839-1937)**
Rockefeller, John Davison, Jr. (industrialist); Cleveland **(1874-1960)**
Rockefeller, John D., 3rd (philanthropist); New York City **(1906-1978)**
Rockefeller, Laurance S. (conservationist); New York City, 5/26/1910
Rockwell, Norman (painter and illustrator); New York City, **(1894-1978)**
Rodgers, Jimmie (singer); Meridian, Miss. **(1897-1933)**
Rodgers, Richard (composer); New York City **(1902-1979)**
Rodin, François Auguste René (sculptor); Paris **(1840-1917)**
Rodzinski, Artur (conductor); Spalato, Dalmatia **(1894-1958)**
Roentgen, Wilhelm Konrad (physicist); Lennep, Prussia **(1845-1923)**
Rogers, Buddy (Charles) (actor); Olathe, Kan., 8/13/1904
Rogers, Fred (Television producer, host); Latrobe, Pa., 3/20/28
Rogers, Ginger (Virginia McMath) (dancer and actress); Independence, Mo., 7/16/1911
Rogers, Kenny (singer); Houston, 1939(?)
Rogers, Roy (Leonard Slye) (actor); Cincinnati, 11/5/1912
Rogers, Wayne (actor); Birmingham, Ala. 4/7/33
Rogers, Will (William Penn Adair Rogers) (humorist); Oologah, Okla. **(1879-1935)**
Rogers, William P. (ex-Secretary of State); Norfolk, N.Y., 6/23/1913
Roland, Gilbert (actor); Juarez, Mexico, 12/11/1905
Rolland, Romain (author); Clamecy, France **(1866-1944)**
Rollins, Sonny (saxophonist); New York City, 9/7/1930
Romberg, Sigmund (comp oser); Szeged (Hungary) **(1887-1951)**
Rome, Harold (composer); Hartford, Conn., 5/27/1908
Romero, Cesar (actor); New York City, 2/15/1907
Romney, George W. (ex-Secretary of HUD); Chihuahua, Mexico, 7/8/1907
Romulo, Carlos P. (diplomat and educator); Manila **(1899-1985)**
Ronsard, Pierre de (poet); La Possonnière nr. Couture (Couture-sur-Loir, France) **(1524-1585)**
Ronstadt, Linda (singer); Tucson, Ariz., 7/30/1946
Rooney, Andy (TV personality); Albany, N.Y., 1/14/1919
Rooney, Mickey (Joe Yule, Jr.) (actor); Brooklyn, N.Y., 9/23/1920
Roosevelt, Anna Eleanor (reformer and humanitarian); New York City **(1884-1962)**
Rorem, Ned (composer); Richmond, Ind., 10/23/23
Rose, Billy (showman); New York City **(1899-1966)**
Rose, Leonard (concert cellist); Washington, D.C. **(1918-1984)**
Ross, Betsy (Betsey Griscom) (flagmaker); Philadelphia **(1752-1836)**
Ross, Diana (singer); Detroit, 3/26/1944
Ross, Katharine (actress); Hollywood, Calif., 1/29/1943
Rossellini, Isabella (model, actress); Rome, Italy, 6/18/1952
Rossellini, Roberto (film director); Rome **(1906-1977)**
Rossetti, Dante Gabriel (painter and poet); London **(1828-1882)**
Rossini, Gioacchino Antonio (composer); Pesaro (Italy) **(1792-1868)**
Rostand, Edmond (dramatist); Marseilles, France **(1868-1918)**
Rostow, Walt Whitman (economist); New York City, 10/7/1916
Rostropovich, Mstislav (cellist and conductor); Baku, U.S.S.R., 3/27/1927
Roth, Lillian (singer); Boston **(1910-1980)**
Roth, Philip (novelist); Newark, N.J., 3/19/1933
Rothko, Mark (Marcus Rothkovich) (painter); Russia **(1903-1970)**
Rouault, Georges (painter); Paris **(1871-1958)**
Roundtree, Richard (actor); New Rochelle, N.Y., 9/7/1942
Rousseau, Henri (painter); Laval, France **(1844-1910)**
Rousseau, Jean Jacques (philosopher); Geneva **(1712-1778)**
Rovere, Richard H. (journalist); Jersey City, N.J., 5/5/1915
Rowan, Dan (comedian); Beggs, Okla. **(1922-1987)**
Rowlands, Gena (actress); Cambria, Wis., 6/19/1936(?)
Rubens, Sir Peter Paul (painter); Siegen (Germany) **(1577-1640)**
Rubinstein, Arthur (concert pianist); Lódz (Poland) **(1887-1982)**
Rubinstein, Helena (cosmetics executive); Krakow (Poland) **(1882?-1965)**
Rubinstein, John (actor, composer); Los Angeles, 12/8/46
Rudel, Julius (conductor); Vienna, 3/6/1921
Ruffo, Titta (baritone); Italy **(1878-1953)**
Ruggles, Charles (actor); Los Angeles **(1892-1970)**
Rule, Janice (actress); Norwood, Ohio, 8/15/1931
Runcie, Robert (Alexander Kennedy) (Archbishop of Canterbury); Liverpool, England, 10/2/1921
Runyon, (Alfred) Damon (journalist); Manhattan, Kan. **(1884-1945)**
Rusk, Dean (ex-Sec. of State); Cherokee County, Ga., 2/9/1909
Ruskin, John (art critic); London **(1819-1900)**
Russell, Lord Bertrand (Arthur William) (mathematician and philosopher); Trelleck, Wales **(1872-1970)**
Russell, Jane (actress); Bemidji, Minn., 6/21/1921
Russell, Ken (film director); Southhampton, England, 4/3/27
Russell, Leon (pianist and singer); Lawton, Okla., 4/2/1941
Russell, Lillian (Helen Louise Leonard) (soprano); Clinton, Iowa **(1861-1965)**
Russell, Mark (satirist); Buffalo, N.Y., 8/23/32
Russell, Nipsy (comedian); Atlanta, 1924(?)

Russell, Rosalind (actress); Waterbury, Conn. **(1912-1976)**
Rustin, Bayard (civil rights leader); West Chester, Pa. **(1910-1987)**
Rutherford, Dame Margaret (actress); London **(1892-1972)**
Ryan, Robert (actor); Chicago **(1909-1973)**
Rydell, Bobby (singer); Philadelphia, 1942
Rysanek, Leonie (dramatic soprano); Vienna, 11/14/1928

S

Saarinen, Eero (architect); Finland **(1910-1961)**
Sabin, Albert B. (polio researcher); Bialystok (Poland), 8/26/1906
Sabu (Dastagir) (actor); Karapur, India **(1924-1963)**
Sadat, Anwar el- (President); Egypt **(1918-1981)**
Sade, Marquis de (Donatien Alphonse Francois, Comte de Sade) (libertine and writer); Paris **(1740-1814)**
Safer, Morley (TV newscaster); Toronto, 11/8/1931
Sagan, Carl (Edward) (astronomer, astrophysicist); New York City, 11/9/1934
Sagan, Françoise (novelist); Cajarc, France, 6/21/1935
Sahl, Mort (Morton Lyon Sahl) (comedian); Montreal, 5/11/1927
Saint, Eva Marie (actress); Newark, N.J., 7/4/1924
Saint-Gaudens, Augustus (sculptor); Dublin **(1848-1907)**
St. Denis, Ruth (dancer,choreographer); Newark, N.J. **(1878-1968)**
St. James, Susan (Susan Miller) (actress); Los Angeles, 8/14/1946
St. John, Jill (actress); Los Angeles, 8/19/1940
St. Johns, Adela Rogers (journalist and author); Los Angeles **(1894-1988)**
Saint-Laurent, Yves (Henri Donat Mathieu) (fashion designer); Oran, Algeria, 8/1/1936
Saint-Saens, Charles Camille (composer); Paris **(1835-1921)**
Sainte-Marie, Buffy (Beverly) (folk singer); Craven, Saskatchewan, Canada, 2/20/1942(?)
Sales, Soupy (Milton Hines); Franklinton, N.C., 1/6/26
Salinger, J(erome) D(avid) (novelist); New York City, 1/1/1919
Salisbury, Harrison E. (journalist); Minneapolis, 11/14/1908
Salk, Jonas (polio researcher); New York City, 10/28/1914
Salk, Leo (psychologist); New York City, 1926
Salomon, Haym (American Revolution financier); Leszno, Poland **(1740-1785)**
Sand, George (Amandine Lucille Aurore Dudevant, née Dupin) (novelist); Paris **(1804-1876)**
Sandburg, Carl (poet and biographer); Galesburg, Ill. **(1878-1967)**
Sanders, George (actor); St. Petersburg, Russia **(1906-1972)**
Sands, Tommy (singer); Chicago, 8/27/1937
Sanger, Margaret (birth control leader); Corning, N.Y. **(1883-1966)**
Santayana, George (philosopher); Madrid **(1863-1952)**
Sappho (poet); Lesbos (Greece) (lived c. 600 a.c.)
Sargent, John Singer (painter); Florence, Italy **(1856-1925)**
Sarnoff, David (radio executive); Minsk, Russia **(1891-1971)**
Saroyan, William (novelist); Fresno, Calif. **(1908-1981)**
Sarrazin, Michael (actor); Quebec, 5/22/1940
Sarto, Andrea del (Andrea Domenico d'Agnolo di Francesco) (painter); Florence (Italy) **(1486-1531)**
Sartre, Jean-Paul (existentialist writer); Paris **(1905-1980)**
Sassoon, Vidal (hair stylist); London, 1/(?)/1928
Saul (King of Israel) **(11th century** B.C.)
Savalas, Telly (Aristoteles) (actor); Garden City, N.Y., 1/21/1924(?)
Savonarola, Girolamo (religious reformer); Ferrara, Italy **(1452-1498)**
Sawyer, Diane (broadcast journalist); Glasgow, Ky., 12/22/1945
Sayão, Bidú (soprano); Rio de Janeiro, 5/11/1902
Scaasi, Arnold (Arnold Isaacs) (fashion designer); Montreal
Scarlatti, Alessandro (composer); Palermo, Italy **(1659-1725)**
Scarlatti, Domenico (composer); Naples, Italy **(1685-1757)**
Scavullo, Francesco (photographer); Staten Island, N.Y. 1/16/1929
Schary, Dore (producer and writer); Newark, N.J. **(1905-1980)**
Schell, Maria (actress); Vienna, 1/15/1926
Schell, Maximilian (actor); Vienna, 12/8/1930
Schiaparelli, Elsa (fashion designer); Rome **(1890?-1973)**
Schiff, Dorothy (newspaper publisher); New York City **(1903-1989)**
Schildkraut, Joseph (actor); Vienna **(1896-1964)**
Schiller, Johann Christoph Friedrich von (dramatist and poet); Marbach (Germany) **(1759-1805)**
Schipa, Tito (tenor); Lecce, Italy **(1890-1965)**
Schippers, Thomas (conductor); Kalamazoo, Mich. **(1930-1977)**
Schlegel, Friedrich von (philosopher); Hanover? Germany **(1772-1829)**
Schlesinger, Arthur M., Jr. (historian); Columbus, Ohio, 10/15/1917
Schnabel, Artur (pianist,composer); Lipnik, Austria **(1882-1951)**
Schneider, Romy (Rose-Marie Albach) (actress); Vienna **(1938-1982)**
Schoenberg, Arnold (composer); Vienna **(1874-1951)**
Schopenhauer, Arthur (philosopher); Danzig (Poland) **(1788-1860)**
Schubert, Franz Peter (composer); Vienna **(1797-1828)**
Schulberg, Budd (novelist); New York City, 3/27/1914
Schulz, Charles M. (cartoonist); Minneapolis, 11/26/1922

Schuman, Robert (statesman); Luxembourg **(1886-1963)**
Schuman, William (composer); New York City, 8/4/1910
Schumann, Robert Alexander (composer); Zwickau (East Germany) **(1810-1856)**
Schumann-Heink, Ernestine (contralto); near Prague **(1861-1936)**
Schwartz, Arthur (song writer); Brooklyn, N.Y. **(1900-1984)**
Schwarzenegger, Arnold (bodybuilder, actor); Graz, Austria, 7/30/47
Schwarzkopf, Elisabeth (soprano); Jarotschin, Poznán (Poland), 12/9/1915
Schweitzer, Albert (humanitarian); Kaysersburg, Upper Alsace **(1875-1965)**
Scofield, Paul (actor); Hurstpierpoint, England, 1/21/1922
Scorsese, Martin (film director); Flushing, N.Y., 11/17/1942
Scott, George C. (actor); Wise, Va., 10/18/1927
Scott, Hazel (singer, pianist); Port of Spain, Trinidad **(1920-1981)**
Scott, Lizabeth (Emma Matso) (actress); Scranton, Pa., 1923
Scott, Martha (actress); Jamesport, Mo., 9/22/1914
Scott, Randolph (Randolph Crane) (actor); Orange County, Va **(1898-1987)**
Scott, Robert Falcon (explorer); Devonport, England **(1868-1912)**
Scott, Sir Walter (novelist); Edinburgh, Scotland **(1771-1832)**
Scott, Zachary (actor); Austin, Tex. **(1914-1965)**
Scotto, Renata (operatic soprano); Savona, Italy, 2/?/1936?
Scruggs, Earl Eugene (bluegrass musician); Cleveland County, N.C., 1/6/1924
Sebastian, John (composer); New York City, 3/17/1944
Seberg, Jean (actress); Marshalltown, Iowa **(1938-1979)**
Sedaka, Neil (singer); Brooklyn, N.Y., 3/13/1939
Seeger, Pete (folk singer); New York City, 5/3/1919
Segal, Erich (novelist); Brooklyn, N.Y., 6/16/1937
Segal, George (actor); New York City, 2/13/1936
Segovia, Andrés (guitarist); Linares, Spain **(1893-1987)**
Selleck, Tom (actor); Detroit, 1/29/1945
Sellars, Peter (theater director); Pittsburgh, Pa., 1958 (?)
Sellers, Peter (actor); Southsea, England **(1925-1980)**
Selznick, David O. (film producer); Pittsburgh **(1902-1965)**
Sendak, Maurice (Bernard) (children's book author and illustrator); Brooklyn, N.Y., 6/10/1928
Sennett, Mack (Michael Sinnott) (film producer); Richmond, Quebec, Canada **(1880-1960)**
Serkin, Peter (pianist); New York City, 7/24/1947
Serkin, Rudolf (pianist); Eger (Hungary) **(1903–1991)**
Serling, Rod (story writer); Syracuse, N.Y. **(1924-1975)**
Sessions, Roger (composer); Brooklyn, N.Y. **(1896-1985)**
Seurat, Georges (painter); Paris **(1859-1891)**
Seuss, Dr. (Theodor Seuss Geisel) (author and illustrator); Springfield, Mass., 3/2/1904
Sevareid, Eric (TV commentator); Velva, N.D., 11/26/1912
Severinsen, Doc (Carl) (band leader); Arlington, Ore., 7/7/1927
Sexton, Anne (poet); Newton, Mass. **(1928-1974)**
Seymour, Jane (actress); Wimbledon, England, 2/15/51
Shaffer, Peter (playwright); Liverpool, England, 5/15/1926
Shahn, Ben(jamin) (painter); Kaunas, Lithuania **(1898-1969)**
Shakespeare, William (dramatist); Stratford on Avon, England **(1564-1616)**
Shandling, Garry (comedian); Chicago, Ill., 1950
Shankar, Ravi (sitar player); Benares, India, 4/7/1920
Sharif, Omar (Michael Shalhoub) (actor); Alexandria, Egypt, 4/10/1932
Shatner, William (actor); Montreal, 3/22/1931
Shaw, Artie (Arthur Arshawsky) (band leader); New York City, 5/23/1910
Shaw, George Bernard (dramatist); Dublin, **(1856-1950)**
Shaw, Irwin (novelist); Brooklyn, N.Y., **(1913-1984)**
Shaw, Robert (actor); Lancashire, England **(1927-1978)**
Shaw, Robert (chorale conductor); Red Bluff, Calif., 4/30/1916
Shawn, Ted (Edwin Myers Shawn) (dancer,choreographer); Kansas City, Mo. **(1891-1972)**
Shearer, Moira (ballerina); Dunfermline, Scotland, 1/17/1926
Shearer, Norma (actress); Montreal, **(1902?-1983)**
Shearing, George (pianist); London, 8/13/1920
Sheen, Fulton J. (Peter Sheen) (Roman Catholic bishop); El Paso, Ill. **(1895-1979)**
Sheen, Martin (Ramon Estevez) (actor); Dayton, Ohio, 8/3/1940
Shelley, Percy Bysshe (poet); nr. Horsham, England **(1792-1822)**
Shepard, Sam (playwright); Ft. Sheridan, Ill. 11/5/1943
Shepherd, Cybill (actress); Memphis, Tenn., 2/18/50
Sheraton, Thomas (furniture designer); Stockton-on-Tees, England **(1751-1806)**
Sheridan, Ann (actress); Denton, Tex. **(1915-1967)**
Sheridan, Philip (army officer); Albany, N.Y. **(1831-1888)**
Sheridan, Richard Brinsley (dramatist); Dublin, **(1751-1816)**
Sherman, William Tecumseh (army officer); Lancaster, Ohio **(1820-1891)**
Sherwood, Robert Emmet (playwright); New Rochelle, N.Y.

(1896-1955)

Shevardnadze, Eduard Amvrosiyevich (Minister of Foreign Affairs, U.S.S.R.); Mamati, Georgia, U.S.S.R. 1/25/1928

Shields, Brooke (actress); New York City, 5/31/1965

Shire, Talia (Coppola) (actress) Lake Success, N.Y. 4/25/46(?)

Shirer, William L. (journalist and historian); Chicago, 2/23/1904

Shirley, Anne (actress); New York City, 4/17/18

Sholokhov, Mikhail (novelist); Veshenskaya, Russia **(1905-1984)**

Shore, Dinah (Frances Rose Shore) (singer); Winchester, Tenn., 3/1/1917(?)

Short, Bobby (Robert Waltrip Short) (singer and pianist); Danville, Ill., 9/15/1924

Shostakovich, Dmitri (composer); St. Petersburg, Russia **(1906-1975)**

Shriner, Herb (humorist,host); Toledo, Ohio **(1918-1970)**

Shriver, Maria (TV co-host); Chicago, 11/6/1955

Shriver, Sargent (Robert Sargent Shriver, Jr.) (business executive); Westminster, Md., 11/9/1915

Shulman, Max (novelist); St. Paul **(1919-1988)**

Sibelius, Jean (Johann Julius Christian Sibelius) (composer); Tavastehus (Finland) **(1865-1957)**

Siddons, Sarah (Sarah Kemble) (actress); Wales **(1755-1831)**

Sidney, Sylvia (actress); New York City, 8/8/1910

Siepi, Cesare (basso); Milan, Italy, 2/10/1923

Signoret, Simone (Simone Kaminker) (actress); Wiesbaden, Germany **(1921-1985)**

Sikorsky, Igor I. (inventor); Kiev, Russia **(1889-1972)**

Sills, Beverly (Belle Silverman) (soprano, opera director); Brooklyn, N.Y., 5/25/1929

Sills, Milton (actor); Chicago **(1882-1930)**

Silone, Ignazio (Secondo Tranquilli) (novelist); Pescina del Marsi, Italy **(1900-1978)**

Silverman, Fred (broadcasting executive); New York City, 9/13/1937

Silver, Ron (actor); New York City, 7/2/1946

Silvers, Phil (Philip Silversmith) (comedian); Brooklyn, N.Y. **(1912-1985)**

Sim, Alastair (actor); Edinburgh, Scotland **(1900-1976)**

Simenon, Georges (Georges Sim) (mystery writer); Liège, Belgium **(1903-1989)**

Simmons, Jean (actress); Crouch Hill, London, 1/31/1929

Simon, Carly (singer and songwriter); New York City, 6/25/1945

Simon, Neil (playwright); Bronx, N.Y., 7/4/1927

Simon, Norton (business executive); Portland, Ore., 2/5/1907

Simon, Paul (singer and songwriter); Newark, N.J., 11/5/1942

Simon, Simone (actress); Marseilles, France, 4/23/1914

Simone, Nina (Eunice Kathleen Waymoa) (singer and pianist); Tryon, N.C., 2/21/1933

Sinatra, Frank (Francis Albert) (singer and actor); Hoboken, N.J., 12/12/1915

Sinclair, Upton Beall (novelist); Baltimore **(1878-1968)**

Singer, Isaac Bashevis (novelist); Radzymin (Poland) **(1904–1991)**

Siqueiros, David (painter); Chihuahua, Mexico **(1896-1974)**

Sisley, Alfred (painter); Paris **(1839-1899)**

Sitting Bull (Prairie Sioux Indian Chief); on Grand River, S.D. **(c. 1835-1890)**

Skelton, Red (Richard) (comedian); Vincennes, Ind., 7/18/1913

Skinner, B(urrhus) F(rederic) (psychologist); Susquehanna, Pa. **(1904-1990)**

Skinner, Cornelia Otis (writer and actress); Chicago, **(1901-1979)**

Skinner, Otis (actor); Cambridge, Mass. **(1858-1942)**

Slatkin, Leonard (conductor); Los Angeles, 9/1/1944

Slezak, Walter (actor); Vienna **(1902-1983)**

Sloan, Alfred P., Jr. (industrialist); New Haven, Conn. **(1875-1965)**

Sloan, John (painter); Lock Haven, Pa. **(1871-1951)**

Smetana, Bedrich (composer); Litomysl (Czechoslovakia) **(1824-1884)**

Smith, Adam (economist); Kirkaldy, Scotland **(1723-1790)**

Smith, Alexis (actress); Penticon, Canada, 6/8/1921

Smith, Alfred Emanuel (politician); New York City **(1873-1944)**

Smith, Sir C. Aubrey (actor); London **(1863-1948)**

Smith, David (sculptor); Decatur, Ind. **(1906-1965)**

Smith, H. Allen (humorist); McLeansboro, Ill. **(1907-1976)**

Smith, Howard K. (TV commentator); Ferriday, La., 5/12/1914

Smith, Jaclyn (actress); Houston, 10/26/47

Smith, John (American colonist); Willoughby, Lincolnshire, England **(1580-1631)**

Smith, Joseph (religious leader); Sharon, Vt. **(1805-1844)**

Smith, Kate (Kathryn) (singer); Greenville, Va. **(1909-1986)**

Smith, Dame Maggie (actress); Ilford, England, 12/28/1934

Smith, Red (Walter) (sports columnist); Green Bay, Wis. **(1905-1982)**

Smits, Jimmy (actor); New York City, 7/9/58

Smollet, Tobias (novelist); Dalquhurn, Scotland **(1721-1771)**

Smothers, Dick (Richard) (comedian); Governors Island, New York City, 11/20/1939

Smothers, Tom (Thomas) (comedian); Governors Island, New York City, 2/2/1937

Snow, Lord (Charles Percy) (author); Leicester, England **(1905-1980)**

Snowdon, Earl of (Anthony Armstrong-Jones) (photographer); London, 3/7/1930

Snyder, Tom (TV personality); Milwaukee, 5/12/1936

Socrates (philosopher); Athens **(469-399** B.C.)

Solomon (King of Israel); Jerusalem (?) **(died c. 933** B.C.)

Solon (lawgiver); Salamis (Greece) **(638?-559** B.C.)

Solti, Sir Georg (conductor); Budapest, 10/21/1912

Solzhenitsyn, Aleksandr (novelist); Kislovodsk, Russia, 12/11/1918

Somers, Suzanne (Suzanne Mahoney) (actress); San Bruno, Calif., 10/16/1946

Somes, Michael (ballet dancer); Horsley, England, 1917

Sommer, Elke (Elke Schletz) (actress); Berlin, 11/5/1942

Sondheim, Stephen (composer); New York City, 3/22/1930

Sontag, Susan (author and film director); New York City, 1/28/1933

Sophocles (dramatist); nr. Athens **(496?-406** B.C.)

Sothern, Ann (Harriette Lake) (actress); Valley City, N.D., 1/22/1909

Soul, David (David Solberg) (actor); Chicago, 8/28/(?)

Sousa, John Philip (composer); Washington, D.C. **(1854-1932)**

Soyer, Raphael (painter); Borisoglebsk, Russia **(1899-1987)**

Spaak, Paul-Henri (statesman); Brussels **(1899-1972)**

Spacek, Sissy (Mary Elizabeth) (actress); Quitman, Tex., 12/25/1949

Spark, Muriel (novelist); Edinburgh, Scotland, 2/1/1918

Sparks, Ned (actor); Ontario **(1883-1957)**

Spector, Phil (rock producer); Bronx, N.Y., 12/25/1940

Spencer, Herbert (philosopher); Derby, England **(1820-1903)**

Spender, Stephen (poet); nr. London, 2/28/1909

Spengler, Oswald (philosopher); Blankenburg, (East Germany) **(1880-1936)**

Spenser, Edmund (poet); London **(1552?-1599)**

Spewack, Bella (playwright); Hungary **(1899-1990)**

Spiegel, Sam (producer); Jaroslaw (Poland) **(1901-1985)**

Spielberg, Steven (film director); Cincinnati, 12/18/1947

Spillane, Mickey (Frank Spillane) (mystery writer); Brooklyn, N.Y., 3/9/1918

Spinoza, Baruch (philosopher); Amsterdam (Netherlands) **(1632-1677)**

Spitalny, Phil (orchestra leader); **(1890-1970)**

Spivak, Lawrence (TV producer); Brooklyn, N.Y., 1900

Spock, Benjamin (pediatrician); New Haven, Conn., 5/2/1903

Springsteen, Bruce (singer and songwriter); Freehold, N.J., 9/23/1949

Sproul, Robert G. (educator); San Francisco **(1891-1975)**

Stack, Robert (actor); Los Angeles, 1/13/1919

Stafford, Jo (singer); Coalinga, Calif., 1918

Stalin, Joseph Vissarionovich (Iosif V. Dzhugashvili) (Soviet leader); nr. Tiflis, Russia **(1879-1953)**

Stalina, Svetlana Alliluyev a (Stalin's daughter); Moscow, 2/28/1926

Stallone, Sylvester (actor and writer); New York City, 7/6/1946

Stamp, Terrence (actor); London, 1938

Stander, Lionel (actor); New York City, 1/11/08

Standing, Sir Guy (actor); London **(1873-1937)**

Stang, Arnold (comedian); Chelsea, Mass., 1925

Stanislavski (Konstantin Sergeevich Alekseev) (stage producer); Moscow **(1863-1938)**

Stanley, Sir Henry Morton (John Rowlands) (explorer); Denbigh, Wales **(1841-1904)**

Stanley, Kim (Patricia Reid) (actress); Tularosa, N.M., 2/11/1925

Stans, Maurice H. (ex-Secretary of Commerce); Shakope, Minn., 3/22/1908

Stanton, Frank (broadcasting executive); Muskegon, Mich., 3/20/1908

Stanwyck, Barbara (Ruby Stevens) (actress); Brooklyn, N.Y. **(1907-1990)**

Stapleton, Jean (Jeanne Murray) (actress); New York City, 1/19/1923

Stapleton, Maureen (actress); Troy, N.Y., 6/21/1925

Starker, János(cellist);Budapest7/5/126

Starr, Kay (Starks) (singer); Dougherty, Okla., 7/21/1922

Starr, Ringo (Richard Starkey) (singer and songwriter); Liverpool, England, 7/7/1940

Stassen, Harold E. (ex-government official); West St. Paul, Minn., 4/13/1917

Steber, Eleanor (soprano); Wheeling, W. Va., 7/17/16

Steegmuller, Francis (biographer); New Haven, Conn., 7/3/1906

Steele, Tommy (singer); London, 12/17/1936

Stegner, Wallace (Earle) (novelist and critic); Lake Mills, Iowa, 2/18/1909

Steichen, Edward Jean (photographer, artist); Luxembourg **(1879-1973)**

Steiger, Rod (Rodney) (actor); Westhampton, N.Y., 4/14/1925

Stein, Gertrude (author); Allegheny, Pa. **(1874-1946)**

Steinbeck, John Ernst (novelist); Salinas, Calif. **(1902-1968)**

Steinberg, David (comedian); Winnipeg, Manitoba, Canada, 8/19/1942

Steinberg, William (conductor); Cologne, Germany **(1899-1978)**
Steinem, Gloria (feminist); Toledo, Ohio, 3/25/1934
Steinmetz, Charles (electrical engineer); Breslau (Poland) **(1865-1923)**
Stendhal (Marie Henri Beyle) (novelist); Grenoble, France **(1783-1842)**
Sterling, Jan (actress); New York City, 4/3/1923
Stern, Isaac (concert violinist); Kreminlecz, Russia, 7/21/1920
Sterne, Laurence (novelist); Clonmel, Ireland **(1713-1768)**
Stevens, Cat (Steven Georgiou) (singer and songwriter); London, 7/?/1947
Stevens, Connie (Concetta Ingolia) (singer); Brooklyn, N.Y., 8/8/1938
Stevens, George (film director); Oakland, Calif. **(1905-1975)**
Stevens, Risë (mezzo-soprano); New York City, 6/11/1913
Stevens, Stella (actress); Yazoo City, Miss., 10/1/1936
Stevenson, Adlai Ewing (statesman); Los Angeles **(1900-1965)**
Stevenson, McLean (actor); Bloomington, Ill., 11/14/1929(?)
Stevenson, Parker (actor); Philadelphia, Pa., 6/4/52
Stevenson, Robert Louis Balfour (novelist and poet); Edinburgh, Scotland **(1850-1894)**
Stewart, James (actor); Indiana, Pa., 5/20/1908
Stewart, Rod (Roderick David) (singer); London, 1/10/1945
Stickney, Dorothy (actress); Dickinson, N.D. 6/21/1903
Stieglitz, Alfred (photographer); Hoboken, N.J. **(1864-1946)**
Stiers, David Ogden (actor); Peoria, Ill., 10/31/42
Stiller, Jerry (actor); Brooklyn, N.Y., 6/8/29
Stills, Stephen (singer and songwriter); Dallas, 1/3/1945
Sting (Gordon Matthew Sumner) (singer and composer): Wallsend, England, 10/2/1951
Stockwell, Dean (actor); North Hollywood, Calif., 3/5/36
Stokes, Carl (TV newscaster); Cleveland, 6/21/1927
Stokowski, Leopold (conductor); London **(1882-1977)**
Stone, Edward Durell (architect); Fayetteville, Ark. **(1902-1978)**
Stone, I(sidor) F(einstein) (journalist); Philadelphia **(1907-1989)**
Stone, Ezra (actor and producer); New Bedford, Mass., 12/2/1917
Stone, Irving (Irving Tennenbaum) (novelist); San Francisco **(1903-1989)**
Stone, Lewis (actor); Worcester, Mass. **(1879-1953)**
Stone, Lucy (woman suffragist); nr. West Brookfield, Mass. **(1818-1893)**
Stone, Sly (Sylvester) (rock musician); 1944
Stoppard, Tom (Thomas Straussler) (playwright); Zlin, Czechoslovakia, 7/3/1937
Storm, Gale (actress); Bloomington, Tex., 1922
Stout, Rex (mystery writer); Noblesville, Ind. **(1886-1975)**
Stowe, Harriet Elizabeth Beecher (novelist); Litchfield, Conn. **(1811-1896)**
Stradivari, Antonio (violinmaker); Cremona (Italy) **(1644-1737)**
Straight, Beatrice (actress); Old Westbury, N.Y., 8/2/16(?)
Strasberg, Lee (stage director); Budanov, Austria **(1901-1982)**
Strasberg, Susan (actress); New York City, 5/22/1938
Stratas, Teresa (soprana); Toronto, Ont., Canada, 5/26/38
Straus, Oskar (composer); Vienna **(1870-1954)**
Strauss, Johann (composer); Vienna **(1825-1899)**
Strauss, Lewis L. (naval officer and scientist); Charleston, W. Va. **(1896-1974)**
Strauss, Peter (actor); New York City, 2/20/1947
Strauss, Richard (composer); Munich, Germany **(1864-1949)**
Stravinsky, Igor (composer); Orlenbaum, Russia **(1882-1971)**
Streep, Meryl (Mary Louise) (actress); Summit, N.J., 6/22/1949
Streisand, Barbra (singer and actress); Brooklyn, N.Y., 4/24/1942
Stritch, Elaine (actress); Detroit, 2/2/1925(?)
Struthers, Sally Ann (actress); Portland, Ore., 7/28/1948
Stuart, Gilbert Charles (painter); Rhode Island **(1755-1828)**
Stuart, James Ewell Brown (known as Jeb) (Confederate army officer); Patrick County, Va. **(1833-1864)**
Sturges, Preston (director, screenwriter, playwright); Chicago **(1898-1959)**
Stuyvesant, Peter (Governor of New Amsterdam); West Friesland (Netherlands) **(1592-1672)**
Styne, Jule (Julius Kerwin Stein) (songwriter); London, 12/31/1905
Styron, William (William Clark Styron, Jr.) (novelist); Newport News, Va., 6/11/1925
Sullavan, Margaret Brooke (actress); Norfolk, Va. **(1911-1960)**
Sullivan, Sir Arthur Seymour (composer); London **(1842-1900)**
Sullivan, Barry (Patrick Barry) (actor); New York City, 8/29/1912
Sullivan, Ed (columnist and TV personality); New York City **(1901-1974)**
Sullivan, Frank (Francis John) (humorist); Saratoga Springs, N.Y. **(1892-1976)**
Sullivan, Louis Henry (architect); Boston, Mass. **(1856-1924)**
Sulzberger, Arthur Ochs (newspaper publisher); New York City, 2/5/1926
Sumac, Yma (singer); Ichocan, Peru, 9/10/1927
Summer, Donna (La Donna Andrea Gaines) (singer); Boston,

12/31/1948
Summerville, Slim (George) (actor); Albuquerque, N.M. **(1892-1946)**
Sun Yat-sen (statesman); nr. Macao **(1866-1925)**
Susann, Jacqueline (novelist); Philadelphia **(1926?-1974)**
Susskind, David (TV producer); New York City **(1920-1987)**
Sutherland, Donald (actor); St. John, N.B., Canada, 7/17/34
Sutherland, Joan (soprano); Sydney, Australia, 11/7/1926
Suzuki, Pat (actress); Cressey, Calif., 1931
Swados, Elizabeth (composer, playwright); Buffalo, N.Y., 2/5/1951
Swanson, Gloria (Gloria May Josephine Svensson) (actress); Chicago, **(1899-1983)**
Swarthout, Gladys (soprano); Deepwater, Mo. **(1904-1969)**
Swayze, John Cameron (news commentator); Wichita, Kan., 4/4/1906
Swayze, Patrick (actor, dancer); Houston, Tex., 8/18/54
Swendenborg, Emanuel (scientist, philosopher, mystic); Stockholm **(1688-1772)**
Swift, Jonathan (satirist); Dublin **(1667-1745)**
Swinburne, Algernon Charles (poet); London **(1837-1909)**
Swit, Loretta (actress); Passaic, N.J., 11/4/37
Swope, Herbert Bayard (journalist); St. Louis **(1882-1958)**
Sydow, von, Max (Carl Adolf von Sydow) (actor); Lund, Sweden, 4/10/1929
Synge, John Millington (dramatist); nr. Dublin **(1871-1909)**
Szilard, Leo (physicist); Budapest **(1898-1964)**

T

Taft, Robert Alphonso (legislator); Cincinnati **(1889-1953)**
Tagore, Sir Rabindranath (poet); Calcutta **(1861-1941)**
Tallchief, Maria (ballerina); Fairfax, Okla., 1/24/1925
Talleyrand-Pèrigord, Charles Maurice de (statesman); Paris **(1754-1838)**
Talmadge, Norma (actress); Niagara Falls, N.Y. **(1897-1957)**
Talvela, Martti (basso); Hiitola, Finalnd **(1935-1989)**
Tamerlane (Timur) (Mongol conqueror); nr. Samarkand (U.S.S.R.) **(1336?-1405)**
Tamiroff, Akim (actor) Baku, Russia **(1899-1972)**
Tandy, Jessica (actress); London, 6/7/1909
Tarkington, (Newton) Booth (novelist); Indianapolis **(1869-1946)**
Tate, Allen (John Orley) (poet and critic); Winchester, Ky., **(1899-1979)**
Tate, Sharon (actress); Dallas **(1943-1969)**
Tati, Jacques (Jacques Tatischeff) (actor); Pecq, France **(1908-1982)**
Taylor, Deems (composer); New York City **(1885-1966)**
Taylor, Elizabeth (actress); London, 2/27/1932
Taylor, Estelle (actress); Wilmington, Del. **(1899-1958)**
Taylor, Harold (educator); Toronto, 9/28/1914
Taylor, James (singer and songwriter); Boston, 3/12/1948
Taylor, (Joseph) De ems (composer); New York City **(1885-1966)**
Taylor, Laurette (Laurette Cooney) (actress); New York City **(1884-1946)**
Taylor, Gen. Maxwell D. (former Army Chief of Staff); Keytesville, Mo **(1901-1987)**
Taylor, Robert (Spangler Arlington Brugh) (actor); Filley, Neb. **(1911-1969)**
Taylor, Rod (actor); Sydney, Australia, 1/11/1930
Tchaikovsky, Peter (Pëtr) Ilich (composer); Votkinsk, Russia **(1840-1893)**
Teasdale, Sara (poet); St. Louis **(1884-1933)**
Tebaldi, Renata (lyric soprano); Pesaro, Italy, 1/2/1922
Tecumseh (Shawnee Indian chief); nr. Springfield, Ohio **(1768?-1813)**
Te Kanawa, Kiri (soprano); Gisborne, New Zealand, 1946(?)
Telemann, Georg Philipp (composer); Magdeburg (East Germany) **(1681-1767)**
Teller, Edward (atomic physicist); Budapest, 1/15/1908
Temple, Shirley. *See* Black, Shirley Temple
Templeton, Alec Andrew (pianist, composer); Cardiff, Wales **(1910-1963)**
Tennille, Toni (singer); Montgomery, Ala., 5/8/43
Tennyson, Alfred (1st Baron Tennyson) (poet); Somersby, England **(1809-1892)**
Terhune, Albert Payson (novelist and journalist); Newark, N.J. **(1872-1942)**
Terkel, Studs (writer-interviewer); New York City, 5/16/1912
Terry, Ellen Alicia (actress); Coventry, England **(1848-1928)**
Terry-Thomas (Thomas Terry Hoar Stevens) (actor); London, 7/14/1911
Tesla, Nikola (electrical engineer and inventor); Smiljan (Yugoslavia) **(1856-1943)**
Thackeray, William Makepeace (novelist); Calcutta **(1811-1863)**
Thalberg, Irving G. (producer); Brooklyn, N.Y. **(1899-1936)**
Thant, U (U.N. statesman); Pantanaw (Burma) **(1909-1974)**
Tharp, Twyla (dancer and choreographer); Portland,

Ind., 7/1/1941(?)

Thatcher, Margaret (Prime Minister); Grantham, England, 10/13/1925

Thaxter, Phyllis (actress); Portland, Me., 1921

Thebom, Blanche (mezzo-soprano); Monessen, Pa., 9/19/1919

Theodorakis, Mikis (composer); Chios, Greece, 7/29/1925

Thicke, Alan (actor); Kirland Lake, Ont., Canada, 3/1/47

Thieu, Nguyen Van (ex-President of South Vietnam); Trithuy (Vietnam) 4/5/1923

Thomas, Danny (Amos Jacobs) (entertainer and TV producer); Deerfield, Mich. **(1912–1991)**

Thomas, Dylan Marials (poet); Carmarthenshire, Wales **(1914-1953)**

Thomas, Lowell (explorer, commentator); Woodington, Ohio **(1892-1981)**

Thomas, Marlo (actress); Detroit, 11/21/1943

Thomas, Michael Tilson (conductor); Hollywood, Calif., 12/21/1944

Thomas, Norman Mattoon (Socialist leader); Marion, Ohio **(1884-1968)**

Thomas, Philip Michael (actor); Columbus, Ohio, 5/26/49

Thomas, Richard (actor); New York City, 6/13/1951

Thompson, Dorothy (writer); Lancaster, N.Y. **(1894-1961)**

Thompson, Hunter (Stockton) (writer); Louisville, Ky. 7/18/1939

Thompson, Sada (actress); Des Moines, Iowa, 9/27/1929

Thomson, Virgil (Garnett) (composer); Kansas City, Mo. **(1896-1989)**

Thoreau, Henry David (naturalist and author); Concord, Mass. **(1817-1862)**

Thorndike, Dame Sybil (actress); Gainsborough, England **(1882-1976)**

Thurber, James Grover (author and cartoonist); Columbus, Ohio **(1894-1961)**

Tibbett, Lawrence (baritone); Bakersfield, Calif. **(1896-1960)**

Tiegs, Cheryl (model,actress); Minnesota, 9/25/47

Tierney, Gene (actress); Brooklyn, N.Y., 11/20/1920

Tiffin, Pamela (actress); Oklahoma City, 10/13/1942

Tillstrom, Burr (puppeteer); Chicago **(1917-1985)**

Tintoretto, Il (Jacopo Robusti) (painter); Venice **(1518-1594)**

Tiny Tim (Herbert Khaury) (entertainer); New York City, 1923(?)

Tiomkin, Dmitri (composer); St. Petersburg, Russia **(1899-1979)**

Titian (Tiziano Veĉelli) (painter); Pieve di Cadore (Italy) **(1477-1576)**

Tito (Josip Broz or Brozovich) (President of Yugoslavia); Croatia (Yugoslavia) **(1892-1980)**

Tocqueville, Alexis de (writer); Verneuil, France **(1805-1859)**

Todd, Ann (actress); Hartford, England, 1/24/09

Todd, Michael (producer); Minneapolis, Minn. **(1907-1958)**

Todd, Richard (actor); Dublin, Ireland, 6/11/19

Todd, Thelma (actress); Lawrence, Mass. **(1905-1935)**

Tolstoi, Count Leo (Lev) Nikolaevich (novelist); Tula Province, Russia **(1828-1910)**

Tomlin, Lily (comedienne); Detroit, 1939(?)

Tone, Franchot (actor); Niagara Falls, N.Y. **(1905-1968)**

Toomey, Regis (actor); Pittsburg, Pa., 8/13/02

Tormé, Mel (Melvin) (singer); Chicago, 9/13/1925

Torn, Rip (Elmore Torn, Jr.) (actor and director); Temple, Tex., 2/6/1931

Torquamada, Tomásde (Spanish Inquisitor); Vlladolid, Spain **(1420-1498)**

Toscanini, Arturo (orchestra conductor); Parma, Italy **(1867-1957)**

Toulouse-Lautrec (Henri Marie Raymond de Toulouse-Lautrec Monfa) (painter); Albi, France **(1864-1901)**

Toynbee, Arnold J. (historian); London **(1889-1975)**

Tracy, Lee (actor); Atlanta, Ga. **(1898-1968)**

Tracy, Spencer (actor); Milwaukee **(1900-1967)**

Traubel, Helen (Wagnerian soprano); St. Louis **(1903-1972)**

Travanti, Daniel J. (actor); Kenosha, Wis., 3/7/40

Travolta, John (actor); Englewood, N.J., 2/18/1954

Treacher, Arthur (actor); Brighton, England **(1894-1975)**

Tree, Sir Herbert Beerbolm (actor-manager); London **(1853-1917)**

Trevor, Claire (actress); New York City, 1911

Trigère, (Pauline (fashion designer); Paris, 11/4/1912

Trilling, Lionel (author and educator); New York City **(1905-1975)**

Trotsky, Leon (Lev Davidovich Bronstein) (statesman); Elisavetgrad, Russia **(1879-1940)**

Troyanos, Tatiana (mezzo-soprano); New York City, 9/12/38

Trudeau, Garry (cartoonist); New York City, 1948

Trudeau, Pierre Elliott (former Prime Minister); Montreal, 10/18/1919

Truffaut, François (film director); Paris **(1932-1984)**

Trujillo y Molina, Rafael Leonidas (Dominican Republic dictator); San Cristóbal, Dominican Republic **(1891-1961)**

Truman, Margaret (author); Independence, Mo., 2/17/1924

Tryon, Thomas (actor and novelist); Hartford, Conn. **(1926–1991)**

Tsiolkovsky, Konstantin E. (father of cosmonautics); Izhevskoye, Russia **(1857-1935)**

Tuchman, Barbara (Wertheim) (historian, author); New York City **(1912-1989)**

Tucker, Forrest (actor); Plainfield, Ind. **(1919-1986)**

Tucker, Richard (tenor); New York City **(1914-1975)**

Tucker, Sophie (Sophie Abuza) (singer); Europe **(1884?-1966)**

Tudor, Antony (choreographer); London **(1909-1987)**

Tune, Tommy (dancer-choreographer); Wichita Falls, Tex., 2/28/1939

Turgenev, Ivan Sergeevich (novelist); Orel, Russia **(1818-18 83)**

Turner, Ike (singer); Clarksdale, Miss., 11/?/1931

Turner, Joseph M.W. (painter); London **(1775-1851)**

Turner, Kathleen (actress); Springfield, Mo., 1956 (?)

Turner, Lana (Julia Jean Mildred Frances Turner) (actress); Wallace, Idaho, 2/8/1920

Turner, Nat (civil rights leader); Southampton County, Va. **(1800-1831)**

Turner, Tina (Annie Mae Bullock) (singer); nr. Brownsville, Tex., 11/25/1940(?)

Turpin, Ben (comedian); New Orleans **(1874-1940)**

Tushingham, Rita (actress); Liverpool, England, 3/14/1942

Twain, Mark (Samuel Langhorne Clemens) (author); Florida, Mo. **(1835-1910)**

Tweed, William Marcy (politician); New York City **(1823-1878)**

Twiggy (Leslie Hornby) (model); London, 9/19/1949

Twining, Gen. Nathan F. (former Air Force Chief of Staff); Monroe, Wis. **(1897-1982)**

Twitty, Conway (Harold Lloyd Jenkins) (singer and guitarist); Friars Point, Miss., 9/1/1933

Tyson, Cicely (actress); New York City, 12/19/1939(?)

U

Udall, Stewart L. (ex-Secretary of the Interior); St. Johns, Ariz., 1/31/1920

Uggams, Leslie (singer and actress); New York City, 5/25/1943

Ulanova, Galina (ballerina); St. Petersburg, Russia, 1/10/1910

Ullman, Tracey (actress, singer); Slough, England, 12/30/59

Ullmann, Liv (actress); Tokyo, 12/16/1939

Ulric, Lenore (actress); New Ulm, Minn. **(1894-1970)**

Untermeyer, Louis (anthologist and poet); New York City **(1885-1977)**

Updike, John (novelist); Shillington, Pa., 3/18/1932

Urey, Harold C. (physicist); Walkerton, Ind. **(1893-1981)**

Uris, Leon (novelist); Baltimore, 8/3/1924

Ustinov, Peter (actor and producer); London, 4/16/1921

Utrillo, Maurice (painter); Paris **(1883-1955)**

V

Vaccaro, Brenda (actress); Brooklyn, N.Y., 11/18/1939

Vadim, Roger (Roger Vadim Plemiannikov) (film director); Paris, 1/26/1928

Valentine, Karen (actress); Santa Rosa, Calif., 1947

Valentino, Rudolph (Rodolpho d'Antonguolla) (actor); Castellaneta, Italy **(1895-1926)**

Valentino (Valentino Garavani) (fashion designer); nr. Milan, Italy, 5/11/1932

Vallee, Rudy (Hubert Prior Rudy Vallée) (band leader and singer); Island Pond, Vt. **(1901-1986)**

Valli, Frankie (Frank Castellaccio) (singer); Newark, N.J., 5/3/1937

Van Allen, James Alfred (space physicist); Mt. Pleasant, Iowa, 9/7/1914

Van Buren, Abigail (Mrs. Morton Phillips) (columnist); Sioux City, Iowa, 7/4/1918

Vance, Vivian (actress); Cherryvale, Kan. **(1912-1979)**

Vanderbilt, Alfred G. (sportsman); London, 9/22/1912

Vanderbilt, Cornelius (financier); Port Richmond, N.Y. **(1794-1877)**

Vanderbilt, Gloria (fashion designer) New York City, 2/20/1924

Van Doren, Carl (writer and educator); Hope, Ill. **(1885-1950)**

Van Doren, Mamie (actress); Rowena, S.D., 2/6/1933

Van Dyke, Dick (actor); West Plains, Mo., 12/13/1925

Vandyke (or Van Dyck), Sir Anthony (painter); Antwerp (Belgium) **(1599-1641)**

Van Eyck, Jan (painter); Maeseyck (Belgium) **(c.1390-1441)**

Van Fleet, Jo (actress); Oakland, Calif., 12/30/19

van Gogh, Vincent (painter); Groot Zundert, Brabant **(1853-1890)**

van Hamel, Martine (ballerina); Brussels, 11/16/1945

Van Heusen, Jimmy (Edward Chester Babcock) (songwriter); Syracuse, N.Y. **(1913-1990)**

Van Patten, Dick (actor); Richmond Hill, N.Y., 12/9/28

Van Peebles, Melvin (playwright); Chicago, 9/21/1932

Vaughan, Sarah (singer); Newark, N.J. **(1924-1990)**

Vaughan Williams, Ralph (composer); Down Ampney, England **(1872-1958)**

Vaughn, Robert (actor); New York City, 11/22/1932

Veidt, Conrad (actor); Potsdam, Germany **(1893-1943)**

Velázquez, Diego Rodriguez de Silva y (painter); Seville, Spain **(1599-1660)**

Velez, Lupe (Guadelupe Velez de Villalobos) (actress); San Luis Potosi, Mexico **(1908-1944)**

Venturi, Robert (Charles) (architect); Philadelphia, 6/25/1925
Verdi, Giuseppe (composer); Roncole (Italy) **(1813-1901)**
Verdon, Gwen (actress); Culver City, Calif., 1/13/1925
Vereen, Ben (actor and singer); Miami, Fla., 10/10/1946
Vermeer, Jan (or Jan van der Meer van Delft) (painter); Delft (Netherlands) **(1632-1675)**
Verne, Jules (author); Nantes, France **(1828-1905)**
Veronese, Paolo (Paolo Cagliari) (painter); Verona **(1528-1588)**
Verrazano, Giovanni da (navigator); Florence (Italy) **(1485?-1528)**
Verrett, Shirley (mezzo-soprano); New Orleans, 5/31/1933
Vesalius, Andreas (anatomist); Brussels, Belgium **(1515-1564)**
Vespucci, Amerigo (navigator); Florence (Italy) **(1454-1512)**
Vickers, Jon (tenor); Prince Albert, Sask, Canada, 10/29/1926
Vico, Giovanni Battista (philosopher); Naples, Italy **(1668-1744)**
Vidal, Gore (novelist); West Point, N.Y., 10/3/1925
Vidor, King (film director and producer); Galveston, Tex. **(1895-1982)**
Vigoda, Abe (actor); New York City, 2/24/21
Villa, Pancho (Doroteo Arango) (revolutionary); Hacienda de Rio Grande, San Juan del Rio, Meixco **(1877-1923)**
Villella, Edward (ballet dancer); Bayside, Queens, N.Y., 10/1/1936
Villon, François (François de Montcorbier) (poet); Paris **(1431-1463)**
Vincent, Helen (actress); Beaumont, Tex., 9/17/07
Vinton, Bobby (singer); Canonsburg, Pa., 4/16/1935(?)
Virgil (or Vergil) (Publius Vergilius Maro) (poet); nr. Mantua (Italy) **(70-19 B.C.)**
Vishnevskaya, Galina (soprano); Leningrad, 10/25/1926
Vivaldi, Antonio (composer); Venice **(1678-1741)**
Vlaminck, Maurice de (painter); Paris **(1876-1958)**
Voight, Jon (actor); Yonkers, N.Y., 12/29/1938
Volta, Alessandro (scientist); Como, Italy **(1745-1827)**
Voltaire (François Marie-Arouet) (author); Paris **(1694-1778)**
von Aroldingen, Karin (Karin Awny Hannelore Reinbold von Aroedingen and Eltzinger) (ballet dancer); Greiz (East Germany) 7/9/1941
von Braun, Wernher (rocket scientist); Wirsitz, Germany **(1912-1977)**
von Furstenberg, Betsy (Elizabeth Caroline Maria Agatha Felicitas Therese von Furstenberg-Hedringen) (actress); Nelheim-Heusen, Germany, 8/16/1935
von Fürstenberg, Diane (Diane Simone Michelle Halfin) (fashion designer); Brussels, 12/31/1946
von Hindenburg, Paul (statesman); Posen (Poland) **(1847-1934)**
von Karajan, Herbert (conductor); Salzburg (Austria) **(1908-1989)**
Vonnegut, Kurt, Jr. (novelist); Indianapolis, 11/11/1922
Von Stade, Frederica (mezzo-soprano); Somerville, N.J., 1945
Von Stroheim, Erich Oswald Hans Carl Maria von Nordenwall (film actor and director); Vienna **(1885-1957)**
Von Zell, Harry (announcer); Indianapolis, Ind. **(1906-1981)**
Vreeland, Diana (Diana Da Iziel) (fashion journalist and museum consultant); Paris **(1903?-1989)**

W

Wagner, Lindsay (actress); Los Angeles, 6/22/1949
Wagner, Robert (actor); Detroit, 2/10/1930
Wagner, Robert F. (ex-Mayor of New York City); New York City **(1910-1991)**
Wagner, Wilhelm Richard (composer); Leipzig (East Germany) **(1813-1883)**
Waldheim, Kurt (ex-U.N. Secretary-General); St. Andrae-Wörden, Austria, 12/21/1918
Walker, Clint (actor); Hartford, Ill., 5/30/1927
Walker, Nancy (Ann Myrtle Swoyer); (actress and comedienne); Philadelphia, 5/10/1922
Wallace, DeWitt (publisher); St. Paul **(1889-1981)**
Wallace, George C. (ex-govenor); Clio, Ala. 8/25/19
Wallace, Irving (novelist); Chicago **(1916-1990)**
Wallace, Mike (Myron Wallace) (TV interviewer and commentator); Brookline, Mass., 5/9/1918
Wallach, Eli (actor); Brooklyn, N.Y., 12/7/1915
Wallenstein, Alfred (conductor); Chicago **(1898-1983)**
Waller, Thomas "Fats" (pianist); New York City **(1904-1943)**
Wallis, Hal (film producer); Chicago **(1899-1986)**
Walpole, Horace (statesman and novelist); London **(1717-1797)**
Waltari, Mika (novelist); Helsinki, Finland, **(1903-1979)**
Walter, Bruno (Bruno Walter Schlesinger) (orchestra conductor); Berlin **(1876-1962)**
Walters, Barbara (TV commentator); Boston, 9/25/1931
Walton, Izaak (author); Stafford, England **(1593-1683)**
Wambaugh, Joseph (author and screenwriter); East Pittsburgh, Pa., 1/22/1937
Wanamaker, John (merchant); Philadelphia **(1838-1922)**
Wanamaker, Sam (actor,director); Chicago, 6/14/19
Ward, Barbara (economist); York, England **(1914-1981)**

Warhol, Andy (artist and producer); Pennsylvania **(1928(?)-1987)**
Waring, Fred (band leader); Tyrone, Pa., **(1900-1984)**
Warner, H. B. (Henry Bryan Warner Lickford) (actor); London **(1876-1958)**
Warren, Lesley Ann (actress); New York City, 8/16/46
Warren, Robert Penn (novelist); Guthrie, Ky. **(1905-1989)**
Warrick, Ruth (actress) St. Joseph, Mo., 6/29/15
Warwick, Dionne (singer); East Orange, N.J., 1941
Washington, Booker Taliaferro (educator); Franklin County, Va. **(1856-1915)**
Waters, Ethel (actr ess and singer); Chester, Pa. **(1896-1977)**
Waters, Muddy (McKinley Morganfield) (singer and guitarist); Rolling Fork, Miss. **(1915-1983)**
Waterson, Sam (actor); Cambridge, Mass., 11/15/1940
Watson, Thomas John (industrialist); Campbell, N.Y. **(1874-1956)**
Watt, James (inventor); Greenock, Scotland **(1736-1819)**
Watteau, Jean-Antoine (painter); Valanciennes, France **(1684-1721)**
Wattleton, Faye (family planning advocate); St. Louis, Mo., 7/8/43
Watts, André (concert pianist); Nuremberg, Germany, 6/20/1946
Waugh, Alec (Alexander Raban Waugh) (novelist); London **(1898-1981)**
Waugh, Evelyn (satirist); London **(1903-1966)**
Wayne, Anthony (military officer); Waynesboro (family farm), nr. Paoli, Pa. **(1745-1796)**
Wayne, David (David McMeekan); (actor); Traverse City, Mich., 1/30/1914
Wayne, John (Marion Michael Morrison) (actor); Winterset, Iowa, **(1907-1979)**
Weaver, Dennis (actor); Joplin, Mo., 6/4/1925
Weaver, Fritz (actor); Pittsburgh, Pa., 1/19/26
Weaver, Sigourney (actress); New York City, 10/8/1949
Webb, Clifton (Webb Parmelee Hollenbeck) (actor); Indianapolis **(1893-1966)**
Webb, Jack (film actor and producer); Santa Monica, Calif. **(1920-1982)**
Weber, Karl Maria Friedrich Ernst von (composer); nr. Lübeck (Germany) **(1786-1826)**
Webster, Daniel (statesman); Salisbury, N.H. **(1782-1852)**
Webster, Margaret (producer, director, actress); New York City **(1905-1973)**
Webster, Noah (lexicographer); West Hartford, Conn. **(1758-1843)**
Weill, Kurt (composer); Dessau, (East Germany) **(1900-1950)**
Weir, Peter (film director); Sydney, Australia, 8/21/1944
Weizmann, Chaim (statesman); Grodno Province, Russia **(1874-1952)**
Welch, Raquel (Raquel Tejada) (actress); Chicago, 9/5/1942
Weld, Tuesday (Susan) (actress); New York City, 8/27/1943
Welk, Lawrence (band leader); Strasburg, N.D., 3/11/1903
Welles, Orson (actor and producer); Kenosha, Wis. **(1915-1985)**
Wellington, Duke of (Arthur Wellesley) (statesman); Ireland **(1769-1852)**
Wells, H(erbert) G(eorge) (author); Bromley, England **(1866-1946)**
Welty, Eudora (novelist); Jackson, Miss., 4/13/1909
Werfel, Franz (novelist); Prague **(1890-1945)**
Werner, Oskar (Josef Schliessmayer) (film actor and director); Vienna **(1922-1984)**
Wertmuller, Lina (film director); Rome, 1926(?)
Wesley, John (religious leader); Epworth Rectory, Lincolnshire, England **(1703-1791)**
West, Dame Rebecca (Cicily Fairfield); (novelist); County Kerry, Ireland **(1892-1983)**
West, Jessamyn (novelist); nr. North Vernon, Ind. **(1902-1984)**
West, Mae (actress); Brooklyn, N.Y. **(1893-1980)**
West, Nathanael (Nathan Weinstein) (novelist); New York City **(1902-1940)**
Westheimer, Ruth (Karola Ruth Siegel) (psychologist, author, broadcaster); Frankfurt, Germany, 1928
Westinghouse, George (inventor); Central Bridge, N.Y. **(1846-1914)**
Westmoreland, William Childs (ex-Army Chief of Staff); Saxon, S.C., 3/26/1914
Wharton, Edith Newbold (née Jones) (novelist); New York City **(1862-1937)**
Wheeler, Bert (Albert Jerome Wheeler) (comedian); Paterson, N.J. **(1895-1968)**
Whistler, James Abbott McNeill (painter and etcher); Lowell, Mass. **(1834-1903)**
White, Betty (actress); Oak Park, Ill., 1/17/24(?)
White, E(lwyn) B(rooks) (author); Mt. Vernon, N.Y. **(1899-1985)**
White, Pearl (actress); Green Ridge, Mo. **(1889-1938)**
White, Stanford (architect); New York City **(1853-1906)**
White, Theodore H. (historian); Boston **(1915-1986)**
White, Vanna (TV personality); Conway, S.C., 2/18/1957
White, William Allen (journalist); Emporia, Kan. **(1868-1944)**
Whitehead, Alfred North (mathematician and philosopher); Isle of Thanet, England **(1861-1947)**

Whiteman, Paul (band leader); Denver **(1891-1967)**
Whiting, Margaret (singer, actress); Detroit, Mich., 7/22/24
Whitman, Walt (Walter) (poet); West Hills, N.Y. **(1819-1892)**
Whitmore, James (actor); White Plains, N.Y., 10/1/1921
Whitney, Cornelius Vanderbilt (sportsman); New York City, 2/20/1899
Whitney, Eli (inventor); Westboro, Mass. **(1765-1825)**
Whitney, John Hay (publisher); Ellsworth, Me. **(1904-1982)**
Whittier, John Greenleaf (poet); Haverhill, Mass. **(1807-1892)**
Whitty, Dame May (actr ess); Liverpool, England **(1865-1948)**
Widmark, Richard (actor); Sunrise, Minn., 12/26/1914
Wiesel, Elie (Eliezer) (author); Signet, Romania, 9/30/1928
Wilde, Cornel (film actor and producer); New York City **(1915-1989)**
Wilde, Oscar Fingal O'Flahertie Wills (author); Dublin **(1854-1900)**
Wilder, Billy (film producer and director); Vienna, 6/22/1906
Wilder, Gene (Jerome Silberman) (actor); Milwaukee, 6/11/1935(?)
Wilder, Thornton (author); Madison, Wis. **(1897-1975)**
Wilding, Michael (actor); Westcliff, England **(1912-1979)**
Wilkins, Roy (civil rights leader); St. Louis **(1901-1981)**
Williams, Andy (singer); Wall Lake, Iowa, 12/3/1930
Williams, Billy Dee (actor); New York City, 4/6/1937
Williams, Cindy (actress); Van Nuys, Calif., 8/22/(?)
Williams, Edward Bennett (lawyer); Hartford, Conn. **(1920-1988)**
Williams, Emlyn (actor and playwright); Mostyn, Wales **(1905-1987)**
Williams, Esther (actress); Los Angeles, 8/8/1923
Williams, Gluyas (cartoonist); San Francisco **(1888-1982)**
Williams, Hank, Sr. (Hiram King Williams) (singer); Georgiana, Ala. **(1923-1953)**
Williams, Joe (singer); Cordele, Ga., 12/12/1918
Williams, Paul (singer, composer, actor); Omaha, Neb., 9/19/1940
Williams, Robin (comedian); Chicago, 7/7/1952
Williams, Roger (clergyman); London (1603?-1683)
Williams, Tennessee (Thomas L. Williams) (playwright); Columbus, Miss. **(1911-1983)**
Williams, William Carlos (physician and poet); Rutherford, N.J. **(1883-1963)**
Williamson, Nicol (actor); Hamilton, Scotland, 9/14/38
Willkie, Wendell Lewis (lawyer); Elwood, Ind. **(1892-1944)**
Willis, Bruce (actor); Germany, 3/19/1955
Willson, Meredith (composer); Mason City, Iowa **(1902-1984)**
Wilson, August (poet, writer, playwright); Pittsburgh, Pa., 1945
Wilson, Don (radio and TV announcer); Lincoln, Neb. **(1900-1982)**
Wilson, Dooley (actor, musician); Tyler, Tex. **(1894-1953)**
Wilson, Edmund (literary critic and author); Red Bank, N.J. **(1895-1972)**
Wilson, Flip (Clerow) (comedian); Jersey City, N.J., 12/8/1933
Wilson, Harold (ex-Prime Minister); Huddersfield, England, 3/11/1916
Wilson, Marie (actress); Anaheim, Calif. **(1916-1972)**
Wilson, Nancy (singer); Chillicothe, Ohio, 2/20/1937
Wilson, Sloan (novelist); Norwalk, Conn., 5/8/1920
Winchell, Walter (columnist); New York City **(1897-1972)**
Windsor, Duchess of (Bessie Wallis Warfield); Blue Ridge Summit, Pa. **(1896-1986)**
Windsor, Duke of (formerly King Edward VIII of England); Richmond Park, England **(1894-1972)**
Winfrey, Oprah (talk show hostess, actress); Kosciuska, Miss., 1/29/1954
Winger, Debra (actress); Cleveland, Ohio, 1955
Winkler, Henry (actor); New York City, 10/30/1945
Winninger, Charles (actor); Athen, Wis. **(1884-1969)**
Winningham, Mare (actress); Phoenix, Ariz., 5/16/1959
Winter, Johnny (guitarist); Leland, Miss., 2/23/1944
Winters, Jonathan (comedian); Dayton, Ohio, 11/11/1925
Winters, Shelley (Shirley Schrift) (actress); East St. Louis, Ill., 8/18/1922
Winthrop, John (first Governor, Massachusetts Bay Colony); Suffolk, England **(1588-1649)**
Wise, Stephen Samuel (rabbi); Budapest **(1874-1949)**
Withers, Jane (actress); Atlanta, 1927
Wittgenstein, Ludwig (Josef Johann) (philosopher); Vienna **(1889-1951)**
Wodehouse, P(elham) G(renville) (novelist); Guildford, England **(1881-1975)**
Wolfe, Thomas Clayton (novelist); Asheville, N.C. **(1900-1938)**
Wolfe, Tom (journalist); Richmond, Va., 3/2/1931
Wolsey, Thomas (prelate and statesman); Ipswich, England (1475?-1530)
Wonder, Stevie (Steveland Judkins, later Steveland Morris) (singer and songwriter); Saginaw, Mich., 5/13/1950
Wong, Anna May (Lu Tsong Wong) (actress); Los Angeles **(1907-1961)**
Wood, Grant (painter); Anamosa, Iowa **(1892-1942)**
Wood, Natalie (Natasha Gurdin) (film actress); San Francisco **(1938-1981)**
Wood, Peggy (Margaret) (actress); Brooklyn, N.Y. **(1892-1978)**
Woodhouse, Barbara (Blackburn) (dog trainer, author, TV personality); Rathfarnham, Ireland **(1910-1988)**
Woodward, Edward (actor); Croydon, England, 6/1/30
Woodward, Joanne (film actress); Thomasville, Ga., 2/27/1930
Woolf, Adeline Virginia (née Stephens) (novelist); London **(1882-1941)**
Woollcott, Alexander (author-critic); Phalanx, N.J. **(1887-1943)**
Woolley, Monty (Edgar Montillion Woolley) (actor); New York City **(1888-1963)**
Woolworth, Frank (merchant); Rodman, N.Y. **(1852-1919)**
Wopat, Tom (actor); Lodi, Wis., 9/9/50
Wordsworth, William (poet); Cockermouth, England **(1770-1850)**
Wouk, Herman (novelist); New York City, 5/27/1915
Wray, Fay (actress); Alberta, Canada, 1907
Wren, Sir Christopher (architect); East Knoyle, England **(1632-1723)**
Wright, Frank Lloyd (architect); Richland Center, Wis. **(1869-1959)**
Wright, Martha (singer); Seattle, Wash., 3/23/26
Wright, Orville (inventor); Dayton, Ohio **(1871-1948)**
Wright, Richard (novelist); nr. Natchez, Miss. **(1908-1960)**
Wright, Teresa (actress); New York City, 10/27/1918
Wright, Wilbur (inventor); Millvillle, Ind. **(1867-1912)**
Wyatt, Jane (film actress); Campgaw, N.J., 8/12/1912
Wycliffe, John (church reformer); Hipswell, England **(1320-1384)**
Wyeth, Andrew (painter); Chadds Ford, Pa., 7/12/1917
Wyler, William (film director); Mulhouse (France), **(1902-1981)**
Wyman, Jane (Sarah Jane Fulks) (actress); St. Joseph, Mo., 1/4/1914
Wynette, Tammy (Wynette Pugh) (singer); Tupelo, Miss. 5/5/1942
Wynn, Ed (Isaiah Edwin Leopold) (comedian); Philadelphia **(1886-1966)**
Wynn, Keenan (actor); New York City **(1916-1986)**
Wynter, Dana (actress); London, 6/8/1930

X

Xavier, St. Francis (Jesuit missionary); Pamplona, Navarre (Spain) **(1506-1552)**
Xenophon (soldier, historian and essayist): Athens, Greece, **(434(?)-355(?)** B.C.)
Xerxes, the Great (king): Persian Empire, **(519(?)-465** B.C.)

Y

Yeats, William Butler (poet); nr. Dublin **(1865-1939)**
Yevtushenko, Yevgeny (poet); Zima, U.S.S.R., 7/18/1933
York, Alvin Cullun (Sergeant York, World War I hero): Tennessee **(1887-1964)**
York, Michael (actor); Fulmer, England, 3/27/1942
York, Susannah (Fletcher) (actress); London, 1/9/1942
Yorty, Samuel W. (ex-Mayor of Los Angeles); Lincoln, Neb., 10/1/1909
Yothers, Tina (actress); Whittier, Calif., 5/5/73
Young, Alan (actor); North Shield, England, 11/19/1919
Young, Brigham (religi ous leader); Whitingham, Vt. **(1801-1877)**
Young, Gig (Byron Barr) (actor); St. Cloud, Minn. **(1917-1978)**
Young, Loretta (Gretchen Young) (actress); Salt Lake City, Utah, 1/6/1913
Young, Neil (singer and songwriter); Toronto, 11/12/1945
Young, Robert (actor); Chicago, 2/22/1907
Young, Roland (actor); London **(1887-1953)**
Youngman, Henny (comedian); Liverpool, England, 1/12/1906

Z

Zanuck, Darryl F. (film producer); Wahoo, Neb. **(1902-1979)**
Zappa, Frank (Francis Vincent Zappa, Jr.) (singer and songwriter); Baltimore, 12/21/1940
Zeffirelli, Franco (director); Florence, Italy, 2/12/1923
Zenger, John Peter (printer and journalist); Germany, **(1697-1746)**
Zhou Enlai (Premier); Hualyin, China **(1898-1976)**
Ziegfeld, Florenz (theatrical producer); Chicago **(1869-1932)**
Zimbalist, Efrem (concert violinist); Rostov-on-Don, Russia **(1889-1985)**
Zimbalist, Efrem, Jr. (actor); New York City, 11/30/1923
Zimbalist, Stephanie (actress); New York City, 10/8/56
Zola, Emile (novelist); Paris **(1840-1902)**
Zoroaster (religious leader); Persian Empire **(c. 6th century** B.C.)
Zukerman, Pinchas (violinist); Tel Aviv, Israel 7/16/1948
Zukor, Adolph (film executive); Risce, Hungary **(1873-1976)**
Zweig, Stefan (author); Vienna **(1881-1942)**
Zwingli, Huldrych (humanist); Wildaus, Switzerland **(1484-1531)**

AWARDS

Nobel Prizes

The Nobel prizes are awarded under the will of Alfred Bernhard Nobel, Swedish chemist and engineer, who died in 1896. The interest of the fund is divided annually among the persons who have made the most outstanding contributions in the fields of physics, chemistry, and physiology or medicine, who have produced the most distinguished literary work of an idealist tendency, and who have contributed most toward world peace.

In 1968, a Nobel Prize of economic sciences was established by Riksbank, the Swedish bank, in celebration of its 300th anniversary. The prize was awarded for the first time in 1969.

The prizes for physics and chemistry are awarded by the Swedish Academy of Science in Stockholm, the one for physiology or medicine by the Caroline Medical Institute in Stockholm, that for literature by the academy in Stockholm, and that for peace by a committee of five elected by the Norwegian Storting. The distribution of prizes was begun on December 10, 1901, the anniversary of Nobel's death. The amount of each prize varies with the income from the fund and currently is about $190,000. No Nobel prizes were awarded for 1940, 1941, and 1942; prizes for Literature were not awarded for 1914, 1918, and 1943.

PEACE

1901	Henri Dunant (Switzerland); Frederick Passy (France)
1902	Elie Ducommun and Albert Gobat (Switzerland)
1903	Sir William R. Cremer (England)
1904	Institut de Droit International (Belgium)
1905	Bertha von Suttner (Austria)
1906	Theodore Roosevelt (U.S.)
1907	Ernesto T. Moneta (Italy) and Louis Renault (France)
1908	Klas P. Arnoldson (Sweden) and Frederik Bajer (Denmark)
1909	Auguste M. F. Beernaert (Belgium) and Baron Paul H. B. B. d'Estournelles de Constant de Rebecque (France)
1910	Bureau International Permanent de la Paix (Switzerland)
1911	Tobias M. C. Asser (Holland) and Alfred H. Fried (Austria)
1912	Elihu Root (U.S.)
1913	Henri La Fontaine (Belgium)
1915	No award
1916	No award
1917	International Red Cross
1919	Woodrow Wilson (U.S.)
1920	Léon Bourgeois (France)
1921	Karl H. Branting (Sweden) and Christian L. Lange (Norway)
1922	Fridtjof Nansen (Norway)
1923	No award
1924	No award
1925	Sir Austen Chamberlain (England) and Charles G. Dawes (U.S.)
1926	Aristide Briand (France) and Gustav Stresemann (Germany)
1927	Ferdinand Buisson (France) and Ludwig Quidde (Germany)
1928	No award
1929	Frank B. Kellogg (U.S.)
1930	Lars O. J. Söderblom (Sweden)
1931	Jane Addams and Nicholas M. Butler (U.S.)
1932	No award
1933	Sir Norman Angell (England)
1934	Arthur Henderson (England)
1935	Karl von Ossietzky (Germany)
1936	Carlos de S. Lamas (Argentina)
1937	Lord Cecil of Chelwood (England)
1938	Office International Nansen pour les Réfugiés (Switzerland)
1939	No award
1944	International Red Cross
1945	Cordell Hull (U.S.)
1946	Emily G. Balch and John R. Mott (U.S.)
1947	American Friends Service Committee (U.S.) and British Society of Friends' Service Council (England)
1948	No award
1949	Lord John Boyd Orr (Scotland)
1950	Ralph J. Bunche (U.S.)
1951	Léon Jouhaux (France)
1952	Albert Schweitzer (French Equatorial Africa)
1953	George C. Marshall (U.S.)
1954	Office of U.N. High Commissioner for Refugees
1955	No award
1956	No award
1957	Lester B. Pearson (Canada)
1958	Rev. Dominique Georges Henri Pire (Belgium)
1959	Philip John Noel-Baker (England)
1960	Albert John Luthuli (South Africa)
1961	Dag Hammarskjöld (Sweden)
1962	Linus Pauling (U.S.)
1963	Intl. Comm. of Red Cross; League of Red Cross Societies (both Geneva)
1964	Rev. Dr. Martin Luther King, Jr. (U.S.)
1965	UNICEF (United Nations Children's Fund)
1966	No award
1967	No award
1968	René Cassin (France)
1969	International Labour Organization
1970	Norman E. Borlaug (U.S.)
1971	Willy Brandt (West Germany)
1972	No award
1973	Henry A. Kissinger (U.S.); Le Duc Tho (North Vietnam)[1]
1974	Eisaku Sato (Japan); Sean MacBride (Ireland)
1975	Andrei D. Sakharov (U.S.S.R.)
1976	Mairead Corrigan and Betty Williams (both Northern Ireland)
1977	Amnesty International
1978	Menachem Begin (Israel) and Anwar el-Sadat (Egypt)
1979	Mother Teresa of Calcutta (India)
1980	Adolfo Pérez Esquivel (Argentina)
1981	Office of the United Nations High Commissioner for Refugees
1982	Alva Myrdal (Sweden) and Alfonso García Robles (Mexico)
1983	Lech Walesa (Poland)
1984	Bishop Desmond Tutu (South Africa)
1985	International Physicians for the Prevention of Nuclear War
1986	Elie Wiesel (U.S.)
1987	Oscar Arias Sánchez (Costa Rica)
1988	U.N. Peacekeeping Forces
1989	Dalai Lama (Tibet)
1990	Mikhail S. Gorbachev (U.S.S.R)

1. Le Duc Tho refused prize, charging that peace had not yet been really established in South Vietnam.

LITERATURE

1901 René F. A. Sully Prudhomme (France)
1902 Theodor Mommsen (Germany)
1903 Björnstjerne Björnson (Norway)
1904 Frédéric Mistral (France) and José Echegaray (Spain)
1905 Henryk Sienkiewicz (Poland)
1906 Giosuè Carducci (Italy)
1907 Rudyard Kipling (England)
1908 Rudolf Eucken (Germany)
1909 Selma Lagerlöf (Sweden)
1910 Paul von Heyse (Germany)
1911 Maurice Maeterlinck (Belgium)
1912 Gerhart Hauptmann (Germany)
1913 Rabindranath Tagore (India)
1915 Romain Rolland (France)
1916 Verner von Heidenstam (Sweden)
1917 Karl Gjellerup (Denmark) and Henrik Pontoppidan (Denmark)
1919 Carl Spitteler (Switzerland)
1920 Knut Hamsun (Norway)
1921 Anatole France (France)
1922 Jacinto Benavente (Spain)
1923 William B. Yeats (Ireland)
1924 Wladyslaw Reymont (Poland)
1925 George Bernard Shaw (Ireland)
1926 Grazia Deledda (Italy)
1927 Henri Bergson (France)
1928 Sigrid Undset (Norway)
1929 Thomas Mann (Germany)
1930 Sinclair Lewis (U.S.)
1931 Erik A. Karlfeldt (Sweden)
1932 John Galsworthy (England)
1933 Ivan G. Bunin (Russia)
1934 Luigi Pirandello (Italy)
1935 No award
1936 Eugene O'Neill (U.S.)
1937 Roger Martin du Gard (France)
1938 Pearl S. Buck (U.S.)
1939 Frans Eemil Sillanpää (Finland)
1944 Johannes V. Jensen (Denmark)
1945 Gabriela Mistral (Chile)
1946 Hermann Hesse (Switzerland)
1947 André Gide (France)
1948 Thomas Stearns Eliot (England)
1949 William Faulkner (U.S.)
1950 Bertrand Russell (England)
1951 Pär Lagerkvist (Sweden)
1952 François Mauriac (France)
1953 Sir Winston Churchill (England)
1954 Ernest Hemingway (U.S.)
1955 Halldór Kiljan Laxness (Iceland)
1956 Juan Ramón Jiménez (Spain)
1957 Albert Camus (France)
1958 Boris Pasternak (U.S.S.R.) (declined)
1959 Salvatore Quasimodo (Italy)
1960 St-John Perse (Alexis St.-Léger Léger) (France)
1961 Ivo Andric (Yugoslavia)
1962 John Steinbeck (U.S.)
1963 Giorgios Seferis (Seferiades) (Greece)
1964 Jean-Paul Sartre (France) (declined)
1965 Mikhail Sholokhov (U.S.S.R.)
1966 Shmuel Yosef Agnon (Israel) and Nelly Sachs (Sweden)
1967 Miguel Angel Asturias (Guatemala)
1968 Yasunari Kawabata (Japan)
1969 Samuel Beckett (Ireland)
1970 Aleksandr Solzhenitsyn (U.S.S.R.)
1971 Pablo Neruda (Chile)
1972 Heinrich Böll (Germany)
1973 Patrick White (Australia)
1974 Eyvind Johnson and Harry Martinson (both Sweden)
1975 Eugenio Montale (Italy)
1976 Saul Bellow (U.S.)
1977 Vicente Aleixandre (Spain)
1978 Isaac Bashevis Singer (U.S.)
1979 Odysseus Elytis (Greece)
1980 Czeslaw Milosz (U.S.)
1981 Elias Canetti (Bulgaria)
1982 Gabriel García Márquez (Colombia)
1983 William Golding (England)
1984 Jaroslav Seifert (Czechoslovakia)
1985 Claude Simon (France)
1986 Wole Soyinka (Nigeria)
1987 Joseph Brodsky (U.S.)
1988 Naguib Mahfouz (Egypt)
1989 Camilo José Cela (Spain)
1990 Octavio Paz (Mexico)

PHYSICS

1901 Wilhelm K. Roentgen (Germany), for discovery of Roentgen rays
1902 Hendrik A. Lorentz and Pieter Zeeman (Netherlands), for work on influence of magnetism upon radiation
1903 A. Henri Becquerel (France), for work on spontaneous radioactivity; and Pierre and Marie Curie (France), for study of radiation
1904 John Strutt (Lord Rayleigh) (England), for discovery of argon in investigating gas density
1905 Philipp Lenard (Germany), for work with cathode rays
1906 Sir Joseph Thomson (England), for investigations on passage of electricity through gases
1907 Albert A. Michelson (U.S.), for spectroscopic and metrologic investigations
1908 Gabriel Lippmann (France), for method of reproducing colors by photography
1909 Guglielmo Marconi (Italy) and Ferdinand Braun (Germany), for development of wireless
1910 Johannes D. van der Waals (Netherlands), for work with the equation of state for gases and liquids
1911 Wilhelm Wien (Germany), for his laws governing the radiation of heat
1912 Gustaf Dalén (Sweden), for discovery of automatic regulators used in lighting lighthouses and light buoys
1913 Heike Kamerlingh-Onnes (Netherlands), for work leading to production of liquid helium
1914 Max von Laue (Germany), for discovery of diffraction of Roentgen rays passing through crystals
1915 Sir William Bragg and William L. Bragg (England), for analysis of crystal structure by X rays
1916 No award
1917 Charles G. Barkla (England), for discovery of Roentgen radiation of the elements
1918 Max Planck (Germany), discoveries in connection with quantum theory
1919 Johannes Stark (Germany), discovery of Doppler effect in Canal rays and decomposition of spectrum lines by electric fields
1920 Charles E. Guillaume (Switzerland), for discoveries of anomalies in nickel steel alloys
1921 Albert Einstein (Germany), for discovery of the law of the photoelectric effect
1922 Niels Bohr (Denmark), for investigation of structure of atoms and radiations emanating from them
1923 Robert A. Millikan (U.S.), for work on elementary charge of electricity and photoelectric phenomena

1924 Karl M. G. Siegbahn (Sweden), for investigations in X-ray spectroscopy

1925 James Franck and Gustav Hertz (Germany), for discovery of laws governing impact of electrons upon atoms

1926 Jean B. Perrin (France), for work on discontinuous structure of matter and discovery of the equilibrium of sedimentation

1927 Arthur H. Compton (U.S.), for discovery of Compton phenomenon; and Charles T. R. Wilson (England), for method of perceiving paths taken by electrically charged particles

1928 In 1929, the 1928 prize was awarded to Sir Owen Richardson (England), for work on the phenomenon of thermionics and discovery of the Richardson Law

1929 Prince Louis Victor de Broglie (France), for discovery of the wave character of electrons

1930 Sir Chandrasekhara Raman (India), for work on diffusion of light and discovery of the Raman effect

1931 No award

1932 In 1933, the prize for 1932 was awarded to Werner Heisenberg (Germany), for creation of the quantum mechanics

1933 Erwin Schrödinger (Austria) and Paul A. M. Dirac (England), for discovery of new fertile forms of the atomic theory

1934 No award

1935 James Chadwick (England), for discovery of the neutron

1936 Victor F. Hess (Austria), for discovery of cosmic radiation; and Carl D. Anderson (U.S.), for discovery of the positron

1937 Clinton J. Davisson (U.S.) and George P. Thomson (England), for discovery of diffraction of electrons by crystals

1938 Enrico Fermi (Italy), for identification of new radioactivity elements and discovery of nuclear reactions effected by slow neutrons

1939 Ernest Orlando Lawrence (U.S.), for development of the cyclotron

1943 Otto Stern (U.S.), for detection of magnetic momentum of protons

1944 Isidor Isaac Rabi (U.S.), for work on magnetic movements of atomic particles

1945 Wolfgang Pauli (Austria), for work on atomic fissions

1946 Percy Williams Bridgman (U.S.), for studies and inventions in high-pressure physics

1947 Sir Edward Appleton (England), for discovery of layer which reflects radio short waves in the ionosphere

1948 Patrick M. S. Blackett (England), for improvement on Wilson chamber and discoveries in cosmic radiation

1949 Hideki Yukawa (Japan), for mathematical prediction, in 1935, of the meson

1950 Cecil Frank Powell (England), for method of photographic study of atom nucleus, and for discoveries about mesons

1951 Sir John Douglas Cockcroft (England) and Ernest T. S. Walton (Ireland), for work in 1932 on transmutation of atomic nuclei

1952 Edward Mills Purcell and Felix Bloch (U.S.), for work in measurement of magnetic fields in atomic nuclei

1953 Fritz Zernike (Netherlands), for development of "phase contrast" microscope

1954 Max Born (England), for work in quantum mechanics; and Walther Bothe (Germany), for work in cosmic radiation

1955 Polykarp Kusch and Willis E. Lamb, Jr. (U.S.), for atomic measurements

1956 William Shockley, Walter H. Brattain, and John Bardeen (U.S.), for developing electronic transistor

1957 Tsung Dao Lee and Chen Ning Yang (China), for disproving principle of conservation of parity

1958 Pavel A. Cherenkov, Ilya M. Frank, and Igor E. Tamm (U.S.S.R.), for work resulting in development of cosmic-ray counter

1959 Emilio Segre and Owen Chamberlain (U.S.), for demonstrating the existence of the anti-proton

1960 Donald A. Glaser (U.S.), for invention of "bubble chamber" to study subatomic particles

1961 Robert Hofstadter (U.S.), for determination of shape and size of atomic nucleus; Rudolf Mössbauer (Germany), for method of producing and measuring recoil-free gamma rays

1962 Lev D. Landau (U.S.S.R.), for his theories about condensed matter

1963 Eugene Paul Wigner, Maria Goeppert Mayer (both U.S.), and J. Hans D. Jensen (Germany), for research on structure of atom and its nucleus

1964 Charles Hard Townes (U.S.), Nikolai G. Basov, and Aleksandr M. Prochorov (both U.S.S.R.), for developing maser and laser principle of producing high-intensity radiation

1965 Richard P. Feynman, Julian S. Schwinger (both U.S.), and Shinichiro Tomonaga (Japan), for research in quantum electrodynamics

1966 Alfred Kastler (France), for work on energy levels inside atom

1967 Hans A. Bethe (U.S.), for work on energy production of stars

1968 Luis Walter Alvarez (U.S.), for study of subatomic particles

1969 Murray Gell-Mann (U.S.), for study of subatomic particles

1970 Hannes Alfvén (Sweden), for theories in plasma physics; and Louis Néel (France), for discoveries in antiferromagnetism and ferrimagnetism

1971 Dennis Gabor (England), for invention of holographic method of three-dimensional imagery

1972 John Bardeen, Leon N. Cooper, and John Robert Schrieffer (all U.S.), for theory of superconductivity, where electrical resistance in certain metals vanishes above absolute zero temperature

1973 Ivar Giaever (U.S.), Leo Esaki (Japan), and Brian D. Josephson (U.K.), for theories that have advanced and expanded the field of miniature electronics

1974 Antony Hewish (England), for discovery of pulsars; Martin Ryle (England), for using radiotelescopes to probe outer space with high degree of precision

1975 James Rainwater (U.S.) and Ben Mottelson and Aage N. Bohr (both Denmark), for showing that the atomic nucleus is asymmetrical

1976 Burton Richter and Samuel C. C. Ting (both U.S.), for discovery of subatomic particles known as J and psi

1977 Philip W. Anderson and John H. Van Vleck (both U.S.), and Nevill F. Mott (U.K.), for work underlying computer memories and electronic devices

1978 Arno A. Penzias and Robert W. Wilson (both U.S.), for work in cosmic microwave radiation; Piotr L. Kapitsa (U.S.S.R.), for basic inventions and discoveries in low-temperature physics

1979 Steven Weinberg and Sheldon L. Glashow (both U.S.) and Abdus Salam (Pakistan), for developing theory that electromagnetism and the "weak" force, which causes radioactive decay in some atomic nuclei, are facets of the same phenomenon

1980 James W. Cronin and Val L. Fitch (both U.S.), for work concerning the assymetry of subatomic particles

1981 Nicolaas Bloembergen and Arthur L. Schawlow (both U.S.) and Kai M. Siegbahn (Sweden), for developing technologies with lasers and other devices to probe the secrets of complex forms of matter

1982 Kenneth G. Wilson (U.S.), for analysis of changes in matter under pressure and temperature

1983 Subrahmanyam Chandrasekhar and William A. Fowler (both U.S.) for complementary research on processes involved in the evolution of stars

1984 Carlo Rubbia (Italy) and Simon van der Meer (Netherlands), for their role in discovering three subatomic particles, a step toward developing a single theory to account for all natural forces

1985 Klaus von Klitzing (Germany), for developing an exact way of measuring electrical conductivity

1986 Ernst Ruska, Gerd Binnig (both Germany) and Heinrich Rohrer (Switzerland) for work on microscopes

1987 K. Alex Müller (Switzerland) and J. Georg Bednorz (Germany) for their discovery of high-temperature superconductors.

1988 Leon M. Lederman, Melvin Schwartz, and Jack Steinberger (all U.S.) for research that improved the understanding of elementary particles and forces.

1989 Norman F. Ramsey (U.S.), for work leading to development of the atomic clock, and Hans G. Dehmelt (U.S.) and Wolfgang Paul (Germany) for developing methods to isolate atoms and subatomic particles.

1990 Dr. Richard E. Taylor (Canada) and Dr. Jerome I. Friedman and Dr. Henry W. Kendall (both U.S.), for their "breakthrough in our understanding of matter" which confirmed the reality of quarks.

CHEMISTRY

1901 Jacobus H. van't Hoff (Netherlands), for laws of chemical dynamics and osmotic pressure in solutions

1902 Emil Fischer (Germany), for experiments in sugar and purin groups of substances

1903 Svante A. Arrhenius (Sweden), for his electrolytic theory of dissociation

1904 Sir William Ramsay (England), for discovery and determination of place of inert gaseous elements in air

1905 Adolf von Baeyer (Germany), for work on organic dyes and hydroaromatic combinations

1906 Henri Moissan (France), for isolation of fluorine, and introduction of electric furnace

1907 Eduard Buchner (Germany), discovery of cell-less fermentation and investigations in biological chemistry

1908 Sir Ernest Rutherford (England), for investigations into disintegration of elements

1909 Wilhelm Ostwald (Germany), for work on catalysis and investigations into chemical equilibrium and reaction rates

1910 Otto Wallach (Germany), for work in the field of alicyclic compounds

1911 Marie Curie (France), for discovery of elements radium and polonium

1912 Victor Grignard (France), for reagent discovered by him; and Paul Sabatier (France), for methods of hydrogenating organic compounds

1913 Alfred Werner (Switzerland), for linking up atoms within the molecule

1914 Theodore W. Richards (U.S.), for determining atomic weight of many chemical elements

1915 Richard Willstätter (Germany), for research into coloring matter of plants, especially chlorophyll

1916 No award

1917 No award

1918 Fritz Haber (Germany), for synthetic production of ammonia

1919 No award

1920 Walther Nernst (Germany), for work in thermochemistry

1921 Frederick Soddy (England), for investigations into origin and nature of isotopes

1922 Francis W. Aston (England), for discovery of isotopes in nonradioactive elements and for discovery of the whole number rule

1923 Fritz Pregl (Austria), for method of microanalysis of organic substances discovered by him

1924 No award

1925 In 1926, the 1925 prize was awarded to Richard Zsigmondy (Germany), for work on the heterogeneous nature of colloid solutions

1926 Theodor Svedberg (Sweden), for work on disperse systems

1927 In 1928, the 1927 prize was awarded to Heinrich Wieland (Germany), for investigations of bile acids and kindred substances

1928 Adolf Windaus (Germany), for investigations on constitution of the sterols and their connection with vitamins

1929 Sir Arthur Harden (England) and Hans K. A. S. von Euler-Chelpin (Sweden), for research of fermentation of sugars

1930 Hans Fischer (Germany), for work on coloring matter of blood and leaves and for his synthesis of hemin

1931 Karl Bosch and Friedrich Bergius (Germany), for invention and development of chemical high-pressure methods

1932 Irving Langmuir (U.S.), for work in realm of surface chemistry

1933 No award

1934 Harold C. Urey (U.S.), for discovery of heavy hydrogen

1935 Frédéric and Irène Joliot-Curie (France), for synthesis of new radioactive elements

1936 Peter J. W. Debye (Netherlands), for investigations on dipole moments and diffraction of X rays and electrons in gases

1937 Walter N. Haworth (England), for research on carbohydrates and Vitamin C; and Paul Karrer (Switzerland), for work on carotenoids, flavins, and Vitamins A and B

1938 Richard Kuhn (Germany), for carotinoid study and vitamin research (declined)

1939 Adolf Butenandt (Germany), for work on sexual hormones (declined the prize); and Leopold Ruzicka (Switzerland), for work with polymethylenes

1943 Georg Hevesy De Heves (Hungary), for work on use of isotopes as indicators

1944 Otto Hahn (Germany), for work on atomic fission

1945 Artturi Illmari Virtanen (Finland), for research in the field of conservation of fodder

1946 James B. Sumner (U.S.), for crystallizing enzymes; John H. Northrop and Wendell M. Stanley (U.S.), for preparing enzymes and virus proteins in pure form

1947 Sir Robert Robinson (England), for research in plant substances

1948 Arne Tiselius (Sweden), for biochemical discoveries and isolation of mouse paralysis virus

1949 William Francis Giauque (U.S.), for research in thermodynamics, especially effects of low temperature

1950 Otto Diels and Kurt Alder (Germany), for discovery of diene synthesis enabling scientists to study structure of organic matter

1951 Glenn T. Seaborg and Edwin H. McMillan (U.S.), for discovery of plutonium

1952 Archer John Porter Martin and Richard Laurence Millington Synge (England), for development of partition chromatography

1953 Hermann Staudinger (Germany), for research in giant molecules

1954 Linus C. Pauling (U.S.), for study of forces holding together protein and other molecules

1955 Vincent du Vigneaud (U.S.), for work on pituitary hormones

1956 Sir Cyril Hinshelwood (England) and Nikolai N. Semenov (U.S.S.R.), for parallel research on chemical reaction kinetics

1957 Sir Alexander Todd (England), for research with chemical compounds that are factors in heredity

1958 Frederick Sanger (England), for determining molecular structure of insulin

1959 Jaroslav Heyrovsky (Czechoslovakia), for development of polarography, an electrochemical method of analysis

1960 Willard F. Libby (U.S.), for "atomic time clock" to measure age of objects by measuring their radioactivity

1961 Melvin Calvin (U.S.), for establishing chemical steps during photosynthesis

1962 Max F. Perutz and John C. Kendrew (England), for mapping protein molecules with X-rays

1963 Carl Ziegler (Germany) and Giulio Natta (Italy), for work in uniting simple hydrocarbons into large molecule substances

1964 Dorothy Mary Crowfoot Hodgkin (England), for determining structure of compounds needed in combating pernicious anemia

1965 Robert B. Woodward (U.S.), for work in synthesizing complicated organic compounds

1966 Robert Sanderson Mulliken (U.S.), for research on bond holding atoms together in molecule

1967 Manfred Eigen (Germany), Ronald G. W. Norrish, and George Porter (both Eng land), for work in high-speed chemical reactions

1968 Lars Onsager (U.S.), for development of system of equations in thermodynamics

1969 Derek H. R. Barton (England) and Odd Hassel (Norway), for study of organic molecules

1970 Luis F. Leloir (Argentina), for discovery of sugar nucleotides and their role in biosynthesis of carbohydrates

1971 Gerhard Herzberg (Canada), for contributions to knowledge of electronic structure and geometry of molecules, particularly free radicals

1972 Christian Boehmer Anfinsen, Stanford Moore, and William Howard Stein (all U.S.), for pioneering studies in enzymes

1973 Ernst Otto Fischer (W. Germany) and Geoffrey Wilkinson (U.K.), for work that could solve problem of automobile exhaust pollution

1974 Paul J. Flory (U.S.), for developing analytic methods to study properties and molecular structure of long-chain molecules

1975 John W. Cornforth (Australia) and Vladimir Prelog (Switzerland), for research on structure of biological molecules such as antibiotics and cholesterol

1976 William N. Lipscomb, Jr. (U.S.), for work on the structure and bonding mechanisms of boranes

1977 Ilya Prigogine (Belgium), for contributions to nonequilibrium thermodynamics, particularly the theory of dissipative structures

1978 Peter Mitchell (U.K.), for contributions to the understanding of biological energy transfer

1979 Herbert C. Brown (U.S.) and Georg Wittig (West Germany), for developing a group of substances that facilitate very difficult chemical reactions

1980 Paul Berg and Walter Gilbert (both U.S.) and Frederick Sanger (England), for developing methods to map the structure and function of DNA, the substance that controls the activity of the cell

1981 Roald Hoffmann (U.S.) and Kenichi Fukui (Japan), for applying quantum-mechanics theories to predict the course of chemical reactions

1982 Aaron Klug (U.K.), for research in the detailed structures of viruses and components of life

1983 Henry Taube (U.S.), for research on how electrons transfer between molecules in chemical reactions

1984 R. Bruce Merrifield (U.S.) for research that revolutionized the study of proteins

1985 Herbert A. Hauptman and Jerome Karle (both U.S.) for their outstanding achievements in the development of direct methods for the determination of crystal structures

1986 Dudley R. Herschback, Yuan T. Lee (both U.S.), and John C. Polanyi (Canada) for their work on "reaction dynamics"

1987 Donald J. Cram and Charles J. Pedersen (both U.S.) and Jean-Marie Lehn (France), for wide-ranging research that has included the creation of artificial molecules that can mimic vital chemical reactions of the processes of life.

1988 Johann Deisenhofer, Robert Huber, and Hartmut Michel (all West Germany) for unraveling the structure of proteins that play a crucial role in photosynthesis

1989 Thomas R. Cech and Sidney Altman (both U.S.) for their discovery, independently, that RNA could actively aid chemical reactions in the cells.

1990 Dr. Elias James Corey (U.S.) for developing new ways to synthesize complex molecules ordinarily found in nature.

PHYSIOLOGY OR MEDICINE

1901 Emil A. von Behring (Germany), for work on serum therapy against diptheria

1902 Sir Ronald Ross (England), for work on malaria

1903 Niels R. Finsen (Denmark), for his treatment of lupus vulgaris with concentrated light rays

1904 Ivan P. Pavlov (U.S.S.R.), for work on the physiology of digestion

1905 Robert Koch (Germany), for work on tuberculosis

1906 Camillo Golgi (Italy) and Santiago Ramón y Cajal (Spain), for work on structure of the nervous system

1907 Charles L. A. Laveran (France), for work with protozoa in the generation of disease

1908 Paul Ehrlich (Germany), and Elie Metchnikoff (U.S.S.R.), for work on immunity

1909 Theodor Kocher (Switzerland), for work on the thyroid gland

1910 Albrecht Kossel (Germany), for achievements in the chemistry of the cell

1911 Allvar Gullstrand (Sweden), for work on the dioptrics of the eye

1912 Alexis Carrel (France), for work on vascular ligature and grafting of blood vessels and organs

1913 Charles Richet (France), for work on anaphylaxy

1914 Robert Bárány (Austria), for work on physiology and pathology of the vestibular system

1915-1918 No award

1919 Jules Bordet (Belgium), for discoveries in connection with immunity

1920 August Krogh (Denmark), for discovery of regulation of capillaries' motor mechanism

1921 No award

1922 In 1923, the 1922 prize was shared by Archibald V. Hill (England), for discovery relating to heat-production in muscles; and Otto Meyerhof (Germany), for correlation between consumption of oxygen and production of lactic acid in muscles

1923 Sir Frederick Banting (Canada) and John J. R. Macleod (Scotland), for discovery of insulin

1924 Willem Einthoven (Netherlands), for discovery of the mechanism of the electrocardiogram

1925 No award

1926 Johannes Fibiger (Denmark), for discovery of the Spiroptera carcinoma

1927 Julius Wagner-Jauregg (Austria), for use of malaria inoculation in treatment of dementia paralytica

1928 Charles Nicolle (France), for work on typhus exanthematicus

1929 Christiaan Eijkman (Netherlands), for discovery of the antineuritic vitamins; and Sir Frederick Hopkins (England), for discovery of growth-promoting vitamins

1930 Karl Landsteiner (U.S.), for discovery of human blood groups

1931 Otto H. Warburg (Germany), for discovery of the character and mode of action of the respiratory ferment

1932 Sir Charles Sherrington (England) and Edgar D. Adrian (U.S.), for discoveries of the function of the neuron

1933 Thomas H. Morgan (U.S.), for discoveries on hereditary function of the chromosomes

1934 George H. Whipple, George R. Minot, and William P. Murphy (U.S.), for discovery of liver therapy against anemias

1935 Hans Spemann (Germany), for discovery of the organizer-effect in embryonic development

1936 Sir Henry Dale (England) and Otto Loewi (Germany), for discoveries on chemical transmission of nerve impulses

1937 Albert Szent-Györgyi von Nagyrapolt (Hungary), for discoveries on biological combustion

1938 Corneille Heymans (Belgium), for determining importance of sinus and aorta mechanisms in the regulation of respiration

1939 Gerhard Domagk (Germany), for antibacterial effect of prontocilate

1943 Henrik Dam (Denmark) and Edward A. Doisy (U.S.), for analysis of Vitamin K

1944 Joseph Erlanger and Herbert Spencer Gasser (U.S.), for work on functions of the nerve threads

1945 Sir Alexander Fleming, Ernst Boris Chain, and Sir Howard Florey (England), for discovery of penicillin

1946 Herman J. Muller (U.S.), for hereditary effects o f X-rays on genes

1947 Carl F. and Gerty T. Cori (U.S.), for work on animal starch metabolism; Bernardo A. Houssay (Argentina), for study of pituitary

1948 Paul Mueller (Switzerland), for discovery of insect-killing properties of DDT

1949 Walter Rudolf Hess (Switzerland), for research on brain control of body; and Antonio Caetano de Abreu Freire Egas Moniz (Portugal), for development of brain operation

1950 Philip S. Hench, Edward C. Kendall (both U.S.), and Tadeus Reichstein (Switzerland), for discoveries about hormones of adrenal cortex

1951 Max Theiler (South Africa), for development of anti-yellow-fever vaccine

1952 Selman A. Waksman (U.S.), for co-discovery of streptomycin

1953 Fritz A. Lipmann (Germany-U.S.) and Hans Adolph Krebs (Germany-England), for studies of living cells

1954 John F. Enders, Thomas H. Weller, and Frederick C. Robbins (U.S.), for work with cultivation of polio virus

1955 Hugo Theorell (Sweden), for work on oxidation enzymes

1956 Dickinson W. Richards, Jr., André F. Cournand (both U.S.), and Werner Forssmann (Germany), for new techniques in treating heart disease

1957 Daniel Bovet (Italy), for development of drugs to relieve allergies and relax muscles during surgery

1958 Joshua Lederberg (U.S.), for work with genetic mechanisms; George W. Beadie and Edward L. Tatum (U.S.), for discovering how genes transmit hereditary characteristics

1959 Severo Ochoa and Arthur Kornberg (U.S.), for discoveries related to compounds within chromosomes, which play a vital role in heredity

1960 Sir Macfarlane Burnet (Australia) and Peter Brian Medawar (England), for discovery of acquired immunological tolerance

1961 Georg von Bekesy (U.S.), for discoveries about physical mechanisms of stimulation within cochlea

1962 James D. Watson (U.S.), Maurice H. F. Wilkins, and Francis H. C. Crick (England), for determining structure of deoxyribonucleic acid (DNA)

1963 Alan Lloyd Hodgkin, Andrew Fielding Huxley (both England), and Sir John Carew Eccles (Australia), for research on nerve cells

1964 Konrad E. Bloch (U.S.) and Feodor Lynen (Germany), for research on mechanism and regulation of cholesterol and fatty acid metabolism

1965 François Jacob, André Lwolff, and Jacques Monod (France), for study of regulatory activities in body cells

1966 Charles Brenton Huggins (U.S.), for studies in hormone treatment of cancer of prostate; Francis Peyton Rous (U.S.), for discovery of tumor-producing viruses

1967 Haldan K. Hartline, George Wald, and Ragnar Granit (U.S.), for work on human eye

1968 Robert W. Holley, Har Gobind Khorana, and Marshall W. Nirenberg (U.S.), for studies of genetic code

1969 Max Delbruck, Alfred D. Hershey, and Salvador E. Luria (U.S.), for study of mechanism of virus infection in living cells

1970 Julius Axelrod (U.S.), Ulf S. von Euler (Sweden), and Sir Bernard Katz (England), for studies of how nerve impulses are transmitted within the body

1971 Earl W. Sutherland, Jr. (U.S.), for research on how hormones work
1972 Gerald M. Edelman (U.S.), and Rodney R. Porter (U.K.), for research on the chemical structure and nature of antibodies
1973 Karl von Frisch and Konrad Lorenz (Austria), and Nikolaas Tinbergen (Netherlands), for their studies of individual and social behavior patterns
1974 George E. Palade and Christian de Duve (both U.S.) and Albert Claude (Belgium), for contributions to understanding inner workings of living cells
1975 David Baltimore, Howard M. Temin, and Renato Dulbecco (all U.S.), for work in interaction between tumor viruses and genetic material of the cell
1976 Baruch S. Blumberg and D. Carleton Gajdusek (U.S.), for discoveries concerning new mechanisms for the origin and dissemination of infectious diseases
1977 Rosalyn S. Yalow, Roger C. L. Guillemin, and Andrew V. Schally (all U.S.), for research in role of hormones in chemistry of the body
1978 Daniel Nathans and Hamilton Smith (both U.S.) and Werner Arber (Switzerland), for discovery of restriction enzymes and their application to problems of molecular genetics
1979 Allan McLeod Cormack (U.S.) and Godfrey Newbold Hounsfield (England), for developing computed axial tomography (CAT scan) X-ray technique
1980 Baruj Benacerraf and George D. Snell (both U.S.) and Jean Dausset (France), for discoveries that explain how the structure of cells relates to organ transplants and diseases
1981 Roger W. Sperry and David H. Hubel (both U.S.) and Torsten N. Wiesel (Sweden), for studies vital to understanding the organization and functioning of the brain
1982 Sune Bergstrom and Bengt Samuelsson (Sweden) and John R. Vane (U.K.), for research in prostaglandins, a hormonelike substance involved in a wide range of illnesses
1983 Barbara McClintock (U.S.), for her discovery of mobile genes in the chromosomes of a plant that change the future generations of plants they produce
1984 Cesar Milstein (U.K./Argentina) Georges J.F. Kohler (West Germany), and Niels K. Jerne (U.K./Denmark) for their work in immunology
1985 Michael S. Brown and Joseph L. Goldstein (both U.S.) for their work which has drastically widened our understanding of the cholesterol metabolism and increased our possibilities to prevent and treat atherosclerosis and heart attacks
1986 Rita Levi-Montalcini (dual U.S./Italy) and Stanley Cohen (U.S.) for their contributions to the understanding of substances that influence cell growth
1987 Susumu Tonegawa (Japan), for his discoveries of how the body can suddenly marshal its immunological defenses against millions of different disease agents that it has never encountered before.
1988 Gertrude B. Elion, George H. Hitchings (both U.S.) and Sir James Black (U.K.) for their discoveries of important principles for drug treatment.
1989 J. Michael Bishop and Harold E. Varmus (both U.S.) for their unifying theory of cancer development.

1990 Dr. Joseph E. Murray and Dr. E. Donnall Thomas (both U.S.), for their pioneering work in transplants.

ECONOMIC SCIENCE

1969 Ragnar Frisch (Norway) and Jan Tinbergen (Netherlands), for work in econometrics (application of mathematics and statistical methods to economic theories and problems)
1970 Paul A. Samuelson (U.S.), for efforts to raise the level of scientific analysis in economic theory
1971 Simon Kuznets (U.S.), for developing concept of using a country's gross national product to determine its economic growth
1972 Kenneth J. Arrow (U.S.) and Sir John R. Hicks (U.K.), for theories that help to assess business risk and government economic and welfare policies
1973 Wassily Leontief (U.S.), for devising the input–output technique to determine how different sectors of an economy interact
1974 Gunnar Myrdal (Sweden) and Friedrich A. von Hayek (U.K.), for pioneering analysis of the interdependence of economic, social and institutional phenomena
1975 Leonid V. Kantorovich (U.S.S.R.) and Tjalling C. Koopmans (U.S.), for work on the theory of optimum allocation of resources
1976 Milton Friedman (U.S.), for work in consumption analysis and monetary history and theory, and for demonstration of complexity of stabilization policy
1977 Bertil Ohlin (Sweden) and James E. Meade (U.K.), for contributions to theory of international trade and international capital movements
1978 Herbert A. Simon (U.S.), for research into the decision-making process within economic organizations
1979 Sir Arthur Lewis (England) and Theodore Schultz (U.S.), for work on economic problems of developing nations
1980 Lawrence R. Klein (U.S.), for developing models for forecasting economic trends and shaping policies to deal with them
1981 James Tobin (U.S.), for analyses of financial markets and their influence on spending and saving by families and businesses
1982 George J. Stigler (U.S.), for work on government regulation in the economy and the functioning of industry
1983 Gerard Debreu (U.S.), in recognition of his work on the basic economic problem of how prices operate to balance what producers supply with what buyers want.
1984 Sir Richard Stone (U.K.), for his work to develop the systems widely used to measure the performance of national economics
1985 Franco Modigliani (U.S.) for his pioneering work in analyzing the behavior of household savers and the functioning of financial markets
1986 James M. Buchanan (U.S.) for his development of new methods for analyzing economic and political decision-making
1987 Robert M. Solow (U.S.), for seminal contributions to the theory of economic growth.
1988 Maurice Allais (France) for his pioneering development of theories to better understand market behavior and the efficient use of resources.
1989 Trygve Haavelmo (Norway) for his pioneering work in methods for testing economic theories.

1990 Harry M. Markowitz, William F. Sharpe, and Merton H. Miller (all U.S.), whose work provided new tools for weighing the risks and rewards of different investments and for valuing corporate stocks and bonds.

Motion Picture Academy Awards (Oscars)

1928

Picture: *Wings,* Paramount
Director: Frank Borzage, *Seventh Heaven;* Lewis Milestone, *Two Arabian Nights*
Actress: Janet Gaynor, *Seventh Heaven, Street Angel, Sunrise*
Actor: Emil Jannings, *The Way of All Flesh, The Last Command*

1929

Picture: *The Broadway Melody,* M–G–M
Director: Frank Lloyd, *The Divine Lady*
Actress: Mary Pickford, *Coquette*
Actor: Warner Baxter, *In Old Arizona*

1930

Picture: *All Quiet on the Western Front,* Universal
Director: Lewis Milestone, *All Quiet on the Western Front*
Actress: Norma Shearer, *The Divorcee*
Actor: George Arliss, *Disraeli*

1931

Picture: *Cimarron;* RKO Radio
Director: Norman Taurog, *Skippy*
Actress: Marie Dressler, *Min and Bill*
Actor: Lionel Barrymore, *A Free Soul*

1932

Picture: *Grand Hotel,* M–G–M
Director: Frank Borzage, *Bad Girl*
Actress: Helen Hayes, *The Sin of Madelon Claudet*
Actor: Fredric March, *Dr. Jekyll and Mr. Hyde,* and Wallace Beery, *The Champ*

1933

Picture: *Cavalcade,* Fox
Director: Frank Lloyd, *Cavalcade*
Actress: Katharine Hepburn, *Morning Glory*
Actor: Charles Laughton, *The Private Life of Henry VIII*

1934

Picture: *It Happened One Night,* Columbia
Director: Frank Capra, *It Happened One Night*
Actress: Claudette Colbert, *It Happened One Night*
Actor: Clark Gable, *It Happened One Night*

1935

Picture: *Mutiny on the Bounty,* MGM
Director: John Ford, *The Informer*
Actress: Bette Davis, *Dangerous*
Actor: Victor McLaglen, *The Informer*

1936

Picture: *The Great Ziegfeld,* M–G–M
Director: Frank Capra, *Mr. Deeds Goes to Town*
Actress: Luise Rainer, *The Great Ziegfeld*
Actor: Paul Muni, *The Story of Louis Pasteur*
Supporting Actress: Gale Sondergaard, *Anthony Adverse*
Supporting Actor: Walter Brennan, *Come and Get It*

1937

Picture: *The Life of Emile Zola,* Warner Bros.
Director: Leo McCarey, *The Awful Truth*
Actress: Luise Rainer, *The Good Earth*
Actor: Spencer Tracy, *Captains Courageous*
Supporting Actress: Alice Brady, *In Old Chicago*
Supporting Actor: Joseph Schildkraut, *The Life of Emile Zola*

1938

Picture: *You Can't Take It with You,* Columbia
Director: Frank Capra, *You Can't Take It with You*
Actress: Bette Davis, *Jezebel*
Actor: Spencer Tracy, *Boys Town*
Supporting Actress: Fay Bainter, *Jezebel*
Supporting Actor: Walter Brennan, *Kentucky*

1939

Picture: *Gone with the Wind,* SelznickM–G–M
Director: Victor Fleming, *Gone with the Wind*
Actress: Vivien Leigh, *Gone with the Wind*
Actor: Robert Donat, *Goodbye, Mr. Chips*
Supporting Actress: Hattie McDaniel, *Gone with the Wind*
Supporting Actor: Thomas Mitchell, *Stagecoach*

1940

Picture: *Rebecca,* Selznick–UA
Director: John Ford, *The Grapes of Wrath*
Actress: Ginger Rogers, *Kitty Foyle*
Actor: James Stewart, *The Philadelphia Story*
Supporting Actress: Jane Darwell, *The Grapes of Wrath*
Supporting Actor: Walter Brennan, *The Westerner*

1941

Picture: *How Green Was My Valley,* 20th Century-Fox
Director: John Ford, *How Green Was My Valley*
Actress: Joan Fontaine, *Suspicion*
Actor: Gary Cooper, *Sergeant York*
Supporting Actress: Mary Astor, *The Great Lie*
Supporting Actor: Donald Crisp, *How Green Was My Valley*

1942

Picture: *Mrs. Miniver,* M–G–M
Director: William Wyler, *Mrs. Miniver*
Actress: Greer Garson, *Mrs. Miniver*
Actor: James Cagney, *Yankee Doodle Dandy*
Supporting Actress: Teresa Wright, *Mrs. Miniver*
Supporting Actor: Van Heflin, *Johnny Eager*

1943

Picture: *Casablanca,* Warner Bros.
Director: Michael Curtiz, *Casablanca*
Actress: Jennifer Jones, *The Song of Bernadette*
Actor: Paul Lukas, *Watch on the Rhine*
Supporting Actress: Katina Paxinou, *For Whom the Bell Tolls*
Supporting Actor: Charles Coburn, *The More the Merrier*

1944

Picture: *Going My Way,* Paramount
Director: Leo McCarey, *Going My Way*
Actress: Ingrid Bergman, *Gaslight*
Actor: Bing Crosby, *Going My Way*
Supporting Actress: Ethel Barrymore, *None But the Lonely Heart*
Supporting Actor: Barry Fitzgerald, *Going My Way*

1945

Picture: *The Lost Weekend,* Paramount
Director: Billy Wilder, *The Lost Weekend*

Actress: Joan Crawford, *Mildred Pierce*
Actor: Ray Milland, *The Lost Weekend*
Supporting Actress: Anne Revere, *National Velvet*
Supporting Actor: James Dunn, *A Tree Grows in Brooklyn*

1946

Picture: *The Best Years of Our Lives,* Goldwyn–RKO Radio
Director: William Wyler, *The Best Years of Our Lives*
Actress: Olivia de Havilland, *To Each His Own*
Actor: Fredric March, *The Best Years of Our Lives*
Supporting Actress: Anne Baxter, *The Razor's Edge*
Supporting Actor: Harold Russell, *The Best Years of Our Lives*

1947

Picture: *Gentleman's Agreement,* 20th Century-Fox
Director: Elia Kazan, *Gentleman's Agreement*
Actress: Loretta Young, *The Farmer's Daughter*
Actor: Ronald Colman, *A Double Life*
Supporting Actress: Celeste Holm, *Gentleman's Agreement*
Supporting Actor: Edmund Gwenn, *Miracle on 34th Street*

1948

Picture: *Hamlet,* Rank–Two Cities–UI
Director: John Huston, *Treasure of Sierra Madre*
Actress: Jane Wyman, *Johnny Belinda*
Actor: Laurence Olivier, *Hamlet*
Supporting Actress: Claire Trevor, *Key Largo*
Supporting Actor: Walter Huston, *Treasure of Sierra Madre*

1949

Picture: *All the King's Men,* Rossen–Columbia
Director: Joseph L. Mankiewicz, *A Letter to Three Wives*
Actress: Olivia de Havilland, *The Heiress*
Actor: Broderick Crawford, *All the King's Men*
Supporting Actress: Mercedes McCambridge, *All the King's Men*
Supporting Actor: Dean Jagger, *Twelve O'Clock High*

1950

Picture: *All About Eve,* 20th Century–Fox
Director: Joseph L. Mankiewicz, *All About Eve*
Actress: Judy Holliday, *Born Yesterday*
Actor: José Ferrer, *Cyrano de Bergerac*
Supporting Actress: Josephine Hull, *Harvey*
Supporting Actor: George Sanders, *All About Eve*

1951

Picture: *An American in Paris,* M–G–M
Director: George Stevens, *A Place in the Sun*
Actress: Vivien Leigh, *A Streetcar Named Desire*
Actor: Humphrey Bogart, *The African Queen*
Supporting Actress: Kim Hunter, *A Streetcar Named Desire*
Supporting Actor: Karl Malden, *A Streetcar Named Desire*

1952

Picture: *The Greatest Show on Earth,* DeMille–Paramount
Director: John Ford, *The Quiet Man*
Actress: Shirley Booth, *Come Back, Little Sheba*
Actor: Gary Cooper, *High Noon*
Supporting Actress: Gloria Grahame, *The Bad and the Beautiful*
Supporting Actor: Anthony Quinn, *Viva Zapata]*

1953

Picture: *From Here to Eternity,* Columbia

Director: Fred Zinnemann, *From Here to Eternity*
Actress: Audrey Hepburn, *Roman Holiday*
Actor: William Holden, *Stalag 17*
Supporting Actress: Donna Reed, *From Here to Eternity*
Supporting Actor: Frank Sinatra, *From Here to Eternity*

1954

Picture: *On the Waterfront,* Horizon–American Corp., Columbia
Director: Elia Kazan, *On the Waterfront*
Actress: Grace Kelly, *The Country Girl*
Actor: Marlon Brando, *On the Waterfront*
Supporting Actress: Eva Marie Saint, *On the Waterfront*
Supporting Actor: Edmond O'Brien, *The Barefoot Contessa*

1955

Picture: *Marty,* Hecht and Lancaster, United Artists
Director: Delbert Mann, *Marty*
Actress: Anna Magnani, *The Rose Tattoo*
Actor: Ernest Borgnine, *Marty*
Supporting Actress: Jo Van Fleet, *East of Eden*
Supporting Actor: Jack Lemmon, *Mister Roberts*

1956

Picture: *Around the World in 80 Days,* Michael Todd Co., Inc.–U.A.
Director: George Stevens, *Giant*
Actress: Ingrid Bergman, *Anastasia*
Actor: Yul Brynner, *The King and I*
Supporting Actress: Dorothy Malone, *Written on the Wind*
Supporting Actor: Anthony Quinn, *Lust for Life*

1957

Picture: *The Bridge on the River Kwai,* Horizon Picture, Columbia
Director: David Lean, *The Bridge on the River Kwai*
Actress: Joanne Woodward, *The Three Faces of Eve*
Actor: Alec Guinness, *The Bridge on the River Kwai*
Supporting Actress: Miyoshi Umeki, *Sayonara*
Supporting Actor: Red Buttons, *Sayonara*

1958

Picture: *Gigi,* Arthur Freed Productions, Inc., M–G–M
Director: Vincente Minnelli, *Gigi*
Actress: Susan Hayward, *I Want to Live!*
Actor: David Niven, *Separate Tables*
Supporting Actress: Wendy Hiller, *Separate Tables*
Supporting Actor: Burl Ives, *The Big Country*

1959

Picture: *BenHur,* M–G–M
Director: William Wyler, *BenHur*
Actress: Simone Signoret, *Room at the Top*
Actor: Charlton Heston, *BenHur*
Supporting Actress: Shelley Winters, *The Diary of Anne Frank*
Supporting Actor: Hugh Griffith, *BenHur*

1960

Picture: *The Apartment,* Mirisch Co., Inc., United Artists
Director: Billy Wilder, *The Apartment*
Actress: Elizabeth Taylor, *Butterfield 8*
Actor: Burt Lancaster, *Elmer Gantry*
Supporting Actress: Shirley Jones, *Elmer Gantry*
Supporting Actor: Peter Ustinov, *Spartacus*

1961

Picture: *West Side Story,* Mirisch Pictures, Inc., and B and P Enterprises, Inc., United Artists
Director: Robert Wise and Jerome Robbins, *West Side Story*
Actress: Sophia Loren, *Two Women*
Actor: Maximillian Schell, *Judgment at Nuremberg*
Supporting Actress: Rita Moreno, *West Side Story*
Supporting Actor: George Chakiris, *West Side Story*

1962

Picture: *Lawrence of Arabia,* Horizon Pictures, Ltd.–Columbia
Director: David Lean, *Lawrence of Arabia*
Actress: Anne Bancroft, *The Miracle Worker*
Actor: Gregory Peck, *To Kill a Mockingbird*
Supporting Actress: Patty Duke, *The Miracle Worker*
Supporting Actor: Ed Begley, *Sweet Bird of Youth*

1963

Picture: *Tom Jones,* A Woodfall Production, UA–Lopert Pictures
Director: Tony Richardson, *Tom Jones*
Actress: Patricia Neal, *Hud*
Actor: Sidney Poitier, *Lilies of the Field*
Supporting Actress: Margaret Rutherford, *The V.I.P.s*
Supporting Actor: Melvyn Douglas, *Hud*

1964

Picture: *My Fair Lady,* Warner Bros.
Director: George Cukor, *My Fair Lady*
Actress: Julie Andrews, *Mary Poppins*
Actor: Rex Harrison, *My Fair Lady*
Supporting Actress: Lila Kedrova, *Zorba the Greek*
Supporting Actor: Peter Ustinov, *Topkapi*

1965

Picture: *The Sound of Music,* Argyle Enterprises Production, 20th CenturyFox
Director: Robert Wise, *The Sound of Music*
Actress: Julie Christie, *Darling*
Actor: Lee Marvin, *Cat Ballou*
Supporting Actress: Shelley Winters, *A Patch of Blue*
Supporting Actor: Martin Balsam, *A Thousand Clowns*

1966

Picture: *A Man for All Seasons,* Highland Films, Ltd., Production, Columbia
Director: Fred Zinnemann, *A Man for All Seasons*
Actress: Elizabeth Taylor, *Who's Afraid of Virginia Woolf?*
Actor: Paul Scofield, *A Man for All Seasons*
Supporting Actress: Sandy Dennis, *Who's Afraid of Virginia Woolf?*
Supporting Actor: Walter Matthau, *The Fortune Cookie*

1967

Picture: *In the Heat of the Night,* Mirisch Corp. Productions, United Artists
Director: Mike Nichols, *The Graduate*
Actress: Katharine Hepburn, *Guess Who's Coming to Dinner*
Actor: Rod Steiger, *In the Heat of the Night*
Supporting Actress: Estelle Parsons, *Bonnie and Clyde*
Supporting Actor: George Kennedy, *Cool Hand Luke*

1968

Picture: *Oliver!,* Columbia Pictures
Director: Sir Carol Reed, *Oliver!*
Actress: Katharine Hepburn, *The Lion in Winter* and Barbara Streisand, *Funny Girl*
Actor: Cliff Robertson, *Charly*
Supporting Actress: Ruth Gordon, *Rosemary's Baby*
Supporting Actor: Jack Albertson, *The Subject Was Roses*

1969

Picture: *Midnight Cowboy,* Jerome Hellman-John Schlesinger Production, United Artists
Director: John Schlesinger, *Midnight Cowboy*
Actress: Maggie Smith, *The Prime of Miss Jean Brodie*
Actor: John Wayne, *True Grit*
Supporting Actress: Goldie Hawn, *Cactus Flower*
Supporting Actor: Gig Young, *They Shoot Horses Don't They?*

1970

Picture: *Patton,* Frank McCarthy–Franklin J. Schaffner Production, 20th Century Fox
Director: Franklin J. Schaffner, *Patton*
Actress: Glenda Jackson, *Women in Love*
Actor: George C. Scott, *Patton*
Supporting Actress: Helen Hayes, *Airport*
Supporting Actor: John Mills, *Ryan's Daughter*

1971

Picture: *The French Connection,* D'Antoni Productions, 20th CenturyFox
Director: William Friedkin, *The French Connection*
Actress: Jane Fonda, *Klute*
Actor: Gene Hackman, *The French Connection*
Supporting Actress: Cloris Leachman, *The Last Picture Show*
Supporting Actor: Ben Johnson, *The Last Picture Show*

1972

Picture: *The Godfather,* Albert S. Ruddy Production, Paramount
Director: Bob Fosse, *Cabaret*
Actress: Liza Minnelli, *Cabaret*
Actor: Marlon Brando, *The Godfather*
Supporting Actress: Eileen Heckart, *Butterflies Are Free*
Supporting Actor: Joel Gray, *Cabaret*

1973

Picture: *The Sting,* Universal-Bill-Phillips-George Roy Hill Production, Universal
Director: George Roy Hill, *The Sting*
Actress: Glenda Jackson, *A Touch of Class*
Actor: Jack Lemmon, *Save the Tiger*
Supporting Actress: Tatum O'Neal, *Paper Moon*
Supporting Actor: John Houseman, *The Paper Chase*

1974

Picture: *The Godfather, Part II,* Coppola Co. Production, Paramount
Director: Francis Ford Coppola, *The Godfather, Part II*
Actress: Ellen Burstyn, *Alice Doesn't Live Here Anymore*
Actor: Art Carney, *Harry and Tonto*
Supporting Actress: Ingrid Bergman, *Murder on the Orient Express*
Supporting Actor: Robert De Niro, *The Godfather, Part II*

1975

Picture: *One Flew Over the Cuckoo's Nest,* Fantasy Films Production, United Artists
Director: Milos Forman, *One Flew Over the Cuckoo's Nest*

Actress: Louise Fletcher, *One Flew Over the Cuckoo's Nest*
Actor: Jack Nicholson, *One Flew Over the Cuckoo's Nest*
Supporting Actress: Lee Grant, *Shampoo*
Supporting Actor: George Burns, *The Sunshine Boys*

1976

Picture: *Rocky,* Robert Chartoff–Irwin Winkler Production, United Artists
Director: John G. Avildsen, *Rocky*
Actress: Faye Dunaway, *Network*
Actor: Peter Finch, *Network*
Supporting Actress: Beatrice Straight, *Network*
Supporting Actor: Jason Robards, *All the President's Men*

1977

Picture: *Annie Hall,* Jack Rollins–Charles H. Joffe Production, United Artists
Director: Woody Allen, *Annie Hall*
Actress: Diane Keaton, *Annie Hall*
Actor: Richard Dreyfuss, *The Goodbye Girl*
Supporting Actress: Vanessa Redgrave, *Julia*
Supporting Actor: Jason Robards, *Julia*

1978

Picture: *The Deer Hunter,* Michael Cimino Film Production, Universal
Director: Michael Cimino, *The Deer Hunter*
Actress: Jane Fonda, *Coming Home*
Actor: Jon Voight, *Coming Home*
Supporting Actress: Maggie Smith, *California Suite*
Supporting Actor: Christopher Walken, *The Deer Hunter*

1979

Picture: *Kramer vs. Kramer,* Stanley Jaffe Production, Columbia Pictures
Director: Robert Benton, *Kramer vs. Kramer*
Actress: Sally Field, *Norma Rae*
Actor: Dustin Hoffman, *Kramer vs. Kramer*
Supporting Actress: Meryl Streep, *Kramer vs. Kramer*
Supporting Actor: Melvyn Douglas, *Being There*

1980

Picture: *Ordinary People,* Wildwood Enterprises Production, Paramount
Director: Robert Redford, *Ordinary People*
Actress: Sissy Spacek, *Coal Miner's Daughter*
Actor: Robert De Niro, *Raging Bull*
Supporting Actress: Mary Steenburgen, *Melvin and Howard*
Supporting Actor: Timothy Hutton, *Ordinary People*

1981

Picture: *Chariots of Fire,* Enigma Productions, Ladd Company/Warner Bros.
Director: Warren Beatty, *Reds*
Actress: Katharine Hepburn, *On Golden Pond*
Actor: Henry Fonda, *On Golden Pond*
Supporting Actress: Maureen Stapleton, *Reds*
Supporting Actor: John Gielgud, *Arthur*

1982

Picture: *Gandhi,* Indo–British Films Production/Columbia
Director: Richard Attenborough, *Gandhi*
Actress: Meryl Streep, *Sophie's Choice*
Actor: Ben Kingsley, *Gandhi*

Supporting Actress: Jessica Lange, *Tootsie*
Supporting Actor: Louis Gossett, Jr., *An Officer and a Gentleman*

1983

Picture: *Terms of Endearment,* Paramount
Director: James L. Brooks, *Terms of Endearment*
Actress: Shirley MacLaine, *Terms of Endearment*
Actor: Robert Duvall, *Tender Mercies*
Supporting Actress: Linda Hunt, *The Year of Living Dangerously*
Supporting Actor: Jack Nicholson, *Terms of Endearment*

1984

Picture: *Amadeus,* Orion Pictures
Director: Milos Forman, *Amadeus*
Actress: Sally Field, *Places in the Heart*
Actor: F. Murray Abraham, *Amadeus*
Supporting Actress: Dame Peggy Ashcroft, *A Passage to India*
Supporting Actor: Haing S. Ngor, *The Killing Fields*

1985

Picture: *Out of Africa,* Universal
Director: Sydney Pollack, *Out of Africa*.
Actress: Geraldine Page, *The Trip to Bountiful*
Actor: William Hurt, *Kiss of the Spider Woman*
Supporting Actress: Anjelica Huston, *Prizzi's Honor*
Supporting Actor: Don Ameche, *Cocoon*

1986

Picture: *Platoon,* Orion Pictures
Director: Oliver Stone, *Platoon*
Actress: Marlee Matlin, *Children of a Lesser God*
Actor: Paul Newman, *The Color of Money*
Supporting Actress: Dianne Wiest, *Hannah and Her Sisters*
Supporting Actor: Michael Caine, *Hannah and Her Sisters*

1987

Picture: *The Last Emperor,* Columbia Pictures
Director : Bernardo Bertolucci, *The Last Emperor*
Actress: Cher, *Moonstruck*
Actor: Michael Douglas, *Wall Street*
Supporting Actress: Olympia Dukakis, *Moonstruck*
Supporting Actor: Sean Connery, *The Untouchables*

1988

Picture: *Rain Man,* United Artists
Director: Barry Levinson, *Rain Man*
Actress: Jodie Foster, *The Accused*
Actor: Dustin Hoffman, *Rain Man*
Supporting Actress: Geena Davis, *The Accidental Tourist*
Supporting Actor: Kevin Kline: *A Fish Named Wanda*

1989

Picture: *Driving Miss Daisy,* Warner Brothers
Director: Oliver Stone, *Born on the Fourth of July*
Actress: Jessica Tandy, *Driving Miss Daisy*
Actor: Daniel Day-Lewis, *My Left Foot*
Supporting Actress: Brenda Fricker, *My Left Foot*
Supporting Actor: Denzel Washington, *Glory*

1990

Picture: *Dances With Wolves,* Orion
Director: Kevin Costner, *Dances With Wolves*
Actress: Kathy Bates, *Misery*
Actor: Jermy Irons, *Reveral of Fortune*
Supporting Actress: Whoopi Goldberg, *Ghost*
Supporting Actor: Joe Pesci, *Goodfellas*

Other Academy Awards for 1990

Art direction: Jeffrey Beecroft, art direction, and Lisa Dean, set decoration, *Dick Tracy*

Cinematography: Dean Semler, *Dances With Wolves*

Costume design: Franca Squarciapino, *Cyrano de Bergerac*

Documentary (feature): *American Dream;* (short subject): *Days of Waiting*

Editing: Neil Travis, *Dances With Wolves*

Foreign-language film: *Journey of Hope*, Switzerland

Makeup: John Caglione Jr., Doug Drexler, *Dick Tracy*

Music (original score): John Barry, *Dances With Wolves;* (song): Stephen Sondheim, *Sooner or Later (I Always Get My Man)* from *Dick Tracy*

Screenplay, Original: Bruce Joel Rubin, *Ghost*

Screenplay, Adapted: Michael Blake, *Dances With Wolves*

Short subject (live action): *The Lunch Date;* (animated): *Creature Comforts*

Sound: Russell Williams 2d, Jeffrey Perkins, Bill W. Benton, and Greg Watkins, *Dances With Wolves*

Sound effects editing: Cecilia Hall and George Watters 2d, *The Hunt for Red October*

Honorary Awards: Myrna Loy and Sophia Loren

Irving J. Thalberg Award: Richard D. Zanuck and David Brown

Special Achievement in Special Effects: *Total Recall*

Academy Award of Merit: The Eastman Kodak Company

Gordon Sawyer Technical Achievement Award: Stefan Kudelski

George Foster Peabody Awards for Broadcasting, 1990

Radio

KQED-FM, San Francisco: *HEAT with John Hockenberry* produced by Murray Street Enterprise, N.Y., in association with KQED-FM

Connecticut Public Radio, New Haven: *The Schubert Theater: 75 Years of Memories.*

WXPN-FM, Philadelphia: *Kid's Corner.*

Vermont Folklife Center, Middlebury: *Journey's End: The Memories and Traditions of Daisy Turner and Family.*

National Public Radio, Washington, D.C.: *Manicu's Story: The War in Mozambique.*

The Southern Center for International Studies, Atlanta, Ga.: for providing an invaluable forum for the important decisionmakers of our time, and, through its broadcasting and recordings has created an irreplaceable record for generations to come.

Young Visions, Inc., Robin Young, Los Angeles, and the Rotary Club of Los Altos: *Rotary and AIDS: The Los Altos Story.*

Television

KPTV News, Portland, Ore.: *Mount St. Helens: A Decade Later.*

Blackside, Inc., Boston: *Eyes on the Prize II: America at the Racial Crossroads (1965–1985).*

WETA, Washington D.C., and Florentine Films: *The Civil War.*

CBS Music Video Enterprises and American Masters in association with **Perry Films:** *John Hammond: From Bessie Smith to Bruce Springsteen.*

ABC News and Koppel Communications, New York: *The Koppel Report: Death of a Dictator.*

Mouchette Films/P.O.V. and co-presented by the National Asian American Telecommunications Association, New York: *P.O.V.: Days of Waiting.*

ABC News/TIME, New York: *Peter Jennings Reporting: Guns.*

KCTS, Seattle, and MacNeil/Lehrer NewsHour, New York: *Backhauling*

WKYC, Cleveland: *Dick Feagler Commentaries.*

Cable News Network, Atlanta, Ga.: for its unique 24-hour global coverage from the scene of the Persian Gulf crisis.

ABC and Lynch/Frost Productions in association with **Propaganda Films** in association with **Worldvision Enterprises, Inc.:** *Twin Peaks*, premiere episode.

NBC, New York: *Saturday Night Live.*

American Playhouse series, New York: for an outstanding record of achievement over nine seasons.

FASE Productions, Los Angeles: *Futures.*

Think Entertainment and The Disney Channel: *Mother Goose Rock 'N' Rhyme.*

John D. and Catherine T. MacArthur Foundation, Chicago: for its distinguished record of achievement in support of quality television.

Personal Awards

Red Barber, for his six decades as a broadcaster and his ten years as a commentator for NPR's *Morning Edition.*

Frederick Wiseman, whose body of work and personal approach to documentary television have set the standard for generations of film and video producers to follow.

Paul and Holly Fine, whose signatures of impassioned and personal reporting span two decades of local and network television.

National Society of Film Critics Awards, 1990

Best Film: *Goodfellas,* Martin Scorcese

Best Actress: Anjelica Huston, *The Grifters* and *The Witches*

Best Actor: Jeremy Irons, *Reversal of Fortune*

Best Supporting Actress: Annette Bening, *The Grifters*

Best Supporting Actor: Bruce Davidson, *Longtime Companion*

Best Screenplay: *To Sleep With Anger,* Charles Burnett

Poets Laureate of the United States

The post was established in 1985. Appointment is for a one-year term, but is renewable.

Robert Penn Warren	1986–1987	Mark Strand	1990–1991
Richard Wilbur	1987–1988	Joseph Brodsky	1991–
Howard Nemerov	1988–1990		

Pulitzer Prize Awards

(For years not listed, no award was made.)

Source: Columbia University.

Pulitzer Prizes in Journalism

MERITORIOUS PUBLIC SERVICE

1918 *New York Times;* also special award to Minna Lewinson and Henry Beetle Hough
1919 *Milwaukee Journal*
1921 *Boston Post*
1922 *New York World*
1923 *Memphis Commercial Appeal*
1924 *New York World*
1926 *Columbus* (Ga.) *Enquirer Sun*
1927 *Canton* (Ohio) *Daily News*
1928 *Indianapolis Times*
1929 *New York Evening World*
1931 *Atlanta Constitution*
1932 *Indianapolis News*
1933 *New York World-Telegram*
1934 *Medford* (Ore.) *Mail Tribune*
1935 *Sacramento Bee*
1936 *Cedar Rapids* (Iowa) *Gazette*
1937 *St. Louis Post-Dispatch*
1938 *Bismarck* (N.D.) *Tribune*
1939 *Miami Daily News*
1940 *Waterbury* (Conn.) *Republican* and *American*
1941 *St. Louis Post-Dispatch*
1942 *Los Angeles Times*
1943 *Omaha World-Herald*
1944 *New York Times*
1945 *Detroit Free Press*
1946 *Scranton* (Pa.) *Times*
1947 *Baltimore Sun*
1948 *St. Louis Post-Dispatch*
1949 (Lincoln) *Nebraska State Journal*
1950 *Chicago Daily News;* and *St. Louis Post-Dispatch*
1951 *Miami Herald;* and *Brooklyn Eagle*
1952 *St. Louis Post-Dispatch*
1953 *Whiteville* (N.C.) *News Reporter;* and *Tabor City* (N.C.) *Tribune*
1954 *Newsday* (Garden City, L.I.)
1955 *Columbus* (Ga.) *Ledger* and *Sunday Ledger-Enquirer*
1956 *Watsonville* (Calif.) *Register-Pajaronian*
1957 *Chicago Daily News*
1958 (Little Rock) *Arkansas Gazette*
1959 *Utica* (N.Y.) *Observer Dispatch* and *Utica Daily Press*
1960 *Los Angeles Times*
1961 *Amarillo* (Tex.) *Globe-Times*
1962 *Panama City* (Fla.) *News-Herald*
1963 *Chicago Daily News*
1964 *St. Petersburg* (Fla.) *Times*
1965 *Hutchinson* (Kan.) *News*
1966 *Boston Globe*
1967 *Louisville Courier-Journal* and *Milwaukee Journal*
1968 *Riverside* (Calif.) *Press-Enterprise*
1969 *Los Angeles Times*
1970 *Newsday* (Garden City, L.I.)
1971 *Winston-Salem* (N.C.) *Journal and Sentinel*
1972 *New York Times*
1973 *Washington Post*
1974 *Newsday* (Garden City, L.I.)
1975 *Boston Globe*
1976 *Anchorage* (Alaska) *Daily News*
1977 *Lufkin* (Tex.) *News*
1978 *Philadelphia Inquirer*

1979 *Point Reyes* (Calif.) *Light*
1980 Gannett News Service
1981 *Charlotte* (N.C.) *Observer*
1982 *Detroit News*
1983 *Jackson* (Miss.) *Clarion-Ledger*
1984 *Los Angeles Times*
1985 *The Fort Worth Star-Telegram*
1986 *Denver Post*
1987 Andrew Schneider and Matthew Brelis, *Pittsburgh Press*
1988 *Charlotte* (N.C.) *Observer*
1989 *Anchorage Daily News*
1990 *Philadelphia Inquirer* and *Washington* (N.C.) *Daily News*
1991 *Des Moines Register,* reporting by Jane Schorer

EDITORIAL

1917 *New York Tribune*
1918 *Louisville Courier-Journal*
1920 Harvey E. Newbranch *(Omaha Evening World-Herald)*
1922 Frank M. O'Brien *(New York Herald)*
1923 William Allen White *(Emporia* [Kan.] *Gazette)*
1924 *Boston Herald* (Frank Buxton); special prize: Frank I. Cobb *(New York World)*
1925 *Charleston* (S.C.) *News and Courier*
1926 *New York Times* (Edward M. Kingsbury)
1927 *Boston Herald* (F. Lauriston Bullard)
1928 Grover Cleveland Hall *(Montgomery* [Ala.] *Advertiser)*
1929 Louis Isaac Jaffe *(Norfolk Virginian-Pilot)*
1931 Charles S. Ryckman *(Fremont* [Neb.] *Tribune)*
1933 *Kansas City* (Mo.) *Star*
1934 E. P. Chase *(Atlantic* [Iowa] *News Telegraph)*
1936 Felix Morley *(Washington Post);* George B. Parker (Scripps-Howard Newspapers)
1937 John W. Owens *(Baltimore Sun)*
1938 W. W. Waymack *(Des Moines Register and Tribune)*
1939 Ronald G. Callvert *(Portland Oregonian)*
1940 Bart Howard *(St. Louis Post-Dispatch)*
1941 Reuben Maury *(New York Daily News)*
1942 Geoffrey Parsons *(New York Herald Tribune)*
1943 Forrest W. Seymour *(Des Moines Register and Tribune)*
1944 *Kansas City* (Mo.) *Star* (Henry J. Haskell)
1945 George W. Potter *(Providence* [R.I.] *Journal-Bulletin)*
1946 Hodding Carter ([Greenville, Miss.] *Delta Democrat-Times)*
1947 William H. Grimes *(Wall Street Journal)*
1948 Virginius Dabney *(Richmond Times-Dispatch)*
1949 John H. Crider *(Boston Herald);* Herbert Elliston *(Washington Post)*
1950 Carl M. Saunders *(Jackson* [Mich.] *Citizen Patriot)*
1951 William H. Fitzpatrick *(New Orleans States)*
1952 Louis LaCoss *(St. Louis Globe-Democrat)*
1953 Vermont C. Royster *(Wall Street Journal)*
1954 *Boston Herald* (Don Murray)
1955 *Detroit Free Press* (Royce Howes)
1956 Lauren K. Soth *(Des Moines Register and Tribune)*
1957 Buford Boone *(Tuscaloosa* [Ala.] *News)*

1958 Harry S. Ashmore *(Arkansas Gazette)*
1959 Ralph McGill *(Atlanta Constitution)*
1960 Lenoir Chambers *(Virginian-Pilot)*
1961 William J. Dorvillier *(San Juan* [P.R.] *Star)*
1962 Thomas M. Storke *(Santa Barbara* [Calif.] *News-Press)*
1963 Ira B. Harkey, Jr. *(Pascagoula* [Miss.] *Chronicle)*
1964 Hazel Brannon Smith *(Lexington* [Miss.] *Advertiser)*
1965 John R. Harrison *(Gainesville* [Fla.] *Daily Sun)*
1966 Robert Lasch *(St. Louis Post-Dispatch)*
1967 Eugene Patterson *(Atlanta Constitution)*
1968 John S. Knight *(Knight Newspapers)*
1969 Paul Greenberg *(Pine Bluff* [Ark.] *Commercial)*
1970 Phillip L. Geyelin *(Washington Post)*
1971 Horance G. Davis, Jr. *(Gainesville* [Fla.] *Sun)*
1972 John Strohmeyer *(Bethlehem* [Pa.] *Globe Times)*
1973 Roger Bourne Linscott *(Berkshire Eagle* [Pittsfield, Mass.])
1974 F. Gilman Spencer *(Trenton* [N.J.] *Trentonian)*
1975 John Daniell Maurice *(Charleston* [W. Va.] *Daily Mail)*
1976 Philip P. Kerby *(Los Angeles Times)*
1977 Warren L. Lerude, Foster Church and Norman F. Cardoza *(Reno* [Nev.] *Gazette* and *Nevada State Journal)*
1978 Meg Greenfield *(Washington Post)*
1979 Edwin M. Yoder, Jr. *(Washington Star)*
1980 Robert L. Bartley *(Wall Street Journal)*
1981 Not awarded
1982 Jack Rosenthal *(New York Times)*
1983 *Miami Herald*
1984 Albert Scardino *(Georgia Gazette)*
1985 Richard Aregood *(Philadelphia Daily News)*
1986 Jack Fuller *(Chicago Tribune)*
1987 Jonathan Freedman *(San Diego Tribune)*
1988 Jane E. Healy *(Orlando* Fla. *Sentinel)*
1989 Lois Wille *(Chicago Tribune)*
1990 Thomas J. Hylton *(Pottstown* [Pa.] *Mercury)*
1991 Ron Casey, Harold Jackson, and Joey Kennedy *(Birmingham* [Ala.] *News)*

CORRESPONDENCE

1929 Paul Scott Mowrer *(Chicago Daily News)*
1930 Leland Stowe *(New York Herald Tribune)*
1931 H. R. Knickerbocker *(Philadelphia Public Ledger* and *New York Evening Post)*
1932 Walter Duranty *(New York Times);* Charles G. Ross *(St. Louis Post-Dispatch)*
1933 Edgar Ansel Mowrer *(Chicago Daily News)*
1934 Frederick T. Birchall *(New York Times)*
1935 Arthur Krock *(New York Times)*
1936 Wilfred C. Barber *(Chicago Tribune)*
1937 Anne O'Hare McCormick *(New York Times)*
1938 Arthur Krock *(New York Times)*
1939 Louis P. Lochner (Associated Press)
1940 Otto D. Tolischus *(New York Times)*
1941 Group award[1]
1942 Carlos P. Romulo *(Philippines Herald)*
1943 Hanson W. Baldwin *(New York Times)*
1944 Ernie Pyle (Scripps-Howard Newspaper Alliance)
1945 Harold V. (Hal) Boyle (Associated Press)
1946 Arnaldo Cortesi *(New York Times)*
1947 Brooks Atkinson *(New York Times)*
1948 Discontinued

EDITORIAL CARTOONING

1922 Rollin Kirby *(New York World)*
1924 Jay Norwood Darling *(New York Tribune)*
1925 Rollin Kirby *(New York World)*

1926 D. R. Fitzpatrick *(St. Louis Post-Dispatch)*
1927 Nelson Harding *(Brooklyn Eagle)*
1928 Nelson Harding *(Brooklyn Eagle)*

1. For the public services and the individual achievements of American news reporters in the war zones.

1929 Rollin Kirby *(New York World)*
1930 Charles R. Macauley *(Brooklyn Eagle)*
1931 Edmund Duffy *(Baltimore Sun)*
1932 John T. McCutcheon *(Chicago Tribune)*
1933 H. M. Talburt *(Washington Daily News)*
1934 Edmund Duffy *(Baltimore Sun)*
1935 Ross A. Lewis *(Milwaukee Journal)*
1937 C. D. Batchelor *(New York Daily News)*
1938 Vaughn Shoemaker *(Chicago Daily News)*
1939 Charles G. Werner *(Daily Oklahoman* [Oklahoma City]*)*
1940 Edmund Duffy *(Baltimore Sun)*
1941 Jacob Burck *(Chicago Times)*
1942 Herbert L. Block (NEA Service)
1943 Jay Norwood Darling *(New York Herald Tribune)*
1944 Clifford K. Berryman *(Washington Evening Star)*
1945 Bill Mauldin (United Features Syndicate)
1946 Bruce Alexander Russell *(Los Angeles Times)*
1947 Vaughn Shoemaker *(Chicago Daily News)*
1948 Reuben L. Goldberg *(New York Sun)*
1949 Lute Pease *(Newark Evening News)*
1950 James T. Berryman *(Washington Evening Star)*
1951 Reg (Reginald W.) Manning *(Arizona Republic* [Phoenix]*)*
1952 Fred L. Packer *(New York Mirror)*
1953 Edward D. Kuekes *(Cleveland Plain Dealer)*
1954 Herbert L. Block *(Washington Post* and *Times-Herald)*
1955 Daniel R. Fitzpatrick *(St. Louis Post-Dispatch)*
1956 Robert York *(Louisville Times)*
1957 Tom Little *(Nashville Tennessean)*
1958 Bruce M. Shanks *(Buffalo Evening News)*
1959 Bill Mauldin *(St. Louis Post-Dispatch)*
1961 Carey Orr *(Chicago Tribune)*
1962 Edmund S. Valtman *(Hartford Times)*
1963 Frank Miller *(Des Moines Register)*
1964 Paul Conrad (formerly of *Denver Post,* later on *Los Angeles Times)*
1966 Don Wright *(Miami News)*
1967 Patrick B. Oliphant *(Denver Post)*
1968 Eugene Gray Payne *(Charlotte* [N.C.] *Observer)*
1969 John Fischetti *(Chicago Daily News)*
1970 Thomas F. Darcy *(Newsday* [Garden City, L.I.]*)*
1971 Paul Conrad *(Los Angeles Times)*
1972 Jeffrey K. MacNelly *(Richmond* [Va.] *News Leader)*
1974 Paul Szep *(Boston Globe)*
1975 Garry Trudeau (Universal Press Syndicate)
1976 Tony Auth *(Philadelphia Inquirer)*
1977 Paul Szep *(Boston Globe)*
1978 Jeffrey K. MacNelly *(Richmond* [Va.] *News Leader)*
1979 Herbert L. Block *(Washington Post)*
1980 Don Wright *(Miami News)*
1981 Mike Peters *(Dayton* [Ohio] *Daily News)*
1982 Ben Sargent *(Austin* [Tex.] *American-Statesman)*
1983 Richard Locher *(Chicago Tribune)*
1984 Paul Conrad *(Los Angeles Times)*
1985 Jeff MacNelly *(Chicago Tribune)*
1986 Jules Feiffer *(Village Voice)*
1987 Berke Breathed *(Washington Post* Writers Group)
1988 Doug Marlette *(Atlanta Constitution* and *Charlotte* [N.C.] *Observer)*

1989 Jack Higgins *(Chicago Sun-Times)*
1990 Tom Toles *(Buffalo News)*
1991 Jim Borgman *(Cincinnati Inquirer)*

NEWS PHOTOGRAPHY

1942 Milton Brooks *(Detroit News)*
1943 Frank Noel (Associated Press)
1944 Frank Filan (Associated Press); Earle L. Bunker *(Omaha World-Herald)*
1945 Joe Rosenthal (Associated Press)
1947 Arnold Hardy
1948 Frank Cushing *(Boston Traveler)*
1949 Nat Fein *(New York Herald Tribune)*
1950 Bill Crouch *(Oakland Tribune)*
1951 Max Desfor (Associated Press)
1952 John Robinson and Don Ultang *(Des Moines Register & Tribune)*
1953 William M. Gallagher *(Flint* [Mich.] *Journal)*
1954 Mrs. Walter M. Schau
1955 John L. Gaunt, Jr. *(Los Angeles Times)*
1956 *New York Daily News*
1957 Harry A. Trask *(Boston Traveler)*
1958 William C. Beall *(Washington Daily News)*
1959 William Seaman *(Minneapolis Star)*
1960 Andrew Lopez (United Press International)
1961 Yasushi Nagao (Mainichi Newspapers, Tokyo)
1962 Paul Vathis (Harrisburg [Pa.] bureau of Associated Press)
1963 Hector Rondon *(La Republica,* Caracas, Venezuela)
1964 Robert H. Jackson *(Dallas Times Herald)*
1965 Horst Faas (Associated Press)
1966 Kyoichi Sawada (United Press International)
1967 Jack R. Thornell (Associated Press)
1968 News: Rocco Morabito *(Jacksonville* [Fla.] *Journal);* features: Toshio Sakai (United Press International)
1969 Spot news: Edward T. Adams (Associated Press); features: Moneta Sleet, Jr.
1970 Spot news: Steve Starr (Associated Press); features: Dallas Kinney *(Palm Beach Post)*
1971 Spot news: John Paul Filo *(Valley Daily News and Daily Dispatch* [Tarentum and New Kensington, Pa.]); features: Jack Dykinga *(Chicago Sun-Times)*
1972 Spot news: Horst Faas and Michel Laurent (Associated Press); features: Dave Kennerly (United Press International)
1973 Spot news: Huynh Cong Ut *(Associated Press);* features: Brian Lanker *(Topeka Capital-Journal)*
1974 Spot news: Anthony K. Roberts (Associated Press); features: Slava Veder (Associated Press)
1975 Spot news: Gerald H. Gay *(Seattle Times);* features: Matthew Lewis *(Washington Post)*
1976 Spot news: Stanley J. Forman *(Boston Herald-American);* features: photographic staff of *Louisville Courier-Journal* and *Times*
1977 Spot news: Neal Ulevich (Associated Press) and Stanley J. Forman *(Boston Herald-American);* features: Robin Hood *(Chattanooga News-Free Press)*
1978 Spot news: John Blair, freelance, Evansville, Ind.; features: J. Ross Baughman (Associated Press)
1979 Spot news: Thomas J. Kelly, 3rd *(Pottstown* [Pa.] *Mercury);* features: photographic staff of *Boston Herald-American*
1980 Features: Erwin H. Hagler *(Dallas Times Herald)*
1981 Spot news: Larry C. Price *(Fort Worth Star-Telegram);* features: Taro M. Yamasaki *(Detroit Free Press)*

1982 Spot news: Ron Edmonds (Associated Press); features: John H. White *(Chicago Sun-Times)*
1983 Spot news: Bill Foley (Associated Press); features: James B. Dickman *(Dallas Times Herald)*
1984 Spot news: Stan Grossfeld *(Boston Globe);* features: Anthony Suau *(Denver Post)*
1985 Spot news: photographic staff of *Register,* Santa Ana, Calif.; features: Stan Grossfeld *(Boston Globe)*
1986 Spot news: Michel duCille and Carol Guzy *(Miami Herald);* features: Tom Gralish *(Philadelphia Inquirer)*
1987 Spot news: Kim Komenich *(San Francisco Examiner);* features: David Peterson *(Des Moines Register)*
1988 Spot news: Scott Shaw *(Odessa* [Texas] *American);* features: Michel duCille *(Miami Herald)*
1989 Spot news: Ron Olshwanger *(St. Louis Post-Dispatch);* features: Manny Crisostomo *(Detroit Free Press)*
1990 Spot news: *Oakland Tribune;* features: David C. Turnley *(Detroit Free Press)*
1991 Spot news: Greg Marinovich (Associated Press); features: William Snyder *(Dallas Morning News)*

NATIONAL TELEGRAPHIC REPORTING

1942 Louis Stark *(New York Times)*
1944 Dewey L. Fleming *(Baltimore Sun)*
1945 James Reston *(New York Times)*
1946 Edward A. Harris *(St. Louis Post-Dispatch)*
1947 Edward T. Folliard *(Washington Post)*

NATIONAL REPORTING

1948 Bert Andrews *(New York Herald Tribune);* Nat S. Finney *(Minneapolis Tribune)*
1949 C. P. Trussell *(New York Times)*
1950 Edwin O. Guthman *(Seattle Times)*
1952 Anthony Leviero *(New York Times)*
1953 Don Whitehead (Associated Press)
1954 Richard Wilson (Cowles Newspapers)
1955 Anthony Lewis *(Washington Daily News)*
1956 Charles L. Bartlett *(Chattanooga Times)*
1957 James Reston *(New York Times)*
1958 Relman Morin (Associated Press) and Clark Mollenhoff *(Des Moines Register & Tribune)*
1959 Howard Van Smith *(Miami News)*
1960 Vance Trimble (Scripps-Howard Newspaper Alliance)
1961 Edward R. Cony *(Wall Street Journal)*
1962 Nathan G. Caldwell and Gene S. Graham *(Nashville Tennessean)*
1963 Anthony Lewis *(New York Times)*
1964 Merriman Smith (United Press International)
1965 Louis M. Kohlmeier *(Wall Street Journal)*
1966 Haynes Johnson *(Washington Evening Star)*
1967 Stanley Penn and Monroe Karmin *(Wall Street Journal)*
1968 Howard James *(Christian Science Monitor);* Nathan K. (Nick) Kotz *(Des Moines Register and Minneapolis Tribune)*
1969 Robert Cahn *(Christian Science Monitor)*
1970 William J. Eaton *(Chicago Daily News)*
1971 Lucinda Franks and Thomas Powers (United Press International)
1972 Jack Anderson *(United Feature Syndicate)*
1973 Robert Boyd and Clark Hoyt *(Knight Newspapers)*
1974 Jack White *(Providence* [R.I.] *Journal-Bulletin);* and James R. Polk *(Washington Star-News)*
1975 Donald L. Barlett and James B. Steele *(Philadelphia Inquirer)*
1976 James Risser *(Des Moines Register)*

1977 Walter Mears (Associated Press)
1978 Gaylord D. Shaw (Los Angeles Times)
1979 James Risser (Des Moines Register)
1980 Bette Swenson Orsini and Charles Stafford (St. Petersburg Times)
1981 John M. Crewdson (New York Times)
1982 Rick Atkinson (Kansas City [Mo.] Times)
1983 Boston Globe
1984 John N. Wilford (New York Times)
1985 Thomas J. Knudson (Des Moines Register)
1986 Craig Flournoy and George Rodrigue (Dallas Morning News) and Arthur Howe (Philadelphia Inquirer)
1987 Miami Herald, staff; New York Times, staff
1988 Tim Weiner (Philadelphia Inquirer)
1989 Donald L. Barlett and James B. Steele (Philadelphia Inquirer)
1990 Ross Anderson, Bill Dietrich, Mary Ann Gwinn, and Eric Nalder (Seattle Times)
1991 Marjie Lundstrom and Rochelle Sharpe (Gannett News Service)

INTERNATIONAL TELEGRAPHIC REPORTING

1942 Laurence Edmund Allen (Associated Press)
1943 Ira Wolfert (North American Newspaper Alliance, Inc.)
1944 Daniel De Luce (Associated Press)
1945 Mark S. Watson (Baltimore Sun)
1946 Homer W. Bigart (New York Herald Tribune)
1947 Eddy Gilmore (Associated Press)

INTERNATIONAL REPORTING

1948 Paul W. Ward (Baltimore Sun)
1949 Price Day (Baltimore Sun)
1950 Edmund Stevens (Christian Science Monitor)
1951 Keyes Beech and Fred Sparks (Chicago Daily News); Homer Bigart and Marguerite Higgins (New York Herald Tribune); Relman Morin and Don Whitehead (Associated Press)
1952 John M. Hightower (Associated Press)
1953 Austin C. Wehrwein (Milwaukee Journal)
1954 Jim G. Lucas (Scripps-Howard Newspapers)
1955 Harrison E. Salisbury (New York Times)
1956 William Randolph Hearst, Jr. and Frank Conniff (Hearst Newspapers) and Kingsbury Smith (INS)
1957 Russell Jones (United Press)
1958 New York Times
1959 Joseph Martin and Philip Santora (New York Daily News)
1960 A. M. Rosenthal (New York Times)
1961 Lynn Heinzerling (Associated Press)
1962 Walter Lippmann (New York Herald Tribune Syndicate)
1963 Hal Hendrix (Miami News)
1964 Malcolm W. Browne (Associated Press) and David Halberstam (New York Times)
1965 J. A. Livingston (Philadelphia Bulletin)
1966 Peter Arnett (Associated Press)
1967 R. John Hughes (Christian Science Monitor)
1968 Alfred Friendly (Washington Post)
1969 William Tuohy (Los Angeles Times)
1970 Seymour M. Hersh (Dispatch News Service)
1971 Jimmie Lee Hoagland (Washington Post)
1972 Peter R. Kann (Wall Street Journal)
1973 Max Frankel (New York Times)
1974 Hedrick Smith (New York Times)
1975 William Mullen and Ovie Carter (Chicago Tribune)
1976 Sydney H. Schanberg (New York Times)
1978 Henry Kamm (New York Times)
1979 Richard Ben Cramer (Philadelphia Inquirer)
1980 Joel Brinkley and Jay Mather (Louisville Courier-Journal)
1981 Shirley Christian (Miami Herald)
1982 John Darnton (New York Times)
1983 Thomas L. Friedman (New York Times)
1984 Karen E. House (Wall Street Journal)
1985 Josh Friedman, Dennis Bell, and Ozier Muhammad (Newsday)
1986 Lewis M. Simons, Pete Carey, and Katherine Ellison (San Jose Mercury News)
1987 Michael Parks (Los Angeles Times)
1988 Thomas L. Friedman (New York Times)
1989 Bill Keller (New York Times); Glenn Frankel (Washington Post)
1990 Nicholas D. Kristof and Sheryl WuDunn (New York Times)
1991 Caryle Murphy (Washington Post) and Serge Schmemann (New York Times)

REPORTING

1917 Herbert B. Swope (New York World)
1918 Harold A. Littledale (New York Evening Post)
1920 John J. Leary, Jr. (New York World)
1921 Louis Seibold (New York World)
1922 Kirke L. Simpson (Associated Press)
1923 Alva Johnston (New York Times)
1924 Magner White (San Diego Sun)
1925 James W. Mulroy and Alvin H. Goldstein (Chicago Daily News)
1926 William Burke Miller (Louisville Courier-Journal)
1927 John T. Rogers (St. Louis Post-Dispatch)
1929 Paul Y. Anderson (St. Louis Post-Dispatch)
1930 Russell D. Owen (New York Times); special award: W. O. Dapping (Auburn [N.Y.] Citizen)
1931 A. B. MacDonald (Kansas City [Mo.] Star)
1932 W. C. Richards, D. D. Martin, J. S. Pooler, F. D. Webb, J. N. W. Sloan (all of Detroit Free Press)
1933 Francis A. Jamieson (Associated Press)
1934 Royce Brier (San Francisco Chronicle)
1935 William H. Taylor (New York Herald Tribune)
1936 Lauren D. Lyman (New York Times)
1937 John J. O'Neill (New York Herald Tribune); William Leonard Laurence (New York Times); Howard W. Blakeslee (Associated Press); Gobind Behari Lal (Universal Service); David Dietz (Scripps-Howard Newspapers)
1938 Raymond Sprigle (Pittsburg Post-Gazette)
1939 Thomas L. Stokes (New York World-Telegram)
1940 S. Burton Heath (New York World-Telegram)
1941 Westbrook Pegler (New York World-Telegram)
1942 Stanton Delaplane (San Francisco Chronicle)
1943 George Weller (Chicago Daily News)
1944 Paul Schoenstein and associates (New York Journal-American)
1945 Jack S. McDowell (San Francisco Call-Bulletin)
1946 William Leonard Laurence (New York Times)
1947 Frederick Woltman (New York World-Telegram)
1948 George E. Goodwin (Atlanta Journal)
1949 Malcolm Johnson (New York Sun)
1950 Meyer Berger (New York Times)
1951 Edward S. Montgomery (San Francisco Examiner)
1952 George de Carvalho (San Francisco Chronicle)
1953 Editorial staff (Providence Journal and Evening Bulletin);[1] Edward J. Mowery (New York World-Telegram and Sun)[2]
1954 Vicksburg (Miss.) Sunday Post-Herald;[1] Alvin Scott McCoy (Kansas City [Mo.] Star)[2]
1955 Mrs. Caro Brown (Alice [Tex.] Daily Echo);[1] Roland Kenneth Towery (Cuero [Tex.] Record)[2]
1956 Lee Hills (Detroit Free Press);[1] Arthur Daley (New York Times)[2]
1957 Salt Lake Tribune;[1] Wallace Turner and Wil-

liam Lambert *(Portland Oregonian)*[2]
1958 *Fargo* [N.D.] *Forum;*[1] George Beveridge *(Washington* [D.C.] *Evening Star)*[2]
1959 Mary Lou Werner *(Washington* [D.C.] *Evening Star);*[1] John Harold Brislin *(Scranton* [Pa.] *Tribune & Scrantonian)*[2]
1960 Jack Nelson *(Atlanta Constitution);*[1] Miriam Ottenberg *(Washington Evening Star)*[2]
1961 Sanche de Gramont *(New York Herald Tribune);*[1] Edgar May *(Buffalo Evening News)*[2]
1962 Robert D. Mullins *(Deseret News,* Salt Lake City);[1] George Bliss *(Chicago Tribune)*[2]
1963 Sylvan Fox, Anthony Shannon, and William Longgood *(New York World-Telegram and Sun);*[1] Oscar Griffin, Jr. (former editor of *Pecos* [Tex.] *Independent and Enterprise,* now on staff of *Houston Chronicle)*[2]

1. Reporting under pressure of edition deadlines. 2. Reporting not under pressure of edition deadlines.

GENERAL LOCAL REPORTING

1964 Norman C. Miller *(Wall Street Journal)*
1965 Melvin H. Ruder *(Hungry Horse News,* Columbia Falls, Mont.)
1966 Staff of *Los Angeles Times*
1967 Robert V. Cox *(Chambersburg* [Pa.] *Public Opinion)*
1968 Staff of *Detroit Free Press*
1969 John Fetterman *(Louisville Times* and *Courier-Journal)*
1970 Thomas Fitzpatrick *(Chicago Sun-Times)*
1971 Staff of *Akron* (Ohio) *Beacon*
1972 Richard Cooper and John Machacek *(Rochester* [N.Y.] *Times-Union)*
1973 *Chicago Tribune*
1974 Arthur M. Petacque and Hugh F. Hough *(Chicago Sun-Times)*
1975 *Xenia* (Ohio) *Daily Gazette*
1976 Gene Miller *(Miami Herald)*
1977 Margo Huston *(Milwaukee Journal)*
1978 Richard Whitt *(Louisville Courier-Journal)*
1979 Staff of *San Diego* (Calif.) *Evening Tribune*
1980 Staff of *Philadelphia Inquirer*
1981 *Longview* (Wash.) *Daily News*
1982 *Kansas City* (Mo.) *Star* and *Kansas City* (Mo.) *Times*
1983 *Fort Wayne* (Ind.) *News-Sentinel*
1984 *Newsday*

GENERAL NEWS REPORTING

1985 Thomas Turcol *(Virginian-Pilot and Ledger-Star)*
1986 Edna Buchanan *(Miami Herald)*
1987 *Akron Beacon Journal,* staff
1988 *Alabama Journal* (Montgomery), staff, *Lawrence* (Mass.) *Eagle-Tribune,* staff
1989 *Louisville Courier-Journal* staff
1990 *San Jose* (Calif.) *Mercury News*

SPOT NEWS REPORTING

1991 *Miami Herald* staff

SPECIAL LOCAL REPORTING

1964 James V. Magee, Albert V. Gaudiosi, and Frederick A. Meyer *(Philadelphia Bulletin)*
1965 Gene Goltz *(Houston Post)*
1966 John A. Frasca *(Tampa Tribune)*
1967 Gene Miller *(Miami Herald)*
1968 J. Anthony Lukas *(New York Times)*
1969 Albert L. Delugach and Denny Walsh *(St. Louis Globe-Democrat)*
1970 Harold Eugene Martin *(Montgomery Advertiser)*

1971 William Hugh Jones *(Chicago Tribune)*
1972 Timothy Leland, Gerard N. O'Neill, Stephen A. Kurkjian, and Ann DeSantis *(Boston Globe)*
1973 Sun Newspapers of Omaha, Neb.
1974 William Sherman *(New York Daily News)*
1975 *Indianapolis Star*
1976 *Chicago Tribune*
1977 Acel Moore and Wendell Rawls, Jr. *(Philadelphia Inquirer)*
1978 Anthony R. Dolan *(Stamford* [Conn.] *Advocate)*
1979 Gilbert M. Gaul and Elliot G. Jaspin *(Pottsville* [Pa.] *Republican)*
1980 Nils J. Bruzelius, Alexander B. Hawes, Jr., Stephen A. Kurkjian, Robert M. Porterfield, and Joan Vennochi *(Boston Globe)*
1981 Clark Hallas and Robert B. Lowe *(Arizona Daily Star,* Tucson)
1982 Paul Henderson *(Seattle Times)*
1983 Loretta Tofani *(Washington Post)*
1984 *Boston Globe*

INVESTIGATIVE REPORTING

1985 Lucy Morgan and Jack Reed (*St. Petersburg* [Fla.] *Times)* and William K. Marimow *(Philadelphia Inquirer)*
1986 Jeffrey A. Marx and Michael M. York *(Lexington* [Ky.] *Herald Leader)*
1987 Daniel R. Biddle, H.G. Bissinger, and Fredric N. Tulsky *(Philadelphia Inquirer)*
1988 Dean Baquet, William C. Gaines, and Ann Marie Lipinski *(Chicago Tribune)*
1989 Bill Dedman *(Atlanta Journal and Constitution)*
1990 Lou Kilzer and Chris Ison *(Minneapolis-St. Paul Star Tribune)*
1991 Joseph T. Hallinan and Susan M. Headden *(Indianapolis Star)*

FEATURE WRITING

1979 Jon D. Franklin *(Baltimore Evening Sun)*
1980 Madeleine Blais *(Miami Herald)*
1981 Teresa Carpenter *(Village Voice,* New York)
1982 Saul Pett (Associated Press)
1983 Nan Robertson *(New York Times)*
1984 Peter M. Rinearson *(Seattle Times)*
1985 Alice Steinbach *(Baltimore Sun)*
1986 John Camp *(St. Paul Pioneer Press and Dispatch)*
1987 Steve Twomey *(Philadelphia Inquirer)*
1988 Jacqui Banasz ynski *(St. Paul Pioneer Press Dispatch)*
1989 David Zucchino *(Philadelphia Inquirer)*
1990 Dave Curtin *(Colorado Springs Gazette Telegraph)*
1991 Sheryl James, *(St. Petersburg* (Fla.) *Times*

COMMENTARY

1970 Marquis W. Childs *(St. Louis Post-Dispatch)*
1971 William A. Caldwell *(Record* [Hackensack, N.J.])
1972 Mike Royko *(Chicago Daily News)*
1973 David S. Broder *(Washington Post)*
1974 Edwin A. Roberts, Jr. *(National Observer)*
1975 Mary McGrory *(Washington Star)*
1976 Walter W. (Red) Smith *(New York Times)*
1977 George F. Will *(Washington Post* Writers Group)
1978 William Safire *(New York Times)*
1979 Russell Baker *(New York Times)*
1980 Ellen H. Goodman *(Boston Globe)*
1981 Dave Anderson *(New York Times)*
1982 Art Buchwald *(Los Angeles Times* Syndicate)
1983 Claude Sitton *(Raleigh* [N.C.] *News & Observer)*
1984 Vermont Royster *(Wall Street Journal)*

1985 Murray Kempton (*Newsday*)
1986 Jimmy Breslin *(New York Daily News)*
1987 Charles Krauthammer (*Washington Post* Writers Group)
1988 Dave Barry *(Miami Herald)*
1989 Clarence Page *(Chicago Tribune)*
1990 Jim Murray *(Los Angeles Times)*
1991 Jim Hoagland *(Washington Post)*

CRITICISM

1970 Ada Louise Huxtable *(New York Times)*
1971 Harold C. Schonberg *(New York Times)*
1972 Frank Peters, Jr. *(St. Louis Post-Dispatch)*
1973 Ronald Powers *(Chicago Sun-Times)*
1974 Emily Genauer (Newsday Syndicate)
1975 Roger Ebert *(Chicago Sun-Times)*
1976 Alan M. Kriegsman *(Washington Post)*
1977 William McPherson *(Washington Post)*
1978 Walter Kerr *(New York Times)*
1979 Paul Gapp *(Chicago Tribune)*
1980 William A. Henry, 3rd *(Boston Globe)*
1981 Jonathan Yardley *(Washington Star)*
1982 Martin Bernheimer *(Los Angeles Times)*
1983 Manuela Hoelterhoff *(Wall Street Journal)*
1984 Paul Goldberger *(New York Times)*
1985 Howard Rosenberg (*Los Angeles Times*)
1986 Donal Henahan *(New York Times)*
1987 Richard Eder *(Los Angeles Times)*
1988 Tom Shales *(Washington Post)*
1989 Michael Skube (*News and Observer*, Raleigh, N.C.)
1990 Allan Temko *(San Francisco Chronicle)*
1991 David Shaw *(Los Angeles Times)*

EXPLANATORY JOURNALISM

1985 Jon Franklin *(Baltimore Evening Sun*)
1986 *New York Times*
1987 Jeff Lyon and Peter Gorner *(Chicago Tribune)*
1988 Daniel Hertzberg and James B. Stewart *(Wall Street Journal)*
1989 David Hanners, William Snyder, and Karen Blessen *(Dallas Morning News)*
1990 David A. Vise and Coll *(Washington Post)*
1991 Susan C. Faludi *(Wall Street Journal)*

SPECIALIZED REPORTING

1985 Randall Savage and Jackie Crosby (*Macon* [Ga.] *Telegraph and News*)
1986 Andrew Schneider and Mary Pat Flaherty *(Pittsburgh Press)*
1987 Alex S. Jones *(New York Times)*
1988 Walt Bogdanich *(Wall Street Journal)*
1989 Edward Humes *(Orange County Register)*
1990 Tamar Stieber *(Albuquerque* (N.M.) *Journal)*

BEAT REPORTING

1991 Natalie Angier *(New York Times)*

SPECIAL CITATIONS

1938 *Edmonton* (Alberta) *Journal,* special bronze plaque for editorial leadership in defense of freedom of press in Province of Alberta.
1941 *New York Times* for the public educational value of its foreign news report.
1944 Byron Price, Director of the Office of Censorship, for the creation and administration of the newspaper and radio codes. Mrs. William Allen White, for her husband's interest and services during the past seven years as a member of the Advisory Board of the Graduate School of Journalism, Columbia University. Richard Rodgers and Oscar Hammerstein II for their musical *Oklahoma!*
1945 The cartographers of the American press for their war maps.
1947 (Pulitzer centennial year.) Columbia University and the Graduate School of Journalism for their efforts to maintain and advance the high standards governing the Pulitzer Prize awards. The *St. Louis Post-Dispatch* for its unswerving adherence to the public and professional ideals of its founder and its leadership in American journalism.
1948 Dr. Frank D. Fackenthal for his interest and service.
1951 Cyrus L. Sulzberger *(New York Times)* for his exclusive interview with Archbishop Stepinac in a Yugoslav prison.
1952 *Kansas City Star* for coverage of 1951 floods; Max Kase *(New York Journal-American)* for exposures of bribery in college basketball.
1953 *New York Times* for its 17-year publication of "News of the Week in Review"; and Lester Markel, its founder.
1957 Kenneth Roberts for his historical novels.
1958 Walter Lippmann *(New York Herald Tribune)* for his "wisdom, perception and high sense of responsibility" in his commentary on national and international affairs.
1960 Garrett Mattingly, for *The Armada.*
1961 *American Heritage Picture History of the Civil War,* as distinguished example of American book publishing.
1964 Gannett Newspapers, Rochester, N.Y.
1973 James Thomas Flexner for his biography *George Washington.*
1974 Roger Sessions for his "life's work in music."
1976 John Hohenberg for "services for 22 years as administrator of the Pulitzer Prizes"; Scott Joplin for his contributions to American music.
1977 Alex Haley for his novel, *Roots.*
1978 E.B. White of *New Yorker* magazine and Richard L. Strout of *Christian Science Monitor.*
1982 Milton Babbitt, "for his life's work as a distinguished and seminal American composer."
1984 Theodor Seuss Geisel (Dr. Seuss) for "books full of playful rhymes, nonsense words and strange illustrations."
1985 William H. Schuman for "more than a half century of contribution to American music as a composer and educational leader."
1987 Joseph Pulitzer Jr., "for extraordinary services to American journalism and letters during his 31 years as chairman of the Pulitzer Prize Board and for his accomplishments as an editor and publisher."

Pulitzer Prizes in Letters

FICTION[1]

1918 *His Family.* Ernest Poole
1919 *The Magnificent Ambersons.* Booth Tarkington
1921 *The Age of Innocence.* Edith Wharton
1922 *Alice Adams.* Booth Tarkington
1923 *One of Ours.* Willa Cather
1924 *The Able McLaughlins.* Margaret Wilson
1925 *So Big.* Edna Ferber
1926 *Arrowsmith.* Sinclair Lewis
1927 *Early Autumn.* Louis Bromfield
1928 *The Bridge of San Luis Rey.* Thornton Wilder
1929 *Scarlet Sister Mary.* Julia Peterkin
1930 *Laughing Boy.* Oliver La Farge
1931 *Years of Grace.* Margaret Ayer Barnes

1932 *The Good Earth.* Pearl S. Buck
1933 *The Store.* T. S. Stribling
1934 *Lamb in His Bosom.* Caroline Miller

1. Before 1948, award was for novels only.
1935 *Now in November.* Josephine Winslow Johnson
1936 *Honey in the Horn.* Harold L. Davis
1937 *Gone With the Wind.* Margaret Mitchell
1938 *The Late George Apley.* John Phillips Marquand
1939 *The Yearling.* Marjorie Kinnan Rawlings
1940 *The Grapes of Wrath.* John Steinbeck
1942 *In This Our Life.* Ellen Glasgow
1943 *Dragon's Teeth.* Upton Sinclair
1944 *Journey in the Dark.* Martin Flavin
1945 *A Bell for Adano.* John Hersey
1947 *All the King's Men.* Robert Penn Warren
1948 *Tales of the South Pacific.* James A. Michener
1949 *Guard of Honor.* James Gould Cozzens
1950 *The Way West.* A. B. Guthrie, Jr.
1951 *The Town.* Conrad Richter
1952 *The Caine Mutiny.* Herman Wouk
1953 *The Old Man and the Sea.* Ernest Hemingway
1955 *A Fable.* William Faulkner
1956 *Andersonville.* MacKinlay Kantor
1958 *A Death in the Family.* James Agee
1959 *The Travels of Jaimie McPheeters.* Robert Lewis Taylor
1960 *Advise and Consent.* Allen Drury
1961 *To Kill a Mockingbird.* Harper Lee
1962 *The Edge of Sadness.* Edwin O'Connor
1963 *The Reivers.* William Faulkner
1965 *The Keepers of the House.* Shirley Ann Grau
1966 *Collected Stories of Katherine Anne Porter.* Katherine Anne Porter
1967 *The Fixer.* Bernard Malamud
1968 *The Confessions of Nat Turner.* William Styron
1969 *House Made of Dawn.* N. Scott Momaday
1970 *Collected Stories.* Jean Stafford
1972 *Angle of Repose.* Wallace Stegner
1973 *The Optimist's Daughter.* Eudora Welty
1975 *The Killer Angels.* Michael Shaara
1976 *Humboldt's Gift.* Saul Bellow
1978 *Elbow Room.* James Alan McPherson
1979 *The Stories of John Cheever.* John Cheever
1980 *The Executioner's Song.* Norman Mailer
1981 *A Confederacy of Dunces.* John Kennedy Toole
1982 *Rabbit Is Rich.* John Updike
1983 *The Color Purple.* Alice Walker
1984 *Ironweed.* William Kennedy
1985 *Foreign Affairs,* Alison Lurie
1986 *Lonesome Dove,* Larry McMurtry
1987 *A Summons to Memphis,* Peter Taylor
1988 *Beloved,* Toni Morrison
1989 *Breathing Lessons,* Anne Tyler
1990 *The Mambo Kings Play Songs of Love,* Oscar Hijeulos
1991 *Rabbit at Rest,* John Updike

DRAMA

1918 *Why Marry?* Jesse Lynch Williams
1920 *Beyond the Horizon.* Eugene O'Neill
1921 *Miss Lulu Bett.* Zona Gale
1922 *Anna Christie.* Eugene O'Neill
1923 *Icebound.* Owen Davis
1924 *Hell-Bent Fer Heaven.* Hatcher Hughes
1925 *They Knew What They Wanted.* Sidney Howard
1926 *Craig's Wife.* George Kelly
1927 *In Abraham's Bosom.* Paul Green
1928 *Strange Interlude.* Eugene O'Neill
1929 *Street Scene.* Elmer L. Rice
1930 *The Green Pastures.* Marc Connelly
1931 *Alison's House.* Susan Glaspell

1932 *Of Thee I Sing.* George S. Kaufman, Morrie Ryskind, and Ira Gershwin
1933 *Both Your Houses.* Maxwell Anderson
1934 *Men in White.* Sidney Kingsley
1935 *The Old Maid.* Zöe Akins
1936 *Idiot's Delight.* Robert E. Sherwood
1937 *You Can't Take It With You.* Moss Hart and George S. Kaufman
1938 *Our Town.* Thornton Wilder
1939 *Abe Lincoln in Illinois.* Robert E. Sherwood
1940 *The Time of Your Life.* William Saroyan
1941 *There Shall Be No Night.* Robert E. Sherwood
1943 *The Skin of Our Teeth.* Thornton Wilder
1945 *Harvey.* Mary Chase
1946 *State of the Union.* Russel Crouse and Howard Lindsay
1948 *A Streetcar Named Desire.* Tennessee Williams
1949 *Death of a Salesman.* Arthur Miller
1950 *South Pacific.* Richard Rodgers, Oscar Hammerstein II, and Joshua Logan
1952 *The Shrike.* Joseph Kramm
1953 *Picnic.* William Inge
1954 *The Teahouse of the August Moon.* John Patrick
1955 *Cat on a Hot Tin Roof.* Tennessee Williams
1956 *The Diary of Anne Frank.* Frances Goodrich and Albert Hackett
1957 *Long Day's Journey Into Night.* Eugene O'Neill
1958 *Look Homeward, Angel.* Ketti Frings
1959 *J.B.* Archibald MacLeish
1960 *Fiorello!* George Abbott, Jerome Weidman, Jerry Bock, and Sheldon Harnick
1961 *All the Way Home.* Tad Mosel
1962 *How to Succeed in Business Without Really Trying.* Frank Loesser and Abe Burrows
1965 *The Subject Was Roses.* Frank D. Gilroy
1967 *A Delicate Balance.* Edward Albee
1969 *The Great White Hope.* Howard Sackler
1970 *No Place to Be Somebody.* Charles Gordone
1971 *The Effect of Gamma Rays on Man-in-the-Moon Marigolds.* Paul Zindel
1973 *That Championship Season.* Jason Miller
1975 *Seascape.* Edward Albee
1976 *A Chorus Line.* Conceived by Michael Bennett
1977 *The Shadow Box.* Michael Cristofer
1978 *The Gin Game.* Donald L. Coburn
1979 *Buried Child.* Sam Shepard
1980 *Talley's Folly.* Lanford Wilson
1981 *Crimes of the Heart.* Beth Henley
1982 *A Soldier's Play.* Charles Fuller
1983 *'Night, Mother.* Marsha Norman
1984 *Glengarry Glen Ross.* David Mamet
1985 *Sunday in the Park with George.* Stephen Sondheim and James Lapine
1987 *Fences.* August Wilson
1988 *Driving Miss Daisy.* Alfred Uhry
1989 *The Heidi Chronicles.* Wendy Wasserstein
1990 *The Piano Lesson,* August Wilson
1991 *Lost in Yonkers,* Neil Simon

HISTORY OF UNITED STATES

1917 *With Americans of Past and Present Days.* J. J. Jusserand, Ambassador of France to United States
1918 *A History of the Civil War, 1861–1865.* James Ford Rhodes
1920 *The War With Mexico.* Justin H. Smith
1921 *The Victory at Sea.* William Sowden Sims in collaboration with Burton J. Hendrick
1922 *The Founding of New England.* James Truslow Adams
1923 *The Supreme Court in United States History.* Charles Warren
1924 *The American Revolution—A Constitutional*

Interpretation. Charles Howard McIlwain
1925 *A History of the American Frontier.* Frederic L. Paxson
1926 *The History of the United States.* Edward Channing
1927 *Pinckney's Treaty.* Samuel Flagg Bemis
1928 *Main Currents in American Thought.* Vernon Louis Parrington
1929 *The Organization and Administration of the Union Army, 1861–1865.* Fred Albert Shannon
1930 *The War of Independence.* Claude H. Van Tyne
1931 *The Coming of the War: 1914.* Bernadotte E. Schmitt
1932 *My Experiences in the World War.* John J. Pershing
1933 *The Significance of Sections in American History.* Frederick J. Turner
1934 *The People's Choice.* Herbert Agar
1935 *The Colonial Period of American History.* Charles McLean Andrews
1936 *The Constitutional History of the United States.* Andrew C. McLaughlin
1937 *The Flowering of New England.* Van Wyck Brooks
1938 *The Road to Reunion, 1865–1900.* Paul Herman Buck
1939 *A History of American Magazines.* Frank Luther Mott
1940 *Abraham Lincoln: The War Years.* Carl Sandburg
1941 *The Atlantic Migration, 1607–1860.* Marcus Lee Hansen
1942 *Reveille in Washington.* Margaret Leech
1943 *Paul Revere and the World He Lived In.* Esther Forbes
1944 *The Growth of American Thought.* Merle Curti
1945 *Unfinished Business.* Stephen Bonsal
1946 *The Age of Jackson.* Arthur M. Schlesinger, Jr.
1947 *Scientists Against Time.* James Phinney Baxter, 3rd
1948 *Across the Wide Missouri.* Bernard DeVoto
1949 *The Disruption of American Democracy.* Roy Franklin Nichols
1950 *Art and Life in America.* Oliver W. Larkin
1951 *The Old Northwest, Pioneer Period 1815–1840.* R. Carlyle Buley
1952 *The Uprooted.* Oscar Handlin
1953 *The Era of Good Feelings.* George Dangerfield
1954 *A Stillness at Appomattox.* Bruce Catton
1955 *Great River: The Rio Grande in North American History.* Paul Horgan
1956 *The Age of Reform.* Richard Hofstadter
1957 *Russia Leaves the War: Soviet-American Relations, 1917–1920.* George F. Kennan
1958 *Banks and Politics in America: From the Revolution to the Civil War.* Bray Hammond
1959 *The Republican Era: 1869–1901.* Leonard D. White, assisted by Jean Schneider
1960 *In the Days of McKinley.* Margaret Leech
1961 *Between War and Peace: The Potsdam Conference.* Herbert Feis
1962 *The Triumphant Empire, Thunder-Clouds Gather in the West.* Lawrence H. Gipson
1963 *Washington, Village and Capital, 1800–1878.* Constance McLaughlin Green
1964 *Puritan Village: The Formation of a New England Town.* Sumner Chilton Powell
1965 *The Greenback Era.* Irwin Unger
1966 *Life of the Mind in America.* Perry Miller
1967 *Exploration and Empire: The Explorer and Scientist in the Winning of the American West.* William H. Goetzmann
1968 *The Ideological Origins of the American Revolution.* Bernard Bailyn
1969 *Origins of the Fifth Amendment.* Leonard W. Levy
1970 *Present at the Creation: My Years in the State Department.* Dean Acheson
1971 *Roosevelt: The Soldier of Freedom.* James McGregor Burns
1972 *Neither Black Nor White. Slavery and Race Relations in Brazil and the United States.* Carl N. Degler
1973 *People of Paradox: An Inquiry Concerning the Origin of American Civilization.* Michael Kammen
1974 *The Americans: The Democratic Experience, Vol. 3.* Daniel J. Boorstin
1975 *Jefferson and His Time.* Dumas Malone
1976 *Lamy of Santa Fe.* Paul Horgan
1977 *The Impending Crisis: 1841–1861.* David M. Potter (posth)
1978 *The Invisible Hand: The Managerial Revolution in American Business.* Alfred D. Chandler, Jr.
1979 *The Dred Scott Case: Its Significance in Law and Politics.* Don E. Fehrenbacher
1980 *Been in the Storm So Long.* Leon F. Litwack
1981 *American Education: The National Experience; 1783–1876.* Lawrence A. Cremin
1982 *Mary Chestnut's Civil War.* C. Vann Woodward, editor
1983 *The Transformation of Virginia, 1740–1790.* Rhys L. Isaac
1985 *The Prophets of Regulation.* Thomas K. McCraw
1986 *. . . the Heavens and the Earth: A Political History of the Space Age.* Walter A. McDougall
1987 *Voyagers to the West: A Passage in the Peopling of America on the Eve of the Revolution.* Bernard Bailyn
1988 *The Launching of Modern American Science 1846–1876.* Robert V. Bruce
1989 *Parting the Waters,* Taylor Branch; *Battle Cry of Freedom,* James M. McPherson
1990 *In Our Image: America's Empire in the Philippines,* Stanley Karnow
1991 *A Midwife's Tale: The Life of Martha Ballard, Based on Her Diary 1785–1812,* Laurel Thatcher Ulrich

BIOGRAPHY OR AUTOBIOGRAPHY

1917 *Julia Ward Howe.* Laura E. Richards and Maude Howe Elliott, assisted by Florence Howe Hall
1918 *Benjamin Franklin, Self-Revealed.* William Cabell Bruce
1919 *The Education of Henry Adams.* Henry Adams
1920 *The Life of John Marshall.* Albert J. Beveridge
1921 *The Americanization of Edward Bok.* Edward Bok
1922 *A Daughter of the Middle Border.* Hamlin Garland
1923 *The Life and Letters of Walter H. Page,* Burton J. Hendrick
1924 *From Immigrant to Inventor.* Michael Idvorsky Pupin
1925 *Barrett Wendell and His Letters.* M. A. DeWolfe Howe
1926 *The Life of Sir William Osler.* Harvey Cushing
1927 *Whitman.* Emory Holloway
1928 *The American Orchestra and Theodore Thomas.* Charles Edward Russell
1929 *The Training of an American. The Earlier Life and Letters of Walter H. Page.* Burton J. Hendrick
1930 *The Raven.* Marquis James

1931 *Charles W. Eliot.* Henry James
1932 *Theodore Roosevelt.* Henry F. Pringle
1933 *Grover Cleveland.* Allan Nevins
1934 *John Hay.* Tyler Dennett
1935 *R. E. Lee.* Douglas S. Freeman
1936 *The Thought and Character of William James.* Ralph Barton Perry
1937 *Hamilton Fish.* Allan Nevins
1938 *Pedlar's Progress.* Odell Shepard; *Andrew Jackson.* Marquis James
1939 *Benjamin Franklin.* Carl Van Doren
1940 *Woodrow Wilson. Life and Letters,* Vols. VII and VIII. Ray Stannard Baker
1941 *Jonathan Edwards.* Ola E. Winslow
1942 *Crusader in Crinoline.* Forrest Wilson
1943 *Admiral of the Ocean Sea.* Samuel Eliot Morison
1944 *The American Leonardo: The Life of Samuel F. B. Morse.* Carleton Mabee
1945 *George Bancroft: Brahmin Rebel.* Russel Blaine Nye
1946 *Son of the Wilderness.* Linnie Marsh Wolfe
1947 *The Autobiography of William Allen White*
1948 *Forgotten First Citizen: John Bigelow.* Margaret Clapp
1949 *Roosevelt and Hopkins.* Robert E. Sherwood
1950 *John Quincy Adams and the Foundations of American Foreign Policy.* Samuel Flagg Bemis
1951 *John C. Calhoun: American Portrait.* Margaret Louise Coit
1952 *Charles Evans Hughes.* Merlo J. Pusey
1953 *Edmund Pendleton, 1721–1803.* David J. Mays
1954 *The Spirit of St. Louis.* Charles A. Lindbergh
1955 *The Taft Story.* William S. White
1956 *Benjamin Henry Latrobe.* Talbot F. Hamlin
1957 *Profiles in Courage.* John F. Kennedy
1958 *George Washington.* Douglas Southall Freeman (Vols. 1–6) and John Alexander Carroll and Mary Wells Ashworth (Vol. 7)
1959 *Woodrow Wilson, American Prophet.* Arthur Walworth
1960 *John Paul Jones.* Samuel Eliot Morison
1961 *Charles Sumner and the Coming of the Civil War.* David Donald
1963 *Henry James: Vol. II, The Conquest of London, 1870–1881; Vol. III, The Middle Years, 1881–1895.* Leon Edel
1964 *John Keats.* Walter Jackson Bate
1965 *Henry Adams* (3 Vols.). Ernest Samuels
1966 *A Thousand Days.* Arthur M. Schlesinger, Jr.
1967 *Mr. Clemens and Mark Twain.* Justin Kaplan
1968 *Memoirs, 1925–1950.* George F. Kennan
1969 *The Man From New York.* B. L. Reid
1970 *Huey Long.* T. Harry Williams
1971 *Robert Frost: The Years of Triumph, 1915–1938.* Lawrence Thompson
1972 *Eleanor and Franklin: The Story of Their Relationship Based on Eleanor Roosevelt's Private Papers.* Joseph P. Lash
1973 *Luce and His Empire.* W. A. Swanberg
1974 *O'Neill, Son and Artist.* Louis Sheaffer
1975 *The Power Broker: Robert Moses and the Fall of New York.* Robert A. Caro
1976 *Edith Wharton: A Biography.* Richard W. B. Lewis
1977 *A Prince of Our Disorder.* John E. Mack
1978 *Samuel Johnson.* Walter Jackson Bate
1979 *Days of Sorrow and Pain: Leo Baeck and the Berlin Jews.* Leonard Baker
1980 *The Rise of Theodore Roosevelt.* Edmund Morris
1981 *Peter the Great.* Robert K. Massie

1982 *Grant: A Biography.* William S. McFeely
1983 *Growing Up.* Russell Baker
1984 *Booker T. Washington.* Louis R. Harlan
1985 *The Life and Times of Cotton Mather,* Kenneth Silverman
1986 *Louise Bogan: A Portrait,* Elizabeth Frank
1987 *Bearing the Cross: Martin Luther King Jr. and the Southern Christian Leadership Conference,* David J. Garrow
1988 *Look Homeward: A Life of Thomas Wolfe.* David Herbert Donald
1989 *Oscar Wilde.* Richard Ellmann
1990 *Machiavelli in Hell,* Sebastian de Grazia
1991 *Jackson Pollock: An American Saga,* Steven Naifeh and Gregory White Smith

POETRY[1]

1918 *Love Songs.* Sara Teasdale
1919 *Old Road to Paradise.* Margaret Widdemer; *Corn Huskers.* Carl Sandburg
1922 *Collected Poems.* Edwin Arlington Robinson
1923 *The Ballad of the Harp-Weaver; A Few Figs from Thistles;* eight sonnets in *American Poetry, 1922, A Miscellany.* Edna St. Vincent Millay
1924 *New Hampshire: A Poem With Notes and Grace Notes.* Robert Frost
1925 *The Man Who Died Twice.* Edwin Arlington Robinson
1926 *What's O'Clock.* Amy Lowell
1927 *Fiddler's Farewell.* Leonora Speyer
1928 *Tristram.* Edwin Arlington Robinson
1929 *John Brown's Body.* Stephen Vincent Benét
1930 *Selected Poems.* Conrad Aiken
1931 *Collected Poems.* Robert Frost
1932 *The Flowering Stone.* George Dillon
1933 *Conquistador.* Archibald MacLeish
1934 *Collected Verse.* Robert Hillyer
1935 *Bright Ambush.* Audrey Wurdemann
1936 *Strange Holiness.* Robert P. T. Coffin
1937 *A Further Range.* Robert Frost
1938 *Cold Morning Sky.* Marya Zaturenska
1939 *Selected Poems.* John Gould Fletcher
1940 *Collected Poems.* Mark Van Doren
1941 *Sunderland Capture.* Leonard Bacon
1942 *The Dust Which Is God.* William Rose Benét
1943 *A Witness Tree.* Robert Frost
1944 *Western Star.* Stephen Vincent Benét
1945 *V-Letter and Other Poems.* Karl Shapiro
1947 *Lord Weary's Castle.* Robert Lowell
1948 *The Age of Anxiety.* W. H. Auden
1949 *Terror and Decorum.* Peter Viereck
1950 *Annie Allen.* Gwendolyn Brooks
1951 *Complete Poems.* Carl Sandburg
1952 *Collected Poems.* Marianne Moore
1953 *Collected Poems, 1917–1952.* Archibald MacLeish
1954 *The Waking.* Theodore Roethke
1955 *Collected Poems.* Wallace Stevens
1956 *Poems—North & South.* Elizabeth Bishop
1957 *Things of This World.* Richard Wilbur
1958 *Promises: Poems, 1954–1956.* Robert Penn Warren
1959 *Selected Poems, 1928–1958.* Stanley Kunitz
1960 *Heart's Needle.* William Snodgrass
1961 *Times Three: Selected Verse From Three Decades.* Phyllis McGinley
1962 *Poems.* Alan Dugan
1963 *Pictures From Breughel.* William Carlos Williams
1964 *At the End of the Open Road.* Louis Simpson

1. This prize was established in 1922. The 1918 and 1919 awards were made from gifts provided by the Poetry Society.

1965 *77 Dream Songs.* John Berryman
1966 *Selected Poems.* Richard Eberhart
1967 *Live or Die.* Anne Sexton
1968 *The Hard Hours.* Anthony Hecht
1969 *Of Being Numerous.* George Oppen
1970 *Untitled Subjects.* Richard Howard
1971 *The Carrier of Ladders.* William S. Merwin
1972 *Collected Poems.* James Wright
1973 *Up Country.* Maxine Winokur Kumin
1974 *The Dolphin.* Robert Lowell
1975 *Turtle Island.* Gary Snyder
1976 *Self-Portrait in a Convex Mirror.* John Ashbery
1977 *Divine Comedies.* James Merrill
1978 *Collected Poems.* Howard Nemerov
1979 *Now and Then: Poems, 1976–1978.* Robert Penn Warren.
1980 *Selected Poems.* Donald Rodney Justice
1981 *The Morning of the Poem.* James Schuyler
1982 *The Collected Poems.* Sylvia Plath
1983 *Selected Poems.* Galway Kinnell
1984 *American Primitive.* Mary Oliver
1985 *Yin,* Carolyn Kizer
1986 *The Flying Change,* Henry Taylor
1987 *Thomas and Beulah,* Rita Dove
1988 *Partial Accounts: New and Selected Poems.* William Meredith
1989 *New and Collected Poems.* Richard Wilbur
1990 *The World Doesn't End,* Charles Simic070
1991 *Near Changes,* Mona Van Duyn

GENERAL NONFICTION

1962 *The Making of the President, 1960.* Theodore H. White
1963 *The Guns of August.* Barbara W. Tuchman
1964 *Anti-Intellectualism in American Life.* Richard Hofstadter
1965 *O Strange New World.* Howard Mumford Jones
1966 *Wandering Through Winter.* Edwin Way Teale
1967 *The Problem of Slavery in Western Culture.* David Brion Davis
1968 *Rousseau and Revolution.* Will and Ariel Durant
1969 *So Human an Animal.* Rene Jules Dubos; *The Armies of the Night.* Norman Mailer
1970 *Gandhi's Truth.* Erik H. Erikson
1971 *The Rising Sun.* John Toland
1972 *Stilwell and the American Experience in China, 1911–1945.* Barbara W. Tuchman
1973 *Fire in the Lake: The Vietnamese and the Americans in Vietnam.* Frances FitzGerald; and *Children of Crisis* (Vols. 1 and 2). Robert M. Coles
1974 *The Denial of Death.* Ernest Becker
1975 *Pilgrim at Tinker Creek.* Annie Dillard
1976 *Why Survive? Being Old in America.* Robert N. Butler
1977 *Beautiful Swimmers: Watermen, Crabs and the Chesapeake Bay.* William W. Warner
1978 *The Dragons of Eden.* Carl Sagan
1979 *On Human Nature.* Edward O. Wilson
1980 *Gödel, Escher, Bach: An Eternal Golden Braid.* Douglas R. Hofstadter
1981 *Fin-de-Siecle Vienna: Politics and Culture.* Carl E. Schorske
1982 *The Soul of a New Machine.* Tracy Kidder
1983 *Is There No Place on Earth for Me?* Susan Sheehan
1984 *Social Transformation of American Medicine.* Paul Starr
1985 *The Good War: An Oral History of World War II,* Studs Terkel

1986 *Move Your Shadow: South Africa, Black and White,* Joseph Lelyveld; *Common Ground: A Turbulent Decade in the Lives of Three American Families,* J. Anthony Lukas
1987 *Arab and Jew: Wounded Spirits in a Promised Land,* David K. Shipler
1988 *The Making of the Atomic Bomb.* Richard Rhodes
1989 *A Bright Shining Lie.* Neil Sheehan
1990 *And Their Children After Them,* Dale Maharidge and Michael Williamson
1991 *The Ants,* Bert Holldobler and Edward O. Wilson

PULITZER PRIZES IN MUSIC

1943 *Secular Cantata No. 2, A Free Song.* William Schuman
1944 *Symphony No. 4* (Op. 34). Howard Hanson
1945 *Appalachian Spring.* Aaron Copland
1946 *The Canticle of the Sun.* Leo Sowerby
1947 *Symphony No. 3.* Charles Ives
1948 *Symphony No. 3.* Walter Piston
1949 *Louisiana Story* music. Virgil Thomson
1950 *The Consul.* Gian Carlo Menotti
1951 Music for opera *Giants in the Earth.* Douglas Stuart Moore
1952 *Symphony Concertante.* Gail Kubik
1954 *Concerto for Two Pianos and Orchestra.* Quincy Porter
1955 *The Saint of Bleecker Street.* Gian Carlo Menotti
1956 *Symphony No. 3.* Ernst Toch
1957 *Meditations on Ecclesiastes.* Norman Dello Joio
1958 *Vanessa.* Samuel Barber
1959 *Concerto for Piano and Orchestra.* John La Montaine
1960 *Second String Quartet.* Elliott Carter
1961 *Symphony No. 7.* Walter Piston
1962 *The Crucible.* Robert Ward
1963 *Piano Concerto No. 1.* Samuel Barber
1966 *Variations for Orchestra.* Leslie Bassett
1967 *Quartet No. 3.* Leon Kirchner
1968 *Echoes of Time and the River.* George Crumb
1969 *String Quartet No. 3.* Karel Husa
1970 *Time's Encomium.* Charles Wuorinen
1971 *Synchronisms No. 6 for Piano and Electronic Sound.* Mario Davidowsky
1972 *Windows.* Jacob Druckman
1973 *String Quartet No. 3.* Elliott Carter
1974 *Notturno.* Donald Martino
1975 *From the Diary of Virginia Woolf.* Dominick Argento
1976 *Air Music.* Ned Rorem
1977 *Visions of Terror and Wonder.* Richard Wernick
1978 *Déjà Vu for Percussion Quartet and Orchestra.* Michael Colgrass
1979 *Aftertones of Infinity.* Joseph Schwantner
1980 *In Memory of a Summer Day.* David Del Tredici
1981 Not awarded
1982 *Concerto for Orchestra.* Roger Sessions
1983 *Three Movements for Orchestra.* Ellen T. Zwilich
1984 *Canti del Sole.* Bernard Rands
1985 *Symphony RiverRun,* Stephen Albert
1986 *Wind Quintet IV,* Georg e Perle
1987 *The Flight Into Egypt,* John Harbison
1988 *12 New Etudes for Piano.* William Bolcom
1989 *Whispers Out of Time,* Roger Reynolds
1990 *Duplicates: A Concerto for Two Pianos and Orchestra,* Mel Powell
1991 *Symphony,* Shulamit Ran

New York Drama Critics' Circle Awards

1935–36
Winterset, Maxwell Anderson
1936–37
High Tor, Maxwell Anderson
1937–38
Of Mice and Men, John Steinbeck
Shadow and Substance, Paul Vincent Carroll[1]
1938–39
(No award) The White Steed, Paul Vincent Carroll[1]
1939–40
The Time of Your Life, William Saroyan
1940–41
Watch on the Rhine, Lillian Hellman
The Corn Is Green, Emlyn Williams[1]
1941–42
(No award) Blithe Spirit, Noel Coward[1]
1942–43
The Patriots, Sidney Kingsley
1943–44
(No award) Jacobowsky and the Colonel. Franz Werfel and S. N. Behrman[1]
1944–45
The Glass Menagerie, Tennessee Williams
1945–46
(No award) Carousel, Richard Rodgers and Oscar Hammerstein II[2]
1946–47
All My Sons, Arthur Miller
No Exit, Jean-Paul Sartre[1]
Brigadoon, Alan Jay Lerner and Frederick Loewe[2]
1947–48
A Streetcar Named Desire, Tennessee Williams
The Winslow Boy, Terence Rattigan[1]
1948–49
Death of a Salesman, Arthur Miller
The Madwoman of Chaillot, Jean Giraudoux and Maurice Valency[1]
South Pacific, Richard Rodgers, Oscar Hammerstein II, and Joshua Logan[2]
1949–50
The Member of the Wedding, Carson McCullers
The Cocktail Party, T. S. Eliot[1]
The Consul, Gian Carlo Menotti[2]
1950–51
Darkness at Noon, Sidney Kingsley[3]
The Lady's Not for Burning, Christopher Fry[1]
Guys and Dolls, Abe Burrows, Jo Swerling, and Frank Loesser[2]
1951–52
I Am a Camera, John Van Druten[4]
Venus Observed, Christopher Fry[1]
Pal Joey, Richard Rodgers, Lorenz Hart, and John O'Hara[2]
Don Juan in Hell, George B. Shaw[5]
1952–53
Picnic, William Inge The Love of Four Colonels, by Peter Ustinov[1]
Wonderful Town, Joseph Fields, Jerome Chodorov, Betty Comden, Adolph Green, and Leonard Bernstein[2]
1953–54
The Teahouse of the August Moon, John Patrick
Ondine, Jean Giraudoux[1]
The Golden Apple, John Latouche and Jerome Moross[2]
1954–55
Cat on a Hot Tin Roof, Tennessee Williams
Witness for the Prosecution, Agatha Christie[1]
The Saint of Bleecker Street, Gian Carlo Menotti[2]
1955–56
The Diary of Anne Frank, Frances Goodrich and Albert Hackett
Tiger at the Gates, Jean Giraudoux and Christopher Fry[1]
My Fair Lady, Frederick Loewe and Alan Jay Lerner[2]
1956–57
Long Day's Journey Into Night, Eugene O'Neill
Waltz of the Toreadors, Jean Anouilh[1]
The Most Happy Fella, Frank Loesser[2 6]
1957–58
Look Homeward, Angel, Ketti Frings[7]
Look Back in Anger, John Osborne[1]
The Music Man, Meredith Willson[2]
1958–59
A Raisin in the Sun, Lorraine Hansberry
The Visit, Friedrich Duerrenmatt-Maurice Valency[1]
La Plume de ma Tante, Robert Dhery and Gerard Calvi[2]
1959–60
Toys in the Attic, Lillian Hellman
Five Finger Exercise, Peter Shaffer[1]
Fiorello], Jerome Weidman, George Abbott, Jerry Bock, and Sheldon Harnick[2]
1960–61
All the Way Home, Tad Mosel[3]
A Taste of Honey, Shelagh Delaney[1]
Carnival, Michael Stewart[2]
1961–62
The Night of the Iguana, Tennessee Williams
A Man for All Seasons, Robert Bolt[1]
How to Succeed in Business Without Really Trying, Abe Burrows, Jack Weinstock, Willie Gilbert, and Frank Loesser[2 9]
1962–63
Who's Afraid of Virginia Woolf?, Edward Albee
Beyond the Fringe, Alan Bennett, Peter Cook, Jonathan Miller, and Dudley Moore[10]
1963–64
Luther, John Osborne
Hello, Dolly], Michael Stewart and Jerry Herman[2 11]
The Trojan Women, Euripides[10 12]
1964–65
The Subject Was Roses, Frank D. Gilroy
Fiddler on the Roof, Joseph Stein, Jerry Bock, and Sheldon Harnick[2 13]
1965–66
The Persecution and Assassination of Marat as Performed by the Inmates of the Asylum of Charenton Under the Direction of the Marquis de Sade, Peter Weiss
The Man of La Mancha, Dale Wasserman, Mitch Leigh, and Joe Darion
1966–67
The Homecoming, Harold Pinter
Cabaret, Joe Masteroff, John Kander, and Fred Ebb[2 14]
1967–68
Rosencrantz and Guildenstern Are Dead, Tom Stoppard
Your Own Thing, Donald Driver, Hal Hester, and Danny Apolinar[2]
1968–69
The Great White Hope, Howard Sackler
1776, Sherman Edwards and Peter Stone[2]
1969–70
Borstal Boy, Frank McMahon[15]
The Effect of Gamma Rays on Man-in-the-Moon Marigolds, Paul Zindel[16]
Company, George Furth and Stephen Sondheim[2]
1970–71
Home, David Storey
The House of Blue Leaves, John Guare[16]

Follies, James Goldman and Stephen Sondheim[2]
1971–72
That Championship Season, Jason Miller
Two Gentlemen of Verona, adapted by John Guare and Mel Shapiro[2]
The Screens, Jean Genet[1]
1972–73
The Changing Room, David Storey
The Hot l Baltimore, by Lanford Wilson[16]
A Little Night Music, Hugh Wheeler and Stephen Sondheim[2]
1973–74
The Contractors, David Storey
Short Eyes, Miguel Piñero[16]
Candide, Leonard Bernstein, Hugh Wheeler, and Richard Wilbur[2]
1974–75
Equus, Peter Shaffer
The Taking of Miss Janie, Ed Bullins[16]
A Chorus Line, James Kirkwood and Nicholas Dante[2]
1975–76
Travesties, Tom Stoppard
Streamers, David Rabe[16]
Pacific Overtures, Stephen Sondheim, John Weidman, and Hugh Wheeler[2]
1976–77
Otherwise Engaged, Simon Gray
American Buffalo, David Mamet[16]
Annie, Thomas Meehan, Charles Strouse, and Martin Charnin[2]
1977–78
Da, Hugh Leonard
Ain't Misbehavin', conceived by Richard Maltby, Jr.[2]
1978–79
The Elephant Man, Bernard Pomerance
Sweeney Todd, Hugh Wheeler and Stephen Sondheim[2]
1979–80
Talley's Folly, Lanford Wilson
Evita,[2] Andrew Lloyd Webber and Tim Rice
Betrayal, Harold Pinter[1]
1980–81
A Lesson From Aloes, Athol Fugard
Crimes of the Heart, Beth Henley[16]
1981–82
The Life and Adventures of Nicholas Nickleby, adapted by David Edgar
A Soldier's Play, Charles Fuller[16]
1982–83
Brighton Beach Memoirs, Neil Simon
Plenty, David Hare[1]
Little Shop of Horrors, Alan Menken and Howard Ashman[2 17]

1983–84
The Real Thing, Tom Stoppard
Glengarry Glen Ross, David Mamet[16]
Sunday in the Park with George, Stephen W Sondheim and James Lapine[2]
1984–85
Ma Rainey's Black Bottom, August Wilson
(No award for best musical or foreign play)
1985–86
Lie of the Mind, Sam Shepard
Benefactors, Michael Frayn[1]
The Search for Signs of Intelligent Life in the Universe, Lily Tomlin and Jane Wagner[10]
(No award for best musical)
1986–87
Fences, August Wilson
Les Liaisons Dangereuses, Christopher Hampton[1]
Les Miserables, Claude-Michel Schonberg and Alain Boublil[2]
1987–88
Joe Turner's Come and Gone, August Wilson
The Road to Mecca, Athol Fugard[1]
Into the Woods, Stephen Sondheim and James Lapine[2]
1988–89
The Heidi Chronicles, Wendy Wasserstein
Aristocrats, Brian Friel[1]
Largely New York, Bill Irwin[18]
(No award for best musical)
1989–90
The Piano Lesson, August Wilson
Privates on Parade, Peter Nichols[1]
City of Angels, Larry Gelbart, Cy Coleman, and David Zippel[2]
1990–91
Six Degrees of Separation, John Guare
Our Country's Good, Timberlake Wertenbaker[1]
The Will Rogers Follies, Cy Coleman, Peter Stone, Betty Comden, and Adolph Green[2]
Eileen Atkins, *A Room of One's Own*[10]

1. Citation for best foreign play. 2. Citation for best musical. 3. Based on a novel by Arthur Koestler. 4. Based on Christopher Isherwood's *Berlin Stories.* 5. For "distinguished and original contribution to the theater." 6. Based on Sidney Howard's *They Knew What They Wanted.* 7. Based on a novel by Thomas Wolfe. 8. Based on James Agee's *A Death in the Family.* 9. Based on a book by Shepherd Mead. 10. Special citation. 11. Based on Thornton Wilder's *The Matchmaker.* 12. Translated by Edith Hamilton. 13. Based on Sholem Aleichem's Tevye stories, translated by Arnold Perl. 14. Based on John Van Druten's *I Am a Camera,* which won the award for best play in 1951–52. 15. Based on Brendan Behan's autobiography. 16. Citation for best American play. 17. Based on a story by Roger Corman. 18. Special citation.

Antoinette Perry (Tony) Awards, 1991

Dramatic Play: *Lost in Yonkers,* Neil Simon
Musical: *The Will Rogers Follies*
Actor (play): Nigel Hawthorne, *Shadowlands*
Acress (play): Mercedes Ruehl, *Lost in Yonkers*
Actor, featured (play): Kevin Spacey, *Lost in Yonkers*
Acress, featured (play): Irene Worth, *Lost in Yonkers*
Actor, musical: Jonathan Pryce, *Miss Saigon*
Actress, musical: Lea Salonga, *Miss Saigon*
Actor, featured (musical): Hinton Battle, *Miss Saigon*
Actress, featured (musical): Daisy Eagan, *The Secret Garden*
Director (play): Jerry Zaks, *Six Degrees of Separation*

Director (musical): Tommy Tune, *The Will Rogers Follies*
Best book of a musical: Marsha Norman, *The Secret Garden*
Best original musical score: Cy Coleman, Betty Comden, and Adloph Green, *The Will Rogers Follies*
Scenic design: Heidi Landesman, *The Secret Garden*
Costume design: Willa Kim, *The Will Rogers Follies*
Lighting: Jules Fisher, *The Will Rogers Follies*
Choreography: Tommy Tune, *The Will Rogers Follies*
Revival: *Fiddler on the Roof*
Regional theater: Yale Repertory Theater

1991 Obie Award Winners

Best New Play: Wallace Shawn, *The Fever*
Performance: Eileen Atkins, *A Room of One's Own;* Stockard Channing, *Six Degrees of Separation;* Joan Copeland, *The American Plan;* Angela Goethals, *The Good Times Are Killing Me;* Tony Goldwyn, *The Sum of Us;* Jan Leslie Harding, *Sincerity Forever;* John Leguizamo, *Mambo Mouth;* Michael Lombard, *What's Wrong With This Picture?;* Jodie Markell, *Machinal;* Anne Pitoniak, *Pygmalion;* Ron Rifkin, *The Substance of Fire;* Kathleen Widdoes, *Tower of Evil;* Bette Bourne, Precious Pearl, Peggy Shaw, and Lois Weaver, ensemble performance in *Belle Reprieve*
Directon: Michael Greif, *Machinal;* Lisa Peterson, *Light Shining in Buckinghamshire*
Sustained Excellence of Lighting Design: Frances Aronson
Sustained Excellence of Set Design: Mark Beard
Sustained Excellence of Costume Design: William Ivey Long
Sound Design: John Gromada, *Machinal*
Special Citations: Blue Man Group; John Kelly, *Love of a Poet;* BACA Downtown; New York Theatre Workshop; New York Shakespeare Festival, 1990–91 season; Lori E. Seid, stage management; Theatre for the New City, "Stop the War: A Festival for Peace in the Middle East"
Playwriting: John Guare, *Six Degrees of Separation;* Mac Wellman, *Sincerity Forever*
Sustained Achivement: The Wooster Group
Off-Broadway Grants: En-Gare Arts, Hearts and Voices, and Mettawee River Theater Company

Winners of Bollingen Prize in Poetry

($5,000[1] award is given biennially. It is administered by Yale University and the Bollingen Foundation.)

1949	Ezra Pound	1963	Robert Frost
1950	Wallace Stevens	1965	Horace Gregory
1951	John Crowe Ransom	1967	Robert Penn Warren
1952	Marianne Moore	1969	John Berryman and Karl Shapiro
1953	Archibald MacLeish and William Carlos Williams	1971	Richard Wilbur and Mona Van Duyn
1954	W. H. Auden	1973	James Merrill
1955	Léonie Adams and Louise Bogan	1975	Archie Randolph Ammons
1956	Conrad Aiken	1977	David Ignatow
1957	Allen Tate	1979	W. S. Merwin
1958	E.E. Cummings	1981	Howard Nemerov and May Swenson
1959	Theodore Roethke	1983	Anthony Hecht and John Hollander
1960	Delmore Schwartz	1985	John Ashbery and Fred Chappell
1961	Yvor Winters	1987	Stanley Kunitz
1962	John Hall Wheelock and Richard Eberhart	1989	Edgar Bowers
		1991	Laura Riding Jackson and Donald Justin

1. Beginning 1989 award increased to $10,000.

National Book Critics Circle Awards, 1991

Fiction: *Rabbit at Rest* by John Updike (Knopf)
General nonfiction: *The Content of Our Character* by Shelby Steele (St. Martin's)
Poetry: *Bitter Angel* by Amy Gerstler (North Point)
Criticism: *Encounters and Reflections: Art in the Historical Present* by Arthur Danto (FSG)
Biography/Autobiography: *Means of Ascent: The Years of Lyndon Johnson* by Robert A. Caro (Knopf)

American Library Association Awards for Children's Books, 1991

(For books published in 1990)

John Newbery Medal for best book: *Maniac Magee,* Jerry Spinelli (Little Brown)
Newbery Honor Book: *The True Confessions of Charlotte Doyle,* Avi (Orchard Books/Watts)
Randolph Caldecott Medal for best picture book: *Black and White,* illustrated and written by David Macaulay (Houghton Mifflin)
Caldecott Honor Books: *Puss in Boots,* illustrated by Fred Marcellino (Farrar, Straus & Giroux); *"More, More, More," Said the Baby: 3 Love Stories,* illustrated and written by Vera B. Williams (Greenwillow Books/Morrow)

National Book Awards, 1990

Established by Association of American Publishers

(American Book Awards 1980–86. Reverted to original name in 1987.)

Fiction: *The Middle Passage,* by Charles Johnson (Atheneum)
Nonfiction: *The House of Morgan, An American Banking Dynasty and the Rise of Modern Finance* by Ron Chernow (Atlantic Monthly Press)
The National Book Foundation Medal for Distinguished Contribution to American Letters: Saul Bellow, a Nobel Prize winner

1991 Bancroft Prizes in American History

Making a New Deal: Industrial Workers in Chicago, 1919–1939, by Lizabeth Cohen (Cambridge University Press)
A Midwife's Tale: The Life of Martha Ballard Based on Her Diary, 1785–1812, Laurel Thatcher Ulrich (Alfred A. Knopf)

726 Awards—British Poet Laureat–Journalist–du Pont–Fermi

Poet Laureate of England

Edmund Spenser	1591–1599	Laurence Eusden	1718–1730	Alfred Lord Tennyson	1850–1892
Samuel Daniel	1599–1619	Colley Cibber	1730–1757	Alfred Austin	1896–1913
Ben Jonson	1619–1637	William Whitehead	1757–1785	Robert Bridges	1913–1930
William Davenant	1638–1668	Thomas Warton	1785–1790	John Masefield	1930–1967
John Dryden[1]	1670–1689	Henry James Pye	1790–1813	C. Day Lewis	1967–1972
Thomas Shadwell	1689–1692	Robert Southey	1813–1843	Sir John Betjeman	1972–1984
Nahum Tate	1692–1715	William Wordsworth	1843–1850	Ted Hughes	1984–
Nicholas Rowe	1715–1718				

1. First to bear the title officially. Source: Encyclopaedia Britannica.

Awards of the Society of Professional Journalists, 1990

(Sigma Delta Chi)

Deadline reporting: New York Newsday
Non-deadline reporting: Susan Taylor Martin, St. Petersburg Times (Fla.)
Investigative reporting: John T. Wark and David Farrell, The Detroit News
Feature writing: Elizabeth Leland, The Charlotte (N.C.) Observer
Editorial writing: Eric Breindel, New York Post
Washington correspondence: Marie Cocco and Earl Lane, New York Newsday
Foreign correspondence: David Remnick, The Washington Post
Public service in newspaper journalism: The Orange County (Calif.) Register (circulation greater than 100,000); The News Tribune (Woodbridge, N.J.) (circulation less than 100,000)
News photography: Michael Wirtz, Philadelphia Inquirer
Editorial cartoons: Jeff MacNelly, Chicago Tribune
Magazine reporting: Peter Cary, U.S. News & World Report

Public service in magazine journalism: Family Circle Magazine
Radio spot-news: WBBM-AM, Chicago
Editorializing on radio: Nicholas DeLuca, KCBS Radio, San Francisco
Radio investigative reporting: Bob Sands, WKY Radio, Oklahoma City
Public service in radio journalism: KRTH-FM, Los Angeles
Television spot-news reporting: WHDH, Boston
Public service in television journalism: WRAL, Raleigh, N.C. (top 40 markets and networks); KGW, Portland, Ore. (all other markets)
Television editorials: KGTV, San Diego, Calif.
Television investigative reporting: ABC Prime-Time Live
Public service newsletter: Mine Regulation Reporter
Research about journalism: Marc Cooper and Lawrence C. Soley, Mother Jones Magazine
Bicentennial Print Award: No award made
Bicentennial Broadcast Award: Nicholas DeLuca, KCBS Radio, San Francisco

Alfred I. du Pont-Columbia University Broadcast News Awards

(For work broadcast between July 1, 1989, and June 30, 1990)

Gold Baton Award: Inside Gorbachev's U.S.S.R., PBS
Silver Baton Awards: CBS Evening News, for coverage of the fall of Communism in Eastern Europe; ABC News special "Peter Jennings Reporting: From the Killing Fields"; NBC News, for Betty Rollin's "Tragedy at Pine Ridge"; KQED in San Francisco for an examination of police brutality; WJLA in Washington for an investigative report by Roberta Baskin into the National Football League's drug-testing procedures; KING in Seattle for an examination of differences in health care and costs

between the United States and Canada; WCBD in Charleston, S.C. for coverage of Hurricane Hugo; WKYC in Cleveland for news commentary by Dick Feagler. Awards for independent productions went to Henry Hampton for "Eyes on the Prize II"; Christine Choy and Renee Tajima for "Who Killed Vincent Chin?"; and Frederic Wiseman for "Near Death."
Silver Baton Awards for Radio News: KCBS-AM in San Francisco for coverage of the October 1989 earthquake and to National Public Radio for "And Justice for All."

Enrico Fermi Award

Named in honor of Enrico Fermi, the atomic pioneer, the $100,000 award is given in recognition of "exceptional and altogether outstanding" scientific and technical achievement in atomic energy.

1954	Enrico Fermi	1971	Shields Warren and Stafford L. Warren	1984	Robert R. Wilson and Georges Vendryès
1956	John von Neumann				
1957	Ernest O. Lawrence	1972	Manson Benedict	1985	Norman C. Rasmussen and Marshall N. Rosenblath
1958	Eugene P. Wigner	1976	William L. Russell		
1959	Glenn T. Seaborg	1978	Harold M. Agnew and Wolfgang K.H. Panofsky	1986	Ernest D. Courant and M. Stanley Livingston
1961	Hans A. Bethe				
1962	Edward Teller	1980	Alvin M. Weinberg and Rudolf E. Peirls	1987	Luis W. Alvarez and Gerald F. Tape
1963	J. Robert Oppenheimer				
1964	Hyman G. Rickover	1981	W. Bennett Lewis	1988	Richard B. Setlow and Victor F. Weisskopf
1966	Otto Hahn, Lise Meitner, and Fritz Strassman	1982	Herbert Anderson and Seth Neddermeyer		
1968	John A. Wheeler	1983	Alexander Hollaender and John Lawrence	1989	Award not given
1969	Walter H. Zinn			1990	George A. Cowan and Robley D. Evans
1970	Norris E. Bradbury				

Presidential Medal of Freedom

The nation's highest civilian award, the Presidential Medal of Freedom, was established in 1963 by President John F. Kennedy to continue and expand Presidential recognition of meritorious service which, since 1945, had been granted as the Medal of Freedom. Kennedy selected the first recipients, but was assassinated before he could make the presentations. They were made by President Johnson. NOTE: An asterisk following a year denotes a posthumous award.

SELECTED BY PRESIDENT KENNEDY

Marian Anderson (contralto)	1963
Ralph J. Bunche (statesman)	1963
Ellsworth Bunker (diplomat)	1963
Pablo Casals (cellist)	1963
Genevieve Caulfield (educator)	1963
James B. Conant (educator)	1963
John F. Enders (bacteriologist)	1963
Felix Frankfurter (jurist)	1963
Karl Horton (youth authority)	1963
Robert J. Kiphuth (athletic director)	1963
Edwin H. Land (inventor)	1963
Herbert H. Lehman (statesman)	1963*
Robert A. Lovett (statesman)	1963
J. Clifford MacDonald (educator)	1963*
John J. McCloy (banker and statesman)	1963
George Meany (labor leader)	1963
Alexander Meiklejohn (philosopher)	1963
Ludwig Mies van der Rohe (architect)	1963
Jean Monnet (European statesman)	1963
Luis Muñoz-Marin (Governor of Puerto Rico)	1963
Clarence B. Randall (industrialist)	1963
Rudolf Serkin (pianist)	1963
Edward Steichen (photographer)	1963
George W. Taylor (educator)	1963
Alan T. Waterman (scientist)	1963
Mark S. Watson (journalist)	1963
Annie D. Wauneka (public health worker)	1963
E. B. White (author)	1963
Thornton N. Wilder (author)	1963
Edmund Wilson (author and critic)	1963
Andrew Wyeth (artist)	1963

AWARDED BY PRESIDENT JOHNSON

Dean G. Acheson (statesman)	1964
Eugene R. Black (banker)	1969
Detlev W. Bronk (neurophysiologist)	1964
McGeorge Bundy (government service)	1969
Ellsworth Bunker (diplomat)	1968
Clark Clifford (statesman)	1969
Aaron Copland (composer)	1964
Michael E. DeBakey (surgeon)	1969
Willem de Kooning (artist)	1964
Walt Disney (cartoon film producer)	1964
J. Frank Dobie (author)	1964
David Dubinsky (labor leader)	1969
Lena F. Edwards (physician and humanitarian)	1964
Thomas Stearns Eliot (poet)	1964
Ralph Ellison (author)	1969
Lynn Fontanne (actress)	1964
Henry Ford II (industrialist)	1969
John W. Gardner (educator)	1964
W. Averell Harriman (statesman)	1969
Rev. Theodore M. Hesburgh (educator)	1964
Bob Hope (comedian)	1969
John XXIII (Pope)	1963*
Clarence L. Johnson (aircraft engineer)	1964
Edgar F. Kaiser (industrialist)	1969
Frederick R. Kappel (telecommunications executive)	1964
Helen A. Keller (educator)	1964
John Fitzgerald Kennedy (U.S. President)	1963*
Robert W. Komer (government service)	1968
Mary Lasker (philanthropist)	1969
John L. Lewis (labor leader)	1964
Walter Lippmann (journalist)	1964
Eugene M. Locke (diplomat)	1968

Alfred Lunt (actor)	1964
John W. Macy, Jr. (government service)	1969
Ralph McGill (journalist)	1964
Robert S. McNamara (government service)	1968
Samuel Eliot Morison (historian)	1964
Lewis Mumford (urban planner and critic)	1964
Edward R. Murrow (radio-TV commentator)	1964
Reinhold Niebuhr (theologian)	1964
Gregory Peck (actor)	1969
Leontyne Price (soprano)	1964
A. Philip Randolph (labor leader)	1964
Laurance S. Rockefeller (conservationist)	1969
Walt Whitman Rostow (government service)	1969
Dean Rusk (statesman)	1969
Carl Sandburg (poet and biographer)	1964
Merriman Smith (journalist)	1969
John Steinbeck (author)	1964
Helen B. Taussig (pediatrician)	1964
Cyrus R. Vance (government service)	1969
Carl Vinson (legislator)	1964
Thomas J. Watson, Jr. (industrialist)	1964
James E. Webb (NASA administrator)	1968
Paul Dudley White (physician)	1964
William S. White (journalist)	1969
Roy Wilkins (social welfare executive)	1969
Whitney M. Young, Jr. (social welfare executive)	1969

AWARDED BY PRESIDENT NIXON

Edwin E. Aldrin (astronaut)	1969
Apollo 13 Mission Operations Team	1970
Neil A. Armstrong (astronaut)	1969
Earl Charles Behrens (journalist)	1970
Manlio Brosio (NATO secretary general)	1971
Michael Collins (astronaut)	1969
Edward K. (Duke) Ellington (musician)	1969
Edward T. Folliard (journalist)	1970
John Ford (film director)	1973
Samuel Goldwyn (film producer)	1971
Fred Wallace Haise, Jr. (astronaut)	1970
William M. Henry (journalist)	1970*
Paul G. Hoffman (statesman)	1974
William J. Hopkins (White House service)	1971
Arthur Krock (journalist)	1970
Melvin R. Laird (government service)	1974
David Lawrence (journalist)	1970
George Gould Lincoln (journalist)	1970
James A. Lovell, Jr. (astronaut)	1970
Dr. Charles L. Lowman (orthopedist)	1974
Raymond Moley (journalist)	1970
Eugene Ormandy (conductor)	1970
William P. Rogers (diplomat)	1973
Adela Rogers St. Johns (journalist)	1970
John Leonard Swigert, Jr. (astronaut)	1970
John Paul Vann (adviser, Vietnam war)	1972*
DeWitt and Lila Wallace (founders, *Reader's Digest*)	1972

AWARDED BY PRESIDENT FORD

I. W. Abel (labor leader)	1977
John Bardeen (physicist)	1977
Irving Berlin (composer)	1977
Norman Borlaug (agricultural scientist)	1977
Gen. Omar N. Bradley (soldier)	1977
David K. E. Bruce (diplomat)	1976
Arleigh Burke (national security)	1977
Alexander Calder (sculptor)	1977
Bruce Catton (historian)	1977

Joseph P. DiMaggio (baseball star)	1977
Ariel Durant (author)	1977
Will Durant (author)	1977
Arthur Fiedler (conductor)	1977
Henry J. Friendly (jurist)	1977
Martha Graham (dancer-choreographer)	1976
Claudia "Lady Bird" Johnson (service to U.S. scenic beauty)	1977
Henry A. Kissinger (statesman)	1977
Archibald MacLeish (poet)	1977
James A. Michener (author)	1977
Georgia O'Keeffe (artist)	1977
Jesse Owens (track champion)	1976
Nelson A. Rockefeller (government service)	1977
Norman Rockwell (illustrator)	1977
Arthur Rubinstein (pianist)	1976
Donald H. Rumsfeld (government service)	1977
Katherine Filene Shouse (service to the performing arts)	1977
Lowell Thomas (radio-TV commentator)	1977
James D. Watson (biochemist)	1977

AWARDED BY PRESIDENT CARTER

Ansel Adams (photographer)	1980
Horace M. Albright (government service)	1980
Roger Baldwin (civil libertarian)	1981
Harold Brown (government service)	1981
Zbigniew Brzezinski (government service)	1981
Rachel Carson (author)	1980 *
Lucia Chase (ballet director)	1980
Warren M. Christopher (government service)	1981
Walter Cronkite (TV newscaster)	1981
Kirk Douglas (actor)	1981
Arthur J. Goldberg (government service)	1978
Hubert H. Humphrey (government service)	1980 *
Archbishop Iakovos (churchman)	1980
Lyndon B. Johnson (U.S. President)	1980 *
Rev. Dr. Martin Luther King, Jr. (civil rights leader)	1977 *
Margaret Craig McNamara (educator)	1981
Margaret Mead (anthropologist)	1979 *
Karl Menninger (psychiatrist)	1981
Clarence Mitchell, Jr. (civil rights leader)	1980
Edmund S. Muskie (government service)	1981
Esther Peterson (government service)	1981
Roger Tory Peterson (ornithologist)	1980
Adm. Hyman Rickover (national security)	1980
Jonas Salk (medical research)	1977
Beverly Sills (opera singer)	1980
Gerard C. Smith (government service)	1981
Robert S. Strauss (government service)	1981
Elbert Parr Tuttle (government service)	1981
Earl Warren (government service)	1981 *
Robert Penn Warren (author and poet)	1980
John Wayne (actor)	1980 *
Eudora Welty (author)	1980
Tennessee Williams (playwright)	1980
Andrew M. Young (government service)	1981

AWARDED BY PRESIDENT REAGAN

Walter H. Annenberg (publisher and diplomat)	1986
Anne L. Armstrong (diplomat)	1987
Howard H. Baker, Jr. (government service)	1984
George Balanchine (choreographer)	1983
Malcolm Baldrige (government service)	1988 *
Count Basie (jazz pianist)	1985 *
Pearl Bailey Bellson (entertainer and humanitarian)	1988
Earl (Red) Blaik (football coach)	1986
James H. (Eubie) Blake (composer-pianist)	1981
Irving Brown (labor leader)	1988
Paul W. (Bear) Bryant (football coach)	1983 *
Warren Burger (former Chief Justice)	1987
James Burnham (editor-historian)	1983
James Francis Cagney (actor)	1984

The Right Honorable Lord Carrington (Secretary General of NATO)	1988
Whittaker Chambers (public servant)	1984 *
James Cheek (educator)	1983
Leo Cherne (economist-humanitarian)	1984
Terence Cardinal Cooke, His Eminence (theologian)	1984 *
Denton Arthur Cooley, M.D. (heart surgeon)	1984
Jacques-Yves Cousteau (marine explorer)	1985
Justin W. Dart Sr. (businessman)	1987 *
Tennessee Ernie Ford (singer)	1984
Milton Friedman (economist)	1988
R. Buckminster Fuller (architect-geometrician)	1983
Hector P. Garcia, M.D. (humanitarian)	1984
Barry Goldwater (government service)	1986
Gen. Andrew J. Goodpaster (soldier-diplomat)	1984
Rev. Billy Graham (evangelist)	1983
Ella T. Grasso (Connecticut governor)	1981 *
Philip C. Habib (diplomat)	1982
Bryce N. Harlow (government service)	1981
Helen Hayes (actress)	1986
Eric Hoffer (philosopher-longshoreman)	1983
Jerome Holland (educator and ambassador)	1985 *
Sidney Hook (philosopher-educator)	1985
Vladimir Horowitz (pianist)	1985
Henry Martin Jackson (government service)	1984 *
Jacob K. Javits (government service)	1983
Walter H. Judd (government service)	1981
Irving Kaufman (jurist)	1987
Danny Kaye (actor)	1987 *
Jeane J. Kirkpatrick (government service)	1985
Lincoln Kirstein (ballet director)	1984
Louis L'Amour (author)	1984
Morris I. Leibman (lawyer)	1981
Gen. Lyman L. Lemnitzer (soldier)	1987
George M. Low (educator and administrator NASA)	1985 *
Clare Boothe Luce (author-diplomat)	1983
Joseph M.A.H. Luns (diplomat-NATO)	1984
Jean Faircloth MacArthur (patriot)	1988
Dumas Malone (historian)	1983
Michael Mansfield (government service)	1989
J. Willard Marriott (businessman)	1988 *
John A. McCone (government service)	1987
Mabel Mercer (jazz singer)	1983
Paul Nitze (government service)	1985
David Packard (public service, businessman)	1988
Frederick Patterson (educator)	1987
Norman Vincent Peale (theologian)	1984
Nathan Perlmutter (public service)	1987
Simon Ramo (industrialist)	1983
Frank Reynolds (TV anchor)	1985 *
Gen. Matthew B. Ridgway (soldier)	1986
S. Dillon Ripley (cultural and public service)	1985
James Stewart (actor)	1985
Jack Roosevelt Robinson (baseball player)	1984 *
Gen. Carlos P. Romulo (Philippino statesman)	1984
Mstislav Rostropovich (cellist-conductor)	1987
Vermont Royster (journalist)	1986
Albert B. Sabin (medical research)	1986
Mohamed Anwar el-Sadat (statesman)	1984 *
George P. Shultz (gov. service)	1989
Eunice Kennedy Shriver (humanitarian)	1984
Frank Sinatra (entertainer)	1985
Kate Smith (singer)	1982
Roger L. Stevens (theatrical producer)	1988
James Stewart (actor)	1985
Mother Teresa (humanitarian)	1985
Charles B. Thornton (industrialist)	1981
William B. Walsh (humanitarian)	1987
Gen. Albert Coady Wedemeyer (national security)	1985
Casper W. Weinberger (government service)	1987
Meredith Willson (composer)	1987 *
Albert and Roberta Wohlstetter (government service)	1985
Charles E. Yeager (public service)	1985

AWARDED BY PRESIDENT BUSH

Lucille Ball (entertainer)	1989 *
C. Douglas Dillon (public servant)	1989
James H. Doolittle (aviation pioneer)	1989
George F. Kennen (public servant and author)	1989
Claude D. Pepper (public servant)	1989
Margaret Chase Smith (public servant)	1989

Lech Walesa (human rights champion)	1989
Margaret Thatcher (former Prime Minister of U.K.)	1991
Gen. Colin L. Powell (soldier)	1991
Gen. H. Norman Schwarzkopf (soldier)	1991
James A. Baker 3d (government service)	1991
Dick Cheney (government service)	1991
Brent Scowcroft (government service)	1991

Recipients of Kennedy Center Honors

The Kennedy Center for the Performing Arts in Washington, D.C., created its Honors awards in 1978 to recognize the achievements of five distinguished contributors to the performing arts. Following are the recipients:

1978: Marian Anderson (contralto), Fred Astaire (dancer-actor), Richard Rodgers (Broadway composer), Arthur Rubinstein (pianist), George Balanchine (choreographer).

1979: Ella Fitzgerald (jazz singer), Henry Fonda (actor), Martha Graham (dancer-choreographer), Tennessee Williams (playwright), Aaron Copland (composer).

1980: James Cagney (actor), Leonard Bernstein (composer-conductor), Agnes de Mille (choreographer), Lynn Fontanne (actress), Leontyne Price (soprano).

1981: Count Basie (jazz composer-pianist), Cary Grant (actor), Helen Hayes (actress), Jerome Robbins (choreographer), Rudolf Serkin (pianist).

1982: George Abbott (Broadway producer), Lillian Gish (actress), Benny Goodman (jazz clarinetist), Gene Kelly (dancer-actor), Eugene Ormandy (conductor).

1983: Katherine Dunham (dancer-choreographer), Elia Kazan (director-author), James Stewart (actor), Virgil Thomson (music critic-composer), Frank Sinatra (singer).

1984: Lena Horne (singer), Danny Kaye (comedian-actor), Gian Carlo Menotti (composer), Arthur Miller (playwright), Isaac Stern (violinist).

1985: Merce Cunningham (dancer-choreographer), Irene Dunne (actress), Bob Hope (comedian), Alan Jay Lerner (lyricist-playwright), Frederick Loewe (composer), Beverly Sills (soprano and opera administrator).

1986: Lucille Ball (comedienne), Ray Charles (musician), Yehudi Menuhin (violinist), Antony Tudor (choreographer), Hume Cronyn and Jessica Tandy (husband-and-wife acting team).

1987: Perry Como (singer), Bette Davis (actress), Sammy Davis Jr. (entertainer), Nathan Milstein (violinist), Alwin Nikolais (choreographer).

1988: Alvin Ailey (choreographer), George Burns (comedian-actor), Myrna Loy (actress), Alexander Schneider (violinist), Roger L. Stevens (theatrical producer and the Kennedy Center's founding chairman).

1989: Harry Belafonte (singer-actor), Claudette Colbert (actress), Alexandra Danilova (ballerina-teacher), Mary Martin (actress), William Schuman (composer)

1990: Dizzy Gillespie (jazz trumpeter), Katharine Hepburn (actress), Risë Stevens (mezzo-soprano), Jule Styne (composer), Billy Wilder (director-author)

1991 Christopher Awards

Adult Books

Anton the Dove Fancier: And Other Tales of the Holocaust, by Vernard Gotfryd (Washington Square Press)

The Boy Who Felt No Pain, by Robert Marion, M.D. (Addison Wesley)

Harvest of Hope: The Pilgrimage of a Mexican-American Physician, by Jorge Prieto, M.D. (University of Notre Dame Press)

House of Light, by Mary Oliver (Beacon)

In Mysterious Ways: The Death and Life of a Parish Priest, by Paul Wilkes (Random House)

In the Lion's Den: The Life of Oswald Rufeisen, by Nechama Tec (Oxford University Press)

Inside Riker's Island: A Chaplain's Search for God, by Pierre Raphael (Orbis)

Risking Hope: Fragile Faith in the Healing Process, by Kathleen O'Connell Chesto (Sheed & Ward)

Road Song, by Natalie Kusz (Farrar Straus Giroux)

The Spiritual Life of Children, by Robert Coles (Houghton Mifflin)

Young People's Books

Mississippi Bridge, by Mildred D. Taylor, illustrated by Max Ginsburg (Dial)

Paul Revere's Ride, Henry Wadsworth Longfellow's poem as illustrated by Ted Rand (Dutton)

Television Specials

Amazing Grace (PBS)

America's Toughest Assignment: Solving the Education Crisis (CBS)

Athletes and Addiction: It's Not a Game (ABC Sports)

The Civil War (PBS/WETA)

Decoration Day (NBC)

The Dreamer of Oz (NBC)

The Incident (CBS)

The Last Best Year (ABC)

The Love She Sought (NBC)

Nobody's Children: The Shame of a Nation (ABC News 20/20)

Weapons of the Spirit/Bill Moyers Interviews Filmmaker Pierre Sauvage (PBS/KTCA)

When You Remember Me (ABC)

Films

Akira Kurasawa's Dreams (Warner Bros.)

Avalon (Tri-Star Pictures)

Awakenings (Columbia Pictures)

Come See the Paradise (Twentieth Century Fox)

The James Keller Award

Clara McBride Hale for decades of devotion to children in crisis.

Major Grammy Awards for Recording in 1990

Source: National Academy of Recording Arts and Sciences.

Record: "Another Day in Paradise," Phil Collins

Album: "Back on the Block," Quincy Jones

Song: "From a Distance," Julie Gold

New Artist: Mariah Carey

Pop Vocalists: (Female) Mariah Carey, "Vision of Love"; (Male) Roy Orbison, "Oh Pretty Woman (From a Black and White Night Live)"

Pop Duo or Group: Linda Ronstadt with Aaron Neville, "All My Life"

Pop Instrumental: Angelo Badalamenti, "Twin Peaks Theme"

Rock Vocalists: (Female) Alannah Myles, "Black Velvet"; (Male) Eric Clapton, "Bad Love"

Rock Duo or Group: Aerosmith, "Janie's Got a Gun"

Rock Instrumental: Vaughan Brothers, "D-FW"

Hard Rock: Living Colour, "Time's Up"

Metal: Metallica, "Stone Cold Crazy"

Rhythm-and-Blues Vocalists: (Female) Anita Baker, "Compositions"; (Male) Luther Vandross, "Here and Now"

Rhythm-and-Blues Duo or Group: Ray Charles and Chaka Khan, "I'll Be Good to You"

Rhythm-and-Blue Song: "U Can't Touch This," James Miller and M.C. Hammer

Traditional Blues: B.B. King, "Live at San Quentin"

Contemporary Blues: Vaughn Brothers, "Family Style"

Rap: M.C. Hammer, "U Can't Touch This"

Rap Duo or Group: Ice-T, Melle Mel, Big Daddy Kane, and Kool Moe Dee, "Back on the Block" (track from Quincy Jones' "Back on the Block")

New Age: Mark Isham, "Mark Isham"

Jazz Fusion: Quincy Jones (various artists) "Birdland" (track from "Back on the Block")

Jazz Vocalists: (Female) Ella Fitzgerald, "All That Jazz"; (Male) Harry Connick Jr., "We Are In Love"

Jazz Instrumentalists: (Soloist) Oscar Peterson, "The Legendary Oscar Peterson Trio Live at the Blue Note"; (Group) Oscar Peterson Trio, "The Legendary Oscar Peterson Trio Live at the Blue Note"

Jazz Big Band: Count Basie Orchestra, "Basie's Bag" (track from "Big Boss Band")

Country Vocalists: (Female) Kathy Mattea, "Where You've Been"; (Male) Vince Gill, "When I Call Your Name"

Country Duo or Group: Kentucky Headhunters, "Pickin' on Nashville"

Country Instrumental: Chet Atkins and Mark Knopfler, "So Soft, Your Goodbye"

Country Song: "Where've You Been," Kathy Mattea

Rock-Contemporary Gospel: Petra, "Beyond Belief"

Pop Gospel: Sandi Patti, "Another Time . . . Another Place"

Southern Gospel: Bruce Carroll, "The Great Exchange"

Traditional Soul Gospel: Tramaine Hawkins, "Tramaine Hawkins Live"

Contemporary Soul Gospel: Take Six, "So Much 2 Say"

Gospel Choir or Chorus: The Rev. James Cleveland and the Southern California Community Choir, "Having Church"

Latin Pop: José Feliciano, "Por Que Te Tengo Que Olvidar?" (track from "Nina")

Tropical Latin: Tito Puente and Millie P. "Tito Puente Presents Millie P"

Mexican-American Performance: Texas Tornados, "Soy de San Luis" (track from "Texas Tornados")

Traditional Folk: Doc Watson, "On Praying Ground"

Contemporary Folk: Shawn Colvin, "Steady On"

Best Polka: Jimmy Sturr and His Orchestra, "When It's Polka Time at Your House"

Reggae: Bunny Wailer, "Time Will Tell: A Tribute to Bob Marley"

For Children: "The Little Mermaid: Original Motion Picture Soundtrack: (songs and instrumental score) Howard Ashman and Alan Menken, composers

Comedy: "P.D.Q. Bach: Oedipus Tex and Other Choral Calamities," Prof. Peter Schickele

Spoken Word: "Gracie: A Love Story," George Burns

Cast Show Album: "Les Misérables: The Complete Symphonic Recording," David Caddick, producer

Instrumental Composition: Pat Metheny, "Change of Heart" (track from "Question and Answer")

Instrumental Composition Written for a Motion Picture or for Television: "Glory," James Horner

Insstrumental Arrangement: "Birdland," (track from "Back on the Block") Quincy Jones, Ian Prince, Rod Templeton, and Jerry Hey

Music Video—Short Form: "Opposites Attract," Paula Abdul; Michael Patterson and Candice Reckinger, directors; Sharon Oreck, producer

Music Video—Long Form: "Please Hammer Don't Hurt 'Em, the Movie," M.C. Hammer; Rupert Wainwright, director, John Oetjen, producer

Historical Album: "The Complete Recordings, Robert Johnson," Lawrence Cohn, producer

Classical Album: Ives, "Symphony No. 2, The Gong on the Hook and Ladder (Fireman's Parade on Main Street)," "Central Park in the Dark," "The Unanswered Question," Leonard Bernstein, conductor; Han Weber, producer

Classical Orchestral Performance: Shostakovich, "Symphonies No. 1 and No. 7," Leonard Bernstein, conductor, Chicago Symphony

Classical Soloist with Orchestra: Itzhak Perlman, violinist (Zubin Mehta, conductor, Israel Philharmonic), Shostakovich: "Violin Concerto No. 1 in A minor" and Glazunov: Violin Concerto in A minor (Op. 82); **Without Orchestra:** Vladimir Horowitz, pianist, "The Last Recording" (Chopin, Haydn, Liszt, Wagner)

Chamber Music or Other Small Ensemble Performance: Itzhak Perlman, violinist; Daniel Barenboim, pianist, Brahms: "The Three Violin Sonatas"

Classical Vocal Performance: "Carreras, Domingo, Pavarotti in Concert," José Carreras, Plácido Domingo, Luciano Pavarotti, tenors

Classical Choral: Walton: "Belshazzar's Feast," Bernstein: "Chichester Psalms," "Missa Brevis," Robert Shaw, conductor, Atlanta Symphony Chorus and Orchestra

Opera: Wagner: "Das Rheingold," James Levine, conductor, Metropolitan Opera Orchestra

Contemporary Composition: "Arias and Barcarolles," Leonard Bernstein

Producers: Non-Classical, Quincy Jonees; **Classical,** Adam Stern

Engineers: Non-Classical, Bruce Swedien, "Back on the Block"; **Classical:** Jack Renner, Rachmaninoff: "Vespers"

ENTERTAINMENT & CULTURE

U.S. Symphony Orchestras and Their Music Directors

(With expenses over $1,050,000)

Source: American Symphony Orchestra League.

Alabama Symphony: Paul Polivnick
Atlanta Symphony: Yoel Levi
Austin Symphony: Sung Kwak
Baltimore Symphony: David Zinman
Boston Symphony: Seiji Ozawa
Buffalo Philharmonic: Maximiano Valdez
Charleston Symphony: David Stahl
Charlotte Symphony: Leo B. Driehuys
Chattanooga Symphony & Opera Assn.: Vakhtang Jordania[1]
Chicago Symphony: Daniel Barenboim
Cincinnati Symphony: Jesus Lopez-Cobos
Cleveland Orchestra: Christoph von Dohnanyi
Colorado Springs Symphony: Christopher P. Wilkins
Columbus Symphony: Christian Badea[1]
Dallas Symphony: Eduardo Mata
Dayton Philharmonic: Isaiah Jackson
Delaware Symphony: Stephen Gunzenhauser
Detroit Symphony: Gunther Herbig
Philharmonic Orchestra of Florida: James Judd
Florida Orchestra: Jahja Ling
Florida Symphony: Kenneth Jean
Florida Symphonic Pops: Mark Azzolina[2]
Fort Wayne Philharmonic: Ronald Ondrejka
Fort Worth Symphony: John Giordano
Grand Rapids Symphony: Catherine Comet
Hartford Symphony: Michael Lankester
Honolulu Symphony Society: Donald Johanos
Houston Symphony: Christoph Eschenbach
Indianapolis Symphony: Raymond Leppard
Jacksonville Symphony: Roger Nierenberg
Kansas City Symphony: William McGlaughlin
Knoxville Symphony: Kirk Trevor
Little Orchestra Society of New York: Dino Anagnost
Long Beach Symphony: JoAnn Falletta[3]
Long Island Philharmonic: Marin Alsop
Los Angeles Chamber Orchestra: Iona Brown
Los Angeles Philharmonic: Esa-Pekka Salonen
Louisville Orchestra: Lawrence Leighton Smith
Memphis Symphony: Alan Balter
Milwaukee Symphony: Zdenek Macal
Minnesota Orchestra: Edo de Waart
Mississippi Symphony: Colman Pearce
Nashville Symphony: Kenneth D. Schermerhorn

National Symphony (D.C.): Mstislav Rostropovich
New Haven Symphony: Michael Palmer
New Jersey Symphony: Hugh Wolff
New Mexico Symphony: Neal H. Stulberg
New Orleans Symphony: Maxim Shostakovich[4]
New World Symphony (Fla.): Michael Tilson Thomas[1]
New York Philharmonic: Kurt Masur
North Carolina Symphony: Gerhardt Zimmermann
Oklahoma City Philharmonic: Joel A. Levine
Omaha Symphony: Bruce B. Hangen
Oregon Symphony: James DePreist
Pacific Symphony (Calif.): Carl St. Clair
Philadelphia Orchestra: Riccardo Muti
Philharmonic Baroque Orchestra (Calif.): Nicholas McGegan
Phoenix Symphony: James Sadares
Pittsburgh Symphony: Lorin Maazel
Portland Symphony: Toshi Shimada
Rhode Island Philharmonic: Andrew Massey
Richmond Symphony: George Manahan
Rochester Philharmonic: Mark Elder
Sacramento Symphony: Carter Nice
St. Louis Symphony: Leonard Slatkin
St. Paul Chamber Orchestra: Christopher Hogwood
San Antonio Symphony: Zdenek Macal[1]
San Diego Symphony: Yoav Talmi
San Francisco Symphony: Herbert Blomstedt
San Jose Symphony: George Cleve
Savannah Symphony: Philp B. Greenberg
Seattle Symphony: Gerard Schwarz
Spokane Symphony: Bruce Ferden
Springfield Symphony (Mass.): Raymond C. Harvey
Syracuse Symphony: Kazuyoshi Akiyama
Toledo Symphony: Andrew Massey
Tucson Symphony: Robert E. Bernhardt
Tulsa Philharmonic: Bernard Rubenstein
Utah Symphony: Joseph Silverstein
West Virginia Symphony: Thomas B. Conlin
Wichita Symphony: Zuohuang Chen
Winston-Salem Symphony Assn.: Peter J. Perret

1. Artistic Director. 2. President/Conductor. 3. Conductor. 4. Principal conductor. James Paul is artistic director.

Major U.S. Dance Companies

(Figure in parentheses is year of founding)

Alvin Ailey American Dance Theatre (1958): Dir.: Judith Jamison
American Ballet Theatre (1940): Dirs.: Jane Hermann and Oliver Smith
Ballet West (1968[1]): Art. Dir.: John Hart
Boston Ballet (1964): Art. Dir.: Bruce Marks
Dance Theatre of Harlem (1968): Art. Dir.: Arthur Mitchell
Feld Ballet, The (1974): Dir.: Eliot Feld
Houston Ballet (1968): Art. Dir.: Ben Stevenson
Joffrey Ballet (1954): Art. Dir.: Gerald Arpino
Jose Limon Dance Company (1946): Art. Dir.: Carla Maxwell
Lar Lubovitch Dance Company (1968): Dir.: Lar Lubovitch
Laura Dean Dancers and Musicians (1974): Dir.: Laura Dean
Lucinda Childs Dance Company (1973): Dir.: Lucinda Childs

Martha Graham Dance Company (1927): Gen. Dir.: Ron Protas
Merce Cunningham Dance Company (1952): Dir.: Merce Cunningham
Miami City Ballet (1986): Art. Dir.: Edward Villella
New York City Ballet (1948): Peter Martins, Ballet Master in Chief
Nikolais Dance Theatre (1948): Dir.: Alvin Nikolais
Pacific Northwest Ballet (1972): Art. Dirs.: Kent Stowell and Francia Russell
Pennsylvania Ballet (1963): Art. Dir.: Christopher d'Amboise
Pilobolus Dance Theatre (1971): Manager: Susan Mandler
Pittsburgh Ballet Theater (1970): Art. Dir.: Patricia Wilde
San Francisco Ballet (1933): Art. Dir.: Helgi Tomasson
Washington Ballet (1962): Dir.: Mary Day

1. Prior company founded 1963, name changed to Ballet West in 1968.

Major Public Libraries

City (branches)	Volumes	Circulation	Budget (in millions)	City (branches)	Volumes	Circulation	Budget (in millions)
Akron-Summit County, Ohio (17)	1,407,000	2,919,962	$12.8	Los Angeles (County) (96)	5,360,000 [4]	12,000,000	77.7
Albuquerque, N.M. (12)	733,311	2,756,342	6.1	Louisville, Ky. (14)	657,000	2,830,500	$7.8
Annapolis, Md. (14)	1,620,159	4,669,584	9.8	Madison, Wis. (7)	699,100	2,584,658	5.4
Atlanta-Fulton County (25)	1,977,157	3,164,014	17.3	Memphis, Tenn. (22)	1,499,018	2,587,331	12.0
Austin, Tex. (16)	969,620	2,331,961	8.5	Miami-Dade County, Fla. (30)	3,106,802	4,300,197	31.2
Baltimore (29)	2,197,362	1,600,232	-16.7	Milwaukee (12)	2,151,896	3,352,002	14.2
Baton Rouge, La. (9)	747,865	2,053,254	8.7	Minneapolis (14)	1,923,967	3,071,444	14.2
Birmingham, Ala. (19)	1,104,700	1,976,895	9.0	Nashville-Davidson County, Tenn. (16)	657,279	1,820,188	7.6
Boston (29)	5,992,634	2,086,071	28.6	Newark, N.J. (11)	1,288,590	1,210,000	9.8
Buffalo-Erie County, N.Y. (58)	4,514,901 [1]	7,147,642	18.4	New Orleans (15)	1,040,708	1,207,346	6.1
Charleston-Kanawha County, W.Va. (8)	570,754	870,486	3.4	*New York City:*			
Charlotte, N.C. (20)	1,233,936	2,989,000	11.2	*The New York Public Library			
Chicago (80)	5,588,103	7,657,392	68.0	Branches (82)	3,524,696	10,384,453	74.5
Cincinnati (41)	4,142,458	9,588,347	27.0	Research	9,834,933		54.0
Cleveland (28)	2,978,283	5,522,839	33.4	Brooklyn Public Library (60)	5,107,737	8,898,599	39.3
Columbus Metropolitan, Ohio (21)	1,774,748	6,721,896	29.8	Queens Borough Public Library (62)	7,046,589	13,202,363	46.6
Dallas (19)	2,229,127	4,617,168	16.7	Norfolk, Va. (11)	889,629	742,131	4.2
Dayton-Montgomery County, Ohio (19)	1,559,865	5,866,960	13.0	Oklahoma City-County (10)	950,376	4,237,844	9.5
Denver (21)	3,979,896	3,393,902	14.9	Omaha, Neb. (9)	602,561	2,281,780	6.6
Des Moines, Iowa (5)	544,449	1,246,350	3.7	Philadelphia (52)	5,056,302	5,103,446	43.3
Detroit (25)	2,760,003	1,633,971	21.4	Phoenix, Ariz. (10)	1,618,390	5,574,950	13.0
D.C. (27)	1,719,116	2,070,739	20.4	Pittsburgh (20)	1,911,402	2,832,251	13.8
El Paso (9)	703,690	1,268,435	5.4 [2]	Portland-Multnomah County, Ore. (14)	1,333,607	4,925,376	13.7
Erie, Pa. (6)	569,533	1,494,308	2.4	Providence, R.I. (9)	1,023,886	622,916	4.3
Evansville-Vanderburgh County, Ind. (7)	870,105	1,434,375	4.5	Richmond, Va. (10)	784,235	824,160	3.6
Fairfax County, Va. (22)	1,900,000	8,500,000	18.7	Rochester, N.Y. (11)	1,542,038	1,653,708	10.3
Fort Wayne-Allen County, Ind. (14)	2,094,789	3,150,922	9.2	Sacramento, Calif. (24)	1,663,893	4,124,258	18.5
Fort Worth (10)	2,102,812	3,708,764	5.9	St. Louis (14)	1,203,960	1,538,296	10.0
Grand Rapids, Mich. (5)	1,048,885	1,006,631	3.7	St. Paul (12)	588,944	2,620,722	6.9
Greenville City-County, S.C. (11)	570,139	1,353,385	5.2	St. Petersburg, Fla. (5)	445,000	1,300,000	2.8
Hawaii State Public Library System (49) [3]	2,388,106	6,187,214	21.1	Salt Lake City-County, Utah (15)	1,110,409	3,758,876	10.1
Houston (33)	3,737,734	6,284,971	19.4	San Antonio (17)	1,907,772	3,301,174	8.5
Independence, Mo. (26)	1,810,000	4,463,723	14.4	San Diego, Calif. (31)	1,642,520	5,138,179	18.5 [5]
Indianapolis-Marion County (21)	1,646,018	6,630,043	18.2	San Francisco (26)	1,972,809	2,986,523	20.1
Jackson-Hinds County, Miss. (12)	644,039	900,418	2.4	San Jose, Calif. (18)	1,364,000	3,936,300	17.0
Jacksonville, Fla. (13)	1,976,589	2,758,564	11.3	Seattle (22)	1,957,251	5,379,319	19.6
Kansas City, Mo. (9)	1,724,945	1,867,000	9.8	Springfield, Mass. (8)	655,761	1,096,477	3.5
Knoxville, Tenn. (16)	653,480	1,637,705	3.9	Tampa, Fla. (17)	1,840,000	3,128,160	13.4
Lincoln, Neb. (7)	562,666	1,709,648	3.3	Tucson, Ariz. (19)	1,226,900	4,890,795	9.8
Long Beach, Calif. (11)	1,052,672	2,783,132	11.3	Tulsa City-County, Okla. (20)	850,044	3,270,709	9.0
				Wichita, Kan. (11)	900,943	1,591,080	4.2
				Winston-Salem-Forsyth County, N.C. (8)	380,000	2,100,000	5.0
				Worcester, Mass. (1)	512,521	779,470	2.7
				Youngstown-Mahoning County, Ohio (22)	702,376	1,395,876	7.0

1. Includes books, periodicals, musical scores, recordings, CDs, films, videos, maps, posters. 2. Budget includes both general and bond funds for books. 3. State-wide system. 4. Includes books, audiovisual materials, government documents, musical scores, etc. 5. Includes $3.3 million capital improvements and $1.3 million grant-funded services. *Includes Manhattan, Bronx, and Staten Island.

Glossary of Art Movements

Abstract Expressionism. American art movement of the 1940s that emphasized form and color within a nonrepresentational framework. Jackson Pollock initiated the revolutionary technique of splattering the paint directly on canvas to achieve the subconscious interpretation of the artist's inner vision of reality.

Art Deco. A 1920s style characterized by setbacks, zigzag forms, and the use of chrome and plastic ornamentation. New York's Chrysler Building is an architectural example of the style.

Art Nouveau. An 1890s style in architecture, graphic arts, and interior decoration characterized by writhing forms, curving lines, and asymmetrical organization. Some critics regard the style as the first stage of modern architecture.

Ashcan School. A group of New York realist artists, formed in 1908, who abandoned decorous subject matter and portrayed the more common as well as the sordid aspects of city life.

Assemblage (Collage). Forms of modern sculpture and painting utilizing readymades, found objects, and pasted fragments to form an abstract composition. Louise Nevelson's boxlike enclosures, each with its own composition of assembled objects, illustrate the style in sculpture. Pablo Picasso developed the technique of cutting and pasting natural or manufactured materials to a painted or unpainted surface.

Barbizon School (Landscape Painting). A group of painters who, around the middle of the 19th century, reacted against classical landscape and advocated a direct study of nature. They were influenced by English and Dutch landscape masters. Theodore Rousseau, one of the principal figures of the group, led the fight for outdoor painting. In this respect, the school was a forerunner of Impressionism.

Baroque. European art and architecture of the 17th and 18th centuries. Giovanni Bernini, a major exponent of the style, believed in the union of the arts of architecture, painting, and sculpture to overwhelm the spectator with ornate and highly dramatized themes. Although the style originated in Rome as the instrument of the Church, it spread throughout Europe in such monumental creations as the Palace of Versailles.

Beaux Arts. Elaborate and formal architectural style characterized by symmetry and an abundance of sculptured ornamentation. New York's old Custom House at Bowling Green is an example of the style.

Black or Afro-American Art. The work of American artists of African descent produced in various styles characterized by a mood of protest and a search for identity and historical roots.

Classicism. A form of art derived from the study of Greek and Roman styles characterized by harmony, balance, and serenity. In contrast, the Romantic Movement gave free rein to the artist's imagination and to the love of the exotic.

Constructivism. A form of sculpture using wood, metal, glass, and modern industrial materials expressing the technological society. The mobiles of Alexander Calder are examples of the movement.

Cubism. Early 20th-century French movement marked by a revolutionary departure from representational art. Pablo Picasso and Georges Bracque penetrated the surface of objects, stressing basic abstract geometric forms that presented the object from many angles simultaneously.

Dada. A product of the turbulent and cynical post-World War I period, this anti-art movement extolled the irrational, the absurd, the nihilistic, and the nonsensical. The reproduction of Mona Lisa adorned with a mustache is a famous example. The movement is regarded as a precursor of Surrealism. Some critics regard HAPPENINGS as a recent development of Dada. This movement incorporates environment and spectators as active and important ingredients in the production of random events.

Expressionism. A 20th-century European art movement that stresses the expression of emotion and the inner vision of the artist rather than the exact representation of nature. Distorted lines and shapes and exaggerated colors are used for emotional impact. Vincent Van Gogh is regarded as the precursor of this movement.

Fauvism. The name "wild beasts" was given to the group of early 20th-century French painters because their work was characterized by distortion and violent colors. Henri Matisse and Georges Rouault were leaders of this group.

Futurism. This early 20th-century movement originating in Italy glorified the machine age and attempted to represent machines and figures in motion. The aesthetics of Futurism affirmed the beauty of technological society.

Genre. This French word meaning "type" now refers to paintings that depict scenes of everyday life without any attempt at idealization. Genre paintings can be found in all ages, but the Dutch productions of peasant and tavern scenes are typical.

Impressionism. Late 19th-century French school dedicated to defining transitory visual impressions painted directly from nature, with light and color of primary importance. If the atmosphere changed, a totally different picture would emerge. It was not the object or event that counted but the visual impression as caught at a certain time of day under a certain light. Claude Monet and Camille Pissarro were leaders of the movement.

Mannerism. A mid-16th century movement, Italian in origin, although El Greco was a major practitioner of the style. The human figure, distorted and elongated, was the most frequent subject.

Neoclassicism. An 18th-century reaction to the excesses of Baroque and Rococo, this European art movement tried to recreate the art of Greece and Rome by imitating the ancient classics both in style and subject matter.

Neoimpressionism. A school of painting associated with George Seurat and his followers in late 19th-century France that sought to make Impressionism more precise and formal. They employed a technique of juxtaposing dots of primary colors to achieve brighter secondary colors, with the mixture left to the eye to complete (pointillism).

Op Art. The 1960s movement known as Optical Painting is characterized by geometrical forms that create an optical illusion in which the eye is required to blend the colors at a certain distance.

Pop Art. In this return to representational art, the artist returns to the world of tangible objects in a reaction against abstraction. Materials are drawn from the everyday world of popular culture—comic strips, canned goods, and science fiction.

Realism. A development in mid-19th-century France lead by Gustave Courbet. Its aim was to depict the customs, ideas, and appearances of the time using scenes from everyday life.

Rococo. A French style of interior decoration developed during the reign of Louis XV consisting mainly of asymmetrical arrangements of curves in paneling, porcelain, and gold and silver objects. The characteristics of ornate curves, prettiness, and gaiety can also be found in the painting and sculpture of the period.

Surrealism. A further development of Collage, Cubism, and Dada, this 20th-century movement stresses the weird, the fantastic, and the dreamworld of the subconscious.

Symbolism. As part of a general European movement in the latter part of the 19th century, it was closely allied with Symbolism in literature. It marked a turning away from painting by observation to transforming fact into a symbol of inner experience. Gauguin was an early practitioner.

Top 10 Videocassettes
Sales, 1990

1. **Bambi** (Walt Disney Home Video)
2. **New Kids on the Block: Hangin' Tough Live** (CBS Music Video Enterprises)
3. **The Little Mermaid** (Walt Disney Home Video)
4. **Lethal Weapon 2** (Warner Home Video)
5. **The Wizard of Oz: The Fiftieth Anniversary Edition** (MGM/UA Home Video)
6. **Batman** (Warner Home Video)
7. **Honey, I Shrunk the Kids** (Walt Disney Home Video)
8. **The Land Before Time** (MCA/Universal Home Video)
9. **Who Framed Roger Rabbit?** (Touchstone Home Video)
10. **Teenage Mutant Ninja Turtles: Cowabunga, Shredhead** (Family Home Entertainment)

Source: © 1991 BPI Communications, Inc. Used with permission from *Billboard.*

Top 10 Classical Crossover
Albums, 1990

1. **1712 Overture,** P.D.Q. Bach (Telarc)
2. **Henry V Soundtrack,** City of Birmingham Symphony (Rattle) (Angel)
3. **Anything Goes,** Criswell, Groenendall, Von Stade (McGlinn) (Angel)
4. **Music of the Night,** Boston Pops (Williams) (Sony Classical)
5. **Fantastic Journey,** Cincinnati Pops (Kunzel) (Telarc)
6. **The Enchanted Forest,** James Galway (RCA)
7. **Trumpet Spectacular,** Doc Severinsen with the Cincinnati Pops (Kunzel) (Telarc)
8. **Show Boat Highlights,** Von Stade, Hadley, Stratas (McGlinn) (Angel)
9. **Happy Trails,** Cincinnati Pops (Kunzel) (Telarc)
10. **James Galway's Greatest Hits,** James Galway (RCA)

Source: © 1991 BPI Communications, Inc. Used with permission from *Billboard.*

Top 10 Kid Videocassettes, 1990

1. **Bambi** (Walt Disney Home Video)
2. **The Land Before Time** (MCA/Universal Home Video)
3. **Teenage Mutant Ninja Turtles: Killer Pizzas** (Family Home Entertainment)
4. **Cinderella** (Walt Disney Home Video)
5. **Charlotte's Web** (Paramount Home Video)
6. **Teenage Mutant Ninja Turtles: Hot Rodding** . . . (Family Home Entertainment)
7. **Teenage Mutant Ninja Turtles: The Shredder** . . . (Family Home Entertainment)
8. **Dumbo** (Walt Disney Home Video)
9. **Teenage Mutant Ninja Turtles: Heros** . . . (Family Home Entertainment)
10. **Winnie the Pooh: New Found Friends** (Walt Disney Home Video)

Source: © 1991 BPI Communications, Inc. Used with permission from *Billboard.*

VCR & TV Sales to Retailers, 1990

Color TV[1]	21,058,000
Projection TV	351,000
Total TV	21,409,000
Home VCR	10,119,000
Camcorders	2,962,000

1. Includes LCD (liquid crystal displays). *Source:* Electronic Industries Association Consumer Electronics Group.

Top 10 Videocassettes
Rentals, 1990

1. **Look Who's Talking** (RCA/Columbia Picture Home Video)
2. **When Harry Met Sally** . . . (Nelson Home Entertainment)
3. **Parenthood** (MCA/Universal Home Video)
4. **K-9** (MCA/Universal Home Video)
5. **Dead Poets Society** (Touchstone Home Video)
6. **Steel Magnolias** (RCA/Columbia Home Video)
7. **Sea of Love** (MCA/Universal Home Video)
8. **Turner & Hooch** (Touchstone Home Video)
9. **Black Rain** (Paramount Home Video)
10. **Internal Affairs** (Paramount Home Video)

Source: © 1991 BPI Communications, Inc. Used with permission from *Billboard.*

Top 10 Music Videocassettes, 1990

1. **Hangin' Tough** (CBS Music Video Enterprise)
2. **Hangin' Tough Live** (CBS Music Video Enterprise)
3. **Janet Jackson's Rhythm Nation 1814** (A&M Video)
4. **Straight Up** (Virgin Music Video)
5. **Milli Vanilli in Motion** (6 West Home Video)
6. **25×5: Continuing Adventures of Rolling Stones** (CBS Music Video Enterprises)
7. **Step by Step** (CBS Music Video Enterprises)
8. **Kenny G Live** (6 West Home Video)
9. **Barry Manilow: Live on Broadway** (6 West Home Video)
10. **His Prerogative** (MCA Music Video)

Source: © 1991 BPI Communications, Inc. Used with permission from *Billboard.*

15 Top-Grossing Concerts

1. **Paul McCartney,** $3,550,580, Memorial Stadium, University of California, Berkeley, March 31–April 1.
2. **The Rolling Stones & Living Colour,** $3,490,126, Olympic Stadium, Montreal, Dec. 13–14, 1989.
3. **Paul McCartney,** $3,415,165, Giants Stadium, East Rutherford, N.J., July 9 and 11.
4. **Billy Joel,** $3,390,000, Giants Stadium, East Rutherford, N.J. Aug. 18–19.
5. **The Rolling Stones & Living Colour,** $3,262,757, Skydome, Toronto, Dec. 3–4, 1989.
6. **Paul McCartney,** $3,107,980, Veterans Stadium, Philadelphia, July 14–15.
7. **Billy Joel,** $3,101,010, Yankee Stadium, New York, N.Y., June 22–23.
8. **The Rolling Stones & Living Colour,** $2,976,592, Metrodome, Minneapolis, Nov. 29–30, 1989.
9. **The Rolling Stones & Living Colour,** $2,958,834, Pontiac Silverdome, Pontiac, Mich., Dec. 9–19, 1989.
10. **Paul McCartney,** $2,862,300, Joe Robbie Stadium, Miami, April 14–15.
11. **Paul McCartney,** $2,756,760, Robert F. Kennedy Memorial Stadium, Washington, D.C., July 4 and 6.
12. **Paul McCartney,** $2,578,110, Foxboro Stadium, Foxboro, Mass., July 24 and 26.
13. **New Kids on the Block, Rick Wes, Tommy Page, Perfect Gentlemen,** $2,542,125, Giants Stadium, East Rutherford, N.J., July 20–21.
14. **The Rolling Stones & Living Colour,** $2,533,955, Hoosier Dome, Indianapolis, Ind., Dec. 6–7, 1989.
15. **Billy Joel,** $2,489,947, The Spectrum, Philadelphia, Dec. 17–18, Jan. 14–15 and 29–30.

Source: © 1990 by *Amusement Business* magazine. Reprinted by permission.

Top 10 Classical Albums, 1990

1. **Horowitz at Home,** Vladimir Horowitz (DG)
2. **Horowitz: The Last Recording,** Vladimir Horowitz (Sony Classical)
3. **Horowitz in Moscow,** Vladimir Horowitz (DG)
4. **Beethoven: Symphony No. 9,** Leonard Bernstein (DG)
5. **Tutto Pavarotti,** Luciano Pavarotti (London)
6. **Handel: Arias,** Kathleen Battle (Angel)
7. **Verdi & Puccini: Arias,** Kiri Te Kanawa (Sony Classical)
8. **The Moves Go to the Opera,** Various artists (Angel)
9. **Black Angels,** Kronos Quartet (Nonesuch)
10. **Beethoven: 9 Symphonies,** Arturo Toscanini (RCA)

Source: © 1990 BPI Communications, Inc. Used with permission from *Billboard.*

Artists of the Year, 1990

Single of the Year: Hold On, Wilson Phillips
Album of the Year: Janet Jackson's Rhythm Nation 1814, Janet Jackson
Female Artist of the Year: Paula Abdul
Male Artist of the Year: Phil Collins
Group of the Year: New Kids on the Block
New Artist of the Year: Bell Biv Devoe
Country Artist of the Year: Randy Travis
Rhythm & Blues Artist of the Year: Janet Jackson
Adult Contemporary Artist of the Year: Phil Collins
Jazz Artist of the Year: Harry Connick, Jr.
Classical Artist of the Year: Vladimir Horowitz
Soundtrack of the Year: Pretty Woman

Source: © 1990 BPI Communications, Inc. Used with permission from *Billboard.*

Top 10 Pop Single Recordings, 1990

1. **Hold On,** Wilson Phillips (SBK)
2. **It Must Have Been Love (from "Pretty Woman"),** Roxette (EMI)
3. **Nothing Compares 2 U,** Sinead O'Connor (Ensign)
4. **Poison,** Bell Biv Devoe (MCA)
5. **Vogue,** Madonna (Sire)
6. **Vision of Love,** Mariah Carey (Columbia)
7. **Another Day in Paradise,** Phil Collins (Atlantic)
8. **Hold On,** En Vogue (Atlantic)
9. **Cradle of Love (from "Ford Fairlane"),** Billy Idol (Chrysalis)
10. **Blaze of Glory (from "Young Guns II"),** Jon Bon Jovi (Mercury)

Source: © 1990 BPI Communications, Inc. Used with permission from *Billboard.*

Top 10 Country Single Recordings, 1990

1. **Nobody's Home,** Clint Black (RCA)
2. **Hard Rock Bottom of Your Heart,** Randy Travis (Warner Bros.)
3. **On Second Thought,** Eddie Rabbitt (Capitol)
4. **Love Without End, Amen,** George Strait (MCA)
5. **Walkin' Away,** Clint Black (RCA)
6. **I've Cried My Last Tear for You,** Ricky Van Shelton (Columbia)
7. **No Matter How High,** The Oak Ridge Boys (MCA)
8. **Help Me Hold On,** Travis Tritt (Warner Bros.)
9. **Chains,** Patty Loveless (MCA)
10. **Here in the Real World,** Alan Jackson (Arista)

Source: © 1990 BPI Communications, Inc. Used with permission from *Billboard.*

Top 10 Pop Albums, 1990

1. **Janet Jackson's Rhythm Nation 1814,** Janet Jackson (A&M)
2. **. . . But Seriously,** Phil Collins (Atlantic)
3. **Soul Provider,** Michael Bolton (Columbia)
4. **Pump,** Aerosmith (Geffen)
5. **Please Hammer Don't Hurt 'Em,** M.C. Hammer (Capitol)
6. **Forever Your Girl,** Paula Abdul (Virgin)
7. **Dr. Feelgood,** Motley Crüe (Electra)
8. **The End of the Innocence,** Don Henley (Geffen)
9. **Cosmic Thing,** The B-52's (Reprise)
10. **Storm Front,** Billy Joel (Columbia)

Source: © 1990 BPI Communications, Inc. Used with permission from *Billboard.*

Manufacturers' Dollar[1] Shipments of Recordings
(in millions)

	1987	1988	1989	1990
Singles	203	180.4	116.4	94.4
LP's/EP's	793	532.3	220.3	86.5
CD's	1,593	2,089.9	2,587.7	3,451.6
Cassettes	2,959	3,385.1	3,345.8	3,472.4
Cassette singles	14[2]	57.3	194.6	257.9
CD singles	—	9.8	−.7	6.0
Music videos	—	—	115.4	172.3

1. List price value. 2. New configuration represents six month sales only. *Source:* Recording Industry Association of America, Inc.

Top 10 Rhythm & Blues Single Recordings, 1990

1. **Hold On,** En Vogue (Atlantic)
2. **Make It Like It Was,** Regina Belle (Columbia)
3. **Real Love,** Skyy (Atlantic)
4. **Feels Good,** Tony! Toni! Tone! (Wing)
5. **Vision of Love,** Mariah Carey (Columbia)
6. **All Around the World,** Lisa Stansfield (Arista)
7. **I'll Be Good to You,** Quincy Jones featuring Ray Charles & Chaka Khan (Qwest)
8. **My, My, My,** Johnny Gill (Motown)
9. **Ready or Not,** After 7 (Virgin)
10. **Poison,** Bell Biv Devoe (MCA)

Source: © 1990 BPI Communications, Inc. Used with permission from *Billboard.*

Top 15 Regularly Scheduled Network Programs, Nov. 1990

Rank	Program name (network)	Total percent of TV households
1.	Cheers (NBC)	24.0
2.	60 Minutes (CBS)	21.8
3.	Murder, She Wrote (CBS)	18.2
3.	Roseanne (ABC)	18.2
5.	America's Funniest People (ABC)	18.0
5.	America's Funniest Home Videos (ABC)	18.0
7.	Murphy Brown (CBS)	17.8
8.	Designing Women (CBS)	17.7
9.	Empty Nest (NBC)	17.6
10.	Bill Cosby Show (NBC)	17.5
11.	Golden Girls (NBC)	17.2
12.	A Different World (NBC)	17.0
13.	NFL Monday Night Football (ABC)	16.7
14.	Unsolved Mysteries (NBC)	16.6
15.	Matlock (NBC)	16.3
Total U.S. TV households 93,100,000		

NOTE: Percentages are calculated from average audience viewings, 5 minutes or longer and 2 or more telecasts. *Source:* Nielsen Media Research, copyright 1991, Nielsen Media Research.

Top Sports Shows 1990–91[1]

Rank	Program name (network)	Rating (% of TV households)
1.	Super Bowl XXV (ABC)	41.9
2.	NFC Championship Game (CBS)	28.5
3.	AFC Playoff Bengals vs. Raiders (NBC)	24.7
4.	NFC Playoff Saints vs. Bears (CBS)	24.2
5.	NFC Playoff Bears vs. Giants (CBS)	22.6

1. Sept. 17, 1990, through July 14, 1991. *Source:* Nielsen Media Research, copyright 1991, Nielsen Media Research.

Persons Viewing Prime Time[1]
(in millions)

	Total persons
Monday	99.2
Tuesday	97.2
Wednesday	89.7
Thursday	95.9
Friday	86.7
Saturday	87.8
Sunday	107.2
Total average	**95.4**

1. Average minute audiences Nov. 1990. NOTE: Prime time is 8–11 p.m. (EST) except Sun. 7–11 p.m. *Source:* Nielsen Media Research, copyright 1991, Nielsen Media Research.

Top 15 Syndicated TV Programs 1990–91 Season

Rank	Program	Rating (% U.S.)[1]
1.	Wheel of Fortune, M-F	13.4
2.	Jeopardy	12.0
3.	Star Trek	10.7[2]
4.	Oprah Winfrey Show	9.0
5.	Cosby Show	8.3[2]
5.	Entertainment Tonight	8.3[2]
7.	Warner Brothers Volume 28	8.2[2]
8.	A Current Affair	7.9[2]
9.	MGM Premiere Network III	7.5[2]
9.	Wheel of Fortune, Weekend	7.5
11.	Universal Pictures Debut Network	6.7[2]
12.	Orion Galaxy Network	6.2[2]
12.	Republic Color Movies	6.2[2]
12.	Warner Brothers Premiere Edition	6.2[2]
15.	Donahue	5.9

1. 8/27/90–12/30/90. 2. Includes multiple exposures. *Source:* Nielsen Syndication Service National TV Ratings. Copyright 1991, Nielsen Media Research.

Top Specials 1990–91[1]

Rank	Program name (network)	Rating (% of TV households)
1.	63rd Academy Awards (ABC)	28.4
2.	Best of Ed Sullivan (CBS)	21.3
3.	American Music Awards (ABC)	20.4
4.	Grammy Awards (CBS)	18.8
5.	Barbara Walters Special with Jeremy Irons, Sophia Loren, and Whoopi Goldberg (ABC)	18.5

1. Sept. 17, 1990, through June 9, 1991. *Source:* Nielsen Media Research, copyright 1991, Nielsen Media Research.

Top Rated Movies 1990–91[1]

Rank	Program name (network)	Rating (% of TV households)
1.	Sarah, Plain and Tall (CBS)	23.1
2.	Stephen King's "It" (Part 2) (ABC)	20.6
3.	Kaleidoscope (NBC)	20.3
4.	Love, Lies and Murder (Part 2) (NBC)	20.3
5.	And the Sea Will Tell (Part 1) (CBS)	20.1

1. Sept. 17, 1990, through April 14, 1991. *Source:* Nielsen Media Research, copyright 1991, Nielsen Media Research.

Museum of Television and Radio Opens

At a ribbon-cutting ceremony on September 12, 1991, The Museum of Television & Radio opened to the public the doors of its new building at 25 West 52nd Street in New York City. Four times the size of its previous facility, the building houses a collection of over 40,000 radio and television programs—local, national, and international. It provides 96 radio and television consoles that the public can use to watch or listen to programs. In addition there are two theaters in the building, one of 200 seats, one of 90 seats, and two 45-seat screening rooms, as well as gallery space for exhibits.

Average Hours of Household TV Usage

(In hours and minutes per day)

	Yearly average	February	July
1981–82	6 h 48 min	7 h 22 min	6 h 09 min
1982–83	6 h 55 min	7 h 33 min	6 h 23 min
1983–84	7 h 08 min	7 h 38 min	6 h 26 min
1984–85	7 h 07 min	7 h 49 min	6 h 34 min
1985–86	7 h 10 min	7 h 48 min	6 h 37 min
1986–87	7 h 05 min	7 h 35 min	6 h 32 min
1987–88	6 h 55 min	7 h 38 min	6 h 31 min
1988–89	7 h 02 min	7 h 32 min	6 h 27 min
1989–90	6 h 55 min	7 h 16 min	6 h 24 min

Source: Nielsen Media Research, copyright 1991, Nielsen Media Research.

Weekly TV Viewing by Age

(in hours and minutes)

	Time per week	
	Nov. 1990	Nov. 1989
Women 18–24 years old	23 h 38 min	25 h 10 min
Women 25–54	30 h 34 min	31 h 31 min
Women 55 and over	40 h 48 min	41 h 19 min
Men 18–24	20 h 50 min	22 h 29 min
Men 25–54	26 h 44 min	27 h 16 min
Men 55 and over	38 h 05 min	38 h 22 min
Female Teens	23 h 25 min	21 h 16 min
Male Teens	23 h 01 min	22 h 18 min
Children 6–11	21 h 19 min	23 h 39 min
Children 2–5	26 h 14 min	27 h 49 min
Total Persons (2+)	**29 h 05 min**	**29 h 52 min**

Source: Nielsen Media Research, copyright 1991, Nielsen Media Research.

Television Network Addresses

American Broadcasting Companies (ABC)
77 W. 66th Street
New York, N.Y. 10023
Cable News Network (CNN)
1 World Trade Center
New York, N.Y. 10048
Canadian Broadcasting Corporation (CBC)
1500 Bronson Avenue
Ottawa, Ontario, Canada K1G 3J5
Columbia Broadcasting System (CBS)
51 W. 52nd Street
New York, N.Y. 10019
Fox Television (WNYW)
205 E. 67th Street
New York, N.Y. 10021
National Broadcasting Company (NBC)
30 Rockefeller Plaza
New York, N.Y. 10020
Public Broadcasting Service (PBS)
1320 Braddock Place
Alexandra, Va. 22314
Turner Network Television (TNT)
575 Madison Avenue
New York, N.Y. 10022
Westinghouse Broadcasting (Group W)
90 Park Avenue
New York, N.Y. 10016

Television Set Ownership

(Nielsen estimate as of Jan. 1, 1991)

Homes with	Number	Percent
Color TV sets	91,300,000	98.0
B&W only	1,800,000	02.0
2 or more sets	60,000,000	64.0
One set	33,100,000	35.0
Cable[1]	56,072,270	60.3
Total TV households	**93,100,000**	**98.0**

1. May 1991. *Source:* Nielsen Media Research, copyright 1991, Nielsen Media Research.

Audience Composition by Selected Program Type[1]

(Average Minute Audience)

	General drama	Suspense and mystery drama	Situation comedy	Informational[2] 6-7 p.m.	Feature films	All regular network programs 7–11 p.m.
Women (18 and over)	8,570,000	9,180,000	10,050,000	5,170,000	10,980,000	9,440,000
Men (18 and over)	5,430,000	6,330,000	6,150,000	4,140,000	7,450,000	6,780,000
Teens (12–17)	760,000	600,000	1,750,000	410,000	1,670,000	1,250,000
Children (2–11)	1,250,000	990,000	2,690,000	690,000	1,700,000	1,800,000
Total persons (2+)	**16,010,000**	**17,100,000**	**20,640,000**	**13,670,000**	**21,800,000**	**19,270,000**

1. All figures are estimated for the period Nov. 1990. 2. Multiweekly viewing. *Source:* Nielsen Media Research, copyright 1991, Nielsen Media Research.

Hours of TV Usage Per Week by Household Income

	Under $30,000	$30,000+	$40,000+	$50,000+	$60,000+
Nov. 1988	52 h 43 min	49 h 22 min	48 h 44 min	48 h 26 min	47 h 49 min
Nov. 1989	52 h 59 min	48 h 47 min	48 h 19 min	46 h 54 min	46 h 20 min
Nov. 1990	n.a.	48 h 03 min	47 h 35 min	47 h 24 min	46 h 12 min

Source: Nielsen Media Research, copyright 1991, Nielsen Media Research. NOTE: n.a. = not available.

Source of Household Viewing—Prime Time
Pay Cable, Basic Cable, and Non-Cable Households
(Mon.-Sun. 8–11 pm)

	Nov. 1990			Nov. 1989			Nov. 1988		
	Pay cable	Basic cable	Non-cable	Pay cable	Basic cable	Non-cable	Pay cable	Basic cable	Non-cable
% TV Usage	66.3	59.6	54.5	65.6	60.3	56.5	67.7	63.1	57.7
Pay Cable	9.9	—	—	9.7	—	—	11.8	—	—
Cable-originated programming	15.9	15.5	—	14.8	14.1	—	13.5	13.1	—
Other-on-air stations	14.1	14.0	17.5	14.2	14.0	15.8	14.2	14.7	16.1
Network affiliated stations	37.0	35.8	42.0	37.5	37.5	44.9	38.1	40.9	46.0
Network share	(56)	(60)	(75)	(57)	(62)	(79)	(56)	(65)	(80)

Source: Nielsen Media Research, copyright 1991, Nielsen Media Research.

Major U.S. Fairs and Expositions

1853 Crystal Palace Exposition, New York City: modeled on similar fair held in London.
1876 Centennial Exposition, Philadelphia: celebrating 100th year of independence.
1893 World's Columbian Exposition, Chicago: commemorating 400th anniversary of Columbus' voyage to America.
1894 Midwinter International Exposition, San Francisco: promoting business revival after Depression of 1893.
1898 Trans-Mississippi and International Exposition, Omaha, Neb.: exhibiting products, resources, industries, and civilization of states and territories west of the Mississippi River.
1901 Pan-American Exposition, Buffalo, N.Y.: promoting social and commercial interest of Western Hemisphere nations.
1904 Louisiana Purchase Exposition, St. Louis: marking 100th anniversary of major land acquisition from France and opening up of the West.
1905 Lewis and Clark Centennial Exposition, Portland, Ore.: commemorating 100th anniversary of exploration of a land route to the Pacific.
1907 Jamestown Ter Centennial Exposition, Hampton Roads, Va.: marking 300th anniversary of first permanent English settlement in America.
1909 Alaska-Yukon-Pacific Exposition, Seattle: celebrating growth of the Puget Sound area.
1915–16 Panama-Pacific International Exposition, San Francisco: celebrating opening of the Panama Canal.

1915–16 Panama-California Exposition, San Diego: promoting resources and opportunities for development and commerce of the Western states.
1926 Sesquicentennial Exposition, Philadelphia: marking 150th year of independence.
1933–34 Century of Progress International Exposition, Chicago: celebrating 100th anniversary of incorporation of Chicago as a city.
1935 California Pacific International Exposition, San Diego: marking 400 years of progress since the first Spaniard landed on the West Coast.
1939–40 New York World's Fair, New York City: "The World of Tomorrow," symbolized by Trylon and Perisphere. Officially commemorating 150th anniversary of inauguration of George Washington as President in New York.
1939–1940 Golden Gate International Exposition, Treasure Island, San Francisco: celebrating new Golden Gate Bridge and Oakland Bay Bridge.
1962 The Century 21 Exposition, Seattle: "Man in the Space Age," symbolized by 600-foot steel space needle.
1964–65 New York World's Fair, New York City: "Peace Through Understanding."
1974 Expo '74, Spokane: "Tomorrow's Fresh, New Environment."
1982 World's Fair, Knoxville, Tenn.: "Energy Turns the World," symbolized by the bronze-globed Sunsphere.
1984 Louisiana World Exposition, New Orleans: "The World of Rivers."

Longest Broadway Runs[1]

1. A Chorus Line (M) (1975–90)	6,137	
2. Oh, Calcutta (M) (1976–89)	5,959	
3. Cats (M) (1982–)	3,693	
4. 42nd Street (M) (1980–89)	3,486	
5. Grease (M) (1972–80)	3,388	
6. Fiddler on the Roof (1964–72)	3,242	
7. Life with Father (1939–47)	3,224	
8. Tobacco Road (1933–41)	3,182	
9. Hello, Dolly! (M) (1964–71)	2,844	
10. My Fair Lady (M) (1956–62)	2,717	
11. Annie (M) (1977–83)	2,377	
12. Oklahoma (M) (1943–48)	2,377	
13. Man of La Mancha (M) (1965–71)	2,328	
14. Abie's Irish Rose (1922–27)	2,327	
15. Pippin (M) (1971–77)	1,994	
16. South Pacific (M) (1949–54)	1,925	
17. Magic Show (M) (1974–78)	1,920	
18. Deathtrap (1978–82)	1,792	
19. Gemini (1977–81)	1,788	
20. Les Miserables (M) (1987–)	1,780	
21. Harvey (1944–49)	1,775	
22. Dancin' (M) (1978–82)	1,774	
23. Cage aux Folles (M) (1983–87)	1,761	
24. Hair (M) (1968–72)	1,750	
25. The Wiz (M) (1975–79)	1,672	

1. As of Aug. 11, 1991. M = musical. Years are those of opening and closing.

Motion Picture Revenues

All-Time Top Money Makers[1]	
1. E.T. The Extra-Terrestrial (Universal, 1982)	$228,618,939
2. Star Wars (20th Century-Fox, 1977)	193,500,000
3. Return of the Jedi (20th Century-Fox, 1983)	168,002,414
4. Batman (Warner Brothers, 1989)	150,500,000
5. The Empire Strikes Back (20th Century-Fox, 1980)	141,600,000
6. Ghostbusters (Columbia, 1984)	132,720,000
7. Jaws (Universal, 1975)	129,549,325
8. Raiders of the Lost Ark (Paramount, 1981)	115,598,000
9. Indiana Jones and the Last Crusade (Paramount, 1989)	115,500,000
10. Indiana Jones and the Temple of Doom (Paramount, 1984)	109,000,000
11. Beverly Hills Cop (Paramount, 1984)	108,000,000
12. Back to the Future (Universal, 1985)	105,493,534
13. Grease (Paramount, 1978)	96,300,000
14. Tootsie (Columbia, 1982)	94,910,000
15. Ghost (Paramount, 1990)	94,000,000
16. The Exorcist (Warner Brothers, 1973)	89,000,000
17. Rain Man (United Artists, 1988)	86,813,000
18. The Godfather (Paramount, 1972)	86,275,000
19. Superman (Warner Brothers, 1978)	82,800,000
20. Close Encounters of the Third Kind (Columbia, 1977)	82,750,000
21. Pretty Woman (Buena Vista, 1990)	81,903,000
22. Three Men and a Baby (Buena Vista, 1987)	81,356,000
23. Who Framed Roger Rabbit (Buena Vista, 1988)	81,244,000
24. Beverly Hills Cop II (Paramount, 1987)	80,857,776
25. Home Alone (20th Century-Fox, 1990)	80,000,000

Top Rentals 1990[2]	
1. Ghost (Paramount)	$94,000,000
2. Pretty Woman (Buena Vista)	81,903,000
3. Home Alone (20th Century-Fox)	80,000,000
4. Die Hard 2 (20th Century-Fox)	66,500,000
5. Total Recall (Tri-Star)	65,000,000
6. Teenage Ninja Mutant Turtles (New Line)	62,000,000
7. Dick Tracy (Buena Vista)	59,526,000
8. The Hunt for Red October (Paramount)	58,500,000
9. Driving Miss Daisy (continuing 1990 run)	49,500,000
10. Back to the Future, Part III (Universal)	48,951,109
11. Presumed Innocent (Warner Brothers)	43,800,000
12. Another 48 Hrs. (Paramount)	40,100,000
13. Days of Thunder (Paramount)	40,000,000
14. Bird on a Wire (Universal)	38,402,931
15. Born on the Fourth of July (Universal)	36,789,000
16. Arachnophobia (Buena Vista)	31,019,000
17. Hard to Kill (Warner Brothers)	30,000,000
18. Dances With Wolves (Orion)	29,000,000
19. Flatliners (Columbia)	28,800,000
20. The Godfather, Part III (Paramount)	28,000,000
21. Three Men and a Little Lady (Buena Vista)	25,000,000
22. Problem Child (Universal)	24,368,353
23. Robocop 2 (Orion)	22,317,000
24. The Jungle Book (reissue)	21,464,000
25. Gremlins 2: The New Batch (Warner Brothers)	20,800,000

NOTE: United States and Canada only. 1. Figures are not to be confused with gross box-office receipts from sale of tickets. 2. Figures are total rentals collected by film distributors as of Dec. 31, 1990. *Source:* Reprinted with permission from *Variety Inc.*

Miss America Winners

1921 Margaret Gorman, Washington, D.C.	1962 Maria Fletcher, Asheville, N.C.
1922-23 Mary Campbell, Columbus, Ohio	1963 Jacquelyn Mayer, Sandusky, Ohio
1924 Ruth Malcolmson, Philadelphia, Pa.	1964 Donna Axum, El Dorado, Ark.
1925 Fay Lamphier, Oakland, Calif.	1965 Vonda Kay Van Dyke, Phoenix, Ariz.
1926 Norma Smallwood, Tulsa, Okla.	1966 Deborah Irene Bryant, Overland Park, Kan.
1927 Lois Delaner, Joliet, Ill.	1967 Jane Anne Jayroe, Laverne, Okla.
1933 Marion Bergeron, West Haven, Conn.	1968 Debra Dene Barnes, Moran, Kan.
1935 Henrietta Leaver, Pittsburgh, Pa.	1969 Judith Anne Ford, Belvidere, Ill.
1936 Rose Coyle, Philadelphia, Pa.	1970 Pamela Anne Eldred, Birmingham, Mich.
1937 Bette Cooper, Bertrand Island, N.J.	1971 Phyllis Ann George, Denton, Texas
1938 Marilyn Meseke, Marion, Ohio	1972 Laurie Lea Schaefer, Columbus, Ohio
1939 Patricia Donnelly, Detroit, Mich.	1973 Terry Anne Meeuwsen, DePere, Wis.
1940 Frances Marie Burke, Philadelphia, Pa.	1974 Rebecca Ann King, Denver, Colo.
1941 Rosemary LaPlanche, Los Angeles, Calif.	1975 Shirley Cothran, Fort Worth, Texas
1942 JoCaroll Dennison, Tyler, Texas	1976 Tawney Elaine Godin, Yonkers, N.Y.
1943 Jean Bartel, Los Angeles, Calif.	1977 Dorothy Kathleen Benham, Edina, Minn.
1944 Venus Ramey, Washington, D.C.	1978 Susan Perkins, Columbus, Ohio
1945 Bess Myerson, New York, N.Y.	1979 Kylene Baker, Galax, Va.
1946 Marilyn Buferd, Los Angeles, Calif.	1980 Cheryl Prewitt, Ackerman, Miss.
1947 Barbara Walker, Memphis, Tenn.	1981 Susan Powell, Elk City, Okla.
1948 BeBe Shopp, Hopkins, Minn.	1982 Elizabeth Ward, Russellville, Ark.
1949 Jacque Mercer, Litchfield, Ariz.	1983 Debra Maffett, Anaheim, Calif.
1951 Yolande Betbeze, Mobile, Ala.	1984 Vanessa Williams, Milwood, N.Y.[1]
1952 Coleen Kay Hutchins, Salt Lake City, Utah	Suzette Charles, Mays Landing, N.J.
1953 Neva Jane Langley, Macon, Ga.	1985 Sharlene Wells, Salt Lake City, Utah
1954 Evelyn Margaret Ay, Ephrata, Pa.	1986 Susan Akin, Meridian, Miss.
1955 Lee Meriwether, San Francisco, Calif.	1987 Kellye Cash, Memphis, Tenn.
1956 Sharon Ritchie, Denver, Colo.	1988 Kaye Lani Rae Rafko, Toledo, Ohio
1957 Marian McKnight, Manning, S.C.	1989 Gretchen Elizabeth Carlson, Anoka, Minn.
1958 Marilyn Van Derbur, Denver, Colo.	1990 Debbye Turner, Mexico, Mo.
1959 Mary Ann Mobley, Brandon, Miss.	1991 Marjorie Judith Vincent, Oak Park, Ill.
1960 Lynda Lee Mead, Natchez, Miss.	1992 (*See* Current Events)
1961 Nancy Fleming, Montague, Mich.	1. Resigned July 23, 1984.

U.S. STATES & CITIES

States and Territories

Sources for state populations, populations under 18, over 65, median age, largest cities and counties, and population by race are latest data provided by the U.S. Census Bureau. NOTE: Persons of Hispanic origin can be of any race. The population counts set forth herein by the Census Bureau are subject to possible correction for undercount or overcount. They include Armed Forces residing in each state. Largest cities include incorporated places only, as defined by the U.S. Census Bureau. They do not include adjacent or suburban areas as do the Metropolitan Statistical Areas found in the "U.S. Statistics" section of this Almanac. For secession and readmission dates of the former Confederate states, *see* Index. For lists of Governors, Senators, and Representatives, *see* Index. For additional state information, *see* the sections on "Business and the Economy," "Elections," "Taxes," and "U.S. Statistics."

ALABAMA

Capital: Montgomery
Governor: Guy Hunt, R (to Jan. 1995)
Lieut. Governor: Jim E. Folsom, Jr., R (to Jan. 1995)
Secy. of State: Billy Joe Camp, D (to Jan. 1995)
Treasurer: George C. Wallace, Jr., D (to Jan. 1995)
Atty. General: James H. Evans, D (to Jan. 1995)
Auditor: Terry Ellis, D (to Jan. 1995)
Organized as territory: March 3, 1817
Entered Union & (rank): Dec. 14, 1819 (22)
Present constitution adopted: 1901
Motto: *Audemus jura nostra defendere* (We dare defend our rights)
STATE SYMBOLS: flower, Camellia (1959); **bird,** Yellowhammer (1927); **song,** "Alabama" (1931); **tree,** Southern pine (longleaf) (1949); **salt water fish,** Tarpon (1955); **fresh water fish,** Largemouth bass (1975); **horse,** Racking horse; **mineral,** Hematite (1967); **rock,** Marble (1969); **game bird,** Wild turkey (1980); **dance,** Square dance (1981); **nut,** Pecan (1982); **fossil,** species *Basilosaurus Cetoides* (1984).
Nickname: Yellowhammer State
Origin of name: May come from Choctaw meaning "thicket-clearers" or "vegetation-gatherers"
10 largest cities (1990 census): Birmingham, 265,968; Mobile, 196,278; Montgomery, 187,106; Huntsville, 159,789; Tuscaloosa, 77,759; Dothan, 53,589; Decatur, 48,761; Gadsden, 42,523; Hoover, 39,788; Florence, 36,426
Land area & (rank): 50,767 sq mi. (131,487 sq km) (28)
Geographic center: In Chilton Co., 12 mi. SW of Clanton
Number of counties: 67
Largest county (1990 census): Jefferson, 651,525
State forests: 21 (48,000 ac.)
State parks: 22 (45,614 ac.)
1980 resident population (1980) census) & (rank): 3,893,888 (22)
1990 census population, sex, & (rank): 4,040,587 (22). **Male:** 1,936,162; **Female:** 2,104,425. **White:** 2,975,797 (73.6%); **Black:** 1,020,705 (25.3%); **American Indian, Eskimo, or Aleut:** 16,506 (0.4%); **Asian or Pacific Islander:** 21,797 (0.5%); **Other race:** 5,782 (0.1%); **Hispanic:** 24,629 (0.6%). **1990 percent population under 18:** 26.2; **65 and over:** 12.9; **median age:** 33.0.

Spanish explorers are believed to have arrived at Mobile Bay in 1519, and the territory was visited in 1540 by the explorer Hernando de Soto. The first permanent European settlement in Alabama was founded by the French at Fort Louis in 1702. The British gained control of the area in 1763 by the Treaty of Paris, but had to cede almost all the Alabama region to the U.S. after the American Revolution. The Confederacy was founded at Montgomery in February 1861 and, for a time, the city was the Confederate capital.

During the last part of the 19th century, the economy of the state slowly improved. At Tuskegee Institute, founded in 1881 by Booker T. Washington, Dr. George Washington Carver carried out his famous agricultural research.

In the 1950s and '60s, Alabama was the site of such landmark civil-rights actions as the bus boycott in Montgomery (1955–56) and the "Freedom March" from Selma to Montgomery (1965).

Today paper, chemicals, rubber and plastics, apparel and textiles, and primary metals comprise the leading industries of Alabama. Continuing as a major manufacturer of coal, iron, and steel, Birmingham is also noted for its world-renowned medical center, especially for heart surgery. The state ranks high in the production of poultry, soybeans, milk, vegetables, livestock, wheat, cattle, cotton, peanuts, fruits, hogs, and corn.

Points of interest include the Space and Rocket Center at Huntsville, the White House of the Confederacy, and Shakespeare Festival Theater Complex in Montgomery, and Russell Cave near Bridgeport, and the Gulf Coast area.

ALASKA

Capital: Juneau
Governor: Walter J. Hickel, Ind-R[1] (to Dec. 1994)
Lieut. Governor: John B. "Jack" Coghill, Ind.-R[1] (to Dec. 1994)
Commissioner of Administration: Millett Keller, R (to Dec. 1994)
Atty. General: Charles E. Cole,R (to Dec. 1994)
Organized as territory: 1912
Entered Union & (rank): Jan. 3, 1959 (49)
Constitution ratified: April 24, 1956
Motto: North to the Future
STATE SYMBOLS: flower, Forget-me-not (1949); **tree,** Sitka spruce (1962); **bird,** Willow ptarmigan (1955); **fish,** King salmon (1962); **song,** "Alaska's Flag" (1955); **gem,** Jade (1968); **marine mammal,** Bowhead Whale (1983); **fossil,** Woolly Mammoth (1986); **mineral,** Gold (1968); **sport,** Dog Mushing (1972)
Nickname: The state is commonly called "The Last Frontier" or "Land of the Midnight Sun"
Origin of name: Corruption of Aleut word meaning "great land" or "that which the sea breaks against"
10 largest cities: Anchorage, 226,338; Fairbanks, 30,843; Juneau, 26,751; Sitka, 8,588; Ketchikan, 8,263; Kodiak, 6,365; Kenai, 4,028
Land area & (rank): 570,833 sq mi (1,478,458 sq km) (1)
Geographic center: 60 mi. NW of Mt. McKinley
Number of boroughs: 12
Largest borough (1990 census): Fairbanks North Star, 77,720

State forests: None
State parks: 5; 59 waysides and areas (3.3 million ac.)
1980 resident census population & (rank): 401,851 (50)
1990 resident census populationm, sex, & (rank):
550,043 (49). **Male:** 289,867; **Female:** 260,176. **White:** 415,492 (75.5%); **Black:** 22,451 (4.1%); **American Indian, Eskimo, or Aleut:** 85,698 (15.6%); **Asian or Pacific Islander:** 19,728 (3.6%); **Other race:** 6,675 (1.2%); **Hispanic:** 17,803 (3.2%). **1990 percent population under 18:** 31.3; **65 and over:** 4.1; **median age:** 29..4

---

1. Independent–Republican.

Vitus Bering, a Dane working for the Russians, and Alexei Chirikov discovered the Alaskan mainland and the Aleutian Islands in 1741. The tremendous land mass of Alaska—equal to one fifth of the continental U.S.—was unexplored in 1867 when Secretary of State William Seward arranged for its purchase from the Russians for $7,200,000. The transfer of the territory took place on Oct. 18, 1867. Despite a price of about two cents an acre, the purchase was widely ridiculed as "Seward's Folly." The first official census (1880) reported a total of 33,426 Alaskans, all but 430 being of aboriginal stock. The Gold Rush of 1898 resulted in a mass influx of more than 30,000 people. Since then, Alaska has returned billions of dollars' worth of products to the U.S.

In 1968, a large oil and gas reservoir near Prudhoe Bay on the Arctic Coast was found. The Prudhoe Bay reservoir, with an estimated recoverable 10 billion barrels of oil and 27 trillion cubic feet of gas, is twice as large as any other oil field in North America. The Trans-Alaska pipeline was completed in 1977 at a cost of $7.7 billion. On June 20, oil started flowing through the 800-mile-long pipeline from Prudhoe Bay to the port of Valdez.

Other industries important to Alaska's economy are fisheries, wood and wood products, and furs, and tourism.

Denali National Park and Mendenhall Glacier in North Tongass National Forest are of interest, as is the large totem pole collection at Sitka National Historical Park. The Katmai National Park includes the "Valley of Ten Thousand Smokes," an area of active volcanoes.

ARIZONA

Capital: Phoenix
Governor: Fife Symington, R (to Jan. 1995)
Secy. of State: Richard Mahoney, D (to Jan. 1995)
Atty. General: Grant Woods, R (to Jan. 1995)
State Treasurer: Tony West, R (to Jan. 1995)
Organized as territory: Feb. 24, 1863
Entered Union & (rank): Feb. 14, 1912 (48)
Present constitution adopted: 1911
Motto: *Ditat Deus* (God enriches)
STATE SYMBOLS: flower: Flower of saguaro cactus (1931); **bird:** Cactus wren (1931); **colors:** Blue and old gold (1915); **song:** "Arizona March Song" (1919); **tree:** Palo Verde (1957); **neckwear,** Bolo tie (1973); **fossil,** Petrified wood (1988); **gemstone,** Turquoise (1974); **animals, mammal,** Ringtail; **reptile,** Arizona ridgenose rattlesnake; **fish,** Arizona trout; **amphibian,** Arizona tree frog (1986)
Nickname: Grand Canyon State
Origin of name: From the Indian "Arizonac," meaning "little spring"
10 largest cities (1990 census): Phoenix, 983,403; Tucson, 405,390; Mesa, 288,091; Glendale, 148,134; Tempe,

141,865; Scottsdale, 130,069; Chandler, 90,533; Yuma, 54,923; Peoria, 50,618; Flagstaff, 45,857
Land area & (rank): 113,508 sq mi. (293,986 sq km) (6)
Geographic center: In Yavapai Co., 55 mi. ESE of Prescott
Number of counties: 15
Largest county (1990 census): Maricopa, 2,122,101
State forests: None
State parks: 24
1980 resident census population & (rank): 2,718,215 (29)
1990 resident census population, sex, & (rank):
3,665,228 (24). **Male:** 1,810,691; **Female:** 1,854,537. **White:** 2,963,186 (80.8%); **Black:** 110,524 (3.0%); **American Indian, Eskimo, or Aleut:** 203,527 (5.6%); **Asian or Pacific Islander:** 55,206 (1.5%); **Other race:** 332,785 (9.1%); **Hispanic:** 688,338 (18.8%). **1990 percent population under 18:** 26.8; **65 and over:** 13.1; **median age:** 32.2

Marcos de Niza, a Spanish Franciscan friar, was the first European to explore Arizona. He entered the area in 1539 in search of the mythical Seven Cities of Gold. Although he was followed a year later by another gold seeker, Francisco Vásquez de Coronado, most of the early settlement was for missionary purposes. In 1776 the Spanish established Fort Tucson. In 1848, after the Mexican War, most of the Arizona territory became part of the U.S., and the southern portion of the territory was added by the Gadsden Purchase in 1853.

In 1973 the world's biggest dam, the New Cornelia Tailings, was completed near Ajo.

Arizona history is rich in legends of America's Old West. It was here that the great Indian chiefs Geronimo and Cochise led their people against the frontiersmen. Tombstone, Ariz., was the site of the West's most famous shoot-out—the gunfight at the O.K. Corral. Today, Arizona has the largest U.S. Indian population; more than 14 tribes are represented on 19 reservations.

Manufacturing has become Arizona's most important industry. Principal products include electrical, communications, and aeronautical items. The state produces over half the country's copper. Agriculture is also important to the state's economy.

State attractions include such famous scenery as the Grand Canyon, the Petrified Forest, and the Painted Desert. Hoover Dam, Lake Mead, Fort Apache, and the reconstructed London Bridge at Lake Havasu City are of particular interest.

ARKANSAS

Capital: Little Rock
Governor: Bill Clinton, D (to Jan. 1995)
Lieut. Governor: Jim Guy Tucker, D (to Jan. 1995)
Secy. of State: W. J. McCuen, D (to Jan. 1995)
Atty. General: Winston Bryant, D (to Jan. 1995)
Auditor of State: Julia Hughes Jones, D (to Jan. 1995)
Treasurer of State: Jimmie Lou Fisher Lumpkin, D (to Jan. 1995)
Land Commissioner: Charles Daniels, D (to Jan. 1995)
Organized as territory: March 2, 1819
Entered Union & (rank): June 15, 1836 (25)
Present constitution adopted: 1874
Motto: *Regnat populus* (The people rule)
STATE SYMBOLS: flower, Apple Blossom (1901); **tree,** Pine (1939); **bird,** Mockingbird (1929); **insect,** Honeybee (1973); **song,** "Arkansas" (1963)

Nickname: Land of Opportunity
Origin of name: From the Quapaw Indians
10 largest cities (1990 census): Little Rock, 175,795; Fort Smith, 72,798; North Little Rock, 61,741; Pine Bluff, 57,140; Jonesboro, 46,535; Fayetteville, 42,099; Hot Springs, 32,462; Springdale, 29,941; Jacksonville, 29,101; West Memphis, 28,259
Land area & (rank): 52,078 sq mi. (134,883 sq km) (27)
Geographic center: In Pulaski Co., 12 mi. NW of Little Rock
Number of counties: 75
Largest county (1990 census): Pulaski, 349,660
State forests: None
State parks: 44
1980 resident census population & (rank): 2,286,435 (33)
1990 resident population, sex, & rank: 2,350,725 (33).
Male: 1,133,076; **Female:** 1,217,649. **White:** 1,944,744 (82.7%); **Black:** 373,912 (15.9%); **American Indian, Eskimo, or Aleut:** 12,773 (0.5%); **Asian or Pacific Islander:** 12,530 (0.5%); **Other race:** 6,766 (0.3%); **Hispanic:** 19,876 (0.8%). **1990 percent population under 18:** 26.4; **65 and over:** 14.9; **median age:** 33.8.

Hernando de Soto, in 1541, was among the early European explorers to visit the territory. It was a Frenchman, Henri de Tonti, who in 1686 founded the first permanent white settlement—the Arkansas Post. In 1803 the area was acquired by the U.S. as part of the Louisiana Purchase.

Food products are the state's largest employing sector, with lumber and wood products a close second. Arkansas is also a leader in the production of cotton, rice, and soybeans. The state produces 97% of the nation's high-grade domestic bauxite ore—the source of aluminum. It also has the country's only active diamond mine; located near Murfreesboro, it is operated as a tourist attraction.

Hot Springs National Park, and Buffalo National River in the Ozarks are major state attractions.

Blanchard Springs Caverns, the Arkansas Territorial Restoration at Little Rock, and the Arkansas Folk Center in Mountain View are of interest.

CALIFORNIA

Capital: Sacramento
Governor: Pete Wilson, R (to Jan. 1995)
Lieut. Governor: Leo McCarthy, D (to Jan. 1995)
Secy. of State: March Fong Eu, D (to Jan. 1995)
Controller: Gray Davis, D (to Jan. 1995)
Atty. General: Dan Lungren, R (to Jan. 1995)
Treasurer: Kathleen Brown, D (to Jan. 1995)
Supt. of Public Instruction: Bill Honig, non-partisan (to 1995)
Entered Union & (rank): Sept. 9, 1850 (31)
Present constitution adopted: 1879
Motto: *Eureka* (I have found it)
STATE SYMBOLS: flower, Golden poppy (1903); **tree,** California redwoods (*Sequoia sempervirens & Sequoia gigantea*) (1937 % 1953); **bird,** California valley quail (1931); **animal,** California grizzly bear (1953); **fish,** California golden trout (1947); **colors,** Blue and gold (1951); **song,** "I Love You, California" (1951)
Nickname: Golden State
Origin of name: From a book, *Las Sergas de Esplandián*, by Garcia Ordóñez de Montalvo, c. 1500
10 largest cities (1990 census): Los Angeles, 3,485,398; San Diego, 1,110,549; San Jose, 782,248; San Francisco, 723,959; Long Beach, 429,433; Oakland, 372,242; Sacramento, 369,365; Fresno, 354,202; Santa Ana, 293,742; Anaheim, 266,406

Land area & (rank): 156,299 sq mi. (404,815 sq km) (3)
Geographic center: In Madera Co., 35 mi. NE of Madera
Number of counties: 58
Largest county (1990 census): Los Angeles, 8,863,164
State forests: 8 (70,283 ac.)
State parks and beaches: 180 (723,000 ac.)
1980 resident census population & (rank): 23,667,902 (1)
1990 resident population, sex, & (rank): 29,760,021 (1).
Male: 14,897,627; **Female:** 14,862,394. **White:** 20,524,327 (69.9%); **Black:** 2,208,801 (7.4%); **American Indian, Eskimo, or Aleut:** 242,164 (0.8%); **Asian or Pacific Islander,** 2,845,659 (9.6%); **Other race:** 3,939,070 (13.2%); **Hispanic,** 7,687,938 (25.8%). **1990 percent population under 18:** 26.0; **65 and over:** 10.5; **median age:** 31.5.

Although California was sighted by Spanish navigator Juan Rodríguez Cabrillo in 1542, its first Spanish mission (at San Diego) was not established until 1769. California became a U.S. Territory in 1847 when Mexico surrendered it to John C. Frémont. On Jan. 24, 1848, James W. Marshall discovered gold at Sutter's Mill, starting the California Gold Rush and bringing settlers to the state in large numbers.

In 1964, the U.S. Census Bureau estimated that California had become the most populous state, surpassing New York. California also leads the country in personal income and consumer expenditures.

Leading industries include manufacturing (transportation equipment, machinery, and electronic equipment), agriculture, biotechnology, and tourism. Principal natural resources include timber, petroleum, cement, and natural gas.

More immigrants settle in California than any other state—more than 30% of the nation's total in 1990. Asian-Pacific Islanders led the influx.

Death Valley, in the southeast, is 282 feet below sea level, the lowest point in the nation; and Mt. Whitney (14,491 ft) is the highest point in the contiguous 48 states. Lassen Peak is one of two active U.S. volcanos outside of Alaska and Hawaii; its last eruptions were recorded in 1917. The General Sherman Tree in Sequoia National Park is estimated to be about 3,500 years old and a stand of bristlecone pine trees in the White Mountains may be over 4,000 years old.

Other points of interest include Yosemite National Park, Disneyland, Hollywood, the Golden Gate bridge, San Simeon State Park, and Point Reyes National Seashore.

COLORADO

Capital: Denver
Governor: Roy Romer, D (to Jan. 1995)
Lieut. Governor: Michael Callihan, D (to Jan. 1995)
Secy. of State: Natalie Meyer, R (to Jan 1995)
Treasurer: Gail Schoettler, D (to Jan. 1995)
Controller: Cliff Hall, R (appointed)
Atty. General: Gale Norton, R (to Jan. 1995)
Organized as territory: Feb. 28, 1861
Entered Union & (rank): Aug. 1, 1876 (38)
Present constitution adopted: 1876
Motto: *Nil sine Numine* (Nothing without Providence)
STATE SYMBOLS: flower, Rocky Mountain columbine (1899); **tree,** Colorado blue spruce (1939); **bird,** Lark bunting (1931); **animal,** Rocky Mountain bighorn sheep (1961); **gemstone,** Aquamarine (1971); **colors,** Blue and white (1911); **song,** "Where the Columbines Grow" (1915); **fossil,** Stegosaurus (1991)

Nickname: Centennial State
Origin of name: From the Spanish, "ruddy" or "red"
10 largest cities (1990 census): Denver, 467,610; Colorado Springs, 281,140; Aurora, 222,103; Lakewood, 126,481; Pueblo, 98,640; Arvada, 89,235; Fort Collins, 87,758; Boulder, 83,312; Westminster, 74,625; Greeley, 60,536
Land area & (rank): 103,595 sq mi. (268,311 sq km) (8)
Geographic center: In Park Co., 30 mi. NW of Pikes Peak
Number of counties: 63
Largest county (1990 census): Denver, 467,610
State forests: 1 (71,000 ac.)
State parks: 44
1980 resident census population & (rank): 2,889,964 (28)
1990 resident census population, sex, & (rank): 3,294,394 (26). **Male:** 1,631,295; **Female:** 1,663,099. **White:** 2,095,474 (88.2%); **Black:** 133,146 (4.0%); **American Indian, Eskimo, or Aleut:** 27,776 (0.8%); **Asian or Pacific Islander:** 59,862 (1.8%); **Other race:** 168,136 (5.1%); **Hispanic:** 424,302 (12.9%). **1990 percent population under 18:** 26.1; **65 and over:** 10.0; **median age:** 32.5

First visited by Spanish explorers in the 1500s, the territory was claimed for Spain by Juan de Ulibarri in 1706. The U.S. obtained eastern Colorado as part of the Louisiana Purchase in 1803, the central portion in 1845 with the admission of Texas as a state, and the western part in 1848 as a result of the Mexican War.

Colorado has the highest mean elevation of any state, with more than 1,000 Rocky Mountain peaks over 10,000 feet high and 54 towering above 14,000 feet. Pikes Peak, the most famous of these mountains, was discovered by U.S. Army Lieut. Zebulon M. Pike in 1806.

Once primarily a mining and agricultural state, Colorado's economy is now driven by the service-producing industries, which provide jobs for more than four-fifths of the state's non-farm work force. In addition, tourism is extremely important to the state's economy. The ski industry accounts for approximately one-third of the state's tourism market. The main tourist attractions in the state include Rocky Mountain National Park, Curecanti National Recreation Area, Mesa Verde National Park, and the Great Sand Dunes and Dinosaur National Monuments.

The two primary facets of Colorado's manufacturing industry are advanced technology and defense.

The mining industry, which includes oil and gas, coal, and metal mining, was important to Colorado's economy, but it now employs only 1.3 percent of the state's workforce. Denver is home to companies that control half of the nation's gold production. The farm industry, which is primarily concentrated in livestock, is also an important element of the state's economy. The primary crops in Colorado are corn, hay, and wheat.

CONNECTICUT

Capital: Hartford
Governor: Lowell P. Weicker, Jr., ACP[1] (to Jan. 1995)
Lieut. Governor: Eunice S. Groark, ACP[1] (to Jan. 1995)
Secy. of State: Pauline R. Kezer, R (to Jan. 1995)
Comptroller: William E. Curry, Jr., D (to Jan. 1995)
Treasurer: Francisco L. Borges, D (to Jan. 1995)
Atty. General: Richard Blumenthal, D (to Jan. 1995)
Entered Union & (rank): Jan. 9, 1788 (5)
Present constitution adopted: Dec. 30, 1965
Motto: *Qui transtulit sustinet* (He who transplanted still

sustains)
STATE SYMBOLS: flower, mountain laurel (1907); **tree,** White Oak (1947); **animal,** Sperm whale (1975); **bird,** American robin (1943); **hero,** Nathan Hale (1985); **insect,** Praying mantis (1977); **mineral,** Garnet (1977); **song,** "Yankee Doodle" (1978); **ship,** USS Nautilus (SSN571) (1983)
Official designation: *Constitution State* (1959)
Nickname: Nutmeg State
Origin of name: From an Indian word (Quinnehtukqut) meaning "beside the long tidal river"
10 largest cities (1990 census): Bridgeport, 141,686; Hartford, 139,739; New Haven, 130,474; Waterbury, 108,961; Stamford, 108,056; Norwalk, 78,331; New Britain, 75,491; Danbury, 65,585; Bristol, 60,640; Meriden, 59,479
Land area & (rank): 4,872 sq mi. (12,618 km) (48)
Geographic center: In Hartford Co., at East Berlin
Number of counties: 8
Largest town (1990 census): West Hartford 60,110
State forests: 30 (139,377 ac.)
State parks: 89 (30,647 ac.)
1980 resident census population & (rank): 3,107,576 (25)
1990 resident population, sex, & (rank): 3,287,116 (27). **Male:** 1,592,873; **Female:** 1,694,243. **White:** 2,859,353 (87.0%); **Black:** 274,269 (8.3%); **American Indian, Eskimo, or Aleut:** 6,654 (0.2%); **Asian or Pacific Islander:** 50,698 (1.5%); **Other race:** 96,142 (2.9%); **Hispanic:** 213,116 (6.5%). **1990 percent population under 18:** 22.8; **65 and over:** 13.6; **median age:** 34.4.

---

1. A Connecticut Party.

The Dutch navigator, Adriaen Block, was the first European of record to explore the area, sailing up the Connecticut River in 1614. In 1633, Dutch colonists built a fort and trading post near presentday Hartford, but soon lost control to English Puritans migrating south from the Massachusetts Bay Colony.

English settlements, established in the 1630s at Windsor, Wethersfield, and Hartford, united in 1639 to form the Connecticut Colony and adopted the *Fundamental Orders,* considered the world's first written constitution.

The colony's royal charter of 1662 was exceptionally liberal. When Gov. Edmund Andros tried to seize it in 1687, it was hidden in the Hartford Oak, commemorated in Charter Oak Place.

Connecticut played a prominent role in the Revolutionary War, serving as the Continental Army's major supplier. Sometimes called the "Arsenal of the Nation," the state became one of the most industrialized in the nation.

Today, Connecticut factories produce weapons, sewing machines, jet engines, helicopters, motors, hardware and tools, cutlery, clocks, locks, ball bearings, silverware, and submarines. Hartford, which has the oldest U.S. newspaper still being published—the *Courant,* established 1764—is the insurance capital of the nation.

Poultry, fruit, and dairy products account for the largest portion of farm income, and Connecticut shade-grown tobacco is acknowledged to be the nation's most valuable crop, per acre.

Connecticut is a popular resort area with its 250-mile Long Island Sound shoreline and many inland lakes. Among the major points of interest are Yale University's Gallery of Fine Arts and Peabody Museum. Other famous museums include the P.T. Barnum, Winchester Gun, and American Clock and Watch. The town of Mystic features a recreated 19th-century New England seaport and the Mystic Marinelife Aquarium.

DELAWARE

Capital: Dover
Governor: Michael N. Castle, R (to Jan. 1993)
Lieut. Governor: Dale E. Wolf, R (to Jan. 1993)
Secy. of State: Michael Harkins, R (Pleasure of Governor)
State Treasurer: Janet C. Rzewnicki, R (to Jan. 1995)
Atty. General: Charles M. Oberly III, D (to Jan. 1995)
Entered Union & (rank): Dec. 7, 1787 (1)
Present constitution adopted: 1897
Motto: Liberty and independence
STATE SYMBOLS: colors, Colonial blue and buff; **flower,** Peach blossom (1895); **tree,** American holly (1939); **bird,** Blue Hen chicken (1939); **insect,** Ladybug (1974); **fish,** Weakfish, *Cynoscion regalis* (1981); **song,** "Our Delaware"
Nicknames: Diamond State; First State; Small Wonder
Origin of name: From Delaware River and Bay; named in turn for Sir Thomas West, Lord De La Warr
10 largest cities (1990 census): Wilmington, 71,529; Dover, 27,630; Newark, 25,098; Milford, 6,040; Elsmere Town, 5,935; Seaford, 5,689; Smyrna Town, 5,213; New Castle 4,837; Middletown Town, 3,834; Georgetown Town, 3,732
Land area & (rank): 1,932 sq mi. (5,005 sq km) (49)
Geographic center: In Kent Co., 11 mi. S of Dover
Number of counties: 3
Largest county (1990 census): New Castle, 441,946
State forests: 3 (6,149 ac.)
State parks: 10
1980 resident census population & (rank): 594,338 (47)
1990 resident census population, sex, & (rank): 666,168 (46). **Male:** 322,968; **Female:** 343,200. **White:** 535,094 (80.3%); **Black:** 112,460 (16.9%); **American Indian, Eskimo, or Aleut:** 2,019 (0.3%); **Asian or Pacific Islander:** 9,057 (1.4%); **Other race:** 7,538 (1.1%); **Hispanic:** 15,820 (2.4%). **1990 percent population under 18:** 24.5; **65 and over:** 12.1; **median age:** 32.9.

Henry Hudson, sailing under the Dutch flag, is credited with Delaware's discovery in 1609. The following year, Capt. Samuel Argall of Virginia named Delaware for his colony's governor, Thomas West, Baron De La Warr. An attempted Dutch settlement failed in 1631. Swedish colonization began at Fort Christina (now Wilmington) in 1638, but New Sweden fell to Dutch forces led by New Netherlands' Gov. Peter Stuyvesant in 1655.

England took over the area in 1664 and it was transferred to William Penn as the southern Three Counties in 1682. Semiautonomous after 1704, Delaware fought as a separate state in the American Revolution and became the first state to ratify the constitution in 1787.

During the Civil War, although a slave state, Delaware did not secede from the Union.

In 1802, Éleuthère Irénée du Pont established a gunpowder mill near Wilmington that laid the foundation for Delaware's huge chemical industry. Delaware's manufactured products now also include vulcanized fiber, textiles, paper, medical supplies, metal products, machinery, machine tools, and automobiles.

Delaware also grows a great variety of fruits and vegetables and is a U.S. pioneer in the food-canning industry. Corn, soybeans, potatoes, and hay are important crops. Delaware's broiler chicken farms supply the big Eastern markets, fishing and dairy products are other important industries.

Points of interest include the Fort Christina Monument, Hagley Museum, Holy Trinity Church (erected in 1698, the oldest Protestant church in the United States still in use) and Winterthur Museum, in and near Wilmington; central New Castle, an almost unchanged late 18th-century capital; and the Delaware Museum of Natural History.

Popular recreation areas include Cape Henlopen, Delaware Seashore, Trapp Pond State Park, and Rehoboth Beach.

DISTRICT OF COLUMBIA

See listing at end of *50 Largest Cities of the United States.*

FLORIDA

Capital: Tallahassee
Governor: Lawton Chiles, D (to Jan. 1995)
Lieut. Governor: Buddy McKay, D (to Jan. 1995)
Secy. of State: Jim Smith, R (to Jan. 1995)
Comptroller: Gerald Lewis, D (to Jan. 1995)
Commissioner of Agriculture: Bob Crawford, D (to Jan. 1995)
Atty. General: Bob Butterworth, D (to Jan. 1995)
Organized as territory: March 30, 1822
Entered Union & (rank): March 3, 1845 (27)
Present constitution adopted: 1969
Motto: In God we trust (1868)
STATE SYMBOLS: flower, Orange blossom (1909); **bird,** Mockingbird (1927); **song,** "Suwannee River" (1935)
Nickname: Sunshine State (1970)
Origin of name: From the Spanish, meaning "feast of flowers" (Easter)
10 largest cities (1990 census): Jacksonville (CC[1]), 672,971; Miami, 358,548; Tampa, 280,015; St. Petersburg, 238,629; Hialeah, 188,004; Orlando, 164,693; Fort Lauderdale, 149,377; Tallahassee, 124,773; Hollywood, 121,697; Clearwater, 98,784
Land area & (rank): 54,153 sq mi. (140,256 sq km) (26)
Geographic center: In Hernando Co., 12 mi. NNW of Brooksville
Number of counties: 67
Largest county (1990 census): Dade, 1,937,094
State forests: 3 (306,881 ac.)
State parks: 105 (215,820 ac.)
1980 resident census population & (rank): 9,746,324 (7)
1990 resident census population, sex, & (rank): 12,937,926 (4). **Male:** 6,261,719; **Female:** 6,676,207. **White:** 10,749,285 (83.1%); **Black:** 1,759,534 (13.6%); **American Indian, Eskimo, or Aleut:** 36,335 (0.3%); **Asian or Pacific Islander:** 154,302 (1.2%); **Other race:** 238,470 (1.8%); **Hispanic:** 1,574,143 (12.2%). **1990 percent population under 18:** 22.2; **65 and over:** 18.3; **median age:** 36.4.

1. Consolidated City (Coextensive with Duval County).

In 1513, Ponce De Leon, seeking the mythical "Fountain of Youth," discovered and named Florida, claiming it for Spain. Later, Florida would be held at different times by Spain and England until Spain finally sold it to the United States in 1819. (Incidentally, France established a colony named Fort Caroline in 1564 in the state that was to become Florida.)

Florida's early 19th-century history as a U.S. territory was marked by wars with the Seminole Indians that did not end until 1842, although a treaty was actually never signed.

One of the nation's fastest-growing states, Florida's population has gone from 2.8 million in 1950 to more than 12.9 million in 1990.

Florida's economy rests on a solid base of tourism (in 1989 the state entertained more than 41.7 million visitors from all over the world), manufacturing, and agriculture.

In recent years, oranges and grapefruit lead Florida's crop list, followed by vegetables, potatoes, melons, strawberries, sugar cane, dairy products, cattle and calves, and forest products.

Major tourist attractions are Miami Beach, Palm Beach, St. Augustine (founded in 1565, thus the oldest permanent city in the U.S.), Daytona Beach, and Fort Lauderdale on the East Coast. West Coast resorts include Sarasota, Tampa, Key West and St. Petersburg. Disney World, located on a 27,000-acre site near Orlando, is a popular attraction.

Also drawing many visitors are the NASA Kennedy Space Center's Spaceport USA, located in the town of Kennedy Space Center, Everglades National Park, and the Epcot Center.

GEORGIA

Capital: Atlanta
Governor: Zell Miller, D (to Jan. 1995)
Lieut. Governor: Pierre Howard, D (to Jan. 1995)
Secy. of State: Max Cleland, D (to Jan. 1995)
Insurance Commissioner: Tim Ryles, D (to Jan. 1995)
Atty. General: Michael J. Bowers, D (to Jan. 1995)
Entered Union & (rank): Jan. 2, 1788 (4)
Present constitution adopted: 1977
Motto: Wisdom, justice, and moderation
STATE SYMBOLS: flower, Cherokee rose (1916); **tree,** Live oak (1937); **bird,** Brown thrasher (1935); **song,** "Georgia on My Mind" (1922)
Nicknames: Peach State, Empire State of the South
Origin of name: In honor of George II of England
10 largest cities (1990 census): Atlanta, 394,017; Columbus[1], 179,278; Savannah, 137,560; Macon, 106,612; Albany, 78,122; Roswell, 47,923; Athens, 45,734; Augusta, 44,639; Marietta, 44,129; Warner Robins, 43,726.
Land area & (rank): 58,910 sq mi. (152,577 sq km) (21)
Geographic center: In Twiggs Co., 18 mi. SE of Macon
Number of counties: 159
Largest county (1990 census): Fulton, 648,951
State forests: 25,258,000 ac. (67% of total state area)
State parks: 53 (42,600 ac.)
1980 resident census population & (rank): 5,463,105 (13)
1990 resident census population, sex, & (rank): 6,478,216 (11). **Male:** 3,144,503; **Female:** 3,333,713. **White:** 4,600,148 (71.0%); **Black:** 1,746,565 (27.0%); **American Indian, Eskimo, or Aleut:** 13,348 (0.2%); **Asian or Pacific Islander:** 75,781 (1.2%); **Other race:** 42,374 (0.7%); **Hispanic:** 108,922 (1.7%). **1990 percent population under 18:** 26.7; **65 and over:** 10.1; **median age:** 31.6.

1. Consolidated City (Coextensive with Muscogee County).

Hernando de Soto, the Spanish explorer, first traveled parts of Georgia in 1540. British claims later conflicted with those of Spain. After obtaining a royal charter, Gen. James Oglethorpe established the first permanent settlement in Georgia in 1733 as a refuge for English debtors. In 1742, Oglethorpe defeated Spanish invaders in the Battle of Bloody Marsh.

A Confederate stronghold, Georgia was the scene of extensive military action during the Civil War. Union General William T. Sherman burned Atlanta and destroyed a 60-mile wide path to the coast where he captured Savannah in 1864.

The largest state east of the Mississippi, Georgia is typical of the changing South with an ever-increasing industrial development. Atlanta, largest city in the state, is the communications and transportation center for the Southeast and the area's chief distributor of goods.

Georgia leads the nation in the production of paper and board, tufted textile products, and processed chicken. Other major manufactured products are transportation equipment, food products, apparel, and chemicals.

Important agricultural products are corn, cotton, tobacco, soybeans, eggs, and peaches. Georgia produces twice as many peanuts as the next leading state. From its vast stands of pine come more than half the world's resins and turpentine and 74.4% of the U.S. supply. Georgia is also a leader in the production of marble, kaolin, barite, and bauxite.

Principal tourist attractions in Georgia include the Okefenokee National Wildlife Refuge, Andersonville Prison Park and National Cemetery, Chickamauga and Chattanooga National Military Park, the Little White House at Warm Springs where Pres. Franklin D. Roosevelt died in 1945, Sea Island, the enormous Confederate Memorial at Stone Mountain, Kennesaw Mountain National Battlefield Park, and Cumberland Island National Seashore.

HAWAII

Capital: Honolulu (on Oahu)
Governor: John Waihee, D (to Dec. 1994)
Lieut. Governor: Ben Cayetano, D (to Dec. 1994)
Comptroller: Russel S. Nagata (to Dec. 1994)
Atty. General: Warren Price (to Dec. 1994)
Organized as territory: 1900
Entered Union & (rank): Aug. 21, 1959 (50)
Motto: *Ua Mau Ke Ea O Ka Aina I Ka Pono* (The life of the land is perpetuated in righteousness)
STATE SYMBOLS: flower, Hibiscus (yellow) 1988; **song,** "Hawaii Ponoi" (1967); **bird,** Nene (hawaiian goose) (1957); **tree,** Kukui (Candlenut) (1959)
Nickname: Aloha State (1959)
Origin of name: Uncertain. The islands may have been named by Hawaii Loa, their traditional discoverer. Or they may have been named after Hawaii or Hawaiki, the traditional home of the Polynesians.
10 largest cities[1] (1990 census): Honolulu, 365,272; Hilo, 37,808; Kailua, 36,818; Kaneohe, 35,448; Waipahu, 31,435; Pearl City, 30,993; Waimalu, 29,967; Mililani Town, 29,359; Schofield Barracks, 19,597; Wahiawa, 17,386

Land area & (rank): 6,425 sq mi. (16,641 sq km) (47)
Geographic center: Between islands of Hawaii and Maui
Number of counties: 4 plus one non-functioning county (Kalawao)
Largest county (1990 census): Honolulu, 836,231
State parks and historic sites: 77
1980 resident census population & (rank): 964,691 (39)
1990 resident census population, sex, & (rank): 1,108,229 (40). **Male:** 563,891; **Female:** 544,338. **White:** 369,616 (33.4%); **Black:** 27,195 (2.5%); **American Indian, Eskimo, or Aleut:** 5,099 (0.5%); **Asian or Pacific Islander:** 685,236 (61.8%); **Other race:** 21,083 (1.9%); **Hispanic:** 81,390 (7.3%). **1990 percent population under 18:** 25.3; **65 and over:** 11.3; **median age:** 32.6

1. Census Designated Place. There are no political boundaries to Honolulu or any other place, but statistical boundaries are assigned under state law.

First settled by Polynesians sailing from other Pacific islands between 300 and 600 A.D., Hawaii was visited in 1778 by British Captain James Cook who called the group the Sandwich Islands.

Hawaii was a native kingdom throughout most of the 19th century when the expansion of the vital sugar industry (pineapple came after 1898) meant increasing U.S. business and political involvement. In 1893, Queen Liliuokalani was deposed and a year later the

Republic of Hawaii was established with Sanford B. Dole as president. Then, following its annexation in 1898, Hawaii became a U.S. Territory in 1900.

The Japanese attack on the naval base at Pearl Harbor on Dec. 7, 1941, was directly responsible for U.S. entry into World War II.

Hawaii, 2,397 miles west-southwest of San Francisco, is a 1,523-mile chain of islets and eight main islands—Hawaii, Kahoolawe, Maui, Lanai, Molokai, Oahu, Kauai, and Niihau. The Northwestern Hawaiian Islands, other than Midway, are administratively part of Hawaii.

The temperature is mild and Hawaii's soil is fertile for tropical fruits and vegetables. Cane sugar and pineapple are the chief products. Hawaii also grows coffee, bananas and nuts. The tourist business is Hawaii's largest source of outside income.

Hawaii's highest peak is Mauna Kea (13,796 ft.). Mauna Loa (13,679 ft.) is the largest volcanic mountain in the world in cubic content.

Among the major points of interest are Hawaii Volcanoes National Park (Hawaii), Haleakala National Park (Maui), Puuhonua o Honaunau National Historical Park (Hawaii), Polynesian Cultural Center (Oahu), the U.S.S. *Arizona* Memorial at Pearl Harbor, and Iolani Palace (the only royal palace in the U.S.), Bishop Museum, and Waikiki Beach (all in Honolulu).

IDAHO

Capital: Boise
Governor: Cecil D. Andrus, D (to Jan. 1995)
Lieut. Governor: C. L. "Butch" Otter, R (to Jan. 1995)
Secy. of State: Pete T. Cenarrusa, R (to Jan. 1995)
State Auditor: J.D. Williams, D (to Jan. 1995)
Atty. General: Larry Echohawk, D (to Jan. 1995)
Treasurer: Lydia Justice Edwards, R (to Jan. 1995)
Organized as territory: March 3, 1863
Entered Union & (rank): July 3, 1890 (43)
Present constitution adopted: 1890
Motto: *Esto perpetua* (It is forever)
STATE SYMBOLS: flower, Syringa (1931); **tree,** White pine (1935); **bird,** Mountain bluebird (1931); **horse,** Appaloosa (1975); **gem,** Star garnet (1967); **song,** "Here We Have Idaho"; **folk dance,** Square Dance
Nicknames: Gem State; Spud State; Panhandle State
Origin of name: Unknown. It is an invented name and has no Indian translation meaning "Gem of the Mountains." Meaning of name, if any, is unknown.
10 largest cities (1990 census): Boise, 125,738; Pocatello, 46,080; Idaho Falls, 43,929; Nampa, 28,365; Lewiston, 28,082; Twin Falls, 27,591; Coeur d'Alene, 24,563, Moscow, 18,519; Caldwell, 18,400; Rexburg, 14,302
Land area & (rank): 82,412 sq mi. (213,449 sq km) (11)
Geographic center: In Custer Co., at Custer, SW of Challis
Number of counties: 44, plus small part of Yellowstone National Park
Largest county (1990 census): Ada, 205,775
State forests: 881,000 ac.
State parks: 21 (42,161) ac.
1980 resident census population & (rank): 943,935 (41)
1990 resident census population, sex, & (rank):
1,006,749 (42). **Male:** 500,956; **Female:** 505,793. **White:** 950,451 (94.4%); **Black:** 3,370 (0.3%); **American Indian, Eskimo, or Aleut:** 13,780 (1.4%); **Asian or Pacific Islander:** 9,365 (0.9%); **Other race:** 29,783 (3.0%); **Hispanic:** 52,927 (5.3%). **1990 percent population under 18:** 30.6; **65 and over:** 12.0; **median age:** 31.5.

After its acquisition by the U.S. as part of the Lou-

isiana Purchase in 1803, the region was explored by Meriwether Lewis and William Clark in 1805–06. Northwest boundary disputes with Great Britain were settled by the Oregon Treaty in 1846 and the first permanent U.S. settlement in Idaho was established by the Mormons at Franklin in 1860.

After gold was discovered on Orofino Creek in 1860, prospectors swarmed into the territory, but left little more than a number of ghost towns.

In the 1870s, growing white occupation of Indian lands led to a series of battles between U.S. forces and the Nez Percé, Bannock, and Sheepeater tribes.

Mining, lumbering, and irrigation farming have been important for years. Idaho produces more than one fifth of all the silver mined in the U.S. It also ranks high among the states in antimony, lead, cobalt, garnet, phosphate rock, vanadium, zinc, mercury, molybdenum, and gold.

Idaho's most impressive growth began when World War II military needs made processing agricultural products a big industry, particularly the dehydrating and freezing of potatoes. The state produces about one fourth of the nation's potato crop, as well as wheat, apples, corn, barley, sugar beets, and hops.

With the growth of winter sports, tourism now outranks mining in dollar revenue. Idaho's many streams and lakes provide fishing, camping, and boating sites. The nation's largest elk herds draw hunters from all over the world and the famed Sun Valley resort attracts thousands of visitors to its swimming and skiing facilities.

Other points of interest are the Craters of the Moon National Monument; Nez Percé National Historic Park, which includes many sites visited by Lewis and Clark; and the State Historical Museum in Boise.

ILLINOIS

Capital: Springfield
Governor: Jim Edgar, R (to Jan. 1995)
Lieut. Governor: Bob Kustra, R (to Jan. 1995)
Atty. General: Roland W. Burris, D (to Jan. 1995)
Secy. of State: George H. Ryan, R (to Jan. 1995)
Comptroller: Dawn Clark Netsch, D (to Jan. 1995)
Treasurer: Patrick Quinn, D (to Jan. 1995)
Organized as territory: Feb. 3, 1809
Entered Union & (rank): Dec. 3, 1818 (21)
Present constitution adopted: 1970
Motto: State sovereignty, national union
STATE SYMBOLS: flower, Violet (1908); **tree,** White oak (1973); **bird,** Cardinal (1929); **animal,** White-tailed deer (1982); **fish,** Bluegill (1987); **insect,** Monarch butterfly (1975); **song,** "Illinois" (1925); **mineral,** Fluorite (1965)
Nickname: Prairie State
Origin of name: From an Indian word and French suffix meaning "tribe of superior men"
10 largest cities (1990 census): Chicago, 2,783,726; Rockford, 139,426; Peoria, 113,504; Springfield, 105,227; Aurora, 99,581; Naperville, 85,351; Decatur, 83,885; Elgin, 77,010; Joliet, 76,836; Arlington Heights Village, 75,460
Land area & (rank): 55,645 sq mi. (144,120 sq km) (24)
Geographic center: In Logan County 28 mi. NE of Springfield
Number of counties: 102
Largest county (1990 census): Cook, 5,105,067
Public use areas: 187 (275,000 ac.), incl. state parks, memorials, forests and conservation areas
1980 resident census population & (rank): 11,426,518 (5)
1990 resident census population, sex, & (rank):
11,430,602 (6). **Male:** 5,552,233; **Female:** 5,878,369.
White: 8,952,978 (78.3%); **Black:** 1,694,273 (14.8%);

American Indian, Eskimo, or Aleut: 21,836 (0.2%); **Asian or Pacific Islander:** 285,311 (2.5%); **Other race:** 476,204 (4.2%); **Hispanic:** 904,446 (7.9%). **1990 percent population under 18:** 25.8; **65 and over:** 12.6; **median age:** 32.8.

French explorers Marquette and Joliet, in 1673, were the first Europeans of record to visit the region. In 1699 French settlers established the first permanent settlement at Cahokia, near present-day East St. Louis.

Great Britain obtained the region at the end of the French and Indian War in 1763. The area figured prominently in frontier struggles during the Revolutionary War and in Indian wars during the early 19th century.

Significant episodes in the state's early history include the growing migration of Eastern settlers following the opening of the Erie Canal in 1825; the Black Hawk War, which virtually ended the Indian troubles in the area; and the rise of Abraham Lincoln from farm laborer to President-elect.

Today, Illinois stands high in manufacturing, coal mining, agriculture, and oil production. The sprawling Chicago district (including a slice of Indiana) is a great iron and steel producer, meat packer, grain exchange, and railroad center. Chicago is also famous as a Great Lakes port.

Illinois ranks first in the nation in export of agricultural products and second in hog production. An important dairying state, Illinois is also a leader in corn, oats, wheat, barley, rye, truck vegetables, and the nursery products.

The state manufactures a great variety of industrial and consumer products: railroad cars, clothing, furniture, tractors, liquor, watches, and farm implements are just some of the items made in its factories and plants.

Central Illinois is noted for shrines and memorials associated with the life of Abraham Lincoln. In Springfield are the Lincoln Home, the Lincoln Tomb, and the restored Old State Capitol. Other points of interest are the home of Mormon leader Joseph Smith in Nauvoo and, in Chicago: the Art Institute, Field Museum, Museum of Science and Industry, Shedd Aquarium, Adler Planetarium, Merchandise Mart, and Chicago Portage National Historic Site.

INDIANA

Capital: Indianapolis
Governor: Birch Evans Bayh III, D (to Jan. 1993)
Lieut. Governor: Frank O'Bannon, D (to Jan. 1993)
Secy. of State: Joseph H. Hogsett, D (to Dec. 1994)
Treasurer: Majorie H. O'Laughlin, R (to Feb. 1995)
Atty. General: Linley E. Pearson, R (to Jan. 1993)
Auditor: Ann G. Devore, R (to Dec. 1994)
Organized as territory: May 7, 1800
Entered Union & (rank): Dec. 11, 1816 (19)
Present constitution adopted: 1851
Motto: The Crossroads of America
STATE SYMBOLS: flower, Peony (1957); **tree,** Tulip tree (1931); **bird,** Cardinal (1933); **song,** "On the Banks of the Wabash, Far Away" (1913)
Nickname: Hoosier State
Origin of name: Meaning "land of Indians"
10 largest cities (1990 census): Indianapolis, 731,327; Fort Wayne, 173,072; Evansville, 126,272; Gary, 116,646; South Bend, 105,511; Hammond, 84,236; Muncie, 71,035; Bloomington, 60,633; Anderson, 59,459; Terre Haute, 57,483
Land area & (rank): 35,932 sq mi. (93,064 sq km) (38)

Geographic center: In Boone Co., 14 mi. NNW of Indianapolis
Number of Counties: 92
Largest county (1990 census): Marion, 797,159
State parks: 19 (54,126 ac.)
State memorials: 16 (941.977 ac.)
1980 resident census population & (rank): 5,490,224 (12)
1990 census population, sex, & (rank): 5,544,159 (14). **Male:** 2,688,281; **Female:** 2,855,878. **White:** 5,020,700 (90.6%); **Black:** 432,092 (7.8%); **American Indian, Eskimo, or Aleut:** 12,720 (0.2%); **Asian or Pacific Islander:** 37,617 (0.7%); **Other race:** 41,030 (0.7%); **Hispanic:** 98,788 (1.8%). **1990 percent population under 18:** 26.3; **65 and over:** 12.6; **median age:** 32.8.

First explored for France by La Salle in 1679–80, the region figured importantly in the Franco-British struggle for North America that culminated with British victory in 1763.

George Rogers Clark led American forces against the British in the area during the Revolutionary War and, prior to becoming a state, Indiana was the scene of frequent Indian uprisings until the victory of Gen. William Henry Harrison at Tippecanoe in 1811.

Indiana's 41-mile Lake Michigan waterfront—one of the world's great industrial centers—turns out iron, steel, and oil products. Products include automobile parts and accessories, mobile homes and recreational vehicles, truck and bus bodies, aircraft engines, farm machinery, and fabricated structural steel. Phonograph records, wood office furniture, and pharmaceuticals are also manufactured.

The state is a leader in agriculture with corn the principal crop. Hogs, soybeans, wheat, oats, rye, tomatoes, onions, and poultry also contribute heavily to Indiana's agricultural output. Much of the building limestone used in the U.S. is quarried in Indiana which is also a large producer of coal.

Wyandotte Cave, one of the largest in the U.S., is located in Crawford County in southern Indiana and West Baden and French Lick are well known for their mineral springs. Other attractions include Indiana Dunes National Lakeshore, Indianapolis Motor Speedway, Lincoln Boyhood National Memorial, and the George Rogers Clark National Historical Park.

IOWA

Capital: Des Moines
Governor: Terry E. Branstad, R (to Jan. 1995)
Lieut. Governor: Joy Corning, R (to Jan. 1995)
Secy. of State: Elaine Baxter, D (to Jan. 1995)
Treasurer: Michael L. Fitzgerald, D (to Jan. 1995)
Atty. General: Bonnie Campbell, D (to Jan. 1995)
Organized as territory: June 12, 1838
Entered Union & (rank): Dec. 28, 1846 (29)
Present constitution adopted: 1857
Motto: Our liberties we prize and our rights we will maintain
STATE SYMBOLS: flower, Wild rose (1897); **bird,** Eastern goldfinch (1933); **colors,** Red, white, and blue (in state flag); **song,** "Song of Iowa"
Nickname: Hawkeye State
Origin of name: Probably from an Indian word meaning "I-o-w-a, this is the place," or "The Beautiful Land"
10 largest cities (1990 census): Des Moines, 193,187; Cedar Rapids, 108,751; Davenport, 95,333; Sioux City, 80,505; Waterloo, 66,467; Iowa City, 59,738; Dubuque, 57,546; Council Bluffs, 54,315; Ames, 47,198; Cedar Falls, 34,298
Land area & (rank): 55,965 sq mi. (144,950 sq km) (24)

Geographic center: In Story Co., 5 mi. NE of Ames
Number of counties: 99
Largest county (1990 census): Polk, 327,140
State forests: 5 (28,000 ac.)
State parks: 84 (49,237)
1980 resident census population & (rank): 2,913,808 (27)
1990 resident census population, sex, & (rank):
2,776,755 (30). Male: 1,344,802; Female: 1,431,953.
White: 2,683,090 (96.6%); Black: 48,090 (1.7%); American Indian, Eskimo, or Aleut: 7,349 (0.3%); Asian or Pacific Islander: 25,476 (0.9%); Other race: 12,750 (0.5%); Hispanic: 32,647 (1.2%). 1990 percent population under 18: 25.9; 65 and over: 15.3; median age: 34.0

The first Europeans to visit the area were the French explorers, Father Jacques Marquette and Louis Joliet in 1673. The U.S. obtained control of the area in 1803 as part of the Louisiana Purchase.

During the first half of the 19th century, there was heavy fighting between white settlers and Indians. Lands were taken from the Indians after the Black Hawk War in 1832 and again in 1836 and 1837.

When Iowa became a state in 1846, its capital was Iowa City; the more centrally located Des Moines became the new capital in 1857. At that time, the state's present boundaries were also drawn.

Although Iowa produces a tenth of the nation's food supply, the value of Iowa's manufactured products is twice that of its agriculture. Major industries are food and associated products, non-electrical machinery, electrical equipment, printing and publishing, and fabricated products.

Iowa stands in a class by itself as an agricultural state. Its farms sell over $9 billion worth of crops and livestock annually. Iowa is second in the nation in all livestock and hog marketings, with about 25% of the pork supply and 8% of the grain-fed cattle. Iowa's forests produce hardwood lumber, particularly walnut, and its mineral products include cement, limestone, sand, gravel, gypsum, and coal.

Tourist attractions include the Herbert Hoover birthplace and library near West Branch; the Amana Colonies; Fort Dodge Historical Museum, Fort, and Stockade; the Iowa State Fair at Des Moines in August; and the Effigy Mounds National Monument at Marquette, a prehistoric Indian burial site.

KANSAS

Capital: Topeka
Governor: Joan Finney, D (to Jan. 1995)
Lieut. Governor: James Francisco, D (to Jan. 1995)
Secy. of State: Bill Graves, R (to Jan. 1995)
Treasurer: Sally Thompson, D (to Jan. 1995)
Atty. General: Robert T. Stephan, R (to Jan. 1995)
Commission of Insurance: Ron Todd, D (to Jan. 1995)
Organized as territory: May 30, 1854
Entered Union & (rank): Jan. 29, 1861 (34)
Present constitution adopted: 1859
Motto: *Ad astra per aspera* (To the stars through difficulties)
STATE SYMBOLS: flower, Sunflower (1903); tree, Cottonwood (1937); bird, Western meadowlark (1937); animal, Buffalo (1955); song, "Home on Range" (1947)
Nicknames: Sunflower State; Jayhawk State
Origin of name: From a Siouan word meaning "people of the south wind"
10 largest cities (1990 census): Wichita, 304,011; Kansas City, 149,767; Topeka, 119,883; Overland Park, 111,790; Lawrence, 65,608; Olathe, 63,352; Salina, 42,303;

Hutchinson, 39,308; Leavenworth, 38,495; Shawnee, 37,993
Land area & (rank): 81,778 sq mi. (211,805 sq km) (13)
Geographic center: In Barton Co., 15 mi. NE of Great Bend
Number of counties: 105
Largest county (1990 census): Sedgwick, 403,662
State parks: 22 (14,394 ac.)
1980 resident census population & (rank): 2,363,679 (32)
1990 resident census population, sex, & (rank):
2,477,574 (32). Male: 1,214,645; Female: 1,262,929.
White: 2,231,986 (90.1%); Black: 143,076 (5.8%); American Indian, Eskimo, or Aleut: 21,965 (0.9%); Asian or Pacific Islander: 31,750 (1.3%); Other race: 48,797 (2.0%); Hispanic: 93,670 (3.8%). 1990 percent population under 18: 26.7; 65 and over: 13.8; median age: 32.9

Spanish explorer Francisco de Coronado, in 1541, is considered the first European to have traveled this region. La Salle's extensive land claims for France (1682) included present-day Kansas. Ceded to Spain by France in 1763, the territory reverted back to France in 1800 and was sold to the U.S. as part of the Louisiana Purchase in 1803.

Lewis and Clark, Zebulon Pike, and Stephen H. Long explored the region between 1803 and 1819. The first permanent settlements in Kansas were outposts—Fort Leavenworth (1827), Fort Scott (1842), and Fort Riley (1853)—established to protect travelers along the Santa Fe and Oregon Trails.

Just before the Civil War, the conflict between the pro- and anti-slavery forces earned the region the grim title "Bleeding Kansas."

Today, wheat fields, oil well derricks, herds of cattle, and grain storage elevators are chief features of the Kansas landscape. A leading wheat-growing state, Kansas also raises corn, sorghums, oats, barley, soy beans, and potatoes. Kansas stands high in petroleum production and mines zinc, coal, salt, and lead. It is also the nation's leading producer of helium.

Wichita is one of the nation's leading aircraft manufacturing centers, ranking first in production of private aircraft. Kansas City is an important transportation, milling, and meat-packing center.

Points of interest include the new Kansas Museum of History at Topeka, the Eisenhower boyhood home and the new Eisenhower Memorial Museum and Presidential Library at Abilene, John Brown's cabin at Osawatomie, recreated Front Street in Dodge City, Fort Larned (once the most important military post on the Santa Fe Trail), and Fort Leavenworth and Fort Riley.

KENTUCKY

Capital: Frankfort
Governor: Wallace G. Wilkinson, D (to Dec. 1991)
Lieut. Governor: Brereton C. Jones, D (to Dec. 1991)
Secy. of State: Bremer Ehrler, D (to Jan. 1992)
State Treasurer: Robert Meade, D (to Jan. 1992)
State Auditor: Bob Babbage, D (to Jan. 1992)
Atty. General: Fred Cowan, D (to Jan. 1992)
Entered Union & (rank): June 1, 1792 (15)
Present constitution adopted: 1891
Motto: United we stand, divided we fall
STATE SYMBOLS: tree, Coffeetree; flower, Goldenrod; bird, Kentucky cardinal; song, "My Old Kentucky Home"
Nickname: Bluegrass State
Origin of name: From an Iroquoian word "Ken-tah-ten" meaning "land of tomorrow"

10 largest cities (1990 census): Louisville, 269,063; Lexington-Fayette, 225,366; Owensboro, 53,549; Covington, 43,264; Bowling Green, 40,641; Hopkinsville, 29,809; Paducah, 27,256; Frankfort, 25,968; Henderson, 25,945; Ashland, 23,622
Land area & (rank): 39,669 sq mi. (102,743 sq km) (37)
Geographic center: In Marion Co., 3 mi. NNW of Lebanon
Number of counties: 120
Largest county (1990 census): Jefferson, population 664,937
State forests: 9 (44,173 ac.)
State parks: 43 (40,574 ac.)
1980 resident census population & (rank): 3,660,777 (23)
1990 resident census population, sex, & (rank): 3,685,296 (23). **Male:** 1,785,235; **Female:** 1,900,061. **White:** 3,391,832 (92.0%); **Black:** 262,907 (7.1%); **American Indian, Eskimo, or Aleut:** 5,769 (0.2%); **Asian or Pacific Islander:** 17,812 (0.5%); **Other race:** 6,976 (0.2%); **Hispanic:** 21,984 (0.6%). **1990 percent population below age 18:** 25.9; **65 and over:** 12.7; **median age:** 33.0.

Kentucky was the first region west of the Allegheny Mountains settled by American pioneers. James Harrod established the first permanent settlement at Harrodsburg in 1774; the following year Daniel Boone, who had explored the area in 1767, blazed the Wilderness Trail and founded Boonesboro.

Politically, the Kentucky region was originally part of Virginia, but early statehood was gained in 1792.

During the Civil War, as a slaveholding state with a considerable abolitionist population, Kentucky was caught in the middle of the conflict, supplying both Union and Confederate forces with thousands of troops.

In recent years, manufacturing has shown important gains, but agriculture and mining are still vital to Kentucky's economy. Kentucky prides itself on producing some of the nation's best tobacco, horses, and whiskey. Corn, soybeans, wheat, fruit, hogs, cattle, and dairy farming are also important.

Among the manufactured items produced in the state are furniture, aluminum ware, brooms, shoes, lumber products, machinery, textiles, and iron and steel products. Kentucky also produces significant amounts of petroleum, natural gas, fluorspar, clay, and stone. However, coal accounts for 90% of the total mineral income.

Louisville, the largest city, famed for the Kentucky Derby at Churchill Downs, is also the location of a large state university, whiskey distilleries, and cigarette factories. The Bluegrass country around Lexington is the home of some of the world's finest race horses. Other attractions are Mammoth Cave, the George S. Patton, Jr., Military Museum at Fort Knox, and Old Fort Harrod State Park.

LOUISIANA

Capital: Baton Rouge
Governor: Buddy Roemer, R (to Jan. 1992)
Lieut. Governor: Paul J. Hardy, R (to Jan. 1992)
Secy. of State: W. Fox McKeithen, R (to Jan. 1992)
Treasurer: Mary Landrieu, D (to Jan. 1992)
Atty. General: Gen. Wm. J. Guste, Jr., D (to Jan. 1992)
Organized as territory: March 26, 1804
Entered Union & (rank): April 30, 1812 (18)
Present constitution adopted: 1974
Motto: Union, justice, and confidence
STATE SYMBOLS: flower, Magnolia (1900); **tree,** Bald cypress (1963); **bird,** Pelican (1958); **songs,** "Give Me Louisiana" and "You Are My Sunshine"

Nicknames: Pelican State; Sportsman's Paradise; Creole State; Sugar State
Origin of name: In honor of Louis XIV of France
10 largest cities (1990 census): New Orleans, 496,938; Baton Rouge, 219,531; Shreveport, 198,525; Lafayette, 94,440; Kenner, 72,033; Lake Charles, 70,580; Monroe, 54,909; Bossier City, 52,721; Alexandria, 49,188; New Iberia, 31,828
Land area & (rank): 44,521 sq mi. (115,309 sq km) (33)
Geographic center: In Avoyelles Parish, 3 mi. SE of Marksville
Number of parishes (counties): 64
Largest parish (1990 census): Jefferson, 448,306
State forests: 1 (8,000 ac.)
State parks: 30 (13,932 ac.)
1980 resident census population & (rank): 4,205,900 (19)
1990 resident census population, sex, & (rank): 4,219,973 (21). **Male:** 2,031,386; **Female:** 2,188,587. **White:** 2,839,138 (67.3%); **Black:** 1,299,281 (30.8%); **American Indian, Eskimo, or Aleut:** 18,541 (0.4%); **Asian or Pacific Islander:** 41,099 (1.0%); **Other race:** 21,914 (0.5%); **Hispanic:** 93,044 (2.2%). **1990 percent population under 18:** 29.1; **65 and over:** 11.1; **median age:** 31.0.

Louisiana has a rich, colorful historical background. Early Spanish explorers were Piñeda, 1519; Cabeza de Vaca, 1528; and de Soto in 1541. La Salle reached the mouth of the Mississippi and claimed all the land drained by it and its tributaries for Louis XIV of France in 1682.

Louisiana became a French crown colony in 1731, was ceded to Spain in 1763, returned to France in 1800, and sold by Napoleon to the U.S. as part of the Louisiana Purchase (with large territories to the north and northwest) in 1803.

In 1815, Gen. Andrew Jackson's troops defeated a larger British army in the Battle of New Orleans, neither side aware that the treaty ending the War of 1812 had been signed.

As to total value of its mineral output, Louisiana is a leader in natural gas, salt, petroleum, and sulfur production. Much of the oil and sulfur comes from offshore deposits. The state also produces large crops of sweet potatoes, rice, sugar cane, pecans, soybeans, corn, and cotton.

Leading manufactures include chemicals, processed food, petroleum and coal products, paper, lumber and wood products, transportation equipment, and apparel.

Louisiana marshes supply most of the nation's muskrat fur as well as that of opossum, raccoon, mink, and otter, and large numbers of game birds.

Major points of interest include New Orleans with its French Quarter and Superdome, plantation homes near Natchitoches and New Iberia, Cajun country in the Mississippi delta region, Chalmette National Historical Park, and the state capital at Baton Rouge.

MAINE

Capital: Augusta
Governor: John R. McKernan, Jr., R (to Jan. 1995)
Secy. of State: G. William Diamond, D (to Jan. 1993)
Controller: David A. Bourne, R (term indefinite)
Atty. General: Michael E. Carpenter, D (to Jan. 1995)
Entered Union & (rank): March 15, 1820 (23)
Present constitution adopted: 1820
Motto: *Dirigo* (I direct)
STATE SYMBOLS: flower, White pine cone and tassel (1895); **tree,** White pine tree (1945); **bird,** Chickadee

(1927); **fish,** Landlocked salmon (1969); **mineral,** Tourmaline (1971); **song,** "State of Maine Song" (1937)
Nickname: Pine Tree State
Origin of name: First used to distinguish the mainland from the offshore islands. It has been considered a compliment to Henrietta Maria, Queen of Charles I of England. She was said to have owned the province of Mayne in France.
10 largest cities (1990 census): Portland, 64,358; Lewiston, 39,757; Bangor, 33,181; Auburn, 24,309; South Portland, 23,163; Augusta, 21,325; Biddeford, 20,710; Waterville, 17,173; Westbrook, 16,121; Saco, 15,181
Land area & (rank): 30,995 sq mi. (80,277 sq km) (39)
Geographic center: In Piscataquis Co., 18 mi. N of Dover—Foxcroft
Number of counties: 16
Largest town (1990 census): Brunswick, 20,906
State forests: 1 (21,000 ac.)
State parks: 26 (247,627 ac.)
State historic sites: 18 (403 ac.)
1980 resident census population & (rank): 1,124,660 (38)
1990 resident census population, sex, & (rank): 1,227,928 (38). **Male:** 597,850; **Female:** 630,078. **White:** 1,208,360 (98.4%); **Black:** 5,138 (0.4%); **American Indian, Eskimo, or Aleut:** 5,998 (0.5%); **Asian or Pacific Islander:** 6,683: (0.5%); **Other race:** 1,749 (0.1%); **Hispanic:** 6,829 (0.6%).

John Cabot and his son, Sebastian, are believed to have visited the Maine coast in 1498. However, the first permanent English settlements were not established until more than a century later, in 1623.

The first naval action of the Revolutionary War occurred in 1775 when colonials captured the British sloop *Margaretta* off Machias on the Maine coast. In that same year, the British burned Falmouth (now Portland).

Long governed by Massachusetts, Maine became the 23rd state as part of the Missouri Compromise in 1820.

Maine produces 98% of the nation's low-bush blueberries. Farm income is also derived from apples, potatoes, dairy products, and vegetables, with poultry and eggs the largest items.

The state is one of the world's largest pulp-paper producers. It ranks fifth in boot-and-shoe manufacturing. With almost 89% of its area forested, Maine turns out wood products from boats to toothpicks.

Maine leads the world in the production of the familiar flat tins of sardines, producing more than 100 million of them annually. Lobstermen normally catch 80–90% of the nation's true total of lobsters.

A scenic seacoast, beaches, lakes, mountains, and resorts make Maine a popular vacationland. There are more than 2,500 lakes and 5,000 streams, plus 26 state parks, to attract hunters, fishermen, skiers, and campers.

Major points of interest are: Bar Harbor, Allagash National Wilderness Waterway, the Wadsworth-Longfellow House in Portland, Roosevelt Campobello International Park, and the St. Croix Island National Monument.

MARYLAND

Capital: Annapolis
Governor: William Donald Schaefer, D (to Jan. 1995)
Lieut. Gov.: Melvin A. Steinberg, D (to Jan. 1995)
Secy. of State: Winfield M. Kelly, Jr., D (appointed by governor) (to Jan. 1995)
Comptroller of the Treasury: Louis L. Goldstein, D (to Jan. 1995)

Treasurer: Lucille Maurer, D (to Jan. 1995)
Atty. General: J. Joseph Curran, Jr., D (to Jan. 1995)
Entered Union & (rank): April 28, 1788 (7)
Present constitution adopted: 1867
Motto: *Fatti maschii, parole femine* (Manly deeds, womanly words)
STATE SYMBOLS: flower, Black-eyed susan (1918); **tree,** White oak (1941); **bird,** Baltimore oriole (1947); **dog,** Chesapeake Bay retriever (1964); **fish,** Rockfish (1965); **crustacean,** Maryland Blue Crab (1989); **insect,** Baltimore checkerspot butterfly (1973); **boat,** Skipjack (1985); **sport,** Jousting (1962); **song,** "Maryland! My Maryland!" (1939)
Nicknames: Free State; Old Line State
Origin of name: In honor of Henrietta Maria (Queen of Charles I of England)
10 largest cities (1990 census): Baltimore, 736,014; Rockville, 44,835; Frederick, 40,148; Gaithersburg, 39,542; Bowie, 37,589; Hagerstown, 35,445; Annapolis, 33,187; Cumberland, 23,706; College Park, 21,927; Greenbelt, 21,096
Land area & (rank): 9,837 sq mi. (25,477 sq km) (42)
Geographic center: In Prince Georges Co., 4 1/2 mi. NW of Davidsonville
Number of counties: 23, and 1 independent city
Largest county (1990 census): Montgomery, 757,027
State forests: 13 (132,944 ac.)
State parks: 47 (87,670 ac.)
1980 resident census population & (rank): 4,216,975 (18)
1990 resident census population, sex, & (rank): 4,781,468 (19). **Male:** 2,318,671; **Female:** 2,462,797. **White:** 3,393,964 (71.0%); **Black:** 1,189,899 (24.9%); **American Indian, Eskimo, or Aleut:** 12,972 (0.3%); **Asian or Pacific Islander:** 139,719 (2.9%); **Other race:** 44,914 (0.9%); **Hispanic:** 125,102 (2.6%). **1990 percent population under 18:** 24.3; **65 and over:** 10.8; **median age:** 33.0

In 1608, Chesapeake Bay was explored by Capt. John Smith. Charles I granted a royal charter to Cecil Calvert, Lord Baltimore, in 1632 and English Roman Catholics landed on St. Clement's (now Blakistone Island) in 1634. Religious freedom, granted all Christians in the Toleration act passed by the Maryland assembly in 1649, was ended by a Puritan revolt, 1654–58.

From 1763 to 1767, Charles Mason and Jeremiah Dixon surveyed Maryland's northern boundary line with Pennsylvania. In 1791, Maryland ceded land to form the District of Columbia.

In 1814, when the British unsuccessfully tried to capture Baltimore, the bombardment of Fort McHenry inspired Francis Scott Key to write *The Star Spangled Banner.*

The Baltimore clipper ship trade developed during the 19th Century. The battles of South Mountain and Antietam (1862) and Monocacy (1864) were fought in this state.

In 1904, the Great Fire of Baltimore occurred. In 1937, the City of Greenbelt, a New Deal model community, was chartered.

Maryland is almost cut in two by the Chesapeake Bay, and the many estuaries and rivers create one of the longest waterfronts of any state. The Bay produces more seafood—oysters, crabs, clams, fin fish—than any comparable body of water. Important agricultural products, in order of cash value, are chickens, dairy products, cattle, soy beans, eggs, corn, hogs, vegetables, and tobacco. Maryland is a leader in vegetable canning. Sand, gravel, lime and cement, stone, coal, and clay are the chief mineral products.

Manufacturing industries produce missiles, airplanes, steel, clothing, and chemicals. Baltimore, home of The Johns Hopkins University and Hospital, ranks as the nation's second port in foreign tonnage. Annapolis, site of the U.S. Naval Academy, has one of the earliest state houses (1772–79) still in regular use by a State government.

Among the popular attractions in Maryland are the Fort McHenry National Monument, Harpers Ferry and Chesapeake and Ohio Canal, National Aquarium, and Maryland Science Center at Baltimore's Inner Harbor, National Historical Parks, Historic St. Mary's City restoration near Leonardtown, USS *Constellation* at Baltimore, U.S. Naval Academy in Annapolis, Goddard Space Flight Center at Greenbelt, Assateague Island National Seashore, Ocean City beach resort, and Catoctin Mountain, Ft. Frederick, and Piscataway parks.

MASSACHUSETTS

Capital: Boston
Governor: William F. Weld, R (to Jan. 1995)
Lieut. Governor: Paul Cellucci, R (to Jan. 1995)
Secy. of the Commonwealth: Michael Joseph Connolly, D (to Jan. 1995)
Treasurer & Receiver-General: Joseph Malone, R (to Jan. 1995)
Auditor of the Commonwealth: A. Joseph DeNucci, D (to Jan. 1995)
Atty. General: L. Scott Harshbarger, D (to Jan. 1995)
Present constitution drafted: 1780 (oldest U.S. state constitution in effect today)
Entered Union & (rank): Feb. 6, 1788 (6)
Motto: *Ense petit placidam sub libertate quietem* (By the sword we seek peace, but peace only under liberty)
STATE SYMBOLS: flower, Mayflower (1918); **tree.** American elm (1941); **bird,** Chickadee (1941); **colors,** Blue and gold; **song,** "All Hail to Massachusetts" (1966); **beverage,** Cranberry juice (1970); **insect,** Ladybug (1974)
Nicknames: Bay State; Old Colony State
Origin of name: From two Indian words meaning "Great mountain place"
10 largest cities (1990 census): Boston, 574,283; Worcester, 169,759; Springfield, 156,983; Lowell, 103,439; New Bedford, 99,922; Cambridge, 95,802; Brockton, 92,788; Fall River, 92,703; Quincy, 84,985; Newton, 82,585
Land area & (rank): 7,824 sq mi. (20,265 sq km) (45)
Geographic center: In Worcester Co., in S part of city of Worcester
Number of counties: 14
Largest county (1990 census): Framingham, 64,989
State forests and parks: 129 (242,000 ac.)[1]
1980 resident census population & (rank): 5,737,037 (11)
1990 resident census population, sex, & (rank): 6,016,425 (13). **Male:** 2,888,745; **Female:** 3,127,680. **White:** 5,405,374 (89.8%); **Black:** 300,130 (5.0%); **American Indian, Eskimo, or Aleut:** 12,241 (0.2%); **Asian or Pacific Islander:** 143,392 (2.4%); **Other race:** 155,288 (2.6%); **Hispanic:** 287,549 (4.8%). **1990 percent population under 18:** 22.5; **65 and over:** 13.6; **median age:** 33.6.

1. The Metropolitan District Commission, an agency of the Commonwealth serving municipalities in the Boston area, has about 14,000 acres of parkways and reservations under its jurisdiction.

Massachusetts has played a significant role in American history since the Pilgrims, seeking religious freedom, founded Plymouth Colony in 1620.

As one of the most important of the 13 colonies, Massachusetts became a leader in resisting British oppression. In 1773, the Boston Tea Party protested unjust taxation. The Minutemen started the American Revolution by battling British troops at Lexington and Concord on April 19, 1775.

During the 19th century, Massachusetts was famous for the vigorous intellectual activity of famous writers and educators and for its expanding commercial fishing, shipping, and manufacturing interests.

Massachusetts pioneered in the manufacture of textiles and shoes. Today, these industries have been replaced in importance by activity in the electronics and communications equipment fields.

The state's cranberry crop is the nation's largest. Also important are dairy and poultry products, nursery and greenhouse produce, vegetables, and fruit.

Tourism has become an important factor in the economy of the state because of its numerous recreational areas and historical landmarks.

Cape Cod has summer theaters, water sports, and an artists' colony at Provincetown. Tanglewood, in the Berkshires, features the summer concerts of the Boston Symphony.

Among the many other points of interest are Old Sturbridge Village, Minute Man National Historical Park between Lexington and Concord, and, in Boston: Old North Church, Old State House, Faneuil Hall, the USS *Constitution* and the John F. Kennedy Library.

MICHIGAN

Capital: Lansing
Governor: John M. Engler, R (to Jan. 1995)
Lieut. Governor: Connie Binsfeld, R (to Jan. 1995)
Secy. of State: Richard H. Austin, D (to Jan. 1995)
Atty. General: Frank J. Kelley, D (to Jan. 1995)
Organized as territory: Jan. 11, 1805
Entered Union & (rank): Jan. 26, 1837 (26)
Present constitution adopted: April 1, 1963, (effective Jan. 1, 1964)
Motto: *Si quaeris peninsulam amoenam circumspice* (If you seek a pleasant peninsula, look around you)
STATE SYMBOLS: flower, Apple blossom (1897); **bird,** Robin (1931); **fishes,** Trout (1965), Brook trout (1988); **gem,** Isle Royal Greenstone (Chlorastrolite) (1972); **stone,** Petoskey stone (1965)
Nickname: Wolverine State
Origin of name: From two Indian words meaning "great lake"
10 largest cities (1990 census): Detroit, 1,027,974; Grand Rapids, 189,126; Warren, 144,864; Flint, 140,761; Lansing, 127,321; Sterling Heights, 117,810; Ann Arbor, 109,592; Livonia, 100,850; Dearborn, 89,286; Westland, 84,724
Land area & (rank): 56,954 sq mi. (147,511 sq km) (22)
Geographic center: In Wexford Co., 5 mi. NNW of Cadillac
Number of counties: 83
Largest county (1990 census): Wayne, 2,111,687
State parks and recreation areas: 92 (250,000 ac.)
1980 resident census population & (rank): 9,262,078 (8)
1990 resident census population, sex, & (rank): 9,295,297 (8). **Male:** 4,512,781; **Female:** 4,787,516. **White:** 7,756,086 (83.4%); **Black:** 1,291,706 (13.9%); **American Indian, Eskimo, or Aleut:** 55,638 (0.6%); **Asian or Pacific Islander:** 104,983 (1.1%); **Other race:** 86,884 (0.9%); **Hispanic:** 201,596 (2.2%). **1990 percent population under 18:** 26.5; **65 and over:** 11.9; **median age:** 32.6.

Indian tribes were living in the Michigan region when the first European, Etienne Brulé of France, arrived in 1618. Other French explorers, including Marquette, Joliet, and La Salle, followed, and the first permanent settlement was established in 1668 at Sault Ste. Marie. France was ousted from the territory by Great Britain in 1763, following the French and Indian War.

After the Revolutionary War, the U.S. acquired most of the region, which remained the scene of constant conflict between the British and U.S. forces and their respective Indian allies through the War of 1812.

Bordering on four of the five Great Lakes, Michigan is divided into Upper and Lower Peninsulas by the Straits of Mackinac, which link Lakes Michigan and Huron. The two parts of the state are connected by the Mackinac Bridge, one of the world's longest suspension bridges. To the north, connecting Lakes Superior and Huron are the busy Sault Ste. Marie Canals.

While Michigan ranks first among the states in production of motor vehicles and parts, it is also a leader in many other manufacturing and processing lines including prepared cereals, machine tools, airplane parts, refrigerators, hardware, steel springs, and furniture.

The state produces important amounts of iron, copper, iodine, gypsum, bromine, salt, lime, gravel, and cement. Michigan's farms grow apples, cherries, pears, grapes, potatoes, and sugar beets and the 1987 value of its forest products was estimated at $3.2 billion. With over 36,000 miles of streams, some 11,000 lakes, and a 2,000 mile shoreline, Michigan is a prime area for both commercial and sport fishing.

Points of interest are the automobile plants in Dearborn, Detroit, Flint, Lansing, and Pontiac; Mackinac Island; Pictured Rocks and Sleeping Bear Dunes National Lakeshores, Greenfield Village in Dearborn; and the many summer resorts along both the inland and Great Lakes.

MINNESOTA

Capital: St. Paul
Governor: Arne Carlson, R (to Jan. 1995)
Lieut. Governor: Joanell Dyrstad, R (to Jan. 1995)
Secy. of State: Joan Anderson Growe, D (to Jan. 1995)
State Auditor: Mark Dayton, D (to Jan. 1995)
Atty. General: Hubert H. Humphrey III, D (to Jan. 1995)
State Treasurer: Michael McGrath, D (to Jan. 1995)
Organized as territory: March 3, 1849
Entered Union & (rank): May 11, 1858 (32)
Present constitution adopted: 1858
Motto: L'Etoile du Nord (The North Star)
STATE SYMBOLS: flower, Showy lady slipper (1902); **tree,** Red (or Norway) pine (1953); **bird,** Common loon (also called Great Northern Diver) (1961); **song,** "Hail Minnesota" (1945); **fish,** Walleye (1965); **mushroom,** Morel (1984)
Nicknames: North Star State; Gopher State; Land of 10,000 Lakes
Origin of name: From a Dakota Indian word meaning "sky-tinted water"
10 largest cities (1990 census): Minneapolis, 368,383; St. Paul, 272,235; Bloomington, 86,335; Duluth, 85,493; Rochester, 70,745; Brooklyn Park, 56,381; Coon Rapids, 52,978; Burnsville, 51,288; Plymouth, 50,889; St. Cloud, 48,812
Land area & (rank): 79,548 sq mi. (206,030 sq km) (14)
Geographic center: In Crow Wing Co., 10 mi. SW of Brainerd
Number of counties: 87
Largest county (1990 census): Hennepin, 1,032,431
State forests: 56 (3,200,000+ ac.)

State parks: 66 (226,000 ac.)
1980 resident census population & (rank): 4,075,970 (21)
1990 resident census population, sex, & (rank): 4,375,099 (20). **Male:** 2,145,183; **Female:** 2,229,916. **White:** 4,130,395 (94.4%); **Black:** 94,944 (2.2%); **American Indian, Eskimo, or Aleut:** 49,909 (1.1%); **Asian or Pacific Islander:** 77,886 (1.8%); **Other race:** 21,965 (0.5%); **Hispanic:** 53,884 (1.2%). **1990 percent population under 18:** 26.7; **65 and over:** 12.5; **median age:** 32.5.

Following the visits of several French explorers, fur traders, and missionaries, including Marquette and Joliet and La Salle, the region was claimed for Louis XIV by Daniel Greysolon, Sieur Duluth, in 1679.

The U.S. acquired eastern Minnesota from Great Britain after the Revolutionary War and 20 years later bought the western part from France in the Louisiana Purchase of 1803. Much of the region was explored by U.S. Army Lt. Zebulon M. Pike before cession of the northern strip of Minnesota bordering Canada by Britain in 1818.

The state is rich in natural resources. A few square miles of land in the north in the Mesabi, Cuyuna, and Vermillion ranges, produce more than 75% of the nation's iron ore. The state's farms rank high in yields of corn, wheat, rye, alfalfa, and sugar beets. Other leading farm products include butter, eggs, milk, potatoes, green peas, barley, soy beans, oats, and livestock.

Minnesota's factory production includes nonelectrical machinery, fabricated metals, flour-mill products, plastics, electronic computers, scientific instruments, and processed foods. It is also one of the nation's leaders in the printing and paper products industries.

Minneapolis is the trade center of the Northwest; and the headquarters of the world's largest super computer and grain distributor. St. Paul is the nation's biggest publisher of calendars and law books. These "twin cities" are the nation's third largest trucking center. Duluth has the nation's largest inland harbor and now handles a significant amount of foreign trade. Rochester is the home of the Mayo Clinic, an internationally famous medical center.

Today, tourism is a major revenue producer in Minnesota, with arts, fishing, hunting, water sports, and winter sports bringing in millions of visitors each year.

Among the most popular attractions are the St. Paul Winter Carnival; the Tyrone Guthrie Theatre, the Institute of Arts, Walker Art Center, and Minnehaha Park, in Minneapolis; Boundary Waters Canal Area; Voyageurs National Park; North Shore Drive; and the Minnesota Zoological Gardens and the state's more than 10,000 lakes.

MISSISSIPPI

Capital: Jackson
Governor: Ray Mabus, D (to Jan. 1992)
Lieut. Governor: Brad Dye, D (to Jan. 1992)
Secy. of State: Dick Molpus, D (to Jan. 1992)
Treasurer: Marshall Bennett, D (to Jan. 1992)
Atty. General: Mike Moore, D (to Jan. 1992)
Organized as Territory: April 7, 1798
Entered Union & (rank): Dec. 10, 1817 (20)
Present constitution adopted: 1890
Motto: *Virtute et armis* (By valor and arms)
STATE SYMBOLS: flower, Flower or bloom of the magnolia or evergreen magnolia (1952); **tree,** Magnolia (1938); **bird,** Mockingbird (1944); **song,** "Go, Mississippi" (1962); **stone,** Petrified wood (1976); **fish,** Largemouth or black bass (1974); **insect,** Honeybee (1980); **shell,** Oyster shell (1974); **water mammal,** Bottlenosed dolphin or porpoise (1974); **fossil,** Prehistoric

whale (1981); **land mammal,** White-tailed deer (1974); **waterfowl,** Wood duck (1974); **beverage,** Milk (1984)

Nickname: Magnolia State

Origin of name: From an Indian word meaning "Father of Waters"

10 largest cities (1990 census): Jackson, 196,637; Biloxi, 46,319; Greenville, 45,226; Hattiesburg, 41,882; Meridian, 41,036; Gulfport, 40,775; Tupelo, 30,685; Pascagoula, 25,899; Columbus, 23,799; Clinton, 21,847

Land area & (rank): 47,233 sq mi. (122,333 sq km) (31)

Geographic center: In Leake Co., 9 mi. WNW of Carthage

Number of counties: 82

Largest county (1990 census): Hinds, 254,441

State forests: 1 (1,760 ac.)

State parks: 27 (16,763 ac.)

1980 resident census population & (rank): 2,520,638 (31)

1990 resident census population, sex, & (rank): 2,573,216 (31). **Male:** 1,230,617; **Female:** 1,342,599. **White:** 1,633,461 (63.5%); **Black:** 915,057 (35.6%); **American Indian, Eskimo, or Aleut:** 8,525 (0.3%); **Asian or Pacific Islander:** 13,016 (0.5%); **Other race:** 3,157 (0.1%); **Hispanic:** 15,931 (0.6%). **1990 percent population under 18:** 29.0; **65 and over:** 12.5; **median age:** 31.2.

First explored for Spain by Hernando de Soto who discovered the Mississippi River in 1540, the region was later claimed by France. In 1699, a French group under Sieur d'Iberville established the first permanent settlement near present-day Biloxi.

Great Britain took over the area in 1763 after the French and Indian War, ceding it to the U.S. in 1783 after the Revolution. Spain did not relinquish its claims until 1798, and in 1810 the U.S. annexed West Florida from Spain, including what is now southern Mississippi.

For a little more than one hundred years, from shortly after the state's founding through the Great Depression, cotton was the undisputed king of Mississippi's largely agrarian economy. Over the last half-century, however, Mississippi has progressively deepened its commitment to diversification by balancing agricultural output with increased industrial activity.

Today, agriculture continues as a major segment of the state's economy. Soybeans have supplanted cotton as the largest crop—Mississippi is now third in cotton production—and the state's farmlands yield important harvests of corn, peanuts, pecans, rice, sugar cane, sweet potatoes, and hay, as well as poultry and eggs. Mississippi is also the world's leading producer of pond-raised catfish.

The state abounds in historical landmarks and is the home of the Vicksburg National Military Park. Other National Park Service areas are Brices Cross Roads National Battlefield Site, Tupelo National Battlefield, and part of Natchez Trace National Parkway. Pre-Civil War mansions are the special pride of Natchez, Oxford, Columbus, Vicksburg, and Jackson.

MISSOURI

Capital: Jefferson City
Governor: John D. Ashcroft, R (to Jan. 1993)
Lieut. Governor: Mel Carnahan, D (to Jan. 1993)
Secy. of State: Roy D. Blunt, R (to Jan. 1993)
Auditor: Margaret Kelly, R (to Jan. 1995)
Treasurer: Wendell Bailey, R (to Jan. 1993)
Atty. General: William L. Webster, R (to Jan. 1993)
Organized as territory: June 4, 1812

Entered Union & (rank): Aug. 10, 1821 (24)

Present constitution adopted: 1945

Motto: *Salus populi suprema lex esto* (The welfare of the people shall be the supreme law)

STATE SYMBOLS: flower, Hawthorn (1923); **bird,** Bluebird (1927); **colors,** Red, white, and blue (1913); **song,** "Missouri Waltz" (1949); **fossil,** Crinoidea (1989); **musical instrument,** Fiddle (1987); **rock,** Mozarkite (1967); **mineral,** Galena (1967); **insect,** Honeybee (1985)

Nickname: Show-me State

Origin of name: Named after a tribe called Missouri Indians. "Missouri" means "town of the large canoes."

10 largest cities (1990 census): Kansas City, 435,146; St. Louis, 396,685; Springfield, 140,494; Independence, 112,301; St. Joseph, 71,852; Columbia, 69,101; St. Charles, 54,555; Florissant, 51,206; Lee's Summit, 46,418; St. Peter's, 45,779

Land area & (rank): 68,945 sq mi. (178,568 sq km) (18)

Geographic center: In Miller Co., 20 mi. SW of Jefferson City

Number of counties: 114, plus 1 independent city

Largest county (1990 census): St. Louis, 993,529

State forests and Tower sites: 134 (308,978 ac.)

State parks: 73 (105,325 ac.)[1]

1980 resident census population & (rank): 4,916,686 (15)

1990 resident census population, sex, & (rank): 5,117,073 (15). **Male:** 2,464,315; **Female:** 2,652,758. **White:** 4,486,228 (87.7%); **Black:** 548,208 (10.7%); **American Indian, Eskimo, or Aleut:** 19,835 (0.4%); **Asian or Pacific Islander:** 41,277 (0.8%); **Other race:** 21,525 (0.4%); **Hispanic:** 61,702 (1.2%). **1990 percent population under 18:** 25.7; **65 and over:** 14.0; **median age:** 33.5.

1. Includes 45 historic sites.

De Soto visited the Missouri area in 1541. France's claim to the entire region was based on La Salle's travels in 1682. French fur traders established Ste. Genevieve in 1735 and St. Louis was first settled in 1764.

The U.S. gained Missouri from France as part of the Louisiana Purchase in 1803, and the territory was admitted as a state following the Missouri Compromise of 1820. Throughout the pre-Civil War period and during the war, Missourians were sharply divided in their opinions about slavery and in their allegiances, supplying both Union and Confederate forces with troops. However, the state itself remained in the Union.

Historically, Missouri played a leading role as a gateway to the West, St. Joseph being the eastern starting point of the Pony Express, while the much-traveled Santa Fe and Oregon Trails began in Independence. Now a popular vacationland, Missouri has 11 major lakes and numerous fishing streams, springs, and caves. Bagnell Dam, across the Osage River in the Ozarks, completed in 1931, created one of the largest man-made lakes in the world, covering 65,000 acres of surface area.

Manufacturing, paced by the aerospace industry, provides more income and jobs than any other segment of the economy. Missouri is also a leading producer of transportation equipment, shoes, lead, and beer. Among the major crops are corn, soybeans, wheat, oats, barley, potatoes, tobacco, and cotton.

Points of interest include Mark Twain's boyhood home and Mark Twain Cave (Hannibal), the Harry S. Truman Library and Museum (Independence), the house where Jesse James was killed in St. Joseph, Jefferson National Expansion Memorial (St. Louis), and the Ozark National Scenic Riverway.

MONTANA

Capital: Helena
Governor: Stanley Stephens, R (to Jan. 1993)
Lieut. Governor: Allen Kolstad, R (to Jan. 1993)
Secy. of State: Mike Cooney, D (to Jan. 1993)
Auditor: Andrea Bennett, R (to Jan. 1993)
Atty. General: Marc Racicot, R (to Jan. 1993)
Organized as territory: May 26, 1864
Entered Union & (rank): Nov. 8, 1889 (41)
Present constitution adopted: 1972
Motto: *Oro y plata* (Gold and silver)
STATE SYMBOLS: flower, Bitterroot (1895); **tree,** Ponderosa pine (1949); **stones,** Sapphire and agate (1969); **bird,** Western meadowlark (1981); **song,** "Montana" (1945)
Nickname: Treasure State
Origin of name: Chosen from Latin dictionary by J. M. Ashley. It is a Latinized Spanish word meaning "mountainous."
10 largest cities (1990 census): Billings, 81,151; Great Falls, 55,097; Missoula, 42,918; Butte-Silver Bow[1], 33,941; Helena, 24,569; Bozeman, 22,660; Kalispell, 11,917; Anaconda-Deer Lodge County, 10,278; Havre, 10,201; Miles City, 8,461
Land area & (rank): 145,388 sq mi. (376,554 sq km) (4)
Geographic center: In Fergus Co., 12 mi. W of Lewistown
Number of counties: 56, plus small part of Yellowstone National Park
Largest county (1990 census): Yellowstone, 113,419
State forests: 7 (214,000 ac.)
State parks and recreation areas: 110 (18,273 ac.)
1980 resident census population & (rank): 786,690 (44)
1990 resident census population, sex, & (rank): 799,065 (44). **Male:** 395,769; **Female:** 403,296. **White:** 741,111 (92.7%); **Black:** 2,381 (0.3%); **American Indian, Eskimo, or Aleut:** 47,679 (6.0%); **Asian or Pacific Islander:** 4,259 (0.5%); **Other race:** 3,635 (0.5%); **Hispanic:** 12,174 (1.5%). **1990 percent population under 18:** 27.8; **65 and over:** 13.3; median age: 33.8.

1. Consolidated City.

First explored for France by François and Louis-Joseph Verendrye in the early 1740s, much of the region was acquired by the U.S. from France as part of the Louisiana Purchase in 1803. Before western Montana was obtained from Great Britain in the Oregon Treaty of 1846, American trading posts and forts had been established in the territory.

The major Indian wars (1867–1877) included the famous 1876 Battle of the Little Big Horn, better known as "Custer's Last Stand," in which Cheyennes and Sioux killed George A. Custer and more than 200 of his men in southeastern Montana.

Much of Montana's early history was concerned with mining with copper, lead, zinc, silver, coal, and oil as principal products.

Butte is the center of the area that once supplied half of the U.S. copper.

Fields of grain cover much of Montana's plains; it ranks high among the states in wheat and barley, with rye, oats, flaxseed, sugar beets, and potatoes other important crops. Sheep and cattle raising make significant contributions to the economy.

Tourist attractions include hunting, fishing, skiing, and dude ranching. Glacier National Park, on the Continental Divide, is a scenic and vacation wonderland with 60 glaciers, 200 lakes, and many streams with good trout fishing.

Other major points of interest include the Custer Battlefield National Monument, Virginia City, Yellowstone National Park, Museum of the Plains Indians at Browning, and the Fort Union Trading Post and Grant-Kohr's Ranch National Historic Sites.

NEBRASKA

Capital: Lincoln
Governor: Ben Nelson, D (to Jan. 1995)
Lieut. Governor: Maxine Moul, D (to Jan. 1995)
Secy. of State: Allen J. Beermann, R (to Jan. 1995)
Atty. General: Don Stenberg, R (to Jan. 1995)
Auditor: John Breslow, R (to Jan. 1995)
Treasurer: Dawn Rockey, D (to Jan. 1995)
Organized as territory: May 30, 1854
Entered Union & (rank): March 1, 1867 (37)
Present constitution adopted: Nov. 1, 1875 (extensively amended 1919–20)
Motto: Equality before the law
STATE SYMBOLS: flower, Goldenrod (1895); **tree,** Cottonwood (1972); **bird,** Western meadowlark (1929); **insect,** Honeybee (1975); **gemstone,** Blue agate (1967); **rock,** Prairie agate (1967); **fossil,** Mammoth (1967); **song,** "Beautiful Nebraska" (1967); **soil,** Typie Arguistolls, Holdrege Series (1979); **mammal,** Whitetail deer (1981)
Nicknames: Cornhusker State (1945); Beef State; The Tree Planter State (1895)
Origin of name: From an Oto Indian word meaning "flat water"
10 largest cities (1990 census): Omaha, 335,795; Lincoln, 191,972; Grand Island, 39,386; Bellevue, 30,982; Kearney, 24,396; Fremont, 23,680; Hastings, 22,837; North Platte, 22,605; Norfolk, 21,476; Columbus, 19,480
Land area & (rank): 76,644 sq mi. (198,508 sq km) (15)
Geographic center: In Custer Co., 10 mi. NW of Broken Bow
Number of counties: 93
Largest county (1990 census): Douglas, 416,444
State forests: None
State parks: 78 areas, historical and recreational; 7 major areas
1980 resident census population & (rank): 1,569,825 (35)
1990 resident census population, sex, & (rank): 1,578,385 (36). **Male:** 769,439; **Female:** 808,946. **White:** 1,480,558 (93.8%); **Black:** 57,404 (3.6%); **American Indian, Eskimo, or Aleut:** 12,410 (0.8%); **Asian or Pacific Islander:** 12,422 (0.8%); **Other race:** 15,591 (1.0%); **Hispanic:** 36,969 (2.3%). **1990 percent population under 18:** 27.2; **65 and over:** 14.1; median age: 33.0.

French fur traders first visited Nebraska in the early 1700s. Part of the Louisiana Purchase in 1803, Nebraska was explored by Lewis and Clark in 1804–06.

Robert Stuart pioneered the Oregon Trail across Nebraska in 1812–13 and the first permanent settlement was established at Bellevue in 1823. Western Nebraska was acquired by treaty following the Mexican War in 1848. The Union Pacific began its transcontinental railroad at Omaha in 1865. In 1937, Nebraska became the only state in the Union to have a unicameral (one-house) legislature. Members are elected to it without party designation.

Nebraska is a leading grain-producer with bumper crops of rye, corn, and wheat. More varieties of grass, valuable for forage, grow in this state than in any other in the nation.

The state's sizable cattle and hog industries make Dakota City and Lexington the nation's largest meat-packing center and the largest cattle markets in the world.

Manufacturing has become diversified in Nebraska, strengthening the state's economic base. Firms making electronic components, auto accessories, pharmaceuticals, and mobile homes have joined such older industries as clothing, farm machinery, chemicals, and transportation equipment. Oil was discovered in 1939 and natural gas in 1949.

Among the principal attractions are Agate Fossil Beds, Homestead, and Scotts Bluff National Monuments; Chimney Rock National Historic Site; a recreated pioneer village at Minden; SAC Museum at Bellevue; the Stuhr Museum of the Prairie Pioneer with 57 original 19th-century buildings near Grand Island; the Sheldon Memorial Art Gallery at the University of Nebraska in Lincoln; and the Lied Center for the Performing Arts located on the University of Nebraska campus in Lincoln.

NEVADA

Capital: Carson City
Governor: Robert J. Miller, D (to Jan. 1995)
Lieut. Governor: Sue Wagner, R (to Jan. 1995)
Secy. of State: Cheryl Lau, R (to Jan. 1995)
Treasurer: Bob Seale, R (to Jan. 1995)
Controller: Darrel R. Daines, R (to Jan. 1995)
Atty. General: Frankie Sue Del Papa, D (to Jan. 1995)
Organized as territory: March 2, 1861
Entered Union & (rank): Oct. 31, 1864 (36)
Present constitution adopted: 1864
Motto: All for Our Country
STATE SYMBOLS: flower, Sagebrush (1959); **trees,** Single-leaf pinon (1953) and Bristlecone pine (1987); **bird,** Mountain bluebird (1967); **animal,** Desert bighorn sheep (1973); **colors,** Silver and blue (1983); **song,** "Home Means Nevada" (1933); **rock,** Sandstone (1987); **precious gemstone,** Virgin Valley Black Fire Opal (1987); **semiprecious gemstone,** Nevada Turquoise (1987); **grass,** Indian Ricegrass (1977); **metal,** Silver (1977); **fossil,** Ichthyosaur (1977); **fish,** Lahontan Cutthroat Trout (1981); **reptile,** Desert tortoise (1989)
Nicknames: Sagebrush State; Silver State; Battle-born State
Origin of name: Spanish: "snowcapped"
10 largest cities (1990 census): Las Vegas, 258,295; Reno, 133,850; Henderson, 64,942; Sparks, 53,367; North Las Vegas, 47,707; Carson City, 40,443; Elko, 14,736; Boulder City, 12,567; Fallon, 6,438; Winnemucca, 6,134
Land area & (rank): 109,894 sq mi. (284,624 sq km) (7)
Geographic center: In Lander Co., 26 mi. SE of Austin
Number of counties: 16, plus 1 independent city
Largest county (1990 census): Clark, 741,459
State forests: None
State parks: 20 (150,000 ac., including leased lands)
1980 resident census population & (rank): 800,493 (43)
1990 resident census population, sex, & (rank): 1,201,833 (39). **Male:** 611,880; **Female:** 589,953. **White:** 1,012,695 (84.3%); **Black:** 78,771 (6.6%); **American Indian, Eskimo, or Aleut:** 19,637 (1.6%); **Asian or Pacific Islander:** 38,127 (3.2%); **Other race:** 52,603 (4.4%); **Hispanic:** 124,419 (10.4%). **1990 percent population under 18:** 24.7; **65 and over:** 10.6; **median age:** 33.3.

Trappers and traders, including Jedediah Smith, and Peter Skene Ogden, entered the Nevada area in the 1820s. In 1843–45, John C. Fremont and Kit Carson explored the Great Basin and Sierra Nevada.

In 1848 following the Mexican War, the U.S. obtained the region and the first permanent settlement was a Mormon trading post near present-day Genoa.

The driest state in the nation with an average annual rainfall of only about 7 inches,[1] much of Nevada is uninhabited, sagebrush-covered desert.

Nevada was made famous by the discovery of the fabulous Comstock Lode in 1859 and its mines have produced large quantities of gold, silver, copper, lead, zinc, mercury, barite, and tungsten. Oil was discovered in 1954. Gold now far exceeds all other minerals in value of production.

In 1931, the state created two industries, divorce and gambling. For many years, Reno and Las Vegas were the "divorce capitals of the nation." More liberal divorce laws in many states have ended this distinction, but Nevada is the gambling and entertainment capital of the U.S. State gambling taxes account for 61.3% of general fund tax revenues. Although Nevada leads the nation in per capita gambling revenue, it ranks only fourth in total gambling revenue.

Near Las Vegas, on the Colorado River, stands Hoover Dam, which impounds the waters of Lake Mead, one of the world's largest artificial lakes.

The state's agricultural crop consists mainly of hay, alfalfa seed, barley, wheat, and potatoes.

Nevada manufactures gaming equipment; lawn and garden irrigation devices; titanium products; seismic and machinery monitoring devices; and specialty printing.

Major resort areas flourish in Lake Tahoe, Reno, and Las Vegas. Recreation areas include those at Pyramid Lake, Lake Tahoe, and Lake Mead and Lake Mohave, both in Lake Mead National Recreation Area. Among the other attractions are Hoover Dam, Virginia City, and Great Basin National Park (includes Lehman Caves).

1. Wettest part of state receives about 40 inches of precipitation per year, while driest spot has less than four inches per year.

NEW HAMPSHIRE

Capital: Concord
Governor: Judd A. Gregg, R (to Jan. 1993)
Treasurer: Georgie A. Thomas, R (to Dec. 1992)
Secy. of State: William M. Gardner, D (to Dec. 1992)
Commissioner: Elliot D. Lerner, R
Atty. General: John P. Arnold, R (to March 1993)
Entered Union & (rank): June 21, 1788 (9)
Present constitution adopted: 1784
Motto: Live free or die
STATE SYMBOLS: flower, Purple lilac (1919); **tree,** White birch (1947); **bird,** Purple finch (1957); **songs,** "Old New Hampshire" (1949) and "New Hampshire, My New Hampshire" (1963)
Nickname: Granite State
Origin of name: From the English county of Hampshire
10 largest cities (1990 census): Manchester, 99,567; Nashua, 79,662; Concord, 36,006; Rochester, 26,630; Portsmouth, 25,925; Dover, 25,042; Keene, 22,430; Laconia, 15,743; Claremont, 13,902; Lebanon, 12,183
Land area & (rank): 8,993 sq mi. (23,292 sq km) (44)
Geographic center: In Belknap Co., 3 mi. E of Ashland
Number of counties: 10
Largest county (1990 census): Derry, 29,603
State forests & parks: 175 (96,975 ac.)
1980 resident census population & (rank): 920,610 (42)
1990 resident census population, sex, & (rank): 1,109,252 (41). **Male:** 543,544; **Female:** 565,708. **White:** 1,087,433 (98.0%); **Black:** 7,198 (0.6%); **American Indian, Eskimo, or Aleut:** 2,134 (0.2%); **Asian or Pacific Islander:** 9,343 (0.8%); **Other race:** 3,144 (0.3%); **Hispanic:** 11,333 (1.0%). **1990 percent population under 18:** 25.1; **65 and over:** 11.3; **median age:** 32.8.

Under an English land grant, Capt. John Smith sent settlers to establish a fishing colony at the mouth of the Piscataqua River, near present-day Rye and Dover, in 1623. Capt. John Mason, who participated in the founding of Portsmouth in 1630, gave New Hampshire its name.

After a 38-year period of union with Massachusetts, New Hampshire was made a separate royal colony in 1679. As leaders in the revolutionary cause, New Hampshire delegates received the honor of being the first to vote for the Declaration of Independence on July 4, 1776. New Hampshire is the only state that ever played host at the formal conclusion of a foreign war when, in 1905, Portsmouth was the scene of the treaty ending the Russo-Japanese War.

Abundant water power early turned New Hampshire into an industrial state and manufacturing is the principal source of income in the state. The most important industrial products are electrical and other machinery, textiles, pulp and paper products, and stone and clay products.

Dairy and poultry farming and growing fruit, truck vegetables, corn, potatoes, and hay are the major agricultural pursuits.

Tourism, because of New Hampshire's scenic and recreational resources, now brings over $2.2 billion into the state annually.

Vacation attractions include Lake Winnipesaukee, largest of 1,300 lakes and ponds; the 724,000-acre White Mountain National Forest; Daniel Webster's birthplace near Franklin; Strawbery Banke, restored building of the original settlement at Portsmouth; and the famous "Old Man of the Mountain" granite head profile, the state's official emblem, at Franconia.

NEW JERSEY

Capital: Trenton
Governor: James J. Florio, D (to Jan. 1994)
Secy. of State: Joan Haberle, D (to Jan. 1994)
Treasurer: Douglas Berman, D (to Jan. 1994)
Atty. General: Robert Del Tufo, D (to Jan. 1994)
Entered Union & (rank): Dec. 18, 1787 (3)
Present constitution adopted: 1947
Motto: Liberty and prosperity
STATE SYMBOLS: flower, Purple violet (1913); **bird,** Eastern goldfinch (1935); **insect,** Honeybee (1974); **tree,** Red oak (1950); **animal,** Horse (1977); **colors,** Buff and blue (1965)
Nickname: Garden State
Origin of name: From the Channel Isle of Jersey
10 largest cities (1990 census)[1]: Newark, 275,221; Jersey City, 228,537; Paterson, 140,891; Elizabeth, 110,002; Edison[2], 88,680; Trenton, 88,675; Camden, 87,492; East Orange, 73,552; Clifton, 71,742; Cherry Hill[2], 69,319
Land area & (rank): 7,468 sq mi. (19,342 sq km) (46)
Geographic center: In Mercer Co., 5 mi. SE of Trenton
Number of counties: 21
Largest county (1990 census): Bergen, 825,380
State forests: 11
State parks: 35 (67,111 ac.)
1980 resident census population & (rank): 7,364,823 (9)
1990 resident census population, sex, & (rank): 7,730,188 (9). **Male:** 3,735,685; **Female:** 3,994,503. **White:** 6,130,465 (79.3%); **Black:** 1,036,825 (13.4%); **American Indian, Eskimo, or Aleut:** 14,970 (0.2%); **Asian or Pacific Islander:** 272,521 (3.5%); **Other race:** 275,407 (3.6%); **Hispanic:** 739,861 (9.6%). **1990 percent population under 18:** 23.3; **65 and over:** 13.4; **median age:** 34.5.

1. These are the official 1990 census largest cities. However, the township of Woodbridge, 93,086, is also a legal municipality or city. 2. Census Designated Place.

New Jersey's early colonial history was involved with that of New York (New Netherlands), of which it was a part. One year after the Dutch surrender to England in 1664, New Jersey was organized as an English colony under Gov. Philip Carteret.

In the late 1600s the colony was divided between Carteret and William Penn; later it would be administered by the royal governor of New York. Finally, in 1738, New Jersey was separated from New York under its own royal governor, Lewis Morris.

Because of its key location between New York City and Philadelphia, New Jersey saw much fighting during the American Revolution.

Today, New Jersey, an area of wide industrial diversification, is known as the Crossroads of the East. Products from over 15,000 factories can be delivered overnight to almost 60 million people, representing 12 states and the District of Columbia. The greatest single industry is chemicals and New Jersey is one of the foremost research centers in the world. Many large oil refineries are located in northern New Jersey and other important manufactures are pharmaceuticals, instruments, machinery, electrical goods, and apparel.

Of the total land area, 37% is forested. Farmland is declining. In 1990 there were about 8,100 farms, with over 870,000 acres under harvest. The state ranks high in production of almost all garden vegetables. Tomatoes, asparagus, corn, and blueberries are important crops, and poultry farming and dairying make significant contributions to the state's economy.

Tourism is the second largest industry in New Jersey. The state has numerous resort areas on 127 miles of Atlantic coastline. In 1977, New Jersey voters approved legislation allowing legalized casino gambling in Atlantic City. Points of interest include the Walt Whitman House in Camden, the Delaware Water Gap, the Edison National Historic Site in West Orange, and Princeton University.

NEW MEXICO

Capital: Santa Fe
Governor: Bruce King, D (to Jan. 1995)
Lieut. Governor: Casey Luna, D (to Jan. 1995)
Secy. of State: Stephanie Gonzales, D (to Jan. 1995)
Atty. General: Robert E. Vigil, D (to Jan. 1995)
State Auditor: David W. King, D (to Jan. 1995)
State Treasurer: Tom Udall, D (to Jan. 1995)
Commissioner of Public Lands: Jim Baca, D (to Jan. 1995)
Organized as territory: Sept. 9, 1850
Entered Union & (rank): Jan. 6, 1912 (47)
Present constitution adopted: 1911
Motto: *Crescit eundo* (It grows as it goes)
STATE SYMBOLS: flower, Yucca (1927); **tree,** Pinon (1949); **animal,** Black bear (1963); **bird,** Roadrunner (1949); **fish,** Cutthroat trout (1955); vegetables, Chili and frijol (1965); **gem,** Turquoise (1967); **colors,** Red and yellow of old Spain (1925); **song,** "O Fair New Mexico" (1917); **Spanish language song,** "Asi Es Nuevo Méjico" (1971); **poem,** A Nuevo México (1991); **grass,** Blue gramma; **fossil,** Coelophysis; **cookie,** Bizcochito (1989); **insect,** Tarantula hawk wasp (1989)
Nicknames: Land of Enchantment; Sunshine State
Origin of name: From the country of Mexico
10 largest cities (1990 census): Albuquerque, 384,736; Las Cruces, 62,126; Santa Fe, 55,859; Roswell, 44,654; Farmington, 33,997; Rio Rancho, 32,505; Clovis, 30,954;

Hobbs, 29,115; Alamogordo, 27,596; Carlsbad, 24,952
Land area & (rank): 121,335 sq mi. (314,258 sq km) (5)
Geographic center: In Torrance Co., 12 mi. SSW of Willard
Number of counties: 33
Largest county (1990 census): Bernalillo, 480,577
State-owned forested land: 933,000 ac.
State parks: 29 (105,012 ac.)
1980 resident census population & (rank): 1,302,894 (37)
1990 resident census population, sex, & (rank): 1,515,069 (37). **Male:** 745,253; **Female:** 769,816. **White:** 1,146,028 (75.6%); **Black:** 30,210 (2.0%); **American Indian, Eskimo, or Aleut:** 134,355 (8.9%); **Asian or Pacific Islander:** 14,124 (0.9%); **Other race:** 190,352 (12.6%); **Hispanic:** 579,224 (38.2%). **1990 percent population under 18:** 29.5; **65 and over:** 10.8; **median age:** 31.3.

Francisco Vásquez de Coronado, Spanish explorer searching for gold, traveled the region that became New Mexico in 1540–42. In 1598 the first Spanish settlement was established on the Rio Grande River by Juan de Onate and in 1610 Santa Fe was founded and made the capital of New Mexico.

The U.S. acquired most of New Mexico in 1848, as a result of the Mexican War, and the remainder in the 1853 Gadsden Purchase. Union troops captured the territory from the Confederates during the Civil War. With the surrender of Geronimo in 1886, the Apache Wars and most of the Indian troubles in the area were ended.

Since 1945, New Mexico has been a leader in energy research and development with extensive experiments conducted at Los Alamos Scientific Laboratory and Sandia Laboratories in the nuclear, solar, and geothermal areas.

Minerals are the state's richest natural resource and New Mexico is one of the U.S. leaders in output of uranium and potassium salts. Petroleum, natural gas, copper, gold, silver, zinc, lead, and molybdenum also contribute heavily to the state's income.

The principal manufacturing industries include food products, chemicals, transportation equipment, lumber, electrical machinery, and stone-clay-glass products. More than two thirds of New Mexico's farm income comes from livestock products, especially sheep. Cotton, pecans, and sorghum are the most important field crops. Corn, peanuts, beans, onions, chile, and lettuce are also grown.

Tourist attractions in New Mexico include the Carlsbad Caverns National Park, Inscription Rock at El Morro National Monument, the ruins at Fort Union, Billy the Kid mementos at Lincoln, the White Sands and Gila Cliff Dwellings National Monuments, and the Chaco Culture National Historical Park.

NEW YORK

Capital: Albany
Governor: Mario M. Cuomo, D (to Jan. 1995)
Lieut. Governor: Stan Lundine, D (to Jan. 1995)
Secy. of State: Gail S. Shaffer, D (to Jan. 1995)
Comptroller: Edward V. Regan, R (to Jan. 1995)
Atty. General: Robert Abrams, D (to Jan. 1995)
Entered Union & (rank): July 26, 1788 (11)
Present constitution adopted: 1777 (last revised 1938)
Motto: *Excelsior* (Ever upward)
STATE SYMBOLS: animal, Beaver (1975); **fish,** Brook trout (1975); **gem,** Garnet (1969); **flower,** Rose (1955); **tree,** Sugar maple (1956); **bird,** Bluebird (1970); **insect,** Ladybug (1989); **song,** "I Love New York" (1980)
Nickname: Empire State

Origin of name: In honor of the English Duke of York
10 largest cities (1990 census): New York, 7,322,564; Buffalo, 328,123; Rochester, 231,636; Yonkers, 188,082; Syracuse, 163,860; Albany, 101,082; Utica, 68,637; New Rochelle, 67,265; Mount Vernon, 67,153; Schenectady, 65,566
Land area & (rank): 47,377 sq mi. (122,707 sq km) (30)
Geographic center: In Madison Co., 12 mi. S of Oneida and 26 mi. SW of Utica
Number of counties: 62
Largest county (1990 census): Kings, 2,300,664
State forest preserves: Adirondacks, 2,500,000 ac., Catskills, 250,000 ac.
State parks: 150 (250,000 ac.)
1980 resident census population & (rank): 17,558,072 (2)
1990 resident census population, sex, & (rank): 17,990,455 (2). **Male:** 8,625,673; **Female:** 9,364,782. **White:** 13,385,255 (74.4%); **Black:** 2,859,055 (15.9%); **American Indian, Eskimo, or Aleut:** 62,651 (0.3%); **Asian or Pacific Islander:** 693,760 (3.9%); **Other race:** 989,734 (5.5%); **Hispanic:** 2,214,026 (12.3%). **1990 percent population under 18:** 23.7; **65 and over:** 13.1; **median age:** 33.9,.

Giovanni da Verrazano, Italian-born navigator sailing for France, discovered New York Bay in 1524. Henry Hudson, an Englishman employed by the Dutch, reached the bay and sailed up the river now bearing his name in 1609, the same year that northern New York was explored and claimed for France by Samuel de Champlain.

In 1624 the first permanent Dutch settlement was established at Fort Orange (now Albany); one year later Peter Minuit is said to have purchased Manhattan Island from the Indians for trinkets worth about $24 and founded the Dutch colony of New Amsterdam (now New York City), which was surrendered to the English in 1664.

For a short time, New York City was the U.S. capital and George Washington was inaugurated there as first President on April 30, 1789.

New York's extremely rapid commercial growth may be partly attributed to Governor De Witt Clinton, who pushed through the construction of the Erie Canal (Buffalo to Albany), which was opened in 1825. Today, the 559-mile Governor Thomas E. Dewey Thruway connects New York City with Buffalo and with Connecticut, Massachusetts, and Pennsylvania express highways. Two toll-free superhighways, the Adirondack Northway (linking Albany with the Canadian border) and the North-South-Expressway (crossing central New York from the Pennsylvania border to the Thousand Islands) have been opened.

New York, with the great metropolis of New York City, is the spectacular nerve center of the nation. It is a leader in manufacturing, foreign trade, commercial and financial transactions, book and magazine publishing, and theatrical production.

New York City is not only a national but an international leader. A leading seaport, its John F. Kennedy International Airport is one of the busiest airports in the world. It is the largest manufacturing center in the country and its apparel industry is the city's largest manufacturing employer, with printing and publishing second.

Nearly all the rest of the state's manufacturing is done on Long Island, along the Hudson River north to Albany and through the Mohawk Valley, Central New York, and Southern Tier regions to Buffalo. The St. Lawrence seaway and power projects have opened the North Country to industrial expansion and have given the state a second seacoast.

The state ranks second in the nation in manufacturing with 1,192,400 employees in 1989. The principal industries are apparel, printing and publishing, leather products, instruments and electronic equipment.

The convention and tourist business is one of the state's most important sources of income.

New York farms are famous for raising cattle and calves, producing corn for grain, poultry, and the raising of vegetables and fruits. The state is a leading wine producer.

Among the major points of interest are Castle Clinton, Fort Stanwix, and Statue of Liberty National Monuments; Niagara Falls; U.S. Military Academy at West Point; National Historic Sites that include homes of Franklin D. Roosevelt at Hyde Park and Theodore Roosevelt in Oyster Bay and New York City; National Memorials, including Grant's Tomb and Federal Hall in New York City; Fort Ticonderoga; the Baseball Hall of Fame in Cooperstown; and the United Nations, skyscrapers, museums, theaters, and parks in New York City.

NORTH CAROLINA

Capital: Raleigh
Governor: James G. Martin, R (to Jan. 1993)
Lieut. Governor: James C. Gardner, R (to Jan. 1993)
Secy. of State: Rufus L. Edmisten, D (to Jan. 1993)
Treasurer: Harlan E. Boyles (to Jan. 1993)
Auditor: Edward Renfrow, D (to Jan. 1993)
Atty. General: Lacey H. Thornburg, D (to Jan. 1993)
Entered Union & (rank): Nov. 21, 1789 (12)
Present constitution adopted: 1971
Motto: *Esse quam videri* (To be rather than to seem)
STATE SYMBOLS: flower, Dogwood (1941); **tree,** Pine (1963); **bird,** Cardinal (1943); **mammal,** Gray squirrel (1969); **insect,** Honeybee (1973); **reptile,** Turtle (1979); **gemstone,** Emerald (1973); **shell,** Scotch bonnet (1965); **historic boat,** Shad Boat (1987); **beverage,** Milk (1987); **rock,** Granite (1979); **dog,** Plott Hound (1989); **song,** "The Old North State" (1927); **colors,** Red and blue (1945)
Nickname: Tar Heel State
Origin of name: In honor of Charles I of England
10 largest cities (1990 census): Charlotte, 395,934; Raleigh, 207,951; Greensboro, 183,521; Winston-Salem, 143,485; Durham, 136,611; Fayetteville, 75,695; High Point, 69,496; Asheville, 61,607; Wilmington, 55,530; Gastonia, 54,732
Land area & (rank): 48,843 sq mi. (126,504 sq km) (29)
Geographic center: In Chatham Co., 10 mi. NW of Sanford
Number of counties: 100
Largest county (1990 census): Mecklenburg, 511,433
State forests: 1
State parks: 30 (125,000 ac.)
1980 resident census population & (rank): 5,881,766 (10)
1990 resident census population, sex, & (rank): 6,628,637 (10). **Male:** 3,214,290; **Female:** 3,414,347. **White:** 5,008,491 (75.6%); **Black:** 1,456,323 (22.0%); **American Indian, Eskimo, or Aleut:** 80,155 (1.2%); **Asian or Pacific Islander:** 52,166 (0.8%); **Other race:** 31,502 (0.5%); **Hispanic:** 76,726 (1.2%). **1990 percent population under 18:** 24.2; **65 and over:** 12.1; **median age:** 33.1.

English colonists, sent by Sir Walter Raleigh, unsuccessfully attempted to settle Roanoke Island in 1585 and 1587. Virginia Dare, born there in 1587, was the first child of English parentage born in America.

In 1653 the first permanent settlements were established by English colonists from Virginia near the Roanoke and Chowan Rivers.

The region was established as an English proprietary colony in 1663–65 and its early history was the scene of Culpepper's Rebellion (1677), the Quaker-led Cary Rebellion of 1708, the Tuscarora Indian War in 1711–13, and many pirate raids.

During the American Revolution, there was relatively little fighting within the state, but many North Carolinians saw action elsewhere. Despite considerable pro-Union, anti-slavery sentiment, North Carolina joined the Confederacy.

North Carolina is the nation's largest furniture, tobacco, brick, and textile producer. It holds second place in the Southeast in population and first place in the value of its industrial and agricultural production. This production is highly diversified, with metalworking, chemicals, and paper constituting enormous industries. Tobacco, corn, cotton, hay, peanuts, and truck and vegetable crops are of major importance. It is the country's leading producer of mica and lithium.

Tourism is also important, with travelers and vacationers spending more than $1 billion annually in North Carolina. Sports include year-round golfing, skiing at mountain resorts, both fresh and salt water fishing, and hunting.

Among the major attractions are the Great Smoky Mountains, the Blue Ridge National Parkway, the Cape Hatteras and Cape Lookout National Seashores, the Wright Brothers National Memorial at Kitty Hawk, Guilford Courthouse and Moores Creek National Military Parks, Carl Sandburg's home near Hendersonville, and the Old Salem Restoration in Winston-Salem.

NORTH DAKOTA

Capital: Bismarck
Governor: George A. Sinner, D (to Dec. 1992)
Lieut. Governor: Lloyd Omdahl, D (to Jan. 1993)
Secy. of State: Jim Kusler, D (to Jan. 1993)
Auditor: Robert W. Peterson, R (to Jan. 1993)
State Treasurer: Robert Hanson, D (to Jan. 1993)
Atty. General: Nicholas Spaeth, D (to Jan. 1993)
Organized as territory: March 2, 1861
Entered Union & (rank): Nov. 2, 1889 (39)
Present constitution adopted: 1889
Motto: Liberty and union, now and forever: one and inseparable
STATE SYMBOLS: tree, American elm (1947); **bird,** Western meadowlark (1947); **song,** "North Dakota Hymn" (1947)
Nickname: Sioux State; Flickertail State, Peace Garden State
Origin of name: From the Dakotah tribe, meaning "allies"
10 largest cities (1990 census): Fargo, 74,111; Grand Forks, 49,425; Bismarck, 49,256; Minot, 34,544; Dickinson, 16,097; Jamestown, 15,571; Mandan, 15,177; Williston, 13,131; West Fargo, 12,287; Wahpeton, 8,751
Land area & (rank): 70,665 sq mi. (183,022 sq km) (17)
Geographic center: In Sheridan Co., 5 mi. SW of McClusky
Number of counties: 53
Largest county (1990 census): Cass, 102,874
State forests: None
State parks: 14 (14,922.6 ac.)
1980 resident census population & (rank): 652,717 (46)
1990 resident census population, sex, & (rank): 638,800 (47). **Male:** 318,201; **Female:** 320,599. **White:** 604,142

(94.6%); **Black:** 3,524 (0.6%); **American Indian, Eskimo, or Aleut:** 25,917 (4.1%); **Asian or Pacific Islander:** 3,462 (0.5%); **Other race:** 1,755 (0.3%); **Hispanic:** 4,665 (0.7%). **1990 percent population under 18:** 27.5; **65 and over:** 14.3; **median age:** 32.4.

North Dakota was explored in 1738–40 by French Canadians led by La Verendrye. In 1803, the U.S. acquired most of North Dakota from France in the Louisiana Purchase. Lewis and Clark explored the region in 1804–06 and the first settlements were made at Pembina in 1812 by Scottish and Irish families while this area was still in dispute between the U.S. and Great Britain.

In 1818, the U.S. obtained the northeastern part of North Dakota by treaty with Great Britain and took possession of Pembina in 1823.

North Dakota is the most rural of all the states, with farms covering more than 90% of the land. North Dakota ranks first in the Nation's production of spring and durum wheat, and the state's coal and oil reserves are plentiful.

Other agricultural products include barley, rye, sunflowers, dry edible beans, honey, oats, flaxseed, sugar beets, and hay; beef cattle, sheep, and hogs.

Recently, manufacturing industries have grown, especially food processing and farm equipment. The state also produces natural gas, lignite, salt, clay, sand, and gravel.

The Garrison Dam on the Missouri River provides extensive irrigation and produces 400,000 kilowatts of electricity for the Missouri Basin areas.

Known for its waterfowl, grouse, and deer hunting and bass, trout, and northern pike fishing, North Dakota has 20 state parks and recreation areas. Points of interest include the International Peace Garden near Dunseith, Fort Union Trading Post National Historic Site, the State Capitol at Bismarck, the Badlands, and Fort Lincoln, now a state park, from which Gen. George Custer set out on his last campaign in 1876.

OHIO

Capital: Columbus
Governor: George V. Voinovich, R (to Jan. 1995)
Lieut. Governor: R. Michael DeWine, R (to Jan. 1995)
Secy. of State: Bob Taft, R (to Jan. 1995)
Auditor: Thomas E. Ferguson, D (to Jan. 1995)
Treasurer: Mary Ellen Withrow, D (to Jan. 1995)
Atty. General: Lee I. Fisher, D (to Jan. 1995)
Entered Union & (rank): March 1, 1803 (17)
Present constitution adopted: 1851
Motto: With God, all things are possible
STATE SYMBOLS: flower, Scarlet carnation (1904); **tree,** Buckeye (1953); **bird,** Cardinal (1933); **insect,** Ladybug (1975); **gemstone,** Flint (1965); **song,** "Beautiful Ohio" (1969); **drink,** Tomato juice (1965)
Nickname: Buckeye State
Origin of name: From an Iroquoian word meaning "great river"
10 largest cities (1990 census): Columbus, 632,910; Cleveland, 505,616; Cincinnati, 364,040; Toledo, 332,943; Akron, 223,019; Dayton, 182,044; Youngstown, 95,732; Parma, 87,876; Canton, 84,161; Lorain, 71,245
Land area & (rank): 41,004 sq mi. (106,201 sq km) (35)
Geographic center: In Delaware Co., 25 mi. NNE of Columbus
Number of counties: 88
Largest county (1990 census): Cuyahoga, 1,412,140
State forests: 19 (172,744 ac.)
State parks: 71 (198,027 ac.)
1980 resident census population & (rank): 10,797,630 (6)

1990 resident census population, sex, & (rank): 10,847,115 (7). **Male:** 5,226,340; **Female:** 5,620,775. **White:** 9,521,756 (87.8%); **Black:** 1,154,826 (10.6%); **American Indian, Eskimo, or Aleut:** 20,358 (0.2%); **Asian or Pacific Islander:** 91,179 (0.8%); **Other race:** 58,996 (0.5%); **Hispanic:** 139,696 (1.3%). **1990 percent population under 18:** 25.8; **65 and over:** 13.0; **median age:** 33.3.

First explored for France by La Salle in 1669, the Ohio region became British property after the French and Indian War. Ohio was acquired by the U.S. after the Revolutionary War in 1783 and, in 1788, the first permanent settlement was established at Marietta, capital of the Northwest Territory.

The 1790s saw severe fighting with the Indians in Ohio; a major battle was won by Maj. Gen. Anthony Wayne at Fallen Timbers in 1794. In the War of 1812, Commodore Oliver H. Perry defeated the British in the Battle of Lake Erie on Sept. 10, 1813.

Ohio is one of the nation's industrial leaders, ranking third in the value of manufactured products. Important manufacturing centers are located in or near Ohio's major cities. Akron is known for rubber; Canton for roller bearings; Cincinnati for jet engines and machine tools; Cleveland for auto assembly and parts, refining, and steel; Dayton for office machines, refrigeration, and heating and auto equipment; Youngstown and Steubenville for steel; and Toledo for glass and auto parts.

The state's thousands of factories almost overshadow its importance in agriculture and mining. Its fertile soil produces soybeans, corn, oats, grapes, and clover. More than half of Ohio's farm receipts come from dairying and sheep and hog raising. Ohio is the top state in lime production and among the leaders in coal, clay, salt, sand, and gravel. Petroleum, gypsum, cement, and natural gas are also important.

Tourism is a valuable revenue producer, bringing in over $3 billion annually. Attractions include the Indian burial grounds at Mound City Group National Monument, Perry's Victory International Peace Memorial, the Pro Football Hall of Fame at Canton, and the homes of Presidents Grant, Taft, Hayes, Harding, and Garfield.

OKLAHOMA

Capital: Oklahoma City
Governor: David Walters, D (to Jan. 1995)
Lieut. Governor: Jack Mildren, D (to Jan. 1995)
Secy. of State: John Kennedy, D (to Jan. 1995)
Treasurer: Claudette Henry, R (to Jan. 1995)
Atty. General: Susan Brimer-Loving, D (to Jan. 1995)
Organized as territory: May 2, 1890
Entered Union & (rank): Nov. 16, 1907 (46)
Present constitution adopted: 1907
Motto: *Labor omnia vincit* (Labor conquers all things)
STATE SYMBOLS: flower, Mistletoe (1893); **tree,** Redbud (1937); **bird,** Scissor-tailed flycatcher (1951); **animal,** Bison (1972); **reptile,** Mountain boomer lizard (1969); **stone,** Rose Rock (barite rose) (1968); **colors,** Green and white (1915); **song,** "Oklahoma" (1953)
Nickname: Sooner State
Origin of name: From two Choctaw Indian words meaning "red people"
10 largest cities (1990 census): Oklahoma City, 444,719; Tulsa, 367,302; Lawton, 80,561; Norman, 80,071; Broken Arrow, 58,043; Edmond, 52,315; Midwest City, 52,267; Enid, 45,309; Moore, 40,318; Muskogee, 37,708
Land area & (rank): 68,655 sq mi. (177,817 sq km) (19)

Geographic center: In Oklahoma Co., 8 mi. N of Oklahoma City
Number of counties: 77
Largest county (1990 census): Oklahoma, 599,611
State forests: None
State parks: 36 (57,487 ac.)
1980 resident census population & (rank): 3,025,290 (26)
1990 resident census population, sex, & (rank): 3,145,585 (28). **Male:** 1,530,819; **Female:** 1,614,766. **White:** 2,583,512 (82.1%); **Black:** 233,801 (7.4%); **American Indian, Eskimo, or Aleut:** 252,420 (8.0%); **Asian or Pacific Islander:** 33,563 (1.1%); **Other race:** 42,289 (1.3%); **Hispanic:** 86,160 (2.7%). **1990 percent population under 18:** 26.6; **65 and over:** 13.5; **median age:** 33.2.

Francisco Vásquez de Coronado first explored the region for Spain in 1541. The U.S. acquired most of Oklahoma in 1803 in the Louisiana Purchase from France; the Western Panhandle region became U.S. territory with the annexation of Texas in 1845.

Set aside as Indian Territory in 1834, the region was divided into Indian Territory and Oklahoma Territory on May 2, 1890. The two were combined to make a new state, Oklahoma, on Nov. 16, 1907.

On April 22, 1889, the first day homesteading was permitted, 50,000 people swarmed into the area. Those who tried to beat the noon starting gun were called "Sooners." Hence the state's nickname.

Oil made Oklahoma a rich state, but natural gas production has now surpassed it. Oil refining, meat packing, food processing, and machinery manufacturing (especially construction and oil equipment) are important industries.

Other minerals produced in Oklahoma include helium, gypsum, zinc, cement, coal, copper, and silver.

Oklahoma's rich plains produce bumper yields of wheat, as well as large crops of sorghum, hay, cotton, and peanuts. More than half of Oklahoma's annual farm receipts are contributed by livestock products, including cattle, dairy products, and broilers.

Tourist attractions include the National Cowboy Hall of Fame in Oklahoma City, the Will Rogers Memorial in Claremore, the Cherokee Cultural Center with a restored Cherokee village, the restored Fort Gibson Stockade near Muskogee, and the Lake Texoma recreation area, Pari-Mutuel horse racing at Remington Park in Oklahoma City, and Blue Ribbon Downs in Sallisaw.

OREGON

Capital: Salem
Governor: Barbara Roberts, D (to Jan. 1995)
Secy. of State: Phil Keisling, D (to Jan. 1993)
Treasurer: Tony Meeker, R (to Jan. 1993)
Atty. General: David B. Frohnmayer, R (to Jan. 1993)
Organized as territory: Aug. 14, 1848
Entered Union & (rank): Feb. 14, 1859 (33)
Present constitution adopted: 1859
Motto: "Alis volat Propriis" ("She flies with her own wings") (1987)
STATE SYMBOLS: flower, Oregon grape (1899); **tree,** Douglas fir (1939); **animal,** Beaver (1969); **bird,** Western meadowlark (1927); **fish,** Chinook salmon (1961); **rock,** Thunderegg (1965); **colors,** Navy blue and gold (1959); **song,** "Oregon, My Oregon" (1927)
Nickname: Beaver State
Poet Laureate: William E. Stafford (1974)
Origin of name: Unknown. However, it is generally accepted that the name, first used by Jonathan Carver in 1778, was taken from the writings of Maj. Robert Rogers, an English army officer.

10 largest cities (1990 census): Portland, 437,319; Eugene, 112,669; Salem, 107,786; Gresham, 68,235; Beaverton, 53,310; Medford, 46,951; Corvallis, 44,757; Springfield, 44,683; Hillsboro, 37,520; Lake Oswego, 30,576
Land area & (rank): 96,184 sq mi. (249,117 sq km) (10)
Geographic center: In Crook Co., 25 mi. SSE of Prineville
Number of counties: 36
Largest county (1990 census): Multnomah, 583,887
State forests: 820,000 ac.
State parks: 240 (93,330 ac.)
1980 resident census population & (rank): 2,633,105 (30)
1990 resident census population, sex, & (rank): 2,842,321 (29). **Male:** 1,397,073; **Female:** 1,445,248. **White:** 2,636,787 (92.8%); **Black:** 46,178 (1.6%); **American Indian, Eskimo, or Aleut:** 38,496 (1.4%); **Asian or Pacific Islander:** 69,269 (2.4%); **Other race:** 51,591 (1.8%); **Hispanic:** 112,707 (4.0%). **1990 percent population under 18:** 25.5; **65 and over:** 13.8; **median age:** 34.5.

Spanish and English sailors are believed to have sighted the Oregon coast in the 1500s and 1600s. Capt. James Cook, seeking the Northwest Passage, charted some of the coastline in 1778. In 1792, Capt. Robert Gray, in the *Columbia*, discovered the river named after his ship and claimed the area for the U.S.

In 1805 the Lewis and Clark expedition explored the area and John Jacob Astor's fur depot, Astoria, was founded in 1811. Disputes for control of Oregon between American settlers and the Hudson Bay Company were finally resolved in the 1846 Oregon Treaty in which Great Britain gave up claims to the region.

Oregon has a $5.5 billion wood processing industry. Its salmon-fishing industry is one of the world's largest.

In agriculture, the state leads in growing peppermint, winter pears, fresh plums, prunes, blackberries, boysenberries, filberts, Blue Lake beans, and cover seed crops, and also raises strawberries, hops, wheat and other grains, sugar beets, potatoes, green peas, fiber flax, dairy products, livestock and poultry, apples, pears, and cherries. Oregon is the source of all the nickel produced in the U.S.

With the low-cost electric power provided by Bonneville Dam, McNary Dam, and other dams in the Pacific Northwest, Oregon has developed steadily as a manufacturing state. Leading manufactures are lumber and plywood, metalwork, machinery, aluminum, chemicals, paper, food packing, and electronic equipment.

Crater Lake National Park, Mount Hood, and Bonneville Dam on the Columbia are major tourist attractions. Oregon Dunes National Recreation Area has been established near Florence. Other points of interest include the Oregon Caves National Monument, Cape Perpetua in Siuslaw National Forest, Columbia River Gorge between The Dalles and Troutdale, and Hells Canyon.

PENNSYLVANIA

Capital: Harrisburg
Governor: Robert P. Casey, D (to Jan. 1995)
Lieut. Governor: Mark S. Singel, D (to Jan. 1995)
Secy. of the Commonwealth: Christopher A. Lewis, D (at the pleasure of the Governor)
Auditor General: Barbara Hafer, R (to Jan. 1993)
Atty. General: Ernest D. Preate, Jr., R (to Jan. 1993)
Entered Union & (rank): Dec. 12, 1787 (2)
Present constitution adopted: 1874
Motto: Virtue, liberty, and independence
STATE SYMBOLS: flower, Mountain laurel (1933); **tree,** Hemlock (1931); **bird,** Ruffled grouse (1931); **dog,** Great

Dane (1965); **colors,** Blue and gold (1907); **song,** None
Nickname: Keystone State
Origin of name: In honor of Adm. Sir. William Penn, father of William Penn. It means "Penn's Woodland."
10 largest cities (1990 census): Philadelphia, 1,585,577; Pittsburgh, 369,879; Erie, 108,718; Allentown, 105,090; Scranton, 81,805; Reading, 78,380; Bethlehem, 71,428; Lancaster, 55,551; Harrisburg, 52,376; Altoona, 51,881
Land area & (rank): 44,888 sq mi. (116,260 sq km) (32)
Geographic center: In Centre Co., 2 1/2 mi. SW of Bellefonte
Number of counties: 67
Largest county (1990 census): Allegheny, 1,336,449
State forests: 1,930,108 ac.
State parks: 120 (297,438 ac.)
1980 resident census population & (rank): 11,863,895 (4)
1990 resident census population, sex, & (rank): 11,881,643 (5). **Male:** 5,694,265; **Female:** 6,187,378. **White:** 10,520,201 (88.5%); **Black:** 1,089,795 (9.2%); **American Indian, Eskimo, or Aleut:** 14,733 (0.1%); **Asian or Pacific Islander:** 137,438 (1.2%); **Other race:** 119,476 (1.0%); **Hispanic:** 232,262 (2.0%). **1990 percent population under 18:** 23.5; **65 and over:** 15.4; **median age:** 35.

Rich in historic lore, Pennsylvania territory was disputed in the early 1600s among the Dutch, the Swedes, and the English. England acquired the region in 1664 with the capture of New York and in 1681 Pennsylvania was granted to William Penn, a Quaker, by King Charles II.

Philadelphia was the seat of the federal government almost continuously from 1776 to 1800; there the Declaration of Independence was signed in 1776 and the U.S. Constitution drawn up in 1787. Valley Forge, of Revolutionary War fame, and Gettysburg, the turning-point of the Civil War, are both in Pennsylvania. The Liberty Bell is located in a glass pavilion across from Independence Hall in Philadelphia.

With the decline of the coal, steel and railroad industries, Pennsylvania's industry has diversified, though the state still leads the country in the production of specialty steel. Pennsylvania is a leader in the production of chemicals, food, and electrical machinery and produces 10% of the nation's cement. Also important are brick and tiles, glass, limestone, and slate. Data processing is also increasingly important.

Pennsylvania's nine million agricultural acres produce a wide variety of crops and its 55,535 farms are the backbone of the state's economy. Leading products are milk, poultry and eggs, a variety of fruits, sweet corn, potatoes, mushrooms, cheese, beans, hay, maple syrup, and even Christmas trees.

Pennsylvania has the largest rural population in the nation. The state's farmers sell more than $3 billion in crops and livestock annually and agribusiness and food-related industries account for another $35 billion in economic activity annually.

Tourists now spend approximately $6 billion in Pennsylvania annually. Among the chief attractions: the Gettysburg National Military Park, Valley Forge National Historical Park, Independence National Historical Park in Philadelphia, the Pennsylvania Dutch region, the Eisenhower farm near Gettysburg, and the Delaware Water Gap National Recreation Area.

RHODE ISLAND

Capital: Providence
Governor: Bruce Sundlun, D (to Jan. 1993)
Lieut. Governor: Roger N. Begin (to Jan. 1993)

Secy. of State: Kathleen S. Connell, D (to Jan. 1993)
Controller: Lawrence Franklin, Jr. (civil service)
Atty. General: James E. O'Neil, D (to Jan. 1993)
Entered Union & (rank): May 29, 1790 (13)
Present constitution adopted: 1843
Motto: Hope
STATE SYMBOLS: flower, Violet (unofficial) (1968); **tree,** Red maple (official) (1964); **bird,** Rhode Island Red (official) (1954); **shell,** Quahog (official); **mineral,** Bowenite; **stone,** Cumberlandite; **colors,** Blue, white, and gold (in state flag); **song,** "Rhode Island" (1946)
Nickname: The Ocean State
Origin of name: From the Greek Island of Rhodes
10 largest cities (1990 census): Providence, 160,728; Warwick, 85,427; Cranston, 70,060; Pawtucket, 72,644; East Providence, 50,380; Woonsocket, 43,877; Newport, 28,227; Central Falls, 17,637
Land area & (rank): 1,055 sq mi. (2,732 sq km) (50)
Geographic center: In Kent Co., 1 mi. SSW of Crompton
Number of counties: 5
Largest town (1990 census): North Providence, 32,090
State forests: 11 (20,900 ac.)
State parks: 17 (8,200 ac.)
1980 resident census population & (rank): 947,154 (40)
1990 resident census population, sex, & (rank): 1,003,464 (43). **Male:** 481,496; **Female:** 521,968. **White:** 917,375 (91.4%); **Black:** 38,861 (3.9%); **American Indian, Eskimo, or Aleut:** 4,071 (0.4%); **Asian or Pacific Islander:** 18,325 (1.8%); **Other race:** 24,832 (2.5%). **Hispanic:** 45,752 (4.6%). **1990 percent population under 18:** 22.5; **65 and over:** 15.0; **median age:** 34.

From its beginnings, Rhode Island has been distinguished by its support for freedom of conscience and action, started by Roger Williams, who was exiled by the Massachusetts Bay Colony Puritans in 1636, and was the founder of the present state capital, Providence. Williams was followed by other religious exiles who founded Pocasset, now Portsmouth, in 1638 and Newport in 1639.

Rhode Island's rebellious, authority-defying nature was further demonstrated by the burnings of the British revenue cutters *Liberty* and *Gaspee* prior to the Revolution, by its early declaration of independence from Great Britain in May 1776, its refusal to participate actively in the War of 1812, and by Dorr's Rebellion of 1842, which protested property requirements for voting.

Rhode Island, smallest of the fifty states, is densely populated and highly industrialized. It is a primary center for jewelry manufacturing in the United States. Electronics, metal, plastic products, and boat and ship construction are other important industries. Non-manufacturing employment includes research in health and medical areas, and the ocean environment. Providence is a wholesale distribution center for New England.

Two of New England's fishing ports are at Galilee and Newport. Rural areas of the state support small-scale farming including grapes for local wineries, dairy, and poultry products.

Tourism is one of Rhode Island's largest industries, generating over a billion dollars a year in revenue.

Newport became famous as the summer capital of society in the mid-19th century. Touro Synagogue (1763) is the oldest in the U.S. Other points of interest include the Roger Williams National Memorial in Providence, Samuel Slater's Mill in Pawtucket, the General Nathanael Greene Homestead in Coventry and Block Island.

SOUTH CAROLINA

Capital: Columbia
Governor: Carroll A. Campbell, Jr., R (to Jan. 1995)
Lieut. Governor: Nick Theodore, D (to Jan. 1995)
Secy. of State: Jim Miles, R (to Jan. 1995)
Comptroller General: Earle E. Morris, Jr., D (to Jan. 1995)
Atty. General: T. Travis Medlock, D (to Jan. 1995)
Entered Union & (rank): May 23, 1788 (8).
Present constitution adopted: 1895
Mottoes: *Animis opibusque parati* (Prepared in mind and resources) and *Dum spiro spero* (While I breathe, I hope)
STATE SYMBOLS: flower, Carolina yellow jessamine (1924); **tree,** Palmetto tree (1939); **bird,** Carolina wren (1948); **song,** "Carolina" (1911)
Nickname: Palmetto State
Origin of name: In honor of Charles I of England
10 largest cities (1990 census): Columbia, 98,052; Charleston, 80,414; North Charleston, 70,218; Greenville, 58,282; Spartanburg, 43,467; Sumter, 41,943; Rock Hill, 41,643; Mount Pleasant Town, 30,108; Florence, 29,813; Anderson, 26,184
Land area & (rank): 30,203 sq mi. (78,227 sq km) (40)
Geographic center: In Richland Co., 13 mi. SE of Columbia
Number of counties: 46
Largest county (1990 census): Greenville, 320,167
State forests: 4 (124,052 ac.)
State parks: 50 (61,726 ac.)
1980 resident census population & (rank): 3,121,820 (24)
1990 resident census population, sex, & (rank): 3,486,703 (25). **Male:** 1,688,510; **Female:** 1,798,193. **White:** 2,406,974 (69.0%); **Black:** 1,039,884 (29.8%); **American Indian, Eskimo, or Aleut:** 8,246 (0.2%); **Asian or Pacific Islander:** 22,382 (0.6%); **Other race:** 9,217 (0.3%); **Hispanic:** 30,551 (0.9%) **1990 percent population under 18:** 26.4; **65 and over:** 11.4; **median age: 32.0**

Following exploration of the coast in 1521 by De Gordillo, the Spanish tried unsuccessfully to establish a colony near present-day Georgetown in 1526 and the French also failed to colonize Parris Island near Fort Royal in 1562.

The first English settlement was made in 1670 at Albemarle Point on the Ashley River, but poor conditions drove the settlers to the site of Charleston (originally called Charles Town). South Carolina, officially separated from North Carolina in 1729, was the scene of extensive military action during the Revolution and again during the Civil War. The Civil War began in 1861 as South Carolina troops fired on federal Fort Sumter in Charleston Harbor and the state was the first to secede from the Union.

Once primarily agricultural, South Carolina has built so many large textile and other mills that today its factories produce eight times the output of its farms in cash value. Charleston makes asbestos, wood, pulp, and steel products; chemicals, machinery, and apparel are also important.

Farms have become fewer but larger in recent years. South Carolina grows more peaches than any other state except California; it ranks third in tobacco. Other farm products include cotton, peanuts, sweet potatoes, soybeans, corn, and oats. Poultry and dairy products are also important revenue producers.

Points of interest include Fort Sumter National Monument, Fort Moultrie, Fort Johnson, and aircraft carrier USS *Yorktown* in Charleston Harbor; the Middleton, Magnolia, and Cypress Gardens in Charleston; Cowpens National Battlefield; and the Hilton Head resorts.

SOUTH DAKOTA

Capital: Pierre
Governor: George S. Mickelson, R (to Jan. 1995)
Lieut. Governor: Walter Dale Miller, R (to Jan. 1995)
Atty. General: Mark Barnett, R (to Jan. 1995)
Secy. of State: Joyce Hazeltine, R (to Jan. 1995)
State Auditor: Vern Larson, R (to Jan. 1995)
State Treasurer: G. Homer Harding, R (to Jan. 1995)
Organized as territory: March 2, 1861
Entered Union & (rank): Nov. 2, 1889 (40)
Present constitution adopted: 1889
Motto: Under God the people rule
STATE SYMBOLS: flower, American pasqueflower (1903); **grass,** Western wheat grass (1970); **soil,** Houdek (1990); **tree,** Black Hills spruce (1947); **bird,** Ring-necked pheasant (1943); **insect,** Honeybee (1978); **animal,** Coyote (1949); **mineral stone,** Rose quartz (1966); **gemstone,** Fairburn agate (1966); **colors,** Blue and gold (in state flag); **song,** "Hail! South Dakota" (1943); **fish,** Walleye (1982); **musical instrument,** Fiddle (1989)
Nicknames: Sunshine State; Coyote State
Origin of name: Same as for North Dakota
10 largest cities (1990 census): Sioux Falls, 100,814; Rapid City, 54,523; Aberdeen, 24,927; Watertown, 17,592; Brookings, 16,270; Mitchell, 13,798; Pierre, 12,906; Yankton, 12,703; Huron, 12,448; Vermillion, 10,034
Land area & (rank): 75,952 sq mi. (196,715 sq km) (16)
Geographic center: In Hughes Co., 8 mi. NE of Pierre
Number of counties: 67 (64 county governments)
Largest county (1990 census): Minnehaha, 123,809
State forests: None[1]
State parks: 13 plus 39 recreational areas (87,269 ac.)[2]
1980 resident census population & (rank): 690,768 (45)
1990 resident census population, sex, & (rank): 696,004 (45). **Male:** 342,498; **Female:** 353,506. **White:** 637,515 (91.6%); **Black:** 3,258 (0.5%); **American Indian, Eskimo, or Aleut:** 50,575 (7.3%); **Asian or Pacific Islander:** 3,123 (0.4%); **Other race:** 1,533 (0.2%); **Hispanic:** 5,252 (0.8%). **1990 percent population under 18:** 28.5; **65 and over:** 14.7; **median age:** 32.5.

1. No designated state forests; about 13,000 ac. of state land is forestland. 2. Acreage includes 39 recreation areas and 80 roadside parks, in addition to 12 state parks.

Exploration of this area began in 1743 when Louis-Joseph and François Verendrye came from France in search of a route to the Pacific.

The U.S. acquired the region as part of the Louisiana Purchase in 1803 and it was explored by Lewis and Clark in 1804–06. Fort Pierre, the first permanent settlement, was established in 1817 and, in 1831, the first Missouri River steamboat reached the fort.

Settlement of South Dakota did not begin in earnest until the arrival of the railroad in 1873 and the discovery of gold in the Black Hills the following year.

Agriculture is the state's leading industry. South Dakota is a leading state in the production of rye, wheat, alfalfa, sunflower seed, flaxseed, and livestock.

South Dakota is the nation's second leading producer of gold and the Homestake Mine is the richest in the U.S. Other minerals produced include berylium, bentonite, granite, silver, petroleum, and uranium.

Processing of foods produced by farms and ranches is the largest South Dakota manufacturing industry, followed by lumber, wood products, and machinery, including farm equipment.

The Black Hills are the highest mountains east of the Rockies. Mt. Rushmore, in this group, is famous for the likenesses of Washington, Jefferson, Lincoln, and Theodore Roosevelt, which were carved in granite by Gutzon Borglum. A memorial to Crazy Horse is also being carved in granite near Custer.

Other tourist attractions include the Badlands; the World's Only Corn Palace in Mitchell; and the city of Deadwood where Wild Bill Hickok was killed in 1876 and where gambling was recently legalized to truly recapture the city's Old West flavor.

TENNESSEE

Capital: Nashville
Governor: Ned Ray McWherter, D (to Jan. 1995)
Lieut. Governor: John S. Wilder, D (to Jan. 1993)
Secy. of State: Bryant Millsaps, D (to Jan. 1993)
Atty. General: Charles W. Burson, D (to Aug. 1998)
State Treasurer: Steve Adams, D (to Jan. 1993)
Entered Union & (rank): June 1, 1796 (16)
Present constitution adopted: 1870; amended 1953, 1960, 1966, 1972, 1978
Motto: "Agriculture and Commerce" (1987)
Slogan: "Tennessee—America at its best!" (1965)
STATE SYMBOLS: flower, Iris (1933); **tree,** Tulip poplar (1947); **bird,** Mockingbird (1933); **horse,** Tennessee walking horse; **animal,** Raccoon (1971); **wild flower,** Passion flower (1973); **song,** "Tennessee Waltz" (1965)
Nickname: Volunteer State
Origin of name: Of Cherokee origin; the exact meaning is unknown
10 largest cities (1990 census): Memphis, 610,337; Nashville-Davidson (CC[1]), 510,784; Knoxville, 165,121; Chattanooga, 152,466; Clarksville, 75,494; Johnson City, 49,381; Jackson, 48,949; Murfreesboro, 44,922; Kingsport, 36,365; Germantown, 32,893
Land area & (rank): 41,155 sq mi. (106,591 sq km) (34)
Geographic center: In Rutherford Co., 5 mi. NE of Murfreesboro
Number of counties: 95
Largest county (1990 census): Shelby, 826,330
State forests: 14 (155,752 ac.)
State parks: 21 (130,000 ac.)
1980 resident census population & (rank): 4,591,120 (17)
1990 resident census population, sex, & (rank): 4,877,185 (17). **Male:** 2,348,928; **Female:** 2,528,257. **White:** 4,048,068 (83.0%); **Black:** 778,035 (16.0%); **American Indian, Eskimo, or Aleut:** 10,039 (0.2%); **Asian or Pacific Islander:** 31,839 (0.7%); **Other race:** 9,204 (0.2%); **Hispanic:** 32,741 (0.7%). **1990 percent population under 18:** 24.9; **65 and over:** 12.7; **median age:** 33.6.

1. Consolidated City.

First visited by the Spanish explorer de Soto in 1540, the Tennessee area would later be claimed by both France and England as a result of the 1670s and 1680s explorations of Marquette and Joliet, La Salle, and the Englishmen James Needham and Gabriel Arthur.

Great Britain obtained the region following the French and Indian War in 1763 and it was rapidly occupied by settlers moving in from Virginia and the Carolinas.

During 1784–87, the settlers formed the "state" of Franklin, which was disbanded when the region was allowed to send representatives to the North Carolina legislature. In 1790 Congress organized the territory south of the Ohio River and Tennessee joined the Union in 1796.

Although Tennessee joined the Confederacy during the Civil War, there was much pro-Union sentiment in the state, which was the scene of extensive military action.

The state is now predominantly industrial; the majority of its population lives in urban areas. Among the most important products are chemicals, textiles, apparel, electrical machinery, furniture, and leather goods. Other lines include food processing, lumber, primary metals, and metal products. The state is known as the U.S. hardwood-flooring center and ranks first in the production of marble, zinc, pyrite, and ball clay.

Tennessee is one of the leading tobacco-producing states in the nation and its farming income is also derived from livestock and dairy products as well as corn, cotton, and soybeans.

With six other states, Tennessee shares the extensive federal reservoir developments on the Tennessee and Cumberland River systems. The Tennessee Valley Authority operates a number of dams and reservoirs in the state.

Among the major points of interest: the Andrew Johnson National Historic Site at Greenville, American Museum of Atomic Energy at Oak Ridge, Great Smoky Mountains National Park, The Hermitage (home of Andrew Jackson near Nashville), Rock City Gardens near Chattanooga, and three National Military Parks.

TEXAS

Capital: Austin
Governor: Ann Richards, D (to Jan. 1995)
Lieut. Governor: Bob Bullock, D (to Jan. 1995)
Secy. of State: John Hannah, Jr., D (Apptd. by Gov.)
Treasurer: Kay Bailey Hutchison (to Jan. 1995)
Comptroller: John Sharp, D (to Jan. 1995)
Atty. General: Dan Morales, D (to Jan. 1995)
Entered Union & (rank): Dec. 29, 1845 (28)
Present constitution adopted: 1876
Motto: Friendship
STATE SYMBOLS: flower, Bluebonnet (1901); **tree,** Pecan (1919); **bird,** Mockingbird (1927); **song,** "Texas, Our Texas" (1930); **fish,** Guadalupe bass (1989); **seashell,** Lightning whelk (1987)
Nickname: Lone Star State
Origin of name: From an Indian word meaning "friends"
10 largest cities (1990 census): Houston, 1,630,553; Dallas, 1,006,877; San Antonio, 935,933; Austin, 465,622; Fort Worth, 447,619; Arlington, 261,721; Corpus Christi, 257,453; Lubbock, 186,206; Garland, 180,650
Land area & (rank): 262,017 sq mi. (678,623 sq km) (2)
Geographic center: In McCulloch Co., 15 mi. NE of Brady
Number of counties: 254
Largest county (1990 census): Harris, 2,818,199
State forests: 4 (6,306 ac.)
State parks: 83 (64 developed)
1980 resident census population & (rank): 14,229,191 (3)
1990 resident census population, sex, & (rank): 16,986,510 (3). **Male:** 8,365,963; **Female:** 8,620,547. **White:** 12,774,762 (75.2%); **Black:** 2,021,632 (11.9%); **American Indian, Eskimo, or Aleut:** 65,877 (0.4%); **Asian or Pacific Islander:** 319,459 (1.9%); **Other race:** 1,804,780 (10.6%); **Hispanic:** 4,339,905 (25.5%). **1990 percent population under 18:** 28.5; **65 and over:** 10.1; **median age:** 30.8.

Spanish explorers, including Cabeza de Vaca and Coronado, were the first to visit the region in the 16th and 17th centuries, settling at Ysleta near El Paso in 1682. In 1685, La Salle established a short-lived French colony at Matagorda Bay.

Americans, led by Stephen F. Austin, began to

settle along the Brazos River in 1821 when Texas was controlled by Mexico, recently independent from Spain. In 1836, following a brief war between the American settlers in Texas and the Mexican government, and famous for the battles of the Alamo and San Jacinto, the Independent Republic of Texas was proclaimed with Sam Houston as president.

After Texas became the 28th U.S. state in 1845, border disputes led to the Mexican War of 1846–48.

Today, Texas, second only to Alaska in land area, leads all other states in such categories as oil, cattle, sheep, and cotton. Possessing enormous natural resources, Texas is a major agricultural state and an industrial giant.

Sulfur, salt, helium, asphalt, graphite, bromine, natural gas, cement, and clays give Texas first place in mineral production. Chemicals, oil refining, food processing, machinery, and transportation equipment are among the major Texas manufacturing industries.

Texas ranches and farms produce beef cattle, poultry, rice, pecans, peanuts, sorghum, and an extensive variety of fruits and vegetables.

Millions of tourists spend well over $2 billion annually visiting more than 70 state parks, recreation areas, and points of interest such as the Gulf Coast resort area, the Lyndon B. Johnson Space Center in Houston, the Alamo in San Antonio, the state capital in Austin, and the Big Bend and Guadalupe Mountains National Parks.

UTAH

Capital: Salt Lake City
Governor: Norman H. Bangerter, R (to Jan. 1993)
Lieut. Governor: W. Val Oveson, R (to Jan. 1993)
Atty. General: Paul Van Dam, D (to Jan. 1993)
Organized as territory: Sept. 9, 1850
Entered Union & (rank): Jan. 4, 1896 (45)
Present constitution adopted: 1896
Motto: Industry
STATE SYMBOLS: flower, Sego lily (1911); **tree,** Blue spruce (1933); **bird,** Seagull (1955); **emblem,** Beehive (1959); **song,** "Utah, We Love Thee" (1953)
Nickname: Beehive State
Origin of name: From the Ute tribe, meaning "people of the mountains"
10 largest cities (1990 census): Salt Lake City, 159,936; West Valley City, 86,976; Provo, 86,835; Sandy, 75,058; Orem, 67,561; Ogden, 63,909; Taylorsville-Bennion, 52,351; West Jordan, 42,892; Layton, 41,784; Bountiful, 36,659
Land area & (rank): 82,073 sq mi. (212,569 sq km) (12)
Geographic center: In Sanpete Co., 3 mi. N. of Manti
Number of counties: 29
Largest county (1990 census): Salt Lake, 725,956
National parks: 5
National monuments: 6
State parks/forests: 44 (64,097 ac.)
1980 resident census population & (rank): 1,461,037 (36)
1990 resident census population, sex, & (rank): 1,722,850 (35). **Male:** 855,759; **Female:** 867,091. **White:** 1,615,845 (93.8%); **Black:** 11,576 (0.7%); **American Indian, Eskimo, or Aleut:** 24,283 (1.4%); **Asian or Pacific Islander:** 33,371 (1.9%); **Other race:** 37,775 (2.2%); **Hispanic:** 84,597 (4.9%). **1990 percent population under 18:** 36.4; **65 and over:** 8.7; **median age:** 26.2.

The region was first explored for Spain by Franciscan friars, Escalante and Dominguez in 1776. In 1824 the famous American frontiersman Jim Bridger discovered the Great Salt Lake.

Fleeing the religious persecution encountered in eastern and middle-western states, the Mormons reached the Great Salt Lake in 1847 and began to build Salt Lake City. The U.S. acquired the Utah region in the treaty ending the Mexican War in 1848 and the first transcontinental railroad was completed with the driving of a golden spike at Promontory Summit in 1869.

Mormon difficulties with the federal government about polygamy did not end until the Mormon Church renounced the practice in 1890, six years before Utah became a state.

Rich in natural resources, Utah has long been a leading producer of copper, gold, silver, lead, zinc, and molybdenum. Oil has also become a major product; with Colorado and Wyoming, Utah shares what have been called the world's richest oil shale deposits.

Ranked eighth among the states in number of sheep in 1989, Utah also produces large crops of alfalfa, winter wheat, and beans. Utah's farmlands and crops require extensive irrigation.

Utah's traditional industries of agriculture and mining are being complemented by increased tourism business and growing aerospace, biomedical, and computer-related businesses. Utah is home to computer software giants Novell and WordPerfect.

Utah is a great vacationland with 11,000 miles of fishing streams and 147,000 acres of lakes and reservoirs. Among the many tourist attractions are Arches, Bryce Canyon, Canyonlands, Capitol Reef, and Zion National Parks; Dinosaur, Natural Bridges, and Rainbow Bridge National Monuments; the Mormon Tabernacle in Salt Lake City; and Monument Valley.

VERMONT

Capital: Montpelier
Governor: Howard B. Dean, D (to Jan. 1993)
Lieut. Governor: (vacant) (to Jan. 1993)
Secy. of State: James H. Douglas, R (to Jan. 1993)
Treasurer: Paul W. Ruse, Jr., D (to Jan. 1993)
Auditor of Accounts: Alexander V. Acebo, R (to Jan. 1993)
Atty. General: Jeffrey L. Amestoy, R (to Jan. 1993)
Entered Union & (rank): March 4, 1791 (14)
Present constitution adopted: 1793
Motto: Vermont, Freedom, and Unity
STATE SYMBOLS: flower, Red clover (1894); **tree,** Sugar maple (1949); **bird,** Hermit thrush (1941); **animal,** Morgan horse (1961); **insect,** Honeybee (1978); **song,** "Hail, Vermont!" (1938)
Nickname: Green Mountain State
Origin of name: From the French "vert mont," meaning "green mountain"
10 largest cities (1990 census): Burlington, 39,127; Rutland, 18,230; South Burlington, 12,809; Barre, 9,482; Essex Junction, 8,396; Montpelier, 8,247; St. Albans, 7,339; Winooski, 6,649; Newport, 4,434; Bellows Falls, 3,313
Land area & (rank): 9,273 sq mi. (24,017 sq km) (43)
Geographic center: In Washington Co., 3 mi. E of Roxbury
Number of counties: 14
Largest county (1990 census): Addison, 32,953
State forests: 34 (113,953 ac.)
State parks: 45 (31,325 ac.)
1980 resident census population & (rank): 511,456 (48)
1990 resident census population, sex, & (rank): 562,758 (48). **Male:** 275,492; **Female:** 287,266. **White:** 555,088 (98.6%); **Black:** 1,951 (0.3%); **American Indian, Eskimo, or Aleut:** 1,696 (0.3%); **Asian or Pacific Islander:** 3,215 (0.6%); **Other race:** 808 (0.1%); **Hispanic:** 3,661 (0.7%). **1990 percent population under 18:** 25.4; **65 and over:** 11.8; **median age:** 33.0.

The Vermont region was explored and claimed for France by Samuel de Champlain in 1609 and the first French settlement was established at Fort Ste. Anne in 1666. The first English settlers moved into the area in 1724 and built Fort Drummer on the site of present-day Brattleboro. England gained control of the area in 1763 after the French and Indian War.

First organized to drive settlers from New York out of Vermont, the Green Mountain Boys, led by Ethan Allen, won fame by capturing Fort Ticonderoga from the British on May 10, 1775, in the early days of the Revolution.

In 1777 Vermont adopted its first constitution abolishing slavery and providing for universal male suffrage without property qualifications. In 1791 Vermont became the first state after the original 13 to join the Union.

Vermont leads the nation in the production of monument granite, marble, and maple syrup. It is also a leader in the production of asbestos and talc.

In ratio to population, Vermont keeps more dairy cows than any other state. Vermont's soil is devoted to dairying, truck farming, and fruit growing because the rugged, rocky terrain discourages extensive farming.

Principal industrial products include electrical equipment, fabricated metal products, printing and publishing, and paper and allied products.

Tourism is a major industry in Vermont. Vermont's many famous ski areas include Stowe, Killington, Mt. Snow, Bromley, Jay Peak, and Sugarbush. Hunting and fishing also attract many visitors to Vermont each year. Among the many points of interest are the Green Mountain National Forest, Bennington Battle Monument, the Calvin Coolidge Homestead at Plymouth, and the Marble Exhibit in Proctor.

VIRGINIA

Capital: Richmond
Governor: L. Douglas Wilder, D (to Jan. 1994)
Lieut. Governor: Donald S. Beyer, Jr., D (to Jan. 1994)
Secy. of the Commonwealth: Pamela M. Wornack (apptd. by governor)
Comptroller: Edward J. Mazur (apptd. by governor)
Atty. General: Mary Sue Terry, D (to Jan. 1994)
Entered Union & (rank): June 25, 1788 (10)
Present constitution adopted: 1970
Motto: *Sic semper tyrannis* (Thus always to tyrants)
STATE SYMBOLS: flower, American dogwood (1918); **bird,** Cardinal (1950); **dog,** American foxhound (1966); **shell,** Oyster shell (1974); **song,** "Carry Me Back to Old Virginia" (1940)
Nicknames: The Old Dominion; Mother of Presidents
Origin of name: In honor of Elizabeth "Virgin Queen" of England
10 largest cities (1990 census): Virginia Beach, 393,069; Norfolk, 261,229; Richmond, 203,056; Newport News, 170,045; Chesapeake, 151,976; Hampton, 133,793; Alexandria, 111,183; Portsmouth, 103,907; Roanoke, 96,907; Lynchburg, 66,049
Land area & (rank): 39,704 sq mi. (102,832 sq km) (36)
Geographic center: In Buckingham Co., 5 mi. SW of Buckingham
Number of counties: 95, plus 41 independent cities
Largest county (1990 census): Fairfax, 818,384
State forests: 8 (49,566 ac.)
State parks and recreational parks: 27, plus 3 in process of acquisition and/or development (42,722 ac.)[1]
1980 resident census population & (rank): 5,346,818 (14)
1990 resident census population, sex, & (rank): 6,187,358 (12). **Male:** 3,033,974; **Female:** 3,153,384. **White:** 4,791,739 (77.4%); **Black:** 1,162,994 (18.8%); **American Indian, Eskimo, or Aleut:** 15,282 (0.2%); **Asian or Pacific Islander:** 159,053 (2.6%); **Other race:**

58,290 (0.9%); **Hispanic:** 160,288 (2.6%). **1990 percent population under 18:** 24.3; **65 and over:** 10.7; **median age:** 32.6.

1. Does not include portion of Breaks Interstate Park (Va.-Ky., 1,200 ac.) which lies in Virginia.

The history of America is closely tied to that of Virginia, particularly in the Colonial period. Jamestown, founded in 1607, was the first permanent English settlement in North America and slavery was introduced there in 1619. The surrenders ending both the American Revolution (Yorktown) and the Civil War (Appomattox) occurred in Virginia. The state is called the "Mother of Presidents" because eight chief executives of the United States were born there.

Today, Virginia has a large number of diversified manufacturing industries including transportation equipment, textiles, food processing and printing. Other important lines are electronic and other electric equipment, chemicals, apparel, lumber and wood products, and furniture.

Agriculture remains an important sector in the Virginia economy and the state ranks among the leaders in the U.S. in tobacco, peanuts, apples, and tomatoes. Other crops include corn, vegetables, and barley. Famous for its turkeys and Smithfield hams, Virginia also has a large dairy industry.

Coal mining accounts for roughly 75% of Virginia's mineral output, and lime, kyanite, and stone are also mined.

Points of interest include Mt. Vernon and other places associated with George Washington; Monticello, home of Thomas Jefferson; Stratford, home of the Lees; Richmond, capital of the Confederacy and of Virginia; and Williamsburg, the restored Colonial capital.

The Chesapeake Bay Bridge-Tunnel spans the mouth of Chesapeake Bay, connecting Cape Charles with Norfolk. Consisting of a series of low trestles, two bridges and two mile-long tunnels, the complex is 18 miles (29 km) long. It was opened in 1964.

Other attractions are the Shenandoah National Park, Fredericksburg and Spotsylvania National Military Park, the Booker T. Washington birthplace near Roanoke, Arlington House (the Robert E. Lee Memorial), the Skyline Drive, and the Blue Ridge National Parkway.

WASHINGTON

Capital: Olympia
Governor: Booth Gardner, D (to 1993)
Lieut. Governor: Joel Pritchard, R (to 1993)
Secy. of State: Ralph Munro, R (to 1993)
State Treasurer: Daniel K. Grimm, D (to 1993)
Atty. General: Kenneth O. Eikenberry, R (to 1993)
Organized as territory: March 2, 1853
Entered Union & (rank): Nov. 11, 1889 (42)
Present constitution adopted: 1889
Motto: *Al-Ki* (Indian word meaning "by and by")
STATE SYMBOLS: flower, Rhododendron (1949); **tree,** Western hemlock (1947); **bird,** Willow goldfinch (1951); **fish,** Steelhead trout (1969); **gem,** Petrified wood (1975); **colors,** Green and gold (1925); **song,** "Washington, My Home" (1959); **dance,** Square dance (1979)
Nicknames: Evergreen State; Chinook State
Origin of name: In honor of George Washington
10 largest cities (1990 census): Seattle, 516,259; Spokane, 177,196; Tacoma, 176,664; Bellevue, 86,874; Everett, 69,961; Yakima, 54,827; Bellingham, 42,155; Renton, 41,688
Land area & (rank): 66,511 sq mi (172,264 sq km) (20)
Geographic center: In Chelan Co., 10 mi. WSW of Wenatchee

Number of counties: 39
Largest county (1990 census): King, 1,507,319
State forest lands: 1,922,880 ac.
State parks: 202 (171,700 ac.)[1]
1980 resident census population & (rank): 4,132,156 (18)
1990 resident census population, sex, & (rank):
4,866,692 (18). **Male:** 2,413,747; **Female:** 2,452,945.
White: 4,308,937 (88.5%); **Black:** 149,801 (3.1%); **American Indian, Eskimo, or Aleut,** 81,483 (1.7%); **Other race:** 115,513 (2.4%); **Hispanic:** 214,570 (4.4%). **1990 percent population under 18:** 25.9% **65 and over:** 11.8; **median age:** 33.1.

---

1. Parks and undeveloped areas administered by Parks and Recreation Dept. Game Dept. administers wildlife and recreation areas totaling 762,895 acres.

As part of the vast Oregon Country, Washington territory was visited by Spanish, American, and British explorers—Bruno Heceta for Spain in 1775, the American Capt. Robert Gray in 1792, and Capt. George Vancouver for Britain in 1792–94. Lewis and Clark explored the Columbia River region and coastal areas for the U.S. in 1805–06.

Rival American and British settlers and conflicting territorial claims threatened war in the early 1840s. However, in 1846 the Oregon Treaty set the boundary at the 49th parallel and war was averted.

Washington is a leading lumber producer. Its rugged surface is rich in stands of Douglas fir, hemlock, ponderosa and white pine, spruce, larch, and cedar. The state holds first place in apples, blueberries, hops, and red raspberries and it ranks high in potatoes, winter wheat, pears, grapes, apricots, and strawberries. Livestock and livestock products make important contributions to total farm revenue and the commercial fishing catch of salmon, halibut, and bottomfish makes a significant contribution to the state's economy.

Manufacturing industries in Washington include aircraft and missiles, shipbuilding and other transportation equipment, lumber, food processing, metals and metal products, chemicals, and machinery.

The Columbia River contains one third of the potential water power in the U.S., harnessed by such dams as the Grand Coulee, one of the greatest power producers in the world. Washington has 90 dams throughout the state built for irrigation, power, flood control, and water storage. Its abundance of electrical power makes Washington the nation's largest producer of refined aluminum.

Among the major points of interest: Mt. Rainier, Olympic, and North Cascades. In 1980, Mount St. Helens, a peak in the Cascade Range in Southwestern Washington erupted on May 18th. Also of interest are National Parks; Whitman Mission and Fort Vancouver National Historic Sites; and the Pacific Science Center and Space Needle in Seattle.

WEST VIRGINIA

Capital: Charleston
Governor: Gaston Caperton, D (to Jan. 1993)
Secy. of State: Ken Heckler, D (to Jan. 1993)
State Auditor: Glen Gainer, D (to Jan. 1993)
Atty. General: Mario Palumbo, D (to Jan. 1993)
Entered Union & (rank): June 20, 1863 (35)
Present constitution adopted: 1872
Motto: *Montani semper liberi* (Mountaineers are always free)
STATE SYMBOLS: flower, Rhododendron (1903); **tree,** Sugar maple (1949); **bird,** Cardinal (1949); **animal,** Black bear (1973); **colors,** Blue and gold (official) (1863); **songs,** "West Virginia, My Home Sweet

Home," "The West Virginia Hills," and "This Is My West Virginia" (adopted by Legislature in 1947, 1961, and 1963 as official state songs)
Nickname: Mountain State
Origin of name: Same as for Virginia
10 largest cities (1990 census): Charleston, 57,287; Huntington, 54,844; Wheeling, 34,882; Parkersburg, 33,862; Morgantown, 25,879; Weirton, 22,124; Fairmont, 20,210; Beckley, 18,296; Clarksburg, 18,059; Martinsburg, 14,073
Land area & (rank): 24,282 sq mi. (62,890 sq km) (41)
Geographic center: In Braxton Co., 4 mi. E of Sutton
Number of counties: 55
Largest county (1990 census): Kanawha, 207,619
State forests: 9 (79,081 ac.)
State parks: 34 (72,599 ac.)
1980 resident census population & (rank): 1,949,644 (34)
1990 resident census population, sex, & (rank):
1,793,477 (34). **Male:** 861,536; **Female:** 931,941. **White:** 1,725,523 (96.2%); **Black:** 56,295 (3.1%); **American Indian, Eskimo, or Aleut:** 2,458 (0.1%); **Asian or Pacific Islander:** 7,459 (0.4%); **Other race:** 1,742 (0.1%); **Hispanic:** 8,489 (0.5%). **1990 percent population under 18:** 24.7; **65 and over:** 15.0; **median age:** 35.4.

West Virginia's early history from 1609 until 1863 is largely shared with Virginia, of which it was a part until Virginia seceded from the Union in 1861. Then the delegates of 40 western counties formed their own government, which was granted statehood in 1863.

First permanent settlement dates from 1731 when Morgan Morgan founded Mill Creek. In 1742 coal was discovered on the Coal River, an event that would be of great significance in determining West Virginia's future.

The state usually ranks 3rd in total coal production with about 15% of the U.S. total. It also is a leader in steel, glass, aluminum, and chemical manufactures; natural gas, oil, quarry products, and hardwood lumber.

Major cash farm products are poultry and eggs, dairy products, apples, and feed crops. More than 75% of West Virginia is covered with forests.

Tourism is increasingly popular in mountainous West Virginia and visitors spent $2.475 billion in 1990. More than a million acres have been set aside in 34 state parks and recreation areas and in 9 state forests, and national forests.

Major points of interest include Harpers Ferry and New River Gorge National River, The Greenbrier and Berkeley Springs resorts, the scenic railroad at Cass, and the historic homes in the Eastern Panhandle.

WISCONSIN

Capital: Madison
Governor: Tommy G. Thompson, R (to Jan. 1995)
Lieut. Governor: Scott McCallum, R (to Jan. 1995)
Secy. of State: Douglas J. La Follette, D (to Jan. 1995)
State Treasurer: Cathy S. Zeuske, R (to Jan. 1995)
Atty. General: James E. Doyle, D (to Jan. 1995)
Superintendent of Public Instruction: Herbert J. Grover, Nonpartisan (to July 1993)
Organized as territory: July 4, 1836
Entered Union & (rank): May 29, 1848 (30)
Present constitution adopted: 1848
Motto: Forward
STATE SYMBOLS: flower, Wood violet (1949); **tree,** Sugar maple (1949); **grain,** corn (1990); **bird,** Robin (1949); **animal, Badger; "wild life" animal,** White-tailed deer (1957); **"domestic" animal,** Dairy cow (1971); **insect,** Honeybee (1977); **fish,** Musky (Muskellunge) (1955);

song, "On Wisconsin"; **mineral,** Galena (1971); **rock,** Red Granite (1971); **symbol of peace:** Mourning Dove (1971); **soil,** Antigo Silt Loam (1983); **fossil,** Trilobite (1985); **dog,** American Water Spaniel (1986); **beverage,** Milk (1988)

Nickname: Badger State

Origin of name: French corruption of an Indian word whose meaning is disputed

10 largest cities (1990 census): Milwaukee, 628,088; Madison, 191,262; Green Bay, 96,466; Racine, 84,298; Kenosha, 80,352; Appleton, 65,695; West Allis, 63,221; Waukesha, 56,958; Eau Claire, 56,856; Oshkosh, 55,006

Land area & (rank): 54,426 sq mi. (140,964 sq km) (25)

Geographic center: In Wood Co., 9 mi. SE of Marshfield

Number of counties: 72

Largest county (1990 census): Milwaukee, 959,275

State forests: 9 (476,004 ac.)

State parks & scenic trails: 49 parks, 13 trails (66,185 ac.)

1980 resident census population & (rank): 4,705,767 (16)

1990 resident census population, sex, & (rank): 4,891,769 (16). **Male:** 2,392,935; **Female:** 2,498,834. **White:** 4,512,523 (92.2%); **Black:** 244,539 (5.0%); **American Indian, Eskimo, or Aleut:** 39,387 (0.8%); **Asian or Pacific Islander:** 53,583 (1.1%); **Other race:** 41,737 (0.9%); **Hispanic:** 93,194 (1.9%). **1980 percent population under 18:** 26.4; **65 and over:** 13.3; **median age:** 32.9.

The Wisconsin region was first explored for France by Jean Nicolet, who landed at Green Bay in 1634. In 1660 a French trading post and Roman Catholic mission were established near present-day Ashland.

Great Britain obtained the region in settlement of the French and Indian War in 1763; the U.S. acquired it in 1783 after the Revolutionary War. However, Great Britain retained actual control until after the War of 1812. The region was successively governed as part of the territories of Indiana, Illinois, and Michigan between 1800 and 1836, when it became a separate territory.

Wisconsin leads the nation in milk and cheese production. In 1989 the state ranked first in the number of milk cows (1,760,000) and produced 17.3% of the nation's total output of milk. Other important farm products are peas, beans, corn, potatoes, oats, hay, and cranberries.

The chief industrial products of the state are automobiles, machinery, furniture, paper, beer, and processed foods. Wisconsin ranks second among the 47 paper-producing states.

Wisconsin pioneered in social legislation, providing pensions for the blind (1907), aid to dependent children (1913), and old-age assistance (1925). In labor legislation, the state was the first to enact an unemployment compensation law (1932) and the first in which a workman's compensation law actually took effect. Wisconsin had the first state-wide primary-election law and the first successful income-tax law. In April 1984, Wisconsin became the first state to adopt the Uniform Marital Property Act. The act took effect on January 1, 1986.

The state has over 8,500 lakes, of which Winnebago is the largest. Water sports, ice-boating, and fishing are popular, as are skiing and hunting. Public parks and forests take up one seventh of the land, with 49 state parks, 9 state forests, 13 state trails, 3 recreational areas, and 2 national forests.

Among the many points of interest are the Apostle Islands National Lakeshore; Ice Age National Scientific Reserve; the Circus World Museum at Baraboo; the Wolf, St. Croix, and Lower St. Croix national scenic riverways; and the Wisconsin Dells.

WYOMING

Capital: Cheyenne

Governor: Michael J. Sullivan, D (to Jan. 1995)

Secy. of State: Kathy Karpan, D (to Jan. 1995)

Auditor: Dave Ferri, R (to Jan. 1995)

Supt. of Public Instruction: Diana Ohman, R (to Jan. 1995)

Treasurer: Stanford S. Smith, R (to Jan. 1995)

Atty. General: Joseph B. Meyer, D (apptd. by Governor)

Organized as territory: May 19, 1869

Entered Union & (rank): July 10, 1890 (44)

Present constitution adopted: 1890

Motto: Equal rights (1955)

STATE SYMBOLS: flower, Indian paintbrush (1917); **tree,** Cottonwood (1947); **bird,** Meadowlark (1927); **gemstone,** Jade (1967); **insignia,** Bucking horse (unofficial); **song,** "Wyoming" (1955)

Nickname: Equality State

Origin of name: From the Delaware Indian word, meaning "mountains and valleys alternating"; the same as the Wyoming Valley in Pennsylvania

10 largest cities (1990 census): Cheyenne, 50,008; Casper, 46,742; Laramie, 26,687; Rock Springs, 19,050; Gillette, 17,635; Sheridan, 13,900; Green River, 12,711; Evanston, 10,903; Rawlins, 9,380; Riverton, 9,202

Land area & (rank): 96,989 sq mi. (251,201 sq km) (9)

Geographic center: In Fremont Co., 58 mi. ENE of Lander

Number of counties: 23, plus Yellowstone National Park

Largest county (1990 census): Laramie, 73,142

State forests: None

State parks and historic sites: 17 (58,498 ac.)

1980 resident census population & (rank): 469,557 (49)

1990 resident census population, sex, & (rank): 453,588 (50). **Male:** 227,007; **Female:** 226,581. **White:** 427,061 (94.2%); **Black:** 3,606 (0.8%); **American Indian, Eskimo, or Aleut:** 9,479 (2.1%); **Asian or Pacific Islander:** 2,806 (0.6%); **Other race:** 10,636 (2.3%); **Hispanic:** 25,751 (5.7%). **1990 percent population under 18:** 29.9; **65 and over:** 10.4; **median age:** 32.0.

The U.S. acquired the territory from France as part of the Louisiana Purchase in 1803. John Colter, a fur-trapper, is the first white man known to have entered present Wyoming. In 1807 he explored the Yellowstone area and brought back news of its geysers and hot springs.

Robert Stuart pioneered the Oregon Trail across Wyoming in 1812–13 and, in 1834, Fort Laramie, the first permanent trading post in Wyoming, was built. Western Wyoming was obtained by the U.S. in the 1846 Oregon Treaty with Great Britain and as a result of the treaty ending the Mexican War in 1848.

When the Wyoming Territory was organized in 1869 Wyoming women became the first in the nation to obtain the right to vote. In 1925 Mrs. Nellie Tayloe Ross was elected first woman governor in the United States.

Wyoming's towering mountains and vast plains provide spectacular scenery, grazing lands for sheep and cattle, and rich mineral deposits.

Mining, particularly oil and natural gas, is the most important industry. In 1990, Wyoming led the nation in sodium carbonate (natrona) and bentonite production, and was second in uranium.

Wyoming ranks second among the states in wool production. In January 1989, its sheep numbered 837,000, exceeded only by Texas and California; it also had 1,330,000 cattle. Principal crops include wheat, oats, sugar beets, corn, potatoes, barley, and alfalfa.

Second in mean elevation to Colorado, Wyoming has many attractions for the tourist trade, notably Yellowstone National Park. Cheyenne is famous for its annual "Frontier Days" celebration. Flaming Gorge, the Fort Laramie National Historic Site, and Devils Tower and Fossil Butte National Monuments are other National points of interest.

U.S. Territories and Outlying Areas

PUERTO RICO

(Commonwealth of Puerto Rico)
Governor: Rafael Hernández-Colón, Popular Democratic Party (1989)
Capital: San Juan
Land area: 3,459 sq mi. (8,959 sq km)
Song: "La Borinqueña"
1990 census population: 3,522,037
Language: Spanish (official), English is understood.
Literacy rate: 89%
Labor force (1988): 1,062,000; 23% government, 20% trade, 18% manufacturing, 4% agriculture, 35% other.
Ethnic divisions: Almost entirely Hispanic.
10 largest municipios (1990 census): San Juan, 437,745; Bayamón, 220,262; Ponce, 187,749; Carolina, 177,806; Caguas, 133,447; Mayagüez, 100,371; Arecibo, 93,385; Guaynabo, 92,886; Toa Baja, 89,454; Trujillo Alto, 61,120
Gross national product (FY 1988): $18.4 billion, per capita $5,574; real growth rate: 4.9%
Land use: 8% arable land; 9% permanent crops; 51% meadows and pastures; 25% forest and woodland; 7% other.
Environment: many small rivers and high central mountains ensure land is well watered; south coast relatively dry; fertile coastal plain belt in north.

Puerto Rico is an island about 100 miles long and 35 miles wide at the northeastern end of the Caribbean Sea. Columbus discovered the island on his second voyage to America in 1493. It is a self-governing Commonwealth freely and voluntarily associated with the U.S. Under its Constitution, a Governor and a Legislative Assembly are elected by direct vote for a four-year period. The judiciary is vested in a Supreme Court and lower courts established by law. The people elect a Resident Commissioner to the U.S. House of Representatives, where he has a voice but no vote. The island was formerly an unincorporated territory of the U.S. after being ceded by Spain as a result of the Spanish-American War.

The Commonwealth, established in 1952, has one of the highest standards of living in Latin America. Featuring Puerto Rican economic development is Operation Bootstrap. There are now over 1,600 manufacturing plants which have been created by this program. It has also greatly increased transportation and communications facilities, electric power, housing, and other industries.

The island's chief exports are chemicals, apparel, fish products and electronic products.

Puerto Rico is importantly located between the Dominican Republic and the Virgin Islands group along the Mona Passage—a key shipping lane to the Panama Canal. San Juan is one of the biggest and best natural harbors in the Caribbean.

GUAM

(Territory of Guam)
Governor: Joseph F. Ada
Capital: Agaña
Land area: 209 sq mi. (541 sq km)
1990 population prel.: 132,726
1989 net migration: 7 migrants per 1,000 population
Ethnic divisions: Chamorro, 50%; Filipino, 25%; Caucasian, 10%; Chinese, Japanese, Korean, and other, 15%
Language: English and Chamorro, most residents bilingual; Japanese also widely spoken
Literacy rate: 90%

Labor force (1990): 59,030; 32% government, 68% private
Gross national product (1988 est.): $1.0 billion, per capita $7,675; real growth rate 20%

Guam, the largest of the Mariana Islands, is independent of the trusteeship assigned to the U.S. in 1947. It was acquired by the U.S. from Spain in 1898 (occupied 1899) and was placed under the Navy Department.

In World War II, Guam was seized by the Japanese on Dec. 11, 1941; but on July 21, 1944, it was once more in U.S. hands.

On Aug. 1, 1950, President Truman signed a bill which granted U.S. citizenship to the people of Guam and established self-government. However, the people do not vote in national elections. In 1972 Guam elected its first delegate to the U.S. Congress. The Executive Branch of the Guam government is under the general supervision of the U.S. Secretary of the Interior. In November 1970, Guam elected its first Governor.

Currently, Guam is an unincorporated, organized territory of the United States. It is "unincorporated" because not all of the provisions of the U.S. constitution apply to the territory. It is an "organized" territory because the Congress provided the territory with an Organic Act in 1950 which organized the government much as a constitution would.

Guam's economy is based on two main sources of revenue: tourism and U.S. military spending (U.S. Naval and Air Force bases on Guam). Federal expenditures (most military) in 1989 amounted to more than $680 million, of which more than $300 million went for salaries and more than $100 million for purchases in the local economy.

U.S. VIRGIN ISLANDS

(Virgin Islands of the United States)
Governor: Alexander A. Farrelly
Capital: Charlotte Amalie (on St. Thomas)
1990 est. population: 96,947 (St. Croix, 45,399; St. Thomas, 47,083; St. John, 3,465)
Land area: 132 sq mi (342 sq km): St. Croix, 84 sq. mi. (218 sq km), St. Thomas, 32 sq mi (83 sq km), St. John, 20 sq mi. (52 sq km)
1989 net migration rate: –1 migrants per 1,000 population
Ethnic divisions: West Indian, 74% (45% born in the Virgin Islands and 29% born elsewhere in the West Indies), U.S. mainland, 13%; Puerto Rican, 5%; other, 8%; black, 80%, white, 15%, other, 5%; 14% of Hispanic origin.
Language: English (official), but Spanish and Creole are widely spoken.
Literacy rate: 90%
Labor force (1987): 45,000
Gross domestic product (1985): $1.03 billion, per capita $9,030
Aid: Western (non-U.S.) countries, official development assistance and other official flows, and bilateral commitments (1970–1987): $33.5 million.

The Virgin Islands, consisting of nine main islands and some 75 islets, were discovered by Columbus in 1493. Since 1666, England has held six of the main islands; the other three (St. Croix, St. Thomas, and St. John), as well as about 50 of the islets, were eventually acquired by Denmark, which named them the Danish West Indies. In 1917, these islands were purchased by the U.S. from Denmark for $25 million. Congress granted U.S. citizenship to Virgin Islanders in 1927; and, in 1931, administration was transferred from the Navy to the Department of the Interior. Universal suffrage was given in 1936 to all persons who could read and write the English language. The Governor was elected by popular vote for the first time in 1970; previously he had been appointed by the President of the U.S. A unicameral 15-man legislature serves the Virgin Islands, and Congressional legislation gave the islands a non-voting Representative in Congress.

The "Constitution" of the Virgin Islands is the Revised Organic Act of 1954 in which the U.S. Congress defines the three branches of the territorial government, i.e., the Executive Branch, the Legislative Branch, and the Judicial Branch. Residents of the islands substantially enjoy the same rights as those enjoyed by mainlanders with one important exception: citizens of the U.S. who are residents may not vote in presidential elections.

Tourism is the primary economic activity, accounting for more than 70% of the GDP and 70% of employment. Tourist expenditures are estimated to be over $500 million annually. In 1990, 1,837,642 tourists arrived in the Virgin Islands; about two-thirds were day visitors on cruise ships. The manufacturing sector consists of textile, electronics, pharmaceutical, and watch assembly plants. The agricultural sector is small with most food imported. International business and financial services are a small but growing component of the economy. The world's largest petroleum refinery is at St. Croix.

AMERICAN SAMOA

(Territory of American Samoa)
Governor: Peter T. Coleman
Lieut. Governor: Galeai Poumele
Capital: Pago Pago
1990 census population: 46,638
1989 net migration rate: −11 migrants per 1,000 population
Ethnic divisions: Samoan (Polynesian) 90%; Caucasian, 2%; Tongan 2%; other 6%
Language: Samoan (closely related to Hawaiian and other Polynesian languages) and English; most people are bilingual
Literacy rate: 99%
Labor force (1990): 13,250
Land area: 77 sq mi (199 sq km)
Gross national product (1985): $190 million; per capita, $5,210
Aid (1989): $20.1 million in operational funds and $5.8 million in construction for capital-improvement projects from the U.S. Department of Interior.

American Samoa, a group of five volcanic islands and two coral atolls located some 2,600 miles south of Hawaii in the South Pacific Ocean, is an unincorporated, unorganized territory of the U.S., administered by the Department of the Interior.

By the Treaty of Berlin, signed Dec. 2, 1899, and ratified Feb. 16, 1900, the U.S. was internationally acknowledged to have rights extending over all the islands of the Samoa group east of longitude 1715 west of Greenwich. On April 17, 1900, the chiefs of Tutuila and Aunu'u ceded those islands to the U.S. In 1904, the King and chiefs of Manu'a ceded the islands of Ofu, Olosega and Tau (composing the Manu'a group) to the U.S. Swains Island, some 214 miles north of Samoa, was included as part of the territory by Act of Congress March 4, 1925; and on Feb. 20, 1929, Congress formally accepted sovereignty over the entire group and placed the responsibility for administration in the hands of the President. From 1900 to 1951, by Presidential direction, the Department of the Navy governed the territory. On July 1, 1951, administration was transferred to the Department of the Interior.

The first Constitution for the territory was signed on April 27, 1960, and was revised in 1967.

Congress has provided for a non-voting delegate to sit in the House of Representatives in 1981.

The people of American Samoa are U.S. nationals, not U.S. citizens. Like U.S. citizens, they owe allegiance to the United States.

Fish processing is the main economic activity. In 1988, American Samoa generated approximately $368 million worth of exports, almost exclusively by tuna canneries located in Pago Pago. The canneries are the second largest employer on the islands. Other principal products are fish, pet food, fish meal, mats, and handicrafts.

BAKER, HOWLAND, AND JARVIS ISLANDS

These Pacific islands were not to play a role in the extraterritorial plans of the U.S. until May 13, 1936. President F. D. Roosevelt, at that time, placed them under the control and jurisdiction of the Secretary of the Interior for administration purposes.

The three islands have a tropical climate with scant rainfall, constant wind, and a burning sun.

Baker Island is a saucer-shaped atoll with an area of approximately one square mile. It is about 1,650 miles from Hawaii.

Howland Island, 36 miles to the northwest, is approximately one and a half miles long and half a mile wide. It is a low-lying, nearly level, sandy, coral island surrounded by a narrow fringing reef.

Howland Island is related to the tragic disappearance of Amelia Earhart and Fred J. Noonan during the round-the-world flight in 1937. They left New Guinea on July 2, 1937, for Howland, but were never seen again.

Jarvis Island is several hundred miles to the east and is approximately one and three quarter miles long by one mile wide. It is a sandy coral island surrounded by a narrow fringing reef.

Baker, Howland, and Jarvis have been uninhabited since 1942. In 1974, these islands became part of the National Wildlife Refuge System, administered by the U.S. Fish & Wildlife Service, Department of the Interior.

CANTON AND ENDERBURY ISLANDS

Canton and Enderbury islands, the largest of the Phoenix group, are jointly administered by the U.S. and Great Britain after an agreement signed April 6, 1939. The status of Canton and Enderbury was the subject of negotiations between the U.S., U.K., and Gilbert Islands Governments in 1979. The negotiations resulted in the signing on September 20, 1979, of a Treaty of Friendship between the U.S. and the Republic of Kiribati. The Republic of Kiribati declared its independence on July 12, 1979.

Canton is triangular in shape and is the largest of the eight islands of this group. It lies about 1,600 miles southwest of Hawaii and was discovered at the turn of the 18th century by U.S. whalers. After World War II it served as an aviation support facility, and later as a missile tracking station.

Enderbury is rectangular in shape and is 2.75 miles long by 1 mile wide. It is unpopulated and lies about 35 miles southeast of Canton.

JOHNSTON ATOLL

Johnston is a coral atoll about 700 miles southwest of Hawaii. It consists of four small islands—Johnston Island, Sand Island, Hikina Island, and Akau Island—which lie on a reef about 9 miles long in a northeast-southwest direction.

The atoll was discovered by Capt. Charles James Johnston of *H.M.S. Cornwallis* in 1807. In 1858 it was claimed by Hawaii, and later became a U.S. possession.

Johnston Atoll is a Naval Defense Sea Area and Airspace Reservation and is closed to the public. The administration of Johnston Atoll is under the jurisdiction of the Defense Nuclear Agency, Commander, Johnston Atoll (FCDNA), APO San Francisco, CA 96305.

KINGMAN REEF

Kingman Reef, located about 1,000 miles south of Hawaii, was discovered by Capt. E. Fanning in 1798, but named for Capt. W. E. Kingman, who rediscovered it in 1853. The reef, drying only on its northeast, east and southeast edges, is of atoll character. The reef is triangular in shape, with its apex northward; it is about 9.5 miles long, east and west, and 5 miles wide, north and south, within the 100-fathom curve. The island is uninhabited.

A United States possession, Kingman Reef is a Naval Defense Sea Area and Airspace Reservation, and is closed to the public. The Airspace Entry Control has been suspended, but is subject to immediate reinstatement without notice. No vessel, except those authorized by the Secretary of the Navy, shall be navigated in the area within the 3-mile limit.

MIDWAY ISLANDS

Midway Islands, lying about 1,150 miles west-northwest of Hawaii, were discovered by Captain N. C. Brooks of the Hawaiian bark *Gambia* on July 5, 1859, in the name of the United States. The atoll was formally declared a U.S. possession in 1867, and in 1903 Theodore Roosevelt made it a naval reservation. The island was renamed "Midway" by the U.S. Navy in recognition of its geographic location on the route between California and Japan.

Midway Islands consist of a circular atoll, 6 miles in diameter, and enclosing two islands. Eastern Island, on its southeast side, is triangular in shape, and about 1.2 miles long. Sand Island on its south side, is about 2.25 miles long in a northeast-southwest direction.

A National Wildlife Refuge was set up on Midway under an agreement with the Fish and Wildlife Service of the U.S. Dept. of the Interior.

The Midway Islands are within a Naval Defense Sea Area. The Navy Department maintains an installation and has jurisdiction over the atoll. Permission to enter the Naval Defense Sea Area must be obtained in advance from the Commander Third Fleet (N31), Pearl Harbor, HI 96860.

Midway has no indigenous population. It is currently populated with several U.S. military personnel.

WAKE ISLAND

Total area: 2.5 sq mi. (6.5 sq km)
Comparative size: about 11 times the size of The Mall in Washington, D.C.
Population (Jan. 1990): no indigenous inhabitants; temporary population consists of 11 U.S. Air Force personnel, 27 U.S. civilians, and 151 Thai contractors.
Economy: The economic activity is limited to providing services to U.S. military personnel and contractors on the island. All food and manufactured goods must be imported.

Wake Island, about halfway between Midway and Guam, is an atoll comprising the three islets of Wilkes, Peale, and Wake. They were discovered by the British in 1796 and annexed by the U.S. in 1899. The entire area comprises 3 square miles and has no native population. In 1938, Pan American Airways established a seaplane base and Wake Island has been used as a commercial base since then. On Dec. 8, 1941, it was attacked by the Japanese, who finally took possession on Dec. 23. It was surrendered by the Japanese on Sept. 4, 1945.

The President, acting pursuant to the Hawaii Omnibus Act, assigned responsibility for Wake to the Secretary of the Interior in 1962. The Department of Transportation exercised civil administration of Wake through an agreement with the Department of the Interior until June 1972, at which time the Department of the Air Force assumed responsibility for the Territory.

FEDERATED STATES OF MICRONESIA

Capital: Kolonia (on the island of Pohnpei. A new capital is being built about 6.2 miles (10 km) southwest in the Palikir valley.
Total area: 271 sq mi (703 sq km). Land area, same (includes islands of Pohnpei, Truk, Yap, and Kosrae.
President: Bailey Olter (1991)
Government: A constitutional government in free association with the United States since November 1986.
Population (1990): 104,937, growth rate (1990): 2.6%
Ethnic divisions: Nine ethnic Micronesian and Polynesian groups.
Language: English is the official and common language; major indigenous languages are Trukese, Pohnpeian, Yapase, and Kosrean.
Gross national product (1989 est.): $150 million, per capita $1,500
Economy: Financial assistance from the U.S. is the primary source of revenue, with the U.S. pledged to spend $1 billion in the islands in the 1990s. Micronesia also earns about $4 million a year in fees from foreign fishing concerns. Economic activity consists primarily of subsistence farming and fishing.
Unemployment rate: 80%
Aid: Under the terms of the Compact of Free Association, the U.S. will provide $1.3 billion in grand aid during the period 1986–2001.

On April 2, 1947, the United Nations Security Council created the Trust Territory of the Pacific Islands under which the Northern Mariana, Caroline, and Marshall Islands were placed under the administration of the United States. These islands comprised what is now called the Federated States of Micronesia and only the Republic of Palau is still administered as a Trust Territory. Micronesia was admitted to the United Nations on September 17, 1991.

The Micronesian islands vary geologically from high mountainous islands to low, coral atolls; volcanic outcroppings on Pohnpei, Kosrae, and Truk. The climate is tropical with heavy, year-round rainfall. The islands are located 3,200 miles (5,150 km) west-southwest of Honolulu in the North Pacific Ocean, about three-quarters of the way between Hawaii and Indonesia.

CAROLINE ISLANDS

The Caroline Islands, east of the Philippines and south of the Marianas, include the Yap, Truk, and the Palau groups and the islands of Ponape and Kusqie, as well as many coral atolls.

The islands are composed chiefly of volcanic rock, and their peaks rise 2,000 to 3,000 feet above sea level. Chief exports of the islands are copra, fish products, and handicrafts.

Formerly members of the U.S. Trust Territory of the Pacific, all of the group but Palau joined the Federated States of Micronesia.

MARIANA ISLANDS

(The Commonwealth of The Northern Mariana Islands)

Governor: Lorenzo I. De Leon Guerrero (1989)

1990 population: 43,345. The population of the Commonwealth of the Northern Mariana Islands (CNMI) is concentrated on the three largest inhabited islands: Saipan, the government seat and commerce center, 39,090; Rota, 2,311; and Tinian, 2,118. The CNMI's northern islands have a population of 36. Of the CNMI's total population, approximately 22,063 are registered aliens, a 670% increase since 1980.

Language: English is the official language, but Chamorro and Carolinian are the spoken native tongues. Japanese is also spoken in many of the hotels and shops, reflecting a heavy tourism industry.

Gross Island Product (1989): $512 million

Economy: The government of the CNMI benefits substantially from U.S. financial assistance. A seven-year financial agreement with the U.S.for the years 1986–1992 entitles the Commonwealth to $228 million for capital development, government operations, and special programs. In addition, the CNMI is eligible for categorical federal programs provided to the 50 states.

The Mariana Islands, east of the Philippines and south of Japan, include the islands of Guam, Rota, Saipan, Tinian, Pagan, Guguan, Agrihan, and Aguijan. Guam, the largest, is independent of the trusteeship, having been acquired by the U.S. from Spain in 1898. (For more information, *see* the entry on Guam in this section.) The remaining islands, referred to as the Commonwealth of the Northern Mariana Islands (CNMI) became part of the United States pursuant to P.L. 94-241 as of November 3, 1986.

Tourism is the leading earning export with total visitor expenditures equaling about 37% of the GIP. Seventy-five percent of the tourists are Japanese.

Agricultural products are coffee, coconuts, fruits, tobacco, and cattle.

REPUBLIC OF THE MARSHALL ISLANDS

Capital: Majuro

President: Amata Kabua (1979)

Government: Constitutional government in free association with the United States

Ethnic divisions: almost entirely Micronesian

Religion: predominantly Christian, mostly Protestant

Language: Both Marshallese and English are official languages. Marshallese is a dialect of the Malayo-Polynesian family

1990 population: 43,417, growth rate: 3.2%

Net migration rate (1990): −1 migrant/1000 population

Total land area: 70 sq mi (181.3 sq km), includes the atolls of Bikini, Eniwetok, and Kwajalein

Comparative land area: slightly larger than Washington, D.C.

Economy: Total exports from the Marshall Islands are some $2 million annually, of which copra products account for some 90 percent. Agriculture, marine resources, and tourism are the top development priorities for the Republic of the Marshall Islands (RMI). The government of the RMI is the largest employer with some 2,000 workers. Direct U.S. aid under the Compact of Free Association accounts for some two-thirds of the RMI's 1990 budget of $69 million. The United States and Japan are major trading partners.

GDP (1989 est.): $64 million, per capita: $1,500

The Government of the United States and the RMI signed a Compact of Free Association on October 15, 1986, which became effective as of October 21, 1986. The termination of the Trusteeship Agreement became effective on November 3, 1986. The Marshall Islands were admitted to the United Nations on Sept. 17, 1991.

The Marshall Islands, east of the Carolines, are divided into two chains: the western or Ralik group, including the atolls Jaluit, Kwajalein, Wotho, Bikini, and Eniwetok; and the eastern or Ratak group, including the atolls Mili, Majuro, Maloelap, Wotje, and Likiep. The islands are of the coral-reef type and rise only a few feet above sea level.

Bikini and Eniwetok were the scene of several atom-bomb tests after World War II. In April 1977, some 55 original inhabitants, the forerunner of 450 returnees, were resettled after an absence of 30 years.

Trust Territory of the Pacific Islands

REPUBLIC OF PALAU

Capital: Koror

Total area: 177 sq mi (458 sq km)

Comparative size: slightly more than 2.5 times the size of Washington, D.C.

1990 population: 15,122, growth rate: 0.7%

Gross domestic product (1986): $31.6 million, per capita $2,260

Economy: The economy consists primarily of subsistence agriculture and fishing. Tourism provides some foreign exchange. The Government relies heavily on financial assistance from the United States.

Ethnic divisions: Palauans are a composite of Polynesian, Malayan, and Melanesian races.

Language: Palauan is the official language, though English is commonplace.

Palau is the last member of the Trust Territory of the Pacific Islands and is administered by the United States. The islands are located 528 mi. (850 km) southeast of the Philippines.

The islands vary geologically from the high mountainous main island of Babelthuap to low, coral islands usually fringed by large barrier reefs.

Tabulated Data on State Governments

State	Governor		Legislature[1]					Highest Court[2]		
	Term, years	Annual salary	Membership U[3] L[4]		Term, U[3]	yrs. L[4]	Salaries of members[5]		Members	Term, years	Annual salary[4]
Alabama	4 [10]	70,222 [16]	35	105	4	4	50.00	per diem[21]	9	6	83,880 [6]
Alaska	4	81,648	20	40	4	2	22,872	per annum	5	([9])	99,504
Arizona	4	75,000	30	60	2	2	15,000	per annum	5	6	75,000
Arkansas	4	35,000	35	100	4	2	7,500	per annum	7	8	76,351 [6]
California	4	120,000 [30]	40	80	4 [35]	2 [36]	52,500	per annum	7	12	121,207 [6]
Colorado	4	70,000	35	65	4	2	17,500	per annum	7	10	84,000 [6, 25]

State	Governor Term, years	Governor Annual salary	Legislature[1] Membership U[3]	L[4]	Term, yrs. U[3]	L[4]	Salaries of members[5]		Highest Court[2] Members	Term, years	Annual salary[4]
Connecticut	4[9]	78,000	36	151	2	2	16,760	per biennium	7	8	96,647[6]
Delaware	4[9]	80,000	21	41	4	2	22,173	per annum	5	12	102,600
Florida	4[10]	103,909	40	120	4	2	21,684	per annum	7	6	100,444
Georgia[10]	4	91,092	56	180	2	2	10,509	per annum	7	6	92,778
Hawaii	4	94,780	25	51	4	2	27,000	per year	5	10	78,500[6]
Idaho	4	75,000	42	84	2	2	12,000	per annum[5]	5	6	71,144[6]
Illinois	4	93,266	59	118	4-2	2	35,661	per annum	7	10	93,266
Indiana	4[10]	77,200	50	100	4	2	11,600	per annum	5	(24)	72,765
Iowa	4	72,500	50	100	4	2	16,600	per annum	9	8	72,900[6]
Kansas	4	65,000	40	125	4	2	169	per diem[22]	7	6	59,143[31]
Kentucky	4[7]	79,255	38	100	4	2	100	per diem[22]	7	8	77,497[6]
Louisiana	4	73,440	39	105	4	4	16,800	per annum	7	10	66,566
Maine	4	70,000[16]	35	151	2	2	10,500	per annum[16]	7	7	77,300
Maryland	4[10]	120,000	47	141	4	4	27,000[5]	per annum	7	10	99,000[6]
Massachusetts	4	75,000	40	160	2	2	30,000	per annum	7	(13)	90,450[6]
Michigan	4	106,690[16]	38	110	4	2	45,450[16]	per annum[16]	7	8	106,610
Minnesota	4	109,053	67	134	4[34]	2	27,979[5]	per annum[16]	7	6	89,052[6]
Mississippi	4	63,000	52	122	4	4	10,000	per session[5]	9	8	76,000[6]
Missouri	4	90,312	34	163	4	2	22,862[5]	per annum[5]	7	12	91,594
Montana	4	53,006	50	100	4	2	52.13	per diem[16]	7	8	56,452
Nebraska	4[10]	65,000	49[11]	—	4[11]	—	12,000	per annum	7	6	77,000
Nevada	4	90,000	21	42	4	2	7,800	per biennium	5	6	85,000
New Hampshire	2	79,541	24	(12)	2	2	200	per biennium	5	(13)	88,200[6]
New Jersey[28]	4[10]	130,000	40	80	4[14]	2	35,000[32]	per annum	7	7[15]	112,000[6]
New Mexico	4[7]	90,000	42	70	4	2	75	per diem	5	8	75,000[6]
New York	4	130,000	61	150	2	2	57,500	per annum	7	14	120,000[6]
North Carolina	4[9]	116,316[16]	50	120	2	2	11,124	per annum[16]	7	8	84,456[6]
North Dakota	4	65,200[16]	53	106	4	2	90	per diem[16 23]	5	10	68,342[6]
Ohio	4	100,000	33	99	4	2	38,483[38]	per annum	7	6	96,338
Oklahoma	4	70,000	48	101	4	2	32,000[16]	per annum	(19)	6	77,550[6]
Oregon	4[10]	75,000	30	60	4	2	937[31]	per annum	7	6	74,172[6]
Pennsylvania	4[10]	105,000	50	203	4	2	47,000	per annum	7	10	91,500
Rhode Island	2	69,900	50	100	2	2	5	per diem[17]	5	(18)	117,373
South Carolina	4	99,960	46	124	4	2	10,400	per annum	5	10	91,163[6]
South Dakota	4[10]	63,232	35	70	2	2	8,000	per biennium	5	3[27]	67,288
Tennessee	4	85,000	33	99	4	2	16,500	per annum	5	8	89,772[26]
Texas	4	93,432	31	150	4	2	7,200[5]	per annum	(20)	6	82,000
Utah	4	72,800	29	75	4	2	65	per diem[16]	5	(37)	80,300[6]
Vermont	2	85,977	30	150	2	2	510	per week[29]	5	6	71,355[6]
Virginia	4[7]	108,000	40	100	4	2	17,640[33]	per annum	7	12	99,709[6]
Washington	4	99,600	49	98	4	2	19,900	per annum	9	6	89,300
West Virginia	4[10]	72,000	34	100	4	2	6,500[16]	per annum	5	12	55,000
Wisconsin	4	92,283	33	99	4	2	33,622	per annum	7	10	82,706
Wyoming	4	70,000	30	64	4	2	75[16]	per diem[16]	5	8	66,500

1. General Assembly in Ark., Colo., Conn., Del., Ga., Ind., Ky., Md., Mo., N.C., Ohio, Pa., R.I., S.C., Tenn., Vt., Va., Legislative Assembly in N.D., Ore.; General Court in Mass., N.H.; Legislature in other states. Meets biennially in Calif., Ky., Me., Mont., Nev., N.J., N.C., N.D., Ore., Pa., Texas, Wash. Wyo Legislature meets annually. Regular general session on odd numbered years and a budget session on even numbered years. Ark. General Assembly meets every other year for 60 days in odd numbered years.; meets annually in other states. 2. Court of Appeals in Md., N.Y., Supreme Court of Virginia in Va.; Supreme Judicial Court in Me.; Mass.; Supreme Court in other states. 3. Upper house: Senate in all states. 4. Lower house: Assembly in Calif., Nev., N.Y., Wis.; House of Delegates in Md., Va., W.Va.; General Assembly in N.J.; House of Representatives in other states. 5. Does not include additional payments for expenses, mileage, special sessions, etc., or additional per diem payments beyond salary shown. 6. In some states, Chief Justice receives a higher salary. 7. Cannot succeed himself. 8. Appointed for 3 years; thereafter subject to approval or rejection on a nonpartisan ballot for 10-year term. 9. May serve only 2 terms, consecutive or otherwise. 10. May not serve 3rd consecutive term. 11. Unicameral legislature. 12. Constitutional number: 375-400. 13. Until 70 years old. 14. When term begins in Jan. of 2nd year following U.S. census, term shall be 2 years. 15. 2nd term receive tenure, mandatory retirement at 70. 16. Plus additional expenses. 17. For 60 days only. 18. Term of good behavior. 19. 9 members in Supreme Court, highest in civil cases; 5 in Court of Criminal Appeals. 20. 9 members in Supreme Court, highest in civil cases; 9 in Court of Criminal Appeals. 21. Five days a week when the Legislature is in session plus $2,280 per month in expenses. 22. When in session. 23. Plus $180 per month when not in session. 24. Appointed for 2 years; thereafter elected popularly for 10-year term. 25. Beginning FY 1993. 26. Adjusted annually according to increase in Consumer Price Index. 27. Subsequent terms, 8 years. 28. Governor has refused to accept the raise because of budget crisis. 29. To limit of $13,000 per biennium; $100 per diem for Special Session. 30. Governor remitted $6,000 for his salary to the state for current fiscal year. 31. Plus $400 monthly when not in session and per diem allowance when in session. 32. Each legislator receives $60,000 annually for appointment of personal staff aides. 33. Senate $18,000. 34. Every 10 years (the year after census) term is only for 2 years. 35. From 1991 onwards 2 terms or 8-year limit. 36. From 1991 onwards 3 terms or 6-year limit. 37. Appointed by governor. Up for re-election at first general election that takes place at least 3 years after appointment. After that, face a retention election every 10 years. 38. Senator's salary higher. NOTE: Salaries are rounded to nearest dollar. *Source: Information Please* questionnaires to the states.

50 Largest Cities of the United States

(According to the 1990 Census.)

Data supplied by Bureau of the Census and by the cities in response to *Information Please* questionnaires. Ranking of 50 largest cities (April 1990 census data). Civilian labor force (April 1991); Percent employed and unemployed (April 1991); Per capita personal income (1989); avg. daily temp.: *(County and City Data Book).* NOTE: Persons of Hispanic origin may be of any race.

ALBUQUERQUE, N.M.

Incorporated as city: 1891
Mayor: Louis E. Saavedra (to Dec. 1993)
1980 population (1980 census) & (rank): 332,920 (44)
1990 census population, sex & (rank): 384,736 (38); **% change,** 15.6; **Male,** 186,584; **Female,** 198,152; **White,** 301,010; **Black,** 11,484 (3.0%); **American Indian, Eskimo, or Aleut,** 11,708 (3.0%0; **Asian or Pacific Islander,** 6,660 (1.7%); **Other race,** 53.874; **Hispanic origin,** 132,706 (34.5%). **1990 percent population under 18:** 25.0%; **65 and over:** 11.1%; **median age:** 32.5.
Land area: 135 sq mi. (350 sq km)
Altitude: 4,958 ft.
Avg. daily temp: Jan., 34.8° F; July, 78.8° F
Location: Central part of state on Rio Grande River
County: Bernalillo
Churches: 211
City-owned parks: 160
Radio stations: 43 (AM, 19; FM, 24)
Television stations: 11
CIVILIAN LABOR FORCE: 215,752
Unemployed: 11,779, **Percent:** 5.5
Per capita personal income: $15,806
Chamber of Commerce: Greater Albuquerque Chamber of Commerce, 401 2nd St., N.W., Albuquerque, N.M. 87102. Albuquerque Hispano Chamber of Commerce, 1520 Central Ave., S.E., Albuquerque, N.M. 87106

ATLANTA, GA.

Incorporated as city: 1847
Mayor: Maynard Jackson (to Jan. 1994)
1980 population (1980 census) & (rank): 425,022 (29)
1990 census population, sex, & (rank): 394,017 (32); **% change,** −7.3; **Male,** 187,877; **Female,** 206,140; **White,** 122,327; **Black,** 264,262 (67.1%); **American Indian, Eskimo, or Aleut,** 563 (0.1%); **Asian or Pacific Islander,** 3,498 (0.9%); **Other race,** 3,367; **Hispanic origin,** 7,525 (1.9%). **1990 percent population under 18:** 24.1; **65 and over:** 11.3; **median age:** 31.5.
City land area: 136 sq mi. (352.2 sq km)
Altitude: Highest, 1,050 ft; lowest, 940
Avg. daily temp.: Jan., 41.9° F; July, 78.6° F
Location: In northwest central part of state, on Chattahoochee River
Counties: Fulton and DeKalb
Churches (18-county area): 1,500
City-owned parks: 277 (3,178 ac.)
Radio stations (18-county area): AM, 7; FM, 20
Television stations (18-county area): 7 commercial; 2 PBS
CIVILIAN LABOR FORCE: 223,205
Unemployed: 15,477, **Percent:** 6.9
Per capita personal income: $19,055
Chamber of Commerce: Atlanta Chamber of Commerce, 235 International Blvd., Atlanta, Ga. 30301; Information is gathered on the 18-county MSA

AUSTIN, TEX.

Incorporated as city: 1839
Mayor: Bruce Todd (to May 1994)
1980 population (1980 census) & (rank): 345,890 (42)
1990 census population, sex, & (rank): 465,622 (27); **% change,** 34.6; **Male,** 232,473; **Female,** 233,149; **White,** 328,542; **Black,** 57,868 (12.4%); **American Indian, Eskimo, or Aleut:,** 1,756 (0.4%); **Asian or Pacific Islander,** 14,141 (3.0%); **Other race,** 63,315; **Hispanic origin,** 106,868 (23.0%). **1990 percent population under 18:** 23.1%; **65 and over:** 7.4%; **median age:** 28.9
Land area: 116 sq mi. (300 sq km)
Altitude: From 425 ft. to over 1000 ft. elevation
Avg. daily temp.: Jan., 49.1° F; July, 84.7° F
Location: In south central part of state, on the Colorado River
County: Seat of Travis Co.
Churches: 353 churches, representing 45 denominations
City-owned parks and playgrounds: 169 (11,800 ac.)
Radio stations: AM, 6; FM, 12
Television stations: 3 commercial; 1 PBS; 1 independent
CIVILIAN LABOR FORCE: 286,392
Unemployed: 14,279, **Percent:** 5.0
Per capita personal income: $16,113
Chamber of Commerce: Greater Austin Chamber of Commerce, P.O. Box 1967, Austin, Tex. 78767

BALTIMORE, MD.

Incorporated as city: 1797
Mayor: Kurt L. Schmoke (to Dec. 1991)
1980 population (1980 census) & (rank): 786,741 (10)
1990 census population, sex, & (rank): 736,014 (13); **% change,** −6.4; **Male,** 343,513; **Female,** 392,501; **White,** 287,753; **Black,** 435,768 (59.2%); **American Indian, Eskimo, or Aleut,** 2,555 (0.3%); **Asian or Pacific Islander,** 7,942 (1.1%); **Other race,** 1,996; **Hispanic origin,** 7,602 (1.0%). **1990 percent population under 18:** 24.4; **65 and over:** 13.7; **Median age:** 32.6.
Land area: 80.3 sq mi. (208 sq km)
Altitude: Highest, 490 ft; lowest, sea level
Avg. daily temp.: Jan., 35.5° F; July, 79.9° F
Location: On Patapsco River, about 12 mi. from Chesapeake Bay
County: Independent city
Churches: Roman Catholic, 72; Jewish, 50; Protestant and others, 344
City-owned parks: 347 park areas and tracts (6,314 ac.)
Radio stations: AM, 10; FM, 11
Television stations: 7 (including Home Shopping Network)
CIVILIAN LABOR FORCE: 346,187
Unemployed: 29,775, **Percent:** 8.6
Per capita personal income: $20,267
Chamber of Commerce: Greater Baltimore Committee, 111 S. Calvert St., Ste. 1500, Baltimore, Md. 21202

BOSTON, MASS.

Incorporated as city: 1822
Mayor: Raymond L. Flynn (to Jan. 1992)
1980 population (1980 census) & (rank): 562,994 (20)
1990 census population, sex, & (rank): 574,283 (20); **% change,** 2.0; **Male,** 275,972; **Female,** 298,311; **White,** 360,875; **Black,** 146,945 (25.6%); **American Indian, Eskimo, or Aleut,** 1,884 (0.3%); **Asian or Pacific Islander,** 30,388 (5.3%); **Other race,** 34,191; **Hispanic**

origin, 61,955 (10.8%). **1990 percent population under 18:** 19.1; **65 and over:** 11.5; **median age:** 30.3.
Land area: 47.2 sq mi. (122 sq km)
Altitude: Highest, 330 ft; lowest, sea level
Avg. daily temp.: Jan., 29.6° F; July, 73.5° F
Location: On Massachusetts Bay, at mouths of Charles and Mystic Rivers
County: Seat of Suffolk Co.
Churches: Protestant, 187; Roman Catholic, 72; Jewish, 28; others, 100
City-owned parks, playgrounds, etc.: 2,276.36 ac.
Radio stations: AM, 9; FM, 12
Television stations: 10
CIVILIAN LABOR FORCE: 297,200
Unemployed: 22,917, **Percent:** 7.7
Per capita personal income: $23,746[1]
Chamber of Commerce: Boston Chamber of Commerce, 600 Atlantic Ave., Boston, Mass. 02210
1. Boston-Lawrence-Salem-Lowell-Brockton NECMA.

BUFFALO, N.Y.

Incorporated as city: 1832
Mayor: James Griffin (to Dec. 1993)
1980 population (1980 census) & (rank): 357,870 (39)
1990 census population, sex, & (rank): 328,123 (50); **% change,** –8.3; **Male,** 153,050; **Female,** 175,073; **White,** 212,449; **Black,** 100,579 (30.7%); **American Indian, Eskimo, or Aleut,** 2,547 (0.8%); **Asian or Pacific Islander,** 3,261 (1.0%); **Other race,** 9,287; **Hispanic origin,** 16,129 (4.9%). **1990 percent population under 18:** 24.2%; **65 and over:** 14.8%; **median age:** 32.0.
Land area: 42.67 sq. mi. (109 sq. km)
Altitude: Highest 705 ft; lowest 571.84 ft
Avg. daily temp.: Jan., 23.5° F; July, 70.7° F
Location: At east end of Lake Erie, on Niagara River
County: Seat of Erie Co.
Churches: 60 denominations, with over 1,100 churches
County-owned parks: 9 public parks (3,000 ac.)
Radio stations: AM 10; FM 13
Television stations: 8 (plus reception from 3 Canadian stations)
CIVILIAN LABOR FORCE: 147,794
Unemployed: 14,252, **Percent:** 9.6
Per capita personal income: $17,724[1]
Chamber of Commerce: Greater Buffalo Chamber of Commerce, 107 Delaware Avenue, Buffalo, N.Y. 14202
1. PMSA.

CHARLOTTE, N.C.

Incorporated as city: 1768
Mayor: Sue Myrick (to Nov. 1991)
1980 population (1980 census) & (rank): 315,474 (47)
1990 census population, sex, & (rank): 395,934 (35); **% change,** 25.5; **Male,** 188,088; **Female,** 207,846; **White,** 259,760; **Black,** 125,827 (31.8%); **American Indian, Eskimo, or Aleut,** 1,425 (0.4%); **Asian or Pacific Islander,** 7,211 (1.8%); **Other race,** 1,711; **Hispanic origin,** 5,571 (1.4%). **1990 percent population under 18:** 24.2%; **65 and over:** 9.8%; **median age:** 32.1.
Land area: 175.59 sq mi. (455 sq km)
Altitude: 765 ft
Avg. daily temp.: Jan., 40.5° F; July, 78.5° F
Location: In the southern part of state near the border of South Carolina
County: Seat of Mecklenburg Co.
Churches: Protestant, over 400; Roman Catholic, 8; Jewish, 3; Greek Orthodox, 1
City-owned parks and parkways: 120
Radio stations: AM, 8; FM, 12

Television stations: 4 commercial; 2 PBS
CIVILIAN LABOR FORCE: 220,378
Unemployed: 9,402, **Percent:** 4.3
Per capita personal income: $17,377[1]
Chamber of Commerce: Charlotte Chamber, P.O. Box 32785, Charlotte, N.C., 28232
1. Charlotte-Gastonia Rock Hill, N.C.-S.C. MSA.

CHICAGO, ILL.

Incorporated as city: 1837
Mayor: Richard M. Daley (to April 1995)
1980 population (1980 census) & (rank): 3,005,072 (2)
1990 census population, sex, & (rank): 2,783,726 (3); **% change,** –7.4; **Male,** 1,334,705; **Female,** 1,449,021; **White,** 1,263,524; **Black,** 1,087,711 (39.1%); **American Indian, Eskimo, or Aleut,** 7,064 (0.3%); **Asian or Pacific Islander,** 104,118 (3.7%); **Other race,** 321,309; **Hispanic origin,** 545,852 (19.6%). **1990 percent population under 18:** 26.0%; **65 and over:** 11.9%; **median age:** 31.3.
Land area: 228.475 sq mi. (592 sq km)
Altitude: Highest, 672 ft; lowest, 578.5
Avg. daily temp.: Jan., 21.4° F; July, 73.0° F
Location: On lower west shore of Lake Michigan
County: Seat of Cook Co.
Churches: Protestant, 850; Roman Catholic, 252; Jewish, 51
City-owned parks: 563
Radio stations: AM, 17; FM, 23
Television stations: 12
CIVILIAN LABOR FORCE: 1,434,029
Unemployed: 108,833, **Percent:** 7.6
Per capita personal income: $20,349[1]
Chamber of Commerce: Chicago Association of Commerce & Industry, 200 N. LaSalle, Chicago, Ill. 60601
1. PMSA.

CINCINNATI, OHIO

Incorporated as city: 1819
Mayor: David Mann (to Nov. 1991)
City Manager: Gerald Newfarmer
1980 population (1980 census) & (rank): 385,409 (32)
1990 census population, sex, & (rank): 364,040 (45); **% change,** –5.5; **Male,** 169,305; **Female,** 194,735; **White,** 220,285; **Black,** 138,1312 (37.9%); **American Indian, Eskimo, or Aleut,** 660 (0.2%); **Asian or Pacific Islander,** 4,030 (1.1%); **Other race,** 933; **Hispanic origin,** 2,386 (0.7%). **1990 percent population under 18:** 25.1%; **65 and over:** 13.9%; **median age:** 30.9.
Land area: 78.1 sq mi. (202 sq km)
Altitude: Highest, 960 ft; lowest, 441
Avg. daily temp.: Jan., 30.3° F; July, 76.1° F
Location: In southwestern corner of state on Ohio River
County: Seat of Hamilton Co.
Churches: 850
City-owned parks: 96 (4,345 ac.)
Radio stations: AM, 10; FM, 15 (Greater Cincinnati)
Television stations: 8
CIVILIAN LABOR FORCE: 207,221
Unemployed: 12,709, **Percent:** 6.1
Per capita personal income: $17,624[1]
Chamber of Commerce: Cincinnati Chamber of Commerce, 441 Vine St. Suite 300, Cincinnati, Ohio 45202
1. PMSA.

CLEVELAND, OHIO

Incorporated as city: 1836
Mayor: Michael R. White (to Dec. 1993)
1980 population (1980 census) & (rank): 573,822 (18)

1990 census population, sex, & (rank): 505,616 (24); % change, −11.9; **Male,** 237,211; **Female,** 268,405; **White,** 250,234; **Black,** 235,405 (46.6%); **American Indian, Eskimo, or Aleut,** 1,562 (0.3%); **Asian or Pacific Islander,** 5,115 (1.0%); **Other race,** 13,300; **Hispanic origin,** 23,197 (4.6%). **1990 percent population under 18:** 26.9; **65 and over:** 14.0; **median age:** 31.9.
Land area: 79 sq mi. (205 sq km)
Altitude: Highest, 1048 ft.; lowest, 573
Avg. daily temp.: Jan., 25.5° F; July, 71.6° F
Location: On Lake Erie at mouth of Cuyahoga River
County: Seat of Cuyahoga Co.
Churches: [1] Protestant, 980; Roman Catholic, 187; Jewish, 31; Eastern Orthodox, 22
City-owned parks: 41 (1,930 ac.)
Radio stations: AM, 15; FM, 17
Television stations: 7
CIVILIAN LABOR FORCE: 246,086
Unemployed: 22,208, **Percent:** 9.0
Per capita personal income: $19,395[1]
Chamber of Commerce: Greater Cleveland Growth Association, 690 Huntington Building, Cleveland, Ohio 44115
1. PMSA.

COLUMBUS, OHIO

Incorporated as city: 1834
Mayor: Dana G. Rinehart (to Jan. 1992)
1980 population (1980 census) & (rank): 565,021 (19)
1990 census population, sex, & (rank): 632,910 (16); % change, 12.0; **Male,** 305,574; **Female,** 327,336; **White,** 471,025; **Black,** 142,748 (22.6%); **American Indian, Eskimo, or Aleut,** 1,469 (0.2%); **Asian or Pacific Islander,** 14,993 (2.4%); **Other race,** 2,675; **Hispanic origin,** 6,741 (1.1%). **1990 percent population under 18:** 23.7; **65 and over:** 9.2; **median age:** 29.4.
Land area: 196.151 sq mi. (508 sq km)
Altitude: Highest, 902 ft; lowest, 702
Avg. daily temp.: Jan., 27.1° F; July, 73.8° F
Location: In central part of state, on Scioto River
County: Seat of Franklin Co.
Churches: Protestant, 436; Roman Catholic, 62; Jewish, 5; Other, 8
City-owned parks: 200 (12,293 ac.)
Radio stations: AM, 10; FM, 15
Television stations: 8 commercial, 3 PBS
CIVILIAN LABOR FORCE: 343,288
Unemployed: 17,267, **Percent:** 5.0
Per capita personal income: $17,178
Chamber of Commerce: Columbus Area Chamber of Commerce, P.O. Box 1527, Columbus, Ohio 43216

DALLAS, TEX.

Incorporated as city: 1856
Mayor: Annette Strauss (to Nov. 1991)
City Manager: Jan Hart (apptd. April 1990)
1980 population (1980 census) & (rank): 904,599 (7)
1990 census population, sex, & (rank): 1,006,877 (8); % change, 11.3; **Male,** 495,141; **Female,** 511,736; **White,** 556,760; **Black,** 296,994 (29.5%); **American Indian, Eskimo, or Aleut,** 4,792 (0.5%); **Asian or Pacific Islander,** 21,952 (2.2%); **Other race,** 126,379; **Hispanic origin,** 210,240 (20.9%). **1990 percent population under 18:** 25.0; **65 and over:** 9.7; **median age:** 30.6.
Land area: 378 sq mi. (979 sq km)
Altitude: Highest, 750 ft; lowest, 375
Avg. daily temp.: Jan., 45.0° F; July, 86.3° F
Location: In northeastern part of state, on Trinity River
County: Seat of Dallas Co.

Churches: 1,974 (in Dallas Co.)
City-owned parks: 296 (47,025 ac.)
Radio stations: AM, 19; FM, 30
Television stations: 10 commercial, 1 PBS
CIVILIAN LABOR FORCE: 649,527
Unemployed: 46,410, **Percent:** 7.1
Per capita personal income: $19,485[1]
Chamber of Commerce: Dallas Chamber of Commerce, 1201 Elm, Dallas, Tex. 75270
1. PMSA.

DENVER, COLO.

Incorporated as city: 1861
Mayor: Wellington Webb (to July 1995)
1980 population (1980 census) & (rank): 492,686 (24)
1990 census population, sex, & (rank): 467,610 (26); % change, −5.1; **Male,** 227,517; **Female,** 240,093; **White,** 337,198; **Black,** 60,046 (12.8%); **American Indian, Eskimo, or Aleut,** 5,381 (1.2%); **Asian or Pacific Islander,** 11,005 (2.4%); **Other race,** 53,980; **Hispanic origin,** 107,382 (23.0%); **1990 percent population under 18:** 22.0; **65 and over:** 13.9; **median age:** 33.9
Land area: 154.63 sq mi. (400.5 sq km)
Altitude: Highest, 5,494 ft; lowest, 5,140
Avg. daily temp.: Jan., 29.5° F; July, 73.3° F
Location: In northeast central part of state, on South Platte River
County: Contiguous boundaries with city of Denver
Churches: [1] Protestant, 859; Roman Catholic, 60; Jewish, 13
City-owned parks: 205 (4,166 ac.)
City-owned mountain parks: 40 (13,600 ac.)
Radio stations: AM, 23; FM, 20[1]
Television stations: 17[1]
CIVILIAN LABOR FORCE: 267,965[2]
Unemployed: 14,464[1], **Percent:** 5.4[3]
Per capita personal income: $19,231[3]
Chamber of Commerce: Greater Denver Chamber of Commerce, 1445 Market Street, Denver, Colo. 80202
1. Metropolitan area. 2. Denver City/County. 3. PMSA.

DETROIT, MICH.

Incorporated as city: 1815
Mayor: Coleman A. Young (to Jan. 1994)
1980 population (1980 census) & (rank): 1,203,368 (6)
1990 census population, sex, & (rank): 1,027,974 (7); % change, −14.6; **Male,** 476,814; **Female,** 551,160; **White,** 222,316; **Black,** 777,916 (75.7%); **American Indian, Eskimo, or Aleut,** 3,655 (0.4%); **Asian or Pacific Islander,** 8,461 (0.8%); **Other race,** 15,626; **Hispanic origin,** 28,473 (2.8%). **1990 percent population under 18:** 29.4; **65 and over:** 12.2; **median age:** 30.8.
Land area: 143 sq mi. (370 sq km)
Altitude: Highest, 685 ft; lowest, 574
Avg. daily temp.: Jan., 23.4° F; July, 71.9° F
Location: In southeastern part of state, on Detroit River
County: Seat of Wayne Co.
Churches: [1] Protestant, 1,165; Roman Catholic, 89; Jewish, 2
City-owned parks: 56 parks (3,843 ac.); 393 sites (5,838 ac.)
Radio stations: AM, 27; FM, 30 (includes 3 in Windsor, Ont.)
Television stations: 8[2] (includes 1 in Windsor, Ont.)
CIVILIAN LABOR FORCE: 441,736
Unemployed: 61,030, **Percent:** 13.8
Per capita personal income: $19,660
Chamber of Commerce: Greater Detroit Chamber of Commerce, 622 W. Lafayette, Detroit, Mich. 48226
1. Six-county metropolitan area. 2. Within four counties of Metro Detroit.

EL PASO, TEX.

Incorporated as city: 1873
Mayor: Bill Tilney
1980 population (1980 census) & (rank): 425,259 (28)
1990 census population, sex, & (rank): 515,342 (22); % change, 21.2; **Male**, 247,163; **Female**, 268,179; **White**, 396,122; **Black**, 17,708 (3.4%); **American Indian, Eskimo, or Aleut**, 2,239 (0.4%); **Asian or Pacific Islander**, 5,956 (1.2%); **Other race**, 93,317; **Hispanic origin**, 355,669 (69.0%). **1990 percent population under 18:** 31.9; **65 and over:** 8.7; **median age:** 28.7
Land area: 247.4 sq mi. (641 sq km)
Altitude: 4,000 ft
Avg. daily temp.: Jan., 44.2° F; July, 82.5° F
Location: In far western part of state, on Rio Grande
County: Seat of El Paso Co.
Churches: Protestant, 320; Roman Catholic, 39; Jewish, 3; others, 20
City-owned parks: 116[1] (1,180 ac.)
Radio Stations: AM, 18; FM, 17
Television stations: 6
CIVILIAN LABOR FORCE: 237,107
Unemployed: 26,379, **Percent:** 11.1
Per capita personal income: $10,735
Chamber of Commerce: El Paso Chamber of Commerce, 10 Civic Center Plaza, El Paso, Tex. 79944
1. Includes 109 developed and 7 undeveloped parks.

FORT WORTH, TEX.

Incorporated as city: 1873
Mayor: Kay Granger (to May 1993)
City Manager: David Ivory
1980 population (1980 census) & (rank): 385,164 (33)
1990 census population, sex, & (rank): 447,619 (28); % change, 16.2; **Male**, 220,268; **Female**, 227,351; **White**, 285,549; **Black**, 98,532 (22.0%); **American Indian, Eskimo, or Aleut**, 1,914 (0.4%); **Asian or Pacific Islander**, 8,910 (2.0%); **Other race**, 52,714; **Hispanic origin**, 87,345 (19.5%). **1990 percent population under 18:** 26.6; **65 and over:** 11.2; **median age:** 30.3.
Land area: 295.301 sq mi. (765 sq km)
Altitude: Highest, 780 ft; lowest, 520
Avg. daily temp.: Jan., 44.2° F; July, 82.5° F
Location: In north central part of state, on Trinity River
County: Seat of Tarrant Co.
Churches: 941, representing 72 denominations
City-owned parks: 171 (8,189 ac.; 3,500 ac. in Nature Center)
Radio stations: AM, 5; FM, 20
Television stations: 15 (9 local)
CIVILIAN LABOR FORCE: 285,465
Unemployed: 24,660, **Percent:** 8.6
Per capita personal income: $17,259[1]
Chamber of Commerce: Fort Worth Chamber of Commerce, 777 Taylor Street, Suit 900, Fort Worth, Tex. 76102
1. Fort Worth–Arlington MSA.

FRESNO, CALIF.

Incorporated as city: 1885
Mayor: Karen Humphrey (to May 1993)
City Manager: Michael A. Bierman
1980 population (1980 census) & (rank): 217,491 (65)
1990 census population, sex, & (rank): 354,202 (47); % change, 62.9; **Male**, 172,241; **Female**, 181,961; **White**, 209,604; **Black**, 29,409 (8.3%); **American Indian, Eskimo, or Aleut**, 3,729 (1.1%); **Asian or Pacific Islander**, 44,358 (12.5%); **Other race**, 67,102; **Hispanic origin**,

105,787 (29.9%). **1990 percent population under 18:** 31.7; **65 and over:** 10.1; **median age:** 28.4.
Land area: 99.38 sq mi. (257.39 sq km)
Altitude: 328 ft
Avg. daily temp.: Jan., 45.5° F; July, 81.0° F
Location: 184 miles southeast of San Francisco and 222 miles northwest of Los Angeles
County: Seat of Fresno County
Churches: 450 (approximate)
City-owned parks: 38 (690 ac.)
Radio stations: AM 11[1]; FM 13[1]; Bilingual 1
Television stations: 8[1]
CIVILIAN LABOR FORCE: 141,133
Unemployed: 16,439, **Percent:** 11.6
Per capita personal income: $15,927
Chamber of Commerce: Fresno County and City Chamber of Commerce, P.O. Box 1469, 2331 Fresno St., Fresno, CA 93716
1. Metropolitan area.

HONOLULU, HAWAII

Incorporated as city and county: 1907
Mayor: Frank F. Fasi (to Jan. 1993)
1980 population (1980 census) & (rank): 365,048 (36)
1990 census population, sex, & (rank): 365,272 (44)[1]; % change, 0.1; **Male**, 180,357; **Female**, 184,915; **White**, 97,527; **Black**, 4,821 (1.3%); **American Indian, Eskimo, or Aleut**, 1,126 (0.3%); **Asian or Pacific Islander**, 257,552 (70.5%); **Other race**, 4,246; **Hispanic origin**, 16,704 (4.6%). **1990 percent population under 18:** 19.1; **65 and over:** 16.0; **median age:** 36.9.
Land area: 600 sq mi. (1,554 sq km)[1]
Altitude: Highest, 4,025 ft; lowest, sea level
Avg. daily temp.: Jan., 72.6° F; July, 80.1° F
Location: The city and county government's jurisdiction includes the entire island of Oahu
Churches: Roman Catholic, 34; Buddhist, 35; Jewish, 2; Protestant and others, 329
City-owned parks: 5,835 ac.
Radio stations: AM, 17; FM, 14
Television stations: 12
CIVILIAN LABOR FORCE: 399,517[1]
Unemployed: 7,984[1], **Percent:** 2.0[1]
Per capita personal income: $19,171
Chamber of Commerce: Chamber of Commerce of Hawaii, 735 Bishop St., Honolulu, Hawaii 96813
1. City and county area. The census bureau does not include the entire city and county in its census of Honolulu. If it did, the 1990 census and rank would be 836,231 (12).

HOUSTON, TEX.

Incorporated as city: 1837
Mayor: Kathryn J. Whitmire (to Dec. 1991)
1980 population (1980 census) & (rank): 1,595,138 (5)
1990 census population, sex, & (rank): 1,630,553 (4); % change, 2.2; **Male**, 809,048; **Female**, 821,505; **White**, 859,069; **Black**, 457,990 (28.1%); **American Indian, Eskimo, or Aleut**, 4,126 (0.3%); **Asian or Pacific Islander**, 67,113 (4.1%); **Other race**, 242,255; **Hispanic origin**, 450,483 (27.6%). **1990 percent population under 18:** 26.7; **65 and over:** 8.3; **median age:** 30.4.
Land area: 581.44 sq mi. (1,506 sq km)
Altitude: Highest, 120 ft; lowest, sea level
Avg. daily temp.: Jan., 51.4° F; July, 83.1° F
Location: In southeastern part of state, near Gulf of Mexico
County: Seat of Harris Co.
Churches: 1,750[2]
City-owned parks: 334 (32,500 ac.)
Radio stations: AM, 25; FM, 29[1]

Television stations: 10 commercial, 1 PBS
Poet Laureate: HUY-LUC Khoi Tien Bui
CIVILIAN LABOR FORCE: 1,049,300
Unemployed: 64,026, **Percent:** 6.1
Per capita personal income: $17,598[3]
Chamber of Commerce: Greater Houston Partnership,
1100 Milam Building, 25th Fl., Houston, Tex. 77002
1. Includes annexations since 1970. 2. Harris County. 3.
PSMA

INDIANAPOLIS, IND.

Incorporated as city: 1832 (reincorporated 1838)
Mayor: William H. Hudnut III (to Jan. 1992)
1980 population (1980 census) & (rank): 711,539 (12)
1990 census population, sex, & (rank)[2]: 744,952 (12); %
change, 4.3; **Male,** 352,309; **Female,** 389,643; **White,**
564,447; **Black,** 166,031 (22.4%); **American Indian,
Eskimo, or Aleut,** 1,580 (0.2%); **Asian or Pacific Is-
lander,** 6,943 (0.9%); **Other race,** 2,951; **Hispanic ori-
gin,** 7,790 (1.0%). **1990 percent population under 18:**
25.6%; **65 and over:** 11.5; **median age:** 31.8.
Land area: 352 sq mi. (912 sq km)
Altitude: Highest, 840 ft; lowest, 700
Avg. daily temp.: Jan., 26.0 F; July, 75.1° F
Location: In central part of the state, on West Fork of
White River
County: Seat of Marion Co.
Churches: 1,200[1]
City-owned parks: 167 (10,753 ac.)
Radio stations: AM, 8[3]; FM, 17[3]
Television stations: 7[1]
CIVILIAN LABOR FORCE: 405,829
Unemployed: 17,720, **Percent:** 4.4
Per capita personal income: $18,080
Chamber of Commerce: Indianapolis Chamber of Com-
merce, 320 N Meridian St., Indianapolis, Ind. 46204
1. Marion County. 2. Consolidated city. 3. Metropolitan
area.

JACKSONVILLE, FLA.

Incorporated as city: 1822
Mayor: Ed Austin (to June 30, 1995)
1980 population (1980 census) & (rank)[1]: 571,003 (19)
1990 census population, sex, & (rank)[1]: 672,971 (15); %
change, 17.9; **Male,** 328,737; **Female,** 344,234; **White,**
489,604; **Black,** 163,902 (24.4%); **American Indian,
Eskimo, or Aleut,** 1,904 (0.3%); **Asian or Pacific Is-
lander,** 12,940 (1.9%); **Other race,** 4,621; **Hispanic ori-
gin,** 17,333 (2.6%). **1990 percent population under 18:**
25.9; **65 and over:** 10.7; **median age:** 31.5.
Land area: 759.6 sq mi. (1,967 sq km)
Altitude: Highest, 71 ft; lowest, sea level
Avg. daily temp.: Jan., 53.2° F; July, 81.3° F
Location: On St. Johns River, 20 miles from Atlantic
Ocean
County: Duval
Churches: Protestant, 771; Roman Catholic, 27; Jewish,
5; others, 21
City-owned parks and playgrounds: 138 (1,522 ac.)
Radio stations: AM, 13; FM, 15
Television stations: 6 commercial, 1 PBS
CIVILIAN LABOR FORCE: 325,187
Unemployed: 20,216, **Percent:** 6.2
Per capita personal income: $16,215
Chamber of Commerce: Jacksonville Area Chamber of
Commerce, Jacksonville, Fla. 32202
1. Consolidated city.

KANSAS CITY, MO.

Incorporated as city: 1850
Mayor: Emanuel Cleaver II (to April 1995)
City Manager: David H. Olson (apptd. Nov. 1984)
1980 population (1980 census) & (rank): 448,028 (27)
1990 census population, sex, & (rank): 435,146 (31); %
change, −2.9; **Male,** 206,965; **Female,** 228,181; **White,**
290,572; **Black,** 128,768 (29.6%); **American Indian,
Eskimo, or Aleut,** 2,144 (0.5%); **Asian or Pacific Is-
lander,** 5,239 (1.2%); **Other race,** 8,423; **Hispanic ori-
gin,** 17,017 (3.9%). **1990 percent population under 18:**
24.8; **65 and over:** 12.9; **median age:** 32.8.
Land area: 317 sq mi. (821 sq km)
Altitude: Highest, 1,014 ft; lowest, 722
Avg. daily temp.: Jan., 28.4° F; July, 80.9 F
Location: In western part of state, at juncture of Mis-
souri and Kansas Rivers
County: Located in Jackson, Clay, and Platte & Cass Co.
Churches: 1,100 churches of all denominations
City-owned parks and playgrounds: 180 (7,799 ac.)
Radio stations: AM, 15; FM, 14[1]
Television stations: 6[1]
CIVILIAN LABOR FORCE: 260,401
Unemployed: 16,871, **Percent:** 6.5
Per capita personal income: $17,899[2]
Chamber of Commerce: Chamber of Commerce of
Greater Kansas City, 920 Main St., Kansas City, Mo.
64105
1. Metropolitan area. 2. Kansas City, Mo.–Kan. MSA.

LONG BEACH, CALIF.

Incorporated as city: 1888
Mayor: Ernie Kell (to third Tuesday of 1994)
City Manager: James C. Hankla
1980 population (1980 census) & (rank): 361,498 (37)
1990 census population, sex, & (rank): 429,433 (32); %
change, 18.8; **Male,** 216,685; **Female,** 212,748; **White,**
250,716; **Black,** 58,761 (13.7%); **American Indian, Eski-
mo, or Aleut,** 2,781 (0.6%); **Asian or Pacific Islander,**
58,266 (13.6%); **Other race,** 58,909; **Hispanic origin,**
101,419 (23.6%). **1990 percent population under 18:**
25.5; **65 and over:** 10.8; **median age:** 30.0.
Land area: 49.8 sq mi. (129 sq km)
Altitude: Highest, 170 ft; lowest, sea level
Avg. daily temp.: Jan., 55.2 F; July, 72.8° F
Location: On San Pedro Bay, south of Los Angeles
County: Los Angeles
Churches: 236
City-owned parks: 42 (1,182 ac.)
Radio stations: AM, 2; FM, 2
Television stations: 8 (metro area)
CIVILIAN LABOR FORCE: 206,552
Unemployed: 14,460, **Percent:** 7.0
Per capita personal income: $19,906[1]
Chamber of Commerce: Long Beach Area Chamber of
Commerce, One World Trade Center, Suite 350, Long
Beach, CA 90831-0350
1. Los Angeles-Long Beach MSA.

LOS ANGELES, CALIF.

Incorporated as city: 1850
Mayor: Tom Bradley (to June 1993)
1980 population (1980 census) & (rank): 2,968,528 (3)
1990 census population, sex, & (rank): 3,485,398 (2); %
change, 17.4; **Male,** 1,750,055; **Female,** 1,735,343;
White, 1,841,182; **Black,** 487,674 (14.0%); **American
Indian, Eskimo, or Aleut,** 16,379 (0.5%); **Asian or Pacific Islander,** 341,807 (9.8%); **Other race,** 798,356;
Hispanic origin, 1,391,411 (39.9%). **1990 percent popu-**

lation under 18: 24.8; 65 and over: 10.0; median age: 30.7.
Land area: 467.4 sq mi. (1,210.57 sq km)
Altitude: Highest, 5,081 ft; lowest, sea level
Avg. daily temp.: Jan., 57.2° F; July, 74.1° F
Location: In southwestern part of state, on Pacific Ocean
County: Seat of Los Angeles Co.
Churches: 2,000 of all denominations
City-owned parks: 355 (15,357 ac.)
Radio stations: AM, 35; FM, 53
Television stations: 19
CIVILIAN LABOR FORCE: 1,791,011
Unemployed: 145,356, **Percent:** 8.1
Per capita personal income: $19,906[1]
Chamber of Commerce: Los Angeles Chamber of Commerce, 404 S Bixel St., Los Angeles, Calif. 90017
1. Los Angeles-Long Beach MSA.

MEMPHIS, TENN.

Incorporated as city: 1826
Mayor: Richard C. Hackett (to Dec. 1991)
1980 population (1980 census) & (rank): 646,174 (14)
1990 census population, sex, & (rank): 610,337 (18); % change, −5.5; **Male,** 285,010; **Female,** 325,327; **White,** 268,600; **Black,** 334,737 (54.8%); **American Indian, Eskimo, or Aleut,** 960 (0.2%); **Asian or Pacific Islander,** 4,805 (0.8%); **Other race,** 1,235; **Hispanic origin,** 4,455 (0.7%). **1990 percent population under 18:** 26.9; **65 and over:** 12.2; **median age:** 31.5.
Land area: 281 sq mi. (728 sq km)
Altitude: Highest, 331 ft
Avg. daily temp.: Jan., 39.6° G; July, 82.1° F
Location: In southwestern corner of state, on Mississippi River
County: Seat of Shelby Co.
Churches: 800
Parks and playgrounds: 172 (5,363 ac.)
Radio stations: AM, 12; FM, 8
Television stations: 6
CIVILIAN LABOR FORCE: 337,450
Unemployed: 15,317, **Percent:** 4.5
Per capita personal income: $16,484[1]
Chamber of Commerce: Memphis Area Chamber of Commerce, P.O. Box 224, Memphis, Tenn. 38103
1. Memphis, Tenn.–Ark.–Miss. MSA.

MIAMI, FLA.

Incorporated as city: 1896
Mayor: Xavier L. Suarez (to Nov. 1993)
City manager: Cesar Odio (apptd. Dec. 1985)
1980 population (1980 census) & (rank): 346,681 (41)
1990 census population, sex, & (rank): 358,548 (46); % change, 3.4; **Male,** 173,223; **Female,** 185,325; **White,** 235,358; **Black,** 98,207 (27.4%); **American Indian, Eskimo, or Aleut,** 545 (0.2%); **Asian or Pacific Islander,** 2,272 (0.6%); **Other race,** 22,166; **Hispanic origin,** 223,964 (62.5%). **1990 percent population under 18:** 23.0; **65 and over,** 16.6; **median age,** 36.0.
Land area: 34.3 sq mi. (89 sq km)
Water area: 19.5 sq mi.
Altitude: Average, 12 ft
Avg. daily temp.: Jan., 67.1° F; July, 82.4° F
Location: In southeastern part of state, on Biscayne Bay
County: Seat of Dade Co.
Churches: Protestant, 258; Roman Catholic, 12; Jewish, 4
City-owned parks: 103

Radio stations: AM, 9; FM, 9
Television stations: 8 commercial, 2 PBS
CIVILIAN LABOR FORCE: 204,602
Unemployed: 20,438, **Percent:** 10.0
Per capita personal income: $17,963[1]
Chamber of Commerce: Greater Miami Chamber of Commerce, 1601 Biscayne Blvd., Miami, Fla. 33132
1. Miami-Hialeah PMSA.

MILWAUKEE, WIS.

Incorporated as city: 1846
Mayor: John O. Norquist (to April 1992)
1980 population (1980 census) & (rank): 636,297 (16)
1990 census population, sex, & (rank): 628,088 (17); % change, −1.3; **Male,** 296,837; **Female,** 331,251; **White,** 398,033; **Black,** 191,255 (30.5%); **American Indian, Eskimo, or Aleut,** 5,858 (0.9%); **Asian or Pacific Islander,** 11,817 (1.9%); **Other race,** 21,125; **Hispanic origin,** 39,409 (6.3%). **1990 percent population under 18:** 27.4; **65 and over:** 12.4; **median age:** 30.3.
Land area: 95.8 sq mi. (248 sq km)
Altitude: 580.60 ft
Avg. daily temp.: Jan., 18.7° F; July, 70.5° F
Location: In southeastern part of state, on Lake Michigan
County: Seat of Milwaukee Co.
Churches: 411
County-owned parks: 14,758 ac.
Radio stations: AM, 15; FM, 8
Television stations: 10
CIVILIAN LABOR FORCE: 306,256
Unemployed: 19,166, **Percent:** 6.3
Per capita personal income: $18,842[1]
Chamber of Commerce: Metropolitan Milwaukee Association of Commerce, 828 N. Broadway, Milwaukee, Wis. 53202; Milwaukee Minority Chamber of Commerce, 2821 N. 4th St., Milwaukee, Wis. 53212; Hispanic Chamber of Commerce, 1125 W. National Ave., Milwaukee, Wis. 53204
1. PMSA.

MINNEAPOLIS, MINN.

Incorporated as city: 1867
Mayor: Donald M. Fraser (to Jan. 1994)
1980 population (1980 census) & (rank): 370,951 (34)
1990 census population, sex, & (rank): 368,383 (42); % change, −0.7; **Male,** 178,671; **Female,** 189,712; **White,** 288,967; **Black,** 47,948 (13.0%); **American Indian, Eskimo, or Aleut,** 12,335 (3.3%); **Asian or Pacific Islander,** 15,723 (4.3%); **Other race,** 3,410; **Hispanic origin,** 7,900 (2.1%). **1990 percent population under 18:** 20.6; **65 and over:** 13.0; **median age:** 31.7
Land area: 55.1 sq mi. (143 sq km)
Altitude: Highest, 945 ft; lowest, 695
Avg. daily temp.: Jan., 11.2° F; July, 73.1° F
Location: In southeast central part of state, on Mississippi River
County: Seat of Hennepin Co.
Churches: 419
City-owned parks: 153
Radio stations: AM, 17; FM, 15 (metro area)
Television stations: 6 (metro area)
CIVILIAN LABOR FORCE: 206,921
Unemployed: 9,189, **Percent:** 4.4
Per capita personal income: $20,227[1]
Chamber of Commerce: Greater Minneapolis Chamber of Commerce, 15 S Fifth Street, Minneapolis, Minn. 55402
1. Minneapolis-St. Paul Minn.–Wis. MSA.

NASHVILLE-DAVIDSON, TENN.

Incorporated as city: 1806
Mayor: Bill Boner (to August, 1991)
1980 population (1980 census) & (rank)[1]: 477,811 (25)
1900 census population, sex, & (rank)[1]: 510,784 (23); % change, 6.9; **Male,** 242,492; **Female,** 268,292; **White,** 381,740; **Black,** 119,273 (23.4%); **American Indian, Eskimo, or Aleut,** 1,162 (0.2%); **Asian or Pacific Islander,** 7,081 (1.4%); **Other race,** 1,528; **Hispanic origin,** 4,775 (0.9%). **1900 percent population under 18:** 22.8; **65 and over:** 11.6; **median age:** 32.6.
Land area: 533 sq mi. (1,380 sq km)
Altitude: Highest, 1,100 ft; lowest, approx. 400 ft
Avg. daily temp.: Jan., 36.7° F; July, 76.6° F
Location: In north central part of state, on Cumberland River
County: Davidson
Churches: Protestant, 781; Roman Catholic, 18; Jewish, 3
City-owned parks: 76 (6,650 ac.)
Radio stations: AM, 11; FM, 8
Television stations: 7
CIVILIAN LABOR FORCE: 276,131
Unemployed: 10,652, **Percent:** 3.9
Per capita personal income: $17,134
Chamber of Commerce: Nashville Area Chamber of Commerce, 161 Fourth Ave. North, Nashville, Tenn. 37219
1. Consolidated city.

NEW ORLEANS, LA.

Incorporated as city: 1805
Mayor: Sidney J. Barthelemy (to May 1994)
1980 population (1980 census) & (rank): 557,927 (21)
1990 census population, sex, & (rank): 496,938 (25); % change, –10.9; **Male,** 230,883; **Female,** 266,055; **White,** 173,554; **Black,** 307,728 (61.9%); **American Indian, Eskimo, or Aleut,** 759 (0.2%); **Asian or Pacific Islander,** 9,678 (1.9%); **Other race,** 5,219; **Hispanic origin,** 17,238 (3.5%). **1990 percent population under 18:** 27.5; **65 and over,** 13.0; **median age,** 31.6.
Land area: 199.4 sq mi. (516 sq km)
Altitude: Highest, 15 ft; lowest, –4
Avg. daily temp.: Jan., 52.4° F; July, 82.1° F
Location: In southeastern part of state, between Mississippi River and Lake Ponchartrain
Parish: Seat of Orleans Parish
Churches: 644
City-owned parks: 266 (4,460 ac.)
Radio stations: AM, 12; FM, 13
Television stations: 8
CIVILIAN LABOR FORCE: 225,315[1]
Unemployed: 12,470[1], **Percent:** 5.5[1]
Per capita personal income: $14,745
Chamber of Commerce: The Chamber/New Orleans and the River Region, 301 Camp Street, New Orleans, La. 70130
1. New Orleans City/Orleans Parish.

NEW YORK, N.Y.

Chartered as "Greater New York": 1898
Mayor: David N. Dinkins (to Dec. 31, 1993)
Borough Presidents: Bronx, Fernando Ferrer; Brooklyn, Howard Golden; Manhattan, Ruth W. Messinger; Queens, Claire Shulman; Staten Island, Guy V. Molinari
1980 population (1980 census) & (rank): 7,071,639 (1)
1990 census population, sex, & (rank): 7,322,564 (1)[1]; % change, 3.5; **Male,** 3,437,687; **Female,** 3,884,877; **White,** 3,827,088; **Black,** 2,102,512 (28.7%); **American Indian, Eskimo, or Aleut,** 27,531 (0.4%); **Asian or Pacific Islander,** 512,719 (7.0%); **Other race,** 852,714; **Hispanic origin,** 1,783,511 (24.4%). **1990 percent population under 18:** 23.0; **65 and over:** 13.0; **median age:** 33.7.
Land area: 314.7 sq mi. (815 sq km) (Queens, 112.83; Brooklyn, 74.45; Staten Island, 60.06; Bronx, 43.63; Manhattan, 23.73)
Altitude: Highest, 410 ft; lowest, sea level
Avg. daily temp.: Jan., 31.8° F; July, 76.7° F
Location: In south of state, at mouth of Hudson River (also known as the North River as it passes Manhattan)
Counties: Consists of 5 counties: Bronx, Kings (Brooklyn), New York (Manhattan), Queens, Richmond (Staten Island)
Churches: Protestant, 1,766; Jewish, 1,256; Roman Catholic, 437; Orthodox, 66
City-owned parks: 1,701 (26,138 ac.)
Radio stations: AM, 13; FM, 18
Television stations: 6 commercial, 1 public
CIVILIAN LABOR FORCE: 3,314,000
Unemployed: 296,000, **Percent:** 8.9
Per capita personal income: $22,0645[2]
Chamber of Commerce: New York Chamber of Commerce and Industry, 65 Liberty St., New York, N.Y. 10005
1. For population of boroughs, *see* Index. 2. PMSA.

OAKLAND, CALIF.

Incorporated as city: 1854
Mayor: Elihu Mason Harris (to Jan. 1995)
City Manager: Henry L. Gardner (apptd. June 1981)
1980 population (1980 census) & (rank): 339,337 (43)
1990 census popultion, sex, & (rank): 372,242 (39); % change, 9.7; **Male,** 178,824; **Female,** 193,418; **White,** 120,849; **Black,** 163,335 (43.9%); **American Indian, Eskimo, or Aleut,** 2,371 (0.6%); **Asian or Pacific Islander,** 54,931 (14.8%); **Other race,** 30,756; **Hispanic origin,** 51,711 (13.9%). **1990 percent population under 18,** 24.9; **65 and over,** 12.0; **median age:** 32.7.
Land area: 53.9 sq mi. (140 sq km)
Altitude: Highest, 1,700 ft; lowest, sea level
Avg. daily temp.: Jan., 49.0° F; July, 63.7° F
Location: In west central part of state, on east side of San Francisco Bay
County: Seat of Alameda Co.
Churches: 374, representing over 78 denominations in the City; over 500 churches in Alameda County
City-owned parks: 2,196 ac.
Radio stations: AM, 1
Television stations: 1 commercial
CIVILIAN LABOR FORCE: 190,884
Unemployed: 13,753, **Percent:** 7.2
Per capita personal income: $22,249[1]
Chamber of Commerce: Oakland Chamber of Commerce, 475 Fourteenth St., Oakland, Calif. 94612-1903
1. PMSA.

OKLAHOMA CITY, OKLA.

Incorporated as city: 1890
Mayor: Ron Norick (to April 1993)
City Manager: Don Brown
1980 population (1980 census) & (rank): 404,014 (31)
1990 census population, sex, & (rank): 444,719 (29); % change, 10.1; **Male,** 214,466; **Female,** 230,253; **White,** 332,539; **Black,** 71,064 (16.0%); **American Indian, Eskimo, or Aleut,** 18,794 (4.2%); **Asian or Pacific Islander,**

10,491 (2.4%); **Other race,** 11,831; **Hispanic origin,** 22,033 (5.0%). **1990 percent population under 18:** 26.0; **65 and over:** 11.9; **median age:** 32.4.
Land area: 623 sq mi. (1,614 sq km)
Altitude: Highest, 1,320 ft; lowest, 1,140
Avg. daily temp.: Jan., 35.9° F; July, 82.1° F
Location: In central part of state, on North Canadian River
County: Seat of Oklahoma Co.
Churches: Roman Catholic, 25; Jewish, 2; Protestant and others, 741
City-owned parks: 138 (3,944 ac.)
Television stations: 8
Radio stations: AM, 10; FM, 14
CIVILIAN LABOR FORCE: 226,927
Unemployed: 11,976, **Percent:** 5.3
Per capita personal income: $15,536
Chamber of Commerce: Oklahoma City Chamber of Commerce, 1 Santa Fe Plaza, Oklahoma City, Okla. 73102

OMAHA, NEB.

Incorporated as city: 1857
Mayor: P.J. Morgan (to June 1993)
1980 population (1980 census) & (rank): 313,939 (48)
1990 census population, sex, & (rank): 335,795 (48); % change, 7.0; **Male,** 160,392; **Female,** 175,403; **White,** 281,603; **Black,** 43,989 (13.1%); **American Indian, Eskimo, or Aleut,** 2,274 (0.7%); **Asian or Pacific Islander,** 3,412 (1.0%); **Other race,** 4,517; **Hispanic origin,** 10,288 (3.1%). **1990 percent population under 18:** 25.4; **65 and over:** 12.9; **median age:** 32.2.
Land area: 102.98 sq mi. (267 sq km)
Altitude: Highest, 1,270 ft
Avg. daily temp.: Jan., 20.2° F; July, 77.7° F
Location: In eastern part of state, on Missouri River
County: Seat of Douglas Co.
Churches: Protestant, 246; Roman Catholic, 44; Jewish, 4
City-owned parks: 159 (over 7,000 ac.)
Radio stations: AM, 7; FM, 13
Television stations: 4
CIVILIAN LABOR FORCE: 193,056
Unemployed: 5,748, **Percent:** 3.0
Per capita personal income: $16,753[1]
Chamber of Commerce: Omaha Chamber of Commerce, 1301 Harway St., Omaha, Neb. 68102
1. Omaha, Neb.–Iowa MSA.

PHILADELPHIA, PA.

First charter as city: 1701
Mayor: W. Wilson Goode (to first Monday, January 1992)
1980 population (1980 census) & (rank): 1,688,210 (4)
1990 census population, sex, & (rank): 1,585,577 (5); % change, –6.1; **Male,** 737,763; **Female,** 847,814; **White,** 848,586; **Black,** 631,936 (39.9%); **American Indian, Eskimo, or Aleut,** 3,454 (0.2%); **Asian or Pacific Islander,** 43,522 (2.7%); **Other race,** 58,079; **Hispanic origin,** 89,193 (5.6%). **1990 percent population under 18:** 23.9; **65 and over:** 15.2; **median age:** 33.2.
Land area: 136 sq mi. (352 sq km)
Altitude: Highest, 440 ft; lowest, sea level
Avg. daily temp.: Jan., 31.2° F; July, 76.5° F
Location: In southeastern part of state, at junction of Schuylkill and Delaware Rivers
County: Seat of Philadelphia Co. (coterminous)
Churches: Roman Catholic, 133; Jewish, 55; Protestant and others, 830

City-owned parks: 630 (10,252 ac.)
Radio stations: AM, 40[1]; FM, 43[1]
Television stations: 14[1]
CIVILIAN LABOR FORCE: 736,895[2]
Unemployed: 57,433[1], **Percent:** 7.8[2]
Per capita personal income: $19,750[1]
Chamber of Commerce: Philadelphia Chamber of Commerce, 1234 Market Street, Suite 1800, Philadelphia, Pa. 19107
1. PMSA. 2. Philadelphia City/County.

PHOENIX, ARIZ.

Incorporated as city: 1881
Mayor: Paul Johnson (to Jan. 1992)
City Manager: Frank Fairbanks (appt. May 1990)
1980 population (1980 census) & (rank): 789,704 (9)
1990 census population, sex, & (rank): 983,403 (9); % change, 24.5; **Male,** 487,589; **Female,** 495,814; **White,** 803,332; **Black,** 51,053 (5.2%); **American Indian, Eskimo, or Aleut,** 18,225 (1.9%); **Asian or Pacific Islander,** 16,303 (1.7%); **Other race,** 94,490; **Hispanic origin,** 197,103 (20.0%). **1990 percent population under 18:** 27.2; **65 and over,** 9.7; **median age,** 31.1.
Land area: 426.1 sq mi. (1,104 sq km)
Altitude: Highest, 2,740 ft.; lowest, 1,017
Avg. daily temp.: Jan., 52.3° F; July, 92.3° F
Location: In center of state, on Salt River
County: Seat of Maricopa Co.
City-owned parks: 140 (30,314 ac.)
Radio stations: AM, 22; FM, 18
Television stations: 9 commercial; 1 PBS
CIVILIAN LABOR FORCE: 591,142
Unemployed: 23,639, **Percent:** 4.0
Per capita personal income: $17,705
Chamber of Commerce: Phoenix Chamber of Commerce, 34 W. Monroe St., Phoenix, Ariz. 85003

PITTSBURGH, PA.

Incorporated as city: 1816
Mayor: Sophie Masloff (to Jan. 1994)
1980 population (1980 census) & (rank): 423,959 (30)
1990 census population, sex, & (rank): 369,879 (40); % change, –12.8; **Male,** 171,722; **Female,** 198,157; **White,** 266,791; **Black,** 95,362 (25.8%); **American Indian, Eskimo, or Aleut,** 671 (0.2%); **Asian or Pacific Islander,** 5,937 (1.6%); **Other race,** 1,118; **Hispanic origin,** 3,468 (0.9%). **1990 percent population under 18:** 19.8; **65 and over,** 17.9; **median age:** 34.6.
Land area: 55.5 sq mi. (144 sq km)
Altitude: Highest, 1,240 ft; lowest, 715
Avg. daily temp.: Jan., 26.7° F; July, 72.0° F
Location: In southwestern part of state, at beginning of Ohio River
County: Seat of Allegheny Co.
Churches: Protestant, 348; Roman Catholic, 86; Jewish, 28; Orthodox, 26
City-owned parks and playgrounds: 270 (2,572 ac.)
Radio stations: AM, 12; FM, 20
Television stations: 8
CIVILIAN LABOR FORCE: 172,507
Unemployed: 8,650, **Percent:** 5.0
Per capita personal income: $17,763[1]
Chamber of Commerce: The Chamber of Commerce of Greater Pittsburgh, 3 Gateway Center, Pittsburgh, Pa. 15222
1. PMSA.

PORTLAND, ORE.

Incorporated as city: 1851
Mayor: John (Bud) Clark (till Jan. 1993)
1980 est. population (1980 census) & rank: 368,148 (35)
1990 census population, sex, & (rank): 437,319 (30); % change, 18.8; **Male,** 211,914; **Female,** 225,405; **White,** 370,135; **Black,** 33,530 (7.7%); **American Indian, Eskimo, or Aleut,** 5,399 (1.2%); **Asian or Pacific Islander,** 23,185 (5.3%); **Other race,** 5,070; **Hispanic origin,** 13,874 (3.2%). **1990 percent population under 18:** 21.9; **65 and over,** 14.6; **median age:** 34.5.
Land area: 136.7 sq mi. (354 sq km.)
Altitude: Highest, 1073 ft; lowest, sea level
Avg. daily temp.: Jan., 38.9° F; July, 67.7° F
Location: In northwestern part of the state on Willamette River
County: Seat of Multnomah Co.
Churches: Protestant, 450; Roman Catholic, 48; Jewish, 9; Buddhist, 6; other, 190
City-owned parks: 200 (over 9,400 ac.)
Radio stations: AM: 14, FM: 14
Television stations: 5 commercial, 1 public
CIVILIAN LABOR FORCE: 217,156
Unemployed: 10,195, **Percent:** 4.7
Per capita personal income: $18,163[1]
Chamber of Commerce: Portland Chamber of Commerce, 221 NW 2nd Ave., Portland, Ore. 97209
1. PMSA.

SACRAMENTO, CALIF.

Incorporated as city: 1849
Mayor: Anne Rudin (to Sept. 1992)
1980 population (1980 census) & (rank): 275,741 (52)
1990 census population, sex, & (rank): 369,365 (41); % change, 34.0; **Male,** 178,737; **Female,** 190,628; **White,** 221,963; **Black,** 56,521 (15.3%); **American Indian, Eskimo, or Aleut,** 4,561 (1.2%); **Asian or Pacific Islander,** 55,426 (15.0%); **Other race,** 30,894; **Hispanic origin,** 60,007 (16.2%). **1990 percent population under 18:** 26.2; **65 and over,** 12.1; **median age:** 31.8.
Land area: 98 sq mi. (254 sq km)
Avg. daily temp.: Jan., 47.1° F; July, 76.6° F
County: Seat of Sacramento Co.
City park & recreational facilities: 131+ (1,427+ ac.)
Television stations: 7
CIVILIAN LABOR FORCE: 174,892
Unemployed: 13,061, **Percent:** 7.5
Per capita personal income: $18,299
Chamber of Commerce: Sacramento Chamber of Commerce, 917 7th St., Sacramento, Calif. 95814; West Sacramento Chamber of Commerce, 834-C Jefferson Blvd., Sacramento, Calif. 95691

ST. LOUIS, MO.

Incorporated as city: 1822
Mayor: Vincent Schoemehl, Jr. (to April 1993)
1980 population (1980 census) & (rank): 452,801 (26)
1990 census population, sex, & (rank): 396,685 (34); % change, −12.4; **Male,** 180,680; **Female,** 216,005; **White,** 202,085; **Black,** 188,408 (47.5%); **American Indian, Eskimo, or Aleut,** 950 (0.2%); **Asian or Pacific Islander,** 3,733 (0.9%); **Other race,** 1,509; **Hispanic origin,** 5,124 (1.3%). **1990 percent population under 18:** 25.2; **65 and over:** 16.6; **median age:** 32.8.
Land area: 61.4 sq mi. (159 sq km)
Altitude: Highest, 616 ft; lowest, 413
Avg. daily temp.: Jan., 28.8° F; July, 78.9° F

Location: In east central part of state, on Mississippi River
County: Independent city
Churches: 900[1]
City-owned parks: 89 (2,639 ac.)
Radio stations: AM, 21; FM 27[1]
Television stations: 6 commercial; 1 PBS
CIVILIAN LABOR FORCE: 190,688
Unemployed: 15,419, **Percent:** 8.1
Per capita personal income: $18,957[2]
Chamber of Commerce: St. Louis Regional Commerce and Growth Association, 100 S. Fourth St., Ste. 500, St. Louis, Mo. 63102
1. Metropolitan area. 2. St. Louis, Mo.–Ill. MSA.

SAN ANTONIO, TEX.

Incorporated as city: 1837
Mayor: Nelson Wolff (to May 1993)
City Manager: Alexander J. Briseno (apptd. April 27, 1990)
1980 population (1980 census) & (rank): 785,940 (11)
1990 census population, sex, & (rank): 935,933 (10); % change, 19.1; **Male,** 450,695; **Female,** 485,238; **White,** 676,082; **Black,** 65,884 (7.0%); **American Indian, Eskimo, or Aleut,** 3,303 (0.4%); **Asian or Pacific Islander,** 10,703 (1.1%); **Other race,** 179,961; **Hispanic origin,** 520,282 (55.6%). **1990 percent population under 18:** 29.0; **65 and over:** 10.5; **median age:** 29.8.
Land area: 341.23 sq mi. (884 sq km)
Altitude: 700 ft
Avg. daily temp.: Jan., 50.4° F; July, 84.6° F
Location: In south central part of state, on San Antonio River
County: Seat of Bexar Co.
City-owned parks: Approximately 6,385 ac.
Radio stations: AM; FM, 19
Television stations: 9
CIVILIAN LABOR FORCE: 446,701
Unemployed: 33,631, **Percent:** 7.5
Per capita personal income: $14,144
Chamber of Commerce: Greater San Antonio Chamber of Commerce, P.O. Box 1628, 602 E Commerce, San Antonio, Tex. 78296

SAN DIEGO, CALIF.

Incorporated as city: 1850
Mayor: Maureen O'Connor (to Dec. 11, 1992)
City Manager: Jack McGrory (apptd. April 1991)
1980 population (1980 census) & (rank): 875,538 (8)
1990 census population, sex, & (rank): 1,110,549 (6); % change, 26.8; **Male,** 566,464; **Female,** 544,085; **White,** 745,406; **Black,** 104,261 (9.4%); **American Indian, Eskimo, or Aleut,** 6,800 (0.6%); **Asian or Pacific Islander,** 130,945 (11.8%); **Other race,** 123,137; **Hispanic origin,** 229,519 (20.7%). **1990 percent population under 18:** 23.1; **65 and over:** 10.2; **median age:** 30.5.
Land area: 330.7 sq miles (857 sq km)
Altitude: Highest, 1,591 ft; lowest, sea level
Avg. daily temp.: Jan., 56.8° F; July, 70.3° F
Location: In southwesternmost part of state, on San Diego Bay
County: Seat of San Diego Co.
Churches: Roman Catholic, 39; Jewish, 9; Protestant, 334; Eastern Orthodox, 8; other, 18
City park and recreation facilities: 164 (17,207 ac.)
Radio stations: AM, 8; FM, 18
Television stations: 9
CIVILIAN LABOR FORCE: 553,612

Unemployed: 33,629, **Percent:** 6.1
Per capita personal income: $18,651
Chamber of Commerce: San Diego Chamber of Commerce, 402 West Broadway, Suite 1000, San Diego, Calif. 92101

SAN FRANCISCO, CALIF.

Incorporated as city: 1850
Mayor: Art Agnos (to Jan. 1992)
1980 population (1980 census) & (rank): 678,974 (13)
1990 census population, sex, & (rank): 723,959 (14); % change, 6.6; **Male,** 362,497; **Female,** 361,462; **White,** 387,783; **Black,** 79,039 (10.9%); **American Indian, Eskimo, or Aleut,** 3,456 (0.5%); **Asian or Pacific Islander,** 210,876 (29.1%); **Other race,** 42,805; **Hispanic origin,** 100,717 (13.9%). **1990 percent population under 18:** 16.1; **65 and over:** 14.6; **median age:** 35.8.
Land area: 46.1 sq mi. (120 sq km)
Altitude: Highest, 925 ft; lowest, sea level
Avg. daily temp.: Jan., 48.5° F; July, 62.2° F
Location: In northern part of state between Pacific Ocean and San Francisco Bay
County: Coextensive with San Francisco Co.
Churches: 540 of all denominations
City-owned parks and squares: 225
Radio stations: 29
Television stations: 10
CIVILIAN LABOR FORCE: 390,877[1]
Unemployed: 19,039[1], **Percent:** 4.9[1]
Per capita personal income: $28,170[2]
Chamber of Commerce: Greater San Francisco Chamber of Commerce, 465 California St., San Francisco, Calif. 94104
1. San Francisco City/County. 2. PMSA.

SAN JOSE, CALIF.

Incorporated as city: 1850
Mayor: Susan Hammer (to Dec. 31, 1994)
City Manager: Leslie R. White (apptd. May 1989)
1980 population (1980 census) & (rank): 629,400 (17)
1990 census population, sex, & (rank): 782,248 (11); % change, 24.3; **Male,** 397,709; **Female,** 384,539; **White,** 491,280; **Black,** 36,790 (4.7%); **American Indian, Eskimo, or Aleut,** 5,416 (0.7%); **Asian or Pacific Islander,** 152,815 (19.5%); **Other race,** 95,947; **Hispanic origin,** 208,388 (26.6%). **1990 percent population under 18:** 26.7; **65 and over:** 7.2; **median age:** 30.4.
Land area: 173.6 sq mi. (450 sq km)
Altitude: Highest, 4,372 ft.; lowest, sea level
Avg. daily temp.: Jan., 49.5° F; July, 68.8° F
Location: In northern part of state, on south San Francisco Bay, 50 miles south of San Francisco
County: Seat of Santa Clara County
Churches: 403
City-owned parks and playgrounds: 152 (3,136 ac.)
Radio stations: 14
Television stations: 4
CIVILIAN LABOR FORCE: 375,309
Unemployed: 24,183, **Percent:** 6.4
Per capita personal income: $24,581[1]
Chamber of Commerce: San Jose Chamber of Commerce, One Paseo de San Antonio, San Jose, Calif. 95113
1. PMSA.

SEATTLE, WASH.

Incorporated as city: 1869
Mayor: Norman B. Rice (to Dec. 31, 1993)
1980 population (1980 census) & (rank): 493,846 (23)
1990 census population, sex, & (rank): 516,259 (21); % change, 4.5; **Male,** 252,042; **Female,** 264,217; **White,** 388,858; **Black,** 51,948 (10.1%); **American Indian, Eskimo, or Aleut,** 7,326 (1.4%); **Asian or Pacific Islander,** 60,819 (11.8%); **Other race,** 7,308; **Hispanic origin,** 18,349 (3.6%). **1990 percent population under 18:** 16.5; **65 and over:** 15.2; **median age:** 34.9.
Land area: 144.6 sq mi. (375 sq km)
Altitude: Highest, 540 ft; lowest, sea level
Avg. daily temp.: Jan., 40.6° F; July, 65.3° F
Location: In west central part of state, on Puget Sound
County: Seat of King Co.
Churches: Roman Catholic, 36; Jewish, 13; Protestant and others, 535
City-owned parks, playgrounds, etc.: 278 (4,773.4 ac.)
Radio stations: AM, 22; FM, 26
Television stations: 3 commercial; 1 educational
CIVILIAN LABOR FORCE: 349,072
Unemployed: 17,901, **Percent:** 5.1
Per capita personal income: $21,137[1]
Chamber of Commerce: Seattle Chamber of Commerce, 1200 One Union Square, Seattle, Wash. 98101
1. PMSA.

TOLEDO, OHIO

Incorporated as city: 1837
Mayor: John McHugh (to Dec. 1991)
City Manager: Thomas R. Hoover
1980 population (1980 census) & (rank): 354,635 (40)
1990 census population, sex, & (rank): 332,943 (45); % change, –6.1; **Male,** 157,941; **Female,** 175,002; **White,** 256,239; **Black,** 65,598 (19.7%); **Americn Indian, Eskimo, or Aleut,** 920 (0.3%); **Asian or Pacific Islander,** 3,487 (1.0%); **Other race,** 6,699; **Hispanic origin,** 13,207 (4.0%). **1990 percent population under 18:** 26.2; **65 and over:** 13.6; **median age:** 31.7.
Land area: 84.2 sq mi. (218 sq km)
Altitude: 630 ft
Avg. daily temp.: Jan., 23.1° F; July, 71.8° F
Location: In northwestern part of state, on Maumee River at Lake Erie
County: Seat of Lucas Co.
Churches: Protestant, 301; Roman Catholic, 55; Jewish, 4; others, 98
City-owned parks and playgrounds: 134 (2,650.90 ac.)
Radio stations: AM, 8; FM, 8
Television stations: 6
CIVILIAN LABOR FORCE: 177,701
Unemployed: 21,010, **Percent:** 11.8
Per capita personal income: $16,893
Chamber of Commerce: Toledo Area Chamber of Commerce, 218 Huron St., Toledo, Ohio 43604

TUCSON, ARIZ.

Incorporated as city: 1877
Mayor: Thomas J. Volgy (to Dec. 1991)
1980 population (1980 census) & (rank): 330,537 (45)
1990 census population, sex, & (rank): 405,390 (33); % change, 22.6; **Male,** 197,319; **Female,** 208,071; **White,** 305,055; **Black,** 17,366 (4.3%); **American Indian, Eskimo, or Aleut,** 6,464 (1.6%); **Asian or Pacific Islander,** 8,901 (2.2%); **Other race,** 67,604; **Hispanic origin,** 118,595 (29.3%). **1990 percent population under 18:** 24.5; **65 and over:** 12.6; **median age:** 30.6.
Land area: 156.04 sq mi. (404 sq km)
Altitude: 2,400 ft
Avg. daily temp.: Jan., 51.1° F; July, 86.2° F

Location: In southeastern part of state, on the Santa Cruz River
County: Seat of Pima Co.
Churches: Protestant, 325; Roman Catholic, 40; other, 74
City-owned parks and parkways: (25,349 ac.)
Radio stations: AM, 16; FM, 11
Television stations: 3 commercial; 1 educational; 3 other
CIVILIAN LABOR FORCE: 206,197
Unemployed: 6,450, **Percent:** 3.1
Per capita personal income: $15,203
Chamber of Commerce: Tucson Metropolitan Chamber of Commerce, P.O. Box 991, Tucson, Ariz. 85702

TULSA, OKLA.

Incorporated as city: 1898
Mayor: Rodger Randle (to May 1994)
1980 population (1980 census) & (rank): 360,919 (38)
1990 census population, sex, & (rank): 367,302 (43); % change, 1.8; **Male,** 175,538; **Female,** 191,764; **White,** 291,444; **Black,** 49,825 (13.6%); **American Indian, Eskimo, or Aleut,** 17,091 (4.7%); **Asian or Pacific Islander,** 5,133 (1.4%); **Other race,** 3,809; **Hispanic origin,** 9,564 (2.6%). **1990 percent population under 18:** 24.4; **65 and over:** 12.7; **median age:** 33.1.
Land area: 192.459 sq mi. (499 sq km)
Altitude: 674 ft
Avg. daily temp.: Jan., 35.2° F; July, 83.2° F
Location: In northeastern part of state, on Arkansas River
County: Seat of Tulsa Co.
Churches: Protestant, 593; Roman Catholic, 32; Jewish, 2; others, 4
City parks and playgrounds: 113 (5,338 ac.)
Radio stations: AM, 7; FM, 6
Television stations: 5 commercial; 1 PBS; 1 cable
CIVILIAN LABOR FORCE: 197,107
Unemployed: 11,262, **Percent:** 5.7
Per capita personal income: $16,016
Chamber of Commerce: Metropolitan Tulsa Chamber of Commerce, 616 S Boston, Tulsa, Okla. 74119

VIRGINIA BEACH, VA.

Incorporated as city: 1963
Mayor: Meyera E. Obendorf (to June 30, 1992)
1980 population (1980 census) & (rank): 262,199 (56)
1990 census population, sex, & (rank): 393,069 (37); % change, 49.9; **Male,** 199,571; **Female,** 193,498; **White,** 316,408; **Black,** 54,671 (13.9%); **American Indian, Eskimo, or Aleut,** 1,384 (0.4%); **Asian or Pacific Islander,** 17,025 (4.3%); **Other race,** 3,581; **Hispanic origin,** 12,137 (3.1%); **1990 percent population under 18:** 28.0; **65 and over:** 5.9; **median age:** 28.9.
Land area: 258.7 sq mi. (670 sq km)
Altitude: 12 ft
Avg. daily temp.: Jan., 39.9° F; July, 78.4° F
Location: Southeastern most portion of state, on Atlantic coastline
County: None
Churches: Protestant, 159; Catholic, 8; Jewish, 4
City-owned parks: 151 (1,748 ac.)
Radio stations: AM 18, FM 22
Television stations: 4 commercial, 1 PBS, 1 cable
CIVILIAN LABOR FORCE: 171,089
Unemployed: 8,525, **Percent:** 5.0
Per capita personal income: $15,721[1]
Chamber of Commerce: Hampton Roads Chamber of Commerce, 4512 Virginia Beach Blvd., Virginia Beach, Va., 23456
1. Norfolk-Virginia Beach-Newport News MSA.

WASHINGTON, D.C.

Land ceded to Congress: 1788 by Maryland; 1789 by Virginia (retroceded to Virginia Sept. 7, 1846)
Seat of government transferred to D.C.: Dec. 1, 1800
Created municipal corporation: Feb. 21, 1871
Mayor: Sharon Pratt Dixon (to Jan. 1995)
Motto: *Justitia omnibus* (Justice to all)
Flower: American beauty rose
Tree: Scarlet oak
Origin of name: In honor of Columbus
1980 population (1980 census) & (rank): 638,432 (15)
1990 census population, sex, & (rank): 606,900 (19); % change, –4.9; **Male,** 282,970; **Female,** 323,930; **White,** 179,667; **Black,** 399,604 (65.8%); **American Indian, Eskimo, or Aleut,** 1,466 (0.2%); **Asian or Pacific Islander,** 11,214 (1.8%); **Other race,** 14,949; **Hispanic origin,** 32,710 (5.4%)
Land area: 68.25 sq mi. (177 sq km)
Geographic center: Near corner of Fourth and L Sts., NW
Altitude: Highest, 420 ft; lowest, sea level
Location: Between Virginia and Maryland, on Potomac River
Churches: Protestant, 610; Roman Catholic, 132; Jewish, 9
City parks: 753 (7,725 ac.)
Radio stations: AM, 9; FM, 38
Television stations: 19
CIVILIAN LABOR FORCE: 283,702
Unemployed: 19,725, **Percent:** 7.0
Per capita personal income: $24,845[1]
Board of Trade: Greater Washington Board of Trade, 1129 20th Street, N.W., Washington, D.C. 20036
Chamber of Commerce: D.C. Chamber of Commerce, 1319 F St., NW, Washington, D.C. 20004
1. Washington, D.C.–Md.–Va. MSA.

The District of Columbia—identical with the City of Washington—is the capital of the United States and the first carefully planned capital in the world.

D.C. history began in 1790 when Congress directed selection of a new capital site, 100 miles square, along the Potomac. When the site was determined, it included 30.75 square miles on the Virginia side of the river. In 1846, however, Congress returned that area to Virginia, leaving the 68.25 square miles ceded by Maryland.

The city was planned and partly laid out by Major Pierre Charles L'Enfant, a French engineer. This work was perfected and completed by Major Andrew Ellicott and Benjamin Banneker, a freeborn black man, who was an astronomer and mathematician. In 1814, during the War of 1812, a British force fired the capital, and it was from the white paint applied to cover fire damage that the President's home was called the White House.

Until Nov. 3, 1967, the District of Columbia was administered by three commissioners appointed by the President. On that day, a government consisting of a mayor-commissioner and a 9-member Council, all appointed by the President with the approval of the Senate, took office. On May 7, 1974, the citizens of the District of Columbia approved a Home Rule Charter, giving them an elected mayor and 13-member council—their first elected municipal government in more than a century. The District also has one non-voting member in the House of Representatives and an elected Board of Education.

On Aug. 22, 1978, Congress passed a proposed constitutional amendment to give Washington, D.C., voting representation in the Congress. The amendment had to be ratified by at least 28 state legislatures within seven years to become effective. As of 1985 it died.

A petition asking for the District's admission to the Union as the 51st State was filed in Congress on September 9, 1983. The District is continuing this drive for statehood.

Largest Cities in the United States
(Over 100,000 population,)

City and State	1990 Population	Rank 1990	Rank 1980
New York, N.Y.	7,322,564	1	1
Los Angeles, Calif.	3,485,398	2	3
Chicago, Ill.	2,783,726	3	2
Houston, Tex.	1,630,553	4	5
Philadelphia, Pa.	1,585,577	5	4
San Diego, Calif.	1,110,549	6	8
Detroit, Mich.	1,027,974	7	6
Dallas, Tex.	1,006,877	8	7
Phoenix, Ariz.	983,403	9	9
San Antonio, Tex.	935,933	10	11
San Jose, Calif.	782,248	11	17
Indianapolis, Ind.[2]	741,952	12	12
Baltimore, Md.	736,014	13	10
San Francisco, Calif.	723,959	14	13
Jacksonville, Fla.[2]	672,971	15	19
Columbus, Ohio	632,910	16	20
Milwaukee, Wis.	628,088	17	16
Memphis, Tenn.	610,337	18	14
Washington, D.C.	606,900	19	15
Boston, Mass.	574,283	20	21
Seattle, Wash.	516,259	21	23
El Paso, Tex.	515,342	22	28
Nashville-Davidson, Tenn[2]	510,784	23	25
Cleveland, Ohio	505,616	24	18
New Orleans, La.	496,938	25	22
Denver, Colo.	467,610	26	24
Austin, Tex.	465,622	27	42
Fort Worth, Tex.	447,619	28	33
Oklahoma City, Okla.	444,719	29	31
Portland, Ore.	437,319	30	35
Kansas City, Mo.	435,146	31	27
Long Beach, Calif.	429,433	32	37
Tucson, Ariz.	405,390	33	45
St. Louis, Mo.	396,685	34	26
Charlotte, N.C.	395,934	35	47
Atlanta, Ga.	394,017	36	29
Virginia Beach, Va.	393,069	37	56
Albuquerque, N.M.	384,736	38	44
Oakland, Calif.	372,242	39	43
Pittsburgh, Pa.	369,879	40	30
Sacramento, Calif.	369,365	41	52
Minneapolis, Minn.	368,383	42	34
Tulsa, Okla.	367,302	43	38
Honolulu, Hawaii[1]	365,272	44	36
Cincinnati, Ohio	364,040	45	32
Miami, Fla.	358,548	46	41
Fresno, Calif.	354,202	47	65
Omaha, Neb.	335,795	48	48
Toledo, Ohio	332,943	49	40
Buffalo, N.Y.	328,123	50	39
Wichita, Kan.	304,011	51	51
Santa Ana, Calif.	293,742	52	69
Mesa, Ariz.	288,091	53	102
Colorado Springs, Colo.	281,140	54	66
Tampa, Fla.	280,015	55	53
Newark, N.J.	275,221	56	46
St. Paul, Minn.	272,235	57	54
Louisville, Ky.	269,063	58	49
Anaheim, Calif.	266,406	59	63
Birmingham, Ala.	265,968	60	50
Arlington, Tex.	261,721	61	94
Norfolk, Va.	261,229	62	55
Las Vegas, Nev.	258,295	63	89
Corpus Christi, Tex.	257,453	64	60
St. Petersburg, Fla.	238,629	65	58
Rochester, N.Y.	231,636	66	57
Jersey City, N.J.	228,537	67	61
Riverside, Calif.	226,505	68	84
Anchorage, Alaska	226,338	69	78
Lexington-Fayette, Ky.	225,366	70	68
Akron, Ohio	223,019	71	59
Aurora, Colo.	222,103	72	97
Baton Rouge, La.	219,531	73	62
Stockton, Calif.	210,943	74	107
Raleigh, N.C.	207,951	75	105
Richmond, Va.	203,056	76	64
Shreveport, La.	198,525	77	67
Jackson, Miss.	196,637	78	70
Mobile, Ala.	196,278	79	71
Des Moines, Iowa	193,187	80	74
Lincoln, Nebr.	191,972	81	81
Madison, Wis.	191,262	82	83
Grand Rapids, Mich.	189,126	83	75
Yonkers, N.Y.	188,082	84	72
Hialeah, Fla.	188,004	85	108
Montgomery, Ala.	187,106	86	76
Lubbock, Tex.	186,206	87	79
Greensboro, N.C.	183,521	88	100
Dayton, Ohio	182,044	89	73
Huntington Beach, Calif.	181,519	90	85
Garland, Tex.	180,650	91	115
Glendale, Calif	180,038	92	114
Columbus, Ga.[2]	179,278	93	86
Spokane, Wash.	177,196	94	82
Tacoma, Wash.	176,664	95	98
Little Rock, Ark.	175,795	96	96
Bakersfield, Calif.	174,820	97	152
Fremont, Calif.	173,339	98	119
Fort Wayne, Ind.	173,072	99	80
Arlington, Va.[3]	170,936	100	—
Newport News, Va.	170,045	101	109
Worcester, Mass.	169,759	102	91
Knoxville, Tenn.	165,121	103	77
Modesto, Calif.	164,730	104	147
Orlando, Fla.	164,693	105	124
San Bernardino, Calif.	164,164	106	131
Syracuse, N.Y.	163,860	107	87
Providence, R.I.	160,728	108	99
Salt Lake City, Utah	159,936	109	90
Huntsville, Ala.	159,789	110	111
Amarillo, Tex.	157,615	111	106
Springfield, Mass.	156,983	112	103
Irving, Tex.	155,037	113	142
Chattanooga, Tenn.	152,466	114	88
Chesapeake, Va.	151,976	115	137
Kansas City, Kan.	149,767	116	92
Metairie, La.[3]	149,428	117	—
Fort Lauderdale, Fla.	149,377	118	101
Glendale, Ariz.	148,134	119	—
Warren, Mich.	144,864	120	93
Winston-Salem, N.C.	143,485	121	120
Garden Grove, Calif.	143,050	122	127
Oxnard, Calif.	142,216	123	145
Tempe, Ariz.	141,865	124	148
Bridgeport, Conn.	141,686	125	110
Paterson, N.J.	140,891	126	116
Flint, Mich.	140,761	127	95

City and State	1990 Population	Rank 1990	Rank 1980	City and State	1990 Population	Rank 1990	Rank 1980
Springfield, Mo.	140,494	128	118	Overland Park, Kan.	111,790	165	—
Hartford, Conn.	139,739	129	117	Hayward, Calif.	111,498	166	—
Rockford, Ill.	139,426	130	113	Concord, Calif.	111,348	167	155
Savannah, Ga.	137,560	131	112	Alexandria, Va.	111,183	168	160
Durham, N.C.	136,611	132	168	Orange, Calif.	110,658	169	—
Chula Vista, Calif.	135,163	133	—	Santa Clarita, Calif.	110,642	170	—
Reno, Nev.	133,850	134	169	Irvine, Calif.	110,330	171	—
Hampton, Va.	133,793	135	128	Elizabeth, N.J.	110,002	172	150
Ontario, Calif.	133,179	136	—	Inglewood, Calif.	109,602	173	—
Torrance, Calif.	133,107	137	123	Ann Arbor, Mich.	109,592	174	146
Pomona, Calif.	131,723	138	—	Vallejo, Calif.	109,199	175	—
Pasadena, Calif.	131,591	139	134	Waterbury, Conn.	108,961	176	158
New Haven, Conn.	130,474	140	125	Salinas, Calif.	108,777	177	—
Scottsdale, Ariz.	130,069	141	—	Cedar Rapids, Iowa	108,751	178	141
Plano, Tex.	128,713	142	—	Erie, Pa.	108,718	179	130
Oceanside, Calif.	128,398	143	—	Escondido, Calif.	108,635	180	—
Lansing, Mich.	127,321	144	122	Stamford, Conn.	108,056	181	161
Lakewood, Colo.	126,481	145	138	Salem, Ore.	107,786	182	—
East Los Angeles, Calif.[3]	126,379	146	—	Citrus Heights, Calif.[3]	107,439	183	—
Evansville, Ind.	126,272	147	121	Abilene, Tex.	106,654	184	—
Boise, Idaho	125,738	148	162	Macon, Ga.	106,612	185	135
Tallahassee, Fla.	124,773	149	—	El Monte, Calif.	106,209	186	—
Paradise, Nev.[3]	124,682	150	—	South Bend, Ind.	105,511	187	143
Laredo, Tex.	122,899	151	—	Springfield, Ill.	105,227	188	171
Hollywood, Fla	121,697	152	129	Allentown, Pa.	105,090	189	156
Topeka, Kan.	119,883	153	132	Thousand Oaks, Calif.	104,352	190	—
Pasadena, Tex.	119,363	154	139	Portsmouth, Va.	103,907	191	154
Moreno Valley, Calif.	118,779	155	—	Waco, Tex.	103,590	192	166
Sterling Heights, Mich.	117,810	156	144	Lowell, Mass.	103,439	193	—
Sunnyvale, Calif.	117,229	157	149	Berkeley, Calif.	102,724	194	157
Gary, Ind.	116,646	158	104	Mesquite, Tex.	101,484	195	—
Beaumont, Tex.	114,323	159	133	Rancho Cucamonga, Calif.	101,409	196	—
Fullerton, Calif.	114,144	160	163	Albany, N.Y.	101,082	197	164
Peoria, Ill.	113,504	161	126	Livonia, Mich.	100,850	198	153
Santa Rosa, Calif.	113,313	162	—	Sioux Falls, S.D.	100,814	199	—
Eugene, Ore.	112,669	163	151	Simi Valley, Calif.	100,217	200	—
Independence, Mo.	112,301	164	140				

1. The estimates shown here are for Honolulu census designated place, which is treated as the city by the Census Bureau, rather than the Honolulu city/county governmental unit. 2. Consolidated city. 3. Census designated place. Data are latest Census Bureau report. *Source:* U.S. Department of Commerce, Bureau of the Census, April 1990.

Total Homeless Not Counted

Source: "Census and You," U.S. Department of Commerce, Bureau of the Census.

On the night of March 20–21, 1990, The Census Bureau conducted a special Shelter and Street Night (S-Night) operation as part of the over-all effort to count the Nation's population in the 1990 census. This tabulation was not intended to officially count the homeless population of the United states for the 1990 census.

Census Bureau Director Barbara Everitt Bryant had cautioned the Congress: "As we have been careful to point out since the inception of planning for Shelter and Street Night, these figures do not represent a count of the total population of homeless persons at the national, State, or local levels, nor were they intended to. They should not be characterized as such. There will be no count of the homeless population from the 1990 census. Even when all the results from the 1990 census have been released, a complete count of the total homeless population will not exist that can be identified at any level of geography."

S-Night is best described as a count of persons who sought emergency shelter, or who were visible to census takers in pre-identified open street and public locations, on the night of March 20 and early morning hours of March 21, 1990.

The S-Night operation reported a count of 178,828 persons in emergency shelters for the homeless and a total of 49,793 persons visible in pre-identified street locations.

The Census Bureau did not attempt to adjust the final totals for overcounts or undercounts because of the mobile nature of the homeless population. □

Tabulated Data on City Governments

City	Mayor			Council or Commission			
	Term, years	Salary[1]	City manager's salary[2]	Name	Members	Term, years	Salary[3]
Albuquerque, N.M.	4	$59,509	—	Council	9	4	$5,951
Atlanta*	4	100,000	—	Council	19	4	22,000 [27]
Austin, Tex.	3	35,006	113,880	Council	6	3	30,014
Baltimore	4	60,000	—	Council	19	4	29,000 [21]
Boston	4	100,000	—	Council	13	2	45,000
Buffalo, N.Y.	4	72,000	—	Council	13	2 [5]	38,000
Charlotte, N.C.	2	14,800	106,780	Council	11	2	8,000
Chicago	4	115,000	—	Council	50	4	55,000
Cincinnati	2	42,600	132,500	Council	9	2	39,100
Cleveland	4	85,000	—	Council	21	4	35,683
Columbus, Ohio	4	85,000	—	Council	7	4	25,000 [15]
Dallas	2	50 [6]	—	Council	11	2	50 [6]
Denver	4	79,500	—	Council	13	4	33,402 [28]
Detroit	4	130,000	—	Council	9	4	60,000 [29]
El Paso	2	25,000	—	Council	7 [7]	2	15,000
Fort Worth	2	75 [8]	96,000	Council	8	2	75 [8]
Fresno, Calif.	4	49,800	120,000	Council	7 [7]	4	28,800 [23]
Honolulu	4	84,725	84,550 [9]	Council	9	4	35,000 [3]
Houston	2	130,516	—	Council	14	2	34,804
Indianapolis	4	86,300	—	Council	29	4	14,072 [10, 11]
Jacksonville, Fla.	4	92,448	80,800 [11]	Council	19	4	21,174 [3]
Kansas City, Mo.	4	54,000	101,220	Council	13	4	21,000
Long Beach, Calif.	4	74,438	150,667 [25]	Council	9	4	19,837
Los Angeles	4	117,884	152,508 [4]	Council	15	4	90,680
Memphis, Tenn.	4	82,500	72,800	Council	13	4	6,000
Miami, Fla.	4	5,000 [13]	106,260	Commission	5	4	5,000
Milwaukee	4	85,178	—	Council	16	4	37,800
Minneapolis	4	67,000	86,835	Council	13	4	49,500
Nashville, Tenn.	4	75,000	—	Council	41	4	5,400
New Orleans	4	85,879	71,028	Council	7	4	42,500
New York	4	130,000	112,000 [14]	Council	51	4	55,000 [26]
Oakland, Calif.	4	80,000	120,998	Council	9 [7]	4	15,000
Oklahoma City	4	2,000	100,000	Council	8	4	20 [17]
Omaha, Neb.	4	69,165	—	Council	7	4	17,791 [3]
Philadelphia	4	110,000	95,000 [18]	Council	17	4	65,000 [16]
Phoenix, Ariz.	2	37,500	119,860	Council	9 [7]	4	18,000
Pittsburgh	4	69,007	—	Council	9	4	39,347
Portland, Ore.	4	72,592	—	Council	4	4	61,131
Sacramento	4	8,100 [30]	119,000	Council	9 [12]	4	8,100 [31]
St. Louis	4	71,266	—	Board of Aldermen	29	4	18,500 [32]
San Antonio	2	3,000 [19]	102,000	Council	11 [7]	2	20 [20]
San Diego, Calif.	4	60,000	121,000	Council	8	4	45,000
San Francisco	4	122,356	121,212 [33]	Board of Supervisors	11	4	23,924
San Jose, Calif.	4	80,000 [34]	133,971 [34]	Council	10	4	52,800 [34]
Seattle	4	95,398	—	Council	9	4	63,892
Toledo, Ohio	2	36,000	83,320	Council	9 [12]	2	7,800 [36]
Tucson, Ariz.	4	24,000	100,000	Council	7 [7]	4	12,000
Tulsa, Okla.	4	70,000	—	Council	9	2	12,000
Virginia Beach, Va.	4	20,000	100,000 [24]	Council	11	4	18,000
Washington, D.C.	4	90,705	90,600 [35]	Council	13	4	71,885 [22]

1. Annual salary unless otherwise indicated. 2. Annual salary. City Manager's term is indefinite and at will of Council (or Mayor). 3. Annual salary unless otherwise indicated. In some cities, President of Council receives a higher salary. 4. City Administrative Officer appointed by Mayor, approved by Council. 5. For 9 District Councilmen; 4 years for President and 3 Councilmen-at-Large. 6. Per Council meeting; not over $2,600 per year. 7. Including Mayor. 8. Per week and per Council meeting. 9. Managing Director appointed by Mayor; Council approval required. 10. $107 per council meeting at a maxium of 21 meetings. $59 per committee meeting at a maximum of 40 meetings. President gets $1,1879 extra. 11. Chief Administrative Officer appointed by Mayor; not subject to Council confirmation. 12. Including Mayor and Vice-Mayor. 13. Plus $2,500 expense account. 14. No City Manager; salary is for Deputy Mayor. 15. Per member. President earns $30,000. 16. Per member. President earns $80,000. 17. Per Council meeting; not to exceed 5 meetings a month. 18. Appointed by Mayor, with title of Managing Director. 19. Plus Council pay. 20. Per Council meeting; not over $1,040 per year. 21. Per member. President earns $53,000. 22. Council Chairman receives $81,885. 23. Mayor Pro Tempore, $31,200. 24. Plus $4,000 in travel expenses. 25. Plus $1,200 per month expense account. 26. Council President receives $105,000. 27. Council earns $53,000; Vice President earns $30,500. 28. Council President receives $38,402. 29. Council President receives $63,000. 30. Plus $4,800 annual expense account, $4,800 annual secretary expense allowance and $4,800 annual vehicle expense allowance. 31. Plus $3,600 annual expense account and $4,800 annual vehicle expense allowance. 32. For 12 Aldermen $18,500, 16 Aldermen $21,460. 33. Chief Administrative Officer, $121,212. 34. Plus $4,200 annual vehicle expense allowance for Mayor/Council and $6,000 for City Manager. 35. City Administrator/Deputy Mayor for operations. 36. Members of Council get $1,200 per year expense account. NOTE: Salaries are given to the nearest dollar. *Source: Information Please* questionnaires to the cities.

U.S. Cities 25,000–100,000, by Rank

Rank	City and State	Population	Rank	City and State	Population
200	Simi Valley city, CA	100,217	269	Newton city, MA	82,585
201	New Bedford city, MA	99,922	270	Carrollton city, TX	82,169
202	Grand Prairie city, TX	99,616	271	Alhambra city, CA	82,106
203	Aurora city, IL	99,581	272	Scranton city, PA	81,805
204	Manchester city, NH	99,567	273	Lynn city, MA	81,245
205	Brownsville city, TX	98,962	274	Billings city, MT	81,151
206	Clearwater city, FL	98,784	275	Lawton city, OK	80,561
207	Pueblo city, CO	98,640	276	Sioux City city, IA	80,505
208	Columbia city, SC	98,052	277	Charleston city, SC	80,414
209	Lancaster city, CA	97,291	278	Kenosha city, WI	80,352
210	Green Bay city, WI	96,466	279	Kalamazoo city, MI	80,277
211	Roanoke city, VA	96,397	280	Norman city, OK	80,071
212	Costa Mesa city, CA	96,357	281	Nashua city, NH	79,662
213	Wichita Falls city, TX	96,259	282	Coral Springs city, FL	79,443
214	West Covina city, CA	96,086	283	Reading city, PA	78,380
215	Cambridge city, MA	95,802	284	Norwalk city, CT	78,331
216	Youngstown city, OH	95,732	285	Albany city, GA	78,122
217	Sunrise Manor CDP, NV	95,362	286	Westminster city, CA	78,118
218	Davenport city, IA	95,333	287	Tuscaloosa city, AL	77,759
219	Lafayette city, LA	94,440	288	Whittier city, CA	77,671
220	Norwalk city, CA	94,279	289	Fairfield city, CA	77,211
221	Burbank city, CA	93,643	290	Elgin city, IL	77,010
222	Santa Clara city, CA	93,613	291	Joliet city, IL	76,836
223	Brockton city, MA	92,788	292	Alameda city, CA	76,459
224	Fall River city, MA	92,703	293	Somerville city, MA	76,210
225	Miami Beach city, FL	92,639	294	Corona city, CA	76,095
226	San Buenaventura (Ventura) city, CA	92,575	295	Cranston city, RI	76,060
227	Daly City city, CA	92,311	296	Silver Spring CDP, MD	76,046
228	Arden-Arcade CDP, CA	92,040	297	Columbia CDP, MD	75,883
229	Downey city, CA	91,444	298	Southfield city, MI	75,728
230	Chandler city, AZ	90,533	299	Fayetteville city, NC	75,695
231	Compton city, CA	90,454	300	Visalia city, CA	75,636
232	Odessa city, TX	89,699	301	Clarksville city, TN	75,494
233	Midland city, TX	89,443	302	New Britain city, CT	75,491
234	Dearborn city, MI	89,286	393	Arlington Heights village, IL	75,460
235	Arvada city, CO	89,235	304	Tyler city, TX	75,450
236	El Cajon city, CA	88,693	305	Sandy city, UT	75,058
237	Edison CDP, NJ	88,680	306	Cape Coral city, FL	74,991
238	Trenton city, NJ	88,675	307	Richardson city, TX	74,840
239	Parma city, OH	87,876	308	Farmington Hills city, MI	74,652
240	Fort Collins city, CO	87,758	309	Westminster city, CO	74,625
241	Fontana city, CA	87,535	310	Fargo city, ND	74,111
242	Camden city, NJ	87,492	311	Lakewood city, CA	73,557
243	Richmond city, CA	87,425	312	East Orange city, NJ	73,233
244	Kendall CDP, FL	87,271	313	Evanston city, IL	73,233
245	West Calley City city, UT	86,976	314	Troy city, MI	72,884
246	Santa Monica city, CA	86,905	315	Mission Viejo city, CA	72,820
247	Bellevue city, WA	86,874	316	Fort Smith city, AR	72,798
248	Provo city, UT	86,835	317	Pawtucket city, RI	72,644
249	Bloomington city, MN	86,335	318	Pompano Beach city, FL	72,411
250	South Gate city, CA	86,284	319	Rialto city, CA	72,388
251	Clinton CDP, MI	85,866	320	Kenner city, LA	72,033
252	Santa Barbara city, CA	85,571	321	Vista city, CA	71,872
253	Duluth city, MN	85,493	322	St. Joseph city, MO	71,852
254	San Mateo city, CA	85,486	323	Clifton city, NJ	71,742
255	Warwick city, RI	85,427	324	Wilmington city, DE	71,529
256	Naperville city, IL	85,531	325	Vacaville city, CA	71,479
257	Quincy city, MA	84,985	326	Bethlehem city, PA	71,428
258	Gainesville city, FL	84,770	327	Hawthorne city, CA	71,349
259	Westland city, MI	84,724	328	Lorain city, OH	71,245
260	San Angelo city, TX	84,474	329	Pontiac city, MI	71,166
261	Cheektowaga CDP, NY	84,387	330	Muncie city, IN	71,035
262	Racine city, WI	84,298	331	Taylor city, MI	70,811
263	Hammon city, IN	84,236	332	Rochester city, MN	70,745
264	Canton city, OH	84,161	333	Lake Charles city, LA	70,580
265	McAllen city, TX	84,021	334	Lakeland city, FL	70,576
266	Carson city, CA	83,995	335	Springfield city, OH	70,487
267	Decatur city, IL	83,885	336	Longview city, TX	70,311
268	Boulder city, CO	93,312	337	North Charleston city, SC	70,218

Rank	City and State	Population
338	Lawrence city, MA	70,207
339	Everett city, WA	69,961
340	Saginaw city, MI	69,512
341	High Point city, NC	69,496
342	Waukegan city, IL	69,392
343	Baldwin Park city, CA	69,330
344	Cherry Hill city, NJ	69,319
345	Columbia city, MO	69,101
346	Palmdale city, CA	68,842
347	Buena Park city, CA	68,784
348	Utica city, NY	68,637
349	Schaumburg village, IL	68,586
350	Gresham city, OR	68,235
351	San Leandro city, CA	68,223
352	St. Clair Shores city, MI	68,107
353	Sandy Springs CDP, GA	67,842
354	West Palm Beach city, FL	67,643
355	Orem city, UT	67,561
356	Federal Way CDP, WA	67,554
357	Mountain View city, CA	67,460
358	Cicero town, IL	67,436
359	New Rochelle city, NY	67,265
360	Mount Vernon city, NY	67,153
361	Plantation city, FL	66,692
361	Waterford CDP, MI	66,692
363	Newport Beach city, CA	66,643
364	Brick Township CDP, NJ	66,473
365	Waterloo city, IA	66,467
366	Redding city, CA	66,462
367	Denton city, TX	66,270
368	Redwood City city, CA	66,072
369	Lynchburg city, VA	66,049
370	Dundalk CDP, MD	65,800
371	Appleton city, WI	65,695
372	Largo city, FL	65,674
373	Lawrence city, KS	65,608
374	Danbury city, CT	65,585
375	Schenectady city, NY	65,566
376	Pembroke Pines city, FL	65,452
377	Royal Oak city, MI	65,410
378	Tonawanda CDP, NY	65,284
379	Framingham CDP, MA	64,994
380	Henderson city, NV	64,942
381	Sunrise city, FL	64,407
382	Portland city, ME	64,358
383	Ogden city, UT	63,909
384	Wyoming city, MI	63,891
385	Baytown city, TX	63,850
386	Killeen city, TX	63,535
387	Champaign city, IL	63,502
388	Upland city, CA	63,374
389	Olathe city, KS	63,352
390	West Allis city, WI	63,221
391	Carlsbad city, CA	63,126
392	Bethesda CDP, MD	62,936
393	El Toro CDP, CA	62,685
394	Palm Bay city, FL	62,632
395	Antioch city, CA	62,195
396	Las Cruces city, NM	62,126
397	Lynwood city, CA	61,945
398	Daytona Beach city, FL	61,921
399	Napa city, CA	61,842
400	Niagara Falls city, NY	61,840
401	Bellflower city, CA	61,815
402	Rochester Hills city, MI	61,766
403	North Little Rock city, AR	61,741
404	Asheville city, NC	61,607
405	Boca Raton city, FL	61,492
406	Bayonne city, NJ	61,444
407	Hamilton city, OH	61,368

Rank	City and State	Population
408	Santa Maria city, CA	61,284
409	Town 'n' Country CDP, FL	60,946
410	Dearborn Heights city, MI	60,838
411	Monterey Park city, CA	60,738
412	Bristol city, CT	60,640
413	Bloomington city, IN	60,633
414	Walnut Creek city, CA	60,569
414	Kettering city, OH	60,569
416	Greeley city, CO	60,536
417	Redlands city, CA	60,394
418	Redondo Beach city, CA	60,167
419	West Hartford CDP, CT	60,110
420	Irvington CDP, NJ	59,774
421	Iowa City city, IA	59,738
422	Lakewood city, OH	59,718
423	Chino city, CA	59,682
424	Melbourne city, FL	59,646
425	Montebello city, CA	59,564
426	Meriden city, CT	59,479
427	Anderson city, IN	59,459
428	Skokie village, IL	59,432
429	Pico Rivera city, CA	59,177
430	Galveston city, TX	59,070
431	Port Arthur city, TX	58,724
432	Lakewood CDP, WA	58,412
433	Greenville city, SC	58,282
434	Pensacola city, FL	58,165
435	Broken Arrow city, OK	58,043
436	Passaic city, NJ	58,041
437	Union City city, NJ	58,012
438	Brandon CDP, FL	57,985
439	Waltham city, MA	57,878
440	Burke CDP, VA	57,734
441	Dubuque city, IA	57,546
442	Terre Haute city, IN	57,483
443	Medford city, MA	57,407
444	Charleston city, WV	57,287
445	Florence-Graham CDP, CA	57,147
446	Pine Bluff city, AR	57,140
447	Canton CDP, MI	57,047
448	Waukesha city, WI	56,958
449	Eau Claire city, WI	56,856
450	Elyria city, OH	56,746
451	Livermore city, CA	56,741
452	Chicopee city, MA	56,632
453	Brooklyn Park city, MN	56,381
454	Merced city, CA	56,216
455	Oak Lawn village, IL	56,182
456	Huntington Park city, CA	56,065
457	South Augusta CDP, GA	55,998
458	Palo Alto city, CA	55,900
459	Port St. Lucie city, FL	55,866
460	Santa Fe city, NM	55,859
461	Lancaster city, PA	55,551
462	Wilmington city, NC	55,530
463	Encinitas city, CA	55,386
464	Levittown CDP, PA	55,362
465	Spring Valley CDP, CA	55,331
466	Great Falls city, MT	55,097
467	Victoria city, TX	55,076
468	Thornton city, CO	55,031
469	Oshkosh city, WI	55,006
470	Bryan city, TX	55,002
471	Yuma city, AZ	54,923
472	Monroe city, LA	54,909
473	Euclid city, OH	54,875
474	Huntington city, WV	54,844
475	West Bloomfield Township CDP, MI	54,843
476	Yakima city, WA	54,827
477	Vineland city, NJ	54,780

Rank	City and State	Population	Rank	City and State	Population
478	Gastonia city, NC	54,732	548	Pleasanton city, CA	50,553
479	Brookline CDP, MA	54,718	549	East Hartford CDP, CT	50,452
480	St. Charles city, MO	54,555	550	Hesperia city, CA	50,418
481	Rapid City city, SD	54,523	551	East Providence city, RI	50,380
482	Redford CDP, MI	54,387	552	Clovis city, CA	50,323
483	Council Bluffs city, IA	54,315	553	Palm Harbor CDP, FL	50,256
484	South San Francisco city, CA	54,312	554	Union CDP, NJ	50,024
485	Troy city, NY	54,269	555	Cheyenne city, WY	50,008
486	National City city, CA	54,249	556	North Miami city, FL	49,998
487	Weymouth CDP, MA	54,063	557	Gardena city, CA	49,847
488	Cleveland Heights city, OH	54,052	558	Taunton city, MA	49,832
489	West Haven city, CT	54,021	559	Lauderhill city, FL	49,708
490	Malden city, MA	53,884	560	Sheboygan city, WI	49,676
491	Union City city, CA	53,762	561	South Whittier CDP, CA	49,514
492	Wheaton-Glenmont CDP, MD	53,720	562	Hempstead village, NY	49,453
493	Fountain Valley city, CA	53,691	563	Towson CDP, MD	49,445
494	Diamond Bar city, CA	53,672	564	Grand Forks city, ND	49,425
495	Oak Park village, IL	53,648	565	Stratford CDP, CT	49,389
496	Dothan city, AL	53,589	566	Johnson City city, TN	49,381
497	Owensboro city, KY	53,549	567	Wauwatosa city, WI	49,366
498	Battle Creek city, MI	53,540	568	Bismarck city, ND	49,256
499	Sparks city, NV	53,367	569	Alexandria city, LA	49,188
500	Carol City CDP, FL	53,331	570	Santa Cruz city, CA	49,040
501	Beaverton city, OR	53,310	571	Rocky Mount city, NC	48,997
502	Levittown CDP, NY	53,286	572	Cuyahoga Falls city, OH	48,950
503	Cerritos city, CA	53,240	573	Jackson city, TN	48,949
504	Des Plaines city, IL	53,223	574	St. Cloud city, MN	48,812
505	Mount Prospect village, IL	53,170	575	Decatur city, AL	48,761
506	Danville city, VA	53,056	576	Harlingen city, TX	48,735
507	Binghamton city, NY	53,008	577	Rancho Cordova CDP, CA	48,731
508	Coon Rapids city, MN	52,978	578	White Plains city, NY	48,718
509	La Mesa city, CA	52,931	579	Carmichael CDP, CA	48,702
510	Santee city, CA	52,902	580	Shelby CDP, MI	48,655
511	Bossier City city, LA	52,721	581	Pittsfield city, MA	48,622
512	College Station city, TX	52,456	582	Castro Valley CDP, CA	48,619
513	Yorba Linda city, CA	52,422	583	Reston CDP, VA	48,556
514	Harrisburg city, PA	52,376	584	Kendale Lakes CDP, FL	48,524
515	Hacienda Heights CDP, CA	52,354	585	Parsippany-Troy Hills township, NJ	48,478
516	Taylorsville-Bennion CDP, UT	52,351	586	North Bergen CDP, NJ	48,414
517	Irondequoit CDP, NY	52,322	587	San Rafael city, CA	48,404
518	Edmond city, OK	52,315	588	Minnetonka city, MN	48,370
519	Camarillo city, CA	52,303	589	Arcadia city, CA	48,290
520	Midwest City city, OK	52,267	590	Milford city (remainder), CT	48,168
521	Bellingham city, WA	52,179	591	Rosell city, GA	47,923
522	Suffolk city, VA	52,141	592	West Seneca CDP, NY	47,866
523	Janesville city, WI	52,133	593	Glendora city, CA	47,828
524	Bloomington city, IL	51,972	594	North Las Vegas city, NV	47,707
525	Altoona city, PA	51,881	595	Paramount city, CA	47,669
526	Lodi city, CA	51,874	596	Novato city, CA	47,585
527	Spring Valley CDP, NV	51,726	597	Pittsburg city, CA	47,564
528	Rosemead city, CA	51,638	598	Wilkes-Barre city, PA	47,523
529	Longmont city, CO	51,555	599	Eagan city, MN	47,409
530	Wheaton city, IL	51,464	600	Mentor city, OH	47,358
531	Penn Hills CDP, PA	51,430	601	Davie town, FL	47,217
532	Haverhill city, MA	51,418	602	Ames city, IA	47,198
533	Roseville city, MI	51,412	603	Delray Beach city, FL	47,181
534	Burnsville city, MN	51,288	604	Dale City CDP, VA	47,170
535	La Habra city, CA	51,266	605	Peabody city, MA	47,039
536	Florissant city, MO	51,206	606	Wayne CDP, NJ	47,025
537	La Crosse city, WI	51,003	607	Medford city, OR	46,951
538	Annandale CDP, VA	50,975	608	Downers Grove village, IL	46,858
539	Sarasota city, FL	50,961	609	Casper city, WY	46,742
540	Plymouth city, MN	50,889	610	Laguna Hills CDP, CA	46,731
541	Deltona CDP, FL	50,828	611	Plainfield city, NJ	46,567
542	Warren city, OH	50,793	612	Hoffman Estates village, IL	46,561
543	Tustin city, CA	50,689	613	Jonesboro city, AR	46,535
544	Milpitas city, CA	50,686	614	Lewisville city, TX	46,521
545	East Lansing city, MI	50,677	615	Lee's Summit city, MO	46,418
546	Mansfield city, OH	50,627	616	Vancouver city, WA	46,380
547	Peoria city, AZ	50,618	617	Deerfield Beach city, FL	46,325

Rank	City and State	Population	Rank	City and State	Population
618	Biloxi city, MS	46,319	688	Salina city, KS	42,303
619	Davis city, CA	46,209	689	Turlock city, CA	42,198
620	Boynton Beach city, FL	46,194	690	York city, PA	42,192
621	Temple city, TX	46,109	691	Kennewick city, WA	42,155
622	Pocatello city, ID	46,080	692	Bloomfield Township CDP, MI	42,137
623	Apple Valley town, CA	46,079	693	North Highlands CDP, CA	42,105
624	Edina city, MN	46,070	694	Fayetteville city, AR	42,099
625	Middletown city, OH	46,022	695	Ocala city, FL	42,045
626	North Richland Hills city, TX	45,895	696	Elmhurst city, IL	42,029
627	Flagstaff city, AZ	45,857	697	Perth Amboy city, NJ	41,967
628	St. Peters city, MO	45,779	698	San Luis Obispo city, CA	41,958
629	Athens city, GA	45,734	699	Sumter city, SC	41,943
630	Potomac CDP, MD	45,634	700	Hattiesburg city, MS	41,882
631	Lima city, OH	45,549	701	Chester city, PA	41,856
632	Aspen Hill CDP, MD	45,494	702	Lincoln Park city, MI	41,832
633	Berwyn city, IL	45,426	703	Layton city, UT	41,784
634	Enid city, OK	45,309	704	New Brunswick city, NJ	41,711
635	Greenville city, MS	45,226	705	Renton city, WA	41,688
636	Brentwood CDP, NY	45,218	706	Rancho Palos Verdes city, CA	41,659
637	Fort Myers city, FL	45,206	707	Rock Hill city, SC	41,643
638	Bloomfield CDP, NJ	45,061	708	Port Charlotte CDP, FL	41,535
639	Greenville city, NC	44,972	709	Ellicott City CDP, MD	41,396
640	Kokomo city, IN	44,962	710	Azusa city, CA	41,333
641	Murfreesboro city, TN	44,922	711	Placentia city, CA	41,259
642	Rockville city, MD	44,835	712	Fitchburg city, MA	41,194
643	Tamarac city, FL	44,822	713	Germantown CDP, MD	41,145
644	Corvallis city, OR	44,757	714	San Clemente city, CA	41,100
645	Roseveille city, CA	44,685	715	Portage city, MI	41,042
646	Springfield city, OR	44,683	716	Meridian city, MS	41,036
647	Rosell city, NM	44,654	717	Joplin city, MO	40,961
648	Augusta city, GA	44,639	718	East St. Louis city, IL	40,944
649	Arlington CDP, MA	44,630	719	Essex CDP, MD	40,872
650	Laguna Niguel city, CA	44,400	720	Bolingbrook village, IL	40,843
651	Newark city, OH	44,389	721	Texas City city, TX	40,822
652	Rome city, NY	44,350	722	Gulfport city, MS	40,775
653	Marietta city, GA	44,129	723	Manteca city, CA	40,773
654	Idaho Falls city, ID	43,929	724	Goldsboro city, NC	40,709
655	Woonsocket city, RI	43,877	725	Victorville city, CA	40,764
656	Cary town, NC	43,858	726	Miramar city, FL	40,663
657	St. Louis Park city, MN	43,787	727	Bowling Green city, KY	40,641
658	Bradenton city, FL	43,779	728	Rock Island city, IL	40,552
659	Lafayette city, IN	43,764	729	La Mirada city, CA	40,452
660	Bedford city, TX	43,762	730	Carson City, NV	40,443
661	Warner Robins city, GA	43,726	731	Charlottesville city, VA	40,341
662	Holyoke city, MA	43,704	732	Moore city, OK	40,318
663	Elkhart city, IN	43,627	733	Muskegon city, MI	40,283
664	East Brunswick CDP, NJ	43,548	734	Cupertino city, CA	40,263
665	Poway city, CA	43,516	735	Colton city, CA	40,213
666	Spartanburg city, SC	43,467	736	Palm Springs city, CA	40,181
667	Pinellas Park city, FL	43,426	737	Hicksville CDP, NY	40,174
668	Covington city, KY	43,264	738	Blue Springs city, MO	40,153
669	Covina city, CA	43,207	739	Frederick city, MD	40,148
670	Moline city, IL	43,202	740	Coral Gables city, FL	40,091
671	Petaluma city, CA	43,184	741	University City city, MO	40,087
672	Southglenn CDP, CO	43,087	742	Chico city, CA	40,079
673	Margate city, FL	42,985	743	Kirkland city, WA	40,052
674	Missoula city, MT	42,918	744	Normal town, IL	40,023
675	West Jordan city, UT	42,892	745	Freeport village, NY	39,894
676	Revere city, MA	42,786	746	Valdosta city, GA	39,806
677	Belleville city, IL	42,785	747	Woodland city, CA	39,802
678	Middletown city, CT	42,762	748	Hoover city, AL	39,788
679	East Hill-Meridian CDP, WA	42,696	749	Lewiston city, ME	39,757
680	Altadena CDP, CA	42,658	750	Fairfield city, OH	39,729
681	Cypress city, CA	42,655	751	Quincy city, IL	39,681
682	Rowland Heights CDP, CA	42,647	752	Gaithersburg city, MD	39,542
683	Tuckahoe CDP, VA	42,629	753	Burlington city, NC	39,498
684	Mishawaka city, IN	42,608	754	Lakeside CDP, CA	39,412
685	Gadsden city, AL	42,523	755	Lombard village, IL	39,408
686	West Babylon CDP, NY	42,410	756	Titusville city, FL	39,394
687	Bell Gardens city, CA	42,355	757	Grand Island city, NE	39,386

Rank	City and State	Population	Rank	City and State	Population
758	Eden Prairie city, MN	39,311	828	Florence city, AL	36,426
759	Hutchinson city, KS	39,308	829	Kingsport city, TN	36,365
758	Palatine village, IL	39,253	830	Urbana city, IL	36,344
761	Burlington city, VT	39,127	831	Rohnert Park city, CA	36,326
762	West Orange CDP, NJ	39,103	832	New Albany city, IN	36,322
763	Blaine city, MN	38,975	833	Willingboro CDP, NJ	36,291
764	San Marcos city, CA	38,974	834	Missouri City city, TX	36,176
765	San Bruno city, CA	38,961	835	Park Ridge city, IL	36,175
766	Bay City city, MI	38,936	836	Commack CDP, NY	36,124
767	State College borough, PA	38,923	837	West Hollywood city, CA	36,118
768	Seaside city, CA	38,901	838	Hemet city, CA	36,094
769	Culver City city, CA	38,793	839	Campbell city, CA	36,048
770	Maple Grove city, MN	38,736	840	Concord city, NH	36,006
771	Chapel Hill town, NC	38,719	841	Woburn city, MA	35,943
772	Richmond city, IN	38,705	842	Redmond city, WA	35,800
773	Huber Heights city, OH	38,696	843	Oxon Hill-Glassmanor CDP, MD	35,794
774	Boardman CDP, OH	38,596	844	Monrovia city, CA	35,761
775	Leavenworth city, KS	38,495	845	Duncanville city, TX	35,748
776	Petersburg city, VA	38,386	846	Orland Park village, IL	35,720
777	Attleboro city, MA	38,383	847	Richfield city, MN	35,710
778	Westfield city, MA	38,372	848	Findlay city, OH	35,703
779	Beverly city, MA	38,195	849	Everett city, MA	35,701
780	McLean CDP, VA	38,168	849	South Valley CDP, NM	35,701
781	Euless city, TX	38,149	851	Fort Hood CDP, TX	35,580
782	Leominster city, MA	38,145	852	Beloit city, WI	35,573
783	Bremerton city, WA	38,142	853	Jefferson City city, MO	35,481
784	Sun City CDP, AZ	38,126	854	Kaneohe CDP, HI	35,448
785	West New York town, NJ	38,125	855	Hagerstown city, MD	35,445
786	Salem city, MA	38,091	856	Shelton city, CT	35,418
787	Midland city, MI	38,053	857	North Miami Beach city, FL	35,359
788	Shawnee city, KS	37,993	858	Pine Hills CDP, FL	35,322
789	Chesterfield city, MO	37,991	859	Port Orange city, FL	35,317
790	Atlantic City city, NJ	37,986	860	Strongsville city, OH	35,308
791	Kent city, WA	37,960	861	San Ramon city, CA	35,303
792	Newark city, CA	37,861	862	East Detroit city, MI	35,283
793	Calumet City city, IL	37,840	863	Catonsville CDP, MD	35,233
794	Kentwood city, MI	37,826	864	Brookfield city, WI	35,184
795	Teaneck CDP, NJ	37,825	865	Suitland-Silver Hill CDP, MD	35,111
796	Hilo CDP, HI	37,808	866	North Tonawanda city, NY	34,989
797	Olympia Heights CDP, FL	37,792	867	Sayreville borough, NJ	34,986
798	Fond du Lac city, WI	37,757	868	North Chicago city, IL	34,978
799	Montclair CDP, NJ	37,729	869	De Kalb city, IL	34,925
800	Manhattan city, KS	37,712	870	Wheeling city, WV	34,882
801	Muskogee city, OK	37,708	871	Altamonte Springs city, FL	34,879
802	Pacifica city, CA	37,670	872	Kearny town, NJ	34,874
803	Lompoc city, CA	37,649	873	Fort Bragg CDP, NC	34,744
804	Bowie city, MD	37,589	874	Pennsauken CDP, NJ	34,733
805	Hillsboro city, OR	37,520	875	Jamestown city, NY	34,681
806	Jackson city, MI	37,446	876	Apple Valley city, MN	34,598
807	Kingwood CDP, TX	37,397	877	Blacksburg town, VA	34,590
808	Norwich city, CT	37,391	878	Minot city, ND	34,544
809	Loveland city, CO	37,352	879	Lancaster city, OH	34,507
810	Glen Burnie CDP, MD	37,305	880	Brighton CDP, NY	34,455
811	Tinley Park village, IL	37,121	881	Highland city, CA	34,439
812	San Gabriel city, CA	37,120	882	Cape Girardeau city, MO	34,438
813	Glenview village, IL	37,093	883	East Point city, GA	34,402
814	Wausau city, WI	37,060	884	Panama City city, FL	34,378
815	Hackensack city, NJ	37,049	885	Bell city, CA	34,365
816	La Puente city, CA	36,955	886	Prichard city, AL	34,311
817	Wilson city, NC	36,930	887	Cedar Falls city, IA	34,298
818	East Meadow CDP, NY	36,909	888	Aloha CDP, OR	34,284
819	Fort Pierce city, FL	36,830	889	Bartlesville city, OK	34,256
820	Kailua CDP, HI	36,818	890	Belleville CDP, NJ	34,213
821	Indio city, CA	36,793	891	North Olmsted city, OH	34,204
822	Camp Lejeune Central CDP, NC	36,716	892	Ewing CDP, NJ	34,185
823	Linden city, NJ	36,701	893	Upper Arlington city, OH	34,128
824	Stillwater city, OK	36,676	894	Marion city, OH	34,075
825	Marrero CDP, LA	36,671	895	Lenexa city, KS	34,034
826	Bountiful city, UT	36,659	896	Dunedin city, FL	34,012
827	Buffalo Grove village, IL	36,427	897	Farmington city, NM	33,997

Rank	City and State	Population	Rank	City and State	Population
898	Valley Stream village, NY	33,946	968	Hendersonville city, TN	32,188
899	East Chicago city, IN	33,892	969	North Providence CDP, RI	32,090
900	Parkersburg city, WV	33,862	970	Manhattan Beach city, CA	32,063
901	Tamiami CDP, FL	33,845	971	Addison village, IL	32,058
902	Olympia city, WA	33,840	972	Trumbull CDP, CT	32,000
903	Braintree CDP, MA	33,836	973	Fort Lee borough, NJ	31,997
904	Auburn city, AL	33,830	974	Beverly Hills city, CA	31,971
905	Danville city, IL	33,828	975	Monterey city, CA	31,954
906	Bethel Park borough, PA	33,823	976	Williamsport city, PA	31,933
907	Michigan City city, IN	33,822	977	Parkway-South Sacramento CDP, CA	31,903
908	Martinez CDP, GA	33,731	978	Dana Point city, CA	31,896
909	Elmira city, NY	33,724	979	Chalmette CDP, LA	31,860
910	Port Huron city, MI	33,694	980	Garden City city, MI	31,846
911	Torrington city, CT	33,687	981	New Iberia city, LA	31,828
912	Littleton city, CO	33,685	982	Marlborough city, MA	31,813
913	New City CDP, NY	33,673	983	Martinez city, CA	31,808
914	Beavercreek city, OH	33,626	984	Columbus city, IN	31,802
915	New Berlin city, WI	33,592	985	Oakville CDP, MO	31,750
916	West Little River CDP, FL	33,575	986	Garfield Heights city, OH	31,739
917	Hurst city, TX	33,574	987	Carol Stream village, IL	31,716
918	Tracy city, CA	33,558	988	West Des Moines city, IA	31,702
919	Galesburg city, IL	33,530	989	Texarkana city, TX	31,656
920	Long Beach city, NY	33,510	990	Parkville CDP, MD	31,617
921	Bessemer city, AL	33,497	991	Sherman city, TX	31,601
922	Roseville city, MN	33,485	992	Pleasant Hill city, CA	31,585
923	Ross Township CDP, PA	33,482	993	Longview city, WA	31,499
924	Elk Grove Village village, IL	33,429	994	Gilroy city, CA	31,487
925	Greenfield city, WI	33,403	995	Mankato city, MN	31,477
926	Hoboken city, NJ	33,397	996	Waipahu CDP, HI	31,435
927	Mount Lebanon CDP, PA	33,362	997	El Centro city, CA	31,384
928	Butte-Silver Bow, (remainder) MT	33,336	998	Chillum CDP, MD	31,309
929	Watertown CDP, MA	33,284	999	Danville city, CA	31,306
930	Tulare city, CA	33,249	1000	Fairborn city, OH	31,300
931	Annapolis city, MD	33,187	1001	North Brunswick Township CDP, NJ	31,287
932	Bangor city, ME	33,181	1002	Murray city, UT	31,282
933	Spring CDP, TX	33,111	1003	Auburn city, NY	31,258
934	Auburn city, WA	33,102	1004	Spring Hill CDP, FL	31,117
935	East Cleveland city, OH	33,096	1005	Temple City city, CA	31,100
936	Chicago Heights city, IL	33,072	1006	Watsonville city, CA	31,099
937	Novi city, MI	32,998	1007	Allen Park city, MI	31,092
938	Sierra Vista city, AZ	32,983	1008	Westmont CDP, CA	31,044
939	Pharr city, TX	32,921	1009	Massillon city, OH	31,007
940	Woodlawn CDP, MD	32,907	1010	Hallandale city, FL	30,996
941	Alton city, IL	32,905	1011	Pearl City CDP, HI	30,993
942	Hanover Park village, IL	32,895	1012	Streamwood village, IL	30,987
943	Germantown city, TN	32,893	1013	Bellevue city, NE	30,982
944	Merritt Island CDP, FL	32,886	1014	Smyrna city, GA	30,981
945	Brea city, CA	32,873	1015	Maplewood city, MN	30,954
946	Granite City city, IL	32,862	1015	Clovis city, NM	30,954
947	Haltom City city, TX	32,856	1017	Wyandotte city, MI	30,938
948	Yucaipa city, CA	32,824	1018	Central Manchester CDP, CT	30,934
949	Willowbrook CDP, CA	32,772	1019	Round Rock city, TX	30,923
950	Logan city, UT	32,762	1020	La Verne city, CA	30,897
951	Marion city, IN	32,618	1020	Hanford city, CA	30,897
952	Manitowoc city, WI	32,520	1022	Nacogdoches city, TX	30,872
953	Rio Rancho city, NM	32,505	1023	Fairbanks city, AK	30,843
954	Claremont city, CA	32,503	1024	Shaker Heights city, OH	30,831
955	Hot Springs city, AR	32,462	1025	Inkster city, MI	30,772
956	Oceanside CDP, NY	32,423	1026	Southgate city, MI	30,771
957	San Dimas city, CA	32,397	1027	Norristown borough, PA	30,749
958	Chelmsford CDP, MA	32,388	1028	Holland city, MI	30,745
959	Sanford city, FL	32,387	1029	Edmonds city, WA	30,744
960	Austintown CDP, OH	32,371	1030	Casa de Oro-Mount Helix CDP, CA	30,727
961	Montgomery Village CDP, MD	32,315	1031	Harrisonburg city, VA	30,707
961	Richland city, WA	32,315	1032	Del Rio city, TX	30,705
963	Northbrook village, IL	32,308	1033	Tupelo city, MS	30,685
964	Moorehead city, MN	32,295	1034	Naugatuck borough, CT	30,625
965	Pekin city, IL	32,254	1035	Raytown city, MO	30,601
966	Millcreek CDP, UT	32,230	1036	Lake Oswego city, OR	30,576
967	Madison Heights city, MI	32,196	1037	Highland Park city, IL	30,575

Rank	City and State	Population
1038	Fair Lawn borough, NJ	30,548
1039	DeSoto city, TX	30,544
1040	Shaler Township CDP, PA	30,533
1041	Houma city, LA	30,495
1042	Stanton city, CA	30,491
1043	Oak Park city, MI	30,462
1044	Cleveland city, TN	30,354
1045	Rome city, GA	30,326
1046	Westerville city, OH	30,269
1047	Lufkin city, TX	30,206
1048	League City city, TX	30,159
1049	Coram CDP, NY	30,111
1050	Mount Pleasant town, SC	30,108
1051	Cascade-Fairwood CDP, WA	30,107
1052	Randolph CDP, MA	30,093
1053	Cathedral City city, CA	30,085
1054	Kissimmee city, FL	30,050
1055	South Miami Heights CDP, FL	30,030
1056	North Fort Myers CDP, FL	30,027
1057	Jacksonville city, NC	30,013
1058	Waimalu CDP, HI	29,967
1059	Springdale city, AR	29,941
1060	Orange CDP, NJ	29,925
1061	Wheeling village, IL	29,911
1062	Edinburg city, TX	29,885
1063	Westchester CDP, FL	29,883
1064	Florence city, SC	29,813
1065	Hopkinsville city, KY	29,809
1066	Folsom city, CA	29,802
1067	Harvey city, IL	29,771
1068	Sandusky city, OH	29,764
1069	Drexel Hill CDP, PA	29,744
1070	Ormond Beach city, FL	29,721
1071	Kannapolis city, NC	29,696
1072	North Bethesda CDP, MD	29,656
1073	Porterville city, CA	29,563
1074	Ithaca city, NY	29,541
1075	Candler-McAfee CDP, GA	29,491
1076	Albany city, OR	29,462
1077	Watertown city, NY	29,429
1078	Wheat Ridge city, CO	29,419
1079	Englewood city, CO	29,387
1080	Mililani Town CDP, HI	29,359
1081	Tigard city, OR	29,344
1082	Chantilly CDP, VA	29,337
1083	Northampton city, MA	29,289
1084	Madera city, CA	29,281
1085	West Warwick CDP, RI	29,268
1086	Newington CDP, CT	29,208
1087	The Woodlands CDP, TX	29,205
1088	Grapevine city, TX	29,202
1089	Clinton city, IA	29,201
1090	Gilbert town, AZ	29,188
1091	Municipality of Monroe borough, PA	29,169
1092	Lakeside CDP, FL	29,137
1093	Inglewood-Finn Hill CDP, WA	29,132
1094	Hobbs city, NM	29,115
1095	Walnut city, CA	29,105
1096	Jacksonville city, AR	29,101
1097	Portage city, IN	29,060
1098	Mason City city, IA	29,040
1099	Grand Junction city, CO	29,034
1100	Lexington city, MA	28,974
1101	West Sacramento city, CA	28,898
1102	Brooklyn Center city, MN	28,887
1103	Westfield town, NJ	28,870
1104	Poughkeepsie city, NY	28,844
1105	Deer Park CDP, NY	28,840
1106	Kent city, OH	28,835
1107	McCandless Township CDP, PA	28,781
1108	Cottonwood Heights CDP, UT	28,766
1109	Powellhurst-Centennial CDP, OR	28,756
1110	San Marcos city, TX	28,743
1111	St. Charles CDP, MD	28,717
1112	Gloucester city, MA	28,716
1113	Chelsea city, MA	28,710
1114	Radnor Township CDP, PA	28,705
1115	Norwood CDP, MA	28,700
1116	Lynnwood city, WA	28,695
1117	Long Branch city, NJ	28,658
1118	Mission city, TX	28,653
1119	Elmont CDP, NY	28,612
1120	Columbia city, TN	28,583
1121	Lake Worth city, FL	28,564
1122	New London city, CT	28,540
1123	St. George city, UT	28,502
1124	Montclair city, CA	28,434
1125	West Islip CDP, NY	28,419
1126	Kearns CDP, UT	28,374
1127	Nampa city, ID	28,365
1128	Fridley city, MN	28,335
1129	New Castle city, PA	28,334
1130	Hickory city, NC	28,301
1131	Niles village, IL	28,284
1132	West Memphis city, AR	28,259
1133	Huntington Station CDP, NY	28,247
1134	Brunswick city, OH	28,230
1135	Newport city, RI	28,227
1136	Franklin Square CDP, NY	28,205
1137	Foster City city, CA	28,176
1137	Bowling Green city, OH	28,176
1139	Melrose city, MA	28,150
1140	Johnstown city, PA	28,134
1141	Bettendorf city, IA	28,132
1142	West Springfield CDP, VA	28,126
1143	Lansing village, IL	28,086
1144	Lewiston city, ID	28,082
1145	Saratoga city, CA	28,061
1146	Menlo Park city, CA	28,040
1147	Glendale Heights village, IL	27,973
1148	Manassas city, VA	27,957
1149	Huntsville city, TX	27,925
1150	La Porte city, TX	27,910
1151	Maywood city, CA	27,850
1152	North Atlanta CDP, GA	27,812
1153	Gahanna city, OH	27,791
1154	Ridgecrest city, CA	27,725
1155	Stow city, OH	27,702
1156	University Place CDP, WA	27,701
1157	Deer Park city, TX	27,652
1158	Riviera Beach city, FL	27,639
1159	West Augusta CDP, GA	27,637
1160	Dover city, DE	27,630
1161	Barberton city, OH	27,623
1162	Burton city, MI	27,617
1163	Conroe city, TX	27,610
1164	Chino Hills CDP, CA	27,608
1165	Burbank city, IL	27,600
1166	Alamogordo city, NM	27,596
1167	Twin Falls city, ID	27,591
1168	Kankakee city, IL	27,575
1169	South Gate CDP, MD	27,564
1170	Needham CDP, MA	27,557
1170	Mehlville CDP, MO	27,557
1172	West Springfield CDP, MA	27,537
1173	Coconut Creek city, FL	27,485
1173	Mount Vernon CDP, VA	27,485
1175	Yuba City city, CA	27,437
1176	Los Gatos town, CA	27,357
1177	Concord city, NC	27,347

Rank	City and State	Population	Rank	City and State	Population
1178	Lauderdale Lakes city, FL	27,341	1238	Oak Forest city, IL	26,203
1179	New Braunfels city, TX	27,334	1239	Anderson city, SC	26,184
1180	Lawndale city, CA	27,331	1240	San Juan Capistrano city, CA	26,183
1181	Oak Ridge city, TN	27,310	1241	San Carlos city, CA	26,167
1182	Kirkwood city, MO	27,291	1242	East Haven CDP, CT	26,144
1183	Merrillville town, IN	27,257	1243	Lakewood CDP, NJ	26,095
1184	Paducah city, KY	27,256	1244	Richmond Highlands CDP, WA	26,037
1185	Burlington city, IA	27,208	1245	Central Islip CDP, NY	26,028
1186	Northglenn city, CO	27,195	1246	Shawnee city, OK	26,017
1187	Maywood village, IL	27,139	1247	McKeesport city, PA	26,016
1188	Superior city, WI	27,134	1248	Millville city, NJ	25,992
1189	Temecula city, CA	27,099	1249	Frankfort city, KY	25,968
1189	Nutley CDP, NJ	27,099	1250	Henderson city, KY	25,945
1191	Maple Heights city, OH	27,089	1251	Portsmouth city, NH	25,925
1192	Carbondale city, IL	27,033	1252	West Lafayette city, IN	25,907
1193	Eureka city, CA	27,025	1253	Pascagoula city, MS	25,899
1194	Westlake city, OH	27,018	1254	Fort Dodge city, IA	25,894
1195	Bartlett town, TN	26,989	1255	Severna Park CDP, MD	25,879
1196	Lindenhurst village, NY	28,879	1255	Morgantown city, WV	25,879
1197	Mercerville-Hamilton Square CDP, NJ	26,873	1257	Dix Hills CDP, NY	25,849
1198	Fair Oaks CDP, CA	26,867	1258	Freeport city, IL	25,840
1199	Homestead city, FL	26,866	1259	Jefferson CDP, VA	25,782
1200	Menomonee Falls village, WI	26,840	1260	Tucker CDP, GA	25,781
1201	Burlingame city, CA	26,801	1261	Reynoldsburg city, OH	25,748
1202	Zanesville city, OH	26,778	1262	Mableton CDP, GA	25,725
1203	Lawrence city, IN	26,763	1262	Milton CDP, MA	25,725
1204	Juneau city, AK	26,751	1264	St. Andrews CDP, SC	25,692
1205	Garfield city, NJ	26,727	1265	Wethersfield CDP, CT	25,651
1206	Centereach CDP, NY	26,720	1266	Smithtown CDP, NY	25,638
1207	Wilmette village, IL	26,690	1267	Plum borough, PA	25,609
1208	Laramie city, WY	26,687	1268	La Grange city, GA	25,597
1209	Rochester city, NH	26,630	1269	Carney CDP, MD	25,578
1210	Anniston city, AL	26,623	1270	Channelview CDP, TX	25,564
1211	Wellesley CDP, MA	26,615	1271	Saugus CDP, MA	25,549
1212	Livingston CDP, NJ	26,609	1272	Emporia city, KS	25,512
1213	Centreville CDP, VA	26,585	1273	Moorpark city, CA	25,494
1214	Oildale CDP, CA	26,553	1274	Golden Glades CDP, FL	25,474
1215	Coronado city, CA	26,540	1275	West Milford CDP, NJ	25,430
1216	Imperial Beach city, CA	26,512	1276	Paradise town, CA	25,408
1217	North Lauderdale city, FL	26,506	1277	Maryland Heights city, MO	25,407
1218	Conway city, AR	26,481	1278	Winona city, MN	25,399
1219	Walla Walla city, WA	26,478	1279	Carmel city, IN	25,380
1220	Prescott city, AZ	26,455	1280	Rahway city, NJ	25,325
1221	Newburgh city, NY	26,454	1281	Phenix City city, AL	25,312
1222	Marina city, CA	26,436	1282	Kinston city, NC	25,295
1223	Bel Air South CDP, MD	26,421	1283	Kingsville city, TX	25,276
1224	Woodbridge CDP, VA	26,401	1284	Holbrook CDP, NY	25,273
1225	Ponca City city, OK	26,359	1285	Lochearn CDP, MD	25,240
1226	Oakland Park city, FL	26,326	1286	Marshalltown city, IA	25,178
1227	Ceres city, CA	26,314	1287	San Pablo city, CA	25,158
1228	Los Altos city, CA	26,303	1288	Pleasure Ridge Park CDP, KY	25,131
1229	Dunwoody city, GA	26,302	1289	Seal Beach city, CA	25,098
1230	Ferry Pass CDP, FL	26,301	1289	Neward city, DE	25,098
1231	Randallstown CDP, MD	26,277	1291	Burien CDP, WA	25,089
1232	Easton city, PA	26,276	1292	Ferndale city, MI	25,084
1233	Orangevale CDP, CA	26,266	1293	Paramus borough, NJ	25,067
1234	Greenwood city, IN	26,265	1294	Santa Paula city, CA	25,062
1235	Woodridge village, IL	26,256	1295	Dover city, NH	25,042
1236	Gladstone city, MO	26,243	1296	Saratoga Springs city, NY	25,001
1237	Plainview CDP, NY	26,207			

NOTE: **Census Designated Place (CDP)**—A statistical area comprising a densely settled concentration of population that is not incorporated but which resembles an incorporated place in that local people can identify it with a name.

The Nation's Ten Largest Counties

The 1990 census found 30 counties with populations over one million. Los Angeles County is the nation's largest, with 8.9 million people, followed by Cook (Chicago), with 5.1 million, and Harris (Houston), with 2.8 million. Others were San Diego County, 2.5 million; Orange County, Calif., 2.4 million; Kings County, N.Y., 2.3 million; Maricopa County, Ariz., and Wayne County, Mich., with 2.1 million; and Queens County, N.Y., and Dade County, Fla., with 1.9 million. □

U.S. STATISTICS

1990 Census Profile

Source: U.S. Department of Commerce, Economics and Statistics Administration, Bureau of the Census.

Population Trends

The resident population of the United States as of April 1, 1990, was 248.7 million persons. This is 9.8% above the 1980 census count of 226.5 million.

The growth rate for the 1980–90 decade is the second lowest in census history. The rate exceeded only the 7.3% increase of the Depression decade of the 1930s, when the rate of childbearing dropped close to two births per woman and net immigration from abroad was negligible. In contrast, the growth rate reached 18.5% in the 1950s, which included the peak of the post-World War II baby boom (1946–64) and a rate of childbearing averaging over three births per woman.

Despite an increase in net immigration since the 1950s, the growth rate has been lower subsequently. The decline is due primarily to the drop in the rate of childbearing, which averaged about two births per woman during the past two decades.

The numerical growth in the 1980–90 decade was 22.2 million. The numerical growth also exceeded 20 million in the three preceding decades, with a peak figure of 28.0 million in the 1950s.

The population growth rate exceeded 30% in each decade from 1790 to 1860 and remained above 20% in each decade from 1860 to 1910, before dropping to 7.3% in the 1930s. The decrease is due primarily to the long-term decline in the average rate of childbearing from about seven births per woman at the beginning of the 19th century. The effect of declining fertility on the growth rate was offset in part by declining mortality, and by large-scale immigration during most of the period from the 1840s to the 1920s.

Fastest Growing Regions

The West had the highest growth rate (22.3%) among the four census regions of the United States during the 1980s. This was down slightly from the 1970s (23.9%), but still more than twice the national rate. The South's growth rate fell more sharply (20.0% to 13.4%), but remained above the national rate. The growth rate rose in the Northeast (0.2% to 3.4%) and fell in the Midwest (4.0% to 1.4%). These two regions had growth rates far below the national rate in both the 1970s and 1980s.

The difference in growth rates among the regions in the 1980s reflect differences in migration among States and immigration, and in rates of natural increase (birth rates minus death rates). There was net migration into the South and West, negligible net migration in the Northeast, and net migration out of the Midwest. The rate of natural increase was highest in the West and lowest in the Northeast.

The South and West together accounted for 89% of national population growth in the 1980s and 90% in the 1970s. Their combined share of the national population increased from 48.0% in 1970 to 52.3% in 1980 and to 55.6% in 1990.

Fastest Growing States

The five States with the highest percent increases in population during the 1980–90 decade were Ne-

vada (50.1), Alaska (36.9), Arizona (34.8), Florida (32.7), and California (25.7).

During the past five decades (the 1940s through the 1980s), five states have dominated the list of most rapidly growing states. Arizona, Florida, and Nevada were included in each decade, while Alaska and California missed only in the 1970s. Nevada had the highest growth rate in each of the last three decades.

The only Northeastern or Midwestern States with growth rates above the national figure during the 1980s were New Hampshire (20.5%) and Vermont (10.0%), while Maine's growth rate was slightly lower (9.2%). These three were the only Northeastern or Midwestern States with growth rates above the national rate in the 1970s.

Four states lost population during the 1980s after increases in the 1970s: Iowa, North Dakota, West Virginia, and Wyoming. New York and Rhode Island gained population in the 1980s after losses in the 1970s. The District of Columbia lost population in both decades.

California, Florida, and Texas

The combined population growth in California (6.1 million), Florida (3.2 million), and Texas (2.8 million) in the 1980–90 decade totaled 12.0 million, or 54% of the 22.2-million national population increase. This is the first time in the nation's 200-year census history that as few as three states accounted for over half of the national population growth.

California's numerical growth of 6.1 million and its 27% share of U.S. population growth during the 1980s are record highs for a single State. Its population of 29.8 million in 1990 was larger than that of the 21 least populous States combined, and its 12.0% share of U.S. population was the highest in one State since 1860 when New York had 12.3%.

Congressional Apportionment

As a result of population changes from 1980 to 1990, eight states will have more representatives in the 103rd Congress, which will convene in January 1993.[1] The largest gains will be in California (+7), Florida (+4), and Texas (+3), while five other states will each gain one seat: Arizona, Georgia, North Carolina, Virginia, and Washington. Thirteen states will have fewer representatives. The largest losses will be in New York (−3), and in Illinois, Michigan, Ohio, and Pennsylvania (−2 each). Eight other states will each lose one seat: Iowa, Kansas, Kentucky, Louisiana, Massachusetts, Montana, New Jersey, and West Virginia.

In the upcoming reapportionment, the new increase of 7 seats in the South reflects a gain of 10 seats and a loss of 1 seat each in Kentucky, Louisiana, and West Virginia. The net increase of 8 seats in the West reflects a gain of 9 seats and a loss of 1 seat in Montana. □

---

1. The 1990 census apportionment population was 249.0 million. This number includes 0.9 million overseas military and Federal civilian employees and their dependents and excludes the District of Columbia.

Population

Colonial Population Estimates (in round numbers)

Year	Population	Year	Population	Year	Population	Year	Population
1610	350	1660	75,100	1710	331,700	1760	1,593,600
1620	2,300	1670	111,900	1720	466,200	1770	2,148,100
1630	4,600	1680	151,500	1730	629,400	1780	2,780,400
1640	26,600	1690	210,400	1740	905,600		
1650	50,400	1700	250,900	1750	1,170,800		

National Censuses[1]

Year	Resident population[2]	Land area, sq mi.	Pop. per sq mi.	Year	Resident population[2]	Land area, sq mi.	Pop. per sq mi.
1790	3,929,214	864,746	4.5	1900	75,994,575	2,969,834	25.6
1800	5,308,483	864,746	6.1	1910	91,972,266	2,969,565	31.0
1810	7,239,881	1,681,828	4.3	1920	105,710,620	2,969,451	35.6
1820	9,638,453	1,749,462	5.5	1930	122,775,046	2,977,128	41.2
1830	12,866,020	1,749,462	7.4	1940	131,669,275	2,977,128	44.2
1840	17,069,453	1,749,462	9.8	1950	150,697,361	2,974,726	50.7
1850	23,191,876	2,940,042	7.9	1960	179,323,175	3,540,911	50.6
1860	31,443,321	2,969,640	10.6	1970	203,302,031	3,540,023	57.4
1870	39,818,449	2,969,640	13.4	1980	226,545,805	3,539,289	64.0
1880	50,155,783	2,969,640	16.9	1990	248,709,873	n.a.	n.a.
1890	62,947,714	2,969,640	21.2				

1. Beginning with 1960, figures include Alaska and Hawaii. 2. Excludes armed forces overseas. n.a. = not available.
Source: Department of Commerce, Bureau of the Census.

Population Distribution by Age, Race, Nativity, and Sex

							Race and Nativity				
		Age					White[1]				
Year	Total	Under 5	5–19	20–44	45–64	65 and over	Total	Native born	Foreign born	Black	Other races[1]
PERCENT DISTRIBUTION											
1860[2]	100.0	15.4	35.8	35.7	10.4	2.7	85.6	72.6	13.0	14.1	0.3
1870[2]	100.0	14.3	35.4	35.4	11.9	3.0	87.1	72.9	14.2	12.7	0.2
1880[2]	100.0	13.8	34.3	35.9	12.6	3.4	86.5	73.4	13.1	13.1	0.3
1890[3]	100.0	12.2	33.9	36.9	13.1	3.9	87.5	73.0	14.5	11.9	0.3
1900	100.0	12.1	32.3	37.7	13.7	4.1	87.9	74.5	13.4	11.6	0.5
1910	100.0	11.6	30.4	39.0	14.6	4.3	88.9	74.4	14.5	10.7	0.4
1920	100.0	10.9	29.8	38.4	16.1	4.7	89.7	76.7	13.0	9.9	0.4
1930	100.0	9.3	29.5	38.3	17.4	5.4	89.8	78.4	11.4	9.7	0.5
1940	100.0	8.0	26.4	38.9	19.8	6.8	89.8	81.1	8.7	9.8	0.4
1950	100.0	10.7	23.2	37.6	20.3	8.1	89.5	82.8	6.7	10.0	0.5
1960	100.0	11.3	27.1	32.2	20.1	9.2	88.6	83.4	5.2	10.5	0.9
1970[2]	100.0	8.4	29.5	31.7	20.6	9.8	87.6	83.4	4.3	11.1	1.4
1980	100.0	7.2	24.8	37.1	19.6	11.3	83.1	n.a.	n.a.	11.7	5.2
MALES PER 100 FEMALES											
1860[2]	104.7	102.4	101.2	107.9	111.5	98.3	105.3	103.7	115.1	99.6	260.8
1870[2]	102.2	102.9	101.2	99.2	114.5	100.5	102.8	100.6	115.3	96.2	400.7
1880[2]	103.6	103.0	101.3	104.0	110.2	101.4	104.0	102.1	115.9	97.8	362.2
1890[3]	105.0	103.6	101.4	107.3	108.3	104.2	105.4	102.9	118.7	99.5	165.2
1900	104.4	102.1	100.9	105.8	110.7	102.0	104.9	102.8	117.4	98.6	185.2
1910	106.0	102.5	101.3	108.1	114.4	101.1	106.6	102.7	129.2	98.9	185.6
1920	104.0	102.5	100.8	102.8	115.2	101.3	104.4	101.7	121.7	99.2	156.6
1930	102.5	103.0	101.4	100.5	109.1	100.5	102.9	101.1	115.8	97.0	150.6
1940	100.7	103.2	102.0	98.1	105.2	95.5	101.2	100.1	111.1	95.0	140.5

				Age				White[1]				
												Race and Nativity
Year	Total	Under 5	5–19	20–44	45–64	65 and over	Total	Native born	Foreign born	Black	Other races[1]	
1950	98.6	103.9	102.5	96.2	100.1	89.6	99.0	98.8	102.0	93.7	129.7	
1960	97.1	103.4	102.7	95.6	95.7	82.8	97.4	97.6	94.2	93.3	109.7	
1970[2]	94.8	104.0	103.3	95.1	91.6	72.1	95.3	95.9	83.8	90.8	100.2	
1980	94.5	104.7	104.0	98.1	90.7	67.6	94.8	n.a.	n.a.	89.6	100.3	

1. The 1980 census data for white and other races categories are not directly comparable to those shown for the preceding years because of the changes in the way some persons reported their race, as well as changes in 1980 procedures relating to racial classification. 2. Excludes persons for whom age is not available. 3. Excludes persons enumerated in the Indian Territory and on Indian reservations. NOTES: Data exclude Armed Forces overseas. Beginning in 1960, includes Alaska and Hawaii. n.a. = not available. 1990 Census data not available at press time. *Source:* Department of Commerce, Bureau of the Census.

Population and Rank of Large Metropolitan Areas, 1990

(over 100,000)

Rank	Standard metropolitan statistical area	Population
1	New York–Northern New Jersey–Long Island–NY–NJ–CT	18,087,251
	New York, NY	8,546,846
	Nassau–Suffolk, NY	2,609,212
	Newark, NJ	1,824,321
	Bergen–Passaic, NJ	1,278,440
	Middlesex–Somerset–Hunterdon, NJ	1,019,835
	Monmouth–Ocean, NJ	986,327
	Jersey City, NJ	553,099
	Bridgeport–Milford, CT	443,772
	Orange County, NY	307,647
	Stamford, CT	202,557
	Danbury, CT	187,867
	Norwalk, CT	127,378
2	Los Angeles–Anaheim–Riverside, CA	14,531,529
	Los Angeles–Long Beach, CA	8,863,164
	Riverside–San Bernardino, CA	2,588,793
	Anaheim–Santa Ana, CA	2,410,556
	Oxnard–Ventura, CA	669,016
3	Chicago–Gary–Lake County, IL–IN–WI	8,065,633
	Chicago, IL	6,069,974
	Gary–Hammond, IN	604,526
	Lake County, IL	516,418
	Joliet, IL	389,650
	Aurora–Elgin, IL	356,884
	Kenosha, WI	128,181
4	San Francisco–Oakland–San Jose, CA	6,253,311
	Oakland, CA	2,082,914
	San Francisco, CA	1,603,678
	San Jose, CA	1,497,577
	Vallejo–Fairfield–Napa, CA	451,186
	Santa Rosa–Petaluma, CA	388,222
	Santa Cruz, CA	229,734
5	Philadelphia–Wilmington–Trenton, PA–NJ–DE–MD	5,899,345
	Philadelphia, PA–NJ	4,856,881
	Wilmington, DE–NJ–MD	578,587
	Trenton, NJ	325,824
	Vineland–Millville–Bridgeton, NJ	138,053
6	Detroit–Ann Arbor, MI	4,665,236
	Detroit, MI	4,382,299
	Ann Arbor, MI	282,937
7	Boston–Lawrence–Salem, MA–NH	4,171,643
	Boston, MA	2,870,669
	Lawrence–Havervill, MA–NH	393,516
	Lowell, MA–NH	273,067
	Salem–Gloucester, MA	264,356
	Brockton, MA	189,478
	Nashua, NH	180,557
8	Washington, DC–MD–VA	3,923,574
9	Dallas–Fort Worth, TX	3,885,415
	Dallas, TX	2,553,362
	Fort Worth–Arlington, TX	1,332,053
10	Houston–Galveston–Brazoria, TX	3,711,043
	Houston, TX	3,301,937
	Galveston–Texas City, TX	217,399
	Brazoria, TX	191,707
11	Miami–Fort Lauderdale, FL	3,192,582
	Miami–Hialeah, FL	1,937,094
	Fort Lauderdale–Hollywood–Pompano Beach, FL	1,255,488
12	Atlanta, GA	2,833,511
13	Cleveland–Akron–Lorain, OH	2,759,823
	Cleveland, OH	1,831,122
	Akron, OH	657,575
	Lorain–Elyria, OH	271,126
14	Seattle–Tacoma, WA	2,559,164
	Seattle, WA	1,972,961
	Tacoma, WA	586,203
15	San Diego, CA	2,498,016
16	Minneapolis–St. Paul, MN–WI	2,464,124
17	St. Louis, MO–WI	2,444,099
18	Baltimore, MD	2,382,172
19	Pittsburgh–Beaver Valley, PA	2,242,798
	Pittsburgh, PA	2,056,705
	Beaver County, PA	186,093
20	Phoenix, AZ	2,122,101
21	Tampa–St. Petersburg–Clearwater, FL	2,067,959
22	Denver–Boulder, CO	1,848,319
	Denver, CO	1,622,980
	Boulder–Longmont, CO	225,339
23	Cincinnati–Hamilton, OH–KY–IN	1,744,124
	Cincinnati, OH–KY–IN	1,452,645
	Hamilton–Middletown, OH	291,479
24	Milwaukee–Racine, WI	1,607,183
	Milwaukee, WI	1,432,149
	Racine, WI	175,034
25	Kansas City, MO–KS	1,566,280
26	Sacramento, CA	1,481,102
27	Portland–Vancouver, OR–WA	1,477,895
	Portland, OR	1,239,842
	Vancouver, WA	238,053
28	Norfolk–Virginia Beach–Newport News, VA	1,396,107
29	Columbus, OH	1,377,419

Rank	Standard metropolitan statistical area	Population	Rank	Standard metropolitan statistical area	Population
30	San Antonio, TX	1,302,099	86	York, PA	417,848
31	Indianapolis, IN	1,249,822	87	Lakeland–Winter Haven, FL	405,382
32	New Orleans, LA	1,238,816	88	Saginaw–Bay City–Midland, MI	399,320
33	Buffalo–Niagara Falls, NY	1,189,288	89	Melbourne–Titusville–Palm Bay, FL	398,978
	Buffalo, NY	968,532	90	Colorado Springs, CO	397,014
	Niagara Falls, NY	220,756	91	Augusta, GA–SC	396,809
34	Charlotte–Gastonia–Rock Hill, NC–SC	1,162,093	92	Jackson, MS	395,396
35	Providence–Pawtucket–Fall		93	Canton, OH	394,106
	River, RI–MA	1,141,510	94	Des Moines, IA	392,928
	Providence, RI	654,854	95	McAllen–Edinburg–Mission, TX	383,543
	Pawtucket–Woonsocket–		96	Daytona Beach, FL	370,712
	Attleboro, RI–MA	329,384	97	Modesto, CA	370,522
	Fall River, MA–RI	157,272	98	Santa Barbara–Santa Maria–	
36	Hartford–New Britain–			Lompoc, CA	369,608
	Middletown, CT	1,085,837	99	Madison, WI	367,085
	Hartford, CT	767,841	100	Fort Wayne, IN	363,811
	New Britain, CT	148,188	101	Spokane, WA	361,364
	Middletown, CT	90,320	102	Beaumont–Port Arthur, TX	361,226
	Bristol, CT	79,488	103	Salinas–Seaside–Monterey, CA	355,660
37	Orlando, FL	1,072,748	104	Davenport–Rock Island–	
38	Salt Lake City–Ogden, UT	1,072,227		Moline, IA–IL	350,861
39	Rochester, NY	1,002,410	105	Corpus Christi, TX	349,894
40	Nashville, TN	985,026	106	Lexington–Fayette, KY	348,428
41	Memphis, TN–AR–MS	981,747	107	Pensacola, FL	344,406
42	Oklahoma City, OK	958,839	108	Peoria, IL	339,172
43	Louisville, KY–IN	952,662	109	Reading, PA	336,523
44	Dayton–Springfield, OH	951,270	110	Fort Myers–Cape Coral, FL	335,113
45	Greensboro–Winston-Salem–		111	Shreveport, LA	334,341
	High Point, NC	942,091	112	Atlantic City, NJ	319,416
46	Birmingham, AL	907,810	113	Utica–Rome, NY	316,633
47	Jacksonville, FL	906,727	114	Appleton–Oshkosh–Neenah, WI	315,121
48	Albany–Schenectady–Troy, NY	874,304	115	Huntington–Ashland, WV–KY–OH	312,529
49	Richmond–Petersburg, VA	865,640	116	Visalia–Tulare–Porterville, CA	311,921
50	West Palm Beach–Boca Raton–		117	Montgomery, AL	292,517
	Delray Beach, FL	863,518	118	Rockford, IL	283,719
51	Honolulu, HI	836,231	119	Eugene–Springfield, OR	282,912
52	Austin, TX	781,572	120	Macon–Warner Robins, GA	281,103
53	Las Vegas, NV	741,459	121	Evansville, IN–KY	278,990
54	Raleigh–Durham, NC	735,480	122	Salem, OR	278,024
55	Scranton–Wilkes-Barre, PA	734,175	123	Sarasota, FL	277,776
56	Tulsa, OK	708,954	124	Erie, Pa	275,572
57	Grand Rapids, MI	688,399	125	Fayetteville, NC	274,566
58	Allentown–Bethlehem–Easton, PA–NJ	686,688	126	New London–Norwich, CT–RI	266,819
59	Fresno, CA	667,490	127	Binghamton, NY	264,497
60	Tucson, AZ	666,880	128	Provo–Orem, UT	263,590
61	Syracuse, NY	659,864	129	Brownsville–Harlingen, TX	260,120
62	Greenville–Spartanburg, SC	640,861	130	Poughkeepsie, NY	259,462
63	Omaha, NE–IA	618,262	131	Killeen–Temple, TX	255,301
64	Toledo, OH	614,128	132	Reno, NV	254,667
65	Knoxville, TN	604,816	133	Fort Pierce, FL	251,071
66	El Paso, TX	591,610	134	Charleston, WV	250,454
67	Harrisburg–Lebanon–Carlisle, PA	587,986	135	South Bend–Mishawaka, IN	247,052
68	Bakersfield, CA	543,477	136	Columbus, GA–AL	243,072
69	New Haven–Meriden, CT	530,180	137	Savannah, GA	242,622
70	Springfield, MA	529,519	138	Johnstown, PA	241,247
71	Baton Rouge, LA	528,264	139	Sprinfield, MO	240,593
72	Little Rock–North Little Rock, AR	513,117	140	Duluth, MN–WI	239,971
73	Charleston, SC	506,875	141	Huntsville, AL	238,912
74	Youngstown–Warren, OH	492,619	142	Tallahassee, FL	233,598
75	Wichita, KS	485,270	143	Anchorage, AK	226,338
76	Stockton, CA	480,628	144	Roanoke, VA	224,477
77	Albuquerque, NM	480,577	145	Portsmouth–Dover–	
78	Mobile, AL	476,923		Rochester, NH–ME	223,578
79	Columbia, SC	453,331	146	Kalamazoo, MI	223,411
80	Worcester, MA	436,905	147	Lubbock, TX	222,636
81	Johnson City–Kingsport–		148	Hickory–Morganton, NC	221,700
	Bristol, TN–VA	436,047	149	Waterbury, CT	221,629
82	Chattanooga, TN–GA	433,210	150	Portland, ME	215,281
83	Lansing–East Lansing, MI	432,674	151	Lincoln, NE	213,641
84	Flint, MI	430,459	152	Bradenton, FL	211,707
85	Lancaster, PA	422,822	153	Lafayette, LA	208,740

Rank	Standard metropolitan statistical area	Population	Rank	Standard metropolitan statistical area	Population
154	Boise City, ID	205,775	207	Joplin, MO	134,910
155	Gainesville, FL	204,111	208	Laredo, TX	133,239
156	Biloxi–Gulfport, MS	197,125	209	Greeley, CO	131,821
157	Ocala, FL	194,833	210	Decatur, AL	131,556
158	Green Bay, WI	194,594	211	Alexandria, LA	131,556
159	St. Cloud, MN	190,921	212	Burlington, VT	131,439
160	Bremerton, WA	189,731	213	Florence, AL	131,327
161	Springfield, IL	189,550	214	Charlottesville, VA	131,107
162	Waco, TX	189,123	215	Dothan, AL	130,964
163	Yakima, WA	188,823	216	Terre Haute, IN	130,812
164	Amarillo, TX	187,547	217	Anderson, IN	130,669
165	Fort Collins–Loveland, CO	186,136	218	Lafayette–West Lafayette, IN	130,598
166	Houma–Thibodaux, LA	182,842	219	Altoona, PA	130,542
167	Chico, CA	182,120	220	Bloomington–Normal, IL	129,180
168	Merced, CA	178,403	221	Bellingham, WA	127,780
169	Fort Smith, AR–OK	175,911	222	Panama City, FL	126,994
170	New Bedrofd, MA	175,641	223	Mansfield, OH	126,137
171	Asheville, NC	174,821	224	Sioux Falls, SD	123,809
172	Champaign–Urbana–Rantoul, IL	173,025	225	State College, PA	123,786
173	Clarksville–Hopkinsville, TN–KY	169,439	226	Pueblo, CO	123,051
174	Cedar Rapids, IA	168,767	227	Yuba City, CA	122,643
175	Lake Charles, LA	168,134	228	Wichita Falls, TX	122,378
176	Longview–Marshall, TX	162,431	229	Bryan–College Station, TX	121,862
177	Benton Harbor, MI	161,378	230	Hagerstown, MD	121,393
178	Olympia, WA	161,238	231	Sharon, PA	121,003
179	Topeka, KS	160,976	232	Wilmington, NC	120,284
180	Wheeling, WV–OH	159,301	233	Texarkana, TX–Texarkana, AR	120,132
181	Muskegon, MI	158,983	234	Muncie, IN	119,659
182	Athens, GA	156,267	235	Abilene, TX	119,655
183	Elkhart–Goshen, IN	156,198	236	Odessa, TX	118,934
184	Lima, OH	154,340	237	Williamsport, PA	118,710
185	Fargo–Moorhead, ND–MN	153,296	238	Glens Falls, NY	118,539
186	Naples, FL	152,099	239	Decatur, IL	117,206
187	Tyler, TX	151,309	240	Santa Fe, NM	117,043
188	Tuscaloosa, AL	150,522	241	Anniston, AL	116,034
189	Richland–Kennewick–Pasco, WA	150,033	242	Wausau, WI	115,400
190	Jacksonville, NC	149,838	243	Pascagoula, MS	115,243
191	Jackson, MI	149,756	244	Sioux City, IA–NE	115,018
192	Parkersburg–Marietta, WV–OH	149,169	245	Florence, SC	114,344
193	Manchester, NH	147,809	246	Billings, MT	113,419
194	Redding, CA	147,036	247	Fayetteville–Springdale, AR	113,409
195	Waterlook–Cedar Falls, IA	146,611	248	Albany, GA	112,561
196	Medford, OR	146,389	249	Columbia, MO	112,379
197	Anderson, SC	145,196	250	Lawton, OK	111,486
198	Fort Walton Beach, FL	143,776	251	Bloomington, IN	108,978
199	Stebuenville–Weirton, OH–WV	142,523	252	Danville, VA	108,711
200	Lynchburg, VA	142,199	253	Burlington, NC	108,213
201	Monroe, LA	142,191	254	Yuma, AZ	106,895
202	Jamestown–Dunkirk, NY	141,895	255	Midland, TX	106,611
203	Janesville–Beloit, WI	139,510	256	Rochester, MN	106,470
204	Eau Claire, WI	137,543	257	Sheboygan, WI	103,877
205	Battle Creek, MI	135,982	258	Fitchburg–Leominster, MA	102,797
206	Las Cruces, NM	135,510	259	Cumberland, MD–WV	101,643

NOTE: A standard metropolitan statistical area (SMSA) is one of a large population nucleus together with adjacent communities that have a high degree of economic and social integration with that nucleus.—Source does not list rank separately. It is given for the Consolidated Metropolitan Statistical Area of which this area is a part. *Source:* Bureau of the Census.

Half of the U.S. Population Lives in the Largest Metro Areas

Final 1990 census figures show that the Nation has 39 metropolitan areas of at least one million people. These 39 areas have 124.8 million inhabitants or 50.2% of the United States total population.

The census figures show that the U.S. population living in all of the metro areas has reached 192,725,741, an increase of 20 million (11.6%) since 1980.

The metropolitan population now constitutes 77.5% of the U.S. total, compared with 76.2% in 1980. Ninety percent of the Nation's growth in the 1980s took place in metropolitan areas.

Only five metropolitan areas as large as one million lost population in the 1980s, compared with eight in the 1970s. However, many middle-sized and smaller metro areas grew more slowly in the 1980s than in the 1970s.

The Los Angeles–Anaheim–Riverside metropolitan area gained three million inhabitants for a total of over 14.5 million. The increase brings that area to within 3.5 million of the New York metropolitan area, the Nation's largest, which gained about 550,000 people for a total of 18.1 million. □

Population by State

State	1990	Percent change, 1980-90	Pop. per sq mi., 1990	Pop. rank, 1990	1980	1950	1900	1790
Alabama	4,040,587	+3.8	79.6	22	3,893,888	3,061,743	1,828,697	—
Alaska	550,403	+36.9	1.0	49	401,851	128,643	63,592	—
Arizona	3,665,228	+34.8	32.3	24	2,718,215	749,587	122,931	—
Arkansas	2,350,725	+2.8	45.1	33	2,286,435	1,909,511	1,311,564	—
California	29,760,021	+25.7	190.4	1	23,667,902	10,586,223	1,485,053	—
Colorado	3,294,394	+14.0	31.8	26	2,889,964	1,325,089	539,700	—
Connecticut	3,287,116	+5.8	674.7	27	3,107,576	2,007,280	908,420	237,946
Delaware	666,168	+12.1	344.8	46	594,338	318,085	184,735	59,096
D.C.	606,900	−4.9	—	—	638,333	802,178	278,718	—
Florida	12,937,926	+32.7	238.9	4	9,746,324	2,771,305	528,542	—
Georgia	6,478,216	+18.6	109.9	11	5,463,105	3,444,578	2,216,331	82,548
Hawaii	1,108,229	+14.9	172.5	41	964,691	499,794	154,001	—
Idaho	1,006,749	+6.7	12.2	42	943,935	588,637	161,772	—
Illinois	11,430,602	0.0	205.4	6	11,426,518	8,712,176	4,821,550	—
Indiana	5,544,159	+1.0	154.2	14	5,490,224	3,934,224	2,516,462	—
Iowa	2,776,755	−4.7	49.6	30	2,913,808	2,621,073	2,231,853	—
Kansas	2,477,574	+4.8	30.3	32	2,363,679	1,905,299	1,470,495	+EMD
Kentucky	3,685,296	+0.7	92.9	23	3,660,777	2,944,806	2,147,174	73,677
Louisiana	4,219,973	+0.3	94.8	21	4,205,900	2,683,516	1,381,625	—
Maine	1,227,928	+9.2	39.6	38	1,124,660	913,774	694,466	96,540
Maryland	4,781,468	+13.4	486.0	19	4,216,975	2,343,001	1,188,044	319,728
Massachusetts	6,016,425	+4.9	768.9	13	5,737,037	4,690,514	2,805,346	378,787
Michigan	9,295,297	+0.4	163.2	8	9,262,078	6,371,766	2,420,982	—
Minnesota	4,375,099	+7.3	55.0	20	4,075,970	2,982,483	1,751,394	—
Mississippi	2,573,216	+2.1	54.5	31	2,520,638	2,178,914	1,551,270	—
Missouri	5,117,073	+4.1	74.2	15	4,916,686	3,954,653	3,106,665	—
Montana	799,065	+1.6	5.5	44	786,690	591,024	243,329	—
Nebraska	1,578,385	+0.5	20.6	36	1,569,825	1,325,510	1,066,300	—
Nevada	1,201,833	+50.1	10.9	39	800,493	160,083	42,335	—
New Hampshire	1,109,252	+20.5	123.3	40	920,610	533,242	411,588	141,885
New Jersey	7,730,188	+5.0	1,035.1	9	7,364,823	4,835,329	1,883,669	184,139
New Mexico	1,515,069	+16.3	12.5	37	1,302,894	681,187	195,310	—
New York	17,990,455	+2.5	379.7	2	17,558,072	14,830,192	7,268,894	340,120
North Carolina	6,628,637	+12.7	135.7	10	5,881,766	4,061,929	1,893,810	393,751
North Dakota	638,800	−2.1	9.0	47	652,717	619,636	319,146	—
Ohio	10,847,115	+0.5	264.5	7	10,797,630	7,946,627	4,157,545	—
Oklahoma	3,145,585	+4.0	45.8	28	3,025,290	2,233,351	790,391[1]	—
Oregon	2,842,321	+7.9	29.5	29	2,633,105	1,521,341	413,536	—
Pennsylvania	11,881,643	+0.1	264.7	5	11,863,895	10,498,012	6,302,115	434,373
Rhode Island	1,003,464	+5.9	951.1	43	947,154	791,896	428,556	68,825
South Carolina	3,486,703	+11.7	115.4	25	3,121,820	2,117,027	1,340,316	249,073
South Dakota	696,004	+0.8	9.1	45	690,768	652,740	401,570	—
Tennessee	4,877,185	+6.2	118.5	17	4,591,120	3,291,718	2,020,616	35,691
Texas	16,986,510	+19.4	64.8	3	14,229,191	7,711,194	3,048,710	—
Utah	1,722,850	+17.9	20.9	35	1,461,037	688,862	276,749	—
Vermont	562,758	+10.0	60.7	48	511,456	377,747	343,641	85,425
Virginia	6,187,358	+15.7	155.8	12	5,346,818	3,318,680	1,854,184	747,610[2]
Washington	4,866,692	+17.8	73.1	18	4,132,156	2,378,963	518,103	—
West Virginia	1,793,477	−8.0	73.8	34	1,949,644	2,005,552	958,800	—
Wisconsin	4,891,769	+4.0	89.9	16	4,705,767	3,434,575	2,069,042	—
Wyoming	453,588	−3.4	4.7	50	469,557	290,529	92,531	—
Total U.S.	248,709,873	+9.8	—	—	226,545,805	151,325,798	76,212,168	3,929,214

1. Includes population of Indian Territory: 1900, 392,960. 2. Until 1863, Virginia included what is now West Virginia. *Source:* Department of Commerce, Bureau of the Census.

The U.S. Population Grows Older

According to the 1990 census, the nation's median age is 32.9 years, up 2.9 years from 1980. Regionally the Northeast has the oldest median, 34.2 years, followed by the Midwest with 33.0 years, and the South with a median of 32.8 years. The West has a median age of 31.8 years, the nation's lowest and below the national median.

In addition the percent of people over the age of 65 has increased from 11 percent in 1980 to 13 percent in 1990. Again the Northeast leads the other regions, with 14 percent of its population aged 65 and over. The Midwest and South have 13 percent of their population in the older group and the West again has the smallest proportion of the elderly, 11 percent.

Persons of Hispanic Origin[1] by Nationality

State	Mexican	Puerto Rican	Cuban	Other	Total
Alabama	9,509	3,553	1,463	10,104	24,629
Alaska	9,321	1,938	277	6,267	17,803
Arizona	616,195	8,256	2,079	61,808	688,338
Arkansas	12,496	1,176	494	5,710	19,876
California	6,118,996	126,417	71,977	1,370,548	7,687,938
Colorado	282,478	7,225	2,058	132,541	424,302
Connecticut	8,393	146,842	6,386	51,495	213,116
Delaware	3,083	8,257	728	3,752	15,820
District of Columbia	2,981	2,204	1,241	26,284	32,710
Florida	161,499	247,010	674,052	491,582	1,574,143
Georgia	49,182	17,443	7,818	34,479	108,922
Hawaii	14,367	25,778	558	40,687	81,390
Idaho	43,213	665	164	8,885	52,927
Illinois	623,688	146,059	18,204	116,495	904,446
Indiana	66,736	14,021	1,853	16,178	98,788
Iowa	24,386	1,270	488	6,503	32,647
Kansas	75,798	3,570	1,403	12,899	93,670
Kentucky	8,692	3,682	1,075	8,535	21,984
Louisiana	23,452	6,180	8,569	54,843	93,044
Maine	2,153	1,250	350	3,076	6,829
Maryland	18,434	17,528	6,367	82,773	125,102
Massachusetts	12,703	151,193	8,106	115,547	287,549
Michigan	138,312	18,538	5,157	39,589	201,596
Minnesota	34,691	3,286	1,539	14,368	53,884
Mississippi	6,718	1,304	497	7,412	15,931
Missouri	38,274	3,959	2,108	17,361	61,702
Montana	8,362	437	124	3,251	12,174
Nebraska	29,665	1,159	480	5,665	36,969
Nevada	85,287	4,272	5,988	28,872	124,419
New Hampshire	2,362	3,299	578	5,094	11,333
New Jersey	28,759	320,133	85,378	305,591	739,861
New Mexico	328,836	2,635	903	246,850	579,224
New York	93,244	1,086,601	74,345	959,836	2,214,026
North Carolina	32,670	14,620	3,723	25,713	76,726
North Dakota	2,878	386	63	1,338	4,665
Ohio	57,815	45,853	3,559	32,469	139,696
Oklahoma	63,226	4,693	1,043	17,198	86,160
Oregon	86,632	2,764	1,333	22,978	112,707
Pennsylvania	24,220	148,988	7,485	51,569	232,262
Rhode Island	2,437	13,016	840	29,459	45,752
South Carolina	11,028	6,423	1,652	11,448	30,551
South Dakota	3,438	377	44	1,393	5,252
Tennessee	13,879	4,292	2,012	12,558	32,741
Texas	3,890,820	42,981	18,195	387,909	4,339,905
Utah	56,842	2,181	456	25,118	84,597
Vermont	725	659	168	2,109	3,661
Virginia	33,044	23,698	6,268	97,278	160,288
Washington	155,864	9,345	2,281	47,080	214,570
West Virginia	2,810	897	261	4,521	8,489
Wisconsin	57,615	19,116	1,679	14,784	93,194
Wyoming	18,730	325	63	6,633	25,751
United States	**13,495,938**	**2,727,754**	**1,043,932**	**5,086,435**	**22,354,059**

1. Persons of Hispanic origin may be of any race. *Source:* Department of Commerce, Bureau of the Census.

Young Adults Delay Marriage

America's young adults are delaying marriage and continuing to live at home with their parents, according to a March 1990 survey by the Commerce Department's Census Bureau.

The survey, which does not reflect results of the 1990 census, found that 77 percent of persons aged 18 to 24 have never married. About two-thirds of these 19.6 million never-married persons were residing with their parents.

The estimated median age at first marriage was 26.1 years for men and 23.9 years for women, up from 23.2 and 20.8 years, respectively, in 1970. The proportion of women aged 30 to 34 who had never married nearly tripled, from 6 percent in 1970 to 16 percent in 1990.

The EXPANSION of the UNITED STATES

CANADA

Atlantic Ocean

limit of British claim

BAHAMA ISLANDS (British)

CUBA

THE UNITED STATES 1783

ORIGINAL THIRTEEN STATES

FLORIDA

Purchased from Spain, 1819

Claimed by Spain to 1795

St. Mary's R.

Gulf of Mexico

L. Superior

L. Huron

L. Michigan

Mississippi R.

LOUISIANA PURCHASE Purchased from France 1803

Missouri R.

REPUBLIC OF TEXAS

Annexed 1845

Area claimed by Texas and ceded by Mexico 1848

Rio Grande

MEXICO

ROCKY MOUNTAINS

OREGON COUNTRY U.S. Claim recognized by Great Britain, by Treaty of 1846

Ceded by Mexico ~ 1848

Gila R.

Gadsden Purchase 1853

Colorado R.

Columbia R.

Pacific Ocean

- - - Present State Boundaries

Scale of Miles

0 100 300 500

Map from AN ENCYCLOPEDIA OF WORLD HISTORY by William L. Langer, The Fifth Edition, Copyright 1940, 1948, 1952 and © 1967, 1972 by Houghton Mifflin Company. Reprinted by permission of Houghton Mifflin Company.

Territorial Expansion

Accession	Date	Area[1]
United States	—	3,618,770
Territory in 1790	—	891,364
Louisiana Purchase	1803	831,321
Florida	1819	69,866
Texas	1845	384,958
Oregon	1846	283,439
Mexican Cession	1848	530,706
Gadsden Purchase	1853	29,640
Alaska	1867	591,004
Hawaii	1898	6,471
Other territory	—	4,664
Philippines	1898	115,600 [2]
Puerto Rico	1899	3,515
Guam	1899	209
American Samoa	1900	77
Canal Zone[3]	1904	553
Virgin Islands of U.S.	1917	132
Trust Territory of Pacific Islands	1947	717 [4]
All other	—	14
Total, 1980	—	**3,623,434**

1. Total land and water area in square miles. 2. Became independent in 1946. 3. Reverted to Panama. 4. Land area only; includes Northern Mariana Islands. NOTE: 1990 Census data not available at press time. *Source:* Department of Commerce, Bureau of the Census.

Total Population

Area	1980	1970	1960
50 states of U.S.	226,545,805	203,302,031	179,323,175
48 conter-			
minous	225,179,263	202,229,535	178,464,236
Alaska	401,851	302,583	226,167
Hawaii	964,691	769,913	632,772
American Samoa	32,297	27,159	20,051
Canal Zone	([1])	44,198	42,122
Canton Island	—	n.a.	320
Corn Islands	—	([2])	1,872
Guam	105,979	84,996	67,044
Johnston Atoll	327	1,007	156
Midway	453	2,220	2,356
Puerto Rico	3,196,520	2,712,033	2,349,544
Swan Islands	n.a.	22	28
Trust Ter. of Pac. Is.	132,929 [3]	90,940	70,724
Virgin Is. of U.S.	96,569	62,468	32,099
Wake Island	302	1,647	1,097
Population abroad	995,546	1,737,836	1,374,421
Armed forces	515,408	1,057,776	609,720
Other[4]	n.a.	n.a.	n.a.
Total	**231,106,727**	**208,066,557**	**183,285,009**

1. Granted independence on Oct. 1, 1979. 2. Returned to Nicaragua April 25, 1971. 3. Includes Northern Mariana Islands. 4. Includes Baker Island, Enderbury Island, Howland Island, and Jarvis Island, all uninhabited. NOTE: n.a.= unavailable. 1990 Census data not available at press time. *Source:* Department of Commerce, Bureau of the Census.

Resident Population by Age, Sex, Race, and Hispanic Origin, 1989[1]
(in thousands)

Age	White Male	White Female	Black Male	Black Female	Other races Male	Other races Female	Hispanic origin[2] Male	Hispanic origin[2] Female	All persons Male	All persons Female
Under 5	7,716	7,335	1,469	1,421	414	399	1,131	1,091	9,598	9,155
5–9	7,504	7,124	1,423	1,378	394	389	1,019	977	9,321	8,891
10–14	6,973	6,601	1,362	1,318	355	342	957	920	8,689	8,260
15–19	7,327	7,015	1,394	1,365	371	341	905	868	9,091	8,721
20–24	7,731	7,628	1,279	1,372	357	335	996	928	9,368	9,334
25–29	9,142	8,960	1,342	1,485	381	389	1,159	1,029	10,865	10,834
30–34	9,385	9,182	1,289	1,455	404	420	1,026	933	11,078	11,058
35–39	8,342	8,283	1,035	1,225	354	382	779	757	9,731	9,890
40–44	7,229	7,321	782	945	283	322	582	603	8,294	8,588
45–49	5,758	5,915	626	769	217	237	427	457	6,601	6,920
50–54	4,791	4,998	544	679	174	189	346	380	5,509	5,866
55–59	4,480	4,830	508	608	133	167	293	329	5,121	5,605
60–64	4,498	5,071	467	567	113	150	249	291	5,079	5,788
65–69	4,130	4,899	402	515	100	125	181	220	4,631	5,538
70–74	3,120	4,074	274	386	69	89	110	153	3,464	4,549
75–79	2,147	3,282	187	299	51	66	77	120	2,385	3,648
80–84	1,189	2,220	91	165	26	37	46	74	1,306	2,422
85 and over	761	2,000	72	165	17	27	32	59	850	2,192
All ages	102,223	106,738	14,545	16,115	4,213	4,404	10,317	10,188	120,982	127,258
16 and over	78,686	84,404	10,027	11,743	2,979	3,208	7,027	7,024	91,693	99,354
18 and over	75,862	81,725	9,466	11,200	2,832	3,072	6,666	6,678	88,160	95,997
65 and over	11,347	16,475	1,025	1,529	264	344	447	626	12,636	18,348
Median age	32.5	34.7	26.3	29.1	27.9	30.1	25.7	26.5	31.6	33.8
Mean age	34.6	37.4	29.3	32.0	29.7	31.7	27.4	29.0	33.8	36.5

1. July 1, 1989. 2. Persons of Hispanic origin may be of any race. NOTE: 1990 Census data not available at press time. *Source:* U.S. Bureau of the Census.

Who Can Afford to Buy a House?

The American dream of owning a home is still possible but it is difficult for some Americans. Only 43 percent of families and unrelated individuals could afford to buy a median-priced house in spring, 1988. However, 52 percent could afford a modestly priced home at that time.

Current homeowners have a better chance of purchasing a median-priced home than do current renters. So do people living in the Midwest and South than those living in the Northeast or West.

Immigration to U.S. by Country of Origin

(Figures are totals, not annual averages, and were tabulated as follows: 1820–67, alien passengers arrived; 1868–91 and 1895–97, immigrant aliens arrived; 1892–94 and 1898 to present, immigrant aliens admitted. 1989 and 1990 totals include legalized immigrants. (Data before 1906 relate to country whence alien came; 1906–80, to country of last permanent residence; 1981 to present data based on country of birth.)

Countries	1990	1820–1990	1981–90	1971–80	1961–70	1951–60	1941–50	1820–1940
Europe: Albania[1]	78	3,090	479	329	98	59	85	2,040
Austria[2]	675	2,661,318	4,636	9,478	20,621	67,106	24,860	2,534,617
Belgium	682	209,196	5,706	5,329	9,192	18,575	12,189	158,205
Bulgaria[3]	428	70,484	2,342	1,188	619	104	375	65,856
Czechoslovakia[1]	1,412	150,074	11,500	6,023	3,273	918	8,347	120,013
Denmark	666	370,422	5,380	4,439	9,201	10,984	5,393	335,025
Estonia[1]	20	1,294	137	91	163	185	212	506
Finland[1]	369	37,346	3,265	2,868	4,192	4,925	2,503	19,593
France	2,849	778,358	23,124	25,069	45,237	51,121	38,809	594,998
Germany[2]	7,493	7,061,615	70,111	74,414	190,796	477,765	226,578	6,021,951
Great Britain	15,928	5,102,100	142,123	137,374	213,822	202,824	139,306	4,266,561
Greece	2,742	694,657	29,130	92,369	85,969	47,608	8,973	430,608
Hungary[2]	1,655	1,670,979	9,764	6,550	5,401	36,637	3,469	1,609,158
Ireland	10,333	4,725,987	32,823	11,490	32,966	48,362	14,789	4,580,557
Italy	3,287	5,338,478	32,894	129,368	214,111	185,491	57,661	4,719,223
Latvia[1]	45	2,981	359	207	510	352	361	1,192
Lithuania[1]	67	4,418	482	248	562	242	683	2,201
Luxembourg[1]	31	3,166	234	307	556	684	820	565
Netherlands	1,424	373,952	11,958	10,492	30,606	52,277	14,860	253,759
Norway[4]	524	753,456	3,901	3,941	15,484	22,935	10,100	697,095
Poland[5]	20,537	620,474	97,390	37,234	53,539	9,985	7,571	414,755
Portugal	4,035	500,850	40,020	101,710	76,065	19,588	7,423	256,044
Romania[6]	4,647	212,947	39,963	12,393	2,531	1,039	1,076	156,945
Spain	1,886	280,413	15,698	39,141	44,659	7,894	2,898	170,123
Sweden[4]	1,196	1,391,428	10,211	6,531	17,116	21,697	10,665	1,325,208
Switzerland	845	357,666	7,076	8,235	18,453	17,675	10,547	295,680
U.S.S.R.[7]	25,524	3,470,110	84,081	38,961	2,465	671	571	3,343,361
Yugoslavia[3]	2,828	136,691	19,182	30,540	20,381	8,225	1,576	56,787
Other Europe	195	60,920	2,661	4,049	4,904	9,799	3,447	36,060
Total Europe	112,401	37,045,140	705,630	800,368	1,123,492	1,325,727	621,147	32,468,776
Asia: China[8]	46,966	956,315	388,686	124,326	34,764	9,657	16,709	382,173
India	30,667	466,771	261,841	164,134	27,189	1,973	1,761	9,873
Israel	4,664	129,620	36,353	37,713	29,602	25,476	476	
Japan[9]	5,734	458,407	43,248	49,775	39,988	46,250	1,555	277,591
Turkey	2,468	409,937	20,843	13,399	10,142	3,519	798	361,236
Other Asia	248,082	3,677,389	2,042,025	1,198,831	285,957	66,374	15,729	44,053
Total Asia[10]	338,581	6,098,449	2,066,455	1,588,178	427,642	153,249	37,028	1,074,926
America: Canada and Newfoundland[11]	16,812	4,257,851	119,204	169,939	413,310	377,952	171,718	3,005,728
Central America	146,202	810,293	458,753	134,640	101,330	44,751	21,665	49,154
Mexico[12]	679,068	3,886,136	1,653,250	640,294	453,937	299,811	60,589	778,255
South America	85,819	1,244,433	455,977	295,741	257,954	91,628	21,831	121,302
West Indies	115,065	2,723,518	892,392	741,126	470,213	123,091	49,725	446,971
Other America[12]	411	111,020	1,352	995	19,630	59,711	29,276	56
Total America	1,043,377	13,033,251	3,580,928	1,982,735	1,716,374	996,944	354,804	4,401,466
Africa	35,893	349,464	192,212	80,779	28,954	14,092	7,367	26,060
Australia and New Zealand	2,583	143,627	20,169	23,788	19,562	11,506	13,805	54,437
Pacific Islands[13]	3,599	57,460	21,041	17,454	5,560	1,470	746	11,089
Countries not specified[14]	49	266,623	196	12	93	12,491	142	253,689
Total all countries	1,536,483	56,994,014	7,338,062	4,493,314	3,321,677	2,515,479	1,035,039	38,290,443

1. Countries established since beginning of World War I are included with countries to which they belonged. 2. Data for Austria–Hungary not reported until 1861. Austria and Hungary recorded separately after 1905, Austria included with Germany 1938–45. 3. Bulgaria, Serbia, Montenegro first reported in 1899. Bulgaria reported separately since 1920. In 1920, separate enumeration for Kingdom of Serbs, Croats, Slovenes; since 1922, recorded as Yugoslavia. 4. Norway included with Sweden 1820–68. 5. Included with Austria–Hungary, Germany, and Russia 1899–1919. 6. No record of immigration until 1880. 7. From 1931–63, the U.S.S.R. was broken down into European U.S.S.R. and Asian U.S.S.R. Since 1964, total U.S.S.R. has been reported in Europe. 8. Beginning in 1957, China includes Taiwan. 9. No record of immigration until 1861. 10. From 1934, Asia included Philippines; before 1934, recorded in separate tables as insular travel. 11. Includes all British North American possessions, 1820–98. 12. No record of immigration, 1886–93. 13. Included with "Countries not specified" prior to 1925. 14. Includes 32,897 persons returning in 1906 to their homes in U.S. *Source:* Department of Justice, Immigration and Naturalization Service. NOTE: Data are latest available.

Immigrant and Nonimmigrant Aliens Admitted to U.S.

Period[1]	Immigrants	Non–immigrants	Total	Period[1]	Immigrants	Non–immigrants	Total
1901–10	8,795,386	1,007,909	9,803,295	1983[2]	559,763	9,849,458	10,409,221
1911–20	5,735,811	1,376,271	7,112,082	1984	543,903	9,426,759	9,970,662
1921–30	4,107,209	1,774,896	5,882,090	1985	570,009	9,675,650	10,245,659
1931–40	528,431	1,574,071	2,102,502	1986	601,708	10,471,024	11,072,732
1941–50	1,035,039	2,461,359	3,496,398	1987	601,516	12,272,866	12,874,382
1951–60	2,515,479	7,113,023	9,628,502	1988	643,025	14,591,735	15,234,760
1961–70	3,321,677	24,107,224	27,428,901	1989	1,090,924[3]	16,144,576	17,235,500
1971–77	2,797,209	45,236,597	48,033,806	1990	1,536,483[3]	17,145,680	18,682,163

1. Fiscal year ending June 30 prior to 1977. After 1977 for fiscal year ending Sept. 30. 2. Nonimmigrant figures for calendar year 1983. Nonimmigrant aliens include visitors for business or pleasure, students, foreign government officials, and others temporarily in the U.S. 3. Includes immigrants and legalized immigrants. *Source:* Department of Justice, Immigration and Naturalization Service.

Persons Naturalized Since 1907

Period[1]	Civilian	Military	Total	Period[1]	Civilian	Military	Total
1907–30	2,713,389	300,506	3,013,895	1985	238,394	3,266	244,717[2]
1930–40	1,498,573	19,891	1,518,464	1986	275,352	2,901	280,623[3]
1941–50	1,837,229	149,799	1,987,028	1987	224,100	2,402	227,008[4]
1951–60	1,148,241	41,705	1,189,946	1988	239,541	2,296	242,063[5]
1961–70	1,084,195	36,068	1,120,263	1989	231,198	1,954	233,777[6]
1971–80	1,397,846	66,926	1,464,772	1907–89	11,588,147	641,582	12,238,532[7]

1. Fiscal year ending June 30. Starting 1977, fiscal year ending Sept. 30. 2. Including 3,057 unidentified. 3. Including 2,370 unidentified. 4. Including 506 unidentified. 5. Including 226 unidentified. 6. Including 625 unidentified. 7. Including 8,803 unidentified. *Source:* Department of Justice, Immigration and Naturalization Service. NOTE: Data are latest available.

Population of Largest Indian Reservations, Jan. 1989

Navajo (Ariz., N.M., Utah)	185,661	Rosebud (S.D.)	17,128	Zuni (N.M.)	8,244
Cherokee (Okla.)	87,059	Gila River (Ariz.)	11,700	Pawnee (Okla.)	2,229
Creek (Okla.)	56,244	Tohono O'odham (Ariz.)	16,531	Northern Pueblos (N.M.)	6,866
Choctaw (Okla.)	26,884	Turtle Mountain (N.D.)	12,312	Shawnee (Okla., Texas)	1,034
Pine Ridge (S.D.)	20,206	Hopi (Ariz.)	9,617	Blackfeet (Mont.)	7,179
Southern Pueblos (N.M.)	18,837	Standing Rock (N.D., S.D.)	10,306	Yakima (Wash.)	6,706
Chicksaw (Okla.)	12,369	Fort Apache (Ariz.)	8,726	Wind River (Wyo.)	4,935

NOTE: The Bureau of Indian Affairs lists 861,500 Indians residing on or near Federal reservations as of January 1987. The total Indian population of the United States, according to the 1980 updated census, is 1,534,000, including Aleuts and Eskimos. *Source:* Department of the Interior, Bureau of Indian Affairs. NOTE: Figures are most recent available.

Persons Below Poverty Level
by Age, Region, Race, and Hispanic Origin, 1989

Age and region	Number below poverty level				Percent below poverty level			
	All races[2]	White	Black	Hispanic origin[1]	All races[2]	White	Black	Hispanic origin[1]
Under 18 years	12,590	7,599	4,375	2,603	19.6	14.8	43.7	36.2
18 to 21	2,201	1,456	611	425	15.3	12.4	29.8	27.0
22 to 44	9,447	6,471	2,505	1,684	10.3	8.4	22.7	20.9
45 to 54	1,883	1,323	462	289	7.4	6.1	17.4	17.0
55 to 59	1,027	693	309	111	9.7	7.6	28.6	17.4
60 to 64	1,017	705	277	107	9.5	7.5	27.0	18.8
65 and over	3,369	2,542	766	211	11.4	9.6	30.8	20.6
Northeast	5,061	3,502	1,303	958	10.0	8.0	24.7	29.6
Midwest	7,043	4,718	2,181	352	11.9	9.0	36.4	24.7
South	12,943	7,498	5,220	1,855	15.4	11.4	31.6	28.7
West	6,487	5,070	601	2,266	12.5	11.3	23.5	23.6
Total	**31,534**	**20,788**	**9,305**	**5,430**	**12.8**	**10.0**	**30.7**	**26.2**

1. Persons of Hispanic origin may be of any race. 2. Includes race not shown separately. *Source:* U.S. Bureau of the Census.

Revised Population Projections to 2080[1,2]
(in millions)

Sex, race, age group	2000	2050	2070	2080	Sex, race, age group	2000	2050	2070	2080
MALE, WHITE	108.8	110.3	105.6	103.6	**FEMALE, BLACK**	18.3	24.7	25.0	25.0
Up to 19 years	29.7	37.3	23.9	23.4	Up to 19 years	5.8	5.6	5.3	5.2
20 to 39 years	31.4	27.4	25.9	25.3	20 to 39 years	5.6	6.2	5.9	5.7
40 to 59 years	30.7	27.6	26.7	25.7	40 to 59 years	4.4	6.0	6.1	6.0
60 to 79 years	14.2	22.8	21.7	21.6	60 to 79 years	2.0	5.0	5.4	5.6
80 and over	2.8	7.4	7.5	7.6	80 and over	0.4	1.8	2.2	2.4
FEMALE, WHITE	112.7	116.2	110.9	108.7	**TOTALS**[3]	268.3	299.8	294.6	292.2
Up to 19 years	28.2	24.0	22.7	22.2	Up to 19 years	73.3	66.7	64.0	63.0
20 to 39 years	30.6	26.7	25.2	24.6	20 to 39 years	76.6	73.1	70.4	69.2
40 to 59 years	31.0	27.6	26.6	25.6	40 to 59 years	72.8	73.0	72.5	70.9
60 to 79 years	17.2	25.1	23.8	23.5	60 to 79 years	36.2	62.0	61.7	62.2
80 and over	5.7	12.9	12.5	12.7	80 and over	9.3	24.9	25.9	26.9
MALE, BLACK	16.7	22.4	22.7	22.6	Males	131.2	145.3	142.9	141.7
Up to 19 years	6.1	5.9	5.6	5.4	Females	137.1	154.5	151.7	150.5
20 to 39 years	5.2	5.8	5.5	5.4	White	221.5	226.6	216.5	212.3
40 to 59 years	3.7	5.3	5.4	5.3	Black	35.1	47.1	47.7	47.6
60 to 79 years	1.6	4.3	4.8	5.0	Median age	36.4	42.7	43.6	43.9
80 and over	0.2	1.1	1.4	1.5					

1. Based on Population Report issued January 1989 revising prior Report issued May 1984. 2. Based on average of 1.8 lifetime births per woman. 3. Includes all races. NOTE: Zero population growth is expected to be reached by 2050. Details may not add because of rounding. *Source:* Department of Commerce, Bureau of the Census.

Marriage and Divorce

Marriages and Divorces

	Marriage		Divorce[1]			Marriage		Divorce[1]	
Year	Number	Rate[2]	Number	Rate[2]	Year	Number	Rate[2]	Number	Rate[2]
1900	709,000	9.3	55,751	.7	1967	1,927,000	9.7	523,000	2.6
1905	842,000	10.0	67,976	.8	1968	2,069,258	10.4	584,000	2.9
1910	948,166	10.3	83,045	.9	1969	2,145,438	10.6	639,000	3.2
1915	1,007,595	10.0	104,298	1.0	1970	2,158,802	10.6	708,000	3.5
1920	1,274,476	12.0	170,505	1.6	1971	2,190,481	10.6	773,000	3.7
1925	1,188,334	10.3	175,449	1.5	1972	2,282,154	11.0	845,000	4.1
1930	1,126,856	9.2	195,961	1.6	1973	2,284,108	10.9	915,000	4.4
1935	1,327,000	10.4	218,000	1.7	1974	2,229,667	10.5	977,000	4.6
1940	1,595,879	12.1	264,000	2.0	1975	2,152,662	10.1	1,036,000	4.9
1945	1,612,992	12.2	485,000	3.5	1976	2,154,807	10.0	1,083,000	5.0
1950	1,667,231	11.1	385,144	2.6	1977	2,178,367	10.1	1,091,000	5.0
1954	1,490,000	9.2	379,000	2.4	1978	2,282,272	10.5	1,130,000	5.2
1955	1,531,000	9.3	377,000	2.3	1979	2,341,799	10.6	1,181,000	5.4
1956	1,585,000	9.5	382,000	2.3	1980	2,406,708	10.6	1,182,000	5.2
1957	1,518,000	8.9	381,000	2.2	1981	2,438,000	10.6	1,219,000	5.3
1958	1,451,000	8.4	368,000	2.1	1982	2,495,000	10.8	1,180,000	5.1
1959	1,494,000	8.5	395,000	2.2	1983	2,444,000	10.5	1,179,000	5.0
1960	1,523,000	8.5	393,000	2.2	1984	2,487,000	10.5	1,155,000	4.9
1961	1,548,000	8.5	414,000	2.3	1985	2,425,000	10.2	1,187,000	5.0
1962	1,577,000	8.5	413,000	2.2	1986	2,400,000	10.0	1,159,000	4.8
1963	1,654,000	8.8	428,000	2.3	1987	2,421,000	9.9	1,157,000	4.8
1964	1,725,000	9.0	450,000	2.4	1988	2,389,000	9.7	1,183,000	4.8
1965	1,800,000	9.3	479,000	2.5	1989	2,404,000	9.7	1,163,000	4.7
1966	1,857,000	9.5	499,000	2.5	1990[3]	2,448,000	9.8	1,175,000	4.7

1. Includes annulments. 2. Per 1,000 population. Divorce rates for 1941–46 are based on population including armed forces overseas. Marriage rates are based on population excluding armed forces overseas. 3. Provisional. NOTE: Marriage and divorce figures for most years include some estimated data. Alaska is included beginning 1959, Hawaii beginning 1960. *Source:* Department of Health and Human Services, National Center for Health Statistics.

Percent of Population Ever Married

Age group, years[1]	1990	1980	1970	1960	1950	1940	1930	1920	1910	1900
Males: 15 to 19	1.5	2.7	2.6	3.3	2.9	1.5	1.5	1.8	1.0	0.9
20 to 24	20.7	31.2	45.3	46.9	41.0	27.8	29.0	29.1	24.7	22.2
25 to 29	54.8	67.0	80.9	79.2	76.2	64.0	63.2	60.5	57.1	54.1
30 to 34	73.0	84.1	90.6	88.1	86.8	79.3	78.8	75.8	73.9	72.3
35 to 44	87.2	92.5	93.3	91.9	90.4	86.0	85.7	83.8	83.3	83.0
45 to 54	93.7	93.9	92.5	92.6	91.5	88.9	88.6	88.0	88.8	89.7
Females: 15 to 19	5.0	8.8	9.7	13.5	14.4	10.0	10.9	10.8	9.8	9.4
20 to 24	37.2	49.8	64.2	71.6	67.7	52.8	53.9	54.4	51.5	48.4
25 to 29	68.9	79.1	89.5	89.5	86.7	77.2	78.3	76.9	75.0	72.4
30 to 34	83.6	90.5	93.8	93.1	90.7	85.3	86.8	85.1	83.8	83.4
35 to 44	90.7	94.5	94.8	93.9	91.7	89.6	90.0	88.6	88.6	88.9
45 to 54	95.0	95.3	95.1	93.0	92.2	91.3	90.9	90.4	91.4	92.2

1. Prior to 1980 data are for persons 14 years and older. *Source:* Department of Commerce, Bureau of the Census.

Persons Living Alone, by Sex and Age
(numbers in thousands)

Sex and Age[1]	1990 Number	1990 Percent	1980 Number	1980 Percent	1975 Number	1975 Percent	1970 Number	1970 Percent	1960 Number	1960 Percent
BOTH SEXES										
15 to 24 years	1,210	5.3	1,726	9.4	1,111	8.0	556	5.1	234	3.3
25 to 44 years	7,110	30.9	4,729	25.8	2,744	19.7	1,604	14.8	1,212	17.2
45 to 64 years	5,502	23.9	4,514	24.7	4,076	29.2	3,622	33.4	2,720	38.5
65 years and over	9,176	39.9	7,328	40.1	6,008	43.1	5,071	46.7	2,898	41.0
Total, 15 years and over	**22,999**	**100.0**	**18,296**	**100.0**	**13,939**	**100.0**	**10,851**	**100.0**	**7,063**	**100.0**
MALE										
15 to 24 years	674	7.4	947	13.6	610	4.4	274	2.5	124	1.8
25 to 44 years	4,231	46.8	2,920	41.9	1,689	12.1	933	8.6	686	9.7
45 to 64 years	2,203	24.3	1,613	23.2	1,329	9.5	1,152	10.6	965	13.7
65 years and over	1,942	21.5	1,486	21.3	1,290	9.3	1,174	10.8	853	12.1
Total, 15 years and over	**9,049**	**100.0**	**6,966**	**100.0**	**4,918**	**35.3**	**3,532**	**32.5**	**2,628**	**37.2**
FEMALE										
15 to 24 years	536	3.8	779	6.9	501	3.6	282	2.6	110	1.6
25 to 44 years	2,881	20.7	1,809	16.0	1,055	7.6	671	6.2	526	7.4
45 to 64 years	3,300	23.7	2,901	25.6	2,747	19.7	2,470	22.8	1,755	24.8
65 years and over	7,233	51.8	5,842	51.6	4,718	33.8	3,897	35.9	2,045	29.0
Total, 15 years and over	**13,950**	**100.0**	**11,330**	**100.0**	**9,021**	**64.7**	**7,319**	**67.5**	**4,436**	**62.8**

1. Prior to 1980, data are for persons 14 years and older. NOTE: Details may not add because of rounding. *Source:* Department of Commerce, Bureau of the Census.

Characteristics of Unmarried–Couple Households, 1990
(number in thousands)

Characteristics	Number	Percent	Characteristics	Number	Percent
Unmarried–couple households	2,856	100.0	Presence of children:		
			No children under 15 years	1,966	68.8
Age of householders:			Some children under 15 years	891	31.2
Under 25 years	596	20.0			
25–44 years	1,775	62.1	Sex of householders:		
45–64 years	358	12.5	Male	1,651	57.8
65 years and over	127	4.4	Female	1,205	42.2

Source: U.S. Bureau of the Census.

Households, Families, and Married Couples

Date	Households		Families		Maried couples
	Number	Average population per household	Number	Average population per family	Number
June 1890	12,690,000	4.93	—	—	—
April 1930	29,905,000	4.11	—	—	25,174,000
April 1940	34,949,000	3.67	32,166,000	3.76	28,517,000
March 1950	43,554,000	3.37	39,303,000	3.54	36,091,000
April 1955	47,874,000	3.33	41,951,000	3.59	37,556,000
March 1960[1]	52,799,000	3.33	45,111,000	3.67	40,200,000
March 1965	57,436,000	3.29	47,956,000	3.70	42,478,000
March 1970	63,401,000	3.14	51,586,000	3.58	45,373,000
March 1975	71,120,000	2.94	55,712,000	3.42	47,547,000
March 1980	80,776,000	2.76	59,550,000	3.29	49,714,000
March 1985	86,789,000	2.69	62,706,000	3.23	51,114,000
March 1988	91,066,000	2.64	65,133,000	3.17	52,613,000
March 1989	92,830,000	2.62	65,837,000	3.16	52,517,000
March 1990	93,347,000	2.63	66,090,000	3.17	53,256,000

1. First year in which figures for Alaska and Hawaii are included. *Source:* Department of Commerce, Bureau of the Census.

Families Maintained by Women, With No Husband Present
(numbers in thousands)

	1990		1980		1975		1970		1960	
	Number	Percent	Number	Percent	Number	Percent	Number	Percent	Number	Percent
Age of women:										
Under 35 years	3,699	34.0	3,015	34.6	2,356	32.5	1,364	24.4	796	17.7
35 to 44 years	2,929	26.9	1,916	22.0	1,510	20.9	1,074	19.2	940	20.9
45 to 64 years	2,790	25.6	2,514	28.9	2,266	31.3	2,021	36.1	1,731	38.5
65 years and over	1,471	13.5	1,260	14.5	1,108	15.3	1,131	20.2	1,027	22.9
Median age	40.7	—	41.7	—	43.4	—	48.5	—	50.1	—
Presence of children:										
No own children under 18 years	4,290	39.4	3,260	37.4	2,838	39.2	2,665	47.7	2,397	53.3
With own children under 18 years	6,599	60.6	5,445	62.6	4,404	60.8	2,926	52.3	2,097	46.7
Total own children under 18 years	11,378	—	10,204	—	9,227	—	6,694	—	4,674	—
Average per family	1.04	—	1.17	—	1.27	—	1.20	—	1.04	—
Average per family with children	1.72	—	1.87	—	2.10	—	2.29	—	2.24	—
Race:										
White	7,306	67.1	6,052	69.5	5,212	72.0	4,165	74.5	3,547	78.9
Black[1]	3,275	30.1	2,495	28.7	1,940	26.8	1,382	24.7	947	21.1
Other	309	2.8	158	1.8	90	1.2	44	0.8	n.a.	n.a.
Marital status:										
Married, husband absent	1,947	17.9	1,769	20.3	1,647	22.7	1,326	23.7	1,099	24.5
Widowed	2,536	23.3	2,570	29.5	2,559	35.3	2,396	42.9	2,325	51.7
Divorced	3,949	36.3	3,008	34.6	2,110	29.1	1,259	22.5	694	15.4
Never married	2,457	22.6	1,359	15.6	926	12.8	610	10.9	376	8.4
Total families maintained by women	10,890	100.0	8,705	100.0	7,242	100.0	5,591	100.0	4,494	100.0

1. Includes other races in 1960. NOTE: n.a. = not available. (—) as shown in this table, means "not applicable." *Source:* Department of Commerce, Bureau of the Census.

Median Age at First Marriage

Year	Males	Females	Year	Males	Females	Year	Males	Females	Year	Males	Females
1900	25.9	21.9	1930	24.3	21.3	1960	22.8	20.3	1988	25.9	23.6
1910	25.1	21.6	1940	24.3	21.5	1970	23.2	20.8	1989	26.2	23.8
1920	24.6	21.2	1950	22.8	20.3	1980	24.7	22.0	1990	26.1	23.9

Source: Department of Commerce, Bureau of the Census.

Selected Family Characteristics

Characteristics[1]	1989 Number (thous.)	Median income	Characteristics[1]	1989 Number (thous.)	Median income
ALL RACES			Type of residence		
All families	66,090	34,213	Nonfarm	55,225	36,104
Type of residence			Farm	1,365	31,020
Nonfarm	64,701	34,300	Location of residence		
Farm	1,390	30,809	Inside metropolitan areas	42,592	39,103
Location of residence			1,000,000 or more	26,080	41,719
Inside metropolitan areas	50,619	36,896	Inside central cities	7,946	34,758
1,000,000 or more	31,836	39,265	Outside central cities	18,134	44,686
Inside central cities	11,535	30,578	Under 1,000,000	16,512	35,182
Outside central cities	20,301	43,801	Inside central cities	6,018	33,684
Under 1,000,000	18,783	33,280	Outside central cities	10,493	35,848
Inside central cities	7,499	30,832	Outside metropolitan areas	13,999	28,154
Outside central cities	11,284	35,118			
Outside metropolitan areas	15,471	26,979	Region		
			Northeast	11,837	40,990
Region			Midwest	14,370	35,789
Northeast	13,494	39,484	South	18,746	32,939
Midwest	16,059	34,613	West	11,638	36,144
South	23,244	30,499			
West	13,293	35,698	Type of family		
			Married–couple family	46,918	39,208
Type of family			Wife in paid labor force	26,829	45,803
Married–couple family	52,317	38,547	Wife not in paid labor force	20,153	29,689
Wife in paid labor force	30,188	45,266	Male householder, no wife present	2,303	30,487
Wife not in paid labor force	22,129	28,747	Female householder, no husband present	7,306	18,946
Male householder, no wife present	2,884	27,847			
Female householder, no husband present	10,890	16,442	Number of earners		
			No earners	7,816	16,360
Number of earners			1 earner	14,970	27,145
No earners	9,439	14,285	2 earners	25,737	41,429
1 earner	18,146	25,226	3 earners	5,832	52,582
2 earners	29,235	40,658	4 earners or more	2,236	66,890
3 earners	6,724	51,758			
4 earners or more	2,546	65,722	**BLACK**		
Size of family			All families	7,470	20,209
2 persons	27,606	28,834	Type of residence		
3 persons	15,353	35,963	Nonfarm	7,453	20,248
4 persons	14,026	40,763	Farm	17	(B)
5 persons	5,938	39,077	Location of residence		
6 persons	1,997	35,801	Inside metropolitan areas	6,256	21,593
7 persons or more	1,170	32,259	1,000,000 or more	4,416	22,986
			Inside central cities	2,949	19,472
Occupation group of longest job of householder (No longer available)			Outside central cities	1,467	32,270
			Under 1,000,000	1,839	19,037
Tenure status			Inside central cities	1,248	18,531
Owner occupied	n.a.	n.a.	Outside central cities	591	20,001
Renter occupied	n.a.	n.a.	Outside metropolitan areas	1,215	14,370
Occupier paid no cash rent	n.a.	n.a.			
Educational attainment of householder			Region		
Elementary	n.a.	n.a.	Northeast	1,279	25,391
High school	n.a.	n.a.	Midwest	1,446	18,301
College	n.a.	n.a.	South	4,147	19,029
1 to 3 years	n.a.	n.a.	West	598	25,670
4 years or more	n.a.	n.a.			
4 years	n.a.	n.a.	Type of family		
5 years or more	n.a.	n.a.	Married–couple family	3,750	30,650
Total, 25 years and over	n.a.	n.a.	Wife in paid labor force	2,400	37,787
			Wife not in paid labor force	13,450	18,727
WHITE			Male householder, no wife present	446	18,395
All families	56,590	35,975	Female householder, no husband present	3,275	11,630

Characteristics[1]	1989 Number (thous.)	1989 Median income	Characteristics[1]	1989 Number (thous.)	1989 Median income
Number of earners			Region		
No earners	1,396	6,166	Northeast	815	22,627
1 earner	2,601	15,440	Midwest	330	26,359
2 earners	2,609	32,171	South	1,596	20,520
3 earners	659	43,693	West	2,101	25,511
4 earners or more	205	53,258			
			Type of family		
HISPANIC ORIGIN OF HOUSEHOLDER[2]			Married–couple family	3,395	27,382
All families	4,840	23,446	Wife in paid labor force	1,763	34,821
Type of residence			Wife not in paid labor force	1,633	20,717
Nonfarm	4,813	23,456	Male householder, no		
Farm	28	(B)	wife present	329	25,176
Location of residence			Female householder, no		
Inside metropolitan areas	4,463	24,050	husband present	1,116	11,745
1,000,000 or more	3,353	25,304			
Inside central cities	1,898	21,662	Number of earners		
Outside central cities	1,456	31,213	No earners	615	7,486
Under 1,000,000	1,110	20,373	1 earner	1,554	17,250
Inside central cities	625	19,347	2 earners	1,860	29,420
Outside central cities	485	21,996	3 earners	541	40,480
Outside metropolitan areas	377	18,343	4 earners or more	271	46,858

1. Family data as of March 1990. 2. Persons of Hispanic origin may be of any race. n.a. = not available. (B) Base less than 75,000. *Source:* Department of Commerce, Bureau of the Census. NOTE: Data are the latest available.

Births

Live Births and Birth Rates

Year	Births[1]	Rate[2]	Year	Births[1]	Rate[2]	Year	Births[1]	Rate[2]
1910	2,777,000	30.1	1956[3]	4,218,000	25.2	1973	3,136,965	14.9
1915	2,965,000	29.5	1957[3]	4,308,000	25.3	1974	3,159,958	14.9
1920	2,950,000	27.7	1958[3]	4,255,000	24.5	1975	3,144,198	14.8
1925	2,909,000	25.1	1959[3]	4,295,000	24.3	1976	3,167,788	14.8
1930	2,618,000	21.3	1960[3]	4,257,850	23.7	1977	3,326,632	15.4
1935	2,377,000	18.7	1961[3]	4,268,326	23.3	1978	3,333,279	15.3
1940	2,559,000	19.4	1962[3]	4,167,362	22.4	1979	3,494,398	15.9
1945	2,858,000	20.4	1963[3]	4,098,020	21.7	1980	3,612,258	15.9
1947	3,817,000	26.6	1964[3]	4,027,490	21.0	1982	3,680,537	15.9
1948	3,637,000	24.9	1965[3]	3,760,358	19.4	1983	3,638,933	15.5
1949	3,649,000	24.5	1966[3]	3,606,274	18.4	1984	3,669,141	15.5
1950	3,632,000	24.1	1967[4]	3,520,959	17.8	1985	3,760,561	15.8
1951[3]	3,823,000	24.9	1968[3]	3,501,564	17.5	1986	3,731,000	15.5
1952[3]	3,913,000	25.1	1969[3]	3,600,206	17.8	1987	3,829,000	15.7
1953[3]	3,965,000	25.1	1970[3]	3,731,386	18.4	1988	3,913,000	15.9
1954[3]	4,078,000	25.3	1971[3]	3,555,970	17.2	1989	4,021,000	16.2
1955	4,104,000	25.0	1972	3,258,411	15.6	1990[5]	4,179,000	16.7

1. Figures through 1959 include adjustment for underregistration; beginning 1960, figures represent number registered. For comparison, the 1959 registered count was 4,245,000. 2. Rates are per 1,000 population estimated as of July 1 for each year except 1940, 1950, 1960, 1970, and 1980, which are as of April 1, the census date; for 1942–46 based on population including armed forces overseas. 3. Based on 50% sample of births. 4. Based on a 20 to 50% sample of births. 5. Provisional. NOTE: Alaska is included beginning 1959; Hawaii beginning 1960. Since 1972, based on 100% of births in selected states and on 50% sample in all other states. *Sources:* Department of Health and Human Services, National Center for Health Statistics.

Divorce Ratio Quadruples Since 1960

Divorce, once an anomaly, has become more commonplace. According to the March 1990 Current Population Survey, there were 15.1 million currently divorced adults who hadn't remarried—8 percent of the total adult population. The 1990 divorce ratio is four times higher than the 1960 ratio.

The divorce ratio is the ratio of persons currently divorced to those currently married and living with their spouse at the time of the survey. There were 142 divorced persons per 1,000 married persons living with their spouse.

Live Births by Age of Mother

Year[1] and race	Total	Age of Mother							
		Under 15 yr	15–19 yr	20–24 yr	25–29 yr	30–34 yr	35–39 yr	40–44 yr	45 yr and over
1940	2,558,647	3,865	332,667	799,537	693,268	431,468	222,015	68,269	7,558
1945	2,858,449	4,028	298,868	832,746	785,299	554,906	296,852	78,853	6,897
1950	3,631,512	5,413	432,911	1,155,167	1,041,360	610,816	302,780	77,743	5,322
1955	4,014,112	6,181	493,770	1,290,939	1,133,155	732,540	352,320	89,777	5,430
1960	4,257,850	6,780	586,966	1,426,912	1,092,816	687,722	359,908	91,564	5,182
1965	3,760,358	7,768	590,894	1,337,350	925,732	529,376	282,908	81,716	4,614
1970	3,731,386	11,752	644,708	1,418,874	994,904	427,806	180,244	49,952	3,146
1975	3,144,198	12,642	582,238	1,093,676	936,786	375,500	115,409	26,319	1,628
1980	3,612,258	10,169	552,161	1,226,200	1,108,291	550,354	140,793	23,090	1,200
1985	3,760,561	10,220	467,485	1,141,320	1,201,350	696,354	214,336	28,334	1,162
1986	3,756,547	10,176	461,905	1,102,119	1,199,519	721,395	230,335	29,847	1,251
1987	3,809,394	10,311	462,312	1,075,856	1,216,080	760,695	247,984	34,781	1,375
1988	3,909,510	10,588	478,353	1,067,472	1,239,256	803,547	269,518	39,349	1,427
White	3,046,162	4,073	315,471	804,622	1,010,748	661,414	217,754	31,068	1,012
Black	671,976	6,182	146,326	220,301	167,684	93,765	32,534	4,981	203
Other	191,372	333	16,556	42,549	60,824	48,368	19,230	3,300	212

1. Data for 1940–55 are adjusted for underregistration. Beginning 1960, registered births only are shown. Data for 1960–70 based on a 50% sample of births. For 1972–84, based on 100% of births in selected states and on 50% sample in all other states. Beginning 1960, including Alaska and Hawaii. NOTE: Data refer only to births occurring within the U.S. Figures are shown to the last digit as computed for convenience in summation. They are not assumed to be accurate to the last digit. Figures for age of mother not stated are distributed. *Source:* Department of Health and Human Services, National Center for Health Statistics.

Births to Unmarried Women
(in thousands, except as indicated)

Age and race	1988	1985	1980	1975	1970	1965	1960	1955	1950
By age of mother:									
Under 15 years	9.9	9.4	9.0	11.0	9.5	6.1	4.6	3.9	3.2
15–19 years	312.5	270.9	262.8	222.5	190.4	123.1	87.1	68.9	56.0
20–24 years	350.9	300.4	237.3	134.0	126.7	90.7	68.0	55.7	43.1
25–29 years	196.4	152.0	99.6	50.2	40.6	36.8	32.1	28.0	20.9
30–34 years	94.9	67.3	41.0	19.8	19.1	19.6	18.9	16.1	10.8
35–39 years	34.4	24.0	13.2	8.1	9.4	11.4	10.6	8.3	6.0
40 years and over	6.3	4.1	2.9	2.3	3.0	3.7	3.0	2.4	1.7
By race:									
White	539.7	433.0	320.1	186.4	175.1	123.7	82.5	64.2	53.5
Black and other	465.6	395.2	345.7	261.6	223.6	167.5	141.8	119.2	88.1
Total of above births	**1,005.3**	**828.2**	**665.8**	**447.9**	**398.7**	**291.2**	**224.3**	**183.4**	**141.6**
Percent of all births[1]	25.7	22.0	18.4	14.2	10.7	7.7	5.3	4.5	3.9
Rate[2]	38.6	32.8	29.4	24.8	26.4	23.4	21.8	19.3	14.1

1. Through 1955, based on data adjusted for underregistration; thereafter, registered births. 2. Rate per 1,000 unmarried (never married, widowed, and divorced) women, 15–44 years old. *Source:* Department of Health and Human Services, National Center for Health Statistics. NOTE: Data are latest available.

Women, Work, and Pregnancy

Between 1961 and 1985, the proportion of women having work experience before the birth of their first child increased. Among women who had their first births in 1961–65, 60 percent worked six or more months continuously before the birth of their first child; by 1981–85, 75 percent had reported a similar work experience.

Employment during pregnancy also became increasingly common; it rose from 44 percent in 1961–65 to 65 percent in 1981–85. The women most likely to work during first pregnancy are relatively older women, White women, and women who had at least a high school education.

Most women who work during pregnancy are full–time workers: since 1961, between 80 and 90 percent of pregnant workers reported that the last job they held before their child's birth was a full–time job (35 or more hours worked per week). Among women who worked during their first pregnancy in 1981–85, 78 percent worked during their last trimester (less then three months before their child's birth), and 47 percent were still at work less than one month before their child's birth.

Live Births and Birth Rates

State	1989[1] number	1989[1] rate	1988 number	1988 rate	State	1989[1] number	1989[1] rate	1988 number	1988 rate
Alabama	58,360	14.2	60,745	14.8	Montana	11,394	14.1	11,692	14.5
Alaska	11,545	21.9	11,232	21.4	Nebraska	24,317	15.1	23,907	14.9
Arizona	67,609	19.0	65,623	18.8	Nevada	18,297	16.5	18,008	17.1
Arkansas	34,997	14.5	35,035	14.6	New Hampshire	17,946	16.2	17,364	16.0
California	557,003	19.2	533,148	18.8	New Jersey	116,554	15.1	117,764	15.3
Colorado	52,863	15.9	53,367	16.2	New Mexico	27,324	17.9	27,015	17.9
Connecticut	47,560	14.7	48,077	14.9	New York	291,145	16.2	280,650	15.7
Delaware	11,492	17.1	10,406	15.8	North Carolina	102,817	15.6	97,579	15.0
D.C.[2]	122,549	37.3	10,540	17.1	North Dakota	10,862	16.5	10,103	15.1
Florida	192,813	15.2	184,119	14.9	Ohio	162,793	14.9	160,529	14.8
Georgia	109,905	17.1	105,923	16.7	Oklahoma	46,455	14.4	47,408	14.6
Hawaii	19,545	17.6	19,045	17.3	Oregon	43,835	15.5	40,052	14.5
Idaho	15,459	15.2	15,741	15.7	Pennsylvania	170,261	14.1	165,639	13.8
Illinois	186,500	16.0	184,841	15.9	Rhode Island	15,302	15.3	14,224	14.3
Indiana	82,764	14.8	81,643	14.7	South Carolina	55,214	15.7	55,114	15.9
Iowa	37,241	13.1	38,119	13.5	South Dakota	10,991	15.4	11,194	15.7
Kansas	35,632	14.2	38,792	15.5	Tennessee	76,780	15.5	70,711	14.4
Kentucky	52,591	14.1	51,058	13.7	Texas	301,360	17.7	303,418	18.0
Louisiana	68,813	15.7	73,902	16.8	Utah	36,208	21.2	36,055	21.3
Maine	16,842	13.8	17,172	14.3	Vermont	7,920	14.0	8,111	14.6
Maryland	67,550	14.4	75,768	16.4	Virginia	93,453	15.3	93,127	15.5
Massachusetts	96,457	16.3	88,194	15.0	Washington	73,261	15.4	72,503	15.6
Michigan	142,673	15.4	139,714	15.1	West Virginia	23,079	12.4	21,846	11.6
Minnesota	66,593	15.3	66,748	15.5	Wisconsin	72,100	14.8	70,817	14.6
Mississippi	42,263	16.1	42,074	16.1	Wyoming	6,491	13.7	7,162	15.0
Missouri	80,126	15.5	76,492	14.9	**Total**	**4,021,000**	**16.2**	**3,909,510**	**15.9**

1. Provisional. 2. The anomaly in the 1988 and 1989 figures is due to the District's unique situation. The 1988 figures refer to place of residence whereas the 1989 figure (as noted) refers to place of occurrence which for D.C. residents can be Maryland or Virginia. NOTE: Provisional data by place of occurrence. Rates are per 1,000 population. *Source:* Department of Health and Human Services, National Center for Health Statistics.

Live Births by Race or National Origin

Race	1988	1987	Race	1988	1987
White	3,046,162	2,992,488	Chinese	22,904	19,293
Black	671,976	641,567	Filipino	24,612	23,636
American Indian[1]	45,871	43,707	Other[2]	84,259	75,880
Japanese	10,483	9,822	Total[3]	3,909,510	3,809,394

1. Includes Eskimos and Aleuts. 2. Hawaiian and other Asian or Pacific Islander. 3. Includes births of other races not shown separately. Data are latest available. *Source:* Department of Health and Human Services, National Center for Health Statistics.

Live Births by Sex and Sex Ratio[1]

Year	Total[2] Male	Total[2] Female	Total[2] Males per 1,000 females	White Male	White Female	White Males per 1,000 females	Black Male	Black Female	Black Males per 1,000 females
1979[3]	1,791,267	1,703,131	1,052	1,442,981	1,365,439	1,057	293,013	284,842	1,029
1980[3]	1,852,616	1,759,642	1,053	1,490,140	1,408,592	1,058	299,033	290,583	1,029
1981[3]	1,860,272	1,768,966	1,052	1,494,437	1,414,232	1,057	297,864	289,933	1,027
1982[3]	1,885,676	1,794,861	1,051	1,509,704	1,432,350	1,054	301,121	291,520	1,033
1983[3]	1,865,553	1,773,380	1,052	1,492,385	1,411,865	1,057	297,011	289,016	1,028
1984[3]	1,879,490	1,789,651	1,050	1,500,326	1,423,176	1,054	300,951	291,794	1,031
1985	1,927,983	1,832,578	1,052	1,536,646	1,454,727	1,056	308,575	299,618	1,030
1986	1,924,868	1,831,679	1,051	1,523,914	1,446,525	1,053	315,788	305,433	1,034
1987	1,951,153	1,858,241	1,050	1,535,517	1,456,971	1,054	325,259	316,308	1,028
1988	2,002,424	1,907,086	1,050	1,562,675	1,483,487	1,053	341,441	330,535	1,033

1. Excludes births to nonresidents of U.S. 2. Includes races other than white and black. 3. Based on 100% of births for selected states and 50% sample in all others. *Source:* Department of Health and Human Services, National Center for Health Statistics. NOTE: Data are latest available.

Abortions and Abortion Rates

State	Number of Abortions 1988	1987	1985	Abortion occurrence rate[1] 1988	1987	1985	Change 1985–88
Alabama	18,220	19,630	19,380	18.7	20.2	20.2	−1.5
Alaska	2,390	2,560	3,450	18.2	19.7	27.7	−9.5
Arizona	23,070	22,130	22,330	28.8	28.2	29.9	−1.1
Arkansas	6,250	7,030	5,420	11.6	13.1	10.1	1.5
California	311,720	300,830	304,130	45.9	45.0	47.9	−2.1
Colorado	18,740	18,850	24,350	22.4	22.4	28.8	−6.4
Connecticut	23,630	22,380	21,850	31.2	29.4	29.3	1.8
Delaware	5,710	5,680	4,590	35.7	35.9	30.9	4.8
District of Columbia	26,120	25,840	23,910	163.3	158.5	145.9	17.4
Florida	82,850	80,560	76,650	31.5	31.2	31.8	−0.3
Georgia	36,720	36,030	38,340	23.5	23.3	26.1	−2.6
Hawaii	11,170	11,290	11,160	43.0	44.1	43.7	−0.7
Idaho	1,920	1,980	2,660	8.2	8.5	11.1	−2.8
Illinois	72,570	72,180	64,960	26.4	26.2	23.8	2.6
Indiana	15,760	14,750	16,090	11.9	11.2	12.2	−0.2
Iowa	9,420	8,900	9,930	14.6	13.8	15.0	−0.4
Kansas	11,440	11,430	10,150	20.1	20.2	18.2	2.0
Kentucky	11,520	11,550	9,820	13.0	13.1	11.0	2.0
Louisiana	17,340	16,550	19,240	16.3	15.4	17.4	−1.1
Maine	4,620	4,950	4,960	16.2	17.7	18.6	−2.4
Maryland	32,670	31,240	29,480	28.6	27.6	26.9	1.7
Massachusetts	43,720	41,490	40,310	30.2	28.7	29.3	0.9
Michigan	63,410	61,060	64,390	28.5	27.3	28.7	−0.3
Minnesota	18,580	17,810	16,850	18.2	17.5	16.6	1.6
Mississippi	5,120	5,430	5,890	8.4	8.9	9.7	−1.3
Missouri	19,490	20,190	20,100	16.4	17.0	17.3	−0.9
Montana	3,050	3,280	3,710	16.5	17.7	19.0	−2.5
Nebraska	6,490	6,580	6,680	17.7	18.0	18.2	−0.4
Nevada	10,190	10,710	9,910	40.3	43.9	40.5	−0.2
New Hampshire	4,710	4,680	7,030	17.5	17.8	29.0	−11.5
New Jersey	63,900	63,570	69,190	35.1	34.9	39.6	−4.5
New Mexico	6,810	6,650	6,110	19.1	18.6	17.4	1.8
New York	183,980	184,420	195,120	43.3	43.3	47.4	−4.0
North Carolina	39,720	37,630	34,180	25.4	24.2	22.6	2.8
North Dakota	2,230	2,560	2,850	14.9	17.0	18.5	−3.6
Ohio	53,400	51,490	57,360	21.0	20.2	22.4	−1.4
Oklahoma	12,120	11,000	13,100	16.2	14.5	17.1	−0.9
Oregon	15,960	14,370	15,230	23.9	21.8	22.3	1.7
Pennsylvania	51,830	51,800	57,370	18.9	18.9	21.3	−2.4
Rhode Island	7,190	7,390	7,770	30.6	31.3	35.5	−4.9
South Carolina	14,160	12,770	11,200	16.7	15.2	13.7	3.1
South Dakota	900	860	1,650	5.7	5.5	10.6	−4.9
Tennessee	22,090	22,050	22,350	18.9	18.9	19.1	−0.2
Texas	100,690	100,210	100,820	24.8	24.7	25.5	−0.7
Utah	5,030	4,830	4,440	12.8	12.4	11.1	1.7
Vermont	3,580	3,690	3,430	25.8	26.9	26.2	−0.5
Virginia	35,420	34,410	34,180	23.7	23.3	24.0	−0.3
Washington	31,220	29,840	30,990	27.6	26.9	28.0	−0.4
West Virginia	3,270	2,990	4,590	7.5	6.8	10.1	−2.6
Wisconsin	18,040	18,330	17,830	16.0	16.3	15.7	0.2
Wyoming	600	680	1,070	5.1	5.7	7.9	−2.8
Total	**1,590,750**	**1,559,110**	**1,588,550**	**27.3**	**26.9**	**28.0**	**−0.7**

1. Rate per 1,000 women aged 15–44. NOTES: Number of abortions are rounded to nearest 10. *Source:* Stanley K. Henshaw and Jennifer Van Vort, "Abortion Services in the United States, 1987 and 1988," *Family Planning Perspectives*, Volume 22, Number 3, May/June 1990, p. 104. © The Alan Guttmacher Institute. NOTE: Data are latest available.

Abortion Rates Are Falling

In 1988 there were 297,251 abortions reported as having been obtained by residents within the 14 states reporting the information to the National Center for Health Statistics, a decrease of 3,059 (1 percent) from the number for the previous year. The abortion ratio of 325.4 abortions per 1,000 live births in 1988 decreased from the ratio of 337.8 for the previous year, and continued the decline observed since 1985.

From 1987 to 1988, ratios decreased for both white and black women. Decreases for both were greater among married than unmarried women.

One-fourth of the induced abortions in 1988 in the 14-state area were to women under 20. One-third occurred to women 20-24 years of age. The remaining 42 percent were to women 25 years of age and over.

Mortality
Death Rates for Selected Causes

Cause of death	Death rates per 100,000							
	1990[1]	1989[1]	1985	1980	1950	1945–49	1920–24[4]	1900–04[4]
Typhoid fever	n.a.	n.a.	—	0.0	0.1	0.2	7.3	26.7
Communicable diseases of childhood	n.a.	n.a.	n.a.	0.0	1.3	2.3	33.8	65.2
Measles	0.0	0.0	—	0.0	0.3	0.6	7.3	10.0
Scarlet fever	n.a.	n.a.	1.0	0.0	0.2	0.1	4.0	11.8
Whooping cough	0.0	0.0	—	0.0	0.7	1.0	8.9	10.7
Diphtheria	n.a.	n.a.	—	0.0	0.3	0.7	13.7	32.7
Pneumonia and influenza	31.4	30.3	27.9	23.3	31.3	41.3	140.3	184.3
Influenza	0.8	0.5	0.8	1.1	4.4	5.0	34.8	22.8
Pneumonia	30.6	29.7	27.1	22.0	26.9	37.2	105.5	161.5
Tuberculosis	0.7	0.7	0.7	0.8	22.5	33.3	96.7	184.7
Cancer	202.1	199.9	191.7	182.5	139.8	134.0	86.9	67.7
Diabetes mellitus	19.0	18.7	16.2	15.0	16.2	24.1	17.1	12.2
Major cardiovascular diseases	366.2	375.3	410.7	434.5	510.8	493.1	369.9	359.5
Diseases of the heart	288.5	295.9	325.0	335.2	356.8	325.1	169.8	153.0
Cerebrovascular diseases	57.5	58.9	64.0	74.6	104.0	93.8	93.5	106.3
Nephritis and nephrosis	8.5	8.9	9.4	7.6	16.4	48.4	81.5	84.3
Syphilis	0.0	0.0	0.0	0.1	5.0	8.4	17.6	12.9
Appendicitis	0.2	0.2	0.2	0.3	2.0	3.5	14.0	9.4
Accidents, all forms	36.5	37.2	38.6	46.0	60.6	67.6	70.8	79.2
Motor vehicle accidents	18.6	18.9	18.8	23.0	23.1	22.3	12.9	n.a.
Infant mortality[2]	n.a.	n.a.	10.6	12.5	29.2	33.3	76.7	n.a.
Neonatal mortality[2]	n.a.	n.a.	7.0	8.4	20.5	22.9	39.7	n.a.
Fetal mortality[3]	n.a.	n.a.	7.9	9.2	19.2	21.6	n.a	n.a.
Maternal mortality[2]	n.a.	n.a.	0.1	0.1	0.8	1.4	6.9	n.a.
All causes	**861.9**	**868.1**	**890.8**	**883.4**	**960.1**	**1,000.6**	**1,157.4**	**1,621.6**

1. Provisional, based on a 10% sample of deaths. 2. Rates per 1,000 live births. 3. Ratio per 1,000 births. 4. Includes only deaths occurring within the registration areas. Beginning with 1933, area includes the entire United States; Alaska included beginning in 1959 and Hawaii in 1960. Rates per 100,000 population residing in areas, enumerated as of April 1 for 1940, 1950, and 1980 and estimated as of July 1 for all other years. Due to changes in statistical methods, death rates are not strictly comparable. n.a. = not available. *Source:* Department of Health and Human Services, National Center for Health Statistics.

Accident Rates, 1989

Class of accident		One every	Class of accident		One every
All accidents	Deaths	6 minutes	Workers off-job	Deaths	14 minutes
	Injuries	4 seconds		Injuries	11 seconds
Motor-vehicle	Deaths	11 minutes	Home	Deaths	23 minutes
	Injuries	19 seconds		Injuries	9 seconds
Work	Deaths	51 minutes	Public non-motor-	Deaths	28 minutes
	Injuries	19 seconds	vehicle	Injuries	13 seconds

NOTE: Data are latest available. *Source:* National Safety Council.

Improper Driving as Factor in Accidents, 1989

Kind of improper driving	Fatal accidents			Injury accidents			All accidents		
	Total	Urban	Rural	Total	Urban	Rural	Total	Urban	Rural
Improper driving	**61.9**	**61.3**	**62.3**	**73.7**	**75.3**	**70.5**	**72.7**	**74.2**	**68.9**
Speed too fast[1]	26.7	27.5	26.3	23.1	21.3	26.8	18.9	17.4	22.5
Right of way	12.2	15.4	10.5	25.4	29.8	16.3	23.4	26.5	15.7
Failed to yield	8.4	10.1	7.5	18.2	20.6	13.2	17.8	19.8	13.1
Passed stop sign	2.1	1.7	2.3	2.0	2.2	1.7	1.6	1.6	1.4
Disregarded signal	1.7	3.6	0.7	5.2	7.0	1.4	4.0	5.1	1.2
Drove left of center	4.5	2.4	5.6	1.5	0.9	2.7	1.7	1.2	2.8
Improper overtaking	6.2	3.9	7.3	2.0	1.5	3.2	2.4	2.1	3.3
Made improper turn	0.4	0.6	0.4	1.5	1.6	1.2	2.6	2.9	1.8
Followed too closely	0.7	0.7	0.7	6.1	6.9	4.5	6.4	7.0	5.0
Other improper driving	11.2	10.8	11.5	14.1	13.3	15.8	17.3	17.1	17.8
No improper driving stated	**38.1**	**38.7**	**37.7**	**26.3**	**24.7**	**29.5**	**27.3**	**25.8**	**31.1**
Total	**100.0%**	**100.0%**	**100.0%**	**100.0%**	**100.0%**	**100.0%**	**100.0%**	**100.0%**	**100.0%**

1. Includes "speed too fast for conditions." *Source:* Motor-vehicle reports from six state traffic authorities to National Safety Council. NOTE: Figures are latest available.

Motor–Vehicle Deaths by Type of Accident

Year	Pedes-trians	Other motor vehicles	Railroad trains	Street cars	Pedalcycles	Animal-drawn vehicle or animal	Fixed objects	Deaths from non-collision accidents	Total deaths[1]
				Deaths from collisions with—					
1975	8,400	19,550	979	1	1,000	100	3,130	12,700	45,853
1980	9,700	23,000	739	1	1,200	100	3,700	14,700	53,172
1985	8,300	19,900	500	(2)	1,100	100	2,800	12,900	45,600
1986	8,300	20,500	600	(2)	1,200	100	3,300	13,900	47,900
1987	8,500	20,500	600	(2)	1,400	100	3,400	14,200	48,700
1988	8,800	21,200	600	(2)	1,100	100	3,300	13,900	49,000
1989	7,200	19,900	700	(2)	1,000	100	13,100	4,900	46,900

1. Totals do not equal sums of various types because totals are estimated. 2. Data not available for these years. NOTE: Figures are latest available. *Source:* National Safety Council.

Accidental Deaths by Principal Types

Year	Motor vehicle	Falls	Drown-ing	Fire burns	Ingestion of food or object	Fire-arms	Poison (solid, liquid)	Poison by gas
1982	45,779	12,077	6,351	5,210	3,254	1,756	3,474	1,259
1983	44,452	12,024	6,353	5,028	3,387	1,695	3,382	1,251
1984	46,263	11,937	5,388	5,010	3,541	1,668	3,808	1,103
1985	45,600	11,700	5,300	4,900	3,600	1,800	3,600	1,000
1986	47,900	11,000	5,600	4,800	3,600	1,800	4,000	900
1987	48,700	11,300	5,300	4,800	3,200	1,400	4,400	1,000
1988	49,000	12,000	5,000	5,000	3,600	1,400	5,300	1,000
1989	46,900	12,400	4,600	4,400	3,900	1,600	5,600	900

NOTE: Figures are latest available. *Source:* National Safety Council.

Deaths and Death Rates

State	Total deaths 1989 number	Total deaths 1989 rate[1]	Motor vehicle traffic deaths 1989 number	Motor vehicle traffic deaths 1989 rate[2]	State	Total deaths 1989 number	Total deaths 1989 rate[1]	Motor vehicle traffic deaths 1989 number	Motor vehicle traffic deaths 1989 rate[2]
Alabama	37,420	9.1	1,025	2.4	Montana	6,682	8.3	181	2.3
Alaska	2,052	3.9	84	2.3	Nebraska	15,226	9.5	296	2.2
Arizona	28,882	8.1	884	2.6	Nevada	9,094	8.2	307	3.3
Arkansas	24,519	10.2	648	3.3	New Hampshire	8,391	7.6	190	2.0
California	217,489	7.5	5,105	2.1	New Jersey	69,393	9.0	890	1.5
Colorado	21,764	6.6	522	1.9	New Mexico	10,525	6.9	538	3.5
Connecticut	28,170	8.7	406	1.6	New York	169,634	9.5	2,239	2.1
Delaware	5,968	8.9	118	1.8	North Carolina	57,859	8.8	1,464	2.5
D.C.	9,862	16.3	75	2.2	North Dakota	5,865	8.9	81	1.4
Florida	133,897	10.6	3,016	2.8	Ohio	98,224	9.0	1,700	2.1
Georgia	53,761	8.4	1,632	2.5	Oklahoma	28,779	8.9	655	2.0
Hawaii	6,708	6.0	147	1.9	Oregon	27,469	9.7	630	2.5
Idaho	7,150	7.1	238	2.8	Pennsylvania	124,149	10.3	1,877	2.3
Illinois	100,686	8.6	1,748	2.2	Rhode Island	9,757	9.8	100	1.7
Indiana	49,421	8.8	973	1.9	South Carolina	28,958	8.2	996	3.2
Iowa	25,201	8.9	511	2.3	South Dakota	6,535	9.1	151	2.3
Kansas	21,519	8.6	426	2.1	Tennessee	47,454	9.6	1,081	2.3
Kentucky	34,005	9.1	782	2.4	Texas	125,622	7.4	3,361	2.2
Louisiana	36,221	8.3	857	2.4	Utah	9,483	5.6	303	2.4
Maine	11,029	9.0	190	1.7	Vermont	4,501	7.9	116	2.1
Maryland	38,078	8.1	750	2.0	Virginia	46,342	7.6	999	1.7
Massachusetts	55,472	9.4	700	1.7	Washington	36,341	7.6	781	1.8
Michigan	77,660	8.4	1,633	2.1	West Virginia	19,472	10.5	468	3.3
Minnesota	34,484	7.9	605	1.6	Wisconsin	42,640	8.8	817	1.9
Mississippi	24,370	9.3	728	3.3	Wyoming	3,065	6.5	127	2.3
Missouri	55,648	10.8	1,052	2.3	**Total**	**2,153,896**	**8.6**	**46,900**	**2.3**

1. Provisional rates per 1,000 population, by place of occurrence. 2. Per 100 million vehicle–miles. *Sources:* Department of Health and Human Services, National Center for Health Statistics; National Safety Council.

Annual Death Rates

Year	Rate		Year	Rate		Year	Deaths	Rate
1900	17.2		1943	10.9		1967	1,851,323	9.4
1905	15.9		1944	10.6		1968	1,930,082	9.7
1910	14.7		1945	10.6		1969	1,921,990	9.5
1915	13.2		1946	10.0		1970[1]	1,921,031	9.5
1920	13.0		1947	10.1		1971	1,927,542	9.3
1925	11.7		1948	9.9		1972	1,963,944	9.4
1926	12.1		1949	9.7		1973	1,973,003	9.3
1927	11.3		1950	9.6		1974	1,934,388	9.1
1928	12.0		1951	9.7		1975	1,892,879	8.8
1929	11.9		1952	9.6		1976	1,909,440	8.8
1930	11.3		1953	9.6		1977	1,899,597	8.6
1931	11.1		1954	9.2		1978	1,927,788	8.7
1932	10.9		1955	9.3		1979	1,913,841	8.5
1933	10.7		1956	9.4		1980	1,989,841	8.7
1934	11.1		1957	9.6		1982	1,974,797	8.5
1935	10.9		1958	9.5		1983	2,019,201	8.6
1936	11.6		1959	9.4		1984	2,039,369	8.6
1937	11.3		1960	9.5		1985	2,086,440	8.7
1938	10.6		1962	9.5		1986	2,099,000	8.7
1939	10.6		1963	9.6		1987	2,127,000	8.7
1940	10.8		1964	9.4		1988	2,171,000	8.8
1941	10.5		1965	9.4		1989	2,155,000	8.7
1942	10.3		1966	9.5		1990[2]	2,162,000	8.6

1. First year for which deaths of nonresidents are excluded. 2. Provisional. NOTE: Includes only deaths occurring within the registration states. Beginning with 1933, area includes entire U.S.; with 1959 includes Alaska, and with 1960 includes Hawaii. Excludes fetal deaths. Rates per 1,000 population residing in area, as of April 1 for 1940, 1950, 1960, 1970, and 1980, and estimated as of July 1 for all other years. *Sources:* Department of Health and Human Services, National Center for Health Statistics.

Death Rates by Age, Race, and Sex

Age	1989[1]	1988	1987	1980	1970[2]	1960	1989[1]	1988	1987	1980	1970[2]	1960
	White males						**White females**					
Under 1 year	9.1	9.3	9.4	12.3	21.1	26.9	7.1	7.2	7.4	9.6	16.1	20.1
1–4	0.4	0.5	0.5	0.7	0.8	1.0	0.3	0.4	0.4	0.5	0.8	0.9
5–14	0.3	0.2	0.3	0.4	0.5	0.5	0.1	0.1	0.2	0.2	0.3	0.3
15–24	1.3	1.3	1.4	1.7	1.7	1.4	0.5	0.4	0.5	0.5	0.6	0.5
25–34	1.7	1.6	1.7	1.7	1.8	1.6	0.6	0.6	0.6	0.7	0.8	0.9
35–44	2.6	2.5	2.5	2.6	3.4	3.3	1.2	1.1	1.2	1.2	1.9	1.9
45–54	5.6	5.6	5.8	7.0	8.8	9.3	3.0	3.1	3.3	3.7	4.6	4.6
55–64	14.9	15.3	15.5	17.3	22.0	22.3	8.4	8.5	8.5	8.8	10.1	10.8
65–74	33.4	35.0	35.5	40.4	48.1	48.5	19.4	19.9	20.0	20.7	24.7	27.8
75–84	79.3	82.0	82.1	88.3	101.0	103.0	50.7	51.2	50.8	54.0	67.0	77.0
85 and over	181.1	188.1	184.3	191.0	185.5	217.5	140.3	147.5	144.9	149.8	159.8	194.8
	All other males						**All other females**					
Under 1 year	17.5	18.9	19.4	23.5	40.2	51.9	15.6	16.0	15.7	19.4	31.7	40.7
1–4	0.6	0.7	0.8	1.0	1.4	2.1	0.6	0.6	0.7	0.8	1.2	1.7
5–14	0.4	0.3	0.4	0.4	0.6	0.8	0.2	0.2	0.2	0.3	0.4	0.5
15–24	2.0	2.0	1.9	2.0	3.0	2.1	0.6	0.6	0.6	0.7	1.1	1.1
25–34	3.6	3.4	3.3	3.6	5.0	3.9	1.3	1.3	1.3	1.4	2.2	2.6
35–44	5.6	5.8	5.7	5.9	8.7	7.3	2.5	2.5	2.5	2.9	4.9	5.5
45–54	10.6	10.6	10.6	13.1	16.5	15.5	5.0	5.4	5.6	6.9	9.8	11.4
55–64	21.0	21.8	21.8	26.1	30.5	31.5	11.9	12.7	12.7	14.2	18.9	24.1
65–74	39.8	41.7	42.3	47.5	54.7	56.6	24.0	25.5	25.7	28.6	36.8	39.8
75–84	80.1	84.0	83.4	86.9	89.8	86.6	52.0	56.2	55.4	58.6	63.9	67.1
85 and over	141.0	145.5	145.1	157.7	114.1	152.4	115.0	119.6	118.1	119.2	102.9	128.7

1. Provisional. Based on a 10% sample of deaths. 2. Beginning 1970 excludes deaths of nonresidents of U.S. NOTE: Excludes fetal deaths. Rates are per 1,000 population in each group, enumerated as of April 1 for 1960, 1970, and 1980, and estimated as of July 1 for all other years. *Sources:* Department of Health and Human Services, National Center for Health Statistics.

Expectation of Life

Expectation of Life in the United States

Calendar period	Age								
	0	10	20	30	40	50	60	70	80
WHITE MALES									
1850[1]	38.3	48.0	40.1	34.0	27.9	21.6	15.6	10.2	5.9
1890[1]	42.50	48.45	40.66	34.05	27.37	20.72	14.73	9.35	5.40
1900–1902[2]	48.23	50.59	42.19	34.88	27.74	20.76	14.35	9.03	5.10
1909–1911[2]	50.23	51.32	42.71	34.87	27.43	20.39	13.98	8.83	5.09
1919–1921[3]	56.34	54.15	45.60	37.65	29.86	22.22	15.25	9.51	5.47
1929–1931	59.12	54.96	46.02	37.54	29.22	21.51	14.72	9.20	5.26
1939–1941	62.81	57.03	47.76	38.80	30.03	21.96	15.05	9.42	5.38
1949–1951	66.31	58.98	49.52	40.29	31.17	22.83	15.76	10.07	5.88
1959–1961[5]	67.55	59.78	50.25	40.98	31.73	23.22	16.01	10.29	5.89
1969–1971[6]	67.94	59.69	50.22	41.07	31.87	23.34	16.07	10.38	6.18
1979–1981	70.82	61.98	52.45	43.31	34.04	25.26	17.56	11.35	6.76
1986	72.0	62.9	53.4	44.2	34.9	26.1	18.2	11.7	6.9
1987	72.2	63.1	53.6	44.3	35.1	26.2	18.3	11.8	6.9
1988	72.3	63.2	53.6	44.4	35.2	26.3	18.4	11.8	6.8
WHITE FEMALES									
1850[1]	40.5	47.2	40.2	35.4	29.8	23.5	17.0	11.3	6.4
1890[1]	44.46	49.62	42.03	35.36	28.76	22.09	15.70	10.15	5.75
1900–1902[2]	51.08	52.15	43.77	36.42	29.17	21.89	15.23	9.59	5.50
1909–1911[2]	53.62	53.57	44.88	36.96	29.26	21.74	14.92	9.38	5.35
1919–1921[3]	58.53	55.17	46.46	38.72	30.94	23.12	15.93	9.94	5.70
1929–1931	62.67	57.65	48.52	39.99	31.52	23.41	16.05	9.98	5.63
1939–1941	67.29	60.85	51.38	42.21	33.25	24.72	17.00	10.50	5.88
1949–1951	72.03	64.26	54.56	45.00	35.64	26.76	18.64	11.68	6.59
1959–1961[5]	74.19	66.05	56.29	46.63	37.13	28.08	19.69	12.38	6.67
1969–1971[6]	75.49	66.97	57.24	47.60	38.12	29.11	20.79	13.37	7.59
1979–1981	78.22	69.21	59.44	49.76	40.16	30.96	22.45	14.89	8.65
1986	78.8	69.6	59.9	50.1	40.5	31.2	22.6	15.1	8.8
1987	78.9	69.7	59.9	50.2	40.6	31.3	22.7	15.1	8.8
1988	78.9	69.7	59.9	50.2	40.6	31.2	22.6	15.0	8.7
ALL OTHER MALES[4]									
1900–1902[2]	32.54	41.90	35.11	29.25	23.12	17.34	12.62	8.33	5.12
1909–1911[2]	34.05	40.65	33.46	27.33	21.57	16.21	11.67	8.00	5.53
1919–1921[3]	47.14	45.99	38.36	32.51	26.53	20.47	14.74	9.58	5.83
1929–1931	47.55	44.27	35.95	29.45	23.36	17.92	13.15	8.78	5.42
1939–1941	52.33	48.54	39.74	32.25	25.23	19.18	14.38	10.06	6.46
1949–1951	58.91	52.96	43.73	35.31	27.29	20.25	14.91	10.74	7.07
1959–1961[5]	61.48	55.19	45.78	37.05	28.72	21.28	15.29	10.81	6.87
1969–1971[6]	60.98	53.67	44.37	36.20	28.29	21.24	15.35	10.68	7.57
1979–1981	65.63	57.40	47.87	39.13	30.64	22.92	16.54	11.36	7.22
1986	67.2	58.7	49.1	40.3	31.8	23.9	17.0	11.5	7.1
1987	67.3	58.8	49.2	40.4	32.0	24.1	17.2	11.6	7.2
1988	67.1	58.6	49.1	40.3	32.0	24.1	17.2	11.6	7.2
ALL OTHER FEMALES[4]									
1900–1902[2]	35.04	43.02	36.89	30.70	24.37	18.67	13.60	9.62	6.48
1909–1911[2]	37.67	42.84	36.14	29.61	23.34	17.65	12.78	9.22	6.05
1919–1921[3]	46.92	44.54	37.15	31.48	25.60	19.76	14.69	10.25	6.58
1929–1931	49.51	45.33	37.22	30.67	24.30	18.60	14.22	10.38	6.90
1939–1941	55.51	50.83	42.14	34.52	27.31	21.04	16.14	11.81	8.00
1949–1951	62.70	56.17	46.77	38.02	29.82	22.67	16.95	12.29	8.15
1959–1961[5]	66.47	59.72	50.07	40.83	32.16	24.31	17.83	12.46	7.66
1969–1971[6]	69.05	61.49	51.85	42.61	33.87	25.97	19.02	13.30	9.01
1979–1981	74.00	65.64	55.88	46.39	37.16	28.59	20.49	14.44	9.17
1986	75.1	66.4	56.6	47.1	37.8	29.1	21.2	14.5	8.9
1987	75.2	66.5	56.7	47.2	38.0	29.2	21.3	14.6	8.9
1988	75.1	66.4	56.7	47.1	37.9	29.2	21.3	14.5	8.8

1. Massachusetts only; white and nonwhite combined, the latter being about 1% of the total. 2. Original Death Registration States. 3. Death Registration States of 1920. 4. Data for periods 1900–1902 to 1929–1931 relate to blacks only. 5. Alaska and Hawaii included beginning in 1959. 6. Deaths of nonresidents of the United States excluded starting in 1970. *Sources:* Department of Health and Human Services, National Center for Health Statistics.

Expectation of Life and Mortality Probabilities, 1988

	Expectation of life in years				Mortality probability per 1,000				
		White		All other			White		All other	
Age	Total persons	Male	Female	Male	Female	Total persons	Male	Female	Male	Female
0	74.9	72.3	78.9	67.1	75.1	10.0	9.5	7.5	16.3	13.9
1	74.7	72.0	78.5	67.3	75.1	0.7	0.7	0.5	1.0	0.8
2	73.8	71.0	77.5	66.3	74.2	0.5	0.5	0.4	0.8	0.7
3	72.8	70.1	76.6	65.4	73.2	0.4	0.4	0.3	0.7	0.5
4	71.8	69.1	75.6	64.4	72.3	0.3	0.3	0.3	0.6	0.4
5	70.8	68.1	74.6	63.5	71.3	0.3	0.3	0.2	0.5	0.4
6	69.9	67.1	73.6	62.5	70.3	0.3	0.3	0.2	0.4	0.3
7	68.9	66.2	72.7	61.5	69.4	0.2	0.3	0.2	0.4	0.3
8	67.9	65.2	71.7	60.5	68.4	0.2	0.2	0.2	0.3	0.2
9	66.9	64.2	70.7	59.6	67.4	0.2	0.2	0.1	0.3	0.2
10	65.9	63.2	69.7	58.6	66.4	0.2	0.2	0.1	0.2	0.2
11	64.9	62.2	68.7	57.6	65.4	0.2	0.2	0.1	0.2	0.2
12	64.0	61.2	67.7	56.6	64.4	0.2	0.2	0.2	0.3	0.3
13	63.0	60.2	66.7	55.6	63.5	0.3	0.4	0.2	0.5	0.3
14	62.0	59.3	65.7	54.6	62.5	0.5	0.6	0.3	0.7	0.3
15	61.0	58.3	64.8	53.7	61.5	0.6	0.8	0.4	1.0	0.4
16	60.1	57.3	63.8	52.7	60.5	0.8	1.1	0.5	1.3	0.4
17	59.1	56.4	62.8	51.8	59.6	0.9	1.2	0.5	1.5	0.5
18	58.2	55.5	61.8	50.9	58.6	1.0	1.4	0.5	1.8	0.5
19	57.2	54.6	60.9	50.0	57.6	1.0	1.4	0.5	2.0	0.6
20	56.3	53.6	59.9	49.1	56.7	1.1	1.5	0.5	2.2	0.7
21	55.3	52.7	58.9	48.2	55.7	1.1	1.6	0.5	2.5	0.7
22	54.4	51.8	58.0	47.3	54.7	1.2	1.6	0.5	2.6	0.8
23	53.5	50.9	57.0	46.4	53.8	1.2	1.6	0.5	2.8	0.9
24	52.5	50.0	56.0	45.5	52.8	1.2	1.6	0.5	2.8	0.9
25	51.6	49.0	55.0	44.7	51.9	1.2	1.6	0.5	2.8	1.0
26	50.6	48.1	54.1	43.8	50.9	1.2	1.5	0.5	2.9	1.1
27	49.7	47.2	53.1	42.9	50.0	1.2	1.5	0.5	3.0	1.1
28	48.8	46.3	52.1	42.1	49.0	1.2	1.6	0.6	3.1	1.2
29	47.8	45.3	51.2	41.2	48.1	1.3	1.6	0.6	3.3	1.3
30	46.9	44.4	50.2	40.3	47.1	1.3	1.7	0.6	3.5	1.4
31	45.9	43.5	49.2	39.5	46.2	1.4	1.7	0.6	3.7	1.4
32	45.0	42.6	48.3	38.6	45.3	1.5	1.8	0.7	3.9	1.5
33	44.1	41.6	47.3	37.7	44.3	1.5	1.9	0.7	4.2	1.7
34	43.1	40.7	46.3	36.9	43.4	1.6	2.0	0.8	4.5	1.8
35	42.2	39.8	45.4	36.1	42.5	1.7	2.0	0.8	4.8	1.9
36	41.3	38.9	44.4	35.2	41.6	1.8	2.1	0.9	5.1	2.1
37	40.4	37.9	43.4	34.4	40.7	1.9	2.2	1.0	5.4	2.2
38	39.4	37.0	42.5	33.6	39.8	2.0	2.4	1.0	5.7	2.4
39	38.5	36.1	41.5	32.8	38.8	2.1	2.5	1.1	5.8	2.5
40	37.6	35.2	40.6	32.0	37.9	2.2	2.6	1.2	6.0	2.6
41	36.7	34.3	39.6	31.2	37.0	2.3	2.8	1.3	6.2	2.8
42	35.8	33.4	38.7	30.4	36.1	2.5	2.9	1.4	6.5	3.0
43	34.9	32.5	37.7	29.6	35.3	3.0	3.1	1.6	6.9	3.2
44	33.9	31.6	36.8	28.8	34.4	3.0	3.4	1.8	7.3	3.4
45	33.0	30.7	35.8	28.0	33.5	3.1	3.6	1.9	7.8	3.7
46	32.1	29.8	34.9	27.2	32.6	3.4	4.0	2.2	8.3	4.0
47	31.3	28.9	34.0	26.4	31.7	3.8	4.3	2.4	8.8	4.3
48	30.4	28.0	33.1	25.6	30.9	4.1	4.7	2.6	9.5	4.7
49	29.5	27.2	32.1	24.9	30.0	4.5	5.2	2.9	10.2	5.2
50	28.6	26.3	31.2	24.1	29.2	5.0	5.7	3.2	10.9	5.6
51	27.8	25.5	30.3	23.4	28.3	5.5	6.3	3.6	11.8	6.2
52	26.9	24.6	29.5	22.7	27.5	6.0	7.0	4.0	12.6	6.7
53	26.1	23.8	28.6	21.9	26.7	6.6	7.8	4.4	13.5	7.3
54	25.3	23.0	27.7	21.1	25.9	7.3	8.6	4.9	14.4	7.9
55	24.4	22.2	26.8	20.5	25.1	8.0	9.6	5.4	15.3	8.5
56	23.6	21.4	26.0	19.8	24.3	8.7	10.6	5.9	16.3	9.2
57	22.8	20.6	25.1	19.2	23.5	9.6	11.7	6.5	17.5	10.0
58	22.0	19.8	24.3	18.5	22.7	10.5	12.9	7.1	18.9	10.9
59	21.3	19.1	23.5	17.9	22.0	11.5	14.2	7.9	20.6	12.0
60	20.5	18.4	22.6	17.2	21.3	12.6	15.6	8.6	22.5	13.2
61	19.8	17.6	21.8	16.6	20.5	13.8	17.2	9.5	24.3	14.5
62	19.0	16.9	21.0	16.0	19.8	15.0	18.7	10.3	26.2	15.6
63	18.3	16.3	20.2	15.4	19.1	16.2	20.3	11.2	27.9	16.7
64	17.6	15.6	19.5	14.9	18.4	17.4	21.9	12.2	29.6	17.7
65	16.9	14.9	18.7	14.3	17.8	18.7	23.6	13.2	31.3	18.7

		Expectation of life in years					Mortality probability per 1,000			
		White		All other			White		All other	
Age	Total persons	Male	Female	Male	Female	Total persons	Male	Female	Male	Female
66	16.2	14.3	17.9	13.7	17.1	20.1	25.4	14.3	33.2	19.8
67	15.6	13.6	17.2	13.2	16.4	21.8	27.6	15.6	35.3	21.1
68	14.9	13.0	16.5	12.7	15.8	23.7	30.2	17.0	37.6	22.6
69	14.2	12.4	15.7	12.1	15.1	25.8	33.1	18.7	40.2	24.4
70	13.6	11.8	15.0	11.6	14.5	28.2	36.3	20.5	42.9	26.3
71	13.0	11.2	14.3	11.1	13.9	30.7	39.7	22.5	45.9	28.4
72	12.4	10.7	13.7	10.6	13.3	33.4	43.4	24.7	49.0	30.6
73	11.8	10.1	13.0	10.2	12.7	36.2	47.2	27.0	52.4	32.9
74	11.2	9.6	12.3	9.7	12.1	39.2	51.3	29.5	56.1	35.3
75	10.7	9.1	11.7	9.2	11.5	42.4	55.8	32.2	60.1	37.9
76	10.1	8.6	11.1	8.8	10.9	46.1	60.7	35.3	64.5	40.9
77	9.6	8.2	10.4	8.4	10.4	50.1	66.0	38.9	69.4	44.4
78	9.0	7.7	9.8	8.0	9.9	54.6	72.0	42.9	74.8	48.5
79	8.5	7.3	9.3	7.6	9.3	59.7	78.5	47.5	81.0	53.3
80	8.1	6.8	8.7	7.2	8.8	65.5	85.9	52.9	88.0	58.9
81	7.6	6.4	8.2	6.8	8.4	72.1	94.0	59.1	95.9	65.5
82	7.1	6.0	7.6	6.5	7.9	79.7	103.0	66.3	105.1	73.2
83	6.7	5.7	7.2	6.2	7.5	88.5	113.2	75.0	115.9	82.5
84	6.3	5.4	6.7	6.0	7.1	98.8	124.4	85.3	128.7	93.8
85	6.0	5.1	6.3	5.8	8.8	—	—	—	—	—

Source: Department of Health and Human Services, National Center for Health Statistics.

Living Arrangements of the Elderly: 1980 and 1990
(in thousands)

Living arrangement and age	1990			1980		
	Total	Men	Women	Total	Men	Women
65 years and over	29,566	12,334	17,232	24,157	9,889	14,268
Living						
Alone	9,176	1,942	7,233	7,067	1,447	5,620
With spouse	16,003	9,158	6,845	12,781	7,441	5,340
With other relatives	3,734	953	2,782	3,892	832	3,060
With nonrelatives only[1]	653	281	372	417	169	248
65 to 74 years	17,979	8,013	9,966	15,302	6,621	8,681
Living						
Alone	4,350	1,042	3,309	3,750	797	2,953
With spouse	11,353	6,265	5,089	9,436	5,285	4,151
With other relatives	1,931	528	1,401	1,890	436	1,454
With nonrelatives only[1]	345	178	167	226	103	123
75 to 84 years	9,354	3,562	5,792	7,172	2,708	4,464
Living						
Alone	3,774	688	3,086	2,664	505	2,159
With spouse	4,145	2,537	1,607	2,977	1,882	1,095
With other relatives	1,237	264	974	1,394	271	1,123
With nonrelatives only[1]	198	73	125	137	50	87
85 years and over	2,233	758	1,475	1,683	560	1,123
Living						
Alone	1,051	213	838	653	145	508
With spouse	505	356	150	368	274	94
With other relatives	567	160	406	608	125	483
With nonrelatives only[1]	110	29	81	54	16	38

1. 1980 data include a small number of persons in unrelated subfamilies. *Source:* U.S. Bureau of the Census, Current Population Reports, Series P-20, No. 450, *Material Status and Living Arrangements: March 1990.*

The Elderly

In 1990, there were 29.6 million persons in the noninstitutional population 65 years and older. Their living arrangements vary by age and sex. In the 65-to-74 group, 63 percent are married and living with their spouse, and 24 percent are living alone. As age increases, the proportion living with a spouse declines and the proportion living alone increases. By the age of 85 and over, 23 percent lived with their spouse and 47 percent lived alone.

SPECIAL REPORT

The Columbian Exchange

Forget 1492. The year that Columbus changed the world was 1493, when he took 17 ships to America, hauling 1,200 immigrants and such alien creatures as horses, cows, pigs, and sheep. His voyage started the Columbian Exchange, a hemispherical swap of peoples, plants, animals, and diseases that transformed not only the new world that he discovered but also the old one he left.

The New World

Potato

With 4,000 years of experience, the Indians of the Andes knew their potatoes. When the Spanish arrived in Peru a few years after Columbus's landfall, Incan farmers were growing 3,000 varieties. The conquistadors, looking for gold and silver, were unimpressed, but a few tubers wound up on ships and sprouted in sailors' gardens on the Spanish coast. One 16th-century writer praised the potato as a love potion, but most Europeans greeted it with disdain. The didn't find roots particularly appetizing.

But the potato proved to be ideal for northern Europe's soil and climate. The vegetable saved the Irish from starvation after Oliver Cromwell's Roundheads pushed Ireland's natives into barren Connacht province. Packing more calories per acre than any European grain, the potato eventually became the dominant food of northern Europe's working class and facilitated Germany's rise to industrial power. Two results, says historian William McNeill, were World War I and World War II.

Tobacco

Columbus provided the first account of what would become a global habit. The Indians, he reported, strolled along with "a firebrand in the hand, and herbs to drink the smoke thereof." What Columbus saw in the Caribbean were cigars. Indians on the mainland puffed pipes, a practice soon copied from England to Japan. During the 16th century, when snuff sniffing caught on among the gentry, tobacco became more popular than tea.

King James I loathed tobacco as a "stinking weed . . . harmful to the braine, dangerous to the Lungs," but his addicted subjects made it the No. 1 product of England's American colonies. George Washington grew the leaf, as did an unenthusiastic Thomas Jefferson, who called it "a culture productive of infinite wretchedness." Tobacco, he noted, exhausted land as well as people. By 1800, tens of thousands of farmers were abandoning the sterile and gullied soil of Virginia and Maryland and heading across the Appalachians. A young nation's westward movement was under way.

Quinine

For thousands of years, malaria was as destructive as any plague. Blacks in West Africa had built an immunity, but Europeans who ventured into warm, swampy areas infested with mosquitoes courted death. Yet the New World remained malaria-free—until American mosquitoes tasted infected Europeans and became carriers.

The disease killed huge numbers of Americans—Indians and whites alike—before Indian medicine men found a cure in the 17th century. It was quinine, derived from the bark of the cinchona tree that dotted the slopes of the Peruvian Andes.

Quinine, says British author Henry Hobhouse, enabled Europeans to colonize the tropics and develop empires in Asia and Africa in the 19th century. The Indians' cure even helped Abraham Lincoln win the Civil War. Union troops had plentiful supplies of quinine, but the Confederacy, deprived of the wonder drug by a Union blockade, lost divisions' worth of men to malarial fevers.

The Old World

Sugar Cane

Most of the first people who settled the New World didn't want to come. They were slaves form Africa, brought to America because Europeans wanted to sweeten their coffee and tea.

Before Columbus carried a few pieces of sugar cane to the Caribbean, sugar was a luxury. Most Europeans got it from their apothecaries to help make medicine taste better. But by the middle of the 16th century, tropical American forests were giving way to

New World to Old			Old World to New		
Corn	Pole, Navy,	Pineapple	Horse	Lettuce	Daffodil
Sweet Potato	Kidney	Sunflower	Cow	Peach and	Tulip
Tomato	Squash	Petunia	Sheep	Pear	Daisy
Bell, Chili	Pumpkin	Black-eyed	Chicken	Lemon and	Crab Grass
Pepper	Cassava Root	Susan	Honeybee	Orange	Dandelion
Pimento	Avocado	Dahlia	Coffee	Banana	
Cacao for	Peanut	Marigold	Wheat, Rice,	Olive	
Chocolate	Pecan	Zinnia	Barley	Gladiolus	
Vanilla	Cashew	Poinsettia	Cabbage	Lilac	
Beans: Lima,	Guava	Turkey	Turnip	Carnation	

Nina. Columbus's favorite ship, is depicted as she looked on his third voyage to the New World in 1498. Drawing by Richard Schlecht © 1986 National Geographic Society.

vast colonies of cane-growing plantations. Europe was hooked on sugar.

Scholars estimate that each ton of sugar cost the life of one worker in the New World. As Indians perished, African slaves were ferried in. Though many died, others took their place, soon outnumbering whites on some islands 20 to 1. The slave-based plantation system that sugar started spread to the Carolinas and Georgia to raise rice, indigo, and cotton. Over nearly four centuries, almost 12 million Africans were enslaved. Nearly 10 million reached the New World. Most of the others died en route.

Pig

Columbus never kept track of the eight pigs he took to the Caribbean settlement of Hispaniola in 1493. But Diego Valázquez de Cuéllar saw what happened to the two dozen he unloaded on Cuba in 1498. Within 16 years, they had increased to 30,000. Hogs were "seeded" on nearly ever island. Reproducing at an average rate of three big litters a year, they guaranteed a steady supply of protein for Old World immigrants. They also fundamentally altered the ecology of the Caribbean.

Omnivorous swine gobbled roots, snakes, grasses, lizards, fruit, and baby birds and probably contributed to the extinction of hundreds of plants and animals never even recorded. Much of the Caribbean's new flora, like the fauna, came from the Old World.

Hernando DeSoto brought pigs to what is now the United States. The 13 hogs that landed in Florida with him in 1539 multiplied to 700 in the three years he crisscrossed the South. Descendants of DeSoto's swine are still devouring wild plants and animals. In the Arkansas Ozarks, they are "razorbacks." In Georgia's Okefenokee Swamp, they are called "piney woods rooters."

Disease

Early Americans suffered their share of ailments before Columbus arrived, including tuberculosis, parasitism, and dysentery. But the Indians had never known such Old World diseases as smallpox, measles, and diphtheria. What had been childhood illnesses in Europe turned into mass killers in the Americas. Up and down the Western Hemisphere, native communities lost between 50 and 90 percent of their people. Most Indians died from the white man's germs without even seeing a white man.

The exporting of infection was not completely one-sided. Syphilis showed up in Spain shortly after Columbus's men returned, and a lethal epidemic swept Europe within five years. Some scholars believe a mild form of syphilis had existed for centuries in the Old World and mutated into a virulent form with the arrival of the American strain. But whatever its pathology, syphilis wreaked what some called "the vengeance of the vanquished."

A Ship for a Distance

The desire for empire created a new breed of ocean ships, making the 15th century the Age of Discovery.

A 1493 woodcut illustrates a rare Florentine edition of Christopher Columbus's letter of discovery, written to the Spanish court of sovereigns after his first voyage across the Atlantic. Columbus left Spain's Canary Islands in early September 1492 for Asia and landed on October 12th in the Bahama Islands. A five-year investigation by the National Geographic Society has concluded that the site of his landfall was Samana Cay in the eastern Bahamas. Courtesy, British Library.

Until the mid-1400s, European ships sailed mainly in spring and summer and stayed close to shore. Columbus's caravels not only moved swiftly before a following wind but also were easily handled in foul weather.

Why He Went

Columbus never tried to show that the Earth wasn't flat. Educated people already knew it was round. The question Columbus sought to answer with three of his four voyages was how long it would take to reach Asia by sailing west. In 1492, he discovered in the Caribbean what he thought was the Indies below China and Japan. In 1493, he brought over boatloads of men and animals to start a colony. In 1498, he resumed his search for Asia—and found Venezuela, which he was convinced lay only a short distance southeast of China. He looked again in 1502—and hit Honduras. He died in 1506 never knowing he had discovered America.

The New World Portrait

Population: Perhaps 40 million throughout the Western Hemisphere, including 10 million to 12 million in central Mexico, 9 million in Peru, and 2 million in the U.S. and Canada.

Work: Men hunted and fished. Women made clothes and pottery, cooked and did much of the farming.

Play: Thirty-mile footraces were popular in the Southwest. Choctaws played lacrosse with a deerskin ball.

Religion: Belief in a personally acquirable magic power was common. Many Indians sought the help of spirits in the green corn ceremony of the forests and the buffalo dances of the plains.

Language: Most Indian languages had at least 20,000 words.

Housing: Adobe apartments were common in the Southwest. New York's Iroquois occupied elm-bark long houses, with up to 20 families and their dogs in a single smoky room 50 to 100 feet long.

Property: Women owned the houses in many villages, but land was deemed the property of everyone in the tribe.

Food: In New England, corn and lima beans formed succotash. In the Carolinas, corn and squirrel meat became brunswick stew. Fattened bear cubs were a California delicacy, along with boiled caterpillars.

Infant mortality: High, like Europe's.

Life expectancy: Around 35, roughly the same as in Europe.

Cures: Herbal remedies included willow bark, which contains salicin, the drug now used in synthetic form in aspirin.

Power: Dogs were the only beasts of burden. Windmills and water wheels, common in Europe, were still unknown.

Rivals: The Arawaks were friendly to Columbus but feared the man-eating Caribs. The Crows fought the Blackfeet, who fought the Sioux, who fought the Chippewas. The Apaches got their name from the oft-raided Zunis, who called them "Apachu," or "enemy."

Old World Portrait

Population: Probably 60 million to 70 million. Roughly 9 of 10 were peasants.

Literacy: Barely 1 person in 20 could read.

Health: Poor grain harvest caused frequent famines. Rat-transmitted plagues were chronic. One in seven persons died of smallpox. Half of the newborn never reached the age of 15.

Medicine: Barely changed from the Roman era. Bloodletting was a common treatment.

Food: Peasants ate bread, salt pork, and a watery porridge called gruel. The rich feasted on mounds of beef, pork, mutton, and poultry.

Manners: Rich and poor alike ate with their fingers.

Housing: A wooden hut with a thatched roof and one smoky room was the usual peasant's quarters. Even in cities, most houses were made of wood.

Possessions: The average person had a few old clothes, a pot, a pan, and a few sacks of straw. Some peasants owned a table and a straw-covered plank bed, but many ate and slept on the floor.

Luxuries: Some peasants had a bench or a stool, but chairs remained rare even among the well-to-do.

Industry: Agriculture ranked No. 1, but an interest in fashion among the nobility and the bourgeoisie created a boom in textiles.

Buildings: Cathedrals at Chartres, Winchester, and Bourges had stood for centuries, but Seville Cathedral was new and King's College chapel in Cambridge was still under construction.

Religion: With Martin Luther only 8 years old, all of Western Europe remained Roman Catholic.

Most significant trend: The Renaissance, which stretched from 1300 to 1600. Leonardo da Vinci was 40 years old in 1492; Michelangelo, a teenager.

Judging Juries

By Seth Shulman

The notion of a jury of one's peers originated in twelfth-century Britain. Only people who knew the defendant and the case at hand were believed to be able to reach a just verdict.

In the twentieth-century United States, however, both the prosecution and the defense go to extreme lengths to seek out jurors entirely unfamiliar with the case, excluding anyone who might be prejudiced either for or against the defendants. And in highly publicized trials, that task is not easy. The events leading to the trial of Washington, D.C., mayor Marion Barry inundated the air waves. Through coverage of legal battles, the public also learned intimate details of the lives of Manual Noriega, Zsa Zsa Gabor, and televangelist Jim Bakker—details that would qualify us as peers but that, by the current thinking, threaten our impartiality.

Last year [1990], Newton Minow and Fred Cate, respectively director and senior fellow at the Annenberg Washington Program in Communications Policy Studies, convened a meeting to address a provocative question: With instant and pervasive mass communications, "must ignorance be a virtue in our search for impartial juries?" A distinguished collection of judges, attorneys, social scientists, and journalists concluded that excluding large numbers of jurors simply on the basis of exposure to press coverage is neither desirable nor necessary.

Pointing to the fact that "satellites, mobile equipment, broadcast and cable television, and other new technologies ... have led to an explosion in news coverage and dramatic reenactments of criminal activities," Minow and Cate say it's time to reassess the way juries are selected. The two lawyers are most concerned about the caliber of jurors, and claim that in the quest for impartiality, our legal system empanels less-qualified juries and wastes valuable court resources.

Consider Oliver North, whose testimony in televised congressional hearings couldn't be used in the case against him. Although jury selection took weeks and excluded dozens of candidates who had been "tainted" by the media, the chosen few earned little recognition as well-rounded members of society. Bruce Fein, former general counsel of the Federal Communications Commission, even called them incompetent. He contended that people who had missed every word off the televised hearings were either "understudies of Rip Van Winkle or congenitally somnolent in the world of government."

The Myth of Impartiality

Cate suggests that an issue of fairness is involved as well, since courts exclude a whole class of people from sitting as jurors in high-visibility trials. The Supreme Court has struck down rules denying women

and African Americans the right to be jurors, but "now we are excluding informed members of our society from judging such cases," he says.

Ronald Olson, a defense lawyer and former president of the American Bar Association Litigation Section, agrees. At the Annenberg meeting, he told his colleagues that excluding people exposed to press coverage "is every bit as prejudicial as the elimination based on race." And, Cate adds, no one proposes applying such a standard to judges who must preside over the cases—it is assumed they will be impartial.

In fact, no research strongly indicates that publicity impairs impartiality, says University of Washington psychologist Elizabeth Loftus. On the contrary, she notes, excluding people based on pre-trial questioning can prejudice a trial's outcome. For example, a conviction-prone jury results when people who express doubts about capital punishment are excluded from trials that could result in a death sentence. Jurors who are in favor of the death penalty are simply more likely to return a guilty verdict—regardless of the ultimate sentence, according to studies done at the universities of Michigan and California.

Nonetheless, research findings do not easily translate to changes in practice. Loftus says changing the rules about jury selection is a low priority in our criminal-justice system. For one thing, few lawyers would forgo any chance to dismiss prospective jurors who could be biased against their clients. And even fewer lawyers would relinquish the right to appeal on such grounds.

Moreover, despite dissatisfaction with shortcomings in the jury-selection process, many members of the legal community think that, overall, the system works. Appellate court justice Abner Mikva, who led a University of Chicago research team on jury performance, argues that usually "a good judge with a good charge to the jury and [an] appropriately conducted trial can get you a jury that is dispassionate and impartial and will do justice."

Even advocates of change acknowledge that some remedies raise serious questions of their own. Britain protects a defendant's right to impartial jurors in large measure by censoring the media's right to publish pre-trial material. That would be virtually unthinkable to the U.S. public or media.

Thus, for now, the situation is likely to remain much like the one Mark Twain ridiculed in 1875: "We have a criminal jury system which is superior to any other in the world; and its efficiency is only marred by the difficulty of finding 12 everyday men who don't know anything and can't read." □

Crime in The United States

Source: Uniform Crime Reports, 1990.

On an average, there is one violent crime every 17 seconds, one property crime every 2 seconds, one murder every 22 minutes, one forcible rape every 5 minutes, one robbery every 49 seconds, one aggravated assault every 30 seconds, one burglary ever ten seconds, one larceny-theft every 4 seconds, and one motor vehicle theft every 19 seconds.

This is the most aggregate representation of the latest *Uniform Crime Reports* data published August 1991, and shows the relative frequency of occurrence of the crime index offenses. It does not imply a regularity in the commission of the offenses, but represents the annual ratio of crime to fixed time intervals.

Rape Statistics

According to the latest *National Crime Survey (NCS) Report,* June 1991, an estimated 155,000 women were raped each year between 1973 and 1987. During this period, there were annually 1.6 rapes per 1,000 women age 12 or older, meaning that one out of every 600 women was raped each year. The average annual number of male victims reported to the NCS for those years was 13,200.

Almost two-thirds of all rapes occurred at night, and most rapes took place at the victim's home.

Black women were significantly more likely to be raped than white women, although a larger number of white women than the total of black, American Indian, Aleut, Eskimo, Asian, and Pacific Islander women were rape victims each year.

Hispanic and non-Hispanic women were equally likely to be raped.

Unemployed women were three times more likely and students one-and-one-half times more likely than women as a whole to be raped.

About half of all victims and almost three-quarters of black victims were in the lowest third of the income distribution.

Black women with low incomes were more likely to be raped than black women with medium or high incomes: they were also more likely to become victims than white women in any income category. Middle and upper-income women of all races had about the same chances of being raped.

According to the report, rapists and their victims were likely to be of the same race. In rapes with one offender, seven of every ten white victims were raped by a white offender, and eight out of ten black victims were raped by a black offender. In rapes with two or more offenders, victims and offenders were of the same race 49% of the time for white women and 72% for black women.

A previous study by the Bureau of Justice Statistics reported that although it is impossible to know exactly how many rapes go unreported, law enforcement agencies estimate that, for each reported rape, there are actually 1,200 rapes or attempted rapes that go unreported.

A February 1991 report entitled "Rape and Sexual Assault: Meeting the Crisis," a New York State Senate Republican study on sex crimes, noted that research indicates a vast majority of sexual attacks are planned in advance by the attacker. Moreover, the victim's attire and actions often have nothing at all to do with the attack itself. In other words, sex itself can often have little to do with the motivation for the attack. Rather, revenge, frustration, displaced anger, or power can often be the real factors behind a sexual attack. ☐

Record Prison Population

According to the Bureau of Justice Statistics, the nation's prison population has increased by almost 134% since 1980. For every 100,000 U.S. residents in 1990 there were 293 prisoners with sentences greater than one year. At the end of 1990, a record number of 771,243 inmates were in state or federal prisons.

The imprisonment rate was highest in South Carolina with 451 per 100,000 residents, followed by Nevada with 444, and Louisiana with 427.

Record Number Under Care or Custody

At the end of 1989, an estimated 4.1 million adults or about one in every 46 were under the care or custody of a corrections agency. A record 2,520,000 adults in the United States were on probation and 456,479 were on parole. About 75% of all convicted offenders are being supervised in the community, not in prisons or jails.

During 1989, the greatest number of adult probationers were in the following states: Texas, 291,156; California, 285,018; Florida, 192,495; New York, 128,707; and Georgia with 125,441. The highest increase of persons on probation was in the West (9.4%) and the lowest increase was in the Northeast (1.2%).

Violent Crimes Against Teenagers

In April 1991, the Bureau of Justice Statistics reported that, each year from 1985 to 1988, youths age 12 to 19 were victims of 1.9 million rapes, robberies, and assaults. On an average every 1,000 teenagers experienced 67 violent crimes each year, compared to 26 violent crimes for every 1,000 persons age 20 or older. About half of these crimes occurred in school buildings, or school property, or on the street. ☐

Recidivism of Prisoners

In April 1989, the Bureau of Justice Statistics released a special report on the recidivism of 108,580 persons in 11 states in 1983, representing more than half of all released state prisoners that year.

According to the study, an estimated 62.5% of the released prisoners had been rearrested for a felony or serious misdemeanor; 46.8% had been reconvicted; and 41.4% returned to prison or jail within three years after their release.

An estimated 67,898 of the prisoners were rearrested and charged with 326,746 new offenses by year–end 1986. More than 50,000 of the new charges were violent offenses, including 2,282 homicides, 1,451 kidnappings, 1,291 rapes, 2,262 other sexual assaults, 17,060 robberies, and 22,633 other assaults.

Released prisoners were often rearrested for the same type of crime for which they had served time in prison. Within three years, 31.9% of released burglars were rearrested for burglary; 24.8% of drug offenders were rearrested for a drug offense; and 19.6% of robbers were rearrested for robbery.

Released rapists were 10.5 times more likely than nonrapists to be rearrested for rape, and released murderers were about five times more likely than other offenders to be rearrested for homicide. ☐

Estimated Arrests, 1990[1]

Murder and non–negligent manslaughter	22,990	Weapons—carrying, possession, etc.	221,200
Forcible rape	39,160	Prostitution and commercial vice	111,400
Robbery	167,990	Sex offenses, except forcible rape	
Aggravated assault	475,330	and prostitution	107,600
Burglary	432,600	Drug abuse violations	1,089,500
Larceny—theft	1,554,800	Gambling	19,300
Motor vehicle theft	211,300	Offenses against family and children	85,800
Arson	19,100	Driving under the influence	1,810,800
Total violent crime	705,500	Liquor laws	714,700
Total property crime	2,217,800	Drunkenness	910,100
Other assaults	1,014,100	Disorderly conduct	733,000
Forgery and counterfeiting	94,800	Vagrancy	38,500
Fraud	291,600	All other offenses, except traffic	3,267,800
Embezzlement	15,300	Curfew and loitering law violations	80,800
Stolen property—buying, receiving, possessing	165,200	Runaways	174,200
Vandalism	326,000	**Total**[2]	**14,195,100**

1. Arrest totals based on all reporting agencies and estimates for unreported areas. 2. Because of rounding, items may not add to totals. *Source:* Department of Justice, Federal Bureau of Investigation, *Uniform Crime Reports for the United States,* 1990, released 1991.

Number of Arrests by Sex and Age

	Male				Female			
	Total		Under 18		Total		Under 18	
Offense	1990	1989	1990	1989	1990	1989	1990	1989
Murder[1]	16,387	14,852	2,423	1,955	1,911	1,989	132	131
Forcible rape	30,630	27,796	4,546	4,229	336	325	82	97
Robbery	125,015	113,833	30,168	26,762	11,285	10,682	2,799	2,472
Aggravated assault	326,780	281,196	43,454	36,948	50,137	43,215	7,713	6,360
Burglary—breaking or entering	311,220	301,083	103,314	97,063	29,972	29,332	9,123	8,450
Larceny—theft	843,851	807,350	266,916	245,167	397,385	351,647	105,217	89,319
Motor vehicle theft	151,449	152,777	65,029	62,373	16,889	17,502	7,901	7,169
Arson	13,024	11,637	5,940	5,315	1,950	1,826	620	581
Violent crime[2]	498,812		80,591		63,669		10,726	
Other assaults	672,455	601,494	91,334	81,513	128,970	111,903	27,724	24,154
Forgery and counterfeiting	48,667	47,584	4,532	3,829	25,726	24,458	2,228	1,755
Fraud	156,120	140,787	6,629	6,305	123,656	116,831	2,839	2,655
Embezzlement	7,083	7,029	532	574	4,972	4,658	332	485
Stolen property—buying, receiving, possessing	115,864	113,096	30,813	28,972	15,792	15,106	3,274	2,901
Vandalism	228,872	201,279	95,070	82,112	27,686	24,949	8,684	8,094
Weapons—carrying, possessing, etc.	163,055	154,504	30,055	27,698	13,082	12,925	1,936	1,929
Prostitution and com-mercialized vice	32,770	25,483	587	490	58,323	57,315	694	709
Sex offenses, except forcible rape and prostitution	78,291	70,737	12,594	11,632	6,561	5,810	913	896
Drug abuse violations	723,329	825,247	57,457	73,379	145,826	161,102	7,283	9,565
Gambling	13,314	13,455	761	796	2,129	2,437	37	33
Offenses against family and children	54,216	42,724	1,700	1,181	11,776	9,366	911	656
Driving under the influence	1,213,216	1,054,789	13,567	11,981	117,690	147,565	2,205	1,930
Liquor laws	448,898	377,973	87,646	77,985	103,141	87,729	34,401	29,958
Drunkenness	644,594	543,426	16,379	13,187	71,910	58,270	2,965	2,666
Disorderly conduct	469,055	477,016	76,246	73,141	110,619	108,625	19,753	17,863
Vagrancy	27,307	24,008	2,116	1,822	3,930	3,063	415	322
All other offenses, except traffic	2,144,717	1,911,497	196,664	185,607	427,774	372,711	52,071	48,525
Curfew and loitering law violations	46,471	46,040	46,471	46,040	18,097	15,888	18,097	15,888
Runaways	60,189	52,067	60,189	52,067	77,966	65,978	77,966	65,978
Total	**9,181,930**	**8,440,759**	**1,355,638**	**1,260,123**	**2,068,153**	**1,863,207**	**398,904**	**351,541**

1. Includes non–negligent manslaughter. 2. Violent crimes are offenses of murder, forcible rape, robbery, and aggravated assault. NOTE: 10,206 agencies reporting; 1990 estimated population 193,507,000. *Source:* Department of Justice, Federal Bureau of Investigation, *Uniform Crime Reports for the United States, 1990,* released 1991.

Arrests by Race, 1990

Offense	White	Black	Other[1]	Total	Offense	White	Black	Other[1]	Total
Murder[2]	7,942	9,952	296	18,190	Sex offenses,				
Forcible rape	16,973	13,309	520	30,802	except forcible				
Robbery	51,229	83,165	1,510	135,904	rape and				
Aggravated					prostitution	65,798	16,271	1,542	83,611
assault	223,952	143,540	6,380	373,872	Drug abuse				
Burglary	230,310	101,855	5,931	338,096	violation	503,315	349,965	6,736	860,016
Larceny–theft	827,860	374,968	28,427	1,231,255	Gambling	7,251	7,294	804	15,349
Motor vehicle					Offenses against				
theft	99,821	64,526	3,561	167,908	family and				
Arson	11,154	3,410	269	14,833	children	42,469	19,602	2,535	64,606
Violent crime[3]	300,096	249,966	8,706	558,768	Driving under				
All other					the influence	1,227,221	118,729	25,286	1,371,236
Other assaults	510,552	269,560	15,795	795,907	Liquor laws	478,873	52,831	16,588	548,292
Forgery and					Drunkenness	566,075	130,226	17,298	713,599
counterfeiting	47,330	24,839	958	73,127	Disorderly conduct	379,324	186,671	10,631	576,626
Fraud	180,671	90,708	2,120	273,499	Vagrancy	17,617	12,644	733	30,994
Embezzlement	7,900	3,816	190	11,906	All other				
Stolen property–					offenses				
buying, receiving,					except				
possessing	74,517	53,482	1,699	129,698	traffic	1,619,001	886,880	49,622	2,555,503
Vandalism	191,269	57,253	4,751	253,273	Suspicion	7,462	10,125	159	17,746
Weapons–					Curfew and				
carrying,					loitering law				
possession, etc.	102,228	69,331	2,772	174,331	violations	50,721	11,379	2,160	64,260
Prostitution and					Runaways	109,159	22,331	4,541	136,031
commercial vice	54,345	35,398	1,155	90,898	Total	7,712,339	3,224,060	214,969	11,151,368

1. Includes American Indian, Alaskan Native, and Asian or Pacific Islander. 2. Includes non–negligent manslaughter. 3. Violent crims are offenses of murder, forcible rape, robbery, and aggravated assault. NOTE: Figures represent arrests reported by 10,110 agencies serving a total 1990 population of 192,939,000 as estimated by FBI. *Source:* Department of Justice, Federal Bureau of Investigation, *Uniform Crime Reports for the United States, 1990,* released 1991.

Total Arrests, by Age Groups, 1990

Age	Arrests	Age	Arrests	Age	Arrests	Age	Arrests	Age	Arrests
Under 15	593,869	18	532,947	22	439,599	30–34	1,600,910	50–54	197,357
15	322,836	19	565,273	23	422,658	35–39	1,053,593	55 and	
16	390,418	20	526,051	24	423,683	40–44	622,896	over	283,435
17	447,419	21	475,213	25–29	2,008,308	45–49	343,618	Total	11,250,083

NOTE: Based on reports furnished to the FBI by 10,206 agencies covering a 1990 estimated population of 193,507,000. *Source:* Department of Justice, Federal Bureau of Investigation, *Uniform Crime Reports for the United States, 1990,* released 1991.

Federal Prosecutions of Public Corruption: 1979 to 1988

(Prosecution of persons who have corrupted public office in violation of Federal Criminal Statutes. As of Dec. 31, 1988)

Prosecution status	1988	1987	1986	1985	1984	1983	1982	1981	1980	1979
Total:[1] Indicted	1,274	1,340	1,192	1,182	936	1,073	729	878	721	687
Convicted	1,067	1,075	1,027	997	934	972	671	730	552	555
Awaiting trial	288	368	246	256	269	222	186	231	213	187
Federal officials: Indicted	629	651	596	563	408	460[2]	158	198	123	128
Convicted	529	545	523	470	429	424[2]	147	159	131	115
Awaiting trial	86	118	83	90	77	58	38	23	16	21
State officials: Indicted	66	102	88	79	58	81	4	87	72	58
Convicted	69	76	71	66	52	65	43	66	51	32
Awaiting trial	14	26	24	20	21	26	18	36	28	30
Local officials: Indicted	276	246	232	248	203	270	257	244	247	212
Convicted	229	204	207	221	196	226	232	211	168	156
Awaiting trial	79	89	55	49	74	61	58	102	82	67

1. Includes individuals who are neither public officials nor employees, but who were involved with public officials or employees in violating the law, now shown separately. 2. Increases in the number indicted and convicted between 1982 and 1983 resulted from a greater focus on federal corruption nationwide and more consistent reporting of cases involving lower–level employees. NOTE: Figures are latest available. *Source:* U.S. Department of Justice, *Federal Prosecutions of Corrupt Public Officials, 1970–1980,* and *Report to Congress on the Activities and Operations of the Public Integrity Section,* annual.

Law Enforcement Officers Killed or Assaulted: 1979 to 1988

(Covers officers killed feloniously and accidentally in line of duty; includes federal officers.)

	1988	1987	1986	1985	1984	1983	1982	1981	1980	1979
Northeast	17	24	15	19	21	20	17	17	31	21
Midwest	18	31	19	23	22	26	41	29	23	28
South	77	51	62	64	69	64	75	80	72	77
West	39	40	29	29	32	34	27	27	32	32
Puerto Rico	1	1	6	10	3	6	3	3	6	4
Total killed	**155**[7]	**147**	**131**	**148**[6]	**147**	**152**[5]	**164**[4]	**157**[3]	**165**[1]	**164**[2]
Assaults:										
Population (1,000)[8]	186,418	190,025	196,030	198,935	195,794	198,341	176,563	177,836	182,288	182,027
Number of—										
Agencies	8,866	8,957	9,755	9,906	10,002	9,908	8,829	9,019	9,235	9,638
Police officers	369,743	378,977	380,249	389,808	372,268	377,620	319,101	332,856	345,554	340,764
Firearm	2,759	2,789	2,852	2,793	2,654	3,067	2,642	3,330	3,295	3,237
Knife or cutting instrument	1,367	1,561	1,614	1,715	1,662	1,829	1,452	1,733	1,653	1,720
Other dangerous weapon	5,573	5,685	5,721	5,263	5,148	5,527	4,879	4,800	5,415	5,543
Hands, fists, feet, etc.	49,053	53,807	54,072	51,953	50,689	51,901	46,802	47,253	47,484	48,531
Total assaulted	**58,752**	**63,842**	**64,259**	**61,724**	**60,153**	**62,324**	**55,775**	**57,116**	**57,847**	**59,031**

1. Includes one officer in Virgin Islands. 2. Includes 2 officers in Guam. 3. Includes one officer in American Samoa. 4. Includes one officer in Mariana Islands. 5. Includes one officer each in Guam and Mariana Islands. 6. Includes one officer in Guam and 2 in foreign locations. 7. Includes one officer in American Samoa and 2 in foreign locations. 8. Represents the number of persons covered by agencies shown. NOTE: Data are latest available. *Source: Statistical Abstract of the United States, 1990.*

Full–Time Law Enforcement Employees, 1990

City	Officers	Civilians	Total	1989 Total	City	Officers	Civilians	Total	1989 Total
Atlanta	1,569	364	1,933	1,849	Minneapolis	794	105	899	872
Baltimore	2,839	551	3,390	3,455	New Orleans	n.a.	n.a.	1,734	n.a.
Birmingham, Ala.	723	214	937	893	New York	26,844	9,563	36,407	35,605
Boston	1,979	683	2,662	n.a.	Newark, N.J.	1,070	155	1,225	1,256
Buffalo, N.Y.	1,029	142	1,171	1,180	Norfolk, Va.	677	91	768	710
Chicago	12,048	1,487	13,535	13,469	Oakland, Calif.	627	331	958	986
Cincinnati	959	225	1,184	1,152	Oklahoma City	882	300	1,182	1,029
Cleveland	1,724	358	2,082	2,116	Omaha, Neb.	606	149	755	779
Columbus, Ohio	1,394	341	1,735	1,670	Philadelphia	6,651	935	7,586	7,190
Dallas	2,747	845	3,592	3,316	Phoenix, Ariz.	1,940	688	2,628	2,614
Denver	1,302	260	1,562	1,567	Pittsburgh	1,147	34	1,181	1,114
Detroit	4,508	605	5,113	5,391	Portland, Ore.	811	195	1,006	932
El Paso	799	251	1,050	980	Rochester, N.Y.	646	119	765	762
Fort Worth	953	307	1,260	1,285	St. Louis	1,574	698	2,272	2,189
Honolulu	1,827	430	2,257	2,185	St. Paul	528	146	674	704
Houston	4,104	1,549	5,653	5,454	San Antonio	1,565	290	1,855	1,812
Indianapolis	984	385	1,369	1,352	San Diego, Calif.	1,882	686	2,568	2,554
Jacksonville, Fla.	1,208	876	2,084	2,023	San Francisco	1,783	493	2,276	2,482
Kansas City, Mo.	1,178	586	1,764	1,704	San Jose, Calif.	1,112	357	1,469	1,284
Long Beach, Calif.	641	340	981	1,021	Seattle	1,264	555	1,819	1,589
Los Angeles	8,381	2,809	11,190	10,478	Tampa, Fla.	848	278	1,126	980
Louisville, Ky.	649	180	829	849	Toledo, Ohio	671	52	723	761
Memphis, Tenn.	1,379	419	1,798	1,781	Tucson, Ariz.	757	246	1,003	n.a.
Miami, Fla.	1,080	338	1,418	1,550	Tulsa, Okla.	699	178	87	822
Milwaukee	1,867	414	2,281	2,343	Washington, D.C.	4,740	781	5,521	4,716

NOTE: As of Oct. 31, 1990. n.a. = not available. *Source:* Department of Justice, Federal Bureau of Investigation, *Uniform Crime Reports for the United States, 1990*, released 1991.

Adolescent Drug Dealers

Most of them are not necessarily involved in other or more serious criminal activity. Most sell marijuana, amphetamines, and tranquilizers less than once a month to support their own use. Their buyers are almost always known to them and they typically distribute drugs in homes or cars, not in public places. They do not consider these activities "serious crimes." □

U.S. District Courts—Criminal Cases Commenced and Defendants Disposed of, by Nature of Offense: 1985 and 1988

[For years ending June 30]

Nature of offense	1988 cases commenced[1]	Disposition of Defendants, 1988									1985
		Not convicted		Convicted[2]			Sentenced			Cases commenced[1]	Defendants disposed of
		Total	Acquitted	Total	Guilty plea[3]	Court or jury	Imprisonment	Probation	Fine and other		
General offenses:											
Homicide	147	40	16	110	86	24	94	6	10	160	170
Robbery	1,283	131	27	1,064	927	137	990	72	2	1,236	1,387
Assault	617	163	37	436	338	98	267	138	31	552	555
Burglary	124	19	1	92	84	8	75	15	2	158	165
Larceny—theft	3,531	706	103	3,159	2,899	260	1,161	1,701	297	3,571	4,108
Embezzlement and fraud	9,433	1,571	240	9,609	8,736	873	4,004	5,334	271	7,912	9,044
Auto theft	293	59	14	323	291	32	224	92	7	300	461
Forgery, counterfeiting	1,674	293	39	1,777	1,666	111	853	910	14	2,118	2,372
Sex offenses	511	64	20	374	315	59	215	154	5	266	200
DAPCA[4]	10,291	2,588	420	13,162	11,044	2,118	9,983	3,042	137	6,690	11,177
Misc. general offenses	15,599	4,255	604	12,796	11,128	1,668	4,607	4,593	3,596	15,583	17,721
Total	**43,503**	**9,889**	**1,521**	**42,902**	**37,514**	**5,388**	**22,473**	**16,057**	**4,372**	**38,546**	**47,360**

1. Excludes transfers. 2. Convicted and sentenced. 3. Includes nolo contendere. 4. All marijuana, narcotics, and controlled substances under the Drug Abuse Prevention and Control Act. NOTE: Data are latest available. *Source: Statistical Abstract of the United States,* 1990.

Murder Victims by Weapons Used

Year	Murder victims, total	Weapons used or cause of death						
		Guns		Cutting or stabbing	Blunt object[1]	Strangulation, hands, fists, feet or pushing	Arson[3]	All other[2]
		Total	Percent					
1965	8,773	5,015	57.2	2,021	505	894	226	112
1970	13,649	9,039	66.2	2,424	604	1,031	353	198
1971	16,183	10,712	66.2	3,017	645	1,295	314	200
1972	15,832	10,379	65.6	2,974	672	1,291	331	185
1973	17,123	11,249	65.7	2,985	848	1,445	173	423
1974	18,632	12,474	66.9	3,228	976	1,417	153	384
1975	18,642	12,061	64.7	3,245	1,001	1,646	193	496
1980	21,860	13,650	62.0	4,212	1,094	1,666	291	947
1981	20,053	12,523	62.4	3,886	1,038	1,469	258	658
1982	19,485	11,721	60.2	4,065	957	1,657	279	630
1983	18,673	10,895	58.0	4,075	1,062	1,656	216	769
1984	16,689	9,819	58.8	3,540	973	1,407	192	758
1985	17,545	10,296	58.7	3,694	972	1,491	243	849
1986	19,257	11,381	59.1	3,957	1,099	1,651	230	939
1987	17,963	10,612	59.1	3,643	1,045	1,525	200	938
1988	17,971	10,895	60.6	3,457	1,126	1,426	255	812
1989	18,954	11,832	62.4	3,458	1,128	1,416	234	886
1990	20,045	12,847	64.1	3,503	1,075	1,424	287	909

1. Refers to club, hammer, etc. 2. Includes poison, explosives, unknown, drowning, asphyxiation, narcotics, other means, and weapons not stated. 3. Before 1973, includes drowning. *Source:* Department of Justice, Federal Bureau of Investigation, *Uniform Crime Reports for the United States, 1990,* released 1991.

Women Drug Offenders

Women offenders are not likely to be high–rate robbers or assaulters, but about one–third of addicted women offenders are prostitutes. Others commit many thefts. Few become top–level or even mid–level drug dealers. Over half, however, play an active role in the lowest levels of the drug trade and facilitate as many sales as men also involved at the lowest levels.

Many of the seriously drug–involved women have children. Those who continue to inject drugs during pregnancy may have infants born addicted. Additionally, because they frequently share needles with other addicts, they are at high risk of contracting AIDS and their children are also at high risk of contracting AIDS.

Crime Rates for Population Groups and Selected Cities, 1988

(offenses known to the police per 100,000 population, as of July 1)

Group and City	Violent Crime					Property crime				Total all crimes
	Mur-der	Forc-ible rape	Rob-bery	Aggra-vated assault	Total	Bur-glary—break-ing or enter-ing	Lar-ceny—theft	Motor vehicle theft	Total	
Total 7,434 cities	**10.5**	**47**	**318**	**462**	**836**	**1,539**	**3,967**	**788**	**6,295**	**7,130**
MSA's (Metropolitan Statistical Areas)	9	43	278	422	752	1,457	3,506	713	5,676	6,428
Other Cities	4	25	55	286	371	1,042	3,298	210	4,550	4,921
Rural Areas	5	18	15	141	180	672	973	114	1,759	1,938
Selected Cities:										
Baltimore	30.6	68	968	861	1,927	1,866	4,268	1,105	7,239	9,166
Chicago	22.0	([1])	968	1,202	([1])	1,739	4,295	1,503	7,537	([1])
Dallas	36.0	128	948	964	2,077	4,180	8,092	2,393	14,665	16,742
Detroit	57.9	133	1,194	989	2,375	2,958	3,981	2,772	9,711	12,085
Houston	25.5	70	582	471	1,149	2,908	4,491	1,763	9,163	10,311
Indianapolis	16.3	87	303	760	1,166	1,596	2,640	740	4,977	6,143
Los Angeles	21.6	59	770	1,111	1,961	1,499	3,531	1,685	6,714	8,676
Memphis	26.0	129	667	511	1,333	2,436	3,307	2,067	7,810	9,143
New York	25.8	46	1,179	967	2,218	1,731	4,199	1,633	7,562	9,780
Philadelphia	22.4	55	537	421	1,035	1,231	2,544	1,227	5,002	6,037
Phoenix	11.1	47	265	568	891	2,190	5,374	695	8,259	9,150
San Antonio	15.3	57	306	186	564	2,957	7,548	1,411	11,916	12,479
San Diego	13.4	36	298	506	854	1,634	4,278	2,247	8,159	9,013
San Francisco	12.2	60	646	560	1,278	1,346	4,863	1,270	7,479	8,757
Washington, D.C.	59.5	27	918	918	1,921	1,983	4,610	1,392	7,985	9,907

1. The rates for 1988 forcible rape, violent crime, and total crime are not shown because the forcible rape figures were not in accordance with national Uniform Crime Reporting guidelines. NOTE: Data are latest available. *Source: Statistical Abstract of the United States 1990.*

Percent of Firearms Usage in Selected Crimes, by Region: 1987–1989

Region	Murder[1]			Aggravated assault			Robbery		
	1989	1988	1987	1989	1988	1987	1989	1988	1987
Northeast	60.1	57.3	54.8	16.3	15.9	14.9	29.0	27.1	25.3
Midwest	58.8	59.0	57.7	23.6	23.1	24.4	33.0	33.4	32.6
South	65.8	64.4	62.9	25.3	26.3	25.6	39.2	40.8	39.7
West	61.6	59.2	56.4	19.5	18.4	17.7	32.4	33.1	33.8
U.S. Total	**62.4**	**60.7**	**59.1**	**21.5**	**21.1**	**21.4**	**33.2**	**33.4**	**33.0**

1. Murder includes non-negligent manslaughter. NOTE: Data are latest available. *Source:* U.S. Federal Bureau of Investigation, *Crime in the United States,* annual.

Reported Child Neglect and Abuse Cases: 1985 to 1987

Division	Percent change 1986–87	Total number of reports (1,000)			Reports per 1,000 population		
		1987	1986	1985	1987	1986	1985
New England	4.0	99.8	95.8	59.9	7.8	7.5	4.7
Middle Atlantic	6.3	242.5	228.1	152.2	6.5	6.1	4.1
North Central	−1.2	515.2	521.4	316.4	18.2	19.3	11.1
South Atlantic	−1.9	293.4	299.2	225.0	7.0	7.3	5.6
South Central	−3.0	302.4	311.7	249.9	14.8	15.1	12.9
Mountain	29.6	128.2	98.9	77.6	9.7	7.6	6.1
Pacific	6.1	443.7	418.3	218.4	12.1	11.7	6.2
U.S. Total	**2.6**	**2,025.2**	**1,973.4**	**1,299.4**	**8.3**	**8.2**	**5.4**

NOTE: Figures are latest available. *Source:* American Humane Association, *National Analysis of Official Child Neglect and Abuse Reporting,* annual.

Gang Violence: A National Problem

Source: National Institute of Justice Reports.

Gang violence is a growing problem across the Nation. It cuts across ethnic and cultural lines, involves youths and increasingly, adults, and is spreading at an alarming rate. It is responsible for an urban gang warfare that has resulted in drive-in shootings, turf battles, and killings of informers.

Two of the most violent youth gangs in America are the Los Angeles-based Crips and Bloods. Their activity in the Los Angeles sub-culture is well known and widely reported in the media. According to a recent Drug Enforcement Administration report, conflict between these two groups has escalated into open guerilla warfare. Youth gang members are readily armed with AK-47's, AK-15's, and other fully automatic weapons.

But more significant is the fact that the California gang members are spreading out into such areas as Shreveport, Louisiana; Kansas City, Missouri; and Seattle, Washington.

That the gang problem involves adults as well as juveniles is well documented. The average age of the gang homicide offender in Los Angeles is between 19 and 20 years of age; gang homicide reports from Chicago show that nearly 50% of the offenders are over the age of nineteen. Similarly, research by the Office of Juvenile Justice and Delinquency Prevention has shown that it is adults who adopt leadership roles and engage in the greatest violence: homicides, aggravated assaults, robberies, and drug trafficking. Their victims may include innocent members of the public, other gang members, and some professional community members such as police officers and teachers in schools. Prison gangs constitute a serious though separate problem as well, noticeably in Illinois, New York, California, and Texas.

Evidence further suggests that gang youths are particularly susceptible to being recruited into larger criminal organizations involved in drug trafficking. The link between organized crime and youth gangs, however, remains to be fully researched and reported.

A 1989 survey of law enforcement officials in 45 cities across the country produced the startling estimate of nearly 1,500 youth gangs nationwide, with more than 120,500 members.

African Americans and Hispanics make up 87% of gang membership, far in excess of their representation in the general population. Many of these gangs were involved in serious crimes. The rate of violent offenses for gang members was three times as high as that for non-gang delinquents.

But while African Americans and Hispanics seem to dominate in memberships in criminal gangs, the problem embraces other ethnic groups and cultures. Chinese, Vietnamese, Cambodian, and Laotian youth gangs have emerged in New York City, Chicago, and Los Angeles. In particular, recent news reports have detailed the involvement of Chinese youth gangs in a resurgent heroin trade in New York City.

In 1990, the number of gang homicides reached an all-time high of 329 in Los Angeles and 98 in Chicago, with gang homicide, as a proportion of total homicides, ranging from 11% in Chicago to 34% in Los Angeles.

Unfortunately, no national data on gangs or gang activity are collected; only gross estimates based on law enforcement perceptions are available in most cities. The definition of the term "gang" and what constitutes gang-related crimes varies from jurisdiction to jurisdiction, as well as in the research literature. This frequently renders problematic the development of laws and subsequent policies and strategies for dealing with the gang problem.

In order to meet this challenge, a new Office of Justice Programs study is now under way to fill in this important gap, and by coordinating their efforts with other concerned agencies will recommend effective ways to address this growing national problem. □

Drug Offenses Rise Sharply

During 1989, the latest year complete Bureau of Justice Statistics are available, drug offenses accounted for 23% of the charges against the nearly 400,000 men and women held in local jails. Of all convicted jail inmates in 1989, more than four in ten said that they had been using an illegal drug during the month before committing the offense for which they were jailed. One in four had used heroin, cocaine, crack, LSD, or PCP that month.

Women were more likely than men and Hispanics were more likely than non-Hispanics to be jailed on drug charges. About a third of female and Hispanic inmate were in jail for drugs.

Of all jail inmates in 1989, 46% were on probation, parole, bail, or in some other criminal justice status at the time of their arrest. More than 75% had a prior sentence to probation, or incarceration, and at least a third were in jail for a violent offense or had previously been sentenced for a violent crime.

State courts convicted about 112,000 persons of felony drug trafficking in 1988, about 50% more than in 1986. The number of adults arrested for serious drug trafficking offenses was about 185,000 in 1986 and 290,000 in 1988. □

Personal and Household Crimes Fall

Personal and household crimes declined from about 35.8 million in 1989 to about 34.8 million in 1990, a drop of one million. The over-all decline resulted from an 8% fall in the 1989 rate of personal thefts without direct contact between the victim and the offender.

About 95% of all personal thefts and about 66% of all cimes against persons involved such offenses as stealing personal belongings from public places or from an unattended automobile parked away from home.

There was a 19% increase in motor vehicle theft, the only crime to rise significantly in 1990. In all there were 1.4 million completed auto thefts and 770,000 attempted thefts—the highest number since the National Crime Survey began in 1977.

About 13.3 million personal and household crimes were reported to the police in 1990—not a statistically significant change from 1989. □

Regional Crime Statistics

According to a National Crime Survey report published in July 1991, the West showed the highest victimization rate for both crimes of violence and crimes of theft. The Northeast had the lowest rates for these crimes, though the violent crime rate in the Midwest was only marginally higher than the rate in the Northeast. The South had a higher violent crime rate than the Midwest, but the rate of personal thefts was not measurably different. □

Prisoners Under Sentence of Death

Characteristic	1988	1987	1986	Characteristic	1988	1987	1986
White	1,238	1,128	1,006	Marital status:			
Black and other	886	839	775	Never married	898	856	772
Under 20 years	11	10	19	Married	594	571	525
20–24 years	195	222	217	Divorced or separated[2]	632	557	484
25–34 years	1,048	969	872	Time elapsed since sentencing:			
35–54 years	823	744	639	Less than 12 months	293	295	293
55 years and over	47	39	34	12–47 months	812	804	757
				48–71 months	409	412	376
Schooling completed:				72 months and over	610	473	355
7 years or less	180	181	164	Legal status at arrest:			
8 years	184	183	174	Not under sentence	1,207	1,123	992
9–11 years	692	650	577	On parole or probation	545[3]	480[3]	409[3]
12 years	657	591	515	In prison or escaped	93	91	82
More than 12 years	180	168	143	Unknown	279	290	298
Unknown	231	211	208	**Total**	**2,124**	**1,967**[1]	**1,781**

1. Revisions to the total number of prisoners were not carried to the characteristics except for race. 2. Includes widows, widowers, and unknown. 3. Includes 20 persons on mandatory conditional release, work release, leave, AWOL, or bail for 1986; 22 for 1987; 24 for 1988. NOTE: As of Dec. 31. Excludes prisoners under sentence of death confined in local correctional systems pending appeal or who had not been committed to prison. *Source:* U.S. Bureau of Justice Statistics, *Capital Punishment,* annual.

Methods of Execution[1]

State	Method	State	Method
Alabama[2]	Electrocution	Nevada[2]	Lethal injection
Alaska	No death penalty	New Hampshire[2]	Lethal injection
Arizona[2]	Lethal gas	New Jersey	Lethal injection[5]
Arkansas[2]	Lethal injection or electrocution	New Mexico	Lethal injection
California*	Lethal gas	New York	No death penalty
Colorado[2]	Lethal injection[7]	North Carolina[2]	Lethal gas or injection
Connecticut[2]	Electrocution	North Dakota	No death penalty
Delaware	Lethal injection[3]	Ohio[2]	Electrocution
D.C.	No death penalty	Oklahoma	Lethal injection
Florida	Electrocution	Oregon	Lethal injection[5]
Georgia[2]	Electrocution	Pennsylvania[2]	Lethal injection
Hawaii	No death penalty	Rhode Island	No death penalty
Idaho[2]	Lethal injection[9]	South Carolina[2]	Electrocution
Illinois	Lethal injection	South Dakota	Lethal injection
Indiana[2]	Electrocution	Tennessee[2]	Electrocution
Iowa	No death penalty	Texas[2]*	Lethal injection
Kansas	No death penalty	Utah[2]*	Firing squad or lethal injection
Kentucky[2]	Electrocution	Vermont	No death penalty
Louisiana[2]	Electrocution[10]	Virginia	Electrocution
Maine	No death penalty	Washington[2]*	Hanging or lethal injection
Maryland[2]	Lethal gas	West Virginia	No death penalty
Massachusetts*	No death penalty	Wisconsin	No death penalty
Michigan	No death penalty	Wyoming	Lethal injection
Minnesota	No death penalty	U.S. (Fed. Govt.)	([4])
Mississippi[2]	Lethal injection[8]	American Samoa	No death penalty
Missouri	Lethal injection	Guam	No death penalty
Montana[2]	Hanging, or lethal injection[6]	Puerto Rico	No death penalty
Nebraska[2]	Electrocution	Virgin Islands	No death penalty

1. On July 1, 1976, by a 7–2 decision, the U.S. Supreme Court upheld the death penalty as not being "cruel or unusual." However, in another ruling the same day, the Court, by a 5–4 vote, stated that states may not impose "mandatory" capital punishment on every person convicted of murder. These decisions left uncertain the fate of condemned persons throughout the U.S. On Oct. 4, the Court refused to reconsider its July ruling, which allows some states to proceed with executions of condemned prisoners. The first execution in this country since 1967 was in Utah on Jan. 17, 1977. Gary Mark Gilmore was executed by shooting. 2. Voted to restore death penalty after June 29, 1972, Supreme Court decision ruling capital punishment unconstitutional. 3. Prisoners originally sentenced to death prior to June 1986 may opt instead to hang. Those sentenced after June 1986 have no choice but lethal injection. 4. Is that of the state in which the execution takes place. 5. Death penalty has been passed, but not been used. 6. Defendant may choose between hanging and a lethal injection. 7. Applies to offenses committed on or after July, 1 1988. Prior to that date the method of execution is lethal gas. 8. Prisoners sentenced prior to July 1, 1984, shall be executed by lethal gas. 9. If the director of the Idaho Department of Corrections finds it impractical to carry out a lethal injection, he may instead use a firing squad. 10. Lethal injection for those individuals sentenced to death after January 1, 1991. *Source: Information Please* questionnaires to the states. NOTE: An asterisk after the name of the state indicates non–reply.

Motor Vehicle Laws, 1991

State	Age for license		Age for driver's license[1]			Driver's license duration	Fee	Annual safety inspection required
	Motorcycle	Moped	Regular	Learner's	Restrictive			
Alabama	14	14	16	15 [5]	14 [11]	4 yrs.	$15.00	no[17]
Alaska	14	14	16	14	14 [6,11]	5	10.00	no[17]
Arizona	16	16	18	15 7 mo [5,6]	16 [6]	4	7.00	no[18]
Arkansas	16	10[10]	18	(5)	14 [6,9]	4	14.25	yes
California	18	15 1/2	18	15 [4,7]	16 [4]	4	10.00	no[19]
Colorado	16	16	21	15 1/2 [5]	16 [6]	5	15.00	no[19]
Connecticut	16	16	18		16 [4]	2 or 4	24.75/38	yes[20]
Delaware	16	16	18	15 7 mo [5,6]	16 [4,6]	5	12.50	yes
D. C.	16	16	18	(5)	16 [6]	4	15.00	yes
Florida	15	15	16	(5)	15 [6]	4 or 6	15.00	no[19]
Georgia	16	15	21	15	16 [6]	4	4.50	no[19]
Hawaii	15	15	18	(5)	15 [6]	4[13]	3–12.00	yes
Idaho	16	16	16	(5)	14 [4]	3	19.50	no
Illinois	18	16[2]	18	(5)	16 [4,6]	4 or 5	10.00	no[19]
Indiana	16	15	18	15 [8]	16 1 mo. [4,6]	4[14]	6.00	no[19]
Iowa	16	14	18	14	16 [4]	4[2]	8/16.00	no[17]
Kansas	14	14	16	(5)	14	4	8/12.00	no[17]
Kentucky	16	16	18	(5)	16 [6]	4	8.00	no
Louisiana	15	15	17	(6)	15 [15]	4	18.00	yes
Maine	17	16	17	(5,7)	16 [4]	4	18.00	yes
Maryland	18[23]	16	18	15 9 mo.	16 [4,6]	4	20.00	no[24]
Massachusetts	17	16	17	(5)	16 1/2 [4,6]	4	35.00	yes[21]
Michigan	18	15	18	(5)	16 [4,6]	2 or 4	6/12.00	no[16]
Minnesota	18[23]	15	18	(5)	16 [4]	4	15.00	no[17]
Mississippi	15[23]	15	15	(5)		4	13.00	yes
Missouri	16[22]	16	16		15 [4]	3	7.50	yes[19]
Montana	16	16[23]	18	(5)	15 [4,6]	4	16/24.00	no
Nebraska	16	16	16	15	14	4	10.00	no
Nevada	16	15 1/2	16	15 1/2 [5]	14 [6]	4	9.00[15]	no[19]
New Hampshire	18	16[26]	18	(5)	16 [4]	4	30.00	yes[21]
New Jersey	17	15	17		16	4	16/17.50	yes
New Mexico	16	13	16	15	14 [12]	4	10.00	no
New York	17	16	17[4]		16 [6]	4	17.50	yes
North Carolina	18	16	18	15 [6]	16 [4]	4	15.00	yes
North Dakota	16	14	16	(5)	14 [4,6]	4	10.00	no[17]
Ohio	18	14	18	16 [5,6]	14 [3]	4	5.00	no[19]
Oklahoma	16	16	16	(8)	15 1/2 [4]	4	18.00	yes
Oregon	16[23]	16	16	15 [5]	14	4	25.00	no[17]
Pennsylvania	18	16	18	16 [6,7]	16 [6]	4	5.00	yes
Rhode Island	18	16	16	16 [6]	16 [4]	5	20.00	yes
South Carolina	16	14	16	15 [9]	15	4	10.00	yes
South Dakota	16	14	16	(5)	14 [9]	4	6.00	yes
Tennessee	16	14	16	15	15	4	16.00	no
Texas	18[23]	15	16[4]	15	15 [4,7]	4	16.00	yes
Utah	16	16	16[4]	(5)		4	10.00	yes[19]
Vermont	18	16	18	15 [22]	16 [7]	2 or 4	12/20.00	yes
Virginia	18[23]	16	18	15 8 mo. [5,6,7]	16 [4,6]	5	12.00	yes
Washington	18[23]	16	18	15 [8]	16 [4]	4	14.00	no[25]
West Virginia	16	16	18	(5)	16 [6]	4	10.00	yes
Wisconsin	18	16	16[4]	(5)	16 [6]	4	9.00	no[16]
Wyoming	16	15[26]	16	15 [6,7]	14 [6,7]	4	10.00	no

1. Full driving privileges at age given in "Regular" column. A license restricted or qualified in some manner may be obtained at age given in "Restricted" column. 2. 2 years if under 18 or over 70. 3. Upon proof of hardship. 4. Must have completed approved driver education course. 5. Learner's permit required. 6. Guardian's or parental consent required. 7. Driver with learner's permit must be accompanied by locally licensed operator 18 years or older. 8. Must be enrolled in driver education course. 9. Driver with learner's permit must be accompanied by locally licensed operator 21 years or older. 10. Up to 50 cc. 11. Restricted to mopeds. 12. For use while enrolled in driver education course. Must be accompanied by instructor. 13. 2 years if 15–24 or over 65. 14. 3 years if over 75. 15. If 65 or over, a $4 fee. 16. Individual inspection upon reasonable grounds. 17. State troopers are authorized to inspect at their discretion. 18. Arizona emission inspection fee $5.40. 19. Annual emissions test in some counties. 20. Used motor vehicles being registered in Connecticut from out–of–state are required to be inspected and approved and Connecticut cars 10 years old and older must be inspected upon being sold or transferred. 21. Annual emissions test. 22. Must be accompanied by licensed operator 25 years or older or a school driver training instructor. 23. 18; 16, if approved driver training course completed. 24. All used vehicles upon resale or transfer. 25. Required on out–of–state or salvaged vehicles. Emissions tested in some counties. 26. May obtain instruction permit with motorcycle endorsement. NOTES: A driver's license is required in every state. All states have an *implied consent* Chemical Test Law for alcohol. *Source:* American Automobile Association.

EDUCATION

School Enrollment, October 1990
(in thousands)

Age	White		Black		Hispanic origin[1]		All races	
	Enrolled	Percent	Enrolled	Percent	Enrolled	Percent	Enrolled	Percent
3 and 4 years	2,700	44.9	452	41.6	249	29.8	3,292	44.4
5 and 6 years	5,750	96.5	1,129	96.3	835	94.8	7,207	96.5
7 to 9 years	8,848	99.7	1,628	99.9	1,296	99.6	10,976	99.7
10 to 13 years	11,228	99.6	2,204	99.9	1,498	99.2	14,040	99.6
14 to 15 years	5,265	99.1	1,023	99.2	739	99.0	6,555	99.0
16 and 17 years	4,858	92.5	962	91.7	592	85.4	6,098	92.5
18 and 19 years	3,271	57.1	596	55.2	329	44.1	4,044	57.3
20 and 21 years	2,402	41.0	305	28.4	213	27.2	2,852	39.7
22 to 24 years	1,781	20.2	274	20.0	121	9.9	2,231	21.0
25 to 29 years	1,706	9.9	162	6.1	130	6.3	2,013	9.7
30 to 34 years	1,090	5.9	119	4.4	72	3.6	1,281	5.8
Total	48,899	49.5	8,854	51.9	6,073	47.4	60,588	50.2

1. Persons of Hispanic origin may be of any race. NOTE: Figures include persons enrolled in nursery school, kindergarten, elementary school, high school, and college. *Source:* Department of Commerce, Bureau of the Census.

Persons Not Enrolled in School, October 1990
(in thousands)

Age	Population	Total not enrolled		High school graduate		Not high school graduate (dropouts)[1]	
		Number	Percent	Number	Percent	Number	Percent
14 and 15 years	6,620	64	1.0	12	0.2	57	0.9
16 and 17 years	6,591	493	7.5	248	3.8	418	6.3
18 and 19 years	7,064	3,020	42.8	5,037	71.3	1,003	14.2
20 and 21 years	7,183	4,331	60.3	6,180	86.0	918	12.8
22 to 24 years	10,605	8,374	79.0	9,094	85.8	1,458	13.8

1. Persons who are not enrolled in school and who are not high school graduates are considered dropouts. *Source:* Department of Commerce, Bureau of the Census.

School Enrollment by Grade, Control, and Race
(in thousands)

Grade level and type of control	White			Black			All races[1]		
	Oct. 1990[3]	Oct. 1980[4]	Oct. 1970	Oct. 1990[3]	Oct. 1980[4]	Oct. 1970	Oct. 1990[3]	Oct. 1980[4]	Oct. 1970
Nursery school: Public	896	432	198	283	180	129	1,212	633	333
Private	1,961	1,205	695	148	115	49	2,188	1,354	763
Kindergarten: Public	2,609	2,172	2,233	574	440	374	3,332	2,690	2,674
Private	472	423	473	62	50	53	567	486	536
Grades 1–8: Public	20,997	19,743	24,923	4,431	4,058	4,668	26,615	24,398	30,001
Private	2,359	2,768	3,715	199	202	200	2,676	3,051	3,949
Grades 9–12: Public	9,429	12,056[2]	11,599	1,937	2,200[2]	1,794	11,911	14,556[2]	13,545
Private	810	—	1,124	65	—	41	906	—	1,170
College: Public	9,049	8,875[2]	5,168	1,120	1,007[2]	422	10,754	10,180[2]	5,699
Private	2,439	—	1,591	274	—	100	2,869	—	1,714
Total: Public	42,954	—	44,121	8,344	—	7,387	53,823	—	52,225
Private	8,041	—	7,598	748	—	443	9,204	—	8,132
Grand Total	50,995	47,673	51,719	9,092	8,251	7,830	63,027	57,348	60,357

1. Includes persons of Spanish origin. 2. Total public and private. Breakdown not available. 3. Estimates controlled to 1980 census base. 4. Estimates controlled to 1970 census base. *Source:* Department of Commerce, Bureau of the Census.

State Compulsory School Attendance Laws, November 1989

State	Enactment[1]	Age limits	State	Enactment[1]	Age limits
Alabama	1915	7–16	Montana[4]	1883	7–16
Alaska[2]	1929	7–16	Nebraska	1887	7–16
Arizona	1899	8–16	Nevada	1873	7–17
Arkansas	1909	5–17	New Hampshire	1871	6–16
California	1874	6–16	New Jersey	1875	6–16
Colorado	1889	7–16	New Mexico	1891	6–18
Connecticut	1872	7–16	New York[5]	1874	6–16
Delaware	1907	5–16	North Carolina	1907	7–16
D. C.	1864	7–17	North Dakota	1883	7–16
Florida	1915	6–16	Ohio	1877	6–18
Georgia	1916	7–16	Oklahoma	1907	7–18
Hawaii	1896	6–18	Oregon	1889	7–18
Idaho	1887	7–16	Pennsylvania	1895	8–17
Illinois	1883	7–16	Rhode Island	1883	6–16
Indiana	1897	7–16	South Carolina[6]	1915	5–17
Iowa	1902	7–16	South Dakota[4]	1883	7–16
Kansas	1874	7–16	Tennessee	1905	7–17
Kentucky[3]	1896	6–16	Texas[7]	1915	7–17
Louisiana	1910	7–17	Utah	1890	6–18
Maine	1875	7–17	Vermont	1867	7–16
Maryland	1902	6–16	Virginia	1908	5–17
Massachusetts	1852	6–16	Washington	1871	8–18
Michigan	1871	6–16	West Virginia	1897	6–16
Minnesota	1885	7–16	Wisconsin	1879	6–18
Mississippi	1918	6–14	Wyoming	1876	7–16
Missouri	1905	7–16			

1. Date of enactment of first compulsory attendance law. 2. Ages 7 to 16 or high school graduation. 3. Must have parental signature for leaving school between ages of 16 and 18. 4. May leave after completion of eighth grade. 5. The ages are 6 to 17 for New York City and Buffalo. 6. Permits parental waiver of kindergarten at age 5. 7. Must complete academic year in which 16th birthday occurs. *Source:* Department of Education, National Center for Educational Statistics.

High School and College Graduates

School Year	High School			College[1]		
	Men	Women	Total	Men	Women	Total
1900	38,075	56,808	94,883	22,173	5,237	27,410
1910	63,676	92,753	156,429	28,762	8,437	37,199
1920	123,684	187,582	311,266	31,980	16,642	48,622
1929–30	300,376	366,528	666,904	73,615	48,869	122,484
1939–40	578,718	642,757	1,221,475	109,546	76,954	186,500
1949–50	570,700	629,000	1,199,700	328,841	103,217	432,058
1959–60	898,000	966,000	1,864,000	254,063	138,377	392,440
1964–65	1,314,000	1,351,000	2,665,000	316,286	213,717	530,003
1969–70	1,433,000	1,463,000	2,896,000	484,174	343,060	827,234
1970–71	1,456,000	1,487,000	2,943,000	511,138	366,538	877,676
1971–72	1,490,000	1,518,000	3,008,000	541,313	389,371	930,684
1972–73	1,501,000	1,536,000	3,037,000	564,680	407,700	972,380
1973–74	1,515,000	1,565,000	3,080,000	575,843	423,749	999,592
1974–75	1,541,000	1,599,000	3,140,000	533,797	425,052	978,849
1975–76	1,554,000	1,601,000	3,155,000	557,817	430,578	988,395
1976–77	1,548,000	1,606,000	3,154,000	547,919	435,989	983,908
1977–78	1,535,000	1,599,000	3,134,000	487,000	434,000	921,000
1978–79	1,531,800	1,602,400	3,134,200	529,996	460,242	990,238
1979–80	1,500,000	1,558,000	3,058,000	526,327	473,221	999,548
1980–81	1,483,000	1,537,000	3,020,000	470,000	465,000	935,000
1981–82	1,474,000	1,527,000	3,001,000	473,000	480,000	953,000
1982–83	1,437,000	1,451,000	2,888,000	479,140	490,370	969,510
1983–84	n.a.	n.a.	2,767,000	482,319	491,990	974,309
1984–85	n.a.	n.a.	2,677,000	482,528	496,949	979,477
1985–86	n.a.	n.a.	2,643,000	485,923	501,900	987,823
1986–87	n.a.	n.a.	2,694,000	480,854	510,485	991,339
1987–88	n.a.	n.a.	2,801,000	476,842[2]	516,520[2]	993,362[2]
1988–89	n.a.	n.a.	2,787,000[3]	483,613[3]	533,115[3]	1,016,728[3]

1. Includes bachelor's and first-professional degrees for years 1900–1960. 2. Preliminary data. 3. Estimated. n.a. = not available. NOTE: Includes graduates from public and private schools. Beginning in 1959–60, figures include Alaska and Hawaii. Because of rounding, details may not add to totals. Most recent data available. *Source:* Department of Education, Center for Education Statistics.

Federal Funds for Some Major Programs for Education, Fiscal Year 1992[1]

Program	Amount in thousands	Program	Amount in thousands
Elementary-secondary		College housing loans	53,072
Educationally disadvantaged	$6,424,344	**Vocational and adult education**	1,261,667
School improvement programs	1,500,528	**Education for the handicapped**	
Bilingual education	200,789	Special education	2,729,853
School assistance in federally		Rehabilitation services and	
affected areas	620,130	disability research	2,003,380
Higher education		All other	114,208
Student financial assistance	6,713,681	**Indian education**	77,400
Guaranteed student loans	3,025,952	**Education research and improvement**	295,751
Higher education facliities loans	9,023	**Total**	**$25,029,778**

1. Estimated outlay for fiscal year 1992. *Source: Budget of the United States Government,* Fiscal Year 1992.

Funding for Public Elementary and Secondary Education, 1981–82 to 1987–88

(In thousands except percent)

School year	Total	Federal	State	Local[1]	% Federal	& State	% Local[1]
1981–82	110,191,257	8,186,466	52,436,435	49,568,356	7.4	47.6	45.0
1982–83	117,497,502	8,339,990	56,282,157	52,875,354	7.1	47.9	45.0
1983–84	126,055,419	8,576,547	60,232,981	57,245,892	6.8	47.8	45.4
1984–85	137,294,678	9,105,569	67,168,684	61,020,425	6.6	48.9	44.4
1985–86	149,127,779	9,975,622	73,619,575	65,532,582	6.7	49.4	43.9
1986–87	158,523,693	10,146,013	78,830,437	69,547,243	6.4	49.7	43.9
1987–88	169,650,907	10,719,821	84,042,408	74,888,679	6.3	49.5	44.1

1. Includes a relatively small amount from nongovernmental sources (gifts and tuition and transportation fees from patrons). *Source:* U.S. Department of Education, National Center for Education Statistics.

Major U.S. College and University Libraries

(Top 50 based on number of volumes in library)

Institution	Volumes	Microforms[1]	Institution	Volumes	Microforms[1]
Harvard	11,874,148	5,557,388	Iowa	3,104,621	3,381,454
Yale	8,862,768	3,393,479	Pennsylvania State	3,095,863	3,125,463
U of Illinois–Urbana	7,748,736	3,502,629	New York	3,092,620	2,039,077
U of California–Berkeley	7,540,234	4,455,669	U of Florida	2,892,301	2,704,717
U of Michigan	6,369,490	4,063,879	U of Georgia	2,889,108	4,518,130
U of Texas	6,265,236	4,413,304	U of Pittsburgh	2,878,713	2,525,370
U of California–Los Angeles	6,156,761	5,618,652	U of Kansas	2,868,223	2,218,777
Columbia	6,032,545	4,094,213	Johns Hopkins	2,835,664	1,548,084
Stanford	5,871,063	3,709,144	Rochester	2,686,996	1,214,830
Cornell	5,216,501	5,036,410	U of Southern California	2,626,271	2,987,801
U of Chicago	5,191,998	1,535,955	Arizona State	2,599,701	3,371,362
U of Wisconsin	5,036,144	3,413,874	SUNY–Buffalo	2,591,006	3,761,902
U of Washington	4,908,988	5,337,134	U of Missouri	2,486,014	4,777,547
U of Minnesota	4,651,111	3,141,452	Louisiana State	2,460,219	2,144,615
Ohio State	4,430,132	3,248,867	South Carolina	2,431,129	3,467,747
Princeton	4,276,086	2,395,378	U of Massachusetts	2,409,946	1,781,928
Indiana	4,133,331	1,754,286	U of Hawaii	2,385,601	3,640,718
Duke	3,846,295	1,481,804	U of California–Davis	2,376,157	2,828,257
North Carolina	3,751,660	3,159,522	Wayne State	2,374,831	2,099,908
U of Pennsylvania	3,665,786	2,427,600	Syracuse	2,332,676	3,654,447
U of Arizona	3,549,281	4,020,838	U of Oklahoma	2,297,087	2,903,183
Northwestern	3,474,423	2,215,175	U of Colorado	2,286,736	1,290,062
Michigan State	3,417,388	3,526,349	Washington U–St. Louis	2,277,203	1,849,845
Rutgers	3,219,823	3,705,472	U of Connecticut	2,271,849	2,842,144
U of Virginia	3,193,260	4,302,386	Brown	2,227,301	1,116,626

1. Includes reels of microfilm and number of microcards, microprint sheets, and microfiches. *Source:* Association of Research Libraries.

College and University Endowments, 1989–90
(top 75 in millions of dollars)

Institution	Endowment (market value)	Voluntary support[1]	Expenditures[2]	Institution	Endowment (market value)	Voluntary support[1]	Expenditures[2]
Harvard U	$4,683.2	$213.5	$1,025.7	Ohio State U	321.9	63.3	771.2
Yale U	2,585.3	130.0	617.3	Wake Forest U	318.0	21.7	230.9
Princeton U	2,475.1	75.2	276.4	U of Cincinnati	314.5	27.4	366.1
Stanford U	2,053.1	202.2	864.0	Texas Christian U	314.4	11.7	74.8
Columbia U	1,515.8	123.2	789.7	U of California–Los Angeles	304.3	96.5	0.0
Texas A&M	1,485.9	50.8	307.8	Carnegie–Mellon U	299.2	36.1	250.7
Massachusetts Inst. of Tech.	1,404.6	117.6	606.3	George Washington U	296.7	15.5	247.2
Washington U	1,386.9	49.6	542.2	Pomona C	296.0	21.4	36.8
Northwestern U	1,202.6	68.1	427.3	Grinnell C	286.8	6.5	28.5
Emory U	1,106.0	38.8	322.8	Indiana U	285.9	79.1	815.0
U of Chicago	1,074.5	67.1	556.7	Trinity U	285.6	10.3	44.8
Rice U	1,068.5	25.8	118.2	U of Richmond	283.0	13.6	49.1
Cornell U	926.9	161.3	789.6	Loyola U of Chicago	278.4	36.3	150.5
U of Pennsylvania	808.4	140.0	685.3	U of Pittsburgh	278.1	36.6	504.4
Dartmouth C	653.8	51.1	197.2	Boston C	277.1	20.0	159.3
U of Notre Dame	605.6	53.8	124.0	Berea C	271.1	14.6	18.8
Vanderbilt U	604.0	43.3	329.5	Wesleyan U	271.0	12.3	71.3
U of Rochester	589.0	34.8	349.2	Amherst C	269.4	10.9	45.0
Johns Hopkins U	560.5	111.8	684.8	Lehigh U	260.4	21.7	113.2
New York U	546.7	74.7	696.2	Baylor U	250.5	23.0	99.4
Rockefeller U	544.9	24.9	92.2	Oberlin C	244.6	10.4	63.0
Duke U	505.0	108.0	428.5	Vassar C	242.5	13.4	53.2
U of Michigan	495.9	83.6	929.4	Georgetown U	242.3	28.6	283.5
U of Southern California	495.6	126.1	689.3	Tulane U	233.4	22.8	219.9
U of Virginia	487.5	51.3	364.9	Rensselaer Poly. Inst.	230.2	23.6	147.9
California Inst. of Tech.	467.0	37.2	184.8	Lafayette C	228.9	13.9	44.1
U of Minnesota	466.3	105.3	965.7	Middlebury C	227.8	9.7	53.3
Brown U	440.7	42.0	200.7	U of Kansas	226.0	23.7	220.0
Case Western Reserve U	420.0	40.8	242.6	Boston U	218.0	28.9	494.8
Princeton Theol. Sem.	379.0	4.3	21.8	U of Wisconsin–Madison	217.5	124.4	802.5
Wellesley C	374.1	29.2	64.4	U of Tennessee System	210.0	33.5	587.6
U of Texas–Austin	355.6	56.7	544.2	Georgia Inst. of Tech.	200.4	28.5	282.0
Southern Methodist U	352.3	22.0	131.5	U of North Carolina at Chapel Hill	200.2	54.2	496.5
Purdue U	350.4	27.5	539.9	U of Illinois	190.5	86.6	1,153.9
Smith C	341.9	35.3	88.8	Saint Louis U	188.1	29.5	174.8
Swarthmore C	336.0	13.3	40.6	Pennsylvania State U	186.3	62.4	825.5
Williams C	333.1	20.0	55.5	U of Florida	185.1	54.8	712.3
Macalester C	326.3	5.5	29.7				

1. Gifts from business, alumni, religious denominations, and others. 2. Figure represents about 80% of typical operating budget. Does not include auxiliary enterprises and capital outlays. NOTE: C = College; U = University. *Source:* Council for Aid to Education.

Institutions of Higher Education—Average Salaries and Fringe Benefits for Faculty Members, 1970–1989[1]
(in thousands of dollars)

Control and Acadmic Rank	1989	1988	1987	1986	1985	1984	1983	1982	1980	1975	1970
Average Salaries											
Public: All ranks	39.6	37.2	35.8	33.4	31.2	29.4	28.6	26.2	22.1	16.6	13.1
Professor	50.1	47.2	45.3	42.3	39.6	37.1	36.0	33.7	28.8	21.7	17.3
Associate professor	37.9	35.6	34.2	32.2	30.2	28.4	27.5	25.7	21.9	16.7	13.2
Assistant professor	31.7	29.6	28.5	26.7	25.0	23.5	22.6	21.2	18.0	13.7	10.9
Instructor	23.9	22.2	21.8	20.9	19.5	19.1	17.7	16.7	14.8	11.2	9.1
Private:[2] All ranks	42.4	39.7	37.8	35.4	33.0	31.1	29.2	26.8	22.1	16.6	13.1
Professor	55.9	52.2	50.3	47.0	44.1	41.5	38.8	35.8	30.1	22.4	17.8
Associate professor	38.8	36.6	34.9	32.9	30.9	29.4	27.5	25.4	21.0	16.0	12.6
Assistant professor	31.9	28.3	26.8	25.0	23.7	22.1	20.4	17.0	13.0	10.3	
Instructor	24.1	22.7	20.4	19.8	19.0	18.4	17.6	15.9	13.3	10.9	8.6
Average Fringe Benefits—All Ranks Combined											
Public	9.0	8.2	7.8	7.3	7.0	6.0	5.4	5.1	3.9	2.5	1.9
Private[2]	10.0	9.2	8.6	8.0	7.2	6.4	5.7	5.4	4.1	2.8	2.2

1. Figures are for 9 months teaching for full-time faculty members in four-year colleges and universities. 2. Excludes church-related colleges and universities. *Source:* U.S. Bureau of the Census, *Statistical Abstract of the United States: 1990.* NOTE: Data are latest available.

Accredited U.S. Senior Colleges and Universities

Source: The Guidance Information System™, a product of The Riverside Publishing Company, a Houghton Mifflin Company.

Schools listed are four-year institutions that offer at least a Bachelor's degree and are fully accredited by one of the institutional and professional accrediting associations. Included are accredited colleges outside the U.S.

Tuition, room, and board listed are average annual figures (including fees) subject to fluctuation, usually covering two semesters, two out of three trimesters,

or three out of four quarters, depending on the school calendar.

For further informmation, write to the Registrar of the school concerned.

NOTE: n.a. = information not available. — = does not apply. Enrollment figures are approximate. (C) = Coeducational, (M) = primarily for men, (W) = primarily for women.

Abbreviations used for controls:

P	Private	Pub	Public

Institution and location	Enrollment	Control	Tuition ($) Res.	Nonres.	Rm/Bd ($)
Abilene Christian University; Abilene, Tex. 79699	3,529 (C)	P	6,944	6,944	3,200
Academy of Art College; San Francisco, Calif. 94108	2,156 (C)	P	4,800	4,800	5,400
Academy of the New Church College; Bryn Athyn, Pa. 19009	139 (C)	P	3,483	3,483	3,039
Adams State College; Alamosa, Colo. 81102	2,161 (C)	Pub	1,445	3,792	2,632
Adelphi University; Garden City, N.Y. 11530	4,813 (C)	P	9,450	9,450	4,520
Adrian College; Adrian, Mich. 49221	1,180 (C)	P	9,340	9,340	3,175
Aeronautics, College of; Flushing, N.Y. 11371	1,333 (C)	P	5,600	5,600	n.a.
Aero-Space Institute; Chicago, Ill. 60605-10717	103 (C)	P	6,000	6,000	n.a.
Agnes Scott College; Decatur, Ga. 30030	591 (W)	P	10,575	10,575	4,180
Akron, University of; Akron, Ohio 44325	24,665 (C)	Pub	2,431	5,971	3,200
Alabama, University of; Tuscaloosa, Ala. 35487-0132	15,910 (C)	Pub	1,936	4,800	3,288
Alabama, University of-Birmingham; Birmingham, Ala. 35294	10,616 (C)	Pub	1,920	3,660	2,545
Alabama, University of-Huntsville; Huntsville, Ala. 35899	10,616 (C)	Pub	2,019	4,038	2,705
Alabama A&M University; Normal, Ala. 35762	3,710 (C)	Pub	1,248	2,236	2,036
Alabama State University; Montgomery, Ala. 36101-0271	4,024 (C)	Pub	1,268	2,428	2,110
Alaska, University of-Anchorage; Anchorage, Alas. 99508	12,860 (C)	Pub	1,300	3,900	3,600
Alaska, University of-Fairbanks; Fairbanks, Alas. 99701	6,989 (C)	Pub	1,490	4,090	2,880
Alaska Southeast, University of-Juneau; Juneau, Alas. 99801	2,158 (C)	Pub	1,300	3,900	3,850
Alaska Bible College; Glennallen, Alas. 99588	111 (C)	P	2,100	2,100	3,200
Alaska Pacific University; Anchorage, Alas. 99508	1,267 (C)	P	6,330	6,330	4,050
Albany College of Pharmacy; Albany, N.Y. 12208	651 (C)	P	7,375	7,375	4,000
Albany State College; Albany, Ga. 31705	2,355 (C)	Pub	1,680	4,260	2,484
Albertus Magnus College; New Haven, Conn. 06511	540 (C)	P	10,120	10,120	4,930
Albion College; Albion, Mich. 49224	1,616 (C)	P	11,134	11,134	4,064
Albright College; Reading, Pa. 19603	1,306 (C)	P	13,560	13,560	4,015
Alcorn State University; Lorman, Miss. 39096	2,853 (C)	Pub	3,700	4,882	1,900
Alderson-Broaddus College; Philippi, W. Va. 26416	760 (C)	P	8,666	8,666	2,860
Alfred University; Alfred, N.Y. 14802	2,086 (C)	P	13,960	13,960	4,470
Alice Lloyd College; Pippa Passes, Ky. 41844	534 (C)	P	3,240	3,240	2,664
Allegheny College; Meadville, Pa. 16335	1,810 (C)	P	14,850	14,850	4,120
Allentown College of St. Francis De Sales; Center Valley, Pa. 18034	873 (C)	P	7,200	7,200	4,150
Alma College; Alma, Mich. 48801	1,227 (C)	P	10,635	10,635	3,878
Alvernia College; Reading, Pa. 19607	1,113 (C)	P	6,932	6,932	3,600
Alverno College; Milwaukee, Wis. 53215	2,414 (W)	P	6,792	6,792	3,030
Ambassador College; Big Sandy, Tex. 75755	635 (C)	P	1,925	1,925	2,450
Amber University; Garland, Tex. 75041	722 (C)	P	3,938	3,938	n.a.
American Baptist College; Nashville, Tenn. 37207	163 (C)	P	2,012	2,012	784
American University of Paris; 75007 Paris, France	1,024 (C)	P	13,526	13,526	n.a.
American College of Switzerland; Switzerland	320 (C)	P	18,600	18,600	3,900
American Conservatory of Music; Chicago, Ill. 60602	124 (C)	P	6,800	6,800	n.a.
American International College; Springfield, Mass. 01109	1,384 (C)	P	8,079	8,079	3,762
American University; Washington, D.C. 20016	5,373 (C)	P	13,506	13,506	6,014
American University in Cairo; New York, N.Y. 10017	2,872 (C)	P	6,860	6,860	3,220
American University of Beirut; Beirut, Lebanon	4,500 (C)	P	3,200	3,200	2,925
American Universtity of Puerto Rico; Bayamon, PR 00621	4,208 (C)	P	2,100	2,100	n.a.
Amherst College; Amherst, Mass. 01002	1,570 (C)	P	15,515	15,515	4,400
Anderson College; Anderson, SC 29621	1,038 (C)	P	5,500	5,500	3,530
Anderson University; Anderson, Ind. 46012	2,015 (C)	P	8,060	8,060	2,870
Andrews University; Berrien Springs, Mich. 49104	2,009 (C)	P	9,105	9,105	3,675
Angelo State University; San Angelo, Tex. 76909	6,003 (C)	Pub	975	4,095	3,280
Anna Maria College for Men and Women; Paxton, Mass. 01612	633 (C)	P	9,480	9,480	4,380
Antillian College; Mayaguez, P.R. 00709	775 (C)	P	2,620	2,620	2,300
Antioch College; Yellow Springs, Ohio 45387	557 (C)	P	14,430	14,430	2,880

Institution and location	Enrollment	Control	Tuition ($) Res.	Tuition ($) Nonres.	Rm/Bd ($)
Antioch Los Angeles; Marina Del Rey, Calif. 90292	157 (C)	P	7,500	7,500	n.a.
Antioch Santa Barbara; Santa Barbara, Calif. 93101	66 (C)	P	6,750	6,750	n.a.
Antioch School for Adult & Experiential Learning; Yellow Springs, Ohio 45387	222 (C)	P	5,580	5,580	n.a.
Antioch Seattle; Seattle, Wash. 98121	115 (C)	P	7,575	7,575	n.a.
Appalachian Bible College; Bradley, W. Va. 25818	186 (C)	P	1,820	1,820	1,300
Appalachian State University; Boone, N.C. 28608	9,785 (C)	Pub	1,465	6,351	2,550
Aquinas College; Grand Rapids, Mich. 49506	2,218 (C)	P	8,960	8,960	3,950
Arizona, University of; Tucson, Ariz. 85721	27,932 (C)	Pub	1,540	6,546	3,192
Arizona College of the Bible; Phoenix, Ariz. 85021	177 (C)	P	4,370	4,370	3,020
Arizona State University; Tempe, Ariz. 85287-0112	32,027 (C)	Pub	1,590	6,996	4,100
Arkansas, Univ. of; Fayetteville, Ark. 72701	11,513 (C)	Pub	1,598	3,950	2,750
Arkansas, Univ. of-Little Rock; Little Rock, Ark. 72204	9,405 (C)	Pub	1,550	3,850	n.a.
Arkansas, Univ. of-Monticello; Monticello, Ark. 71655	1,854 (C)	Pub	1,410	3,230	1,880
Arkansas, Univ. of-Pine Bluff; Pine Bluff, Ark. 71601	3,333 (C)	Pub	1,320	3,140	1,300
Arkansas Baptist College; Little Rock, Ark. 72202	233 (C)	P	4,670	4,670	2,200
Arkansas College; Batesville, Ark. 72501	855 (C)	P	7,040	7,040	3,140
Arkansas State University; State University, Ark. 72467	8,429 (C)	Pub	1,400	2,650	2,010
Arkansas Tech. University; Russellville, Ark. 72801	3,453 (C)	Pub	1,200	2,400	3,280
Arlington Baptist College; Arlington, Tex. 76012	179 (C)	P	2,250	2,250	2,350
Armstrong College; Berkeley, Calif. 94704	100 (C)	P	4,500	4,500	n.a.
Armstrong State College; Savannah, Ga. 31419	4,170 (C)	Pub	1,467	4,047	2,850
Arnold & Marie Schwartz College of Pharmacy & Health Sciences. *See* Long Island University Center, Brooklyn Center					
Art Academy of Cincinnati; Cincinnati, Ohio 45202	247 (C)	P	7,200	7,200	n.a.
Art Center College of Design; Pasadena, Calif. 91103	1,268 (C)	P	11,780	11,780	n.a.
Art Institute of Chicago, School of the; Chicago, Ill. 60603	2,066 (C)	P	11,500	11,500	n.a.
Art Institute of Southern California; Laguna Beach, Calif. 92651	130 (C)	P	7,700	7,700	n.a.
Arts, The University of the; Philadelphia, Pa. 19102	1,245 (C)	P	10,775	10,775	3,570
Asbury College; Wilmore, Ky. 40390	1,053 (C)	P	7,350	7,350	2,476
Ashland University; Ashland, Ohio 44805	1,651 (C)	P	9,965	9,965	4,120
Assumption College; Worcester, Mass. 01615-0005	1,787 (C)	P	9,835	9,835	5,370
Athens State College; Athens, Ala. 35611	2,770 (C)	Pub	1,700	3,400	2,800
Atlanta Christian College; East Point, Ga. 30344	169 (C)	P	3,620	3,620	2,600
Atlanta College of Art; Atlanta, Ga. 30309	368 (C)	P	7,500	7,500	2,720
Atlantic, College of the; Bar Harbor, Maine 04609	226 (C)	P	11,625	11,625	3,295
Atlantic Christian College; Wilson, N.C. 27893	1,434 (C)	P	6,173	6,173	2,814
Atlantic Union College; South Lancaster, Mass. 01561	782 (C)	P	9,800	9,800	3,300
Auburn University; Auburn University, Ala. 36849	18,645 (C)	Pub	1,596	4,788	3,000
Auburn University-Montgomery; Montgomery, Ala. 36193	5,286 (C)	Pub	1,428	4,284	6,660
Augsburg College; Minneapolis, Minn. 55454	2,872 (C)	P	10,233	10,233	3,832
Augusta College; Augusta, Ga. 30910	5,205 (C)	Pub	1,431	3,909	3,175
Augustana College; Rock Island, Ill. 61201	2,235 (C)	P	11,118	11,118	3,666
Augustana College; Sioux Falls, S.D. 57197	1,952 (C)	P	9,330	9,330	3,100
Aurora University; Aurora, Ill. 60506	1,602 (C)	P	8,730	8,730	3,405
Austin College; Sherman, Tex. 75090	1,203 (C)	P	9,465	9,465	3,745
Austin Peay State University; Clarksville, Tenn. 37040	4,784 (C)	Pub	1,353	3,241	2,450
Averett College; Danville, Va. 24541-3692	1,042 (C)	P	8,750	8,750	4,200
Avila College; Kansas City, Mo. 64145	1,397 (C)	P	7,300	7,300	3,200
Azusa Pacific University; Azusa, Calif. 91702	1,720 (C)	P	8,900	8,900	3,590
Babson College; Wellesley, Mass. 02157	1,584 (C)	P	14,838	14,838	6,498
Baker University; Baldwin City, Kan. 66006	870 (C)	P	6,850	6,850	4,450
Baldwin-Wallace College; Berea, Ohio 44017	4,138 (C)	P	9,945	9,945	3,900
Ball State University; Muncie, Ind. 47306	18,993 (C)	Pub	2,110	4,870	2,790
Baltimore, University of; Baltimore, Md. 21201	3,216 (C)	Pub	2,047	3,635	n.a.
Baltimore Hebrew University; Baltimore, Md. 21215	612 (C)	P	1,920	1,920	n.a.
Baptist Bible College; Springfield, Mo. 65803	793 (C)	P	1,600	1,600	2,190
Baptist Bible College of Pennsylvania; Clarks Summit, Pa. 18411	494 (C)	P	8,590	8,590	5,510
Baptist Christian College; Shreveport, La. 71108	350 (C)	P	2,100	2,100	n.a.
Barat College; Lake Forest, Ill. 60045	685 (C)	P	8,640	8,640	3,300
Barber-Scotia College; Concord, N.C. 28025	370 (C)	P	4,000	4,000	2,487
Bard College; Annandale-on-Hudson, N.Y. 12504	1,023 (C)	P	16,790	16,790	5,565
Barnard College of Columbia University; New York, N.Y. 10027	2,200 (W)	P	16,468	16,468	6,892
Barry University; Miami Shores, Fla. 33161	4,442 (C)	P	8,490	8,490	3,340
Bartlesville Wesleyan College; Bartlesville, Okla. 74003	489 (C)	P	5,650	5,650	2,900
Bassist College; Portland, Ore. 97201	157 (C)	P	7,900	7,900	4,100
Bates College; Lewiston, Maine 04240	1,500 (C)	P	21,400	21,400	—
Baylor University; Waco, Tex. 76798-7032	10,389 (C)	P	6,060	6,060	3,658
Beaver College; Glenside, Pa. 19038	1,215 (C)	P	10,820	10,820	4,750
Behrend College. *See* Pennsylvania State University					
Beirut University College; Beirut, Lebanon	2,438 (C)	P	1,300	1,300	500
Belhaven College; Jackson, Miss. 39202	693 (C)	P	5,880	5,880	2,310
Bellarmine College; Louisville, Ky. 40205	1,853 (C)	P	6,615	6,615	2,450
Bellevue College; Bellevue, Neb. 68005	1,956 (C)	P	2,916	2,916	n.a.

Institution and location	Enrollment	Control	Tuition ($) Res.	Tuition ($) Nonres.	Rm/Bd ($)
Bellin College of Nursing; Green Bay, Wis. 54305-3400	180 (C)	P	5,222	5,222	n.a.
Belmont Abbey College; Belmont, N.C. 28012	1,023 (C)	P	6,870	7,870	3,804
Belmont College; Nashville, Tenn. 37203	2,508 (C)	P	6,100	6,100	3,150
Beloit College; Beloit, Wis. 53511	1,152 (C)	P	13,050	13,050	3,300
Bemidji State University; Bemidji, Minn. 56601	4,642 (C)	Pub	1,944	2,976	2,259
Benedict College; Columbia, S.C. 29204	1,448 (C)	P	5,084	5,084	2,292
Benedictine College; Atchison, Kan. 66002	788 (C)	P	7,150	7,150	3,060
Bennett College; Greensboro, N.C. 27401	572 (W)	P	4,850	4,850	2,600
Bennington College; Bennington, Vt. 05201	570 (C)	P	19,400	19,400	3,800
Bentley College; Waltham, Mass. 02254	5,503 (C)	P	11,390	11,390	4,768
Berea College; Berea, Ky. 40404	1,535 (C)	P	177	177	2,457
Berklee College of Music; Boston, Mass. 02215	2,734 (C)	P	9,085	9,085	6,190
Bernard M. Baruch Coll. See New York, City Univ. of					
Berry College; Mount Berry, Ga. 30149	1,714 (C)	P	6,990	6,990	3,360
Bethany Bible College; Santa Cruz, Calif. 95066	533 (C)	P	5,850	5,850	3,000
Bethany College; Bethany, W. Va. 36032	844 (C)	P	11,170	11,170	4,000
Bethany College; Lindsborg, Kan. 67456	653 (C)	P	7,028	7,028	3,241
Bethel College; McKenzie, Tenn. 38201	469 (C)	P	4,100	4,100	2,350
Bethel College; Mishawaka, Ind. 46545	679 (C)	P	7,200	7,200	2,750
Bethel College; North Newton, Kan. 67117	605 (C)	P	6,990	6,990	2,800
Bethel College; St. Paul, Minn. 55112	1,832 (C)	P	9,950	9,950	3,590
Bethune-Cookman College; Daytona Beach, Fla. 32015	2,351 (C)	P	4,944	4,944	2,787
Biola University; La Mirada, Calif. 90639	1,834 (C)	P	9,902	9,902	4,060
Birmingham-Southern College; Birmingham, Ala. 35254	1,846 (C)	P	8,900	8,900	4,135
Blackburn College; Carlinville, Ill. 62626	508 (C)	P	7,070	7,070	3,400
Black Hills State University; Spearfish, S.D. 57783	2,545 (C)	Pub	1,949	3,402	2,355
Bloomfield College; Bloomfield, N.J. 07003	1,701 (C)	P	7,300	7,300	3,700
Bloomsburg State Coll. See Bloomsburg Univ. of Pennsylvania					
Bloomsburg University of Pennsylvania; Bloomsburg, Pa. 17815	6,808 (C)	Pub	2,278	4,312	2,466
Bluefield College; Bluefield, Va. 24605	435 (C)	P	5,400	5,400	3,620
Bluefield State College; Bluefield, W. Va. 24701	2,706 (C)	Pub	1,454	3,424	n.a.
Blue Mountain College; Blue Mountain, Miss. 38610	364 (W)	P	3,434	3,434	2,040
Bluffton College; Bluffton, Ohio 45817	684 (C)	P	8,100	8,100	3,324
Bob Jones University; Greenville, S.C. 29614	4,003 (C)	P	3,660	3,660	3,360
Boca Raton, College of; Boca Raton, Fla. 33431	1,100 (C)	P	10,900	10,900	4,400
Boise State University; Boise, Idaho 83725	10,725 (C)	Pub	1,378	3,578	2,923
Boricua College; New York, N.Y. 10032	1,100 (C)	P	4,900	4,9900	n.a.
Boston Architecture Center School of Architecture; Boston, Mass. 02115	653 (C)	P	2,280	2,280	n.a.
Boston College; Chestnut Hill, Mass. 02167	8,649 (C)	P	13,925	13,925	6,150
Boston Conservatory; Boston, Mass. 02215	385 (C)	P	9,650	9,650	5,151
Boston University; Boston, Mass. 02215	14,572 (C)	P	16,190	16,190	6,320
Bowdoin College; Brunswick, Maine 04011	1,350 (C)	P	16,380	16,380	5,590
Bowie State University; Bowie, Md. 20715	2,879 (C)	Pub	2,254	4,179	3,418
Bowling Green State University; Bowling Green, Ohio 43403	15,847 (C)	Pub	2,162	2,162	2,514
Bradford College; Bradford, Mass. 01835	456 (C)	P	10,650	10,650	5,450
Bradley University; Peoria, Ill. 61625	5,255 (C)	P	9,060	9,060	3,950
Brandeis University; Waltham, Mass. 02254	2,920 (C)	P	16,535	16,535	6,250
Brenau: The Women's College; Gainesville, Ga. 30501	477 (W)	P	7,242	7,242	5,658
Brescia College; Owensboro, Ky. 42301	756 (C)	P	5,600	5,600	2,700
Brewton-Parker College; Mount Vernon, Ga. 30445	1,350 (C)	P	3,150	3,150	2,130
Briar Cliff College; Sioux City, Iowa 51104	1,131 (C)	P	8,760	8,760	3,147
Bridgeport, University of; Bridgeport, Conn. 06601	2,903 (C)	P	11,465	11,465	5,300
Bridgeport Engineering Institute; Bridgeport, Conn. 06606	830 (C)	P	5,450	5,450	n.a.
Bridgewater College; Bridgewater, Va. 22812	1,007 (C)	P	9,195	9,195	4,295
Bridgewater State College; Bridgewater, Mass. 02325	5,262 (C)	Pub	1,250	4,325	3,675
Brigham Young University; Provo, Utah 84602	25,812 (C)	P	2,850	2,850	3,120
Brigham Young University-Hawaii; Laie, Oahu, Hawaii 96762	2,040 (C)	P	2,280	2,280	2,530
Brooklyn Center. See Long Island University Center					
Brooklyn College. See New York, City University of					
Bristol University; Bristol, Tenn. 37621	700 (C)	P	4,360	4,360	n.a.
Brooks Institute of Photography; Santa Barbara, Calif. 93108	665 (C)	P	9,900	9,900	n.a.
Brown University; Providence, R.I. 02912	5,804 (C)	P	16,860	16,860	5,220
Bryan College; Dayton, Tenn. 37321	551 (C)	P	6,410	6,410	3,520
Bryant College; Smithfield, R.I. 02917	2,923 (C)	P	10,993	10,993	5,932
Bryn Mawr College; Bryn Mawr, Pa. 19010	1,177 (W)	P	15,750	15,750	5,850
Bucknell University; Lewisburg, Pa. 17837	3,373 (C)	P	15,650	15,650	3,825
Buena Vista College; Storm Lake, Iowa 50588	1,032 (C)	P	10,900	10,900	3,110
Burlington College; Burlington, Vt. 05401	206 (C)	P	6,865	6,864	n.a.
Butler University; Indianapolis, Ind. 46208	2,457 (C)	P	10,500	10,500	3,840
Cabrini College; Radnor, Pa. 19087	832 (C)	P	7,860	7,860	4,700
Caldwell College; Caldwell, N.J. 07006	1,186 (C)	P	7,600	7,600	4,000

Institution and location	Enrollment	Control	Tuition ($) Res.	Tuition ($) Nonres.	Rm/Bd ($)
California, University of; Berkeley, Calif. 94720:					
UC-Berkeley; Berkeley, Calif. 94720	22,262 (C)	Pub	1,640	7,556	5,134
UC-Davis; Davis, Calif. 95616	18,395 (C)	Pub	1,829	8,373	4,655
UC-Irvine; Irvine, Calif. 92717	13,150 (C)	Pub	1,796	7,712	5,350
UC-Los Angeles; Los Angeles, Calif. 90024	24,284 (C)	Pub	2,200	8,050	3,700
UC-Riverside; Riverside, Calif. 92521	6,747 (C)	Pub	1,644	7,560	4,850
UC-San Diego; La Jolla, Calif. 92093	14,105 (C)	Pub	2,284	7,650	5,250
UC-Santa Barbara; Santa Barbara, Calif. 93106	15,975 (C)	Pub	1,638	5,916	5,338
UC-Santa Cruz; Santa Cruz, Calif. 95064	8,883 (C)	Pub	1,813	7,729	4,787
California Baptist College; Riverside, Calif. 92504	617 (C)	P	5,076	5,076	4,198
California College of Arts and Crafts; Oakland, Calif. 94618	1,039 (C)	P	9,760	9,760	3,700
California Institute of Technology; Pasadena, Calif. 91125	810 (C)	P	13,300	13,300	5,422
California Institute of the Arts; Valencia, Calif. 91355	640 (C)	P	12,200	12,200	3,725
California Lutheran University; Thousand Oaks, Calif. 91360	1,636 (C)	P	9,450	9,450	4,200
California Maritime Academy; Vallejo, Calif. 94590	431 (C)	Pub	1,391	1,391	4,002
California Polytechnic State University; San Luis Obispo, Calif. 93407	16,530 (C)	Pub	948	5,604	3,960
California State Coll. (Pa.). *See* California Univ. of Pennsylvania					
California State Polytechnic University-Pomona; Pomona, Calif. 91768	17,933 (C)	Pub	820	5,670	4,116
California State University-Bakersfield; Bakersfield, Calif. 93311-1099	3,679 (C)	Pub	878	5,548	3,475
California State University-Chico; Chico, Calif. 95929	14,491 (C)	Pub	914	6,654	3,720
California St. Univ.-Dominguez Hills; Carson, Calif. 90747	6,158 (C)	Pub	876	5,796	4,480
California State Univ.-Fresno; Fresno, Calif. 93740	15,854 (C)	Pub	906	6,123	3,633
California State Univ.-Fullerton; Fullerton, Calif. 92634	21,210 (C)	Pub	916	6,586	4,056
California State Univ.-Hayward; Hayward, Calif. 94542	9,405 (C)	Pub	894	5,826	4,605
California State Univ.-Long Beach; Long Beach, Calif. 90840	27,131 (C)	Pub	862	6,526	4,400
California State Univ.-Los Angeles; Los Angeles, Calif. 90032	16,094 (C)	Pub	961	5,345	4,602
California State Univ.-Northridge; Northridge, Calif. 91330	24,664 (C)	Pub	972	5,892	5,500
California State Univ.-Sacramento; Sacramento, Calif. 95819	20,846 (C)	Pub	1,050	8,430	3,944
California State Univ.-San Bernardino; San Bernardino, Calif. 92407	7,914 (C)	Pub	845	5,670	4,043
California State Univ.-Stanislaus; Turlock, Calif. 95380	4,268 (C)	Pub	870	5,406	3,845
California Univ. of Pennsylvania; California, Pa. 15419	5,995 (C)	Pub	2,648	4,682	2,940
Calumet College of St. Joseph; Whiting, Ind. 46394	976 (C)	P	3,600	3,600	n.a.
Calvary Bible College; Kansas City, Mo. 64147	305 (C)	P	3,400	3,400	2,570
Calvin College; Grand Rapids, Mich. 49506	4,097 (C)	P	8,150	8,150	3,350
Cameron University; Lawton, Okla. 73505	4,894 (C)	Pub	1,209	2,965	1,862
Campbellsville College; Campbellsville, Ky. 42718	760 (C)	P	4,500	4,500	2,760
Campbell University; Buies Creek, N.C. 27506	3,941 (C)	P	7,296	7,296	2,690
Canisius College; Buffalo, N.Y. 14208	3,753 (C)	P	8,800	8,800	4,650
Capital University; Columbus, Ohio 43209	2,015 (C)	P	11,085	11,085	3,700
Capitol College; Laurel, Md. 20708	737 (C)	P	6,588	6,588	4,230
Cardinal Stritch College; Milwaukee, Wis. 53217	2,125 (C)	P	6,960	6,960	3,150
Carleton College; Northfield, Minn. 55057	1,850 (C)	P	16,290	16,290	3,330
Carlow College; Pittsburgh, Pa. 15213	1,125 (W)	P	8,336	8,336	4,000
Carnegie-Mellon University; Pittsburgh, Pa. 15213	4,327 (C)	P	15,350	15,350	5,110
Carroll College; Helena, Mont. 59625	1,234 (C)	P	6,570	6,570	3,230
Carroll College; Waukesha, Wis. 53186	1,495 (C)	P	11,068	11,068	3,560
Carson-Newman College; Jefferson City, Tenn. 37760	2,031 (C)	P	6,670	6,670	2,790
Carthage College; Kenosha, Wis. 53140	1,116 (C)	P	10,640	10,640	3,350
Case Western Reserve University; Cleveland, Ohio 44106	3,067 (C)	P	13,600	13,600	4,930
Castleton State College; Castleton, Vt. 05735	1,461 (C)	Pub	3,300	6,850	4,300
Catawba College; Salisbury, N.C. 28144	1,000 (C)	P	7,700	7,700	3,700
Catholic University of America; Washington, D.C. 20064	2,950 (C)	P	10,850	10,850	5,400
Catholic University of Puerto Rico; Ponce, P.R. 00732	11,598 (C)	P	2,457	2,457	2,265
Cayey University College. *See* Puerto Rico, University of					
Cazenovia College; Cazenovia, N.Y. 13035	1,070 (C)	P	7,654	7,654	3,832
Cedar Crest College; Allentown, Pa. 18104-6196	497 (W)	P	12,210	12,210	4,911
Cedarville College; Cedarville, Ohio 45314	1,923 (C)	P	5,710	5,710	3,390
Centenary College; Hackettstown, N.J. 07840	388 (C)	P	10,390	10,390	4,890
Centenary College of Louisiana; Shreveport, La. 71104	849 (C)	P	6,500	6,500	2,910
Center for Creative Studies, College of Art and Design; Detroit, Mich. 48202	953 (C)	P	8,900	8,900	4,950
Central Arkansas, University of; Conway, Ark. 72032	6,670 (C)	Pub	1,260	2,520	2,156
Central Baptist College; Conway, Ark. 72032	201 (C)	P	2,190	2,190	1,785
Central Bible College; Springfield, Mo. 65803	1,042 (C)	P	3,120	3,120	2,600
Central Christian College of the Bible; Moberly, Mo. 65270	79 (C)	P	2,815	2,815	2,200
Central College; Pella, Iowa 50219	1,695 (C)	P	9,198	9,198	3,417
Central Connecticut State University; New Britain, Conn. 06050	11,250 (C)	Pub	2,414	6,144	3,830
Central Florida, University of; Orlando, Fla. 32816	16,548 (C)	Pub	1,471	4,782	3,360
Central Methodist College; Fayette, Mo. 65248	824 (C)	P	6,710	6,710	3,270
Central Michigan University; Mt. Pleasant, Mich. 48859	15,628 (C)	Pub	2,065	5,110	3,350
Central Missouri State University; Warrensburg, Mo. 64093	9,755 (C)	Pub	1,870	3,580	2,982
Central Oklahoma, University of; Edmond, Okla. 73034-0419	11,165 (C)	Pub	1,065	2,811	1,992

Institution and location	Enrollment	Control	Tuition ($) Res.	Tuition ($) Nonres.	Rm/Bd ($)
Central State University; Wilberforce, Ohio 45384	2,550 (C)	Pub	2,247	4,788	3,753
Central Texas, University of; Killeen, Tex. 76540	336 (C)	P	3,660	3,660	2,484
Central Washington University; Ellensburg, Wash. 98926	7,298 (C)	Pub	1,674	5,712	2,993
Central Wesleyan College; Central, S.C. 29630	934 (C)	P	7,090	7,090	2,980
Centre College; Danville, Ky. 40422	859 (C)	P	10,110	10,110	3,930
Chadron State College; Chadron, Neb. 69337	2,062 (C)	Pub	1,457	2,273	2,614
Chaminade University of Honolulu; Honolulu, Hawaii 96816	2,704 (C)	P	5,930	6,680	3,715
Chapman College; Orange, Calif. 92666	1,489 (C)	P	11,910	11,910	4,640
Charleston, College of; Charleston, S.C. 29424	6,663 (C)	Pub	2,400	4,650	3,000
Charleston Southern University; Charleston, S.C. 29411	2,036 (C)	P	6,522	6,522	2,990
Charleston, University of; Charleston, W. Va. 25304	1,510 (C)	P	7,840	7,840	3,500
Charter Oak College; Farmington, Conn. 06032-1909	884 (C)	Pub	615	855	n.a.
Chatham College; Pittsburgh, Pa. 15232	686 (W)	P	11,065	11,065	4,745
Chestnut Hill College; Philadelphia, Pa. 19118-2695	850 (W)	P	8,250	8,250	4,800
Cheyney University of Pennsylvania; Cheyney, Pa. 19319	1,314 (C)	Pub	2,588	4,622	2,956
Chicago, University of—The College; Chicago, Ill. 60637	3,478 (C)	P	15,945	15,945	5,685
Chicago State University; Chicago, Ill. 60628	5,129 (C)	Pub	1,772	4,916	n.a.
Christ College-Irvine; Irvine, Calif. 92715	574 (C)	P	8,800	8,800	4,170
Christian Brothers College; Memphis, Tenn. 38104	1,678 (C)	P	7,640	7,640	2,960
Christian Heritage College; El Cajon, Calif. 92019	328 (C)	P	6,877	6,877	3,522
Christian Life College; Stockton, Calif. 95210	173 (C)	P	2,140	2,140	2,400
Christopher Newport College; Newport News, Va. 23606—2998	4,861 (C)	Pub	2,010	4,460	n.a.
Church College of Hawaii. *See* Brigham Young University— Hawaii Campus					
Cincinnati, University of; Cincinnati, Ohio 45221	13,885 (C)	Pub	3,008	7,180	4,185
Cincinnati Bible College; Cincinnati, Ohio 45204	633 (C)	P	3,762	3,762	2,966
Cincinnati College of Mortuary Science Cohen Center; Cincinnati, Ohio 45212	120 (C)	P	6,080	6,080	4,200
Circleville Bible College; Circleville, Ohio 43113	162 (C)	P	3,514	3,514	2,580
Citadel-The Military College of South Carolina; Charleston, S.C. 29409	1,960 (M)	Pub	8,607	11,945	—
City College (NYC). *See* New York, City University of					
City University; Bellevue, Wash. 98008	2,222 (C)	P	6,030	6,030	n.a.
Claflin College; Orangeburg, S.C. 29115	756 (C)	P	6,413	6,413	2,140
Claremont Colleges:					
Claremont McKenna College; Claremont, Calif. 91711	847 (C)	P	13,850	13,850	4,840
Claremont Men's College. *See* Claremont McKenna College					
Harvey Mudd College; Claremont, Calif. 91711-5990	568 (C)	P	14,490	14,490	5,990
Pitzer College; Claremont, Calif. 91711	750 (C)	P	15,428	15,428	5,742
Pomona College; Claremont, Calif. 91711	1,375 (C)	P	14,030	14,030	5,700
Scripps College; Claremont, Calif. 91711	607 (W)	P	13,920	13,920	6,000
Clarion State College. *See* Clarion University of Pennsylvania					
Clarion University of Pennsylvania; Clarion, Pa. 16214	5,789 (C)	Pub	2,278	4,438	2,558
Clark Atlanta University; Atlanta, Ga. 30314	2,339 (C)	P	6,600	6,600	3,500
Clarke College; Dubuque, Iowa 52001	820 (C)	P	8,780	8,780	3,000
Clarkson College of Technology. *See* Clarkson University					
Clarkson University; Potsdam, N.Y. 13676	3,035 (C)	P	13,675	13,675	4,732
Clark University; Worcester, Mass. 01610	2,200 (C)	P	15,200	15,200	4,500
Clearwater Christian College; Clearwater, Fla. 33519	295 (C)	P	4,575	4,575	3,220
Cleary College; Ypsilanti, Mich. 48197	940 (C)	P	5,790	5,790	n.a.
Clemson University; Clemson, S.C. 29634	13,010 (C)	Pub	2,623	7,001	3,153
Cleveland College of Jewish Studies; Beachwood, Ohio 44122	350 (C)	P	3,015	3,015	n.a.
Cleveland Institute of Art; Cleveland, Ohio 44106	495 (C)	P	10,800	10,800	4,310
Cleveland Institute of Music; Cleveland, Ohio 44106	173 (C)	P	11,800	11,800	4,875
Cleveland State University; Cleveland, Ohio 44115	13,408 (C)	Pub	2,538	5,076	3,069
Clinch Valley College. *See* Virginia, University of					
Coe College; Cedar Rapids, Iowa 52402	1,217 (C)	P	10,280	10,280	3,940
Cogswell College; Cupertino, Calif. 95014	275 (C)	P	6,240	6,240	n.a.
Coker College; Hartsville, S.C. 29550	778 (C)	P	8,339	8,339	3,818
Colby College; Waterville, Me. 04901	1,695 (C)	P	16,460	16,460	5,350
Colby-Sawyer College; New London, N.H. 03257	550 (C)	P	12,185	12,185	4,715
Coleman College; La Mesa, Calif. 92041	1,080 (C)	P	7,990	7,990	n.a.
Colgate University; Hamilton, N.Y. 13346	2,680 (C)	P	16,102	16,102	5,070
College for Human Services; New York, N.Y. 10014. *See* Human Services, College for					
College Misericordia; Dallas, Pa. 18612	900 (C)	P	8,650	8,650	4,446
College of Great Falls; Great Falls, Mont. 59405. *See* Great Falls, College of					
Colorado, University of; Boulder, Colo. 80309:					
U. of Colorado-Boulder; Boulder, Colo. 80309	18,927 (C)	Pub	2,346	4,875	3,340
U. of Colorado-Colorado Springs; Colorado Springs, Colo. 80933	4,216 (C)	Pub	1,942	5,856	n.a.
U. of Colorado-Denver; Denver, Colo. 80204	5,843 (C)	Pub	1,891	6,991	n.a.
Colorado Christian University; Lakewood, Colo. 80226	658 (C)	P	5,030	5,030	2,990
Colorado College; Colorado Springs, Colo. 80903	1,880 (C)	P	12,710	12,710	3,410

Institution and location	Enrollment	Control	Tuition ($)		Rm/Bd ($)
			Res.	Nonres.	
Colorado School of Mines; Golden, Colo. 80401	1,623 (C)	Pub	3,540	9,812	3,400
Colorado State University; Fort Collins, Colo. 80523	16,911 (C)	Pub	2,223	6,589	3,915
Colorado Technical College; Colorado Springs, Colo. 80907	1,200 (C)	P	5,670	5,670	n.a.
Colorado Women's College. *See* Denver, Univ. of					
Columbia Bible College and Seminary; Columbia, S.C. 29230	518 (C)	P	5,025	5,025	2,913
Columbia Christian College; Portland, Ore. 97216	250 (C)	P	5,952	5,952	2,872
Columbia College; Chicago, Ill. 60605	6,535 (C)	P	5,828	5.828	n.a.
Columbia College; Columbia, Mo. 65216	714 (C)	P	6,844	6,844	3,082
Columbia College; Columbia, S.C. 29203	1,147 (W)	P	8,725	8,725	3,255
Columbia College-Hollywood; Los Angeles, Calif. 90038	233 (C)	P	6,350	6,350	n.a.
Columbia Union College; Takoma Park, Md. 20912	1,356 (C)	P	8,200	8,200	2,900
Columbia University-Columbia College; New York, N.Y. 10027	3,200 (C)	P	14,793	14,793	5,735
Columbus College; Columbus, Ga. 31993	3,661 (C)	Pub	1,413	3,891	n.a.
Columbus College of Art and Design; Columbus, Ohio 43215	1,631 (C)	P	8,550	8,550	4,500
Conception Seminary College; Conception, Mo. 64433	76 (M)	P	4,254	4,254	2,736
Concord College; Athens, W. Va. 24712	2,651 (C)	Pub	1,622	3,642	2,894
Concordia College; Ann Arbor, Mich. 48105	416 (C)	P	7,812	7,812	3,580
Concordia College; Bronxville, N.Y. 10708	560 (C)	P	8,370	8,370	4,200
Concordia College; Moorhead, Minn. 56560	2,948 (C)	P	8,690	8,690	2,710
Concordia College; Portland, Ore. 97211	555 (C)	P	8,707	8,707	2,550
Concordia College; St. Paul, Minn. 55104	1,235 (C)	P	8,268	8,268	2,910
Concordia College; Seward, Neb. 68434	818 (C)	P	6,600	6,600	2,790
Concordia Lutheran College; Austin, Tex. 78705	603 (C)	P	6,090	6,090	3,200
Concordia University; River Forest, Ill. 60305	952 (C)	P	7,328	7,328	3,603
Concordia University Wisconsin; Mequon, Wis. 53092	1,606 (C)	P	7,400	7,400	3,100
Connecticut, University of; Storrs, Conn. 06269	13,715 (C)	Pub	3,463	9,173	4,522
Connecticut College; New London, Conn. 06320	1,650 (C)	P	16,270	16,270	5,370
Conservatory of Music of Puerto Rico; Hato Rey, P.R. 00918	264 (C)	Pub	210	210	n.a.
Converse College; Spartanburg, S.C. 29301	860 (W)	P	10,368	10,368	3,240
Cooper Union; New York, N.Y. 10003	973 (C)	P	300	300	5,250
Coppin State College; Baltimore, Md. 21216	2,325 (C)	Pub	2,281	4,045	n.a.
Corcoran School of Art; Washington, D.C. 20006	302 (C)	P	9,500	9,500	4,955
Cornell College; Mt. Vernon, Iowa 52314	1,155 (C)	P	12,360	12,360	3,960
Cornell University; Ithaca, N.Y. 14853	7,600 (C)	P	16,192	16,192	5,414
Cornish College of the Arts; Seattle, Wash. 98102	598 (C)	P	8,010	8,010	n.a.
Corpus Christi State Univ.; Corpus Christi, Tex. 78412	2,070 (C)	Pub	958	4,286	3,500
Covenant College; Lookout Mountain, Ga. 30750	606 (C)	P	8,130	8,130	3,480
Creighton University; Omaha, Neb. 68178	3,576 (C)	P	8,996	8,996	3,798
Crichton College; Memphis, Tenn. 38175-7830	358 (C)	P	3,899	3,899	3,050
Culver-Stockton College; Canton, Mo. 63435	1,129 (C)	P	6,650	6,650	2,600
Cumberland College; Williamsburg, Ky. 40769	1,712 (C)	P	5,280	5,280	3,076
Cumberland University of Tennessee; Lebanon, Tenn. 37087	707 (C)	P	4,700	4,700	2,830
Curry College; Milton, Mass. 02186	1,001 (C)	P	11,125	11,125	5,810
Curtis Institute of Music; Philadelphia, Pa. 19103	119 (C)	P	450	450	n.a.
C. W. Post Center. *See* Long Island Univ. Center					
D'Youville College; Buffalo, N.Y. 14201	1,166 (C)	P	7,750	7,750	3,730
Daemen College; Amherst, N.Y. 14226	1,962 (C)	P	7,920	7,920	3,950
Dakota State University; Madison, S.D. 57042	1,311 (C)	Pub	7,822	7,822	2,176
Dakota Wesleyan University; Mitchell, S.D. 57301	706 (C)	P	6,250	6,250	2,530
Dallas, University of; Irving, Tex. 75062	1,101 (C)	P	8,600	8,600	4,000
Dallas Baptist University; Dallas, Tex. 75211	2,333 (C)	P	5,100	5,100	2,928
Dallas Christian College; Dallas, Tex. 75234	114 (C)	P	2,040	2,040	2,500
Dana College; Blair, Neb. 68008	507 (C)	P	7,370	7,370	2,770
Daniel Webster College; Nashua, N.H. 03063	550 (C)	P	9,710	9,710	4,140
Dartmouth College; Hanover, N.H. 03755	3,752 (C)	P	16,335	16,335	5,160
David Lipscomb University; Nashville, Tenn. 37203	2,284 (C)	P	6,165	6,165	3,020
Davidson College; Davidson, N.C. 28036	1,406 (C)	P	13,280	13,280	4,160
Davis and Elkins College; Elkins, W. Va. 26241	890 (C)	P	7,820	7,820	3,930
Dayton, University of; Dayton, Ohio 45469	6,737 (C)	P	9,410	9,410	3,760
Defiance College; Defiance, Ohio 43512	1,006 (C)	P	8,690	8,690	3,290
Delaware, University of; Newark, Del. 19716	14,615 (C)	P	2,890	7,680	3,571
Delaware State College; Dover, Del. 19901	2,510 (C)	Pub	1,295	3,170	4,182
Delaware Valley College of Science and Agriculture; Doylestown, Pa. 18901	1,050 (C)	P	8,500	8,500	3,900
Delta State University; Cleveland, Miss. 38732	3,330 (C)	Pub	1,706	2,888	1,690
Denison University; Granville, Ohio 43023	2,024 (C)	P	14,700	14,700	3,980
Denver, University of; Denver, Colo. 80208	2,765 (C)	P	12,990	12,990	4,206
CWC Campus Weekend College- Women's Program; Denver, Colo. 80220	419 (W)	P	6,300	6,300	n.a
DePaul University; Chicago, Ill. 60604	9,416 (C)	P	9,342	9,342	5,843
DePauw University; Greencastle, Ind. 46135	2,347 (C)	P	12,288	12,288	4,420
Deree College-Division of the American College of Greece; Athens, Greece GR-153 42	4,081 (C)	P	2,400	2,400	n.a.
Design Institute of San Diego; San Diego, Calif. 92121	190 (C)	P	5,700	5,700	n.a.

Institution and location	Enrollment	Control	Tuition ($) Res.	Tuition ($) Nonres.	Rm/Bd ($)
Detroit Bible College. *See* William Tyndale College					
Detroit College of Business; Dearborn, Mich. 48126	4,528 (C)	P	4,248	4,248	n.a.
Detroit Mercy, University of; Detroit, Mich. 48221	3,206 (C)	P	8,850	8,850	3,300
DeVry Institute of Technology; Chicago, Ill. 60618-5994	3,261 (C)	P	5,015	5,015	n.a.
DeVry Institute of Technology; City of Industry, Calif. 91744-3495	1,886 (C)	P	5,012	5,012	n.a.
DeVry Institute of Technology; Columbus, Ohio 43209-2764	2,715 (C)	P	5,015	5,015	n.a.
DeVry Institute of Technology; Decatur, Ga. 30030-2198	3,121 (C)	P	5,015	5,015	n.a.
DeVry Institute of Technology; Irving, Tex. 75038-4299	2,292 (C)	P	5,015	5,015	n.a.
DeVry Institute of Technology; Kansas City, Mo. 64131-3626	1,748 (C)	P	5,015	5,015	n.a.
DeVry Institute of Technology; Lombard, Ill. 60148-4299	2,453 (C)	P	5,012	5,012	n.a.
DeVry Institute of Technology; Phoenix, Ariz. 85021	2,647 (C)	P	5,012	5,012	n.a.
Dickinson College; Carlisle, Pa. 17013	2,003 (C)	P	15,565	15,565	4,530
Dickinson State University; Dickinson, N.D. 58601	1,429 (C)	Pub	1,659	4,731	1,750
Dillard University; New Orleans, La. 70122	1,200 (C)	P	5,500	5,500	3,250
District of Columbia, Univ. of the; Washington, D.C. 20008	11,280 (C)	Pub	664	2,464	n.a.
Divine Word College; Epworth, Iowa 52045	62 (M)	P	5,200	5,200	1,200
Doane College; Crete, Neb. 68333	651 (C)	P	8,320	8,320	2,600
Dr. Martin Luther College; New Ulm, Minn. 56073	443 (C)	P	3,132	3,132	1,770
Dominican College of Blauvelt; Orangeburg, N.Y. 10962	1,480 (C)	P	6,890	6,890	5,150
Dominican College of San Rafael; San Rafael, Calif. 94901	430 (C)	P	10,390	10,390	5,150
Dominican School of Philosophy and Theology; Berkeley, Calif. 94709	8 (C)	P	4,500	4,500	n.a.
Dordt College; Sioux Center, Iowa 51250	1,038 (C)	P	7,900	7,900	2,250
Dowling College; Oakdale, N.Y. 11769	3,242 (C)	P	7,130	7,130	2,500
Drake University; Des Moines, Iowa 50311	4,352 (C)	P	11,040	11,040	4,215
Drew University-College of Liberal Arts; Madison, N.J. 07940	1,485 (C)	P	16,502	16,502	4,840
Drexel University; Philadelphia, Pa. 19104	7,100 (C)	P	10,859	10,859	5,400
Drury College; Springfield, Mo. 65802	1,130 (C)	P	7,510	7,510	3,184
Dubuque, University of; Dubuque, Iowa 52001	836 (C)	P	9,105	9,105	3,100
Duke University; Durham, N.C. 27706	5,950 (C)	P	15,101	15,101	5,050
Duquesne University; Pittsburgh, Pa. 15282	4,200 (C)	P	8,850	8,850	4,317
Dyke College; Cleveland, Ohio 44115	1,261 (C)	P	4,900	4,900	n.a.
Earlham College; Richmond, Ind. 47374	1,200 (C)	P	13,479	13,479	3,726
East Carolina University; Greenville, N.C. 27834	12,982 (C)	Pub	1,140	5,512	2,720
East Central University; Ada, Okla. 74820-6899	3,459 (C)	Pub	1,215	3,210	1,988
Eastern College; St. Davids, Pa. 19087	1,115 (C)	P	9,500	9,500	3,786
Eastern Connecticut State Univ.; Willimantic, Conn. 06226	4,190 (C)	Pub	2,406	6,136	3,434
Eastern Illinois University; Charleston, Ill. 61920	9,352 (C)	Pub	2,114	5,258	2,574
Eastern Kentucky University; Richmond, Ky. 40475	15,371 (C)	Pub	1,440	4,040	3,046
Eastern Mennonite College; Harrisonburg, Va. 22801	969 (C)	P	7,900	7,900	3,300
Eastern Michigan University; Ypsilanti, Mich. 48197	19,700 (C)	Pub	2,116	5,189	3,951
Eastern Montana College; Billings, Mont. 59101	3,533 (C)	Pub	1,308	2,991	2,839
Eastern Nazarene College; Quincy, Mass. 02170	746 (C)	P	7,020	7,020	3,100
Eastern New Mexico University; Portales, N.M. 88130	3,187 (C)	Pub	1,233	4,251	2,594
Eastern Oregon State College; La Grande, Ore. 97850	1,767 (C)	Pub	1,755	1,755	2,840
Eastern Washington University; Cheney, Wash. 99004	7,465 (C)	Pub	1,611	5,649	2,971
Eastman School of Music; Rochester, N.Y. 14604	411 (C)	P	14,039	14,039	5,996
East Stroudsburg University of Pennsylvania; East Stroudsburg, Pa. 18301	4,735 (C)	Pub	2,278	4,676	3,065
East Tennessee State University; Johnson City, Tenn. 37614	9,761 (C)	Pub	1,390	4,594	2,400
East Texas Baptist University; Marshall, Tex. 75670	924 (C)	P	4,050	4,050	2,750
East Texas State University; Commerce, Tex. 75428	4,881 (C)	Pub	1,022	4,082	3,082
East-West University; Chicago, Ill. 60605	238 (C)	P	5,360	5,360	n.a.
Eckerd College; St. Petersburg, Fla. 33711	1,350 (C)	P	13,040	13,040	3,210
Edgewood College; Madison, Wis. 53711	1,067 (C)	P	6,950	6,950	3,330
Edinboro University of Pennsylvania; Edinboro, Pa. 16444	6,750 (C)	Pub	2,590	4,624	2,904
Edward Waters College; Jacksonville, Fla. 32209	686 (C)	P	3,476	3,476	3,400
Electronic Data Processing College of Puerto Rico; Hato Rey, P.R. 00918	1,176 (C)	P	2,334	2,334	n.a.
Elizabeth City State University; Elizabeth City, N.C. 27909	1,694 (C)	Pub	1,273	5,261	2,549
Elizabethtown College; Elizabethtown, Pa. 17022	1,451 (C)	P	11,650	11,650	3,950
Elmhurst College; Elmhurst, Ill. 60126-3296	1,758 (C)	P	7,532	7,532	3,442
Elmira College; Elmira, N.Y. 14901	1,002 (C)	P	11,380	11,380	3,900
Elms College; Chicopee, Mass. 01013-2839	600 (W)	P	9,650	9,650	4,400
Elon College; Elon College, N.C. 27244	3,205 (C)	P	7,320	7,320	3,550
Embry-Riddle Aeronautical Univ.-Daytona Beach Campus; Daytona Beach, Fla. 32114	4,975 (C)	P	6,400	6,400	3,550
Prescott Campus; Prescott, Ariz. 86301	1,676 (C)	P	6,390	6,390	3,550
Emerson College; Boston, Mass. 02116	2,065 (C)	P	12,096	12,096	6,832
Emmanuel College; Boston, Mass. 02115	902 (W)	P	10,345	10,345	5,420
Emmanuel College School of Christian Ministries; Franklin Springs, Ga. 30639	51 (C)	P	3,501	3,501	2,610
Emory and Henry College; Emory, Va. 24327	853 (C)	P	7,270	7,270	3,956
Emory University; Atlanta, Ga. 30322	4,747 (C)	P	14,700	14,700	4,532

Institution and location	Enrollment	Control	Tuition ($) Res.	Tuition ($) Nonres.	Rm/Bd ($)
Emporia State University; Emporia, Kan. 66801	4,472 (C)	Pub	1,490	4,005	2,695
Endicott College; Beverly, Mass. 01915	755 (W)	P	9,640	9,640	5,310
Erskine College; Due West, S.C. 29639	514 (C)	P	9,650	9,650	3,340
Esther Boyer College of Music, Temple University; Philadelphia, Pa. 19122	350 (C)	Pub	4,294	7,892	4,400
ETI Technical College; Cleveland, Ohio 44114	900 (C)	P	4,080	4,080	2,995
Eugene Bible College; Eugene, Ore. 97405	145 (C)	P	3,192	3,192	2,250
Eureka College; Eureka, Ill. 61530	478 (C)	P	9,425	9,425	3,160
Evangel College; Springfield, Mo. 65802	1,540 (C)	P	6,064	6,064	2,880
Evansville, University of; Evansville, Ind. 47722	3,006 (C)	P	9,710	9,710	3,750
Evergreen State College; Olympia, Wash. 98505	3,250 (C)	Pub	1,611	5,649	3,600
Fairfield University; Fairfield, Conn. 06430	2,928 (C)	P	12,650	12,650	5,350
Fairhaven College-Western Washington University; Bellingham, Wash. 98225	282 (C)	Pub	1,611	5,649	3,550
Fairleigh Dickinson Univ.-Madison; Madison, N.J. 07940	2,501 (C)	P	10,178	10,178	6,104
Fairleigh Dickinson Univ.-Rutherford; Rutherford, N.J. 07070	1,505 (C)	P	10,184	10,184	4,596
Fairleigh Dickinson Univ.-Teaneck; Teaneck, N.J. 07666	4,402 (C)	P	10,184	10,184	5,273
Fairmont State College; Fairmont, W. Va. 26554	6,306 (C)	Pub	1,424	3,454	2,720
Faith Baptist Bible College and Theological Seminary; Ankeny, Iowa 50021	263 (C)	P	4,206	4,206	2,622
Faulkner University; Montgomery, Ala. 36193	1,690 (C)	P	4,150	4,150	2,700
Fayetteville State University; Fayetteville, N.C. 28301	2,307 (C)	Pub	1,354	5,670	2,147
Felician College; Lodi, N.J. 07644	750 (C)	P	6,950	6,950	n.a.
Ferris State University; Big Rapids, Mich. 49307	11,813 (C)	Pub	2,412	4,896	3,018
Ferrum College; Ferrum, Va. 24088	1,238 (C)	P	7,725	7,725	3,075
Findlay, University of; Findlay, Ohio 45840	2,215 (C)	P	9,005	9,005	3,895
Finlay Engineering College; Kansas City, Mo. 64114	100 (C)	P	3,500	3,500	n.a.
Fisk University; Nashville, Tenn. 37203	520 (C)	P	5,050	5,050	3,050
Fitchburg State College; Fitchburg, Mass. 01420	6,030 (C)	Pub	2,530	5,605	3,104
Flagler College; St. Augustine, Fla. 32085	1,187 (C)	P	4,550	4,550	2,840
Flaming Rainbow University; Stilwell, Okla. 74960	129 (C)	P	3,400	3,400	n.a.
Florida, University of; Gainesville, Fla. 32611	26,435 (C)	Pub	1,320	4,640	3,330
Florida A&M University; Tallahassee, Fla. 32307	8,082 (C)	Pub	1,295	4,606	2,482
Florida Atlantic University; Boca Raton, Fla. 33431-0991	8,498 (C)	Pub	1,300	4,040	3,345
Florida Baptist Theological College; Graceville, Fla. 32440	386 (C)	P	1,463	1,463	2,725
Florida Christian College; Kissimmee, Fla. 34744	123 (C)	P	3,296	3,296	3,076
Florida Institute of Technology; Melbourne, Fla. 32901	3,865 (C)	P	11,526	11,526	3,465
Florida International University; Miami, Fla. 33199	14,814 (C)	Pub	1,324	4,627	5,422
Florida Memorial College; Miami, Fla. 33054	1,750 (C)	P	4,450	4,450	2,800
Florida Southern College; Lakeland, Fla. 33801	1,770 (C)	P	6,600	6,600	4,200
Florida State University; Tallahassee, Fla. 32306	21,341 (C)	Pub	1,307	4,619	3,419
Fontbonne College; St. Louis, Mo. 63105	821 (C)	P	7,470	7,470	3,500
Fordham Univ.-Rose Hill Campus; New York, N.Y. 10458	7,020 (C)	P	11,254	11,254	6,525
Forsyth School for Dental Hygienists; Boston, Mass. 02115	117 (C)	P	10,130	10,130	6,249
Fort Hays State University; Hays, Kan. 67601	3,792 (C)	Pub	1,470	3,600	2,502
Fort Lauderdale College; Fort Lauderdale, Fla. 33301	1,300 (C)	P	4,500	4,500	4,600
Fort Lewis College; Durango, Colo. 81301	3,842 (C)	Pub	1,420	5,048	2,520
Fort Valley State College; Fort Valley, Ga. 31030	1,748 (C)	Pub	1,650	4,230	2,310
Framingham State College; Framingham, Mass. 01701	3,248 (C)	Pub	2,329	5,404	3,160
Franciscan University of Steubenville; Steubenville, Ohio 43952	1,419 (C)	P	7,190	7,190	3,925
Francis Marion College; Florence, S.C. 29501	3,687 (C)	Pub	2,140	4,280	3,078
Franklin and Marshall College; Lancaster, Pa. 17604-3003	1,876 (C)	P	16,905	16,905	3,980
Franklin College; Franklin, Ind. 46131	811 (C)	P	8,250	8,250	3,110
Franklin College; Switzerland	225 (C)	P	15,150	15,150	3,450
Franklin Pierce College; Rindge, N.H. 03461	1,300 (C)	P	11,325	11,325	4,160
Franklin University; Columbus, Ohio 43215-5399	4,005 (C)	P	4,371	4,371	n.a.
Freed-Hardeman University; Henderson, Tenn. 38340	1,150 (C)	P	5,040	5,040	2,810
Free Will Baptist Bible College; Nashville, Tenn. 37205	269 (C)	P	3,074	3,074	2,970
Fresno Pacific College; Fresno, Calif. 93702	488 (C)	P	8,200	8,200	3,300
Friends Bible College; Haviland, Kan. 67059	106 (C)	P	5,400	5,400	2,500
Friends University; Wichita, Kan. 67213	1,135 (C)	P	7,260	7,260	2,520
Friends World College; Huntington, N.Y. 11743	300 (C)	P	9,000	9,000	4,750
Frostburg State University; Frostburg, Md. 21532	4,127 (C)	Pub	2,016	3,666	3,690
Furman University; Greenville, S.C. 29613	2,522 (C)	P	10,922	10,922	3,728
Gallaudet University; Washington, D.C. 20002	1,558 (C)	P	3,334	3,334	4,160
Gannon University; Erie, Pa. 16541	3,975 (C)	P	8,744	8,744	3,800
Gannon University–Willa Marie Campus; Erie, Pa. 16505	699 (W)	P	8,830	8,830	3,500
Gardner-Webb College; Boiling Springs, N.C. 28017	824 (C)	P	6,720	6,720	3,580
General Motors Institute. *See* GMI Engineering and Management Institute					
Geneva College; Beaver Falls, Pa. 15010	1.264 (C)	P	7,565	7,565	3,680
George Fox College; Newberg, Ore. 97132	820 (C)	P	8,950	8,950	3,440
George Mason University; Fairfax, Va. 22030	13,371 (C)	Pub	2,988	7,464	4,910
Georgetown College; Georgetown, Ky. 40324	1,188 (C)	P	6,250	6,250	3,286

Institution and location	Enrollment	Control	Tuition ($) Res.	Tuition ($) Nonres.	Rm/Bd ($)
Georgetown University; Washington, D.C. 20057	5,906 (C)	P	15,510	15,510	6,550
George Washington University; Washington, D.C. 20052	6,532 (C)	P	14,902	14,902	6,356
Georgia, University of; Athens, Ga. 30602	21,494 (C)	Pub	2,076	5,520	3,438
Georgia College; Milledgeville, Ga. 31061	4,703 (C)	Pub	1,461	2,448	2,205
Georgia Institute of Technology; Atlanta, Ga. 30332	9,270 (C)	Pub	2,913	7,074	3,855
Georgia Southern University; Statesboro, Ga. 30458	12,250 (C)	Pub	1,563	4,041	2,730
Georgia Southwestern College; Americus, Ga. 31709	1,873 (C)	Pub	1,527	4,005	2,220
Georgian Court College; Lakewood, N.J. 08701	1,672 (W)	P	7,180	7,180	3,750
\Georgia State University; Atlanta, Ga. 30303	16,470 (C)	Pub	1,812	5,780	n.a.
Gettysburg College; Gettysburg, Pa. 17325	1,900 (C)	P	16,500	16,500	3,470
Glassboro State College; Glassboro, N.J. 08208	5,427 (C)	Pub	2,302	3,200	4,105
Glenville State College; Glenville, W. Va. 26351	2,238 (C)	Pub	1,280	3,150	2,590
GMI Engineering & Management Institute; Flint, Mich. 48504	2,505 (C)	P	9,490	9,490	2,840
Goddard College; Plainfield, Vt. 05667	225 (C)	P	15,344	15,344	—
Golden Gate University; San Francisco, Calif. 94105	2,049 (C)	P	4,500	4,500	n.a.
God's Bible School and College; Cincinnati, Ohio 45201	203 (C)	P	2,670	2,670	2,140
Goldey Beacom College; Wilmington, Del. 19808	1,920 (C)	P	5,600	5,600	4,189
Gonzaga University; Spokane, Wash. 99258	2,567 (C)	P	10,300	10,300	3,650
Gordon College; Wenham, Mass 01984	1,146 (C)	P	11,400	11,400	3,630
Goshen College; Goshen, Ind. 46526	1,107 (C)	P	7,720	7,720	3,275
Goucher College; Baltimore, Md. 21204	909 (C)	P	11,750	11,750	5,380
Governors State University; University Park, Ill. 60466	2,770 (C)	Pub	1,646	4,838	n.a.
Grace Bible College; Grand Rapids, Mich. 49509	127 (C)	P	3,600	3,600	2,750
Grace College; Winona Lake, Ind. 46590	665 (C)	P	7,011	7,011	3,328
Grace College of the Bible; Omaha, Neb. 68108	256 (C)	P	3,780	3,780	2,400
Graceland College; Lamoni, Iowa 50140	935 (C)	P	7,850	7,850	2,650
Grambling State University; Grambling, La. 71245	5,896 (C)	Pub	1,812	3,362	2,612
Grand Canyon University; Phoenix, Ariz. 85017	1,835 (C)	P	6,730	6,730	2,800
Grand Rapids Baptist College; Grand Rapids, Mich. 49505	752 (C)	P	5,852	5,852	3,630
Grand Valley State University; Allendale, Mich. 49401-9401	9,529 (C)	Pub	2,132	4,910	3,300
Grand View College; Des Moines, Iowa 50316	1,349 (C)	P	7,750	7,750	2,900
Gratz College; Melrose Park , Pa. 19126	92 (C)	P	3,500	3,500	n.a.
Great Falls, College of; Great Falls, Mont. 59405	1,127 (C)	P	3,790	3,790	n.a.
Great Lakes Bible College; Lansing, Mich. 48901	150 (C)	P	5,600	5,600	3,675
Green Mountain College; Poultney, Vt. 05764	600 (C)	P	7,495	7,495	4,690
Greensboro College; Greensboro, N.C. 27401	1,116 (C)	P	6,830	6,830	3,280
Greenville College; Greenville, Ill. 62246	753 (C)	P	8,960	8,960	3,730
Griffin College; Seattle, Wash. 98121	1,700 (C)	P	5,200	5,200	n.a.
Grinnell College; Grinnell, Iowa 50112	1,251 (C)	P	13,724	13,724	3,868
Grove City College; Grove City, Pa. 16127	2,139 (C)	P	4,630	4,630	2,670
Guam, University of; Mangilao, Guam 96913	2,057 (C)	Pub	1,408	2,016	3,805
Guilford College; Greensboro, N.C. 27410	1,154 (C)	P	10,510	10,510	4,514
Gustavus Adolphus College; St. Peter, Minn. 56082	2,371 (C)	P	11,900	11,900	2,900
Gwynedd-Mercy College; Gwynedd Valley, Pa. 19437	1,861 (C)	P	8,600	8,600	4,500
Hahnemann University School of Health Sciences and Humanities; Philadelphia, Pa. 19102	793 (C)	P	7,150	7,150	5,164
Hamilton College; Clinton, N.Y. 13323	1,673 (C)	P	16,650	16,650	4,550
Hamline University; St. Paul, Minn. 55104	1,507 (C)	P	11,725	11,725	3,631
Hampden-Sydney College; Hampden-Sydney, Va. 23943	950 (M)	P	11,685	11,685	3,797
Hampshire College; Amherst, Mass. 01002	1,253 (C)	P	16,000	16,000	4,240
Hampton University; Hampton, Va. 23668	4,490 (C)	P	6,550	6,550	3,000
Hannibal-LeGrange College; Hannibal, Mo. 63401	830 (C)	P	4,980	4,980	2,110
Hanover College; Hanover, Ind. 47243	1,060 (C)	P	6,450	6,450	2,885
Harding University; Searcy, Ark. 72143	3,311 (C)	P	4,500	4,500	2,850
Hardin-Simmons University; Abilene, Tex. 79698	1,636 (C)	P	4,950	4,950	2,436
Harrington Institute of Interior Design; Chicago, Ill. 60605	404 (C)	P	7,565	7,565	n.a.
Harris-Stowe State College; St. Louis, Mo. 63103	1,480 (C)	Pub	1,407	2,800	n.a.
Hartford, University of; West Hartford, Conn. 06117	5,858 (C)	P	12,990	12,990	6,018
Hartwick College; Oneonta, N.Y. 13820	1,498 (C)	P	13,450	13,450	4,350
Harvard and Radcliffe Colleges; Cambridge, Mass. 02138	6,601 (C)	P	16,560	16,560	5,520
Harvey Mudd College. *See* Claremont Colleges					
Hastings College; Hastings, Neb. 68901	925 (C)	P	8,090	8,090	2,910
Haverford College; Haverford, Pa. 19041	1,147 (C)	P	16,275	16,275	5,400
Hawaii, Univ. of-Hilo Colleges of Arts and Sciences and Agriculture; Hilo, Hawaii 96720-4091	1,408 (C)	Pub	450	2,510	3,254
Hawaii, University of-Manoa; Honolulu, Hawaii 96822	12,763 (C)	Pub	1,230	3,680	3,276
Hawaii, University of-West Oahu; Pearl City, Hawaii 96782	652 (C)	Pub	850	2,590	n.a.
Hawaii Loa College; Kaneohe, Hawaii 96744	597 (C)	P	7,800	7,800	4,200
Hawaii Pacific University; Honolulu, Hawaii 96813	5,025 (C)	P	4,950	4,950	n.a.
Health Sciences, University of-School of Related Health Sciences; North Chicago, Ill. 60064	65 (C)	P	10,280	10,280	n.a.
Hebrew Theological College; Skokie, Ill. 60077	266 (C)	P	4,795	4,795	3,790
Heidelberg College; Tiffin, Ohio 44883	1,200 (C)	P	11,680	11,680	3,730
Hellenic College; Brookline, Mass. 02146	41 (C)	P	7,260	7,260	3,800

Institution and location	Enrollment	Control	Tuition ($) Res.	Nonres.	Rm/Bd ($)
Henderson State University; Arkadelphia, Ark. 71923	3,223 (C)	Pub	1,200	2,400	2,092
Hendrix College; Conway, Ark. 72032	1,029 (C)	P	6,653	6,653	2,595
Herbert H. Lehman College. See New York, City University of					
Heritage College; Toppenish, Wash. 98948	383 (C)	P	4,923	4,923	n.a.
High Point College; High Point, N.C. 27261	2,023 (C)	P	6,085	6,085	2,985
Hillsdale College; Hillsdale, Mich. 49242	1,080 (C)	P	9,400	9,400	3,900
Hillsdale Free Will Baptist College; Moore, Okla. 73153	170 (C)	P	2,738	2,738	2,740
Hiram College; Hiram, Ohio 44234	900 (C)	P	11,800	11,800	3,780
Hobart and William Smith Colleges; Geneva, N.Y. 14456	1,838 (C)	P	16,477	16,477	5,166
Hofstra University; Hempstead, N.Y. 11550	8,541 (C)	P	8,507	8,507	5,992
Hollins College; Roanoke, Va. 24020	919 (W)	P	10,810	10,810	4,350
Holy Apostles College and Seminary; Cromwell, Conn. 06416	54 (C)	P	3,400	3,400	4,320
Holy Cross, College of the; Worcester, Mass. 01610	2,684 (C)	P	15,530	15,530	5,700
Holy Family College; Philadelphia, Pa. 19914	986 (C)	P	7,000	7,000	n.a.
Holy Names College; Oakland, Calif. 94619	596 (C)	P	9,256	9,256	4,422
Hong Kong Baptist College; Kowloon, Hong Kong	3,028 (C)	Pub	1,100	1,100	n.a.
Hood College; Frederick, Md 21701	1,161 (W)	P	12,208	12,208	5,675
Hope College, Holland, Mich. 49423	2,813 (C)	P	10,086	10,086	3,826
Houghton College, Houghton, N.Y. 14744	1,164 (C)	P	8,676	8,676	3,134
Houghton College-Buffalo Suburban Campus; West Seneca, N.Y. 14225	86 (C)	P	7,056	7,056	3,020
Houston, Univ. of; Houston, Tex. 77284-2161	25,052 (C)	Pub	990	3,438	3,770
Houston, Univ. of-Clear Lake; Houston, Tex. 77058	3,957 (C)	Pub	914	4,154	n.a.
Houston, Univ. of-Downtown; Houston, Tex .77002	8,056 (C)	Pub	1,010	4,310	3,034
Houston, Univ. of-Victoria; Victoria, Tex. 77901	480 (C)	Pub	648	4,392	n.a.
Houston Baptist University; Houston, Tex. 77074	1,868 (C)	P	4,695	4,695	2,590
Howard Payne University; Brownwood, Tex. 76801	1,247 (C)	P	4,160	4,160	2,710
Howard University; Washington, D.C. 20059	8,820 (C)	P	6,446	6,446	3,540
Human Services, College for; New York, N.Y. 10014	911 (C)	P	8,400	8,400	n.a.
Humboldt State University; Arcata, Calif. 95521	6,245 (C)	Pub	904	5,440	3,945
Humphreys College; Stockton, Calif. 95207	414 (C)	P	3,730	3,730	3,730
Hunter College. See New York, City University of					
Huntingdon College; Montgomery, Ala. 36194	866 (C)	P	6,500	6,500	3,200
Huntington College; Huntington, Ind. 46750	545 (C)	P	7,770	7,770	3,100
Huron University; Huron, S.D. 57350	602 (C)	P	6,150	6,150	2,816
Husson College; Bangor, Me. 04401	1,846 (C)	P	7,320	7,320	3,770
Huston-Tillotson College; Austin, Tex. 78702	502 (C)	P	4,230	4,230	3,679
Idaho, College of; Caldwell, Idaho 83605	581 (C)	P	10,152	10,152	2,710
Idaho, University of; Moscow, Idaho 83843	7,210 (C)	Pub	1,236	3,746	2,808
Idaho State University; Pocatello, Idaho 83209	6,047 (C)	Pub	1,086	2,986	2,667
Illinois, Univ. of, at Chicago; Chicago, Ill. 60680	16,465 (C)	Pub	2,730	6,270	4,100
Illinois, Univ. of, at Urbana-Champaign; Urbana, Ill. 61801	26,445 (C)	Pub	2,846	6,385	3,658
Illinois Benedictine College; Lisle, Ill. 60532	1,623 (C)	P	8,850	8,850	3,605
Illinois College; Jacksonville, Ill. 62650	813 (C)	P	6,600	6,600	3,250
Illinois Institute of Technology; Chicago, Ill. 60616	2,612 (C)	P	12,690	12,690	4,350
Illinois State University; Normal, Ill. 61761	19,651 (C)	Pub	2,306	5,734	2,560
Illinois Wesleyan University; Bloomington, Ill. 61702	1,744 (C)	P	11,015	11,015	3,695
Immaculata College; Immaculata, Pa. 19345	2,100 (W)	P	8,500	8,500	4,400
Incarnate Word College; San Antonio, Tex. 78209	2,141 (C)	P	7,200	7,200	3,500
Indiana Institute of Technology; Fort Wayne, Ind. 46803	936 (C)	P	5,850	5,850	3,030
Indianapolis, University of; Indianapolis, Ind. 46227	2,788 (C)	P	9,020	9,020	3,470
Indiana Institute of Technology; Fort Wayne, Ind. 46803	936 (C)	P	7,200	7,200	3,500
Indiana State University; Terre Haute, Ind. 47809	10,308 (C)	Pub	2,104	5,056	3,332
Indiana University of Pennsylvania; Indiana, Pa. 15705	13,000 (C)	Pub	2,524	4,380	2,350
Indiana University-Bloomington; Bloomington, Ind. 47405	26,685 (C)	Pub	2,368	6,900	3,370
Indiana University-East; Richmond, Ind. 47374	1,860 (C)	Pub	1,490	3,668	n.a.
Indiana University-Kokomo; Kokomo, Ind. 46902	2,857 (C)	Pub	1,790	4,512	n.a.
Indiana University-Northwest; Gary, Ind. 46408	4,325 (C)	Pub	1,836	4,177	n.a.
Indiana University-Purdue University at Fort Wayne; Fort Wayne, Ind. 46805	10,961 (C)	Pub	2,216	3,934	n.a.
Indiana University-Purdue University at Indianapolis; Indianapolis, Ind. 46202-5143	20,087 (C)	Pub	1,971	5,777	n.a.
Indiana University-South Bend; South Bend, Ind. 46634	5,799 (C)	Pub	1,895	4,617	n.a.
Indiana University-Southeast; New Albany, Ind. 47150	5,182 (C)	Pub	1,790	4,512	n.a.
Indiana Wesleyan University; Marion, Ind. 46953	1,656 (C)	P	7,590	7,590	3,392
Industrial Engineering College of Chicago; Chicago, Ill. 60601	120 (C)	P	4,420	4,420	n.a.
Insurance, College of; New York, N.Y. 10007	650 (C)	P	8,790	8,790	6,280
Inter-American University-Arecibo Regional College; Arecibo, P.R. 00612	3,715 (C)	P	2,445	2,445	n.a.
International Bible College; Florence, Ala. 35630	119 (C)	P	2,920	2,920	2,500
International Institute of A.C.E.; Lewisville, Tex. 75067	75 (C)	P	2,000	2,000	2,800
International Institute of the Americas of World University; Carolina, P.R. 00628	4,600 (C)	P	2,280	2,280	n.a.
International Training, School for; Brattleboro, Vt. 05301	60 (C)	P	9,820	9,820	3,578

Institution and location	Enrollment	Control	Tuition ($) Res.	Nonres.	Rm/Bd ($)
Iona College; New Rochelle, N.Y. 10801	3,420 (C)	P	9,090	9,090	5,900
Iowa, University of; Iowa City, Iowa 52242	20,160 (C)	Pub	1,952	6,470	2,920
Iowa State University; Ames, Iowa 50011	21,188 (C)	Pub	1,952	6,406	2,870
Iowa Wesleyan College; Mount Pleasant, Iowa 52641	914 (C)	P	7,800	7,800	3,000
Ithaca College; Ithaca, N.Y. 14850	6,267 (C)	p	12,040	12,040	5,100
ITT Technical Institute; West Covina, Calif. 91790-2767	700 (C)	P	6,490	6,490	n.a.
Jackson College for Women. *See* Tufts University					
Jackson State Universityi; Jackson, Miss. 39217	6,051 (C)	Pub	1,786	2,968	2,424
Jacksonville State University; Jacksonville, Ala. 36265	7,272 (C)	Pub	1,420	2,130	2,354
Jacksonville University; Jacksonville, Fla. 32211	2,099 (C)	P	8,245	8,245	3,840
James Madison University; Harrisonburg, Va. 22807	9,860 (C)	Pub	3,298	6,650	4,102
Jamestown College; Jamestown, N.D. 58401	841 (C)	P	6,670	6,670	2,980
Jarvis Christian College; Hawkins, Tex. 75765	560 (C)	P	4,015	4,015	2,999
Jersey City State College; Jersey City, N.J. 07305	5,728 (C)	Pub	2,212	2,902	4,450
Jewish Theological Seminary of America; New York, N.Y. 10027	134 (C)	P	5,910	5,910	5,720
John Brown University; Siloam Springs, Ark. 72761	912 (C)	P	5,390	5,390	3,060
John Carroll University; University Heights, Ohio 44118	3,400 (C)	P	9,253	9,253	5,050
John F. Kennedy University-Evenings; Orinda, Calif. 94563	327 (C)	P	5,160	5,160	n.a.
John Jay Coll. of Criminal Justice. *See* New York, City Univ. of					
Johns Hopkins Universtiy; Baltimore, Md. 21218	2,898 (C)	P	16,400	16,400	6,120
Johnson and Wales University; Providence, R.I. 02903	7,019 (C)	P	8,235	8,235	4,000
Johnson Bible College; Knoxville, Tenn. 37998	409 (C)	P	3,350	3,350	2,645
Johnson C. Smith University; Charlotte, N.C. 28216	1,197 (C)	P	5,876	5,876	2,158
Johnson State College; Johnson, Vt. 05656	1,200 (C)	Pub	2,870	6,152	4,086
Johnston College, Calif. *See* Redlands, University of					
John Wesley College; High Point, N.C. 27260	67 (C)	P	3,639	3,639	4,400
Jones College—Jacksonville; Jacksonville, Fla. 32211	1,700 (C)	P	3,240	3,240	n.a.
Jordan College; Cedar Springs, Mich. 49319	2,322 (C)	P	4,340	4,340	n.a.
Judson College; Elgin, Ill. 60120	498 (C)	P	8,090	8,090	4,090
Judson College; Marion, Ala. 36756	411 (W)	P	4,750	4,750	3,090
Juilliard School; New York, N.Y. 10023	485 (C)	P	10,350	10,350	5,830
Juniata College; Huntingdon, Pa. 16652	1,134 (C)	P	12,470	12,470	3,690
Kalamazoo College; Kalamazoo, Mich. 49007	1,265 (C)	P	12,719	12,719	4,053
Kansas, University of; Lawrence, Kan. 66045	19,261 (C)	Pub	1,546	4,670	2,500
Kansas, University of, Medical Center; Kansas City, Kan. 66103	597 (C)	Pub	1,358	4,482	n.a.
Kansas City Art Institute; Kansas City, Mo. 64111	533 (C)	P	11,260	11,260	3,500
Kansas City College and Bible School; Overland Park, Kan. 66204	49 (C)	P	2,275	2,275	2,450
Kansas Newman College; Wichita, Kan. 67213	756 (C)	P	6,523	6,523	3,168
Kansas State University; Manhattan, Kan. 66506	20,110 (C)	Pub	1,699	5,377	2,680
Kansas Wesleyan College; Salina, Kan. 67401	550 (C)	P	6,220	6,220	2,900
Kean College of New Jersey; Union, N.J. 07083	10,907 (C)	Pub	1,950	2,640	2,920
Keene State College; Keene, N.H. 03431	3,512 (C)	Pub	2,544	6,394	3,430
Kendall College; Evanston, Ill. 60201	371 (C)	P	7,005	7,005	4,473
Kendall College of Art and Design; Grand Rapids, Mich. 49503	742 (C)	P	8,124	8,124	n.a.
Kennesaw College, Marietta, Ga. 30061	8,404 (C)	Pub	1,461	4,041	n.a.
Kent State University; Kent, Ohio 44242	19,636 (C)	Pub	3,006	6,006	3,008
Kentucky, University of; Lexington, Ky. 40506	17,300 (C)	Pub	1,844	5,084	3,534
Kentucky Christian College; Grayson, Ky. 41143	479 (C)	P	3,250	3,250	2,950
Kentucky State University; Frankfurt, Ky. 40601	2,425 (C)	Pub	1,452	4,051	2,468
Kentucky Wesleyan College; Owensboro, Ky. 42301	711 (C)	P	6,690	6,690	3,760
Kenyon College; Gambier, Ohio 43022	1,530 (C)	P	16,050	16,050	3,375
Keuka College; Keuka Park, N.Y. 14478	651 (C)	P	7,660	7,660	3,580
King College; Bristol, Tenn. 37620	535 (C)	P	6,650	6,650	3,050
Kings College; Briarcliff Manor, N.Y. 10510	508 (C)	P	8,310	8,310	3,820
King's College; Wilkes-Barre, Pa 18711	2,257 (C)	P	8,500	8,500	4,120
Knox College; Galesburg, Ill. 61401	1,000 (C)	P	12,765	12,765	3,675
Knoxville College; Knoxville, Tenn. 37921	1,225 (C)	P	5,100	5,100	3,600
Kutztown University; Kutztown, Pa. 19530	6,883 (C)	Pub	2,552	4,586	2,548
Laboratory Institute of Merchandising; New York, N.Y. 10022	258 (C)	P	8,300	8,300	n.a.
Lafayette College; Easton, Pa. 18042	2,323 (C)	P	15,475	15,475	4,900
LaGrange College; LaGrange, Ga. 30240	961 (C)	P	5,127	5,127	3,000
Lake Erie College; Painesville, Ohio 44077	613 (C)	P	8,480	8,480	4,000
Lake Forest College; Lake Forest, Ill. 60045	1,121 (C)	P	13,885	13,885	3,155
Lakeland College; Sheboygan, Wis. 53082	1,967 (C)	P	8,050	8,050	3,250
Lake Superior State University; Sault Ste. Marie, Mich. 49783	3,078 (C)	Pub	1,998	4,119	3,454
Lamar University; Beaumont, Tex. 77710	11,174 (C)	Pub	890	3,400	2,800
Lambuth College; Jackson, Tenn. 38301	804 (C)	P	4,600	4,600	3,000
Lancaster Bible College; Lancaster, Pa. 17601	395 (C)	P	6,560	6,560	2,940
Lander College; Greenwood S.C. 29649	2,309 (C)	Pub	3,180	3,180	2,430
Lane College; Jackson, Tenn. 38301	525 (C)	P	4,357	4,357	2,473
Langston University; Langston, Okla. 73050	2,103 (C)	Pub	1,103	3,041	2,192
Laredo State University; Laredo, Tex. 78040-9960	541 (C)	Pub	1,338	4,398	n.a.
La Roche College; Pittsburgh, Pa. 15237	1,868 (C)	P	7,138	7,138	3,878
La Salle University; Philadelphia, Pa. 19141	3,396 (C)	P	10,250	10,250	4,800

Institution and location	Enrollment	Control	Tuition ($) Res.	Tuition ($) Nonres.	Rm/Bd ($)
Lasell College; Newton, Mass. 02166	444 (W)	P	8,575	8,575	5,175
La Verne, University of; La Verne, Calif 91750	1,485 (C)	P	10,060	10,060	3,646
Lawrence Technological University; Southfield, Mich. 48075	5,182 (C)	P	5,826	5,826	4,246
Lawrence University; Appleton, Wis. 54912	1,176 (C)	P	14,685	14,685	3,363
Lebanon Valley College; Annville, Pa. 17003	1,211 (C)	P	11,750	11,750	4,325
Lee College; Cleveland, Tenn. 37311	1,738 (C)	P	4,379	4,379	2,774
Lee College of the University of Judaism; Los Angeles, Calif. 90077	70 (C)	P	7,200	7,200	5,140
Lehigh University; Bethlehem, Pa. 18015	4,493 (C)	P	15,650	15,650	4,940
Le Moyne College; Syracuse, N.Y. 13214-1399	2,354 (C)	P	9,270	9,270	4,220
Le Moyne-Owen College; Memphis, Tenn. 38126	955 (C)	P	3,650	3,650	n.a.
Lenoir-Rhyne College; Hickory, N.C. 28603	1,544 (C)	P	8,584	8,584	3,326
Lesley College; Cambridge, Mass. 02138-2790	571 (W)	P	10,140	10,140	4,770
LeTourneau University; Longview, Tex. 75607	773 (C)	P	7,250	7,250	3,640
Lewis and Clark College; Portland, Ore. 97219	1,896 (C)	P	13,470	13,470	4,653
Lewis-Clark State College; Lewiston, Idaho 83501	2,275 (C)	Pub	1,118	2,206	2,700
Lewis University; Romeoville, Ill. 60441	3,091 (C)	P	7,850	7,850	3,965
Liberty University; Lynchburg, Va. 24506	8,367 (C)	P	6,045	6,045	3,970
L.I.F.E. Bible College; Los Angeles, Calif. 90086-2529	370 (C)	P	4,090	4,090	2,800
L.I.F.E. Bible College East; Christiansburg, V.A. 24073	112 (C)	P	2,160	2,160	2,240
Limestone College, Gaffney, S.C. 29340	295 (C)	P	6,464	6,464	3,122
Lincoln Christian College; Lincoln, Ill. 62656	327 (C)	P	3,965	3,965	2,470
Lincoln Memorial University; Harrogate, Tenn. 37752	1,609 (C)	P	4,780	4,780	2,430
Lincoln University; San Francisco, Calif. 94118	159 (C)	P	1,000	1,000	n.a.
Lincoln University; Jefferson City, Mo. 65101	3,242 (C)	Pub	1,930	3,840	2,728
Lincoln University; Lincoln University, Pa. 19352	1,180 (C)	Pub	2,510	3,730	2,700
Lindenwood College; St. Charles, Mo. 63301	1,412 (C)	P	8,180	8,180	4,400
Lindsey Wilson College; Columbia, Ky. 42728	1,060 (C)	P	5,168	5,168	3,280
Linfield College; McMinnville, Ore. 97128	1,590 (C)	P	11,050	11,050	3,500
Livingstone College; Salisbury, N.C. 28144	580 (C)	P	5,028	5,028	3,140
Livingstone University; Livingston, Ala. 35470	1,641 (C)	Pub	1,524	1,524	2,055
Lock Haven University of Pennsylvania; Lock Haven, Pa. 17745	3,521 (C)	Pub	2,318	4,214	2,274
Lockyear College; Evansville, Ind. 47706	721 (C)	P	2,850	2,850	n.a.
Loma Linda University; Loma Linda, Calif. 92350	2,322 (C)	P	9,360	9,360	3,246
Loma Linda University-La Sierra; Riverside, Calif. 92515	1,800 (C)	P	9,360	9,360	3,246
Long Island University; Greenvale, N.Y. 11548:					
Brooklyn Campus; Brooklyn, N.Y. 11201	3,441 (C)	P	8,100	8,100	6,000
C.W. Post Campus; Greenvale, N.Y. 11548	4,906 (C)	P	8,700	8,700	4,580
Southampton Campus; Southampton, N.Y. 11968	1,162 (C)	P	9,100	9,100	4,500
Longwood College; Farmville, Va. 23901	2,947 (C)	Pub	3,190	6,790	3,554
Loras College; Dubuque, Iowa 52001	1,807 (C)	P	9,115	9,115	3,200
Louisiana College; Pineville, La. 71359	1,017 (C)	P	3,300	3,300	2,808
Louisiana State Univ. and A&M Coll.; Baton Rouge, La. 70803	20,792 (C)	Pub	2,043	5,243	2,710
LSU-Shreveport; Shreveport, La. 71115	3,594 (C)	Pub	1,910	4,830	n.a.
Louisiana Tech University; Ruston, La. 71272	9,078 (C)	Pub	1,841	2,996	2,115
Louisville, University of; Louisville, Ky, 40292	17,835 (C)	Pub	1,740	4,980	3,040
Lourdes College; Sylvania, Ohio 43560	886 (C)	P	4,680	4,680	n.a.
Lowell, University of; Lowell, Mass. 01854	11,328 (C)	Pub	3,168	6,685	3,990
Loyola College; Baltimore, Md. 21210	3,134 (C)	P	9,640	9,640	5,080
Loyola Marymount University; Los Angeles, Calif. 90045	4,076 (C)	P	11,367	11,367	5,671
Loyola University; New Orleans, La. 70118	3,642 (C)	P	9,370	9,370	4,848
Loyola University of Chicago; Chicago, Ill. 60611	6,037 (C)	P	9,270	9,270	4,908
Lubbock Christian University; Lubbock, Tex. 79407	1,035 (C)	P	5,630	5,630	2,330
Lutheran Bible Institute of Seattle; Issaquah, Wash. 98027	148 (C)	P	2,455	2,455	3,240
Luther College; Decorah, Iowa 52101	2,265 (C)	P	10,600	10,600	3,300
Lycoming College; Williamsport, Pa. 17701	1,271 (C)	P	11,000	11,000	3,975
Lynchburg College; Lynchburg, Va. 24501	1,958 (C)	P	10,330	10,330	5,050
Lyndon State College; Lyndonville, Vt. 05851	1,067 (C)	Pub	4,801	7,033	4,290
Macalester College; St. Paul, Minn. 55105	1,744 (C)	P	13,331	13,331	3,970
MacMurray College; Jacksonville, Ill. 62650	569 (C)	P	8,150	8,150	3,350
Madonna College; Livonia, Mich. 48150	4,055 (C)	P	4,050	4,050	3,200
Maharishi International University; Fairfield, Iowa 52556	360 (C)	P	7,250	7,250	2,532
Maine, Univ. of, at Augusta; Augusta, Me. 04330	4,773 (C)	Pub	1,920	4,650	n.a.
Maine, Univ. of, at Farmington; Farmington, Me. 04938	2,438 (C)	Pub	2,410	5,470	3,586
Maine, Univ. of, at Fort Kent; Fort Kent, Me. 04743-1292	576 (C)	Pub	1,920	4,650	3,395
Maine, Univ. of, at Machias; Machias, Me. 04654	1,008 (C)	Pub	1,920	4,650	3,090
Maine, Univ. of, at Orono; Orono, Me. 04469	11,262 (C)	Pub	2,679	6,843	4,241
Maine, Univ. of, at Presque Isle; Presque Isle, Me. 04769	1,394 (C)	Pub	1,920	4,650	3,090
Maine Maritime Academy—College of Engineering, Transportation, and Management; Castine, Me. 04420	555 (C)	Pub	3,320	3,320	4,000
Malone College; Canton, Ohio 44709	1,515 (C)	P	7,860	7,860	3,000
Manchester College; North Manchester, Ind. 46962	1,113 (C)	P	8,270	8,270	3,246
Manhattan Christian College; Manhattan, Kan. 66502	206 (C)	P	3,180	3,180	2,434
Manhattan College; Riverdale, N.Y. 10471	3,146 (C)	P	11,100	11,100	5,800

Institution and location	Enrollment	Control	Tuition ($) Res.	Tuition ($) Nonres.	Rm/Bd ($)
Manhattan School of Music; New York, N.Y. 10027	398 (C)	P	10,250	10,250	n.a.
Manhattanville College; Purchase, N.Y. 10577	1,004 (C)	P	12,690	12,690	5,600
Mankato State University; Mankato, Minn. 56001	13,141 (C)	Pub	1,976	3,224	2,388
Mannes College of Music; New York, N.Y. 10024	14 (C)	P	10,030	10,030	6,200
Mansfield University of Pennsylvania; Mansfield, Pa. 16933	2,661 (C)	Pub	2,908	4,764	2,316
Marian College; Indianapolis, Ind. 46222	1,233 (C)	P	7,584	7,584	3,104
Marian College of Fond du Lac; Fond du Lac, Wis. 54935	1,168 (C)	P	7,400	7,400	3,300
Marietta College; Marietta, Ohio 45750	1,285 (C)	P	16,817	16,817	5,155
Marist College; Poughkeepsie, N.Y. 12601	2,941 (C)	P	9,195	9,195	5,100
Marlboro College; Marlboro, Vt. 05344	275 (C)	P	15,000	15,000	5,150
Marquette University; Milwaukee, Wis. 53233	9,053 (C)	P	8,284	8,284	3,450
Mars Hill College; Mars Hill, N.C. 28754	1,097 (C)	P	6,650	6,650	3,300
Marshall University; Huntington, W. Va. 25705	10,581 (C)	Pub	2,712	4,042	3,630
Martin University; Indianapolis, Ind. 46218	475 (C)	P	4,500	4,500	n.a.
Mary, University of; Bismarck, N.D. 58504	1,190 (C)	P	5,568	5,568	2,448
Mary Baldwin College; Staunton, Va. 24401	677 (W)	P	9,165	9,165	6,175
Marygrove College; Detroit, Mich. 48221	1,099 (C)	P	6,420	6,420	3,360
Mary Hardin-Baylor, University of; Belton, Tex. 76513	1,812 (C)	P	4,400	4,400	2,680
Maryland, Univ. of-Baltimore County; Baltimore, Md. 21228	8,542 (C)	Pub	2,380	6,330	3,860
Maryland, Univ. of-College Park; College Park, Md. 20742	22,553 (C)	Pub	2,269	6,325	4,712
Maryland, Univ. of-Eastern Shore; Princess Anne, Md. 21853	1,925 (C)	Pub	2,114	5,764	3,534
Maryland, Univ. of, University College; College Park, Md. 20742	11,715 (C)	Pub	3,865	4,015	n.a.
Maryland Institute-College of Art; Baltimore, Md. 21217	850 (C)	P	10,600	10,600	4,125
Marylhurst College; Marylhurst, Ore. 97036	865 (C)	P	7,200	7,200	n.a.
Marymount College; Tarrytown, N.Y. 10591	1,108 (W)	P	10,200	10,200	5,750
Marymount Manhattan College; New York, N.Y. 10021	1,484 (W)	P	9,258	9,258	4,200
Marymount Univ.; Arlington, Va. 22207	1,878 (C)	P	9,707	9,707	4,650
Maryville College; Maryville, Tenn. 37801	855 (C)	P	7,750	7,750	3,550
Maryville College-St. Louis; St. Louis, Mo. 63141	3,143 (C)	P	7,800	7,800	3,850
Mary Washington College; Fredericksburg, Va. 22401	3,395 (C)	Pub	2,618	6,076	4,250
Marywood College; Scranton, Pa. 18509	2,052 (C)	P	8,250	8,250	3,800
Massachusetts, Univ. of-Amherst; Amherst, Mass. 01003	17,961 (C)	Pub	3,200	8,222	3,640
Massachusetts, Univ. of-Boston; Boston, Mass. 02125	10,336 (C)	Pub	2,200	6,400	n.a.
Massachusetts College of Art; Boston, Mass. 02115	1,109 (C)	Pub	3,311	7,101	5,142
Massachusetts College of Pharmacy and Allied Health Sciences; Boston, Mass. 02115	785 (C)	P	8,500	8,500	6,115
Massachusetts Institute of Technology; Cambridge, Mass. 02139	4,242 (C)	P	16,900	16,900	4,076
Massachusetts Maritime Academy; Buzzards Bay, Mass. 02532	600 (C)	Pub	2,010	5,980	3,800
Master's College, The; Newhall, Calif. 91322	845 (C)	P	7,180	7,180	3,810
Mayville State University; Mayville, N.D. 58257	764 (C)	Pub	1,482	3,954	2,054
McKendree College; Lebanon, Ill. 62258	1,100 (C)	P	6,626	6,626	3,420
McMurry College; Abilene, Tex. 79697	1,711 (C)	P	6,255	6,255	3,371
McNeese State University; Lake Charles, La. 70609	6,662 (C)	Pub	1,626	3,176	2,160
McPherson College; McPherson, Kan. 67460	462 (C)	P	6,660	6,660	3,110
Medaille College; Buffalo, N.Y. 14214	1,105 (C)	P	3,590	3,590	n.a.
Medical College of Georgia; Augusta, Ga. 30912	780 (C)	Pub	1,962	5,406	2,590
Medical College of South Carolina; Charleston, S.C. 29425	964 (C)	Pub	1,750	3,500	3,300
Memphis College of Art; Memphis, Tenn. 38112	251 (C)	P	8,140	8,140	4,000
Memphis State University; Memphis, Tenn. 38152	16,207 (C)	Pub	1,472	4,675	2,740
Menlo College; Atherton, Calif. 94027-4185	490 (C)	P	12,100	12,100	6,320
Mercer University; Macon, Ga. 31207	2,596 (C)	P	9,450	9,450	3,780
Mercer University-Atlanta; Atlanta, Ga. 30341	1,405 (C)	P	5,600	5,600	n.a.
Mercy College; Dobbs Ferry, N.Y. 10522	5,283 (C)	P	6,990	6,990	n.a.
Mercyhurst College; Erie, Pa. 16546	2,086 (C)	P	8,754	8,754	3,345
Meredith College; Raleigh, N.C. 27607	2,038 (W)	P	5,720	5,720	2,820
Merrimack College; North Andover, Mass. 01845	2,240 (C)	P	10,350	10,350	5,700
Mesa State College; Grand Junction, Colo. 81502	3,242 (C)	Pub	1,546	4,094	3,144
Messiah College; Grantham, Pa. 17027	2,252 (C)	P	8,700	8,700	4,380
Methodist College; Fayetteville, N.C. 28311-1499	1,190 (C)	P	7,700	7,700	3,100
Metropolitan State College; Denver, Colo. 80204	16,262 (C)	Pub	1,710	4,435	n.a.
Metropolitan State University; St. Paul, Minn. 55101	5,535 (C)	Pub	1,740	1,740	n.a.
Miami, University of; Coral Gables, Fla. 33124	8,714 (C)	P	14,095	14,095	5,575
Miami Christian College; Miami, Fla. 33167	173 (C)	P	5,170	5,170	2,760
Miami University; Oxford, Ohio 45056	14,467 (C)	Pub	6,880	6,880	3,460
Michigan, Univ. of-Ann Arbor; Ann Arbor, Mich. 48109	21,811 (C)	Pub	3,366	11,874	3,853
Michigan, Univ. of-Dearborn; Dearborn, Mich. 48128	6,737 (C)	Pub	3,744	11,988	n.a.
Michigan, Univ. of-Flint; Flint, Mich. 48502	6,174 (C)	Pub	2,104	6,860	n.a.
Michigan Christian College; Rochester Hills, Mich. 48307	282 (C)	P	4,200	4,200	3,030
Michigan State University; East Lansing, Mich. 48824	34,829 (C)	Pub	3,302	8,143	3,168
Michigan Technological University; Houghton, Mich. 49931	6,107 (C)	Pub	2,436	5,907	3,186
Mid-America Bible College; Oklahoma City, Okla. 73170	236 (C)	P	3,640	3,640	2,936
Mid-America Nazarene College; Olathe, Kan. 66061	1,189 (C)	P	5,090	5,090	2,990
Middlebury College; Middlebury, Vt. 05753	1,950 (C)	P	20,460	20,460	—

Institution and location	Enrollment	Control	Tuition ($) Res.	Tuition ($) Nonres.	Rm/Bd ($)
Middle Tennessee State University; Murfreesboro, Tenn. 37132	12,744 (C)	Pub	1,346	4,550	1,914
Midland Lutheran College; Fremont, Neb. 68025	960 (C)	P	8,100	8,100	2,550
Midway College; Midway, Ky. 40347	335 (W)	P	5,840	5,840	3,550
Midwestern State University; Wichita Falls, Tex. 76308	4,805 (C)	Pub	1,190	4,430	2,830
Miles College; Birmingham, Ala. 35208	566 (C)	P	3,760	3,760	2,300
Millersville University of Pennsylvania; Millersville, Pa. 17551	6,996 (C)	Pub	2,536	4,392	2,810
Milligan College; Milligan College, Tenn. 37682	600 (C)	P	6,214	6,214	2,736
Millikin University; Decatur, Ill. 62522	1,805 (C)	P	10,081	10,081	3,784
Millsaps College; Jackson, Miss. 39210	1,325 (C)	P	9,720	9,720	4,620
Mills College; Oakland, Calif. 94613	789 (W)	P	13,005	13,005	5,400
Milwaukee Institute of Art and Design; Milwaukee, Wis. 53202	408 (C)	P	7,600	7,600	n.a.
Milwaukee School of Engineering; Milwaukee, Wis. 53201-0644	1,808 (C)	P	9,150	9,150	3,225
Minneapolis Coll. of Art and Design; Minneapolis, Minn. 55404	629 (C)	P	10,300	10,300	3,610
Minnesota, Univ. of-Duluth; Duluth, Minn. 55812	7,800 (C)	Pub	2,614	5,000	3,066
Minnesota, Univ. of-Morris; Morris, Minn. 56267	2,021 (C)	Pub	2,585	6,089	2,835
Minnesota, Univ. of-Twin Cities; Minneapolis, Minn. 55455	29,082 (C)	Pub	2,337	5,341	2,900
Minnesota Bible College; Rochester, Minn. 55902	96 (C)	P	3,940	3,940	2,770
Minot State University; Minot, N.D. 58701	3,236 (C)	Pub	1,703	4,249	1,746
Mississippi, University of; University, Miss. 38677	7,589 (C)	Pub	2,059	3,240	2,934
Mississippi, Univ. of, Medical Center; Jackson, Miss. 39216	472 (C)	Pub	1,595	2,777	2,600
Mississippi College; Clinton, Miss. 39058	2,078 (C)	P	5,403	5,403	2,550
Mississippi State University; Mississippi State, Miss. 39762	11,123 (C)	Pub	2,223	3,685	2,800
Mississippi University for Women; Columbus, Miss. 39701	2,407 (C)	Pub	2,043	3,503	2,092
Mississippi Valley State University; Itta Bena, Miss. 38941	1,848 (C)	Pub	1,750	2,932	1,924
Missouri, Univ. of-Columbia; Columbia, Mo. 65211	18,763 (C)	Pub	2,230	6,253	3,004
Missouri, Univ. of-Kansas City; Kansas City, Mo. 64110	6,703 (C)	Pub	2,217	6,240	3,270
Missouri, Univ. of-Rolla; Rolla, Mo. 65401	4,126 (C)	Pub	2,340	6,138	3,100
Missouri, Univ. of-St. Louis; St. Louis, Mo. 63121	10,737 (C)	Pub	2,310	6,333	n.a.
Missouri Baptist College; St. Louis, Mo. 63141	951 (C)	P	5,820	5,820	2,650
Missouri Southern State College; Joplin, Mo. 64801	6,012 (C)	Pub	1,784	3,056	2,340
Missouri Valley College; Marshall, Mo. 65340	1,130 (C)	P	8,178	8,178	4,656
Missouri Western State College; St. Joseph, Mo. 64507	4,338 (C)	Pub	1,648	3,112	2,154
Mobile College; Mobile, Ala. 36613	1,032 (C)	P	4,650	4,650	2,900
Molloy College; Rockville Centre, N.Y. 11570	1,476 (C)	P	8,164	8,164	n.a.
Monmouth College; Monmouth, Ill. 61462	655 (C)	P	12,450	12,450	3,350
Monmouth College; West Long Branch, N.J. 07764	3,078 (C)	P	10,470	10,470	5,000
Montana, University of; Missoula, Mont. 59812	8,135 (C)	Pub	1,447	3,520	3,029
Montana College of Mineral Science and Technology; Butte, Mont. 59701	1,690 (C)	Pub	1,309	3,382	3,000
Montana State University; Bozeman, Mont. 59717	10,024 (C)	Pub	1,764	3,837	3,000
Montclair State College; Upper Montclair, N.J. 07043	10,200 (C)	Pub	2,400	3,392	4,132
Monterey Institute of Intl. Studies; Monterey, Calif. 93940	108 (C)	P	11,345	11,345	n.a.
Montevallo, University of; Montevallo, Ala. 35115	2,648 (C)	Pub	1,954	3,784	2,820
Montreat-Anderson College; Montreat, N.C. 28757	386 (C)	P	5,250	5,250	3,000
Moody Bible Institute; Chicago, Ill. 60610	1,434 (C)	P	900	900	3,750
Moore College of Art and Design; Philadelphia, Pa. 19103	590 (W)	P	10,700	10,700	4,600
Moorhead State University; Moorhead, Minn. 56560	8,709 (C)	Pub	1,758	3,062	2,256
Moravian College; Bethlehem, Pa. 18018	1,215 (C)	P	12,698	12,698	4,044
Morehead State University; Morehead, Ky. 40351	7,083 (C)	Pub	1,420	4,020	2,900
Morehouse College; Atlanta, Ga. 30314	2,720 (M)	P	6,210	6,210	4,462
Morgan State University; Baltimore, Md. 21239	3,878 (C)	Pub	2,124	4,048	4,380
Morningside College; Sioux City, Iowa 51106	1,282 (C)	P	9,206	9,206	2,980
Morris Brown College; Atlanta, Ga. 30314	1,500 (C)	P	6,550	6,550	3,800
Morris College; Sumter, S.C. 29150	760 (C)	P	3,939	3,939	2,387
Morrison College/Reno Business College; Reno, Nev. 89503	400 (C)	P	8,235	8,235	n.a.
Mount Angel Seminary; St. Benedict, Ore. 97373	27 (M)	P	3,300	3,300	2,900
Mount Holyoke College; South Hadley, Mass. 01075	1,954 (W)	P	15,050	15,050	4,600
Mount Ida College; Newton Centre, Mass. 02159	1,400 (C)	P	8,300	8,300	5,865
Mount Marty College; Yankton, S.D. 57078	685 (C)	P	6,690	6,690	2,705
Mount Mary College; Milwaukee, Wis. 53222	1,418 (W)	P	6,950	6,950	2,447
Mount Mercy College; Cedar Rapids, Iowa 52402	1,529 (C)	P	7,750	7,750	3,150
Mount Olive College; Mount Olive, N.C. 28365	756 (C)	P	6,600	6,600	2,550
Mount St. Joseph, College of; Mount St. Joseph, Ohio 45051	2,398 (C)	P	8,170	8,170	3,810
Mount Saint Mary College; Newburgh, N.Y. 12550	1,239 (C)	P	7,335	7,335	4,300
Mount Saint Mary's College; Emmitsburg, Md. 21727	1,413 (C)	P	9,875	9,875	5,700
Mount St. Clare College; Clinton, Iowa 52732	325 (C)	P	7,267	7,267	3,230
Mount St. Mary's College; Los Angeles, Calif. 90049	910 (W)	P	9,250	9,250	4,535
Mount Saint Vincent, College of; New York, N.Y. 10471	1,043 (C)	P	9,920	9,920	4,900
Mount Senario College; Ladysmith, Wis. 54848	403 (C)	P	6,300	6,300	2,625
Mount Union College; Alliance, Ohio 44601	1,360 (C)	P	11,320	11,320	3,280
Mount Vernon College; Washington, D.C. 20007	528 (W)	P	12,510	12,510	6,090
Mount Vernon Nazarene College; Mount Vernon, Ohio 43050	1,061 (C)	P	5,750	5,750	3,350
Muhlenberg College; Allentown, Pa. 18104	1,615 (C)	P	15,180	15,180	4,260
Multnomah School of the Bible; Portland, Ore. 97220	508 (C)	P	5,090	5,090	3,056

Institution and location	Enrollment	Control	Tuition ($) Res.	Tuition ($) Nonres.	Rm/Bd ($)
Mundelein College; Chicago, Ill. 60660	917 (W)	P	9,260	9,260	4,730
Murray State University; Murray, Ky. 42071	6,296 (C)	Pub	1,410	5,000	2,490
Museum of Fine Arts, School of the-Tufts University; Boston, Mass. 02115	690 (C)	P	10,355	10,355	n.a.
Museum Art School, Portland. *See* Pacific Northwest College of Art					
Muskingum College; Concord, Ohio 43762	1,092 (C)	P	11,855	11,855	3,510
NAES College; Chicago, Ill. 60659	119 (C)	P	4,300	4,300	n.a.
Naropa Institute; Boulder, Colo. 80302	135 (C)	P	7,580	7,580	n.a.
Nathaniel Hawthorne College. *See* Hawthorne College					
National College-Albuquerque; Albuquerque, N.M. 87108-7439	134 (C)	P	5,472	5,472	n.a.
National College, Colorado Springs Branch; Colorado Springs, Colo. 80909	207 (C)	P	3,800	3,800	n.a.
National College; Rapid City, S.D. 57709	585 (C)	P	5,460	5,460	2,790
National-Louis University; Evanston, Ill. 60201	2,910 (C)	P	6,975	6,975	4,065
National University; San Diego, Calif. 92108	7,121 (C)	P	5,950	5,950	n.a.
Nazareth College in Kalamazoo; Nazareth, Mich. 49001-1282	564 (C)	P	7,664	7,664	3,076
Nazareth College of Rochester; Rochester, N.Y. 14610	1,370 (C)	P	8,750	8,750	4,480
Nebraska, University of-Kearney; Kearney, Neb. 68849	7,458 (C)	Pub	1,415	2,135	2,030
Nebraska, University of-Lincoln; Lincoln, Neb. 68588-0415	19,791 (C)	Pub	1,284	3,492	3,125
Nebraska, University of-Omaha; Omaha, Neb. 68182	14,057 (C)	Pub	1,358	3,669	n.a.
Nebraska Christian College; Norfolk, Neb. 68701	139 (C)	P	2,600	2,600	2,240
Nebraska Wesleyan University; Lincoln, Neb. 68504	1,682 (C)	P	8,227	8,227	2,950
Neumann College; Aston, Pa. 19014	1,206 (C)	P	7,800	7,800	n.a.
Nevada, University of-Las Vegas; Las Vegas, Nev. 89154	16,320 (C)	Pub	1,426	4,726	4,200
Nevada, University of-Reno; Reno, Nev. 89557	7,507 (C)	Pub	1,593	3,600	3,720
Newberry College; Newberry, S.C. 29108	701 (C)	P	7,400	7,400	3,000
New College of California; San Francisco, Calif. 94110	200 (C)	P	5,850	5,850	n.a.
New College of the University of South Florida; Sarasota, Fla. 34243-2197	525 (C)	Pub	1,419	4,730	3,300
New England, University of; Biddeford, Me. 04005	801 (C)	P	9,750	9,750	4,300
New England College; Henniker, N.H. 03242	1,073 (C)	P	11,290	11,290	4,700
New England College-Arundel Campus; England	220 (C)	P	10,570	10,570	3,420
New England Conservatory of Music; Boston, Mass. 02115	348 (C)	P	12,840	12,840	6,150
New England Institute of Technology; Warwick, R.I. 02886	1,950 (C)	P	7,425	7,425	n.a.
New Hampshire, University of; Durham, N.H. 03824	10,121 (C)	Pub	3,014	8,804	3,276
New Hampshire College; Manchester, N.H. 03104	1,897 (C)	P	10,008	10,008	4,635
New Haven, University of; West Haven, Conn. 06516	3,839 (C)	P	9,640	9,640	5,000
New Jersey Institute of Technology; Newark, N.J. 07102	4,957 (C)	Pub	4,000	4,000	4,632
New Mexico, University of; Albuquerque, N.M. 87131	19,927 (C)	Pub	1,554	5,520	3,123
New Mexico Highlands University; Las Vegas, N.M. 87701	1,889 (C)	Pub	1,248	4,488	2,230
New Mexico Inst. of Mining & Technology; Socorro, N.M. 87801	1,311 (C)	Pub	1,393	4,842	3,026
New Mexico State University; Las Cruces, N.M. 88003-0001	12,312 (C)	Pub	1,488	5,184	2,588
New Orleans, University of; New Orleans, La. 70148	12,609 (C)	Pub	1,924	4,616	2,368
New Rochelle, College of-School of Arts & Sciences and School of Nursing; New Rochelle, N.Y. 10805	766 (W)	P	10,150	10,150	4,420
New School for Social Research Eugene Lang College; New York, N.Y. 10011	400 (C)	P	11,794	11,794	7,346
New York, City University of; New York, N.Y. 10021:					
Bernard M. Baruch College; New York, N.Y. 10010	12,835 (C)	Pub	1,250	4,050	n.a.
Brooklyn College; Brooklyn, N.Y. 11210	12,000 (C)	Pub	1,250	4,050	n.a.
City College; New York, N.Y. 10031	11,206 (C)	Pub	1,450	4,050	n.a.
College of Staten Island; Staten Island, N.Y. 10301	11,000 (C)	Pub	1,450	4,050	n.a.
Hunter College; New York, N.Y. 10021	14,866 (C)	Pub	1,450	4,050	3,200
John Jay College of Criminal Justice; New York, N.Y. 10019	8,090 (C)	Pub	1,316	4,150	n.a.
Lehman College; Bronx, N.Y. 10468	8,298 (C)	Pub	1,250	4,050	n.a.
Medgar Evers College; Brooklyn, N.Y. 11225	2,823 (C)	Pub	1,225	2,025	n.a.
New York City Technical College; Brooklyn, N.Y. 11201	10,323 (C)	Pub	1,274	4,054	n.a.
Queens College; Flushing, N.Y. 11367	17,500 (C)	Pub	1,433	4,233	n.a.
York College; Jamaica, N.Y. 11451	5,455 (C)	Pub	1,532	4,132	n.a.
New York, State University of; Albany, N.Y. 12246:					
SUNY-Albany; Albany, N.Y. 12222	11,870 (C)	Pub	1,350	4,700	3,301
SUNY-Buffalo; Buffalo, N.Y. 14214	18,831 (C)	Pub	1,525	4,875	4,020
SUNY-College at Brockport; Brockport, N.Y. 14420	7,096 (C)	Pub	1,586	4,936	3,690
SUNY-College at Buffalo; Buffalo, N.Y. 14222	10,520 (C)	Pub	1,465	4,815	3,090
SUNY-College at Cortland; Cortland, N.Y. 13045	3,467 (C)	Pub	1,350	4,700	3,610
SUNY-College at Fredonia; Fredonia, N.Y. 14063	4,473 (C)	Pub	1,529	4,879	3,580
SUNY-College at Geneseo; Geneseo, N.Y. 14454-1471	4,968 (C)	Pub	1,500	4,900	3,050
SUNY-College at New Paltz; New Paltz, N.Y. 12561	4,728 (C)	Pub	1,495	4,095	3,360
SUNY-College at Old Westbury; Old Westbury, N.Y. 11568	3,999 (C)	Pub	1,475	4,825	3,898
SUNY-College at Oneonta; Oneonta, N.Y. 13820	5,218 (C)	Pub	1,350	4,700	3,500
SUNY-College at Oswego; Oswego, N.Y. 13126	6,574 (C)	Pub	1,475	4,825	3,236
SUNY-College at Plattsburgh; Plattsburgh, N.Y. 12901	5,754 (C)	Pub	1,475	3,825	3,400
SUNY-College at Potsdam; Potsdam, N.Y. 13676	4,194 (C)	Pub	1,475	4,825	4,225

Institution and location	Enrollment	Control	Tuition ($) Res.	Tuition ($) Nonres.	Rm/Bd ($)
SUNY-College of Agriculture and Life Sciences at Cornell University; Ithaca, N.Y. 14853	2,970 (C)	Pub	6,472	11,972	5,414
SUNY-College of Environmental Science and Forestry; Syracuse, N.Y. 13210	942 (C)	Pub	1,460	4,760	5,210
SUNY-College of Human Ecology at Cornell University; Ithaca, N.Y. 14853	1,225 (C)	Pub	6,472	11,972	5,414
SUNY-College of Technology-Farmingdale; Farmingdale, N.Y. 11735	11,106 (C)	Pub	1,650	5,000	3,850
SUNY-Empire State College; Saratoga Springs, N.Y. 12866	7,072 (C)	Pub	2,081	7,106	n.a.
SUNY-Fashion Institute of Technology; New York, N.Y. 10001-5992	4,443 (C)	Pub	1,570	3,920	4,500
SUNY-Health Science Center at Syracuse; Syracuse, N.Y. 13210	304 (C)	Pub	1,475	4,825	4,102
SUNY-Institute of Technology at Utica/Rome; Utica, N.Y. 13054-3050	2,344 (C)	Pub	1,510	4,860	n.a.
SUNY-Maritime College; Throggs Neck, N.Y. 10465	688 (C)	Pub	1,350	4,700	3,632
SUNY-Purchase; Purchase, N.Y. 10577	4,587 (C)	Pub	1,650	5,000	3,590
SUNY-School of Industrial and Labor Relations at Cornell University; Ithaca, N.Y. 14853	625 (C)	Pub	6,472	11,972	5,414
SUNY-Stony Brook; Stony Brook, N.Y. 11794	11,403 (C)	Pub	1,350	4,700	3,894
SUNY-University Center at Binghamton; Binghamton, N.Y. 13901	9,310 (C)	Pub	1,943	5,293	4,474
New York City Technical Coll. See New York, City Univ. of					
New York Institute of Technology; Old Westbury, N.Y. 11568	6,428 (C)	P	6,700	6,700	n.a.
New York Institute of Technology Central Islip Campus; Central Islip, N.Y. 11722	1,616 (C)	P	6,770	6,770	4,400
New York Institute of Technology, Metropolitan Center; New York, N.Y. 10023	2,841 (C)	P	6,700	6,700	n.a.
New York School of Interior Design; New York, N.Y. 10022	643 (C)	P	10,115	10,115	n.a.
New York University; New York, N.Y. 10011	15,801 (C)	P	15,820	15,820	7,064
New York, University of the State of, Regents College Degrees; Albany, N.Y. 12230	13,305 (C)	Pub	425	425	n.a.
Niagara University; Niagara University, N.Y. 14109	2,425 (C)	P	9,030	9,030	2,060
Nicholls State University; Thibodaux, La. 70310	6,639 (C)	Pub	1,590	3,390	2,350
Nichols College; Dudley, Mass. 01570	848 (C)	P	7,130	7,130	4,100
Norfolk State University; Norfolk, Va. 23504	7,241 (C)	Pub	2,330	5,160	3,320
North Adams State College; North Adams, Mass. 01247	2,204 (C)	Pub	2,202	5,277	3,460
North Alabama, University of; Florence, Ala. 35632	5,006 (C)	Pub	1,620	1,914	4,000
North Carolina, Univ. of-Asheville; Asheville, N.C. 28804	3,259 (C)	Pub	1,116	4,958	2,990
North Carolina, Univ. of-Chapel Hill; Chapel Hill, N.C. 27514	15,251 (C)	Pub	1,084	5,584	3,472
North Carolina, Univ. of-Charlotte; Charlotte, N.C. 28223	11,143 (C)	Pub	1,035	5,565	2,456
North Carolina, Univ. of-Greensboro; Greensboro, N.C. 27412	9,191 (C)	Pub	1,364	5,978	3,345
North Carolina, Univ. of-Wilmington; Wilmington, N.C. 28403	6,642 (C)	Pub	1,188	5,719	3,034
North Carolina Agricultural and Technical State University; Greensboro, N.C. 27411	5,716 (C)	Pub	1,040	5,412	2,188
North Carolina Central University; Durham, N.C. 27707	4,070 (C)	Pub	1,121	5,652	2,764
North Carolina School of the Arts; Winston-Salem, N.C. 27127-2189	502 (C)	Pub	1,848	5,918	3,039
North Carolina State University-Raleigh; Raleigh, N.C. 27695	22,121 (C)	Pub	1,044	5,546	2,900
North Carolina Wesleyan College; Rocky Mount, N.C. 27801	724 (C)	P	7,160	7,160	3,540
North Central Bible College; Minneapolis, Minn. 55404	1,182 (C)	P	4,768	4,768	3,110
North Central College; Naperville, Ill. 60566-7063	2,216 (C)	P	9,960	9,960	3,735
North Dakota, University of; Grand Forks, N.D. 58202	10,086 (C)	Pub	2,040	5,058	2,190
North Dakota State University; Fargo, N.D. 58105	8,518 (C)	Pub	1,890	5,046	2,178
Northeastern Illinois University; Chicago, Ill. 60625	7,457 (C)	Pub	1,706	4,870	n.a.
Northeastern State Univ.; Tahlequah, Okla. 74464	6,985 (C)	Pub	1,255	3,268	1,880
Northeastern University; Boston, Mass. 02115	13,788 (C)	P	10,178	10,178	2,410
Northeast Louisiana University; Monroe, La. 71209	9,522 (C)	Pub	1,615	3,199	1,950
Northeast Missouri State University; Kirksville, Mo. 63501	5,610 (C)	Pub	1,800	3,504	2,584
Northern Arizona University; Flagstaff, Ariz. 86011	11,029 (C)	Pub	1,580	6,246	2,714
Northern Colorado, University of; Greeley, Colo. 80639	8,442 (C)	Pub	1,820	5,190	3,211
Northern Illinois University; DeKalb, Ill. 60115	18,220 (C)	Pub	2,650	6,250	2,900
Northern Iowa, University of; Cedar Falls, Iowa 50614	11,495 (C)	Pub	1,991	5,012	2,455
Northern Kentucky University; Highland Heights, Ky. 41076	10,195 (C)	Pub	1,410	4,010	2,920
Northern Michigan University; Marquette, Mich. 49855	7,656 (C)	Pub	1,987	3,907	3,157
Northern Montana College; Havre, Mont. 59501	1,489 (C)	Pub	1,272	2,955	2,910
Northern State University; Aberdeen, S.D. 57401	3,100 (C)	Pub	1,735	3,094	1,798
North Florida, University of; Jacksonville, Fla. 32216	6,497 (C)	Pub	1,200	3,800	2,800
North Georgia College; Dahlonega, Ga. 30579	2,180 (C)	Pub	1,650	4,230	2,295
Northland College; Ashland, Wis. 54806	547 (C)	P	8,380	8,380	3,450
North Park College; Chicago, Ill. 60625	1,083 (C)	P	10,665	10,665	4,035
Northrop University; Los Angeles, Calif. 90045	954 (C)	P	11,706	11,706	4,952
North Texas, University of; Denton, Tex. 76203	19,970 (C)	Pub	1,036	4,156	3,304
Northwest Christian College; Eugene, Ore. 97401	279 (C)	P	5,130	5,130	3,072
Northwest College; Kirkland, Wash. 98083-0579	681 (C)	P	5,277	5,277	2,900
Northwestern College; Orange City, Iowa 51041	1,047 (C)	P	8,000	8,000	2,800
Northwestern College; St. Paul, Minn. 55113	1,115 (C)	P	9,096	9,096	2,640
Northwestern Oklahoma State University; Alva, Okla. 73717	1,642 (C)	Pub	1,277	3,282	1,772
Northwestern State Univ. of Louisiana; Natchitoches, La. 71497	6,594 (C)	Pub	1,767	3,567	2,143
Northwestern University; Evanston, Ill. 60201-3060	7,360 (C)	P	14,370	14,370	4,827
Northwest Missouri State University; Maryville, Mo. 64468	4,997 (C)	Pub	1,590	2,880	2,645

Institution and location	Enrollment	Control	Tuition ($) Res.	Tuition ($) Nonres.	Rm/Bd ($)
Northwest Nazarene College; Nampa, Idaho 83651	1,095 (C)	P	5,823	5,823	2,529
Northwood Institute of Florida; West Palm Beach, Fla. 33409	528 (C)	P	7,770	7,770	4,725
Northwood Institute of Michigan; Midland, Mich. 48640	1,850 (C)	P	7,500	7,500	3,555
Northwood Institute of Texas; Cedar Hill, Tex. 75104	290 (C)	P	7,290	7,290	3,891
Norwich University; Northfield, Vt. 05663	1,900 (C)	P	11,800	11,800	4,500
Notre Dame, College of, Belmont, Calif. 94002	667 (C)	P	10,165	10,165	5,100
Notre Dame, University of; Notre Dame, Ind. 46556	7,500 (C)	P	13,500	13,500	3,600
Notre Dame College; Manchester, N.H. 03104	600 (C)	P	8,376	8,376	4,635
Notre Dame of Maryland, College of; Baltimore, Md. 21210	672 (W)	P	9,500	9,500	4,800
Notre Dame College of Ohio; Cleveland, Ohio 44121	849 (W)	P	6,850	6,850	3,460
Nova University; Ft. Lauderdale, Fla. 33314	3,560 (C)	P	7,050	7,050	3,265
Nyack College; Nyack, N.Y. 10960	519 (C)	P	7,430	7,430	2,940
Oakland City College; Oakland City, Ind. 47660	636 (C)	P	6,300	6,300	2,840
Oakland University; Rochester, Mich. 48063	9,472 (C)	Pub	2,200	6,000	3,200
Oakwood College; Huntsville, Ala. 35896	1,223 (C)	P	5,925	5,925	3,486
Oberlin College; Oberlin, Ohio 44074	2,850 (C)	P	15,220	15,220	4,890
Oblate College; Washington, D.C. 20017	8 (C)	P	3,750	3,750	n.a.
Occidental College; Los Angeles, Calif. 90041	1,677 (C)	P	14,640	14,640	5,216
Oglala Lakota College; Kyle, S.D. 57752	800 (C)	Pub	1,720	1,720	n.a.
Oglethorpe University; Atlanta, Ga. 30319	1,092 (C)	P	10,250	10,250	4,000
Ohio Dominican College; Columbus, Ohio 43219	1,365 (C)	P	7,020	7,020	3,740
Ohio Institute of Technology; Columbus. *See* DeVry Institute of Technology, Columbus					
Ohio Northern University; Ada, Ohio 45810	2,225 (C)	P	12,255	12,255	3,390
Ohio State University; Columbus, Ohio 43210	41,161 (C)	Pub	2,343	6,295	3,750
Ohio State University-Lima; Lima, Ohio 45804	1,312 (C)	Pub	2,253	6,852	n.a.
Ohio State University-Mansfield; Mansfield, Ohio 44906	1,236 (C)	Pub	2,106	6,195	n.a.
Ohio State University-Marion; Marion, Ohio 43302	1,021 (C)	Pub	2,253	6,852	n.a.
Ohio State University-Newark; Newark, Ohio 43055	1,499 (C)	Pub	2,253	6,852	n.a.
Ohio University; Athens, Ohio 45701	14,500 (C)	Pub	2,730	5,922	3,549
Ohio University-Lancaster; Lancaster, Ohio 43130	1,500 (C)	Pub	2,070	4,929	n.a.
Ohio University-Zanesville; Zanesville, Ohio 43701	985 (C)	Pub	2,199	5,283	n.a.
Ohio Valley College; Parkersburg, W.Va. 26101	224 (C)	P	4,435	4,435	3,005
Ohio Wesleyan University; Delaware, Ohio 43015	2,055 (C)	P	13,610	13,610	4,884
Oklahoma, University of-Norman; Norman, Okla. 73019	14,709 (C)	Pub	1,513	4,420	3,172
Oklahoma, University of-Health Sciences Center; Oklahoma City, Okla. 73190	1,186 (C)	Pub	1,419	4,581	n.a.
Oklahoma Baptist University; Shawnee, Okla. 74801	2,208 (C)	P	5,390	5,390	2,800
Oklahoma Christian University of Science and Arts; Oklahoma City, Okla. 73136-1100	1,645 (C)	P	4,715	4,715	2,720
Oklahoma City University; Oklahoma City, Okla. 73106	1,882 (C)	P	5,500	5,500	3,520
Oklahoma Panhandle State University; Goodwell, Okla. 73939	1,276 (C)	Pub	1,382	3,320	1,800
Oklahoma State University; Stillwater, Okla. 74078	15,141 (C)	Pub	1,568	4,525	2,876
Old Dominion University; Norfolk, Va. 23529-0050	11,679 (C)	Pub	2,848	6,928	4,134
Olivet College; Olivet, Mich. 49076	766 (C)	P	7,890	7,890	2,860
Olivet Nazarene University; Kankakee, Ill. 60901	1,566 (C)	P	6,476	6,476	3,510
O'More College of Design; Franklin, Tenn. 37604	147 (C)	P	5,900	5,900	n.a.
Oral Roberts University; Tulsa, Okla. 74171	3,250 (C)	P	6,025	6,025	3,495
Oregon, University of; Eugene, Ore. 97403	14,018 (C)	Pub	1,782	5,043	3,389
Oregon Coll. of Education. *See* Western Oregon State Coll.					
Oregon Health Sciences University; Portland, Ore. 97201	400 (C)	Pub	2,061	4,929	2,849
Oregon Institute of Technology; Klamath Falls, Ore. 97601	2,873 (C)	Pub	1,890	5,592	3,180
Oregon State University; Corvallis, Ore. 97331	12,419 (C)	Pub	1,833	5,541	2,810
Orlando College; Orlando, Fla. 32810	810 (C)	P	4,300	4,300	n.a.
Otis Art Institute of Parsons School of Design; Los Angeles, Calif. 90057	735 (C)	P	10,050	10,050	4,600
Ottawa University; Ottawa, Kan. 66067	536 (C)	P	6,450	6,450	2,998
Ottawa University-Phoenix Center; Phoenix, Ariz. 85021	560 (C)	P	3,000	3,000	n.a.
Otterbein College; Westerville, Ohio 43081	2,352 (C)	P	10,800	10,800	3,912
Ouachita Baptist University; Arkadelphia, Ark. 71923	1,284 (C)	P	5,210	5,210	2,300
Our Lady of Angels College. *See* Neumann College					
Our Lady of Holy Cross College; New Orleans, La. 70131-7399	1,033 (C)	P	4,600	4,600	n.a.
Our Lady of the Lake-University of San Antonio; San Antonio, Tex. 78285	2,101 (C)	P	5,992	5,992	4,000
Ozark Christian College; Joplin, Mo. 64801	538 (C)	P	2,866	2,866	2,600
Ozarks, College of the; Point Lookout, Mo. 65726	1,512 (C)	P	—	—	1,700
Ozarks, University of the; Clarksville, Ark. 72830	616 (C)	P	3,520	3,520	2,330
Pace University; New York, N.Y. 10038	6,148 (C)	P	8,754	8,754	4,180
Pace University-College of White Plains; White Plains, N.Y. 10603	1,431 (C)	P	8,754	8,754	4,180
Pace University-Pleasantville-Briarcliff; Pleasantville, N.Y. 10570	3,937 (C)	P	8,754	8,754	4,180
Pacific, University of the; Stockton, Calif. 95211	3,802 (C)	P	14,480	14,480	5,100
Pacific Christian College; Fullerton, Calif. 92631	466 (C)	P	5,000	5,000	4,000
Pacific Lutheran University; Tacoma, Wash. 98447	3,049 (C)	P	11,075	11,075	3,890

Institution and location	Enrollment	Control	Tuition ($) Res.	Nonres.	Rm/Bd ($)
Pacific Northwest College of Art; Portland, Ore. 97205					
Pacific Oaks College; Pasadena, Calif. 91103	150 (C)	P	9,945	9,945	n.a.
Pacific States University; Los Angeles, Calif. 90006	300 (C)	P	3,600	3,600	n.a.
Pacific Union College; Angwin, Calif. 94508	1,676 (C)	P	9,595	9,595	3,335
Pacific University; Forest Grove, Ore. 97116	899 (C)	P	10,200	10,200	3,175
Paier College of Art, Inc.; Hamden, Conn. 06511	309 (C)	P	8,700	8,700	n.a.
Paine College; Augusta, Ga. 30910	581 (C)	P	5,256	5,256	2,660
Palm Beach Atlantic College; West Palm Beach, Fla. 33401	1,375 (C)	P	5,600	5,600	3,170
Pan American University; Edinburg, Tex. 78539	9,000 (C)	Pub	762	1,629	2,288
Park College; Parkville, Mo. 64152	450 (C)	P	6,820	6,820	3,300
Parks College of St. Louis University; Cahokia, Ill. 62206	1,100 (C)	P	7,000	7,000	3,700
Parsons School of Design; New York, N.Y. 10011	1,760 (C)	P	12,050	12,050	6,200
Patten College; Oakland, Calif. 94601	333 (C)	P	3,490	3,490	3,695
Paul Quinn College; Waco, Tex. 76704	509 (C)	P	3,635	3,635	2,975
Peabody Conservatory of Music; Baltimore, Md. 21202	256 (C)	P	11,480	11,480	4,770
Pembroke State University; Pembroke, N.C. 28372	2,712 (C)	Pub	800	4,642	1,920
Pennsylvania, University of; Philadelphia, Pa. 19104	9,949 (C)	P	15,894	15,894	6,030
Pennsylvania State Erie –The Behrend College; Erie, Pa. 16563	2,648 (C)	Pub	4,048	8,444	3,510
Pennsylvania State Harrisburg–The Capital College; Middletown, Pa. 17057	1,959 (C)	Pub	3,754	7,900	3,610
Pennsylvania State University Park; University Park, Pa. 16802	31,621 (C)	Pub	3,754	7,900	3,570
Pepperdine University School of Business and Management; Culver City, Calif. 90230	520 (C)	P	13,500	13,500	n.a.
Pepperdine University-Seaver College; Malibu, Calif. 90265	2,562 (C)	P	15,230	15,230	6,070
Peru State College; Peru, Neb. 68421	1,724 (C)	Pub	1,489	2,305	2,450
Pfeiffer College; Misenheimer, N.C. 28109	830 (C)	P	7,295	7,295	3,050
Pharmacy, School of (Ga.). *See Mercer Univ.*					
Philadelphia College of Bible; Langhorne, Pa. 19047	647 (C)	P	6,245	6,245	3,580
Philadelphia College of Pharmacy and Science; Philadelphia, Pa. 19104	1,543 (C)	P	9,250	9,250	4,266
Philadelphia College of Textiles and Science; Philadelphia, Pa. 19144	1,711 (C)	P	9,735	9,735	4,500
Philander Smith College; Little Rock, Ark. 72202	572 (C)	P	2,350	2,350	2,300
Phillips University; Enid, Okla. 73702	828 (C)	P	8,530	8,530	2,770
Phoenix, University of; Phoenix, Ariz. 85040	3,023 (C)	P	5,588	5,588	n.a.
Piedmont Bible College; Winston-Salem, N.C. 27101	298 (C)	P	3,190	3,190	2,500
Piedmont College; Demorest, Ga. 30535	495 (C)	P	3,600	3,600	3,050
Pikeville College; Pikeville, Ky. 41501	753 (C)	P	4,200	4,200	2,400
Pillsbury Baptist Bible College; Owatonna, Minn. 55060	367 (C)	P	3,672	3,672	2,700
Pine Manor College; Chestnut Hill, Mass. 02167	525 (W)	P	13,700	13,700	5,700
Pittsburgh, University of; Pittsburgh, Pa. 15260	18,475 (C)	Pub	4,314	8,886	3,514
Pittsburgh, University of-Bradford; Bradford, Pa. 16701-2898	1,204 (C)	Pub	4,298	8,870	3,460
Pittsburgh, University of-Greensburg; Greensburg, Pa. 15601	1,504 (C)	Pub	4,278	8,850	3,120
Pittsburgh, University of-Johnstown; Johnstown, Pa. 15904	3,210 (C)	Pub	4,262	8,834	3,186
Pittsburg State University; Pittsburg, Kan. 66762	4,476 (C)	Pub	1,450	3,964	2,600
Pitzer College. *See Claremont Colleges.*					
Plymouth State College; Plymouth, N.H. 03264	4,000 (C)	Pub	2,574	5,934	3,442
Point Loma Nazarene College; San Diego, Calif. 92106	1,837 (C)	P	8,058	8,058	3,624
Point Park College; Pittsburgh, Pa. 15222	2,881 (C)	P	7,980	7,980	3,940
Polytechnic University; Brooklyn, N.Y. 11201	1,655 (C)	P	12,800	12,800	4,500
Pomona College. *See Claremont Colleges.*					
Pontifical College Josephinum; Columbus, Ohio 43235-1498	58 (M)	P	4,500	4,500	3,000
Portland, University of; Portland, Ore. 97203	2,084 (C)	P	9,250	9,250	3,580
Portland School of Art; Portland, Me. 04101	305 (C)	P	8,300	8,300	5,085
Portland State University; Portland, Ore. 97207	11,504 (C)	Pub	1,917	5,676	3,434
Post College; Waterbury, Conn. 06708	2,082 (C)	P	10,075	10,075	4,180
Potsdam Coll. of Arts & Science. *See New York, State Univ. of*					
Prairie View A&M University; Prairie View, Tex. 77446	5,240 (C)	Pub	931	4,051	2,938
Pratt Institute; Brooklyn, N.Y. 11205	2,687 (C)	P	11,184	11,184	6,130
Presbyterian College; Clinton, S.C. 29325	1,126 (C)	P	10,326	10,326	3,184
Prescott College; Prescott, Ariz. 86301	320 (C)	P	7,200	7,200	n.a.
Presentation College; Aberdeen, S.D. 57401	464 (C)	P	5,146	5,146	2,535
Princeton University; Princeton, N.J. 08544	4,524 (C)	P	16,570	16,570	5,311
Principia College; Elsah, Ill. 62028	622 (C)	P	11,310	11,310	4,590
Providence College; Providence, R.I. 02918	3,805 (C)	P	12,290	12,290	5,300
Puerto Rico, University of-Cayey University College; Cayey, P.R. 00633	3,332 (C)	Pub	662	2,000	n.a.
Puerto Rico, University of-Humacao University College; Humacao, P.R. 00661	3,982 (C)	Pub	707	2,257	n.a.
Puerto Rico, University of-Mayaguez Campus; Mayaguez, P.R. 00708	9,123 (C)	Pub	838	2,838	2,950
Puerto Rico, University of-Medical Science; San Juan, P.R. 00936	1,037 (C)	Pub	[2]	[3]	n.a.

Institution and location	Enrollment	Control	Tuition ($) Res.	Tuition ($) Nonres.	Rm/Bd ($)
Puget Sound, University of; Tacoma, Wash. 98416	3,214 (C)	P	12,690	12,690	3,980
Puget Sound Christian College; Edmonds, Wash. 98020	70 (C)	P	4,485	4,485	3,000
Purdue University; West Lafayette, Ind. 47907	29,537 (C)	Pub	2,152	6,764	3,320
Purdue University-Calumet; Hammond, Ind. 46323	7,710 (C)	Pub	1,789	4,504	n.a.
Purdue University-North Central; Westville, Ind. 46391	3,013 (C)	Pub	1,789	4,504	n.a.
Queens College; Charlotte, N.C. 28274	1,369 (C)	P	9,300	9,300	4,400
Queens College (NYC). *See* New York, City University of					
Quincy College; Quincy, Ill. 62301	1,559 (C)	P	8,604	8,604	3,440
Quinnipiac College; Hamden, Conn. 06518	2,950 (C)	P	10,350	10,350	4,990
Rabbinical College of America; Morristown, N.J. 07960	230 (M)	P	4,100	4,100	3,400
Rabbinical Seminary of America; Forest Hills, N.Y. 11375	200 (M)	P	3,000	3,000	3,000
Radcliffe College. *See* Harvard and Radcliffe Colleges					
Radford University; Radford, Va. 24142	9,175 (C)	Pub	2,436	5,584	3,718
Ramapo College of New Jersey; Mahwah, N.J. 07403	4,525 (C)	Pub	3,644	3,644	4,782
Randolph-Macon College; Ashland, Va. 23005	1,141 (C)	P	10,810	10,810	4,600
Randolph-Macon Woman's College; Lynchburg, Va. 24503	750 (W)	P	11,680	11,680	5,140
Redlands, University of; Redlands, Calif. 92373-0999	1,220 (C)	P	12,960	12,960	5,070
Reed College; Portland, Ore. 97202	1,261 (C)	P	16,700	16,700	4,640
Reformed Bible College; Grand Rapids, Mich. 49506	193 (C)	P	5,166	5,166	3,000
Regis College; Denver, Colo. 80221	1,041 (C)	P	10,340	10,340	6,100
Regis College; Weston, Mass. 02193	1,145 (W)	P	10,650	10,650	5,200
Rensselaer Polytechnic Institute; Troy, N.Y. 12180	4,436 (C)	P	15,625	15,625	5,150
Research College of Nursing; Kansas City, Mo. 64132	133.(C)	P	6,850	6,850	3,200
Rhode Island, University of; Kingston, R.I. 02881	12,646 (C)	Pub	2,437	6,819	4,230
Rhode Island, University of, College of Continuing Education; Providence, R.I. 02908-5090	4,400 (C)	Pub	(4)	(5)	n.a.
Rhode Island College; Providence, R.I. 02908	5,433 (C)	Pub	2,000	5,119	5,200
Rhode Island School of Design; Providence, R.I. 02903	1,809 (C)	P	14,121	14,121	5,892
Rhodes College Memphis; Memphis, Tenn. 38112	1,407 (C)	P	12,958	12,958	4,516
Rice University; Houston, Tex. 77251	2,741 (C)	P	8,125	8,125	4,900
Richmond, University of; Richmond, Va. 23173	2,749 (C)	P	11,695	11,695	2,865
Richmond College; Surrey, TW10 6JP England	1,044 (C)	P	9,550	9,550	4,745
Rider College; Lawrenceville, N.J. 08648	3,080 (C)	P	10,900	10,900	4,650
Ringling School of Art and Design; Sarasota, Fla. 34234	578 (C)	P	8,900	8,900	4,700
Ripon College; Ripon, Wis. 54971	854 (C)	P	12,740	12,740	3,150
Rivier College; Nashua, N.H. 03060	778 (C)	P	9,050	9,050	4,310
Roanoke Bible College; Elizabeth City, N.C. 27909	114 (C)	P	5,280	5,280	2,400
Roanoke College; Salem, Va. 24153	1,668 (C)	P	11,250	11,250	4,000
Robert Morris College; Coraopolis, Pa. 15108	4,945 (C)	P	5,100	5,100	3,800
Roberts Wesleyan College; Rochester, N.Y. 14624	969 (C)	P	8,508	8,508	2,976
Rio Grande, University of; Rio Grande, Ohio 45674	2,000 (C)	P	2,865	4,620	3,000
Rochester, University of; Rochester, N.Y. 14627	4,823 (C)	P	15,651	15,651	5,750
Rochester Institute of Technology; Rochester, N.Y. 14623	10,789 (C)	P	11,952	11,952	5,100
Rockford College; Rockford, Ill. 61108	1,168 (C)	P	9,400	9,400	3,400
Rockhurst College; Kansas City, Mo. 64110	3,085 (C)	P	8,560	8,560	3,750
Rocky Mountain College; Billings, Mont. 59102	769 (C)	P	7,197	7,197	3,328
Roger Williams College; Bristol, R.I. 02809	2,111 (C)	P	10,560	10,560	5,120
Rollins College; Winter Park, Fla. 32789	1,500 (C)	P	12,800	13,900	4,295
Roosevelt University; Chicago, Ill. 60605	4,293 (C)	P	7,470	7,470	4,500
Rosary College; River Forest, Ill. 60305-1099	1,042 (C)	P	9,276	9,276	4,176
Rose-Hulman Institute of Technology; Terre Haute, Ind. 47803	1,300 (M)	P	10,785	10,785	3,600
Rosemont College; Rosemont, Pa. 19010	627 (W)	P	9,445	9,445	5,400
Rush University Colleges of Nursing and Health Sciences; Chicago, Ill. 60612	175 (C)	P	9,800	9,800	5,920
Russell Sage College; Troy, N.Y. 12180	1,000 (W)	P	10,470	10,470	4,240
Rust College; Holly Springs, Miss. 38635	936 (C)	P	4,152	4,152	1,948
Rutgers, The State University of New Jersey–Camden College of Arts and Sciences; Camden, N.J. 08102	2,695 (C)	Pub	3,279	6,237	3,826
Rutgers, The State University of New Jersey–College of Engineering; New Brunswick, N.J. 08903	2,537 (C)	Pub	3,740	7,026	3,826
Rutgers, The State University of New Jersey–College of Nursing-Newark; Newark, N.J. 07102	401 (C)	Pub	3,274	6,232	3,826
Rutgers, The State University of New Jersey–College of Pharmacy; New Brunswick, N.J. 08903	783 (C)	Pub	3,595	6,881	3,826
Rutgers, The State Universit of New Jersey–Cook College; New Brunswick, N.J. 08903	2,874 (C)	Pub	3,766	7,052	3,826
Rutgers, The State University of New Jersey–Douglass College; New Brunswick, N.J. 08903	3,227 (W)	Pub	3,424	6,382	3,826
Rutgers, The State University of New Jersey–Livingston College; New Brunswick, N.J. 08903	3,776 (C)	Pub	3,444	6,402	3,826
Rutgers, The State University of New Jersey–Mason Gross School of the Arts; New Brunswick, N.J. 08903	428 (C)	Pub	3,281	6,239	3,826

Institution and location	Enrollment	Control	Tuition ($) Res.	Tuition ($) Nonres.	Rm/Bd ($)
Rutgers, The State University of New Jersey–Newark College of Arts and Sciences; Newark, N.J. 07102	3,396 (C)	Pub	3,281	6,239	3,826
Rutgers, The State University of New Jersey–Rutgers College; New Brunswick, N.J. 08903	8,377 (C)	Pub	3,432	6,390	3,826
Rutgers, The State University of New Jersey–University College–Camden; Camden, N.J. 08102	872 (C)	Pub	(6)	(7)	n.a.
Rutgers, The State University of New Jersey–University College–New Brunswick; New Brunswick, N.J. 08903	3,087 (C)	Pub	(6)	(7)	n.a.
Rutgers, The State University of New Jersey–University College–Newark; Newark, N.J. 07102	1,758 (C)	Pub	(6)	(7)	n.a.
Sacred Heart, Univ. of the; Santurce, P.R. 00924	7,044 (C)	P	3,130	3,130	3,340
Sacred Heart Seminary; Detroit, Mich. 48206	194 (C)	P	2,900	2,900	2,400
Sacred Heart University; Fairfield, Conn. 06432	3,218 (C)	P	8,970	8,970	5,010
Saginaw Valley State University; University Center, Mich. 48710	5,263 (C)	Pub	2,344	4,672	3,200
Saint Ambrose University; Davenport, Iowa 52803	1,700 (C)	P	8,530	8,530	3,420
Saint Andrews Presbyterian College; Laurinburg, N.C. 28352	794 (C)	P	8,875	8,875	3,920
Saint Anselm College; Manchester, N.H. 03102	1,890 (C)	P	10,160	10,160	5,000
Saint Augustine's College; Raleigh, N.C. 27611	1,716 (C)	P	5,000	5,000	3,200
St. Benedict, College of; St. Joseph, Minn. 56374-2099	1,916 (W)	P	10,135	10,135	3,750
St. Bonaventure University; St. Bonaventure, N.Y. 14778	2,396 (C)	P	9,067	9,067	4,510
St. Catherine, College of; St. Paul, Minn. 55105	2,463 (W)	P	10,140	10,140	3,674
St. Cloud State University; St. Cloud, Minn. 56301	14,454 (C)	Pub	1,977	2,990	2,300
St. Edward's University; Austin, Tex. 78704	2,524 (C)	P	7,764	7,764	3,644
St. Elizabeth, College of; Convent Station, N.J. 07961	1,068 (W)	P	9,600	9,600	4,400
St. Francis, College of; Joliet, Ill. 60435	1,080 (C)	P	7,980	7,980	3,580
St. Francis College; Brooklyn Heights, N.Y. 11201	1,743 (C)	P	5,250	5,250	n.a.
St. Francis College; Fort Wayne, Ind. 46808	751 (C)	P	7,158	7,158	3,450
St. Francis College; Loretto, Pa. 15940	1,001 (C)	P	9,596	9,596	4,490
St. Hyacinth College and Seminary; Granby, Mass. 01033	25 (M)	P	3,600	3,600	4,000
St. John Fisher College; Rochester, N.Y. 14618	1,668 (C)	P	9,320	9,320	5,094
St. John's College; Annapolis, Md. 21404	444 (C)	P	14,262	14,262	4,696
St. John's College; Santa Fe, N.M. 87501	409 (C)	P	13,040	13,040	4,410
St. John's Seminary; Camarillo, Calif. 93012	86 (M)	P	4,012	4,012	—
St. John's Seminary College of Liberal Arts; Brighton, Mass. 02135	70 (M)	P	3,600	3,600	2,600
St. John's University; Collegeville, Minn. 56321	1,971 (M)	P	10,135	10,135	3,680
St. John's University–Queens–Staten Island; Jamaica, N.Y. 11439	14,154 (C)	P	7,530	7,530	n.a.
St. John Vianney College Seminary; Miami, Fla. 33165	47 (M)	P	5,600	5,600	3,000
St. Joseph College; West Hartford, Conn. 06117	1,215 (W)	P	10,400	10,400	4,264
St. Joseph in Vermont, College of; Rutland, Vt. 05701	377 (C)	P	6,085	6,085	3,550
St. Joseph's College; Brooklyn, N.Y. 11205	827 (C)	P	6,156	6,156	n.a.
St. Joseph's College–Suffolk; Patchogue, N.Y. 11772	1,936 (C)	P	6,356	6,356	n.a.
Saint Joseph's College; Rensselaer, Ind. 47978	1,032 (C)	P	9,410	9,410	3,570
Saint Joseph's College; Windham, Me. 04062-1198	660 (C)	P	8,500	8,500	4,300
St. Joseph Seminary College; St. Benedict, La. 70457	55 (M)	P	5,400	5,400	3,500
Saint Joseph's University; Philadelphia, Pa. 19131	3,884 (C)	P	10,150	10,150	4,962
St. Lawrence University; Canton, N.Y. 13617	1,967 (C)	P	15,951	15,951	5,050
Saint Leo College; Saint Leo, Fla. 33574	6,000 (C)	P	7,230	7,230	3,480
St. Louis Christian College; Florissant, Mo. 63033	142 (C)	P	3,343	3,343	2,360
St. Louis College of Pharmacy; St. Louis, Mo. 63110	701 (C)	P	5,935	5,935	3,750
St. Louis Conservatory of Music; St. Louis, Mo. 63130	70 (C)	P	7,750	7,750	n.a.
St. Louis University; St. Louis, Mo. 63103	7,729 (C)	P	9,160	9,160	4,242
St. Martin's College; Lacey, Wash. 98503	577 (C)	P	9,605	9,605	3,720
Saint Mary College; Leavenworth, Kan. 66048	1,133 (W)	P	3,880	3,880	3,160
St. Mary of the Plains College; Dodge City, Kan. 67801	566 (C)	P	6,450	6,450	3,250
St. Mary-of-the-Woods Coll.; St. Mary-of-the-Woods, Ind. 47876	911 (C)	P	5,800	5,800	3,100
St. Mary's College; Notre Dame, Ind. 46556	858 (W)	P	9,110	9,110	3,775
St. Mary's College; Orchard Lake, Mich. 48033	1,798 (W)	P	9,390	9,390	4,096
St. Mary's College; Winona, Minn. 55987	307 (C)	P	3,850	3,850	2,800
St. Mary's College of California; Moraga, Calif. 94575	1,275 (C)	P	9,225	9,225	3,150
St. Mary's College of Maryland; St. Mary's City, Md. 20686	2,583 (C)	P	10,294	10,294	5,058
St. Mary's University of San Antonio; San Antonio, Tex. 78284	1,568 (C)	Pub	2,860	4,660	4,100
Saint Meinrad College; St. Meinrad, Ind. 47577	2,404 (C)	P	7,300	7,300	3,346
Saint Michael's College; Colchester, Vt. 05439	96 (M)	P	5,413	5,413	4,064
St. Norbert College; De Pere, Wis. 54115	1,710 (C)	P	11,265	11,265	5,090
St. Olaf College; Northfield, Minn. 55057	1,936 (C)	P	10,225	10,225	3,900
St. Paul Bible College; Bible College, Minn. 55375	3,097 (C)	P	12,080	12,080	3,345
Saint Paul's College; Lawrenceville, Va. 23868	526 (C)	P	6,240	6,240	3,318
Saint Peter's College; Jersey City, N.J. 07306	736 (C)	P	4,806	4,806	3,180
	3,152 (C)	P	7,590	7,590	3,100
Saint Rose, The College of; Albany, N.Y. 12203	2,361 (C)	P	8,530	8,530	5,010
St. Scholastica, College of; Duluth, Minn. 55811	1,741 (C)	P	9,921	9,921	3,255
St. Thomas, College of; St. Paul, Minn. 55105	5,129 (C)	P	10,625	10,625	3,543
St. Thomas, University of; Houston, Tex. 77006	1,105 (C)	P	6,090	6,09	3,240

Institution and location	Enrollment	Control	Tuition ($) Res.	Tuition ($) Nonres.	Rm/Bd ($)
St. Thomas Aquinas College; Sparkill, N.Y. 10968	1,875 (C)	P	6,750	6,750	4,200
Saint Thomas University; Miami, Fla. 33054	1,383 (C)	P	8,125	8,125	4,100
Saint Vincent College; Latrobe, Pa. 15650	1,238 (C)	P	9,080	9,080	3,520
St. Xavier College; Chicago, Ill. 60655	2,177 (C)	P	8,820	8,820	3,692
Salem College; Winston-Salem, N.C. 27108	694 (W)	P	8,950	8,950	5,600
Salem State College; Salem, Mass. 01970	5,388 (C)	Pub	1,250	3,930	2,841
Salem-Teikyo University; Salem, W.Va. 26426	400 (C)	P	6,380	6,380	4,320
Salisbury State University, Salisbury, Md. 21801	5,183 (C)	Pub	2,444	4,498	4,090
Salve Regina University; Newport, R.I. 02840-4192	1,830 (C)	P	11,700	11,700	5,500
Samford University; Birmingham, Ala. 35229	3,203 (C)	P	6,540	6,540	3,576
Sam Houston State University; Huntsville, Tex. 77341	12,750 (C)	Pub	1,060	4,360	2,490
San Diego, University of; San Diego, Calif. 92110	3,886 (C)	P	11,360	11,360	5,000
San Diego State University; San Diego, Calif. 92182	28,712 (C)	Pub	894	5,430	3,968
Imperial Valley Campus; Calexico, Calif. 92231	253 (C)	Pub	838	5,500	n.a.
San Francisco, University of; San Francisco, Calif. 94117	3,326 (C)	P	10,960	10,960	5,214
San Francisco Art Institute; San Francisco, Calif. 94133	514 (C)	P	11,350	11,350	n.a.
San Francisco Conservatory of Music; San Francisco, Calif. 94122	155 (C)	P	8.550	8,550	n.a.
San Francisco State Univ.; San Francisco, Calif. 94132	22,251 (C)	Pub	864	5,670	3,904
Sangamon State University; Springfield, Ill. 62708	2,342 (C)	Pub	1,644	5,218	2,554
San Jose Christian College; San Jose, Calif. 95108	235 (C)	P	5,361	5,361	3,240
San Jose State University; San Jose, Calif. 95192-0009	24,001 (C)	Pub	1,056	7,356	4,550
Santa Clara University; Santa Clara, Calif. 95053	3,830 (C)	P	11,271	11,271	5,292
Santa Fe, College of; Santa Fe, N.M. 87501	1,652 (C)	P	7,506	7,506	2,580
Sarah Lawrence College; Bronxville, N.Y. 10708	902 (C)	P	15,530	15,530	5,960
Savannah College of Art and Design; Savannah, Ga. 31401	1,835 (C)	P	7,575	7,575	4,800
Savannah State College; Savannah, Ga. 31404	1,754 (C)	Pub	1,635	4,215	2,145
Schiller International University; 6900 Heidelberg, Germany	1,345 (C)	P	9,740	9,740	4,400
Schreiner College; Kerrville, Tex. 78028	658 (C)	P	6,975	6,975	4,800
Science and Arts, University of, of Oklahoma; Chickasha, Okla. 73018	1,551 (C)	Pub	1,317	3,616	1,820
Scranton, University of; Scranton, Pa. 18510	3,849 (C)	P	9,700	9,700	4,500
Scripps College. *See* Claremont Colleges					
Seattle Pacific University; Seattle, Wash. 98119	2,268 (C)	P	10,630	10,630	3,969
Seattle University; Seattle, Wash. 98122	3,406 (C)	P	10,770	10,770	4,251
Seaver College. *See* Pepperdine University					
Selma University; Selma, Ala. 36701	217 (C)	P	2,380	2,380	1,740
Seton Hall University; South Orange, N.J. 07079	5,380 (C)	P	11,110	11,110	5,517
Seton Hill College; Greensburg, Pa. 15601	1,037 (W)	P	9,030	9,030	3,760
Shawnee State University; Portsmouth, Ohio 45662	2,900 (C)	Pub	1,893	2,697	3,400
Shaw University; Raleigh, N.C. 27611	1,500 (C)	P	4,894	4,894	3,282
Sheldon Jackson College; Sitka, Alaska 99835	300 (C)	P	5,960	5,960	4,215
Shenandoah College and Conservatory; Winchester, Va. 22601-9986	818 (C)	P	7,900	7,900	4,100
Shepherd College; Shepherdstown, W. Va. 25443	3,700 (C)	Pub	1,894	4,314	3,690
Shimer College; Waukegan, Ill. 60085	100 (C)	P	8,800	8,800	3,150
Shippensburg University of Pennsylvania; Shippensburg, Pa. 17257	5,324 (C)	Pub	2,396	3,818	2,282
Shorter College; Rome, Ga. 30161	858 (C)	P	5,810	5,810	3,450
Siena College; Loudonville, N.Y. 12211	3,551 (C)	P	8,850	8,850	4,465
Siena Heights College; Adrian, Mich. 49221	1,493 (C)	P	7,170	7,170	3,550
Sierra Nevada College; Incline Village, Nev. 89450	300 (C)	P	6,750	6,750	4,400
Silver Lake College; Manitowoc, Wis. 54220	748 (C)	P	7,480	7,480	n.a.
Simmons Bible College; Louisville, Ky. 40210	103 (C)	P	520	520	n.a.
Simmons College; Boston, Mass. 02115	1,417 (W)	P	13,632	13,632	6,000
Simon's Rock of Bard College; Great Barrington, Mass. 01230	298 (C)	P	14,450	14,450	4,810
Simpson College; Indianola, Iowa 50125	1,735 (C)	P	9,585	9,585	3,375
Simpson College; Redding, Calif. 96003	356 (C)	P	6,388	6,388	3,480
Sinte Gleska College; Rosebud, S.D. 57570	485 (C)	P	1,927	1,927	n.a.
Sioux Falls College; Sioux Falls, S.D. 57105	937 (C)	P	7,496	7,496	2,927
Skidmore College; Saratoga Springs, N.Y. 12866	2,174 (C)	P	16,000	16,000	5,090
Slippery Rock State College. *See* Slippery Rock University of Pennsylvania					
Slippery Rock Univ. of Pennsylvania; Slippery Rock, Pa. 16057	7,084 (C)	Pub	2,668	4,702	2,794
Smith College; Northampton, Mass. 01063	2,662 (W)	P	15,770	15,770	6,100
Sojourner-Douglass College; Baltimore, Md. 21205	298 (C)	P	4,515	4,515	n.a.
Sonoma State University; Rohnert Park, Calif. 94928	4,983 (C)	Pub	882	5,418	4,820
South, University of the; Sewanee, Tenn. 37375	1,096 (C)	P	13,505	13,505	3,510
South Alabama, University of; Mobile, Ala. 36688	9,658 (C)	Pub	1,905	2,505	2,565
Southampton College. *See* Long Island Univ. Center					
South Carolina, University of; Columbia, S.C. 29208	16,017 (C)	Pub	3,328	7,168	2,700
South Carolina, Univ. of-Aiken; Aiken, S.C. 29801	2,967 (C)	Pub	1,800	4,500	2,470
South Carolina, Univ. of-Coastal Carolina; Conway, S.C. 29526	4,080 (C)	Pub	1,920	4,800	4,000
South Carolina, Univ. of-Spartanburg; Spartanburg, S.C. 29303	3,501 (C)	Pub	1,920	4,800	2,540
South Carolina State College; Orangeburg, S.C. 29117	3,531 (C)	Pub	3,470	5,500	1,216
South Dakota, University of; Vermillion, S.D. 57069	5,501 (C)	Pub	2,089	3,802	2,270

Institution and location	Enrollment	Control	Tuition ($)		Rm/Bd ($)
			Res.	Nonres.	
South Dakota School of Mines and Technology; Rapid City, S.D. 57701	2,015 (C)	Pub	3,555	4,676	2,300
South Dakota State University; Brookings, S.D. 57007	6,816 (C)	Pub	1,936	3,539	1,722
Southeast Missouri State Univ.; Cape Girardeau, Mo. 63701	7,810 (C)	Pub	1,836	3,276	2,825
Southeastern Baptist College; Laurel, Miss. 39440	70 (C)	P	2,200	2,200	1,700
Southeastern Bible College; Birmingham, Ala. 35243	138 (C)	P	3,400	3,400	2,400
Southeastern College; Lakeland, Fla. 33801	1,192 (C)	P	3,168	3,168	2,948
Southeastern Louisiana University; Hammond, La. 70402	9,500 (C)	Pub	1,703	3,503	2,280
Southeastern Massachusetts University; North Dartmouth, Mass. 02747	5,354 (C)	Pub	1,600	5,485	3,822
Southeastern Oklahoma State Univ.; Durant, Okla. 74701	3,546 (C)	Pub	1,200	3,000	2,330
Southeastern University; Washington, D.C. 20024	559 (C)	P	5,190	5,190	n.a.
Southern Arkansas University; Magnolia, Ark. 71753	2,388 (C)	Pub	1,155	1,848	2,310
Southern California, Univ. of; Los Angeles, Calif. 90089	16,113 (C)	P	14,375	14,375	5,650
Southern California College; Costa Mesa, Calif. 92626	828 (C)	P	6,720	6,720	3,300
Southern California Institute of Architecture; Santa Monica, Calif. 90404	310 (C)	P	7,960	7,960	n.a.
Southern College of Seventh-Day Adventists; Collegedale, Tenn. 37315	1,534 (C)	P	7,100	7,100	3,040
Southern College of Technology; Marietta, Ga. 30060	3,829 (C)	Pub	1,431	3,909	3,215
Southern Colorado, University of; Pueblo, Colo. 81001	4,246 (C)	Pub	1,720	5,525	3,370
Southern Connecticut State Univ.; New Haven, Conn. 06515	6,723 (C)	Pub	2,199	5,929	3,986
Southern Illinois Univ.-Carbondale; Carbondale, Ill. 62901	19,888 (C)	Pub	2,332	5,452	3,764
Southern Illinois Univ.-Edwardsville; Edwardsville, Ill. 62026	8,841 (C)	Pub	1,821	4,743	3,619
Southern Indiana, University of; Evansville, Ind. 47714	6,480 (C)	Pub	1,800	7,212	2,860
Southern Maine, University of; Gorham, Me. 04038	8,819 (C)	Pub	2,214	5,994	3,844
Southern Methodist University; Dallas, Tex. 75275	5,749 (C)	P	11,768	11,768	4,832
Southern Missionary College. *See* Southern College of Seventh-Day Adventists					
Southern Mississippi, Univ. of; Hattiesburg, Miss. 39406	10,118 (C)	Pub	3,087	5,460	3,420
Southern Nazarene Univ.; Bethany, Okla. 73008	1,254 (C)	P	5,588	5,588	3,256
Southern Oregon State College; Ashland, Ore. 97520	4,453 (C)	Pub	2,400	5,600	3,300
Southern University-Baton Rouge; Baton Rouge, La. 70813	9,448 (C)	Pub	1,576	5,482	2,350
Southern University-New Orleans; New Orleans, La. 70126	3,200 (C)	Pub	1,452	3,010	n.a.
Southern Utah State College; Cedar City, Utah 84720	3,600 (C)	Pub	1,345	3,596	2,070
Southern Vermont College; Bennington, Vt. 05201	676 (C)	P	7,230	7,230	3,828
South Florida, University of; Tampa, Fla. 33620	21,565 (C)	Pub	1,410	4,750	3,100
Southwest, College of the; Hobbs, N.M. 88240	277 (C)	P	2,700	2,700	2,755
Southwest Baptist University; Bolivar, Mo. 65613	2,920 (C)	P	6,204	6,204	2,340
Southwestern Adventist College; Keene, Tex. 76059	785 (C)	P	6,552	6,552	3,242
Southwestern Assemblies of God College; Waxahachie, Tex. 75165	686 (C)	P	3,540	3,540	2,762
Southwestern College; Winfield, Kan. 67156	653 (C)	P	5,050	5,050	2,810
Southwestern Conservative Baptist Bible College; Phoenix, Ariz. 85032	146 (C)	P	5,160	5,160	2,090
Southwestern Louisiana, University of; Lafayette, La. 70504	14,103 (C)	Pub	1,490	3,140	1,945
Southwestern Oklahoma State Univ.; Weatherford, Okla. 73096	5,401 (C)	Pub	1,172	2,928	1,770
Southwestern University; Georgetown, Tex. 78626	1,219 (C)	P	9,400	9,400	4,081
Southwest Missouri State Univ.; Springfield, Mo. 65804	17,037 (C)	Pub	1,718	1,718	3,024
Southwest State University; Marshall, Minn. 56258	3,035 (C)	Pub	1,800	3,000	2,400
Southwest Texas State Univ.; San Marcos, Tex. 78666	20,511 (C)	Pub	1,042	4,178	2,968
Spalding University; Louisville, Ky. 40203	735 (C)	P	6,696	6,696	2,760
Spelman College; Atlanta, Ga. 30314	1,757 (W)	P	6,707	6,707	4,770
Spring Arbor College; Spring Arbor, Mich. 49283	847 (C)	P	7,556	7,556	3,100
Spring Garden College; Philadelphia, Pa. 19119	1,465 (C)	P	8,800	8,800	3,850
Spring Hill College; Mobile, Ala. 36608	1,160 (C)	P	10,114	10,114	4,060
Stanford University; Stanford, Calif. 94305	6,505 (C)	P	14,280	14,280	5,930
Staten Island, Coll. of (NYC). *See* New York, City Univ. of					
Stephen F. Austin State Univ. Nacogdoches, Tex. 75962	11,471 (C)	Pub	900	3,262	2,950
Stephens College; Columbia, Mo. 65215	1,191 (W)	P	11,475	11,475	4,500
Sterling College; Sterling, Kan. 67579	468 (C)	P	6,785	6,785	3,000
Stetson University; Deland, Fla. 32720	2,113 (C)	P	10,020	10,020	4,070
Stevens Institute of Technology; Hoboken, N.J. 07030	1,600 (C)	P	16,285	16,285	4,595
Stillman College; Tuscaloosa, Ala. 35403	770 (C)	P	4,260	4,260	2,640
Stockton State College; Pomona, N.J. 08240	5,639 (C)	Pub	2,456	3,096	4,332
Stonehill College; North Easton, Mass. 02357	1,964 (C)	P	10,290	10,290	5,366
Strayer College; Washington, D.C. 20036	2,288 (C)	P	4,950	4,950	n.a.
Suffolk University; Boston, Mass. 02108	2,845 (C)	P	8,535	8,535	n.a.
Sul Ross State University; Alpine, Texas 79832	1,580 (C)	Pub	985	4,252	2,730
Sul Ross State University–Uvalde Study Center; Uvalde, Texas 78801	347 (C)	Pub	708	3,204	n.a.
Summit Christian College; Fort Wayne, Ind. 46807	376 (C)	P	6,625	6,625	2,860
Susquehanna University; Selinsgrove, Pa. 17870	1,465 (C)	P	13,950	13,950	4,030
Swarthmore College; Swarthmore, Pa. 19081	1,302 (C)	P	16,640	16,640	5,520
Sweet Briar College; Sweet Briar, Va. 24595	539 (W)	P	12,500	12,500	4,850
Syracuse University; Syracuse, N.Y. 13210	12,577 (C)	P	12,958	12,958	5,570
Tabor College; Hillsboro, Kan. 67063	436 (C)	P	6,160	6,160	2,760
Talladega College; Talladega, Ala. 35160	615 (C)	P	4,449	4,449	2,364

Institution and location	Enrollment	Control	Tuition ($) Res.	Tuition ($) Nonres.	Rm/Bd ($)
Tampa, University of; Tampa, Fla. 33606	2,026 (C)	P	10,100	10,100	3,720
Tampa College; Tampa, Fla. 33614	1,350 (C)	P	4,725	4,725	n.a.
Tarleton State University; Stephensville, Tex. 76402	5,585 (C)	Pub	1,132	3,120	2,592
Taylor University; Upland, Ind. 46989	1,740 (C)	P	9,353	9,353	3,542
Teikyo Westmar University; Le Mars, Iowa 51031	658 (C)	P	8,397	8,397	3,339
Teikyo Marycrest University; Davenport, Iowa 52804	1,309 (C)	P	8,440	8,440	3,100
Temple University, Philadelphia, Pa. 19122	22,336 (C)	Pub	4,294	7,892	4,398
Temple University-Ambler; Ambler, Pa. 19002	4,242 (C)	Pub	3,996	7,258	4,056
Tennessee, Univ. of-Chattanooga; Chattanooga, Tenn. 37402	6,698 (C)	Pub	1,493	4,696	4,748
Tennessee, Univ. of-Knoxville; Knoxville, Tenn. 37996	19,532 (C)	Pub	1,712	4,916	2,964
Tennessee, Univ. of-Martin; Martin, Tenn. 38238	5,056 (C)	Pub	1,546	4,750	2,440
Tennessee, Univ. of-Memphis, The Health Science Center; Memphis, Tenn. 38163	315 (C)	Pub	1,644	4,650	2,892
Tennessee State University; Nashville, Tenn. 37203	7,012 (C)	Pub	1,400	4,604	2,290
Tennessee Technological Univ.; Cookeville, Tenn. 38505	6,954 (C)	Pub	1,462	4,666	1,300
Tennessee Temple University; Chattanooga, Tenn. 37404	1,400 (C)	P	3,700	3,700	3,180
Tennessee Wesleyan College; Athens, Tenn. 37303	605 (C)	P	5,569	5,569	3,144
Texas, University of-Arlington; Arlington, Tex. 76019	20,735 (C)	Pub	1,700	6,692	3,852
Texas, University of-Austin; Austin, Tex. 78712	37,152 (C)	Pub	1,100	4,220	3,400
Texas, University of-Dallas; Richardson, Tex. 75083-0688	4,493 (C)	Pub	950	4,070	n.a.
Texas, University of-El Paso; El Paso, Tex. 79968	14,047 (C)	Pub	990	4,230	3,300
Texas, University of-Health Science Center-San Antonio; San Antonio, Tex. 78284	810 (C)	Pub	733	3,973	n.a.
Texas, University of, Medical Branch-Galveston; Galveston, Tex. 77550	655 (C)	Pub	864	5,760	5,400
Texas, University of-Permian Basin; Odessa, Tex. 79762	1,258 (C)	Pub	960	4,080	3,175
Texas, University of-San Antonio; San Antonio, Tex. 78285	12,459 (C)	Pub	930	4,050	3,345
Texas, University of, Southwestern Medical Center at Dallas; Dallas, Tex. 75235	356 (C)	Pub	990	5,400	n.a.
Texas, University of-Tyler; Tyler, Tex. 75701	2,579 (C)	Pub	900	4,020	n.a.
Texas A&I University-Kingsville; Kingsville, Tex. 78363	4,911 (C)	Pub	910	4,030	2,624
Texas A&M University; College Station, Tex. 77843	32,204 (C)	Pub	1,200	4,362	3,884
Texas A&M University-Galveston; Galveston, Tex. 77553	1,075 (C)	Pub	970	4,395	3,119
Texas Christian University; Fort Worth, Tex. 76129	5,415 (C)	P	8,166	8,166	2,735
Texas College; Tyler, Tex. 75702	450 (C)	P	3,275	3,275	2,430
Texas Lutheran College; Seguin, Tex. 78155	1,014 (C)	P	5,820	5,820	2,820
Texas Southern University; Houston, Tex. 77004	7,179 (C)	Pub	1,098	4,360	3,320
Texas Tech University; Lubbock, Tex. 79409	20,990 (C)	Pub	1,198	4,258	3,348
Texas Wesleyan University; Fort Worth, Tex. 76105	1,300 (C)	P	5,600	5,600	3,230
Texas Woman's University; Denton, Tex. 76204	4,992 (W)	Pub	964	4,084	2,678
Thiel College; Greenville, Pa. 16125	918 (C)	P	9,355	9,355	4,230
Thomas Aquinas College; Santa Paula, Calif. 93060	196 (C)	P	10,350	10,350	4,420
Thomas College; Waterville, Me. 04901	822 (C)	P	8,050	8,050	4,150
Thomas Edison State College, Trenton, N.J. 08608-1176	7,811 (C)	Pub	220	365	n.a.
Thomas Jefferson University, College of Allied Health Sciences; Philadelphia, Pa. 19107	1,333 (C)	P	10,600	10,600	4,650
Thomas More College; Crestview Hills, Ky. 41017	1,297 (C)	P	7,430	7,430	3,400
Tiffin University; Tiffin, Ohio 44883	854 (C)	P	6,100	6,100	3,380
Toccoa Falls College; Toccoa Falls, Ga. 30598	840 (C)	P	4,894	4,894	3,333
Toledo, University of; Toledo, Ohio 43606	21,585 (C)	Pub	2,526	5,781	2,805
Tougaloo College; Tougaloo, Miss. 39174	788 (C)	P	4,190	4,190	1,690
Touro College; New York, N.Y. 10001	4,298 (C)	P	6,730	6,730	6,050
Towson State University; Towson, Md. 21204-7097	13,519 (C)	Pub	2,458	4,380	2,205
Transylvania University; Lexington, Ky. 40508	1,076 (C)	P	9,619	9,619	4,048
Trenton State College; Trenton, N.J. 08650	6,760 (C)	Pub	2,720	3,795	4,400
Trevecca Nazarene College; Nashville, Tenn. 37210	1,051 (C)	P	4,896	4,896	2,660
Tri-State University; Angola, Ind. 46703	1,185 (C)	P	7,272	7,272	3,333
Trinity Bible College; Ellendale, N.D. 58436	394 (C)	P	4,088	4,088	3,098
Trinity Christian College; Palos Heights, Ill. 60463	546 (C)	P	8,250	8,250	3,340
Trinity College; Burlington, Vt. 05401	1,108 (W)	P	8,850	8,850	4,452
Trinity College; Deerfield, Ill. 60015	849 (C)	P	8,610	8,610	3,850
Trinity College; Hartford, Conn. 06106	1,969 (C)	P	16,960	16,960	4,820
Trinity College; Washington, D.C. 20017	884 (W)	P	10,600	10,600	6,280
Trinity University; San Antonio, Tex. 78284	2,383 (C)	P	9,676	9,676	4,340
Troy State University; Troy, Ala. 36802	3,642 (C)	Pub	1,470	2,172	2,632
Troy State University-Dothan; Dothan, Ala. 36303	1,169 (C)	Pub	1,419	1,824	n.a.
Troy State University-Montgomery; Montgomery, Ala. 36195-4419	2,242 (C)	Pub	1,370	2,090	n.a.
Tufts University; Medford, Mass. 02155	4,556 (C)	P	17,179	17,179	5,300
Tulane University; New Orleans, La. 70118	7,369 (C)	P	16,980	16,980	5,505
Tulsa, University of; Tulsa, Okla. 74104	2,980 (C)	P	8,700	8,700	3,600
Tusculum College; Greeneville, Tenn. 37743	720 (C)	P	5,700	5,700	3,100
Tuskegee University; Tuskegee, Ala. 36088	3,096 (C)	P	6,250	6,250	3,000
Union College; Barbourville, Ky. 40906	781 (C)	P	5,590	5,590	2,560
Union College; Lincoln, Neb. 68506	627 (C)	P	8,200	8,200	1,970
Union College; Schenectady, N.Y. 12308	1,957 (C)	P	15,579	15,579	5,395

Institution and location	Enrollment	Control	Tuition ($) Res.	Tuition ($) Nonres.	Rm/Bd ($)
Union Institute, The; Cincinnati, Ohio 45202-2407	300 (C)	P	7,284	7,284	n.a.
Union University; Jackson, Tenn. 38305	1,638 (C)	P	4,550	4,550	2,540
U.S. Air Force Academy; Colorado Springs, Colo. 80840	4,443 (C)	Pub	1,500	1,500	—
U.S. Coast Guard Academy; New London, Conn. 06320	951 (C)	Pub	1,500	1,500	—
U.S. International University; San Diego, Calif. 92131	1,254 (C)	P	8,550	8,550	4,155
U.S. Merchant Marine Academy; Kings Point, N.Y. 11024	844 (C)	Pub	2,980	2,980	—
U.S. Military Academy; West Point, N.Y. 10996	4,322 (C)	Pub	1,000	1,000	—
U.S. Naval Academy; Annapolis, Md. 21402	4,000 (C)	Pub	1,500	1,500	—
Unity College; Unity, Me. 04988	410 (C)	P	7,150	8,300	4,400
Universidad de las Américas—Puebla; Puebla, Mexico 72820	4,488 (C)	P	4,000	4,000	1,000
Universidad Politecnica de Puerto Rico; Hato Rey, San Juan, P.R. 00918	3,116 (C)	P	(8)	(8)	n.a.
Upper Iowa University; Fayette, Iowa 52142	2,215 (C)	P	8,540	8,540	2,860
Upsala College; East Orange, N.J. 07019	1,228 (C)	P	10,079	10,079	4,528
Urbana Univ.; Urbana, Ohio 43078	852 (C)	P	7,130	7,130	3,710
Ursinus College; Collegeville, Pa. 19426	1,128 (C)	P	12,530	12,530	4,500
Ursuline College; Pepper Pike, Ohio 44124	1,460 (C)	P	6,600	6,600	3,380
Utah, University of; Salt Lake City, Utah 84112	21,009 (C)	Pub	2,008	5,695	3,200
Utah State University; Logan, Utah 84322	10,030 (C)	Pub	1,686	4,668	2,790
Utica College of Syracuse University; Utica, N.Y. 13502	1,700 (C)	P	10,490	10,490	4,450
Valdosta State College; Valdosta, Ga. 31698	6,033 (C)	Pub	1,638	4,218	2,760
Valley City State University; Valley City, N.D. 58072	1,085 (C)	Pub	1,638	4,110	1,920
Valley Forge Christian College; Phoenixville, Pa. 19460	511 (C)	P	3,346	3,346	2,700
Valparaiso University; Valparaiso, Ind. 46383	3,243 (C)	P	9,110	9,110	2,700
Vanderbilt University; Nashville, Tenn. 37212	5,097 (C)	P	15,483	15,483	5,420
VanderCook College of Music; Chicago, Ill. 60616	104 (C)	P	7,545	7,545	3,992
Vassar College; Poughkeepsie, N.Y. 12601	2,306 (C)	P	14,950	14,950	4,980
Vennard College; University Park, Iowa 52595	153 (C)	P	4,172	4,172	2,310
Vermont, University of; Burlington, Vt. 05401-3596	8,032 (C)	Pub	4,200	12,800	4,026
Villa Julie College; Stevenson, Md. 21153	1,596 (C)	P	5,770	5,700	n.a.
Villanova University; Villanova, Pa. 19085	6,400 (C)	P	12,050	12,050	5,420
Virginia, University of; Charlottesville, Va. 22906	11,304 (C)	Pub	3,350	9,550	3,450
Virginia, University of—Clinch Valley College; Wise, Va. 24293	1,528 (C)	Pub	2,056	3,716	2,900
Virginia Commonwealth University; Richmond, Va. 23284-2526	15,920 (C)	Pub	2,719	6,698	3,350
Virginia Intermont College; Bristol, Va. 24201	521 (C)	P	6,570	6,570	3,930
Virginia Military Institute; Lexington, Va. 24450	1,300 (M)	Pub	4,325	9,865	3,525
Virginia Polytechnic Institute and State University; Blacksburg, Va. 24061	18,574 (C)	Pub	3,304	8,152	2,754
Virginia State University; Petersburg, Va. 23803	3,308 (C)	Pub	2,908	6,628	3,977
Virginia Union University; Richmond, Va. 23220	1,165 (C)	P	6,131	6,131	3,162
Virginia Wesleyan College; Norfolk-Virginia Beach, Va. 23502	1,390 (C)	P	8,740	8,740	4,425
Virgin Islands, University of the; St. Thomas, V.I. 00802	2,432 (C)	Pub	1,122	3,336	3,600
Visual Arts, School of; New York, N.Y. 10010	2,035 (C)	P	9,950	9,950	5,100
Viterbo College; La Crosse, Wis. 54601	1,122 (C)	P	7,900	7,900	3,100
Voorhees College; Denmark, S.C. 29042	574 (C)	P	6,292	6,292	2,522
Wabash College; Crawfordsville, Ind. 47933	850 (M)	P	10,700	10,700	3,665
Wadhams Hall Seminary—College; Ogdensburg, N.Y. 13669-9308	43 (M)	P	3,550	3,550	3,400
Wagner College; Staten Island, N.Y. 10301	1,290 (C)	P	10,050	10,050	4,850
Wake Forest University; Winston-Salem, N.C. 27109	3,483 (C)	P	10,800	10,800	3,900
Walla Walla College; College Place, Wash. 99324	1,534 (C)	P	9,540	9,540	2,985
Walsh College; Canton, Ohio 44720	1,315 (C)	P	6,528	6,528	3,350
Walsh College of Accountancy and Business Administration; Troy, Mich. 48007	1,734 (C)	P	4,034	4,034	n.a.
Warner Pacific College; Portland, Ore. 97215	496 (C)	P	7,472	7,472	3,298
Warner Southern College; Lake Wales, Fla. 33853	423 (C)	P	5,320	5,320	2,090
Warren Wilson College; Swannanoa, N.C. 28778	502 (C)	P	8,515	8,515	2,852
Wartburg College; Waverly, Iowa 50677	1,440 (C)	P	9,640	9,640	3,080
Warwick, University of; Coventry, CV4 7AL, England	5,626 (C)	Pub	3,071	3,071	2,456
Washburn University; Topeka, Kan. 66621	5,492 (C)	Pub	2,342	3,632	2,734
Washington, University of; Seattle, Wash. 98195	24,566 (C)	Pub	1,941	5,421	3,918
Washington and Jefferson College; Washington, Pa. 15301	1,205 (C)	P	12,850	12,850	3,290
Washington and Lee University; Lexington, Va. 24450	1,624 (C)	P	11,575	11,575	4,068
Washington Bible College; Lanham, Md. 20706	325 (C)	P	5,143	5,143	2,210
Washington College; Chestertown, Md. 21620	899 (C)	P	11,400	11,400	4,600
Washington State University; Pullman, Wash. 99164	13,814 (C)	Pub	1,954	5,434	3,300
Washington University; St. Louis, Mo. 63130	4,916 (C)	P	16,110	16,110	5,127
Wayland Baptist University; Plainview, Tex. 79072	2,052 (C)	P	4,654	4,654	3,073
Waynesburg College; Waynesburg, Pa. 15370	1,196 (C)	P	7,490	7,490	3,050
Wayne State College; Wayne, Neb. 68787	2,714 (C)	Pub	1,421	2,186	2,290
Wayne State University; Detroit, Mich. 48202	21,085 (C)	Pub	2,128	4,702	4,860
Webber College; Babson Park, Fla. 33827	247 (C)	P	5,390	5,390	2,730
Webb Institute of Naval Architecture; Glen Cove, N.Y. 11542	78 (C)	P	—	—	4,200
Weber State College; Ogden, Utah 84408	12,783 (C)	Pub	1,400	3,753	2,535

Institution and location	Enrollment	Control	Tuition ($) Res.	Tuition ($) Nonres.	Rm/Bd ($)
Webster University; St. Louis, Mo. 63119	2,275 (C)	P	7,340	7,340	3,650
Wellesley College; Wellesley, Mass. 02181	2,279 (W)	P	15,966	15,966	5,657
Wells College; Aurora, N.Y. 13026	400 (W)	P	11,690	11,690	4,300
Wentworth Institute of Technology; Boston, Mass. 02115	3,034 (C)	P	7,716	7,716	5,954
Wesleyan College; Macon, Ga. 31297	511 (W)	P	9,845	9,845	3,950
Wesleyan University; Middletown, Conn. 06457	2,671 (C)	P	16,250	16,250	4,990
Wesley College; Dover, Del. 19901	1,295 (C)	P	8,055	8,055	3,800
Wesley College; Florence, Miss. 39073	65 (C)	P	1,740	1,740	1,980
West Chester Univ. of Pennsylvania; West Chester, Pa. 19383	9,770 (C)	Pub	2,279	4,562	3,194
West Coast Christian College; Fresno, Calif. 93710	274 (C)	P	2,880	2,880	2,640
West Coast University; Los Angeles, Calif. 90020-1765	850 (C)	P	8,250	8,250	n.a.
Western Baptist College; Salem, Ore. 97301	358 (C)	P	7,150	7,150	3,350
Western Carolina University; Cullowhee, N.C. 28723	5,106 (C)	Pub	1,213	5,744	2,180
Western Connecticut State University; Danbury, Conn. 06810	5,163 (C)	Pub	2,490	6,202	3,200
Western Illinois University; Macomb, Ill. 61455	11,004 (C)	Pub	2,229	5,541	2,869
Western International University; Phoenix, Ariz. 85021	1,173 (C)	P	4,370	4,370	n.a.
Western Kentucky University; Bowling Green, Ky. 42101	13,130 (C)	Pub	1,440	4,040	2,570
Western Maryland College; Westminster, Md. 21157	1,315 (C)	P	12,505	12,505	4,740
Western Michigan University; Kalamazoo, Mich. 49008	20,598 (C)	Pub	2,270	5,370	3,375
Western Montana College; Dillon, Mont. 59725	905 (C)	Pub	1,364	3,035	3,010
Western New England College; Springfield, Mass. 01119	2,232 (C)	P	7,982	7,982	4,900
Western New Mexico University; Silver City, N.M. 88061	1,546 (C)	Pub	1,122	4,352	2,110
Western Oregon State College; Monmouth, Ore. 97361	3,461 (C)	Pub	1,806	4,566	2,940
Western State College of Colorado; Gunnison, Colo. 81230	2,500 (C)	Pub	1,599	4,693	2,958
Western Washington University; Bellingham, Wash. 98225	8,882 (C)	Pub	1,611	5,649	3,200
Westfield State College; Westfield, Mass. 01085	3,043 (C)	Pub	1,250	4,325	2,160
West Florida, University of; Pensacola, Fla. 32514	6,625 (C)	Pub	1,321	4,632	3,204
West Georgia College; Carrollton, Ga. 30118	5,269 (C)	Pub	1,587	4,065	2,304
West Liberty State College; West Liberty, W. Va. 26074	2,386 (C)	Pub	1,500	3,470	2,650
West Los Angeles, University of, School of Paralegal Studies; Los Angeles, Calif. 90066	319 (C)	P	2,904	2,904	n.a.
Westminster Choir College; Princeton, N.J. 08540	230 (C)	P	11,100	11,100	4,780
Westminster College; Fulton, Mo. 65251	761 (C)	P	8,200	8,200	3,350
Westminster College; New Wilmington, Pa. 16172	1,392 (C)	P	10,580	10,580	3,150
Westminster Coll. of Salt Lake City; Salt Lake City, Utah 84105	1,609 (C)	P	7,254	7,254	3,550
Westmont College; Santa Barbara, Calif. 93108	1,264 (C)	P	10,900	10,900	4,650
West Oahu College. *See* Hawaii, University of					
West Texas State University; Canyon, Tex. 79016	4,813 (C)	Pub	1,060	4,128	2,686
West Virginia Institute of Technology; Montgomery, W. Va. 25136	2,883 (C)	Pub	3,082	3,082	3,010
West Virginia State College; Institute, W. Va. 25112	4,834 (C)	Pub	1,432	3,542	2,800
West Virginia University; Morgantown, W. Va. 26506	14,984 (C)	Pub	1,850	5,000	3,846
West Virginia Wesleyan College; Buckhannon, W. Va. 26201	1,461 (C)	P	11,930	11,930	3,150
Wheaton College; Norton, Mass. 02766	1,264 (C)	P	16,040	16,040	5,300
Wheaton College; Wheaton, Ill. 60187	2,235 (C)	P	9,500	9,500	3,800
Wheeling Jesuit College; Wheeling, W. Va. 26003	1,224 (C)	P	8,550	8,550	3,840
Wheelock College; Boston, Mass. 02215	750 (C)	P	11,212	11,212	5,078
White Plains, Coll. of, of Pace Univ. *See* Pace Univ.					
Whitman College; Walla Walla, Wash. 99362	1,239 (C)	P	13,210	13,210	4,340
Whittier College; Whittier, Calif. 90608	1,029 (C)	P	14,632	14,632	4,966
Whitworth College; Spokane, Wash. 99251	1,237 (C)	P	10,415	10,415	3,850
Wichita State University; Wichita, Kan. 67208	17,419 (C)	Pub	1,608	4,715	3,127
Widener University; Chester, Pa. 19013	2,403 (C)	P	10,500	10,500	4,560
Wilberforce University; Wilberforce, Ohio 45384	779 (C)	P	6,346	6,346	3,686
Wiley College; Marshall, Tex. 75670	505 (C)	P	4,146	4,146	2,544
Wilkes University; Wilkes-Barre, Pa. 18766	1,886 (C)	P	9,275	9,275	4,700
Willamette University; Salem, Ore. 97301	1,535 (C)	P	12,480	12,480	3,950
William and Mary, College of; Williamsburg, Va. 23185	5,286 (C)	Pub	3,730	10,450	3,746
William Carey College; Hattiesburg, Miss. 39401	1,546 (C)	P	4,555	4,555	2,250
William Jewell College; Liberty, Mo. 64068	1,477 (C)	P	7,450	7,450	2,560
William Paterson College; Wayne, N.J. 07470	7,370 (C)	Pub	2,385	3,135	2,085
William Penn College; Oskaloosa, Iowa 52577	737 (C)	P	9,190	9,190	2,720
Williams Baptist College; Walnut Ridge, Ark. 72476	504 (C)	P	3,110	3,110	2,220
Williams College; Williamstown, Mass. 01267	2,060 (C)	P	15,535	15,535	4,975
William Smith College. *See* Hobart and William Smith Colleges					
William Tyndale College; Farmington Hills, Mich. 48108	396 (C)	P	5,060	5,060	3,400
William Woods College; Fulton, Mo. 65251	750 (W)	P	8,208	8,208	3,560
Wilmington College; New Castle, Del. 19720	1,796 (C)	P	4,945	4,945	n.a.
Wilmington College of Ohio; Wilmington, Ohio 45177	890 (C)	P	8,780	8,780	3,250
Wilson College; Chambersburg, Pa. 17201-1285	853 (W)	P	10,582	10,582	4,936
Wingate College; Wingate, N.C. 28174	1,791 (C)	P	5,900	5,900	3,120
Winona State University; Winona, Minn. 55987	7,100 (C)	Pub	2,000	3,200	2,450
Winston-Salem State University; Winston-Salem, N.C. 27110	2,517 (C)	Pub	896	4,268	2,265
Winthrop College; Rock Hill, S.C. 29733	4,173 (C)	Pub	2,568	4,612	2,668
Wisconsin, University of-Eau Claire; Eau Claire, Wis. 54701	10,003 (C)	Pub	1,829	5,476	2,420

Institution and location	Enrollment	Control	Tuition ($) Res.	Tuition ($) Nonres.	Rm/Bd ($)
Wisconsin, University of-Green Bay; Green Bay, Wis. 54302	4,590 (C)	Pub	1,754	5,300	2,350
Wisconsin, University of-La Crosse; La Crosse, Wis. 54601	8,120 (C)	Pub	1,970	5,830	2,130
Wisconsin, University of-Madison; Madison, Wis. 53706	29,248 (C)	Pub	2,107	6,831	3,445
Wisconsin, University of-Milwaukee; Milwaukee, Wis. 53201	20,686 (C)	Pub	2,054	6,881	3,476
Wisconsin, University of-Oshkosh; Oshkosh, Wis. 54901	9,543 (C)	Pub	1,850	5,700	2,110
Wisconsin, University of-Parkside; Kenosha, Wis. 53141	4,896 (C)	Pub	1,781	5,059	2,916
Wisconsin, University of-Platteville; Platteville, Wis. 53818	5,213 (C)	Pub	1,877	5,524	2,260
Wisconsin, University of-River Falls; River Falls, Wis. 54022	4,583 (C)	Pub	1,760	5,120	2,292
Wisconsin, University of-Stevens Point; Stevens Point, Wis. 54481	8,429 (C)	Pub	1,879	5,526	2,614
Wisconsin, University of-Stout; Menomonie, Wis. 54751	6,889 (C)	Pub	1,866	5,513	2,263
Wisconsin, University of-Superior; Superior, Wis. 54880	2,112 (C)	Pub	1,677	5,401	2,200
Wisconsin, University of-Whitewater; Whitewater, Wis. 53190	9,147 (C)	Pub	1,800	5,493	2,100
Wisconsin Lutheran College; Milwaukee, Wis. 53226	283 (C)	P	7,578	7,578	3,200
Wittenberg University; Springfield, Ohio 45501	2,341 (C)	P	13,491	13,491	4,044
Wofford College; Spartanburg, S.C. 29303-3663	1,076 (C)	P	9,790	9,790	4,150
Woodbury University; Burbanks, Calif. 91510-7846	865 (C)	P	9,342	9,342	5,100
Wooster, College of; Wooster, Ohio 44691	1,891 (C)	P	13,410	13,410	4,240
Worcester Polytechnic Institute; Worcester, Mass. 01609	2,820 (C)	P	14,295	14,295	4,590
Worcester State College; Worcester, Mass. 01602	3,600 (C)	Pub	1,812	4,506	3,630
World College West; Petaluma, Calif. 94952	125 (C)	P	8,850	8,850	3,900
Wright State University; Dayton, Ohio 45435	13,783 (C)	Pub	2,469	4,938	3,642
Wyoming, University of; Laramie, Wyo. 82071	9,408 (C)	Pub	1,293	4,097	3,262
Xavier University; Cincinnati, Ohio 45207	3,912 (C)	P	9,000	9,000	3,910
Xavier University of Louisiana; New Orleans, La. 70125	2,563 (C)	P	5,500	5,500	2,900
Yale University; New Haven, Conn. 06520	5,182 (C)	P	16,300	16,300	5,900
Yeshiva University; New York, N.Y. 10033-3299	1,754 (C)	P	10,310	10,310	5,130
York College of Pennsylvania; York, Pa. 17405	2,746 (C)	P	4,448	4,448	2,972
Youngstown State Univ.; Youngstown, Ohio 44555	13,647 (C)	Pub	2,190	3,390	3,405

1. Graduate school only. 2. $15 per credit. 3. $50 per credit. 4. $86 per credit. 5. $273 per credit. 6. $93 per credit. 7. $188 per credit. 8. $65 per credit.

Public Education Expenditures Exceeded $286 Billion in 1989

Source: U.S. Department of Commerce, Bureau of the Census.

Federal, state, and local governments spent more than $286 billion in 1989 to fund higher education institutions and provide elementary-secondary education according to a report issued by the Commerce Department's Census Bureau.

The federal government spent $38.5 billion, or 13 percent of the total public education costs, to fund programs such as school lunch and milk, impact aid, education for the handicapped, and project Head Start. The federal share increased by 9.2 percent over 1988.

State governments contributed nearly $159 billion, or 55 percent of the total, for public education. This included more than $91.5 billion to elementary-secondary school systems and $67 billion to state-operated higher education institutions, special schools, and scholarship/fellowship payments.

Local school systems, the primary recipients of federal and state intergovernmental payments for education, supplied an additional $89 billion, or 31 percent.

The report also shows that:

• State support for elementary-secondary education increased by 7.2 percent from 1988 to 1989, and local tax support by 8.2 percent.

• Local funding for elementary-secondary education ranged from a high of 89 percent in New Hampshire to a low of 13 percent in New Mexico.

• Systems with the greatest percentage of state funding were Hawaii (100 percent), New Mexico (76 percent), and Washington (70 percent).

• The federal government's funding share was highest in Mississippi (16 percent).

• Of the $194 billion spent by public school systems for elementary-secondary education, $106 billion—almost 55 percent—was allocated to instructional programs, while $78 billion was spent on teachers and other instructional salaries. Although instructional salaries increased by 5.2 percent from the $74 billion spent in 1988, its share of total elementary-secondary expenditures shrank from 41.7 to 40.4 percent.

• Spending per pupil for instruction averaged $2,635 in 1989.

Selected Degree Abbreviations

A.B. Bachelor of Arts
AeEng. Aeronautical Engineer
A.M.T. Master of Arts in Teaching
B.A. Bachelor of Arts
B.A.E. Bachelor of Arts in Education, or Bachelor of Art Education, Aeronautical Engineering, Agricultural Engineering, or Architectural Engineering
B.Ag. Bachelor of Agriculture
B.A.M. Bachelor of Applied Mathematics
B.Arch. Bachelor of Architecture
B.B.A. Bachelor of Business Administration
B.C.E. Bachelor of Civil Engineering
B.Ch.E. Bachelor of Chemical Engineering
B.C.L. Bachelor of Canon Law
B.D. Bachelor of Divinity
B.E. Bachelor of Education or Bachelor of Engineering
B.E.E. Bachelor of Electrical Engineering
B.F. Bachelor of Forestry
B.F.A. Bachelor of Fine Arts
B.J. Bachelor of Journalism
B.L.S. Bachelor of Liberal Studies or Bachelor of Library Science
B.Lit. Bachelor of Literature
B.M. Bachelor of Medicine or Bachelor of Music
B.M.S. Bachelor of Marine Science
B.N. Bachelor of Nursing
B.Pharm. Bachelor of Pharmacy
B.R.E. Bachelor of Religious Education
B.S. Bachelor of Science
B.S.Ed. Bachelor of Science in Education
C.E. Civil Engineer
Ch.E. Chemical Engineer
D.B.A. Doctor of Business Administration
D.C. Doctor of Chiropractic
D.D. Doctor of Divinity[1]
D.D.S. Doctor of Dental Surgery or Doctor of Dental Science
D.L.S. Doctor of Library Science
D.M.D. Doctor of Dental Medicine
D.O. Doctor of Osteopathy
D.M.S. Doctor of Medical Science
D.P.A. Doctor of Public Administration[2]
D.P.H. Doctor of Public Health
D.R.E. Doctor of Religious Education
D.S.W. Doctor of Social Welfare or Doctor of Social Work
D.Sc. Doctor of Science[3]
D.V.M. Doctor of Veterinary Medicine
Ed.D. Doctor of Education[2]
Ed.S. Education Specialist
E.E. Electrical Engineer

E.M. Engineer of Mines
E.Met. Engineer of Metallurgy
I.E. Industrial Engineer or Industrial Engineering
J.D. Doctor of Laws[2]
J.S.D. Doctor of Juristic Science
L.H.D. Doctor of Humane Letters[3]
Litt.B. Bachelor of Letters
Litt.M. Master of Letters[4]
LL.B. Bachelor of Laws
LL.D. Doctor of Laws[3]
LL.M. Master of Laws
M.A. Master of Arts
M.Aero.E. Master of Aeronautical Engineering
M.B.A. Master of Business Administration
M.C.E. Master of Christian Education or Master of Civil Engineering
M.C.S. Master of Computer Science
M.D. Doctor of Medicine
M.Div. Master of Divinity
M.E. Master of Engineering
M.Ed. Master of Education
M.Eng. Master of Engineering
M.F.A. Master of Fine Arts
M.H.A. Master of Hospital Administration
M.L.S. Master of Library Science
M.M. Master of Music
M.M.E. Master of Mechanical Engineering or Master of Music Education
M.Mus. Master of Music
M.N. Master of Nursing
M.R.E. Master of Religious Education
M.S. Master of Science
M.S.W. Master of Social Work
M.Th. Master of Theology
Nuc.E. Nuclear Engineer
O.D. Doctor of Optometry
Pharm.D. Doctor of Pharmacy[2]
Ph.B. Bachelor of Philosophy
Ph.D. Doctor of Philosophy
S.B. Bachelor of Science
Sc.D. Doctor of Science[3]
S.J.D. Doctor of Juridical Science or Doctor of the Science of Law
S.Sc.D. Doctor of Social Science
S.T.B. Bachelor of Sacred Theology
S.T.D. Doctor of Sacred Theology
S.T.M. Master of Sacred Theology
Th.B. Bachelor of Theology
Th.D. Doctor of Theology
Th.M. Master of Theology

1. Honorary. 2. Earned and honorary. 3. Usually honorary.
4. Sometimes honorary.

Academic Costume: Colors Associated With Fields

Field	Color	Field	Color
Agriculture	Maize	Medicine	Green
Arts, Letters, Humanities	White	Music	Pink
Commerce, Accountancy,		Nursing	Apricot
Business	Drab	Oratory (Speech)	Silver gray
Dentistry	Lilac	Pharmacy	Olive green
Economics	Copper	Philosophy	Dark blue
Education	Light blue	Physical Education	Sage green
Engineering	Orange	Public Admin. including Foreign Service	Peacock blue
Fine Arts, Architecture	Brown	Public Health	Salmon pink
Forestry	Russet	Science	Golden yellow
Journalism	Crimson	Social Work	Citron
Law	Purple	Theology	Scarlet
Library Science	Lemon	Veterinary Science	Gray

SPORTS

THE OLYMPIC GAMES

(W)—Site of Winter Games. (S)—Site of Summer Games

1896	Athens	1936	Berlin (S)	1972	Munich (S)
1900	Paris	1948	St. Moritz (W)	1976	Innsbruck, Austria (W)
1904	St. Louis	1948	London (S)	1976	Montreal (S)
1906	Athens	1952	Oslo (W)	1980	Lake Placid (W)
1908	London	1952	Helsinki (S)	1980	Moscow (S)
1912	Stockholm	1956	Cortina d'Ampezzo, Italy (W)	1984	Sarajevo, Tugoslavia (W)
1920	Antwerp	1956	Melbourne (S)	1984	Los Angeles (S)
1924	Chamonix (W)	1960	Squaw Valley, Calif. (W)	1988	Calgary, Alberta (W)
1924	Paris (S)	1960	Rome (S)	1988	Seoul, South Korea (S)
1928	St. Moritz (W)	1964	Innsbruck, Austria (W)	1992	Albertville, France (W)
1928	Amsterdam (S)	1964	Tokyo (S)	1992	Barcelona, Spain (S)
1932	Lake Placid (W)	1968	Grenoble, France (W)	1994	Lillehammer, Norway (W)
1932	Los Angeles (S)	1968	Mexico City (S)	1996	Atlanta, Ga. (S)
1936	Garnisch–Partenkirchen (W)	1972	Sapporo, Japan (W)		

The first Olympic Games of which there is record were held in 776 B.C., and consisted of one event, a great foot race of about 200 yards held on a plain by the River Alpheus (now the Ruphia) just outside the little town of Olympia in Greece. It was from that date the Greeks began to keep their calendar by "Olympiads," the four–year spans between the celebrations of the famous games.

The modern Olympic Games, which started in Athens in 1896, are the result of the deveotion of a French educator, Baron Pierre de Coubertin, to the idea that, since young people and athletics have gone together through the ages, educaiton and athletics might go hand–in–hand toward a better international understanding.

The principal organization responsible for the staging of the Games every four years is the International Olympic Committee (IOC). Other important roles are played by the National Olympic Committees in each participating country, international sports federations, and the organizing committee of the host city.

The headquarters of the 89–member International Olympic Committee are in Lausanne, Switzerland. The president of the IOC is Juan Antonio Samaranch of Spain.

The Olympic motto is "Citius, Altius, Fortius,"–"Faster, Higher, Stronger." The Olympic symbol is five interlocking circles colored blue, yellow, black, green, and red, on a white background, representing the five continents. At least one of those colors appears in the national flag of every country.

The ideal of peaceful international athletic competition has been severely tested in past Olympiads, dating back to the 1972 raid by Arab terrorists on the Olympic village in Munich, Germany. Eleven Israelis, five terrorists, and a German police officer were all killed in the seige.

In 1976, political problems kept one–quarter of the IOC–member nations from competing. The most pressing was the conflict over recognition of Taiwan or Mainland China as the correct representative of that country. An additional 31 nations withdrew over the failure to bar New Zealand, which had a soccer team touring apartheid South Africa.

A total of 66 nations, including the United States, did not participate in 1980, over the Soviet Union's invasion of Afghanistan. Those Summer Games were scheduled for Moscow.

Considering this action, it was almost inevitable that the Soviet Union would take some similar action for the 1984 games, held in Los Angeles. Officially, the Soviet Union, and nearly the entire Soviet–comunist bloc, withdrew over dissatisfaction with security measures in Los Angeles.

The 1988 Summer Olympics were held in Seoul, South Korea. For the first time since 1976, all the Eastern bloc countries competed against the nations of the West.

Winter Games

FIGURE SKATING–MEN

1908	Ulrich Salchow, Sweden
1920	Gillis Grafstrom, Sweden
1924	Gillis Grafstrom, Sweden
1928	Gillis Grafstrom, Sweden
1932	Karl Schaefer, Austria
1936	Karl Schaefer, Austria
1948	Richard Button, United States
1952	Richard Button, United States
1956	Hayes Alan Jenkins, United States
1960	David Jenkins, United States
1964	Manfred Schnelldorfer, Germany
1968	Wolfgang Schwartz, Austria
1972	Ondrej Nepela, Czechoslovakia
1976	John Curry, Great Britain
1980	Robin Cousins, Great Britain
1984	Scott Hamilton, United States
1988	Brian Boitano, United States

FIGURE SKATING–WOMEN

1908	Madge Syers, Britain
1920	Magda Julin–Maurey, Sweden
1924	Herma Szabo–Planck, Austria
1928	Sonja Henie, Norway
1932	Sonja Henie, Norway
1936	Sonja Henle, Norway
1948	Barbara Ann Scott, Canada
1952	Jeannette Altwegg, Great Britain
1956	Tenley Albright, United States
1960	Carol Heiss, United States
1964	Sjoukje Dijkstra, Netherlands
1968	Peggy Fleming, United States

1972	Beatrix Schuba, Austria	
1976	Dorothy Hamill, United States	
1980	Anett Poetzsch, East Germany	
1984	Katarina Witt, East Germany	
1988	Katarina Witt, East Germany	

SPEED SKATING–MEN

(U.S. winners only)

500 Meters

1924	Charles Jewtraw	44.0
1932	John A. Shea	43.4
1952	Kenneth Henry	43.2
1964	Terrence McDermott	40.1
1980	Eric Heiden	38.03

1,000 Meters

1976	Peter Mueller	1:19.32
1980	Eric Heiden	1:15.18

1,500 Meters

1932	John A. Shea	2:57.5
1980	Eric Heiden	1:55.44

5,000 Meters

1932	Irving Jaffee	9:40.8
1980	Eric Heiden	7:02.29

10,000 Meters

1932	Irving Jaffee	19:13.6
1980	Eric Heiden	14:28.13

SPEED SKATING–WOMEN

500 Meters

1972	Anne Henning	43.33
1976	Sheila Young	42.76
1988	Bonnie Blair,	39.10 [1]

1,500 Meters

1972	Dianne Holum	2:20.85

1. World Record

SKIING, ALPINE–MEN

Downhill

1948	Henri Oreiller, France	2m55.0s
1952	Zeno Colo, Italy	2m30.8s
1956	Anton Sailer, Austria	2m52.2s
1960	Jean Vuarnet, France	2m06.2s
1964	Egon Zimmermann, Austria	2m18.16s
1968	Jean–Claude Killy, France	1m59.85s
1972	Bernhard Russi, Switzerland	1m51.43s
1976	Franz Klammer, Austria	1m45.72s
1980	Leonhard Stock, Austria	1m45.50s
1984	Bill Johnson, United States	1m45.59s
1988	Pirmin Zurbriggen, Switzerland	1m59.63s

Slalom

1948	Edi Reinalter, Switzerland	2m10.3s
1952	Othmar Schneider, Austria	2m00.0s

DISTRIBUTION OF MEDALS
1988 WINTER GAMES

(Calgary, Alberta)

	Gold	Silver	Bronze	Total
Soviet Union	11	9	9	29
East Germany	9	10	6	25
Switzerland	5	5	5	15
Austria	3	5	2	10
West Germany	2	4	2	8
Finland	4	1	2	7
Netherlands	3	2	2	7
Sweden	4	0	2	6
United States	2	1	3	6
Italy	2	1	2	5
Norway	0	3	2	5
Canada	0	2	3	5
Yugoslavia	0	2	1	3
Czechoslovakia	0	1	2	3
France	1	0	1	2
Japan	0	0	1	1
Liechtenstein	0	0	1	1

1956	Anton Sailer, Austria	194.7 pts.
1960	Ernst Hinterseer, Austria	2m08.9s
1964	Josef Stiegler, Austria	2m10.13
1968	Jean–Claude Killy, France	1m39,73s
1972	Francisco Fernandez Ochoa, Spain	1m49.27s
1976	Piero Gros, Italy	2m03.29s
1980	Integmar Stenmark, Sweden	1m44.26s
1984	Phil Mahre, United States	1m39.41s
1988	Alberto Tomba, Italy	1m39.47s

Giant Slalom

1952	Stein Eriksen, Norway	2m25.0s
1956	Anton Sailer, Austria	3m00.1s
1960	Roger Staub, Switzerland	1m48.3s
1964	François Bonlieu, France	1m46.71s
1968	Jean-Claude Killy, France	3m29.28s
1972	Gustavo Thoeni, Italy	3m09.52s
1976	Heini Hemmi, Switzerland	3m26.97s
1980	Ingemar Stenmark, Sweden	2m40.74s
1984	Max Julen, Switzerland	1m20.54s
1988	Alberto Tomba, Italy	2m06.37s

SKIING, ALPINE–WOMEN

Downhill

1948	Hedi Schlunegger, Switzerland	2m28.3s
1952	Trude Jochum–Beiser, Austria	1m47.1s
1956	Madeleine Berthod, Switzerland	1m40.1s
1960	Heidi Biebl, Germany	1m37.6s
1964	Christi Haas, Austria	1m55.39s
1968	Olga Pall, Austria	1m40.87s
1972	Marie–Therese Nadig, Switzerland	1m36.68s
1976	Rosi Mittermeier, West Germany	1m46.16s
1980	Annemarie Proell Moser, Austria	1m37.52s
1984	Michela Figini, Switzerland	1m13.36s
1988	Marina Kiehl, West Germany	1m25.86s

Slalom

1948	Gretchen Fraser, United States	1m57.2s
1952	Andrea Mead Lawrence, United States	2m10.6s
1956	Renee Colliard, Switzerland	112.3 pts.
1960	Anne Heggtveigt, Canada	1m49.6s
1964	Christine Goitschel, France	1m29.86s
1968	Marielle Goitschel, France	1m25.86s
1972	Barbara Cochran, United States	1m31.24s

1976	Rosi Mittermeier, West Germany	1m30.54s
1980	Hanni Wenzel, Liechtenstein	1m25.09s
1984	Paoletta Magoni, Italy	1m36.47s
1988	Vreni Schneider, Switzerland	1m36.69s

Giant Slalom

1952	Andrea M. Lawrence, United States	2m06.8s
1956	Ossi Reichert, Germany	1m56.5s
1960	Yvonne Ruegg, Switzerland	1m39.9s
1964	Marielle Goitschel, France	1m52.24s
1968	Nancy Greene, Canada	1m51.97s
1972	Marie–Therese Nadig, Switzerland	1m29.90s
1976	Kathy Kreiner, Canada	1m29.13s
1980	Hanni Wenzel, Liechtenstein	2m41.66s
1984	Debbie Armstrong, United States	2m20.98s
1988	Vreni Schneider, Switzerland	2m06.49s

SKIING, NORDIC, JUMPING

90–Meter Hill

1924	Jacob T. Thams, Norway	227.5
1928	Alfred Andersen, Norway	230.5
1932	Birger Ruud, Norway	228.0
1936	Birger Ruud, Norway	232.0
1948	Peter Hugsted, Norway	228.1
1952	A. Bergmann, Norway	226.0
1956	Antii Hyvarinen, Finland	227.0
1960	Helmut Recknagel, Germany	227.2
1964	Toralf Engan, Norway	230.7
1968	Vladimir Beloussov, U.S.S.R.	231.3
1972	Wojciech Fortuna, Poland	219.9
1976	Karl Schnabl, Austria	234.8
1980	Jouko Tormanen, Finland	271.0
1984	Matti Nykanen, Finland	231.2
1988	Matti Nykanen, Finland	224.0

Small Hil (70 meters)

1964	Veikko Kankkonen, Finland	229.9
1968	Jiri Raska, Czechoslovakia	216.5
1972	Yukio Kasaya, Japan	244.2
1976	Hans–Georg Aschenbach, East Germany	252.0
1980	Anton Innauer, Austria	266.3
1984	Jens Weissflog, East Germany	215.2
1988	Matti Nykanen, Finland	229.1

ICE HOCKEY

1920	Canada	1960	United States
1924	Canada	1964	U.S.S.R.
1928	Canada	1968	U.S.S.R.
1932	Canada	1972	U.S.S.R.
1936	Great Britain	1976	U.S.S.R.
1948	Canada	1980	United States
1952	Canada	1984	U.S.S.R.
1956	U.S.S.R.	1988	U.S.S.R.

FINAL OVER-ALL 1988 OLYMPIC HOCKEY STANDINGS

	W	L	T	Pts	GF	GA
1. Soviet Union	4	1	0	8	25	7
2. Finland	3	1	1	7	18	10
3. Sweden	2	1	2	6	16	18
Canada	2	2	1	5	17	14
West Germany	1	4	0	2	8	26
Czechoslovakia	1	4	0	2	12	22

1. won gold medal 2. won silver medal 3. won bronze medal

Championship
Soviet Union 7, Sweden 1

Second Place
Finland 2, Soviet Union 1

Third Place
Sweden 3, West Germany 2

Fourth Place
Canada 6, Czechoslovakia 3

Seventh Place
United States 8, Switzerland 4

Ninth Place
Austria 3, Poland 2

Other 1988 Winter Olympic Games Champions

Biathlon

10–kilometer—Frank-Peter Roetsch, East Germany
20–kilometer—Frank-Peter Roetsch, East Germany
30–kilometer relay—Soviet Union

Bobsledding

2–man—U.S.S.R. I
4–man—Switzerland I

Figure Skating

Pairs—Ekaterina Gordeeva and Sergeir Grinkov, U.S.S.R.
Dance—Natalia Berstemianova and Andrei Boukine,
U.S.S.R.

Speed Skating–Men

500m—Jens-Uew Mey, East Germany
1,000m—Nikolai Gouliaev, U.S.S.R.
1,500m—Andre Hoffmann, East Germany
5,000m—Tomas Gustafson, Sweden
10,000m—Tomas Gustafson, Sweden

Speed Skating–Women

500m—Bonnie Blair, United States
1,000m—Christa Rothenberger, East Germany

1,500m—Yvonne Van Gennip, The Netherlands
3,000m—Yvonne Van Gennip, The Netherlands
5,000m—Yvonne Van Gennip, The Netherlands

Luge

Men's singles—Jens Mueller, East Germany
Men's doubles—Joerg Hoffmann and Jochen Pietzsch,
East Germany

Skiing, Nordic–Men

Combined team—West Germany
Combined—Hippolyt Kempf, Switzerland
Men's 15-kilometer—Mikhail Deviatiarov, U.S.S.R.
Men's 30-kilometer—Alexei Prokourorov, U.S.S.R.
Men's 50-kilometer—Gunde Svan, Sweden
40-kilometer relay—Sweden
70–m jump—Matti Nykaenen, Finland
90–m jump—Matti Nykaenen, Finland

Skiing, Nordic–Women

Women's 5–kilometer—Marjo Matikainen, Finland
Women's 10–kilometer—Vida Ventsene, U.S.S.R.
Women's 20–kilometer—Tamara Tikhonova, U.S.S.R.
20–kilometer relay—U.S.S.R.

Summer Games

TRACK AND FIELD–MEN

100–Meter Dash

1896	Thomas Burke, United States	12s
1900	Francis W. Jarvis, United States	10.8s
1904	Archie Hahn, United States	11s
1906	Archie Hahn, United States	11.2s
1908	Reginald Walker, South Africa	10.8s
1912	Ralph Craig, United States	10.8s
1920	Charles Paddock, United States	10.8s
1924	Harold Abrahams, Great Britain	10.6s
1928	Percy Williams, Canada	10.8s
1932	Eddie Tolan, United States	10.3s
1936	Jesse Owens, United States	10.3s
1948	Harrison Dillard, United States	10.3s
1952	Lindy Remigino, United States	10.4s
1956	Bobby Morrow, United States	10.5s
1960	Armin Hary, Germany	10.2s
1964	Robert Hayes, United States	10s
1968	James Hines, United States	9.9s
1972	Valery Borzow, U.S.S.R.	10.14s
1976	Hasely Crawford, Trinidad and Tobago	10.06s
1980	Allan Wells, Britain	10.25s
1984	Carl Lewis, United States	9.99s
1988	Carl Lewis, United States	9.92s

1. wind assisted. 2. Lewis was awarded the gold medal when Ben Johnson of Canada, the original winner in 09.79s, was stripped of the medal after testing positive for steroid use.

200–Meter Dash

1900	John Tewksbury, United States	22.2s
1904	Archie Hahn, United States	21.6s
1908	Robert Kerr, Canada	22.6s
1912	Ralph Craig, United States	21.7s
1920	Allan Woodring, United States	22s
1924	Jackson Scholz, United States	21.6s
1928	Percy Williams, Canada	21.8s
1932	Eddie Tolan, United States	21.2s
1936	Jesse Owens, United States	20.7s
1948	Melvin E. Patton, United States	21.1s
1952	Andrew Stanfield, United States	20.7s
1956	Bobby Morrow, United States	20.6s
1960	Livio Berruti, Italy	20.5s
1964	Henry Carr, United States	20.3s
1968	Tommie Smith, United States	19.8s
1972	Vallery Borzov, U.S.S.R.	20s
1976	Don Quarrie, Jamaica	20.23s
1980	Pietro Mennea, Italy	20.19s
1984	Carl Lewis, United States	19.80s
1988	Joe DeLoach, United States	19.75s

400–Meter Dash

1896	Thomas Burke, United States	54.2s
1900	Maxwell Long, United States	49.4s
1904	Harry Hillman, United States	49.2s
1906	Paul Pilgrim, United States	53.2s
1908	Wyndham Halswelle, Great Britain (walkover)	50s
1912	Charles Reidpath, United States	48.2s
1920	Bevil Rudd, South Africa	49.6s
1924	Eric Liddell, Great Britain	47.6s
1928	Ray Barbuti, United States	47.8s
1932	William Carr, United States	46.2s
1936	Archie Williams, United States	46.5s
1948	Arthur Wint, Jamaica, B.W.I.	46.2s
1952	George Rhoden, Jamaica, B.W.I.	45.9s
1956	Charles Jenkins, United States	46.7s
1960	Otis Davis, United States	44.9s
1964	Mike Larrabee, United States	45.1s
1968	Lee Evans, United States	43.8s
1972	Vincent Matthews, United States	44.66s

1976	Alberto Juantorena, Cuba	44.26s
1980	Viktor Markin, U.S.S.R.	44.60s
1984	Alonzo Babers, United States	44.27s
1988	Steve Lewis, United States	43.87s

800–Meter Run

1896	Edwin Flack, Australia	2m11s
1900	Alfred Tysoe, Great Britain	2m1.4s
1904	James Lightbody, United States	1m56s
1906	Paul Pilgrim, United States	2m1.2s
1908	Mel Sheppard, United states	1m52.8s
1912	Ted Meredith, United States	1m51.9s
1920	Albert Hill, Great Britain	1m53.4s
1924	Douglas Lowe, Great Britain	1m52.4s
1928	Douglas Lowe, Great Britain	1m51.8s
1932	Thomas Hampson, Great Britain	1m49.8s
1936	John Woodruff, United States	1m52.9s
1948	Malvin Whitfield, United States	1m49.2s
1952	Malvin Whitfield, United States	1m49.2s
1956	Tom Courtney, United States	1m47.7s
1960	Peter Snell, New Zealand	1m46.3s
1964	Peter Snell, New Zealand	1m45.1s
1968	Ralph Doubell, Australia	1m44.3s
1972	David Wottle, United States	1m45.9s
1976	Alberto Juantorena, Cuba	1m43.5s
1980	Steve Ovett, Britain	1m45.4s
1984	Joaquin Cruz, Brazil	1m43.0s
1988	Paul Ereng, Kenya	1m43.45s

1,500–Meter Run

1896	Edwin Flack, Australia	4m33.2s
1900	Charles Bennett, Great Britain	4m6s
1904	James Lightbody, United States	4m5.4s
1906	James Lightbody, United States	4m12s
1908	Mel Sheppard, United States	4m3.4s
1912	Arnold Jackson, Great Britain	3m56.8s
1920	Albert Hill, Great Britain	4m1.8s
1924	Paavo Nurmi, Finland	3m53.6s
1928	Harry Larva, Finland	3m53.2s
1932	Luigi Becali, Italy	3m51.2s
1936	Jack Lovelock, New Zealand	3m47.8s
1948	Henri Eriksson, Sweden	3m49.8s
1952	Joseph Barthel, Luxembourg	3m45.2s
1956	Ron Delany, Ireland	3m41.2s
1960	Herb Elliott, Australia	3m35.6s
1964	Peter Snell, New Zealand	3m38.1s
1968	Kipchoge Keino, Kenya	3m34.9s
1972	Pekka Vasala, Finland	3m36.3s
1976	John Walker, New Zealand	3m39.17s
1980	Sebastian Coe, Britain	3m38.4s
1984	Sebastian Coe, Britain	3m32.53s
1988	Peter Rono, Kenya	3m35.96s

5,000-Meter Run

1912	Hannes Kolehmainen, Finland	14m36.6s
1920	Joseph Guillemot, France	14m55.6s
1024	Paavo Nurmi, Finland	14m31.2s
1928	Willie Ritola, Finland	14m38s
1932	Lauri Lehtinen, Finland	14m30s
1936	Gunnar Hockert, Finland	14m22.2s
1948	Gaston Reiff, Belgium	14m17.6s
1952	Emil Zatopek, Czechoslovakia	14m6.6s
1956	Vladimir Kuts, U.S.S.R.	13m39.6s
1960	Murray Halberg, New Zealand	13m43.4s
1964	Bob Schul, United States	13m48.8s
1968	Mohamed Gammoudi, Tunisia	14m.05s
1972	Lasse Viren, Finland	13m26.4s
1976	Lasse Viren, Finland	13m24.76s
1980	Miruts Yifter, Ethiopia	13m21s
1984	Saud Aouita, Morocco	13m5.59s

1988 John Ngugi, Kenya   13m11.70s

10,000–Meter Run

1912	Hannes Kolehmainen, Finland	31m20.8s
1920	Paavo Nurmi, Finland	31m45.8s
1924	Willie Ritola, Finland	30m23.2s
1928	Paavo Nurmi, Finland	30m18.8s
1932	Janusz Kusocinski, Poland	30m11.4s
1936	Ilmari Salminen, Finland	30m15.4s
1948	Emil Zatopek, Czechoslovakia	29m59.6s
1952	Emil Zatopek, Czechoslovakia	29ml7s
1956	Vladimir Kuts, U.S.S.R.	28m45.6s
1960	Peter Bolotnikov, U.S.S.R.	28m32.2s
1964	Billy Mills, United States	28m24.4s
1968	Nartali Temu, Kenya	29m27.4s
1972	Lasse Viren, Finland	27m38.4s
1976	Lasse Viren, Finland	27m40.38s
1980	Miruts Yifter, Ethiopia	27m42.7s
1984	Alberto Cova, Italy	27m47.5s
1988	Mly Brahim Boutaib, Morocco	27m21.46s

Marathon

1896	Spiridon Loues, Greece	2h58m50s
1900	Michel Teato, France	2h59m45s
1904	Thomas Hicks, United States	3h28m53s
1906	William J. Sherring, Canada	2h51m23.65s
1908	John J. Hayes, United States	2h55m18.4s
1912	Kenneth McArthur, South Africa	2h36m54.8s
1920	Hannes Kolehmainen, Finland	2h32m35.8s
1924	Albin Stenroos, Finland	2h41m22.6s
1928	A.B. El Ouafi, France	2h32m57s
1932	Juan Zabala, Argentina	2h31m36s
1936	Kitei Son, Japan	2h29m19.2s
1948	Delfo Cabrera, Argentina	2h34m51.6s
1952	Emil Zatopek, Czechoslovakia	2h23m3.2s
1956	Alain Mimoun, France	2h25m
1960	Abebe Bikila, Ethiopia	2h15m16.2s
1964	Abebe Bikila, Ethiopia	2h12m11.2s
1968	Mamo Wold, Ethiopia	2h20m26.4s
1972	Frank Shorter, United States	2h12m19.8s
1976	Walter Cierpinski, East Germany	2h09m55s
1980	Walter Cierpinski, East Germany	2h11m3s
1984	Carlos Lopes, Portugal	2h9m.55s
1988	Gelindo Bordin, Italy	2hr10m47s

110–Meter Hurdles

1896	Thomas Curtis, United States	17.6s
1900	Alvin Kraenzlein, United States	15.4s
1904	Frederick Schule, United States	16s
1906	R.G. Leavitt, United States	16.2s
1908	Forrest Smithson, United States	15s
1912	Frederick Kelly, United States	15.1s
1920	Earl Thomson, Canada	14.8s
1924	Daniel Kinsey, United States	15s
1928	Sydney Atkinson, South Africa	14.8s
1932	George Saling, United States	14.6s
1936	Forrest Towns, United States	14.2s
1948	William Porter, United States	13.9s
1952	Harrison Dillard, United States	13.7s
1956	Lee Calhoun, United States	13.5s
1960	Lee Calhoun, United States	13.8s
1964	Hayes Jones, United States	13.6s
1968	Willie Davenport, United States	13.3s
1972	Rodney Milburn, United States	13.24s
1976	Guy Drut, France	13.30s
1980	Thomas Munkett, East Germany	13.20s
1984	Roger Kingdom, United States	13.20s
1988	Roger Kingdom, United States	12.98s

200–Meter Hurdles

1900	Alvin Kraenzlein, United States	25.4s
1904	Harry Hillman, United States	24.6s

400–Meter Hurdles

1900	John Tewksbury, United States	57.6s
1904	Harry Hillman, United States	53s
1908	Charles Bacon, United States	55s
1920	Frank Loomis, United States	54s
1924	F. Morgan Taylor, United States	52.6s
1928	Lord David Burghley, Great Britain	53.4s
1932	Robert Tisdall, Ireland	51.8s [1]
1936	Glenn Hardin, United States	52.4s
1948	Roy Cochran, United States	51.1s
1952	Charles Moore, United States	50.8s
1956	Glenn Davis, United States	50.1s
1960	Glenn Davis, United States	49.3s
1964	Rex Cawley, United States	49.6s
1968	David Hemery, Great Britain	48.1s
1972	John Akii–Bua, Uganda	47.8s
1976	Edwin Moses, United States	47.64s
1980	Volker Beck, East Germany	48.70s
1984	Edwin Moses, United States	47.75s
1988	Andre Phillips, United States	47.19s

1. Record not allowed.

2,500–Meter Steeplechase

1900	George Orton, United States	7m34s
1904	James Lightbody, United States	7m39.6s

3,000–Meter Steeplechase

1920	Percy Hodge, Great Britain	10m0.4s
1924	Willie Ritola, Finland	9m33.6s
1928	Toivo Loukola, Finland	9m21.8s
1932	Volmari Iso–Hollo, Finland	10m33.4s [1]
1936	Volmari Iso–Hollo, Finland	9m3.8s
1948	Thure Sjoestrand, Sweden	9m4.6s
1952	Horace Ashenfelter, United States	8m45.4s
1956	Chris Brasher, Great Britain	8m41.2s
1960	Zdzislaw Krzyskowiak, Poland	8m34.2s
1964	Gaston Roelants, Belgium	8m30.8s
1968	Amos Biwott, Kenya	8m51s
1972	Kipchoge Keino, Kenya	8m23.6s
1976	Anders Gardervd, Sweden	8m08.02s
1980	Bronislaw Malinowski, Poland	8m9.7s
1984	Julius Korir, Kenya	8m11.80s
1988	Julius Karluki, Kenya	8m05.51s

1. About 3,450 meters–extra lap by error.

10,000–Meter Walk

1912	George Goulding, Canada	46m28.4s
1920	Ugo Frigerio, Italy	48m6.2s
1924	Ugo Frigerio, Italy	47m49s
1948	John Mikaelsson, Sweden	45m13.2s
1952	John Mikaelsson, Sweden	45m2.8s

20,000–Meter Walk

1956	Leonid Spirin, U.S.S.R.	1h31m27.4s
1960	Vladimir Golubnichy, U.S.S.R.	1h34m7.2s
1964	Ken Mathews, Great Britain	1h29m34s
1968	Vladimir Golubnichy, U.S.S.R.	1h33m58.4s
1972	Peter Frenkel, East Germany	1h26m42.4s
1976	Daniel Bautista, Mexico	1h24m40.6s
1980	Maurizio Damiliano, Italy	1h23m35.5s
1984	Ernesto Conto, Mexico	1m23.13s
1988	Jozef Pribilinec, Czechoslovakia	1h19m57s

50,000–Meter Walk

1932	Thomas W. Green, Great Britain	4h50m10s
1936	Harold Whitlock, Great Britain	4h30m41.1s
1948	John Ljunggren, Sweden	4h41m52s
1952	Giuseppe Dordoni, Italy	4h28m7.8s
1956	Norman Read, New Zealand	4h30m42.8s
1960	Donald Thompson, Great Britain	4h25m30s
1964	Abdon Pamich, Italy	4h11m12.4s
1968	Christoph Hohne, East Germany	4h20m13.6s
1972	Bern Kannernberg, West Germany	3h56m11.6s

1980	Hartwig Guader, East Germany	3h49m24s
1984	Raul Gonzalez, Mexico	3hr37m26s
1988	Viacheslau Ivanenko, U.S.S.R.	3h438m29s

400–Meter Relay (4x100)

1912	Great Britain	42.4s
1920	United States	42.2s
1924	United States	41s
1928	United States	41s
1932	United States	40s
1936	United States	39.8s
1948	United States	40.6s
1952	United States	40.1s
1956	United States	39.5s
1960	Germany	39.5s
1964	United States	39s
1968	United States	38.2s
1972	United States	38.19s
1976	United States	38.33s
1980	U.S.S.R.	38.26s
1984	United States	37.83s
1988	U.S.S.R.	38.19s

1,600–Meter Relay (4x400)

1912	United States	3m16.6s
1920	Great Britain	3m22.2s
1924	United States	3m16s
1928	United States	3m14.2s
1932	United States	3m8.2s
1936	Great Britain	3m9s
1948	United States	3m10.4s
1952	Jamaica, B.W.I.	3m3.9s
1956	United States	3m4.8s
1960	United States	3m2.2s
1964	United States	3m0.7s
1968	United States	2m56.1s
1972	Kenya	2m59.8s
1976	United States	2m58.65s
1980	U.S.S.R.	3m01.1s
1984	United States	2m57.91s
1988	United States	2m56.16s

Team Race

		Pts
1900	Great Britain (5,000 meters)	26
1904	United States (4 miles)	27
1908	Great Britain (3 miles)	6
1912	United States (3,000 meters)	9
1920	United States (3,000 meters)	10
1924	Finland (3,000 meters)	9

Standing High Jump

1900	Ray Ewry, United States	5 ft 5 in.
1904	Ray Ewry, United States	4 ft. 11 in.
1906	Ray Ewry, United States	5 ft 1 5/8 in.
1908	Ray Ewry, United States	5 ft 2 in.
1912	Platt Adams, United States	5 ft 4 1/8 in.

Running High Jump

1896	Ellery Clark, United States	5 ft 11 1/4 in.
1900	Irving Baxter, United States	6 ft 2 3/4 in.
1904	Samuel Jones, United States	5 ft 11 in.
1906	Con Leahy, Ireland	5 ft 9 7/8 in.
1908	Harry Porter, United States	6 ft 3 in.
1912	Alma Richards, United States	6 ft 4 in.
1920	Richmond Landon, United States	6 ft 4 1/4 in.
1924	Harold Osborn, United States	6 ft 5 15/16 in.
1928	Robert W. King, United States	6 ft 4 3/8 in.
1932	Duncan McNaughton, Canada	6 ft 5 5/8 in.
1936	Cornelius Johnson, United States	6 ft 7 15/16 in.
1948	John Winter, Australia	6 ft 6 in.
1948	Walter David, United States	6 ft 8 5/16 in.
1956	Charles Dumas, United States	6 ft 11 1/4 in.
1960	Robert Shavlakadze, U.S.S.R.	7 ft 1 in.

1964	Valeri Brumel, U.S.S.R.	7 ft 1 3/4 in.
1968	Dick Fosbury, United States	7 ft 4 1/4 in.
1972	Yuri Tarmak, U.S.S.R.	7 ft 3 3/4 in.
1976	Jacek Wszola, Poland	(2.25m) 7 ft 4 1/2 in.
1980	Gerd Wessig, East Germany	7 ft 8 3/4 in.
1984	Dietmar Mogenburg, West Germany	7 ft 8 1/2 in.
1988	Guennadi Avdeenko, U.S.S.R.	7 ft 9 1/2 in.

Long Jump

1896	Ellery Clark, United States	20 ft 9 3/4 in.
1900	Alvin Kraenzlein, United States	23 ft 6 7/8 in.
1904	Myer Prinstein, United States	24 ft 1 in.
1906	Myer Prinstein, United States	23 ft 7 1/2 in.
1908	Frank Irons, United States	24 ft 6 1/2 in.
1912	Albert Gutterson, United States	24 ft 11 1/4 in.
1920	William Pettersson, Sweden	23 ft 5 1/2 in.
1924	DeHart Hubbard, United States	24 ft 5 1/8 in.
1928	Edward B. Hamm, United States	25 ft 4 3/4 in.
1932	Edward Gordon, United States	25 ft 3/4 in.
1936	Jesse Owens, United States	26 ft 5 5/16 in.
1948	Willie Steele, United States	25 ft 8 in.
1952	Jerome Biffle, United States	24 ft 10 in.
1956	Gregory Bell, United States	25 ft 8 1/4 in.
1960	Ralph Boston, United States	26 ft 7 3/4 in.
1964	Lynn Davies, Great Britain	26 ft 5 3/4 in.
1968	Bob Beamon, United States	29 ft 2 1/2 in.
1972	Randy Williams, United States	27 ft 1/2 in.
1976	Arnie Robinson, United States (8.35m)	24 ft 7 3/4 in.
1980	Lutz Dombrowski, E. Germany	28 ft 1/4 in.
1984	Carl Lewis, United States	28 ft 1/4 in.
1988	Carl Lewis, United States	28 ft 7 1/4 in.

Triple Jump

1896	James B. Connolly, United States	45 ft
1900	Myer Prinstein, United States	47 ft 4 1/4 in.
1904	Myer Prinstein, United States	47 ft
1906	P.G. O'Connor, Ireland	46 ft 2 in.
1908	Timothy Ahearne, Great Britain	48 ft 11 1/4 in.
1912	Gustaf Lindblom, Sweden	48 ft 5 1/8 in.
1920	Vilho Tuulos, Finland	47 ft 6 7/8 in.
1924	Archie Winter, Australia	50 ft 11 1/8 in.
1928	Mikio Oda, Japan	49 ft 10 13/16 in.
1932	Chuhei Nambu, Japan	51 ft 7 in.
1936	Naoto Tajima, Japan	52 ft 5 7/8 in.
1948	Arne Ahman, Sweden	50 ft 6 1/4 in.
1952	Adhemar da Silva, Brazil	53 ft 2 1/2 in.
1956	Adhemar da Silva, Brazil	53 ft 7 1/2 in.
1960	Jozef Schmidt, Poland	55 ft 1 3/4 in.
1964	Jozef Schmidt, Poland	55 ft 3 1/4 in.
1968	Viktor Saneyev, U.S.S.R.	57 ft 3/4 in.
1972	Viktor Saneyev, U.S.S.R.	56 ft 11 in.
1976	Viktor Saneyev, U.S.S.R. (17.29m)	56 ft 8 3/4 in.
1980	Jaak Uudmae, U.S.S.R.	56 ft 11 1/8 in.
1984	Al Joyner, United States	56 ft 7 1/2 in.
1988	Hristo Markov, Bulgaria	57 ft 9 1/4 in.

Pole Vault

1896	William Hoyt, United States	10 ft 9 3/4 in.
1900	Irving Baxter, United States	10 ft 9 7/8 in.
1904	Charles Dvorak, United States	11 ft 6 in.
1906	Fernand Gouder, France	11 ft 6 in.
1908	Alfred Gilbert, United States, and Edward Cook, United States (tie)	12 ft 2 in.
1912	Harry Babcock, United States	12 ft 11 1/2 in.
1920	Frank Foss, United States	13 ft 5 9/16 in.
1924	Lee Barnes, United States	12 ft 11 1/2 in.
1928	Sabin W. Carr, United States	13 ft 9 3/8 in.
1932	William Miller, United States	14 ft 1 7/8 in.
1936	Earle Meadows, United States	14 ft 3 1/4 in.
1948	Guinn Smith, United States	14 ft 1 1/4 in.
1952	Robert Richards, United States	14 ft 11 1/8 in.
1956	Robert Richards, United States	14 ft 11 1/2 in.
1960	Don Bragg, United States	15 ft 5 1/8 in.

1964	Fred Hansen, United States	16 ft 8 3/4 in.
1968	Bob Seagren, United States	17 ft 8 1/2 in.
1972	Wolfgang Nordwig, East Germany	18 ft 1/2 in.
1976	Tadeusz Slusarski, Poland	(5.50m) 18 ft 1/2 in.
1980	Wladyslaw Kozakiewics, Poland	18 ft 11 1/2 in.
1984	Pierre Quinon, France	18 ft 10 1/4 in.
1988	Sergei Bubka, U.S.S.R.	18 ft 4 1/4 in.

16–lb Shot-Put

1896	Robert Garrett, United States	36 ft 9 3/4 in.
1900	Richard Sheldon, United States	46 ft 3 1/8 in.
1904	Ralph Rose, United States	48 ft 7 in.
1906	Martin Sheridan, United States	40 ft 4 4/5 in.
1908	Ralph Rose, United States	46 ft 7 1/2 in.
1912	Pat McDonald, United States	50 ft 4 in.
1920	Ville Porhola, Finland	48 ft 7 1/8 in.
1924	Clarence Houser, United States	49 ft 2 1/2 in.
1928	John Kuck, United States	52 ft 11 11/16 in.
1932	Leo Sexton, United States	52 ft 6 3/16 in.
1936	Hans Woellke, Germany	53 ft 1 3/4 in.
1948	Wilbur Thompson, United States	56 ft 2 in.
1952	Parry O'Brien, United States	57 ft 1 1/2 in.
1956	Parry O'Brien, United States	60 ft 11 in.
1960	Bill Nieder, United States	64 ft 6 3/4 in.
1964	Dallas Long, United States	66 ft 8 1/4 in.
1968	Randy Matson, United States	67 ft 4 3/4 in.
1972	Wladyslaw Komar, Poland	69 ft 6 in.
1976	Udo Beyer, East Germany	(21.05m) 69 ft 3/4 in.
1980	Vladimr KIselyov, U.S.S.R.	70 ft 1/2 in.
1984	Alessandro Andrei, Italy	69 ft 9 in.
1988	Uhf Timmerman, East Germany	73 ft 8 3/4 in.

Discus Throw

1896	Robert Garrett, United States	95 ft 7 1/2 in.
1900	Rudolf Bauer, Hungary	118 ft 2 7/8 in.
1904	Martin Sheridan, United States	128 ft 10 1/2 in.
1906	Martin Sheridan, United States	136 ft 1 1/3 in.
1908	Martin Sheridan, United States	134 ft 2 in.
1912	Armas Taipale, Finland	145 ft 9/16 in.
1920	Elmer Niklander, Finland	146 ft 7 in.
1924	Clarence Houser, United States	151 ft 5 1/4 in.
1928	Clarence Houser, United States	155 ft 2 4/5 in.
1932	John Anderson, United States	162 ft 4 7/8 in.
1936	Ken Carpenter, United States	165 ft 7 3/8 in.
1948	Adolfo Consolini, Italy	173 ft 2 in.
1952	Simeon Iness, United States	180 ft 6 1/2 in.
1956	Al Oerter, United States	184 ft 10 1/2 in.
1960	Al Oerter, United States	194 ft 2 in.
1964	Al Oerter, United States	200 ft 1 1/2 in.
1968	Al Oerter, United States	212 ft 6 in.
1972	Ludvik Danek, Czechoslovakia	211 ft 3 in.
1976	Mac Wilkins, United States	(67.5m) 221 ft 5 in.
1980	Viktor Rashchpukin, U.S.S.R.	218 ft 8 in.
1984	Rolf Dannenberg, West Germany	218 ft 6 in.
1988	Jurgen Schult, East Germany	225 ft 9 1/4 in.

Javelin Throw

1906	Eric Lemming, Sweden	175 ft 6 in.
1908	Eric Lemming, Sweden	179 ft 10 1/2 in.
1912	Eric Lemming, Sweden	198 ft 11 1/4 in.
1920	Jonni Myyra, Finland	215 ft 9 3/4 in.
1924	Jonni Myyra, Finland	206 ft 6 3/4 in.
1928	Eric Lundquist, Sweden	218 ft 6 1/8 in.
1932	Matti Jarvinen, Finland	238 ft 7 in.
1936	Gerhard Stoeck, Germany	235 ft 8 5/16 in.
1948	Kaj Rautavaara, Finland	228 ft 10 1/2 in.
1952	Cy Young, United States	242 ft 3/4 in.
1956	Egil Danielsen, Norway	281 ft 2 1/4 in.
1960	Viktor Tsibuelnko, U.S.S.R.	277 ft 8 3/8 in.
1964	Pauli Nevala, Finland	271 ft 2 1/4 in.
1968	Janis Lusis, U.S.S.R.	295 ft 7 in.
1972	Klaus Wolfermann, West Germany	296 ft 10 in.

1976	Miklos Nemeth, Hungary	(94.58m) 310 ft 4 in.
1980	Dainis Kula, U.S.S.R.	299 ft 2 3/8 in.
1984	Arto Haerkoenen, Finland	284 ft 8 in.
1988	Tapio Korjus, Finland	276 ft 6 in.

16–lb Hammer Throw

1900	John Flanagan, United States	167 ft 4 in.
1904	John Flanagan, United States	168 ft 1 in.
1908	John Flanagan, United States	170 ft 4 1/4 in.
1912	Matt McGrath, United States	179 ft 7 1/8 in.
1920	Pat Ryan, United States	173 ft 5 5/8 in.
1924	Fred Tootell, United States	174 ft 10 1/4 in.
1928	Patrick O'Callaghan, Ireland	168 ft 7 1/2 in.
1932	Patrick O'Callaghan, Ireland	176 ft 11 1/8 in.
1936	Karl Hein, Germany	185 ft 4 in.
1948	Imre Nemeth, Hungary	183 ft 11 1/2 in.
1952	Jozsef Csermak, Hungary	197 ft 11 9/16 in.
1956	Harold Connolly, United States	207 ft 2 3/4 in.
1960	Vasily Rudenkov, U.S.S.R.	220 ft 1 5/8 in.
1964	Romuald Klim, U.S.S.R.	228 ft 9 1/2 in.
1968	Gyula Zsivotzky, Hungary	240 ft 8 in.
1972	Anatoly Bondarchuk, U.S.S.R.	247 ft 8 1/2 in.
1976	Yuri Sedykh, U.S.S.R.	(77.52m) 254 ft 4 in.
1980	Yuri Sedykh, U.S.S.R.	(81.80m 268 ft 4 1/2 in.
1984	Juha Tiainen, Finland	256 ft 2 in.
1988	Sergei Litvinov, U.S.S.R.	278 ft 2 1/2 in.

Decathlon

1912	Jim Thorpe, United States	—
	Hugo Wieslander, Sweden	—
1920	Helge Lovland, Norway	6,804.35 pts.
1924	Harold Osborn, United States	7,710.775 pts.
1928	Paavo Yrjola, Finland	8,053.29 pts.
1932	James Bausch, United States	8,462.23 pts.
1936	Glenn Morris, United States	7,900 pts. [1]
1948	Robert B. Mathias, United States	7,139 pts.
1952	Robert B. Mathias, United States	7,887 pts.
1956	Milton Campbell, United States	7,937 pts.
1960	Rafer Johnson, United States	8,392 pts.
1964	Willi Holdorf, Germany	7,887 pts. [1]
1968	Bill Toomey, United States	8,193 pts.
1972	Nikolai Avilov, U.S.S.R.	8,454 pts.
1976	Bruce Jenner, United States	8,618 pts.
1980	Daley Thompson, Britain	8,495 pts.
1984	Daley Thompson, Britain	8,797 pts.
1988	Christian Schenk, East Germany	8,488 pts.

1. Point system revised.

TRACK AND FIELD–WOMEN

100–Meter Dash

1928	Elizabeth Robinson, United States	12.2s
1932	Stella Walsh, Poland	11.9s
1936	Helen Stephens, United States	11.5s
1948	Fanny Blankers–Koen, Netherlands	11.9s
1952	Marjorie Jackson, Australia	11.5s
1956	Betty Cuthbert, Australia	11.5s
1960	Wilma Rudolph, United States	11s
1964	Wyomia Tyus, United States	11.4s
1968	Wyomia Tyus, United States	11s
1972	Renate Stecher, East Germany	11.07s
1976	Annegret Richter, West Germany	11.08s
1980	Lyudmila Kondratyeva, U.S.S.R.	11.06s
1984	Evelyn Ashford, United States	10.97s
1988	Florence Griffith–Joyner, United States	10.54s

200–Meter Dash

1948	Fanny Blankers–Koen, Netherlands	24.4s
1952	Marjorie Jackson, Australia	23.7s
1956	Betty Cuthbert, Australia	23.4s
1960	Wilma Rudolph, United States	24s
1964	Edith McGuire, United States	23s

1968	Irena Szewinska, Poland	22.5s
1972	Renate Stecher, East Germany	22.4s
1976	Baerbel Eckert, East Germany	22.37s
1980	Barbara Wockel, East Germany	22.03s
1984	Valerie Brisco–Hooks, United States	21.81s
1988	Florence Griffith–Joyner, United States	21.34s

400–Meter Dash

1964	Betty Cuthbert, Australia	52s
1968	Colette Besson, France	52s
1972	Monika Zehrt, East Germany	51.08s
1976	Irena Szewinska, Poland	49.29s
1980	Marita Koch, East Germany	48.88s
1984	Valerie Brisco–Hooks, United States	48.83s
1988	Olga Bryzguina, U.S.S.R.	48.65s

800–Meter Run

1928	Lina Radke, Germany	2m16.8s
1960	Ljudmila Shevcova, U.S.S.R.	2m4.3s
1964	Ann Packer, Great Britain	2m1.1s
1968	Madeline Manning, United States	2m0.9s
1972	Hildegard Falck, West Germany	1m58.6s
1976	Tatiana Kazankina, U.S.S.R.	1m54.94s
1980	Nadezhda Olizarenko, U.S.S.R.	1m53.5s
1984	Doina Melinte, Romania	1m57.60s
1988	Sigrun Wodars, East Germany	1m56.10s

1,500–Meter Run

1972	Ludmila Bragina, U.S.S.R.	4m01.4s
1976	Tatiana Kazankina, U.S.S.R.	4m05.48s
1980	Tatiana Kazankina, U.S.S.R.	3m56.6s
1984	Gabriella Dorio, Italy	4m03.25s
1988	Paula Ivan, Romania	3m53.96s

3,000–Meter Run

1984	Maricica Puica, Romania	8m35.96s
1988	Tatiana Samolenko, U.S.S.R.	8m26.53s

80–Meter Hurdles

1932	Mildred Didrikson, United States	11.7s
1936	Trebisonda Valla, Italy	11.7s
1948	Fanny Blankers–Koen, Netherlands	11.2s
1952	Shirley S. de la Hunty, Australia	10.9s
1956	Shirley S. de la Hunty, Australia	10.7s
1960	Irina Press, U.S.S.R.	10.8s
1964	Karin Balzer, Germany	10.5s [1]
1968	Maureen Caird, Australia	10.3s

1. Wind assisted.

100–Meter Hurdles

1972	Annelie Ehrhardt, East Germany	12.59s
1976	Johanna Schaller, East Germany	12.77s
1980	Vera Komisova, U.S.S.R.	12.56s
1984	Benita Fitzgerald–Brown, United States	12.84s
1988	Jordanka Donkova, Bulgaria	12.38s

400–Meter Hurdle

1984	Nawai El Moutawakel, Morocco	54.61s
1988	Debra Flintoff–King, Australia	53.17s

400–Meter Relay

1928	Canada	48.4s
1932	United States	47s
1936	United States	46.9s
1948	Netherlands	47.5s
1952	United States	45.9s
1956	Australia	44.5s
1960	United States	44.5s
1964	Poland	43.6s
1968	United States	42.8s
1972	West Germany	42.81s

1976	East Germany	42.55s
1980	East Germany	41.60s
1984	United States	41.65s
1988	United States	41.98s

1,600–Meter Relay

1972	East Germany	3m23s
1976	East Germany	3m19.23s
1980	U.S.S.R.	3m20.2s
1984	United States	3m18.29s
1988	U.S.S.R.	3m15.18s

Marathon

1984	Joan Benoit, United States	2 hr 24 m 52s
1988	Rose Mota, Portugal	2 hr 25 m 40s

Running High Jump

1928	Ethel Catherwood, Canada	5 ft 3 in.
1932	Jean Shiley, United States	5 ft 5 1/4 in.
1936	Ibolya Csak, Hungary	5 ft 3 in.
1948	Alice Coachman, United States	5 ft 6 1/8 in.
1952	Ester Brand, South Africa	5 ft 5 3/4 in.
1956	Mildred McDaniel, United States	5 ft 9 1/4 in.
1960	Iolanda Balas, Romania	6 ft 3/4 in.
1964	Iolanda Balas, U.S.S.R.	6 ft 2 3/4 in.
1968	Miloslava Rezkova, Czechoslovakia	5 ft 11 3/4 in.
1972	Ulrike Meyfarth, West Germany	6 ft 3 5/8 in.
1976	Rosemarie Ackerman, E. Germany (1.93m)	6 ft 4 in.
1980	Sara Simeoni, Italy	6 ft 5 1/2 in.
1984	Ulrike Meyfarth, West Germany	6 ft 7 1/2 in.
1988	Louise Ritter, United States	6 ft 8 in.

Long Jump

1948	Olga Gyarmati, Hungary	18 ft 8 1/4 in.
1952	Yvette Williams, New Zealand	20 ft 5 3/4 in.
1956	Elzbieta Krzesinska, Poland	20 ft 9 3/4 in.
1960	Vera Krepkina, U.S.S.R.	20 ft 10 3/4 in.
1964	Mary Rand, Great Britain	22 ft 2 in.
1968	Viorica Ciscopoleanu, Romania	22 ft 4 1/2 in.
1972	Heidemarie Rosendahl, West Germany	22 ft 3 in.
1976	Angela Voigt, East Germany (6.72m)	22 ft 1/2 in.
1980	Tatiana Kolpakova, U.S.S.R.	23 ft 2 in.
1984	Anisoara Stanciu, Romania	22 ft 10 in.
1988	Jackie Joyner–Kersee, United States	24 ft 3 1/2 in.

Shot–Put

1948	Micheline Ostermeyer, France	45 ft 1 1/2 in.
1952	Galina Zybina, U.S.S.R.	50 ft 1 1/2 in.
1956	Tamara Tishkyevich, U.S.S.R.	54 ft 5 in.
1960	Tamara Press, U.S.S.R.	56 ft 9 7/8 in.
1964	Tamara Press, U.S.S.R.	59 ft 6 in.
1968	Margitta Gummel, East Germany	64 ft 4 in.
1972	Nadezhda Chizhova, U.S.S.R.	69 ft
1976	Ivanka Christova, Bulgaria (21.16m)	69 ft 5 in.
1980	Ilona Sluplanek, East Germany	73 ft 6 in.
1984	Claudia Losch, West Germany	67 ft 2 1/4 in.
1988	Natalya Lisovskaya, U.S.S.R.	72 ft 11 1/2 in.

Discus Throw

1928	Helena Konopacka, Poland	129 ft 11 7/8 in.
1932	Lillian Copeland, United States	133 ft 2 in.
1936	Gisela Mauermayer, Germany	156 ft 3 3/16 in.
1948	Micheline Ostermeyer, France	137 ft 6 1/2 in.
1956	Olga Fikotova, Czechoslovakia	176 ft 1 1/2 in.
1960	Nina Ponomareva, U.S.S.R.	180 ft 8 1/4 in.
1964	Tamara Press, U.S.S.R.	187 ft 10 3/4 in.
1968	Lia Manoliu, Romania	191 ft 2 1/2 in.
1972	Faina Melnik, U.S.S.R.	218 ft 7 in.
1976	Evelin Schlaak, East Germany (69.0m)	226 ft 4 in.
1980	Evelin Jahl, East Germany	229 ft 6 1/2 in.
1984	Ria Stalman, Netherlands	214 ft 5 in.
1988	Martina Hellmann, East Germany	237 ft 2 1/4 in.

Javelin Throw

1932	Mildred Didrikson, United States	143 ft 4 in.
1936	Tilly Fleischer, Germany	148 ft 2 3/4 in.
1948	Herma Bauma, Austria	149 ft 6 in.
1952	Dana Zatopek, Czechoslovakia	165 ft 7 in.
1956	Inessa Janzeme, U.S.S.R.	176 ft 8 in.
1960	Elvira Ozolina, U.S.S.R.	183 ft 8 in.
1964	Mihaela Penes, Romania	198 ft 7 1/2 in.
1968	Angela Nemeth, Hungary	198 ft 0 in.
1972	Ruth Fuchs, East Germany	209 ft 7 in.
1976	Ruth Fuchs, East Germany	(65.94m) 216 ft 4 in.
1980	Maria Colon, Cuba	224 ft 5 in.
1984	Tessa Sanderson, Britain	228 ft 2 in.
1988	Petra Felke, East Germany	245 ft

Pentathlon

1964	Irina Press, U.S.S.R.	5,246 pts.
1968	Ingrid Becker, West Germany	5,098 pts.
1972	Mary Peters, Britain	4,801 pts.
1976	Siegrun Siegl, East Germany	4,745 pts.
1980	Nadyeszhda Tkachenko, U.S.S.R.	5,083 pts.
1984	Daniele Masala, Italy	5,469 pts.
1988	Jackie Joyner–Kersee, United States	7,291 pts.

SWIMMING–MEN

50 Meter Freestyle

1988	Matt Biondi, United States	22.14s

100 Meter Freestyle

1896	Alfred Hajos, Hungary	1m22.2s
1904	Zoltan de Halmay, Hungary	1m2.8s [1]
1906	Charles Daniels, United States	1m13s
1908	Charles Daniels, United States	1m5.6s
1912	Duke P. Kahanamoku, United States	1m3.4s
1920	Duke P. Kahanamoku, United States	1m1.4s
1924	John Weissmuller, United States	59s
1928	John Weissmuller, United States	58.6s
1932	Yasuji Miyazaki, Japan	58.2s
1936	Ferenc Csik, Hungary	57.6s
1948	Walter Ris, United States	57.3s
1952	Clarke Scholes, United States	57.4s
1956	Jon Henricks, Australia	55.4s
1960	John Devitt, Australia	55.2s
1964	Don Schollander, United States	53.4s
1968	Michael Wenden, Australia	52.2s
1972	Mark Spitz, United States	51.22s
1976	Jim Montgomery, United States	49.99s
1980	Jorg Woithe, East Germany	50.40s
1984	Rowdy Gaines, United States	49.80s
1988	Matt Biondi, United States	48.63s

1. 100 yards.

200–Meter Freestyle

1900	Frederick Lane, Australia	2m25.2s
1904	Charles Daniels, United States	2m44.2s [1]
1968	Michael Wenden, Australia	1m55.2s
1972	Mark Spitz, United States	1m52.78s
1976	Bruce Furniss, United States	1m50.29s
1980	Sergei Kopiliakov, U.S.S.R.	4m49.81s
1984	Michael Gross, West Germany	1m47.44s
1988	Duncan Armstrong, Australia	1m47.25s

1. 220 yards

400–Meter Freestyle

1896	Paul Neumann, Austria	8m12.6s [1]
1904	Charles Daniels, United States	6m16.2s [2]
1906	Otto Sheff, Austria	6m23.8s
1908	Henry Taylor, Great Britain	5m36.8s
1912	George Hodgson, Canada	5m24.4s
1920	Norman Ross, United States	5m26.8s
1926	John Weissmuller, United States	5m4.2s

1928	Albert Zorilla, Argentina	5m1.6s
1932	Clarence Crabbe, United States	4m48.4s
1936	Jack Medica, United States	4m44.5s
1948	William Smith, United States	4m41s
1952	Jean Boiteux, France	4m30.7s
1956	Murray Rose, Australia	4m27.3s
1960	Murray Rose, Australia	4m18.3s
1964	Don Schollander, United States	4m12.2s
1968	Mike Burton, United States	4m9s
1972	Bradford Cooper, Australia	4m00.27s [3]
1976	Brian Goodell, United States	3m51.93s
1980	Vladimir Salnikov, U.S.S.R.	3m51.31s
1984	George DiCarlo, United States	3m51.23s
1988	Uwe Dassier, East Germany	3m46.95s

1. 500 meters. 2. 440 yards. 3. Rich DeMont, United States, won but was disqualified following day for medical reasons.

1,500 Meter Freestyle

1904	Emil Rausch, Germany	27m18.2s [1]
1906	Henry Taylor, Great Britain	28m28s [2]
1908	Henry Taylor, Great Britain	22m48.4s
1912	George Hodgson, Canada	22m
1920	Norman Ross, United States	22m23.2s
1924	Andrew Charlton, Australia	20m6.6s
1928	Arne Borg, Sweden	19m51.8s
1932	Kusuo Kitamura, Japan	19m12.4s
1936	Noboru Terada, Japan	19m13.7s
1948	James McLane, United States	19m18.5s
1952	Ford Konno, United States	18m30s
1956	Murray Rose, Australia	17m58.9s
1960	Jon Konrads, Australia	17m19.6s
1964	Robert Windle, Australia	17m1.7s
1968	Michael Burton, United States	16m38.9s
1972	Michael Burton, United States	15m52.58s
1976	Brian Goodell, United States	15m02.4s
1980	Vladimir Salnikov, U.S.S.R.	14m58.27s
1984	Michael O'Brien, United States	15m05.2s
1988	Vladimir Salnikov, U.S.S.R.	15m00.4s

1. One mile.   2. 1,600 meters

100–Meter Backstroke

1904	Walter Brack, Germany	1m16.8s [1]
1908	Arno Bieberstein, Germany	1m24.6s
1912	Harry Hebner, United States	1m21.2s
1920	Warren Kealoha, United States	1m15.2s
1924	Warren Kealoha, United States	1m13.2s
1928	George Kojac, United States	1m8.2s
1932	Masaji Kiyokawa, Japan	1m8.6s
1936	Adolph Kiefer, United States	1m5.9s
1948	Allen Stack, United States	1m6.4s
1952	Yoshinobu Oyakawa, United States	1m5.4s
1956	David Thiele, Australia	1m2.2s
1960	David Thiele, Australia	1m1.9s
1968	Roland Matthes, East Germany	58.7s
1972	Roland Matthes, East Germany	56.58s
1976	John Naber, United States	55.49s
1980	Bengt Baron, Sweden	56.53s
1984	Rick Carey, United States	55.79s
1988	Daichi Suzuki, Japan	55.05s

1. 100 yards

200–Meter Backstroke

1900	Ernst Hoppenberg, Germany	2m47s
1964	Jed Graef, United States	2m10.3s
1968	Roland Matthes, East Germany	2m9.6s
1972	Roland Matthes, East Germany	2m2.82s
1976	John Naber, United States	1m59.19s
1980	Sandor Wladar, Hungary	2:01.93s
1984	Rick Carey, United States	2m00.23s
1988	Igor Polianski, U.S.S.R.	1m59.37s

100–Meter Breaststroke

1968	Donald McKenzie, United States	1m7.7s
1972	Nobutaka Taguchi, Japan	1m4.94s
1976	John Hencken, United States	1m03.11s
1980	Duncan Goodhew, Britain	1m03.34s
1984	Steve Lindquist, United States	1m01.65s
1988	Adrian Moorhouse, Great Britain	1m02.04s

200–Meter Breaststroke

1908	Frederick Holman, Great Britain	3m9.2s
1912	Walter Bathe, Germany	3m1.8s
1920	Haken Malmroth, Sweden	3m4.4s
1924	Robert Skelton, United States	2m56.6s
1928	Yoshiyuki Tsuruta, Japan	2m48.8s
1932	Yoshiyuki Tsuruta, Japan	2m45.4s
1936	Tetsuo Hamuro, Japan	2m41.5s
1948	Joseph Verdeur, United States	2m39.3s
1952	John Davies, Australia	2m34.4s
1956	Masaura Furukawa, Japan	2m34.7s
1960	Bill Muliken, United States	2m37.4s
1964	Ian O'Brien, Australia	2m27.8s
1968	Felipe Munoz, Mexico	2m28.7s
1972	John Hencken, United States	2m21.55s
1976	David Willkie, Britain	2m15.11s
1980	Robertas Zulpa, U.S.S.R.	2m15.85s
1984	Victor Davis, Canada	2m13.34s
1988	Jozef Szabo, Hungary	2m13.52s

100–Meter Butterfly

1968	Douglas Russell, United States	55.9s
1972	Mark Spitz, United States	54.27s
1976	Matt Vogel, United States	54.35s
1980	Par Arvidsson, Sweden	54.92s
1984	Michael Gross, West Germany	53.08s
1988	Anthony Nesty, Surinam	53.0s

200–Meter Butterfly

1956	Bill Yorzyk, United States	2m19.3s
1960	Mike Troy, United States	2m12.8s
1964	Kevin Berry, Australia	2m6.6s
1968	Carl Robie, United States	2m8.7s
1972	Mark Spitz, United States	2m00.7s
1976	Mike Bruner, United States	1m59.23s
1980	Sergei Fesenko, U.S.S.R.	1m59.76s
1984	Jon Sieben, Australia	1m57.0s
1988	Michael Gross, East Germany	1m56.94s

200–Meter Individual Medley

1968	Charles Hickcox, United States	2m12s
1972	Gunnar Larsson, Sweden	2m7.17s
1988	Tamas Darnyi, Hungary	2m0.17s

400–Meter Individual Medley

1964	Dick Roth, United States	4m45.4s
1968	Charles Hickox, United States	4m48.4s
1972	Gunnar Larsson, Sweden	4m31.98s
1976	Rod Strachan, United States	4m23.68s
1980	Aleksandr Sidorenko, U.S.S.R.	4m22.8s
1984	Alex Baumann, Canada	4m17.41s
1988	Tamas Darnyi, Hungary	4m14.75s

400–Meter Freestyle Relay

1964	United States	3m32.2s
1968	United States	3m31.7s
1972	United States	3m26.42s
1988	United States	3m16.52s

800–Meter Freestyle Relay

1908	Great Britain	10m55.6s
1912	Australia	10m11.2s
1920	United States	10m4.4s
1924	United States	9m53.4s
1928	United States	9m36.2s
1932	Japan	8m58.4s
1936	Japan	8m51.5s
1948	United States	8m46.1s
1952	United States	8m31.1s
1956	Australia	8m23.6s
1960	United States	8m10.2s
1964	United States	7m52.1s
1968	United States	7m52.3s
1972	United States	7m35.78s
1976	United States	7m23.22s
1980	U.S.S.R.	7m23.50s
1984	United States	7m16.59s
1988	United States	7m12.51s

400–Meter Medley Relay

1960	United States	4m5.4s
1964	United States	3m58.4s
1968	United States	3m54.9s
1972	United States	3m48.16s
1976	United States	3m42.22s
1980	Australia	3m45.70s
1984	United States	3m39.30s
1988	United States	3m36.93s

Springboard Dive

		Points
1908	Albert Zuerner, Germany	85.5
1912	Paul Guenther, Germany	79.23
1920	Louis Kuehn, United States	675
1924	Albert White, United States	696.4
1928	Pete Desjardins, United States	185.04
1932	Michael Galitzen, United States	161.38
1936	Richard Degener, United States	163.57
1948	Bruce Harlan, United States	163.64
1952	David Browning, United States	205.59
1956	Robert Clotworthy, United States	159.56
1960	Gary Tobian, United States	170.00
1964	Ken Sitzberger, United States	159.90
1968	Bernard Wrightson, United States	170.15
1972	Vladimir Vasin, U.S.S.R.	594.09
1976	Phil Boggs, United States	619.05
1980	Alexsandr Portnov, U.S.S.R.	905.02
1984	Greg Louganis, United States	754.41
1988	Greg Louganis, United States	730.80

Platform Dive

		Points
1904	G.E. Sheldon, United States	12.75
1906	Gottlob Walz, Germany	156
1908	Hialmar Johansson, Sweden	83.75
1912	Erik Adlerz, Sweden	73.94
1920	Clarence Pinkston, United States	100.67
1924	Albert White, United States	487.3
1928	Pete Desjardins, United States	98.74
1932	Harold Smith, United States	124.80
1936	Marshall Wayne, United States	113.58
1948	Samuel Lee, United States	130.05
1952	Samuel Lee, United States	156.28
1956	Joaquin Capilla, Mexico	152.44
1960	Bob Webster, United States	165.56
1964	Bob Webster, United States	148.58
1968	Klaus Dibiasi, Italy	164.18
1972	Klaus Dibiasi, Italy	504.12
1976	Klaus Dibiasi, Italy	600.51
1980	Falk Hoffman, E. Germany	835.65
1984	Greg Louganis, United States	710.91
1988	Greg Louganis, United States	638.61

SWIMMING–WOMEN

50–Meter Freestyle

1988	Kristin Otto, East Germany	25.49s

100–Meter Freestyle

1912	Fanny Durack, Australia	1m22.2s
1920	Ethelda Bleibtrey, United States	1m13.6s
1924	Ethel Lackie, United States	1m12.4s
1928	Albina Osipowich, United States	1m11s
1932	Helene Madison, United States	1m6.8s
1936	Hendrika Mastenbroek, Netherlands	1m5.9s
1948	Greta Andersen, Denmark	1m6.3s
1952	Katalin Szoke, Hungary	1m6.8s
1956	Dawn Fraser, Australia	1m2s
1960	Dawn Fraser, Australia	1m1.2s
1964	Dawn Fraser, Australia	59.5s
1968	Marge Jan Henne, United States	1m
1972	Sandra Neilson, United States	58.59s
1976	Kornelia Ender, East Germany	55.65s
1980	Barbara Krause, East Germany	54.79s
1984	Carrie Steinseifer, United States	55.92s
1988	Kristin Otto, East Germany	54.93s

200–Meter Freestyle

1968	Debbie Meyer, United States	2m10.5s
1972	Shane Gould, Australia	2m3.56s
1976	Kornelia Ender, East Germany	1m59.26s
1980	Barbara Krause, East Germany	1m58.33s
1984	Mary Wayle, United States	1m59.23s
1988	Heike Friedrich, East Germany	1m57.65s

400–Meter Freestyle

1920	Ethelda Bleibtrey, United States	4m34s[1]
1924	Martha Norelius, United States	6m2.2s
1928	Martha Norelius, United States	5m42.8s
1932	Helene Madison, United States	5m28.5s
1936	Hendrika Mastenbroek, Netherlands	5m26.4s
1948	Ann Curtis, United States	5m17.8s
1952	Valerie Gyenge, Hungary	5m12.1s
1956	Lorraine Crapp, Australia	4m54.6s
1960	Chris von Saltza, United States	4m50.6s
1964	Ginny Duenkel, United States	4m43.3s
1968	Debbie Meyer, United States	4m31.8s
1972	Shane Gould, Australia	4m19.04s
1976	Petra Thumer, East Germany	4m09.89s
1980	Ines Diers, East Germany	4m08.76s
1984	Tiffany Cohen, United States	4m07.10s
1988	Janet Evans, United States	4m03.85s

1. 300 meters.

800–Meter Freestyle

1968	Debbie Meyer, United States	9m24s
1972	Keena Rothhammer, United States	8m53.68s
1976	Petra Thumer, East Germany	8m37.14s
1980	Michelle Ford, Australia	8m28.90s
1984	Tiffany Cohen, United States	8m24.95s
1988	Janet Evans, United States	8m20.20s

100–Meter Backstroke

1924	Sybil Bauer, United States	1m23.2s
1928	Marie Braun, Netherlands	1m22s
1932	Eleanor Holm, United States	1m19.4s
1936	Dina Senff, Netherlands	1m18.9s
1948	Karen Harup, Denmark	1m14.4s
1952	Joan Harrison, South Africa	1m14.3s
1956	Judy Grinham, Great Britain	1m12.9s
1960	Lynn Burke, United States	1m9.3s
1964	Cathy Ferguson, United States	1m7.7s
1968	Kaye Hall, United States	1m6.2s
1972	Melissa Belote, United States	1m5.78s
1976	Ulrike Richter, East Germany	1m01.83s
1980	Rica Reinisch, East Germany	1m00.86s
1984	Theresa Andrews, United States	1m02.55s
1988	Kristin Otto, East Germany	1m0.89s

200–Meter Backstroke

1968	Pokey Watson–United States	2m24.8s

200–Meter Backstroke (continued)

1972	Melissa Belote, United States	2m19.19s
1976	Ulrike Richter, East Germany	2m13.43s
1980	Rica Reinisch, East Germany	2m11.77s
1984	Jolanda DeRover, Netherlands	2m12.38s
1988	Krisztina Egerszegi, Hungary	2m09.29s

100–Meter Breaststroke

1968	Djurdjica Bjedov, Yugoslavia	1m15.8s
1972	Catherine Carr, United States	1m13.58s
1976	Hannelore Anke, East Germany	1m11.16s
1980	Ute Geweniger, East Germany	1m10.22s
1984	Petra Van Staveren, Netherlands	1m09.88s
1988	Tainia Dangalakova, Bulgaria	1m07.95s

200–Meter Breaststroke

1924	Lucy Morton, Great Britain	3m33.2s
1928	Hilde Schrader, Germany	3m12.6s
1932	Clare Dennis, Australia	3m6.3s
1936	Hideko Maehata, Japan	3m3.6s
1948	Nel van Vliet, Netherlands	2m57.2s
1952	Eva Szekely, Hungary	2m51.7s
1956	Ursala Happe, Germany	2m53.1s
1960	Anita Lonsbrough, Great Britain	2m49.5s
1964	Galina Prozumenschikova, U.S.S.R.	2m46.4s
1968	Sharon Wichman, United States	2m44.4s
1972	Beverly Whitfield, Australia	2m41.71s
1976	Marina Koshevaia, U.S.S.R.	2m33.35s
1980	Lina Kachushite, U.S.S.R.	2m29.54s
1984	Anne Ottenbrite, Canada	2m30.38s
1988	Silke Hoerner, East Germany	2m26.71s

100–Meter Butterfly

1956	Shelley Mann, United States	1m11s
1960	Carolyn Schuler, United States	1m9.5s
1964	Sharon Stouder, United States	1m4.7s
1968	Lynn McClements, Australia	1m5.5s
1972	Mayumi Aoki, Japan	1m3.34s
1976	Kornelia Ender, East Germany	1m00.13s
1980	Caren Metschuck, East Germany	1m00.42s
1984	Mary Meagher, United States	59.26s
1988	Kristin Otto, East Germany	59s

200–Meter Butterfly

1968	Ada Kok, Netherlands	2m24.7s
1972	Karen Moe, United States	2m15.57s
1976	Andrea Pollack, East Germany	2m11.41s
1980	Ines Geissler, East Germany	2m10.44s
1984	Mary Meagher, United States	2m06.90s
1988	Kathleen Nord, East Germany	2m9.51s

200–Meter Individual Medley

1968	Claudia Kolb, United States	2m24.7s
1972	Shane Gould, Australia	2m23.07s
1984	Tracy Caulkins, United States	2m12.64s
1988	Daniela Hunger, East Germany	2m12.59s

400–Meter Individual Medley

1964	Donna de Varona, United States	5m18.7s
1968	Claudia Kolk, United States	5m8.5s
1972	Gail Neall, Australia	5m2.97s
1976	Ulrike Tauber, East Germany	4m42.77s
1980	Petra Schneider, East Germany	4m36.29s
1984	Tracy Caulkins, United States	4m39.21s
1988	Janet Evans, United States	4m37.76s

400–Meter Freestyle Relay

1912	Great Britain	5m52.8s
1920	United States	5m11.6s
1924	United States	4m58.8s
1928	United States	4m47.6s
1932	United States	4m38s
1936	Netherlands	4m36s
1948	United States	4m29.2s
1952	Hungary	4m24.4s

1956	Australia	4m17.1s
1960	United States	4m8.9s
1964	United States	4m3.8s
1968	United States	4m2.5s
1972	United States	3m55.19s
1976	United States	3m44.82s
1980	East Germany	3m42.71s
1984	United States	3m44.43s
1988	East Germany	3m40.63s

400–Meter Medley Relay

1960	United States	4m41.1s
1964	United States	4m33.9s
1968	United States	4m28.3s
1972	United States	4m20.75s
1976	East Germany	4m07.95s
1980	East Germany	4m06.67s
1984	United States	4m08.34s
1988	East Germany	4m03.74s

Springboard Dive

		Points
1920	Aileen Riggin, United States	539.90
1924	Elizabeth Becker, United States	474.5
1928	Helen Meany, United States	78.62
1932	Georgia Coleman, United States	87.52
1936	Marjorie Gestring, United States	89.27
1948	Victoria M. Draves, United States	108.74
1952	Patricia McCormick, United States	147.30
1956	Patricia McCormick, United States	142.36
1960	Ingrid Kramer, Germany	155.81
1964	Ingrid Kramer Engel, Germany	145.00
1968	Sue Gossick, United States	150.77
1972	Micki King, United States	450.03
1976	Jennifer Chandler, United States	506.19
1980	Irina Kalinina, U.S.S.R.	725.91
1984	Sylvie Bernier, Canada	530.70
1988	Gao Min, China	580.23

Platform Dive

		Points
1912	Greta Johansson, Sweden	39.9
1920	Stefani Fryland, Denmark	34.60
1924	Caroline Smith, United States	166
1928	Elizabeth B. Pinkston, United States	31.60
1932	Dorothy Poynton, United States	40.26
1936	Dorothy Poynton Hill, United States	33.92
1948	Victoria M. Draves, United States	68.87
1952	Patricia McCormick, United States	79.37
1956	Patricia McCormick, United States	84.85
1960	Ingrid Kramer, Germany	91.28
1964	Lesley Bush, United States	99.80
1968	Milena Duchkova, Czechoslovakia	109.59
1972	Ulrika Knape, Sweden	390.00
1976	Elena Vaytsekhovskaia, U.S.S.R.	406.59
1980	Martina Jaschke, East Germany	596.25
1984	Zhou Jihong, China	435.51
1988	Xu Yanmei, China	445.20

BASKETBALL–MEN

1904	United States	1968	United States
1936	United States	1972	U.S.S.R.
1948	United States	1976	United States
1952	United States	1980	Yugoslavia
1956	United States	1984	United States
1960	United States	1988	U.S.S.R.
1964	United States		

BASKETBALL–WOMEN

1976	U.S.S.R.	1984	United States
1980	U.S.S.R.	1988	United States

DISTRIBUTION OF MEDALS
1988 SUMMER GAMES

Country	Gold	Silver	Bronze	Total
Soviet Union	55	31	46	132
East Germany	37	35	30	102
United States	36	31	27	94
West Germany	11	14	15	40
Bulgaria	10	12	13	35
South Korea	12	10	11	33
China	5	11	12	28
Romania	7	11	6	24
Britain	5	10	9	24
Hungary	11	6	6	23
France	6	4	6	16
Poland	2	5	9	16
Italy	6	4	4	14
Japan	4	3	7	14
Australia	3	6	5	14
New Zealand	3	2	8	13
Yugoslavia	3	4	5	12
Sweden	0	4	7	11
Canada	3	2	5	10
Kenya	5	2	2	9
The Netherlands	2	2	5	9
Czechoslovakia	3	3	2	8
Brazil	1	2	3	6
Norway	2	3	0	5
Denmark	2	1	1	4
Finland	1	1	2	4
Spain	1	1	2	4
Switzerland	0	2	2	4
Morocco	1	0	2	3
Turkey	1	1	0	2
Jamaica	0	2	0	2
Argentina	0	1	1	2
Belgium	0	0	2	2
Mexico	0	0	2	2
Austria	1	0	0	1
Portugal	1	0	0	1
Suriname	1	0	0	1
Chile	0	1	0	1
Costa Rica	0	1	0	1
Indonesia	0	1	0	1
Iran	0	1	0	1
Neth. Antilles	0	1	0	1
Peru	0	1	0	1
Senegal	0	1	0	1
Virgin Islands	0	1	0	1
Colombia	0	0	1	1
Djibouti	0	0	1	1
Greece	0	0	1	1
Mongolia	0	0	1	1
Pakistan	0	0	1	1
Philippines	0	0	1	1
Thailand	0	0	1	1

BOXING
(U.S. winners only)

(U.S. boycotted Olympics in 1980)

Flyweight–112 pounds (51 kilograms)

1904	George v. Finnegan	1952	Nate Brooks
1920	Frank De Genaro	1976	Leo Randolph
1924	Fidel La Barba	1984	Steve McCrory

Bantamweight–119 (54 kg)

1904	O.L. Kirk	1988	Kennedy McKinney

Featherweight–126 pounds (57 kg)

1904	O.L. Kirk	1984	Meldrick Taylor
1924	Jackie Fields		

Lightweight–132 pounds (60 kg)

1904	H.J. Spanger	1976	Howard Davis
1920	Samuel Mosberg	1984	Pernell Whitaker
1968	Ronnie Harris		

Light Welterweight–140 pounds (63.5 kg)

1952	Charles Adkins	1976	Ray Leonard
1972	Ray Seales	1984	Jerry Page

Welterweight–148 pounds (67 kg)

1904	Al Young	1984	Mark Breland
1932	Edward Flynn		

Light Middleweight–157 pounds (71 kg)

1960	Wilbert McClure	1984	Frank Tate

Middleweight–165 pounds (75 kg)

1904	Charles Mayer	1960	Eddie Cook
1932	Carmen Barth	1976	Michael Spinks
1952	Floyd Patterson		

Light Heavyweight–179 pounds (81 kg)

1920	Edward Eagan	1960	Cassius Clay
1952	Norvel Lee	1976	Leon Spinks
1956	James Boyd	1988	Andrew Maynard

Heavyweight–201 pounds

1904	Sam Berger	1968	George Foreman
1952	Edward Sanders	1984	Henry Tilman
1956	Pete Rademacher	1988	Ray Mercer
1964	Joe Frazier		

Super Heavyweight (unlimited)

1984	Tyrell Biggs

Sixty–one Nations Competed in Seoul Paralympics

The Games of the 8th Seoul Paralympics opened at the Seoul Olympic Stadium on Oct. 15, 1988, with the attendance of 4,278 disabled athletes from 61 nations, the largest turnout in the events' history.

The sports competition for the disabled took place at the games venues in Seoul Sports Complex, Olympic Park and Kyonggi–do area under the ideas of "challenge and overcoming," "peace and friendship," and "participation and equality."

They competed in 16 sports including archery, track and field, fencing, judo, cycling, shooting, soccer, swimming and pingpong.

Other competitions were basketball, weightlifting and powerlifing, lawn bowling, boccia, goal ball, and snooker.

Among the participating nations, the United States fielded the largest number of participants with 376 in 12 games, followed by Britain with 242 in 15 games and host Korea with 239 in 16 games.

The nations participating in the Seoul Paralympics included the Soviet Union, China, Yugoslavia, Hungary, Bulgaria, Poland, and Czechoslovakia.

Koh Kwi–Nam, president of the Seoul Paralympics Organizing Committee (SPOC), said 8,325 people including physically handicapped citizens and their family members as well as those suffering other plights were invited to the Opening Ceremony.

The Seoul Paralympics served as an occasion to enhance the recognition by the Korean people of the physically handicapped and cement friendly relationships among the disabled from around the world, he said.

The Athletes Village for the Seoul Paralympics, consisting of 1,316 apartments in 10 buildings, was built at a 57,666–square–meter site, about 4 kilometers away from the Olympic Stadium.

A total of 5,911 volunteers worked for the Games as interpreter–guides for foreign athletes and officials, and assistants in competition operation, administration, logistics, security, and medical services.

Coubertin Founded Modern Olympics

In the late 1880s, Baron Pierre de Coubertin of France conceived the idea of holding a modern olympics every four years to diminish tensions between world nations through the ennoblement of amateur sports and the general spirit of competition. Accordingly, he organized a conference in Paris in 1884 for this purpose. Thirteen countries sent representatives and 21 other nations sent their message of support.

Baron de Coubertin wanted the first modern olympics to be held in Paris, but a motion was passed to hold them in Athens, Greece in 1896. At that time, most of the games consisted of track and field events.

De Coubertin died in Geneva in 1937, but his heart was buried near the Temple of Hera at Olympia. In honor of this remarkable man who shaped the ideals of the modern games, each olympic torch bearer must visit de Courbertin's tomb with the lighted torch before beginning the run to the host city.

JIM THORPE'S OLYMPIC MEDALS

More than 70 years after he won the pentathlon and decathlon at Stockholm, Sweden, Jim Thorpe's Olympic gold medals were returned posthumously to him by the International Olympic Committee. Thorpe, an Oklahoma Sac and Fox Indian, became one of the greatest all–around athletes ever produced in America. He was an all–American football player at the Carlisle Institute, an Indian trade school in Pennsylvania, and starred in baseball and track and field. After winning the medals in the 1912 Olympics, he was forced to give them up when he admitted he had played two seasons for money as a semipro baseball player in 1909 and 1910. Under the rules, he had lost his amateur status by taking money and thus was theoretically ineligible for the Olympics. In October of 1982, after many years of vigorous efforts by his family and other officials in athletics, the I.O.C. reinstated Thorpe in its archives as a co–winner of the two events. At ceremonies in Los Angeles in January 1983, Antonio Samaranch, president of the I.O.C. presented Thorpe's children with gold medals to replace those he had turned back. Thorpe, who later in his career played major–league baseball and pro football, died at the age of 65 in 1953.

Other 1988 Summer Olympic Games Champions

Archery
Men—Jay Barrs, United States
Men's Team—South Korea
Women—Kim Soo-nyung, South Korea
Women's Team—South Korea

Baseball
Men—Unted States

Canoeing
500 m—Olaf Heukrodt, East Germany
1,000 m—Ivan Klementiev, U.S.S.R.
500—m pairs—U.S.S.R. (Victor Reneiski and Nikolai Jouravski)
1,000—m pairs—U.S.S.R. (Victor Reneiski and Nikolai Jouravski)

Kayak—Women
500 m—Vania Guecheva, Bulgaria
500—m pairs—East Germany (Birgit Schmidt and Anke Nothnagel)
500—m fours—East Germany

Kayak—Men
500 m—Zsolt Gyulay, Hungary
500—m pairs—New Zealand (Ian Ferguson and Paul MacDonald)
1,000—m pairs—Greg Barton, Unitd States
1,000—m pairs—United States (Greg Barton and Norman Bellingham)
1,000—m fours—Hungary

Cycling—Men
196.9–km Individual road race—Olaf Ludwig, East Germany
Individual time trial—Alexander Kirichenko, U.S.S.R.
100–km Team time trial—East Germany
4,000–m Individual pursuit—Gintaoutas Umaras, U.S.S.R.
Match sprint—Lutz Hesslich, East Germany
4,000–m Team Pursuit—U.S.S.R.
Points race—Dan Frost, Denmark

Cycling—Women
Sprint—Erika Salumiae, U.S.S.R.
Individual road race—Monique Knol, Holland

Equestrian
Dressage—Nicole Uphoff, West Germany
Dressage team—West Germany
Jumping—Pierre Durand, France
Jumping team—West Germany
Three–day event—Mark Todd, New Zealand
Team three–day event—West Germany

Fencing
Foil—Stefano Cerioni, Italy
Team foil—U.S.S.R.
Epee—Arnd Schmitt, West Germany
Team epee—France
Sabre—Jeanfrancois Lamour, France
Team sabre—Hungary
Women's foil—Anja Fichtel, West Germany
Women's team foil—West Germany

Gymnastics—Men
All–around—Vladimir Artemov, U.S.S.R.
Floor exercise—Sergei Kharikov, U.S.S.R.
Horizontal bar—Vladimir Artemov, U.S.S.R.
Parallel bars—Vladimir Artemov, U.S.S.R.

Pommel horse—Zsolt Borkai, Hungary; Dmitri Bilozertchev, U.S.S.R.; Lyubomir Gueraskov, Bulgaria
Rings—Holger Berendt, East Germany; Dmitri Bilozertchev, U.S.S.R.
Vault—Lou Yun, China
Team—U.S.S.R.

Gymnastics—Women
All–around—Elena Shoushounova, U.S.S.R.
Balance beam—Daniela Silivas, Romania
Floor exercise—Daniela Silvas, Romania
Rhythmic Gymnastics—Marina Lobatch, U.S.S.R.
Uneven bars—Daniela Silivas, Romania
Vault—Svetlana Boguinskaia, U.S.S.R.
Team—U.S.S.R.

Judo
133 lb—Kim Jae–Yup, South Korea
143 lb—Lee Kyung–keun, South Korea
156 lb—Marc Alexandre, France
171 lb—Waldemar Legien, Poland
189 lb—Peter Seisenbacher, Austria
209 lb—Hitoshi Saito, Japan
Over 209 lb—Hitoshi Saito, Japan

Modern Pentathlon
Individual—Janos Martinek, Hungary
Team—Hungary

Rowing—Men
Singles—Thomas Lange, East Germany
Doubles—Holland
Quadruples—Italy
Pairs—Great Britain
Pairs with coxswain—Italy
Fours—East Germany
Fours with coxswain—East Germany
Eights—West Germany

Rowing—Women
Singles—Jutta Behrendt, East Germany
Doubles—East Germany
Pairs—Romania
Fours with coxswain—East Germany
Quadruple sculls—East Germany
Eights—East Germany

Shooting—Men
Free pistol—Sorin Babii, Romania
Rapid–fire pistol—Afanasi Kouzming, U.S.S.R.
Small–bore rifle—Miroslav Varga, Czechoslovakia
Small–bore rifle, 3–position—Malcolm Cooper, Great Britain
Rifle running game target—Tor Heiestad, Norway
Trap—Dimitri Monakov, U.S.S.R.
Air rifle—Goran Maksimovic, Yugoslavia

Shooting—Women
Air rifle—Irina Chilova, U.S.S.R.
Small–bore rifle—Silvia Sperber, West Germany
Air pistol—Jasna Sekaric, Yugoslavia
Rapid–fire pistol—Nino Saloukvadze, U.S.S.R.

Synchronized Swimming
Solo—Carolyn Waldo, Canada
Duet—Canada (Carolyn Waldo and Michelle Cameron)

Table Tennis
Men's singles—Yoo Nam–kyu, South Korea

Men's doubles—China (Chen Longcan and Wei Qingguang)
Women's singles—Chen Jing, China
Women's doubles—South Korea (Hyun Junghwa and Yang Young–ja)

Tennis
Men's singles—Miloslav Mecir, Czechoslovakia
Men's doubles—United States (Ken Flach and Robert Seguso)
Women's singles—Steffi Graf, West Germany
Women's doubles—United States (Pam Shriver and Zina Garrison)

Weight Lifting
115 lb—Sevdalin Marinov, Bulgaria
126 lb—Oxen Mirzoian, U.S.S.R.
132 lb—Naim Suleymanoglu, Turkey
149 lb—Joachim Kunz, East Germany
165 lb—Borislav Guidikov, Bulgaria
182 lb—Israil Arsamakov, U.S.S.R.
198 lb—Anatoli Khrapatyi, U.S.S.R.
220 lb—Pavel Kousnetzov, U.S.S.R.
242 lb—Yuri Zacharevich
Over 242—Alexandre Kurlovich, U.S.S.R.

Wrestling—Freestyle
105.5 lb—Takashi Kobayashi, Japan
114.5 lb—Mitsuru Sato, Japan
125.5 lb—Sergei Beloglazov, U.S.S.R.
136.5 lb—John Smith, United States
149.5 lb—Arsen Fadzaev, U.S.S.R.
162.5 lb—Kenneth Monday, United States
180 lb—Han Myung–woo, South Korea
198 lb—Makharbek Khadartsev, U.S.S.R.
220 lb—Vasile Puscasu, Romania
286 lb—David Godedjichvili, U.S.S.R.

Wrestling—Greco–Roman
105.5 lb—Vincenzo Maenza, Itlay
114.5 lb—Jon Ronningen, Norway
125.5 lb—Andras Sike, Hungary
135.25 lb—Kamandar Madjivov, U.S.S.R.
149.5 lb—Levon Djoulfalakian, U.S.S.R.
162.75 lb—Kim Young–nam, South Korea
180.25 lb—Mikhail Mamiachvili, U.S.S.R.
198 lb—Atanas Komchev, Bulgaria
220 lb—Andrzej Wronski, Poland
286 lb—Alexandre Kareline, U.S.S.R.

Yachting
Board sailing—Bruce Kendall, New Zealand
Finn—Jose Luis Doreste, Spain
Flying Dutchman—Denmark (Jorgen Bojsen–Moller and Christian Gronborg)
470 Class—France (Thierry Peponnet and Luc Pillot)
Soling—East Germany
Star—Great Britain (Michael McIntyre and Philip Bryn Vaile)
Tornado—France (Jean Yves Le Deroff and Nicolas Henard)
Women's 470—United States (Allison Jolly and Lynne Jewell)

Team Champions
Field hockey, men—Great Britain
Field hockey, women—Australia
Handball, men—U.S.S.R.
Handball, women—South Korea
Soccer—U.S.S.R.
Volleyball, men—United States
Volleyball—U.S.S.R.
Water polo—Yugoslavia

FOOTBALL

The pastime of kicking around a ball goes back beyond the limits of recorded history. Ancient savage tribes played football of a primitive kind. There was a ball-kicking game played by Athenians, Spartans, and Corinthians 2500 years ago, which the Greeks called *Episkuros*. The Romans had a somewhat similar game called *Harpastum* and are supposed to have carried the game with them when they invaded the British Isles in the First Century, B.C.

Undoubtedly the game known in the United States as Football traces directly to the English game of Rugby, though the modifications have been many. Informal football was played on college lawns well over a century ago, and an annual Freshman-Sophomore series of "scrimmages" began at Yale in 1840. The first formal intercollegiate football game was the Princeton-Rutgers contest at New Brunswick, N.J. on Nov. 6, 1869, with Rutgers winning by 6 goals to 4.

In those days, games were played with 25, 20, 15, or 11 men on a side. In 1880, there was a convention at which Walter Camp of Yale persuaded the delegates to agree to a rule calling for 11 players on a side.

The first professional game was played in 1895 at Latrobe, Pa. The National Football League was founded in 1921. The All-American Conference went into action in 1946. At the end of the 1949 season the two circuits merged, retaining the name of the older league. In 1960, the American Football League began operations. In 1970, the leagues merged. The United States Football League played its first season in 1983, from March to July. It suspended spring operation after the 1985 season, and planned a 1986 move to fall, but suspended operations again. It did not function as a league through 1987.

In 1991, another effort at spring football was launched, but this time it had the backing of the National Football League. The World League of American Football debuted in March 1991 with 10 teams. Three of them were in Europe—London, Barcelona, and Frankfurt. The other seven were in North America, including the Montreal Machine in Canada and six United States teams. With television contracts signed with ABC and USA Cable Network, the league seemed to be on sound footing from the beginning.

College Football

NATIONAL COLLEGE FOOTBALL CHAMPIONS

The "National Collegiate A.A. Football Guide" recognizes as unofficial national champion the team selected each year by press association polls. The Associated Press poll (of writers) does not agree with the United Press International poll (of coaches), the guide lists both teams selected.

1937	Pittsburgh	1950	Oklahoma	1960	Minnesota	1971	Nebraska	1981	Clemson
1938	Texas Christian	1951	Tennessee	1961	Alabama	1972	So. California	1982	Penn State
1939	Texas A & M	1952	Mich. State	1962	So. California	1973	Notre Dame	1983	Miami
1940	Minnesota	1953	Maryland	1963	Texas		and U. of Ala.	1984	Brigham Young
1941	Minnesota	1954	Ohio State	1964	Alabama	1974	Oklahoma and	1985	Oklahoma
1942	Ohio State		and U.C.L.A.	1965	Alabama and		So. California	1986	Penn State
1943	Notre Dame	1955	Oklahoma		Mich. State	1975	Oklahoma	1987	Miami
1944	Army	1956	Oklahoma	1966	Notre Dame	1976	Pittsburgh	1988	Notre Dame
1945	Army	1957	Auburn and	1967	So. California	1977	Notre Dame	1989	Miami
1946	Notre Dame		Ohio State	1968	Ohio State	1978	Alabama and	1990	Colorado
1947	Notre Dame	1958	Louisiana	1969	Texas		So. California		
1948	Michigan		State	1970	Texas and	1979	Alabama		
1949	Notre Dame	1959	Syracuse		Nebraska	1980	Georgia		

RECORD OF ANNUAL MAJOR BOWL COLLEGE FOOTBALL GAMES

Rose Bowl

(At Pasadena, Calif.)

1902	Michigan 49, Stanford 0	1932	So. California 21, Tulane 12	1952	Illinois 40, Stanford 7
1916	Washington State 14, Brown 0	1933	So. California 35, Pittsburgh 0	1953	So. California 7, Wisconsin 0
1917	Oregon 14, Pennsylvania 0	1934	Columbia 7, Stanford 0	1954	Michigan State 28, U.C.L.A. 20
1918	Mare Island Marines 19, Camp	1935	Alabama 29, Stanford 13	1955	Ohio State 20, So. California 7
	Lewis 7	1936	Stanford 7, So. Methodist 0	1956	Michigan State 17, U.C.L.A. 14
1919	Great Lakes 17, Mare Island	1937	Pittsburgh 21, Washington 0	1957	Iowa 35, Oregon State 19
	Marines 0	1938	California 13, Alabama 0	1958	Ohio State 10, Oregon 7
1920	Harvard 7, Oregon 6	1939	So. California 7, Duke 3	1959	Iowa 38, California 12
1921	California 28, Ohio State 0	1940	So. California 14, Tennessee 0	1960	Washington 44, Wisconsin 8
1922	Washington and Jefferson 0,	1941	Stanford 21, Nebraska 13	1961	Washington 17, Minnesota 7
	California 0	1942	Oregon State 20, Duke 16[1]	1962	Minnesota 21, U.C.L.A. 3
1923	So. California 14, Penn State 3	1943	Georgia 9, U.C.L.A. 0	1963	So. California 42, Wisconsin 37
1924	Navy 14, Washington 14	1944	So. California 29, Washington 0	1964	Illinois 17, Washington 7
1925	Notre Dame 27, Stanford 10	1945	So. California 25, Tennessee 0	1965	Michigan 34, Oregon State 7
1926	Alabama 20, Washington 19	1946	Alabama 34, So. California 14	1966	U.C.L.A. 14, Michigan State 12
1927	Alabama 7, Stanford 7	1947	Illinois 45, U.C.L.A. 14	1967	Purdue 14, So. California 13
1928	Stanford 7, Pittsburgh 6	1948	Michigan 49, So. California 0	1968	So. California 14, Indiana 3
1929	Georgia Tech 8, California 7	1949	Northwestern 20, California 14	1969	Ohio State 27, So. California 16
1930	So. California 47, Pittsburgh 14	1950	Ohio State 17, California 14	1970	So. California 10, Michigan 3
1931	Alabama 24, Wash. State 0	1951	Michigan 14, California 6	1971	Stanford 27, Ohio State 17

Year	Result
1972	Stanford 13, Michigan 12
1973	So. California 42, Ohio State 17
1974	Ohio State 42, So. California 21
1975	So. California 18, Ohio State 17
1976	U.C.L.A. 23, Ohio State 10
1977	So. California 14, Michigan 6
1978	Washington 27, Michigan 20
1979	So. California 17, Michigan 10
1980	So. California 17, Ohio State 16
1981	Michigan 23, Washington 6
1982	Washington 28, Iowa 0
1983	U.C.L.A. 24, Michigan 14
1984	U.C.L.A. 45, Illinois 9
1985	USC 20, Ohio St. 17
1986	U.C.L.A. 45, Iowa 28
1987	Arizona State 22, Michigan 15
1988	Michigan State 20, USC 17
1989	Michigan 22, So. California 14
1990	USC 17, Michigan 10
1991	Washington 46, Iowa 34

1. Played at Durham, N.C.

Orange Bowl
(At Miami)

Year	Result
1933	Miami (Fla.) 7, Manhattan 0
1934	Duquesne 33, Miami (Fla.) 7
1935	Bucknell 26, Miami (Fla.) 0
1936	Catholic 20, Mississippi 19
1937	Duquesne 13, Mississippi State 12
1938	Auburn 6, Michigan State 0
1939	Tennessee 17, Oklahoma 0
1940	Georgia Tech 21, Missouri 7
1941	Mississippi State 14, Georgetown 7
1942	Georgia 40, Texas Christian 26
1943	Alabama 37, Boston College 21
1944	Louisiana State 19, Texas A&M 14
1945	Tulsa 26, Georgia Tech 12
1946	Miami (Fla.) 13, Holy Cross 6
1947	Rice 8, Tennessee 0
1948	Georgia Tech 20, Kansas 14
1949	Texas 41, Georgia 28
1950	Santa Clara 21, Kentucky 13
1951	Clemson 15, Miami (Fla.) 14
1952	Georgia Tech 17, Baylor 14
1953	Alabama 61, Syracuse 6
1954	Oklahoma 7, Maryland 0
1955	Duke 34, Nebraska 7
1956	Oklahoma 20, Maryland 6
1957	Colorado 27, Clemson 21
1958	Oklahoma 48, Duke 21
1959	Oklahoma 21, Syracuse 6
1960	Georgia 14, Missouri 0
1961	Missouri 21, Navy 14
1962	Louisiana State 25, Colorado 7
1963	Alabama 17, Oklahoma 0
1964	Nebraska 13, Auburn 7
1965	Texas 21, Alabama 17
1966	Alabama 39, Nebraska 28
1967	Florida 27, Georgia Tech 12
1968	Oklahoma 26, Tennessee 24
1969	Penn State 15, Kansas 14
1970	Penn State 10, Missouri 3
1971	Nebraska 17, Louisiana State 12
1972	Nebraska 38, Alabama 6
1973	Nebraska 40, Notre Dame 6
1974	Penn State 16, Louisiana State 9
1975	Notre Dame 13, Alabama 11
1976	Oklahoma 14, Michigan 6
1977	Ohio State 27, Colorado 10
1978	Arkansas 31, Oklahoma 6
1979	Oklahoma 31, Nebraska 24
1980	Oklahoma 24, Florida State 7
1981	Oklahoma 18, Florida State 17
1982	Clemson 22, Nebraska 15
1983	Nebraska 21, Louisiana State 20
1984	Miami 31, Nebraska 30
1985	Washington 28, Oklahoma 17
1986	Oklahoma 25, Penn St. 10
1987	Oklahoma 42, Arkansas 8
1988	Miami 20, Oklahoma 14
1989	Miami 23, Nebraska 3
1990	Notre Dame 21, Colorado 6
1991	Colorado 10, Notre Dame 9

Sugar Bowl
(At New Orleans)

1935	Tulane 20, Temple 14
1936	Texas Christian 3, Louisiana State 2
1937	Santa Clara 21, Louisiana State 14
1938	Santa Clara 6, Louisiana State 0
1939	Texas Christian 15, Carnegie Tech 7
1940	Texas A & M 14, Tulane 13
1941	Boston College 19, Tennessee 13
1942	Fordham 2, Missouri 0
1943	Tennessee 14, Tulsa 7
1944	Georgia Tech 20, Tulsa 18
1945	Duke 29, Alabama 26
1946	Oklahoma A & M 33, St. Mary's (Calif.) 13
1947	Georgia 20, North Carolina 10
1948	Texas 27, Alabama 7
1949	Oklahoma 14, North Carolina 6
1950	Oklahoma 35, Louisiana State 0
1951	Kentucky 13, Oklahoma 7
1952	Maryland 28, Tennessee 13
1953	Georgia Tech 24, Mississippi 7
1954	Georgia Tech 42, West Virginia 19
1955	Navy 21, Mississippi 0
1956	Georgia Tech 7, Pittsburgh 0
1957	Baylor 13, Tennessee 7
1958	Mississippi 39, Texas 7
1959	Louisiana State 7, Clemson 0
1960	Mississippi 21, Louisiana State 0
1961	Mississippi 14, Rice 6
1962	Alabama 10, Arkansas 3
1963	Mississippi 17, Arkansas 13
1964	Alabama 12, Mississippi 7
1965	Louisiana State 13, Syracuse 10
1966	Missouri 20, Florida 18
1967	Alabama 34, Nebraska 7
1968	Louisiana State 20, Wyoming 13
1969	Arkansas 16, Georgia 2
1970	Mississippi 27, Arkansas 22
1971	Tennessee 34, Air Force Academy 13
1972	Oklahoma 40, Auburn 22
1973	Oklahoma 14, Penn State 0
1974	Notre Dame 24, Alabama 23
1975	Nebraska 13, Florida 10
1976	Alabama 13, Penn State 6
1977	Pittsburgh 27, Georgia 3
1978	Alabama 35, Ohio State 6
1979	Alabama 14, Penn State 7
1980	Alabama 24, Arkansas 9
1981	Georgia 17, Notre Dame 10
1982	Pittsburgh 24, Georgia 20
1983	Penn State 27, Georgia 23
1984	Auburn 9, Michigan 7
1985	Nebraska 28, LSU 10
1986	Tennessee 35, Miami, Fla. 7
1987	Nebraska 30, Louisiana State 15
1988	Syracuse 16, Auburn 16 (tie)
1989	Florida State 13, Auburn 7
1990	Miami 33, Alabama 25
1991	Tennessee 23, Virginia 22

Cotton Bowl
(At Dallas)

Year	Result
1937	Texas Christian 16, Marquette 6
1938	Rice 28, Colorado 14
1939	St. Mary's (Calif.) 20, Texas Tech. 13
1940	Clemson 6, Boston College 3
1941	Texas A & M 13, Fordham 12
1942	Alabama 29, Texas A & M 21
1943	Texas 14, Georgia Tech 7
1944	Randolph Field 7, Texas 7
1945	Oklahoma A & M 34, Texas Christian 0
1946	Texas 40, Missouri 27
1947	Louisiana State 0, Arkansas 0
1948	So. Methodist 13, Penn State 13
1949	So. Methodist 21, Oregon 13
1950	Rice 27, North Carolina 13
1951	Tennessee 20, Texas 14
1952	Kentucky 20, Texas Christian 7
1953	Texas 16, Tennessee 0
1954	Rice 28, Alabama 6
1955	Georgia Tech 14, Arkansas 6
1956	Mississippi 14, Texas Christian 13
1957	Texas Christian 28, Syracuse 27
1958	Navy 20, Rice 7
1959	Air Force 0, Texas Christian 0
1960	Syracuse 23, Texas 14
1961	Duke 7, Arkansas 6
1962	Texas 12, Mississippi 7
1963	Louisiana State 13, Texas 0
1964	Texas 28, Navy 6
1965	Arkansas 10, Nebraska 7
1966	Louisiana State 14, Arkansas 7
1967	Georgia 24, So. Methodist 9
1968	Texas A & M 20, Alabama 16
1969	Texas 36, Tennessee 13
1970	Texas 21, Notre Dame 17
1971	Notre Dame 24, Texas 11
1972	Penn State 30, Texas 6
1973	Texas 17, Alabama 13
1974	Nebraska 19, Texas 3
1975	Penn State 41, Baylor 20
1976	Arkansas 31, Georgia 10
1977	Houston 30, Maryland 21
1978	Notre Dame 38, Texas 10
1979	Notre Dame 35, Houston 34
1980	Houston 17, Nebraska 14
1981	Alabama 30, Baylor 2
1982	Texas 14, Alabama 12
1983	Southern Methodist 7, Pittsburgh 3
1984	Georgia 10, Texas 9
1985	Boston College 45, Houston 28
1986	Texas A & M 36, Auburn 16
1987	Ohio State 28, Texas A & M 12
1988	Texas A & M 35, Notre Dame 10
1989	UCLA 17, Arkansas 3
1990	Tennessee 31, Arkansas 27
1991	Miami 46, Texas 3

Gator Bowl
(At Jacksonville, Fla. Played on Saturday nearest New Year's Day of year indicated)

Year	Result
1953	Florida 14, Tulsa 13
1954	Texas Tech 35, Auburn 13
1955	Auburn 33, Baylor 13
1956	Vanderbilt 25, Auburn 13

1957	Georgia Tech 21, Pittsburgh 14	1970	Florida 14, Tennessee 13	1983	Florida State 31, West Virginia 12
1958	Tennessee 3, Texas A & M 0	1971	Auburn 35, Mississippi 28		
1959	Mississippi 7, Florida 3	1972	Georgia 7, North Carolina 3	1984	Florida 14, Iowa 6
1960	Arkansas 14, Georgia Tech 7	1973	Auburn 24, Colorado 3	1985	Oklahoma St. 21, South Carolina 14
1961	Florida 13, Baylor 12	1974	Texas Tech 28, Tennessee 19		
1962	Penn State 30, Georgia Tech 15	1975	Auburn 27, Texas 3	1986	Florida State 34, Oklahoma St. 23
1963	Florida 17, Penn State 7	1976	Maryland 13, Florida 0		
1964	No. Carolina 35, Air Force 0	1977	Notre Dame 20, Penn State 9	1987	Clemson 27, Stanford 21
1965	Florida State 36, Oklahoma 19	1978	Pittsburgh 34, Clemson 3	1988	LSU 30, South Carolina 13
1966	Georgia Tech 31, Texas Tech 21	1979	Clemson 17, Ohio State 15	1989	Georgia 34, Michigan St. 27
1967	Tennessee 18, Syracuse 12	1980	North Carolina 17, Michigan 15	1990	Clemson 27, West Virginia 7
1968	Penn State 17, Florida State 17	1981	Pittsburgh 37, South Carolina 9	1991	Michigan 35, Mississippi 3
1969	Missouri 35, Alabama 10	1982	North Carolina 31, Arkansas 27		

RESULTS OF OTHER 1990 SEASON BOWL GAMES

All–American (Birmingham, Ala., Dec. 28)—North Carolina St. 31, Southern Mississippi 27

Aloha (Honolulu, Dec. 25)—Syracuse 28, Arizona 0

Blockbuster Bowl (Miami, Dec. 28)—Florida St. 24, Penn St. 17

California (Fresno, Dec. 8)—San Jose St. 48, Central Michigan 24

Copper (Tucson, Ariz., Dec. 31)—Calif. 17, Wyoming 15

Fiesta (Tempe, Ariz., Jan 1)—Louisville 34, Alabama 7

Florida Citrus (Orlando, Jan. 1)—Georgia Tech 45, Nebraska 21

Freedom (Anaheim, Calif., Dec. 29)—Colo. St. 32, Oregon 31

Hall of Fame (Tampa, Fla., Jan. 1)—Clemson 30, Illinois 0

Holiday (San Diego, Dec. 29)—Texas A&M 65, Brigham Young 14

Independence (Shreveport, La., Dec. 15)—Louisiana Tech 34, Maryland 34 (tie)

John Hancock Bowl (El Paso, Tex., Dec. 31)—Michigan St. 17, USC 16

Liberty (Memphis, Dec. 27)—Air Force 23, Ohio St. 11

Peach (Atlanta, Dec. 29)—Auburn 27, Indiana 23

HEISMAN MEMORIAL TROPHY WINNERS

The Heisman Memorial Trophy is presented annually by the Downtown Athletic club of New York City to the nation's outsanding college football player, as determined by a poll of sportswriters and sportscasters.

1935	Jay Berwanger, Chicago	1955	Howard Cassady, Ohio State	1974–75	Archie Griffin, Ohio State
1936	Larry Kelley, Yale	1956	Paul Hornung, Notre Dame	1976	Tony Dorsett, Pittsburgh
1937	Clinton Frank, Yale	1957	John Crow, Texas A & M	1977	Earl Campbell, Texas
1938	Davey O'Brien, Texas Christian	1958	Pete Dawkins, Army	1978	Billy Sims, Oklahoma
		1959	Billy Cannon, Louisiana State	1979	Charles White, Southern California
1939	Nile Kinnick, Iowa	1960	Joe Bellino, Navy		
1940	Tom Harmon, Michigan	1961	Ernie Davis, Syracuse	1980	George Rogers, South Carolina
1941	Bruce Smith, Minnesota	1962	Terry Baker, Oregon State		
1942	Frank Sinkwich, Georgia	1963	Roger Staubach, Navy	1981	Marcus Allen, Southern California
1943	Angelo Bertelli, Notre Dame	1964	John Huarte, Notre Dame		
1944	Leslie Horvath, Ohio State	1965	Mike Garrett, Southern California	1982	Hershel Walker, Georgia
1945	Felix Blanchard, Army			1983	Mike Rozier, Nebraska
1946	Glenn Davis, Army	1966	Steve Spurrier, Florida	1984	Doug Flutie, Boston College
1947	Johnny Lujack, Notre Dame	1967	Gary Beban, U.C.L.A.	1985	Bo Jackson, Auburn
1948	Doak Walker, So. Methodist	1968	O.J. Simpson, Southern California	1986	Vinnie Testeverde, Miama
1949	Leon Hart, Notre Dame			1987	Tim Brown, Notre Dame
1950	Vic Janowicz, Ohio State	1969	Steve Owens, Oklahoma	1988	Barry Sanders, Oklahoma State
1951	Dick Kazmaier, Princeton	1970	Jim Plunkett, Stanford		
1952	Billy Vessels, Oklahoma	1971	Pat Sullivan, Auburn		
1953	Johnny Lattner, Notre Dame	1972	Johnny Rodgers, Nebraska	1989	Andre Ware, Houston
1954	Alan Ameche, Wisconsin	1973	John Cappelletti, Penn State	1990	Ty Detmer, Brigham Young

1990 N.C.A.A. CHAMPIONSHIP PLAYOFFS

DIVISION I–AA

Quarterfinals
Boise State 20, Middle Tenn. St. 13
Nevada–Reno 42, Furman 35 (3 OT)
Central Florida 52, William & Mary 38
Georgia Southern 28, Idaho 27

Semifinals
Nevada–Reno 59, Boise State 52 (3 OT)
Georgia Southern 44, Cent. Florida 7

Championship
Georgia Southern 36, Nevada–Reno 13

DIVISION II

Quarterfinals
Pittsburg State 60, East Texas State 28
Indiana (Pa.) 14, Edinboro 7
Mississippi College 14, Jacksonville State 7
North Dakota State 47, Cal Poly 0

Semifinals
Indiana (Pa.) 27, Mississippi College 8
No. Dakota State 39, Pittsburg State 29

Championship
North Dakota State 51, Indiana (Pa.) 11

DIVISION III

Quarterfinals
Hofstra 38, Trenton State 3
Lycoming 24, Washington & Jefferson 0
Allegheny 31, Dayton 23
Central (Iowa) 33, St. Thomas (Minn.) 32

Semifinals
Lycoming 20, Hofstra 10
Allegheny 24, Central (Iowa) 7

Championship
Allegheny 21, Lycoming 14

1990 NATIONAL ASSOCIATION OF INTERCOLLEGIATE ATHLETICS CHAMPIONSHIPS

Division I
Quarterfinals
Central State (Ohio) 48, Fort Hays State (Kan.) 10
Carson–Newman (Tenn.) 35, Southwest State (Minn.) 6
Mesa State (Colo.) 37, Western New Mexico 30 (OT)
Central Arkansas 26, Northeastern State (Okla.) 14

Semifinals
Central State (Ohio) 41, Carson–Newman (Tenn.) 14
Mesa State (Colo.) 10, Central Arkansas 9

Championship
Central State (Ohio) 38, Mesa (Colo.) 16

DIVISION II
Quarterfinals
Baker (Kan.) 56, William Jewell (Mo.) 29
Peru State (Neb.) 38, Dickinson State (N.D.) 34
Central Washington 24, Pacific Lutheran (Wash.) 6
Westminster (Pa.) 19, Tarleton State (Texas) 17

Semifinals
Westminster (Pa.) 24, Central Washington 17
Peru State (Neb.) 27, Baker (Kan.) 3

Championship
Peru State 17, Westminster (Pa.) 7

COLLEGE FOOTBALL HALL OF FAME

(Kings Island, Interstate 71, Kings Mills, Ohio) (Date given is player's last year of competition)

Players

Abell, Earl—Colgate, 1915
Agase, Alex—Purdue/Illinois, 1946
Agganis, Harry—Boston Univ., 1952
Albert, Frank—Stanford, 1941
Aldrich, Chas. (Ki)—T.C.U., 1938
Aldrich, Malcolm—Yale, 1921
Alexander, John—Syracuse, 1920
Alworth, Lance—Arkansas, 1961
Ameche, Alan (Horse)—Wisconsin, 1954
Amling, Warren—Ohio State, 1946
Anderson, Donny—Texas Tech, 1965
Andderson, H. (Hunk)—Notre Dame, 1921
Atkins, Doug—Tennessee, 1952
Bacon, C. Everett—Wesleyan, 1912
Bagnell, Francis (Reds)—Penn, 1950
Baker, Hobart (Hobey)—Princeton, 1913
Baker, John—So. Calif., 1931
Baker, Terry—Oregon State, 1962
Ballin, Harold—Princeton, 1914
Banker, Bill—Tulane, 1929
Banonis, Vince—Detroit, 1941
Barnes, Stanley—S. California, 1921
Barrett, Charles—Cornell, 1915
Baston, Bert—Minnesota, 1916
Battles, Cliff—W. Va. Wesleyan, 1931
Baugh, Sammy—Texas Christian U., 1936
Baughan, Maxie—Georgia Tech, 1959
Bausch, James—Kansas, 1930
Beagle, Ron—Navy, 1955
Beban, Gary—UCLA, 1967
Bechtol, Hub—Texas Tech, 1946
Beckett, John—Oregon, 1913
Bednariok, Chuck—Pennsylvania 1948
Behm, Forrest—Nebraska, 1940
Bell, Bobby—Minnesota, 1962
Bellino, Joe—Navy, 1960
Below, Marty—Wisconsin, 1923
Benbrook, A.—Michigan, 1911
Bertelli, A.—Notre Dame, 1943
Berry, Charlie—Lafayette, 1924
Berwanger, John (Jay)—Chicago, 1935
Bettencourt, Larry—St. Mary's, 1927
Biletnikoff, Fred—Florida State, 1964
Blanchard, Felix (Doc)—Army, 1946
Bock, Ed—Iowa State, 1938
Bomar, Lynn—Vanderbilt, 1924
Bomeisler, Doug (Bo)—Yale, 1913
Booth, Albie—Yale, 1931
Borries, Fred—Navy, 1934
Bosely, Bruce—West Virginia, 1955
Bosseler, Don—Miami, Fla., 1956
Bottari, Vic—California, 1939
Boynton, Ben—Williams, 1920
Bozis, Al—Georgetown, 1941
Brewer, Charles—Harvard, 1895
Bright, John—Drake, 1951
Brodie, John—Stanford, 1956
Brooke, George—Pennsylvania, 1895
Brown, George—Navy, San Diego St., 1947
Brown, Gordon—Yale, 1900
Brown, John, Jr.—Navy, 1913
Brown, Johnny Mack—Alabama, 1925
Brown, Raymond (Tay)—So. Calif., 1932
Bunker, Paul—Army, 1902
Burton, Ron—Northwestern, 1956
Butkus, Dick—Illinois, 1964
Butler, Robert—Wisconsin, 1912
Cafego, George—Tennessee, 1939
Cagle, Chris—SW La./ Army, 1929
Cain, John—Alabama, 1932
Cameron, Eddie—Wash. & Lee, 1924
Campbell, David C.—Harvard, 1901

Campbell, Earl—Texas, 1977
Cannon, Billy—L.S.U., 1959
Cannon, Jack—Notre Dame, 1929
Carideo, Frank—Notre Dame, 1930
Caroline, J.C.—Illinois, 1954
Carney, Charles—Illinois, 1921
Carpenter, Bill—Army, 1959
Carpenter, C. Hunter—VPI, 1905
Carroll, Charles—Washington, 1928
Casey, Edward L.—Harvard, 1919
Cassady, Howard—Ohio State, 1955
Chamberlain, Guy—Nebraska, 1915
Chapman, Sam—Cal.-Berkeley, 1938
Chappuis, Bob—Michigan, 1947
Christman, Paul—Missouri, 1940
Clark, Earl (Dutch)—Colo. College, 1929
Cleary, Paul—USC, 1947
Clevenger, Zora—Indiana, 1903
Cloud, Jack—William & Mary, 1948
Cochran, Gary—Princeton, 1895
Cody, Josh—Vanderbilt, 1920
Coleman, Don—Mich. State, 1951
Conerly, Chuck—Mississippi, 1947
Connor, George—Notre Dame, 1947
Corbin, W.—Yale, 1888
Corbus, William—Stanford, 1933
Cowan, Hector—Princeton, 1889
Coy, Edward H. (Tad)—Yale, 1909
Crawford, Fred—Duke, 1933
Crow, John D.—Texas A&M, 1957
Crowley, James—Notre Dame, 1924
Csonka, Larry—Syracuse, 1967
Cutter, Slade—Navy, 1934
Czarobski, Ziggie—Notre Dame, 1947
Dale, Carroll—Virginia Tech, 1959
Dalrymple, Gerald—Tulane, 1931
Daniell, James—Ohio State, 1941
Dalton, John—Navy, 1912
Daly, Charles—Harvard/Army, 1902
Daniell, Averell—Pittsburgh, 1936
Davies, Tom—Pittsburgh, 1921
Davis, Ernest—Syracuse, 1961
Davis, Glenn—Army, 1946
Davis, Robert T.—Georgia Tech, 1947
Dawkins, Pete—Army, 1958
De Rogatis, Al—Duke, 1940
DesJardien, Paul—Chicago 1914
Devino, Aubrey—Iowa, 1921
DeWitt, John—Princeton, 1903
Ditka, Mike—Pittsburgh, 1960
Dobbs, Glenn—Tulsa, 1942
Dodd, Bobby—Tennessee, 1930
Donan, Holland—Princeton, 1950
Donchess, Joseph—Pittsburgh, 1929
Dougherty, Nathan—Tennessee, 1909
Drahos, Nick—Cornell, 1940
Driscoll, Paddy—Northwestern, 1917
Drury, Morley—So. California, 1927
Dudley, William (Bill)—Virginia, 1941
Easley, Ken—UCLA, 1980
Eckersall, Walter—Chicago, 1906
Edwards, Turk—Washington State, 1931
Edwards, William—Princeton, 1900
Eichenlaub, R.—Notre Dame, 1913
Elliott, Chalmers—Purdue, 1944 & Mich., 1947
Evans, Ray—Kansas, 1947
Exendine, Albert—Carlisle, 1908
Falaschi, Nello—Santa Clara, 1937
Fears, Tom—Santa Clara/UCLA, 1947
Feathers, Beattie—Tennessee, 1933
Fenimore, Robert—Oklahoma State, 1947
Fenton, G.E. (Doc)—La. State U., 1910

Ferraro, John—So. California, 1944
Fesler, Wesley—Ohio State, 1930
Fincher, Bill—Georgia Tech, 1920
Fischer, Bill—Notre Dame, 1948
Fish, Hamilton—Harvard, 1909
Fisher, Robert—Harvard, 1911
Flowers, Abe—Georgia Tech, 1920
Fortmann, Daniel—Colgate, 1935
Francis, Sam—Nebraska, 1936
Franco, Edmund (Ed)—Fordham, 1937
Frank, Clint—Yale, 1937
Franz, Rodney—California, 1949
Friedman, Benny—Michigan, 1926
Gabriel, Roman—North Carolina St., 1961
Gain, Bob—Kentucky, 1950
Galiffa, Arnold—Army, 1949
Gallarneau, Hugh—Stanford, 1941
Garbisch, Edgar—Army, 1924
Garrett, Mike—USC, 1965
Gelbert, Charles—Pennsylvania, 1896
Geyer, Forest—Oklahoma, 1915
Giel, Paul—Minnesota, 1953
Gifford, Frank—So. California, 1951
Gilbert, Walter—Auburn, 1936
Gipp, George—Notre Dame, 1920
Gladchuk, Chet—Boston College, 1940
Glass, Bill—Baylor, 1956
Goldberg, Marshall—Pittsburgh, 1938
Goodreault, Gene—Boston College, 1940
Gordon, Walter—California, 1918
Governale, Paul—Columbia, 1942
Graham, Otto—Northwestern, 1943
Grange, Harold (Red)—Illinois, 1925
Grayson, Roberty—Stanford, 1935
Green, Joe—North Texas State, 1968
Griese, Bob—Purdue, 1966
Griffin, Archie—Ohio State, 1975
Gulick, Merel—Hobart, 1929
Guyon, Joe—Georgia Tech, 1919
Hale, Edwin—Mississippi Col, 1921
Hall, Parker—Mississippi, 1938
Ham, Jack—Penn State, 1970
Hamilton, Robert (Bones)—Stanford, 1935
Hamilton, Tom—Navy, 1925
Hanson, Vic—Syracuse, 1926
Hardwick, H. (Tack)—Harvard, 1914
Hare, T. Truxton—Pennsylvania, 1900
Harley, Chick—Ohio State, 1919
Harmon, Tom—Michigan, 1940
Harpster, Howard—Carnegie Tech, 1928
Hart, Edward J. Princeton, 1911
Hart, Leon—Notre Dame, 1949
Hartman, Bill—Georgia, 1937
Hazel, Homer—Rutgers, 1924
Healey, Ed—Dartmouth, 1916
Heffelfinger, W. (Pudge)—Yale, 1891
Hein, Mel—Washington State, 1930
Heinrich, Don—Washington, 1952
Hendricks, Ted—Miami, 1968
Henry, Wilbur—Wash. & Jefferson, 1919
Herschberger, Clarence—Chicago, 1899
Herwig, Robert—California, 1937
Heston, Willie—Michigan, 1904
Hickman, Herman—Tennessee, 1931
Hickok, William—Yale, 1895
Hill, Dan—Duke, 1938
Hillebrand, A.R. (Doc)—Princeton, 1900
Hinkey, Frank—Yale, 1894
Hinkle, Carl—Vanderbilt, 1937
Hinkle, Clark—Bucknell, 1932
Hirsch, Elroy—Wis./Mich., 1943
Hitchcock, James—Auburn, 1932
Hoffman, Frank—Notre Dame, 1931

Hogan, James J.—Yale, 1904
Holland, Jerome (Brud)—Cornell, 1938
Holleder, Don—Army, 1955
Hollenbeck, William—Penn., 1908
Holovak, Michael—Boston College, 1942
Holub, E.J.—Texas Tech, 1960
Hornung, Paul—Notre Dame, 1956
Horrell, Edwin—California, 1924
Horvath, Les—Ohio State, 1944
Howe Arthur—Yale, 1911
Howell, Millard (Dixie)—Alabama, 1934
Hubbard, Cal—Centenary, 1926
Hubbard, John—Amherst, 1906
Hubert, Allison—Alabama, 1925
Huff, Robert Lee (Sam)—W. Va., 1955
Humble, Weldon G.—Rice, 1946
Hunt, Joel—Texas A&M, 1927
Huntington, Ellery—Colgate, 1914
Hutson, Don—Alabama, 1934
Ingram, James—Navy, 1906
Isbell, Cecil—Purdue, 1937
Jablonsky, Harvey—Wash. U./Army, 1933
Janowicz, Vic—Ohio State, 1951
Jenkins, Darold—Missouri, 1941
Jensen, Jack—Cal-Berkeley, 1948
Joesting, Herbert—Minnesota, 1927
Johnson, James—Carlisle, 1903
Johnson, Robert—Tennessee, 1967
Jones, Calvin—Iowa, 1955
Jones, Gormer—Ohio State, 1935
Jordan, Lee Roy—Alabama, 1962
Juhan, Frank—Univ. of South, 1910
Justice, Charlie—North Carolina, 1949
Kaer, Mort—So. California, 1926
Karras, Alex—Iowa, 1957
Kavanaugh, Kenneth—La. State U., 1939
Kaw, Edgar—Cornell, 1922
Kazmaier, Richard—Princeton, 1951
Keck, James—Princeton, 1921
Kelley, Larry—Yale, 1936
Kelly, William—Montana, 1926
Kenna, Ed—Syracuse, 1946
Kern, George—Boston College, 1941
Ketcham, Henry—Yale, 1913
Keyes, Leroy—Purdue, 1968
Killinger, William—Penn State, 1922
Kimbrough, John—Texas A&M, 1940
Kinard, Frank—Mississippi, 1937
King, Philip—Princeton, 1893
Kinnick, Nile—Iowa, 1939
Kipke, Harry—Michigan, 1923
Kirkpatrick, John Reed—Yale, 1910
Kitzmiller, John—Oregon, 1929
Koch, Barton—Baylor, 1931
Kitner, Malcolm—Texas, 1942
Kramer, Ron—Michigan, 1956
Krueger, Charlie—Texas A&M, 1957
Kwalick, Ted—Penn State, 1968
Lach, Steve—Duke, 1941
Lane, Myles—Dartmouth, 1927
Lattner, Joseph J.—Notre Dame, 1953
Lauricella, Hank—Tennessee, 1952
Lautenschlaeger—Tulane, 1925
Layden, Elmer—Notre Dame, 1924
Layne, Bobby—Texas, 1947
Lea, Langdon—Princeton, 1895
LeBaron, Eddie—Univ. of Pacific, 1949
Leech, James—Va. Mil. Insst., 1920
Lester, Darrell—Texas Christian, 1935
Lilly, Bob—Texas Christian, 1960
Little, Floyd—Syracuse, 1966
Lio, Augie—Georgetown, 1940
Locke, Gordon—Iowa, 1922
Lourie, Don—Princeton, 1921
Lucas, Richard—Penn State, 1959
Luckman, Sid—Columbia, 1938
Lujack, John—Notre Dame, 1947
Lund, J.L. (Pug)—Minnesota, 1934
Macomber, Bart—Illinois, 1915
MacLeod, Robert—Dartmouth, 1938
Maegle, Dick—Rice, 1954
Mahan, Edward W.—Harvard, 1915
Majors, John—Tennessee, 1956
Mallory, William—Yale, 1893

Mancha, Vaughn—Alabama, 1947
Mann, Gerald—So. Methodist, 1927
Manning, Archie—Mississippi, 1970
Manske, Edgar—Northwestern, 1933
Marinaro, Ed—Cornell, 1971
Markov, Vic—Washinton, 1937
Marshall, Robert—Minnesota, 1907
Matson, Ollie—San Fran. U., 1952
Matthews, Ray—Texas Christ. U., 1928
Maulbetsch, John—Michigan, 1914
Mauthe, J.L. (Pete)—Penn State, 1912
Maxwell, Robert—Chi./Swarthmore, 1906
McAfee, George—Duke, 1939
McClung, Thomas L.—Yale, 1891
McColl, William F.—Stanford, 1951
McCormick, James B.—Princeton, 1907
McDonald, Tom—Oklahoma, 1956
McDowall, Jack—No. Car. State, 1927
McElhenny, Hugh—Washington, 1951
McEver, Gene—Tennessee, 1931
McEwan, John—Minn./Army, 1916
McFadden, J.B.—Clemson, 1939
McFadin, Bud—Texas, 1950
McGee, Mike—Duke, 1959
McGinley, Edward—Pennsylvania, 1924
McGovern, J.—Minnesota, 1910
McGraw, Thurman—Colorado State, 1949
McKeever, Mike—USC, 1960
McLaren, George—Pittsburgh, 1918
McMillan, Dan—U.S.C./Calif., 1922
McMillin, A.N. (Bo)—Centre, 1921
McWhorter, Robert—Georgia, 1913
Mercer, Leroy—Pennsylvania, 1912
Meredith, Don—Southern Methodist, 1959
Metzger, Bert—Notre Dame, 1930
Meyland, Wayne—Nebraska, 1967
Mickal, Abe—La. State U., 1935
Miller, Creighton—Notre Dame, 1943
Miller, Don—Notre Dame, 1925
Miller, Edgar (Rip)—Notre Dame, 1924
Miller, Eugene—Penn State, 1913
Miller, Fred—Notre Dame, 1928
Millner, Wayne—Notre Dame, 1935
Milstead, Century—Wabash, Yale, 1923
Minds, John—Pennsylvania, 1897
Minisi, Anthony—Navy, Pennsylvania, 1947
Moffatt, Alex—Princeton, 1884
Molinski, Ed—Tennessee, 1940
Montgomery, Cliff—Columbia, 1933
Moomaw, Donn—U.C.L.A., 1952
Morley, William—Columbia, 1903
Morris, George—Georgia Tech, 1952
Morton, William—Dartmouth, 1931
Moscrip, Monk—Stanford, 1935
Muller, Harold (Brick)—Calif., 1922
Nagurski, Bronko—Minnesota, 1929
Nevers, Ernie—Stanford, 1925
Newell, Marshall—Harvard, 1893
Newman, Harry—Michigan, 1932
Nobis, Tommy—Texas, 1965
Nomellini, Leo—Minnesota, 1949
Oberland, Andrew—Dartmouth, 1925
O'Brien, Davey—Texas Chritst. U., 1938
O'Dea, Pat–Wisconsin, 1899
O'Hearn, J.—Cornell, 1915
Olds, Robin—Army, 1942
Oliphant, Elmer—Purdue/Army, 1917
Olsen, Merlin—Utah State, 1961
Oosterbaan, Ben—Michigan, 1927
O'Rourke, Charles—Boston College, 1940
Orsi, John—Colgate, 1931
Osgood, W.D.—Cornell/Penn, 1895
Osmanski, William—Holy Cross, 1938
Owen, George—Harvard, 1922
Owens, Jim—Oklahoma, 1949
Owens, Steve—Oklahoma, 1969
Pardee, Jack—Texas A&M, 1956
Parilli, Vito (Babe)—Kentucky, 1951
Parker, Clarence (Ace)—Duke, 1936
Parker, Jackie—Miss. State, 1953
Parker, James—Ohio State, 1956
Pazzetti, V.J.—Wes./Lehigh, 1912
Peabody, Endicott—Harvard, 1941
Peck, Robert—Pittsburgh, 1916

Pennock, Stanley B.—Harvard, 1914
Pfann, George—Cornell, 1923
Phillips, H.D.—U. of South, 1904
Pingel, John—Michigan State, 1938
Pihos, Pete—Indiana, 1945
Pinckert, Ernie—So. California, 1931
Plunkett, Jim—Stanford, 1970
Poe, Arthur—Princeton, 1899
Pollard, Fritz—Brown, 1916
Poole, Barney—Miss./Army, 1947
Pregulman, Merv—Michigan, 1943
Price, Eddie—Tulane, 1949
Pund, Henry—Georgia Tech, 1928
Ramsey, Gerrard—Wm. & Mary, 1942
Reeds, Claude—Oklahoma, 1913
Reid, Mike—Penn St., 1970
Reid, Steve—Northwestern, 1936
Reid, William—Harvard, 1900
Renfro, Mel—Oregon, 1963
Rentner, Ernest—Northwestern, 1932
Reynolds, Robert—Nebraska, 1952
Reynolds, Robert—Stanford, 1935
Richter, Les—California, 1951
Riley, John—Northwestern, 1931
Rinehart, Charles—Lafayette, 1897
Rodgers, Ira—West Virginia, 1919
Rogers, Edward L.—Minnesota, 1903
Romig, Joe—Colorado, 1961
Rosenberg, Aaron—So. California, 1934
Rote, Kyle—So. Methodist, 1950
Routt, Joe—Texas A&M, 1937
Salmon, Louis—Notre Dame, 1904
Sauer, George—Nebraska, 1933
Savitsky, George—Pennsylvania, 1947
Sayer's Gale—Kansas, 1964
Scarbath, Jack—Maryland, 1952
Scarlett, Hunter—Pennsylvania, 1909
Schloredt, Bob—Washington, 1960
Schoonover, Wear—Arkansas, 1929
Schreiner, Dave—Wisconsin, 1942
Schultz, Adolf (Germany)—Mich., 1908
Schwab, Frank—Lafayette, 1922
Schwartz, Marchmont—Notre Dame, 1931
Schwegler, Paul—Washington, 1931
Scott, Clyde—Arkansas, 1949
Scott, Richard—Navy, 1947
Scott, Tom—Virginia, 1953
Seibels, HHenry—Sewanee, 1899
Sellers, Ron—Florida State, 1968
Selmon, Lee Roy—Oklahoma, 1975
Shakespeare, Bill—Notre Dame, 1935
Shelton, Murray—Cornell, 1915
Shevlin, Tom—Yale, 1905
Shively, Bernie—Illinois, 1926
Simons, Claude—Tulane, 1934
Simpson, O.J.—So. Calif., 1968
Sington, Fred—Alabama, 1930
Sinkwich, Frank—Georgia, 1942
Sitko, Emil—Notre Dame, 1949
Skladany, Joe—Pittsburgh, 1933
Slater, F.F. (Duke)—Iowa, 1921
Smith, Bruce—Minnesota, 1941
Smith, Bubba—Michigan State, 1966
Smith, Ernie—So. California, 1932
Smith, Harry—So. California, 1939
Smith, Jim Ray—Baylor, 1954
Smith, John (Clipper)—Notre Dame, 1927
Smith, Riley—Alabama, 1935
Smith, Vernon—Georgia, 1931
Snow, Neil—Michigan, 1901
Sparlis, Al—U.C.L.A., 1945
Spears, Clarence W.—Dartmouth, 1915
Spears, W.D.—Vanderbilt, 1927
Sprackling, William—Brown, 1911
Sprague, M. (Bud)—Texas/Army, 1928
Spurrier, Steve—Florida, 1966
Stafford, Harrison—Texas, 1932
Stagg, Amos Alonzo—Yale, 1889
Starcevich, Max—Washington, 1936
Staubach, Roger—Navy, 1963
Steffen, Walter—Chicago, 1908
Steffy, Joe—Army, 1947
Stein, Herbert—Pittsburgh, 1921
Steuber, Robert—Missouri, 1943

Stevens, Mal—Yale, 1923
Stillwagon, Jim—Ohio State, 1970
Stinchcomb, Gaylord—Ohio State, 1920
Stevenson, Vincent—Pennsylvania, 1905
Strom, Brock—Air Force, 1959
Strong, Ken—New York Univ., 1928
Strupper, George—Georgia Tech, 1917
Stuhldreher, Harry—Notre Dame, 1924
Stydahar, Joe—West Virginia, 1935
Suffridge, Robert—Tennessee, 1940
Suhey, Steve—Pennsylvania State, 1947
Sullivan, Pat—Auburn, 1971
Sundstrom, Frank—Cornell, 1923
Swanson, Clarence—Nebraska, 1921
Swiacki, Bill—Holy Cross/Colombia, 1947
Swink, Jim—Texas Christian, 1956
Taliafarro, George—Indiana, 1948
Tarkenton, Fran—Georgia, 1960
Tavener, John—Indiana, 1944
Taylor, Charles—Stanford, 1942
Thomas, Aurelius—Ohio St., 1957
Thompson, Joe—Pittsburgh, 1907
Thorne, Samuel B.—Yale, 1906
Thorpe, Jim—Carlisle, 1912
Ticknor, Ben—Harvard, 1930
Tigert, John—Vanderbilt, 1904
Tinsley, Gaynell—La. State U., 1936
Tipton, Eric—Duke, 1938
Tonnemaker, Clayton—Minnesota, 1949

Torrey, Robert—Pennsylvania, 1906
Travis, Ed Tarkio—Missouri, 1920
Trippi, Charles—Georgia, 1946
Tryon, J. Edward—Colgate, 1925
Utay, Joe—Texas A&M, 1907
Van Brocklin, Norm—Oregon, 1948
Van Sickel, Dale—Florida, 1929
Van Surdam, Henderson—Wesleyan, 1905
Very, Dexter—Penn Stste, 1912
Vessels, Billy—Oklahoma, 1952
Vick, Ernie—Michigan, 1921
Wagner, Huber—Pittsburgh, 1913
Walker, Doak—So. Methodist, 1949
Wallace, Bill—Rice, 1935
Walsh, Adam—Notre Dame, 1924
Warburton, I. (Cotton)—So. Calif., 1934
Ward, Robert (Bob)—Maryland, 1951
Warner, William—Cornell, 1903
Washington, Ken—U.C.L.A., 1939
Webster, George—Michigan St., 1966
Wedemeyer, Herman J.—St. Mary's, 1947
Weekes, Harold—Columbia, 1902
Weir, Ed—Nebraska, 1925
Welch, Gus—Carlisle, 1914
Weller, John—Princeton, 1935
Wendell, Percy—Harvard, 1913
West, D. Belford—Colgate, 1919
Westfall, Bob—Michigan, 1941
Weyand, Alex—Army, 1915

Wharton, Charles—Pennsylvania, 1896
Wheeler, Arthur—Princeton, 1894
White, Byron (Whizzer)—Colorado, 1937
Whitmire, Don—Alabama/Navy, 1944
Wickhorst, Frank—Navy, 1926
Widseth, Ed—Minnesota, 1936
Wildung, Richard—Minnesota, 1942
Williams, Bob—Notre Dame, 1950
Williams, James—Rice, 1949
Willis, William—Ohio State, 1945
Wilson, George—Washington, 1925
Wilson, George—Lafayette, 1928
Wilson, Harry—Penn State/Army, 1923
Wistert, Albert A.—Michigan, 1942
Wistert, Al—Michigan, 1942
Wistert, Frank (Whitey)—Mich., 1933
Wood, Barry—Harvard, 1931
Wojciechowicz, Alex—Fordham, 1936
Wyant, Andrew—Bucknell/Chicago, 1894
Wyatt, Bowden—Tennessee, 1938
Wyckoff, Clint—Cornell, 1896
Yarr, Tom—Notre Dame, 1931
Yary, Ron—USC, 1968
Yoder, Lloyd—Carnegie Tech, 1926
Young, Claude (Buddy)—Illinois, 1946
Young, Harry—Wash. & Lee, 1916
Young, Walter—Oklahoma, 1938
Zarnas, Gus—Ohio State, 1937

Coaches

Bill Alexander
Dr. Ed Anderson
Ike Armstrong
Harry Baujan
Matty Bell
Hugo Bezdek
Dana X. Bible
Bernie Bierman
Bob Blackman
Earl (Red) Blaik
Frank Broyles
Paul "Bear" Bryant
Charles W. Caldwell
Walter Camp
Len Casanova
Frank Cavanaugh
Richard Colman
Fritz Crisler
Duffy Daugherty
Bob Devaney
Dan Devine
Gil Dobie
Michael Donohue

Gus Dorais
Bill Edwards
Charles (Rip) Engle
Don Faurot
Jake Gaither
Sid Gillman
Ernest Godfrey
Ray Graves
Andy Gustafson
Jack Harding
Edward K. Hall
Richard Harlow
Jesse Harper
Percy Haughton
Woody Hayes
John W. Heisman
R.A. (Bob) Higgins
Orin E. Hollingberry
Frank Howard
William Ingram
Morley Jennings
Howard Jones

L. (Biff) Jones
Thomas (Tad) Jones
Ralph (Shug) Jordan
Andy Kerr
Frank Leahy
George E. Little
Lou Little
El (Slip) Madigan
Dave Maurer
Charley McClendon
Herbert McCracken
Daniel McGugin
John McKay
Allyn McKeen
DeOrmond (Tuss) McLaughry
L.R. (Dutch) Meyer
Bernie Moore
Scrappy Moore
Jack Mollenkopf
Ray Morrison
George A. Munger

Clarence Munn
Frank Murray
William Murray
Ed (Hooks) Mylin
Earle (Greasy) Neale
Jess Neely
David Nelson
Robert Neyland
Homer Norton
Frank (Buck) O'Neill
Bennie Owen
Ara Parseghian
Doyt LPerry
James Phalea
Tommy Prothro
E.N. Robinson
Knute Rockne
E.L. (Dick) Romney
William W. Roper
Darrell Royal
George F. Sanford
Francis A. Schmidt

Floyd (Ben) Schwartzwalder
Clark Shaughnessy
Buck Shaw
Andrew L. Smith
Carl Snavely
Amos A. Stagg
Jock Sutherland
James Tatum
Frank W. Thomas
Thad Vann
John H. Vaught
Wallace Wade
Lynn Waldorf
Glenn (Pop) Warner
E.E. (Tad) Wieman
John W. Wilce
Bud Wilkinson
Henry L. Williams
George W. Woodruff
Warren Woodson
Fielding H. Yost
Robert Zuppke

NFL TEAM NICKNAMES AND HOME FIELD CAPACITIES

AMERICAN CONFERENCE

Eastern Division
Buffalo Bills	Rich Stadium (AT)	80,020
Indianapolis Colts[1]	Hoosier Dome (AT)	61,500
Miami Dolphins	Joe Robbie Stadium (G)	75,000
New England Patriots	Sullivan Stadium (ST)	61,297
New York Jets[2]	Giants Stadium (AT)	76,891

Central Division
Cincinnati Bengals	Riverfront Stadium (AT)	59,754
Cleveland Browns	Municipal Stadium (G)	80,322
Houston Oilers	Astrodome (AT)	50,496
Pittsburgh Steelers	Three Rivers Stadium (AT)	59,000

Western Division
Denver Broncos	Mile High Stadium (G)	75,103
Kansas City Chiefs	Arrowhead Stadium (TT)	78,067
Los Angeles Raiders[3]	Memorial Coliseum (G)	92,498
San Diego Chargers	Jack Murphy Stadium (G)	53,675
Seattle Seahawks	Kingdome (AT)	64,757

NATIONAL CONFERENCE

Eastern Division
Dallas Cowboys	Texas Stadium (TT)	65,101
New York Giants	Giants Stadium (AT)[1]	76,891
Philadelphia Eagles	Veterans Stadium (AT)	72,204
Phoenix Cardinals	Sun Devil Stadium (G)	70,491
Washington Redskins	R.F. Kennedy Stadium (G)	55,045

Central Division
Chicago Bears	Soldier Field (AT)	65,793
Detroit Lions	Pontiac Silverdome (AT)	80,638
Green Bay Packers	Lambeau Field (G)	56,189
	Milwaukee Stadium (G)	55,958
Minnesota Vikings	Hubert Humphrey Metrodome (ST)	62,212
Tampa Bay Buccaneers	Tampa Stadium (G)	72,812

Western Division
Atlanta Falcons	Atlanta–Fulton Stadium (G)	60,748
Los Angeles Rams	Anaheim Stadium (G)	69,007
New Orleans Saints	Louisiana Superdome (AT)	71,330
San Francisco 49ers	Candlestick Park (G)	61,185

1. Moved franchise from Baltimore prior to 1984 season.
2. Moved to Giants Stadium; East Rutherford, N.J. prior to 1984 season. 3. Moved franchise to Los Angeles for 1982 season.

1. At East Rutherford, N.J. NOTE: Stadium playing surfaces in parentheses: (AT) Astro Turf; (G) Grass; (ST) Super Turf; (TT) Tartan Turf.

Professional Football

NATIONAL FOOTBALL LEAGUE FINAL REGULAR-SEASON STANDINGS 1990

AMERICAN FOOTBALL CONFERENCE
Eastern Division

	W	L	T	Pct	Pts	Op
Buffalo[1]	13	3	0	.813	428	263
Miami[2]	12	4	0	.750	336	242
Indianapolis	7	9	0	.438	281	353
N.Y. Jets	6	10	0	.375	295	345
New England	1	15	0	.063	181	446

Central Division

	W	L	T	Pct	Pts	Op
Cincinnati[1]	9	7	0	.563	360	352
Houston[2]	9	7	0	.563	405	307
Pittsburgh	9	7	0	.563	292	240
Cleveland	3	13	0	.188	228	462

Western Division

	W	L	T	Pct	Pts	Op
L.A. Raiders[1]	12	4	0	.750	337	268
Kansas City[2]	11	5	0	.688	369	257
Seattle	9	7	0	.563	306	286
San Diego	6	10	0	.375	315	281
Denver	5	11	0	.313	331	374

NATIONAL FOOTBALL CONFERENCE
Eastern Division

	W	L	T	Pct	Pts	Op
N.Y. Giants[1]	13	3	0	.813	335	211
Philadelphia[2]	10	6	0	.625	396	299
Washington[2]	10	6	0	.625	381	301
Dallas	7	9	0	.438	244	308
Phoenix	5	11	0	.313	268	396

Central Division

	W	L	T	Pct	Pts	Op
Chicago[1]	11	5	0	.688	348	280
Tampa Bay	6	10	0	.375	264	367
Detroit	6	10	0	.375	373	413
Green Bay	6	10	0	.375	271	347
Minnesota	6	10	0	.375	351	326

Western Division

	W	L	T	Pct	Pts	Op
San Francisco[1]	14	2	0	.875	353	239
New Orleans[2]	8	8	0	.500	274	275
L.A. Rams	5	11	0	.313	345	412
Atlanta	5	11	0	.313	348	365

1. Division Champion. 2. Wild Card Team. Cincinnati won AFC Central title based on best head-to-head record (3-1) vs. Houston (2-2) and Pittsburgh (1-3). Houston was Wild Card based on better conference record (8-4) than Seattle (7-5) and Pittsburgh (6-6). Philadelphia finished second in NFC East based on better division record (5-3) than Washington (4-4). Tampa Bay was second in NFC Central based on 5-1 record vs. Detroit, Green Bay, and Minnesota. Detroit was third based on best net division points (minus 8) vs. Green Bay (minus 40) in fourth. Minnesota was fifth based on 4-8 conference record. Los Angeles Rams finished third in NFC West based on net points in division (plus 1) vs. Atlanta (minus 31).

LEAGUE CHAMPIONSHIP—SUPER BOWL XXV

(January 27, 1991 at Tampa Stadium, Tampa, Fla.; Attendance: 73,813)

Scoring

	1st Q	2nd Q	3rd Q	4th Q	Final
Buffalo (AFC)	3	9	0	7	— 19
N.Y. Giants (NFC)	3	7	7	3	— 20

First Quarter: NY—FG Bahr 28, 7:14. Drive: 58 yards, 11 plays. Key plays: Meggett 10 run; Hostetler 16 pass to Ingram on 3rd and 7. N.Y. Giants 3, Buffalo 3. Buf—FG Norwood 23, 9:09. Drive: 66 yards, 6 plays. Key play: Kelly 61 pass to Lofton. Buffalo 3, N.Y. Giants 3.

Second Quarter: Buf—D. Smith 1 run (Norwood kick), 2:30. Drive: 80 yards, 12 plays. Key plays: Kelly 20 pass to Reed; Kelly 13 pass to Thomas. Buffalo 10, N.Y. Giants 3. Buf—Safety, Hostetler tackled in end zone, 6:33. Buffalo 12, N.Y. Giants 3. NY—Baker 11 pass from Hostetler (Bahr kick), 14:35. Drive: 87 yards, 10 plays. Key plays: Hostetler 22 pass to Ingram; Hostetler 7 pass to Cross on 3rd and 6. Buffalo 12, N.Y. Giants 10.

Third Quarter: NY—Anderson 1 run (Bahr kick), 9:29. Drive: 75 yards, 14 plays. Key plays: Hostetler 11 pass to Meggett on 3rd and 8; Anderson 24 run on 3rd and 1. N.Y. Giants 17, Buffalo 12.

Fourth Quarter: Buf—Thomas 31 run (Norwood kick), :08. Drive: 63

yards, 4 plays. Key play: Kelly 19 pass to K. Davis. Buffalo 19, N.Y. Giants 17. NY—FG Bahr 21, 7:40. Drive 74 yards, 14 playls. Key plays: Hostetler 16 pass to Bavaro on 3rd and 7; Meggett 6 run on 3rd and 5. N.Y. Giants 20, Buffalo 19.

Statistics of the Game

	Buffalo	N.Y. Giants
First downs	18	24
Third down eff	1–8	9–16
Fourth down eff	0–0	0–1
Total net yards	371	386
Net yards rushing	166	172
Net yards passing	205	214
Punts–avg.	6–39	4–44
Total return yards	114	85
Penalties–yds	6–35	5–31
Fumbles–lost	1–0	0–0
Time of possession	19:27	40:33

SUPER BOWLS I–XXV

Game	Date	Winner	Loser	Site	Attendance
XXV	Jan. 27, 1991	Giants (NFC) 20	Buffalo (AFC) 19	Tampa Stadium, Tampa, Fla.	73,813
XXIV	Jan. 28, 1990	San Francisco (NFC) 55	Denver (AFC) 10	Superdome, New Orleans	72,919
XXIII	Jan. 22, 1989	San Francisco (NFC) 20	Cincinnati (AFC) 16	Joe Robbie Stadium, Miami, Fla.	75,179
XXII	Jan. 31, 1988	Washington (NFC) 42	Denver (AFC) 10	Jack Murphy Stadium, San Diego, Calif.	73,302
XXI	Jan. 25, 1987	Giants (NFC) 39	Denver (AFC) 20	Rose Bowl, Pasadena, Calif.	101,063
XX	Jan. 26, 1986	Chicago (NFC) 46	New England (AFC) 10	Superdome, New Orleans	73,818
XIX	Jan. 20, 1985	San Francisco (NFC) 38	Miami (AFC) 16	Stanford Stadium, Palo Alto, Calif.	84,059
XVIII	Jan. 22, 1984	Los Angeles Raiders (AFC) 38	Washington (NFC) 9	Tampa Stadium, Tampa, Fla	72,920
XVII	Jan. 30, 1983	Washington (NFC) 27	Miami (AFC) 17	Rose Bowl, Pasadena, Calif.	103,667
XVI	Jan. 24, 1982	San Francisco (NFC) 26	Cincinnati (AFC) 21	Silverdome, Pontiac, Mich.	81,270
XV	Jan. 25, 1981	Oakland (AFC) 27	Philadelphia (NFC) 10	Superdome, New Orleans	75,500
XIV	Jan. 20, 1980	Pittsburgh (AFC) 31	Los Angeles (NFC) 19	Rose Bowl, Pasadena	103,985
XIII	Jan. 21, 1979	Pittsburgh (AFC) 35	Dallas (NFC) 31	Orange Bowl, Miami	79,484
XII	Jan. 15, 1978	Dallas (NFC) 27	Denver (AFC) 10	Superdome, New Orleans	75,583
XI	Jan. 9, 1977	Oakland (AFC) 32	Minnesota (NFC) 14	Rose Bowl, Pasadena	103,424

X	Jan. 18, 1976	Pittsburgh (AFC) 21	Dallas (NFC) 17	Orange Bowl, Miami	80,187
IX	Jan. 12, 1975	Pittsburgh (AFC) 16	Minnesota (NFC) 6	Tulane Stadium, New Orleans	80,997
VIII	Jan. 13, 1974	Miami (AFC) 24	Minnesota (NFC) 7	Rice Stadium, Houston	71,882
VII	Jan. 14, 1973	Miami (AFC) 14	Washington (NFC) 7	Memorial Coliseum, Los Angeles	90,182
VI	Jan. 16, 1972	Dallas (NFC) 24	Miami (AFC) 3	Tulane Stadium, New Orleans	81,591
V	Jan. 17, 1971	Baltimore (AFC) 16	Dallas (NFC) 13	Orange Bowl, Miami	79,204
IV	Jan. 11, 1970	Kansas City (AFL) 23	Minnesota (NFL) 7	Tulane Stadium, New Orleans	80,562
III	Jan. 12, 1969	New York (AFL) 16	Baltimore (NFL) 7	Orange Bowl, Miami	75,389
II	Jan. 14, 1968	Green Bay (NFL) 33	Oakland (AFL) 14	Orange Bowl, Miami	75,546
I	Jan. 15, 1967	Green Bay (NFL) 35	Kansas City (AFL) 10	Memorial Coliseum, Los Angeles	61,946

NOTE: Super Bowls I to IV were played before the American Football League and National Football League merged into the NFL, which was divided into two conferences, the NFC and AFC.

NATIONAL LEAGUE CHAMPIONS

Year	Champion (W-L-T)	Year	Champion (W-L-T)	Year	Champion (W-L-T)
1921	Chicago Bears (Staley's) (10-1-1)	1925	Chicago Cardinals (11-2-1)	1929	Green Bay Packers (12-0-1)
1922	Canton Bulldogs (10-0-2)	1926	Frankford Yellow Jackets!(14-1-1)	1930	Green Bay Packers (10-3-1)
1923	Canton Bulldogs (11-0-1)	1927	New York Giants (11-1-1)	1931	Green Bay Packers (12-2-0)
1924	Cleveland Indians (7-1-1)	1928	Providence Steamrollers (8-1-2)	1932	Chicago Bears (7-1-6)

Year	Eastern Conference winners (W-L-T)	Western Conference winners (W-L-T)	League champion playoff results
1933	New York Giants (11-3-0)	Chicago Bears (10-2-1)	Chicago Bears 23, New York 21
1934	New York Giants (8-5-0)	Chicago Bears (13-0-0)	New York 30, Chicago Bears 13
1935	New York Giants (9-3-0)	Detroit Lions (7-3-2)	Detroit 26, New York 7
1936	Boston Redskins (7-5-0)	Green Bay Packers (10-1-1)	Green Bay 21, Boston 6
1937	Washington Redskins (8-3-0)	Chicago Bears (9-1-1)	Washington 28, Chicago Bears 21
1938	New York Giants (8-2-1)	Green Bay Packers (8-3-0)	New York 23, Green Bay 17
1939	New York Giants (9-1-1)	Green Bay Packers (9-2-0)	Green Bay 27, New York 0
1940	Washington Redskins (9-2-0)	Chicago Bears (8-3-0)	Chicago Bears 73, Washington 0
1941	New York Giants (8-3-0)	Chicago Bears (10-1-1)[2]	Chicago Bears 37, New York 9
1942	Washington Redskins (10-1-1)	Chicago Bears (11-0-0)	Washington 14, Chicago Bears 6
1943	Washington Redskins (6-3-1)[2]	Chicago Bears (8-1-1)	Chicago Bears 41, Washington 21
1944	New York Giants (8-1-1)	Green Bay Packers (8-2-0)	Green Bay 14, New York 7
1945	Washington Redskins (8-2-0)	Cleveland Rams (9-1-0)	Cleveland 15, Washington 14
1946	New York Giants (7-3-1)	Chicago Bears (8-2-1)	Chicago Bears 24, New York 14
1947	Philadelphia Eagles (8-4-0)[2]	Chicago Cardinals (9-3-0)	Chicago Cardinals 28, Philadelphia 21
1948	Philadelphia Eagles (9-2-1)	Chicago Cardinals (11-1-0)	Philadelphia 7, Chicago Cardinals 0
1949	Philadelphia Eagles (11-1-0)	Los Angeles Rams (8-2-2)	Philadelphia 14, Los Angeles 0
1950[1]	Cleveland Browns (10-2-0)[2]	Los Angeles Rams (9-3-0)[2]	Cleveland 30, Los Angeles 28
1951[1]	Cleveland Browns (11-1-0)	Los Angeles Rams (8-4-0)	Los Angeles 24, Cleveland 17
1952[1]	Cleveland Browns (8-4-0)	Detroit Lions (9-3-0)[2]	Detroit 17, Cleveland 7
1953	Cleveland Browns (11-1-0)	Detroit Lions (10-2-0)	Detroit 17, Cleveland 16
1954	Cleveland Browns (9-3-0)	Detroit Lions (9-2-1)	Cleveland 56, Detroit 10
1955	Cleveland Browns (9-2-1)	Los Angeles Rams (8-3-1)	Cleveland 38, Los Angeles 14
1956	New York Giants (8-3-1)	Chicago Bears (9-2-1)	New York 47, Chicago Bears 7
1957	Cleveland Browns (9-2-1)	Detroit Lions (8-4-0)[2]	Detroit 59, Cleveland 14
1958	New York Giants (9-3-0)[2]	Baltimore Colts (9-3-0)	Baltimore 23, New York 17[3]
1959	New York Giants (10-2-0)	Baltimore Colts (9-3-0)	Baltimore 31, New York 16
1960	Philadelphia Eagles (10-2-0)	Green Bay Packers (8-4-0)	Philadelphia 17, Green Bay 13
1961	New York Giants (10-3-1)	Green Bay Packers (11-3-0)	Green Bay 37, New York 0
1962	New York Giants (12-2-0)	Green Bay Packers (13-1-0)	Green Bay 16, New York 7
1963	New York Giants (11-3-0)	Chicago Bears (11-1-2)	Chicago 14, New York 10
1964	Cleveland Browns (10-3-1)	Baltimore Colts (12-2-0)	Cleveland 27, Baltimore 0
1965	Cleveland Browns (11-3-0)	Green Bay Packers (11-3-1)[2]	Green Bay 23, Cleveland 12
1966	Dallas Cowboys (10-3-1)	Green Bay Packers (12-2-0)	Green Bay 34, Dallas 27
1967	Dallas Cowboys (9-5-0)[2]	Green Bay Packers (9-4-1)[2]	Green Bay 21, Dallas 17
1968	Cleveland Browns (10-4-0)[2]	Baltimore Colts (13-1-0)[2]	Baltimore 34, Cleveland 0
1969	Cleveland Browns (10-3-1)2	Minnesota Vikings (12-2-0)[2]	Minnesota 27, Cleveland 7

1. League was divided into American and National Conferences, 1950-52 and again in 1970, when leagues merged. 2. Won divisional playoff. 3. Won at 8:15 of sudden death overtime period.

NATIONAL CONFERENCE CHAMPIONS

Year	Eastern Division	Central Division	Western Division	Champion
1970	Dallas Cowboys (10-4-0)	Minnesota Vikings (12-2-0)	San Francisco 49ers (10-3-1)	Dallas
1971	Dallas Cowboys (11-3-0)	Minnesota Vikings (11-3-0)	San Francisco 49ers (9-5-0)	Dallas
1972	Washington Redskins (11-3-0)	Green Bay Packers (10-4-0)	San Francisco 49ers (8-5-1)	Washington
1973	Dallas Cowboys (10-4-0)	Minnesota Vikings (12-2-0)	Los Angeles Rams (12-2-0)	Minnesota
1974	St. Louis Cardinals (10-4-0)	Minnesota Vikings (10-4-0)	Los Angeles Rams (10-4-0)	Minnesota
1975	St. Louis Cardinals (11-3-0)	Minnesota Vikings (12-2-0)	Los Angeles Rams (12-2-0)	Dallas
1976	Dallas Cowboys (11-3-0)	Minnesota Vikings (11-2-1)	Los Angeles Rams (10-3-1)	Minnesota

1977	Dallas Cowboys (12–2–0)	Minnesota Vikings (9–5–0)	Los Angeles Rams (10–4–0)	Dallas
1978	Dallas Cowboys (12–4–0)	Minnesota Vikings (8–7–1)	Los Angeles Rams (12–4–0)	Dallas
1979	Dallas Cowboys (11–5–0)	Tampa Bay Buccaneers (10–6–0)	Los Angeles Rams (9–7–0)	Los Angeles
1980	Philadelphia Eagles (12–4–0)	Minnesota Vikings (9–7–0)	Atlanta Falcons (12–4–0)	Philadelphia
1981	Dallas Cowboys (12–4–0)	Tampa Bay Buccaneers (9–7–0)	San Francisco 49ers (13–3–0)	San Francisco
1982*	Washington Redskins won conference title and also had best regular–season record (8–1–0)			
1983	Washington Redskins (14–2–0)	Detroit Lions (8–8–0)	San Francisco 49ers (10–6–0)	Washington
1984	Washington Redskins (11–5–0)	Chicago Bears (10–6–0)	San Francisco 49ers (15–1–0)	San Francisco
1985	Dallas Cowboys (10–6–0)	Chicago Bears (15–1–0)	Los Angeles Rams (11–5–0)	Chicago
1986	New York Giants (14–2–0)	Chicago Bears (14–2–0)	San Francisco 49ers (10–5–1)	New York
1987	Washington Redskins (11–4–0)	Chicago Bears (11–4–0)	San Francisco 49ers (13–2–0)	Washington
1988	Philadelphia Eagles (10–6–0)	Chicago Bears (12–4–0)	San Francisco 49ers (10–6–0)	San Francisco
1989	New York Giants (12–4–0)	Minnesota Vikings (10–6–0)	San Francisco 49ers (14–2–0)	San Francisco
1990	New York Giants (13–3–0)	Chicago Bears (11–5–0)	San Francisco 49ers (14–2–0)	New York

*Schedule reduced to 9 games from usual 16, with no standings kept in Eastern, Central, and Western Divisions, because of 57–day player strike.

AMERICAN CONFERENCE CHAMPIONS

Year	Eastern Division	Central Division	Western Division	Champion
1970	Baltimore Colts (11–2–1)	Cincinnati Bengals (8–6–0)	Oakland Raiders (8–4–2)	Baltimore
1971	Miami Dolphins (10–3–1)	Cleveland Browns (9–5–0)	Kansas City Chiefs (10–3–1)	Miami
1972	Miami Dolphins (14–0–0)	Pittsburgh Steelers (11–3–0)	Oakland Raiders (10–3–1)	Miami
1973	Miami Dolphins (12–2–0)	Cincinnati Bengals (10–4–0)	Oakland Raiders (9–4–1)	Miami
1974	Miami Dolphins (11–3–0)	Pittsburgh Steelers (10–3–1)	Oakland Raiders (12–2–0)	Pittsburgh
1975	Baltimore Colts (10–4–0)	Pittsburgh Steelers (12–2–0)	Oakland Raiders (12–2–0)	Pittsburgh
1976	Baltimore Colts (11–3–0)	Pittsburgh Steelers (10–4–0)	Oakland Raiders (13–1–0)	Oakland
1977	Baltimore Colts (10–4–0)	Pittsburgh Steelers (9–5–0)	Denver Broncos (12–2–0)	Denver
1978	New England Patriots (11–5–0)	Pittsburgh Steelers (14–2–0)	Denver Broncos (10–6–0)	Pittsburgh
1979	Miami Dolphins (10–6–0)	Pittsburgh Steelers (12–4–0)	San Diego Chargers (12–4–0)	Pittsburgh
1980	Buffalo Bills (11–5–0)	Cleveland Browns (11–5–0)	San Diego Chargers (11–5–0)	Oakland
1981	Miami Dolphins (11–4–1)	Cincinnati Bengals (12–4–0)	San Diego Chargers (10–6–0)	Cincinnati
1982*	Miami Dolphins won the conference title, but the Los Angeles Raiders had best regular–season record (8–1–0).			
1983	Miami (12–4–0)	Pittsburgh (10–6–0)	Los Angeles Raiders (12–4–0)	Los Angeles
1984	Miami (14–2–0)	Pittsburgh (9–7–0)	Denver (13–3–0)	Miami
1985	Miami (12–4–0)	Cleveland (8–8)	Los Angeles Raiders (12–4–0)	New England
1986	New England (11–5–0)	Cleveland (12–4–0)	Denver (11–5–0)	Denver
1987	Indianapolis Colts (9–6–0)	Cleveland Browns (10–5–0)	Denver Broncos (10–4–1)	Denver
1988	Buffalo Bills (12–4–0)	Cincinnati Bengals (12–4–0)	Seattle Seahawks (9–7–0)	Cincinnati
1989	Buffalo Bills (9–7–0)	Cleveland Browns (9–6–1)	Denver Broncos (11–5–0)	Denver
1990	Buffalo Bills (13–3–0)	Cincinnati Bengals (9–7–0)	Los Angeles Raiders (12–4–0)	Buffalo

*Schedule reduced to 9 games from usual 16, with no standings kept in Eastern, Central, and Western Divisions, because of 57–day player strike.

AMERICAN LEAGUE CHAMPIONS

Year	Eastern Division (W–L–T)	Western Division (W–L–T)	League champion, playoff results
1960	Houston Oilers (10–4–0)	Los Angeles Chargers (10–4–0)	Houston 24, Los Angeles 16
1961	Houston Oilers (10–3–1)	San Diego Chargers (12–2–0)	Houston 10, San Diego 3
1962	Houston Oilers (11–3–0)	Dallas Texans (11–3–0)	Dallas 20, Houston 17[1]
1963	Boston Patriots (8–6–1)[2]	San Diego Chargers (11–3–0)	San Diego 51, Boston 10
1964	Buffalo Bills (12–2–0)	San Diego Chargers (8–5–1)	Buffalo 20, San Diego 7
1965	Buffalo Bills (10–3–1)	San Diego Chargers (9–2–3)	Buffalo 23, San Diego 0
1966	Buffalo Bills (9–4–1)	Kansas City Chiefs (11–2–1)	Kansas City 31, Buffalo 7
1967	Houston Oilers (9–4–1)	Oakland Raiders (13–1–0)	Oakland 40, Houston 7
1968	New York Jets (11–3–0)	Oakland Raiders (12–2–0)[2]	New York 27, Oakland 23
1969	New York Jets (10–4–0)	Oakland Raiders (12–1–1)	Kansas City 17, Oakland 7[3]

1. Won at 2:45 of second sudden death overtime period. 2. Won divisional playoff. 3. Kansas City defeated New York, 13–6, and Oakland defeated Houston, 56–7, in interdivisional playoffs.

PRO FOOTBALL HALL OF FAME

(National Football Museum, Canton, Ohio)

Teams named are those with which player is best identified; figures in parentheses indicate number of playing seasons.

Adderley, Herb, defensive back, Packers, Cowboys (12)	1961–72
Alworth, Lance, wide receiver, Chargers, Cowboys (12)	1962–72
Atkins, Doug, defensive end, Browns, Bears, Saints (17)	1953–69
Badgro, Morris, end, N.Y. Yankees, Giants, Bklyn. Dodgers (8)	1927, 1930–36
Battles, Cliff, back, Redskins (6)	1932–37
Bednarik, Chuck, center–lineback, Eagles (14)	1949–62
Bell, Bert, N.F.L. founder, Eagles and Steelers, N.F.L. Commissioner	1946–59
Bell, Bobby, linebacker, Chiefs (12)	1963–74
Berry, Raymond, end, Colts (13)	1955–67
Bidwell, Charles W., owner Chicago Cardinals	1933–47
Biletnikoff, Fred, wide receiver, Raiders (14)	1965–1978
Blanda, George, quarterback–kicker, Bears, Oilers, Raiders (27)	1949–75
Blount, Mel, cornerback, Pittsburgh Steelers (14)	1970–83
Bradshaw, Terry, quarterback, Pittsburgh Steelers (14)	1970–83
Brown, Jim, fullback, Browns (9)	1957–65
Brown, Paul E., coach, Browns (1946–62), Bengals (1968–75)	1946–75

Brown, Roosevelt, tackle, Giants (13)	1953–65
Brown, Willie, cornerback, Broncos, Raiders (16)	1963–78
Buchanan, Buck, tackle, Chiefs (11)	1963–73
Butkus, Dick, linebcker, Bears (9)	1965–73
Campbell, Earl, running back, Oilers, Saints (8)	1978–85
Canadeo, Tony, back, Packers (11)	1941–52
Carr, Joe, president N.F.L. (18)	1921–39
Chamberlin, Guy, end 4 teams (9)	1919–27
Christiansen, Jack, defensive back, Lions (8)	1951–58
Clark, Earl (Dutch), Qback, Spartans, Lions (7)	1931–38
Connor, George, tackle, linebacker, Bears (8)	1948–55
Conzelman, Jimmy, Qback 5 teams (10), owner	1921–48
Csonka, Larry, back, Dolphins, Giants (11)	1968–79
Davis, Willie, defensive end, Packers (10)	1960–69
Dawson, Len, quarterback, Steelers, Browns, Texans, Chiefs (19)	1957–75
Ditka, Mike, tight end, Bears, Eagles, Cowboys (12)	1961–72
Donovan, Art, defensive tackle, Colts (12)	1950–61
Driscoll, John (Paddy), Qback, Cards, Bears (11)	1919–29
Dudley, Bill, back, Steelers, Lions, Redskins (9)	1942–53
Edwards, Albert Glen (Turk), tackle, Redskins (9)	1932–40
Ewbank, Weeb, coach Colts, Jets (20)	1954–73
Fears, Tom, end, Rams (9); coach, Saints	1948–56
Flaherty, Ray, end, Yankees, Giants (9); coach, Redskins, Yankees (14)	1928–49
Ford, Len, end, def. end, Browns, Packers (11)	1948–58
Fortmann, Daniel J., guard, Bears (8)	1936–43
Gatski, Frank, offensive lineman, Browns (12)	1946–57
George, Bill, linebacker, Bears, Rams (15)	1952–66
Gifford, Frank, back, Giants (12)	1952–64
Gillman, Sid, coach, Rams, Chargers, Oilers (18)	1955–70, 73–74
Graham, Otto, quarterback, Browns (10)	1946–55
Grange, Harold (Red), back, Bears, Yankees (9)	1925–34
Greene, Joe, defensive tackle, Steelrs (13)	1968–81
Gregg, Forrest, tackle, Packers (15)	1956–71
Griese, Bob, quarterback, Dolphins (14)	1967–80
Groza, Lou, place–kicker, tackle, Browbns (21)	1946–67
Guyon, Joe, back, 6 teams (8)	1919–27
Halas, George, N.F.L. founder, owner and coach, Staleys and Bears, end (11)	1919–27
Ham, Jack, linebacker, Steelers (13)	1970–82
Hannah, John, guard, Patriots (13)	1973–85
Harris, Franco, running back, Steelers, Seahawks (13)	1972–84
Healey, Ed, Tackle, Bears (8)	1920–27
Hein, Mel, center, Giants (15)	1931–45
Hendricks, Ted, linebacker, Colts, Packers, Raiders (15)	1969–83
Henry, Wilbur (Pete), tackle, Bulldogs, Giants (8)	1920–28
Herber, Arnie, Qback, Packers, Giants (13)	1930–45
Hewitt, Bill, end, Bears, Eagles (9)	1932–43
Hinkle, Clarke, fullback, Packers (10)	1932–41
Hirsch, Elroy (Crazy Legs), back, end, Rams (12)	1946–57
Hornung, Paul, running back, Packers (9)	1957–62, 64–66
Houston, Ken, def. bck, Oilers, Redskins (14)	1967–80
Hubbard, R. (Cal), tackle, Giants, Packers (9)	1927–36
Huff, Sam, linebacker, Giants, Redskins (13)	1956–67, 1969
Hunt, Lamar, Founder A.F.L., owner Texans, Chiefs	1959–
Hutson, Don, end, Packers (11)	1935–45
Johnson, John Henry, back, 49ers, Lions, Steelers, Oilers (13)	1954–66
Jones, David (Deacon), defensive end, Rams, Chargers, Redskins (14)	1961–74
Jones, Stan, defensive tackle, Bears, Redskins (13)	1954–66
Jurgensen, Sonny, quarterback, Eagles, Redskins (18)	1957–74
Kiesling, Walt, guard 6 teams (13)	1926–38
Kinard, Frank (Bruiser), tackle, Dodgers (9)	1938–47
Lambeau, Earl (Curly), N.F.L. founder, coach, end, back, Packers (11)	1919–53
Lambert, Jack, linebcker, Steelers (11)	1974–84
Landry, Tom, coach, Cowboys (29)	1960–88
Lane, Richard (Night Train), defensive back, Rams, Cardinals, Lions (14)	1952–65
Langer, Jim, center, Dolphins, Vikings (12)	1970–81
Lanier, Willie, linebacker, Chiefs (11)	1967–77
Lary, Yale, defensive bck, punter, Lions (11)	1952–64
Laveill, Dante, end, Browns (11)	1946–56
Layne, Bobby, Qback, Bears, Lions, Steelers (15)	1948–62
Leemans, Alphonse (Tuffy), back, Giants (8)	1936–43
Lilly, Bob, defensive tackle, Cowboys (14)	1961–74
Lombardi, Vince, coach, Packers, Redskins (11)	1959–70
Luckman, Sid, quarterback, Bears (12)	1939–50
Lyman, Roy (Link), tackle, Bulldogs, Bears (11)	1922–34
Mara, Tim, N.F.L. founder, owner Giants	1925–59
Marchetti, Gino, defensive end, Colts (14)	1952–66
Marshall, George P., N.F.L. founder, owner, Redskins	1932–65
Matson, Ollie, back, Cardinals, Rams,	
Lions, Eagles (14)	1952–66
Maynard, Don, receiver, Giants, Jets, Cardinals (15)	1958–73
McAfee, George, bck, Bears (8)	1940–50
McCormack, Mike, tackle, N.Y. Yankees, Cleveland Browns (10)	1951–62
McElhenny, Hugh, back, 49ers, Vikings, Giants (13)	1952–64
McNally, John (Blood), back, 7 teams (15)	1925–39
Michalske, August, guard, Yankees, Packers (11)	1926–37
Millner, Wayne, end, Redskins (7)	1936–45
Mitchell, Bobby, wide receiver, Browns, Redskins (11)	1958–68
Mix, Ron, tckle, Chargers (11)	1960–71
Moore, Lenny, back, Colts (12)	1956–67
Motley, Marion, fullback, Browns, Steelers (9)	1946–55
Musso, George, guard–tackle, Bears (12)	1933–44
Nagurski, Bronko, fullback, Bears (9)	1930–43
Namath, Joe, quarterback, Jets, Rams (13)	1965–77
Neale, Earle (Greasy), coach, Eagles	1941–50
Nevers, Ernie, fullback, Chicago Cardinals (5)	1926–31
Nitschke, Ray, linebackers, Packers (15)	1958–72
Nomellini, Leo, defensive tckle, 49ers (14)	1950–63
Olsen, Merlin, defensive tackle, Rams (15)	1962–76
Otto, Jim, center, Raiders (15)	1960–74
Owen, Steve, tackle, Giants (9), coach, Giants (13)	1924–53
Page, Alan, defensive tackle, Vikings, Bears (15)	1967–81
Parker, Clarence (Ace), quarterback, Dodgers (7)	1937–46
Parker, Jim, guard, tackle, Colts (11)	1957–67
Perry, Joe, fullback, 49ers, Colts (16)	1948–63
Pihos, Pete, end, Eagles (9)	1947–55
Ray, Hugh, Shorty, N.F.L. advisor	1938–52
Reeves, Dan, owner Rams	1941–71
Ringo, Jim, center, Packers (15)	1953–67
Robustelli, Andy, def. end, Rams, Giants (14)	1951–64
Rooney, Art, N.F.L. founder, owner Steelers	1933–
Rozelle, Pete, commissioner, NFL,	1960–89
St. Claire, Bob, tackle, 49ers (11)	1953–63
Sayers, Gale, back, Bears (7)	1965–71
Schmidt, Joe, linebacker, Lions (13)	1953–65
Schramm, Tex, administrator Rams, Cowboys (42)	1947–89
Shell, Art, Tackle, Raiders (15)	1968–82
Simpson, O.J., back, Bills, 49ers (11)	1969–79
Starr, Bart, quarterback, coach, Packers (16)	1956–71
Staubach, Roger, quarterback, Cowboys (11)	1969–79
Stautner, Ernie, defensive tackle, Steelres (14)	1950–63
Stenerud, Jan, placekicker, Chiefs, Packers, Vikings (19)	1967–85
Strong, Ken, back, Giants, Yankees (14)	1929–47
Stydahar, Joe, tackle, Bears (9); coach, Rams, Cardinals (5)	1936–54
Tarkenton, Fran, quarterback, Vikings, Giants (18)	1961–78
Taylor, Charlie, wide receiver, Redskins (14)	1964–77
Taylor, Jim, fullback, Packers, Saints (10)	1958–67
Thorpe, Jim, back, 7 teams (12)	1915–28
Tittle, Y.A., Qback, Colts, 49ers, Giants (17)	1948–64
Trafton, George, center, Bears (13)	1920–32
Trippi, Charley, back, Chicago Cardinals (9)	1947–55
Tunnell, Emlen, def. back, Giants, Packers (14)	1948–61
Turner, Clyde (Bulldog), center, Bears (13)	1940–52
Unitas, John, quarterback, Colts (18)	1956–73
Upshaw, Gene, guard, Raiders (15)	1967–81
Van Brocklin, Norm, Qback, Rams, Eagles (12)	1949–60
Van Buren, Steve, back, Eagles (8)	1944–51
Walker, Doak, running back, def. back, kicker, Lions (6)	1950–55
Warfield, Paul, wide receiver, Browns, Dolphins (13)	1964–74, 76–77
Waterfield, Bob, quarterback, Rams (8)	1945–52
Weinmeister, Arnie, tckle, N.Y. Yankees, Giants (6)	1948–53
Willis, Bill, guard, Browns (8)	1946–53
Wilson, Larry, defensive back, Cardinals (13)	1960–72
Wood, Willie, safety, Packers (12)	1960–71
Wojciechowicz, Alex, center, Lions, Eagles (13)	1938–50

N.F.L. INDIVIDUAL LIFETIME, SEASON, AND GAME RECORDS

(American Football League records were incorporated into N.F.L. records after merger of the leagues)

All–Time Leading Touchdown Scorers
(Through 1990 season)

Player	Yrs	Rush.	Rec.	Returns	TD
Jim Brown	9	106	20	0	126
Walter Payton	13	110	15	0	125
John Riggins	14	104	12	0	116
Lenny Moore	12	63	48	2	113
Don Hutson	11	3	99	3	105
Steve Largent	14	1	100	0	101
Franco Harris	13	91	9	0	100
Marcus Allen	9	75	17	1	93
Jim Taylor	10	83	10	0	93
Tony Dorsett	12	77	13	1	91
Bobby Mitchell	11	18	65	8	91

All–Time Leading Receivers
(Through 1990)

Player	Yrs	No.	Yds	Avg	Long	TD
Steve Largent	14	819	13,089	16.0	74	100
Charlie Joiner	18	750	12,146	16.2	87	65
Art Monk	11	730	9,335	13.6	79	52
Ozzie Newsome	13	662	7,980	12.1	74	47
Charley Taylor	13	649	9,110	14.0	88	79
James Lofton	13	642	11,963	18.6	80	61
Don Maynard	15	633	11,834	18.7	87	88
Raymond Berry	13	631	9,275	14.7	70	68
Harold Carmichael	14	590	8,985	15.2	85	79
Fred Biletnikoff	14	589	8,974	15.2	82	76
Harold Jackson	16	579	10,372	17.9	79	76

All–Time Leading Passers
(Minimum 1,500 attempts. Through 1990.)

Rank	Player	Yrs	Att	Comp	Yds	TD	Int	Rating
1.	Joe Montana[1]	12	4,579	2,914	34,998	242	123	93.4
2.	Dan Marino[1]	8	4,181	2,480	31,416	241	136	88.5
3.	Jim Kelly[1]	5	2,088	1,251	15,730	105	72	85.8
4.	Boomer Esiason[1]	7	2,687	1,520	21,381	150	98	85.8
5.	Roger Staubach	11	2,958	1,685	22,700	153	109	83.4
6.	Neil Lomax	8	3,153	1,817	22,771	136	90	82.7
7.	Sonny Jergensen	18	4,262	2,433	32,224	255	189	82.6
8.	Len Dawson	19	3,741	2,136	28,711	239	183	82.6
9.	Dave Krieg[1]	11	3,291	1,909	24,052	184	136	82.3
10.	Jim Everett[1]	5	2,038	1,154	15,345	101	73	82.2
11.	Ken O'Brien[1]	8	2,878	1,697	20,444	109	78	82.2
12.	Ken Anderson	16	4,475	2,654	32,838	197	160	81.9
13.	Danny White	13	2,950	1,761	21,959	155	132	81.7
14.	Bart Starr	16	3,149	1,808	24,718	152	138	80.5
15.	Fran Tarkenton	18	6,467	3,686	47,003	342	266	80.4
16.	Bernie Kosar[1]	6	2,363	1,364	16,450	85	62	80.3
17.	Dan Fouts	15	5,604	3,297	43,040	254	242	80.2
18.	Warren Moon[1]	7	3,025	1,701	22,989	134	112	79.9
19.	Tony Eason[1]	8	1,564	911	11,142	61	51	79.7
20.	Jim McMahon[1]	9	1,840	1,056	13,398	77	66	79.3

1. Active in 1991 season.

All–Time Leading Scorers
(Through 1990)

Rank	Player	Yrs	TD	FG	PAT	Pts
1.	George Blanda	26	9	335	943	2,002
2.	Jan Stenrud	19	0	373	580	1,699
3.	Jim Turner	16	1	304	521	1,439
4.	Mark Mosley	16	0	300	482	1,382
5.	Jim Bakken	17	0	282	534	1,380
6.	Fred Cox	15	0	282	519	1,365
7.	Pat Leahy[1]	17	0	278	528	1,362
8.	Lou Groza	17	1	234	641	1,349
9.	Chris Bahr[1]	14	0	241	490	1,213
10.	Nick Lowery	12	0	259	375	1,152
11.	Gino Capalletti	11	42	176	350	1,130
12.	Ray Wersching	15	0	222	456	1,122
13.	Don Cockroft	13	0	216	432	1,080
14.	Garo Yepremian	14	0	210	444	1,074
15.	Jim Breech	12	0	201	459	1,062

1. Active in 1991 season.

All–Time Leading Rushers
(Through 1990)

Rank	Player	Yrs	Att.	Yds	Avg	TD
1.	Walter Payton	13	3,838	16,726	4.4	110
2.	Tony Dorsett[1]	12	2,936	12,739	4.3	77
3.	Jim Brown	9	2,359	12,312	5.2	106
4.	Franco Harris	13	2,949	12,120	4.1	91
5.	Eric Dickerson[1]	8	2,616	11,903	4.6	86
6.	John Riggins	14	2,916	11,352	3.9	104
7.	O.J. Simpson	11	2,404	11,236	4.7	61
8.	Otis Anderson[1]	12	2,499	10,101	4.0	80
9.	Earl Campbell	8	2,187	9,407	4.3	74
10.	Jim Taylor	10	1,941	8,597	4.4	83
11.	Joe Perry	14	1,737	8,378	4.8	53
12.	Larry Csonka	11	1,891	8,081	4.3	64
13.	Marcus Allen[1]	9	1,960	7,957	4.1	75
14.	Gerald Riggs	9	1,911	7,940	4.2	58
15.	Freeman McNeil[1]	10	1,704	7,604	4.5	36

1. Active in 1991 season.

Scoring

Most points scored, lifetime—2,002, George Blanda, Chicago Bears, 1949–58; Baltimore, 1950; Houston, 1960–66; Oakland, 1967–75 (9tds, 943 pat, 335 fgs).

Most points, season—176, Paul Hornung, Green Bay, 1960 (15 td, 41 pat, 15 fg).

Most points, game—40, Ernie Nevers, Chicago Cardinals, 1929 (6 td, 4 pat).

Most points, per quarter—29, Don Hutson, Green Bay, 1945 (4 td, 5 pat).

Most touchdowns, lifetime—126, Jim Brown, Cleveland, 1957–65

Most touchdowns, season—24, John Riggins, Washington, 1983

Most touchdowns, game—6, Ernie Nevers, Chicago Cardinals, 1929; William Jones, Cleveland, 1951; Gale Sayers, Chicago Bears, 1965.

Most points after touchdown, lifetime—943, George Blanda, Chicago Bears, 1949–58; Baltimore, 1950; Houston, 1960–66; Oakland, 1967–75.

Most points after touchdown, game—9, Pat Harder, Chicago Cardinals, 1948; Bob Waterfield, Los Angeles, 1950; Charlie Gogolak, Washington, 1966.

Most consecutive points after touchdown—234, Tommy Davis, San Francisco, 1959–65.

Most points after touchdown, no misses, season—56, Danny Villanueva, Dallas, 1966.

Most field goals, lifetime—373, Jan Stenerud, Kansas City Chiefs, 1967–79; Green Bay Packers, 1980–84; Minnesota Vikings, 1985.

Most field goals, season—35, Ali Haji-Sheikh, N.Y. Giants, 1983.

Most field goals, game—7, Jim Bakken, St. Louis, 1967; and Rick Karlis, Minnesota, 1989.

Longest field goal—63 yards, Tom Dempsey, New Orleans, 1970.

Rushing

Most yards gained, lifetime—16,726, Walter Payton, Chicago Bears, 1975–1987.

Most yards gained, season—2,105, Eric Dickerson, Los Angeles, 1984.

Most yards gained, game—275, Walter Payton, Chicago, 1977.

Most touchdowns, lifetime—110, Walter Payton, Chicago, 1975–1987.

Most touchdowns, season—24, John Riggins, Washington, 1983.

Most touchdowns, game—6, Ernie Nevers, Chicago Cardinals, 1929; Dub Jones, Cleveland Browns, 1951; Gale Sayers, Chicago Bears, 1968.

Longest run from scrimmage—99 yards, Tony Dorsett, Dallas, 1982 (touchdown).

Passing

Most touchdown passes, lifetime—342, Fran Tarkenton, Minnesota, 1961–66, 72–78; New York Giants, 1967–71.

Most touchdown passes, season—48, Dan Marino, Miami, 1984.

Most touchdown passes, game—7, Sid Luckman, Chicago Bears, 1943; Adrian Burk, Philadelphia, 1954; George Blanda, Houston, 1961; Y.A. Tittle, New York Giants, 1963; Joe Kapp, Minnesota, 1969.

Most consecutive games, touchdown passes—47, John Unitas, Baltimore.

Most consecutive passes attempted, none intercepted—294, Bart Starr, Green Bay, 1964–65.

Longest pass completion—99 yards, Frank Filchock (to Andy Farkas), Washington, 1939; George Izo (to Bob Mitchell), Washington, 1963; Karl Sweetan (to Pat Studstill), Detroit, 1966; Sonny Jurgensen (to Gerry Allen), Washington, 1968; Jim Plunkett (to Cliff Branch) L.A. Raiders, 1985; Ron Jaworksi (to Mike Quick), Philadelphia, 1985.

Receiving

Most pass receptions, lifetime—819, Steve Largent, Seattle Seahawks, 1976–1989.

Most pass receptions, season—106, Art Monk, Washington, 1984.

Most pass receptions, game—18, Tom Fears, Los Angeles, 1950.

Most consecutive games, pass receptions—177, Steve Largent, 1976–1989.

Most yards gained, pass receptions, lifetime—13,089, Steve Largent, Seattle, 1976–1989.

Most yards gained receptions, season—1,746, Charley Hennigan, Houston, 1961.

Most yards gained receptions, game—336, Willie Anderson, Los Angeles Rams, Nov. 26, 1989 vs. New Orleans.

Most touchdown receptions, lifetime—100, Steve Largent, Seattle, 1976–1989.

Most touchdown pass receptions, season—22, Jerry Rice, San Francisco 49ers, 1987.

Most touchdown pass receptions, game—5, Bob Shaw, Chicago Cards, 1950; Kellen Winslow, San Diego Chargers, 1981; Jerry Rice, San Francisco 49ers, 1990.

Most consecutive games, touchdown pass receptions—13, Jerry Rice, San Francisco 49ers, 1986–87.

Most pass interceptions, lifetime—81, Paul Krause, Washington, 1964–67; Minnesota, 1968–79.

Most pass interceptions, season—14, Richard (Night Train) Lane, Los Angeles, 1952.

Most pass interceptions, game—4, by 17 players.

Longest pass interception return—103 yards, Venice Glenn, San Diego, vs. Denver, Nov. 29, 1987.

Kicking

Longest punt—98 yrds, Steve O'Neal, New York Jets, 1969.

Highest average punting, lifetime—45.16 yards, Sammy Baugh, Washington, 1937–52.

Longest punt return—98 yards, Gil LeFebvre, Cincinnati Reds, 1933; Charlie West, Minnesota, 1968; Dennis Morgan, Dallas, 1974.

Longest kick-off return—106 yards, Roy Green, St. Louis, 1979; Al Carmichael, Green Bay, 1956; Noland Smith, Kansas City, 1967.

Most punts lifetime—1,154, Dave Jennings, N.Y. Giants 1974–84; N.Y. Jets, 1985–87.

Passing

Most passes completed, lifetime—3,686, Fran Tarkenton, Minnesota, 1961–66, 72–78; New York Giants, 1967–71.

Most passes completed, season—378, Dan Marino, 1986.

Most passes completed, game—42, Richard Todd, New York Jets, 1980.

Most consecutive passes completed—22, Joe Montana, San Francisco, 1987.

Most yards gained, lifetime—47,003, Fran Tarkenton, Minnesota, 1961–66, 72–78; New York Giants, 1967–71.

Most yards gained, season—5,084, Dan Marino, Miami, 1984.

Most yards gained, game—554, Norm Van Brocklin, Los Angeles, 1951.

NFL GOVERNMENT

Paul Tagliabue, Commissioner; Neil Austrian, President; Jay Moyer, Executive Vice President and League Counsel; Harold Henderson, Executive Vice President for Labor Relations/Chairman NFLMC; Joe Browne, Vice President of Communications & Development; Val Pinchbeck, Jr., Vice President of Broadcasting & Productions; Tom Sullivan, Treasurer; Jim Steeg, Executive Director for Special Events; Roger Goodell, Executive Director for Club Relations and International Development; Dennis Curran, General Counsel/Management Council; Pete Abitante, Director of Information; Greg Aiello, Director of Communications; Phil Ayoub, Comptroller; Nancy Behar, Assistant Director of Broadcasting and Productions; Joel Bussert, Director of Player Personnel; John Buzzeo, Director of Administration; David Cornwell, Director of Equal Emploument and Assistant Counsel; Joe Ellis, Assistant Director of Club Administration; Bill Granholm, Director of Special Projects; Leslie Hammond, Director of Information, AFC; Charlie Jackson, Assistant Director of Security; John Jones, Director of Labor Operations; Dick Maxwell, Director of Broadcasting Services; Susan McCann Minogue, Assistant Director of Special Events; Jack Reader, Assistant Director of Officiating; Reggie Roberts, Director of Information, NFC; Peter Ruocco, Director of Planning for Player Employment; Jerry Seeman, Director of Officiating; Jan Van Duser, Director of Game Operations; Don Weiss, Director of Planning; Warren Welsh, Director of Security.

BASKETBALL

Basketball may be the one sport whose exact origin is definitely known. In the winter of 1891–92, Dr. James Naismith, an instructor in the Y.M.C.A. Training College (now Springfield College) at Springfield, Mass., deliberately invented the game of basketball in order to provide indoor exercise and competition for the students between the closing of the football season and the opening of the baseball season. He affixed peach baskets overhead on the walls at opposite ends of the gymnasium and organized teams to play his new game in which the purpose was to toss an association (soccer) ball into one basket and prevent the opponents from tossing the ball into the other basket. The game is fundamentally the same today, though there have been improvements in equipment and some changes in rules.

Because Dr. Naismith had eighteen available players when he invented the game, the first rule was: "There shall be nine players on each side." Later the number of players became optional, depending upon the size of the available court, but the five-player standard was adopted when the game spread over the country. United States soldiers brought basketball to Europe in World War I, and it soon became a worldwide sport.

College Basketball

NATIONAL COLLEGIATE A.A. CHAMPIONS

1939	Oregon	1951	Kentucky	1963	Loyola (Chicago)	1981	Indiana
1940	Indiana	1952	Kansas	1964	U.C.L.A.	1982	North Carolina
1941	Wisconsin	1953	Indiana	1965	U.C.L.A.	1983	North Carolina
1942	Stanford	1954	La Salle	1966	Texas Western		State
1943	Wyoming	1955	San Francisco	1967–73	U.C.L.A.	1984	Georgetown
1944	Utah	1956	San Francisco	1974	No. Carolina State	1985	Villanova
1945	Oklahoma A & M	1957	North Carolina	1975	U.C.L.A.	1986	Louisville
1946	Oklahoma A & M	1958	Kentucky	1976	Indiana	1987	Indiana
1947	Holy Cross	1959	California	1977	Marquette	1988	Kansas
1948	Kentucky	1960	Ohio State	1978	Kentucky	1989	Michigan
1949	Kentucky	1961	Cincinnati	1979	Michigan State	1990	Nevada–Las Vegas
1950	C.C.N.Y.	1962	Cincinnati	1980	Louisville	1991	Duke

NATIONAL INVITATION TOURNAMENT (NIT) CHAMPIONS

1939	Long Island U.	1953	Seton Hall	1966	Brigham Young	1979	Indiana
1940	Colorado	1954	Holy Cross	1967	So. Illinois	1980	Virginia
1941	Long Island U.	1955	Duquesne	1968	Dayton	1981	Tulsa
1942	West Virginia	1956	Louisville	1969	Temple	1982	Bradley
1943–44	St. John's (N.Y.C.)	1957	Bradley	1970	Marquette	1983	Fresno State
1945	DePaul	1958	Xavier (Cincinnati)	1971	North Carolina	1984	Michigan
1946	Kentucky	1959	St. John's (N.Y.C.)	1972	Maryland	1985	U.C.L.A.
1947	Utah	1960	Bradley	1973	Virginia Tech	1986	Ohio State
1948	St. Louis	1961	Providence	1974	Purdue	1987	So. Mississippi
1949	San Francisco	1962	Dayton	1975	Princeton	1988	Connecticut
1950	C.C.N.Y.	1963	Providence	1976	Kentucky	1989	St. John's
1951	Brigham Young	1964	Bradley	1977	St. Bonaventure	1990	Vanderbilt
1952	La Salle	1965	St. John's (N.Y.C.)	1978	Texas	1991	Stanford

N.C.A.A. MAJOR COLLEGE INDIVIDUAL SCORING RECORDS

Single Season Averages

Player, Team	Year	G	FG [1]	FT	Pts	Avg
Pete Maravich, Louisiana State	1969–70	31	522 [1]	337	1381 [1]	44.5 [1]
Pete Maravich	1968–69	26	433	282	1148	44.2
Pete Maravich	1967–68	26	432	274	1138	43.8
Frank Selvy, Furman	1953–54	29	427	355 [1]	1209	41.7
Johnny Neumann, Mississippi	1970–71	23	366	191	923	40.1
Freeman Williams, Portland State	1976–77	26	417	176	1010	38.8
Billy McGill, Utah	1961–62	26	394	221	1009	38.8
Calvin Murphy, Niagara	1967–68	24	337	242	916	38.2
Austin Carr, Notre Dame	1969–70	29	444	218	1106	38.1

1. Record.

N.C.A.A. CAREER SCORING TOTALS

Division I

Player, Team	Last year	G	FG	FT	Pts	Avg
Pete Maravich, Louisiana State	1970	83	1387 [1]	893 [1]	3667 [1]	44.2 [1]
Austin Carr, Notre Dame	1971	74	1017	526	2560	34.6
Oscar Robertson, Cincinnati	1960	88	1052	869	2973	33.8
Calvin Murphy, Niagara	1970	77	947	654	2548	33.1
Dwight Lamar [2]	1973	57	768	326	1862	32.7
Frank Selvy, Furman	1954	78	922	694	2538	32.5
Rick Mount, Purdue	1970	72	910	503	2323	32.3
Darrel Floyd, Furman	1956	71	868	545	2281	32.1
Nick Werkman, Seton Hall	1964	71	812	649	2273	32.0

1. Record. 2. Also played two seasons in college division.

Division II

Player, Team	Last year	G	FG	FT	Pts	Avg
Travis Grant, Kentucky State	1972	121	1760 [1]	525	4045 [1]	33.4 [1]
John Rinka, Kenyon	1970	99	1261	729	3251	32.8
Florindo Vierira, Quinnipiac	1957	69	761	741	2263	32.8
Willie Shaw, Lane	1964	76	960	459	2379	31.3
Mike Davis, Virginia Union	1969	89	1014	730	2758	31.0
Henry Logan, Western Carolina	1968	107	1263	764	3290	30.7
Willie Scott, Alabama State	1969	103	1277	601	3155	30.6
Gregg Northington, Alabama State	1972	75	894	403	2191	29.2
Bob Hopkins, Grambling	1956	126	1403	953	3759	29.8

1. Record.

TOP SINGLE–GAME SCORING MARKS

Player, Team (Opponent)	Yr	Pts	Player, Team (Opponent)	Yr	Pts
Selvy, Furman (Newberry)	1954	100 [1]	Floyd, Furman (Morehead)	1955	67
Williams, Portland State (Rocky Mtn.)	1978	81	Maravich, LSU (Tulane)	1969	66
Mlkvy, Temple (Wilkes)	1951	73	Handlan, W & L (Furman)	1951	66
Williams, Portland State (So. Oregon)	1977	71	Roberts, Oral Roberts (N.C. A&T)	1977	66
Maravich, LSU (Alabama)	1970	69	Williams, Portland State (Geo. Fox Coll.)	1978	66
Murphy, Niagara (Syracuse)	1969	68	Roberts, Oral Roberts (Oregon)	1977	65

1. Record.

MEN'S N.C.A.A. BASKETBALL CHAMPIONSHIPS—1991

DIVISION I

First Round—East
North Carolina 101, Northeastern 66
Villanova 50, Princeton 48
Eastern Michigan 76, Mississippi St. 56
Penn State 74, UCLA 69
No. Carolina St. 114, So. Mississippi 85
Oklahoma State 67, New Mexico 54
Temple 80, Purdue 63
Richmond 73, Syracuse 69

First Round—Southeast
Arkansa 117, Georgia State 76
Arizona State 79, Rutgers 76
Wake Forest 71, Louisana Tech 65
Alabama 89, Murray State 79
Pittsburgh 76, Georgia 68 (OT)
Kansas 55, New Orleans 49
Florida State 75, USC 72
Indiana 79, Coastal Carolina 69

First Round—Midwest
Ohio State 97, Towson State 86
Georgia Tech 87, DePaul 70
Texas 73, St. Peter's 65
St. John's 75, Northern Illinois 68
Connecticut 79, LSU 62
Xavier 89, Nebraska 84
Iowa 76, East Tennessee State 73
Duke 102, Northeast Louisiana 73

First Round—West
UNLV 99, Montana 65
Georgetown 70, Vanderbilt 60
Michigan State 60, Wisc.–Green Bay 58
Utah 82, South Alabama 72
Creighton 64, New Mexico State 56

Seton Hall 71, Pepperdine 51
BYU 61, Virginia 48
Arizona 93, St. Francis (Pa.) 80

Second Round—East
North Carolina 84, Villanova 69
East Michigan 84, Penn State 68 (OT)
Oklahoma 85, No. Carolina State 64
Temple 77, Richmond 64

Second Round—Southeast
Arkansas 97, Arizona State 90
Alabama 96, Wake Forest 88
Kansas 77, Pittsburgh 66
Indiana 82, Florida State 60

Second Round—Midwest
Ohio State 65, Georgia Tech 61
St. John's 84, Texas 76
Connecticut 66, Xavier 50
Duke 85, Iowa 70

Second Round—West
UNLV 62, Georgetown 54
Utah 85, Michigan State 84 (2 OT)
Seton Hall 81, Creighton 69
Arizona 76, BYU 61

Third Round—East
North Carolina 93, Eastern Michigan 67
Temple 72, Oklahoma State 63 (OT)

Third Round—Southeast
Arkansas 93, Alabama 70
Kansas 83, Indiana 65

Third Round—Midwest
St. John's 91, Ohio State 74
Duke 81, Connecticut 67

Third Round—West
UNLV 83, Utah 66
Seton Hall 81, Arizona 77

Regional Finals
East—North Carolina 75, Temple 72
Southeast—Kansas 93, Arkansas 81
Midwest—Duke 78, St. John's 61
West—UNLV 77, Seton Hall 65

National Semifinals
(Saturday, March 30, 1991 at Indianapolis, Ind.)
Kansas 79, North Carolina 73
Duke 79, UNLV 77

National Final
(Monday, April 1, 1991 at Indianapolis, Ind.)
Duke 72, Kansas 65

DIVISION II
Semifinals
Northern Alabama 97, Virginia Union 76
Bridgeport (Conn.) 73, Cal State Bakersfield 66 (OT)

Championship
Northern Alabama 79, Bridgeport 72

DIVISION III
Semifinals
Franklin & Marshall 109, Ramapo 56
Wisconsin–Platteville 96, Otterbein 94

Championship
Wisconsin–Platteville 81, Franklin & Marshall 74

WOMEN'S N.C.A.A. BASKETBALL CHAMPIONSHIPS—1991

DIVISION I

First Round—East
Geoerge Washington 73, Richmond 62
Providence 88, Fairfield 87
James Madison 70, Kentucky 62
Toledo 83, Rutgers 65

First Round—Mideast
Florida State 96, Appalachian State 57
Holy Cross 81, Maryland 74
Southwest Missouri 94, Tenn. Tech 64
Vanderbilt 73, South Carolina 64

First Round—Midwest
Stephen F. Austin 73, Mississippi 62
Oklahoma State 81, DePaul 80
Northwestern 82, Washington State 62
Lamar 77, Texas 63

First Round—West
USC 63, Utah 52
Iowa 64, Montana 53
UNLV 70, Texas Tech 65
Fullerton State 84, Louisiana Tech 80

Second Round—East
James Madison 73, Penn State 71
No. Carolina State 94, George Washington 83
Clemson 103, Providence 91
Connecticut 81, Toledo 80

Second Round—Mideast
Tennessee 55, SW Missouri State 47
Western Kentucky 72, Florida State 69
Vanderbil 69, Purdue 63
Auburn 84, Holy Cross 58

Second Round—Midwest
Arkansas 105, Northwestern 68
Oklahoma St. 96, Michigan St. 94 (3 OT)
Virginia 74, Stephen F. Austin 72
Lamar 93, Louisiana State 73

Second Round—West
Georgia 86, UNLV 62
Long Beach State 83, USC 58
Washington 70, Iowa 53
Stanford 91, Fullerton State 67

Third Round—East
Connecticut 82, North Carolina State 71
Clemson 57, James Madison 55

Third Round—Mideast
Tennessee 68, Western Kentucky 61
Auburn 58, Vanderbilt 45

Third Round—Midwest
Virginia 76, Oklahoma State 61
Lamar 91, Arkansas 75

Third Round—West
Stanford 73, Washington 47
Georgia 87, Long Beach State 77

Regional Finals
East—Connecticut 60, Clemson 57
Mideast—Tennessee 69, Auburn 65
Midwest—Virginia 85, Lamar 70
West—Stanford 75, Georgia 67

National Semifinals
(Sat., March 30, at New Orleans, La.)
Tennessee 68, Stanford 60
Virginia 61, Connecticut 55

National Championship
(Sun., March 31, at New Orleans, La.)
Tennessee 70, Virginia 67 (OT)

DIVISION II
Semifinals
North Dakota State 83, Bentley 76
SE Missouri State 85, Norfolk State 52

Championship
North Dakota State 81, Southeast Missouri State 74

DIVISION III
Semifinals
St. Thomas (Minn.) 91, East. Conn. St. 55
Muskingum (Ohio) 85, Washinngton (Mo.) 60

Championship
St. Thomas 73, Muskingum 55

LEADING N.C.A.A. SCORERS—1990–91

Division I

		FG	3-PT FG	Pts	Avg
1.	Kevin Bradshaw, U.S. Intl.	60	190	1054	37.6
2.	Alphonso Ford, Miss. Valley	86	260	915	32.7
3.	Von McDade, Wis.-Milwaukee	96	242	830	29.6
4.	Steve Rogers, Alabama St.	56	147	852	29.4
5.	Terrell Lowery, Loyola (Cal.)	103	257	884	28.5
6.	Bobby Phills, Southern-B.R.	123	353	795	28.4
7.	Shaquille O'Neal, LSU	0	0	774	27.6
8.	John Taft, Marshall	82	197	764	27.3
9.	Rodney Monroe, N.Caro. St.	104	239	836	27.0
10.	Terrell Brandon, Oregon	40	119	745	26.6
11.	Kenny Anderson, Georgia Tech	65	185	776	25.9
12.	Eric Murdock, Providence	56	160	818	25.6
13.	Keith Gailes, Loyola (Ill.)	50	145	657	25.3
14.	Curtis Stuckey, Bradley	55	147	702	25.1
15.	Steve Smith, Michigan St.	66	162	752	25.1
16.	Rod Parker, Chicago St.	33	95	621	24.8
17.	Tom Davis, Delaware St.	0	3	740	24.7
18.	Michael Ervin, Prairie View	20	88	612	24.5
19.	Robert Youngblood, Southern-B.R.	3	10	679	24.3
20.	Mike Iuzzolino, St. Fran. (Pa.)	103	195	772	24.1
21.	Larry Stewart, Coppin St.	1	1	716	23.9
22.	Desi Wilson, FDU-Teaneck	2	10	738	23.8
23.	Reggie Isaac, Coppin St.	83	197	712	23.7
24.	Terry Boyd, Western Caro.	65	172	664	23.7
25.	Allan Houston, Tennessee	99	231	806	23.7

NATIONAL ASSOCIATION OF INTERCOLLEGIATE ATHLETICS—1991

MEN'S TOURNAMENT

First Round
Pfeiffer 96, St. Vincent 82

Rio Grande (Ohio) 111, Campbellsville 92
Taylor (Ind.) 68, Francis Marion 67
Northern State (S.D.) 80, Georgia Southwestern 67
Oklahoma City 80, Concordia (Neb.) 77
Wisconsin–Eau Claire 78, Maine–Machias 49
Briar Cliff (Iowa) 72, Park (Mo.) 60
Central Arkansas 75, Olivet Nazarene 66
St. Mary's (Mich.) 77, Wayland Baptist 68
Concord (W. Va.) 106, Southern Colorado 91
College of Idaho 96, St. Rose (N.Y.) 91
Athens State (Ala.) 85, Whitworth (Wash.) 65
Minnesota–Duluth 76, Xavier (La.) 68
David Lipscomb (Tenn.) 106, Holy Family (Pa.) 75
Westmont (Calif.) 65, Emporia State (Kan.) 65
St. Mary's (Texas) 96, Hawaii–Loa 94 (OT)

Round of 16
Taylor 60, Northern State 59
Central Arkansas 99, Rio Grande 72
St. Mary's (Mich.) 83, College of Idaho 78
Oklahoma City 107, Concord 85
Athens State 62, Minnesota–Duluth 56 (OT)
David Lipscomb 89, Briar Cliff 87
Wisconsin–Eau Claire 55, Westmont 52
Pfeiffer 83, St. Mary's (Texas) 71

Quarterfinals
Taylor 64, Wisconsin–Eau Claire 57
Central Arkansas 95, Athens State 64
Pfeiffer 105, David Lipscomb 95
Oklahoma City 112, St. Mary's (Mich.) 94

Semifinals
Central Arkansas 66, Taylor 60
Oklahoma City 100, Pfeiffer 83

Championship
(Monday, March 17, at Kansas City, Mo.)
Oklahoma City 77, Central Arkansas 74

WOMEN'S TOURNAMENT

Round of 16
St. Edward's (Texas) 92, Rosary (Ill.) 51
Fort Hays State (Kansas) 70, Northern Montana 53
Wingate (N.C.) 81, Central State (Ohio) 78
IU–PU–Indianapolis 99, Midland Lutheran (Neb.) 79
Southwest Oklahoma 67, Western Oregon 55
Wayland Baptist (Texas) 58, Minnesota–Duluth 51
Belmont (Tenn.) 99, Mount Mercy 83
Claflin (S.C.) 93, Central Arkansas 77

Quarterfinals
IU–PU–Indianapolis 99, Wingate 96
Fort Hays State 78, Wayland Baptist 65
Southwest Oklahoma 70, Belmont 65 (OT)
Claflin 67, St. Edward's 66

Semifinals
Southwest Oklahoma 69, IU–PU–Indianapolis 49
Fort Hays State 75, Claflin 63

Championship
Fort Hays State 57, Southwest Oklahoma 53

NATIONAL INVITATION TOURNAMENT (N.I.T.)—1991

Semifinals
(March 25, 1991 at Madison Square Garden, N.Y.)

Stanford 73, Massachusetts 71
Oklahoma 88, Colorado 78

Championship
(March 27, 1991 at Madison Square Garden, N.Y.)

Stanford 78, Oklahoma 72

N.C.A.A. LEADING REBOUNDERS— 1990–91

		Games	No.	Avg
1.	Shaquille O'Neal, LSU	28	411	14.7
2.	Popeye Jones, Murray St.	33	469	14.2
3.	Larry Stewart, Coppin St.	30	403	13.4
4.	Tim Burroughs, Jacksonville	27	350	13.0
5.	Warren Kidd, Middle Tenn. St.	30	370	12.3
6.	Clarence Weatherspoon, South. Miss.	29	355	12.2
7.	Ervin Johnson, New Orleans	30	367	12.2
8.	Tom Davis, Delaware St.	30	366	12.2
9.	Dikembe Mutombo, Georgetown	32	389	12.2
10.	Dale Davis, Clemson	28	340	12.1
11.	Dwayne Tanka, Southern–B.R.	28	337	12.0
12.	Tommy Brown, Austin Peay	29	344	11.9
13.	Travis Williams, So. Caro. St.	28	325	11.6
14.	Billy Owens, Syracuse	32	371	11.6
15.	Steve Carney, Northeastern	31	356	11.5
16.	Drew Henderson, Fairfield	25	284	11.4
17.	Chris Gatling, Old Dominion	32	356	11.1
18.	Kevin Roberson, Vermont	28	311	11.1
19.	Ron Reis, Santa Clara	29	320	11.0
20.	Larry Johnson, Nevada–Las Vegas	35	380	10.9
21.	Malcolm Mackey, Georgia Tech.	30	321	10.7
22.	Jarvis Lang, N.C.–Charlotte	28	298	10.6
23.	Chris Collier, Georgia St.	31	328	10.6
24.	Byron Houston, Oklahoma St.	32	336	10.5
25.	Byron Tucker, George Mason	30	314	10.5
26.	Vinnie Baker, Hartford	29	302	10.4
27.	Doug Smith, Missouri	30	311	10.4
28.	Reginald Slater, Wyoming	32	331	10.3
29.	Brian Clifford, Niagara	28	289	10.3
30.	Gary Alexander, So. Fla.	30	307	10.2

Professional Basketball

NATIONAL BASKETBALL ASSOCIATION CHAMPIONS

Source: National Basketball Association.

The National Basketball Association was originally the Basketball Association of America. It took its current name in 1949 when it merged with the National Basketball League.

Season	Eastern Conference (W–L)	Western Conference (W–L)	Playoff Champions[1]
1946–47	Washington Capitols (49–11)	Chicago Stags (39–22)	Philadelphia Warriors
1947–48	Philadelphia Warriors (27–21)	St. Louis Bombers (29–19)	Baltimore Bullets
1948–49	Washington Capitols (38–22)	Rochester Royals (45–15)	Minneapolis Lakers
1949–50	Syracuse Nationals (51–13)	Indianapolis Olympians (39–25)	Minneapolis Lakers
1950–51	Philadelphia Warriors (40–26)	Minneapolis Lakers (44–24)	Rochester Royals
1951–52	Syracuse Nationals (40–26)	Rochester Royals (41–25)	Minneapolis Lakers
1952–53	New York Knickerbockers (47–23)	Minneapolis Lakers (48–22)	Minneapolis Lakers
1953–54	New York Knickerbockers (44–28)	Minneapolis Lakers (46–26)	Minneapolis Lakers
1954–55	Syracuse Nationals (43–29)	Ft. Wayne Pistons (43–29)	Syracuse Nationals
1955–56	Philadelphia Warriors (45–27)	Ft. Wayne Pistons (37–35)	Philadelphia Warriors
1956–57	Boston Celtics (44–28)	St. Louis Hawks (38–34)	Boston Celtics
1957–58	Boston Celtics (48–23)	St. Louis Hawks (41–31)	St. Louis Hawks
1958–59	Boston Celtics (52–20)	St. Louis Hawks (49–23)	Boston Celtics
1959–60	Boston Celtics (59–16)	St. Louis Hawks (46–29)	Boston Celtics
1960–61	Boston Celtics (57–22)	St. Louis Hawks (51–28)	Boston Celtics
1961–62	Boston Celtics (60–20)	Los Angeles Lakers (54–26)	Boston Celtics
1962–63	Boston Celtics (58–22)	Los Angeles Lakers (53–27)	Boston Celtics
1963–64	Boston Celtics (59–21)	San Francisco Warriors (48–32)	Boston Celtics
1964–65	Boston Celtics (62–18)	Los Angeles Lakers (49–31)	Boston Celtics
1965–66	Philadelphia 76ers (55–25)	Los Angeles Lakers (45–35)	Boston Celtics
1966–67	Philadelphia 76ers (68–13)	San Francisco Warriors (44–37)	Philadelphia 76ers
1967–68	Philadelphia 76ers (62–20)	St. Louis Hawks (56–26)	Boston Celtics
1968–69	Baltimore Bullets (57–25)	Los Angeles Lakers (55–27)	Boston Celtics
1969–70	New York Knickerbockers (60–22)	Atlanta Hawks (48–34)	New York Knicks
1970–71	Baltimore Bullets (42–40)	Milwaukee Bucks (66–16)	Milwaukee Bucks
1971–72	New York Knickerbockers (48–34)	Los Angeles Lakers (69–13)	Los Angeles Lakers
1972–73	New York Knickerbockers (57–25)	Los Angeles Lakers (60–22)	New York Knicks
1973–74	Boston Celtics (56–26)	Milwaukee Bucks (59–23)	Boston Celtics
1974–75	Washington Bullets (60–22)	Golden State Warriors (48–34)	Golden State Warriors
1975–76	Boston Celtics (54–28)	Phoenix Suns (42–40)	Boston Celtics

Season	Eastern Conference (W–L)	Western Conference (W–L)	Playoff Champions[1]
1976–77	Philadelphia 76ers (50–32)	Portland Trail Blazers (49–33)	Portland Trail Blazers
1977–78	Washington Bullets (44–38)	Seattle Super Sonics (47–35)	Washington Bullets
1978–79	Washington Bullets (54–28)	Seattle Super Sonics (52–30)	Seattle Super Sonics
1979–80	Philadelphia 76ers (59–23)	Los Angeles Lakers (60–22)	Los Angeles Lakers
1980–81	Boston Celtics (62–20)	Houston Rockets (40–42)	Boston Celtics
1981–82	Philadelphia 76ers (58–24)	Los Angeles Lakers (57–25)	Los Angeles Lakers
1982–83	Philadelphia 76ers (65–17)	Los Angeles Lakers (58–24)	Philadelphia 76ers
1983–84	Boston Celtics (56–26)	Los Angeles Lakers (58–24)	Boston Celtics
1984–85	Boston Celtics (63–19)	Los Angeles Lakers (62–20)	Los Angeles Lakers
1985–86	Boston Celtics (67–15)	Houston Rockets (51–31)	Boston Celtics
1986–87	Boston Celtics (59–23)	Los Angeles Lakers (65–17)	Los Angeles Lakers
1987–88	Detroit Pistons (54–28)	Los Angeles Lakers (62–20)	Los Angeles Lakers
1988–89	Detroit Pistons (63–18)	Los Angeles Lakers (57–25)	Detroit Pistons
1989–90	Detroit Pistons (59–23)	Portland Trail Blazers (59–23)	Detroit Pistons
1990–91	Chicago Bulls (61–21)	Los Angeles Lakers (58–24)	Chicago Bulls

1. Playoffs may involve teams other than conference winners.

INDIVIDUAL N.B.A. SCORING CHAMPIONS

Season	Player, Team	G	FG	FT	Pts	Avg
1953–54	Neil Johnston, Philadelphia Warriors	72	591	577	1759	24.4
1954–55	Neil Johnston, Philadelphia Warriors	72	521	589	1631	22.7
1955–56	Bob Pettit, St. Louis Hawks	72	646	557	1849	25.7
1956–57	Paul Arizin, Philadelphia Warriors	71	613	591	1817	25.6
1957–58	George Yardley, Detroit Pistons	72	673	655	2001	27.8
1958–59	Bob Pettit, St. Louis Hawks	72	719	667	2105	29.2
1959–60	Wilt Chamberlain, Philadelphia Warriors	72	1065	577	2707	37.6
1960–61	Wilt Chamberlain, Philadelphia Warriors	79	1251	531	3033	38.4
1961–62	Wilt Chamberlain, Philadelphia Warriors	80	1597	835	4029	50.4
1962–63	Wilt Chamberlain, San Francisco Warriors	80	1463	660	3586	44.8
1963–64	Wilt Chamberlain, San Francisco Warriors	80	1204	540	2948	36.9
1964–65	Wilt Chamberlain, San Francisco Warriors–Phila. 76ers	73	1063	408	2534	34.7
1965–66	Wilt Chamberlain, Philadelphia 76ers	79	1074	501	2649	33.5
1966–67	Rick Barry, San Francisco Warriors	78	1011	753	2775	35.6
1967–68	Dave Bing, Detroit Pistons	79	835	472	2142	27.1
1968–69	Elvin Hayes, San Diego Rockets	82	930	467	2327	28.4
1969–70	Jerry West, Los Angeles Lakers	74	831	647	2309	31.2
1970–71	Lew Alcindor,[1] Milwaukee Bucks	82	1063	470	2596	31.7
1971–72	Kareem Abdul–Jabbar, Milwaukee Bucks	81	1159	504	2822	34.8
1972–73	Nate Archibald, Kansas City–Omaha Kings	80	1028	663	2719	34.0
1973–74	Bob McAdoo, Buffalo Braves	74	901	459	2261	30.8
1974–75	Bob McAdoo, Buffalo Braves	82	1095	641	2831	34.5
1975–76	Bob McAdoo, Buffalo Braves	78	934	559	2427	31.1
1976–77	Pete Maravich, New Orleans Jazz	73	886	501	2273	31.1
1977–78	George Gervin, San Antonio Spurs	82	864	504	2232	27.2
1978–79	George Gervin, San Antonio Spurs	80	947	471	2365	29.6
1979–80	George Gervin, San Antonio Spurs	78	1024	505	2585	33.1
1980–81	Adrian Dantley, Utah Jazz	80	909	632	2452	30.7
1981–82	George Gervin, San Antonio Spurs	79	993	555	2551	32.3
1982–83	Alex English, Denver Nuggets	82	959	406	2326	28.4
1983–84	Adrian Dantley, Utah Jazz	79	802	813	2418	30.6
1984–85	Bernard King, New York Knicks	55	691	426	1809	32.9
1985–86	Dominique Wilkins, Atlanta Hawks	78	888	527	2366	30.3
1986–87	Michael Jordan, Chicago Bulls[2]	82	1098	833	3041	37.1
1987–88	Michael Jordan, Chicago Bulls[3]	82	1069	723	2868	35.0
1988–89	Michael Jordan, Chicago Bulls[4]	81	966	674	2633	32.5
1989–90	Michael Jordan, Chicago Bulls[5]	82	1034	593	2753	33.6
1990–91	Michael Jordan, Chicago Bulls[6]	82	990	571	2580	31.5

1. (Kareem Abdul–Jabbar). 2. Also had 12 3–point field goals. 3. Also had 7 3–point field goals. 4. Also had 27 3–point field goals. 5. Also had 92 3–point field goals. 6. Also had 29 3-point-field goals.

N.B.A. LIFETIME LEADERS

(Through 1990–91 season)

Most Games Played

Kareem Abdul–Jabbar	1,560
Elvin Hayes	1,303
John Havlicek	1,270
Paul Silas	1,254
Alex English	1,193
Robert Parish	1,181
Moses Malone	1,164
Hal Greer	1,122
Dennis Johnson	1,100
Len Wilkens	1,077

Steals

Maurice Cheeks	2,194
Magic Johnson	1,698
Gus Williams	1,638
Isiah Thomas	1,552
Julius Erving	1,508

Larry Bird	1,504
Dennis Johnson	1,477
Michael Ray Richardson	1,463
Lafayette Lever	1,461
Randy Smith	1,403

BLOCKED SHOTS

Kareem Abdul–Jabbar	3,189
Mark Eaton	2,780
Wayne Rollins	2,394
George T. Johnson	2,082
Robert Parish	1,952
Akeem Olajuwon	1,798
Elvin Hayes	1,771
Artis Gilmore	1,747
Moses Malone	1,641
Caldwell Jones	1,517

FREE THROW PERCENTAGE

(1,200 free throws made, minimum)

	FTA	FTM	Pct
Rick Barry	4,242	3,818	.900
Calvin Murphy	3,864	3,445	.892
Larry Bird	4,309	3,810	.884
Bill Sharman	3,559	3,143	.883
Chris Mullin	2,508	2,208	.880
Jeff Malone	2,483	2,170	.874
Kiki Vandeweghe	3,850	3,367	.873
Mike Newlin	3,456	3,005	.870
John Long	2,076	1,789	.862
Fred Brown	2,211	1,896	.858

SCORING AVERAGE

(400 games or 10,000 points minimum)

	Games	Pts	Avg
Michael Jordan	509	16,596	32.6
Wilt Chamberlain	1045	31,419	30.1
Elgin Baylor	846	23,149	27.4
Jerry West	932	25,192	27.0
Bob Pettit	792	20,880	26.4
George Gervin	791	20,708	26.2
Dominique Wilkins	720	18,796	26.1

Oscar Robertson	1040	26,710	25.7
Karl Malone	489	12,498	25.6
Larry Bird	852	20,883	24.5

REBOUNDS

Wilt Chamberlain	23,924
Bill Russell	21,620
Kareem Abdul–Jabbar	17,440
Elvin Hayes	16,279
Moses Malone	15,150
Nate Thurmond	14,464
Walt Bellamy	14,241
Wes Unseld	13,769
Jerry Lucas	12,942
Bob Pettit	12,849

FIELD GOAL PERCENTAGE

(2,000 field goals made, minimum)

	FGA	FGM	Pct.
Artis Gilmore	9,570	5,732	.599
Charles Barkley	7,596	4,403	.580
James Donaldson	5,109	2,941	.576
Steve Johnson	4,965	2,841	.572
Darryl Dawkins	6,079	3,477	.572
Jeff Ruland	3,685	2,080	.564
Kevin McHale	11,051	6,209	.562
Kareem Abdul–Jabbar	28,307	15,837	.559
Larry Nance	9,347	5,128	.549
James Worthy	10,217	5,578	.546

ASSISTS

Magic Johnson	9,921
Oscar Robertson	9,887
Isiah Thomas	7,431
Len Wilkens	7,211
Maurice Cheeks	7,100
Bob Cousy	6,955
Guy Rodgers	6,917
Nate Archibald	6,476
John Lucas	6,454
Norm Nixon	6,386

N.B.A. MOST VALUABLE PLAYERS

1956	Bob Pettit	1973	Dave Cowens
1957	Bob Cousy	1974	Kareem Abdul–Jabbar, Milwaukee
1958	Bill Russell		
1959	Bob Pettit	1975	Bob McAdoo, Buffalo
1960	Wilt Chamberlain	1976–77	Kareem Abdul–Jabbar, Los Angeles
1961–63	Bill Russell		
1964	Oscar Robertson	1978	Bill Walton, Portland
1965	Bill Russell	1979	Moses Malone, Houston
1966–68	Wilt Chamberlain	1980	Kareem Abdul–Jabbar, Los Angeles
1969	Wes Unseld		
1970	Willis Reed	1981	Julius Erving, Philadelphia
1971–72	Lew Alcindor (Kareem Abdul–Jabbar)	1982	Moses Malone, Houston

1983	Moses Malone, Philadelphia
1984	Larry Bird, Boston
1985	Larry Bird, Boston
1986	Larry Bird, Boston
1987	Earvin Johnson, Los Angeles
1988	Michael Jordan, Chicago
1989	Earvin Johnson, Los Angeles
1990	Earvin Johnson, Los Angeles
1991	Michael Jordan, Chicago

N.B.A. TEAM RECORDS

Most points, game—186, Detroit vs. Denver, 3 overtimes, 1983
Most points, quarter—58, Buffalo vs. Boston, 1968
Most points, half—97, Atlanta vs. San Diego, 1970
Most points, overtime period—22, Detroit vs. Cleveland, 1973
Most field goals, game—74, Detroit, 1983
Most field goals, quarter—23, Boston, 1959; Buffalo, 1972
Most field goals, half—40, Boston, 1959; Syracuse, 1963; Atlanta, 1979
Most assists, game—53, Milwaukee, 1978
Most rebounds, game—109, Boston, 1960
Most points, both teams, game—370 (Detroit 186, Denver 184)

3 overtimes, Denver, December 13, 1983
Most points, both teams, quarter—96 (Boston 52, Minneapolis 44), 1959; (Detroit 53, Cincinnati 43), 1972
Most points, both teams, half—170 (Philadelphia 90, Cincinnati 80), Philadelphia, 1971
Longest winning streak—33, Los Angeles, 1971–72
Longest losing streak—20, Philadelphia, 1973
Longest winning streak at home—36, Philadelphia, 1966–67
Most games won, season—69, Los Angeles, 1971–72
Most games lost, season—73, Philadelphia, 1972–73
Highest average points per game—126.5, Denver, 1981–82

N.B.A. INDIVIDUAL RECORDS

Most points, game—100, Wilt Chamberlain, Philadelphia vs. New York at Hershey, Pa. 1962
Most points, quarter—33, George Gervin, San Antonio, 1978
Most points, half—59, Wilt Chamberlain, Philadelphia, 1962
Most free throws, game—28, Wilt Chamberlain, Philadelphia vs. New York at Hershey, Pa. 1962; 28, Adrian Dantley, Utah vs. Houston, 1984
Most free throws, quarter—14, Rick Barry, San Francisco, 1966

Most free throws, half—19, Oscar Robertson, Cincinnati, 1964
Most field goals, game—36, Wilt Chamberlain, Philadelphia, 1962
Most consecutive gield goals, game—18, Wilt Chamberlain, San Franciscco, 1963; Wilt Chamberlain, Philadelphia, 1967
Most assists, game—29, Kevin Porter, New Jersey Nets, 1978
Most rebounds, game—356, Wilt Chamberlain, Philadelphia, 1963

NATIONAL BASKETBALL ASSOCIATION
FINAL STANDINGS OF THE CLUBS—1990–91

EASTERN CONFERENCE

Atlantic Division

	W	L	Pct	Games behind
Boston Celtics	56	26	.683	—
Philadelphia 76ers	44	38	.537	12
New York Knicks	39	43	.476	17
Washington Bullets	30	52	.366	26
New Jersey Nets	26	56	.317	30
Miami Heat	24	58	.293	32

Central Division

	W	L	Pct	Games behind
Chicago Bulls	61	21	.744	—
Detroit Pistons	50	32	.610	11
Milwaukee Bucks	48	34	.585	13
Atlanta Hawks	43	39	.524	18
Indiana Pacers	41	41	.500	20
Cleveland Cavaliers	33	49	.402	28
Charlotte Hornets	26	56	.317	35

WESTERN CONFERENCE

Midwest Division

	W	L	Pct	Games behind
San Antonio Spurs	55	27	.671	—
Utah Jazz	54	28	.659	1
Houston Rockets	52	30	.634	3
Orlando Magic	31	51	.378	24
Minnesota Timberwolves	29	53	.354	26
Dallas Mavericks	28	54	.341	27
Denver Nuggets	20	62	.244	35

Pacific Division

	W	L	Pct	Games behind
Portland Trail Blazers	63	19	.768	—
Los Angeles Lakers	58	24	.707	5
Phoenix Suns	55	27	.671	8
Golden State Warriors	44	38	.537	19
Seattle SuperSonics	41	41	.500	22
Los Angeles Clippers	31	51	.378	32
Sacramento Kings	25	57	.305	38

N.B.A. PLAYOFFS—1991

EASTERN CONFERENCE

First Round

Chicago defeated New York 3 games to 0
Detroit defeated Atlanta, 3 games to 3
Philadelphia defeated Milwaukee, 3 games to 0
Boston defeated Indiana, 3 games to 2

Semifinal Round

Chicago defeated Philadelphia, 4 games to 1
Detroit defeated Boston, 4 games to 2

Conference Finals

Chicago defeated Detroit, 4 games to 0
  May 19—Chicago 94, Detroit 83
  May 21—Chicago 105, Detroit 97
  May 25—Chicago 113, Detroit 107
  May 27—Chicago 115, Detroit 94

WESTERN CONFERENCE

First Round

Los Angeles Lakers defeated Houston, 3 games to 0
Golden State defeated San Antonio, 3 games to 1
Utah defeated Phoenix, 3 games to 1
Portland defeated Seattle, 3 games to 2

Semifinal Round

Los Angeles Lakers defated Golden State, 4 games to 1
Portland defeated Utah, 4 games to 1

Conference Finals

L.A. Lakers defeated Portland, 4 games to 2
  May 18—L.A. Lakers 111, Portland 106
  May 21—Portland 109, L.A. Lakers 98
  May 24—L.A. Lakers 106, Portland 92
  May 26—L.A. Lakers 116, Portland 95
  May 28—Portland 95, L.A. Lakers 84
  May 30—L.A. Lakers 91, Portland 90

CHAMPIONSHIP

Chicago defeated L.A. Lakers, 4 games to 1
  June 2—L.A. Lakers 93, Chicago 91
  June 5—Chicago 107, L.A. Lakers 86
  June 7—Chicago 104, L.A. Lakers 96 (OT)
  June 9—Chicago 97, L.A. Lakers 82
  June 12—Chicago 108, L.A. Lakers 101

LEADING SCORERS—1990–1991

	G	FG	FT	Pts	Avg
Jordan, Chi.	82	990	571	2580	31.5
K. Malone, Utah	82	847	684	2382	29.0
King, Wash.	64	713	383	1817	28.4
Barkley, Phil.	67	665	475	1849	27.6
Ewing, N.Y.	81	845	464	2154	26.6
Adams, Den.	66	560	465	1752	26.5
Wilkins, Atl.	81	770	476	2101	25.9
Mullin, G.S.	82	777	513	2107	25.7
Robinson, S.A.	82	754	592	2101	25.6
Richmond, G.S.	77	703	394	1840	23.9
Hardaway, G.S.	82	739	306	1881	22.9
Miller, Ind.	82	596	551	1855	22.6
K. Johnson, Phoe.	77	591	519	1710	22.2
Hawkins, Phil.	80	590	479	1767	22.1
Campbell, Minn.	77	652	358	1678	21.8
Daugherty, Clev.	76	605	435	1645	21.6
Drexler, Port.	82	645	416	1767	21.5
Worthy, LAL	78	716	212	1670	21.4
Pierce, Sea.	78	561	430	1598	20.5
Dumars, Det.	80	622	371	1629	20.4

STEALS LEADERS—1990–1991

(minimum 70 games or 125 steals)

	G	Stl	Avg
Robertson, Milwaukee	81	246	3.04
Stockton, Utah	82	234	2.85
Jordan, Chicago	82	223	2.72
Hardaway, Golden State	82	214	2.61
Pippen, Chicago	82	193	2.35
Blaylock, New Jersey	72	169	2.35
Adams, Denver	66	147	2.23
Hawkins, Philadelphia	80	178	2.23
K. Johnson, Phoenix	77	163	2.12
Mullin, Golden State	82	173	2.11

ASSISTS LEADERS—1990–91

(minimum 70 games or 400 assists)

	G	No.	Avg
Stockton, Utah	82	1164	14.2
Johnson, LAL	79	989	12.5
Adams, Den.	66	693	10.5
K. Johnson, Phoe.	77	781	10.1
Hardaway, G.S.	82	793	9.7
Thomas, Det.	48	446	9.3
Richardson, Minn.	82	734	9.0
Grant, LAC	68	587	8.6
Douglas, Mia.	73	624	8.5
Skiles, Orl.	79	660	8.4

BLOCKED–SHOTS LEADERS—1990–91

(minimum 70 games or 100 blocked shots)

	G	No.	Avg
Olajuwon, Houston	56	221	3.95
Robinson, San Antonio	82	320	3.90
Ewing, New York	81	258	3.19
Bol, Philadelphia	82	247	3.01
Dudley, New Jersey	61	153	2.51
Nance, Cleveland	80	200	2.50
Eaton, Utah	80	188	2.35
McHale, Boston	68	146	2.15
Benjamin, Seattle	70	145	2.07
Ellison, Washington	76	157	2.07

FIELD GOAL LEADERS—1990–91

(minimum 300 FG made)

	FG	FGA	Pct
Williams, Port.	358	595	.602
Parish, Bos.	485	811	.598
Gamble, Bos.	548	933	.587
Barkley, Phil.	665	1167	.570
Divac, LAL	360	637	.565
Polynice, LAC	316	564	.560
Thorpe, Hou.	549	988	.556
McHale, Bos.	504	912	.553
Robinson, S.A.	754	1366	.552
Paxson, Chi.	317	578	.548

FREE–THROW LEADERS—1990–91

(minimum 125 FT made)

	FTM	FTA	Pct
Miller, Indiana	551	600	.918
J. Malone, Utah	231	252	.917
Pierce, Seattle	430	471	.913
Tripuka, Charlotte	153	168	.910
Johnson, L.A. Lakers	519	573	.906
Skiles, Orlando	340	377	.902
Vandeweghe, New York	259	288	.899
Hornacek, Phoenix	201	224	.897
Johnson, Seattle	229	257	.891
Bird, Boston	163	183	.891

REBOUND LEADERS—1990–91

(minimum 70 games or 700 rebounds)

	G	Off	Def	Tot	Avg
Robinson, S.A.	82	335	728	1063	13.0
Rodman, Det.	82	361	665	1026	12.5
Oakley, N.Y.	76	305	615	920	12.1
K. Malone, Utah	82	236	731	967	11.8
Ewing, N.Y.	81	194	711	905	11.2
Daugherty, Clev.	76	177	653	830	10.9
Parish, Bos.	81	271	585	856	10.6
Benjamin, Sea.	70	157	566	723	10.3
Thorpe, Hou.	82	287	559	846	10.3
Coleman, N.J.	74	269	490	759	10.3

3–POINT FIELD–GOAL LEADERS 1990–91

(minimum 25 made)

	3FG	3FGA	Pct
Les, Sacramento	71	154	.461
Tucker, New York	64	153	.418
Hornacek, Phoenix	61	146	.418
Porter, Portland	130	313	.415
Skiles, Oregon	93	228	.408
Ainge, Portland	102	251	.406
Hawkins, Philadelphia	108	270	.400
Bird, Boston	77	198	.389
Rice, Miami	71	184	.386
Hardaway, Golden State	97	252	.385

Sports Personalities

A name in parentheses is the original name or form of name. Localities are places of birth. Dates of birth appear as month/day/year. **Boldface** years in parentheses are dates of **(birth–death)**.
Information has been gathered from many sources, including the individuals themselves. However, the *Information Please Almanac* cannot guarantee the accuracy of every individual item.

Aaron, Hank (Henry) (baseball); Mobile, Ala., 2/5/1934
Aaron, Tommie (baseball); Mobile, Ala., **(1939–1984)**
Abdul-Jabbar, Kareem (Lewis Ferdinand Alcindor, Jr.) (basketball); New York City, 4/16/1947
Adderly, Herbert A. (football); Philadelphia, 6/8/1939
Affleck, Francis (auto racing) **(1951–1985)**
Alcindor, Lew. *See* Abdul–Jabbar.
Ali, Muhammad (Cassius Clay) (boxing); Louisville, Ky., 1/18/1942
Allen, Dick (Richard Anthony) (baseball); Wampum, Pa., 3/8/1942
Allen, George (football) **(1918–1990)**
Allison, Bobby (Robert Arthur) (auto racing); Hueytown, Ala., 12/3/1937
Alston, Walter (baseball); Venice, Ohio **(1911–1984)**
Alworth, Lance (football); Houston, 8/3/1940
Ameche, Alan (football); Houston, Tex., **(1933–1988)**
Anderson, Donny (Gary Donny) (football); Brooklyn, N.Y., 4/3/1949
Anderson, Ken (football); Batavia, Ill., 2/15/1949
Anderson, Sparky (George) (baseball); Bridgewater, S.D., 2/22/1934
Andretti, Mario (auto racing); Montona, Trieste, Italy, 2/28/1940
Anthony, Earl (bowling); Kent, Wash., 4/27/1938
Appling, Luke (baseball); High Point, N.C **(1907–1990)**
Arcaro, Eddie (George Edward) (jockey); Cincinnati, 2/19/1916
Ashe, Arthur (tennis); Richmond, Va., 7/10/1943
Austin, Tracy (tennis); Rolling Hills, Calif., 12/2/1962
Averill, Earl (baseball); Everett, Wash. **(1915–1983)**
Babashoff, Shirley (swimming); Whittier, Calif., 1/31/1957
Baer, Max (boxing); Omaha, Neb. **(1909–1959)**
Bakken, Jim (James Leroy) (football); Madison, Wis., 11/2/1940
Banks, Ernie (baseball); Dallas, 1/31/1931
Bannister, Roger (runner); Harrow, England, 3/24/1929
Barkley, Charles (basketball); Leeds, Ala., 2/20/1963
Barry, Rick (Richard) (basketball); Elizabeth, N.J., 3/28/1944
Bauer, Hank (Henry) (baseball); East St. Louis, Ill., 7/31/1922
Baugh, Sammy (football); Temple, Tex., 3/17/1914
Bayi, Filbert (runner); Karratu, Tanganyika, 6/23/1953
Baylor, Elgin (basketball); Washington, D.C., 9/16/1934
Beamon, Bob (long jumper); New York City, 8/22/1946
Becker, Boris (tennis); Leiman, W. Germany, 11/22/1967
Bee, Clair (basketball); Cleveland, Ohio **(1896–1983)**
Beliveau, Jean (hockey); Three Rivers, Quebec, Canada, 8/31/1931
Bell, Rickey (football); Inglewood, Calif. **(1949–1984)**
Beman, Deane (golf); Washington, D.C., 4/22/1938
Bench, Johnny (Johnny Lee) (baseball); Oklahoma City, 12/7/1947
Berg, Patty (Patricia Jane) (golf); Minneapolis, 2/13/1918
Berning, Susie Maxwell (golf); Pasadena, Calif., 7/22/1941
Berra, Yogi (Lawrence) (baseball); St. Louis, 5/12/1925
Biletnikoff, Frederick (football); Erie, Pa., 2/23/1943
Bing, Dave (basketball); Washington, D.C., 11/24/1943
Bird, Larry (basketball); French Lick, Ind., 12/7/1956
Blaik, Earl H. (football); Detroit, 2/15/1897
Blanda, George Frederick (football); Youngwood, Pa., 9/17/1927
Blue, Vida (baseball); Mansfield, La., 7/28/1949
Borg, Björn (tennis); Stockholm, 6/6/1956
Boros, Julius (golf); Fairfield, Conn., 3/3/1920
Bossy, Mike (hockey); Montreal, 1/22/1957
Boston, Ralph (long jumper); Laurel, Miss., 5/9/1939
Bradley, Bill (William Warren) (basketball); Crystal City, Mo., 7/28/1943
Bradshaw, Terry (football); Shreveport, La., 9/2/1948
Brathwaite, Chris (track); Eugene, Ore. **(1949–1984)**
Breedlove, Craig (Norman) (speed driving); Los Angeles, 3/23/1938
Brett, George (baseball); Glendale, W. Va., 5/15/1953
Brewer, James (Jim) (baseball); Merced, Calif. **(1937–1987)**
Brock, Louis Clark (baseball); El Dorado, Ark., 6/18/1939
Brown, Jimmy (football); St. Simon Island, Ga., 2/17/1936
Brown, Larry (football); Clairton, Pa., 9/19/1947
Brumel, Valeri (high jumper); Tolbuzino, Siberia, 4/14/1942
Bryant, Paul "Bear" (football); Tuscaloosa, Ala., **(1913–1983)**
Bryant, Rosalyn Evette (track); Chicago, 1/7/1956
Burton, Michael (swimming); Des Moines, Iowa, 7/3/1947
Butkus, Dick (Richard Marvin) (football); Chicago, 12/9/1942
Campanella, Roy (baseball); Homestead, Pa., 11/19/1921
Campbell, Earl (football); Tyler, Tex., 3/29/1955
Caponi, Donna Maria (golf); Detroit, 1/29/1945
Cappelletti, Gino (football); Keewatin, Minn., 3/26/1934
Carew, Rod (Rodney Cline) (baseball); Gatun, Panama, 10/1/1945

Carlos, John (sprinter); New York City, 6/5/1945
Carlton, Steven Norman (baseball); Miami, Fla., 12/22/1944
Carner, Joanne Gunderson, Mrs. Don (golf); Kirkland, Wash., 3/4/1939
Casals, Rosemary (tennis); San Francisco, 9/16/1948
Casper, Billy (golf); San Diego, Calif., 6/24/1931
Caulkins, Tracy (swimming); Winona, Minn., 1/11/1963
Cauthen, Steve (jockey); Covington, Ky., 5/1/1960
Chamberlain, Wilt (Wilton) (basketball); Philadelphia, 8/21/1936
Chandler, Spud (baseball); Commerce, Ga., **(1907–1990)**
Chapot, Frank (equestrian); Camden, N.J., 2/24/1934
Chinaglia, Giorgio (soccer); Carrara, Italy, 1/24/1947
Clarke, Bobby (Robert Earle) (hockey); Flin Flon, Manitoba, Canada, 8/13/1949
Clay, Cassius. *See* Ali, Muhammad
Clemente, Roberto Walker (baseball); Carolina, Puerto Rico **(1934–1972)**
Cobb, Ty (Tyrus Raymond) (baseball); Narrows, Ga., **(1886–1961)**
Cochran, Barbara Ann (skiing); Claremont, N.H., 1/14/1951
Cochran, Marilyn (skiing); Burlington, Vt., 2/7/1950
Cochran, Robert (skiing); Claremont, N.H., 12/11/1951
Coe, Sebastian Newbold (track); London, England, 9/29/1956
Colavito, Rocky (Rocco Domenico) (baseball); New York City, 8/10/1933
Comaneci, Nadia (gymnast); Onesti, Romania, 11/12/1961
Conigliaro, Tony (baseball); Revere, Mass., **(1945–1990)**
Connors, Jimmy (James Scott) (tennis); East St. Louis, Ill., 9/2/1952
Cordero, Angel (jockey); Santurce, Puerto Rico, 5/8/1942
Cournoyer, Yvan Serge (hockey); Drummondville, Quebec, Canada, 11/22/1943
Court, Margaret Smith (tennis); Albury, New South Wales, Australia, 7/16/1942
Cousy, Bob (basketball); New York City, 8/9/1928
Crabbe, Buster (swimming); Scottsdale, Ariz. **(1908–1983)**
Crenshaw, Ben (golf); Austin, Tex., 1/11/1952
Cronin, Joe (baseball executive); San Francisco, **(1906–1984)**
Cruyff, Johan (soccer); Amsterdam, Netherlands, 4/25/47
Csonka, Larry (Lawrence Richard) (football); Stow, Ohio, 12/25/1946
Dancer, Stanley (harness racing); New Egypt, N.J., 7/25/1927
Dantley, Adrian (basketball); Washington, D.C., 2/28/1956
Dark, Alvin (baseball); Comanche, Okla., 1/7/1922
Davenport, Willie (track); Troy, Ala., 6/6/1943
Dawson, Leonard Ray (football); Alliance, Ohio, 6/20/1935
Dean, Dizzy (Jay Hanna) (baseball); Lucas, Ark. **(1911–1974)**
DeBusschere, Dave (basketball); Detroit, 10/16/1940
Delvecchio, Alex Peter (hockey); Fort William, Ontario, Canada, 12/4/1931
Demaret, Jim (golf); Houston **(1910–1983)**
Dempsey, Jack (William H.) (boxing); Manassa, Colo. **(1895–1983)**
DeVicenzo, Roberto (golf); Buenos Aires, 4/14/1923
Dibbs, Edward George (tennis); Brooklyn, New York, 2/23/1951
Dietz, James W. (rowing); New York, N.Y., 1/12/1949
DiMaggio, Joe (baseball); Martinez, Calif., 11/25/1914
Dionne, Marcel (hockey); Drummondville, Quebec, Canada, 8/3/1951
Dominguín, Luis Miguel (matador); Madrid, 12/9/1926
Dorsett, Tony (football); Rochester, Pa., 4/7/1954
Dryden, Kenneth (hockey); Hamilton, Ontario, Canada, 8/4/1947
Drysdale, Don (baseball); Van Nuys, Calif., 7/23/1936
Duran, Roberto (boxing); Panama City, 6/16/1951
Durocher, Leo (baseball); West Springfield, Mass., 7/27/1906
Durr, Francois (tennis); Algiers, Algeria, 12/25/1942
El Cordobés (Manuel Benitez Pérez) (matador); Palma del Rio, Córdoba, Spain, 5/4/1936(?)
Elder, Lee (golf); Dallas, 7/14/1934
Emerson, Roy (tennis); Kingsway, Australia, 11/3/1936
Ender, Kornelia (swimming); Plauen, East Germany, 10/25/1958
Erving, "Dr. J" (Julius) (basketball); Roosevelt, N.Y., 2/22/1950
Espinosa, Nino (baseball); Villa Altagracia, Dominican Republic **(1953–1988)**
Esposito, Phil (Philip Anthony) (hockey); Sault Ste. Marie, Ontario, Canada, 2/20/1942
Evans, Lee (runner); Mendena, Calif., 2/25/1947
Ewbank, Weeb (football); Richmond, Ind., 5/6/1907
Ewing, Patrick (basketball); Kingston, Jamaica, 8/5/1962
Feller, Robert (Bobby) (baseball); Van Meter, Iowa, 11/3/1918

Feuerbach, Allan Dean (track); Preston, Iowa, 1/12/1948
Finley, Charles O. (sportsman); Ensley, Ala., 2/22/1918
Fischer, Bobby (chess); Chicago, 3/9/1943
Fitzsimmons, Bob (Robert Prometheus) (boxing); Cornwall, England **(1862–1917)**
Fleming, Peggy Gale (ice skating); San Jose, Calif., 7/27/1948
Ford, Whitey (Edward) (baseball); New York City, 10/21/1928
Foreman, George (boxing); Marshall, Tex., 1/10/1949
Fosbury, Richard (high jumper); Portland, Ore., 3/6/1947
Fox, Nellie (Jacob Nelson) (baseball); St. Thomas, Pa. **(1927–1975)**
Foxx, James Emory (baseball); Sudlersville, Md. **(1907–1967)**
Foyt, A. J. (auto racing); Houston, 1/16/1935
Francis, Emile (hockey); North Battleford, Sask., Canada, 9/13/1926
Fratianne, Linda (figure skating); Los Angeles, 8/2/1960
Frazier, Joe (boxing); Beauford, S.C., 1/17/1944
Frazier, Walt (basketball); Atlanta, 3/29/1945
Frick, Ford C. (baseball); Wawaka, Ind. **(1894–1978)**
Furillo, Carl (baseball); Stony Creek Mills, Pa. **(1922–1989)**
Furniss, Bruce (swimming); Fresno, Calif., 5/27/1957
Gable, Dan (wrestling); Waterloo, Iowa, 10/25/1945
Gabriel, Roman (football); Wilmington, N.C., 8/5/1940
Gallagher, Michael Donald (skiing); Yonkers, N.Y., 10/3/1941
Garms, Debs (baseball); Glen Rose, Tex. **(1908–1984)**
Garvey, Steve (baseball); Tampa, Fla., 12/22/1948
Gehrig, Lou (Henry Louis) (baseball); New York City **(1903–1941)**
Gehringer, Charlie (baseball); Fowlerville, Mich., 5/11/1903
Geoffrion, "Boom Boom" (Bernie) (hockey); Montreal, 2/14/1931
Gerulaitis, Vitas (tennis); Brooklyn, N.Y., 7/26/1954
Giacomin, Ed (hockey); Sudbury, Ontario, Canada, 6/6/1939
Giamatti, A. Bartlett (baseball); South Hadley, Mass. **(1938–1989)**
Gibson, Bob (baseball); Omaha, Neb., 11/9/1935
Gifford, Frank (football); Santa Monica, Calif., 8/16/1930
Gilbert, Rod (Rodrique) (hockey); Montreal, 7/1/1941
Giles, Warren (baseball executive); Tiskilwa, Ill. **(1896–1979)**
Gilmore, Artis (basketball); Chipley, Fla., 9/21/1949
Glance, Harvey (track); Phenix City, Ala., 3/28/1957
Gonzalez, Pancho (tennis); Los Angeles, 5/9/1928
Goodell, Brian Stuart (swimming); Stockton, Calif., 4/2/1959
Gooden, Dwight (baseball); Tampa, Fla., 11/16/1964
Goodrich, Gail (basketball); Los Angeles, 4/23/1943
Goolagong, Cawley, Evonne (tennis); Griffith, Australia, 7/31/1951
Gossage, Rich "Goose" (baseball); Colorado Springs, Colo., 4/5/1951
Gottfried, Brian (tennis); Baltimore, Md., 1/27/1952
Graf, Steffi (tennis); Mannheim, W. Germany, 6/14/1969
Graham, David (golf); Windsor, Australia, 5/23/1946
Graham, Otto Everett (football); Waukegan, Ill., 12/6/1921
Grange, Red (Harold) (football); Forksville, Pa. **(1904–1991)**
Green, Hubert (golf); Birmingham, Ala., 12/28/1946
Greene, Charles E. (sprinter); Pine Bluff, Ark., 3/21/1945
Greene, "Mean" (Joe); (football); Temple, Tex., 9/24/1946
Gretzky, Wayne (hockey); Brantford, Ont., 1/26/1961
Griese, Bob (Robert Allen) (football); Evansville, Ind., 2/3/1945
Groebli, "Mr. Frick" (Werner) (ice skating); Basil, Switzerland, 4/21/1915
Grove, Lefty (Robert Moses) (baseball); Lonaconing, Md., **(1900–1975)**
Groza, Lou (football); Martins Ferry Ohio, 1/25/1924
Guidry, Ronald Ames (baseball); Lafayette, La., 8/28/1950
Gunter, Nancy Richey (tennis); San Angelo, Tex., 8/23/1942
Halas, George (football); Chicago **(1895–1983)**
Hall, Gary (swimming); Fayetteville, N.C., 8/7/1951
Hamill, Dorothy (figure skating); Chicago, 1956(?)
Hamilton, Scott (figure skating); Bowling Green, Ohio, 8/28/1958
Hammond, Kathy (runner); Sacramento, Calif., 11/2/1951
Harris, Franco (football); Ft. Dix, N.J., 3/7/1950
Hartack, William, Jr. (jockey); Colver, Pa., 12/9/1932
Haughton, William (harness racing); Gloversville, N.Y. **(1923–1986)**
Havlicek, John (basketball); Martins Ferry, Ohio, 4/8/1940
Hayes, Elvin (basketball); Rayville, La., 11/17/1945
Hayes, Woody (football); Upper Arlington, Ohio **(1913–1987)**
Haynie, Sandra (golf); Fort Worth, 6/4/1943
Heiden, Eric (speed skating); Madison, Wis., 6/14/1958
Hencken, John (swimming); Culver City, Calif., 5/29/1954
Henderson, Rickey (baseball); Chicago, 12/25/1958
Henie, Sonja (ice skater); Oslo **(1912–1969)**
Herman, Floyd Caves (Babe) (baseball); Buffalo, N.Y. **(1903–1987)**
Hernandez, Keith (baseball); San Francisco, 10/20/1953
Hershiser, Orel (baseball); Buffalo, N.Y., 9/16/1958
Hickcox, Charles (swimming); Phoenix, Ariz., 2/6/1947
Hines, James (sprinter); Dumas, Ark., 9/10/1946
Hodges, Gil (baseball); Princeton, Ind. **(1924–1972)**
Hogan, Ben (golf); Dublin, Tex., 8/13/1912
Holmes, Larry (boxing); Cuthert, Ga., 11/3/1949

Hornsby, Rogers (baseball); Winters, Tex. **(1896–1963)**
Hornung, Paul (football); Louisville, Ky., 12/23/1935
Houk, Ralph (baseball); Lawrence, Kan., 8/9/1919
Howard, Elston (baseball); St. Louis **(1929–1980)**
Howe, Gordon (hockey); Floral, Sask., Canada, 3/31/1928
Howell, Jim Lee (football); Lonoke, Ark., 9/27/1914
Howser, Dick (baseball); Miami, Fla. **(1937–1987)**
Hubbell, Carl (baseball); Carthage, Mo., 6/22/1903
Huff, Sam (Robert Lee) (football); Morgantown, W. Va., 10/4/1934
Hull, Bobby (hockey); Point Anne, Ontario, Canada, 1/3/1939
Hunter, "Catfish" (Jim) (baseball); Hertford, N.C., 4/8/1946
Huntley, Joni (track); McMinnville, Ore., 8/4/1956
Hutson, Donald (football); Pine Bluff, Ark., 1/31/1913
Insko, Del (harness racing); Amboy, Minn., 7/10/1931
Irwin, Hale (golf); Joplin, Mo., 6/3/1945
Jackson, Reggie (baseball); Wyncote, Pa., 5/18/1946
Jeffries, James J. (boxing); Carroll, Ohio **(1875–1953)**
Jenkins, Ferguson Arthur (baseball); Chatham, Ontario, Canada, 12/13/1943
Jenner, (W.) Bruce (track); Mt. Kisco, N.Y., 10/28/1949
Jezek, Linda (swimming); Palo Alto, Calif., 3/10/1960
Johnson, "Magic" (Earvin) (basketball); E. Lansing, Mich., 8/14/1959
Johnson, Anthony (rowing); Washington, D.C., 11/16/1940
Johnson, Jack (John Arthur) (boxing); Galveston, Tex. **(1876–1946)**
Johnson, Rafer (decathlon); Hillsboro, Tex., 8/18/1935
Johnson, Wilham Julius (Judy) (baseball); Wilmington, Del. **(1899–1989)**
Jones, Deacon (David) (football); Eatonville, Fla., 12/9/1938
Jordan, Michael (basketball); Brooklyn, N.Y., 2/17/1963
Joyner, Florence Griffith (sprinter); Mojave Desert, Calif., 12/21/1959
Juantoreno, Alberto (track); Santiago, Cuba, 12/3/1951
Jurgensen, Sonny (football); Wilmington, N.C., 8/23/1934
Kaat, Jim (baseball); Zeeland, Mich., 11/7/1938
Kaline, Al (Albert) (baseball); Baltimore, 12/19/1934
Keino, Kipchoge (runner); Kapchemoiymo, Kenya 1/?/1940
Kelly, Leroy (football); Philadelphia, 5/20/1942
Kelly, Red (Leonard Patrick) (hockey); Simcoe, Ontario, Canada, 7/9/1927
Killebrew, Harmon (baseball); Payette, Idaho, 6/29/1936
Killy, Jean–Claude (skiing); Saint–Cloud, France, 8/30/1943
Kilmer, Bill (William Orland) (football); Topeka, Kan., 9/5/1939
King, Billie Jean (Bille Jean Moffitt) (tennis); Long Beach, Calif., 11/22/1943
Kinsella, John (swimming); Oak Park, Ill., 8/26/1952
Kluszeewski, Ted (baseball); Argo, Ill. **(1924–1988)**
Kodes, Jan (tennis); Prague, 3/1/1946
Kolb, Claudia (swimming); Hayward, Calif., 12/19/1949
Koosman, Jerry Martin (baseball); Appleton, Minn., 12/23/1942
Korbut, Olga (gymnast); Grodno, Byelorussia, U.S.S.R., 5/16/1955
Koufax, Sandy (Sanford) (baseball); Brooklyn, N.Y., 12/30/1935
Kramer, Jack (tennis); Las Vegas, Nev., 8/1/1921
Kramer, Jerry (football); Jordan, Mont., 1/23/1936
Kuenn, Harvey (baseball); West Allis, Wis. **(1930–1988)**
Kuhn, Bowie Kent (baseball); Takoma Park, Md., 10/28/1926
Kwalik, Ted (Thaddeus John) (football); McKees Rocks, Pa., 4/15/1947
Lafleur, Guy Damien (hockey); Thurson, Quebec, Canada, 8/20/1951
Laird, Ronald (walker); Louisville, Ky., 5/31/1935
Lamonica, Daryle (football); Fresno, Calif., 7/17/1941
Landis, Kenesaw Mountain (1st baseball commissioner); Millville, Ohio **(1866–1944)**
Landry, Tom (football); Mission, Tex., 9/11/1924
Landy, John (runner); Australia, 4/4/1930
Larrieu, Francie (track); Palo Alto, Calif., 11/28/1952
Lasorda, Tom (baseball); Norristown, Pa., 9/22/1927
Laver, Rod (tennis); Rockhampton, Australia, 8/9/1938
Layne, Bobby (football); Lubbock, Texas **(1927–1986)**
Lemieux, Mario (hockey); Montreal, Quebec, Canada, 10/5/1965
Lendl, Ivan (tennis); Prague, 3/7/1960
Leonard, Benny (Benjamin Leiner) (boxing); New York City **(1896–1947)**
Leonard, Sugar Ray (boxing); Wilmington, N.C., 5/17/1956
Lewis, Carl (track); Willingboro, N.J., 7/1/1961
Linehan, Kim (swimming); Bronxville, N.Y., 12/11/1962
Liquori, Marty (runner); Montclair, N.J., 9/11/1949
Little, Floyd Douglas (football); New Haven, Conn., 7/4/1942
Little, Lou (football); Leominster, Mass., **(1893–1979)**
Littler, Gene (golf); La Jolla, Calif., 7/21/1930
Lloyd, Chris Evert (Christine Marie) (tennis); Fort Lauderdale, Fla., 12/21/1954
Lombardi, Vince (football); Brooklyn, N.Y. **(1913–1970)**
Longden, Johnny (horse racing); Wakefield, England, 2/14/1907

Lopez, Al (baseball); Tampa, Fla., 8/20/1908
Lopez, Nancy (golf); Torrance, Calif., 1/6/1957
Louis, Joe (Joe Louis Barrow) (boxing); Lafayette, Ala. **(1914–1981)**
Lynn, Frederic Michael (baseball); Chicago, Ill., 2/3/1952
Lynn, Janet (figure skating); Rockford, Ill., 4/6/1953
Mack, Connie (Cornelius Alexander McGillicuddy) (baseball executive); East Brookfield, Mass. **(1862–1956)**
Mackey, John (football); New York City, 9/24/1941
Mahovlich, Frank (Francis William) (hockey); Timmins, Ontario, Canada, 1/10/1938
Mahre, Phil (skiiing); White Pass, Wash., 5/10/1957
Malone, Moses (basketball); Petersburg, Va., 3/23/1955
Mandlikova, Hana (tennis); Prague, Czechoslovakia, 2/1962
Mann, Carol (golf); Buffalo, N.Y., 2/3/1941
Manning, Madeline (runner); Cleveland, 1/11/1948
Mantle, Mickey Charles (baseball); Spavinaw, Okla., 10/20/1931
Maravich, "Pistol Pete" (Peter); Aliquippa, Pa. **(1948–1988)**
Marble, Alice (tennis); Palm Springs, Calif. **(1913–1990)**
Marciano, Rocky (boxing); Brockton, Mass. **(1923–1969)**
Marichal, Juan (baseball); Laguna Verde, Montecristi, Dominican Republic, 10/20/1937
Maris, Roger (baseball); Hibbing, Minn. **(1934–1985)**
Martin, Billy (Alfred Manuel) (baseball); Berkeley, Calif. **(1928–1989)**
Martin, Rick (Richard Lionel) (hockey); Verdun, Quebec, Canada, 7/26/1951
Mathews, Ed (Edwin) (baseball); Texarkana, Tex., 10/13/1931
Matson, Randy (shot putter); Kilgore, Tex., 3/5/1945
Mays, Willie (baseball); Westfield, Ala., 5/6/1931
McAdoo, Bob (basketball); Greensboro, N.C., 9/25/1951
McCarthy, Joe (Joseph Vincent) (baseball); Philadelphia **(1887–1978)**
McCovey, Willie Lee (baseball); Mobile, Ala., 1/10/1938
McDonald, Lanny (hockey); Hanna, Alberta, Canada, 2/16/1953
McEnroe, John Patrick, Jr. (tennis); Wiesbaden, Germany, 2/16/1959
McGraw, John Joseph (baseball); Truxton, N.Y. **(1873–1934)**
McLain, Dennis (baseball); Chicago, 3/24/1944
McMillan, Kathy Laverne (track); Raeford, N.C., 11/7/1957
Merrill, Janice (track); New London, Conn., 6/18/1962
Meyer, Deborah (swimming); Haddonfield, N.J., 8/14/1952
Middlecoff, Cary (golf); Halls, Tenn., 1/6/1921
Mikita, Stan (hockey); Sokolce, Czechoslovakia, 5/20/1940
Milburn, Rodney, Jr. (hurdler); Opelousas, La., 5/18/1950
Miller, Johnny (golf); San Francisco, 4/29/1947
Montgomery, Jim (swimming); Madison, Wis., 1/24/1955
Moore, Archie (boxing); Benoit, Miss., 12/13/1916
Morgan, Joe Leonard (baseball); Bonham, Tex., 9/19/1943
Morrall, Earl (football); Muskegon, Mich., 5/17/1934
Morton, Craig L. (football); Flint, Mich., 2/5/1943
Mosconi, Wilie (pocket billiards); Philadelphia, 6/27/1913
Moser, Annemarie. *See* Proell, Annemarie.
Moses, Edward Corley (track); Dayton, Ohio, 8/31/1958
Mungo, Van Lingo (baseball); Pageland, S.C. **(1911–1985)**
Munson, Thurman (baseball); Akron, Ohio **(1947–1979)**
Murphy, Calvin (basketball); Norwalk, Conn., 5/9/1948
Musial, Stan (baseball); Donora, Pa., 11/21/1920
Myers, Linda (archery); York, Pa., 6/19/1947
Naber, John (swimming); Evanston, Ill., 1/20/1956
Namath, Joe (Joseph William) (football); Beaver Falls, Pa., 5/31/1943
Nastase, Ilie (tennis); Bucharest, 7/19/1946
Navratilova, Martina (tennis); Prague, 10/18/1956
Nehemiah, Renaldo (track); Newark, N.J., 3/24/1959
Nelson, Cindy (skiing); Lutsen, Minn., 8/19/1955
Newcombe, John (tennis); Sydney, Australia, 5/23/1943
Niekro, Phil (baseball); Lansing, Ohio, 4/1/1939
Nicklaus, Jack (golf); Columbus, Ohio, 1/21/1940
Norman, Greg(ory) (golf); Mount Isa, Australia, 2/10/1955
North, Lowell (yachting); Springfield, Mo., 12/2/1929
Oerter, Al (discus thrower); New York City, 9/19/1936
Okker, Tom (tennis); Amsterdam, 2/22/1944
Oldfield, Barney (racing driver); Fulton County, Ohio **(1878–1946)**
Oliva, Tony (Pedro) (baseball); Pinar Del Rio, Cuba, 7/20/1940
Olsen, Merlin Jay (football); Logan, Utah, 9/15/1940
O'Malley, Walter (baseball executive); New York City **(1903–1979)**
Orantes, Manuel (tennis); Granada, Spain, 2/6/1949
Orr, Bobby (hockey); Parry Sound, Ontario, Canada, 3/20/1948
Ovett, Steve (track); Brighton, England, 10/9/1955
Owens, Jesse (track); Decatur, Ala. **(1914–1980)**
Pace, Darrell (archery); Cincinnati, 10/23/1956
Paige, Satchell (Leroy) (baseball); Mobile, Ala. **(1906–1982)**
Palmer, Arnold (golf); Latrobe, Pa., 9/10/1929
Palmer, James Alvin (baseball); New York City, 10/15/1945

Parent, Bernard Marcel (hockey); Montreal, 4/3/1945
Park, Brad (Douglas Bradford) (hockey); Toronto, Ontario, Canada, 7/6/1948
Parseghian, Ara (football); Akron, Ohio, 5/21/1923
Pasarell, Charles (tennis); San Juan, Puerto Rico, 2/12/1944
Patterson, Floyd (boxing); Waco, N.C., 1/4/1935
Peete, Calvin (golf); Detroit, Mich., 7/18/1943
Pelé (Edson Arantes do Nascimento) (soccer); Tres Coracoes, Brazil, 10/23/1940
Perry, Gaylord (baseball); Williamston, N.C., 9/15/1938
Perry, Jim (baseball); Williamston, N.C., 9/15/1938
Pettit, Bob (basketball); Baton Rouge, La., 12/12/1932
Petty, Richard Lee (auto racing); Randleman, N.C., 7/2/1937
Pincay, Laffit, Jr. (jockey); Panama City, Panama, 12/29/1946
Plager, Barclay (ice hockey); Kirkland Lake, Ontario **(1941–1988)**
Plante, Jacques (hockey); Sahwinigan Falls, Quebec, Canada, 1/17/1929
Player, Gary (golf); Johannesburg, South Africa, 11/1/1935
Plunkett, Jim (football); San Jose, Calif., 12/5/1947
Potvin, Denis Charles (hockey); Hull, Quebec, Canada, 10/29/1953
Powell, Boog (John) (baseball); Lakeland, Fla., 8/17/1941
Prefontaine, Steve Roland (runner); Coos Bay, Ore. **(1951–1975)**
Prince, Bob (baseball announcer); Pittsburgh **(1917–1985)**
Proell, Annemarie Moser (Alpine skier); Kleinarl, Austria, 3/27/1953
Ralston, Dennis (tennis); Bakersfield, Calif., 7/27/1942
Rankin, Judy Torluemke (golf); St. Louis, Mo., 2/18/1945
Raschi, Vic (baseball); West Springfield, Mass. **(1919–1988)**
Ratelle, Jean (Joseph Gilbert Yvon Jean) (hockey); St. Jean, Quebec, Canada, 10/29/1953
Rawls, Betsy (Elizabeth Earle) (golf); Spartanburg, S.C., 5/4/1928
Reed, Willis (basketball); Hico, La., 6/25/1942
Reese, Pee Wee (Harold) (baseball); Ekron, Ky., 7/23/1919
Resch, Glenn "Chico" (hockey); Moose Jaw, Saskatchewan, Canada, 7/10/1948
Richard, Maurice (hockey); Montreal, 8/14/1924
Riessen, Martin (tennis); Hinsdale, Ill., 12/4/1941
Rigney, William (baseball); Alameda, Calif., 1/29/1918
Rizzuto, Phil (baseball); New York City, 9/25/1918
Roark, Helen Wills Moody (tennis); Centerville, Calif., 10/6/1906
Robertson, Oscar (basketball); Charlotte, Tenn., 11/24/1938
Robinson, Arnie (track); San Diego, Calif., 4/7/1948
Robinson, Brooks (baseball); Little Rock, Ark., 5/18/1937
Robinson, Frank (baseball); Beaumont, Tex., 8/31/1935
Robinson, Jackie (baseball); Cairo, Ga. **(1919–1972)**
Robinson, Larry Clark (hockey); Marvelville, Ontario, Canada, 6/2/1951
Robinson, "Sugar" Ray (boxing); Detroit **(1920–1989)**
Rockne, Knute Kenneth (football); Voss, Norway **(1888–1931)**
Rockwell, Martha (skiing); Providence, R.I., 4/26/1944
Rono, Harry (track); Kiptaragon, Kenya, 2/12/1952
Rooney, Art (football); Pittsburgh, Pa. **(1901–1988)**
Rose, Pete (Peter Edward) (baseball); Cincinnati, 4/14/1942
Rosenbloom, Maxie (boxing); New York City **(1904–1976)**
Rosewall, Ken (tennis); Sydney, Australia, 11/2/1934
Rote, Kyle (football); San Antonio, 10/27/1928
Roush, Edd (baseball); Oakland City, Ind. **(1893–1988)**
Rozelle, Pete (Alvin Ray) (commissioner of National Football League); South Gate, Calif., 3/1/1926
Rudolph, Wilma Glodean (sprinter); St. Bethlehem, Tenn., 6/23/1940
Russell, Bill (basketball); Monroe, La., 2/12/1934
Ruth, Babe (George Herman Ruth) (baseball); Baltimore **(1895–1948)**
Rutherford, Johnny (auto racing); Fort Worth, 3/12/1938
Ryan, Nolan (Lynn Nolan, Jr.) (baseball); Refugio, Tex., 1/31/1947
Ryon, Luann (archery); Long Beach, Calif., 1/13/1953
Ryun, Jim (runner); Wichita, Kan., 4/29/1947
Salazar, Alberto (track); Havana, 8/7/1958
Samuels, Howard (horse racing soccer); New York City **(1920–1984)**
Santana, Manuel (Manuel Santana Martinez) (tennis); Chamartin, Spain, 5/10/1938
Sayers, Gale (football); Wichita, Kan., 5/30/1943
Schmidt, Mike (baseball); Dayton, Ohio, 9/27/1949
Shoendienst, Al (Albert) (baseball); Germantown, Ill., 2/2/1923
Schollander, Donald (swimming); Charlotte, N.C., 4/30/1946
Seagren, Bob (Robert Lloyd) (pole vaulter); Pomona, Calif., 10/17/1946
Seaver, Tom (baseball); Fresno, Calif., 11/17/1944
Seidler, Maren (track); Brooklyn, N.Y., 6/11/1962
Selke, Frank (ice hockey); Canada **(1893–1985)**
Sewell, Joe (baseball); Titus, Ala., **(1898–1990)**
Shepherd, Lee (auto racing) **(1945–1985)**
Shero, Fred (hockey); Camden, N.J. **(1945–1990)**

Shoemaker, Willie (jockey); Fabens, Tex., 8/19/1931
Shore, Eddie (ice hockey); Saskatchewan, Canada (1902–1985)
Shorter, Frank (runner); Munich, Germany, 10/31/1947
Shriver, Pam (tennis); Baltimore, 7/4/1962
Shula, Don (Donald Francis) (football); Grand River, Ohio, 1/4/1930
Silvester, Jay (discus thrower); Tremonton, Utah, 2/27/1937
Simpson, O.J. (Orenthal James) (football); San Francisco, 7/9/1947
Sims, Billy (football); St. Louis, 9/18/1955
Smith, Bubba (Charles Aaron) (football); Orange, Tex., 2/28/1945
Smith, Ronnie Ray (sprinter); Los Angeles, 3/28/1949
Smith, Stanley Roger (tennis); Pasadena, Calif., 12/14/1946
Smith, Tommie (sprinter); Clarksville, Tex., 6/5/1944
Smoke, Marcia Jones (canoeing); Oklahoma City, 7/18/1941
Snead, Sam (golf); Hot Springs, Va., 5/27/1912
Sneva, Tom (auto racing); Spokane, Wash., 6/1/1948
Snider, Duke (Edwin) (baseball); Los Angeles, 9/19/1926
Solomon, Harold (tennis); Washington, D.C., 9/17/1952
Spahn, Warren (baseball); Buffalo, N.Y., 4/23/1921
Speaker, Tristram (baseball); Hubbard City, Tex. (1888–1958)
Spencer, Brian (ice hockey); Fort St. James, British Columbia (1949–1988)
Spinks, Leon (boxing); St. Louis, 7/11/1953
Spitz, Mark (swimming); Modesto, Calif., 2/10/1950
Stabler, Kenneth (football); Foley, Ala., 12/25/1945
Stagg, Amos Alonzo (football); West Orange, N.J. (1862–1965)
Stargell, Willie (Wilver Dornell) (baseball); Earlsboro, Okla., 3/6/1941
Starr, Bart (football); Montgomery, Ala., 1/9/1934
Staub, "Rusty" (Daniel) (baseball); New Orleans, 4/4/1944
Staubach, Roger (football); Cincinnati, 2/5/1942
Steinkraus, William C. (equestrian); Cleveland, 10/12/1925
Stenerud, Jan (football); Fetsund, Norway, 11/26/1942
Stengel, Casey (Charles Dillon) (baseball); Kansas City, Mo. (1891–1975)
Stenmark, Ingemar (Alpine skier); Tarnaby, Sweden, 3/18/1956
Stockton, Richard LaClede (tennis); New York City, 2/18/1951
Stones, Dwight Edwin (track); Los Angeles, 12/6/1953
Strawberry, Darryl (baseball); Los Angeles, 3/12/1962
Sullivan, John Lawrence (boxing); Boston (1858–1918)
Sutton, Don (Donald Howard) (baseball); Clio, Ala., 4/2/1945
Swann, Lynn (football); Alcoa, Tenn., 3/7/1952
Tanner, Leonard Roscoe III (tennis); Chattanooga, Tenn., 10/15/1951
Tarkenton, Fran (Francis) (football); Richmond, Va., 2/3/1940
Tebbetts, Birdie (George R.) (baseball); Nashua, N.H., 11/10/1914
Theismann, Joe (football); New Brunswick, N.J., 9/9/1946
Thoeni, Gustavo (Alpine skier); Trafoi, Italy, 2/28/1951
Thomas, Isiah (basketball); Chicago, Ill., 4/30/1961
Thompson, David (basketball); Shelby, N.C., 7/13/1954
Thorpe, Jim (James Francis) (all–around athlete); nr. Prague, Okla. (1888–1953)
Tilden, William Tatem II (tennis); Philadelphia (1893–1953)
Tittle, Y. A. (Yelberton Abraham) (football); Marshall, Tex., 10/24/1926
Tooney, William (decathlon); Philadelphia, 1/10/1939
Trevino, Lee (golf); Dallas, 12/1/1939
Trottier, Bryan (hockey); Val Marie, Sask., Canada, 7/17/1956

Tunney, Gene (James J.) (boxing); New York City (1898–1978)
Tyus, Wyomia (runner); Griffin, Ga., 8/29/1945
Ueberroth, Peter (baseball); Evanston, Ill., 9/2/1937
Unitas, John (football); Pittsburgh, 5/7/1933
Unser, Al (auto racing); Albuquerque, N. Mex., 5/29/1939
Unser, Bobby (auto racing); Albuquerque, N. Mex., 2/20/1934
Valenzuela, Fernando (baseball); Sonora, Mexico, 11/1/1960
Van Brocklin, Norm (football); Eagle Butte, S. Dak. (1926–1983)
Vilas, Guillermo (tennis); Mar del Plata, Argentina, 8/17/1952
Viola, Frank (baseball); Hempstead, N.Y., 4/19/1960
Viren, Lasse (track); Myrskyla, Finland, 7/12/1949
Wade, Virginia (tennis); Bournemouth, England, 7/10/1945
Wagner, Honus (John Peter Honus) (baseball); Carnegie, Pa. (1867–1955)
Waitz, Grete (Andersen) (running); Oslo, Norway, 10/1/1953
Wakefield, Dick (baseball); Chicago (1921–1985)
Walcott, Jersey Joe (Arnold Cream) (boxing); Merchantville, N.J., 1/31/1914
Walsh, Adam (football) (1902–1985)
Walton, Bill (basketball); La Mesa, Calif., 11/5/1952
Waterfield, Bob (football); Burbank, Calif (1921–1983)
Watson, Martha Rae (track); Long Beach, Calif., 8/19/1946
Watson, Tom (golf); Kansas City, Mo., 9/4/1949
Weaver, Earl (baseball); St. Louis, 8/14/1930
Webster, Alex (football); Kearny, N.J., 4/19/1931
Weiskopf, Tom (golf); Massillon, Ohio, 11/9/1942
Weiss, George (baseball executive); New Haven, Conn. (1895–1972)
Weissmuller, Johnny (swimmer and actor); Windber, Pa. (1904–1984)
Weld, Philip (sailing); Cambridge, Mass. (1915–1984)
West, Jerry (basketball); Cheylan, W. Va., 5/28/1938
White, Willye B. (long jumper); Money, Miss., 1/1/1936
Whitworth, Kathy (golf); Monahans, Tex., 9/27/1939
Widing, Juha (ice hockey); Vancouver, Canada (1948–1985)
Wilkens, Mac Maurice (track); Eugene, Ore., 11/15/1950
Wilkins, Lennie (basketball); 11/25/1937
Wilkinson, Bud (football); Minneapolis, 4/23/1916
Williams, Del (football); New Orleans (1945–1984)
Williams, Dick (baseball); St. Louis, 5/7/1929
Williams, Ted (baseball); San Diego, Calif., 8/30/1918
Wills, Maury (baseball); Washington, D.C., 10/2/1932
Winfield, Dave (baseball); St. Paul, Minn., 10/3/1951
Wohlhuter, Richard C. (runner); Geneva, Ill., 12/23/1945
Wood, "Smokey" (Joseph) (baseball); Kansas City, Mo. (1890–1985)
Woodhead, Cynthia (swimming); Riverside, Calif., 2/7/1964
Wottle, David James (runner); Canton, Ohio, 8/7/1950
Wright, Mickey (Mary Kathryn) (golf); San Diego, Calif., 2/14/1935
Yarborough, Cale (William Caleb) (auto racing); Timmonsville, S.C., 3/27/1939
Yarbrough, Leeroy (auto racing); Jacksonville, Fla. (1938–1984)
Yastrzemski, Carl (baseball); Southampton, N.Y., 8/22/1939
Young, Cy (Denton True) (baseball); Gilmore, Ohio (1867–1955)
Young, Shelia (speed skater, bicycle racer); Detroit, 10/14/1950
Zaharias, Babe Didrikson (golf); Port Arthur, Tex. (1913–1956)

Yachting

The word "yacht" is of Dutch origin and the first "yacht race" of record in the English language was a sailing contest from Greenwich to Gravesend and return in 1662 between a Dutch yacht and an English yacht designed and, at some part of the race, sailed by Charles II of England. The royal yacht won the contest.

The first yacht club was organized at Cork, Ireland, in 1720 under the name of the Cork Harbour Water Club, later changed to the Royal Cork Yacht Club. The Royal Yacht Squadron was organized at Cowes in 1812 and the name changed to the Royal Yacht Club in 1820. The New York Yacht Clue was organized aboard the Stevens schooner "Gimcrack" on July 30, 1844, and a clubhouse erected at Elysian Fields, Hoboken, N.J., the following year.

Bowling

The game of bowling in the United States is an indoor development of the more ancient outdoor game that survives as lawn bowling. The outdoor game is prehistoric in origin and probably goes back to Primitive Man and round stones that were rolled at some target. It is believed that a game something like nine-pins was popular among the Dutch, Swiss and Germans as long ago as A.D. 1200 at which time the game was played outdoors with an alley consisting of a single plank 12 to 18 inches wide along which was rolled a ball toward three rows of three pins each placed at the far end of the alley. When the first indoor alleys were built and how the game was modified from time to time are matters of dispute.

It is supposed that the early settlers of New Amsterdam (New York City) being Dutch, they brought their two bowling games with them. About a century ago the game of nine-pins was flourishing in the United States but so corrupted by gambling on matches that it was barred by law in New York and Connecticut. Since the law specifically barred "nine-pins," it was eventually evaded by adding another pin and thus legally making it a new game.

Various organizations were formed to make rules for bowling and supervise competition in the United States but none was successful until the American Bowling Congress, organized Sept. 9, 1895, became the ruling body.

HOCKEY

Ice hockey, by birth and upbringing a Canadian game, is an offshoot of field hockey. Some historians say that the first ice hockey game was played in Montreal in December 1879 between two teams composed almost exclusively of McGill University students, but others assert that earlier hockey games took place in Kingston, Ontario, or Halifax, Nova Scotia. In the Montreal game of 1879, there were fifteen players on a side, who used an assortment of crude sticks to keep the puck in motion. Early rules allowed nine men on a side, but the number was reduced to seven in 1886 and later to six.

The first governing body of the sport was the Amateur Hockey Association of Canada, organized in 1887. In the winter of 1894–95, a group of college students from the United States visited Canada and saw hockey played. They became enthused over the game and introduced it as a winter sport when they returned home. The first professional league was the International Hockey League,

which operated in northern Michigan in 1904–06.

Until 1910, professionals and amateurs were allowed to play together on "mixed teams," but this arrangement ended with the formation of the first "big league," the National Hockey Association, in eastern Canada in 1910. The Pacific Coast League was organized in 1911 for western Canadian hockey. The league included Seattle and later other American cities. The National Hockey League replaced the National Hockey Association in 1917. Boston, in 1924, was the first American city to join that circuit. The league expanded to include western cities in 1967. The Stanley Cup was competed for by "mixed teams" from 1894 to 1910, thereafter by professionals. It was awarded to the winner of the N.H.L. playoffs from 1926–67 and now to the league champion. The World Hockey Association was organized in October 1972 and was dissolved after the 1978–79 season when the N.H.L. absorbed four of the teams.

STANLEY CUP WINNERS

Emblematic of World Professional Championship; N.H.L. Championship after 1967

1894	Montreal A.A.A.	1924	Montreal Canadiens	1952	Detroit Red Wings
1895	Montreal Victorias	1925	Victoria Cougars	1953	Montreal Canadiens
1896	Winnipeg Victorias	1926	Montreal Maroons	1954–55	Detroit Red Wings
1897–99	Montreal Victorias	1927	Ottawa Senators	1956–60	Montreal Canadiens
1900	Montreal Shamrocks	1928	N.Y. Rangers	1961	Chicago Black Hawks
1901	Winnipeg Victorias	1929	Boston Bruins	1962–64	Toronto Maple Leafs
1902	Montreal A.A.A.	1930–31	Montreal Candiens	1965–66	Montreal Canadiens
1903–05	Ottawa Silver Seven	1932	Toronto Maple Leafs	1967	Toronto Maple Leafs
1906	Montreal Wanderers	1933	N.Y. Rangers	1968–69	Montreal Canadiens
1907	Kenora Thistles[1]	1934	Chicago Black Hawks	1970	Boston Bruins
1907	Mont. Wanderers[2]	1935	Montreal Maroons	1971	Montreal Canadiens
1908	Montreal Wanderers	1936–37	Detroit Red Wings	1972	Boston Bruins
1909	Ottawa Senators	1938	Chicago Red Hawks	1973	Montreal Canadiens
1910	Montreal Wanderers	1939	Boston Bruins	1974–75	Philadelphia Flyers
1911	Ottawa Senators	1940	N.Y. Rangers	1976–79	Montreal Canadiens
1912–13	Quebec Bulldogs	1941	Boston Bruins	1980–83	New York Islanders
1914	Toronto	1942	Toronto Maple Leafs	1984	Edmonton Oilers
1915	Vancouver Millionaires	1943	Detroit Red Wings	1985	Edmonton Oilers
1916	Montreal Canadiens	1944	Montreal Canadiens	1986	Montreal Canadiens
1917	Seattle Metropolitans	1945	Toronto Maple Leafs	1987	Edmonton Oilers
1918	Toronto Arenas	1946	Montreal Canadiens	1988	Edmonton Oilers
1919	No champion	1947–49	Toronto Maple Leafs	1989	Calgary Flames
1920–21	Ottawa Senators	1950	Detroit Red Wings	1990	Edmonton Oilers
1922	Toronto St. Patricks	1951	Toronto Maple Leafs	1991	Pittsburgh Penguins
1923	Ottawa Senators				1. January. 2. March.

NATIONAL HOCKEY LEAGUE YEARLY TROPHY WINNERS

The Hart Trophy—Most Valuable Player

1924	Frank Nighbor, Ottawa	1939	Toe Blake, Montreal Canadiens	1957–58	Gordon Howe, Detroit
1925	Billy Burch, Hamilton	1940	Eddie Goodfellow, Detroit	1959	Andy Bathgate, N.Y. Rangers
1926	Nels Stewart, Montreal Maroons	1941	Bill Cowley, Boston	1960	Gordon Howe, Detroit
		1942	Tom Anderson, N.Y. Americans	1961	Bernie Geoffrion, Montreal Canadiens
1927	Herb Gardiner, Montreal Canadiens	1943	Bill Cowley, Boston		
		1944	Babe Pratt, Toronto	1962	Jacques Plante, Montreal Canadiens
1928	Howie Morenz, Montreal Canadiens	1945	Elmer Lach, Montreal Canadiens		
				1963	Gordon Howe, Detroit
1929	Roy Worters, N.Y. Americans	1946	Max Bentley, Chicago	1964	Jean Beliveau, Montreal Canadiens
1930	Nels Stewart, Montreal Maroons	1947	Maurice Richard, Montreal Canadiens		
				1965–66	Bobby Hull, Chicago
1931–32	Howie Morenz, Montreal Canadiens	1948	Buddy O'Connor, N.Y. Rangers	1967–68	Stan Mikita, Chicago
		1949	Sid Abel, Detroit	1969	Phil Esposito, Boston
1933	Eddie Shore, Boston	1950	Chuck Rayner, N.Y. Rangers	1970–72	Bobby Orr, Boston
1934	Aurel Joliat, Montreal Canadiens	1951	Milt Schmidt, Boston	1973	Bobby Clarke, Philadelphia
		1952–53	Gordon Howe, Detroit	1974	Phil Esposito, Boston
1935–36	Eddie Shore, Boston	1954	Al Rollins, Chicago	1975–76	Bobby Clarke, Philadelphia
1937	Babe Siebert, Montreal Canadiens	1955	Ted Kennedy, Toronto	1977–78	Guy Lafleur, Montreal
1938	Eddie Shore, Boston	1956	Jean Belveau, Montreal Canadiens	1979	Bryan Trottier, N.Y. Islanders

1980	Wayne Gretzky, Edmonton
1981	Wayne Gretzky, Edmonton
1982	Wayne Gretzky, Edmonton
1983	Wayne Gretzky, Edmonton
1984	Wayne Gretzky, Edmonton
1985	Wayne Gretzky, Edmonton
1986	Wayne Gretzky, Edmonton
1987	Wayne Gretzky, Edmonton
1988	Mario Lemieux, Pittsburgh
1989	Wayne Gretzky, Los Angeles
1990	Mark Messier, Edmonton
1991	Brett Hull, St. Louis

Vezina Trophy—Leading Goalkeeper

1956–60	Jacques Plante, Montreal
1961	Johnny Bower, Toronto
1962	Jacques Plante, Montreal
1963	Glenn Hall, Chicago
1964	Charlie Hodge, Montreal
1965	Terry Sawchuk—Johnny Bower, Toronto
1966	Lorne Worsley—Charlie Hodge, Montreal
1967	Glen Hall—Denis DeJordy, Chicago
1968	Lorne Worsley—Rogatien Vachon, Montreal
1969	Glen Hall—Jacques Plante, St. Louis
1970	Tony Esposito, Chicago
1971	Ed Giacomin—Gilles Villemure, New York
1972	Tony Esposito—Gary Smith, Chicago
1973	Ken Dryden, Montreal
1974	Bernie Parent, Philadelphia and Tony Esposito, Chicago
1975	Bernie Parent, Philadelphia
1976	Ken Dryden, Montreal
1977–79	Ken Dryden—Michel Larocque, Montreal
1980	Bob Sauve—Don Edwards, Buffalo
1981	Richard Sevigny, Denis Herron and Michel Larocque, Montreal
1982	Billy Smith, New York Islanders
1983	Pete Peeters, Boston
1984	Tom Barrasso, Buffalo
1985	Pelle Lindbergh, Philadelphia
1986	John Vanbiesbrouck, New York Rangers
1987	Ron Hextall, Philadelphia
1988	Grant Fuhr, Edmonton
1989	Patrick Roy, Montreal
1990	Patrick Roy, Montreal
1991	Ed Belfour, Chicago

James Norris Trophy— Defenseman

1954	Red Kelly, Detroit
1955–58	Doug Harvey, Montreal
1959	Tom Johnson, Montreal
1960–62	Doug Harvey, Montreal; New York (62)
1963–65	Pierre Pilote, Chicago
1966	Jacques Laperriere, Montreal
1967	Harry Howell, New York
1968–75	Bobby Orr, Boston
1976	Denis Potvin, N.Y. Islanders
1977	Larry Robinson, Montreal
1978–79	Denis Potvin, N.Y. Islanders
1980	Larry Robinson, Montreal
1981	Randy Carlyle, Pittsburgh
1982	Doug Wilson, Chicago
1983–84	Rod Langway, Washington
1985	Paul Coffey, Edmonton
1986	Paul Coffey, Edmonton
1987	Ray Bourque, Boston
1988	Ray Bourque, Boston
1989	Chris Chelios, Montreal
1990	Ray Bourque, Boston
1991	Ray Bourque, Boston

Lady Byng Trophy— Sportsmanship

1960	Don McKenney, Boston
1961	Red Kelly, Detroit
1962–63	Dave Keon, Toronto
1964	Ken Wharram, Chicago
1965	Bobby Hull, Chicago
1966	Alex Delvecchio, Detroit
1967–68	Stan Mikita, Chicago
1969	Alex Delvecchio, Detroit
1970	Phil Goyette, St. Louis
1971	John Bucyk, Boston
1972	Jean Ratelle, New York
1973	Gil Perrault, Buffalo
1974	John Bucyk, Boston
1975	Marcel Dionne, Detroit
1976	Jean Ratelle, N.Y. Rangers—Boston
1977	Marcel Dionne, Los Angeles
1978	Butch Goring, Los Angeles
1979	Bob MacMillan, Atlanta
1980	Wayne Gretzky, Edmonton
1981	Rick Kehoe, Pittsburgh
1982	Rick Middleton, Boston
1983–84	Mike Bossy, N.Y. Islanders
1985	Jari Kurri, Edmonton
1986	Mike Bossy, N.Y. Islanders
1987	Joe Mullen, Calgary
1988	Mats Naslund, Montreal
1989	Joe Mullen, Calgary
1990	Brett Hull, St. Louis
1991	Wayne Gretzky, Los Angeles

Calder Trophy—Rookie

1962	Bobby Rousseau, Montreal
1963	Kent Douglas, Toronto
1964	Jacques Laperriere, Montreal
1965	Roger Crozier, Detroit
1966	Brit Selby, Toronto
1967	Bobby Orr, Boston
1968	Derek Sanderson, Boston
1969	Danny Grant, Minnesota
1970	Tony Esposito, Chicago
1971	Gilbert Perrault, Buffalo
1972	Ken Dryden, Montreal
1973	Steve Vickers, New York Rangers
1974	Denis Potvin, N.Y. Islanders
1975	Eric Vail, Atlanta
1976	Bryan Trottier, N.Y. Islanders
1977	Willi Plett, Atlanta
1978	Mike Bossy, N.Y. Islanders
1979	Bobby Smith, Minnesota
1980	Ray Bourque, Boston
1981	Peter Stastny, Quebec
1982	Dale Hawerchuk, Winnipeg
1983	Steve Larmer, Chicago
1984	Tom Barrasso, Buffalo
1985	Mario Lemieux, Pittsburgh
1986	Gary Suter, Calgary
1987	Luc Robitaille, Los Angeles
1988	Joe Nieuwendyk, Calgary
1989	Brian Leetch, N.Y. Rangers
1990	Sergei Makarov, Calgary
1991	Ed Belfour, Chicago

Art Ross Trophy—Leading scorer

1955	Bernie Geoffrion, Montreal
1956	Jean Beliveau, Montreal
1957	Gordie Howe, Detroit
1958–59	Dickie Moore, Montreal
1960	Bobby Hull, Chicago
1961	Bernie Geoffrion, Montreal
1962	Bobby Hull, Chicago
1963	Gordie Howe, Detroit
1964–65	Stan Mikita, Chicago
1966	Bobby Hull, Chicago
1967–68	Stan Mikita, Chicago
1969	Phil Esposito, Boston
1970	Bobby Orr, Boston
1971–74	Phil Esposito, Boston
1975	Bobby Orr, Boston
1976–78	Guy Lafleur, Montreal
1979	Bryan Trottier, N.Y. Islanders
1980	Marcel Dionne, Los Angeles
1981–87	Wayne Gretzky, Edmonton
1988	Mario Lemieux, Pittsburgh
1989	Mario Lemieux, Pittsburgh
1990	Wayne Gretzky, Los Angeles
1991	Wayne Gretzky, Los Angeles

N.H.L. CHAMPIONS
Wales Trophy

1939	Boston
1940	Boston
1941	Boston
1942	New York
1943	Detroit
1944–47	Montreal
1948	Toronto
1948–55	Detroit
1956	Montreal
1957	Detroit
1958–62	Montreal
1963	Toronto
1964	Montreal
1965	Detroit
1966	Montreal
1967	Chicago

Eastern Division

1968–69	Montreal
1970	Chicago
1971	Boston
1972	Boston
1973	Montreal
1974	Boston

Wales Conference

1975	Buffalo
1976–79	Montreal
1980	Buffalo
1981	Montreal
1982	New York Islanders
1983	New York Islanders
1984	New York Islanders

1985	Philadelphia
1986	Montreal
1987	Philadelphia
1988	Boston
1989	Montreal
1990	Boston
1991	Pittsburgh

CAMPBELL BOWL

Western Division

1968	Philadelphia
1969	St. Louis
1970	St. Louis
1971–73	Chicago
1974	Philadelphia

Campbell Conference

1975	Philadelphia
1976–77	Philadelphia
1978–79	N.Y. Islanders
1980	Philadelphia
1981	New York Islanders
1982	Edmonton
1983	Edmonton
1984	Edmonton
1985	Edmonton
1986	Calgary
1987	Edmonton
1988	Edmonton Oilers
1989	Calgary
1990	Edmonton
1991	Minnesota

NATIONAL HOCKEY LEAGUE
FINAL STANDING OF THE CLUBS—1990–91

PRINCE OF WALES CONFERENCE
Patrick Division

	W	L	T	Pts	GF	GA
Pittsburgh	41	33	6	88	342	305
N.Y. Rangers	36	31	13	85	297	265
Washington	37	36	7	81	258	258
New Jersey	32	33	15	79	272	264
Philadelphia	33	37	10	76	252	267
N.Y. Islanders	25	45	10	60	223	290

Adams Division

	W	L	T	Pts	GF	GA
Boston Bruins	44	24	12	100	299	264
Montreal Canadiens	39	30	11	89	273	249
Buffalo Sabres	31	30	19	81	292	278
Hartford Whalers	31	38	11	73	238	276
Quebec Nordiques	16	50	14	46	236	354

CLARENCE CAMPBELL CONFERENCE
Norris Division

	W	L	T	Pts	GF	GA
Chicago Black Hawks	49	23	8	106	284	211
St. Louis Blues	47	22	11	105	310	250
Detroit Red Wings	34	38	8	76	273	298
Minnesota North Stars	27	39	14	68	256	266
Toronto Maple Leafs	23	46	11	57	241	318

Smythe Division

	W	L	T	Pts	GF	GA
Los Angeles Kings	46	24	10	102	340	254
Calgary Flames	46	26	8	100	344	263
Edmonton Oilers	37	37	6	80	272	272
Vancouver Canucks	28	43	9	65	243	315
Winnipeg Jets	26	43	11	63	260	288

Stanley Cup Playoffs—1991

DIVISION SEMIFINALS
Patrick Division

Pittsburgh Penguins defeated New Jersey Devils, 4 games to 3

Washington Capitals defated New York Rangers, 4 games to 2

Adams Division

Boston Bruins defeated Hartford Whalers, 4 games to 2

Montreal Canadiens defeated Buffalo Sabres, 4 games to 2

Norris Division

Minnesota North Stars defeated Chicago Black Hawks, 4 games to 2

St. Louis Blues defeated Detroit Red wings, 4 games to 3

Smythe Division

Los Angeles Kings defeated Vancouver Canucks, 4 games to 2

Edmonton Oilers defeated Calgary Flames, 4 games to 3

DIVISION FINALS
Patrick Division

Pittsburgh Penguins defeated Washington Capitals, 4 games to 1

Adams Division

Boston Bruins defeated Montreal Canadiens, 4 games to 3

Norris Division

Minnesota North Stars defeated St. Louis Blues, 4 games to 2

Smythe Division

Edmonton Oilers defeated Los Angeles Kings, 4 games to 2

CONFERENCE FINALS (League Semifinals)
Prince of Wales Conference

Pittsburgh Penguins defeated Boston Bruins, 4 games to 2

May 1—Boston 6, Pittsburgh 3
May 3—Boston 5, Pittsburgh 4 (OT)
May 5—Pittsburgh 4, Boston 1
May 7—Pittsburgh 4, Boston 1
May 9—Pittsburgh 7, Boston 2
May 11—Pittsburgh 5, Boston 3

Clarence Campbell Conference

Minnesota North Stars defeated Edmonton Oilers, 4 games to 1

May 2—Minnesota 3, Edmonton 1
May 4—Edmonton 7, Minnesota 2
May 6—Minnesota 7, Edmonton 3
May 8—Minnesota 5, Edmonton 1
May 10—Minnesota 3, Edmonton 2

STANLEY CUP CHAMPIONSHIP FINALS

Pittsburgh defeated Minnesota, 4 games to 2

May 15—Minnesota 5, Pittsburgh 4
May 17—Pittsburgh 4, Minnesota 1
May 19—Minnesota 3, Pittsburgh 1
May 21—Pittsburgh 5, Minnesota 3
May 23—Pittsburgh 6, Minnesota 4
May 25—Pittsburgh 8, Minnesota 0

N.H.L. LEADING GOALTENDERS—1990–91
(Minimum 1,300 minutes played)

	Mins	Avg	SO	GA
Belfour, Chicago	4127	2.47	4	170
Beaupre, Washington	2572	2.64	5	113
Roy, Montreal	2835	2.71	1	128
Moog, Boston	2844	2.87	4	136
Peeters, Philadelphia	1270	2.88	1	61
Hrudey, Los Angeles	2730	2.90	3	132
Terreri, New Jersey	2970	2.91	1	144
Casey, Minnesota	3185	2.98	3	158
Riendeau, St. Louis	2671	3.01	3	134
Wamsley, Calgary	1670	3.05	0	85
Joseph, St. Louis	1710	3.12	0	89
Richter, N.Y. Rangers	2596	3.12	0	135
Hextall, Philadelphia	2035	3.13	0	106
Hayward, Minnesota	1473	3.14	2	77
Essensa, Winnipeg	2916	3.15	4	153
Ranford, Edmonton	3415	3.20	0	182
Berthiaume, Los Angeles	2119	3.31	1	117
Vernon, Calgary	3121	3.31	1	172
Healy, N.Y. Islanders	2999	3.32	0	166
Sidorkiewicz, Hartford	2953	3.33	1	164

OTHER NHL AWARDS—1991

Frank Selke Trophy (Top defensive forward)—Dirk Graham, Chicago

King Clancy Award (Humanitarian)—Dave Taylor, Los Angeles

James Adam Trophy (Coach of the Year)—Brian Sutter, St. Louis

N.H.L. LEADING SCORERS—1990–91

	GP	G	A	Pts
Gretzky, Los Angeles	78	41	122	163
Hull, St. Louis	78	86	45	131
Oates, St. Louis	61	25	90	115
Recchi, Pittsburgh	78	40	73	113
Cullen, Pitts–Hartford	78	39	71	110
Sakic, Quebec	80	48	61	109
Yzerman, Detroit	80	51	57	108
Fleury, Calgary	79	51	53	104
MacInnis, Calgary	78	28	75	103
Larmer, Chicago	80	44	57	101
Roenick, Chicago	79	41	53	94
Bourque, Boston	76	21	73	94
Coffey, Pittsburgh	76	24	69	93
Janney, Boston	77	26	66	92
Neely, Boston	69	51	40	91
Robitaille, Los Angeles	76	45	46	91
Sandstrom, Los Angeles	68	45	44	89
Hawerchuk, Buffalo	80	31	58	89
Leetch, N.Y. Rangers	80	16	72	88
Francis, Hart–Pittsburgh	81	23	64	87

N.H.L. CAREER SCORING LEADERS

(Through 1990–91 season)

(Number in parentheses is standing among all-time leading goal scorers)

	Yrs	Games	G	A	Pts
Wayne Gretzky (3)[1]	12	925	718	1,424	2,316
Gordie Howe (1)	26	1,767	801	1,049	1,850
Marcel Dionne (2)	18	1,348	731	1,040	1,771
Phil Esposito (4)	18	1,282	717	873	1,590
Stan Mikita (9)	22	1,394	541	926	1,467
Bryan Trottier[1]	16	1,175	509	872	1,381
John Bucyk (8)	23	1,540	556	813	1,369
Guy Lafleur (9)	17	1,126	560	793	1,363
Gilbert Perreault	17	1,191	512	814	1326
Alex Delvecchio	24	1,549	456	825	1,281
Jean Ratelle	21	1,281	491	776	1,267
Norm Ullman	20	1,410	490	739	1,229
Jean Beliveau	20	1,125	507	712	1,219
Bobby Clarke	15	1,144	358	852	1,210
Bobby Hull (5)	16	1,063	610	560	1,170
Bernie Federko	14	1,000	389	761	1,130
Mike Bossy (6)	10	752	573	553	1,126
Darryl Sittler	15	1,096	484	637	1,121
Peter Stasny[1]	11	826	403	716	1,119
Frank Mahovlich (10)	18	1,181	533	570	1,103

1. Still active in the N.H.L.

BOWLING

AMERICAN BOWLING CONGRESS CHAMPIONS

Year	Singles	All–events	Year	Singles	All–events
1959	Ed Lubanski	Ed Lubanski	1976	Mike Putzer	Jim Lindquist
1960	Paul Kulbaga	Vince Lucci	1977	Frank Gadaleto	Bud Debenham
1961	Lyle Spooner	Luke Karen	1978	Rich Mersek	Chris Cobus
1962	Andy Renaldo	Billy Young	1979	Rick Peters	Bob Basacchi
1963	Fred Delello	Bus Owalt	1980	Mike Eaton	Steve Fehr
1964	Jim Stefanich	Les Zikes, Jr.	1981	Rob Vital	Rod Toft
1965	Ken Roeth	Tom Hathaway	1982	Bruce Bohm	Rich Wonders
1966	Don Chapman	John Wilcox	1983	Rick Kendrick	Tony Cariello
1967	Frank Perry	Gary Lewis	1984	Bob Antczak and	
1968	Wayne Kowalski	Vince Mazzanti		Neal Young (tie)	Bob Goike
1969	Greg Campbell	Eddie Jackson	1985	Glen Harbison	Barry Asher
1970	Jake Yoder	Mike Berlin	1986	Jess Mackey	Ed Marazka
1971	Al Cohn	Al Cohn	1987	Terry Taylor	Ryan Schafer
1972	Bill Pointer	Mac Lowry	1988	Steve Hutkowski	Rick Steelsmith
1973	Ed Thompson	Ron Woolet	1989	Paul Tetreault	George Hall
1974	Gene Krause	Bob Hart	1990	Bob Hochrein	Mike Neumann
1975	Jim Setser	Bobby Meadows	1991	Ed Deines	Tom Howery

PROFESSIONAL BOWLERS ASSOCIATION

National Championship Tournament

1960	Don Carter	1968	Wayne Zahn	1976	Paul Colwell	1984	Bob Chamberlain
1961	Dave Soutar	1969	Mike McGrath	1977	Tommy Hudson	1985	Mike Aulby
1962	Carmen Salvino	1970	Mike McGrath	1978	Warren Nelson	1986	Tom Crites
1963	Billy Hardwick	1971	Mike Lemongello	1979	Mike Aulby	1987	Randy Pedersen
1964	Bob Strampe	1972	Johnny Guenther	1980	Johnny Petraglia	1988	Brian Voss
1965	Dave Davis	1973	Earl Anthony	1981	Earl Anthony	1989	Pete Weber
1966	Wayne Zahn	1974	Earl Anthony	1982	Earl Anthony	1990	Jim Pencak
1967	Dave Davis	1975	Earl Anthony	1983	Earl Anthony	1991	Mike Miller

BOWLING PROPRIETORS' ASSOCIATION OF AMERICA—MEN

United States Open[1]

1971	Mike Lemongello	1977	Johnny Petraglia	1983	Gary Dickinson	1989	Mike Aulby
1972	Don Johnson	1978	Nelson Burton, Jr.	1984	Mark Roth	1990	Ron Palumbi, Jr.
1973	Mike McGrath	1979	Joe Berardi	1985	Marshall Holman	1991	Pete Weber
1974	Larry Laub	1980	Steve Martin	1986	Steve Cook		
1975	Steve Neff	1981	Marshall Holman	1987	Del Ballard		
1976	Paul Moser	1982	Dave Husted	1988	Pete Weber		

1. Replaced All–Star tournament and is rolled as part of B.P.A. tour.

WOMEN'S INTERNATIONAL BOWLING CONGRESS CHAMPIONS

Year	Singles	All–events	Year	Singles	All–events
1959	Mae Bolt	Pat McBride	1977	Akiko Yamaga	Akiko Yamaga
1960	Marge McDaniels	Judy Roberts	1978	Mae Bolt	Annese Kelly
1961	Elaine Newton	Evelyn Teal	1979	Betty Morris	Betty Morris
1962	Martha Hoffman	Flossie Argent	1980	Betty Morris	Cheryl Robinson
1963	Dot Wilkinson	Helen Shablis	1981	Virginia Norton	Virginia Norton
1964	Jean Havlish	Jean Havlish	1982	Gracie Freeman	Aleta Rzepecki
1965	Doris Rudell	Donna Zimmerman	1983	Aleta Rzepecki	Virginia Norton
1966	Gloria Bouvia	Kate Helbig	1984	Freida Gates	Shinobu Saitoh
1967	Gloria Paeth	Carol Miller	1985	Polly Schwarzel	Aleta Sill
1968	Norma Parks	Susie Reichley	1986	Dana Stewart	Robin Romeo
1969	Joan Bender	Helen Duval			Maria Lewis (tie)
1970	Dorothy Fothergill	Dorothy Fothergill	1987	Regi Junak	Leanne Barrette
1971	Mary Scruggs	Lorrie Nichols	1988	Michelle Meyer–Welty	Lisa Wagner
1972	D. D. Jacobson	Mildred Martorella	1989	Lorraine Anderson	Nancy Fehn
1973	Bobby Buffaloe	Toni Calvery	1990	Dana Miller–Mackie	
1974	Shirley Garms	Judy C. Soutar		and Paula Carter	Carol Norman
1975	Barbara Leicht	Virginia Norton	1991	Debbie Kuhn	Debbie Kuhn
1976	Bev Shonk	Betty Morris			

WIBC QUEENS TOURNAMENT CHAMPIONS

1961	Janet Harman	1969	Ann Feigel	1977	Dana Stewart	1985	Aleta Sill
1962	Dorothy Wilkinson	1970	Mildred Martorella	1978	Loa Boxberger	1986	Cora Fiebig
1963	Irene Monterosso	1971	Mildred Martorella	1979	Donna Adamek	1987	Cathy Almeida
1964	D.D. Jacobson	1972	Dorothy Fothergill	1980	Donna Adamek	1988	Wendy McPherson
1965	Betty Kuczynski	1973	Dorothy Fothergill	1981	Katsuko Sugimoto	1989	Carol Gianotti
1966	Judy Lee	1974	Judy Soutar	1982	Katsuko Sugimoto	1990	Patty Ann
1967	Mildred Martorella	1975	Cindy Powell	1983	Aleta Rzepecki	1991	Dede Davidson
1968	Phyllis Massey	1976	Pamela Buckner	1984	Kazue Inahashi		

BOWLING PROPRIETORS' ASSOCIATION OF AMERICA—WOMEN

United States Open

1971	Paula Carter	1977	Betty Morris	1982	Shinobu Saitoh	1987	Carol Nurman
1972	Lorrie Nichols	1978	Donna Adamek	1983	Dana Miller	1988	Lisa Wagner
1973	Mildred Martorella	1979	Diana Silva	1984	Karen Ellingsworth	1989	Robin Romeo
1974	Pat Costello (Calif.)	1980	Pat Costello (Calif.)	1985	Pat Mercatanti	1990	Dana Miller–Mackie
1975	Paula Carter	1981	Donna Adamek	1986	Wendy MacPherson	1991	Anne Marie Duggan
1976	Patty Costello (Pa.)						

WOMEN'S INTERNATIONAL BOWLING CONGRESS QUEENS TOURNAMENT

(May 12–16, 1991 Cedar Rapids, Iowa)

Winner—Dede Davidson, San Jose, Calif., defeated Jeanne Maiden, Tacoma, Wash., 231–159 in final.
3. Laurie Soto, Canyon County, Calif.
4. Kristy Whitcher, Bremerton, Wash.
5. Lynda Norry, Concord, Calif.

AMERICAN BOWLING CONGRESS TOURNAMENT—1991

(Toledo, Ohio, Feb. 9–June 1, 1991)

Regular Division

Singles—Ed Deines, Fort Collins, Colo.	826
Doubles—Jimmy Johnson and Dan Nadeau, Las Vegas, Nev.	1,505
All-Events—Tom Howery, Madison, Wis.	2,216
Team—Tri-State Lanes, No. 1, Chattanooga, Tenn.	3,410

Booster Division

Lewis Marine Supply, Ft. Lauderdale, Fla.	2,974

PROFESSIONAL BOWLERS ASSOCIATION
Championship Tournament—1991

(Toledo, Ohio, March 24–30, 1991)

Winner—Mike Miller, Albuquerque, N.M., defeated Norm Duke, Albuquerque, N.M., 218–214 in final
3. Martin Lestcher, Bel Air, Md.
4. David Ozio, Vidor, Texas
5. Brian Brazeau, Milwaukee

WOMEN'S INTERNATIONAL BOWLING CONGRESS TOURNAMENT—1991

(Cedar Rapids, Iowa, April 4–June 20, 1991)

Open Division

Singles—Debbie Kuhn, Baltimore, Md.	773
Doubles—Lucy Giovinco, Tampa, Fla. and Cindy Coburn-Carroll, Tonawanda, N.Y.	1,318
Team—Clear-Vu Window Cleaning Inc., Milwaukee, Wis.	2,984
All-Events—Debbie Kuhn, Baltimore, Md.	2,036 [1]

1. Record

Division I

Singles—Kelly Smith, Faribault, Minn.	660
Doubles—Lina Rincon, San Antonio, Tex., and Bonnie Van Steenburg, Universal, Tex.	1,227
Team—Jolly Ladies, Philadelphia, Pa.	2,751
All-Events—Chris Crow, Prospect, Ky.	1,803

Division III

Singles—Darlene Schoon, Freeman, S.D.	656
Doubles—Shirley Piper and Rhonda Custer, Waynesboro, Pa.	1,150
Team—Lindberg Shelter Insurance, Albia, Iowa	2,598
All-Events—Ruth Reimer, St. Catherine, Ont., Canada	1,661

SKIING

ALPINE WORLD CUP OVERALL WINNERS

Year	Men	Women	Team
1967	Jean–Claude Killy, France	Nancy Greene, Canada	France
1968	Jean–Claude Killy, France	Nancy Greene, Canada	France
1969	Karl Schranz, Austria	Gertrude Gabl, Austria	Austria
1970	Karl Schranz, Austria	Michel Jacot, France	France
1971	Gustavo Thoeni, Italy	Annemarie Proell, Austria	France
1972	Gustavo Thoeni, Italy	Annemarie Proell, Austria	France
1973	Gustavo Thoeni, Italy	Annemarie Proell Moser, Austria	Austria
1974	Piero Gros, Italy	Annemarie Proell Moser, Austria	Austria
1975	Gustavo Thoeni, Italy	Annemarie Proell Moser, Austria	Austria
1976	Ingemar Stenmark, Sweden	Rosi Mittermaier, West Germany	Austria
1977	Ingemar Stenmark, Sweden	Lise–Marie Morerod, Switzerland	Austria
1978	Ingemar Stenmark, Sweden	Hanni Wenzel, Liechtenstein	Austria
1979	Peter Luescher, Switzerland	Annemarie Proell Moser, Austria	Austria
1980	Andreas Wenzel, Liechtenstein	Hanni Wenzel, Liechtenstein	Liechtenstein
1981	Phil Mahre, United States	Marie–Theres Nadig, Switzerland	Switzerland
1982	Phil Mahre, United States	Erika Hess, Switzerland	Austria
1983	Phil Mahre, United States	Tamara McKinney, United States	
1984	Pirmin Zurbriggen, Switzerland	Erika Hess, Switzerland	
1985	Màrc Girardelli, Luxembourg	Michela Figini, Switzerland	
1986	Marc Girardelli, Luxembourg	Maria Walliser, Switzerland	Switzerland
1987	Pirmin Zubriggen, Switzerland	Maria Walliser, Switzerland	Switzerland
1988	Pirmin Zubriggen, Switzerland	Michela Figini, Switzerland	Switzerland
1989	Marc Girardelli, Luxembourg	Vreni Schneider, Switzerland	Switzerland
1990	Pirmin Zubriggen, Switzerland	Petra Kronberger, Austria	Austria
1991	Marc Girardelli, Luxembourg	Petra Kronberger, Austria	Austria

ALPINE WORLD CUP—1991

Overall—Men

1. Marc Girardelli, Luxembourg — 242
2. Alberto Tomba, Italy — 222
3. Rudolf Nierlich, Austria — 201
4. Franz Heinzer, Switzerland — 199
5. Ole Christian Furuseth, Norway — 156
Best U.S.A. finisher—none

Overall—Women

1. Petra Kronberger, Austria — 312
2. Sabine Ginther, Austria — 195
3. Vreni Schneider, Switzerland — 185
4. Chantal Bournissen, Switzerland — 181
5. Carole Merle, France — 176
Best U.S.A. finisher—14. Eva Twardokens — 83

Event Leaders—Men

Downhill—Franz Heinzer, Switzerland — 159
  2. Atle Skaardal, Norway — 125
  3. Daniel Mahrer, Switzerland — 81
Best American finish—29. Tommy Moe — 7

Slalom—Marc Girardelli, Luxembourg — 110
  2. Ole Christian Furuseth, Norway — 102
  3. Rudolf Nierlich, Austria — 100
Best American finish—none

Giant Slalom—Alberto Tomba, Italy — 152
  2. Rudolf Nierlich, Austria — 101
  3. Marc Girardelli, Luxembourg — 84
Best American finish—none

Super Giant Slalom—Franz Heinzer, Switzerland — 40
  2. Stefan Eberharter, Austria — 33
  3. Atle Skaardal, Norway — 28
Best American finish—none

Event Leaders—Women

Downhill—Chantal Bournissen, Switzerland — 140
  2. Sabine Ginther, Austria — 122
  3. Petra Kronberger, Austria — 90
Best American finish—20. Kristin Krone — 16

Slalom—Petra Kronberger, Austria — 83
  2. Pernilla Wiberg, Sweden — 79
  3. Blanca Fernandez Ochoa, Spain — 76
Best American finish—19. Heidi Voelker — 12

Gian Slalom—Vreni Schneider, Switzerland — 113
  2. Anita Wachter, Austria — 79
  3. Pernilla Wiberg, Sweden — 61
  4. Eva Twardokens, United States — 57

Super Giant Slalom—Carole Merle, France — 88
  2. Petra Kronberger, Austria — 70
  3. Michaela Gerg, Germany — 44

UNITED STATES CHAMPIONSHIPS—1991

ALPINE

Men's Events

Downhill—A.J. Kitt	1:26.78
Slalom—Joe Levins	1:30.41
Giant Slalom—Alain Feutrier	2:08.10
Super Giant Slalom—A.J. Kitt	1:23.74

Women's Events

Downhill—Megan Gerety	1:26.76
Slalom—Eva Twardokens	1:48.90
Giant Slalom—Eva Twardokens	2:39.99
Super Giant Slalom—Julie Parisien	1:12.93

NORDIC
Men's Cross Country

10 kilometers—John Farra	0:27:39.3
15 kilometers—John Bauer	0:39:57.3
30 kilometers—Todd Boonstra	1:27:34.5

Women's Cross Country

5 kilometers—Nancy Fiddler	0:15:38.0
10 kilometers—Leslie Thompson	0:29:27.9
15 kilometers—Nancy Fiddler	0:49:15.4
20 kilometers—Nancy Fiddler	1:29:04.9

NCAA RESULTS—1991

Men

Slalom—Einar Boehmer, Vermont	1:11.26
Giant Slalom—Toni Standteiner, Colorado	1:24.76
Freestyle cross country—Bjorn Svensson, Colorado	0:25:46.3
Diagonal cross country—Stig Matteon, Alaska–Anchorage	1:11:55.7

Women

Slalom—Heather Flood, Middlebury	1:14.62
Giant Slalom—Keri Schlopy, Vermont	1:27.55
Freestyle cross country—Laura Wilson, Vermont	0:15:09.6
Diagonal cross country—Laura Wilson, Vermont	1:07:15.1

Team (men & women)

1. Colorado	713
2. Vermont	682
3. Utah	615
4. Wyoming	574
5. Dartmouth	492

WORLD CUP SKI JUMPING—1991

1. Andreas Felder, Austria	260
2. Stefan Zund, Switzerland	206
3. Dieter Thoma, Germany	201
4. Stefan Horngacher, Austria	179
5. Ari Pekka Nikkola, Finland & Mikael Martinsson, Sweden	158

Ski Jumping
Nations Cup Standings

1. Austria	886
2. Germany	691
3. Finland	347

WORLD CUP NORDIC COMBINED—1991

Final Standings

1. Andreas Felder, Austria	260
2. Dieter Thoma, Germany	191
3. Stefan Zhuend, Switzerland	181
4. Stefan Horngacher, Austria	176
5. Ari Pekka Nikkola	158

Overall
Nations Cup Standings

1. Austria	2,405
2. Switzerland	1,330
3. Germany	755
4. Norway	702
5. France	569
United States—8th	307

UNITED STATES JUMPING AND NORDIC COMBINED CHAMPIONSHIPS

Seniors 70-meter jump

	Pts
1. Jim Holland Mark Konopacke (tie)	210.9
3. Kris Severson	190.7
4. Tad Langlos	187.3
5. Eric Haitt	183.7

Juniors 70-meter jump

1. Eric Hiatt	183.7
2. Ryan Heckman	181.8
3. Randy Weber	124.1
4. Kip Kopelke	117.9
5. John Keck	110.3

Seniors 90-meter jump

1. Ryan Heckman	207.6
2. Reed Zuehlke	205.4
3. Mark Hammel	203.6
4. Mark Konopacke	200.9
5. Kris Severson	197.8

10-kilometers cross country

1. Todd Wilson	0:29.25
2. Mason Dwinell	0:29.27
3. Tim Tetrault	0:29.30
4. Kris Lodwick	0:29.53
5. Jim Leggett	0:30.03

Longest Standing Jump

1. Ryan Heckman	111.5
2. Kris Severson	110.0
3. Jim Holland	105.5
Eric Hiatt	
Mark Konopacke (tie)	

Final Nordic Combined (jumping and cross country)

1. Jim Holland
2. Dan Williams
3. Matt Laue
4. Ryan Heckman
5. Blue Teramoto

HISTORY OF SKIING IN THE UNITED STATES

Skis were devised for utility, to aid those who had to travel over snow. The Norwegians, Swedes, Lapps, and other inhabitants of northern lands used skis for many centuries before skiing became a sport. Emigrants from these countries brought skis to the United States with them. The first skier of record in the United States was a mailman by the name of "Snowshoe" Thompson, born and raised in Telemarken, Norway, who came to the United States and, beginning in 1850, used skis through 20 successive winters in carrying mail from Northern California to Carson Valley, Idaho.

Ski clubs sprang up over 100 years ago where there were Norwegian and Swedish settlers in Wisconsin and Minnesota and ski contests were held in that territory in 1886. On Feb. 21, 1904, at Ishpenning, Mich., a small group of skiers organized the National Ski Association. In 1961 it was renamed the United States Ski Association.

FISHING

SELECTED WORLD ALL-TACKLE FISHING RECORDS

Source: International Game Fish Association

Caught with Rod and Reel in Fresh Water (as of June 12, 1991)

Species	lb–oz	Where caught	Year	Angler
Bass, Largemouth	22–4	Montgomery Lake, Ga.	1932	George W. Perry
Bass, Peacock	26–8	Mataveni River, Columbia	1982	Rod Neubert
Bass, Redeye	8–3	Flint River, Ga.	1977	David A. Hubbard
Bass, Rock	3–0	York River, Ontario	1974	Peter Gulgin
Bass, Smallmouth	11–15	Dale Hollow Lake, Ky.	1955	David L. Hayes
Bass, Spotted	9–4	Parris Lake, Calif.	1987	Steven West[1] & Gilbert Rowe
Bass, Striped	60–8	Anderson County, Tenn.	1988	Gary Everett Helms
Bass, Striped (landlocked)	66–0	O'Neill Forebay, Los Banos, Calif.	1988	Ted Furnish
Bass, White	6–13	Lake Orange, Orange, Va.	1989	Ronald L. Sprouse
Bass, Whiterock	24–3	Leesville Lake, Va.	1989	David Lambert
Bass, Yellow	2–4	Lake Monroe, Ind.	1977	Donald L. Stalker
Bluegill	4–12	Ketona Lake, Ala.	1950	T.S. Hudson
Bowfin	21–8	Florence, S.C.	1980	Robert L. Harmon
Buffalo, Bigmouth	70–5	Bussey Brake, Bastrop, La.	1980	Delbert Sisk
Buffalo, Smallmouth	68–8	Lake Hamilton, Ark.	1984	Jerry L. Dolezal
Bullhead, Black	8–0	Lake Waccabuc, N.Y.	1951	Kani Evans
Bullhead, Brown	5–8	Veal Pond, Ga.	1975	Jimmy Andrews
Burbot	18–4	Pickford, Mich.	1980	Tom Courtemanche
Carp	57–13	Potomac River, Wash., D.C.	1983	David Nikolow
Catfish, Blue	109–4	Cooper River, S.C.	1991	George Lijewski
Catfish, Channel	58–0	Santee–Cooper Res., S.C.	1964	W.B. Whaley
Catfish, Flathead	98–0	Lewisville, Tex.	1986	William Stevens
Char, Arctic	32–9	Tree River, Canada	1981	Jeffery Ward
Crappie, Black	4–8	Kerr Lake, Va.	1981	L. Carl Herring, Jr.
Crappie, White	5–3	Enid Dam, Mississippi	1957	Fred L. Bright
Dolly Varden	12–0	Noatak River, Alaska	1987	Kenneth Alt
Drum, Freshwater	54–8	Nickajack Lake, Tenn.	1972	Benny E. Hull
Gar, Alligator	279	Rio Grande River, Tex.	1951	Bill Valverde
Gar, Longnose	50–5	Trinity River, Texas	1954	Townsend Miller
Gar, Shortnose	5–0	Vian, Okla.	1985	Buddy Croslin
Inconnu	38–2	Kobuk River, Alaska	1982	Mark L. Feldman
Muskellunge	69–15	St. Lawrence River, N.Y.	1957	Arthur Lawton
Muskellunge, Tiger	51–3	Lac–Vieux–Desert, Wisc.–Mich.	1919	John A. Knobla
Perch, White	4–12	Messalonskee Lake, Maine	1949	Mrs. Earl Small
Perch, Yellow	4–3	Bordentown, N.J.	1865	Dr. C.C. Abbot
Pickerel, Eastern Chain	9–6	Homerville, Ga.	1961	Baxley McQuaig, Jr.
Redhorse, Northern	3–11	Missouri River, S.D.	1977	Phillip Laumeyer
Redhorse, Silver	11–7	Plum Creek, Wisconsin	1985	Neal D.G. Long
Salmon, Atlantic	79–2	Tana River, Norway	1928	Henrik Henriksen
Salmon, Chinook	97–4	Kenai River, Alaska	1985	Les Anderson
Salmon, Chum	27–3	Raymond Cove, Alaska	1977	Robert A. Jahnke
Salmon, Coho	33–4	Pulaski, N.Y.	1989	Jerry Lifton
Salmon, Landlocked	22–8	Sebago Lake, Maine	1907	Edward Blakely
Salmon, Pink	12–9	Moose & Kenai Rivers, Alaska	1974	Steven Alan Lee
Salmon, Sockeye	15–3	Kenai River, Alaska	1987	Stan Roach
Shad, American	11–1	Delaware River, N.J.	1984	Charles J. Mower
Sturgeon	468–0	Benicia, Calif.	1983	Joey Pallotta III
Sturgeon, White	380–0	Snake River, Idaho	1973	Del Canty
Sunfish, Green	2–2	Stockton Lake, Missouri	1971	Paul M. Dilley
Sunfish, Redbreast	1–12	Suwannee River, Fla.	1984	Alvin Buchanan
Sunfish, Redear	4–10	Mill Pond, Fla.	1985	C.L. Windham
Tigerfish	61–11	Lake Tanganyika, Zambia	1984	Don Hunter
Trout, Brook	14–8	Nipigon River, Ontario	1916	Dr. W.J. Cook
Trout, Brown	35–15	Nahuel Huapi, Argentina	1952	Eugenio Cavaglia
Trout, Bull	32–0	Lake Pend Orielle, Idaho	1949	N.L. Higgins
Trout, Cutthroat	41–0	Pyramid Lake, Nev.	1925	John Skimmerhorn
Trout, Golden	11–0	Cook's Lake, Wyoming	1948	Charles S. Reed
Trout, Lake	65–0	Great Bear Lake, N.W.T., Canada	1970	Larry Daunis
Trout, Rainbow	42–2	Bell Island, Alaska	1970	David Robert White
Trout, Tiger	20–13	Lake Michigan, Wisc.	1978	Peter M. Friedland
Walleye	25–0	Old Hickory Lake, Tenn.	1960	Mabry Harper
Whitefish, Lake	14–6	Meaford, Ontario, Canada	1984	Dennis M. Laycock
Whitefish, Mountain	5–0	Athabasca River, Alberta, Canada	1963	Orville Welch
Whitefish, Round	6–0	Putahow River, Manitoba, Canada	1984	Allan J. Ristori

1. West and Rowe caught same size record spotted bass in 1987 in same location, Parris Lake, Calif. 3 months apart—West in Feb. and Rowe in April.

Caught With Rod and Reel in Salt Water (as of July 12, 1991)

Species	lb–oz	Where caught	Year	Angler
Albacore	88–2	Canary Islands	1977	Siegfried Dickemann
Amberjack	155–10	Challenger Bank, Bermuda	1981	Joseph Dawson
Barracuda	83	Lagos, Nigeria	1952	K. J. W. Hackett
Bass, Black Sea	9–8	Virginia Beach, Va.	1987	Joe Mizelle, Jr.
Bass, Black Sea	9–8	Virginia Beach, Va.	1990	Jack G. Stallings, Jr.
Bass, Giant Sea	563–8	Anacapa Island, Calif.	1968	J. D. McAdam, Jr.
Bass, Striped	78–8	Atlantic City, N.J.	1982	Albert R. McReynolds
Blackfish (Tautog)	21–8	Wachapreague, Virginia	1984	Tommy Wood
Bluefish	31–12	North Carolina	1972	James M. Hussey
Bonefish	19	Zululand, S. Africa	1962	Brian W. Batchelor
Bonito, Atlantic	18–4	Fayal Island, Azores	1984	D. Gama Higgs
Bonito, Pacific	23–8	Victoria, Mahe	1975	Mrs. Anne Cochain
Cobia	135–9	Shark Bay, Australia	1985	Peter Goulding
Cod, Atlantic	98–12	Isle of Shoals, N.H.	1969	Alphonse Bielevich
Cod, Pacific	30–0	Andrew Bay, Alaska	1984	Donald R. Vaughn
Conger	102–8	Plymouth, Devon, England	1983	Raymond Ewart Street
Dolphin	87	Papagallo Gulf, Costa Rica	1976	Manual Salazar
Drum, Black	113–1	Lewes, Del.	1975	G. M. Townsend
Drum, Red	94–2	Avon, North Carolina	1984	David G. Deuel
Flounder, Summer	22–7	Montauk, N.Y.	1975	Charles Nappi
Flounder, Winter	4–3	Perkins Cove, Maine	1989	Lisa Boughner
Haddock	9–15	Perkins Cove, Maine	1988	Jim Donohue
Halibut, Atlantic	255	Gloucester, Mass.	1989	Sonny Manley
Halibut, California	53–4	Santa Rosa Island, Calif.	1988	Russ Harmon
Hailbut, Pacific	350	Homer, Alaska	1982	Vern S. Foster
Jack, Crevalle	54–7	Port Michel, Gabon	1982	Thomas F. Gibson, Jr.
Jack, Horse–eye	24–8	Miami, Fla.	1982	Tito Schnau
Jack, Pacific Crevalle	24–0	Cabo San Lucas, Mexico	1987	Sharon Swanson
Jewfish	680	Fernandina Beach, Fla.	1961	Lynn Joyner
Lingcod	64–0	Elfin Cove, Alaska	1988	David Bauer
Mackerel, King	90	Key West, Florida	1976	Norton I. Thomton
Mackerel, Spanish	13–0	Ocracoke Inlet, N.C.	1987	Robert Cranton
Marlin, Atlantic Blue	1282	St. Thomas, Virgin Islands	1977	Larry Martin
Marlin, Black	1560	Cabo Blanco, Peru	1953	A. C. Glassel, Jr.
Marlin, Pacific Blue	1376	Kaaiwi Point, Kona, Hawaii	1982	Jay Wm. deBeaubien
Marlin, Striped	494	Tutukaka, New Zealand	1986	Bill Boniface
Marlin, White	181–14	Victoria, Brazil	1979	Evandro Luiz Coser
Permit	51–8	Lake Worth, Fla.	1978	William M. Kenney
Pollack	26–7	Salcombe, England	1984	Robert Perry
Pollack (Virens)	46–7	Brielle, N.J.	1975	John T. Holton
Pompano, African	41–8	Fort Lauderdale, Fla.	1979	Wayne Sommers
Sailfish, Atlantic	128–1	Luanda, Angola, Africa	1974	Harm Steyn
Sailfish, Pacific	221	Santa Cruz Is., Galapagos Is.	1947	C. W. Stewart
Seabass, White	83–12	San Felipe, Mexico	1953	L. C. Baumgardner
Shark, Blue	437	Catherine Bay, Australia	1976	Peter Hyde
Shark, Hammerhead	991	Sarasota, Fla.	1982	Allen Ogle
Shark, Mako	1115–0	Black River, Mauritius	1988	Patrick Guillanton
Shark, Porbeagle	465	Padstow, Cornwall, England	1976	Jorge Potier
Shark, Thresher	802	Tutukaka, New Zealand	1981	Dianne North
Shark, Tiger	1780	Cherry Grove, S.C.	1964	Walter Maxwell
Shark, White	2664	South Australia	1959	Alfred Dean
Snapper, Cubera	121–8	Cameron, La.	1982	Mike Hebert
Snook	53–10	Costa Rica	1978	Gilbert Ponzi
Spearfish	90–13	Madeira Island, Portugal	1980	Joseph Larkin
Swordfish	1182	Iquique, Chile	1953	L. E. Marron
Tanguigue	99	Scottburgh, Natal, South Africa	1982	Michael John Wilkinson
Tarpon	283	Lake Maracalbo, Venezuela	1956	M. Salazar
Trevally, Bigeye	15–0	Isla Coiba, Panama	1984	Sally S. Timms
Trevally, Giant	137–9	McKenzie State Park, Hawaii	1983	Roy K. Gushiken
Tuna, Atlantic Bigeye	375–8	Ocean City, Md.	1977	Cecil Browne
Tuna, Blackfin	42	Bermuda	1978	Alan J. Card (tie)
Tuna, Blackfin	42	Challenger Bank, Bermuda	1989	Gilbert C. Pearman (tie)
Tuna, Bluefin	1496	Nova Scotia, Canada	1979	Ken Fraser
Tuna, Dog–tooth	194	Kwan–Tall Island, Korea	1980	Kim Chul
Tuna, Longtail	79–2	Montague Island, Australia	1982	Tim Simpson
Tuna, Pacific Bigeye	435	Cobo Blanco, Peru	1957	R.V. A. Lee
Tuna, Skipjack	41–12	Black River, Mauritius	1982	Bruno de Ravel
Tuna, Southern Bluefin	348–5	Whakatane, New Zealand	1981	Rex Wood
Tuna, Yellowfin	388–12	Mexico	1977	Curt Wiesenmutter
Wahoo	149	Cat Cay, Bahamas	1962	John Pirovano
Weakfish	19–2	Jones Beach Inlet, N.Y.	1984	Dennis Roger Rooney
Yellowtail, California	78–0	Rocas Alijos, Mexico	1987	Richard Cresswell
Yellowtail, Southern	114–10	Tauranga, New Zealand	1984	Mike Godfrey

SPEED SKATING

U.S. OUTDOOR CHAMPIONS (LONG TRACK)

Men

1959–60	Ken Bartholomew	1983	Michael Ralston	1970–71	Sheila Young
1961	Ed Rudolph	1984	Michael Ralston	1972	Ruth Moore, Nancy Thorne
1962	Floyd Bedbury	1985	Andy Gabel	1973	Nancy Class
1963	Tom Gray	1986	Eric Klein	1974	Kris Garbe
1964	Neil Blatchford	1987	Dave Paulicic	1975	Nancy Swider
1965–66	Rich Wurster	1988	Patrick Wentland	1976	Connie Carpenter
1967	Mike Passarella	1989	Matt Trimble	1977	Liz Crowe
1968–70	Peter Cefalu	1990	Andy Zak	1978	Paula Class, Betsy Davis
1971	Jack Walters	1991	Pat Seltsam	1979	Gretchen Byrnes
1972	Barth Levy			1980	Shari Miller
1973	Mike Woods	**Women**		1981	Lisa Merrifield
1974	Leigh Barczewski, Mike	1960	Mary Novak	1982	Lisa Merrifield
	Passarella	1961	Jean Ashworth	1983	Janet Hainstock
1975	Rich Wurster	1962	Jean Omelenchuk	1984	Janet Hainstock
1976	John Wurster	1963	Jean Ashworth	1985	Betsy Davis
1977	Jim Chapin	1964	Diane White	1986	Deb Perkins
1978	Bill Heinkel	1965	Jean Omelenchuk	1987	Laura Zuckerman
1979	Erik Henriksen	1966	Diane White	1988	Elise Brinich
1980	Greg Oly	1967	Jean Ashworth	1989	Liza Merrifield
1981	Tom Grannes	1968	Helen Lutsch	1990	Jane Eickhoff
1982	Greg Oly	1969	Sally Blatchford	1991	Liza Dennehy

WORLD SPEED SKATING RECORDS

Men

Distance	Time	Skater	Place	Year
500m	0:36.45	Jens–Uwe Mey, East Germany	Calgary, Canada	1988
1000m	1:12.58	Pavel Pegov, Soviet Union	Medeo, U.S.S.R.	1983
1000m	1:12.58	Igor Zhelezovski	Heerenveea, The Netherlands	1989
1500m	1:52.50	Andre Hoffmann, East Germany	Calgary, Canada	1988
3000m	3:57.52	Johann Olav Koss, Norway	Heerenveen, The Netherlands	1990
5000m	6:41.73	Johann Olav Koss, Norway	Heerenveen, The Netherlands	1991
10,000m	13:43.54	Johann Olav Koss, Norway	Heerenveen, The Netherlands	1991
All–around	160.807	Victor Shasherin, Soviet Union	Medeo, U.S.S.R.	1984

Women

Distance	Time	Skater	Place	Year
500m	0:39.10	Bonnie Blair, United States	Calgary, Canada	1988
1000m	1:17.65	Christa Rothenburger, E. Germany	Calgary, Canada	1988
1500m	2:00.68	Yvonne Van Gennip, Netherlands	Calgary, Canada	1988
3000m	4:11.94	Yvonne Van Gennip, Netherlands	Calgary, Canada	1988
5000m	7:14:13	Yvonne Van Gennip, Netherlands	Calgary, Canada	1988
All–around	171.760	Andrea Schone, East Germany	Medeo, U.S.S.R.	1984

U.S. INDOOR (SHORT TRACK) CHAMPIONS—1991

Men—Patrick Wentland, Scituate, Mass.
Women—Kristen Talbot, Schuylerville, N.Y.
Intermediate men—Timothy Quinn, Westlake, Ohio
Intermediate women—Karen Cashman, Quincy, Mass.
Junior boys—Leif Ahlgren, St. Paul, Minn.
Junior girls—Nicole Ziegelmeyer, Imperial, Mo.

WORLD SPRINT CHAMPIONSHIPS—1991
(Inzell, Germany Feb. 23–24, 1991)

Men
(Two races in both 500m and 1000m. Overall winner on points)

500m—	Uwe Jens Mey, Germany	0:36.96
	Uwe Jens Mey, Germany	0:36.64
1000m—	Igor Zhelezouski, Soviet Union	1:13.85
	Igor Zhelezovski, Soviet Union	1:13.90
Overall—	Igor Zhelezouvski, Soviet Union	147.905 points

Women
(Two races in both 500m and 1000m. Overall winnter on points)

500m—	Christine Aaftink, Netherlands	0:40.70
	Monique Garbrecht, Germany	0:40.01
1000m—	Angela Hauck, Germany	1:22.17
	Monique Garbrecht, Germany	1:21.26
Overall—	Monique Garbrecht, Germany	162.660 points

U.S. OUTDOOR (LONG TRACK) CHAMPIONS—1991

Men—Pat Seltsam, Pembroke, Mass.
Women—Liza Dennehy, Butte, Mont.
Intermediate men—Kurt Luedke, Shorewood, Wis.
Intermediate women—not held in 1991
Junior boys—Casey FitzRandolph, Verona, Wis.
Junior girls—Becky Sundstrom, Glen Ellyn, Ill.

WORLD CHAMPIONSHIPS—1991
Men
(Heerenveen, The Netherlands, Feb. 9–10, 1991)

Overall champion—Johann Olav Koss, Norway	157.396
500m—Peter Adeberg, Germany	0:37.52
1500m—Johann Olav Koss, Norway	1:52.76
5000m—Johann Olav Koss, Norway	6:41.73 [1]
10,000m—Johann Olav Koss, Norway	13:43.54 [1]

Women
(Hamar, Norway, Feb. 2–3, 1991)

Overall champion—Gunda Kleeman, Germany	177.263
500m—Qiaobo Ye, China	0:41.85
1500m—Gunda Kleeman, Germany	2:09.45
3000m—Gunda Kleeman, Germany	4:32.00
5000m—Gunda Kleeman, Germany	7:43.10

1. World Record.

FIGURE SKATING

WORLD CHAMPIONS

Men

1960	Alain Giletti, France	1983	Scott Hamilton, United States	1974	Christine Errath, East Germany
1961	No competition	1984	Scott Hamilton, United States	1975	Dianne de Leeuw, Netherlands
1962	Donald Jackson, Canada	1985	Alexandr Fadeev, U.S.S.R.	1976	Dorothy Hamill, United States
1963	Don McPherson, Canada	1986	Brian Boitano, United States	1977	Linda Fratianne, United States
1964	Manfred Schnelldorfer, West Germany	1987	Brian Orser, Canada	1978	Anett Poetzsch, East Germany
		1988	Brian Boitano, United States	1979	Linda Fratianne, United States
1965	Alain Calmat, France	1989	Kurt Browning, Canada	1980	Anett Poetzsch, East Germany
1966–68	Emmerich Danzer, Austria	1990	Kurt Browning, Canada	1981	Denise Beillmann, Switzerland
1969–70	Tim Wood, United States	1991	Kurt Browning, Canada	1982	Elaine Zayak, United States
1971–73	Ondrej Nepela, Czechoslovakia			1983	Rosalynn Sumners, United States
1974	Jan Hoffman, East Germany	**Women**			
1975	Sergei Yolkov, U.S.S.R.	1956–60	Carol Heiss, United States	1984	Katarina Witt, East Germany
1976	John Curry, Britain	1961	No competition	1985	Katarina Witt, East Germany
1977	Vladimir Kovalev, U.S.S.R.	1962–64	Sjoukje Dijkstra, Netherlands	1986	Debi Thomas, United States
1978	Charles Tickner, United States	1965	Petra Burka, Canada	1987	Katarina Witt, East Germany
1979	Vladimir Kovalev, U.S.S.R.	1966–68	Peggy Fleming, United States	1988	Katarina Witt, East Germany
1980	Jan Hoffman, East Germany	1969–70	Gabriele Seyfert, East Germany	1989	Midori Ito, Japan
1981	Scott Hamilton, United States	1971–72	Beatrix Schuba, Austria	1990	Jill Trenary, United States
1982	Scott Hamilton, United States	1973	Karen Magnusson, Canada	1991	Kristi Yamaguchi, United States

U.S. CHAMPIONS

Men

1946–52	Richard Button	1982	Scott Hamilton	1961	Laurence Owen
1953–56	Hayes Jenkins	1983	Scott Hamilton	1962	Barbara Roles Pursley
1957–60	David Jenkins	1984	Scott Hamilton	1963	Lorraine Hanlon
1961	Bradley Lord	1985	Brian Boitano	1964–68	Peggy Fleming
1962	Monty Hoyt	1986	Brian Boitano	1969–73	Janet Lynn
1963	Tommy Liz	1987	Brian Boitano	1974–76	Dorothy Hamill
1964	Scott Allen	1988	Brian Boitano	1977–80	Linda Fratianne
1965	Gary Visconti	1989	Christopher Bowman	1981	Elaine Zayak
1966	Scott Allen	1990	Todd Eldredge	1982	Rosalynn Sumners
1967	Gary Visconti	1991	Todd Eldredge	1983	Rosalynn Sumners
1968–70	Tim Wood			1984	Rosalynn Sumners
1971	John M. Petkevich	**Women**		1985	Tiffany Chin
1972	Ken Shelley	1943–48	Gretchen Merrill	1986	Debi Thomas
1973–75	Gordon McKellen	1949–50	Yvonne Sherman	1987	Jill Trenary
1976	Terry Kubicka	1951	Sonya Klopfer	1988	Debi Thomas
1977–80	Charles Tickner	1952–56	Tenley Albright	1989	Jill Trenary
1981	Scott Hamilton	1957–60	Carol Heiss	1990	Jill Trenary
				1991	Tonya Harding

WORLD CHAMPIONS—1991
(Munich, Germany, March 11–16, 1991)

Men's singles—Kurt Browning, Canada
Women's singles—Kristi Yamaguchi, United States
Pairs—Natalia Mishkuteniok and Artur Bmitriev, Soviet Union
Dance—Isabelle and Paul Duchesnay, France

UNITED STATES CHAMPIONSHIPS—1991
(Minneapolis, Minn., Feb. 12–17, 1991)

Senior men—Todd Eldredge, Los Angeles, Calif.
Senior women—Tonya Harding, Portland, Ore.
Senior pairs—Natasha Kuchiki and Todd Sand, Los Angeles, Calif.
Senior dance—Elizabeth Punsalan and Jerod Swallow, Colorado Springs, Colo.
Junior men—Damon Allen, Rockford, Ill.
Junior women—Lisa Ervin, Lakewood, Ohio
Junior pairs—Aimee Offner, Norristown Pa., and Brian Helgenberg, Philadelphia, Pa.

Junior dance—Kimberly Callahan, Oak Park, Ill., and Robert Peale, Chicago, Ill.
Novice men—John Bevan, Spokane, Wash.
Novice women—Tanya Street, Chicago, Ill.

CURLING

United States Championships—1991
Men (Utica, N.Y., March 3–9, 1991)—Madison, Wis., Steve Brown, skip (defeated Seattle, Wash., Doug Jones, skip, 6–3 in final)
Women (Utica, N.Y., March 3–9, 1991)—Houston, Texas, Maymar Gemmell, skip (defeated Madison, Wis., Lisa Schoeneberg, skip, 7–5 in final)

World Championships—1991
Men (Winnipeg, Canada, March 23–31)—Scotland, David Smith, skip (defeated Canada, Kevin Martin, skip, 7–2 in final)
Women (Winnipeg, Canada, March 23–31, 1991)—Norway, Dordi Norddy, skip (defeated Canada, Julie Sutton, skip, 4–3 in final)

SWIMMING

WORLD RECORDS—MEN

(Through September 19, 1991)
Approved by the International Swimming Federation (F.I.N.A.)
(F.I.N.A. discontinued acceptance of records in yards in 1968)
Source: United States Swim Team

Distance	Record	Holder	Country	Date
Freestyle				
50 meters	0:21.81	Tom Jager	United States	March 24, 1990
100 meters	0:48.42	Matt Biondi	United States	August 9, 1988
200 meters	1:46.69	Georgio Lamberti	Italy	Aug. 15, 1989
400 meters	3:46.95	Uwe Dussler	East Germany	Sept. 23, 1988
800 meters	7:47.85	Kieren Perkins	Austria	Aug. 25, 1991
1,500 meters	14:50.36	Jorg Hoffman	Germany	Jan. 13, 1991
Backstroke				
100 meters	0:53.93	Jeff Rouse	United States	Aug. 25, 1991
200 meters	1:57.30	Martin Zubero	Spain	Aug. 13, 1991
Breaststroke				
100 meters	1:01.29	Norbert Rosza	Hungary	Aug. 20, 1991
200 meters	2:11.53	Mike Barrowman	United States	July 20, 1990
Butterfly				
100 meters	0:52.84	Pablo Morales	United States	June 23, 1986
200 meters	1:55.69	Melvin Stewart	United States	Jan. 12, 1991
Individual Medley				
200 meters	1:59.36	Tamas Darnyi	Hungary	Jan. 13, 1991
400 meters	4:12.36	Tamas Darnyi	Hungary	Jan. 18, 1991
Freestyle Relay				
400 meters	3:16.53	United States	National Team	Sept. 23, 1988
800 meters	7:12.51	United States	National Team	Sept. 21, 1988
Medley Relay				
400 meters	3:36.93	United States	National Team	Sept. 25, 1988

WORLD RECORDS—WOMEN

Distance	Record	Holder	Country	Date
Freestyle				
50 meters	0:24.98	Yang Wenyi	China	April 11, 1988
100 meters	0:54.73	Kristin Otto	East Germany	Aug. 19, 1986
200 meters	1:57.55	Heike Friedrich	East Germany	June 16, 1986
400 meters	4:03.85	Janet Evans	United States	Sept. 22, 1988
800 meters	8:16.22	Janet Evans	United States	Aug. 20, 1989
1,500 meters	15:52.10	Janet Evans	United States	March 26, 1988
Backstroke				
100 meters	1:00.31	Kristina Egerszegi	Hungary	Aug. 20, 1991
200 meters	2:06.62	Kristina Egerszegi	Hungary	Aug. 26, 1991
Breaststroke				
100 meters	1:07.91	Silke Hoerner	East Germany	Aug. 21, 1987
200 meters	2:26.71	Silke Hoerner	East Germany	Sept. 21, 1988
Butterfly				
100 meters	0:57.93	Mary T. Meagher	United States	Aug. 16, 1981
200 meters	2:05.96	Mary T. Meagher	United States	Aug. 13, 1981
Individual Medley				
200 meters	2:11.73	Ute Geweniger	East Germany	July 4, 1981
400 meters	4:36.10	Petra Schneider	East Germany	Aug. 1, 1982

Freestyle Relay

400 meters	3:40.57	East German National Team	East Germany	Aug. 19, 1986
800 meters	7:55.47	East German National Team	East Germany	Aug. 18, 1987

Medley Relay

400 meters	4:03.69	East German National Team	East Germany	Aug. 24, 1984

AMERICAN SWIMMING RECORDS
(As of September 19, 1991)

Distance	Holder	Record	Date
MEN			
Freestyle			
50 meters	Tom Jager	0:21.81	March 24, 1990
100 meters	Matt Biondi	0:48.42	August 10, 1988
200 meters	Matt Biondi	1:47.72	August 15, 1989
400 meters	Matt Cetlinski	3:48.06	August 11, 1988
800 meters	Sean Killion	7:52.45	July 27, 1987
1500 meters	George DiCarlo	15:01.51	June 30, 1984
Backstroke			
100 meters	Jeff Rouse	0:53.93	August 25, 1991
200 meters	Rick Carey	1:58.86	June 27, 1984
Breaststroke			
100 meters	Steve Lundquist	1:01.65	July 29, 1984
200 meters	Mike Barrowman	2:11.53	July 20, 1990
Butterfly			
100 meters	Pablo Morales	0:52.84	June 23, 1986
200 meters	Melvin Stewart	1:55.69	January 12, 1991
Individual Medley			
200 meters	David Wharton	2:00.11	August 20, 1989
400 meters	Eric Namesnik	4:15.21	January 8, 1991
Freestyle Relay			
400 meters	US National Team	3:16.53	September 23, 1988
800 meters	US National Team	7:12.51	September 21, 1988
Medley Relay			
400 meters	US National Team	3:36.93	September 25, 1988

Distance	Holder	Record	Date
WOMEN			
Freestyle			
50 meters	Leigh Ann Fetter	0:25.50	January 13, 1991
100 meters	Angel Martino	0:55.14	August 23, 1991
200 meters	Cynthia Woodhead	1:58.23	September 3, 1979
400 meters	Janet Evans	4:03.85	September 22, 1988
800 meters	Janet Evans	8:16.22	August 20, 1989
1500 meters	Janet Evans	15:52.10	March 26, 1988
Backstroke			
100 meters	Betsy Mitchell	1:01.20	June 24, 1986
200 meters	Betsy Mitchell	2:08.60	June 27, 1986
Breaststroke			
100 meters	Tracey McFarlane	1:08.91	August 11, 1988
200 meters	Anita Nall	2:27.08	April 4, 1991
Butterfly			
100 meters	Mary T. Meagher	0:57.93	August 16, 1981
200 meters	Mary T. Meagher	2:05.96	August 13, 1981
Individual Medley			
200 meters	Tracy Caulkins	2:12.64	August 3, 1984
400 meters	Janet Evans	4:37.76	September 19, 1988

Distance	Holder	Record	Date
Freestyle Relay			
400 meters	US National Team	3:43.43	August 26, 1978
	US National Team	3:43.43	July 31, 1984
800 meters	US National Team	8:02.12	August 17, 1986
Medley Relay			
400 meters	USA Pan Pacific Team	4:05.98	August 25, 1991

U.S. SWIMMING SENIOR NATIONALS—1991

(April 3–7, 1991, Federal Way, Washington)

Women's Events

50-meter freestyle—Angel Martino	0:25.88
100-meter freestyle—Nicole Haislett	0:55.42
200-meter freestyle—Nicole Haislett	2:00.91
400-meter freestyle—Janet Evans	4:09.11
800-meter freestyle—Janet Evans	8:30.75
1,500-meter freestyle—Janet Evans	16:11.22
100-meter backstroke—Janie Wagstaff	1:01.22
200-meter backstroke—Janie Wagstaff	2:09.09
100-meter breaststroke—Anita Nall	1:09.83
200-meter breaststroke—Anita Nall	2:27.08
100-meter butterfly—Summer Sanders	1:00.47
200-meter butterfly—Erika Hansen	2:13.52
200-meter individual medley—Nicole Haislett	2:16.34
400-meter individual medley—Janet Evans	4:44.07
400-meter medley relay—Texas Aquatics	4:17.29
400-meter freestyle relay—Texas Aquatics	3:48.57
800-meter freestyle relay—Texas Aquatics	8:14.50

Team standings: 1. Texas Aquatics 563.5
2. Stanford 348
3. Mission Viejo 152

Men's Events

50-meter freestyle—Stephen Crocker	0:22.41
100-meter freestyle—Shaun Jordan	0:49.61
200-meter freestyle—Joe Hudepohl	1:49.71
400-meter freestyle—Lawrence Frostad	3:53.33
800-meter freestyle—Keith Frostad	8:01.17
1,500-meter freestyle—Lawrence Frostad	15:18.40
100-meter backstroke—Dave Berkoff	0:55.57
200-meter backstroke—Royce Sharp	1:59.26
100-meter breaststroke—Seth Van Neerden	1:01.67
200-meter breaststroke—Mike Barrowman	2:12.61
100-meter butterfly—Brian Alderman	0:53.50
200-meter butterfly—Melvin Stewart	1:58.33
200-meter individual medley—Dave Wharton	2:01.99
400-meter individual medley—Dave Wharton	4:16.90
400-meter medley relay—Peddie Aquatics	3:45.87
400-meter freestyle relay—Fort Lauderdale	3:24.23
800-meter freestyle relay—Peddie Aquatics	7:28.39

Team Standings—1. Texas Aquatics 347.5
2. Peddie Aquatics 222.0
3. University of Michigan 137

Combined Team Champions—1. Texas Aquatics 911
2. Peddie Aquatics 373
3. Mission Viejo 281

PHILLIPS 66 NATIONAL SWIMMING CHAMPIONSHIPS—1991

(Aug. 12–16, 1991)

Women's Events

50-meter freestyle—Sara Perroni	0:26.00
100-meter freestyle—Paige Zemina	0:56.09
200-meter freestyle—Sara Torres	2:01.68
400-meter freeslyte—Julie Kole	4:15.54
800-meter freestyle—Sarah Anderson	8:48.12
1,500-meter freestyle—Kathy Hoffman	16:40.40
100-meter backstroke—B.J. Bedford	1:02.43
200-meter backstroke—Paige Wilson	2:14.68
100-meter breaststroke—Emily Short	1:10.79

200-meter breaststroke—Megan Kleine	2:33.71
100-meter butterfly—Paige Wilson	1:01.03
200-meter butterfly—Julie Kole	2:11.70
200-meter individual medley—Mary Ellen Blanchard	2:17.91
400-meter individual medley—Sheila Taormina	4:51.29
400-meter freestyle relay—Florida Aquatic "A"	3:45.49
800-meter freestyle relay—Florida Aquatic "A"	8:14.00

Men's Events

50-meter freestyle—Del Cerney	0:23.09
100-meter freestyle—Doug Gjertsen	0:50.48
200-meter freestyle—Doug Gjertsen	1:49.69
400-meter freestyle—Lars Jorgensen	3:54.12
800-meter freestyle—Lars Jorgensen	8:02.56
1,500-meter freestyle—Lars Jorgensen	15:22.75
100-meter backstroke—Derek Weatherford	0:56.25
200-meter backstroke—Martin Zubero	1:58.85
100-meter breaststroke—Seth Van Neerden	1:02.11
200-meter breaststroke—Mike Bartrowman	2:10.60
100-meter butterfly—Trip Zedlitz	0:54.53
200-meter butterfly—Melvin Stewart	1:56.69
200-meter individual medley—Trip Zedlitz	2:02.81
400-meter individual medley—Derek Weatherford	4:22.39
400-meter medley relay—Texas Aquatics "A"	3:47.59
400-meter freestyle relay—Texas Aquatics "A"	3:22.39
800-meter freestyle relay—Texas Aquatics "A"	7:28.94

U.S. DIVING CHAMPIONSHIPS—1991

(April 17–21, 1991, Minneapolis, Minn.)

INDOOR

Men's Events

1-meter—Pat Evans, Stingray Diving Cub	606.51
3-meter—Mark Lenzi, Ohio State Diving Club	710.04
Platform—Pat Evans, Stingray Diving Club	614.13

Team—1. Ohio State Diving 176
2. Fort Lauderdale 95
3. Kimball Divers 71.5

Women's Events

1-meter—Wendy Lucero, Kimball Divers	452.73
3-meter—Wendy Lucero, Kimball Divers	507.21
Platform—Cokey Smith, Kimball Divers	412.44

Team—1. Kimball Divers 151
2. Fort Lauderdale 106
3. Hurricane Diving 76

Combined Champion—Kimball Divers 222.5

OUTDOOR

Men's Events

1-meter—Mark Lenzi, unattached	659.46
3-meter—Patrick Jeffrey, Ft. Lauderdale Diving	634.47
Platform—Scott Donie, Ft. Lauderdale Diving	562.68

Team—1. Ft. Lauderdale 121
2. Kimball Divers 65
3. (tie) Cincinnati Stingrays
Miami Hurricanes 55

Women's Events

1-meter—Wendy Lucero, Kimball Divers	458.16
3-meter—Krista Klein, Mustang Diving	490.14
Platform—Ellen McGrath, Emerald City Divers	377.01

Team—1. Kimball Divers 105
2. Stanford Diving 58
3. Ft. Lauderdale 54

Combined Champion—Kimball Divers 220

BOXING

Whether it be called pugilism, prize fighting or boxing, there is no tracing "the Sweet Science" to any definite source. Tales of rivals exchanging blows for fun, fame or money go back to earliest recorded history and classical legend. There was a mixture of boxing and wrestling called the "pancratium" in the ancient Olympic Games and in such contests the rivals belabored one another with hands fortified with heavy leather wrappings that were sometimes studded with metal. More than one Olympic competitor lost his life at this brutal exercise.

There was little law or order in pugilism until Jack Broughton, one of the early champions of England, drew up a set of rules for the game in 1743. Broughton, called "the father of English boxing," also is credited with having invented boxing gloves. However, these gloves—or "mufflers" as they were called—were used only in teaching "the manly art of self-defense" or in training bouts. All professional championship fights were contested with "bare knuckles" until 1892, when John L. Sullivan lost the heavyweight championship of the world to James J. Corbett in New Orleans in a bout in which both contestants wore regulation gloves.

The Broughton rules were superseded by the London Prize Ring Rules of 1838. The 8th Marquis of Queensberry, with the help of John G. Chambers, put forward the "Queensberry Rules" in 1866, a code that called for gloved contests. Amateurs took quickly to the Queensberry Rules, the professionals slowly.

HISTORY OF WORLD HEAVYWEIGHT CHAMPIONSHIP FIGHTS

(Bouts in which a new champion was crowned)

Source: Nat Fleischer's Ring *Boxing Encyclopedia and Record Book,* published and copyrighted by The Ring Book Shop, Inc., 120 West 31st St., New York, N.Y. 10001.

Date	Where held	Winner, weight, age	Loser, weight, age	Rounds	Referee
Sept. 7, 1892	New Orleans, La.	James J. Corbett, 178 (26)	John L. Sullivan, 212 (33)	21	Prof. John Duffy
March 17, 1897	Carson City, Nev.	Bob Fitzsimmons, 167 (34)	James J. Corbett, 183 (30)	KO 14	George Siler
June 9, 1899	Coney Island, N.Y.	James J. Jeffries, 206 (24)[1]	Bob Fitzsimmons, 167 (37)	KO 11	George Siler
Feb. 23, 1906	Los Angeles	Tommy Burns, 180 (24)[2]	Marvin Hart, 188 (29)	20	James J. Jeffries
Dec. 26, 1908	Sydney, N.S.W.	Jack Johnson, 196 (30)	Tommy Burns, 176 (27)	KO 14	Hugh McIntosh
April 5, 1915	Havana, Cuba	Jess Willard, 230 (33)	Jack Johnson, 205 1/2 (37)	KO 26	Jack Welch
July 4, 1919	Toledo, Ohio	Jack Dempsey, 187 (24)	Jess Willard, 245 (37)	KO 3	Ollie Pecord
Sept. 23, 1926	Philadelphia	Gene Tunney, 189 (28)[3]	Jack Dempsey, 190 (31)	10	Pop Reilly
June 12, 1930	New York	Max Schmeling, 188 (24)	Jack Sharkey, 197 (27)	WF 4	Jim Crowley
June 21, 1932	Long Island City	Jack Sharkey, 205 (29)	Max Schmeling, 188 (26)	15	Gunboat Smith
June 29, 1933	Long Island City	Primo Carnera, 260 1/2 (26)	Jack Sharkey, 201 (30)	KO 6	Arthur Donovan
June 14, 1934	Long Island City	Max Baer, 209 1/2 (25)	Primo Carnera, 263 1/4 (27)	KO 11	Arthur Donovan
June 13, 1935	Long Island City	Jim Braddock, 193 3/4 (29)	Max Baer, 209 1/2 (26)	15	Jack McAvoy
June 22, 1937	Chicago	Joe Louis, 197 1/4 (23)	Jim Braddock, 197 (31)	KO 8	Tommy Thomas
June 22, 1949	Chicago	Ezzard Charles, 181 3/4 (27)[4]	Joe Walcott, 195 1/2 (35)	15	Davey Miller
Sept. 27, 1950	New York	Ezzard Charles, 184 1/2 (29)[5]	Joe Louis, 218 (36)	15	Mark Conn
July 18, 1951	Pittsburgh	Joe Walcott, 194 (37)	Ezzard Charles, 182 (30)	KO 7	Buck McTiernan
Sept. 23, 1952	Philadelphia	Rocky Marciano, 184 (29)[6]	Joe Walcott, 196 (38)	KO13	Charley Daggett
Nov. 30, 1956	Chicago	Floyd Patterson, 182 1/4 (21)	Archie Moore, 187 3/4 (42)	KO 5	Frank Sikora
June 26, 1959	New York	Ingemar Johansson, 196 (26)	Floyd Patterson, 182 (24)	KO 3	Ruby Goldstein
June 20, 1960	New York	Floyd Patterson, 190 (25)	Ingemar Johansson, 194 3/4 (27)	KO 5	Arthur Mercante
Sept. 25, 1962	Chicago	Sonny Liston, 214 (28)	Floyd Patterson, 189 (27)	KO 1	Frank Sikora
Feb. 25, 1964	Miami Beach, Fla.	Cassius Clay, 210 (22)[7]	Sonny Liston, 218 (30)	KO 7	Barney Felix
March 4, 1968	New York	Joe Frazier, 204 1/2 (24)[8]	Buster Mathis, 243 1/2 (23)	KO 11	Arthur Mercante
April 27, 1968	Oakland, Calif.	Jimmy Ellis, 197 (28)[9]	Jerry Quarry, 195 (22)	15	Elmer Costa
Feb. 16, 1970	New York	Joe Frazier, 205 (26)[10]	Jimmy Ellis, 201 (29)	KO 5	Tony Perez
Jan. 22, 1973	Kingston, Jamaica	George Foreman, 217 1/2 (24)	Joe Frazier, 214 (29)	KO 2	Arthur Mercante
Oct. 30, 1974	Kinshasa, Zaire	Muhammad Ali, 216 1/2 (32)	George Foreman, 220 (26)	KO 8	Zack Clayton
Feb. 15, 1978	Las Vegas, Nev.	Leon Spinks, 197 (25)	Muhammad Ali, 224 1/2 (36)	15	Howard Buck
June 9, 1978	Las Vegas, Nev.	Larry Holmes, 212 (28)[11]	Ken Norton, 220 (32)	15	Mills Lans
Sept. 15, 1978	New Orleans	Muhammad Ali, 221 (36)[12]	Leon Spinks, 201 (25)	15	Lucien Joubert
Oct. 20, 1979	Pretoria, S. Africa	John Tate, 240 (24)[13]	Gerrie Coetzee, 222 (24)	15	Carlos Berrocal
March 31, 1980	Knoxville, Tenn.	Mike Weaver, 207 1/2 (27)	John Tate, 232 (25)	KO 15	Ernesto Magana Ansorena
Dec. 10, 1982	Las Vegas, Nev.	Michael Dokes, 216 (24)	Mike Weaver, 209 1/2 (30)	KO 1	Joey Curtis
Sept. 23, 1983	Richfield, Ohio	Gerrie Coetzee, 215 (28)	Michael Dokes, 217 (25)	KO 10	Tony Perez
March 9, 1984	Las Vegas, Nev.	Tim Witherspoon, 2201/2 (26)[14]	Greg Page, 239 1/2 (25)	12	Mills Lane
August 31, 1984	Las Vegas, Nev.	Pinklon Thomas, 216 (26)	Tim Witherspoon, 217 (26)	12	Richard Steele
Nov. 9, 1984	Las Vegas, Nev.	Larry Holmes, 221 1/2 (35)[15]	James Smith 227 (31)	KO 12	Dave Pearl
Dec. 1, 1984	Sun City, S. Africa	Greg Page, 236 (25)[16]	Gerry Coetzee, 217 (29)	KO 8	unavailable
April 29, 1985	Buffalo, N.Y.	Tony Tubbs, 229 (26)[16]	Greg Page, 239 1/2 (26)	15	unavailable.
Sept. 21,1985	Las Vegas, Nev.	Michael Spinks, 200 (29)	Larry Holmes, 221 (35)	15	Carlos Padilla
Jan. 17, 1986	Atlanta, Ga.	Tim Witherspoon, 227 (28)	Tony Tubbs, 229 (27)	15	unavailable
Nov. 23, 1986	Las Vegas, Nev.	Mike Tyson, 217 (20)[17]	Trevor Berbick, 220 (29)	KO 2	unavailable
Dec. 12, 1986	New York, N.Y.	James Smith, 230 (33)[16]	Tim Witherspoon, 218 (29)	KO 1	unavailable
March 7, 1987	Las Vegas, Nev.	Mike Tyson, 217 (20)[16]	James Smith, 230 (33)	12	unavailable
Feb. 10, 1990	Tokyo	James "Buster" Douglas,[18] 231 1/2 (29)	Mike Tyson (220) (23)	KO 10	Octavio Meyrom
Oct. 25, 1990	Las Vegas, Nev.	Evander Holyfield, 208 (28)	James "Buster" Douglas, 246 (30)	KO 3	Mills Lane

1. Jeffries retired as champion in March 1905. He named Marvin Hart and Jack Root as leading contenders and agreed to referee their fight in Reno, Nev., on July 3, 1905, with the stipulation that he would term the winner the champion. Hart, 190 (28), knocked out Root, 171 (29), in the 12th round. 2. Burns claimed the title after defeating Hart. 3. Tunney retired as champion after defeating Tom Heeney on July 26, 1928. 4. After Louis announced his retirement as champion on March 1, 1949, Charles won recognition from the National Boxing Association as champion by defeating Walcott. 5. Charles gained undisputed recognition as champion by defeating Louis, who came out of retirement. 6. Retired as Champion April 27, 1956. 7. The World Boxing Association later withdrew its recognition of Clay as champion and declared the winner of a bout between Ernie Terrell and Eddie Machen would gain its version of the title. Terrell, 199 (25), won a 15–round decision from Machen, 192 (32), in Chicago on March 5, 1965. Clay, 212 1/4 (25) and Terrell, 212 1/2 (27) met in Houston on Feb. 6, 1967, Clay winning a 15–round decision. 8. Winner recognized by New York, Massachusetts, Maine, Illinois, Texas and Pennsylvania to fill vacated title when Clay was stripped of championship for failing to accept U. S. Induction. 9. Bout was final of eight–man tournament to fill Clay's place and is recognized by World Boxing Association. 10. Bout settled controversy over title. 11. Holmes won World Boxing Council title after WBC had withdrawn recognition of Spinks, March 18, 1978, and awarded its title to Norton. WBC said Spinks had reneged on agreement to fight Norton 12. Ali regained World Boxing Association championship. 13. Tate won WBA title after Ali retired and left it vacant. 14. Tim Witherspoon and Greg Page fought for the WBC heavyweight title vacated by Larry Holmes, who could not come to agreement on a deal to fight Page, the No. 1 contender. Holmes declared he would fight under the banner of the International Boxing Federation. Several dates were set and postponed for fights between Holmes and Gerry Coetzee, the WBA champ, the latest being Nov. 16, 1984. 15. First fight under banner of International Boxing Federation. 16. New W.B.A. champion. 17. New W.B.C. champion. 18. New undisputed champion.

OTHER WORLD BOXING TITLEHOLDERS
(Through Aug. 15, 1991)

Light Heavyweight

Year	Holder
1903	Jack Root, George Gardner
1903–05	Bob Fitzsimmons
1905–12	Philadelphia Jack O'Brien[1]
1912–16	Jack Dillon
1916–20	Battling Levinsky
1920–22	Georges Carpentier
1923	Battling Siki
1923–25	Mike McTigue
1925–26	Paul Berlenbach
1926–27	Jack Delaney[2]
1927	Mike McTigue
1927–29	Tommy Loughran
1930	Jimmy Slattery
1930–34	Maxie Rosenbloom
1934–35	Bob Olin
1935–39	John Henry Lewis
1939	Melio Bettina
1939–41	Billy Conn[2]
1941	Anton Christoforidis (NBA)
1941–48	Gus Lesnevich
1948–50	Freddie Mills
1950–52	Joey Maxim
1952–61	Archie Moore[3]
1961–63	Harold Johnson
1963–65	Willie Pastrano
1965–66	José Torres
1966–67	Dick Tiger
1968	Dick Tiger, Bob Foster
1969–70	Bob Foster
1971	Vicente Rondon (WBA), Bob!Foster (WBC)
1972-73	Bob Foster (WBA, WBC)
1974	John Conteh (WBA), Bob Foster (WBC)[1,4]
1975–76	Victor Galindez (WBA), John Conteh (WBC)
1977	Victor Galindez (WBA), John Conteh (WBC)[4] Miguel Cuello (WBC)
1978	Victor Galindez (WBA), Mike Rossman (WBA), Miguel Cuello (WBC), Mate Parlov (WBC), Marvin Johson (WBC)
1979	Mike Rossman (WBA), Victor Galindez (WBA), Marvin Johnson (WBC), Matthew (Franklin) Saad Muhammad (WBC)
1980	Matthew Saad Muhammad (WBC), Marvin Johnson (WBA), Eddie (Gregory), Mustafa Muhammad (WBA)
1981	Matthew Saad Muhammad (WBC), Eddie Mustafa Muhammad (WBA), Michael Spinks (WBA), Dwight Braxton (WBC)
1982	Dwight Braxton (WBC), Michael Spinks (WBA)
1983	Michael Spinks (undisputed)
1984	Michael Spinks (undisputed)
1985	Michael Spinks (undisputed)[5]
1986	Marvin Johnson (WBA) Dennis Andries (WBC)
1987	Thomas Hearns (WBC), Virgil Hill (WBA), Bobby Czyz (IBF)
1988	Charles Williams (IBF), Virgil Hill (WBA), Donny LaLonde (WBC), Sugar Ray Leonard (WBC)
1989	Dennis Andries (WBC), Virgil Hill (WBA), Charles Williams (IBF), Jeff Harding (WBC)
1990	Virgil Hill (WBA), Charles Williams (IBF), Jeff Harding (WBC), Dennis Andries (WBC)
1991	Virgil Hall (WBA), Thomas Hearns (WBA), Dennis Andries (WBC), Charles Williams (IBF)

1. Retired. 2. Abandoned title. 3. NBA withdrew recognition in 1961, New York Commission in 1962; recognized thereafter only by California and Europe. 4. WBC withdrew recognition. 5. Spinks relinquished title in 1985 to fight for heavyweight title.

Middleweight

Year	Holder
1867–72	Tom Chandler
1872–81	George Rooke
1881–82	Mike Donovan[1]
1884–91	Jack (Nonpareil) Dempsey
1891–97	Bob Fitzsimmons[2]
1908	Stanley Ketchel, Billy Papke
1908–10	Stanley Ketchel[3]
1913	Frank Klaus
1913–14	George Chip
1914–17	Al McCoy
1917–20	Mike O'Dowd
1920–23	Johnny Wilson
1923–26	Harry Greb
1926	Tiger Flowers
1926–31	Mickey Walker[2]
1931–41	Gorilla Jones, Ben Jeby, Marcel Thil, Lou Brouillard, Vince Dundee, Teddy Yarosz, Babe Risko, Freddy Steele, Al Hostak, Solly Kreiger, Fred Apostoli, Cerferino Garcia, Ken Overlin, Billy Soose, Tony Zale[4]
1941–47	Tony Zale
1947–48	Rocky Graziano
1948	Tony Zale
1948–49	Marcel Cerdan
1949–51	Jake LaMotta
1952	Ray Robinson, Randy Turpin
1951–52	Ray Robinson[1]
1953–55	Carl Olson
1955–57	Ray Robinson[5]
1957	Gene Fullmer, Ray Robinson
1957–58	Carmen Basilio
1958–60	Ray Robinson[6]
1960–61	Paul Pender[7]
1959–62	Gene Fullmer (NBA)
1961–62	Terry Downes[1]
1962	Paul Pender[1]
1962–63	Dick Tiger
1963–65	Joey Giardello
1965–66	Dick Tiger
1966	Emile Griffith
1967	Nino Benvenuti, Emile Griffith
1968	Emile Griffith, Nino Benvenuti
1969	Nino Benvenuti
1970	Nino Benvenuti, Carlos Monzon
1971–73	Carlos Monzon
1974–75	Carlos Monzon (WBA), Rodrigo Valdez (WBC)
1976	Carlos Monzon (WBA, WBC), Rodrigo Valdez (WBC)
1977	Carlos Monzon (WBA,WBC)[1], Rodrigo Valdez (WBA, WBC)
1978	Rodrigo Valdez, Hugo Corro
1979	Hugo Corro, Vito Antuofermo

1980	Vito Antuofermo, Alan Minter, Marvin Hagler
1981	Marvin Hagler
1982–86	Marvelous Marvin Hagler (undisputed)
1987	Marvin Hagler (undisputed) Sugar Ray Leonard (undisputed)
1988	Sumbu Kalambay (WBA), Thomas Hearns (WBC), Iran Barkley (WBC), Frank Tate (IBF), Michael Nunn (IBF), James Kinchen (NABF)
1989	Michael Nunn (IBF), Mike McCallum (WBA), Iran Barkley (WBC), Roberto Duran (WBC)
1990	Michael McCallum (WBA), Michael Nunn (IBF), Iran Barkley (WBC)
1991	Michael Nunn (IBF), James Toney (IBF), Michael McCallum (WBA)

1. Retired. 2. Abandoned title. 3. Died. 4. National Boxing Association and New York Commission disagreed on champions. Those listed were accepted by one or the other until Zale gained world-wide recognition. 5. Ended retirement in 1954. 6. NBA withdrew recognition. 7. Recognized by New York, Massachusetts, and Europe.

Welterweight

1892–94	Mysterious Billy Smith
1894–96	Tommy Ryan
1896	Kid McCoy[2]
1896–	
1900	Mysterious Billy Smith
1900	Rube Ferns
1900–01	Matty Matthews
1901	Ruby Ferns
1901–04	Joe Walcott
1904	Dixie Kid[2]
1904–06	Joe Walcott
1906–07	Honey Mellody
1907	Mike (Twin) Sullivan[2]
1915–19	Ted Lewis
1919–22	Jack Britton
1922–26	Mickey Walker
1926–27	Pete Latzo
1927–29	Joe Dundee
1929–30	Jackie Fields
1930	Young Jack Thompson
1930–31	Tommy Freeman
1931	Young Jack Thompson
1931–32	Lou Brouillard
1932–33	Jackie Fields
1933	Young Corbett 3rd
1933–34	Jimmy McLarnin, Barney Ross
1934–35	Jimmy McLarnin
1935–38	Barney Ross
1938–40	Henry Armstrong
1940–41	Fritzie Zivic
1941–46	Freddie Cochrane
1946	Marty Servo[1]
1946–51	Ray Robinson[2]
1951	Johnny Bratton (NBA)
1951–54	Kid Gavilan
1954–55	Johnny Saxton
1955	Tony DeMarco
1955–56	Carmen Basilio

1956	Johnny Saxton
1956–57	Carmen Basilio[2]
1958	Virgil Akins
1959–60	Don Jordan
1960–61	Benny (Kid) Paret
1961	Emile Griffith
1961–62	Benny (Kid) Paret
1962–63	Emile Griffith, Luis Rodriguez
1963–66	Emile Griffith[2]
1966-69	Curtis Cokes
1969	Curtis Cokes, José Napoles
1970	José Napoles, Billy Backus
1971	Billy Backus, José Napoles
1972–74	José Napoles
1975	José Napoles (WBA, WBC),[3] Angel Espada (WBA), John Stracey (WBC)
1976	Angel Espada (WBA), José Cuevas (WBA), John Stracey (WBC), Carlos Palomino (WBC)
1977–78	José Cuevas (WBA), Carlos Palomino (WBC)
1979	José Cuevas (WBA), Carlos Palomino (WBC), Wilfredo Benitez (WBC)
1980	José Cuevas (WBA), Ray Leonard (WBC), Roberto Duran (WBC), Thomas Hearns (WBA)
1981	Ray Leonard (WBC), Thomas Hearns (WBA), Ray Leonard (WBC,WBA)
1982	Ray Leonard
1983–85	Donald Curry (WBA)
1983–85	Milton McCrory (WBC)
1985–86	Donald Curry (undisputed)
1987	Mark Breland (WBA) Marlon Starling (WBA) Lloyd Honeychan (IBF)
1988	Marlon Starling (WBA), Tomas Molinares (WBA), Lloyd Honeyghan (WBC), Simon Brown (IBF)
1989	Mark Breland (WBA), Marlon Starling (WBC), Simon Brown (IBF)
1990	Mark Breland (WBA), Aaron Davis (WBA), Simon Brown (WBC), Marlon Starling (WBC), Maurice Blocker (WBC)
1991	Meldrick Taylor (WBA), Simon Brown (IBF, WBC)

1. Retired. 2. Abandoned title. 3. WBA withdrew recognition.

Lightweight

1869–99	Kid Lavigne
1899–	
1902	Frank Erne
1902–08	Joe Gans
1908–10	Battling Nelson
1910–12	Ad Wolgast
1912–14	Willie Ritchie
1914–17	Freddy Welsh
1917–25	Benny Leonard[1]
1925	Jimmy Goodrich
1925–26	Rocky Kansas
1926–30	Sammy Mandell
1930	Al Singer
1930–33	Tony Canzoneri
1933–35	Barney Ross[2]

1935–36	Tony Canzoneri
1936–38	Lou Ambers
1938–39	Henry Armstrong
1939–40	Lou Ambers
1940–41	Lew Jenkins
1941–42	Sammy Angott[1]
1943–47	Beau Jack (N.Y.), Bob Montgomery (N.Y.), Sammy Angott (NBA), Juan Zurita (NBA), Ike Williams (NBA)
1947–51	Ike Williams
1951–52	James Carter
1952	Lauro Salas
1952–54	James Carter
1954	Paddy DeMarco
1954–55	James Carter
1955–56	Wallace Smith
1956–62	Joe Brown
1962–65	Carlos Ortiz
1965	Ismael Laguna
1965–68	Carlos Ortiz
1968	Teo Cruz
1969	Teo Cruz, Mando Ramos
1970	Mando Ramos, Ismael Laguna, Ken Buchanan
1971	Ken Buchanan (WBA), Mando Ramos (WBC), Pedro Carrasco (WBC)
1972	Ken Buchanan (WBA), Roberto Duran (WBA), Pedro Carrasco (WBC), Mando Ramos (WBC), Chango Carmona (WBC), Rodolfo Gonzalez (WBC)
1973	Roberto Duran (WBA), Rodolfo Gonzalez (WBC)
1974	Roberto Duran (WBA), Rodolfo Gonzalez (WBC), Guts Ishimatsu (WBC)
1975	Roberto Duran (WBA), Guts Ishimatsu (WBC)
1976	Roberto Duran (WBA), Guts Ishimatsu (WBC), Esteban!De Jesus (WBC)
1977	Roberto Duran (WBA), Esteban De Jesus (WBC)
1978	Roberto Duran (WBA, WBC)
1979	Roberto Duran[2], Jim Watt (WBC), Ernesto Espana (WBA)
1980	Ernesto Espana (WBA), Hilmer Kenty (WBA), Jim Watt (WBC)
1981	Hilmer Kenty (WBA), Sean O'Grady (WBA), James Watt (WBC), Alexis Arguello (WBC), Arturo Frias (WBA)
1982	Arturo Frias (WBA), Ray Mancini (WBA), Alexis Arguello (WBC)
1983	Edwin Rosario (WBC), Ray Mancini (WBA)
1984	Edwin Rosario (WBC), Livingstone Bramble (WBA)
1985	Jose Luis Ramirez (WBC) Hector Camacho (WBC) Livingstone Bramble (WBA)
1986	Hector Camacho (WBC) Livingstone Bramble (WBA) Jim Paul (IBF)

1987	Edwin Rosario (WBA) Jose Luis Ramirez (WBC), Greg Haugen (IBF)
1988	Jose Luis Ramirez (WBC), Julio Cesar Chavez (WBA), Greg Haugen (IBF), Julius Cesar Chavez (WBC & WBA title unified)
1989	Pernell Whitaker (IBF, WBC), Edwin Rosario (WBA)
1990	Pernell Whitaker (IBF, WBC) Juan Nazario (WBA)
1991	Pernell Whitaker (IBF, WBA, WBC)

1. Retired. 2. Abandoned title.

Featherweight

1889	Dal Hawkins[1]
1890	Billy Murphy
1892–	
1900	George Dixon
1900–01	Terry McGovern
1901	Young Corbett[1]
1901–12	Abe Attell
1912–23	Johnny Kilbane
1923	Eugene Criqui
1923–25	Johnny Dundee[1]
1925–27	Louis (Kid) Kaplan[1]
1927–28	Benny Bass
1928	Tony Canzoneri
1928–29	Andre Routis
1929–32	Battling Battalino[1]
1932	Tommy Paul (NBA), Kid Chocolate (N.Y.)
1933–36	Freddie Miller
1936–37	Petey Sarron
1937–38	Henry Armstrong[1]
1938–40	Joey Archibald
1940–41	Harry Jefra, Joey Archibald
1941–42	Chalky Wright
1942–48	Willie Pep
1948–49	Sandy Saddler[2]
1949–50	Willie Pep
1950–57	Sandy Saddler
1957–59	Kid Bassey
1959–63	Davey Moore
1963–64	Sugar Ramos
1964–67	Vicente Saldivar[2]
1968	Howard Winstone, José Legra,[3] Paul Rojas (WBA), Sho Saijo (WBA)
1969	Sho Saijo (WBA), Johnny Famechon[3]
1970	Sho Saijo (WBA), Johnny Famechon,[3] Vicente Salvidar,[3] Kuniaki Shibata[3]
1971	Sho Saijo (WBA), Antonio Gomez (WBA), Kuniaki Shibata (WBC)
1972	Antonio Gomez (WBA), Ernesto Marcel (WBA), Kuniaki Shibata (WBC), Clemente Sanchez (WBC), José Legra (WBC)
1973	Ernesto Marcel (WBA), José Legra (WBC), Eder Jofre (WBC)
1974	Ernesto Marcel (WBA)[2], Ruben Olivares (WBA), Alexis Arguello (WBA), Eder Jofre (WBC), Bobby Chacon (WBC)

1975	Alexis Arguello (WBA), Bobby Chacon (WBC), Ruben Olivares (WBC), David Kotey (WBC)
1976	Alexis Arguello (WBA),[2] David Kotey (WBC), Danny Lopez (WBC)
1977	Rafael Ortega (WBA), Danny Lopez (WBC)
1978	Rafael Ortega (WBA), Cecilio Lastra (WBA), Eusebio Pedroza (WBA), Danny Lopez (WBC)
1979	Eusebio Pedroza (WBA), Danny Lopez (WBC)
1980	Eusebio Pedroza (WBA), Danny Lopez (WBC), Salvador Sanchez (WBC)
1981	Eusebio Pedroza (WBA), Salvador Sanchez (WBC)
1982	Eusebio Pedroza (WBA), Salvador Sanchez (WBC)[4]
1983	Juan Laporte (WBC), Eusebio Pedroza (WBA)
1984	Wilfred Gomez (WBC), Eusebio Pedroza (WBA)
1985	Eusebio Pedroza (WBA) Barry McGuigan (WBA) Azumah Nelson (WBC)
1986	Barry McGuigan (WBA) Stevie Cruz (WBA) Azumah Nelson (WBC)
1987	Azumah Nelson (WBC) Antonio Esparragoza (WBA)
1988	Calvin Grove (IBF), Jorge Paez (IBF), Antonio Esparragoza (WBA), Jeff Fenech (WBC)
1989	Jorge Paez (IBF), Antonio Esparragoza (WBA), Jeff Fenech (WBC)
1990	Marcos Villasana (WBC), Antonio Esparragoza (WBA), Jorge Paez (IBF)
1991	Park Young-Kyun (WBA), Troy Dorsey (IBF), Marcos Villagana (WBC)

1. Abandoned title. 2. Retired. 3. Recognized in Europe, Mexico, and Orient. 4. Killed in auto accident.

Bantamweight

1890–92	George Dixon[1]
1894–99	Jimmy Barry[2]
1899–	
1900	Terry McGovern[1]
1901	Harry Harris[1]
1902–03	Harry Forbes
1903–04	Frankie Neil
1904	Joe Bowker[1]
1905–07	Jimmy Walsh[1]
1910–14	Johnny Coulon
1914–17	Kid Williams
1917–20	Pete Herman
1920	Joe Lynch
1920–21	Joe Lynch, Pete Herman, Johnny Buff
1922	Johnny Buff, Joe Lynch
1923	Joe Lynch
1924	Joe Lynch, Abe Goldstein
1924	Abe Goldstein, Eddie (Cannonball) Martin
1925	Eddie (Cannonball) Martin, Charlie (Phil) Rosenberg[3]
1927–28	Bud Taylor (NBA)[1]

1929–34	Al Brown
1935	Al Brown, Baltazar Sangchili
1936	Baltazar Sangchili, Tony Marino, Sixto Escobar
1937	Sixto Escobar, Harry Jeffra
1938	Harry Jeffra, Sixto Escobar
1939–40	Sixto Escobar[2]
1940–42	Lou Salica
1942–46	Manuel Ortiz
1947	Manuel Ortiz, Harold Dade
1948–50	Manuel Ortiz
1950–52	Vic Toweel
1952–54	Jimmy Carruthers[2]
1954–55	Robert Cohen
1956	Robert Cohen, Mario D'Agata, Raul Macias (NBA)
1957	Mario D'Agata, Alphonse Halimi
1958–59	Alphonse Halimi
1959–60	Jose Becerra[2]
1960–61	Alphonse Halimi[4]
1961–62	Johnny Caldwell[4]
1961–65	Eder Jofre
1965–68	Masahika (Fighting) Harada
1968	Masahika (Fighting) Harada, Lionel Rose
1969	Lionel Rose, Ruben Olivares
1970	Ruben Olivares, Chucho Castillo
1971	Chucho Castillo, Ruben Olivares
1972	Ruben Olivares, Rafael Herrera, Enrique Pinder
1973	Enrique Pinder (WBA), Romeo Anaya (WBA), Arnold Taylor (WBA), Rodolfo Martinez (WBC), Rafael Herrera
1974	Arnold Taylor (WBA), Soo Hwan Hong (WBA), Rafael Herrera (WBC), Rodolfo Martinez (WBC)
1975	Soo Hwan Hong (WBA), Alfonso Zamora (WBA), Rodolfo Martinez (WBC)
1976	Alfonso Zamora (WBA), Rodolfo Martinez (WBC), Carlos Zarate (WBC)
1977	Alfonso Zamora (WBA), Jorge Lujan (WBA), Carlos Zarate (WBC)
1978	Jorge Lujan (WBA), Carlos Zarate (WBC)
1979	Jorge Lujan (WBA), Carlos Zarate (WBC), Lupe Pintor (WBC)
1980	Jorge Lujan (WBA), Lupe Pintor (WBC), Julian Solis (WBA), Jeff Chandler (WBA)
1981	Lupe Pintor (WBC), Jeff Chandler (WBA)
1982	Lupe Pintor (WBC), Jeff Chandler (WBA)
1983	Jeff Chandler (WBA), Albert Dauila (WBC)
1984	Richie Sandqual (WBA), Albert Dauila (WBC)
1985	Richard Sandoval (WBA) Daniel Zaragoza (WBC) Miguel Lora (WBC)
1986	Richard Sandoval (WBA) Bernardo Pinango (WBA) Jeff Fenech (IBF)

1987	Bernardo Pinango (WBA) Takuya Muguruma (WBA) Miguel Lora (WBC)	
1988	Wilfred Vasquez (WBA), Jibaro Perez (WBC), Moon Sung-gil (WBA) Orlando Canizales (IBF)	
1989	Jibaro Perez (WBC), Moon Sung-gil (WBA), Orlando Canizales (IBF) Kaokor Galaxy (WBA), Luis Espinosa (WBA)	
1990	Orlando Canizales (IBF), Jibaro Perez (WBC), Luis Espinosa (WBA)	
1991	Greg Richardson (WBC), Orlando Canizales (IBF), Luis Espinosa (WBA)	

1. Abandoned title. 2. Retired. 3. Deprived of title for failing to make weight. 4. Recognized in Europe.

Flyweight

1916–23	Jimmy Wilde
1923–25	Pancho Villa[1]
1925	Frankie Genaro
1925–27	Fidel La Barba[2]
1927–31	Corporal Izzy Schwartz, Frankie Genaro, Emile (Spider) Pladner, Midget Wolgast, Young Perez[3]
1932–35	Jackie Brown
1935–38	Bennie Lynch[4]
1939	Peter Kane[4]
1943–47	Jackie Paterson[1]
1947–50	Rinty Monaghan[2]
1950	Terry Allen
1950–52	Dado Marino
1952–54	Yoshio Shirai
1954–60	Pascual Perez
1960–62	Pone Kingpetch

1962–63	Masahika (Fighting) Harada
1963–64	Hiroyuki Ebihara
1964–65	Pone Kingpetch
1965–66	Salvatore Burrini
1966	Walter McGown, Chartchai Chionoi
1966–68	Charchai Chionoi
1969	Bernabe Villacampa, Efran Torres (WBA)
1970	Bernabe Villacampa, Chartchai Chionoi, Erbito Salavarria, Berkrerk Chartvanchai (WBA) Masao Ohba (WBA)
1971	Masao Ohba (WBA), Erbito Salavarria (WBC)
1972	Masao Ohba (WBA), Erbito Salavarria (WBC), Betulio Gonzalez (WBC), Venice Borkorsor (WBC)
1973	Masao Ohba (WBA), Chartchai Chionoi (WBA), Venice Borkorsor (WBC), Betulio Gonzalez (WBC)
1974	Chartchai Chionoi (WBA), Susumu Hanagata (WBA), Betulio Gonzalez (WBC), Shoji Oguma (WBC)
1975	Susumu Hanagata (WBA), Erbito Salavarria (WBA), Shoji Oguma (WBC), Miguel Canto (WBC)
1976	Erbito Salavarria (WBA), Alfonso Lopez (WBA), Guty Espadas (WBA), Miguel Canto (WBC)
1977	Guty Espadas (WBA), Miguel Canto (WBC)
1978	Guty Espadas (WBA), Betulio Gonzalez (WBA), Miguel Canto (WBC)

1979	Betulio Gonzalez (WBA), Miguel Canto (WBC), Park Chan–Hee (WBC)
1980	Luis Ibarra (WBA), Kim Tae Shik (WBA), Park Chan–Hee (WBC), Shoji Oguma (WBC)
1983	Frank Cedeno (WBC), Santos Lacia (WBA)
1984	Koji Kobayashy (WBA), Gabriel Bernal (WBC), Santos Laciar (WBA)
1985	Sot Chitlada (WBC) Santos Laciar (WBA)
1986	Hilario Zapata (WBA) Julio Cesar–Chevez (WBC)
1987	Shin Hi Sop (IBF) Chang Ho Choi (IBF) Sot Chitlada (WBC)
1988	Sot Chitlada (WBC), Kim Young Kang (WBC), Duke McKenzie (IBF), Fidel Bassa (WBA)
1989	Kim Young–gang (WBC), Sot Chitlada (WBC), Lee Yol–woo (WBA), Duke McKenzie (IBF), Dave McAuley (IBF) Jesus Rojas (WBA)
1990	Sot Chitlada (WBC), Kim Bong–Jung (WBA), Lee Yul–woo (WBA), Dave McAuley (IBF), Leopard Tamakuma (WBA)
1991	Muangchai Kittasem (WBC), Kim-Yong-gang (WBC), Elvis Alvarez (WBA), Dave McAuley (IBF)

1. Died. 2. Retired. 3. Claimants to NBA and New York Commission titles. 4. Abandoned title.

FENCING

World Champions—1991

Source: United States Fencing Association.

Men's epee—Andrei Chouvalov, Soviet Union
Men's foil—Ingo Weissenborn, Germany
Men's sabre—Gregory Kirienko, Soviet Union
Women's foil—Giovanna Trillini, Italy
Women's epee—Marianne Horvath, Hungary
Men's foil team—Cuba
Men's epee team—Soviet Union
Men's sabre team—Hungary
Women's foil team—Italy
Women's epee team—Hungary

United States Champions—1991

Men's foil—Nick Bravin
Women's foil—Mary Jane O'Neill

Men's epee—Jon Normile
Women's epee—Margo Miller
Men's sabre—Michael Lofton

World University Games—1991

Men's foil—Nick Bravin
Women's foil—Isabelle Hamori
Men's epee—Ben Atkins
Women's epee—Jennifer Gilbert
Men's sabre—Robert Cottingham

World Cadet Championships—1991

Men's foil—Sean McClain
Women's foil—Felicia Zimmerman
Men's epee—Sean McClain
Women's epee—Bettina Burleigh
Men's sabre—George Kalmar

HORSE RACING

Ancient drawings on stone and bone prove that horse racing is at least 3000 years old, but Thoroughbred Racing is a modern development. Practically every thoroughbred in training today traces its registered ancestry back to one or more of three sires that arrived in England about 1728 from the Near East and became known, from the names of their owners, as the Byerly Turk, the Darley Arabian, and the Godolphin Arabian. The Jockey Club (English) was founded at Newmarket in 1750 or 1751 and became the custodian of the Stud Book as well as the court of last resort in deciding turf affairs.

Horse racing took place in this country before the Revolution, but the great lift to the breeding industry came with the importation in 1798, by Col. John Hoomes of Virginia, of Diomed, winner of the Epsom Derby of 1780. Diomed's lineal descendants included such famous stars of the American turf as American Eclipse and Lexington. From 1800 to the time of the Civil War there were race courses and breeding establishments plentifully scattered through Virginia, North Carolina, South Carolina, Tennessee, Kentucky, and Louisiana.

The oldest stake event in North America is the Queen's Plate, a Canadian fixture that was first run in the Province of Quebec in 1836. The oldest stake event in the United States is The Travers, which was first run at Saratoga in 1864. The gambling that goes with horse racing and trickery by jockeys, trainers, owners, and track officials caused attacks on the sport by reformers and a demand among horse racing enthusiasts for an honest and effective control of some kind, but nothing of lasting value to racing came of this until the formation in 1894 of The Jockey Club.

"TRIPLE CROWN" WINNERS IN THE UNITED STATES[1]
(Kentucky Derby, Preakness and Belmont Stakes)

Year	Horse	Owner	Year	Horse	Owner
1919	Sir Barton	J. K. L. Ross	1946	Assault	Robert J. Kleberg
1930	Gallant Fox	William Woodward	1948	Citation	Warren Wright
1935	Omaha	William Woodward	1973	Secretariat	Meadow Stable
1937	War Admiral	Samuel D. Riddle	1977	Seattle Slew	Karen Taylor
1941	Whirlaway	Warren Wright	1978	Affirmed	Louis Wolfson
1943	Count Fleet	Mrs. John Hertz			

KENTUCKY DERBY
Churchill Downs; 3–year-olds; 1 1/4 miles.

Year	Winner	Jockey	Wt.	Win val.	Year	Winner	Jockey	Wt.	Win val.
1875	Aristides	O. Lewis	100	$2,850	1913	Donerail	R. Goose	117	$5,475
1876	Vagrant	R. Swim	97	2,950	1914	Old Rosebud	J. McCabe	114	9,125
1877	Baden Baden	W. Walker	100	3,300	1915	Regret	J. Notler	112	11,450
1878	Day Star	J. Carter	100	4,050	1916	George Smith	J. Loftus	117	9,750
1879	Lord Murphy	C. Schauer	100	3,550	1917	Omar Khayyam	C. Borel	117	16,600
1880	Fonso	G. Lewis	105	3,800	1918	Exterminator	W. Knapp	114	14,700
1881	Hindoo	J. McLaughlin	105	4,410	1919	Sir Barton	J. Loftus	1121/2	20,825
1882	Apollo	B. Hurd	102	4,560	1920	Paul Jones	T. Rice	126	30,375
1883	Leonatus	W. Donohue	105	3,760	1921	Behave Yourself	C. Thompson	126	38,450
1884	Buchanan	I. Murphy	110	3,990	1922	Morvich	A. Johnson	126	46,775
1885	Joe Cotton	E. Henderson	110	4,630	1923	Zev	E. Sande	126	53,600
1886	Ben Ali	P. Duffy	118	4,890	1924	Black Gold	J. D. Mooney	126	52,775
1887	Montrose	I. Lewis	118	4,200	1925	Flying Ebony	E. Sande	126	52,950
1888	Macbeth II	G. Covington	115	4,740	1926	Bubbling Over	A. Johnson	126	50,075
1889	Spokane	T. Kiley	118	4,970	1927	Whiskery	L. McAtee	126	51,000
1890	Riley	I. Murphy	118	5,460	1928	Reigh Count	C. Lang	126	55,375
1891	Kingman	I. Murphy	122	4,680	1929	Clyde Van Dusen	L. McAtee	126	53,950
1892	Azra	A. Clayton	122	4,230	1930	Gallant Fox	E. Sande	126	50,725
1893	Lookout	E. Kunze	122	4,090	1931	Twenty Grand	C. Kurtsinger	126	48,725
1894	Chant	F. Goodale	122	4,020	1932	Burgoo King	E. James	126	52,350
1895	Halma	J. Perkins	122	2,970	1933	Brokers Tip	D. Meade	126	48,925
1896	Ben Brush	W. Simms	117	4,850	1934	Cavalcade	M. Garner	126	28,175
1897	Typhoon H	F. Garner	117	4,850	1935	Omaha	W. Saunders	126	39,525
1898	Plaudit	W. Simms	117	4,850	1936	Bold Venture	I. Hanford	126	37,725
1899	Manuel	F. Taral	117	4,850	1937	War Admiral	C. Kurtsinger	126	52,050
1900	Lieut. Gibson	J. Boland	117	4,850	1938	Lawrin	E. Arcaro	126	47,050
1901	His Eminence	J. Winkfield	117	4,850	1939	Johnstown	J. Stout	126	46,350
1902	Alan–a–Dale	J. Winkfield	117	4,850	1940	Gallahadion	C. Bierman	126	60,150
1903	Judge Himes	H. Booker	117	4,850	1941	Whirlaway	E. Arcaro	126	61,275
1904	Elwood	F. Prior	117	4,850	1942	Shut Out	W. D. Wright	126	64,225
1905	Agile	J. Martin	122	4,850	1943	Count Fleet	J. Longden	126	60,725
1906	Sir Huon	R. Troxler	117	4,850	1944	Pensive	C. McCreary	126	64,675
1907	Pink Star	A. Minder	117	4,850	1945	Hoop Jr.	E. Arcaro	126	64,850
1908	Stone Street	A. Pickens	117	4,850	1946	Assault	W. Mehrtens	126	96,400
1909	Wintergreen	V. Powers	117	4,850	1947	Jet Pilot	E. Guerin	126	92,160
1910	Donau	F. Herbert	117	4,850	1948	Citation	E. Arcaro	126	83,400
1911	Meridian	G. Archibald	117	4,850	1949	Ponde	S. Brooks	126	91,600
1912	Worth	C. H. Shilling	117	4,850	1950	Middleground	W. Boland	126	92,650

Year	Winner	Jockey	Wt.	Win val.	Year	Winner	Jockey	Wt.	Win val.
1951	Count Turf	C. McCreary	126	$98,050	1972	Riva Ridge	R. Turcotte	126	$140,300
1952	Hill Gail	E. Arcaro	126	96,300	1973	Secretariat	R. Turcotte	126	155,050
1953	Dark Star	H. Moreno	126	90,050	1974	Cannonade	A. Cordero, Jr.	126	274,000
1954	Determine	R. York	126	102,050	1975	Foolish Pleasure	J. Vasquez	126	209,600
1955	Swaps	W. Shoemaker	126	108,400	1976	Bold Forbes	A. Cordero, Jr.	126	165,200
1956	Needles	D. Erb	126	123,450	1977	Seattle Slew	J. Cruguet	126	214,700
1957	Iron Liege	W. Hartack	126	107,950	1978	Affirmed	S. Cauthen	126	186,900
1958	Tim Tam	I. Valenzuela	126	116,400	1979	Spectacular Bid	R. Franklin	126	228,650
1959	Tomy Lee	W. Shoemaker	126	119,650	1980	Genuine Risk	J. Vasquez	126	250,550
1960	Venetian Way	W. Hartack	126	114,850	1981	Pleasant Colony	J. Velasquez	126	317,200
1961	Carry Back	J. Sellers	126	120,500	1982	Gato del Sol	E. Delahoussaye	126	417,600
1962	Decidedly	W. Hartack	126	119,650	1983	Sunny's Halo	E. Delahoussaye	126	426,000
1963	Chateaugay	B. Baeza	126	108,900	1984	Swale	L. Pincay, Jr.	126	537,400
1964	Northern Dancer	W. Hartack	126	114,300	1985	Spend a Buck	A. Cordero, Jr.	126	406,800
1965	Lucky Debonair	W. Shoemaker	126	112,000	1986	Ferdinand	W. Shoemaker	126	609,400
1966	Kauai King	D. Brumfield	126	120,500	1987	Alysheba	C. McCarron	126	618,600
1967	Proud Clarion	R. Ussery	126	119,700	1988	Winning Colors	Gary Stevens	126	611,200
1968	Forward Pass[1]	I. Valenzuela	126	122,600	1989	Sunday Silence	Patrick Valenzuela	126	574,200
1969	Majestic Prince	W. Hartack	126	113,200					
1970	Dust Commander	M. Manganello	126	127,800	1990	Unbridled	Craig Perret	126	581,000
1971	Canonero II	G. Avila	126	145,500	1991	Strike the Gold	Chris Antley	126	655,800

1. Dancer's Image finished first but was disqualified after traces of drug were found in system.

PREAKNESS STAKES

Pimlico; 3–year–olds; 1 3/16 miles; first race 1873.

Year	Winner	Jockey	Wt.	Win val.	Year	Winner	Jockey	Wt.	Win val.
1919	Sir Barton	J. Loftus	126	$24,500	1961	Carry Back	J. Sellers	126	$126,200
1930	Gallant Fox	E. Sande	126	51,925	1962	Greek Money	J. Rotz	126	135,800
1931	Mate	G. Ellis	126	48,225	1963	Candy Spots	W. Shoemaker	126	127,500
1932	Burgoo King	E. James	126	50,375	1964	Northern Dancer	W. Hartack	126	124,200
1933	Head Play	C. Kurtsinger	126	26,850	1965	Tom Rolfe	R. Turcotte	126	128,100
1934	High Quest	R. Jones	126	25,175	1966	Kauai King	D. Brumfield	126	129,000
1935	Omaha	W. Saunders	126	25,325	1967	Damascus	W. Shoemaker	126	141,500
1936	Bold Venture	G. Woolf	126	27,325	1968	Forward Pass	I. Valenzuela	126	142,700
1937	War Admiral	C. Kurtsinger	126	45,600	1969	Majestic Prince	W. Hartack	126	129,500
1938	Dauber	M. Peters	126	51,875	1970	Personality	E. Belmonte	126	151,300
1939	Challedon	G. Seabo	126	53,710	1971	Canonero II	G. Avila	126	137,400
1940	Bimelech	F.A. Smith	126	53,230	1972	Bee Bee Bee	E. Nelson	126	135,300
1941	Whirlaway	E. Arcaro	126	49,365	1973	Secretariat	R. Turcotte	126	129,900
1942	Alsab	B. James	126	58,175	1974	Little Current	M. Rivera	126	156,000
1943	Count Fleet	J. Longden	126	43,190	1975	Master Derby	D. McHargue	126	158,100
1944	Pensive	C. McCreary	126	60,075	1976	Elocutionist	J. Lively	126	129,700
1945	Polynesian	W.D. Wright	126	66,170	1977	Seattle Slew	J. Cruguet	126	138,600
1946	Assault	W. Mehrtens	126	96,620	1978	Affirmed	S. Cauthen	126	136,200
1947	Faultless	D. Dodson	126	98,005	1979	Spectacular Bid	R. Franklin	126	165,300
1948	Citation	E. Arcaro	126	91,870	1980	Codex	A. Cordero	126	180,600
1949	Capot	T. Atkinson	126	79,985	1981	Pleasant Colony	J. Velasquez	126	270,800
1950	Hill Prince	E. Arcaro	126	56,115	1982	Aloma's Ruler	J. Kaenel	126	209,900
1951	Bold	E. Arcaro	126	83,110	1983	Deputed Testimony	D. Miller	126	251,200
1952	Blue Man	C. McCreary	126	86,135					
1953	Native Dancer	E. Guerin	126	65,200	1984	Gate Dancer	A. Cordero	126	243,600
1954	Hasty Road	J. Adams	126	91,600	1985	Tank's Prospect	Pat Day	126	423,200
1955	Nashua	E. Arcaro	126	67,550	1986	Snow Chief	A. Solis	126	411,900
1956	Fabius	W. Hartack	126	84,250	1987	Alysheba	C. McCarron	126	421,100
1957	Bold Ruler	E. Arcaro	126	65,250	1988	Risen Star	E. Delahoussaye	126	413,700
1958	Tim Tam	I. Valenzuela	126	97,900	1989	Sunday Silence	P. Valenzuela	126	438,230
1959	Royal Orbit	W. Harmatz	126	136,200	1990	Summer Squall	Pat Day	126	445,900
1960	Bally Ache	R. Ussery	126	121,000	1991	Hansel	Jerry Bailey	126	432,770

BELMONT STAKES

Belmont Park; 3–year–olds; 1 1/2 miles.

Run at Jerome Park 1867 to 1890; at Morris Park 1890–94; at Belmont Park 1905–62; at Aqueduct 1963–67. Distance 1 5/8 miles prior to 1874; reduced to 1 1/2 miles, 1874; reduced to 1 1/4 miles, 1890; reduced to 1 1/8 miles, 1893; increased to 1 1/4 miles, 1895; increased to 1 3/8 miles, 1896; reduced to 1 1/4 miles in 1904; increased to 1 1/2 miles, 1926.

Year	Winner	Jockey	Wt.	Win val.	Year	Winner	Jockey	Wt.	Win val.
1919	Sir Barton	J. Loftus	126	$11,950	1932	Faireno	T. Malley	126	$55,120
1930	Gallant Fox	E. Sande	126	66,040	1933	Hurryoff	M. Garner	126	49,490
1931	Twenty Grand	C. Kurtsinger	126	58,770	1934	Peace Chance	W.D. Wright	126	43,410

Year	Winner	Jockey	Wt.	Win val.	Year	Winner	Jockey	Wt.	Win val.
1935	Omaha	W. Saunders	126	$35,480	1965	Hail to All	J. Sellers	126	$104,150
1936	Granville	J. Stout	126	29,800	1966	Amberoid	W. Boland	126	117,700
1937	War Admiral	C. Kurtsinger	126	38,020	1967	Damascus	W. Shoemaker	126	104,950
1938	Pasteurized	J. Stout	126	34,530	1968	Stage Door			
1939	Johnstown	J. Stout	126	37,020		Johnny	H. Gustines	126	117,700
1940	Bimelech	F.A. Smith	126	35,030	1969	Arts and Letters	B. Baeza	126	104,050
1941	Whirlaway	E. Arcaro	126	39,770	1970	High Echelon	J. Rotz	126	115,000
1942	Shut Out	E. Arcaro	126	44,520	1971	Pass Catcher	R. Blum	126	97,710
1943	Count Fleet	J. Longden	126	35,340	1972	Riva Ridge	R. Turcotte	126	93,540
1944	Bounding Home	G.L. Smith	126	55,000	1973	Secretariat	R. Turcotte	126	90,120
1945	Pavot	E. Arcaro	126	56,675	1974	Little Current	M. Rivera	126	101,970
1946	Assault	W. Mehrtens	126	75,400	1975	Avatar	W. Shoemaker	126	116,160
1947	Phalanx	R. Donoso	126	78,900	1976	Bold Forbes	A. Cordero, Jr.	126	117,000
1948	Citation	E. Arcaro	126	77,700	1977	Seattle Slew	J. Cruguet	126	109,080
1949	Capot	T. Atkinson	126	60,900	1978	Affirmed	S. Cauthen	126	110,580
1950	Middleground	W. Boland	126	61,350	1979	Coastal	R. Hernandez	126	161,400
1951	Counterpoint	D. Gorman	126	82,000	1980	Temperence Hill	E. Maple	126	176,220
1952	One Count	E. Arcaro	126	82,400	1981	Summing	G. Martens	126	170,580
1953	Native Dancer	E. Guerin	126	82,500	1982	Conquistador			
1954	High Gun	E. Guerin	126	89,000		Cielo	L. Pincay, Jr.	126	159,720
1955	Nashua	E. Arcaro	126	83,700	1983	Caveat	L. Pincay, Jr.	126	215,100
1956	Needles	D. Erb	126	83,600	1984	Swale	L. Pincay, Jr.	126	310,020
1957	Gallant Man	W. Shoemaker	126	77,300	1985	Creme Fraiche	Eddie Maple	126	307,740
1958	Cavan	P. Anderson	126	73,440	1986	Danzig Connec-			
1959	Sword Dancer	W. Shoemaker	126	93,525		tion	C. McCarron	126	338,640
1960	Celtic Ash	W. Hartack	126	96,785	1987	Bet Twice	C. Perret	126	329,160
1961	Sherluck	B. Baeza	126	104,900	1988	Risen Star	E. Delahoussaye	126	303,720
1962	Jaipur	W. Shoemaker	126	109,550	1989	Easy Goer	P. Day	126	413,520
1963	Chateauguay	B. Baeza	126	101,700	1990	Go And Go	Michael Kinane	126	411,600
1964	Quadrangle	M. Ycaza	126	110,850	1991	Hansel	Jerry Bailey	126	417,480

TRIPLE CROWN RACES—1991

Kentucky Derby (Churchill Downs, Louisville, Ky., May 4, 1991). Gross purse: $908,800. Distance: 1 1/4 miles. Order of finish: 1. Strike the Gold (Antley), mutuel return: $11.60, $6.20, $5.40. 2. Best Pal (Stevens), $6.40, $5.40; Mane Minister (Solis), $25.60. 4. Green Alligator (Nakatani). 5. Fly So Free (Santos). 6. Paulrus (Sellers). 7. Sea Cadet (McCarron). 8. Corporate Report (Day). 9. Hansel (Bailey). 10. Happy Jazz Band (Asmussen). 11. Lost Mountain (McCauley). 12. Another Review (Madrid Jr.). 13. Wilder Than Ever (Deegan). 14. Forty Something (Seefeldt). Winner's purse: $655,800. Margin of Victory: 1 3/4 lengths. Time of race: 2:03. Attendance: 135,554.

Preakness Stakes (Pimlico, Md., May 18, 1991). Gross purse: $665,800. Distance: 1 3/16 miles. Order of finish: 1. Hansel (Bailey), mutuel return: $20.20, $10.80, $80. 2. Corporate Report (Day), $11.00, $6.40. 3. Maine Minister (Solis), $5.80. 4. Olympio (Delahoussaye). 5. Best Pal (Stevens). 6. Strike The Gold (Antley). 7. Whadjathink (Velasquez). 8. Honor Grades (McCarron). Winner's purse: $432,770. Margin of victory: Seven lengths. Time of race: 1:54. Attendance: 87,245.

Belmont Stakes (Elmont, N.Y., June 8, 1991). Gross purse: $695,800. Distance: 1 1/2 miles. Order of finish: 1. Hansel (Bailey), mutuel return: $10.20, $6.40, $5.00. 2. Strike The Gold (Antley), $5.00, $4.00. 3. Mane Minister (Solis), $4.00. 4. Cor-

porate Report (Day). 5. Scan (McCarron). 6. Quintana (Cordero). 7. Lost Mountain (Perret). 8. Smooth Performance (Kinane). 9. Subordinated Debt (Krone). 10. Green Alligator (Nakatani). 11. Another Review (Migliore). Winner's purse: $417,480. Margin of victory: Nose. Time of race: 2:28. Attendance: 51,766.

ECLIPSE AWARDS—1990

(Presented February 1991)

Horse of the Year	Criminal Type
Two—year—old colt	Fly So Free
Two—year—old filly	Meadow Star
Three—year—old colt	Unbridled
Three—year—old filly	Go For Wand
Older male horse	Criminal Type
Older filly or mare	Bayakoq
Male turf horse	Itsallgreektome
Female turf horse	Laugh and Be Merry
Sprinter	Housebuster
Steeplechaser	Morley Street
Owner	Frances D. Genter
Trainer	Carl Nafzger
Breeder	Calumet Farm
Jockey	Craig Perret
Apprentice Jockey	Mark Johnston

RODEO

PROFESSIONAL RODEO COWBOY ASSOCIATION, ALL AROUND COWBOY

1953	Bill Linderman	1963–65	Dean Oliver	1976–79	Tom Ferguson	1985	Lewis Field
1954	Buck Rutherford	1966–70	Larry Mahan	1980	Paul Tierney	1986	Lewis Field
1955	Casey Tibbs	1971–72	Phil Lyne	1981	Jimmie Cooper	1987	Lewis Field
1956–59	Jim Shoulders	1973	Larry Mahan	1982	Chris Lybbert	1988	Dave Appleton
1960	Harry Tompkins	1974	Tom Ferguson	1983	Roy Cooper	1989	Ty Murray
1961	Benny Reynolds	1975	Leo Camarillo and	1984	Dee Pickett	1990	Ty Murray
1962	Tom Nesmith		Tom Ferguson				

1. 1991 championship scheduled December 1991 after *Information Please Almanac* went to press.

TRACK AND FIELD

Running, jumping, hurdling and throwing weights—track and field sports, in other words—are as natural to young people as eating, drinking and breathing. Unorganized competition in this form of sport goes back beyond the Cave Man era. Organized competition begins with the first recorded Olympic Games in Greece, 776 b.c, when Coroebus of Elis won the only event on the program, a race of approximately 200 yards. The Olympic Games, with an ever–widening program of events, continued until "the glory that was Greece" had faded and "the grandeur that was Rome" was tarnished, and finally were abolished by decree of Emperor Theodosius I of Rome in a.d. 394. The Tailteann Games of Ireland are supposed to have antedated the first Olympic Games by some centuries, but we have no records of the specific events and winners thereof.

Professional contests of speed and strength were popular at all times and in many lands, but the widespread competition of amateur athletes in track and field sports is a comparatively modern development. The first organized amateur athletic meet of record was sponsored by the Royal Military Academy at Woolwich, England, in 1849. Oxford and Cambridge track and field rivalry began in 1864, and the English amateur championships were established in 1866. In the United States such organizations as the New York Athletic Club and the Olympic Club of San Francisco conducted track and field meets in the 1870s, and a few colleges joined to sponsor a meet in 1874. The success of the college meet led to the formation of the Intercollegiate Association of Amateur Athletes of America and the holding of an annual set of championship games beginning in 1876. The Amateur Athletic Union, organized in 1888, has been the ruling body in American amateur athletics since that time. In 1980, The Athletics Congress of the U.S.A. took over the governing of track and field from the A.A.U.

WORLD RECORDS—MEN

(Through Sept. 10, 1991)

Recognized by the International Athletic Federation.
The I.A.A.F. decided late in 1976 not to recognize records in yards except for the one–mile run.
The I.A.A.F. also requires automatic timing for all records for races of 400 meters or less.

Event	Record	Holder	Home Country	Where Made	Date
Running					
100 m	0:09.86	Carl Lewis	United States	Tokyo, Japan	Aug. 25, 1991
200 m	0:19.72	Pietro Mennea	Italy	Mexico City	Sept. 17, 1979
400 m	0:43.29	Butch Reynolds	United States	Indianapolis, Ind.	Aug. 17, 1988
800 m	1:41.8	Sebastian Coe	England	Florence, Italy	June 10, 1981
1,000 m	2:12.40	Sebastian Coe	England	Oslo, Norway	July 11, 1981
1,500 m	3:29.45	Said Aouita	Morocco	Berlin	August 23, 1985
1 mile	3:46.31	Steve Cram	Great Britain	Oslo	July 27, 1985
2,000 m	4:50.81	Said Aouita	Morocco	Paris	July 16, 1987
3,000 m	7:29.45	Said Aouita	Morocco	Cologne, W. Germany	Aug. 20, 1989
3,000 m steeplechase	8:05.35	Peter Koech	Kenya	Stockholm	July 3, 1989
5,000 m	12:58.39	Said Aouita	Morocco	Rome	July 22, 1987
10,000 m	27:08.23	Arturo Barrios	Mexico	Berlin	Aug. 18, 1989
25,000 m	1:13:55.8	Toshihiko Seko	Japan	Christchurch, N.Z.	March 22, 1981
30,000 m	1:29:18.8	Toshihiko Seko	Japan	Christchurch, N.Z.	March 22, 1981
20,000 m	56:55.60	Arturo Barrios	Mexico	La Fleche, France	March 30, 1991
1 hour	21,101 m	Arturo Barrios	Mexico	La Fleche, France	March 30, 1991
Marathon	2:06.50	Belayneh Densimo	Ethiopia	Rotterdam	April 17, 1988
Walking					
20,000 m	1:18:39.9	Ernesto Canto	Mexico	Fana, Norway	May 5, 1984
2 hours	17 mi. 1,092 yd	Ralph Kowalsky	East Germany	East Berlin	March 28, 1982
30,000 m	2:06:27.0	Maurizio Damilano	Italy	Milanese, Italy	May 5, 1985
50,000 m	3:41.39	Raul Gonzales	Mexico	Bergen, Norway	May 25, 1979
Hurdles					
110 m	0:12.92	Roger Kingdom	United States	Berlin	Aug. 16, 1989
400 m	0:47.02	Edwin Moses	United States	Koblenz, W. Ger.	Aug. 31, 1983
Relay Races					
400 m (4 × 100)	0:37.50	National Team	United States	Tokyo, Japan	Sept. 1, 1991
800 m (4 × 200)	1:19.38	Santa Monica Track Club	United States	Koblenz, W. Germany	Aug. 23, 1989
(Danny Everett, Leroy Burrell, Floyd Heard, Carl Lewis)					
1,600 m (4 × 400)	2:56.16	National Team	United States	Mexico City	Oct. 20, 1968
(Vince Matthews, Ron Freeman, Larry James, Lee Evans)					
1,600 m (4 × 400)	2:56.16	Olympic Team	United States	Seoul, South Korea	Oct. 1, 1988
3,200 m (4 × 800)	7:03.89	National Team	Britain	London	Aug. 30, 1982
(Peter Elliot, Garry Cook, Steve Cram, Sebastian Coe)					

Field Events

Event	Record	Holder	Home Country	Where Made	Date
High Jump	8 ft 0 in.	Javier Sotomayor	Cuba	San Juan, P.R.	July 29, 1989
Long jump	29 ft 4 1/2 in.	Mike Powell	United States	Tokyo, Japan	Aug. 30, 1991
Triple Jump	58 ft 11 1/2 in.	Willie Banks	Los Angeles, Ca.	Indianapolis	June 16, 1985
Pole vault	20 ft 0 in.	Sergey Bubka	Soviet Union	Malmo, Sweden	Aug. 5, 1991
Shot—put	75 ft 10 1/4 in.	Randy Barnes	United States	Los Angeles	May 20, 1990
Discus throw	243 ft 0 in.	Juergen Schult	East Germany	Neubrandenburg	June 6, 1986
Hammer throw	284 ft 7 in.	Yuriy Syedikh	U.S.S.R.	Stuttgart	Aug. 28, 1986
Javelin throw	318 ft 1 in.	Seppo Raty	Finland	Punkalaidun	June 3, 1991
Decathlon	8,798 pts.	Jurgen Hingsen	W. Germany	Mannheim, W. Ger.	June 8–9, 1984

WORLD RECORDS—WOMEN

(Through Sept. 10, 1991)

Event	Record	Holder	Home Country	Where Made	Date
Running					
100 m	0:10.49	Florence Griffith-Joyner	United States	Indianapolis, Ind.	July 16, 1988
200 m	0:21.56	Florence Griffith-Joyner	United States	Seoul, South Korea	Oct. 1, 1988
400 m	0:47.60	Martina Koch	East Germany	Canberra	Oct. 6, 1985
800 m	1:53.28	Jarmila Kratochvilova	Czechoslovakia	Munich, W. Ger.	July 26, 1983
1,500 m	3:52.47	Tatyana Kazankina	U.S.S.R.	Zurich, Switz.	Aug. 13, 1980
1 mile	4:15.61	Paula Ivan	Romania	Nice, Italy	July 10, 1989
3,000 m	8:22.62	Tatyana Kazankina	U.S.S.R.	Moscow	Aug. 26, 1984
5,000 m	14:37.33	Ingrid Kristiansen	Norway	Stockholm	Aug. 5, 1986
10,000 m	30:13.74	Ingrid Kristiansen	Norway	Oslo	July 5, 1986
Marathon	2:21:06.0	Ingrid Kristiansen	Norway	London	April 21, 1985
Walking					
5,000 m	20:07.52	Beate Anders	East Germany	Rostock	June 23, 1990
10,000 m	41:46.21	Nadyezhda Ryashkina	Soviet Union	Seattle, Wash.	July 24, 1990
Hurdles					
100—m hurdles	0:12.25	Ginka Zagorcheva	Bulgaria	Greece	August 8, 1987
400 m	0:53.33	Maria Stepanova	U.S.S.R.	Stuttgart	Aug. 28, 1986
Relay Races					
400 m (4 × 100)	0:41.53	East Germany	E. Germany	Berlin, E. Ger.	July 31, 1983
800 m (4 × 200)	1:28.15	East Germany	E. Germany	Jena, E. Ger.	Aug. 9, 1980
1,600 m (4 × 400)	3:15.18	Soviet Union	Soviet Union	Seoul, South Korea	Oct. 1, 1988
3,200 m (4 × 800)	7:52.3	U.S.S.R.	U.S.S.R.	Podolsk, U.S.S.R.	Aug. 16, 1976
Field Events					
High jump	6 ft 10 1/4 in.	Stefka Kostadinova	Bulgaria	Rome	August 30, 1987
Long jump	24 ft 8 1/4 in.	Galina Chistyakova	Soviet Union	Leningrad	June 11, 1988
Triple jump	49 ft 3/4 in.	Inessa Kravets	Soviet Union	Moscow	June 10, 1991
Shot—put	74 ft 3 in.	Natalya Lisovskaya	U.S.S.R.	Moscow	June 7, 1987
Discus throw	252 ft 0 in.	Gabriele Reinsch	East Germany	Neubrandenburg, E. Ger.	July 9, 1988
Javelin throw	262 ft 5 in.	Petra Felke	East Germany	Potsdam	Sept. 9, 1988
Heptathlon	7,291 pts	Jackie Joyner–Kersee	United States	Seoul, South Korea	Sept. 24, 1988

AMERICAN RECORDS—MEN

(Through Sept. 10, 1991)
Officially approved by The Athletics Congress.

Event	Record	Holder	Where Made	Date
Running				
100 m	0:09.86	Carl Lewis	Tokyo, Japan	Aug. 25, 1991
200 m	0:19.75	Carl Lewis	Indianapolis, Ind.	June 19, 1983
200 m	0:19.75	Jue De Loach	Seoul, South Korea	Sept. 28, 1988
400 m	0:43.29	Butch Reynolds	Indianapolis, Ind.	Aug. 17, 1988
800 m	1:42.60	Johnny Gray	Koblenz, W. Ger.	Aug. 29, 1985
1,000 m	2:13.9	Richard Wohlhuter	Oslo, Norway	July 30, 1974
1,500 m	3:29.77	Sydney Maree	Cologne, W. Ger.	Aug. 25, 1985
1 mile	3:47.69	Steve Scott	Oslo, Norway	July 7, 1982
2,000 m	4:54.71	Steve Scott	Ingelhem, W. Ger.	Aug. 31, 1982
3,000 m	7:35.84	Doug Padilla	Oslo, Norway	July 9, 1983
5,000 m	13:01.15	Sydney Maree	Oslo, Norway	July 27, 1985
10,000 m	27:20.56	Mark Nenow	Brussels	Sept. 5, 1986
20,000 m	58:15.0	Bill Rodgers	Boston, Mass.	Aug. 9, 1977
25,000 m	1:14:11.8	Bill Rodgers	Saratoga, Cal.	Feb. 21, 1979
30,000 m	1:31:49.0	Bill Rodgers	Saratoga, Cal.	Feb. 21, 1979

| 1 hour | 12 mi., 1351 yds | Bill Rodgers | Boston, Mass. | Aug. 9, 1977 |
| 3,000–m steeplechase | 8:09.17 | Henry Marsh | Koblenz, W. Ger. | Aug. 29, 1985 |

Hurdles

| 110 m | 0:12.92 | Roger Kingdom | Berlin | Aug. 16, 1989 |
| 400 m | 0:47.02 | Edwin Moses | Koblenz, W. Ger. | Aug. 31, 1983 |

Relay Races

400 m (4 × 100)	0:37.50	U.S. National Team	Tokyo, Japan	Sept. 1, 1991
800 m (4 × 200)	1:20.26	Southern California	Tempe, Ariz.	May 27, 1978
1,600 m (4 × 400)	2:56.16	U.S. Olympic Team	Seoul, South Korea	Oct. 1, 1988
3,200 m (4 × 800)	7:06.50	Santa Monica Track Club	Walnut	Apr. 26, 1986

Field Events

High jump	7 ft 10 1/2 in.	Charles Austin	Zurich	Aug. 7, 1991
Long jump	29 ft 4 1/2 in.	Mike Powell	Tokyo, Japan	Aug. 30, 1991
Triple jump	58 ft 11 1/2 in.	Willie Banks	Indianapolis, Ind.	June 16, 1985
Pole vault	19 ft 6 1/2 in.	Joe Dial	Norman	June 18, 1987
Shot-put	75 ft 10 1/4 in.	Randy Barnes	Los Angeles	May 20, 1990
Discus throw	237 ft 4 in.	Ben Plucknett	Stockholm, Swe.	July 7, 1981
Javelin throw	280 ft 1 in.	Tom Petranoff	Helsinki	July 7, 1986
Hammer throw	268 ft 8 in.	Judd Logan	University Park, Pa.	April 23, 1988
Decathlon	8,812 pts	Dan O'Brien	Tokyo, Japan	Aug. 29–30, 1991

AMERICAN RECORDS—WOMEN

(Through Sept. 10, 1991)

Event	Record	Holder	Where Made	Date
Running				
100 m	0:10.49	Florence Griffith–Joyner	Indianapolis, Ind.	July 16, 1988
200 m	0:21.56	Florence Griffith–Joyner	Seoul, South Korea	Oct. 1, 1988
400 m	0:48.83	Valerie Brisco–Hooks	Los Angeles, Cal.	Aug. 6, 1984
800 m	1:56.90	Mary Decker Slaney	Bern	Aug. 16, 1985
1,500 m	3:57.12	Mary Decker Slaney	Stockholm, Swe.	July 26, 1983
1000 m	2:34.8	Mary Decker Slaney	Eugene, Ore.	July 4, 1985
1 mile	4:16.71	Mary Decker Slaney	Zurich	Aug. 21, 1985
3,000 m	8:29.69	Mary Decker Slaney	Cologne	Aug. 25, 1985
5,000 m	14:59.99	PattiSue Plummer	Stockholm	July 3, 1989
10,000 m	31:28.92	Francie L. Smith	Austin, Texas	April 4, 1991
Hurdles				
100 m hurdles	0:12.48	Gail Devers	Berlin	Sept. 10, 1991
400 m hurdles	0:53.37	Sandra Farmer–Patrick	New York	July 23, 1989
Relay Races				
400 m (4 × 100)	0:41.61	U.S. National Team	Colorado Springs, Col.	July 3, 1983
800 m (4 × 200)	1:32.57	Louisiana State	Des Moines, Iowa	April 28, 1989
1,600 m (4 × 400)	3:15.51	U.S. Olympic Team	Seoul, South Korea	Oct. 1, 1988
Field Events				
High jump	6 ft 8 in.	Louise Ritter	Austin, Tex.	July 9, 1988
Long jump	24 ft. 5 1/2 in.	Jackie Joyner–Kersee	Indianapolis	August 12, 1987
Triple jump	46 ft. 0 3/4 in.	Sheila Hudson	Durham, N.C.	June 2, 1990
Shot-put	66 ft. 2 1/2 in.	Ramon Pagel	San Diego, Calif.	June 25, 1988
Discus throw	216 ft 10 in.	Carol Cady	San Jose, Calif.	May 31, 1986
Javelin throw	227 ft 5 in.	Kate Schmidt	Furth, W. Ger.	Sept. 10, 1977
Heptathlon	7,291 pts	Jackie Joyner–Kersee	Seoul, South Korea	Sept. 23–24, 1988

HISTORY OF THE RECORD FOR THE MILE RUN

Time	Athlete	Country	Year	Location
4:36.5	Richard Webster	England	1865	England
4:29.0	William Chinnery	England	1868	England
4:28.8	Walter Gibbs	England	1868	England
4:26.0	Walter Slade	England	1874	England
4:24.5	Walter Slade	England	1875	London
4:23.2	Walter George	England	1880	London
4:21.4	Walter George	England	1882	London
4:18.4	Walter George	England	1884	Birmingham, England
4:18.2	Fred Bacon	Scotland	1894	Edinburgh, Scotland
4:17.0	Fred Bacon	Scotland	1895	London

4:15.6	Thomas Conneff	United States	1895	Travers Island, N.Y.
4:15.4	John Paul Jones	United States	1911	Cambridge, Mass.
4:14.4	John Paul Jones	United States	1913	Cambridge, Mass.
4:12.6	Norman Taber	United States	1915	Cambridge, Mass.
4:10.4	Paavo Nurmi	Finland	1923	Stockholm
4:09.2	Jules Ladoumegue	France	1931	Paris
4:07.6	Jack Lovelock	New Zealand	1933	Princeton, N.J.
4:06.8	Glenn Cunningham	United States	1934	Princeton, N.J.
4:06.4	Sydney Wooderson	England	1937	London
4:06.2	Gundar Hägg	Sweden	1942	Goteborg, Sweden
4:06.2	Arne Andersson	Sweden	1942	Stockholm
4:04.6	Gunder Hägg	Sweden	1942	Stockholm
4:02.6	Arne Andersson	Sweden	1943	Goteborg, Sweden
4:01.6	Arne Andersson	Sweden	1944	Malmo, Sweden
4:01.4	Gunder Hägg	Sweden	1945	Malmo, Sweden
3:59.4	Roger Bannister	England	1954	Oxford, England
3:58.0	John Landy	Australia	1954	Turku, Finland
3:57.2	Derek Ibbotson	England	1957	London
3:54.5	Herb Elliott	Australia	1958	Dublin
3:54.4	Peter Snell	New Zealand	1962	Wanganui, N.Z.
3:54.1	Peter Snell	New Zealand	1964	Auckland, N.Z.
3:53.6	Michel Jazy	France	1965	Rennes, France
3:51.3	Jim Ryun	United States	1966	Berkeley, Calif.
3:51.1	Jim Ryun	United States	1967	Bakersfield, Calif.
3:51.0	Filbert Bayi	Tanzania	1975	Kingston, Jamaica
3:49.4	John Walker	New Zealand	1975	Goteborg, Sweden
3:49.0	Sebastian Coe	England	1979	Oslo
3:48.8	Steve Ovett	England	1980	Oslo
3:48.53	Sebastian Coe	England	1981	Zurich, Switzerland
3:48.40	Steve Ovett	England	1981	Koblenz, W. Ger.
3:47.33	Sebastian Coe	England	1981	Brussels
3:46.31	Steve Cram	England	1985	Oslo

TOP TEN WORLD'S FASTEST OUTDOOR MILES

Time	Athlete	Country	Date	Location
3:46.31	Steve Cram	England	July 27, 1985	Oslo
3:47.33	Sebastian Coe	England	Aug. 28, 1981	Brussels
3:47.69	Steve Scott	United States	July 7, 1982	Oslo
3:47.79	Jose Gonzalez	Spain	July 27, 1985	Oslo
3:48.40	Steve Ovett	England	Aug. 26, 1981	Koblenz, W. Ger.
3:48.53	Sebastian Coe	England	Aug. 19, 1981	Zurich
3:48.53	Steve Scott	United States	June 26, 1982	Oslo
3:48.8	Steve Ovett	England	July 1, 1980	Oslo
3:48.83	Sydney Maree	United States	Sept. 9, 1981	Rieti, Italy
3:48.85	Sydney Maree[1]	United States	June 26, 1982	Oslo

1. Finished second. NOTE: Professional marks not included.

TOP TEN WORLD'S FASTEST INDOOR MILES

Time	Athlete	Country	Date	Location
3:49.78	Eamonn Coghlan	Ireland	Feb. 27, 1983	East Rutherford, N.J.
3:50.6	Eamonn Coghlan	Ireland	Feb. 20, 1981	San Diego
3:50.94	Marcus O'Sullivan	Ireland	Feb. 13, 1988	East Rutherford, N.J.
3:51.2	Ray Flynn[1]	Ireland	Feb. 27, 1983	East Rutherford, N.J.
3:51.66	Marcus O'Sullivan	Ireland	Feb. 10, 1989	East Rutherford, N.J.
3:51.8	Steve Scott[1]	United States	Feb. 20, 1981	San Diego
3:52.28	Steve Scott[2]	United States	Feb. 27, 1983	East Rutherford, N.J.
3:52.30	Frank O'Mara	Ireland	Feb. , 1986	New York
3:52.37	Eamonn Coughlan	Ireland	Feb. 9, 1985	East Rutherford, N.J.
3:52.40	Sydney Maree	United States	Feb. 9, 1985	East Rutherford, N.J.

1. Finished second. 2. Finished third.

TOP TEN POLE VAULT DISTANCES

Source: The Athletes Congress.

Fiberglas Poles

1991	Sergey Bubka	20 ft 0 in.	1987	Sergey Bubka	19 ft 9 1/4 in.
1991	Sergey Bubka	19 ft 11 3/4 in.	1986	Sergey Bubka	19 ft 8 1/2 in.
1991	Sergey Bubka	19 ft 11 1/4 in.	1985	Sergey Bubka	19 ft 8 1/4 in.
1991	Sergey Bubka	19 ft 11 in.	1984	Sergey Bubka	19 ft 5 3/4 in.
1988	Sergey Bubka	19 ft 10 1/2 in.	1984	Thierry Vigneron	19 ft 4 3/4 in.

THE ATHLETICS CONGRESS NATIONAL INDOOR CHAMPIONSHIPS—1991

(Feb. 22, 1991, Madison Square Garden, New York)

Men's Events

60 m—Andres Simon, Cuba	0:06.58
400 m—Michael Johnson, Waco, Texas	0:46.70
500 m—Andrew Valmon, Mazda Track Club	1:04.21
800 m—Ray Brown, Nike Atlantic	1:48.68
Mile—Noureddine Morceli, Algeria	3:52.99
3,000 m—Terry Brahm, Nike Indians	7:50.08
60 m hurdles—Greg Foster, World Class	0:07.49
5,000 m walk—Doug Fournier, Parkside	20:03.74
1,600 m relay—Seton Hall University	3:18.35
3,200 m relay—New York Athletic Club	7:33.83
High jump—Javier Sotomayor, Cuba	7 ft 6 1/2 in.
Pole vault—Kory Tarpenning, Nike International	18 ft 4 1/2 in.
Long jump—Llewellyn Starks, Sports Track Club	26 ft 4 1/2 in.
Triple jump—Frank Rutherford, Houston Track Club	54 ft 8 1/4 in.
Shot-put—Ronald Backes, New York Athletic Club	67 ft 1 1/4 in.
35-pound weight throw—Lance Deal, New York Athletic Club	79 ft 3 3/4 in.

(Held at Princeton University.)*

Team—1. New York Athletic Club, 25; 2. Nike International, 16; 3. Shore Athletic Club, 9.

Most Valuable Athlete—Lance Deal, N.Y. Athletic Club

Women's Events

60 m—Michelle Finn, Mazda Track Club	0:07.16
200 m—Rochelle Stevens, Nike International	0:23.65
400 m—Diane Dixon, Atoms Track Club	0:52.38
800 m—Meredith Rainey, Atoms Track Club	2:03.07
Mile—Suzy Favor, Reebok Running Club	4:37.55
3,000 m—Margareta Keszeg, Romania	8:49.61
60 m hurdles—Kim McKenzie, Mazda Track Club	0:08.12
3,000 m walk—Teresa Vaill, Natural Sport	12:49.95
1,600 m relay—Seton Hall University	3:49.03
High jump—Yolanda Henry, Mazda Track Club	6 ft 5 in.
Long jump—Carol Lewis, Santa Monica Track Club	21 ft 6 1/4 in.
Triple jump—Juliana Yendork, Walnut, Calif.	43 ft 1/2 in.
Shot-put—Connie Price Smith, Nike North	61 ft 10 1/2 in.
20-pound weight throw—Sonja Fitts, St. John's University	59 ft 7 3/4 in.

(Held at Princeton University.)

Team—1. Mazda Track Club, 18; 2. Nike International, 12; 3. Atoms Track Club, 10; Reebok Running Club, 10.

Most Valuable Athlete—Diane Dixon, Atoms Track Club

*World record.

THE ATHLETICS CONGRESS NATIONAL OUTDOOR CHAMPIONSHIPS

(June 13–15, 1991, New York City)

Men's Events

100 m—Leroy Burrell, Santa Monica Track Club	0:09.90
200 m—Michael Johnson, Nike Internatioanl	0:20.31
400 m—Antonio Pettigrew, St. Augustine's College	0:44.36
800 m—Mark Everett, Nike International	1:44.28
1,500 m—Terrance Herrington, Nike Atlantic Coast	3:40.72
3,000-m steeplechase—Mark Croghan, Ohio St. University	8:21.64
5,000 m—John Trautman, New York Athletic Club	13:55.26
10,000 m—Shannon Butler, Montana St. Univ.	28:09.40
100-m hurdles—Greg Foster, Chino Hills, Calif.	0:13.29
400-m hurdles—Danny Harris, Nike Internatioanl	0:47.62
20-km walk—Tim Lewis, Reebok Running Club	1 hr 29 min 55 sec

Long jump—Carl Lewis, Santa Monica Track Club	28 ft 4 1/4 in.
Triple jump—Kenny Harrison, Mizuno Track Club	56 ft 10 in.
High jump—Hollis Conway, Nike Internatioanl	7 ft 7 1/2 in.
Pole vault—Tim Bright, Mizuno Track Club	18 ft 8 1/2 in.
Shot put—Ron Backes, N.Y. Athletic Club	64 ft 11 1/2 in.
Discuss—Tony Washington, Stars & Stripes Track Club	211 ft 11 in.
Hammer throw—Jud Logan, New York Athletic Club	244 ft 10 in.
Javelin—Mike Barnett, N.Y. Athletic Club	262 ft 0 in.
Decathlon—Dan O'Brien, Reebok Running Club	8,844 pts

Team—1. New York Athletic Club, 86; 2. Santa Monica Track Club, 85; 3. Nike International, 50 1/3.

Women's Events

100 m—Carlette Guidry, University of Texas	0:10.94
200 m—Gwen Torrance, Nike South Track Club	0:22.38
400 m—Lillie Leatherwood, Reebok Running Club	0:49.66
800 m—Delisa Floyd, Sports Track Club	1:59.82
1,500 m—Suzy Favor Hamilton, Reebok Running Club	4:06.13
3,000 m—Sally Steely, Mizuno Track Club	8:49.00
5,000 m—PattiSue Plummer, Nike International	16:24.72
10,000 m—Lynn Jennings, Nike International	32:45.88
10,000 m walk—Debbi Lawrence, Propet Walkers	46:06.36
100-m hurdles—Gail Devers-Roberts, World Class A.C.	0:12.83
400-m hurdles—Kim Batten, Florida St. Univ.	0:54.18
Long jump—Jackie Joyner-Kersee, McDonald's Track Club	22 ft 8 in.
High jump—Yolanda Henry, Mazda Track Club	6 ft 4 3/4 in.
Triple jump—Carla Shannon, unattached	44 ft 4 1/4 in.
Shot-put—Ramona Pagel, Mazda Track Club	60 ft 2 1/2 in.
Discus—Lacy Barnes, Nike Track Club	199 ft 10 in.
Javelin throw—Karin Smith, Nike Coast Track Club	197 ft 6 in.
Hammer throw—Bonnie Edmondson, Hebron, Conn.	169 ft 0 in.
200-m steeplechase—Teressa DiFerna, State College, Pa.	7:12.76
Heptathlon—Jackie Joyner-Kersee, McDonald's Track Club	6,878 points

Team—1. Nike Coast Track Club, 78; 2. Nike International, 53; 3. Reebok Running Club, 40.

N.C.A.A. CHAMPIONSHIPS—1991

INDOOR

(University of Indiana, Indianapolis, Ind., March 8–9, 1991)

Men's Events

55 m—Augustine Olobia, Washington St.	0:06.17
55-m hurdles—Tony Li, Washington St.	0:07.08
200 m—Frank Fredericks, Brigham Young	0:20.68
400 m—Gabriel Luke, Rice	0:46.52
800 m—George Kersh, Mississippi	1:46.19
Mile run—Robert Kennedy, Indiana	3:58.11
3,000 m—Reuben Reina, Arkansas	7:50.00
5,000 m—Jonah Koech, Iowa St.	13:36.64
1,600 m relay—Baylor	3:08.28
3,200 m relay—Georgetown	7:19.86
High jump—Tony Barton, George Mason	7 ft 6 1/2 in.
Pole vault—Istvan Bagyula, George Mason	19 ft 5 1/4 in.
Long jump—Alan Turner, Indiana	26 ft 5 1/4 in.
Triple jump—Eugene Greene, Boise St.	53 ft 3 3/4 in.
Shot-put—Eric Bergeen, UCLA	62 ft 10 3/4 in.
35-pound weight throw—Christophe Epalle, SMU	74 ft 6 3/4 in.

Team—1. Arkansas, 34; 2. Georgetown, 27; 3. Washington St., 26.

Division II champion—St. Augustine, Raleigh, N.C.

Division III champion—University of Wisconsin at LaCrosse

Women's Events

55 m—Carlette Guidry, Texas	0:06.74
55-m hurdles—Mary Cobb, Louisiana St.	0:07.61
200 m—Carlette Guidry, Texas	0:23.23
400 m—Maicel Malone, Arizona	0:51.05
800 m—Edith Nakiyingi, Iowa St.	2:04.84
Mile run—Jennifer Lanctot, Boston University	4:35.65
3,000 m—Patty Wiegand, Tennessee	9:09.83
5,000 m—Sonia O'Sullivan, Villanova	15:49.46
1,600-m relay—Arizona St.	3:32.46
3,200-m relay—Tennessee	8:36.32
High jump—Tanya Hughes, Arizona	6 ft 2 in.
Long jump—Diane Guthrie, George Mason	20 ft 9 1/2 in.
Triple jump—Leah Kirklin, Florida	43 ft 5 1/4 in.
Shot-put—Tracie Millett, UCLA	54 ft 3 1/4 in.
Team—1. Louisiana St.	48
2. Texas	39
3. Villanova	35

Division II champion—Abilene Christian University, Abilene, Texas
Division III champion—Cortland State Univ., Cortland, N.Y.

OUTDOOR

(Univ. of Oregon, Eugene, Ore., May 29–June 1, 1991)

Men's Events

100 m—Frank Fredericks, Brigham Young	0:10.03
200 m—Frank Fredericks, Brigham Young	0:19.90
400 m—Gabriel Luke, Rice	0:45.32
800 m—George Kersh, Mississippi	1:45.82
1,500 m—Samuel Kibiri, Washington St.	3:39.53
3,000-m steeplechase—Mark Croghan, Ohio St.	8:22.26
5,000 m—Shannon Butler, Montana St.	13:41.61
10,000 m—Terry Thorton, Louisiana St.	28:25.92
110-m hurdles—Greg Williams, Texas A&M	0:13.55
400-m hurdles—Samuel Matete, Auburn	0:49.12
400-m relay—Texas Christian	0:38.88
1,600-m relay—Baylor	3:02.52
High jump—Darrin Plab, Southern Illinois	7 ft 6 1/2 in.
Pole vault—Istvan Bagyula, George Mason	19 ft 1/4 in.
Long jump—George Ogbeide, Washington St.	26 ft 8 1/4 in.
Triple jump—Brian Wellman, Arkansas	56 ft 10 1/4 in.
Shot-put—Simon Williams, Louisiana St.	61 ft 4 in.
Discus—Kamy Kashmiri, Nevada-Reno	218 ft 5 in.
Hammer throw—Christophe Epalle, SMU	238 ft 6 in.
Javelin—Patrik Boden, Texas	260 ft 4 in.
Decathlon—Aric Long, Tennessee	7,916 points
Team—1. Tennessee	51
2. Washington St.	42
3. Oregon	36

Division II champion—St. Augustine's College, Raleigh, N.C.
Division III champion—Univ. of Wisconsin at LaCrosse

Women's Events

100 m—Carlette Guidry, Texas	0:10.91
200 m—Carlette Guidry, Texas	0:22.44
400 m—Ximena Restropo, Nebraska	0:51.01
800 m—Nekita Beasly, Florida	2:03.29
1,500 m—Darcy Arreola, Cal. St. Northridge	4:11.46
3,000 m—Sonia O'Sullivan, Villanova	8:56.74
5,000 m—Laurie Gomez, N.C. State	16:07.96
10,000 m—Jamie Park, Arkansas	33:15.08
100-m hurdles—Dawn Bowles, Louisiana St.	0:12.70
400-m hurdles—Janeene Vickers, UCLA	0:55.65
400-m relay—Texas	0:42.88
1,600-m relay—Nebraska	3:29.87
High jump—Tanya Hughes, Arizona	6 ft 4 1/4 in.
Long jump—Diane Guthrie, George Mason	21 ft 10 in.
Triple jump—Donna Crumety, St. Joseph's	44 ft 0 in.
Shot-put—Eileen Vanisi, Texas	57 ft 9 in.
Discus—Anna Mosdell, Brigham Young	183 ft 10 in.
Javelin—Paula Berry, Oregon	188 ft 5 in.
Heptathlon—Sharon Jaklofsky, Louisiana St.	5,732 points
Team—1. Louisiana State	78
2. Texas	67
3. Nebraska	43

Division II champion—California Polytechnic University, San Luis Obispo, Calif.
Division III champion—University of Wisconsin–Oshkosh

WORLD CHAMPIONSHIPS—1991

(Aug. 23–Sept. 1, Tokyo, Japan)

Men's Events

100 m—Carl Lewis, United States	0:09.86*
200 m—Michael Johnson, United States	0:20.01
400 m—Antonio Pettigrew, United States	0:44.57
800 m—Bill Konchellah, Kenya	1:43.99
1,500 m—Noureddine Morceli, Algeria	3:32.84
5,000 m—Yobes Ondeiki, Kenya	13:14.45
10,000 m—Moses Tanui, Kenya	27:38.74
Marathon—Hiromi Taniguchi, Japan	2 hr 14 min 57 sec
110-m hurdles—Greg Foster, United States	0:13.06
400-m hurdles—Samuel Matete, Zambia	0:46.64
High jump—Charles Austin, United States	7 ft 9 3/4 in.
Pole vault—Sergei Bubka, Soviet Union	19 ft 6 1/4 in.
Long jump—Mike Powell, United States	29 ft 4 1/2 in.*
Triple jump—Kenny Harrison, United States	58 ft 4 in.
Shot-put—Werner Gunthor, Switzerland	71 ft 11 1/4 in.
Discus—Lars Riedel, Germany	217 ft 2 in.
Hammer throw—Yuriy Sedikh, Soviet Union	268 ft 0 in.
Javelin—Kimmo Kinnunen, Finland	297 ft 11 in.
Decathlon—Dan O'Brien, United States	8,812 points
20-kilometer walk—Maurizio Damilano, Italy	1 hr 19 min 37 sec
400-m relay—United States	0:37.50*
1,600-m relay—Great Britain	2:57.53

Women's Events

100 m—Katrin Krabbe, Germany	0:10.99
200 m—Katrin Krabbe, Germany	0:22.09
400 m—Marie Josee Perec, France	0:49.13
800 m—Lilia Nurutdinova, Soviet Union	1:57.50
1,500 m—Hassiba Boulmerka, Algeria	4:02.58
3,000 m—Tatyana Dorovskikh, Soviet Union	8:35.82
10,000 m—Liz McColgan, Great Britain	31:14.31
Marathon—Wanda Panfill, Poland	2 hrs 29 min 53 sec
100-m hurdles—Lyudmila Narozhhilenko, Soviet Union	0:12.59
400-m hurdles—Tatyana Ledovskaya, Soviet Union	0:53.11
High jump—Heike Henkel, Germany	6 ft 8 3/4 in.
Long jump—Jackie Joyner-Kersee, United States	24 ft 1/4 in.
Shot-put—Zhiong Huang, China	68 ft. 4 1/4 in.
Discus—Tsvetanka Khristova, Bulgaria	233 ft 0 in.
Javelin—Demei Xu, China	225 ft 8 in.
Heptathlon—Sabine Braun, Germany	6,672 points
10-kilometer walk—Alina Ivanova, Soviet Union	42 min 57 sec
400-m relay—Jamaica	0:41.94
1,600-m relay—Soviet Union	3:18.43

Final medals leaders:

1. Soviet Union	28		6. Jamaica	5
2. United States	26		7. China	4
3. Germany	17		8. Algeria	3
4. Kenya	8		Finland	3
5. Great Britain	7			

* World record.

SPORTS ORGANIZATIONS AND BUREAUS

(Note: Addresses are subject to change)

Amateur Athletic Union of the U.S. 3400 West 86th St., P.O. Box 68207, Indianapolis, Ind. 46268–0207

Amateur Hockey Association of the U.S. Inc. USA Hockey, 2997 Broadmoor Valley Road, Colorado Springs, Colo. 80906

Amateur Softball Association. 2801 N.E. 50th St., Oklahoma City, Okla. 73111

American Amateur Racquetball Association/International Racquetball Federation/Pan American Racquetball Confederation. 815 N. Weber St., Colorado Springs, Colo. 80903-2947

American Association of Professional Baseball Clubs. P.O. Box 608, 3860 Broadway, Grove City, Ohio 43123

American Bowling Congress. 5301 South 76th St., Greendale, Wis. 53129–0500

American Hockey League. 425 Union St., Springfield, Mass. 01089

American Horse Shows Association. 220 E. 42nd St., New York, N.Y. 10017–5806

American Kennel Club Inc. 51 Madison Ave., New York, N.Y. 10010

American League (baseball). 350 Park Ave., New York, N.Y. 10022

American Sportcasters Association, The. 5 Beekman St., New York, N.Y. 10038

Athletics Congress/USA, The. One Hoosier Dome, Suite 140, Indianapolis, Ind. 46225.

Baseball Hall of Fame. P.O. Box 590, Cooperstown, N.Y. 13326

Football Hall of Fame (college). Kings Island, Ohio 45034

Big Ten Conference, Inc. (1896). 1500 W. Higgins Rd., Park Ridge, Ill. 60068-6300

International Game Fish Association. 3000 E. Las Olas Blvd., Fort Lauderdale, Fla. 33316

International League of Professional Baseball Clubs, Inc. Box 608, Grove City, Ohio 43123

International Olympic Committee. Chateau de Vidy, 1007 Lausanne, Switzerland

International Tennis Hall of Fame. National Historic Landmark, Newport Casino, 194 Bellevue Ave., Newport, R.I. 02840

Little League Baseball. P.O. Box 3485, Williamsport, Pa. 17701

National Archery Association. 1750 E. Boulder St., Colorado Springs, Colo. 80909

National Association for Stock Car Auto Racing. P.O. Box 2875, Daytona Beach, Fla. 32120-2875

National Association of Intercollegiate Athletics. 1221 Baltimore Ave., Kansas City, Mo. 64105

National Baseball Congress. P.O. Box 1420, Wichita, Kan. 67201

National Collegiate Athletic Association. 6201 College Blvd., Overland Park, Kan. 66211-2422

National Duckpin Bowling Congress. 4991 Fairview Ave., Linthicum, Md. 29090

National Field Archery Association. 31407 Outer I–10, Redlands, Calif. 92373

National Football Foundation and College Hall of Fame. 1865 Palmer Ave., Larchmont, N.Y. 10538. *See also:* Football Hall of Fame (college)

National Football League. 410 Park Ave., New York, N.Y. 10022

National Hockey League. 1155 Metcalfe St., Suite 960, Montreal, Que., Canada H3B 2W2

National Horseshoe Pitchers Association. Box 7927, Columbus, Ohio 43207

National Hot Rod Association. P.O. Box 5555,

National Junior College Athletic Association. P.O. Box 7305, Colorado Springs, Colo. 80933-7305

National Rifle Association of America. 1600 Rhode Island Ave., N.W., Washington, D.C. 20036

National Shuffleboard Association. 3816 Norbrook Dr., Columbus, Ohio 43220

National Skeet Shooting Association. P.O. Box 680007, San Antonio, Tex. 78268–0007

National Sporting Clays Association. P.O. Box 680007, San Antonio, Tex. 78268-0007

New York Racing Association. P.O. Box 90, Jamaica, N.Y. 11417

New York State Athletic Commission (boxing and wrestling). 270 Broadway, New York, N.Y. 10007

North American Yacht Racing Union. *See* United States Yacht Racing Union

PGA TOUR, Inc. 112 TPC Blvd., Sawgrass, Ponte Vedra, Fla. 32082

Pro Football Hall of Fame. 2121 George Halas Drive, N.W., Canton, Ohio 44708

Roller Skating Associations. P.O. Box 81846, Lincoln, Neb. 68501

Thoroughbred Racing Assns. of N. America. 3000 Marcus Ave., Lake Success, N.Y. 11042

United States Amateur Confederation of Roller Skating. P.O. Box 6579, Lincoln, Neb. 68506

United States Auto Club. 4910 West 16th St., Speedway, Ind. 46224

United States Gymnastics Federation. 201 S. Capitol, Ste. 300, Indianapolis, Ind. 46225

United States-International Professional Shuffleboard. 1901 S.W. 87th Terrace, Fort Lauderdale, Fla. 33324

U.S. Baseball Federation. 2160 Greenwood Ave., Trenton, N.J. 08609

U.S. Chess Federation. 186 Route 9W, New Windsor, N.Y. 12553

U.S. Cycling Federation. 1750 East Boulder St., Colorado Springs, Colo. 80909

U.S. Fencing Assn. 1750 E. Boulder St., Colorado Springs, Colo. 80909

U.S. Figure Skating Association. 20 First St., Colorado Springs, Colo. 80906

U.S. Golf Association. Golf House, P.O. Box 708, Far Hills, N.J. 07931–0708

U.S. Handball Association. 930 N. Benton Ave., Tucson, Ariz. 85711

U.S. Olympic Committee. 1750 East Boulder St., Colorado Springs, Colo. 80909

U.S. Orienteering Federation. Box 1444, Forest Park, Ga. 30051

U.S. Rowing Assn. Pan American Plaza, 201 S. Capitol Ave., Ste. 400, Indianapolis, Ind. 46225

U.S. Soccer Federation. 1750 East Boulder St., Colorado Springs, Colo. 80909-5791

U.S. Tennis Association. 1212 Avenue of the Americas, New York, N.Y. 10036-9998

U.S. Trotting Association. 750 Michigan Ave., Columbus, Ohio 43215

U.S. Yacht Racing Union. P.O. Box 209, Goat Island, Newport, R.I. 02840

USA Amateur Boxing Federation. 1750 East Boulder St., Colorado Springs, Colo. 80909

U.S.A. Basketball. 1750 East Boulder St., Colorado Springs, Colo. 80909

Women's International Bowling Congress. 5301 S. 76th St., Greendale, Wis. 53129-1191

TENNIS

Lawn tennis is a comparatively modern modification of the ancient game of court tennis. Major Walter Clopton Wingfield thought that something like court tennis might be played outdoors on lawns, and in December, 1873, at Nantclwyd, Wales, he introduced his new game under the name of *Sphairistike* at a lawn party. The game was a success and spread rapidly, but the name was a total failure and almost immediately disappeared when all the players and spectators began to refer to the new game as "lawn tennis." In the early part of 1874, a young lady named Mary Ewing Outerbridge returned from Bermuda to New York, bringing with her the implements and necessary equipment of the new game, which she had obtained from a British Army supply store in Bermuda. Miss Outerbridge and friends played the first game of lawn tennis in the United States on the grounds of the Staten Island Cricket and Baseball Club in the spring of 1874.

For a few years, the new game went along in haphazard fashion until about 1880, when standard measurements for the court and standard equipment with in definite limits became the rule. In 1881, the U.S. Lawn Tennis Association (whose name was changed in 1975 to U.S. Tennis Association) was formed and conducted the first national championship at Newport, R.I. The international matches for the Davis Cup began with a series between the British and United States players on the courts of the Longwood Cricket Club, Chestnut Hill, Mass., in 1900, with the home players winning.

Professional tennis, which got its start in 1926 when the French star Suzanne Lenglen was paid $50,000 for a tour, received full recognition in 1968. Staid old Wimbledon, the London home of what are considered the world championships, let the pros compete. This decision ended a long controversy over open tennis and changed the format of the competition. The United States championships were also opened to the pros and the site of the event, long held at Forest Hills, N.Y., was shifted to the National Tennis Center in Flushing Meadows, N.Y., in 1978. Pro tours for men and women became worldwide in play that continued throughout the year.

DAVIS CUP CHAMPIONSHIPS

No matches in 1901, 1910, 1915–18, and 1940–45.

1900	United States 3, British Isles 0	1933	Great Britain 3, France 2	1966	Australia 4, India 1
1902	United States 3, British Isles 2	1934	Great Britain 4, United States 1	1967	Australia 4, Spain 1
1903	British Isles 4, United States 1	1935	Great Britain 5, United States 0	1968	United States 4, Australia 1
1904	British Isles 5, Belgium 0	1936	Great Britain 3, Australia 2	1969	United States 5, Romania 0
1905	British Isles 5, United States 0	1937	United States 4, Great Britain 1	1970	United States 5, West
1906	British Isles 5, United States 0	1938	United States 3, Australia 2		Germany 0
1907	Australasia 3, British Isles 2	1939	Australia 3, United States 2	1971	United States 3, Romania 2
1908	Australasia 3, United States 2	1946	United States 5, Australia 0	1972	United States 3, Romania 2
1909	Australasia 5, United States 0	1947	United States 4, Australia 1	1973	Australia 5, United States 0
1911	Australasia 5, United States 0	1948	United States 5, Australia 0	1974	South Africa (Default by India)
1912	British Isles 3, Australasia 2	1949	United States 4, Australia 1	1975	Sweden 3, Czechoslovakia 2
1913	United States 3, British Isles 2	1950	Australia 4, United States 1	1976	Italy 4, Chile 1
1914	Australasia 3, United States 2	1951	Australia 3, United States 2	1977	Australia 3, Italy 1
1919	Australasia 4, British Isles 1	1952	Australia 4, United States 1	1978	United States 4, Britain 1
1920	United States 5, Australasia 0	1953	Australia 3, United States 2	1979	United States 5, Italy 0
1921	United States 5, Japan 0	1954	United States 3, Australia 2	1980	Czechoslovakia 3, Italy 2
1922	United States 4, Australasia 1	1955	Australia 5, United States 0	1981	United States 3, Argentina 1
1923	United States 4, Australasia 1	1956	Australia 5, United States 0	1982	United States 3, France 0
1924	United States 5, Australasia 0	1957	Australia 3, United States 2	1983	Australia 3, Sweden 2
1925	United States 5, France 0	1958	United States 3, Australia 2	1984	Sweden 4, United States 1
1926	United States 4, France 1	1959	Australia 3, United States 2	1985	Sweden 3, West Germany 2
1927	France 3, United States 2	1960	Australia 4, Italy 1	1986	Australia 3, Sweden 2
1928	France 4, United States 1	1961	Australia 5, Italy 0	1987	Sweden 5, Austria 0
1929	France 3, United States 2	1962	Australia 5, Mexico 1	1988	West Germany 4, Sweden 1
1930	France 4, United States 1	1963	United States 3, Australia 2	1989	West Germany 3, Sweden 2
1931	France 3, Great Britain 2	1964	Australia 3, United States 2	1990	United States 3, Australia 2
1932	France 3, United States 2	1965	Australia 4, Spain 1		

FEDERATION CUP CHAMPIONSHIPS

World team competition for women conducted by International Lawn Tennis Federation.

1963	United States 2, Australia 1	1974	Australia 2, United States 1	1984	Czechoslovakia 2, Australia 1
1964	Australia 2, United States 1	1975	Czechoslovakia 3, Australia 0	1985	Czechoslovakia 2, United
1965	Australia 2, United States 1	1976	United States 2, Australia 1		States 1
1966	United States 3, West	1977	United States 2, Australia 1	1986	United States 3,
	Germany 0	1978	United States 2, Australia 1		Czechoslovakia 0
1967	United States 2, Britain 0	1979	United States 3, Australia 0	1987	West Germany 2, United
1968	Australia 3, Netherlands 0	1980	United States 3, Australia 0		States 1
1969	United States 2, Australia 1	1981	United States 3, Britain 0	1988	Czechoslovakia 2, Soviet
1970	Australia 3, West Germany 0	1982	United States 3, West		Union 1
1971	Australia 3, Britain 0		Germany 0	1989	United States 3, Spain 0
1972	South Africa 2, Britain 1	1983	Czechoslovakia 2, West	1990	United States 2, Soviet Union 1
1973	Australia 3, South Africa 0		Germany 1	1991	Spain 2, United States 1

U.S. CHAMPIONS
Singles—Men

NATIONAL

1881–87	Richard D. Sears	1919	William Johnston	1950	Arthur Larsen	1969	Rod Laver
1888–89	Henry Slocum, Jr.	1920–25	Bill Tilden	1951–52	Frank Sedgman	1970	Ken Rosewall
1890–92	Oliver S. Campbell	1926–27	Jean Rene	1953	Tony Trabert	1971	Stan Smith
1893–94	Robert D. Wrenn		Lacoste	1954	Vic Seixas	1972	Ilie Nastase
1895	Fred H. Hovey	1928	Henri Cochet	1955	Tony Trabert	1973	John Newcombe
1896–97	Robert D. Wrenn	1929	Bill Tilden	1956	Ken Rosewall	1974	Jimmy Connors
1898–		1930	John H. Doeg	1957	Mal Anderson	1975	Manuel Orantes
1900	Malcolm Whitman	1931–32	Ellsworth Vines	1958	Ashley Cooper	1976	Jimmy Connors
1901–02	William A. Larned	1933–34	Fred J. Perry	1959–60	Neale Fraser	1977	Guillermo Vilas
1903	Hugh L. Doherty	1935	Wilmer L. Allison	1961	Roy Emerson	1978	Jimmy Connors
1904	Holcombe Ward	1936	Fred J. Perry	1962	Rod Laver	1979	John McEnroe
1905	Beals C. Wright	1937–38	Don Budge	1963	Rafael Osuna	1980–81	John McEnroe
1906	William J. Clothier	1939	Robert L. Riggs	1964	Roy Emerson	1982	Jimmy Connors
1907–11	William A. Larned	1940	Donald McNeill	1965	Manuel Santana	1983	Jimmy Connors
1912–13	Maurice	1941	Robert L. Riggs	1966	Fred Stolle	1984	John McEnroe
	McLoughlin[1]	1942	Fred Schroeder	1967	John Newcombe	1985–87	Ivan Lendl
1914	R. N. Williams II	1943	Joseph Hunt	1968	Arthur Ashe	1988	Mats Wilander
1915	William Johnston	1944–45	Frank Parker	1969	Rod Laver	1989	Boris Becker
1916	R. N. William II	1946–47	Jack Kramer	**OPEN**		1990	Pete Sampras
1917–18	R. Lindley	1948–49	Richard Gonzales	**19**68	Arthur Ashe	1991	Stefan Edberg
	Murray[2]						

Singles—Women

NATIONAL

1887	Ellen F. Hansel	1906	Helen Homans	1941	Sarah Palfrey	**OPEN**	
1888–89	Bertha Townsend	1907	Evelyn Sears		Cooke	1968	Virginia Wade
1890	Ellen C. Roosevelt	1908	Maud	1942–44	Pauline Betz	1969–70	Margaret Court
1891–92	Mabel E. Cahill		Bargar–Wallach	1945	Sarah Cooke	1971–72	Billie Jean King
1893	Aline M. Terry	1909–11	Hazel V.	1946	Pauline Betz	1973	Margaret Court
1894	Helen R. Helwig		Hotchkiss	1947	Louise Brough	1974	Billie Jean King
1895	Juliette P.	1912–14	Mary K. Browne	1948–50	Margaret Osborne	1975–78	Chris Evert
	Atkinson	1915–18	Molla Bjurstedt		duPont	1979	Tracy Austin
1896	Elisabeth H.	1919	Hazel Hotchkiss	1951–53	Maureen Connolly	1980	Chris Evert–Lloyd
	Moore		Wightman	1954–55	Doris Hart	1981	Tracy Austin
1897–98	Juliette P.	1920–22	Molla Bjurstedt	1956	Shirley Fry	1982	Chris Evert–Lloyd
	Atkinson		Mallory	1957–58	Althea Gibson	1983–84	Martina Navratilova
1899	Marion Jones	1923–25	Helen N. Wills	1959	Maria Bueno	1985	Hana Mandlikova
1900	Myrtle McAteer	1926	Molla B. Mallory	1960–61	Darlene Hard	1986–87	Martina Navratilova
1901	Elisabeth H.	1927–29	Helen N. Wills	1962	Margaret Smith	1988	Steffi Graf
	Moore	1930	Betty Nuthall	1963–64	Maria Bueno	1989	Steffi Graf
1902	Marion Jones	1931	Helen Wills Moody	1965	Margaret Smith	1990	Grabriela Sabatini
1903	Elisabeth H.	1932–35	Helen Jacobs	1966	Maria Bueno	1991	Monica Seles
	Moore	1936	Alice Marble	1967	Billie Jean King		
1904	May Sutton	1937	Anita Lizana	1968–69	Margaret Smith		
1905	Elisabeth H.	1938–40	Alice Marble		Court[3]		
	Moore						

Doubles—Men

NATIONAL

1920	Bill Johnston–C. J. Griffin	1942	Gardnar Mulloy–Bill Talbert	1955	Kosei Kamo–Atsushi Miyagi
1921–22	Bill Tilden–Vincent Richards	1943	Jack Kramer–Frank Parker	1956	Lewis Hoad–Ken Rosewall
1923	Bill Tilden–B. I. C. Norton	1944	Don McNeill–Bob	1957	Ashley Cooper–Neale Fraser
1924	H. O. Kinsey—R. G. Kinsey		Falkenburg	1958	Ham Richardson–Alex
1925–26	Vincent Richards—R. N.	1945	Gardnar Mulloy–Bill Talbert		Olmedo
	Williams II	1946	Gardnar Mulloy–Bill Talbert	1959–60	Neale Fraser–Roy Emerson
1927	Bill Tilden—Frank Hunter	1947	Jack Kramer–Fred	1961	Chuck McKinley–Dennis
1928	G. M. Lott, Jr.–V. Hennessy		Schroeder		Ralston
1929–30	G. M. Lott, Jr.–J. H. Doeg	1948	Gardnar Mulloy–Bill Talbert	1962	Rafael Osuna–Antonio
1931	W. L. Allison–John Van Ryn	1949	John Bromwich–William		Palafox
1932	E. H. Vines, Jr.–Keith Gledh		Sidwell	1963–64	Chuck McKinley–Dennis
1933–34	G. M. Lott, Jr.–L. R. Stoefen	1950	John Bromwich–Frank		Ralston
1935	W. L. Allison–John Van Ryn		Sedgman	1965–66	Fred Stolle–Roy Emerson
1936	Don Budge–Gene Mako	1951	Frank Sedgman–Ken	1967	John Newcombe–Tony
1937	G. von Cramm–H. Henkel		McGregor		Roche
1938	Don Budge–Gene Mako	1952	Vic Seixas–Mervyn Rose	1968	Stan Smith–Bob Lutz[3]
1939	A. K. Quist–J. E. Bromwich	1953	Mervyn Rose–Rex Hartwig	1969	Richard Crealy–Allan Stone[3]
1940–41	Jack Kramer–F. R. Schroeder	1954	Vic Seixas–Tony Trabert		

OPEN

1968	Stan Smith–Bob Lutz	1977	Frew McMillan–Bob Hewitt	1985	Ken Flach–Robert Seguso
1969	Fred Stolle–Ken Rosewall	1978	Bob Lutz–Stan Smith	1986	Andres Gomez–Slobodan
1970	Nikki Pilic–Fred Barthes	1979	John McEnroe–Peter		Zivojinovic
1971	John Newcombe–Roger		Fleming	1987	Stefan Edberg–Anders
	Taylor	1980	Stan Smith–Bob Lutz		Jarryd
1972	Cliff Drysdale–Roger Taylor	1981	John McEnroe–Peter	1988	Sergio Casal–Emilio
1973	John Newcombe–Owen		Fleming		Sanchez
	Davidson	1982	Kevin Curren–Steve Denton	1989	John McEnroe—Mark
1974	Bob Lutz–Stan Smith	1983	John McEnroe–Peter		Woodforde
1975	Jimmy Connors–Ilie		Fleming	1990	Pieter Aldrich–Danie Visser
	Nastase	1984	John Fitzgerald–Tomas	1991	John Fitzgerald–Anders
1976	Marty Riessen–Tom Okker		Smid		Jarryd

1. Challenge round abandoned in 1912. 2. Patriotic Tournament in 1917. 3. With the inaugural of the Open Tournament in 1968, the United States Lawn Tennis Association held a national championship at Longwood, Chestnut Hill, Mass. which barred contract professionals in 1968 and 1969.

Doubles—Women

NATIONAL

1924	G. W. Wightman–Helen Wills	1958–59	Darlene Hard–Jeanne Arth	1975	Margaret Court–Virginia
1925	Mary K. Browne–Helen Wills	1960	Darlene Hard–Maria Bueno		Wade
1926	Elizabeth Ryan–Eleanor Goss	1961	Darlene Hard–Lesley Turner	1976	Linky Boshoff–Ilana Kloss
1927	L. A. Godfree–Ermyntrude	1962	Darlene Hard–Maria Bueno	1977	Martina Navratilova–Betty
	Harvey	1963	Margaret Smith–Robyn		Stove
1928	Hazel Hotchkiss Wightman–		Ebbern	1978	Billie Jean King–Martina
	Helen Wills	1964	Karen Hantze Susman–Billie		Navratilova
1929	Phoebe Watson–L. R. C.		Jean Moffitt	1979	Betty Stove–Wendy Turnbull
	Michell	1965	Nancy Richey–Carole	1980	Billie Jean King–Martina
1930	Betty Nuthall–Sarah Palfrey		Caldwell Graebner		Navratilova
1931	Betty Nuthall–E. B.	1966	Nancy Richey–Maria Bueno	1981	Kathy Jordan–Anne Smith
	Wittingstall	1967	Billie Jean King–Rosemary	1982	Rosemary Casals–Wendy
1932	Helen Jacobs–Sarah Palfrey		Casals		Turnbull
1933	Betty Nuthall–Freda James	1968	Margaret Court–Maria	1983–84	Martina Navratilova–Pam
1934	Helen Jacobs–Sarah Palfrey		Bueno[3]		Shriver
1935	Helen Jacobs–Sarah Palfrey	1969	Margaret Court–Virginia	1985	Claudia Khode–Kilsch–
	Fabyan		Wade[3]		Helena Sukova
1936	Marjorie G. Van Ryn–Carolin			1986–87	Martina Navratilova–Pam
	Babcock	**OPEN**			Shriver
1937–40	Sarah Palfrey Fabyan–Alice	1968	Maria Bueno–Margaret	1988	Gigi Fernandez–Robin White
	Marble		Court	1989	Hana Mandlikova–Martina
1941	Sarah Palfrey Cooke–	1969	Darlene Hard–Francoise Durr		Navratilova
	Margaret Osborne	1970	Margaret Court–Judy Dalton	1990	Gigi Fernandez–Martina
1942–47	A. Louise Brough–Margaret	1971	Rosemary Casals–Judy		Navratilova
	Osborne		Dalton	1991	Pam Shriver–Natalia Zvereva
1948–50	A. Louise Brough–Margaret	1972	Francoise Durr–Betty Stove		
	O. duPont	1973	Margaret Court–Virginia		
1951–54	Doris Hart–Shirley Fry		Wade		
1955–57	A. Louise Brough–Margaret	1974	Billie Jean King–Rosemary		
	O. duPont		Casals		

1. Challenge round abandoned in 1912. 2. Patriotic Tournament in 1917. 3. With the inaugural of the Open Tournament in 1968, the United States Lawn Tennis Association held a national championship at Longwood, Chestnut Hill, Mass. which barred contract professionals in 1968 and 1969.

BRITISH (WIMBLEDON) CHAMPIONS

(Amateur from inception in 1877 through 1967)

Singles—Men

1908–09	Arthur Gore	1931	S. B. Wood	1954	Jaroslav Drobny	1973	Jan Kodes
1910–13	A. F. Wilding	1932	Ellsworth Vines	1955	Tony Trabert	1974	Jimmy Connors
1914	N. E. Brookes	1933	J. H. Crawford	1956–57	Lewis Hoad	1975	Arthur Ashe
1919	G. L. Patterson	1934–36	Fred Perry	1958	Ashley Cooper	1976–80	Bjorn Borg
1920–21	Bill Tilden	1937–38	Don Budge	1959	Alex Olmedo	1981	John McEnroe
1922	G. L. Patterson	1939	Robert L. Riggs	1960	Neale Fraser	1982	Jimmy Connors
1923	William Johnston	1946	Yvon Petra	1961–62	Rod Laver	1983–84	John McEnroe
1924	Jean Borotra	1947	Jack Kramer	1963	Chuck McKinley	1985–86	Boris Becker
1925	Rene Lacoste	1948	R. Falkenburg	1964–65	Roy Emerson	1987	Pat Cash
1926	Jean Borotra	1949	Fred Schroeder	1966	Manuel Santana	1988	Stefan Edberg
1927	Henri Cochet	1950	Budge Patty	1967	John Newcombe	1989	Boris Becker
1928	Rene Lacoste	1951	Richard Savitt	1968–69	Rod Laver	1990	Stefan Edberg
1929	Jean Cochet	1952	Frank Sedgman	1970–71	John Newcombe	1991	Michael Stich
1930	Bill Tilden	1953	Vic Siexas	1972	Stan Smith		

Singles—Women

1919–23	Lenglen	1938	Helen Wills Moody	1962	Karen Susman	1976	Chris Evert
1924	Kathleen McKane	1939	Alice Marble	1963	Margaret Smith	1977	Virginia Wade
1925	Lenglen	1946	Pauline M. Betz	1964	Maria Bueno	1978–79	Martina Navratilova
1926	Godfree	1947	Margaret Osborne	1965	Margaret Smith	1980	Evonne Goolagong
1927–29	Helen Wills	1948–50	A. Louise Brough	1966–67	Billie Jean King		Cawley
1930	Helen Wills Moody	1951	Doris Hart	1968	Billie Jean King	1981	Chris Evert–Lloyd
1931	Frl. C. Aussen	1952–54	Maureen Connolly	1969	Ann Jones	1982–87	Martina Navratilova
1932–33	Helen Wills Moody	1955	A. Louise Brough	1970	Margaret Court	1988–89	Steffi Graf
1934	D. E. Round	1956	Shirley Fry	1971	Evonne Goolagong	1990	Martina Navratilova
1935	Helen Wills Moody	1957–58	Althea Gibson	1972–73	Billie Jean King	1991	Steffi Graf
1936	Helen Jacobs	1959–60	Maria Bueno	1974	Chris Evert		
1937	D. E. Round	1961	Angela Mortimer	1975	Billie Jean King		

Doubles—Men

1953	K. Rosewall–L. Hoad	1967	Bob Hewitt–Frew McMillan	1981	John McEnroe–Peter Fleming
1954	R. Hartwig–M. Rose	1968–70	John Newcombe–Tony Roche	1982	Paul McNamee–Peter
1955	R. Hartwig–L. Hoad	1971	Rod Laver–Roy Emerson		McNamara
1956	L. Hoad–K. Rosewall	1972	Bob Hewitt–Frew McMillan	1983–84	John McEnroe–Peter Fleming
1957	Gardnar Mulloy–Budge Patty	1973	Jimmy Connors–Ilie Nastase	1985	Heinz Gunthardt–Balazs
1958	Sven Davidson–Ulf Schmidt	1974	John Newcombe–Tony Roche		Taroczy
1959	Roy Emerson–Neale Fraser	1975	Vitas Gerulaitis–Sandy Mayer	1986	Joakim Nystrom–Mats
1960	Dennis Ralston–Rafael Osuna	1976	Brian Gottfried–Raul Ramirez		Wilander
1961	Roy Emerson–Neale Fraser	1977	Ross Case–Geoff Masters	1987	Ken Flach–Robert Seguso
1962	Fred Stolle–Bob Hewitt	1978	Fred McMillan–Bob Hewitt	1988	Ken Flach–Robert Seguso
1963	Rafael Osuna–Antonio Palafox	1979	Peter Fleming–John McEnroe	1989	John Fitzgerald–Anders Jarryd
1964	Fred Stolle–Bob Hewitt	1980	Peter McNamara–Paul	1990	Rick Leach–Jim Pugh
1965	John Newcombe–Tony Roche		McNamee	1991	Anders Jarryd–John Fitzgerald
1966	John Newcombe–Ken Fletcher				

Doubles–Women

1956	Althea Gibson–Angela Buxton	1969	Margaret Court–Judy Tegart	1980	Kathy Jordan–Anne Smith
1957	Althea Gibson–Darlene Hard	1970–71	Billie Jean King–Rosemary	1981	Martina Navratilova–Pam
1958	Althea Gibson–Maria Bueno		Casals		Shriver
1959	Darlene Hard–Jeanne Arth	1972	Billie Jean King–Betty Stove	1982–84	Pam Shriver–Martina
1960	Darlene Hard–Maria Bueno	1973	Billie Jean King–Rosemary		Navratilova
1961	Karen Hantze–Billie Jean		Casals	1985	Kathy Jordan–Elizabeth Smylie
	Moffitt	1974	Evonne Goolagong–Peggy	1986	Pam Shriver–Martina
1962	Karen Hantze Susman–Billie		Michel		Navratilova
	Jean Moffitt	1975	Ann Kiyomura–Kazuko	1987	Claudia Khode-Kilsch–Helena
1963	Darlene Hard–Maria Bueno		Sawamatsu		Sukova
1964	Margaret Smith–Les Turnerley	1976	Chris Evert–Martina	1988	Steffi Graf–Gabriela Sabatini
1965	Billie Jean Moffitt–Maria		Navratilova	1989	Jana Novotna–Helena Sukova
	Bueno	1977	Helen Cawley–JoAnne Russell	1990	Jana Novotna–Helena Sukova
1966	Nancy Richey–Maria Bueno	1978	Wendy Turnbull–Kerry Reid	1991	Pam Shriver–Natalia Zvereva
1967–68	Billie Jean King–Rosemary	1979	Billie Jean King–Martina		
	Casals		Navratilova		

UNITED STATES CHAMPIONS—1991

United States Open
(Flushing Meadow, Aug. 26–Sept. 8, 1991)

Men's singles—Stefan Edberg (2), Sweden, defeated Jim Courier (4), Dade City, Fla., 6–2, 6–4, 6–0.

Men's doubles—John Fitzgerald, Australia, and Anders Jarryd, Sweden (1), defeated Scott Davis, Davie, Fla., and David Pate, Las Vegas (2), 6–3, 3–6, 6–3, 6–3.

Women's singles—Monica Seles (2), Yugoslavia, defeated Martina Navratilova (6), Aspen, Colo., 7–6, (7–1), 6–1.

Women's doubles—Pam Shriver, Lutherville, Md., and Natalia Zvereva, Soviet Union (6), defeated Jana Novotna, Czechoslovakia, and Larisa Savchenko, Soviet Union (1), 6–4, 4–6, 7–6 (7–5).

Mixed doubles—Manon Bollegraf and Tom Nijssen, Netherlands, defeated Arantxa Sanchez Vicario and Emilio Sanchez, Spain (2), 6–2, 7–6 (7–2).

Boys singles—Leander Paes (2), India, defeated Karim Alami (4), Morocco, 6–4, 6–4.

Girls' singles—Karina Habsudova (2), Czechoslovakia, defeated Anne Mall, Laguna Niguel, Calif., 6–1, 6–3.

Senior men's singles—Hank Pfister (4), Bakersfield, Calif., defeated Tom Gullikson (2), Palm Coast, Fla., 1–6, 7–6 (11–9), 6–4.

United States Hardcourts—Men
(Aug. 12–18, 1991, Indianapolis, Ind.)

Men's singles—Peter Sempras, Rancho Palos Verdes, Calif., defeated Boris Becker, Germany 7–6 (7–2), 3–6, 6–3.

Men's doubles—Ken Flach, Sebring, Fla., and Robert Seguso, Boca Raton, Fla., defeated Kent Kinnear, Greenwood, Ind., and Sven Salumaa, Bloomington, Ind., 7–6 (7–3), 6–4.

United States Hardcourts—Women
(March 25–31, 1991, San Antonio, Texas)

Women's singles—Steffi Graf, Germany, defeated Monica Seles, Yugoslavia, 6–4, 6–3.

Women's doubles—Patty Fendick, Sacramento, Calif., and Monica Seles, Yugoslavia, defeated Jill Heatherington, Canada, and Kathy Rinaldi, Amelia Island, Fla., 7–5, 6–2.

U.S. Pro Championships
(July 29–Aug. 4, 1991))

Men's singles—Andrei Cherkasov, Soviet Union, defeated Jimmy Arias, Buffalo, N.Y., 7–5, 6–4.

Men's doubles—Peter Nyborg, Sweden, and Luke Jensen, Ludington, Mich., defeated Layden Decker, Boston, and Richey Reneberg, Houston, 6–4, 6–3.

U.S. Clay Court Championships

(May 6–12, 1991, Charlotte, N.C.)

Men's singles—Jaime Yzaga, Peru, defeated Jimmy Arias, Buffalo, N.Y., 6–3, 7–5.

International Players Championships

(March 15–24, 1991, Key Biscayne, Fla.)

Men's singles—Jim Courier, Dade City, Fla., defeated David Wheaton, Deephaven, Minn., 4–6, 6–3, 6–4.
Women's singles—Monica Seles, Yugoslavia, defeated Gabriela Sabatini, Argentina, 6–3, 7–5.
Men's doubles—Wayne Ferreira, South Africa, and Piet Norval, South Africa, defeated Ken Frach, St. Louis, and Robert Seguso, Boca Raton, Fla., 5–7, 7–6, 6–2.
Women's doubles—Mary Joe Fernandez, Miami, and Zina Garrison, Houston, defeated Gigi Fernandez, Aspen, Colo., and Jana Novotna, Czechoslovakia, 7–5, 6–2.

United States Pro Indoor

(Feb. 11–17, 1991, Philadelphia, Pa.)

Singles final—Ivan Lendl, Czechoslovakia, defeated Peter Sampras, Rancho Palos Verdes, Calif., 5–7, 6–4, 6–4, 3–6, 6–3.
Doubles final—Rich Leach, Laguna Beach, Calif., and Jim Pugh, Rancho Palos Verdes, Calif., defeated Udo Riglewski and Michael Stich, Germany, 6–4, 6–4.

OTHER 1991 CHAMPIONS

Australian Open

Men's singles—Boris Becker, Germany, defeated Ivan Lendl, Czechslovakia, 1–6, 6–4, 6–4, 6–4.
Women's singles—Monica Seles, Yugoslavia, defeated Jana Novotna, Czechoslovakia, 5–7, 6–3, 6–1.
Men's doubles—Scott Davis, Davie, Fla., and David Pate, Las Vegas, defeated Patrick McEnroe, Oyster Bay, N.Y., and David Wheaton, Deephaven, Minn., 6–7 (4–7), 7–6 (10–8).
Women's doubles—Patty Fendick, Sacramento, Calif., and Mary Joe Fernandez, Miami, defeated Gigi Fernandez, Aspen, Colo., and Jana Novotna, Czechoslovakia, 7–6 (7–4), 6–1.
Mixed doubles—Jeremy Bates and Jo Durie, Britain, defeated Scott Davis, Davie, Fla., and Robin White, San Diego, 2–6, 6–4, 6–4.

Wimbledon Open

Men's singles—Michael Stich, Germany, defeated Boris Becker, Germany, 6–4, 7–6 (7–4), 6–4.
Women's singles—Steffi Graf, Germany, defeated Gabriela Sabatini, Argentina, 6–4, 3–6, 8–6.
Men's doubles—John Fitzgerald, Australia, and Anders Jarryd, Sweden, defeated Javier Frana, Argentina, and Leonardo Lavalle, Mexico, 6–3, 6–4, 6–7 (7–9), 6–1.

Women's doubles—Larisa Savchenko and Natalia Zvereva, Soviet Union, defeated Gigi Fernandez, Aspen, Colo., and Jana Novotna, Czechoslovakia, 6–4, 3–6, 6–4.
Mixed doubles—John Fitzgerald and Elizabeth Smylie, Australia, defeated Jim Pugh, Rancho Palos Verdes, Calif., and Natalia Zvereva, Soviet Union, 7–6 (7–4), 6–2.

French Open

Men's singles—Jim Courier, Dade City, Fla., defeated Andre Agassi, Las Vegas, 3–6, 6–4, 2–6, 6–1, 6–4.
Women's singles—Monica Seles, Yugoslavia, defeated Arantxa Sanchez Vicario, Spain, 6–3, 6–4.
Men's doubles—John Fitzgerald, Australia, and Anders Jarryd, Sweden, defeated Rick Leach, Laguna Beach, Calif., and Jim Pugh, Rancho Palos Verdes, Calif., 6–0, 7–6 (7–2).
Women's doubles—Gigi Fernandez, Aspen, Colo., and Jana Novotna, Czechoslovakia, defeated Larisa Savchenko and Natalia Zvereva, Soviet Union, 6–4, 6–0.
Mixed doubles—Helena Sukova and Cyril Suk, Czechoslovakia, defeated Carolina Vis and Paul Haarhuis, Netherlands, 3–6, 6–4, 6–1.

DAVIS CUP RESULTS—1990

United States 3, Australia 2 (at St. Petersburg, Fla., Nov. 30–Dec. 2, 1990)

Singles—Andre Agassi, United States, defeated Richard Fromberg, Australia, 4–6, 6–2, 6–2, 6–4; Michael Chang, United States, defeated Darren Cahil, Australia, 6–2, 7–6 (7–4), 6–0; Fromberg, Australia, defeated Chang, United States, 7–5, 2–6, 6–3; Cahil, Australia, defeated Agassi, United States, 6–4, 4–6 retired.
Doubles—Rick Leach and Jim Pugh, United States, defeated Pat Cash and John Fitzgerald, Australia, 6–4, 6–2, 3–6, 7–6 (7–2).

MEN'S FINAL TENNIS EARNINGS—1990

Men—1. Stefan Edberg (Sweden), $1,995,901. 2. Andre Agassi (United States), $1,741,382. 3. Boris Becker (Germany), $1,587,502. 4. Ivan Lendl (Czechoslovakia), $1,145,742. 5. Peter Sampras (United States), $900,057. 6. Andres Gomez (Ecuador), $874,605. 7. Emilio Sanchez (Spain), $734,291. 8. Goran Ivanisevic (Soviet Union), $720,945. 9. Jakob Hlasek (Sweden), $661,671. 10. Guy Forget, $638,358.

WOMEN'S FINAL TENNIS EARNINGS—1990

Women—1. Steffi Graf (Germany), $1,921,853. 2. Monica Seles (Yugoslavia), $1,637,222. 3. Martina Navratilova (United States), $1,330,794. 4. Gabriela Sabatini (Argentina), $975,490. 5. Jana Novotna (Czechoslovakia), $645,500. 6. Zina Garrison (United States), $602,203. 7. Helena Sulcova (Czechoslovakia), $562,715. 8. Mary Joe Fernandez (United States), $518,366. 9. Arantxa Sanchez-Vicario (Spain), $517,662. 10. Natalia Zvereva (Soviet Union), $462,770.

COLLEGE SOCCER

(1990 NCAA PLAYOFFS)

DIVISION I
MEN

Quarterfinals
Rutgers 1, Dartmouth 0
Evansville 1, Indiana 0
N.C. State 2, Virginia 1 (2OT, penalty kicks)
UCLA 2, Southern Methodist 0

Semifinals
(at University of South Florida, Tampa, Fla., Dec. 1, 1990))
Rutgers 1, Evansville 0

UCLA 1, N.C. State 0 (2 OT, penalty kicks)

Championship
(at University of South Florida, Tampa, Fla., Dec. 2, 1990)
UCLA 1, Rutgers 0 (2 OT, penalty kicks)

DIVISION I—WOMEN

Quarterfinals
North Carolina 4, N.C. State 3 (2 OT)
Colorado College 2, Wisconsin 1
Santa Clara 2, Cal–Santa Barbara 0
Connecticut 1, Virginia 0

Semifinals
(at University of North Carolina, Chapel Hill, N.C., Nov. 17, 1990)

North Carolina 2, Colorado College 1
Connecticut 2, Santa Clara 1 (2 OT, penalty kicks)

Championship
(at Unitersity of North Carolina, Chapel Hill, N.C., Nov. 18, 1990)
North Carolina 6, Connecticut 0

ROWING

Rowing goes back so far in history that there is no possibility of tracing it to any particular aboriginal source. The oldest rowing race still on the calendar is the "Doggett's Coat and Badge" contest among professional watermen of the Thames (England) that began in 1715. The first Oxford-Cambridge race was held at Henley in 1829. Competitive rowing in the United States began with matches between boats rowed by professional oarsmen of the New York waterfront. They were oarsmen who rowed the small boats that plied as ferries from Manhattan Island to Brooklyn and return, or who rowed salesmen down the harbor to meet ships arriving from Europe. Since the first salesman to meet an incoming ship had some advantage over his rivals, there was keen competition in the bidding for fast boats and the best oarsmen. This gave rise to match races.

Amateur boat clubs sprang up in the United States between 1820 and 1830 and seven students of Yale joined together to purchase a four-oared lap-streak gig in 1843. The first Harvard-Yale race was held Aug. 3, 1852, on Lake Winnepesaukee, N.H. The first time an American college crew went abroad was in 1869 when Harvard challenged Oxford and was defeated on the Thames. There were early college rowing races on Lake Quinsigamond, near Worcester, Mass., and on Saratoga Lake, N.Y., but the Intercollegiate Rowing Association in 1895 settled on the Hudson, at Poughkeepsie, as the setting for the annual "Poughkeepsie Regatta." In 1950 the I.R.A. shifted its classic to Marietta, Ohio, and in 1952 it was moved to Syracuse, N.Y. The National Association of Amateur Oarsmen, organized in 1872, has conducted annual championship regattas since that time.

INTERCOLLEGIATE ROWING ASSOCIATION REGATTA

(Varsity Eight-Oared Shells)

Rowed at 4 miles, Poughkeepsie, N.Y., 1895–97, 1899–1916, 1925–32, 1934–41. Rowed at 3 miles, Saratoga, N.Y., 1898; Poughkeepsie, 1921–24, 1947–49; Syracuse, N.Y., 1952–1963, 1965–67. Rowed at 2,000 meters, Syracuse, N.Y., 1964 and from 1968 on. Rowed at 2 miles, Ithaca, N.Y., 1920; Marietta, Ohio, 1950–51. Suspended 1917–19, 1933, 1942–46.

Year	Time	First	Second	Year	Time	First	Second
1895	21:25	Columbia	Cornell	1948	14:06 2/5	Washington	California
1896	19:59	Cornell	Harvard	1949	14:42 3/5	California	Washington
1897	20:47 4/5	Cornell	Columbia	1950	8:07.5	Washington	California
1898	15:51 1/2	Pennsylvania	Cornell	1951	7:50.5	Wisconsin	Washington
1899	20:04	Pennsylvania	Wisconsin	1952	15:08.1	Navy	Princeton
1900	19:44 3/5	Pennsylvania	Wisconsin	1953	15:29.6	Navy	Cornell
1901	18:53 1/5	Cornell	Columbia	1954	16:04.4	Navy[1]	Cornell
1902	19:03 3/5	Cornell	Wisconsin	1955	15:49.9	Cornell	Pennsylvania
1903	18:57	Cornell	Georgetown	1956	16:22.4	Cornell	Navy
1904	20:22 3/5	Syracuse	Cornell	1957	15:26.6	Cornell	Pennsylvania
1905	20:29	Cornell	Syracuse	1958	17:12.1	Cornell	Navy
1906	19:36 4/5	Cornell	Pennsylvania	1959	18:01.7	Wisconsin	Syracuse
1907	20:02 2/5	Cornell	Columbia	1960	15:57	California	Navy
1908	19:24 1/5	Syracuse	Columbia	1961	16:49.2	California	Cornell
1909	19:02	Cornell	Columbia	1962	17:02.9	Cornell	Washington
1910	20:42 1/5	Cornell	Pennsylvania	1963	17:24	Cornell	Navy
1911	20:10 4/5	Cornell	Columbia	1964	6:31.1	California	Washington
1912	19:31 2/5	Cornell	Wisconsin	1965	16:51.3	Navy	Cornell
1913	19:28 3/5	Syracuse	Cornell	1966	16:03.4	Wisconsin	Navy
1914	19:37 4/5	Columbia	Pennsylvania	1967	16:13.9	Pennsylvania	Wisconsin
1915	19:36 3/5	Cornell	Stanford	1968	6:15.6	Pennsylvania	Washington
1916	20:15 2/5	Syracuse	Cornell	1969	6:30.4	Pennsylvania	Dartmouth
1920	11:02 3/5	Syracuse	Cornell	1970	6:39.3	Washington	Wisconsin
1921	14:07	Navy	California	1971	6:06	Cornell	Washington
1922	13:33 3/5	Navy	Washington	1972	6:22.6	Pennsylvania	Brown
1923	14:03 1/5	Washington	Navy	1973	6:21	Wisconsin	Brown
1924	15:02	Washington	Wisconsin	1974	6:33	Wisconsin	M.I.T.
1925	19:24 4/5	Navy	Washington	1975	6:08.2	Wisconsin	M.I.T.
1926	19:28 3/5	Washington	Navy	1976	6:31	California	Princeton
1927	20:57	Columbia	Washington	1977	6:32.4	Cornell	Pennsylvania
1928	18:35 4/5	California	Columbia	1978	6:39.5	Syracuse	Brown
1929	22:58	Columbia	Washington	1979	6:26.4	Brown	Wisconsin
1930	21:42	Cornell	Syracuse	1980	6:46	Navy	Northeastern
1931	18:54 1/5	Navy	Cornell	1981	5:57.3	Cornell	Navy
1932	19:55	California	Cornell	1982	5:57.5	Cornell	Princeton
1934	19:44	California	Washington	1983	6:14.4	Brown	Navy
1935	18:52	California	Cornell	1984	5:54.7	Navy	Pennsylvania
1936	19:09 3/5	Washington	California	1985	5:49.9	Princeton	Brown
1937	18:33 3/5	Washington	Navy	1986	5:50.2	Brown	Pennsylvania
1938	18:19	Navy	California	1987	6:02.9	Brown	Wisconsin
1939	18:12 3/5	California	Washington	1988	6:14.0	Northeastern	Brown
1940	22:42	Washington	Cornell	1989	5:56.0	Penn	Wisconsin
1941	18:53 3/10	Washington	California	1990	5:55.5	Wisconsin	Pennsylvania
1947	13:59 1/5	Navy	Cornell	1991	6:05.2	Northeastern	Pennsylvania

1. Disqualified.

HARNESS RACING

Oliver Wendell Holmes, the famous Autocrat of the Breakfast Table, wrote that the running horse was a gambling toy but the trotting horse was useful and, furthermore, "horse–racing is not a republican institution; horse–trotting is." Oliver Wendell Holmes was a born–and–bred New Englander, and New England was the nursery of the harness racing sport in America. Pacers and trotters were matters of local pride and prejudice in Colonial New England, and, shortly after the Revolution, the Messenger and Justin Morgan strains produced many winners in harness racing "matches" along the turnpikes of New York, Connecticut, Rhode Island, Massachusetts, Vermont, and New Hampshire.

There was English thoroughbred blood in Messenger and Justin Morgan, and, many years later, it was blended in Rysdyk's Hambletonian, foaled in 1849. Hambletonian was not particularly fast under harness but his descendants have had almost a monopoly of prizes, titles, and records in the harness racing game. Hambletonian was purchased as a foal with its dam for a total of $124 by William Rysdyk of Goshen, N.Y., and made a modest fortune for the purchaser.

Trotters and pacers often were raced under saddle in the old days, and, in fact, the custom still survives in some places in Europe. Dexter, the great trotter that lowered the mile record from 2:19 3/4 to 2:17 1/4 in 1867, was said to handle just as well under saddle as when pulling a sulky. But as sulkies were lightened in weight and improved in design, trotting under saddle became less common and finally faded out in this country.

WORLD RECORDS

Established in a Race or Against Time at One Mile *Source:* United States Trotting Association
(Through Aug. 1, 1991)

Trotting on Mile Track

	Record	Holder	Driver	Where Made	Year
All Age	1:52 1/5	Mack Lobell	John Campbell	Springfield, Ill.	1987
	1:52 4/5	Peace Corps	John Campbell	Du Quoin, Ill.	1989
	* 1:54	Arndon	Del Miller	Lexington, Ky.	1982
	* 1:55 1/4	Greyhound	Sep Palin	Lexington, Ky.	1938
2–year–old	* 1:55	Noxie Hanover	Jim Simpson	Lexington, Ky.	1988
	1:55 3/5	Mack Lobell	John Campbell	Lexington, Ky.	1986
	1:57 2/5	I'm Impeccable	Dave Rankin	Lexington, Ky.	1989
3–year–old	1:52 1/5	Mack Lobell	John Campbell	Springfield, Ill.	1987
	1:52 4/5	Peace Corps	John Campbell	Du Quoin, Ill.	1989
	1:56	Nuclear Arsenal	Dave Magee	Springfield, Ill.	1989
4–year–old	1:53	Express Ride	Berndt Lindstedt	Lexington, Ky.	1987
	* 1:55 2/5	Classical Way	John Simpson Jr.	Lexington, Ky.	1980
	1:56	Delray Lobell	John Campbell	East Rutherford, N.J.	1989
5–year–old and older	1:54 1/5	Napoletano	Stig Johansson	East Rutherford, N.J.	1989
	1:54 4/5	Kit Lobell	Berndt Lindstedt	East Rutherford, N.J.	1990
	1:55	Franconia	John Campbell	East Rutherford, N.J.	1987
	* 1:55 1/4	Greyhound	Sep Palin	Lexington, Ky.	1938

Trotting on Five-Eighths-Mile Track

All Age	1:54 1/5	Mack Lobell	John Campbell	Pompano Beach, Fla.	1987
2–year–old	1:57 3/5	Royal Troubador	Carl Allen	Pompano Beach, Fla.	1989
3–year–old	1:54 1/5	Mack Lobell	John Campbell	Pompano Beach, Fla.	1987
4–year–old	1:54 4/5	Mack Lobell	John Campbell	Solvalla, Sweden	1988
5–year–old and older	1:55	Minou Du Donjon	Olle Goop	Solvalla, Sweden	1985

Trotting on Half-Mile Track

All Age	1:56	Mack Lobell	John Campbell	Saratoga Springs, N.Y.	1988
2–year–old	1:58 1/5	Royal Troubador	Carl Allen	Delaware, Ohio	1989
3–year–old	1:56 4/5	Editor In Chief	John Campbell	Delaware, Ohio	1988
4–year–old	1:56	Mack Lobell	John Campbell	Saratoga Springs, N.Y.	1988
5–year–old and older	1:57 4/5	Lakewater Glory	Valery Tanishin	Northfield, Ohio	1989

Pacing on a Mile Track

All Age	* 1:48 2/5	Matt's Scooter	Michel Lachance	Lexington, Ky.	1988
	* 1:50 4/5	Fan Hanover	Glen Garnsey	Lexington, Ky.	1982
	1:51 1/5	Indian Alert	Jack Moiseyev	East Rutherford, N.J.	1988
2–year–old	1:52	L Dees Trish	Michel Lachance	Lexington, Ky.	1988
	1:52 1/5	Raque Bogart	Bill Fahy	Lexington, Ky.	1988
3–year–old	* 1:48 2/5	Matt's Scooter	Michel Lachance	Lexington, Ky.	1988
	* 1:51 2/5	Trini Hanover	Ron Waples	Springfield, Ill.	1987
	1:51 4/5	Indian Alert	Larry Noggle	Lexington, Ky.	1987
4–year–old	* 1:49 2/5	Jaguar Spur	Dick Stillings	Lexington, Ky.	1988
	* 1:50 4/5	Fan Hanover	Glen Garnsey	Lexington, Ky.	1982
	1:51 1/5	Indian Alert	Jack Moiseyev	East Rutherford, N.J.	1988
5–year–old and older	1:50 1/5	Ramblin' Storm	Michel Lachance	East Rutherford, N.J.	1988

Pacing on Five-Eighths-Mile Track

All Age	1:50 4/5	In the Pocket	John Campbell	Meadow Lands, Pa.	1990
2–year–old	1:53 2/5	Kentucky Spur	Dick Stillings	Pompano Beach, Fla.	1988
3–year–old	1:50 4/5	In the Pocket	John Campbell	Meadow Lands, Pa.	1990
	1:51 1/5	Goalie Jeff	Michel Lachance	Montreal, Canada	1989

4–year–old	1:51	Falcon Seelster	Tom Harmer	Meadow Lands, Pa.	1986
	1:51	Matt's Scooter	Michel Lachance	Campbellville, Ont., Canada	1989
5–year–old and older	1:52 2/5	Ring of Light	James Morand	Laurel, Md.	1988

Pacing on a Half-Mile Track

All Age	1:51	Falcon Seelster	Tom Harmer	Delaware, Ohio	1985
2–year–old	1:54.3	OK Bye	John Campbell	Freehold, N.J.	1989
3–year–old	1:51	Falcon Seelster	Tom Harmer	Delaware, Ohio	1985
4–year–old	1:53 1/5	Falcon Seelster	Tom Harmer	Maywood, Ill.	1986
5–year–old and older	1:54 1/5	Port Stanley	John Reese	Maywood, Ill.	1988

*Set in a time trial.

HARNESS RACING RECORDS FOR THE MILE

Trotters

Pacers

Time	Trotter, age, driver	Year	Time	Pacer, age, driver	Year
2:00	Lou Dillon, 5, Millard Sanders	1903	2:00 1/2	John R. Gentry, 7, W.J. Andrews	1896
1:58 1/2	Lou Dillon, 5, Millard Sanders	1903	1:59 1/4	Star Pointer, 8, D. McClary	1897
1:58	Uhlan, 8, Charles Tanner	1912	1:59	Dan Patch, 7, M. E. McHenry	1903
1:58	Peter Manning, 5, T. W. Murphy	1921	1:56 1/4	Dan Patch, 7, M. E. McHenry	1903
1:57 3/4	Peter Manning, 5, T. W. Murphy	1921	1:56	Dan Patch, 8, H. C. Hersey	1904
1:57	Peter Manning, 6, T. W. Murphy	1922	1:55	Billy Direct, 4, Vic Fleming	1938
1:56 3/4	Peter Manning, 6, T. W. Murphy	1922	1:55	Adios Harry, 4, Luther Lyons	1955
1:56 3/4	Greyhound, 5, Sep Palin	1937	1:54 3/5	Adios Butler, 4, Paige West	1960
1:56	Greyhound, 5, Sep Palin	1937	1:54	Bret Hanover, 4, Frank Ervin	1966
1:55 1/4	Greyhound, 6, Sep Palin	1938	1:53 3/5	Bret Hanover, 4, Frank Ervin	1966
1:54 4/5	Nevele Pride, 4, Stanley Dancer	1969	1:52	Steady Star, 4, Joe O'Brien	1971
1:54 4/5	Lindy's Crown, 4, Howard Beissinger	1980	1:49 1/5	Niatross, 3, Clint Galbraith	1980
1:54	Arndon, 3, Del Miller	1982	1:48 2/5	Matt's Scooter, 3, Michel Lachance	1989
1:52 1/5	Mack Lobell, 3, John Campbell	1987			

HISTORY OF TRADITIONAL HARNESS RACING STAKES

The Hambletonian

Three–year–old trotters. One mile. Guy McKinney won first race at Syracuse in 1926; held at Goshen, N.Y., 1930–1942, 1944–1956; at Yonkers, N.Y., 1943; at Du Quoin, Ill., 1957–1980. Since 1981, the race has been held at The Meadowlands in East Rutherford, N.J.[

Year	Winner	Driver	Best time	Total purse
1967	Speedy Streak	Del Cameron	2:00	$122,650
1968	Nevele Pride	Stanley Dancer	1:59 2/5	116,190
1969	Lindy's Pride	Howard Beissinger	1:57 3/5	124,910
1970	Timothy T.	John Simpson, Jr.	1:58 2/5[1]	143,630
1971	Speedy Crown	Howard Beissinger	1:57 2/5	129,770
1972	Super Bowl	Stanley Dancer	1:56 2/5	119,090
1973	Flirth	Ralph Baldwin	1:57 1/5	144,710
1974	Christopher T	Billy Haughton	1:58 3/5	160,150
1975	Bonefish	Stanley Dancer	1:59[2]	232,192
1976	Steve Lobell	Billy Haughton	1:56 3/5	263,524
1977	Green Speed	Billy Haughton	1:55 3/5	284,131
1978	Speedy Somolli	Howard Beissinger	1:55[3]	241,280
1979	Legend Hanover	George Sholty	1:56 1/5	300,000
1980	Burgomeister	Billy Haughton	1:56 3/5	293,570
1981	Shiaway St. Pat	Ray Remmen	2:01 1/5[4]	838,000
1982	Speed Bowl	Tommy Haughton	1:56 4/5	875,750
1983	Duenna	Stanley Dancer	1:57 2/5	1,000,000
1984	Historic Free	Ben Webster	1:56 2/5	1,219,000
1985	Prakas	Bill O'Donnell	1:54 3/5	1,272,000
1986	Nuclear Kosmos	Ulf Thoresen	1:56	1,172,082
1987	Mack Lobell	John Campbell	1:53 3/5	1,046,300
1988	Armbro Goal	John Campbell	1:54 3/5	1,156,800
1989	Park Avenue Joe	Ron Wayples	1:55 3/5	1,131,000
1990	Embassy Lobell	Michel Lachance	1:56 1/5	1,346,000
1991	Giant Victory	Jack Moiseyev	1:54 4/5	1,238,000

1. By Formal Notice. 2. By Yankee Bambino. 3. By Speedy Somolli and Florida Pro. 4. By Super Juan.

Little Brown Jug

Three–year–old pacers. One Mile. Raced at Delaware County Fair Grounds, Delaware, Ohio.

Year	Winner	Driver	Best time	Total purse
1967	Best of All	Jim Hackett	1:59[1]	S84,778
1968	Rum Customer	Billy Haughton	1:59 3/5	104,226
1969	Laverne Hanover	Billy Haughton	2:00 2/5	109,731
1970	Most Happy Fella	Stanley Dancer	1:57 1/5	100,110
1971	Nansemond	Herve Filion	1:57 2/5	102,994
1972	Strike Out	Keith Waples	1:56 3/5	104,916

Year	Winner	Driver	Best time	Total purse
1973	Melvin's Woe	Joe O'Brien	1:57 3/5	120,000
1974	Ambro Omaha	Billy Haughton	1:57	132,630
1975	Seatrain	Ben Webster	1:57[2]	147,813
1976	Keystone Ore	Stanley Dancer	1:56 4/5[3]	153,799
1977	Governor Skipper	John Chapman	1:56 1/5	150,000
1978	Happy Escort	William Popfinger	1:55 2/5[4]	186,760
1979	Hot Hitter	Herve Filion	1:55 3/5	226,455
1980	Niatross	Clint Galbraith	1:54 4/5	207,361
1981	Fan Hanover	Glen Garnsey	1:56[5]	243,799
1982	Merger	John Campbell	1:56 3/5	328,900
1983	Ralph Hanover	Ron Waples	1:55 3/5	358,800
1984	Colt 46	Norman Boring	1:53 3/5	366,717
1985	Nihilator	Bill O'Donnell	1:52 1/5	350,730
1986	Barberry Spur	Bill O'Donnell	1:52 4/5	407,684
1987	Jaguar Spur	Richard Stillings	1:55 3/5	412,330
1988	B.J. Scoot	Michel Lachance	1:52 3/5	486,050
1989	Goalie Jeff	Michel Lachance	1:54 1/5	500,200
1990	Beach Towel	Ray Remmen	1:53 3/5	253,049
1991	Precious Bunny	Jack Moiseyev	1:54 1/5	575,150

1. By Nardin's Byrd. 2. By Albert's Star. 3. By Armbro Ranger. 4. By Falcon Almahurst. 5. By Seahawk Hanover.

HARNESS HORSE OF THE YEAR

Chosen in poll conducted by United States Trotting Association in conjunction with the U.S. Harness Writers Assn.

1959	Bye Bye Byrd, Pacer	1970	Fresh Yankee, Trotter	1981	Fan Hanover, Pacer
1960	Adios Butler, Pacer	1971	Albatross, Pacer	1982	Cam Fella, Pacer
1961	Adios Butler, Pacer	1972	Albatross, Pacer	1983	Cam Fella, Pacer
1962	Su Mac Lad, Trotter	1973	Sir Dalrae, Pacer	1984	Fancy Crown, Trotter
1963	Speedy Scot, Trotter	1974	Delmonica Hanover, Trotter	1985	Nihilator, Trotter
1964	Bret Hanover, Pacer	1975	Savoir, Trotter	1986	Forrest Skipper
1965	Bret Hanover, Pacer	1976	Keystone Ore, Pacer	1987	Mack Lobell
1966	Bret Hanover, Pacer	1977	Green Speed, Trotter	1988	Mack Lobell
1967	Nevele Pride, Trotter	1978	Abercrombie, Pacer	1989	Matt's Scooter
1968	Nevele Pride, Trotter	1979	Niatross, Pacer	1990	Beach Towell
1969	Nevele Pride, Trotter	1980	Niatross, Pacer		

WRESTLING

N.C.A.A. CHAMPIONSHIPS—1991

(March 14–16, 1991, University of Iowa, Iowa City, Iowa)

Division I
118 lb—Jeff Prescott, Penn State
126 lb—Jason Kelber, Nebraska
134 lb—Tom Brands, Iowa
142 lb—Scott Collins, West Virgina
150 lb—Matt Demaray, Wisconsin
158 lb—Pat Smith, Oklahoma State
167 lb—Mark Reiland, Iowa
177 lb—Marty Norgan, Minnesota
190 lb—Paul Keysaw, California State–Bakersffield
Heavyweight—John Llewellyn, Illinois

Team Champions
Division I—University of Iowa
Division II—University of Nebraska at Omaha
Division III—Augsburg College, Minneapolis, Minn.

WORLD CUP—1991

Freestyle
105.5 lb (48 kg)—Kim Jong–Shin, Korea
114.5 lb (52 kg)—Zeke Jones, United States
125.5 lb (57 kg)—Sergei Smal, Soviet Union
136.5 lb (62 kg)—John Smith, United States
149.5 lb (68 kg)—John Glura, United States
163.0 lb (74 kg)—Gamzat Khazamov, Soviet Union
180.5 lb (82 kg)—Royce Alger, United States
198.0 lb (90 kg)—Chris Campbell, United States
220.0 lb (100 kg)—Lari Khabelov, Soviet Union
Unlimited—Bruce Baumgartner, United States
NOTE: 1991 World Champions and 1991 Greco-Roman World Cup were scheduled after *Information Please Almanac* went to press.

U.S.A. NATIONAL CHAMPIONSHIPS—1991

(May 8–11, 1991 at Las Vegas, Nev.)

Freestyle
105.5 lb (48 kg)—Tim Vanni, Sunkist
114.5 lb (52 kg)—Zeke Jones,, Sunkist
125.5 lb (57 kg)—Brad Penrith, Sunkist
136.5 lb (62 kg)—John Smith, Sunkist
149.5 lb (68 kg)—Townsend Saunders, Sunkist
163.0 lb (74 kg)—Kenny Monday, Sunkist
180.5 lb (82 kg)—Kevin Jackson, Foxcatcher
198.0 lb (90 kg)—Chris Campbell, Sunkist
220.0 lb (100 kg)—Mark Campbell, N.Y. Athletic Club
Unlimited—Bruce Baumgartner, N.Y. Athletic Club

Greco-Roman
105.5 lb (48 kg)—Eric Wetzel, Armed Forces
114.5 lb (52 kg)—Shawn Sheldon, Jets
125.5 lb (57 kg)—Frank Famiano, Jets
136.5 lb (62 kg)—Buddy Lee, Armed Forces
149.5 lb (68 kg)—Andy Seras, Jets
163.0 lb (74 kg)—Gordy Morgan, Jets
180.5 lb (82 kg)—John Morgan, Jets
198.0 lb (90 kg)—Michael Foy, Sunkist
220.0 lb (100 kg)—Dennis Koslowski, Jets
Unlimited—Craig Pittman, Armed Forces

GOLF

It may be that golf originated in Holland—historians believe it did—but certainly Scotland fostered the game and is famous for it. In fact, in 1457 the Scottish Parliament, disturbed because football and golf had lured young Scots from the more soldierly exercise of archery, passed an ordinance that "futeball and golf be utterly cryit doun and nocht usit." James I and Charles I of the royal line of Stuarts were golf enthusiasts, whereby the game came to be known as "the royal and ancient game of golf."

The golf balls used in the early games were leather–covered and stuffed with feathers. Clubs of all kinds were fashioned by hand to suit individual players. The great step in spreading the game came with the change from the feather ball to the guttapercha ball about 1850. In 1860, formal competition began with the establishment of an annual tournament for the British Open championship. There are records of "golf clubs" in the United States as far back as colo-

nial days but no proof of actual play before John Reid and some friends laid out six holes on the Reid lawn in Yonkers, N.Y., in 1888 and played there with golf balls and clubs brought over from Scotland by Robert Lockhart. This group then formed the St. Andrews Golf Club of Yonkers, and golf was established in this country.

However, it remained a rather sedate and almost aristocratic pastime until a 20-year-old ex-caddy, Francis Ouimet of Boston, defeated two great British professionals, Harry Vardon and Ted Ray, in the United States Open championship at Brookline, Mass., in 1913. This feat put the game and Francis Ouimet on the front pages of the newspapers and stirred a wave of enthusiasm for the sport. The greatest feat so far in golf history is that of Robert Tyre Jones, Jr., of Atlanta, who won the British Open, the British Amateur, the U.S. Open, and the U.S. Amateur titles in one year, 1930.

THE MASTERS TOURNAMENT WINNERS

Augusta National Golf Club, Augusta, Ga.

Year	Winner	Score	Year	Winner	Score	Year	Winner	Score
1934	Horton Smith	284	1955	Cary Middlecoff	279	1974	Gary Player	278
1935	Gene Sarazen[1]	282	1956	Jack Burke	289	1975	Jack Nicklaus	276
1936	Horton Smith	285	1957	Doug Ford	283	1976	Ray Floyd	271
1937	Byron Nelson	283	1958	Arnold Palmer	284	1977	Tom Watson	276
1938	Henry Picard	285	1959	Art Wall, Jr.	284	1978	Gary Player	277
1939	Ralph Guldahl	279	1960	Arnold Palmer	282	1979	Fuzzy Zoeller[1]	280
1940	Jimmy Demaret	280	1961	Gary Player	280	1980	Severiano Ballesteros	275
1941	Craig Wood	280	1962	Arnold Palmer[1]	280	1981	Tom Watson	280
1942	Byron Nelson[1]	280	1963	Jack Nicklaus	286	1982	Craig Stadler[1]	284
1943–45	No Tournaments		1964	Arnold Palmer	276	1983	Severiano Ballesteros	280
1946	Herman Keiser	282	1965	Jack Nicklaus	271	1984	Ben Crenshaw	277
1947	Jimmy Demaret	281	1966	Jack Nicklaus[1]	288	1985	Bernhard Langer	282
1948	Claude Harmon	279	1967	Gay Brewer, Jr.	280	1986	Jack Nicklaus	279
1949	Sam Snead	282	1968	Bob Goalby	277	1987	Larry Mize[1]	285
1950	Jimmy Demaret	283	1969	George Archer	281	1988	Sandy Lyle	281
1951	Ben Hogan	280	1970	Billy Casper[1]	279	1989	Nick Faldo[1]	283
1952	Sam Snead	286	1971	Charles Coody	279	1990	Nick Faldo	278
1953	Ben Hogan	274	1972	Jack Nicklaus	286	1991	Ian Woosnam	277
1954	Sam Snead[1]	289	1973	Tommy Aaron	283			

1. Winner in playoff.

U.S. OPEN CHAMPIONS

Year	Winner	Score	Where played	Year	Winner	Score	Where played
1895	Horace Rawlins	173	Newport	1919	Walter Hagen[2]	301	Brae Burn
1896	James Foulis	152	Shinnecock Hills	1920	Edward Ray	295	Inverness
1897	Joe Lloyd	162	Chicago	1921	Jim Barnes	289	Columbia
1898[3]	Fred Herd	328	Myopia	1922	Gene Sarazen	288	Skokie
1899	Willie Smith	315	Baltimore	1923	R. T. Jones, Jr.[1 2]	296	Inwood
1900	Harry Vardon	313	Chicago	1924	Cyril Walker	297	Oakland Hills
1901	Willie Anderson[1]	331	Myopia	1925	Willie Macfarlane[1]	291	Worcester
1902	Laurie Auchterlonie	307	Garden City	1926	R. T. Jones, Jr.[2]	293	Scioto
1903	Willie Anderson[1]	307	Baltusrol	1927	Tommy Armour[1]	301	Oakmont
1904	Willie Anderson	303	Glen View	1928	Johnny Farrell[1]	294	Olympia Fields
1905	Willie Anderson	314	Myopia	1929	R. T. Jones, Jr.[1 2]	294	Winged Foot
1906	Alex Smith	295	Onwentsia	1930	R. T. Jones, Jr.[2]	287	Interlachen
1907	Alex Ross	302	Philadelphia	1931	Billy Burke[1]	292	Inverness
1908	Fred McLeod[1]	322	Myopia	1932	Gene Sarazen	286	Fresh Meadow
1909	George Sargent	290	Englewood	1933	John Goodman[2]	287	North Shore
1910	Alex Smith[1]	298	Philadelphia	1934	Olin Dutra	293	Merion
1911	John McDermott[1]	307	Chicago	1935	Sam Parks, Jr.	299	Oakmont
1912	John McDermott	294	Buffalo	1936	Tony Manero	282	Baltusrol
1913	Francis Ouimet[1 2]	304	Brookline	1937	Ralph Guldahl	281	Oakland Hills
1914	Walter Hagen	290	Midlothian	1938	Ralph Guldahl	284	Cherry Hills
1915	Jerome D. Travers[2]	297	Baltusrol	1939	Byron Nelson[1]	284	Philadelphia
1916	Charles Evans, Jr.[2]	286	Minikahda	1940	Lawson Little[1]	287	Canterbury
1917–18	No tournaments[4]			1941	Craig Wood	284	Colonial

Year	Winner	Score	Where played	Year	Winner	Score	Where played
1942–45	No tournaments[5]			1969	Orville Moody	281	Champions G. C.
1946	Lloyd Mangrum[1]	284	Canterbury	1970	Tony Jacklin	281	Hazeltine
1947	Lew Worsham[1]	282	St. Louis	1971	Lee Trevino[1]	280	Merion
1948	Ben Hogan	276	Riviera	1972	Jack Nicklaus	290	Pebble Beach
1949	Cary Middlecoff	286	Medinah	1973	Johnny Miller	279	Oakmont
1950	Ben Hogan[1]	287	Merion	1974	Hale Irwin	287	Winged Foot
1951	Ben Hogan	287	Oakland Hills	1975	Lou Graham[1]	287	Medinah
1952	Julius Boros	281	Northwood	1976	Jerry Pate	277	Atlanta A.C.
1953	Ben Hogan	283	Oakmont	1977	Hubert Green	278	Southern Hills
1954	Ed Furgol	284	Baltusrol	1978	Andy North	285	Cherry Hills
1955	Jack Fleck[1]	287	Olympic	1979	Hale Irwin	284	Inverness
1956	Cary Middlecoff	281	Oak Hill	1980	Jack Nicklaus	272	Baltusrol
1957	Dick Mayer[1]	298	Inverness	1981	David Graham	273	Merion
1958	Tommy Bolt	283	Southern Hills	1982	Tom Watson	282	Pebble Beach
1959	Bill Casper, Jr.	282	Winged Foot	1983	Larry Nelson	280	Oakmont
1960	Arnold Palmer	280	Cherry Hills	1984	Fuzzy Zoeller[1]	276	Winged Foot
1961	Gene Littler	281	Oakland Hills	1985	Andy North	279	Oakland Hills
1962	Jack Nicklaus[1]	283	Oakmont	1986	Ray Floyd	279	Shinnecock Hills
1963	Julius Boros[1]	293	Country Club	1987	Scott Simpson	277	Olympic Golf Club
1964	Ken Venturi	278	Congressional	1988	Curtis Strange[1]	278	The Country Club
1965	Gary Player[1]	282	Bellerive	1989	Curtis Strange	278	Oak Hill Country Club
1966	Bill Casper[1]	278	Olympic	1990	Hale Irwin[1]	280	Medinah C.C.
1967	Jack Nicklaus	275	Baltusrol	1991	Payne Stewart[1]	282	Hazeltine
1968	Lee Trevino	275	Oak Hill				

1. Winner in playoff. 2. Amateur. 3. In 1898, competition was extended to 72 holes. 4. In 1917, Jock Hutchison, with a 292, won an Open Patriotic Tournament for the benefit of the American Red Cross at Whitemarsh Valley Country Club. 5. In 1942, Ben Hogan, with a 271 won a Hale American National Open Tournament for the benefit of the Navy Relief Society and USO at Ridgemoor Country Club.

U.S. AMATEUR CHAMPIONS

1895	Charles B. Macdonald	1922	Jess W. Sweetser	1950	Sam Urzetta	1972	Vinny Giles 3d
1896–97	H. J. Whigham	1923	Max R. Marston	1951	Billy Maxwell	1973[3]	Craig Stadler
1898	Findlay S. Douglas	1924–25	R. T. Jones, Jr.	1952	Jack Westland	1974	Jerry Pate
1899	H. M. Harriman	1926	George Von Elm	1953	Gene Littler	1975	Fred Ridley
1900–01	Walter J. Travis	1927–28	R. T. Jones, Jr.	1954	Arnold Palmer	1976	Bill Sander
1902	Louis N. James	1929	H. R. Johnston	1955–56	Harvie Ward	1977	John Fought
1903	Walter J. Travis	1930	R. T. Jones, Jr.	1957	Hillman Robbins	1978	John Cook
1904–05	H. Chandler Egan	1931	Francis Ouimet	1958	Charles Coe	1979	Mark O'Meara
1906	Eben M. Byers	1932	Ross Somerville	1959	Jack Nicklaus	1980	Hal Sutton
1907–08	Jerome D. Travers	1933	G. T. Dunlap, Jr.	1960	Deane Beman	1981	Nathaniel Crosby
1909	Robert A. Gardner	1934–35	Lawson Little	1961	Jack Nicklaus	1982	Jay Sigel
1910	W. C. Fownes, Jr.	1936	John W. Fischer	1962	Labron Harris, Jr.	1983	Jay Sigel
1911	Harold H. Hilton	1937	John Goodman	1963	Deane Beman	1984	Scott Verplank
1912–13	Jerome D. Travers	1938	Willie Turnesa	1964	Bill Campbell	1985	Sam Randolph
1914	Francis Ouimet	1939	Marvin H. Ward	1965[2]	Robert Murphy, Jr.	1986	Buddy Alexander
1915	Robert A. Gardner	1940	R. D. Chapman	1966	Gary Cowan[1]	1987	Bill Mayfair
1916	Charles Evans, Jr.	1941	Marvin H. Ward	1967	Bob Dickson	1988	Eric Meeks
1919	S. D. Herron	1946	Ted Bishop	1968	Bruce Fleisher	1989	Chris Patton
1920	Charles Evans, Jr.	1947	Robert Riegel	1969	Steven Melnyk	1990	Phil Mickelson
1921	Jesse P. Guilford	1948	Willie Turnesa	1970	Lanny Wadkins	1991	Mitch Voges
		1949	Charles Coe	1971	Gary Cowan		

1. Winner in playoff. 2. Tourney switched to medal play through 1972. 3. Return to match play.

U.S. P.G.A. CHAMPIONS

1916	Jim Barnes	1939	Henry Picard	1955	Doug Ford	1970	Dave Stockton
1919	Jim Barnes	1940	Byron Nelson	1956	Jack Burke, Jr.	1971	Jack Nicklaus
1920	Jock Hutchison	1941	Victor Ghezzi	1957	Lionel Hebert	1972	Gary Player
1921	Walter Hagen	1942	Sam Snead	1958[2]	Dow Finsterwald	1973	Jack Nicklaus
1922–23	Gene Sarazen	1944	Bob Hamilton	1959	Bob Rosburg	1974	Lee Trevino
1924–27	Walter Hagen	1945	Byron Nelson	1960	Jay Hebert	1975	Jack Nicklaus
1928–29	Leo Diegel	1946	Ben Hogan	1961	Jerry Barber[1]	1976	Dave Stockton
1930	Tommy Armour	1947	Jim Ferrier	1962	Gary Player	1977	Lanny Wadkins[1]
1931	Tom Creavy	1948	Ben Hogan	1963	Jack Nicklaus	1978	John Mahaffey
1932	Olin Dutra	1949	Sam Snead	1964	Bobby Nichols	1979	David Graham[1]
1933	Gene Sarazen	1950	Chandler Harper	1965	Dave Marr	1980	Jack Nicklaus
1934	Paul Runyan	1951	Sam Snead	1966	Al Geiberger	1981	Larry Nelson
1935	Johnny Revolta	1952	Jim Turnesa	1967	Don January[1]	1982	Ray Floyd
1936–37	Denny Shute	1953	Walter Burkemo	1968	Julius Boros	1983	Hal Sutton
1938	Paul Runyan	1954	Chick Harbert	1969	Ray Floyd	1984	Lee Trevino

1. Winner in playoff. 2. Switched to medal play.

1985	Hubert Green	1987	Larry Nelson	1989	Payne Stewart	1991	John Daly
1986	Bob Tway	1988	Jeff Sluman	1990	Mac Grady		

U.S. WOMEN'S AMATEUR CHAMPIONS

1916	Alexa Stirling	1938	Patty Berg	1960	JoAnne Gunderson	1974	Cynthia Hill
1919–20	Alexa Stirling	1939–40	Betty Jameson			1975	Beth Daniel
1921	Marion Hollins	1941	Mrs. Frank Newell	1961	Anne Quast Decker	1976	Donna Horton
1922	Glenna Collett	1946	Mildred Zaharias			1977	Beth Daniel
1923	Edith Cummings	1947	Louise Suggs	1962	JoAnne Gunderson	1978	Cathy Sherk
1924	Dorothy Campbell .Hurd	1948	Grace Lenczyk			1979	Carolyn Hill
		1949	Mrs. D. G. Porter	1963	Anne Quast Welts	1980	Juli Inkster
1925	Glenna Collett	1950	Beverly Hanson	1964	Barbara McIntire	1981	Juli Inkster
1926	Helen Stetson	1951	Dorothy Kirby	1965	Jean Ashley	1982	Juli Inkster
1927	Mrs. M. B. Horn	1952	Jacqueline Pung	1966	JoAnne Gunderson	1983	Joanne Pacillo
1928–30	Glenna Collett	1953	Mary Lena Faulk			1984	Deb Richard
1931	Helen Hicks	1954	Barbara Romack	1967	Lou Dill	1985	Michiko Hattori
1932–34	Virginia Van Wie	1955	Patricia Lesser	1968	JoAnne G. Carner	1986	Kay Cockerill
1935	Glenna Collett Vare	1956	Marlene Stewart	1969	Catherine LaCoste	1987	Kay Cockerill
		1957	JoAnne Gunderson	1970	Martha Wilkinson	1988	Pearl Sinn
1936	Pamela Barton			1971	Laura Baugh	1989	Vicki Goetze
1937	Mrs. J. A. Page, Jr.	1958	Anne Quast	1972	Mary Ann Budke	1990	Pat Hurst
		1959	Barbara McIntire	1973	Carol Semple	1991	Amy Fruhwirth

U.S. WOMEN'S OPEN CHAMPIONS

Year	Winner	Score	Year	Winner	Score	Year	Winner	Score
1946	Patty Berg (match play)	—	1962	Murle Lindstrom	301	1978	Hollis Stacy	289
1947	Betty Jameson	295	1963	Mary Mills	289	1979	Jerilyn Britz	284
1948	Mildred D. Zaharias	300	1964	Mickey Wright[1]	290	1980	Amy Alcott	280
1949	Louise Suggs	291	1965	Carol Mann	290	1981	Pat Bradley	279
1950	Mildred D. Zaharias	291	1966	Sandra Spuzich	297	1982	Janet Alex	283
1951	Betsy Rawls	293	1967	Catherine LaCoste[2]	294	1983	Jan Stephenson	290
1952	Louise Suggs	284	1968	Susie Berning	289	1984	Hollis Stacy	290
1953	Betsy Rawls[1]	302	1969	Donna Caponi	294	1985	Kathy Baker	280
1954	Mildred D. Zaharias	291	1970	Donna Caponi	287	1986	Jane Geddes[1]	287
1955	Fay Crocker	299	1971	JoAnne Carner	288	1987	Laura Davies[1]	285
1956	Katherine Cornelius[1]	302	1972	Susie Berning	299	1988	Liselotte Neumann	277
1957	Betsy Rawls	299	1973	Susie Berning	290	1989	Betsy King	278
1958	Mickey Wright	290	1974	Sandra Haynie	295	1990	Betsy King	284
1959	Mickey Wright	287	1975	Sandra Palmer	295	1991	Meg Mallon	283
1960	Betsy Rawls	291	1976	JoAnne Carner[1]	292			
1961	Mickey Wright	293	1977	Hollis Stacy	292			

1. Winner in playoff. 2. Amateur.

BRITISH OPEN CHAMPIONS

(First tournament, held in 1860, was won by Willie Park, Sr.)

Year	Winner	Score	Year	Winner	Score	Year	Winner	Score
1920	George Duncan	303	1948	Henry Cotton	283	1970	Jack Nicklaus[1]	283
1921	Jock Hutchison[1]	296	1949	Bobby Locke[1]	283	1971	Lee Trevino	278
1922	Walter Hagen	300	1950	Bobby Locke	279	1972	Lee Trevino	278
1923	A. G. Havers	295	1951	Max Faulkner	285	1973	Tom Weiskopf	276
1924	Walter Hagen	301	1952	Bobby Locke	287	1974	Gary Player	282
1925	Jim Barnes	300	1953	Ben Hogan	282	1975	Tom Watson[1]	279
1926	R. T. Jones, Jr.	291	1954	Peter Thomson	283	1976	Johnny Miller	279
1927	R. T. Jones, Jr.	285	1955	Peter Thomson	281	1977	Tom Watson	268
1928	Walter Hagen	292	1956	Peter Thomson	286	1978	Jack Nicklaus	281
1929	Walter Hagen	292	1957	Bobby Locke	279	1979	Severiano Ballesteros	283
1930	R. T. Jones, Jr.	291	1958	Peter Thomson[1]	278	1980	Tom Watson	271
1931	Tommy Armour	296	1959	Gary Player	284	1981	Bill Rogers	276
1932	Gene Sarazen	283	1960	Kel Nagle	278	1982	Tom Watson	284
1933	Denny Shute1	292	1961	Arnold Palmer	284	1983	Tom Watson	275
1934	Henry Cotton	283	1962	Arnold Palmer	276	1984	Severiano Ballesteros	276
1935	A. Perry	283	1963	Bob Charles[1]	277	1985	Sandy Lyle	282
1936	A. H. Padgham	287	1964	Tony Lema	279	1986	Greg Norman	280
1937	Henry Cotton	290	1965	Peter Thomson	285	1987	Nick Faldo	279
1938	R. A. Whitcombe	295	1966	Jack Nicklaus	282	1988	Seve Ballesteros	273
1939	R. Burton	290	1967	Roberto de Vicenzo	278	1989	Mark Calcavecchia	275
1940	Sam Snead	290	1968	Gary Player	289	1990	Nick Faldo	270
1947	Fred Daly	294	1969	Tony Jacklin	280	1991	Ian Baker-Finch	272

1. Winner in playoff.

OTHER 1991 PGA TOUR WINNERS

(Through Sept. 2, 1991)

Tournament of Champions—Tom Kite (272)	$144,000
Telecom Tucson Open—Phil Mickelson (272)	
amateur, two tied for second earned	144,000
Hawaiian Open—Lanny Wadkins (270)	198,000
Phoenix Open—Nolan Henke (268)	180,000
Pebble Beach National Pro-Am—Paul Azinger (274)	198,000
Bob Hope Classic—Corey Pavin (331)	198,000
Shearson Lehman Hutton Open—J.D. Blake (268)	180,000
Doral Open—Rocco Mediate (278)	252,000
Honda Classic—Steve Date (279)	180,000
Nestle Invitational—Andrew Magee (203)	180,000
USF&G Classic—Ian Woosnam (275)	180,000
PGA Players Championship—Steve Elkington (276)	288,000
Heritage Classic—Davis Love III (271)	180,000
Greater Greensboro Open—Mark Brocks (275)	225,000
Byron Nelson Classic—Nick Price (270)	198,000
Atlanta Classic—Corey Pavin (272)	180,000
Memorial Tournament—Kenny Perry (273)	216,000
Colonial—Tom Purtzer (267)	216,000
Kemper Open—Billy Andrade (263)	180,000
Buick Classic—Billy Andrade (273)	180,000
St. Jude Classic—Fred Couples (269)	180,000
Western Open—Russ Cochran (275)	180,000
Greater Hartford Open—Billy Ray Brown (271)	180,000
Buick Open—Brad Faxon (271)	180,000
World Series—Tom Purtzer (279)	216,000
International—Jose Maria Olazabal (10 points)	198,000
Milwaukee Open—Mark Brocks (270)	180,000

OTHER 1991 LPGA TOUR WINNERS

(Through Sept. 3, 1991)

Jamaica Open—Jane Geddes (207)	$75,000
LPGA Classic—Meg Mallon (276)	60,000
Phar-Mor Classic—Beth Daniel (209)	75,000
Inamori Classic—Laura Davies (277)	60,000
Desert Invitational—Penny Hammel (211)	60,000
Standard Register—Meg Mallon (285)	44,000
Nabisco Dinah Shore—Amy Alcott (273)	90,000
Tucson Open—Chris Johnson (273)	52,500
Sara Lee Classic—Nancy Lopez (206)	63,750
Konica Cup—Beth Daniel (278)	66,600
Crestar Classic—Hollis Stacy (282)	60,000
Centel Classic—Pat Bradley (278)	65,000
Corning Classic—Betsy King (273)	60,000
Rochester International—Rosie Jones (276)	60,000
Atlantic City Classic—Jane Geddes (208)	45,000
Lady Keystone Open—Colleen Walker (207)	60,000
LPGA McDonald's Championship—Beth Daniel (273)	112,500
LPGA Championship—Meg Mallon (274)	150,000
Jamie Farr Classic—Alice Miller (205)	52,500
Big Apple Classic—Betsy King (279)	75,000
Bay State Classic—Juli Inkster (275)	60,000
LPGA Phar-Mor—Deb Richard (207)	75,000
Stratton Mountain Classic—Melissa McNamara (278)	67,500
LPGA Shootout—Martha Nause (275)	63,750
Northgate—Cindy Rarick (211)	60,000
Rail Classic—Pat Bradley (197)[1]	160,000

1. LPGA record for a 54-hole event.

JAMES E. SULLIVAN MEMORIAL AWARD WINNERS

(Amateur Athlete of Year Chosen in Amateur Athletic Union Poll)

1930	Robert Tyre Jones, Jr.	Golf	1961	Wilma Rudolph Ward	Track and field
1931	Bernard E. Berlinger	Track and field	1962	Jim Beatty	Track and field
1932	James A. Bausch	Track and field	1963	John Pennel	Track and field
1933	Glenn Cunningham	Track and field	1964	Don Schollander	Swimming
1934	William R. Bonthron	Track and field	1965	Bill Bradley	Basketball
1935	W. Lawson Little, Jr.	Golf	1966	Jim Ryun	Track and field
1936	Glenn Morris	Track and field	1967	Randy Matson	Track and field
1937	J. Donald Budge	Tennis	1968	Debbie Meyer	Swimming
1938	Donald R. Lash	Track and field	1969	Bill Toomey	Decathlon
1939	Joseph W. Burk	Rowing	1970	John Kinsella	Swimming
1940	J. Gregory Rice	Track and field	1971	Mark Spitz	Swimming
1941	Leslie MacMitchell	Track and field	1972	Frank Shorter	Marathon
1942	Cornelius Warmerdam	Track and field	1973	Bill Walton	Basketball
1943	Gilbert L. Dodds	Track and field	1974	Rick Wohlhuter	Track
1944	Ann Curtis	Swimming	1975	Tim Shaw	Swimming
1945	Felix (Doc) Blanchard	Football	1976	Bruce Jenner	Track and field
1946	Y. Arnold Tucker	Football	1977	John Naber	Swimming
1947	John B. Kelly, Jr.	Rowing	1978	Tracy Caulkins	Swimming
1948	Robert B. Mathias	Track and field	1979	Kurt Thomas	Gymnastics
1949	Richard T. Button	Figure skating	1980	Eric Heiden	Speed skating
1950	Fred Wilt	Track and field	1981	Carl Lewis	Track and field
1951	Robert E. Richards	Track and field	1982	Mary Decker Tabb	Track and field
1952	Horace Ashenfelter	Track and field	1983	Edwin Moses	Track and field
1953	Major Sammy Lee	Diving	1984	Greg Louganis	Diving
1954	Malvin Whitfield	Track and field	1985	Joan Benoit—Samuelson	Marathon
1955	Harrison Dillard	Track and field	1986	Jackie Joyner—Kersee	Heptathlon
1956	Patricia McCormick	Diving	1987	Jim Abbott	Baseball
1957	Bobby Jo Morrow	Track and Field	1988	Florence Griffith—Joyner	Track and field
1958	Glenn Davis	Track and field	1989	Janet Evans	Swimming
1959	Parry O'Brien	Track and field	1990	John Smith	Wrestling
1960	Rafer Johnson	Track and field			

SOCCER

WORLD CUP

1930	Uruguay	1950	Uruguay	1970	Brazil	1990	West Germany
1934	Italy	1954	West Germany	1974	West Germany	1994	To be held in United
1938	Italy	1958	Brazil	1978	Argentina		States
1942	No competition	1962	Brazil	1982	Italy		
1946	No competition	1966	England	1986	Argentina		

WORLD CUP—1990

SEMIFINALS

1. (at Naples, Italy, July 3, 1990)

Argentina 1, Italy 1 (Argentina wins, on 4–3 penalty kick shootout)

2. (at Turin, Italy, July 4, 1990)

West Germany 1, England 1 (West Germany wins, on 4–3 penalty kick shootout)

THIRD PLACE

(at Bari, Italy, July 7, 1990)

Italy 2, England 1

FINALS

(at Rome, Italy, July 8, 1990)

West Germany 1, Argentina 0

West Germany (Group D)	Argentina (Group B)
	Cameroon 1, Argentina 0
W. Germany 4, Yugoslavia 1	Argentina 2, Soviet Union 0
W. Germany 5, United Arab Emirates 1	Argentina 1, Romania 1 (tie)
	Argentina 1, Brazil 0
W. Germany 1, Colombia 1 (tie)	Argentina 0, Yugoslavia 0
	(Argentina wins, 3–2, on a
West Germany 2, Netherlands 1	penalty shootout)
West Germany 1, Czechoslovakia 0	

England (Group F)	Italy (Group A)
England 1, Ireland 1 (tie)	Italy 1, Austria 0
England 0, Netherlands 0 (tie)	Italy 1, United States 0
England 1, Egypt 0	Italy 2, Czechoslovakia 0
England 1, Belgium 0 (extra time)	Italy 2, Uruguay 0
England 3, Cameroon 2 (OT)	Italy 1, Ireland 0

WEST GERMANY WINS WORLD CUP ON A PENALTY KICK

Andreas Brehme's penalty kick in the 84th minute gave West Germany a 1–0 victory over Argentina in the World Cup championship game played in Rome, Italy. The championship was West Germany's third in the 60–year history of the event, tying that country for first in the all–time World Cup standings with Brazil.

West Germany dominated the final against an Argentine team crippled by injuries and the eventual expulsion of two players, which forced the defending champions to play with nine men at the end.

The shutout was the first in World Cup championship game history. Argentina had defeated West Germany, 3–2, in the 1986 World Cup championship game.

A crowd of 73,603 witnessed the championship, televised in America by Turner Network Television, a cable company.

The winning goal came with six minutes remaining in regulation. Midfielder Lothar Mattheaus passed the ball to forward Rudi Voeller. Voeller carried the ball into the box with Argentina's Roberto Sensini shadowing him. When Sensini reached in with his right leg, he was called for tripping Voeller, and West Germany was awarded the penalty kick.

Brehme was the choice to take it. He pushed the ball up, just inside the left post and just beyond the reach of Argentina's goalkeeper, Sergio Goycoechea.

The United States made a bit of World Cup history by qualifying for the first time since 1950. Though the U.S. went winless in the tournament's first round—losing to Czechoslovakia 5–1, Italy 1–0, and Austria 2–1—the experience gave the American team much–needed help in getting ready for its role as host of the 1994 World Cup.

U.S. GAINS 1994 WORLD CUP

It was both fitting and a bit ironic that the Federation Internationale de Football Association picked July 4, 1989, to award the United States the 1994 World Cup competition.

The World Cup, arguably the No. 1 sports event in the world, thus comes to a country where soccer has struggled for a national foothold.

The 1990 World Cup was held in Italy, and 113 countries from around the world competed, including the United States.

The right to stage the World Cup was a prize the United States Soccer Federation had been seeking for many years. In 1983, the U.S. Federation bid for the 1986 tournament, but it was rejected by FIFA, which did not feel the necessary fan support existed in the United States.

What likely put the United States over the top was the total attendance of more than 1.4 million for soccer at the 1984 Summer Olympics in Los Angeles.

A new organization, World Cup USA 1994 was formed, with Paul Stiehl as director and financial backing from sponsors including Coca-Cola, Gillette, Anheuser-Busch, and American Express.

MAJOR SOCCER LEAGUE TEAM STANDINGS—1991[1]

EASTERN DIVISION

	W	L	Pct	GB
Cleveland	29	23	.558	—
Kansas City	26	26	.500	3.0
Baltimore	21	31	.404	8.0
Wichita	21	31	.404	8.9

WESTERN DIVISION

	W	L	Pct	GB
San Diego	34	18	.654	—
St. Louis	32	20	.615	2.0
Tacoma	25	27	.481	9.0
Dallas	20	32	.385	14.0

1991 PLAYOFF RESULTS
SAN DIEGO VS. CLEVELAND, MSL CHAMPIONSHIP SERIES

Date		Result	
Game 1—May 10, 1991	Cleveland	4	at San Diego 8
Game 2—May 12, 1991	Cleveland	4	at San Diego 3
Game 3—May 17, 1991	San Diego	6	at Cleveland 5
Game 4—May 19, 1991	San Diego	5	at Cleveland 4
Game 5—May 21, 1991	San Diego	6	at Cleveland 1
Game 6—May 23, 1991	Cleveland	6	at San Diego 8

San Diego wins series 4–2 and seventh Major Soccer League Championship.

1. League officially changed its name from Major Indoor Soccer League in 1991.

NORTH AMERICAN SOCCER LEAGUE CHAMPIONS

1968—Atlanta Chiefs	1973—Philadelphia Atoms	1978—New York Cosmos	1982—New York Cosmos
1969—Kansas City Stars	1974—Los Angeles Aztecs	1979—Vancouver Whitecaps	1983—Tulsa Roughnecks
1970—Rochester Lancers	1975—Tampa Bay Rowdies	1980—New York Cosmos	1984—Chicago Sting
1971—Dallas Tornado	1976—Toronto Metro–Croatia	1981—Chicago Sting	
1972—New York Cosmos	1977—New York Cosmos		

YACHTING

AMERICA'S CUP RECORD

First race in 1851 around Isle of Wight, Cowes, England. First defense and all others through 1920 held 30 miles off New York Bay. Races since 1930 held 30 miles off Newport, R.I. Conducted as one race only in 1851 and 1870; best four-of-seven basis, 1871; best two-of-three, 1876–1887; best three-of-five, 1893–1901; best four-of-seven, since 1930. Figures in parentheses indicate number of races won.

Year	Winner and owner	Loser and owner
1851	AMERICA (1), John C. Stevens, U.S.	AURORA, T. Le Marchant, England[1]
1870	MAGIC (1), Franklin Osgood, U.S.	CAMBRIA, James Ashbury, England[2]
1871	COLUMBIA (2), Franklin Osgood, U.S[3]	LIVONIA (1), James Ashbury, England
	SAPPHO (2), William P. Douglas, U.S.	
1876	MADELEINE (2), John S. Dickerson, U.S.	COUNTESS OF DUFFERIN, Chas. Gifford, Canada
1881	MISCHIEF (2), J. R. Busk, U.S.	ATALANTA, Alexander Cuthbert, Canada
1885	PURITAN (2), J. M. Forbes–Gen. Charles Paine, U.S.	GENESTA, Sir Richard Sutton, England
1886	MAYFLOWER (2), Gen. Charles Paine, U.S.	GALATEA, Lt. William Henn, England
1887	VOLUNTEER (2), Gen. Charles Paine, U.S.	THISTLE, James Bell et al., Scotland
1893	VIGILANT (3), C. Oliver Iselin et al., U.S.	VALKYRIE II, Lord Dunraven, England
1895	DEFENDER (3), C. O. Iselin–W. K. Vanderbilt–E. D. Morgan, U.S	VALKYRIE III, Lord Dunraven–Lord Lonsdale–Lord Wolverton, England
1899	COLUMBIA (3), J. P. Morgan–C. O. Iselin, U.S.	SHAMROCK I, Sir Thomas Lipton, Ireland
1901	COLUMBIA (3), Edwin D. Morgan, U.S.	SHAMROCK II, Sir Thomas Lipton, Ireland
1903	RELIANCE (3), Cornelius Vanderbilt et al., U.S.	SHAMROCK III, Sir Thomas Lipton, Ireland
1920	RESOLUTE (3), Henry Walters et al., U.S.	SHAMROCK IV (2), Sir Thomas Lipton, Ireland
1930	ENTERPRISE (4), Harold S. Vanderbilt et al., U.S.	SHAMROCK V, Sir Thomas Lipton, Ireland
1934	RAINBOW (4), Harold S. Vanderbilt, U.S.	ENDEAVOUR (2), T. O. M. Sopwith, England
1937	RANGER (4), Harold S. Vanderbilt, U.S.	ENDEAVOUR II, T. O. M. Sopwith, England
1958	COLUMBIA (4), Henry Sears et al., U.S.	SCEPTRE, Hugh Goodson et al., England
1962	WEATHERLY (4), Henry D. Mercer et al., U.S.	GRETEL (1), Sir Frank Packer et al., Australia
1964	CONSTELLATION (4), New York Y.C. Syndicate, U.S.	SOVEREIGN (0), J. Anthony Bowden, England
1967	INTREPID (4), New York Y.C. Syndicate, U.S.	DAME PATTIE (0), Sydney (Aust.) Syndicate
1970	INTREPID (4), New York Y.C. Syndicate, U.S.	GRETEL II (1), Sydney (Aust.) Syndicate
1974	COURAGEOUS (4), New York, N.Y. Syndicate, U.S.	SOUTHERN CROSS (0), Sydney (Aust.) Syndicate
1977	COURAGEOUS (4), New York, N.Y. Syndicate, U.S.	AUSTRALIA (0), Sun City (Aust.) Syndicate
1980	FREEDOM (4), New York, N.Y. Syndicate, U.S.	AUSTRALIA (1), Alan Bond et al, Australia
1983	AUSTRALIA II (4) Alan Bond et al., Australia,	LIBERTY (3) New York, N.Y. Syndicate, U.S.
1987	STARS & STRIPES (4), Dennis Conner et al., United States	KOOKABURRA III (0), Iain Murray et al., Australia
1988[4]	NEW ZEALAND Michael Fay, et al., New Zealand	STARS & STRIPES, Dennis Conner, et al., United States

1. Fourteen British yachts started against America; Aurora finished second. 2. Cambria sailed against 23 U.S. yachts and finished tenth. 3. Columbia was disabled in the third race, after winning the first two; Sappho substituted and won the fourth and fifth. 4. Shortly after Dennis Conner and his 60-foot, twin-hulled catamaran easily defeated the challenge of the New Zealand, a 133-foot, single-hulled yacht in the waters off San Diego in early September 1988, a New York State Supreme Court judge ruled that the Americans did not live up to the America's Cup Deed of Gift, which means competing boats must be similar. The judge ruled that the Americans had an unfair advantage over the monohulled ship, and awarded the Cup to New Zealand. However, an Appeal awarded the Cup to the United States. The next challenge was scheduled to take place in 1992.

WEIGHTLIFTING

U.S. WEIGHTLIFTING FEDERATION MEN'S NATIONAL CHAMPIONSHIPS
(Blaine, Minn., April 26–28, 1991)

	Snatch	C&J[1]	Total[2]
52 kg—Chad Ikel	85.0	100.0	185.0
56 kg—Robert Gilsdorf	87.5	115.0	202.5
60 kg—Bryan Jacob	120.0[3]	140.0	260.0
67.5 kg—Timothy McRae	122.5	152.5	275.0
75 kg—Jeffrey Macy	130.0	160.0	290.0
82.5 kg—Roberto Urrutia	140.0	185.0	325.0
90 kg—Bret Brian	150.0	192.5	342.5
100 kg—David Langon	155.0	190.0	345.0
110 kg—Richard Schutz	160.0	200.0	360.0
Over 110 kg—Mario Martinez	167.5	200.0	367.5

WOMEN'S NATIONAL CHAMPIONSHIPS
(Blaine, Minn., April 26–28, 1991)

	Snatch	C&J[3]	Total[2]
44 kg—Andrea Tibeau	55.0	75.0[3]	130.0
48 kg—Victoria L. Futch	62.5	75.0[3]	137.5
52 kg—Robin Byrd	72.5	92.5	165.0
56 kg—Melanie J. Getz	75.0	85.0	160.0
60 kg—Giselle Shepatin	77.5	92.5	170.0
67.5 kg—Diana M. Fuhrman	90.0	107.5	197.5
75 kg—Decia J. Agnew	80.0	97.5	177.5
82.5 kg—Karyn S. Marshall	90.0	105.0	195.0
Over 82.5 kg—Carla Garrett	90.0	125.0	215.0

1. Clean and jerk. 2. All results in kilograms. 3. American record.

AUTO RACING

INDIANAPOLIS 500

Year	Winner	Car	Time	mph	Second place
1911	Ray Harroun	Marmon	6:42:08	74.59	Ralph Mulford
1912	Joe Dawson	National	6:21:06	78.72	Teddy Tetzloff
1913	Jules Goux	Peugeot	6:35:05	75.93	Spencer Wishart
1914	René Thomas	Delage	6:03:45	82.47	Arthur Duray
1915	Ralph DePalma	Mercedes	5:33:55.51	89.84	Dario Resta
1916[1]	Dario Resta	Peugeot	3:34:17	84.00	Wilbur D'Alene
1919	Howard Wilcox	Peugeot	5:40:42.87	88.05	Eddie Hearne
1920	Gaston Chevrolet	Monroe	5:38:32	88.62	René Thomas
1921	Tommy Milton	Frontenac	5:34:44.65	89.62	Roscoe Sarles
1922	Jimmy Murphy	Murphy Special	5:17:30.79	94.48	Harry Hartz
1923	Tommy Milton	H. C. S. Special	5:29.50.17	90.95	Harry Hartz
1924	L. L. Corum–Joe Boyer	Dusenberg Special	5:05:23.51	98.23	Earl Cooper
1925	Peter DePaolo	Dusenberg Special	4:56:39.45	101.13	Dave Lewis
1926[2]	Frank Lockhart	Miller Special	4:10:14.95	95.904	Harry Hartz
1927	George Souders	Dusenberg Special	5:07:33.08	97.54	Earl DeVore
1928	Louis Meyer	Miller Special	5:01:33.75	99.48	Lou Moore
1929	Ray Keech	Simplex Special	5:07:25.42	97.58	Louis Meyer
1930	Billy Arnold	Miller–Hartz Special	4:58:39.72	100.448	Shorty Cantlon
1931	Louis Schneider	Bowes Special	5:10:27.93	96.629	Fred Frame
1932	Fred Frame	Miller–Hartz Special	4:48:03.79	104.144	Howard Wilcox
1933	Louis Meyer	Tydol Special	4:48:00.75	104.162	Wilbur Shaw
1934	Bill Cummings	Boyle Products Special	4:46:05.20	104.863	Mauri Rose
1935	Kelly Petillo	Gilmore Special	4:42:22.71	106.240	Wilbur Shaw
1936	Louis Meyer	Ring Free Special	4:35:03.39	109.069	Ted Horn
1937	Wilbur Shaw	Shaw–Gilmore Special	4:24:07.80	113.580	Ralph Hepburn
1938	Floyd Roberts	Burd Piston Ring Special	4:15:58.40	117.200	Wilbur Shaw
1939	Wilbur Shaw	Boyle Special	4:20:47.39	115.035	Jimmy Snyder
1940	Wilbur Shaw	Boyle Special	4:22:31.17	114.277	Rex Mays
1941	Floyd Davis–Mauri Rose	Noc–Out Hose Clamp Special	4:20:36.24	115.117	Rex Mays
1946	George Robson	Thorne Engineering Special	4:21:26.71	114.820	Jimmy Jackson
1947	Mauri Rose	Blue Crown Special	4:17:52.17	116.338	Bill Holland
1948	Mauri Rose	Blue Crown Special	4:10:23.33	119.814	Bill Holland
1949	Bill Holland	Blue Crown Special	4:07:15.97	121.327	Johnny Parsons
1950[3]	Johnnie Parsons	Wynn's Friction Proof Special	2:46:55.97	124.002	Bill Holland
1951	Lee Wallard	Belanger Special	3:57:38.05	126.244	Mike Nazaruk
1952	Troy Ruttman	Agajanian Special	3:52:41.88	128.922	Jim Rathmann
1953	Bill Vukovich	Fuel Injection Special	3:53:01.69	128.740	Art Cross
1954	Bill Vukovich	Fuel Injection Special	3:49:17.27	130.840	Jim Bryan
1955	Bob Sweikert	John Zink Special	3:53:59.13	128.209	Tony Bettenhausen
1956	Pat Flaherty	John Zink Special	3:53:28.84	128.490	Sam Hanks
1957	Sam Hanks	Belond Exhaust Special	3:41:14.25	135.601	Jim Rathmann
1958	Jimmy Bryan	Belond A–P Special	3:44:13.80	133.791	George Amick
1959	Rodger Ward	Leader Card 500 Roadster	3:40:49.20	135.857	Jim Rathmann
1960	Jim Rathmann	Ken–Paul Special	3:36:11.36	138.767	Rodger Ward
1961	A. J. Foyt	Bowes Special	3:35:37.49	139.130	Eddie Sachs
1962	Rodger Ward	Leader Card Special	3:33:50.33	140.293	Len Sutton
1963	Parnelli Jones	Agajanian Special	3:29:35.40	143.137	Jim Clark
1964	A. J. Foyt	Sheraton–Thompson Spl.	3:23:35.83	147.350	Rodger Ward
1965	Jim Clark	Lotus–Ford	3:19:05.34	150.686	Parnelli Jones
1966	Graham Hill	Red Ball Lola–Ford	3:27:52.53	144.317	Jim Clark
1967[4]	A. J. Foyt	Sheraton-Thompson Coyote–Ford	3:18:24.22	151.207	Al Unser
1968	Bobby Unser	Rislone Eagle–Offenhauser	3:16:13.76	152.882	Dan Gurney
1969	Mario Andretti	STP Hawk–Ford	3:11:14.71	156.867	Dan Gurney
1970	Al Unser	Johnny Lightning P. J. Colt–Ford	3:12:37.04	155.749	Mark Donohue
1971	Al Unser	Johnny Lightning P. J. Colt–Ford	3:10:11.56	157.735	Peter Revson
1972	Mark Donohue	Sunoco McLaren–Offenhauser	3:04:05.54	162.962	Al Unser
1973[5]	Gordon Johncock	STP Eagle–Offenhauser	2:05:26.59	159.036	Bill Vukovich
1974	Johnny Rutherford	McLaren–Offenhauser	3:09:10.06	158.589	Bobby Unser
1975[6]	Bobby Unser	Jorgensen Eagle–Offenhauser	2:54:55.08	149.213	Johnny Rutherford
1976[7]	Johnny Rutherford	Hy-gain McLaren–Offenhauser	1:42:52.48	148.725	A. J. Foyt
1977	A. J. Foyt	Gilmore Coyote–Foyt	3:05:57.16	161.331	Tom Sneva
1978	Al Unser	1st Nat'l City Lola–Cosworth	3:05:54.99	161.363	Tom Sneva
1979	Rick Mears	Gould Penske–Cosworth	3:08:27.97	158.899	A. J. Foyt
1980	Johnny Rutherford	Pennzoil Chaparral–Cosworth	3:29:59.56	142.862	Tom Sneva
1981[8]	Bobby Unser	Norton Penske–Cosworth	3:35:41.78	139.029	Mario Andretti
1982	Gordon Johncock	STP Wildcat–Cosworth	3:05:09.14	162.029	Rick Mears
1983	Tom Sneva	Texaco Star March–Cosworth	3:05:03.06	162.117	Al Unser
1984	Rick Mears	Pennzoil March–Cosworth	3:03:21.00	162.962	Roberto Guerrero

1985	Danny Sullivan	Miller March–Cosworth	3:16:06.069	152.982	Mario Andretti
1986	Bobby Rahal	Budweiser March–Cosworth	2:55:43.48	170.722	Kevin Cogan
1987	Al Unser, Sr.	Cummins March–Cosworth	3:04:59.147	162.175	Roberto Guerrero
1988	Rick Mears	Pennzoil Penske P.C.17–Chevrolet	3:27:10.204	144.809	Emerson Fittipaldi
1989	Emerson Fittipaldi	Marlboro Penske-Cosworth	2:59:01.04	167.581	Al Unser, Jr.
1990	Arie Luyendyk	Domino's Pizza Lola–Cosworth	2:41:18.248	185.987	Bobby Rahal
1991	Rick Mears	Marlboro Penske–Cosworth	2:50:01.018	176.460	Michael Andretti

1. 300 miles. 2. Race ended at 400 miles because of rain. 3. Race ended at 345 miles because of rain. 4. Race, postponed after 18 laps because of rain on May 30, was finished on May 31. 5. Race postponed May 28 and 29 was cut to 332.5 miles because of rain, May 30. 6. Race ended at 435 miles because of rain. 7. Race ended at 255 miles because of rain. 8. Andretti was awarded the victory the day after the race after Bobby Unser, whose car finished first, was penalized one lap and dropped from first place to second for passing other cars illegally under a yellow caution flag. Unser appealed the decision to the U.S. Auto Club and was upheld. A panel ruled the penalty was too severe and instead fined Unser $40,000, but restored the victory to him.

INDY CAR NATIONAL CHAMPIONS

1910	Ray Harroun	1927	Peter DePaolo	1952	Chuck Stevenson	1973	Roger McCluskey
1911	Ralph Mulford	1928–29	Louis Meyer	1953	Sam Hanks	1974	Bobby Unser
1912	Ralph DePalma	1930	Billy Arnold	1954	Jimmy Bryan	1975	A. J. Foyt
1913	Earl Cooper	1931	Louis Schneider	1955	Bob Sweikert	1976	Gordon Johncock
1914	Ralph DePalma	1932	Bob Carey	1956–57	Jimmy Bryan	1977–78	Tom Sneva
1915	Earl Cooper	1933	Louis Meyer	1958	Tony Bettenhausen	1979	Rick Mears (CART)
1916	Dario Resta	1934	Bill Cummings	1959	Rodger Ward		A.J. Foyt (USAC)[1]
1917	Earl Cooper	1935	Kelly Petillo	1960–61	A. J. Foyt	1980	Johnny Rutherford
1918	Ralph Mulford	1936	Mauri Rose	1962	Rodger Ward	1981–82	Rick Mears
1919	Howard Wilcox	1937	Wilbur Shaw	1963–64	A. J. Foyt	1983	Al Unser
1920	Gaston Chevrolet	1938	Floyd Roberts	1965–66	Mario Andretti	1984	Mario Andretti
1921	Tommy Milton	1939	Wilbur Shaw	1967	A. J. Foyt	1985	Al Unser
1922	James Murphy	1940–41	Rex Mays	1968	Bobby Unser	1986–87	Bobby Rahal
1923	Eddie Hearne	1946–48	Ted Horn	1969	Mario Andretti	1988	Danny Sullivan
1924	James Murphy	1949	Johnnie Parsons	1970	Al Unser	1989	Emerson Fittipaldi
1925	Peter DePaolo	1950	Henry Banks	1971–72	Joe Leonard	1990	Al Unser Jr.
1926	Harry Hartz	1951	Tony Bettenhausen				

1. Two separate series were held in 1979. NOTE: There have been three sanctioning bodies for the series: the Automobile Association of America (1909–1955), the U.S. Auto Club (1956–1979), and the Championship Auto Racing Team (CART), 1979–present.

NATIONAL ASSOCIATION FOR STOCK CAR AUTO RACING
WINSTON CUP CHAMPIONS

1949	Red Byron	1960	Rex White	1971–72	Richard Petty	1984	Terry Labonte
1950	Bill Rexford	1961	Ned Jarrett	1973	Benny Parsons	1985	Darrell Waltrip
1951	Herb Thomas	1962–63	Joe Weatherly	1974–75	Richard Petty	1986	Dale Earnhardt
1952	Tim Flock	1964	Richard Petty	1976–78	Cale Yarborough	1987	Dale Earnhardt
1953	Herb Thomas	1965	Ned Jarrett	1979	Richard Petty	1988	Bill Elliott
1954	Lee Petty	1966	David Pearson	1980	Dale Earnhardt	1989	Rusty Wallace
1955	Tim Flock	1967	Richard Petty	1981	Darrell Waltrip	1990	Dale Earnhardt
1956–57	Buck Baker	1968–69	David Pearson	1982	Darrell Waltrip		
1958–59	Lee Petty	1970	Bobby Isaac	1983	Bobby Allison		

WORLD GRAND PRIX DRIVER CHAMPIONS

1950	Giuseppe Farina, Italy, Alfa Romeo	1971	Jackie Stewart, Scotland, Tyrrell–Ford
1951	Juan Fangio, Argentina, Alfa Romeo	1972	Emerson Fittipaldi, Brazil, Lotus–Ford
1952	Alberto Ascari, Italy, Ferrari	1973	Jackie Stewart, Scotland, Tyrrell–Ford
1953	Alberto Ascari, Italy, Ferrari	1974	Emerson Fittipaldi, Brazil, McLaren–Ford
1954	Juan Fangio, Argentina, Maserati, Mercedes–Benz	1975	Niki Lauda, Austria, Ferrari
1955	Juan Fangio, Argentina, Mercedes–Benz	1976	James Hunt, Britain, McLaren–Ford
1956	Juan Fangio, Argentina, Lancia–Ferrari	1977	Niki Lauda, Austria, Ferrari
1957	Juan Fangio, Argentina, Maserati	1978	Mario Andretti, United States, Lotus
1958	Mike Hawthorn, England, Ferrari	1979	Jody Scheckter, South Africa, Ferrari
1959	Jack Brabham, Australia, Cooper	1980	Alan Jones, Australia, Williams–Ford
1960	Jack Brabham, Australia, Cooper	1981	Nelson Piquet, Brazil, Brabham–Ford
1961	Phil Hill, United States, Ferrari	1982	Kiki Rosberg, Finland, Williams–Ford
1962	Graham Hill, England, BRM	1983	Nelson Piquet, Brazil, Brabham–BMW
1963	Jim Clark, Scotland, Lotus–Ford	1984	Nikki Lauda, Austria, McLaren–Porsche
1964	John Surtees, England, Ferrari	1985	Alain Prost, France, McLaren–Porsche
1965	Jim Clark, Scotland, Lotus–Ford	1986	Alain Prost, France, McLaren–Porsche
1966	Jack Brabham, Australia, Brabham–Repco	1987	Nelson Piquet, Brazil, Williams–Honda
1967	Denis Hulme, New Zealand, Brabham–Repco	1988	Aryton Senna, Brazil, McLaren–Honda
1968	Graham Hill, England, Lotus–Ford	1989	Alain Prost, France, McLaren–Honda
1969	Jackie Stewart, Scotland, Matra–Ford	1990	Ayrton Senna, Brazil, McLaren–Honda
1970	Jochen Rindt, Austria, Lotus–Ford		

1990 NASCAR LEADING MONEY WINNERS

1. Dale Earnhardt	$3,083,056
2. Mark Martin	1,302,958
3. Geoff Bodine	1,131,222
4. Bill Elliott	1,090,730
5. Rusty Wallace	954,129
6. Ken Schrader	769,934
7. Kyle Petty	746,326
8. Morgan Shepherd	666,915
9. Davey Allison	640,684
10. Ricky Rudd	573,650

1990 WINSTON CUP POINT LEADERS

1. Dale Earnhardt	4430	11. Kyle Petty	3501
2. Mark Martin	4404	12. Brett Bodine	3440
3. Geoff Bodine	4017	13. Davey Allison	3423
4. Bill Elliott	3999	14. Sterling Marlin	3387
5. Morgan Shepherd	3689	15. Terry Labonte	3371
6. Rusty Wallace	3676	16. Michael Waltrip	3251
7. Ricky Rudd	3601	17. Harry Gant	3182
8. Alan Kulwicki	3599	18. Derrike Cope	3140
9. Ernie Ivan	3593	19. Bobby Hillin	3048
10. Ken Schrader	3572	20. Darrell Waltrip	3013

TOP 25 1990 INDY CAR WORLD SERIES PERFORMANCES

Driver	Points	Purse	Driver	Points	Purse
1. Al Unser Jr.	210	$1,936,833	14. Teo Fabi	33	$614,335
2. Michael Andretti	181	1,303,526	15. Scott Brayton	28	592,442
3. Rick Mears	168	1,414,744	16. Roberto Guerrero	24	471,375
4. Bobby Rahal	153	1,462,458	17. Mike Groff	17	257,628
5. Emerson Fittipaldi	144	1,513,176	18. Didier Theys	15	452,218
6. Danny Sullivan	139	965,161	19. Dominic Dobson	12	325,390
7. Mario Andretti	136	976,721	20. Pancho Carter	9	323,967
8. Arie Luyendyk	90	1,747,984	21. Jon Beekhuis	7	127,024
9. Eddie Cheever	80	869,720	22. Jeff Wood	7	117,269
10. John Andretti	51	456,594	23. Kevin Cogan	4	164,630
11. A.J. Foyt Jr.	42	578,744	24. Tony Bettenhausen	4	345,710
12. Raul Boesel	42	579,913	25. Dean Hall	4	444,735
13. Scott Goodyear	36	429,724			

LACROSSE

NATIONAL INTERCOLLEGIATE CHAMPIONS

1946	Navy	1961	Army, Navy	1978–80	Johns Hopkins
1947–48	Johns Hopkins	1962–66	Navy	1981	North Carolina
1949	Johns Hopkins, Navy	1967	Johns Hopkins, Maryland, Navy	1982	North Carolina
1950	Johns Hopkins	1968	Johns Hopkins	1983	Syracuse
1951	Army, Princeton	1969	Army, Johns Hopkins	1984	Johns Hopkins
1952	Virginia, R.P.I.	1970	Johns Hopkins, Navy, Virginia	1985	Johns Hopkins
1953	Princeton	1971[1]	Cornell	1986	North Carolina
1954	Navy	1972	Virginia	1987	Johns Hopkins
1955–56	Maryland	1973	Maryland	1988	Syracuse
1957	Johns Hopkins	1974	Johns Hopkins	1989	Syracuse
1958	Army	1975	Maryland	1990	Syracuse
1959	Army, Johns Hopkins, Maryland	1976–77	Cornell	1991	North Carolina
1960	Navy				

1. First year of N.C.A.A. Championship Tournaments.

1991 N.C.A.A. LACROSSE

DIVISION I
Men's Championships
Quarterfinals
North Carolina 11, Loyola–Maryland 9
Towson State 14, Princeton 13
Syracuse 11, Johns Hopkins 8
Maryland 16, Brown 13

Semifinals
North Carolina 19, Syracuse 13
Towson State 15, Maryland 11

Championship
(at Syracuse University, Syracuse, N.Y., May 25–27, 1991)
North Carolina 18, Towson State 13

Women's Championships
Semifinals
Virginia 10, Penn State 5
Maryland 4, New Hampshire 3

Championship
(at Trenton State College, Trenton, N.J., May 19, 1991)
Virginia 8, Maryland 6

BOBSLEDDING

WORLD CHAMPIONSHIPS—1991
(Altenburgh, Germany, Feb. 1991)

1. Germany (Wolfgang Hoppe, driver)
2. Switzerland (Gustuf Weder, driver)
3. Germany (H. Czudaj, driver)
4. Austria (I. Appelt, driver)
5. Italy (G. Huber, driver)
6. Canada (Chris Lori, driver)
7. United States (Brian Shimer, driver)

World Two–Man Championships
(Altenburgh, Germany, February 1991)

1. Germany (Rudy Lochner, driver)
2. Switzerland (Gustaf Weder, driver)
3. Germany (Wolfgang Hoppe, driver)
4. Canada (Greg Haydenluck, driver)
5. Austria (I. Appelt, driver)
6. Italy (G. Huber, driver)
7. United States (Brian Shimer, driver)

SOFTBALL

Source: Amateur Softball Association.

AMATEUR CHAMPIONS

1959	Aurora (Ill.) Sealmasters	
1960	Clearwater (Fla.) Bombers	
1961	Aurora (Ill.) Sealmasters	
1962–63	Clearwater (Fla.) Bombers	
1964	Burch Gage & Tool, Detroit	
1965	Aurora (Ill.) Sealmasters	
1966	Clearwater (Fla.) Bombers	
1967	Aurora (Ill.) Sealmasters	
1968	Clearwater (Fla.) Bombers	
1969–70	Raybestos Cardinals, Stratford, Conn.	
1971	Welty Way, Cedar Rapids, Iowa	
1972	Raybestos Cardinals, Stratford, Conn.	
1973	Clearwater (Fla.) Bombers	
1974	Santa Rosa (Calif.)	
1975	Rising Sun Hotel, Reading, Pa.	
1976	Raybestos Cardinals, Stratford, Conn.	
1977	Billard Barbell, Reading, Pa.	
1978	Reading, Pa.	
1979	Midland, Mich.	
1980	Peterbilt Western, Seattle	
1981	Archer Daniels Midland, Decatur, Ill.	
1982	Peterbilt Western, Seattle	
1983	Franklin Cardinals, West Haven, Conn.	
1984	California Coors Kings, Merced, Calif.	
1985	Pay 'n Pak, Bellevue, Wash.	
1986	Pay 'n Pak, Bellevue, Wash.	
1987	Pay 'n Pak, Bellevue, Wash.	
1988	TransAire, Elkhart, Ind.	
1989	Penn Corp., Sioux City, Iowa	
1990	Penn Corp., Sioux City, Iowa	
1991	Guanella Brothers, Rohnert Park, Calif.	

ASA NATIONAL CHAMPIONS—1991

Adult Champions

Men's Major FP: Guanella Brothers, Rohnert Park, Calif.
Women's Major FP: Raybestos Brakettes, Stratford, Conn.
Men's Super SP: Sunbelt/Worth, Centerville, Ga.
Men's Major SP: Riverside Paving, Louisville, Ky.
Women's Major SP: Cannan's Illusion, San Antonio, Texas
Men's Class A SP: Lee Roy's Framing, Claremont, N.C.
Women's Class A FP: Destin Roofing, Destin, Fla.
Men's Class A FP: Springers, Boulder, Colo.
Women's Class A FP: Nor Cal Chargers, Antioch, Calif.
Men's Major Industrial SP: County Fed Meats/Delta, Riverside, Ga.
Men's Class A Industrial SP: Peterson AFB Sabres, Colorado Springs, Colo.
Men's Major Modified Pitch: Hialeah Stings, Hialeah, Fla.
Women's Class A Industrial SP: Springhill Heartbeats, Mobile, Ala.
Men's Major Church SP: Oakview Presbyterian, Burlington, N.C.
Women's Major Church SP: First Baptist Red, Milton, Fla.
Men's Class A Church SP: First Freewill Baptist, Albany, Ga.
Women's Major Modified Pitch: The House That Jack Built, Lakewood, N.Y.
Men's Class A Modified Pitch: Hawks, Roxbury, Mass.
Men's Masters 40-and-over FP: Superior Office, Sikeston, Miss.
Women's Masters 35-and-over FP: C.T. Timers, Savannah, Mo.
Women's Class A Church SP: Mount Olive, Cleveland, Tenn.
Men's Masters 35-and-over SP: Virginia Pets, Annandale, Va.
Men's Masters 55-and-over SP: Wiggins Iron Works, Savannah, Ga.
Men's Masters 40-and-over SP: Old A's, El Sombrante, Calif.
Men's Masters 45-and-over SP: Nothdurft Tool, Clinton, Mich.

FP: Fast Pitch. SP: Slow Pitch.

Coed Class A SP: Chick's Crew, Ardmore, Okla.
Women's Class B FP: Golden State Royals, San Mateo, Calif.
Women's Class C FP: Creative Awards, Tucson, Ariz.
Men's 23-and-under FP: Page Brake, Salt Lake City, Utah
Men's 16-inch SP: Splinter Sports Club, Mt. Prospect, Ill.
Coed Major SP: South Florida Softball, Hollywood, Fla.
Men's Class A 16-inch SP: The Stickmen, Chicago, Ill.
Men's C SP: Pudley's, Redwood City, Calif.
Men's D SP: Red's Sporting Goods, Brandon, Fla.
Women's D SP: Rohnert Park Pirates, Rohnert Park, Calif.
Men's B FP: Orlando Athletics, St. Cloud, Fla.

Junior Champions

Boys' 12-and-under SP: Covington Turners, Hebron, Ky.
Boys' 14-and-under SP: Tifton Mustangs, Tifton, Ga.
Boys' 16-and-under SP: Cane's Softball Club, Tifton, Ga.
Boys' 18-and-under SP: Renegades, Tifton, Ga.
Boys 12-and-under FP: California Quake, Westminister, Calif.
Boys' 14-and-under FP: South Sioux Kiwanis, Sioux Falls, S.D.
Boys 16-and-under FP: Cameron Fastballers, Rice Lake, Wisc.
Boys' 18-and-under FP: Charles Bailly, Sioux Falls, S.D.
Girls' 12-and-under FP: Batbusters, Orange County, Calif.
Girls' 14-and-under FP: Outlaws, Huntington Beach, Calif.
Girls' 16-and-under FP: California Thunder, Glendora, Calif.
Girls' 18-and-under FP: California Raiders, Moreno Valley, Calif.
Girls' 12-and-under SP: Peaches, Peachtree City, Ga.
Girls' 14-and-under SP: Thunder, Pembroke Pines, Fla.
Girls' 16-and-under SP: Tony's Angels, Semmes, Ala.
Girls' 18-and-under SP: Gwinnett Lady Panthers, Lilburn, Ga.

HANDBALL

U.S.H.A. NATIONAL FOUR–WALL CHAMPIONS

Singles

1960	Jimmy Jacobs
1961	John Sloan
1962–63	Oscar Obert
1964–65	Jimmy Jacobs
1966–67	Paul Haber
1968	Simon (Stuffy) Singer
1969–71	Paul Haber
1972	Fred Lewis
1973	Terry Muck
1974	Fred Lewis
1975	Jay Bilyeu
1976	Vern Roberts, Jr.
1977	Naty Alvarado
1978	Fred Lewis
1979	Naty Alvarado
1980	Naty Alvarado
1981	Fred Lewis
1982	Naty Alvarado
1983	Naty Alvarado
1984	Naty Alvarado
1985	Naty Alvarado
1986	Naty Alvarado
1987	Naty Alvarado
1988	Naty Alvarado[1]
1989	Ponch Monreal
1990	Naty Alvarado
1991	John Bike

Doubles

1960	Jimmy Jacobs–Dick Weisman
1961	John Sloan–Vic Hershkowitz
1962–63	Jimmy Jacobs–Marty Decatur
1964	John Sloan–Phil Elbert
1965	Jimmy Jacobs–Marty Decatur
1966	Pete Tyson–Bob Lindsay
1967–68	Jimmy Jacobs–Marty Decatur
1969	Lou Kramberg–Lou Russo
1970	Karl and Ruby Obert
1971	Ray Neveau–Simie Fein
1972	Kent Fusselman–Al Drews
1973–74	Ray Neveau–Simie Fein
1975	Marty Decatur–Steve Lott
1976	Gary Rohrer–Dan O'Connor
1977	Skip McDowell–Matt Kelly
1978	Stuffy Singer–Marty Decatur
1979	Stuffy Singer–Marty Decatur
1980	Skip McDowell–Harry Robertson
1981	Tom Kopatich–Jack Roberts
1982	Naty Alvarado–Vern Roberts
1983	Naty Alvarado–Vern Roberts
1984	Naty Alvarado–Vern Roberts
1985	Naty Alvarado–Vern Roberts
1986–87	Jon Kemdler–Poncho Monreal
1988	Doug Glatt–Dennis Haynes
1989	Danny Bell—Charlie Kalil
1990	Doug Glatt–Rod Prince
1991	John Bike–Octavio Silveyra

1. 10th time—American record.

BASEBALL

The popular tradition that baseball was invented by Abner Doubleday at Cooperstown, N.Y., in 1839 has been enshrined in the Hall of Fame and National Museum of Baseball erected in that town, but research has proved that a game called "Base Ball" was played in this country and England before 1839. The first team baseball as we know it was played at the Elysian Fields, Hoboken, N.J., on June 19, 1846, between the Knickerbockers and the New York Nine. The next fifty years saw a gradual growth of baseball and an improvement of equipment and playing skill.

Historians have it that the first pitcher to throw a curve was William A. (Candy) Cummings in 1867. The Cincinnati Red Stockings were the first all-professional team, and in 1869 they played 64 games without a loss. The standard ball of the same size and weight, still the rule, was adopted in 1872. The first catcher's mask was worn in 1875. The National League was organized in 1876. The first chest protector was worn in 1885. The three-strike rule was put on the books in 1887, and the four-ball ticket to first base was instituted in 1889. The pitching distance was lengthened to 60 feet 6 inches in 1893, and the rules have been modified only slightly since that time.

The American League, under the vigorous leadership of B. B. Johnson, became a major league in 1901. Judge Kenesaw Mountain Landis, by action of the two major leagues, became Commissioner of Baseball in 1921, and upon his death (1944), Albert B. Chandler, former United States Senator from Kentucky, was elected to that office (1945). Chandler failed to obtain a new contract and was succeeded by Ford C. Frick (1951), the National League president. Frick retired after the 1965 season, and William D. Eckert, a retired Air Force lieutenant general, was named to succeed him. Eckert resigned under pressure in December, 1968. Bowie Kuhn, a New York attorney, became interim commissioner for one year in February. His appointment was made permanent with two seven-year contracts until August 1983. In August 1983, Kuhn's contract was not renewed, and a search was begun for his successor. Peter Ueberroth was named new Commissioner and took office Oct. 1, 1984.

Ueberroth did not seek a new term in 1989 and was succeeded by Bart Giamatti who died suddenly on Sept. 1, 1989. Francis T. Vincent, Jr., replaced him on Sept. 13, 1989.

MAJOR LEAGUE ALL-STAR GAME

Year	Date	Winning league and manager	Runs	Losing league and manager	Runs	Winning pitcher	Losing pitcher	Site	Paid attendance
1933	July 6	A.L. (Mack)	4	N.L. (McGraw)	2	Gomez	Hallahan	Chicago A.L.	47,595
1934	July 10	A.L. (Cronin)	9	N.L. (Terry)	7	Harder	Mungo	New York N.L.	48,363
1935	July 8	A.L. (Cochrane)	4	N.L. (Frisch)	1	Gomez	Walker	Cleveland A.L.	69,831
1936	July 7	N.L. (Grimm)	4	A.L. (McCarthy)	3	J. Dean	Grove	Boston N.L.	25,556
1937	July 7	A.L. (McCarthy)	8	N.L. (Terry)	3	Gomez	J. Dean	Washington A.L.	31,391
1938	July 6	N.L. (Terry)	4	A.L. (McCarthy)	1	Vander Meer	Gomez	Cincinnati N.L.	27,067
1939	July 11	A.L. (McCarthy)	3	N.L. (Hartnett)	1	Bridges	Lee	New York A.L.	62,892
1940	July 9	N.L. (McKechnie)	4	A.L. (Cronin)	0	Derringer	Ruffing	St. Louis N.L.	32,373
1941	July 8	A.L. (Baker)	7	N.L. (McKechnie)	5	E. Smith	Passeau	Detroit A.L.	54,674
1942	July 6	A.L. (McCarthy)	3	N.L. (Durocher)	1	Chandler	Cooper	New York N.L.	34,178
1943	July 13	A.L. (McCarthy)	5	N.L. (Southworth)	3	Leonard	Cooper	Philadelphia A.L.	31,938
1944	July 11[1]	N.L. (Southworth)	7	A.L. (McCarthy)	1	Raffensberger	Hughson	Pittsburgh N.L.	29,589
1946	July 9	A.L. (O'Neill)	12	N.L. (Grimm)	0	Feller	Passeau	Boston A.L.	34,906
1947	July 8	A.L. (Cronin)	2	N.L. (Dyer)	1	Shea	Sain	Chicago N.L.	41,123
1948	July 13	A.L. (Harris)	5	N.L. (Durocher)	2	Raschi	Schmitz	St. Louis A.L.	34,009
1949	July 12	A.L. (Boudreau)	11	N.L. (Southworth)	7	Trucks	Newcombe	Brooklyn N.L.	32,577
1950	July 11	N.L. (Shotton)	4	A.L. (Stengel)	3[3]	Blackwell	Gray	Chicago A.L.	46,127
1951	July 10	N.L. (Sawyer)	8	A.L. (Stengel)	3	Maglie	Lopat	Detroit A.L.	52,075
1952	July 8	N.L. (Durocher)	3	A.L. (Stengel)	2[4]	Rush	Lemon	Philadelphia N.L.	32,785
1953	July 14	N.L. (Dressen)	5	A.L. (Stengel)	1	Spahn	Reynolds	Cincinnati N.L.	30,846
1954	July 13	A.L. (Stengel)	11	N.L. (Alston)	9	Stone	Conley	Cleveland A.L.	68,751
1955	July 12	N.L. (Durocher)	6	A.L. (Lopez)	5[5]	Conley	Sullivan	Milwaukee N.L.	45,643
1956	July 10	N.L. (Alston)	7	A.L. (Stengel)	3	Friend	Pierce	Washington A.L.	28,843
1957	July 9	A.L. (Stengel)	6	N.L. (Alston)	5	Bunning	Simmons	St. Louis N.L.	30,693
1958	July 8	A.L. (Stengel)	4	N.L. (Haney)	3	Wynn	Friend	Baltimore A.L.	48,829
1959[2]	July 7	N.L. (Haney)	5	A.L. (Stengel)	4	Antonelli	Ford	Pittsburgh N.L.	35,277
	Aug. 3	A.L. (Stengel)	5	N.L. (Haney)	3	Walker	Drysdale	Los Angeles N.L.	55,105
1960[2]	July 11	N.L. (Alston)	5	A.L. (Lopez)	3	Friend	Monbouquette	Kansas City A.L.	30,619
	July 13	N.L. (Alston)	6	A.L. (Lopez)	0	Law	Ford	New York A.L.	38,362
1961[2]	July 11	N.L. (Murtaugh)	5	A.L. (Richards)	4[6]	Miller	Wilhelm	San Francisco N.L.	44,115
	July 31	N.L. (Murtaugh)	1	A.L. (Richards)	1[7]	—	—	Boston A.L.	31,851
1962[2]	July 10	N.L. (Hutchinson)	3	A.L. (Houk)	1	Marichal	Pascual	Washington A.L.	45,480
	July 30	A.L. (Houk)	9	N.L. (Hutchinson)	4	Herbert	Mahaffey	Chicago N.L.	38,359
1963	July 9	N.L. (Dark)	5	A.L. (Houk)	3	Jackson	Bunning	Cleveland A.L.	44,160
1964	July 7	N.L. (Alston)	7	A.L. (Lopez)	4	Marichal	Radatz	New York N.L.	50,850
1965	July 13	N.L. (March)	6	A.L. (Lopez)	5	Koufax	McDowell	Minnesota A.L.	46,706
1966	July 12	N.L. (Alston)	2	A.L. (Mele)	1[6]	Perry	Rickert	St. Louis N.L.	49,926
1967	July 11	N.L. (Alston)	2	A.L. (Bauer)	1[8]	Drysdale	Hunter	Anaheim A.L.	46,309
1968	July 9	N.L. (Schoendienst)	1	A.L. (Williams)	0	Drysdale	Tiant	Houston N.L.	48,321
1969	July 23	N.L. (Schoendienst)	9	A.L. (M. Smith)	3	Carlton	Stottlemyre	Washington A.L.	45,259
1970	July 14	N.L. (Hodges)	5	A.L. (Weaver)	4	Osteen	Wright	Cincinnati N.L.	51,838
1971	July 13	A.L. (Weaver)	6	N.L. (Anderson)	4	Blue	Ellis	Detroit A.L.	53,559

Year	Date	N.L.	A.L.		Win	Lose	Location	Att.
1972	July 25	N.L. (Murtaugh)	4 A.L. (Weaver)	3[6]	McGraw	McNally	Atlanta N.L.	53,107
1973	July 24[1]	N.L. (Anderson)	7 A.L. (Williams)	1	Wise	Blyleven	Kansas City A.L.	40,849
1974	July 23[1]	N.L. (Berra)	7 A.L. (Williams)	2	Brett	Tiant	Pittsburgh N.L.	50,706
1975	July 15[1]	N.L. (Alston)	6 A.L. (Dark)	3	Matlack	Hunter	Milwaukee A.L.	51,540
1976	July 13	N.L. (Anderson)	7 A.L. (D. Johnson)	1	R. Jones	Fidrych	Philadelphia N.L.	63,974
1977	July 19[1]	N.L. (Anderson)	7 A.L. (Martin)	5	Sutton	Palmer	New York A.L.	56,683
1978	July 11[1]	N.L. (Lasorda)	7 A.L. (Martin)	3	Sutter	Gossage	San Diego N.L.	51,549
1979	July 17[1]	N.L. (Lasorda)	7 A.L. (Lemon)	6	Sutter	Kern	Seattle A.L.	58,905
1980	July 8[1]	N.L. (Tanner)	4 A.L. (Weaver)	2	Reuss	John	Los Angeles N.L.	56,088
1981	Aug. 9[1]	N.L. (Green)	5 A.L. (Frey)	4	Blue	Fingers	Cleveland* A.L.	72,086
1982	July 13[1]	N.L. (Lasorda)	4 A.L. (Martin)	1	Rogers	Eckersley	Montreal N.L.	59,057
1983	July 6[1]	A.L. (Kuenn)	13 N.L. (Herzog)	3	Steib	Soto	Chicago A.L.	43,801
1984	July 11[1]	N.L. (Owens)	3 A.L. (Altobelli)	1	Leg	Steib	San Francisco, N.L.	57,756
1985	July 16[1]	N.L. (Williams)	6 A.L. (Anderson)	1	Hoyt	Morris	Minneapolis, A.L.	54,960
1986	July 15[1]	A.L. (Howser)	3 N.L. (Herzog)	2	Clemens	Gooden	Houston, N.L.	45,774
1987	July 14[1]	N.L. (Johnson)	2 A.L. (McNamara)	0	Smith	Howell	Oakland, A.L.	49,671
1988	July 12[1]	A.L. (Kelly)	2 N.L. (Herzog)	1	Viola	Gooden	Cincinnati, N.L	55,837
1989	July 11[1]	A.L. (LaRussa)	5 N.L. (Lasorda)	3	Ryan	Smoltz	California, A.L.	64,036
1990	July 10[1]	A.L. (LaRussa)	2 N.L. (Craig)	0	Saberhagen	Brantley	Chicago, N.L.	39,071
1991	July 9[1]	A.L. (LaRussa)	4 N.L. (Piniella)	2	Key	Martinez	Toronto, A.L.	52,383

1. Night game. 2. Two games. 3. Fourteen innings. 4. Five innings, rain. 5. Twelve innings. 6. Ten innings. 7. Called because of rain after nine innings. 8. Fifteen innings. NOTE: No game in 1945. *Game was originally scheduled for July 14, but was put off because of players' strike.

NATIONAL BASEBALL HALL OF FAME

Cooperstown, N.Y.

Fielders

Member	Active years
Aaron, Henry (Hank)	1954–1976
Anson, Adrian (Cap)	1876–1897
Aparicio, Luis	1956–1973
Appling, Lucius (Luke)	1930–1950
Averill, H. Earl	1929–1941
Baker, J. Frank (Home Run)	1908–1922
Bancroft, David	1915–1930
Banks, Ernest	1953–1971
Beckley, Jacob	1888–1907
Bell, James (Cool Papa)[1]	1920–1947
Bench, John	1967–1983
Berra, Lawrence (Yogi)	1946–1965
Bottomley, James	1922–1937
Boudreau, Louis	1938–1952
Bresnahan, Roger	1897–1915
Brock, Lou	1961–1980
Brouthers, Dennis	1879–1896
Burkett, Jesse	1890–1905
Campanella, Roy	1948–1957
Carew, Rod	1967–1985
Carey, Max	1910–1929
Chance, Frank	1898–1914
Charleston, Oscar[1]	1915–1954
Clarke, Fred	1894–1915
Clemente, Roberto	1955–1972
Cobb, Tyrus	1905–1928
Cochrane, Gordon (Mickey)	1925–1937
Collins, Edward	1906–1930
Collins, James	1895–1908
Comiskey, Charles	1882–1894
Combs, Earle	1924–1935
Connor, Roger	1880–1897
Crawford, Samuel	1899–1917
Cronin, Joseph	1926–1945
Cuyler, Hazen (Kiki)	1921–1938
Dandridge, Ray[1]	1933–1953
Delahanty, Edward	1888–1903
Dickey, William	1928–1946
Dihigo, Martin[1]	1923–1945
DiMaggio, Joseph	1936–1951
Doerr, Bobby	1937–1951

Member	Active years
Duffy, Hugh	1888–1906
Ewing, William	1880–1897
Eyers, John	1902–1919
Flick, Elmer	1898–1910
Foxx, James	1925–1945
Frisch, Frank	1919–1937
Gehrig, H. Louis (Lou)	1923–1939
Gehringer, Charles	1924–1942
Gibson, Josh[1]	1929–1946
Goslin, Leon (Goose)	1921–1938
Greenberg, Henry (Hank)	1933–1947
Hafey, Charles (Chick)	1924–1937
Hamilton, William	1888–1901
Hartnett, Charles (Gabby)	1922–1941
Heilmann, Harry	1914–1932
Herman, William	1931–1947
Hooper, Harry	1909–1925
Hornsby, Rogers	1915–1937
Irvin, Monford (Monte)[1]	1939–1956
Jackson, Travis	1922–1936
Jennings, Hugh	1891–1918
Johnson, William (Judy)[1]	1921–1937
Kaline, Albert W.	1953–1974
Keeler, William (Wee Willie)	1892–1910
Kell, George	1943–1957
Kelley, Joseph	1891–1908
Kelly, George	1915–1932
Kelly, Michael (King)	1878–1893
Killebrew, Harmon	1954–1975
Kiner, Ralph	1946–1955
Klein, Charles H. (Chuck)	1928–1944
Lajoie, Napoleon	1896–1916
Lazzeri, Tony	1926–1939
Leonard, Walter (Buck)[1]	1933–1955
Lindstrom, Frederick	1924–1936
Lloyd, John Henry[1]	1905–1931
Lombardi, Ernie	1932–1947
Mantle, Mickey	1951–1968
Manush, Henry (Heinie)	1923–1939
Maranville, Walter (Rabbit)	1912–1935
Matthews, Edwin	1952–1968

Member	Active years
Mays, Willie	1951–1973
McCarthy, Thomas	1884–1896
McGraw, John J.	1891–1906
McCovey, Willie	1959–1980
Medwick, Joseph (Ducky)	1932–1948
Mize, John (The Big Cat)	1936–1953
Morgan, Joe	1963–1984
Musial, Stanley	1941–1963
O'Rourke, James	1876–1894
Ott, Melvin	1926–1947
Reese, Harold (Pee Wee)	1940–1958
Rice, Edgar (Sam)	1915–1934
Robinson, Brooks	1955–1977
Robinson, Frank	1956–1976
Robinson, Jack	1947–1956
Robinson, Wilbert	1886–1902
Roush, Edd	1913–1931
Ruth, George (Babe)	1914–1935
Schalk, Raymond	1912–1929
Schoendienst, Red	1945–1963
Sewell, Joseph	1920–1933
Simmons, Al	1924–1944
Sisler, George	1915–1930
Slaughter, Enos	1938–1959
Snider, Edwin D. (Duke)	1947–1964
Speaker, Tristram	1907–1928
Stargell, Willie	1962–1982
Terry, William	1923–1936
Thompson, Samuel	1885–1906
Tinker, Joseph	1902–1916
Traynor, Harold (Pie)	1920–1937
Vaughan, Arky	1932–1948
Wagner, John (Honus)	1897–1917
Wallace, Roderick (Bobby)	1894–1918
Waner, Lloyd	1927–1945
Waner, Paul	1926–1945
Ward, John (Monte)	1878–1894
Wheat, Zachariah	1909–1927
Williams, Billy	1959–1976
Williams, Theodore	1939–1960
Wilson, Lewis R. (Hack)	1923–1934
Yastrzemski, Carl	1961–1983
Youngs, Ross (Pep)	1917–1926

1. Negro League player selected by special committee.

Pitchers

Alexander, Grover	1911–1930	Grove, Robert (Lefty)	1925–1941	Palmer, Jim	1965–1984
Bender, Charles (Chief)	1903–1925	Haines, Jesse	1918–1937	Pennock, Herbert	1912–1934
Brown, Mordecai (3–Finger)	1903–1916	Hoyt, Waite	1918–1938	Perry, Gaylord	1962–1983
Chesbro, John	1899–1909	Hubbell, Carl	1928–1943	Plank, Edward	1901–1917
Clarkson, John	1882–1894	Hunter, Jim (Catfish)	1965–1979	Radbourn, Charles (Hoss)	1880–1891
Coveleski, Stanley	1912–1928	Jenkins, Ferguson	1965–1983	Rixey, Eppa	1912–1933
Dean, Jerome (Dizzy)	1930–1947	Johnson, Walter	1907–1927	Roberts, Robert (Robin)	1948–1966
Drysdale, Don	1956–1969	Joss, Adrian	1902–1910	Ruffing, Charles (Red)	1924–1947
Faber, Urban (Red)	1914–1933	Keefe, Timothy	1880–1893	Rusie, Amos	1889–1901
Feller, Robert	1936–1956	Koufax, Sanford (Sandy)	1955–1966	Spahn, Warren	1942–1965
Ferrell, Rick	1929–1947	Lemon, Robert	1946–1958	Vance, Arthur (Dazzy)	1915–1935
Ford, Edward (Whitey)	1950–1967	Lyons, Theodore	1923–1946	Waddell, George	1897–1910
Foster, Andrew (Rube)	1897–1926	Marichal, Juan	1960–1975	Walsh, Edward	1904–1917
Galvin, James (Pud)	1876–1892	Marquard, Richard (Rube)	1908–1924	Welch, Michael (Mickey)	1880–1892
Gibson, Bob	1959–1975	Mathewson, Christopher	1900–1916	Wilhelm, Hoyt	1952–1972
Gomez, Vernon (Lefty)	1930–1943	McGinnity, Joseph	1899–1908	Wynn, Early	1939–1963
Griffith, Clark	1891–1914	Nichols, Charles (Kid)	1890–1906	Young, Denton (Cy)	1890–1911
Grimes, Burleigh	1916–1934	Paige, Leroy (Satchel)[1]	1926–1965		

Officials and Others

Alston, Walter[2]	Cummings, William A.[6]	Johnson, B. Bancroft[3]	Rickey, W. Branch[2][3]
Barrow, Edward[2][3]	Evans, William G.[5][3]	Klem, William[5]	Spalding, Albert G.[5]
Bulkeley, Morgan G.[3]	Frick, Ford C.[7][3]	Landis, Kenesaw M.[7]	Stengel, Charles D.[8]
Cartwright, Alexander[3]	Giles, Warren C.[3]	Lopez, Alfonso R.[8]	Veeck, Bill[3]
Chadwick, Henry[4]	Harridge, William[3]	Mack, Connie[2][3]	Weiss, George M.[3]
Chandler, A.B.[7]	Harris, Stanley R.[8]	MacPhail, Leland S.[3]	Wright, George[6]
Conlan, John[3]	Hubbard, R. Calvin[5]	McCarthy, Joseph V.[2]	Wright, Harry[6][2]
Connolly, Thomas[5]	Higgins, Miller J.[2]	McKechnie, William B.[2]	Yawkey, Thomas[3]

1. Negro league player selected by special committee. 2. Manager. 3. Executive. 4. Writer–statistician. 5. Umpire. 6. Early player. 7. Commissioner. 8. Player–manager.

BASEBALL SUFFERS THROUGH TWO STRIKES AND A LOCKOUT

Major League baseball endured a strike by players for the second time since 1981 in August 1985. Unlike the 1981 strike, which lasted seven weeks and canceled 713 games, this one was ended quickly. The players walked on Aug. 6, and were back on the field three days later.

While in 1981 the major issue was over compensation for free agent signings to the club losing players, the 1985 strike was primarily over the pension fund, and how much of the reported $1.1 billion the owners receive through network television agreements would go into the plan.

The players were seeking an increase of $45 million over the $15 million they'd been receiving under the contract signed in 1981. The owners were adamant in refusing such a large increase.

There were other matters at question, including the issue of arbitration. Under the 1981 agreement, a player with two years of major league service who couldn't come to terms with ownership could take his case to binding arbitration. The owners were looking to increase the number of years vested service required to three years, and pointed to substantial operating losses caused, in part, by large salaries granted by arbitrators and the increasing spiral of free agent salaries.

In the end, the players wound up with approximately $35 million for their pension fund, and the owners got their desired three years for arbitration, albeit the rule did not take effect until 1987.

The games canceled by the strike were rescheduled for later in the season, unlike the 1981 affair when far too many games were lost to be made up.

The 1981 strike settlement had been complicated by the decision to play a split season—awarding divisional championships to the teams in first place before the strike began, and starting a new second season to crown four additional champions. Those eight teams played off in a preliminary series. The survivors played for the league title and the right to move on to the World Series.

With the contract up at the end of the 1989 season, there was serious threat of another strike before the 1990 season. Instead, the owners locked the players out of spring training camps and the regular season was delayed a week in starting. Spring training was reduced to three weeks. A new three-year contract guaranteed baseball labor peace through 1992.

LIFETIME BATTING, PITCHING, AND BASE–RUNNING RECORDS

(An asterisk indicates active player)

Source: The Complete Handbook of Baseball, published and copyrighted by New American Library, New York, N.Y. 10019. All records through 1990 unless noted.

(Records Through 1990)

Hits (3,000 or more)

Pete Rose	4,256
Ty Cobb	4,190
Henry Aaron	3,771
Stan Musial	3,630
Tris Speaker	3,515
Honus Wagner	3,430
Carl Yastrzemski	3,419
Eddie Collins	3,311
Willie Mays	3,283
Nap Lajoie	3,251
Paul Waner	3,152
Rod Carew	3,053
Lou Brock	3,023
Cap Anson	3,022
Al Kaline	3,007
Roberto Clemente	3,000

Earned Run Average

(Minimum 1,500 innings pitched)

Ed Walsh	1.82
Addie Joss	1.88
Joe Wood	2.03
Three Finger Brown	2.06
Christy Mathewson	2.13
Rube Waddell	2.16
Walter Johnson	2.17
Orvie Overall	2.23
Ed Ruelbach	2.28
Jim Scott	2.32
Ed Plank	2.34
Ed Cicotte	2.37
Ed Killian	2.38
Doc White	2.38
Nap Rucker	2.42
Jeff Tesreau	2.43
Chief Bender	2.46
Sam Leaver	2.47

Runs Scored

Ty Cobb	2,245
Henry Aaron	2,174
Babe Ruth	2,174
Pete Rose	2,165
Willie Mays	2,062
Stan Musial	1,949
Lou Gehrig	1,888
Tris Speaker	1,881
Mel Ott	1,859
Frank Robinson	1,829
Eddie Collins	1,816
Carl Yastrzemski	1,816
Ted Williams	1,798
Charlie Gehringer	1,774
Jimmie Foxx	1,751
Honus Wagner	1,740
Willie Keeler	1,720
Cap Anson	1,712
Jesse Burkett	1,708
Billy Hamilton	1,690
Mickey Mantle	1,677
John McPhee	1,674
George Van Haltren	1,650

Strikeouts, Pitching

Nolan Ryan**	5,308
Steve Carlton	4,136
Tom Seaver	3,640
Don Sutton	3,569
Bert Blyleven	3,562
Gaylord Perry	3,534
Walter Johnson	3,509
Phil Niekro	3,342
Ferguson Jenkins	3,192
Bob Gibson	3,117
Jim Bunning	2,855
Mickey Lolich	2,832
Cy Young	2,819
Warren Spahn	2,583
Bob Feller	2,581
Tim Keefe	2,538
Christy Mathewson	2,505

**Active through 1990.

Home Runs (350 or More)

Henry Aaron	755
Babe Ruth	714
Willie Mays	660
Frank Robinson	586
Harmon Killebrew	573
Reggie Jackson	563
Mike Schmidt	548
Mickey Mantle	536
Jimmie Foxx	534
Ted Williams	521
Willie McCovey	521
Eddie Mathews	512
Ernie Banks	512
Mel Ott	511
Lou Gehrig	493
Stan Musial	475
Willie Stargell	475
Carl Yastrzemski	452
Dave Kingman	442
Billy Williams	426
Darrell Evans	414
Duke Snider	406
Al Kaline	399
Johnny Bench	389
Frank Howard	382
Jim Rice	382
Orlando Cepeda	379
Norm Cash	377
Rocky Colavito	374
Tony Perez	371
Gil Hodges	370
Ralph Kiner	369
Joe DiMaggio	361
Lee May	360
Johnny Mize	359
Yogi Berra	358
Dick Allen	351

Shutouts

Walter Johnson	110
Grover Alexander	90
Christy Mathewson	83
Cy Young	77
Ed Plank	64
Warren Spahn	63
Tom Seaver	60
Ed Walsh	58
Don Sutton	58
James Galvin	57
Bob Gibson	56
Steve Carlton	55
Bert Blyleven	55
Jim Palmer	53
Gaylord Perry	53
Juan Marichal	52

Strikeouts, Batting

Reggie Jackson	2,597
Willie Stargell	1,936
Mike Schmidt	1,883
Tony Perez	1,867
Dave Kingman	1,816
Bobby Bonds	1,757
Lou Brock	1,730
Mickey Mantle	1,710
Harmon Killebrew	1,699
Lee May	1,570
Darrell Evans	1,570
Dick Allen	1,566
Willie McCovey	1,550
Frank Robinson	1,532
Willie Mays	1,526

Bases on Balls

Babe Ruth	2,056
Ted Williams	2,019
Carl Yastrzemski	1,844
Mickey Mantle	1,734
Mel Ott	1,708
Eddie Yost	1,614
Darrell Evans	1,605
Stan Musial	1,599
Harmon Killebrew	1,559
Lou Gehrig	1,510
Mike Schmidt	1,507
Willie Mays	1,463
Jimmie Foxx	1,452
Eddie Mathews	1,444
Frank Robinson	1,426
Henry Aaron	1,402

BASEBALL'S PERFECTLY PITCHED GAMES[1]

(no opposing runner reached base)

John Richmond—Worcester vs. Cleveland (NL) June 12, 1880 (1–0)

John M. Ward—Providence vs. Buffalo (NL) June 17, 1880 (5–0)

Cy Young—Boston vs. Philadelphia (AL) May 5, 1904 (3–0)

Addie Joss—Cleveland vs. Chicago (AL) Oct. 2, 1908 (1–0)

Ernest Shore[2]—Boston vs. Washington (AL) June 23, 1917 (4–0)

Charles Robertson—Chicago vs. Detroit (AL) April 30, 1922 (2–0)

Don Larsen[3]—New York (AL) vs. Brooklyn (NL) Oct. 8, 1956 (2–0)

Jim Bunning—Philadelphia vs. New York (NL) June 21, 1964 (6–0)

Sandy Koufax—Los Angeles vs. Chicago (NL) Sept. 9, 1965 (1–0)

Jim Hunter—Oakland vs. Minnesota (AL) May 8, 1968 (4–0)

Len Barker—Cleveland vs. Toronto (AL) May 15, 1981 (3–0)

Mike Witt—California vs. Texas (AL) Sept. 30, 1984 (1–0)

Tom Browning—Cincinnati vs. Los Angeles (NL) Sept. 16, 1988 (1–0)

Dennis Martinez—Montreal vs. Los Angeles (NL) July 28, 1991 (2–0)

1. Harvey Haddix, of Pittsburgh, pitched 12 perfect innings against Milwaukee (NL), May 26, 1959 but lost game in 13th on error and hit. 2. Shore, relief pitcher for Babe Ruth who walked first batter before being ejected by umpire, retired 26 batters who faced him and baserunner was out stealing. 3. World Series.

RECORD OF WORLD SERIES GAMES
(Through 1990)

Source: The Book of Baseball Records, published by Seymour Siwoff, New York City.

Figures in parentheses for winning pitchers (WP) and losing pitchers (LP) indicate the game number in the series.

1903—Boston A.L. 5 (Jimmy Collins); Pittsburgh N.L. 3 (Fred Clarke). WP—Bos.: Dinneen (2, 6, 8), Young (5, 7); Pitts.: Phillippe (1, 3, 4). LP—Bos.: Young (1), Hughes (3), Dinneen (4); Pitts.: Leever (2, 6), Kennedy (5), Phillippe (7, 8).

1904—No series.

1905—New York N.L. 4 (John J. McGraw); Philadelphia A.L. 1 (Connie Mack). WP—N.Y.: Mathewson (1, 3, 5); McGinnity (4); Phila.: Bender (2). LP—N.Y.: McGinnity (1); Phila.: Plank (1, 4), Coakley (3), Bender (5).

1906—Chicago A.L. 4 (Fielder Jones); Chicago N.L. 2 (Frank Chance). WP—Chi.: A.L.: Altrock (1), Walsh (3, 5), White (6); Chi.: N.L.: Reulbach (2), Brown (4). LP—Chi. A.L.: White (2), Altrock. (4); Chi.: N.L.: Brown (1, 6), Pfeister (3, 5).

1907—Chicago N.L. 4 (Frank Chance); Detroit A.L. 0 (Hugh Jennings). First game tied 3–3, 12 innings. WP—Pfeister (2), Reulbach (3), Overall (4), Brown (5). LP—Mullin (2, 5), Siever (3), Donovan (4).

1908—Chicago N.L. 4 (Frank Chance); Detroit A.L. 1 (Hugh Jennings). WP—Chi.: Brown (1, 4), Overall (2, 5); Det.: Mullin (3). LP—Chi.: Pfeister (3); Det.: Summers (1, 4), Donovan (2, 5).

1909—Pittsburgh N.L. 4 (Fred Clarke); Detroit A.L. 3 (Hugh Jennings). WP—Pitts.: Adams (1, 5, 7), Maddox (3); Det.: Donovan (2), Mullin (4, 6). LP—Pitts.: Camnitz (2), Leifield (4), Willis (6); Det.: Mullin (1), Summers (3, 5), Donovan (7).

1910—Philadelphia A.L. 4 (Connie Mack); Chicago N.L. 1 (Frank Chance). WP—Phila.: Bender (1), Coombs (2, 3, 5); Chi.: Brown (4). LP—Phila.: Bender (4); Chi.: Overall (1), Brown (2, 5), McIntyre (3).

1911—Philadelphia A.L. 4 (Connie Mack); New York N.L. 2 (John J. McGraw). WP—Phila.: Plank (2), Coombs (3), Bender (4, 6); N.Y.: Mathewson (1), Crandall (5). LP—Phila.: Bender (1), Plank (5); N.Y.: Marquard (2), Mathewson (3, 4), Ames (6).

1912—Boston A.L. 4 (J. Garland Stahl); New York N.L. 3 (John J. McGraw). Second game tied, 6–6, 11 innings. WP—Bos.: Wood (1, 4, 8), Bedient (5); N.Y.: Marquard (3, 6), Tesreau (7). LP—Bos.: O'Brien (3, 6), Wood (7); N.Y.: Tesreau (1, 4), Mathewson (5, 8).

1913—Philadelphia A.L. 4 (Connie Mack); New York N.L. 1 (John J. McGraw). WP—Phila.: Bender (1, 4), Bush (3), Plank (5); N.Y.: Mathewson (2); LP—Phila.: Plank (2); N.Y.: Marquard (1), Tesreau (3), Demaree (4), Mathewson (5).

1914—Boston N.L. 4 (George Stallings); Philadelphia A.L. 0 (Connie Mack). WP—Rudolph (1, 4), James (2, 3). LP—Bender (1), Plank (2), Bush (3), Shawkey (4).

1915—Boston A.L. 4 (Bill Carrigan); Philadelphia N.L. 1 (Pat Moran). WP—Bos.: Foster (2, 5), Leonard (3), Shore (4); Phila.: Alexander (1). LP—Bos.: Shore (1); Phila.: Mayer (2), Alexander (3), Chalmers (5), Rixey (5).

1916—Boston A.L. 4 (Bill Carrigan); Brooklyn N.L. 1 (Wilbert Robinson). WP—Bos.: Shore (1, 5), Ruth (2), Leonard (4); Bklyn.: Coombs (3). LP—Bos.: Mays (3); Bklyn.: Marquard (1, 4), Smith (2), Pfeffer (5).

1917—Chicago A.L. 4 (Clarence Rowland); New York N.L. 2 (John J. McGraw). WP—Chi.: Cicotte (1), Faber (2, 5, 6); N.Y.: Benton (3), Schupp (4). LP—Chi.: Cicotte (3), Faber (4); N.Y.: Sallee (1, 5), Anderson (2), Benton (6).

1918—Boston A.L. 4 (Ed Barrow); Chicago N.L. 2 (Fred Mitchell). WP—Bos.: Ruth (1, 4), Mays (3, 6); Chi.: Tyler (2), Vaughn (5). LP—Bos.: Bush (2), Jones (5); Chi.: Vaughn (1, 3), Douglas (4), Tyler (6).

1919—Cincinnati N.L. 5 (Pat Moran); Chicago A.L. 3 (William Gleason). WP—Cin.: Ruether (1), Sallee (2), Ring (4), Eller (5, 8); Chi.: Kerr (3, 6), Cicotte (7). LP—Cin.: Fisher (3), Ring (6), Sallee (7); Chi.: Cicotte (1, 4), Williams (2, 5, 8).

1920—Cleveland A.L. 5 (Tris Speaker); Brooklyn N.L. 2 (Wilbert Robinson). WP—Cleve.: Coveleski (1, 4, 7), Bagby (5), Mails (6); Bklyn.: Grimes (2), Smith (3). LP—Cleve.: Bagby (2), Caldwell (3). Bklyn.: Marquard (1), Cadore (4), Grimes (5, 7), Smith (6).

1921—New York N.L. 5 (John J. McGraw); New York A.L. 3 (Miller Huggins). WP—N.Y. N.L.: Barnes (3, 6), Douglas (4, 7), Nehf (8); N.Y. A.L.: Mays (1), Hoyt (2, 5). LP—N.Y. N.L.: Nehf (2, 5), Douglas (1). N.Y. A.L.: Quinn (3), Mays (4, 7), Shawkey (6), Hoyt (8).

1922—New York N.L. 4 (John J. McGraw); New York A.L. 0 (Miller Huggins). Second game tied 3–3, 10 innings. WP—Ryan (1), Scott (3), McQuillan (4), Nehf (5); LP—Bush (1, 5), Hoyt (3), Mays (4).

1923—New York A.L. 4 (Miller Huggins); New York N.L. 2 (John J. McGraw). WP—N.Y. A.L.: Pennock (2, 6), Shawkey (4), Bush (5); N.Y. N.L.: Ryan (1), Nehf (3). LP—N.Y. A.L.: Bush (1), Jones (3); N.Y. N.L.: McQuillan (2), Scott (4), Bentley (5), Nehf (6).

1924—Washington A.L. 4 (Bucky Harris); New York N.L. 3 (John J. McGraw). WP—Wash.: Zachary (2, 6), Mogridge (4), Johnson (7); N.Y.: Nehf (1), McQuillan (3), Bentley (5). LP—Wash.: Johnson (1, 5), Marberry (3); N.Y.: Bentley (2, 7), Barnes (4), Nehf (6).

1925—Pittsburgh N.L. 4 (Bill McKechnie); Washington A.L. 3 (Bucky Harris). WP—Pitts.: Aldridge (2, 5), Kremer (6, 7); Wash.: Johnson (1, 4), Ferguson (3). LP—Pitts.: Meadows (1), Kremer (3), Yde (4); Wash.: Coveleski (2, 5), Ferguson (6), Johnson (7).

1926—St. Louis N.L. 4 (Rogers Hornsby); New York A.L. 3 (Miller Huggins). WP—St. L.: Alexander (2, 6), Haines (3, 7); N.Y.: Pennock (1, 5), Hoyt (4). LP—St. L.: Sherdel (1, 5), Reinhart (4); N.Y.: Shocker (2), Ruether (3), Shawkey (6), Hoyt (7).

1927—New York A.L. 4 (Miller Huggins); Pittsburgh N.L. 0 (Donie Bush). WP—Hoyt (1), Pipgras (2), Pennock (3), Moore (4). LP—Kremer (1), Aldridge (2), Meadows (3), Miljus (4).

1928—New York A.L. 4 (Miller Huggins); St. Louis N.L. 0 (Bill McKechnie). WP—Hoyt (1, 4), Pipgras (2), Zachary (3). LP—Sherdel (1, 4), Alexander (2), Haines (3).

1929—Philadelphia A.L. 4 (Connie Mack); Chicago N.L. 1 (Joe McCarthy). WP—Phila.: Ehmke (1), Earnshaw (2), Rommel (4), Walberg (5); Chi.: Bush (3). LP—Phila.: Earnshaw (3) Chi.: Root (1), Malone (2, 5), Blake (4).

1930—Philadelphia A.L. 4 (Connie Mack); St. Louis N.L. 2 (Gabby Street). WP—Phila.: Grove (1, 5), Earnshaw (2, 6); St. L.: Hallahan (3), Haines (4). LP—Phila.: Walberg (3), Grove (4); St. L.: Grimes (1, 5), Rhem (2), Hallahan (6).

1931—St. Louis N.L. 4 (Gabby Street); Philadelphia A.L. 3 (Connie Mack). WP—St. L.: Hallahan (2, 5), Grimes (3, 7); Phila.: Grove (1, 6), Earnshaw (4). LP—St. L.: Derringer (1, 6), Johnson (4); Phila.: Earnshaw (2, 7), Grove (3), Hoyt (5).

1932—New York A.L. (Joe McCarthy); Chicago N.L. 0 (Charles Grimm). WP—Ruffing (1), Gomez (2), Pipgras (3), Moore (4). LP—Bush (1), Warneke (2), Root (3), May (4).

1933—New York N.L. 4 (Bill Terry); Washington A.L. 1 (Joe Cronin). WP—N.Y.: Hubbell (1, 4), Schumacher (2), Luque (5); Wash.: Whitehill (3). LP—N.Y.: Fitzsimmons (3); Wash.: Stewart (1), Crowder (2), Weaver (4), Russell (5).

1934—St. Louis N.L. 4 (Frank Frisch); Detroit A.L. 3 (Mickey Cochrane). WP—St. L.: J. Dean (1, 7), P. Dean (3, 6); Det.: Rowe (2), Auker (4), Bridges (5). LP—St. L.: W. Walker (2, 4), J. Dean (5); Det.: Crowder (1), Bridges (3), Rowe (6), Auker (7).

1935—Detroit A.L. 4 (Mickey Cochrane); Chicago N.L. 2 (Charles Grimm). WP—Det.: Bridges (2, 6), Rowe (3), Crowder (4); Chi.: Warneke (1, 5); LP—Det.: Rowe (1, 5), Chi.: Root (2), French (3, 6), Carleton (4).

1936—New York A.L. 4 (Joe McCarthy); New York N.L. 2 (Bill Terry). WP—N.Y. A.L.: Gomez (2, 6), Hadley (3), Pearson (4); N.Y. N.L.: Hubbell (1), Schumacher (5); LP—N.Y. A.L.: Ruffing (1), Malone (5); N.Y. N.L.: Schumacher (2), Fitzsimmons (3, 6), Hubbell (4).

1937—New York A.L. 4 (Joe McCarthy); New York N.L. 1 (Bill Terry). WP—N.Y. A.L.: Gomez (1, 5), Ruffing (2), Pearson (3); N.Y. N.L.: Hubbell (4). LP—N.Y. A.L.: Hadley (4); N.Y. N.L.: Hubbell (1), Melton (2, 5), Schumacher (3).

1938—New York A.L. 4 (Joe McCarthy); Chicago N.L. 0 (Gabby Hartnett). WP—Ruffing (1, 4), Gomez (2), Pearson (3) LP—Lee (1, 4), Dean (2), Bryant (3).

1939—New York A.L. 4 (Joe McCarthy); Cincinnati N.L. 0 (Bill McKechnie). WP—Ruffing (1), Pearson (2), Hadley (3), Murphy (4). LP—Derringer (1), Walters (2, 4), Thompson (3).

1940—Cincinnati N.L. 4 (Bill McKechnie); Detroit A.L. 3

(Del Baker). WP—Cin.: Walters (2, 6), Derringer (4, 7); Det.: Newsom (1, 5), Bridges (3). LP—Cin.: Derringer (1), Turner (3), Thompson (5); Det.: Rowe (2, 6), Trout (4), Newsom (7).

1941—New York A.L. 4 (Joe McCarthy); Brooklyn N.L. 1 (Leo Durocher). WP—N.Y.: Ruffing (1), Russo (3), Murphy (4), Bonham (5); Bklyn: Wyatt (2). LP—N.Y.: Chandler (2); Bklyn: Davis (1), Casey (3, 4), Wyatt (5).

1942—St. Louis N.L. 4 (Billy Southworth); New York A.L. 1 (Joe McCarthy). WP—St. L.: Beazley (2, 5), White (3), Lanier (4); N.Y.: Ruffing (1). LP—St. L.: Cooper (1); N.Y.: Bonham (2), Chandler (3), Donald (4), Ruffing (5).

1943—New York A.L. 4 (Joe McCarthy); St. Louis N.L. 1 (Billy Southworth). WP—N.Y.: Chandler (1, 5), Borowy (3), Russo (4); St. L.: Cooper (2). LP—N.Y.: Bonham (2); St. L.: Lanier (1), Brazle (3), Brecheen (4), Cooper (5).

1944—St. Louis N.L. 4 (Billy Southworth); St. Louis A.L. 2 (Luke Sewell). WP—St. L. N.L.: Donnelly (2), Brecheen (4), Cooper (5), Lanier (6); St. L. A.L.: Galehouse (1), Kramer (3). LP—St. L.: Cooper (1), Wilks (3); St. L. A.L.: Muncrief (2), Jakucki (4), Galehouse (5), Potter (6).

1945—Detroit A.L. 4 (Steve O'Neill); Chicago N.L. 3 (Charles Grimm). WP—Det.: Trucks (2), Trout (4), Newhouser (5, 7); Chi.: Borowy (1, 6), Passeau (3). LP—Det.: Newhouser (1), Overmire (3), Trout (6); Chi.: Wyse (2), Prim (4), Borowy (5, 7).

1946—St. Louis N.L. 4 (Eddie Dyer); Boston A.L. 3 (Joe Cronin). WP—St. L.: Brecheen (2, 6, 7), Munger (4); Bos.: Johnson (1), Ferriss (3), Dobson (5). LP—St. L.: Pollet (1), Dickson (3), Brazle (5); Bos.: Harris (2, 6), Hughson (4), Klinger (7).

1947—New York A.L. 4 (Bucky Harris); Brooklyn N.L. 3 (Burt Shotton). WP—N.Y.: Shea (1, 5), Reynolds (2), Page (7); Bklyn.: Casey (3, 4), Branca (6). LP—N.Y.: Newsom (5), Bevens (4), Page (6); Bklyn.: Branca (1), Lombardi (2), Barney (5), Gregg (7).

1948—Cleveland A.L. 4 (Lou Boudreau); Boston N.L. 2 (Billy Southworth). WP—Cleve.: Lemon (2, 6), Bearden (3), Gromek (4); Bos.: Sain (1), Spahn (5). LP—Cleve.: Feller (1, 5); Bos.: Spahn (2), Bickford (3), Sain (4), Voiselle (6).

1949—New York A.L. 4 (Casey Stengel); Brooklyn N.L. 1 (Burt Shotton). WP—N.Y.: Reynolds (1), Page (3), Lopat (4), Raschi (5); Bklyn.: Roe (2). LP—N.Y.: Raschi (2); Bklyn.: Newcombe (1, 4), Branca (3), Barney (5).

1950—New York A.L. 4 (Casey Stengel); Philadelphia N.L. 0 (Eddie Sawyer). WP—Raschi (1), Reynolds (2), Ferrick (3), Ford (4). LP—Konstanty (1), Roberts (2), Meyer (3), Miller (4).

1951—New York A.L. 4 (Casey Stengel); New York N.L. 2 (Leo Durocher). WP—N.Y. A.L.: Lopat (2, 5), Reynolds (4), Raschi (6); N.Y. N.L.: Koslo (1), Hearn (3). LP—N.Y. A.L.: Reynolds (1), Raschi (3); N.Y. N.L.: Jansen (2, 5), Maglie (4), Koslo (6).

1952—New York A.L. 4 (Casey Stengel); Brooklyn N.L. 3 (Chuck Dressen). WP—N.Y.: Raschi (2, 6), Reynolds (4, 7); Bklyn.: Black (1), Roe (3), Erskine (5). LP—N.Y.: Reynolds (1), Lopat (3), Sain (5); Bklyn.: Erskine (2), Black (4, 7), Loes (6).

1953—New York A.L. 4 (Casey Stengel); Brooklyn N.L. 2 (Chuck Dressen). WP—N.Y.: Sain (1), Lopat (2), McDonald (5), Reynolds (6); Bklyn.: Erskine (3), Loes (4). LP—N.Y.: Raschi (3), Ford (4); Bklyn.: Labine (1, 6), Roe (2), Podres (5).

1954—New York N.L. 4 (Leo Durocher); Cleveland A.L. 0 (Al Lopez). WP—Grissom (1), Antonelli (2), Gomez (3), Liddie (4). LP—Lemon (1, 4), Wynn (2), Garcia (3).

1955—Brooklyn N.L. 4 (Walter Alston); New York A.L. 3 (Casey Stengel). WP—Bklyn.: Podres (3, 7), Labine (4), Craig (5); N.Y.: Ford (1, 6), Byrne (2). LP—Bklyn.: Newcombe (1), Loes (2), Spooner (6); N.Y.: Turley (3), Larsen (4), Grim (5), Byrne (7).

1956—New York A.L. 4 (Casey Stengel); Brooklyn N.L. 3 (Walter Alston). WP—N.Y.: Ford (1), Sturdivant (4), Larsen (5), Kucks (7); Bklyn.: Maglie (1), Bessent (2), Labine (6). LP—N.Y.: Ford (1), Morgan (2), Turley (6); Bklyn.: Craig (3), Erskine (4), Maglie (5), Newcombe (7).

1957—Milwaukee N.L. 4 (Fred Haney); New York A.L. 3 (Casey Stengel). WP—Mil.: Burdette (2, 5, 7), Spahn (4); N.Y.: Ford (1), Larsen (3), Turley (6). LP—Mil.: Spahn (1), Buhl (3), Johnson (6); N.Y.: Shantz (2), Grim (4), Ford (5), Larsen (7).

1958—New York A.L. 4 (Casey Stengel); Milwaukee N.L. 3 (Fred Haney). WP—N.Y.: Larsen (3), Turley (5, 7), Duren (6); Mil.: Spahn (1, 4), Burdette (2). LP—N.Y.: Duren (1), Turley (2), Ford (4); Mil.: Rush (3), Burdette (5, 7), Spahn (6).

1959—Los Angeles N.L. 4 (Walter Alston); Chicago A.L. 2 (Al Lopez). WP—L.A.: Podres (2), Drysdale (3), Sherry (4, 6); Chi.: Wynn (1), Shaw (5). LP—L.A.: Craig (1), Koufax (5); Chi.: Shaw (2), Donovan (3), Staley (4), Wynn (6).

1960—Pittsburgh N.L. 4 (Danny Murtaugh); New York A.L. 3 (Casey Stengel). WP—Pitts.: Law (1, 4), Haddix (5, 7); N.Y.: Turley (2), Ford (3, 6). LP—Pitts.: Friend (2, 6), Mizell (3); N.Y.: Ditmar (1, 5), Terry (4, 7).

1961—New York A.L. 4 (Ralph Houk); Cincinnati N.L. 1 (Fred Hutchinson). WP—N.Y.: Ford (1, 4), Arroyo (3), Daley (5); Cin.: Jay (2). LP—N.Y.: Terry (2); Cin.: O'Toole (1, 4), Purkey (3), Jay (5).

1962—New York A.L. 4 (Ralph Houk); San Francisco N.L. 3 (Al Dark). WP—N.Y.: Ford (1), Stafford (3), Terry (5, 7); S.F. Sanford (2), Larsen (4), Pierce (6). LP—N.Y.: Terry (2), Coates (4), Ford (6); S.F.: O'Dell (1), Pierce (3), Sanford (5, 7).

1963—Los Angeles N.L. 4 (Walter Alston); New York A.L. 0 (Ralph Houk). WP—Koufax (1, 4), Podres (3), Drysdale (3). LP—Ford (1, 4), Downing (2), Bouton (3).

1964—St. Louis N.L. 4 (Johnny Keane); New York A.L. 3 (Yogi Berra). WP—St. L.: Sadecki (1), Craig (4), Gibson (5, 7); N.Y.: Stottlemyre (2), Bouton (3, 6). LP—St. L.: Gibson (2), Schultz (3), Simmons (6); N.Y.: Ford (1), Downing (4), Mikkelsen (5), Stottlemyre (7).

1965—Los Angeles N.L. 4 (Walter Alston); Minnesota N.L. 3 (Sam Mele). WP—L.A.: Osteen (3), Drysdale (4), Koufax (5, 7); Minn.: Grant (1, 6), Kaat (2). LP—L.A.: Drysdale (1), Koufax (2), Osteen (6); Minn.: Pascual (3), Grant (4), Kaat (5, 7).

1966—Baltimore A.L. 4 (Hank Bauer); Los Angeles N.L. 0 (Walter Alston). WP—Drabowsky (1), Palmer (2), Bunker (3), McNally (4). LP—Drysdale (1, 4), Koufax (2), Osteen (3).

1967—St. Louis N.L. 4 (Red Schoendienst); Boston A.L. 3 (Dick Williams). WP—St. L.: Gibson (1, 4, 7), Briles (3); Bos.: Lonborg (2, 5); Wyatt (6). LP—St. L.: Hughes (2), Carlton (5), Lamabe (6); Bos.: Santiago (1, 4), Bell (3), Lonborg (7).

1968—Detroit A.L. 4 (Mayo Smith); St. Louis N.L. 3 (Red Schoendienst). WP—Det.: Lolich (2, 5, 7), McLain (6); St. L.: Gibson (1, 4), Washburn (3). LP—Det.: McLain (1, 4), Wilson (3); St. L.: Briles (2), Hoerner (5), Washburn (6), Gibson (7).

1969—New York N.L. 4 (Gil Hodges); Baltimore A.L. 1 (Earl Weaver). WP—N.Y.: Koosman (2, 5), Gentry (3), Seaver (4); Balt.: Cuellar (1). LP—N.Y.: Seaver (1); Balt.: McNally (2), Palmer (3), Hall (4), Watt (5).

1970—Baltimore A.L. 4 (Earl Weaver); Cincinnati N.L. 1 (Sparky Anderson) 1. WP—Balt.: Palmer (1), Phoebus (2), McNally (3), Cuellar (5); Cin.: Carroll (4). LP—Cin.: Nolan (1), Wilcox (3), Cloninger (3), Merritt (5); Balt.: Watt (4).

1971—Pittsburgh N.L. 4 (Danny Murtaugh); Baltimore A.L. 3 (Earl Weaver). WP—Pitts.: Blass (3, 7), Kison (4), Briles (5); Balt.: McNally (1, 6), Palmer (2). LP—Pitts.: Ellis (1), R. Johnson (2), Miller (6); Balt.: Cuellar (3, 7), Watt (4) McNally (5).

1972—Oakland A.L. 4 (Dick Williams); Cincinnati N.L. (Sparky Anderson) 3. WP—Oakland: Holtzman (1), Hunter (2, 7), Fingers (4); Cincinnati: Billingham (3), Grimsley (5, 6). LP—Oakland: Odom (3), Fingers (5), Blue (6); Cincinnati: Nolan (1), Grimsley (2), Carroll (4), Borbon (7).

1973—Oakland A.L. 4 (Dick Williams); New York N.L. 3 (Yogi Berra). WP—Oakland: Holtzman (1, 7), Lindblad (3), Hunter (6). New York: McGraw (2), Matlack (4), Koosman (5). LP—Oakland: Fingers (2), Holtzman (4), Blue (5). New York: Matlack (1, 7) Parker (3), Seaver (6).

1974—Oakland A.L. 4 (Al Dark); Los Angeles N.L. 1 (Walter Alston). WP—Oakland: Fingers (1), Hunter (3), Holtzman (4), Odom (5). Los Angeles: Sutton (2). LP—Oakland: Blue (2), Los Angeles: Messersmith (1, 4), Downing (3), Marshall (5).

1975—Cincinnati N.L. 4 (Sparky Anderson); Boston A.L. 3 (Darrell Johnson). WP—Cincinnati: Eastwick (2, 3), Gullett (5), Carroll (7); Boston: Tiant (1, 4), Wise (6). LP—Cincinnati: Gullett (1), Norman (4), Darcy (6); Boston: Drago (2), Willoughby (3), Cleveland (5), Burton (7).

1976—Cincinnati N.L. 4 (Sparky Anderson); New York A.L. 0 (Billy Martin). WP—Gullett (1), Billingham (2), Zachry (3), Nolan (4). LP—Alexander (1), Hunter (2), Ellis (3), Figueroa (4).

1977—New York A.L. 4 (Billy Martin); Los Angeles N.L. 2

(Tom Lasorda). WP—New York: Lyle (1), Torrez (3, 6), Guidry (4); Los Angeles: Hooton (2), Sutton (5). LP—New York: Hunter (2), Gullett (5); Los Angeles: Rhoden (1), John (3), Rau (4), Hooton (6).

1978—New York A.L. 4 (Bob Lemon), Los Angeles N.L. 2 (Tom Lasorda); WP—New York: Guidry (3), Gossage (2); Beattie (5), Hunter (6); Los Angeles: John (1), Hooton (2). LP—New York: Figueroa (1), Hunter (2); Los Angeles: Sutton (3, 6), Welch (4), Hooton (5).

1979—Pittsburgh N.L. 4 (Chuck Tanner), Baltimore A.L. 3 (Earl Weaver); WP—Pittsburgh: D. Robinson (2), Blyleven (5); Candelaria (6), Jackson (7); Baltimore: Flanagan (1), McGregor (3), Stoddard (4). LP—Pittsburgh: Kison (1), Candelaria (3), Tekulve (4); Baltimore: Stanhouse (2), Flanagan (5), Palmer (6), McGregor (7).

1980—Philadelphia N.L. 4 (Dallas Green), Kansas City A.L. 2 (Jim Frey); WP—Philadelphia: Walk (1), Carlton (2), McGraw (5), Carlton (6); Kansas City: Quisenberry (3), Leonard (4). LP—Philadelphia: McGraw (3), Christenson (4); Kansas City: Leonard (1), Quisenberry (2), Quisenberry (5), Gale (6).

1981—Los Angeles N.L. 4 (Tom Lasorda), New York A.L. 2 (Bob Lemon); WP—Los Angeles: Valenzuela (3), Howe (4), Reuss (5), Hooton (6); New York: Guidry (1), John (2). LP—Los Angeles: Reuss (1), Hooton (2); New York: Frazier (3), Frazier (4), Guidry (5), Frazier (6).

1982—St. Louis N.L. 4 (Whitey Herzog), Milwaukee A.L. 3 (Harvey Kuenn); WP—St. Louis: Sutter (2), Andujar (3), Stuper (6), Andujar (7). Milwaukee: Caldwell (1), Slaton (4), Caldwell (5). LP—St. Louis: Forsch (1), Bair (4), Forsch (5). Milwaukee: McClure (2), Vuckovich (3), Sutton (6), McClure (7).

1983—Baltimore A.L. 4 (Joe Altobelli), Philadelphia N.L. 1 (Paul Owens); WP—Baltimore: Boddicker (2), Palmer (3), Davis (4),

McGregor (5). Philadelphia: Denny (1).

1984—Detroit A.L. 4 (Sparky Anderson), San Diego N.L. 1 (Dick Williams); WP—Det.: Morris (1,4), Wilcox (3), Lopez (5), San Diego: Hawkins (2). LP—Det.: Petry (2), San Diego: Thurmond (1), Lollar (3), Show (4), Hawkins (5).

1985—Kansas City A.L. 4 (Dick Howser), St. Louis N.L. 3 (Whitey Herzog); WP—KC: Saberhagen (3,7) Quisenberry (6), Jackson (5). St. Louis: Tudor (1,4) Dayley (2). LP—KC: Jackson (1), Leibrandt (2), Black (4); St. Louis: Andujar (3), Forsch (5), Worrell (6), Tudor (7).

1986—New York N.L. 4 (Dave Johnson); Boston A.L. (John McNamara) 3 WP—N.Y.—Ojeda (3), Darling (4), Aguilera (6), McDowell (7), Bos: Hurst (1), (5), Crawford (2). LP—N.Y. Darling (1), Gooden (2, 5).

1987—Minnesota, A.L. 4 (Tom Kelly); St. Louis N.L. (Whitey Herzog) 3. WP—Minn. Viola (1, 7), Blyleven (2), Schatzeder (6); St. Louis: Tudor (3), Forsch (4), Cox (5). LP—Minn. Berenguer (3), Viola (4), Blyleven (5); St. Louis: Magrane (1), Cox (2, 7), Tudor (6).

1988—Los Angeles N.L. 4 (Tommy Lasorda); Oakland A.L. (Tony LaRussa) 1. WP—Los Angeles: Hershiser (2, 5), Pena (1), Belcher (4); Oakland: Honeycutt (3). LP—Los Angeles: Howell (3); Oakland: Davis (2, 5), Eckersley (1), Stewart (4).

1989—Oakland, A.L. 4 (Tony LaRussa); San Francisco N.L. 0 (Roger Craig). WP—Oakland: Dave Stewart (1, 3), Mike Moore (2, 4). LP—San Francisco: Scott Garrelts (1, 3), Don Robinson (4), Rick Reuschel (2).

1990—Cincinnati N.L. 4 (Lou Piniella); Oakland A.L. 0 (Tony LaRussa). WP—Cincinnati: Jose Rijo (1, 4), Rob Dibble (2), Tom Browning (3). LP—Oakland: Dave Stewart (1, 4), Dennis Eckersley (2), Mike Moore (3).

Before the World Series

Source: Information Please Sports Almanac, 1990 edition

The NL–American Assn. Series, 1882–90

When the National League met the American League for the first time in the 1903 World Series, it was not the N.L.'s first venture into post–season play.

From 1882–90, the N.L. pennant winner engaged in a championship series with the champion of the American Association. The Nationals won four of the eight series, lost once, and tied three times.

Year	Champion	Loser	Series	Year	Champion	Loser	Series
1882	Chicago (NL) &			1886	St. Louis (AA)	Chicago (NL)	4–2
	Cincinnati (AA)	—	1–1	1887	Detroit (NL)	St. Louis (AA)	10–5
1883	No series			1888	New York (NL)	St. Louis (AA)	6–4
1884	Providence (NL)	New York (AA)	3–0	1889	New York (NL)	Brooklyn (AA)	6–3
1885	Chicago (NL) &			1890	Brooklyn (NL) &		
	St. Louis (AA)	—	3–3–1		Louisville (AA)	—	3–3–1

Early NL and AL Pennant Winners

The National League had been around 27 years before the 1903 World Series. The AL, however, was only in its third season when the two leagues met. The following lists account for the pennant winners in those pre–World Series years and in 1904 when the NL champion New York Giants refused to play Boston.

NL Pennant Winners, 1876–1902, '04

Year	Winner	Manager	Year	Winner	Manager	Year	Winner	Manager
1876	Chicago	Al Spalding	1885	Chicago	Cap Anson	1895	Baltimore	Ned Hanlon
1877	Boston	Harry Wright	1886	Chicago	Cap Anson	1896	Baltimore	Ned Hanlon
1878	Boston	Harry Wright	1887	Detroit	Bill Watkins	1897	Boston	Frank Selee
1879	Providence	George Wright	1888	New York	Jim Mutrie	1898	Boston	Frank Selee
1880	Chicago	Cap Anson	1889	New York	Jim Mutrie	1899	Brooklyn	Ned Hanlon
1881	Chicago	Cap Anson	1890	Brooklyn	Bill McGunnigle	1900	Brooklyn	Ned Hanlon
1882	Chicago	Cap Anson	1891	Boston	Frank Selee	1901	Pittsburgh	Fred Clarke
1883	Boston	John Morrill	1892	Boston	Frank Selee	1902	Pittsburgh	Fred Clarke
1884	Providence	Frank Bancroft	1893	Boston	Frank Selee	1904	New York	John McGraw
			1894	Baltimore	Ned Hanlon			

AL Pennant Winners, 1901–02, '04

Year	Winner	Manager	Year	Winner	Manager	Year	Winner	Manager
1901	Chicago	Clark Griffith	1902	Philadelphia	Connie Mack	1904	Boston	Jimmy Collins

WORLD SERIES CLUB STANDING
(Through 1990)

	Series	Won	Lost	Pct.		Series	Won	Lost	Pct.
Pittsburgh (N)	7	5	2	.714	Kansas City (A)	2	1	1	.500
New York (A)	33	22	11	.667	Detroit (A)	9	4	5	.444
Oakland (A)	6	4	2	.667	New York (N–Giants)	14	5	9	.357
Cleveland (A)	3	2	1	.667	Washington (A)	3	1	2	.333
New York (N–Mets)	3	2	1	.667	Philadelphia (N)	4	1	3	.250
Philadelphia (A)	8	5	3	.625	Chicago (N)	10	2	8	.200
St. Louis (N)	15	9	6	.600	Brooklyn (N)	9	1	8	.111
Boston (A)	9	5	4	.550	St. Louis (A)	1	0	1	.000
Los Angeles (N)	9	5	4	.550	San Francisco (N)	2	0	2	.000
Cincinnati (N)	9	5	4	.550	Milwaukee (A)	1	0	1	.000
Milwaukee (N)	2	1	1	.500	San Diego (N)	1	0	1	.000
Boston (N)	2	1	1	.500					
Chicago (A)	4	2	2	.500	**Recapitulation**				
Baltimore (A)	6	3	3	.500					Won
Minnesota (A)	2	1	1	.500	American League				49
					National League				36

LIFETIME WORLD SERIES RECORDS
(Through 1990)

Most hits—71, Yogi Berra, New York A.L., 1947, 1949–53, 1955–58, 1960–63.

Most runs—42, Mickey Mantle, New York A.L., 1951–53, 1955–58, 1960–64.

Most runs batted in—40, Mickey Mantle, New York A.L., 1951–53, 1955–58, 1960–64.

Most home runs—18, Mickey Mantle, New York A.L., 1951–53, 1955–58, 1960–64.

Most bases on balls—43, Mickey Mantle, New York A.L., 1951–53, 1955–58, 1960–64.

Most strikeouts—54, Mickey Mantle, New York A.L., 1951–53, 1955–58, 1960–64.

Most stolen bases—14, Eddie Collins, Philadelphia A.L. 1910–11, 13–14; Chicago A.L., 1917, 1919. Lou Brock, St. Louis N.L., 1964, 67–68.

Most victories, pitcher—10, Whitey Ford, New York A.L., 1950, 1953, 1955–58, 1960–64.

Most times member of winning team—10, Yogi Berra, New York A.L., 1947, 1949–53, 1956, 1958, 1961–62.

Most victories, no defeats—6, Vernon Gomez, New York A.L., 1932, 1936(2), 1937(2), 1938.

Most shutouts—4, Christy Mathewson, New York N.L., 1905 (3), 1913.

Most innings pitched—146, Whitey Ford, New York A.L., 1950, 1953, 1955–58, 1960–64.

Most consecutive scoreless innings—33 2/3, Whitey Ford, New York A.L., 1960 (18), 1961 (14), 1962 (1 2/3).

Most strikeouts by pitcher—94, Whitey Ford, New York A.L., 1950, 1953, 1955–58, 1960–64.

SINGLE GAME AND SINGLE SERIES RECORDS
(Through 1990)

Most hits game—5, Paul Molitor, Milwaukee A.L., first game vs. St. Louis, N.L., 1982.

Most 4–hit games, series—2, Robin Yount, Milwaukee A.L., first and fifth games vs. St. Louis N.L., 1982.

Most hits inning—2, held by many players.

Most hits series—13 (7 games) Bobby Richardson, New York A.L., 1964; Lou Brock, St. Louis N.L., 1968; 12 (6 games) Billy Martin, New York A.L., 1953; 12 (8 games) Buck Herzog, New York N.L., 1912; Joe Jackson, Chicago A.L., 1919; 10 (4 games) Babe Ruth, New York A.L., 1928; 9 (5 games) held by 8 players.

Most home runs, series—5 (6 games) Reggie Jackson, New York A.L., 1977; 4 (7 games) Babe Ruth, New York A.L., 1926; Duke Snider, Brooklyn N.L., 1952, 1955; Hank Bauer, New York A.L., 1958; Gene Tenace, Oakland A.L., 1972; 4 (4 games) Lou Gehrig, New York A.L., 1928; 3 (6 games) Babe Ruth, New York A.L., 1923; Ted Kluszewski, Chicago A.L., 1959; 3 (5 games) Donn Clendenon, New York Mets N.L., 1969.

Most home runs, game—3, Babe Ruth, New York A.L., 1926 and 1928; Reggie Jackson, New York A.L., 1977.

Most strikeouts, series—12 (6 games) Willie Wilson, Kansas City A.L., 1980; 11 (7 games) Ed Mathews, Milwaukee N.L., 1958; Wayne Garrett, New York N.L., 1973; 10 (8 games) George Kelly, New York N.L., 1921; 9 (6 games) Jim Bottom-

ley, St. Louis N.L., 1930; 9 (5 games) Carmelo Martinez, San Diego, N.L., 1984; Duke Snider, Brooklyn N.L., 1949; 7 (4 games) Bob Muesel, New York N.L., 1927.

Most stolen bases, game—3, Honus Wagner, Pittsburgh N.L., 1909; Willie Davis, Los Angeles N.L., 1965; Lou Brock, St. Louis N.L., 1967 and 1968.

Most strikeouts by pitcher, game—17, Bob Gibson, St. Louis N.L. 1968.

Most strikeouts by pitcher in succession—6, Horace Eller, Cincinnati N.L., 1919; Moe Drabowsky, Baltimore A.L., 1966.

Most strikeouts by pitcher, series—35 (7 games) Bob Gibson, St. Louis N.L., 1968; 28 (8 games) Bill Dinneen, Boston A.L., 1903; 23 (4 games) Sandy Koufax, Los Angeles, 1963; 20 (6 games) Chief Bender, Philadelphia A.L., 1911; 18 (5 games) Christy Mathewson, New York N.L., 1905.

Most bases on balls, series—11 (7 games) Babe Ruth, New York A.L., 1926; Gene Tenace, Oakland A.L., 1973; 9 (6 games) Willie Randolph, New York A.L., 1981; 7 (5 games) James Sheckard, Chicago N.L., 1910; Mickey Cochrane, Philadelphia A.L., 1929; Joe Gordon, New York A.L., 1941; 7 (4 games) Hank Thompson, New York N.L., 1954.

Most consecutive scoreless innings one series—27, Christy Mathewson, New York N.L., 1905.

AMERICAN LEAGUE HOME RUN CHAMPIONS

Year	Player, team	No.	Year	Player, team	No.	Year	Player, team	No.
1901	Nap Lajoie, Phila.	13	1933	Jimmy Foxx, Phila.	48	1966	Frank Robinson, Balt.	49
1902	Ralph Seybold, Phila.	16	1934	Lou Gehrig, N.Y.	49	1967	Carl Yastrzemski, Bost., and	
1903	Buck Freeman, Bost.	13	1935	Jimmy Foxx, Phila., and			Harmon Killebrew, Minn.	44
1904	Harry Davis, Phila.	10		Hank Greenberg, Det.	36	1968	Frank Howard, Wash.	44
1905	Harry Davis, Phila.	8	1936	Lou Gehrig, N.Y.	49	1969	Harmon Killebrew, Minn.	49
1906	Harry Davis, Phila.	12	1937	Joe DiMaggio, N.Y.	46	1970	Frank Howard, Wash.	44
1907	Harry Davis, Phila.	8	1938	Hank Greenberg, Det.	58	1971	Bill Melton, Chicago	33
1908	Sam Crawford, Det.	7	1939	Jimmy Foxx, Bost.	35	1972	Dick Allen, Chicago	37
1909	Ty Cobb, Det.	9	1940	Hank Greenberg, Det.	41	1973	Reggie Jackson, Oak.	32
1910	J. Garland Stahl, Bost.	10	1941	Ted Williams, Bost.	37	1974	Dick Allen, Chicago	32
1911	Franklin Baker, Phila.	9	1942	Ted Williams, Bost.	36	1975	Reggie Jackson, Oak., and	
1912	Franklin Baker, Phila.	10	1943	Rudy York, Det.	34		George Scott, Mil.	36
1913	Franklin Baker, Phila.	12	1944	Nick Etten, N.Y.	22	1976	Graig Nettles, N.Y.	32
1914	Franklin Baker, Phila., and		1945	Vern Stephens, St. L.	24	1977	Jim Rice, Boston	39
	Sam Crawford, Det.	8	1946	Hank Greenberg, Det.	44	1978	Jim Rice, Boston	46
1915	Robert Roth, Chi.–Cleve.	7	1947	Ted Williams, Bost.	32	1979	Gorman Thomas, Milwaukee	45
1916	Wally Pipp, N.Y.	12	1948	Joe DiMaggio, N.Y.	39	1980	Reggie Jackson, N.Y., and	
1917	Wally Pipp, N.Y.	9	1949	Ted Williams, Bost.	43		Ben Oglivie, Mil.	41
1918	Babe Ruth, Bost., and		1950	Al Rosen, Cleve.	37	1981*	Tony Armas, Oak., Dwight	
	Clarence Walker, Phila.	11	1951	Gus Zernial, Chi.–Phila.	33		Evans, Bost., Bobby Grich,	
1919	Babe Ruth, Bost.	29	1952	Larry Doby, Cleve.	32		Calif., and Eddie	
1920	Babe Ruth, N.Y.	54	1953	Al Rosen, Cleve.	43		Murray, Balt. (tie)	22
1921	Babe Ruth, N.Y.	59	1954	Larry Doby, Cleve.	32	1982	Gorman Thomas, Mil., and	
1922	Ken Williams, St. L.	39	1955	Mickey Mantle, N.Y.	37		Reggie Jackson, Calif.	39
1923	Babe Ruth, N.Y.	41	1956	Mickey Mantle, N.Y.	52	1983	Jim Rice, Boston	39
1924	Babe Ruth, N.Y.	46	1957	Roy Sievers, Wash.	42	1984	Tony Armas, Boston	43
1925	Bob Meusel, N.Y.	33	1958	Mickey Mantle, N.Y.	42	1985	Darrell Evans, Detroit	40
1926	Babe Ruth, N.Y.	47	1959	Rocky Colavito, Cleve., and		1986	Jesse Barfield, Toronto	40
1927	Babe Ruth, N.Y.	60		Harmon Killebrew, Wash.	42	1987	Mark McGwire, Oakland	49
1928	Babe Ruth, N.Y.	54	1960	Mickey Mantle, N.Y.	40	1988	Jose Canseco, Oakland	42
1929	Babe Ruth, N.Y.	46	1961	Roger Maris, N.Y.	61	1989	Fred McGriff, Toronto	36
1930	Babe Ruth, N.Y.	49	1962	Harmon Killebrew, Minn.	48	1990	Cecil Fielder, Detroit	51
1931	Lou Gehrig, N.Y., and		1963	Harmon Killebrew, Minn.	45	1991	Jose Canseco, Oakland	
	Babe Ruth, N.Y.	46	1964	Harmon Killebrew, Minn.	49		Cecil Fielder, Detroit (tie)	44
1932	Jimmy Foxx, Phila.	58	1965	Tony Conigliaro, Bost.	32			

AMERICAN LEAGUE BATTING CHAMPIONS

Year	Player, team	Avg	Year	Player, team	Avg	Year	Player, team	Avg
1901	Nap Lajoie, Phila.	.422	1932	Dale Alexander, Det.–Bost.	.367	1962	Pete Runnels, Bost.	.326
1902	Ed Delahanty, Wash.	.376	1933	Jimmy Foxx, Phila.	.356	1963	Carl Yastrzemski, Bost.	.321
1903	Nap Lajoie, Cleve.	.355	1934	Lou Gehrig, N.Y.	.363	1964	Tony Oliva, Minn.	.323
1904	Nap Lajoie, Cleve.	.381	1935	Buddy Myer, Wash.	.349	1965	Tony Oliva, Minn.	.321
1905	Elmer Flick, Cleve.	.306	1936	Luke Appling, Chi.	.388	1966	Frank Robinson, Balt.	.316
1906	George Stone, St. L.	.358	1937	Charley Gehringer, Det.	.371	1967	Carl Yastrzemski, Bost.	.326
1907	Ty Cobb, Det.	.350	1938	Jimmy Foxx, Bost.	.349	1968	Carl Yastrzemski, Bost.	.301
1908	Ty Cobb, Det.	.324	1939	Joe DiMaggio, N.Y.	.381	1969	Rod Carew, Minn.	.332
1909	Ty Cobb, Det.	.377	1940	Joe DiMaggio, N.Y.	.352	1970	Alex Johnson, Calif.	.329
1910	Ty Cobb, Det.	.385	1941	Ted Williams, Bost.	.406	1971	Tony Oliva, Minn.	.337
1911	Ty Cobb, Det.	.420	1942	Ted Williams, Bost.	.356	1972	Rod Carew, Minn.	.318
1912	Ty Cobb, Det.	.410	1943	Luke Appling, Chi.	.328	1973	Rod Carew, Minn.	.350
1913	Ty Cobb, Det.	.390	1944	Lou Boudreau, Cleve.	.327	1974	Rod Carew, Minn.	.364
1914	Ty Cobb, Det.	.368	1945	George Sternweiss, N.Y.	.309	1975	Rod Carew, Minn.	.359
1915	Ty Cobb, Det.	.369	1946	Mickey Vernon, Wash.	.353	1976	George Brett, Kansas City	.333
1916	Tris Speaker, Cleve.	.386	1947	Ted Williams, Bost.	.343	1977	Rod Carew, Minn.	.388
1917	Ty Cobb, Det.	.383	1948	Ted Williams, Bost.	.369	1978	Rod Carew, Minn.	.333
1918	Ty Cobb, Det.	.382	1949	George Kell, Det.	.343	1979	Fred Lynn, Boston	.333
1919	Ty Cobb, Det.	.384	1950	Billy Goodman, Bost.	.354	1980	George Brett, Kansas City	.390
1920	George Sisler, St. L.	.407	1951	Ferris Fain, Phila.	.344	1981*	Carney Lansford, Bost.	.336
1921	Harry Heilmann, Det.	.394	1952	Ferris Fain, Phila.	.327	1982	Willie Wilson, Kansas City	.332
1922	George Sisler, St. L.	.420	1953	Mickey Vernon, Wash.	.337	1983	Wade Boggs, Boston	.361
1923	Harry Heilmann, Det.	.403	1954	Bobby Avila, Cleve.	.341	1984	Don Mattingly, New York	.343
1924	Babe Ruth, N.Y.	.378	1955	Al Kaline, Det.	.340	1985	Wade Boggs, Boston	.368
1925	Harry Heilmann, Det.	.393	1956	Mickey Mantle, N.Y.	.353	1986	Wade Boggs, Boston	.357
1926	Heinie Manush, Det.	.378	1957	Ted Williams, Bost.	.388	1987	Wade Boggs, Boston	.363
1927	Harry Heilmann, Det.	.398	1958	Ted Williams, Bost.	.328	1988	Wade Boggs, Boston	.366
1928	Goose Goslin, Wash.	.379	1959	Harvey Kuenn, Det.	.353	1989	Kirby Puckett, Minnesota	.339
1929	Lew Fonseca, Cleve.	.369	1960	Pete Runnels, Bost.	.320	1990	George Brett, Kansas City	.328
1930	Al Simmons, Phila.	.381	1961	Norman Cash, Det.	.361	1991	Julio Franco, Texas	.341
1931	Al Simmons, Phila.	.390						

*Split season because of player strike.

NATIONAL LEAGUE HOME RUN CHAMPIONS

Year	Player, team	No.
1876	George Hall, Phila. Athletics	5
1877	George Shaffer, Louisville	3
1878	Paul Hines, Providence	4
1879	Charles Jones, Bost.	9
1880	James O'Rourke, Bost., and Harry Stovey, Worcester	6
1881	Dan Brouthers, Buffalo	8
1882	George Wood, Det.	7
1883	William Ewing, N.Y.	10
1884	Ed Williamson, Chi.	27
1885	Abner Dalrymple, Chi.	11
1886	Arthur Richardson, Det.	11
1887	Roger Connor, N.Y., and Wm. O'Brien, Wash.	17
1888	Roger Connor, N.Y.	14
1889	Sam Thompson, Phila.	20
1890	Tom Burns, Bklyn, and Mike Tiernan, N.Y.	13
1891	Harry Stovey, Bost., and Mike Tiernan, N.Y.	16
1892	Jim Holliday, Cin.	13
1893	Ed Delahanty, Phila.	19
1894	Hugh Duffy, Bost., and Robert Lowe, Bost.	18
1895	Bill Joyce, Wash.	17
1896	Ed Delahanty, Phila., and Sam Thompson, Phila.	13
1897	Nap Lajoie, Phila.	10
1898	Jim Colins, Bost.	14
1899	John Freeman, Wash.	25
1900	Herman Long, Bost.	12
1901	Sam Crawford, Con.	16
1902	Tom Leach, Pitts.	6
1903	James Sheckard, Bklyn.	9
1904	Harry Lumley, Bklyn.	9
1905	Fred Odwell, Cin.	9
1906	Tim Jordan, Bklyn	12
1907	David Brain, Bost.	10
1908	Tim Jordan, Bklyn.	12
1909	John Murray, N.Y.	7
1910	Fred Beck, Bost., and Frank Schulte, Chi.	10
1911	Frank Schulte, Chi.	21
1912	Henry Zimmerman, Chi.	14
1913	Cliff Cravath, Phila.	19
1914	Cliff Cravath, Phila.	19
1915	Cliff Cravath, Phila.	24
1916	Davis Robertson, N.Y., and Fred Williams, Chi.	12
1917	Davis Robertson, N.Y., and Cliff Cravath, Phila.	12
1918	Cliff Cravath, Phila.	8
1919	Cliff Cravath, Phila.	12
1920	Cy Williams, Phila.	15
1921	George Kelly, N.Y.	23
1922	Rogers Hornsby, St. L.	42
1923	Cy Williams, Phila.	41
1924	Jacques Fournier, Bklyn.	27
1925	Rogers Hornsby, St. L.	39
1926	Hack Wilson, Chi.	21
1927	Hack Wilson, Chi., and Cy Williams, Phila.	30
1928	Hack Wilson, Chi., and Jim Bottomley, St. L.	31
1929	Chuck Klein, Phila.	43
1930	Hack Wilson, Chi.	56
1931	Chuck Klein, Phila.	31
1932	Chuck Klein, Phila., and Mel Ott, N.Y.	38
1933	Chuck Klein, Phila.	28
1934	Mel Ott, N.Y., and Rip Collins, St. L.	35
1935	Wally Berger, Bost.	34
1936	Mel Ott, N.Y.	33
1937	Mel Ott, N.Y., and Joe Medwick, St. L.	31
1938	Mel Ott, N.Y.	36
1939	John Mize, St. L.	28
1940	John Mize, St. L.	43
1941	Dolph Camilli, Bklyn.	34
1942	Mel Ott, N.Y.	30
1943	Bill Nicholson, Chi.	29
1944	Bill Nicholson, Chi.	33
1945	Tommy Holmes, Bost.	28
1946	Ralph Kiner, Pitts.	23
1947	Ralph Kiner, Pitts., and John Mize, N.Y.	51
1948	Ralph Kiner, Pitts., and John Mize, N.Y.	40
1949	Ralph Kiner, Pitts.	54
1950	Ralph Kiner, Pitts.	47
1951	Ralph Kiner, Pitts.	42
1952	Ralph Kiner, Pitts., and Hank Sauer, Chi.	37
1953	Ed Mathews, Mil.	47
1954	Ted Kluszewski, Cin.	49
1955	Willie Mays, N.Y.	51
1956	Duke Snider, Bklyn.	43
1957	Henry Aaron, Mil.	44
1958	Ernie Banks, Chi.	47
1959	Ed Mathews, Mil.	46
1960	Ernie Banks, Chi.	41
1961	Orlando Cepeda, San Fran.	46
1962	Willie Mays, San Fran.	49
1963	Henry Aaron, Mil., and Willie McCovey, San Fran.	44
1964	Willie Mays, San Fran.	47
1965	Willie Mays, San Fran.	52
1966	Henry Aaron, Atlanta	44
1967	Henry Aaron, Atlanta	39
1968	Willie McCovey, San Fran.	36
1969	Willie McCovey, San Fran.	45
1970	Johnny Bench, Cin.	45
1971	Willie Stargell, Pitts.	48
1972	Johnny Bench, Cin.	40
1973	Willie Stargell, Pitts.	44
1974	Mike Schmidt, Phila.	36
1975	Mike Schmidt, Phila.	38
1976	Mike Schmidt, Phila.	38
1977	George Foster, Cin.	52
1978	George Foster, Cin.	40
1979	Dave Kingman, Chicago	48
1980	Mike Schmidt, Phila.	48
1981*	Mike Schmidt, Phila.	31
1982	Dave Kingman, N.Y.	37
1983	Mike Schmidt, Phila.	40
1984	Mike Schmidt, Phila. and Dale Murphy, Atlanta	36
1985	Dale Murphy, Atlanta	37
1986	Mike Schmidt, Phila.	37
1987	Andre Dawson, Chicago	49
1988	Darryl Strawberry, N.Y.	39
1989	Kevin Mitchell, San Francisco	47
1990	Ryne Sandberg, Chicago	40
1991	Howard Johnson, N.Y.	38

*Split season because of player strike.

NATIONAL LEAGUE BATTING CHAMPIONS

Year	Player, Team	Avg
1876	Roscoe Barnes, Chicago	.404
1877	Jim White, Boston	.385
1878	Abner Dalrymple, Mil.	.356
1879	Cap Anson, Chicago	.407
1880	George Gore, Chicago	.365
1881	Cap Anson, Chicago	.399
1882	Dan Brouthers, Buffalo	.367
1883	Dan Brouthers, Buffalo	.371
1884	James O'Rourke, Buffalo	.350
1885	Roger Connor, N.Y.	.371
1886	King Kelly, Chicago	.388
1887	Cap Anson, Chicago	.421
1888	Cap Anson, Chicago	.343
1889	Dan Brouthers, Boston	.373
1890	John Glasscock, N.Y.	.336
1891	William Hamilton, Phila.	.338
1892	Dan Brouthers, Bklyn., and Clarence Childs, Cleve.	.335
1893	Hugh Duffy, Boston	.378
1894	Hugh Duffy, Boston	.438
1895	Jesse Burkett, Cleveland	.423
1896	Jesse Burkett, Cleveland	.410
1897	Willie Keeler, Baltimore	.432
1898	Willie Keeler, Baltimore	.379
1899	Ed Delahanty, Phila.	.408
1900	Honus Wagner, Pittsburgh	.381
1901	Jesse Burkett, St. Louis	.382
1902	Clarence Beaumont, Pitts.	.357
1903	Honus Wagner, Pittsburgh	.355
1904	Honus Wagner, Pittsburgh	.349
1905	Cy Seymour, Cincinnati	.377
1906	Honus Wagner, Pittsburgh	.339
1907	Honus Wagner, Pittsburgh	.350
1908	Honus Wagner, Pittsburgh	.354
1909	Honus Wagner, Pittsburgh	.339
1910	Sherwood Magee, Phila.	.331
1911	Honus Wagner, Pittsburgh	.334
1912	Henry Zimmerman, Chicago	.372
1913	Jake Daubert, Brooklyn	.350
1914	Jake Daubert, Brooklyn	.329
1915	Larry Doyle, New York	.320
1916	Hal Chase, Cincinnati	.339
1917	Edd Roush, Cincinnati	.341
1918	Zack Wheat, Brooklyn	.335
1919	Edd Roush, Cincinnati	.321
1920	Rogers Hornsby, St. Louis	.370
1921	Rogers Hornsby, St. Louis	.397
1922	Rogers Hornsby, St. Louis	.401
1923	Rogers Hornsby, St. Louis	.384
1924	Rogers Hornsby, St. Louis	.424
1925	Rogers Hornsby, St. Louis	.403
1926	Gene Hargrave, Cincinnati	.353
1927	Paul Waner, Pittsburgh	.380
1928	Rogers Hornsby, Boston	.387
1929	Lefty O'Doul, Phila.	.398
1930	Bill Terry, N.Y.	.401
1931	Chick Hafey, St. Louis	.349
1932	Lefty O'Doul, Brooklyn	.368
1933	Chuck Klein, Phila.	.368

960 *Sports—Baseball*

Year	Player, team	Avg	Year	Player, team	Avg	Year	Player, team	Avg
1934	Paul Waner, Pittsburgh	.362	1954	Willie Mays, N. Y.	.345	1973	Pete Rose, Cincinnati	.338
1935	Arky Vaughan, Pittsburgh	.385	1955	Richie Ashburn, Phila.	.338	1974	Ralph Garr, Atlanta	.353
1936	Paul Waner, Pittsburgh	.373	1956	Henry Aaron, Mil.	.328	1975	Bill Madlock, Chicago	.354
1937	Joe Medwick, St. Louis	.374	1957	Stan Musial, St. Louis	.351	1976	Bill Madlock, Chicago	.339
1938	Ernie Lombardi, Cin.	.342	1958	Richie Ashburn, Phila.	.350	1977	Dave Parker, Pittsburgh	.338
1939	John Mize, St. Louis	.349	1959	Henry Aaron, Mil.	.355	1978	Dave Parker, Pittsburgh	.334
1940	Debs Garms, Pittsburgh	.355	1960	Dick Groat, Pittsburgh	.325	1979	Keith Hernandez, St. Louis	.344
1941	Pete Reiser, Brooklyn	.343	1961	Roberto Clemente, Pitts.	.351	1980	Bill Buckner, Chicago	.324
1942	Ernie Lombardi, Boston	.330	1962	Tommy Davis, L. A.	.346	1981*	Bill Madlock, Pittsburgh	.341
1943	Stan Musial, St. Louis	.357	1963	Tommy Davis, L. A.	.326	1982	Al Oliver, Montreal	.331
1944	Dixie Walker, Brooklyn	.357	1964	Roberto Clemente, Pitts.	.339	1983	Bill Madlock, Pittsburgh	.323
1945	Phil Cavarretta, Chicago	.355	1965	Roberto Clemente, Pitts.	.329	1984	Tony Gwynn, San Diego	.351
1946	Stan Musial, St. Louis	.365	1966	Matty Alou, Pittsburgh	.342	1985	Willie McGee, St. Louis	.353
1947	Harry Walker, St. L.–Phila.	.363	1967	Roberto Clemente, Pitts.	.357	1986	Tim Raines, Montreal	.334
1948	Stan Musial, St. Louis	.376	1968	Pete Rose, Cincinnati	.335	1987	Tony Gwynn, San Diego	.370
1949	Jackie Robinson, Brooklyn	.342	1969	Pete Rose, Cincinnati	.348	1988	Tony Gwynn, San Diego	.313
1950	Stan Musial, St. Louis	.346	1970	Rico Carty, Atlanta	.366	1989	Tony Gwynn, San Diego	.336
1951	Stan Musial, St. Louis	.355	1971	Joe Torre, St. Louis	.363	1990	Willie McGee, St. Louis	.335
1952	Stan Musial, St. Louis	.336	1972	Billy Williams, Chicago	.333	1991	Terry Pendleton, Atlanta	.319
1953	Carl Furillo, Brooklyn	.344						

AMERICAN LEAGUE PENNANT WINNERS

Year	Club	Manager	Won	Lost	Pct
1901	Chicago	Clark C. Griffith	83	53	.610
1902	Philadelphia	Connie Mack	83	53	.610
1903[1]	Boston	Jimmy Collins	91	47	.659
1904[2]	Boston	Jimmy Collins	95	59	.617
1905	Philadelphia	Connie Mack	92	56	.622
1906[1]	Chicago	Fielder A. Jones	93	58	.616
1907	Detroit	Hugh A. Jennings	92	58	.613
1908	Detroit	Hugh A. Jennings	90	63	.588
1909	Detroit	Hugh A. Jennings	98	54	.645
1910[1]	Philadelphia	Connie Mack	102	48	.680
1911[1]	Philadelphia	Connie Mack	101	50	.669
1912[1]	Boston	J. Garland Stahl	105	47	.691
1913[1]	Philadelphia	Connie Mack	96	57	.627
1914	Philadelphia	Connie Mack	99	53	.651
1915[1]	Boston	William F. Carrigan	101	50	.669
1916[1]	Boston	William F. Carrigan	91	63	.591
1917[1]	Chicago	Clarence H. Rowland	100	54	.649
1918[1]	Boston	Ed Barrow	75	51	.595
1919	Chicago	William Gleason	88	52	.629
1920[1]	Cleveland	Tris Speaker	98	56	.636
1921	New York	Miller J. Huggins	98	55	.641
1922	New York	Miller J. Huggins	94	60	.610
1923[1]	New York	Miller J. Huggins	98	54	.645
1924[1]	Washington	Stanley R. Harris	92	62	.597
1925	Washington	Stanley R. Harris	96	55	.636
1926	New York	Miller J. Huggins	91	63	.591
1927[1]	New York	Miller J. Huggins	110	44	.714
1928[1]	New York	Miller J. Huggins	101	53	.656
1929[1]	Philadelphia	Connie Mack	104	46	.693
1930[1]	Philadelphia	Connie Mack	102	52	.662
1931	Philadelphia	Connie Mack	107	45	.704
1932[1]	New York	Joseph V. McCarthy	107	47	.695
1933	Washington	Joseph E. Cronin	99	53	.651
1934	Detroit	Gordon Cochrane	101	53	.656
1935[1]	Detroit	Gordon Cochrane	93	58	.616
1936[1]	New York	Joseph V. McCarthy	102	51	.667
1937[1]	New York	Joseph V. McCarthy	102	52	.662
1938[1]	New York	Joseph V. McCarthy	99	53	.651
1939[1]	New York	Joseph V. McCarthy	106	45	.702
1940	Detroit	Delmar D. Baker	90	64	.584
1941[1]	New York	Joseph V. McCarthy	101	53	.656
1942	New York	Joseph V. McCarthy	103	51	.669
1943[1]	New York	Joseph V. McCarthy	98	56	.636
1944	St. Louis	Luke Sewell	89	65	.578
1945[1]	Detroit	Steve O'Neill	88	65	.575
1946	Boston	Joseph E. Cronin	104	50	.675
1947[1]	New York	Stanley R. Harris	97	57	.630
1948[1]	Cleveland	Lou Boudreau	97	58	.626
1949[1]	New York	Casey Stengel	97	57	.630
1950[1]	New York	Casey Stengel	98	56	.636
1951[1]	New York	Casey Stengel	98	56	.636
1952[1]	New York	Casey Stengel	95	59	.617
1953[1]	New York	Casey Stengel	99	52	.656
1954	Cleveland	Al Lopez	111	43	.721
1955[1]	New York	Casey Stengel	96	58	.623
1956[1]	New York	Casey Stengel	97	57	.630
1957	New York	Casey Stengel	98	56	.636
1958[1]	New York	Casey Stengel	92	62	.597
1959	Chicago	Al Lopez	94	60	.610
1960	New York	Casey Stengel	97	57	.630
1961[1]	New York	Ralph Houk	109	53	.673
1962[1]	New York	Ralph Houk	96	66	.593
1963	New York	Ralph Houk	104	57	.646
1964	New York	Yogi Berra	99	63	.611
1965	Minnesota	Sam Mele	102	60	.630
1966[1]	Baltimore	Hank Bauer	97	53	.606
1967	Boston	Dick Williams	92	70	.568
1968[1]	Detroit	Mayo Smith	103	59	.636
1969	Baltimore[3]	Earl Weaver	109	53	.673
1970[1]	Baltimore[3]	Earl Weaver	108	54	.667
1971	Baltimore[4]	Earl Weaver	101	57	.639
1972[1]	Oakland[5]	Dick Williams	93	62	.600
1973[1]	Oakland[6]	Dick Williams	94	68	.580
1974[1]	Oakland[6]	Alvin Dark	90	72	.556
1975	Boston[4]	Darrell Johnson	95	65	.594
1976	New York[7]	Billy Martin	97	62	.610
1977[1]	New York[7]	Billy Martin	100	62	.617
1978[1]	New York[7]	Billy Martin and Bob Lemon	100	63	.613
1979	Baltimore[8]	Earl Weaver	102	57	.642
1980	Kansas City[9]	Jim Frey	97	65	.599
1981	New York[10]	Gene Michael– Bob Lemon	59	48	.551*
1982	Milwaukee[11]	Harvey Kuenn	95	67	.586
1983[1]	Baltimore[12]	Joe Altobelli	98	64	.605
1984[1]	Detroit[13]	Sparky Anderson	104	58	.642
1985[1]	Kansas City[14]	Dick Howser	91	71	.562
1986	Boston[11]	John McNamara	95	66	.590
1987[1]	Minnesota[15]	Tom Kelly	85	77	.525
1988	Oakland[16]	Tony LaRussa	104	58	.642
1989[1]	Oakland[17]	Tony LaRussa	99	63	.611
1990	Oakland[18]	Tony LaRussa	103	59	.636
1991[1]	Minnesota[19]	Tom Kelly	95	67	.586

*Split season because of player strike. 1. World Series winner. 2. No World Series. 3. Defeated Minnesota, Western Division winner, in playoff. 4. Defeated Oakland, Western Division Leader, in playoff. 5. Defeated Detroit, Eastern Division winner, inplayoff. 6. Defeated Baltimore, Eastern Division winner, in playoff. 7. Defeated Kansas City, Western Division winner, in playoff. 8. Defeated California, Western Division winner, in playoff. 9. Defeated New York, Eastern Division winner, in playoff. 10. Defeated Oakland, Western Division winner, in playoff. 11. Defeated California, Western Division winner, in playoff. 12. Defeated Chicago, Western Division winner in playoff. 13. Defeated Kansas City, Western Division winner, in playoff. 14. Defeated Toronto, Eastern Division winner, in playoff. 15. Defeated Detroit, Eastern winner, in playoff. 16. Defeated Boston, Eastern division winner, in playoffs. 17. Defeated Toronto, Eastern Division winner, in playoffs. 18. Defeated Boston, Eastern Division winner, in playoffs. 19. Defeated Toronto, Eastern Division winner, in playoffs.

NATIONAL LEAGUE PENNANT WINNERS

Year	Club	Manager	Won	Lost	Pct	Year	Club	Manager	Won	Lost	Pct
1876	Chicago	Albert G. Spalding	52	14	.788	1934	St. Louis[1]	Frank F. Frisch	95	58	.621
1877	Boston	Harry Wright	31	17	.646	1935	Chicago	Charles J. Grimm	100	54	.649
1878	Boston	Harry Wright	41	19	.683	1936	New York	William H. Terry	92	62	.597
1879	Providence	George Wright	55	23	.705	1937	New York	William H. Terry	95	57	.625
1880	Chicago	Adrian C. Anson	67	17	.798	1938	Chicago	Gabby Hartnett	89	63	.586
1881	Chicago	Adrian C. Anson	56	28	.667	1939	Cincinnati	Wm. B. McKechnie	97	57	.630
1882	Chicago	Adrian C. Anson	55	29	.655	1940	Cincinnati[1]	Wm. B. McKechnie	100	53	.654
1883	Boston	John F. Morrill	63	35	.643	1941	Brooklyn	Leo E. Durocher	100	54	.649
1884	Providence	Frank C. Bancroft	84	28	.750	1942	St. Louis[1]	Wm. H. Southworth	106	48	.688
1885	Chicago	Adrian C. Anson	87	25	.777	1943	St. Louis	Wm. H. Southworth	105	49	.682
1886	Chicago	Adrian C. Anson	90	34	.726	1944	St. Louis[1]	Wm. H. Southworth	105	49	.682
1887	Detroit	W. H. Watkins	79	45	.637	1945	Chicago	Charles J. Grimm	98	56	.636
1888	New York	James J. Mutrie	84	47	.641	1946	St. Louis[1]	Edwin H. Dyer	98	58	.628
1889	New York	James J. Mutrie	83	43	.659	1947	Brooklyn	Burton E. Shotton	94	60	.610
1890	Brooklyn	Wm. H. McGunnigle	86	43	.667	1948	Boston	Wm. H. Southworth	91	62	.595
1891	Boston	Frank G. Selee	87	51	.630	1949	Brooklyn	Burton E. Shotton	97	57	.630
1892	Boston	Frank G. Selee	102	48	.680	1950	Philadelphia	Edwin M. Sawyer	91	63	.591
1893	Boston	Frank G. Selee	86	44	.662	1951	New York	Leo E. Durocher	98	59	.624
1894	Baltimore	Edward H. Hanlon	89	39	.695	1952	Brooklyn	Charles W. Dressen	96	57	.630
1895	Baltimore	Edward H. Hanlon	87	43	.669	1953	Brooklyn	Charles W. Dressen	105	49	.682
1896	Baltimore	Edward H. Hanlon	90	39	.698	1954	New York[1]	Leo E. Durocher	97	57	.630
1897	Boston	Frank G. Selee	93	39	.705	1955	Brooklyn[1]	Walter Alston	98	55	.641
1898	Boston	Frank G. Selee	102	47	.685	1956	Brooklyn	Walter Alston	93	61	.604
1899	Brooklyn	Edward H. Hanlon	88	42	.677	1957	Milwaukee1	Fred Haney	95	59	.617
1900	Brooklyn	Edward H. Hanlon	82	54	.603	1958	Milwaukee	Fred Haney	92	62	.597
1901	Pittsburgh	Fred C. Clarke	90	49	.647	1959	Los Angeles[1]	Walter Alston	88	68	.564
1902	Pittsburgh	Fred C. Clarke	103	36	.741	1960	Pittsburgh[1]	Danny Murtaugh	95	59	.617
1903	Pittsburgh	Fred C. Clarke	91	49	.650	1961	Cincinnati	Fred Hutchinson	93	61	.604
1904	New York[2]	John J. McGraw	106	47	.693	1962	San Francisco	Alvin Dark	103	62	.624
1905	New York[1]	John J. McGraw	105	48	.686	1963	Los Angeles[1]	Walter Alston	99	63	.611
1906	Chicago	Frank L. Chance	116	36	.763	1964	St. Louis[1]	Johnny Keane	93	69	.574
1907	Chicago[1]	Frank L. Chance	107	45	.704	1965	Los Angeles[1]	Walter Alston	97	65	.599
1908	Chicago[1]	Frank L. Chance	99	55	.643	1966	Los Angeles	Walter Alston	95	67	.586
1909	Pittsburgh[1]	Fred C. Clarke	110	42	.724	1967	St. Louis[1]	Red Schoendienst	101	60	.627
1910	Chicago	Frank L. Chance	104	50	.675	1968	St. Louis	Red Schoendienst	97	65	.599
1911	New York	John J. McGraw	99	54	.647	1969	New York[1,3]	Gil Hodges	100	62	.617
1912	New York	John J. McGraw	103	48	.682	1970	Cincinnati[4]	Sparky Anderson	102	60	.630
1913	New York	John J. McGraw	101	51	.664	1971	Pittsburgh[1,5]	Danny Murtaugh	97	65	.599
1914	Boston[1]	George T. Stallings	94	59	.614	1972	Cincinnati[4]	Sparky Anderson	95	59	.617
1915	Philadelphia	Patrick J. Moran	90	62	.592	1973	New York[6]	Yogi Berra	82	79	.509
1916	Brooklyn	Wilbert Robinson	94	60	.610	1974	Los Angeles[4]	Walter Alston	102	60	.630
1917	New York	John J. McGraw	98	56	.636	1975	Cincinnati[1]	Sparky Anderson	108	54	.667
1918	Chicago	Fred L. Mitchell	84	45	.651	1976	Cincinnati[7,1]	Sparky Anderson	102	60	.630
1919	Cincinnati[1]	Patrick J. Moran	96	44	.686	1977	Los Angeles[7]	Tom Lasorda	98	64	.605
1920	Brooklyn	Wilbert Robinson	93	61	.604	1978	Los Angeles[7]	Tom Lasorda	95	67	.586
1921	New York[1]	John J. McGraw	94	59	.614	1979[1]	Pittsburgh[6]	Chuck Tanner	98	64	.605
1922	New York[1]	John J. McGraw	93	61	.604	1980[1]	Philadelphia[8]	Dallas Green	91	71	.562
1923	New York	John J. McGraw	95	58	.621	1981	Los Angeles[1,9]	Tom Lasorda	63	47	.573
1924	New York	John J. McGraw	93	60	.608	1982[1]	St. Louis[3]	Whitey Herzog	92	70	.568
1925	Pittsburgh[1]	Wm. B. McKechnie	95	58	.621	1983	Philadelphia[11]	Paul Owens	90	72	.556
1926	St. Louis[1]	Rogers Hornsby	89	65	.578	1984	San Diego[12]	Dick Williams	92	70	.568
1927	Pittsburgh	Donie Bush	94	60	.610	1985	St. Louis[11]	Whitey Herzog	101	61	.623
1928	St. Louis	Wm. B. McKechnie	95	59	.617	1986	New York[8]	Dave Johnson	108	54	.667
1929	Chicago	Joseph V. McCarthy	98	54	.645	1987	St. Louis[5]	Whitey Herzog	95	67	.586
1930	St. Louis	Gabby Street	92	62	.597	1988	Los Angeles[10]	Tom Lasorda	94	67	.584
1931	St. Louis[1]	Gabby Street	101	53	.656	1989	San Francisco[12]	Roger Craig	92	70	.568
1932	Chicago	Charles J. Grimm	90	64	.584	1990	Cincinnati[4]	Lou Piniella	91	71	.562
1933	New York[1]	William H. Terry	91	61	.599	1991	Atlanta[4]	Bobby Cox	94	68	.580

*Split season because of player strike. 1. World Series winner. 2. No World Series. 3. Defeated Atlanta, Western Division winner, in playoff. 4. Defeated Pittsburgh, Eastern Division winner, in playoff. 5. Defeated San Francisco, Western Division winner, in playoff. 6. Defeated Cincinnati, Western Division winner, in playoff. 7. Defeated Philadelphia, Eastern Division winner, in playoff. 8. Defeated Houston, Western Division winner, in playoff. 9. Defeated Montreal, Eastern Division winner, in playoff. 10. Defeated New York, Eastern Division winner, in playoff. 11. Defeated Los Angeles, Western Division in playoff. 12. Defeated Chicago, Eastern Division champion in playoff.

MOST VALUABLE PLAYERS

(Baseball Writers Association selections)

American League

1931	Lefty Grove, Philadelphia
1932–33	Jimmy Foxx, Philadelphia
1934	Mickey Cochrane, Detroit
1935	Hank Greenberg, Detroit
1936	Lou Gehrig, New York
1937	Charlie Gehringer, Detroit
1938	Jimmy Foxx, Boston
1939	Joe DiMaggio, New York
1940	Hank Greenberg, Detroit
1941	Joe DiMaggio, New York
1942	Joe Gordon, New York
1943	Spurgeon Chandler, New York
1944–45	Hal Newhouser, Detroit
1946	Ted Williams, Boston
1947	Joe DiMaggio, New York
1948	Lou Boudreau, Cleveland
1949	Ted Williams, Boston
1950	Phil Rizzuto, New York
1951	Yogi Berra, New York
1952	Bobby Shantz, Philadelphia
1953	Al Rosen, Cleveland
1954–55	Yogi Berra, New York
1956–57	Mickey Mantle, New York
1958	Jackie Jensen, Boston
1959	Nellie Fox, Chicago
1960–61	Roger Maris, New York
1962	Mickey Mantle, New York
1963	Elston Howard, New York
1964	Brooks Robinson, Baltimore
1965	Zoilo Versalles, Minnesota
1966	Frank Robinson, Baltimore
1967	Carl Yastrzemski, Boston
1968	Dennis McLain, Detroit
1969	Harmon Killebrew, Minnesota
1970	John (Boog) Powell, Baltimore
1971	Vida Blue, Oakland
1972	Dick Allen, Chicago
1973	Reggie Jackson, Oakland
1974	Jeff Burroughs, Texas
1975	Fred Lynn, Boston
1976	Thurman Munson, New York
1977	Rod Carew, Minnesota
1978	Jim Rice, Boston
1979	Don Baylor, California
1980	George Brett, Kansas City
1981	Rollie Fingers, Milwaukee
1982	Robin Yount, Milwaukee
1983	Cal Ripken, Jr., Baltimore
1984	Willie Hernandez, Detroit
1985	Don Mattingly, New York
1986	Roger Clemens, Boston
1987	George Bell, Toronto
1988	Jose Canseco, Oakland
1989	Robin Yount, Milwaukee
1990	Rickey Henderson, Oakland

National League

1931	Frank Frisch, St. Louis
1932	Chuck Klein, Philadelphia
1933	Carl Hubbell, New York
1934	Dizzy Dean, St. Louis
1935	Gabby Hartnett, Chicago
1936	Carl Hubbell, New York
1937	Joe Medwick, St. Louis
1938	Ernie Lombardi, Cincinnati
1939	Bucky Walters, Cincinnati
1940	Frank McCormick, Cincinnati
1941	Dolph Camilli, Brooklyn
1942	Mort Cooper, St. Louis
1943	Stan Musial, St. Louis
1944	Marty Marion, St. Louis
1945	Phil Cavarretta, Chicago
1946	Stan Musial, St. Louis
1947	Bob Elliott, Boston
1948	Stan Musial, St. Louis
1949	Jackie Robinson, Brooklyn
1950	Jim Konstanty, Philadelphia
1951	Roy Campanella, Brooklyn
1952	Hank Sauer, Chicago
1953	Roy Campanella, Brooklyn
1954	Willie Mays, New York
1955	Roy Campanella, Brooklyn
1956	Don Newcombe, Brooklyn
1957	Henry Aaron, Milwaukee
1958–59	Ernie Banks, Chicago
1960	Dick Groat, Pittsburgh
1961	Frank Robinson, Cincinnati
1962	Maury Wills, Los Angeles
1963	Sandy Koufax, Los Angeles
1964	Ken Boyer, St. Louis
1965	Willie Mays, San Francisco
1966	Roberto Clemente, Pittsburgh
1967	Orlando Cepeda, St. Louis
1968	Bob Gibson, St. Louis
1969	Willie McCovey, San Francisco
1970	Johnny Bench, Cincinnati
1971	Joe Torre, St. Louis
1972	Johnny Bench, Cincinnati
1973	Pete Rose, Cincinnati
1974	Steve Garvey, Los Angeles
1975–76	Joe Morgan, Cincinnati
1977	George Foster, Cincinnati
1978	Dave Parker, Pittsburgh
1979	Willie Stargell, Pittsburgh
1979	Keith Hernandez, St. Louis
1980	Mike Schmidt, Philadelphia
1981	Mike Schmidt, Philadelphia
1982	Dale Murphy, Atlanta
1983	Dale Murphy, Atlanta
1984	Ryne Sandberg, Chicago
1985	Willie McGee, St. Louis
1986	Mike Schmidt, Philadelphia
1987	Andre Dawson, Chicago
1988	Kirk Gibson, Los Angeles
1989	Kevin Mitchell, San Francisco
1990	Bobby Bonds, Pittsburgh

CY YOUNG AWARD

1956	Don Newcombe, Brooklyn N.L.
1957	Warren Spahn, Milwaukee N.L.
1958	Bob Turley, New York A.L.
1959	Early Wynn, Chicago A.L.
1960	Vernon Law, Pittsburgh, N.L
1961	Whitey Ford, New York A.L.
1962	Don Drysdale, Los Angeles N.L.
1963	Sandy Koufax, Los Angeles N.L.
1964	Dean Chance, Los Angeles A.L.
1965	Sandy Koufax, Los Angeles N.L.
1966	Sandy Koufax, Los Angeles N.L.
1967	Jim Lonborg, Boston A.L.; Mike McCormick, San Francisco N.L.
1968	Dennis, McLain, Detroit A.L.; Bob Gibson, St. Louis N.L.
1969	Mike Cuellar, Baltimore, and Dennis McLain, Detroit, tied in A.L.; Tom Seaver, N.Y. N.L.
1970	Jim Perry, Minnesota A.L.; Bob Gibson, St. Louis N.L.
1971	Vida Blue, Oakland A.L.; Ferguson Jenkins, Chicago N.L.
1972	Gaylord Perry, Cleveland A.L.; Steve Carlton, Phila. N.L.
1973	Jim Palmer, Baltimore A.L.; Tom Seaver, New York N.L.
1974	Catfish Hunter, Oakland A.L.; Mike Marshall, Los Angeles N.L.
1975	Jim Palmer, Baltimore A.L.; Tom Seaver, New York N.L.
1976	Jim Palmer, Baltimore A.L.; Randy Jones, San Diego N.L.
1977	Sparky Lyle, N.Y., A.L.; Steve Carlton, Philadelphia N.L.
1978	Ron Guidry, N.Y., A.L.; Gaylord Perry, San Diego N.L.
1979	Mike Flanagan, Baltimore A.L.; Bruce Sutter, Chicago, N.L.
1980	Steve Stone, Baltimore, A.L.; Steve Carlton, Philadelphia, N.L.
1981	Rollie Fingers, Milwaukee, A.L.; Fernando Valenzuela, Los Angeles, N.L.
1982	Pete Vuckovich, Milwaukee, A.L.; Steve Carlton, Philadelphia, N.L.
1983	LaMarr Hoyt, Chicago, A.L.; John Denny, Philadelphia, N.L.
1984	Willie Hernandez, Detroit, A.L.; Rick Sutcliffe, Chicago, N.L.
1985	Bret Saberhagen, A.L.; Dwight Gooden, N.L.
1986	Roger Clemens, A.L.; Mike Scott, N.L.
1987	Roger Clemens, A.L.; Steve Bedrosian, N.L.
1988	Frank Viola, A.L.; Orel Hershiser, N.L.
1989	Bret Saberhagen, A.L.; Mark Davis, N.L.
1990	Bob Welch, A.L.; Doug Drabek, N.L.

ROOKIE OF THE YEAR
(Baseball Writers Association selections)

American League

1949	Roy Sievers, St. Louis
1950	Walt Dropo, Boston
1951	Gil McDougald, New York
1952	Harry Byrd, Philadelphia
1953	Harvey Kuenn, Detroit
1954	Bob Grim, New York
1955	Herb Score, Cleveland
1956	Luis Aparicio, Chicago
1957	Tony Kubek, New York
1958	Albie Pearson, Washington
1959	Bob Allison, Washington
1960	Ron Hansen, Baltimore
1961	Don Schwall, Boston
1962	Tom Tresh, New York
1963	Gary Peters, Chicago
1964	Tony Oliva, Minnesota
1965	Curt Blefary, Baltimore
1966	Tommy Agee, Chicago
1967	Rod Carew, Minnesota
1968	Stan Bahnsen, New York
1969	Lou Piniella, Kansas City
1970	Thurman Munson, New York
1971	Chris Chambliss, Cleveland
1972	Carlton Fisk, Boston
1973	Alonzo Bumbry, Baltimore
1974	Mike Hargrove, Texas
1975	Fred Lynn, Boston
1976	Mark Fidrych, Detroit
1977	Eddie Murray, Baltimore
1978	Lou Whitaker, Detroit
1979	Alfredo Griffin, Toronto
1979	John Castino, Minnesota
1980	Joe Charboneau, Cleveland
1981	Dave Righetti, New York
1982	Cal Ripken, Jr., Baltimore
1983	Ron Kittle, Chicago
1984	Alvin Davis, Seattle
1985	Ozzie Guillen, Chicago
1986	Jose Canseco, Oakland
1987	Mark McGwire, Oakland
1988	Walter Weiss, Oakland
1989	Gregg Olson, Baltimore
1990	Sandy Alomar Jr., Cleveland

National League

1949	Don Newcombe, Brooklyn
1950	Sam Jethroe, Boston
1951	Willie Mays, New York
1952	Joe Black, Brooklyn
1953	Jim Gilliam, Brooklyn
1954	Wally Moon, St. Louis
1955	Bill Virdon, St. Louis
1956	Frank Robinson, Cincinnati
1957	Jack Sanford, Philadelphia
1958	Orlando Cepeda, San Francisco
1959	Willie McCovey, San Francisco
1960	Frank Howard, Los Angeles
1961	Billy Williams, Chicago
1962	Ken Hubbs, Chicago
1963	Pete Rose, Cincinnati
1964	Richie Allen, Philadelphia
1965	Jim Lefebvre, Los Angeles
1966	Tommy Helms, Cincinnati
1967	Tom Seaver, New York
1968	Johnny Bench, Cincinnati
1969	Ted Sizemore, Los Angeles
1970	Carl Morton, Montreal
1971	Earl Williams, Atlanta
1972	Jon Matlack, New York
1973	Gary Matthews, San Francisco
1974	Bake McBride, St. Louis
1975	John Montefusco, San Francisco
1976	Pat Zachry, Cincinnati
1976	Bruce Metzger, San Diego
1977	Andre Dawson, Montreal
1978	Bob Horner, Atlanta
1979	Rick Sutcliffe, Los Angeles
1980	Steve Howe, Los Angeles
1981	Fernando Valenzuela, Los Angeles
1982	Steve Sax, Los Angeles
1983	Darryl Strawberry, New York
1984	Dwight Gooden, New York
1985	Vince Coleman, St. Louis
1986	Todd Worrell, St. Louis
1987	Benito Santiago, San Diego
1988	Chris Sabo, Cincinnati
1989	Jerome Walton, Chicago
1990	Dave Justice, Atlanta

MAJOR LEAGUE LIFETIME RECORDS
(Through 1991)

Leading Batters, by Average

(Minimum 10 major league seasons and 4,000 at bats)

	Years	At Bats	Hits	Avg
Ty Cobb	24	11,436	4,190	.366
Rogers Hornsby	23	8,173	2,930	.358
Joe Jackson	13	4,981	1,774	.356
Pete Browning	13	4,795	1,664	.347
Ed Delahanty	16	7,493	2,593	.346
Willie Keeler	19	8,570	2,955	.345
Billy Hamilton	14	6,262	2,157	.344
Ted Williams	19	7,706	2,654	.344
Tris Speaker	22	10,208	3,515	.344
Dan Brouthers	19	6,682	2,288	.342
Jesse Burkett	16	8,389	2,872	.342
Babe Ruth	22	8,399	2,873	.342
Harry Heilmann	17	7,787	2,660	.342
Bill Terry	14	6,428	2,193	.341
George Sisler	15	8,267	2,812	.340
Lou Gehrig	17	8,001	2,721	.340
Nap Lajoie	21	9,590	3,251	.339
Riggs Stephenson	14	4,508	1,515	.336
Al Simmons	20	8,761	2,927	.334
Cap Anson	22	9,067	3,022	.333
Paul Waner	20	9,459	3,152	.333
Eddie Collins	25	9,949	3,311	.333
Sam Thompson	15	5,972	1,984	.332
Stan Musial	22	10,972	3,630	.331
Heinie Manush	17	7,653	2,524	.330
Hugh Duffy	17	7,026	2,313	.329
Honus Wagner	21	10,427	3,430	.329
Rod Carew	19	9,315	3,053	.328
Top O'Neill	10	4,254	1,389	.327
Jimmie Foxx	20	8,134	2,646	.325
Earle Combs	12	5,748	1,866	.325
Joe DiMaggio	13	6,821	2,214	.325

Leading Pitchers
(More than 250 career victories)

	Years	W	L	Pct
Cy Young	22	511	315	.619
Walter Johnson	21	416	279	.599
Christy Mathewson	17	374	187	.667
Grover Cleveland Alexander	20	373	208	.642
Warren Spahn	21	363	245	.597
James Galvin	15	361	309	.542
Kid Nichols	17	361	208	.634
Tim Keefe	14	341	224	.604
Steve Carlton	24	329	244	.574
John Clarkson	12	327	176	.650
Eddie Plank	17	325	193	.627
Don Sutton	24	324	256	.559
Phil Niekro	24	318	274	.537
Gaylord Perry	22	314	265	.542
Nolan Ryan**	24	314	278	.530
Tom Seaver	20	311	205	.603
Mickey Welch	13	309	209	.597
Hoss Radbourne	21	308	191	.617
Lefty Grove	20	300	141	.680
Early Wynn	23	300	244	.551

	Years	W	L	Pct		Years	W	L	Pct
Tommy John	27	288	231	.555	Bob Feller	18	266	162	.621
Robin Roberts	19	286	245	.539	Eppa Rixey	21	266	251	.515
Tony Mullane	14	286	213	.573	Gus Weyhing	14	266	229	.537
Ferguson Jenkins	19	284	226	.557	Jim McCormick	10	264	214	.562
Jim Kaat	25	283	236	.545	Ted Lyons	21	260	230	.531
Bert Blyleven	21	279	238	.540	Red Faber	20	254	212	.545
Red Ruffing	22	273	225	.548	Carl Hubbell	16	253	154	.622
Burleigh Grimes	19	270	212	.560	Bob Gibson	17	251	174	.591
Jim Palmer	18	268	149	.643	**Active through 1991.				

MAJOR LEAGUE ALL–TIME PITCHING RECORDS
(Through 1991)

Most Games Won—511, Cy Young, Cleveland N.L., 1890–98, St. Louis N.L., 1899–1900, Boston A.L., 1901–08, Cleveland A.L., 1909–11, Boston N.L., 1911.

Most Games Won, Season—60, Hoss Radbourne, Providence N.L., 1884. (Since 1900—41, Jack Chesbro, New York A.L., 1904.)

Most Consecutive Games Won—24, Carl Hubbell, New York N.L., 1936 (16) and 1937 (8).

Most Consecutive Games Won, Season—19, Tim Keefe, New York N.L., 1888; Rube Marquard, New York N.L., 1912.

Most Years Won 20 or More Games—16, Cy Young, Cleveland N.L., 1891–98, St. Louis N.L., 1899–1900, Boston A.L., 1901–04, 1907–08.

Most Shutouts—113, Walter Johnson, Wash. A.L., 1907–27.

Most Shutouts, Season—16, Grover Alexander, Philadelphia N.L., 1916.

Most Consecutive Shutouts—6, Don Drysdale, Los Angeles, N.L., 1968.

Most Consecutive Scoreless Innings—59, Orel Hershiser, Los Angeles Dodgers, 1988.

Most Strikeouts—5,511, Nolan Ryan, New York N.L., California A.L., Houston N.L., 1968–1988 Texas, 1989–91 (still active).

Most Strikeouts, Season—505, Matthew Kilroy, Baltimore A.A., 1886. (Since 1900—383, Nolan Ryan, California, A.L., 1973.)

Most Strikeouts, Game—21, Tom Cheney, Washington A.L., 1962, 16 innings. Nine innings: 20, Roger Clemens, Boston, A.L., 1986; 19, Charles McSweeney, Providence N.L., 1884; Hugh Dailey, Chicago U.A., 1884. (Since 1900—19, Steve Carlton, St. Louis N.L. vs. New York, Sept. 15, 1969; Tom Seaver, New York N.L. vs. San Diego, April 22, 1970; Nolan Ryan, California A.L. vs. Boston, Aug. 12, 1974; David Cone, New York N.L. vs. Philadelphia, Oct. 6, 1991.)

Most Consecutive Strikeouts—10, Tom Seaver, New York N.L. vs. San Diego, April 22, 1970.

Most Games, Season—106, Mike Marshall, Los Angeles, N.L., 1974.

Most Complete Games, Season—74, William White, Cincinnati N.L., 1879. (Since 1900—48, Jack Chesbro, New York A.L., 1904.)

MAJOR LEAGUE INDIVIDUAL ALL–TIME RECORDS
(Through 1991)

Highest Batting Average—.442, James O'Neill, St. Louis, A.A., 1887; .438, Hugh Duffy, Boston, N.L., 1894 (Since 1900—.424, Rogers Hornsby, St. Louis, N.L., 1924; .422, Nap Lajoie, Phil., A.L., 1901)

Most Times at Bat—12,364, Henry Aaron, Milwaukee N.L., 1954–65; Atlanta N.L., 1966–74; Milwaukee A.L., 1975–76.

Most Years Batted .300 or Better—23, Ty Cobb, Detroit A.L., 1906–26, Philadelphia A.L., 1927–28.

Most hits—4,256, Pete Rose, Cincinnati 1963–79, Philadelphia 1980–83, Montreal 1984, Cincinnati 1984–86.

Most Hits, Season—257, George Sisler, St. Louis A.L., 1920.

Most Hits, Game (9 innings)—7, Wilbert Robinson, Baltimore N.L., 6 singles, 1 double, 1892. Rennie Stennett, Pittsburgh N.L., 4 singles, 2 doubles, 1 triple, 1975.

Most Hits, Game (extra innings)—9, John Burnett, Cleveland A.L., 18 innings, 7 singles, 2 doubles, 1932.

Most Hits in Succession—12, Mike Higgins, Boston A.L., in four games, 1938; Walt Dropo, Detroit A.L., in three games, 1952.

Most Consecutive Games Batted Safely—56, Joe DiMaggio, New York A.L., 1941.

Most Runs—2,244, Ty Cobb, Detroit A.L., 1905–26, Philadelphia A.L., 1927–28.

Most Runs, Season—196, William Hamilton, Philadelphia N.L., 1894. (Since 1900—177, Babe Ruth, New York A.L., 1921.)

Most Runs, Game—7, Guy Hecker, Louisville A.A., 1886. (Since 1900—6, by Mel Ott, New York N.L., 1934, 1944; Johnny Pesky, Boston A.L., 1946; Frank Torre, Milwaukee N.L., 1957.)

Most Runs Batted in—2,297, Henry Aaron, Milwaukee N.L., 1954–1965; Atlanta N.L., 1966–74; Milwaukee A.L., 1975–76.

Most Runs Batted in, Season—190, Hack Wilson, Chicago N.L., 1930.

Most Runs Batted In, Game—12, Jim Bottomley, St. Louis N.L., 1924.

Most Home Runs—755, Henry Aaron, Milwaukee N.L., 1954–1965; Atlanta N.L., 1966–74; Milwaukee A.L., 1975–76.

Most Home Runs, Season—61, Roger Maris, New York A.L., 1961 (162–game season); 60, Babe Ruth, New York A.L., 1927 (154–game season)

Most Home Runs with Bases Filled—23, Lou Gehrig, New York A.L., 1927–39.

Most 2–Base Hits—793, Tris Speaker, Boston A.L., 1907–15, Cleveland A.L., 1916–26, Washington A.L., 1927, Philadelphia A.L., 1928.

Most 2–Base Hits, Season—67, Earl Webb, Boston A.L., 1931.

Most 2–base Hits, Game—4, by many.

Most 3–Base Hits—312, Sam Crawford, Cincinnati N.L., 1899–1902, Detroit A.L., 1903–17.

Most 3–Base Hits, Season—36, Owen Wilson, Pittsburgh N.L., 1912.

Most 3–Base Hits, Game—4, George Strief, Philadelphia A.A., 1885; William Joyce, New York N.L., 1897. (Since 1900—3, by many.)

Most Games Played—3,298, Henry Aaron, Milwaukee N.L., 1954–1965; Atlanta, N.L., 1966–74; Milwaukee A.L., 1975–76.

Most Consecutive Games Played—2,130, Lou Gehrig, New York A.L., 1925–39.

Most Bases on Balls—2,056, Babe Ruth, Boston A.L., 1914–19; New York A.L., 1920–34, Boston N.L., 1935.

Most Bases on Balls, Season—170, Babe Ruth, New York A.L., 1923.

Most bases on Balls, Game—6, Jimmy Foxx, Boston A.L., 1938.

Most Strikeouts, Season—189, Bobby Bonds, San Francisco N.L., 1970.

Most Strikeouts, Game (9 innings)—5, by many.

Most Strikeouts, Game (extra innings)—6, Carl Weilman, St. Louis A.L., 15 innings, 1913; Don Hoak, Chicago N.L., 17 innings, 1956; Fred Reichardt, California A.L., 17, innings, 1966; Billy Cowan, California A.L., 20, 1971; Cecil Cooper, Boston A.L., 15, 1974.

Most pinch—hits, lifetime—150, Manny Mota, S.F., 1962; Pitt., 1963–68; Montreal, 1969; L.A., 1969–80, N.L.

Most Pinch-hits, season—25, Jose Morales, Montreal N.L., 1976.

Most consecutive pinch–hits—9, Dave Philley, Phil., N.L., 1958 (8), 1959 (1).

Most pinch–hit home runs, lifetime—18, Gerald Lynch, Pitt.–Cin. N.L., 1957–66.

*Still active coming into 1992 season.

Most pinch–hit home runs, season—6, Johnny Frederick, Brooklyn, N.L., 1932.

Most stolen bases, lifetime (since 1900)—994, Rickey Henderson,* 1979–84 Oakland, 1985–89 New York (A.L.), 1989–91 Oakland

Most stolen bases, season—156, Harry Stovey, Phil., A.A., 1888. Since 1900: 130, Rickey Henderson, Oak., A.L., 1982; 118, Lou Brock, St. Louis, N.L., 1974.

Most stolen bases, game—7, George Gore, Chicago N.L. 1881; William Hamilton, Philadelphia N.L. 1894. (Since 1900—6, Eddie Collins, Philadelphia A.L., 1912.)

Most time stealing home, lifetime—35, Ty Cobb, Detroit–Phil. A.L., 1905–28.

MAJOR LEAGUE BASEBALL EXPANDS PLAYOFFS TO BEST 4–OF–7

After 16 years of five–game league championship playoffs, baseball expanded to a seven–game format in 1985 for the purpose of reaping a reported additional $9 million in network television revenue.

An agreement was reached between management and players to expand the series for 1985. The decision immediately increased baseball's revenue from $20 to $29 million for the playoffs.

The formula for splitting that money was part of the agreement with the players which settled the Aug. 6–8, 1985 major league players strike.

The playoffs had been a best 3–of–5 affair since 1969, when divisional play was first initiated. The World Series remained a best 4–of–7 format.

MAJOR LEAGUE ATTENDANCE RECORDS
(Through 1991)

Single game—78,672, San Francisco at Los Angeles (N.L.), April 18, 1958. (At Memorial Coliseum.)

Doubleheader—84,587, New York at Cleveland (A.L.), Sept. 12, 1954.

Night—78,382, Chicago at Cleveland (A.L.), Aug. 20, 1948.

Season, home—4,001,526, Toronto (A.L.), 1991.

Season, league—32,148,198, American League, 1991

Season, both leagues—56,888,512, 1991

Season, road—2,461,240, New York (A.L.), 1980.

World Series, single game—92,706, Chicago (A.L.) at Los Angeles (N.L.), Oct. 6, 1959.

World Series, all games (6)—420,784, Chicago (A.L.) and Los Angeles (N.L.), 1959.

MOST HOME RUNS IN ONE SEASON
(45 or More)

HR	Player/Team	Year	HR	Player/Team	Year
61	Roger Maris, New York (AL)	1961	48	Jimmy Foxx, Philadelphia (AL)	1933
60	Babe Ruth, New York (AL)	1927	48	Harmon Killebrew, Minnesota (AL)	1962
59	Babe Ruth, New York (AL)	1921	48	Willie Stargell, Pittsburgh (NL)	1971
58	Jimmy Foxx, Philadelphia (AL)	1932	48	Dave Kingman, Chicago (NL)	1979
58	Hank Greenberg, Detroit (AL)	1938	48	Mike Schmidt, Philadelphia (NL)	1980
56	Hack Wilson, Chicago (NL)	1930	47	Babe Ruth, New York (AL)	1926
54	Babe Ruth, New York (AL)	1920	47	Ralph Kiner, Pittsburgh (NL)	1950
54	Babe Ruth, New York (AL)	1928	47	Ed Mathews, Milwaukee (NL)	1953
54	Ralph Kiner, Pittsburgh (NL)	1949	47	Ernie Banks, Chicago (NL)	1958
54	Mickey Mantle, New York (AL)	1961	47	Willie Mays, San Francisco (NL)	1964
52	Mickey Mantle, New York (AL)	1956	47	Henry Aaron, Atlanta (NL)	1971
52	Willie Mays, San Francisco (NL)	1965	47	Reggie Jackson, Oakland (AL)	1969
52	George Foster, Cincinnati (NL)	1977	47	George Bell, Toronto (AL)	1987
51	Ralph Kiner, Pittsburgh (NL)	1947	47	Kevin Mitchell, San Francisco (NL)	1989
51	John Mize, New York (NL)	1947	46	Babe Ruth, New York (AL)	1924
51	Willie Mays, New York (NL)	1955	46	Babe Ruth, New York, (AL)	1929
51	Cecil Fielder (AL)	1990	46	Babe Ruth, New York (AL)	1931
50	Jimmy Foxx, Boston (AL)	1938	46	Lou Gehrig, New York (AL)	1931
49	Babe Ruth, New York (AL)	1930	46	Joe DiMaggio, New York (AL)	1937
49	Lou Gehrig, New York (AL)	1934	46	Ed Mathews, Milwaukee (NL)	1959
49	Lou Gehrig, New York (AL)	1936	46	Orlando Cepeda, San Francisco (NL)	1961
49	Ted Kluszewski, Cincinnati (NL)	1954	46	Jim Rice, Boston (AL)	1978
49	Willie Mays, San Francisco (NL)	1962	45	Harmon Killebrew, Minnesota (AL)	1963
49	Harmon Killebrew, Minnesota (AL)	1964	45	Willie McCovey, San Francisco (NL)	1969
49	Frank Robinson, Baltimore (AL)	1966	45	Johnny Bench, Cincinnati (NL)	1970
49	Harmon Killebrew, Minnesota (AL)	1969	45	Gorman Thomas, Milwaukee (AL)	1979
49	Mark McGwire, Oakland (AL)	1987	45	Henry Aaron, Milwaukee (NL)	1962
49	Andre Dawson, Chicago (NL)	1987			

MAJOR LEAGUE BASEBALL—1991

AMERICAN LEAGUE

(Final Standing—1991)

EASTERN DIVISION

Team	W	L	Pct	GB
Toronto Blue Jays	91	71	.562	—
Boston Red Sox	84	78	.519	7
Detroit Tigers	84	78	.519	7
Milwaukee Brewers	83	79	.512	8
New York Yankees	71	91	.438	20
Baltimore Orioles	67	95	.414	24
Cleveland Indians	57	105	.352	34

WESTERN DIVISION

Team	W	L	Pct	GB
Minnesota Twins	95	67	.586	—
Chicago White Sox	87	75	.537	8
Texas Rangers	85	77	.525	10
Oakland Athletics	84	78	.519	11
Seattle Mariners	83	79	.512	12
Kansas City Royals	82	80	.506	13
California Angels	81	81	.500	14

AMERICAN LEAGUE LEADERS—1991

Batting—Julio Franco, Texas	.341
Runs—Paul Molitor, Milwaukee	133
Hits—Paul Molitor, Milwaukee	216
Runs batted in—Cecil Fielder, Detroit	133
Triples—Lance Johnson, Chicago	13
Doubles—Rafael Palmeiro, Texas	49
Home runs—Jose Canseco, Oakland	
Cecil Fielder, Detroit (tie)	44
Stolen bases—Rickey Henderson, Oakland	58
Total bases—Cal Ripken Jr., Baltimore	368
Slugging percentage—Danny Tartabull, Kansas City	.593
On-base percentage—Frank Thomas, Chicago	.453

Pitching

Victories—Scott Erickson, Minnesota and	
Bill Gullickson, Detroit (tie)	20
Earned run average—Roger Clemens, Boston	2.62
Strikeouts—Roger Clemens, Boston	241
Shutouts—Roger Clemens, Boston	4
Complete games—Jack McDowell, Chicago	15
Saves—Bryan Harvey, California	46
Innings pitched—Roger Clemens, Boston	271 1/3

NATIONAL LEAGUE

(Final Standing—1991)

EASTERN DIVISION

Team	W	L	Pct	GB
Pittsburgh Pirates	98	64	.605	—
St. Louis Cardinals	84	78	.519	14
Philadelphia Phillies	78	84	.481	20
Chicago Cubs	77	83	.481	20
New York Mets	77	84	.475	20 1/2
Montreal Expos	71	90	.441	26 1/2

WESTERN DIVISION

Team	W	L	Pct	GB
Atlanta Braves	94	68	.580	—
Los Angeles Dodgers	93	69	.574	1
San Diego Padres	84	78	.519	10
San Francisco Giants	75	87	.463	19
Cincinnati Reds	74	88	.457	20
Houston Astros	65	97	.401	29

NATIONAL LEAGUE LEADERS—1991

Batting—Terry Pendleton, Atlanta	.319
Runs—Brett Butler, Los Angeles	112
Hits—Terry Pendleton, Atlanta	187
Runs batted in—Howard Johnson, N.Y.	117
Triples—Ray Lankford, St. Louis	15
Doubles—Bobby Bonilla, Pittsburgh	44
Home runs—Howard Johnson, N.Y.	38
Stolen bases—Marquis Grissom, Montreal	76
Total bases—Terry Pendleton, Atlanta	303
Slugging percentage—Will Clark, San Francisco	.536
On-base percentage—Barry Bonds, Pittsburgh	.410

Pitching

Victories—John Smiley, Pittsburgh and	
Tom Glavine, Atlanta (tie)	20
Earned run average—Dennis Martinez, Montreal	2.39
Strikeouts—David Cone, New York	241
Shutouts—Dennis Martinez, Montreal	5
Complete games—Tom Glavine, Atlanta and	
Dennis Martinez, Montreal (tie)	9
Saves—Lee Smith, St. Louis	47
Innings pitched—Greg Maddux, Chicago	263

AMERICAN LEAGUE AVERAGES—1991

Team Batting

	AB	R	H	HR	RBI	Pct
Minnesota	5556	776	1557	140	733	.280
Milwaukee	5611	799	1523	115	750	.271
Texas	5703	829	1539	177	774	.269
Boston	5530	731	1486	126	691	.268
Kansas City	5584	727	1475	117	689	.264
Chicago	5594	758	1464	139	722	.261
Toronto	5489	684	1412	133	649	.257
New York	5541	674	1418	147	630	.255
California	5470	653	1396	115	607	.255
Seattle	5494	702	1400	126	665	.254
Cleveland	5470	576	1390	79	546	.254
Baltimore	5604	686	1421	170	660	.253
Oakland	5410	760	1342	159	716	.247
Detroit	5547	817	1372	209	778	.247

Individual Batting

(Based on 405 plate appearances.)

Player/Team	AB	R	H	HR	RBI	Pct
Franco Tex	589	108	201	5	78	.341
Boggs Bsn	546	93	181	8	51	.332
Griffey Jr Sea	548	76	179	22	100	.327
Randolph Mil	431	60	141	0	54	.327

Player/Team	AB	R	H	HR	RBI	Pct
Molitor Mil	665	133	216	17	75	.325
CRipken Blt	650	99	210	34	114	.323
Palmeiro Tex	631	115	203	26	88	.322
Puckett Min	611	92	195	15	89	.319
Thomas Chi	559	104	178	32	109	.318
Tartabull KC	484	78	153	31	100	.316
Hamilton Mil	405	64	126	1	57	.311
Harper Min	441	54	137	10	69	.311
Mack Min	442	79	137	18	74	.310
EMartinez Sea	544	98	167	14	52	.307
Sierra Tex	661	110	203	25	116	.307
Sax NY	652	85	198	10	56	.304
Joyner Cal	551	79	166	21	96	.301
Greenwell Bsn	544	76	163	9	83	.300
Polonia Cal	604	92	179	2	50	.296
ACole Cle	387	58	114	0	21	.295
RAlomar Tor	637	88	188	9	69	.295
Quintana Bsn	478	69	141	11	71	.295
Baines Oak	488	76	144	20	90	.295
Surhoff Mil	505	57	146	5	68	.289
Baerga Cle	593	80	171	11	69	.288
Mattingly NY	587	64	169	9	68	.288
Pecota KC	398	53	114	6	45	.286
Hall NY	492	67	140	19	80	.285

Individual Pitching
(Based on 10 decisions)

Player/Club	IP	H	BB	SO	W	L	ERA
Frohwirth Blt	96	64	29	77	7	3	1.87
Radinsky Chi	71	53	23	49	5	5	2.02
Farr NY	70	57	20	60	5	5	2.19
Clemens Bsn	271	219	65	241	18	10	2.62
Willis Min	89	76	19	53	8	3	2.63
Candiotti Tor	238	202	73	167	13	13	2.65
DWard Tor	107	80	33	132	7	6	2.77
Wegman Mil	193	176	40	89	15	7	2.84
Henneman Det	84	81	34	61	10	2	2.88
JAbbott Cal	243	222	73	158	18	11	2.89
Ryan Tex	173	102	72	203	12	6	2.91
MMoore Oak	210	176	105	153	17	8	2.96
Tapani Min	244	225	40	135	16	9	2.99
JuGuzman Tor	138	98	66	123	10	3	2.99
Langston Cal	246	190	96	183	19	8	3.00
Key Tor	209	207	44	125	16	12	3.05
Saberhagen KC	196	165	45	136	13	8	3.07
JoGuzman Tex	169	152	84	125	13	7	3.08
MPerez Chi	135	111	52	128	8	7	3.12
Timlin Tor	108	94	50	85	11	6	3.16
Olson Blt	73	74	29	72	4	6	3.18
Erickson Min	204	189	71	108	20	8	3.18
Bosio Mil	204	187	58	117	14	10	3.25
MJackson Sea	88	64	34	74	7	7	3.25
JeRussell Tex	79	71	26	52	6	4	3.29
Hesketh Bsn	153	142	53	104	12	4	3.29
McDowell Chi	253	212	82	191	17	10	3.41
Appler KC	207	205	61	158	13	10	3.42

Team Pitching

	ERA	H	ER	BB	SO	ShO	SA
Toronto	3.50	1301	569	523	971	16	60
California	3.68	1351	591	543	990	10	50
Minnesota	3.69	1402	595	488	876	12	53
Chicago	3.78	1302	622	601	923	8	40
Seattle	3.78	1387	616	628	823	13	48
Kansas City	3.92	1473	639	529	924	12	41
Boston	4.01	1405	642	530	999	13	45
Milwaukee	4.14	1498	674	527	859	11	41
Cleveland	4.23	1551	678	441	862	8	33
New York	4.41	1510	709	506	936	11	37
Texas	4.46	1486	734	662	922	10	41
Detroit	4.50	1570	726	593	739	8	38
Oakland	4.57	1425	734	655	892	10	49
Baltimore	4.58	1534	743	504	868	8	42

NATIONAL LEAGUE AVERAGES—1991

Team Batting

	AB	R	H	HR	RBI	Pct
Pittsburgh	5449	768	1433	126	725	.262
Cincinnati	5501	689	1419	164	654	.257
Atlanta	5456	749	1407	141	704	.257
St. Louis	5362	651	1366	68	599	.254
Los Angeles	5408	665	1366	108	605	.252
Chicago	5522	695	1395	159	654	.252
San Francisco	5463	695	1345	141	605	.246
Montreal	5412	579	1329	95	536	.245
San Diego	5408	636	1321	121	591	.244
Houston	5504	605	1345	79	570	.244
New York	5359	640	1305	117	605	.243
Philadelphia	5521	629	1332	111	590	.241

Individual Batting
(405 or more at bats)

Player/Team	AB	R	H	HR	RBI	Pct
Pendleton Atl	586	94	187	22	86	.319
Morris Cin	478	72	152	14	59	.318
TGwynn SD	530	69	168	4	62	.317
McGee SF	497	67	155	4	43	.312
Jose StL	568	69	173	8	77	.305
Larkin Cin	464	88	140	20	69	.302
Bonilla Pit	577	102	174	18	100	.302
Sabo Cin	582	91	175	26	88	.301
WClark SF	565	84	170	29	116	.301
Calderon Mon	470	69	141	19	75	.300
Nixon Atl	401	81	119	0	26	.297
Butler LA	615	112	182	2	38	.296
Biggio Hou	546	79	161	4	46	.295
DaMartinez Mon	396	47	117	7	42	.295
Bagwell Hou	554	79	163	15	82	.294
Kruk Phi	538	84	158	21	92	.294
Bonds Pit	510	95	149	25	116	.292
Sandberg Chi	585	104	170	26	100	.291
LWalker Mon	487	59	141	16	64	.290
LHarris LA	429	59	123	3	38	.287
Finley Hou	596	84	170	8	54	.285
GBell Chi	558	63	159	25	86	.285
OSmith StL	550	96	157	3	50	.285
Roberts SD	424	66	119	3	32	.281
Zeile StL	565	76	158	11	81	.280
Doran Cin	361	51	101	6	35	.280
McGriff SD	528	84	147	31	106	.278

Individual Pitching
(Based on 10 decisions)

Player/Team	IP	H	BB	SO	W	L	ERA
GHarris SD	133	116	27	95	9	5	2.23
MiWilliams Phi	88	56	62	84	12	5	2.34
DeMartinez Mon	222	187	62	123	14	11	2.39
Rijo Cin	204	165	55	172	15	6	2.51
Glavine Atl	246	201	69	192	20	11	2.55
Belcher LA	209	189	75	156	10	9	2.62
Harnisch Hou	216	169	89	172	12	9	2.70
DeLeon StL	162	144	61	118	5	9	2.71
Morgan LA	236	197	61	140	14	10	2.78
Stanton Atl	78	62	21	54	5	5	2.88
Franco NY	55	61	18	45	5	9	2.93
McDowell LA	101	100	48	50	9	9	2.93
Tomlin Pit	175	170	54	104	8	7	2.98
Benes SD	223	194	59	167	15	11	3.03
Drabek Pit	234	245	62	142	15	14	3.07
Smiley Pit	207	194	44	129	20	8	3.08
JHowell LA	51	39	11	40	6	5	3.18
Ojeda LA	189	181	70	120	12	9	3.18
ZSmith Pit	228	234	29	120	16	10	3.20
Assenmacher Chi	102	85	31	117	7	8	3.24
Tewksbury StL	191	206	38	75	11	12	3.25
RMartinez LA	220	190	69	150	17	13	3.27
Melendez SD	93	77	24	60	8	5	3.27
Hurst SD	221	301	59	141	15	8	3.29
Cone NY	232	204	73	241	14	14	3.29
GMaddux Chi	263	232	66	198	15	11	3.35
BJones Mon	88	76	33	46	4	9	3.35
Burke NY	101	96	26	59	6	7	3.36

Team Pitching

	ERA	H	ER	BB	SO	ShO	SA
Los Angeles	3.06	1312	496	500	928	14	40
Pittsburgh	3.44	1411	557	401	919	11	51
Atlanta	3.48	1304	563	481	969	7	48
New York	3.55	1403	568	410	928	11	39
San Diego	3.57	1385	577	457	921	11	47
Montreal	3.64	1304	583	584	909	14	39
St. Louis	3.68	1367	588	454	822	5	51
Cincinnati	3.83	1372	613	560	997	11	43
Philadelphia	3.86	1346	628	670	988	11	35
Houston	4.00	1347	646	651	833	13	36
Chicago	4.03	1415	653	542	927	4	40
San Francisco	4.03	1397	646	544	905	10	45

MAJOR LEAGUE BASEBALL—1991

NATIONAL LEAGUE PLAYOFFS—1991

1st game, Pittsburgh, Pa., Oct. 9, 1991

Atlanta	000	000	001	—	1	5	0
Pittsburgh	102	001	01X	—	5	8	2

Glavine, Wohlers, Stanton; Drabek, Walk.
Winner: Drabek. Loser: Glavine. Attendance: 57,347.

2nd game, Pittsburgh, Pa., Oct. 10, 1991

Atlanta	000	001	000	—	1	8	0
Pittsburgh	000	000	000	—	0	6	0

Avery, Pena; Z. Smith, Mason, Belinda.
Winner: Avery. Loser: Z. Smith. Attendance: 57,533.

3rd game, Atlanta, Ga., Oct. 12, 1991

Pittsburgh	100	100	100	—	3	10	2
Atlanta	411	000	13X	—	10	11	0

Smiley, Landrum, Patterson, Kipper, Rodriguez; Smoltz, Stanton, Wohlers, Pena.
Winner: Smoltz. Loser: Smiley. Attendance: 50,905.

4th game, Atlanta, Ga., Oct. 13, 1991

Pittsburgh	010	010	000	1 — 3	11	1
Atlanta	200	000	000	0 — 3	7	1

Tomlin, Walk, Belinda; Leibrandt, Clancy, Stanton, Mercker, Wohlers.
Winner: Belinda. Loser: Mercker. Attendance: 51,109.

5th game, Atlanta, Ga., Oct. 14, 1991

Pittsburgh	000	010	000	—	1	6	2
Atlanta	000	000	000	—	0	9	1

Z. Smith, Mason; Glavine, Pena.
Winner: Z. Smith. Loser: Glavine. Attendance: 51,109.

6th game, Pittsburgh, Pa., Oct. 16, 1991

Atlanta	000	000	001	—	1	7	0
Pittsburgh	000	000	000	—	0	4	0

Avery, Pena; Drabek.
Winner: Avery. Loser: Drabek. Attendance: 54,508.

7th game, Pittsburgh, Pa., Oct. 17, 1991

Atlanta	300	010	000	—	4	6	1
Pittsburgh	000	000	000	—	0	6	0

Smoltz; Smiley, Walk, Mason, Belinda.
Winner: Smoltz. Loser: Smiley. Attendance: 46,932.
Atlanta wins series, 4 games to 3.

AMERICAN LEAGUE PLAYOFFS—1991*

1st game, Minneapolis, Minn., Oct. 8, 1991

Toronto	000	103	000	—	4	9	3
Minnesota	221	000	00X	—	5	11	0

Candiotti, Wells, Timlin; Morris, Willis, Aguilera.
Winner: Morris. Loser: Candiotti. Attendance: 54,766.

2nd game, Minneapolis, Minn., Oct. 9, 1991

Toronto	102	000	200	—	5	9	0
Minnesota	001	001	000	—	2	5	1

Guzman, Henke, Ward; Tapani, Bedrosian, Guthrie.
Winner: Guzman. Loser: Tapani. Attendance: 54,816.

3rd game, Toronto, Canada, Oct. 11, 1991

Minnesota	000	011	000	1 — 3	7	0
Toronto	200	000	000	0 — 2	11	1

Erickson, West, Willis, Guthrie, Aguilera; Key, Wells, Henke, Timlin.
Winner: Guthrie. Loser: Timlin. Attendance: 51,454.

4th game, Toronto, Canada, Oct. 12, 1991

Minnesota	000	402	111	—	9	13	1
Toronto	010	001	001	—	3	11	2

Morris, Bedrosian, Stottlemyre, Wells, Acker, Timlin, MacDonald.
Winner: Morris. Loser: Stottlemyre. Attendance: 51,526.

5th game, Toronto, Canada, Oct. 13, 1991

Minnesota	110	003	030	—	8	14	2
Toronto	003	200	000	—	5	9	1

Tapani, West, Willis, Aguilera; Candiotti, Timlin, Ward, Wells.
Winner: West. Loser: Ward. Attendance: 51,425.
Minnesota wins series, 4 games to 1.

*First playoff series played entirely in indoor stadiums.

WORLD SERIES—1991

1st Game—Minneapolis, Oct. 19

ATLANTA (N)

	AB	R	H	RBI
LoSmith dh	3	1	0	0
Treadway 2b	3	1	1	0
Pendleton 3b	4	0	0	0
Justice rf	2	0	1	0
Gant cf	4	0	3	2
Bream 1b	4	0	0	0
Hunter lf	4	0	0	0
Olson c	3	0	1	0
Belliard ss	1	0	0	0
Blauser ph-ss	2	0	0	0
Totals	**30**	**2**	**6**	**2**

MINNESOTA (A)

	AB	R	H	RBI
Gladden lf	2	1	0	0
Knoblauch 2b	3	0	3	1
Puckett cf	4	0	0	0
CDavis dh	3	0	0	0
Harper c	4	0	2	0
Mack rf	4	0	0	0
Hrbek 1b	4	2	2	1
Leius 3b	2	1	1	0
Pagliarulo ph-3b1	1	0	0	0
Gagne ss	3	1	1	3
Totals	**30**	**5**	**9**	**5**

Atlanta	000	001	010	—	2	6	1
Minnesota	001	031	00x	—	5	9	1

E—Treadway (1), Gladden (1). LOB—Atlanta 7, Minnesota 5. 2B—Harper (1), Gladden (1). HR—Hrbek (1) off Clancy, Gagne (1) off Leibrandt. RBI—Gant 2 (2), Knoblauch (1), Hrbek (1), Gagne 3 (3). SB—Gladden (1), Knoblauch 2 (2). CS—Gladden (1). S—Belliard (1). DB—Atlanta 2, Minnesota 2.

Atlanta

	IP	H	R	ER	BB	SO
Leibrandt L, 0–1	4	7	4	4	1	3
Clancy	2	1	1	1	2	0
Wohlers	1	1	0	0	1	1
Stanton	1	0	0	0	0	2

Minnesota

	IP	H	R	ER	BB	SO
Morris W, 1–0	7	5	2	2	4	3
Guthrie	2/3	0	0	0	1	0
Aguilera S, 1	1 1/3	1	0	0	0	0

Leibrandt pitched to 3 batters in the 5th, Morris pitched to 2 batters in the 8th.. Time of game: 3:00. Attendance: 55,108.

2nd Game—Minneapolis, Oct. 20

ATLANTA (N)

	AB	R	H	RBI
LoSmith dh	3	0	0	0
Pendleton 3b	4	0	2	0
Gant cf	4	0	1	0
Justice rf	4	1	1	0
Bream 1b	4	0	1	0
Hunter lf	3	0	1	1
Olson c	4	1	1	0
Lemke 3b	3	0	0	0
Gregg ph	1	0	0	0
Belliard ss	2	0	1	1
Totals	**32**	**2**	**8**	**2**

MINNESOTA (A)

	AB	R	H	RBI
Gladden lf	4	0	0	0
Knoblauch 2b	3	1	0	0
Puckett cf	4	0	0	0
CDavis dh	3	1	1	2
Harper c	2	0	1	0
Mack rf	3	0	0	0
Hrbek 1b	2	0	0	0
Leius 3b	3	1	1	1
Gagne ss	3	0	1	0
Totals	**27**	**3**	**4**	**3**

Atlanta	010	010	000	—	2	8	1
Minnesota	200	000	01x	—	3	4	1

E—Justice (1), Leius (1). LOB—Atlanta 6, Minnesota 3. 2B—Bream (1), Olson (1). HR—CDavis (1) off Glavine, Leius (1) off Glavine. RBI—Hunter (1), Belliard (1), CDavis 2 (2), Leius (1). S—LoSmith. SF—Hunter, Belliard. DP—Atlanta 2.

	IP	H	R	ER	BB	SO
Atlanta						
Glavine L, 0–1	8	4	3	3	3	6
Minnesota						
Tapani W, 1–0	8	7	2	2	0	3
Aguilera S, 2	1	1	0	0	0	3

Balk—Glavine. Time of game: 2:37. Attendance: 55,145.

3rd Game—Atlanta, Oct. 22, 1991

MINNESOTA (A)

	AB	R	H	RBI
Gladden lf	6	1	3	0
Knoblauch 2b	5	0	1	1
Hrbek 1b	6	0	1	0
Puckett cf	4	1	1	1
Mack rf	4	0	0	0
Willis p	0	0	0	0
Sorrento ph	1	0	0	0
Guthrie p	0	0	0	0
Aguilera ph-p	1	0	0	0
Leius 3b	3	0	0	0
Pagliarulo ph-3b	1	0	0	0
Newman ph-3b	1	0	0	0
Gagne ss	5	0	0	0
Ortiz c	2	0	1	0
Harper ph-c	3	1	1	0
Erickson p	1	0	0	0
West p	0	0	0	0
Leach p	0	0	0	0
Larkin ph	1	0	1	0
Bedrosian p	0	0	0	0
CDavis ph	1	1	1	2
JBrown rf	0	0	0	0
Bush ph-rf	2	0	0	0
Totals	47	4	10	4

ATLANTA (N)

	AB	R	H	RBI
LoSmith lf	4	1	1	1
KtMitchell lf	0	0	0	0
Pendleton 3b	4	1	0	0
Gant cf	6	0	0	0
Justice rf	6	2	2	1
Bream 1b	3	0	1	0
Hunter ph-1b	2	0	0	0
Olson c	3	1	1	1
Lemke 2b	5	0	2	1
Belliard ss	3	0	1	1
Blauser ph-ss	1	0	0	0
Avery p	3	0	0	0
Pena p	0	0	0	0
Treadway ph	0	0	0	0
Stanton p	0	0	0	0
Cabrera ph	1	0	0	0
Wohlers p	0	0	0	0
Mercker p	0	0	0	0
Clancy p	0	0	0	0
Totals	43	5	8	5

Minnesota 100 000 120 000—4 10 1
Atlanta 010 120 000 001—5 8 2

E—Knoblauch (1), Pendleton (1), Lemke (1). LOB—Minnesota 10, Atlanta 12. 2B—Bream (2), Olson (2). 3B—Gladden (1). HR—LoSmith (1), Justice (1), Puckett (1), CDavis (4). RBI—Knoblauch (2), Puckett (1), CDavis 2 (4), LoSmith (1), Justice (1), Olson (1), Lemke (1), Belliard (2). SB—Knoblauch (3), Justice (1). S—Treadway. SF—Knoblauch.

	IP	H	R	ER	BB	SO
Minnesota						
Erickson	4 2/3	5	4	3	2	3
West	0	0	0	0	2	0
Leach	1/3	0	0	0	0	1
Bedrosian	2	0	0	0	0	1
Willis	2	0	0	0	2	0
Guthrie	2	1	0	0	1	1
Aguilera, L, 0-1	2/3	2	1	1	1	0
Atlanta						
Avery	7	4	3	2	0	5
Pena	2	4	1	1	0	4
Stanton	2	1	0	0	1	3
Wohlers	1/3	1	0	0	0	0
Mercker	1/3	0	0	0	0	1
Clancy W, 1-0	1/3	0	0	0	1	0

WP—Erickson, Pena. Time of game: 4:04. Attendance: 50,878.

4th Game—Atlanta, Oct. 23, 1991

MINNESOTA (A)

	AB	R	H	RBI
Gladden lf	4	0	0	0
Knoblauch 2b	4	0	1	0
Puckett cf	4	0	1	0
Hrbek 1b	4	0	0	0
Harper c	4	1	2	0
Mack rf	4	0	0	0
Pagliarulo 3b	3	1	3	2
Leius ph-3b	1	0	0	0
Bedrosian p	0	0	0	0
Gagne ss	3	0	0	0
Morris p	2	0	0	0
Larkin ph	1	0	0	0
Willis p	0	0	0	0
Guthrie p	0	0	0	0
Newman 3b	0	0	0	0
Totals	33	2	7	2

ATLANTA (N)

	AB	R	H	RBI
LoSmith lf	4	1	2	1
Pendleton 3b	4	1	1	1
Gant cf	3	0	1	0
Justice rf	3	0	0	0
Bream 1b	3	0	0	0
Hunter ph-1b	1	0	0	0
Olson c	3	0	0	0
Lemke 2b	4	1	3	0
Belliard ss	2	0	0	0
Treadway ph	1	0	0	0
Blauser ss	0	0	0	0
Smoltz p	2	0	0	0
Gregg ph	1	0	0	0
Wohlers p	0	0	0	0
Stanton p	0	0	0	0
Cabrera ph	0	0	0	0
Williard ph	0	0	0	1
Totals	31	3	8	3

Minnesota 010 000 100 — 2 7 0
Atlanta 001 000 101 — 3 8 0

LOB—Minnesota 5, Atlanta 7. 2B—Knoblauch (1), Harper (2), Pendleton (1), Lemke (1). 3B—Lemke (1). HR—LoSmith (2), Pendleton (1). RBI—Pagliarulo (1), LoSmith (2), Pendleton (1), Willard (1). SB—Knoblauch (4), LoSmith (1), Gant (1). CS—Mack (1). SF—Willard.

	IP	H	R	ER	BB	SO
Minnesota						
Morris	6	6	1	1	3	4
Willis	1 1/3	1	1	1	0	1
Guthrie L, 0-1	1/3	1	1	1	1	1
Bedrosian	1/3	0	0	0	0	0
Atlanta						
Smoltz	7	7	2	2	2	7
Wohlers	1/3	0	0	0	1	0
Stanton W, 1-0	1 2/3	0	0	0	0	1

WP—Morris. Time of Game: 2:57. Attendance: 50,878.

5th Game—Atlanta, Oct. 24, 1991

MINNESOTA (A)

	AB	R	H	RBI
Gladden lf	5	1	1	0
Knoblauch 2b	3	1	1	0
Bedrosian p	0	0	0	0
Ortiz c	1	0	0	1
Puckett cf	2	1	1	0
JBrown ph-cf	2	0	0	0
CDavis rf	3	2	1	0
Willis p	0	0	0	0
Harper c	2	0	0	1
Bush ph-rf	1	0	0	0
Leius 3b	2	0	1	1
West p	0	0	0	0
Newman 2b	1	0	1	1
Hrbek 1b	3	0	0	0
Sorrento ph-1b	0	0	0	0
Gagne ss	4	0	1	0
Tapani p	0	0	0	0
Larkin ph	1	0	0	0
Leach p	0	0	0	0
Pagliarulo ph-3b	2	0	0	0
Totals	33	5	7	5

ATLANTA (N)

	AB	R	H	RBI
LoSmith lf	5	1	1	1
KtMitchell lf	0	0	0	0
Pendleton 3b	4	3	2	0
Gant cf	4	3	3	1
Justice rf	5	2	2	5
Bream 1b	2	0	0	0
Hunter ph-1b	2	2	2	2
Olson c	5	1	3	0
StClaire p	0	0	0	0
Lemke 2b	4	2	2	3
Belliard ss	4	0	2	2
Glavine p	2	0	0	0
Mercker p	0	0	0	0
Gregg ph	1	0	0	0
Clancy p	1	0	0	0
Cabrera c	0	0	0	0
Totals	39	14	17	14

Minnesota 000 003 011 — 5 7 1
Atlanta 000 410 63x — 14 17 1

E—Harper (1), Pendleton (2). LOB—Minnesota 7, Atlanta 5. 2B—Gagne (1), Pendleton (2), Belliard (1). 3B—Gladden (1), Newman (1), Gant (1), Lemke 2 (3). HR—LoSmith (3), Justice (2), Hunter (1). RBI—Ortiz (1), Harper (1), Leius (2), Newman (1), Hrbek (2), LoSmith (3), Gant (3), Justice 5 (6), Hunter 2 (3), Lemke 3 (4), Belliard 2 (4). SB—Justice (2), Olson (1). CS—Leius (1). S—Puckett.

	IP	H	R	ER	BB	SO
Minnesota						
Tapani L, 1-1	4	6	4	4	2	4
Leach	2	2	1	1	0	1
West	0	2	4	4	2	0
Bedrosian	1	3	2	2	0	1
Willis	1	4	3	3	0	0
Atlanta						
Glavine W, 1-1	5 1/3	3	3	3	4	2
Mercker	2/3	0	0	0	0	0
Clancy	2	2	1	1	1	1
StClaire	1	1	1	1	0	0

WP—Bedrosian. Time of game: 2:59. Attendance: 50,878.

6th Game—Minneapolis, Oct. 26, 1991

ATLANTA (N)	AB	R	H	RBI	MINNESOTA (A)	AB	R	H	RBI
LoSmith dh	3	1	0	0	Gladden lf	4	1	0	0
Pendleton 3b	5	1	4	2	Knoblauch 2b	5	1	1	0
Gant cf	5	0	0	1	Puckett cf	4	2	3	3
Justice rf	4	0	0	0	CDavis dh	4	0	2	1
Bream 1b	4	0	1	0	Mack rf	4	0	2	1
KtMitchell pr-lf	0	0	0	0	Leius 3b	3	0	2	0
Hunter lf-1b	5	0	0	0	Pagliarulo ph-3b	1	0	0	0
Olson c	5	0	0	0	Hrbek 1b	4	0	0	0
Lemke 2b	4	1	2	0	Ortiz c	2	0	0	0
Belliard ss	2	0	1	0	Harper ph-c	2	0	0	0
Gregg ph	0	0	0	0	Gagne ss	4	0	1	0
Blauser ph-ss	2	0	1	0					
Totals	**39**	**3**	**9**	**3**	**Total**	**37**	**4**	**9**	**4**

Atlanta	000		020		100	00 —3	9	1
Minnesota	200		010		000	01 —4	9	0

E—Hunter (1). LOB—Atlanta 7, Minnesota 5. 2B—Mack (1). 3B—Puckett (1). HR—Puckett (2), Pendleton (2). RBI—Pendleton 2 (3), Gant (4), Puckett 3 (4), Mack (1). SB—Gladden (2), Puckett (1). CS—KtMitchell (1). SF—Puckett. DP—Atlanta 2, Minnesota 2.

Atlanta	IP	H	R	ER	BB	SO
Avery	6	6	3	3	1	3
Stanton	2	2	0	0	0	1
Pena	2	0	0	0	0	2
Leibrandt L, 0-2	0	1	1	1	0	0
Minnesota						
Erickson	6	5	3	3	2	2
Guthrie	1/3	1	0	0	1	1
Willis	2 2/3	1	0	0	0	1
Aguilera W, 1-1	2	2	0	0	0	0

HBP—by Erickson (LoSmith). WP—Guthrie. Time of game: 3:36. Attendance: 55,155.

7th Game—Minneapolis, Oct. 27, 1991

ATLANTA (N)	AB	R	H	RBI	MINNESOTA (A)	AB	R	H	RBI
LoSmith dh	4	0	2	0	Gladden lf	5	1	3	0
Pendleton 3b	5	0	1	0	Knoblauch 2b	4	0	1	0
Gant cf	4	0	0	0	Puckett cf	2	0	0	0
Justice rf	3	0	1	0	Hrbek 1b	3	0	0	0
Bream 1b	4	0	0	0	CDavis dh	4	0	1	0
Hunter lf	4	0	1	0	JBrown pr-ph	0	0	0	0
Olson c	4	0	0	0	Larkin ph	1	0	1	1
Lemke 2b	4	0	1	0	Harper c	4	0	2	0
Belliard ss	2	0	1	0	Mack rf	3	0	0	0
Blauser ph-ss	1	0	0	0	Gagne ss	2	0	0	0
					Bush ph	1	0	1	0
					Newman pr-ss	0	0	0	0
					Sorrento ph	1	0	0	0
					Leius ss	0	0	0	0
Totals	**35**	**0**	**7**	**0**	**Total**	**34**	**1**	**10**	**1**

Atlanta	000	000	000	0 —0	7	0
Minnesota	000	000	000	1 —1	10	0

LOB—Atlanta 8, Minnesota 12. 2B—Pendleton (3), Hunter (1), Gladden 2 (2). RBI—Larkin (1). S—Pendleton, Knoblauch. DP—Atlanta 3, Minnesota 1.

Atlanta	IP	H	R	ER	BB	SO
Smoltz	7 1/3	6	0	0	1	4
Stanton	2/3	2	0	0	1	0
Pena L, 0-1	1 1/3	2	1	1	3	1
Minnesota						
Morris W, 2-0	10	7	0	0	2	8

HBP—by Smoltz (Hrbek). PB—Harper. Time of game: 3:23. Attendance: 55,118.

Minnesota wins series, 4 games to 3.

IDITAROD

IDITAROD TRAIL SLED DOG RACE—1991

(Alaska, March 1991)

Course: 1,163 miles Anchorage to Nome.

Rick Swensen defeated Susan Butcher to win for a record fifth time. Both had won four previous races.

BICYCLING

TOUR DE FRANCE

(July 6–28, 1991)

Race in 22 stages covering 2,462 miles in 23 days around France.

Final standings

1. Miguel Indurain, Spain, Banesto, 101 hours, 1 minute, 20 seconds. 2. Gianni Bugno, Italy, Chateau d'Ax, 3 minutes, 36 seconds behind. 3. Claudio Chiappucci, Italy, Carrera, 5:56. 4. Charly Mottet, France, RMO, 7:37. 5. Luc Leblanc, France, Castorama, 10:10. 6. Laurent Fignon, France, Castorama, 11:27. 7. Greg LeMond, Wayzata, Minn., Z, 13:13. 8. Andrew Hampsten, Boulder, Colo., Motorola, 13:40. 9. Pedro Delgado, Spain, Banesto, 20:10. 10. Gerard Rue, France, Helvetia, 20:13. 11. Eduardo Chozas, Spain, ONCE, 21:00. 12. Abelardo Rondon, Colombia, Banesto, 26:47. 13. Gert-Jan Theunisse, Netherlands, 27:10. 14. Jean-Francois Bernard, France, Banesto, 28:57. 15. Maurizio Fondriest, Italy, RMO, 30:09.

HENDERSON OF ATHLETICS SETS CAREER STOLEN BASE MARK

Rickey Henderson of the Oakland A's broke the major league record for career stolen bases ending the 1991 season with 58 stolen bases making his career total 994. The previous record was held by Lou Brock with 938.

Henderson broke the major league record for stolen bases in one season on Aug. 27, 1982, at Milwaukee when he stole his 119th base in the third inning. The previous record of 118 was held by Lou Brock of St. Louis and was set in 1974. In 1982 he completed the season with 130.

TABLE TENNIS

WORLD CHAMPIONSHIPS

(Chiba, Japan, April 25–30, 1991)

Sweden defeated Yugoslavia, 3–2.

Singles

Joren Persson, Sweden, defeated Ilija Lupuleski, Yugoslavia, 21–18, 23–21; Mikael Appelgren, Sweden, defeated Zoran Kalinic, 21–13, 18–21, 21–0; Jan-ove Walldner, Sweden, defeated Zoran Kalinic, 21–19, 21–8; Zoran Primorac, Yugoslavia, defeated Jan-ove Waldner, 21–14, 21—11

Doubles

Zoran Primorac and Ilija Lupuleski, Yugoslavia, defeated Mikael Appelgren and Jorgen Persson, 21–16, 21–19.

Third place match—Czechoslovakia defeated Belgium, 3 games to 1.

Fifth place match—Germany defeated Korea, 3–0.

Seventh place match—China defeated Canada, 3–0.

Ninth place match—Austria defeated Britain, 3–0.

Eleventh place match—France defeated Soviet Union, 3–1.

Thirteenth place match—Japan defeated Italy, 3–0.

Fifteenth place match—United States defeated China, 3–0.

Women's Championship—Korea defeated China, 3–2.

CHESS

WORLD CHAMPIONS

1894–1921	Emanuel Lasker, Germany
1921–27	Jose R. Capablanca, Cuba
1927–35	Alexander A. Alekhine, U.S.S.R.
1935–37	Dr. Max Euwe, Netherlands
1937–46	Alexander A. Alekhine, U.S.S.R.[1]
1948–57	Mikhail Botvinnik, U.S.S.R.
1957–58	Vassily Smyslov, U.S.S.R.
1958–60	Mikhail Botvinnik, U.S.S.R.
1960–61	Mikhail Tal, U.S.S.R.
1961–63	Mikhail Botvinnik, U.S.S.R.
1963–68	Tigran Petrosian, U.S.S.R.
1969–71	Boris Spassky, U.S.S.R.
1972–74	Bobby Fischer, Los Angeles
1975	Bobby Fischer[2], Anatoly Karpov, U.S.S.R.
1976–85	Anatoly Karpov, U.S.S.R.[3]
1985–91[4]	Gary Kasparov, U.S.S.R.

1. Alekhine, a French citizen, died while champion. 2. Relinquished title. 3. In 1978, Karpov defeated Viktor Korchnoi 6 games to 5. 4. Next World Championship scheduled for October, 1993.

UNITED STATES CHAMPIONS

1909–36	Frank J. Marshall, New York
1936–44	Samuel Reshevsky, New York[1]
1944–46	Arnold S. Denker, New York
1946	Samuel Reshevsky, Boston
1948	Herman Steiner, Los Angeles
1951–52	Larry Evans, New York
1954–57	Arthur Bisguier, New York
1958–61	Bobby Fischer, Brooklyn, N.Y.

1962	Larry Evans, New York
1963–67	Bobby Fischer, New York
1968	Larry Evans, New York
1969–71	Samuel Reshevsky, Spring Valley, N.Y.
1972	Robert Byrne, Ossining, N.Y.
1973	Lubomir Kavelek, Washington; John Grefe, San Francisco
1974–77	Walter Browne, Berkeley, Calif.
1978–79	Lubomir Kavalek, New York
1980	Tie, Walter Browne, Berkeley, Calif. Larry Christiansen, Modesto, Calif. Larry Evans, Reno, Nev.
1981–82[2]	Tie, Walter Browne, Berkeley, Calif. Yasser Seirawan, Seattle, Wash.
1983	Tie, Walter Browne, Berkeley, Calif. Larry Christiansen, Los Angeles, Calif., Roman Dzindzichashvili, Corona, N.Y.
1984–85	Lev Alburt, New York City
1986	Yasser Seirawan, Seattle, Wash.
1987	Tie—Nick Defirmian, San Francisco, and Joel Benjamin, Brooklyn, N.Y.
1988	Michael Wilder, Princeton, N.J.
1989	Tie, Stuart Rachels, Birmingham, Ala. Yasser Seirawan, Seattle, Wash. Roman Dzindzichashvili, New York, N.Y.
1990–91	Lev Alburt, New York, N.Y.

1. In 1942, Isaac I. Kashdan of New York was co-champion for a while because of a tie with Reshevsky in that year's tournament. Reshevsky won the play-off. 2. Championship not contested in 1982.

GYMNASTICS

WORLD CHAMPIONSHIPS—1991
(Sept. 6–15, 1991, Indianapolis, Ind.)

Men	Pts
All–around—1. Grigori Misutin, Soviet Union	59.050
2. Vitaly Scherbo, Soviet Union	58.950
3. Valeri Liukin, Soviet Union	58.550
Vault—1. Ok You You, Korea	9.700
2. Vitaly Scherbo, Soviet Union	9.699
3. Yutaka Alhara, Japan	9.631
Parallel bars—1. Jing Li, China	9.862
2. Igor Korobchinski, Soviet Union	9.825
3. Linyao Guo, China	9.812
Floor exercise—1. Igor Korobchinski, Soviet Union	9.875
2. Vitaly Scherbo, Soviet Union	9.800
3. Daisuke Nishikawa, Japan	9.787
Pommel horse—1. Valeri Belenki, Soviet Union	9.912
2. Linyao Guo, China	9.887
3. Jing Li, China	9.875
Still rings—1. Grigori Misutin, Soviet Union	9.875
2. Andreas Wecker, Germany	9.982
3. Yuri Chechi, Italy	9.837
High bar—1. (tie) Chungyang Li, China and Ralf Buechner, Germany	9.787
2. Vitaly Scherbo, Soviet Union	9.775

Women	Pts
All–Around—1. Kim Zmeskal, United States	39.848
2. Svetlana Boguinskala, Soviet Union	39.736
3. Christina Bontas, Romania	39.711
Vault—1. Lavinia Milosovici, Romania	9.949
2. (tie) Henrietta Onodi, Hungary and Oksana Tchusovitina, Soviet Union	9.918
Uneven bars—1. Gwang Suk Kim, North Korea	10.000
2. (tie) Shannon Miller, United States, and Tatiana Gutsu, Soviet Union	9.950
Beam—1. Svetlana Boguinskala, Soviet Union	9.962
2. Tatiana Gutso, Soviet Union	9.950
3. (tie) Betty Okino, United States, and Lavinia Milosovici, Romania	9.900
Floor exercise—1. (tie) Christina Bontas, Romania, and Oksana Tchusovitini, Soviet Union	9.962
3. Kim Zmesdkal, United States	9.950

UNITED STATES CHAMPIONSHIPS
(June 6–9, 1991, Cincinnati, Ohio)

Men	Pts
All–around—1. Chris Waller, Mount Prospect, Ill.	114.62
2. Patrick Kirksey, Tucker, Ga.	114.58
Chainey Umphrey, Albuquerque, N.M. (tie)	114.58
Vault—1. Scott Keswick, Las Vegas, Nev.	9.625
2. John Roethlisberger, Afton, Minn.	9.600
3. Lance Ringnald, Albuquerque, N.M.	9.425
Parallel bars—1. Scott Keswick, Las Vegas, Nev.	9.850
2. John Roethlisberger, Afton, Minn.	9.725
3. Jarrod Hanks, University of Oklahoma	9.700
Floor exercise—1. Mike Racanelli, West Babylon, N.Y.	9.800
2. Tom Schlesinger, Boulder, Colo.	9.700
3. Lance Ringnald, Albuquerque, N.M.	9.675
Pommel horse—1. Chris Waller, Mount Prospect, Ill.	9.825
2. (tie) Jarrod Hanks, University of Oklahoma Dominick Minicucci, Temple University	9.675
Still rings—1. Scott Keswick, Las Vegas, Nev.	9.825
2. Chainey Umphrey, Albuquerque, N.M.	9.775
3. Bob Steller, University of Nebraska	9.725
High bar—1. Lance Ringnald, Albuquerque, N.M.	9.800
2. Tim Ryan, Stanford University	9.500
3. Dominick Minicucci, Temple University	9.400

Women	Pts
All–around—1. Kim Zmeskal, Houston, Texas	78.42
2. Sandy Woolsey, Tempe, Ariz.	78.08
3. Kerri Strug, Houston, Texas	77.97
Vault—1. Kerri Strug, Houston, Texas	9.825
2. Sandy Woolsey, Tempe, Ariz.	9.743
3. Shannon Miller, Edmond, Okla.	9.687
Uneven bars—1. Elisabeth Crandall, Woodland Hills, Ca.	9.875
2. Sandy Woolsey, Tempe, Ariz.	9.850
3. (tie) Kerri Strug, Houston Texas, and Chelle Stack, Cypress Academy	9.762
Beam—1. Shannon Miller, Edmond, Okla.	9.867
2. Kim Zmeskal, Houston, Texas	9.812
3. Shelley Engel, Los Angeles, Calif.	9.750
Floor exercise—1. (tie) Kim Zmeskal, Houston, Texas, and Dominique Dawes, Silver Spring, Md.	9.912
3. (tie) Sandy Woolsey, Tempe, Ariz., and Kim Kelley, King of Prussia, Pa.	9.850

The Baltic Republics Regain Their Independence

The three Baltic republics—Estonia, Latvia, and Lithuania—received recognition of their independence just past our final deadline for inclusion in our regular Countries of the World section. Therefore, rather than choosing not to include these nations in the 1992 *Almanac*, we are presenting them one-time only as a Special Current Events item in order to honor them with the recognition they deserve. □

ESTONIA

Republic of Estonia
President: Arnold Ruutel (1990)
Prime Minister: Edgar Savisaar (1990)
Area: 18,370 sq mi. (47,549 sq km)
Population: (1990): 1.5 million (Estonians, 61.5%; Russians, 30.3%; Ukrainians, 3.1%; Byelorussians, 1.8%; Finns, 1.1%); (avg. annual growth rate, ethnic Estonians: 1.6%); density per square mile: 82
Capital and largest city (1990): Tallinn, 506,000. Other important cities: Tartu, Kohtla-Järve, Narva, and Pärnu
Monetary unit: Ruble, Estonian currency to be created
Languages: Estonian is official; also Russian
Religions (1937): Lutheran, 78%; Orthodox, 19%
National name: Esti
Literacy: (n.a., there was a high literacy rate before the Soviet occupation)
Economic survey (1989): Gross national product: n.a. Per capita income: $6,240. Labor force (1987): urban areas, 72%, rural, 28%. Major industries: oil shale processing (World's No. 2 producer), mineral fertilizers, wood processing, pulp, and peat. Fishing, farming, and shipbuilding are also important. Trade: exports to over 30 countries, (sold for rubles to Moscow, who exported the products to West for hard currency).

Geography: Estonia borders on the Baltic Sea in the west, the gulfs of Riga and Finland in the southwest and north, respectively, Latvia in the south, and Russia in the east. It is mainly a lowland country with numerous lakes. Lake Chudskoye is the largest and is important to the fishing and shipping industries.

Government: Transitional, from a Moscow-directed occupation government to an anticipated Western-style democratic government.

History: Born out of World War I, this small Baltic state enjoyed a mere two short decades of independence before it was absorbed again by its powerful neighbor, Russia. In the 13th century, the Estonians had been conquered by the Teutonic Knights of Germany, who reduced them to serfdom. In 1521, the Swedes took over, and the power of the German (Balt) landowning class was curbed somewhat. But after 1721, when Russia succeeded Sweden as the ruling power, the Estonians were subjected to a double bondage—the Balts and the tsarist officials. The oppression lasted until the closing months of World War I, when Estonia finally achieved independence.

Shortly after the start of World War II, the nation was occupied by Russian troops and was incorporated as the 16th republic of the U.S.S.R. in 1940. Germany occupied the nation from 1941 to 1944, when it was retaken by the Russians. Most of the nations of the world, including the United States and Great Britain, never recognized the Soviet incorporation of Estonia.

Soon after Lithuania's declaration of independence from the Soviet Union in March 1990, the Estonian congress renamed its country on May 8 and omitted the words "Soviet Socialist" and adopted the former (1918) Coat of Arms of the Republic of Estonia. Thereafter, the government cautiously promoted national autonomy.

After the attempted Soviet coup to remove President Gorbachev failed, Estonia formally declared its independence from the U.S.S.R. on August 20, 1991. Recognition by European and other countries followed, and on Sept. 2, 1991, President Bush announced that the United States was giving full diplomatic recognition to the Baltic nations. The Soviet Union recognized Estonia's independence on September 6 and it received UN membership on Sept. 17, 1991.

LATVIA

The Republic of Latvia
President: Anatolijs Gorbunovos (1990)
Prime Minister: Ivars Jodmanis
Area: 25,400 sq mi. (65,786 sq km)
Population (1990): 2,700,000 (Latvian, 53%; Russian, 33%; Ukrainians, Byelorussians, other 14%); density per square mile: 106
Capital and largest city (1990): Riga, 915,000. Other important cities: Daugavpils, 127,000; Liepaja, 114,000
Monetary unit: Ruble (from 1940–1991). Will convert to "Lat" in mid-1992.
Language: Latvian
Religions: Lutheran, Catholic, and Baptist
National name: Latvija
Literacy: very high
Economic survey: Most industrialized of the Baltic states. Gross national product and per capita income: n.a. Natural resources: Peat, sapropel, timber, limestone, dolomite, and clay. Major industries: Machinery and metalworking, electrical equipment, agricultural engineering, light industry, timber and paper, building materials, and chemicals and pharmaceuticals. Latvia also has a large dairy industry. About 80% of trade is with the Soviet Union; other countries are Poland, Germany, Sweden, and Czechoslovakia.

Geography: Latvia borders Estonia on the north, Lithuania in the south, the Baltic Sea with the Gulf of Riga in the west, Russia in the east, and Byelorussia in the southeast. Latvia is largely a fertile lowland with numerous lakes and hills to the east.

Government: Latvia is a parliamentary democracy.

History: Descended from Aryan stock, the Latvians were early tribesmen who settled along the Baltic Sea and, lacking a central government, fell an easy prey to more powerful peoples. The German Teutonic knights first conquered them in the 13th century and ruled the area, consisting of Livonia and Courland, until 1562.

Poland conquered the territory in 1562 and ruled until 1795 in Courland; control of Livonia was disputed between Sweden and Poland from 1562 to 1629. Sweden controlled Livonia from 1629 to 1721. Russia took over Livonia in the latter year and Courland after the third partition of Poland in 1795.

From that time until 1918, the Latvians remained Russian subjects, although they preserved their language, customs, and folklore. The Russian Revolution of 1917 gave them their opportunity for freedom, and the Latvian republic was proclaimed on Nov. 18, 1918.

The republic lasted little more than 20 years. It was occupied by Russian troops in 1939 and incorporated into the Soviet Union in 1940. German armies occupied the nation from 1941 to 1943–44, when they were driven out by the Russians. Most countries, including the United States, refused to recognize the Soviet annexation of Latvia.

In September 1989, the Central Committee of the Soviet Communist Party accused the independence movements of the three Baltic republics of trying to disintegrate the cohesion of the Soviet Union and warned them of "impending disaster." Despite continued threats from the Kremlin, the leaders of the movements continued to protest and demand a peaceful transition to self-determination.

When the coup against Soviet President Mikhail Gorbachev failed, the Baltic nations saw a historic opportunity to free themselves from Soviet domination and, following the actions of Lithuania and Estonia, Latvia declared its independence on Aug. 21, 1991.

European and most other nations quickly recognized their independence, and on Sept. 2, 1991, President Bush announced full diplomatic recognition for Latvia, Estonia, and Lithuania. The Soviet Union recognized Latvia's independence on September 6, and UN membership followed on Sept. 17, 1991.

LITHUANIA

Republic of Lithuania
President: Vytautas Landsbergis (1990)
Prime Minister: Gediminas Vatnorius (1991)
Area: 25,174 sq mi. (64,445 sq km)
Population (1989): 3,690,000 (Lithuanian, 80.1%; Russian, 8.6%); density per square mile: 82
Capital and largest city: Vilnius, 582,000
Monetary unit: Ruble; Lithuanian currency will replace it
Languages: Lithuanian
Religion (1939): Catholic, 85%
National name: Lietuva
Literacy: very high
Economic survey: Gross national product: n.a. Per capita income (1989): $3,000. Labor force: 1,653,000. Employment: Industry and construction, 40%; agriculture and forestry, 20%. Lithuania has many mineral resources. About 55% of trade is with the Soviet Union. Also trades with Germany, Great Britain, Belgium, Denmark, Poland, Cuba, Czechoslovakia, and Hungary.

Geography: Lithuania is situated on the eastern shore of the Baltic Sea and borders Latvia on the north, Russia on the east, and Poland on the south. It is a country of gently rolling hills, many forests, rivers and streams, and lakes. Its principal natural resource is agricultural land.

Government: Lithuania is a parliamentary democracy. The head of state is the chairman of the Supreme Council (parliament). The president chooses the prime minister with the approval of the parliament.

History: Southernmost of the three Baltic states, Lithuania in the Middle Ages was a grand duchy joined to Poland through royal marriage. Poles and Lithuanians merged forces to defeat the Teutonic knights of Germany at Tannenberg in 1410 and extended their power far into Russian territory. In 1795, however, following the third partition of Poland, Lithuania fell into Russian hands and did not regain its independence until 1918, toward the end of the first World War.

The republic was occupied by the Soviet Union in 1939 and annexed outright the following year. From 1940 to 1944 it was occupied by German troops and then was retaken by Russia. Western countries, including the United States, never recognized the Russian annexation of Lithuania.

Nineteen eighty-eight saw a re-emergence of the Lithuanian independence movement. On March 11, 1990, Vytautas Landsbergis, the non-communist head of the largest Lithuanian popular movement (Sajudis) was elected president, and his party swept the Lithuanian parliament. On the same day, the Supreme Council rejected Soviet rule and declared the restoration of Lithuania's independence, the first Baltic republic to take this action.

Confrontation with the Soviet Union ensued along with economic sanctions, but they were lifted after which the Lithuanian government agreed to freeze its declaration. However, the growing split with Moscow led to increasing popular demands for self-determination.

After an abortive coup to depose Soviet President Mikhail Gorbachev, President Landsbergis called his country's independence a formality.

Lithuania's independence was quickly recognized by major European and other nations, and on Sept. 2, 1991, President Bush announced full diplomatic recognition for the Baltic republics. The Soviet Union finally recognized the independence of the Baltic states on September 6. UN admittance followed on Sept. 17, 1991.

The Nazi-Soviet Non-Aggression Pact

On Aug. 23, 1939, a week before Germany invaded Poland, Soviet Foreign Commissar, Vyacheslav Molotov and Joachim von Ribbintrop, Germany's Foreign Minister, signed a mutual non-aggression pact in Moscow that guaranteed the security of the Soviet Union's borders.

However, it was never announced to the public that the pact included a secret protocol in which Germany agreed to recognize a Soviet-sphere of influence that gave Russia a free hand to annex the Baltic republics—Estonia, Latvia, and Lithuania, the eastern half of Poland, Finland, and the Rumanian province of Bessarabia. Moscow also agreed to provide Germany with strategic raw materials in exchange for industrial products.

Germany invaded Poland on Sept. 1, 1939, and the Soviet Union secured its part of the bargain by invading eastern Poland on September 17. On September 28, a German-Russian agreement was signed dividing Poland between Russia and Germany.

The mere existence of the secret protocol remained a secret until after the war when a copy of the text fell into British hands in Germany. The Soviet government strongly denied its authenticity until very recently. ☐

The Gulf War and Its Aftermath

By Arthur P. Reed, Jr.

From the euphoria of a quick Persian Gulf victory early in 1991, the United States and its allies reeled under the impact of a troubled postwar era.

Americans' preoccupation with the "Vietnam syndrome" had soon faded and they were still proud of the achievements of their armed forces, many of them young reservists torn from their families, jobs, and studies, many of them women who shared the hardships and dangers of "Operation Desert Storm."

But at home, the pressure of domestic troubles mounted—recession, civil rights, city and state financial woes, crime. The euphoria that returned briefly for massive victory parades could not mask those worries.

And victory was not bloodless, particularly for civilians. Relentless bombing of Iraqi targets cost thousands of lives and crippled one of the most advanced nations of the Middle East. When the war was over, the accounting was not all one-sided. Yes, Kuwait, still with its royal family in power, had been liberated—with heavy damage and hundreds of oil wells still smoldering and darkening the skies—and a feared invasion of Saudi Arabia had been averted. But the despot Saddam Hussein still swaggered among his war-weakened people ravaged by disease.

In the north, some two million Kurdish refugees—estimates varied—many of then infants, suffered and died under squalid conditions that sickened a compassionate world.

During months of inaction after the invasion of Kuwait on Aug. 2,1991, President Bush forged a coalition of some Arab states, nations of West Europe, and even Japan. Every day fresh troops, armor, ships, and planes arrived at the Persian Gulf to build the massive force that ultimately drove Saddam Hussein from conquered Kuwait. On Aug. 6, 1990, the U.N. Security Council outlawed trade with Iraq unless it withdrew from Kuwait by Jan. 15, 1991. As the deadline drew near, Congress, on Jan. 12, authorized the President to take military action. This, with some misgivings as to whether sanctions had been given sufficient time to prove effective.

At the U.N. deadline, the Allied forces launched air attacks against Iraq and occupied Kuwait. The next day Iraq fired the first Scud missiles at Israel in what was to prove a futile attempt to bait Israel into retaliation with the possible weakening of the Arab segment of the coalition.

Among early highlights of the conflict an ecological disaster loomed as Iraq spilled millions of gallons of Kuwaiti oil into the Persian Gulf, creating a spill 40 miles long and 8 miles wide that dwarfed the *Exxon Valdez* disaster in Alaska. The United States bombed Iraqi-controlled oil installations along the Kuwaiti coastline seeking to contain the spill. In late January Hussein fulfilled his threat to set Kuwaiti oil refineries ablaze, the smoke from more than 500 wells darkening the Kuwaiti skies long after the end of the war.

When the war began, U.S. officials insisted that their policy was to aim only at military targets. However, bombardments took a heavy toll of Iraqi civilians and crippled vital services. One of the worst disasters came on Feb. 13. An American Stealth fighter-bomber dropped two bombs on a reinforced concrete building in a residential section of Baghdad identified by the Allies as a military command and control center. More than 500 civilians were reported to have been killed. The next day the Iraqi Government denounced the attack on what they contended was merely an air-raid shelter; Western reporters said they could find no signs of military use. Washington, however, blamed Hussein's placement of civilians in the building with the ensuing loss of lives.

The role of the Allied Patriot missiles in countering the Soviet-built Iraqi Scuds was equivocal. Early in the short war, Scuds attacked Israel and Saudi Arabia with some casualties and building damage.

Reports at the time said American Patriots had successfully intercepted many Scuds high above Tel Aviv, Haifa, and Riyadh. However, on Feb. 26, despite a Patriot response, a Scud demolished a barracks in Dhahran, Saudi Arabia, housing about 100 American troops, with 28 deaths reported. Much later the Pentagon conceded that a computer software defect had caused the Patriot's radar aiming system to shut down, and that a similar problem had been encountered in another Patriot battery in Israel. It was noted, however, that the Patriot had not been designed for the defense of cities but as an antiaircraft weapon that could be operated up to 14 hours at a time, far shorter than was the wartime practice.

Long after the war, the Pentagon and the press—print and audio-visual—remained at odds over restrictions that had been placed on news coverage through the requirement for escorted reporter pools and close censoring of reports. The issue, of course, was whether military operations required such extreme restrictions.

The Pentagon laid down the rules on Jan. 9. News executives immediately denounced them as intolerable censorship.

Later, 17 top news executives said in a report to Defense Secretary Dick Cheney that the news restrictions in the Gulf had amounted to "real censorship" "and confirmed the worst fears of reporters in a democracy."

On Feb. 27 President Bush declared the war ended—"Kuwait is liberated"; "Iraq's army is defeated"—and suspended offensive operations.

And on April 3 the U.N. Security Council formally offered to end the war but only if Saddam Hussein accepted tough military and financial conditions, among them that he renounce terrorism, pay billions of dollars in compensation for the occupation of Kuwait, and accept borders that he had earlier rejected.

The U.N. also stipulated that Hussein allow the destruction of all chemical and biological weapons and Scud and other missiles, and the monitoring of atomic potential. On April 6 Hussein accepted those terms although he branded them unjust.

Allied war strategy was unexpectedly effective against what had been feared were superior odds in combat troops, tanks, and artillery. And Allied casualties were relatively low. The U.S. command in the Gulf, Gen. H. Norman Schwarzkopf, attributed the Allied victory to deception, mobility, and overwhelming air superiority (although at a later hearing he questioned over-all intelligence). Thus, troops were deployed to fool Hussein as to the sites of planned assaults. The massive troop movements—both deceptive and real—went undetected by the enemy, whose planes had been grounded and who lacked spy satellites.

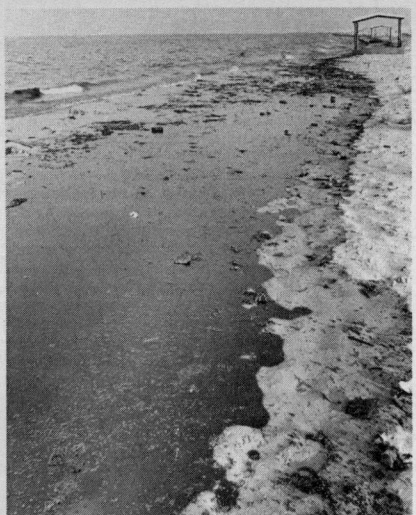

World nations were shocked by Iraq's deliberate acts of ecological terrorism during the Gulf war. Above—Crude oil washes ashore at Kafji, Saudi Arabia, polluting once pristine beaches and killing sea birds. Military authorities claim that Iraq released the oil from Kuwaiti refineries. AP/Wide World photo.

In a postwar survey, a United Nations inspection team declared that the Allied bombardment had had a "near apocalyptic impact" on Iraq and that it had relegated it to being a "pre-industrial age nation" which "had been until January a rather highly urbanized and mechanized society."

Later, a Harvard medical team reported after a survey that public health in Iraq was rapidly worsening with postwar epidemics, power disruptions, and the closing of many overloaded hospitals and clinics.

And in June Administration analysts reported that Iraq remained seriously incapacitated with a health catastrophe at hand and years of rebuilding the civilian economy. As the year drew on, there were more and more reports of the harsh effect of the continuing embargo on Iraq's economy.

In Washington the quick success of the war was a setback for the Democrat's 1992 hopes. The Republicans sought to portray them as weak and unpatriotic, since many had opposed the war. The Democrats tried to turn the focus onto domestic and economic issues. The White House downplayed reported statements by General Schwarzkopf that questioned the decision to end the war without advancing farther into Iraq to crush Hussein's armies. And there were reports that Gen. Colin L. Powell, Chairman of the Joint Chiefs of Staff, had favored further reliance on economic pressure.

But in the postbellum era the plight of the refugees, north and south, remained a festering sore. Some specialists in disaster relief ranked the crisis among the major disasters of recent years, but with its horrors compressed into a record short time.

By early April, the Iraqi Government appeared to have crushed a Shiite rebellion in the south and Kurdish outbreaks in the north. Earlier, anarchy prevailed in the cities of Basra, Iraq's second largest, and Safwan, near the Kuwaiti border. Troops and vehicles driven from Kuwait had engulfed the area. Crowds cheered anti-Hussein slogans. But Government forces were reported to have regained major cities. Kurdish rebels in the north fled across the mountain borders with Iran and Turkey.

After their month-long revolt had collapsed, Kurdish civilians fleeing Hussein's vengeance began a mass exodus in a human tide by car, truck, and mule along twisting mountain roads.

In freezing shelterless mountain "camps," especially in Turkey, starvation and disease were rampant. Countless infants, dehydrated, died after wrenching bouts of diarrhea.

The plight of the refugees aroused the world's compassion; in April Bush ordered Air Force transports to begin dropping food, water, tents, blankets, and clothing to the Kurds in northern Iraq. He also promised aid to Turkey and Iran, havens for most of the fleeing Kurds.

In agreeing to safe zones in the north, the Administration dealt gingerly with the problems of international law and regional feelings. The relief effort involved plans for feeding 700,000 persons a day and setting up refugee settlements. Until the terrified Kurds could be persuaded that returning home was safe, American, British, and French troops erected secure camps to shelter thousands.

On April 20 a battalion of 500 American marines landed in northern Iraq to establish the first camp, and set up a safe perimeter to assure safety for Kurds returning from Turkey and other havens.

A mass repatriation began in early May, with thousands returning to Iraq in Allied vehicles and on their own. On June 1 the Allies closed the last refugee camp in Turkey.

As the refugee crisis seemed to be winding down, it became the focus of criticism of Bush and his overall war policies. He was accused by some of having encouraged anti-Hussein uprisings and then of having failed to support them. Some even charged the President with betrayal for having failed to ground Hussein's gunships that harassed the refugees. In reply, the Administration displayed reluctance to interfere in the internal affairs of Iraq.

There was also disquiet about the internal situation in liberated Kuwait, where mass trials of alleged collaborators, followed by Draconian death sentences, drew worldwide criticism for neglect of ordinary standards of fairness and due process.

Over-all, as the year drew on, the consequences of the war were unfathomable—for Kuwait, Iraq, Saudi Arabia, and the whole Middle East—and may remain so for years. For Kuwait, still a feudal fiefdom, the cost of reconstruction was estimated at $100 billion. And the Herculean task of quenching the hundreds of oil well fires seems likely to take years. But stirring of democracy augurs change.

Tension between Israel and the Arab states remained high even as Secretary of State James H. Baker 3rd sought to mediate with persistent shuttle diplomacy.

A further complication arose with charges to the U.N. by the Bush Administration that Iraq was trying to hide equipment for making nuclear weapons in violation of the Security Council resolution ending the war.

Only time will vindicate the wisdom of the decision to go to war and the judgments of those who waged it—as well as the integrity of those for and against it. Meanwhile, the bands played, confetti showered, and fireworks dazzled at mammoth parades in New York, Washington, and across the nation, giving millions a short respite from the gritty peacetime life around them. □

The New Face of Eastern Europe

By Arthur P. Reed, Jr.

Like the burst of an H-bomb, events in the Soviet Union exploded over the world in a single week of August 1991. When the blast was over, the Soviet Union was crumbling, the Communist Party was rapidly dissolving and a new leadership was in the ascendance.

The week began with an abortive coup to unseat Soviet President Mikhail S. Gorbachev, itself earth-shaking and enough for banner headlines in the conservative press. Gorbachev was reported under house arrest at his vacation retreat in the Crimea; right-wing diehards seemed to have triumphed. But within days Gorbachev was back in his Moscow office after Russians by the thousands had mobilized to thwart a threatened takeover of their Republic's Government by the military. Russian President Boris Yeltsin was emerging as the Union's hero, with Gorbachev seemingly relegated to a minor role. This though he had sealed the Communist Party's doom by resigning as its Secretary general and ordering its Central Committee to dissolve. And Republic after Republic began proclaiming independence.

Almost immediately, Western Governments began recognizing the secession of the three Baltic republics. And on September 2 President Bush gave them the full prestigious diplomatic recognition of the United States.

The final outcome? It will be years before the world knows. But nothing will be the same.

The Russian explosion dwarfed all blips on the thermometer of East Europe's health, as measured in medical terms.

Otherwise, East Europe's state fluctuated wildly during 1991. Its temperatures ranged from a mild fever—99 or 100, perhaps—in the relatively calm states of Poland, Hungary, Bulgaria and Romania—to a feverish (?) in a Yugoslavia torn by ethnic strife that approached outright civil war.

But for all nations of East Europe, the demise of the Warsaw pact on July 1 signaled the end, with its consequent benefits, of the belligerent Cold War era.

In the Soviet Union the forces of democracy and a free economy had earlier seemed to gain, if haltingly, against the entrenched reaction of the diehard Communist bureaucracy, the KGB, and the military after 70 years of a mindless, doctrinaire, and ruthless Marxist dictatorship.

One milestone was the election in June of Boris Yeltsin as President of the dominant Russian Republic in the first free Western-style ballot. Another was the success, modest but real, of Soviet President Gorbachev in winning more than token acceptance as an associate of the Group of Seven of the world's leading democracies at their London meeting in July.

A splintered Yugoslavia was on the brink of full-scale civil war. Alarmed, the European Community sent more than 100 observers to seek a cease-fire in the battles between Serbs and Croatians. Indeed, in mid-summer the Yugoslav Prime Minister warned of a conflagration with millions of victims and threatened to resign if his peace program was not accepted. Already the death toll had mounted into the hundreds in clashes between Serbs and Croats, the two largest ethnic groups.

The tide of nationalism, rooted both in ancient rivalries and bitter memories of World War II, ran high. Serbia, the largest and most powerful republic, Croatia, and Slovenia all took steps to secede from the Yugoslav federation.

Elsewhere in the erstwhile Soviet zone, progress toward democracy stumbled forward. A key step toward a new era was taken when the Soviet Union and five other nations formally dissolved the Warsaw pact, a Cold War hangover.

Progress toward reform seemed greatest in Poland, Czechoslovakia, and Hungary. But even there strikes and protests mounted over the hardships of transition.

On the political side events included: Czechoslovakia's law returning hundreds of thousands of business and other property confiscated by the old Communist regime to the original owners or their heirs; the signing by the leaders of Germany and Poland of a treaty of cooperation and friendship.

In once hard-line Stalinist Albania, the winds of change blew freshest during 1991. For four decades or more, the tiny Balkan nation had been a textbook bastion of the most rigid Marxist orthodoxy, isolated not only from the West but also from liberalizing influences in the East.

The prognosis for an ailing or recuperating East Europe? Perhaps examining physicians might guardedly find its health somewhat improved despite some tragic and major relapses.   ☐

The Strategic Arms Limitation Treaty

A solemn 30-minute ceremony in St. Vladimir's Hall in the Kremlin on July 31 marked the signing of the long-awaited Strategic Arms Reduction Treaty (Start).

With their pen-strokes on the 700-page document, Presidents Bush and Gorbachev agreed, after nine years of negotiations, on a compact to scale down their stocks of long-range nuclear weapons. Their two legislatures are expected to approve.

The goal of the treaty is to reduce strategic offensive arms over seven years by approximately 30 percent.

Key Features: Limits of 1,600 delivery vehicles, intercontinental ballistic missiles, submarine-launched ballistic missiles and launchers, and heavy bombers.

Limits of 6,000 "accountable" strategic warheads on these systems: no more than 4,900 on ballistic missiles; no more than 1,100 on mobile intercontinental ballistic missiles; no more than 1,540 on SS-18s (the Soviet's 154 heavy intercontinental ballistic missiles).

Detailed rules for counting are specified. Ballistic missile warheads will count as one warhead each under the 6,000 limit.

General Effects: The Soviet Union must cut its ballistic missile warheads by more than 35 percent, to about 7,000 from 11,000. The U.S. must reduce its own arsenal by about 25 percent, to 9,000 from 12,000. The Soviets must destroy half of their heavy SS-18 intercontinental ballistic missiles; the U.S. has none and is banned from building any.

Verification: Complicated procedures are stipulated. These include spot inspections of strategic weapons emplacements.

Despite the reductions both superpowers will retain tremendous nuclear strength, with thousands of warheads trained on each others' major cities.

But in sum, Gorbachev described the Start treaty as a "moral achievement." To Bush, it represented a major step "forward toward world peace."   ☐

What Happened in 1991

Highlights of the important events of the year from January to October 1991, organized month by month, in three categories for easy reference. The Countries of the World section (starting on page 147) covers specific international events, country by country.

JANUARY 1991
International

Israelis Open Consulate in Moscow (Jan. 3): Raise flag in major step toward restoring full relations.

Troops Defeat Coup in Haiti (Jan. 7): Storm Presidential palace and seize Duvalier-era official after he had declared martial law.

Lithuanian Government Resigns (Jan. 8): Prime Minister and Cabinet quit in dispute with Parliament over economic and political policy.

South Africa Schools Integrated (Jan. 9): Black children admitted for first time to previously all-white classes in 33 schools where parents approved.

Pentagon Adopts Rules for Gulf News (Jan. 9): Orders war coverage by pools of reporters and security review of dispatches. Media protest strongly.

Congress Votes Authority for War (Jan. 12): After three days of debate authorizes Bush to use military force against Iraq. Vote in Senate is 52–47. In House it is 250–183.

Moscow Moves Against Baltic States (Jan. 13): Soviet Army seizes power for faceless Communist Party loyalists, National Salvation Committee. Fourteen dead and more than 100 wounded. Bush deplores action but takes no steps against Kremlin. **(Jan. 14):** Gorbachev blames leaders of separatist Lithuanian Parliament for attack. **(Jan. 20):** Soviet commandos raid government building in Riga, Latvia. At least four dead. **(Jan. 30):** Kremlin says most troops involved in attack in Lithuania have been withdrawn.

U.N. Head Fails in Iraqi Talks (Jan. 13): Secretary General talks for two and a half hours with President Saddam Hussein but reports no progress in getting his forces to pull out of Kuwait.

Two P.L.O. Leaders Slain in Tunis (Jan. 14): Bodyguard also shot dead. Rival Arab leader later blamed.

U.S. and Allies at War With Iraq—Highlights: (Jan. 15): Planes batter Baghdad and other targets in Iraq and Kuwait to start campaign to oust President Saddam Hussein's army from Kuwait. **(Jan. 17):** Eight Iraqi Scud missiles strike Israel, all in Tel Aviv-Haifa area. **(Jan. 19):** Allied planes fail to wipe out all Scuds. **(Jan. 21):** American Patriot missiles destroy most of Iraqi Scud attack on Saudi Arabia. **(Jan. 25):** Iraq releases millions of gallons of Kuwaiti crude oil into Persian Gulf, creating huge slick endangering desalination plants. **(Jan. 27):** U.S. bombs oil installations in effort to check flow. **(Jan. 31):** Saudi troops supported by U.S. Marines drive Iraqi invaders from coastal town of Kharfji after 36-hour battle. Eleven Marines reported killed.

Soviet Foreign Minister Named (Jan. 15): Aleksandr A. Bessmertnykh, Ambassador to U.S., succeeds Eduard A. Shevardnadze.

Turkey Authorizes Use of Air Base (Jan. 17): Parliament allows U.S. fighters and bombers to launch strikes on Iraq from Incirlik, on Mediterranean.

Soviet Withdraws Currency (Jan. 22): Takes 50- and 100-ruble notes out of circulation in move to bolster failing economy and fight black market.

China Sentences Human Rights Leader (Jan. 26): Ren Wanding punished as agitator for democracy and role in Tiananmen Square demonstration. Student leader gets four years. Other rights militants also sentenced.

Black Factions Reach Accord in South Africa (Jan. 27): Agreement between National Congress and rival Inkatha Freedom Party a step for unity against apartheid.

National

F.D.A. Approves Portable Heart Pump (Jan. 3): Sanctions experimental use of battery-powered mechanical device.

U.S. Seizes One of Largest Banks (Jan. 6): Acts to prevent run on Bank of New England Corporation and says it will protect all depositors.

Justices Approve End of Busing (Jan. 15): Supreme Court rules, 5–3, that formerly segregated school districts may be released after all "practicable" steps to eliminate legacy of segregation.

A 29-cent Postage Stamp Approved (Jan. 22): U.S. Postal Service accepts four-cent increases for first-class letters and for postal cards.

New Agriculture Secretary Nominated (Jan. 25): President names Representative Edward Madigan of Illinois to succeed Clayton K. Yeutter. Republican National committee picks Yeutter as chairman.

President's State of Union Address (Jan. 30): Bush tells Congress "indomitable" American character will prevail against Iraq and economic troubles at home.

General

Rhode Island Acts in Banking Crisis (Jan. 1): Governor closes 45 banks and credit unions until they arrange Federal insurance for deposits.

Arts Endowment Approves Grants (Jan. 4): Two controversial performers among more than 1,000 artists included in awards of Federal funds.

Death Toll Heavy in British Isles Gales (Jan. 6): At least 28 dead or missing at sea as storms sweep across Ireland and Britain. Tourists among victims.

N.C.A.A. Orders Reductions (Jan. 9): National Collegiate Athletic Association votes to reduce number of football and basketball scholarships and to limit time demands for student athletes.

Pete Rose Barred From Hall of Fame (Jan. 10): Special committee recommends exclusion of star hitter by banning anyone eliminated from baseball.

Space Telescope "Sees" Massive Stars (Jan. 16): Astronomers report exciting images and data by Hubble Telescope showing two extremely large and hot stars.

Father Wins Life Decision (Jan. 17): Missouri judge rules he has right to end comatose daughter's treatment even if end of feeding means her death.

Utah Gets Strict Anti-Abortion Law (Jan. 25): Governor signs toughest measure in nation.

FEBRUARY 1991

International

South Africa Moves Against Apartheid (Feb. 1): President de Klerk announces he will scrap remaining laws supporting racial discrimination policy. Includes Population Registration Act, setting up four racial groups.

Italy Communist Party Transformed (Feb. 3): Becomes Democratic Party of the Left. Abandons Marxism and red flag with hammer and sickle emblem.

U.N. Forces Win Persian Gulf War—Highlights: (Feb. 4): Powerful guns of U.S. battleship *Missouri* pound Iraqi targets. **(Feb. 5):** Iraq suspends fuel sales for a land already suffering shortages of food, water, electricity, and gasoline because of Allied air attacks. **(Feb. 13):** U.S. Stealth fighter-bomber drops two bombs in residential Baghdad, killing hundreds of civilians in building Iraqis say is an air-raid shelter, Americans contend is a military command center. **(Feb. 19):** Bush cool to Moscow's proposals for Iraqi withdrawal from Kuwait. **(Feb. 22):** President Saddam Hussein accepts later Soviet formula but Bush voices concerns. **(Feb. 24):** Ground war opens. Allied forces drive into Kuwait and reach outskirts of Kuwait City, encountering light resistance. **(Feb. 27):** Iraqi troops in headlong retreat. Allied forces enter ravaged Kuwait City. Bush declares "Kuwait is liberated" and orders suspension of offensive military operations. Says Iraq must observe all conditions of U.N. resolutions as condition of permanent cease-fire.

I.R.A. Fires at 10 Downing Street (Feb. 7): Three rounds aimed at Prime Minister's residence as he presides over War Cabinet meeting. No officials injured.

New President of Haiti Sworn In (Feb. 7): Jean-Bertrand Aristide, 37, liberal Roman Catholic priest, becomes nation's first democratically elected executive.

Lithuanians Vote for Independence (Feb. 9): Margin is 9–1 as nationwide plebiscite turns into gesture of defiance of Kremlin.

China Punishes Two Dissidents (Feb. 12): Court sentences longtime advocates of democracy to 13 years, longest sentences in Tiananmen Square protests.

Soviet Plans to Raise Retail Prices (Feb. 13): Decides on average increase of two to three times. Will end subsidies on most consumer goods and compensate for food price increases.

Latin America Fights Cholera (Feb. 14): Peru's neighbors halt food imports and restrict arrivals.

Soviet Consumer Prices Going Up (Feb. 18): Kremlin warns of 60 percent increase under latest plan to revive critically troubled economy.

I.R.A. Bombs Two London Rail Stations (Feb. 18): One killed and 40 injured in attacks on Victoria and Paddington terminals.

Yugoslavia's Unity Shattered (Feb. 20): Slovenia, most affluent republic, takes over banking and defense functions from Belgrade government. **(Feb. 21):** Croatia adopts veto power over federal laws.

Warsaw Pact Ending Military Alliance (Feb. 25): Budapest conference of Eastern European nations agrees to dissolve 36-year-old alliance because of collapse of Soviet power in the region.

National

Federal Reserve Moves to Spur Economy (Feb. 1): Sharply reduces interest rates in view of recession. Large banks across country promptly slash prime rate.

President Submits 1992 Budget (Feb. 4): Sends Congress request for $1.45 trillion. Understates cost of Persian Gulf War. Seeks to cut benefits for upper- and middle-income families, an explosive issue.

Sweeping Overhaul of Banking Proposed (Feb. 5): Bush Administration would eliminate many barriers and regulations with incentives to competition.

Former Thornburgh Aide Convicted (Feb. 7): Henry G. Barr, 47, found guilty in Pennsylvania court on four counts involving use of cocaine and lying about it to get high-ranking job in Justice Department.

White House Offers Highway Bill (Feb. 13): Sends Congress proposal for five-year $105-billion program of Federal aid to states for roads and mass transit.

High Court Backs Immigration Suits (Feb. 20): Justices rule, 7–2, Government can face action over way it administers amnesty provisions of 1986 law.

Arts Agency Drops Obscenity Pledge (Feb. 20): National Endowment ends controversial policy on grants.

New Labor Secretary Sworn In (Feb. 22): Lyn Martin, former Illinois Congresswoman, takes oath.

Ethics Committee Accuses Cranston (Feb. 27): Senate unit warns California Democrat of disciplinary action for conduct in savings and loan scandal. Committee criticizes conduct of four others.

U.S. Witness in Noriega Case Killed (Feb. 28): Crash in Miami fatal to Ramon A. Navarro, 41, paid informer.

General

Pakistan–Afghan Earthquake Kills 300 (Feb. 1): At least 500 injured in mountain villages. Shock felt in neighboring Soviet Central Asian republics.

Plane Crash Kills 34 in Los Angeles (Feb. 2): U.S. Air jet, Boeing 737, collides with small commuter craft, Skywest Airlines Fairchild Metro III, on runway at International Airport. **(Feb. 4):** Federal investigators cite error by controller and longstanding communications problems.

Ex-F.B.I. Agent Sentenced as Spy (Feb. 4): U.S. judge in Los Angeles metes 20 years to Richard Miller, 54, only serving agent ever convicted of espionage.

Use of Suicide Machine Barred (Feb. 5): Michigan court enjoins Dr. Jack Kevorkian from helping the terminally ill kill themselves with his invention.

Judge Upsets Jim Bakker's Term (Feb. 12): U.S. Appeals Court in Richmond, Va., rules sentencing judge improperly emphasized religion in meting 45 years to TV evangelist after conviction for fraud.

Unmarried Couples Register on Coast (Feb. 14): Heterosexual and homosexual partners enroll under new law at San Francisco City Hall.

Alzheimer's Disease Clue Discovered (Feb. 15): Researchers in London find pinpoint mutation in a single gene can cause neurological illness.

Car Bomb Kills 22 in Colombia (Feb. 16): Blast injures 140 near bullfighting ring at Medellín. Drug traffickers claim responsibility.

Maryland Law Protects Abortion Rights (Feb. 18): Governor signs measure voted by Legislature.

Crash Kills 19 on Antarctica Flight (Feb. 20): Chilean chartered BAE-146 was carrying 72, mostly American tourists, off southern coast of Chile.

Agreement on Sale of New York Giants (Feb. 20): Preston Robert Tisch, billionaire president of Loews Corporation, to purchase 50 percent of Super Bowl champions for reported price of $50 million.

High-Rise Philadelphia Building Burns (Feb. 24): Three firefighters killed as 38-story structure in downtown area next to City Hall is damaged.

MARCH 1991

International

Highlights of Persian Gulf War (March 3): Iraqi military leaders accept stringent Allied terms for ending conflict, including prompt return of all prisoners and civilian detainees. **(March 5):** Saddam Hussein government voids annexation of Kuwait. **(March 6):** Bush plans to start returning troops. Pledges to keep strong diplomatic presence in Middle East. **(March 10):** Six Arab countries support Bush's Middle East plans. **(March 21):** U.N. survey calls civilian damage in Iraq "near apocalyptic." **(March 26):** Schwarzkopf says he recommended continued warfare. **(March 27):** Bush disputes his assertion. **(March 28–29):** President and general resolve differences.

Baltic Voters Support Independence (March 3): Plebiscites in Estonia and Latvia demonstrate popular desire to be free of Soviet Union. Ballot result has heavy support of Russian minorities.

Unrest Breaks Out in Yugoslavia (March 9): Two killed in Belgrade as police break up demonstration by thousands demanding ouster of Communist heading Republic of Serbia. **(March 12):** Serbia gives in to protesters and removes TV officials blamed for propaganda in news programs. **(March 15):** Borisav Jovic, leader of Yugoslav 8-member presidency, resigns after failure of effort to gain approval for army intervention in rivalries among nationalities.

Erich Honecker Moved to Soviet Union (March 14): Bonn demands return of ill longtime East German Prime Minister to face trial for crimes committed as head of former Communist regime.

Britain Frees Six Jailed Irishmen (March 14): Court of Appeal (cq) acts after prosecutors admit confessions and police evidence were discredited in 1974 bombing of two Birmingham pubs by Irish Republican Army.

Polish Foreign Debt Reduced (March 15): Western governments agree to forgive about half $33 billion owed to help transition to market economy.

U.S. and Albania Resume Ties (March 15): Full diplomatic relations will end 52 years of nonrecognition, aiding democratic process.

Gorbachev Wins Partial Election Victory (March 18): Voters nationwide generally support Soviet leader in ballot on national unity. But many voters endorse greater autonomy in such regions as the republics of Russia and the Ukraine.

Envoy Tells of Warning to Hussein (March 20): April C. Glaspie, U.S. Ambassador to Iraq, at Senate hearing, recalls warning president of American reaction if he attacked Kuwait.

Britain to Scrap Unpopular "Poll Tax" (March 21): In face of year of protests, Conservative Government decides to return to some property tax by 1993.

Soviet Coal Miners Strike (March 27): Nationwide walkout demands resignation of Gorbachev, his government, and Parliament. Workers coordinate tactics.

Moscow Marchers Defy Kremlin (March 28): Soviet President Gorbachev forbids demonstrations for rival, Boris Yeltsin. **(March 28):** More than 100,000 Muscovites defy ban and huge display of police and military force to rally behind Yeltsin. Gorbachev setback seen.

National

Justices Uphold Punitive Damages (March 4): Supreme Court, 7–1, rejects constitutional attack, upholding discretion of juries over awards.

New Education Secretary Confirmed (March 14): Senate unanimously approves Lamar Alexander, former Tennessee Governor. **(March 18):** He stresses intent to help Bush as "education President."

Justices Back Woman Workers (March 20): Supreme Court rules unanimously that employers cannot exclude them from jobs in which exposure to toxic substances could harm a developing fetus.

Senate Confirms Anti-Drug Chief (March 21): Approves former Florida Gov. Bob Martinez as co-ordinator despite Democratic attacks on policies.

High Court Upsets Confession Rule (March 26): Justices decide, 5–4, that use of coerced statement in criminal trial does not automatically void conviction.

General

TV Tape of Police Beating Shocks Nation (March 3): Amateur's pictures revive charges that Los Angeles department has failed to confront pattern of brutality. Tape shows officers taking turns clubbing and kicking black motorist. **(March 15):** Four white policemen indicted on charges of assault with deadly weapon. False reports also charged.

Jet Crash Kills 25 in Colorado (March 3): United Airlines 737 plunges into neighborhood park at Colorado Springs, barely missing housing development and apartment complex.

U.S.–Britain Airline Accord (March 11): Agreement will allow United Airlines and American Airlines to fly to London's Heathrow Airport, with major impact on trans-Atlantic travel.

Donation for Metropolitan Museum (March 11): Walter H. Annenberg, 83, publisher and former Ambassador to Britain, bequeaths painting collection valued at $1 billion to New York institution.

Exxon to Pay $1.1-Billion Settlement (March 12): A $100-million criminal penalty included in arrangement for settling civil and criminal cases from record oil spill in Alaska.

New York Daily News Strike Ends (March 14): Robert Maxwell, British publisher, signs final agreement to take over city's largest tabloid, crippled by 20-week tie-up. Unions make concessions.

Plane Crash Kills Seven Country Musicians (March 16): Members of singer Reba McIntire's band with road manager and two pilots victims as private aircraft crashes in California mountain area.

Two Noriega Codefendants Guilty (March 19): Convicted of plotting with former Panama leader to trade M-16 automatic rifles for cocaine.

Twenty-seven Missing as Navy Planes Crash (March 21): Two antisubmarine aircraft on routine training mission collide over Pacific Ocean near San Diego.

Drug Raids Hit Fraternities (March 22): Federal, state, and local officers arrest 11 students at University of Virginia and seize bags of drugs.

New Harvard President Chosen (March 23): Neil L. Rudenstine, 56, former provost of Princeton University, selected to succeed Derek C. Bok.

Reagan Backs Gun Control Measure (March 29): Shifting position, former President endorses legislation for seven-day waiting period for purchases. Urges Bush to drop his opposition.

Oil Spill Contaminates Caribbean (March 30): Fouls 300 miles of shoreline with 570,000 gallons dumped by barge that sank off island of St. Kitts.

Storms Kill at Least 23 in South (March 30): Heavy storms rage from East Texas across Louisiana, Arkansas, and Mississippi and northeast into North Carolina and Virginia over several days.

APRIL 1991
International

Cease-Fire Ends Persian Gulf War (April 3): U.N. Security Council votes tough financial and military conditions requiring Iraqi President Saddam Hussein to renounce terrorism, pay billions of dollars for damage to Kuwait, and accept borders with Kuwait negotiated in 1963. Iraq also required to destroy chemical and biological weapons. **(April 6):** Iraq accepts terms, but brands them unjust.

Thousands of Kurds Flees Iraqi Army (April 3): Civilians cross borders to Iran and Turkey after month-old revolt collapses. Most are hungry, wounded, or dying. **(April 7):** Six U.S. Air Force cargo planes parachute food, water, and medical supplies to refugees striving to reach Turkey. Iran shuts borders. **(April 16):** President Bush says U.S., British, and French troops will set up secure camps in northern Iraq to shelter refugees. **(April 20):** U.S. Marines start erecting first camp. **(April 21):** Iraqi troops begin withdrawal in north as camps rise.

Workers Protest Soviet Price Rises (April 4): Tens of thousands jam streets of Minsk, capital of Byelorussia, in first such mass protest.

Yeltsin Expands His Powers (April 5): Opponent of Kremlin wins right to rule by decree in Russian republic and establishment of republican presidency.

Thousands Defy Gorbachev Injunction (April 9): Soviet President orders republics to halt strikes and demonstrations, warning of economic collapse and paralysis of power. **(April 10):** Tens of thousands rally in Minsk, Georgian leaders call for widespread strikes, and Siberian miners step up demands.

Georgia Breaks With Moscow (April 9): Soviet republic's parliament unanimously declares independence in new rebuff to President Gorbachev.

Europeans End Sanctions on South Africa (April 15): Twelve nations of Community agree to drop economic penalties in recognition of Pretoria Government's continuing moves to dismantle apartheid.

Iran Reports on Chemical Arsenal (April 19): Tells U.N. much of supply of chemical and ballistics weapons survived Persian Gulf War. Denies nuclear stocks.

New Cabinet Named in Kuwait (April 20): Members of ruling Sabah family keep major posts in move for more democratic government.

Gorbachev Yields to Republics (April 24): Agrees to enhance their role in governing. Pact worked out with leaders, including Boris Yeltsin, Russian president and chief opposition critic. Gorbachev promises to revise unpopular tax and price programs.

Thousands Dead in Bangladesh Cyclone (April 30): Powerful storm batters nation for eight hours. **(May 10):** Poverty with lack of shelters and embankments blamed for high toll. **(May 11):** Official death toll set at 138,868. **(May 16):** Nearly 8,000 U.S. troops land in helicopters for massive relief effort to bring food and medicine to even remote areas.

National

Justices Limit Race in Jury Selection (April 1): Supreme Court, 7–2, expands ban on use of racial criteria to affect defendant and jurors.

***Atlantis* Shuttle Flies Six-Day Mission (April 5):** Five astronauts in orbit on first shuttle launching of year and 39th in 10 years of reusable spaceships. Crew: Air Force Col. Steven R. Nagel, 44, mission commander; Marine Lieut. Col. Kenneth D. Cameron, 41, pilot. Mission specialists: Dr. Linda M. Godwin, 38, physicist; Air Force Lieut. Col. Jerry L. Ross,

43; Dr. Jerome Apt, 41, NASA engineer. **(April 7):** Two astronauts walk in space to free jammed antenna to deploy $600-million astronomy satellite. **(April 11):** *Atlantis* lands safely at Edwards Air Force Base, Calif., after winds force day's delay.

Senate Unit Rejects Court Nominee (April 11): Judiciary Committee votes against U.S. Judge Kenneth L. Ryskamp of Florida for Court of Appeals because of complaints about attitude toward minorities.

Death Row Appeals Curbed (April16): Supreme Court, 6–3, in Georgia case, limits right of state prisoners to bring multiple Federal court challenges to constitutionality of convictions or sentences.

Congress Stops Nationwide Rail Strike (April 17): Halts walkout after one day. Creates special three-member board to hear differences between railroads and workers and impose settlement in 65 days.

Washington Cheers Dalai Lama (April 18): Tibet's exiled spiritual leader addresses Congress and pleads for U.S. aid in struggle against Chinese rule. Earlier he had met President Bush. China files formal protest against Dalai Lama's travels.

Bush Campaigns for Better Schools (April 18): Calls for national testing and Federal funds for students who choose private and parochial schools.

Supreme Court Backs Labor (April 23): Unanimously upholds N.L.R.B. regulation making it easier for unions to organize workers at thousands of community hospitals throughout the nation.

Air Force Chooses Lockheed Plane (April 23): Ends five-year competition by accepting design for F-22, new generation of agile radar-evading fighters.

Senate Rejects Social Security Tax Cut (April 24): Vote of 60 to 38 kills Moynihan proposal opposed by Bush Administration as threatening bankruptcy of Social Security System.

Shuttle *Discovery* Ends "Star Wars" Mission (April 28): Launched at Cape Canaveral, Fla., on first military flight without secrecy. Members of crew—Navy Capt. Michael L. Coats, 45, mission commander; Air Force Lieut. Col. L. Blaine Hammond, Jr., 39, pilot; mission specialists: Air Force Col. Guion S. Bluford, Jr., 48; Gregory J. Harbaugh, 35, civilian astronaut; Richard J. Hieb, 35, civilian engineer; Air Force Lieut. Col. Donald R. McMonagle, 38; Charles Lacy Veach, 46, Air Force veteran. **(May 6):** *Discovery* lands safely at Cape Canaveral, diverted from California by high winds. Most of research tasks completed despite series of equipment problems.

Federal Reserve Cuts Interest Rates (April 30): Moves to revive economy by lowering discount rate from 6 percent to 5 1/2 percent.

General

Ozone Loss Exceeds Forecasts (April 4): E.P.A. Reports depletion of protective layer in U.S. is twice as great as scientists had predicted.

Senator Killed in Plane Crash (April 4): John Heinz, 52, of Pennsylvania, and six others perish near Philadelphia when chartered plane collides with helicopter. Senator a moderate Republican.

Ex-Senator Tower Dies in Plane Crash (April 5): Texan among 23 killed as commuter aircraft crashes and burns approaching Brunswick airport on Georgia coast.

Burning Tanker Spills Oil in Gulf of Genoa (April 14): Cypriot ship rocked by explosions; three dead, three missing. **(April 14):** Sinks in shallow water off northwest coast of Italy.

Cholera Kills Thousands in South America (April 18): Epidemic spreads after killing 1,100 in Peru and making 150,000 ill. Hits Ecuador and Colombia, with isolated cases reported in Chile and U.S. Greatest concern is for heavily populated Brazil.

Conviction Upheld in Cocaine Baby Case (April 18): Florida appeals court affirms nation's first verdict in a case of mother charged with delivering drug to baby through the umbilical cord.
Central America Quake Kills Scores (April 22): At least 50 reported dead in Costa Rica, 23 in Panama. At least 500 injured in both countries. Relief is rushed.
Midwest Tornadoes Kill More Than 20 (April 26): Some

70 twisters tear through seven states. Most victims in small town of Andover, Kan. Thousands homeless and damage is heavy.
Soviet Earthquake Kills More than 100 (April 29): Temblor rocks mountain area in central Georgia. Tens of thousands left homeless, communications severed, buildings razed.

MAY 1991

International

Cease-Fire Reached in Angola (May 1): Leftist Government and U.S.-backed rebels agree to hold nation's first free elections in second half of 1992.
Lebanese Army Tightens Control (May 2): Opens roads in mountain districts. Traffic moves smoothly through Christian and Muslim areas for first time since civil war erupted in 1975. Sense of security spreads.
Russia Gets Coal Mine Control (May 6): Kremlin transfers Siberian industry to republic, a gain for Boris Yeltsin in fight for autonomy.
Yugoslavia Fights Ethnic Tensions (May 9): Leadership agrees on plan to disarm paramilitary units, averting martial law sought by army.
Winnie Mandela Sentenced (May 13): Johannesburg justice finds wife of African National Congress leader guilty of kidnapping four youths taken to her home and beaten. (May 14): She is sentenced to six years in prison.
Soviet Republics Agree on Crisis Program (May 16): Thirteen of 15 accept ban on strikes, budget cuts, and assurances for foreign investors.
Abortion Ban Rejected in Poland (May 17): Parliament deals Roman Catholic Church first political setback since fall of Communism in 1989.
Soviet Liberalizes Travel Regulations (May 20): Parliament approves nation's first law granting citizens right to go abroad and emigrate freely. Resolution will be effective in January 1993.
Ethiopian Dictator Resigns and Flees (May 21): Departure of President Mengistu Haile Mariam after 17 years heralds end of hard-line Marxist government. Rebels advance on Addis Ababa. Government seeks intervention of U.S. to arrange settlement.
Rajiv Gandhi Assassinated (May 22): Former prime minister of India killed by bomb at Madras as he campaigns to be elected to return to power. Armed forces on "red alert" as gangs seek scapegoats. Gandhi, 46, is second political martyr in family dynasty. (May 23): Widow, Italian-born Sonia Gandhi, rejects Congress Party bid to succeed him as president. Party in disarray.
Ethiopian Rebels Seize Capital (May 24): Israel begins transporting 16,000 Ethiopian Jews to Israel under secret agreement with besieged government. (May 25): Separatists seize Red Sea port, last controlled by government. Embassies evacuated. (May 27): Acting president surrenders Addis Ababa, capital, to rebels. (May 28): Rebels take full control of capital with display of force.
NATO to Cut U.S. Troop Strength (May 28): Agrees on 50 percent reduction, with smaller over-all cut in radical reorganization.
Pope Appoints 22 Cardinals (May 29): Two Americans among them. Pontiff reveals secret appointment of Chinese archbishop 12 years previously, who had been imprisoned for loyalty to Vatican.

National

Bush Treated for Abnormal Heartbeat (May 4): President stricken by erratic rhythms while jogging at Camp David. (May 5): President found not to have suffered heart attack. Responds to drug treatment. (May 6): Two drugs control condition. President returns to work at White House. Overactive thyroid blamed for condition. Caused by same noncontagious ailment wife has.
Intelligence Chief Retires (May 8): Director William H. Webster leaving after four years. (May 14): Bush designates Robert M. Gates, career intelligence analyst, to succeed him.
Supreme Court Revises Arrest Deadline (May 13): Rules, 5–4, police may hold suspect up to 48 hours without warrant pending judicial finding on charge.
Queen and Husband Visit U.S. (May 14): Elizabeth II and Prince Philip arrive in Washington for 13-day visit including tours of Florida and Texas. (May 16): In address to Congress, Queen stresses common aims and ties of U.S. and Britain. (May 20): Queen awards honorary knighthood to Gen. H. Norman Schwarzkopf in simple Florida ceremony.
U.S. Trade Deficit at Eight-Year Low (May 17): Narrowed to $4.05 billion in March by increase in exports and decline in demand for imports.
Court Upholds U.S. Curb on Abortion Advice (May 23): Justices, 5–4, approve pending regulations barring federally-financed clinics from providing basic information. Many family planning agencies across nation to continue to provide services even though they sacrifice Government financial aid.
North Conviction To Be Reviewed (May 28): Supreme Court lets stand ruling that Iran-Contra prosecutors must re-examine witnesses against Oliver L. North for prejudice from hearing Capitol testimony.
Justices Broaden Car Search Rules (May 30): Supreme Court, 6–3, decides police can inspect bags and packages with warrant whether with or without reason to search vehicle. Twelve-year precedent overturned.

General

Oil Spill Settlement Blocked (May 3): Exxon and Alaska withdraw from $1-billion agreement on civil complaints. State and Federal officials plan court move. Criminal charges still pending.
Portable Mechanical Heart Implanted (May 9): For first time, surgeons install device to help failing organ pump until replacement is found.
Kennedy Nephew Charged With Rape (May 9): William K. Smith, 30, accused of attack on woman who drove him home to Kennedy estate March 30. Police account made public.
New Cancer Drug Found in Tree (May 12): Only source is bark of rarely distributed yew in Pacific Northwest. Drug melts tumors resistant to other treatment.
Organ Transplants Cause AIDS (May 17): Three deaths reported among nearly 50 persons who received donations from Virginia man infected with virus.
Jet Crash Kills 223 in Thailand (May 26): All aboard dead as Austrian airliner, Boeing 767-300, explodes over jungle. Cause is a mystery.

JUNE 1991

International

Angola and Rebels End 16-Year War (June 1): Cease-fire in effect after government and opponents sign agreement to prepare African nation for democracy.

U.S. and Soviet Reach Arms Accord (June 1): Settle differences on treaty to reduce conventional forces in Europe. Talks on strategic weapons facilitated.

Last Kurdish Camp in Turkey Closed (June 1): Humanitarian mission along Iraq border ends successfully. U.S. troops prepare to withdraw. Hundreds of thousands still in Iran camps.

France Accepts Nuclear Arms Pact (June 3): Agrees to sign 1968 treaty banning spread of atomic weapons, joining U.S., Britain, Soviet Union, and 139 other nations.

Communist Government of Albania Resigns (June 4): Bows to general strike and street demonstrations. Opposition hails "step to democracy." **(June 12):** Parliament approves first non-Communist government in postwar era, breaking hard-line rule.

Pentagon Estimates Iraqi Toll (June 4): Gives tentative figures of 100,000 soldiers killed and 300,000 wounded in Persian Gulf conflict.

Widow of Mao Commits Suicide (June 4): Jiang Qing, 77, herself a leader in tumultuous years in China, was serving prison sentence for role as leader of Gang of Four in Cultural Revolution.

Apartheid Legislation Repealed (June 5): South African Parliament scraps racial discrimination laws in property ownership and residential selection.

Pope Crusades in Poland (June 10): Ends 13-day pilgrimage after dynamic appeal for evangelical role of Roman Catholic Church in post-Communist Europe and warning to Poles against abortion and Western decadence.

Boris Yeltsin Wins Russian Election (June 12): Leading Soviet political and economic reformer gains about 60 percent of votes in republic, first popularly elected leader in Russian history. In another rebuff to Communists, Leningrad voters vote to restore St. Petersburg name.

U.N. Charges Iraqi Nuclear Deceit (June 14): Officials report Iraq understates weapons program and amount of weapons-grade nuclear material. **(June 28):** Iraqi soldiers fire over heads of U.N. inspectors and bar them from inspecting suspicious machinery.

South Africa Scraps Apartheid Base (June 17): Parliament repeals Population Registration Act more than four decades after enactment.

Gandhi's Party Leads in India Election (June 17): Congress ahead by narrow margin after most violent campaign in history of independence. Party short of parliamentary majority needed to rule without coalition. **(June 21):** P.V. Narasimha Rao, 70, elected by party as India's ninth Prime Minister.

Volcano Erupts in Philippines (June 18): Cities and villages across thousands of square miles dig out after week of eruptions by Mount Pinatubo spreads thick blanket of volcanic ash. Death toll mounts well above 100. U.S. evacuates thousands from Clark Air Force Base.

Berlin Again the German Capital (June 20): Parliament votes to return seat of Federal Government 350 miles eastward from Bonn.

Two Yugoslav States Vote to Secede (June 25): Slovenia and Croatia declare independence unless Belgrade agrees to looser federated nation.

National

Court Widens Jury Exclusion Rule (June 3): Justices, 6–3, decide that ban on race as cause applies to civil cases as well as to criminal prosecutions.

Bush Grants Soviet Trade Benefits (June 3): Approves extension to allow $1.5 billion in credits for additional food purchases by Moscow.

Ambassador to Moscow Nominated (June 4): Bush chooses Robert S. Strauss, 72, close friend and Democratic leader, in move to cement ties with Gorbachev and emphasize business and economic issues.

Parades Celebrate Gulf Victory (June 8): Thousands in Washington jam route lined by patriotic monuments to cheer display of armed might. **(June 10):** Enormous tickertape celebration greets U.S. and allied forces in march up Broadway.

Bush Approves Soviet Farm Loan (June 11): Orders $1.5 billion in agricultural guarantees for Soviet to buy feed grain and other essentials.

Voting Rights Act Covers Judges (June 20): Supreme Court rules, 6–3, in two cases, on decisions that could change makeup of state courts throughout the South, with slender minority makeup.

Bush Praises Yeltsin (June 20): Acclaims new President of Russian republic, visiting Washington, for commitment to democracy and free market, but emphasizes support for Soviet President Gorbachev.

High Court Backs Nude Dancing Ban (June 21): Justices, 5–4, rule that, while it is protected expression, states may allow it to guard morality.

Sununu's Travel Restricted (June 22): White House imposes strict regulations on Chief of Staff after review of criticism of use of Government and private transport for political and personal use.

Justices Rule on Press Sources (June 24): Supreme Court, 5–4, decides First Amendment does not protect a news organization from lawsuit if it discloses a name it promised to keep secret.

Justice Thurgood Marshall Resigns (June 27): Announces retirement from Supreme Court after 24 years. A hero of civil rights movement and one of last liberal voices on high bench.

General

Lesbian Ordained Episcopal Priest (June 5): Bishop of Washington ordains Elizabeth L. Carl in move that upsets Presiding Bishop Edmund L. Browning.

Shuttle *Columbia* Carries Space Experiments (June 5): Takes off from Cape Canaveral, Fla., with rats and jellyfish for tests of adjustments to weightlessness and return to gravity. The crew: Marine Col. Bryan D. O'Connor, commander; Air Force Lieut. Col. Sidney M. Gutierrez, pilot; Dr. Tamara E. Jernigan, physicist, mission specialist. Scientists are three physicians—James P. Bagian, Margaret Rhea Seddon, and Francis A. Gaffney—and a chemist, Dr. Millie Hughes-Fulford. **(June 14):** *Columbia* lands safely at Edwards Air Force Base, Calif., with 21,000-pound Spacelab science module.

Presbyterians Reject Sex Report (June 10): General Assembly turns down appeal for church to relax traditional stand against sexual relations among homosexuals and unmarried heterosexuals.

Baseball Expansion Race Settled (June 10): National League committee recommends Miami and Denver for new franchises costing $95 million apiece.

Pigs Yield Key Part of Human Blood (June 15): Genetic techniques create hemoglobin, essential-oxygen-carrying component, scientists report.

Strictest Abortion Law Enacted (June 19): Louisiana Legislature overrides veto of measure outlawing all abortions except for few conditions.

JULY 1991

International

Opposition Group in Soviet Union (July 1): Reformists organize in nationwide challenge to Communist Party, led by Eduard A. Shevardnadze.

Warsaw Pact Dissolved at Prague (July 1): Soviet and five other nations agree to end Cold War political and military alliance in Eastern Europe.

Soviet Breaks Government Monopoly (July 1): For first time in seven decades, Parliament allows individuals, including foreigners, to buy and own industrial enterprises.

Northern Ireland Talks Collapse (July 3): Leaders of four major political parties fail to agree on form of regional government for Ulster.

Private Banking Empire Seized (July 5): Regulators of seven countries take control of Bank of Credit and Commerce International after charges of "widespread fraud" over period of years.

Iraq Admits Atomic Program (July 8): Reports three clandestine programs to produce enriched uranium, which could be used to make a nuclear bomb.

Olympics Ban on South Africa Ended (July 9): International Committee lifts 21-year sanction, satisfied that nation is committed to abolishing discrimination in sports. Way clear for 1992 Summer Games.

Bush Lifts Economic Ban on South Africa (July 10): Ends U.S. economic sanctions imposed in 1986. Says Pretoria has taken "irreversible" steps to end racial separation and white minority rule.

Boris N. Yeltsin Inaugurated (July 10): Takes oath as first freely elected President of Russian Republic before Kremlin assembly in ceremony attended by Gorbachev and Orthodox Patriarch.

Rushdie Translator Slain in Japan (July 12): Prof. Hitoshi Igarashi, 44, found stabbed to death outside office at Tsukuba University.

Strategic Arms Accord Reached (July 17): U.S. and Soviet Union agree after nine years of negotiating on treaty to reduce each nation's stocks of nuclear weapons. Bush agrees to Moscow summit.

Technical Aid Promised Soviet Union (July 17): Group of Seven industrialized democracies, at London conference, pledge large-scale assistance but no substantial financial contributions to assist in transition to market economy. Moscow also offered associate membership in International Monetary Fund and World Bank.

Syria Agrees to Mideast Peace Talks (July 18): Accepts U.S. proposal for conference opening direct discussion between Israel and Arab neighbors.

Israeli Police Blamed in Shootings (July 18): Judge concludes they and not Palestinians provoked violence in October 1990 in which 17 Palestinians were shot and killed in Jerusalem's Old City.

Pretoria Aided Mandela's Rivals (July 19): South African regime admits it secretly funded black political organization Inkatha in frequently violent rivalry with African National Congress.

Gorbachev Backed on Power Sharing (July 24): Reports agreement with nine of 15 Soviet republics on draft of drastic decentralization plan.

Gorbachev Challenges Party (July 25): Urges Communist leaders to reject hallowed tenets, including the sanctity of Marxism-Leninism.

Yugoslavia Fears All-Out Civil War (July 28): Prime Minister Markovic says strife could claim millions. Threatens to resign after weekend of worst clashes between Serbs and Croatians, two largest ethnic groups, since World War II. At least 50 killed in three days of fighting between Serbs, Croats and Yugoslav Army units after weeks of unrest.

Strategic Arms Treaty Signed (July 30): Fourth Bush-Gorbachev summit meeting opens in Moscow. Bush promises to seek most-favored-nation tariff status for Soviet Union. **(July 31):** Two Presidents sign strategic arms treaty designed to scale down their nations' stocks of long-range nuclear weapons. Legislators of both countries must approve. They join in calling for Middle East peace conference in October.

Six Lithuanian Border Guards Killed (July 31): Gunmen attack customs station, a symbol of Lithuania's claim to independence from Soviet Union.

National

Conservative Picked for High Court (July 1): Bush names Appeals Court Judge Clarence Thomas, 43, black Republican, to succeed Supreme Court Justice Thurgood Marshall. Would be second black on Court.

Federal Reserve Head Reappointed (July 19): President Bush to nominate Alan Greenspan for another four-year term in important policy post.

Revision of Census Rejected (July 15): Commerce Secretary overrules Census Bureau Director and experts in refusing to adjust figures to add about five million persons missed in 1990 count.

U.S. to Abandon Clark Air Base (July 15): Notifies Philippine Government of decision because of damage from eruption of Mount Pinatubo.

Senate Votes Curbs on Trade With China (July 23): Approves long list of conditions, including ban on certain arms sales and release of some political prisoners. Vote, 55–44, not big enough to override expected veto and is setback for Senate Democratic leadership.

U.S. Limits Referrals by Doctors (July 25): New rules by Department of Health and Human Services will restrict practice of sending Medicare and Medicaid patients to agencies in which they invest.

Curbs on Covert Action Voted (July 26): Senate-House conferees agree on bill to clarify and limit President's power to order secret operations by intelligence agents abroad.

Senate Rejects Curb on Women in Combat (July 31): Votes overwhelmingly to overturn 43-year-old law that prohibits them from flying warplanes in combat. Similar measure already passed by House.

General

Crash Kills 261 at Saudi Airport (July 11): DC-8 jetliner plunges in flames attempting emergency landing at Jidda. Was carrying Muslim pilgrims.

Total Eclipse of Sun Observed (July 11): It blacks out 150-mile-wide swath across Pacific Ocean and Central America. Most spectacular in memory.

Astronomers Report Distant Planet (July 25): British scientists say they have detected object in orbit around remnant of collapsed star outside solar system, first such discovery.

Doctor Who Aided Suicide Is Free (July 26): Grand jury in Rochester, N.Y., declines to indict physician who prescribed barbiturates for terminally ill leukemia patient to kill herself.

Oil Spill Fouls Northwest Beaches (July 30): Ships collide off Olympic National Park. Vast population of sea birds and mammals threatened.

AUGUST 1991

International

Iraq Reveals Plutonium (Aug. 5): U.N. informed that scientists extracted small amount of weapons-grade material from spent nuclear fuel.

U.N. Lets Iraq Sell Oil (Aug. 7): Security Council retains sanctions but permits one-time exception for sale of up to $1.6 billion worth, with part to be spent on food and medical supplies.

Hostage Freed After Five Years (Aug. 8): Pro-Iranian militants in Lebanon release John McCarthy, 34, British journalist. Diplomats in many capitals intensify efforts to free other hostages. **(Aug. 11):** Lebanon kidnappers release Edward Austin Tracy, American held captive for five years, hours after Jèrome Leyraud, Frenchman abducted week previously, is released. Israel under pressure.

Former Iran Prime Minister Slain (Aug. 9): Shahpur Bakhtiar, 75, stabbed to death outside Paris. Long opponent of Shah. Last Iranian premier before Islamic revolution of 1979.

China Accepts Nuclear Accord (Aug. 10): Decides "in principle" to sign Nuclear Non-Proliferation Treaty as last major nuclear power to commit itself to agreement to curb spread of atomic weapons.

Coup Fails to Dislodge Gorbachev (Aug. 18): Eight diehard Communists isolate Soviet President in Crimea dacha, unleashing cataclysmic changes. The leaders, dominated by KGB and military, move swiftly to seize power. Russian President Boris Yeltsin rallies opposition. **(Aug. 20):** Gorbachev placed under house arrest as he prepares to fly to Moscow. Russian leaders and military hold out in republic's headquarters. **(Aug. 22):** After rescue, Gorbachev betrayed by trusted aides, credits Yeltsin for thwarting coup. Thousands cheer Yeltsin. KGB and military chiefs replaced.

Gorbachev Seals Communist Party Doom (Aug. 24): Soviet President surrenders to liberal and democratic forces. Resigns as Communist Secretary General, disbands leadership, ending party's decades of iron rule.

Baltic Republics Win Independence (Aug. 25): Denmark, Norway, and Finland first to recognize secession of Estonia, Latvia, and Lithuania from Soviet Union. **(Aug. 27):** European Economic Community grants unconditional recognition to three Baltic states after five decades as part of Soviet Union under Hitler-Stalin treaty. Other republics join in drive for independence. **(Sept. 2):** President Bush extends full diplomatic recognition. **(Sept. 6):** Soviet Union's new ruling council formally frees three republics, incorporated forcibly in 1940.

Gorbachev Appeals for Soviet Unity (Aug. 26): In wake of foiled coup, he recognizes that old tight order cannot be sustained, but calls on restive republics to seek greater autonomy through proposed new union treaty with Kremlin. Majority of 15 republics pursue campaigns for independence. Around the Soviet Union, statues of Lenin are destroyed.

Serbia Accepts Europe's Peace Plan (Aug. 31): Agrees to let foreign observers oversee Croatian cease-fire and arbitrate over-all Yugoslav crisis.

National

AIDS Panel Backs Needle Exchange (Aug. 6): National Commission approves program to reduce spread of disease among drug users.

Dioxin Danger Downgraded (Aug. 14): Federal Health officials retreat from position that chemical compound is top toxic menace.

U.S. Trade Deficit at Eight-Year Low (Aug. 16): Drop laid to increased exports of manufactured goods, low oil prices, and drop in demand for imports.

General

***Atlantis* Shuttle Mission Successful (Aug. 2):** Spacecraft launched at Cape Canaveral after technical problems and postponements. Members of crew: Mission commander, Air Force Col. John E. Blaha, 48; pilot, Navy Comdr. Michael A. Baker, 37; mission specialists: Dr. Shannon W. Lucid, 48; G. David Low, 35; Army Col. James C. Adamson, 45. **(Aug. 11):** *Atlantis* lands safely at Cape Canaveral, Fla., after nine days in orbit. It carried 22 scientific experiments and launched giant communications satellite to expedite data from spacecraft.

Louisiana Anti-Abortion Law Overruled (Aug. 7): U.S. judge finds strict new statute unconstitutional under Supreme Court Roe v. Wade decision.

Abortion Foes Demonstrate in Kansas (Aug. 9): Scores storm gates of clinic in defiance of Federal Court order against blocking entry as massive demonstrations grow. U.S. District Judge Patrick F. Kelly has reported death threats after preventing hundreds from shutting down three clinics.

Clark Clifford Quits as Bank Head (Aug. 13): A leading Washington figure resigns as chairman of First American Bankshares Inc., Washington's largest bank holding company. Federal regulators have linked it to Bank of Credit and Commerce International, under investigation for criminal activity.

Hurricane Sweeps Eastern Seaboard (Aug. 19): First of season causes at least two deaths, cuts off electrical power to nearly a million homes and businesses, and floods low-lying areas from North Carolina to Maine. Damage in millions.

U.S. Agents Free Prison Hostages (Aug. 30): Stage three-minute raid at Talladega, Ala., Federal Correctional Institution. Release nine hostages and seize 121 inmates who had rebelled 10 days previously in effort to block deportation to Cuba.

Major Emmy Awards for TV, 1991

(August 25, 1991)

Drama series: *L.A. Law* (NBC)
　Actress: Patricia Wettig, *thirtysomething* (ABC)
　Actor: James Earl Jones, *Gabriel's Fire* (ABC)
　Supporting actress: Madge Sinclair, *Gabriel's Fire* (ABC)
　Supporting actor: Timothy Busfield, *thirtysomething* (ABC)

Comedy series: *Cheers* (NBC)
　Actress: Kirstie Alley, *Cheers* (NBC)
　Actor: Burt Reynolds, *Evening Shade* (CBS)
　Supporting actress: Bebe Neuwirth, *Cheers* (NBC)
　Supporting actor: Jonathan Winters, *Davis Rules* (ABC)

Variety, Music or Comedy Program: *The 63rd Annual Academy Awards* (ABC)

Drama/comedy special and mini-series: *Separate But Equal* (ABC)

Actress in a mini-series or special: Lynn Whitfield, *The Josephine Baker Story* (HBO)

Actor in a mini-series or special: John Gielgud, *Masterpiece Theater: Summer's Lease* (PBS)

Supporting actress in a mini-series or special: Ruby Dee, *Hallmark Hall of Fame: Decoration Day* (NBC)

Supporting actor in a mini-series or special: James Earl Jones, *Heatwave* (TNT)

Individual performance in a variety or music program: Billy Crystal, *The 63rd Annual Academy Awards* (ABC)

Governor's Award: *Masterpiece Theater* (PBS)

SEPTEMBER 1991

International

Bush recognizes Baltic Republics (Sept. 2): Gives full diplomatic status to Latvia, Estonia, and Lithuania.

South Africa Gets Voting Rights Plan (Sept. 4): President de Klerk outlines Government's proposals for constitution with universal suffrage.

Lithuania Voids War Crime Convictions (Sept. 4): Starts exonerating thousands condemned by Soviet courts as collaborators with Nazis.

Soviet Central Power Collapses (Sept. 5): Gorbachev ultimatum forces all-Soviet Congress to surrender power to new government largely controlled by republics. Congress thus dissolves itself as highest legislative authority in Soviet Union.

Three Baltic Republics Gain Independence (Sept. 6): New Soviet ruling council recognizes Lithuania, Estonia, and Latvia after long struggle.

Israel Frees 51 Arab Prisoners (Sept. 11): Returns bodies of nine guerrillas in return for word that Israeli soldier missing in Lebanon is dead.

A-Bomb Capacity Laid to Iraqis (Sept. 13): United Nations finds Hussein had enough nuclear explosives to have built two or three atomic weapons a year in 1990s before plants were bombed.

Peace Agreement in South Africa (Sept. 14): Two main black groups and Government accept comprehensive plan to end black factional violence that has cost thousands of lives.

Swedish Socialists Defeated (Sept. 15): Suffer worst election defeat in more than 60 years as voters rebel against expensive welfare state. Five rival parties are divided.

Democracy Backers Win in Hong Kong (Sept. 16): Liberals take 16 of 18 legislative seats in message to Britain and China of people's feelings.

Soviet Exonerates Solzhenitsyn (Sept. 17): Chief prosecutor drops treason charges, last obstacle to Russian writer's return after 17 years' exile.

Soviet Doubles Estimate of Food-Aid Needs (Sept. 19): Officials, after review of stagnant economy, call for $14.7 billion for coming year in request to European Commission in Brussels.

U.N. Authorizes Oil Sales by Iraq (Sept. 19): Allows sales of $1.6 billion over six months to buy food and other civilian supplies and compensate victims of Iraq's invasion of Kuwait.

Iraq Frees Nuclear Inspectors (Sept. 23): Forty U.N. officials detained after discovering secret Iraqi plans for making nuclear weapons at building in Baghdad and trying to remove them. **(Sept. 27):** Iraq bows to Security Council and releases team and allows them to remove secret document.s

Germans Arrest East's Master Spy (Sept. 24): Markus Wolf, long head of efficient intelligence agency for Communists, surrenders to Berlin prosecutors after year-long refuge in Soviet Union and an unsuccessful bid for asylum in Austria.

British Hostage Released in Beirut (Sept. 24): Pro-Iranian abductors hand Jack Mann, 77, over to Syrian officials after his more than two years in captivity. Mann, in frail health, is fourth Western prisoner released in six weeks.

Salvador and Rebels Reach Accord (Sept. 25): President and five guerrilla commanders achieve breakthrough on country's political and economic future.

Prime Minister of Romania Resigns (Sept. 26): Petre Roman responds to protests against his economic reforms. Thousands of miners and others continue to demonstrate for resignation of President Ion Iliescu. Major outbreak feared.

Bush Abandons Short-Range Nuclear Arms (Sept. 27): Announces U.S. will eliminate all tactical weapons on land and at sea in Europe and Asia. He offers to negotiate with Soviet Union for sharp reductions. Unilateral reduction most one-sided such cut by any power. It reflects dramatic change in global relations since end of Soviet dominance in Eastern Europe and breakup of centralized Soviet Union. **(Sept. 28):** Gorbachev welcomes action but sees need for further discussions. Defense Secretary Cheney orders military to eliminate about 2,400 tactical nuclear weapons and end 24-hour alert by long-range bombers and some long-range missiles.

Yugoslav Army Moves on Croatia (Sept. 30): Serb-dominated armored forces drive toward secessionist area in offensive to take besieged Vukovar.

Haitian Troops Seize President in Uprising (Sept. 30): Mutinous soldiers arrest Jean-Bertrand Aristide, 38, victor in nation's first democratic election.

Colonel Guilty in El Salvador Deaths (Sept. 30): Nation hails jury verdict convicting Guillermo Benevides Moreno in killing of six Jesuit priests, their cook, and her daughter, shot in 1989.

National

Former High C.I.A. Official Indicted (Sept. 6): Clair E. George, once in third position, accused of perjury, false statements, and obstruction of inquiries in Iran-Contra investigation.

Federal Reserve Cuts Interest Rates (Sept. 13): Reduces discount rate from 5 1/2% to 5%, lowest since 1970s, in move to stimulate weak economy.

Charges Against Oliver North Dropped (Sept. 16): Federal judge ends case against former National Security Council aide. Independent prosecutor finds evidence in Iran-Contra conviction possibly contaminated by testimony given under immunity.

Senators Deadlocked on Thomas Nomination (Sept. 27): Judiciary Committee, 7–7, refuses to endorse Clarence Thomas, Bush choice for Supreme Court, but sends nomination to Senate floor.

General

Blaze Kills 25 in Factory (Sept. 3): Forty injured in fire at North Carolina chicken-processing plant believed to have started in grease-filled vat. Some charge exits were blocked

Computer Deciphers Dead Sea Scrolls (Sept. 4): Hackers devise programs to use concordance to unravel secrets held tightly by coterie of scholars.

Space Shuttle *Discovery* Successful (Sept. 12): Launched at Cape Canaveral, Fla. Members of crew: Mission commander, Navy Capt. John O. Creighton, 48; pilot, Navy Cmdr. Kenneth S. Reightler, Jr., 40; mission specialists—Army Maj. Charles D. Gemar, 36; Army Col. James F. Buchli, 46; Air Force Col. Mark N. Brown, 40. **(Sept. 18):** Shuttle lands safely at Edwards Air Force Base, Calif., after releasing 14,500-pound Upper Atmosphere Research Satellite for study of how pollutants are depleting ozone layer shielding Earth from radiation.

Six Arrested in Buddhist Temple Killings (Sept. 13): Held by Arizona police in nine deaths near Phoenix. Motive believed rage at failed robbery attempt.

Miss America Receives Crown (Sept. 14): Carolyn Suzanne Sapp, a native of Honolulu, Hawaii, is the new title-holder.

Dead Seas Scrolls Unveiled (Sept. 21): Huntington Library in California reveals it has nearly complete set of photographs of rare biblical documents and decides to make them generally available.

OCTOBER 1991
(Through October 18)

International

Fighting Worsens in Croatia (Oct. 1): Heavy clashes occur along virtually all of the front as the nine-day-old cease-fire steadily eroded. **(Oct. 2):** Croatia's president appeals to federal army for a new cease-fire. **(Oct. 3):** Yugoslavia's navy renews blockade of Croatian ports. **(Oct. 4):** The eight-member presidency split in half, each asserting sovereignty. **(Oct. 7):** Slovenia and Croatia both formally declare their independence.

U.S. Suspends Assistance to Haiti (Oct. 1): The United States cuts off economic aid and refuses to recognize the military junta that ousted President Aristide. **(Oct. 2):** The Organization of American States agrees to apply pressure to restore Aristide. **(Oct. 3):** Aristide asks U.N. Security Council for help in restoring democracy to Haiti. **(Oct. 5):** O.A.S. mission learns junta is willing to relinquish power to an interim administration headed by the chief justice of the Haitian Supreme Court. **(Oct. 8):** The Haitian National Assembly swears in Joseph Nerette as provisional president.

Philippines Settle on Three-Year U.S. Pullout (Oct. 2): President Corazon C. Aquino and a majority of senators reach a compromise, agreeing to negotiate a pullout of American troops by 1994.

Pact Bans Oil Exploration in Antarctica (Oct. 4): The United States joins 23 other countries in banning mineral and oil exploration in Antarctica for at least 50 years. The agreement also includes new regulations for wildlife protection, waste disposal, marine pollution, and continued monitoring of the region.

Soviets Match U.S. on Nuclear Arms Cut (Oct. 5): In response to President Bush's nuclear arms reduction initiative, President Gorbachev goes along announcing the elimination or reduction of a range of tactical weapons. He also pledges to cut the number of strategic warheads beyond the requirement of the new strategic arms treaty and to halt nuclear testing for a year.

U.N. Inspectors Discover Hidden Atom Arms Center (Oct. 7): Inspection team reports that a top-secret document they found indicates the hub of Iraq's weapons development program was a scientific research installation about 40 miles south of Baghdad. It was only lightly hit during the war.

Peace Talks Set for Madrid (Oct. 18): The United States and the Soviet Union extend invitations to Israel, Arab states, and Palestinians for a Middle East peace conference in Madrid on October 30.

Israel and Soviets Renew Ties (Oct. 18): After 24 years Israel and the Soviets restore full diplomatic relations.

National

Congress Approves Jobless Benefits (Oct. 1): Both houses of Congress vote to extend unemployment benefits to workers who have been jobless for six months of more. **(Oct. 11):** Bush vetos bill. **(Oct. 16):** Senate fails to override veto by two votes.

Senate Passes Family Leave Bill (Oct. 2): By a 65-to-32 margin the Senate votes to require many employers to grant up to 12 weeks of unpaid leave for workers to attend to family emergencies.

House Bank to Close (Oct. 3): Responding to criticism about the bank's covering members' bad checks, Speaker Thomas S. Foley announces the bank will close by the end of the year. The announcement was later ratified by a vote of the House.

Congress Votes to Replace Moscow Embassy (Oct. 5): On voice votes the House and Senate approve a plan to build a new $220-million embassy to replace the unfinished wiretapped structure erected by Soviet crews. That building will be used for unclassified activities and unused space rented to American companies seeking office space in Moscow.

Professor Accuses Thomas of Sexual Harassment (Oct. 6): Anita F. Hill, tenured professor of law at the University of Oklahoma, says Judge Thomas sexually harassed her while she served as his personal assistant in the Federal Government. **(Oct. 9):** Senate agrees to postpone vote on Thomas confirmation and hold hearings into the harassment charge. **(Oct. 15):** Senate confirms Judge Thomas by a 52–48 vote.

General

Massachusetts A-Plant Closes (Oct. 1): The Yankee Rowe, the nation's oldest nuclear power plant, begins shutting down after Nuclear Regulatory staff questions it safety.

Researchers Link New Gene Defect to Alzheimer's (Oct. 4): Following discovery of the first genetic defect that causes Alzheimer's disease, another research team finds a second defect in the same spot.

Judge Accepts Exxon Settlement (Oct. 8): Federal Judge H. Russel Holland approves a $1-billion package of criminal and civil settlements ending state and Federal cases arising from the *Exxon Valdez* oil spill.

F.D.A. Approves Second AIDS Drug (Oct. 9): The Federal Food and Drug Administration clears dideoxyinosine (DDI) for use by AIDS patients who are not helped by AZT.

1991 Nobel Prize Winners

Peace: Daw Aung San Suu Kyi (Burmese), an opposition leader held under house arrest, "for her nonviolent struggle for democracy and human rights."

Literature: Nadine Gordimer (South African), novelist and short story writer, "who through her magnificent epic writing has—in the words of Alfred Nobel—been of very great benefit to humanity."

Medicine: Dr. Erwin Neher and Dr. Bert Sakmann (German) for their research, particularly the development of a technique called patch clamp, which allows the detection of electrical currents of a trillionth of an ampere in the membrane, or surface, of a cell, has "revolutionized modern biology and facilitated research" in many areas. Dr. Neher is a physicist at the Max Planck Institute for Biophysical Chemistry in Göttingen, Germany. Dr. Sakmann is a medical doctor at the Max Planck Institute for Medical Research in Heidelberg, Germany.

Economics: Ronald Coase (American), a professor emeritus at the University of Chicago Law School, for his pioneering work in how property rights and the cost of doing business affect the economy.

Physics: Dr. Pierre-Gilles de Gennes (French), a professor at the Collège de France, Paris, for his discoveries about the ordering of molecules in substances ranging from "super" glue used in aircraft construction to an exotic form of liquid helium.

Chemistry: Dr. Richard R. Ernst (Swiss), a professor at the Eidgenössische Technische Hochscule in Zürich, for the refinements he developed in nuclear magnetic resonance spectroscopy—a powerful method of chemical analysis.

Deaths in 1990–1991

(As of September 1, 1991)

Anderson, Carl D., 85: co-winner of Nobel Prize in Physics in 1936 for discovery of positron, one of tiniest particles in nature. Jan. 11, 1991.

Arden, Eve, 83: sardonic and caustic film and stage actress. Popular in television series "Our Miss Brooks." Nov. 12, 1990.

Arrau, Claudio, 88: one of great pianists of 20th century known for aristocratic interpretations of great works of 19th century. June 9, 1991.

Arrupe, Rev. Pedro, 83: retired Superior General of Society of Jesus. Guided Jesuits through period of controversy over liberal positions. Feb. 1, 1991.

Arthur, Jean, 90: buoyant screen actress of 1930s and 1940s. Starred in comedy dramas including "Mr. Deeds Goes to Town" and "Mr. Smith Goes to Washington." June 19, 1991.

Ashcroft, Dame Peggy, 83: outstanding British actress. Appeared in Shakespearean roles and in mid-70s won acclaim in films with India as theme.

Atwater, Lee, 40: former chairman of Republican National Committee. Guided Bush's 1988 Presidential campaign as aggressive and ruthless tactician. March 29, 1991.

Bardeen, Dr. John, 82: co-inventor of transistor, which led to modern electronics. Twice winner of Nobel Prize in Physics. Jan. 30, 1991.

Barrett, Dr. Alan H., 64: authority and pioneer in radio astronomy, professor emeritus of physics at M.I.T. July 3, 1991.

Bennett, Joan, 80: screen actress who played blonde ingenues in 1930s films and later became brunette femme fatale in film classics of 1940s. Dec. 7, 1990.

Bernstein, Leonard, 72: world-famous American composer, conductor, pianist, writer, and educator. At 40 became youngest music director ever engaged by New York Philharmonic. Oct. 14, 1990.

Blakey, Art, 71: drummer and band leader, one of most influential figures in jazz. Oct. 16, 1990.

Bliss, Anthony A., 78: lawyer who was an active executive in New York's opera and dance world for four decades. Aug. 10, 1991.

Bolet, Jorge, 75: Cuban-born piano virtuoso, one of leading contemporary exponents of Romantic music. Oct. 16, 1990.

Boyle, Andrew, 71: British author and broadcaster whose book "The Climate of Treason" led to the exposure of the "fourth man" in a Soviet spy ring. April 22, 1991.

Broyard, Anatole, 70: book critic, essayist, and editor for *The New York Times* for 18 years. Oct. 11, 1990.

Chandler, A.B. (Happy), 92: former Governor of Kentucky and U.S. Senator. As outstanding baseball commissioner, supported breaking of color line. June 15, 1991.

Chang, Dr. M.C., 82: scientist in reproductive biology and co-developer of birth control pill. June 5, 1991.

Cooper, John Sherman, 89: liberal Republican Senator from Kentucky. One of first in Senate G.O.P. to stand up against anti-Communist smear tactics of Senator Joseph R. McCarthy, Feb. 21, 1991.

Copland, Aaron, 90: nation's best-known composer of classical music, both serious and popular, and a champion of American music in every style. Dec. 2, 1990.

Cousins, Norman, 75: Editor-in-Chief of *Saturday Review* for more than 30 years. His "Anatomy of an Illness: As Perceived by the Patient" became bestseller late in life. Nov. 30, 1990.

Cugat, Xavier, 90: Spanish-born bandleader. Introduced Latin-American rhythms to North America. Oct. 27, 1990.

Dahl, Roald, 74: best-selling British author of macabre children's stories and books for adults and films. Nov. 23, 1990.

Daly, John Charles, Jr., 77: reporter and television news executive. Was affable host of popular quiz show "What's My Line?" Feb. 25, 1991.

Delacorte, George T., 97: founded Dell publishing house. As philanthropist gave millions to New York City for fountains, statues, theaters, and schools. May 4, 1991.

Dewhurst, Colleen, 67: a leading American actress. In 40-year career on stage, screen and in television, earned two Tony Awards and three Emmys. Identified with Eugene O'Neill plays. Aug. 2, 1991.

Doe, Samuel K., 38: President of Liberia. Seized power in 1980 in coup that triumphed over descendants of American slaves. Administration had reputation for abuse of human rights. Sept. 9, 1990.

Dunne, Irene, 91: film actress known for her patrician manner in madcap comedies, sentimental dramas, and Jerome Kern musicals of 1930s and 40s. Awarded Kennedy Center honors in performing arts in 1985. Sept. 4, 1990.

Durrell, Lawrence, 78: British novelist and poet, author of sensuous and exotic fiction, notably the "Alexandria Quartet." Nov. 7, 1990.

Dürrenmatt, Friedrich, 69: Swiss playwright, novelist, and essayist. Author of plays "The Visit" and "The Physicist." Dec. 14, 1990.

Edwards, Douglas, 73: network television's first anchorman. Covered close of World War II with Edward R. Murrow in London. Oct. 13, 1990.

Engle, Paul, 82: poet and author. Developed writers' program at University of Iowa to point of international recognition. March 22, 1991.

Fish, Hamilton, 102: was conservative Republican Congressman from upstate New York who opposed U.S. involvement in World War II. Jan. 18, 1991.

Flexner, Stuart Berg, 62: editor, author, and lexicographer. Editor of second edition of unabridged Random House Dictionary of the English Language and author of books on language. Dec. 3, 1990.

Fodor, Eugene, 85: producer of travel guides used for half a century by tourists around the world. Feb. 18, 1991.

Fonteyn, Dame Margot, 71: famed British ballerina, international idol. She redefined 20th century ballet style. Feb. 21, 1991.

Getz, Stan, 64: influential jazz musician noted for tenor saxophone improvisations. June 6, 1991.

Gobel, George, 71: TV, radio, and nightclub comedian. Won Emmy in 1954 after outstanding success of "The George Gobel Show" on NBC. Feb. 24, 1991.

Goren, Charles H., 90: world expert on contract bridge, known to millions as "Mr. Bridge," as author of books, columns, and articles. Held world title. April 3, 1991.

Graham, Martha, 96: pioneer American dancer and choreographer. Revolutionary forms of expression ranked her with Joyce, Picasso, and Stravinsky. April 1, 1991.

Grange, Harold (Red), 78: "Galloping Ghost" of football, famed for exploits as running back for University of Illinois and Chicago Bears more than 60 years previously. Jan. 28, 1991.

Greene, Graham, 86: British author with 60-year writing career. Novels plumbed sordid politics of modern world and inner torments of mankind. April 3, 1991.

Groff, Brig. Gen. John, 100: oldest surviving general in U.S. Marine Corps. Rose from private in 34 years' service. Oct. 3, 1990.

Hammer, Armand, 92: Chairman of Occidental Petroleum Corporation. For years sought peace between U.S. and Soviet Union. Known as philanthropist and art collector. Dec. 10, 1990.

Hofstadter, Dr. Robert, 75: Nobel prize winner in physics in 1961 for pioneer research into heart of nuclear particles. Nov. 17, 1990.

Holley, Major (Mule) (Major Quincy Holley, Jr.), 66: one of great jazz bass players. Oct. 28, 1990.

Honda, Soichiro, 84: Japanese mechanic who defied Government and built one of world's largest and most innovative auto companies. Aug. 5, 1991.

Jagger, Dean, 87: character actor who appeared in more than 120 films over half a century. Won 1950 Academy Award as best supporting actor for role in "Twelve O'Clock High." Feb. 1,1991.

Kaganovitch, Lazar Moyseyevich, 97: once regarded as No. 2 man in Soviet Union because of close ties to Stalin. Last surviving Communist leader who joined party before 1917 Revolution, July 25, 1991.

Kiviat, Abel, 99: former world-record holder in 1,500-meter run. Won silver medal in 1912 Olympics. Was oldest living Olympian. Aug. 24, 1991.

Klopsteg, Paul E., 101 (cq): scientist and inventor. Helped organize National Science Foundation and was president of American Association for the Advancement of Science. April 28, 1991.

Kohler, Foy D., 82: veteran diplomat who, as Ambassador to Moscow, was intermediary between U.S. and Soviet at height of Cuban missile crisis in 1961. Dec. 23, 1990.

Kosinski, Jerzy, 57: Polish-born novelist who emigrated to U.S. Won greatest fame with first novel, "The Painted Bird," a classic of Holocaust fiction. May 3, 1991.

Land, Dr. Edwin H., 81: inventor of instant camera. Head of Polaroid Corporation for decades. March 3, 1991.

Landon, Michael, 54: creator, writer, and director of television hits. Won fame as Little Joe Cartwright in TV series "Bonanza." July 1, 1991.

Lean, Sir David, 83: British director whose films won 28 Academy Awards. Works ranged from intimate films like "Brief Encounter" to epics like "Bridge on the River Kwai." April 17, 1991.

Le Gallienne, Eva, 92: a leading figure of American stage as actress, producer, director, writer, and teacher. June 3, 1991.

LeMay, Gen. Curtis E., 83: former Air Force Chief of Staff and architect of strategic air power. Oct. 1, 1990.

Luke, Keye, 86: Chinese-born actor in more than 100 films. Was No. 1 son in old Charlie Chan detective films. Jan. 12, 1991.

Mannes, Marya, 85: versatile author, journalist, and critic of radio, television, and theater. Sept. 13, 1990.

Manzù, Giacomo, 82: a leading Italian sculptor. Famed for monumental bronze doors for St. Peter's Basilica. Jan. 17, 1991.

Marble, Alice, 77: nation's top female tennis player. Won U.S. women's amateur singles title four times between 1936 and 1940. Dec. 14, 1990.

Martin, Mary, 76: favorite leading lady of musical comedy, famed for roles in "Peter Pan," "South Pacific," and "The Sound of Music." Nov. 3, 1990.

McCone, John A., 89: chairman of Atomic Energy Commission from 1958 to 1960. Director of Central Intelligence from 1961 to 1965. Feb. 14, 1991.

McCrea, Joel, 84: Hollywood actor known for ruggedly handsome roles in 80 movies, many of them Westerns. Oct. 20, 1990.

McKissick, Floyd B., 69: an early leader in civil rights movement. April 28, 1991.

Moravia, Alberto, 82: Italian novelist who explored alienation and other conditions in works focusing on human sexuality. Sept. 26, 1990.

Motherwell, Robert, 76: a leader in American art for nearly 50 years. One of last giants of Abstract Expressionist movement. July 16, 1991.

Muggeridge, Malcolm, 87: British journalist, foreign correspondent, once editor of *Punch,* and writer known as caustic social critic. Nov. 14, 1990.

Murray, Arthur, 95: world's best-known teacher of ballroom dancing. Known for skills as promoter and executive as well as expert in varied dances. March 3, 1991.

Nemerov, Howard, 71: conservative, formalist poet, Pulitzer Prize winner, and a former poet laureate of the United States. July 5, 1991.

O'Faolain, Sean, 91: Irish writer, considered master of short story. Works blended lyricism, humor, and irony. April 20, 1991.

Olaf V. King of Norway, 87: as crown prince, was national symbol of resistance to occupation by Nazi Germany. Jan. 17, 1991.

Page, Ruth, 92: pioneer American ballet dancer and one of ballet choreographers to use American themes. April 7, 1991.

Paley, William S., 89: built CBS Inc. empire into powerful communications force. Company revolutionized recording industry. Oct. 26, 1990.

Penney, Lord William George, 81: father of British atomic bomb in 1950s, and adviser on earlier American atomic projects.

Porter, Sylvia F., 72: author and newspaper columnist who interpreted business and financial news for general readers. June 5, 1991.

Reasoner, Harry, 68: newscaster who spent most of four-decade career at CBS News. Known for wit and low-key delivery. Aug. 6, 1991.

Remick, Lee, 55: versatile and elegant actress who appeared in dozens of films and many stage and television plays. July 2, 1991.

Rizzo, Frank L., 70: former Philadelphia Mayor and police commissioner. One of city's dominant political forces for quarter of a century. July 16, 1991.

Robinson, Earl, 81: versatile composer known for "Joe Hill" and other songs about labor movement. Also wrote "Ballad for Americans" and "The House I Live In." July 20, 1991.

Roosevelt, Elliott, 80: third child of President Franklin D. Roosevelt. World War II Air Corps general and author of mystery novels. Oct. 27, 1990.

Roosevelt, James, 83: eldest son of President Franklin D. Roosevelt. Was a six-term Congressman and former delegate to United Nations. Aug. 13, 1991.

Scribner, David, 84: lawyer who specialized in civil rights law and labor cases. On defense team for Scottsboro Boys in famed case in 1930s. April 10, 1991.

Serkin, Rudolf, 88: renowned piano virtuoso. A founder of Marlboro Festival, summer music series in Vermont. May 8, 1991.

Seton, Anya, 86: author of popular historical and biographical novels. Two, "Dragonwyck" and "Foxfire," made into successful films. Nov. 8, 1990.

Steber, Eleanor, 76: a leading soprano at Metropolitan Opera in 1940s and '50s. Oct. 3, 1990.

Tho, Le Duc, 79: chief North Vietnamese negotiator in Paris talks that led to 1973 cease-fire and withdrawal of U.S. troops. Oct. 13, 1990.

Thomas, Danny, 79: television comedian, star of "Make Room for Daddy," later "The Danny Thomas Show." Also philanthropist who founded St. Jude Children's Research Hospital in Memphis. Feb. 6, 1991.

Tower, John G., 65: served 24 years in U.S. Senate as first Republican senator from Texas since Reconstruction. Rejected by Senate as nominee for post of Secretary of Defense. April 5, 1991.

Zwicker, Ralph W., 88: retired Army major general. Was a central figure in Senate's censure of Senator Joseph R. McCarthy in 1954. Aug. 11, 1991.

POSTAL REGULATIONS

Domestic Mail Service 1991

First Class

First-class consists of letters and written and sealed matter. The rate is 29¢ for the first oz; 23¢ for each additional oz, or fraction of an oz, up to 11 oz. Pieces over 11 oz are subject to priority-mail (heavy pieces) rates. Single postcards, 19¢; double postcards, 38¢ (19¢ for each half). The post office sells prestamped single and double postal cards. Consult your postmaster for information on business-reply mail and presort rates.

The weight limit for first-class mail is 70 lb.

Weight not exceeding	Rates
1 oz	$ .29
2 oz	.52
3 oz	.75
4 oz	.98
5 oz	1.21
6 oz	1.44
7 oz	1.67
8 oz	1.90
9 oz	2.13
10 oz	2.36
11 oz	2.59
Over 11 ounces, *see* Priority Mail.	

Priority Mail (over 11 oz to 70 lb)

The zone rate applies to mailable matter over 11 oz of any class carried by air. Your local post office will supply free official zone tables appropriate to your location.

Airmail

First-class and priority mail receive airmail service.

Express Mail

Express Mail Service is available for any mailable article up to 70 lb in weight and 108 in. in combined length and girth, 7 days a week, 365 days a year. Call 800-333-8777 for pick-up service; there is a single charge of $4.50, no matter how many pieces. Flat rates: letter rate (up to 8 ounces), $9.95; up to 2 lb, $13.95; over 2 lb and up to 70 lb, consult your postmaster.

The flat-rate envelope (whatever the weight, the item goes for the same 2-lb rate) may be used by paying the appropriate 2-lb postage rate for the level of service desired. Other service features include: noon delivery between major business markets; merchandise and document reconstruction insurance; Express Mail shipping containers; shipment receipt; special collection boxes; and such options as return receipt service; COD service; waiver of signature; and pickup service. Consult Postmaster for other Express Mail Services and rates.

The Postal Service will refund, upon application to originating office, the postage for any Express Mail shipments not meeting the service standard, except for those delayed by strike or work stoppage.

Second Class

Second-class mail is used primarily by newspapers, magazines, and other periodicals with second-class mailing privileges. For copies mailed by the public, the rate is the applicable Express Mail, Priority Mail, or single-piece first-, third- or fourth-class rate.

Third Class (under 16 oz)

Third-class mail is used for circulars, books, catalogs, printed matter, merchandise, seeds, cuttings, bulbs, roots, scions, and plants. There are two rate structures for this class, a single-piece and a bulk rate. Regular and special bulk rates are available only to authorized mailers—consult postmaster for details.

Third-Class, Single-Piece Rates

Weight not exceeding	Rates	Weight not exceeding	Rates
1 oz	$ .29	10 oz	$ 1.44
2 oz	.52	12 oz	1.56
3 oz	.75	14 oz	1.67
4 oz	.98	Over 14 oz but	
6 oz	1.21	less than 16 oz	1.79
8 oz	1.33		

Fourth Class (Parcel Post— 16 oz and over)

Fourth-class mail is used for merchandise, books, printed matter, and all other mailable matter not in first, second, or third class. Special fourth-class rates apply to books, library books, publications or records for the blind, and certain controlled-circulation publications.

Packages should be taken to your local post office, where the postage will be determined according to the weight of the package and the distance it is being sent. Information on weight and size limits for fourth-class mail may be obtained there.

Special Services

Registered Mail. When you use registered mail service, you are buying security—the safest way to send valuables. The full value of your mailing must be declared when mailed. You receive a receipt and the movement of your mail is controlled throughout the postal system. For an additional fee, a return receipt showing to whom, when, and where delivered may be obtained.

Fees for articles (in addition to postage)

Value			With insurance	Without insurance
$ 0.01	to	$ 100	$4.50	$4.40
100.01	to	500	4.85	4.70
500.01	to	1,000	5.25	5.05

For higher values, consult your postmaster.

Certified Mail. Certified mail service provides for a receipt to the sender and a record of delivery at the post office of address. No record is kept at the post office where mailed. It is for First-Class and Priority Mail only.

Fee in addition to postage, $1.00

Return Receipts. Available for COD, Express Mail, and certified, insured (for over $50), and registered mail. Requested at time of mailing:

Showing to whom and date delivered	$1.00
Showing to whom, date, and address where delivered	1.35
Requested after mailing:	
Showing to whom and date delivered	6.00

C.O.D. Mail. Maximum value for service is $600. Consult your postmaster for fees and conditions of mailing.

Insured Mail. Fees, in addition to postage, for coverage against loss or damage:

Liability			Fees
$ .01	to	$50	$ .75
$ 50.01	to	$100	1.60
$ 100.01	to	$200	2.40
$ 200.01	to	$300	3.50
$ 300.01	to	$400	4.60
$ 400.01	to	$500	5.40
$ 500.01	to	$600	6.20

Special Delivery. The payment of the special-delivery fee entitles mail to the most expeditious transportation and delivery. The fee is in addition to the regular postage.

	Weight/Fees		
Class of mail	Not more than 2 lb	More than 2 lb but not more than 10 lb	More than 10 lb
First-class	$7.65	$7.95	$8.55
All other classes	8.05	8.65	9.30

Special Handling. Payment of the special-handling fee entitles third- and fourth-class matter to the most expeditious handling and transportation, but not special delivery. The fee is in addition to the regular postage.

Weight	Fees
Not more than 10 lb	$1.80
More than 10 lb	2.50

Money Orders. Money orders are used for the safe transmission of money.

Amount of money order	Fees
$ .01 to $700	$1.00

Minimum Mail Sizes

All mail must be at least 0.007 in. thick and mail that is 1/4 in. or less in thickness must be at least 3 1/2 in. in height, at least 5 in. long, and rectangular in shape (except keys and identification devices). NOTE: Pieces greater than 1/4 in. thick can be mailed even if they measure less than 3 1/2 by 5 inches.

Adhesive Stamps Available

Purpose	Form	Prices and denomination
Regular postage	Single or sheet	1, 2, 3, 4, 5, 6, 7, 8, 9, 10, 15, 19, 20, 22, 23, 25, 28, 29, 30, 35, 40, 45, 50, 52, 65, 75¢, $1, $2, $2.90, $5, $9.95.
	Booklets	10 at 29 cents ($2.90) 20 at 29 cents ($5.80) 20 at 19 cents ($3.80)
	Coil of 100	19, 25, and 29¢ (dispenser and stamp affixer for use with these coils are also available).
	Coil of 500	1, 2, 3, 4, 5, 10, 15, 19, 20, 23, 25, 29¢, and $1.
	Coil of 3000	1, 2, 3, 4, 5, 10, 15, 19, 20, 23, 25, 29¢.
	Coil of 10,000	29¢.
International airmail postage	Single or sheet	40 and 50¢

Note: Denominations listed are currently in stock. Others may be available until supplies are exhausted.

Regular envelopes are available prestamped for 29¢ and 34¢ each (less than 500). For bulk prices, consult postmaster.

Single postcards are available prestamped for 19¢ each. Reply postcards (19¢ each half) are 38¢ each.

Non-Standard Mail

All first-class mail (except presort first-class and carrier route first-class weighing one ounce or less) and all single-piece rate third-class mail weighing one ounce or less is nonstandard (and subject to a 10¢ surcharge in addition to the applicable postage and fees) if any of the following dimensions are exceeded: length—11 1/2 inches; height—6 1/8 inches; thickness—1/4 inch, or the piece has a height to length (aspect) ratio which does not fall between 1 to 1.3 and 1 to 2.5 inclusive. (The aspect ratio is found by dividing the length by the height. If the answer is between 1.3 and 2.5 inclusive, the piece has a standard aspect ratio).

International Mail Service, 1991

Letters and Letter Packages

Items of mail containing personal handwritten or typewritten communications having the character of current correspondence must be sent as letters or letter packages. Unless prohibited by the country of destination, merchandise or other articles within the applicable weight and size limits may also be mailed at the letter rate of postage. Weight limit for all countries, 4 pounds. For rates, consult your local post office.

Letters and Letter Packages— Airmail Rates

All Countries other than Canada & Mexico

Weight not over	Rate	Weight not over	Rate
Oz		*Oz*	
0.5	$ 0.50	24.5	$19.28
1.0	0.95	25.0	19.67
1.5	1.34	25.5	20.06
2.0	1.73	26.0	20.45
2.5	2.12	26.5	20.84
3.0	2.51	27.0	21.23
3.5	2.90	27.5	21.62
4.0	3.29	28.0	22.01
4.5	3.68	28.5	22.40
5.0	4.07	29.0	22.79
5.5	4.46	29.5	23.18
6.0	4.85	30.0	23.57
6.5	5.24	30.5	23.96
7.0	5.63	31.0	24.35
7.5	6.02	31.5	24.74
8.0	6.41	32.0	25.13
8.5	6.80	33	25.52
9.0	7.19	34	25.91
9.5	7.58	35	26.30
10.0	7.97	36	26.69
10.5	8.36	37	27.08
11.0	8.75	38	27.47
11.5	9.14	39	27.86
12.0	9.53	40	28.25
12.5	9.92	41	28.64
13.0	10.31	42	29.03
13.5	10.70	43	29.42
14.0	11.09	44	29.81
14.5	11.48	45	30.20
15.0	11.87	46	30.59
15.5	12.26	47	30.98
16.0	12.65	48	31.37
16.5	13.04	49	31.76
17.0	13.43	50	32.15
17.5	13.82	51	32.54
18.0	14.21	52	32.93
18.5	14.60	53	33.32
19.0	14.99	54	33.71
19.5	15.38	55	34.10
20.0	15.77	56	34.49
20.5	16.16	57	34.88
21.0	16.55	58	35.27
21.5	16.94	59	35.66
22.0	17.33	60	36.05
22.5	17.72	61	36.44
23.0	18.11	62	36.83
23.5	18.50	63	37.22
24.0	18.89	64	37.61

Post and Postal Cards

Canada	$0.30	All other—surface	$0.35
Mexico	$0.30	All other—air	$0.40

Aerogrammes—$0.45 each.

Canada and Mexico—Surface Rates

All Countries other than Canada & Mexico

Weight not over		Canada	Mexico	Weight not over		Canada	Mexico
Lb	*Oz*			*Lb*	*Oz*		
0	0.5	$.40	$.35	0	10	2.47	2.65
0	1	.40	.45	0	11	2.70	2.90
0	1.5	.63	.55	0	12	2.93	3.15
0	2	.63	.65	1	0	3.25	4.15
0	3	.86	.90	1	8	3.85	6.15
0	4	1.09	1.15	2	0	4.45	8.15
0	5	1.32	1.40	2	8	5.38	10.15
0	6	1.55	1.65	3	0	6.31	12.15
0	7	1.78	1.90	3	8	7.24	14.15
0	8	2.01	2.15	4	0	8.17	16.15
0	9	2.24	2.40				
			Weight Limit—4 Pounds*				

Note: Mail paid at this rate receives First-Class service in the United States and air service in Canada and Mexico. *Registered letters to Canada may weigh up to 66 pounds. The rate for over 4 pounds to 66 pounds is $1.80 per pound or fraction of a pound.

Countries Other Than Canada and Mexico—Surface Rates

Letters and Letter Packages

Weight not over		Rate	Weight not over		Rate
Lb	*Oz*		*Lb*	*Oz*	
0	1	0.70	0	11	3.95
0	2	0.95	0	12	3.95
0	3	1.20	1	0	5.55
0	4	1.45	1	8	7.65
0	5	1.70	2	0	9.75
0	6	1.95	2	8	11.85
0	7	2.20	3	0	13.95
0	8	2.45	3	8	16.05
0	9	3.95	4	0	18.15
0	10	3.95			

Weight limit—4 pounds.

International Surface Parcel Post

Other Than Canada

Weight through lb	Mexico Central America, Caribbean Islands, Bahamas, Bermuda, St. Pierre and Miquelon	All other countries
2	$ 6.00	$ 6.55
	$1.85 each additional lb or fraction	$2.10 each additional lb or fraction

Consult your postmaster for weight/size limits of individual countries.

For other international services and rates consult your local postmaster.

Canada Surface Parcel Post

Up to 2 lb $4.85, $1.45 for each additional lb up to the maximum weight of 66 lb. Minimum weight is 1 lb.

International Money Order Fees

This service available only to certain countries. Consult post office. Fee: $3.00. Maximum amount for a single money order is $700.

United Nations Stamps

United Nations stamps are issued in three different currencies, namely, U.S. dollars, Swiss francs, and Austrian schillings. Stamps in all three currencies are available at face value at each of the U.N. Postal Administration offices in New York, Geneva, and Vienna. They may be purchased over the counter, by mail, or by opening a Customer Deposit Account.

Mail orders for mint (unused) stamps and postal stationery may be sent to the U.N. Postal Administration in New York, Geneva, and Vienna. Write to: United Nations Postal Administration, P.O. Box 5900, Grand Central Station, New York, N.Y. 10017.

How to Complain About a Postal Problem

When you have a problem with your mail service, complete a Consumer Service Card which is available from letter carriers and at post offices. This will help your postmaster respond to your problem. If you wish to telephone a complaint, a postal employee will fill out the card for you.

The Consumer Advocate represents consumers at the top management level in the Postal Service. If your postal problems cannot be solved by your local post office, then write to the Consumer Advocate. His staff stands ready to serve you.

Write to: The Consumer Advocate, U.S. Postal Service, Washington, D.C. 20260-6320. Or phone: 1-202-268-2284.

The Mail Order Merchandise Rule

The mail order rule adopted by the Federal Trade Commission in October 1975 provides that when you order by mail:

You must receive the merchandise when the seller says you will.

If you are not promised delivery within a certain time period, the seller must ship the merchandise to you no later than 30 days after your order comes in.

If you don't receive it shortly after that 30-day period, you can cancel your order and get your money back.

How the Rule Works

The seller must notify you if the promised delivery date (or the 30-day limit) cannot be met. The seller must also tell you what the new shipping date will be and give you the option to cancel the order and receive a full refund or agree to the new shipping date. The seller must also give you a free way to send back your answer, such as a stamped envelope or a postage-paid postcard. *If you don't answer, it means that you agree to the shipping delay.*

The seller must tell you if the shipping delay is going to be more than 30 days. You then can agree to the delay or, if you do not agree, the seller must return your money by the end of the first 30 days of the delay.

If you cancel a prepaid order, the seller must mail you the refund within seven business days. Where there is a credit sale, the seller must adjust your account within one billing cycle.

It would be impossible, however, for one rule to apply uniformly to such a varied field as mail order merchandising. For example, the rule does not apply to mail order photo finishing, magazine subscriptions, and other serial deliveries (except for the initial shipment); to mail order seeds and growing plants; to COD orders; or to credit orders where the buyer's account is not charged prior to shipment of the merchandise.

Authorized 2-Letter State Abbreviations

When the Post Office instituted the ZIP Code for mail in 1963, it also drew up a list of two-letter abbreviations for the states which would gradually replace the traditional ones in use. Following is the official list, including the District of Columbia, Guam, Puerto Rico, and the Virgin Islands (note that only capital letters are used):

Alabama	AL	Kentucky	KY	Ohio	OH
Alaska	AK	Louisiana	LA	Oklahoma	OK
Arizona	AZ	Maine	ME	Oregon	OR
Arkansas	AR	Maryland	MD	Pennsylvania	PA
California	CA	Massachusetts	MA	Puerto Rico	PR
Colorado	CO	Michigan	MI	Rhode Island	RI
Connecticut	CT	Minnesota	MN	South Carolina	SC
Delaware	DE	Mississippi	MS	South Dakota	SD
Dist. of Columbia	DC	Missouri	MO	Tennessee	TN
Florida	FL	Montana	MT	Texas	TX
Georgia	GA	Nebraska	NE	Utah	UT
Guam	GU	Nevada	NV	Vermont	VT
Hawaii	HI	New Hampshire	NH	Virginia	VA
Idaho	ID	New Jersey	NJ	Virgin Islands	VI
Illinois	IL	New Mexico	NM	Washington	WA
Indiana	IN	New York	NY	West Virginia	WV
Iowa	IA	North Carolina	NC	Wisconsin	WI
Kansas	KS	North Dakota	ND	Wyoming	WY